Current Biography Yearbook 2010

EDITOR
Clifford Thompson

SENIOR EDITORS
Miriam Helbok
Mari Rich

PRODUCTION EDITOR
Bertha Muteba

ASSISTANT EDITOR
Margaret R. Mead

STAFF WRITERS
Christopher Cullen
William Dvorak
Dmitry Kiper
Joanna Padovano
Hallie Rose Waxman

CONTRIBUTING WRITERS
Nicholas W. Malinowski
Majid Mozaffari
Margaret R. Mead
Tracy O'Neill
Kenneth J. Partridge
Jamie E. Peck
Maria A. Suarez

EDITORIAL ASSISTANT
Carolyn Ellis

THE H.W. WILSON COMPANY
NEW YORK • DUBLIN

SEVENTY-FIRST ANNUAL CUMULATION—2010

PRINTED IN THE UNITED STATES OF AMERICA

International Standard Serial No. (0084-9499)

International Standard Book No. – 978-0-8242-1113-4

Library of Congress Catalog Card No. (40-27432)

Table of Contents

PREFACE

The aim of *Current Biography Yearbook 2010*, like that of the preceding volumes in this series of annual dictionaries of contemporary biography, now in its eighth decade of publication, is to provide reference librarians, students, and researchers with objective, accurate, and well documented biographical articles about living leaders in all fields of human accomplishment. Whenever feasible, obituary notices appear for persons whose biographies have been published in Current Biography.

Current Biography Yearbook 2010 carries on the policy of including new and updated biographical profiles that supersede earlier articles. Profiles have been made as accurate and objective as possible through careful researching of newspapers, magazines, the World Wide Web, authoritative reference books, and news releases of both government and private agencies. Immediately after they are published in the 11 monthly issues, articles are submitted to biographees to give them an opportunity to suggest additions and corrections in time for publication of the *Current Biography Yearbook*. To take account of major changes in the careers of biographees, articles are revised before they are included in the yearbook.

Classification by Profession–2010 and *2001–2010 Index* are at the end of this volume. *Current Biography Cumulated Index 1940–2005* cumulates and supersedes all previous indexes.

For their assistance in preparing *Current Biography Yearbook 2010*, I thank the staff of *Current Biography* and also the staffs of the company's Computer and Manufacturing departments.

Current Biography welcomes comments and suggestions. Please send your comments to: The Editor, *Current Biography*, The H. W. Wilson Company, 950 University Ave., Bronx, NY 10452; fax: 7185904566; Email: cthompson@hwwilson.com.

Clifford Thompson

List of Biographical Sketches

ix

x

Current Biography Yearbook 2010

David Silverman/Getty Images

Agassi, Shai

(AH-gass-ee, shy)

Apr. 19, 1968– Founder and CEO of Better Place; former software developer

Address: Better Place, 1070 Arastradero Rd., Suite 220, Palo Alto, CA 94304

Shai Agassi is the founder and chief executive officer (CEO) of Better Place, a California-based company launched in October 2007, whose mission is to end global dependency on petroleum to fuel cars and trucks. In the hundreds of interviews, talks, and meetings large and small in which he has participated the world over, Agassi has argued that ending reliance on petroleum and introducing alternative sources of energy as soon as possible is vital for several compelling reasons. One is that, in light of the expected increase in Earth's human population and rise in demand for energy from people in India, China, and other industrializing nations, by 2050 there will be a severe shortage of energy; according to some experts, without major changes in technology and behavior, less than half of the needed energy will be available. Another reason is the danger to the well-being of all living organisms posed by global warming, which the overwhelming majority of scientists believe is real and which stems mostly from the emission of gases produced by the burning of petroleum and other fossil fuels. A third reason is connected to the economic, social, and political ramifications of the interdependence of oil-importing and oil-exporting nations, which range from crippling cost-of-living increases to armed conflicts and the financing of terrorist groups. Agassi proposes to inaugurate the era of the clean, or "green," car by not only introducing vehicles that run solely on electricity but making them affordable, efficient, and convenient. To cite earlier examples of such an approach, Thomas Edison introduced not only the electric lightbulb but also a system of generators, transmission lines, electrical substations, and other facilities necessary to make lightbulbs practical; the age of the automobile came about not only because Henry Ford introduced the assembly-line manufacture of moderately priced cars but also because a nationwide highway system was created and gas stations and repair shops arrived on the scene. Similarly, Agassi and his colleagues at Better Place have come up not only with a design for electric-powered vehicles with switchable batteries but also a many-faceted system to support their widespread use.

Agassi earned an undergraduate degree in computer science in 1990 at the Technion–Israel Institute of Technology, one of the most prestigious universities in Israel, his native land. Immediately afterward, in partnership with his father, he embarked on a half-dozen software ventures. In 2001 the German firm SAP—currently Europe's largest software company and the world's fourth-biggest, after Microsoft, IBM, and Oracle—acquired the most successful of the Agassis' start-ups, TopTier, for $400 million, and Shai Agassi joined SAP as the chief executive officer of a new subsidiary called SAP Portals. He joined SAP's executive committee in 2002 and later became the president of SAP's products and technology group. In that post he was guided by the belief, as he put it to Chris Taylor for *Time* (December 1, 2003), that "training people on computer systems is stupid. We need to train the systems to work with people." His proposal for what became one of SAP's most innovative and useful creations, NetWeaver, contributed to his growing reputation as a visionary leader. When, in 2007, contrary to his expectation, he was not named SAP's co-CEO, he left the company to devote himself full-time to his ideas for making gasoline-powered vehicles obsolete. Urged on by Shimon Peres, a former prime minister of Israel who is now the country's president, he secured $200 million in investments in Project Better

Place, as it was originally called, and has since raised hundreds of millions more in private capital. The Nissan and Renault automakers (which have been partners since 1999) have agreed to produce 100,000 cars to Agassi's specifications, to go to Israel and Denmark, Better Place's first two commercial markets. In addition to those countries, Better Place has focused on bringing the cars to Australia, Japan, China, and parts of North America.

"Shai's genius is not really the technology, it's the business model," the conservationist Robert F. Kennedy Jr. told Matt Nauman for the *San Jose (California) Mercury News* (January 16, 2009). Alan Salzman, a managing partner of VantagePoint Venture Partners, a backer of Better Place, told Nauman, "What's overlooked in Shai's long list of capabilities is his ability to get diverse groups in diverse countries to coalesce over changing the auto industry." The prospect of making a historic, worldwide change that will improve lives and slow climate change thrills Agassi, Daniel Roth wrote for *Wired* (September 2008, on-line). "I get to shift multiple markets," Agassi told him. "I get to shift economies. It's extremely liberating. I breathe differently." When Roth asked him if he worried about "a competitor stealing his idea," Agassi looked incredulous. "The mission is to end oil," he said, "not create a company."

Shai Agassi was born on April 19, 1968 in Ramat-Gan, Israel, a suburb of Tel Aviv, to Reuvan Agassi, an electrical engineer, and his wife, a fashion designer. His father's family had immigrated to Israel from Iraq, his mother's family from Morocco. Agassi's siblings work at Better Place—his younger brother, Tal Agassi, manages the firm's global-deployment operations, and his younger sister, Dafna Barazovsky, handles the company's marketing in Israel. Agassi spent his childhood in Argentina, where his parents moved shortly after his birth. While on a visit to Israel when he was seven, he learned the fundamentals of programming in a computer-science course for children held at Tel Aviv University. He took to programming immediately, in part because he had always liked to build things and be in control. "Other kids collected baseball cards," Agassi told Chris Taylor. "I collected punch cards." Agassi earned his high-school diploma at 15, at Lincoln, the American International School of Buenos Aires. He then enrolled at the Technion–Israel Institute of Technology, in Haifa, his father's alma mater. As an undergraduate Agassi was struck by a car while crossing a street in Tel Aviv, severely damaging a leg. The accident (which left the leg an inch shorter than the other) set his graduation back by a year and led officials to reduce the length of his mandatory service in the Israeli Armed Forces. He served an abbreviated stint as a computer programmer for the Israeli Defense Force Intelligence before earning a B.A. degree, with honors in computer science, from the Technion in 1990.

In 1991 Agassi and his father launched a software company called QuickSoft. Over the next several years, they set up QuickSoft Media, TopTier Software, and TopManage, among other software companies. As the head of each start-up, Shai Agassi was directly involved in all phases of the companies' development, including strategic planning, technical direction, and financing, and he negotiated agreements with SAP, Baan, Microsoft, and other firms. He eventually became the CEO of TopTier, the Agassis' most successful venture, which provided companies with the technology to build enterprise portals, internal Web sites that provide employees with corporate information and access to select public sites. Unlike most of its competitors, TopTier focused its efforts on small and medium-size businesses.

In April 2001 the Walldorf, Germany–based SAP (pronounced "ess-aye-pee"), then the world's third-largest software company, bought TopTier from Agassi for $400 million. SAP combined TopTier with its software-integration division, My-SAP, and its other e-business software division, e-SAP, to form a new subsidiary, SAP Portals. With Agassi as the CEO, SAP Portals focused on the creation of improved enterprise portals (also called enterprise information portals or simply portals)—customized Web sites that serve as one-stop gateways into databases and anything else particular users might need to conduct their businesses. Agassi told a writer for the *Red Herring* (March 2003) that he did not sell his company to SAP for the money but for the additional resources that became available to him. "I had a vision of enterprise computing that was too big for a small company to execute. To fulfill this vision, I need[ed] to ally TopTier with a much bigger player." As the CEO of SAP Portals, Agassi was charged with developing new ways to customize and improve enterprise portals.

At the first high-level strategy meeting that he attended, in February 2002, Agassi made a dozen unconventional suggestions for creating better intranets (private Internet sites) and applications for companies, to replace "ad hoc combination[s] of spreadsheets and email," as he put it to *Red Herring*. His presentation included a PowerPoint slide showing a hand whose fingers represented the five major SAP operations that required software applications: enterprise resource planning (ERP), customer-relationship management (CRM), supplier-relationship management, supply-chain management, and product-life-cycle management. Threaded among the fingers was a rainbow, which, Agassi explained, represented a proposed computer platform—called NetWeaver—designed to run all of SAP's applications. Agassi's bold proposal sparked a "four-hour argument," he recalled to *Red Herring*. "The gist of the other side boiled down to, 'That is not the way we do things here.' Fortunately, I was able to overcome those objections." Agassi won the support of SAP's co-founder Hasso Plattner, who made Agassi's suggestion the company's focus. NetWeaver was introduced in 2003. According to sapgeek.net (May 25, 2010), NetWeaver greatly reduced the cost of producing, managing, storing, and disseminating information and developing and using "composite applications." In February 2003 Agassi joined SAP's executive board; later that year he became the president of SAP's product and technology group.

Over the next few years, SAP began redesigning all of its software products to make them simpler and more user-friendly and harmonious. Agassi oversaw the development of xApps, an array of business-software applications. Each xApp was geared toward helping companies manage one or more aspects of the five business processes that Agassi had outlined on his original NetWeaver slide. One application enabled companies to collect information from various departments—for instance, project management, human resources, or finance—and assemble it into "dashboards," to provide managers with real-time status reports, thus making sure, for example, that projects proceeded according to schedule. Agassi also helped develop smaller-scale applications, or "snap apps," which addressed more specific functions. In November 2003 SAP introduced a Web-services software called Enterprise Services Architecture (ESA). According to searchsaptechtarget.com, ESA "facilitates deployment of Web services at the business level."

Meanwhile, SAP had also begun to offer financial incentives to sell NetWeaver to companies that agreed to leave other software providers. Agassi also made overtures to Microsoft and IBM; in July 2003 SAP announced that IBM would begin selling NetWeaver communications software. SAP's main targets were small and midsize companies, an underserved market; by June 2004 SAP had created two software suites tailored for such companies, Business One and mySAP All-in-One, and sold them to more than 8,000 customers. By then NetWeaver was widely thought to be the biggest player in what became known as the new IT ecosystem. Referring to SAP's investment in NetWeaver, Agassi told an audience at Sapphire, the SAP users' annual conference, "We believe in this so much that we have bet the company," according to the London, England, *Information Age* (November 10, 2004).

In 2006 Agassi announced SAP's next area of innovation, service-oriented architecture (SOA), infrastructure that aims to loosely couple services with operating systems and provide IT infrastructure that allows for further integration and communication between applications and processes. At Microsoft's TechEd conference in 2006, Agassi outlined the plan that positioned SAP's enterprise resources planning (ERP) as the core component of its SOA business-software plan. He explained that customers would be able to innovate their own ERP systems by using pluggable "enhancement packages," or collections of enterprise services that would be released incrementally. A departure from the previous methods of software upgrading, by which customers had to purchase upgraded versions of software and accept all of the applications that came with them, Agassi's enhancement packages offered customers "the flexibility to choose and add new functionality at their own pace," Agassi said, as quoted by Madan Sheina in *Computer Wire* (September 14, 2006). In December 2006 Agassi announced that over the next year, SAP planned to release enough SOA-based products to complete the company's transformation to NetWeaver-compatible ESA software.

Earlier, in 2005, Agassi had joined the Young Global Leaders, an invitation-only group of politicians, businesspeople, and intellectuals under the age of 40, organized by the World Economic Forum. During the induction seminar the group was asked the question, "How do you make the world a better place by 2020?" With the environment as his assigned topic, Agassi focused on climate change and devoted his free time to learning about worldwide energy consumption. "When you get a question in your head and you're an engineer, you want to solve the engineering problem," Agassi told Matt Nauman for the *San Jose (California) Mercury News* (January 16, 2009, on-line). He talked about the need to end dependence on petroleum as a speaker at the annual Saban Forum (supported by the Israeli-American billionaire Haim Saban), held in December 2006 at the Brookings Institute, in Washington, D.C., and devoted to the subject "America and Israel Confronting a Middle East in Turmoil." Agassi suggested that governments create agencies to ensure the widespread use of electric cars, with private dealerships selling such cars to consumers. While at the conference he chatted with Shimon Peres, a member of the Israeli Cabinet at that time, who described Israel's determination to reduce its use of foreign oil. Another attendee, former U.S. president Bill Clinton, advised Agassi to take into account the millions of Americans who never buy new cars. As Agassi recalled to Stephanie N. Mehta for *CNNMoney.com* (July 8, 2009) in describing the best advice he had ever received, Clinton told him that the "average Joe . . . buys a nine-year-old used car and drives it into the ground, and then he buys another nine-year-old car. You need to figure out how to get the average Joe in an electric car for free and still make money." When Agassi asked Clinton to suggest a way to do that, Clinton responded, "You're the smart guy—you figure it out." Clinton's words helped Agassi realize that for his plan to succeed, cars would have to be either free or far less expensive than they were. Instead of paying for cars, owners would pay for electricity, choosing among so-called mile plans, including, for example, plans for an unlimited number or a maximum number of miles per month or a "pay as you go" plan. The costs of the plans would total less than the costs of gasoline for similar numbers of miles traveled. Several weeks after the conference, Agassi received a telephone call from Peres, who said to him, as he recalled to Mehta, "Agencies don't do things. Entrepreneurs do things. You have to start a company. Otherwise, this is just an idea. You have a good job, but this is a better job because you can save the world."

Agassi and another SAP executive, Leo Apotheker, were said to be in line to become the company's co-CEOs, succeeding Henning Kagermann in early 2007. But in March of that year, SAP announced that Kagermann would remain as CEO. A few days later Agassi, with Peres's advice fresh in his mind, resigned from SAP. His publicly expressed reason for his departure, as Angela Eager paraphrased it for *Computer Wire* (March 30, 2007), was his desire to "more quickly commit himself to his personal agenda of environmental policy and alternative energy sources and other issues."

When Better Place launched, in October 2007, its staff included several of Agassi's former SAP colleagues. By that time Agassi had concluded that the best way to end the world's dependency on petroleum, and thereby slow global warming, would be to end the use of gasoline in transportation, starting with the introduction of fully electric cars. Electric vehicles date from as early as 1840, but none proved to be practical, because after relatively short distances their batteries would lose their charge, and recharging them took hours. Hybrid gas/electric cars contain "range extenders"—gasoline engines that are activated when the batteries give out; when that happens they emit the gases that contribute to global warming. Agassi's idea for avoiding those problems is not only to introduce state-of-the-art electric cars but also to install an infrastructure to support them. The network would have three main components. The first is an extensive network of charging stations, at residential and commercial sites, where drivers could plug in their cars to recharge their batteries; the necessary electricity would be generated from the sun, wind, geothermal heat, rain, or tides (depending on available resources) and would thus be renewable. The second main component of the infrastructure is designed for drivers who do not have time to wait for their batteries to recharge via standard measures: a network of battery-exchange stations, where, in less than three minutes, robot-like mechanical devices would remove depleted batteries and install fully charged replacements. The third element, reflecting Agassi's work in software, would manage the overall network. The electric cars would be equipped with software whose functions include energy monitoring and global positioning; thus, drivers would be alerted to the need to recharge or replace their batteries and told the nearest locations for doing so, even receiving directions for getting there. Software would also keep track of the system as a whole, to ensure that electricity is available where needed.

Immediately upon starting Better Place, Agassi sought private funding and government support to make his vision a reality. In June 2007 he secured an agreement from Idan Ofer, Israel's richest citizen, to provide $130 million toward building an electric grid in Israel. (Ofer was attracted to Agassi's plan in part because he had invested in the Chinese firm Chery Automobile, which he anticipated would begin to manufacture electric cars, in light of China's stated intention of becoming a global leader in clean energy.) Within Better Place's first year, Agassi had raised an additional $70 million from Morgan Stanley, VantagePoint Venture Partners, and Maniv Energy Capital. He also won a commitment from Peres and Israel's prime minister, Ehud Olmert, that Israel would be Better Place's first market. (It was already Israel's policy to reduce its petrol consumption by offering significant tax breaks to Israelis who bought electric cars within the first few years of their introduction.) The Better Place proposal is particularly well-suited for Israel, which (excluding the West Bank and the Gaza Strip) is smaller than New Hampshire; moreover, since virtually all car travel occurs within its borders, one-day trips of hundreds of miles are rare. Although setting up the system in Israel would require in the neighborhood of $700 million, the cost would be "insignificant compared to what foreign oil costs the economy," Roth wrote. Earlier, at the annual World Economic Forum, held in Davos, Switzerland, in January 2007, Agassi had met Carlos Ghosn, the CEO of Renault–Nissan, which together constitute the world's fourth-largest automaker. Later that year Ghosn, eager to see Renault–Nissan emerge as the number-one maker of electric cars, committed $200 million to developing by 2011 an electric car whose battery remains charged for up to 100 miles. In March 2008 Better Place entered its second market, Denmark, and partnered with that country's largest utility, Danish Oil and Natural Gas (DONG), to create an electric-car network powered by Denmark's excess wind energy. In October 2008 the Macquarie Capital Group of Australia pledged to raise $1 billion for an electric grid in that country; that month the mayors of San Francisco, California, and other major Bay Area communities endorsed the Better Place plan, and in December 2008 the government of Hawaii, with the support of the Hawaiian Electric Co., agreed to take the necessary steps for introducing the Better Place system. On April 26, 2010, in an on-line press release, Better Place announced the start of a three-month trial of three switchable-battery electric taxis in Tokyo, Japan, where some 60,000 taxis operate—more than the number in New York, London, and Paris combined. On August 25, 2010 Better Place announced plans to extend the trial through the end of the year, in order to "gain further insights into the battery performance and durability of the switch station itself, which will be invaluable as we move towards commercial launch later next year in Israel and Denmark," according to Kiyotaka Fuji, the president of Better Place Japan, as quoted in a press release on the Better Place Web site. One month later Better Place announced a partnership with General Electric (GE). To supplement Better Place's existing battery-swapping service, GE will provide WattStation charging stations, which, according to GE, will recharge an electric-vehicle battery in four hours.

The main criticism of the Better Place plan is that in order to succeed, every car must use batteries with precisely the same specifications, necessitating the collaboration of all car makers. In addition, the technology for car batteries is still evolving; thus, sooner or later, a more efficient battery may supplant the one chosen by Better Place. Nevertheless, Daniel Roth wrote in 2008, "everyone who meets [Agassi] already believes he can see the future."

Agassi lives in Israel. He and his wife have two young sons.

—M.R.M.

Suggested Reading: Better Place Web Site; *Computer Wire* (on-line) Sep. 14, 2006, Mar. 30, 2007; *Jerusalem Report* Business p34 Mar. 17, 2008; (London) *Information Age* Nov. 10, 2004; *New York Times* (on-line) Dec. 2, 2008; *Red Herring* p40 Mar. 2003; *San Francisco Business Times* p3 May 18, 2001; *Time* p81 Dec. 1, 2003; *Wired* Features p118+ Sep. 2008

Neil Abramson, courtesy of Kim Smith PR

Allen, J. D.

Dec. 11, 1972– Jazz saxophonist

Address: c/o Sunnyside Records, 348 W. 38th St., New York, NY 10018

The tenor saxophonist and composer J. D. Allen has borrowed from jazz greats including John Coltrane, Sonny Rollins, and Ornette Coleman and, with skill and confidence, incorporated those influences in his own ecstatic style. His two recent releases with his main band, the J. D. Allen Trio, *I Am I Am* (2008) and *Shine!* (2009), have earned Allen a great deal of notice and praise from National Public Radio (NPR), allaboutjazz.com, the *New York Times*, and many other sources; NPR's "Take Five" segment named *Shine!* one of the top 10 jazz records of 2009. Allen's playing is high-spirited and powerful, and the relative shortness of his compositions—they average about four minutes each—separates him from the many jazz musicians who have embraced more drawn-out forms over the last few decades. After arriving in New York, in 1993, at the age of 20, Allen played with the venerable jazz vocalist Betty Carter and later joined the jazz group led by the drummer Cindy Blackman. During the time of those early successes, personal problems—caused or exacerbated by New York's many distractions—kept him from focusing on his work. With his recent albums, however, in the opinion of many jazz critics, he has begun to fulfill his potential.

John Daniel Allen 3d was born on December 11, 1972 in Detroit, Michigan, and raised primarily by his mother, Shirley. After Allen's birth his mother gave up her career as a professional singer to work as an administrator at an area hospital. In an interview with *Current Biography*, the source of quotes for this article unless otherwise noted, Allen said that he loved his father, though he was not around much, due largely to the unpredictable nature of his work—robbing banks. (He was eventually sent to prison and later released.) While growing up in Detroit's poor, majority-black east side, Allen and his two younger sisters were given singing lessons—usually involving Motown classics—by their mother, who was a tough disciplinarian. When he was seven or eight, he recalled, "I couldn't sing in tune. So my mother would always hit me in the mouth every time I would go flat." A few years later, having made little progress with his singing, Allen decided to give the clarinet a try. Because the family did not have much money, at one point his mother had to sell his instrument. Too embarrassed to tell his teacher what had happened, Allen skipped the music class at his public school; when he returned, the teacher told him that the only instrument available for him to play was an alto saxophone. Six months later Allen switched from that horn to the tenor saxophone, because, he said, "I figured, if I'm gonna have an instrument, I'm gonna have one bigger, so I can get noticed. I was pretty short. So I got the biggest thing

I could get that I could carry home. . . . I fell in love with it immediately."

Allen, who could not read music, would play by ear along with the symphonic music the school band was performing; for example, he would listen to a melody from the trumpet section and improvise a harmony. "You know," Allen's teacher told him, "there is a kind of music where you can improvise, and it's called jazz." That teacher helped Allen enroll in Northwestern High School, in Detroit, which had an excellent jazz program. One class, taught by the saxophonist James Carter—who would become a big name in the jazz world in the 1990s—was literally a school of hard knocks. For most of the week the students studied improvisation and played composed music. On Fridays there would be a test of sorts: the drummer and the bassist would play a rhythm, and everybody else in the class, one at a time, would have to improvise. "And if you didn't improvise [well]," Allen recalled, "then you got a punch in the chops. So everybody was trying to figure out what they were going to do by Friday so the classmates wouldn't jump him. It was kind of like a fraternity, now that I look back on it." A bad improvisation could lead Carter to exit the room, leaving the improviser vulnerable to the wrath of his classmates. (At the time Allen thought that his teacher's behavior was normal; in retrospect, although he laughed while telling the story, he called it negligent and illegal.) "But I got it together," he added. "Look, it wasn't politically correct at all. It was like, look man, we got the baddest band in the country, so you gotta play if you're up in here." Carter also served as Allen's mentor and unofficial music teacher outside school. After school or during weekends, Allen would go to Carter's house, and together they would listen to records by jazz artists—among them Frank Lowe, Albert Ayler, John Coltrane, and Sonny Rollins—as well as other artists, such as Jimi Hendrix and Frank Zappa.

After graduating from high school, in 1991, Allen studied music education at Hampton University, a historically black college in Hampton, Virginia. One day a friend of his sent a music tape—which featured Allen on saxophone—to the lauded jazz singer Betty Carter, who then invited both of them to participate in her Jazz Ahead program for young musicians. Allen went to New York City not expecting to stay, but Carter, who enjoyed helping talented young musicians to hone their skills, soon asked Allen to join her band.

Allen said that although he learned a lot during his time with Betty Carter, he did not take full advantage of her expertise and connections, and he missed many opportunities to improve as a musician and further his career. At the time he was 21 years old and "wild," as he has often described himself then. "Mentally I wasn't ready to be in New York City," he said. "I wanted to experience the life. I would stay up for two or three days just because I was afraid of missing something. I thought, sleep—I can't sleep. Everything is going

on 24 hours a day, and I tried to be part of *every 24 hours of that day*. I was more immersed in *the life* of being a musician than actually taking care of business—being better and making connections." Allen spent much of his time at the West Village jazz club Small's, often staying from nine in the evening until eight in the morning. After that he would sometimes go to the top of the Empire State Building and take in the view of Manhattan, or play pool, or hang out in the diamond district with his friends and "look at the ladies go by." After about two years of playing with Carter, he was fired. He understood why: in addition to staying up for days at a time, he drank a lot, so he would often feel tired during the sets. After running out of money, he went to Carter for a loan; instead, she offered him his job back. But after about six months, Allen and Carter's musical relationship "dissipated."

With his album *In Search Of . . .* (1999), Allen debuted as a leader. "That was a fluke," he said, laughing. "I don't know how that happened." (The album was recorded during what he called his "wild" period.) The trumpet player Fabio Morgera, a friend who had a connection at a record company, asked Allen if he wanted to record an album, and the saxophonist agreed. Steve Loewy, writing for allmusic.com, wrote that the songs—all but one of which Allen composed—are "surprisingly mature and memorable." Allen was happy to make the recording, but he ultimately thought it was "a failure"; still, he said, he can now hear the potential he displayed. That year Allen made a significant step in his career when he joined the band led by the jazz and rock drummer Cindy Blackman, best known for playing with the rocker Lenny Kravitz. Allen performed on three of Blackman's recordings and accompanied her on tour. Blackman taught Allen how to be a frontman and how to rehearse. Allen said that each rehearsal—which could last as long as six hours—was like a "laboratory," a setting in which to experiment and fine-tune arrangements. Blackman also insisted that the band perform live without sheet music; everyone had to memorize the songs. (To this day Allen and the musicians in his trio perform without sheet music.) Reviewing a Blackman concert for the *Washington Post* (February 20, 2001), Mike Joyce wrote that in Allen, Blackman had "found both a worthy collaborator and a cunning foil."

After about a year of playing with Blackman, Allen said, he "woke up" and changed his bad personal and professional habits. Soon afterward he began working on the album *Pharoah's Children* (2002), whose lineup included Orrin Evans on piano, Eric Revis on bass, and Gene Jackson on drums. Allen considered the record to be "a step in the right direction." The influences of John Coltrane and Sonny Rollins were obvious on the record, and Allen also borrowed from the "free jazz" approach of the avant-garde saxophonist/composer Ornette Coleman. At that point Allen did not want to have any single recognizable style. Paraphrasing a quote from the late martial artist and actor Bruce Lee, whom Allen greatly admires, the saxophonist said, "You have to be like water. Whatever the shape is of the container the water is in, that's what water becomes." David R. Adler, in his review of *Pharoah's Children* for allmusic.com, nonetheless observed that Allen is "clearly beginning to make significant, up-to-date statements of his own." Despite that success and some steady work, Allen still sometimes had financial trouble because, he said, he was "having too much fun." He was even homeless for a time, during which he slept on subway trains, at friends' houses, and at the jazz club Small's. "I still played," Allen said. "I kept myself together."

Thanks in part to the advice of a pastor, Allen made another turnaround: "I stopped believing the negativity about myself." He also drew inspiration from the work of other musicians. One of the qualities Allen admires in Coltrane is "the intensity and the intent behind his music. Of course, what he does technically, but also spiritually—for lack of a better word, an overused word today. *A Love Supreme* [Coltrane's influential 1965 album], listening to it for the first time, it seemed like it was music for a purpose."

Following his epiphany Allen toured and recorded with Blackman's band and played with Revis, Evans, the saxman David Murray, the bassists Ron Carter and Joseph Lepore, the drummers Jack DeJohnette and Marcus Gilmore, and others. In a review of a Brooklyn, New York, performance by a trio in which Allen led Lepore and Gilmore, Ben Ratliff wrote for the *New York Times* (May 20, 2005), "Allen has superb rhythm, and he plays eighth-note patterns with a fast, on-the-beat buoyancy; though there was some Coltrane in the improvised melodic material and the group's surging energy, the notes never came out husky or smeared. They were popping and on-the-beat, and more like Cannonball Adderley's, full and individuated." Allen also made a significant contribution to *November* (2008), a record by the highly regarded young trumpeter Jeremy Pelt, who had played on three tracks of *Pharoah's Children*.

As time passed Allen became more serious about recording as the leader of a sax-bass-drum trio, and he looked for musicians who wanted to help him develop a distinctive sound. *I Am I Am* (2008), the recording debut of the J. D. Allen Trio, with Gregg August on bass and Rudy Royston on drums, was met with much critical praise. In the studio, Allen recalled, he told August and Royston "not to play like they're relaxed. I didn't want any calm. I wanted it to be intense." The songs—energetic but focused—were mostly four or five minutes long. "And if you've listened to much serious jazz lately," Ratliff wrote for the *New York Times* (April 13, 2008), "that alone is a reason to be curious." Ratliff added: "Balanced somewhere between études and collective workouts, all the tracks contain nuggets of song, and Mr. Allen's even, balanced sound works through them with remarkable care, never revealing too much or stiffing

you on a good melody." The following year the J. D. Allen Trio released *Shine!* (2009), which brought Allen more attention and praise. That album, in his opinion, is stronger, wider in range, and more experimental than his previous record. On *Shine!* he sounds more confident, he said, because "I did exactly what I wanted to do. . . . Not that I don't care about listeners. But I'm sure that when an artist is painting something of value he doesn't care who buys it. He just does it." The songs on the album, most of them four minutes or shorter, were again dense and powerful. "I believe in getting to the point," Allen explained. "This brevity in solos squeezes the cream to the top," Mark Corroto wrote for allaboutjazz.com (June 7, 2009). "Still, the compact presentation never feels incomplete or abbreviated. Even the title track, a gentle ballad played wistfully, completes its pensiveness without lingering too long."

Two months after the album's release, the J. D. Allen Trio played at the Village Vanguard, a famous club, founded in 1935, where Coltrane, Rollins, the pianist Bill Evans, the saxophonist Dexter Gordon, and many other jazz greats played and recorded live albums. Prior to the show, nearly every story and listing announcing the event alluded to those icons, particularly Rollins, whose album *A Night at the Village Vanguard* (1957) featured a tenor saxophone, bass, and drums. Playing at the same venue with the same kind of lineup, Allen had a lot to live up to. "And judging by Tuesday night's set," Nate Chichen wrote in a review of the show for the *New York Times* (August 13, 2009), "Mr. Allen has found a way to address that legacy in his own voice, and on his own terms." Chichen also wrote, "The J. D. Allen Trio takes a fearless approach to a formidable tradition. It's a tenor saxophone trio, with bass and drums but no piano or guitar, which means that the burden of exposition falls squarely on the shoulders of its namesake bandleader." Under Allen's direction the band, as always, played without a set list. "I like to read the crowd," he explained. "When I get on the stage, I like to feel what's going on and act accordingly." Also as usual, Allen played without breaks between songs and did not announce the songs—not even to his bandmates. (Because they know the material so well, after a bar or two of his playing, they simply join in—or "fall in," as Allen put it.) Allen is used to playing 45- to 60-minute sets, but at the Village Vanguard he had to play for 75 minutes straight. To give the audience a bit of relief from his energy and speed, he played two ballads. Allen likes ballads including "Where Are You?" and "Stardust." (The latter is his favorite song.) "I think people are appreciative of the ballads once we get to them," he said. Comparing the rest of the set to working up a lather, he said that the ballads provide a "rinse." The trio performed at the Vanguard for a week. Allen recalled that at the end of the last show, he thought, "Wow. That was wild. I just played a whole week at the Vanguard with my own music, with my own band."

The following year, after a performance, Allen talked with a photographer who mentioned knowing Ornette Coleman, one of Allen's musical idols. Soon Allen and Coleman had a phone conversation, and Allen later went to Coleman's home, in Midtown Manhattan, where he spent six hours with the jazz legend. "He said, 'I'm going to give you something that's not gonna make you sound like a saxophone player.' He gave me three chords . . . and we played around with that. When he said, play it in this key, now play it in this key, I realized that this isn't a man with a random thought. This is a man with a plan." Meeting Coleman gave Allen a greater appreciation of the older musician's experimentation. "It was one of the most intense experiences of my life," Allen said about the meeting. "It was so intense, I had to leave. I was dizzy." His meeting with Coleman inspired Allen to write several songs, some of which he plans to record.

With his trio Allen is currently working on an album, tentatively titled "Victory," that he expects to be released in early 2011. He is also planning to work on a project with two bassists, a drummer, and a pianist, a lineup he would like to take to the Village Vanguard. In addition, he hopes to write film scores.

Allen lives in the New York City borough of Brooklyn.

—D.K.

Suggested Reading: allaboutjazz.com Feb. 27, 2010; allmusic.com; *New York Times* E p4 May 20, 2005, (on-line) Apr. 13, 2008, Aug. 13, 2009; npr.org Aug. 12, 2009, Dec. 6, 2009

Selected Albums: *In Search Of . . .* , 1999; *Pharoah's Children*, 2002; *I Am I Am*, 2008; *Shine!*, 2009

Frederick M. Brown/Getty Images

Anderson, Chris

July 9, 1961– Magazine editor; writer

Address: Wired, *520 Third St., #305, San Francisco, CA 94107-6805*

Few magazines cover the world of technology the way *Wired* does. Not surprisingly, *Wired* carries stories about such technology giants as Apple and Google, networking services including Facebook and Twitter, and such high-tech gadgets as touch-screen phones and digital cameras; what makes those stories unusual, though, is their analysis not only of the technology but of how it relates to our world and why it is important. Recent stories in *Wired* have also looked into such topics as how inmates in U.S. prisons managed to get access to cell phones; why placebos seem to be getting more effective (information of particular interest to drug companies); and how multitasking, with or without computers, befogs our brains. Since 2001 Chris Anderson has been the editor in chief of *Wired*, whose Web site gets 120 million page views per month. (Although Anderson wrote for *Science* and *Nature* magazines before covering business and technology for the *Economist* from 1994 to 2001, he was hired at *Wired* not only because of his professional experience—but also because of his personal history: his having joined a punk band as a college dropout in his 20s helped him form a bond with officials at *Wired*'s parent company, Condé Nast Publications.) In addition to making *Wired* more accessible to mainstream readers, Anderson has won several National Magazine Awards and authored two best-selling books—*The Long Tail: Why the Future of Business Is Selling Less of More* (2006) and *Free: The Future of a Radical Price* (2009)—in the process becoming an acknowledged (albeit occasionally controversial) guru of the digital age.

Chris W. Anderson was born in London, England, on July 9, 1961. When he was five years old, his family moved to the United States, settling in Washington, D.C., when Anderson was eight. His family had roots in the U.S.: Anderson's great-grandfather Jo Labadie was one of the founders of the American anarchist movement in the late 19th century; his grandfather Fred Hauser, who invented the automatic-sprinkler system, had a workshop in Los Angeles, California, where Anderson spent summers as a boy; and his father, Jim Anderson, who came from Wisconsin, worked for the U.S. Army's newspaper in La Rochelle, France, during the Korean War, and continued to work as a journalist in Europe until the 1960s. In 1998 Anderson's mother, Carlotta, published a biography of her grandfather, *All-American Anarchist: Joseph A. Labadie and the Labor Movement.*

After failing his college courses, Anderson dropped out and found work as a bike messenger in Washington. At night he performed as a member of a punk band called R.E.M., which, unbeknownst to its members, had the same name as another group. In 1982, when Anderson and his bandmates were making their first recording, their producer told them about the other R.E.M., from Athens, Georgia. The owner of the well-known 9:30 Club, a Washington music venue, invited both groups to participate in a battle-of-the-bands in which the winner would get to keep the name R.E.M.—and rename the loser. Winning a coin toss, Anderson's band performed first and, as he noted on his blog, longtail.com, "played a killer set" and "got a lot of applause." After the performance the band members sat drinking at the bar as the group from Athens took the stage. From the first song on, Anderson wrote, the other R.E.M. played an "incredible set," winning the competition. Mike Mills, the bass player of the victorious R.E.M., gave Anderson's group the name "Egoslavia." (In 2007 the group that retained the name "R.E.M.," led by Michael Stipe, was inducted into the Rock and Roll Hall of Fame.)

Anderson later went back to college to study physics. He received a B.S. degree from George Washington University, in Washington, D.C., and then studied quantum mechanics and science journalism at the University of California at Berkeley. During those years he worked at the Los Alamos National Laboratory, in New Mexico, soon realizing that writing about science and technology held more appeal for him. Anderson next moved back to Washington and found work as a technology reporter, starting at *Nature* in 1988 and moving on to *Science.* In 1994 he left Washington and became a writer for the *Economist,* a prestigious British weekly, where he held a variety of positions, including technology editor and U.S. business editor. During his seven years with the magazine, he worked in London, New York City, and Hong Kong, China.

At the age of 39, Anderson accepted the position of editor in chief at *Wired,* starting his duties in the summer of 2001. (*Wired* was founded in 1993 by the journalist Louis Rossetto, the editor John Battelle, and the businesswoman Jane Metcalfe.) During the first few months of 2000, the Internet-technology "bubble"—whose epicenter was the San Francisco Bay Area—had burst, and matters had not improved by 2001; given that *Wired*'s focus was digital-technology innovation, Anderson had taken the magazine's reins at a tough time. But it was soon apparent that he had a vision for *Wired*: to make the magazine accessible to intelligent lay

readers as well as computer and technology "nerds." Anderson reasoned that since technology—ubiquitous in music, movies, cars, gadgets, military operations, medicine, education, and many other areas—affected nearly everyone, the number of potential new readers was enormous. As Stephanie Clifford wrote for the *New York Times* (May 18, 2009), Anderson "expanded *Wired*'s coverage from fringe technology to daily-life technology." Soon Anderson was winning praise and awards, most notably the National Magazine Award in various categories in every year from 2001 through 2009, except 2003. After winning the editor-of-the-year award from *Advertising Age* (October 17, 2005), Anderson was praised by the magazine's writer Scott Donaton for "his drive to reinvent and revive *Wired,* elevating the magazine to its rightful role as The Essential (Don't Even Think of Missing an Issue) Guide to the Digital Age."

For the October 2004 issue of *Wired,* Anderson wrote an article that he would later expand into a best-selling book. The article, "The Long Tail," opened with an anecdote: "In 1988, a British mountain climber named Joe Simpson wrote a book called *Touching the Void,* a harrowing account of near death in the Peruvian Andes. It got good reviews but, only a modest success, it was soon forgotten. Then, a decade later, a strange thing happened. Jon Krakauer wrote *Into Thin Air,* another book about a mountain-climbing tragedy, which became a publishing sensation. Suddenly *Touching the Void* started to sell again. Random House rushed out a new edition to keep up with demand. Booksellers began to promote it next to their *Into Thin Air* displays, and sales rose further. A revised paperback edition . . . spent 14 weeks on the *New York Times* bestseller list. That same month, IFC Films released a docudrama of the story to critical acclaim. Now *Touching the Void* outsells *Into Thin Air* more than two to one. What happened? In short, Amazon.com recommendations. The online bookseller's software noted patterns in buying behavior and suggested that readers who liked *Into Thin Air* would also like *Touching the Void.* People took the suggestion, agreed wholeheartedly, wrote rhapsodic reviews. More sales, more algorithm-fueled recommendations, and the positive feedback loop kicked in. Particularly notable is that when Krakauer's book hit shelves, Simpson's was nearly out of print. A few years ago, readers of Krakauer would never even have learned about Simpson's book—and if they had, they wouldn't have been able to find it. Amazon changed that. It created the *Touching the Void* phenomenon by combining infinite shelf space with real-time information about buying trends and public opinion. The result: rising demand for an obscure book." Anderson's point was that "assumptions about popular taste are actually artifacts of poor supply-and-demand matching." Anderson explained that there is now, thanks to the Internet, a new economy: it is driven by information about, rather than ignorance of, potential demand, and is based not on scarcity but on abundance. Actual stores, such as Blockbuster Video, Virgin Megastore, and Barnes & Noble, however big they may be, are still limited by the economics of space: it is too costly to stock titles that do not sell reasonably well. By contrast, such services as Netflix, Amazon, and iTunes can offer a seemingly infinite selection.

Anderson challenged the assumption that "if something isn't a hit"—whether the "something" is a book, song, or movie—"it won't make money." To illustrate his point he cited the example of bookstores. "The average Barnes & Noble carries 130,000 titles," he wrote. "Yet more than half of Amazon's book sales come from *outside* its top 130,000 titles. Consider the implication: If the Amazon statistics are any guide, the market for books that are not even sold in the average bookstore is larger than the market for those that are. In other words, the potential book market may be twice as big as it appears to be, if only we can get over the economics of scarcity." Companies and services that have gotten over the "economics of scarcity"—Netflix, Amazon, and iTunes—make a significant percentage of their profits from what Anderson called "the long tail," an extraordinarily large number of products outside the mainstream. Therefore, a company can maximize its profits, according to Anderson, by selling or renting products or providing services from every point on the popularity spectrum, from the wildly popular to the highly obscure.

The publication of *The Long Tail: Why the Future of Business Is Selling Less of More* (2006) brought a lot of attention and debate. Anderson was both praised for illuminating the ramifications of a seemingly simple idea and criticized for trying to apply the idea too broadly. Many reviewers agreed with Lorne Manly, who wrote for the *New York Times* (August 10, 2006) that "Anderson's thesis suffers at times from overextending itself," attempting to encompass areas as disparate as national security and gang violence. Echoing many other critics, Tim Wu pointed out in his review for *Slate* (July 21, 2006) that Anderson's overreaching weakened his theory, which applies mainly to e-commerce and entertainment—particularly, Wu wrote, to businesses "1) where the price of carrying additional inventory approaches zero and 2) where consumers have strong and heterogeneous preferences." Despite—or because of—Anderson's broad application of his theory, *The Long Tail* became a best-seller. Manly wrote that like *The Tipping Point*, by Malcolm Gladwell, "Mr. Anderson's book does an excellent job of spotting trends and fitting them into an easily accessible theoretical framework that helps explain the changing culture around us."

In his next book, *Free: The Future of a Radical Price* (2009), Anderson argued that technology has made the cost of storing and transmitting digital text, audio files, video, photos, and software so low

that it can be done successfully for free. "Despite its subtitle, the book is less about the future than the present and recent past, which Anderson surveys in a cheerful, can-do voice," Virginia Postrel wrote for the *New York Times* (July 12, 2009). Postrel went on to quote Anderson: "People are making lots of money charging nothing. Not nothing for everything, but nothing for enough that we have essentially created an economy as big as a good-sized country around the price of $0.00." Providers of goods and services can make profits, Anderson suggested, through what he called a "freemium" strategy. For example, Web sites such as Yahoo! Mail offer a free service with ads as well as a paid, premium service without ads; and musicians, accepting that people will try to get their music online for free, simply give it away, using it to promote concerts and merchandise. "Indeed," Rob Pegoraro wrote for the *Washington Post* (July 26, 2009), "a good chunk of what [Anderson] advocates has nothing to do with giving products away and everything to do with shifting costs to interested parties who have better reasons to pay. But *Cost-Shifted* doesn't make for as catchy a title as *Free*."

Free received mixed, largely negative reviews. Malcolm Gladwell, the author of the best-sellers *The Tipping Point* (2000), *Blink* (2005), and *Outliers* (2008), had praised Anderson (for the "Big Idea" expressed in *The Long Tail*) in a short piece for the April 30, 2007 issue of *Time*, in which Anderson was named one of "The *Time* 100." Two years later, reviewing *Free* for the *New Yorker* (July 6, 2009), Gladwell acknowledged that Anderson's "advice is pithy, his tone uncompromising, and his subject matter perfectly timed for a moment when old-line providers are desperate for answers." Still, he attacked Anderson's "insistence that the relentless downward pressure on prices represents an iron law of the digital economy. Why is it a law? Free is just another price, and prices are set by individual actors, in accordance with the aggregated particulars of marketplace power."

Gladwell did not deny the power of free products to attract people. Indeed, he pointed to a study—which Anderson mentioned in his book—conducted by the behavioral economist Dan Ariely, the author of *Predictably Irrational* (2009), in which, when Ariely offered his subjects Lindt truffles for 15 cents each and Hershey's Kisses for one cent each, three-quarters of the subjects chose the truffles; but when Ariely dropped the price of both chocolates by one cent, thereby making the truffles 14 cents and the kisses free, 69 percent of the participants chose the kisses. Still, the issue, as it relates to Anderson's book, was not people's attraction to free products but the ability to parlay that attraction into profit. Accordingly, Gladwell pointed ed out what he saw as flaws in Anderson's argument that many companies can make money by giving away much of their content. The video-sharing Web site YouTube, for example, allows users to upload and watch video content for free, but the site is losing hundreds of millions of dollars per year—not because people are not watching the videos, but because it is hard to persuade advertisers to associate their products with videos that are often of very low quality or otherwise objectionable. Furthermore, the cost of streaming hundreds of millions of videos is not negligible. Gladwell noted, "An estimated seventy-five billion videos will be served up by YouTube this year. Although . . . the cost of serving up each video is 'close enough to free to round down,' 'close enough to free' multiplied by seventy-five billion is still a very large number."

As he did in *The Long Tail*, Anderson expanded his principle beyond the digital world. Genetic engineering, he argued, will allow the pharmaceutical industry to sell drugs at ever-lower prices. "The expensive part of making drugs has never been what happens in the laboratory," Gladwell countered. "It's what happens after the laboratory, like the clinical testing, which can take years and cost hundreds of millions of dollars. In the pharmaceutical world, what's more, companies have chosen to use the potential of new technology to do something very different from their counterparts in Silicon Valley. They've been trying to find a way to serve smaller and smaller markets—to create medicines tailored to very specific subpopulations and strains of diseases—and smaller markets often mean higher prices."

Around the time that *Free* was published, a controversy broke out when the *Virginia Quarterly Review* blogger Waldo Jaquith discovered that various parts of Anderson's new book had been taken from the on-line encyclopedia Wikipedia without attributions. After being alerted to the situation, Anderson made a well-publicized apology, explaining that he and his publisher had not been able to agree on a method of citation and that the lack of attributions had resulted from late revisions of the book. A copy of *Free* later posted on Google Books includes attributions.

The September 2010 issue of *Wired* featured an article titled "The Web Is Dead. Long Live the Internet," co-written by Anderson and Michael Wolff. The difference between the Web and the Internet, the authors noted, is "not a trivial distinction." They continued, "Over the past few years, one of the most important shifts in the digital world has been the move from the wide-open Web to semiclosed platforms [such as Facebook] that use the Internet for transport but not the browser for display. It's driven primarily by the rise of the iPhone model of mobile computing, and it's a world Google can't crawl, one where HTML doesn't rule. And it's the world that consumers are increasingly choosing, not because they're rejecting the idea of the Web but because these dedicated platforms often just work better or fit better into their lives (the screen comes to them, they don't have to go to the screen). The fact that it's easier for companies to make money on these platforms only cements the trend."

Anderson is the non-executive chairman and a shareholder of BookTour, which he co-founded in 1997; BookTour offers a free directory of readings, tours, and other events involving writers. (In 2009 Amazon bought a minority share in the company.) Anderson is also the founder of DIY Drones and 3D Robotics, a company that makes robotics equipment. Anderson noted in a disclosure on longtail.com, "I am, unavoidably, conflicted because I live in the world I write about. I have friends, sometimes close, in many of the companies I discuss. I've run brainstorming sessions for some of them and spoken at others. Although I own no shares in any company mentioned on this blog, the book, or *Wired* Magazine (aside from [BookTour and DIY Drones and 3D Robotics]), I do speak for hire. . . . When I feel that my connection to a company, whether through a friendship or a business relationship, risks coloring my judgment as an editor, I usually recuse myself from that story. (I do so with Amazon, for instance.) When it risks doing the same as a writer, I try not to write about the company at all. But there are plenty of examples, such as Google, Yahoo! or eBay, where this is not possible—I can't avoid writing about them nor can I not associate with their people (let that be a disclosure, then; I have friends at all three). I frankly don't know what to do about that. The list of my potential and real conflicts is impossibly long and I find it arbitrary to only list the conflicts that involve money (such as a paid speaking gig), since the friendships are much more likely to influence me."

Anderson lives in Berkeley, California, with his wife and five children.

—D.K.

Suggested Reading: longtail.com; *New Yorker* p78 July 6, 2009; *San Francsico Chronicle* B p1 Apr. 12, 2001; *Slate.com* July 21, 2006; *wired.com*

Selected Books: *The Long Tail: Why the Future of Business Is Selling Less of More*, 2006; *Free: The Future of a Radical Price*, 2009

Arellano, Gustavo

Feb. 3, 1979– Journalist; columnist

Address: OC Weekly, 1666 N. Main St., Suite 500, Santa Ana, CA 92701

"In a way, it's scary that Mexicans still remain such a mystery, such an exotic species, to so many people," the journalist and writer Gustavo Arellano told Sam McManis for the *Sacramento (California) Bee* (October 19, 2007). "I could either weep and moan about how misunderstood we are or I could do something about it and have fun." Arellano opt-

Michael Buckner/Getty Images

Gustavo Arellano

vember 29, 2007). Arellano has said that whenever "¡Ask a Mexican!" enters a new market, it takes time for readers to get used to his sense of humor. "I know how the reaction goes: Hate, puzzlement, calls and letters to the newspaper, meetings with the editors, and then eventually, people settle down and start reading the column," he told Steffen. "And more often than not, I'm able to convert those people into being fans of the column." "A movie director told me, 'You can be the next Cantinflas,'" he told Mireya Navarro for the *New York Times* (June 24, 2007), referring to the Mexican comic icon Mario Moreno (1911–93). "I just said 'No, no, you're missing the point. This is satire. Outrageousness mixed in with jarring truth.'" In August 2010 Arellano was named the *OC Weekly*'s managing editor.

Arellano is a *Los Angeles Times* contributing editor and the author of two books: *¡Ask a Mexican!* (2007), a compilation of his columns, and *Orange County: A Personal History* (2008), which blends reminiscence with history and sociology. He earned the Association of Alternative Newsweeklies Award for the best column in a large-circulation weekly in 2006, the Presidents Award from the Los Angeles Press Club in 2007, and, in 2008, both the Impact Award from the National Hispanic Media Coalition and the Latino Spirit Award from the California Latino Legislative Caucus. He was the keynote speaker at the commencement ceremony of the University of California–Los Angeles (UCLA) College of Letters and Science in June 2010.

The first of four children, Gustavo Arellano was born to Lorenzo Arellano and Maria De La Luz Arellano on February 3, 1979 in Anaheim, a city in Orange County, California, which borders Los Angeles County to the south. He has two sisters, Elsa and Alejandrina; Elsa is a high-school administrator. His brother, Gabriel, is about 10 years his junior. Arellano's paternal grandfather and great-grandfather were born in Mexico and spent portions of their lives working in Orange County, beginning around 1918. At that time, Arellano wrote in his book *Orange County*, "many restaurants barred Mexicans from entering; there were [separate] restrooms for Mexicans and whites. In the orange groves, the few white pickers always received better pay and tools than the Mexicans. Once, my grandfather and his friends tried to enter a movie theater, only to be chased out by the manager because they were Mexican." Arellano's father, a truck driver, was also born in Mexico; in 1968 he crossed the border into the U.S. illegally, hiding in the trunk of a car. He was granted amnesty in 1986, thanks to a provision of the federal Immigration Control and Reform Act of that year. Arellano's mother, who was also born in Mexico and had relatives in California, arrived in the U.S. when she was 12. Her schooling ended with ninth grade. Thereafter she worked as a strawberry picker before taking a job in a tomato-canning facility. For his first 10 years, Gustavo lived with his family in

ed for the latter alternative, and about a year and a half after he joined the *OC Weekly*, as a reporter and food critic, he launched "¡Ask a Mexican!," a column that offers answers to readers' questions regarding Mexican people and culture. His first column for the *OC Weekly*, an alternative newspaper based in Orange County, California, appeared on November 11, 2004. It was meant as a joke—Arellano, who is of Mexican descent, supplied the question, "Why do Mexicans call white people gringos?," as well as the answer. The column quickly caught on, and readers began submitting their queries. Nearly six years later, "¡Ask a Mexican!" appears in some 40 newspapers, with a combined circulation of more than two million. "I'm still astounded," Arellano told McManis. "We really expected the column just to be an [Orange County] thing. I never thought any other newspaper would have the guts to carry it." Arellano is a much-in-demand guest on TV and radio talk and news shows, among them the *Today* show, *Nightline*, *The Situation with Tucker Carlson*, *The Colbert Report*, and National Public Radio's *On the Media*.

Using sarcasm, satire, and biting humor as well as solid facts to debunk Mexican stereotypes, Arellano has courted controversy from the start. He is not averse to using racial slurs, and each installment runs alongside a cartoon portrait of a sombrero-wearing, mustachioed Mexican—a crude caricature many of Arellano's detractors have mentioned when speaking out against the column. "I'm trying to reappropriate that image to castrate it of its power, publish it again and again and again until people no longer see that as a Mexican," Arellano told Suzi Steffen for the *Eugene (Oregon) Weekly* (No-

La Fabrica, a poor neighborhood near the railroad tracks in Anaheim. He has often likened his experience to that of a child growing up in Mexico, since there were so few white people around. "We didn't have to go outside of our little enclave to experience Mexican culture," he told Daniel Hernandez for the *Los Angeles Times* (February 23, 2006). Through hard work his parents saved enough to buy a three-bedroom house with a backyard swimming pool in a more prosperous section of Anaheim. "No one in our family has ever viewed ourselves as victims," he told Gwendolyn Driscoll for the *Orange County Register* (May 1, 2007).

As a child Arellano developed a love for reading, and by the time he reached Anaheim High School, he had earned the nickname "Nerdo." One of his favorite pastimes was reading biographies of notable Americans, and he dreamed of becoming a history professor at Harvard University, in Cambridge, Massachusetts. He graduated from high school in 1997, then attended Chapman University, a private school in Anaheim, where he earned a B.A. degree in film studies in 2001. "I have no love lost for Chapman University, . . . for which I have no respect since President Jim Doti doesn't give a s**t about letting a free press do its job," he wrote for an *OC Weekly* blog (February 6, 2009), referring to the campus newspaper. As an undergraduate he joined the student group MEChA (Chicano Student Movement of Aztlán), propelled by his fury regarding the plan of an Anaheim police officer, Harold Martin, to "sue Mexico for $50 million for the cost of educating the children of illegal immigrants . . . ," as he wrote in *Orange County*. "I encountered some extremist rhetoric at my first MEChA meeting at Chapman—wild ideas such as increasing Latino enrollment on our minority-deficient campus and mentoring at-risk high school students. All the hype about MEChA as the storm troopers for the coming Reconquista [the forced return to Mexico of Texas and other formerly Mexican territory] was gibberish." Also while at Chapman Arellano began reading the *OC Weekly*, a sister newspaper of the *LA Weekly* and the *Village Voice*; launched in 1995, the award-winning weekly is free and generates income from advertising. Arellano sent suggestions for stories to Will Swaim, the founding editor and then-publisher. Swaim liked Arellano's ideas and suggested that he try writing articles himself. Arellano began to do so at around the time he enrolled in the graduate program in Latin American studies at UCLA, where he earned a master's degree in 2003.

After he completed his formal education, Arellano joined the *OC Weekly* as a full-time food critic and investigative reporter, writing on a wide range of topics, including immigration. In November 2003 his editors asked him to cover a sex-abuse scandal involving the Catholic Diocese of Orange County. Arellano had been raised in the Roman Catholic faith, and the assignment triggered a crisis of conscience. "To think, let alone write, anything remotely negative about the church, I felt, would be as serious a sin as adultery," he said in a report for the National Public Radio (NPR) program *Day by Day* (June 14, 2004). Arellano prayed for a sign, and one day a person who had been sexually abused by a Catholic priest came into the newspaper office with a stack of confidential documents. "I knew what I had to do," Arellano told NPR. "I've penned damaging story after damaging story on the Orange County Diocese since. I've written about cover-ups, I've interviewed police officers who complained that their investigations were hampered by uncooperative priests and I've talked to sex abuse survivors whose own parishes ignore their pain." On the strength of Arellano's investigations, the *OC Weekly* revealed that Tod D. Brown, the bishop of the Roman Catholic Diocese of Orange County, had failed to report molestation charges leveled against him and two other priests. Many more cases of abuse and subsequent failures to act upon them later came to light. "I continue to believe in Jesus, Mary and the saints, but I stopped attending Mass around the time I latched onto the Orange diocese sex-abuse scandal in 2004," Arellano wrote for the *OC Weekly* (December 27, 2007). "I couldn't stand praying among county Catholics since they haven't yet overthrown the amoral hierarchy of Bishop Tod D. Brown." (In 2005 the diocese paid $100 million to settle 90 reported cases of sexual abuse. Bishop Brown has kept his post.)

One day early in November 2004, while Arellano and Swaim were driving together, they passed a billboard advertising Eduardo Sotelo's radio show. Arellano was amazed that Swaim had never heard of Sotelo, a disc jockey known as "Piolin" or "Tweety Bird," who has a huge Latino following. The ensuing conversation led to the idea for "¡Ask a Mexican!," a column in which Arellano would answer questions about Mexican culture. For the first column, published on November 11, 2004, which was intended as a joke, Arellano posed the question "Why do Mexicans call white people gringos?" His answer was that Mexicans do not use that word; rather, they call white people "*gabachos*," a slightly more cutting ethnic slur (although, he noted in his column of June 11, 2009, "in the grand Rolodex of Racism, *gabacho* is as soft a jab as calling someone a scoundrel"). He concluded the column—which was accompanied by a cartoon portrait of a stereotypical, overweight Mexican man, complete with sombrero, black mustache, five-o'clock shadow, toothy smile, and gold tooth—with the line, "Hey, got a spicy question about Mexicans? Ask a Mexican." "We knew we'd get some reaction because the logo for the column is the grossest stereotype of a Mexican," he told McManis. "But people went crazy about it, both in a good way and bad way. What we didn't expect, though, was for people to actually start sending in questions about Mexicans. They called us on our bluff." Arellano began to develop a signature style for answering questions. He would offer statistics to back up many of his points, while commenting in an ironic, satirical tone on the racist attitudes inherent in many of the questions. "The people who write in—they have this preconceived notion of what a Mexican is," Arellano told Hernandez. "I answer their question, but in a way that's either going to flip the stereotype or going to explode it." When one reader asked (February 3, 2005) why Mexicans always sell oranges on the side of California freeways, Arellano responded, "What do you want them to sell—Steinways?" In response to a question (December 8, 2005) concerning Mexican people's penchant for displaying paintings of the Virgin of Guadalupe—the Virgin Mary, as an image of her is said to have appeared on a Mexican peasant's cloak in 1531—Arellano wrote, "We can display our saints as comfortably in a cathedral as we do on hubcaps."

For a while "¡Ask a Mexican!" puzzled many readers in Orange County, a politically conservative area where immigration is a major issue. "Satire is the hardest form of humor to do," Arellano told McManis. "After a couple of months in Orange County, the column became accepted." He added, "I already had been an investigative reporter at the paper, and you have to have a thick skin. One of the issues I covered was immigration, so I was used to anti-immigrant, Orange County whack jobs leaving me rambling messages. In doing the column, I was ready for all the hate coming my way. As long as people are reading, I'm doing my job." In March 2006 Village Voice Media announced that Arellano had signed a syndication deal, paving the way for "¡Ask a Mexican!" to run in newspapers across the country. By that time Arellano had already been featured in the *Los Angeles Times* and on NBC's *Today* show, and he had been a guest commentator on a number of radio programs. Driscoll described Arellano's columns as "sarcastic yet erudite, salted with at least one obscure pop-cultural reference and typically involving the frequent and ripe use of invective." Some columns included the term "wetback," a derogatory word that refers to Mexican immigrants. "As a journalist, free speech is very important to me, and I'm all for people using whatever words they may want to use," Arellano told Kerry Lengel for the *Arizona Republic* (July 8, 2007). "That said, they better be prepared to deal with the repercussions."

As "¡Ask a Mexican!" began to appear in more newspapers—as of mid-2010, it ran in 39 publications—Arellano received growing numbers of angry letters, many from readers who accused him of being racist. In Eugene, Oregon, a city where the column caused a big stir (though fewer than 5 percent of its residents identify themselves as being of Mexican origin), a member of the local human-rights community charged that Arellano's work "is based upon purposely exploiting the dominant culture's racial cruel streak," according to Steffen. Carmine Urbina, a Latina political activist, wrote to the editors of the *Eugene Weekly* complaining about Arellano's use of the term "*un nopal en la frente*," which Mexicans living in the U.S. use to describe those immigrants who have very recently crossed the border or who look stereotypically Mexican or have stereotypically Mexican attitudes. (In English it means "a prickly-pear cactus growing from the forehead.") "Reading this column, seeing those words, do you know what this means?" Urbina wrote, as quoted by Camilla Mortensen in the *Eugene Weekly* (December 6, 2007). "It hits to the core of demeaning stereotypes." In addressing such accusations, Arellano said people living in other cities—including those with large Latin American populations, such as El Paso, Texas—had responded similarly to his columns, but that once readers adjusted to his style of humor, they tended to become fans. "The column, it's really multifaceted," he told Steffen. "It's combating hate, providing a forum for people to learn about Mexicans and attempting to really destroy the Mexican of the American imagination. We're not all rapist-criminals, but we're also not all saints. We're humans like everybody else. We have the good, the bad, the goofy, and I want to talk about all of that."

The column's popularity earned Arellano a book contract (reportedly worth a six-figure amount) with Scribner Publishing. *¡Ask a Mexican!*, a compilation of his columns, was published in 2007. His second book, *Orange County: A Personal History*, appeared the next year. In a glowing review for *Aztlán: A Journal of Chicano Studies* (Fall 2009), Richard T. Rodriguez, an associate professor of English and Latina/Latino studies at the University of Illinois at Urbana-Champaign, wrote, "Arellano's book provides a witty and illuminating history of Latinos, including his own family, in Orange County, California, over the past one hundred years. . . . *Orange County* is scholarly in its precise approach to research. It is also elegantly written and a pleasure to read." The author "paints a vivid picture of the composite and often contradictory reality that was, and continues to be, Orange County . . . ," Rodriguez continued. "Arellano names names, cites statistics, and exposes the discrepancies behind Orange County's grossly generalized image." That image has been presented in various television shows, among them *The Real Housewives of Orange County*, *The O.C.*, and *Laguna Beach: The Real Orange County*; Arellano discussed those programs in a chapter called "The 'Real' Real Orange County Reel, or: About Those Stupid Television Shows, Why Orange County Is 'Hip,' and What's Really Real and What's Somewhat Real—for Real!" Rodriguez concluded, "In a moment when, as Arellano notes, more minorities than whites occupy the space of Orange County, it is indeed time to 'wake up and smell the tacos, *cabrones*'"—using a word that means "male goat" and is used as a slur.

In 2005, in recognition of a piece he wrote about a veteran of the Iraq War, Arellano was named a finalist for the PEN USA Literary Awards for Journalism. That same year he was a finalist for the "best public-service article" prize at the Maggie Awards—an honor that stemmed from his coverage of the Catholic Church scandals. In 2006 "¡Ask a Mexican!" won the Association of Alternative Weeklies prize for best column. It won again in 2008, and Arellano hosted the awards ceremony. In the fall 2010 semester, he began teaching a new course, called "History of the Chicano—The Mexican OC," at the California State University at Fullerton.

Arellano has been described as a quick-witted self-promoter. "He's a very ambitious guy, and I mean that in the best sense of the word," Will Swaim told Gwendolyn Driscoll. "He told me early on: I want to make a difference in the world." A one-time homophobe, Arellano now supports gay rights and has urged others to "learn from him" regarding attitudes toward homosexuals, Richard Rodriguez wrote. Arellano shared a room with his brother in his parents' house until he was 27, when he moved in with a friend in Santa Ana, California. He admits to having a poor grasp of Spanish, despite its being his primary language until kindergarten. In many of his columns, he has asserted that Mexicans will eventually assimilate into American culture—providing as one piece of evidence the fact that his father, a former illegal immigrant, now favors stricter immigration laws. "If that's not assimilation, I don't know what it is," he told David Puente for *ABC News Now* (May 3, 2007). "Assimilation in this country has never been pretty," he told Steffen, adding that he understands why some people fear the growing influence of Mexicans in the U.S. "There is going to be curiosity; there is going to be skepticism. As a member of the 'invading army,' I can tell people: Look, it's going to be OK."

—K.J.P.

Suggested Reading: *Los Angeles Times* A p1 Feb. 23, 2006, E p1 May 19, 2007; *New York Times* ST p1+ June 24, 2007; (Orange County, California) *OC Weekly* Dec. 27, 2007; *Orange County (California) Register* May 1, 2007; *Sacramento (California) Bee* Oct. 19, 2007; Arellano, Gustavo. *Orange County: A Personal History*, 2008

Selected Books: *¡Ask a Mexican!*, 2007; *Orange County: A Personal History*, 2008

Arena, Bruce

Sep. 21, 1951– Soccer coach

Address: Los Angeles Galaxy, Home Depot Ctr., 18400 Avalon Blvd., Carson, CA 90746

In January 2010 Bruce Arena was elected to the U.S. National Soccer Hall of Fame, an honor recognizing him as one of the most successful soccer coaches in the nation's history. A veteran of college, professional, and international play, Arena headed the soccer program—and carved out a stellar record—during 18 seasons at the University of Virginia, beginning in the late 1970s. He skippered U.S. national men's teams through Olympic competition in 1996 and two World Cup tournaments, in 2002 and 2006, and he has coached three teams in Major League Soccer (MLS), which has twice named him Coach of the Year. Through it all Arena has demonstrated his belief in the potential of U.S.-born players, in contrast to coaches who make a habit of recruiting foreign athletes, and he has contributed substantially to soccer's growing popularity in the U.S.

Nearly as well-known as Arena's coaching success is his reputation for saying what he thinks. "One of the ways Bruce deals with people is to challenge people, and he often does that by being sarcastic," Bob Bradley, an assistant under Arena at Virginia and the current coach of the U.S. men's soccer team, told John Jeansonne for *Newsday* (December 12, 1995). "He puts heat on people. He picks on people a little bit." Claudio Reyna, who played under Arena in the 1990s, said to Ronald

Otto Greule Jr./Getty Images

Blum for the Cincinnati *Enquirer* (June 1, 2002, online) about the Brooklyn-born coach, "He says what's on his mind. He doesn't hold back anything. He still has that brash New York attitude. That's never left him." Since 2008 Arena has served as the coach and general manager of the Los Angeles Galaxy, which competed in the 2009 MLS championship final.

ARENA

Bruce Arena was born on September 21, 1951 in Brooklyn, New York, and raised in Franklin Square, on Long Island, New York. He has two older brothers, Paul and Mike; his twin sister, Barbara, died of cancer. Arena's father, Vincent, was a butcher, and his mother, Adeline, drove a school bus. Arena began playing sports at an early age. "Our view of things those days was pretty simple," he told Michael Lewis for the Web site ENYSoccer.com (June 16, 2004). "Give me a ball, a baseball bat, a glove and I'll be back in about eight or 10 hours. We didn't need any of the [video] games, the computers and that kind of stuff. . . . Everyday was fun, hanging out with the guys in the neighborhood, playing games." His older brothers played quarterback on the football team at Frank Carey High School. For one year Arena, too, played quarterback at the school, but he was too small to make the varsity team. "I was 5-2 and 100 pounds," Arena recalled to John Jeansonne. "That's how I became a soccer player." After his freshman year Arena began playing lacrosse and soccer and excelled at both sports. In soccer he started out as a midfielder but soon replaced the goalie, who was suspended from competition for a season after hitting an opposing player. During that time Arena joined a youth team run by Hota, a club in the German-American Soccer League (now the Cosmopolitan League). "I picked up the game far too late. I was 15, and you can't start at 15 and hope to compete [at the top level]," Arena told Clive Gammon for Sports Illustrated (November 8, 1982). "But I was a good athlete. . . . I was born too early for soccer [in the U.S.]."

Arena graduated from high school in 1969 and spent two years at Nassau Community College (NCC), near his hometown, earning All-American honors in both lacrosse and soccer. In 1971 he transferred to Cornell University, in Ithaca, New York, where he earned All-American honors for his skills at lacrosse and All-Ivy League distinction for soccer. Arena was also named most valuable defensive player for his efforts in the National Collegiate Athletic Association (NCAA) Division I Soccer Championships in 1972. While attending Cornell, Arena was drafted by the New York Cosmos of the North American Soccer League (NASL), but their contract offer of about $4,000 per season was not as appealing to Arena as a college degree. He remained at Cornell, graduating with a business degree in 1973. That year he made his first and only appearance as a soccer player in international competition, with the United States national team, when he substituted as the goalkeeper near the end of a 2–0 loss to Israel.

Following his graduation Arena stayed on with the Cornell soccer team as an assistant coach; he held that position for two years. In 1975 he played one season of professional lacrosse for the Montreal Quebecois and the following year played a single season of professional soccer for the Tacoma Tides of the now-defunct American Soccer League.

Arena's unremarkable professional playing career ended in 1976, when he accepted the head-coaching position with the soccer team at the University of Puget Sound, in Washington State. After one season he returned to Cornell as an assistant coach on the lacrosse team. He was hired in 1978 as an assistant coach for the lacrosse team at the University of Virginia, as the heir apparent to the Hall of Fame coach Jim Adams; essentially as an afterthought, he was also given the responsibility of coaching the soccer team, the Cavaliers. "The soccer program here [at Virginia] was basically an intramural program," Arena explained to Doug Doughty for the Roanoke (Virginia) Times (December 3, 1995). Despite the unglamorous tradition of soccer at Virginia, Arena discovered that he was more inclined toward coaching soccer than retaining a position with the highly lauded lacrosse team. Because of the regional nature of lacrosse, Arena found it limiting as a coach. By 1985 Arena had stepped down from the lacrosse team to concentrate full-time on soccer.

While at Virginia Arena often butted heads with the university's administration. He fought successfully to get soccer scholarships, as his team had lagged behind other schools in the Atlantic Coast Conference (ACC) in that regard. Virginia had plush facilities for its other sports teams, most noticeably the football and basketball squads, and Arena believed that for the soccer team to be as successful it would need its own grass-surfaced stadium. (The team played home games in the football stadium, which had Astroturf rather than grass.) Arena eventually persuaded school administrators to finance the $1.2 million stadium, which was completed in 1992 and bolstered the school's reputation as a growing college sports powerhouse. He was also committed to recruiting high-school players in the U.S. rather than foreign athletes, as many of his peers were doing. (Soccer was less popular in the United States than abroad, and there was a perception that U.S.-born players could never compete at the highest level of collegiate play.)

As early as 1979 Arena had displayed a knack for recruiting, and the Cavaliers quickly became competitive, reaching the NCAA tournament in Arena's second year with a 12–4–1 regular-season record. The team took a step backward in 1980, posting an 8–9–1 record, but that would prove to be the only season during Arena's tenure at Virginia in which the Cavaliers lost more games than they won. Initially, despite posting successful regular-season records, Arena found difficulty succeeding in the NCAA play-offs. In Virginia's first three trips to the NCAA tournament under Arena, the team failed to win a single game and was outscored one goal to four. The 1983 season, Arena's fifth as head coach, saw the team advance for the first time into the semifinal round at the NCAA tournament. Beginning in 1981 the Cavaliers completed 15 straight seasons with a winning record and a berth in the NCAA tournament. They dominated ACC play, winning the conference tournament on numerous occasions. Finally, in 1989, the team competed in its first-ever NCAA championship game, which ended after four overtime periods in a 1–1 draw. With no tie-breaking procedure in place, Virginia and Santa Clara were named co-champions. In 1991 Arena again led the team to the final game, which again resulted in a tie against Santa Clara, this time 0–0. A penalty-kick shootout had been adopted as a tie-breaking measure, and Virginia prevailed. Arena and the Virginia team won the national championship for the next three years. The Cavaliers were unseated in 1995, but their string of five championships in six seasons was as impressive a run as any in NCAA sports at that time. Arena came to be known as a "player's coach." George Galnovatch, who played for Arena from 1983 to 1986 and later succeeded him as head coach at Virginia, said to Steven Goff for the *Washington Post* (December 7, 1995) that that approach was central to Arena's success. "Away from the field, Bruce is the biggest micromanager you've ever seen," Galnovatch explained. "But on the field, he gives the players the freedom to play and he allows them to be themselves. It's a unique combination and obviously it has worked." Virginia was widely regarded as having the best college soccer program in the country, and Arena received many accolades during the 1990s for the team's success. He won the ACC Coach of the Year Award seven times and in 1993 received the National Coach of the Year Award from the NCAA. John Jeansonne described Arena's influence on the Virginia teams for *Newsday* (December 12, 1995): "He created teams that went beyond sheer dominance—four straight NCAA titles—to critically acclaimed aesthetics, playing what was universally described as 'attacking, attractive, sophisticated soccer.'" During his time as head coach at Virginia, Arena compiled a record of 295–58–32. His .808 career winning percentage is among the best ever in collegiate sports history.

In an article for *Sports Illustrated* (May 15, 2003, on-line) devoted largely to the subject of Arena's plainspokenness, Grant Wahl reported that Arena had learned a great deal about coaching by eavesdropping on basketball coaches before and during games at the University of Virginia. Sitting in his office, he could hear coaches talking to their players. Wahl wrote, referring to legendary coaches at the University of North Carolina, North Carolina State University, and the University of Maryland, respectively, "What [Arena] heard wafting through the air vents was an education in coaching: Dean Smith's scholarly pep talks, Jim Valvano's comedic ramblings, Lefty Driesell's Southern plaints." Arena told Wahl, "Coaching is teaching, and for a long time I got a chance to listen to the elite coaches teaching the elite athletes of this country. Other soccer coaches were making trips to Europe, but I don't think that was half as educational as what I was doing."

Despite Arena's success at the University of Virginia and his interest in coaching a national soccer team, the U.S. Soccer Federation—the country's governing body for soccer, including U.S. participation in international competition—regarded him warily, perceiving him as arrogant. "A lot of people misread Bruce because he's been critical of the [U.S. soccer] system," Sampson explained to Jeansonne. "Bruce has had the guts to challenge the system to change." (Among other things, he had called the U.S. Soccer Federation a "good ol' boy network," or an organization marked by cronyism.) Then, in 1995, Arena was approached about coaching the men's under-23 national team, which would represent the United States at the 1996 Olympics, in Atlanta, Georgia. In the end, as some observed, Arena's success at Virginia made him hard to ignore. Arena was granted a leave of absence from Virginia to coach the under-23 team.

Coaching the Olympic soccer team presented an enormous challenge. The team's 1996 appearance would be only its third at the Olympics since 1956; U.S. teams had failed to qualify for competition in most of the 10 prior Olympic contests. The age restriction of 23 years, imposed on Olympic soccer by the sport's world governing body, FIFA (Fédération Internationale de Football Association), further limited the potential of the U.S. team. (The team would be allowed only three overage players.) While most of the qualifying U.S. players were just out of college, where NCAA rules dictated that teams could play only during the fall season, other nations had players who had been competing professionally year-round. In the lead-up to the Olympics, the team had a winning record, which made Arena optimistic about its potential. At the Olympics, however, the team received an unfavorable draw due to its low international stature and faced the difficult task of having to beat either Argentina or Portugal in order to advance. The U.S. finished third in Group A with a 1–1–1 record, defeating Tunisia, ending in a draw with Portugal, and losing to Argentina, which meant that the team was unable to advance. Though the U.S. had not made it past the first round, Arena refused to describe his players' performance as unsuccessful. "No way this is a failure," Arena told Jerry Lindquist for the *Richmond Times Dispatch* (July 26, 1996). "If we stunk it up over three games, then it would be a failure. This is nothing but positive. We made great progress." Particularly with its 1–1 draw against favored Portugal, the United States had proved capable of playing competitively on the international level. Arena was widely credited with accelerating the development of soccer in the U.S.

During the under-23 team's 1995–96 season, Arena accepted a job as head coach of the D.C. United, one of 10 teams in the inaugural season of Major League Soccer, the new professional soccer league in the U.S. Arena had immediate success with D.C. United, winning the first two MLS Cups, in 1996 and 1997. He earned the MLS Coach of the Year Award in 1997 and was elected to coach the

MLS All-Star games in 1997 and 1998. In the latter year D.C. United lost in the final game of the MLS Cup. Perhaps Arena's most significant accomplishments during that period took place on the international stage. In 1997 Arena took D.C. United to the CONCACAF Champions Cup semifinals. (CONCACAF, or the Confederation of North, Central American and Caribbean Association Football, is the governing body of soccer in North America and the Caribbean. The CONCACAF Champions Cup goes to the association's winning team.) In 1998 D.C. United won the CONCACAF Champions Cup and advanced to the Interamerican Cup, which pits the CONCACAF club champion against the winning South American team. D.C. United faced Brazil's Vasco Da Gama, winning with a two-game aggregate score of 2–1. With that victory D.C. United was crowned the best club team in the Western Hemisphere. Arena's CONCACAF wins, combined with his four NCAA titles and two MLS Cup victories, made him the most successful U.S. soccer coach of the 1990s.

Arena left D.C. United in 1998 to become the head coach of the U.S. men's national team. (He succeeded Steve Sampson after the U.S. team's disastrous showing at the 1998 World Cup, in which it failed to win a single game.) In his eight years in the position, Arena became one of the most successful coaches in U.S. Soccer history; his 71 victories and .658 winning percentage are both records. He had a successful debut year, taking the team to a 7–4–2 record in 1999, which included wins over the soccer powers Germany, Argentina, and Chile. Arena had four years to organize his team for the 2002 World Cup competition. Heading into that competition, held in South Korea, the national team had a record of 33–17–11, and the U.S. Soccer Federation anticipated a better showing than the U.S. had had in 1998. Nonetheless, because the team's sterling record was a result of having played inferior teams that did not qualify for the World Cup, the U.S. was considered an underdog. The team thus surprised many in the first game of the tournament, beating the favored Portuguese team, 3–2. In the next game the U.S. played the host nation, South Korea, to a 1–1 draw, which was considered a success for the Americans. In its third game the U.S. lost to Poland, 1–3, but nonetheless qualified for the quarterfinal round, where it fell 0–1 to Germany, despite dominating the field for large portions of the game. The eighth-place finish at the 2002 World Cup was deemed an extraordinary success for U.S. Soccer, as it marked the best performance by the U.S. at the World Cup since 1930.

The year 2002 began the most successful period for the U.S. soccer team in recent memory. The team won the CONCACAF Gold Cup that year, repeating that feat in 2005, in the midst of qualifying matches for the 2006 World Cup. The U.S. went unbeaten in 16 games in 2003–04, and its 14 wins in 2005 were its most ever during a calendar year. Arena led the team to its then-highest-ever FIFA ranking (fourth) in April 2006.

In June of that year, the U.S. went into the World Cup ranked second in its pool, which was considered one of the most competitive in the tournament and was frequently referred to as the "Group of Death." Besides the Czech Republic, ranked second by FIFA, the U.S. had to play the eventual champion, Italy, and Ghana, which had allowed only four goals during its 12 qualifying matches. The U.S. was thoroughly overmatched against the Czech Republic, losing its first game 3–0. Against Italy, a game marred by player ejections, the U.S. managed a 1–1 draw. Needing to beat Ghana in order to stay in the tournament, the U.S. struggled again, losing 2–1. Most analysts put the blame on Arena, for failing to change his strategies during games once they proved to be unsuccessful. Soon after the U.S. team returned from its disappointing World Cup performance, Arena, whose contract was set to expire at the end of 2006, was told by the U.S. Soccer president, Sunil Gulati, that his contract would not be renewed. Some of the players thought that Arena was being scapegoated for the team's poor performance.

Arena next accepted the head-coach position with the New York Red Bulls, an MLS team (formerly known as the New York/New Jersey MetroStars). Despite strong attendance and such star players as Alexi Lalas, Clint Mathis, Eddie Pope, Tony Meola, and Giovanni Savarese, the Red Bulls had consistently underachieved and had compiled a 125–146–35 record over nine years of MLS play. "This will be fun," Arena said to Jane Havsy for the *Asbury Park (New Jersey) Press* (August 8, 2006). "It will be a great challenge, and it's not going to happen overnight. There's a lot of work to be done here." As it turned out, Arena appeared to find his stint with the Red Bulls more challenging than fun. After replacing the interim coach, Richie Williams, in 2006, Arena led the team to a 4–5–3 record for the year. The Red Bulls began 2007 with three straight losses, an MLS record for the longest losing streak at the beginning of a season. (The team was not helped by being without a permanent training facility.) Through it all, Paul Gardner noted for the *New York Sun* (October 31, 2007), Arena conveyed "the public image . . . of a man not enjoying his work." In November 2007, after the Red Bulls failed for the second straight year to make it past the first round of the play-offs, Arena announced his resignation.

In August 2008 Arena signed on as both head coach and general manager of MLS's Los Angeles Galaxy. In the Galaxy he found another underachieving team that looked to him for a reversal of its fortunes. The strength of its offense—which boasted two superstars of the sport, David Beckham and Landon Donovan—was more than offset by a defense that allowed more goals than the team scored; the result was a losing streak that had stretched to eight games by the time Arena arrived. That year the Galaxy finished last in the Western Conference, with a record of 8–13–9. In the following season, in addition to boosting the Galaxy's defense, Arena brought in new players and helped the team work well together, an effort that included smoothing over public differences between Beckham and Donovan. The team made it to the 2009 MLS championship game, which it lost to Real Salt Lake, 5–4, in penalty kicks. Arena won the MLS Coach of the Year Award, and in January 2010 he was elected to the U.S. Soccer Hall of Fame. "I think 2009 was a real challenge, from the start all the way through to the end," Arena told Grahame L. Jones for the *Los Angeles Times* (March 27, 2010). "It was constant tinkering and everything else. I think this year we're a little bit more estab- lished and there's not so much experimenting and juggling lineups. We're a little bit more settled in. Hopefully, that means we have a good team."

Arena and his wife, Phyllis, have a son, Kenny, a former professional soccer player who is current- ly an assistant coach with the University of Califor- nia–Los Angeles (UCLA) Bruins soccer team.

—N.W.M.

Suggested Reading: *Newsday* A p68 Dec. 12, 1995; *Roanoke (Virginia) Times* C p1 Dec. 3, 1995; *Sports Illustrated* p76 Nov. 8, 1982; *Washington Post* B p5 Dec. 7, 1995

Frazer Harrison/Getty Images

Atwood, Colleen

Sep. 25, 1948– Costume designer

Address: c/o IATSE, 1430 Broadway, 20th Fl., New York, NY 10018

The Hollywood costume designer Colleen Atwood is "the person in charge of one of the most impor- tant moments in every movie," Stephen B. Hunt wrote for *Moving Pictures Magazine* (2005, on- line): filmgoers' first impressions of the characters. Since 1984 Atwood has dressed the casts of some 50 feature films, designing apparel that evokes the personalities of the characters as well as the peri- ods and atmospheres of the stories, in movies rang- ing from historical and contemporary dramas to musicals to adult and juvenile fantasies. "My cos- tumes are part of the whole film, not just what I think they should be," she told Jamie Diamond for the *New York Times* (February 24, 2005). Atwood's success in reflecting the visions of filmmakers has led three directors to work with her repeatedly: Tim Burton, on the films *Sleepy Hollow, Ed Wood, Edward Scissorhands, Mars Attacks!*, the remake of *Planet of the Apes, Big Fish, Sweeney Todd: The Demon Barber of Fleet Street*, and the latest remake of *Alice in Wonderland*; Jonathan Demme, on *Mar- ried to the Mob, Beloved, That Thing You Do!, Phil- adelphia*, and *The Silence of the Lambs* (the last of which won the Academy Award for best picture of 1991); and Rob Marshall, on *Chicago* (the Oscar winner for best picture in 2002), *Memoirs of a Gei- sha*, and *Nine*.

Atwood has also collaborated with directors in- cluding Michael Mann, on *Manhunter*; Paul Bo- gart, on *Torch Song Trilogy*; Lawrence Kasdan, on *Wyatt Earp*; Ridley Scott, on *Someone to Watch Over Me*; Gillian Armstrong, on the latest big- screen adaptation of *Little Women*; John Patrick Shanley, on *Joe Versus the Volcano*; George Miller, on *Lorenzo's Oil*; Brad Silberling, on *Lemony Sni- ckets' A Series of Unfortunate Events*; and J.J. Abrams, on *Mission: Impossible III*. Films with her clothing designs have premiered on the silver screen in 22 of the past 26 years, and three times— in 1988, 1994, and 2001—her name has appeared in the credits for four motion pictures in a single year. In the 1980s Atwood created wardrobes for the musicians Sting and Elton John, and in 2005– 06 she redesigned all the costumes worn by per- formers with the Ringling Bros. and Barnum & Bai- ley Circus. Among her three-dozen honors, she won Academy Awards for her designs for *Chicago* and *Memoirs of a Geisha* and Oscar nominations for her work on *Little Women, Beloved, Sleepy Hol- low, Lemony Snickets' A Series of Unfortunate Events*, and *Sweeney Todd*. Nominated for seven awards from BAFTA (the British Academy of Film and Television Arts), she has won two, for *Mem- oirs of a Geisha* and *Sleepy Hollow*, and of the sev- en awards from the Costume Designers Guild (CDG) for which she has been nominated, she has won five. She was named Costume Designer of the Year at the 2005 Hollywood Film Festival, and the next year she received a Career Achievement

Award from the CDG. In 2007 she won an Emmy Award for the clothing she designed for the television special *Tony Bennett: An American Classic.*

Colleen Atwood was born on September 25, 1948 in Ellensburg, Washington, and raised in Quincy, a farm town in that state. (Some sources list her year of birth as 1949 or 1950 and the place as Yakima, Washington.) "I always loved clothes, just not clothes that were appropriate to the place I grew up in," she told Jamie Diamond, referring to the white-buck shoes and preppy white blazer she wore in elementary school. She also said to Diamond, "I grew up in the age of polyester. When I got to touch real silk, cotton and velvet, the feel of nonsynthetic fabrics blew me away. I know it's important how clothing looks, but it's equally important how it feels on your skin." As a child Atwood dreamed of a career as a painter. While in high school she became a wife and mother. She divorced soon afterward and moved with her child to Seattle, Washington. There, she found a job in sales at a Marshall Field's department store, where she gained familiarity with upscale apparel. She furthered her knowledge of clothing design in the 1970s through courses she took at the Cornish College of Fine Arts, in Seattle. For some years she worked as a fashion adviser.

In 1980 Atwood moved to New York City, where she briefly attended New York University's film school. Her academic training ended around that time, when she got a job as a production assistant for the films *Ragtime* (1981), after the first person hired failed to show up, and *A Little Sex* (1982). Her supervisor was Patrizia Von Brandenstein, who served as the production designer for the former and costume designer for the latter. Soon afterward Atwood was hired to design costumes for Elton John and Sting. Her costumes for Sting may be seen in the Michael Apted–directed documentary *Bring on the Night* (1985), as can Atwood herself, in a scene in which Sting's manager, Miles Copeland III, complains that the clothing she designed for Sting's backup musicians looks "boring." Atwood's first solo design credit came with another of Apted's movies, *Firstborn* (1984), whose cast included Teri Garr, Peter Weller, Sarah Jessica Parker, and Robert Downey Jr. The cast of the comedy *Critical Condition* (1987), Atwood's third project with Apted, included Richard Pryor, Rubén Blades, Bob Dishy, Joe Mantegna, and Sylvia Miles. Her next assignments included designs for the well-received screwball farce *Married to the Mob* (1988), her first collaboration with Jonathan Demme. In *Married to the Mob*, Mafiosos (portrayed by Alec Baldwin and Dean Stockwell) strut in flamboyant suits, a doorman at a Mafia-frequented nightspot wears a coat of armor, and a Mafia widow (Michelle Pfeiffer) "looks utterly ravishing" in garish sequined dresses and other outfits "that set the teeth on edge," Janet Maslin wrote for the *New York Times* (August 19, 1988). With the "junkiest of jewelry," Maslin wrote, and "costumes so frightening they take your breath away, Mr.

Demme may joke, but he's also capable of suggesting that the very fabric of American life may be woven of such things, and that it takes a merry and adventurous spirit to make the most of them."

In 1990 Atwood created the costumes for Tim Burton's *Edward Scissorhands*, a dark fantasy set in a 1960s American subdivision. Its hero is Edward (played by Johnny Depp), a sweet, quiet, melancholy man, whose creator, a mad inventor, dies before replacing the 10 long pairs of shears that serve as Edward's hands and fingers. Edward also has a huge mop of tangled black hair, a sickly complexion, and dark, punk-style clothing, which Atwood created with found objects and pieced fabric, echoing the nature of its wearer. (Costume designers provide guidance for makeup and hair as well as apparel.) In stark contrast, Edward's female neighbors wear plain pastel clothing. For the anti-hero of Demme's next film, *The Silence of the Lambs* (1991), based on a novel by Thomas Harris, Atwood designed clothes to mirror his qualities— those of a deeply depraved but brilliant serial killer and cannibal, Hannibal Lecter (Anthony Hopkins). "Sometimes a contemporary film like *Silence of the Lambs* is difficult," she told Keith Bush for his Web site (2002). "To make it look real but interesting is always a challenge. You try . . . to serve the story by creating characters. Hannibal Lecter's costumes were tailored to fit him in a minutely kind of tight way to help show he was a totally controlling person even though he was in the confines of a prison." BAFTA nominated Atwood for awards for best costume design for both *Edward Scissorhands* and *The Silence of the Lambs.*

Two period films released in 1994, *Wyatt Earp* and *Little Women*, featured Atwood's costumes. For *Wyatt Earp*, a blend of biography and Western whose title character lived from 1848 to 1929, Atwood conducted research at the libraries at the Western Costume Co., in Los Angeles, California, the Metropolitan Museum of Art, in New York City, and the Angels and Bermans costume house, in London, England. She dressed the men in dark, dusty-looking outerwear and the women in dresses including plain or fringed Victorian styles or ornate, beaded silk gowns. "This was a huge, but great challenge," Atwood told Betty Goodwin for the *Los Angeles Times* (June 23, 1994). "After a year when *The Piano* comes out, which is so strict [in keeping with the period], you have to make a choice. Do you do costumes with a basis in history and try to stick to it, or do you bend it? We had a strong historical basis, but we bent it sometimes." Most of the costumes for Wyatt Earp were made specifically for the actors; others were rented or bought from more than five dozen suppliers.

Atwood's costumes for *Little Women*, adapted from the classic 1868 novel by Louisa May Alcott, more faithfully reflected the setting—Concord, Massachusetts, during the American Civil War period. Atwood's inspirations included paintings and drawings by such American artists as Winslow Homer and James McNeill Whistler as well as photos from that time. She told Betty Goodwin for the *Los Angeles Times* (December 29, 1994) that she and the director, Gillian Armstrong, decided that the film should be "more realistic" than earlier adaptations of *Little Women*—in particular, George Cukor's and Mervyn LeRoy's versions, in 1933 and 1949, respectively, which "were much more Hollywood." Atwood and Armstrong's female characters (played by actresses including Winona Ryder, Claire Danes, and Susan Sarandon) wore drab dresses made of rough wools or cottons, some with patches. "We made little holes . . . in some things, like a glove or a collar, then repaired them," Atwood told Goodwin. Many of the antique articles of clothing were obtained from the Helen Larson Collection at the FIDM (Fashion Institute of Design and Merchandising) Museum, in Los Angeles, and similar sources. The women's gloves, however, were mostly made to fit the actresses who would be wearing them, because so many of the available period gloves were too small, reflecting the smaller sizes of average women's hands in the mid-1800s.

For Tim Burton's *Sleepy Hollow* (1999), the lighting director and special-effects team made nearly every scene look dark and foggy. The story, based on a classic tale by Washington Irving, is set in a small New York town in 1799, when few people bathed regularly or owned more than a minimum of clothing and when heavy rains transformed roads into seas of mud. Atwood's costumes reflected both the somber atmosphere of the film and the characters' lack of cleanliness. An exception was the character portrayed by Christina Ricci. "As a daughter of the richest man in town . . . , Ricci had to wear costumes with an angelic, pure look to them," Lorenza Munoz wrote for the *Los Angeles Times* (November 22, 1999). "So Atwood worked with fine velvet in silvery tones for most of her outfits. She also found antique silks, which have a lighter texture than contemporary silk, to give her dresses an airy, almost dreamlike bounce." For *Sleepy Hollow*'s Headless Horseman, Munoz wrote, "Atwood invented a special process (that she won't divulge) that gave his costume the look of clothing worn by someone literally rising from the dead." To convey the Headless Horseman's scariness, Atwood made the character's boots, spurs, and buckles significantly bigger than usual, "because sometimes in fear, we amplify things," she told Karin Lipson for *Newsday* (March 26, 2000).

Atwood won her first Academy Award for costume design for Rob Marshall's blockbuster film *Chicago* (2002), the latest incarnation of a 1920s play. (*Chicago* was also a 1970s Broadway musical. The Broadway revival of that musical, which opened in late 1996, is still running.) Set in Chicago during the 1920s, the story follows two fame-seeking, vaudeville-loving murderesses: the audacious and alluring Velma Kelly (played by Catherine Zeta-Jones) and the dreamer Roxie Hart (Renee Zellweger). Other leading characters are the fast-talking lawyer Billy Flynn (Richard Gere), Roxie's

clueless husband, Amos (John C. Reilly), and the tough prison warden Matron Mama Morton (Queen Latifah). Referring to William Ivey Long, the costume designer for the 1996 Broadway revival of *Chicago*, Lisa Lenoir wrote for the *Chicago Sun-Times* (September 3, 2003), "*Chicago* revs up audiences with its sassy songs, acrobatic dance moves, and pithy dialogue. But it's the costumes that punctuate the storyline. Atwood . . . and Long . . . know how to paint a picture in their respective genres, defining mood with fabrics, color, and design." According to a *Los Angeles Times* (March 24, 2003) writer, "Velma Kelly's strength and gutsiness suggested black colors and bold styles, while Roxie Hart's dull flesh-toned attire segued to flashy, silver-and-fringe costumes for her fantasy life. Lawyer Billy Flynn moved from the straw-hat song-and-dance-man outfit to elegant pinstripes for the courtroom. Sad-sack Amos wore a baggy-pants vaudeville costume for his 'Mr. Cellophane' number, and Matron Mama shifted from prison gray to shimmering gold for her show-stopping stage number."

The main characters in the fantasy *Lemony Snicket's A Series of Unfortunate Events* (2004), based on children's novels by Daniel Handler, are three orphaned siblings in the custody of the evil Count Olaf. In designing their wardrobes, Atwood studied the illustrations of insects, animals, and plants in the book *Cabinet of Natural Curiosities*, by Albertus Seba (1665–1736). "I felt the people in the books and film were extensions of that sort of caricature," she told Jamie Diamond. "So it worked to have the clothing look like illustrations." The apparel for Jim Carrey, who played Count Olaf, includes many vertical stripes to create the illusion of great height. "I wanted him to intimidate the kids, to appear to tower over them, as if he were miles taller than they were," Atwood told Diamond.

Atwood earned her second Oscar and a bevy of other honors for her costumes for Rob Marshall's *Memoirs of a Geisha* (2005). The screenplay was based on Arthur Golden's same-titled novel of 1997, a first-person narration in which Sayuri, the title character, describes her life in 1930s and 1940s Japan. Atwood had only five months to design, acquire materials for, and rent or supervise the construction of the costumes worn by the six main characters and some 200 extras. A crew of 30 fabricated more than 250 kimonos, mostly with expensive silks custom-painted for the film; each kimono required about eight yards of fabric. In the course of her extensive research regarding geishas' kimonos, Atwood traveled to the 1,200-year-old city of Kyoto, Japan, where she perused museum collections and books and hired Japanese fashion consultants. "You go in the front door knowing nothing, and six months later you go out the back having [created] an entire world," she told Missy Schwartz for *Entertainment Weekly* (November 18, 2005). She also told Schwartz, "The art of the kimono is a very complicated art form. What I learned was minuscule compared to what a real expert would know." Atwood altered the traditional form of the kimono slightly, making the waist more defined and the neck more exposed. "We were taking an art form that is a huge part of Japanese culture, but it was important to remember that we were making a movie, based on a book of fiction, written by a guy, about a geisha," Atwood told Mimi Avins for the *Los Angeles Times* (November 6, 2005). "It's not a documentary film. . . . [Marshall's] vision was that this movie is a grand story about a woman's life, a sort of *Gone with the Wind* set in another time and place. His vision freed all of us to create a theatrical world together."

Marshall and Atwood most recently collaborated for the movie-musical *Nine* (2009), an adaptation of Federico Fellini's *8¹/₂* and the Broadway musical reimagining of that film, which premiered in 1982 and had a revival in 2003. The story is set in 1960s Rome, Italy, and centers on a famous, narcissistic movie director, Guido Contini (Daniel Day-Lewis); while grappling with an ill-timed creative block, Contini juggles the many women in his life, both past and present, among them his wife (portrayed by Marion Cotillard), his mistress (Penélope Cruz), the film star who used to serve as his muse (Nicole Kidman), his confidante and costume designer (Judi Dench), and a prostitute from his youth (Stacy Ferguson, known as Fergie). The glittery dresses on view required for their creation "more than a million crystals in 31 variations of cut and size and 22 colors" and "roughly 1,640 feet of crystal mesh," Venessa Lau wrote for *WWD* (December 15, 2009). Atwood also designed many fancy corsets and other types of undergarments—"Women [back] then didn't just wear a bra and panties," she noted to Lau—using stretch fabrics and double-sewn seams so that they remained intact during vigorous dances. During one dance number Cruz wore three different pairs of shoes, which looked the same but had subtle variations in heel height and arch construction, to facilitate trouble-free footwork. The fabrics for two of Cruz's dresses came from Atwood's large personal collection of vintage materials.

Atwood designed the costumes for two 2010 films—Tim Burton's *Alice in Wonderland* and Florian Henckel von Donnersmarck's *The Tourist*—and two scheduled for release in 2011: Bruce Robinson's *The Rum Diary* and Christian Keller's *Trevi*.

In part because her continually bustling workroom is also a storeroom for thousands of fabrics and other items used in costume construction, Atwood's home, in Pacific Palisades, California, is minimally decorated, conveying airiness and peacefulness. Atwood has two daughters.

—T.O.

Suggested Reading: *Chicago Sun-Times* p59 Sep. 3, 2003; *Entertainment Weekly* p60 Nov. 18, 2005; imdb.com; *Los Angeles Magazine* p78+ Feb. 2006; *Los Angeles Times* E p6 June 23, 1994; *MovingPicturesMagazine.com*; *New York Times* (on-line) Feb. 24, 2005; *Newsday* D p23 Mar. 26, 2000; *USA Today* D p7 Mar. 18, 1992; *Who's Who in America*

Selected Films: *Firstborn*, 1984; *Out of the Darkness*, 1985; *Bring on the Night*, 1985; *Manhunter*, 1986, *Critical Condition*, 1987, *Someone to Watch Over Me*, 1987, *The PickUp Artist*, 1987; *Torch Song Trilogy*, 1988; *Married to the Mob*, 1988; *Fresh Horses*, 1988; *For Keeps*, 1988; *Hider in the House*, 1989; *The Handmaid's Tale*, 1989; *Joe Versus the Volcano*, 1990; *Edward Scissorhands*, 1990; *The Silence of the Lambs*, 1991; *Rush*, 1991; *Lorenzo's Oil*, 1992; *Love Field*, 1992; *Philadelphia*, 1993; *Born Yesterday*, 1993; *Cabin Boy*, 1994; *Wyatt Earp*, 1994; *Ed Wood*, 1994; *Little Women*, 1994; *Mars Attacks!*, 1996; *That Thing You Do!*, 1996; *Beloved*, 1998; *Mumford*, 1998; *Sleepy Hollow*, 1999; *Golden Dreams*, 2001; *The Mexican*, 2001; *Planet of the Apes*, 2001; *The Tick*, 2001; *CinéMagique*, 2002; *Chicago*, 2002; *Big Fish*, 2003; *Lemony Snicket's A Series of Unfortunate Events*, 2004; *Memoirs of a Geisha*, 2005; *Mission: Impossible III*, 2006; *Sweeney Todd: The Demon Barber of Fleet Street*, 2007; *Public Enemies*, 2009; *Nine*, 2009; *Alice in Wonderland*, 2010; *The Tourist*, 2010

Bair, Sheila C.

Apr. 3, 1954– Chairperson of the FDIC; former New York Stock Exchange executive; educator; lawyer; writer

Address: Federal Deposit Insurance Corp., 550 17th St., N.W., Washington, DC 20429

Sheila C. Bair, the chairperson of the Federal Deposit Insurance Corp. (FDIC), "is one of the few government officials whose reputation has actually improved during the financial crisis," Jim Puzzanghera wrote for the *Los Angeles Times* (November 18, 2008, on-line). Bair is at the forefront of the U.S. government's strenuous efforts to return the American banking industry to health, end the credit crunch that has stymied businesses and individuals since the start of the current economic downturn, in 2008, and prevent millions of families and individuals from losing their homes to foreclosure. Selected by President George W. Bush and confirmed by the U.S. Senate, Bair began her five-year term as head of the FDIC in June 2006. For more than a quarter-century before that, Bair, who has a degree in law, acquired firsthand knowledge of the worlds of both finance and government and politics. She held several positions straddling those worlds, as an adviser at the U.S. Department of Health, Education, and Welfare and in the office of

Courtesy of the FDIC

Sheila C. Bair

U.S. senator Bob Dole of Kansas; as the legislative counselor and senior vice president for government relations at the New York Stock Exchange; and as an assistant secretary for financial institutions at the U.S. Department of the Treasury. In addition, for four years she served on the Commodity Futures Trading Commission, and for another four she held a named professorship at the University of Massachusetts at Amherst, where, in addition to teaching courses in financial regulatory policy, she conducted in-depth studies related to the insurance industry, the federal home-loan bank system, borrowing patterns by people with low incomes, and access to U.S. financial institutions by recent Hispanic immigrants—all issues pertaining to consumer protection. At the FDIC Bair has made the needs and well-being of ordinary depositors as high a priority as those of banks—sometimes in the face of public opposition by the secretary of the treasury and other prominent members of the administrations of President Bush and, now, President Barack Obama.

Bair was among the financial experts who first warned publicly that the considerable weakening of standards among mortgage lenders in the late 1990s, during the expansion of the so-called housing bubble, would have dire consequences. She also correctly predicted the flood of foreclosures that would ensue among people who had been lured to buy homes by such lenders' deceptively affordable adjustable-rate mortgages—people who soon discovered that they did not have the means to keep up their payments after their rates jumped. As the chair of the FDIC, Bair has strenuously pushed for the use of federal funds to enable the millions of homeowners facing foreclosure to hold onto their property through debt relief and the lowering of their mortgage rates. Her suggestions were rebuffed by Bush administration officials but met with the approval of many Democrats, among them Barack Obama, Bush's successor in the White House. Obama chose not to ask Bair, a registered Republican, to step down from her post with the beginning of his new, Democratic administration, as he had the prerogative to do. "I do think that the F.D.I.C. and Sheila Bair have had the sense of urgency about the problem that I want to see . . . ," Obama told Stephen Labaton for the *New York Times* (January 7, 2009), two weeks before his inauguration as president. "I think generally they've been on the case with the resources that they have to try to shore up the system." Binyamin Appelbaum, who has reported extensively about the housing bubble and the crisis in the banking industry, described Bair for the *Washington Post* (October 2, 2008) as being "principled and blunt without being confrontational." "She has the talent, more often observed in diplomats than in banking regulators, for simultaneously communicating opposition to an idea and personal warmth for the holder of the idea," he continued. "And she knows how to make a deal." In 2009 Bair won a John F. Kennedy Profile in Courage Award from the John F. Kennedy Library Foundation, "in recognition of the political courage [she] demonstrated in sounding early warnings about conditions that contributed to the current global financial crisis," according to a foundation press release (March 25, 2009, online).

Sheila Colleen Bair was born to Albert E. Bair and the former Clara F. Brenneman on April 3, 1954 in Wichita, Kansas (Independence, Kansas, according to some sources). She has recalled accompanying her father to a local Wichita bank each week as a small child. "I would wait for him in the lobby as he transacted business," she told a writer for the quarterly *NeighborWorks Bright Ideas* (Fall 2007). "My interest in banks and finance only grew, as I did." She attended the University of Kansas, where she received a B.A. degree in philosophy in 1975. She then entered the University of Kansas School of Law, in Lawrence, earning a J.D. degree in 1978. During her college years she worked as a bank teller.

After law school Bair held a one-year teaching fellowship at the University of Arkansas School of Law, in Fayetteville. From 1979 to 1981 she worked as an attorney/adviser at the U.S. Department of Health, Education, and Welfare (now the Department of Health and Human Services) in Kansas City, Missouri. She then moved to Washington, D.C., to serve as a legal and policy adviser to Bob Dole, a Kansas Republican who was in his third term as a U.S. senator. She left Dole in 1986 to work for the law firm Kutak, Rock & Campbell, whose specialties include corporate and public finance. In 1987 and 1988 she directed research for Dole's presidential-primary campaign, which he lost to then–Vice President George H. W. Bush.

From 1989 to 1991 she served the New York Stock Exchange (NYSE) as a counsel for legislative affairs; she acted as a liaison between the exchange and federal lawmakers and state legislatures. During that period she ran in the 1990 Republican primary for the seat from Kansas's Fifth Congressional District. In the course of her campaign, she bicycled to homes in small towns and spoke in favor of abortion rights. She lost to Dick Nichols, who outspent her by a large margin. (Because of the drop in population revealed by the 1990 census, since 1992 Kansas has had only four seats in the House.)

In 1991 Bair changed jobs again, this time becoming one of the five commissioners who comprise the Commodity Futures Trading Commission (CFTC), a federal agency that acts independently of the government. At the time of the CFTC's creation, in 1974, futures contracts involved agricultural products—wheat, soybean oil, and pork bellies, for example. When Bair arrived at the CFTC, a significant portion of such contracts involved bond, stock index, and other financial futures, some of them highly complex. In 1993 Bair was the commission's acting chairman. In 1995 she left the CFTC to return to the NYSE as a senior vice president for government relations.

Bair left the NYSE in 2000. Soon afterward, in 2001, as an appointee of President George W. Bush, she joined the U.S. Treasury Department as assistant secretary for financial institutions. She worked closely with the Treasury Department's banking regulatory bureaus—the Office of the Comptroller of the Currency and the Office of Thrift Supervision—as well as the Federal Reserve Board and the FDIC. With the Federal Reserve's governor, Edward Gramlich, she tried without success to persuade mortgage lenders to agree on a set of "best practices" for subprime loans. She was among the first to recognize potential problems in the subprime-lending industry and wrote and spoke openly about her belief that some lenders were taking advantage of borrowers' lack of financial savvy. "This is somebody who was focused on the mortgage issue long before the real bubble had built up," Ellen Seidman, a financial-policy expert at the New America Foundation and a former head of the Office of Thrift Supervision, told Jonathan Peterson for the Los Angeles Times (December 23, 2007, on-line). After the September 11, 2001 terrorist attacks, Bair switched her focus to security issues.

In 2002 Bair left the Treasury Department to join the faculty of the Isenberg School of Management at the University of Massachusetts at Amherst, as the dean's professor of financial regulatory policy (a formal title). She and Thomas O'Brien, the school's dean, taught a course in that subject. "She was terrific in demonstrating why the history of the policy is important to the shaping of the policy itself," O'Brien recalled to Binyamin Appelbaum. "She showed how ideas got shaped and how policy came from those discussions and compromises." He told Theresa Howard for USA Today (October

2, 2008, on-line), "I was the color man . . . the old ballplayer, and she was the substance, the play-by-play. She fascinated the students but was not lighthearted. She was a pretty serious analyst of the issues and problems but was not dour." While at the Isenberg School, Bair, with the help of several graduate students, also engaged in research on "the structure and policies of the financial regulatory environment" and on "expanding access to financial services by low-income groups," according to a University of Massachusetts press release (June 16, 2006, on-line). In one of her reports for the school, published in 2004, she concluded that oversight of life insurers by individual states is insufficient, that "federal action is necessary to prompt needed improvements in the regulation of life insurance," and that "properly structured federal regulation of insurance patterned after the dual banking system could provide significant benefits to consumers." (The dual banking system that has existed in the U.S. since 1863 allows new banks to be chartered either by a state or by the federal government.) In a second report, published in 2005, Bair offered alternatives to so-called payday loans, which typically impose on borrowers interest rates of more than 300 percent (computed annually). During her years at Isenberg, Bair also served on the FDIC's Advisory Committee on Banking Policy and on advisory boards of the Center for Responsible Lending, the Investor Education Board, and the Insurance Marketplace Standards Association.

In 2006 Bair was summoned back to Washington, when President Bush nominated her to head the FDIC. The U.S. Senate voted to confirm her, and she was sworn in to a five-year term as chair on June 26, 2006. On the same day she began a seven-year term as a member of the FDIC board of directors. That year Bair topped the Wall Street Journal's annual list of the "50 Women to Watch," and Forbes magazine ranked her the second-most-powerful woman in the world, behind Chancellor Angela Merkel of Germany.

The FDIC was created by Congress in 1933, at the height of the Great Depression and the beginning of the presidency of Franklin D. Roosevelt. It was established in response to the failure of thousands of banks in the previous four years, during the administration of President Herbert Hoover, and the almost certain imminent failures of thousands more. Its mission, as stated on its Web site, is to "maintain stability and public confidence in the nation's financial system," by insuring the money deposited in banks and promoting "safe and sound business practices." The FDIC also manages receiverships—that is, it assumes control of failed banks and oversees activities arising from their failures. According to its Web site, between 1883 and 1933 lawmakers made 150 unsuccessful attempts to establish a federal mechanism for insuring bank deposits. Thousands of banks had failed in the U.S. since the early 1800s; in the 1920s more than 5,700 banks failed—over 10 times the number that had succumbed in the previous decade. In the four years beginning in 1930, some 9,000 banks were shuttered. Losses to depositors between 1929 and 1933 amounted to $1.3 billion (more than $21 billion in 2008 dollars). With the passage by Congress of the Bank Act of 1933, signed by President Roosevelt on June 16, 1933, the FDIC was created; it was intended to be a temporary government entity. When it began operating, on January 1, 1934, it guaranteed insurance of up to $2,500 per bank account; within six months that sum was doubled. (Currently, it insures deposits of up to $250,000 in each account in every bank.) The Bank Act of 1933 also made the FDIC responsible for regulating state-chartered banks that were not members of the Federal Reserve system; it also made the FDIC the receiver for failed national banks and (with the agreement of the particular states) failed state banks. As of mid-October 2010, the FDIC insured the deposits in 7,770 banks and savings institutions. It receives no federal tax dollars; its salaries and operations are funded entirely by fees collected from the financial institutions whose deposits it insures. To date no depositor has ever lost any money insured by the FDIC.

When Bair became the FDIC's head, two years had passed since the last bank failure (the longest period in the corporation's history), and consequently many FDIC employees had been laid off. Although the housing market was still booming, Bair again became concerned about subprime loans and the aggressive practices that enabled people without sufficient income or savings to acquire mortgages. Noting to Jonathan Peterson that she was "astonished" at the lenders' weak standards, she warned publicly of the potential dangers of subprime lending, not only to consumers but also to the banking industry. At Bair's urging, the FDIC and other regulators bought a database of information about securitized loans. They soon discovered that there had been an alarming pattern of disregard for traditional underwriting and that many subprime borrowers whose loans were set to skyrocket in cost could have been offered safer, fixed-rate mortgages. Mortgage originators, they found, lured buyers with no-money-down loans and required little or no financial information about the borrowers; other lenders failed to provide crucial information while using high-pressure tactics to persuade potential home buyers to sign mortgage contracts. As the number of foreclosures increased, Bair began pushing the Bush administration to facilitate efforts by lenders to modify broad categories of loans on a "fast-track" basis. The mass modifications of loans, she reasoned, would not only help homeowners to avoid foreclosure, but would also help banks and other companies (those that renovate houses, for example) avoid the consequences of those foreclosures. "Foreclosures hurt not only individual homeowners but entire neighborhoods and the American economy . . . ," Joe Nocera reminded *New York Times* (November 1, 2008) readers. "Until housing

prices stabilize, the financial crisis won't end, because housing is at the root of it. . . . Keeping people in their homes is the quickest, most compassionate way to begin stabilizing home prices." In a speech given in early October 2007, Bair said that in the next few years over $300 billion worth of adjustable-rate mortgages (ARMs) were due to be reset. "For owner-occupied housing where the loan is current," she advised, as quoted in *Mortgage News Daily* (November 21, 2008, on-line), "just convert the sub-prime hybrid A.R.M. into a fixed-rate mortgage. Keep it at the starter rate. Convert it into a fixed rate. Make it permanent. And get on with it."

Bair's words made little impact. That situation changed marginally after the failure on July 11, 2008 of IndyMac BanCorp, a federal savings bank in Pasadena, California, that had been among the nation's four biggest subprime-mortgage lenders. The FDIC took control of IndyMac, and the next month it authorized the bank to help borrowers who had fixed-rate mortgages, and who were 60 or more days in default of their payments, by lowering their rates to no more than 38 percent of their monthly household incomes while maintaining their debt at their current levels. If a borrower defaulted a second time, the government would assume half of the bank's losses. "The plan, bold but not radical, has succeeded in earning wide praise from pundits as well as the Democratic majority in the House," according to *Mortgage News Daily*. In November 2008 the FDIC posted on-line a detailed guide to its loan-modification program and urged lenders to adopt it.

The previous month had seen the passage of the Emergency Economic Stabilization Act of 2008; widely referred to as a bailout of the nation's financial system, it aimed to lift from banks the burden of so-called distressed assets (also known as toxic assets and legacy assets) and enable and encourage banks to resume or continue making loans to home buyers and businesses. Distressed assets include mortgages in default and securities backed by such mortgages in a complex process known as bundling. (At that time the bundling and selling of loans accounted for "almost half of the credit going to Main Street as well as Wall Street," according to an FDIC fact sheet.) The law created the Troubled Assets Relief Program (TARP), which authorized payments by the federal government (as represented by the U.S. secretary of the treasury) of up to $700 billion to buy distressed assets. It also set up the Capital Assistance Program, whereby financial institutions deemed to be sufficiently sound would have access to a "capital buffer" to "help absorb losses and serve as a bridge to receiving increased private capital," according to the fact sheet, and the Public-Private Investment Fund, through which private investors would join the government in buying toxic assets, with the government insuring any future losses to some extent. Bair publicly criticized TARP as heavily weighted in favor of bankers rather than consumers; she recommended that

$24.4 billion be allocated for preventing 1.5 million foreclosures, with the funds paid directly to homeowners. The Treasury Department and the finance industry strongly opposed that approach, which also drew fire from some of the many people who had kept up their mortgage payments without interruption. "Yes, maybe we're helping somebody who shouldn't have taken that mortgage—maybe they should have known better," Bair explained to Yuki Noguchi for National Public Radio (November 18, 2008, on-line). "But at the end of the day, it's in our collective economic interest to get those mortgages fixed and keep those people in their homes." None of the provisions of the Emergency Economic Stabilization Act forces lenders to act, and as of the end of 2009, according to Michael Powell, writing for the *New York Times* (December 30, 2009), only 31,000 homeowners had received new permanent mortgages; in thousands of other cases, banks refused to lower rates to affordable levels, used delaying tactics in renegotiating mortgages, or in other ways failed to help homeowners avoid foreclosure. A *New York Times* editorial published six days later offered evidence that neither the new law nor a temporary federal tax credit for new-home buyers had alleviated the housing crisis: if, as anticipated, 2.4 million homes enter foreclosure this year, the number of single-family homes on the market will grow to 5.6 million; with the number of unsold houses greatly exceeding the number of prospective buyers, the average price of houses nationwide will continue to decline, to about 60 percent of the average price at the peak of the housing market in 2006. "Already an estimated one-third of homeowners with a mortgage—nearly 16 million people—owe more than their homes are worth . . . ," the editorial reported. "Research suggests that the greater the loss of home equity, the greater the likelihood that borrowers will decide to turn in the keys and find a cheaper place to rent."

Because of the failures of 25 banks in 2008 (among them Washington Mutual, which held $182 billion in deposits) and 140 banks in 2009, the FDIC insurance fund declined from $50 billion before the recession to a negative balance of $8.2 billion at the end of the third quarter of 2009, Eric Dash wrote for the *New York Times* (November 25, 2009). In late September of that year, the FDIC estimated that its losses would total $100 billion within a year or two. A large reason for its slide into the red is that for more than 10 years beginning in 1996, most banks had not been obligated to pay any premiums, or fees, to the FDIC, because the agency's deposit-guarantee fund exceeded the amount required by law—at least 1.5 percent of the total amount deposited. During that period Bair and others had repeatedly petitioned Congress, without success, to allow the FDIC to resume the collection of fees in case of a financial crisis. In May 2009, in the belief that many more banks were headed for trouble, the FDIC reimposed the fees and also imposed an additional, temporary assessment of five cents for every $100 in deposits. In November the FDIC announced that banks would be required to prepay fees that normally would have been due through 2012. Currently, the highest premiums amount to 12 to 16 cents on every $100 in deposits.

Between January 1 and mid-October 2010, 132 U.S. banks failed. At the end of the second quarter of 2010, the FDIC insurance fund carried a negative balance of $15.2 billion, Eric Dash reported for the *New York Times* (August 31, 2010, on-line), and agency officials expected an additional $20 billion in losses stemming from bank failures in the next three years. Nevertheless, Bair said that the agency would recoup those losses, by means of higher premium fees and other assessments. The banking industry has continued to recover, with $21.6 billion in earnings in the second quarter of 2010, the best results since the beginning of the credit crisis in late 2007. Bair warned, however, according to Dash, that "the industry still faces challenges" and that the FDIC expected the recovery to remain "sluggish and slow."

Bair is married to Scott P. Cooper, the vice president of government relations at the American National Standards Institute, an organization whose members include government agencies, organizations, companies, academic institutions, and international entities. The couple have two children: a teenage son, Preston, and a daughter, Colleen, who is in elementary school. Bair has written short stories for the magazine *Highlights for Children* and two children's books: *Rock, Brock and the Savings Shock* (2006) and *Isabel's Car Wash* (2008). She has been a member of the Insurance Marketplace Standards Association, Women in Housing and Finance, the Center for Responsible Lending, the American Bar Association, and the Society of Children's Book Writers and Illustrators. Her honors include the Treasury Department's Treasury Medal (2002), the Association of Education Publishers' Distinguished Achievement Award (2005), and the Burton Foundation's Regulatory Innovation Award (2009).

—C.C.

Suggested Reading: *Economist* (on-line) Oct. 9, 2008; FDIC Web site; *Los Angeles Times* C p2 Dec. 23, 2007; *New York Times* C p1 Dec. 15, 2007, C p1 Aug. 27, 2008; National Public Radio (on-line) Nov. 18, 2008; *USA Today* (on-line) Oct. 2, 2008; *Washington Post* D p1 Oct. 2, 2008

Selected Books: *Rock, Brock, and the Savings Shock*, 2006; *Isabel's Car Wash*, 2008

Frederick M. Brown/Getty Images

Baumbach, Noah

Sep. 3, 1969– Filmmaker

Address: c/o United Talent Agency, 9560 Wilshire Blvd., Suite 500, Beverly Hills, CA 90212

With *The Squid and the Whale, Margot at the Wedding, Greenberg*, and his other works for the silver screen, the award-winning independent filmmaker Noah Baumbach has sought to create "a cinematic world where pain and humor exist simultaneously . . . rather than, I suppose, a comedy that takes a 'time out' to have a 'serious moment,'" as he told Jordana Horn for *New York* (March 26, 2010). "You can laugh or cringe or slowly sink into a quiet depression, all at the same moment." A son of film critics and an avid moviegoer since childhood, Baumbach has been writing and directing motion pictures since the age of 26, and he has acted in four of his own: *Kicking and Screaming*, his first, which was released in 1995; *Highball*; *Mr. Jealousy*; and *The Squid and the Whale*, which won the award for best direction of a drama at the 2005 Sundance Film Festival and prizes for best screenplay from several other institutions. With the filmmaker Wes Anderson, he wrote the screenplays for two Anderson-directed motion pictures: *The Life Aquatic with Steve Zissou* and a stop-motion adaptation of Raoul Dahl's story *Fantastic Mr. Fox*. The latter film, to which George Clooney, Bill Murray, and Meryl Streep lent their voices, earned screenwriting honors from the San Diego, San Francisco, and Online Film Critics societies. While *Fantastic Mr. Fox* is the only one among Baumbach's films to be based on a story for young readers, all of

Baumbach's screenplays—according to Anthony Kaufman, writing for *indieWIRE* (March 18, 2010, on-line)—show the filmmaker's "knack for capturing the regressive, self-absorbed, juvenile side of the adult human condition." Baumbach's adaptation of Claire Messud's novel *The Emperor's Children* is scheduled to arrive at theaters in 2011. He has also been recruited by DreamWorks to rewrite the script for the animated film *Madagascar 3*, which is due to be released in 2012.

The first of the two children of Jonathan Baumbach and Georgia Brown, Noah Baumbach was born on September 3, 1969 in Brooklyn, New York. He has an older stepbrother and stepsister; his father was married and divorced twice before he married Baumbach's mother, and after he and Brown divorced, he married his fourth wife. Jonathan Baumbach has written 14 novels and has had more than 90 short stories published; he chaired the National Society of Film Critics from 1984 to 1986 and wrote film criticism for the *Partisan Review*. Georgia Brown was a film critic for the *Village Voice* in the 1970s and 1980s. "I have a great respect for criticism . . . as an art form," Noah Baumbach told Walter Chaw for *Film Freak Central* (November 6, 2005, on-line). "I grew up in that sort of environment, with the critical eye being the way to look at things and in a way I had to, when I started making movies, I had to learn to trust a more emotional way of doing things." Baumbach was raised in the Park Slope section of Brooklyn with his younger brother, Nicholas (called Nico), who was born in 1975. "Growing up in Brooklyn felt like being outside of the action," he told Noel Murray for the *A.V. Club* (November 9, 2005, on-line). "It's isolated from Manhattan, and Manhattan seemed like this incredible place where really interesting people had dinner parties." He told Ann J. Kolson for the *New York Times* (May 31, 1998), "All of my memories are associated with movies. I remember where I saw every movie and who I was with. I remember the experience of going to them." As a youngster Baumbach drew comics and wrote short stories. He attended the private, nonsectarian Saint Ann's Middle School and the public Midwood High School, both in Brooklyn. After his high-school graduation, in 1987, he entered Vassar College, in Poughkeepsie, New York, where he wrote and directed his own plays. He earned a B.A. degree in English in 1991.

Baumbach spent the summer of 1991 as a messenger for the *New Yorker* magazine. He also worked on the script for his debut film, *Kicking and Screaming*, based on a story he had written with Oliver Berkman. Raising enough money to make that motion picture—$1.3 million—took Baumbach four years. On the first of the 24 days of shooting, Baumbach found himself on a movie set for the first time. "I'd convinced myself in my head that I'd been doing this before," he recalled to Ann J. Kolson. "Now, when I think about that, I'm sort of terrified for myself retroactively. If you have that kind of ambition and confidence, I think, combined with being naïve, it's great because you don't know how hard it is." *Kicking and Screaming* is about four college graduates who lack the motivation to move forward. "They prefer a pleasant limbo filled with witty asides, trivia contests and hairsplitting arguments about matters of no consequence," Janet Maslin wrote for the *New York Times* (October 4, 1995). Baumbach told Noel Murray, "Sort of the point of *Kicking and Screaming*, I always felt, was that college equalizes people from different economic backgrounds, and once you graduate, you're put back where you were." The film starred Carlos Jacott, Jason Wiles, Josh Hamilton, and Chris Eigeman as the four students; Eric Stoltz, Elliot Gould, Parker Posey, and Olivia d'Abo were also in the cast, as were Baumbach, his father, and his brother.

Kicking and Screaming premiered at the New York Film Festival in 1995. Janet Maslin, who saw it there, wrote that the film "occupies its postage-stamp size terrain with confident comic style . . . [and] strikes a cheerfully solipsistic note," and she noted its characters' "archly literate verbal style." Maslin concluded, "*Kicking and Screaming* . . . benefits from an appealing cast and Mr. Baumbach's keen recollection of what it's like to be smart, promising and temporarily adrift. He himself clearly isn't drifting anymore." Hal Hinson, writing for the *Washington Post* (November 17, 1995), called the film "hilariously insightful" and wrote, "In general, Baumbach's eye for generational detail is impeccable—he knows what's on these kids' minds, and has found a language to express it." The film had a very limited distribution and earned little at the box office, but it became an art-house hit, and Baumbach was nominated for a director's award at the 1995 Moscow International Film Festival.

Baumbach's second project was *Mr. Jealousy* (1997). That film is about the insecure, paranoid Lester (Stoltz), who joins the psychotherapy group of Dashiell (Eigeman), the previous lover of his current girlfriend, Ramona (Annabelle Sciorra), in hopes of discovering how to strengthen her affection for him. Written and directed by Baumbach, it was filmed for $2 million in 30 days and distributed by Lions Gate in Seattle, Washington; Los Angeles, California; and Toronto, Ontario. In a glowing assessment, Kenneth Turan wrote for the *Los Angeles Times* (June 23, 1998, on-line) that *Mr. Jealousy*'s "easygoing and engaging quality masks how rare an accomplishment it is to create something achingly true as well as amusing, as wise about people as it is about the craft of film. For a gambit like *Mr. Jealousy* to succeed, the writer-director has to be a matchmaker several times over. He has to first mediate between his characters and his actors, getting the performers to understand his off-center people as well as he does. Even harder is the mediation between the characters and the audience, the creation of a bond that makes viewers empathetic instead of dismissive when multiple quirks develop. Baumbach and his cast manage to do all this and make it seem easy. . . . It's the writer-director's gift for truly seeing people, for imagining them whole, foibles and all, that is the critical element. And deciding to build the piece around a sophisticated, knowing voice-over that is bemused as well as caring is a structure that makes everything possible." By contrast, Marc Savlov wrote for the *Austin (Texas) Chronicle* (July 10, 1998), "*Mr. Jealousy* dives deep into the foamy green waters of emotional malaise and surfaces with nary a clue, although some fine performances . . . manage to keep things interesting," and he dismissed the film as "a slight contrivance."

Working with some of the same actors and crew, Baumbach next focused on *Highball*. Directed by Baumbach from a screenplay that he co-wrote with Carlos Jacott and Christopher Reed, the low-budget *Highball* is about a couple who throw a series of three parties in an attempt to bolster their social life. "Over the course of one year, . . . friendships and relationships are formed, dissolved, and re-formed amidst witty banter," Keith Phipps wrote for *All Movie Guide*. Collaborating for a third time with the cinematographer/director of photography Steven Bernstein, Baumbach shot a rough copy of *Highball* in six days in 1997 and then abandoned the project after a dispute with the producers. "It really was an experiment, and kind of a foolish experiment because I didn't think about what the ramifications would be if it didn't work," Baumbach told Murray. "But it was made with all the best intentions. And it was a funny script. But it was just too ambitious. We didn't have enough time, we didn't finish it, it didn't look good, it was just a whole . . . mess." The movie came out on DVD without Baumbach's approval in 2000, with the writer listed as "Jesse Carter" and the director as "Ernie Fusco." In a brief assessment for *filmcritic.com* (March 16, 2001), Christopher Null wrote, "Mostly consisting of recycled jokes that didn't make it into [Baumbach's] earlier films, *Highball* is still frequently funny while it's perpetually random."

Baumbach next created the pilot for an ABC sitcom that never aired. He also developed a friendship and professional partnership with the writer and director Wes Anderson. He told Noel Murray that he and Anderson "go out to dinner and talk about movies and things we like and don't like, and we introduce each other to things and read each other's scripts, and then we actually work together off of that." Baumbach and Anderson co-wrote, and Anderson directed, *The Life Aquatic with Steve Zissou* (2004), about an aging, cranky oceanographer who has become internationally known in the manner of the real-life Jacques Cousteau. The cast included such A-list performers as Bill Murray (as Zissou), Owen Wilson, Cate Blanchett, Anjelica Huston, Willem Dafoe, Jeff Goldblum, and Michael Gambon. In a representative mixed review, Stephanie Zacharek wrote for *Salon.com* (December 10, 2004), "*The Life Aquatic* gives us some wowee visuals. But there's no emotional texture to them, and the story . . . meanders in such a meaningless way that the visual details, as carefully wrought as they are, come off as mere props." Despite what A.O. Scott derided as Anderson's "self-indulgent make-believe" and the film's "wispy story," that *New York Times* (December 10, 2004) reviewer called *The Life Aquatic* "mostly delightful." "If you allow yourself to surrender" to the movie, he suggested, "you may find that its slow, meandering pace and willful digressions are inseparable from its pleasures."

The Squid and the Whale, the next film that Baumbach wrote and directed, is about the disintegration of the marriage of a Brooklyn couple and the effect on their sons, 12-year-old Frank and 16-year-old Walt. The father, Bernard Berkman, is a self-important English professor whose writing career is on the decline; his seemingly laid-back wife, Joan, has entered into an affair with Frank's tennis instructor and is about to have her first book published. The title of the movie refers to a diorama at the American Museum of Natural History, in Manhattan, which Walt remembers from repeated childhood visits with his mother. During the course of the film, the Berkmans' complicated arrangements for sharing custody of the boys (and even the family cat) grow still more complex when Walt, who closely identifies with his father, develops a crush on Bernard's new love interest (one of his students), and Frank, whose sympathies lie with his mother, becomes aware of his budding sexuality. After *The Squid and the Whale* debuted, at the 2005 Sundance Film Festival, interviewers invariably questioned Baumbach about its seemingly autobiographical aspects, given that he and his brother had also witnessed the breakup of their parents' marriage—though at the ages of eight and four. (The Baumbach brothers' parents divorced years after they separated.) "Someone would ask me if something was true, and I'd say no, and then they'd ask me a follow-up question under the assumption that it was true," the filmmaker told Dennis Lim for the *New York Times* (November 11, 2007). "I'd get tripped up answering a question about my real father based on something in the movie that wasn't real." He added, "If I'm using something that's familiar or from my life, it's only to ground me so I can invent off of that." "The only thing I want to make sure people know is that I invented the stuff the younger brother . . . does, the drinking and the masturbation," he told M. Faust for *Artvoice* (December 2, 2005, on-line). "My brother didn't do those things. Even if he had, I don't know that I would have had access to that information, and if I had I wouldn't betray a trust like that." By his own account, the making of *The Squid and the Whale* powerfully affected Baumbach's professional development. "I started making movies pretty young; I had a lot of preconceived ideas about who I was as a filmmaker and the kind of career I wanted to have that were still connected, I think, to the teenager I was rather that the person I was becoming," he told Jonathan Lethem for

Bomb (Fall 2005). "I discovered here who I really am as a writer and then as a director." *The Squid and the Whale* was widely acclaimed, and its screenplay earned an Academy Award nomination.

In 2005 Baumbach married the actress Jennifer Jason Leigh. Leigh had a leading role in his next film, *Margot at the Wedding* (2007), which is set right before the wedding of Pauline (Leigh) to Malcolm (Jack Black). Unexpectedly, Pauline's long-estranged, highly neurotic, and caustically judgmental sister, Margot (Nicole Kidman), whose own marriage is collapsing, arrives with her 13-year-old son; she proceeds to criticize and insult Malcolm and leads Pauline to question the wisdom of marrying him. In an assessment of the movie for *Hollywood.com*, Jenny Peters wrote that Baumbach had proved that "he is still a sharply observant author who explores dysfunctional family relationships with insight and verve." "The best thing about Baumbach's work . . . ," she declared, "is his dialogue. The conversations the family members engage in are multilayered, with the things they don't say as obvious as the things they do. He's one of the few writers working in film today who can draw a cringe of compassion out of even the most jaded viewer. With *Margot at the Wedding*, Baumbach forces us to think about the words we say to our own loved ones—and how harmful they can be if uttered without thinking them through." By contrast, Anton Bitel, writing for the British Web site *Eye for Film*, found *Margot at the Wedding*—and *The Squid and the Whale*—to be irritatingly "static," and Kidman's depiction of Margot struck him as "irksome."

"Everyone I know, myself included, deals with this conflict between who you think you are—and how you'd like to be seen, and the kind of person you want to be—and then how you may actually be in the world," Baumbach said to Jordana Horn in reference to the troubled title character of his next directorial effort, *Greenberg* (2010). *Greenberg*'s screenplay was co-written by Baumbach and Leigh, the latter of whom also had a role in the film. The story follows Roger Greenberg, an unmarried, jobless carpenter (portrayed by Ben Stiller) of about 40 who has recently received treatment for obsessive-compulsive disorder. Roger leaves New York for Los Angeles to house-sit for his rich brother. Over the course of the next few weeks, he embarks on an awkward romantic relationship with his brother's assistant, the 25-year-old Florence (Greta Gerwig), who "exists in the same provisionally, painfully self-conscious not-quite-there-ness as Greenberg," Ann Hornaday wrote for the *Washington Post* (March 26, 2010); elsewhere in that review, Hornaday described the film as "a quietly funny portrait of grown-ups growing up" and "a compassionate tribute to all the people on [Hollywood's] star-strewn avenues" who are "alone with their dreams." According to Clint O'Connor, a Cleveland, Ohio, *Plain Dealer* (March 26, 2010, on-line) critic, *Greenberg* "is an easy film to admire.

It's just not easy to like." Baumbach, O'Connor wrote, "has an amazing ear for how people actually talk," and with *Greenberg*, O'Connor suggested, he wanted viewers "to feel uncomfortable, to feel the heat of his main character's burning anxiety. And we do. It's a movie that's palpable, and funny. . . . But I still found myself asking questions like, Is this entertaining? Am I having fun? I've known enough people in real life like Greenberg; do I really want to hang out with them for two hours in a theater?" *Greenberg* was nominated for the Golden Bear Award at the 60th Berlin International Film Festival in 2010.

The 41-year-old Baumbach was 40 when he got his driver's license. "It's kind of major, learning to drive. I feel like it kicked up other stuff in my life," he told Karina Longworth for the *Village Voice* (March 9, 2010). According to various sources, Baumbach is co-directing an as-yet-untitled documentary in collaboration with Jake Paltrow. He and his wife have residences in Brooklyn and Los Angeles.

—J.P.

Suggested Reading: *Bomb* p32+ Fall 2005; *indieWIRE.com* Dec. 20, 2009; *Los Angeles Times* (on-line) Mar. 21, 2010; *New York* (on-line) Mar. 26, 2010; *New York Times* II p13 May 31, 1998; *Variety* p46 Feb. 9–15, 2004

Selected Films: as writer and director—*Kicking and Screaming*, 1995; *Mr. Jealousy*, 1997; *The Squid and the Whale*, 2005; *Margot at the Wedding*, 2007; *Greenberg*, 2010; as writer—*The Life Aquatic with Steve Zissou* (with Wes Anderson), 2004; *Fantastic Mr. Fox* (with Wes Anderson), 2009; as actor—*Kicking and Screaming*, 1995; *Mr. Jealousy*, 1997; *The Life Aquatic with Steve Zissou*, 2004

Tim Sloan/AFP/Getty Images

Benjamin, Regina

Oct. 26, 1956– U.S. surgeon general; internist

Address: Office of the Surgeon General, 5600 Fishers Ln., Rm. 18-66, Rockville, MD 20857

"I am a firm believer that you bloom wherever you're planted," Regina Benjamin, the new surgeon general of the U.S., told an interviewer for *Ebony* (March 1997). The 53-year-old Benjamin, a family physician, bloomed where she planted *herself* in 1990: in Bayou La Batre, a fishing village on

the Gulf Coast of Alabama, near where she grew up. As the founder and chief executive officer of the Bayou La Batre Rural Health Clinic, Benjamin often worked 17-hour days, seven days a week, ministering to a community of about 2,500 people, most of them very poor and lacking medical insurance. To her patients, some of whom paid for her services in seafood from their catches, she was "an angel in a white coat," as the headline of an article by Rick Bragg for the *New York Times* (April 3, 1995) put it. Benjamin, Bragg wrote, was "a throwback long thought to be extinct: a country doctor with a heart." Two months after Bragg's article was published, Benjamin became the first African-American woman, and the first physician under 40, to be elected to the board of the American Medical Association (AMA). "She gave us a perspective in her role as a young, solo, rural practitioner dedicated to educating her patients," Timothy Flaherty, another AMA board member, told Mark Taylor for *Modern Healthcare* (May 22, 2000). "Regina has unique skills, and she made the board more aware of and sensitive to minority issues. She was listened to very carefully." Benjamin is the first black woman to hold the top post of a U.S. state medical society—that of Alabama, in 2002. Thanks to her many years as a family doctor and her activities not only with the AMA and other physicians' groups but also with local, state, and federal legislators and agencies, health-maintenance organizations (HMOs) and other medical insurers, and medical regulatory boards, Benjamin has gained wide experience in dealing with politicians, bureaucrats, powerful members of the medical community, and representatives of the medical-insurance industry.

On July 13, 2009, when President Barack Obama announced that he had chosen Benjamin for the post of U.S. surgeon general, he spoke about the need to reform the country's health-care system to cover the approximately 50 million Americans who were uninsured and the estimated additional 25 million people who were underinsured. "I am acutely aware of the national scope of the problem," Benjamin had written 13 years earlier in an article, called "Feeling Poorly," for the *National Forum* (Summer 1996). "It has been said that a country can be judged by how it treats it neediest citizens," she declared in her article. "If that judgment extends to health care, the United States and its people may not want to hear the verdict." She concluded, "Addressing the health-care needs of our poor and underserved not only will improve their health, but also the health of the country." (In March 2010 Obama signed into law the Patient Protection and Affordable Care Act.) "For all the tremendous obstacles that she has overcome, Regina Benjamin also represents what's best about health care in America, doctors and nurses who give and care and sacrifice for the sake of their patients," Obama said when he announced her nomination, according to the Associated Press (July 13, 2009). In addition to the Bayou La Batre clinic's chronic shortage of funds, which for some years was so severe that Benjamin could not pay herself a salary, those obstacles included the destruction of the facility by Hurricane Georges in 1998, by Hurricane Katrina in 2005, and by fire in 2006. For months or years at a stretch after each of those disasters, Benjamin cared for her patients without interruption by working out of temporary quarters, including the back of her pickup truck and a trailer, and making daily house calls. Her dedication and her successful efforts to rebuild the clinic three times—with loans, donations, volunteer labor, and, once, by mortgaging her home and borrowing to the limit on each of her credit cards—have earned her international recognition and honors, among them the $500,000 so-called genius grant from the John D. and Catherine T. MacArthur Foundation in 2008. Benjamin assumed the post of surgeon general on October 29, 2009, after the U.S. Senate voted unanimously for her confirmation.

The younger of the two children of Clarence and Millie Benjamin, Regina Marcia Benjamin was born on October 26, 1956 in Mobile, Alabama. She was raised with her brother in the Roman Catholic faith in Daphne, a small town on the east coast of Mobile Bay, which empties into the Gulf of Mexico. Her father moved to the Pacific Coast after he and his wife separated, when their daughter was two; they later divorced. Benjamin's mother worked as a waitress (or a domestic worker, according to some sources); although the family was poor, they always had enough to eat—including the gulf's plentiful shrimp, mullet, oysters, and other seafood—and Benjamin never felt deprived of anything, as she told a reporter for *Ebony* (March 1997). Her maternal grandmother, who died when Benjamin was nine, "was very strong willed and very compassionate," Benjamin said in an interview for a profile of her posted in 2002 on the Web site of the National Library of Medicine (NLM), a division of the National Institutes of Health (NIH). Her grandmother was the principal mover in the founding and building of a Catholic church for African-Americans in Daphne. In the 1930s, during the Great Depression, she routinely provided food and drink for vagabonds, both black and white, who happened to pass by her home. "Those values she passed on to my mother and ultimately to my brother and to me," Benjamin recalled. Her mother, Benjamin said for the NLM profile, "was truly my mentor. . . . She was very intelligent, very bright, witty and extremely social and outgoing, very much a team and consensus builder, and was very opinionated. Many of those traits I inherited." Benjamin's parents and brother have all died—her father from diabetes and hypertension, her brother from HIV-related causes, and her mother, a longtime smoker, from lung cancer. "While I cannot change my family's past, I can be a voice in the movement to improve our nation's healthcare and our nation's health for the future," Benjamin told Steve Holland and Maggie Fox for Reuters (July 13, 2009, on-line).

Benjamin attended Fairhope High School, in a nearby town. An excellent student, she was active in the drama club and a member of the student council and the school honor society. An article she read about international lawyers led her to apply to Yale University's law school while still in high school. "They sent me a reply politely telling me that I needed my undergraduate degree first," she told the *Ebony* reporter. Benjamin won a scholarship to Xavier University of Louisiana, in New Orleans, "the only historically Black, Catholic University in the Western Hemisphere," according to its Web site. There she joined the school's pre-med club, where she could observe doctors at work and where, for the first time, she saw a black physician. She told *Ebony* that she was fascinated by "how the doctors enjoyed what they were doing and how they impacted the lives of their patients." As a student in Xavier's pre-med program, she participated in a training course for student interns run by the Central Intelligence Agency. She earned a B.S. degree in chemistry from Xavier in 1979. She then entered the Morehouse School of Medicine, in Atlanta, Georgia, which at that time offered only a two-year course for prospective physicians. At Morehouse she studied community medicine under David Satcher (who later, from 1998 to 2002, served as the nation's surgeon general) and hematology under Louis Sullivan (later, from 1989 to 1993, the secretary of the U.S. Department of Health and Human Services). While at Morehouse, she said for the NLM profile, she became aware of "the importance of being politically active." In 1981 Benjamin entered the University of Alabama School of Medicine at Birmingham. She earned an M.D. degree in 1984. She completed her internship and residency in family medicine at the Medical Center of Central Georgia, in Macon, in 1987. During that period she campaigned in support of an AMA resolution to require that medical schools offer a class on sexually transmitted diseases. By 1986 every medical school in the country had added such classes to their curricula. Also in 1986 Benjamin helped to organize the AMA's Young Physicians Section; two years later she helped to set up a similar subgroup of the Alabama Medical Association.

Benjamin's medical-school tuition, fees, and loans had been paid by the National Health Service Corps (NHSC), an arm of the Department of Health and Human Services. In return for the corps's financial assistance, Benjamin had agreed to serve for three years as a primary-care physician in an NHSC-approved area suffering from an acute shortage of doctors. In 1987 the NHSC sent Benjamin to work at Mostellar Medical Center in Irvington, Alabama, near Mobile. When she completed her NHSC service, she decided to remain in the area. In 1990 she set up a medical practice in Bayou La Batre, on the Gulf Coast of Alabama about 30 miles southwest of Daphne (and on the west side of Mobile Bay). Pronounced as one name—"Baylabatray"—by residents, Bayou La Batre had no local doctor in 1990; its population then was about 2,300 (it is now about 2,700). A majority of its residents are African-American; the others are primarily Cajuns or immigrants or their descendants from Vietnam, Laos, and Cambodia. Most of them earn their livings from fishing and shrimping; then, as now, the incomes of most were below the poverty level. Benjamin had a sliding scale for payments from her patients. "Most pay me what they can, when they can," she wrote for the *National Forum*. "It is not uncommon for payments to come in five, ten dollars at a time—if at all." For the many who could not pay, she accepted shrimp, smoked fish, oysters, or other edibles in lieu of money. "I wanted to allow people to keep their dignity . . . ," she told Bob Dart for the *Atlanta Journal-Constitution* (June 4, 2006). "They work for a living and they're proud."

In addition to seeing patients, usually beginning at 7:00 a.m., Benjamin moonlighted as the medical director of several nursing homes and on the late-night shifts at emergency rooms in Mobile and Fairhope. Even with those extra jobs, it was virtually impossible for her to earn enough to cover her expenses. Determined to find ways to make her practice financially stable, she enrolled in the M.B.A. program at Tulane University, in New Orleans. Making the 250-mile round-trip commute to the school twice weekly, she completed the degree in 1991. While at Tulane she learned that, thanks to a 1977 law, the federal government provided funds to health clinics in economically depressed rural areas. With minimal changes to her office, her practice became the Bayou La Batre Rural Health Clinic Inc.

In 1995 Benjamin became the first African-American woman to be elected to the board of trustees of the American Medical Association. Two years later the CBS program *This Morning* (a precursor to *The Early Show*) named Benjamin "Woman of the Year." In 1998 the Henry J. Kaiser Family Foundation honored her with a Nelson Mandela Award for Health and Human Rights. In articles whose titles drew attention to her achievements, Benjamin was profiled in the magazines *Southern Living* (June 1999), in "Mending Souls and Bones"; *Modern Healthcare* (May 22, 2000), in "A Voice for Patients: At Home in Rural Ala., She's Still Setting Milestones in Medicine"; *People* (May 13, 2002), in "Always on Call"; *Reader's Digest* (January 2003), in "The Doctor Is Always In" (reprinted in the same periodical in February 2006 as "A Healing Force"); and *U.S. News & World Report* (December 1–8, 2008), as one of "America's Best Leaders 2008," in "Big-City Healthcare in a Tiny Rural Town." Although as of July 1, 2008 the number of African-Americans living in the U.S. was 41.1 million, or 13.5 percent of the total population, only about 47,700, or 5.6 percent, of the nation's physicians were African-American, and of that 47,700, only 47.4 percent were women. Thus, Benjamin is among the fewer than 2.5 percent of physicians in the U.S. who are both black and female.

On July 13, 2009 President Obama announced his nomination of Benjamin to the post of U.S. surgeon general. The surgeon general works for the U.S. Public Health Service (USPHS) under the auspices of the Department of Health and Human Services. He or she is in charge of the 6,000-member quasi-military commissioned corps of the USPHS—physicians, dentists, nurses, pharmacists, dietitians, environmental-health officers, mental-health specialists, veterinarians, and scientists. Those medical professionals staff health centers on Native American reservations, serve in areas of the country where there is a shortage of medical personnel, conduct quarantine inspections in U.S. ports, help out during national medical emergencies, engage in basic research, and provide various other services. The surgeon general also articulates the nation's health-care goals, issues warnings to the public about specific dangers to health, and acts as the president's spokesperson on health-related issues. In introducing Benjamin to the press, President Obama said, "For nearly two decades, Dr. Regina Benjamin has seen—in a very personal way—what is broken about our health-care system," according to Jane Zhang in the *Wall Street Journal* (July 14, 2009). Benjamin, too, said that she intended to push for more-affordable health care for all Americans. "I want to ensure that no one, no one falls through the cracks as we improve our healthcare system," she declared.

A few health experts criticized Obama's choice of Benjamin because she is overweight. Marcia Angell, for example, a former editor of the *New England Journal of Medicine* and a senior lecturer at the Harvard University Medical School, told Susan Donaldson James for abcnews.go.com (July 21, 2009) that Benjamin's size "tends to undermine her credibility." But Angell's was a minority opinion. An editorial supporting Benjamin for the job appeared in the *Chicago Tribune* (July 30, 2009):

"There's nothing in a doctor's training or contract that suggests they are put on Earth to model all the correct behaviors for the rest of us. If that were the case, you wouldn't find doctors sneaking a smoke outside the hospital. Bulletin: Doctors are human. Some of them are overweight, just like much of the rest of America. . . . What makes a surgeon general credible—any doctor—is her understanding of the science behind medical advice and the ability to explain it to people so they take action. No, it's not easy to lose weight. With Benjamin, however, many Americans might recognize a fellow combatant in that relentless battle."

Benjamin's stance regarding abortion rights did not become an issue during the discussion of her nomination, as has happened with nominees for the post in the past; indeed, her position on abortion has never been made public. No abortions have ever been performed at the Bayou La Batre clinic. Although the clinic dispenses birth-control information and devices, in 2006 Pope Benedict XVI, the head of the Catholic Church worldwide, which forbids the use by its followers of any devices or substances for contraception, honored her with the Pro Ecclesia et Pontifice, the highest papal award for laypeople. Benjamin's nomination was confirmed by the U.S. Senate on October 29, 2009.

In April 2010 the offshore-oil-drilling rig Deepwater Horizon—owned by Transocean Ltd. and licensed by British Petroleum (BP)—exploded at its location in the Gulf of Mexico, about 41 miles off the coast of Louisiana. For five months afterward, until the source of the leak was permanently capped, some 206 million gallons of oil spewed into the gulf. The disaster caused widespread devastation of wildlife habitats and crippled the area's fishing and tourism industries. In September 2010 Benjamin joined the newly created Alabama Coastal Recovery Commission, whose mission is to design a plan to help Louisiana recover from the impact of the spill. Benjamin visited the region in July, and in a speech in New Orleans, she directed attention to the possible long-term mental-health effects of the spill on residents. "It's hard to explain what the water means to us," she said, as quoted by Sharmila Devi in the *Lancet* (August 14–20, 2010). "The biggest factor is the uncertainty. With hurricanes, you wait for it to strike, it hits, then you move on with the recovery. . . . With this, you continue to ask every day: 'When will our oyster beds be back? When will our jobs come back?'" Benjamin noted that the Obama administration would work to require BP to fund mental-health services for those affected.

In June 2010 Benjamin, along with First Lady Michelle Obama and Kathleen Sebelius, the secretary of the U.S. Department of Health and Human Services, launched "The Surgeon General's Vision for a Healthy and Fit Nation," a program aimed at encouraging people to exercise and otherwise lead more healthful lives. To promote the program Benjamin took part in community walks around the nation. In October 2010 she launched the "Young and Mobile" program, which aims to end the epidemic of obesity among children.

Benjamin joined the faculty of the University of South Alabama College of Medicine, in Mobile, as an associate professor of family medicine in 1997. She was named assistant dean and then associate dean for rural-health programs at that medical school in 1998 and 1999, respectively, and held the latter title until 2004. From May 2008 until she assumed the surgeon general's post, Benjamin chaired the Federation of State Medical Boards (FSMB); she has also served on the FSMB's board of directors and on many of the group's committees, including one that drew up guidelines for the treatment of drug addicts in internists' offices. Among the many other groups on which she has served, she sat on Alabama's board of medical examiners for 12 years and for some years on the National Board of Medical Examiners. She also served as president of the American Medical Association Education and Research Foundation and chaired the AMA Council on Ethical and Judicial Affairs.

Benjamin is single. Her leisure interests include environmental issues and travel.

—W.D.

Suggested Reading: *Contemporary Black Biography* Dec. 1998; *Ebony* p86+ Mar. 1997; *Jet* p8 Aug. 3, 2009; *Modern Healthcare* p34+ May 22, 2000; *National Catholic Reporter* p9 Aug. 7, 2009; National Library of Medicine Web site; *New York Times* A p12 Apr. 3, 1995, (on-line) July 14, 2009; *People* p219+ May 13, 2002; *Reader's Digest* p23+ Jan. 2003, p144+ Feb. 2006; *Southern Living* p130+ June 1999; *U.S. News & World Report* p43+ Dec. 18, 2008; *Wall Street Journal* (on-line) July 14, 2009

Bewkes, Jeffrey L.

(BYOO-kess)

May 25, 1952– Chairman and chief executive officer of Time Warner Inc.

Address: One Time Warner Center, New York, NY 10019-8016

When Jeffrey Bewkes—the chief executive officer (CEO) of Time Warner Inc. since 2008 and chairman since 2009—began his career there at 27 as a junior finance officer in its HBO division in 1979, HBO was a single channel offering previously released films, standup comedy, and boxing matches, and only about 10 percent of American households had cable TV. By the time of his promotion to chairman of Time Warner's entertainment and networks group, in 2002, Bewkes had served as an HBO executive for more than a dozen years and had built Home Box Office (its full name) into a

Peter Kramer/Getty Images

Jeffrey L. Bewkes

highly profitable family of cable-television networks catering to some 40 million subscribers worldwide. He had also transformed it into a television treasure, with award–winning sports programs; original feature films including documentaries, docudramas, and biopics; and very popular dramatic or comedic series, among them *The Sopranos*, *Sex and the City*, *Curb Your Enthusiasm*, and *Six Feet Under*. During the approximately four years that Bewkes guided Warner Bros. Entertainment, the firm produced or co-produced films including the first three *Harry Potter* movies (2002, 2004, 2005); *Mystic River* (2003); *Million Dollar Baby* and *Aviator* (both 2004); and *Good Night and Good Luck* and *Syriana* (both 2005). From 2005 to 2007 Bewkes served as Time Warner's president and chief operating officer.

As Time Warner's top executive, Bewkes oversees the HBO and Cinemax networks and the multifaceted Turner Broadcasting System, which includes the Cartoon Network, such channels as TCM (Turner Classic Movies), TBS, and CNN/U.S., Web sites including CNNMoney.com, NASCAR.com, and PGA Tour.com, and radio stations. The Time Warner umbrella also covers Warner Bros. Entertainment, whose parts include Warner Bros. Pictures, New Line Cinema, Warner Home Video, and the Warner Bros. Television Group, which produces series for NBC, ABC, Fox, and other networks as well as its own programming. Bewkes also oversees Time Inc., the largest publisher of magazines in the U.S. and one of the biggest in Great Britain and Mexico. Time Inc.'s nearly 120 magazines include *Time*, *People*, *Fortune*, *Sports Illustrated*, *Entertainment Weekly*, *Essence*, *Advertising Age*, *Marie Claire*, *InStyle*, *Money*,

Country Life, *Southern Living*, *Hi-Fi News*, *Horse & Hound*, *Model Collector*, *Rugby World*, and *Shooting Times*. In each month of the first quarter of 2010, according to the Time Warner Web site, Time Inc.'s 26 on-line sites in the U.S. attracted an average of 52 million different visitors.

According to Georg Szalai, writing for the *Hollywood Reporter* (November 6, 2007), Bewkes is known as a "hard-driven, bottom-line enforcer with a penetrating gaze." David Joyce, an analyst with the brokerage firm Miller Takab, told Szalai that Bewkes "is generally well liked on [Wall] Street and in Hollywood as he is known for having a good mix of business and creative thinking. That is a potent mix that is, unfortunately, not always present" among those in comparable positions of corporate power.

Bewkes strongly disapproved of Time Warner's sale to AOL, which went into effect in January 2000. For reasons still in dispute (among them discord between Time Warner veterans and AOL decision makers), the mega-merger led to tremendous losses in revenues and stock value. Unlike Richard Parsons, his predecessor as CEO and chairman, who was said to feel attached to Time Warner's multiple arms, Bewkes was seen as being unafraid to make major changes in order to improve the company's finances, including dismemberment. On November 5, 2007, when Time Warner announced that Bewkes would succeed Parsons, the consensus among industry observers, Szalai wrote, was that Bewkes "puts excellence of execution and pragmatism over big visions." "We have a lot to do," Bewkes said, according to Szalai, "and I'm intensely focused on building shareholder value." Toward that end, on March 12, 2009 Time Warner divested itself of Time Warner Cable, and the following December it spun off AOL Inc. On August 4, 2010 Time Warner reported on its Web site that during the second quarter of 2010, the company's revenues rose 8 percent, to $6.4 billion—the highest rate of growth in two years—and advertising revenues rose 11 percent. Its stock price is currently slightly lower than it was when Bewkes became Time Warner's head.

The second of the three sons of Eugene Garrett Bewkes Jr. and Marjorie (Klent) Bewkes, Jeffrey Lawrence Bewkes was born on May 25, 1952 in Paterson, New Jersey. His older brother, Eugene III (called Gar), is an investment banker; his brother Robert (Bobby) co-owns a real-estate firm. Bewkes's paternal grandfather was the president of St. Lawrence University, in Canton, Ohio, for nearly two decades. His father earned a J.D. degree from Yale Law School and held executive positions with large corporations including Canada Dry Inc. Bewkes and his brothers grew up in Darien, Connecticut, an affluent suburb about 40 miles northeast of New York City. Like their father, all three boys attended the prestigious Deerfield Academy, in Deerfield, Massachusetts. As a boarding student there, Bewkes was a member of the debate team. One year he persuaded the administration to end the requirement that students appear for breakfast in the dining hall at 7:30 a.m., on the grounds that their schoolwork often kept them up past midnight.

After graduating from Deerfield, in 1970, Bewkes enrolled at Yale University, in New Haven, Connecticut. He was "a somewhat romantic figure of countercultural élan—a tad scruffy and artistic-looking in a battered leather jacket," Lloyd Grove, a fellow Yale alumnus, wrote for *New York* (January 2, 2008). During the summer after his junior year, Bewkes opted against relaxing at the family beach house on Nantucket, a Massachusetts island; instead, he worked as a gofer for the TV and film writer and producer Leonard B. Stern, who was then the vice president of Talent Associates/Norton Simon and the co-owner of a company in which Bewkes's father owned shares. While on that job Bewkes chauffeured the British actress Diana Rigg. He graduated from Yale with a B.A. degree in philosophy in 1974. With the idea of becoming a TV reporter, he took a research position with the documentary division of NBC News, but he was laid off soon after, when he completed his assignment. He then applied to law and business schools and chose to attend the graduate program in business at Stanford University, in Palo Alto, California. At Yale Bewkes had not struck others as a serious scholar, "but when he got to Stanford, things changed dramatically," James Angell, a friend from his Yale years, told Grove. "Once he decided that he was going to undertake a business career, he became very focused." While at Stanford Bewkes worked as the operations director of a California winery.

After he earned an M.B.A. degree, in 1977, Bewkes moved to New York City and took a job as an accounting officer with Citibank. While friends of his took advantage of the city's nightlife, Bewkes devoted himself to work. "We'd all be having dinner, and we'd say, 'Come with us to the Mudd Club, we're going to see Talking Heads,' and Jeff would say, 'No, I've got to be at work in the morning,'" Angell told Grove. Another of Bewkes's Yale friends, Laurie Frank, told Grove, "Jeff was always very close to his dad. And some of his drive comes from wanting to be acknowledged by him—to be viewed as an equal." She also said, "I think Jeff was always being groomed to be a CEO, to be the head of a company like Time Warner." According to Grove, however, "Bewkes bristles at the suggestion that he's a member of a privileged East Coast elite—preferring to align himself with his father's salt-of-the-earth forebears who emigrated to New Jersey from the Netherlands in the late-nineteenth century, and to reminisce about a childhood spent hanging out in his German maternal grandfather's dry-goods store in Phoenixville," a small town in Pennsylvania.

After two years with Citibank, Bewkes turned down the company's offer of a position in Hong Kong and accepted a job with HBO, a fledgling cable station owned by Time Inc. In his early days there, as a marketing manager, he was charged with persuading hotel chains to sign up for HBO, which at that time specialized in showing feature films, boxing events, and standup comedy. He found a mentor in Michael J. Fuchs, the forceful, abrasive executive whom many have credited with making HBO the media giant it eventually became. Guided by Fuchs, Bewkes steadily climbed the corporate ladder, becoming HBO's chief financial officer in 1986 and president and chief operating officer five years later. The latter promotion positioned him directly under Fuchs, who was then HBO's chairman and chief executive officer. Bewkes began negotiating with movie studios, overseeing HBO's expansion into foreign markets, and increasing the budget for original programming, which was then sold to other networks.

In 1995 clashes with Time Warner higher-ups led to Fuchs's ouster, and Bewkes succeeded him as HBO's chairman and CEO. A dozen years later Fuchs told Grove, "You see a lot of ass-kissing out there, but Jeff did not do that. . . . Jeff has a certain grace about him. It reminds me of what they used to say about [the legendary baseball player] Joe DiMaggio. He never looked like he was running in the outfield, but he would catch the ball nevertheless." Building on a strategy that Fuchs had introduced, Bewkes tripled HBO's budget for original programming, allocating more than $700 million for in-house productions. Bewkes routinely spent large amounts of money for projects that he believed had great merit, such as the 10-part World War II miniseries *Band of Brothers*, which cost $120 million to produce. While *Band of Brothers*, which debuted two days before 9/11, attracted relatively few viewers, it proved to be highly profitable as a DVD release. Other profitable HBO programs that aired under Bewkes included *Sex and the City* (1998–2004), *The Sopranos* (1999–2007), *Curb Your Enthusiasm* (2000–), and *Six Feet Under* (2001–05), all of which gained large, loyal audiences. *The Sopranos*, an immensely popular drama about a New Jersey Mafia family, came to HBO after the Fox network rejected it. Bewkes championed it after watching the pilot episode. "I showed it to Jeff and basically he asked, 'Can we keep making it this good?,'" Chris Albrecht, HBO's president of original programming/New York at that time, told Grove. *The Sopranos*' creator, David Chase, recalled to Grove, "The show didn't test all that well. Jeff had to be party to disregarding the research and saying, 'Who cares what these focus groups say? We like this.' That takes something special." In 1997 HBO won 15 Emmy Awards. It had received 90 nominations, "marking the first time a cable network had garnered more nominations than any broadcast network," according to fundinguniverse.com; in 2002 it was nominated for 93 Emmys and won 22.

On another front, Bewkes challenged HBO's competitors by creating multiple HBO channels, thus establishing a network of specialized stations, among them HBO Family, HBO Latino, and HBO

Comedy. He also worked to implement video-on-demand technology and pushed for increased DVD sales. Under his leadership HBO became the most profitable TV network in the world, quintupling in value to $10 billion. "What Jeff did there is a great case study of taking an organization that people thought was at its prime and taking it someplace they didn't think it could go," Tom Freston, then an executive with Viacom, told Richard Siklos for the *New York Times* (October 9, 2005).

In 1999 Bewkes learned that Gerald Levin, Time Warner's CEO, was negotiating a deal in which AOL, a major global Internet service, would purchase Time Warner. He expressed his fierce opposition to the sale, but Levin dismissed his concerns. The deal, worth about $164 billion (widely different figures have been cited), was completed on January 10, 2000; Stephen M. "Steve" Case, AOL's founder and head, became the chairman of the merged conglomerate, christened AOL Time Warner, and share prices rose from $71.84, at the end of 2001, to $97.50 on January 11, 2001. By January 11, 2002, however, the stock's value had dropped to $63.36, as many subscribers had switched from AOL's dial-up service to high-speed Internet providers and AOL ad revenues had plummeted. One year later the price for a share of AOL Time Warner stock was $30.72. Earlier, at a top-management meeting in the spring of 2002, Bewkes had bluntly criticized Case; in the book *Stealing Time* (2003), Alec Klein, its author, who had been covering AOL since 2000 for the *Washington Post*, quoted Bewkes as saying, "I'm tired of this. This is bull****. The only division that's not performing is yours. Every one of us is growing, making the numbers. The only problem in this construct is AOL." (Some insiders told Klein that Richard Parsons, who in 2002 succeeded Levin, had urged Bewkes to attack Case, but Parsons denied doing so.) Klein's *Washington Post* reports of questionable business and accounting practices within AOL spurred investigations of AOL by the U.S. Justice Department and the Securities and Exchange Commission as well as an internal AOL probe, which led to AOL's admission that it had inflated its reported advertising revenues by some $190 million.

In July 2002 Bewkes was named chairman of AOL Time Warner's newly created entertainment division, encompassing Warner Bros. film and television studios; New Line Cinema; CNN, HBO, Turner Networks, and the WB Network; and Warner Music. Bewkes's promotion came after the company's board of directors pressured Robert Pittman, the chief operating officer of AOL Time Warner and chief executive officer of AOL, to step down. In a management reorganization, the board tapped Bewkes and Don Logan, who had been named AOL Time Warner's chair of new media and communications, to replace Pittman and function as AOL Time Warner's co–chief operating officers. "Although the unassuming Mr. Logan and the outspoken Mr. Bewkes are stylistic opposites, both are very popular at Time Warner, in part because their divisions have reputations for producing quality products and consistent profits," David Carr and Jim Rutenberg wrote for the *New York Times* (July 19, 2002); the reporters cited the 42 percent increase in the number of HBO subscribers between 1995 and 2002 (from 27 million to 38.5 million) and the growth in gross earnings during that period to a compounded annual rate of 16 percent. According to Carr and Rutenberg, Bewkes's accomplishments at HBO gave him "an aura of invincibility. . . . His independence from the new management [Case and Pittman] reinforced Mr. Bewkes's image as a different kind of corporate executive, one with a wicked sense of humor that matched the earthy comedy of his network and a streak of confident anti-authoritarianism." They also reported, "Some associates said they were surprised he was taking the new corporate job, one that takes him into areas like ad-supported television networks where he has little experience. He has previously rebuffed overtures to head other units of the company (including AOL) and to work at other companies (ABC). But some associates said they wondered if he was perhaps more ambitious than he had let on. 'I always wondered, did he stick it out because he wanted to be C.E.O. of AOL Time Warner, or was he risk-averse and liked what he was doing,' said one competing executive, who said he had once tried to offer Mr. Bewkes a major job and was quickly turned down. What few dispute is that he was unhappy with the way things were going and did not hesitate to tell top AOL Time Warner executives when he disagreed with them."

In 2003 the "AOL" part of the corporate name was discarded. The next year Time Warner sold its music division to a group of investors led by Edgar Bronfman Jr. for $2.6 billion. In 2005 the "corporate raider" Carl Icahn joined forces with three hedge funds and bought 2.6 percent of Time Warner's stock. Like many others Icahn believed that Time Warner had grown to an unwieldy size, and he hoped to force the media conglomerate to sell more of its divisions. Icahn publicly criticized the board of directors, most of whom had voted for the ill-fated AOL merger, and he lambasted Parsons for selling the Warner Music division for what he deemed to be too low a price. Parsons resisted calls to carve up Time Warner, explaining to Richard Siklos, "No one has made a persuasive case to me that having these businesses together somehow diminishes value, as opposed to enhances value." Through a stock-buyback program, Time Warner succeeded in blocking Icahn's takeover attempt. Sources differ as to whether Bewkes approved of the way Parsons had gone about repurchasing shares. An unnamed media investor and confidant of Bewkes's told Grove, "Money was foolishly squandered. . . . Jeff thinks [Parsons] got rolled." Edward Adler, Time Warner's executive vice president for corporate communications, disputed that assertion, maintaining to Grove that Bewkes "strongly believed in the stock buyback throughout the Icahn period."

In January 2006 Bewkes was named Time Warner's president and chief operating officer. The next month Time Warner sold its book-publishing division to the Hachette Book Group, a subsidiary of Hachette Livre, one of the world's largest publishing companies. In response to continually falling AOL subscription rates, Bewkes implemented a new strategy for Time Warner's on-line division. Instead of being a subscription-driven Internet provider, AOL became a free "portal," like Yahoo! or Google, offering users e-mail and search capabilities. Bewkes hoped that ad revenue on the site would make up for lost subscriptions, but while AOL saw 40 percent ad growth in the first quarter of 2007, the number fell to 13 percent by the third quarter.

On November 5, 2007, shortly after Parsons had announced that, as of January 1, 2008, he would step down as president and CEO (while remaining chairman), the Time Warner board announced that Bewkes would succeed him. Immediately, Wall Street observers predicted that Bewkes would try to turn Time Warner into a company "both smaller and more focused on producing content rather than distributing it," David Carr and Brian Stelter wrote for the *New York Times* (November 6, 2007). He would do so, word had it, by selling parts of the company. "Now Bewkes will maybe get license from the board to stir things up a little," the investment manager Lawrence Haverty told Thomas S. Mulligan for the *Los Angeles Times* (November 6, 2007). When Parsons disclosed his intention to step down, the value of Time Warner's stock was about $37.00, about 10 percent lower than its worth one year earlier. Asked days later what he would do if he were in Bewkes's position, Parsons joked, according to Grove, "If I were Jeff, I would shoot myself." Later that month Bewkes appeared at the Nielsen and Dow Jones Media and Money Conference, in New York City; asked by the *Wall Street Journal* on-line editor Alan Murray how he intended to reverse Time Warner's fortunes, he said, "Every option is on the table," according to Grove. When Murray asked Bewkes if he would make the stock price rise, he replied, "Yes," drawing laughter from the audience for his unwillingness to elaborate. "Whether [Time Warner] is the biggest is not the main thing," Bewkes said. "It needs to be the most profitable." He added, "We're not waiting three years for the stock to go up. It has to go up now."

Bewkes officially assumed leadership of Time Warner on January 1, 2008. In late February, in what was widely seen as his first major corporate move, he announced that the film studio New Line Cinema would merge with Warner Bros., eliminating hundreds of positions in New York City and Los Angeles, California. The following month, while speaking at the Bear Stearns Media Conference, he said Time Warner would likely sell its 84 percent ownership of Time Warner Cable Inc.'s

common stock, insisting that the division would fare better as a standalone entity. "It doesn't matter whether Time Warner as a conglomerate is larger or smaller," Bewkes said, according to Gillian Wee, writing for bloomberg.com (March 11, 2008). "It matters that the return on capital is high." The spinoff, which generated about $9.25 billion for Time Warner, was completed in March 2009. Earlier, in January 2009, Bewkes had gained the title of chairman, Parsons having relinquished that position at the end of 2008.

On May 28, 2009 a share of Time Warner stock was worth $21.93. That day, in an e-mail message sent to Time Warner employees, as quoted by Kara Swisher on the All Things Digital Web site, Bewkes announced that the company's board of directors had "authorized management to proceed with plans for the complete legal and structural separation of AOL from Time Warner. . . . The separation will be another important step in the process we began last year of refocusing Time Warner to an even greater degree on our core content businesses." AOL became independent on December 9, 2009. On December 10, 2009 the price of one share of Time Warner stock was $30.45; on September 14, 2010, $31.80—almost precisely the amount when trading closed on January 10, 2003.

On August 4, 2010 Time Warner reported on its Web site that during the second quarter of 2010 the company's revenues rose 8 percent, to $6.4 billion—the highest rate of growth in two years—and advertising revenues rose 11 percent. Revenues from Time Warner's TV networks and "filmed entertainment" were greater during that period than they had been during the corresponding three months one year earlier, while revenues from publishing decreased slightly. The networks generated $2.855 billion in 2009 and $3.17 billion in 2010; films generated $2.333 billion and $2.516 billion in 2009 and 2010, respectively; and publishing, $919 million and $915 million in 2009 and 2010, respectively. In the same second-quarter financial report, Bewkes stated, "HBO achieved impressive audience growth for its returning shows, and it has more original series in development than at any time in its history. Last week, Warner Bros. became the only studio in history whose films surpassed $1 billion at the domestic box office for ten straight years, while its TV production business extended its streak as the #1 provider of broadcast network programming."

The six-foot one-inch Bewkes is unusually thin and, by all accounts, can be extremely funny. According to various sources, he seldom takes advantage of the limousines and corporate jets at his disposal or of other privileges common among executives of huge businesses. Sheila Nevins, HBO's president for documentaries and family programming, told Grove in 2008, "He still has a tuna sandwich for lunch, and he doesn't even eat the whole thing." According to Grove, between 2000 and 2002, when Parsons, Case, and Pittman profited greatly by selling their Time Warner stock, Bewkes held on to his shares. While the decision cost him "tens of millions of dollars," Grove wrote, Bewkes believed that unloading his stock would have sent a bad message to the public.

Bewkes is a trustee of Yale University and a member of various advisory councils and boards. In 2009 the Stanford Business School honored him with its Excellence in Leadership Award.

Bewkes's first marriage, to a trusts lawyer, ended in divorce. He and his second wife, the Emmy Award–winning TV-news writer, director, and producer Margaret "Peggy" Brim, maintain homes in New York City and Greenwich, Connecticut. Ac-

cording to one source, Bewkes and Brim each brought one son to their marriage; according to another, they have three children between them.

—K.J.P.

Suggested Reading: *Business Wire* Jan. 25, 2007; *Hollywood Reporter* Nov. 6, 2007; *Los Angeles Times* C p1+ Nov. 6, 2007, (on-line) May 16, 2003; *New York* p30+ Jan. 21–28, 2008; *New York Times* III p1+ Oct. 9, 2005, C p1+ Dec. 22, 2005, C p1+ Nov. 6, 2007, (on-line) Dec. 30, 1996; timewarner.com

Jason Merritt/Getty Images for VH1

Bigelow, Kathryn

Nov. 27, 1951– Filmmaker

Address: c/o Creative Artists Agency, 2000 Ave. of the Stars, Los Angeles, CA 90067

"I think I'll probably always be making movies with dark underpinnings and a main character who's trapped in a situation from which he can't extract himself . . . a fatalism combined with an adrenalin aspect," the director Kathryn Bigelow told Marcia Froelke Coburn for the *Chicago Tribune* (October 11, 1987). "I'm interested in high-impact, high-velocity movie-making." *The Hurt Locker* (2009), Bigelow's eighth and most recent feature film, shows that that interest has continued to fuel her work. Widely considered to be the best motion picture about the war in Iraq to reach theaters since the U.S. and its allies invaded that

country, in 2003, *The Hurt Locker* is also her greatest critical success to date; it earned an Academy Award as the year's best motion picture, and Bigelow won the Oscar as best director. Three decades ago, while in her 20s, she studied painting and mingled with conceptual artists. The experience of shooting footage for a friend's performance piece inspired her to pursue a graduate degree in film. "My movement from painting to film was a very conscious one," she told Veronica Webb for *Interview* (November 1995). "Whereas painting is a more rarefied art form, with a limited audience, I recognized film as this extraordinary social tool that could reach tremendous numbers of people."

Bigelow made her debut as an independent filmmaker with *The Loveless* (1982), about a motorcycle gang. That and her second work for the big screen, the Western/horror film *Near Dark* (1987), have become cult classics. With her next films—among them *Blue Steel*, *Point Break*, and *Strange Days*—Bigelow maintained her intellectual approach to portrayals of aggression and violence; free of preachiness or moralizing, her fast-paced, engaging thrillers and action films provocatively twist their respective genres. Her sixth and seventh films are *The Weight of Water* and *K-19: The Widowmaker*. "Ms. Bigelow, whose body of work . . . has been uneven but never uninteresting, has an almost uncanny understanding of the circuitry that connects eyes, ears, nerves and brain," A.O. Scott wrote in his review of *The Hurt Locker* for the *New York Times* (June 26, 2009). "She is one of the few directors for whom action-movie-making and the cinema of ideas are synonymous."

"I've spent a fair amount of time thinking about what my aptitude is, and I really think it's to explore and push the medium," Bigelow told Jennie Yabroff for *Newsweek* (June 19, 2009). "It's not about breaking gender roles or genre traditions." Nevertheless, among directors of "high-impact, high-velocity" films, Bigelow is the sole female. "The take on Kathryn Bigelow is that she is a great female director of muscular action movies . . . ," Manhola Dargis wrote for the *New York Times* (June 21, 2009). "Sometimes, more simply, she's called a great female director. But here's a radical thought: She is, simply, a great filmmaker."

The only child of a librarian and a paint-factory manager, Kathryn Bigelow was born on November 27, 1951 in San Carlos, a rural suburb of San Francisco, California. At an early age she came to love horses and art. "My dad used to draw these great cartoon figures," she told Yabroff. "His dream was being a cartoonist, but he never achieved it, and it kind of broke my heart. I think part of my interest in art had to do with his yearning for something he could never have." She has said that she also turned to art because she was introverted and felt awkward, in part because of her height. (She is five feet 11 inches tall.) Drawing, she told Jamie Diamond for the *New York Times* (October 22, 1995), "was an arena in which you could have tremendous confidence because you were the architect of your own universe." In her early teens she became fascinated with the works of Raphael and other old masters of European painting and would paint details from their paintings—a hand or a foot, for example—on wall-size canvases in the family garage. "I don't know why I was interested in magnification—maybe because I'm large, the Big People Syndrome," she told Diamond. "It was also disassociative, taking something and making it yours." In the early 1970s Bigelow spent two years at the San Francisco Art Institute, majoring in painting. She was attracted to abstract expressionism, she told Dargis, and to "big, gestural, visceral, raw, immediate pieces. . . . Nothing really struck me that was tight and precise and patient and careful and perhaps more introspective. Perhaps it's just a sensibility defect." "In painting, there are no preconceived notions of what's possible," she told Richard Natale for the *Los Angeles Times* (July 14, 2002). "You're always starting with a blank canvas. And that's what's given me strength."

On the strength of work that one of her teachers submitted to the Independent Study Program of the Whitney Museum, in New York City, Bigelow was accepted into the program with a scholarship. She moved to the city in around 1972 and remained there for the next 12 years. During the nine-month Whitney program, Bigelow had her own studio; established artists, writers, and others recruited by the museum to serve as mentors would visit her there to discuss her work. "You were constantly thinking, what statement am I trying to make? And then [the essayist and novelist] Susan Sontag would come in and ask you the same question and you'd go, now wait a minute, I thought I had a logic for this," she told Diamond. With one of her pieces—sections of pipes set out on the floor, accompanied by "a recording of pipes clanging against one another"—Bigelow explored "potentiality," according to Diamond. New York's vibrant downtown art scene gave Bigelow the opportunity to exchange ideas with conceptual artists and musicians, including Lawrence Weiner, Vito Acconci, John Baldessari, Laurie Anderson, Richard Serra, and Philip Glass. She became fascinated

with poststructuralism and the writings and theories of Guy Debord, Jacques Lacan, Jean Baudrillard, and other French critics and began working with the Art & Language conceptual-art collective, whose members made performance pieces and short films. "They were really interested in working against the commodification of culture, looking at how art works within the art itself," she told Steve Rose for the London *Guardian* (August 19, 2009).

The possibilities and appeal of filmmaking, Bigelow told Gerald Peary for the Toronto, Canada, *Globe and Mail* (March 30, 1990), came as "a revelation" when Acconci hired her to shoot some film to accompany one of his performance pieces. "Film became the interchange where all these ideas were intersecting," she told Dargis. She said to Natale, "Painting is a bit elitist, while film crosses culture and class. It's a populist medium that people can access in different ways. That's difficult to do with a painting. To understand it requires a background. In art, context is everything."

Bigelow won a scholarship to Columbia University's Graduate Film School. While there she saw Sam Peckinpah's *The Wild Bunch* (1969) and Martin Scorsese's *Mean Streets* (1973) as a double feature—an experience that marked "a turning point in my film consciousness," she told Veronica Webb. "I realized that [*The Wild Bunch*] isn't a film about violence per se; Peckinpah just used violence as a language to discuss honor and as a means of catharsis. That's the kind of thing I'm still responding to." She said to Yabroff, "It took all my semiotic Lacanian deconstructivist saturation and [twisted] it. I realized there's a more muscular approach to filmmaking that I found very inspiring." Bigelow made her first short film, *The Set Up* (1978), at Columbia. Dargis described it as a 20-minute deconstruction of violence, "in which two men (Gary Busey included) fight each other as the semioticians Sylvère Lotringer and Marshall Blonsky deconstruct the images in voice-over." Bigelow told Dargis, "The piece ends with Sylvère talking about the fact that in the 1960s you think of the enemy as outside yourself, in other words, a police officer, the government, the system, but that's not really the case at all, fascism is very insidious, we reproduce it all the time." Bigelow earned a master's degree in film criticism and theory at Columbia in 1979.

With Monty Montgomery, Bigelow co-wrote and co-directed her first feature film, *The Loveless* (1982). It starred Willem Dafoe (in his first screen role) as a member of a motorcycle gang. In the *New York Times* (January 20, 1984), Janet Maslin panned the movie as "a slavish homage to *The Wild Bunch*" whose "evocation of tough-guy glamour is ridiculously stilted." More recently, in an undated blurb for *Time Out Film Guide* (on-line), a reviewer hailed it as "one of the most original American independents in years: a bike movie which celebrates the '50s through '80s eyes. Where earlier bike films like *The Wild One* were forced to concentrate on plot, *The Loveless* deliberately slips its story into the background in order to linger over all the latent erotic material of the period that other films could only hint at in their posters." After the release of *The Loveless*, according to Dargis, Bigelow received—and turned down—scripts for high-school comedies, which were considered the domain of female directors. In 1983, for financial reasons, she accepted a teaching job at the California Institute of the Arts, in Valencia, offered to her by her friend John Baldessari, a prominent conceptual artist who taught there. Also in 1983 Bigelow appeared in the role of a newspaper editor in Lizzie Borden's feminist film *Born in Flames*.

Through the director and producer Walter Hill, who admired *The Loveless*, Bigelow landed a deal to develop a film, but nothing came of it. "She, of course, had the extreme disadvantage of being an intellectual, which does you no good in Hollywood, but she wanted to be a film director," Hill told Diamond. It took Bigelow four years to find a producer who agreed to let her direct her next feature, *Near Dark*, which she co-wrote with Eric Red. A vampire/Western hybrid, *Near Dark* (1987) has been described as a cult classic. "I don't know if [the characters] were vampires," Bigelow told Clifford Terry for the *Oregonian* (April 10, 1990). "They're kind of modern creatures of the night. It was a way to take a convention, a horror movie, and turn it on its head. You erase all the gothic elements. It was a way to redefine it."

The year after *Near Dark* was released, Bigelow talked with Clarke Taylor for the *Los Angeles Times* (October 9, 1988) about the tension between creative fulfillment and the business of filmmaking: "I've been very fortunate, getting producers, and it helps to write your own material—you've invented it. But I've had very limited access, in terms of audience, finances, options, and in film making, you have to justify the expenditures with wider audiences in order to continue. So I want more access. I can't just ask for money to fulfill my own creative desires. And yet I want to be able to continue to make films I can live with."

In 1989 Bigelow married the filmmaker James Cameron; they divorced in 1991, after the release the year earlier of Bigelow's next film, the fast-paced police thriller *Blue Steel* (1990). Co-written with Eric Red, it starred Jamie Lee Curtis as Megan Turner, an ambitious rookie cop who is alternately seduced and stalked by a psychotic killer (Ron Silver). In seeking producers for *Blue Steel*, Bigelow told Terry, she had to overcome "pretty significant resistance" to the idea of a woman in such a role. "We've seen this genre, but we've seen it with a man at the center of it, not a woman," studio executives told her. "My response was, 'That's the reason to make it.' I understand their point, though. I'm asking them to commit a significant amount of money ($7 million) to film a story that they hadn't seen. But it would have been unthinkable to make a film that I had seen already. Very simply, I wanted to make a woman's action film. I'd seen it in a science-fiction context, I'd seen it in the context of comedy, but I'd never seen it in an action film."

Point Break (1991), originally intended for the director Ridley Scott, became Bigelow's next project. A novel fusion of the crime and surfer genres written by Peter Iliff, it follows an undercover FBI agent, played by Keanu Reeves, who infiltrates and is then seduced by a gang of adrenalin-addicted surfers who dress as former U.S. presidents and execute daring bank robberies. "It's a little more complicated when your good guy—your 'hero'—is seduced by the darkness inside him and your 'villain' is no villain whatsoever, he's more of an anti-hero," Bigelow told Mark Salisbury for the London *Guardian* (November 21, 1991). "The ocean in this particular context serves as a crucible for the main characters through which they define, test and challenge themselves. It's a film about self-realisation; they could have been doing anything. The unique thing about surfing is that it kind of exists outside the system, the people that embody it are of their own mindset, they have their own language, dress code, conduct, behaviour and it's very primal, very tribal. I tried to use the surfing as a landscape that could offer a subversive mentality." "The surfers, like the motorcycle gang in *The Loveless* and the roving vampires in *Near Dark*," Dave Kehr wrote for the *Chicago Tribune* (June 12, 1991), "are portrayed as a kind of improvised alternative family, bound together by an all-consuming common obsession. This obsession, also shared by the loner heroine of *Blue Steel*, lies in extreme degrees of stimulation and excitement, of adrenalin as a drug. It is a sensation closely linked to the experience of death, of killing or being killed, and it is clear for Bigelow that this is also the experience of the movies—that of losing yourself in the pure sensation, the kinetic rush, of well-filmed action." *Point Break* proved to be one of Bigelow's most commercially successful movies.

Cameron co-wrote, with Jay Cocks, and produced Bigelow's next directorial endeavor, *Strange Days* (1995), a highly original, surrealistic science-fiction thriller. Its subtle genre-bending approach to technology and spectatorship in contemporary society bears traces of Bigelow's influence. Set on New Year's Eve 1999 in a chaotic Los Angeles, California, where doomsday seems not far off, the film is about Lenny Nero (Ralph Fiennes), who deals in black-market virtual-reality tapes, mostly sex clips. The story changes direction after a film of a man raping and murdering a woman falls into Lenny's hands. "*Strange Days* delivers a heady and far-reaching critique of the society of the spectacle that presciently foretells the intoxicating appeal of reality television," according to a review posted on the Web site of the Harvard Film Archive. "In the film's darkly metaphorical future, the most fashionable drug is a cunning new technology that allows users to fully enter into the lives and experiences of others, be they emotional, physical, sexual or traumatic. The superbly conjured science-fiction world of *Strange Days* is nevertheless grounded in very real tensions—especially around race and police brutality—at work in turn-of-the-millennium America." "There's a reflexive element in *Strange Days*," Bigelow told Diamond. "The spectacle is both medium and subject . . . [reminding] the audience that there's a participatory relationship being created here, as opposed to voyeuristic."

The screenplay for Bigelow's next film, *The Weight of Water* (2000), a melodramatic psychological thriller, was adapted by Alice Arlen and Christopher Kyle from Anita Shreve's novel of the same name. *The Weight of Water* interweaves two narratives: one is a present-day drama, set on a sailboat as a hurricane approaches, involving a husband and wife and the predatory new girlfriend of the married man's brother; the other is a murder mystery, set in the U.S. in 1873, involving married and single Norwegian immigrants. "*The Weight of Water* had a lot to do with the fact that my heritage on my mother's side is Norwegian, and this is a piece about immigrants," Bigelow told Kevin Lally for *Film Journal International* (July 1, 2002). "My great-grandparents came from Norway. They ended up in the Dakotas and the people in this story end up in New Hampshire, but it's the same kind of immigrant spirit of a brave new world with no return ticket, regardless of what you're met with. The tremendous amount of courage I always felt from my relatives, and imagining what that might have been like, I rediscovered in the pages of the book. That was what drew me to it, in an effort to understand what their journey was by recreating it." Released in November 2002, two years after its completion and several months after the opening of Bigelow's next film, *K-19: The Widowmaker*, *The Weight of Water* was not a commercial or critical success.

With a story by Louis Nowra and a filmscript by Christopher Kyle, the action thriller *K-19: The Widowmaker* (2002) is a fictionalized account of a real event: a disastrous voyage of the first Soviet nuclear submarine in 1961, during the Cold War, when both the Soviet Union and the U.S. were stockpiling thermonuclear weapons. Improper construction led the submarine's nuclear reactor to overheat by hundreds of degrees; attempts by seven members of the crew to contain radiation within the reactor—and prevent a possibly catastrophic confrontation between the two nuclear powers—led to their deaths from radiation poisoning within a week and the deaths of 20 other crew members within the next few years. The commander of the submarine rejected the offer of help extended by a nearby American ship. Starring Harrison Ford and Liam Neeson as the submarine's feuding current and previous captains, *K-19* was among the first mainstream American films to humanize Soviet citizens and present them as heroes. Bigelow, who directed and produced the film, worked on it on and off for a half-dozen years. She began with extensive research, meeting in Russia with members of the crew and relatives of those who died. She

worked closely with Kyle and produced the storyboards herself before pitching the project. After Bigelow learned that another film set on a submarine (*U-571*) was being made, she set aside *K-19*, returning to it after she completed *The Weight of Water*.

While studying art Bigelow had heeded a teacher's advice to students to determine their "most productive weakness." Hers, she told Richard Natale, was her difficulty in handling pressure. "I learned to treat the reality of constant pressure on a movie set abstractly, like it was a mental process," she told him. That skill enabled her to handle the myriad tasks involved in the making of *K-19*. "It was a huge logistical undertaking," Harrison Ford told Natale. "But I don't remember ever facing the feeling of chaos. Directors have to be able to think on their feet when the time isn't there, the light isn't there, when the capacity of an actor to perform isn't there—and they have to find a way to make it work anyway. Kathryn never would have survived if she hadn't been able to do that." In his review of *K-19* for the *New York Times* (July 19, 2002), A. O. Scott wrote, "*K-19* acquits itself honorably." Bigelow, he continued, "is one of the most gifted pure-action directors working in movies today, and she piles up one nerve-racking crisis after another, interspersed with moments of ethereal, almost otherworldly beauty. . . . She takes hold of a sturdily conventional plot and makes it into a tense, swift drama of mechanical catastrophe and dueling egos." Peter Travers, the *Rolling Stone* (July 19, 2002, on-line) reviewer, agreed: "A salute is in order for Bigelow, a director who knows how to navigate macho terrain . . . without losing her human compass." At box offices in the U.S. and overseas, *K-19* recouped only two-thirds of the $100 million it cost to make.

The Hurt Locker (2009) was based on observations and experiences of the journalist Mark Boal during the two weeks he spent embedded with an elite, three-man U.S. Army bomb squad in Baghdad, Iraq's capital, in 2004. The men paid little attention to relations between the U.S. and Iraq or other such issues connected with the war; in one of the world's most dangerous jobs, they were bent on survival. With guidance from Bigelow, Boal wrote the script in 2005; the next year Bigelow raised the money to make it independently. She shot it, in Jordan in 2007, with little-known actors (Jeremy Renner, Anthony Mackie, and Brian Geraghty) in the leading roles. "War's dirty little secret is that some men love it," Bigelow told Yabroff. "I'm trying to unpack why, to look at what it means to be a hero in the context of 21st-century combat." In a review for the *New Yorker* (June 29, 2009), David Denby wrote, "By the mid-nineties, I had [Bigelow] figured as a violence junkie with a strong tendency to stylize everything into stunning images that didn't always mean much. As a filmmaker, Bigelow is still obsessed with violence, but she's become a master at staging it. In *The Hurt Locker*, there are no wasted shots or merely beautiful images. . . . Unlike so many directors today, who jam together crashes, explosions, and people sailing through the air in nonsensical montages of fantasy movement, Bigelow keeps the space tight and coherent. . . . *The Hurt Locker* is quite a feat: in this period of antic fragmentation, Bigelow has restored the wholeness of time and space as essentials for action." Distribution of the film was limited almost entirely to art-house cinemas, because executives at the major studios "in effect," James Surowiecki wrote for the *New Yorker* (August 14, 2009), decided that "Americans weren't going to watch this kind of movie, and then made sure they wouldn't." Nevertheless, in 2009 and in January 2010, the film and its director won prestigious awards at festivals around the world—including four for Bigelow at the Venice Film Festival. Bigelow won best-director honors from the Directors Guild of America and a half-dozen film-critics' associations. Among dozens of other nominations for prizes, *The Hurt Locker* earned nine Academy Award nominations. It won the Oscar for best motion picture, and Bigelow won the Oscar for best director, becoming the first woman to win in that category.

Bigelow has directed music videos and episodes of the TV series *Homicide: Life on the Street* and *Wild Palms* and has appeared in Gap commercials. She lives in Los Angeles and is discreet about her private life.

—M.M.

Suggested Reading: *Chicago Tribune* Arts p10 Oct. 11, 1987; *Film Comment* p46+ Sep./Oct. 1995; Harvard Film Archive (on-line); *Interview* p42+ Nov. 1995; (London) *Guardian* (on-line) Aug. 19, 2009; *Los Angeles Times* Sunday Calendar p5+ July 14, 2002; *New York Times* II p13 Oct. 22 1995; *Newsweek* p64+ June 29, 2009

Selected Films: as actress—*Born in Flames*, 1983; as director—*Point Break*, 1991; *Strange Days*, 1995; *The Weight of Water*, 2000; as co-director and co-writer—*The Loveless*, 1982; as director and co-writer—*Near Dark*, 1987; *Blue Steel*, 1990; *The Hurt Locker*, 2009; as director and producer—*K19: The Widowmaker*, 2002

Blackman, Cindy

Nov. 18, 1959– Drummer

Address: c/o Four Quarters Entertainment, 555 Eighth Ave., New York, NY 10018

With her outsized Afro, Cindy Blackman, best known for recording and touring with the retro funk rocker Lenny Kravitz, is one of the most recognizable contemporary drummers. She is also regarded as one of the most talented: influenced by the legendary jazz drummer Tony Williams, she has won acclaim for her creativity and versatility, which have enabled her to move seamlessly between the worlds of jazz and rock. Owen McNally wrote for the *Hartford (Connecticut) Courant* (September 11, 2008), "Cindy Blackman can make rhythms surge for virtually any genre, whether jazz, rock, funk or fusion," and Zan Stewart, writing for the Newark, New Jersey, *Star-Ledger* (August 31, 2007), described Blackman as "an imaginative, invigorating musician who plays with creative fire and dexterity." Raised in Ohio and Connecticut, Blackman moved to New York in 1982 to pursue a career in jazz. Early in the following decade, she joined Kravitz's band, with which she toured extensively over the next 14 years. Blackman has also performed with such acclaimed jazz artists as Wallace Roney, Jackie McLean, Joe Henderson, Don Pullen, and Kenny Barron and has recorded 11 jazz albums under her own name. A master of an instrument women have often been discouraged from playing, Blackman has not let gender discrimination get in the way of her music.

Jimmy Bruch, courtesy of Four Quarters Entertainment

She explained to Ashnate Infantry for the *Toronto (Canada) Star* (June 7, 2008, on-line), "In the past, there were a lot of stigmas attached to women playing certain instruments. I think a lot of women stick to particular instruments, like piano, that are acceptable, so that lessens the playing field in terms of how many women are out there. And let's face it, boys' clubs still exist. But I care nothing about that at all. I'm going to do what I'm going to do musically anyway." She added, "God forbid I should be limited to only play my drums in my basement; but if that's all I had, that's what I would do. Any woman, or anyone facing race prejudice, weight prejudice, hair prejudice . . . if you let somebody stop you because of their opinions, then the only thing you're doing is hurting yourself. I don't want to give somebody that power over me." In the liner notes of her 2004 album, *Music for the New Millennium*, Blackman stated the purpose of her music: "The goal is to reach the apex of creativity, to push the envelope and to move musical sound beyond the constraints of commercialism and conservatism. The goal is intelligent freedom. The goal is love. The goal is life."

Cindy Blackman was born on November 18, 1959 in Yellow Springs, Ohio. She was raised in a musical family. Blackman's mother played the violin in classical orchestras, and her maternal grandmother was a classically trained pianist; her uncle was a vibraphonist. She grew up listening to an eclectic assortment of music, from her father's Miles Davis and Ahmad Jamal jazz records to her siblings' Beatles, John Coltrane, Jimi Hendrix, and Sly and the Family Stone albums. Blackman also listened to the music of such artists as the Jackson 5, the Sylvers, Kansas, and Tower of Power, which she described to Renee Graham for the *Boston Globe* (February 22, 2000) as "the teeny-bop music of the time." Commenting on her rich musical upbringing, she said to Graham, "It was just a collage of sounds. I feel blessed to have been able to hear such a variety of stuff." When Blackman was seven years old, she came across a drum set while walking through a friend's house during a pool party. Drawn to it, she sat down to try to play. "It was incredible," she recalled to Stina Sieg for the Glenwood Springs, Colorado, *Post Independent* (July 16, 2008, on-line). "Just looking at them struck something in my core, and it was completely right from the second I saw them. And then, when I hit them, it was like, wow, that's me. That's completely natural for me. It's like breathing for me. It didn't feel awkward at all."

Blackman started playing the drums at the age of eight and began performing in school bands shortly thereafter. She received her first drum set at 12, after spending several years trying to convince her parents that she was serious about playing the instrument. Blackman has said that because of her gender, she was frequently discouraged during her youth from learning to play the drums. Disregarding advice that she take up other, supposedly more feminine instruments, such as the flute or the violin, she "learned very early on—when I was 13—that when I concentrate on those attitudes, I don't make progress for myself," as she told Patrick Cole for the *Windsor (Canada) Star* (February 8, 2008, on-line). "If they're not paying my mortgage, I don't care what they think." Blackman began her formal drum training at the age of 13, after moving with her family to Hartford, Connecticut. Her passion for jazz was sparked around that time, when

she was introduced to the music of the pioneering jazz percussionists Max Roach and Tony Williams; both artists, particularly Williams, heavily influenced her style of drumming. Commenting on her discovery of Williams, best known for his landmark recordings with Miles Davis in the 1960s (beginning when he was a teenager), Blackman recalled to Ken Micallef for *Modern Drummer* (June 2008, on-line), "When I first heard Tony on Miles Davis' *Four & More*, I was trippin'.' A friend who played it for me told me Tony was sixteen when he recorded it. He was my age and playing like that?! Then he put on Miles' *Live in Europe*. I was completely hooked into Tony from that moment on." When she was 16 she heard Williams play at a drum clinic in Hartford. She recalled to Zan Stewart, "His technique, his intelligence, his feel, his concept—it blew my mind. I was so in awe of what I saw, when I tried to ask a question, I couldn't speak. That day set me in the direction that I had to follow."

After taking lessons during high school at the Hart College of Music at the University of Hartford, Blackman enrolled at the Berklee College of Music, in Boston, Massachusetts. There, she studied classical percussion under Alan Dawson, who had also taught Williams. Blackman spent three semesters at Berklee before moving to New York in 1982 to become the drummer for the singing group the Drifters. Next she played gigs around the city with others, at one point joining a group of street musicians who included the trumpet player Tommy Turrentine. She told Stacey Daniels for *Alice Magazine* (January 2000), "It wasn't easy, but it was cool for musical development. I mean, we were playing from noon to six or seven with very few, if any, breaks. The more you play, the better. . . . It was a lot of fun." While honing her skills during the 1980s, Blackman sought the counsel of numerous jazz luminaries, including Miles Davis, Dizzy Gillespie, Max Roach, Woody Shaw, Kenny Clarke, and Art Blakey—all of whom were still active on the New York jazz scene at the time. (With the exception of Roach, who died in 2007, all of those artists had passed away by the early 1990s.) Blakey—credited as one of the inventors of the hard-bop style of drumming—became a major influence and mentor for Blackman. She recalled to Renee Graham, "He taught me a lot about drumming, about music, about life. He was the kind of guy you would go hang out with, and you'd leave feeling like you were on top of the world. He loved music and jazz so much, you couldn't be in his presence and not carry that with you."

Blackman first made her mark in New York at after-hours jam sessions organized by the trumpeter Ted Curson at the Blue Note jazz club. Her first two compositions were heard on the trumpeter Wallace Roney's debut album as a bandleader, *Verses* (1987). Those compositions, which bore traces of the style of Tony Williams, helped her land a recording contract with Muse Records. In 1988 Blackman made her debut as a bandleader with *Ar-*

cane. That album's lineup included Roney, the saxophonists Kenny Garrett and Joe Henderson, the pianist Larry Willis, and the bassists Buster Williams and Clarence Seay. Blackman next performed session work for a quartet led by the saxophonist Jackie McLean and later played for a group led by Joe Henderson at the Mount Fuji Jazz Festival, in Japan. She subsequently played on Roney's *Intuition* (1988), *The Standard Bearer* (1989), and *Obsession* (1990), all released on the Muse label. Blackman also recorded an album, *Autumn Leaves* (1989), with the folk singer-songwriter Marc Cohen and the bassist Charnett Moffett, and played with a trio led by the pianist Don Pullen at several festivals in 1990. Also that year Blackman released two albums: the hard-bop solo effort *Trio + Two*, on Freelance Records, with the bassist Santi Debriano and the guitarist Dave Fiuczynski, and *Code Red*, on the Muse label. The latter album featured Roney, the saxophonist Steve Coleman, the pianist Kenny Barron, and the bassist Lonnie Plaxico. (Blackman dedicated *Code Red* to Art Blakey, who died in October 1990.)

In 1993 Blackman was introduced to the rock singer-songwriter Lenny Kravitz, who was looking for a drummer to tour with his band. After hearing her play over the phone, Kravitz immediately arranged for her to fly to Los Angeles to audition for the coveted job—which she won, beating out dozens of other players. She remained in Los Angeles for the next two weeks, during which she shot the video for Kravitz's hit song "Are You Gonna Go My Way," the title track from his eponymous 1993 album. In the now-classic video, Blackman showcased her ferocious style of play while wearing a 1970s-style Afro wig and black wraparound sunglasses, which "made her a role model for women who wanted to crash the male-dominated club of power drumming," in the words of Adam Budofsky, the managing editor of *Modern Drummer*, according to Patrick Cole. Budofsky added, "Cindy is one of the few artists who is able to live in both the jazz and rock worlds at the same time. She knew that when she played a gig like Lenny's that there's a whole different set of rules, and she could provide what's needed." *Are You Gonna Go My Way* became a major critical and commercial success, reaching number 12 on the *Billboard* 200 album chart and selling more than four million copies worldwide. Blackman spent most of the next year and a half touring with Kravitz, which helped establish her in the rock world.

The transition from small clubs to big concert venues was initially difficult for Blackman. She said, as quoted on ultimatesantana.com, "The first time I played in a really large concert with Lenny was at an outdoor festival . . . for 70,000 people . . . I almost lost it, my equilibrium was teetering. I wasn't used to seeing that many people; I was disoriented; I just had to stop looking and start focusing." Blackman explained to Rumeysa Ozel for the Istanbul, Turkey, *Today's Zaman* (November 27, 2007, on-line): "In the concert hall you have thou-

sands and thousands of screaming fans, people are creating a lot of energy, that's very exciting. . . . When you play in a small club or in a small venue, people can see you better. The focus is [not] necessarily on partying, but on the music. So it is a little more intense in terms of listening and nuance. Because it is not some big roaring stage, people can hear you better." Blackman has said that there are benefits to playing both jazz and rock. She explained to Rick Mark for the Manhattan *Villager* (August 24–30, 2005, on-line), "I can appreciate the simplicity of playing one beat for a long time [with rock music], and focusing on making that feel so good you don't care to hear anything else. By the same token, I still hear things while I'm playing that groove, so when I get to a situation that's more creative [with jazz], I get to interject things that I'm hearing." Blackman stated, as quoted by Cole, "To me, jazz is the highest form of music that you can play because of the creative requirements." She told Zan Stewart, "Jazz is part street, part heart, part intellect. Those things change and evolve, so if the music isn't changing and evolving, it's not jazz."

Blackman maintained a busy touring schedule with Kravitz throughout the remainder of the 1990s and far into the 2000s. While achieving mainstream success with Kravitz, she remained dedicated to jazz and frequently took time off from touring to record her own music. In 1994 Blackman released her third album on the Muse label, *Telepathy*, which included interpretations of Thelonious Monk's "Well, You Needn't" and Miles Davis's "Tune Up" as well as the original songs "Spank," "Missing You," and "Persuasion." In a review for the All Music Guide, Ron Wynn wrote, "Blackman's third Muse album shows a maturity, confidence, and assertiveness that her two previous sessions lacked. She is the unquestioned leader, sparkling in her playing and punctuating the songs with the vigor you'd expect from a veteran percussionist." In 1995 Blackman released, on the Muse label, *The Oracle*, whose lineup included Kenny Barron, the bassist Ron Carter, and the saxophonist Gary Bartz. Her next album, *In the Now*, was released in 1998 on the High Note label. That album featured Carter, the saxophonist Ravi Coltrane, and the pianist Jacky Terrasson. Also in 1998 Blackman made the instructional video *Multiplicity*, on which she gave demonstrations of various drum styles and suggested how to avoid getting hurt while playing.

In 1999 Blackman recorded *Works on Canvas* for the High Note label. With performances by the saxophonist J.D. Allen, the bassist George Mitchell, and the pianist Carlton Holmes, the album was inspired by three paintings by the Dutch artist Vincent van Gogh. It included original interpretations of Bronislau Kaper's "On Green Dolphin Street," Kurt Weill and Ira Gershwin's "My Ship," and Vernon Duke and E.Y. Harburg's "April in Paris," in addition to the original numbers "My Isha," "Spanish Colored Romance," "Ballad Like," "Sword of the Painter," and three versions of "The Three Van Goghs." In a review for *Jazz Times* (June 2000, on-line), John Murph wrote that Blackman's arrangement of "On Green Dolphin Street" is "one of the most magical interpretations of the Kaper composition in recent years." He added, "The record is also a great indicator of Blackman's growth as a composer and bandleader. True to its name, *Works on Canvas* proceeds like an impressionistic suite in which she not only functions as the main rhythmic engine of the music, but also a magnificent colorist. As a composer, many of the compositions here have the electric/acoustic vibe of Miles Davis' transitional period in the late '60s, thanks to Holmes' subtle Fender Rhodes shading on the 'Three Van Goghs' interludes and 'Sword of the Painter.' The music also benefits greatly from the wonderful cohesion of the quartet, especially when they craft the thrilling elastic tension atop hypnotic grooves on songs like 'Ballad Like' and 'Sword of the Painter.'" Murph declared, "*Works on Canvas* is an amazing portrait of one of this generation's most colorful drummers." Blackman's next recording as bandleader, *Someday* (2001), her last for the High Note label, again included Allen, Mitchell, and Holmes. The album included reworkings of tunes recorded by Miles Davis—"My Funny Valentine," "Someday My Prince Will Come," and "Walkin'"—and five original songs in a post-bop style.

In 2004 Blackman took a hiatus from Kravitz's band to focus more on her jazz career. That year she recorded her 10th album, *Music for the New Millennium*, with the other members of her regular quartet—Allen, Mitchell, and Holmes. The album, released on her own label, Sacred Sounds, was inspired by traditional African music. (Blackman dedicated the album to her grandmother Martha Blackman-Higby.) Patrick Cole wrote that the album "embodies the rhythm and feel of acoustic jazz with a touch of 1970s fusion," and Owen McNally described the album as "a wide-ranging compendium of Blackman originals whose boldness and energy relentlessly push, pound, and pummel the conventional boundaries of acoustic jazz and fusion." McNally added, "With her explosive drum kit, Blackman's solo salvos and kinetic backup add not just a stream of kaleidoscope rhythms, but also a variety of textures to her band." Ken Micallef observed, "Serial jazz and rock drum killer Cindy Blackman is the kind of ultra-talented, well-trained, and dynamically inspired musician who could only exist in the new millennium. Her tenth, double CD, *Music for the New Millennium*, shows a creative force to be reckoned with, revealed in the album's amalgam of late-'60s Miles Davis–inspired compositions (in classic quartet format) fired by drumming that could fairly be described as jazz toxic shock therapy."

With her quartet Blackman has performed at jazz venues and festivals all over the world. Commenting on the style and objective of their music, she told Rick Mark, "It's rooted in tradition, but it's not traditional music. It's explorative, very creative, very expressive, and we really try to expand any ideas we have that everything is played over the forms, but we like to stretch it, and really see the colors and make the music grow and move. We experiment—but it's never free. Everything is written out. I have charts for all the songs. We expand on what's there, and stretch harmonies and note choices." In 2007 Blackman conducted a series of drum workshops in South America, making stops in Argentina, Chile, and Brazil. Since she left Kravitz's band, in June of that year, she has continued to tour and record with various other bands and jazz ensembles. Blackman's latest solo album, *Another Lifetime*, was released on the Four Quarters Entertainment label in 2010. The album pays homage to Lifetime, a pioneering jazz-rock fusion group led by Tony Williams.

On July 9, 2010 Blackman became engaged to the Latin rock legend Carlos Santana, who proposed to her onstage at a concert in Tinley Park, Illinois. (Blackman is currently Santana's touring drummer.) She makes her home in the New York City borough of Brooklyn, where she owns a chicly designed loft. Blackman stays in shape for drumming by practicing yoga and karate. She is a follower of the Baha'i faith and is a student of the Kabbalah. Commenting on spirituality as expressed through music, she told Infantry, "I believe that music is so sacred that once you're playing music you are doing the work of prayer, whether you're conscious of it or not, because you have a focused intent. You transcend, because you're crossing barriers that a lot of people and even us as musicians don't normally venture to, because we don't think about it."

—C.C.

Suggested Reading: *Alice Magazine* p45 Jan. 2000; All Music Guide (on-line); *Boston Globe* F p1 Feb. 22, 2000; drummerworld.com; (Glenwood Springs, Colorado) *Post Independent* (on-line) July 16, 2008; *Hartford (Connecticut) Courant* p24 Sep. 11, 2008; (Istanbul, Turkey) *Today's Zaman* (on-line) Nov. 27, 2007; *Modern Drummer* (on-line) June 2008; (Newark, New Jersey) *Star-Ledger* p16 Aug. 31, 2007; *Santa Fe New Mexican* p50 May 11, 2001; *Windsor (Canada) Star* (on-line) Feb. 8, 2008

Selected Recordings: with Lenny Kravitz—*Are You Gonna Go My Way*, 1993; as solo artist—*Arcane*, 1988; *Autumn Leaves*, 1989; *Trio + Two*, 1990; *Code Red*, 1990; *Telepathy*, 1994; *The Oracle*, 1995; *In the Now*, 1998; *Works on Canvas*, 1999; *Someday*, 2001; *Music for the New Millennium*, 2004; *Another Lifetime*, 2010

Selected Videos: *Multiplicity*, 1998

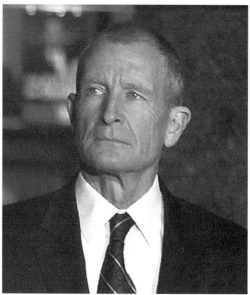

Ron Sachs-Pool/Getty Images

Blair, Dennis C.

Feb. 4, 1947– Former director of national intelligence; former U.S. Navy officer

Address: National Bureau of Asian Research, George F. Russell Jr. Hall, 1414 N.E. 42d St., Suite 300, Seattle, WA 98105; NBAR, 1301 Pennsylvania Ave, N.W., Suite 305, Washington, DC 20004

On May 28, 2010, 16 months after he was sworn in as the nation's third director of national intelligence (DNI), Dennis C. Blair resigned from his post. In a statement distributed to members of the intelligence community, Blair gave no reason for his departure, and although his announcement was not unexpected, he stepped down before President Barack Obama had selected a replacement. It was widely believed that the Obama administration had become increasingly dissatisfied with his performance; his tenure, Greg Miller wrote for the *Washington Post* (May 21, 2010), had been "marred by the recent failures of U.S. spy agencies to detect terrorist plots and by political missteps that undermined his standing with the White House." In response to Blair's resignation, Representative Silvestre Reyes of Texas, the chairman of the House Intelligence Committee, noted, as quoted by *FederalTimes.com* (May 20, 2010), "The job description of Director of National Intelligence continues to evolve, even five years after its creation." In words that reflected that continuing evolution, Miller wrote, "[Blair's] departure is likely to renew debate over whether the DNI position, a daunting job created amid sweeping intelligence reforms after the Sept. 11, 2001, attacks, is fundamentally flawed."

The job of DNI came into being in 2005 through the Intelligence Reform and Terrorism Prevention Act of 2004. It was created as a means of coordinating the country's 16 federal intelligence agencies and improving the performance of each. "What we're trying to do is work on a process in which we all contribute, rather than trying to invent new diagrams of who reports to whom," Blair told Alex Kingsbury for *USNews.com* (April 8, 2009). As the DNI, Blair, who retired from the U.S. Navy in 2002 as a four-star admiral, was the principal adviser to President Barack Obama on intelligence matters and had authority over the intelligence community's budget (about $45 billion annually) and personnel (more than 100,000 people). During his 34-year career in the navy, he commanded guided-missile destroyers in the Atlantic and Pacific fleets and served as the commander in chief of the U.S. Pacific Command, which encompasses half the world's surface and 36 nations (among them Russia, India, China, Japan, South Korea, and North Korea) that, together, are home to more than half the world's people. Blair is known as "an intellectual who values straightforwardness and has mastered the byzantine interagency process during his various government stints," Dana Priest wrote for the *Washington Post* (December 20, 2008). Those stints included time with the Central Intelligence Agency (CIA); the National Security Council; and the Joint Staff, which assists the Joint Chiefs of Staff. T. L. McCreary, a retired rear admiral and one-time colleague of his, told Kingsbury that Blair "has an incredible capacity for interpreting a complex set of facts and storing them in his head like a file cabinet, sometimes for months, before bringing them out." A press release issued on September 15, 2009 from Blair's department—the Office of the Director of National Intelligence (ODNI)—announced the release of the latest four-year National Intelligence Strategy and listed its objectives, which include combatting violent extremism, preventing the proliferation of weapons of mass destruction, enhancing cybersecurity, and coming up with "wise national security policies" that address "global trends related to forces like economics, the environment, emerging technology, and pandemic disease."

An attempt by a Nigerian man to blow up an American plane with an explosive device hidden in his underwear on December 25, 2009 pointed up the continuing deficiencies in the U.S. intelligence network: various U.S. authorities had known that the man posed a potential threat but had not acted on that knowledge. "A systemic failure has occurred, and I consider that totally unacceptable," President Obama declared at a news conference, referring to the thwarted bombing as a "potential catastrophic breach of security," as Peter Baker and Carl Hulse reported for the *New York Times* (December 29, 2009). In a statement issued by the ODNI on January 5, 2010, Blair declared, "We must be able to stop such attempts. The Intelligence Community has made considerable progress in developing collection and analysis capabilities and improving collaboration, but we need to strengthen our ability to stop new tactics such as the efforts of individual suicide terrorists. . . . We can and we must outthink, outwork and defeat the enemy's new ideas."

A sixth-generation naval officer, Dennis Cutler Blair was born on February 4, 1947 in Kittery, Maine. He is a great-great-great grandson of William Price Williamson, a chief engineer in the Confederate Navy during the Civil War, who was recognized for suggesting that the hull of the frigate USS *Merrimack* be used to build the ironclad warship CSS *Virginia*. Blair's father served at the Portsmouth, Maine, naval shipyard. Following family tradition, Blair attended St. Andrews School, an exclusive preparatory school, in Middletown, Delaware, and then entered the U.S. Naval Academy. When he graduated, in 1968, he had a grade-point average of 4.0 and ranked second in his class of 836. The "legendary leadership class of 1968," as it has been called, also included Oliver North, who became a member of the administration of President Ronald Reagan; the future U.S. senator Jim Webb of Virginia; and the future chairman of the Joint Chiefs of Staff Mike Mullen.

Upon his graduation Blair was assigned to the guided-missile destroyer USS *Tattnall*. Shortly afterward he earned a Rhodes scholarship to Oxford University, in England. At Oxford, where he met the Rhodes scholar and future U.S. president Bill Clinton, Blair completed a master's degree in history and languages. From 1975 to 1976 he served as a White House fellow, with assignments at the federal Department of Housing and Urban Development. Blair then landed a series of intelligence jobs, among them a staff position on the National Security Council (NSC) during the Reagan administration. "He went everywhere with a pad, constantly writing notes," one of Blair's NSC colleagues told James Kirchick for the *New Republic* (January 25, 2010). "I thought to myself, 'This guy's writing a book.'" (Blair has not published any books.)

In the 1980s and 1990s, Blair rose rapidly through the ranks of the navy. From 1984 to 1986 he served as the commander of the guided-missile destroyer USS *Cochrane*, whose home port was Yokosuka, Japan. He later served as commander of Naval Station Pearl Harbor (1989–90) and of the USS *Kitty Hawk* Battle Group (1993–95). In 1995 Blair was named the first associate director of military support for the CIA. In that position he worked to facilitate better cooperation between the CIA and the Pentagon. Around that time he also served as a budget and policy adviser on the NSC. In 1996 he was named director of the Joint Staff at the Pentagon. Serving under General Hugh Shelton, the chairman of the Joint Chiefs of Staff, Blair was responsible for overseeing dozens of officers and many military programs. He helped in the execution of the first Quadrennial Defense Review, which assessed every facet of the entire U.S. armed forces.

In his last military assignment (1999–2002), Blair was the commander in chief of the U.S. Pacific Command (USPACOM). He had authority over all U.S. Army, Navy, Air Force, and Marine forces in the Asia-Pacific region (about 300,000 people); he communicated with commanding officers of each branch of the military, transmitting to them objectives and strategies, and maintained relations with the militaries of 43 countries, among them China, India, North Korea, and South Korea. Among other accomplishments, he helped to expand the Joint Intelligence Center Pacific, in Hawaii, which provides intelligence to USPACOM. One of the projects he directed entailed gathering information on all of China's recent military acquisitions—a job that "took thousands of man-hours," an unidentified officer recalled to Richard Halloran for the *Washington Times* (January 18, 2009). "Some of the staff had to work so hard they started calling it the 'Blair Witch Project'"—the title of a popular 1999 horror movie.

While with USPACOM, Blair became the subject of media scrutiny regarding the struggle for independence by East Timor, which had gained independence from Portugal in 1975, then lost its sovereignty days later, when troops from its neighbor Indonesia (headed by President Suharto from 1967 until 1998) invaded it. The years that followed Indonesia's annexation of East Timor, in 1976, were marked by oppression and brutality; Indonesian troops killed upwards of 60,000 civilians, and many thousands of other East Timorese were forced to flee their homes. In January 1999 Suharto's successor, B. J. Habibie, announced that a referendum on independence would be held in East Timor on August 30 of that year. Violence—perpetrated by Indonesian troops as well as pro-Indonesia militias supported by the Indonesian Army (known as the TNI)—increased in the months preceding and following the referendum, in which more than 78 percent of nearly all eligible voters cast their ballots for independence. "The US government has publicly reprimanded the Indonesian Army for the militias," Allan Nairn wrote for the *Nation* (September 27, 1999, on-line), but "the US military"—as represented by Blair—"has, behind the scenes and contrary to Congressional intent, been backing the TNI." In April 1999 Blair had met with Indonesia's top military commander, General Wiranto, ostensibly to persuade him to put an end to the violence; instead, Nairn wrote, a classified cable that had come to his attention revealed that in April 1999, Blair had offered Wiranto "promises of new US assistance," including "new riot-control training for the Indonesian armed forces." On January 22, 2009, in testimony before the U.S. Senate Select Committee on Intelligence during hearings on his confirmation, Blair described such charges as "flatly inaccurate." The American ambassador to Indonesia had been present at all his meetings with Indonesian military officials, he said, as was a note taker, who cabled reports of those meetings to officials in Washington,

D.C. "My support of U.S. policy is a matter of record," Blair declared. "My conversations specifically included strong opposition to violence against civilians. I emphasized the importance of respect for human rights."

Blair made full use of his diplomatic skills in his response to what became known as the Hainan Island incident, in which, on April 1, 2001, a U.S. Navy EP-3 spy plane collided with a Chinese interceptor fighter jet. The Chinese pilot was killed, and the American plane was forced to make an emergency landing on Hainan Island. While the U.S. insisted that the EP-3 had been flying in international airspace, the Chinese insisted that it had entered Chinese airspace, and they held the EP-3's 21-person crew for 11 days. Although theoretically U.S. military planes have "sovereign immunity"—"that is, no other country can go aboard them or keep them," as Blair explained at a press conference a few hours after the plane landed on Hainan Island—the Chinese kept the aircraft for nearly four months and returned it to the U.S. in pieces. Although having American spy equipment fall into Chinese hands was damaging to U.S. security to some extent, the repercussions from the confrontation between China and the U.S. could have been far worse. Stephen Haines, Blair's roommate at the U.S. Naval Academy, commented to David Wood for the *Baltimore Sun* (December 22, 2008), "What could have been a huge problem disappeared because Denny knew the generals over there and called and said, 'Hey, we know each other, let's work this thing out.'"

On February 27, 2002, 11 months after the collision over the South China Sea, Blair told members of two subcommittees of the House International Relations Committee that "military-to-military relations" between China and the U.S. were "resuming slowly." He added, "It is in the interests of the United States to interact with the PLA [China's army] to address common interests, such as combating terrorism, peacekeeping operations, search and rescue, counterdrug, counterpiracy, and humanitarian assistance. These interactions should be reciprocal and transparent and serve to reduce misunderstandings and the risk of miscalculations on both sides." Blair told Michael R. Gordon for the *New York Times* (June 4, 2001) that such contacts enabled him to get a "sense of what is going on on the other side. I think that this is a fundamentally safer situation, even if it does not lead to a nice, neat solution of a crisis, than a situation in, say, North Korea, where none of us know who those people are. On the Chinese side, although they don't much like it, they are generally impressed with the superiority of our armed forces. That is a useful antidote to their self-propaganda." Secretary of Defense Donald Rumsfeld, however, felt differently; in response to the EP-3 affair, he had personally banned the majority of "seminars, visits, and other contacts with China," Gordon reported. Rumsfeld regarded Blair's views on Asia as evidence of his being "too independent," according to

the *New York Times* (June 9, 2009, on-line), and led Rumsfeld, on October 31, 2001, to name the air-force general Richard B. Myers rather than Blair to succeed General Shelton as the chairman of the Joint Chiefs of Staff.

Blair was praised for his counterterrorism efforts in Southeast Asia in the wake of the 9/11 attacks on the U.S., in particular for leading a coalition of special-operations forces and CIA agents in tracking down members of the Abu Sayyaf, an Al Qaeda–linked terrorist group based in the Philippines. The aim of the coalition was to aid the Philippine army in neutralizing members of the Abu Sayyaf and to rescue two American missionaries and a Filipino nurse whom they were holding hostage. In a shootout that erupted during a rescue mission, one American missionary, Gracia Burnham, was rescued; the other two hostages were killed. The coalition was credited with diminishing Abu Sayyaf's power and influence.

Blair held the rank of four-star admiral when he retired from the navy, in 2002. Upon becoming a civilian he joined the Institute for Defense Analyses (IDA), a nonprofit, independent, government-funded think tank that studies national-security issues, particularly from technological and scientific standpoints; it does not work directly with private industry or the military but issues reports to the Pentagon. Blair rose from senior fellow to president and CEO of the IDA in 2003. He was forced to resign in 2006, after the Pentagon's inspector general ruled that his membership on the boards of directors of two Pentagon subcontractors—the EDO Corp. and Tyco International Ltd.—presented conflicts of interest, because both companies were involved in the F-22 Raptor stealth-fighter program, which the IDA had assessed. The inspector general found that Blair had not influenced the outcome of the IDA's evaluation, however. At the time Blair said, as quoted by R. Jeffrey Smith in the *Washington Post* (December 20, 2006), "With due respect to the inspector general, I find it difficult to understand how I can be criticized for a conflict of interest involving a study in which I had no involvement." He told members of the Senate Intelligence Committee during his confirmation hearing as national intelligence director, according to Caitlin Webber and Tim Starks in *CQ Politics* (January 28, 2009), "It was a mistake not to have recused myself from those two studies when I was president of IDA. . . . I did not in fact try to influence the study nor . . . did I do so. There were not good procedures for the [president] of IDA to review and recuse himself when appropriate, and I instituted those procedures before . . . I left."

In 2007 Blair joined the National Bureau of Asian Research as the John M. Shalikashvili Chair in National Security Studies, an endowed position that "provides a distinguished scholar in the national security field with an opportunity to inform, strengthen, and shape the understanding of U.S. policymakers on critical current and long-term national security issues related to the Asia-Pacific," according to the organization's Web site. Concurrently, during the 2007–08 academic year, he held the Omar N. Bradley Chair in Strategic Leadership, with residencies at both Dickinson College and the U.S. Army War College, in Carlisle, Pennsylvania. Along with General Wesley Clark, the former national-security adviser Brent Scowcroft, and 19 others, he was a member of the committee that prepared the report *Forging a New Shield* (November 2008) as participants in the Project on National Security Reform, sponsored by the Center for the Study of the Presidency. Blair, the deputy executive director of the project, and his fellow committee members affirmed unanimously "that the national security of the United States of America is fundamentally at risk," in part because of "the increasing misalignment of the national security system with a rapidly changing global security environment." The committee recommended a multipronged redesign of the national-security system, ranging from the establishment of a President's Security Council, which would replace the National Security Council and the Homeland Security Council, to the creation of a National Security Professional Corps, "specifically trained for interagency assignments." For the most part, the recommendations have yet to be implemented.

When, on January 9, 2009, Obama announced that he had chosen Blair to serve as the director of national intelligence, the president-elect said that "as someone who has handled intelligence as a sailor at sea and strategic thinker in Washington, he will have the expertise and authority to ensure that our sixteen intelligence agencies act with unity of effort and purpose." During his Senate confirmation hearings later that month, Blair denounced the interrogation tactics condoned by the George W. Bush administration and stated that he would not support "any surveillance activities that circumvent" the law, as Walter Pincus reported for the *Washington Post* (January 23, 2009). Blair added, "There will be no waterboarding on my watch. There will be no torture on my watch." On January 28, 2009 the U.S. Senate approved Blair's appointment, and he was sworn into office the next day.

In matters involving intelligence—information about the nation's enemies or potential enemies or situations that threaten the nation's security—Blair had authority over the Federal Bureau of Investigation (FBI); the CIA; the Departments of Energy, Homeland Security, State, and the Treasury; the U.S. Army, Air Force, Navy, Marine Corps, and Coast Guard; the Drug Enforcement Administration; the National Security Agency; the Defense Intelligence Agency; the National Geospacial Intelligence Agency; and the National Reconnaissance Office. He also dealt with a large number of private contractors. He provided President Obama with a daily report (often face-to-face) that included updates on everything from drug-cartel activities in Mexico to the current conflicts in Iraq and Afghanistan. "I try to put myself in the president's shoes and make the intelligence useful to him," Blair told Alex Kingsbury.

Among Blair's greatest challenges was the long-standing failure of many of the 16 intelligence agencies under his purview to share information adequately, mostly for territorial reasons and fear of decreased powers but also because of ineffective or nonexistent procedures. Blair tried to build better lines of communication among the agencies and also to establish sharply defined lines of authority. In an example of the difficulties he faced, early on he clashed with Leon Panetta, whom Obama appointed to head the CIA, because Panetta thought that he, not Blair, had the authority to choose the top U.S. intelligence officials in countries overseas, just as his predecessors had. Blair, however, believed that in the intelligence hierarchy, he was above Panetta; in addition, he argued in favor of increasing the responsibilities of such officials to include jobs not directly linked with CIA activities. (To date, Panetta has retained control in that area.) Blair also tried in vain to gain a more active role regarding covert actions; the White House, however, directed the CIA to keep ODNI better informed about such matters.

A would-be suicide bomber's near-success at destroying a Northwest Airlines passenger jet with 279 people aboard on December 25, 2009 provided chilling evidence of continuing serious problems within the intelligence community. The public soon learned that intelligence officials had been warned earlier about a possible terrorist attack by a Nigerian man associated with Al Qaeda in Yemen. In addition, in November 2009 a Nigerian man had sought assistance from the American Embassy in Nigeria in locating his son, the 23-year-old Umar Farouk Abdulmutallab, who, the father said, had recently embraced radical Islam. Suspicions about Abdulmutallab had led the British government to refuse to issue him a visa, but he had acquired an American visa. Abdulmutallab had paid cash for his Northwest flight from Switzerland to Detroit, Michigan, and had checked no baggage, but neither airport-security workers nor anyone else had alerted authorities about that unusual behavior. Abdulmutallab's attempt to detonate an explosive device (hidden in his underwear) failed, but the device began to burn and smoke under his clothes, leading one of the passengers to tackle and subdue Abdulmutallab.

On January 7, 2010, in a message from the ODNI, Blair called Abdulmutallab's success in boarding a U.S.-bound plane "a failure of the counterterrorism system." "The Intelligence Community analysts who were working hard on immediate threats to Americans in Yemen did not understand the fragments of intelligence on what turned out later to be Mr. Abdulmutallab, so they did not push him onto the 'no fly' list," he acknowledged. Blair also said that he would be overseeing and managing work in four areas: "assigning clear lines of responsibility for investigating all leads on high-priority threats, so they are pursued more aggressively; distributing intelligence reports more quickly and widely, especially those suggesting specific threats against the U.S.; applying more rigorous standards to analytical tradecraft to improve intelligence integration and action; and enhancing the criteria for adding individuals to the terrorist watchlist and 'no fly' watchlist."

Four and a half months later, on May 20, 2010, Blair announced that he was stepping down from his post. Congressman Silvestre Reyes, the chairman of the House Ingelligence Committee, said in response to Blair's announcement, as quoted by the *FederalTimes.com* article of May 20, 2010, "Not one to back down in the face of a challenge, Director Blair worked hard to make the work-in-progress of intelligence reform and integration a reality. One of the lasting legacies of Director Blair's tenure will be his efforts to establish credibility with Congress. He was willing to give it straight to Congress, which I always appreciated." Congressman Bennie Thompson of Mississippi, the chairman of the House Homeland Security Committee, commented, according to the same article, "The ODNI is at a critical juncture. It now needs strong presidential leadership to help realize its potential as envisioned by Congress and the 9-11 Commission, or it will sink into irrelevance. The ODNI will only be effective if the President clarifies its authorities and defines its roles and responsibilities." In early June 2010 President Obama named James R. Clapper, a retired U.S. Air Force lieutenant general, as the next DNI. The Senate confirmed Clapper's appointment the following August.

Blair's honors include four Defense Distinguished Service Medals and other awards from the governments of Japan, Thailand, South Korea, Taiwan, and Australia as well as the U.S. He enjoys fishing and is famous in navy circles for once trying to water ski behind the USS *Cochrane* when he was its commander. Blair and his wife, the former Diane Everett, live in Washington, D.C. The couple have two adult children, Duncan and Pamela.

—C.C.

Suggested Reading: *Baltimore Sun* A p1+ Dec. 22, 2008; *Los Angeles Times* A p10 Dec. 20, 2008; *New Republic* (on-line) Jan. 25, 2010; *New York Times* A p38 Dec. 21, 2008, A p14 Feb. 13, 2009, (on-line) Nov. 22, 2008; *Time* (on-line) Jan. 12, 2009; *USNews.com* Feb. 13, 2009, Apr. 8, 2009, Feb. 3, 2010; *Washington Post* A p4+ Dec. 20, 2008; *Washington Times* M p10 Jan. 18, 2009

Bolden, Charles F. Jr.

Aug. 19, 1946– Administrator of NASA; former astronaut

Address: Public Affairs, NASA, 200 E St., S.W., Mailstop 9P39, Washington, DC 20546

Charles F. Bolden Jr.'s appointment as the 12th administrator of the National Aeronautics and Space Administration (NASA), on July 17, 2009, represented a breaking of new ground as well as the culmination of an already high-profile career with the agency. Bolden, who was an astronaut for 14 years and has been to space four times, is NASA's first black administrator and the second former astronaut (after Richard Truly) to man the post in the agency's 50-plus-year history. Bolden's nomination comes at a critical moment for NASA. As the agency undergoes a major transition that will determine the near future of the space program, it also must deal with problems that threaten the U.S.'s standing as a world leader in space exploration—perhaps most urgently, the retirement of the space-shuttle fleet in 2011, which will leave American astronauts dependent on Russian spacecraft for at least five years. Bolden also faces a challenge in implementing the government–private industry partnership that he and the Barack Obama administration have proposed as the most viable way of getting American space exploration back on track.

Charles F. Bolden Jr. was born in Columbia, South Carolina, on August 19, 1946. His mother, Ethel, was a teacher and high-school librarian; his

Courtesy of NASA

father, Charles Sr., a World War II veteran, taught high-school social studies and also served as a counselor and sports coach. The Charles F. Bolden Stadium, in Columbia, was named for the astronaut's father. Charles Jr. and his brother, Warren, grew up at a time when most South Carolina schools were still racially segregated. Despite that obstacle Bolden excelled as a student and proved to be a capable athlete, playing quarterback on his high-school football team under the direction of his father, the team's head coach. A former classmate said of Bolden to the *State*, a South Carolina newspaper, as quoted in *Time* (May 19, 2009), "He could get along with everyone. You never did see Charles mad. He always had that way about him to smooth things over, with his calming voice and rational thinking." Although he attended all-black schools close to his home, the young Bolden's involvement in various out-of-state summer programs, often as one of only a handful of African-American participants, exposed him to people, places, and ideas that broadened his perspective.

Bolden said in a 2004 interview with Sandra Johnson, as part of the NASA Johnson Space Center Oral History Project, that he knew he wanted to go into the military since the seventh or eighth grade, when he saw a TV program called *Men of Annapolis*, about the U.S Naval Academy. He "fell in love with the uniform" and noted that the military men in movies and on television "seemed to get all the good-looking girls." During his middle- and high-school years, getting an appointment to the U.S. Naval Academy became Bolden's goal.

Bolden graduated from C.A. Johnson High School in 1964, and then, with the help of a former federal judge and a recommendation from U.S. congressman William L. Dawson of Illinois, received an appointment to the U.S. Naval Academy. He revealed to Sandra Johnson that his first year there was "bad, horrible. . . . I cried all the time. I wanted to go home, and my father kept me there. Every time I'd call on weekends, he's say, 'Stay one more week and then we'll talk about it.' And so that's the way I went through the first year." He entered the academy with the intention of becoming a Navy SEAL, but by the time he graduated, in 1968, with a degree in electrical science, Bolden—following the example of one of his company commanders—had decided to become an infantry officer; he entered the Marine Corps soon afterward, with the rank of second lieutenant. That same year Bolden married his childhood friend and fellow Columbia native Alexis "Jackie" Walker.

Bolden changed his mind about entering the infantry after being given the chance to fly with an instructor. "It was like magic, and I knew that I wanted to fly. So I stumbled into it, to be quite honest," Bolden said in his interview with Johnson. After completing a series of flight-training programs, Bolden became a naval aviator in 1970. He was sent to Southeast Asia, where he flew more than 100 combat missions during the early 1970s, the height of the Vietnam War. Upon his return to the U.S., Bolden held various positions with the Marine Corps, including that of recruiting officer, before pursuing his master's degree in systems management at the University of Southern California. After receiving his degree, in 1977, Bolden attended the U.S. Pilot Test School, in Patuxent River, Maryland, graduating in 1979. Meanwhile, he had attained the rank of colonel in the Marine Corps.

In 1980, while working at the Naval Air Test Center's Systems Engineering and Strike Aircraft Test Directorates, testing ground-attack aircraft, Bolden applied to NASA's astronaut corps, even though he did not think he would be accepted. "Not in my wildest imagination could someone like me become an astronaut, because they were all white, Anglo-Saxon, Protestant, all test pilots, all about five-feet-ten. They all looked alike. And I was none of those," the five-foot seven-inch Bolden recalled to Johnson. To his surprise, Bolden was selected, becoming the first African-American Marine chosen as a NASA astronaut. By 1981 he had moved his family to Houston, Texas, and begun training as an astronaut.

Bolden made his first trip to space as part of a seven-member crew aboard the space shuttle *Columbia* when it embarked on mission STS-61-C from Kennedy Space Center on January 12, 1986. Bolden, who piloted *Columbia*, became NASA's first African-American shuttle pilot. Among those on board were Franklin Chang-Diaz, the first Hispanic in space, and a payload specialist, Bill Nelson—now a U.S. senator from Florida and one of Bolden's strongest supporters. During the six-day flight, while the shuttle completed 96 orbits of Earth, crew members deployed the SATCOM KU communications satellite and conducted experiments in astrophysics and materials processing. *Columbia* returned to Earth on January 18, 1986, landing at Edwards Air Force Base, in California. That was only 10 days before the launch of the space shuttle *Challenger*, which exploded 73 seconds into its 10th mission, on January 28, resulting in the deaths of all seven crewmembers on board (including Bolden's close friend Ronald McNair). The *Challenger* disaster led to a two-and-a-half-year grounding of the shuttle fleet, during which Bolden, as the chief of the Safety Division at Johnson Space Center (JSC), oversaw the safety efforts undertaken at NASA in order to resume space flight.

On April 24, 1990 Bolden made his second trip to space, aboard the space shuttle *Discovery*'s mission STS-31, again serving as pilot. On the second day of the mission, the *Discovery*'s crew launched the Hubble Space Telescope into Earth's orbit. *Discovery* landed at Edwards Air Force Base on April 29, 1990. For his final two missions, STS-45 (March 24–April 2, 1992), aboard the *Atlantis*, and STS-60 (February 3–11, 1994), aboard the *Discovery*, Bolden was the mission commander. STS-60 was the first mission of the Shuttle-Mir Program, a joint effort of the U.S. and Russia, and included the first Russian cosmonaut to fly aboard an American space shuttle.

Bolden's technical assignments during his first stint at NASA included: Astronaut Office safety officer; technical assistant to the director of flight-crew operations; special assistant to the director of the Johnson Space Center; Astronaut Office liaison to the Safety, Reliability and Quality Assurance Directorates of the Marshall Space Flight Center and the Kennedy Space Center; chief of the Safety Division at JSC; lead astronaut for vehicle test and checkout at the Kennedy Space Center; and assistant deputy administrator, NASA Headquarters. He was also the first person to ride the Launch Complex 39 slidewire baskets, which allow astronauts to escape quickly from a space shuttle on the launch pad if danger threatens. (A human test was deemed necessary following an aborted launch.)

After his final space flight, in 1994, Bolden left NASA and returned to active duty in the Marine Corps. He served as deputy commander of midshipmen at the U.S. Naval Academy until 1997, when he was assigned as deputy commander general of the 1st Marine Expeditionary Force in the Pacific. He held that post in support of Operation Desert Thunder, in Kuwait, before being promoted to his final rank, major general, and named deputy commander of U.S. forces in Japan in 1998. When Bolden retired from the Marine Corps, in 2004, his many military decorations included the Distinguished Flying Cross, the Defense Superior Service Medal, and two NASA Exceptional Service medals. In 2006 Bolden was inducted into the Astronaut Hall of Fame, in Cape Canaveral, Florida.

In 2002 President George W. Bush had nominated Bolden to serve as NASA's deputy administrator. With the "war on terror" having been launched in the aftermath of the September 11, 2001 terrorist attacks, however, the Department of Defense issued a policy in March 2002 limiting the placement of experienced military officers in civilian jobs, and the Bush administration withdrew Bolden's nomination. On May 23, 2009 Bolden was again nominated—this time by President Barack Obama—for an important NASA post: that of administrator. Confirmed unanimously by the U.S. Senate, Bolden began his duties as the 12th administrator of NASA on July 19, 2009, becoming the first African-American to head the agency on a permanent basis. (Frederick D. Gregory, another African-American astronaut and former deputy administrator, served as acting administrator for a brief period in 2005, following the resignation of Sean O'Keefe.) Bolden is only the second former astronaut to head NASA.

Bolden has taken on a number of challenges in his post. NASA is in some ways a very different agency from the one Bolden entered in 1981, and he has admitted that a lack of both funds and interest has prevented the program from progressing the way he then thought it would. "If you told me back in 1980 when I was a young astronaut candidate that we wouldn't be back on the moon today . . . I would have told you that you were smoking some bad stuff. I thought I was going up on the shuttle and coming back to train to go to the moon," Bolden said at a NASA policy talk on January 5, 2010, as quoted by *Science News* (February 13, 2010). "We became risk averse after the space shuttle *Challenger*, and we have not recovered from that. That has got to stop." First and foremost, the agency must find a way to deal with the five-year gap

between the scheduled retirement of its space-shuttle fleet, in 2011, and the implementation of its successor, the *Ares I* rocket, originally intended for use in moon missions. The NASA science program continues to suffer from cuts to funding made by the Bush administration—funds that had been intended to pay for NASA's Constellation program, of which *Ares* and *Orion*, its crew capsule, are a part. On February 1, 2010 President Obama proposed a $19 billion budget that would invest in new technology and partnerships with private companies to send astronauts to Mars and other destinations beyond low-Earth orbit—while cancelling most of the Constellation program, which the president has called costly and inefficient. (In April Obama announced changes to the proposal, including reviving the *Orion* capsule for use at the International Space Station as a rescue spacecraft.) The budget request would set aside $6 billion over the next five years to support the development of commercial spaceships capable of carrying American astronauts into space. That development would take time, and with the remaining three space shuttles pegged for retirement in 2011, American astronauts will be forced to depend on the Russian *Soyuz* spacecraft to get to and from the International Space Station until a replacement, NASA-built or otherwise, is available. The looming gap and subsequent layoffs will force NASA to let go of talented engineers, posing a threat to the very future of the agency and possibly eroding the United States' status as a leader in space exploration.

At a February 2010 meeting with the Senate's Commerce, Science, and Transportation Subcommittee members and space experts regarding NASA's 2011 budget proposal, a number of senators complained about the proposal's lack of specifics, and Senator David Vitter of Louisiana asked Bolden what he planned to tell NASA employees who lose their jobs as a result of the retirement of the space-shuttle program. Bolden grew visibly upset and began to tear up before replying, as quoted by Tariq Malik on SPACE.com (February 24, 2010), "I can tell them, as I have, that I'm going to do everything in my power to try to make sure that we develop some programs that are going to get to where we all want to go as soon as possible." What that means, according to Bolden, is increased funding for research into new technologies, especially those meant to ensure astronaut safety (including measures to combat the radiation and health dangers presented by deep-space travel) and those aimed at expediting missions to Mars. Eugene Levy, a space scientist at Rice University, remarked to *New Scientist* (May 24, 2009) that with the current NASA budget, money is so tight that "little or nothing can be done well, compromising the entire programme."

Some of Bolden's critics have warned that his ties to the aerospace industry may present a conflict of interest. Prior to his nomination as administrator, Bolden was the chief executive officer of a small firm, JackandPanther LLC, that provides military and aerospace consulting services. Bolden served on the board of directors at Gencorp Inc., whose subsidiary Aerojet has a contract to build engines for the *Orion* space capsule currently in development at NASA. In 2005 Bolden was a registered lobbyist for the firm ATK, which manufactures rocket boosters for NASA projects. Because of those affiliations, Bolden has been granted a two-year limited waiver with regard to the administration's ethics policy, which prohibits appointees from taking part in matters "directly and substantially related" to their former employers, according to the *New York Times* on-line profile of Bolden. Through that measure Bolden will be able to participate in major policy decisions related to program capabilities and objectives but will be excused from making any contractual decisions involving ATK or Gencorp.

Bolden's goals for the agency in the next five years include safely completing the space-shuttle fleet's last flight to the International Space Station, developing a viable commercial space industry, and improving job security and conditions for NASA employees. His long-term goals include sending humans and robots to Earth's moon, the moons of Mars, and Mars itself. Accomplishing those goals would call for a new era of invention at NASA. "We have not done anything in the past decade for basic research," Bolden noted while speaking at the Massachusetts Institute of Technology (MIT) on May 10, 2010, as quoted in *Technology Review* (May 11, 2010, on-line). "The frustration for me is that when I go to Congress, all we talk about is Constellation and human spaceflight. We forget that the president's plan is to spend a lot of money on basic research." Ultimately, Bolden wants humans to colonize Mars; he believes that the first step should be more robotic exploration. "Robots can help us understand everything there is to know about the planet's harsh environment," he said at MIT. As for a time frame, Bolden said in an interview with Andrew Williams for the British publication *Metro* (December 21, 2006, on-line), "The ultimate goal is to get a person to Mars in 25 years. Our governments need to invest more in the exploration of our universe. I won't do it but I'd like to pave the way for my granddaughters to set foot on Mars. There's evidence Mars may sustain life today and we need to see that."

Bolden and his wife live near the Johnson Space Center, in Houston. Their two children are Anthony Che, a lieutenant colonel in the Marine Corps, and Kelly Michelle, a physician. The couple also have three grandchildren. Bolden's hobbies include playing racquetball and running.

—H.R.W.

Suggested Reading: Associated Press Oct. 23, 2009; *NASA Johnson Space Center Oral History Project* Jan. 6, 2004; *New York Times* (on-line) Feb. 25, 2010; (South Carolina) *State* May 24, 2009; *Space.com* (on-line) Feb. 24, 2010; *Technology Review* (on-line) May 11, 2010

Charley Gallay/Getty Images

Boll, Uwe

(bowl, OO-vay)

June 22, 1965– Filmmaker

Address: Brightlight Pictures, Bridge Studios, 2400 Boundary Rd., Burnaby, BC V5M 3Z3, Canada

The name of the independent director, producer, and screenwriter Uwe Boll has become virtually synonymous with bad filmmaking. "Uwe Boll is to directing what cirrhosis is to the liver," Reed Tucker wrote for the *New York Post* (January 6, 2008, on-line). "Or so his critics would have you believe. His movies—popcorn-action flicks based on video games like 'BloodRayne'—have been eviscerated by reviewers and earned him the title of 'world's worst director.'" A native of Germany, Boll has directed 19 feature films; he also wrote or co-wrote the screenplays for some of them and, since 1999, has produced them as the head of his own company, Boll KG. *BloodRayne*, *Heart of America*, *House of the Dead*, *Postal*, *Rampage*, and all of Boll's other films have been panned (though not universally) for their cinematic clichés, faulty plotting, one-dimensional characters, nonsensical dialogue, wooden acting, and general air of schlock. Boll has also come under fire from fans of the video games he has adapted for straying far afield from his sources and sullying them in the process; aficionados of horror films, too, have attacked him, for "tarnishing the movie-making art" with films "whose ancillary purpose, Boll will tell you, is to offer a tax benefit to his high-end German investors," Paul Brownfield wrote for the *Los Angeles Times* (May

23, 2008). Despite such indictments, the casts of some of Boll's films have included such respected actors as Ben Kingsley, Christian Slater, and Ray Liotta, and Boll has attracted a following among those who view him as a pop-culture provocateur.

Boll has argued that critics treat him unfairly because he works outside the Hollywood system. He has also complained that while reviewers judge film adaptations of comic books on their merits, they automatically dismiss movies based on video games. In addition, in his view, it is unfair that his low-cost films are compared unfavorably with films whose budgets exceed his many times over. "Any ***hole can make a good movie for $100 million," he told Sean O'Neal for the *A.V. Club* (September 20, 2007). "I think it's way harder to make a movie with no money, and to start with no contacts and work your way up to international productions." (Boll made his first film in Germany in 1991 for the equivalent of about $30,000 and nine of his last films in British Columbia, Canada, in collaboration with the Vancouver-based Brightlight Pictures, for a total of $200 million, including the $60 million he spent for the 2007 movie *Postal.*) Boll has often responded to his detractors with personal attacks; in 2006 he generated a lot of publicity by defeating five of his critics in public boxing matches. According to Peter Hartlaub, writing for the *San Francisco Chronicle* (May 30, 2008, on-line), "Boll's films have been so despised that the idea of reviewing them has become all but moot. A new Boll film becomes less of a piece of art to be judged subjectively than a foregone conclusion—a cinematic pinata to test a writer's ability to write a snarky rant." Boll told Aaron Thompson for the *Las Vegas Weekly* (May 22, 2008, online) that the 19th-century British writer Oscar Wilde "said at one point that the only thing you'll regret is the things you didn't do, and I agree with it. I do what I want, and I don't regret that I did it this way. . . . I totally regret nothing."

Uwe Boll was born on June 22, 1965 in Wermelskirchen, a town in what was then West Germany. He has said that his passion for film took root when, at age 10, he saw the version of *Mutiny on the Bounty* (1962) starring Marlon Brando. He has cited the work of the filmmakers Martin Scorsese, John Ford, Orson Welles, Stanley Kubrick, William Wyler, François Truffaut, and John Carpenter as particularly influential in his thinking about cinema; Carpenter directed and/or wrote the screenplays for horror movies including *Eyes of Laura Mars*, *The Thing*, and *Halloween* and its many sequels. As a teenager Boll made home movies and videos. He later took courses in film in Munich, Germany, and Vienna, Austria. He abandoned his studies in 1985. "I wanted to make movies, not talk about movies," he recalled to Luke Y. Thompson for *LA Weekly* (May 22, 2008, on-line). "I was talking about movies in my free time with my buddies nonstop, so the thing was like, what am I doing here?" By his own account, in 1995 he earned a Ph.D. degree in literature from the University of Cologne. He described that accomplishment to Jim Slotek for the *Toronto Sun* (May 23, 2008) as "absurd if you make movies like *House of the Dead.*" When Sean O'Neal asked him why, as the holder of a doctorate in literature, he favors adaptations from video games, Boll responded, "Of course there are a lot of books that are interesting to make movies out of, but on the other hand, I think video games are also kind of like bestselling books for the younger generation, and the younger generation is the one going to the theaters." He also noted that he typically paid about $500,000 for the rights to a video game, while the rights to books by such writers as Stephen King or John Grisham typically cost millions of dollars each.

With borrowed equipment and 60,000 German marks (about $30,000 in 1991) contributed by family members and friends, and a cast willing to work for free, Boll made his first film, *German Fried Movie*. Written by Boll and Frank Lustig, it was designed as an homage to John Landis's crude comedy *Kentucky Fried Movie* (1977); like that film, it poked fun at everything from sitcoms to religion. It was relatively well received in Germany, where it played in a series of theaters for six months and earned enough to finance Boll's next film, *Barschel—Murder in Geneva* (1993). Co-written with Lustig and directed by Boll, that film was about the mysterious death of the real-life German politician Uwe Barschel in 1987. Boll wrote and directed his first horror film, *Amoklauf* ("To Run Amok"), in 1994.

During his first few years as a filmmaker, Boll supplemented his income with factory work. For about five years beginning in 1995, he worked as a producer of television and music shows for a German company, TaunusFilm Produktions. He co-wrote, directed, and produced his next film, *Das Erste Semester* ("The First Semester," 1997), a comedy about a student's struggles in his classes and in finding a steady girlfriend. Distributed by United International Pictures, a London–based company owned jointly by Paramount and Universal, the film fared poorly at the box office. Boll's first English-language film was the made-for-television *Sanctimony*, which he wrote and directed. *Sanctimony* was the first film financed by Boll's recently launched production company, Boll KG, and it marked the first time Boll used a German tax loophole to raise funds. He told Luke Y. Thompson, "I created this thing of going to investors, dentists, whomever [asking them to] give me $50,000 and you can write it off on the taxes, and I started collecting money for *Sanctimony* . . . in 1999. It was a long process." Contrary to widespread rumors, Boll has never financed his work with "Nazi gold"—money and property stolen and hidden by the Nazi government during World War II; the tax loophole he exploited was recently closed. *Sanctimony* aired in the U.S. and Germany in 2000. It starred Casper Van Dien as a serial killer who, guided by the maxim "See no evil, hear no evil, speak no evil," removes his victims' eyes, ears, and tongues.

Boll's next venture was the psychological thriller *Blackwoods* (2002), starring the B-list actors Patrick Muldoon, Michael Paré, and Clint Howard. Muldoon's character, racked with guilt over having killed a young girl when he was driving while drunk, is pursued by angry, deranged members of the girl's family. Most critics considered the film derivative and the plot outlandish. Stephen Holden, however, wrote for the *New York Times* (May 10, 2002) that although the movie was "far from a future cult classic, it turns out to be smarter and more diabolical than you could have guessed at the beginning."

Boll next served as the producer, director, and writer (with Robert Dean Klein) of *Heart of America* (2003), about a suburban high-school shooting. Some critics condemned the film for exploiting such tragedies as the killing of 12 students and a teacher by two other students at Columbine High School, in Colorado, in 1999. Dennis Harvey, referring to the director of the film *Kids*, wrote for *Variety* (March 3, 2003) that Boll's film "lands between Larry Clark–style teensploitation and a preachy after-school special—watchable but hardly laudable." An unnamed writer for the *Entertainment Weekly* Web site wrote, "*Heart of America* is what Gus Van Zant's Columbine-inspired *Elephant* might have looked like had Van Zant never directed a film before, or, indeed, . . . never seen one."

In 2003 Boll secured the film-adaptation rights to the Sega Corp.'s popular video game *House of the Dead* (1996). The events of Boll's *House of the Dead* take place on an island where a group of teenagers (played by virtual unknowns) come under attack by bloodthirsty zombies and seek refuge in a creepy house. The film's box-office receipts placed it barely in the black, and it was critically panned for its weak plot, acting, and dialogue, bad make-up, and distracting use of clips from the video game. "To properly convey the jaw-dropping shoddiness of this videogame-based 'horror' 'movie,' one must approach what scientists call Absolute Stupid," Scott Brown wrote for *Entertainment Weekly* (October 24, 2003). A few words of praise came from Kevin Thomas, who acknowledged in a review for the *Los Angeles Times* (October 13, 2003) that the film offered "scarcely a whiff of originality" but added, "Boll has directed it with enough energy and style that it adds up to passably mindless if grisly fun."

Boll's next cinematic adaptation of a zombie-themed video game was *Alone in the Dark* (2005). Based on a 1989 product from Atari that had become a cult classic, the picture starred Christian Slater and Tara Reid. Critics scorned it for its non-existent plot, stiff acting, and senseless shoot-out sequences, none of which reflected the aesthetic of the video game. One of Boll's most vociferous critics, known as Quint, a writer for the film and video-game Web site Ain't It Cool News, wrote, "Once again we have a video game movie that completely throws out everything that made the game great."

For his next effort Boll secured the rights to *BloodRayne*, a video game about the half-vampire, half-woman Rayne. Boll's *BloodRayne* (2005) starred the Academy Award–winning actor Ben Kingsley as the evil vampire king Kagan, alongside Kristanna Lokan (as Rayne), Billy Zane, and Michael Madsen. "The Pepto-abysmal horror tale *BloodRayne* provides us yet one more argument for why no moviemaker should ever, ever, ever be allowed to base a film on a video game—ever," Dann Gire wrote for the Chicago, Illinois, *Daily Herald* (January 7, 2006). "The dialogue borders on gibberish . . . and the furiously edited, unfocused footage looks like someone put the film together with a Cuisinart."

Boll told Baker that he became disgusted "with all these Internet geeks hiding behind nicknames saying they want to kick my *ss." In a June 2006 press release, Boll, a former amateur boxer, challenged his detractors to fight him in the boxing ring. (He mentioned the filmmakers Roger Avary and Quentin Tarantino specifically, but neither responded.) Choosing from among those who sent him two of their published negative assessments of his work, he picked Richard "Lowtax" Kyanka, the creator of the blog "Something Awful"; Chris Alexander, a *Rue Morgue* magazine contributor; Carlos Palencia Jimenez-Arguello, the Webmaster of Cinecutre.com; and the Ain't It Cool News writer Jeff Sneider. He also agreed to fight Chance Minter, a 17-year-old amateur boxer. All of his opponents signed a waiver absolving Boll of responsibility for injuries. In the first bout, held on September 5, 2006 in Malaga, Spain, Boll knocked out Arguello in three rounds. Calling himself "Teutonic Terror," Boll defeated the others on September 23 before an audience at the Plaza of Nations, in Vancouver. The event was filmed and later included as an extra feature on the DVD of Boll's film *Postal*.

Boll cast Ray Liotta, Burt Reynolds, John Rhys-Davies, Leelee Sobieksi, Jason Statham, and Matthew Lillard in his adventure epic *In the Name of the King: A Dungeon Siege Tale* (2007). Based on the video game *Dungeon Siege*, the film follows Statham's character, a farmer bent on avenging the death of his son at the hands of the Krugs, a race of animal warriors. Critics found little to praise in it. Scott Tobias wrote for the *A.V. Club* (January 11, 2008, on-line), "Cultists will be happy to discover that *In The Name of the King* bears all the so-bad-it's-good hallmarks of a classic Boll production: A bizarre ensemble cast of fallen stars and incorrigible hams . . . ; the stunning vistas of non-union locales (here, British Columbia); clumsily patched-in CGI [computer-generated imagery] backdrops; hilariously stilted dialogue; and action sequences as tightly choreographed as a demolition derby." "*In The Name of the King* . . . was my opportunity to do my epic, *Braveheart*, *Lord of the Rings*, *Gladiator* movie," Boll told Sean O'Neal. "I try not to repeat myself in genres too much. Everybody says video-game adaptations are all the same, but I disagree. . . . I think I've [covered] a wide range of genres and time periods, like Transylvania in 1700 and now a Western with *BloodRayne II*, . . . or comedy and satire with *Postal*." Boll characterized his 2008 film *Far Cry*, which was based on the same-named video game, as "a real, pure action movie—like *Die Hard* on an island."

Postal (2007) was based on the video game *Running with Scissors* and its sequel, in which players control the "Postal Dude" as he goes berserk. Boll and the game's creators "had a huge dispute about what direction the movie should go," he told Luke Y. Thompson. "They saw it more as a real rampage movie"—like a "super-brutal" successor to the film *Taxi Driver* (1976), directed by Martin Scorsese, in which Robert De Niro starred as a mentally unbalanced former marine who becomes a killer. "And I said, 'I don't want to do it. I want to make a comedy, and I have to do my thing here.'" Boll sought to make a comedic satire to mock President George W. Bush, the so-called war on terror, religious cults, and himself. "I used that movie to finish up a lot, to make a political statement, and to make a statement about my whole career, showing myself as that lederhosen Nazi guy . . . ," he told Luke Y. Thompson. "I wanted to wash the past away in a way, it was one big hammer hit, and I think I definitely reached my goal in the way that it is a ridiculous, ruthless, over-the-top movie." The film, which opens with a joke about 9/11, follows the Postal Dude (the actor Zack Ward) and his uncle (the comedian Dave Foley), the leader of a religious cult, as they attempt to fight terrorists led by Osama bin Laden (Larry Thomas), who is being protected by his best friend, George W. Bush (Brent Mendenhall). The film includes a brief appearance by Boll as the owner of a Nazi theme park. In the U.S. *Postal* was barred from the 5,325-odd theaters in the AMC chain and the approximately 6,775 theaters in the Regal Entertainment chain and opened in less than a dozen other theaters. When Sean O'Neal asked Boll if he thought the U.S. was "ready for a 9/11 parody," Boll said, "I think it's better to be too early and disturb a few people . . . than to do it way after the fact. . . . I think it's important to have a movie like *Postal* now, where we are on the peak of the Iraq War, on the peak of terrorist attacks, where everything is actually happening." He noted that Charlie Chaplin's movie *The Great Dictator*, which satirizes Adolf Hitler, was released in 1940, during World War II, and Stanley Kubrick's *Dr. Strangelove*, which satirizes the Cold War, was released in 1964, during the fierce nuclear-arms race between the Soviet Union and the U.S.

Boll's attempts at political satire in *Postal* struck most critics as futile. Mark Olsen wrote for the *Los Angeles Times* (May 23, 2008), "Boll's rampant narcissistic showmanship creates such a bizarre, garish spectacle that it is almost tempting to give him credit for being something of a misunderstood artist after all. Almost, but not quite. *Postal* is largely just a byproduct of Boll's self-promotion, rendering the film itself, in essence, beside the point." Peter Hartlaub, however, disagreed, declaring,

"The much-delayed low-budget movie may be completely beyond the bounds of mainstream taste, but it's also funny, and criticizes our government's hypocrisy and political correctness in a way that's refreshingly pointed. If this movie had been made by an unknown young director, a lot of critics would still be panning the movie for its inconsistencies—but many others would be praising his courage." In audience balloting at the 2008 Hoboken International Film Festival, in New Jersey, *Postal* was named the best film and Boll the best director.

Boll's film *Seed*, released in early 2008, received little press. Also largely overlooked were *1968 Tunnel Rats* (2008), about American soldiers hunting down the Vietcong in their vast network of underground tunnels during the Vietnam War; *Rampage* (2009), about a sociopath who embarks on a killing spree; *Final Storm*, an apocalyptic thriller involving a married couple and a weird stranger; *Stoic* (2009), about rape, torture, and suicide in a prison; and *Darfur* (2009), about three American journalists in war-ravaged Sudan. Boll's 2010 films include *BloodRayne 3: The Third Reich* and *Max Schmeling*, both of which he produced and directed. He also served as writer, producer, and director of *Auschwitz*, which was scheduled for release in Germany at the end of the year. A trailer for the film that was posted on the Internet in September 2010 generated criticism for its depiction of Boll as a Nazi police officer guarding a concentration-camp gas chamber filled with civilian captives. Boll is the subject of the documentary *Raging Boll*, directed by Dan Lee West, which premiered at the Austin Film Festival, in Texas, in October 2010. His upcoming projects as a director include the film "Bennie," scheduled for a 2012 release. He has reportedly been working since 2007 on a motion-picture adaptation of the video game *Zombie Massacre7*.

A petition posted on the Web since 2006 calls upon Boll to "stop directing, producing, or taking any part in the creation of feature films." "Boll has repeatedly shown a complete lack of comprehension regarding the videogames he has dragged, kicking and screaming, to the silver screen and his ham-fisted approach to horror has soiled future possibilities for anyone else who may attempt to bring videogames to film," it states. As of late October 2010, the petition had more than 360,000 signatures—far fewer than the one million necessary to persuade Boll to retire, the filmmaker told a London *Guardian* (April 7, 2008, on-line) reporter.

Boll has written two books, one about making movies in Germany and the other about television serials; to date both are available only in German. A citizen of both Germany and Canada, Boll is married to a Canadian.

—W.D.

Suggested Reading: *GQ* p208+ Mar. 2008; imdb.com; *LA Weekly* (on-line) May 22, 2008; *Los Angeles Times* E p2 May 23, 2008; *Ottawa*

Citizen D p7 Jan. 11, 2008; *San Francisco Chronicle* (on-line) May 30, 2008; *Wired* p256+ Dec. 2006

Selected Films: *German Fried Movie*, 1991; *Barschel—Murder in Geneva*, 1993; *Amoklauf*, 1994; *The First Semester*, 1997; *Sanctimony*, 2000; *Blackwoods*, 2002; *Heart of America*, 2003; *House of the Dead*, 2003; *Alone in the Dark*, 2005; *Bloodrayne*, 2005; *In the Name of the King: A Dungeon Siege Tale*, 2007; *Postal*, 2007; *Seed*, 2008; *1968 Tunnel Rats*, 2008; *Rampage*, 2009; *Stoic*, 2009; *Darfur*, 2009; *Final Storm*, 2010; *BloodRayne 3: The Third Reich*, 2010; *Max Schmeling*, 2010

Chris Graythen/Getty Images

Bosh, Chris

Mar. 24, 1984– Basketball player

Address: Miami Heat, American Airlines Arena, 601 Biscayne Blvd., Miami, FL 33132

"Chris Bosh doesn't have the cachet of a [LeBron] James or a Dwyane Wade or even a Carmelo Anthony . . . ," Doug Smith wrote for the *Toronto (Canada) Star* (February 17, 2008), toward the end of Bosh's seven-year stint as a power forward for the Toronto Raptors of the National Basketball Association (NBA). He is "hardly ever mentioned in the same sentence with James, Wade and Anthony," Smith continued, "all members of a 2003 draft class that will go down in NBA history as one of the best of all time. He doesn't have the flash or the style or the success of the others, and to casual fans

he's just a good, young big man playing on a team held in little regard. Bosh is denied some of the hype and publicity simply by his style, but less is more when it comes to the 6-foot-10 native of Dallas." Smith concluded that with such celebrated players as Kevin Garnett and Shaquille O'Neal "get[ting] older and closer to the end of their careers, Bosh is among the next wave of great big men." In his freshman season as a Raptor, Bush flew under the radar, finishing behind his fellow draftees James, Anthony, and Wade in the league's rookie-of-the-year voting, despite having played impressively—all the more so since he played out of position. Following the trade of the six-year veteran Vince Carter, in 2004, Bosh was moved from center back to his natural position—power forward—and quickly became the team's leading scorer and rebounder. Ranked with his league's leaders in scoring and rebounding since the 2005–06 season, he helped to secure the franchise's first play-off appearance in five years in 2006–07. And while James, Wade, and Anthony may get more publicity, in 2009 *Sporting News* and *Slam Online* named Bosh on their lists of the top 50 NBA players. Along with James, Wade, and several other basketball superstars, Bosh became a free agent after the 2009–10 season. On July 7, 2010 he announced that he would be signing with the Miami Heat. (James and Wade also joined the Heat.)

Christopher Wesson Bosh was born on March 24, 1984 to Noel and Freida Bosh in Dallas, Texas, and grew up in the nearby town of Hutchins. He has a younger brother, Joel. Bosh's father was a plumbing engineer who also served as a volunteer church youth minister and counselor; his mother worked as a computer-systems analyst. According to Bosh's mother, his athletic talents were evident even before his birth. "I knew [Chris] was going to be special when I was pregnant [with him]," Freida Bosh told Richie Whitt for the *Dallas Observer* (September 28, 2006). "Some moms say they feel a kick. I felt jumps." When he was three years old, Bosh's parents enrolled him in gymnastics and karate classes. A year later he was dribbling a basketball at the gym where his father played in weekly pickup games, and when he was eight, he began honing his basketball skills at a neighborhood playground. "I wasn't old enough to run with the big boys yet. So I was just out there working on my moves," Bosh told Glen Colbourn for the *Toronto Star* (January 13, 2004). Growing up, the highly competitive Bosh, who often spent his summer weekends playing basketball with his father at a local recreation center, would challenge his younger brother to one-on-one games in their shared bedroom, using the miniature Nerf basketball set their mother had bought for them. Although Bosh's parents encouraged their sons' love of sports, they also stressed the importance of education. Bosh consistently earned straight A's in middle school while playing on the basketball and baseball teams.

During his freshman year at Lincoln High School in Dallas, Bosh joined the Tigers, the varsity basketball team. In his sophomore year, in 1999, under a new coach, Leonard Bishop, Bosh won the starting power-forward position. Because of his wiry frame, however, he was often out-muscled under the basket by larger, more physical opponents. Determined to improve his overall game, Bosh assiduously studied Bishop's weekly handout sheets, on which the coach pointed out areas of improvement for team members. He developed a variety of jumpshots, including his fadeaway, his turnaround shot, and his pull-up jumper. Bosh's efforts helped the Tigers reach the 1999 regional finals of the University Interscholastic League (UIL) Conference 4A championship, where his team lost, 78–75, to James Madison High School. In Bosh's junior year the Tigers returned to the Conference 4A championship and advanced one step further, to the state semifinals, which they narrowly lost, 50–48, to Sidney Lanier High School, in San Antonio. Bosh had his best year during the 2001–02 season, averaging 20 points, 9.5 rebounds, and four blocked shots per game. Lincoln High ended the season with a 40–0 record, capturing the Texas state championship and *USA Today*'s number-one national ranking. At the 2002 Texas State Tournament, the Tigers won their third state championship (the others were in 1990 and 1993) with a 71–51 victory against Ozen High School, in Beaumont, Texas. Bosh's dominant performance—21 points, 11 rebounds, and seven blocked shots—earned him Most Valuable Player (MVP) honors. In his senior year Bosh was named the high-school player of the year by Basketball America and designated a first team All-American by McDonald's and *Parade* magazine. In international competition Bosh represented the U.S. at the third annual Global Games, where his squad won the gold medal and he was named MVP. Bosh also played on the bronze-medal-winning USA men's team at the 2002 International Basketball Association (FIBA) Americas under-18 Championship (formerly the FIBA Americas Junior World Championship Qualifier). He graduated with honors from Lincoln High School in 2002.

Bosh, who had been pursued by many college recruiters, chose to attend the Georgia Institute of Technology (better known as Georgia Tech), in Atlanta. He cited the fast-paced transition offense employed by Paul Hewitt, the head coach of the Georgia Tech Yellow Jackets, as a big draw, along with the challenge of competing in the Atlantic Coast Conference (ACC). (Widely considered to be the premier college basketball conference in the U.S., the ACC is known for its members' quick-paced, guard-oriented style of play.) In his debut game, on November 23, 2002, Bosh scored 26 points and a game-high 14 rebounds for the Yellow Jackets in their 113–75 victory against the University of Arkansas Golden Lions. By the end of the season, Bosh had started all 31 regular-season games at the power-forward position and averaged

15.6 points, nine rebounds, and 2.2 blocks per game. Georgia Tech clinched the fifth seed in the ACC tournament and advanced to the March 14, 2003 quarterfinal game, in which they lost to North Carolina State, 71–65; Bosh scored a team-high 14 points and 10 rebounds. Later in March the Yellow Jackets played in the National Invitation Tournament (NIT), where they suffered a quarterfinal loss (80–72) to the Texas Tech Red Raiders.

In 2003 Bosh was named ACC Rookie of the Year by the Atlantic Coast Sports Media, having led the conference in blocks (67) and field-goal percentage (.560) that season; he became only the second freshman to lead the ACC in the latter category. The conference's second-leading rebounder (with 278), he was voted to the All-ACC second team, the ACC All-Defensive and rookie teams, and the U.S. Basketball Writers Association's (USBWA) Freshman All-America Team.

In May 2003 Bosh was announced as an early-entry candidate for the following month's highly anticipated NBA draft, which also included the future NBA superstars LeBron James, Carmelo Anthony, and Dwyane Wade. Bosh was the fourth overall pick of the Toronto Raptors, who signed him in July 2003 and moved him to the starting-center position. Despite missing several games in January and February, due to a sprained right knee and a sprained left ankle, Bosh averaged 11.5 points, 7.4 rebounds, and 1.4 blocks per game in his first year with the Raptors, who ended the regular season with 33 wins and 49 losses—sixth-best in the Eastern Conference's Central Division—and failed to make the play-offs. In his freshman NBA season, Bosh finished first among rookies in rebounding and blocks, while also setting a franchise record for total rebounds (557) and being named to the 2003–04 All-Rookie first team. At the NBA's 2004 All-Star Rookie Challenge, he scored eight points for the rookies in a game won by the sophomore team, 142–118.

Prior to the 2004–05 season, the Raptors underwent several changes, moving from the Eastern Conference's Central Division to its Atlantic Division and making shifts in personnel. In June Rob Babcock was appointed the Raptors' new general manager (GM), succeeding Glen Grunwald, who had been fired two months earlier (Jack McCloskey had served in the interim); in July Sam Mitchell replaced Kevin O'Neill as the head coach. Bosh moved back to the forward position, following Toronto's acquisition of the center Loren Woods in August. Within the first four months of the 2004–05 season, Bosh had emerged as the face of the franchise. His offense improved significantly that season, in which he started 81 regular-season games and averaged 16.8 points and a team-high 8.9 rebounds per game, surpassing his previous year's numbers in both categories. Bosh earned Eastern Conference Player of the Week honors (for January 3–9, 2005) after averaging 20.5 points, 13 rebounds, and 1.3 blocks per game while also shooting 60 percent (30 out of 50 in field-goal attempts).

He recorded his 1,000th career rebound during a February 22, 2005 victory (100–82) against the New Jersey Nets, becoming the third-youngest NBA player to accomplish that feat. Also in February Bosh participated in the annual All-Star Rookie Challenge, this time as a starting member of the sophomore team, which boasted game-MVP Carmelo Anthony, LeBron James, and Dwyane Wade; Bosh scored 26 points and was the game leader in rebounds (14) and steals (four), contributing to his team's win (133–106). The Raptors, however, had a disappointing year, duplicating the previous season's record (33–49)—good enough for a fourth-place finish in the Atlantic Division but not for a play-off spot.

Bosh entered the 2005–06 NBA season as the newly anointed captain of the Raptors, whose roster included several new draft picks, among them the Croatian point guard Roko Ukic and three forwards—Charlie Villanueva, Joey Graham, and the Slovenian Uros Slokar. The point guards Mike James and Jose Calderon were other additions. Bosh continued to play well. He recorded his 2,500th career point during a 117–91 loss to the Golden State Warriors, on November 26, and snagged his 1,500th career rebound during a 107–80 loss to the Philadelphia 76ers, on December 18. In January 2006 Bosh was named the Eastern Conference Player of the Week for the second time, after he averaged 30.3 points, 12 rebounds, and four assists per game, while shooting 53 percent from the field from January 30 to February 5. In late February Bosh made his first appearance at an NBA All-Star Game, scoring eight points as a reserve player for the Eastern Conference squad, which narrowly beat the West (122–120). After suffering a severely sprained left thumb during a March 26, 2006 overtime loss (125–116) to the Milwaukee Bucks, Bosh missed the final 12 games of the regular season. In his absence the Raptors lost 10 of the 11 last games, finished in fourth place in the Atlantic Division (with a 27–55 record), and again failed to make the play-offs. In 70 regular-season games, Bosh averaged 22.5 points, 9.2 rebounds, and 2.6 assists; he ranked among the league's top 15 players in all three categories. In July 2006 he signed a three-year contract extension with a fourth-year option, reportedly worth more than $60 million. A month later Bosh played for the USA Basketball men's senior national team at the FIBA World Championships in Japan; he led his team in field-goal percentage (.654), helping the U.S. win the bronze-medal match against Argentina (96–81).

The Raptors revamped their roster prior to the 2006–07 season, selecting Andrea Bargnani, the 2006 top NBA draft pick, while also signing the shooting guard Anthony Parker, the small forward Jorge Garbajosa, the point guard T.J. Ford, and the center Radoslav Nesterovic. After some early struggles the team finished the season with an overall record of 47 wins and 35 losses and an impressive 30–11 home record, clinching their first-ever Atlantic Division title and marking one of the best turnaround seasons in the history of the NBA. In the 2007 play-offs—their first postseason appearance in five years—the third-seeded Raptors suffered a first-round defeat, losing four games in the best-of-seven series against the sixth-seeded Nets, despite having home-court advantage. Bosh averaged a team-leading 22.6 points and 10.7 rebounds per game. He also received the second-highest number of fan votes (1,091,263) among Eastern Conference forwards and was a first-time starter for the Eastern Conference squad at the 2007 All-Star Game, won by the Western Conference, 153–132. In his second All-Star appearance, Bosh had 11 points and seven rebounds. Additionally, he was named to the All-NBA Second Team and earned Eastern Conference Player of the Month honors in January 2007, after averaging 25.4 points and 9.1 rebounds per game.

In an attempt to build on the previous season's success, the Raptors made several changes to their roster, acquiring the shooting guard/small forward Carlos Delfino from the Detroit Pistons. They also signed the small forwards Jamario Moon and Jason Kapono and traded a second-round pick in the 2008 draft to the San Antonio Spurs to acquire Georgios Printezis, the 58th overall pick in the 2007 draft. During the 2007–08 season, however, the Raptors were plagued by injuries among several of their key players, including Bosh and T.J. Ford, as well as the inconsistent play of Bargnani, the runner-up in the 2007 rookie-of-the-year voting. Nevertheless, the team ended the regular season with a 41–41 record and earned another berth at the NBA play-offs, where they suffered a first-round loss to the Orlando Magic. Bosh, who amassed an average of 22.3 points (10th-best in the league) and 8.7 rebounds per game during the regular season, appeared in his third All-Star Game. He had finished third in the fan voting, helped by a video he made that became popular with Internet viewers and landed him his own channel on YouTube. Selected as a reserve player on the Eastern Conference team, Bosh replaced an injured Kevin Garnett at one of the starting power-forward positions; Bosh scored 14 points and seven rebounds in the 134–128 victory by the East. At the 2008 Olympic Games, in Beijing, China, Bosh averaged a team-leading 6.1 rebounds per game for the gold-medal-winning U.S. men's basketball squad, which defeated Spain, 118–107.

In late June 2008 the Raptors acquired the forward/center Jermaine O'Neal and the forward Nathan Jawai in exchange for Ford, Nesterovic, the forward Maceo Baston, and the draft rights to the center Roy Hibbert. After the Raptors opened the 2008–09 season with eight wins and nine losses, the GM, Bryan Colangelo, replaced Mitchell with Jay Triano as head coach. The team continued to struggle after the February 13, 2009 trade of Jermaine O'Neal and Jamario Moon to the Miami Heat for the small forward Shawn Marion and the guard Marcus Banks; the Raptors finished the regular season with a 33–49 record—fourth-best in the Atlantic Division—and failed to advance to the play-offs. Bosh was ranked among the league's top-10 players in average number of points (a career-best 22.7) and rebounds per game (10). He was selected as a reserve player for the 2009 All-Star Game, but a knee injury forced him to sit it out.

Before the 2009–10 season, with the aim of improving the team's offense, Colangelo signed the forward Hedo Turkoglu, re-signed Nesterovic, and acquired other players including the forward/center Antoine Wright, the forward Devean George, and the guard Greg Buckner. Bosh made headlines in June 2009, when he refused to sign a contract extension with the Raptors, leading to speculation that he would be traded or that he would leave the team. (Bosh was among a highly touted group of players who became free agents after the 2009–10 season.)

By the start of the 2009–10 season, thanks to a vigorous workout regime, Bosh had added 20 pounds of muscle to his six-foot 10-inch frame. He finished the year with career-high averages of 24.0 points and 10.8 rebounds per game, good for ninth and sixth places in the league, respectively. Bosh earned his fifth All-Star Game appearance and served as an assistant bench coach for the sophomore team in the Rookie Challenge. The Raptors, meanwhile, missed out on the play-offs again, with a 40–42 record. As many expected, Bosh began courting offers from several NBA clubs when the free-agency period began, on July 1, 2010. He announced on July 7 that he would be joining the Miami Heat; two days later he completed a deal with that team. When he left the Raptors, Bosh was the franchise's all-time leader in points, rebounds, blocks, minutes played, and free throws. Soon afterward Dwyane Wade, the Heat's longtime franchise player, re-signed with the Heat, followed by LeBron James's much-publicized decision to join that team. Many in the media have referred to the Heat's new superstar trio as the "Big Three" (casting a shadow on another "Big Three"—the Boston Celtics' Ray Allen, Paul Pierce, and Kevin Garnett). The Heat immediately became the favorite to win the NBA championship in 2010–11.

Bosh, who has an endorsement deal with Nike, is the co-founder of Max Deal Technologies, a digital-marketing, Web-design, and consulting firm; among its most recent projects is *First Ink* (2009), a documentary about him during the summer of 2009. He has established an eponymous nonprofit organization "with branches in Toronto, Detroit and Dallas that provides mentoring and education programs for children ages 5 to 18 at schools and community centers," according to Michael Lee, writing for the *Washington Post* (February 5, 2009). Bosh has also donated his time to the Boys and Girls Clubs of Canada and the Toronto Special Olympics. He received his league's Community Assist Award in 2005 and a 2007–08 NBA Sportsmanship Award.

Bosh's personal life received considerable media attention in March 2009, when his former girlfriend Allison Mathis sued him for financial support for their daughter, Trinity, and herself.

—B.M.

Suggested Reading: *Dallas Morning News* C p9 June 25, 2003; *Fort Worth (Texas) Star-Telegram* D p6 Feb. 25, 2006; Raptors.com; *Sports Illustrated* p94+ Jan. 30, 2006, p58 Dec. 22, 2003

Courtesy of Alan Boss

Boss, Alan P.

July 20, 1951– Astrophysicist; writer

Address: Carnegie Institution for Science, Dept. of Terrestrial Magnetism, 5241 Broad Branch Rd., N.W., Washington, DC 20015

Until the mid-1990s astronomers had no evidence for the existence of extrasolar planets—planets that orbit stars other than our sun—and thus could not know whether they are plentiful or scarce or exist at all among the approximately 100 billion stars in our galaxy, the Milky Way. Thus, the only planetary system available to them for study was our own—the solar system, which consists of the sun and the eight planets and other objects and substances that orbit it. Then, in 1995, thanks to advances in technology, two Swiss astronomers, Michel Mayor and Didier Queloz, detected the presence of a planet orbiting the star 51 Pegasi; since then, more than 400 extrasolar planets have been discovered—not directly (except in an extremely few cases), but through measurable effects on their stars. The highly varied characteristics of the extra-solar planets detected to date have greatly surprised astronomers, astrophysicists, and others who study outer space; previously, they would have dismissed some of them as theoretically impossible. Many scientists now think it likely that Earth-like planets with some form of life exist elsewhere in the Milky Way (or in the hundreds of billions of other galaxies in the universe). Among them is the astrophysicist Alan P. Boss, a theoretician who has worked at the Carnegie Institution, in Washington, D.C., since 1982 and has served as an adviser on many National Air and Space Administration (NASA) panels. "From ground-based observations, we know that Earth-like planets are going to be quite common," Boss told Claudia Dreifus for the *New York Times* (July 20, 2009, on-line). "Estimates are that 'earths' probably occur [with] 10 to 20 percent of the stars. My feeling is that if you have that many earths and you have some prebiotic soup, comets that bring in the organic chemicals that you need to have life, something is going to grow. You might not always end up with dinosaurs and cavemen, but there are going to be planets out there that will have primitive life. Life on Earth is so vigorous and so able to thrive and fill every niche, how could it not be elsewhere? Give life a few billion years and, under the right conditions, something is going to happen, at the very least some sort of primitive bacteria like what we find in the geysers at Yellowstone [National Park, in Wyoming]."

Boss's theories about extrasolar planets are inextricably linked to another of his primary research interests: the events, starting some 4.6 billion years ago, that led to the formation of the planets of our solar system. The solar system consists of the sun and its eight major planets—Mercury, Venus, Earth, and Mars, which are nearest to the sun, and the more-distant Jupiter, Saturn, Uranus, and Neptune. (The solar system also contains a total of more than 140 moons, every planet except Mercury and Venus having at least one, and hundreds of thousands of comets, asteroids, and meteoroids. Pluto, discovered in 1930, was thought to be the ninth planet until 2006, when its status was reduced to that of a dwarf planet.) Theories about how the planets came to be must take into account the differences between the four planets nearest to the sun, known as the terrestrial planets, whose surfaces and topmost layers are solid and rocky, and the other four, the gas giants, whose surfaces and topmost layers are gaseous; they must also explain why the compositions of Uranus and Neptune differ significantly from those of Jupiter and Saturn. Boss believes that neither of the two theories of planet formation most commonly held among scientists—the core-accretion theory and the gas-accretion theory—adequately explains the formation of the solar system's gas giants or the extrasolar planets so far discovered, nearly all of which are gas giants. Boss is prominent among the few astrophysicists who have promoted the theory

that the gas giants formed by a third process, dubbed disk instability. "Understanding how our solar system formed—that's my wild dream . . . ," Boss told Corey S. Powell for *Discover* (January 12, 2009, on-line). "It's taken 30 years, but I'm starting to think I understand what happened. I expected at some point I'd get old and not care anymore. But I care more and more. It's just amazing."

The University of Arizona astrophysicist Steven Kortenkamp told Keay Davidson for the *San Francisco Chronicle* (June 17, 2002) that the discoveries of extrasolar planets and the disk-instability theory "are making it very difficult to stick to the party line endorsing the so-called standard model" of planetary formation. "Alan Boss is one of the very few mavericks going out on a limb with a totally new theory . . . ," Kortenkamp declared. "Hopefully, we will know if Alan is right in a matter of a few years, maybe a decade." Harold F. Levison, at the Southwest Research Institute, in Boulder, Colorado, who studies the behavior of planets and other objects in the solar system, told Robert Roy Britt for Space.com (July 9, 2002), "The thing we've learned in the last couple years is that the standard model [for the formation of planets] cannot work. I applaud Alan for trying to think in a new direction. I happen to think it's not right. But it's ideas like this that the science needs to evolve to the right answer." Boss is the author of *Looking for Earths: The Race to Find New Solar Systems* (1998) and *The Crowded Universe: The Search for Living Planets* (2009).

The son of Paul Boss and Marguerite May (Gehringer) Boss, Alan Paul Boss was born on July 20, 1951 in Lakewood, Ohio, and raised in Florida. His sister, Barbara, he told *Current Biography*, "was just as much of a science nerd as I was, and with her being three years older, I followed in her footsteps in high school and college as an overachiever." After Boss completed all the science courses offered at his high school, he volunteered to assist a teacher in the chemistry lab. He was not interested in space then, he told *Current Biography*, because the "the bright lights, clouds, and night fogs" where he lived "mostly limited one's view of objects in the sky to the Sun and the moon." After high school he enrolled at the University of South Florida, with the intention of majoring in oceanography. He abandoned that plan as a freshman, when he decided that the oceanography curriculum was boring. He studied physics instead, earning a B.S. degree in that subject in 1973.

Boss then entered the University of California at Santa Barbara (UCSB), where he received an M.S. degree in 1975 and a Ph.D. degree in 1979, both in physics. He had intended to concentrate on high-energy physics, but during his second year there, he so impressed the astrophysicist Stanton J. Peale that Peale chose him to be his research assistant. Peale, whom Boss has described as a "celestial mechanician," "wanted me to work on the formation of the Solar System, and that sounded like even more of a challenge than deciphering particle physics, so off I dove into the then uncharted waters of star and planet formation," Boss told *Current Biography*. He began by reading a book by the Soviet astronomer Viktor Safronov called *The Evolution of the Protoplanetary Cloud and Formation of the Earth and the Planets*. "Safronov's book simply started off with a young star and a rotating disk and then addressed the problem of planet formation," he told *Current Biography*. "I wanted to know how that star and disk formed in the first place, and that meant studying how rotating clouds collapse to form not only single stars with disks, but also binary and multiple star systems." (By "disk," Safronov and Kirk were referring to the cloud of gas that orbits a developing star and gets flattened into a disk as the cloud rotates.)

From 1973 to 1974 Boss was a teaching assistant, and for the next five years a research assistant, at UCSB; his title was changed to postdoctoral researcher after he earned his Ph.D. That year he left UCSB to join the division of space science at NASA's Ames Research Center, in Moffett Field, California, where he worked as a resident research associate. He told *Current Biography* that his "main accomplishment" at Ames was the creation of a three-dimensional model of radiative transfer, the transport of electromagnetic radiation from one molecule or other object to another. In 1982 he took on the post of staff associate in the Department of Terrestrial Magnetism at the Carnegie Institution. He has worked there as a full-fledged member of the staff since 1983. Grants from NASA, since 1982, and from the National Science Foundation, since 1984, have funded his research, which has focused on the formation of planetary and stellar systems and extrasolar planets.

Astronomers believe that our star, the sun, and its planets started to form around 4.6 billion years ago. The process is believed to have begun when shock waves produced by a supernova—an exploding star—squeezed a nearby nebula, a gigantic cloud of gas (primarily hydrogen and helium) and dust, causing it to start to collapse. As the cloud collapsed, gravity pulled its contents closer together, and it began to spin (just as a spinning ice skater rotates faster as she pulls her arms closer to her body); as it spun, it flattened into a disk. Much of the matter in the disk was pulled into its center, where it became hot and formed the sun. Most of the remaining matter in the disk formed the eight planets of the solar system.

According to the core-accretion theory, the dust particles in the disk collided to form increasingly larger particles, growing to boulder size and then, as more matter stuck to them, to about six miles in diameter, when they became what are known as planetesimals; at that point their gravity had increased to the point that they experienced "runaway" growth. Their final sizes depended on their distance from the sun and their particular compositions and densities. According to the gas-accretion theory, as Boss explained to Corey S. Powell, "If there's gas around and the bodies get large enough, perhaps something on the order of 10 Earth masses or so, then you can start pulling some gas in on top of your rocky core and make something that looks like a gas giant planet, like Jupiter. You just have to build that core fast enough to be able to pull in gas while the gas is still there." Boss believes that in the cases of some gas giants, the core cannot form rapidly enough to retain the surrounding gas. In the late 1980s, after working with computerized three-dimensional models, he offered another theory. The flattened disk, he proposed, had spiral arms, which, he told *Current Biography*, might have formed "self-gravitating clumps that could go on to form gas giant planets, rather than merely move gas and dust around the disk." Since then, he said, "I have been working to see if this serendipitous prediction might actually work in the real world. While disk instability is unlikely to explain the formation of all giant planets, the evidence is gathering that it forms at least a fraction of them."

The disk-instability theory has stirred a mixed response among scientists. Jack Lissauer, an astrophysicist at the Ames Research Center, told Keay Davidson that the "idea is hardly advanced enough to call it a model" and added, "Although Alan may believe that a paradigm shift has occurred, few others in the field agree with him." Steven Kortenkamp, on the other hand, told Davidson that Boss "is on to something interesting that is causing a much-needed shakeup in the field." In defense of his theory, Boss told Corey S. Powell, "Disk instability can form planets that look like Saturn and Jupiter just as well as core accretion can. So from that point of view, we now have two ways of making gas giant planets. And I think we need both of them. One or the other is not going to do it because there's such a wide range of systems." The discovery of the planet orbiting 51 Pegasi led Boss to conclude that yet another mechanism had been at work in its formation, because the planet, which is the size of Jupiter, is "too close to its sun to have formed there," he told Powell; it completely orbits the star in only 4.2 days. "One night I was lying in bed at 2 a.m. staring at the ceiling and it just sort of came to me," Boss recalled to Powell. "The damn thing must have migrated in and gotten left behind. There's just no way to understand its forming there."

In a review of Boss's first book, *Looking for Earths: The Race to Find New Solar Systems* (1998), Mira Dougherty-Johnson wrote for *Astronomy* (April 1999) that the author "possesses a unique insider's perspective that allows him to portray the reality of modern discovery. With the sympathy of a humble narrator, Boss takes readers on a thrilling journey of discovery. He details the actions of scientists who have created a new way of thinking about our solar system. And he shows how these remarkable finds have transformed this scientific field. . . . His book is full of humor, heartbreak, and a deep understanding of the ardor and luck that compose years of research. . . . As

Boss looks upward and outward, he never loses sight of where he stands, grounded in humanity. As a result, the reader becomes not merely a receiver of Boss's vision, but a fellow explorer." David Morrison, who was then the director of astrobiology and space research at the Ames Research Center, was similarly enthusiastic; in his review of *Looking for Earths* for *Natural History* (February 1999), he described Boss as "a gifted writer who gives us a detailed account of nearly a century of effort directed to distinguishing planets from stars, understanding how planetary systems form and evolve, and searching for the elusive evidence of extrasolar planets. . . . You will find no better introduction to one of the truly revolutionary developments in modern astronomy." In an assessment for *Science* (December 4, 1998), Jack J. Lissauer found fault with the book: among other flaws, Lissauer wrote, "Boss has not written a comprehensive review. Some of his terminology is quite unconventional. His presentation of the theory of planet formation is not balanced . . . and his interpretation of some observations differs from that of most observers and theorists in the field." Nevertheless, Lissauer praised the book for providing "a substantial amount of information about the search for extrasolar planets, as well as a good story."

In *The Crowded Universe: The Search for Living Planets* (2009), Boss discussed the probability that astronomers will find planets in the Milky Way hospitable to life. In a review for *Natural History* (May 2009, on-line), Laurence A. Marschall, an astronomer and physicist, wrote, "The tone of Boss's book . . . is excited and hopeful, but there's also a note of wry irony in his descriptions of the political trials astronomers have gone through trying to promote their research. And despite the successes of the past decade, Boss senses that it may be increasingly difficult for astronomers to attract the sums needed to continue the search for habitable planets. Readers of this book, I am certain, will hope his fears are unsubstantiated." The astrobiologist Lewis Dartnell wrote for *New Scientist* (March 14, 2009), "Boss recounts the exhilarating tale of the race to discover the first truly Earth-like exoplanet [extrasolar planet]. As *The Crowded Universe* unfolds, it brings alive the thrills and disappointments of bleeding-edge science, the fierce competition between American and European planet-hunting teams and the politics of billion-dollar research. Along the way we learn the latest theories on how planets form and just how astronomers detect distant worlds too faint to see. Frustratingly, the book is written as a series of chronologically dated sections which often lack cohesion. As a result, it feels as if Boss has simply lent us notes from his diary."

Boss is a member of the Science Working Group of NASA's Kepler Mission (named for the 16th–17th-century German astronomer Johannes Kepler), whose spacecraft, launched in March 2009, is searching for Earth-like exoplanets among approximately 150,000 stars in the constellation Cygnus,

in the Milky Way. In particular, Boss is helping to "interpret [the craft's] discoveries in terms of the theory of planet formation," he told *Current Biography*. "The most certain discovery in the next five years is the determination of the fraction of Earth-like planets in our galaxy," he said.

Boss is a member of the American Academy of Arts and Sciences and a fellow of the American Association for the Advancement of Science, the Meteoritical Society, and the American Geophysical Union. He was the founding chairman of the International Astronomical Union's (IAU) Working Group on Extra-Solar Planets (WGESP) and is currently the president of WGESP's successor, known as IAU Commission 53 on Extrasolar Planets. Boss has been married to the former Catherine Ann Starkie since 1979. His wife is an accountant and has her own practice. The couple have two children, Margaret and Nicholas, and live in a Washington, D.C., suburb. Of the 400,000 known asteroids, one—minor planet number 29137—bears the name Alanboss.

—W.D.

Suggested Reading: ciw.edu/boss; CNN.com Feb. 25, 2009; *Discover* (on-line) Jan. 12, 2009; *New York Times* (on-line) July 20, 2009; *San Francisco Chronicle* A p6 June 17, 2002; Boss, Alan P. *Looking for Earths: The Race to Find New Solar Systems*, 1998, *The Crowded Universe: The Search for Living Planets*, 2009

Selected Books: *Looking for Earths: The Race to Find New Solar Systems*, 1998; *The Crowded Universe: The Search for Living Planets*, 2009

Bradley, Bob

Mar. 3, 1958– Soccer coach

Address: c/o U.S. Soccer Federation, 1801 S. Prairie Ave., Chicago, IL 60616

As a high-school and college soccer player, Robert "Bob" Bradley—the coach who led the U.S. men's national soccer team to the 2010 World Cup—was notable for neither speed nor strength. Instead, what struck observers as unusual was his disciplined, insightful approach and superlative understanding of the game. After he earned his bachelor's degree, Bradley developed his coaching philosophy while working with the undergraduate soccer teams at Ohio University, the University of Virginia, and then Princeton, his alma mater. He later served as the head coach of a series of three Major League Soccer (MLS) teams: the Chicago Fire, the MetroStars, and Chivas USA. The winningest coach during his nine years with the MLS, the first to achieve 100 wins, and the only one to be named MLS Coach of the Year twice,

Kevork Djansezian/Getty Images

Bob Bradley

Bradley is famous for his uncompromising principles. Jeffrey Stout, a professor of religion at Princeton and a longtime friend of his, told Rich Fisher for the New Jersey *Trentonian* (June 9, 2010, on-line) that Bradley "doesn't care a whole lot about what other people think of him. He's intense about the things he cares about, and that has to do with achieving excellence in all the things he does." Perhaps above all else Bradley's success as a player and coach has been shaped by his passion for soccer. Aled Lalas, the general manager of the Metro-Stars during Bradley's tenure as coach, said in an interview with Jeré Longman for the *New York Times* (June 6, 2010), "I have this gut feeling that Bob would be in his utopia if he could coach and his team could play without any fans, no media, no distractions, just the sport in the purest sense." Under Bradley the U.S. Men's National Team (USMNT)—which he has coached and managed since 2006—reached the finals of the Confederations Cup and the Confederation of North, Central American and Caribbean Association Football (CONCACAF) Gold Cup, both in 2009; in recognition of his accomplishments, the U.S. Olympic Committee named Bradley the 2009 National Coach of the Year. The USMNT was eliminated from World Cup competition in June 2010 after a loss to Ghana.

The oldest of three brothers, Robert Bradley (called "Rob" or "Robbie" by family members and close friends) was born on March 3, 1958 to Gerald and Mary Bradley in Montclair, New Jersey. He grew up in Essex Falls, New Jersey. "Our lives revolved around sports," Bradley's brother Scott told Longman. "Our nickname around town was the All-American boys. Goody two-shoes. We came home, did our homework, went to the school field,

and we played." Scott Bradley had a successful career as a Major League Baseball catcher (1984–92), mostly with the Seattle Mariners; he currently coaches Princeton University's men's baseball team. Jeff Bradley, the youngest brother, is a senior sportswriter with *ESPN The Magazine*. Scott, who by all accounts was the most talented athlete of the three, has said that early on, his older brother displayed an unusual understanding of sports strategy. Every time the boys played soccer, "I'd have five or six breakaways and I'd be lucky if I scored once," Scott recalled to Wayne Drehs for *ESPN Soccernet* (June 9, 2010, on-line). "And he would find himself in the right spot four different times and have a hat trick. It drove me crazy. I remember wondering, 'How the hell is he scoring all these goals?' But looking back, that was the beginning of his ability to analyze games and slow things down in his mind. He was very aware that there were things more important than being 100 percent the best athlete. And he wasn't even 10 years old."

Bradley attended West Essex High School, in North Caldwell, New Jersey, where he played on the soccer team. After his graduation, in 1976, he enrolled at Princeton University, in New Jersey, and joined the school's soccer team, the Tigers. During his sophomore year he suffered a compound fracture of his ankle. Mark Mulert, Bradley's college roommate and teammate, told Drehs, "If the doctors told him to rehab for an hour, he'd do an hour and a half. If they told him to walk, he'd run. If they told him it would take six weeks until the cast came off, he would make sure it only took four. He's relentless. Once he decides to do something, it's complete and utter over-the-top dedication. And he won't stop." The next season, when Bradley returned to the field, he scored four goals in the first game. He tied for Tigers top scorer in 1979, the team's most successful year up to that point. (The college soccer season runs from August to late November or early December.) Jack Blair, one of Bradley's teammates, told Rich Fisher that Bradley "always made the correct run, was in the right place. I would have told you then that if Bob committed to the sport of soccer, he would be a natural coach and his attitude and knowledge of the game would take him far. He was supremely confident in his approach and what he wanted from the game." Blair also said, "He had his own moral compass which he followed intensely and without concern of what others thought. He believed that his approach was the best and he followed his own path religiously without regard to what he might be 'missing.' He was never sucked into wanting to please others or do something he felt was not to his benefit." While at Princeton Bradley also played varsity baseball and was a broadcaster for WPRB, the school's radio station. Bradley majored in history; his senior thesis was titled "The History of Intercollegiate Athletics at Princeton." He earned a bachelor's degree in 1980.

At that time there were few opportunities for Americans to become professional soccer players. Shortly after he completed college, Bradley enrolled in a managerial training program at Procter & Gamble. One of his tasks involved "going from store to store, peddling cake mix," according to Longman, who reported that Bradley hated the work, repeatedly telling his brother Scott, "I've got to get back into sports." Before the year was out, the 22-year-old Bradley left Procter & Gamble to take the job of head men's soccer coach at Ohio University, in Athens. In 1983 Bruce Arena, widely considered to be one of the best coaches in U.S. soccer history, recruited him to serve as his assistant coach at the University of Virginia, in Charlottesville. Bradley remained in Virginia until 1984, when he took the position of head men's soccer coach at Princeton.

In his 12 seasons as the Tigers' coach, Bradley led the team to win two Ivy League titles and to compete in the National Collegiate Athletic Association (NCAA) Final Four in 1993; that year he was named the NCAA Division I Men's Coach of the Year. Bradley's successor as the Tigers' coach, Jim Barlow, who was named the 1987 Ivy League Rookie of the Year and the 1990 Ivy League Player of the Year when he played for the team under Bradley, told Longman, "I've never had a coach who could recall in such detail and point out what you were feeling so accurately. Bob cuts through the feel-good stuff to the core of what he's seeing." Barlow told Fisher, "I always felt the things that Bob said really resonated with me as a player. He had a great way of being able to see something, put it into words and you could say 'Yeah, that's exactly what it was.'" During the 1990s, according to Fisher, Bradley studied closely the tactics of the celebrated Italian soccer team A.C. Milan.

In 1995 Bradley left Princeton for Washington, D.C., to serve as assistant coach under Bruce Arena for the D.C. United of the newly established MLS. After two years under Arena, Bradley changed jobs again, becoming the manager of the newly formed Chicago Fire, an MLS expansion team. In their inaugural season the Fire won both the MLS Cup and the U.S. Open Cup, and Bradley was named the 1998 MLS Coach of the Year. In 2000 he again led the Fire to win the Open Cup.

After the close of the 2002 MLS season (late March or early April to November), Bradley resigned as manager of the Fire to take over as coach of the MetroStars (known earlier as the New York/New Jersey MetroStars and currently as the Red Bulls), one of the MLS's original teams. In an indication of the MetroStars' trouble-filled history, he was the seventh person to coach the team since its debut, in 1996. In his first season (2003), the team racked up 11 wins, 10 losses, nine ties, and a total of 42 points and reached the finals of the U.S. Open Cup for the first time. The next year it had 11 wins, 12 losses, seven ties, and a total of 42 points. In October 2005, when a losing streak had brought the MetroStars' win/loss/tie record to 11,

12, and seven with only three games left in the regular season, Bradley was fired. Shortly after the close of that season, Bradley was hired to coach Chivas USA, a Los Angeles, California, club that had fared poorly in its first and second seasons (2004 and 2005). Bradley, the team's third coach, succeeded in leading Chivas USA to a third-place finish at the Western Conference Championships in 2006.

The defeat of the U.S. Men's National Team in the first round of the 2006 World Cup led the U.S. Soccer Federation (USSF) to refuse to renew the contract of Bruce Arena, the team's coach since 1998, despite his record number of wins during his nine seasons in that job. Bradley was one of only a handful of coaches whom the federation considered as Arena's successor. The federation's first choice was Jurgen Klinsmann, the former manager of the German national team, but negotiations with Klinsmann fell through, and Bradley was tapped to fill the vacancy; the federation appointed him interim coach on December 8, 2006. At the time of his appointment, Bradley was the all-time winningest coach in the history of the MLS.

In his new position Bradley immediately began to recruit young talent. He also scheduled a series of friendlies—matches of no competitive value arranged by national-team managers that help to introduce new players to the international stage and test tactics and formations. On May 15, 2007, after a successful friendlies run that included the U.S.'s 2–0 win over Mexico, the USSF officially named Bradley the USMNT manager and coach. The team's success under Bradley continued into the summer, with Bradley leading the players to the 2007 Gold Cup Final, where, on June 24, they beat Mexico, 2–1. The team's Copa America 2007 run ended after losses to Argentina, Paraguay, and Colombia during the group stage. Bradley found himself criticized by some observers for using what they viewed as a second-tier lineup in the Copa America. As the USMNT coach, however, he has made a practice of giving as many members of the team as possible the chance to play, and many fans welcomed the resulting diversity of the player pool. In his first year as manager, Bradley compiled a record of 12 wins, five losses, and one draw.

Bradley's dedication and professionalism quickly earned him respect among the USMNT players. The USMNT forward Landon Donovan said to Drehs, "When we're in camp together this appears like a 24–7 job for Bob. Aside from sleeping, he's working on what he needs to do to make us successful that week, that camp, that trip, that tournament, whatever. He cares a lot about what he does. And he cares about his team being successful." The USMNT midfielder DeMarcus Beasley, who had played for Bradley on the Chicago Fire, told Kelly Whiteside for *USA Today* (June 17, 2010) that Bradley was "very detailed, watches a lot of tape, very organized in the way he goes about everything. Every player knows what they're supposed to do." Donovan told Filip Bondy and Michael Lewis for the New York *Daily News* (June 22, 2010), "A lot of coaches pull players to embarrass them. Bob only does things he thinks will make a difference. Not necessarily that someone isn't playing well or poorly. More what the game needs is very clear to him. Over the course of time I've been here, almost all his decisions have worked out in a way. So we trust that."

Early in 2008, to prepare for the 2010 World Cup qualification matches, Bradley scheduled another series of friendlies. In contests with some of the world's best teams, the U.S. ended with a 2–2 draw against Mexico, a 2–0 loss to England, a 1–0 loss to Spain, and a 0–0 draw with Argentina. During the second round of the CONCACAF qualification matches in July 2008, the U.S. achieved the biggest victory in the history of U.S. national soccer, with an 8–0 blowout against Barbados. As one of the 12 teams to make it to the third round, the U.S. men dominated their group, which included Guatemala, Cuba, and Trinidad and Tobago, advancing along with Trinidad and Tobago to the fourth and final CONCACAF qualification group. The U.S. then secured first place in the fourth round, after a dramatic 2–2 draw against Costa Rica, thus assuring the team's presence at the World Cup. (The U.S. had a total of 20 points to Costa Rica's 16 points.)

In the months leading to the World Cup, American interest in soccer, Bradley, and the USMNT grew considerably, but Bradley avoided interviews with members of the media. Instead, he concentrated on training and instructed his players to do the same. For that reason an image of Bradley as stoic, distant, and cold emerged in printed and broadcast reports. According to Jim Barlow and Charlie Inverso, a New Jersey community-college Hall of Fame soccer coach and longtime friend of Bradley's, that perception is false. Barlow told Fisher that Bradley "doesn't show a lot of his personality to the media and the media gets turned off that he doesn't share as much with them as they'd like. But for Bob, that isn't what's important. The team building is important." Charlie Inverso told Fisher that Bradley is "a very funny guy. He tells great stories and has a great laugh."

The 2010 World Cup began on June 11, 2010 in South Africa. The U.S. tied with England (1–1) and Slovenia (2–2) and then defeated Algeria to win in its group—for the first time since 1930. On June 26 the U.S. lost, 2–1, in overtime, to Ghana in an elimination game, thus ending the American team's chances of winning the cup. The defeat led some observers to cast doubt on Bradley's future as the USMNT coach. In an interview with Michelle Kaufman for the *Miami (Florida) Herald* (June 28, 2010), Sunil Gulati, the president of the U.S Soccer Federation, said, "I think the team is capable of more. I think the players know it. I think Coach Bob Bradley knows it. At that level, we are disappointed we didn't get to play another 90 minutes, at least. . . . It is a missed opportunity to stay in the public eye for another four, five, six days, maybe

10 days, when interest is at an all-time high." For his part, shortly after the USMNT's loss against Ghana, Bradley told Filip Bondy and Michael Lewis for the New York *Daily News* (June 27, 2010), "I don't think it's the time to talk about my situation. We culminated a four-year cycle in Africa and we're disappointed." In late August 2010 Bradley and U.S. Soccer agreed to a four-year contract extension that will secure Bradley's position as coach of the USMNT through August 31, 2014; thus, he will remain with the team through the 2014 FIFA World Cup qualifying cycle and the Cup itself.

Jeffrey Stout told Drehs, "There are other people who care about the truth, who are intense, who understand what it means to be a man and build a team. There are other people who care about their players and their families and the communities in which they live. But I can't think of anybody who cares as relentlessly and passionately as [Bradley] does. There just aren't many people like him." Bradley and his wife, Lindsey, live in Manhattan Beach, California. The couple's two daughters, Kerry and Ryan, are college students; their son, Michael, is a midfielder with the USMNT. Neither father nor son welcome discussions about their professional relationship. When asked about being coached by his father, Michael has dismissed the subject as a nonissue. Pete Grathoff, writing for the *Kansas City Star* (June 19, 2010), quoted Michael as saying, "He's the coach, he's my dad. I'm a player, I'm his son. There's not much else to it." Following the U.S. team's loss to Ghana, in a rare public expression of pride, the elder Bradley told Grathoff that his son "gives everything he has in every game. His commitment to try to do whatever is needed in the game to help his team is pretty clear." Since December 2009, through the organization Oasis for Orphans, the Bradleys have helped to support a child in Kenya. During the 2010 World Cup events, Kerry and Ryan Bradley visited the girl, who is about eight years old.

—H.R.W.

Suggested Reading: *ESPN Soccernet* (on-line) June 9, 2010, June 24, 2010; (Mercer County, New Jersey) *Trentonian* (on-line) June 9, 2010; (New York) *Daily News* (on-line) June 27, 2010; *New York Times* Sports p1+ June 6, 2010; Reuters June 27, 2010; *Sports Illustrated Inside Soccer* (on-line) Sep. 8, 2009; *USA Today* Dec. 18, 2006

Ben Krain, courtesy of Random House

Brockmeier, Kevin

Dec. 6, 1972– Writer

Address: c/o Vintage/Anchor Books Publicity, 1745 Broadway, New York, NY 10019

Pointing to the huge followings of the television series *Lost* and the Harry Potter books and films, whose stories include supernatural elements, Gwenda Bond wrote for *Publishers Weekly* (April 3, 2006), "Fantasy has conquered popular culture, and the successes are continuing to build in the final frontier: literary fiction." Among the "serious" writers whose works deal with the fantastical, Bond singled out Kevin Brockmeier. The 38-year-old Brockmeier has published two acclaimed novels, *The Truth About Celia* (2003) and *The Brief History of the Dead* (2006); two short-story collections, *Things That Fall from the Sky* (2002) and *The View from the Seventh Layer* (2008); and two children's novels, *City of Names* (2002) and *Grooves: A Kind of Mystery* (2006)—all of which stray beyond the bounds of the ordinary to illuminate the universal. The Little Rock, Arkansas–based writer, whose work is known for its lyrical prose as well as its strains of fantasy, told Bond, "I grew up reading mainstream literary fiction, but also fantasy and science fiction. As my own tastes matured, the first literary fiction writers I responded to were people who were playing with the fantastic, like Italo Calvino and Gabriel García Márquez." Brockmeier has had short stories published in such esteemed journals as the *New Yorker*, *McSweeney's*, and the *Georgia Review*, and his work has been selected for the annual collections *O. Henry Prize Stories* and *Best American Short Sto-*

ries. He has received numerous honors, including the *Chicago Tribune*'s Nelson Algren Award, an Italo Calvino Short Fiction Award, and a Guggenheim Fellowship. In 2007 Brockmeier was chosen as one of the British literary magazine *Granta*'s 21 "Best Young American Novelists."

Kevin John Brockmeier was born on December 6, 1972 in Hialeah, Florida, just outside Miami. His father, Jack Brockmeier, worked as an insurance agent, and his mother, Sally Brockmeier, was a legal secretary. His parents later divorced. When Kevin Brockmeier was four years old, his father's employer transferred him to Little Rock, and the family, which includes Kevin's younger brother, Jeff, moved there.

Brockmeier's mother has said that Kevin was an intelligent child who began speaking in full sentences at the age of two and could usually be found with a book. He began crafting stories when he was eight. In elementary school he amused his friends by writing stories about them, "most of them funny ones," as his mother told Ron Wolfe for the Little Rock *Arkansas Democrat-Gazette* (April 4, 2002). Brockmeier told Lynn Carey for the *Contra Costa (California) Times* (March 4, 2007), "I was the smart kid in class, but I was also the sensitive kid in class. If I was reprimanded by the teacher, I just started crying. I couldn't help myself."

Brockmeier attended Little Rock's Parkview Arts and Science Magnet High School (which he described to Carey as "wonderful"), where he participated in speech tournaments, performed in plays, and studied creative writing. Judy Goss, who was a writing teacher at Parkview, told Scott A. Johnson for the *Arkansas Democrat-Gazette* (March 5, 2006) about Brockmeier, "What was clear was his commitment to writing. He loved to write, and he was curious about everything. . . . Kevin, even at that time, was an intriguing combination of confidence and humility."

After graduating with honors from Parkview, in 1991, Brockmeier attended Southwest Missouri State University, in Springfield, on a full scholarship; he studied creative writing, philosophy, and theater, receiving a B.A. degree in 1995. That year he enrolled in the prestigious University of Iowa Writers' Workshop, in Iowa City. One of his professors there was Marilynne Robinson, who later won the Pulitzer Prize for fiction for her novel *Gilead* (2004). She recalled to Johnson, "[Brockmeier has] one of the most original minds I have ever encountered. There is absolutely nothing mannered or superficial about his originality, nothing facile or edgy about it. . . . Kevin can, in fact, re-imagine reality, make it shine and float, and he does it by means of strength of observation, erudition, a rather courtly generosity of spirit and a grave joy in the workings of language."

Brockmeier completed his M.F.A. degree in 1997 and returned to Little Rock. He supported himself by teaching English composition and creative writing at the University of Arkansas and the Pulaski Technical College. He also worked part-time for the property-management company his mother had started. Brockmeier's short story "A Day in the Life of Half of Rumpelstiltskin," his first published work, appeared in *Writing on the Edge* (Spring/Summer 1997). Written while he attended Southwest Missouri State University, the story begins after the end of the classic fairy tale; having torn himself in two after the queen correctly guessed his name, Rumpelstiltskin carries on with his life while wondering what has happened to his other half. Soon after that work appeared, Brockmeier's short story "These Hands," in which a 34-year-old male babysitter describes his love for his two-year-old charge, was accepted by the *Georgia Review*, and his story "Apples"—which recounts a day in the life of a 13-year-old boy, during which he receives his first kiss and his Bible teacher is struck and killed by a falling metal bucket—appeared in the *Chicago Tribune*. The stories garnered several awards, including, for "Half of Rumpelstiltskin," an Italo Calvino Short Fiction Prize, an annual award sponsored by the Creative Writing Program at the University of Louisville, in Kentucky. "These Hands" was also published in *Prize Stories 1997: The O. Henry Awards.*

Brockmeier signed a two-book contract with Random House in 2000, and *Things That Fall from the Sky*, a collection of his short stories, went on sale in March 2002. Discussing the collection, Brockmeier said in an interview with the literary blog *Avery Anthology* (January 25, 2009), "I finished the earliest story in the book, 'A Day in the Life of Half of Rumpelstiltskin,' when I was 22 and a senior in college, and the last, 'The Jesus Stories,' when I was 28. That's six years. . . . By the time the book saw print, it had been so long since I had written some of the stories in the collection that I felt slightly estranged from them." Still, his stories were well-received, and one, "The Ceiling," in which a marriage falls apart as a dark spot in the sky grows and descends upon a small town, won an O. Henry Award.

In 2002 Brockmeier received a $20,000 grant from National Endowment for the Arts. That May, Viking Children's Books, an imprint of Penguin, published his first children's book, *City of Names*. While a student at Southwest Missouri State University, Brockmeier had returned to Little Rock every summer to work at a day-care center; there, he entertained the children by making up fantastical stories. "You never knew exactly what direction the stories were going to take, but [the children] loved it and I loved doing it," Brockmeier recalled to Scott A. Johnson. "[After college] I just missed it and that's how I ended up writing the first children's book. Some years had passed, and all of these kids were 10, 11, 12 years old, and I felt like I wanted to be able to continue speaking in some way to those particular children. So I sat down to write *City of Names* as a gift to them."

City of Names tells the story of Howie, a fifth-grader who receives a mysterious book that contains a map of his hometown, in which the buildings are labeled with their "true names"; by reciting the names Howie is able to travel through portals to other locations in his hometown. Eventually, he goes to the underground Hall of Babies, where he meets his unborn sister and learns her true name. A writer for *Publishers Weekly* (2002) wrote of *City of Names*, as quoted on amazon.com, "Unfortunately, digressions and dull dialogue may discourage readers, and while the contrivances are clever, the author fails to use them to exciting or meaningful effect." Echoing that sentiment, Elaine E. Knight wrote in her review for the *School Library Journal* (2002), "While the premise has potential, the author doesn't carry it off successfully. Story elements are introduced but not resolved and plot threads are left dangling everywhere."

Brockmeier's first adult novel, *The Truth About Celia* (2003), examines the life of Christopher Brooks, a science-fiction and fantasy writer who lives in a small, sleepy town with his wife, Janet, and their seven-year-old daughter, Celia. One day Celia vanishes from their backyard without a trace. Unable to explain her disappearance, Christopher tries to cope with the tragedy by writing a series of stories that reimagine her disappearance and place her in a parallel dimension, where she lives on. Meanwhile, Christopher's marriage crumbles, and the residents of the town try to make sense of Celia's disappearance.

The novel received widespread praise. Describing Brockmeier's writing as "lyrical and near hypnotic," David Wiegand wrote in his review of the book for the *San Francisco Chronicle* (July 12, 2003), "Lest anyone think Brockmeier is merely parading a clever conceit here, *The Truth About Celia* is emotional, heartbreaking and beautifully styled. It's by turning the cliché of the missing child into a provocative meditation on the perception of reality as affected by time that Brockmeier pulls us into the quiet tragedy of this story."

Many critics found *The Truth About Celia* to be reminiscent of the 2002 best-selling novel *The Lovely Bones*, written by Alice Sebold, which tells the story of a murdered teenage girl who watches over her family as they try to cope with her death. Gregory Kirschling wrote for *Entertainment Weekly* (July 25, 2003, on-line), "Shake the story line of *The Lovely Bones* like a snow globe and you might get Kevin Brockmeier's equally affecting miniaturist's take on a little girl's vanishing, *The Truth About Celia*. . . . Told in short, fine-tuned chapters, Brockmeier's [novel] is a dazzling fantasia on grief and time." Many critics felt that Brockmeier's novel, when compared with the many others that examine the lives of families in which a child goes missing, proved to be—as Gail Caldwell wrote for the *Boston Globe* (August 10, 2003)—"the finest of the form."

Two Brockmeier novels were published in February 2006: *Grooves: A Kind of Mystery* and *The Brief History of the Dead*. *Grooves*, the writer's second children's book, follows a seventh-grader, Dwayne Ruggles, who after running a phonograph needle across his jeans discovers that the grooves of his pants contain a hidden call for help. When Ruggles and his friends learn that the jeans were produced at a factory owned by a wealthy entrepreneur, Howard Thigpen, they set out to find the source of the message. *The Brief History of the Dead* evolved from a short story of the same name published in the September 8, 2003 issue of the *New Yorker*. The story, which became the novel's first chapter, received an O. Henry Award in 2005.

The Brief History of the Dead begins in "the city," a place where the recently deceased reside until every person on Earth who remembers them has died. (Brockmeier was inspired by a passage in James W. Loewen's book *Lies My Teacher Told Me: Everything Your American History Textbook Got Wrong*, which explains that many African cultures believe there are three categories of people: those who are still living on Earth; the *sasha*, who remain in the memories of the living; and the *zamani*, whose last human links to the living world have died.) Brockmeier's novel alternates between the city—in which people continue to work and live as they did on Earth—and the world of the living, where Laura Byrd, a wildlife specialist, is stranded in a research station at the South Pole, unable to communicate with the outside world. When the population of the city expands and then rapidly depletes, those left discover that a plague has killed off most of the world's population. Byrd, isolated from the rest of the world, is soon the last surviving human. When the city dwindles to a small number of inhabitants, the only ones who remain realize that they exist only by way of Byrd's memories. "I wanted [*The Brief History of the Dead*] to be about human connection and the way we carry around the people we remember," Brockmeier told Lynn Carey for the *Contra Costa Times* (March 4, 2007).

Most critics praised *The Brief History of the Dead* for its complexity and vividly imagined story. *The Brief History of the Dead* "ingeniously investigates how mythology or fantasy can reshape the way we think about memory . . . ," Meghan O'Rourke wrote for *Slate* (February 22, 2006, on-line). "Brockmeier's obsession with metaphors means that his writing can seem airless at times, as if we've been taken inside a glass-blown object, where everything is finely wrought but nothing can breathe or move. *The Brief History of the Dead* certainly suffers from this a bit. . . . But maybe the lack of plot pyrotechnics is precisely the point. This is a story, after all, about the stories that will no longer be told; a story about the end of a world, which necessarily leaves one feeling disappointed. Even so, Brockmeier's vision is essentially compassionate and humanistic." Laurel Maury, in her review for the *Los Angeles Times* (March 11, 2006), proclaimed, "*The Brief History of the Dead* strips the thriller to its bones, presenting the end of humanity undiluted, without any comforting distractions." She added, "Although Brockmeier's writing is clunky in places, he creates an enduring

sense of dread. I had nightmares after reading *Brief History*. . . . [His] book is the only modern thriller I've read that's literary and scary too." The novel won the 2007 PEN USA award for fiction.

Brockmeier's short-story collection *The View from the Seventh Layer* was published in March 2008. Its 13 stories include the title piece, about a lonely woman who lives on a tropical island and believes she has been visited by an unknown figure she refers to as "The Entity." Among the other stories are "The Lady with Pet Tribble," which reimagines Anton Chekhov's story "The Lady with the Little Dog" as set in the futuristic world of the *Star Trek* television series, and "The Human Soul as a Rube Goldberg Device," an homage to the once-popular children's books that allowed readers to choose the actions of the characters. In "The Human Soul," the reader is the main character and can construct a day in his or her life, choosing among more than 60 pages' worth of mundane activities (going to McDonald's, for example, or calling a friend on the telephone). Any choice ends with the reader dying of a heart attack.

Most recently Brockmeier served as the editor of the book *Real Unreal: Best American Fantasy 3* (2010), which brings together 20 stories by writers including Stephen King, Jeffrey Ford, and Lisa Goldstein.

Brockmeier has said that on a productive day he completes a single page of writing. "I can't remember who said that writing a story is like cleaning a kitchen floor . . . [but] I really do treat a story square by square, sentence by sentence, attempting to remove each minute speck of dirt, so that when I finally reach the end I can look back and see a shining white floor behind me," he said to Gregory Cowles for the *New York Times*' blog Paper Cuts (November 13, 2009, on-line). A bibliophile, he has been known to read up to 170 books a year. He does not, however, reread his own work. He told *Avery Anthology,* "Whenever I try, I feel a discomfiting blend of intimacy and alienation; I still recognize what I'm reading as a product of my own imagination, and I remember the labor that went into it, but I've become divorced enough from it that I can only see the flaws."

Brockmeier keeps, and constantly updates, lists of his 50 favorite books, movies, and albums. His list's top 10 novels, as reported in 2006, included Gabriel García Márquez's *One Hundred Years of Solitude*, Italo Calvino's *The Baron in the Trees*, Mikhail Bulgakov's *The Master and Margarita*, and Philip Pullman's *His Dark Materials* trilogy. His favorite books of 2009 included Victor LaValle's novel *Big Machine* and Dino Buzzati's graphic novel *Poem Strip*. His favorite body of work is that of the Arkansas novelist Donald Harington, who completed 15 books before his death, in November 2009.

Brockmeier lives in Little Rock. "One of the advantages of working as a writer . . .," he said, as quoted by the *Encyclopedia of Arkansas History & Culture* (on-line), "is that you don't have to live anywhere in particular to participate in the strongest currents of your art form . . . When it comes to literature, there's no such thing as the provinces."

—M.A.S.

Suggested Reading: *Arkansas Democrat-Gazette* E p1 Apr. 4, 2002, High Profile Mar. 5, 2006; (California) *Contra Costa Times* F p4 Mar. 4, 2007; *Publishers Weekly* p29 Apr. 3, 2006; randomhouse.com

Selected Books: *Things That Fall from the Sky*, 2002; *City of Names*, 2002; *The Truth About Celia*, 2003; *Grooves: A Kind of Mystery*, 2006; *The Brief History of the Dead*, 2006; *The View from the Seventh Layer*, 2008; as editor—*Real Unreal: Best American Fantasy 3*, 2010

Alex Wong/Getty Images for *Meet the Press*

Broder, David

Sep. 11, 1929– Political columnist; reporter

Address: Washington Post Writers Group, 1150 15th St., N.W., Washington, DC 20071

In a career that has spanned the years from the John F. Kennedy era to the presidency of Barack Obama, the *Washington Post* political columnist and reporter David S. Broder has often been singled out for his fairness and integrity. Kim Isaac Eisler, compiling a list for the *Washingtonian* magazine (March 2001) of "Washington's 50 best and most influential journalists," ranked Broder fourth, calling him "the most unpredictable, reliable, and intellectually honest columnist working today." Eis-

ler added, "While the journalistic pack is pestering a flack, Broder is out with the people; no one gets a better sense of the pulse of American opinion. In a profound sense, Broder is the moral compass of the press." Broder, who won a Pulitzer Prize in 1973, has been labeled alternately as liberal and conservative, and in his columns—published twice weekly in more than 300 newspapers around the world—he has been known to criticize Democrats and Republicans alike. Writing for the *New Yorker* (August 21, 2006, on-line), Hendrik Hertzberg called Broder "relentlessly centrist." "He is the absolute antithesis of the hey-lookit-me ethos that—sadly—permeates our popular culture, and has crept into the effusions of some hot, hip, happening newsies," Brooks Peterson wrote for the *Corpus Christi (Texas) Caller-Times* (September 11, 2006). "Broder's copy doesn't sizzle; neither does it pulsate with pizzazz. Where others foam and froth, Broder just gives us the goods—straight, no seltzer, no tiny paper umbrellas. What it all boils down to is: If Broder writes it, you can take it to the bank. Solid, solid, solid."

David Salzer Broder was born to Albert and Nina (Salzer) Broder on September 11, 1929 in Chicago Heights, Illinois. His father was a dentist, and during Broder's childhood, which coincided with the Great Depression, his father would often barter services with patients who did not have enough money to pay for dental care. "I remember that we got fresh milk right from the cooling shed at the Niedtfeldt family farm," Broder wrote for the *Chicago Tribune* (March 6, 1994). "In return, my father took care of their dental needs." Broder attended Roosevelt Elementary School before moving on to Washington Junior High School and Bloom Township High School. As a boy he loved athletics, but due to his thinness, poor eyesight, and lack of coordination, he was better at writing about sports than playing them. "The only area where I wasn't at risk to myself and a total embarrassment was track," he wrote. "I was a slow low-hurdler and a low high-jumper." Broder was a fan of the Chicago Cubs baseball team and also enjoyed the Chicago Symphony; his mother frequently took him to concerts.

Broder attended the University of Chicago, where he earned both a B.A. degree (1947) and an M.A. degree (1951) in political science. As an undergraduate he wrote for the *Maroon*, the campus newspaper, and before long he worked his way up to editor. While on the newspaper staff he met Ann Creighton Collar, whom he married in 1951. Broder has described his years at the University of Chicago as exciting, since servicemen returning from World War II were becoming activists and raising awareness of important political issues. When the university's Billings Hospital was accused of discriminating against African-American patients, Broder was among those who joined the picket lines. He took his first journalism job, an editing position at the *Hyde Park Herald*, in Chicago, while he was studying for his master's degree.

From 1951 to 1953 Broder served in the U.S. Army. After his discharge he moved to Bloomington, Illinois, where both he and his wife had been hired to work for the *Bloomington Pantagraph*. Ann gave birth to the couple's first child in 1955. Broder spent two years reporting for the newspaper, during which he developed his interest in covering politics. In 1955 he moved to Washington, D.C., to begin writing for *Congressional Quarterly*. That publication had not been his first choice; according to Joe Strupp, writing for *Editor & Publisher Magazine* (November 1, 2005), Broder took the job after the *Washington Post*'s associate editor, Ben Gilbert, told him, "We don't hire people like you"—referring to Broder's lack of experience. After five years with *Congressional Quarterly*, Broder became a political reporter for the *Washington Star*, where he remained until 1965. In 1960 he covered his first presidential election, the contest between the Republican nominee, then–Vice President Richard Nixon, and U.S. senator John F. Kennedy, a Massachusetts Democrat. As he traveled with Kennedy, Broder learned that members of the press sometimes become biased toward the candidates they are following. "As a young reporter, the Kennedy campaign shocked me," Broder told Ken Adelman for the *Washingtonian* (August 1996). "I watched the reporters I most admired act almost as deputy campaign managers for Kennedy. They identified totally with him and his politics." Alan Otten, a reporter for the *Wall Street Journal*, acted as Broder's mentor, giving him tips on how to remain impartial. "Deliberately lean a bit against the candidate you're traveling with," Broder told Adelman, recalling what Otten told him. "Hope that your counterpart traveling with the other candidate does likewise. That way the coverage stays balanced." In November 1963 Broder was sent to cover President Kennedy's trip to Dallas, Texas, and he was a block away when Kennedy was assassinated. "I can tell how shook up I was because I can barely read my notes from that day," he told Strupp.

In 1965 Broder became a reporter for the *New York Times*. He worked in the newspaper's Washington, D.C., bureau, covering national politics, for 15 months. He left "5 minutes before I would have been fired as a small pawn in a large power struggle between the paper's New York and Washington bureaus," he wrote for the *Chicago Tribune*. In 1967 Broder co-wrote (with Stephen Hess) his first book, *The Republican Establishment: The Present and Future of the GOP*. In the meantime he had taken a job with the *Washington Post*, where he reported on politics before being offered his own column. "It was probably in lieu of money that I made him a columnist," the paper's then–executive ditor, Ben Bradlee, jokingly told Strupp. "He was the best young political reporter at the time."

Broder wrote in the *Chicago Tribune* piece that his column is "really just the tail of the dog," adding that he devotes 90 percent of his time to reporting. Even his column tends to be based on re-porting, and he has said that he refrains from spouting raw opinion. "It is what I've practiced and what I enjoy," he told Strupp. "It is a reporting-based column because that is all I can do." Discussing influences on his work, Broder said to Adelman, referring to Theodore H. White, "My generation of reporters was deeply influenced by Teddy White, the greatest political journalist of our time. He showed us how far inside a campaign you could go. We naturally emulated him, at least as far as our skills would take us." As the oldest of his four sons prepared for college, Broder asked Bradlee if his column might become syndicated. Bradlee, hoping he could avoid raising Broder's pay by selling his column to other newspapers, established an in-house syndication company, the Washington Post Writers Group. Broder's column went national in 1970. Two years later he published his second book, *The Party's Over: The Failure of Politics in America*. The book "lamented the decline of political parties as forces in disciplining legislators," according to Martin Gottlieb, writing for the *Dayton (Ohio) Daily News* (June 5, 2005). Writing for *Roll Call* (April 2, 1990), Glenn R. Simpson called the work "influential."

In 1973 Broder won the Pulitzer Prize for Distinguished Commentary. Around that time President Nixon was being investigated for his role in the Watergate scandal—named for a Washington, D.C., hotel, office, and apartment complex and home to the Democratic National Headquarters, which Republican operatives burglarized in 1972. "As a reporter in the newsroom of the *Washington Post*, when Nixon and his agents were doing their damndest to discredit the paper and cover up the crime, I found his actions unforgivable," Broder wrote in his column (April 26, 1994). "For no reason except his inability to own up to what had happened, he subjected the American people to almost two years of unnecessary turmoil and division. He caused long-term damage to the bond of trust between the government and the citizenry without which democracy cannot survive." In 1975 Broder became an associate editor at the *Washington Post*.

In 1980 Broder published his third book, *Changing of the Guard: Power and Leadership in America*. For that volume he asked hundreds of people involved in American politics, including members of Congress and of the White House staff, to share their experiences and opinions. "Reading *Changing of the Guard* by David Broder is like eavesdropping on the conversations of people who wonder why they are so successful when the system still doesn't seem to be working," Aaron Wildavsky wrote in an assessment for the *New York Times* (August 31, 1980). "Always the last to know, they barely suspect that they may be the problem to which they seek a solution." Wildavsky went on to call the book "fascinating."

In 1980 Broder covered what he has since called one of the most interesting presidential elections of his career. In particular, he has said that he was impressed with the Republican Ronald Reagan's ability to communicate with voters on the campaign trail. Referring to Reagan's defeat in the Iowa caucuses, Broder told Adelman, "After he was sandbagged in Iowa by George [H. W.] Bush, his crew put him on the bus, and Reagan worked every day from sunup 'til well into the night. He never cheated on a speech. No matter how few people were there, he'd give the full dose." Broder added, "Reagan was a terrific campaigner. He was the best I've ever seen giving a speech on television." Broder has also said that the best convention he has covered was the 1980 Republican National Convention, which was made interesting by rumors that Reagan, having won the party's nomination, would select former president Gerald Ford as his running mate. (In the end he chose Bush.) "It was wild," Broder told Strupp. "Television went crazy with it, but we were working our sources and being cautious because it was not a done deal, and it ended up not happening." In 1981 Broder was named "Washington's most highly regarded columnist" in a survey of newspaper editors conducted by the *Washingtonian*.

Broder had the idea for his fourth book, *Behind the Front Page: A Candid Look at How the News Is Made* (1987), while giving a speech in 1979 that criticized the way newspapers operated. "Not only has [Broder] read virtually every bit of important political reporting over the last 20 years, but he has also listened to both the champions and the critics of that reporting; and he proves himself as tireless and as well-sourced when it comes to analyzing the coverage as he is in sizing up the politicians and campaigns themselves," Charles Fountain wrote for the *Christian Science Monitor* (June 9, 1987). "Like his newspaper work, his book is a combination of peerless reporting and keen commentary."

In 1988 Broder covered what he later dubbed the worst campaign he has ever witnessed—Democratic Massachusetts governor Michael Dukakis's presidential run. "Churchill once said, 'This pudding lacks a theme,'" Broder told Adelman. "Well, that campaign lacked a theme." He added, "Dukakis could never say what his campaign was about. I'd thought he'd do better than he did." In 1990 the *Washingtonian* conducted a survey of newspaper editorial-page editors, and Broder was named "best reporter," "least ideological," and "hardest working." In 1991 the cable-news network CNN announced that Broder would join the political analyst Jack Germond in covering the following year's presidential election.

In 1992 Broder collaborated with his famed *Washington Post* colleague Bob Woodward on *The Man Who Would Be President: Dan Quayle*, a biography of the vice president under George H. W. Bush. In a review for the *Los Angeles Times* (June 14, 1992), Jefferson Morley blasted the book, writing, "When two good journalists can produce a book this bad, all students of journalism should pay attention." In particular, Morley accused Woodward and Broder of practicing "access jour-

nalism"—a trend whereby reporters, in exchange for being granted access to high-level politicians, write simplistic, flattering stories that will not offend their subjects. In a piece for the *Chicago Sun-Times* (May 25, 1994), Steve Neal took a more favorable view of the book, writing of Broder and Woodward, "Their book was perhaps the most insightful portrait of a sitting vice president since Earl Mazo's 1960 biography of Richard M. Nixon."

While covering the 1996 presidential election, Broder told Bob Greene for the *Chicago Tribune* (November 13, 1996), he engaged in what had long been a favorite journalistic practice: "door-knocking," or going from house to house and canvassing opinions from ordinary citizens. Broder told Greene that that talking to voters gives him ideas for his columns. "I don't have the skill to sit in the study and think great thoughts," he said. "And besides, you get a lot out of this. You get to meet some people who are enjoyable to talk to and unpredictable in their opinions. Once they begin to have a conversation with you, it's often wonderful.What gets reaffirmed for me every time is the realization that the American people don't always have all the information in their hands—but their judgment is just about always sharp. You'll find that they don't make a hell of a lot of mistakes."

Also in 1996 Broder and his fellow *Washington Post* reporter Haynes Johnson published *The System: The American Way of Politics at the Breaking Point*, a book detailing the government's failure to pass a health-care reform bill. In the book Broder and Johnson cite President Bill Clinton; First Lady Hillary Clinton; special-interest groups; former Republican Speaker of the House Newt Gingrich; and the press as being partially responsible for derailing efforts to revamp the health-care system. (Such a bill was passed in 2010.) In a review for the *Los Angeles Times* (July 21, 1996), Larry Bensky called the book "one of the most thoroughly detailed studies of a single legislative issue ever written."

In 1999, after President Bill Clinton was impeached by the U.S. House of Representatives for lying under oath about having an affair with Monica Lewinsky, a White House intern, Broder implied in his February 10, 1999 column that the president should resign, calling it an "honorable course of action." (Clinton refused to step down and was later acquitted by the U.S. Senate.) Broder said in a widely quoted interview that Clinton had "trashed" Washington, and in his column of January 1, 1999, he wrote that he was "appalled" by the president's refusal to answer the question, "Does it matter if you have committed perjury or . . . broken the law?"

Broder published his seventh book, *Democracy Derailed: Initiative Campaigns and the Power of Money*, in 2000. The book deals with ballot initiatives—issues that are put before voters rather than decided by elected officials—and criticizes the role that special-interest groups and, especially, money play in influencing their outcomes. "What makes the book important is not merely the story Broder tells, but the very fact that Broder, *The Washington Post*'s widely respected national political correspondent and columnist, is telling it with so much passion—for Broder is nothing if not thorough and scrupulously evenhanded," Peter Schrag wrote for the *American Prospect* (July 17, 2000). In a review for the *New York Times* (April 16, 2000), David Brooks took issue with Broder's central argument—that ballot initiatives are corrupted by money—writing, "The essential problem with *Democracy Derailed* is that the system Broder uncovers is not that appalling. Sure, money shapes referendum campaigns, but not less so than it does Congressional races or legislative lobbying." Brooks called Broder "utterly convincing" with regard to his predictions, however, and he praised the author for warning that so-called "direct democracy" could eventually supercede representative government.

In the immediate aftermath of the 2000 presidential election, when contested results in Florida meant that no winner had been declared in the race between Vice President Al Gore, the Democratic candidate, and George W. Bush, the Republican, Broder said that the large divide between Democrats and Republicans was the result of issues the baby-boom generation had not resolved. "It's almost like there are two different nations," Broder told Duane Schuman for the *Fort Wayne (Indiana) News Sentinel* (November 13, 2000). "We're going through a generational change. The formative experiences for older Americans—the Great Depression and World War II—were unifying experiences. For the Boomers, the 1960s divided them with the racial revolution, the feminist revolution and the Vietnam War. They never really settled those quarrels, so it's not surprising there are really strong differences." Broder has expounded on those ideas in recent years, telling Bernard Schoenburg for the *State-Journal Register* (October 19, 2007) that Barack Obama, then a Democratic U.S. senator from Illinois and declared presidential candidate, was "probably one of the advance guard" of politicians young enough to be unaffected by the tumultuous 1960s. Broder called the new breed of politicians "much more inclusive and less doctrinaire."

Throughout President George W. Bush's two terms in office (2001–09), Broder drew criticism for being too conservative, particularly when he defended Karl Rove, the polarizing figure who served as the president's deputy chief of staff before resigning in 2007. (In particular Broder chastised the media for attempting to implicate Rove in the scandal surrounding Valerie Plame, a CIA agent whose identity was revealed to the public in an effort to punish her husband, Joseph Wilson; Wilson had criticized as faulty the intelligence that the Bush administration used to justify the war in Iraq.) In April 2007 Broder drew flak for a column he wrote about Senate majority leader Harry Reid, a Democrat, who had declared the war in Iraq to be "lost." "The Democrats deserve better, and the country needs more, than Harry Reid has offered as

Senate majority leader," Broder wrote for the *Washington Post* (April 26, 2007). In response to that column, the 50-member Senate Democratic Caucus sent a letter to the *Washington Post* in defense of Reid, calling him "an extraordinary leader who has effectively guided the new Democratic majority through these first few months with skill and aplomb," according to Ken Silverstein, writing for *Harper's* magazine (April 30, 2007, on-line). Silverstein lambasted Broder for questioning Reid's assertion that the war was lost, calling that particular view "mainstream opinion." He also called Broder "hilariously ill-informed." Some pundits came to Broder's defense; in a column for the *Salt Lake Tribune* (May 4, 2007), Kathleen Parker wrote, "In fact, what Broder said was not remotely outrageous. It's hardly crazy to think it inappropriate when the leader of the most powerful governing body in the world declares in the midst of a war that the war is lost."

Broder ends each year by writing a column admitting to what he considers his mistakes during the previous 12 months. He has said that he rarely rereads his columns, telling Dennis Lythgoe for the *Deseret News* (July 17, 1997), "I'd much rather contradict myself, which I do all the time, than to try to square today's opinion with yesterday's." Broder also said, "I still have absolutely no idea what . . . a newspaper column is supposed to be. I've never known why a particular editor buys the column or drops the column. I've never been able to figure out why they run some and don't run others. I figured out a long time ago that if you really tried to figure out how to write a column that would satisfy the tastes and biases of 300 or more separate editors, you would go bonkers."

In his recent columns Broder has continued to criticize politicians on both the left and the right. In the wake of President Obama's appearance on national television to address the British Petroleum (BP) oil spill in the Gulf of Mexico the previous April, Broder wrote for the *Washington Post* (June 17, 2010), "If there is any value in President Obama's knocking himself out to dramatize on prime-time television his impotence in the face of the Gulf of Mexico oil leak calamity, I wish someone would explain it. His multiple inspection trips to the afflicted and threatened states, his Oval Office TV address to the nation, and now his sit-down with the executives of BP have certainly established his personal connection with one of the worst environmental disasters in history. But the only thing people want to hear from him is word that the problem is on its way to being solved—and this message he cannot deliver." Broder urged the president to focus on other matters: "Obama may be excused for impotence in the gulf," he wrote. "But no president can escape responsibility for the budget and the economy." Writing in his column of July 11, 2010 about the Tea Party movement, some of whose followers have expressed extreme right-wing views, Broder pointed to the presidential campaigns of the conservative Barry Goldwater, the Republican standard bearer in 1964, and the Democrat William Jennings Bryan, who campaigned in the late 19th/early 20th century. Both men failed, Broder wrote, by allowing extremists to define their agendas. "Building a majority coalition will require a strong, sensible platform," Broder wrote. "And a clear separation from the [sorts of] kooks and cranks who sank both Bryan and Goldwater." On the subject of the Internet, which has replaced print journalism as a source of news for many people, Broder said in a speech at Samford University, in Alabama, in 2006 that while many seek news on the Web because of its quick availability, "speed is the opposite of care. The editing responsibility [in journalism] is critical."

In addition to writing columns, news stories, and books, Broder has been a regular guest on PBS's *Washington Week in Review* and CNN's *Inside Politics*. He has made more than 400 appearances—more than any other political pundit—on NBC's *Meet the Press*, and Tim Russert, the show's host for nearly two decades, called him "a superb analyst," according to Strupp. In February 2001 Broder joined the journalism faculty at the University of Maryland, signing on to teach a weekly seminar on political reporting. In May 2005 he won the University of Chicago Alumni Association's Alumni Medal, the organization's highest honor. In 1997 the National Society of Newspaper Columnists

honored Broder with its Lifetime Achievement Award. He has earned nearly two dozen honorary doctoral degrees. Broder lives with his wife in Arlington, Virginia. After decades of reporting he told Carly Hemphill for *University Wire* (March 29, 2001) that he still enjoys covering the political process: "It gives you an opportunity to watch what I still think is the most exciting part of our country, the chance to govern ourselves," he said. "The chance to watch it close up is a great pleasure."

—K.J.P.

Suggested Reading: *Chicago Tribune* C p6 Mar. 6, 1994, p1 Nov. 13, 1996; *Editor & Publisher News* Nov. 2005; (Salt Lake City) *Deseret News* C p1 July 17, 1997; *Washingtonian* p23 Aug. 1996

Selected Books: *The Republican Establishment: The Present and Future of the GOP* (with Stephen Hess), 1967; *The Party's Over: The Failure of Politics in America*, 1972; *Changing of the Guard: Power and Leadership in America*, 1980; *Behind the Front Page: A Candid Look at How the News is Made*, 1987; *The Man Who Would Be President: Dan Quayle* (with Bob Woodward), 1992; *The System: The American Way of Politics at the Breaking Point* (with Haynes Johnson), 1996; *Democracy Derailed: Initiative Campaigns and the Power of Money*, 2000

Brown, Dustin

Dec. 8, 1984– Tennis player

Address: c/o ATP Tour, 201 ATP Tour Blvd., Ponte Vedra, FL 32082-3211

Dustin Brown is "the most exciting and controversial tennis player to emerge from the Caribbean in a long time," Kevin Mitchell wrote for the London *Observer* (June 20, 2010). Mitchell expressed that view the day before Brown made his Grand Slam singles debut at the Wimbledon Championships, in England. Brown thus became the first person since Richard Russell, in 1970, to play for Jamaica in that tournament, the world's oldest, most prestigious professional tennis competition. Brown's ancestry is British and German as well as Jamaican. He spent his first dozen years in Germany and competed there in junior tennis competitions. During the next eight years or so, he lived in Jamaica, where tennis generates much less interest—and receives far less financial and other support—than the sports most popular among Jamaicans: track, soccer, and cricket. Frustrated by the cold shoulder he felt he was getting from the Jamaican Tennis Federation, he left Jamaica for Europe in 2004, two years after he turned professional. There, while traveling—and living—in a camper van, he com-

peted on the International Tennis Federation (ITF) futures circuit and then on Association of Tennis Professionals (ATP) circuits, mainly the ATP Challenger Tour. In the past two years, he has risen nearly 400 places in both the ATP singles and the ATP doubles rankings. On May 17, 2010, at age 25, Brown reached a singles ranking of 99—his first appearance in the top 100. At Wimbledon he lost in the first round to Jürgen Melzer of Austria (a semifinalist in the 2010 French Open).

In the world of tennis, the six-foot five-inch Brown is distinguished by his dreadlocks, which reach his lower back; his style of play, in which, Kevin Mitchell wrote, "a booming serve" and "a curious slice on a viciously whipped forehand" are prominent; and shoelaces of different colors—a fluorescent orange lace for his left sneaker and a fluorescent apple-green lace for the right. Due to a continuing conflict with Jamaican tennis officials, Brown has considered playing for Great Britain rather than Jamaica. Nevertheless, he told Christopher Torchia for the Associated Press (June 21, 2010), referring to the rarity of high-ranking Jamaican tennis players, "Going to a tournament and you see the Jamaican flag, OK, it's there for me and not for another 20 guys. So that's definitely a nice thing." On July 26, 2010 Brown reached a career-high singles ranking of 98. As of October 2010 he placed 109th and 69th (a career high) on the ATP

Matthew Stockman/Getty Images

Dustin Brown

singles and doubles rankings, respectively, and his total career earnings had reached $298,377.

Dustin Brown was born on December 8, 1984 in Celle (pronounced "TSEH-lee"), a town in north-central Germany, to a Jamaican father, Leroy Brown, and a German mother, Inge. His paternal grandmother is British. According to the ATP World Tour Web site, he has two half-brothers. Brown began playing tennis at age five with a Jamaican friend of his parents who coached at a tennis club near their home. He recalled to a writer for menstennisblog.com (June 21, 2010), "I did football, soccer, judo, swimming, tennis, and actually sometimes even more than one thing in a day. I'd go from judo to swimming and then from swimming to tennis practice." Brown excelled in soccer and tennis, the latter of which appealed to him more because it is an individual, not a team, sport. He trained with Kim Michael Wittenberg, a prominent American juniors coach who worked in Germany for many years. He told Greg Bishop, writing for the *New York Times* (June 20, 2010), that Wittenberg taught him everything he knows about tennis. Brown played in junior tournaments throughout Germany. At that time, as he told the menstennisblog interviewer, "I would have days when I would, for example, play against a top junior in my age group where I would do really well or beat them or almost beat them, and then the next day I would play against a kid who basically couldn't hold a racquet and I would lose."

In 1996 the Brown family moved to Jamaica, where his mother and father found work in that island nation's tourism industry. While living with his parents in Montego Bay, Brown continued to hone his tennis skills, usually on dilapidated pub-

lic courts; he told Bishop that he would play against any willing partners and use any ball "that was yellow and would bounce." "It was good to see a harder side of life," he told a writer for ATPworldtour.com (March 2, 2010). "In Germany as a 10 or 11 year old you have a computer, a Gameboy, but in Jamaica [you do not]. . . . It was good for me personally, mentally and also for my game to get a little tougher and not to whine about everything, which you tend to do if you get pampered all the time. In Jamaica there was not a lot of pampering." Although Brown fared well in some junior tournaments, he was granted access to well-maintained courts in resorts only sporadically. The Jamaican Tennis Federation covered none of his expenses.

Brown completed high school in 2002. That year he turned professional and made his debut on the ITF Futures circuit. Also in 2002 Brown, a right-hander who uses both hands on backhand strokes, played in the Davis Cup for Jamaica's national team. (He did so only once more, in 2007.) In 2003 Brown made an ATP International Series appearance, at the Hall of Fame Tennis Championships in Newport, Rhode Island, where he lost in the first round to Bob Bryan, an ATP World Tour doubles champion. He continued to compete in ITF Futures tournaments in Jamaica until 2004, when he returned to Europe. He took that step after his mother concluded that his chances of advancing his career would be greater overseas. By her own account, she was sitting on a beach one day, pondering how her son might be able to afford to participate in pro tennis overseas, when suddenly the idea came to her of buying a fully equipped camper that would serve as Dustin Brown's home as well as his means of transportation. She and her husband bought such a vehicle for Brown as a gift.

"Money was pretty tight" in Europe, Brown told Mitchell. "I was playing Futures, on the road all over Europe, and making $170 to lose in the first-round match is not exactly good money. But with the camper, it was possible, it [enabled] me, if I lost in the first round, to have enough money to play the next tournament. That pretty much saved my career." He also said to Mitchell, "At the beginning it certainly was not very easy, but that was my last option to keep going with tennis. It took me a while to get used to it. But, after all, it got me to where I am, so I am very thankful to be given that opportunity by my parents." For a while he often felt lonely. Later, friends of his on the tennis circuit sometimes accompanied him in his van (which has three beds as well as a kitchen) from one tournament to another. He told Greg Bishop that he kept reminding himself to "just keep going and going and never stopping, just trying and believing and hoping that, you know, sooner or later something, anything would happen."

At the start of the years 2004, 2005, 2006, 2007, and 2008, Brown placed 627th, 820th, 636th, 566th, and 456th, respectively, on the ATP singles rankings. In 2008 Air Berlin, Germany's second-largest airline, began paying for his flights to tournaments. In Futures events that year, he reached the finals in a competition in Antalya, Turkey, in March. The following June, in Trier, Germany, he won the singles title in a match with Tobias Clemens of Germany, 7–5, 6–7(6), 6–0, and also the doubles title, along with Stefan Seifert of Germany. At the end of 2008, he ranked 499th among ATP singles players. Brown won his first contest on the ATP Challenger circuit on August 10, 2009 in Samarkand, Uzbekistan, defeating Jonathan Dasnieres de Veigy of France in straight sets, 7–6(3), 6–3. Also in 2009 he reached the final in four other Challenger tournaments, in three German cities (Karlsruhe, as a qualifier; Eckental; and Aachen) and Almaty, Kazakhstan. He ended 2009 with a record of 29–16 on the ATP Challenger circuit and an ATP singles ranking of 144.

Based on his performances in ATP Challenger events, Brown earned enough points to become eligible for events on the top-tier ATP World Tour. In January 2010 he failed to qualify for the Chennai Open, in India, and the Australian Open, in Melbourne. The next month he achieved a career breakthrough, at the SA Tennis Open, in Johannesburg, South Africa: he defeated the number-four-seeded Marco Chiudinelli of Switzerland in the first round (6–4, 3–6, 6–4) and Laurent Recouderc of France in the second round (6–4, 6–4). In the quarterfinals he lost, 7–6(5), 6–3, to Stephane Robert of France, the number-eight seed and eventual runner-up. With that quarterfinals appearance, Brown became only the second Jamaican since Doug Burke, in 1989, to reach the quarterfinals of an ATP Tour event. In April 2010 Brown captured his first ATP Challenger title ever, when he defeated Izak van der Merwe of South Africa in straight sets (7–6, 6–3) at the Soweto Open in Johannesburg. With that victory Brown reached the 99th spot on the ATP's singles list, the highest ranking ever for a Jamaican player.

In June 2010 Brown competed in his third ATP World Tour event—the Aegon Championships, held at the Queen's Club in London, England. He defeated Frank Dancevic of Canada in the first round, 7–5, 6–7(4), 6–4, then lost in the second round to Denis Istomin of Uzbekistan, 7–6(7), 6–4. In June Brown took part in the Boodles Challenge, an international exhibition competition traditionally held at the Stoke Park Club in Buckinghamshire, England, one week before the Wimbledon Championships. He defeated two Spaniards, Fernando Verdasco and Tommy Robredo—whose career-high ATP rankings are seven and 16, respectively—before losing to Gael Monfils of France (whose career-high ranking is seven). Based on his ATP world ranking (then 105)—and dropouts due to injuries of several players who ranked higher than he did—Brown secured an entry to the Wimbledon Championships, in which 128 singles players compete. On June 21, 2010, in his first Grand Slam singles appearance, Brown was defeated by Jürgen Melzer of Austria in the first round in four sets (6–3, 4–6, 6–2, 6–3). (Melzer's career-high ATP ranking on August 13, 2010 was 15.)

On July 7, 2010 Brown upset the number-one-seeded Sam Querrey of the U.S. in straight sets (6–4, 6–3) at the Hall of Fame Tennis Championships. In his second career ATP World Tour quarterfinals appearance, he was defeated by Brian Dabul of Argentina, 6–4, 6–4. Later that month he reached a career-high singles ranking of 98. On the ATP doubles circuit, in April 2010 he won the Ixian Grand Aegean Tennis Cup title on the island of Rhodos, Greece, with the German player Simon Stadler as his partner, and the next month he recorded a runner-up finish at the Palm Hills International in Cairo, Egypt, with another German partner, Andre Begemann. In September of that year, Brown won the Open de Moselle tournament in Metz, France, with his doubles partner Rogier Wassen of the Netherlands. That victory gave him his first ATP World Tour doubles title.

Brown has repeatedly spoken out against Tennis Jamaica, the official tennis governing body in that nation, for its failure to support him. "The Jamaican federation are not doing their job," he told a reporter for the *Jamaica Observer*, as quoted on *Radio West Indies* (June 22, 2010, on-line). "Everybody knows it. They have given me no funds, no coaching, no help." He added, "It doesn't really help getting an e-mail from the president of the federation . . . telling me, 'Congratulations on your wildcard for Wimbledon.'" (Brown was not a wildcard player—one who is allowed entry into a competition despite the absence of proper qualifications.) According to Jamie Jackson, writing for the London *Guardian* (June 24, 2010, on-line), Phillip Gore, the president of Tennis Jamaica, told the *Jamaica Gleaner*, "When I took over five years ago I met with Brown and asked him to let bygones be bygones. But he refused and said he would not play for Jamaica again as long as Dougie Burke remains as national technical director. He needs to apologise to the directors of Tennis Jamaica for his public comments against us; and secondly, accept Mr Burke as our technical director." Jackson reported that in an angry post on Brown's Facebook page, Brown accused Tennis Jamaica officials of having refused to offer him financial support years earlier because his mother is white, "meaning that we have money."

Brown lives in the town of Winsen an der Aller, Germany, near Celle. He is fluent in English, German, and the patois spoken in Jamaica. In his leisure time Brown enjoys watching movies, listening to music, and surfing the Internet. Currently, he is sponsored by the French racquet maker Babolat and the American clothing company Topspin. From time to time he still uses his camper. He told Greg Bishop, "When I see that van, I think that everything is possible."

—C.C.

Suggested Reading: Associated Press June 21, 2010; Association of Tennis Professionals (ATP) Web site; dustinbrown.de.tl; (London) *Guardian* (on-line) June 20, 2010; (London) *Observer*

Sports p8 June 20, 2010; menstennisblog.com June 21, 2010; *New York Times* D p4 June 21, 2010

Chip Somodevilla/Getty Images

Brown, Scott

Sep. 12, 1959– U.S. senator from Massachusetts (Republican)

Address: 317 Russell Senate Office Bldg., Washington, DC 20510

On January 19, 2010 Scott Brown became the first Republican in nearly 40 years to be elected to the U.S. Senate from Massachusetts when he defeated the Democratic candidate, state attorney general Martha Coakley. Brown's victory was especially surprising since it came in the special election for the seat made vacant by the death of Edward M. "Ted" Kennedy, the Senate's most famous liberal, in a state where only 13 percent of voters are registered Republicans. Brown's election also ended the Democrats' 60-vote majority in the Senate, which had enabled the party to pass key legislation without threat of a filibuster from Republicans.

A lawyer and former model, Brown steadily worked his way up the political ranks in Massachusetts, serving as a member of the state House of Representatives (1999–2004) and state Senate (2004–10) prior to his election to the U.S. Senate. Though he is fiscally conservative and promised in his campaign to fight for smaller government, Brown is known for being more liberal than many of his Republican colleagues. Explaining his brand of Republicanism in an interview for the *Today*

show (January 20, 2010), Brown told Meredith Vieira that when he calls himself "a Scott Brown Republican," he means that he is "somebody who's always been accountable and attentive, an independent thinker and voter and looking at every single issue . . . on its merits, whether it's a good Democrat idea or a good Republican idea." He continued, "I'm a different kind of Republican. I've always just wanted to go down and solve the problem, regardless of party."

Many Republicans saw Brown's election as part of a backlash against President Barack Obama's domestic agenda. Brown, however, felt that his victory indicated something "bigger than that," as he told Vieira. Residents of Massachusetts, he said, "have three speakers that were indicted, three senators that have resigned in disgrace. We have out-of-control taxation and spending in Massachusetts. You couple that with what's being proposed nationally, people are angry, they're tired of the backroom deals. They want transparency, they want good government, they want fairness and they want people to start working and solving their problems."

While he has been celebrated for his charm, populist message, and good looks, Brown is also known for his occasional gaffes. He was heavily criticized by gay-rights supporters in 2001 when he said that it was "not normal" for Massachusetts state senator Cheryl Jacques, a lesbian, to have a baby with her partner. (Brown, who opposes same-sex marriage but supports civil unions for gays, has since apologized for the comment.) In 2007 his appearance at a student assembly at King Philip Regional High School in Wrentham, Massachusetts, drew controversy when he quoted and identified students who had made vulgar comments on the Facebook page of one of his daughters. After his victory speech in January 2010, he received some flak for having blurted out that his daughters were "both available" to date. "I can't believe I said that," Brown later told Frank Bruni for the *New York Times Magazine* (February 28, 2010).

Brown, whose childhood was marred by divorce and poverty, has said that his past made him who he is today. "I don't think I would have changed a thing," he told John McCormack for the *Weekly Standard* (February 1, 2010). "Because if I changed one thing it affects everything else. If I wasn't on welfare or wasn't from a broken home, I never would have learned from my parents' mistakes."

Scott Philip Brown was born in Kittery, Maine, on September 12, 1959 to C. Bruce and Judith Ann (Rugg) Brown. His parents divorced when he was about a year old. Afterward he lived with his mother in Wakefield, north of Boston, Massachusetts. Katie Curley Katzman reported for the Newburyport, Massachusetts, *Daily News* (January 15, 2010) that Brown spent summers at his father's home near Plum Island, on the northeastern coast of Massachusetts; Bruni, however, wrote that Brown was often left alone in Wakefield even during the summers, as his mother struggled to support him and his younger half-sister. The family relied on welfare for a brief period, and Brown lived at different times with an aunt and his grandmother. During Brown's boyhood his mother remarried three times (as did his father), and her husbands sometimes abused her; Brown recalled to Bruni that he woke one night to hear his mother being beaten and ran to defend her, getting struck himself as a result.

Brown's difficulties at home led him into trouble elsewhere. As a 12-year-old Brown was arrested in Salem, Massachusetts; when he tried to smuggle some records out of a music store. He was sent to the Salem District Court, where a judge ordered him to write a 1,500-word essay on how his younger half-siblings would feel if they saw him in prison. "That was the last time I ever stole, the last time I ever thought about stealing," Brown told Brian C. Mooney for the *Boston Globe* (November 20, 2009).

In junior high school Brown received encouragement from the basketball coach, Brad Simpson, and became one of the school's best players. "I dribbled the basketball everywhere," Brown told Bruni. "I'd take it on dates. I'd dribble it up and down town. I was the guy—you know, every town has one of those—just dribble, dribble. 'Oh, there's Scott: dribble, dribble, dribble.'" During his senior year at Wakefield High School—where he was mentored by another coach, Ellis Lane—Brown was co-captain of the Wakefield Warriors basketball team and led the team in scoring. Through basketball, and the guidance of Simpson and Lane, Brown grew disciplined and became a good student. After graduating from high school, in 1977, he enrolled at Tufts University, in Medford, Massachusetts, largely because the school provided him with significant financial aid and was located close to home. "I'd get calls—'you've got to come home!'—and I could be there in 20 minutes," Brown explained to Bruni. In his family, he said, he was "always being the responsible one, always being the one to solve problems."

During his four years at Tufts, Brown continued to play basketball—serving as co-captain of the team during his senior year—and studied history. He also joined the Army National Guard ROTC program, training at Fort Dix, New Jersey, in the summer after his junior year. After earning his B.A. degree, in 1981, he went on to study at Boston College Law School. Then, in 1982, Brown's half-sister secretly sent his picture to the women's fashion magazine *Cosmopolitan* for its "America's Sexiest Man" competition; Brown won, having been personally approved by the magazine's editor, Helen Gurley Brown. He agreed to pose nude for the magazine—though with one hand strategically placed—and earned $1,000. Seeing an opportunity to save money for school, Brown took a year off from his law studies and moved to New York City to pursue modeling and acting work. (He also enrolled part-time at Yeshiva University's Benjamin N. Cardozo School of Law, in Manhattan.) Brown was represented by the renowned Wilhelmina

modeling agency and worked primarily as a fashion and commercial model, in addition to hand modeling and appearing in television commercials. One of his more prominent jobs had him working as a hand model in a bank commercial featuring the former Boston Bruins hockey player Bobby Orr. "When you would see Bobby Orr's hands, you're actually looking at mine," Brown told Robert Preer for the *Boston Globe* (November 16, 2003). During his time as a model in New York, he met his future wife, Gail Huff, who at the time modeled for catalogs and appeared in television commercials and a music video.

During those years Brown enrolled in the Reserve Officers' Training Corps at Northeastern University, in Boston. In 1983 he completed airborne training at Fort Bragg, North Carolina. By the time he received his law degree, in 1985, he had obtained the rank of second lieutenant. (Brown, who was trained in infantry, airborne, and quartermaster duties, has never been assigned to a war zone.) He joined the Judge Advocate General's Corps in 1994 and served as a military lawyer assigned to the Massachusetts National Guard headquarters, in Milford. In that post he has defended soldiers facing disciplinary action and has lent his expertise in real-estate transactions to soldiers being deployed overseas. He attained the rank of lieutenant colonel in 2006.

Brown was first exposed to politics by his father, who served as a city-council member in Newburyport for 18 years. After graduating from law school, Brown settled in Wrentham, Massachusetts, about 30 miles southwest of Boston, and worked as an attorney for a private practice. In 1992 he was elected tax assessor in Wrentham, a position that put him in charge of determining and recording the market value of all real estate in the town. He then served as a selectman from 1995 to 1998, the year he won election to the state House of Representatives. Throughout his local and state political career, Brown continued to work as a lawyer.

In March 2004 Brown beat the Democrat Angus McQuilken by fewer than 350 votes in a special election for the Massachusetts state Senate seat representing the Ninth District of Norfolk, which includes the towns of Wrentham, Norfolk, and Plainville and portions of Medfield, Millis, and Walpole. (The seat had been left vacant after Senator Cheryl Jacques resigned to become president of the Human Rights Campaign, a lesbian, gay, bisexual, and transgender advocacy group.) That July Brown introduced legislation for the Joanne and Alyssa Act, which was aimed at toughening laws against sex offenders. The bill sought to prohibit all level-two and level-three offenders (levels indicate the individual's estimated risk of repeat offense) from living or working within 1,000 feet of a school or day-care facility. It also called for prohibiting those offenders in state-owned or state-funded housing from living within a mile and a half of a school, child-care facility, or residence of a minor. Brown's work on the legislation earned him the

Public Servant of the Year award from the United Chamber of Commerce. (Although the Joanne and Alyssa Act was never signed into law, key provisions of that bill were incorporated into another sex-offender bill that was made into law in September 2006.) Brown was elected to a full state Senate term in November 2004, beating McQuilken a second time, and again two years later, running without opposition. In 2008 he defeated the Democrat Sara Orozco with 59 percent of the vote to Orozco's 41 percent. At that time Brown was one of only five Republicans in the 40-seat Massachusetts Senate.

The death of Ted Kennedy from brain cancer on August 25, 2009 left open the U.S. Senate seat that the Democratic politician had held since 1964. Brown was quick to admit his desire to run for the seat but stated that he would not enter the race if the Republican Andrew H. Card Jr., a former chief of staff under President George W. Bush, decided to do so. After Card declined, Brown formally announced his candidacy, on September 12. From the start Brown tried to appeal to voters in the famously Democratic state by casting himself as an independent thinker. In his speech announcing that he would enter the race, mentioning the neighborhood associated with the Massachusetts state government, Brown insisted that he was "not part of the Beacon Hill insider club." "This Senate seat doesn't belong to any one person, or political party," he said. "It belongs to you, the people, and the people deserve a U.S. senator who will always put your interests first."

Brown easily won the Republican primary on December 8, 2009, defeating the lawyer and businessman Jack E. Robinson with 89 percent of the vote. He then went on to face Attorney General Martha Coakley, his main rival, in the January 19, 2010 special election. (The race also included a third candidate, the Independent Joseph L. Kennedy—no relation to Ted Kennedy.) Brown and Coakley held strikingly different political views. While Brown supported President Barack Obama's decision to send 30,000 additional troops to Afghanistan, Coakley opposed the move. Coakley was vocal about her support of a "cap-and-trade" program, which would use market incentives to encourage companies to reduce greenhouse-gas emissions. Brown, however, voiced opposition to that approach, claiming that it would result in higher energy costs. As for immigration, Coakley supported measures that would provide a path to citizenship for undocumented immigrants currently within the U.S., while Brown believed that those immigrants should apply for citizenship and return to their native lands until they became legal citizens. Both candidates favored abortion rights; Brown, however, stated his opposition to late-term abortions and to the use of public money for abortions.

A fiscal conservative, Brown focused much of his campaign on his stance on taxes. Years earlier he had signed a "no-new-taxes" pledge sponsored by Citizens for Limited Taxation, the largest taxpayers' association in Massachusetts, and was vocal about his opposition to higher taxes. He told Jim Braude on the December 10, 2009 installment of *Broadside*, a program that airs on the New England Cable News network, that he had signed the no-tax pledge "12 years ago when I ran for the state senate and I haven't voted for a tax increase while in elective office." While Brown's campaign painted Coakley as a "big-spending Democrat," Coakley's campaign criticized Brown for saying that he had never voted for tax increases, claiming that his votes for several state budgets had in fact resulted in such hikes. Brown also concentrated on the controversial health-care bill then before the U.S. Senate, pledging to cast the 41st vote against the bill (the Republicans needed 41 votes to block the legislation). Though he has expressed support for health-care reform, he was opposed to the federal bill because he believed it would negatively affect Medicare and increase taxes and spending. "[In Massachusetts] we passed our [health-care] plan without cutting Medicare. We didn't raise taxes. It was all self-sufficient. It was done through a free-market system where people could go in and [comparison shop] for a plan, and if they couldn't afford it, they would get a form of government subsidy," Brown explained to Karen Tumulty for *Time* (January 20, 2010, on-line). "But this [federal] plan that they are pushing has so many special-interest carve-outs right now [that] people have lost faith in it. There is no tort reform in it. There's certainly the cuts in Medicare and the taxes on medical-device companies. It's totally different as to how they get to the final product." After the election many conservative politicians and pundits claimed that Brown's victory represented a referendum on the health-care bill, but analysts pointed to a number of other factors that contributed to his victory, namely the effectiveness of his campaign relative to Coakley's and voters' concerns about the U.S. economy.

Despite the fact that Brown was, for a Republican, seen as something of a liberal in his left-leaning state, the majority of news media portrayed Coakley as the sure winner. Coakley enjoyed greater name recognition than Brown, who had to do much of his campaigning during major holidays (Thanksgiving, Christmas, and New Year's), when voters tend to pay less attention to politics. Wayne Woodlief wrote an op-ed piece for the *Boston Herald* (December 10, 2009) calling for Brown to run for attorney general after his inevitable loss to Coakley, saying that "it's almost impossible to beat a Democrat in this still-predominantly Democratic state with such a short run-up" to the election. Even the national Republican committees donated very little to Brown's campaign. Those groups' lack of support angered local Republicans, but Brown was not visibly bothered by it. He and his campaign staff were "doing very, very well on our own, and I don't want to be beholden to anybody at this point," he was quoted as saying by Hillary Chabot in the *Boston Herald* (December 29, 2009). Indeed, Brown's campaign raised nearly $2.5 million in the weeks prior to the election. In all, he raised $15.2 million.

Brown campaigned vigorously, running radio and television commercials and depicting himself as an "everyman" who drove his pickup truck to all parts of the state to speak with the public. Coakley, apparently not viewing Brown as a threat, held very few public events and took time off during the holiday season. With strong grassroots support, Brown attracted a significant number of independent voters, and on Election Day he stunned Democrats by winning nearly 52 percent of the ballots. (Coakley won 47 percent, and Kennedy garnered less than one percent. Among independent voters, Brown won 64 percent to Coakley's 32 percent.) Brown was sworn in as senator, a post that had been filled temporarily by Paul G. Kirk, on February 4, 2010. The following month Brown was assigned to the Senate Committees on Armed Services, Homeland Security and Governmental Affairs, and Veterans' Affairs. He will be up for re-election in 2012.

Since his election to the Senate, Brown's voting record seems to confirm his self-described independent thinking—from his unpopular votes against an extension of unemployment benefits to his siding with Democrats to pass a jobs bill that provides tax breaks to companies hiring new employees. Despite Brown's persistent opposition to the health-care bill, Congressional Democrats were able to pass the legislation in March without a single vote from Republicans, using the simple-majority reconciliation process, which requires only 51 votes in the Senate.

Brown is six feet two inches tall, trim, and handsome, with graying brown hair. A self-described Type A personality, he regularly swims, bikes, and runs and keeps a collection of trophies from the various triathlons and duathlons in which he has participated. Brown married Gail Huff in 1986. Huff was a general-assignment news reporter for WCVB-TV in Boston for 17 years, beginning in 1993; she left in mid-2010 to work part-time as a reporter for WJLA-TV, an ABC affiliate in Washington, D.C. "My marriage has lasted 23 years because my wife and I don't talk politics," Brown told Robert Z. Nemeth for the Worcester, Massachusetts, *Sunday Telegram* (November 22, 2009). The Browns have two grown daughters, Ayla and Arianna. Ayla, a Boston College graduate, gained local fame after appearing as a contestant on the popular television singing competition *American Idol* during the show's fifth season (2005–06). Arianna is a premed student at Syracuse University, in New York. The Browns live in Wrentham, Massachusetts, and Washington, D.C., with their dogs, Snuggles and Koda. They also own a summer home on Rye Beach in Rye, New Hampshire.

The publishing company HarperCollins disclosed that it had bought the rights to Brown's currently untitled memoir. The book is scheduled to be published in early 2011.

—M.A.S.

Suggested Reading: *Boston Globe* H p2 Feb. 1, 2001, Metro p1 Nov. 20, 2009, Metro p1 Jan. 7, 2010; *New York Times* A p24 Dec. 10, 2009; *New York Times Magazine* p24+ Feb. 28, 2010; scottbrown.senate.gov

Cameron Spencer/Getty Images

Bryce, Quentin

Dec. 23, 1942– Governor-general of Australia

Address: Government House, Dunrossil Dr., Yarralumla ACT 2600, Australia

"A day will come when the appointment or election of a woman to a significant public position will be triumphed first for the achievement of the individual involved," an editorial writer for the *Canberra (Australia) Times* (April 15, 2008) predicted, "rather than as a first for women, an achievement of womanhood, or as some sort of milepost on the way to complete social, political and economic equality of women in the community. When that day happens, one of those who will be credited for helping establish the conditions in which the sex of the office-taker is scarcely even mentioned, and certainly not highlighted, will be Quentin Bryce, the new Governor-General of Australia." Bryce is the first woman to serve as her nation's governor-general (a largely ceremonial post). "I grew up in the '50s and '60s and we didn't have role models, we didn't have women in senior positions at all," she said in a speech the day following the announcement of her appointment, as quoted in many Australian newspapers. "There weren't women in the amazing diversity of positions that we see today—we couldn't have dreamt of it really."

Bryce began her professional life in 1968, as a lecturer in law at the University of Queensland. During the 15 years that she taught there, she also raised five children. In her next jobs she concentrated on human rights, most notably those affecting the lives of Australian women and children: first as the inaugural director of the Queensland Women's Information Service (1984–87), then as the director of the Human Rights and Equal Opportunity Commission in Queensland (1987–88), the federal sex-discrimination commissioner (1988–93), and the founding chair and chief executive officer of the National Childcare Accreditation Council Inc. (1993–96). "I feel very committed to working to see that things are easier for young women, particularly combining work and family and responsibilities . . . ," she told Deborah McIntosh for the *Sydney (Australia) Sun Herald* (April 10, 1994). "There are enormous expectations on young women and they put them on themselves. I want things to be easier for them, not harder." She added, "I suppose when I did law I chose it because I had all these noble ideals about justice and equality and fairness and making the world a better place. And I like to think that's what I'm doing." In 2003, after six years as the principal and chief executive officer of the Women's College, University of Sydney, Bryce was appointed governor of Queensland. She was serving an extended term in that post when she was named the nation's next governor-general. She assumed that position on September 5, 2008. Bryce has never been linked to a particular political party. "I deliberately chose a course of political independence in my earliest days as an advocate and social and legal reformer," she told Damien Murphy, Deborah Snow, and Tim Dick for the *Sydney Morning Herald* (April 19, 2008). "It was a carefully considered choice which I made in my 20s and a course which I have followed ever since."

Bryce was born Quentin Alice Louise Strachan on December 23, 1942 in Brisbane, Queensland. She is the second of the four daughters of Norman and Naida (Wetzel) Strachan. (The sibling born immediately before her died in infancy.) Bryce and her older sister, Diane, and sisters Revelyn and Helene spent their earliest years in Ilfracombe, a tiny sheep-farming community in Queensland. Their father managed the town's wool-scour facility (where wool is washed to remove contaminants) and served as an Ilfracombe Shire councilor. Their mother was a schoolteacher before becoming a full-time homemaker; she was also active in the Country Women's Association and the local Red Cross chapter. As little girls the Strachan sisters did not attend the Infracombe school; rather, they began their education at home, in part through correspondence courses. From a young age Bryce

learned to maintain a polished appearance. "My mother was very stylish. She made all our clothes," she told Matthew Condon for the Brisbane *QWeekend* (May 10, 2008). "She went to a lot of trouble to see we were beautifully dressed in hand-smocked dresses and lovely Swiss fabrics. It's what mothers did." As a family the Strachans often discussed historical and current events and talked about the importance of social responsibility, and Bryce's parents regularly held parties for their neighbors in their large house. Partygoers could fish in the Strachans' pond, play tennis on their court, and relax in their evergreen garden.

In 1949 the Strachans moved to Launceston, on the island of Tasmania, an Australian state. There Bryce's father worked for L.W. Smith, a wealthy wool merchant. His job ended after a year, and the family returned to Queensland, settling in Belmont, a Brisbane suburb. Bryce attended Camp Hill State School, a primary school (kindergarten through seventh grade) in nearby Camp Hill. By 1956 her father had bought a sheep farm, outside Tenterfield, in New South Wales, just south of the Queensland border and Brisbane. That same year Bryce enrolled at Moreton Bay Girls' High School (now Moreton Bay College), a small Methodist-Presbyterian boarding school in Brisbane. She performed well academically, participated in sports and in student drama productions, and served as a school prefect.

In 1960, with a Commonwealth scholarship, Bryce entered the University of Queensland at St. Lucia. After two years she abandoned plans to become a social worker and focused on law. She lived near the campus with her family (their sheep farm had failed and they had sold their land) and worked during school holidays in jobs including babysitter and sales assistant. In 1962 she began dating Michael Bryce, an architecture student. They married on December 12, 1964. The next year Quentin Bryce graduated with a bachelor of arts and laws degree and was admitted to the Queensland bar. (Although several sources claim that she was the first woman to be admitted to that state's bar, in reality she was the seventh. She never practiced law, though.) In the mid-1960s she gave birth to her first child.

Bryce and her family lived in London, England, for some time, then returned to St. Lucia. In 1968 Michael Bryce launched his own architectural firm, building it into a highly successful, award-winning nationally active concern. In the same year Quentin Bryce joined the University of Queensland Faculty of Law as a part-time tutor; when she left the university, in 1983, she had been promoted to full-time lecturer. (Sources differ as to whether she was the first female part-time lecturer on the law-school faculty or the first female full-time lecturer.) Meanwhile, by 1972 she had also become the mother of four more children. "I was flat out on the superwoman track," Bryce told Amanda Ellis for Ellis's book *Women's Business, Women's Wealth* (2002), as posted on wbww.com.au. "I had five little ones under seven and I wanted to be the perfect everything—wife, mother, neighbor, worker, activist, hostess. . . . I had this sense of madness, chaos and exhaustion balancing too many competing priorities. Women like me were struggling with guilt and anxiety about the double bind of being a working mother. It was a no-win situation: working extraordinary hours equated to being a bad mother and not working extraordinary hours equated to not being serious about [a] career." According to Murphy, Snow, and Dick, Bryce told participants in a 2004 mental-health forum that once, during her 20s, she experienced a near emotional collapse while physically ill: "I remember lying in my bed, shrouded in fear, asking myself how would I ever cope with my little baby, two toddlers, keeping my household running, my job, my marriage, my life. How easily I could have travelled down another road. I learnt many lessons during that time. I gained my first insight into mental health: how vulnerable we are, that we are more so at particular times. I had heard and read about breakdowns. Suddenly I had a glimpse, and an unforgettable one, of what the word means."

While at the university Bryce helped start Campus Kindy, a day-care center for children of staff members and students. Starting in 1978 she also served on the newly established National Women's Advisory Council.

In 1984 Bryce became the founding director of the Queensland Women's Information Service in the Office of the Status of Women in Brisbane. She strived to improve conditions for Australian women in the workplace, by addressing such issues as maternity leave, affirmative action, and educational opportunities. In 1987 she was appointed director of the Human Rights and Equal Opportunity Commission in Queensland. The following year she assumed the post of federal sex-discrimination commissioner, with an office in Sydney, New South Wales, and responsibility for ensuring compliance with Australia's Sex Discrimination Act of 1984. Bryce spoke out forcefully against sexual harassment and urged women to report any sexual abuse. "We only see the tip of the iceberg. The most disadvantaged women in Australia don't come to the commission—it's my challenge to reach those women," she told a reporter for the Hobart, Tasmania, Mercury (April 12, 1988). Ironically, she herself was accused of sexual harassment in 1991, three months after she rejected a complaint by a physician, Alex Proudfoot, about inequities in gender-specific health centers in Canberra, where he practiced: while women-only health clinics were relatively abundant, none existed for men. After a federal court ruled that the Human Rights and Equal Opportunity Commission was wrong not to look into the complaint, an internal memorandum Bryce had written about Proudfoot's complaint surfaced. In it she had characterized his grievance as "another example of a male wasting our time with trivia." Proudfoot then charged her with bias

against men, but Bryce denied that claim, explaining that she had written the memo out of frustration stemming from the large number of frivolous claims that had been made during that time. An investigation ensued, clearing Bryce of bias.

From 1993 to 1996 Bryce served as the founding chairwoman and chief executive officer of the National Childcare Accreditation Council (NCAC) Inc. Based in Sydney, the NCAC implements the Child Care Quality Assurance system of accreditation for Australia's child-care services. Accreditation depends on whether certain criteria, including activities offered, nutritional content of meals provided, and safety precautions, meet NCAC's standards. In 1997 Bryce accepted the position of principal and chief executive officer of the Women's College at the University of Sydney. "People said it was a funny career move," she told Sandra McLean for the Brisbane Courier-Mail (March 15, 2003), "but it did bring together all the life skills and attributes I have acquired, and to be influencing the future of young women—I knew I would love it." "Bryce is fondly remembered by most students for deep involvement in college life, and an outstanding mentoring program for the girls there," according to Damien Murphy, Deborah Snow, and Tim Dick. Dale Spender, a feminist writer and one of Bryce's friends, told Matthew Condon, "It was amazing what [Bryce] did" there. "The college was dowdy, rundown and stuffy, and by the time she left there were scholarships and a chef!," which helped to boost the college's public profile.

Ever since 1988, when her youngest child was in his mid-teens, Bryce had commuted regularly between her family's home in Brisbane and her office in Sydney, 450 miles away. For six years during that period, she lived during the week in the home of her close friend Wendy McCarthy, a feminist, educator, and corporate adviser who is widely described as an "agent for change" in Australia. Bryce told Deirdre Macken for the Sydney Morning Herald (July 25, 1998), "You miss the family and feel guilty about the choice you've made. It's a deeply embedded trait in women to put their families first. It's very hard to put yourself at the top of the family agenda. It's something I urge women to do but it's very hard. I talk about it here [at the Women's College] with students because I want them to see that everything is possible. This issue of being mobile in the workforce shouldn't be seen as a barrier to having a rich family life as well." When Macken asked Bryce's husband how he felt about her absences, he said that he and his wife "have quite different personalities. The types of things she likes to eat and do and speak about are quite boring to me and she thinks the same of many of my interests, but we do enjoy each other. It is also more exciting. When you get back together, you're pleased to see each other, you've got a lot to talk about. I've never taken her for granted; she's a unique woman." Her husband's help, along with that of Bryce's mother, mother-in-law, and housekeepers, was crucial to her success as a career woman, as was what she has termed "extraordinary organization."

Although, officially, a commission appoints the governor-general, in reality Peter Beattie, a leader of the Australian Labor Party in Queensland who was then Queensland's premier, appointed Bryce governor of Queensland, in 2003; the appointment won the virtually automatic approval of Queen Elizabeth II, who represents the 54 nations that make up the British Commonwealth. The governor serves for five years. According to the governor's Web site, the person holding that post "does not participate in the political process. It is the main constitutional responsibility of the Governor to ensure that the State continues to have a stable government which commands the popular support of the Parliament." Bryce was only the second woman to govern the state. (The first was Leneen Forde, who was the first female governor of any Australian state and who served from 1992 to 1997.) "I hope being governor will send a really important message to women about what is possible for women," Bryce told Sandra McLean. "The issue of leadership is very important, but I see that many boards and committees and places of influence are still largely dominated by men. Our leadership needs to be more diverse so that it includes not only women but also indigenous people as well. Diversity is strength." (Inhabitants of the island for at least 40,000 years, the indigenous people of Australia are identified as Aborigines or Torres Strait Islanders. The hundreds of Aboriginal groups include the Ngunnawal, the Murrdi, the Noongar, and the Anangu. Aborigines and Torres Strait Islanders comprise about 2.5 percent of the total population of Australia, which in 2008 was 21,374,000.)

In April 2005 the public learned that several senior staff members of the governor's official residence, Government House, including three chefs, a chauffeur, a house manager, and a personal assistant, had quit their jobs since Bryce's arrival. As reported by Natasha Bita for the *Sydney Weekend Australian* (August 30, 2008), one former staff member called Bryce "a control freak. The way it normally works is the governor does governor things, and the office of the governor looks after the Government House estate. But she wanted to be involved in everything, from what type of flowers were being planted, to the type of furniture being purchased, to the exact menu being served. She's all sweet and understanding in public, but in private it was a whole different ball game." It was also reported that the staff disapproved of her using the house for personal gatherings, among them the wedding reception held for one of her sons. "A friend alleges [that the resignations occurred] because she was busy breaking the stuffy mould set by her predecessors, among other things inviting indigenous Australians to be guests at her table," Murphy, Snow, and Dick wrote. Boni Robertson, a professor of indigenous policy at Griffith University, in Queensland, told the same reporters that Aborigines felt welcome with Bryce as host. "It

doesn't matter whether she's standing there in Dior, she treats everybody the same," Robertson said. "She makes you feel as if you are standing there in Dior, too."

Bryce remained popular with the public, and in January 2008 Queen Elizabeth II approved an extension of her term as governor to 2010. Her governorship ended sooner, however: on April 13, 2008 the queen, on the recommendation of the prime minister of Australia, Kevin Rudd, selected her to be the country's next governor-general. "It's a great day for Australian women," she said in a speech the following day. "I grew up in a little bush town in Queensland with 200 people and what this day says to Australian women and Australian girls is that you can do anything, you can be anything and it makes my heart sing to see women in so many diverse roles across our country in Australia." Hugh Macken, president of the Law Society of New South Wales, told Zoe Lyon for the *Australian Lawyer Weekly* (April 18, 2008), "Quentin Bryce has contributed greatly to the legal community both academically and professionally and through her own successes has helped elevate the standing and calibre of the profession. Her appointment as governor general is not only a testament to her extraordinary skill and expertise, but it also recognizes the extraordinary work she has done in helping to pave the way for women within the legal profession." Bryce officially succeeded Governor-General Michael Jeffery on September 5, 2008. At her inauguration she swore her allegiance to the queen, as was required. Like the governors of Australian states, she represents the queen. Though the job is largely ceremonial, the governor-general has the authority to appoint a prime minister if an election results in a "hung parliament" and to dismiss a prime minister who has acted unlawfully or who no longer enjoys the confidence of Parliament. The Australian constitution states that the governor-general is the commander in chief of the Australian military, but in practice the defense minister makes all military decisions, and the governor-general acts only in accordance with the minister's advice. Bryce has set as one of her priorities wiping out the vestiges of the discriminatory and unfair treatment from which Aboriginal Australians have suffered since the first British settlement on the island continent, in 1788. Another item on her agenda is to promote the hiring or appointment of women to senior positions in the private and public spheres.

In her 2003 interview with Sandra McLean, Bryce said, "I think Australia is very well served by our system of government, and I certainly have the greatest admiration and respect for the Queen." Members of the Australian Republican Movement, a lobbying group, who want to change Australia from a constitutional monarchy into a republic and end ties with the British Commonwealth of Nations, hope that Bryce will be Australia's last governor-general. Although Bryce has identified herself as a monarchist, she has not taken a stand regarding total independence from the commonwealth but has said that the issue should be widely discussed among Australians.

"How can Quentin Bryce be a feminist and wear lipstick?," the writer of an article published in the University of Queensland student magazine *Semper Floreat* in 1970 asked. Bryce, who has a penchant for red lipstick, colorful clothing, and stilettos, is known for her sense of style. *Harper's Bazaar* named her among Australia's best-dressed women in 2006, and the Queensland fashion designer Daniel Lightfoot described her to Matthew Condon as "the closest we have" to the actress and princess of Monaco Grace Kelly and First Lady Jacqueline Kennedy, both of whom were considered fashion icons. "As I work with the public it's important to be well-groomed, neat and clean . . . ," Bryce told R. Murray for the Brisbane *Courier-Mail* (September 12, 1985). "I think that's good manners." She also said, "One thing I'm not good at is casual clothes. But I resist the attitude of dressing for success in business—wearing parodies of men's clothes. For me I prefer something a little softer."

In addition to her salaried jobs, Bryce has aided some 30 governmental, quasi-governmental, and private agencies and groups; among others, she was a member of the National Committee on Discrimination in Employment and Occupation, the Intellectually Handicapped Citizens Council, the National Institute for Law, Ethics, and Public Affairs, and the Network of Enterprising Women in Business, an arm of the New South Wales Chamber of Commerce. Bryce was named an officer, in 1988, and a companion, in 2003, of the Order of Australia for her service to her community, especially its women and children. Also in 2003 she was honored as a dame of grace by the Most Venerable Order of the Hospital of St. John of Jerusalem. In 2010 the University of Sydney awarded Bryce an honorary doctoral degree.

In her leisure time Bryce enjoys reading, running, practicing yoga, and being with her three sons, Michael, Rupert, and Tom, two daughters, Revelyn and Chlothilde, and six grandchildren. In 2008 her husband relinquished the chairmanship of his firm (now called Minale Bryce Design Strategy), in order to avoid any possible conflicts of interest during his wife's term as governor-general.
—M.A.S.

Suggested Reading: (Brisbane, Queensland) *Courier-Mail* p31 Mar. 15, 2003; (Brisbane, Queensland) *QWeekend* p14 May 10, 2008; gg.gov.au/governorgeneral; Marquis Who's Who on the Web; *Sydney (Australia) Morning Herald* p1+ Apr. 14, 2008; (Sydney, Australia) *Sun Herald* p125 Apr. 10, 1994; (Sydney, Australia) *Weekend Australian* p25 Aug. 30, 2008

Brzezinski, Mika

(bruh-ZHIN-skee, MEE-kuh)

May 2, 1967– Television journalist; co-host of MSNBC's Morning Joe

Address: MSNBC/NBC News, 30 Rockefeller Plaza, New York, NY 10112

Mika Brzezinski has co-hosted the weekday-morning news-and-talk show *Morning Joe* since May 2007, when it debuted on the cable-news network MSNBC. The format of the show includes news segments; interviews with politicians, analysts, and other newsmakers; and leisurely conversation and banter among the show's co-hosts, who also include Joe Scarborough and Willie Geist. "On *Morning Joe*, shouting is discouraged, the teleprompter has been largely banished, and the overarching mood, despite an almost exclusive focus on the day's political fisticuffs, is chatty bonhomie," Mark Binelli wrote for *New York* magazine (July 21, 2008). Observers have attributed a large part of the show's success to the on-air chemistry between Scarborough, an outspoken conservative, and Brzezinski, who acts as his "gentle liberal foil," as Binelli put it. In an interview with Amanda Robb for *More* magazine (September 2009), Brzezinski described her reaction to her first day of

Andrew H. Walker/Getty Images

working with Scarborough on *Morning Joe*: "I was, like, 'Wow. Of all the thousands of wavelengths out there, [Joe and I] are on the same one.' I felt I'd known him for 20 years and he was like one of my brothers at the dinner table, fighting the way we fought in our family." "Joe is extraordinary, but Mika makes him even better," Rick Kaplan, the executive producer of *CBS Evening News*, told Robb. "She gets under his skin. She is a catalyst for some of the show's most interesting conversations." Brzezinski earned international attention about a month after the show's debut when she refused to lead the show's news segment with a story about the socialite and hotel heiress Paris Hilton, instead attempting to set the script on fire and, later, putting it through a shredder. Clips of the episode spread through the Internet, and Brzezinski was praised for taking a stand against the pop culture–centric stories that have become standard in today's news. Brzezinski told Meredith Nelson for *Newsmax* magazine (May 2009, on-line), "[The Paris Hilton incident] made me realize that we do what we want to do and have developed a format where we are not pressured to fall into the typical patterns of TV." Since December 2008 Brzezinski and Scarborough have also co-hosted the radio program *The Joe Scarborough Show*, which airs on ABC Radio stations across the country.

Mika Emilie Leonia Brzezinski was born in New York City on May 2, 1967 and grew up in Virginia with her two older brothers, Mark and Ian. Her father, Zbigniew Brzezinski, who was born in Warsaw, Poland, is a political scientist and a foreign-policy expert; he served as the U.S. national-security adviser to President Jimmy Carter from 1977 to 1981 and received a 1981 Presidential Medal of Freedom for his role in normalizing relations between the U.S. and China and helping formulate U.S. human-rights and national-security policies. Zbigniew Brzezinski, currently a professor of American foreign policy at Johns Hopkins University's School of Advanced International Studies, in Washington, D.C., has made several appearances on *Morning Joe*. Mika's mother, Emilie Benes Brzezinski, was born to Czech parents in Geneva, Switzerland, and is a sculptor whose work has been exhibited in museums across the U.S. and Europe. Mika Brzezinski's maternal grandfather was a nephew of Eduard Benes, a president of pre-Communist Czechoslovakia from 1935 to 1938. Brzezinski told Howard Kurtz for the *Washington Post* (December 22, 2008) that for years "people made fun of me and assumed doors were opened because of my last name. In some cases it was true and in others it wasn't. I had to triple-prove myself and compensate for inbred resentment in newsrooms." Her brother Mark Brzezinski, now a lawyer, previously served as the director of Southeast European affairs and Russian/Eurasian affairs in the National Security Council during President Bill Clinton's administration, and her brother Ian Brzezinski, who is currently a consultant for the strategy and technology consulting firm Booz Allen Hamilton, once served as the U.S. deputy assistant secretary of defense for NATO and European policy in the George W. Bush administration.

As a young girl Brzezinski was friends with Amy Carter, the daughter of then-President Jimmy Carter, and often slept at the White House. She accompanied her father when he met with world leaders—once joining him on a secret meeting in Tunisia with the Palestinian leader Yasir Arafat—and when he gave interviews with members of the media. "I would go with my dad when he was interviewed on the *Today* show, *Nightline*, and *Meet the Press*, and he thought I was listening to him," Brzezinski told Nelson. "But I was totally wrapped up in what was going on around me." Uninterested in pursuing a career in politics, Brzezinski set her sights on a career as a television reporter. As a teenager she and a friend co-hosted a talk show, called *The Mika and Melissa Show*, that focused on teen issues and aired on a public-access channel in Fairfax, Virginia.

Brzezinski graduated from the private, all-girls Madeira School in McLean, Virginia, in 1985 and applied to Williams College, in Williamstown, Massachusetts, but was not accepted. (She had been drawn to Williams after visiting her brother Ian while he was a student there.) She instead enrolled at Georgetown University, in Washington, D.C. "Look, I've never been a great student, in fact math and biology were trouble for me, but I was willing to work at it," she told an interviewer for the Williams College Athletics Web site (November 3, 2008). "I spent my first two years at Georgetown hoping to do well enough to transfer into Williams." Brzezinski transferred to Williams College as a junior. There she excelled as a long-distance runner for the Ephs, lettering in both cross-country and indoor and outdoor track and winning the 5,000-meter race at the New England Small College Athletic Conference (NESCAC) Championships one year. She also hosted a show on a public-access station in North Adams, Massachusetts, called *Hidden Issues—The High Rate of Teen Pregnancy in Northern Berkshire County*. Brzezinski spent her summers working as a page on Capitol Hill and volunteering at such local-news stations as WUSA and WRC. After graduating from Williams with a degree in English, in 1989, she was hired as a desk assistant for WTIC-TV, a FOX-affiliated television station based in Hartford, Connecticut; two years later she became a general-assignment reporter. In 1992 she joined the CBS affiliate WFSB-TV, also based in Hartford, and soon became its weekday-morning news anchor.

Brzezinski left WFSB in 1997 and moved to New York City to join CBS News as the co-anchor of its late-night news program *Up to the Minute*, along with Rick Jackson. She also worked as a CBS News correspondent and contributed to *CBS Sunday Morning* and *60 Minutes*. In 2000 she took a short hiatus from CBS to co-host MSNBC's *Homepage* news program, with Ashleigh Banfield. She returned to CBS News in September 2001 to become the network's principal "Ground Zero" reporter during and in the aftermath of the 9/11 terrorist attacks. Brzezinski was broadcasting live in front of the World Trade Center when the South Tower collapsed.

In 2006 Brzezinski signed a contract with CBS to contribute to the *Sunday Evening News* and *60 Minutes*. During that time she took pride in her ability to balance motherhood and work. "I would bring my kids to work with me. . . . If I did the Sunday evening news, chances are one of my kids were under that desk for the entire show," she told Lesley Stahl for the Web site Women on the Web (February 18, 2009). "I made them a part of my work life and I made my work life a part of my home life. And I thought I was doing the right thing." Later that year, however, Sean McManus, who had become CBS News president in October 2005, made a number of changes to the network; he hired Katie Couric to anchor the *CBS Evening News* and fired Brzezinski along with a handful of other correspondents. The news came as a shock to Brzezinski. "The bottom line is, I tried to be everything to everybody and I ended up being nothing, ultimately," she told Stahl. "And it was very public, it was very painful and a lot of women in our industry, and in any industry where you go up really fast and you get ahead really fast, you start to drink your own Kool-Aid and you think you're untouchable."

Brzezinski initially used her time away from television to focus on her family, becoming a stay-at-home mother, but she soon realized that both she and her family would be happier if she were working. Brzezinski wrote in her official biography, posted on the MSNBC Web site (2009), "After 20 years of working up to and becoming a roving reporter, correspondent and anchor, the adjustment was, let's say, a challenge. After suffering through my horrible, and I mean absolutely terrible home cooking for a few months, my husband said, 'Boy you better hurry up and get a job before we all get sick!'" Finding a new job, however, was more difficult than Brzezinski had expected, and she spent a year looking without success for a full-time position. She told Kurtz, "You spend 10 years at a place, you gave your heart and soul and blood for it, and all of a sudden it's over? I was 40 and, quote, fired, and I'm sure people were thinking, what's wrong with her?" Brzezinski eventually accepted a freelance position, preparing and delivering four 30-second news cut-ins (news updates inserted into national broadcasts) each evening for MSNBC. After delivering the cut-ins, Brzezinski would reintroduce MSNBC's weeknight opinion-and-analysis show *Scarborough Country*, hosted by Joe Scarborough.

Though Brzezinski was happy to be working again, she was also frustrated, knowing that her experience and skills qualified her for a better position. She has admitted that during the reintroductions to *Scarborough Country*, she would playfully lower her voice in order to make the show's title sound ironic. Scarborough explained to Binelli, "Whenever [Brzezinski] tossed it back to [my show], she'd always say, 'Now back to Scarrrrbo-

rough Country.' I started to think, 'Damn it, she's making fun of me.'" Scarborough and Brzezinski met at the MSNBC offices in New York City in the spring of 2007; Scarborough was there to record *Morning Joe*, the morning show he had created as a possible replacement for the three-hour program *Imus in the Morning*, which had been cancelled in April 2007 following the controversy over host Don Imus's racially offensive on-air comments about the Rutgers University women's basketball team. "Finally we met in New York, and I said, 'Hey, I'm onto you. I know you're mocking the show,'" Scarborough told Binelli. "And she said, 'How can I mock a show I've never seen?' I said, 'But you're here every night. You're paid to watch this network.' She said, 'When you're on, I use the time to call my friends.'" Scarborough admired Brzezinski's brazen honesty and sense of humor, recalling to Kurtz, "I could tell she was not a talking head. She wasn't like anyone I'd met in television news. She didn't take herself too seriously and was obviously very quick on her feet." Scarborough asked producers to hire Brzezinski as a co-host for *Morning Joe*. (John Ridley had quit his co-host position after a couple of installments, opting instead to be a frequent guest.) After initial resistance from producers, who had been looking for either a more traditional newsreader or a youthful reporter, Brzezinski became a co-host shortly after the program's debut, in May 2007.

On June 26, just over a month after the show's debut, Brzezinski made headlines when she refused to read a story about the socialite Paris Hilton's release from prison after a short stay for violating her probation. "I hate this story," Brzezinski declared on-air, before attempting to set the script on fire with a lighter and then ripping it to pieces. When she was handed another copy of the script later in the broadcast, Brzezinski ran it through a nearby paper shredder. Referring to the day's other news stories, such as the Republican U.S. senator Richard Lugar's declaration that President Bush's Iraq War strategy was not working, Brzezinski later told David Bauder for the Associated Press (July 8, 2007), "I could not get through the first three words [of the Paris Hilton story] without crumbling. My skin was crawling. This was our lead? On a day like this? To me, it was just the ultimate Paris Hilton out-of-control moment. We've gone too far and we've got to stop." Footage of Brzezinski's on-air reaction to the story was posted on the video-sharing Web site YouTube and has since been viewed more than 3.8 million times. Although some have questioned whether Brzezinski's behavior was scripted or spontaneous, viewers applauded her refusal to include the trivial celebrity story in the news segment. The incident caught the attention of media outlets from around the world, and Brzezinski was even named "woman of the week" by the British Web site Dollymix.tv. Megan Gibb wrote for the *New Zealand Herald* (June 29, 2007, on-line), "Deliberate or not, there is no denying the incident struck a chord with viewers the world over. When it comes to Paris, we've all had enough."

In July 2007 *Morning Joe* was chosen to fill MSNBC's morning time slot permanently. Over the next year or so, the show continued to gain viewers who tuned in for coverage of the 2008 election. By May 2008 *Morning Joe* averaged 365,000 viewers, surpassing Imus's ratings for his last month on the air. In March 2009 *Morning Joe* was watched by more viewers between the ages of 25 and 54 (173,000) than its rival, CNN's *American Morning* (168,000), marking the first time in more than seven years that an MSNBC morning show had attracted more viewers in that demographic than a CNN morning show. Between March 2008 and March 2009, *Morning Joe* increased its viewership by 33 percent (431,000 vs. 324,000). In the third quarter of 2009 (July–September), *Morning Joe* attracted an average of 357,000 viewers per installment.

In contrast to the conservative views held by Scarborough, Brzezinski's political perspective is difficult to categorize. "I would say I'd lean to the left [politically], but it's not necessarily my role [on *Morning Joe*]," Brzezinski told Stahl. "My role is to challenge Joe when necessary and for the two of us to try our best to create an accessible show." She continued, "And I would say my role is far less ideological and on one side than Joe's, although I'm happy to lean left when necessary, because that feels more natural to me." Indeed, Brzezinski has been known to side with Scarborough on certain issues and has expressed views that have been unpopular within the liberal establishment. During the 2008 presidential race she often defended the Republican vice-presidential nominee, Sarah Palin, against criticisms advanced by the political left and by some members of the media. "When Sarah Palin first came on the scene . . . this is what [the media] knew about her: She was a woman, she was pro-life, and she had some very, very conservative views on other issues," Brzezinski stated on her radio program with Scarborough, *The Joe Scarborough Show*, as quoted by Michael van der Galien for PoliGazette (May 12, 2009). "And all I could hear from my friends in the network media elite was, 'Let's bring her down.' I hope these rumors bring her down' . . . . They did not know her. They didn't know anything about her. But they wanted to bring her down." Brzezinski has also criticized what she perceives as the media's infatuation with President Obama, stating on *The Joe Scarborough Show*, as quoted by van der Galien, "I still don't think it's right to be in love with [Obama] . . . and to be acting like a little girl at a Beatles concert." Brzezinski has also criticized some of Obama's policies; she expressed her opposition to Obama's stimulus package, noting, as quoted by Nelson, "I feel as a taxpayer that we are getting completely hoodwinked all over again, just like with the bailout."

Morning Joe has been criticized for signing a marketing deal with the Starbucks Coffee Co. in June 2009. Starbucks coffee had been a part of the show since its debut—both Scarborough and Brzezinski can often be seen drinking from Starbucks cups. The show's logo now features the Starbucks brand, and its introduction includes a voice-over telling viewers that *Morning Joe* is "brewed by Starbucks." Although MSNBC's president, Phil Griffin, has insisted that the marketing will have no effect on the show's content, critics have asserted that the deal threatens to violate journalistic standards.

Brzezinski, who has said that she regularly sleeps less than five hours at night, wakes at 3:30 in the morning. She reads the day's major news stories and op-ed pieces on her Blackberry while being chauffeured to *Morning Joe*'s studio, in Manhattan, and while her hair and makeup are being done. Until recently, after filming *Morning Joe*, from 6:00 to 9:00 a.m., Brzezinski traveled to a separate studio to record *The Joe Scarborough Show*, Scarborough and Brzezinski's radio show, which debuted in December 2008 and aired weekdays from 10:00 a.m. to noon. On April 26, 2010 Citadel Media announced that *The Joe Scarborough Show* had been placed on hold. (Citadel Media owns WABC, the station that carried the show.) According to Citadel, the radio show is currently being retooled; its run time will be extended to three hours to allow more time for guests' and listeners' participation. A date for the new radio show's debut has not been determined. Brzezinski also occasionally reports for *NBC Nightly News* and NBC's *Weekend Today*.

In January 2010 Brzezinski published *All Things at Once*, a motivational tome about the challenges women face as they try to balance family and career. Written with Daniel Paisner, the book includes a description of a particularly traumatic moment in Brzezinski's life when, overworked and exhausted from working nights and trying to raise two young children, she fell down the stairs of her home while holding her four-month-old daughter. Her daughter, who suffered a broken femur, later made a complete recovery. The accident, Brzezinski wrote, forced her to reevaluate her priorities. *All Things at Once* received mixed reviews; some readers felt that Brzezinski's message to career-minded women—"Don't wait to have children"—was unrealistic for those who cannot afford proper child care. James Srodes, writing for the *Washington Times* (January 29, 2010), claimed, "The Mika Brzezinski . . . in this memoir is a person almost totally consumed by ambition, but with a startling naiveté about the real world of work." He added, "The clear message of this book is that, despite the title, one cannot have 'all things at once.' There are prices to pay for each choice, and the goal ought to be worth the sacrifice for it will be paid."

Brzezinski married James Patrick "Jim" Hoffer on October 23, 1993. Hoffer, a television-news reporter for WABC in New York City, has won numerous honors for his investigative reports, including five Emmy Awards and a 2002 National

Edward R. Murrow Award. Brzezinski and Hoffer have two daughters, Emilie and Carlie, and reside in Bronxville, in Westchester County, New York. In her scant spare time, Brzezinski enjoys long-distance running.

—M.A.S.

Suggested Reading: *Creative Review* p36+ June 1999; *More* (on-line) Sep. 2009; MSNBC Web site; *New York* July 21, 2008; *Newsmax* (on-line) May 2009; *Washington Post* C p1 Dec. 22, 2008; Williams College Athletics Web site Nov. 3, 2008; Women on the Web (on-line) Feb. 18, 2009

Selected Television Programs: *CBS News Up to the Minute*, 1997–2000; *Homepage*, 2000; *Morning Joe*, 2007–

Selected Radio Shows: *The Joe Scarborough Show*, 2008–

Selected Books: *All Things at Once* (with Daniel Paisner), 2010

Burch, Tory

June 15, 1966– Fashion entrepreneur; philanthropist

Address: Tory Burch, 11 W. 19th St., Ninth Fl., New York, NY 10011-4275

In less than seven years, Tory Burch's eponymous label has become one of the most sought-after American brands in fashion. Before she opened her first store, at the age of 37, Burch had no formal training in fashion design or business. But as a member of wealthy, sophisticated families through birth and marriage, she had always lived among people who, like her, appreciated and talked about style and quality in dress. Also, after graduating from college, Burch had worked in a series of fashion-related jobs, with *Harper's Bazaar* magazine and firms including those founded by Ralph Lauren and Vera Wang. Later, feeling unfulfilled as a full-time homemaker and volunteer worker for charitable organizations, Burch studied the fashion business with the aim of launching her own line of clothing and accessories—products that would reflect her personal style and taste. In the course of her research, she detected what she identified as a gap in the marketplace between extremely expensive designer brands—Chanel, Christian Dior, and Givenchy, for example—and far lower-priced brands: everything from Benetton and Levi Strauss to Nine West and J. C. Penney. "I felt what was needed—what I was missing—were clothes that were classic, but had some intricate and original detailing, an undercurrent of retro or bohemia, but that were available for a fairly manageable price," Burch told Vanessa Friedman for the *Financial Times* (January 15, 2005). "I wanted to do something that was different . . . ," she told Jeffrey Podolsky for the London *Times Magazine* (March 11, 2006): "a lifestyle concept that was luxury in spirit, but well-priced."

The original Tory Burch boutique, located in Lower Manhattan, in New York City, made its debut in February 2004, with about $100,000 worth of merchandise, nearly all of which sold out in one day. Her appearance on Oprah Winfrey's television talk show in April 2005 gave a huge boost to her business, as did photos of Winfrey wearing Tory Burch designs on the covers of the June 2005 and July 2006 issues of Winfrey's magazine, *O*. The slim, blond, photogenic Burch has become the face of her company, both in the print media and on television. The firm has also benefited from a great deal of free publicity from such celebrities as the singer Mariah Carey, who wore one of Burch's signature tunics in the music video of her Grammy Award–winning single "We Belong Together" (2005), and the actresses Reese Witherspoon, Cameron Diaz, Uma Thurman, and Julia Roberts, all of whom have been photographed in public while wearing Burch shoes or apparel. In mid-October 2010 there were 36 Tory Burch boutiques in the U.S., Japan, South Korea, Taiwan, and the Philippines, and items bearing her label were being sold in upwards of 450 department and specialty stores worldwide as well as through her Web site. Her products, which she has described as timeless classics distinguished by fun, flair, and edge, include women's clothing, much of it designed to be suitable for both casual daytime activities and fancier evening events—"great for moms who don't have time to change," Witherspoon told a *People* (August 1, 2005) interviewer. Burch's line of clothing and accessories also includes swimwear; shoes; eyewear; scarves; belts; jewelry; handbags; wallets; and a limited collection of clothing and shoes for girls.

"What took Ralph Lauren decades—developing brand signatures such as the Polo pony, Polo shirt, concho belt and blanket coat—Burch has done in a handful of years. The tunic top, the sequin knit dress, the dickey sweater and the $195 Reva ballet flat . . . have become classic designs," the fashion critic Booth Moore wrote for the *Los Angeles Times* (June 1, 2008). Anna Wintour, the editor in chief of U.S. *Vogue*, told Michael Shnayerson for *Vanity Fair* (February 2007), "Tory has been very smart about branding herself. I think she completely understands the power of image and marketing and branding. . . . Women find her clothes accessible and now they're buying into Tory herself." Wintour described Burch as "hardworking . . . not a socialite who puts her name on something and goes to lunch." "The genius of Burch's entire line is how designer it looks—but how down-to-earth it sells," Shnayerson wrote. "Working women can splurge on a Tory Burch polo dress for a little over $200. Wealthy women can grab the same dress to fill out a wardrobe of far more expensive clothes."

Tory Burch

Stephen Lovekin/Getty Images

Burch won the Rising Star Award from the Fashion Group International in 2005 and, for her Reva line of shoes, the Accessory Brand Launch of the Year Award from the Accessories Council in 2007. In the latter year, by invitation, she became a member of the Council of Fashion Designers of America, and in 2008 the council named her Accessories Designer of the Year. Also in 2008 she launched the Tory Burch Foundation, which, in partnership with Accion USA, provides microloans to would-be businesswomen in the U.S. "After realizing my own dream of starting a company, I wanted to find a way to help other women entrepreneurs accomplish their own goals," Burch wrote for *Fortune* (September 17, 2009, on-line).

The only daughter of Buddy and Reva Robinson, Burch was born Tory Robinson on June 15, 1966 in Valley Forge, Pennsylvania, near Philadelphia. She grew up there in a 250-year-old farmhouse that sits on a 30-acre plot, where her family kept horses and bred German shepherds. She has two older brothers, Robert and James, and considers Leonard Lopez, the son of her family's housekeeper, a brother as well. (He and his mother lived with the Robinsons.) Burch's paternal grandfather held a stock-exchange seat and owned a paper-cup-manufacturing company that brought him great wealth. Her father (who died a few years ago) inherited both; he sold the company and worked as an investor. Burch's ancestors were Jewish, but her family did not maintain any Jewish traditions.

The Robinsons socialized with Philadelphia's Main Line elite. Both of Burch's parents enjoyed dressing fashionably. Most of her father's clothing was custom-made, and her mother owned many outfits with haute-couture or high-end labels; her

favorite designers included Zoran Ladicorbic (known simply as Zoran). She loved tunics, adding to her collection during the six-week trips she and her husband took overseas every year. "I developed an interest in design watching my mother get dressed for an evening out and seeing the way my father . . . lined his dinner jackets with Hermès scarves," Burch told Amanda FitzSimons for *WWD Scoop* (March 24, 2008). "The people I grew up around in Philadelphia had a classic American sensibility in the way they dressed, which has definitely been incorporated into my designs."

Something of a tomboy, Burch was athletic and liked to climb trees. She attended the Agnes Irwin School, an exclusive, private all-girls school in nearby Rosemont, Pennsylvania, where she was captain of the varsity tennis team and rode horses. At her senior prom she wore a dress designed by Yves Saint Laurent. As an undergraduate at the University of Pennsylvania, in Philadelphia, she was known for having a distinctive fashion sense. Hayley Boesky, who knew Burch in college, told Michael Shnayerson, "She was very bohemian, listening to Janis Joplin, burning incense, wearing Grateful Dead T-shirts. But she also had this equestrian-Hermes thing going on as well. She was always accessorized, like a French or Italian woman." Burch told Shnayerson that other students called her wardrobe "Torywear." "My friend Patrick used to say, 'Half preppy and half jock—or prock,'" she recalled. She earned a B.A. degree in art history in 1988.

For at least eight years after her graduation, Burch worked at a series of fashion-related jobs. The first, which she landed with her mother's help, was in the public-relations office of Zoran, in New York City. She next worked as a sittings assistant (or assistant fashion editor, according to some sources) for the fashion magazine *Harper's Bazaar*; in the public-relations department and as a copywriter for the designer Ralph Lauren; and in the public-relations departments of the designer Vera Wang and the Spanish luxury brand Loewe, then headed by the designer Narciso Rodríguez. While with Ralph Lauren, she told an interviewer for *Fortune* (July 6, 2009), she learned "the importance of having a complete vision for the company, from product to marketing to store visuals."

During that period, in 1993, Burch married William Macklowe, the son of a real-estate mogul. That union ended in divorce in less than a year. In 1996 Burch married the venture capitalist and entrepreneur John Christopher "Chris" Burch, who owned a successful sportswear company called Eagle's Eye, which he had started as a college student in the early 1970s with his brother. Tory Burch became the stepmother to Chris Burch's three daughters (the oldest then 12, the youngest six) from his previous marriage. Her new family grew to include twin sons, Henry and Nicholas, born in 1997, and a third son, Sawyer, born in 2001. She managed three homes: a 9,000-square-foot apartment created from three suites and part of a corridor in the

Hotel Pierre in New York City, a summer house in Southhampton, on Long Island, New York, and a house in Pennsylvania. She joined New York's prominent social set and worked for several charitable groups.

Burch has traced her decision to start a fashion-related business to the restlessness she was feeling as a stay-at-home mother, her excitement during the process of renovating and redecorating her family's Hotel Pierre apartment, and an inspirational commercial about pursuing one's dreams that aired after the 9/11 terrorist attacks. She undertook an exhaustive study of the fashion industry and surveyed the sorts of women's clothing available at various price levels. She thought of reviving Jax, a popular 1960s brand of sportswear that her mother had liked, but the surviving owner, Sally Hanson, "wasn't willing to give me the Jax name," Burch told Sarah Haight for W (March 2010). She began to sketch ideas for her own line, taking inspiration from her mother's decades-old apparel and items she herself had bought at flea markets and vintage-clothing stores around the world. "When I was researching my business plan, I came up with the idea of what was missing from the market. I wanted beautifully made but accessibly priced clothing," Burch told Katie Weisman for the International Herald Tribune (October 20, 2009). "Since I had worked in the business, I knew what kind of margins and markups were being made. I knew that price was going to be a challenge." She told the Fortune interviewer that many people advised her against launching a retail business "because it was too big a risk. They told me to launch as a wholesaler to test the waters—because that was the traditional way." Such warnings did not faze her; instead, she heeded the words of Glen T. Senk, the chief executive officer of Urban Outfitters (now a member of her firm's board), who "told me to follow my instincts and take the risk."

Earlier, in 1999, Burch's husband had reaped tens of millions of dollars through the sale of their last holdings in Eagle's Eye. Although he expressed skepticism regarding his wife's plans, Chris Burch invested $2 million in her project, and she secured additional funding from other family members and friends. She hired a small team of designers, made an arrangement with a Chinese manufacturer whom her husband had known during his Eagle's Eye days, and recruited her friend Fiona Kotur Marin, an accessories designer, to set up a production office in Hong Kong. She bought a 1,900-square-foot space in an upscale section of Lower Manhattan and, with the architect David Mann, transformed it into a colorful, homey shop, with orange walls, vintage chandeliers, Moroccan rugs, and white couches. In February 2004, after eight months of her nearly round-the-clock work—including a last-minute all-nighter in which her stepdaughters helped—Burch's boutique made its debut. Tory by TRB, as her line was known until 2006, offered 230 designs in 15 categories, among

them pants, shirts, jackets, tunics, and accessories. On its opening day more than 400 customers came, mostly by invitation, and nearly every item in the store sold out. Through word of mouth and rave reviews in national fashion magazines and elsewhere, Tory Burch designs quickly become popular. "When an elegant style arbiter talks of dressing well, chances are what she means is dressing correctly—choosing unobjectionable, usually unassuming, garments from a handful of socially sanctioned design houses," Robert Haskell wrote for W (March 1, 2004). "It's precisely in this way that, all too often, New York's swans become sheep. . . . But no one could accuse [Burch] of blindly following the fold. In fact, Burch is that rare socialite . . . with sharply honed individual style."

The high-end Manhattan department store Bergdorf Goodman opened a Tory Burch section in September 2004. On April 4, 2005 Burch appeared on The Oprah Winfrey Show, and her label—billed as "the next big thing in fashion"—reached a national audience. Within one day of her appearance on Oprah, Burch's Web site received eight million hits. "It changed our business overnight," Burch told Podolsky.

Winfrey had become a fan of the designer's clothes when one of her producers gave her a Tory Burch tunic for Christmas in 2004. A staple in all Burch collections, the tunic is a long, loose-fitting top with a collarless neckline slit several inches vertically in its center and wide, three-quarter-length sleeves. Burch has cited as inspirations for her tunic designs an old photograph showing one of her grandmothers wearing one, her mother's collection, and a 1960s polyester tunic that Burch bought at a flea market in Paris, France.

In 2006 Burch introduced another of her signature products: Reva ballet flats—brightly colored shoes decorated with Burch's logo (two serifed, sculpted T's, one upside down atop the other). Named for Burch's mother, the style was an immediate hit: more than 300,000 pairs were sold within its first year. In July 2010 a pair of the standard leather version—one of 22 variations—was selling for $195 on the firm's Web site. Also in 2006 Tory Burch shops opened in Harvey Nichols (a luxury British retailer) in London and Dubai, and Tory Burch boutiques opened in Dallas, Texas; Costa Mesa, California; and Greenwich, Connecticut. A sales office and showroom opened in Milan, Italy, in 2008. As of mid-July 2010, there were six boutiques in California; four in New York; four in Florida; two in Nevada; two in Texas; and one each in Arizona, Connecticut, Georgia, Illinois, Michigan, New Jersey, Pennsylvania, Washington State, Japan, and the Philippines. Representative products sold via toryburch.com included a pair of women's flip-flops ($45), a tank top ($85), a pair of enamel-frame aviator sunglasses ($195), a fabric and patent-leather beach tote ($250), a high-heeled boot ($475), a short tweed jacket ($525), a leather tote with chain strap ($550), a gold and enamel bib necklace ($695), and a sequined blazer ($895).

In an article posted on the Web site of the Pennsylvania Center for the Book at Pennsylvania State University (Summer 2008), Urja Davé wrote that by 2008, Burch's annual sales had climbed to $200 million. Brigitte Kleine, the president of Tory Burch since early 2005, described the Tory Burch brand in an interview for *BaseNow* (October 20 and 27, 2008, on-line) as "a billion dollar megabrand, arguably making it THE fashion success story of the last decade." Kleine, formerly an executive with Michael Kors, Alexander McQueen, and Donna Karan, has played a major role in the company's expansion. Burch holds the title of creative director. Although her second marriage ended in divorce in 2006, Chris Burch continues as the firm's chairman and chief executive officer. In July 2009 the Mexico City–based investment company Tresalia Capital acquired a minority stake (an estimated 20–25 percent) in the company. Burch and Kleine expressed the expectation that Tresalia would bolster their plans for expansion overseas.

When it comes to her business, Brigitte Kleine told the *BaseNow* interviewer, Burch is "incredibly passionate and incredibly focused" but still "manages to stay calm at all times." Kleine added that she "encourages all of us to have balanced lives, spend time with our families and do things for others." Pictures of Burch at fund-raising events appear regularly in magazines and newspapers; photo spreads of her New York City apartment have appeared in *Vogue*, *Vanity Fair*, *House Beautiful*, and *Elle*. In addition to her own designs, she favors apparel by Michael Kors, Marc Jacobs, Carolina Herrera, and Narciso Rodríguez. She has been linked romantically with the cyclist Lance Armstrong, the New York hotelier Andre Balázs, and the Warner Music Group executive Lyor Cohen. Burch maintains that her children remain her top priority. "I work my tail off, because it's important to show my children that a working mother can be independent," she told Jeffrey Podolsky. "But if I can help women get dressed more efficiently, then I'm even more thrilled."

—M.A.S.

Suggested Reading: *InStyle* p201+ Apr. 2008; *New York Times* IX p1+ Oct. 3, 2004; *Philadelphia Magazine* (on-line) Feb. 2004; toryburch.com; *Vanity Fair* p174+ Feb. 2007; *W* p264+ Sep. 2006, p148 Mar. 2010; *Wall Street Journal* B p1+ Sep. 8, 2009; *Women's Wear Daily* p1 Dec. 18, 2009; *WWD Scoop* (on-line) Mar. 24, 2008

Cameron, David

Oct. 9, 1966– Prime minister of Great Britain

Address: 10 Downing St., London SW1A 2AA, England

When David Cameron emerged as the leader of Great Britain's coalition government, following the parliamentary elections of May 2010, he became—at 43—his nation's youngest prime minister since Robert Jenkinson, in 1812. Cameron's ascension to Britain's top leadership position surprised few political analysts, as he had been steadily working his way through his party's ranks since he was first elected to the House of Commons, the lower house of Parliament, in 2001. A self-described "compassionate conservative," Cameron became the leader of the Conservative Party in 2005 and immediately began to modernize the party, which had struggled to regain popularity since it was voted out of power in favor of the Labour Party in 1997. Cameron's youthful optimism and relatively liberal take on social issues appealed to younger citizens and moderates who had previously viewed the Conservative Party as being out of touch with an increasingly multicultural Britain. The political biographer Anthony Seldon told Sarah Lyall for the *New York Times* (May 11, 2010, on-line) that Cameron's rise to power can be ascribed to his understanding of the Conservatives' place in modern Britain. "He hasn't tried to be what he's not," Seldon said. "He

Leon Neal WPA Pool/Getty Images

speaks to a country as it is at the moment, when it needs to recover its belief in politics." Cameron himself, as quoted by James Hanning in the London *Independent* (May 12, 2010), explained that his party aims to "reflect the country we aspire to govern, and the sound of modern Britain is a complex harmony, not a male voice choir."

Although the Conservative Party won more seats in the 2010 parliamentary elections than its chief rivals—the Labour Party and the Liberal Democrats—it did not secure a majority; the coalition government formed by the Conservatives and the Liberal Democrats made Nick Clegg, of the latter party, deputy prime minister. In contrast to the traditional fiscal and social conservatism of the Conservative Party (often referred to as the Tory Party, or Tories), the Liberal Democrats espouse a form of social liberalism that includes increased taxes for social services, government reform, and an emphasis on civil liberties and rights. Those fundamental differences between the two parties, critics argue, could make it difficult for the coalition to tackle the U.K.'s most pressing problems, which include an ongoing financial crisis and a massive deficit. In his first speech as prime minister, quoted by Carsten Volkery on the ABC News Web site (May 12, 2010), Cameron agreed that cooperation within the coalition was "going to be hard and difficult work." He noted, however, that in his new role as prime minister, he was determined to push the country to "face up to our really big challenges, to confront our problems, to take difficult decisions, to lead people through those difficult decisions so that together we can reach better times ahead."

David William Duncan Cameron was born on October 9, 1966 in London, England, the third of the four children of Ian Donald Cameron and Mary Fleur (Mount) Cameron. He is a direct descendant of King William IV (1765–1837) and a distant relative of Queen Elizabeth II. (Cameron is the queen's fifth cousin twice removed.) His great-great-great-uncle was the Duke of Fife, who married a daughter of King Edward VII (1841–1910). According to Cahal Milmo, writing for the London *Independent* (December 5, 2005, on-line), Cameron's "noble lineage" "comes with a faint whiff of early 19th-century scandal," as William IV had an affair with a stage actress, Dorothy Jordan (spelled Dorothea in some sources), with whom he fathered 10 illegitimate children.

Ian Cameron, who died in 2010, was the director of the real-estate agency John D. Wood & Co. as well as a stockbroker with Panmure Gordon & Co., where David Cameron's paternal grandfather and great-grandfather had worked; he was also chairman of the elite London gentlemen's club White's. Ian was born with deformed legs that were later amputated and also lost sight in one eye, but he was nonetheless able to live a normal life and raise children. In an interview with Sir Trevor McDonald for ITV, as quoted by Patrick Foster in the London *Times* (March 15, 2010, on-line), David Cameron described his father as a "huge hero figure" and an "amazingly brave man." He added, "I hope I have got my sense of optimism from him." He said to Mick Brown for the London *Telegraph* (May 1, 2010, on-line), "My father always used to say that

nothing in life is fair, but both he and Mum were very much of the view that you had to muck in and get on with things and deal with the difficult stuff that comes your way." Cameron's mother, the daughter of a baronet, served as a justice of the peace for 30 years. Cameron has a brother, Alec, and two sisters, Clare and Tania. After Cameron's birth his family lived for three years in Phillimore Gardens, in Kensington, West London, before moving to Peasemore, in the county of Berkshire.

Writing for the London *Daily Mail* (May 17, 2010), Richard Pendlebury observed that Cameron "is not an aristocrat. But his family tree is socially distinguished, with both noble lineage and royal connections." He noted that "the Cameron children enjoyed an idyllic upper middle-class country home life" that included cricket, horse riding, shooting, tennis, and more. "I've never tried to hide anything about who I am or my background or where I come from. I've been really lucky," Cameron told McDonald. "I totally accept that in the eyes of many people that is . . . [a] very posh, very privileged upbringing."

When Cameron was seven he was sent to Heatherdown, an exclusive preparatory school in Winkfield, Berkshire. As part of a family tradition, he then attended the prestigious Eton College (often referred to as Eton), a school for boys also located in Berkshire. In a profile for BBC News (May 11, 2010, on-line), Brian Wheeler wrote, "School friends say Mr Cameron was never seen as a great academic—or noted for his interest in politics, beyond the 'mainstream Conservative' views held by most of his classmates." Cameron was reportedly almost expelled for smoking marijuana while at Eton, but he has refused to discuss the incident with the media. At a 2007 press conference, he told reporters, as quoted by Jennifer Quinn in the London *Independent* (February 11, 2007, on-line), "Like many people, I did things when I was young that I shouldn't have done and that I regret. But I do believe that politicians are entitled to a past that is private and that remains private, and so I won't be making any commentary on what's in the newspapers."

Toward the end of his time at Eton, in the sixth form (the last two years of secondary schooling), Cameron began to distinguish himself academically. He gained acceptance to Oxford University's Brasenose College, where he studied philosophy, politics, and economics. Before he enrolled he took a year off, working as a researcher for his godfather, the conservative Parliament member John Rankin "Tim" Rathbone, then working for three months in Hong Kong for a shipping agent. At Oxford he became captain of the tennis team and joined the Bullingdon dining club, which is infamous for the drinking binges and sometimes destructive behavior of its members. (Cameron has refused to discuss his time in the club.)

In a London *Daily Telegraph* article (May 13, 2010) consisting of interviews with those who knew Cameron before he entered politics, several acquaintances noted that he demonstrated leadership abilities as a young adult. His headmaster at Eton observed, "You can't draw too many parallels between school and later life, but he did show leadership qualities early on as an excellent House captain. Boys in his Boarding House thought him firm and fair. They liked him and knew that he cared about making it a happy House." A classmate from Brasenose recalled, "He showed none of the nervousness you'd expect from a fresher. On the contrary, he was as confident then as he is now. Not conceited, not even particularly cocky, just in possession of that bottomless self-assurance that characterises Old Etonians at Oxford." Although he did not become involved in student government at Oxford, Cameron still harbored an interest in politics, which he had developed at Eton. His politics teacher from Eton, John Clarke, told Hanning, "I'm pretty sure I viewed him as politically ambitious even then. He was articulate and politically motivated and interested. He was interested in the business of politics, in politics as a profession, even at that stage. . . . He was intrigued by politics as an art, as a way of resolving problems."

Cameron graduated from Oxford with a first-class honors degree in philosophy, politics, and economics in 1988. He initially considered journalism or banking but was hired as a researcher with the Conservative Research Department (CRD), a Conservative Party think tank. He rose through the ranks of the CRD and became responsible for briefing party politicians, including Prime Minister John Major, for their media appearances. Cameron, along with several conservative colleagues known collectively as the "Brat Pack," worked on Major's successful campaign in the 1992 general election, which brought victory for Conservatives. He also spent time as a political adviser to Norman Lamont, then the chancellor of the exchequer (a cabinet minister responsible for the country's financial affairs), and then–Home Secretary Michael Howard. In 1992, while working with Lamont, Cameron was present for the events of September 16, known as "Black Wednesday," when the government had to withdraw the weakened pound from the European Exchange Rate Mechanism (ERM). The events of Black Wednesday and their aftermath caused Lamont's popularity to decline, but the relatively unknown Cameron remained unaffected politically.

By 1993 Cameron had decided on a career in politics. However, understanding that experience in the private sector would later help his political career, he worked in the public-relations department of the ITV television company Carlton Communications. He obtained the job through his then-girlfriend and future wife, Samantha Sheffield, whose mother was friendly with Carlton's executive chairman, Michael Green. With one brief break Cameron worked with Carlton from 1994 to 2001, eventually becoming director of corporate affairs. In that post he often traveled with the notoriously short-tempered Green. He also reportedly alienated several journalists with his brusque manner and unwillingness to discuss company initiatives. An unnamed business journalist told James Robinson and David Teather for the London *Guardian* (February 20, 2010, on-line) that Cameron was "thoroughly unpleasant" and noted that "a good PR man will tell you stuff and give you insights and he never did that—which is why Carlton had rings run round it." Cameron's often curt dealings with reporters have been ascribed to the difficulty of his situation. Robinson and Teather wrote, "As a conduit between Green and the media, Cameron had a job that must have seemed impossible at times," and Leslie Hill, a former director with the company, told Robinson and Teather that Cameron had "the hardest job at Carlton. Michael was prickly about the press and about communications; he wasn't good at it and he didn't like it so David fulfilled a more vital role than he would have done at another company. He handled Michael brilliantly."

Cameron waged his first campaign for elective office in 1997, running unsuccessfully for the House of Commons seat representing Stafford; the Labour Party triumphed all around, as a result of recent scandals in the Conservative government. Cameron then returned to Carlton until 2001, when he was elected to a "safe" seat as the member of Parliament for the Witney constituency in West Oxfordshire. In Parliament Cameron served on the Home Affairs Select Committee, which recommended loosening drug laws. In 2003 he was appointed shadow minister in the Privy Council Office. Later that year, when Michael Howard became leader of the Conservative Party, he made Cameron a deputy chairman of the party. In 2004 Cameron won his first frontbench position, as the opposition party's local government spokesperson. He was then promoted into the shadow cabinet as the head of policy coordination. (The shadow cabinet, formally known as the Official Loyal Opposition Shadow Cabinet, consists of senior members of the opposition party.) After only three months Cameron became the shadow education secretary.

In 2005, when Howard announced his resignation after a Labour Party victory in the general election, Cameron announced his candidacy for his party's top leadership post. He found support from several major party figures, including former party head William Hague, but did not become a popular contender until he gave an unscripted and impassioned speech at the 2005 Conservative Party conference in Blackpool. Speaking about his party's failures in the past decade, he said, as quoted by BBC News (October 4, 2005, on-line), that he wished to see citizens "feel good about being Conservatives again. . . . I want to switch on a whole new generation." He also said that he would bring forward "modern, compassionate Conservatism." After his speech he received a three-minute ovation. Later, in the final round of voting for party leader, Cameron trumped then–shadow home secretary David Davis with 68 percent of the vote.

As leader of the Conservative Party and leader of the opposition, Cameron successfully worked to push his party past the stigma associated with it since the late 1990s. He presented an optimistic demeanor and a more moderate ideology, championing environmental stewardship and working to recruit more women and minorities to the Conservative Party. The party soon began to see higher ratings in opinion polls than the Labour Party. Discussing the party's turnaround under Cameron, Lyall wrote, "The Conservative Party that David Cameron inherited in 2005 was a disoriented shadow of its once mighty self, riven by ideological disarray, wounded by endless power struggles and facing the bleak prospect of long-term unelectability. As leader, the smooth, self-assured Mr. Cameron . . . moved swiftly to weed out the old guard, replacing the party's mean-spirited image with a kinder, more socially progressive philosophy that he called compassionate Conservatism. That he succeeded is a reflection of his toughness, acumen and resolve." The media and political analysts often compared Cameron to the youthful and popular Tony Blair, then the prime minister and Labour Party leader, who had similarly succeeded in turning around his party's fortunes when he was elected to its top leadership post in 1994.

The Conservative Party's newfound popularity began to wane in 2007, however, with the resignation of Blair and the rise of the new Labour Party leader and prime minister, Gordon Brown. May 2010 brought a general election, in preparation for which the leaders of the Conservative, Labour, and Liberal Democrat Parties participated in televised debates—the first televised prime-ministerial debates in British history. After the first debate, opinion polls suggested that Nick Clegg, the leader of the Liberal Democrats, had come out on top. However, in the two subsequent debates, Cameron was considered the strongest performer. Critics in the media and some politicians attacked Cameron's privileged background, but the future prime minister successfully countered the criticism with a down-to-earth persona that won over many skeptics.

In the election the Conservative Party aspired to secure a majority of seats—326—but came up 20 seats short of its goal; the Tories nonetheless saw their largest increase in seats in several decades, enough to make Cameron the country's prime minister. The hung Parliament required that a coalition government be formed, and after Brown announced his resignation as head of the Labour Party, a coalition of the Conservative Party and the Liberal Democrats was formed, with Clegg as deputy prime minister and a cabinet comprising members of both parties. In total, 306 seats went to the Conservatives and 57 to the Liberal Democrats— enough to give the coalition a majority. On May 12, after several days of talks, the formation of the coalition, the U.K.'s first since World War II, was announced.

The coalition government—already a shaky pairing of two very disparate parties—faces several immediate concerns that may harden its divisions, including the ongoing European financial crisis and a high level of national debt. "It's going to be a very interesting and hairy ride," Steven Fielding, the director of the Center for British Politics at Nottingham University, told Lyall. "We've got a set of politicians who aren't used to coalition government and who are going to have to learn on the job, in the midst of one of the worst economic crises we've ever lived through." Once in office the coalition government moved quickly to make changes, canceling many Labour Party initiatives, creating a new department—the National Security Council—and renaming another (the Department for Children, Schools, and Families became the Department for Education). It also announced that it would implement significant public-spending cuts to rein in the growing deficit. The resignation of David Laws, the chief secretary to the treasury, in late May, after disclosures of his misuse of funds, came as a blow to the coalition.

The government's spending cuts were announced to the public by George Osborne, the chancellor of the exchequer, on October 20, 2010. They include decreases affecting many government departments and cuts in funding for welfare, education, defense, health care, and more. The retirement age was raised by four years, and beginning in 2013 child-benefit payments will be limited to those earning less than £44,000 ($70,000) a year. Osborne also noted that about 490,000 public-sector jobs would be eliminated. In the months leading up to Osborne's announcement, Cameron's government had been subjected to heated criticism over the expected cuts and warnings that they might push the country into a so-called double-dip recession. Cameron defended the cuts as painful but necessary at a time when the country faced the largest deficit ever seen during peacetime. In public appearances he explained that the cuts would not disproportionately affect the poor, and he emphasized his "big society" plan, in which communities would be encouraged to organize volunteers to run libraries, post offices, and museums and to find ways to fund important projects. "The cuts are so momentous that they could determine the coalition's fate as Britons face politically charged austerity after years of growing prosperity before the financial meltdown in 2008," Sarah Lyall and Alan Cowel wrote for the *New York Times* (October 20, 2010, on-line).

According to Christopher Caldwell, writing for the *New York Times* (July 12, 2009, on-line), "There are really two strands of modernizers in the Tory party. There are the green-friendly, diversity-oriented, welfare-state-defending ones—the ones who simply want to move the party to the left. And there is a smaller group, centered on the former party leader Iain Duncan Smith, that is equally troubled by the [Margaret] Thatcher era's undue focus on economic matters but that has a very different idea of what the party's real focus ought to be. Heavily influenced by American conservative Christianity, this wing of the party often speaks of 'compassionate conservatism.'" Cameron, Caldwell observed, "has managed to straddle the two camps." He has a conservative take on social issues, but as leader of his party he has shown a willingness to compromise. Although generally an opponent of gay rights, for example, he voiced support for same-sex civil unions once he became party leader.

Cameron's willingness to compromise and bring to the forefront issues that conservatives have generally declined to discuss helped his party in the election. His approach, however, has also alienated some of his party members. Caldwell wrote, "Older Thatcherites generally look on Cameronism as merely a set of clever public-relations stunts." Robin Harris, a conservative-policy analyst and a former boss of Cameron's, told Caldwell that the "modernization" of the party is merely an attempt to push it away from its core values. "Modernizing was never about technical changes," he said. "Modernizing was basically being unconservative in a deliberate manner. It implies Conservatism has failed." According to Caldwell, though, "Cameron aides counter that the new approach has allowed the party to make conservative arguments that in the past would have been misunderstood or misrepresented. They can now talk about welfare reform without being called heartless, immigration without being called racist and marriage without being called prudish."

In response to criticism of his brand of "compassionate conservatism," Cameron told Mick Brown, "I've always found it very condescending, this idea that you have to be left-wing in order to be compassionate. I think the Conservatives are deeply compassionate because we understand that the things that actually deliver a more compassionate society are things like families and good schools. The party has modernised and is more in connection with the country it seeks to govern, but the core beliefs that the good society is the responsible society, that government can't do everything, that communities need to pull together, that is as old as the hills." In fact, Caldwell observed that Cameron's politics are "closer to the traditions of Conservatism than most of his contemporaries tend to realize." He has expressed admiration for the policies of the Conservative prime ministers Margaret Thatcher (who served from 1979 to 1990) and Harold Macmillan (1957 to 1963). Although not a diehard Thatcherite, Cameron supported Thatcher's efforts to privatize state utilities and reform trade unions. "The 1980s was a fascinating decade—strikes and unions and privatisations and CND [Campaign for Nuclear Disarmament] marches and all the rest of it," Cameron told Brown. "I wasn't particularly a Thatcher fan, but I just thought, on these themes, of course we shouldn't be on strike the whole time, and should have business that could compete and succeed, and that if the Russians have the bomb we

probably ought to have it too. So I thought, on all those arguments Mrs Thatcher is probably making the right decisions." The journalist Charles Moore told Caldwell that Cameron is "temperamentally and mentally the absolute classic British Tory. His faith is in adaptation, in changing your spots. The reason he was a Thatcherite was not because he was a true believer in Thatcherism, but because it seemed to be working. Because of the economic crisis we're in now, he has returned to some extent to a more Thatcherite approach. He genuinely respects her. He's certainly not an anti-Thatcher person. But it's got to be expressed in a different way. He is more, by temperament, character or attitude, what used to be called a trimmer, rather than a sort of die-in-the-ditch man." Cameron told Brown that he is not "a deeply ideological person" but a "practical person, and pragmatic. I know where I want to get to, but I'm not ideologically attached to one particular method."

Cameron's wife, Samantha Gwendoline Cameron, is the former creative director of Smythson, a London-based manufacturer of stationery and leather products. Her father is Sir Reginald Sheffield, Eighth Baronet, a landowner and descendant of Charles II (1630–85). Her mother, Annabel Jones, is a successful businesswoman. Cameron and his wife have three young children: Arthur, Nancy, and Florence, the last of whom was born in August 2010. The couple's first child, Ivan, was born with cerebral palsy and epilepsy. He died in February 2009, at age six, a tragedy about which Cameron was candid in public, prompting an outpouring of sympathy. "It is probably true," Brown wrote, to say that Cameron's son's death "is the defining event" in the prime minister's life. In his spare time Cameron enjoys reading and watching what he described to Brown as "boys' films"—*The Godfather* (1972), *Carlito's Way* (1993), and *Where Eagles Dare* (1968), among others. He also listens to the music of the alternative rock bands Radiohead, the Smiths, Pulp, and Blur and the folk-rock icon Bob Dylan.

Opinions on Cameron's personality vary. Brown wrote, "You do not have to spend long with David Cameron to recognise that he is extremely clever, astute, quick on the uptake and with a ready, jocular humour. But he is not, at first blush, a particularly warm man. He answers questions readily, but in a determinedly businesslike manner, on his own terms. He is personable, but in a guarded way." Michael Gove, the shadow secretary of state for children, schools and families and a friend of Cameron's, told Brown that the prime minister is "a very English person. He's not someone—and most Englishmen aren't—who talks freely and easily in the open-hearted Oprah-esque fashion that some do. But he's extremely good company. Over a drink or over dinner he does open up, and enjoys talking about issues and friends and people in common as much as, in fact even more than, shop." Cameron is known for having numerous friends and hosting gatherings at his home. "He's naturally someone who relaxes in company," Gove said. "There are people who need to spend time on their own in order to recharge their batteries, and people whose batteries are recharged by being around others. He's the latter."

—W.D.

Suggested Reading: BBC News (on-line) May 11, 2010; (London) *Daily Mail* (on-line) May 17, 2010; (London) *Guardian* (on-line) Feb. 20, 2010; (London) *Independent* News p4 May 12, 2010, (on-line) Dec. 5, 2005; (London) *Telegraph* (on-line) May 1, 2010; *New York Times* (on-line) May 11, 2010, (on-line) July 12, 2009, Oct. 20, 2010

Gabriel Bouys/AFP/Getty Images

Catlin, Don H.

June 4, 1938– Drug-testing expert; physician; educator

Address: Anti-Doping Research Inc., 3873 Grand View Blvd., Los Angeles, CA 90066

In recent years the use of steroids and other banned strength-and-endurance aids among athletes has become common, so much so that outstanding feats in sports often trigger suspicion. Don H. Catlin, a physician, is one of the founding fathers of drug testing in sports. Over the last quarter-century, he has developed numerous drug-identification techniques and helped lead the fight against athletes' use of performance-enhancing substances. Catlin is the founder (in 1982) and former director of the UCLA Olympic Analytical Lab-

oratory, the first drug-testing lab in the United States to be accredited by the International Olympic Committee (IOC). Under his 25-year stewardship, the lab grew to become the largest testing facility for performance-enhancing drugs in the world, processing approximately 40,000 urine samples a year and providing drug education and tests for many national and international sports organizations, including the U.S. Olympic Committee, the National Collegiate Athletic Association (NCAA), the National Football League (NFL), and Minor League Baseball. During that time Catlin developed the groundbreaking carbon-isotope ratio (CIR) test, which determines whether testosterone in athletes' bodies is natural or has come from a prohibited performance-enhancing drug. He also led efforts to get the IOC to ban androstenedione and other male-hormone supplements. Catlin's greatest achievement came in 2003, when he cracked the code for the previously undetectable "designer" steroid tetrahydrogestrinone (THG), popularly known as "the Clear." That breakthrough led to the decoding of other steroids and played a key role in the Bay Area Laboratory Cooperative (BALCO) investigation, which linked such high-profile athletes as Barry Bonds, Jason Giambi, Marion Jones, and a slew of other professional athletes to use of a wide array of performance-enhancing drugs; Catlin was honored by the *Chicago Tribune* as sportsman of the year for his contribution to that investigation.

In 2005 Catlin became the founder and chief executive officer of Anti-Doping Research Inc., a nonprofit organization based in Los Angeles, California. There, he has continued to develop new testing methods, including one aimed at detecting the human-growth hormone (hGH). Commenting on the proliferation of drug use in sports, Catlin explained to Dan Shaughnessy for the *Boston Globe* (July 16, 2006), "People think of this as cops and robbers. That's not really it. I look at any positive test as a failure of the system. A failure to explain things. A lot of [those who test positive] are innocent. They get stuff that's contaminated and they get whacked even though they have no intention to cheat. Those guys don't bother me. We want to catch the cheaters. If you believe that sport is good for life and society and is worth preserving, you have to do something about it." He also said, "I think a clever crook can beat us. Once we get [the test for] growth hormone, they'll just shift a few degrees and start doing something else. There is so much money involved, there is so much desire to win, whether it be a pennant, a World Cup, the Tour de France. It doesn't matter. People want to win and they're going to do what they have to do and they might consider cheating. It's part of a way of life for an athlete. And that's tough." Catlin said to Jill Lieber Steeg for *USA Today* (February 28, 2007), "I can't think of anything more exciting than the Olympic model, where 220 countries in the world participate and every four years they send their best to compete against the best from other countries and the best man or woman wins. That's gorgeous. What could be nicer?" He told Steeg, "You should care about preserving something natural and beautiful."

Don H. Catlin was born on June 4, 1938 in New Haven, Connecticut, and was raised near the Berkshire Mountains of western Massachusetts. His father, Kenneth, was an insurance executive; his mother, Hilda, was a homemaker. An avid sports fan from youth, Catlin grew up "rooting for Ted Williams and the Boston Red Sox," as Steeg noted. One of his family's close friends was the pioneering surgeon and Yale University professor Gustaf Lindskog. "Private chats with him convinced me to go to medical school," Catlin told *Current Biography*. "That made sense to me because I feared boredom and medicine seemed to guarantee a lifetime of challenges." After graduating from high school, he attended Yale, in New Haven, where he received a bachelor's degree in statistics and psychology in 1960. Catlin then attended medical school at the University of Rochester, in New York. He earned an M.D. degree in 1965.

Upon completing his medical studies, Catlin joined the U.S. Army and became a specialist in internal medicine at the Walter Reed Army Medical Center, in Washington, D.C. During that time he read an account of a Washington, D.C., man who took drug addicts from the streets to his treatment center and helped them overcome their habits. "He had the right approach," Catlin recalled to Steeg. "He would dry them out, physically keep them away from drugs. He would literally hold them, then sing, play music, and talk to them." After the government threatened to close the center because it had no doctor on staff, Catlin offered to fill that position. On the strength of his reputation for working with addicts, he was put in charge of an army treatment program. He clashed with generals at the Pentagon over plans to jail soldiers who had turned to heroin to deal with the stress of the war in Vietnam. He recalled to Steeg, "I said, 'Wait, let's try the medical model.' But they locked 'em up anyway."

In 1972 Catlin joined the faculty of the University of California at Los Angeles (UCLA), beginning as an assistant professor in the Department of Pharmacology. He had been teaching at UCLA for nine years when the IOC recruited him to set up and run its drug-testing lab for the 1984 Summer Olympics, which were being held in Los Angeles. At the time only three labs in the world (in London, England; Paris, France; and Cologne, Germany) were conducting sports-doping research. While the IOC had started using limited doping tests at the 1968 Summer Olympics, in Mexico City, not much other drug testing had been done. Catlin confessed to T. J. Quinn for the New York *Daily News* (June 11, 2006) that at first "the idea made no sense to me. Why would a young, healthy athlete want to take a drug? It seemed so stupid." He nonetheless took the assignment, in part because UCLA would keep the lab equipment after the Games. In 1982 he

founded the UCLA Olympic Analytical Laboratory, the first anti-doping lab in the United States. At the behest of the IOC, he began educating athletes a year prior to the 1984 Olympics to give them a chance to experience the drug-testing process. Shortly afterward he tested a series of urine samples that, he discovered, contained a banned drug in decreasing amounts and realized that someone was using the program to figure out how long it took for the drug to disappear from athletes' systems. Catlin recalled to Steeg, "[The U.S. Olympic Committee] wanted to do testing, and for us to tell them the answers, meaning whether their guys and girls test positive or not. But they didn't want any consequences. It would just be an educational experience. And already we could see that, well, what kind of education is this? We shouldn't be doing this. . . . That program stopped real fast."

After the 1984 Olympics Catlin approached Manfred Donike, a pioneer in drug testing for sports, about the lack of a test for Stanozolol, a synthetic anabolic steroid that Catlin had suspected athletes of using in the Los Angeles Games. Catlin said to Steeg, "[Donike] hands me a pill—Stanozolol—and says, 'Here, take this.' So, I took it, and I gave him my urine, and he couldn't find it." A year later Donike discovered a way to detect the drug. Throughout the 1980s Catlin made repeated pleas to the IOC to establish a code of ethics for Olympic drug-testing labs; the code was eventually adopted as a requirement for accreditation by the IOC. In 1988 Catlin persuaded the IOC to remove norethisterone, a substance common in birth-control pills, from its list of banned drugs; it had been barred because of its potential to generate a by-product also created by the banned anabolic steroid nandralone, which made it impossible for drug testers to know whether a female athlete had taken nandralone, a birth-control pill, or both. Catlin and his team of scientists found a method of determining which substance a female athlete had consumed. Also that year, in a development that rocked the sporting world, the Canadian sprinter Ben Johnson tested positive for Stanozolol, just days after winning the gold medal and breaking the world record in the 100 meters at the 1988 Summer Olympics, in Seoul, South Korea. Catlin, who was in Seoul when the scandal erupted, told Dan Shaughnessy, "That changed things a lot. It woke up a lot of sports people. When I came home from Seoul, my friends said, 'We're going to send our kids out for baseball. They don't have drugs in baseball.' That was 1988. People like sports and they don't like to believe how dirty it can be. So they put blinders on. It's hard for me to do that. When you get into my field, everything looks very different."

In the 1990s Catlin developed the CIR test, which differentiates between testosterone produced naturally and that introduced through drugs. During that period, in efforts to set stricter drug-testing policies, Catlin suggested to the IOC that approval by the International Organization for

Standardization be a prerequisite to IOC lab accreditation, an idea that the IOC adopted years later. Meanwhile, in 1998 Catlin got the IOC to ban other performance-enhancing drugs, including androstenedione and other male-hormone supplements. (Androstenedione, commonly known as "andro," was widely used throughout the 1990s by Major League Baseball players. Prior to its banning it could be purchased over the counter.)

The year 2000 saw the establishment of both the World Anti-Doping Agency (WADA) and the U.S. Anti-Doping Agency (USADA). The former was created in the wake of the 1998 doping scandal involving Tour de France riders from the French Festina cycling team, which exposed many of the failings of the old drug-testing system. (The team was found to have doped their riders with everything from anabolic steroids to the red-blood-cell-boosting endurance drug erythropoietin, or EPO.) Up until then each of the various sports organizations had run its own anti-doping operation, which made it easier for athletes to cheat the system. The IOC created the WADA as an independent body that would establish a universal list of prohibited substances. The WADA does no testing of its own but comprises a global chain of accredited laboratories that do so. The UCLA Olympic Analytical Laboratory is currently one of 35 laboratories that conduct tests for the WADA. The USADA, by contrast, sends its own officers to collect urine samples and request tests from labs. Athletes who test positive for performance-enhancing drugs are then charged and punished by the agency. Catlin, for his part, has maintained that what he calls the cop-and-robber approach to drug testing is ultimately futile. "People are following this old model—run 'em down, chase 'em, find 'em, assume they are guilty, drag them into testing," he explained to Brian Alexander for *Outside* magazine (July 2005, online). "And athletes still get away with stuff, and I maintain you can get away with stuff with everybody looking *right* at you." He added, "The system has failed to deal with the problem. And it will fail now."

Despite his skepticism, Catlin continued to lead the charge against drug misuse in sports and developed a number of new tests. In 2000 the scientists in his lab learned to distinguish between natural testosterone and that produced by a drug made from yams. Then, prior to the 2002 Winter Olympics, in Salt Lake City, Utah, Catlin used the French EPO test (developed by the scientist Françoise Lasne) to detect darbepoetin, a variety of EPO that increases endurance. That test helped expose three cross-country skiers who used darbepoetin while competing in the Games, including the gold medalists Johann Muehlegg of Spain and Larissa Lazutina of Russia. Later that year, after analyzing data from an athlete's urine sample, Catlin cracked the code for norbolethone, the first reported "designer" steroid, or synthetic steroid created to enable its users to evade existing drug laws. (The drug, aimed at increasing weight, was first synthe-

sized by the pharmaceutical company Wyeth in 1966 but was never marketed, out of fear of harmful side effects.) Catlin explained to Steeg that his lab's discovery "proved beyond a shadow of a doubt that our suspicions were true, that there were designer steroids out there that we couldn't find and that people were getting a hold of them." In the same year the U.S. track cyclist Tammy Thomas was found to have used norbolethone and was banned for life from competing in the sport.

In 2003 Catlin cracked the code for another designer steroid. The circumstances of the discovery brought to mind "a B-movie mystery plot," as Brian Alexander noted. In June of that year, a syringe was mailed anonymously to the USADA. (The source was later revealed to be Trevor Graham, a former track-and-field coach who received a lifetime ban from his sport in 2008 for supplying many athletes with performance-enhancing drugs.) The USADA sent some of the syringe's contents to Catlin, who with his team of about 40 researchers concluded that the substance was a previously undetectable, custom-made steroid, which they called tetrahydrogestrinone, or THG. Catlin then developed a special test for the drug. He noted to Steeg, "It was a wonderful time for us because it was a kind of project that took all the skills that are represented in this lab, in terms of PhDs, chemists . . . it took everybody."

Through his research Catlin was able to advise Jeff Novitzky, an agent of the Internal Revenue Service (IRS), who opened the BALCO case, leading to perhaps the biggest doping investigation in the history of sports. Headquartered in Burlingame, California, BALCO provided blood and urine analysis and food supplements for professional athletes. An investigation revealed that BALCO's owner and founder, Victor Conte, was working with a network of rogue chemists and steroid dealers to supply professional athletes with performance-enhancing drugs. Catlin, who had long suspected that bodybuilders and other athletes were being supplied with undetectable steroids from clandestine labs around the country, helped expose BALCO by testing more than 550 existing urine samples from athletes, 20 of which contained traces of THG. He was the first witness to testify before the grand jury in the BALCO case. Among the athletes named in connection with the BALCO case were the baseball players Barry Bonds, Jason Giambi, Gary Sheffield, Benito Santiago, and Jeremy Giambi; the football players Bill Romanowski, Tyrone Wheatley, Barrett Robbins, Chris Cooper, and Dana Stubblefield; the boxer Shane Mosley; and the sprinters Dwain Chambers, Marion Jones, Tim Montgomery, Raymond J. Smith, and Kelli White and many other track-and-field stars, including the shot putters Kevin Toth and C.J. Hunter. The scandal foreshadowed the findings of the Mitchell Report, the result of former U.S. senator George J. Mitchell's 21-month investigation into the use of anabolic steroids and human-growth hormone in Major League Baseball (MLB). The report, released on December

13, 2007, named 85 MLB players who were alleged to have used steroids or other banned drugs, including such superstars as Roger Clemens, Andy Pettitte, Miguel Tejada, and Eric Gagne. A number of other athletes have since come forth about their steroid use, most notably the baseball players Alex Rodriguez and Mark McGwire.

In 2004 Catlin cracked the code for madol (commonly known as DMT), the third reported designer anabolic steroid; in January 2010 the drug became a controlled substance, meaning that U.S. federal law governs its manufacture, distribution, and use. In 2005 Catlin became the founder, president, and CEO of Anti-Doping Research Inc., a nonprofit research organization focused on performance-enhancing drugs. The organization has led efforts to uncover new drugs being used illegally by athletes and worked toward developing new tests to detect them. In 2007 Catlin stepped down from his directorship at the UCLA Olympic Analytical Laboratory to work exclusively with Anti-Doping Research. Over the last several years, the organization has attempted to produce an effective urine test for hGH, a hormone that has been used in the past primarily to treat abnormally short children. Many believe that the use of human-growth hormone is still common among professional athletes, making a successful hGH test highly sought-after by sports leagues worldwide. In the meantime Catlin and his researchers have been successful in developing tests for other drugs. Most recently, in late 2009, he and his team developed an equine test for the potent blood-boosting drug CERA (sold under the brand name Mircera), a long-acting form of EPO.

Catlin's organization has also worked to set up programs that will dissuade athletes at all levels from using performance-enhancing drugs. Catlin has long advocated the establishment of a volunteer program, through which athletes would submit to tests to create a set of "biomarkers" for each participant, showing what is normal and abnormal (regarding levels of testosterone or insulin, for example). The participants would have ongoing checkups to ensure that no banned drugs are in their systems and would be recognized as honest athletes. While the idea has been called far-fetched because it would rely on voluntary actions, Catlin believes that social pressure would ultimately lead most athletes to volunteer. He told T. J. Quinn, "We're fundamentally optimists; we have to be in this field. We're not proposing that there's a solution, we're proposing that it needs to be tried."

Brian Alexander described Catlin as tall and balding with "a handsomely craggy face." Catlin is professor emeritus of molecular and medical pharmacology at the UCLA David Geffen School of Medicine. He serves as chairman of the Equine Drug Research Institute's Scientific Advisory Committee and is a member of the Federation Equestre Internationale Commission on Equine Anti-Doping & Medication. In addition, he is a member of the International Olympic Committee Medical Commission. Catlin's wife, Bernadette, a nurse

whom he met at UCLA, died of melanoma in 1989. He has two sons from that marriage: Bryce, a software engineer in San Francisco, California, and Oliver, who is vice president of Anti-Doping Research. According to Steeg, Catlin has gotten hate mail from athletes caught using drugs, and on one occasion his car was firebombed. Catlin has remained undeterred, however. Oliver Catlin told Steeg that since he started working with his father, he has become "fully aware of how dedicated he is to his field. He doesn't stop thinking about this stuff. He eats, drinks, and sleeps this stuff. It's his life. It's his cause. It makes him tick."

—C.C.

Suggested Reading: *Boston Globe* C p1 July 16, 2006; *Christian Science Monitor* p25 Aug. 5, 2008; *Cycling Weekly* (on-line) Nov. 6, 2008; *Los Angeles Times* D p1+ Nov. 6, 2003, D p1 Nov. 11, 2008; *New Scientist* p44+ Aug. 11, 2007; (New York) *Daily News* p62+ June 11, 2006; *Outside* (on-line) July 2005; *San Francisco Chronicle* A p1+ Oct. 26, 2003, B p3 Apr. 2, 2008; *Time* p60 Mar. 1, 2004; *USA Today* C p9 Feb. 28, 2007; *Washington Post* D p1+ Mar. 8, 2003, E p1 Oct. 18, 2005; Fainaru-Wada, Mark, and Lance Williams. *Game of Shadows*, 2006

Chang, David

Aug. 5, 1977– Chef; restaurateur; writer

Address: Momofuku Offices, 853 Broadway, New York, NY 10003

"David Chang is a terrific cook, a pork-loving, pickle-happy individualist whose integration of Asian flavors and his own unbound sense of what's delectable makes for some deliriously enjoyable meals . . . ," the restaurant critic Frank Bruni wrote for the *New York Times* (February 21, 2007). "He has proven himself one of this city's brightest culinary talents." Similarly, Rob Patronite and Robin Raisfeld, writing for *New York* magazine (January 15, 2007), called Chang "something of a culinary rebel." "In a town overflowing with precious temples of gastronomy and $2.50 falafel shacks," they wrote, "he has defiantly carved out a tasty, idiosyncratic middle ground with inventive new riffs on traditional Asian flavors. His food is more than cheap and delicious—it is the unique synthesis of his highbrow training with his lowbrow appetites." Bruni, Patronite, and Raisfeld wrote those words after dining at the Momofuku Noodle Bar and the Momofuku Ssäm Bar, which Chang opened in New York City in 2004 and 2006, respectively. Chang has since added four more establishments to the chain—Momofuku Ko, two Momofuku Milk Bars, and Má Pêche, all in New York. ("Momofuku" means "lucky peach" in Japa-

Courtesy of Gabriele Stabile

David Chang

nese; "má pêche" means "mother peach" in *tay boi*, a Vietnamese-French slang spoken in Vietnam.) In only six years Chang has gained a remarkable reputation: Katy McLaughlin, writing for the *Wall Street Journal* (October 23, 2009, on-line), called him "the anointed star of the current dining scene" and "the young gun that other chefs world-wide are watching and copying." He has also accumulated an extraordinary number of the culinary world's highest honors, among them three awards from the James Beard Foundation—the "Oscars of the food world," as *Time* magazine put it—which named him rising star chef of the year in 2007 and best chef in New York in 2008 and named Momofuku Ko the best new restaurant in 2009.

As a teenager Chang, a second-generation Korean-American, worked in the restaurants his father owned, but, at his father's insistence, he never cooked. He gained his knowledge of food preparation at the French Culinary Institute, in New York City, and to a much greater extent, he has said, in the kitchens of a series of restaurants in New York and Japan in which he worked after he completed the institute's six-month program. In a conversation with the food writer Alan Richman for *GQ* (December 2007), Chang described his signature Momofuku ramen, Momofuku pork buns, and other dishes as "American food." Other culinary experts, though, have viewed them somewhat differently, since the cuisines not only of Korea and Japan but also of the southern U.S., Vietnam, and France have influenced his recipes. For example, according to *Esquire* (October 2008), whose editors included Chang on their list of the "most influential persons of the 21st century," he "transforms known flavors . . . into a new kind of American

comfort cuisine that somehow seems strange and familiar at the same time. His food exploits our reference points and creates new ones. It repackages flavors we already understand and gives us a new understanding of their possibilities. And it is satisfying in ways that are unprecedented." Chang has also earned praise for championing the use of fresh produce and other items for sale at farmers' markets. "Dave's importance is that he serves delicious, really well-executed food at a great price . . . ," the chef Wylie Dufresne, the owner of the New York City restaurant wd'50, told Helin Jung for IAmKoreAm.com (June 1, 2009). "A lot of people espouse locally-sourced American ingredients, but Dave is doing it in an unpretentious and approachable way. He doesn't hit you over the head with it, which makes the whole idea more attractive."

Chang is the co-author, with the food writer Peter Meehan, of *Momofuku* (2009), a cookbook cum memoir that also offers glimpses of Chang's philosophy as a chef, entrepreneur, and employer. Katy McLaughlin paraphrased Chang as saying that in writing the book, he made "a conscious attempt to capture the brutal, gritty and exhilarating tone of the restaurant kitchen." The "cooking world," he told her, is "hard, hot and grueling." McLaughlin described Chang's approach in the recipes as that of an encouraging coach. In judging any dish, according to Chang, the main criterion is whether it tastes delicious. In 2010 the James Beard Foundation nominated *Momofuku* (2009) for one of its book awards, in the category "cooking from a professional point of view."

The youngest of the four children of Joe and Sherri Chang, David Chang was born on August 5, 1977 in Arlington, Virginia. His mother immigrated to the U.S. from South Korea, his father from North Korea. Joe Chang arrived in the U.S. in 1963 with only $50 to his name; he worked as a dishwasher in New York City restaurants for years, then became a successful businessman, as the owner of a couple of restaurants in the Washington, D.C., area and, later, a golf-equipment company. Because of his heavy workload, he was rarely at home. Chang has described his mother (who has always spoken Korean with him) and maternal grandmother as excellent cooks; his grandfather, who is fluent in Japanese, introduced him to the pleasures of Japanese cuisine. Chang grew up in an upscale suburb in the D.C. metropolitan area. He started playing golf at an early age. "My early childhood was strange . . . ," he told an interviewer for Bigthink.com (January 25, 2008). Other than going to school, "all I did literally every day, 365 days a year was play golf." When he was 10 years old, Chang won two Virginia state championships in his age group. In his early teens, though, he "flamed out," he told Richman, remarking that "in golf you're never good enough." Meanwhile, he developed a strong desire to cook in a restaurant. "I was fascinated by it. There's no real food memories or anything like that that drew me to it," he told the

Bigthink.com interviewer. His father, however, after decades as a restaurant worker and restaurateur, wanted his children to work in other fields and tried (in vain) to squelch David's interest in cooking by having him wait tables and perform menial jobs in the restaurants he owned.

Chang attended a private high school, where he became a star football player. In about 1995 he entered Trinity College, in Hartford, Connecticut. During his freshman year, he told Richman, "I had a 1.9 grade point average. . . . I smoked pot every day. I was drinking. I was going out every night. I was a total waste." Nevertheless, he graduated after seven semesters. He spent one of them studying in London, England, where Alan Yau's Wagamama noodle bars reignited his dream of a culinary career. While overseas he applied, without success, for admission to Le Cordon Bleu, a famous cooking school in Paris, France. After he earned his bachelor's degree from Trinity, in religious studies, in January 1999, he taught English in Japan for two months, then worked briefly in the U.S. for a financial firm.

That same year Chang completed the six-month, 600-hour course offered by the French Culinary Institute in New York City, which accepts only two dozen students per day or evening session. He told Stewart Oksenhorn for the *Aspen (Colorado) Times* (June 16, 2006) that the institute's teachers "hated" him but that he learned a lot. He quickly found work, first at Jean-Georges Vongerichten's Mercer Kitchen and then at Tom Colicchio's Craft, both highly acclaimed New York restaurants. Craft, he told an *Art Culinaire* (December 22, 2006) interviewer, "was the only place I wanted to be"; to get his foot in the door, he accepted a job answering the telephone. After a month he began working in Craft's kitchen full-time. "I felt like I'd hit the lottery," he told the *Art Culinaire* writer. He remarked to Oksenhorn, "A lot of students want to take the shortcut route to being a top chef, a celebrity chef. I'm not a fan of the short-term, super-expensive cooking course. It's not like you go to, say, journalism school and call yourself a journalist. . . . I think it's better to work in kitchens."

After about two years at Craft, Chang returned to Japan with the goal of deepening and broadening his knowledge of Japanese cuisine. He worked at Sobaya Fuyu-rin, a noodle shop, and for shorter times at an *izakaya* and at the *kaiseki* restaurant at the Park Hyatt Tokyo, an extremely fancy hotel. (An *izakaya* is a Japanese-style bar that serves food; a *kaiseki* restaurant serves traditional, multi-course Japanese meals.) He also frequented other types of eateries. "Japan changed the way I think about food," he told Rob Patronite and Robin Raisfeld. "It's a food culture. And food didn't have to be great on just a fine-dining level. You could eat really well. Even fast-food chains were awesome." Back in New York eight months later, he tried without success to get a job at the popular Tex-Mex fast-food chain Chipotle, as a way to learn the ins and outs of that chain, which is known for good

food at affordable prices. Soon afterward he landed work as a line cook in "a kitchen full of ninjas," as he put it to Oksenhorn, at Café Boulud, under the much-praised chef Andrew Carmellini. He left Café Boulud after less than a year, to help take care of his mother, who had become ill, and also because, as he explained to Oksenhorn, "I didn't like cooking that food anymore. I liked the atmosphere—it's raw, intense, busy. But there's too many fine-dining restaurants, and everyone's doing the same thing. And they [the other line cooks] were all better than me. None of my friends came in there. I was thinking, what does the future hold for me? The chance of getting my own kitchen [in such a restaurant] was slim to none. For me, fine dining was dead."

Chang resolved to open a moderately priced, cafeteria-style noodle bar. "People told me I was crazy, that I didn't know enough," he recalled to the *Art Culinaire* interviewer. Friends of his who promised to help finance his venture later backed out, saying that he was bound to fail. His father lent him about $130,000 of the $250,000 he needed, and through an ad that he posted on Monster.com, he found a partner—Joaquin Baca, an aspiring chef. (The two co-owned the Momofuku chain, with Chang as the main recipe creator, until 2008, when Baca left to start a restaurant of his own.) In August 2004, after Chang apprenticed at a noodle shop called Rai Rai Ken for a week, he and Baca opened the 650-square-foot, 27-seat Momofuku Noodle Bar, with no employees but themselves. "We didn't have servers," Chang told the *Art Culinaire* writer. "We had to learn how to run the cash register. We didn't have a bookkeeper, a manager, nothing. We didn't have a dishwasher. We bought enough plateware that we could just stack it up and wash it all at the end of the night. We were pretty naïve to think that we could do it all on our own for very long."

During the noodle bar's difficult early days, when customers were few, Chang and Baca concocted new recipes, thinking that if they were destined to fail, they might as well enjoy themselves until then. Through word of mouth—and "good decision making, luck, perseverance or most likely a combination of all three," Mark Bittman wrote for the *New York Times* (April 5, 2006)—Momofuku's clientele grew. Over the next six months, Chang hired three more cooks, expanded and diversified the menu (which now offers more than two-dozen items, including seasonal dishes), and began using fresh fruits, vegetables, pork, and other products from Greenmarket farmers' markets. "I love that we use crazy small farmers. I'll do anything I can to promote pork guys in Kansas. We found Allan Benton, who does smoked country hams in Madisonville, Tennessee," Chang noted to an interviewer for *Food & Wine* (on-line). He told Oksenhorn, "From day one, the goal was to serve great food at an affordable price. I couldn't cook better than my peers in a fine-dining room. But I could do better than the neighborhood restaurant"—a reference to a nearby Japanese dining place—"which doesn't necessarily use the best ingredients. I just try to get the better ingredients. At the end of the day, it's how good your ingredients are." Chang has also attributed Momofuku's survival to the strong support of his friends. In one instance, when the worker who handled the dishwashing failed to arrive, his friends from Café Boulud helped him wash the dishes. Peter Meehan sampled the menu of the noodle bar soon after it opened and again eight months later; after the latter visit he wrote for the New York Times (April 13, 2005) that Chang had "taken Momofuku from a neighborhoody near-ramen shop to a plywood-walled diamond in the rough."

Two of Momofuku's best-known dishes are its ramen and pork buns. (Ramen is wheat noodles—made by Chang's supplier to his specifications—served in a broth made with roasted pork bones, shiitake mushrooms, and bacon, to which are added a poached egg, bamboo shoots, scallions, peas, and braised pork. Pork buns are steamed buns stuffed with pork belly, an Asian flavoring sauce called hoisin, and pieces of scallions and cucumbers.) On the blog communaltable.com (May 23, 2007), Adrian Hale described Momofuku's ramen as "transcendent" and concluded, "David Chang has a way of downing a huge helping of authenticity, slurping it around in his imagination, and dishing it back up with feisty charm." Patronite and Raisfeld expressed similar enthusiasm: "No one expects to linger over ramen: The proper etiquette, of course, is to bend the noggin troughlike over the bowl and in an ecstasy of feverish slurping shovel it in at a rate that should qualify you for a seat at the Nathan's Fourth of July hot-dog-eating contest. But the young crew at Momofuku . . . creates its own dynamic atmosphere, navigating the open kitchen with a balletic grace that becomes hypnotic, shimmying by each other to drain noodles out of simmering vats, carefully composing soups as tantalizing still lifes almost too beautiful to touch." Writing for the New Yorker (May 22, 2006), Lauren Collins described Momofuku as "the best place in town to end up after a long day's schlep."

In early 2006, using two new lines of credit and Momofuku Noodle Bar as collateral for a $1 million loan, Chang signed a $10,000-a-month long-term lease for a second space, a few blocks from the noodle bar and twice as large, with room for 55 diners. During its first year the Momofuku Ssäm Bar, as he named it, specialized in Asian-style burritos, or ssam—the Korean word for "wrap" or "wrapped food." Chang's ssam was a flour-based wrap stuffed with pork, rice, pickled shiitake mushrooms, roasted onions, edamame (young green soybeans), and kimchi puree. (Kimchi, also spelled "kimchee" or "gimchee," is the Korean national dish; along with rice, it is eaten at virtually every meal. There are thousands of recipes for kimchi, a mixture of Napa cabbage and/or Korean radishes, salt, sugar, garlic, ginger, Korean red pepper ground up or in threads, green onions,

and, often, Korean fish sauce or bits of shrimp. It is usually fermented for several days; according to Mark Bittman, Chang's method of making kimchi "produces a super-flavorful result that has the distinct advantage of being delicious the instant it is done.") Momofuku Ssäm Bar opened in August 2006, with a party whose attendees included Martha Stewart, Michael and Ariane Batterberry, the founders of Food Arts and Food & Wine magazines, and the food writer Ruth Reichl. Like its predecessor, it experienced a slow start; during its first several weeks, it sold barely 100 ssams a day. Business soon picked up, however, and at patrons' requests, Chang added more choices, including customized ssams, fish-sauce-dressed fried cauliflower with chili peppers and mint, and bo ssam. (That dish is a large roasted chunk of fatty pork butt, made to be eaten by at least eight people using tongs to pull off pieces of the meat, which is then wrapped in lettuce leaves along with rice, kimchi, salted shrimp, and pickled chilis, among other ingredients.) Business further increased with expanded hours.

Six months after it opened, Frank Bruni wrote for the New York Times (February 21, 2007) that Momofuku Ssäm Bar had "emerged as much, much more than the precocious fast-food restaurant it initially was. By bringing sophisticated, inventive cooking and a few high-end grace notes to a setting that discourages even the slightest sense of ceremony, Ssäm Bar answers the desires of a generation of savvy, adventurous diners with little appetite for starchy rituals and stratospheric prices." Bruni, declaring that Chang had a "wicked grasp of flavor and unerring sense of balance," recommended dishes including the grilled rice cakes, "which are slathered with a sauce of pork sausage and kimchi and taste like gnocchi with a Korean passport," and raw-seafood compositions, among them scallops with pineapple and sea urchin with whipped tofu, and he praised the young waiters, who, he wrote, exhibited "more knowledge and palpable enthusiasm about the menu than many of their counterparts at more conventionally polished establishments." Adam Platt wrote for New York (April 2, 2007) that like the American chef Mario Batali and the British chef Fergus Henderson, Chang has "a knack for creating big, addictive flavor combinations that get under your skin." Momofuku Ssäm Bar was named the best new restaurant at the James Beard Awards ceremony in 2007.

Momofuku Ko (or simply Ko, as it is better known, "ko" meaning "child of" in Japanese) opened in March 2008 at the site of Chang's noodle bar. (The noodle bar moved to another location.) Ko was Chang's "first attempt at ambitious, haute cuisine cooking," Adam Platt wrote for New York (April 21, 2008, on-line). To eat at Ko, which seats only 12, diners must make reservations (for at most four people) on-line, with seating on a first-come, first-served basis. The on-line calendar shows a full week's worth of reservations for dinner and two weeks' worth for lunch, beginning on the current day. The Web site opens at 10:00 a.m., and generally, Brendan Spiegel wrote for Wired.com (July 2, 2008), reservations are filled within seconds; for that reason, he reported, the attempt to get a reservation immediately became "a frenzied morning ritual for thousands of obsessive fans," many of whom recruited others to try in their stead. Both lunch and dinner are multi-course meals; patrons get a similar series of eight to 10 dishes at each meal (nothing can be ordered à la carte) and are advised to allow three hours for lunch and two for dinner. In late June 2010 lunch, served on Fridays, Saturdays, and Sundays, cost $175; dinner, served every day, cost $125. The menu varies according to the availability of fresh ingredients and the whims of the chefs, who cook in front of the diners and also serve. One frequently mentioned dish is a chunk of short rib, braised for two days in a marinade devised by Chang's mother (soy sauce, sugar, and a sweet Japanese rice wine called mirin) and then deep-fried. "Dish after dish dazzles with class, innovation and balance . . . ," Randall Lane wrote for *Time Out New York* (May 22–28, 2008, on-line). "I witnessed the hyperactively perfectionist Chang chastise one chef for how she wrung out a washcloth. It's great theater, and the show will constantly change: Ko promises to continually alter the menu, one dish at a time, with nothing sacred and anything game. I came in doubting Chang could match the hype—I left plotting how I can win the Ko lottery again." Ko earned two stars in the 2009 Michelin guide, indicating that Michelin's judges found that the restaurant offered "excellent cooking" and was "worth a detour."

The first Momofuku Milk Bar, which opened in the East Village in early 2009, was, "as with all things Momofuku-related . . . greeted with an apostolic fervor," Ligaya Mishan wrote for the *New York Times* (April 8, 2009). Overseen by Christina Tosi, a pastry chef, the menu includes baked goods (breads, pies, cakes, cookies), soft ice creams with toppings, pork buns, shakes, coffee, and so-called cereal milk. A trademarked Momofuku specialty, cereal milk is derived from toasted corn flakes that are soaked in milk; the mixture is then strained to produce the cereal milk (to which a pinch of sugar and salt is added). In mid-June 2010 the milk bar offered several flavors of soft ice cream, among them cantaloupe honey, peach tea, and raspberry lemonade; "compost" cookies, made with pretzels, potato chips, coffee, oats, butterscotch, and chocolate chips; candy-bar pie—chocolate crust, caramel, peanut-butter nougat, and pretzels; grasshopper pie—graham crust with a filling of mint cheesecake and brownie; kimchi and blue-cheese croissants; and apple and cheddar cornbread. Chang's second milk bar is in Midtown Manhattan.

The latest addition to the Momofuku chain is Má Pêche, which opened in November 2009 in the Chambers Hotel, in Midtown Manhattan. Its co-owner and executive chef is Tien Ho, a native of Vietnam. According to its Web site, the menu has "a French-Vietnamese focus" and changes regularly. One of its specialties is "beef seven ways," a "Vietnamese celebratory feast, comprised of seven different courses of beef."

"I finally understand what it's like to be an A+ student, when in the past, I only understood from having known or dated girls that were always the best," Chang told Helin Jung. "I never understood the pressure of success. How does one cope with that?" According to Alan Richman, Chang is "a humanitarian, post-hippie, blasphemous idealist" who resembles "a burly, slightly overweight judo competitor"; Jung described him as "passionate and funny and blunt." Chang rejects all forms of snobbism and elitism and, as a restaurateur, rarely extends special favors to celebrities or people of influence. He provides health insurance for his workers, pays them well, and encourages their creativity in the kitchen. By all accounts he has not only made many new friends in recent years but has retained all his old ones.

Chang lives alone in the Chelsea section of Manhattan. He told Cara Buckley for the *New York Times* (July 12, 2009) that he keeps nothing in his refrigerator, never uses his stove, and on Sundays, likes to stay home and do nothing.

—C.C.

Suggested Reading: *Art Culinaire* p24+ Dec. 22, 2006; *Aspen (Colorado) Times* (on-line) June 16, 2006; *GQ* (on-line) Dec. 2007; IAmKoreAm.com June 1, 2009; *New York* p180+ Oct. 6, 2008, (on-line) May 21, 2005, Jan. 15, 2007, Apr. 2, 2007; *New York Press* (on-line) July 12, 2006, Sep. 13, 2006; *New York Times* (on-line) Feb. 21, 2007; *New Yorker* May 22, 2006

Selected Books: *Momofuku* (with Peter Meehan), 2009

Cheney, Liz

(CHAY-nee)

July 28, 1966– Lawyer; political activist; organization official

Address: Keep America Safe, 1718 M St., N.W., #351, Washington, DC 20036

Within the Republican Party and elsewhere, Elizabeth "Liz" Cheney is considered one of the GOP's most influential up-and-comers. A daughter of Dick Cheney, the vice president in the George W. Bush White House, she has moved in political circles since her early years, and she has had a long and varied career as an attorney and federal-government official. In the public sector she has worked for the United States Agency for International Development; the Bureau of Near Eastern Affairs, an arm of the U.S. State Department; and a division of the quasi-governmental World Bank

Courtesy of David Bohrer

Liz Cheney

Group. Cheney, whose father served five terms in the U.S. House of Representatives (1979–89) as well as two terms in the White House (2001–09), has also held important positions in GOP election campaigns, among them the Bush/Cheney campaigns of 2000 and 2004 and the unsuccessful presidential runs of former U.S. senator Fred Thompson of Tennessee and former governor Mitt Romney of Massachusetts.

Two weeks after Barack Obama's inauguration as president, in January 2009, Cheney appeared on television by her father's side as he argued that the new administration's foreign policy would place the nation in grave danger of another terrorist attack. Since then Liz Cheney has made dozens of other appearances on television, primarily on cable news shows, defending her father's record as vice president and speaking in support of neoconservative positions while criticizing President Obama and his administration. Since 2009 she has done so as the co-founder and chair of Keep America Safe, a neoconservative advocacy group that focuses on what its members deem the failures and dangers of Obama's policies and actions. In an address at the Southern Republican Leadership Conference held in April 2010 in New Orleans, Louisiana, Cheney accused the Obama administration of "arrogance and incompetence" and of "putting [the U.S.] on the path to decline," as quoted by David Weigel in the *Washington Post* (April 8, 2010, online). She also said, according to Weigel, "When it comes to foreign policy, it looks increasingly like there are three pillars to the 'Obama Doctrine'—(1) Apologize for America, (2) Abandon our allies, and (3) Appease our enemies."

Liz Cheney is known for her outspokenness and combativeness and for standing her ground in conversations, or confrontations, with those who oppose her views. "She doesn't back away from unpopular positions . . . ," Joe Scarborough, a former Republican congressman and currently the co-host of MSNBC's *Morning Joe*, told Matthew Duss for the *Nation* (March 18, 2010). "She gives absolutely no quarter." Cheney has said that she agrees with her father on every political issue, and by all accounts there is no record of her publicly offering an opinion or version of historical events that differs with his in any substantive way. Barton Gellman, who expanded his Pulitzer Prize–winning series of *Washington Post* articles about the Bush–Cheney White House for his book *Angler: The Cheney Vice Presidency* (2008), told Duss, "From everything I can tell," Liz Cheney is "a little bit to the right of her father." Cheney is currently helping her father write a memoir, and commentators on the left of the political spectrum view her recent activities as attempts to secure a respected place for him in history and possibly to position herself for a campaign for public office.

Elizabeth L. Cheney was born on July 28, 1966 in McLean, Virginia. She is the first of the two daughters of Richard "Dick" Cheney and Lynne (Vincent) Cheney. The couple's second child, Mary, was born in 1969. The Cheneys maintained homes in McLean, an affluent suburb of Washington, D.C., and Casper, Wyoming, where Dick and Lynne Cheney grew up. Liz and Mary were exposed to politics as children, accompanying their father during his successful campaign for Wyoming's sole seat in the U.S. House of Representatives in 1978.

Cheney was captain of the cheerleading team at McLean High School. After her graduation, in 1984, she entered her mother's alma mater, Colorado College, a private liberal-arts school in Colorado Springs. Cheney's conservative views were uncommon among her peers there, but she retained her convictions. "Liz was very engaged, espousing her worldview and what was best for America, even in a context where most listeners wouldn't have shared her worldview," a Cheney family friend, D. J. Gribbin, told Joe Hagan for *New York* (March 15, 2010). In her senior thesis, "The Evolution of Presidential War Powers," Cheney argued that presidents' powers during times of war should be virtually unchecked, so as to keep the country safe at all costs. She received a B.A. degree in political science in 1988.

The following year, after President George H. W. Bush appointed her father secretary of defense, Cheney got a job with the United States Agency for International Development (USAID), the federal agency responsible for providing economic, agricultural, health-related, and humanitarian assistance to developing nations. She worked first for USAID's Asia and Middle East bureau; later, she was stationed in the American embassies in Warsaw, Poland, and Budapest, Hungary, handling aspects of assistance for those former Communist states. For a while her supervisor was Richard Armitage, who, as a so-called ambassador for Europe, oversaw distribution of aid to nations in the former Soviet bloc. Armitage told Joe Hagan that Dick Cheney asked him to keep close tabs on his daughter, saying, "You know, she's got a will of her own, [but] she does have my name, so I'd appreciate it if you'd vet where she's going." In 1993 Armitage left government service, and Liz Cheney joined his Arlington, Virginia–based international consulting firm, Armitage Associates, which specialized in business matters.

That same year the newly married Cheney moved to Chicago, Illinois, to attend the University of Chicago Law School. (Barack Obama taught constitutional law there at that time, but the two never crossed paths.) In addition to courses in law, Cheney took classes in Middle Eastern history at the University of Chicago's Oriental Institute. She received a J.D. degree in 1996. Upon graduation she joined the international law firm White & Case LLP in Washington, D.C. In 1999 she went to work for the International Financial Corp. (IFC), the private-sector lending arm of the World Bank Group, which provides financial services to businesses investing in developing nations. In that job Cheney focused on investments in the Middle East and central Asia.

Cheney went on maternity leave in early 2000, when her third child was born. She then extended her leave to work as an unpaid volunteer for the presidential campaign of Republican governor George W. Bush of Texas, who selected Dick Cheney as his vice-presidential running mate in the race against the Democratic presidential nominee, Al Gore. During the campaign Liz Cheney managed debate preparation for her father, which entailed coordinating research and compiling briefing books. After a close and heavily disputed election, the Supreme Court declared Bush the winner. He and Dick Cheney took office on January 20, 2001, and Liz Cheney returned to her job at the IFC.

Cheney had been back with the IFC for only a few months when, in March 2002, she was appointed to a State Department job, as a deputy assistant secretary of state in the Bureau of Near Eastern Affairs. Critics argued that Cheney's post had been created specifically to accommodate the vice president's daughter, but Secretary of State Colin Powell stated that the position had been left vacant and that he had appointed her based on her high level of competency. According to friends of hers, she had been reluctant to accept the job. Margaret D. Tutwiler, a former U.S. ambassador to Morocco who has known her for years, told Elisabeth Bumiller for the New York Times (June 16, 2003), "She was concerned: how could she be treated normally? Her father is not just the sitting vice president, but an extremely influential one." In her new position Cheney designed and launched the Middle East Partnership Initiative, a $393 million program that seeks to "expand political participation, strengthen civil society and the rule of law, empower women and youth, create educational opportunities, and foster economic reform throughout the Middle East and North Africa," according to the initiative's Web site. She echoed ideas voiced by her father, including, for instance, the belief that democratizing Iraq would be the key to winning the "war on terror." "The impact of a free Iraq is something that will have repercussions across the rest of the Middle East," she told Susan Baer for the Baltimore Sun (April 1, 2004). Referring to the U.S. invasion of Iraq under the Bush administration, in 2003, she said, "There's no question but that liberating Iraq was absolutely the right thing to do and that they [the Bush administration] would do it again if faced with the same decision today." (The invasion was launched for the stated purpose of ridding Iraq of so-called weapons of mass destruction; no such weapons were found there.)

Some of Cheney's former colleagues have spoken fondly of her. One of them, Catherine A. Novelli, a former assistant U.S. trade representative for Europe and the Mediterranean, told Bumiller, "She is completely a team player. She is somebody who wants to be recognized on her own merits." Others recalled that they felt uncomfortable working alongside the daughter of the vice president. "It was very awkward, and people had to be careful in front of her," a former official told Michael Isikoff and Michael Hirsh for Newsweek (March 22, 2010). "How do you conduct a viable meeting if you think one of the people is going to turn around and tell all to the vice president?"

Cheney left the State Department in 2003 to work on the Bush–Cheney reelection campaign. Starting in May 2004 she helped lead the campaign's "W Stands for Women" initiative, aimed at persuading women to vote for Republicans. Cheney took issue with the Democratic candidates for president and vice president, U.S. senators John Kerry and John Edwards, respectively, for their speaking publicly about her sister's homosexuality. During one televised vice-presidential debate, Edwards said that he respected the Cheney family for acknowledging and accepting their daughter's lifestyle. Later, Kerry, in a televised presidential debate with Bush, responded to a question about whether he considered homosexuality to be a choice by saying, "I think if you were to talk to Dick Cheney's daughter, who is a lesbian, she would tell you that she's being who she was." Liz Cheney, echoing the sentiments of her parents, told Steven K. Paulson, an Associated Press (October 19, 2004) reporter, that she was "surprised" that Kerry had mentioned her sister's sexual orientation. "I think it is unprecedented for a candidate for the presidency to sort of exploit the child of one of his opponents for political gain . . . ," she asserted. "I thought that was out of bounds, and I think what you have seen as a result of that is a lot of folks across the country really wondering what sort of a person would do that."

Andrew Sullivan, a gay journalist who has described himself as a libertarian conservative, criticized the Cheney family's reaction, noting to Hank Stuever for the *Washington Post* (October 19, 2004) that nobody in that family had responded to remarks by the Republican senatorial candidate Alan Keyes, who, Sullivan said, had aimed a "direct insult" at Mary Cheney. (Keyes had accused her of "selfish hedonism.") "But they are outraged that Kerry mentioned the simple fact of their daughter's openly gay identity. What complete b.s. . . . The GOP is run, in part, by gay men and women, its families are full of gay people, and yet it is institutionally opposed to even the most basic protections for gay couples. You can keep up a policy based on rank hypocrisy for only so long. And then it tumbles like a house of cards." (While Dick Cheney expressed his support for gay marriage, as long as it is legalized by individual states, President Bush backed legislation during their time in the White House that would have banned gay marriage.)

Bush and Dick Cheney were reelected in November 2004. Three months later, after turning down offers to become a television commentator, Liz Cheney was appointed principal deputy assistant secretary of state (PDAS, as it is known in the White House) for Near Eastern affairs, making her the second-ranking State Department official responsible for U.S. policy in the Middle East. As PDAS under C. David Walsh, Cheney was largely responsible for the management and administration of the State Department's Bureau of Near Eastern Affairs. Again, several Washington insiders criticized her appointment, but others felt she had earned the position. Edward S. Walker Jr., a predecessor of Walsh's and the president and CEO of the Middle East Institute, a private research group, from 2001 to 2006, told Todd S. Purdum for the *New York Times* (May 31, 2005), "Sometimes [political appointees] are good, and sometimes they are bad. . . . Liz is a little different, obviously, because of the name. But the name doesn't bother anybody I know, simply because she did her job. She could have been a disaster, given her father, given the fact that she knew all the players, she could have run roughshod [over career Foreign Service officers]. But she didn't."

In 2005 Cheney oversaw the launch of two government-financed, semi-independent foundations set up to help increase prosperity and strengthen democracy in the Middle East and North Africa. One, the Fund of the Future, provided capital for small businesses in those regions; the other, the Foundation of the Future, attempted to strengthen freedom of the press and democracy by awarding grants to nongovernmental organizations. "In many ways we're seeing that veil of fear is lifting," Cheney said, according to Steven R. Weisman, writing for the *New York Times* (November 20, 2005). "I think that we're seeing something very real happening across the region in terms of progress toward opening up societies, opening up political systems and economic systems." Others, speaking to Weisman anonymously, criticized the Bush administration's efforts to promote democracy. "The cause has not been helped, they say, by what sounds like preaching from American officials," Weisman wrote.

Cheney also headed the Iran-Syria Policy and Operations Group (ISOG), established within the bureau in 2006. The secrecy that surrounded ISOG, as well as its partial resemblance to the Office of Special Plans, a Pentagon unit that laid the groundwork for the U.S. invasion of Iraq, led ISOG's critics to fear that the group intended to plot covert actions that might lead to a military conflict with Iran or Syria. In May 2007, after it came to light that the ISOG sought to provide military aid to neighbors of Iran and Syria and support groups that opposed the two nations' leaders, the Bush administration disbanded the ISOG.

Cheney left the State Department in May 2006, shortly before the birth of her fifth child. In June 2007 she signed on to work for the 2008 presidential campaign of the Republican candidate Fred Thompson, a former U.S. senator from Tennessee. Later, she was appointed co-chair of his national campaign leadership team. After he dropped out of the race, in January 2008, she became a senior foreign-policy adviser for the presidential campaign of another Republican, former governor Mitt Romney of Massachusetts.

Soon after Barack Obama entered the White House, in January 2009, Cheney began to make increasingly frequent appearances on talk shows as an unofficial spokesperson for the neoconservative wing of the Republican Party. In his profile of her for *New York*, Joe Hagan wrote, "She has been waging a scorched-earth campaign to characterize Obama as 'misguided' and 'dangerous' and defend her father as a man of backbone in a world of wafflers and wimps. Unabashed and stunningly direct, Liz called Obama's Nobel [Peace] Prize a 'farce' and the Democrats' attacks on her father's policies 'incredibly irresponsible' and 'appalling.'" Liz Cheney has repeatedly defended the use of "enhanced interrogation" tactics in the questioning of suspected terrorists during the Bush-Cheney administration, maintaining that such techniques, including waterboarding, are not torture and that President Obama has endangered the U.S. by revealing to the public information about their use after 9/11. "I think taking the step of releasing the legal memos that laid out in great detail exactly what techniques we used in our enhanced interrogation program gave, as my dad said . . . the terrorists a new insert for their training manual," Cheney declared on the ABC news show *Good Morning America* (May 22, 2009). At the same time she called upon the Obama White House to disclose top-secret documents that would purportedly show the effectiveness of waterboarding in persuading captives to disclose information vital to U.S. interests. Cheney has also decried Obama's promise to close the controversial detention center at Guantánamo Bay, Cuba—a plan supported by Colin Powell, a retired four-star U.S. Army general as well as a former secretary of state; General David H. Petraeus, who headed the Central Command and now oversees the U.S. war in Afghanistan; and, among others, the dozen retired generals and admirals who witnessed Obama, on January 22, 2009, as he signed the executive order calling for the center's dismantling. Like Dick Cheney, Liz Cheney has claimed that its closure would make the U.S. unsafe, because some detainees would be released and would immediately resume their terrorist activities.

In October 2009 Cheney co-founded the organization Keep America Safe, along with Bill Kristol, the editor of the conservative publication the *Weekly Standard*, and Debra Burlingame, whose brother, a pilot, was killed in the 9/11 attacks. The Keep America Safe Web site states that its mission is to "provide information for concerned Americans about critical national security issues." In a section called "Recent News," the site posted an opinion column about hunger strikes written by Jay Nordliner for the *National Review* (April 6, 2010); a transcription of a Radio Free Europe piece (October 10, 2009) entitled "Necessary Gesture Or Bad Decision? U.S. Cuts Funds To Iran Rights Group"; and articles from the *New York Times*, the *Washington Post*, and the Associated Press on such subjects as the Chinese and Iranian governments' imprisonment of political protesters. Critics of Keep America Safe include Matthew Duss, who wrote that the group's "main goal seems to be to Keep America Scared S**tless. [Its] website is a clearinghouse for anti-Islamic paranoia; it features numerous scary stories related to terrorism . . . and a daily 'detainee spotlight' bio of the various Guantanamo Bay prisoners President Obama presumably wants to release into your neighborhood."

In March 2010 Keep America Safe aired a television advertisement that overtly questioned the ethics and patriotism of seven U.S. Justice Department lawyers—whose identities had been withheld from the public—who had provided legal representation for Guantánamo Bay detainees. The commercial, which called the Department of Justice the "Department of Jihad," dubbed the lawyers the "Al Qaeda 7" and asked, "Whose values do they share?," while showing an image of the Al Qaeda leader Osama bin Laden. The ad sparked outrage even within the Republican Party; more than 20 politically conservative lawyers signed an open letter denouncing Keep America Safe's suggestion that lawyers who defend unpopular suspects are somehow disloyal to the U.S. They included the former U.S. solicitor general Kenneth Starr and such top officials from the George W. Bush administration as Charles Stimson, who resigned from his job as deputy assistant secretary of defense for detainee affairs in 2007 after criticism arising from his suggestion that corporations should not hire law firms whose staffs included lawyers representing people charged with terrorist activities. "To suggest that the Justice Department should not employ talented lawyers who have advocated on behalf of detainees maligns the patriotism of people who have taken honorable positions on contested questions and demands a uniformity of background and view in government service from which no administration would benefit," the letter declared. Some view the "Al Qaeda 7" ad as an attempt to weaken President Obama's credibility with the American public. "This is really part of a death-by-a-thousand-cuts strategy to wound President Obama politically," Eugene Robinson wrote in his *Washington Post* (March 9, 2010) column. "The charge of softness on terrorism—or terrorist suspects—is absurd; Obama has brought far more resources and focus to the war against Al Qaeda in Afghanistan than the Bush-Cheney administration cared to summon. Since Obama's opponents can't attack him on substance, they resort to atmospherics. They distort. They insinuate. They sully. They blow smoke."

Many political reporters have suggested that Keep America Safe is readying Liz Cheney for a congressional run in Wyoming or Virginia or the Virginia governor's office, a move that Dick Cheney has endorsed publicly. Lawrence B. "Larry" Lindsey, who directed the National Economic Council under President George W. Bush in 2001 and 2002 and who worked alongside Liz Cheney on Fred Thompson's presidential campaign in 2008, told Joe Hagan, "I think she's a better politician than her dad. She's really outgoing, connects with people, very quick with a response, which the vice-president often wasn't."

Described as "personable but tough-minded" by Tamara Lipper and Evan Thomas, writing for *Newsweek* (July 26, 2004), the petite Cheney is a senior fellow at the American Enterprise Institute for Public Policy Research, a conservative think tank with which she has been associated since 1994. In 1993 she married Philip J. Perry, an attorney who served as the general counsel to the U.S. Department of Homeland Security from 2005 to 2007. The couple live near Cheney's parents and her sister's family in McLean. They have three daughters, Kate, Elizabeth, and Grace, and two sons, Philip and Richard, who range in age from four to about 16.

—M.A.S.

Suggested Reading: *Baltimore Sun* E p1 Apr. 1, 2004; *Nation* (on-line) Mar. 18, 2010; *New York* p38+ Mar. 15, 2010; *New York Times* A p16 June 16, 2003, A p15 May 31, 2005; *Newsweek* p32+ Mar. 22, 2010

Andy Lyons/Getty Images

Cink, Stewart

(sink)

May 21, 1973– Golfer

Address: 2195 Lockett Ct., Duluth, GA 30097

Stewart Cink, Stan Awtrey wrote for the *Atlanta Journal-Constitution* (May 14, 2008), is the "Everyman" of the Professional Golfers' Association (PGA) Tour, "with one exception: he's better than almost every man out there." In a sport largely dominated by one name—Tiger Woods—Cink has quietly emerged as one of the top competitors in the world. "I'm usually the guy that the crowd, they appreciate, but they're not behind me 100 percent of the way," Cink told Christopher Clarey for the *New York Times* (July 20, 2009). "You know, they aren't. So you know, that's the sort of role I've been cast into for my whole career. And hey, that's not the worst. It's O.K." Since he turned professional, in 1995, Cink has amassed six victories on the PGA Tour and more than $29 million in career earnings; he has also collected eight top-10 finishes in majors and played several times in golf's two top international competitions, earning spots on five Ryder Cup teams and three Presidents Cup teams. As with most other contemporary golfers not named Woods, however, Cink's stature in his sport was uncertain—until 2009, when he captured his first major title, that year's British Open Championship, defeating the 59-year-old golfing legend Tom Watson in a four-hole play-off. While Cink's victory was bittersweet—he prevented the fan favorite, Watson, from becoming the oldest major-championship winner in history—it marked a

bright spot in a career that had been as well known for blunders as for triumphs. His reputation as a "choke artist" crystallized during the 2001 U.S. Open, when Cink famously missed a seemingly surefire 18-inch putt on the 72d hole of the competition, which prevented him from joining Mark Brooks and the eventual champion, Retief Goosen, in a three-way play-off for the major title. Shortly after that disappointment, which highlighted the uncertainty he had been feeling in competition, Cink sought out psychotherapy to improve his mental approach to the game. He has since brought a higher level of concentration and aggressiveness to high-pressure tournaments, as exemplified by his British Open victory. Commenting on the feeling of winning or losing at golf, Cink explained to Jeff Jacobs for the *Hartford (Connecticut) Courant* (June 23, 2008), "It's definitely something that snowballs either way. You go the way that Tiger [Woods] goes any time he is sniffing the lead. He seems to just will it through. Or you go the way I was, where it seems like any time there's a chance to lose, you lose. . . . It's a crazy game, this game of golf."

Stewart Ernest Cink was born on May 21, 1973 in Huntsville, Alabama. His father, Robert, was a building-materials salesman, and his mother, Anne, worked as a bookkeeper at a junior high school. Cink has a sister, Danielle, who is four years his junior. When he was six years old, his family moved to Florence, Alabama, where his parents, both avid golfers, soon joined the Florence Country Club. It was there that Cink learned to play golf by imitating the motions of his parents. Despite being too young to play on the course, he was allowed to practice on the driving range while his parents played; he would also chip balls on a putting green for hours on end. As a boy, Cink, who played in his first tournament at the age of eight, trained under Chris Burns, the country club's head golf professional and a lifetime member of the PGA of America. Under Burns he quickly developed into one of the country's top junior golfers, taking the prize for his age group at the State Junior Championships on several occasions and winning the overall title in 1990. "It was obvious from an early age that he was so talented, so eager to learn and he loved competition," Burns noted to Ian Thompson for the *Birmingham (Alabama) News* (July 23, 2009).

Cink attended Bradshaw High School, in Florence, where he was a straight-A student and a member of the National Honor Society. On the golf course he took home the Press Thornton Future Masters title in 1991 and was named the Junior Rolex Player of the Year by the Alabama Junior Golf Association. He went on to win the Alabama state amateur title in 1992. Recruited by 40 colleges, Cink enrolled at the Georgia Institute of Technology (also known as Georgia Tech), in Atlanta, a school renowned for its golf program. There, he became a teammate of another highly touted amateur, David Duval, now an accomplished PGA Tour veteran who held the number-one spot in the official golf rankings in April 1999. At Georgia Tech Cink earned first-team All-American honors in the National Collegiate Athletic Association (NCAA) Division I competition for three consecutive years. During his senior year he defeated Tiger Woods, then a freshman at Stanford University, in an exhibition match at the Druid Hills Golf Club in Atlanta. While working constantly to improve his golf game during that time, he also started a family; he married his high-school sweetheart, Lisa, at the age of 20, and the couple had a son, Connor, while they were still in college. "I learned how to manage my time a lot better because I knew I had responsibilities at home," Cink told Bruce Berlet for the *Hartford Courant* (June 28, 1998). "And, because of that, I learned to squeeze a lot of good work into a little bit of time on the practice range." Cink's added responsibilities notwithstanding, he managed to finish college with a 2.9 grade-point average and was named the 1995 Georgia Tech golfer of the year.

Upon graduating from Georgia Tech with a business-management degree, in 1995, Cink turned pro. He made his professional debut at that year's Canon Greater Hartford Open (now known as the Travelers Championship), finishing in 18th place and winning $15,120. Cink competed in several more PGA Tour events that season but did not qualify for the tour in 1996, having failed to finish well in key events. Nevertheless, he earned a spot on the Nike Tour (now known as the Nationwide Tour), which serves as a proving ground for golfers aspiring to play on the PGA Tour; players earn their PGA Tour cards based on placement in events and earnings. Cink wasted no time proving his worth, winning three times and earning a record $251,699 during the 1996 season. He finished first overall in total earnings on the Nike Tour and was named player of the year, automatically ensuring him a PGA Tour card for the 1997 season.

Cink won his first tour event in the summer of 1997, at the Canon Greater Hartford Open in Cromwell, Connecticut, taking home a $270,000 purse. He finished the season with $809,580 in winnings, good for 29th place on the 1997 money list, and was named rookie of the year. Over the next two seasons, Cink performed consistently on the tour, notching six top-10 finishes in 1998 and eight in 1999. He also finished second in two tournaments, the 1998 Canon Greater Hartford Open and the 1999 BellSouth Classic, and posted his best showing in a major, garnering a third-place finish at the 1999 PGA Championship. Cink had an even better season in 2000, picking up his second career tour victory at the MCI Classic and nine top-10 finishes. He earned a roster spot on the Presidents Cup team and finished 10th in prize earnings that year, with $2,169,727.

While Cink had established a reputation as a solid if unspectacular player in his first five seasons on the tour, his accomplishments paled in comparison with those of his former teammate David Du-

val, who for a time in the late 1990s rivaled Tiger Woods as the best player in the world. At tournaments during that period, Cink often performed poorly under pressure, routinely blowing leads he had either held or shared going into the final rounds. That was most evident at the 2001 U.S. Open, held at the Southern Hills Country Club in Tulsa, Oklahoma. Going into the final round tied for the lead, he botched an 18-inch bogey putt on the 72d hole, costing him a spot in a play-off with Mark Brooks and Retief Goosen. (Goosen went on to win the tournament.) "I can handle this," Cink said at the time, as noted by Paul Newberry for the Associated Press Worldstream. "This is golf. This is a game. I can handle it." By the end of the 2001 season, he had slipped to 26th place on the earnings list, with $1,743,028.

Despite being chosen for the 2002 U.S. Ryder Cup team, Cink continued to see his game hampered by anxiety and mental lapses. "I was dreading tournament golf," he recalled to John Garrity for *Sports Illustrated* (April 5, 2005). "I was a mess." After several discussions with his wife, Cink came to accept that he had what is known in golf as the "yips"—a chronic inability to perform well due to nervousness, especially when it came to short putts. "Yips is a word you don't want to ever talk about as a golfer," Cink noted to Jeff Jacobs. Eschewing traditional sports psychology, he sought out psychotherapy to gain a better understanding of his problem. He began having weekly sessions with a renowned psychoanalyst, Preston Waddington, who helped him revamp his mental approach to the game. Cink told Garrity, "The sports psychologist will tell you to totally focus on the target, and if you do, there's no room for other thoughts. If you shut everything out, stay in the moment and follow directions, you'll be invincible. You'll never stand on the tee and be afraid." Cink adopted a different approach: instead of viewing each golf shot as a gravely important matter, he took Waddington's advice and gradually learned not to measure his self-worth by his success in a given day's golf game. During that time he also started working on the mechanics of his play, for both his driving and putting games, with the help of a noted golf instructor, Butch Harmon. Commenting on the resulting improvement in his game, Cink explained to Glenn Sheeley for the *Atlanta Journal-Constitution* (September 13, 2004), "The easiest way to put it is that I learned that where your golf ball goes really doesn't affect the way you feel about yourself. It's a golf shot. It's not a self-esteem thing. And that's basically the way it was with me. Everything in my body and in my mind—everything about myself—was all riding on my golf shots: my scores, my results, where I finished."

Cink dropped to 74th place on the earnings list in 2002. Then, in 2003, his game improved dramatically. He finished second in two tournaments, the Bay Hill Classic and the Funai Classic, and went up to number 36 on the money list. Cink's rebound continued in 2004, the best season of his career. That year he recorded 10 top-10 finishes and doubled his victory total by winning two tournaments. In the MCI Heritage (now known as the Verizon Heritage) at the Harbour Town Golf Links in Hilton Head Island, South Carolina, he broke a four-year winless streak, coming from nine strokes back to beat Ted Purdy on the fifth hole of a play-off, but his dramatic victory raised questions: after hitting his ball into a waste bunker on the final play-off hole, Cink removed several small rocks from behind the ball to set up his next shot, which landed six feet from the cup and was followed by a winning birdie. Purdy publicly complained, arguing that Cink should not have been allowed to move the rocks, but Cink's win was upheld. Cink's second tournament win that year, the prestigious WGC-NEC Invitational at the Firestone Country Club in Akron, Ohio, was indisputable, as he won by four strokes and took home a $1.2 million purse. Making his second Ryder Cup team, Cink reached a career-high world ranking of fifth that season and also finished fifth on the earnings list, with $4.45 million. He led the tour in putting average that year as well.

Cink's 2005 season included four top-10 finishes in his first 12 tournaments, but his play faltered during the second half of the season, and he dropped to 43d place in earnings. He remained a consistent force on the tour during the following two seasons, notching 13 top-10 finishes and finishing 15th and 24th on the money list, respectively. However, Cink's inability to clinch events continued to haunt him, and he entered the 2008 season without having won a tournament in four years. After an impressive runner-up finish to Tiger Woods in the WGC-Accenture Match Play Championship, he infamously blew a two-stroke lead going into the final round of the PODS Championship, playing the final six holes three over par to hand the title to Sean O'Hair and finish in a six-way tie for second place. Then, thanks to some "tough love" from his wife, who suggested that he work to shed his inhibitions and think less about others' opinions of him, Cink again retooled psychologically and adopted a new pre-putt routine that helped to keep his mind clear during high-pressure situations. Returning to form, he posted his best-ever finish at the Masters tournament, placing third. Two months later he ended his second four-year victory drought by winning the Travelers Championship (formerly known as the Canon Greater Hartford Open) at River Highlands in Hartford, Connecticut. The victory came with a $1,080,000 purse and marked his seventh top-10 finish of the year, which at the time made him the PGA Tour leader. (Cink is only the sixth player in the 56-year history of the tournament to win it twice; the other two-time winners are Arnold Palmer, Billy Casper, Peter Jacobsen, Paul Azinger, and Phil Mickelson.) By the end of the 2008 season, Cink had cracked the top 10 of the money list for the second time of his career, finishing in ninth place, with nearly $4 million in earnings.

Cink got off to a rough start in 2009. In the first 11 events of the season, he missed the cut three times and finished better than 24th only once. By July, when he reached the British Open—held at the Turnberry golf resort in Ayrshire, Scotland—he was the 33d-ranked player in the world and not expected to be among the top contenders in the tournament. Despite feeling ill for most of the week leading up to the event, Cink battled his way through the first 54 holes and finished in a tie for sixth going into the final round, trailing Tom Watson by three strokes. He then shot a 69 during the final round, birdying a 15-footer, to force Watson, who had bogeyed the 72d hole, into a play-off. In the four-hole play-off, Cink dominated and won by a commanding six strokes to claim the first major title of his career. Though his British Open win garnered little fanfare, as the aging Watson had been the fans' sentimental favorite, it quieted those who doubted his chances of ever winning a major tournament. Cink commented to Christopher Clarey, "It's all paid off, you know, everything I've changed. When you're having a solid career, and you go and just make massive changes, it's a leap of faith to some extent, and I trusted other people. I trusted myself that I would be able to transform myself into a new type of golfer. And that transformation . . . it's now complete." In 2010 Cink recorded three top-10 finishes and earned a spot on a Ryder Cup team for the fifth time. As of late October of that year, he ranked 39th on the PGA Tour official world golf rankings.

Cink and his wife, Lisa, live in Duluth, Georgia, a suburb of Atlanta, with their two sons, Connor, 15, and Reagan, 12. Cink, a devout Christian who is known for his genial nature and calm demeanor, is widely regarded as one of the nicest players on the tour. In his spare time he enjoys skiing, being in the outdoors, and watching hockey. A frequent user of the social-networking service Twitter, Cink has developed a substantial on-line fan base, with more than a million "followers." He quipped to Christopher Clarey, "It's like the only legacy I have. One day, on my gravestone it's going to say: 'STEWART CINK, TWITTER PIONEER OF PGA TOUR. AND ALSO, PLAYER.'"

—C.C.

Suggested Reading: *Atlanta (Georgia) Journal-Constitution* D p1 May 14, 2008; *Golf World* p33 June 14, 2002, p22 June 27, 2008; *Hartford (Connecticut) Courant* K p7 June 28, 1998; *Los Angeles Times* C p1 July 21, 2009; *New York Times* D p1 July 20, 2009; *Sports Illustrated* p50+ Apr. 5, 2005, G p6+ Mar. 3, 2008, G p4+ July 27, 2009; *USA Today* C p1 July 20, 2009

Courtesy of Juan Cole

Cole, Juan R. I.

1952– Historian; creator of the blog Informed Comment: Thoughts on the Middle East, History, and Religion

Address: University of Michigan, Dept. of History, 1029 Tisch Hall, 435 S. State St., Ann Arbor, MI 48109

Juan R. I. Cole, a professor of Middle Eastern studies at the University of Michigan, in Ann Arbor, was little-known outside academic circles until his personal blog—Informed Comment: Thoughts on the Middle East, History, and Religion—became one of the most visited Web sites for information on the Middle East in the wake of the 2003 U.S.–led invasion of Iraq. The subsequent insurgency and outbreak of sectarian violence among the country's two opposing Islamic denominations—Sunni and Shia—created a complicated scenario that saw ordinary news readers and seasoned journalists alike turning to experts for clarification; Cole, who is fluent in Urdu, Persian, Turkish, and colloquial Arabic and the author of many books on the region, emerged as one such expert. His ability to quickly translate Arabic news sources into English and to post about unfolding events made Informed Comment a trove of information not readily available in the mainstream Western media. The blog continued to gain in visibility, and Doug Ireland wrote for the *Los Angeles Times* (December 24, 2004) that it soon became "a must-read for anyone seriously interested in Iraq." By 2006, according to the University of Oklahoma Middle Eastern studies professor Joshua Landis, who discussed Informed Comment's creator with

Philip Weiss for the *Nation* (July 3, 2006, on-line), Cole had "done something that no other Middle East academic has done since [the Princeton professor] Bernard Lewis. . . . He [became] a household word."

Despite his undisputable success as a blogger, which has led to appearances on CNN and National Public Radio, among other media outlets, Cole has proved to be a polarizing and controversial figure. He has frequently criticized the Iraq War, which he believes has led to needless violence and strife, and he often excoriates what he considers to be Israel's aggressive military actions in the territories it shares with Palestinian Arabs. Liel Leibovitz wrote for the New York *Jewish Week* (June 9, 2006), "Often favoring a pugilistic tone and consistently criticizing Israel's policies in the West Bank, Cole has . . . [become] a favorite target of several conservative commentators." Nonetheless, while not popular with right-leaning observers, Cole is generally regarded as being preeminently knowledgeable about the history and religions of the Middle East; Zachary Lockman, a professor of Middle Eastern studies at New York University, told Weiss, "It's fair to say he is probably among the leading historians of the modern Middle East in this country."

John "Juan" Ricardo Irfan Cole was born in 1952 in Albuquerque, New Mexico. His father was a member of the U.S. Army Signal Corps, and as a result, the family relocated frequently, living in New Mexico and France, among other places. In an interview available on the Web site of the University of California's Institute of International Studies, Cole told Harry Kreisler, "Sometimes I would be [educated] in civilian schools, but at other times I would be on the [military] base. . . . I went to twelve different schools in twelve years." Cole attended first grade in North Carolina, sixth grade in California, and a portion of high school in the East African nation of Eritrea (then part of Ethiopia), where his father was stationed for 18 months. Cole's parents were influential in shaping his world views; he told Kreisler that his father was a strong proponent of civil rights and that his mother, who had grown up in a small farming community in Virginia, held populist opinions. "The thing that most outrages her is when she reads a newspaper article about fat cats taking advantage of people," he said.

In 1975 Cole completed his undergraduate studies at Northwestern University, in Chicago, Illinois, earning a B.A. degree in history and the literature of religions. In 1972, while a student there, he had converted to the Baha'i faith, to which he had been introduced while living in Eritrea. Baha'i, one of the world's youngest religions, was founded in 1863 in Iran. Followers of the faith believe that God will, over time, reveal more of himself through a series of messengers. The faith also emphasizes unity and acceptance of other religions; followers believe, for example, that Moses, Buddha, Jesus, and Muhammad are part of a continuing line of prophetic messengers.

During his senior year at Northwestern, Cole had spent two quarters working on a research project in Beirut, Lebanon. After graduating he returned to Lebanon, hoping to earn a master's degree in Shia Islam from the American University of Beirut (AUB). However, that year saw the outbreak of the Lebanese Civil War, and, unable to remain in the country, he decided instead to go to Egypt to pursue Islamic and Middle Eastern studies at the American University in Cairo (AUC). After earning his M.A. degree, in 1978, Cole returned to Beirut to work at a newspaper as a translator. He told Kreisler that the experience "got some of the printer's ink in my blood and taught me how to read quickly and to distill information, to put things in an inverted pyramid form and to work under pressure." Living in the war-torn city of Beirut proved harrowing; he told Kreisler, "Sometimes . . . the electricity would be knocked out, and we wouldn't know whether we'd be able to get the paper out the next morning or not, so we were finishing it up by hand in candlelight in case the electricity would come back on."

Cole returned to the U.S. in 1979 and entered the University of California, Los Angeles (UCLA), where he received his Ph.D. degree in Islamic studies in 1984. While working on his dissertation, he received language training at the University of California's Urdu Program, held in Lahore, Pakistan. In Lahore Cole met and married Shahin Malik, a lawyer.

The first of Cole's many articles, "Rifaà al-Tahtawi and the Revival of Practical Philosophy," was published in 1980 in the *Muslim Word*, a scholarly journal. He followed that with "Feminism, Class, and Islam in Turn-of-the-Century Egypt," for the *International Journal of Middle East Studies* (1981); "Rashid Rida on the Baha'i Faith: A Utilitarian Theory of the Spread of Religions," for *Arab Studies Quarterly* (1983); and "Shi'i Clerics in Iraq and Iran 1722–1780: The Akhbari-Usuli Controversy Reconsidered," for the journal *Iranian Studies* (1985). Cole currently writes articles on the Middle East for various publications; among his most recent are "The Decline of Grand Ayatollah Sistani's Influence," which appeared in 2007 in *Die Friedens-Warte: Journal of International Peace and Organization*; "Iraq and the Israeli-Palestinian Conflict in the Twentieth Century," published in the Spring 2009 issue of *Macalester International*; and "Notes on 'Iran Today,'" published in the Winter 2010 issue of the *Michigan Quarterly Review*.

In 1982 Cole translated a compilation of essays by the Iranian Baha'i scholar Mirzá Abu'l-Fadl Gulpáygáním that addressed universal religious questions and themes; that work was published under the title *Miracles and Metaphors*. Two years later he co-edited and contributed to *From Iran East and West: Studies in Babi and Baha'i History*, a collection of essays. In 1984 he also joined the faculty of the University of Michigan as an assistant professor of history. He was promoted to associate professor in 1990 and full professor in 1995.

Cole began his work with the Middle East Studies Association (MESA) of North America, an organization aimed at educating the public about the region, in 1987, when he joined the Society for Iranian Studies, an affiliated nonprofit research organization. He remained active with the group in several capacities before becoming its president in 2006. For example, he worked from 1988 to 1992 as the book-review editor for the organization's *International Journal of Middle East Studies*, served as a member of the book-award committee in 1991, and was editor of the *International Journal of Middle East Studies* from 1999 to 2004.

In 1991 Cole joined the editorial board of the journal *Iranian Studies*, and the following year he edited *Comparing Muslim Societies: Knowledge and the State in a World Civilization*. In 1992 he also became a member of the board of directors of the American Institute of Iranian Studies, an academic consortium with offices in New York City. Cole's next major project was to translate a group of short stories by the iconic Lebanese-American writer Kahlil Gibran for the collection *Spirit Brides* (1993). The Web site of the book's publisher, White Cloud Press, stated that Cole's "stunning and lyric translation revives Gibran's passionate stories of spiritual transcendence through love and suffering." Cole translated Gibran's prose poems in *The Vision* (1994) and his book *Broken Wings: A Novel* (1998), both published by White Cloud Press.

From 1993 to 1996 Cole served on the joint committee on the Near and Middle East for the Social Science Research Council, a nonprofit organization that studies various issues of social significance. From 1995 to 2000 he was a member of the editorial board of the academic journal *Critique*.

In 1996 Cole left the Baha'i faith after growing dissatisfied with its leadership. He told Barbara McLeod for the *Yukon News* (January 28, 2005), "The longer I was in the community, the more I felt there was something fishy about it, and ultimately, it turns out that the upper administrative reaches of the religion tend to be dominated by what I consider to be somewhat cultish fundamentalists." In an essay available on his personal page at the University of Michigan Web site (January 31, 2000), Cole wrote that he left because he had been accused of going against the faith in his academic pursuits. He asserted that Douglas Martin, then a member of the Universal House of Justice, the Baha'i governing body, "viewed me as a covenant breaker" and "played a very sinister role in making the administration of the faith inhospitable to intellectual and spiritual exploration of the sort [its founder] clearly desired for us. [Martin] has taken what should have been an open-minded faith and made it a crucible for inquisition."

In 1998 Cole published *Modernity and the Millennium: The Genesis of the Baha'i Faith in the Nineteenth-Century Middle East*. *Sacred Space and Holy War: The Politics, Culture and History of Shiite Islam* followed in 2002. In an article for the Michigan-based magazine *Domes* (October 31,

2003), El-Sayed El Asward wrote of the latter volume, "Overall, the book shows great concern with the economic, monetary, political and social conditions that have impacted significantly on Shiites" and noted, "In the last chapter the study provides a number of provocative hypotheses and reaches interesting conclusions regarding modernism, secularism, science, liberalism and religiosity." *Napoleon's Egypt: Invading the Middle East* was published in 2007. Khody Akhavi wrote for the Interpress Service (August 28, 2007, on-line) that *Napoleon's Egypt* "sheds light on the Iraq War through an analysis of Napoleon Bonaparte's military misadventure in Egypt in 1798. It describes Napoleon's invasion and the [George W.] Bush administration's Iraq War as historical bookends to modern imperialism in the Middle East." Akhavi observed, "In Cole's view, the Bush administration's rhetoric of 'liberating Iraq' from the clutches of a tyrannical leader with a hankering for weapons of mass destruction can't mask its long-term neocolonial ambitions. . . . Both invasions deployed rhetoric of liberation. Like the French general, Bush had a desire to create a 'Greater Middle East,' only to face an insurgency that viewed the foreign presence as an occupation, not liberation." Some critics were hesitant to embrace Cole's point of view fully. Simon Caterson, for example, wrote for the *Australian* (February 6, 2008), "Cole's view of the Egyptian expedition is antipathetic to the French. While he offers valuable information about how the French were viewed by various sections of the local population, it is clear he regards the invaders as reprehensible and the Muslim population as misunderstood. The French are condemned for their ignorance of the Muslim world, while local practices such as honor killings, the persecution of non-Muslims and the subjugation of women are just the way things were."

Cole's most recent book, *Engaging the Muslim World*, was published in 2009. In a largely positive notice for the *New York Times* (May 7, 2009, online), David E. Sanger called the volume a "field guide to the politics of modern Islam" and praised Cole's exploration of "what he sees as the twin dynamic of 'Islam Anxiety' in the United States and 'American Anxiety' in the Arab world." In a review for the London *Guardian* (May 9, 2009, on-line), Steven Poole agreed, calling the book "an eloquent corrective that will probably be ignored by those who need it most."

Despite his prolific writing, it was not until Cole started Informed Comment, in 2002, that he gained widespread public attention. After the September 11, 2001 attacks mounted by members of the terrorist group Al Qaeda, Cole had found himself fielding frequent e-mail inquiries from colleagues concerning Middle Eastern terrorism and politics. "Because I was familiar with the terrain from which al Qaeda developed, people would ask questions about what was going on and I would try to answer them," Cole explained to Curt Guyette for the Detroit *Metro Times* (August 25, 2004, on-line). "My

answers were thought well of by my colleagues. My responses would get forwarded very widely. Frankly, I began getting fan mail from places like Denmark. Obviously, there was a lot of interest in what I had to say. People were trying to make sense of the situation." Instead of continuing to answer questions individually, Cole started a blog on which his thoughts and commentary on the Middle East and 9/11 would be accessible to anyone. The result was Informed Consent—later changed to Informed Comment—which Cole wrote from his home in Ann Arbor.

When the United States launched the Iraq War in 2003, the blog began to attract a wider readership, as people turned to the Internet for information. Cole's ability to read Arabic allowed him to quickly relate news and facts directly from the region's own news sources. He told Guyette, "I could get a level of texture and detail that you could never get from the Western press."

When an insurgency broke out in Iraq in 2004, Cole's blog became a major source for information on what was now becoming a war riddled with complicated internal conflict. Informed Comment began to attract up to 250,000 views a month. Brendan I. Koerner wrote for the *Village Voice* (April 27, 2004), "The situation in Iraq can confuse even the most educated of news consumers, especially when it comes to parsing out the intricacies of religious allegiances. If you're not already visiting Juan Cole's Informed Comment on a daily basis, now's the time to get in the habit. The University of Michigan professor, an expert on Iraqi Shiites, knows whereof he speaks, unlike so many TV talking heads."

The commentary on Cole's blog has been both praised and lamented; his critiques of U.S. policy in the Middle East, as well as his opinions of the ongoing conflict between Israelis and Palestinians, have generated much controversy. In one hotly debated post (May 24, 2006) on the Iraq War, Cole wrote, "Bush Administration policies in Iraq have largely been a failure. It has created a failed state in that country, which is in flames and seething with new religious and ethnic nationalist passions of a sort never before seen on this scale in modern Iraqi history. The severe instability in Iraq threatens the peace and security of the entire region, and could easily ignite a regional guerrilla war that might well affect petroleum exports from the Oil Gulf and hence the health of the world economy." Despite his opposition to the Iraq War, Cole had supported the 2001 invasion of Afghanistan, writing on July 14, 2004, "The Afghanistan war was the right war at the right time, and it did break up the network of al-Qaeda training camps from which terrorists would have gone on hitting the United States."

Cole vehemently opposes Israel's policies concerning the Palestinians, and he believes that U.S. support of Israel is one of the main causes of anti-American sentiment in the Middle East. In his blog he has frequently asserted that wealthy Jewish lobbies have contributed to making the U.S. subservient to the interests of Israel. In an August 29, 2004 post, he wrote that supporters of Israel's center-right Likud Party "in the [U.S.] Department of Defense . . . concluded that 9/11 would give them carte blanche to use the Pentagon as Israel's Gurkha regiment, fighting elective wars on behalf of Tel Aviv (not wars that really needed to be fought, but wars that the Likud coalition thought it would be nice to see fought so as to increase Israel's ability to annex land and act aggressively, especially if someone else's boys did the dying)." Such rhetoric has sparked outrage on the part of many readers; in an opinion piece written by Eliana Johnson and Mitch Webber for the New York Sun (April 18, 2006, on-line), Cole was criticized for using "his modicum of fame not to participate in the realm of respectable scholarly debate but to express his deep and abiding hatred of Israel and to opine about the influence of a Zionist cabal on American foreign policy." Efraim Karsh wrote for the New Republic (April 14, 2005, on-line), "Cole's discussion of U.S. foreign policy frequently veers toward conspiratorial anti-Semitism." On being labeled anti-Semitic, Cole told Leibovitz, "The idea that I am any sort of anti-Jewish racist because I think Israel would be better off without the occupied territories is bizarre, but I fear that a falsehood repeated often enough and in high enough places may begin to lose its air of absurdity."

In 2006 Cole was nominated to teach Middle Eastern studies at Yale University, in New Haven, Connecticut. He was initially approved by the school's sociology and history departments, so when a senior appointments committee overruled the nomination, speculation emerged as to whether outside influence from Cole's detractors had played a part in the decision. During the hiring process, opinion pieces critical of Cole had been published in the Yale Standard, the Wall Street Journal, and Slate, among other outlets, and, according to Leibovitz, the Washington Times columnist Joel Mowbray had sent "a letter to a dozen of Yale's major donors, many of whom are Jewish, urging them to call the university and protest Cole's hiring." Mowbray reportedly wrote, "Yale is poised to hire and award tenure to a professor who doubts that the 9/11 attacks had any connection to fundamentalist Islam, blames Israel for causing terror attacks against the U.S. and contends that Iran's nuclear ambitions are only a threat in the minds of American 'neocons' and their Tel Aviv counterparts." Yale officials responded that Cole's political beliefs were only a small factor in the decision not to hire him. An unnamed university insider told Leibovitz, "Most of Cole's scholarship pertains to the Baha'i faith and is limited to the 18th and 19th centuries, a liability for a professor charged with teaching about the contemporary Middle East. Second . . . Cole appears to lack in collegiality, as his penchant for combative blog entries and personal spats with detractors might make him an unnerving fixture [at] Yale."

The Yale controversy did little to affect Cole's standing at the University of Michigan, which awarded him the title of Richard P. Mitchell Collegiate Professor of History in 2007. Still, Cole has expressed pessimism about his future in academia. "I knew when I began to speak out [on certain issues] that I wasn't going to be hired [by Yale]," he told Philip Weiss. "I knew my academic career was over. I knew that I can be in this place, be a professor of Middle Eastern studies at the University of Michigan for the rest of my life. But I would never be a dean. I would never be a provost. I would never be in the Ivy League. I'm not surprised. I'm not upset. Actually, the bizarre thing is that Juan Cole was considered by Yale in the first place."

Cole, who has written opinion pieces and essays for such publications as the London Guardian, the San Jose Mercury News, and Salon, received the James Aronson Award for Social Justice Journalism from New York City's Hunter College in 2006, the first year that bloggers were considered for the honor.

Cole and his wife, Shahin, have one son, Arman, who was born in 1987. Cole's interests include learning languages, bicycling, and exploring the Internet. He is currently the president of the Global Americana Institute, a nonprofit organization that aims to translate important American literary works into Arabic.

—W.D.

Suggested Reading: *Atlantic Free Press* (on-line) Dec. 27, 2007; (Detroit) *Metro Times* (on-line) Aug. 25, 2004; *Foreign Policy* p32 Nov. 1, 2004; juancole.com; *Nation* (on-line) July 3, 2006; New York *Jewish Week* p1 June 9, 2006

Selected Books: *Modernity and the Millennium: The Genesis of the Baha'i Faith in the Nineteenth-Century Middle East*, 1998; *Sacred Space and Holy War: The Politics, Culture and History of Shi'ite Islam*, 2002; *Napoleon's Egypt: Invading the Middle East*, 2007; *Engaging the Muslim World*, 2009

Conde, Cristóbal

(KON-day, cree-STOH-bal)

Apr. 4, 1960– Software executive; president and CEO of SunGard Data Systems

Address: SunGard, 680 E. Swedesford Rd., Wayne, PA 19087

Cristóbal Conde is the president and chief executive officer (CEO) of SunGard Data Systems, one of the world's leading software and technology-services companies, serving upwards of 25,000 corporate, public-sector, and other clients in more than 70 countries. With annual revenues of over

Courtesy of SunGard

Cristóbal Conde

$5 billion, SunGard is the largest privately held business-software and information-technology (IT) provider in the U.S.; in 2010 it ranked 380th on the *Fortune* 500 list of U.S. firms. Conde joined Sun-Gard in 1987, when it acquired Devon Systems International, the software company he co-founded in the mid-1980s. He rose to become SunGard's chief operating officer (COO) in 1999 and president and COO in 2000; he has held his current titles since 2002. The Chilean-born Conde has greatly expanded SunGard and guided the company's return to private ownership after its 20 years as a publicly held firm. Without the constraints imposed by public trading, and thanks to Conde's business savvy, SunGard has suffered far less than many of its competitors during the current economic recession.

SunGard came into being in 1982 as a spin-off of the Sun Oil Co.'s computer-services division, which had been created during a period of diversification in the 1970s, when oil was insufficiently profitable. The "Gard" part of its name is an acronym for Guaranteed Access to Recovered Data, its disaster-recovery operation, now known as Availability Services. ("Disaster recovery" refers to restoring operations after fires, floods, earthquakes, or other calamities, using backup systems, data, and facilities. As *PCMag.com* defines the term, "It includes routine off-site backup as well as a procedure for activating vital information systems in a new location.") In mid-2010, according to its Web site, SunGard owned or leased five million square feet of "secure operations space," to ensure that its customers have "uninterrupted access to their IT systems." SunGard's customers include many banks and other finance-related businesses; non-

profit organizations; 1,600 institutions of higher learning; school districts that serve a total of seven million students in kindergarten through 12th grade; and public-safety and judicial agencies and city and other governments. Every business day its systems process about five million transactions and keep track of assets totaling some $25 trillion.

SunGard's success has also been traced to Conde's adoption of a "flattened" corporate environment rather than one that reflects "top-down" management. In "Thinking Forward," an undated posting on the SunGard Web site, Conde explained, "My approach is very simple: agree on objectives with individuals and then leave them to achieve them. . . . I like to think there are many things I could do well at different levels of the organization, but that's not my role. My role is to create a structure where people can contribute their best and take pride in what they are doing." In an interview with Adam Bryant for the *New York Times* (January 17, 2010, on-line) that was widely quoted on the Internet, Conde likened himself to "the producer of the show, rather than being the lead. I think too many bosses think that their job is to be the lead. . . . By creating an atmosphere of collaboration, the people who are consistently right get a huge following, and their work product is talked about by people they've never met. It's fascinating."

Cristóbal Ignacio Conde was born on April 4, 1960 in Santiago, Chile, to a university professor and his wife. His family left the country soon after the coup of September 11, 1973, in which a military junta led by General Augusto Pinochet overthrew the democratically elected Marxist president, Salvador Allende, and imposed a repressive dictatorship. Conde attended Yale University, in New Haven, Connecticut, where he earned a B.S. degree in astronomy and physics in 1981. His mother, feeling "deeply suspicious of anything financial," Conde told Joann S. Lubin for the *Wall Street Journal* (December 24, 2009, on-line), hoped in vain that he would follow his father's footsteps into academia.

After college Conde started working as a computer programmer and became friendly with Gregory S. "Greg" Bentley, who had earned a bachelor's degree in decision science (1977) and a master's degree in business (1978) from the University of Pennsylvania. In the mid-1980s the two founded Devon Systems International, which specialized in options-trading software. One of Conde and Bentley's programs was designed to compete with the Philadelphia Stock Exchange, in particular regarding the negotiations of currency-options contracts by brokers on the floor of the exchange. (Such contracts allow holders the right to buy or sell currency at specific exchange rates for set periods of time.) Their program usurped a lot of the exchange's business in that area, and soon Devon Systems became a leading supplier of such software to financial institutions. By 1987 Devon had 185 corporate and other customers in Europe and

Asia as well as the U.S. and had established headquarters in New York City and branches in London, England; Zurich, Switzerland; and Philadelphia, Pennsylvania. Its primary product was the Exposure Management System, which provided pricing, risk analyses, and everything else that live trading offered. That year SunGard Data Systems (as it was then known) acquired Devon for $20 million, and Devon became a SunGard unit. Both Conde and Bentley remained with Devon. For several years Conde did not hold an executive position, but he was content because, he told Joseph N. DiStefano for the *Philadelphia Inquirer* (September 27, 1999), "no one was bossing us around." "The way he tells it," DiStefano wrote, "SunGard . . . took care of billing, accounting and other necessary evils, and let Conde focus on improving his software and selling it to big institutions around the world."

In 1991 Conde was named chairman and CEO of SunGard's Devon Systems unit. According to a SunGard press release quoted on PR Newswire (April 26, 1991), at that time Devon was "the world's leading provider of derivative instrument trading and accounting systems" for "swaps, options, futures, and other securities," and Conde was regarded internationally as an authority on derivative instruments. SunGard, the press release stated, was "the only large specialized provider of proprietary investment support systems to the financial services industry" and "the pioneer and a leading provider of comprehensive computer disaster recovery services." Also in 1991 Conde launched SunGard's trading-systems division, which grew to include four groups, devoted to brokerage systems, risk-integration systems, securities and treasury systems, and energy-trading systems. In 1998 SunGard named Conde executive vice president, and the next year he was promoted to the newly created position of COO of SunGard and joined the firm's board of directors. As COO Conde handled SunGard's acquisitions of dozens of firms. He made the Internet one of Devon Systems' basic tools, having recognized early on the profound effect it would have on business.

In 2000 SunGard's board of directors chose Conde as the company's next president. He was named CEO in 2002. Since then he has continued to expand the company through acquisitions, a strategy SunGard has practiced since its inception. Examples include the purchases of FDP Corp., a maker of software for insurance and pension businesses, and the Israel–based Oshap Technologies, which created and licensed financial software and offered consulting services to large corporations. In 2006 the SunGard Financial Systems business acquired both System Access and Kingstar, and SunGard's Higher Education Public Sector Systems group was divided into two separate businesses: SunGard BSR (which had been purchased in 1999) merged with the more recently acquired SCT and Collegis to become the company's higher-education arm, and a new public-sector business was formed from five companies acquired between 1995 and 2005.

In 2005 Conde led SunGard's return to private ownership. In a widely publicized leveraged buyout (LBO), SunGard was purchased for $11.4 billion by a consortium of seven private-equity firms, among them Kohlberg Kravis Roberts, the Blackstone Group, and Goldman Sachs Capital Partners. In the "Thinking Forward" piece, Conde said, "I've been involved in about 100 M&A [mergers and acquisitions] negotiations over the years, and I know that the vast majority of deals never happen. So it wasn't until about five days before we signed that I realized it was actually going to happen." The purchase was the second-largest deal of its kind up to that time; in the *New York Times* blog "The Deal Professor" (April 4, 2008), Steven M. Davidoff wrote, "In the history of the latest private equity bubble," the acquisition was "a milestone." According to Conde in "Thinking Forward," "It changed people's views about the size and kind of business that can be taken private. More important, it left SunGard a much stronger company than it was before the LBO," because "we are now able to focus more strongly on the long term. When you are running a public company, you are forced to focus on the volatility of earnings. You spend a lot of time worrying about being able to predict results quarter-to-quarter, which by itself adds no value to the business. Now we focus on growth and can tolerate volatility." Returning to private ownership led directly to SunGard's larger presence in Asia and the Pacific Rim countries and to a huge increase in research and development.

Conde told Doreen Hemlock for *Poder 360°* (August 26, 2009, on-line) that SunGard anticipated the current recession: "Before the crisis started, I brought together senior leadership and asked just one question, 'When was the last time you saw so many warning signs and had it turn out well?' None of us could think of such a time. So, we created a contingency case: yellow for a downturn and red for a severe downturn. And we said, 'Let's bring expenses down to the red level and hope revenues will be in the yellow.' We ended up having revenues at red and expenses at the black level, which didn't even exist at that time. By taking action early, we avoided massive layoffs." During the downturn Conde retained all but a few employees. "We wanted products ready to go at the end of the cycle," he told Lubin. "I saw a huge competitive opportunity to protect programmers when others weren't." Although SunGard was hurt by the loss of major customers that did not survive the economic downturn, such as Bear Stearns, in May 2010 it reported that its first-quarter revenues were only 6 percent less than those for the same period in 2009. Its second-quarter revenues, made public three months later, were only 5 percent less than those of the same period the year before. In an interview with Bloomberg TV in October, Conde predicted that 2011 would prove to be another difficult year for financial IT markets. Nevertheless, SunGard appeared to be financially strong, as it had added 3,500 new employees since the market hit bottom in 2009.

In mid-2010 SunGard introduced what it called "one-stop-shop" capabilities. "What this means is that if you are a SunGard customer—a broker-dealer, for example—and want to expand into new trading services such as dark pool access or options trading, everything you need to make the shift into a new trading area will now be at your fingertips," Raj Mahajan, the president of SunGard's trading business, explained to Katherine Heires for *Securities Industry News* (June 7, 2010). Heires wrote, "Mahajan wants securities firms to think of Sun-Gard as morphing into the trading equivalent of an Apple iPhone, providing access to an ever-expanding array of applications."

Conde has talked frankly about what he has learned from his past management mistakes, such as attempts to micromanage his employees. He told Adam Bryant, "Collaboration is one of the most difficult challenges in management. I think top-down organizations got started because the bosses either knew more or they had access to more information. None of that applies now. Everybody has access to identical amounts of information." Conde has brought to SunGard a system created by David Sacks—an in-house Web service, similar to Facebook and Twitter, known as a real-time communication platform; christened Yammer, it allows SunGard employees to communicate directly to the entire staff simultaneously. "You have to work on the structure of collaboration," Conde explained. "How do people get recognized? How do you establish a meritocracy in a highly dispersed environment? The answer is to allow employees to develop a name for themselves that is irrespective of their organizational ranking or where they sit in the org chart. And it actually is not a question about monetary incentives. They do it because recognition from their peers is, I think, an extremely strong motivating factor, and something that is broadly unused in modern management." Conde also described ways in which he uses Yammer: "I try to see a client every day, and because of my title I get to see more senior people [employed by that client]. And so then they'll tell me things—you know, what are their biggest problems, what are their biggest issues, what are their biggest bets. All this information is incredibly valuable. Now, what could I do with that? I'm not going to send that out in a broadcast voice mail to every employee. I'm not even going to write a long e-mail about it to every employee, because even that is almost too formal. But I can write five lines on Yammer, which is about all it takes. A free flow of information is an incredible tool because I can tell people, 'Look, this is one of our largest clients, and the C.E.O. just told me his top three priorities are X, Y and Z. Think about them.'"

SunGard's many honors include, in 2009, being named by *Global Finance Magazine* as the best treasury and cash-management provider in the categories of accounts-receivable services and treasury-workstation provider. The company was called best banking-technology provider by *Banker*

Middle East magazine and was named top vendor in *Energy Risk* magazine's software rankings, in the categories of operational risk, risk metrics, trade execution, and best customer service. In 2010 Sun-Gard ranked second in the seventh annual Fin-Tech100 listings of the top international technology providers to the financial-services industry.

Conde has three children from his first marriage, which ended in divorce; he has since remarried. He is a member of the Clinton Global Initiative and the Human Rights Watch New York Committee and is on the board of Business Executives for National Security. In his leisure time he enjoys reading literary classics and Latin American novels; he also likes the comic strip *Dilbert* and is a fan of NA-SCAR (National Association for Stock Car Auto Racing) events. He wears bowties rather than neckties because, he said in the "Thinking Forward" interview, "it's practical"—"you roll it in a sock, put it in a suitcase, and it comes out perfect on the other end. Second, it's unconventional. I've always been wary of convention."

Conde was at a meeting on the 33d floor of a tower of the World Trade Center, in New York City, on the morning of September 11, 2001, when the skyscraper was struck by a plane hijacked by Al Qaeda terrorists. His best friend and 41 other friends and colleagues of his died in the attack. "When I was going down to the ground floor . . . all I could keep thinking about was the people in my life and how many I didn't thank," he recalled to Doreen Hemlock. "My parents—when was the last time that I told them they were great? So when I got out, I decided . . . that I would never leave anything unsaid. Now, if somebody has done a good job, I tell them on the spot. I don't want to be again in a position of thinking of all the things I should have said that I didn't'. In the "Thinking Forward" piece, he said that his experience on 9/11 "brought me a new sense of perspective. I value each day. I resolutely refuse to let little things bother me."

—W.D.

Suggested Reading: *New York Times* (on-line) Jan. 17, 2010; *Philadelphia Inquirer* F p1+ Sep. 27, 1999; *Poder 360°* (on-line) Aug. 26, 2009; *Wall Street Journal* (on-line) Dec. 24, 2009; SunGard.com

Critchley, Simon

Feb. 27, 1960– Philosopher; writer; educator

Address: Philosophy Dept., New School, Rm. 1015A, 6 E. 16th St., New York, NY 10003

"I am hugely attracted to the idea of life as a mistake, as a kind of natural error for which we try and find some metaphysical assurance or consolation," the philosopher Simon Critchley told Andrew Gal-

Courtesy of Simon Critchley

Simon Critchley

lix for *3:AM Magazine* (June 26, 2008, on-line). Critchley is a leading thinker in what is called Continental philosophy, which seeks to reveal truths about life through the analysis and comparison of existing texts—literary works as well as books on ethics, politics, and the history of philosophy. Critchley's own works, among them *The Book of Dead Philosophers* (2008)—a *New York Times* best-seller—have established his reputation in academic circles while occasionally finding a niche in the mainstream. Critchley is currently the chairman of the Philosophy Department at the New School, a university in New York City. His other books include *The Ethics of Deconstruction: Derrida and Levinas* (1992), *Very Little, Almost Nothing: Death, Philosophy, and Literature* (1997), *On Humour* (2002), *Infinitely Demanding: Ethics of Commitment, Politics of Resistance* (2007), *On Heidegger's Being and Time* (with Reiner Schürmann, 2008), and *How to Stop Living and Start Worrying* (2010).

Continental philosophy emerged in Europe in the 19th century, and by the late 20th century it had come to encompass the philosophical schools of phenomenology, existentialism, structuralism, and deconstruction, drawing heavily on the works of Martin Heidegger, Jean-Paul Sartre, Michel Foucault, and Jacques Derrida. As Critchley wrote in *A Companion to Continental Philosophy* (1998), "Continental philosophy is a highly eclectic and disparate series of intellectual currents that could hardly be said to amount to a unified tradition." It is, nonetheless, considered to be the contrasting school to analytic philosophy, which emerged as the dominant school of the 20th century. Analytic philosophy concerns the pursuit of truth with an emphasis on precision, independent of history or conventional morality. Laura Miller wrote for *Salon.com* (June 21, 2008), "To put it very roughly (and consequently provoke squalls of protest), the analytic philosophers concern themselves with what the universe is, or rather how we can know what it is, while their continental counterparts are more focused on the question of how we ought to live. Critchley doesn't have much use for the analytic side and its conviction that 'philosophy should aspire to the impersonality of natural science.'"

Simon J. Critchley was born on February 27, 1960 in Hertfordshire, a county in England that borders Greater London. He fell in with the nascent punk-rock scene in London when he was a teenager. In a piece he contributed to Blake Wilson's *New York Times* blog "Paper Cuts" (February 25, 2009, on-line), Critchley wrote, "When I was a boy in England in the 1970s, you had two options: if you were working class, you were a soul [music] boy; if you were middle class, you were a hippy. I fell pretty squarely into the former category, but ended up at an academic high school, surrounded by bell-bottomed, badly-coiffured multitudes listening endlessly to junk like [the bands] Pink Floyd, Yes and Genesis." He went on to write that when he heard a recording by the New York City–based punk band the Ramones in 1976, he felt an immediate affinity for their music. The basic, aggressive three-chord rock and the genre's general disdain for mainstream music and traditional values appealed to him. "Punk was the crucible out of which my paltry subjectivity was formed," Critchley told Gallix. "My years watching bands and performing in bands allowed me the imaginative space to try and conceive of a life a little different from what I was meant to do." He has credited punk's antiestablishment message with pushing him to seek out the works of philosophers, avant-garde writers, among them William S. Burroughs, and radical activists, such as the Situationists. Critchley performed in or was associated with the punk bands the Social Class Five, Panic, the Fur Coughs (later renamed the Bleach Boys), and the Good Blokes.

As a young man Critchley, while working at a series of blue-collar jobs, also tried his hand at poetry and became a political activist. When he was 22 an acquaintance suggested that he apply to college, an idea that, as he explained to Gallix, "had never previously crossed my mind. Something to do with social class, no doubt." In 1985 he earned a B.A. degree from the University of Essex, in Colchester, England. He then attended the University of Nice, in France, where he earned his master of philosophy degree in 1987. He received a Ph.D. in philosophy from the University of Essex in 1988. His dissertation, entitled *The Chiasmus: Levinas, Derrida and the Ethics of Deconstruction Reading*, was about the ethics of deconstruction as discussed by Jacques Derrida and Emmanuel Levinas.

In 1989 Critchley became a lecturer in philosophy at the University of Essex. He went on to become a reader and then professor of philosophy there before his appointment to a post at the New School, in 2004. In 1992 his book *The Ethics of Deconstruction: Derrida and Levinas* was published. Deconstruction evolved from the work of the Algerian-born French philosopher Jacques Derrida (1930–2004), who in the 1960s devised an approach to reading literary texts that reveals their inherent contradictions and ambiguities, allowing multiple meanings to be derived from them. Derrida maintained that ideas can never be expressed in their pure form, without having their meanings altered by the language used to convey them; he even challenged the notion that a text's meaning originates with its author. In his book Critchley argued that deconstruction, which has been criticized by some philosophers and writers for seeking to strip texts of the meanings intended by their authors, has ethical merits.

In his second book, *Very Little, Almost Nothing: Death, Philosophy, and Literature* (1997), Critchley explored ways to find meaning in human finitude, or mortality, in the process citing works by Maurice Blanchot, Stanley Louis Cavell, and Samuel Beckett, among others. Writing for the *Modern Language Review* (October 1, 1999), Lance St. John Butler echoed an occasional criticism of Critchley when he argued that the philosopher had failed to address the nominal topic of his book. He wrote that Critchley "has read an impressive amount, in several languages, but when, having given us copious draughts of his learning, he asks the rhetorical question: 'Where does all this leave us?', the reader cannot help responding with an irreverent 'Where indeed?'." St. John Butler also wrote, "Individual readings form pleasing clearings in the jungle: Blanchot, Levinas, and [Ivan] Turgenev are turned over and exposed in a new light, but the book is none the less virtually unreadable in that it is almost impossible to know where we are going at any point."

In 1998, while still teaching at the University of Essex, Critchley became a program director at the Collège Internationale de Philosophie in Paris, France, a position he held until 2004. His book *Ethics Politics Subjectivity: Essays on Derrida, Levinas and Contemporary French Thought* was published in 1999. In it he discussed ethics in philosophy and the relation of ethics to politics. According to the Verso Books Web site, in the book "Critchley takes up three questions at the centre of contemporary theoretical debate: What is ethical experience? What can be said of the subject who has this experience? What, if any, is the relation of ethical experience to politics?" Critchley's next book was *Continental Philosophy: A Very Short Introduction* (2001), a volume in Oxford University Press's Very Short Introductions series. Critchley discussed the ideas of philosophers including Imannuel Kant, Georg Hegel, Friedrich Nietzsche, and Jean-Paul Sartre and analyzed the concepts of nihilism, existentialism, and phenomenology in relation to Continental philosophy. In *On Humour* (2002) Critchley explored the human concept of humor and sought to address how and why it is used to deal with such phenomena as death, racism, and sexism. The book contains comedic anecdotes, insights, and jokes told by philosophers. A review in the *New Scientist* (June 27, 2002) noted that *On Humour* is "a skinny book that promises much—and delivers. . . . [It] is dripping with sharp quotes and neat jokes. An offer of a second cup of tea to a French intellectual brings the elegant refusal, 'Non, je suis mono-thé-iste.' Critchley shares out the buried joke: philosopher Emmanuel Levinas specialised in monotheism. He follows up with a Tommy Cooper gem: 'So I got home and the phone's ringing. Who's speaking please? A voice down the line says, You are.'"

In 2005 Critchley's book *Things Merely Are: Philosophy in the Poetry of Wallace Stevens* was published. In it Critchley examined the philosophy underlying the work of Stevens, an acclaimed American Modernist poet who died in 1955. He argued that Stevens, in an attempt to find meaning in life through his poetry, came to the conclusion that humans cannot fully comprehend the meaning of reality. Critchley wrote, "Stevens's late poems stubbornly show how the mind cannot seize hold of the ultimate nature of the reality that faces it. Reality retreats before the imagination that shapes and orders it. Poetry is therefore the experience of failure. As Stevens puts it in a famous late poem, the poet gives us ideas about the thing, not the thing itself. The insight towards which I see Stevens's verse making its way is an acceptance of both the necessity of poetry and its limitation, the acknowledgement that things merely are and that we are things too, things endowed with imagination." Gerald L. Bruns wrote for the Web site Notre Dame Philosophical Reviews (February 9, 2006) that Critchley views Stevens "as a philosophical poet preoccupied with classical philosophical questions like 'How is knowledge possible?' and 'How do we know we are not deceived in our natural experience of things?' Critchley's thesis is that in his austere late poetry Stevens puts questions of this sort to rest because he realizes that, as a species of world-making, poetry is a noble failure. The paradox is that only poetry can articulate this fact about itself, which also turns out to be a fact about the world itself: namely, as Critchley's title has it, 'things merely are.' The turn of the screw is that perhaps only poetry can shed interesting light on this fact about things." In the book Critchley also examined the films of the director Terrence Malick, with an emphasis on the war film *The Thin Red Line* (1998). Bruns wrote, "Critchley tries to connect his appreciation of Malick's films with his reading of Stevens' poetry, where the connection appears to lie in an attention to the singularity of things, their resistance to the sense we try to make of them."

In *Infinitely Demanding: Ethics of Commitment, Politics of Resistance* (2007), Critchley touched again on ethics in politics. Tom McCarthy wrote for the Toronto, Canada, *Globe and Mail* (December 29, 2007) that in the book—which McCarthy called one of his favorites of the works he had read that year—Critchley "harnesses the remarkable work of Emmanuel Levinas to suggest ways of both passively understanding and actively navigating the current global political climate: strategies grounded in the belief that we are 'dividuals' rather than individuals, subject to an ethical demand we can never fulfill but must nonetheless respond to." Stephen Poole wrote for the London *Guardian* (June 14, 2007), "The author weaves together a challenging idea of ethics out of Kant, Levinas and [Jacques] Lacan, and marries it to a conception of 'politics' as action taken at a critical distance from the state." Kevin Kuswa wrote for *Argumentation and Advocacy* (June 22, 2007) that *Infinitely Demanding* is "an outstanding series of threads involving ethics, the Other, and subjectivity all woven into a wonderful tapestry of critical theory and guidelines for a new politics."

On Heidegger's Being and Time, by Critchley and Reiner Schürmann, was published in 2008. In the book the two philosophers discussed their interpretations of Martin Heidegger's 1927 work, *Being and Time*. Also in 2008 Critchley received generally favorable reviews for *The Book of Dead Philosophers*. That volume consists of 190 brief entries on the deaths of noteworthy philosophers; in the cases of some, Critchley discussed their final moments in relation to their philosophical views on death. He pointed out the tragic irony in some deaths—for example, that of Francis Bacon, a proponent of scientific methods, who succumbed to pneumonia after conducting an experiment in the cold on the preservative powers of snow—and the banality of others. Critchley was inspired by a quote from the 16th-century French essayist Michel de Montaigne—"To philosophize is to learn how to die"—and attempted in the book to show how the philosophical acceptance of death can free one from the fear of death. He told Gallix, "The idea of the philosophical death is the core teaching of philosophy in antiquity from Socrates and Epicurus onwards: we can go to our death freely and without fear having given up the consolation of any belief in an afterlife." Dinitia Smith wrote for the *New York Times* (January 30, 2009), "As a philosopher dies, so he has lived and believed. And from the manner of his dying we can understand his thinking, or so the philosopher Simon Critchley seems to be saying in his cheekily titled *Book of Dead Philosophers*. . . . To understand the meaning of life the philosopher must try to understand death and its meaning, or possibly its lack of meaning. And for Mr. Critchley you cannot separate the spirit of philosophy from the body of the philosopher. As he says, 'The history of philosophy can be approached as a history of philosophers that proceeds by examples remembered, often no-

ble and virtuous, but sometimes base and comical.' He adds, 'The manner of the death of philosophers humanizes them and shows that, despite the lofty reach of their intellect, they have to cope with the hand life deals them like the rest of us.'" Smith also wrote, "This book is just fun to read."

Others echoed that point; several critics praised Critchley's sense of humor and accessible approach to philosophical discussion. El Bicho wrote for the Web site Blog Critics (February 15, 2009), *"The Book of Dead Philosophers* is an enjoyable read and reference book. It also disarms some of the mystique and stuffiness associated with philosophy, making a great entryway into the field. Like other great works of art, what makes the book so compelling is that it can be returned to many times over, whether in small increments or reread completely, and different perspectives can be taken away each time." Jim Holt wrote for the *New York Times Book Review* (February 15, 2009), "Critchley has a mischievous sense of humor, and he certainly does not shrink from the embodied nature of his subjects. There is arch merrymaking over beans (Pythagoras and Empedocles proscribed them) and flatulence (Metrocles became suicidally distraught over a bean-related gaseous indiscretion during a lecture rehearsal). We are told of Marx's genital carbuncles, Nietzsche's syphilitic coprophagy and Freud's cancerous cheek growth, so malodorous that it repelled his favorite dog, a chow."

Still other critics argued that Critchley had failed to connect philosophy and death in *The Book of Dead Philosophers*. Laura Miller wrote, "The chief difficulty of Critchley's project lies in the paucity of data; we simply don't know that much about how philosophers have died." Carlin Romano wrote for the *Chronicle of Higher Education* (February 13, 2009), "Critchley never argues convincingly for his claim that the question 'What is a philosopher?' is 'indistinguishable' from the question 'How does a philosopher die?' Despite Critchley's assertion that 'the classical philosophical attitude towards death' is that 'it is nothing to be feared,' there doesn't seem to be any uniform philosophical approach to death." Miller and Romano also criticized Critchley's attempts at humor and his inclusion of superfluous information. Miller wrote, "If you want to encourage people to think more seriously about their mortality, it's counterproductive to devote most of your text to jokes about toxic pâté or to devote, say, half the entry on Brahe to the fact that he had a false nose (made of copper, apparently), in lieu of mentioning anything about his work or what he believed." Romano observed, "Critchley can't seem to decide whether he's writing a gimmick book for sale next to the cash register, an introductory trot on the order of *Philosophy for Beginners* (that pioneer graphic text), or a serious book in bite-sized pieces."

The title of Critchley's latest book, *How to Stop Living and Start Worrying*,(2010), pokes fun at that of a famous self-help book by Dale Carnegie, *How to Stop Worrying and Start Living* (1948). In a series of imaginary conversations, Critchley discussed "how to lead a happy and meaningful life," according to a writer for the Web site of the book's publisher (polity.co.uk)—a question that "has been at the heart of philosophical debate since time immemorial." "Today, however," the Polity blurb continued, "these questions seem to be addressed not by philosophers but by self-help gurus, who frantically champion the individual's quest for self-expression and self-realization; the desire to become authentic. Against these new age sophistries, *How to Stop Living and Start Worrying* tackles the question of 'how to live' by forcing us to explore our troubling relationship with death." The book also contains a debate about authenticity between Critchley and the novelist Tom McCarthy.

Critchley is the "chief philosopher" of the International Necronautical Society (INS), a parodic, semi-fictitious organization modeled after early-20th-century avant-garde groups such as the Futurists. Dedicated to the concept of "inauthenticity," the INS holds events and releases publications and manifestos. In January 2009 the INS sponsored a lecture, the "Tate Declaration of Inauthenticity," at the Tate Britain art gallery, in London. The talk was advertised as featuring Critchley and the INS "general secretary," Tom McCarthy, but the two men were played by actors. (McCarthy, a novelist and performer, founded the organization in 1999.) Discussing the lecture, Steve Finbow wrote for *3:AM Magazine* (January 22, 2009, on-line), "Despite some undergraduate humour, [and] the actors' inability to pronounce some of the words . . . the INS is at least questioning how we think about art, literature, and existence. In its acknowledgment of continental philosophy, experimental literature, and the place of the avant-garde in society, the INS—whether wholly serious or tongue in cheek—is a welcome addition to a culture slaloming headlong down lowbrow hill." In 2010 Critchley moderated a series of essays for the *New York Times* (on-line) called "The Stone," in which contemporary philosophers contributed pieces about current and timeless philosophical matters. A half-dozen of the essays were by Critchley himself. He has performed spoken-word pieces over the music of the Australian musician and filmmaker John Simmons. In 2008 the duo released an album, *Humiliation*, under the name Critchley & Simmons.

In 2009 Critchley gave a lecture, titled "The Faith of the Faithless," at Tilburg University, in the Netherlands. In it he discussed the growing links between politics and religion and his belief that those without religious convictions should respond with a proposed "faith of the faithless" that "insists that the utopian impulse in political thinking is not dead." An expanded version of the lecture will be published as a book in 2011.

Critchley has held visiting professorships at several institutions, including the University of Nijmegen, in the Netherlands, in 1997; the University of Sydney, in Australia, in 2000; Notre Dame University, in Indiana, in 2002; Cardozo Law School, in New York, in 2005; and Oslo University, in Norway, in 2006. From 1997 to 2001 Critchley held a Humboldt Research Fellowship in Philosophy at the University of Frankfurt, in Germany, and from 2006 to 2007 he was a scholar at the Getty Research Institute in Los Angeles. He is married and lives in New York City.

—W.D.

Suggested Reading: *3:AM Magazine* (on-line) June 26, 2008; necronauts.org; *New York Times* (on-line) Feb. 25, 2009; newschool.edu

Selected Books: *The Ethics of Deconstruction: Derrida and Levinas*, 1992; *Very Little, Almost Nothing: Death, Philosophy, and Literature*, 1997; *Ethics Politics Subjectivity*, 1999; *Continental Philosophy: A Very Short Introduction*, 2001; *On Humour*, 2002; *Things Merely Are: Philosophy in the Poetry of Wallace Stevens*, 2005; *Infinitely Demanding: Ethics of Commitment, Politics of Resistance*, 2007; *On Heidegger's Being and Time* (with Reiner Schürmann), 2008; *The Book of Dead Philosophers*, 2008; *How to Stop Living and Start Worrying*, 2010

Daniels, Lee

Dec. 24, 1959– Filmmaker

Address: Lee Daniels Entertainment, 315 W. 36th St., Suite 1002, New York, NY 10018

The filmmaker Lee Daniels was in his mid-20s and operating his own health-care agency when, in the mid-1980s, he entered the motion-picture industry. Despite his lack of experience, he soon got work as a casting director. Within a decade he had launched his own production company and become the manager of several major actors and actresses, among them Morgan Freeman, Hilary Swank, and Cuba Gooding Jr. His debut as a film producer came with the critically acclaimed drama *Monster's Ball* (2001), which earned an Academy Award nomination for best screenplay and made history when its female lead, Halle Berry, became the first African-American woman to win an Oscar for best actress. His next project as a producer, *The Woodsman* (2004), was honored at several film festivals and was named best first feature film at the 2005 Independent Spirit Awards ceremony. Daniels's second directorial effort, *Precious: Based on the Novel Push by Sapphire* (2009), which followed the critical and box-office flop *Shadowboxer* (2005), attracted an enormous amount of attention and high praise for its screenplay, cast, and director. "The real star of this show is director Lee Daniels," Chris Vognar wrote in his review of *Pre-*

Jason Merritt/Getty Images for NAACP

Lee Daniels

cious for the *Dallas Morning News* (November 12, 2009). "He's the one who conjures the film's eerie mix of kitchen-sink realism and gothic symbolism, its deft back-and-forth between the horrific and the sublime. A tough film by any measure, *Precious* rides Daniels' nerve to a place near grace. The film marks the arrival of a major filmmaking voice, an artist capable of plumbing lower depths without wallowing in or exploiting them." Daniels received a Career Achievement Award at the 14th annual American Black Film Festival, held in June 2010.

The eldest of the five children born to the former Clara Mae Watson and William Daniels, Leonardo Louis Daniels—"Lenny" to family members—was born on December 24, 1959 in Philadelphia, Pennsylvania. His father, a Philadelphia police officer, abused him physically and psychologically. "One time, I put on my mom's red patent-leather high heels, and he beat me," Daniels recalled to Lynn Hirschberg, writing for the *New York Times Magazine* (October 25, 2009). "I knew he loved me, but he thought I wouldn't survive as a black gay guy." Daniels's Aunt Dot, his father's sister, told Hirschberg, "I think Lenny was gay from the time he was a baby, and his father saw him walking and acting real feminine, and he wanted Lenny to be tough. He tried to get him into boxing. He was verbally cruel. He cracked the whip." In December 1975 William Daniels was shot and killed by one of several young men who robbed a bar where the policeman had gone for an after-work drink. "He was a hero in that moment," Daniels told Hirschberg. "But I knew a different man. It's taken me a long time to forgive him. He wanted me to be a man who's strong and could attack the world, so what does that say? That beating a kid is good? Being

told you're nothing makes you what you are? My father could have been sent to jail for what he did to me, but he also made me tough. I never give up. Never ever ever. I hope that doesn't justify his behavior."

Daniels's mother, suddenly responsible for raising five children 16 years of age and under by herself, held two jobs to make ends meet. Distressed by the increasing violence of their West Philadelphia neighborhood, she sent Daniels to live with relatives on what is known as the Main Line, a string of affluent suburban communities northwest of Philadelphia. He attended Radnor High School, known for its academic excellence. "It was an immediate cultural change," Daniels recalled to Richard Rys for *Philadelphia Magazine* (January 2005). "It was a turning point in my way of being." In a conversation with Hirschberg, he referred to an uncle who "murdered people," adding, "And yet he took care of me too." In a discussion with the directors Norman Jewison and Clement Virgo on race relations in the film industry, posted on Cinematic Passions at wordpress.com (February 10, 2010), Daniels recalled going with his mother, an aunt, an uncle, and a cousin to see Jewison's film *In the Heat of the Night* (1967). In that film a black Philadelphia detective, played by Sidney Poitier, becomes involved in a murder investigation in a racist southern town. Daniels remembered that the film affected his relatives powerfully and led to his realization that he wanted to make movies.

Following his graduation from high school, in 1978, Daniels attended Lindenwood University, in St. Charles, Missouri, on a Hero Scholarship, for children of deceased police officers. After two years he left and moved to Los Angeles, California, to pursue a screenwriting career. To earn money he worked as a receptionist at a nurse-placement agency.

Working in the health-care industry at the start of the AIDS epidemic in the 1980s, Daniels noticed a lack of facilities in Los Angeles devoted to the care of patients with AIDS. In his early 20s he started his own health-care agency, which provided nurses for at-home AIDS patients. The agency was the first to be under contract with the renowned AIDS Project Los Angeles, one of the nation's largest service organizations dedicated to improving the lives of people with HIV/AIDs. (Daniels's agency also held contracts with the American Heart & Lung Association and the American Sickle Cell Anemia Association.) The agency made $1 million in only two years and grew to employ more than 500 people. Daniels went on to sell the company in the late 1980s for $3 million.

During his time as manager and owner of the health-care agency, Daniels found his way into the film industry. After an agency client in the movie business urged Daniels to pursue his dream, he began working as a casting director. He started out as a casting intern for the musician Prince, helping to cast his music videos as well as the films *Purple Rain* (1984) and *Under the Cherry Moon* (1986).

Daniels next became head of minority casting at Warner Bros. films. He left that job to go into business for himself, establishing Lee Daniels Entertainment in 1984. During the next dozen years, Daniels briefly managed the careers of such notable actors as Morgan Freeman, Wes Bentley, Hilary Swank, Marianne Jean-Baptiste, and Cuba Gooding Jr.

In 1997 Daniels moved to New York City to become a film producer. "I felt I needed to go to another level, and I didn't like the type of films my actors were being offered," Daniels explained to a *Jet* (March 18, 2002) reporter. From Wes Bentley he learned about a screenplay titled *Monster's Ball*, about Hank, a bigoted corrections officer guarding death-row inmates. Hank quits his job after his son, who had been following in his footsteps at the prison, commits suicide. Hank later comes to the aid of an African-American woman, Leticia, after her son is hit and killed by a car; bonded by tragedy, Hank and Leticia begin a physical relationship and fall in love. Leticia later discovers the connection between Hank and her husband, who was executed.

The screenplay for *Monster's Ball*, completed by Milo Addica and Will Rokos in 1995, had been rejected by several studios. Around the time that Daniels began to look into acquiring film rights to the story, Bentley and the actor Robert De Niro talked about starring in the proposed film, with Sean Penn as director. Those plans fell through, however. A year later the director Oliver Stone and the actor Tommy Lee Jones became interested, only to pull out as well. After Daniels acquired the film option, he spent several months negotiating with executives at the independent film and television distribution company Lionsgate before they agreed to provide $2.5 million toward the production of *Monster's Ball*. Daniels next worked with the casting crew, which included Daniels's thenboyfriend, Billy Hopkins, to fill the roles; he chose Halle Berry as Leticia, Billy Bob Thornton as Hank, Heath Ledger as his son, Peter Boyle as Hank's rabidly racist father, Sean "P. Diddy" Combs as Leticia's husband, and Coronji Calhoun as her hugely overweight son. Daniels also selected the up-and-coming Swiss filmmaker Marc Forster to direct. Shot in five weeks, *Monster's Ball* went on to gross nearly $45 million worldwide and earned an Academy Award nomination for best original screenplay; Berry won the best-actress Oscar.

Despite that recognition, Daniels found it hard to arouse interest in mainstream Hollywood circles in the kinds of films he wanted to make. "No one of color is signing a check" at the major film studios except to finance stereotypically black films, he told Annette John-Hall for the *Philadelphia Inquirer* (June 12, 2003). "I realized that there is a deep-rooted racism in Hollywood, and I didn't know that before because everyone who had helped me was white." After turning down several offers to work on "urban" films, Daniels chose instead to produce another independent film, *The*

Woodsman, directed by Nicole Kassell and based on a play of the same name by Steven Fechter. Starring Kevin Bacon, Kyra Sedgwick, and Mos Def, *The Woodsman* is about Walter (Bacon), who must deal with his past demons when he returns home after spending 12 years in prison for child molestation. *The Woodsman* premiered in January 2004 at the Sundance Film Festival, in Park City, Utah, where it was nominated for the Grand Jury Prize; it won the Jury Prize at the Deauville International Film Festival, in France, and earned special recognition for excellence in filmmaking from the National Board of Review. It was named best independent picture by the Foundation for the Advancement of African Americans in Film (sponsor of the Black Reel Awards) and best first feature film at the 2005 Independent Spirit Awards.

After he completed *The Woodsman*, Daniels felt "tired of producing because, at the end of the day, I was tired of creating monster movie-star directors," he told Lynn Hirschberg. "I was stuck with, How am I going to find my next $2 million to make my next movie and [those directors are] walking away to jobs that pay them $2 million. I thought, How do I get my voice across? I wanted to direct." For his directorial debut Daniels chose *Shadowboxer*, about two contract killers, Rose and Mikey, a mother and stepson who are also lovers. Hired to kill a gangster's pregnant girlfriend, the two decide to run away with the woman and her newborn baby and protect them. Starring Helen Mirren as Rose, Cuba Gooding Jr. as Mikey, and Stephen Dorff as the gangster, *Shadowboxer* contains a great deal of graphic violence and sex. It received mostly negative reviews. Bill Zwecker, a *Chicago Sun-Times* (July 28, 2006) critic, wrote, "Daniels makes a stab at pushing the envelope and smashing some old taboos, but sadly his efforts lead only to confusion and result in senseless drift. If anything, *Shadowboxer* made me laugh—when I should have been cringing with fear." "*Shadowboxer* was a very humbling experience for me," Daniels told Ethan Alter for *Film Journal International* (October 1, 2009) several years later. Daniels next produced the poorly received film *Tennessee* (2008), about two brothers (portrayed by Adam Rothenberg and Ethan Peck) who set out to find their biological father and, along the way, meet an aspiring singer (Mariah Carey) fleeing from her abusive husband.

Daniels faced opposition from the writer Sapphire when he tried to secure the rights to her novel *Push* (1996). The novel concerns an obese, illiterate, inner-city teenager who endures abuse by her mother and is raped by her mostly absent father, who has recently impregnated her for the second time. *Push* had stirred Daniels's imagination when he first read it, soon after its publication. Sapphire's resistance to having Daniels make a film of *Push* evaporated after she viewed *Monster's Ball* and *Shadowboxer*. She told Michele Norris for the National Public Radio program *All Things Considered* (November 6, 2009) that because Daniels "had gone over the edge in some cases with his own work, the films that I had seen, I felt this would be someone who would not back up from the material and would present something true and vital to the public." Still, Daniels encountered difficulties in raising funds to make the film. "*Shadowboxer* hadn't done so well, so I found myself back at Square 1," he told Lynn Hirschberg. "It was very, very hard to get financing for *Precious*. All the studios said no. They didn't want to make a film about a 350-pound black girl who is abused."

Daniels had partially financed *Shadowboxer* with money from a businessman in Philadelphia. Eighty percent of the $5 million spent to make *Tennessee* had come from a couple in Denver, Colorado: Gary Magness, an investment-group chairman and an owner of TCI, the telecommunications company started by his father, and Sarah Siegel-Magness, an entrepreneur whose parents founded the Celestial Seasonings tea company. The couple also pledged $12 million toward the making of *Precious*. The main character of *Precious*, 16-year-old Clareece Precious Jones, is the daughter of a vicious, rage-filled mother (played by Mo'Nique) who abuses her verbally, physically, and sexually. At 12 Precious gave birth to a baby with Down syndrome, and she is now pregnant again by the same man—her own father, who is HIV positive and is usually absent from her life. To escape her mother's derision and hostility, Precious has created a fantasy world in which she is desirable to good-looking men.

Daniels's search for the actress who would play Precious extended for many weeks. "Do you know how difficult it is to find a 300lb black girl to be great in a movie? They don't exist in Hollywood," Daniels told Stuart Jeffries for the London *Guardian* (January 20, 2010). He held open casting calls in big cities and scouted for likely candidates at McDonald's outlets, movie theaters, welfare offices, and urban college campuses. He interviewed more than 400 teenagers and young women, many of whom, like the character, had been sexually abused and could not read or write. Gabourey Sidibe, the confident 24-year-old Lehman College student from the Harlem section of New York City who won the part, had little in common with Precious except for her size. Daniels later realized, he told Terry Gross for the National Public Radio program *Fresh Air* (November 5, 2009), that "if I had used one of the girls that was really [like] Precious, that I would have been exploiting them." *Precious* was filmed in seven weeks in Harlem and other locations, most in New York City. It premiered at the 2009 Sundance Film Festival, where it won the Audience Award and the Grand Jury Prize, and Mo'Nique won a Special Jury Prize. Lionsgate then agreed to distribute *Precious*, and the television host Oprah Winfrey and filmmaker Tyler Perry signed on as executive producers.

In a review of the film for *Entertainment Weekly* (November 13, 2009), Owen Gleiberman wrote, "*Precious* captures how a lost girl rouses herself from the dead, and Daniels shows unflinching courage as a filmmaker by going this deep into the pathologies that may still linger in the closets of some impoverished inner-city lives. . . . It's a potent and moving experience, because by the end you feel you've witnessed nothing less than the birth of a soul." Amy Biancolli, writing for *sfgate.com* (November 13, 2009), described *Precious* as "depressing, devastating, harrowing and repulsive. But there are lyric flights of hope interspersed among that raw naturalism, and that's what makes this movie amazing. . . . Cynics may be tempted to dismiss [the film] as pop exploitation of a sensitive topic. It isn't. It is, first and foremost, a compassionate, closely observed study of a traumatized adolescent." Among those who found little to admire or like in *Precious* was Anthony Lane, who wrote for the *New Yorker* (November 9, 2009), "What we have here is a fouled-up fairy tale of oppression and empowerment, and it's hard not to be ensnared by its mixture of rank maleficence and easy reverie. The gap between being genuinely stirred and having your arm twisted, however, is narrower than we care to admit." Among many other honors, *Precious* won an Academy Award nomination as best picture, and Daniels was nominated for an Oscar in the best-director category.

Daniels plans to direct a film called "Selma," about the famous march in Alabama organized by the civil rights leader Martin Luther King Jr. in 1965, and another titled "The Butler," about Eugene Allen, a former White House servant.

In October 2005 Daniels suffered a heart attack, which he attributed to a combination of stress, exhaustion, and the residual effects of his longtime use of cocaine. "Before [my heart attack], success was trying to get a movie made," he told Regina R. Robertson for *Essence* (March 2006). "Now it's making sure the bills are covered, and my kids are eating and in school. Honestly, that's what gives me happiness." By contrast, he told Lisa Kennedy for the *Advocate* (November 2009), "I live for my art to the point that my health comes second. . . . I get so wrapped up in my work. When I get into the thick of things, I'm not good for my kids. I'm not good for my boyfriend. I don't care what I eat or if I eat. I can work 17 hours a day—I have." "Much of Daniels's patter . . . sounds both rehearsed and contradictory," Hirschberg noted. "But it's also colorful and strangely persuasive—as long as you don't listen too closely. Daniels is always convincing someone of something, and like any good salesman, he knows that selling is not just about the truth."

In 2004, at the request of former president Bill Clinton, Daniels produced a series of public-service television announcements urging young people of color to vote. He has devoted some of his time to projects that encourage African-American youths to pursue careers in film and to charities that help those stricken with HIV/AIDS.

Daniels is the father of 14-year-old twins, Clara and Liam. Born to one of Daniels's brothers (who was about to go to prison at the time of their birth) and the brother's girlfriend, the twins were adopted by the filmmaker and Billy Hopkins a few days after they were born. Daniels and Hopkins, who separated in 2009, have joint custody of the twins, whose biological parents have never participated in their upbringing. Daniels currently lives in Manhattan with his children and Andy Sforzini, an insurance-company actuary.

—M.A.S.

Suggested Reading: *Film Journal International* p12+ Oct. 2009; Lee Daniels Entertainment Web site; *New York Times Magazine* p28+ Oct. 25, 2009; *Philadelphia Inquirer* D p1 June 12, 2003; *Philadelphia Magazine* Jan. 2005

Selected Films: as producer—*Monster's Ball*, 2001; *The Woodsman*, 2004; *Tennessee*, 2008; as director and producer—*Shadowboxer*, 2005; *Precious: Based on the Novel Push by Sapphire*, 2009

Davis, Glen

Jan. 1, 1986– Basketball player

Address: Boston Celtics, 226 Causeway St., Fourth Fl., Boston, MA 02114

At first glance the 289-pound Glen Davis might trigger thoughts of football—at which he excelled in high school—rather than basketball. But as a power forward with the Boston Celtics of the National Basketball Association (NBA), Davis has won widespread attention thanks to his fiery presence, childlike exuberance, love of the limelight, and gritty style of play. Serving primarily in a back-up role for most of his three complete seasons in the league, Davis emerged as one of the Celtics' most valuable reserve players during the 2010 NBA play-offs, when he came off the bench to deliver several game-changing performances. His intensity helped spur the Celtics' postseason success and contributed to their strong showing in the 2010 NBA championship, which they lost to the Los Angeles Lakers. "Big Baby," as he is known, is "an undersized big man with limited skills, but . . . plays hard on each possession, brings energy and has a passion for the game," according to Frank Zicarelli, writing for the *London (Ontario) Free Press* (June 12, 2010). Kevin Garnett, the Celtics' All-Star power forward, described his teammate to Joseph Schiefelbein for the Baton Rouge, Louisiana, *Advocate* (February 19, 2009) as "a ball of fire. He's like the yin and the yang. He has a soft side to him and he's real pure, but he has an aggressive side that you can't deny him. . . . Big Baby is one of the

purest human beings I've ever met. He has a great heart."

Ronald Glen Davis was born on January 1, 1986 in Baton Rouge to Donald Robertson and Tonya Davis. With his two sisters, he endured a tough upbringing. His father was never present during his early years, and his mother's attempt to raise him was thwarted by her severe drug problem. As a child Davis was shuttled from place to place; he and one of his sisters lived in a foster home for a time. He sometimes resorted to stealing food from the neighborhood store in order to provide for his family. "I was put in a situation to be a man before my time, and I just had to develop character," he told Mark Murphy for the *Boston Herald* (December 27, 2007). "I'm so happy when I think about it, because all of those experiences molded me into a positive person. Everyone should have that view of things—that things are real; use reality in a positive way."

Davis's outlook was partly shaped by his early involvement in basketball and football, which allowed him to escape from his home life. He played on youth-league teams as a boy and also spent a large portion of his time at the Baton Rouge Sports Academy, where he befriended his future Louisiana State University (LSU) teammate Tyrus Thomas, now a member of the NBA's Charlotte Bobcats. Because of his rapid physical growth, Davis's athletic coaches often had him play against children in older age divisions. As a nine-year-old, he was given the nickname "Big Baby" after complaining to his football coaches about being manhandled by players three years older than he was. He was also accused of whining after being fouled in basketball games, which helped the nickname stick. That aside, Davis's athletic talent was evident.

One who recognized Davis's talent early on was Collis Temple Jr., who coached Davis in Amateur Athletic Union (AAU) summer-league teams. (Temple, the first African-American to play varsity basketball at LSU, in 1970, was among only a handful of African-Americans in all of Southeastern Conference—SEC—basketball at that time.) Seeing Davis's unstable home life as an impediment to his athletic and emotional development, Temple stepped in as a mentor and father figure. Davis went to live with the Temples when he was in seventh grade, after his mother was arrested on drug charges. Living with Temple's family, Davis received the structure and guidance that had been lacking earlier in his life. He told Mark Murphy, "The thing that really pushed me was seeing Mr. Temple and the life he lived—the way he treated his kids. That's what I wanted to do. . . . A lot of my friends in the same situation went the opposite way. I'm lucky I had [the Temples]." (Starting when he was a high-school sophomore, Davis also spent some time living with his biological father, a postal worker.) Temple, who had known Davis's mother since high school, told Mark Murphy that Davis "has her personality without the challenges she has. She's an incredibly bright woman, witty,

Elsa/Getty Images

Glen Davis

articulate, very outgoing. . . . He's so sincere and genuine, and he gets it from her." "All my flair, my personality, comes from her," Davis told Mark Canizzaro for the *New York Post* (March 20, 2006).

Davis attended University Laboratory High School in Baton Rouge, which is affiliated with LSU's College of Education. There, he became a standout athlete in both football and basketball. In addition, he was a shot putter on University High's track-and-field team. Due to his then-350-pound frame, Davis initially garnered more attention as a football player, rushing for more than 1,200 yards as a tailback during his high-school career. "He was quite a running back," Davis's high-school basketball coach, Ari Fisher, told Alan Greenberg for the *Hartford (Connecticut) Courant* (March 31, 2006). "He was just bigger and stronger than everyone, and when you tried to tackle him, he'd just drag you." Still, a month before the start of his senior football season at University High, the six-foot eight-inch Davis decided to concentrate solely on basketball, losing weight until he was a slightly more agile 325 pounds. During his senior year he averaged 26.3 points and 14.3 rebounds per game and led University High to a 35–2 record en route to the 2004 Class 2A state championship, which marked his team's second title in three years. At the end of the season, Davis earned *Parade* and McDonald's All-American honors and was named Most Valuable Player (MVP) for the Class 2A Division, in addition to being named MVP of the Top 28 Class 2A tournament. He was also recognized as the Gatorade Player of the Year for Louisiana, Athlete of the Year by the Baton Rouge *Advocate*, and Mr. Basketball by the Louisiana Sports Writers Association.

Despite skipping his senior season of football, Davis was among the 100 football players most heavily recruited by colleges; he received scholarship offers from schools with some of the best football programs in the nation, including Florida State University and the University of Tennessee. However, he turned down those offers to play basketball with the LSU Tigers. Davis recalled to Robin Fambrough for the Associated Press (April 3, 2004), "I just had it on my mind that basketball was my love. After I made the decision to just play basketball, everybody said I was crazy. So I made up my mind to prove them wrong." During his freshman season Davis made an immediate impact, starting 29 games, averaging 13.5 points, 8.8 rebounds, and 1.4 blocked shots per game, and being named the SEC Freshman of the Year. He continued to silence his detractors during his sophomore season, when he led the SEC in scoring and rebounding, with an average of 18.6 points and 9.7 rebounds per game, respectively, becoming only the fifth player in league history and the first since Shaquille O'Neal in 1991 to accomplish that feat. He helped lead LSU to a 14–2 record and an SEC regular-season championship and was a pivotal figure in taking the Tigers to their first NCAA Final Four appearance since 1986. In that year's NCAA tournament, Davis contributed to upset victories over number-one-ranked Duke and number-nine-ranked Texas (in overtime). He then scored 14 points in the national semifinal game against the University of California–Los Angeles (UCLA), which LSU lost, 59–45. At the end of the season, Davis was named the SEC Player of the Year and earned First-Team All-Conference honors. He also earned Second Team All-America honors from the *Sporting News* and Third Team honors from the Associated Press.

Despite being hampered by injuries throughout the 2006–07 season, Davis led the SEC in rebounding for the second consecutive year, with an average of 10.4 rebounds per game, and finished third in the league in scoring, with 17.7 points per game, on average. He was again named to the First-Team All-Conference team and was named First-Team All-District by members of the United States Basketball Writers Association (USBWA). Following his junior year at LSU, Davis entered the 2007 NBA Draft. He finished his college career at LSU ranked 10th of all time in career scoring, with 1,587 points, sixth in rebounds, with 916, and third in blocked shots, with 110. Davis is only the sixth player in LSU history to finish his career with at least 1,500 career points and 900 rebounds and the second (after Shaquille O'Neal) to have at least 1,500 career points, 900 rebounds, and 100 blocked shots. (In 2009 he was one of 16 players named to the LSU All-Century Team.)

Analysts predicted that Davis would be selected in the first round of the 2007 NBA Draft. It was not until the second round, however, that he was chosen as the 35th overall pick by the Seattle Supersonics. He was then traded to the Boston Celtics.

Clearly disappointed, Davis was quoted by Glenn Guilbeau in the Monroe, Louisiana, *News-Star* (June 29, 2007) as saying, "It's the NBA Draft. It's just like a movie. You never know what's going to happen. I've got some mixed emotions right now, but I'm excited about going to the Boston Celtics." Davis's being a second-round pick had financial ramifications: while first-round selections have guaranteed three-year contracts, second-round selections are not guaranteed a contract or roster spot. Nevertheless, Davis entered that off-season on a mission, dropping 30 pounds by overhauling his diet and adding muscle through an intense regimen. He then earned a roster spot after proving himself on the Celtics' 2007 Summer League team, averaging 12 points, 9.8 rebounds, and 1.8 blocked shots in five games. In September of that year, Davis signed a two-year contract with the Celtics. Danny Ainge, the Celtics' executive director of basketball operations, said, as quoted by a writer in the *Providence (Rhode Island) Journal* (September 5, 2007), "I like [Davis's] versatility. He can shoot the ball. He's a terrific rebounder and on defense he's got quick feet."

During his rookie campaign, in 2007–08, Davis served mostly in a reserve role for a Celtics team that had three superstars: Paul Pierce, Ray Allen, and Kevin Garnett. During the course of the season, he backed up Leon Powe at center and the veteran P.J. Brown at power forward. After coming off the bench for the first 19 games of the season, Davis made his first NBA start on December 12, 2007, in a game against the Sacramento Kings. Playing power forward, he recorded 16 points and nine rebounds in the Celtics' 90–78 victory. Davis then had a breakout game against the Detroit Pistons on January 5, 2008, when he scored a then-career-high 20 points (16 in the fourth quarter) with four rebounds (three offensive) to help lead the Celtics to a 92–85 victory. During the regular season he averaged 4.5 points, 3.0 rebounds, and 13.6 minutes in 69 games. The Celtics, meanwhile, finished with a league-best 66–16 regular-season record, after having ended the previous season with the league's second-worst record (24–58). (The Celtics' 42-game improvement from the previous year set an NBA record, eclipsing the 36-game improvement by the San Antonio Spurs during the 1997–98 season.) Anchored by the play of their so-called Big Three (Pierce, Allen, and Garnett), the Celtics carried their momentum into the postseason and reached the NBA Finals, where they defeated the Los Angeles Lakers in six games to win their 17th NBA championship. As a result of a tightened rotation during the postseason, Davis played only sparingly in the play-offs and finals and averaged 8.1 minutes per game. Still, he had the honor of playing on a championship team in his rookie season. (Previously, none of the Celtics' Big Three had made an NBA Finals appearance: Garnett made it in his 13th season, Allen in his 12th, and Pierce in his 10th.)

Gradually earning more time on the court with his solid play, Davis saw his role with the Celtics grow during the 2008–09 season. In a December 2008 game against the Portland Trail Blazers, Davis, living up to his nickname, displayed his emotional side when he was caught on camera crying after Kevin Garnett berated him and fellow bench players for their poor play. "He wasn't yelling at me," he explained to Stan Grossfeld for the *Boston Globe* (March 4, 2009). "He was yelling at the team. Basically, he said we weren't playing together and we weren't playing Celtics basketball. And, you know, I took it to heart because I wanted to go out there and execute. . . . I hold myself up to high expectations." He added, "I'm an emotional player. I feel the game. I love the game, and it gets that way sometimes. It's about what you do after. How do you bounce back? I'm not ashamed. I'm never ashamed." Davis "bounced back" after Garnett and several other players suffered injuries that season. (Garnett missed the final 25 games of the regular season due to knee problems.) He was in the starting lineup on 16 occasions and proved himself to be a valuable asset, averaging 12 points per game after the All-Star break.

In a February 2009 game against the Philadelphia 76ers, Davis recorded his first career "double-double," with 12 points and 11 rebounds, and in a March game against the Memphis Grizzlies, he scored a career-high 24 points. Davis played in a total of 76 games during the regular season and averaged 7.0 points, 4.0 rebounds, and 0.9 assists. The Celtics finished second in the Eastern Conference with a 62–20 record (despite starting off the season at 27–2, the best starting record in NBA history), and advanced to the Eastern Conference semifinals, where they lost to the Orlando Magic in seven games. During the postseason Davis became the Celtics' starting power forward and put up the best numbers of his career, averaging 15.8 points, 5.6 rebounds, and 36.4 minutes in 14 games. He shone particularly in the Orlando series and made the game-winning shot in Game Four to give the Celtics a 95–94 victory. After that game, Davis said, as quoted by John DeShazier in the New Orleans, Louisiana, *Times-Picayune* (March 12, 2009), "I kind of feel myself making game-winning shots all the time. . . . A shot like that, you believe you're going to make it. And you make it."

In August 2009 Davis signed a two-year, $6.5 million contract with the Celtics. Coming off a strong year, he entered the 2009–10 season with high expectations. Then, in October, Davis was suspended by the Celtics after being involved in an altercation with his friend and former University High teammate Shawn Bridgewater two days before the start of the regular season. Davis suffered a broken right thumb in the fight, which forced him to undergo surgery. He was sidelined for the first two months of the season and missed 28 games. Upon returning to competition, he received limited playing time and averaged 6.3 points, 3.8 rebounds, and 17.3 minutes in 54 games. The Celtics, meanwhile, finished fourth in the Eastern Conference, with a 50–32 record. While many expected the Celtics to make an early exit from the play-offs, due to various injuries and a lack of team chemistry throughout the regular season, the team upset the Miami Heat and Cleveland Cavaliers, in the first and second rounds, respectively, to reach the NBA Finals for the second time in three years. In the finals they again squared off against their archrivals, the Los Angeles Lakers, losing the series in seven games. Redeeming himself after his "lost" regular season, as Bob Ryan called it in the *Boston Globe* (June 11, 2010), Davis became one of the Celtics' most valuable bench players in the postseason, averaging 7.3 points, 4.5 rebounds, and 20.1 minutes in 24 games. His biggest impact came in Game Four of the NBA Finals, when he scored 18 points on 7-for-10 shooting and pulled down five rebounds (four offensive) to help guide the Celtics to a crucial 96–89 victory, which evened the series at two games apiece. Describing Davis's performance, Ryan wrote, "He is 6 feet 8 inches (maybe), and he often has a lot of trouble finishing underneath among the NBA redwoods, but he usually finds a way to make an impact on a basketball game, and last night he made one of his biggest. He was at his slashing, marauding, kamikaze best in the fourth quarter, leading the Celtics with his amazing range of skill and inspiring them with his emotion and desire." He added, "When this man has it going, he just about takes your breath away." As quoted by Frank Zicarelli, the Celtics' head coach, Doc Rivers, said, "You know, this incident that happened at the beginning of the season was not the best thing for him or our team. I wouldn't want it to happen to any other player. . . . But in some ways, it may have helped him understand that he had to mature. He also understood that the team was not going to wait for him. We were going to move on. When he came back, he didn't immediately play and in some way that helped him. . . . He still has his days and I think we laugh, but he did earn the name Big Baby and it wasn't from his size. He's growing, he's growing up as a guy in front of our eyes and it's nice."

Davis lives in Waltham, Massachusetts. He has been linked romantically to Jenna Gomez, the former co-captain of the women's basketball team at Tufts University. For conditioning, and to improve his agility and balance, Davis plays soccer and ultimate Frisbee and practices the martial art of muay thai during the off-season.

—C.C.

Suggested Reading: (Baton Rouge, Louisiana) *Advocate* C p1 Feb. 19, 2009; *Boston Globe* C p1+ Mar. 4, 2009; *Boston Herald* p56+ Dec. 27, 2007; *Hartford (Connecticut) Courant* C p1 Mar. 31, 2006; Louisiana State University (LSU) Athletics Web site

---

Dean, Tacita

Nov. 12, 1965– Artist

Address: c/o Frith Street Gallery, 17–18 Golden Sq., London, England W1F 9JJ

The work of the British artist Tacita Dean "has the not-quite-completely-here quality of conceptual art: there is something to look at or at least hear, but it refers to another reality that is uncontainable and cannot be fully comprehended," Jonathan Jones wrote for the London *Guardian* (November 4, 1999). "She makes films, does beautiful drawings, records sounds. But there's always an absent aspect of the work." That "absent" quality is one reason why Dean's 16mm films—which have been hailed as strikingly original and powerfully evocative—are shown in art galleries and museums rather than commercial movie theaters. Although they are based almost entirely on real-life people, stories, and occurrences, her films never chronicle events or proceed as narratives. Rather, their static shots and lengthy takes often merely hint at their subjects and require of viewers long stretches of uninterrupted concentration. "For me," Dean once said, as quoted on the Dia Art Foundation Web site (2008), "making a film is connected to the idea of loss and disappearance." For her series Disappearance at Sea, for example, about the doomed attempt of a weekend boater named Donald Crowhurst to win an around-the-world contest for solo yachtsmen, Dean made one film of a seascape as seen from a single lighthouse, another of only the lighthouse, and a third of Crowhurst's boat, neglected and decaying on a Cayman-island beach three decades after his fatal voyage—all of which, according to various sources, awaken in viewers a sense of the awful circumstances and anguish that led to Crowhurst's death while also stirring thoughts and feelings of a general nature about time, the sea, and human follies. "The vividness of her images and the vibrancy of her soundscapes are a challenge to the desensitised, coarse world of normal experience, where bright lights, movement and noise cheat us into believing that something is happening," the British novelist Jeanette Winterson wrote for the London *Guardian* (September 29, 2005, on-line). "Tacita Dean's slow nothingness is far more rich and strange." Dean's film *A Bag of Air* and others among her works also serve as comments on the process of creating art. "Trained as a painter, Dean operates within the art world rather than the film industry, yet her use of film as a primary medium puts her at an equal remove from the conventions of art and film—a distance that allows her to reflect critically and nostalgically, but above all curiously, on both," the art critic Barry Schwabsky wrote for *ArtForum* (March 1999).

Vittorio Zunino Celotto/Getty Images

Tacita Dean

In the early 1990s Dean was pigeonholed with the so-called Young British Artists, a group that included Rachel Whiteread, Damien Hirst, Marc Quinn, Ron Mueck, Tracey Emin, and Marcus Harvey. Now in their 40s, all are distinguished in part by a "fascination with the real: with how real objects can be incorporated, modified, implied, whatever, in . . . art and made somehow unreal or hyper-real," Michael Kimmelman wrote for the *New York Times* (May 17, 1996). Since 1992, when she won an award for a short film included in the group show BT New Contemporaries, Dean has had dozens of solo shows, at sites including the Tate Britain and the Tate Gallery, in London; the Guggenheim Museum, in New York City; the Hirshhorn Museum, in Washington, D.C.; the National Museum of Art, Architecture, and Design, in Oslo, Norway; and the Musée d'Art Moderne de la Ville de Paris, in France. Dean, who has lived in Berlin, Germany, since 2000, has also participated in several hundred group shows, among them the Venice Biennale, in Italy, in 2003 and 2005, at the latter of which she won the Benesse Prize, sponsored by a Japanese foundation and awarded to artists who are "opening new horizons outside the current paradigm with an experimental spirit," according to the Web site szhkbiennale.org in 2009. In 2006 Dean won the Guggenheim Museum's $50,000 Hugo Boss Prize, one of the most prestigious, and financially munificent, honors in the art world.

Tacita Dean was born on November 12, 1965 in Canterbury, in the county of Kent, England. She has a brother, Ptolemy, a sister, Antigone, and "intellectual parents," she told Jonathan Jones. She studied painting at the Falmouth School of Art (now University College Falmouth), graduating in 1988. Next, she attended the Supreme School of Fine Art in Athens, Greece, for a year, then completed her formal education at the Slade School of Fine Art, in London (1990–92), where she earned a postgraduate degree. While at the Slade, during what she described in an article for *Frieze* (October 2009, on-line) as "a period of awakening," she became intensely interested in experimental film. One that inspired her powerfully was Chantal Akerman's 200-minute *Jeanne Dielman, 23, Quai du Commerce, 1080 Bruxelles* (1975), which follows a prostitute as she cleans her apartment, cooks, tends to her baby son, and engages in "business" transactions, all part of her daily routine. "I remember thinking how radical its length was, and how Akerman created tension through languor and boredom rather than through any sort of action," Dean wrote. "I thought it was an amazing film."

Dean soon began making short films herself. In 1992 she was included in the group exhibition BT New Contemporaries, held at the Newlyn Art Gallery in Penzance, England. Her first solo exhibition, The Martyrdom of St. Agatha and Other Stories, was held in 1994 at Galerija Skuc, in Maribor, Slovenia. The title (also the name of one of the films shown there) refers to a third-century follower of Jesus who chose to remain celibate; after she rejected the sexual advances of a Roman senator, he punished her by having her breasts cut off. Dean's film about St. Agatha shows several nuns "sitting around a table preparing plaster breasts for packaging and sale," Barry Schwabsky wrote. The items being sold by a female shopkeeper in a second film, *The Story of Beard* (1992), are detachable beards. Both films, Schwabsky noted, "imagine the aesthetic object as a relic of sorts (with a peculiarly sexual slant) as well as an item of commerce." *The Story of Beard* is black and white until the end, when, in full color, an image appears of a variation of the French Impressionist painter Edouard Manet's *Dejeuner sur l'herbe*, with the two nude female picnickers having beards. "What counts is the idea of the object of fantasy and desire, something fabulously elusive and alluring—the unobtainable beard, the mystifyingly peripatetic severed breast," Schwabsky wrote.

Dean's three-minute film *A Bag of Air*, made in 1995, debuted that year at a solo show held at a gallery at the School of Fine Arts in Bourges, France. Dean shot it while riding in the basket of a hot-air balloon. The balloon's shadow is visible on the ground; a pair of hands holds a plastic bag over the edge of the basket. Dean's voice is heard explaining that if one travels via a hot-air balloon in March, "you can catch a bag of air . . . intoxicated with the essence of spring." Schwabsky suggested that her words and images conveyed an idea that is "a mainstay of modern art": that "the art object need not be made of intrinsically noble materials but can be the most ordinary thing in the world, as long as it has been transformed by some inspired aesthetic intention." "Wittily yet lyrically," he continued, "Dean's film satirizes this commonplace—sends it up, so to speak—while the dreamily soft yet precise black-and-white photography and succession of beautifully framed shots fulfills it." In 1998 Dean was one of four artists nominated for the Turner Prize. Her entry, a film included at the artists' group exhibition at the Tate Gallery, showed a seascape as dusk arrived; it was accompanied by recorded sounds of the ocean and a revolving lamp. (The winner that year was Chris Ofili.)

Dean used several media to make her series Disappearance at Sea (1999). The inspiration was the real-life tragedy of Donald Crowhurst, a 36-year-old father of four from Teignmouth, England, who, desperately seeking a way to rescue his failing electronics business by means of prize money and publicity, entered the London Sunday Times Golden Globe Race, a nonstop, 27,000-mile, round-the-world contest for solo yachtsmen. With funds from a wealthy retired businessman, Crowhurst, an amateur sailor, commissioned the building of an unusual boat, called a trimaran. Inadequately equipped and unable to handle his flimsy, badly constructed boat, Crowhurst soon ran into serious trouble. Instead of dropping out of the race or struggling on, he remained in the South Atlantic while concocting extremely detailed navigational logs to fool people into thinking that he was making excellent progress. When he learned that his seemingly unbeatable lead had caused the only other remaining racer among the nine competitors to quit, and that Teignmouth officials and others fully expected his victory, he apparently grew fearful that his records would be carefully scrutinized and his hoax discovered. His increasingly irrational and confused log entries degenerated into delusional religious ramblings. In July 1969, several weeks after he was last heard from, his boat—the Teignmouth Electron—was located, but no trace of Crowhurst was ever found; presumably, he had jumped overboard and drowned.

Crowhurst's misplaced hopes and painful end fascinated Dean, who devoted parts of four years to researching and documenting his history. "You imagine that if you met Crowhurst in the Teignmouth Yachting Club, you might find him a bit arrogant, but as a human being, alone in an unremitting seascape trying to come to terms with his deteriorating psychological state and his monumental deception, his story is genuinely tragic and existential," she wrote in the book that is part of her series about him. Disappearance at Sea I (1996), the first work in that series, focuses on the lighthouse at Berwick-upon-Tweed, England, at dusk as its lamp flickers on. Dean thereby used "the device of alluding to a narrative that never actually enters the film," Schwabsky wrote. "What the film presents is less a disappearance than a nonappearance. Crowhurst's tale exists primarily to set up a background of expectation—the light projected by the lighthouse, we feel we have every right to expect, will reveal a clue, a trace, some sign of the eponymous disappearance." For Disappearance at Sea II (Voyage de Guérison) (1997), whose parenthetical

title means "voyage of healing," or "recovery," Dean filmed from inside a lighthouse, the camera facing the ocean. The other two parts in the Crowhurst series are set on Cayman Brac, an island in the Caribbean where the last of the Teignmouth Electron's subsequent owners beached the boat. Some of the footage and many photos she took of the ruined craft appear in her film Teignmouth Electron and her book of the same name, both completed in 1999. The latter also includes stills from several movies made about Crowhurst and Dean's account of her experiences and emotions as she learned about Crowhurst's life.

Other noteworthy 1990s films by Dean include Foley Artist (1996), Trying to Find the Spiral Jetty (1997), Sound Mirrors (1999), Banewl (1999), and Bubble House (1999). A video monitor in the installation Foley Artist, mounted at the Tate Gallery in London, provided views of some of the film-industry specialists of the title at work in their studios. (Foley artists add traffic noise, the squeaks of rusty hinges, bird calls, and myriad other sorts of sounds to films during the postproduction phase.) Eight speakers installed around a room in the gallery projected samples of motion-picture sounds along with bits of dialogue. "Images and noises describe the disjointed narrative of a hallucinatory journey," Jennifer Higgie wrote of the installation for Frieze (November/December 1996, on-line). "Along the way, Dean plays expectation against assumption: as we hear people kiss and murmur on a beach, for example, the startling visual image is of the Foley artists, who, staring blankly into space, lean towards their microphones with gentle indifference as they kiss and tongue their own wrists." Higgie also wrote, "Rather than creating an exhibition about the construction and artifice of cinema . . . Dean uses film's shadowy metaphors to explore the gulf between the idea of something and how to explain it."

Trying to Find the Spiral Jetty shows Dean's futile attempt to follow seemingly explicit directions to find the 1,500-foot-long Spiral Jetty along the shore of Utah's Great Salt Lake. A famous example of "earth art," the jetty is a counterclockwise spiral created with 15-foot-wide arms of basalt rock, soil, salt crystals, and water by the artist Robert Smithson in 1970, when the water level of the lake was unusually low because of drought. Higher water levels have kept the jetty submerged for much of the past four decades. Dean's seven-minute, black-and-white Sound Mirrors was commissioned by the Public Art Development Trust of London. It offers views of several acoustic mirrors—huge, concave, hemispherical concrete sound reflectors—erected by the British prior to World War II, before the advent of radar. Each of the devices reflected the sound waves of approaching aircraft to a microphone and thus served as an early-warning system, albeit one of very limited usefulness. The soundtrack of Dean's film was recorded at decrepit acoustic mirrors still standing near the Lydd Airport, in Kent. Writing for the London Guardian

(February 20, 2001, on-line), Adrian Searle noted the "flat light," "deadpan emotional pitch," and "sense of stalled time, fugue-like boredom, [and] awful grandeur" conveyed in *Sound Mirrors*, which he termed a "terribly somnolent film, . . . of an equally melancholic place . . . a sort of ruin of the near-present."

The title of the 63-minute *Banewl* is the name of a small dairy farm (Burnewhall) in Cornwall, as pronounced by people living in that part of England. *Banewl* was shot from early morning to late afternoon at Burnewhall Farm on the day of a total eclipse of the sun, using four cameras to capture the eclipse, other parts of the changing sky, the land, and farm scenes. (For works requiring more than one camera, and for her so-called anamorphic films, which depend on a variety of lenses, Dean works with other photographers, principally John Adderley and Jamie Cairney.) "The resulting installation is a subtle, contemplative work whose effect is almost that of a traditional British pastoral landscape painting brought to life," according to a press release about *Banewl* posted by the University of California at Berkeley Art Museum/Pacific Film Archive in 2000. *Bubble House* is the name Dean gave to an ovoid house built on Cayman Brac by a wealthy Frenchman; arrested for embezzlement and sentenced to 35 years in prison, he never got a chance to live in it. The Frenchman and Donald Crowhurst "were somehow connected," Dean suggested, as quoted in Briony Fer's book *Tacita Dean: Film Works* (2007). "Both men . . . paid dearly for their fraud, and both boat and 'bubble house' seemed at home, if not all together welcome, in their final Caribbean resting place."

Dean was commissioned to create a work of art for the Millennium Dome in London in 2000. She contributed Friday/Saturday, an installation consisting of recordings of ambient sounds made at coastal locations chosen for their relation to the Greenwich Meridian (also known as the Prime Meridian), which marks zero degrees of longitude and passes through the Millennium Dome site. The places—among them Aden, Yemen, and New Orleans, Louisiana—were 45 degrees of longitude or multiples of 45 degrees east or west of the Prime Meridian. At each site Dean recorded the sounds for 24 hours beginning at midday on a Friday. Noise from a huge vent at the dome made Friday/Saturday inaudible for much of the time, so Dean re-created the installation as a huge, brilliantly lit jukebox containing 192 CDs, each containing one hour's worth of sound from the eight locations.

In 2000 Dean was given a one-year German Academic Exchange Service (DAAD) scholarship to work in Berlin. Her 44-minute film *Fernsehturm* (2001)—the title is German for "television tower"—was shot in the revolving restaurant of what had once been the East Berlin television tower. The film focuses on the diners and waiters in the restaurant as the sun goes down. "For much of the movie, the camera is static," Adrian Searle wrote, "looking across an arc of the cafe, with its stuffy at-

mosphere, the fiddly details, the slanted, light-filled windows. . . . The human activity is desultory, banal, ritualised in cafe time, drinks time, dinner time. Glasses are raised, heads nod, hair haloed in tobacco light. Long and uneventful though it at first seems, *Fernsehturm* is Dean's most accomplished work to date. In fact, I believe it is a masterpiece." Winterson wrote that Dean's "genius, with her slow, steady, held frames, is to allow the viewer to dream the *Fernsehturm*; to enter it without hurry, without expectation, and to accept, as we do in a dream, a different experience of time, and a different relationship to everyday objects."

Winterson also wrote, "Looking—which none of us really does in normal life, has a way of slowing time down, and a way of altering perception through the intensity of the gaze. Looking at things—which is what artists do and what we don't do, both opens the mind to the object, and closes it to unnecessary flotsam. Tacita Dean has a way of making you concentrate—but beware, it is an unsettling experience." Winterson noted that in *Fernsehturm* and in another Dean film, the eight-minute *Pie* (2003), in which magpies hop from branch to branch in the trees outside her window, Dean "uses the time-line of the film to release her subject into its timeless state. . . . This collision of time and timelessness is unfolded through the courage of Tacita Dean's held gaze. It is a bluff and a dare to hold any shot for longer than a few seconds. 'I do not think I am slowing down time, but I am demanding people's time,' she says. In a busy world, that is a big demand, but one of the many reasons why art matters, is its ability to stop the rush. We are the ones speeding things up intolerably. Art is not so much slowing us down as bringing us back to a necessary point of contemplation."

Dean's *Palast* ("Palace," 2005) shows the mirrored-glass façade of the Palast der Republik, which housed the parliament of East Germany and certain cultural events. (The building was dismantled in 2006–07.) During the rule of the brutal Communist government in East Germany (1949–90), the secret police recruited hundreds of thousands of informants to keep tabs on the activities of their neighbors. In *Tacita Dean: Film Works*, Dean explained that as a British expatriate living in Berlin, she was attracted to the monolithic Palast der Republik for its "totalitarian aesthetic." "We, who have no inkling of what the building meant when it had meaning, had no reason to look upon it and know the monster it contained when the copper-tinted mirrored glass was not about catching reflections and deflecting the sun, but about looking in one direction only, about being observed without leave to observe," she said.

Dean's film *Kodak* (2006) was shot at the Kodak factory in Chalon-sur-Saône, France, on the day that the workers processed 16mm celluloid film for the last time. (The factory still processes X-ray film.) As Dean "watches the process of manufacturing X-ray film," Jonathan Jones wrote for the London *Guardian* (April 3, 2007, on-line), "she discovers a secret world of ethereal colour and beauty. Film is not just lovely when projected, it turns out, but even in the way it is treated in a factory." The prevalence of digital video notwithstanding, Dean has continued to work with 16mm film. She told Rina Carvajal in an interview for *Tacita Dean: Film Works* that with video, "there's no depth of field, there's no black," that celluloid "is about light and emulsion and lenses" as opposed to "pixelization and electronic code," and that she loves the tactile process of editing film. "It's just the rapidity with which the digital age has pushed film aside that makes it suddenly look as if I'm working with obsolete technology like a fetishist," she said. "But I'm not; I'm just fighting for the medium I love."

In 2007 Dean was commissioned to create a piece related to the writer W. G. Sebald for the exhibition Waterlog, mounted at the Castle Museum in Norwich, England. The result was *Michael Hamburger*, a film about one of the translators of Sebald's prose and a good friend of his. Hamburger, who, like Sebald, had emigrated from Germany (in Hamburger's case, to escape the Nazis) and settled in England, was also a poet, biographer, and college professor. The 28-minute film focuses on Hamburger's lovingly cultivated apple orchard, some grown from seeds given to him. "The austerity of a writer's life and the ripe sensuality of the fruit merge, in the film, to form something like a Cézanne still life," Karen Rosenberg wrote for the *New York Times* (April 24, 2009), after viewing the film at the Marian Goodman Gallery, which, along with the Frith Street Gallery, represents Dean. A blurb for the Frith gallery, in London, where the film was shown in 2007, reads in part, "[Hamburger's] rambling house and its encroaching garden, the sunlight, the rattling wind and then the appearance of a rainbow all act as metaphor to the man as poet." Also on view at the same show was Dean's film *Darmstädter Werkblock* (2007), whose subject is the gallery in the Hessisches Landesmuseum, in Darmstadt, Germany, that housed an installation by the German artist Joseph Beuys. Prohibited from taking pictures of the objects in the installation, Dean focused on the gallery's old, heavily patched muslim-covered walls and stained carpeting.

In 2007 Dean made six films called *Merce Cunningham Performs Stillness (in Three Movements) to John Cage's Composition 4'33" with Trevor Carlson, New York City, 28 April 2007*. The avant-garde choreographer and dancer Merce Cunningham maintained a creative partnership and personal relationship with the composer John Cage for many years, until Cage's death, in 1992. In the Cage piece that Dean used, a musician on stage in a concert hall sits motionless for the duration of the four-minute-33-second, three-"movement" work, "written" in 1952; the audience hears only the sounds they themselves may produce along with ambient sounds inside the theater and sounds from outside loud enough to penetrate the building's walls.

Dean filmed Cunningham with a stationary camera as he sat on a nondescript chair in the practice studio of his dance company; when Trevor Carlson, the executive director of the dance company, indicated that another "movement" had started, Cunningham changed his position. Each of the six films was shot from a different position in the room, and each was shown so that the viewer saw Cunningham in his full size. The films debuted at the Dia Art Foundation museum in Beacon, New York. "Dean's film of Mr. Cunningham's performance is about the sound and motion of history in action," Holland Cotter wrote for the *New York Times* (August 21, 2009, on-line): "the personal history of one man's fidelity to the memory of another; the cultural history of a living artist transmitting and rejuvenating the creative essence of one who has died; the contemporary history of a younger artist preserving and honoring all this, and the two men (the piece is above all a portrait of Mr. Cunningham) in her art."

The last collaboration between Dean and Cunningham, who died in July 2009, was *Craneway Event* (2009). For that film Dean shot the legendary choreographer rehearsing with his company at a former Ford auto-assembly plant in California. Dean was in the process of editing the film when Cunningham died; she said, as quoted on the Frith Street Gallery Web site, "I realised that I was in the unique position of still being able to work with him and to create something new, not only about him, but also with him. Although I lost the pleasure of imagining him watching the film, I gained a different sort of Muse. Merce's joy in the process was steadfastly there and his enthusiasm seemed to have a directional force. I began to feel that Merce had set up the components that make up the film—the building, the dancers, the light, the ships and the birds, because he knew they would not fail him in absentia."

In 2009 the Nicola Trussardi Foundation commissioned Dean to create a piece on the Italian painter Girgio Morandi (1890–1964), nearly all of whose many still-lifes show plain bottles, jugs, and other vessels from the artist's small collection of such containers arranged linearly, side by side, in one or several rows. Dean shot two films, *Still Life* and *Day for Night*, in Morandi's newly restored studio in Bologna, Italy. Not permitted to touch or move anything in it, she photographed (for *Still Life*) the sheet of paper on which Morandi made preliminary sketches for his paintings—many intersecting penciled outlines of the bottoms of the containers. For *Day for Night* she focused her camera on the objects that served as Morandi's subjects, showing them singly, juxtaposed in time rather than space.

Copies of her films and other works by Dean have been acquired for more than 30 public collections. The Museum of Modern Art in New York City owns one of eight copies of *T&I* (2006), a somber image of sky, land, and water made from an old postcard that Dean magnified and reproduced by a difficult, all-but-forgotten process called photogravure. Each of the 25 sheets in *T&I* is more than two feet high by a bit less than three feet wide and contains text chalked-in by Dean, some alluding to the tragic mythical lovers Tristan and Isolde and others to Donald Crowhurst. According to the museum's Web site, "The rich velvety texture of the photogravure medium contributes a nineteenth-century patina that is ideally suited to the intensity and foreboding melancholy of the subject." The museum also owns a copy of Dean's much-lauded *Crowhurst* (2006), a gelatin silver print about 19 feet by 13 feet, made from another found postcard, that shows a famous tree, said to be 4,000 years old, known in England as the Crowhurst yew.

Analogue: Drawings 1991–2006, edited by Theodora Vischer and Isabel Friedli, contains many of Dean's drawings on paper, blackboards, alabaster, and photographs. Images of many of the postcards Dean found at flea markets appear in her book *FLOH* (2001), written with Martyn Ridgewell. Other books with text by Dean include *Place* (2005), co-written by Jeremy Millar; a contribution to a series called Art Works, it explores such aspects of place as urban and natural settings, political boundaries, fantastical and mythical sites, and itinerary. *An Aside* (2005) accompanied a National Touring Exhibition show that Dean curated in 2005. The 17 artists represented include Peter Fischli, Joseph Beuys, Gerhard Richter, Thomas Schutte, and Kurt Schwitters.

Dean lives and works in Berlin. She has one son, Rufus, who was born in 2005. Rufus's godfather is the novelist Jeffrey Eugenides.

—W.D.

Suggested Reading: *ArtForum* (on-line) Mar. 1999; *Bomb* (on-line) Spring 2006; Frith Street Gallery (on-line); (London) *Guardian* p8 Nov. 4, 1999, (on-line) Feb. 20, 2001, Sep. 29, 2005, Apr. 3, 2007; Dean, Tacita and Briony Fer. *Tacita Dean: Film Works*, 2007

Selected Films: *The Story of Beard*, 1992; *The Martyrdom of St. Agatha*, 1994; *A Bag of Air*, 1995; *Disappearance at Sea I*, 1996; *Disappearance at Sea II (Voyage de Guérison*, 1997; *Teignmouth Electron*, 1999; *Fernsehturm*, 2001; *The Green Ray*, 2001; *Pie*, 2003; *Palast*, 2004; *Kodak*, 2006; *Michael Hamburger*, 2007; *Amadeus*, 2008; *Merce Cunningham Performs Stillness*, 2007; *Still Life*, 2009; *Day for Night*, 2009; *Craneway Event*, 2009

Selected Books: *FLOH* (with Martyn Ridgewell), 2001; *Place* (with Jeremy Millar), 2005; *An Aside*, 2005; *Analogue: Drawings 1991–2006* (edited by Theodora Vischer and Isabel Friedli), 2006

Deen, Paula

Jan. 19, 1947– Cook; restaurateur; writer; television personality

Address: Lady & Sons Restaurant, 102 W. Congress St., Savannah, GA 31401

"I retired at 18 and went to work at 42," the cook, cookbook writer, restaurateur, and entrepreneur Paula Deen remarked to Richard L. Eldredge for the *Atlanta Journal-Constitution* (April 11, 2005). With her folksy language, thick southern drawl, bright blue eyes, silver hair, and warm, boisterous persona, Deen is among the most recognizable and popular cooks in the United States. She owns a celebrated restaurant, the Lady & Sons, in Savannah, Georgia, and co-owns another; hosts three highly rated Food Network television series—*Paula's Home Cooking*, *Paula's Party*, and *Paula's Best Dishes*; has written or co-written a dozen cookbooks, some of them best-sellers, and a memoir; publishes a bimonthly lifestyle magazine, *Cooking with Paula Deen*, whose circulation in early 2009 topped 800,000, with an estimated 7.4 million readers; and markets her own lines of cookware, furniture, rugs, and spices. Deen insists on calling herself a cook, not a chef, because she has no formal training in the culinary arts; indeed, she spent

Dr. Billy Ingram/Getty Images

little time in the kitchen until she got married, in 1965, a few months after her high-school graduation. "It didn't take me long to realize that Mama was not going to show up at my house every day and cook," she told Kate Coyne for *Good Housekeeping* (May 2008). During her more than two decades as a stay-at-home wife and mother, Deen relied on her maternal grandmother's recipes for traditional southern fare and her own ingenuity in the kitchen. For much of that time, Deen left her house as rarely as possible, because she suffered from agoraphobia, an anxiety disorder marked by fear of having a panic attack in a public place or social situation. Until 1989, when she found herself in dire need of money, she told an interviewer for *Good Housekeeping* (November 2009), "I never had to take complete responsibility for myself. And then in my 40s, I had to face the fact, maybe you do have to take care of yourself, Paula, and maybe you can do a better job at it. I made a commitment that I was going to do whatever it took to care for my boys and become financially independent, and I would not let anything stop me." Having conquered her agoraphobia on her own, she began selling her homemade bag lunches to Savannah office workers with the help of her sons, Jamie and Bobby Deen. That humble business was the beginning of what is now the multifaceted corporate entity known as Paula Deen Enterprises, in which Jamie and Bobby Deen play major roles, as managers of the Lady & Sons.

Deen has attributed a large part of the appeal of her recipes to their simplicity. Her style of southern cooking, she said, as quoted by the writer John Behrendt in his introduction to her first book, *The Lady & Sons Savannah Country Cookbook*, "does not require a sophisticated palate. It's poor-man's food. Kids don't have to acquire a taste for it. They love it from the start. Nothing's flown in. It's all home-grown. There's no quail, no pheasant, no filet mignon, no foie gras, no truffles, no snails, no caviar, and no crepes. Southern dishes do not require split-second timing. They do not 'fall' in the oven. We don't go in for ornate presentation, either, or sculpted desserts. We just heap food on the plate." (Behrendt himself figures in Deen's journey to prosperity: his book *Midnight in the Garden of Good and Evil*, which spent four years on the *New York Times* best-seller list in the mid-1990s, is set in Savannah and gave the city's tourism industry an enormous boost.)

Deen's heavy use of butter, mayonnaise, heavy cream, artificial whipped cream, cheese, ham hocks, and other fat- and calorie-laden ingredients contributes to the tastiness of her creations. It has also sparked much criticism at a time when obesity among adults and children in the U.S. has become a major health problem, since diabetes and other life-threatening diseases strike those who are obese with far more frequency than they do those of normal weight. According to Chris Martell, writing for the *Wisconsin State Journal* (January 23, 2010), the Physicians Committee for Responsible Medicine, a nonprofit group, listed *Paula Deen's Kitchen Classics* (2005) among the five worst cookbooks of the 2000s, declaring that its "high-fat recipes help

explain why America's obesity-related medical spending doubled over the past decade." Deen has responded to such criticism by emphasizing the importance of moderation in people's diets and suggesting that her food be included in meal plans only as an occasional treat. "I'm your cook, not your doctor," she has often said. Deen has also been disparaged for including canned and other ready-made foods in her recipes. She has countered that complaint by noting that most contemporary home cooks have far less time to spend in the kitchen than those in earlier generations, and thus they appreciate shortcuts. In November 2008 *Forbes* included Deen among the 100 most powerful celebrities in the world and reported that she had earned $4.5 million in 2007.

Deen was born Paula Ann Hiers on January 19, 1947 in Albany, in southwestern Georgia. Her family lived in River Bend, a few miles from Albany, where her maternal grandparents, John and Irene Paul, owned and operated a motel, a restaurant, a skating rink, and a swimming pool. Her father, Earl Wayne Hiers, worked at a car dealership; her mother, Corrie (Paul) Hiers, helped the Pauls at their restaurant. When Deen was six her parents bought a gas station and a souvenir shop in River Bend; her father operated the gas station, her mother the shop. Her brother, Earl W. Hiers Jr., nicknamed Bubba, was born the next year; he is the co-owner, with Deen, and manager of Uncle Bubba's Oyster House, which opened in 2004, and the author of *Uncle Bubba's Savannah Seafood*.

Deen attended Albany High School, where she was a member of the cheerleading squad. As a teenager she had "a very busy social life . . . ," she told Kate Coyne. "I really didn't have an interest in being in the kitchen until after I was married." After her graduation, in 1965, Deen asked for her parents' permission to attend modeling school in Atlanta; they refused, because they did not want her to live by herself in the city. She vehemently rejected her father's suggestion that, instead, she become a dental hygienist. Unable to think of another option, she married her high-school sweetheart, Jimmy Deen, in November 1965. Her husband worked at a car dealership.

In 1966 Paula Deen's father died. Her first son, Jamie, was born the next year. By the time her second son, Bobby, was born, in 1970, her husband had become a heavy drinker. That same year Deen's mother died, and her brother, then 16, moved into the Deens' home. The loss of her remaining parent, compounded by her domestic troubles, pushed Deen to an emotional low. "My spirit was broken," she wrote in her memoir. "My mind wasn't doing too good either. I felt increasingly fearful when I had to leave my house. So mostly, I stayed in." "An impending sense of doom really hung over me, as if I'd be living in a dark valley forever," she recalled in that book. "Every day I thought I'd die, or, even worse, someone I loved would die. The blackness still didn't have a name. The days dragged by. I hated to leave my home, my comfort zone, but my kids were so small, they were totally dependent on my shopping for them and getting them some fresh air. I got out a little, a very little—and then hurried back home as though something was chasing me." She told Julia Moskin for the *New York Times* (February 27, 2007), "Some days I could get to the supermarket, but I could never go too far inside. I learned to cook with the ingredients they kept close to the door." That limitation notwithstanding, Deen mastered the recipes (fried chicken, collard greens, pickled green beans, fried peach pies, and sour-cream pound cake) that her maternal grandmother had passed down to her.

In 1978 Jimmy Deen's employer went out of business, and Jimmy lost his job. Unable to keep up with their mortgage payments, the Deens lost their home. Although Paula Deen's fear of panic attacks continued to plague her, they varied in severity; when she felt strong enough, she would take entry-level jobs to help make ends meet. She has said that she was cured after forcing herself to drive in incrementally greater distances from her home. In 1986 the Deens moved to Savannah, hundreds of miles east of Albany. In Savannah Deen got a job in the billing department of a medical center. One day in the late 1980s, while watching *The Phil Donahue Show*, a TV talk show, Deen learned that her persistent anxiety was a disorder called agoraphobia and that thousands of others suffered from it. "Finally—it finally had a name. . . . I thought nobody else could be this crazy, and here was Phil Donahue devoting a whole program to it," Deen wrote in her memoir.

Deen enjoyed her job at the medical center, but her salary and her husband's were not enough to pay their bills, and she began to look for a way to earn more money. An account of a woman in Atlanta who sold snacks to beauty-salon customers gave Deen the idea of delivering bag lunches to Savannah office workers. In 1989, with only $200 to spare, she bought a cooler, groceries, and a license to start a business—the Bag Lady. She made sandwiches, salads, and desserts, which her sons sold on-site during workers' lunch breaks. At about the same time, Deen and her husband divorced. "He was a good man, but he was pulling in one direction and I was pulling in the other," she told Jac Chebatoris for *Newsweek* (April 6, 2007, on-line).

Deen soon added catering to her business. By 1991, buoyed by praise from her growing clientele, she opened a full-service restaurant, the Lady, in a Best Western hotel on Savannah's Southside. In the following years she dreamed of moving her business to a site in historic downtown Savannah. When she had saved $20,000, she tried to get a loan to make her dream a reality, but for months every bank she approached rejected her application. Then one loan officer and bank agreed to fund her endeavor (she remains their loyal customer to this day), but not with enough money to enable her to go ahead with it. At that point an aunt and uncle of hers signed over one of their certificates of de-

posit (CDs) to Deen, making up the shortfall. Deen's second restaurant, renamed the Lady & Sons, opened in 1996, and she soon repaid her aunt and uncle, with twice the interest they would have gotten if their CD had remained in their bank. "Bobby would make desserts and Jamie was really talented with cold salads and things like that," Deen told Susan Houston for the Raleigh, North Carolina, *News & Observer* (April 6, 2005). "I didn't want my children to be [uneducated] like me. Neither one was college material. They had no burning passions, and I had no money to send them to school. But I wanted them to have choices." (According to a brief biography posted on the restaurant's Web site, Jamie "attended Valdosta State University and was working in various businesses when the Paula Deen brand was in its infancy.")

In 1997 Deen self-published *The Lady & Sons Savannah Country Cookbook*. She had sold only a few dozen copies when, the next year, a Random House executive ate at Deen's restaurant. (The woman "had my biscuits and hoecakes—which she thoroughly enjoyed," Deen told a reporter for the April 13–19, 2005 issue of *Creative Loafing*.) Soon afterward, at the executive's request, Deen sent her a few copies of the book, and within days Random House had agreed to publish it; the redesigned volume arrived in bookstores with the same title later in 1998. Soon afterward Deen appeared on the home-shopping TV channel QVC to promote her cookbook, and in a single day some 70,000 viewers placed orders for it.

The next year a friend introduced Deen to the reporter and TV personality Gordon Elliott, the host of a reality-TV series called *Door Knock Dinners*, which aired on the Food Network for several seasons. Elliott would arrive without warning at a viewer's house and then—if invited inside—would prepare a meal using only ingredients already in the kitchen, with the help of the celebrity chef who had accompanied him that day. "You show up unannounced and people just throw you out, as they should do," Elliott told Russ Bynum for the Associated Press (January 5, 2002). Deen, however, who joined him on several installments of the series, could charm viewers who balked at his proposal. "Paula was the only chef who could talk her way into a house I couldn't get into," Elliott said.

In December 1999 the *USA Today* food critic Jerry Shriver honored the Lady & Sons for making what he dubbed the International Meal of the Year. "Paula Deen's home-style Southern menu at The Lady & Sons turned me into a ravenous beast unmindful of manners, cholesterol, North-South diplomacy and the dropped jaws of my companions . . . ," Shriver wrote. "I'm not proud of what went down on that sunny Saturday afternoon, but I learned something about myself: Though I had stuffed my face on two continents during the past year, apparently I had starved my soul." The year 2000 saw the publication of Deen's second cookbook, *The Lady & Sons, Too!: A Whole New Batch of Recipes from Savannah*.

In the aftermath of the September 11, 2001 terrorist attacks, Elliott, without much effort, successfully pitched to Food Network executives his idea for a cooking show that Deen would host. "People out there are looking for this kind of comfort," he told them, as Deen recalled to Mary Jane Park for the *St. Petersburg (Florida) Times* (September 8, 2004). On *Paula's Home Cooking*, which has aired since November 2002, Deen demonstrates how to prepare simple southern-style meals featuring traditional "comfort food." The series was an immediate hit. In 2007 it won the Daytime Emmy Award for outstanding lifestyle program, and Deen received the Daytime Emmy for outstanding lifestyle host.

The popularity of Deen's restaurant grew along with that of her show. A year after the debut of *Paula's Home Cooking*, the renovation of the third incarnation of the Lady & Sons was completed, in a 200-year-old, three-story building one block from its predecessor. In the restaurant's far more spacious new location, the seating capacity increased from 85 to about 330.

The first issue of Deen's bimonthly magazine, *Cooking with Paula Deen*, is dated November/December 2005. The publication offers information on such topics as cooking techniques, recipes, gardening tips, and interior decorating. Also in 2005 Deen made her debut on the silver screen, in the small role of the aunt of the main character (played by Orlando Bloom) in Cameron Crowe's *Elizabethtown*. Her second television series, *Paula's Party*, premiered the next year. It was taped in front of a small audience at her brother's restaurant until the spring of 2008, when it began airing from a New York City studio. On that show, in addition to dispensing culinary advice, Deen interacts with audience members; sometimes she flirts with men in the audience, sitting on their laps, blowing kisses to them, or spicing her chat with sexual double-entendres. Members of Deen's family, including her former husband, have appeared on *Paula's Party*, as have such celebrity guests as Michelle Obama (before her husband won the 2008 presidential election), the actor David Hyde Pierce, and the singer Gloria Estefan. In a critique of the show, Susan Stewart wrote for the *New York Times* (October 6, 2006, on-line), "Food has always been secondary to the Deen persona. Paula is about empowerment. Her own hard-luck story . . . comes up again and again in her patter. . . . She offers homespun wisdom—'Anything worth having is not gonna be easy'—and volunteers that when she started her first catering business, she was so poor that she couldn't afford a hairnet and wore her own underwear on her head. You won't remember much about her fake crab cakes, but the underwear anecdote is unforgettable. And it's naughty, at least by Ms. Deen's retro standards." Stewart concluded, "Ms. Deen harks back to a time when sin was a bigger concern than cholesterol, when it was O.K. to

use canned soup, and flirting was an art form. So what if she's started believing her own publicity? She's not the only one."

Deen's memoir, *Paula Deen: It Ain't All About the Cookin'* (written with Sherry Suib Cohen), was published in 2007. "This wonderfully nourishing book will have readers laughing, crying, and hungry for more," John Charles wrote for *Library Journal Review* (March 15, 2007), after noting that Deen had presented her reminiscences and beliefs in a "warm, comfortable, and occasionally salty style." "Anyone who's ever watched, mesmerized, as the author of this memoir pan-fries a porkchop on the Food Network will find lots to savor in her down-home life story . . . ," a *Publishers Weekly* (December 31, 2007) critic advised. "Deen writes the way she talks—lots of ain'ts, darlings and honeys—but the effect is charming and disarmingly upfront. On her early Food Network success, [Deen] says, 'I was not a size 2, but instead a sassy, roundish, white-headed cook. Women could identify with me. . . . I could be them, and they could be me.' She's absolutely right; when Deen has turned the last of life's lemons into Southern-sweet lemonade, readers may want to stand up and cheer, or maybe just tuck into a big, celebratory plate of porkchops."

Deen's third Food Network series, *Paula's Best Dishes*, started in 2008. Her recent books include two for children, *Paula Deen's My First Cookbook* (2008) and *Paula Deen's Cookbook for the Lunch-Box Set* (2009), both written with Martha Nesbit, and *The Deen Family Cookbook* (2009), written with Melissa Clark. Brandon Branch is the co-author of *Paula Deen's Savannah Style* (2010).

Deen's name is associated with the new Horseshoe Southern Indiana Hotel buffet and a Universal Furniture collection. In 2010 she started working with farmers on developing her own brand of fresh produce.

On March 6, 2004 Deen married Michael Anthony Groover, a tugboat pilot nine years her junior, whom she had met by chance three years earlier, after her two Shih Tzus, Otis and Sam, ran into his yard. Their wedding was televised as a one-hour special that remains among the Food Network's highest-rated shows. Deen and Groover live in a 4,800-square-foot house in Savannah. Next to the couple's bed are several carpeted steps, for use by Otis and Sam, who have tiny legs and cannot jump very high. Groover has co-written a book with Sherry Suib Cohen: *My Delicious Life with Paula Deen* (2009), which includes many of his own recipes. Groover has a son, Anthony, and a daughter, Michelle, from his previous marriage. In interviews Deen has talked about the difficulties she had to overcome as a stepmother. Her sons have published three cookbooks and host their own Food Network series, *Road Tasted*. Jamie Deen and his wife are the parents of Deen's grandson, Jack. A company called Old Savannah Tours offers a "Paula Deen tour," which ends with a meal in Bubba's restaurant. Deen herself hosts an annual weeklong cruise, called Paula Cookin' at Sea, which goes round-trip from Seattle, Washington, to Hubbard Glacier, in Alaska. In 2007, in collaboration with Smithfield Foods, Deen and her sons pledged to provide one million meals to local food kitchens.

—M.A.S.

Suggested Reading: Associated Press Jan. 5, 2002, Sep. 6, 2006; foodnetwork.com; *Good Housekeeping* p160 May 1, 2008; *Miami (Florida) Herald* M p1 Feb. 17, 2008; *New York Times* F p1 Feb. 28, 2007; pauladeen.com; (Raleigh, North Carolina) *News & Observer* E p1 Apr. 6, 2005; *Savannah Business Journal* p35 Apr. 1994; Deen, Paula. *Paula Deen: It Ain't All About the Cookin'*, 2007

Selected Television Shows: *Paula's Home Cooking*, 2002– ; *Paula's Party*, 2006– ; *Paula's Best Dishes*, 2008–

Selected Books: *The Lady & Sons Savannah Country Cookbook*, 1998; *The Lady & Sons, Too!: A Whole New Batch of Recipes from Savannah*, 2000; *The Lady & Sons Just Desserts: More Than 120 Sweet Temptations from Savannah's Favorite Restaurant*, 2002; *Paula Deen & Friends: Living It Up, Southern Style* (with Martha Nesbit), 2005; *Paula Deen Celebrates!* (with Martha Nesbit), 2006; *Christmas with Paula Deen: Recipes and Stories from My Favorite Holiday*, 2007; *Paula Deen: It Ain't All About the Cookin'* (with Sherry Suib Cohen), 2007; *Paula Deen's My First Cookbook* (with Martha Nesbit), 2008; *The Deen Family Cookbook* (with Melissa Clark), 2009; *Paula Deen's Cookbook for the Lunch-Box Set* (with Martha Nesbit), 2009; *Paula Deen's Savannah Style* (with Brandon Branch), 2010

Selected Magazines: *Cooking with Paula Deen*, 2005–

Selected Films: *Elizabethtown*, 2005

---

del Potro, Juan Martin

Sep. 23, 1988– Tennis player

Address: c/o ATP Tour, 201 ATP Tour Blvd., Ponte Vedra Beach, FL 32082

Nicknamed the "Tower from Tandil" for his height—six feet six inches—and his hometown, in Argentina, the 22-year-old Juan Martin del Potro earned a number-four ranking from the Association of Tennis Professionals (ATP) Tour in January 2010, four months after he won the U.S. Open, one of the four annual Grand Slam tournaments. Del Potro's unexpected victory in the U.S. Open came after he defeated Spain's Rafael Nadal, then the ATP World Tour's number-two-ranked player, in the semifinals, and Switzerland's Roger Federer, who ranked first, in the finals, in a grueling five-set match that lasted more than four hours. Del Potro began playing ATP World tournaments in 2006. In the summer of 2008, his four back-to-back ATP tournament victories shot his world ranking up to number nine, making him, at 19 years old, the youngest player in the ATP World Tour top 10. (In previous years he had been the youngest player in the ATP top 200, 100, and 50.) Del Potro's height—unusual for a champion tennis player—enhances his chances of returning hard-to-reach shots and enables him to serve with extraordinary power and from an unusual angle; he also has a very strong forehand. His being so tall has also presented challenges: he is prone to certain injuries and has had to work harder than most at developing his quickness on the court. As many observers have noted, del Potro has brilliantly overcome these chal-

Robert Prezioso/Getty Images

lenges. "Del Potro moves with nimble, graceful steps that defy his height," the tennis coach and commentator Brad Gilbert told Greg Bishop for the *International Herald Tribune* (September 8, 2009). "He takes the ball early, moves laterally and uses the leverage created by his long arms to produce power, especially from the baseline."

Of Italian descent, Juan Martin del Potro was born to Daniel and Patricia del Potro on September 23, 1988. His father is a veterinarian who once played semiprofessional rugby; his mother is a literature teacher. He grew up with his younger sister, Julieta, in Tandil, some 400 miles from Buenos Aires, the nation's capital. A surprising number of other notable professional tennis players also come from Tandil—Maximo Gonzalez, Diego Junquiera, Juan Monaco, Guillermo Perez Roldan, and Mariano Zabaleta. Del Potro has described Argentina as "sports-obsessed," especially with regard to soccer (called football there). As a boy he excelled at soccer, his favorite sport, and also played rugby and basketball. While walking home from soccer practice, del Potro often passed tennis courts at Independiente de Tandil, a sports club where the renowned tennis coach Marcelo Gomez worked. When he was seven years old, the boy began taking lessons with Gomez. "Even then you could tell he had nerves of steel and great strengths," Gomez told Vincente L. Panetta for the Queensland, Australia, *Sunday Mail* (September 20, 2009). "His desire, his power and his concentration made me think that this child was going to stand out in tennis just like he did in football." Del Potro's unusually long, thin legs led to his being nicknamed "Little Sticks" and, ironically, "Midget." Because del Potro's size hampered his quickness and mobility on the court at that time, Gomez focused on increasing the young player's power so that he could gain points quickly. "His size was going to limit his movement, so he always thought about the quick, hard-court game. His dream was the U.S. Open," Gomez told Panetta. Del Potro, who idolized the tennis greats Pete Sampras, Lleyton Hewitt, and Marat Safin, soon developed powerful serves and forehand shots.

In 2002, at the age of 13, del Potro won the Orange Bowl, a youth tournament held in Miami, Florida. The next year he earned wild-card spots in three local tournaments on the ATP Futures Tour—a series of tournaments two levels below the World Tour and one level below the Challenger Tour; he was defeated in the first round of each event. In March 2004 del Potro won his first professional match on the International Tennis Federation (ITF) circuit, defeating the Argentinian Matias Niemiz at a Buenos Aires tournament. In the second round del Potro lost to another compatriot, Sebastian Decoud. At the end of 2004, his record was seven wins and eight losses, with his finest performance in the quarterfinals of a tournament held in Campinas, Brazil.

While competing on the Futures circuit at the beginning of 2005, del Potro reached his first career final at a tournament—one held in Mexico, where he lost to the Serbian player Darko Madjarovski. In April of that year, del Potro won his first three Futures tournaments—two in Santiago, Chile, and the third in Argentina. By the spring of 2005, del Potro's improved ranking had allowed him to move up to the ATP Challenger circuit. At the first Challenger tournament in which he competed, a clay-court event held in Reggio Emilia, Italy, in June, del Petro advanced to the semifinals before

being defeated by a fellow Argentinian, Martin Vassallo-Arguello. The next month, at a tournament held in Campos do Jordão, Brazil, del Potro advanced to the final round before being eliminated by Brazil's Andre Sa. Del Potro won his first Challenger tournament in November 2005, at the Petrobras Cup, in Montevideo, Uruguay: he defeated the Serbian-born Boris Pashanski, who was then ranked 112 on the ATP. With that victory, del Potro's world ranking jumped 927 points, from 1,077 to 150. Also that November, with the Costa Rican player Juan Antonio Marin, del Potro won a doubles title at a Challenger tournament in Guayquil, Ecuador. Del Potro's record at the end of the 2005 season was 23–10; at that point he held the distinction of being the youngest player in the ATP's top 200. (The tennis season starts in January and ends in December.)

The 17-year-old del Potro made his debut on the ATP World Tour in January 2006, at the Movistar Open, in Vina del Mar, Chile. He advanced to the second round, where he fell to Fernando Gonzalez of Chile. In June del Potro competed in the 2006 French Open—his first career Grand Slam tournament. He lost in four sets in the first round to the previous year's champion, Juan Carlos Ferrero. Del Potro collected two Challenger-level titles that season, at competitions in Mexico and Spain. In July he advanced to his first ATP World Tour quarterfinals, at a tournament in Umag, Croatia, before losing in three sets to Stanislas Wawrinka of Switzerland, who went on to win the title. Del Potro reached the quarterfinals again at an October indoor tournament in Basel, Switzerland, before losing to the Chilean Fernando Gonzalez. At the end of the 2006 season, he ranked 99th, with a Challenger record of 17–10. At 18 years and two months, he was the youngest player to be ranked in the top 100.

Del Potro began the 2007 season by reaching his first ATP semifinals at the Next Generation Adelaide International, in New Zealand, before losing to Austria's Chris Guccione. In March, at the Sony Ericsson Open, on hard courts in Miami, del Potro defeated such highly ranked players as Marcos Baghdatis (number 17) from Cyprus and Mikhail Youzhny (number 16) from Russia, advancing to the fourth round, where the number-two-ranked Nadal beat him and then went on to finish in second place behind Federer. In June del Potro lost to Nadal again, in the second round of the Stella Artois Championships, on grass courts at the Queen's Club in London, England. That same month he reached the quarterfinals at the Nottingham Open, another grass tournament, before losing to the Croatian player Ivo Karlovic. Del Potro qualified to compete in Wimbledon, held in a suburb of London; he made his first career appearance there in July. After winning in the first round, he was defeated in straight sets (6–2, 7–5, 6–1) by the top-ranked Federer. Del Potro was eliminated in the third round at both the Masters Series Cincinnati tournament and the U.S. Open, both hard-court contests. In October at the Mutua Madrilena Masters, in Madrid, Del Potro captured his first victory over a top-10-ranked player, defeating the number-nine-ranked Tommy Robredo of Spain in the second round; he lost in the next round. By the year's end del Potro had compiled records of 21–9 on hard courts, 4–3 on grass, and 1–2 on clay.

Del Potro struggled at the beginning of the 2008 season, losing in the first round of Australia's Next Generation Adelaide International tournament in January and withdrawing from competition in the second round of the Australian Open, two weeks later, due to back pain and toenail infections; both problems continued to plague him for many months. After he lost several more matches, del Potro's ATP ranking dropped to 81 from the top-50 position he had held before that season began. In March he hired a new coach, Franco Davin, an Argentinian who had coached several successful players and who, at age 15, had set a record as the youngest player to win an ATP Tour match. Davin determined that del Potro's injuries and his sometimes erratic serve had been the result of his failure to condition his body properly. "Sometimes he would serve unbelievably and other times he would just put the ball in court," Davin told Barry Flatman for the London *Sunday Times* (September 13, 2009). "When he gets tired he relaxes and the first thing that goes is his serve. That needed to change." Del Potro, who, Flatman wrote, is "laid-back to the extent that he can quite easily sleep all day," was eager to improve his physical condition. "I knew if I was going to even think about beating Nadal or Federer I needed to be strong and more aggressive but I needed more time," he told Flatman.

After his injuries healed del Potro entered clay-court tournaments and avoided those conducted on hard courts, so as to minimize stress on his joints and back. In May he made headlines when, at the Rome, Italy, Masters tournament, he engaged in a heated exchange during a match against Andy Murray of Scotland, whom he has known since both were junior players. As the two switched sides in the second set, Murray asked del Potro why he had not apologized for hitting a ball toward Murray's head; del Potro reportedly responded by complaining that neither Murray nor his mother had changed and were "always the same." Del Potro and Murray continued yelling when they were sitting on the sidelines of the court, and after the match, Murray said, as quoted in the London *Telegraph* (May 7, 2008, on-line), "He can say whatever he wants about me. . . . Someone saying something about your mother who is one of the nicest ladies you're ever going to meet? I don't think that's really cool." An injury forced del Potro to retire in the middle of that set. At Wimbledon in late June and early July, del Potro lost in the second round to number-13-ranked Stanislas Wawrinka.

Soon afterward del Potro's performance began to improve. In July he won four back-to-back ATP titles. The first win in that series, and the first ATP World title of his career, was at the Mercedes Cup,

held in Stuttgart, Germany, in which del Potro, who was seeded seventh, defeated the sixth-seeded Agustín Calleri of Argentina in the semifinals and bested second-seeded Richard Gasquet of France in the finals. (Del Potro gave his sister his prize: a car.) In the following weeks del Potro won the Austrian Open, defeating the sixth-seeded Jurgen Melzer in the final match in just 59 minutes; the Countrywide Classic in Los Angeles, California, defeating the number-one-seeded American Andy Roddick in the final in straight sets; and the Legg Mason Tennis Classic in Washington, D.C., besting the Serbian Viktor Troicki in straight sets. Del Potro's defeat of Roddick had elevated his ranking to number 19—his first appearance in the top 20. The four straight wins earned him the distinction of being the first player in history to win his first four career titles in as many tournaments.

Del Potro's winning streak came to an end at the 2008 U.S. Open, in part because of continuing left-knee problems that required constant taping. Ranked 17th out of 32 players, he advanced to the quarterfinals, where he faced the number-six-ranked Andy Murray. Though del Potro impressed observers with his fierce forehands and ability to move quickly around the court despite his size, Murray defeated del Potro in four sets. Later in September, at the AIG Japan Open Tennis Championship finals in Tokyo, he lost to the Czech Tomas Berdych. Competing in the four Davis Cup events of 2008, del Potro helped Argentina's national tennis team advance to the finals, held in Argentina in November, where they lost to Spain. The 20-year-old del Potro finished the season with a career-high world ranking of number five, making him the youngest player in the top 10, with a record of 27–11 on hard courts, 15–3 on clay, and 4–2 on grass. At the end of the ATP season, observers identified him as a rising star. "I want to win a Grand Slam next year or in the next two or three years," he said, as quoted by an Associated Press (December 12, 2008) reporter. "I'm living a dream at the moment. When I was young I used to dream of being in the world top 10. But I want more. I want to be better. I still need to do a lot more work."

Del Potro began the 2009 season by securing his fifth ATP victory, beating the American Samuel Querrey in the finals at the Heineken Open in Aukland, New Zealand. He continued his strong performance for several months. He competed in the quarterfinals at several tournaments, including the Australian Open, where he lost to Federer in straight sets; the PNB Paribus Open in Indian Wells, California, where he lost to Nadal; and the Internazionali BNL d'Italia, held in Rome, where he fell to Djokovic. After losing to Federer at the semifinals of the Mutua Madrilena Masters in Madrid in May, del Potro faced him again at the French Open, in del Potro's first career Grand Slam semifinals appearance. The number-one-ranked Federer fell behind del Potro 2–1 after three sets, then went on to win the match in five sets, taking the final two with scores of 6–1 and 6–4. (Federer defeated Sweden's Robin Soderling in the final round.) His loss notwithstanding, del Potro's fierce playing against Federer impressed many observers. Del Potro went on to triumph over two other highly ranked players in the following weeks: he defeated Roddick in defending his title at the Legg Mason Tennis Classic in August and beat Nadal in the quarterfinals and Roddick in the semifinals at the World Masters Tour, in Montreal. In part due to sheer exhaustion, he succumbed to Murray in the World Masters finals.

By the time del Potro entered the U.S. Open, in Forest Hills, New York, in August 2009, the speed of his serve had increased from a bit under 160 kilometers per hour (or just less than 100 miles per hour) in 2007 to about 185 km per hour (about 115 miles per hour). He ranked sixth in the world, and many predicted that he would acquit himself outstandingly on the hard court. Without much apparent struggle he defeated Argentina's Juan Monaco and Austria's Jurgen Melzer and Daniel Kollerer in the first, second, and third rounds, respectively. He won in the fourth round, defeating Ferrero, in straight sets. In the quarterfinals del Potro faced the Croatian Marin Cilic, whose height exactly matched his. In the fourth round Cilic had scored an upset victory over Murray, who was ranked second at the tournament. After losing the first set, 4–6, del Potro handily won the next three. He advanced to the semifinals, where he faced Nadal, who had been troubled by injuries throughout the tournament. After losing his first serving game, del Potro dominated the match and, to the surprise of many, defeated Nadal in three straight sets (6–2, 6–2, 6–2), marking the Spaniard's worst defeat of his career at a Grand Slam tournament.

The next day, in the finals, del Potro faced Federer, who had beaten del Potro in two contests during the year and had set a record earlier in the season by winning his 15th Grand Slam title. There was significant excitement over the match, not least because Federer had held the U.S. Open title for the last five years—every year in which he had competed. As many observers noted, del Potro looked skittish at the beginning of the match and made several wild shots, resulting in a first-set loss, 4–6. In the second set, with the score 5–4 in Federer's favor, del Potro challenged one of the umpire's "out" calls on one of his shots. Federer, a longtime critic of the use of technology in tennis's review system, protested that del Potro had taken too long to make the call, and when the umpire replied, Federer made an uncharacteristically profane response. The "out" call was ultimately overturned, helping del Potro win that point and eventually the set, after the two competed in a lengthy, tie-breaking game. Federer won the third set, 6–4, despite repeatedly failing to keep his first serve in play. Although del Potro came within two points of losing the match during the fourth set, his strong serve and backhand rescued him, as did his saving of 17 out of 22 break points—a remarkable statistic—and he won the fourth set in a tiebreaker.

Del Potro won the final set, 6–2, when one of Federer's shots sailed out of bounds. In addition to raising his ranking, the victory made del Potro the first person to triumph over Nadal and Federer on consecutive days. "I had two dreams this week," del Potro said shortly after the match with Federer, as quoted by Mark Hodgkinson in the London *Telegraph* (September 15, 2009). "One was to win the US Open and the other one was to be like Roger. One is done, but I need to improve a lot to be like Roger. Roger fought until the final point. He is a great champion. I'm very happy to be here with this trophy, with these people, on this court. This will be in my mind forever." When the champion returned to Tandil, he was greeted by a horde of reporters and fans, and a parade was held in his honor.

Despite his outstanding successes, the shy and modest del Potro still thought of himself as an underdog after the U.S. Open. "To me there is Roger, there is Rafa [Nadal]. Then there are other top guys like Murray and Djokovic who are the ones people are expecting to win a big title if the top two don't," he told Barry Flatman for the London *Sunday Times* (October 18, 2009). "Me? I'm still in the pack behind the top guys. Sure I won the US Open, which has always been my greatest ambition, but I've come to the conclusion that it was a big surprise for me to give the performance I did in those matches against Rafa and Roger. I honestly didn't think I was prepared sufficiently to do what I did." Franco Davin, del Potro's coach, told Flatman that his toughest job at that point in del Potro's career had nothing to do with athletic training. "The thing I have to do every day, with almost every conversation, is to repeatedly make him believe that he has now earned the right to believe he is one of the very top players," he told Flatman. "It's a battle to get Juan Martin to believe in himself. He feels hesitant, that's his natural personality, and it's important to change him."

In a Tokyo tournament in October 2009, in his first game after the U.S. Open, del Potro lost to France's Edouard Roer-Vasselin, whose world ranking was 189. The next month, at the ATP Tennis Masters Cup in London, he defeated Federer on his way to the finish, where he lost to Russia's Nikolay Davydenko. Del Potro lost to Davydenko in the finals of the Barclays ATP World Tour, held in London in late November, after defeating Fernando Verdasco Carmona, Federer, and Soderling in the round-robin semifinals. Del Potro finished the season with records of 41–11 on hard courts, 12–4 on clay, and 1–1 on grass. His record against top-10 opponents was 11–9. He earned a career-high $4,753,087 in 2009.

Del Potro won the opening match of the 2010 AAMI Kooyong Classic tournament, in Melbourne, Australia, in January, then was forced to withdraw because of a wrist injury. In mid-January he briefly held a number-four ATP World Tour ranking—the highest of his career—after Murray lost points due to his withdrawal from an ATP Tour event in Doha,

Qatar. At the Australian Open, held in Melbourne in late January, del Potro advanced to the second round after defeating the American Michael Russell in four sets. He then defeated James Blake in the second round, in a lengthy match consisting of five sets and 62 games (6–4, 6–7, 5–7, 6–3, 10–8), and bested Germany's Florian Mayer (6–3, 0–6, 6–4, 7–5) in the third round. He lost to Cilic in the fourth round in five sets. His persistent wrist injury led him to sit out the next several tournaments. Del Potro returned to the court for the 2010 ATP PTT Thailand Open, on September 28 in Bangkok, falling in the first round to the Belgian Olivier Rochus (7–9 in a tiebreaker for the first set and 4–6 in the second). At the ATP Rakuten Japan Open on October 4, del Porto lost (3–6, 0–6) to Feliciano López of Spain in the first round.

Del Potro has half-jokingly expressed his ambition to play professional soccer someday. "He was talented in football despite his height," Horacio Morrone, the president of the club where del Potro began playing tennis, told Vincente L. Panetta. "He was a great goalscorer." Then he added, referring to legendary soccer players from Argentina and Brazil, respectively, "If Juan Martin had stayed with football, he'd be a Maradona or Pele."

—M.R.M.

Suggested Reading: ATP World Tour Web site; *International Herald Tribune* p11 Sep. 8, 2009; (London) *Sunday Times* Sport p15 Sep. 13, 2009, p17 Oct. 18, 2009; (Queensland, Australia) *Sunday Mail* Sport p81 Sep. 20, 2009

Krafft Angerer/Getty Images

Demand, Thomas

1964– Sculptor; photographer; filmmaker

Address: c/o Esther Schipper, Linienstr. 85, D–10119 Berlin, Germany

Often described as one of the most innovative artists of his generation, the German sculptor and photographer Thomas Demand uses a labor-intensive process to produce huge photographs—some more than 16 feet long or high—that strike many viewers as eerie, surreal, or disturbing and throw into question one's perception of reality. That process has remained more or less the same since the early 1990s, when he was in his late 20s

and still a student. Demand starts with a preexisting photograph—typically, a picture of a room or part of an interior that he found in a newspaper, magazine, postcard, or book. He then reproduces with paper and cardboard, in three dimensions, the objects and setting in the photo. Demand's re-created objects and setting, usually life-size, seem at first glance to be faithful reconstructions, but they are not: what was a flat surface in the original photo now has tiny wrinkles, for example, or a surface that looked rough is smooth; the pages of an open book or sheets of paper strewn about are blank; walls, furniture, or other objects that were stained or grimy are now pristine. Since light and shadows greatly affect the appearance of everything we see, Demand then determines how best to light his creation. He takes many photos of it, choosing for exhibition only one (except for his few works that consist of a series of pictures); then he destroys and discards what he has built. Although his photos depict apparently commonplace scenes, and their titles reveal nothing specific, many show re-created settings of historically significant or widely publicized events, known to millions of people through photos: the room in which the last failed attempt to assassinate the German dictator Adolf Hitler took place, in 1944, for example, and the site of the bitterly disputed recount of votes cast by Floridians in the 2000 U.S. presidential election. "I don't see a hierarchy between more truthful and less important images," Demand told James Lindon for *Kulture Flash* (June 29, 2005, on-line). "But as I look more closely at what's left in our memory of a well-circulated image I discover they all enter a stage of fictionality." There is evidence of human occupation or activity in Demand's photos (desks, dishes, potted plants) but never any people.

"Demand's work is concerned with the distance that the act of representation places between the viewer and the often emotionally charged content buried behind his photographs' immaculate surfaces," Ellis Woodman wrote for *Building Design* (January 25, 2008). "Looking at his work is to be caught in a circular game of interpretation and misinterpretation." "There is something both added to and subtracted from these life-sized depictions of an alternate reality . . . ," Sarah Crompton wrote for the London *Telegraph* (May 27, 2006, on-line). "The pictures we see, particularly in the media, give us a collective view of the world. But Demand is also interested in exploring the way in which we imbue places with significance that in themselves they do not have." Demand's art, she continued, is "at once blank and hugely expressive. It forces you to look and look again at places that are at once familiar and alien; he asks you to see and to think." When Crompton told Demand that his photographs seem to have "a sense of expectancy," he responded, "Yes. They are waiting for you to bring your brain into it." Demand's body of work also includes *Parking Garage* (1996), *Balconies* (1997), and other photos of re-creations of ordinary structures of no apparent importance. According to a writer for *Design Week* (June 23, 2000), Demand "pick[s] up on neglected, overlooked features of the cityscape, attempting to create architectural swans out of ugly, utilitarian ducklings."

Demand's work has been exhibited in dozens of solo and group shows around the world, among them the 2004 São Paulo Biennale, in Brazil, where he represented Germany; the 2005 and 2007 Venice Biennales, in Italy; and the 2006 Shanghai Biennale, in China. In 2009 he had solo shows in Austria, Brazil, Spain, and Germany, the last of which was a retrospective at the National Gallery, in Berlin, and he was represented in group shows in eight cities in five countries. In 2010 exhibitions of his work were mounted in venues including the Guggenheim Museum, in New York City; the Whitworth Art Gallery, in Manchester, England; the Museum of Design in Zurich, Switzerland; and the Bucerius Kunst Forum, in Hamburg, and the Kunsthalle in Emden, both in Germany. Major museums on several continents have acquired his photographs for their permanent collections. Currently, Demand is represented by galleries in New York City; Tokyo, Japan; London, England; and Berlin, Germany. Since his first exhibition, in 1992, his work has been the subject of many museum catalogs and books and hundreds of articles published in art journals and other periodicals.

Thomas Cyrill Demand was born in Munich, in what was then West Germany, in 1964. His Web site offers no biographical information other than his year of birth, the years of his attendance at three schools, and his place of residence, Berlin; no information easily accessible in English offers any information about his childhood or youth. From 1987 to 1989 he studied church and theater design at the Akademie der Bildenden Künste (Academy of Fine Arts) in Munich. After that he spent three years (1990–92) at the Kunstakademie Düsseldorf (Dusseldorf Art Academy), also in Germany. There he studied with the German sculptor Fritz Sch-

wegler, who encouraged him to use architectural models as a means of expression. He began to make paper and cardboard sculptures, which he preserved as finished pieces and photographed to document their existence. He then spent a year in Paris, France, at the Cité Internationale des Arts, which provides artists with temporary living quarters and studio space. During that year he had his first solo exhibition, at the Galerie Tanit in Munich. From 1993 to 1994 he attended Goldsmiths' College, University of London (known unofficially as Goldsmiths), in England, where he completed an M.F.A. degree in sculpture. By then he was constructing sculptures for the sole purpose of photographing them and had educated himself in the art and craft of photography. Demand told Matt Watkins for *Tate Online* (Spring 2005) that he chose paper as his medium because of its "strong associative memories." "We know the surfaces, so we have a whole set of experiences about it," he said, "whereas fewer people have those experiences with paint." (Cardboard is heavy-duty, heavyweight paper.) Demand recalled to Watkins that when he started building models based on photos, he strived to make them as similar to the original images as possible; later he decided that "the imperfection is the beauty of it." "You see the seams in every wall, the folding of the corners of the furniture," Barry Schwabsky wrote for the *Nation* (November 9, 2009) about Demand's creations. Schwabsky also wrote that as a photographer, Demand "seems deliberately to cultivate the sense that things are ever so slightly overlit, that just a little bit less of the scene is in perfect focus than might have been possible, that the image could have been rendered with greater crispness and definition. . . . Rather than availing himself of the camera's potential for an inhumanly penetrating apprehension of surfaces, he evokes what one might call a normal, technically competent but unfetishized mode of looking. The photographs pretend to be a little less carefully made than they really are."

Some of Demand's best-known pieces date from the 1990s. Among them are photos of re-created settings of events in Germany, some from the years 1933 through 1945, during the dictatorship of Adolf Hitler, the leader of the Nazi Party. *Room* (1994), for instance, which shows an office strewn with rubble, is based on a photo of the room in Wolf's Lair, Hitler's military headquarters in Poland, in which a planted bomb exploded while Hitler was meeting there with 23 others on July 20, 1944. Four army officers died of injuries suffered in the blast, but Hitler was hurt only slightly. Army colonel Claus Graf Schenk von Stauffenberg, who planned the assassination attempt, and his fellow conspirators were executed within hours of the bombing. The source for Demand's photo *Archive* (1995) is a picture of part of the storage area for films by Leni Riefenstahl, who made propaganda motion pictures for the Nazis—most famously, or notoriously, *Triumph of the Will*, about the party's rally in Nuremberg, Germany, in 1934—and who continued to make films for another seven decades. Another 1995 photograph, *Office,* shows a room with blank sheets of paper scattered everywhere, covering desks and the floor; it represents an office in the headquarters of the East German Secret Service, which was looted by citizens searching for documents about themselves, following the collapse of the Communist regime, in 1989. The inspiration for *Bathroom* (1997) was a widely publicized picture of the bathtub in which the clothed body of the German politician Uwe Barschel was found in 1987. In what remains an unsolved case, evidence indicated that Barschel was probably murdered, by one or more people who tried to make his death look like a suicide.

Aside from the complete absence of print or other writing, logos, or anything else that might offer clues to the events to which the images allude, Demand's photographs appear to reproduce reality—that is, to offer glimpses of places that once existed or still exist. "This leaves the viewer with a disturbingly empty feeling," Donald Miller wrote for the *Pittsburgh Post-Gazette* (October 11, 1997), after attending a group exhibition that included photos by Demand at the Forum Gallery of the Carnegie Museum of Art, in Pittsburgh, Pennsylvania, in 1997. "We are left to re-evaluate our own environment, cherishing the specific over the numbing absence of detail." Writing for *Art in America* (June 1, 2005), Pepe Karmel expressed his belief that Demand wanted his images of sites in Germany to mirror the reactions of average Germans to events in their country under the Nazis and, in East Germany, under Communist regimes. "This willful erasure seems to represent the deliberate amnesia of a society that does not want to remember," Karmel wrote. Writing for *Parachute: Contemporary Worldview* (October 1, 1999), Stephen Horne linked the spotless surfaces and lack of distinguishing details in Demand's photographs to the "utopian worldview" held by modern artists and architects as well as the fascist dictators who came to power in Europe in the first half of the 20th century.

One of Demand's best-known photographs, *Corridor* (1995), shows his re-creation of the hallway that led to the Milwaukee, Wisconsin, apartment of the mass murderer Jeffrey Dahmer. Another, *Corner* (1996), shows the reconstruction of the desk and of a corner of the Harvard University dormitory room where Bill Gates, the co-founder of the Microsoft Corp., came up with a version of the programming language BASIC. *Room* (1996) depicts a model of the squalid hotel room in which L. Ron Hubbard, the founder of the Church of Scientology, wrote *Dianetics* (1950), regarded as Scientology's bible. *Barn* (1997), based on a 1950 photograph by Hans Namuth, shows the interior of the converted barn that the artist Jackson Pollock used as a studio. In a review of Demand's 1998 solo exhibition at 303 Gallery, in New York City, which included *Corridor, Corner,* and *Room,* Stephanie Cash wrote for *Art in America* (November 1, 1998), "Though today's viewer is too savvy to fall for most photographic tricks, Demand still plays with our willingness to believe that photos are proof of reality. . . . Even knowing Demand's technique, you look closer to make sure the images aren't real, that he's not pulling yet another fast one." In a 40-second video, called *Tunnel,* that debuted as part of the same 303 Gallery show, Demand's camera moved through a cardboard reconstruction of the underpass in Paris, France, where Princess Diana of Great Britain was fatally injured in a car crash on August 31, 1997.

A solo Demand exhibition at the 303 Gallery in 2001 included *Poll* (2000), an image of desks and phones in a nondescript work area. *Poll* was based on a picture of the Palm Beach County Emergency Operations Center, where the recount of votes cast by Floridians in the 2000 U.S. presidential election was halted. (Shortly afterward the U.S. Supreme Court, in a 5–4 decision, declared the Republican candidate, George W. Bush, the winner.) *Podium* (2000) shows Demand's reconstruction of the podium at which, on June 28, 1989, as ethnic tensions mounted in what was then Yugoslavia, the Serbian leader Slobodan Milosovic delivered a televised speech in which he referred to "battles" as a way to end the conflicts. Many observers believe that his remarks served an incendiary purpose, fueling antagonisms that later erupted into war in that part of Europe. "Demand's new works depict locations and scenarios in which historical truth is at issue," James Trainor wrote for *International Contemporary Art* (June 22, 2001), "whether sites where history is redrafted, facts selectively ignored, or photographic records given the status of truth."

A major retrospective exhibit of Demand's work was mounted at the Museum of Modern Art in New York City in 2005, when Demand was 40—making him one of the youngest artists so honored by that institution. The exhibition included *Clearing* (2003), a photo inspired by the Giardini in Venice, Italy, the area of parkland, gardens, and pavilions in which the Venice Biennale is held. For *Clearing,* Demand and 30 assistants worked for over three months to make upwards of 270,000 green-paper leaves and affix them to paper trees; light from a 10,000-watt bulb simulated rays of sun filtered through foliage. For *Kitchen* (2004), another photo in the retrospective, Demand re-created the cooking area near the underground hideaway in Tikrit, Iraq, in which a slovenly, unshaven Saddam Hussein, the deposed Iraqi dictator, was discovered by American soldiers in 2003 and photographed by one of them. The exhibition also marked the U.S. premiere of Demand's film *Trick* (2004), a 52-second reenactment of the juggler's act recorded in *Spinning Plates* (1895), by the pioneering French filmmakers Louis and Auguste Lumière. Among the many art critics who praised the retrospective was Pepe Karmel, who described it as an "unsettling alternate universe."

The five photographs in Demand's series *Klause/Tavern* (2006) show the exterior and interior of a building that once housed a bar in a German village. In 2001 a young boy held captive by 13 people, including his mother and stepsister, suffocated in the locked broom closet of the bar. The bar closed, and a pizzeria took its place. By the time the crime came to light, the pizzeria, too, had gone out of business. Police reconstructed the bar and photographed it, for use in their questioning of suspects. During a protracted trial that "scandalised the entire country," Sarah Crompton wrote, the five people who had confessed to the crime denied their involvement, and the woman who had managed the tavern insisted that the alleged events had never occurred; indeed, the boy's body was never found. When Crompton interviewed Demand, he said that the impetus for *Klause/Tavern* was his desire to make "a series of images of something of truly biblical horror," in Crompton's words. He cited as an example of another such project *Apocalypse*, a series of drawings made by the exiled German artist Max Beckmann (1884–1950) in the early 1940s. Pamela Buxton reported for *Building Design* (February 10, 2006, on-line) that in a lecture to Architecture Association members, Demand traced the genesis of *Klause/Tavern* to the feeling of "time standing still" that *Apocalypse* evoked in him: after considering states of mind (senility, for example) or stages of life (early childhood) in which time is "not relevant," he remembered the case of the murdered boy. Demand based his model of the building on published photos of the reconstructed bar along with photos he had commissioned. *Klause/Tavern* offers images of his re-creations of the bar's boarded-up entrance, the broom closet, a dead potted plant, and views of two ivy-covered windows. "I can't really say anything about the crime itself," Demand told Crompton. "I can only say something about the fact that I know about the crime." He told the Architecture Association audience, as quoted by Buxton, "I don't have a clue what you should take from this, nor what I should. . . . It's about putting another code on a message."

Klause/Tavern was included in a 2006 solo exhibition at the Serpentine Gallery in London. Also in that show was *Grotto* (2006), an enormous photograph of Demand's reconstruction of a cave on Majorca, a Spanish island in the Mediterranean Sea. Working from a postcard image, Demand constructed the cave out of 900,000 layers of cardboard, cut with the help of a computer program. He wanted to make part of the photo look out of focus without digitally manipulating the image; he has consistently refused to change his photos in any way (except to enlarge them, sometimes joining several huge sheets of paper for one image). To create the pixilated effect that would mimic lack of focus, Demand had some of his assistants make thousands of densely crowded, tiny holes in portions of the cardboard. The scope of the project and the enormous labor it entailed impressed some art critics more than did the photo itself. "Ironically the complexity of *Grotto* lacks the intensity of Demand's other works, which represent moments of achingly ordinary architecture," Eliza Williams wrote for *Art Monthly* (July 1, 2006). "A kitchen, an institutional stairwell and a barren print store all appear to resonate with an eerie silence, as if something catastrophic is happening just out of frame."

The nine photos in Demand's series *Yellow Cake* were exhibited at the 303 Gallery in 2007. Yellowcake is an enriched form of uranium, quantities of which, the administration of President George W. Bush alleged, Saddam Hussein acquired from Nigerian sources for use in making "weapons of mass destruction"; according to Bush, the probable existence of such weapons justified the invasion of Iraq by the U.S. and its allies in March 2003. The scant evidence for Iraq's purchase of yellowcake—letters on official stationery of the Nigerian Embassy in Rome, Italy—later proved to be forgeries. Demand visited the embassy and took pictures of its exterior; he surreptitiously photographed or committed to memory the appearance of rooms in its interior, which he was not permitted to photograph. "In a stunning congruence of subject matter and methodology, Demand's virtuoso reconstruction of the embassy, with its paper imitations of different kinds of paper, along with walls, doors and furnishings, is the handmade basis for photographs of a true crime scene," Paul Mattick wrote for *Art in America* (May 1, 2008). "Uniting the literal and the metaphorical, these works address both the material effectiveness of representation and the weakness of the knowledge it is purported to provide."

For several months beginning in November 2008, Demand's series Presidency was exhibited at the Spüth Magers Gallery in London. The series consisted of five photographs of models of the Oval Office in the White House. Demand based the models on photos he took during the last year of President George W. Bush's second term.

Peter Kelly wrote for the British magazine *Blueprint* (September 28, 2009, on-line), "In conversation, Demand talks softly, quickly and precisely. Like his artworks, an acute awareness of absurdity underlies almost every statement, but the wit is resolutely deadpan." Demand told Kelly that humor is "an underrated quality" that is present in all his photos. In Demand's studio in Berlin, Kelly saw "a reconstruction of one of Demand's children's bedrooms, which displays [the artist's] lighthearted side." "There's a toy in there, and every time I see it, I laugh because it's just such a very funny object to make," Demand said to him. Demand has a home and workspace in London as well as Berlin. For some years he shared his Berlin studio, in an enormous warehouse, with the artists Olafur Eliasson and Tacita Dean.

—M.R.M.

Suggested Reading: *Art in America* p136 Nov. 1, 1998, p146+ June/July 2005, p193 May 1, 2008; *Art Monthly* p34+ July 1, 2006; *Building Design* p21 Feb. 10, 2006, p16 Jan. 25, 2008; *Design Week* p16 June 23, 2000, p56 Nov. 17, 2000; *International Contemporary Art* p27 June 22, 2001; *Kulture Flash* (on-line) June 29, 2005; *Parachute: Contemporary Art Magazine* p21+ Oct. 1, 1999; *Tate Etc.* (on-line) Spring 2005; thomasdemand.de

Selected Works: photographs—*Room*, 1994; *Archive*, 1995; *Office*, 1995; *Corridor*, 1995; *Corner*, 1996; *Parking Garage*, 1996; *Balconies*, 1997; *Barn*, 1997; *Bathroom*, 1997; *Poll*, 2000; *Podium*, 2000; *Clearing*, 2003; *Kitchen*, 2004; *Klause/Tavern*, 2006; *Grotto*, 2006; Yellow Cake (series), 2007; Presidency (five photographs), 2008; films—*Tunnel*, 1998; *Trick*, 2004; installation—*Nagelhaus, Zurich* (with Caruso St. John), 2010

Courtesy of Nathaniel Dominy

Dominy, Nathaniel J.

May 27, 1976– Anthropologist

Address: University of California, Dept. of Anthropology, 1156 High St., Santa Cruz, CA 95064-1077

Nathaniel J. Dominy's interdisciplinary work combines anthropology, paleontology, genetics, ecology, chemistry, and biomechanics to shed light on some of the most enduring and perplexing questions about human evolution. "What changed?"

Dominy asked, as quoted in a University of California–Santa Cruz (UCSC) press release (September 9, 2007). "Why did our earliest human ancestors deviate from the pattern we see in living apes to evolve this incredibly large brain, which is very energetically expensive to maintain, and to become a much more efficient bipedal organism?" In an attempt to answer such questions, Dominy, who has referred to himself as a "food guy," explores the dietary habits and nutritional profiles of our hominin ancestors. "Diet controls everything—locomotion, social organization, and reproduction," Dominy has said, as quoted in a UCSC press release (May 1, 2007). "Something about our ancestors' diet shifted to favor them becoming bipedal and increasingly brainy. No other organism on the planet evolved that way."

In 2009 Dominy, who spends much of his time conducting field research in Africa, Southeast Asia, and Central America, was named one of *Popular Science* magazine's "Brilliant 10 under 40," an annual list of young scientists the publication believes "will change the future." He is an associate professor of anthropology and human evolution at UCSC, where he heads a laboratory that bears his name. The lab is dedicated, according to its Web site, to researching "primate visual ecology, material properties of foods, orangutan foraging behavior, tubers and cooking in human evolution, [and] molecular evolution of salivary amylase genes."

Nathaniel J. Dominy was born on May 27, 1976 to parents who were both astrophysicists. He has said that he was first attracted to the topic of evolution when he discovered *National Geographic* magazine at the age of nine. Dominy graduated from Central Bucks West High School in Doylestown, Pennsylvania, in 1994 and subsequently entered Johns Hopkins University, in Baltimore, Maryland, where he studied anthropology and literature and played for the university's football team. Dominy discovered his area of interest during a trip to Costa Rica with his anatomy professors for a research project. According to an article by Melinda Wenner for *Popular Science* (October 19, 2009, on-line), Dominy was given "the physically demanding task of catching small, drugged monkeys" as they dropped from trees. "You have this moving target, completely unconscious, and you have a net in your hand," he told Wenner. He returned the following year, in a quest to ascertain the monkeys' eating habits by studying their teeth. "I got this quick introduction to the importance of food and diet in thinking about the adaptation and behaviors of primates and humans," he explained to Wenner. "I just loved every minute."

After he graduated from Johns Hopkins, in 1998, with B.A. degrees in English literature and anthropology, Dominy entered the University of Hong Kong, in China, where he earned a doctoral degree in anatomy three years later. From 2002 to 2004 he served as a National Institutes of Health (NIH) postdoctoral fellow in ecology and evolution at the University of Chicago and then joined the faculty of UCSC as an assistant professor of anthropology.

At UCSC's Dominy Lab, the scientist and his colleagues have studied how humankind's tendency to seek out and digest energy-rich, starchy tubers and bulbs—rather than the low-starch, ripe fruits that apes eat—led to the development of our larger brains and thus to our dominance. While many experts thought that a diet rich in meat was the answer, Dominy was skeptical. "Even when you look at modern human hunter-gatherers, meat is a relatively small fraction of their diet," he explained to a reporter for BBC News (September 9, 2007, on-line). "To think that, two to four million years ago, a small-brained, awkwardly bipedal animal could efficiently acquire meat, even by scavenging, just doesn't make a whole lot of sense." Other scientists believed that the hominin diet consisted primarily of tough grasses and sedges, because of isotopic evidence found on fossilized hominin teeth, but were puzzled because the fossilized teeth were flat—seemingly better for grinding nuts and seeds than grasses. Dominy and his team studied African mole rats and showed that starchy tubers and bulbs produced the same chemical traces on teeth, thereby solving that conundrum. (The word "hominin" replaced "hominid" in the 1980s, when scientists split the Hominoid family into two subfamilies: Ponginae, or orangutans, and Homininae, which comprises three tribes—Hominini, or humans and their ancestors, called hominins; Panini, or chimpanzees; and Gorillini, or gorillas.)

Dominy has proved that humans are better equipped genetically than most nonhuman primates to break down starches because we have many more copies of a gene, AMY1, which results in the increased expression of salivary amylase, the sole enzyme responsible for digesting starch. Dominy and his colleagues found that human populations with high-starch diets tend to have more copies of AMY1 than those with low-starch diets. The BBC reporter gave as examples the Japanese, whose diet includes large amounts of starchy rice, versus the Yakut of the Arctic, whose traditional diet relies on fish.

In an article for scitizen.com (December 11, 2007), Erin K. Digitale asserted that in addition to supplying an explanation for how humans developed large brains, "this strong link between gene copy number and diet . . . shows a new route for evolution: Instead of waiting for a beneficial mutation to pop up, evolution can favor duplicating existing genes with useful functions." She wrote of the tubers and roots, "Not only were the new foods readily available, they had the advantage of being less fibrous than fruits. Reducing dietary fiber seems backwards now. For modern humans, it's a struggle to eat roughage and 'stay regular.' But our ancestors had the opposite problem: they ate so much indigestible plant matter that their bodies had to spend vast amounts of energy just grinding away at their food. The switch to starchy foods saved calories, let early humans grow shorter guts, and left more sugar to feed their brains."

In another set of studies, Dominy and his team showed that cooking or roasting tubers made them easier for our early human ancestors to digest and therefore increased the efficiency of accessing the energy in them. "We roast tubers, and we eat French fries and baked potatoes," Dominy said, as quoted in the UCSC press release of September 9, 2007. "When you cook, you can afford to eat less overall, because the food is easier to digest. Some marginal food resource that you might only eat in times of famine, now you can cook it and eat it. Now you can have population growth and expand into new territories."

Since his time at the University of Hong Kong, Dominy has also been interested in the visual ecology of primates. While still a graduate student, he studied the eating habits of apes and monkeys in Uganda, to learn how their ability to see colors influenced what they chose to eat. He discovered that the animals with the ability to distinguish between red and green found the most nutritious young leaves in times of scarcity. (The youngest, most tender leaves are often tinged with red, which helps them stand out from the surrounding green forest.) "We humans owe our unique color vision to our primate ancestors," Dominy told a Reuters reporter (March 14, 2001).

Dominy continues to spend much of his time in Africa. "You learn more from a week in the forest than a semester in the classroom," he told Jennifer McNulty for the *UC Santa Cruz Review* (Fall 2007). For the past three years, he has been studying the foraging behavior of pygmy hunter-gatherers in Africa and Southeast Asia, hypothesizing that their short stature is advantageous in the humid tropical rain forest, because it reduces heat stress and minimizes the energy cost of walking through dense vegetation. "The classic hypothesis is that short stature is the result of poor nutrition, but then you'd expect to see people of short stature in other habitats where the food supply is limited, like the western desert of Australia," Dominy explained to Jennifer McNulty for the University of California Newsroom Web site (October 9, 2009). "Instead, short stature has arisen multiple times in forests, in Indonesia and northern Australia, as well as in Africa. That makes me think something else is going on."

In a headline-grabbing study in 2009, Dominy and his colleagues used stable-isotope analysis to debunk a longstanding myth. In 1898, after two lions had terrorized railroad workers in Kenya for almost a year, they were shot and killed by a British lieutenant colonel, John H. Patterson. In his best-selling account, *The Man-Eaters of Tsavo*, published in 1907, Patterson claimed that the lions had eaten 135 victims. (The railroad company disputed that figure, claiming that the lions had killed fewer than 30 victims.) The sensationalistic book became the basis for *Bwana Devil* (1952) and *The Ghost and the Darkness* (1996), among other Hollywood films, and the taxidermied remains of the animals have been a popular exhibit at the Field Museum of Natural History, in Chicago, since the mid-1920s. The discrepancy between Patterson's tale and that of the railroad company was not fully addressed until Dominy analyzed the lions' hair and bones and proved that there had been only about 35 victims in total. His research also showed that while one lion ate both humans and grazing mammals, the other fed almost exclusively on the herbivores. Dominy and his collaborators hypothesized that the lions had been working in tandem to hunt strategically—an unusual occurrence probably occasioned by the facts that drought and disease had depleted the lions' conventional prey and that large numbers of people had gathered for the railway project.

In 2002 the University of Hong Kong awarded Dominy its Li Ka-Shing Prize. In 2007 he won the prestigious Packard Fellowship, which comes with a grant of $825,000 over five years. Dominy is known as an exceptionally dedicated and inspirational teacher. Every year he takes a group of students enrolled in his course on field methods in primatology on a trip to Costa Rica to conduct original research projects. "He's one of those faculty members who changes peoples' lives," Alison Galloway, a fellow UCSC professor, told Marissa Cevallos for the *Santa Cruz Sentinel* (October 15, 2009, on-line).

Dominy has been on the editorial board of the *International Journal of Primatology* since 2002. Since 2008 he has been married to Erin Butler, a Stanford University bioengineer. The couple live in Los Gatos, California.

—M.M.

Suggested Reading: *Popular Science* (on-line) Oct. 19, 2009; *Santa Cruz Sentinel* (on-line) Oct. 15, 2009; scitizen.com Dec. 11, 2007; *UC Santa Cruz Review* p22 Fall 2007

Courtesy of Brown University

Donoghue, John

(DON-uh-hew)

Mar. 22, 1949– Neuroscientist

Address: Dept. of Neuroscience, Box GL-N, Brown University, Providence, RI 02912

In 2006 the neuroscientist John Donoghue sent ripples through the scientific community when he unveiled technology that allowed a quadriplegic man to move a computer cursor—using only his thoughts. "If your brain can do it, we can tap into it," Donoghue told Andrew Pollack for the *New York Times* (July 12, 2006, on-line). The experiment was the result of decades of research and a yearlong clinical trial, and the technology was the most sophisticated brain-computer interface (BCI) ever tested on a human. "I think we're at the edge of a new era of neurotechnology where there's a whole armamentarium of devices available to physicians to interact with the nervous system," Donoghue told Joe Palca for the National Public Radio show *Talk of the Nation* (July 14, 2006). "Just like the cochlear implant, which has been implanted in 50,000 or more people to restore hearing, we're going to see a range of devices like this that will be able to couple the brain to the outside world and we hope someday coupling it up to paralyzed muscles and letting people move their muscles again."

Donoghue is the Henry Merritt Wriston professor of neuroscience at Brown University as well as the director of the school's Brain Science Program and chairman of its Neuroscience Department. In 2001 he co-founded Cyberkinetics Neurotechnology Systems Inc. to develop the BrainGate Neural Interface System—commonly referred to as "BrainGate"—the technology that eventually allowed his test subject to move a computer cursor. When Cyberkinetics closed its doors, in 2009, Donoghue and his team of researchers started the BrainGate Co. to continue their work. The BrainGate system consists of a sensor, implanted in the brain, which detects the signals made by neurons—cells that transmit information—when they communicate movement to a part of the body. (As long as the paralyzed individual's brain still functions properly, it can continue to generate the signals for movement.) The sensor is connected to a pedestal on the subject's skull, and the neural signals are then sent out through the wires on the pedestal into a series of computers, which then translate the signals into commands for basic movements, such as that of a hand moving a computer cursor.

Although Donoghue's technology is still in the experimental phase and has yet to win the support of the entire neuroscience community, it has the potential to enable paralyzed individuals to communicate better and control their surroundings to a limited extent. "I don't think we'll see something that's the finished end product fully restoring many, many complex actions for some time," Donoghue told Palca. "But I do think that within a short timeframe, within a few years, we'll begin to see products available that will have substantial impact on the quality of life of individuals with spinal cord injury and other movement disorders."

John Phillip Donoghue was born on March 22, 1949 in Cambridge, Massachusetts, the oldest son of John P. Donoghue, a bricklayer, and Nanette L. (Maxwell) Donoghue. Raised in nearby Arlington, Massachusetts, he is a third-generation Irish-American whose paternal grandfather, Stephen Sidney Donoghue, arrived in the U.S. in the early 20th century from the town of Kilgarvan in County Kerry, Ireland. When Donoghue was a child he developed a degenerative bone disease and spent several years confined to a wheelchair. He told Kyla Dunn and Jennifer Kahn for *Discover* (December 1, 2006, on-line) that that experience helped him understand "what it means to be limited in your mobility and not able to do the things that the rest of the world is doing."

Donoghue attended Boston University, where he received an A.B. degree in 1971. After graduating he found a job at the Fernald School, in Waltham, Massachusetts, a facility for mentally handicapped children. His supervisor at the facility, the Harvard University neuroanatomist Paul Yakovlev, had once studied under the Nobel Prize–winning Russian physiologist Ivan Pavlov (1849–1936), who had conducted famous experiments with conditioned reflexes in dogs. In those experiments Pavlov struck a bell when dogs were given food; because the food stimulated the dogs' salivary glands, and the dogs came to associate the sound of the bell with food, Pavlov was eventually able to make the dogs salivate by ringing the bell even when no food was present. (That result is popularly known as "Pavlov's response.") Through his work with dogs, Pavlov was able to map the motor cortex of the human brain, revealing which areas control movements of which body parts.

At Fernald Donoghue worked with Yakovlev in studying samples of brains, most of them damaged, to understand how they worked. He soon became interested in the brain's plasticity—its formation of neural pathways in response to stimuli. He told Richard Martin for *Wired* (March 2005, on-line), "By understanding how the plasticity of the brain can be captured and controlled, I believed we could promote the recovery of function in severely impaired patients." That belief inspired him to study neural activity. In 1976 he earned an M.S. degree in anatomy from the University of Vermont, and in 1979 he received his Ph.D. in neuroscience from Brown University, in Providence, Rhode Island. In 1984 Donoghue became an assistant professor at Brown's Center for Neural Science, rising to the position of associate professor in 1988. In 1991 he assumed the post of chairman of the Department of Neuroscience of neuroscience. That year he also was named the Henry Merritt Wriston professor of neuroscience. He became the executive director of Brown's Brain Science Program in 1998.

Earlier, in 1984, Donoghue had begun researching how the brain communicates movement commands to other parts of the body. He told a writer for the Business Innovation Factory Web site, "It's one of the great questions. It's sort of the essence of what is man." Describing the type of movement he was seeking to understand, he said to Dunn and Kahn, "I want to pick up my coffee cup, and my hand gets shaped and goes over there, picks it up, and grabs it. How does that happen?" At the time scientists had recorded the activities of only one neuron at a time, in monkeys and rats. Comparing a study of the brain to the experience of hearing an orchestra perform, Donoghue told Martin, "Listening to just one neuron is like hearing only the second violinist." Hoping to find a way to "hear the whole orchestra"—that is, record the activities of many neurons simultaneously—in 1992 Donoghue attended a meeting of the Society for Neuroscience. There, he met the University of Utah professor and bioengineer Richard "Dick" Normann, who had recently developed an electrode array, made of silicon, that could sit above the cerebral cortex and send signals to numerous brain cells at the same time. When Donoghue suggested that the device might also be used to glean information *from* the brain, he and Normann agreed to collaborate and began testing the device on monkeys.

In 2001 Donoghue, along with his fellow researchers Gerhard Friehs, Nicho Hatsopoulos, and Misha Serruya, founded Cyberkinetics Neurotechnology Systems Inc., in a licensing agreement with the Brown University Research Foundation. Donoghue became the company's chief scientific officer. The company aimed to develop a system of brain implants that would translate neural signals into bodily movement. In 2002 researchers at Duke University showed that signals from a monkey's brain could be used to control the movement of the cursor on a computer screen, once wires were inserted into the brain; in 2003 Donoghue reported that he had obtained similar results in monkeys using Normann's device, which was less likely to result in brain scarring. The stage was set for the system of human brain implants to be developed. The BrainGate Neural Interface System, commonly referred to as "BrainGate," won approval from the U.S. Food and Drug Administration in 2004, which allowed Donoghue and his colleagues to test the process on human subjects. By 2004 Cyberkinetics had raised $9 million for the BrainGate project.

For its first human subject, Cyberkinetics settled on 25-year-old Matthew Nagle. A former high-school football star, Nagle was paralyzed from the neck down. In 2001 he and several friends had gone to Wessagussett Beach, roughly 20 miles south of Boston, to witness a fireworks display; as the group prepared to leave, one of Nagle's friends became involved in a scuffle with another group, and when Nagle intervened, he was stabbed in the neck. The knife's eight-inch blade severed his spinal cord, ending his ability to move his limbs and anything else below his neck. He spent four months in rehabilitation and required a respirator to breathe. When Nagle's mother saw an article about Cyberkinetics Neurotechnology Systems in the *Boston Globe*, she brought it to her son's attention. "My mother was scared of what might happen, but what else can they do to me?" Nagle told Martin. "I was in a corner, and I had to come out fighting." (Nagle died in 2007 from a blood infection unrelated to the brain implant, which had been removed much earlier. The man who stabbed him, Nicholas Cirignano, was sentenced to 10 years in prison for assault with intent to kill and assault with a deadly weapon; following Nagle's death he pleaded guilty to manslaughter and received an additional 10 years' probation.)

Nagle's brain was disconnected from his spinal cord, leaving Donoghue and his colleagues to wonder if their patient would still be able to create the neural signals needed for movement. "That was the great unknown," Donoghue explained to Martin. "When he thinks 'move left,' were we going to get one neuron firing one time, 20 the next time? Or maybe not anything? Could he still imagine motion enough to make those cells modulate?" The BrainGate team hoped that if they could "read" sufficient neural activity, they would be able to translate it into commands for movement. In June 2004 the scientists used gamma-knife surgery—which focuses beams of radiation to treat tumors and other diseases of the brain—to attach 100 electrodes to Nagle's motor cortex; the electrodes were placed in the area where it had been determined, through magnetic-resonance imaging (MRI), that his arm-movement signals were generated. Nagle's skull was then closed, with a small opening left for a series of wires connecting the electrodes to a pedestal placed on the top of the skull. A cable, connected to a nearby computer, was then plugged into the pedestal.

After three weeks of recovery from the surgery, Nagle began his first session with Donoghue and his colleagues. He was told to think about moving his arm in various directions. "When we watched the system monitor, we could plainly see that neurons were briskly modulating," Donoghue recalled to Martin. "My reaction was 'This is it!'" He told Dunn and Kahn, "To me it was just incredible because you could see brain cells changing their ac-

tivity. Then I knew that everything could go forward, that the technology could actually work." The next steps involved recording and reading the patterns of Nagle's neurons as he thought about certain actions. After many trials the computer was able to "memorize" the neural patterns associated with specific movements, and when Nagle thought about an action, the computer attached to the pedestal translated the neuron signals into the movement of a cursor on the computer's screen. Soon Nagle was able to move the cursor around the screen, activate a television set, play rudimentary games, open electronic messages, move a robotic arm and a prosthetic hand, and draw shapes (with the cursor). He was also able to manipulate the cursor far sooner than anticipated. "I learned to use it in two or three days—it's supposed to take 11 months," he told Martin. "I totally knew this was going to work."

The results of Donoghue's experiment were published in the scientific journal *Nature* on July 13, 2006, eliciting excitement within the scientific community. The paper marked the first peer-reviewed publication regarding experiments using an implant more sophisticated than those that were merely attached to the scalp. In a commentary in the same issue of *Nature*, as quoted by Pollack, Stephen H. Scott, a professor of anatomy and cell biology at Queen's University in Ontario, Canada, said that Donoghue's paper helped to "shift the notion of such 'implantable neuromotor prosthetics' from science fiction towards reality." The experiment was also significant because it showed that Nagle's neurons were still active years after they had last generated movement.

Donoghue's paper also noted that many obstacles still remained before the BrainGate technology could be perfected and made practical. For example, the device's ability to detect neuron activity began to decrease after several months, and the system needed to be recalibrated daily. In addition, Nagle took longer than the average nonparalyzed person to move the cursor, and his movement was often unsteady. Also, a way had to be found to transmit signals wirelessly, instead of through a hole in the skull, because such a hole could eventually lead to infection. Not all of the scientific community saw BrainGate as a major advancement, either. Jonathan R. Wolpaw, a researcher at the New York State Department of Health, told Pollack that Donoghue's technology was no more effective than other processes that called only for attaching electrodes to the outside of the scalp. "If you are going to have something implanted into your brain, you'd probably want it to be a lot better [than BrainGate]," he said.

After their relative success with Nagle, Donoghue's team tested BrainGate on three other patients, with varying degrees of success. To date none of the test subjects has suffered harm because of the experiments, and all were able to move the cursor. In 2009 Cyberkinetics Neurotechnology Systems shut down, as a result of the faltering economy. That left Donoghue feeling uncertain for a time over the future of his project. "Cyberkinetics accelerated this field tremendously," he told Felice J. Freyer for the *Providence (Rhode Island) Journal-Bulletin* (June 10, 2009). "I figure it would have taken me 20 years to get the kind of money they provided." Donoghue and his team were soon able to obtain federal funding and donations to continue the research, with more than $8 million coming from the Department of Veterans Affairs, the National Institutes of Health, and several charitable foundations. They then formed the privately held BrainGate Co. and purchased the rights and assets for the BrainGate technology and intellectual property from Cyberkinetics. According to the BrainGate Co. Web site, the company's goal is "to create technology that will allow severely disabled individuals—including those with traumatic spinal cord injury and loss of limbs—to communicate and control common every-day functions literally through thought."

The BrainGate Co. is currently working on an improved version of its technology, known as BrainGate 2, at Massachusetts General Hospital (MGH) facilities in Boston. The research is being conducted in collaboration with Brown University's Department of Neuroscience, Division of Engineering, and Institute for Brain Sciences and with the U.S. Department of Veterans Affairs' Rehabilitation Research and Development Service at the Providence VA Medical Center. Members of the research team also include scientists from the Functional Electrical Stimulation Center at Case Western Reserve University, in Cleveland, Ohio, and the Cleveland VA Medical Center. Leigh R. Hochberg, a Brown University engineering professor and a neurologist at MGH, is directing the research alongside Donoghue. (Hochberg was also involved in the first BrainGate project.)

Donoghue's laboratory at Brown is recognized internationally as a leader in brain–computer interface. In 2004 Donoghue was named a runner-up for the "scientist of the year" award from *Discover*. He has written more than 50 papers for top science journals, including *Nature*, *Science*, and the *Journal of Neuroscience*. He has also served on several boards and panels, including the NIH's Neurology and Mental Health Institute board and the National Aeronautics and Space Administration's (NASA's) space-medicine panel. With his wife, Karen, he has two children, Jacob and Noah. The goal of his research, he told Dunn and Kahn, is to enable paralyzed individuals to control their muscles independently through technology. "I'm almost certain I'll never see somebody playing piano," he said. "But feeding themselves, doing simple tasks, I'm hoping that that's one thing that would happen."
—W.D.

Suggested Reading: braingate.com; *Discover* (on-line) Dec. 1, 2006; *Irish America* p72 Apr./May 2007; *New Scientist* p38+ Aug. 29, 2009; *Wired* (on-line) Mar. 2005

Courtesy of Shaun Roberts

Douglas, Emory

May 24, 1943– Artist; activist

Address: 355 Gaven St., San Francisco, CA 94134

An icon of the countercultural and antiestablishment movements of the 1960s, the Black Panther Party was founded in Oakland, California, with the goals of protecting members of African-American communities from police harassment and operating food, health-care, and other programs for poor blacks. Before internal divisions and battles with federal agents led to its demise, in the late 1970s, the party made a large impression on the public's consciousness, in part through its newspaper, the *Black Panther*, which at its height had a circulation of several hundred thousand. The paper's chief artist was Emory Douglas, who served as the Panthers' minister of culture and as one of their spokespersons after the party's founders were jailed or exiled. With distinctive, biting, sometimes incendiary images, Douglas's cartoons and illustrations expressed the frustration of his community and the goals of the Panthers' leadership. Douglas's work was described by Steven Heller for the *New York Times* (April 8, 2007) as "alternately angry and jubilant, yet always defiant." After his time with the Panthers, Douglas served on the staff of a local San Francisco, California–based newspaper for two decades. In 2007 an exhibition of his work led to the publication of the book *Black Panther: The Revolutionary Art of Emory Douglas*, with text by the Panthers' co-founder Bobby Seale, the actor Danny Glover, and others. Exhibits of Douglas's work have since been seen in cities in the U.S. and abroad. "Emory's art was a combination of expressionist agitprop and homeboy familiarity," the poet and playwright Amiri Baraka wrote for the book *Black Panther*. "I always felt that Emory's work functioned as if you were in the middle of a rumble and somebody tossed you a machine pistol. It armed your mind and your demeanor. Ruthlessly funny, but at the same time functional as the .45 slugs pouring out of that weapon."

Emory Douglas was born on May 24, 1943 in Grand Rapids, Michigan. The only child of a legally blind single mother who worked factory jobs, Douglas suffered from asthma attacks as a child. After a doctor suggested that a change in climate would improve Douglas's condition, his mother moved with him to San Francisco, where her sister lived, in 1951. As a child Douglas liked to draw, copying cartoons and other images from magazines; he has said that one of the only black artists he remembers admiring in his youth was Charles White, who made illustrations for the calendars his aunt received yearly from an insurance company. He has recalled experiencing racism, segregation, and police harassment from a young age and identifying with the struggles blacks faced as a group, particularly when he saw television footage of the brutal treatment of nonviolent civil rights demonstrators in the U.S. and South Africa. As a youngster Douglas had little interest in school and soon began to spend more time on the streets than in class. At 13, while watching "older guys" shoot dice in a park, as he told *Current Biography*, he was caught up in a police raid and sent to a juvenile-detention facility. Committing petty crimes, he returned to juvenile prisons repeatedly until the age of 18. When he was about 16, he was incarcerated at the Youth Training School in Ontario, California, where, still fond of drawing, he was shown professional art techniques. "Because I still had this desire for art, I got into the print shop there . . . ," he told *Current Biography*. "So that was basically my . . . introduction to doing something that dealt with the concept of design elements." Some of the more experienced people working in the prison print shop, as well as a counselor, suggested he go to college to study art.

Douglas enrolled at City College, a junior college in San Francisco, in about 1963. While attending classes on and off during that period, he decided to pursue commercial art, in which the school specialized. His studies gave him a solid foundation in creating printed art. By the mid-1960s San Francisco had become a hotbed of radical and protest politics, particularly on college campuses. "When I went there, there was this whole movement of black people to define themselves, and [achieve] self-determination, so it was the whole black power movement moving forward, and negating the name of Negroes . . . to define who we were as black people," Douglas told *Current Biography*. He was involved in the successful effort to change the name of his school's Negro Student Association to the Black Student Association, and he designed and printed posters, flyers, and banners for the group. Douglas also started traveling regularly to nearby San Francisco State University, where he would attend black cultural events and student-union meetings, becoming associated with what came to be known as the Black Arts Movement. In 1967 the poet, playwright, and essayist LeRoi Jones, who later changed his name to Amiri Baraka, took a post as visiting professor at San Francisco State University and pushed for the creation of black-studies programs in colleges; he established the Black Communications Project to develop and organize poetry, theater, and music events, and Douglas became the primary set designer for those performances, creating sets for plays including Baraka's *Madheart* and working with the poet Sonia Sanchez, the playwrights Ed Bullins and Marvin X, and others.

Through his involvement with the Black Arts Movement, Douglas was invited to attend a planning session for the First Annual Malcolm X Grassroots Memorial in January 1967, named for the black nationalist and Nation of Islam leader slain two years earlier. While Douglas was tasked with creating posters for the event, a couple of Oakland residents were said to be organizing a security detail, including an armed escort for Betty Shabazz, Malcolm X's widow. "At this time no one had ever heard of the Black Panther Party," Douglas told an interviewer for *Com-Raid* magazine (May 5, 2009, on-line). "The only thing I had heard were some guys were patrolling the community in Oakland." Huey Newton and Bobby Seale had founded the Black Panther Party for Self-Defense in 1966, in Oakland, heavily influenced by, among several others, Malcolm X (who had called for freedom, equality, and justice for African-Americans "by any means necessary"), the African anticolonial revolutionary Frantz Fanon, and Robert F. Williams, a leader of the National Association for the Advancement of Colored People (NAACP) and the author of *Negroes with Guns*. In addition to calling for armed protection of black neighborhoods against police brutality, which had intensified in the wake of riots in the nation's inner cities in the mid-1960s, the party adopted Marxist ideology in seeking to address poverty, unemployment, and lack of access to health care and education in black communities. Seale and Newton, in investigating legal avenues to impede the police harassment of blacks, had identified a law allowing citizens to carry firearms, which made it legal for the Panthers to patrol their own neighborhoods. The party also organized a free breakfast program for children of poor families, among other services. Douglas was instantly attracted to Newton and Seale's prescriptions for change. "Like many others I respected the civil rights movement, but it just wasn't something I was able to do, to turn the other cheek," he told *Com-Raid*. "Of course, that's a very courageous thing to be able to do but of course I wasn't one of those who felt at that time capable of doing that. So the Black Panther party was more appealing to my desire." The visual image the party projected was another key element of its appeal; members wore berets and black leather jackets. "It was about the self-defense, but it was more than that, because initially when they came over, they came over with the uniforms on and they had the guns with them," Douglas told *Current Biography*. "It just seemed that they had this spirit and organization about them and I wanted to know more about it and that was why I requested to become a member." After the memorial Douglas asked Newton and Seale how he could get involved in the party, then still a local organization.

At the time Douglas lived just three blocks from the apartment of Eldridge Cleaver, which the Panthers often used as an office. Cleaver, a follower of Malcolm X who had helped encourage the murdered leader's widow to attend the memorial, had been writing for *Ramparts* magazine, and Newton and Seale had been urging him to become the head writer and editor of the party newspaper they were planning. Douglas was at Cleaver's apartment to witness the creation of the inaugural issue (published on April 25, 1967), and seeing the crude materials Seale was using, he offered to use his skills to make it look more professional. Impressed with the result, the party's leaders asked him to take a position with the paper immediately, naming him revolutionary artist of the Black Panther Party. (Seale was chairman, Newton minister of defense, and Cleaver minister of information.) Beginning with the weekly paper's second issue, Douglas was involved in all aspects of its production until the final issue was published, 12 years later. He began taking the bus to Oakland, going on armed patrols of the neighborhoods there, participating in the free-breakfast programs, selling the newspaper, and pasting the artwork from leftover copies on walls, lampposts, and telephone poles in surrounding black neighborhoods. Douglas told *Current Biography*, "In those days you didn't have black people . . . going to the art galleries . . . because they were just going about their daily lives trying to survive. So therefore the art became a part of their daily lives as they went on their way to do what they were doing." Douglas said that while he shared the frustration that gripped black communities all across the country during that period, the Black Panther Party helped him develop the ideas that would inform his art. "I'm a young man [who was] apolitical," he told *Current Biography*. "My consciousness was just like everybody else in the 'hood, I didn't come up understanding socialism or communism or any other isms, but I understood the abuse, being confronted by it like many other young people who also came into the party during that time. So [learning the party's ideology] was on-the-job training. . . . It was also a reflection of the community work, and the party members coming back in, talking about the things that went on in the neighborhoods." Douglas told *Com-Raid*, "We enjoyed what we did. We were young people. Initially the original party member ages were from

age 15 to around 23. . . . So it was a very young organization at the time. We still had that arrogance and swagger about ourselves, and at the same time we knew what we were up against, what was going on."

On May 2, 1967, in perhaps their most memorable act, the Panthers appeared in front of the California State Capitol building, in Sacramento, to protest the Mulford Act. Also known as the Panther Bill, the measure—which made it illegal to carry weapons openly—was a direct response by legislators to the Panthers' having armed themselves. The protestors, including Douglas, were arrested, and the incident proved to be a major media event, boosting the party's profile, popularity, and membership considerably. The party grew to include 5,000 members in 48 chapters across the country. Those developments, in turn, brought a sustained government backlash. In the following months and years, as they became the primary targets of the FBI's Counter Intelligence Program, or COINTELPRO, hundreds of party members were imprisoned and dozens were killed in raids or in shootouts with authorities. After Newton was incarcerated, in October 1967, Seale named Douglas minister of culture, and after Seale himself was jailed, Douglas became one of the party's main spokespeople. Douglas explained to *Current Biography* some of the effects of the crackdown on the party: "It had positives and negatives. . . . The money that we were using for the social programs now had to be used, some of it, to help take care of the legal aspect of those party members who were incarcerated during that period. But also what evolved out of that was . . . being able to talk about why you were incarcerated unjustly as political prisoners . . . using that as a way to mobilize and educate people." Taking on increasing responsibilities in the party toward the end of the turbulent year 1967, which included arranging entertainment for fund-raising (he organized benefit concerts by Santana and the Grateful Dead, among other performers and groups), Douglas moved into a communal home and worked for the Black Panther Party full-time.

For the first few issues of the *Black Panther*, Douglas concentrated mainly on such ordinary tasks as layout. But around the fourth or fifth issue, his signature image, a pig—representing abusive police officers—began to appear. While Douglas was not the first to refer to police as "pigs," he was undoubtedly instrumental in popularizing the epithet. As Colette Gaiter wrote for Aiga.org (June 8, 2005), the Web site of the American Institute of Graphic Arts, over time Douglas's cartoons "extended the pig icon to represent the entire capitalist military/industrial complex." While government opposition to the Panthers intensified, the group maintained its uncompromising criticism of capitalism, imperialism, and racism. In an incendiary illustration that appeared in the paper in March 1968, Douglas depicted four lynched pigs identified as President Lyndon Johnson, former attorney general Robert Kennedy, Defense Secretary Robert McNamara, and Secretary of State Dean Rusk. The caption, signed "Emory," read: "ON LANDSCAPE ART: It is good only when it shows the oppressor hanging from a tree by his [expletive] neck." "All those people [depicted in the illustration] were involved in colonization and involved in the overthrowing of governments," Douglas told *Current Biography*. "So that's what that was about. They tried to play it off as these were great American heroes but in reality these were people who were overthrowing governments, assassinating elected leaders of governments all over the world, in particular in South America, during that period." Douglas explained that the combination of a strong ideological message and humor was both a direct way of communicating with the Panthers' followers, many of whom did not read a great deal, and a reflection of the character of the party and its members.

In 1968 the Black Panther Party made the decision to drop "Self-Defense" from its name and refocus its resources on social and community-welfare programs, legal battles to free its jailed members, campaigns to influence electoral politics, and expressions of solidarity with struggles elsewhere in the world against imperialism, racism, and capitalism. While mainstream sources portrayed the Panthers as hoodlums advocating racism, violence, and terrorism, and the FBI director, J. Edgar Hoover, famously declared them to be "the greatest threat to internal security of the country," the party's supporters argued that its main threat to the government consisted of educating people about their rights, preaching and practicing self-sufficiency, and providing social services where elected leaders had failed to do so. By 1971 the *Black Panther* had reached its peak circulation, roughly 400,000. While Douglas continued to write and draw acerbic critiques of the political establishment, he began complementing them with images of ordinary people engaged in quiet, individual acts of political struggle. One illustration, for example, showing a woman wearing a Panther button and holding grocery bags from a free-food program, had a caption that read: "This year, I think I WILL vote." Douglas both inspired and drew inspiration from activist/artists from around the world. Published regularly in poster form by the Organization of the Solidarity of the People of Asia, Africa, and Latin America (OSPAAAL, the acronym for its name in Spanish), Douglas's work reached people in many countries. Douglas has often said that he was inspired by the art then coming out of Vietnam, China, the Middle East, and Cuba. According to Stephen Williams, writing for the *New African* (March 2009), his "graphic style owed much to . . . the 'heroic worker' poster style of the communist bloc." In addition to helping with the party's community programs, Douglas ran a printing service, Emory's Community Printing and Graphics. "We used to do outreach to the community," he told *Current Biography*. "And we did it cheaper than a

regular commercial printer . . . just to make enough money to maintain our operation and to buy new supplies."

By the mid- to late 1970s, the COINTELPRO campaign against the Panthers "had begun to take its toll," as Douglas told *Current Biography*. "And then [began] the decline and demise." Along with pressures from without, internal tensions over ideology and the direction of the party began to weaken the Panthers. Some have argued that while the party leaders' charisma was an effective tool to rally people around causes, it could also account for the party's lack of durability, as a great deal depended on a few individuals who became targets. By the time the *Black Panther* ceased publication, in 1979, the party had virtually disintegrated.

In the early 1980s Douglas held a succession of jobs, including a brief stint at a silkscreen factory, while continuing to do community-related work. In 1984 he joined the staff of the San Francisco *Sun-Reporter*, the city's oldest African-American newspaper, as a production artist and prepress manager; he remained with that publication for the next two decades. During his time with the Panthers, Douglas had developed a good relationship with the *Sun-Reporter*, which published articles on some of the party's programs and received help from Douglas on production and other technical issues. Since he left the *Sun-Reporter*, in 2004, Douglas has continued to work as an artist and activist, holding children's art workshops and providing social commentary through his own art. In recent years he has created pieces about issues including HIV/AIDS, gang activity, the prison system, and the Iraq war. In 2002 the Los Angeles–based artist Sam Durant invited Douglas to deliver a lecture at one of his shows at the Museum of Contemporary Art (MOCA) in Los Angeles. "They had a lot of people who came into the museum who normally don't come to museums, to hear the lecture presentation that I did," Douglas told *Current Biography*. Durant and officials at the MOCA Pacific Design Center then asked Douglas to mount a show of his own work. The book accompanying the show, *Black Panther: The Revolutionary Art of Emory Douglas*, was published in 2007. "It got the artwork to a whole other audience of folks who had never seen it before," Douglas told *Current Biography*.

In 2008 and 2009 Douglas's work was mounted in exhibitions, modeled on the MOCA show, in museums around the world, including venues in Manchester, England; Sydney, Australia; Houston, Texas; and New York City. At around that time the video producer and multi-instrumentalist Doctor L (born Liam Farrell) animated some of Douglas's work and added live music for a show organized by the jazz saxophonist David Murray. The debut of the show, called *Tongues on Fire: A Tribute to the Black Panthers*, featured the band Living Colour and took place at the Festival Sons d'Hiver in Vitry sur Seine, France, in February 2010. The second and third installments took place at the Barbican Center in London and the Jazz à la Villette Festival in Paris, France, the following September.

Douglas is known for his modest and unpretentious attitude about his career. "More of a listener than one of the talkative crowd that gathered in Eldridge's apartment, Emory's own intensity came out in his drawings," Kathleen Cleaver wrote for the book *Black Panther*. Douglas's daughter, Cindy Devesey Douglas, wrote about him, "He himself has never bragged, boasted, or even mentioned [his role with the Panthers] to us in private conversation. My father . . . remains humble in the face of his accomplishments. My [brother] and I are proud of him as a human being, an artist, an activist, and a father." Douglas spent much of the past two decades caring for his ailing mother, who died in 2008, and he still lives in their San Francisco home. In addition to his daughter, he has a son and several grandchildren.

—M.M.

Suggested Reading: aiga.org June 8, 2005; *Black Panther* Oct. 21, 1972; *Com-Raid* (on-line) May 5, 2009; itsabouttimebpp.com; (London) *Times* (on-line) Oct. 18, 2008; *New York Times* (on-line) Apr. 8, 2007

Selected Books: *Black Panther: The Revolutionary Art of Emory Douglas*, 2007

Gabriel Bouys/AFP/Getty Images

Dudamel, Gustavo

Jan. 26, 1981– Orchestra conductor; violinist; educator

Address: Los Angeles Philharmonic, 111 S. Grand Ave., Los Angeles, CA 90012

"Aside from the hair, the first thing you might notice about Gustavo Dudamel is the joy, the exuberance, the passion, the energy, with which he conducts. Watching Dudamel conduct is mesmerizing, and audiences around the world can't get enough of him," Bob Simon said for a profile of Dudamel on the CBS-TV news magazine *60 Minutes* (February 17, 2008). A native of Venezuela, the 29-year-old Dudamel has been the principal conductor (or music director) of the Simón Bolívar Youth Orchestra (SBYO), the country's national youth orchestra, since 1999; of the Gothenburg Symphony Orchestra, the national orchestra of Sweden, since 2007; and of the Los Angeles Philharmonic Orchestra, in California, since 2009. He has also been a much-sought-after guest conductor of major orchestras the world over, and hundreds of thousands of fans have seen him on the podium via YouTube. "There are three main elements behind Dudamel's appeal," Alex Ross wrote for the *New Yorker* (December 14, 2009). "The first is his astonishing natural command of the art of conducting. . . . Second, Dudamel has an infectious emotional energy that tends to win over jaded souls in audiences and orchestras alike. . . . Finally, his Latino background puts a new face on an art that is widely viewed as an all-white affair . . . and his perspective is bracingly different from that of the staid conservatory graduate."

Prominent in Dudamel's background and in the development of his perspective is his long involvement with El Sistema—the State Foundation for the National System of Youth and Children's Orchestras of Venezuela. El Sistema was started in 1975 by the musician, economist, and social activist José Antonio Abreu, with the goal of offering free, early access to music education to all Venezuelan children, particularly those from poor families. Dudamel began to make music with other youngsters when he was four years old and started playing violin at age 10. In his after-school Sistema classes every weekday, most of his tutors were older children with more musical experience. The children's groups with which he played led him to view an orchestra as a community and a conductor as simply a member of that community—one who serves as a bridge between the instrumentalists and the composers whose music they play. "The secret to the success of El Sistema, both musically and socially, is the fact that the children practise and develop in a peer environment," Guy Dixon wrote for the Toronto, Canada, *Globe and Mail* (October 24, 2009). "It's the reverse of North American students practising mostly on their own and then auditioning for orchestras."

When Dudamel was 16 Abreu took him under his wing, and the two have remained extremely close. Dudamel, like Abreu, believes that "the high musical culture of the world has to be a common culture, part of the education of everyone," as Abreu put it to Arthur Lubow, writing for the *New York Times Magazine* (October 28, 2007). Dudamel told Teresa Albano for *People's World* (April 18, 2009), "The System exists not to build musicians so much as to create better citizens. Many of our kids come from neighborhoods where there are drugs and crime, some from broken homes. But when they are playing in the orchestra, they are all the same. It is a model democracy. It sets an example of how a community can function together." The best students become members of the Simón Bolívar Youth Orchestra (also known as the Simón Bolívar Symphony Orchestra), founded by Abreu in 1975—the crème de la crème of El Sistema's 220 youth orchestras. The DVD *El Sistema: Music to Change Life* (2008) shows Dudamel at work with the orchestra, whose concerts in Venezuela and overseas have gotten rave reviews. Dudamel launched a program similar to El Sistema in Los Angeles in 2007.

Dudamel's commitment to furthering the music education of young people is one of several characteristics that have led many to compare him to the conductor Leonard Bernstein (1918–90). Other qualities that evoke the memory of Bernstein, the longtime music director of the New York Philharmonic, are the brilliance Dudamel displayed from an early age; his talents as an instrumentalist (Bernstein was a pianist); his "powerfully intuitive feeling for color and character in music," as Anthony Tommasini wrote for a *New York Times* (December 1, 2007) music review; his spirited and highly animated style of conducting; the enthusiasm he sparks in orchestra members as well as audiences; and his extraordinary charisma. Dudamel, Ross wrote for the *New Yorker* (December 3, 2007), "communicates his ideas with a zeal that even hardened professionals find irresistible." "When he's conducting [a] piece, you're feeling like it's just been composed, it's like he's creating it himself," Michele Zukofsky, the Los Angeles Philharmonic's principal clarinetist, told Lubow. "He throws away the past. You're not bogged down by what's supposed to be. It's like jazz, in a way." Esa-Pekka Salonen, Dudamel's predecessor at the Los Angeles Philharmonic, told Lubow, "Gustavo is not concerned about authority. He is concerned about music, which is exactly the right approach. The orchestra gets seduced into playing well for him, rather than forced. . . . He has had a few years of very professional conducting around the world, and obviously he is a very different kind of guy. What hasn't disappeared is the sense of wonder and awe and discovery. These are wonderful qualities in all human beings, but especially in a conductor." "I need music, like air, like water, like food," Dudamel told an interviewer for CBC News (October 27, 2009, on-line). "When I'm conduct-ing, I like to give every part of my energy. Even if people say it's too much. It's the way that my soul, that my body, is expressing what I want."

The only child of Óscar Dudamel Vásquez, a trombonist, and Solangel Ramírez Viloria, a voice teacher, the conductor was born Gustavo Adolfo Dudamel Ramírez on January 26, 1981 in Barquisimeto, in the state of Lara, in northwestern Venezuela. He and his parents lived with his paternal grandfather, a truck driver, and grandmother. By the age of four, Dudamel had begun to study music through El Sistema. Around that time he taught himself to sight-read music by following the instructions in one of his father's books. At a concert he attended with his parents when he was around seven, he fell in love with conducting. "I thought, how interesting that the conductor uses an instrument that no one hears," he recalled to Chris Kraul and Chris Pasles for the *Los Angeles Times* (December 31, 2006). Young Gustavo would set up an orchestra with toy soldiers and conduct while playing recordings of the Vienna Philharmonic and other great orchestras. His toy orchestra "always played very well, but still I would sometimes stop the record and correct something," he told Joshua Kosman for the *San Francisco Chronicle* (November 3, 2007). He recalled to Sue Fox for the London *Times* (March 28, 2009) that he was also powerfully influenced by a videotape of José Antonio Abreu conducting a performance of Mahler's Second Symphony: "It was like, 'Wow!' An amazing inspiration. He was conducting from memory and I could really feel the deep love he had for the music."

As a youngster Dudamel hoped to become a trombonist and play in salsa bands, as his father did at that time, but his arms proved to be too short; instead, by age 10, he had begun to study the violin, both with El Sistema and at the Jacinto Lara Conservatory. "From the very beginning he showed signs of great talent and learned everything very easily," José Luis Jiménez, his violin teacher and El Sistema's principal administrator in Lara, told Lubow. When Dudamel was 12 his father and mother moved to another city, where his father had found a new job. (Currently, both of his parents work for El Sistema.) Dudamel remained with his grandparents so that he could continue his studies with Jiménez. When the violin teacher José Francisco del Castillo accepted Dudamel as his pupil at the Latin American Academy of Violin, in Caracas, Venezuela, his grandparents would wake up at dawn once a week to take him for lessons. That year Dudamel was named concertmaster of the Lara children's orchestra and of Jiménez's Amadeus Youth Orchestra. One afternoon when Jiménez arrived late for a rehearsal, he found the adolescent Dudamel conducting the students. "He was great, he was like a regular conductor," Jiménez told Lubow. Dudamel was named assistant conductor, which, as Lubow wrote, "meant in practice" that he was handling "much of the conducting" for both the Amadeus Youth Orchestra and the Lara children's orchestra. In 1995 Dudamel began to study under Rodolfo Saglimbeni, one of Venezuela's leading conductors, and he was named music director of the Amadeus Youth Orchestra. By 1997 he was leading ensembles in public every week. The next year, at the suggestion of José Antonio Abreu, the 16-year-old Dudamel moved to Caracas to further his studies under Abreu's tutelage.

When he was 18 Dudamel was named the conductor of the Simón Bolívar Youth Orchestra, most of whose approximately 200 members are between about 15 and 26 years of age and have grown up in poverty. Under his baton the orchestra has gained an international reputation for its professionalism and vivacity; it has performed on several continents and has attracted huge followings on YouTube. During the group's tours of European nations, conductors including Giuseppe Sinopoli, Claudio Abbado, Daniel Barenboim, and Simon Rattle mentored Dudamel. Rattle, the principal conductor of the Berlin Philharmonic, described El Sistema to Ed Vulliamy, writing for the London *Observer Magazine* (July 29, 2007), as "nothing less than a miracle" and as representing "the future of music for the whole world." Lubow wrote, "As an international celebrity whose career was incubated by the sistema, Dudamel is uniquely able to champion its expansion at home and promote its adoption abroad. . . . This dual vision—of hundreds of thousands of young people transformed by the sistema and of a youthful conductor who can bring audiences to their feet cheering—is a powerful sign of vitality to rebut those grim-faced pulse takers who are forever proclaiming the senescence of classical music."

In 2004 Dudamel won the inaugural international Gustav Mahler Conducting Competition, organized by the Bamberg Symphony Orchestra, in Germany, for conductors under 35. In that event, competitors first rehearse with the Bamberg orchestra; then the winner, chosen by a jury of conductors, composers, and orchestra managers, appears in a public performance. Dudamel won "with conspicuous brilliance . . . ," Michael White wrote for the London *Independent* (May 14, 2004). "His technique was sharp, efficient, focused, with an easy self-assurance. And he had . . . vision and charisma." Years later White recalled for the London *Sunday Telegraph* (April 19, 2009), "As the competition was a test of rehearsal technique rather than performance, we watched open-mouthed as the wiry, unpre-possessing 23-year-old from Caracas metamorphosed into a true maestro: not just waving his arms (which anyone can do) but actually making things happen, changing the sound, the shape, the temperature of what we heard. He had ideas and knew how to communicate them. And he could get seasoned players twice his age to do exactly what he wanted."

After his victory in Bamberg, Dudamel received invitations to guest-conduct major orchestras the world over, including one from Esa-Pekka Sa-

lonen, the Los Angeles Philharmonic's music director, who had witnessed the Mahler competition. During the next few years, Dudamel led the Israel Philharmonic Orchestra, the La Scala Theater orchestra, in Milan, Italy, the Chicago Symphony, in Illinois, the Royal Liverpool Philharmonic and the City of Birmingham Symphony, in England, the Dresden State Orchestra, in Germany, and the San Francisco Symphony, in California, among other ensembles. In 2007, two years after he guest-conducted the Gothenburg Symphony at the BBC Proms (a series of summer concerts held at the Royal Albert Hall, in London), he was named that group's principal conductor and signed a contract that runs through 2012. Also in 2007 he conducted the Stuttgart Radio Symphony Orchestra of Germany in a concert at the Vatican that celebrated the 80th birthday of Pope Benedict XVI and was recorded for a DVD. He made his New York City debut in November of that year, with the Bolívar youth orchestra at Carnegie Hall, and his debut with the New York Philharmonic two weeks later. In the latter concert he used one of the three batons owned by Leonard Bernstein—"treasured artifacts . . . rarely lent to visiting conductors," Anthony Tommasini wrote for his December 1, 2007 *New York Times* review. After describing Dudamel as "the most talked about conductor in classical music right now," Tommasini reported that Dudamel had "cut through" all the media hype preceding his New York debut: "Somehow, he withstood the pressure and delivered teeming, impassioned and supremely confident performances of works by Carlos Chávez, Dvorak and Prokofiev. Clearly, the Philharmonic players were inspired by the boundless joy and intensity of his music-making." Henry Fogel, who served as the president of the Chicago Symphony Orchestra Association for 18 years, wrote for his *artsjournal.com* (March 2009) blog, "On the Record," "The New York Philharmonic doesn't give many guest conductors, certainly not many very young ones, solo bows where the musicians refuse to stand and remain seated tapping their bows in admiration. On the two occasions when I've seen [Dudamel] with that orchestra, I've seen that ultimate demonstration of musician respect."

Earlier, in April 2007, the Los Angeles Philharmonic announced that Dudamel had signed a five-year contract to be the orchestra's next music director, beginning in the fall of 2009. (He had guest-conducted that orchestra only twice when he was selected for that post.) Gretchen Nielsen, its director of educational initiatives, told Lucia Brawley for blog.artsusa.org (September 22, 2009) that the philharmonic had lured Dudamel with a promise to support him in introducing in Los Angeles a program modeled on El Sistema. Dudamel launched the initiative, called Youth Orchestra Los Angeles, or YOLA, in 2007. YOLA has two components. One is the EXPO Center Youth Orchestra, whose members—youngsters from 60 schools in South Los Angeles—get free instruments and free group lessons, as do the Venezuelan children involved with El Sistema; in return, they must agree to take care of their instruments, practice, and faithfully attend lessons and rehearsals (one hour three afternoons a week and three hours on Saturday mornings). The other component is the YOLA Stakeholder Network, a consortium of music and arts organizations, whose mission, according to the YOLA Web site, is "to transform lives and inspire social change in the heart of Los Angeles communities by increasing access to quality instrumental and orchestral education for Los Angeles' underserved youth."

On October 3, 2009, a few days after Dudamel's contract with the Los Angeles Philharmonic went into effect, the conductor led the EXPO Center Youth Orchestra in a performance of "Ode to Joy," from Beethoven's Symphony no. 9. The group appeared as part of "Bienvenido Gustavo!," a free event, held at the Hollywood Bowl, that also featured five other performances, including those by the jazz pianist Herbie Hancock with the Los Angeles County High School for the Arts Jazz Band, and David Hidalgo, of the band Los Lobos, with Taj Mahal and the Mexican folk band Los Cenzontles. That night, after an intermission, Dudamel conducted the Los Angeles Philharmonic and the Los Angeles Master Chorale in a performance of the whole of Beethoven's ninth symphony.

Dudamel's official debut concert as the Los Angeles Philharmonic's principal conductor took place one week later. At that much-anticipated, black-tie, celebrity-studded event, held at the Walt Disney Concert Hall (built especially for Los Angeles's orchestra), Dudamel conducted a new work by John Adams, called *City Noir*, and Mahler's Symphony no. 1. In a highly enthusiastic review, Anthony Tommasini, writing for the *New York Times* (October 10, 2009), described the concert as "exceptional and exciting . . . by any standard." In conducting *City Noir*, Tommasini wrote, "Mr. Dudamel, gyrating on the podium and in control at every moment, drew a cranked-up yet subtly colored performance of this challenging score from his eager players. He seemed so confident dispatching this metrically fractured work that I was drawn into the music, confident that a pro was on the podium." Dudamel's reading of the Mahler symphony, he continued, "was not what you might expect from a young conductor. For all the sheer energy of the music-making, here was a probing, rigorous and richly characterized interpretation, which Mr. Dudamel conducted from memory." During the 10-minute ovation that greeted Dudamel and the orchestra at the end of the concert, Tommasini wrote, the conductor "returned to the stage again and again. But he never took a solo bow from the podium. Instead, he stood proudly with his players on stage."

The album *Gustavo Dudamel and the Los Angeles Philharmonic: The Inaugural Concert* was released in 2009 on the Deutsche Grammophon label. For his debut recording on that label, released in 2006, Dudamel had conducted the fifth and seventh symphonies of Beethoven with the SBYO. Three more-recent albums also offer performances by the SBYO under Dudamel: the first (2007) is of Mahler's Symphony no. 5; the second, *Fiesta* (2008), includes pieces by Arturo Marquéz, Silvestre Revueltas, and Antonio Estévez and is an example of Dudamel's efforts to lift the work of Latin American composers out of obscurity in the world of classical music; the third, also in 2008, contains Tchaikovsky's Symphony No. 5 and his symphonic fantasia *Francesca da Rimini*. In a review of the last album for the All Music Guide (online), Blair Sanderson declared that Dudamel "obviously has something important to say in this . . . performance that adds to our understanding of symphony and doesn't just provide a novel twist to extremely familiar music. From the outset, Dudamel treats the score as if it were brand new and not covered in accretions of past performances: the rhythmic details and full orchestration of the Allegro stand out in high relief; the lyricism of the Andante cantabile is touching and hauntingly tragic; the Valse is delicate and picante, yet surprisingly ominous; and the Finale is considerably shorn of bombast thanks to the real explosiveness and fury Dudamel inspires in the musicians. Taken altogether, the pacing of the symphony is also given a makeover, insofar as Dudamel lets it go at its own speed and doesn't rush to get to the big climaxes, but lets the tempos and phrasing develop according to necessity. Of course, some listeners will find Dudamel's interpretation and the orchestra's execution neither daring nor different enough to matter, and for them this symphony has probably already worn out its welcome, along with the popular . . . *Francesca da Rimini*, which is provided as fiery filler. This is a marvelously insightful reading of the 'Fifth' that has genuine emotion and a feeling of organic unfolding and inevitability that makes it feel like great music again." Dudamel's discography also includes a live recording of the Los Angeles Philharmonic performing Béla Bartók's Concerto for Orchestra (2007). His latest album, recorded in 2010 with the SBYO, pairs Stravinsky's *Le Sacre du Printemps* (*The Rite of Spring*) with *La Noche de los Mayas* (*Night of the Mayas*), a score for a 1939 Mexican film by Silvestre Revueltas.

Dudamel's 2010 schedule included dozens of concerts with his three orchestras, in Venezuela, Sweden, and U.S. cities including New York; Phoenix, Arizona; Nashville, Tennessee; Newark, New Jersey; Philadelphia, Pennsylvania; Chicago, Illinois; Washington, D.C.; and San Francisco, California, in addition to Los Angeles. In June he and the SBYO toured Scandinavia and Russia, performing Shostakovich's Symphony no. 5. Others among the many works that Dudamel conducted in 2010 include Rachmaninoff's Piano Concerto no. 4, with Leif Ove Andsnes as the soloist; Leonard Bernstein's *Age of Anxiety*, with Jean-Yves Thibaudet at the piano; and Mozart's Mass in C minor.

Dudamel's honors include the 2006 Pegasus Prize, given at the Festival of Two Worlds in Spoleto, Italy; the 2007 Premio de la Latinidad, given by the 37 member states of the Latin Union for outstanding contributions to Latin cultural life; the 2007 Royal Philharmonic Society Music Award for Young Artists; and the 2009 City of Toronto Glenn Gould Protégé Prize, from the Glenn Gould Foundation. In 2008 he and Abreu jointly earned Harvard University's Q Prize for extraordinary service to children.

Dudamel has been married to Eloísa Maturén, a Venezuelan journalist and former ballet dancer, since 2006. The couple have homes in the Hollywood Hills section of Los Angeles and in Caracas.

—M.M.

Suggested Reading: *60 Minutes* (on-line) Feb. 17, 2008; (London) *Observer* p16 July 29, 2007; (London) *Sunday Telegraph* p26 Apr. 19, 2009; *Los Angeles Times* A p1+ Nov. 23, 2008, D p1+ June 2, 2009; *New York Times Magazine* p32+ Oct. 28, 2007; *New Yorker* p90+ Dec. 14, 2009; *Vogue* p518+ Sep. 2009

Selected Recordings: with the Simón Bolívar Youth Orchestra—Beethoven Symphonies nos. 5 & 7, 2006; Mahler's Symphony no. 5, 2007; *Fiesta*, 2008; Tchaikovsky's Symphony no. 5 and *Francesca da Rimini*, 2008; with the Los Angeles Philharmonic: *Gustavo Dudamel and the Los Angeles Philharmonic: The Inaugural Concert*, 2009; *Rite: Stravinsky / Revueltas* (*Le Sacre du Printemps*; *La Noche de los Mayas*), 2010

Neilson Barnard/Getty Images

Dumas, Marlene

(doo-MAH)

Aug. 3, 1953– Artist

Address: c/o Saatchi Gallery, County Hall, Southbank, London SE1 7PB, England

"Marlene Dumas's provocative paintings of women, children, celebrities and people of colour are as psychologically disturbing as they are violently beautiful," Patricia Ellis wrote about the work of the 56-year-old South African painter for the Saatchi Gallery's Web site. "Championing the under-represented classes, her characters occupy an unholy ground where the viewer's individual morality, ethics and adherence to ideological convention are questioned." Dumas is known for creating masterful renderings of human subjects, mainly in oil or pen and watercolor, that address issues of birth, death, sex, race, violence, politics, grief, and identity with explicit images and "often in troubling combinations," as Robert Ayers wrote for *ArtInfo* (November 29, 2006). Dumas paints almost exclusively from second-hand images—from newspaper clippings, her own photographs, historical paintings, or pornographic magazines. Her paintings are not realistic, though; she distorts and simplifies her images with bold lines and shapes and expressive colors that often bleed into one another or appear faded or "ashy." Her style has been called "intellectual expressionist."

While she is often referred to as a feminist artist, Dumas has been compared to past European male masters for her ability to "secure big effects from small gestures," as Robert Enright wrote for *Border Crossings* (August 2004). Referring to a series of Dumas's sexually explicit works, Enright wrote: "In these erotic works she is giving the guys with the gaze a run for their money; she contests [Gustave] Courbet's claim that the origin of the world is the male domain and wrestles the phallic paintbrush from [Edgar] Degas and [Pablo] Picasso, turning an implement of penetration into a whisk of intimacy." Since the 1970s Dumas has exhibited her paintings in solo shows at major museums all over the world to great critical acclaim and has been been credited with helping to reinvigorate the European painting scene. But it was not until 2005, when her 1987 painting *The Teacher*—which depicts an eerie class portrait in which the teacher's eyes resemble black holes—was auctioned by the art dealer Christie's for $3.34 million, that she gained worldwide prominence and the distinction of being the highest-paid female artist in the world. Despite her prominence in Europe and elsewhere, she has so far received comparatively little recognition in the United States. Though she had previously shown work in the U.S., the Amsterdam-based artist's 2008–09 exhibition Measuring Your Own Grave, shown at venues including the Museum of Contemporary Art (MOCA) in Los Angeles, California, was considered her first major solo exhibit in the U.S.

The younger sister to two brothers, Marlene Dumas was born on August 3, 1953 in Cape Town, South Africa. Her father died when she was 12 years old. Raised on a vineyard near the city of Stellenbosch, Dumas had little opportunity to visit art museums. Still, she drew constantly as a child, often inspired by films and comics; she sometimes made cartoon drawings that she has compared to the paintings of bosomy women by the artist Richard Prince. "We didn't come from an artistic background, but just the fact that I was always drawing such a lot and so quickly made the family think that I must be an artist," she told Carol Kino for the New York Times (March 27, 2005, on-line). From 1948 to 1990 South African society operated under the system of apartheid; brutally enforced by the government, apartheid divided society into racial categories and stripped blacks of their rights. As Dumas grew older she observed that among artists in South Africa, "the theatre people and filmmakers were better at dealing with the actuality of political horrors," as she told Enright. "As painters, no one really knew how to deal with that. And while I didn't want to illustrate anything, I always wanted my paintings to have some political intent or to have them deal with things that actually happened."

From 1972 to 1975 Dumas attended the University of Cape Town's Michaelis School of Fine Art, where she studied ethics and earned her B.A. degree in fine art. There, she developed a passion for the human form, at a time when contemporary art was dominated by abstract expressionism and conceptualism, art movements that are concerned not with representation but with the emotion or—in the case of conceptualism—the idea that drives the artwork. In 1976, at the age of 23, Dumas won a grant from the University of Cape Town that allowed her to spend two years studying art abroad. She chose to attend the art school Atelier 63 in Haarlem, the Netherlands, with the intention of expanding her knowledge of European art history. (Her studies at the University of Cape Town had focused on American art.) In Holland she set about reading books that had been banned in South Africa under apartheid, including works by the antiapartheid activist and future South African president Nelson Mandela and the American black nationalist Malcolm X, as well as works of pornography. Dumas was uninspired by the Dutch art that was being produced at the time, because, as she told Enright, the artists "weren't interested in anything that was even remotely social or political." On the other hand, she became interested in the subjects of intimacy and eroticism, about which Dutch society was very open. Many of her earliest pieces are large collages of drawings in ink, pencil, and crayon, mixed with text as well as newspaper and magazine clippings. In a representative piece, Don't Talk to Strangers (1977), the edges of the canvas contain salutations from letters to the artist, such as "Dear Miss Dumas," followed by phrases such as "How are you getting on?" while the center of the work is blank. "This early work signals Dumas' lasting interest in human relationships often laden with uncertainty, anxiety, sexual tension, and desire," a critic wrote for artnews.com. From 1979 to 1980 Dumas attended the Institute of Psychology at the University of Amsterdam. Around that time she began what would be a five-year hiatus from painting.

Remaining in Amsterdam, Dumas returned to painting again in 1984, showing her work extensively in galleries and museums throughout the city. Her provocative and often subversive work was received warmly. One of her early solo exhibitions, The Private versus the Public, at Galerie Paul Andriesse in Amsterdam in 1987, featured a series of portraits of groups and individuals based on Polaroid photographs, some taken by her. "[Dumas's] emotional involvement with the subjects coupled with her distortion of the original photographs created unnaturalistic renderings that had characteristically a haunting edge," Cecile Johnson wrote for the Web site of the Museum of Modern Art (MoMA) in New York City. In 1988 Dumas presented a series of eight small, expressionist-style drawings and paintings of nude figures, collectively titled Defining in the Negative. Hung alongside or written on the drawings are notes that critique the way women have been historically portrayed in art, such as "I Won't Pose for Mr. Salle," a reference to the figurative artist David Salle. Grace Glueck wrote for the New York Times (March 29, 2002) that Dumas seemed to be "arguing for the importance of a meaningful figurative art as opposed to the use of the figure as a strategy." Dumas explained to Enright: "I always see myself in relation to other people and I was never a bitter or angry person in my reaction to other artists. It was more a question of trying to find out what type of woman I wanted to paint now that I was actually one of these people who make images."

Children, often in ambiguous and disturbingly suggestive contexts, are a frequent subject of Dumas's paintings. Her painting Baby (1985) is a portrait of the head and shoulders of a baby boy, with a mature expression, awash in eerie yellow and blue light. Many critics have taken note of the baby's unsettling aura. Ellis wrote for the Saatchi Gallery's Web site that the baby seems to represent "the unnerving presence of an 'other,' the realisation of an individual with a will and determination of his own. Marlene Dumas confronts the reality of motherhood, with all its natural and terrifying implications." Another oil painting, Young Boys (1993), depicts a mysterious line-up of naked boys standing awkwardly for an unknown purpose. Ellis wrote, "[Dumas] creates a subtle unnerving perversity from an unabashed simplicity. This is a painting with no frills: full on, with nowhere to hide." One of Dumas's best-known paintings, *The Secret* (1994), depicts, as described by Kino, "a childlike figure standing with its back to the viewer against a dark, murky ground . . . everything seems indeterminate, from the child's sex and skin color, which modulates from grayish pink to bluish gray, to the background, which at once suggests deep space and flatness. . . . It's impossible to know whether the child is listening at a door, urinating against a wall, being punished, or simply standing in darkness—or even whether the figure is really a child." About the painting's intended meaning, Dumas told Kino: "I wanted to say, 'You go and figure it out yourself.'" Dumas represented the Netherlands at the Venice Biennale, in Italy, in 1995.

Dumas's paintings often directly reflect her experience with violence and racism in South Africa under apartheid. Several early works included in the retrospective exhibit Name No Names, which premiered at the Centre Pompidou, in Paris, France, in 2001, display the artist's complex feelings toward her home country. Some of the pieces seem to relate satirically to apartheid, including *Self-Portrait as a Black Girl* (1989) and *Mask for a White Man Entering a Black Area* (1980–88). *Black Drawings* (1991–92), which appeared in that exhibition, is a grid containing more than 100 portraits of distinctive black faces, done in ink wash and watercolor on paper and slate. Glueck quoted Dumas as writing that with her exclusion of white faces from the piece, she attempted "to exhibit my own unease, fear and admiration for the individuals grouped together under the term 'Black.'" That show also included paintings containing religious allusions—such as *Jesus Serene* (1994), a series of 21 images—and large nude-figure paintings of women including the performers Mae West and Josephine Baker; the biblical figure Mary Magdalene; and prostitutes from Amsterdam's Red Light District. (Dumas "was brought up in the Dutch Reformed Church," Glueck noted, "and evidently its influence has lasted.") "Dumas asks us to re-see her subjects by magnifying them and abstracting them, by disregarding natural proportions and discarding the comforts of the context," Johanna Burton wrote about the exhibit for postmedia.net. Burton noted that Dumas's painting style made the images "feel like quick bodily utterances: gasps, exclamations, shudders."

Dumas's work also often contains implicit criticism of contemporary violence, war, and sexual exploitation. In her exhibition Suspect, shown at the Palazzetto Tito during the 2003 Venice Biennale, "Dumas deals with the very point at which art and the big questions of life and death converge," Emma Dexter wrote for *Modern Painters* (Autumn 2003), "and she's not afraid to draw parallels between her timeless depictions of the poignancy and magnificence of death and the terrible political and human tragedies of the day." In that show Du-

mas's work was divided into five rooms—the Waiting Room, the Boys' Room, the Lovers' Room, the Girls' Room, and the Drawing Room—each containing paintings that explored the room's theme. For instance, the Boys' Room contained two paintings of young men, apparently Middle Eastern, lying in open coffins. "The viewer is not told that they are Palestinian martyrs, yet somehow it is evident . . . ," Dexter wrote. "Shrouded, almost swaddled, their faces emerge still beautiful, the poignant object of a mother's grief." The Lover's Room contained mostly images drawn from pornography. One small painting, *The Immaculate*, is of a female's naked torso, her vulva at the center, belly and breasts beyond. "This is not a picture of pleasure like the other porno pictures," Dexter wrote; "this is a painting of inescapable fact." The Girls' Room contained an image of tragedy: a painting of four hanged schoolgirls. Departing from her usual approach to paintings, whose subjects are drawn from photographs, Dumas imagined the subjects in that work. "I am not a visionary," Dumas wrote for the exhibit's catalog, as quoted by Dexter. "I am not a witness. I am just afraid." Dumas has said, as quoted by Enright, that one reason she paints images of pain and death is that she is "touched by our bruiseability." Another notable show in 2003, Second Coming, was held at the Frith Street Gallery in London, England. That exhibit included four large-scale close-ups of women's faces, each with an ambiguous expression that could represent either mortality, pain, or erotic pleasure.

In the early 2000s Dumas's paintings fetched increasingly higher prices. As of 2002 the highest price one of her paintings had drawn at auction was $50,000. In June 2003 *Feather Stola* (2000), an oil painting of a woman posing erotically with a black stole, auctioned for $307,633, more than double that house's highest estimate of its sale price. In May 2004 her painting *Young Boys* was purchased from the art dealer Phillips de Pury for $993,600. At that point New York auction houses had begun to sell Dumas's work, and in November 2004 Christie's sold *Jule, die Vrou* (Jule, the Woman), a close-up painting of a transvestite's face, for $1.24 million. In February 2005 Dumas's *The Teacher* sold for $3.34 million, more than prices paid for work by such canonical female artists as Eva Hesse and Agnes Martin. Dumas had mixed feelings about that, telling Kino, "Sometimes its funny, if you see it as indeed a game. Sometimes I think it's nice for a woman painter. And sometimes you don't feel very good, and you get criticized for having much too high prices."

In 2007 Dumas presented her first solo exhibition in her native country of South Africa: Intimate Relations, at the South African National Gallery, in Cape Town. Among the pieces in the exhibit were a 1984 portrait of the artist's grandmother, called *Martha*; a portrait of a fellow South African artist, Moshekwa Langa; and heads of four men recently killed in war, called *Fog of War* (2006). About *Mar-*

tha—which Sean O'Toole described for Frieze.com as "stolid and distant, a liquid blur of dirty blues and hazy emotion"—Dumas wrote for the accompanying catalog, "God cannot be painted. And He isn't a man. But if He had been a woman, He would have looked like this sometimes."

Dumas's show Measuring Your Own Grave, held at the Los Angeles Museum of Contemporary Art from June to October 2008, featured 66 paintings and several dozen works on paper, going back to 1984. Dumas was inspired to create one of her more recent paintings, *Dead Marilyn* (2008)—based on a well-known photograph of the actress Marilyn Monroe taken during her autopsy—shortly after Dumas's mother had died, at a time when the artist was feeling very depressed and had not been motivated to paint. "Suddenly, in this very sad picture, I think my own personal sadness and all kinds of things came together," she told Madeleine Brand for the National Public Radio program *Day to Day* (June 20, 2008). The exhibit's title painting, *Measuring Your Own Grave* (2003), is of a figure bent over forward, dividing the canvas horizontally between light and darkness, his outstretched arms barely touching each side of the painting, in a gesture that makes him appear to bow. Christopher Knight wrote for the *Los Angeles Times* (June 25, 2008) about the painting, "It's a work Dumas probably couldn't have made before racking up some time on the job. Any artist, especially one with her ambition and success, is anxious about the legacy she leaves for the future. In that sense painting is indeed an act of measuring your own grave—passing time from one lived moment to the next while carving out a place in history." The exhibition was held at MoMA in New York City from December 14, 2008 through February 16, 2009, then at the Menil Collection, in Houston, Texas, from March 26 through June 21, 2009. The exhibition elicited mixed responses from those in the art world. Roberta Smith wrote for the *New York Times* (December 12, 2008), "The show suggests that while this amply talented artist has created some riveting images, her work becomes monotonous and obvious when seen in bulk. She has not substantially varied her subjects or her habit of basing her images on photographs in about 25 years. And when you stand in front of her paintings, far too many other photo-dependent artists come to mind for the pictures to qualify as original. Her work tends too much toward well-done pastiches of ideas and tactics from the last 25 years, primarily Conceptualism, appropriation art and Neo-Expressionism." Smith, however, identified the small, oval-shaped painting *Breakfast for Claes Oldenburg*, which Dumas completed in 1975, when she was still an art student, as the show's standout piece. In contrast, a writer for Blogcritics.org (February 10, 2009) commented on the ambiguous message contained in Dumas's works, writing, "Full of verve without joy, her thinly painted, fragmented style, and hallucinatory colors, Dumas's figures toe a borderline of real and imagined that won't quite let the viewer make comfortable assumptions, and this disquieting quality illuminates her work with a chill beauty."

In 2009 Dumas and her work were featured in Catherine Meyburgh's documentary film *Kentridge and Dumas in Conversation*. Dumas's latest solo exhibition, Against the Wall, included 17 paintings inspired by the Israeli-Palestinian conflict. It ran for a month, in March and April 2010, at the David Zwirner Gallery, in New York City.

The attention paid by critics to the explicit nature of Dumas's subject matter, rather than to her technique—which Ayers described as "a highly sophisticated pictorial style that features distortion, simplification, a rough-edged finish and a deeply personal amalgam of painting and drawing"—has been a source of frustration for Dumas. The artist told Enright, "My mother used to say to me, why don't you paint a flower or something like that before I die? Why do you always have to do naked people?"

Dumas's work is in the permanent collections of major museums and institutions in New York; London; Amsterdam; Paris; Frankfurt and Munich, Germany; and Tokyo, Japan. In 1998 she received the Coutts Contemporary Art Foundation Award, established by the Coutts Bank in Zürich, Switzerland, as well as the David Röell prize, presented by the Prince Bernhard Cultural Fund. In 2007 she was awarded the Dusseldorf Art Prize, one of Germany's most prestigious art awards. Dumas, who teaches at De Ateliers (formerly Ateliers '63) in Amsterdam, was honored in the fall of 2006 with the Alex Katz visiting chair in painting at the Cooper Union, in New York City. "In the end, I think that I paint simply because it's quite exciting to make something with the touch of my hand," Dumas told Gioni Massimiliano for Art Press (November 2005). "It is an ancient, primitive urge, the urge of leaving a mark, as to prove that you can exist outside yourself." In 2001 Dumas published a series of drawings that represent the previous 10 years of her work in the book *One Hundred Models and Endless Rejects*. She has published several other books of her work, including *Marlene Dumas: Intimate Relations* (2007), an account of her life and a catalog of her drawings and paintings. Dumas lives in Amsterdam with her companion, the artist Jan Andriesse. The couple have a daughter, Helena.

—M.R.M.

Suggested Reading: ArtInfo.org Nov. 29, 2006; *Border Crossings* p22+ Aug. 2004; *Los Angeles Times* E p1 June 25, 2008; *Modern Painters* p131 Spring 2000, p90+ Autumn 2003; *New York Times* (on-line) Mar. 29, 2002, Mar. 27, 2005; saatchi-gallery.com; Bonacossa, Ilaria, et al. *Marlene Dumas*, 2009

Selected Works: *Breakfast for Claes Oldenburg*, 1975; *Don't Talk to Strangers*, 1977; *Mask for a White Man Entering a Black Area*, 1980–88;

Martha, 1984; Baby, 1985; The Teacher, 1987; Defining in the Negative (series), 1988; Self Portrait as a Black Girl, 1989; The Secret, 1994; Stripper, 1999; Feather Stola, 2000; The Kiss, 2003; Measuring Your Own Grave, 2003; Fog of War, 2006; Dead Marilyn, 2008; Self-Portrait at Noon, 2008

Selected Books: The Question of Human Pink, 1989; Nom de Personne = Name No Names, 2001; Marlene Dumas: Collected Works, 2006; as co-author—Marlene Dumas: Measuring Your Own Grave, 2007; as co-editor—Marlene Dumas: Models, 1995; Marlene Dumas: One Hundred Models and Endless Rejects, 2001; Marlene Dumas: Intimate Relations, 2007

Jonathan Daniel/Getty Images

Durant, Kevin

(der-ANT)

Sep. 29, 1988– Basketball player

Address: Oklahoma City Thunder, Two Leadership Sq., 211 N. Robinson Ave., Suite 300, Oklahoma City, OK 73102

Kevin Durant, a six-foot nine-inch small forward for the Oklahoma City Thunder (who were formerly the Seattle Supersonics), is among the most consistent offensive players in the National Basketball Association (NBA). After gaining national attention during his high-school career and setting records during his single year at the University of Texas, Durant was selected second by the Sonics

in the 2007 draft and went on to earn the Rookie of the Year award. As the Thunder's leading scorer and shot-blocker, he has established himself as the centerpiece of his team, helping to lead it from sub-par play in previous years to a winning record in the 2009–10 season. He is helped by his physique—each of his arms is 36 inches long, nearly the length of the average broomstick—and by his remarkable work ethic, which he developed as a youngster. He earned his first spot on the Western Conference All-Star team in February 2010. In an article for Sports Illustrated (January 25, 2010), Chris Ballard noted that Durant is now "scoring a ton of points for a winning team" and that "players who do that are tagged All-Star and Franchise Player and have names like Kobe [Bryant] and Carmelo [Anthony]. . . . While Durant has not reached their level just yet, there are nights when he comes pretty damn close." On April 14, 2010 Durant became, at 21, the youngest scoring champion in NBA history, with an average of 30.1 points for the 2009–10 season.

Kevin Wayne Durant was born on September 29, 1988 in Suitland, Maryland, a suburb of Washington, D.C. His mother, the former Wanda Durant, was a postal worker, and his father, Wayne Pratt, a federal police officer. When Kevin was born his parents were not married, and his mother's maiden name became his surname. Wayne Pratt was absent for much of his son's childhood; when he and Wanda reunited and married, in 2001, Wanda changed her own last name to Pratt. Chip Brown reported for the Dallas Morning News (November 8, 2006) that when she was a young mother, Wanda Pratt was passed over for a promotion at work and felt angry, until she realized that she simply had not done her best at her job. She told Brown, "I decided right then my kids would never be in the same situation. They were always going to work hard to get what they wanted."

Kevin Durant has a brother, Tony, who is three years his senior; both Durants were attracted to basketball as children. (The six-foot seven-inch Tony Durant later played forward for Towson University, in Maryland.) Durant also has a half-brother, Cliff Dixon, who currently plays basketball for Western Kentucky University, and according to some sources, he also has two sisters. Basketball "was just something I always thought was fun," Durant told Darnell Mayberry for the Oklahoma City Oklahoman (January 29, 2010). "If I got in trouble at home, I could always go to the gym and get my mind off it. Really, that's how it started, just trying to get away from stuff." Durant played basketball for fun in pickup games at the Seat Pleasant Activity Center, situated in a one-story building 15 minutes away from his home. There, his competitiveness emerged when he sought a spot on the recreation center's youth team. When he was about 11 years old, he told his mother that he wanted to play professional basketball. She asked him to spend a day thinking about whether a basketball career was what he truly wanted; when he said the next day that it was, his mother promised to do all she could to help him reach his goal. She enlisted the help of Taras Brown, a basketball coach at the recreation center with a "tough-love," disciplinarian style, who agreed to train Durant for a basketball career.

Between the ages of 11 and 16, Durant spent hours each day practicing with Brown, who ran the boy through intense drills that developed his fundamental skills and mental and physical discipline. Durant was forbidden to play in casual five-on-five pickup games at the recreation center, which Brown feared would adversely affect his form. "Some days I wouldn't pick up a basketball," Durant told Grant Wahl for *Sports Illustrated* (February 19, 2007). "[Brown would] put 60 minutes on the clock and say I had to do defensive drills the whole time." One particularly grueling drill involved Durant's lying on his back with a pillow under his head and holding up a heavy medicine ball with his elbow cocked in a shooting position. "I was supposed to hold it there for an hour. An hour!" Durant recalled to Ballard. After a while holding the ball caused throbbing pain and then numbness in his elbow and shoulder. Angry at what appeared to Durant to be a pointlessly painful exercise, he walked out—marking the only time he ever refused to complete one of Brown's drills. He retreated to the home of his grandmother, who comforted him but encouraged him to return to the gym; he did so two hours later, picking up the medicine ball to try the exercise again. "I was never sure what that drill was for," Durant told Ballard, "but I know it's those types of drills that made me who I am today." Brown also made Durant do sprints up Hunt's Hill, an incline located near the recreation center, which Durant scaled, in his estimation, about a thousand times. His mother would often sit in her car and watch Durant during those runs to make sure he was putting in his full effort. "He worked so hard," Wanda Pratt, who also signed up Kevin's brother Tony to train with Brown, told Mayberry. "That's what people don't get. He worked so hard from 8 years old to the age of when he decided that that's what he wanted to do. And then from there up until now he works non-stop." As a result of his hard work, Durant developed excellent form, including an accurate shot and impressive passing skills.

Durant spent his freshman year of high school at National Christian Academy, a private school in Fort Washington, Maryland. Durant, who stood six feet two inches at that time, played point guard on the junior-varsity team for the season's first five games before coaches moved him to the varsity squad. As a sophomore Durant played guard, forward, and center and was the team's leading scorer, helping to guide them to a 27–3 record, the best in the school's history. Durant spent his junior year at Oak Hill Academy, a private school in Mouth of Wilson, Virginia, known for its elite boys' basketball program. He started in every game of that season, averaging 19.6 points and 8.8 rebounds per game, shooting 65 percent from the field and 43 percent from three-point range, and helping to lead the Warriors to a 34–2 season record and to win the *USA Today* National Championship. Durant transferred again in his senior season to Montrose Christian Academy, in Rockville, Maryland, to play under the school's veteran coach, Stu Vetter, who had helmed a number of championship teams and coached several future NBA stars. During his senior season, Durant—who now measured six feet nine inches and boasted a seven-foot five-inch wingspan—led the team in scoring, averaging 23.6 points and 10.2 rebounds per game. He was named the 2006 All-Met Player of the Year by the *Washington Post* and the Most Valuable Player of the 2006 McDonald's High School All-American Game (an award he shared with Chase Budinger, who currently plays with the Houston Rockets).

Meanwhile, during his teen years Durant also played in Amateur Athletic Union (AAU) basketball games at the Seat Pleasant Activity Center for two decorated teams, the PG Jaguars and the D.C. Blue Devils. During Durant's time with the Jaguars—whose other players included the future standouts Michael Beasley and Chris Braswell—the team won multiple national championships. On the Blue Devils Durant played alongside Tywon Lawson, who currently plays for the Denver Nuggets. In April 2005 Durant's AAU coach, Charles Craig, was murdered at the age of 35; since Craig's death Durant has worn the number 35 to honor him. In addition to league games and practice with Brown, a motivating factor for Durant in those years was the desire to defeat his brother Tony in a one-on-one game, a goal he finally accomplished at 17. "Every time I played against him I just wanted to destroy him," he told Mayberry. "That's how he made me feel and that's what got me better."

As he approached graduation Durant was considered the nation's second-best high-school basketball player in the 2006 class. (Greg Oden, who went on to play for Ohio State University and then the NBA, was generally considered to be the best.) Had he graduated one year earlier, Durant's talents would unquestionably have made him an early selection in the NBA draft, but in 2006 the NBA had increased its age requirement for entrance into the league from 18 to 19, making it mandatory that all new players be at least one year beyond high-school graduation. Durant was heavily recruited by several universities, including the University of North Carolina and the University of Connecticut, but he decided to attend the University of Texas to play for the Longhorns, mainly because of his liking for the school's coaches, Russell Springman and Rick Barnes. The widely held assumption was that Durant would enter the NBA draft the following June.

As a Texas Longhorn Durant was one of four freshmen among the starting five players. He averaged 25.8 points and 11.1 rebounds in 35 games, 28.9 points in Big-12 games, and 12.5 rebounds in conference play, the last two statistics setting Big-

12 single-season records. (The Big-12 is a college athletic conference involving 12 Division I schools in the central U.S. that compete with one another regularly.) He scored more than 20 points each in 30 of his games and more than 30 points in 11 contests. He also set the single-season school and Big-12 records for total points (903) and a single-season school record for total rebounds (390). Durant received the Big-12 Most Valuable Player award and was named the National College Player of the Year by the Associated Press, the National Association of Basketball Coaches, the U.S. Basketball Writers Association, CBS/Chevrolet, and the *Sporting News*. In addition, he won the Adolph Rupp Trophy, the Naismith Award, and the Wooden Award, becoming the first freshman in National Collegiate Athletic Association (NCAA) history to claim any of those honors. "He's the best freshman, and one of the best players, I've ever seen first-hand," Billy Gillespie, the Texas A&M University coach, told Bud Withers for the *Seattle Times* (February 22, 2007). "I think it's going to take NBA players to slow him down. And I doubt if very many of them are going to slow him down, either."

Durant was selected second in the first round of the 2007 NBA draft, by the Seattle Supersonics—also known as the Sonics. (Oden was selected first, by the Portland Trailblazers.) Shortly after his signing, Durant won a lucrative endorsement contract with Nike, worth about $50 million over seven years. He later received endorsement deals with EA Sports and Gatorade. After spending much of the summer practicing with Team USA, which included such NBA superstars as Kobe Bryant, LeBron James, Carmelo Anthony, and Dwight Howard, he was one of two players cut from the 12-person U.S. roster for the 2008 World Championship competition, the qualifying international tournament for the 2008 Olympics. (The other was his fellow Supersonic Nick Collison.) Prior to the 2007–08 season, Durant moved with his mother into a house outside Seattle, Washington. Over the two previous seasons, the Sonics had posted a combined losing record of 66–98. The team boasted no other "marquee players," and it was widely assumed that the offense would be designed around Durant's developing skills. The Sonics' coach, P.J. Carlesimo, who had joined the team that summer, told Jack McCallum for *Sports Illustrated* (November 12, 2007), "Kevin is our focus. We can't hide that. We can't pretend he isn't. He will play 34 to 36 minutes and have a lot of rope."

In 2007–08, although the team finished with a franchise-worst record of 20–62, Durant had an outstanding debut season, proving to be the team's most consistent scorer. By season's end he averaged 20.3 points per game—becoming only the third teenager, after James and Anthony, to achieve a per-game scoring average of 20 or more—and led all 2007 draft rookies in scoring. Durant shot 87.3 percent from the foul line, scored 20 or more points in 44 games and 30-plus points in seven games, and led or co-led the team in points in 47 contests.

He also established his role as a playmaker in clutch situations, scoring several high-pressure, game-winning shots. For instance, in a November 16, 2007 game against the Atlanta Hawks, Durant sank a last-second three-point shot during the second overtime period for a 126–123 victory. Durant also led his team in blocks, with 75. He received the Rookie of the Month award five times during the season and was named to the NBA All-Rookie First Team. Durant participated in the T-Mobile Rookie Challenge on February 15, 2009, where he notched 23 points, eight rebounds, and four assists. He was granted the 2008 Rookie of the Year award, receiving 90 first-place votes—60 more than the second-place finisher, Al Horford of the Hawks—from a panel of 125 sportswriters and broadcasters. Upon receiving the award, in May 2008, Durant donated it to the trophy case of the Seat Pleasant Activity Center and dedicated it to Craig, his late AAU coach. "Yesterday when I found out I won [the award], that was the same day three years ago that my AAU coach died," Durant told Percy Allen for the *Seattle Times* (May 2, 2008). "I just want to give it to him to show how much I worked hard."

Prior to the 2008–09 season, the Sonics relocated to Oklahoma City, Oklahoma, and were renamed the Thunder. Durant continued his strong performance, averaging 39 minutes of play per game as well as 25.3 points, 6.5 rebounds, 2.8 assists, and 1.3 steals. He notched 20 or more points in 57 games, 30 or more points in 21 games (including five straight games from February 1 to February 17, the longest 30-plus-point streak of his career), and 40-plus points in three games. He scored a career-high 47 points on February 10, 2009, in a game against the New Orleans Hornets. (The Thunder ultimately lost the game, however, 100–98.) In a January 23, 2009 game against the Los Angeles Clippers, Durant set a franchise record by sinking 24 free-throw shots, made a career-high 15 rebounds, and scored 46 points. He had his highest steal total against the Dallas Mavericks on December 13, 2008. Despite missing eight games due to an injury, Durant ranked sixth in the NBA in scoring. At the T-Mobile Rookie Challenge & Youth Jam, Durant was the lead scorer, with 46 points, for the sophomore team, which defeated the freshmen, 122–116. He was also crowned Most Valuable Player of that game. The Thunder finished the 2008–09 season with a 23–59 record.

Despite his offensive dominance in his first two years of professional play, Durant has been considered a below-average defender. "Durant admits that when he got out of [defensive] position in the past, it was because 'either I didn't know the schemes or was being lazy,'" Ballard wrote. "This season [2009–10], however, he came to camp determined, as he says, 'to let my defense lead my offense.'" Prior to the beginning of the 2009–10 season, Durant received training from the assistant coach Ron Adams, a defensive specialist, and his improvement soon became evidence: he led the

Thunder in steals and had an easier time making the transition from offense to defense. Whereas during the previous season, statistics indicated that the Thunder was a worse defensive team when Durant was playing than when he was on the bench, in 2010 it was a better defensive team when he was playing, though he continued to struggle with turnovers. In the Thunder's last regular-season game of 2009–10, a victory against the Memphis Grizzlies, Durant scored 31 points, bringing his season average to 30.1—and becoming the NBA's youngest-ever scoring champion. (He replaced Max Zaslofsky of the 1947–48 Chicago Stags, then 22.)

Durant finished second in MVP voting in 2010 (behind LeBron James) and earned his first spot on the Western Conference's All Star team. The Thunder, meanwhile, enjoyed a rapid turnaround and finished with a 50–32 record, more than doubling their win total of the previous season. The team advanced to the postseason, where they lost to the defending-champion Los Angeles Lakers in the first round, four games to two.

In July 2010 Durant signed a five-year, $86 million contract extension with the Thunder.

Durant is known by his teammates and coaches as a hard worker who is eager to please. He typically arrives at practice at least an hour early and stays for two hours afterward. At 21 he has many childlike interests and ways; for instance, he enjoys watching children's movies and playing games such as Jenga, and Ballard reported that he calls Wanda Pratt "Mommy." "There's nothing fake about Kevin; he is who he is," his teammate Collison told Ballard. "It's kind of refreshing, someone with that much talent and ability, a guy who's been on the cover of magazines since he was 18, but all he wants to do is play basketball and hang out. He's not trying to rule the world or become a global marketing icon—he just wants to play ball."

—M.R.M.

Suggested Reading: *Dallas Morning News* Sports Day C p1 Nov. 8, 2006; nba.com; (Oklahoma City) *Oklahoman* Sports C p1 Jan. 29, 2010; *Seattle Times* Sports D p5 Feb. 22, 2007, Sports C p1 May 2, 2008; *Sports Illustrated* p28 Feb. 19, 2007, p52 Nov. 12, 2007, p46 Jan. 25, 2010

Ehrman, Bart D.

Oct. 5, 1955– Biblical scholar; writer; educator

Address: Dept. of Religious Studies, CB # 3225, Saunders 117, University of North Carolina, Chapel Hill, NC 27599

In his best-selling book *Misquoting Jesus: The Story Behind Who Changed the Bible and Why*, the Bible scholar Bart D. Ehrman described for ordinary readers—both those who believe in Jesus and those who do not—many of the contradictions and inconsistencies in the four gospels of the New Testament: discrepancies that have been discussed in college classes, divinity schools, and scholarly works for hundreds of years. In language easily understandable by laypeople, Ehrman explained that some of the most familiar and frequently cited portions of the New Testament do not appear in the earliest versions of the gospels. The thousands of copies of the Bible made afterward but before the invention of the printing press, in the 15th century, were all transcribed by hand from previous copies. Those handwritten copies contain mistakes or changes made deliberately to reflect the scribes' own theological views or views prevalent at the time: the belief that Jesus was human, or divine, or both human and divine; the belief that his death offered or did not offer eternal salvation; the belief that the God of the Old Testament is the same as or different from the Christian God or that the two are aspects of the same higher power. Thus, for cultural and theological reasons as well as because of

Courtesy of R. Baley, via GNU Free Documentation

errors in transcription, the gospels as they currently appear contain differing accounts of the life and teachings of Jesus, the Last Supper, the crucifixion, and the resurrection.

As a student at the Moody Bible Institute and Wheaton College, Ehrman identified himself as a fundamentalist Christian. He still held firm fundamentalist beliefs when he entered the Princeton

Theological Seminary to pursue a graduate degree. There, his historical and literary research and analyses of manuscripts written in Greek, Latin, and other languages led him to conclude that the substantive differences among the Gospels of Matthew, Mark, Luke, and John cannot be explained away, and that all attempts to do so rely on convoluted, specious arguments. By the time he earned a doctoral degree, in 1985, Ehrman had left the Christian fold. In his writing for a general readership, Ehrman's approach is that of an educator, not an ideologue, and aside from a few attacks by conservative Christians, *Misquoting Jesus* was well received. His next two books for lay readers—*God's Problem: How the Bible Fails to Answer Our Most Important Question—Why We Suffer* and *Jesus, Interrupted: Revealing the Hidden Contradictions in the Bible (and Why We Don't Know About Them)*— also earned critical praise and became best-sellers. Ehrman was a faculty member at Rutgers University from 1984 until 1988; he has been an adjunct professor at Duke University since 2000 and has taught since 1988 at the University of North Carolina (UNC) at Chapel Hill, where since 2003 he has held the title of James A. Gray Distinguished Professor in the Department of Religious Studies. He has also taught in the Department of Classics at UNC–Chapel Hill since 2005.

Bart D. Ehrman was born on October 5, 1955 in Lawrence, Kansas. He has a sister and a brother. He and his family attended an Episcopalian church on Sundays and said grace before dinner, but religion played only a small role in their lives. At church and in his Sunday school, the priests and teachers emphasized the importance of doing good deeds; they did not focus on the Bible. One day at a party during his sophomore year in high school, Ehrman met Bruce, a charismatic evangelical Christian in his early 20s—one of several Christian-outreach college students at the gathering—who told him that the most important thing in life was to have a personal relationship with God, and that the only way to do so was to accept Jesus as one's savior. During that period Ehrman, like many other teenagers, had been experiencing feelings of alienation and emptiness, and evangelical Christianity soon filled that void. His conversion brought him a "rush of joy and a sense of oneness with the world," he said in an interview with *Current Biography,* the source of quotes for this article unless otherwise noted. Part of the appeal of his newfound religion, he said, was the comfort that came with having answers to the big questions he had, among them, Why am I here? What will happen after I die? The self-described "gung ho Christian" persuaded his girlfriend and family members to adopt evangelical Christianity. "Like a lot of evangelical Christians," Ehrman recalled, "I thought that if you weren't an evangelical Christian you weren't really a Christian." Although he attended many Bible-study classes and prayer meetings, he continued to pursue activities common among teens—partying and drinking on Saturday nights.

On Sunday mornings he would go to church "to repent," he said.

Conflicted about his behavior and eager to study and memorize large parts of the Bible, as Bruce had, Ehrman enrolled at the Moody Bible Institute, in Chicago, Illinois. A strict evangelical school, the institute prohibited not only drinking alcohol and smoking but also playing card games, seeing movies, dancing, and having physical contact with the opposite sex on campus. The "seriousness" that such rules implied about the school appealed to Ehrman. As a 17-year-old freshman, he began to study the Bible voraciously. "As a committed Bible-believing Christian I was certain that the Bible, down to its very words, had been inspired by God," he wrote in the preface to *Jesus, Interrupted.* "Maybe that's what drove my intense study. These were God's words, the communications of the Creator of the universe and Lord of all, spoken to us, mere mortals. Surely knowing them intimately was the most important thing in life. At least it was for me." He soon learned that what he had assumed to be the "word of God" had many variations: more than 5,500 Greek manuscripts (some only fragments) with upwards of 200,000 differences among them—some minor, some very significant. The knowledge that no original manuscripts of the "word of God" have ever been found made him uneasy. To his surprise, none of his friends seemed to be bothered. Ehrman completed his course work at Moody in three years, graduating at age 20.

He then enrolled at Wheaton College, an evangelical Christian school in the Chicago suburb of Wheaton, where he earned a B.A. degree in English literature magna cum laude in 1978. He also studied philosophy, history, and Greek at the school. "Understanding literature more broadly would help me understand this piece of literature [the Bible]," he wrote in the preface to *Jesus, Interrupted*; "being able to read Greek helped me know the actual words given by the Author of the text." Ehrman excelled in his Greek courses, and, at the suggestion of his professor, he read works by Bruce Metzger, a highly respected scholar of Greek manuscripts of the New Testament. The more he read, the more troubled he became about the abundance of different biblical manuscripts, many written centuries after the death of Jesus. Determined to pursue a graduate degree in New Testament studies, he won admission to the Princeton Theological Seminary, in New Jersey, knowing little more about the school other than that Metzger taught there.

The Princeton Theological Seminary is not an evangelical school, and when he enrolled there, Ehrman prepared himself to defend his beliefs, in part by explaining away any inconsistencies in the four gospels of the New Testament. Thus, for the final assignment for a course on the Gospel of Mark that he took during his second semester, he wrote a 35-page paper in which he tried to account for what he now acknowledges to be an obvious contradiction: in Mark 2:26 Jesus speaks of the time that King David went into the temple as "when Abiathar was the high priest"; according to the Old Testament, however, King David's visit occurred when Ahimelech, Abiathar's father, was the high priest. His professor returned the paper with a note that read, "Maybe Mark just made a mistake." Ehrman was shocked. Soon, though, he admitted to himself that perhaps Mark *had* made a mistake.

Ehrman's acceptance of that possibility marked a turning point for him. Afterward, he no longer felt the need to deny contradictions and inconsistencies in the New Testament. (For example, the Gospel of Mark asserts that Jesus was crucified the day after the first Passover meal, while according to the Gospel of John, the crucifixion occurred before that meal.) Ehrman began to regard the Bible as a book written by various people at different times and then transcribed by others thousands of times over hundreds of years. "If there are inconsistencies in the Bible," Ehrman recalled thinking, "then how can we know what's true about God, Jesus' life, eternal life, or anything?" Over the years he continued to view the Bible as very important historically and socially but not as perfect and unquestionable. He received his Ph.D. from Princeton Theological Seminary in 1985; his doctoral thesis, about the fourth-century scholar Didymus the Blind, who headed a school in Alexandria, Egypt, for Christian theologians and wrote voluminously about the Bible, was published as a book in 1986. In 1988, after a stint as a lecturer at the Department of Religion at Rutgers University, in New Jersey, Ehrman joined the faculty at the Department of Religious Studies at the University of North Carolina at Chapel Hill. His classes there became very popular.

In one of his favorite classroom exercises, Ehrman asks his students if they believe the Bible is the "word of God." Invariably, a great majority raise their hands. Then he asks how many have read one or more of the Harry Potter books from cover to cover. Again, most of them have. His final question is, "Who among you has read the entire Bible?" Very few hands go up. "It's a very effective exercise," Ehrman said. "My students often comment on it after the class. They realize just how inconsistent they are in thinking that the Bible is God's revelation to them, but they haven't even bothered to see what he's trying to reveal." Ehrman requires his students to write about the ways in which the accounts of the Last Supper, the crucifixion, the resurrection, and other events differ in the Gospels of Matthew, Mark, Luke, and John. In Mark, for example, Jesus is silent on the cross until moments before his death, when he cries out, "My God, my God, why have you forsaken me?" In Luke, Jesus is not silent and seems much more composed; he says, "Father, forgive them for they do not know what they are doing." And in Luke his last words are "Father, into your hands I commit my spirit." The reactions of Ehrman's students to differences that cannot be reconciled usually vary: "Almost all my students go into the class thinking that the Bible can't have any contradictions in it. Some students who start seeing that there are contradictions have a radical turnabout where they decide they're willing to give up the faith, which isn't a very common reaction and it isn't a reaction that I encourage. Some students hide their head in the sand and pretend that they're not seeing what they're seeing. But I think most students realize that faith is a more complicated proposition than they were raised to believe."

Since 1983 Ehrman has published, for scholars, more than a dozen books; more than two dozen articles for professional journals; and book chapters on the New Testament and early Christianity. His book *Misquoting Jesus: The Story Behind Who Changed the Bible and Why* (2005) became a *New York Times* best-seller. "*Misquoting Jesus* did not reveal any new information to any scholars," Ehrman explained. "What it did was make this information available to people who aren't scholars." Jesus's disciples Matthew, Mark, Luke, and John were illiterate Aramaic-speaking peasants who never wrote accounts of their leader's life and philosophy. The four earliest known versions of the gospels (the word is derived from an Anglo-Saxon word meaning "good spell" or "good news") were recorded anonymously in Greek on papyrus by obviously well-trained writers between 30 and 60 years after Jesus's death. They were based on oral accounts and were changed repeatedly in the decades and centuries that followed. For example, in the Gospel According to John, when Jesus encounters an adulteress who is about to be stoned by an angry mob, he says, "Let the one who is without sin among you be the first to cast a stone at her." That story is not in the earliest versions of that gospel; it was added many years later. John's statement about the Trinity—"There are three that bear witness in heaven, the Father, the Word, and the Holy Spirit, and these are one"—was also added later, when his gospel was translated from Greek into Latin. The reviews for *Misquoting Jesus* were enthusiastic. Yonat Shimron, writing for the Raleigh, North Carolina, *News & Observer* (January 13, 2006), called Ehrman "one of the most distinguished scholars on the history of the biblical text and the early church." Neely Tucker, a *Washington Post* (March 5, 2006) reporter, wrote that *Misquoting Jesus* "casts doubt on any number of New Testament episodes that most Christians take as, well, gospel." Tucker also noted that it had "become one of the unlikeliest bestsellers of the year."

In his next best-seller, *God's Problem: How the Bible Fails to Answer Our Most Important Question—Why We Suffer* (2008), Ehrman described his serious struggle with the "problem of suffering." It started in the mid-1980s, when he was teaching a class at Rutgers called "The Problem of Suffering in Biblical Traditions." Ehrman wrote that few of his students, most of whom were white and middle-class, had any understanding of the worst kinds of suffering. He showed them photos of victims of the Ethiopian famine of 1984–85, which led to the deaths of an estimated one million people. At the time he still considered himself a Christian and tried to explain to his students that the existence of suffering is a real philosophical problem for those with faith in God. Some philosophers, Ehrman said, have addressed the question of suffering—if there is a God who is good and all-powerful, why does he not prevent or minimize suffering?—as purely theoretical and as being explained by the existence of free will. Humans' having free will, however, cannot explain why hurricanes, floods, and other natural disasters occur. Indeed, the line between acts of nature and acts of humans is not always clear: famines, for example, have followed governments' decisions to devote money and manpower to the building of armaments rather than agriculture; flooding has sometimes followed deforestation or resulted from poorly constructed levees or dikes; autism and many other disorders have or seem to have physiological, neurological, or genetic bases. Furthermore, with regard to free will, the Bible describes many situations in which God interferes in people's daily lives and imposes his will on theirs. No abstract arguments, Ehrman contended, can explain fully why an all-powerful being would allow so many innocent people to suffer so terribly. In *God's Problem* he examined Bible accounts of suffering and biblical reasons for its existence. He analyzed what he considered to be the most important biblical explanations, which treat suffering as punishment for sin, as a test of faith, and as redemptive, and he concluded that they are often contradictory or intellectually and morally unsatisfying. In *God's Problem* he also recorded his personal philosophical struggle with the question of suffering and revealed that he lost his faith completely in the late 1990s. Some reviewers, mostly conservative Christians, dismissed *God's Problem* on the grounds that Ehrman was questioning God and not citing faith as an answer in itself. By contrast, in his *New York Times* blog "Think Again" (November 4, 2007), Stanley Fish, a professor of humanities and law, described *God's Problem* as a serious inquiry that Ehrman had pursued with "an energy and goodwill that invite further conversation with sympathetic and unsympathetic readers alike."

In his next book, *Jesus, Interrupted: Revealing the Hidden Contradictions in the Bible (and Why We Don't Know About Them)*, published in 2009, Ehrman elaborated on the many significant discrepancies and contradictions in the New Testament that biblical scholars have been writing about for hundreds of years. In that book Ehrman wrote that Jesus is rarely described as "God" in the New Testament; only in the Gospel according to John is he characterized as divine. Also, the gospels offer contradictory accounts of the resurrection, including differences in reports of who went to the tomb of Jesus and who or what those people saw there. "This kind of scholarship is taught to pastors in seminary when they're training for ministry," Ehrman said, "but when they go into the church they

appear to forget all about it. So people don't know. That's why this book became a bestseller, because it's giving information that scholars have known for a long time, that pastors learn in seminary, but that nobody bothered to tell people." Rich Barlow, writing for the *Boston Globe* (May 6, 2009), commented on that observation: "I expect that for more than a few folks *Jesus, Interrupted* will be a grenade tossed into their tidy living rooms of religious faith." Although many book reviewers praised Ehrman, some theologians accused him trying to "destroy Christian faith." Regardless of whether reviews of his books are positive or negative, Ehrman is amused that some of them imply that he himself discovered the inconsistencies and contradictions in the Bible. "These aren't my idiosyncratic, weird views of the Bible," he told *Current Biography*. "This stuff is commonly taught in the United States and Europe in colleges, universities, and divinity schools."

Ehrman's other books include *The Orthodox Corruption of Scripture: The Effect of Early Christological Controversies on the Text of the New Testament* (1993); *Jesus: Apocalyptic Prophet of the New Millennium* (1999); *Lost Scriptures: Books That Did Not Become the New Testament* (2003); *Lost Christianities: The Battles for Scripture and the Faiths We Never Knew* (2003); *Truth and Fiction in the DaVinci Code: A Historian Reveals What We Can Really Know about Jesus, Mary, and Constantine* (2004); *Peter, Paul, and Mary Magdalene: The Followers of Jesus in History and Legend* (2006); and *The Lost Gospel of Judas Iscariot: Betrayer and Betrayed Reconsidered* (2006). Ehrman's latest book, *Forged: Writing in the Name of God—Why the Bible's Authors Are Not Who We Think They Are*, is scheduled to be published in early 2011.

Ehrman and his wife, Sarah Beckwith, the Marcello Lotti Professor of English at Duke University, live in Durham, North Carolina. The couple have two children—a daughter, Kelly, and a son, Derek.
—D.K.

Suggested Reading: bartdehrman.com; *Boston Globe* G p11 May 6, 2009; (Raleigh, North Carolina) *News & Observer* E p1 Jan. 13, 2006; *Washington Post* D p1 Mar. 5, 2006

Selected Books: *The Orthodox Corruption of Scripture: The Effect of Early Christological Controversies on the Text of the New Testament*, 1993; *Jesus: Apocalyptic Prophet of the New Millennium*, 1999; *Lost Scriptures: Books That Did Not Become the New Testament*, 2003; *Lost Christianities: The Battles for Scripture and the Faiths We Never Knew*, 2003; *Truth and Fiction in the DaVinci Code: A Historian Reveals What We Can Really Know about Jesus, Mary, and Constantine*, 2004; *Misquoting Jesus: The Story Behind Who Changed the Bible and Why*, 2005; *Peter, Paul, and Mary Magdalene: The Followers of Jesus in History and Legend*, 2006; *God's*

Problem: How the Bible Fails to Answer Our Most Important Question—Why We Suffer, 2008; *The Lost Gospel of Judas Iscariot: Betrayer and Betrayed Reconsidered*, 2006; *Jesus, Interrupted: Revealing the Hidden Contradictions in the Bible (and Why We Don't Know About Them)*, 2009

Shah Marai/AFP/Getty Images

Eikenberry, Karl W.

1951– U.S. ambassador to Afghanistan

Address: USAID/Kabul, 6180 Kabul Pl., Dulles, VA 20189

In May 2009, a day after retiring from the U.S. Army with the rank of lieutenant general, Karl Eikenberry became the U.S. ambassador to Afghanistan. While the appointment of a soon-to-be-retired career army officer to a diplomatic post was "highly unusual," as Eric Schmitt wrote for the *New York Times* (January 30, 2009, on-line), in Eikenberry's case it marked a natural progression: the general had previously served in the war-torn country as commander of the Combined Forces Command, a post in which he trained Afghan police and troops to combat insurgents. As Schmitt noted, Eikenberry's connections to the country's key figures and familiarity with its issues amounted to "a valuable commodity in a year when the United States will send thousands of additional troops to Afghanistan and the country [held] presidential elections."

The U.S. invaded Afghanistan in late 2001, following that year's terrorist attacks on Washington, D.C., and New York City by Al Qaeda, a terrorist group that had used Afghanistan as a safe haven and training ground. Although the U.S. ousted the Taliban, the Islamic fundamentalist group that harbored the terrorists in Afghanistan, its later focus on Iraq—which it invaded in March 2003, ostensibly based on the belief that that country had weapons of mass destruction—allowed the Taliban to regroup. During his successful campaign for the presidency in 2008, Barack Obama promised to reduce the level of U.S. troops in Iraq and concentrate on Afghanistan, whose democratically elected government was struggling with an increasingly violent insurgency. In late 2009, acting on the advice of U.S. Army general Stanley A. McChrystal, the top commander of the International Security Assistance Force (ISAF), Obama committed 30,000 additional troops to Afghanistan. (The ISAF, under NATO command since 2003, is comprised primarily of U.S. troops—along with soldiers from 42 other countries—and is responsible for stabilizing Afghanistan.) Along with defeating the Taliban and other insurgent elements, diplomacy will play a key role in the U.S. efforts to bring security to Afghanistan. In his post as ambassador, Eikenberry is responsible for keeping the U.S. and the Afghan government on the "same page," a task for which the Obama administration has found him well-suited. According to Schmitt, "General Eikenberry has a track record for spotting problems in Afghanistan early. He sounded some of the first alarms about a resurgent Taliban and the need to keep the country from backsliding into anarchy. He was also an early and vigorous champion of building up the Afghan Army to combat the Taliban, a top priority for the Obama administration."

Karl Winfrid Eikenberry was born in 1951 to Harry and Mary Eikenberry. His father was a business executive whose work required him to relocate the family often. In the late 1960s his father took a job at Hevi-Duty Electric, and the family moved to Goldsboro, North Carolina, where the company was located. (Hevi-Duty Electric later merged with Sola Electric; the business is now a division of Waukesha Electric Systems.) Eikenberry entered Goldsboro High School as a sophomore and eventually became the manager of the school's football team. He has credited the former Goldsboro coach Gerald Whisenhunt with teaching him leadership skills. "The idea of managing resources and having to put together a team of managers underneath you, and being given some important responsibilities, was a tremendous experience," he told Turner Walston for the *Goldsboro News-Argus* (April 25, 2005, on-line). Eikenberry also told Walston that his challenging high-school classes helped him greatly later on. As a senior Eikenberry was elected class president.

Eikenberry was also influenced in his career choice by his father, who had served as a combat-engineer officer in World War II. "I think I had a predisposition toward an interest in the military," Eikenberry explained to Walston. After taking a tour of the U.S. Military Academy at West Point, in

New York, Eikenberry was determined to join the armed forces. He graduated from West Point in 1973, then served as commander of an infantry company of roughly 130 soldiers stationed at Fort Stewart, Georgia. From 1979 to 1981 he attended Harvard University, in Cambridge, Massachusetts, earning a master's degree in East Asian studies. (He is fluent in Mandarin Chinese.) He also attended Stanford University, in California, from which he earned a master's degree in political science. From 1992 to 1993 he was a National Security Fellow at the Kennedy School of Government at Harvard.

Eikenberry's experience at Fort Stewart, he told Walston, had "led to a lot of certainty on my part that I wanted to do this for an entire career." He spent over three decades in the military, both in administrative positions and in the field. From 1997 to 2000 he was a defense attaché with the Defense Intelligence Agency, stationed in Beijing, China. From 2000 to 2001 he was assistant division commander for the 25th Infantry Division of the U.S. Army, located at Schofield Barracks, in Hawaii. In 2001 he served in Washington, D.C., as deputy director of strategy, plans, and policy for the army; he had an office at the Pentagon when one of the airplanes taken over by Al Qaeda terrorists crashed into the building on September 11. Since then, as he later said at his confirmation hearing before the U.S. Senate, "Afghanistan has been at the center of my career."

Next, Eikenberry was U.S. security coordinator and chief of the Office of Military Cooperation at the U.S. embassy in Kabul, Afghanistan, from 2002 to 2003. In that post he was responsible for building up Afghan security forces, specifically the Afghan National Army. He then assumed the post of director for strategic planning and policy for the U.S. Pacific Command, at Camp H.M. Smith, Hawaii, in 2003. Beginning in 2005 he had his second tour of duty in Afghanistan, as commander of the Combined Forces Command, a position that put him in charge of all non-NATO U.S. forces stationed in the country. Under Eikenberry's leadership the Combined Forces Command trained Afghan police and military personnel, operated U.S. prisons and interrogation centers, and focused on counterterrorism and reconstruction efforts. In 2007 Eikenberry was transferred to NATO to serve as deputy chairman of the Military Committee in Brussels, Belgium, a post he held until he joined the U.S. State Department as ambassador to Afghanistan.

Eikenberry's good relations with Afghan president Hamid Karzai (who was elected after the U.S. ousted the Taliban), as well as his ties to U.S. allies in Europe, made him an appealing choice for the Obama administration. Admiral Mike Mullen, chairman of the Joint Chiefs of Staff, told Robert Burns for the Associated Press (April 28, 2009), "Karl's experience as a soldier and scholar will be crucial to fostering the strong civil-military relationship required to tip the balance." Eikenberry was confirmed by the Senate on April 3 and began his new post in Kabul in May—at a time when the eight-year-old conflict in Afghanistan had entered a perilous phase of insurgent violence, and the Obama administration was seeking new ways to stabilize the country. Eikenberry said at his Senate confirmation hearing, as quoted by CNN (November 12, 2009, on-line), "There is no silver bullet and no quick, cheap or easy solutions. There is no substitute for more resources and sacrifice." He added, "There is no exclusively military solution to the issues we and our partners confront in Afghanistan."

In his first month in his new post, Eikenberry stressed the need for greater trust between Afghanistan and the U.S. To that end, he worked to win the trust of local Afghan leaders and ordinary citizens. In a Canadian Press article (September 16, 2009), Jason Straziuso observed that Eikenberry felt secure enough to walk the streets of Kabul (with bodyguards) to talk to its residents. "The mission here is to secure the people, secure the community," Eikenberry told him. "You've got to be out here getting a sense of what the people are thinking in order to do that." When a U.S. airstrike in May in the province of Farah resulted in the deaths of dozens of civilians, Eikenberry joined Karzai in a visit to the area to express condolences to the victims' families. After Afghanistan's presidential election in August, when it was revealed that almost one in three votes for Karzai was fraudulent, Eikenberry had the task of encouraging the incumbent president to consider a runoff election. The situation was delicate, as a refusal by Karzai would have jeopardized his partnership with the U.S. and NATO forces and the efforts to stabilize the country's government. Along with U.S. senator John F. Kerry of Massachusetts, the chairman of the Senate Foreign Relations Committee, Eikenberry persuaded Karzai over a series of meetings to accept the findings of the U.N. Electoral Complaints Commission (ECC), which invalidated almost a million of the votes for Karzai. Obama said that Karzai's decision to accept the runoff reflected "a commitment to rule of law and an insistence that the Afghan people's will should be done." The president also praised Eikenberry and Kerry for their efforts.

In November 2009 an anonymous source reported to the media that Eikenberry had come out against a proposal to send 40,000 additional troops to Afghanistan to bolster the 68,000 U.S. military personnel already there. The troop increase, requested by the top military commander in Afghanistan, Stanley McChrystal, was under consideration by the Obama administration as one of several options during a three-month review of the situation in Afghanistan; in opposing the increase, Eikenberry argued that Karzai should first work to end widespread corruption in his country and that more U.S. troops would only make the Afghans more dependent on the U.S. "Sending additional forces will delay the day when Afghans will take over, and make it difficult, if not impossible, to bring our people home on a reasonable timetable," he wrote, as quoted by Eric Schmitt in the *New York Times* (January 26, 2010, on-line). "An increased U.S. and foreign role in security and governance will increase Afghan dependence, at least in the short-term." He also expressed misgivings about Karzai's leadership, noting that the Afghan leader was "not an adequate strategic partner" and that he "continues to shun responsibility for any sovereign burden, whether defense, governance or development. He and much of his circle do not want the U.S. to leave and are only too happy to see us invest further. They assume we covet their territory for a never-ending 'war on terror' and for military bases to use against surrounding powers."

Nonetheless, when Obama announced a commitment of 30,000 additional troops, Eikenberry expressed his support for the decision. As Kevin Whitelaw reported for National Public Radio (December 8, 2009, on-line), Eikenberry threw his support behind a troop surge only after the new direction in Afghanistan was fully fleshed-out. "As a result of this very extensive review, the mission was refined, the ways forward were clarified and the resources now have been committed to allow us to achieve the refined mission," he said. "I am unequivocally in support of this mission."

Although Eikenberry has expressed confidence in the new U.S. efforts in Afghanistan, he has also admitted that there are many challenges ahead. The U.S and its allies, he indicated, need to help boost Afghanistan's economy so that the country can eventually fund its own troops. A transition of combat operations from coalition to Afghani forces is expected to begin in 2011, but Eikenberry acknowledged to Whitelaw, "In spite of everything we do, Afghanistan may struggle to take over the essential task of governance and security on a timely basis." Another issue involves the neighboring country of Pakistan, which terrorists use as a safe haven. "The effort we're undertaking in Afghanistan is likely to fall short of our strategic goals unless there is more progress at eliminating the sanctuaries used by the Afghan Taliban and their associates inside of Pakistan," Eikenberry told Whitelaw. In mid-December 2009 Eikenberry spoke before the Afghan Ministry of Foreign Relations, saying, as quoted by Thomas L. Day for McClatchy Newspapers (December 17, 2009, on-line), "Our military commitment will not end or decline even as our combat forces [withdraw]," and adding that troop withdrawal in 2011 is "entirely based on the conditions that exist at that time." Nonetheless, he said, "After eight years of assistance to Afghanistan, many Americans and many members of Congress are impatient to see results."

According to Alissa H. Rubin, writing for the *New York Times* (June 29, 2010), the Afghan attorney general, Mohammad Ishaq Alako, accused Eikenberry of putting inappropriate pressure on him on two occasions to prosecute cases of alleged corruption. One of the cases involved Rafiullah Azimi, a high-profile executive with the Afghan United Bank. "In this particular case, against all diplomatic norms, the U.S. ambassador told me that 'if you are not arresting him, you should resign,'" Alako said. Although corruption has been a major factor in the fraught relations between the U.S. and Afghanistan, Eikenberry and the U.S. Embassy maintained that they respected personnel decisions made by the Afghan government.

In October 2010 reports from Afghanistan indicated that the situation there was becoming less troubled. "Compared to where we were a year ago, we're seeing some positive trends emerging," Eikenberry told Joshua Parlow for the *Washington Post* (October 17, 2010). "I want to be clear: There are areas with significant insecurity," he said, but he added that the activities of NATO and Afghan forces were "starting to have a cumulative effect."

Eikenberry has won numerous military awards and decorations, including the Defense Distinguished and Superior Service Medals, Legion of Merit, Bronze Star, Ranger Tab, Combat and Expert Infantryman badges, and master parachutist badge. He has also been awarded the Department of State Meritorious and Superior Honor Awards and the Director of Central Intelligence Award. From other countries, Eikenberry has received the Canadian Meritorious Service Cross, the Czech Republic Meritorious Cross, the Hungarian Alliance Medal, the French Legion of Honor, and Afghanistan's Ghazi Amir Amanullah Khan and Akbar Khan Medals. He has published many articles on a variety of topics, including military tactics and strategy, Asia-Pacific security, and ancient Chinese military history. He is a former president of the Foreign Area Officers Association and is a member of the nonprofit Council on Foreign Relations.

Eikenberry holds an Interpreter's Certificate in Mandarin Chinese from the United Kingdom Ministry of Defense Chinese Language School, in Hong Kong, China. He also has an advanced degree in Chinese history from Nanjing University, in China. He is married to Ching Eikenberry. Though State Department rules bar family members of diplomats from accompanying them to dangerous countries, Eikenberry lobbied successfully for his wife to be with him in Afghanistan. Eikenberry has a commercial pilot's license and spends some of his free time sailing and scuba diving.

—W.D.

Suggested Reading: cnn.com Nov. 12, 2009; *Goldsboro (North Carolina) News-Argus* (on-line) Apr. 25, 2005; McClatchy Newspapers (on-line) Dec. 17, 2009; National Public Radio (on-line) Dec. 8, 2009; *New York Times* (on-line) Jan. 30, 2009

Frazer Harrison/Getty Images

Favreau, Jon

(fav-ROH)

Oct. 19, 1966– Actor; screenwriter; director

Address: c/o Directors Guild of America, 7920 Sunset Blvd., Los Angeles, CA 90046

"An indie actor-writer who has successfully shifted to directing big studio films, Jon Favreau is simultaneously all Hollywood, and not Hollywood at all—a pretty amazing feat, all things considered," Amelie Gillette wrote for the A.V. Club (March 7, 2006, on-line), adding that he is "one of the most down-to-earth showbiz insiders around." Favreau began his career in show business as an improvisational actor in Chicago. In 1996, four years after his arrival in Hollywood and the year he turned 30, Favreau starred in *Swingers*, an independent film made for only $250,000 from his own semiautobiographical script. A "retro romance filled with wit, craft and heart" and a "beguiling fantasy of comradeship" that succeeded as "both a guys' movie and a date movie," the film critic Richard Corliss wrote for *Time* (November 4, 1996), *Swingers* lifted Favreau from relative obscurity and provided the foundation for his highly successful career not only as an actor and screenwriter but also as a director and producer, in television as well as in film. With *Made* (2001), which followed his appearances in half a dozen feature films and in such acclaimed TV series as *Friends* and *The Sopranos*, Favreau had an auspicious debut as a director and producer and again displayed his talents as a writer and actor. He gained far more attention with his next directorial effort: the Christmas-

themed *Elf* (2003), starring Will Ferrell, which brought raves from critics and—unlike *Swingers* and *Made*, which have earned more in video and DVD sales than they did at the box office—drew many millions of moviegoers to theaters. His biggest hits to date, in terms of gross earnings, are *Iron Man* (2008), starring Robert Downey Jr., and *Iron Man 2*, with Downey again in the title role; by mid-October 2010 the former had earned more than $585 million in the U.S. and overseas, and the latter, $621 million. From 2001 to 2005 Favreau hosted an unusual TV talk show, *Dinner for Five*, in which he and four others from the entertainment industry (a different four for each installment) chatted about whatever struck their fancies while having a meal together. *Dinner for Five* won an Emmy Award nomination in 2005 in the category of outstanding nonfiction series.

The only son of Charles Favreau, a special-education teacher, and Madeleine Favreau, an elementary-school teacher, Jonathan Kolia Favreau was born on October 19, 1966 in Flushing, a section of the New York City borough of Queens, and grew up in Forest Hills, another Queens neighborhood. His father is an Italian-American Catholic. His mother, who was Jewish, died of leukemia when he was 12. As a youngster he enjoyed science fiction and the role-playing game *Dungeons & Dragons*. Favreau attended the Bronx High School of Science, a New York City public school that admits applicants on the basis of a competitive test. "There were kids there from all over the city, so it really broadened my horizons beyond Queens," Favreau told James Ryan for the *New York Times* (October 13, 1996). One of his English teachers, Arthur Feinberg, helped spark his interest in playwriting and acting, and he performed in several high-school productions. Sometimes, he recalled to Ryan, he and his friends would cut classes and go to Greenwich Village, in Manhattan, to see revivals of old films. In 1984 Favreau enrolled at Queens College, a division of the City University of New York, as a preengineering student. He spent much of his time working with student organizations, mainly the College Union Program Board, which organized extracurricular campus activities, and the Center for Human Relations. "Being involved with clubs and events prepared me for my career . . . ," he told Bob Suter for *Q Magazine* (Fall 2006), a Queens College periodical. "Programming the fests and the bands," he explained, is "very similar to production. For the real world, there's nothing like the boots-on-the-ground experience of getting stuff done, pulling together big events and having budgets and committees and a sense of vision and direction and purpose." As the chairman of the Freshman Weekend committee, he continued, he honed his "interpersonal communications skills"—skills, he added, that are "very helpful when you're working on a film set or dealing with groups of people."

After his junior year, feeling that he needed even more real-world experience, Favreau left college and took a job in "facilities planning" with the Wall Street investment-banking firm Bear Stearns. He soon realized that the work did not suit him, and he quit. He returned to college in 1988 but soon left for good, without completing his degree. That summer he traveled to Los Angeles, California, by motorcycle. On his way back to New York, he stopped in Chicago, Illinois, where one of his college friends had been performing in improvisational theater. Instantly hooked by the improv scene, Favreau stayed in Chicago in hopes of making a career in improvisational comedy. While working as a dishwasher at the famed Second City Theatre and selling cartoons that he drew as a freelance artist, he studied at the ImprovOlympic Theater under Del Close, a master of improvisational techniques. He himself later taught classes at ImprovOlympic. Sometimes he would perform at bars, where he became skilled at making funny comebacks to patrons' heckling. During that period his weight ballooned to about 280 pounds. In one of his rare acting gigs, he appeared at a boat show dressed as Cap'n Crunch, the breakfast-cereal cartoon character. While there he met Ron Livingston, who would later be cast in *Swingers*. Favreau's work in a few TV commercials gained him admission to the Screen Actors Guild.

After four years in Chicago, Favreau won his first part in a feature film—that of a Chicago taxi driver in Ted Kotcheff's flop *Folks!* (1992). His first notable big-screen role came the following year, in David Anspaugh's inspirational sports movie *Rudy*, in which he portrayed the title character's pudgy best friend, D-Bob. The film, based on a true story, was a moderate critical and commercial success that later gained a significantly larger audience in video. During shooting on location, at the University of Notre Dame, in Indiana, Favreau became friends with the then-unknown actor Vince Vaughn, who had a smaller role in the film. At Vaughn's urging he moved to Los Angeles, where he discovered that he had already been typecast, because of *Rudy*, as a lovable fat guy. In 1994 he played a fraternity brother named Gutter in the *Animal House*–like comedy *PCU* and appeared in an episode of *Seinfeld* as Eric the Clown. Then he landed small parts in *Mrs. Parker and the Vicious Circle* (1994), as the playwright Elmer Rice, and in *Batman Forever* (1995), as the assistant to Bruce Wayne, but none of his scenes in either movie survived the editor's ax. During the next year Favreau lost 80 pounds, only to find that when he auditioned for people who had seen *Rudy*, he would be turned down because he was no longer fat. He told a *Time* (May 17, 2010) questioner, "I learn more as a director from [acting] than vice versa. I've had the good fortune of being a de facto apprentice on the movies I'm an actor in. Being on other people's sets and watching the flow of work and watching how to handle people gave me a tremendous leg up on other people who were first-time directors and never had that experience."

Meanwhile, Favreau and Vaughn had begun hanging out at Hollywood locations favored by young out-of-work actors like themselves. In his interview with Ryan, Favreau described the regulars in that so-called neo-lounge scene as "all in black leather jackets and introducing each other like they're saying hello to the Don. But you listen to what they're saying and they're all talking about what kind of products they're using in their hair." His observations inspired him to write *Swingers*, which he completed in two weeks with the help of an on-line screenwriting course his father had paid for as a gift. Favreau's script got a positive reception from film-industry decision-makers, who envisioned marquee actors in the leading roles. Favreau, however, was determined to co-star with Vaughan in any film made with his script. Turning down six-figure offers from producers, he sold the rights to *Swingers* for $1,000 to his friend Doug Liman, who agreed to cast him and Vaughan as Mike and Trent, the main characters. Liman, who served as the cinematographer as well as the director, employed a documentary style that made frequent use of hand-held cameras. To avoid the high costs of permits necessary for sole use of various places, Liman shot the film's party and nightclub scenes during normal business hours, when real patrons were present.

Swingers, completed at a cost of $250,000, turned out to be one of the most critically acclaimed films of 1996. Writing for the *New York Times* (October 18, 1996), Janet Maslin described the film as "irresistible" and "convivial" and Favreau's script as "very funny," and she noted that the camaraderie among the cast, which included Ron Livingston, Patrick Van Horn, and Alex Desert playing three of Mike and Trent's friends, was "appealingly clear." Jeffrey Westhoff, the McHenry County, Illinois, *Northwest Herald* (June 21, 2002) reviewer, wrote, "*Swingers* captures the yearnings and motives—both romantic and pathetic—of guys in their 20s like no film since *Diner*." The actor and director Peter Berg wrote for *Interview* (June 1998), "Favreau possesses a singular talent for penetrating the beige façade of Guydom. He doesn't stop at the hackneyed [*Saturday Night Live*]-dude humor that hasn't evolved since the days of Bill Murray and Chevy Chase (it was funny then); nor does he join the legions of actors emulating Woody Allen's over-therapized, self-obsessed anti-intellectual intellectualism. Favreau finds the soft underbelly of today's guy, and serves it up with wit, irony, affection and humility." Such *Swingers'* exclamations as "You're so money!" became catchphrases among twentysomethings, and Favreau and Liman won the 1997 Florida Film Critics Circle Award in the category of newcomers of the year.

On the heels of *Swingers'* success, Favreau landed several high-profile motion-picture and television roles. In 1997 he appeared in six episodes of the extremely popular TV series *Friends* as the wealthy boyfriend of the Courteney Cox character, Monica. The following year he starred in Mimi

Leder's summer blockbuster *Deep Impact*, as a heroic astronaut, and in Peter Berg's *Very Bad Things*, as a soon-to-be-married man whose friends throw a stag party for him in Las Vegas (a film universally panned for its unthinking racism, bigotry, and violence). Favreau portrayed the legendary boxer Rocky Marciano for a 1999 Showtime TV movie of the same name. For that role the actor bulked up significantly and learned how to box. Favreau "does a good job of getting inside a conflicted character," Michael Speier wrote for *Variety* (May 11, 1999). "Sensitive but fearless, Marciano showed genuine concern and forceful determination, and both components are well expressed by the *Swingers* thespian." In 2000 Favreau played a maniacal linebacker in Howard Deutsch's *The Replacements* and starred opposite Famke Janssen in Valerie Breiman's romantic comedy *Love & Sex*. In the latter film, Stephanie Zacharek wrote for *Salon.com* (July 20, 2001), he "proved himself an immensely appealing actor" in the part of "a grumbly, obnoxious boyfriend harboring an inescapably decent nature. It was the kind of character that stuck with you long after you forgot the plot details." Later in 2000 Favreau played himself in an episode of the HBO series *The Sopranos*.

Also in the years following *Swingers*, Favreau directed two shows for television (one called *Hollywood Tales* and the other a police drama); neither ever aired, but with both he gained important skills. He told Amelie Gillette that he was "pretty experienced behind the camera" by 2001, when he made his debut as a film director, with the comedy *Made*, which he also wrote. Widely seen as a sort of sequel to *Swingers*, the film starred Favreau as Bobby, a down-and-out boxer and part-time laborer, and Vaughn as Ricky, his dim-witted best friend. The men travel to New York at the behest of Bobby's boss, a low-level underworld figure (played by Peter Falk), to carry out a small job for a young mob operative (Sean Combs). The film received mostly mixed reviews. "*Made* is little more than a rambling chain of combative buddy mishaps, but the interplay between Vaughn and Favreau, who does great double takes of thrusting chin frustration, spins you through the weak patches," Owen Gleiberman wrote for *Entertainment Weekly* (July 11, 2001).

For four years beginning in July 2001, Favreau hosted an unscripted program on the Independent Film Channel called *Dinner for Five*. For each of the 50 installments, which aired at irregular intervals, Favreau was joined at a restaurant after-hours by four people connected with the entertainment industry who were not always personally acquainted; the five would order their meals from real menus, and the establishment's regular waiters would serve them. Favreau did not interview his guests beforehand, and he set no guidelines as to subject matter for their dinner-table discussions; the guests talked freely about anything they chose. "I wanted to show them, not in the sensationalized way they're presented in the press, but as normal people," Favreau told Robin Pogrebin for the *New York Times* (April 14, 2002). "There's no audience; there's no monologue. It's not what people are used to seeing on TV." Calling *Dinner for Five* "highly uneven but often fascinating," Anita Gates wrote for the *New York Times* (April 15, 2002), "Maybe the show has just worked out the details about close-ups and microphones, or maybe Mr. Favreau is just finding his way with the format, but *Dinner for Five* seems to improve episode by episode." In examples of Favreau's mixes of guests, Sean Combs, John Leguizamo, Vincent Pastore, and Juliette Lewis sat down with Favreau for the first season's 10th installment; for the second season's fourth installment, Edward Asner, Ed Begley Jr., Carrie Fisher, and Blair Underwood had dinner with him; for the third season's fifth, Janeane Garofalo, David Byrne, Dave Eggers, and Joe Pantoliano; and for the last season's 10th, Rosanna Arquette, Bill Maher, Alanis Morissette, and Bob Odenkirk. In editing their two hours of dinnertime talk for TV, Favreau avoided showing any guest chewing and deleted comments obviously not meant for a wide audience or ones that guests requested that he omit.

In 2003 Favreau had a small role in Nancy Meyers's film *Something's Gotta Give*, starring Jack Nicholson and Diane Keaton; appeared in and produced Steve Anderson's motion picture *The Big Empty;* and played the lawyer Foggy Nelson in the action movie *Daredevil*, based on the Marvel Comics character. He next directed Will Ferrell in the family movie *Elf* (2003). The film, written by David Berenbaum, is about an overgrown human child named Buddy (Ferrell), who, after creeping into Santa's sack as a baby one Christmas Eve, was raised by elves at the North Pole. His inability to fit in with the elf community and his newfound knowledge that his biological father (James Caan) lives in New York spur Buddy to go to the Big Apple in search of his real parents. Favreau told Naomi Pfefferman for the *Jewish Journal* (December 26, 2003) that he had been "looking for a Christmas movie, to allow me to deal with my issues"—a reference to his feelings about the death of his mother, shortly before Christmas 1978. "When I was growing up, we'd have the traditional Christmas Eve dinner with my Catholic grandmother, and then Christmas morning would be lox and bagels with my Jewish side," he recalled to Pfefferman. After his mother died, he said, "Christmas went from a very happy time of the year to a very traumatic time. Over the years, I felt like I had not only lost my mother, I had lost Christmas." *Elf*, whose cast also included Edward Asner as Santa, Bob Newhart as Buddy's adoptive father, Zooey Deschanel as Buddy's love interest, and Favreau in the small role of a physician, won critical acclaim and grossed over $100 million at the box office.

In 2004 Favreau appeared on the big screen in *Wimbledon*, and the following year he directed his third feature film, *Zathura: A Space Adventure*, based on the same-titled children's book by Chris

Van Allsburg. The story is about two brothers (portrayed by Josh Hutcherson and Jonah Bobo) who, in Van Allsburg's previous book *Jumanji*, find the box containing the magical board game *Jumanji* soon after it was discarded by the brother and sister who experienced fantastical, hair-raising events unleashed when they played the game. The brothers' attempt to play another board game, called *Zathura*, which was packed in the same box, sends them on a spine-tingling space adventure. "Favreau is one of those rare directors who remembers his own childhood and can actually re-create what kids might want to see in a film," Jeffrey M. Anderson wrote for the Combustible Celluloid Web site; "he also builds a remarkably accurate portrait of two brothers." Despite that and other enthusiastic reviews, at the box office the movie grossed less than half of the $65 million it cost to produce.

In 2006 Favreau had a small role in the romantic comedy *The Break-Up*, which starred Vince Vaughn and Jennifer Aniston, and voiced a character in the computer-animated film *Open Season*. In 2008 he directed his fourth feature film, *Iron Man*. Based on the Marvel Comics superhero of the same name, it starred Robert Downey Jr. as Iron Man and his playboy alter ego, Tony Stark. The film follows Stark as he fights crime in a custom-made, powered suit of armor. Also starring Gwyneth Paltrow, Terrence Howard, and Jeff Bridges, *Iron Man* was both a critical and commercial success. A. O. Scott, in a representative review for the *New York Times* (May 2, 2008, on-line), called the film "an unusually good superhero picture. Or at least—since it certainly has its problems—a superhero movie that's good in unusual ways. The film benefits from a script . . . that generally chooses clever dialogue over manufactured catchphrases and lumbering exposition, and also from a crackerjack cast that accepts the filmmakers' invitation to do some real acting rather than just flex and glower and shriek for a paycheck." He further commented, "Mr. Favreau . . . wears the genre paradigm as a light cloak rather than a suit of iron. Instead of the tedious, moralizing, pop-Freudian origin story we often get in the first installments of comic-book-franchise movies—childhood trauma; identity crisis; longing for justice versus thirst for revenge; wake me up when the explosions start—*Iron Man* plunges us immediately into a world that crackles with character and incident." Favreau, who had a small part in *Iron Man*, appeared in several comedies—*Four Christmases* (2008), *I Love You, Man* (2009), and *Couples Retreat* (2009)—before returning to the director's chair for the blockbuster sequel *Iron Man 2* (2010). The film continues the story of Stark as he tries to ward off an array of colorful villains and maintain world peace. In addition to Downey and Paltrow, the film starred Don Cheadle, Scarlett Johansson, and Mickey Rourke. Though *Iron Man 2* was criticized for having too many subplots, the film received mostly positive reviews.

Favreau directed Sam Rockwell, Harrison Ford, and Daniel Craig in the science-fiction action movie *Cowboys & Aliens*, which is scheduled for a 2011 release. Referring to the fate of his movies after their theatrical runs are over, he told Scott Hettrick for *Video Business* (November 24, 2003), "I think about DVDs as much as the movies because that's where 90% of the people will see [them]." He also said, "That's why I always chock my DVDs full of extras."

Favreau and his wife, Joya Tillem, a doctor of internal medicine at Cedars Sinai Medical Center, in Los Angeles, have been married since 2000. They have three young children: their son, Max, and daughters Madelaine and Brighton Rose.

—C.C.

Suggested Reading: A.V. Club (on-line) Mar. 7, 2006; All Movie Guide (on-line); imdb.com; *Interview* p106+ June 1998; *Jewish Journal* (on-line) Dec. 26, 2003; *New York Times* II p28 Oct. 13, 1996, Television p1+ Apr. 14, 2002; *People* p153+ Dec. 3, 2007; *Q Magazine* Fall 2006

Selected Films: as actor—*Folks!*, 1992; *Hoffa*, 1992; *Rudy*, 1993; *PCU*, 1994; *Grandpa's Funeral*, 1994; *Deep Impact*, 1998; *Very Bad Things*, 1998; *Rocky Marciano*, 1999; *Love & Sex*, 2000; *The Replacements*, 2000; *Daredevil*, 2003; *Something's Gotta Give*, 2003; *Wimbledon*, 2004; *The BreakUp*, 2006; *Open Season*, 2006; *Four Christmases*, 2008; *I Love You, Man*, 2009; as director—*Life on Parole* (TV), 2003; *Zathura*, 2005; as actor and director—*Elf,* 2003; *Iron Man*, 2008; as actor, director, and executive producer—*Iron Man 2*, 2010; as actor and producer—*The Big Empty*, 2003; as writer, actor, and producer—*Swingers*, 1996; as writer, actor, producer, and director—*Made*, 2001; as writer and actor—*Couples Retreat*, 2009; as writer—*The First $20 Million Is Always the Hardest* (TV), 2002

Selected Television Shows: as actor—*Ain't It Cool News*, 2001; *Seinfeld*, 1994; *Chicago Hope*, 1994; *The Larry Sanders Show*, 1995; *Tracey Takes On . . .*, 1996; *Friends*, 1997; *Hercules*, 1999; *Dilbert*, 2000; *The Sopranos*, 2000; *Buzz Lightyear of Star Command*, 2000; *The King of Queens*, 2004; *My Name Is Earl*, 2006; as producer—*Undeclared*, 2001; as executive producer and host—*Dinner for Five*, 2001–05

Claire Greenway/Getty Images

Fenton, George

Oct. 19, 1950– Composer for film, television, and theater

Address: c/o Gofaine/Schwartz Agency, Suite 509, 4111 W. Almeda Ave., Burbank, CA 91505

The British composer George Fenton is known for creating scores that are tailored with sensitivity, subtlety, and acuity to the plays, films, and television shows they accompany. Over the course of close to four decades, Fenton has scored music for more than 100 works for theater, television, and cinema in genres ranging from romantic comedies to history-based dramas to nature documentaries, set in periods ranging from the 16th century to the present day. An accomplished guitarist, pianist, and organist, Fenton launched his career as an actor right after he completed secondary school. Within a few years he had changed course, having decided that his future lay in music. His big break in composing for the theater came in 1974, when the director Peter Gill hired him to come up with music for a Royal Shakespeare Company (RSC) production of *Twelfth Night*; in film, it came in 1982, when the director Richard Attenborough recruited him to write the score for *Gandhi*. Other directors with whom he has collaborated include Stephen Frears (*Mary Reilly, Mrs. Henderson Presents, Dangerous Liaisons*), Harold Ramis (*Multiplicity, Groundhog Day*), Neil Jordan (*High Spirits, We're No Angels*), Nora Ephron (*You've Got Mail, Bewitched*), and Nicholas Hytner (*Ladybird Ladybird, My Name Is Joe, The Madness of King George*). "I've been lucky enough to have these relationships with directors whose work has been

successful," Fenton told David Whetstone for the Newcastle-upon-Tyne, England, *Journal* (November 28, 2006). "I could have written reasonable music for things nobody liked and that would have got me nowhere." Benton's theme music for the cult BBC-TV detective series *Bergerac* and the BBC-TV News have been heard in Great Britain since 1981. His scores have accompanied a number of David Attenborough's award-winning BBC-TV nature-documentary series, among them *Blue Planet* (2001) and *Planet Earth* (2006). Since 2001 Fenton has toured widely as the conductor of the *Blue Planet Live!* performances. Among other honors, the versatile composer has won three British Academy of Film and Television Arts (BAFTA) Awards, three British Music Industry (BMI) Awards, and two Emmy Awards; he has also received nominations for 11 other BAFTAs, five Academy Awards, two Golden Globe Awards, and two Grammy Awards.

George Fenton was born George Richard Ian Howe on October 19, 1950 in South London, England. (Readily available sources do not reveal when or why he changed his surname.) His father, an engineer, played the drums. Fenton grew up in a village in the Midlands, in central England. He began playing the guitar when he was eight years old. As a child he also learned to play the piano and church organ, the latter of which became his favorite instrument, because it was so "loud" and "dramatic," he told Whetstone. Fenton told Thea Jourdan for the *Scotsman* (November 26, 2001) that he credits his "sponge-like" quality with helping him to understand music from different perspectives even before he learned how to read scores. As a boy he performed in village musicals. In his teens he attended St. Edwards, a private boarding school in Oxford, England. (There, a counselor suggested that he become a policeman because he was tall.)

Determined to pursue an acting career in London, Fenton turned down an offer to attend the University of London's Central School of Speech and Drama when he left St. Edwards. In 1968 he won the part of a schoolboy in the premiere of *Forty Years On*, by the English actor, playwright, and author Alan Bennett; John Gielgud starred in that drama, which opened at a West End theater. Fenton's other London stage appearances included a role in a production of Simon Gray's *Butley* (1971). He had a part in the film *Private Road* (1971) and also composed some of its soundtrack, and the next year he appeared on stage in Bennett's play *A Day Out*. In his highest-profile acting job, he portrayed a minor character, Martin Gimbel, in the British TV soap opera *Emmerdale Farm*, which has aired since 1972.

Meanwhile, Fenton was developing an increasing passion for music. "I generally ended up dodging off every five minutes to play the piano in the wings," he told Jourdan. He also landed some jobs as a session musician. Envisioning a career as a "record producer or a rock star," as he told Whetstone, Fenton abandoned acting. He found regular work as an instrumentalist with a number of British theater companies, including the National Theater, the Royal Court, the Riverside Studios, and the Royal Shakespeare Company, at Stratford-Upon-Avon. One day the director Peter Gill, who had mistaken him for an actor, invited him to audition for the RSC's upcoming, 1974 production of *Twelfth Night.* Fenton thought he was going to be assessed for another orchestra job and arrived at the audition with his guitar. When Gill realized his mistake, he asked Fenton to play for him; he was so impressed that he hired Fenton to arrange the music for *Twelfth Night.* In 1976 Fenton composed his first television score, for *Hitting Town,* a play by Stephen Poliakoff that was directed by Gill and performed for BBC-TV. More TV jobs soon followed, including scores for several plays by Bennett. Fenton composed music for the BBC-TV series *Shoestring* (1979–80), about a computer expert who suffers a nervous breakdown and becomes a detective, and for the film *Bloody Kids* (1979), directed by Stephen Frears from a screenplay by Poliakoff. Fenton was nominated for BAFTA Awards for both *Shoestring* and *Bloody Kids.* In 1981 *Shoestring* was resurrected as *Bergerac,* and in 1982 Fenton won his first BAFTA Award in the category of best original television music for his score for the show.

A year or two earlier, Michael Attenborough, a theater director and a fan of Fenton's work, had introduced Fenton's work to his father, the film director Richard Attenborough. Months later Richard Attenborough recruited Fenton to write the score for his next film, about the life of Mohandas K. Gandhi (1869–1948), the political and spiritual leader of the nonviolent movement that forced Great Britain to relinquish its rule over India, in 1947. Fenton collaborated with the renowned Indian sitarist Ravi Shankar to compose the music for the 188-minute-long *Gandhi* (1982), which starred Ben Kingsley in the title role. Released in the United States and the United Kingdom in December 1982, the film earned high praise from critics and won Academy Awards in eight categories. Fenton and Shankar's score was nominated for an Oscar, a BAFTA Award, and a Grammy Award.

Following the great success of *Gandhi,* Fenton's career as a composer for theater, television, and film advanced rapidly. He received BAFTA nominations for his scores for the television miniseries *The Jewel in the Crown* (1984), the film *The Company of Wolves* (1984), and Bennett's play *Talking Heads* (1987). He earned an Academy Award and BAFTA, Golden Globe, and Grammy Awards for his music for Richard Attenborough's film *Cry Freedom* (1987), about the friendship between the South African newspaper editor Donald Woods (portrayed by Kevin Kline) and Steve Biko (Denzel Washington), a young black leader who was murdered by South African policemen in 1977. He and Attenborough worked together again for *Shadowlands* (1993), *In Love and War* (1996), and *Grey Owl* (1999), a film that failed to find a distributor

in the U.S. In 1993 the London Symphony Orchestra included parts of the score for *Shadowlands* in one of its concerts.

Earlier, Fenton had received his second BAFTA Award for his score for the World War I–era TV miniseries *The Monocled Mutineer* (1987), loosely based on the life of Percy Topliss, a working-class trickster who became an army deserter, was tried for murder in absentia, and succumbed to a bullet while on the run. Fenton joined Stephen Frears to create the score for *Dangerous Liaisons*—one of his five screen credits in 1988—about the cruel games played by bored aristocrats (Glenn Close and John Malkovich played the leads) in 1790s France; for that work he received Oscar and BAFTA nominations. He won a BAFTA TV Award for Michael Caton-Jones's *Memphis Belle* (1990), which combined original tunes with variations on such traditional songs as "Amazing Grace," "Londonderry Air," and "Danny Boy." In 1992 Fenton was nominated for another Academy Award for his score for Terry Gilliam's *The Fisher King* (1991), starring Jeff Bridges and Robin Williams. In 1993 his music accompanied Harold Ramis's romantic comedy-fantasy *Groundhog Day,* in which Bill Murray and Andie McDowell had the leads. "The soundtrack to *Groundhog Day . . .* is illustrative of Fenton's light romantic comedy style (albeit with a darker more philosophical side) and a main title speaking eloquently of small town band with clarinets and brass," an unnamed writer opined on the British Web site Music Files.

Fenton had a setback in 1994 when, after spending nine months putting together a score for Neil Jordan's film *Interview with the Vampire,* with a screenplay by Anne Rice based on her same-titled novel, his music was scrapped and the composer Elliot Goldenthal was hired to replace him. "It destroyed me," Fenton told Jourdan about the experience. "Your score is like one of your babies. Writing 90 minutes of music for a full orchestra, recording it, putting on the film, seeing the film play with it and then having it junked is hard." According to a writer for filmtracks.com (June 6, 2003), the producers of *Interview with the Vampire* thought that Fenton's music "was too understated and slowly paced for the picture." Fenton's adaptations of two classical pieces by the 19th-century composer Frédéric Chopin and two by the 18th-century composer George Frideric Handel (music from his opera *Terpsichore* and his Harp Concerto) were kept in the soundtrack.

In 1994 Fenton collaborated with Bennett, as screenwriter, and Hytner, as director, for the film *The Madness of King George,* about the slow mental disintegration of King George III of Great Britain, who reigned from 1760 to 1820. For that score Fenton drew heavily from music by Handel, who spent most of his adult life in England. "Fenton pieces together snippets of operas, oratorios, anthems and concerti grossi for maximum theatrical effect, only occasionally stepping outside the vocabulary of 18th-century musical practice," James

Chute wrote in a review for the *San Diego Union-Tribune* (February 16, 1995). "That Fenton generally manages not only to stay within Handel's idiom but to speak in Handel's voice is a tribute to adapter and composer." Later in the 1990s his music was heard in films including *Mary Reilly*, *Heaven's Prisoners*, *Multiplicity*, *Carla's Song*, *The Crucible*, and *In Love and War*, all in 1996, and *My Name Is Joe*, *Ever After*, *Living Out Loud*, and *You've Got Mail*, all in 1998. In 1999 Fenton composed the music for the film *Anna and the King*, based on a novel by Margaret Landon (1944); that book drew from the diaries of Anna Leonowens, a widowed British schoolteacher who spent eight years in the 1860s instructing dozens of the children of King Mongkut of Siam (the official name of Thailand until 1939). Fenton considered the project particularly difficult, in part because the celebrated film composer Bernard Hermann had provided the music for the popular 1946 film *Anna and the King of Siam*, starring Irene Dunne and Rex Harrison, and Richard Rodgers's score for the hit 1951 theatrical musical *The King and I* (heard also in the 1956 movie adaptation) was so well known to the public. In addition, Fenton told Jon Burlingame for *Variety* (October 15, 1999), "in an epic film, it's much more complicated to work out the architecture of the score. There are themes that relate to the place, to the political story and to the romantic story." He said that he had aimed to write music "in a style that is consistent with Thai music" while also expressing his own interpretation of the story. Directed by Andy Tennant and starring Jodie Foster and Yun-Fat Chow, *Anna and the King* earned Fenton two Golden Globe nominations in the categories of best original song (for "How Can I Not Love You") and best original score.

Meanwhile, in 1990 Fenton had scored his first nature-documentary series, *The Trials of Life: A Natural History of Animal Behaviour*, hosted by the British naturalist and broadcaster David Attenborough. Produced by the BBC, *The Trials of Life* is one of nine series in the network's Life collection. Each of the dozen 50-minute segments of *The Trials of Life* focuses on a different aspect of animal life (for example, hunting, fighting, mating). Three years later Fenton composed the score for the related series *Life in the Freezer* (1993), which explored aspects of the seasonal cycle in Antarctica in six 30-minute installments. Fenton told Whetstone that he regarded those and other nature-series projects as "an antidote to doing movies," because it freed him from the pressures exerted by film studios.

Fenton walked away from a "big film" he was asked to do in Hollywood, he told Gordon Barr for the Newcastle-upon-Tyne *Evening Chronicle* (December 13, 2006), to take on the job of composing the music for Attenborough's next series, *Blue Planet: Seas of Life* (2001), about the world's oceans and their inhabitants. After viewing many of the series' sequences—described variously by film critics as "awesome," "extraordinary," and "unabashedly poetic"—which were captured by 35 photographers using underwater cameras over the course of five years in nearly 200 marine locations, Fenton took a diving course to experience aquatic life firsthand. "I actually saw a 6-foot-long reef shark on my first dive. It was swimming about 10 to 15 ft above me . . . ," he told Barr. "Being able to dive made me realize more and appreciate more the incredible calm that the camera crew have and just how spectacular it is down there." "I wanted to write a big-screen score," Fenton told Barr. "I didn't want it to be a natural history documentary, but a big old-fashioned Hollywood score." Each of the eight 50-minute segments of *Blue Planet*, all produced by Alastair Fothergill, focuses on a different aspect of sea life. The footage "runs the gamut from tranquility to terror," Richard Jinman wrote for the *Age* (December 11, 2004), a Melbourne, Australia, daily. "Jellyfish, whales and a solitary albatross wheeling above the Southern Ocean provide some of the quieter moments. But a scene in which dolphins, sharks and gannets cut swathes through a boiling shoal of sardines is as pulse-racing as a John Woo-directed car chase." In another scene a pod of orcas, or killer whales (a dolphin species), stalks and attacks a mother gray whale and its calf. Fenton told Michael Granberry for the *Dallas (Texas) Morning News* (July 2, 2008) that, in order to compose music for that scene, he tried "to imagine the sounds of [the struggle]. It's rather like a U-boat and simple in that way. . . . [The music] makes it clear, and I think it's quite emotional for an audience." In an assessment of *Blue Planet* for the *New York Times* (January 27, 2002), Julie Salamon wrote, "The prevailing sense of grandeur is reinforced by George Fenton's emphatic music." *Blue Planet* debuted on BBC-TV in September 2001 and earned Fenton BAFTA and Grammy Awards for its music.

In the recording studio Fenton came up with the idea of creating a theatrical-length feature film with selected footage from *Blue Planet* that would be projected on a big screen and accompanied by live narration and music. The first live performance of *The Blue Planet Live!* took place at London's Royal Festival Hall on October 13, 2001, with Fenton conducting the BBC Concert Orchestra and the Choir of Magdalen College, of Oxford University, and David Attenborough as narrator. "With every twist in the tale, Fenton's music was correspondingly amazing," Michael Church wrote in a review of the concert for the United Kingdom's *Sunday Express* (October 21, 2001). "Massive percussion and rending brass for the destructive work of the whales, graceful flutes for the spinning dolphins, Chinese theatre instruments to illustrate the antics of exotic pink crabs." *The Blue Planet Live!* has since been performed at locations the world over. "If people do come and then leave with a feeling that they would like to go to see an orchestra again, then we have accomplished something," Fenton told Barr. The full-length film *Deep Blue*, released on video in 2003, includes some reedited scenes from *The Blue Planet* as well as never-before-seen footage; the actor Michael Gambon narrates, and the Berlin Philharmonic Orchestra performs Fenton's music. Unlike the *Blue Planet* TV series, whose main purpose was educational, the aim of *Deep Blue* was to "take its audience on an emotional journey," Richard Jinman wrote.

Fenton joined forces with Fothergill and David Attenborough again to compose the score for *Planet Earth*, a series of 11 episodes, each 50 minutes, featuring rare footage of wildlife in some of the most remote places on Earth, struggling to stay alive in habitats undergoing major, manmade changes. Co-produced by the BBC, which broadcast the first episode in the United Kingdom in March 2006, and the Discovery Channel, which showed the series in the United States a year later, *Planet Earth* consistently attracted large audiences; its honors included a Peabody Award for excellence in television broadcasting, a BAFTA Award, and an Emmy Award, and Fenton earned a 2007 Classical Brit Award for best soundtrack. While some critics found Fenton's score overbearing, most praised it as a lively audio backdrop that reflected and enhanced the images onscreen with unusual skill. A feature-length film, called *Earth*, composed of reedited portions of *Planet Earth*, was shown on BBC-TV in 2008. A writer for the *Jakarta Post* (May 4, 2008) described Fenton's score for *Earth* as "uplifting, enchanting and at times sobering," while Iain McKay, writing for the *Sunday Age* (December 14, 2008), declared it to be "one of [Fenton's] finest achievements—a majestic and dramatic tribute to a world which, according to the film's disheartening message on global warming, may not be around in its present form much longer." The 10-part BBC documentary series *Life*, seen on British TV in 2009 and in the U.S. beginning in March 2010 on the Discovery Channel, also has a score by Fenton.

Among Fenton's scores for nondocumentary British or Hollywood films made during the 2000s are those for Ken Loach's *The Navigators* (2001), *Sweet Sixteen* (2002), and *It's a Free World . . .* (2007); Christopher Hampton's *Imagining Argentina* (2003); Richard Eyre's *Stage Beauty* (2004); Gary Chapman's *Valiant* (2005); Frears's *Mrs. Henderson Presents* (2005); Hytner's *The History Boys* (2006); Wayne Wang's *Last Holiday* (2006); and Tennant's *Fool's Gold* (2008) and *The Bounty Hunter* (2010). He won BMI Film Music Awards for his scores for Tennant's *Sweet Home Alabama* (2002) and *Hitch* (2005).

Fenton is a visiting professor at London's Royal College of Music, where, he told Church, he tries to impart to his students "two things: first, there are no fixed career paths in film music—I'm the walking example of that. Second, the best film music is informed by music pure and simple—not by other film music." In 2001 Church described him as "gangling, debonair, [and] youthful." Fenton lives in England; he believes that had he succumbed to pressure to move to Hollywood, his compositions would have been far less musically diverse.

—M.R.M.

Suggested Reading: *Dallas Morning* News E p1 July 2, 2008; *Jakarta (Indonesia) Post* p14 May 4, 2008; Marquis Who's Who on the Web; (Melbourne, Australia) *Age* A2 p4 Dec. 11, 2004; Music Files Web site; (Newcastle-upon-Tyne, England) *Evening Chronicle* p2 Dec. 13, 2006; (Newcastle-upon-Tyne, England) *Journal* p24 Nov. 28, 2006; *Nottingham (England) Evening Post* p2 Dec. 15, 2006; *Scotsman* p11 Nov. 26, 2001; (United Kingdom) *Sunday Express* Features p66 Oct. 21, 2001

Selected Works: for film—*Bloody Kids*, 1979; *Gandhi*, 1982; *The Company of Wolves*, 1984; *East of Ipswich*, 1987; *Cry Freedom*, 1987; *Dangerous Liaisons*, 1988; *Memphis Belle*, 1990; *The Fisher King*, 1991; *Final Analysis*, 1992; *Groundhog Day*, 1993; *Shadowlands*, 1993; *Ladybird Ladybird*, 1994; *The Madness of King George*, 1994; *Land and Freedom*, 1995; *Multiplicity*, 1996; *Mary Reilly*, 1996; *Heaven's Prisoners*, 1996; *Carla's Song*, 1996; *The Crucible*, 1996; *In Love and War*, 1996; *My Name Is Joe*, 1998; *Ever After*, 1998; *Living Out Loud*, 1998; *You've Got Mail*, 1998; *Anna and the King*, 1999; *Center Stage*, 2000; *The Navigators*, 2001; *Sweet Sixteen*, 2002; *Sweet Home Alabama*, 2002; *Deep Blue*, 2003; *Imagining Argentina*, 2003; *Stage Beauty*, 2004; *Hitch*, 2005; *Valiant*, 2005; *Bewitched*, 2005; *Mrs. Henderson Presents*, 2005; *Last Holiday,* 2006; *The History Boys*, 2006; *Earth*, 2007; *It's a Free World . . . ,* 2007; *Love and Death in Shanghai*, 2007; *Fool's Gold*, 2008; *The Bounty Hunter*, 2010; for television— *Hitting Town*, 1976; *ITV Plahouse*, 1977–78; *Shoestring*, 1979–80; *BBC2 Playhouse*, 1981; *Bergerac*, 1981; *Play for Tomorrow*, 1982; *Objects of Affection*, 1982; *The Jewel in the Crown*, 1984; *Call Me Mister*, 1986; *Talking Heads*, 1987; *The Monocled Mutineer*, 1987; *The Trials of Life: A Natural History of Animal Behavior*, 1990; *Life in the Freezer*, 1993; *Talking Heads 2*, 1998; *Blue Planet: Seas of Life*, 2001; *Planet Earth*, 2006; *Life*, 2009; for theater—*Twelfth Night*, 1974; *Much Ado About Nothing*, 1981; *A Month in the Country*, 1981; *The Duchess of Malfi*, 1981; *Don Juan*, 1981; *Good*, 1981; *Antony and Cleopatra*, 1983; *Macbeth*, 1983; *Mother Courage*, 1984; *Bengal Lancer*, 1985

Selected Performances: in theater—*Forty Years On*, 1968; *Butley*, 1971; *A Day Out*, 1972; *The Pleasure Principle*, 1973; *Twelfth Night*, 1975; in film—*Private Road*, 1971; in television— *Emmerdale Farm*, 1972

Joern Pollex/Bongarts/Getty Images

Ferguson, Alex

Dec. 31, 1941– Soccer manager

Address: Manchester United, Sir Matt Busby Way, Old Trafford, Manchester M16 0RA, England

In 1986, when Alex Ferguson became the manager of the Manchester United Football Club, based in Manchester, England, that soccer organization was seen as a "dispirited team of underachievers," according to its own Web site. Since then Ferguson has guided Manchester United, one of the 20 teams in Great Britain's Premier League, to three dozen major trophies, including 11 Premier League championships, four Premier League Cups, five Football Association Cups, two Union of European Football Associations (UEFA) Champions League titles, and a FIFA Club World Cup. Ferguson's accomplishments with the Red Devils, or the Reds, as the team is often called, have made him the most successful manager in the history of British soccer. In 1999 he was granted knighthood by Queen Elizabeth II, and two years later, during its Sports Personality of the Year gala, the British Broadcasting Corp. (BBC) presented him with its Lifetime Achievement Award. Sometimes referred to as "Furious Fergie" by the media, Ferguson has earned a reputation for being a strict disciplinarian. Famously short-tempered, he once threw a tray of teacups at players during a locker-room pep talk. "He put pressure on you to perform all the time and he expected you to have the mental strength to withstand it," Mark McGhee, a former player, told Jim White for the London *Guardian* (May 22, 1999). "If you repaid him, he was incredibly loyal

to you. But if you didn't, he wasn't slow to tell you. He was very honest." Ferguson does not coddle superstars, and his coaching style includes shuffling players in and out of the roster for what he believes is the overall good of the team. Players have dubbed him "the hairdryer," for his tendency to scream at those who have angered him while standing mere inches from their faces. "Sometimes I lose my temper, sometimes I don't. If someone argues with me I have to win the argument," he told Robert Crampton for the London *Times* (February 22, 2003). Ferguson has also often berated reporters during press conferences, and he has refused to speak to any from the BBC since 2004, when the company broadcast a documentary accusing one of his sons, a sports agent, of profiting from his father's influence. According to the Associated Press (April 22, 2010), *Forbes* ranks Manchester United as the most valuable team not only in soccer but in all of professional sports worldwide; in terms of "account revenue growth, profitability and debt levels" in 2008–09, it was worth $1.8 billion, $150 million more than the next-most-valuable team, the Dallas Cowboys of the National Football League, and $200 million more than Major League Baseball's New York Yankees.

Alex Chapman Ferguson was born on December 31, 1941 in Govan, a blue-collar district of Glasgow, Scotland. His father, Alexander, a Protestant, worked in a shipyard; his mother, Elizabeth, a Catholic, was a factory worker. His brother, Martin, is currently a Manchester United scout for foreign talent. Thanks to his parents' mixed-faith marriage, Alex Ferguson rejected the religious bigotry common in Scotland during those years. He also inherited his parents' unrelenting work ethic, and he idolized his father, a quick-tempered man whose workweek often stretched to 48 hours but who earned a relatively small salary. In a conversation with the political strategist and journalist Alasdair Campbell, a friend of his, for *New Statesman* (March 23, 2009), Ferguson said, "I was always very conscious of the sense of community, people and families supporting each other. I grew up believing Labour was the party of the working man, and I still believe that." A bright and argumentative child, Ferguson dreamed of playing soccer. He supported the Glasgow Rangers professional team, and at seven he joined the Govan Rovers, a local youth club. After he completed high school, he became a member of the Drumchapel Amateur Football Club before signing on as a part-time player with Queen's Park at 16. At the same time he worked as a toolmaker in a typewriter factory, his father having insisted that he learn a trade. During that period Ferguson became interested in labor unions, and at 19 he staged a walkout of local apprentices.

In 1960, the same year he led the apprentices' strike, Ferguson began playing for St. Johnstone, a professional team based in Perth, Scotland. He fought with the team's owners over his pay, and for a while he considered abandoning the sport and moving to Canada, where many toolmakers were finding work. His decision to stick with soccer led him to join Dunfermline Athletic Football Club. He quit his job at the factory and became a full-time professional. The team won the Scottish Cup in 1961, and Ferguson led his teammates in scoring for three consecutive seasons. (The soccer season runs from August to the end of March of the following year.) In 1966 he married Cathy Holding, a Catholic, and the next year, fulfilling his boyhood dream, he signed with the Glasgow Rangers, with whom he spent two and a half years. In his first season he scored 19 goals in 29 league contests, a team high. (Some sources say he scored 23 goals.) "He was not the most skillful player, but his effort was always considerable," his former teammate Kai Johansen told Matthew Lindsay for Scotland's *Evening Times* (October 22, 2003). "Nobody would fight harder for your cause than Alex." Ferguson's time with the Rangers ended in 1969, after he was blamed for a 4–0 loss to the team's archrival Celtic Football Club in the Scottish Cup title game. (The player he was assigned to guard scored the opening goal, and the Rangers never recovered.) He later claimed that his leaving had more to do with sectarianism in Glasgow's front office: officials drew support largely from Protestants, and he believed that they were unhappy that he had a Catholic wife.

In 1969 Ferguson signed with Falkirk Football Club; in addition to playing, he helped out with coaching. Four years later he signed with Ayr United Football Club. Concurrently, he ran Fergie's, a pub he had bought in Glasgow. In 1974, when he was on the verge of leaving soccer and opening a restaurant, he was hired as manager of East Stirling Football Club. He remained on that job for only three months. His next managerial stint, with St. Mirren Football Club, was much more successful. In 1976–77 the team won a First Division Championship, and by 1978 the average attendance at matches had risen from 1,200 to 12,000. Nevertheless, that year Ferguson was let go. He sued St. Mirren for what he maintained was his wrongful dismissal, but a tribunal ruled in favor of the team. Meanwhile, Ferguson had taken a coaching job with the Aberdeen Dons. In 1980 the Dons finished the season ahead of Celtic, winning their first of three consecutive Scottish titles. Three years later Ferguson enjoyed what Alex Dowdalls, writing for Scotland's *Daily Record* (December 29, 2001), called "the greatest night in the Dons' history," when he led the team to victory over the Spanish team Real Madrid in the European Cup Winners' Cup. (An international competition, it merged with the UEFA Champions League, or European Cup, in 1999.) Later that year the Dons topped Hamburg to win the European Super Cup. The next season, in 1983–84, Aberdeen achieved a so-called League and Cup double, winning both the Scottish league and Scottish Cup. Ferguson was named Scottish coach of the year in 1983, 1984, and 1985. In the last of those years, his memoir *A Light in the North*, the first of his five books, was published.

In 1986 Ferguson was named the successor to Jock Stein, the manager of the Scottish national team, who had collapsed and died during a World Cup qualifying match. Later that year the team was eliminated in the first round of the World Cup tournament, which was held in Mexico. Rather than continue coaching Team Scotland, Ferguson took the job of managing Manchester United, an English club that, despite a history of greatness, had not won a league title in two decades. The club plays home games in Old Trafford, a UEFA five-star, all-seater facility in Greater Manchester. Ferguson's first three seasons were largely unsuccessful. Then, in 1990, he led Manchester to victory in the Football Association (FA) Cup—an annual competition among English soccer clubs—thus ushering in a decade of "silverware," as soccer trophies are often called. In the 1990–91 season the Red Devils won the European Cup Winners Cup, and on November 19, 1991 the team won the European Super Cup, 1–0, with Red Star Belgrade, in what is now Serbia, taking the loss. At the end of the 1991–92 season, the team won the League Cup, and the following year it finished first in the newly created Premier League, earning its first league championship in 26 years. In 1993–94 Ferguson and the Red Devils won a League and Cup double, finishing first in the Premier League and winning the FA Cup. While 1994–95 was marked with disappointment—the Red Devils narrowly lost both the league and FA Cup titles—the following year brought another League and Cup double, marking the first time in soccer history that a team had won that particular double twice. Manchester earned another Premier League title in 1996–97, the second time since 1992 that the club had finished first in back-to-back seasons.

After finishing second in 1997–98, Manchester United rebounded the following year, winning the Premier League, FA Cup, and European Cup—an unprecedented "treble," which refers to winning a league title and two cup competitions in the same season. Ferguson drew praise for his coaching in the European Cup final, in which he sent in Teddy Sheringham and Ole Gunnar Solskjaer, players who had spent much of the season as substitutes, with minutes to play in the match. Both Sheringham and Solskjaer scored goals, lifting Manchester United over the German team Bayern Munich. The stellar season earned Ferguson a new level of respect, and in 1999, the same year his second memoir, *Managing My Life: The Autobiography*, was published, he was granted knighthood by Queen Elizabeth II. (Earlier, Ferguson had received Order of the British Empire and Commander of the British Empire honors, in 1984 and 1995, respectively.) Also in 1999 the Reds won the International Cup, beating the Palmeiras, from São Paulo, Brazil, 1–0, in a contest held at the National Stadium in Tokyo, Japan. In 2000 Ferguson announced his intention to retire at the end of the 2001–02 season, but after celebrating his 60th birthday, he decided that he was not ready to leave the game and signed a three-year deal worth a reported £11 million (about $15 million then). Ferguson, who had fought with team officials over his salary for much of the 1990s, thus became the highest-paid manager in British soccer.

Manchester United won the Premier League in the 1999–2000, 2000–01, and 2002–03 seasons. In 2003–04, despite its failure to win a league title, the team captured the FA Cup, marking the fourth time Ferguson had led the Red Devils to victory in that competition. In the early 2000s Ferguson publicly butted heads with David Beckham, a star player who, due in part to his marriage to Victoria "Posh Spice" Adams, a member of the pop group the Spice Girls, had become one of England's biggest celebrities. In February 2000 Beckham skipped a practice, claiming that his infant son, Brooklyn, was sick. It was later revealed that Beckham—who, during his nine years for United up until then, had never failed to show up for practice—had watched Brooklyn so that his wife could go shopping, leading Ferguson to bench him for a match against Leeds and to fine him £50,000. In August Ferguson sold Beckham's United teammate Jaap Stam to the Italian team Lazio after the publication of Stam's autobiography, which contained criticism of Ferguson.

In 2003 Beckham signed a deal with Real Madrid, and at around the same time, Ferguson found himself coaching a team that comprised few players from Manchester United's 1990s glory years. He began to rebuild the squad by signing such young standouts as Cristiano Ronaldo and Wayne Rooney, and in 2005–06 the Red Devils won a League Cup. The following season Ferguson captured his ninth Premier League title. In January 2004, meanwhile, he had signed a deal allowing him to renew his contract on a yearly basis. In 2007–08 Ferguson earned two more major trophies, guiding Manchester United to Premier League and European Cup titles. He captured the latter, his 20th major trophy, when his team defeated Chelsea in Moscow, Russia. The game, which was played in heavy rain, ended after a 1–1 tie, when Manchester United won in the decisive penalty-kick shootout. In December 2008, in Yokohama, Japan, the Reds defeated the Ecuadorian club LDU Quito, 1–0, thus becoming the first British team to win the International Federation of Association Football (known by its French acronym, FIFA) Club World Cup. In the Premier League finals, on March 1, 2009, with Ben Foster, Jonny Evans, Darren Gibson, Danny Welbeck, Nani, and Carlos Tevez in the starting lineup, Manchester United triumphed over Tottenham Hotspur (the Spurs), 4–1, in a penalty shootout after a 0–0 draw, to win the League Cup (also called the Carling Cup, for its beer-company sponsor, since 2003). On May 16, 2009 Manchester secured the Premier League title for the third season in a row and the 11th time since Ferguson's arrival, thanks to a 0–0 draw in a match with the North London team Arsenal. On February 29, 2010 the Reds won the League Cup

again, beating Aston Villa by a score of 2–1. That year they missed out on a fourth consecutive Premier League title, having finished one point behind Chelsea in the overall standings.

Under Ferguson, Manchester United has also won nine matches in the annual FA Community Shield games, played between the winners of the FA Cup and the FA Premier League champions (or the league runner-up, if one team has won the Double). The Reds shared the prize with Liverpool in 1990 and won in 1993, 1994, 1996, 1997, 2003, 2007, 2008, and 2010.

Ferguson and his wife live in Wilmslow, an affluent town in the county of Cheshire, England. The coupled named their house Fairfields, after the shipyard where Ferguson's father worked. In addition to Jason, their children are Mark, who works in the financial industry, and Darren, a one-time Manchester United player who, in 2007, was named player-manager of the team Peterborough United. In his leisure time Ferguson enjoys film, food, fine wine, and horseracing. (He owns several horses.) He has read extensively about the U.S. Civil War and the assassination of President John F. Kennedy and owns a copy of the "Warren Commission Report" (1964)—the official document produced by a U.S. government–appointed panel that investigated Kennedy's murder—signed by President Gerald R. Ford. A self-professed socialist, Ferguson supports Labour Party candidates, and during the 1990s he campaigned on behalf of British prime minister Tony Blair. Once, when asked by the party for advice, he replied, as quoted in the London *Sunday Times* (May 30, 1999), "Just keep going on the things that matter—jobs, schools, hospitals, crime—and hold your nerve."

—K.J.P.

Suggested Reading: (Exeter, England) *Express & Echo* p36 Jan. 7, 2005; (Glasgow, Scotland) *Evening Times* p32 Oct. 22, 2003; (London) *Daily Mail* p94 Dec. 29, 2001; (London) *Times* p16 Feb. 22, 2003; (Scotland) *Daily Record* p2 Dec. 29, 2001; (South Africa) *Sunday Times* p8 Oct. 13, 2002; Crick, Michael. *The Boss: The Many Sides of Alex Ferguson*, 2002; Ferguson, Alex. *A Light in the North*, 1985, *Six Years at United*, 1992, *A Will to Win: The Manager's Diary* (with David Meek), 1997, *Managing My Life: My Autobiography*, 1999, *The Unique Treble*, 2000; Taylor, Daniel. *This Is the One: Sir Alex Ferguson—The Uncut Story of a Football Genius*, 2008

Selected Books: *A Light in the North*, 1985; *Six Years at United*, 1992; *A Will to Win: The Manager's Diary* (with David Meek), 1997; *Managing My Life: My Autobiography*, 1999; *The Unique Treble*, 2000

Nina Subin, courtesy of Hachette Book Group

Ferris, Joshua

Nov. 8, 1974– Novelist

Address: c/o Author Mail, Little, Brown and Co., 237 Park Ave., New York, NY 10017

Joshua Ferris was in his early 30s when his debut novel, *Then We Came to the End* (2007), brought him a reputation on the international literary scene as one of the brightest new American fiction writers. (The book has been translated into 24 languages.) Set in an advertising agency and inspired partly by his experiences as an ad-agency copywriter in Chicago, Illinois, for nearly four years, *Then We Came to the End* was seen by several critics as an unusual blend of the horror and satire that distinguishes Joseph Heller's World War II novel, *Catch-22* (1961), and the cringe-worthy humor of the television mockumentary *The Office*. The book, which received an abundance of enthusiastic reviews, won the Hemingway Foundation/PEN Award and was a finalist for the National Book Award. Ferris's second and latest novel, *The Unnamed* (2010), is about a man who has an unexplained, uncontrollable impulse (a disorder that Ferris made up) that forces him to leave his office or his home—suddenly and without warning—and walk outdoors until he can walk no more. Generally regarded as more ambitious than Ferris's first novel, *The Unnamed* polarized critics. "This is a story about a man with a walking problem, but it is also a larger tale about struggling with uncertainty," an admiring *Economist* (January 30, 2010, online) reviewer wrote. "Scattered throughout the novel are some odd events: blizzards, floods, fires, dying bees. Mr Ferris is reminding us of how little

we know about the world we live in, and how little we know about ourselves within it, and yet we persist. This is not to say that Tim's walking is some clunky metaphor. Mr Ferris is wise enough not to teach a lesson. Rather, he has teased ordinary circumstances into something extraordinary, which is exactly what we want our fiction writers to do." While the *Economist* reviewer found the story to be "serious and mysterious," Janet Maslin, writing for the *New York Times* (January 14, 2010), found Tim's ups and downs "cyclical" and the plot seemingly "going nowhere." Juliet Lapidos, however, in her assessment of the book for the on-line magazine *Slate* (January 11, 2010), viewed those aspects of the book as meaningful: "A baggy novel, *The Unnamed* is frustrating to read. Characters drop in, clamor for attention, then vanish. Specific themes fade into more existential explorations. Subplots bend into narrative cul-de-sacs. . . . Perhaps just as frustrating: This frustration is, in itself, a sign of the novel's success. It takes an often-rudderless, unstructured novel to make palpable Tim's rudderless, unstructured existence. You may find yourself compelled, in an inexorable, Tim-like way, to keep turning the pages—to see what happens next to this character trapped 'in the present, above time,' with only the most tenuous grasp of his own future."

Joshua Ferris was born on November 8, 1974 in Danville, Illinois. At the age of 10, along with his mother, brother, sister, and stepfather, Ferris—whose parents had divorced—moved to Cudjoe Key, Florida, where he learned to snorkel, fish, and work. "At ten I had my own landscaping company for Cudjoe residents happy to pay three bucks an hour to have their weeds pulled and lawns mowed," Ferris wrote for the Web site book-browse.com. "I had my first proper job at Godfather's Pizza in 1985, busing tables and washing dishes." By that time Ferris was already writing what he called "imitation Alfred Hitchcock stories." His mother, who tried in vain to get work in her field, social work, landed a job as a prison guard. After several years in the Florida Keys, Ferris returned to Illinois—to Downers Grove, a Chicago suburb—where he attended high school while living with his father, a financial adviser. After high school Ferris attended the University of Iowa, in Iowa City, where he studied English and philosophy.

In college Ferris continued to write stories, imitating the styles of such literary authors as Vladimir Nabokov and Donald Barthelme. He also wrote for the *Daily Iowan*, a student newspaper. One day, on assignment for the paper, Ferris interviewed David Foster Wallace, one of his literary idols. At the time Wallace, whose books include *Girl with Curious Hair* (1989) and *Infinite Jest* (1996), was 33 years old and Ferris 22. "The writers most frequently checklisted in association with Wallace's name—James Joyce, Thomas Pynchon, Don DeLillo—come now to a young writer's attention with a round thick penumbra of myth and aura, properly setting them apart not only from their contemporaries but from mere mortals as well," Ferris wrote for the London *Guardian* (September 21, 2008) two weeks after Wallace's suicide. "Their auras are never so imposing and impenetrable as when one is in college, and when one worships, with all one's wide-eyed heart and overeager soul, at the altar of the novel. When I was in college, I knew well enough that when DeLillo's new novel came out, he was not likely to have a conversation with a sometime-contributor to the *Daily Iowan*. Even less likely Pynchon. And Joyce was of course dead. In my affection and enthusiasm, I did not distinguish a difference between these three writers and Wallace, except to say that Wallace was about my age, wrote characters of about my age, and seemed to know more about My Age than his elder-statesmen counterparts. So I was shocked that he would be so accessible, and so game."

Ferris received a bachelor's degree from the University of Iowa in 1996. Two years later, after teaching English in Japan and working as a technical writer for Pennsylvania State University, he moved to Chicago, where he worked as a copywriter at the advertising firm Davis Harrison Dion and the direct-marketing firm Draft Worldwide. In interviews Ferris has said that he began writing *Then We Came to the End* around 1999, while he was still working in advertising and before Ricky Gervais's *The Office* premiered in England, in 2001. (The American version premiered in 2005.) "I was very impressed by the way [that show] handled what I had initially feared could be a terribly dry subject," Ferris said in an interview with Dave Weich for the Powell's Books Web site (February 22, 2007). "They brought such wonderful comedic moments, and also very touching moments, to that setting. My goal was a little more literary though. It was really to investigate the meaning of a collective voice, the meaning of a collective opinion, and the individual struggles particular characters have when confronted by that collective." Speaking to Terry Gross for the National Public Radio interview program *Fresh Air* (April 23, 2007), Ferris explained his motivation for writing a novel set in a big corporate office: "The real reason that I wanted to write it was because when I first walked into my first office as . . . a 24, 25-year-old guy, I was blown away by this behemoth structure. I mean, not just physically, the building itself, and all of the cubes and offices, but also psychologically, where you had . . . closed doors and protocols, secret protocols, conversations that you . . . were picking up bits and pieces of and . . . strange euphemisms. And it just seemed like it was very good material for a sustained literary effort." After three and a half years as a copywriter, Ferris left the world of advertising. He then enrolled in the M.F.A. program at the University of California at Irvine, where he continued to work on his novel. Ferris earned a master's degree in 2004 and finished the novel around the middle of 2005.

Then We Came to the End (2007) is set in 2000 and 2001 in a struggling Chicago advertising agency, which is peopled by paranoid, eccentric, critical, gossipy, and snarky employees who also, at times, display kindness, empathy, and generosity. As the economy collapses, the agency loses clients and projects, and people get laid off haphazardly. (Ferris completed the book before the start of the current worldwide recession.) To emphasize the collective nature of the work environment, Ferris wrote the novel in the first person plural—"we." The book begins with the words, "We were fractious and overpaid. Our mornings lacked promise. At least those of us who smoked had something to look forward to at ten-fifteen. Most of us liked most everyone, a few of us hated specific individuals, one or two people loved everyone and everything. Those who loved everyone were unanimously reviled. . . . Our benefits were astonishing in comprehensiveness and quality of care. Sometimes we questioned whether they were worth it. We thought moving to India might be better, or going back to nursing school. Doing something with the handicapped or working with our hands. No one ever acted on these impulses, despite their daily, sometimes hourly contractions. Instead we met in conference rooms to discuss the issues of the day."

Ferris told Weich, "It wasn't ever a question, what point of view the story had to be told in. I knew it had to be in the *we*." That certainty came partly from his memories of hearing his father's message on the answering machine in a business he had just started, in which his father was initially the sole employee: "We're not here right now, but leave us a message and we'll call you back." Ferris told Weich, "I would think, *Who the hell is this* we? *It's just you.* But I realized of course that he couldn't say that. He needed to establish the necessary corporate veneer of being a group. From the very beginning, as a young kid, I thought this was interesting, how we use this—as I'm using it right now—use this pronoun to either project a sense of power and unity or use it to subtly manipulate opinion. It's used in advertis[ing] pervasively. There's always an implied *we* somewhere in the message. *We will give you something better. You can be part of this wonderful group that we've created.*" He also recalled to Weich that he "spent a long time trying to figure out how to work the first person plural—and screwing up repeatedly. I spent probably two years in a state of constant anxiety about it. I set it aside and sort of thought, *This is the book I tried to cut my teeth on. It'll never see the light of day.* Then about a year and a half later I got the voice. I got the first two or three sentences in my head, and I just knew that I could write it. I knew how to balance the *we* so it wasn't always just griping about work; it was balanced with what is enjoyable and meaningful about work."

The novel's many, disparate characters include Karen Woo, the smart, gossipy art director; Chris Yop, the copywriter who comes to work even after being fired; Tom Mota, the cynical divorcé with a passion for guns, Ralph Waldo Emerson, and practical jokes; and Lynn Mason, the hardworking, intimidating boss who may or may not have breast cancer. (For most of the novel, the rumor is unconfirmed.) Ferris used the more traditional third-person-singular "she" in a chapter about Mason. "What began as a workplace farce starts transforming the cumulative pathos of everyday tics into something more meaningful," James P. Othmer wrote for the *Washington Post* (March 28, 2007). "With the layoffs and the threat of more to come, we are suddenly walking the halls of an office consumed by fear, insecurity and a compulsive fixation on the quotidian extracurricular details of its co-workers."

The reviews for *Then We Came to the End* were mostly positive. "At times," Othmer observed, "the characters suffer from an excess of eccentricities and tragedies large and small. But Ferris skillfully balances the comic with the authentic, the insightful with the absurd, and we can't help but be transfixed by their stories." Writing for the *New York Times* (March 18, 2007), James Poniewozik described the novel as "expansive, great-hearted and acidly funny." Poniewozik also praised the subtlety with which Ferris constructed his satire: while showing the "soul-killing and pernicious" elements of white-collar work, Ferris acknowledged that such work can also give people "purpose and meaning." Writing for *Slate* (March 8, 2007), Meghan O'Rourke found that although the novel has flaws—in her view, it is too long—Ferris should be commended for taking on the topic of the American workplace: "What is most striking about Ferris' take is that, for all the hype we've heard about how dramatically the workplace has changed in our contemporary era of greater labor mobility (one that has also seen the influx of women and the advent of the computer), not all that much seems different in the industry Ferris depicts. Indeed, stripped of references to the Internet, *Then We Came to the End* could almost be set in the 1950s of [Richard Yates's] *Revolutionary Road* or the 1960s of [Don DeLillo's] *Americana*, driving home that in many industries, the continuities are far more striking than the differences. Perhaps in the era of the professionalization of writing itself, many novelists have avoided chronicling the subtleties of office life because it's not perceived as 'literary' or because they have no experience of it. But as *Then We Came to the End* begins to suggest, it is one of the richest settings of our time."

Ferris's second novel, *The Unnamed* (2010), is about a handsome, wealthy man named Tim Farnsworth. Although Tim has every reason to be happy—he has a prestigious position at a Manhattan law firm, a wife and daughter who love him, and a large house in an upscale suburb—there is something undeniably wrong. Suddenly he develops a condition—which has no name, hence the title of the book—whose primary symptom is the compulsion to drop whatever he is doing and start walking. He wanders on streets and highways and through parks and even forests until he collapses from exhaustion and loses consciousness. Sometimes he walks for months at a stretch. Doctors and therapists cannot determine the cause of his compulsion, which is leading to psychosis. For six months of the three years Ferris devoted to writing *The Unnamed*, he concentrated on "working out how to make the disintegration into madness feel real," he told Eric Konigsberg for *New York* (February 1, 2010). He also said, "I don't think the first [novel] taught me anything about how to write the second—I used tools from two different belts. . . . I had to use everything in my power to make [*The Unnamed*] feel real." Some reviewers praised the first third or first half of the book, whereas others found fault with those parts but lauded what followed. A reviewer for the *New Yorker* (January 18, 2010), for example, criticized the first half as being unfocused but declared the second half to be "a stunner, an unnerving portrait of a man stripped of civilization's defenses. Ferris's prose is brash, extravagant, and, near the end, chillingly beautiful."

Ferris's fiction has appeared in the *New Yorker*, *Granta*, the *Iowa Review*, *Tin House*, and other publications. He has also contributed nonfiction to publications including *New York*, *GQ*, and the *New York Times*. He is currently working on a third novel.

Ferris lives with his wife and their young son in the New York City borough of Brooklyn; the couple also have a home in Hudson, New York, about 100 miles north of the city.

—D.K.

Suggested Reading: *Economist* (on-line) Jan. 30, 2010; joshuaferris.com; *New York* p16 Feb. 1, 2010; *New York Times* VII p1 Mar. 18, 2007; Powells.com Feb. 22, 2007; *Slate.com* Mar. 8, 2007, Jan. 11, 2010; *Washington Post* C p5 Mar. 28, 2007

Selected Novels: *Then We Came to the End*, 2007; *The Unnamed*, 2010

Field, Patricia

Dec. 12, 1942– Costume and apparel designer; stylist; entrepreneur

Address: Patricia Field, 302 Bowery, New York, NY 10012

The stylist, apparel designer, and costume designer Patricia Field has always believed that buying clothes "should be fun, not painful, and you don't wanna have to take a mortgage out on a fabulous dress," as she told Nicola Jeal for the London *Observer* (April 21, 1991). "That doesn't mean you wear it and then trash it. But it has to have energy, at a good price." Field is best known as the costume

Getty Images Entertainment

Patricia Field

designer for the TV series *Sex and the City*, which ran on the HBO cable network for six seasons (1998–2004) and won millions of devoted fans as well as critical plaudits. She became famous for the eclectic ensembles in which she dressed the actresses Sarah Jessica Parker, Kim Cattrall, Cynthia Nixon, and Kristin Davis, who played the main characters on that show. Her imaginative mixtures of vintage, couture, casual, chic, ethnic, and highly unconventional styles attracted an enormous amount of attention (and an Emmy Award for Field); indeed, according to Candace Wedlan, writing for the *Los Angeles Times* (June 30, 2000), the costumes were "practically a fifth character." Field's unusual ideas about fashion reached many more millions with the release of the movie *Sex and the City*, in 2008 (which earned Field an Oscar nomination), and its sequel, in 2010; others have seen Field's work through the syndication of the TV series, which has aired in Australia, England, the Czech Republic, Russia, Saudi Arabia, South Korea, Argentina, and more than two dozen other nations on every continent. Among other honors and awards, in 2006 Field earned an Emmy nomination for the costumes for the sitcom *Ugly Betty*. She has also won five Costume Designers Guild Awards, for her work on *Sex and the City* (on TV) in 2000, 2001, 2004, and 2005 and for *Ugly Betty* in 2009. In addition, she served as the costume designer during the six-year run of the series *Spin City* (1996–2002) and the three-year run of the sitcom *Hope & Faith* (2003–06). Field, according to Adrineh Gregorian, writing for the *Armenian Reporter* (May 31, 2008), "has helped define the fashion landscape of our time. Her story is not just about a person who turned a talent into a ca-

reer. . . . It's about a person whose simple act of living life on her own terms has inspired others to do the same."

Field, who has had a keen interest in clothing from as far back as she can remember, has no formal training in design or styling. "I'm not thinking about fashion when I'm doing it . . . ," she told Gregorian. "Fashion is not my thing. My thing is making things pretty and beautiful and happy. I want everything to be as nice as it can be. That's all I know." Of course, "pretty," "beautiful," and "nice" are subjective terms; according to Nicola Jeal, the merchandise in Field's boutique is "all about dressing up in the best possible bad taste." Field opened her first retail outlet in 1966, when she was 23, in the Greenwich Village district of Manhattan, near New York University, her alma mater. Stocked with sequined miniskirts, hardware-studded vinyl catsuits, and other far-from-the-mainstream apparel and accessories, Patricia Field, as the shop was called, epitomized countercultural sensibilities and New York City as a "fast, zany, multiracial society," in Jeal's words. Still a thriving business, though in a different location, the boutique became "an institution for New York artists, trendsetters, and fashionistas," Gregorian wrote. Since the late 1970s it has sold House of Field apparel and accessories in addition to products bearing other labels. Clothing, shoes, jewelry, and other items are also for sale via the Patricia Field Web site. "The right way to wear my clothes is from an individual point of view using your own creativity," Field told Sylvia Capelaci for the *Toronto (Canada) Sun* (August 23, 1994). "The way not to wear them is in a clone-like fashion. It's the art of dressing as opposed to just putting clothes on."

One of the two daughters of an Armenian father and a Greek mother, Patricia Field was born on December 12, 1942 in New York City and raised in the Astoria section of Queens, a city borough. Field's parents owned several dry-cleaning stores in the borough of Manhattan, and from their example Field grew up with a respect for entrepreneurship and a strong work ethic. After her father died, when she was seven, her mother and her many maternal relatives kept his memory very much alive, often speaking highly of him (as they did of Greek family members). "I was brought up with this pride of being Greek and being Armenian," Field recalled to Adrineh Gregorian. She also told Gregorian that because her parents (and later her widowed mother) were so busy managing their stores, she "didn't have too much parental authority" and "learned to be independent from a very young age. With that independence," she continued, "I established my own style very young. I had my own mind. I wanted to dress this way because I was allowed to." Starting at 13 she worked during summers in one or another of her mother's stores as a replacement for vacationing employees—experience that stood her in good stead when she went into business for herself. Since girlhood she has admired Cleopatra, the alluring, clever, ambitious ruler of Egypt from 69 to 30 B.C., and still regards that queen as her hero, she told Brooke Kosofsky Glassberg for *O Magazine* (June 2010).

In 1959 Field entered New York University (NYU), in Manhattan, where she took liberal-arts courses because, she told Gregorian, she "loved studying"; "I never coupled what I was learning with what I might want to do with my career," she said. She earned a B.A. degree, with a concentration in government, in 1963. Her participation in an executive-training program led to a position as a junior executive at the Bronx branch of Alexander's department stores and then with Petrie Stores, a women's-apparel retail chain. In 1966, with a small trust fund that her father had set up for her—its value had grown to $4,000 by then—Field opened her first boutique, in Greenwich Village, near NYU. "It wasn't 'fashion,' it was . . . 'What could I do now?'" she recalled to Gregorian. She told Brooke Kosofsky Glassberg, "For me, fashion is easy and pleasant, but it was also a means to an end—the bigger goal was always to have an independent career." With such items as polyvinyl-chloride apparel, campy costumes, neon Lycra pants, avant-garde artwear (such as the graffiti artist Jean-Michel Basquiat's painted sweatshirts), fishnet tights, garish wigs, ostentatiously false eyelashes, and sequined cigarette holders, her boutique drew not only NYU students but drag queens, club patrons, and others in the downtown Manhattan set. In 1971 Field moved to a new location two blocks away, in the SoHo district, where the shop remained for the next three decades. Writing for the *New York Times* (March 6, 1986), Michael Gross characterized the boutique as "a mecca for downtown fashion" whose merchandise served as "costumes" for a "theater of life as art." In time it became a popular stopping point even for American tourists. "They come here and they're wide-eyed. It means, they've been entertained, and that's where we're at," Field told Jeal. In 2006 she moved her boutique to a "gritty lower Manhattan area of industrial warehouses" on the Bowery, Suzy Menkes wrote for the *New York Times* (June 5, 2006, on-line). "My real creative outlet is my shop," Field told Gregorian. "I can walk into my place and feel these are my people, these are my kids, they are my philosophy. . . . I have a great store. It's so wonderful really. I love it."

In the late 1970s, frustrated that wholesalers could not supply the variety of funky clothing and accessories she wanted, Field launched her own label, House of Field, serving briefly as its designer. Since then she has relied on a revolving group of aspiring young designers; currently, David Dalrymple is most prominent. Products from her line are carried by other retailers as well and are available through Field's Web site. In September 2010 House of Field apparel and accessories included front-zippered shorts with metal studs ($120), a T-shirt ($38) and a "shredded" tank top ($86) with a huge splotch of black surrounding the words "Fear of Nothing," a sequined fanny pack ($26), and a baseball-style hat with Field's signature embroidered on the front and the words "I'll kick your ass" on one side ($36). Other products with Field's signature prominently displayed (sometimes along with what looks like a stylized portrait of her atop a sketchy Greek column) include hoodies, clutches, and tote bags. In 2007, in an arrangement with the toy manufacturer Mattel, Field added Barbie-themed items, such as a necklace with a Barbie silhouette; in 2009 she introduced apparel inspired by the work of the designer Stephen Sprouse (1953–2004). The most recent additions to her line are decorated with illustrations by the artist Keith Haring (1958–90). What she dubbed the Keith Haring by the House of Field Paradise Garage Collection debuted in early 2010 in a Manhattan hotel, at a huge party attended by an "over-the-top crowd (think exposed breasts, Darth Vader masks, and pancake makeup)," Kristian Laliberte wrote for *Refinery29.com* (February 15, 2010). Field has never offered seasonal collections, because she believes her styles are suitable all year round. Her merchandise comes in bright colors, black, or white—"nothing in between," she told David Graham for the *Toronto Star* (August 18, 1994). "We don't talk beige or gray or camel."

Field's career in television began in 1986, when she designed costumes for the TV series *Crime Story*. Her next job for TV came with *L.A. Takedown*, in 1989. She won an Emmy Award for her costumes for the many actors and singers—among them Jean Stapleton, Shelley Duvall, Bobby Brown, Deborah Harry, Little Richard, Art Garfunkel, and Cyndi Lauper—cast in the made-for-TV musical *Mother Goose Rock 'n' Rhyme*, which aired on the Disney Channel in 1990. Field returned to Hollywood in 1994 to design costumes for *Miami Rhapsody* (1995), starring Sarah Jessica Parker. Field and Parker became close friends, and at Parker's suggestion, Field was hired to dress the actors and actresses cast in the HBO series *Sex and the City*, created by Darren Star. Inspired by the same-titled collection of essays (1997), which Candace Bushnell originally wrote for the *New York Observer*, *Sex and the City* follows four single New York City professional women, with heavy emphasis on their love lives. Field has said that Sarah Jessica Parker's style sense and ways of moving and walking (Parker studied ballet during her childhood), as well as Field and Parker's creative bond, were essential to her success as a designer for the show. Field told the *Miami Herald*'s Lydia Martin, as carried by the *Pittsburgh Post-Gazette* (July 23, 2000), "I use a formula when I do costumes. I see it as a triangle. At one point, there is the actress. At the other is the character. The third is the clothing. You have to combine all three. In order for the actress to represent the character well, she has to feel comfortable with the way she is presented. My job is to help create that character within the actress." Field was assisted by the designer Rebecca Weinberg, her companion, who, during the course of the series, identified herself as Rebecca Field.

By the show's second season, the importance of clothes to the series had become apparent. "One of the major pleasures of watching . . . is to see what the women will be wearing from week to week," Cynthia Robins wrote for the *Chicago Sun-Times* (September 12, 1999). "And their 'looks' are no accident—they're very carefully put together by a pair of women named Field." Fashion became so central to *Sex and the City* that clothes sometimes drove the plotlines. For example, in one episode Charlotte (Kristin Davis) allows a salesman with a foot fetish to touch her feet in exchange for a pair of shoes; in another, Carrie (Sarah Jessica Parker) fights with her boyfriend over space in their closet for a vintage Versace outfit. In a third, Samantha (Kim Cattrall), a publicist whose clients include the actress Lucy Liu, covets a Hermès Birkin bag; to bypass the long waiting list of would-be buyers, she pretends to be purchasing one for Liu.

The Birkin bag was among a bevy of garments and accessories that became widely known thanks to their appearances on *Sex and the City*. Those items included gold personalized necklaces, large flower brooches, a horseshoe charm necklace, the newsboy cap, and short shorts. "Everything that Field selects for Carrie to wear is an instant hit—no matter how eclectic, which is the essential ingredient of the character's style," Melissa Whitworth wrote for the London *Telegraph* (April 9, 2008, online). "No sooner was Carrie spotted carrying a bag in the shape of a horse's head in one episode . . . than thousands of orders from across the world flooded in" to the Beverly Hills office of its designer, Timmy Woods. Field also introduced *Sex and the City* viewers to Fendi handbags, Vivienne Westwood suits, and Jimmy Choo and Manolo Blahnik shoes. Clo Jacobs, a Jimmy Choo spokeswoman, told Madeleine Marr for the *Houston Chronicle* (February 20, 2004), "*Sex and the City* . . . not only gave a platform to so many new designers, but it allowed women all over the world to take chances they might not ordinarily have." When an interviewer for *Allure* (April 30, 2010) asked Field how she avoided selecting styles for *Sex and the City* and *Sex and the City 2* that might seem "too costumey," the designer responded, "I think of it like walking up the very edge of the cliff but not taking that last step. I like to take it to the edge because that's when it becomes exciting. But I don't want to make it look silly." Field's work for *Sex and the City* earned her nominations for Costume Designers Guild and Satellite Awards in 2009.

Earlier, Field had served as costume designer for the *The Devil Wears Prada* (2006). That film was adapted from the same-titled novel by Lauren Weisberger, which she based on her experiences as an assistant to Anna Wintour, the famously demanding and influential editor of *Vogue*. Field did not base the wardrobe of Meryl Streep, who starred as the editor of the fictional magazine *Runway*, on that of Wintour. "What I wanted to do was to create a character who was the biggest editor-in-chief of a fashion magazine," she told Serena French for the *New York Post* (June 21, 2006). "And the only rule I imposed upon myself other than making Meryl look as good as I know how, was that in her position she would wear expensive clothing because she has access to everything." The clothing budget for *The Devil Wears Prada* was not nearly enough to cover the cost of the couture outfits Field wanted Streep to wear, so she turned to some of her many acquaintances in the fashion world for help. Some designers lent outfits for use in the film; others, fearful of Wintour's wrath, declined to do so. Fashion journalists differed in their reactions to Field's wardrobe choices. Anne Slowey, *Elle*'s fashion-news editor, told Ruth La Ferla for the *New York Times* (June 29, 2006) that the costumes were "a caricature of what people who don't work in fashion think fashion people look like." Field rejected such complaints, telling La Ferla, "My job is to present an entertainment, a world people can visit and take a little trip. If they want a documentary, they can watch the History Channel."

Among other projects she has undertaken as a freelancer, Field has designed wearables for Candie's shoes, Payless Shoes, Rocawear, ProKeds, and the Japanese firms Crystal Ball and Ash & Diamonds. For the Home Shopping Network in the U.S., Marks & Spencer in Europe, and the Myer Department Store in Australia, she created a line called Destination Style. For Coca-Cola she has designed bottles and a tote bag made entirely from recycled plastic bottles. She has also provided costumes for the Greek Music Awards ceremony, in Greece, and a fashion and music event organized by American Express Japan.

Field has never married and has no children. (Penelope Green's reference to a son named Steven Field in the August 26, 1990 edition of the *New York Times* was erroneous.) An acknowledged lesbian, she ended her intimate relationship with Rebecca Weinberg in the early 2000s. Said to be unusually approachable, sociable, cheerful, and without airs, she has colored her long hair an unnatural shade of dark, reddish magenta for many years. Field lives in Manhattan with her two poodles.

—T.O.

Suggested Reading: *Armenian Reporter* C p6+ May 31, 2008; (London) *Guardian* (on-line) Oct. 4, 2008; (London) *Observer* p52 Apr. 21, 1991; (London) *Telegraph* (on-line) Apr. 9, 2008; (New York) *Daily News* p49 Sep. 6, 2001; *New York Times* (on-line) June 5, 2006; Patricia Field Web site

Courtesy of Helen Fisher

Fisher, Helen

May 31, 1945– Anthropologist

Address: Apt. 5C, 4 E. 70th St., New York, NY 10021

"Spending 30 years studying why we love hasn't changed my feelings about love at all," the anthropologist Helen Fisher told Jenny Colgan for the London *Independent on Sunday* (July 18, 2004). "In fact, knowing how it works expands my wonder in it—to know how people, and animals, feel all over the world and what's in store for every person in the world, today, tomorrow, a million years ago. It's a basic brain-system response, equally valid at six or sixty. You can know every ingredient of chocolate cake and it can still bring you enormous pleasure. You can know every note of a Beethoven symphony, and it still never takes away from the passion and the fascination. In fact, if anything, this understanding just gives me even more respect for the evolutionary process." Fisher is the author of five books that examine different aspects of the evolution and biology of love, family, and human sexuality. In her 2004 book, *Why We Love: The Nature and Chemistry of Romantic Love*, Fisher presented brain-mapping research to show that love affects the brain along three distinct chemical circuits that can produce feelings of lust, attraction, and attachment. After the publication of that book, Fisher was hired as the chief scientific adviser for the new dating Web site Chemistry.com, which matches people based on the compatibility of their personality types and brain chemistries. In her most recent book, *Why Him? Why Her?: Finding Real Love by Understanding Your Personality*

Type (2009), Fisher explained how people can use biological information to find and maintain romantic love. Asked by Robert Strauss for the *New York Times* (April 9, 2006) whether she considered online dating unnatural, she replied, "Who says going to a bar is natural? Way back to the grasslands of Africa for millions of years, long before you met somebody, you knew their parents, their background, you certainly knew what a lot of people thought of them. Matchmakers are thousands of years old. Meeting through agents of one variety of another is millions of years old. Walking into a bar, where you know nobody, don't know these people's intentions, don't know whether they are married or single, don't know whether they will court you tonight and leave town tomorrow, that is what is odd, strange, unnatural. In many ways this [online dating] is a more natural system."

Fisher has worked as a research associate in the Department of Anthropology at the New School for Social Research (1981–84) and at the American Museum of Natural History (1984–94), both in New York City. She became a research associate in the Department of Anthropology at Rutgers University, in New Brunswick, New Jersey, in 1994, and in 2000 she became a research professor there. Since 1983 she has served as an anthropological commentator and consultant for business and media as well as a national lecturer.

Helen Fisher was born on May 31, 1945 in the New York City borough of Manhattan to Helen Greef Fisher, a poet, sculptor, and flower arranger, and Roswell E. Fisher, an executive at *Time* magazine. She was raised in New Canaan, Connecticut, with her identical twin sister, Lorna, and two other stepsiblings. Fisher recalled to Strauss that as a child, she was naturally drawn to anthropological study. "I grew up in a glass house, a modern house, but it was all glass, and my neighbors had a glass house," she told Strauss. "I used to sit in the woods and watch my neighbors eat dinner. I was always interested in watching people. Since I am also an identical twin, ever since my small childhood, people have been asking us how we were alike. Long before I knew there was a nature-nurture argument, I was observing how much of my nature was biological. It just came naturally to me. I was always interested in why we were all alike, stemming from that childhood." Fisher majored in anthropology and psychology at New York University and received a B.A. degree in 1968. She then attended graduate school at the University of Colorado, in Boulder, where she received her master's degree in physical anthropology, cultural anthropology, linguistics, and archaeology in 1972, and her doctoral degree in physical anthropology in 1975. Her dissertation focused on the evolution of human sexuality and the origin of the nuclear family.

Fisher used the subject of her dissertation as the basis for her first book, *The Sex Contract: The Evolution of Human Behavior* (1982), in which she argued that the institution of family evolved from the utilitarian needs of our simian ancestors some

10 million years ago. At that time, according to Fisher, with the advent of upright walking and the shifting of pelvic positions in females, premature birth became more prevalent. The complications that resulted from premature births necessitated more attentive care giving, leading to a decrease in the time available to females to scavenge for food. Female simians began to secure food and protection from males in exchange for copulation. As a result women bore more children and required the participation of males in their upbringing. Thus the formation of families, according to Fisher, was eminently practical. "If a woman was carrying the equivalent of a 9-kg bowling ball in one arm and a pile of sticks in the other, it was ecologically critical to pair up with a mate to rear the young," Fisher explained, as quoted by Steve Thompson for the Singapore *Straits Times* (February 15, 1993). In his review for the Toronto, Canada, *Globe and Mail* (March 4, 1982), William French noted that Fisher's book was "a feminist revisionist view of evolution. Fisher is subtle about it, but she leaves no doubt that the male role in evolution has been exaggerated. . . . Primitive society was a matriarchy and, if Fisher's theory is correct, pre-historic females cleverly manipulated the males into helping with responsibility for the young. Our evolutionary heritage is that women have a stronger sex drive than men and experience more intense pleasure from its gratification. The women have been very patient, all these eons, in tolerating bragging males who think just the opposite." *The Sex Contract* became a Book-of-the-Month-Club selection and was published in seven languages in addition to English.

In 1992 Fisher published *The Anatomy of Love: The Natural History of Monogamy, Adultery, and Divorce.* (The book appeared in another edition two years later, under the title *The Anatomy of Love: The Natural History of Monogamy, Adultery, and Why We Stray.*) In that book Fisher presented studies of divorce in 62 societies and adultery in 42 societies, as well as research about monogamy and desertion among humans' ancestors and other animals. In her research Fisher discovered what she termed a "four-year itch," a tendency among couples to separate or to stray after approximately four years together. That length of time corresponded with the period that prehistoric simian couples tended to stay together following their child's birth—after which the child was old enough to be cared for by others in the simian social network. The pair would then often separate; the male would seek a younger female with fresher eggs, and the female would seek a male with greater resources. Fisher found a similar pattern in the pairing behavior of many animals and human tribes. "Four years is the usual period between successive births among continually breast-feeding Australian Aborigines and the Gainj of New Guinea," Fisher wrote in her book, as excerpted in an article in the Brisbane, Australia, *Courier-Mail* (August 13, 1993). "Infants also generally are weaned

around the fourth year among the Yanomamo of Amazonia, the Netsilik Eskimos, the Lepcha of Sikkim, and the Dani of New Guinea." Dubbing the frequency of infidelity after four years "a trial of nature over culture," Fisher wrote, as quoted by Janice Turner in the *Toronto Star* (November 26, 1992), "Like the stereotypic flirt, the smile, the brain physiology for infatuation, and our drive to bond with a single mate, philandering seems to be part of our ancient reproductive game."

Fisher's theories sparked strong responses from readers and reviewers. Some saw them as undermining moral responsibility and the institution of marriage. Fisher explained to Turner, "I'm not a moralist. I'm trying to add to people's understanding of who they are. There are some people who have horrible marriages and they probably should break up. There are other people who should work harder at their marriages. But I'm not in the business of telling people what to do with their lives. I'm trying to give them a different perspective." In a review for the London *Guardian* (March 6, 1993), Suzanne Moore dismissed Fisher's theories in *The Anatomy of Love* on the grounds that they oversimplified the evolutionary link between the behavior of our human ancestors and other prehistoric species and that of present-day humans. Moore wrote, "While Fisher accepts that culture sculpts diversity from common human genetic material, her real interest lies in the biological bases of our behavior. Yet this emphasis on unchanging biology, and the similarity of our mating rituals with those of other animals, ignores precisely what separates us from other animals. We have languages, and with languages come immortality, through intergenerational knowledge, abstract symbolic thought, not to mention morality. This is why I am not that much reassured by the cases of adultery she finds amongst baboons and Swedish blackbirds. An instinctual basis for adultery may be just what you have been looking for, but surely it means something different for us than for a redwinged blackbird?" The book was published in 18 languages other than English and was selected as a Notable Book by the *New York Times Book Review* in both 1992 and 1994.

In her next book, *The First Sex: The Natural Talents of Women and How They Are Changing the World* (1999), Fisher examined the natural brain differences between men and women and the effects of those differences on the changing role of women in the 21st century. Fisher argued that women, "because of their unique brain structure and skills developed as gatherers and nurturers, are on the verge of an equality and power they have not enjoyed since humans settled in farming communities nearly 15,000 years ago and women lost considerable status," Peggy O'Crowley wrote for the Newark, New Jersey, *Star-Ledger* (June 27, 1999). Fisher told O'Crowley, "We are really moving out of position as the second sex, and beginning to predominate in not all, but in some of the important parts of the economy that are going to have a profound impact." She continued, "We're moving into a communications age, which is going to be very good for women, because women are so good with words. We're moving into an information economy, and a knowledge economy and a service economy. Those are all going to use women's skills." She explained to John Tierney for the *New York Times* (May 10, 1999, on-line) that the independence of women in today's society is actually a return to an ancient tradition in which women spent the day working outside the home, roaming the savannas to gather food. "The divorce rate is high in Manhattan for the same reason it was high among hunter-gatherers," Fisher told Tierney. "When you have women with careers outside the home who can support themselves and aren't tied to the land, they don't have to remain the subordinate partner in a bad marriage. They can look for a better marriage that's a partnership of equals." Fisher predicted that, although there would likely be a greater number of female CEOs in the near future, women were unlikely to hold those positions in the same numbers as men anytime soon, because women are less likely than men to make major sacrifices in other areas of their lives, such as family and friendships, in order to get those jobs.

The First Sex was selected as a Notable Book by the *New York Times Book Review*. Assessments of the book were mixed. Tierney applauded her work, noting, "Dr. Fisher has gathered so much outside evidence, from the medication techniques of female chimpanzees to the brain structures of male executives, that it's easy to believe her, especially since her observations come without a predictable political agenda." In contrast, Jim Holt, another reviewer for the *New York Times* (July 11, 1999, online), noted that the book "must be read with great caution. The quality of Fisher's evidence is uneven, to say the least; it ranges from scientific studies to quotations from spokeswomen for professional organizations to articles in New York tabloids. A more serious flaw crops up in Fisher's logic. She freely puts her own speculative interpretations on new scientific findings, lets those interpretations harden into seemingly well-established facts, and proceeds to explain these facts by making up a suitable evolutionary story."

Meanwhile, in 1996, Fisher had conducted a study to determine which regions of the brain were associated with feelings of love. Using magnetic resonance imaging (MRI), Fisher observed the brain activity of 17 student volunteers at the State University of New York (SUNY) at Stony Brook who claimed to have recently fallen in love. When the participants were shown images of their loved ones, compared with when they looked at pictures of acquaintances, Fisher observed significantly higher levels of activity in the ventral tegmental area (VTA) of their brains, where the neurotransmitter dopamine is produced, and in the caudate nucleus, a C-shaped region in the brain's center, where dopamine receptor sites are located. The claudate nucleus is also associated with arousal,

pleasure, and motivation to acquire rewards. Dopamine, a chemical tied to feelings of euphoria, addiction, and some psychiatric disorders, has also been linked with heightened attention and short-term memory, sleeplessness, hyperactivity, and goal-oriented behavior. According to Fisher the link between love and dopamine activity can explain the irrational behavior of people who are experiencing romantic love—which Fisher has argued is a much more powerful force than the human sex drive. Fisher said, as quoted on her Web site, "After all, if you casually ask someone to go to bed with you and they refuse, you don't slip into a depression, or commit suicide or homicide; but around the world people suffer terribly from rejection in love." Fisher published her findings from that and numerous other studies in her book *Why We Love: The Nature and Chemistry of Romantic Love* (2004), in which she examined love from biological, chemical, evolutionary, and behavioral standpoints. One of her findings was that intense romantic love, or attraction, is one of three stages of love that affect different chemical circuits in the brain. The first stage, lust, activates the sex hormones estrogen and testosterone; attraction activates dopamine; and attachment, the third stage, is associated with oxytocin in women or vasopressin in men, both of which produce a sense of calm and security. In her review for the *New York Times* (March 7, 2004), Liesl Schillinger called *Why We Love* Fisher's "most controversial book." She noted, "If, as Fisher states, 90 percent of prairie voles stick with one mate for life because they're good dopamine producers and have a sprig of DNA that enhances loyalty, and if norepinephrine automatically floods the brain of a ewe who's on the prowl every time she sees a slide of a ram's face, and those same chemicals burble through the human brain in love, will people one day be able to modify and medicate passions we once regarded as ungovernable? Will not only lust but love be buttressed, cured or even created with a prescription?"

In December 2004 Fisher was recruited to become the chief scientific adviser for Chemistry.com, a new Web site that was being developed by the Internet dating company Match.com. "Before I decided to work with [Chemistry.com], I took all the questionnaires given on the other major [dating] sites," Fisher explained on Chemistry.com. "They all seem to match largely by similarity of background, interests, values, and goals. Chemistry.com does, too, of course, as these are important elements to a good relationship. But matching by similarity is only half the story. Chemistry.com's hypothesis is that you need chemistry as well as compatibility for a successful relationship." Based on copious amounts of research on genetics, neurotransmitters, hormones, and personality types, Fisher created a questionnaire that measured basic aspects of brain and body chemistry that are related to temperament and personality. Users of the site receive a profile based on the answers to those questions that quantifies the test-taker's relationship to four personality types—dubbed "Explorers," "Builders," "Negotiators," and "Directors"—each of which is associated with a particular brain chemical. "Explorers have an excess of dopamine, which makes them curious, energetic, creative and optimistic," Robert Strauss wrote. "Those with more serotonin [Fisher] calls Builders, and they are calm, conscientious, dutiful and loyal. She calls people with high levels of estrogen Negotiators because they are sympathetic, intuitive, imaginative and have good people skills. Those with high testosterone levels, the Directors, are assertive, direct, ambitious and decisive." Fisher explained on Chemistry.com that we are "unconsciously attracted to those who complement ourselves biologically." As of August 2010 Chemistry.com had a total of four million participating singles. Fisher discussed the relationships among personality types, brain chemicals, and love in her book *Why Him? Why Her?: Finding Real Love by Understanding Your Personality Type*, published in January 2009. (A second edition was published a year later, under the title *Why Him? Why Her?: How to Find and Keep Lasting Love*.)

Based on her findings linking dopamine with romantic love, Fisher has speculated that the use of prescription antidepressants that increase serotonin levels in the brain may make it difficult to fall in love. "Serotonin enhancers also suppress the dopamine system in the brain," Fisher wrote in her blog, The Nature of Love (March 28, 2007). "And dopamine circuits become super active when you feel intense romantic love. So, connecting the dots, I hypothesize that when you take these drugs, you can jeopardize your ability to fall in love and/or stay in love." Fisher has stated, however, that she does not dispute the benefit of antidepressants for those with chronic, severe depression. "I'm concerned about well-adjusted men and women who go through a crisis and start taking antidepressants," she told Susan Brink for the *Los Angeles Times* (July 30, 2007). "They continue taking them, not realizing they may be suppressing these other systems."

Fisher delivers lectures all over the world on human sexuality, romantic love, marriage and divorce, gender differences, and other related topics. She is a regular commentator on NBC's *Today* show and many other programs and serves as a consultant for such companies as the Canadian Broadcasting Corp., Reader's Digest, Procter and Gamble, National Starch and Chemical Co., and Leo Burnett. In 1995 Fisher hosted the four-part TV series *Anatomy of Love* for TBS, and in 2004 she was the host of the four-part radio series *What Is Love?* for the BBC World Service. In 1985 Fisher received the Distinguished Service Award from the American Anthropological Association for disseminating anthropological ideas to a broad public audience through books, radio, and television.

Fisher lives on the Upper East Side of Manhattan. She was married once, in her early 20s, but divorced after one year. In an interview with *Current*

Biography on February 28, 2008, Fisher said: "The next man that I fall in love with, I will marry—if he wants to marry me. I am finally ready to wed."

—T.O.

Suggested Reading: (Brisbane, Australia) *Courier-Mail* p13 Aug. 13, 1993; (London) *Guardian* Features p29 Mar. 6, 2003; (New York) *Daily News* p2 Feb. 9, 2005; *New York Times* (on-line) Apr. 9, 2006, May 10, 1999, July 11, 1999; (Newark, New Jersey) *Star-Ledger* Accent p1 June 27, 1999; (Toronto, Canada) *Globe and Mail* (on-line) Mar. 4, 1982; *Toronto Star* Life p1 Nov. 26, 1992; *Washington Post* Z p10 Jan. 20, 1998

Selected Books: *The Sex Contract: The Evolution of Human Behavior*, 1982; *The Anatomy of Love: The Natural History of Monogamy, Adultery, and Divorce*, 1992; *The First Sex: The Natural Talents of Women and How They Are Changing the World*, 1999; *Why We Love: The Nature and Chemistry of Romantic Love*, 2004; *Why Him? Why Her?: Finding Real Love by Understanding Your Personality Type*, 2009

Fleming, Maureen

1955(?)– Dancer; choreographer; educator

Address: 6 E. Second St., New York, NY 10003

"If people watch my work as they watch their dreams, rather than trying to think about what things mean too much, the power of what I'm trying to communicate will come through," the dancer and choreographer Maureen Fleming told Frank Green for the *Cleveland (Ohio) Free Times* (September 1998). Fleming has traced her passion for dance to the day when, as a two-year-old, she suffered damage to her spine in a car accident—an event she knew nothing about until well into adulthood. "I think that experience planted a seed in my body," she told Eri Misaki for the *Arts Cure* (Spring 2005, on-line). She said to Catherine Foster for the *Boston Globe* (February 24, 2002) that as a child, "I would twist and move my body in a way that released any kind of pain." What she has called her "need" for movement, which helps to mute her ever-present, low-level pain, fuels her art, which stems from her rigorous training in classical dance, beginning when she was seven, and her intensive study of butoh, a minimalist style of dance that originated in Japan after World War II. "Watching Maureen Fleming dance is like stepping into a sculptor's mind and seeing clay curve and transform into unexpected shapes and images," Shannon Brady Marin wrote for *Dance Magazine* (November 2007). An on-line blurb announcing an upcoming performance of Fleming's in 2009 at the Cleveland Museum of Art offered a similar analo-

Maureen Fleming

gy: "Fleming invents exquisite movement poetry, sculpting her body into nearly unbelievable, shatteringly beautiful shapes. She pushes the boundaries of the body's expressive potential and challenges the definition of what is physically possible. Part dance, part dream, part sculpture, Fleming explores our never-ending search for what is universal about the journey of the soul." "Maureen Fleming conveys more meaning in one evening than most choreographers put across in an entire career . . . ," Theodore Bale wrote for the *Boston Herald* (November 3, 2007, on-line). "One might think that dances on grand themes such as birth, death, and resurrection would resort to symbol, metaphor, and archetype. Fleming's idiosyncratic style, however, is completely direct. She doesn't dance *about* water. Rather, she *becomes* water. . . . There is nobody else like her." In many of her dances, some of which are of evening length, Fleming performs in the nude. "The female body has been a potent image throughout the history of art," she told Catherine Foster. "One of the reasons it's a strong and expressive image is that it's universal. As soon as clothes are put on, there's a time and place. . . . I've always looked for those elements in dance that point toward what is universal about the journey of the soul. I do this in the hope that at some point in our evolution we can understand that we as humans share more than we are different." Adding to the powerful effects of her movements in some works, yards of diaphanous fabric blown by a wind machine billow and swirl around and above her body as she dances. Her ultimate goal, as posted on her Web site, is "to reveal the transcendent through images which focus on the human body as a vehicle of transformation. I

am specifically interested in finding a universal art which touches the evolutionary traces imbedded in human experience and transcends the limits of nationality and gender . . . [with the] aim of discovering what is truly universal about being human."

Fleming has performed at dozens of festivals and in stand-alone concerts in North and South America, Europe, Asia, and Africa. She has served as dancer-in-residence at Ellen Stewart's LaMaMa Experimental Theatre Club (LaMaMa E.T.C.), Off-Off-Broadway, in New York City, since 1984. In the mid-1990s she founded her own troupe, the Maureen Fleming Company. As a choreographer she has collaborated with the composers Philip Glass, Teiji Ito, and Genji Ito, the playwright David Henry Hwang, the photographers Tadayuki Naitoh, Lois Greenfield, and Spencer Tunic, the videographers Jeff Bush, Hiroshi Onihiro, and Suh Yang Byum, the sound designer Brett Jarvis, the pianists Peter Phillips and Bruce Brubaker, the ikebana artist Gaho Taniguchi, and her husband, the light and visual designer Christopher Odo, among others. The many public and private sources that have supported her work include the National Endowment for the Arts, the Asian Cultural Council, the Japan–U.S. Friendship Commission, the Rockefeller Foundation, the Japan Foundation, the Fulbright Commission, and the Fund for U.S. Artists at International Festivals and Exhibitions.

Maureen Fleming was born to a U.S. Navy officer and his wife in around 1955 on a naval base near Yokohama, Japan. The trauma to her spine happened when, as her mother was driving near the base one day, a bicyclist swerved and stopped on the road a short distance from the approaching car. Her mother immediately floored the brake, stopping the car so suddenly that Fleming and her sister were catapulted through the windshield. As her mother rushed to the aid of her daughters, who were lying bloodied on the road, the bicyclist laughed and rode away. Determined to wipe that horrific image from her memory, her mother never mentioned the accident to the girls. "The accident happened when I was so young it was part of my 'normal' reality, so I don't believe that I recognized [the effects] as pain," Fleming recalled to Julie Mullins for *citybeat.com* (February 18, 2009). "Rather it was like a toothache in my spine that subsided after beginning to move. . . . Movement was as essential to my livelihood as eating. I began twisting my body into different shapes as a way of trying to compensate for the trauma that had happened in my past. Over the years, that twisting became my choreography."

Fleming remained ignorant about her childhood injury until she was 35 (or older, according to some sources), when a doctor whom she consulted about severe neck pain and difficulty in moving one arm detected in X-rays a long bone spur that had replaced the disc between her fourth and fifth vertebrae. Her mother's account of the accident illuminated for Fleming why, from early childhood, "creating dance was an integral part of my identity . . . ," she told Gail Johnson for the Vancouver, Canada, publication *straight.com* (March 3, 2005). "When I looked back at photos, my head was always hanging down. My choreography has these extreme twists; I needed to twist away from the accident. I had to find my own ways to regenerate and heal my body." She noted on her Web site, "The twisting and untwisting of joints increases blood flow and has become a slow method of regeneration." For many years Fleming has engaged in a training regimen of her own design, "Fleming Elastics," to maintain her flexibility and her control over her connective tissue and muscles, including, by her own account, deep muscles normally inaccessible even to professional dancers. The doctor who X-rayed her neck warned her that there would be dire consequences if she did not have surgery to remove the bone spur, consequences that never materialized. Many assessments of her work have alluded to what she has accomplished in the physical realm; a reviewer for the University of Massachusetts–Amherst magazine *Spotlight* (February/March 2004) wrote after seeing her performance of *Decay of the Angel*, "Fleming transforms her body into structural forms that push and break any limitations inherent in a human skeleton. Often compared to that of an invertebrate sea creature, Fleming's body retains the flexibility of an infant."

Fleming was about three when her family returned to the U.S. She attended Catholic schools for 16 years. "I have four uncles who are Catholic priests," she told Daniel Neman for the *Richmond (Virginia) Times Dispatch* (March 14, 1999). "And I really understand that way of thinking, because in Western spiritual thinking the soul is divorced from the body. And that's part of my work: the question of can the soul be transformed from the body?" Fleming's training in classical dance began when she was seven and continued for years, but published accounts reveal little about the chronology of her formal instruction. Her principal teachers include Kazuo Ohno (born in 1906), who, with Tatsumi Hijikata, is considered the co-founder of butoh; the dancer and choreographer Min Tanaka (born in 1945), who studied with Hijikata; and, with a scholarship in the 1980s, the renowned ballet teacher Margaret Craske (1893–1990), a disciple of the great Italian ballet master Enrico Cecchetti (1850–1928). Also prominent in her development as a dancer are Yoshito Ohno, Kazuo Ohno's son, Ellen Stewart, the founder and artistic director of LaMaMa E.T.C., and the mythologist Joseph Campbell, who once said to Fleming after seeing her perform, "Your dance is your transcendence."

Butoh is difficult to define or describe, because it is not based on a theory of dance and is not choreographed as a series of specific steps or movements; thus, it is not repeatable. It rejects the rigidity of classical Japanese dance (most prominently, noh), the strictly defined movements of classical Western ballet, and the narrative elements often present in those genres, and arose in reaction to the materialism (associated with the West) that had begun to supplant long-held Japanese cultural traditions in the wake of World War II. "Butoh was conceived as an art that would continue to rebel, even to rebel against itself," Fleming told Misaki. "It was conceived as an art that would not become an institutionalized form, but rather remain alive and vital, continuously reinvented by innovators inspired by it. So the idea of the initial Butoh artists was to strip away anything that was technique-driven." She told Neman, "What Butoh truly does is reduce movement to an essence, where the motivating inspiration is the spiritual energy in the body"; butoh, she said, is like "paintings that move in slow motion."

Fleming met Min Tanaka in 1984, when he choreographed *Mythos Oedipus* for LaMaMa. Fleming's spiritual leanings and skills, including her knowledge of aikido, a Japanese martial art, impressed Tanaka, and he invited her to perform in *Mythos Oedipus* with his company, Maijuku, at LaMaMa. Afterward Fleming joined Maijuku and toured with the company in Europe. She then trained with Tanaka in Japan for six months, adhering to a routine that was "unbelievably difficult," Fleming told Misaki, explaining that "Min was interested in going to the limit of whatever he was doing." Every morning for about two hours beginning at 8:30 a.m., Fleming and her fellow dancers (all of them Japanese) engaged in "muscle-bone training," which involved jumping continuously from one side of the room to the other. Then came over two hours of "manipulations," in which "the body is stretched to its limit," and several hours of "imagination" exercises. Often, with minimal rest, the dancers then gave performances in Tanaka's theater in Tokyo. The physical demands on Fleming's body were so great that her menstrual periods ceased during those six months. In addition, in a form of mental conditioning, Tanaka would have his dancers spend eight days in isolation in a mountain forest, with no food and nothing to protect them from the elements except one plastic sheet. When Fleming was in the forest, it was bitterly cold. "You just totally shed a comprehension of who you are," she recalled to Misaki. "It makes one lose the armor around the body. You have no choice but to find a way to breathe to make the body warm. . . . The first night I slept in a tree. The space that you get to and the closeness to the earth that you feel . . . on the sixth or seventh day of the fast, I was probably happier than I've ever been in my life. . . . I began to realize how little we need to be happy." During the fast she also had strange visions and auditory sensations and entered "states where the line between conscious and unconscious becomes faint." "Isn't that what Butoh is about?" she added. Tanaka had told the dancers that they could leave the forest at any time, but Fleming remained. Her training under Tanaka, she told Misaki, "was a very important introduction into a way of approaching movement."

Later, after winning a grant from the arts organization Creative Time to choreograph a new work, Fleming returned to Japan to study under Kazuo Ohno; she boarded in his house as well. "Ohno's classes are really different from Min's," Fleming told Misaki. "It's complete improvisation. And it's improvisation based on what he's read that day. If he's read the Bible, for example, about the woman who turned to salt, that day the improvisation is salt becoming water. The snow melting into water." She also trained with Ohno's son, Yoshito.

An image of Fleming in *Birth Song* (1984) is the earliest of the dance photos on her Web site. Far better known among her dances is *Axis Mundi* ("Tree of Life"), which premiered in 1989 at La MaMa E.C.T. and remains in the dancer's repertoire. Long, crooked, forked white branches held in either hand figure in that work. Writing for the Canadian magazine *Dance Current* (March 2005, online), Kaija Pepper described *Axis Mundi* as a "meditation on the human body, gorgeously lit, with huge, engrossing film and photographic images projected on an upstage screen" and wrote that Fleming "most often moves like a slow, natural process—a flower unfolding or landscape shifting." Fleming's *Water on the Moon* also debuted in 1989. At the 1990 Butoh Festival, held in Tokyo, Fleming—the only non-Japanese dancer invited to participate—performed *Axis Mundi* for an audience that included her butoh teachers and mentors. The next year marked the premiere, at LaMaMa, of *Eros*, in which she and Yoshito Ohno appeared on stage separately. Indeed, Ohno had created his solo without consulting her. "Yoshito believed that dancers needed to work independently and that there would be a psychic connection that would join the images," Fleming told Misaki. "I found this to be a profound, mysterious, and important part of understanding what Butoh is about." In 1996 Fleming premiered *After Eros* at the 96th St. Y, in collaboration with the playwright David Henry Hwang and the composer Philip Glass, weaving Fleming's life story into the tale of Psyche and Eros from Greek mythology. Jack Anderson wrote for the *New York Times* (December 25, 1996, on-line) that Fleming "seemed to transcend the material world and enter a realm of pure spirit" and that the work featured "wondrous choreographic metamorphoses."

Fleming's Web site lists her dances in order of the dates they premiered; the posted dance photos bear the dates on which the pictures were shot. In addition to *Birth Song*, *Axis Mundi*, *Water on the Moon*, and *Eros*, there are images of Fleming performing *Mother and Child*, *Sphere*, *Womb Mandala*, *After Eros*, *Flower*, *Flower Revolution*, *The Stairs*, *The Driftwood*, *Dialogue of Self and Soul*, *Decay of the Angel*, *Effulgent Wings*, and *The Immortal Rose*. "One of the principles which underlies my work is the creation of the 'archetype,'" she explained on her Web site. "An archetype is a universal symbol that embodies a pattern of life experience. For example, in *The Sphere*, the universal symbol of a circle forms and deconstructs. The image bespeaks a reality beyond the pairs of opposites such as birth and death or pain and ecstasy and contains them in the same moment. The image, encompassing an interface between music and light, creates a state which allows the observer to reflect on their lives and watch the image like a dream." According to her Web site, in creating a dance—a process that may take her as long as 10 years—Fleming "records her improvisations and begins the process of identifying the archetypal moments. Through a studied process of dissolving original images one into the other, she documents her choreography in her studio on video, establishing the concept, choreography and title of the work." Fleming recently premiered *Dances from Home*, an installation at LaMaMa Galleria. A piece about Fleming in *TimeOut New York* in 2009 featured a photograph she took of herself using natural light.

From the early 1990s through 2010, Fleming performed solo and group works in Italy, France, Germany, Russia, Colombia, Brazil, Venezuela, Mexico, Iceland, and South Korea as well as the U.S. and Japan, at festivals, universities, embassies, museums, arts centers, and other sites. In one representative assessment, posted on her Web site, Massoud Saidpour, the coordinator for performing arts at the Cleveland Museum of Art, wrote in 1998, "There are artists who words cannot describe. You can only recommend 'GO SEE HER!,' and that was all I could say to those who later inquired about her performance. . . . Alone in the presence of others, in the vulnerable state of a naked child, totally disarmed, she began a spellbinding performance. Her total disarmament toward the others, combined with the mastery with which she executes the most unbelievable body movements, her amazingly beautiful use of film, live and taped music, her keen sense of choreography and scenography, all worked together to put . . . a silent spell over the auditorium. Just as in a dream, her work allows for a flight of the psyche."

Fleming has taught in dance-residency programs at the Tisch School of the Arts, a division of New York University, and the Juilliard School, in New York City, and is an artist-in-residence at the Seoul Institute of the Arts, in South Korea (2006–2010). She has conducted workshops at the Kripalu Center, in Stockbridge, Massachusetts, the Flynn Center for the Performing Arts, in Burlington, Vermont, and other places. She lives on the Lower East Side of New York City with her husband, Christopher Odo.

—C.C.

Suggested Reading: *Arts Cure* (on-line) Spring 2005; *Boston Globe* C p6 Feb. 24, 2002, D p15 Feb. 20, 2004, F p3 Nov. 3, 2007; *Boston Herald* S p8 Mar. 1, 2002; *Chicago Reader* (on-line) Apr. 30, 1999; citybeat.com Feb. 18, 2009; *Cleveland (Ohio) Free Times* (on-line) Sep. 1998; Maureen Fleming Web site; (Richmond, Virginia) *Times Dispatch* H p1 Mar. 14, 1999

Selected Works: *Birth Song*, 1984; *Axis Mundi*, 1989; *Water on the Moon*, 1989; *Eros, 1991; Sphere, 1991; Mother and Child, 1993; Flower, 1993; Womb Mandala*, 1995; *After Eros*, 1996; *The Stairs*, 1997; *The Driftwood*, 2001; *Flower Revolution*, 2001; *Decay of the Angel*, 2004; *Dialogue of Self and Soul*, 2006; *Waters of Immortality*, 2007; *The Immortal Rose*, 2007; *Effulgent Wings*, 2008; *Dances from Home*, 2009

Hugo Glendinning, courtesy of Fortier Danse-Création

Fortier, Paul-André

(for-tee-YAY)

Apr. 30, 1948– Choreographer and dancer

Address: Fortier Danse-Création, 2022 Sherbrooke East, Office 301, Montréal, Québec H2K 1B9, Canada

The dancer and choreographer Paul-André Fortier has been influential in the Canadian dance world for over three decades. In 1973, at the age of 25, Fortier abandoned his career as a literature and theater teacher after his introduction to dance via a course for beginners taught by Martine Époque, the co-founder and co-artistic director of the modern-dance company Groupe Nouvelle Aire. Époque immediately recognized his inborn talents, and at her invitation he joined her troupe and devoted himself to dance. In 1981, two years after he formed his own company, Fortier Danse-Création, he gained national recognition as the winner of the Jean A. Chalmers Award, Canada's highest honor for choreographers. In the mid-1980s, with Daniel

Jackson, he co-founded Montréal Danse, serving as its co-artistic director until 1989. From that year until 1999 he was a professor in the Dance Department of the University of Quebec at Montreal.

Fortier has created more than 40 works, some on commission and some for specific dancers; he has performed in most of them himself, as a soloist or with others. His dances have been described variously as highly experimental, beautiful, disturbing, thought-provoking, and mesmerizing. In the 1980s, Pamela Anthony wrote for the *Edmonton (Alberta, Canada) Journal* (November 2, 2000), Fortier "forged his reputation . . . with aggressive, dramatic dances that questioned both society and the dance establishment"; in the 1990s, she wrote, his dances had "a distinctly meditative air." His best-known work from the 2000s is *Solo 30X30* (2006), which he described to Olivia Fincato for *Vogue Italy* (August 24, 2010, on-line) as "a piece about a man trying to find his own place in the city . . . who wants to reconnect with the sky, the ground and the people." Fortier has performed *Solo 30X30* in cities in Canada, England, Italy, France, Japan, and the U.S., in the last as a participant—at age 62—in the annual River to River Festival in New York City in 2010. In each city he danced *Solo 30X30* for 30 minutes on 30 consecutive days, always in the same outdoor location, no matter what the weather. In 2010 the French Ministry of Culture named Fortier a Chevalier of the Order of Arts and Letters of France for his contributions to dance.

Paul-André Fortier was born on April 30, 1948 in Waterville, a small town about 100 miles south of Quebec City in the province of Quebec, in southeastern Canada. He attended the University of Sherbrooke, near Waterville, which conducts classes in French rather than English. He earned a master's degree in arts and education there. Soon afterward he started teaching literature and running a theater program at the Cégep de Granby—Haute-Yamaska, a junior college in Granby, near Montreal, Quebec. At that point he had no dance experience; as he told William Littler for the *New York Times* (September 9, 1990), "I finished my literary studies before I did my first plié"—a basic ballet step. One day in 1973 he shared with a colleague some observations he had made while attending one of her dance rehearsals, and in response she suggested that he take a six-week summer-school dance course offered by Martine Époque, the co-head of Groupe Nouvelle Aire ("New Area Company"). Although Fortier had never danced before and had attended only one dance concert—the *Nutcracker*—he registered for the course. "I have a very good memory of those six weeks, because it was a period of total discovery for me," Fortier told Andrea Rowe for the *Ottawa (Canada) Citizen* (June 11, 2002). "With all the classes and the teachers it was a very, very exciting six weeks. [Époque] was a good pedagogue, and had the instinct to say, that this person can dance, this is a stage person, this person has the desire.

She had that capacity to accept people around her who she instinctively felt would be a plus for the group." At Époque's invitation Fortier joined her troupe that same year.

The French-born and -trained Epoque, who served as co–artistic director of Groupe Nouvelle Aire from 1968 to 1980, nurtured the burgeoning careers of such up-and-coming dancers and choreographers as Édouard Lock, Daniel Léveillé, Louise Lecavalier, and Ginette Laurin as well as Fortier. In an interview with Rowe, Laurin recalled, "The ambience was very open for young choreographers, partly because there weren't a lot of shows, so we had lots of time to explore and do research in the studio." Among the outside artists who taught at Epoque's invitation, the most influential for Fortier was the choreographer Françoise Sullivan. He told Rowe that while Epoque gave him the chance to become a dancer and choreographer, Sullivan was his "artistic mother." He continued, "It was Françoise who made an artist out of me—she gave me my sense of freedom, of being able to go for what I want and not caring about whoever, of doing my thing and not trying to be part of any stream or current." Fortier choreographed several works for Groupe Nouvelle Aire, among them, in 1978, Derrière la porte un mur ("A Wall Behind the Door") and Images Noires ("Black Images" or "Black Frames"). He also "interpreted" Lock's early dances, according to his Web site. He left the company in 1979.

That year Fortier launched his own dance company, Théâtre Danse Paul-André Fortier; two years later he renamed it Fortier Danse Création. (According to some sources, among them the Canada Council for the Arts and one post on the Danse Création Web site, he founded the company in 1981.) Fortier's next dances—Parlez-moi donc du cul de mon enfance ("So Tell Me About My Childhood Arse," 1979) and Violence (1980)—were described as provocative, theatrical, disturbing, and sexual. Chaleurs ("Heat") premiered in Montreal at the 1985 Festival International de Nouvelle Dance. In a critique for the New York Times (September 23, 1985), Anna Kisselgoff wrote that while Fortier had succeeded in creating "an effective theatrical image" in Chaleurs, he "lack[ed] the movement sense and structures to deepen it. . . . There is eventually a sense of life and love dying out." She added, "There is a clever use of sound. . . . There is one wonderful moment of hysteria when men rush in with screaming women on their shoulders. But there is not enough to fill the spaces between." The next year marked the debut of Mythe Décisif ("Decisive Myth"). At around that time, with Daniel Jackson, Fortier co-founded the company Montréal Danse, where he served as artistic co-director for three years.

During his decade as a professor at the University of Quebec, starting in 1989, Fortier continued to dance and choreograph. The first of a three-solo trilogy, Les Males Heures ("The Male Hours," 1989), about a man's internal struggles with sexual temptation and questions of identity, was followed by La Tentation de la transparence ("The Temptation of Transparency," 1991), which again examined the notion of self-discovery. Fortier performed the latter piece on a stage surrounded by audience members. "It is a dance of the arms, liquid, bending—hands curving in Fortier's trademark mudras," Michael Scott wrote for the Vancouver (British Columbia, Canada) Sun (October 16, 1991), referring to symbolic or ritual hand gestures used in some Asian religious ceremonies. "And it leads us through a series of cycles, of tensions invoked and released. On one level there is a line running from innocence to knowledge; others lead from childhood to middle age, from previous incarnations to this one. . . . It is the piece's end, though, that suffuses the imagination with a golden light for days afterward. As Fortier sinks slowly into a crevice of the stage, he places his cupped hand on various parts of his body, on parts of the stage, on the air around him, with each light touch making a gentle kissing sound. The message of peaceful acceptance, of loving the art of dance and all its components—body, stage and audience—is exquisitely beautiful." In 1993, for his work on La Tentation de la transparence, Fortier won Canada's prestigious Dora Mavor Moore Award for choreography. His next solo piece was titled Bras de plomb ("Arms of Lead," 1993), a highly lauded collaboration with the Canadian visual artist Betty Goodwin. That work had four parts: in the first, Fortier's arms, as if without bones, seemed to float above his body; in the second, big metal clips pinned his arms to his sides; in the third, lead sleeves encased his arms, and Fortier danced as if trying to escape entrapment; and in the final solo, with his arms in sleeves with a golden sheen, his movements resembled those in the martial arts, symbolizing strength. Bras de plomb struck Linde Howe-Beck, writing for Dance Magazine (January 1, 1994), as having a "soft, introspective magic with a beauty that transcends urban life."

In 1996, after a decade of creating only solo dances, Fortier choreographed Entre la mémoire et l'oubli ("Between Memory and Oblivion"), to mark the 10th anniversary of Montréal Danse. At its debut it was performed by members of the Society of Contemporary Music of Quebec, with music by the Canadian composer Luc Marcel. The year 1996 also saw the premiere of La Part des anges ("Angels' Portion," 1996), for four performers (originally, Peggy Baker, Robert Meilleur, Gioconda Barbuto, and Fortier). The title refers to the fraction of alcohol that evaporates during the wine-making process; similarly, Fortier suggested, the act of breathing can lead to a kind of spiritual cleansing and transformation. La Part des anges—in which the dancers embraced, lifted, poked, and imitated one another—had no narrative. "The pared-down movement, barren stage, stark lighting and minimalist score recall the astringent esthetic of a Mark Rothko painting," Deirdre Kelly wrote for the Toronto, Canada, Globe and Mail (March 14,

1998). "And like such a work of abstract art, the dance provides for an intense visual experience." Linde Howe-Beck, writing for the *Canadian Encyclopedia*, described *La Part des anges* as "a deeply meditative work about maturity and relationships." Peggy Baker later commissioned Fortier to create a solo dance for her. The result, *Loin, très loin* ("Far, Very Far"), premiered in 2000 in Toronto.

Fortier had choreographed an earlier work, *Jeux de Fous* ("Crazy Games" or "Foolish Games," 1998), for three young dancers close to graduation from the University of Quebec at Montreal. A "raw, edgy work about the contradictions of youth," Howe-Beck wrote for the *Canadian Encyclopedia*, it premiered at Agora de la danse, a venue for contemporary dance in Montreal, and was performed many times during the next several years in Canada and France. In 2002 *Jeux de Fous* was presented at the Canada Dance Festival, in Ottawa, along with *Tensions*, in which Fortier and a much younger dancer engaged in "parallel solos," as Fortier put it on his Web site. Also present, offstage, were three additional collaborators: the composer Alain Thibault, the video artist Patrick Masbourian, and the lighting designer John Munro. "In this case, I think the input of the other creators is so major that though I am the leader, there is something that's close to being a collective experience because the involvement of each of them was so strong and their contribution was so involved at every level," Fortier told Andrea Rowe for the *Ottawa Citizen* (June 11, 2002). Five days earlier Rowe had written for the same publication that Fortier, who was then 54, was "the oldest to dance in the Festival" and then added, "He may be bald and need glasses to read the program, but boy, can his presence pack a wallop."

On commission, Fortier choreographed *Excès* ("Excess," 2002) for LADMMI, the school of contemporary dance in Montreal; *Sparks* (2003), for the School of Contemporary Dance in Winnipeg, the capital of the Canadian province of Manitoba; and *Social Studies* (2005), for Danse Cité, in Montreal, with John Ottmann as the soloist at its premiere. In 2006 Fortier choreographed the dance cum event *Solo 30X30*, for which he eschewed music, theaters, and ticket sales. Rather, he presented the 30-minute piece at outdoor urban sites, performing at each location every day at the same time for 30 days straight, regardless of weather conditions, traffic and other ambient noise, comments from spectators or passersby, or his own moods. The show premiered at 1:00 p.m. on March 1, 2006 on the Gateshead Millennium Bridge, in Newcastle, England. During the next four years, Fortier danced *Solo 30X30* in Ottawa and Montréal; Yamaguchi, Japan; Nancy and Lyon, France; London, England; Bolzano and Rome, Italy; and, most recently, New York City, from July 16 to August 14, 2010, at age 62. *Solo 30X30* is "about a man trying to find his place in the concrete, where you have to fight for your space," Fortier told Susan Reiter

for the *New York Press* (July 16, 2010), "and there is a point where it becomes very difficult. It's really about how you find your space within the city." "This solo is the most demanding thing I've done," he told Gia Kourlas for *Time Out New York* (July 15–21, 2010). "When you dance on a stage, you are protected; when you're outside, the sky is so high! For me, it's been a learning process about focusing."

After Olivia Fincato, an interviewer for *Vogue Italy* (August 24, 2010), saw Fortier perform at One New York Plaza, in Lower Manhattan, she asked him how people reacted to his performances of *Solo 30X30*. "Sometime, when they see me for the first time, they think I am a crazy man. Then if they get closer and see that I am not young anymore, they respect me. If they stay a little longer, suddenly I see some emotions in their faces. They get absorbed and I feel I accomplish something. I took them in a place where they can reconnect to their bodies, their own self." *Solo 30X30* got a tepid reception from the *New York Times* (July 25, 2010, on-line) dance critic Alastair Macaulay, who witnessed Fortier's July 24 performance. "Coolly he shows us one movement after another," Macaulay wrote. "Most of them are fairly interesting or agreeable. . . . Many of his liveliest moments involve the flourishing of his hands." Macaulay concluded, "The carefully measured tone of Mr. Fortier's movements stopped any of this from having any force or from being absorbing. His quality of teacherly reserve places a curious distance between his solo and himself. It's as if he were presenting something in which he didn't quite believe but feels ought to impress us anyway."

Soon after Fortier performed *Solo 30X30* in Japan, in 2006, he choreographed the hour-long *Solo 1X60—Un Jardin d'objets* ("A Garden of Objects"). He introduced that work at the Yamaguchi Center for Arts and Media, in Japan, performing to the accompaniment of electronic music composed by Alain Thibault on a set furnished with many electronic gadgets (designed by the Japanese video artist Takao Minami). For his next project, the duet *Cabane* ("Hut" or "Cabin," 2008), Fortier collaborated with the filmmaker Robert Morin, who created visual imagery for it, such as that of a vulture taking flight, and the artist/writer/performer/musician Rober Racine, who interacted with Fortier onstage and provided sounds and music, by playing a harmonica and a specially altered wire mattress, for example. A mix of art installation and performance art, *Cabane* had no narrative and took place on a stage whose focal point was a small shed. It premiered at the Festival TransAmériques in Montreal in mid-2008. "The piece journeys to unusual places such as an indoor parking lot, a ballroom and a theatre, creating a disturbing universe removed from reality, a place beyond reason . . . ," according to the Canada Council for the Arts (on-line, May 2008). "The shack . . . is a world unto itself—a shelter, a workshop, a screen or perhaps a mausoleum—enmeshed in spaces that have strong connotations and fall between luxury, poverty and artifice." *Cabane*, Giannandrea Poesio wrote for the British weekly the *Spectator* (October 17, 2009), presented ideas in "an unexpectedly quirky and provocative way." Poesio added, "Fortier's elegantly reiterated movements were utterly mesmerising, as if part of a hypnotic ritual or trance dance, contrasting with and complementing the more spirited, sound-making physical performance of Racine."

Fortier served as a dance consultant for the Canada Council of the Arts (1993–95); as president of the influential organization Regroupement québecois de la danse (1994–95); and as vice president of the Conseil des arts et des lettres du Québec (1998–2003). From 2003 to 2007 he was the artist-in-residence at the performing-arts center Place des Arts, in Montreal, and the choreographer-in-residence at the Cinquième Salle, a theater there. He lives in Montreal.

—D.K.

Suggested Reading: *Canadian Encyclopedia* (online); *Dance Magazine* p112 Jan. 1, 1994; fortier-danse.com; *New York Times* C p1 July 26, 2010; *Ottawa (Canada) Citizen* B p7 June 11, 2002; (Toronto, Canada) *Globe and Mail* C p8 Mar. 14, 1998; *Toronto (Canada) Star* D p24 Dec. 9, 1988

Selected Works: *Derriere la porte un mur*, 1978; *Images Noires*, 1978; *Parlez-moi donc du cul de mon enfance*, 1979; *Violence*, 1980; *Fin*, 1981; *Creation*, 1982; *Moi, King Kong*, 1982; *Gravitation*, 1983; *Chaleur*, 1985; *Tell*, 1987; *Sans titre et qui le restera*, 1987; *Les Males Heures*, 1989; *La Tentation de la transparence*, 1991; *Bras de plomb*, 1993; *La Part des anges*, 1996; *Jeux de Fous*, 1998; *Loin, très loin*, 2000; *Tensions*, 2002; *Excès*, 2002; *Sparks*, 2003; *Risque*, 2003; *Lumiere*, 2004; *Social Studies*, 2005; *Spirale*, 2008; *Cabane*, 2008; *She*, 2009; *Solo 1X60*, 2006; *Solo 30X30*, 2006

Kevin Winter/Getty Images

Fox, Megan

May 16, 1986– Actress

Address: c/o International Creative Management, 10250 Constellation Blvd., Los Angeles, CA 90067

Megan Fox is perhaps better known for her stunning looks and provocative persona than for her acting roles. While some observers have characterized her as empowered and refreshingly honest, others have suggested that Fox's image is a carefully crafted combination of sex appeal and controversy. Among the latter group is Lynn Hirschberg, who, in an article for the *New York Times Magazine* (November 15, 2009) entitled "The Self-Manufacture of Megan Fox," wrote, "Megan Fox is a fox. And not just in the way you might think if you've seen her in a tiny bikini in a men's magazine or leaning over the hood of a '76 Camaro in [the movie] *Transformers*. Yes, Fox is beautiful and often scantily clad, but dozens of beautiful girls arrive in Hollywood every day who are more than happy to pose nearly naked. Unlike them, Fox has a quality that sets her apart: Fox is sly. Canny. A devoted student of stardom, past and present, she knows how to provide her own color commentary." Hirschberg continued, "In the age of the 24-hour news cycle and hungry blogs, Fox has supplied a seemingly endless stream of tantalizing quotes. . . . [She] understood instinctively that noise plus naked equals celebrity."

After appearing in 2001 in a straight-to-video release starring the winsome, blond twins Mary-Kate and Ashley Olsen, Fox came to wider attention as the villain in Disney's *Confessions of a Teenage Drama Queen* (2004). In 2007 she attracted a somewhat more mature fan base with the blockbuster Hollywood movie *Transformers*, in which she played the sultry girlfriend of the hero. Fox soon began topping lists compiled by the editors of such publications as *FHM*, *Maxim*, and AskMen.com of the most beautiful women in the world, and she quickly became a fixture of Internet gossip sites for her startling pronouncements about her sexuality, marijuana use, and tattoos. She admitted to Hirschberg, "You have to be put in a box in this industry so they can sell you."

Megan Denise Fox was born in Oak Ridge, Tennessee, on May 16, 1986 to Darlene Tonachio and Franklin Foxx. (Her father later dropped one "x" from the family name.) Many journalists have asserted that her mixed ancestry—Irish, French, and Native American—is responsible for her striking good looks. Fox's parents separated when she was three years old, and Fox and her sister, Vivian, remained with their mother, who later remarried and moved the family to Port St. Lucie, Florida. Fox has said that her mother and stepfather, a staunch Pentecostal Christian, were extremely strict with her as a child, setting the stage for a tumultuous adolescent rebellion.

Fox, who had harbored dreams of becoming an actress since she watched *The Wizard of Oz* as a child, took ballet and acting classes throughout her youth and also swam competitively. She attended Morningside Academy, a small, private Christian school in Port St. Lucie, before enrolling at St. Lucie West Centennial High School. She has told journalists that her fellow female students were especially mean to her, and that her friends were all boys. Uninterested in academics, Fox was frequently grounded by her parents for such antics as driving her mother's car without permission.

Fox, who was working occasionally as a catalog model, made her acting debut in *Holiday in the Sun* (2001), one in a series of pictures made by the hugely popular Olsen twins and aimed at a young, female audience. (Now adults, the twins control a media and fashion empire worth an estimated $100 million.) Fox described her role to Hirschberg as that of "the spoiled, rich, nasty alpha female that picked on the nice sweet blond Olsen twins."

At age 15 Fox was an uncredited extra in *Bad Boys II*, a police drama directed by Michael Bay and released in 2003. "They put me in six-inch heels and a stars-and-stripes bikini," Fox recalled to Hirschberg. "Then they put me in the scene under a waterfall. You got $500 extra if you were willing to get wet, and I was thrilled to get wet. I was still a child, but for those two days I was being treated like a grown woman. I felt like I should be in a bikini dancing under a waterfall: that is where I thought I belonged."

Two years later the 17-year-old Fox moved with her mother to Los Angeles to pursue her acting career. (According to various sources, she completed her high-school requirements via correspondence and received a diploma.) Fox quickly landed a regular role on the critically panned soap opera *Ocean Ave.* and guest spots on such sitcoms as *What I Like About You* and *Two and a Half Men*.

In 2004 Fox appeared in her first major feature-film role, opposite Lindsay Lohan, in *Confessions of a Teenage Drama Queen*. "I played the b**ch, of course . . . ," Fox told Hirschberg. "The light-haired girl is the sweet leading lady, and the dark girl is the sexy b**ch. I didn't know how to act when I did that movie. I just mimicked all the b**ches I'd seen other people play on TV." Those few critics who noticed the picture at all were unimpressed.

That year Fox also landed a recurring role in the ABC sitcom *Hope & Faith*, about two sisters—one a happily married midwestern mother (Faith Ford), the other a diva-like unemployed actress (Kelly Ripa). Fox moved by herself to New York City, where the show was taped, to play the vain teenage daughter of Ford's character. (She replaced the actress Nicole Paggi, who had originated the part during the show's first season.)

Fox appeared on *Hope & Faith* until the show went off the air, in 2006, and was then cast in the film that became the vehicle for her rapid rise to pop-culture ubiquity: *Transformers*, a live-action hit based on the celebrated cartoon series and toy line. Released in 2007, *Transformers* was directed by Michael Bay, whom Fox had met while filming *Bad Boys II*. Fox was cast as Mikaela Banes, the beautiful, machine-savvy love interest of the teenage hero of the film, Sam Witwicky (Shia LaBeouf). A big-budget, effects-laden action movie featuring battling robots, *Transformers* was one of the year's most commercially successful films. While most critics were enthusiastic about the picture's action sequences and its computer-generated imagery (CGI), few took notice of Fox's acting. In her review for the *New York Times* (July 2, 2007, on-line), Manohla Dargis described *Transformers* as "part car commercial, part military recruitment ad, a bumper-to-bumper pileup of big cars, big guns and, as befits its recently weaned target demographic, big breasts." She wrote of Fox and her female co-star, Rachael Taylor, "These walking, talking dolls register as less human and believable than the Transformers, which may be why they were even allowed inside this boy's club."

Fox reprised the role in the 2009 sequel, *Transformers: Revenge of the Fallen*. Her relationship with Bay was troubled, however. In a widely quoted interview with the British magazine *Wonderland* (September/October 2009), she compared the director of *Transformers* to Napoleon and Hitler and claimed that working with him was a "nightmare." In response, an open letter was posted on the Internet—purportedly written by *Transformers* crew members, although some suspected that Bay was the author—criticizing Fox as "dumb as a rock," "unbearable," and "thankless." Fox's character will not appear in the third installment of the *Transformers* series.

Fox's other credits include *How to Lose Friends and Alienate People* (2008), a film adaptation of a memoir by the journalist Toby Young; *Whore* (2008), which follows a group of aspiring young actors who are forced to prostitute themselves on the streets of Hollywood to survive; and the horror movie *Jennifer's Body* (2009), which marked the first time that Fox was billed as a lead. As with most of her other pictures, in *Jennifer's Body* she played a mean beauty—but with a twist: she kills and eats the boys she seduces. "As played by Megan Fox, several orders of magnitude of icy beauty above the mere mortals around her, Jennifer is the worst type of popular high school girl, fully aware of her newfound beauty and confident enough to brandish it like a weapon against one and all," John Patterson wrote for the London *Guardian* (October 31, 2009).

Reviews of the movie varied widely. "Fox's charms, first in *Transformers: Revenge of the Fallen* and now here, elude me," Stephanie Zacharek wrote for *Salon* (September 18, 2009, on-line). "She's a glossy blank, and her character is constructed and played so that her actions are inscrutable. The movie awkwardly frames her predicament as a kind of revenge against the male sex. But her viciousness—she preys mostly on nice, or at least OK, kids—is neither cathartic, nor does it make us recoil in horror. Her evil is shiny, hard and cheap, like something she bought at Forever 21." Roger Ebert, on the other hand, wrote for the *Chicago Sun-Times* (September 17, 2009, on-line), "Megan Fox is an interesting case. We think of her as a star, but this is actually her first leading role. She didn't get to No. 18 on *Maxim*'s Hot 100 list of 2007 for acting. . . . Fox did her career a lot of good with the two *Transformer* movies, but this is her first chance to really perform, and you know what? She comes through. She has your obligatory projectile vomiting scene and somehow survives it, she plays the role straight, and she looks great in a blood-drenched dress with her hair all straggly."

"People expected *Jennifer's Body* to make so much money," Fox told Hirschberg. "But I was doubtful. The movie is about a man-eating, cannibalistic lesbian cheerleader, and that pretty much eliminates middle America. It's obviously a girl-power movie, but it's also about how scary girls are." Fox hosted *Saturday Night Live* (*SNL*) on September 26, 2009 while promoting *Jennifer's Body*, which, as she predicted, failed to attract audiences to the movie theater. Critics generally praised her *SNL* appearance, during which she genially mocked her own image. During her opening monologue, for example, she displayed what she claimed were nude photos of herself—in which her head was poorly grafted onto bodies that were obviously not hers.

Fox was cast as a gun-toting prostitute in the comic-book-inspired *Jonah Hex* (2010), a Western/horror hybrid starring Josh Brolin. She appeared as an angel in Mitch Glazer's *Passion Play*; co-starring Mickey Rourke and Bill Murray, it was shown at the Toronto Film Festival in September of that year.

Fox, who has several tattoos, including one that makes reference to *King Lear* and another that depicts Marilyn Monroe, told an interviewer for *Nylon* magazine (September 26, 2009, on-line) that she is well aware of the pitfalls of quick fame: "I think that I'm really overexposed. I was part of [*Transformers*,] a movie that [the studio] wanted to make sure would make $700 million, so they oversaturated the media with their stars. I don't want to be in magazines every week and on the Internet everyday. I don't want to have people get completely sick of me before I've ever even done something legitimate." Still, Fox, whose resemblance to the actress Angelina Jolie has often been noted by reporters, has admitted that she has contributed greatly to the hype. "When I sit down to talk to men's magazines, there's a certain character that I play," Fox told Hirschberg. "There's something so ridiculous about always being in your underwear in those magazines, and you know the interview is going to run [next to] those pictures." Hirschberg opined, "She seems to think that her constant references to sex are a kind of feminist stance, that while she may seem like a headline-seeking provocateur, she is simply navigating a complex and chauvinistic world."

In June 2010 Fox married Brian Austin Green, a fellow actor best known for his role in the show *Beverly Hills, 90210*. Previously, the couple's rocky relationship had been constant sources of speculation for the tabloid press.

—M.M.

Suggested Reading: *Chicago Sun-Times* (on-line) Sep. 17, 2009; (London) *Guardian* Guide Section p8 Oct. 31, 2009; *New York Times Magazine* p57+ Nov. 15, 2009; *Nylon* (on-line) Sep. 26, 2009; *Salon* (on-line) Sep. 18, 2009; *San Francisco Chronicle* (on-line) Feb. 20, 2004

Selected Films: *Holiday in the Sun*, 2001; *Bad Boys II*, 2003; *Confessions of a Teenage Drama Queen*, 2004; *Transformers*, 2007; *How to Lose Friends and Alienate People*, 2008; *Whore*, 2008; *Transformers: Revenge of the Fallen*, 2009; *Jennifer's Body*, 2009; *Jonah Hex*, 2010; *Passion Play*, 2010

Selected Television Shows: *Ocean Ave.*, 2003; *What I Like About You*, 2003; *Two and a Half Men*, 2004; *Hope & Faith*, 2004–06

Fujii, Satoko

Oct. 9, 1958– Jazz pianist; composer

Address: c/o North Country Distributors, Cadence Bldg., Redwood, NY 13679

"Everyone has a different definition of jazz. I use the word 'jazz' for music that has improvisation and also can include any culture and can develop all the time," the pianist and composer Satoko Fujii told Fred Jung, in an undated interview for the alternative on-line publication *Jazz Weekly*. "'Jazz' is not the thing that we can see in a museum. With this definition, jazz is life and life is jazz." As a member of several major ensembles and with more than 50 albums in her discography, Fujii is one of the most prolific Japanese jazz artists of all time. She is also one of the most versatile, performing everything from avant-garde jazz-rock to original,

Valerie Trucchia, courtesy of Satoko Fujii

Satoko Fujii

jazz-tinged interpretations of traditional Japanese folk music. "Satoko Fujii is a rare breed," Kurt Gottschalk wrote for allaboutjazz.com (July 20, 2007). "The pianist and composer manages to continually defy expectations while remaining solid and eminently musical in her work."

Satoko Fujii was born on October 9, 1958 in Tokyo, Japan. In an interview for allaboutjazz.com (January 1, 2001), she told Wayne Zade, "I was very shy when I was little and was never comfortable playing outside with other kids. I spent all day long with my mother inside. She is a music lover, who likes classical music and some world music like Italian songs and Argentinian tango. Because of her taste, the first music that I listened to was very dramatic and passionate music." Fujii took classical-piano lessons from the age of four until she was 20, when she came to the realization that rigid classical training had diminished her childhood knack for improvisation. "I began to feel that classical music was not the [art] for me," she recalled to Jung. "I was like a well-trained dog that can do anything that [it has been] told to do, but cannot do anything by [its] own decision." She continued, "I wanted to create something from my heart not by music paper that had been written by somebody else. So that was the reason that I became interested in playing jazz improvisation."

Two of Fujii's teachers, Koji Taku and Fumio Itabashi, were essential to her development as a musician. Taku, the chair of the classical-piano department at a Tokyo arts college, had quit his post at the age of 60 to perform jazz at various local venues. "It was not the usual thing that people in Japan do," Fujii told Zade. "But he didn't care about his status in society—he just followed his feeling. I

was so impressed with the example of his life. I never went on to the conservatory because of his influence. I began to listen to jazz because I wanted to see why he was so into it. I listened to a jazz program on FM radio, and was knocked out by [the John Coltrane album] *A Love Supreme*. That was a great experience for me, to be so moved by something that I could not understand." Fujii soon began performing in Tokyo cabarets as a house pianist, covering the music of Count Basie and Duke Ellington, among others.

In 1985 Fujii moved to the U.S., to enroll at the Berklee College of Music, in Boston, Massachusetts. There, she was taught by the jazz artists Herb Pomeroy and Bill Pierce and earned a scholarship during her second semester. After graduating, magna cum laude, in 1987, Fujii returned to Japan, where she played at Tokyo jazz clubs and taught at the Yamaha Music School. After spending six years there, she returned to the U.S. to complete her graduate studies at the New England Conservatory of Music, in Boston. Her teachers there included George Russell, Cecil McBee, and Paul Bley. Bley, a pioneer of free-jazz piano playing, had a particularly large impact on Fujii.

Fujii received a diploma in jazz performance from the New England Conservatory in 1996 and subsequently moved to New York City. She made her recording debut with *Something About Water*, on which Bley contributed to eight of the 11 tracks. (Sources vary as to the release dates of many of Fujii's recordings; *Something About Water*, for example, is listed sometimes as a 1995 album and sometimes as a 1996 recording.) In a review for allaboutjazz.com (May 8, 2008), Budd Kopman wrote, "While this release can be considered her debut recording, it is a fully mature effort where teacher and student interact as equals."

Fujii's next U.S. release was *Indication* (1996). Six of the nine solo tracks on the recording were composed by Fujii, and the album also included her interpretation of a traditional Japanese folk song, "Itsuki no Komoriuta." In a review for *Jazz Times* (December 1997, on-line), Marcela Breton wrote, "Fujii's intros are stately and her approach frequently meditative. . . . She can also startle, though, with sudden, unpredictable changes." In 1997 Fujii and her husband, Natsuki Tamura, a trumpet player, recorded an album of duets, *How Many?* That marked the first of numerous collaborations between the pair. Steve Loewy wrote for the All Music Guide Web site, "Tamura seems stimulated by the virtuosic jabs and undercurrents of Fujii, as the trumpeter covers a wide range of technical and emotional ground. . . . His alternatively weeping, muttering, and wailing blather seem to fit perfectly against Fujii's more traditional approach."

In 1997 Fujii also recorded *South Wind*, an album of original songs performed with a 15-piece orchestra she had put together in New York City the year before. (The group is sometimes referred to as the Satoko Fujii Orchestra West, as Fujii also leads the Satoko Fujii Orchestra East, based in Japan.) Thom Jurek wrote for the All Music Guide Web site that Fujii had created "a palette from which the lines between improvisation and written script blur, and then fade altogether." He continued, "It's not just a bunch of improvisers blowing each other out of the chart, but whistling themselves—and their section members—through them. The texts are adventurous but playful, and austere yet lush in others. This is first-rate big band music." That year Fujii also released the album *Looking Out My Window*, with Mark Dresser and Jim Black. The editors of the magazines *Coda* and *Jazziz* selected *Looking Out My Window* as one of the top 10 albums of the year.

In 1999 Fujii released *Kitsune-Bi*, an album of pieces performed with the soprano saxophonist Sachi Hayasaka, Dresser, and Black. (The Japanese word *kitsune* refers to a fox, generally in the context of folklore or myth. The title of the album can be loosely translated as "Fox Fire.") In a *Jazziz* review from 2000, as posted on Amazon.com, William Stephenson wrote, "Fujii is an instrumentalist in the joyfully aggressive mode of [the free-jazz innovator] Cecil Taylor. She can tear into even the most deftly packaged melody the way a child tears into a brightly wrapped birthday present: headlong, hungry, unstoppable. Also like Taylor, she requires of her accompanists equal parts sensitivity and adventurousness." That year Fujii also released *Past Life*, recorded with a Japanese sextet she had formed in the mid-1990s.

In 2000 Fujii released multiple albums, including *Jo*, which merged traditional Japanese folk with avant-garde jazz, funk, and rock. She explained her late-blooming interest in the music of her native country to Zade: "In Japan, we don't have that many opportunities to listen to Japanese music. This is very sad and it's not right. After the Meiji period [from 1868 to 1912, when the emperor Meiji the Great held power], the government set the school music program and we [studied] Western music mainly. Besides that, most music on TV and radio in Japan is Western music. For many Japanese, Japanese music sounds very exotic." She added that after being urged by an American musician to listen to more Japanese music, she was "very excited" by it—"more than 'very' excited. It felt different in my heart and soul when I listened to it."

Among Fujii's acclaimed 2000 releases was *Double Take*, with her two orchestras on separate discs: the "East" incarnation recorded live in Okegawa, Japan, and the New York–based "West" group recorded its contribution in a studio. Her husband played the trumpet on three tracks. Some critics, while lavishing praise on the double album as a whole, noted a disconnect between the two orchestras. Bob Blumenthal wrote for the *Boston Globe* (July 28, 2000), "The New York edition is filled with more familiar names, but the Japanese crew sounds more like a unit. Should we draw cultural conclusions from this, credit the different re-

cording circumstances, . . . or simply allow that the Tokyo unit apparently had more time with the music?" Martin Wisckol wrote for the *Orange County (California) Register* (July 28, 2000), "It's remarkable how strong the Japanese are—but for this Yankee's dollar, the West unit is more distinctive and forward looking."

In 2001 Fujii released an album with the violinist Mark Feldman entitled *April Shower*, as well as another trio outing, *Junction*. She and her husband also teamed up with members of the jazz-infused progressive rock band Ruins to create the Satoko Fujii Quartet, which recorded *Vulcan*, an album of free-form jazz and rock. Jim Santella wrote for allaboutjazz.com (January 1, 2002): "[Takeharu] Hayakawa's fuzzy electric bass and [drummer Tatsuya] Yoshida's rock beat power the quartet beyond accepted jazz limits. Several times, Fujii stops the action with piano interludes that provide a quiet oasis. Then, the four-pronged high-energy action continues. By moving consistently in and out of the mainstream, Satoko Fujii continues to be one of the most creative voices in contemporary jazz." In 2002 Fujii and her trio released *Bell the Cat!* Another collaboration with her husband, *Clouds*, was also released that year, as well as *Minerva*, her second album with the quartet from *Vulcan*. The following year Fujii's "East" orchestra released the album *Before the Dawn*, and the "West" orchestra came out with *The Future of the Past*.

In 2004 Fujii's third album with her *Vulcan* quartet, *Zephyros*, was released to critical acclaim, and she toured Europe with the group OrkestRova in support of its album *An Alligator in Your Wallet*, on which she performed. She then released her first solo album in a decade, *Sketches*, which was praised by jazz critics. Wisckol described it for the *Orange County Register* (July 18, 2004) as "a moody, dramatically unfurling adventure in postmodern piano improvisation," and Jim Santella wrote for allaboutjazz.com (July 3, 2004), "By employing repetition with each turn of ideas, the artist provides acceptable foundations upon which to build. Hence, the session turns out quite accessible. Fujii's sketches tour the spectrum of natural wonders, from loud depths of darkness to soft cascades that flow like water." That year also saw the release of Fujii's New York orchestra's *Blueprint* and her Nagoya orchestra's debut recording, *Nagoyanian*. (The Nagoya group is an offshoot of the "East" orchestra.) Reviewing the latter album for allaboutjazz.com (January 29, 2005), Eyal Hareuveni wrote, "The U.S.-based West Orchestra is more imbued in the great tradition of jazz and blues and may be more open rhythmically, but this stormy version of the East Orchestra brings forth Fujii as a unique composer who can turn compositions upside down and always find deep and exciting nuances in them."

Fujii continued to record prolifically. In 2005 she played on *In the Tank*, a collaborative improv album featuring Tamura, the guitarist and saxophonist Elliott Sharp, and the guitarist Takayuki

Kato. She also took part in a three-musician collaboration for the album *Yamabuki*, with the accordionist Ted Reichman and folk vocalist Koh Yamabuki. In 2006 the Satoko Fujii Four (Fujii, Dresser, Black, and Tamura) released *When We Were There*, and the album *Fragment* introduced a new trio named Junk Box, which included Tamura and the drummer John Hollenbeck.

In 2007 Fujii joined with Tamura, the trumpeter Angelo Verploegen, and the pianist Misha Mengelberg to form Double Duo, which released the album *Crossword Puzzle*. That year Fujii's eponymous quartet also released the album *Bacchus*, and she delved further into traditional Japanese music with a new group, the Min-Yoh Ensemble, with Tamura on trumpet, Curtis Hasselbring on trombone, and Andrea Parkins on accordion. Of their album *Fujin Raijin*, Dan McClenaghan wrote for allaboutjazz.com (May 26, 2007), "As with every new ensemble Fujii forms, the listener encounters things they've never heard before—calamitous sonic assaults beside gentle yet insistent pushes that are always taking the listener, by force or guile, to new places."

Among Fujii's most recent releases are *Trace a River* (2008), recorded with her eponymous trio; *Cloudy Then Sunny* (2008), with Junk Box; *Under the Water* (2009), with the pianist Myra Melford; *Kuroi Kawa–Black River* (2009), with the violinist Carla Kihlstedt; *Desert Ship* (2010), with the acoustic quartet Ma-Do; *Cut the Rope* (2010), with the newly formed quartet First Meeting, which includes her husband, the drummer Tatsuhisa Yamamoto, and the guitarist Kelly Churko; and *Zakopane* (2010), recorded with the orchestra in Tokyo. Also in 2010 Fujii performed three tracks on the album *All Kinds of People: Love Burt Bacharach*, produced by Jim O'Rourke for the B.J.L. label, and she contributed to the Raymond MacDonald International Big Band's album *Buddy*. Starting in January 2011 Fujii was to serve as the artist-in-residence at the Montalvo Arts Center, in Saratoga, California.

Fujii is a regular member of her husband's acoustic quartet, Gato Libre, playing both piano and accordion in the group. Fujii and Tamura met in 1985, when Fujii was working as a house pianist at a Tokyo cabaret. Fujii told Don Williamson for *Jazz Review* (on-line), "Natsuki [Tamura] and I both think we can derive inspiration from anything when we want to make music."

—W.D.

Suggested Reading: allaboutjazz.com; *Boston Herald* (on-line) Apr. 21, 2002; *Los Angeles Times* (on-line) May 6, 2002; *New York Times* (on-line) Nov. 12, 2007; *Seattle Times* (on-line) June 30, 2005; *Washington Post* (on-line) Mar. 13, 2000

Selected Recordings: *Something About Water*, 1995; *Indication*, 1996; *How Many?*, 1997, *South Wind*, 1997; *Looking Out My Window*, 1997;

Kitsune-Bi, 1999; *Past Life*, 1999; *Jo*, 2000; *Double Take*, 2000; *April Shower*, 2001; *Junction*, 2001; *Vulcan*, 2001; *Clouds*, 2002; *Bell the Cat!*, 2002; *Sketches*, 2004; *Nagoyanian*, 2004; *In the Tank*, 2005; *Yamabuki*, 2005; *Blueprint*, 2005; *When We Were There*, 2006; *Fragment* (with Junk Box), 2006; *Bacchus*, 2007; *Trace a River*, 2008; *Cloudy Then Sunny* (with Junk Box), 2008; *Sanrei*, 2008; *Summer Suite*, 2008; *Under the Water* (with Myra Melford), 2009; *Kuroi Kawa–Black River*, 2009; *Desert Ship*, 2010; *Cut the Rope* (with First Meeting), 2010; *Zakopane*, 2010

Pete Souza, courtesy of the White House

Gaspard, Patrick

1967– White House director of political affairs

Address: Office of Political Affairs, The White House, 1600 Pennsylvania Ave., N.W., Washington, DC 20500

Patrick Gaspard "may very well be the most brilliant strategist and organizer you have never heard of," Sam Stein wrote for the *Huffington Post* (December 4, 2008, on-line). As director of the office of political affairs in the administration of President Barack Obama, Gaspard—who works behind the scenes, avoiding the limelight—is widely considered to be one of the most powerful men in the White House. Since he took that position, upon Obama's inauguration as president, on January 20, 2009, Gaspard has been hailed by his peers in the White House for "persevering in an impossible role" and for finding "his niche as the clearinghouse for information, the liaison to Democratic campaigns and the gateway to the grassroots and labor organizations where he got his political start," Anne E. Kornblut and Jason Horowitz wrote for the *Washington Post* (November 2, 2009). Like Obama, Gaspard began his career as a community organizer and comes from a family with recent ties to Africa. He gained his first political experience as a member of the Reverend Jesse Jackson's 1988 presidential campaign; the following year he worked on the historic campaign of David Dinkins, who became the first African-American mayor of New York. In the 1990s Gaspard emerged as one of the top political strategists in that city, working on Manhattan borough president Ruth Messinger's ultimately unsuccessful mayoral campaign against Rudolph Giuliani in 1997, then serving as chief of staff to city-council member Margarita Lopez, while remaining heavily involved in grassroots organizing. In 1999 he became executive vice president for political and legislative affairs with New York's 1199 SEIU United Health Care Workers East, the nation's largest local union, and played a central role the same year in its "March for Justice" demonstration against police brutality, in the wake of the fatal police shooting of an unarmed 22-year-old Guinean immigrant, Amadou Diallo. Gaspard went on to serve as a registered lobbyist for the union, fighting for health-care and education benefits for members. In 2003 he worked as the deputy national field director for Howard Dean's presidential campaign, and he later served as the national field director for America Coming Together (ACT), a liberal political-action committee (PAC) dedicated to getting out the Democratic vote. In 2006 Gaspard was the acting political director of SEIU International and contributed to Democratic victories in national and local races across the country, as part of the union's successful effort to help Democrats recapture the congressional majority. He next signed on with the Obama campaign, in mid-2008. "President Obama and I met with him and really liked him, because he wasn't your traditional political schmoozer," David Plouffe, Obama's campaign manager, recalled to Jason Horowtiz for the *New York Observer* (June 23, 2009, on-line). "There was a depth to him that we found attractive." Plouffe told Kornblut and Horowitz, "He's got a great dry and ironic sense of humor. He's the kind of guy who's very calm even during a crisis. He doesn't go off the handle—and provides a good balance there. He's very Obamalike in that regard."

Patrick H. Gaspard was born in 1967 in Kinshasa, the capital and largest city of the Democratic Republic of the Congo (known from 1971 until 1997 as Zaire). His parents, who came from Haiti, were unhappy under the dictatorship of François Duvalier, who ruled that country from 1957 until his death, in 1971; they fled to the newly independent Congo when Patrice Lumumba, the country's first and only elected prime minister, invited French-speaking academics of African descent to teach there. (Lumumba was assassinated on January 17, 1961, 200 days after he took office.) Gaspard immigrated with his parents to the United States at the age of three. He was raised, along with his brother, Michael, in the New York City boroughs of Manhattan and Queens. At an early age Gaspard developed a deep interest in Haitian culture and politics and subsequently became drawn to such political radicals as Aimé Césaire, an anticolonialist, Martinique-born poet and politician and the author of a biography of the Haitian revolutionary Toussaint L'Ouverture. Gaspard graduated from Brooklyn Technical High School and briefly attended the School of Visual Arts, a college in Manhattan, before leaving to pursue a career in politics.

Gaspard worked in the mid-1980s as a community organizer. His early efforts included staging demonstrations throughout New York City on behalf of Haitian causes. He cut his teeth on the campaign trail in 1988, while working on the presidential campaign of the Reverend Jesse Jackson, who ran unsuccessfully for the Democratic nomination for president. Gaspard's zeal soon caught the attention of the Harlem, New York–based political consultant Bill Lynch, who recruited him to work the following year on then–Manhattan borough president David Dinkins's first mayoral race. During Dinkins's campaign, which led to his becoming New York City's first African-American mayor, Gaspard "poured himself into behind-the-scenes work, making inroads with different constituencies and offering strategic advice when needed," Sam Stein noted. He remained with the Dinkins administration until 1993, when the Republican Rudolph Giuliani won the New York mayoralty. While Dinkins's tenure was marked by a rise in crime and a deteriorating economy, Gaspard was praised for his handling of administrative affairs. "He has great instincts," Dinkins recalled to Stein. "You were not apt to find him beating his chest and talking about how great a job he did. But anyone who worked for him would make that observation for him." Dinkins said to Horowitz, "He was smart and loyal and really knew his way around."

After leaving City Hall, Gaspard attended Columbia University's School of General Studies, an undergraduate program designed for older, nontraditional students. He studied there from the fall of 1994 until the spring of 1997, leaving without receiving a degree. Gaspard remained steeped in New York politics and organizing throughout the 1990s. In 1995 he worked as an organizer for the New Party, a left-leaning political coalition based in Brooklyn, New York. (Obama, who ran successfully for a seat in the Illinois state Senate the following year, reportedly joined the group at around the same time.) Two years later Gaspard signed on with the outgoing Manhattan borough president, Ruth Messinger, to work on her mayoral campaign against Rudolph Giuliani. In 1999 he became chief of staff to city councilwoman Margarita Lopez, a radical feminist and one of the most outspoken critics of the Giuliani administration. Lopez, noting that the wrong conclusions might be drawn from Gaspard's squeaky-clean lifestyle (he abstains not only from alcohol but even from caffeinated soft drinks), told Horowtiz, "Don't be mistaken about him being a gentleman—don't even go there. When a situation got to a point that there was no resolution I would reach Patrick and say, 'Go for it, and bring me no hostages, this battle is going to be won with no hostages.' And I can tell you Patrick delivered every single time."

In 1999, while Gaspard was working for Lopez, a 22-year-old, unarmed Guinean immigrant named Amadou Diallo was gunned down by four plain-clothes New York City police officers who were searching for an armed serial rapist; fired at 41 times, Diallo was struck by 19 bullets. The subsequent acquittal of the four officers on charges of murder resulted in protest demonstrations all over the city. At that time Lopez had Gaspard help Local 1199 of the Service Employees International Union (SEIU) to organize a march to condemn the shooting. He went on to organize and coordinate the union's "March for Justice" demonstration against police brutality, which brought together a slew of prominent politicians, activists, religious officials, and celebrities. (Diallo's family received a $3 million settlement from the city in March 2004.) Later that year Gaspard was named SEIU's Local 1199 executive vice president for politics and legislation. "He knows what buttons to push and in what order," Jennifer Cunningham, then the union's political director, explained to Horowitz.

While coordinating political activity and government relations for SEIU 1119—which has more than 300,000 members—Gaspard remained active in other political endeavors. In 2003 he served as the acting field director for the presidential campaign of Howard Dean, then the governor of Vermont. When Dean dropped out of the race, in early 2004, Gaspard became the national field director for America Coming Together, a liberal PAC dedicated to get-out-the-vote efforts on behalf of Democratic candidates; the group was founded by the Hungarian-American investor and activist George Soros. As national field director Gaspard was responsible for overseeing officials in every state and helped direct the day-to-day operations of a staff that numbered in the thousands. Gaspard's efforts with ACT were credited with contributing to the solid showing by U.S. senator John Kerry of Massachusetts in the 2004 presidential election, in which he gained 48 percent of the popular vote to President George W. Bush's 51 percent. Steve Rosenthal, ACT's director, told Stein about Gaspard, "He is extremely close to his kids and . . . his wife. Getting him to leave New York to join us was a very big get. But he did it at an enormous sacrifice." In 2006 Gaspard served as the acting political director of SEIU International, which helped Democrats to regain a majority in both houses of Congress in that year's elections.

In early 2007 Gaspard was asked by Barack Obama, then a U.S. senator from Illinois, to join his presidential campaign; in that now-famous ex-change, as Ryan Lizza reported for the *New Yorker* (November 17, 2008), Obama's invitation came with a warning: "I think that I'm a better speech-writer than my speechwriters. I know more about policies on any particular issue than my policy directors. And I'll tell you right now that I'm gonna think I'm a better political director than my political director." Gaspard turned down the offer, instead working on state and local races for 1199-favored candidates in New York. But in June 2008, once Obama had all but officially become the Democratic nominee, Gaspard joined the senator's campaign as political director, taking a leave of absence from his union job. His behind-the-scenes efforts at holding together different groups and constituencies were widely credited with helping Obama run a smooth campaign. "He was dealing with politicians and political organizations from very high-ranking people down the line, all around the country," David Axelrod, Obama's chief strategist, explained to Stein. "So it is fair to say that he had a lot of headaches from morning to night because you can never please everybody. . . . Patrick was, I thought, incredibly deft at making the right judgments and enforcing the right decisions and doing it all in the spirit of our campaign."

On November 4, 2008 Obama was elected the 44th president of the United States, winning 365 electoral votes to John McCain's 173. Afterward Gaspard was put in charge of political affairs for Obama's transition team. On November 21, 2008 he was named political director; he officially took on that position in January 2009. As the director of the Office of Political Affairs, which was established during President Ronald Reagan's administration, Gaspard is responsible for providing the president with "an accurate assessment of the political dynamics affecting the work of his administration, supporting the advancement of his agenda, and ensuring that the White House understands the priorities of and remains in close contact with Americans across the nation," as stated on the White House Web site. Gaspard's low-key demeanor and behind-the-scenes approach stand in stark contrast to the high-profile antics of former White House political directors including Ed Rollins, Rahm Emanuel, and Karl Rove; he rarely grants interviews to the media, and he has been known to downplay his role in the campaigns of others. Horowitz observed that he "is at his most comfortable making his presence felt without actually being seen." In addition to his humility, Gaspard's political acumen has been highly praised. Kevin Sheekey, deputy mayor for government relations for New York City mayor Michael Bloomberg, told Stein, "Patrick is the best political mind of his generation in New York and maybe the nation." Axelrod said to the same writer, "He is one of the most impactful people I have ever met in politics." Jim Messina, the White House deputy chief of staff, told Kornblut and Horowitz, "Patrick has a personality that is such that everyone likes him and respects him. He's one of the most grounded people I've ever met."

Since he became President Obama's political director, Gaspard has wielded his influence to shape the outcome of several important Democratic races. In 2009 he orchestrated key endorsements for Democratic candidates in the gubernatorial races in Virginia and New Jersey, though to limited effect (Republicans won both races). He then played a major behind-the-scenes role in the special election in New York's 23rd Congressional District, when he persuaded the Republican state assemblywoman Dede Scozzafaza to endorse the Democrat Bill Owens rather than the conservative third-party candidate, Doug Hoffman, who received heavy support from right-wing Republicans, including Sarah Palin. Owens captured that House seat.

On January 19, 2010 the Republican Scott Brown defeated the Democrat Martha Coakley, Massachusetts's attorney general, in the special election to fill the U.S. Senate seat of Edward M. Kennedy, a Democrat, who had died in August 2009 after a long struggle with brain cancer. Prior to his death, Kennedy—a longtime advocate of health-care reform—had showed unbending support for Obama's health-care legislation. Coakley's loss to Brown, an avid opponent of health-care reform, ended the Democrats' filibuster-proof majority in the Senate and thus put the legislation in peril. Those events took place in the aftermath of the 7.3-magnitude earthquake that devastated Gaspard's family's homeland, Haiti, a week before. Despite being deeply distraught over that situation, Gaspard traveled to Boston with President Obama a few days before Coakley's loss to Brown in an effort to resurrect her campaign; despite her loss, Obama's landmark health-care bill was signed into law on March 23, 2010. Gaspard has continued to play a part in gubernatorial, Senate, and House races across the country that are vital to Obama's political agenda. An organizer for the Democratic National Committee (DNC), commenting on Gaspard's approach to his work, told Dayo Olopade for the *Daily Beast* (May 12, 2010, on-line), "He builds relationships; he puts out fires; he identifies fires when they're about to start; he's a sounding board for the president whenever something is happening. And he's just never rattled."

Gaspard is married and has two children. He and his family reside in the nation's capital, after living for years in the Park Slope section of Brooklyn. An avid jogger and comic-book collector, Gaspard enjoys writing poetry and reading Russian literature in his spare time.

—C.C.

Suggested Reading: *Huffington Post* (on-line) Dec. 4, 2008; *Journal of Blacks in Higher Education* Fall 2009; *New York Observer* (on-line) June 23, 2009; *Washington Post* C p3 Mar. 30, 2009, C p1 Nov. 2, 2009, C p1 Jan. 19, 2010; WhoRunsGov.com

Geha, Marla

(GEE-ha)

Dec. 10, 1973– Astronomer; astrophysicist; educator

Address: Dept. of Astronomy, Yale University, P.O. Box 208101, New Haven, CT 06520-8101

Marla Geha is an observational astronomer who studies dwarf galaxies—galaxies that are 1/10th the size of the Milky Way (the galaxy that contains our solar system) or smaller. In particular, Geha studies the behavior of satellite dwarf galaxies, which are gravitationally bound to the Milky Way and orbit it. There are many theories, or models, that purport to explain how dwarf galaxies and everything else in the universe came to be, each based on many thousands of observations. Among those theories, the cold-dark-matter (CDM) model provides the best picture of the universe as it appears today. Also known as the Standard Model, the CDM model is a refinement of the Big Bang theory, which proposes that the universe formed nearly 14 billion years ago from an infinitely dense, unimaginably hot entity smaller than all known atomic particles, and that since it exploded into being, it has never stopped expanding. Computer simulations based on the CDM model have delineated with remarkable accuracy the events that occurred after the Big Bang, as manifested by what is detectable in the known universe. In such computer simulations "you can actually see galaxies form and structure a universe that looks really similar to what we see, at least for massive galaxies," Geha said in an interview with *Current Biography*, the source of quotes in this article unless otherwise noted. According to the CDM model, about 90 percent of the universe is composed of cold dark matter, an invisible material that neither emits light nor has magnetic or electromagnetic properties and whose existence is deduced from measurements of visible matter and radiation. Dark matter is "literally the stuff we don't see," Geha explained to Rick Sandella for the *New Haven (Connecticut) Register* (October 19, 2009). "It's not made of protons and electrons that we're used to. It's made of something that we don't know what it is yet. . . . But it's matter. It has mass, it has gravity, all the same physics as regular matter." The presence of cold dark matter explains (theoretically) why the measurable characteristics of galaxies—their masses, rotational speeds, gravitational pull, and temperatures—indicate that those galaxies are significantly larger than they were thought to be accord-

Andrew Geha, courtesy of Marla Geha

Marla Geha

ing to estimates based on the sum of each individual star's estimated mass. The CDM model also makes the case that there are several hundred or as many as 1,000 satellite dwarf galaxies orbiting the Milky Way. Until 2005, though, astronomers had detected only 11. The difference between the known 11 and the theoretical hundreds, the "missing satellite problem," has long been the largest discrepancy between the predictions of the CDM model and the known reality.

An assistant professor of astronomy at Yale University, in New Haven, Connecticut, since late 2007, Geha has made discoveries that may account for that discrepancy. Working since early 2007 with Joshua Simon, currently a Millikan postdoctoral scholar at the California Institute of Technology, she found evidence that the Milky Way may be orbited by hundreds of slow-moving ultra-faint dwarf galaxies, so-called because of the relatively small number of stars and (presumably) the large amount of dark matter within them. Using data from the Sloan Digital Sky Survey—an ongoing project to photograph about one-fifth of the observable sky digitally—as well as images they obtained while working at the W. M. Keck Observatory, in Hawaii, Geha and Simon have identified 12 additional ultra-faint dwarf galaxies orbiting the Milky Way. Geha and Simon published their findings in the November 10, 2007 issue of the *Astrophysical Journal*, in a paper entitled "Kinematics of the Ultra-Faint Milky Way Satellites: Solving the Missing Satellite Problem." Their discoveries have provided significant support for the notion of a universe dominated by dark matter, as the CDM model suggests. They have also led some astronomers to theorize that many more ultra-faint galaxies—and

possibly another type of galaxy, composed entirely of dark matter—are orbiting the Milky Way. "We do think that we're measuring the masses of these very small objects correctly. . . . We think we're seeing . . . the limits of galaxy formation, that we're seeing the smallest galaxies that we know of. And in fact galaxies can't form much smaller, much fainter than that," Geha said in a videotaped lecture she delivered on April 18, 2009 at the Tilde Cafe in Branford, Connecticut, as posted on YouTube.com. "And so these objects, these ultra-faint dwarf galaxies, are giving us information both about how galaxies form and . . . about dark matter and how much there is and what it actually is."

Marla Catherine Geha was born on December 10, 1973 to a physician (who died several years ago) and his wife, an executive with a nonprofit organization. She was raised in Springfield, Massachusetts, with one sibling, a brother. Drawn to science from an early age, Geha briefly envisioned a career as an astronaut after watching the televised space-shuttle launches in the early 1980s. "Somehow, also early, I realized that I was too short or I was too something to actually be an astronaut and that astronomer or astrophysics was a good second choice," she said. With those goals in mind, she took courses in physics in high school and majored in engineering and physics at Cornell University, in Ithaca, New York, "always with an eye toward doing research in astrophysics," she said. Like many undergraduate science programs at that time, Cornell's physics program offered very few opportunities for independent research. One summer, eager to engage in hands-on astronomy research "instead of doing some very dull job," in her words, Geha, on her own initiative, arranged to conduct research under the guidance of James R. "Jim" Houck. A professor of astronomy at Cornell, Houck was a pioneer in the use of mid-infrared spectrometers in astronomy—tools used to measure the physical characteristics of objects in space, ranging from planets to galaxies. Geha and Houck worked on building "a little camera to put on the telescope that was on campus," Geha said. During her last year at Cornell, Geha served as a teaching assistant for an engineering class in computer instrumentation. During the years 1993 and 1995, in the latter of which she earned a B.S. degree, she held Cornell's Academic Excellence Scholarships.

Geha applied to graduate programs only in the southwestern U.S. She won acceptance to New Mexico State University, in Las Cruces, where she studied the ages and chemistries of the stars in the Large Megallanic Cloud, one of the largest dwarf galaxies that orbit the Milky Way and one of only two dwarf galaxies that can be seen from Earth with the naked eye (but, like the other, the Small Megallanic Cloud, only in the Southern Hemisphere). "That [work] definitely got me interested in and moving in the direction of thinking about dwarf galaxies," Geha said. After obtaining her master's degree, in 1998, Geha spent a year as a researcher at the Lawrence Livermore National Laboratory (LLNL), in San Francisco, California. She was assigned to work with the astrophysicist and astronomer Charles Alcock on the MACHO project, a collaboration between scientists at the Mt. Stromblo and Siding Spring Observatories, in Australia, and the Center for Particle Astrophysics at the University of California. The focus of that project was to test the hypothesis that dark matter in the Milky Way is made up of so-called massive compact halo objects (hence the acronym MACHO), including partially formed planets or other celestial objects "that are dark and fairly compact," as Geha put it. Geha and an LLNL research team used a process called microlensing, which involves measuring characteristics of light emitted from a star as it passes around another object's gravitational field. The project ended up disproving the hypothesis. "You can't explain all the dark matter based on dead stars and that kind of stuff . . . ," Geha said. "That's why [astronomers] move on to these really kind of weird and exotic possibilities —that dark matter is some kind of new particle, some sort of physical particle."

Geha then entered a Ph.D. program in astronomy and astrophysics at the University of California at Santa Cruz, where she worked with the astronomer Raja Guhathakurta, whose specialty is dwarf galaxies. For her dissertation, "Kinematics of Dwarf Elliptical Galaxies," Geha studied the movement of stars in dwarf elliptical galaxies—dwarf galaxies that have little or no dust or gas and show little or no evidence of star formation. "Galaxies come basically in two flavors: ones that have gas and ones that don't . . . ," Geha said. "So the ones that have gas are forming stars, they're active, they're creating new generations of stars. The ones that don't have gas are basically dead. The stars that you see are the stars that you get, and that's it. And the idea is that we find these things that don't have gas near big things, like big galaxies. We see galaxies without gas around the Milky Way, but we don't see them off in isolation by themselves, and the idea is that the big galaxies have stripped the gas out of the little ones, and that's why they can't make any stars on their own." In order to better understand the stars in the elliptical galaxies, Geha measured how fast the stars were moving, using a method called spectroscopy, which involves observing a Doppler shift in the wavelength of light being emitted from the stars, arising from the relationship between their motion and Earth's motion. "If stars are moving, the wavelength of light will shift in proportion to how fast it's moving," Geha said. "It's the same idea as the Doppler shift for sounds—an ambulance siren changes pitch as it's moving towards [or] away from you." Once Geha obtained the velocities of individual stars, she used that data to calculate the mass of the galaxy itself (by means of a mathematical formula) and discern other characteristics. "If you know how massive a galaxy is, it gives you an understanding of how stars have formed, why stars aren't forming now. It gives you

a lot of information about the history of what happened [there]," Geha said. "Definitely my experience with my thesis—measuring the velocities of stars and these things—led directly into the work that I'm doing now on these ultra-faint galaxies around the Milky Way."

Geha completed her doctoral thesis while she was a Hubble Fellow at the Observatories of the Carnegie Institution of Washington, in Pasadena, California, from 2003 to 2006. There, she continued her research on the Milky Way's dwarf galaxies, in an attempt to resolve the "missing galaxy problem." In 2006 the Sloan Digital Sky Survey appeared to have uncovered the presence of 15 ultra-faint dwarf galaxies orbiting the Milky Way. "So the question is how in the world did we miss 15 galaxies around the Milky Way when we were searching for some so hard?" Geha said in her Tilde Cafe lecture. Geha and other astronomers theorized that one reason was that the light from the stars in the Milky Way was overwhelming the light being emitted from the smaller, fainter galaxies. In order to filter out the light from the Milky Way and observe the ultra-faint galaxies directly, Geha's research team used a process called reduction. In reduction, a hypothesis is made about the presence of an ultra-faint galaxy in a particular location in a digital image of the sky; then, a computer filters out nearby stars that do not have the color and brightness consistent with the predicted age and distance from Earth of the hypothesized galaxy. Using that technique with images from the Sloan Digital Sky Survey, researchers confirmed the presence of 14 clusters with several hundred stars of about the same age in each. The groups of stars were considered "candidate galaxies," because there was a possibility that the stars were not linked by gravity and were simply near one another.

"Other people have done this technique of filtering these images and finding the candidates," Geha told the audience at the Tilde Cafe, "and my research is to go and look at individual stars, measure their velocities and determine if this object is gravitationally bound and figure out what its mass is." In order to obtain those measurements, Geha had to view each star through a powerful telescope. In September 2006 Geha and Simon wrote a proposal to earn observation time at the Keck Telescope, in Hawaii. With a mirror 10 meters in diameter, the Keck Telescope has the largest lens in the world, and it is equipped with a deep imaging multi-object spectrograph (DEIMOS), the best available tool for measuring star velocity. Geha and Simon's proposal won them three consecutive nights of observation time at the telescope—nights in which the sky proved to be extremely clear. With the data she gathered on those nights, Geha figured out the velocities of the stars and then determined that in 12 of the candidate galaxies, stars were orbiting at the same velocity and thus were bound to one another by gravity. As of 2009 a total of 14 such galaxies had been identified.

GEHA

Although the galaxies Geha observed were both remarkably small and remarkably slow-moving—they were 1/1,000th to 1/10,000th the size of the Milky Way and were moving at about five kilometers per second (km/sec) rather than 200 km/sec, the speed of stars in the Milky Way—they were moving much faster than Geha had expected. Based on the galaxies' masses, Geha had expected the stars to be moving at about 1/10th their actual speed. "The fact that things are moving faster and yet they seem to be all bound together means there must be some kind of mass there that I'm not seeing," Geha said. "And this is where dark matter comes in." If the velocity measurements were accurate, Geha determined, the galaxies would have to be 100 to 1,000 times more massive than they appeared to be; that would be possible only if a substantial amount of dark matter were present. "For each of the galaxies we measure, as the galaxies get fainter and fainter, we need to have more and more dark matter," Geha said. The least luminous and most dark-matter-filled galaxy identified by Geha and Simon, called Segue 1, has only a few hundred stars—making it one billion times less bright than the Milky Way—and has nearly 1,000 times more mass than can be accounted for by that number of stars. To explain the existence of such ultra-faint galaxies, scientists have pointed to simulations of universe formation showing that the first stars created ultraviolet radiation and supernova blasts that appear to have pushed most of the hydrogen out of the dwarf galaxies, causing star production to cease within them and resulting in dark-matter-dominated galaxies.

Though Geha and Simon's findings are widely considered significant, some scientists have suggested that the stars' high velocities may have been caused by phenomena other than high concentrations of dark matter. "The velocities could be produced through interactions with other galaxies, or general tidal effects from M31 [the spiral galaxy nearest to the Milky Way] or the Milky Way," Christopher Conselice, an astronomer and astrophysicist at the University of Nottingham, in England, told *Sky & Telescope* (October 2007). "This is one of the major problems with interpreting these observations."

Geha's work has helped to bring the total number of observable satellite dwarf galaxies to about 24, and astronomers predict that once the Sloan Sky Survey is completed, that number will rise to 60 or 70. Because the Sloan Sky Survey's limited technology allows it to locate ultra-faint galaxies only up to a certain distance from Earth, astronomers will have to wait until the invention of more powerful technology to penetrate farther into space. With more advanced instruments, Geha and others have predicted, astronomers will detect about 200 or 300 ultra-faint dwarf galaxies. "Instead of having a missing satellite problem [as the 'missing galaxy problem' is also known], we probably have a missing satellite mild annoyance, where the numbers actually seem like they may in fact

line up," Geha told the Tilde Cafe audience. "We may actually have some need for dark galaxies that don't have any stars in them, but in fact we think we are seeing most of the things that the predictions suggest, and that our understanding of galaxy formation in these numerical simulations [associated with the CDM model] in fact may be correct and we can believe all of the results that are coming out of them." The information obtained by Geha and her colleagues has helped scientists refine their theories about how the universe began. Geha hopes that her research over the next few years—which will involve obtaining more accurate velocity and mass measurements for stars in the known dwarf galaxies and continuing to search for ultra-faint galaxies around the Milky Way—will continue to uncover mysteries about galaxy formation.

Scientists are also trying to find evidence for dark matter in other ways. "There's one idea that if dark matter is made out of a certain particle, occasionally, [the particles will] bump into each other," Geha said. "The particles will bump into each other and create a photon [a unit of light], which we can actually detect. And that photon, in the models, they tend to be very, very high-energy and you have to look in gamma rays to try and see them." Astronomers are currently using information gathered by satellites to detect gamma rays and then determine which gamma rays contain photons that might have resulted from collisions of dark-matter particles. In other investigations, scientists are attempting to observe dark-matter particles interacting with visible particles on Earth; one such experiment, called the Xenon Dark Matter Project, involves monitoring a quantity of the element xenon in its liquid form, to produce evidence of a dark-matter particle bumping into a stationary xenon atom. (Xenon, like helium and neon, is among the so-called noble gases; it is extremely unlikely to react with other elements.) The newly unveiled Large Hadron Collider (LHC), in Geneva, Switzerland—the world's largest particle accelerator—may allow scientists to see direct evidence of a dark-matter particle.

Since late 2007 Geha has been an assistant professor at Yale University. Previously she was an instructor at the University of Victoria, in British Columbia, Canada, and the California State Summer School for Mathematics and Science, which operates at four University of California campuses. In October 2009 *Popular Science* magazine named her one of its "Brilliant 10," the 10 brightest researchers younger than 40. In 2009 Geha married the travel writer Matthew Edward Polly. Polly's first book, *American Shaolin: Flying Kicks, Buddhist Monks, and the Legend of Iron Crotch: An Odyssey in the New China*, was a best-seller; he is currently working on his second book. Geha lives with her husband in New York City and New Haven. In her leisure time she enjoys surfing and practicing yoga.

—M.R.M.

Suggested Reading: *Discover Magazine* (on-line) Dec. 12, 2007; *Honolulu (Hawaii) Star* Sep. 12, 2007; M2 PressWIRE Sep. 18, 2008; *New Haven (Connecticut) Register* P p111 Oct. 19, 2009; *Popular Science* (on-line) Oct. 19, 2009; *Science Daily* (on-line) Sep. 17, 2007; *Sky & Telescope* p20+ Oct. 2007

Axel Schmidt/AFP/Getty Images

Gerwig, Greta

Aug. 4, 1983– Actress

Address: United Talent Agency, 9560 Wilshire Blvd., Suite 500, Beverly Hills, CA 90212

Writing for *Variety* (February 14, 2010, on-line) about Greta Gerwig's performance in the 2010 film *Greenberg*, Todd McCarthy observed that the independent-film actress "offers no perceptible performance in the popularly received sense; you don't detect impulse, calculation, yearning, hidden feelings or anything else beneath the surface. She just seems completely real, behaving the way people do, just reacting to things as they happen. Either she's a total natural—most likely—or she has the most invisible technique of any modern actor." That seemingly artless approach to acting has made Gerwig one of the independent-film world's top stars. She has appeared in several of the low-budget films that comprise the so-called "mumblecore" movement, which focuses on the ennui and social anxiety experienced by upper-middle-class recent college graduates. Gerwig's work in those movies, notable among them *Hannah Takes the Stairs* (2007) and *Nights and Weekends* (2008), has

made her the unofficial queen of that small film scene. "It's easy to see why Gerwig has become a favorite actress in the [mumblecore] scene," Raven Baker wrote for the Baltimore *City Paper* (April 30, 2008, on-line). "Tom-boy pretty, with an ingénue's wide eyes and sweet smile, she brings a laid-back quirkiness to her roles. Even when her characters are behaving very badly . . . she remains sympathetic and endearingly upbeat." Joan Anderman wrote for the *Boston Globe* (March 21, 2010, on-line), "Tall, blond, awkward, lovely—and unflinchingly, impossibly real—she's the scene's leading lady, queen of the improvised imbroglio, muse to a collective of twentysomething filmmakers ginning up small movies about complicated young people in complicated young love." Gerwig's role alongside Ben Stiller in the more mainstream dark comedy *Greenberg* has won her a wider audience and led critics to predict that she will make the transition from independent-film "it" girl to one of Hollywood's top young actresses.

Greta Gerwig was born on August 4, 1983 in Sacramento, California, and raised in that city's River Park neighborhood, where her parents—Christine, a nurse, and Gordon, who handles small-business loans—still live. In an interview with Baker, Gerwig described herself as having been "an activities kid," explaining, "I kind of thought I had ADD [attention deficit disorder], but my mom didn't want me to be on any medications so she signed me up for lots of stuff." As a girl Gerwig took dance classes at the Sacramento Ballet and with the dance group Celebration Arts. She later turned to acting, appearing in musicals at the Woodland Opera House and performing for a summer in Sacramento City College's Shakespeare in the Park production of *The Merry Wives of Windsor*. "I only said one word, but I memorized everybody else's lines," Gerwig told Marcus Crowder for the *Sacramento Bee* (March 22, 2010, on-line). She also appeared in plays at Sacramento's Jesuit High School and studied acting with Ed Claudio at the Actor's Workshop Theatre of Sacramento. "I worked with her all through high school and helped her with her college auditions, too," Claudio told Crowder. "She had it all the while, you could see that. You can't teach the talent, but you can give them opportunities to explore it. You teach them craft."

After she graduated from St. Francis High School, Gerwig studied English and philosophy at Columbia University's Barnard College, a women's liberal-arts institution in New York City. There, her professors encouraged her nascent interest in playwriting. "I got way more interested in writing plays than acting in them, although I never lost my love for acting," she recalled to Baker. She told Crowder, "It wasn't that I clearly wanted to act or clearly wanted to write. But I was pretty sure I wanted to be in the world of making stories." Gerwig decided to pursue acting after she appeared in the second film by the director Joe Swanberg, the 81-minute, low-budget ($3,000) independent mumblecore movie *LOL*, which was released in

2006. The film focuses on the impact of excessive Internet and cell-phone use on social relations; its three main characters, the recent college graduates Alex, Tim, and Chris, are unable to overcome their chat-room and camera-phone obsessions long enough to pursue real relationships with those around them. Gerwig was brought into the film by chance: her then-boyfriend, C. Mason Wells, played Chris, who is in a long-distance relationship, and Wells asked Gerwig if he could use a voice-mail message she had left on his phone as a message from Chris's girlfriend. Swanberg later expanded the role of the girlfriend and asked Gerwig to play the part via cell-phone photographs and conversations, which Gerwig supplied—long distance—to the Chicago-based production from her home in New York. *LOL* was relatively well-received, earning accolades at the South by Southwest (SXSW) Film Festival in Austin, Texas.

Mumblecore films are generally shot on small budgets and in the less-expensive medium of digital video. They also incorporate improvisation and feature the filmmakers or their friends in lead roles; their unscripted—sometimes inarticulate—dialogue makes for moments of spontaneity not common in Hollywood films. Baker wrote that the mumblecore scene is "so-named for the mush-mouth tendencies of the talk-heavy films" and made up of "a loose but highly interconnected network of young filmmakers working . . . to create naturalistic studies of relationships among educated, artsy twentysomethings." The films have occasionally been compared to the work of the director John Cassavetes, who pioneered independent film in the 1960s and '70s and employed cinema verité (or documentary-style) camera work and improvisation. They also reflect the exhibitionism associated with the social-networking Web sites MySpace and Facebook and the video-sharing site YouTube. Baker noted, "What distinguishes mumblecore from the contrived self-presentations of online social networks, however, are the unflinching, even unflattering, portrayals of characters. There are no clear heroes or villains in the films, and even the most likable characters come off as jerks at times. And while mumblecore flicks dwell on characters' failings to often humorous effect, there is little of the irony that marked films like [Kevin Smith's 1994 'slacker' film] *Clerks.* The films' hyperfocus on mundane matters—say, deciding whether or not to answer a call from an ex-boyfriend—acknowledges that even the most seemingly inconsequential action can have off-the-Richter-scale effects on one's life."

Gerwig met Swanberg in person only when both attended a screening of *LOL*, but she so impressed the director that he cast her as the title character in the 2007 film *Hannah Takes the Stairs*, which she also co-wrote with Swanberg and the actor Kent Osborne. (Additional material in the screenplay was provided by other cast members.) In that comedy-drama Hannah, a recent college graduate with an internship at a Chicago production company, shares an office with two writers, Matt and Paul, both of whom she pursues romantically. Meanwhile, she still has feelings for her former boyfriend, Mike. Throughout the film she contemplates her seemingly aimless existence and struggles to choose among the men in her life. The film featured a "who's who" of mumblecore personalities as Hannah's romantic interests, including Andrew Bujalski, the director of the breakout indie films *Funny Ha Ha* (2002) and *Mutual Appreciation* (2003), and Mark Duplass, the director of *The Puffy Chair* (2005) and (with his brother Jay) *Baghead* (2008).

Matt Zoller Seitz described Gerwig's Hannah for the *New York Times* (August 22, 2007, on-line) as "neurotic, sweet and mildly sarcastic" and observed that "her small-stakes odyssey through three relationships is wryly observed." The film received more publicity and praise from film critics than did *LOL*, and some hailed Gerwig's performance as a standout. Noel Murray wrote for the *A.V. Club* (August 24, 2007, on-line), "The movie would be nothing without Gerwig, one of the rare improvisatory actresses who cuts right to the truth of a scene, and doesn't try to feign confidence by filling her camera time with a lot of chatter. She *lives* in this movie, and while her character's 'type' is annoying, Swanberg frames her in such a way that she becomes, if not likeable, then at least familiar." *Hannah Takes the Stairs* catapulted Gerwig and Swanberg to fame in independent-film circles and helped bring the mumblecore genre closer to mainstream recognition.

In 2008 Gerwig appeared in supporting roles in the low-budget films *Yeast* and *Baghead*, the latter a mock-horror picture. She also served as the lead actress, screenwriter, and co-director (with Swanberg) of *Nights and Weekends*. That film found Gerwig and Swanberg playing a couple, James and Mattie, who struggle through a long-distance relationship. An official selection of the SXSW, Stockholm, and London film festivals, *Nights and Weekends* continues the theme of emotional disconnectedness addressed in Swanberg's previous outings, with the main characters finding it hard to be completely open with each other after so much time spent apart. Critics were divided on the film's merits. Andrew O'Hehir wrote for *Salon.com* (March 10, 2008), "There's an intimacy and a universality to these characters that feels a world away from the post-collegiate claustrophobia of *Hannah Takes the Stairs.*" Murray noted for the *A.V. Club* (October 16, 2008, on-line), "Swanberg and Gerwig . . . have a gift for constructing the kind of moments rarely seen in contemporary American independent film. When Gerwig cheerfully shoos Swanberg out of her apartment so she can change for their not-quite-a-date, then crumples into sobs as soon as he steps out, it's both a powerful, beautifully acted scene and a critical study of what becomes of the noncommittal." Echoing an occasional complaint some critics have lodged against mumblecore films, Nathan Lee wrote for the *New York*

Times (October 10, 2008, on-line), "The subject of the movie is the gulf between persona—how people project an idea of who they are to others—and true self. The problem with the movie is that James and Mattie exhibit little but shallow, infantile neurosis, with next to no hint of a complex—or even legible—inner life. *Nights and Weekends* simultaneously plays like a critique of the mumblecore ethos and an especially obnoxious example of its whimsical tics and insouciant solipsism. Are the filmmakers exposing the insufferable coyness of urban hipsters or merely embodying it?"

Also in 2008 Gerwig had a role in *Quick Feet, Soft Hands*, directed by Paul Harrill. In that 25-minute film she played Lisa, the wife of Jim, a minor-league baseball player. The couple base their economic future on the hope that Jim's career will take off, then get a dose of reality when Jim's performance on the mound begins to falter. In addition, Gerwig appeared in a minor role in Rod Webber's 2008 romantic drama, *I Thought You Finally Completely Lost It*, about a man who tries to win back his ex-girlfriend. In 2009 Gerwig had a supporting role in an independent-film homage to 1980s horror movies, *The House of the Devil*, written and directed by Ti West. Unlike *Baghead*, *The House of the Devil* was not an ironic take on the genre but an attempt to re-create the look and tone of those films, evoking the aesthetic of John Carpenter and Wes Craven. The film, which Peter DeBruge described for *Variety* (October 8, 2009, on-line) as "the best '80s babysitter-in-peril movie never made," became something of a cult hit and broadened Gerwig's fan base.

Gerwig broke into the mainstream with her role in the 2010 film *Greenberg*, directed by the independent filmmaker Noah Baumbach—himself a former underground figure who achieved mainstream recognition for his 2005 sleeper hit *The Squid and the Whale* and the 2007 movie *Margot at the Wedding*. *Greenberg* starred the popular comic actor Ben Stiller as Roger Greenberg, an unemployed, 40-year-old failed musician who arrives in Hollywood to house-sit for his successful brother. There, he meets Florence Marr (Gerwig), his brother's 25-year-old personal assistant, and the two—both adrift in life—begin to form a connection. Although Greenberg harbors insecurities and often lashes out at Florence, she accepts him for who he is and begins to change his negative perception of life. The film is thematically similar to those in the mumblecore genre but commanded greater attention, thanks to its director, lead male actor, and production studio (Focus Films, a division of Universal Pictures). As a result Gerwig received the most intense exposure of her short career, and many critics predicted that she would become a major star over the next few years.

Greenberg also differed from some of Gerwig's prior films in that it did not incorporate improvisation. Gerwig told Sam Adams for the *A.V. Club* (March 23, 2010, on-line), "Everything was word-perfect. I think that's largely because Noah is such a precise writer, and he writes almost more like a playwright. There's internal rhythm and structure to his scenes, so if you miss a word, it sounds off, something akin to how when you speak Shakespeare, you can hear when it doesn't complete itself. So it's an obligation to the character, but also the structure of the words, how they sound." She also noted that while she had improvised dialogue in several of her earlier films, adhering to a script "allows you to be more invested in actually creating a whole person. It's easier when you're not trying to come up with your next line on the spot." To prepare for her role, Gerwig spent a month working as the personal assistant to the screenwriter Barbara Turner, the mother of the actress Jennifer Jason Leigh (Baumbach's wife and a co-writer of the film). Writing for *New York* magazine (March 7, 2010, on-line), Amy Larocca observed, "It's exactly the kind of job someone like Gerwig—26 years old, studied playwriting at Barnard—would have if she had not managed to become, in the four years since graduating, the queen of the film genre known as mumblecore."

Greenberg was generally well-liked by reviewers, and Gerwig was singled out by many for her charm and natural acting style. Ann Hornaday wrote for the *Washington Post* (March 26, 2010, on-line), "Gerwig . . . proves her bona fides here as a fine, engaging young actress. Whether she's singing, smiling or wondering out loud whether the driver in the other lane let her in, she seems lit from within. In many ways, those scenes, featuring just Florence in her car, listening to music, get to the heart that beats so jaggedly within *Greenberg*." A. O. Scott, in an article about Gerwig for the *New York Times* (March 19, 2010, on-line), observed that although the movie "is called *Greenberg* . . . it is equally—maybe even more so—the story of Florence Marr." He added, "What Ms. Gerwig does in *Greenberg* confirms a suspicion that began to bubble up through the diffidence and indirection of movies like *Hannah Takes the Stairs*, *LOL*, and *Nights and Weekends*. . . . Ms. Gerwig, most likely without intending to be anything of the kind, may well be the definitive screen actress of her generation, a judgment I offer with all sincerity and a measure of ambivalence. She seems to be embarked on a project, however piecemeal and modestly scaled, of redefining just what it is we talk about when we talk about acting. Part of her accomplishment is that most of the time she doesn't seem to be acting at all. The transparency of her performances has less to do with exquisitely refined technique than with the apparent absence of any method. The determined artlessness of Mr. Swanberg's films—the wandering camera and meandering stories, the ground-level observations of unfocused young people desultorily negotiating the challenges of romance and friendship—is epitomized by Ms. Gerwig, who carries some of the loose, no-big-deal aesthetic of those movies into *Greenberg*."

Also in 2010 Gerwig appeared in the low-budget independent films *Art House* and *Northern Comfort*. Another independent motion picture starring Gerwig, *The Dish & the Spoon*, was in post-production as of October 2010.

Gerwig is single and lives in the Chelsea neighborhood of Manhattan, in New York City.

—W.D.

Suggested Reading:*A.V. Club* (on-line) Mar. 23, 2010; Baltimore *City Paper* (on-line) Apr. 30, 2008; *Los Angeles Times* E p16 July 26, 2008; *New York Times* (on-line) Mar. 24, 2010; *Sacramento Bee* (on-line) Mar. 22, 2010

Selected Films: *LOL*, 2006; *Hannah Takes the Stairs*, 2007; *Baghead*, 2008; *Yeast*, 2008; *Nights and Weekends*, 2008; *The House of the Devil*, 2009; *Greenberg*, 2010; *Art House*, 2010; *Northern Comfort*, 2010

Courtesy of Andrea Ghez

Ghez, Andrea

June 16, 1965– Astronomer; professor of physics and astronomy

Address: UCLA, PAB 3-911, 405 Hilgard Ave., Los Angeles, CA 90095-9000

"Few people know the center of the Milky Way—some 26,000 light-years from Earth—as intimately as Andrea Ghez," an interviewer for the PBS television series *Nova* (July 31, 2006, on-line) wrote of Ghez, identifying her as a "galactic explorer." An astronomer and physicist who has taught at the

University of California at Los Angeles (UCLA) since 1994, Ghez has made major discoveries regarding the Milky Way, the galaxy that is home to our solar system. She did so by taking full advantage of momentous improvements in telescope technology—in particular, the introduction of high-resolution techniques, in the form of adaptive optics. With far more precise and detailed images of the center of the Milky Way than had previously been possible with terrestrial telescopes, Ghez and the other members of the Galactic Center Group, as her UCLA team is called, made a key discovery: that thousands of bright spots previously thought to be individual stars were in reality binary- or multiple-star systems—that is, two or more stars linked gravitationally. The clarity of the images enabled Ghez and her team to measure the movements of stars clustered near the center of the Milky Way, by painstakingly comparing thousands of images and infrared recordings. That highly labor-intensive work produced evidence that a supermassive black hole approximately three million times the size of the sun lies at the center of the Milky Way. Along with four of her collaborators, Ghez announced the team's discovery in her paper "The Accelerations of Stars Orbiting the Milky Way's Central Black Hole," published in the September 21, 2000 issue of *Nature*. She has also co-authored some 150 articles for the *Astronomical Journal*, the *Astrophysical Journal*, the *Proceedings of the National Academy of Sciences*, *Science*, and other professional journals, and she has contributed chapters to many books.

Ghez's achievements have earned her a bevy of honors, among them a MacArthur Foundation fellowship—the so-called genius grant—in 2008. In addition to investigations regarding star formation, the origins and evolution of galaxies, and other astronomical mysteries, Ghez has dedicated herself to inspiring young women to pursue careers in astronomy and physics, fields in which males have traditionally outnumbered females overwhelmingly. She has done so not only in the classroom and as a mentor to UCLA students but also through the media, including a book for young readers, *You Can Be a Woman Astronomer*, which she co-wrote with Judith Love Cohen (1995). "Research is a wonderful career, because once you've started to do work on one question, what you find is not only the answer to the first question but often new puzzles . . . ," she told the *Nova* interviewer. "Now my work has become one big puzzle, and that's what keeps me going."

Andrea Mia Ghez was born on June 16, 1965 in New York City and grew up in Chicago, Illinois. Her mother, Susanne Ghez, is the director of the Renaissance Society at the University of Chicago, whose mission is the promotion of contemporary art. Her father, Gilbert R. Ghez, is a professor of management and economics at Roosevelt University, which has campuses in Chicago and Schaumburg, Illinois; his publications include the book *The Allocation of Time and Goods Over the Life*

Cycle (1975), co-written with Gary S. Becker, the 1992 Nobel Prize winner in economic sciences. Ghez's parents imbued her with the idea that she would reach a high level in whatever profession she chose; from an early age, she has said, she knew that someday she would earn a doctoral degree. Ghez has recalled dreaming of becoming a ballet dancer. Her aspirations broadened when, in July 1969, she watched televised images of the American astronaut Neil Armstrong walking on the moon; she later saw images of the five subsequent moon landings achieved through the Apollo program of the U.S.'s National Aeronautics and Space Administration (NASA). "I was very struck by this," Ghez told the Nova interviewer. "I think I announced to my mother when I was four that I was going to be the first woman to the moon!" She soon became fascinated by astronomy, a passion that her parents encouraged, not least by giving her a telescope. But Chicago's myriad lights made the sky too bright at night to see much with the telescope, and Ghez "quickly lost interest" in using it, she recalled to the Nova reporter. Other scientific subjects also appealed to her, because science seemed to her like "a game or puzzle" and she "liked the process of solving things," she told an interviewer for the Poster Project (on-line), sponsored by the Math Department of the State University of New York (SUNY) at Stony Brook. She also enjoyed simple arithmetic and, later, mathematics.

From kindergarten through 12th grade, Ghez attended the University of Chicago Laboratory Schools, which are renowned for their ethnic and racial diversity and their academic excellence. The schools "really focused on teaching students how to learn and think independently, without the restricting notion that there might be only one way," Ghez told Douglas Cruickshank for Edutopia.com (April 2009). "I think this allowed me, and many others, to find a personal mode of learning and questioning. It also taught me how to learn (as opposed to just knowing the facts). I have become increasingly aware that this was a really magical school." During her teens Ghez was particularly inspired by a female chemistry teacher.

By the time Ghez graduated from high school, in 1983, she had developed a desire to prove that she was capable of succeeding in a male-dominated field. As a student at the Massachusetts Institute of Technology (MIT), in Cambridge, she focused on math before changing her major to another male-dominated discipline—physics. She earned a B.S. degree in that subject in 1987. She then entered the California Institute of Technology (Caltech), in Pasadena, where she completed her M.S. and Ph.D. degrees in physics in 1989 and 1992, respectively. While at Caltech, at her own request, Ghez taught undergraduates, and she won a Caltech Teaching Award in 1991.

Also during her years at Caltech, Ghez discovered that most stars form not by themselves but along with a companion star, and she deduced that in most planetary systems, the planets must re-

volve around two stars rather than one. But she also determined that planets rarely exist in association with twin stars. Thus our solar system and systems like it, which have only one star, may be rare—relatively rare, that is, since there are believed to be about 100 billion stars in the Milky Way and there are many millions of other galaxies. (The Milky Way contains the sun, which is a star, and Earth and the other planets—and asteroids and other matter—that orbit it.) The number of stars in the observable universe—that is, the part of the universe that humans can see with the most powerful land-based or space telescopes—is estimated to be 70 sextillion, or 70,000 billion billion.

Ghez worked as a Hubble postdoctoral research fellow at the Steward Observatory, at the University of Arizona, from October 1992 to December 1993 and as a visiting research scholar at the Institute of Astronomy of the University of Cambridge, in England, from January to March 1994. Also in January 1994 Ghez joined the UCLA faculty as an assistant professor of physics and astronomy; she was promoted to associate professor in 1997 and full professor in 2000, at age 35. She became a member of UCLA's Institute of Geophysics and Planetary Physics in 1999. For some years she has headed a research team called the Galactic Center Group. One of the group's main projects aimed to ascertain the possible existence of a supermassive black hole at the center of the Milky Way, a possibility that had been suggested three decades earlier but had not gained credence. A black hole is an object in space whose mass and density are so great that light cannot escape its enormously powerful gravitational pull; thus, it appears as black as the space around it and cannot be seen. Black holes reveal their presence by the effects they have on the stars that are nearest to them. "The key to proving that there's a black hole is showing that there's a tremendous amount of mass in a very small volume," Ghez told the Nova interviewer. "And you can do that with the motions of stars. The way the star moves around the center of the galaxy is very much like the way the planets orbit the sun. And the planets orbiting the sun can actually [enable astronomers to] measure the mass of the sun, just the way the stars orbiting the center of the galaxy can tell you what the mass is inside their orbit. So you need to measure the [movements of] stars . . . close to the center to show that there's a lot of mass inside a small volume, which is key to proving the existence of a supermassive black hole."

Unlike images from the Hubble and other space telescopes, which take pictures in outer space, where there are negligible numbers of molecules of oxygen or any other gases found in air, the images gathered by ground-based telescopes are distorted by Earth's atmosphere. (The distortion is analogous to that caused by water. As Ghez explained on the documentary Supermassive Black Holes, broadcast on the British TV channel BBC2 in November 2000, if you "look at a penny at the bottom of a pond and the water's moving, it looks all distorted and it looks different every time you look at it.") Early in her career Ghez helped to develop a technique called speckle imaging, which uses a process known as image stacking to increase the resolution, or clarity, of images produced by ground-based telescopes. Later in the 1990s a far superior technology called adaptive optics became available. (Earlier, it was used in U.S. spy satellites and was considered a military secret.) Adaptive optics (a light-sensitive system that uses a series of multidirectional mirrors, greatly eliminating atmosphere-related distortions) were installed at one of the world's largest telescopes, at the Keck Observatory, 14,000 feet above sea level on Mauna Kea, a mountain in Hawaii. Working with that new technology at Keck, Ghez and her team obtained images of the Milky Way's center that were 30 times clearer than those produced by speckle imaging. By comparing thousands of images recorded over a period of months, Ghez and her team saw that individual stars in the central part of the galaxy were moving unusually rapidly, leading them to deduce that an invisible object was affecting their movements. That object, they concluded, was a supermassive black hole. "When I first started thinking about astronomy it never occurred to me that there might be a supermassive black hole at the center of our galaxy," Ghez said, according to the *Supermassive Black Holes* transcript posted on-line. "The idea was that galaxies rotated just around the mass of the centre, which was just stars and gas and dust and nothing particularly exotic. It's hard to believe that black holes really exist, because it's such an exotic state of the universe. We've been able to demonstrate it, and I find that really profound."

According to Ghez, the black hole at the center of the Milky Way must have formed billions of years ago, possibly when several massive stars died at the same time and formed a single, supermassive object. Moreover, its presence in our galaxy indicates that most, if not all, galaxies also contain supermassive black holes. "There seems to be a strong relationship between the existence of a supermassive black hole at the center of a galaxy and the existence of the galaxy itself. . . . Whatever's responsible for the galaxy had to, as a by-product, produce the supermassive black hole at its center," Ghez said on *Nova*. In an interview with Jorge Salazar for *EarthSky* (September 14, 2009, on-line), she said, "A couple of years ago we might have asked the question, which came first, the chicken or the egg, or rather, the black hole or the galaxy. And today we understand that they had to come together. It wasn't possible for them to form separately." Ghez has noted that greater understanding of black holes will lead to additional insights about the origin and evolution of the universe.

In the *Nova* interview, Ghez said that although the Milky Way's black hole does not affect Earth at present, it may in a few billion years. "Our black hole is quiet [now] simply because there's not a lot of matter falling onto it," she explained. "You could say that our black hole is on a diet. General-

ly, there's a lot more matter in a galaxy when it's young. So you expect a black hole at the center to become more quiet as a galaxy ages. However, we know that galaxies are likely to merge with other galaxies, and when a merger happens, it will provide a new source of fuel or matter to the center of the new galaxy that comes out of the merger. So, in fact, our black hole could become rejuvenated if we merge with a nearby galaxy." To find out how the Milky Way's black hole accumulates mass, Ghez and her team are studying variations in the light emitted from the stars that are being pulled toward it.

At UCLA Ghez often incorporates cartoons in her lectures and exams to help her undergraduate students feel less threatened by mathematics and physics. "My favorite thing to teach is freshmen . . . ," she said on *Nova*. "That's because they're still trying to figure out what they want to do. They haven't declared majors for the most part, and I think the best way to convince them that physics is fun is to have fun doing it." As a successful female researcher in a scientific discipline, Ghez actively tries to awaken the interest of female students in physics, mathematics, and astronomy. She won UCLA Outstanding Teaching Awards in 1997, 1998, and 2005 and the school's Gold Shield Faculty Prize for Academic Excellence in 2004. "I think the most important thing you can do to encourage girls and young women into science is to show them that it's possible, that it's an allowed path . . . ," she said on *Nova*. "The best way to do that is to put role models in front of them, to show them that there are women in these fields." At present about 2,000, or one-fifth, of the 10,000 members of the American Astronomical Society are women.

Outside the classroom and research facilities, Ghez's activities include membership on many UCLA committees (more than two dozen since 1995), federal and organizational committees, and "telescope" committees, such as the one that allocates the times that researchers can use NASA's Spitzer Space Telescope and the Keck telescope. Ghez herself, Linda Copman wrote for *Cosmic Matters* (Winter 2007/Spring 2008, on-line), "has passed up family vacations, high school reunions, lots of holidays, and even a wedding anniversary in order to work at Keck." Ghez's two-dozen honors include a National Science Foundation Young Investigator Award (1994), the Newton Lacy Pierce Prize, from the American Astronomical Society (1998), the Maria Goeppert-Mayer Award, from the American Physical Society (1999), and election to both the National Academy of Sciences and the American Academy of Arts and Sciences in 2004. After she won the $500,000 the MacArthur Foundation fellowship, she told Stuart Wolpert, according to a UCLA press release (September 23, 2008, on-line), "The current shortage of federal funding for science can lead scientists to take fewer risks"; the message she took from the MacArthur Foundation, she said, was that "I should be brave and take risks." She also said that the grant would "definitely help with the balancing act"—that is, balancing her role as an educator and researcher with her responsibilities as a homemaker. Ghez is married to Tom LaTourette, a research scientist and geologist with the Rand Corp. The couple have two young sons, Evan and Miles. In her scarce free time, Ghez enjoys swimming.

—J.P.

Suggested Reading: astro.ucla.edu; *EarthSky* (online) Sep. 14, 2009; *Los Angeles Times* A p11 Dec. 10, 2008; myhero.com (2006); PBS *Nova* (on-line) July 31, 2006; "Science Careers," sciencemag.org; *Smithsonian* p44+ Apr. 2008

Selected Books: *You Can Be a Woman Astronomer* (with Judith Love Cohen), 1995

Courtesy of Ted Gioia

Gioia, Ted

(JOY-uh)

Oct. 21, 1957– Music writer

Address: c/o Author Mail, W. W. Norton & Co., 500 Fifth Ave., New York, NY 10110

Ted Gioia's accomplishments in the jazz world go far beyond his highly acclaimed books, the best known of which is *The History of Jazz* (1997), regarded by some critics as a definitive history of that genre. Gioia, who has been playing the piano and studying music since his childhood, has recorded three jazz albums. In college and graduate school

he concentrated not on music but on literature, philosophy, economics, politics, and business; his wide-ranging interests have contributed to his distinctive viewpoint as a music writer and culture critic. In the mid-1980s he helped to set up the jazz-studies program at his alma mater, Stanford University, in California, where for several years he was a faculty member alongside the school's artist-in-residence at that time, the legendary saxophone player Stan Getz. Gioia's passions and accomplishments also extend to the blues. His book *Delta Blues: The Life and Times of the Mississippi Masters Who Revolutionized American Music* (2008), was published after a decade of research that started with his investigation of the relationship between music and daily life and work. *Delta Blues* has received a lot of praise for its insights and writing; the *New York Times* listed it among its 100 notable books of the year. Gioia has also worked extensively as a business consultant; according to his Web site, he has "undertaken business projects in 25 countries on five continents, and has managed large businesses (up to $200 million in revenues)."

The second of the four children of Michael and Dorothy (Ortiz) Gioia, Theodore Gioia was born on October 21, 1957 and grew up in Hawthorne, a small working-class city in Los Angeles County, California. His father, whose parents came from the Italian island of Sicily, and mother, who was of Mexican and Native American ancestry, were deeply religious Roman Catholics and raised their children in that faith. Gioia has a younger brother, Greg, and a younger sister, Cara. His older brother, Dana, is an award-winning poet, opera librettist, translator, literary critic, and writer; he chaired the National Endowment for the Arts from 2003 to 2009. The Gioias lived very near many of their Sicilian relatives, including Michael Gioia's parents, and as a boy Ted Gioia often heard conversations spoken in a Silician dialect of Italian. Gioia's parents both had full-time jobs but different shifts; when one was at work, the other was at home. Gioia's parents never attended college, but both were determined that their children receive a fine education, not only in academic subjects but also in music and the arts. The Gioias owned a piano, left there by Gioia's maternal uncle Ted Ortiz, a Merchant Marine who lived with the family when he was not on the job. Their apartment also housed the uncle's huge collection of books and classical-music scores, and shelves in their tiny garage held hundreds of his classical albums. In an essay for the *Southern Review* (Winter 2005), Dana Gioia described Ted Ortiz as "an old-style proletarian intellectual" who could read German, Spanish, and Italian as well as English; Ted Gioia described him to Cynthia Haven for *Stanford Magazine* (March/April 2007) as an "extraordinary" person who was unusually curious and had a wealth of knowledge about classical music. Ted Gioia never knew his uncle, however; Ted Ortiz died in a plane crash at the age of 27, shortly before the birth of his namesake.

Ted Gioia began to study the piano at about six years of age. In his teens he "tried a number of different forms of self-expression," he told Haven. "Classical had the sophistication I wanted—but it lacked the immediacy in emotional impact I craved, and it lacked spontaneity and the ability to improvise. Rock lacked sophistication and depth." One night the young man went to a jazz club and heard a band perform. "It changed everything for me," Gioia recalled. "Within ten seconds, I knew this was what I wanted to do. I practiced relentlessly, soaked up music whenever I could."

Gioia was the valedictorian of the class of 1975 at Hawthorne High School. He attended Stanford University, in California, with a National Merit Scholarship. As an undergraduate he studied English literature and edited the student literary magazine, *Sequoia*; he also wrote for the campus newspaper, the *Stanford Daily*. He continued to study jazz and got jobs as a jazz pianist. During his junior year, at age 20, he started teaching courses in jazz at Stanford. He was also a member of Stanford's champion bowling team. He graduated in 1979 with an A.B. degree, and, supported by another scholarship, enrolled at Trinity College, Oxford University, in England, where he studied philosophy, politics, and economics. He earned B.A. and M.A. degrees, with honors, two years later and then returned to Stanford University to pursue an M.B.A. degree. He completed his graduate studies in 1983. In the mid-1980s he worked with Stanford's Department of Music to create a jazz-studies program for which he himself taught courses in jazz history and performance.

Gioia was still on the Stanford faculty when, at the age of 30, he published his first book, *The Imperfect Art: Reflections on Jazz and Modern Culture* (1988). In it he provided musical and cultural analyses of jazz in seven essays, bearing titles including "What Has Jazz to Do with Aesthetics?," "Jazz as Song," "Neoclassicism and Jazz," and "Jazz and the Primitivist Myth." In the last-named essay, Gioia attacked the notion—which he regards as fallacious—that because of its instinctive and improvisational qualities, jazz is primitive, a kind of music "charged with emotion but largely devoid of intellectual content," as he wrote. In jazz, Gioia argued, structure and composition are just as important as improvisation. The essays in *The Imperfect Art*, Peter Keepnews wrote for the *New York Times* (May 15, 1988), "indicate both the scope of [Gioia's] vision and the self-importance that occasionally trip him up." After pointing out that "much of what Mr. Gioia has to say is thoughtful and thought-provoking," Keepnews continued, "What is most unusual about *The Imperfect Art* is the apparent inner conflict it reflects: while the musician in Mr. Gioia obviously loves jazz for its spontaneity and directness, the esthetician in him seems uncomfortable with its intensity, its 'inherent tendency towards excess' and its capacity to bore listeners—the latter being, he suggests in one perceptive essay, a dirty little secret most critics would rather not discuss." *The Imperfect Art* received the ASCAP–Deems Taylor Award from the American Society of Composers, Authors, and Publishers in 1989.

Three years later Gioia published his second book, *West Coast Jazz: Modern Jazz in California 1945–1960*. That book examines the importance of a great variety of musicians who came out of or significantly contributed to the West Coast jazz sound—Dexter Gordon, Wardell Gray, Sonny Criss, Shelly Manne, and Art Pepper, to name a few; the book also focuses on the jazz forms known as bebop, hard bop, and big band. *West Coast Jazz* opens with the arrival of Charlie Parker and Dizzy Gillespie in Los Angeles, in December 1945, and ends with a history and analysis of the experimental jazz of Charles Mingus, Ornette Coleman, and others. "Especially valuable are fresh, prickly chapters on such maligned figures as Dave Brubeck, Jimmy Giuffre, and Stan Kenton," Chris Morris wrote for *Billboard* (May 9, 1992). "Gioia also makes a compelling case for the oft-ignored yet important post-bop work of the Lighthouse All-Stars. Anyone looking for a basic history of the California scene should start with this smart, opinionated book." One of the big themes of the book is the freedom to experiment—with structure, composition, and harmony—that was prevalent on the West Coast. Gioia also discussed other factors that shaped the sound of the West Coast jazz scene: nightclubs, record companies, the press, and the use of illegal drugs—especially heroin. *West Coast Jazz*, John Litweiler wrote for the *Chicago Tribune* (July 6, 1992), "makes a large, disparate, unruly subject not only coherent but also intriguing."

With his next, complex and ambitious undertaking, Gioia set out to create a lively, coherent history of jazz and the musicians who made it what it is. The resulting book, *The History of Jazz* (1997), describes the major movements in jazz (New Orleans, big band, bop, cool jazz, modern jazz, and fusion) and its major figures (Jelly Roll Morton, Duke Ellington, Art Tatum, Louis Armstrong, Charlie Parker, and Miles Davis, among many others) and offers Gioia's insights and analyses. "The title of this book," Jonathan Yardley wrote for the *Washington Post* (November 30, 1997), "is commandingly peremptory: not 'a' history of jazz, but 'the' history of jazz. Yet *The History of Jazz* lives up to that claim. It is a remarkable piece of work, not without its shortcomings or its invitations to argument but, withal, the definitive work: encyclopedic, discriminating, provocative, perceptive and eminently readable. With its publication, it can no longer be said that the literature of jazz falls far short of the music itself. The sweep of Ted Gioia's narrative . . . helps us understand just how grand the story of jazz really is."

Gioia received much similar praise for *The History of Jazz*. Sometimes, however, reviewers also noted what they deemed to be questionable conclusions or inadequate treatment of some aspects of jazz. Greg Tate, writing for the *Village Voice* (December 23, 1997), commended Gioia for the relative brevity—400-odd pages—of such a "coherently and eruditely" compact book, but he took issue with the "astoundingly, incomprehensibly lackluster treatment of jazz drumming and drummers." Tate cited Gioia's brief mention of the drummer Elvin Jones, who played with John Coltrane, among those he felt were given short shrift. Furthermore, Tate wrote, "Gioia also stumbles over the question of whether jazz is exhausted or flourishing under the weight of historical conservation, institutional domestication, and untrammeled eclecticism." Some criticism was even more serious. The complaints in a critique of the book for the *New York Times* (December 28, 1997) by Peter Keepnews, who also writes often about jazz, included Gioia's use of such "vague and unhelpful" adjectives as "solid" and "forward-looking"; insufficient attention to some key figures, such as the trumpeter Roy Eldridge; inconsistencies in the inclusion of recording dates; and his occasional inclusion of musical terms, such as "suspended fourths" (a kind of chord), without definition. Nevertheless, Keepnews acknowledged that *The History of Jazz* "addresses all the major figures, most of them at length and many of them quite informatively. . . . The book is peppered with pithy and thoughtful observations." *The History of Jazz* was selected as one of the 20 best books of the year by the *Washington Post* and as a notable book of the year by the *New York Times*.

For the next decade Gioia immersed himself in research and study of music as it is connected with activities of everyday life. The points of intersection between life and music, Gioia wrote for his official Web site, "are richer and more frequent than most realize—we are so accustomed to thinking of music as something that takes place on a stage or in a recording studio, that we miss our intimate relationships with sound and song. In particular, I am thinking of the use of music in work and play, ritual and worship, healing and social integration, courtship and romance, and other aspects of quotidian life. My interest is motivated by more than just a scholarly curiosity, but from a heartfelt concern that the power and enchantment of music are being lost in our contemporary society. Even the critics and historians of music, who should be our guides and interpreters, are the least sensitive to these realities." Those critics, Gioia added, often miss the "human element" of music.

The year 2006 saw the publication of two books by Gioia about people's day-to-day relationships with music: *Work Songs* and *Healing Songs*. In *Work Songs* he examined the role of songs in lessening the burden of hard work, whether in factories, mines, or fields. In *Healing Songs* he examined the ancient idea that music can help to heal, cure, or relieve physical and psychological conditions. Although those books were not as widely reviewed as *The History of Jazz*, the assessments they received were positive. "These two new books share much beyond a conviction that music speaks most eloquently when it is grounded in human life," Ivan Hewett wrote for the London *Daily Telegraph* (September 9, 2006). "Both break through the cultural and genre boundaries that determine the scope of most books on music, seeking out unsuspected parallels between widely separated cultures. Another similarity is the change through history from music conceived as magic to music judged rationally according to its effectiveness. Magic and music were at first hardly separable; as Gioia reminds us, the Latin word carmen means both song and spell." The third volume of the series will be about love songs and the use of music in courtship and romance.

In *Delta Blues: The Life and Times of the Mississippi Masters Who Revolutionized American Music* (2008), Gioia extended the themes of *Work Songs* and *Healing Songs* to the connection of music to such phenomena as poverty, isolation, and racial discrimination. Unlike Robert Palmer in his book *Deep Blues* (1981), Gioia did not dwell on the blues' West African roots. He identified the Mississippi Delta—the region of the United States between the Mississippi and Yazoo rivers, whose inhabitants were predominantly African-Americans living at or not far above the poverty level—as the birthplace of the blues. In the book he examined the evolution of the blues chronologically, while focusing on legendary figures including Bukka White, Charley Patton, Son House, Robert Johnson, Muddy Waters, Howlin' Wolf, Buddy Guy, and B.B. King. Early bluesmen sang solo, accompanying themselves on acoustic guitar. In the early 1940s some of the greats—Waters, Wolf, and others—took their talents north to Chicago, Illinois, where they created a new kind of blues, full of emotional, sexual energy. The Chicago bluesmen would usually plug their guitars into amplifiers, which allowed them to perform with bands. After World War II ended, blues began to gain popularity; in the 1950s it gave rise to rock and roll—the music of Little Richard, Elvis Presley, and, in the next decade, the Beatles, Rolling Stones, Led Zeppelin, and others. Most reviewers of *Delta Blues* praised Gioia's writing style and insights while noting that he had covered a lot of ground that had already been treated in depth, most notably by the musicologist and blues producer Robert Palmer and the folklorist and ethnomusicologist Alan Lomax. "But Gioia, who has researched thoroughly and listened carefully, does a splendid job of telling the story on a broad canvas, and weaving together the disparate threads of its central characters' lives," Mick Brown wrote for the London *Daily Telegraph* (December 27, 2008). "It is a book that leads you back to the music." *Delta Blues* was selected by the *New York Times* as one of its 100 notable books of the year.

Gioia's latest book, *The Birth (and Death) of the Cool* (2009), examines the notion of "cool"—particularly through the music and histories of Bix Beiderbecke, Lester Young, and Miles Davis—and how it became mainstream and commercial starting in American popular culture in the 1960s and '70s.

In addition to playing jazz piano, Gioia composes music, and he has released three jazz albums: *The End of the Open Road* (1988), *Tango Cool* (1994), and *The City Is a Chinese Vase* (1999). He is the founder of the Web site jazz.com; in 2010 he stepped down as a writer and editor for that site. Gioia reviews books at greatbooksguide.com and blogcritics.com.Gioia lives in Plano, Texas, with his wife, the former Tara Munjee, whom he married in 1991. The couple have two children.

—D.K.

Suggested Reading: allaboutjazz.com; *Economist* p97 Oct. 18, 2008; jazz.com; *New York Times* p27 May 15, 1988, p17 Dec. 28, 1997;

tedgioia.com; *Washington Post* X p3 Nov. 30, 1997

Selected Books: *The Imperfect Art: Reflections on Jazz and Modern Culture*, 1988; *West Coast Jazz: Modern Jazz in California 1945–60*, 1992; *The History of Jazz*, 1997; *Work Songs*, 2006; *Healing Songs*, 2006; *Delta Blues: The Life and Times of the Mississippi Masters Who Revolutionized American Music*, 2008; *The Birth (and Death) of the Cool*, 2009

Selected Recordings: *The End of the Open Road*, 1988; *Tango Cool*, 1994; *The City Is a Chinese Vase*, 1999

Jason Merritt/Getty Images

Goldthwait, Bobcat

May 26, 1962– Comedian; filmmaker

Address: c/o Gersh Agency, 9465 Wilshire Blvd., Beverly Hills, CA 90212; c/o Booking Entertainment, 275 Madison Ave, 6th Fl., New York, NY 10016

In the 1980s the comedian Bobcat Goldthwait was notorious for his loud, seemingly neurosis-driven stand-up routine, featuring what Christopher Wallenberg described for the *Boston Globe* (November 5, 2006) as a "nervous-wreck persona" with a "trademark convulsive caterwaul of a voice—an unsteady mix of Grover from *Sesame Street* and a

coyote in the throes of death." A regular on the cable-TV and club circuits of that era, Goldthwait won popularity for his subversive social and political comedy, which owed much to the edgy, off-the-wall, discomfort-inducing work of Andy Kaufman. While starring in a string of televised comedy specials, Goldthwait also became something of an icon of low-brow humor with his role as Zed in three of the seven Police Academy films; he solidified his cult status with a role in the critically panned talking-horse movie comedy *Hot to Trot* (1988) and through his directorial debut, *Shakes the Clown* (1992), in which he portrayed that film's drunk, misanthropic title character. Goldthwait continued to perform stand-up and act in film and television projects during the 1990s before reinventing himself in the 2000s as an independent filmmaker, winning critical praise for his controversial dark comedies *Sleeping Dogs Lie* (2006) and *World's Greatest Dad* (2009). While the two movies contain some of the sophomoric humor that defines the comedian's earlier work, they have surprised critics with their underlying moral and social themes. J. R. Jones wrote for the *Chicago Reader* (September 3, 2009, on-line), "Perverse sexual adventures may figure prominently in *Sleeping Dogs Lie* and *World's Greatest Dad*, but Goldthwait never goes for the easy laugh. What gives both movies their edge is his honest recognition of his characters' needs, no matter how dark. Honesty in turn becomes a major thematic concern, though in each movie Goldthwait arrives at a radically different morality." Goldthwait told Daniel Neman for the *Richmond (Virginia) Times Dispatch* (January 24, 2008) that his films, like his stand-up work, are intended to make audiences squirm. "I'm not a big fan of joke-driven [movie] comedies," he said. "I'm more a fan of comedy of the uncomfortable."

Robert Francis Goldthwait was born on May 26, 1962 in East Syracuse, New York, a suburb of Syracuse. His mother, Kathleen, was a department-store employee, and his father, Tom, was a sheet-metal worker. Goldthwait's comedic style was influenced by his parents; according to Teri Maddox, writing for the *Belleville (Illinois) News-Democrat* (February 5, 2004), his mother "loved sarcasm," and his father performed "crazy stunts." Goldthwait's later penchant for "making people [feel] awkward" through comedy, as he told Nathan Rabin for the *A.V. Club* (August 20, 2009, on-line), was inspired by his father's antics. He told Rabin, "My dad used to do stuff like threaten to jump off the top of the refrigerator into an open jar of mayonnaise while he had a crash helmet on. . . . And the whole neighborhood would be in our kitchen, and then my dad would climb on top of the fridge, and there would always be some kind of snafu, like it's the wrong brand of mayonnaise: 'Oh, is that Hellmann's? I can't do it with Hellmann's.' So I'm sure that that influenced me at an early age."

Goldthwait began writing his own comedic bits when he was 13. He formed a comedy duo with his childhood friend Tommy Kenny, who went on to voice the character SpongeBob Squarepants in the popular animated children's television show of the same name. Calling themselves the Generic Comics, Goldthwait and Kenny began performing at clubs in the Syracuse area. Goldthwait took his stage name during a performance at a club in the nearby town of Skaneateles. Barry Crimmins, who booked the duo, later became a noted comedian and political satirist; as Goldthwait told Dan Pearson for the *Illinois Pioneer Local* (August 27, 2009, on-line), "Barry was known as Bearcat. And Tom and myself, being jerks, went, 'Well, we're Tomcat and Bobcat,' which was a lie at the time. The joke really backfired because years later they are Tom and Barry and I am Bobcat."

Goldthwait told Neman, "I was influenced by Andy Kaufman when I first started. I didn't have jokes; I'd just go onstage and read a Dear John letter and cry." Other influences included the boundary-pushing comedian George Carlin, the experimental British sketch-comedy troupe Monty Python, and 1970s and 1980s punk-rock bands, which favored a stripped-down sound and confrontational performances. As a teen Goldthwait sang in several punk bands, including one called the Dead Ducks. He told *Entertainment Weekly* (May 15, 1992, on-line) that in the band, "I was using pretty much the same delivery as today. A lot of angst." He told Bill Brownstein for the Montreal *Gazette* (July 25, 1994), "I feel more akin to punk than comedy. Punk deals more with anger."

After graduating from high school, Goldthwait moved to Boston, Massachusetts, to pursue his stand-up career. Crimmins had already moved to Boston and was booking shows at a Chinese restaurant in nearby Cambridge called the Ding Ho, which became the base for the city's nascent comedy scene, with up-and-coming comedians including Denis Leary, Steven Wright, Lenny Clarke, and Janeane Garofalo performing regularly. Goldthwait eventually earned a living through stand-up appearances at the Ding Ho and elsewhere. "While most young comedians were striving for a relaxed delivery of glib one-liners," Larry Hoyt wrote for the Syracuse *Post-Standard* (October 22, 1987), "Goldthwait stuttered and stammered his way on stage through mock terror to manic outrage, giving his audience an uninhibited jolt of modern psycho-comedy."

In 1983 Goldthwait moved to San Francisco, California. There, the actress and comedian Whoopi Goldberg's manager, Barry Josephson, saw one of his performances and promptly signed the young comedian. Later that year Goldthwait, at 20, appeared on the TV program *Late Night with David Letterman*—his big break. "I was terrified," Goldthwait told Maddox. "I think you needed subtitles to understand what I was saying. But it ended up being the thing that opened up the doors for me." Soon nationally recognized for his stand-up work, Goldthwait had his own televised specials in the 1980s, among them *An Evening with Bobcat Goldthwait: Share the Warmth* (1987), and appeared on many TV comedy events, late-night programs, and awards shows.

In 1984 Goldthwait made his film debut, in the drama *Massive Retaliation*, and in 1985 he had a role in George Carlin's fictional day-in-the-life TV comedy *Apt. 2C*. He became best known for his role as the villain in the slapstick comedy *Police Academy 2: Their First Assignment* (1985). That film, the second of seven in the Police Academy series, follows the antics of a dysfunctional group of recent police-academy graduates. Never a favorite of film critics, the series has achieved commercial success with its low-brow humor. Goldthwait adapted his stand-up persona to his role in *Police Academy 2*; Paul Attanasio wrote for the *Washington Post* (April 2, 1985) that Goldthwait "makes the gang leader Zed into the nuttiest psychopath in years; he seems to be trying to wriggle out of his own face, and his voice is a jumble of insane roars and spoiled whininess." Goldthwait reprised his popular character in *Police Academy 3: Back in Training* (1986) and *Police Academy 4: Citizens on Patrol* (1987). Despite the recognition they brought Goldthwait, he has often spoken in interviews about his dissatisfaction with the films, calling them the "Police Lobotomy" movies.

In 1986 Goldthwait appeared alongside Whoopi Goldberg as a flamboyant dog groomer in the crime comedy *Burglar*. In 1988 he starred in *Hot to Trot* as a stockbroker who inherits a talking horse after his mother dies. When he discovers the horse's ability to provide accurate stock tips, Goldthwait's character schemes with the animal (voiced by John Candy) to get rich by playing the stock market. The film's nonsensical plot and gags failed to impress reviewers, who were also appalled by the number of obscenities in what appeared to be intended as a children's film. Also in 1988 Goldthwait appeared in *Scrooged*, very loosely based on Charles Dickens's novella *A Christmas Carol* and starring Bill Murray. Other films in which Goldthwait appeared during that period include *Meet the Hollowheads* (1989) and *Little Las Vegas* (1990).

Goldthwait's first solo comedy album, *Meat Bob*, comprising some of his live performances, was released by Chrysalis Records in 1988. Joe Brown wrote for the *Washington Post* (November 25, 1988), "In the opening moments Goldthwait compresses and tortures every comedy cliché imaginable. He says he doesn't know any 'jokes,' and he doesn't—the laughs in his stream-of-subconsciousness stuff lie almost entirely in his splenetic, frenetic delivery, like multiple personalities wrestling to take control of the same sentence. Goldthwait exploits his own daughter for laughs ('Everyone's going, 'Is that your baby?' Every baby looks like me—no hair and screaming their head off'); pinpoints sports ('I'll tell you what I know about sports: I know that if your team wins later that evening, you can legally do anything you want') . . . and makes a point of mentioning Satan because 'I want the Washington Wives to ban my record so it sells a few million copies.'"

Goldthwait made his feature-film directorial debut with *Shakes the Clown* (1992). A cult hit, the movie—which he also wrote—stars Goldthwait as an alcoholic, womanizing clown who performs at the occasional birthday party and spends the rest of his time drinking with his clown friends at a bar, the Twisted Balloon. When Shakes is framed for the murder of his boss, he faces the difficult challenge of proving himself innocent. The film also features Tommy Kenny as Shakes's nemesis, Binky, and Robin Williams (listed in the credits as "Marty Fromage") as a mime. Critics offered mixed opinions, with some praising the film's eccentric originality and others lambasting its juvenile jokes and outlandish premise. (One reviewer famously called it "the *Citizen Kane* of alcoholic clown movies.") Goldthwait told Maddox about the film, "Folks just really, really like it or really, really hate it. No one's ever impartial. . . . I don't do it on purpose, but it seems that the things I write are dark and odd. It's not very lucrative, but that's OK. That's just how my brain's wired."

In 1994 Goldthwait cemented his reputation as a bizarre and outrageous comedian with two acts on late-night television. In April, during an appearance on the *Arsenio Hall Show*, he threw furniture and spray-painted "Paramount Sucks" on the set to protest Paramount Television's decision to cancel that talk show. A week later he was booked as a guest on the *Tonight Show with Jay Leno*, where he unexpectedly doused his chair with lighter fluid and set it on fire. (Leno and another guest quickly put out the flames.) Later prosecuted, Goldthwait received a $2,700 fine and was ordered to reimburse NBC and record fire-safety public-service announcements. Goldthwait told Brownstein that he set the chair on fire because "I resented them [the show's producers]. The only reason they had me on the show was because I had trashed the *Arsenio Hall* set the week before. Then the *Tonight Show* people tell me not to trash their set because the furniture is brand new. So I said I wouldn't—I'm going to burn it instead."

After *Shakes the Clown*, Goldthwait appeared as a guest actor on many television shows, including *Married . . . with Children*, *Are You Afraid of the Dark?*, and *ER*. From 1992 to 1995 he voiced the character Muggle, a former lab rat, on the cartoon *Capitol Critters*. His other work in the 1990s included a voice-acting assignment for an episode of the cartoon *Beavis and Butt-head* in 1995 and roles in *Tales from the Crypt* (1990, 1996), *Sabrina the Teenage Witch* (1997), and the animated show *Hercules* (1998–99), for which he voiced the character Pain. From 1995 to 1999 he voiced Mr. Floppy, a talking stuffed rabbit and the imaginary friend of the character Jack on the sitcom *Unhappily Ever After*. In 2000 he voiced a character in five episodes of the animated Disney series *Buzz Lightyear of Star Command*, and from 2001 to 2002 he reprised his role as Pain for Disney's *House of Mouse*. In 1998 he hosted the FX cable game show *Bobcat's Big Ass Show*, on which guests performed bizarre stunts.

In the early 2000s, dissatisfied with the direction in which his career was heading, Goldthwait stepped away from acting. He recalled to Rabin in 2009, "About five, six years ago I said, 'I may be broke but I quit, man, I'm not gonna pursue being in movies that I wouldn't watch.' I just turned my back on show business. I jokingly say I retired at the same time people weren't hiring me anymore. And that's true, to an extent. But there's certainly a lot of things out there for me to do if I was interested in continuing to exploit myself, like reality shows and hosting game shows and all that crap." Goldthwait decided to try his hand behind the camera, and from 2000 to 2003 he directed television segments of *The Man Show*, a series, hosted by Adam Carolla and Jimmy Kimmel, that consisted of sketches celebrating stereotypical male behavior. That led to further directing work, and in 2003 Goldthwait directed segments of the popular sketch-comedy program *Chappelle's Show*, hosted by Dave Chappelle. That year he also directed the award-winning made-for-television film *Windy City Heat*, which aired on Comedy Central. Goldthwait's second stand-up album, *I Don't Mean to Insult You, But You Look Like Bobcat Goldthwait*, was released in 2003 by Comedy Central Records. The album contained autobiographical material, with Goldthwait poking fun at episodes from the past decade of his life—from his infamous *Tonight Show* appearance to his getting fired from the game show *Hollywood Squares* for his unpredictability. (He had appeared on that show from 1998 to 2000.) In 2004 Goldthwait began directing taped comedy segments for ABC's *Jimmy Kimmel Live!*, a late-night talk show. Impressed by Goldthwait's directing abilities, Kimmel made him director of the live portion of the program. Goldthwait told Neman that directing was similar to performing stand-up comedy because "you've got a million plates spinning." He directed the show from 2004 to 2006 and returned for a second stint in 2007.

In 2006, after more than a decade, Goldthwait returned to writing and directing feature films with his dark comedy *Sleeping Dogs Lie*. (The film was titled *Stay* when it appeared that year at the Sundance Film Festival, where it was nominated for the Grand Jury Prize.) Goldthwait produced the low-budget film in just two weeks, for $50,000, with a crew he had hired by advertising on the Web site craigslist.com. The film stars Melinda Page Hamilton as Amy, a young schoolteacher who, when pressured by her fiancé to be completely open with him, admits to having engaged in a sexual act with her dog while in college. Amy's unexpected revelation alienates her from her fiancé and family and seriously disrupts her life. Goldthwait told Wallenberg about Amy's confession, "I needed [a secret] that people couldn't get past. It was a little bit like my stand-up. I used to just bring up a topic that would make people uncomfortable, and then spend the next five minutes or next hour trying to dig myself out of that hole. And that's what I think this [film] was like—an experiment to see if I could actually dig myself out." Most critics praised Goldthwait for choosing not to concentrate on the shocking nature of Amy's act but to focus instead on the ramifications of her admission. Wallenberg wrote, "Despite a premise that could have resulted in a sophomoric, Farrelly brothers–type farce, Goldthwait instead delivers a nuanced film that forcefully argues that society's idealization of total honesty in relationships is bunk. *Dogs* has sharply drawn characters and turns out to be surprisingly authentic and sweet." Not all reviewers agreed. Stephen Whitty wrote for Newhouse News Service, in a review published in the *Houston Chronicle* (December 1, 2006), that the film "is worse than offensive, it's boring, and these busy days that's really unforgivable." Due to poor distribution, *Sleeping Dogs Lie* was not commercially successful and was shown primarily at film festivals before its DVD release.

Goldthwait's next feature film was *World's Greatest Dad* (2009). That movie starred the director's longtime friend Robin Williams as Lance Clayton, a single father distraught over his failure as a novelist, his lack of popularity as a high-school poetry teacher, and the disrespect shown by his misanthropic, foul-mouthed teenage son (a student at the school where Lance teaches), who spends much of his time surfing the Internet for pornography. After his son dies in a sex-related accidental suicide, Clayton responds by ghostwriting a suicide note and journal, which portray his son as a gifted writer. The student body, faculty, media, and publishing industry soon take notice of the note and journal, and Clayton's son is posthumously elevated to the status of misunderstood genius. As the film progresses, Clayton struggles with the knowledge that only through deception was he able to find a following for his writing. The film was critically acclaimed, with many calling it, despite its provocative content, Goldthwait's most heartfelt and resonant picture. Steven Rea wrote

for the *Philadelphia Inquirer* (September 4, 2009, on-line), "For a film that trades in weirdos, loners, and the oddest sort of human behavior, *World's Greatest Dad* gets strangely hokey at times. There's satire here, to be sure, and irony, but also an earnestness about the human condition that, well, can get to you." When asked about the dark nature of *World's Greatest Dad*, Goldthwait told Rabin, "I'm not interested in doing movies where your leading man rescues a puppy in the first scene so you can see he's an okay dude. As I keep making movies, I hope they're about flawed people. And if I make the movies that I'm writing right now, they'll actually be a lot more flawed."

Goldthwait married Ann Luly in 1981 (1986, according to some sources). The marriage produced a daughter, Tasha, and Goldthwait helped to raise Luly's son, Taylor. The couple divorced in 1998. Goldthwait then became engaged to his *Unhappily Ever After* co-star Nikki Cox, but the couple split up in 2002. In 2009 he married Sarah de Sa Rego, a costume designer and co-producer of *Sleeping Dogs Lie* and *World's Greatest Dad*.

In 2010 Goldthwait directed installments of *Important Things with Demetri Martin*. When not directing for television or film, the comedian continues to perform his stand-up routine on tour—albeit without the manic persona and voice that gained him his reputation in the 1980s. "I really didn't like doing the persona that people kind of expected of me and one that I totally started using as a crutch," he told Pearson. "So I just jettisoned the character and started going up on stage as myself, which was very hard. In some cities some people were going, 'do the voice' but I kind of stuck to my guns. I made a decision not to do what is easy and expected of me." He told David Germain for the Associated Press (August 24, 2009), "I go out and do standup, and I'm starting to enjoy it again, but I go out and do that to pay bills so I can keep making these really tiny personal movies. I don't really care about being in front of the camera, mostly because I really, really take this seriously. I really want to do a good job. I really want to be concentrating on this."

—W.D.

Suggested Reading: *Belleville (Illinois) News-Democrat* C p1 Feb. 5, 2004; (Montreal, Quebec) *Gazette* B p5 July 25, 1994; *Richmond (Virginia) Times Dispatch* F p18 Jan. 24, 2008; (Syracuse, New York) *Post-Standard* D p1 Oct. 22, 1987

Selected Films: As actor—*Massive Retaliation*, 1984; *Apt. 2C*, 1985; *Police Academy 2: Their First Assignment*, 1985; *Police Academy 3: Back in Training*, 1986; *Burglar*, 1986; *Police Academy 4: Citizens on Patrol*, 1987; *Hot to Trot*, 1988; *Scrooged*, 1988; *Meet the Hollowheads*, 1989; *Little Las Vegas*, 1990; as writer, actor, and director—*Shakes the Clown*, 1992; as writer and director—*Sleeping Dogs Lie*, 2006; *World's Greatest Dad*, 2009; as director—*Windy City Heat*, 2003

Selected Television Specials: *Bob Gold-thwait—Don't Watch This Show*, 1986; *An Evening with Bobcat Goldthwait: Share the Warmth*, 1987; *Bob Goldthwait—Is He Like That All the Time?*, 1988

Selected Albums: *Meat Bob*, 1988; *I Don't Mean to Insult You, But You Look Like Bobcat Gold-thwait*, 2003

Sam Greenwood/Getty Images

Goosen, Retief

(ruh-TEEF)

Feb. 3, 1969– Golfer

Address: c/o IMG, McCormack House, Hogarth Business Park, Burlington Ln., Chiswick, London W4 2TH, England

A native of South Africa, the quiet and unassuming Retief Goosen has at times ranked among the top five golfers in the world, and his swing—which can propel a ball a distance of nearly 300 yards—is widely acknowledged to be one of the best and most beautiful among contemporary players. Nevertheless, his exceptional coolness on the links, as well as his reticence and modesty, has left him largely out of the media spotlight, and most golf fans know little about him. "Goosen has the perfect demeanor for both golf and poker," Jeff Smith wrote for the golf blog thesandtrap.com (August 12, 2005). "Getting a read on him is not unlike looking at a book written in Sanskrit." Known affectionately as "the Goose" by fellow players and

friends, Goosen turned professional in 1990. In 1992 he joined the Professional Golfers' Association (PGA) European Tour. Despite his successes in European Tour competitions, he attracted only modest attention among followers of international golf until 2001, when he won the U.S. Open. That year and the next four, he won events on both the U.S. PGA Tour and the PGA European Tour. His victory at the U.S. Open in 2004 raised his world ranking to a career-high three. In 2009, after several lackluster seasons, he bounced back, with his seventh PGA Tour win. As of October 24, 2010 he was ranked 17th in world golf. Some observers attribute Goosen's accomplishments to his ease during tournaments. "He just gets on with it," the golf agent Guy Kinnings told Tim Rosaforte for *Golf World* (July 13, 2001). "He intimidates others just by being himself." Tom Spousta wrote for *USA Today* (June 16, 2005), "Inside the ropes, Goosen has earned a reputation as a no-nonsense player who rarely makes a mistake to beat himself. His game matches his demeanor: long and straight off the tee, precise with all irons, one of the best putters on any tour."

The youngest of the three sons of Annie and Theo Goosen, Retief Goosen was born on February 3, 1969 in Pietersburg (now Polokwane), South Africa, six years after the second-oldest son. He and his brothers grew up on their family's 4,000-acre cattle farm. His father, a real-estate agent, former amateur rugby player, and amateur golfer as well as a rancher, named him after Retief Waltman, a three-time South African Open champion (1961, 1962, and 1963). Goosen had a strict upbringing; his father told Smith, "I never made life easy for my kids. We never spoiled them. We never pleasurized them." Sources differ as to when Goosen started playing golf. In an interview with Don Riddell for cnn.com (May 4, 2006), he said that since his father and brothers played golf, his introduction to the game came at an early age; he "started playing serious golf," he said, when he was 10. His father helped him hone his skills, even constructing a wooden apparatus that held Goosen's head still while he hit the ball. At school he played several other sports. By the age of 15, Goosen had won many amateur golf tournaments and was seen as having the potential to become one of South Africa's top players.

On January 30, 1985, a few days before his 16th birthday, Goosen had a near-death experience on the course of the Pietersburg Golf Club, where he and his cousin Henri Potgieter had gone to practice. After waiting out a sudden thunderstorm, Goosen and Potgieter resumed their play, thinking that the storm had passed. "Thunder storms in South Africa tend to come in pretty quickly and leave pretty quickly," Goosen explained to Chris Baldwin for *WorldGolf.com* (August 9, 2005). As Goosen walked beside a cluster of trees to retrieve his ball, a lightning bolt struck one of the trees and traveled to the ground, hitting both boys. Potgieter was thrown down but was unhurt, but Goosen was knocked unconscious, his clothing burnt from his body, his skin singed, and some of his golf clubs melted. His cousin's screams attracted several adult golfers, who rushed Goosen to a hospital. He recovered within about three weeks, with a punctured eardrum the only physical remnant of the trauma. Goosen told Baldwin that his mother believes that the accident changed his personality: whereas before he had been an outgoing teenager who liked to tease his brothers, he became introverted, prone to angry outbursts, and more serious and determined. Goosen has acknowledged some personality changes but believes he always had a strong drive to succeed. "I was back on the golf course about three weeks later . . . ," he told Baldwin. "As soon as I got rid of all the burn marks and I could get my shoes back on, I was out there playing again." As for his father, Theo Goosen regarded his son's experience as an omen. "That he was saved was indicative of what might happen in the future," he told Rosaforte. Not long after his recovery, Goosen contracted hepatitis. He regained his strength by means of an exercise regimen.

As an amateur Goosen won 30 titles and was awarded national colors. In 1990 he won the South African Amateur and turned professional. He then entered the South African Sunshine Tour. He took lessons from Ronnie Leviton, the father-in-law of the South African golfer Roger Wessels. In 1991 he won the tour's Iscor Newcastle Classic, and the next year he qualified for the European PGA Tour; he also signed with IMG, a major sports and entertainment management firm. Around that time he started dating Tracy Pittock, a native of Great Britain, who helped him emerge from his shell and regain some of his boyhood cheerfulness. "When I met him, he was much quieter and withdrawn, very negative about people and life in general," she told Rosaforte. "I told him, 'For heaven's sake, if you've got anything to say, say something positive. I'm not going to stay with a guy like you unless you change.'" Goosen and Pittock married in 2001. "She struggled with me," Goosen told Smith. "I was a bit of a tough guy in the beginning. She's changed a lot in me; I was just too serious. I try to enjoy life more now. She knew the potential was there, and I just didn't believe it."

Earlier, in 1995, Goosen captured his first professional win, at the South African Open, at Rand Park, in Johannesburg, South Africa, an unusually difficult course. His victory there brought him to the attention of the golf world. "That was the toughest course you ever saw," the South African golfer Fulton Allem told Rosaforte. "The rough was so deep that if you missed the fairway by one foot you'd be hitting sand iron. That was proof Retief was for real. His temperament was good, and his swing was one of the most compact I'd ever seen." In 1996 Goosen achieved his first win on the European Tour, at the Slaley Hall Northumberland Challenge, in Great Britain. Over the next few years, he finished in first place in several European Tour contests in France—at the Peugeot Open in

1997, the Novotel Perrier Open in 1999, and the Trophée Lancôme in 2000. With his fellow countrymen Ernie Els and David Frost, he won the Alfred Dunhill Cup, a "special approved event" on the European Tour for three-men teams, in 1997 and 1998. In 2000 he tied for 12th at the U.S. Open in Pebble Beach, California.

The year 2001 was one of Goosen's most successful. He won the U.S. Open in Tulsa, Oklahoma, becoming one of only five non-American players to win the U.S. Open since World War II. He won the Scottish Open at Loch Lomond, came in second at the Trophée Lancôme, and snagged his third European Tour win, at the Telefonica Open de Madrid. He also won, with Els, the EMC World Cup in Japan, and he became the European Tour Order of Merit winner, receiving the Harry Vardon Trophy for earning the most money that year. Also for the first time, he ranked among the world's top-10 golfers, at number 10.

In 2002 Goosen won the Order of Merit again. He placed first in the European Tour's Johnnie Walker Classic in Perth, Australia, and in the Southern African Sunshine Tour's Dimension Data Pro Am. He also won the BellSouth Classic, in Atlanta, Georgia, on the PGA Tour. Early in 2003 he took a short sabbatical from playing to spend time with his wife and newborn son. After he returned he had one win on the European Tour, at the Trophée Lancôme, and his third win on the PGA Tour, at the Chrysler Championship in Florida.

In 2004, in Shinnecock Hills, New York, Goosen secured his second U.S. Open title, beating the American golfer Phil Mickelson by two shots. The event was also significant for Goosen because it trumped his boyhood rival Els, who was generally regarded as the better golfer. That year Goosen also won the European Open Title at the K Club in Ireland, and he beat the American golfer Tiger Woods by four shots at the Tour Championships in Atlanta, the final PGA event of the season. He ended that season with a career-high ranking of six on the year's list of top earners; in terms of earnings, he also placed second on the European Tour and third in the Official World Golf Ranking. The 2004 season marked the beginning of the five-year "Big Five" era, in which Vijay Singh, Woods, Els, Mickelson, and Goosen dominated the sport.

Goosen's 2005 victories included wins at the PGA's International, in Colorado; the Asian Tour's Volkswagen Masters, in China; and the German Masters (now the Mercedes-Benz Championship). Although he finished in 11th place at the U.S. Open, he ranked fifth in the world rankings that year. In 2006 he hired a swing coach, Gregor Jamieson, because he had not felt "very happy with the way things have been going," in his words, as quoted on the *Golf News Today* Web site (October 25, 2006). "I had to make a choice. I haven't used [a coach] for nine years. In a way, I've been too scared to go to somebody to work on your swing in case you get more confused. Gregor has been very simple with the way we've worked on things." In 2006

Goosen won again at the Volkswagen Masters and at the Sunshine Tour's South African Open Championship.

His swing work notwithstanding, in 2007 Goosen dropped out of the top 50. According to an Associated Press report carried by the *New York Times* (March 13, 2009), he was hampered by the after-effects of surgery to correct an eye problem. He had only one professional victory in 2007, at the European Tour's Qatar Masters, in Doha. In 2008 he again had only one win, at the Asian Tour's Iskandar Johor Open, in Malaysia. Goosen's career picked up in 2009, when he won the Sunshine Tour's Africa Open at the East London Golf Club and secured a victory in the Transitions Championship, in Florida, his seventh PGA Tour win and his first in about four years. "This year, I feel I'm a little more prepared for the game than over the last couple of years," he wrote for his Web site, after losing about 20 pounds. "I have been working hard on my fitness and everything. I'm probably the fittest now that I've been in the last five years." With his win at the Transitions Championship, he jumped to number 22 in the Official World Golf Ranking.

Goosen continued to perform well in 2010. In March he tied for fourth place in the Arnold Palmer Invitational—his fifth top-10 win in the PGA Tour. That achievement placed him 15th in the Official World Golf Ranking. In April he tied at 38th in the Masters Tournament. Later that month he broke a toe, forcing him to miss the annual Players Championship. He also missed the BMW PGA Championship in May because of a hand injury. He returned to the PGA Tour in July, competing in the St. Jude Classic in Memphis, Tennessee, where he finished in the top 15. At the end of the 2010 PGA Tour season, Goosen had 10 top-10 finishes and more than $3 million in earnings. He ranked 17th in world golf as of October 24, 2010.

Goosen, who is six feet tall and weighs about 175 pounds, has been described as unusually modest and down-to-earth. He has collaborated on the designs of several golf courses and owns a vineyard in the Garden Route region of South Africa, where in 2007 he launched the Goose Wines Co. He supports the South African Disabled Golf Association, which helps handicapped young people learn to play golf, and Make a Difference, a Cape Town–based charity that finances schooling for underprivileged children. In addition to their son, Leo, Goosen and his wife have a daughter, Ella, who was born in 2004. The children attend school in Ascot, in Berkshire County, England, where the Goosens maintain one of their three homes. The others are in Orlando, Florida, and Polokwane.

—W.D.

Suggested Reading: *Golf Monthly* (on-line) Nov. 2007; *Golf World* p34 July 13, 2001; retiefgoosen.com; SouthAfrica.info; thegolfchannel.com; thesandtrap.com Aug. 12, 2005; *USA Today* C p1 June 16, 2005; worldgolf.com Aug. 9, 2005

Courtesy of Morgan Stanley

Gorman, James P.

July 14, 1958– Financial-services company executive

Address: Morgan Stanley, 1585 Broadway, New York, NY 10036

In January 2010 James P. Gorman became the chief executive officer (CEO) of Morgan Stanley, one of the world's biggest financial-services companies. When he agreed to join the firm, in the summer of 2005, Morgan Stanley was perceived by some analysts as inefficient and was in reality the least profitable brokerage on Wall Street. But Gorman soon faced bigger challenges, stemming from the international economic crisis caused in large part by careless and highly risky use of various investment tools and strategies. In 2008 Morgan Stanley's stock price fell drastically, and along with several other major investment firms, the company reached the brink of collapse. That same year Morgan Stanley announced that it would no longer be an investment bank and thus would now be regulated under the Federal Reserve System. The federal government gave the firm $10 billion as part of its economic bailout; the sum has since been repaid. As reported in the *New York Times* (April 12, 2010), Gorman expressed his dissatisfaction over Morgan Stanley's financial performance in 2009, but during the first three months of 2010, under his leadership, the company reported a $1.8 billion profit. Nevertheless, it still ranked behind such competitors as J.P. Morgan Chase and Goldman Sachs.

Before his arrival at Morgan Stanley, Gorman had worked at Merrill Lynch & Co. since 1999; when he left he headed the company's global private-client group. He joined Morgan Stanley as president and chief operating officer of the individual-investment group, and from 2007 to 2009, he was the company's co-president and co-head of strategic planning. Gorman has been commended for his calm, honest approach to leadership.

The sixth of the 10 children of Kevin Gorman, an engineering consultant, and Joan Gorman, James P. Gorman was born on July 14, 1958 in or near Melbourne, in the Australian state of Victoria, and raised in Glen Iris and Armadale, Melbourne suburbs. His older sister Katherine Williams is a Supreme Court judge in Victoria. In an interview with the Melbourne daily the *Age* (2005), quoted by Clive Mathieson in the *Australian* (September 12, 2009, on-line), Gorman said that as a member of such a large family, he learned tolerance, because "you have to decide whether you want to fight your whole life, or fit in. . . . Rather than fight, we talked a lot, particularly over the evening meal, where each had to contribute something specific to a designated topic for discussion. . . . That meant from an early age we were all exposed to the very full range of behaviours, personalities and political beliefs that you could ever expect to get over dinner from a family of 12 very extroverted Australians of Irish descent in Melbourne. We are competitive to a point. We all like to win but none of us particularly enjoys seeing others lose." Gorman described himself as "probably the most shy" of all the siblings.

Gorman attended Xavier College, an all-boys Roman Catholic high school in Kew, another Melbourne suburb, and after his graduation enrolled at the University of Melbourne, where he received a bachelor's of law degree in 1982. He then worked as an insurance litigator at the law firm Phillips Fox & Masel (now called DLA Phillips Fox), in Melbourne. "Those were hectic years" for him, Leonie Wood wrote for the *Age* (October 20, 2001), referring to the large number of lawsuits that followed the devastating, wind-driven bushfires that broke out in Victoria on February 16, 1983 (known ever since in Australia as Ash Wednesday) after a long drought; 75 people died and thousands of homes and huge swathes of forest burned. Since a large number of the fires were traced to electricity power lines' coming in contact with trees or with one another, many of the suits were filed against the State Electricity Commission. Gorman first worked to defend the commission against individual claims and then represented the commission in its attempt to gain compensation from its insurers.

"Absorbed as he was by the intellectual challenge of law," Wood wrote, "Gorman found he had developed a taste for business management, and craved a leadership role." Gorman decided to study business and, in 1985, moved to New York City, where he attended the Columbia University Graduate School of Business. He welcomed instruction from businessmen as well as professors. "If you want to be a financier, it's the place," Gorman told Wood. "I didn't want to just learn; I wanted to enjoy the whole New York world-experience." Gorman received his M.B.A. degree in 1987.

That year Gorman joined the international management-consulting firm McKinsey & Co. as an intern. In 1992 he was made a partner and was named co-head of the North America division of personal financial services. He served as chairman of the New York personnel operating committee from 1996 to 1999 and concurrently, for two years starting in 1997, as both a member of the partner election committee and a senior partner. Earlier, in 1990, he had taken on Merrill Lynch & Co. as one of his clients, and in time he took charge of the whole Merrill Lynch account. During his time with McKinsey, Gorman lived at various times in countries including Mexico, Germany, Japan, China, England, and France as well as the U.S.

In 1999, when David H. Komansky, then the CEO of Merrill Lynch, recruited him, Gorman already had a detailed knowledge of the firm's strengths and weaknesses. His first position at Merrill Lynch was that of executive vice president and chief marketing officer. His responsibilities included developing the firm's Internet-initiated business. A joint venture for on-line banking and investment he negotiated with HSBC proved to be unprofitable and ended in 2002. Earlier, in 2001, Gorman had been appointed head of the U.S. private-client group, a branch of the brokerage division, which was headed by E. Stanley O'Neal, Merrill's CEO. His promotion raised some eyebrows among his colleagues, because Gorman's expertise was in marketing and advising; he had never worked as a broker. Over the next two years, as a cost-cutting measure, he closed one-fourth of the company's retail branches. He also fired one-third of Merrill Lynch's brokers, retaining those whose clients invested the greatest amounts. In shifting the firm's focus to wealthier clients, he ruled that calls from investors whose accounts totaled $100,000 or less must be shunted to call centers. In 2002 Gorman was appointed head of Merrill's global private-client group, a position in which he managed the firm's 14,000 financial advisers. According to the Morgan Stanley Web site, under Gorman's leadership, from 2002 to 2004, the global private-client group more than doubled its pretax profits and "led the industry in terms of revenue and profits per broker."

In the summer of 2005, John J. Mack, who had returned to Morgan Stanley a few weeks earlier as CEO and chairman after an absence of four years, asked Gorman to leave Merrill Lynch and join Morgan Stanley. Mack had been with the firm from 1972 until 2001; that year, after holding the post of president for seven years, he left, in the wake of a fierce power struggle that followed Morgan Stanley's 1997 merger with Dean Witter Reynolds, another major brokerage house, and Discover Inc.,

Sears Roebuck's financial-services spin-off. Landon Thomas Jr. wrote for the *New York Times* (July 1, 2005) that Mack's recruitment of Gorman represented "his first substantial hiring of an executive who had no previous ties to him. More important, it signals to investors and the firm's employees that Mr. Mack is committed to turning the much maligned business around, as opposed to just sprucing it up for a quick disposal." Gorman came on board as president and chief operating officer of Morgan Stanley's individual-investment group in February 2006, after his contractual obligations to Merrill Lynch ended.

As president of Morgan Stanley, Mack had been dubbed "Mack the Knife," for his "cost-cutting prowess and obsessive focus on efficiency," Kamelia Angelova wrote for *businessinsider.com* (September 14, 2009). When he returned, Morgan Stanley was the least profitable of Wall Street's major brokerage houses. In his first two months as CEO and chairman, he laid off about 10 percent of the company's brokers whom he considered to be underperforming. Gorman, too, promptly fired 500 brokers who he believed showed little promise, and he replaced 27 of the top 30 managers.

Within months the effects of those changes were palpable. "By the spring, Mack was starting to see signs of progress," Emily Thornton wrote for *BusinessWeek* (July 3, 2006). "Gorman was making real strides in overhauling the retail brokerage business." In particular, Gorman had begun laying off an additional 700 employees and set about changing numerous aspects of day-to-day business, from the training of brokers to customer statements. Among other moves, he also instructed his team to attract wealthy clients through new investment initiatives and expanded the company's services with regard to retail banking and small-business lending programs. But there were also problems: the firm, Graham Bowley wrote for the *New York Times* (January 17, 2010), was engaged in too much high-risk trading and "factional disputes and internal debates over strategy." Furthermore, Bowley wrote, "Under Mr. Mack, Morgan Stanley made errant mortgage bets and commercial property gambles that cost it billions of dollars and almost destroyed it." The company survived in large part because of funds from Asian investors and $10 billion from the U.S. government (a portion of its October 2008 financial-bailout package). In the summer of 2009, Gorman coordinated Morgan Stanley's acquisition of 51 percent of Citigroup Inc.'s wealth-management firm Smith Barney (for $2.75 billion), which made Morgan Stanley Smith Barney—with its 20,000 financial advisers—one of the world's biggest wealth-management firms.

As Morgan Stanley's CEO, Mack engaged in risky financial activities, in part to keep up with Goldman Sachs and its other competitors. In 2006 he was suspected by the Securities and Exchange Commission of insider trading with his former employer, Pequot Capital Management, but no official charges were filed. Between 2005 and the fall of 2009, when Mack announced that he would be stepping down as CEO, the value of the company's stock fell more than 30 percent. Despite the firm's extensive risk-taking, in the summer of 2009 Mack attributed Morgan Stanley's near-collapse to its being too cautious.

On January 1, 2010 Gorman became the company's CEO. He was unanimously selected by the board, not only for his intellect but also for his calm, thoughtful temperament. (John Mack has stayed on as company chairman.) Speaking to Bowley, Gorman acknowledged that Morgan Stanley had "periods of management turmoil" and "misplaced trading positions." The immediate focus, he said, would be well-grounded advisory services for clients, not big, risky trading. But as Bowley pointed out, Gorman and his firm have a huge task ahead. "Some analysts remain tentative about Morgan Stanley's prospects in a financial landscape littered with corporate wreckage and dominated by a handful of wily survivors. While the firm's traditional investment banking franchise has emerged strongly from the crisis—topping JPMorgan and Goldman in some of its businesses—it has shrunk its fixed-income division and taken piles of money off the table in its broader institutional securities business." In January 2010 Morgan Stanley reported its second annual loss—the second fiscal year during which it did not make a net profit. However, it had earned profits during the last two quarters of 2009.

Gorman expressed his displeasure with the firm's overall performance in 2009. With the new year some good news came: during the first three months of 2010, Morgan Stanley reported a profit of $1.8 billion. Under his leadership as CEO, Gorman has sought to reduce the company's general risk levels. Overall, there was notable growth (for example, in its asset-management business) and some big losses (among others, a $932 million loss on an abandoned casino/hotel project). In the second quarter of 2010, Morgan Stanley reported a profit of $1.4 billion. According to Antony Currie and Rob Cox, writing for the *New York Times* (July 22, 2010), what made the firm stand out among its competitors was Gorman's traders, who showed "greater resilience" than traders at, for example, Citigroup and JPMorgan Chase. Currie and Cox added: "By sidestepping the latest trading pitfalls, Mr. Gorman showed admirable restraint. He didn't give in to the all-too-common Wall Street temptation of chasing the outsize results of rivals. That should give shareholders comfort that the firm's 18-month-old pledge to keep risk in check is more than just talk."

The six-foot two-inch Gorman is "cerebral, circumspect and analytical," according to Bowley. Gorman and his wife, Penny, have two teenage children.

—D.K.

Suggested Reading: *Australian* (on-line) Sep. 12, 2009; bloomberg.com Sep. 11, 2009; (Melbourne, Australia) *Age* Business p1 Oct. 20, 2001; morganstanley.com; *New York Times* C p1+ Aug. 17, 2005, Business p1+ Jan. 17, 2010

Courtesy of William Gray

Gray, William M.

Oct. 9, 1929– Meteorologist

Address: Colorado State University, 205A Atmospheric Science, Fort Collins, CO 80523

"The best way to predict the future is to study the past," the meteorologist William M. Gray told Diane Levick for the *Hartford (Connecticut) Courant* (September 17, 1999). "There are surprising precursor signals that tip off what the coming season will be like." Gray was referring to the hurricane season; long before he spoke to Levick, he had become one of the world's foremost authorities on hurricanes and other tropical storms: how they form, their structure, the paths they take, their frequency, and global factors affecting their intensity. Gray's intensive study of meteorology began during his service in the Korean War, in the early 1950s; later, in graduate school, at the University of Chicago, he became a protégé of Herbert Riehl, "widely regarded as the father of tropical meteorology," according to *Meteorology and Atmospheric Physics* (March 1998). Riehl became Gray's research partner as well as mentor, and after Riehl moved to Colorado State University, Gray followed him, in 1961. Gray has worked there ever since; hundreds of professional meteorologists who hold

jobs at the National Hurricane Center and elsewhere were students of his. For the last few years, he has held the title of professor emeritus of atmospheric sciences at the university.

Although he has repeatedly reminded the public that there is still no foolproof way to anticipate weather conditions with precision, in 1984 Gray began to make annual predictions regarding each year's hurricane season, and he has never been wide of the mark. His predictions have appeared in hundreds of newspapers and on many Internet sites. Reasonable accuracy in forecasting is invaluable to farmers, the most obvious example of people who depend directly on the weather for their livelihoods. Others who depend on accurate weather forecasts are government agencies whose mission is to help people whose lives or property may be imminently endangered by bad weather; companies that insure against weather-related damage to property; and people who engage in futures trading of grains and other agricultural commodities. Millions, if not billions, of ordinary people in the developed world have come to listen to or look at weather reports as a daily ritual, and they, too, rely on the information provided.

In recent years meteorologists—those who study Earth's atmosphere and monitor and forecast the weather—have expanded their field of expertise to the investigation of global warming and its effects. Gray, too, has studied global warming, but unlike most of the scientists whose views have been made public on that subject, he believes that human activities—foremost among them the burning of fossil fuels—have had and will have negligible effect on the increases in the temperatures of the air and the surfaces of the oceans; rather, he believes that such changes constitute evidence of the next in the series of Earth's natural cycles of atmospheric warming and cooling. He has frequently labeled the linking of human activities and global warming a hoax—"one of the greatest hoaxes ever," he has said, as quoted by Nicholas Riccardi in the *Los Angeles Times* (May 30, 2006). He said to Alan Prendergast for *westword.com* (June 29, 2006), "I'm going to give the rest of my life to working on this stuff."

William Mason Gray was born on October 9, 1929 in Detroit, Michigan, and grew up in Washington, D.C. As a young man he loved baseball and was a pitcher of some promise; an injured knee prevented him from pursuing that sport professionally. Gray attended George Washington University, in the nation's capital; he earned a B.S. degree in geography in 1952. The Korean War was about to enter its third year then; wary of being drafted into combat after college, Gray had preemptively signed up for a meteorological program in the air force that would pay for his graduate studies in climatology following three years of military service. During the first year of his service, he studied meteorology at the University of Chicago, in Illinois. After his discharge from the air force, Gray enrolled in the graduate meteorology program at that school. There, he met Herbert Riehl. Gray began to help Riehl with his research, in the course of which they would hire pilots to fly them into or above tropical storms. In 1958, in one of the most memorable of such flights, they traveled in a converted bomber along the coast of North and South Carolina while the 150-mile-an-hour winds of Hurricane Helene—a Category Four hurricane and the strongest of that year's tropical storms—raged below them. (Sustained wind speed is the measurement that determines a hurricane's category, with Category One being the least intense and Category Five the most intense. Only two officially recorded Category Five hurricanes have struck the U.S. mainland: Camille, in 1969, and Andrew, in 1992.)

Historical accounts show that humans have attempted to predict the weather for at least 2,500 years. People probably strived to make accurate long- and short-term forecasts for thousands of years before that, beginning when they turned from hunting and gathering to growing their own crops. The science of forecasting received a huge boost with the invention of the telegraph, in the mid-1800s, which made possible the rapid dissemination of data (regarding air temperature, wind speed, humidity, and precipitation, to name some of the major variables in weather) across long distances. With the dawn of the computer age, meteorology again advanced exponentially, as computers enabled scientists both to cumulate and to analyze, compare, and contrast vast amounts of data rapidly. The third invaluable aid to the field was the invention of the weather satellite; the U.S. government's first successful launch of such a satellite came in 1960. When Gray began working with Riehl, meteorology was still relatively primitive. "Those were the days of pre-satellite data, when the airplane was king and flew into storms," Gray told Deborah Mendez for the Associated Press (September 26, 1994).

Gray earned an M.S. degree in meteorology from the University of Chicago in 1959; his thesis was entitled "On the Balance of Forces in Hurricane Daisy of 1958." He completed a Ph.D. in geophysical sciences in 1964, writing a dissertation entitled "On the Scales of Motion and Internal Stress Characteristics of the Hurricane." Earlier, from 1957 to 1961, he had worked as a research assistant at the University of Chicago, then followed Riehl to Colorado State University in Fort Collins to take the post of assistant meteorologist in the newly founded Department of Atmospheric Science. Gray became a full professor of atmospheric sciences in 1974.

The research of Gray and Riehl focused on storms with paths in the Atlantic Ocean. For some time they made little progress in making sense of their data and thus becoming adept at forecasting such storms. The accuracy of their predictions improved when they began collecting data from further afield. "The problem was that we'd been looking locally," Gray told Alan Prendergast. "You had to look globally." He and Riehl identified several

factors that influenced the patterns and strengths of hurricanes but occurred far from the East Coast of the U.S. They included El Niño, the irregularly occurring warming of seawater in the eastern Pacific; sea-level air pressure in the Caribbean Basin; rainfall in West Africa; and the direction of stratospheric winds above the equator and above the lower Caribbean Basin. (Earth's atmosphere has five layers. The stratosphere is the second; it extends from about 31 to about 34 miles above Earth's surface.) Those factors, Gray told William Fox for the *St. Petersburg Times* (June 2, 1987), account for only about half the variability of hurricane seasons from one year to the next.

In meteorological jargon, a tropical storm has winds of between 34 and 74 miles per hour (mph). Storms whose wind speeds are less than 34 mph are called tropical depressions; those with wind speeds greater than 74 mph are called hurricanes. (In other parts of the world, hurricanes are known as cyclones or typhoons.) In 1984 Gray publicly forecast, for the first time, how many hurricanes (seven) and tropical storms (10) he expected to occur that summer. Five hurricanes developed, along with 12 storms. That prediction was sufficiently on target to attract some attention; more came his way after he improved his methods and launched the University of Colorado's Tropical Meteorology Project. In 1985 he predicted eight hurricanes, and seven occurred; in 1986, he predicted four, and four occurred; in 1987 he predicted four hurricanes and three tropical storms, and there were three hurricanes and four tropical storms. Additionally, in 1987 he forecast that on 35 days a hurricane or tropical storm would be active during the Atlantic hurricane season (which, officially, extends from June 1 through November 30); the actual number was 36. By the early 1990s Gray had made a name for himself as a trustworthy forecaster of hurricanes and tropical storms. The ease with which he won grants and other funding for his research reflected his success.

In his interview with William Fox in 1987, Gray noted that, because of global wind patterns, there had been a smaller than average number of intense storms since 1970. But he expected those patterns to change within the next dozen years or so, and then, he warned, people would need to "watch out." A decade later Gray testified before members of the Subcommittee on Housing and Community Opportunity of the U.S. House of Representatives' Banking and Financial Services Committee regarding the possibilities of hurricanes making landfall in the U.S. "Global observations indicate that we are entering a new era of increased intense or 'major' hurricanes," he said, as quoted by the Federal News Service (June 24, 1997). "If our interpretation of climate trends which are indicating increased intense hurricane activity bear out, then the cost of U.S. hurricane-spawned destruction will be of a magnitude as never before seen." During his testimony he also denounced the theory of manmade global warming, declaring, "These are natural changes."

In an interview with William K. Stevens for the *New York Times* (February 29, 2000), Gray said, "I don't think we're arguing over whether there's any global warming. The question is, 'What is the cause of it?'" According to Gray, rising temperatures are part of a natural cycle of heating and cooling caused by, among other factors, thermohaline circulation (THC), also called the global ocean conveyor. All the world's oceans are connected, and scientists have detected large-scale patterns in the movement of seawater at the surface and at all depths. "Overall, the globe has warmed over the past 120 years," Gray told Alan Prendergast. "That's due, in my view, to a multi-century slowing of the thermohaline. We're coming out of a little ice age, and overall, the thermohaline has been slowing. But that doesn't mean it doesn't speed up for thirty or forty years."

In his conversation with Stevens, Gray also disputed the theory that global warming is connected with an increase in hurricanes. He later presented his evidence for that assertion, and for the role THC plays in climate change, in a paper, "Global Warming and Hurricanes," that he presented in 2006 at the 27th Conference on Hurricanes and Tropical Meteorology, sponsored by the American Meteorological Society. He began his paper with a quote from the Republican U.S. senator James Inhofe of Oklahoma, who declared on the floor of the Senate in 2003, "Global warming caused by human activity might be the greatest hoax ever perpetrated on the American people." Gray ended the paper by referring to the novel *State of Fear* (2004), by Michael Crichton. (One of the chief villains in *State of Fear*, the head of an environmental organization, conspires with ecoterrorists to convince the public of the danger of global warming so as to scare them into donating generously to his group; the hero debunks the global-warming theory, his arguments supported by footnotes in which Crichton cited papers by real-life global-warming deniers such as Gray.) As Gray noted, the American Association of Petroleum Geologists (AAPG) honored Crichton with its Journalism Award for *State of Fear*, a book that, he added, "dismisses global warming as a conspiracy." Gray quoted Larry Nation, an AAPG spokesperson, as saying of *State of Fear*, "It is fiction. But it has the absolute ring of truth."

Several of the climatologists who publish the Web site realclimate.org (April 26, 2006) refuted "a few key points" from Gray's paper that "illustrate the fundamental misconceptions on the physics of climate that underlie most of Gray's pronouncements on climate change and its causes." ("Our discussion is not a point-by-point rebuttal of Gray's claims; there is far more wrong with the paper than we have the patience to detail," they explained.) "None of the assertions are based on rigorous statistical associations, oceanographic observations or physically based simulations," they wrote. "It is all seat-of-the-pants stuff of a sort that was common in the early days of climate studies." The renowned physicist, oceanographer, and climatologist Stefan Rahmstorf, a professor at Potsdam University, in Germany, who specializes in the role of ocean currents in climate change, wrote the next day in a message to realclimate.org (April 27, 2006) that he had met Gray at a conference in 1998 and had "a nice discussion" with him. Gray "described to me in very clear terms how the thermohaline ocean circulation had decreased and increased at various times during the 20th Century," Rahmstorf recalled. "I felt very embarrassed—here I was, a young scientist who had been working already for seven years on the THC, and I had never even heard of these changes—I had thought it was basically unknown how the THC had varied over the 20th Century! Obviously I had a major gap in my grasp of the scientific literature. When I returned home I immediately did an extensive literature search—and to my surprise I found no studies at all that supported the very assured claims made by Gray."

Rahmstorf and others who criticize his views, Gray complained to Prendergast, "want to put me on the fringe. My brain is fossilized. I'm an old curmudgeon who doesn't change with the times. They use anything they can against you." Gray himself has publicly accused scientists of knowingly carrying out flawed experiments, even lying, for the sake of their funding. "It bothers me that my fellow scientists are not speaking out against something they know is wrong," he told Steve Lyttle for the *Sydney (Australia) Morning Herald* (October 14, 2007). "But they also know that they'd never get any grants if they spoke out. I don't care about grants." During the administrations of President Bill Clinton, though, Gray continued to apply for federal grants. "I must have been turned down thirteen times," he told Prendergast, adding that other scientists "were getting money to run these big [computer] models, and they were bending their objectivity to get the money." Greg Holland, the head of the Mesoscale and Microscale Meteorology Division of the National Center for Atmospheric Research, in Boulder, Colorado, who completed his doctoral work under Gray, told Prendergast, "Getting support for research goes through a well-established peer review. . . . The lack of funding for [Gray's] research is related to the quality of his research." Peter Webster, a professor of meteorology at the Georgia Institute of Technology and a former collaborator of Gray's, told Prendergast that he had recently refused to participate in a public panel with Gray because he could not extract from Gray a promise to stick to the science and refrain from ad hominem attacks. "I certainly wasn't going to stand in public and let Bill berate me," Webster said. Holland told Prendergast, "[Gray] has always been a natural thinker, the sort of person who asks difficult questions. The unfortunate difference now is the way personalities are being brought into it—and the denigration of perfectly good scientific techniques."

When Prendergast asked him to consider the possibility that human activities will indeed cause irreversible damage to the environment, Gray replied, "There's nothing we can do about it anyway. We're not going to stop burning fossil fuels. China and India aren't going to stop. The little amount you might be able to cut out is negligible, and it's going to hurt the middle class." With the aim of devoting himself to recording his ideas about global warming in an article that will be accepted for publication in a respected journal, Gray recently passed most of his Tropical Meteorology Project responsibilities to Philip J. Klotzbach, who earned a Ph.D. under his guidance. (Before he ended his teaching career, Gray served as an adviser to more than 70 master's-degree and doctoral-degree students at Colorado State University.) "When I am pushing up daisies, I am very sure that we will find that humans have warmed the globe slightly, but that it's nothing like what they're saying," he told Prendergast. "I just don't want to die and leave all these loose ends."

Gray is a research fellow at the Oakland, California– and Washington, D.C.–based Independent Institute, whose mission, according to its Web site, is "to transcend the all-too-common politicization and superficiality of public policy research and debate, redefine the debate over public issues, and foster new and effective directions for government reform." His honors include the Jule G. Charney Award (1994), from the American Meteorological Association; the Banner I. Miller Award (1994), from the Atlantic Oceanographic and Meteorological Laboratory, a division of the National Oceanic and Atmospheric Administration; and the Neil Frank Award (1995), from the National Hurricane Conference.

The six-foot five-inch Gray is a widower. He has adult children and lives in Fort Collins.

—J.E.P.

Suggested Reading: Colorado State University Web site; (Denver, Colorado) *westword.com* June 29, 2006; *Discover* p15+ Sep. 2005; *Los Angeles Times* A p6 May 30, 2006; *New York Times* F p1 Feb. 29, 2000; realclimate.org; *Who's Who in America*

Gregory, David

Aug. 24, 1970– Broadcast journalist

Address: Meet the Press, MSNBC, 4001 Nebraska Ave., N.W., Washington, DC 20016

Meet the Press, which debuted on NBC on November 6, 1947, is the longest-running series on television, and for decades it has been considered a "leading program for providing political accountability," as the *Encyclopedia of Television* (2004) put it. People in positions of power seldom turn down invitations to appear on *Meet the Press*, where typically they must respond to hard-hitting questions posed in respectful tones. For those reasons, hosting *Meet the Press* is among the most prestigious and influential jobs in journalism. The broadcast journalist David Gregory, who became the program's ninth moderator on December 14, 2008, succeeded two hosts with outsized reputations: Tim Russert, the moderator of *Meet the Press* for more than 17 years, and Tom Brokaw, the anchor and managing editor of *NBC Nightly News* from 1982 to 2004, who served as interim host of *Meet the Press* for six months after Russert's sudden death, on June 13, 2008. Although Gregory was only 38 years old when he took over, he already had 20 years of broadcasting experience, starting in the summer between his freshman and sophomore years of college. He became a roving correspondent for NBC in 1995 and the network's chief White House correspondent in 2001.

Frederick M. Brown/Getty Images

As a member of the White House press corps for eight years, Gregory reported on most domestic or overseas events in which the George W. Bush administration was involved—excellent preparation for his role on *Meet the Press*, which requires in-depth knowledge of government, politics, and national and international affairs. Gregory accompanied the president on Air Force One on nearly all of Bush's 44 trips outside the U.S., which took him to Canada, Mexico, the majority of the countries in Europe, many in Asia, some in Central and South America, and a few in Africa. Gregory reported on dozens of meetings Bush had in the U.S. or overseas with heads of state, royalty, and Popes John Paul II and Benedict XVI; he also covered the president's visits to Iraq and Afghanistan, regarding the ongoing armed conflicts in those nations, and his talks with U.S. military officials and troops and Iraqi and Afghan leaders. In addition, Gregory chronicled Bush's contributions to summit meetings of NATO (North Atlantic Treaty Organization), APEC (Asia-Pacific Economic Cooperation), the G8 (Group of Eight), and the United States–European Union, and he witnessed Bush's participation in celebrations of historical events, such as the 60th anniversary of V.E. (Victory in Europe) Day.

From time to time between January 2001 and December 2008, Gregory filled in as anchor or host of NBC's *Nightly News* and its weekend edition, *Today*, and *Meet the Press*. For nearly 10 months starting in March 2008, he hosted the MSNBC series *Race to the White House* (which was renamed *1600 Pennsylvania Avenue* after Election Day). According to Gary Strauss, writing for *USA Today* (December 8, 2008), in his regular positions and as a substitute, Gregory displayed "a sense of humor and an ability to ask frank questions." After NBC announced that Gregory would be taking the helm of *Meet the Press*, Ari Fleischer, a former press secretary under George W. Bush, told Mike Allen for politico.com (December 2, 2008), "No one was a tougher, more aggressive questioner in the [White House] briefing room than David Gregory. But when it came time to go on the air, he was always nothing but fair." Gregory told Sandra Sobieraj Westfall for *People* (March 16, 2009) that as a *Meet the Press* interviewer, he has been guided by Russert's credo: "Learn everything about your guest, then take the other side—but with a tone of civility." Transcripts of *Meet the Press* are available on the Internet from the Federal Document Clearing House, a private transcription service.

David Michael Gregory was born on August 24, 1970 in Los Angeles, California, where he grew up. His father, Don Gregory, is a theater, television, and film producer; his mother, a business administrator, most recently served as an account manager for Office Depot. According to Eric Fingerhut, writing for *Washington Jewish Week* (March 19, 2008, on-line), at a conference organized by the United Jewish Communities in 2008, Gregory said that as the son of a Jewish father and a non-Jewish mother, he was raised with a sense of "peoplehood and tradition" but with not much "theology or spirituality." As a teenager he studied the techniques of the ABC-TV reporter and anchor Sam Donaldson and other TV newscasters and also read books about broadcast journalism. By age 15 he knew he wanted to pursue a career in that field. In 1988, shortly before his high-school graduation, "my dad and I

had a conversation about how to do it, how to navigate it, how to pursue what I wanted to do," Gregory told Siena Rafter for Scholastic.com (February 20, 2008).

Gregory attended American University, in Washington, D.C. He landed his first television job at 18, after persuading decision-makers at KGUN-TV in Tucson, Arizona, to hire him as a Washington correspondent for the summer. As an undergraduate he worked at ATV, American University's student-run TV station. In 1992 he earned a B.A. degree in international studies. He then worked briefly at a CBS affiliate in Albuquerque, New Mexico. At that time many of the city's employees were being laid off because of a budget crisis, and the relationship between the press and Albuquerque's mayor, Louis Saavedra, had become prickly. On his first day at that job, Gregory told Siena Rafter, he interviewed the mayor. When he asked a question about the then-current conflict between Saavedra and the police union, the mayor declared, "This interview is over," and left the room. The next day Gregory met the mayor by chance; when he tried to speak to Saavedra again, the mayor "grabbed my hand and said, 'You are nothing but disgusting slime, leave me alone.'" Gregory added, "There was a big headline in the afternoon paper that said, 'Disgusting Slime.'" Gregory next worked for NBC's West Coat affiliate KCRA-TV, in Sacramento, California.

Gregory's first big break came in 1995, when KCRA-TV sent him to cover the murder trial of the former football star O. J. Simpson, as a replacement for the regular correspondent, who had been reporting for NBC's video news service for local stations. Gregory's performance impressed his superiors, and later in 1995 he was named a correspondent for NBC News in Los Angeles and Chicago, Illinois. In 1997 he reported on the O. J. Simpson civil trial, in Los Angeles, and then on the trial in Denver, Colorado, of Timothy McVeigh, who was found guilty of setting off the bombs that killed 165 people in a federal office building in Oklahoma City, Oklahoma, in 1995.

In 1998, for MSNBC, Gregory covered the sex scandal involving President Bill Clinton and the former White House intern Monica Lewinsky, the subsequent impeachment of the president by the House of Representatives in December of that year, and Clinton's acquittal by the U.S. Senate in February 1999. Later in 1999 NBC assigned Gregory to its weekly TV newsmagazine *Dateline* as a correspondent. Next, he became the anchor of a short-lived talk show called *News Chat* and appeared occasionally on the daytime programs *Crosstalk NBC* and *Newsfront*. In 2000 Gregory joined the journalists who traveled with Republican governor George W. Bush of Texas during his run for the White House. On the day that Gregory turned 30, Bush, who nicknamed the six-foot five-inch journalist "Stretch," threw a birthday party for him aboard his campaign plane. Bush "is such an affable, personable guy and uses that to his advantage," Gregory told Howard Kurtz years later for the *Washington Post* (March 14, 2006). "A lot of reporters think he's a good guy. I think he's a good guy." During the highly contentious counting of ballots that followed the disputed Election Day results in Florida, Gregory reported from NBC headquarters in Austin, Texas, on the legal battles between Republican and Democratic officials. Those fights ended on December 12, 2000, when the Supreme Court declared Bush the victor over Al Gore.

On the day of Bush's inauguration, NBC named Gregory its chief White House correspondent. In his early weeks in that position, Gregory adopted a pugnacious manner at White House press conferences and while questioning Bush-administration officials elsewhere. He soon realized, he told Kurtz, that "you can't function effectively if you're constantly having a confrontational relationship" with political figures. "You have to balance some access with being tough on them." Nevertheless, in an off-camera incident in February 2006, Gregory exchanged insults with White House press secretary Scott McClellan; he later apologized to McClellan. Many in the press complained that as Bush's press secretary, McClellan either dodged or offered vague, misleading responses to substantive questions; nonetheless, in his memoir, *What Happened: Inside the Bush White House and Washington's Culture of Deception* (2008), McClellan contended that the White House press corps failed to question Bush's policies strongly enough. As a guest on MSNBC's *Hardball with Chris Matthews* on May 29, 2008, according to mediamatters.org, Gregory responded by saying, "I think the questions were asked. I think we pushed. I think we prodded. I think we challenged the president. . . . I think there's a lot of critics—and I guess we can count Scott McClellan as one—who [think] that if we did not debate the president, debate the policy in our role as journalists, if we did not stand up and say, 'This is bogus,' and 'You're a liar,' and 'Why are you doing this?' that we didn't do our job. And I respectfully disagree. It's not our role." In an *American Prospect* blog (December 2, 2008) posted after NBC's announcement that Gregory would host *Meet the Press*, Ezra Klein wrote that Gregory "made his name as an adversarial member of the White House press corps at a time when his colleagues were being oddly deferential, so he's certainly able to ask an angry or tough question in the face of pompous authority. That's a plus. But Gregory's hostility has, in general, been curiously hollow. . . . He would get indignant over the White House's poor treatment of the press, but his actual coverage didn't betray much anger over their substantive assault on the country."

Gregory, like President Bush, was in Florida on September 11, 2001, when Al Qaeda terrorists attacked the World Trade Center, in New York, and the Pentagon, outside Washington, D.C. He was the only television journalist to accompany the president on his visit to Ground Zero three days later. During the remainder of Bush's two terms in the White House, Gregory covered the so-called war on terror day by day, starting with the invasion of Afghanistan by American and British forces in October 2001 and continuing with the invasion of Iraq in March 2003 by American, British, Australian, and Polish forces, which followed months of White House claims that Iraq possessed weapons of mass destruction. (No such weapons were found there.) Gregory's reports on those and related developments led repeatedly to complaints from both sides of the political spectrum. "I've been criticized by the left for being too cozy with Bush and not pushing hard enough in the run-up to the war," he told Kurtz, "and criticized by the right for being disrespectful or hysterical or just going nuts over things that don't matter." Gregory's extensive coverage of the "war on terror" also included his reports on ongoing conflicts between the Bush administration, its Republican supporters, and right-wing organizations, on one side, and Democrats, civil-liberties organizations, and left-leaning groups on the other. Those conflicts concerned such matters as lawful limits regarding domestic federal surveillance, the continuing detention and legal rights of prisoners at Guantánamo Bay, Cuba, and the legality of waterboarding and other coercive interrogation techniques used with captives suspected of terrorist acts.

The hundreds of events and issues on which Gregory reported as NBC's chief White House correspondent also included the deaths of several postal workers in 2001 from anthrax spores and the resulting nationwide panic, and the Bush administration's refusal the same year to support the United Nations' proposed International Criminal Court or to join 178 other nations in signing the Kyoto Treaty to curb global warming. In 2002 Gregory accompanied Vice President Richard B. "Dick" Cheney on a 12-nation tour of the Middle East, in which Cheney attempted to gain Arab support for a possible invasion of Iraq. Also in 2002 Gregory covered the meeting at which Bush and President Vladimir Putin of Russia signed the arms-reduction treaty that called upon the U.S. and Russia to reduce their arsenals of deployed strategic nuclear weapons by about two-thirds within the next 10 years. He reported on the administration's abandonment of the 1972 Antiballistic Missile Treaty signed by the U.S. and the Soviet Union and Bush's signing into law of the Sarbanes–Oxley Act, which called for various corporate reforms in the wake of accounting and other business-related scandals involving Enron, Tyco International, and other companies.

Gregory himself became the subject of news because of an incident at a joint press conference held on May 26, 2002 by Bush and French president Jacques Chirac in Paris, France, where anti-American protests had greeted Bush, as they had several days earlier in Germany. At the press conference, as Bill Sammon reported for the *Washington Times* (May 27, 2002, on-line), Gregory asked Bush, "I wonder why it is you think there are such strong sentiments in Europe against you and against this administration? Why, particularly, there's a view that you and your administration are trying to impose America's will on the rest of the world, particularly when it comes to the Middle East and where the war on terrorism goes next?" Gregory then turned to Chirac and said in French, "And, Mr. President, would you maybe comment on that?" "Very good," Bush said mockingly. "The guy memorizes four words, and he plays like he's intercontinental." "I can go on," Gregory responded. Bush then said, "I'm impressed—*que bueno*"— Spanish for "how wonderful." Later, as Bush turned away from the podium, he said to Gregory, "As soon as you get in front of a camera, you start showing off." On October 13, 2006, as a guest on the *Tonight Show with Jay Leno*, Gregory imitated Bush uttering those remarks and said that Bush had teased him about the incident for a long time afterward.

In 2003, among many other happenings, Gregory covered the White House reaction to the destruction of the space shuttle *Columbia* during its reentry into Earth's atmosphere and the deaths of the seven astronauts it carried; Bush's May 1 speech regarding Iraq while aboard the aircraft carrier USS *Abraham Lincoln*, where a huge banner behind the president read "Mission Accomplished," igniting much controversy as increasing street fighting in Iraq led to mounting numbers of casualties; and Bush's $350 billion, 10-year tax-cut package, enacted in May. In 2004 Gregory reported on the uproar sparked by the public dissemination of photos showing the abuse and torture of prisoners at Abu Ghraib, a prison complex in Iraq that was then under U.S. military control. The White House insisted that neither Bush nor anybody in his administration had ever approved the abuse or torture of captives; that only a few "bad apples" among enlisted soldiers, acting on their own, were guilty of misdeeds at Abu Ghraib; and that, in any case, the "war on terror" made irrelevant the Geneva Conventions or any other treaties or laws forbidding the use of torture. Also that year the Senate Select Intelligence Committee released a report disputing the existence of any credible evidence of weapons of mass destruction in Iraq. The president responded that invading Iraq had nevertheless been the right thing to do and that his policies had made Americans safer, because Saddam Hussein, the dictator of Iraq at the time of the invasion, wanted to possess such weapons and would have built them sooner or later. As Gregory reported, Bush used such arguments in his successful run for a second term in the White House.

Significant events that Gregory covered in 2005 included the Bush administration's response to the enormous destruction and loss of life caused by Hurricane Katrina along the American Gulf Coast—a response widely condemned as both belated and grossly inadequate. Also prominent in the news in 2005 were the confirmations of two of Bush's nominees for the U.S. Supreme Court—

John G. Roberts, who succeeded the deceased William Rehnquist as chief justice, and Samuel Alito, who replaced the retiring Sandra Day O'Connor—and the intense opposition that greeted Bush's nomination of his White House counsel, Harriet Miers, to fill O'Connor's post, which led him to withdraw her name from consideration.

In 2006 Gregory covered the White House reaction to such events as the announcement by President Mahmoud Ahmadinejad of Iran that his nation had successfully enriched uranium; North Korea's firing of a test missile over the Sea of Japan; and the same country's explosion of a nuclear weapon in North Korean mountains. He also reported on the reauthorization of the Patriot Act and Bush's assertion in a so-called signing statement that he would disregard that law's stipulation that he inform Congress about executive use of its provisions. Gregory spoke on NBC-TV news in 2006 about Bush's first veto of congressional legislation—that of a bill designed to expand the federally financed use of stem cells for research. He discussed Bush's veto of a similar bill the next year and, later, the president's 10 other vetoes, including that of a bill reauthorizing the Children's Health Insurance Program, known as CHIP, the Water Resources Development Act of 2007, the 2007 U.S. Farm Bill, and the 2008 Medicare Improvements for Patients and Providers Act—the last three vetoes of which the House and Senate overrode. In November 2006, after the Democrats won sufficient congressional elections to regain control of both the Senate and the House the following January, Gregory reported on Bush's acknowledgment that as head of the GOP, he was responsible to some extent for the "thumping" Republicans had taken at the polls.

In addition to the wars in Iraq and Afghanistan, the news in 2008 was dominated by the global economic recession, described as the worst since the Great Depression of the 1930s; the presidential primary contests; and the campaigns of the eventual Republican and Democratic nominees, U.S. senators John McCain of Arizona and Barack Obama of Illinois, respectively. With regard to the recession, Gregory reported on Bush's approval of the $700 billion Emergency Economic Stabilization Act of 2008—the so-called federal bailout of American financial institutions. Bush was virtually absent from the campaign trails of Republican candidates in 2008, largely because that year, according to various polls, fewer than a third of Americans approved of the way he was handling his job. (His approval rating had reached a high of about 85 percent in the weeks following 9/11.) During 2008 Gregory accompanied Bush on trips overseas, to a total of two dozen countries and the Vatican.

On June 13, 2008 Tim Russert, the highly respected and popular moderator of *Meet the Press* since 1991, suddenly died of a heart attack. During the next half-year, Tom Brokaw served in his place. NBC's announcement that Gregory would succeed Russert as *Meet the Press*'s permanent host was greeted with little surprise. The few reservations included the observation that unlike Russert, Gregory had no hands-on political experience and thus might be at a disadvantage in interviewing government officials. (Between 1977 and 1984 Russert, who had a law degree, served as a special counsel and chief of staff to Democratic U.S. senator Daniel Patrick Moynihan and then as counsel to New York governor Mario Cuomo, also a Democrat.) Gregory's recent guests on *Meet the Press* include Timothy F. Geithner, the U.S. treasury secretary (July 25, 2010); Mike Mullen, the chairman of the Joint Chiefs of Staff (August 1, 2010); David Petraeus, the commander of U.S. forces in Afghanistan (August 15, 2010); Arne Duncan, the U.S. secretary of education (September 26, 2010); and Robert Gibbs, the White House press secretary (October 27, 2010). Currently, *Meet the Press* competes on Sunday mornings with ABC's *This Week*, with Christiane Amanpour; CBS's *Face the Nation*, with Bob Schieffer; *Fox News Sunday*, with Chris Wallace; and CNN's *State of the Nation*, with Candy Crowley. Although *Meet the Press* attracts fewer viewers and a smaller percentage of total viewership for Sunday-morning talk shows than it did during Russert's time, it still tops its competitors in popularity, according to the Nielsen TV-ratings company.

Among journalists Gregory has been distinguished by his prematurely gray hair as well as his height. He met his wife, Beth A. Wilkinson, in 1997, when, as an assistant federal district attorney, she argued for the prosecution in the trial of Timothy McVeigh. The couple, who married in 2001, live in Washington, D.C., with their two sons and one daughter: Max, born in 2003, and twins, Ava and Jed, born in 2006. Gregory prepares all week for his interviews on *Meet the Press*, but he nevertheless has far more time to spend with his family than he had as NBC's White House correspondent. He enjoys cooking breakfast for his children and attending hockey games with Max. Since he became a father, he has studied Judaism regularly with a friend. "I was born into a tradition," he said at the 2008 conference on Judaism. "Who am I to let it slip through my fingers?"

—J.E.P.

Suggested Reading: *Los Angeles Times* E p1+ Dec. 8, 2008; *New Republic* p12+ June 4, 2007; *People* p9+ Mar. 16, 2009; Politico.com Dec. 2, 2008; *USA Today* Life p3 Dec. 8, 2008; *Washington Post* C p1+ Mar. 14, 2006

Greinke, Zack

(GRAIN-kee)

Oct. 21, 1983– Baseball player

Address: Kansas City Royals, Kauffman Stadium, 1 Royal Way, Kansas City, MO 64129-6969

Zack Greinke of the Kansas City Royals is widely considered to be among the best control pitchers in Major League Baseball (MLB)—meaning that he relies more on accuracy than on speed. His pitching repertoire includes a sharp slider, a mystifying curveball, a straight changeup, and a fastball, and he has the ability to vary the speed of pitches by as much as 40 miles per hour, constantly keeping hitters off balance. Mike Arbuckle, a senior adviser in the Royals organization, told Jim Salisbury for the *Philadelphia Inquirer* (May 17, 2009), "He's got four quality pitches, and he can throw any one in any count. He can overpower hitters when he needs to. He can change speeds when he needs to. This guy is fun to watch. When he pitches, people show up thinking they're going to see something special." Greinke was drafted by the Royals after graduating from high school, in 2002, and spent less than two years in the team's farm system before making his major-league debut, in May 2004, at the age of 20. In his rookie season he posted an 8–11 record with a 3.97 earned-run average (ERA) and was named the Royals' Pitcher of the Year. The

Ezra Shaw/Getty Images

sportswriter Joe Posnanski observed for the *Kansas City Star* (April 5, 2009) that during his debut season, Greinke was "unlike any young pitcher I had ever seen. He threw Bugs Bunny slow pitches, he threw ever-varying fastballs (it sometimes seemed he never threw two fastballs at the same speed), he tried all sorts of different windups, he was like a kid who is so bored in a classroom that he finds 101 different uses for a pencil. He was half pitcher, half scientist, and that's just not something you see in 20-year-old pitchers."

Greinke struggled to perform during his sophomore season, posting a 5–17 record and a 5.80 ERA. Greinke, who had long suffered from emotional and social problems, was also struggling internally, having grown increasingly uninterested in baseball and uncomfortable around his teammates. In early 2006 Greinke was granted a two-month leave of absence, during which he sought help from a sports psychologist, who diagnosed him with social-anxiety disorder (SAD) and depression and prescribed medication. Greinke returned to the Royals at the end of the 2006 season with renewed enthusiasm; he rejoined the Royals' starting rotation in 2008 and enjoyed a breakout season, finishing with a 13–10 record and 3.47 ERA. In 2009 he achieved career-high marks in virtually every major statistical category, including a 16–8 record and major-league–leading 2.16 ERA. He also won the American League (AL) Cy Young Award, which recognizes the league's best pitcher, and was named AL Pitcher of the Year by the magazine *Sporting News*. The Royals pitching coach Bob McClure, speaking with Jack Curry for the *New York Times* (April 24, 2009) about Greinke's transformation, noted, "I think there were a lot of expectations for Zack at a young age that it was hard to live up to. Zack is getting comfortable just being Zack."

The older of the two sons of Don and Marsha Greinke, Donald Zackary Greinke was born on October 21, 1983 in Orlando, Florida, and was raised in Apopka, an Orlando suburb. (His younger brother, Luke, also a pitcher, was selected by the New York Yankees in the 12th round of the 2008 MLB draft.) Zack Greinke excelled in golf and tennis as a youth and was, as Posnanski put it for the *Kansas City Star*, "too good to play golf with kids his own age, too good to play tennis with kids his own age." Emotional and social problems were also evident during his boyhood, however. When he was eight years old, for example, Greinke had posted a perfect 50–0 tennis-tournament record when the immense anxiety he felt before matches became too much for him. After intentionally losing a match, he quit the sport for good. He recalled to Wright Thompson for the *Kansas City (Missouri) Star* (April 20, 2006), "I had problems; I'd get real nervous before the games. The last time, I got so nervous and I was like, 'Dad, I can't play anymore.' I was going crazy thinking I was gonna lose. I got so nervous I ended up hitting every ball straight into the net. The second set, I was loose and I beat the guy like 6–2. I ended up quitting in the last one. I hit them into the net again." He told Wright, "I knew there was something wrong with me but I never thought about going to see anyone to talk about it."

Enamored with the thrill of hitting home runs, Greinke found relief from his anxiety problems in baseball. As a freshman at Apopka High School, he earned a spot on the varsity baseball team. He displayed all-around skills as a fielder, alternating between shortstop and first-base positions, and as a hitter, achieving a batting average of .444 or better every year of his high-school career and notching a total of 31 home runs and 144 runs batted in (RBIs). Greinke always took great pride in his hitting skills. While participating in a home-run derby at a high-school tournament in Atlanta, Georgia, Greinke, who bats and throws right-handed, established such a significant lead that he decided to hit the last pitch left-handed just for fun. "He crushed a long home run to the wonder of all," Posnanski wrote for the *Kansas City Star*. "And then he dropped the bat and walked off to the cheers." Though Greinke was always more interested in hitting, coaches recognized his throwing talent and trained him to become a pitcher for his senior year. Greinke proved to be a natural, "with such freakishly good control that he simply did not understand what the big deal was about throwing strikes," as Posnanski wrote for the *Kansas City Star*. That season he pitched 63 innings and posted a 9–2 record, with 118 strikeouts, only eight walks, and an astonishing 0.55 ERA, helping to lead Apopka High to a 30–3 record. He was also named Gatorade National Player of the Year. By the time Greinke graduated, he was one of the most heavily recruited pitchers in the country, with up to three dozen scouts in attendance at each of his games. He signed a letter of intent to attend Clemson University, in South Carolina, before deciding to forgo college to enter the 2002 MLB amateur draft. The Kansas City Royals selected Greinke sixth overall in the draft's first round and provided him a contract that included a signing bonus of about $2.4 million.

Greinke rapidly ascended the Royals' farm system. In the summer of 2002, he pitched three games for the Royals' Rookie League team in Davenport, Florida, before moving up to the organization's single-A affiliate in Spokane, Washington, and, shortly thereafter, to the Wilmington, Delaware, Blue Rocks, an advanced single-A affiliate. Greinke played with the Blue Rocks for the first half of the 2003 season, dominating the competition with a record of 11–1 and a 1.14 ERA in 14 starts. The Royals then sent him to play with the double-A Wichita Wranglers, with whom he went 4–3 with a 3.23 ERA in nine starts. That season he held opponents to three or fewer earned runs in 22 of his 23 starts, and in eight of his starts, he did not allow a single run. Opponents batted just .221 against him for the year. After compiling a combined 15–4 record and 1.93 ERA for the Wilmington and Wichita teams, Greinke was named the Royals' Minor League Pitcher of the Year, the *Sporting News* Minor League Player of the Year, and the Carolina League Player of the Year.

Greinke opened the 2004 season playing with the Omaha Royals, in the triple-A Pacific Coast League. After six starts with the club, Greinke made his major-league debut, on May 22, 2004, in a game against the Oakland Athletics. At 20 years and seven months old, he was the third-youngest pitcher in franchise history to start a game—after Bret Saberhagen, in 1984, and Mark Littell, in 1973. He pitched five innings, allowing two runs on five hits, and earned a no-decision in a 5–4, 11-inning loss. Greinke picked up his first career win (4–2) on June 8, 2004 in a contest against the Montreal Expos. In that game he allowed only three hits in seven innings. He also retired the first 10 batters and allowed only two runners to get as far as second base. Despite the struggles of the franchise—the Royals finished last in the AL Central Division that season, with a 58–104 record—Greinke finished the season with impressive numbers, notching a record of 8–11 and a 3.97 ERA in 24 games and allowing only 64 earned runs in 145 innings. His 3.97 ERA was the best on the team and the best of all major-league rookies. (Greinke's ERA would have earned him a spot on the MLB's list of top-10 pitchers if he had thrown in the requisite 162 innings to qualify for the ranking.) In addition, Greinke finished among the major-league rookie leaders in most statistical categories, including innings pitched (second), wins (third), and strikeouts (second, with 100). The majority of Greinke's losses were widely attributed to the lack of run support he received from the team, which scored only 15 runs in his 11 losses. At the end of the season, Greinke was named the Royals Pitcher of the Year and finished fourth in the voting for AL Rookie of the Year.

Despite his impressive rookie campaign, Greinke had grown increasingly anxious and uncomfortable in the locker room, the dugout, and the bullpen. His aloof attitude and his seeming lack of interest in the game perplexed his teammates and coaches, who came to interpret his behavior as the growing pains of a young player making a difficult transition to the major leagues. After recording solid numbers at the beginning of the 2005 season, posting a 3.09 ERA in his first eight starts, Greinke performed poorly for much of the rest of the year, finishing with a 5–17 record and a 5.80 ERA, while giving up 233 hits in 183 innings. The Royals ended the year with 106 losses, a franchise record high. Signs of Greinke's emotional instability emerged at various points during the season, most notably in a July game against the Arizona Diamondbacks, in which he gave up a franchise-record 11 earned runs and tied a club record by allowing 15 hits in only 4.1 innings. In that game, undoubtedly the worst of his professional career, the pitcher astounded viewers when he recorded the first major-league hit of his career—a home run (his only one to date) off the pitcher Russ Ortiz. Allard Baird, the former general manager of the Royals and now an assistant general manager with the Boston Red Sox, recalled to Posnanski for *Sports Il-*

lustrated (April, 28, 2009, on-line), "I remember when he hit that home run, [manager] Buddy [Bell] walked to the top step and looked up at me in the press box with his hands out. And it was like, 'You have *got* to be kidding me.'" Greinke's sudden burst of power was the result of his pent-up frustration with his poor performance that day and with his experiences on the team. The game was a 12–11 loss for the Royals and a no-decision for Greinke.

In the off-season Greinke's emotional problems became more severe. He missed practices and participated reluctantly in team events; he even quarreled with his coaches. In late February 2006, after a few disastrous bullpen sessions, Greinke realized that he needed a break from baseball. "The way I was throwing," he told Thompson, "it wasn't me throwing. I couldn't throw a strike. I couldn't think about throwing a strike. I couldn't focus. And I had the worst bullpen of my life one day, and the next time [in the bullpen] I was trying to throw my arm off just because I was going crazy. I was throwing everything 100 miles per hour. That's when I was like, I can't keep doing this." After speaking with his coaches and Royals officials, Greinke was granted a two-month leave of absence to sort out his problems. Recalling his discussion with Greinke, Baird told Posnanski for the *Kansas City Star*, "That was one of the most emotional conversations I've ever had with anyone. It had nothing at all to do with baseball. I just saw a young man in a lot of pain." Baird also told Bob Nightengale for *USA Today* (May 1, 2008) that he "never thought [Greinke would] leave baseball forever, anyways." Greinke, who did not initially intend to return to baseball, considered careers in other areas, including professional golf. While staying at his parents' home, near Orlando, Florida, he sought the counsel of a sports psychologist, who diagnosed him with clinical depression and social-anxiety disorder. The latter condition is marked by extreme tension in social settings and affects more than 19 million Americans. (Other high-profile athletes have been diagnosed with the disorder, perhaps most notably the Miami Dolphins running back Ricky Williams.) Greinke, whose family has a history of depression, began receiving treatment that included prescribed medication and soon decided to return to baseball. "The problem I have isn't going to bother me just if I play baseball," Greinke told Thompson. "It's gonna bother me no matter what I'm doing. That's one thing I realized when I left and started talking to some people. I realized that it's not just at the baseball field that [my condition is] like this."

In June 2006 Greinke returned to the double-A Wichita Wranglers and started to rebuild his relationship with the world of professional baseball. He added more velocity to his pitches and made several adjustments to his delivery. He also focused on having more fun on the field. The changes helped: he went 8–3 with a 4.34 ERA in 18 games and was named Wichita Pitcher of the Year. Greinke was called back up to the major leagues in late September and made three relief appearances for the Royals, allowing three runs in six innings and posting a 1–0 record with a 4.26 ERA. Greinke has since credited Baird, who was fired from the Royals in May 2006, for being instrumental in his recovery and return to baseball. "I don't know if I make it back without Allard," he told Nightengale. "He did so much to help me as a person, it was like he was learning about [my illness] along with me. He never once said, 'We need you back.' He never once rushed me. Here he was, knowing his job was on the line, and he was more worried about me than his own job. I'll never forget what he did for me."

Greinke began the 2007 season as the Royals' number-three starting pitcher. In seven starts he went 1–4 with a 5.71 ERA, before his struggles sent him back to the bullpen. He soon found that he excelled in the role of relief pitcher and notched a 4–1 record with one save and a 3.54 ERA in 38 relief appearances. He returned to the Royals' starting rotation in August and finished the season on a strong note, going 2–2 with a 1.85 ERA in his last seven starts. His 1.54 ERA led the majors from August to the end of the season. For the year Greinke posted a 7–7 record with a 3.69 ERA. Greinke had a successful 2008 season, compiling a record of 13–10. (His 13 wins were the most achieved by a Royals pitcher in 11 years.) He also posted a 3.47 ERA—the best of any Royals pitcher since 1997—with 183 strikeouts in 202.1 innings, both career highs. The Royals displayed their renewed faith in Greinke during the 2009 off-season by signing him to a four-year, $38 million contract. During spring training Greinke worked on improving his change-up pitch, which in the past he had struggled to keep low to the ground.

In 2009 Greinke posted what was arguably the greatest pitching season in Royals history. In his first 24 innings, he allowed no runs, extending his total number of consecutive scoreless innings to 38 after having closed out the 2008 season with 14 shutout innings. Greinke also won his first four starts and became the first pitcher in major-league history to post an ERA of 0.00 while recording at least 36 strikeouts during the first four games in a season. After his next two starts (both wins), his ERA of 0.40 was the third-lowest in major-league history that deep into a season. (The first and second lowest ERAs were held by the Washington Senators' Walter Johnson in 1913 and the Los Angeles Dodgers' Fernando Valenzuela in 1981.) Greinke was subsequently named the American League Pitcher of the Month for April after going 5–0 with a 0.50 ERA and 44 strikeouts, while allowing only two earned runs in 36 innings. He was then selected for the AL All-Star team, after receiving 360 votes—more than any other major-league pitcher. In August Greinke broke the Royals' single-game strikeout record by fanning 15 batters in a game against the Cleveland Indians, which the Royals won, 6–2. Greinke followed that performance with a one-hit complete-game shutout win

(3–0) over the Seattle Mariners, in which he retired the last 22 batters. He finished the season with a record of 16–8 and an ERA of 2.16; both marks were the best in the majors. He also finished at or near the top in most other statistical categories for AL pitchers, leading the league in opponent on-base percentage (.276), base runners allowed per nine innings (9.81), and home runs per nine innings (0.43). He finished second in the AL in complete games (six), shutouts (four), strikeouts (242), opponent batting average (.230), opponent slugging average (.336), hits per nine innings (7.65), and strikeout-to-walk ratio (4.75). As had been the case in earlier seasons, most of Greinke's losses could be attributed to poor run support; the Royals scored only 13 total runs in his eight losses (an average of 1.6 per game) and only 34 runs in his 17 combined starts and no-decisions. The Royals again finished in last place in their division, with a 65–97 record. Greinke's stellar regular-season performance, however, did not go overlooked. At the end of the season, he was named AL Pitcher of the Year by the magazine *Sporting News,* and he also won the Cy Young Award, receiving 25 of 28 first-place votes. Greinke was only the third pitcher in Royals history to win a Cy Young Award, after Bret Saberhagen (1985 and 1989) and David Cone (1994), and the fourth pitcher in history to win the award on a team that finished last place in its division.

In 2010 Greinke posted a record of 10–14 and an ERA of 4.17. He finished seventh in the AL in innings (220.0) and eighth in the league in complete games (three). The Royals ended the season with a record of 67–95, finishing last in their division for the sixth time in seven years. Greinke, who has repeatedly voiced his frustration with the Royals' losing ways, was the subject of trade rumors during the 2010 off-season.

Greinke is "the most competitive person I've ever met in my life," the Royals' starting pitcher Brian Bannister, a friend of Greinke's, explained to Jerry Crasnick for ESPN.com (February 21, 2010). "It doesn't matter what it is—he will find a way to claim he's better than you at anything. Like brushing your teeth. He'll find a way to somehow criticize you about your technique and explain how he's better at it." Greinke has been known to be blunt when speaking with members of the press, and for that reason he has sometimes been accused of being arrogant. "It's not that I'm shy," Greinke told Nightengale. "I just don't like talking. I'd rather be by myself than talk to people." He continued, "It's just like now. I'm not going to sit here and say everything is great when sometimes everything is not so great. I may have a bad day or a bad week. But, as I've learned, that's OK, too."

On November 21, 2009, Greinke married his high-school sweetheart, Emily Kuchar, a former Miss Daytona Beach USA and a former Dallas Cowboys cheerleader.

—C.C.

Suggested Reading: ESPN.com Feb. 21, 2010; *Kansas City (Missouri) Star* A p1 Apr. 20, 2006, G p10+ Apr. 5, 2009; Major League Baseball (MLB) Official Web site; *New York Times* B p11 Apr. 24, 2009; *Orlando (Florida) Sentinel* C p1+ June 22, 2009; *Philadelphia Inquirer* E p8+ May 17, 2009; *Sports Illustrated* (on-line) Apr. 28, 2009; *USA Today* C p1 May 1, 2008, C p1 May 4, 2009

Courtesy of PIMCO

Gross, William H.

Apr. 13, 1944– Bond-fund manager

Address: Pacific Investment Management Co., 840 Newport Center Dr., Suite 100, Newport Beach, CA 92660

Described over the years as the "bond king," "the world's most successful bond manager," and "perhaps the savviest bond manager around," William H. Gross is one of the most important financiers in the nation. Gross is co-founder, co–chief investment officer (CIO), and managing director of Pacific Investment Management Co. LLC (PIMCO)—"the world's largest and most influential bond investment house," as Katie Benner reported for *Fortune* (March 2, 2009). The firm is based in Newport Beach, California, and has more than 1,300 employees in offices in New York City; the Netherlands; Singapore; Japan; England; Australia; Germany; Canada; and China. Home of the PIMCO Total Return Fund, the largest mutual fund in the world, the firm had a total of $1.07 trillion in assets under management as of March 31, 2010.

Gross has earned such a reputation in the industry that his monthly "Investment Outlook" column, posted on PIMCO's Web site, has become a must-read for bond investors. Christopher Palmeri wrote for *BusinessWeek* (June 9, 2003, on-line) that Gross is "the guru of the bond market . . . and the most widely quoted and closely watched bond expert in the county."

William Hunt "Bill" Gross was born on April 13, 1944 in Middletown, Ohio, a steel-company town situated between Cincinnati and Dayton. His father, Sewell "Dutch" Gross, worked as a sales executive at the steel manufacturer American Rolling Mills Corp., or Armco. (The company, now known as AK Steel Holding Corp., moved its headquarters from Middletown to West Chester, Ohio, in 2007.) His mother, Shirley, was a homemaker. Gross has an older brother, Craig, and a younger sister, Lyn. The family relocated to San Francisco, California, in 1954, after Dutch Gross was assigned to an office in the area; Monee Fields-White, writing for the Bloomberg financial news Web site (April 30, 2004), reported that Bill Gross was "staggered by the scale" of San Francisco, quoting him as saying, "It was just like another universe." Following his high-school graduation, in 1962, Gross received an academic scholarship to attend Duke University, in Durham, North Carolina. Unsure about his career goals, he majored in psychology. During the summers he managed slot machines at Harrah's casino in Lake Tahoe, Nevada.

During his senior year, in 1966, Gross was involved in a near-fatal car crash when his vehicle skidded on an icy road into incoming traffic. Thrown through his car's windshield, he lost three-quarters of his scalp and suffered a collapsed lung. To pass the time during the months he spent recovering from the accident, he read the mathematician Edward O. Thorp's *Beat the Dealer: A Winning Strategy for the Game of Twenty-One* (1962), a gambling-strategy book about the card game blackjack. That book was the first to prove mathematically that one could win at blackjack—that is, receive cards with a greater numerical value than the dealer's without going over 21—with a card-counting system, which would determine the ratio of high cards to low cards remaining in the deck and reveal a player's chances against the house.

Following his graduation from Duke, in 1966, Gross went to Las Vegas, Nevada, and became a professional blackjack player. Competing for 16 hours every day (while living in a $6-per-night hotel) during his few months there, Gross turned the $200 he started with into $10,000 in less than four months. "It was blackjack that got me interested in securities markets," he told Timothy Middleton for the *New York Times* (July 6, 1997). "When I found out you could beat the house at blackjack—and you can—it encouraged me to test my skills in financial markets."

Meanwhile, upon graduating from college, Gross had enlisted in the U.S. Navy. He reported to the Naval Air Station in Pensacola, Florida, in October 1966, hoping to become a fighter pilot. His flying skills were severely lacking, however, and Gross was instead sent to Vietnam—where war was escalating—to serve as an assistant chief engineer on a World War II destroyer escort being used to transport Navy SEALS. Fields-White paraphrased Gross as saying that he "was never less qualified for a job before or since." Gross wrote about that experience for PIMCO's newsletter, as quoted by E. Scott Reckard for the *Los Angeles Times* (July 8, 1999), "I sweated bullets, even if I didn't fire many." He left the navy in 1969.

Using the money he had earned in Las Vegas, Gross obtained an M.B.A. degree from the University of California at Los Angeles in 1971. Soon afterward he became a junior bond analyst for the Pacific Mutual Insurance Co. "I initially wanted to work on stocks, not bonds," Gross explained to Steve Thomas for the Orange County, California, magazine *OC Metro* (October 30, 2003). He took his position "thinking I could switch to equities after a year or two. But then a passion for bonds set in and I've been hooked, and will continue to be hooked, for the rest of my life."

A bond is a debt security issued by companies and governments. When an investor buys a bond, he or she is essentially lending the issuer money. In exchange, the investor receives a fixed return (interest rate or "coupon rate") on the investment. Bonds are usually issued for a specified time period, which can range from a year to more than 10 years and is known as the bond's maturity. By contrast, when an investor buys stock (or equity), he or she is buying part-ownership in a company. Investment in a certain stock can be indefinite. Generally, stocks can produce greater returns on investments in a shorter time than bonds, but they are also particularly volatile, since their value is heavily dependent on the overall health of the stock market and the economy. Bonds, though they are usually long-term and may not produce as high a return as stocks, are more stable during market fluctuations and economic downturns.

Gross and his colleagues William Podlich and James F. Muzzy persuaded Pacific Mutual to allow them to manage bond investments. Thus, PIMCO was created in 1971, as a division of Pacific Mutual, with $5 million in assets under management. Gross managed the fund while Muzzy dealt with the marketing aspects of the business and Podlich handled administration. Gross was promoted to senior analyst in 1973 and named vice president for fixed-income securities in 1976. Although PIMCO's growth was slow during its first years, the investments handled by the firm, which at the time serviced clients including AT&T and the Bechtel Corp., nearly doubled in the first half of 1978, to $205 million. By 1980 PIMCO, with $1.5 billion in assets under management, was ranked first among all bank and insurance-company bond managers

evaluated by the money-management publication *Pensions & Investments*. Over the preceding five years, PIMCO had averaged an annual total return of 11.2 percent. (In comparison, Salomon Brothers, another top firm, averaged 5.8 percent.)

As PIMCO enjoyed mounting success, Gross and his colleagues demanded independence from their parent company. In 1982 the chief executive officer (CEO) of Pacific Mutual, Walter Gerken, signed the contract granting PIMCO managers autonomy as well as profits from their earnings. PIMCO formally split from Pacific Mutual in 1985. (In May 2000 the German insurance giant Allianz SE bought 70 percent of PIMCO. To keep Gross on board, Allianz paid him $40 million annually—on top of his regular salary—through 2005.)

PIMCO's Total Return Bond Fund, introduced in 1975, has become the crown jewel of the investment firm. Between the time Gross took over the fund, in May 1987, and May 2007, the fund had an average annual return of 8.29 percent, compared with an average of 7.25 percent for similar funds ranked by Morningstar Inc., an independent investment-research company. In 1992 the Total Return fund received the coveted five-star rating by Morningstar, which awards funds between one and five stars based on annual returns and risk.

Although, in 2005, Gross predicted the looming subprime-mortgage crisis and was able to spare his clients the worst when the housing bubble burst the following year, he miscalculated the government's reaction to the crisis. His belief that the Federal Reserve would cut interest rates to boost the U.S. housing market led him to avoid high-yield corporate bonds and buy securities that would gain from a rate cut. The Federal Reserve, however, did not lower rates, and high-yield bonds ended up earning substantial amounts of money. Due to Gross's poor investments, the Total Return Fund earned only 6.22 percent in 2006–07, while similar funds averaged 6.96, and it trailed almost three-quarters of its competitors. Still, among the five largest bond funds in the nation, Total Return retained the best 10-year (1997–2007) annual average, at 5.9 percent. The fund has since rallied; as of October 6, 2010, it held nearly $234 billion in assets. Its annual return has averaged 9.94 percent over the past three years.

Gross has attributed his remarkable track record in part to the firm's annual Secular Forum, a three-day investment summit at which PIMCO's top employees and invited speakers discuss the future of the world's economies and develop plans of action. "We try to take the day-to-day depression and euphoria out of the market," Gross explained to Christopher Palmeri, adding that the summit "provides a road map." Palmeri wrote, "Those maps have led to consistent profitability for [Gross's] clients. Gross's bear-market call in the stagflated 1970s helped PIMCO's funds outperform the pack. A bullish stance in the following two decades boosted the firm's assets from $5 million, when Gross joined the firm in 1973, to over $345 billion [in 2003]." (Writing for the March 4, 2002 issue of *Fortune*, David Rynecki reported that Gross also moderates PIMCO's "Portfolio Manager's Strategy Meeting," which Rynecki described as "a full-on brainiac shoving match that takes place every quarter.") PIMCO has also remained much more diverse than most other bond funds; instead of focusing on specific sectors of the bond market, the firm's employees have become experts in all sectors, including hedged foreign bonds, futures, and options markets. Summing up the firm's strategy, Gross told the PR Newswire Association (January 21, 1993) that PIMCO has achieved success by "taking the long view, where we stay the course in spite of temporary bumps in the road, and by running down every opportunity in the bond market that makes sense for our clients."

Still, Gross and PIMCO have not been without their share of controversy. In February 2004 the New Jersey attorney general, Peter Harvey, filed a lawsuit against PIMCO and PEA Capital LLC, a unit of PIMCO's parent company, Allianz. The suit claimed that the firms had allowed Canary Capital Partners, a Secaucus, New Jersey, hedge-fund firm, to "make rapid trades in and out of certain funds," Monee Fields-White explained. "So-called market-timing trades bilk other investors in funds by saddling them with additional trading fees and illegally giving certain investors an advantage." The suit further alleged, Fields-White wrote, that PEA and PIMCO "also let Canary buy shares of one fund, exchange them for shares of a second and then transfer back to the original fund, a tactic known as round-trip trading." In an effort to prove the firm's innocence, Gross and PIMCO's CEO, William Thompson, published a letter in the form of a full-page advertisement in a number of nationally distributed newspapers. Gross admitted that PIMCO had made an agreement with Canary in 2002 that allowed the hedge fund one "round-trip" trade in PIMCO funds per month, but he contended that the deal was not illegal and that Canary trades had not hurt shareholders in PIMCO's mutual funds. (Gross did not directly manage any of the company's funds that were cited in the lawsuit.) PIMCO was cleared of all charges in June, but PEA and two other Allianz subsidiaries faced federal charges. The Securities and Exchange Commission dropped the charges against the three firms later that month when they agreed to pay a fine.

Recently, Gross and PIMCO have been criticized for what some perceive as their growing sway over the U.S. government. As one of the few healthy financial institutions during the nation's recent economic and financial-market downturns, Katie Benner wrote, PIMCO "has become the U.S. government's partner in reviving the credit markets. It runs the Federal Reserve's $251 billion commercial paper program, which keeps short-term loans flowing to corporate America. It is also one of four asset managers picked to run the government's $500 billion program to purchase mortgage-backed securities. With many traditional bond market players—like investment banks, insurers, and pension funds—on the sidelines, Pimco is serving as a buyer of last resort for hedge funds and others seeking to sell bonds to raise cash."

One critic, the venture capitalist and management consultant Peter Cohan, told Benner, "This is a bilateral monopoly with one big seller and one big buyer. Gross, a famously good gambler, knows that winning in this type of market means threatening not to buy when the government needs to sell. Gross has the government in a weak negotiating position." An example of Gross's influence, critics say, is the government bailout of the mortgage giants Freddie Mac and Fannie Mae. Starting in 2007 Gross was a vocal advocate for the government takeover. By May 2008 he had moved 60 percent of Total Return, a 20 percent increase from the previous year, into mortgages backed by Fannie Mae and Freddie Mac as well as other so-called government-sponsored enterprises (GREs). When the U.S. Treasury took control of Freddie Mac and Fannie Mae on September 7, PIMCO's Total Return Fund earned more than $1.7 billion. "[Gross] convinced the Treasury to keep his bonds from going to zero, or else he would stop lending money to distressed companies that were important to the economy," Cohan alleged. Gross, responding to the criticism, told Benner, "If you're in a marriage, each person has his or her own concept of what the argument is about. That's because they perceive reality differently, and not always because one is right and the other is wrong. The policy prescriptions I've proposed were a realistic attempt to assist the markets. In my eyes, they had nothing to do with bailing out our positions."

Over the past four decades, Gross and PIMCO have received numerous accolades within the industry. In December 1996 Gross became the first portfolio manager inducted into the Fixed Income Analysts Society's Hall of Fame, for his contributions to the advancement of fixed-income analysis and portfolio management. In his speech during Gross's induction, Jack Malvey, former president of the Fixed-Income Analysts Society, noted, referring to the famed stock-market guru who managed Fidelity's Magellan fund from 1977 to 1990, "Bill often has been characterized as the Peter Lynch of the bond markets. But based on his longevity (2.5 times Mr. Lynch) and the size of his assets under management (nearly 5 times the Magellan fund), it would be more appropriate to characterize Peter Lynch as the Bill Gross of the equity markets." Gross and his investment team have been selected as Morningstar's fixed-income manager of the year on three separate occasions (1998, 2000, and 2007), and PIMCO was named the 2007 credit investor of the year by *Derivatives Week*, the 2008 fixed-income provider of the year by *Global Pensions Magazine*, and global fixed-income manager of the year by both *Professional Pensions* (2008) and *Financial News* (2006). In 2003 Gross was number 10 on *Fortune*'s list of the "25 Most Powerful People in Business," and in May 2007 he was named one of the most influential individuals on Wall Street by *Investment Advisor Magazine*. In January 2010 Morningstar named Gross the fixed-income manager of the decade.

Rynecki described Gross as "a man who compartmentalizes and analyzes every action so that it fits into a routine so damn monotonous that it would drive most people to distraction. . . . Spend a week with the man, and against all instincts you come to understand that this might be the most exciting routine in the world." Gross is a tall, lanky man with graying brown hair and is known for wearing his ties unknotted and draped around his neck. He is soft-spoken and self-effacing. "[Gross is] not the typical Wall Street guy who's so full of himself that you get turned off," Raymond Watson, a former longtime member of the board of Pacific Mutual Life Insurance, told E. Scott Reckard. "He doesn't say, 'I know what the bond market will do.' It's more like, 'Here's what I believe might happen—but I've been wrong before.'" Gross has written numerous articles on the bond market and authored two books, *Everything You've Heard About Investing Is Wrong!* (1997) and *Bill Gross on Investing* (1998). He appears frequently on national news programs.

The 66-year-old Gross practices yoga for at least an hour each day and has run in several marathons. Since childhood he has collected stamps. His extensive collection, which includes a complete set of U.S. stamps produced between 1847 and 1869, has been displayed at the Washington Convention Center, in Washington, D.C. In June 2007 Gross auctioned off his collection of classic British stamps, which included a block of Penny Black, the world's first postage stamp, issued in 1840, and an envelope affixed with the world's first three stamps. The collection earned $9.1 million, the highest amount ever paid in a single stamp-auction sale, all of which was donated to the international humanitarian organization Doctors Without Borders/Médecins Sans Frontières. Gross and his wife, Sue, frequently contribute to charities and donate $100,000 annually to Orange County's Teacher of the Year program. They reside in Laguna Beach, California, and have three grown children: two sons, Jeff and Nick, and a daughter, Jennifer.

—M.A.S.

Suggested Reading: *BusinessWeek* (on-line) June 9, 2003; *Forbes* p154+ Sep. 17, 2007; *Fortune* p98 Mar. 4, 2002, p80 Mar. 2, 2009; *New York Times* III p11 July 6, 1997; *Orange County (California) Business Journal* p1 Jan. 6–12, 2003; pimco.com

Selected Books: *Everything You've Heard About Investing Is Wrong!*, 1997; *Bill Gross on Investing*, 1998

Grossman, Lev

June 26, 1969– Writer

Address: Time, *1271 Ave. of the Americas, 23d Fl., New York, NY 10020*

"There was a time—yes my children, the legends are true—when J. R. R. Tolkien was not cool. Really. Very much not cool. Also video games, and Spider-Man, and the X-Men. There was a time, not even that long ago, when you could get beaten up by jocks in the woods behind the backstop for being down with X-Men," Lev Grossman wrote in an essay for *Time* magazine (September 25, 2005, online) called "The Geek Shall Inherit the Earth." The piece examined the cultural shift that has made "nerd culture"—as epitomized by comic books, video games, and the fantasy and science-fiction genres—increasingly fashionable with mainstream audiences as the influence of the Internet has expanded. Grossman, currently a book critic and technology writer for *Time*, has been interested in that culture since he was a child, and he touches upon it in much of his work, which also includes three novels: *Warp* (1997), *Codex* (2004), and *The Magicians* (2009). "*Harry Potter, The Chronicles of Narnia* and *The Lord of the Rings* series are all paid various levels of homage," Henry C. Jackson wrote

Amy Sussman/Getty Images for Tribeca Film Festival

in his Associated Press review of *The Magicians*, as published in the *Missoulian* (September 5, 2009, on-line). "Yet Grossman's performed a nifty trick.

While he borrows heavily from fantasy's canon, he has crafted a work that is strikingly original in plot and construction."

Lev Thomas Grossman was born on June 26, 1969 in Concord, Massachusetts. He grew up in nearby Lexington, a "placid little suburb of Boston," as he described it for his Web site. Grossman's mother, Judith, is a novelist and short-story writer, and his father, Allen, is a poet whose honors include a MacArthur Fellowship and a Bollingen Prize. The two have also taught at such institutions as Johns Hopkins University, Bennington College, and the University of Iowa. Grossman has a twin brother, Austin, a video-game developer and novelist, and a sister, Bathsheba, an artist specializing in sculptures based on mathematical models. He also has two half-brothers from his father's first marriage, which ended in divorce. "My parents were a bit like those tennis parents who start drilling their kids on the court when they're about two, with the idea of creating some kind of inhumanly precocious tennis prodigy," Grossman told an interviewer for BookReporter.com (August 14, 2009). "Mine were very aggressive about exposing me to the finer sorts of books early on, with the idea of turning me—and my brother and sister—into teenage super-literati. Then my father made the mistake of reading me *The Hobbit*, and at a stroke all their careful work was undone."

To his parents' dismay, Grossman gravitated solely to comic books and science-fiction and fantasy novels. "It was an act of very calculated treason," he told Ed Park for the *Los Angeles Times* (August 16, 2009). "I was not a very rebellious child or rebellious teenager—or rebellious adult!—but to the extent that I was, my love of fantasy was it. These were not books my parents approved of or placed values on." He continued, "Growing up in the '70s and '80s, science fiction and especially fantasy had such a stigma attached to them. I felt so punished and exiled for being devoted to these things."

In 1991 Grossman graduated magna cum laude from Harvard University, in Cambridge, Massachusetts, with a B.A. degree in literature. "[I then] spent several aimless years wandering around reading and temping and trying and failing to learn various foreign languages," he wrote on his Web site. Grossman subsequently enrolled in a graduate program in comparative literature at Yale University, in New Haven, Connecticut. He earned a master's degree in 1996 but left before obtaining a doctoral degree, "once I realized that a career in comparing literature was not for me," as he quipped.

Grossman next worked for a string of dot-com companies while writing freelance articles about books, technology, and culture for such periodicals as *Lingua Franca*, the *Village Voice, Entertainment Weekly, Salon,* and the *New York Times.* Concurrently, he began developing ideas for his novels. In 1997 he published *Warp*, whose protagonist is Hollis, a science-fiction–obsessed recent Harvard graduate who is unsure of what to do with his life.

Reviews were largely mixed. "Grossman does not so much tell [Hollis's] story as take a snapshot of him during a time of indecision as he wanders through an evening and a night and a day in search of meaning," a critic wrote for *Kirkus Reviews* (October 15, 1997, on-line). "Hollis is a likable fellow, a smart-ass, though not malicious, always visualizing himself in *Star Trek* episodes; or as a noble knight-errant who must leave beautiful maidens behind as he goes off to serve the king; or as a brave little boy in a children's story, sailing out to capture a sea monster that has been terrorizing the village." The reviewer found the author "reminiscent of the young [F. Scott] Fitzgerald," but concluded, "Grossman can write, but sooner or later he'll have to find a subject." In a review for the British Web site FantasticFiction.co.uk, Doris Lynch called *Warp* "a fun take on life for the twentysomething crowd that doesn't quite succeed but offers entertaining moments."

Unlike the professional reviewers of his book, the reading public was sometimes scathing. Grossman was so hurt by the many negative reviews his book received from customers of Amazon.com that he rashly decided to post his own positive reviews on the site, using fake names. He explained in an article titled "Terrors of the Amazon" for *Salon* (March 2, 1999, on-line), "As a novelist, I'm comfortable with fictional alter egos, so I went undercover. 'I loved this book,' I wrote, posing as a 'reader from' (for some reason) 'Philadelphia.' 'I highly recommend it.' Five stars." Grossman wrote several more such reviews and thereby raised his average Amazon rating to 2.5 (out of five) stars. Grossman's reviews were ultimately revealed as fake. (Some skeptics have suggested that he may have also written the negative reviews, thus orchestrating the entire series of events in an effort to attract publicity.)

In 2004 Grossman published his second novel, *Codex*, which follows Edward Wozny, a talented young investment banker who is recruited by one of his clients, the elderly Duchess of Bowmry, to organize her library. Soon he and his attractive assistant discover that the duchess is competing with her husband to locate an ancient book (or codex) that could destroy the family name. Meanwhile, Wozny is becoming obsessed with a video game that eerily parallels his search for the codex. David Lazarus wrote in his review for the *San Francisco Chronicle* (March 7, 2004), "This is one of those deeply nuanced tales in which small things take on great significance and readers are rewarded for paying close attention to details. It also demonstrates time and again an affection not just for books but also for the pursuit of knowledge. It is, like the manuscript Edward seeks, the story of a quest." Offering a different take in his review for *Newsday* (February 29, 2004), Charles Taylor described the book as "a moderately engrossing time-killer" and wrote, "*Codex* is Lev Grossman's bid at the market that has sprung up for mysteries with historical backgrounds, and for stories about mysteries hidden in old books." The book became a modest best-seller.

In 2007 Grossman's brother, Austin, published a novel, *Soon I Will Be Invincible*, about a group of modern-day superheroes called the Champions and a villain named Dr. Impossible. Impressed and inspired after reading an early draft of the book, Grossman decided to give up trying to write a literary novel. "I always loved [fantasy and science fiction]—I just didn't take it seriously," Grossman told Jason Heller for the *A.V. Club* (August 26, 2009, on-line). "Suddenly I realized that this was my cultural DNA, not [Jonathan Franzen's acclaimed novel] *The Corrections*, but all this nerdy stuff." Grossman told Heller that when he read his brother's book, "I realized I'd been going about writing fiction all wrong. And when I started writing [*The Magicians*], it was like nothing else. It was like I'd been writing in a foreign language my whole life, and I'd decided to write something in my mother tongue."

The protagonist of *The Magicians*, published in 2009, is Quentin Coldwater, a brilliant but socially awkward high-school senior who harbors a secret passion for reading fantasy novels. While on his way to an admissions interview at Princeton University, he is tapped to attend the Brakebills College of Magic. While many reviewers pointed out the plot's similarity to that of J. K. Rowling's first book, *Harry Potter and the Sorcerer's Stone*, Grossman's character is several years older than Harry, who is 11 when Rowling's series begins; thus, Quentin is able to engage in sex, drinking, and other adult pursuits while at Brakebills. (The book also contains a nod to the venerable writer C.S. Lewis; Quentin is obsessed with *Fillory and Further*, a series similar in style to *The Chronicles of Narnia*.)

The Magicians received largely positive reviews. Keith Donahue wrote for the *Washington Post* (August 1, 2009): "Grossman . . . clearly has read his Potter and much more. While this story invariably echoes a whole body of romantic coming-of-age tales, Grossman's American variation is fresh and compelling. Like a jazz musician, he riffs on Potter and Narnia, but makes it his own." Ed Park concurred, writing: "Spells are cast, demons unleashed; indeed, a fairy is present (albeit one who notes that 'pixie' is the technical term). The novel manages a literary magic trick: It's both an enchantingly written fantasy and a moving deconstruction of enchantingly written fantasies." "Even if its author, Lev Grossman, weren't a colleague and friend, I'd be fervently recommending *The Magicians* to any reader who fell under the spell of Narnia or Harry Potter as a child and looks back on it all with an adult's ambivalence," Laura Miller wrote for *Salon* (August 12, 2009, on-line). "*The Magicians* is a grown-up's book, one that reflects on the sort of questions you never think to ask about fantasy narratives as a kid, such as: Is it such a good idea to meddle in the politics of a strange country you barely understand? Wouldn't magical

powers drain much of the challenge—and therefore the purpose—out of life? If animals and trees could really talk, would they have anything especially interesting to say? Instead of deflating the novel's spell, this skepticism liberates the story from the old fantasy clichés and takes it into exhilaratingly uncharted territory."

As a book reviewer for *Time*, a post he has held since 2002, Grossman has written about several of his fellow fantasy authors, including Stephenie Meyer and J. K. Rowling. He received significant attention for an essay he published in the July 12, 2007 issue, shortly before the publication of the seventh and final book in Rowling's series, *Harry Potter and the Deathly Hallows*. In it he wrote, "Rowling's work is so familiar that we've forgotten how radical it really is. Look at her literary forebears. In *The Lord of the Rings*, J. R. R. Tolkien fused his ardent Catholicism with a deep, nostalgic love for the unspoiled English landscape. C. S. Lewis was a devout Anglican whose *Chronicles of Narnia* forms an extended argument for Christian faith. Now look at Rowling's books. What's missing? If you want to know who dies in Harry Potter, the answer is easy: God."

Grossman also writes frequently for *Time* on issues relating to technology. For the August 30, 2007 issue, he penned a now-infamous essay aimed at explaining the culture of video games to a general readership. Grossman angered many insiders by stating, "The cliché about gamers is that they're antisocial, if not sociopathic," and adding, "Those who belong to [the gaming subculture] love it with a lonely, alienated, unironic passion." Grossman contributes regular entries to *Time*'s Techland blog and appears in the humorous on-line videos collectively known as *The Techland Show*, which has included installments titled "The iPhone Porn Episode," "The Giant Xbox Controller Edition," and "Shooting Civilians Is Wrong."

Grossman has been seen on various television shows. He has appeared, for example, on ABC's *Good Morning America* and on CNN, on which he has presented *Time*'s selection of the year's best inventions.

In 2000 Grossman married Heather O'Donnell, whom he had met in a Yale graduate-school course on James Joyce. According to their wedding announcement in the *New York Times* (April 2, 2000, on-line): "One day, in a unisex bathroom frequented mainly by graduate students at Yale's Sterling Library, [O'Donnell] was startled to read on a bathroom stall, 'I'm in love with a girl named Heather, but she doesn't love me.' She hurriedly wrote beneath that sentence: 'I do love you, Lev, but please stop writing about our romance on bathroom walls.'" The couple later divorced. Grossman currently lives in the New York City borough of Brooklyn.

—M.R.M.

Suggested Reading: *A.V. Club* (on-line) Aug. 26, 2009; *Los Angeles Times* E p1 Aug. 16, 2009; *New Yorker* (on-line) Aug. 28, 2009; *Newsday* C p38 Feb. 29, 2004; *San Francisco Chronicle* M p6 Mar. 7, 2004; *Time* (on-line) June 13, 2004, Sep. 25, 2005, Apr. 24, 2008

Selected Books: *Warp*, 1997; *Codex*, 2004; *The Magicians*, 2009

Alex Wong/Getty Images for *Meet the Press*

Haass, Richard N.

July 28, 1951– Organization official; foreign-policy expert; former government official

Address: Council on Foreign Relations, The Harold Pratt House, 58 E. 68th St., New York, NY 10065

Since the summer of 2003, Richard N. Haass has been the president of the Council on Foreign Relations (CFR), an independent, nonpartisan organization that provides research and insight on foreign-policy issues to individuals and institutions, including government officials, business executives, journalists, teachers, students, civic and religious leaders, and CFR members. Prior to joining CFR, Haass served from 2001 to 2003 in the George W. Bush administration as director of policy planning for the U.S. State Department, where he was a key adviser to Secretary of State Colin L. Powell; at the time he was also the U.S. envoy to Northern Ireland and the coordinator of U.S. policy in Afghanistan. Although he was a member of the Bush administration during the planning and early im-

plementation of the Iraq War (launched in March 2003), Haass had relatively little influence on U.S.-Iraq policies at the time, in large part because nearly all members of the administration were neoconservatives, whereas Haass considered himself a foreign-policy "realist"—one who opposed the invasion of foreign countries solely on the basis of those nations' internal conflicts and believed that if a war was deemed necessary, it should involve the support and cooperation of allies. Haass had much more support and influence during his time in the administration of Bush's father, George H. W. Bush. From 1989 to early 1993 Haass was the special assistant to the president for national-security affairs and the senior director of Near East and South Asian affairs for the National Security Council. He was one of a handful of architects of the first Iraq War, in 1991, when the United States and its allies forced Iraqi troops out of Kuwait; in keeping with Haass's realist philosophy, the U.S. did not try to invade Iraq and topple the regime, judging that the political, economic, and military costs of doing so would have far outweighed the benefits. Prior to joining the first Bush administration, Haass served in the Department of State under President Ronald Reagan, from 1981 to 1985, and in the Department of Defense under President Jimmy Carter, from 1979 to 1980. Haass is also the author of many books on foreign policy. His latest is *War of Necessity, War of Choice: A Memoir of Two Iraq Wars* (2009).

Of Jewish descent, Richard Nathan Haass was born on July 28, 1951 in the New York City borough of Brooklyn. When he was a baby, his parents moved to Valley Stream, a small town on Long Island, New York. "Life was innocent and uncomplicated," Haass told Nora Boustany for the *Washington Post* (June 20, 2003) about his growing-up years. His father, Irving, was the vice president for research at the Smilen Investment Co. and a stockbroker who co-founded the firm David J. Greene & Co. His mother, Marcella, was a homemaker. During Haass's teen years the international conflicts in the news involved the Cold War with the former Soviet Union and the Vietnam War. After graduating from Roslyn High School, Haass studied comparative religion at Oberlin College, in Oberlin, Ohio. He changed his focus after spending his junior year in Jerusalem, Israel, participating in archaeological digs, working on a kibbutz, and learning Hebrew and Arabic. "In Israel," Haass told Chris Hedges for the *New York Times* (September 9, 2003), "I could read texts that were thousands of years old and walk in the same places, see the same battlegrounds that had been the site of conflict for centuries. The problems of the past became contemporary. They were no longer just historical." Haass changed his major to modern Middle East studies and received his B.A. degree in 1973. He then won a Rhodes scholarship to pursue graduate studies at Oxford University, in England, where he focused on international relations. He received his master's degree in 1975 and his Ph.D. in 1982.

Meanwhile, Haass had begun working in the world of politics and government. In 1975 he served as a legislative assistant to U.S. senator Claiborne Pell of Rhode Island, a Democrat. Starting in 1977 he worked as a research associate at the International Institute for Strategic Studies, in London, England, which provides information on international issues to politicians, diplomats, military officials, businesspeople, economists, and others. After two years Haass returned to Washington, D.C., where he worked during the last year and a half of the Democrat Jimmy Carter's presidency as a special assistant to the undersecretary at the Department of Defense. In 1981, remaining at the Department of Defense, he began his tenure under Republican president Ronald Reagan as the director of the Office of Regional Security Affairs. The following year, back at the State Department, he became the deputy for European and Canadian Affairs, a post he held until 1985; concurrently, starting in 1983, he also served as the department's Cyprus coordinator, a position he also held until 1985. From that year until 1989 Haass served as a lecturer at the John F. Kennedy School of Government at Harvard University, in Cambridge, Massachusetts.

Haass's entry into the big leagues of foreign policy occurred in 1989, when he joined the Republican George H. W. Bush's administration as a special assistant to the president for national-security affairs and as the senior director of Near East and South Asian affairs for the National Security Council (NSC). His most significant undertaking during that administration was his work before and during the first Iraq War, also known as the Persian Gulf War. On August 2, 1990 Iraq, under the brutal dictator Saddam Hussein, invaded Kuwait, a country that borders Iraq and Saudi Arabia. Haass's work during that time served as a good example of his realist approach to global politics: for the most part, he believed, what a country's leadership does within its borders is less important than its observance of international laws outside them; once it violates those laws, other nations have a right to join forces and engage in tough negotiations—and, if necessary, armed conflict—with the perceived aggressor. Iraq's invasion of Kuwait was condemned by many leaders worldwide and officially criticized by the United Nations, which placed economic sanctions on Iraq. President Bush deployed forces in Saudi Arabia. On November 29, 1990 the U.N. Security Council authorized the use of "all means necessary" to remove Iraqi forces from Kuwait if Hussein did not withdraw his troops by January 15, 1991. He did not, and two days after the deadline, the U.S. and more than 30 other countries began their attack on Iraqi forces. The fighting continued until late February 1991, when Iraqi troops left Kuwait. An official ceasefire was declared on February 28. The execution and conclusion of the Persian Gulf War were also a reflection of Haass's political philosophy: although he saw the need to remove Iraqi forces from Ku-

wait, he did not believe it was necessary—or wise—to follow the troops into Iraq and attempt a regime change there. His views had general support within the Bush administration.

After the election of the Democrat Bill Clinton to the presidency, in November 1992, Haass left government to become, successively, a senior associate at the Carnegie Endowment for International Peace (1993–94), the director of national-security programs and senior fellow at the Council on Foreign Relations (1994–96), and the vice president and director of foreign-policy programs at the Brookings Institution (1996–2001), a think tank based in Washington, D.C.

After Haass concluded his fellowship at the CFR, that group published his book *The Reluctant Sheriff: The United States After the Cold War* (1997). In part, the book provided an analysis of two significant and competing foreign-policy doctrines: hegemony (sometimes called unipolarity), or the belief that the United States must be militarily, economically, and politically dominant in the world, and isolationism, whose adherents are divided into two camps—one saying that the U.S. has no significant interests outside its own borders, the other that the U.S. has important interests but does not have the capacity to promote them. In Haass's view of realpolitik, it did not make sense to pursue either hegemony or isolationism blindly. He argued, for example, that hegemony is not only an unattainable goal but bad foreign policy; the existence of other strong states, he felt, does not mean that those states will be hostile, and they might be necessary allies. At the same time, the promotion of democracy and human rights abroad, while not of primary concern, is sometimes a logical goal. The reviewer for the *Economist* (September 6, 1997) summarized Haass's position thusly: "American diplomats should worry more about instability between states than about instability within them. Their priorities should be to deter aggressors, to prevent nasty weapons getting to nasty people and to maintain international trade treaties. Once these priorities have been seen to, Mr. Haass says, there is no harm in speaking up for human rights and democracy. . . . This realism-plus should be pursued, says Mr Haass, through a series of temporary alliances. Standing alliances, such as NATO, have lost their cohesion as the threats that gave rise to them have gone; fleeting coalitions, like the one that won the Gulf war, have come to matter more. . . . America should act as sheriff, assembling posses as needed: hence the title of Mr Haass's book."

In 2001, under the administration of the newly elected Republican president George W. Bush, Haass returned to government, this time as the director of policy planning for the U.S. Department of State, under Secretary of State Colin L. Powell. The ideological environment he encountered in the new Bush administration was significantly different from—and, for Haass, more difficult than—what he had dealt with during the presidency of

Bush's father a decade earlier. This time he was one of only a handful of "realists" in an administration otherwise full of neoconservatives. The terrorist attacks on the United States on September 11, 2001, less than a year after Bush took office, created a new level of public awareness, and fear, of foreign governments and international developments and made for a climate of support for bold moves abroad. In response to the attacks, the U.S. invaded Afghanistan, whose government, led by the Muslim-fundamentalist Taliban faction, had provided a haven for the terrorists, members of the group Al Qaeda; later, in 2003, the U.S. invaded Iraq for the stated purpose of ridding it of so-called weapons of mass destruction (which never materialized). Even before the 9/11 terrorist attacks, however, there had already been talk in White House circles of using military force to remove Saddam Hussein from power. Haass publicly acknowledged that line of thought while seeking other approaches to dealing with Iraq. On the National Public Radio (NPR) program *Morning Edition* (January 2, 2001), Haass said that the incoming Bush administration would seek to make the economic sanctions against Iraq less harmful to the country's general population but more burdensome for Hussein; if Iraq became a threat to the region, he said, invasion was not out of the question.

A few months into Bush's presidency, it appeared that Haass was emerging as an influential member of the foreign-policy team. In his position as director of policy planning, which carried an ambassadorial rank, he wrote speeches for the State Department and helped steer Middle East policy, diplomacy between the Republic of Ireland and Northern Ireland, and the implementing of economic sanctions against other countries. One of the reasons Haass received so much responsibility was that President Bush cut more than 20 foreign-policy positions in the name of efficiency—a move that was criticized by some, including then–U.S. senator Joseph R. Biden of Delaware, the ranking Democrat on the Senate Foreign Relations Committee. Haass himself also received some criticism. In a particularly stinging essay for the *New Republic* (March 26, 2001), Lawrence F. Kaplan acknowledged Haass's belief that economic sanctions against Iraq and North Korea promoted anti-Americanism and hurt the citizens of those countries, and that Haass wanted to make those sanctions more effective and less harmful. On the other hand, Kaplan argued, Haass was concerned not just with the well-being of the citizens of those countries but with the effects of sanctions and embargoes on the oil industry. Kaplan wrote: "So it's perhaps no surprise that oil companies such as Conoco and Arco fund a chunk of Haass's sanctions project at Brookings. . . . According to Conoco representatives, Haass has also consulted for the oil company, which the U.S. government barred from doing business in Iran in 1995. USA*Engage, the anti-sanctions business coalition, tirelessly promotes Haass's work. And another oil firm, the Santa Fe International Corporation, whose parent company helps pay for his sanctions project, even installed him on its board of directors."

A month after the 9/11 attacks, around the time of the United States invasion of Afghanistan, Secretary Powell appointed Haass to be his special coordinator for U.S. policy regarding that nation. Powell, like Haass, was seen as a believer in multilateralism; meanwhile, Nicholas Lemann, writing for the *New Yorker* (April 1, 2002), cited as an indication of Bush's ideology the fact that the neoconservative, hawkish Paul Wolfowitz, then deputy secretary of defense, had a higher-ranking post in the administration than did Haass. Still, there were also signs that Haass was shifting ideologically. Lemann observed that Haass "seems to have become more hawkish" with regard to Iraq. Although Haass still opposed unilateral warfare and what he saw as unjust sanctions, he conveyed a greater willingness to go to war. He told Lemann, alluding to reports of Iraq's abuse of its citizens and allegations of contact between Iraq and Al Qaeda, "Sovereignty entails obligations. One is not to massacre your own people. Another is not to support terrorism in any way. If a government fails to meet these obligations, then it forfeits some of the normal advantages of sovereignty, including the right to be left alone inside your own territory. Other governments, including the United States, gain the right to intervene. In the case of terrorism, this can even lead to a right of preventive self-defense. You essentially can act in anticipation if you have grounds to think it's a question of when, and not if, you're going to be attacked." With regard to the notion of preemptive war, Haass mentioned the Iraqi leader by name: "I don't think the American public needs a lot of persuading about the evil that is Saddam Hussein."

Ultimately, Haass's influence in the administration proved to be limited. In a July 2002 meeting, he asked Condoleezza Rice, then Bush's national-security adviser, whether the administration truly wanted to make Iraq its foreign-policy priority, despite the ongoing war in Afghanistan and other serious terrorist threats. Rice told him that the decision to do so had already been made. In another interview with Lemann for the *New Yorker* (March 31, 2003), Haass elaborated: "For me, it was that meeting with Condi that made me realize [that the plan to invade Iraq] was farther along than I had realized. So then when Powell had his famous dinner with the President, in early August, 2002"—during which Powell persuaded President Bush to take the matter to the United Nations—"the agenda was not whether [to invade] Iraq, but how." The U.S. invaded Iraq on March 19, 2003, based on intelligence—which critics later argued was selectively used at best and purposely misleading at worst—indicating that Hussein had weapons of mass destruction.

In the summer of 2003, Haass left the Bush administration to run the Council on Foreign Relations. The CFR's Web site lists Haass's areas of expertise at the organization as U.S. foreign policy; international security; globalization; Asia; and the Middle East.

In the summer of 2009, after Bush had left the White House, Haass published an insider's view of the roads to and implementation of the first and second Iraq wars. In *War of Necessity, War of Choice: A Memoir of Two Iraq Wars* (2009), he recounted his involvement in the 1991 conflict, which he called a "war of necessity," and in the 2003 invasion, which he argued was a "war of choice." With regard to the latter, Haass wrote that he was surprised by the unverified claims Vice President Dick Cheney made to the media about Saddam Hussein's nuclear weapons; Haass also observed that the Bush administration exploited Secretary of State Powell's popularity with the international community and general public, having him speak to media outlets and make a case for the war before the United Nations Security Council. In addition, Haass claimed that the administration often disregarded the advice and intelligence of the State Department. He retold the story of his meeting with Rice in July 2002, saying, contrary to what he had indicated earlier, that the decision to go to war had not been finalized by then. "Altogether Haass emerges as an intelligent and honest man, but a little rarefied and maybe indecisive," Geoffrey Wheatcroft wrote for the *New York Times* (June 28, 2009). "He gives too many people the benefit of the doubt and has few really bad words for anyone." Haass admitted in the book that at first he had not been entirely opposed to the war, and that once the decision to invade Iraq had been made, he saw it as his duty to help plan for that course of action. He revealed that one of the reasons he began to oppose the war, as he did in the end, was that his wife called him an "enabler" of the decision to invade. Haass left the administration three months after the launch of the war. "His book will be of some interest to students of the Washington bureaucracy, but of much more to those who worry about when public servants should resign," a reviewer wrote for the *Economist* (June 20, 2009). "It is a tale of a good man doggedly working for a bad end."

In his capacity as president of the Council on Foreign Relations, Haass has continued to write and speak about the wars in Iraq and Afghanistan and other foreign-policy issues, such as relations with Iran. After President Barack Obama called the war in Afghanistan "a war of necessity" and prepared to elevate U.S. troop levels there, Haass provided his own analysis of the situation on the op-ed page of the *New York Times* (August 21, 2009). A "war of necessity," he argued, implies two conditions: that the war involves "vital national interest" and that there is "a lack of viable alternatives to the use of military force to protect those interests." As examples of "necessary" war, Haass cited World War II, the Korean War, and the first Iraq War. Haass concluded that the war in Afghanistan is a "war of choice," comparable to U.S. engagements in Vietnam, Bosnia, Kosovo, and Iraq in 2003. "Wars of choice are not inherently good or bad," Haass wrote. "It depends on whether military involvement would probably accomplish more than it would cost and whether employing force is more promising than the alternatives. Making this assessment in Afghanistan is difficult. The Taliban are resourceful and patient and can use Pakistan as a sanctuary. It is not obvious that Afghans can overcome ethnic and tribal loyalties, corruption and personal rivalries. . . . The risk of ending our military effort in Afghanistan is that [its capital city] Kabul could be overrun and the government might fall. The risk of the current approach (or even one that involves dispatching another 10,000 or 20,000 American soldiers, as the president appears likely to do) is that it might produce the same result in the end, but at a higher human, military and economic cost. All of which makes Afghanistan not just a war of choice but a tough choice. My judgment is that American interests are sufficiently important, prospects for achieving limited success are sufficiently high and the risks of alternative policies are sufficiently great to proceed, for now, with Mr. Obama's measured strategy." However, Haass concluded, the president, Congress, and the American people should continually analyze the costs and benefits of the Afghan war.

The following year Haass published a piece in *Newsweek* (February 1, 2010) in which he maintained that while he initially supported Obama's choice to negotiate with Iran over its nuclear-weapons program, "I've changed my mind. The nuclear talks are going nowhere. The Iranians appear intent on developing the means to produce a nuclear weapon; there is no other explanation for the secret uranium-enrichment facility discovered near the holy city of Qum. Fortunately, their nuclear program appears to have hit some technical snags, which puts off the need to decide whether to launch a preventive strike. Instead we should be focusing on another fact: Iran may be closer to profound political change than at any time since the revolution that ousted the shah 30 years ago." Haass urged American, European, and other world leaders to speak out for the rights of Iranian people; he acknowledged that outsiders' promotion of regime change in Iran would allow that country's leadership to attack its political opponents as "pawns of the West" but argued that the regime is doing that already. Stephen M. Walt, writing for *Foreign Policy* (January 25, 2010, on-line), argued that because Iran is so insolated, outsiders simply do not have enough information about the country's internal political and ideological tensions to speak specifically about its domestic politics. More importantly, he argued, many leaders of the current opposition to Iran's regime support the nuclear program, making it unlikely that regime change would mean the end of the program. He called

Haass's position "misguided." Haass has continued to advocate his position on Iran.

Haass is also the author of *Congressional Power: Implications for American Security Policy* (1979), *Beyond the INF Treaty: Arms, Arms Control and the Atlantic Alliance* (1988), *Conflicts Unending: The United States and Regional Disputes* (1990), *The Power to Persuade* (1994), *Intervention: The Use of American Military Force in The Post-Cold War World* (1994), *The Bureaucratic Entrepreneur* (1999), and *The Opportunity: America's Moment to Alter History's Course* (2005).

For his work in the George W. Bush administration, Haass received the State Department's Distinguished Honor Award. During the George H. W. Bush administration, Haass received the Presidential Citizens Medal for his work on Persian Gulf War policy.

Haass and his wife, Susan Mercandetti, have been married since 1990. The couple have two children, Francesca and Sam. Mercandetti served as a White House intern during the presidency of Gerald R. Ford. A former independent television producer, she is currently an executive editor at Random House.

—D.K.

Suggested Reading: cfr.org; *New Republic* p17 Mar. 26, 2001; *New York Times* A p8 Aug. 7, 1990; *New York Times Book Review* p11 June 28, 2009; *New Yorker* p42+ Apr. 1, 2002, p36+ Mar. 31, 2003; *Washington Post* A p22 June 20, 2003

Selected Books: *Congressional Power: Implications for American Security Policy*, 1979; *Beyond the INF Treaty: Arms, Arms Control and the Atlantic Alliance*, 1988; *Conflicts Unending: The United States and Regional Disputes*, 1990; *The Power to Persuade*, 1994; *Intervention: The Use of American Military Force in The Post-Cold War World*, 1994; *The Reluctant Sheriff: The United States After the Cold War*, 1997; *The Bureaucratic Entrepreneur*, 1999; *The Opportunity: America's Moment to Alter History's Course*, 2005; *War of Necessity, War of Choice: A Memoir of Two Iraq Wars*, 2009

Handler, Chelsea

Feb. 25, 1975– Comedian; talk-show host; writer

Address: 2118 Wilshire Blvd., Suite 1053, Santa Monica, CA 90403

Chelsea Handler has parlayed her barely supervised childhood, passion for vodka, and love-hate relationship with Hollywood into a career as one of the most successful women in comedy. In addition to writing, producing, and hosting her own late-night talk show, *Chelsea Lately*, since 2007, Handler is a touring stand-up comedian, the owner of a production company, and the author of three best-selling books. Handler's signature is to insult Hollywood's elite without fear and—perhaps because she often turns her stinging wit on herself—seemingly without reprisal. Only the second woman to have her own late-night talk show (the first was Joan Rivers), Handler has won the support of her fellow late-night fixture Jay Leno, who has frequently had her as a guest on the *Tonight Show.* Leno told Brooks Barnes for the *New York Times* (April 9, 2010, on-line), "What I love about Chelsea is that she shows we've reached a point where comedy is comedy—it's not male comedy or female comedy. When I was a kid, it was Phyllis Diller. To be a comedian she had to make herself more unattractive than she was. But Chelsea Handler can walk out onstage looking like a *Playboy* centerfold if she wants and still be funny." Handler's appeal seems to lie in her ability to speak her mind regardless of the consequences. "Every once in a while, a person comes along and gets a following for saying what everyone is thinking," Blake Han-

Alberto E. Rodriguez/Getty Images

non wrote for the *McClatchy–Tribune Business News* (April 30, 2010). "For our tabloid-flooded, celebrity-obsessed culture, that person is acid-tongued comedienne Chelsea Handler." "She's the king of hot, drunk blondes," Handler's fellow comedian Heather McDonald said in an interview with Ari Karpel for *Entertainment Weekly* (July 11, 2008, on-line). "They've been wandering the earth, they've never had a leader, until Chelsea arrived . . . and they're like, 'She's me!'"

The youngest of six children, Chelsea Joy Handler (some sources list her middle name as "Jane") was born on February 25, 1975 in Livingston, New Jersey, to Melvin Handler, a used-car dealer, and Rita Sylvia Handler, a homemaker. Her mother was a Mormon, and her father is Jewish. "They asked me to choose between Judaism and Mormonism," Handler said in an April 1, 2010 interview on the CNN program *Larry King Live*. "My one sister told me that with Mormonism, you can't drink, you can't have caffeine, and you can't really have sex. So I was like, I'll take the dreidel." She told an interviewer for the Minneapolis *Star-Tribune* (July 25, 2008), "I consider myself Jewish, but I don't really practice it. I'm not a very religious person, although I do believe in God and karma and tipping well." Handler's parents gave her a lot of freedom from a young age, perhaps contributing to her independent spirit. "I think my parents just realized that if they had another kid, she'd just raise herself, which is what happened," Handler was quoted as saying in an article for *Harper's Bazaar* (April 2010). "They were not your typical middle-class parents that I was surrounded by. They didn't ask for anybody's phone numbers when I went out. They weren't interested in where I spent the night."

Handler developed a sarcastic sense of humor as a way to differentiate herself from her siblings. Humor also served as a coping mechanism for Handler and her family after her oldest brother died in a hiking accident when she was nine. "People cope through humor," Chelsea's sister Simone Handler-Hutchinson said to Brooks Barnes, "but it also meant that Chelsea grew up very quickly." Handler's quick wit proved to be an asset in other areas of her life as well. "She was always able to tell some elaborate tale to get out of homework," Handler-Hutchinson recalled. In her second book, *Are You There, Vodka? It's Me, Chelsea* (2008), Handler wrote about one such tall tale: the time she told her third-grade teacher that she had not completed her homework because she had spent the night before in negotiations with the actors Kurt Russell and Goldie Hawn over a sequel to the film *Private Benjamin*, in which Chelsea would play the couple's daughter. For a time, Handler wrote, her teachers and classmates believed her. The older girls who had once teased her suddenly regarded Handler with awe. "With that wave of confidence came the feeling that I was, in a way, impenetrable. I was the exact same person I had been the day before, but now I was being treated better and the older kids wanted to be friends with me. . . . I had found myself engaging, charismatic—even sublime at times. I had all the charm I believed a true movie star to have," she wrote. In her profile of Handler for the *New Yorker* (May 24, 2010), Nancy Franklin noted, "That's how an actor, if not a star, is born." Still, "when that movie never came out they realized I was lying," Handler told Rick Bentley for the *McClatchy-Tribune Business News* (January 8, 2009). "It was easy to make friends with lies, but then when the truth came out, I would lose them."

Handler attended college for one semester before dropping out and moving to Los Angeles, California, hoping to become an actress. When her plans did not work out, she ended up waiting tables. At 21 she was arrested for drunk driving, a development that led her to a revelation. As a result of her arrest, Handler was forced to attend a driver's-safety course for drunk-driving offenders, at the end of which she was asked to recount the circumstances of her arrest to the rest of the group. Mortified, she attempted to ease the tension the best way she knew how, as she recalled to Brian Stelter for the *New York Times* (January 15, 2009): "I called the officer a racist; we were both white; my sister turned me in." By the time she was done, the whole class was laughing. Handler told Stelter that that "was the most orgasmic moment of my life."

Inspired, Handler began writing material, recording videos of herself performing stand-up routines in her home, and sending the videos to various venues and promoters. At 23 she was booked for her first gig, at a club called the Improv. With 20 or so friends in attendance for support, Handler pretended she was telling jokes at a party. That approach worked. "I've been doing it ever since," Handler said to Marcia Manna for the *San Diego Union-Tribune* (June 9, 2008). "I was always this way, whether I was on stage or not. I guess it worked out like it should have."

For Handler, being an attractive woman has not always been an asset in the world of comedy. From the beginning she had to fight the assumption that women could not be pretty and funny at the same time. At times the blond, blue-eyed comedian endured heckling from rowdy male audience members. Handler recalled one incident to Edward Lewine for the *New York Times Magazine* (December 16, 2007): "I had just started in stand-up. My brothers and father came. Everybody was screaming, 'Take your top off!' My father was just staring at me. It was one of the most humiliating experiences of my life." By the same token, Handler has said that she does not think women should use their attractiveness to get ahead in their careers. "I don't have a lot of respect for women who play up their sexuality," she told Greg Braxton for the *Los Angeles Times* (August 24, 2008). "I know I'm attractive, but that's not my best feature. What's up here in my head is more important."

After several years of performing stand-up comedy, Handler was chosen for the Oxygen cable channel's hidden-camera show, *Girls Behaving Badly* (2002–05). The show, which was described by the channel as "*Sex and the City* meets *Candid Camera*," followed four female comedians as they played pranks on unsuspecting victims. Before long Handler was getting offers to appear in small roles on a number of popular television shows, including *The Bernie Mac Show*, *The Practice*, and *My Wife and Kids*. In 2004 she was recruited to host installments of the E! Channel's celebrity-culture programs, among them *101 Most Awesome Moments in Entertainment* and *50 Shocking Celebrity Confessions*. E! producers found her acerbic sense of humor to be a perfect fit for the channel and offered Handler her own show. *The Chelsea Handler Show*, a late-night half-hour program that combined Handler's stand-up routines with roundtable discussions, interviews, and pretaped skits, debuted on April 21, 2006 and ran for 12 installments on E! before being transformed the following year into *Chelsea Lately*. That show is produced by Handler's company, Borderline Amazing Productions, and was recently renewed to run through 2012. The half-hour *Chelsea Lately* airs Monday through Thursday at 11 p.m. The show usually opens with a short monologue by Handler, followed by a discussion of the latest news in pop culture by a panel of three commentators referred to as "the round table." In a 2007 article for *Broadcasting & Cable*, Ben Grossman wrote: "E! spends 23.5 hours a day genuflecting in front of Hollywood. Handler punches the town in the groin for the remaining half-hour."

Handler is most celebrated for mercilessly ripping into the likes of Britney Spears, Paris Hilton, and Lindsey Lohan, among other tabloid-cover regulars. In a sample post from the *Inside Chelsea* blog portion of E!'s *Chelsea Lately* Web site (February 19, 2010, on-line), Handler wrote, "Paris Hilton and her boyfriend, Doug Reinhardt, recently took a romantic trip to Brazil. In between tweeting about her outfits, she seemed to have had a good time. At the end of the trip she obviously didn't want to leave, and posted on her Twitter: 'Sad to leave, but ready to go home and get back to work. :)' Work then responded on its Twitter: 'I've never heard of Paris Hilton.'" Handler frequently refers to Tori Spelling, an actress and the daughter of the late television producer Aaron Spelling, as "he," because she thinks Spelling looks "like a man," and to the reality-TV couple Heidi Montag and Spencer Pratt as "Herpes Simplex 1 and 2." But it often seems that Handler's favorite target is herself. "If you're going to pay attention to celebrities so much you have to make fun of yourself," she said to John Wenzel for the *Denver Post* (October 17, 2008). "If I wanted to make a show seriously . . . well, I would never do that. I want to make fun of the fact that we care about this. As long as you know where you're coming from on that level and how ridiculous it all is, it's just a free-for-all." Handler's on-air sidekick on *Chelsea Lately* is a chubby dwarf named Chuy, whom she refers to as her "little nugget." Chuy, who participated in the 2010 Comedians of Chelsea Lately Tour, published the book *Little Nuggets of Wisdom: Big Advice from the Small Star of Chelsea Lately* in 2010. When asked by Allison Kugel for *PR.com* (February 20, 2008, on-line) if Chuy was "in" on the joke, Handler said, "Oh, yeah, yeah, yeah! He gets it."

In 2007 Handler traveled the U.S. with Comedy Central's Hour Stand-Up Comedy Tour and hosted the premiere episode of the ill-fated Fox reality-television series *On the Lot*. Handler did not return for the second installment; hosting duties were taken over by Adrianna Costa for the remainder of the show's single season. "I actually quit that show," Handler said at a 2007 press conference, as quoted in the *Pittsburgh Post-Gazette* (July 15, 2007). "I wasn't replaced. I quit because I smelled the disaster happening before it did." Handler has appeared as a commentator on other E! network shows and on the media personality Joe Scarborough's political opinion and analysis show *Scarborough County* on MSNBC. She has been a frequent guest and sometime correspondent on the *Tonight Show with Jay Leno*, a guest co-host on *The View*, and a guest on a number of other programs, including the game show *Million Dollar Password*, the reality-TV dating show *Real Chance of Love*, and a 2009 episode of the legal drama *The Good Wife*. On *The Good Wife* she played herself to interview one of the show's characters on a fictional installment of *Chelsea Lately*.

Starting in 2007 Handler, along with Leah Remini and Jenny McCarthy, starred in *In the Motherhood*, a popular Web-based series following the day-to-day lives of three mothers. That show was adapted for television by ABC in 2009. Originally slated to appear in the series, Handler backed out because of scheduling conflicts with *Chelsea Lately*. Currently, she is developing a half-hour TV show, tentatively called "After Lately," that will reveal activities backstage on the set of *Chelsea Lately*. To be produced by Borderline Amazing Productions, it will rely heavily on improvisation.

Handler is the author of three books, all of them *New York Times* best-sellers. *My Horizontal Life: A Collection of One-Night Stands* (2005) chronicles, with much candor and detail, Handler's sex life in the period after she arrived in Los Angeles. *Are You There, Vodka? It's Me, Chelsea* (2008) is primarily about Handler's quirky life, family, and friends, from childhood to young adulthood; that book had a print run of close to half a million copies. Handler's latest book, *Chelsea Chelsea Bang Bang* (2010), debuted at number one on the *New York Times* nonfiction best-seller list. Handler said to Hector Saldna for the *San Antonio Express* (June 15, 2008), "I was the only one in my family [who] didn't graduate from college, and I'm like, 'By the way you guys, I have a book deal.' My brothers and sisters were like, 'A book deal about what?' I'm, like, 'Don't worry about it.'" Although Handler does not paint her family and friends in the most flattering light, she has said that anyone close to her is used to such treatment, and some of her friends were hurt that they were not mentioned in her books. "My dad already thinks he's a celebrity," Handler told Megan Friedman for *Time* (March 9, 2010, on-line), shortly before *Chelsea Chelsea Bang Bang* was published. "He's like, 'I can't even go to the supermarket without being recognized.'

I'm like, 'Dad, the book's not out [yet], and no one knows who you are unless you're introducing yourself as Chelsea Handler's father. And if you are doing that, please stop.'" Handler joked that her father wanted to sue her for the way she portrayed him in her books but would first have to borrow money from her to hire a lawyer. Although some of Handler's stories are outrageous, the comedian has insisted that most of them are true. "There's not a lot of exaggeration in my stories . . . ," she told Friedman. "I don't have to exaggerate a lot, because my life is ridiculous."

In 2006 Handler began dating the president and CEO of Comcast Entertainment Group, Ted Harbert. Comcast owns the E! Network, making Harbert Handler's boss. Handler has said that their relationship interfered very little with their professional lives. (Handler and Harbert work in separate buildings, and Harbert is said to have recused himself from negotiations over Handler's salary and the running of her show.) In January 2010 Handler confirmed on her show that, after living together for three years, she and Harbert had split. Much of the book *Chelsea Chelsea Bang Bang* is dedicated to mocking Harbert, but he claims not to take offense. "It's funny—that's why I signed the damn release," Harbert said to Barnes.

Handler lives in a three-bedroom condominium in Marina del Rey, California, with her dog, Chunk. In addition to writing, producing, and hosting her show, Handler continues to tour as a stand-up comedian. She told Larry King that she does not necessarily want to have children: "I have a lot of nieces and nephews. . . . I love them so much, and they give me . . . a lot of joy and happiness. A lot of that joy and happiness comes from walking away when they are in a bad mood." Handler has expressed interest in having a more well-rounded show, one that would include discussion of books and politics. Still, "I don't really want to work my whole life," she said to Tom Teodorczuk for the London *Guardian* (July 25, 2009, on-line). "I would love to be able to make a ton of money and go live on an island and drink margaritas for the rest of my life. Hopefully I'll be able to do it by 40." When asked by Blake Hannon of the *McClatchy-Tribune Business News* (April 30, 2010) about the secret to her success in comedy, the 35-year-old Handler responded, "I can hold my liquor better than most women."

—H.R.W.

Suggested Reading: *Boston Globe* C p1 Aug. 15, 2008; *Finance Wire* (on-line) Apr. 12, 2010; *Los Angeles Times* E p1 Aug. 24, 2008; *McClatchy Business-Tribune News* (on-line) Jan. 8, 2009; *New Yorker* (on-line) May 24, 2010; *New York Times* (on-line) Apr. 9, 2010; *New York Times Magazine* (on-line) Dec. 16, 2007; *San Antonio Express-News* H p3 June 15, 2008; *Time* (on-line) Mar. 9, 2010

Selected Television Shows: *Girls Behaving Badly*, 2002–05; *101 Most Awesome Moments in Entertainment*, 2004; *50 Shocking Celebrity Confessions*, 2004; *The Chelsea Handler Show*, 2006; *On the Lot*, 2007; *Chelsea Lately*, 2007–

Selected Books: *My Horizontal Life: A Collection of One-Night Stands*, 2005; *Are You There, Vodka? It's Me, Chelsea*, 2008; *Chelsea Chelsea Bang Bang*, 2010

Rob Loud/Getty Images

Hansen, Chris

Mar. 26, 1959– Investigative journalist

Address: NBC News, 30 Rockefeller Plaza, New York, NY 10112

The Emmy Award–winning Chris Hansen "has supplanted Mike Wallace as the TV journalist you'd least like to see emerge from behind a closed door," David Bauder wrote for the Associated Press (April 2, 2007). Hansen, a correspondent for the NBC television newsmagazine *Dateline*, served from 2004 to 2008 as the host of that show's series of special investigative reports "To Catch a Predator," which helped apprehend some 250 suspected or potential child molesters through staged, hidden-camera sting operations. Hansen was sometimes accused of unfairly entrapping hapless men, and the show was often derided for its sensationalism, but "To Catch a Predator" nonetheless attracted a reported seven million to 11 million viewers per installment. "The 'Predator' segments are as seedy and fascinatingly repellant as the suspected predators they showcase," Alessandra Stanley wrote for the *New York Times* (May 17, 2006). Hansen told a writer for the Morristown, New Jersey, *Daily Record* (April 25, 2007), "It's undeniably compelling television to see these guys from all walks of life—doctors, police, teachers—engaging in this . . . behavior." Hansen has also hosted such spin-offs as "To Catch a Con Man" and "To Catch an ID Thief" and has additionally reported for *Dateline* on such topics as terrorist groups and counterfeit prescription drugs.

Christopher Edward Hansen was born on March 26, 1959 in Lansing, Michigan. Affirming the loyalty and affection he feels for his network, he has told interviewers that his was a "Huntley-Brinkley family," referring to NBC's long-running nightly news show *The Huntley-Brinkley Report.* After graduating from Brother Rice High School, a Catholic institution in Bloomfield Hills, Michigan, Hansen attended Michigan State University (MSU), in East Lansing. In addition to being active at the campus radio station, he began working at WJIM, a small television and radio station in Lansing. Hansen earned a bachelor's degree from MSU's College of Communication Arts and Sciences in 1981. Upon graduating he worked for various local radio stations and newspapers in Michigan before landing a job with WFLA-TV, an NBC affiliate in Tampa, Florida.

Hansen subsequently returned to Michigan, and in 1988 he found work as an anchor and investigative reporter for WDIV-TV, an NBC affiliate based in Detroit. During his time in that city, Hansen helped break a number of important stories, including one about the notorious Chambers Brothers gang, which was heavily involved in the distribution of crack cocaine during the 1980s. (The 1991 film *New Jack City*, starring Wesley Snipes, was loosely based on the Chambers Brothers' activities.)

In May 1993 Hansen became a correspondent for *Now with Tom Brokaw and Katie Couric*, a prime-time NBC newsmagazine, which in 1994 was incorporated into the network's popular program *Dateline*. Although perhaps most widely recognized for his "To Catch a Predator" segments, Hansen has worked on a wide variety of reports for *Dateline*, including coverage of the 1995 Oklahoma City terrorist bombing, the arrest of Ted Kaczynski (the Unabomber), the Columbine massacre, and the TWA Flight 800 disaster. Hansen served as *Dateline*'s lead correspondent during the 9/11 terrorist attacks, and he contributed numerous stories on the operations of Al Qaeda. One of those reports exposed how a group connected to Osama bin Laden and Al Qaeda tried to buy stinger missiles and other weapons of mass destruction from American citizens. In connection with the 9/11 terrorist attacks, Hansen worked on a hidden-camera series that examined the inadequate security at American airports, which led the Federal Aviation Administration (FAA) to conduct an investigation that resulted in an immediate change in policy. Another

of his aviation-related reports included an interview with the Alaska Airlines pilot John Liotine, whose revelations about the company helped launch an investigation into the airline's maintenance policies.

In 2002 Hansen launched a hidden-camera investigation into India's lucrative silk trade. The series, which earned international acclaim, revealed that countless Indian children under the age of 14 were being treated as slaves in unsanitary silk factories. Two years later Hansen conducted a hidden-camera report on child sex trafficking in Cambodia, going undercover to rescue some of the children with assistance from members of the International Justice Mission. His *Dateline* exposé was honored with two Emmy Awards.

The first installment of "To Catch a Predator" aired in September 2004. The staff of the series worked with Perverted-Justice, a civilian group, as well as local police to catch suspected or potential pedophiles through Internet sting operations. An adult, pretending on-line to be a teenager, would arrange a tryst with a suspect; the latter, as Alessandra Stanley phrased it, would enter "a cozy suburban kitchen filled with snacks, only to discover the *Dateline* correspondent Chris Hansen and hidden cameras lying in wait." The operation ensnared a variety of men, including a rabbi seeking sex with a teenage boy. "Many suspects are passive and astonishingly candid when confronted," Stanley wrote, "a testimony, perhaps, to the hypnotic powers of a television camera. These raw, unscripted spectacles of men caught sweaty-handed were such a hit that *Dateline* has made 'Predator' a recurring feature, usually timed to a sweeps week."

During the show's run, from 2004 to 2008, its hidden-camera investigations helped expose more than 250 would-be predators. David Bauder admitted that the program "shed light on a 21st century crime and, either through the arrests of potential sex fiends or deterrence, probably saved some youths from being victims." "Yet," he continued, "'To Catch a Predator' is also an ethical minefield." The show's creators were frequently accused of participating in "checkbook journalism," which included paying members of Perverted-Justice a consulting fee of about $70,000 per installment. Marsha Bartel, a former *Dateline* producer, filed a lawsuit against the network, contending that she had been fired because of her opposition to the program's production practices, which she found unethical. The suit also claimed that Perverted-Justice did not keep accurate transcripts of its chats with potential predators. (The suit was dismissed.)

Another lawsuit was filed in 2007 by Patricia Conradt, who accused *Dateline* of contributing to the suicide of her brother, Louis Conradt Jr. of Texas, who was the subject of one of the show's hidden-camera investigations. When Conradt refused to be lured to the house *Dateline*'s producers had rigged with cameras, the television crew followed Kaufman County law officials to his own home. When the police stormed in to arrest him for soliciting minors over the Internet, Conradt fatally shot himself. In her suit, his sister accused NBC of being "concerned more with its own profits than with pedophilia" and claimed that a policeman at the scene of the suicide had told a producer, "That'll make good TV." In 2008 NBC "amicably resolved" the $108 million lawsuit; the details of the settlement were not publicized. Hansen has remained unapologetic over the incident. He told Bauder, "If it had happened to my brother, I'd be sad that he had decided to commit suicide. But to say it's our fault, I just don't think that's true."

The last installment of "To Catch a Predator" aired in December 2008; the series had been the victim, according to most observers, of the bad publicity surrounding the lawsuits. Still, before going off the air, the segments had inspired the spin-offs "To Catch an ID Thief" (which involved bait credit cards and a fake on-line store), "To Catch a Con Man" (in which Hansen hunted down Internet scammers), and "To Catch an iJacker" (about iPod thieves).

Hansen's many professional honors include seven Emmy Awards, four Edward R. Murrow Awards, three Clarion Awards from the Association for Women in Communications, an Overseas Press Club Award, a National Press Club Award,

and an International Consortium of Investigative Journalists Award.

The author of the book *To Catch a Predator: Protecting Your Kids from Online Enemies Already in Your Home* (2007), Hansen lives in Stamford, Connecticut, with his wife, Mary Joan, and their two sons. Among his most recent work for *Dateline* is "America Now: City of Heartbreak and Hope," a special report on Detroit's "economic blight, population flight and political scandals and also on the people who are pouring their hearts into improving the situation," as Julie Hinds wrote for the *Detroit Free Press* (April 17, 2010, on-line).

—C.C.

Suggested Reading: Associated Press Apr. 2, 2007; *Detroit Free Press* (on-line) Apr. 17, 2010; *Esquire* p232+ Sep. 1, 2007; (Morristown, New Jersey) *Daily Record* Apr. 25, 2007; *New York Observer* p2+ June 12, 2006; *New York Times* C p1 Aug. 27, 2007

Selected Books: *To Catch a Predator: Protecting Your Kids from Online Enemies Already in Your Home*, 2007

Selected Television Shows: *Dateline*, 1994–

Hastreiter, Kim

(HASS-try-ter)

Nov. 12, 1951– Magazine editor and publisher

Address: Paper, *15 E. 32d St., New York, NY 10016*

"The coolest person in New York may well be a large 58-year-old woman who wears cherry-colored glasses and a linen smock, and is planning a hip replacement." That is how Guy Trebay, writing for the *New York Times* (April 8, 2010), described Kim Hastreiter, the co-founder, co-editor, and co-publisher of *Paper* magazine. Hastreiter and her business partner, David Hershkovits, launched *Paper* in May 1984, two years after their employer, the alternative New York City paper the *SoHo Weekly News*, ceased publication and both lost their jobs. *Paper*, which currently publishes eight issues annually, is devoted to fashion, music, film, theater, art, and other cultural pursuits, and it also covers restaurants, clubs, and after-hours events. It began as a fold-out poster and over the years became a big, colorful magazine; in 1995 a Web version, too, became available. *Paper* is widely regarded as unique, in large part because of Hastreiter's rare ability to see styles, artworks, and other phenomena as cool before they catch the eye of anyone else, let alone become trends. For example, *Paper* included a column by the New York

Dimitrios Kambouris/Getty Images

City hip-hop pioneer Afrika Bambaataa in its first issue—many years before his name appeared in mainstream periodicals or even in the city's well-known alternative weekly the *Village Voice*—and it was among the earliest chroniclers of the spread of hip-hop culture. A 1985 cover story was about the baggy clothing that later became ubiquitous in hip-hop fashion, and years before tattooing became a popular form of self-expression among young American men and women and the New York city council legalized the practice, in 1997, an image of a local waitress covered with tattoos appeared on a cover of *Paper*. In 1994, the year *Paper* celebrated its 10th anniversary, four dozen editors of such Condé Nast publications as *Glamour*, *GQ*, *Details*, and *Vogue* were subscribers. "From the very beginning I have read every issue and I read every word," the veteran fashion editor Polly Allen Mellen, the creative director of *Allure* magazine from 1991 to 1999, told Alex Kuczynski for the *New York Times* (September 20, 1999). "I love its streetness. And everyone reads [it]. If people at the big magazines say very smugly that they do not, then they are lying. A lot of things you see in fashion magazines have been in *Paper* first."

Ahead of many others, Hastreiter recognized the growing interconnectedness, both calculated and serendipitous, between fashion and the arts, especially music and film. Moreover, she herself has connected many people in those fields—she introduced the filmmakers John Waters and Pedro Almodóvar; Almodóvar and the fashion designers Ruben and Isabel Toledo; the Toledos and the Latin-jazz-pop band Pink Martini—acting as a catalyst for friendships and, in some cases, professional collaborations. "To say that Kim Hastreiter knows practically everyone who matters in the cultural life of this city is an understatement . . . ," Guy Trebay wrote. "A lot of people here know practically everyone, or anyway claim they do. What separates Kim Hastreiter from the run of ordinary power people is that no imaginary velvet rope cordons off her cohort of acquaintances and friends. Like a lot of this town's celebrity brokers and society hostesses and fame wranglers, she keeps a mental list of interesting types. Unlike the average power snob, though, she shares her list freely and it is never closed." Sally Singer, *Vogue's* fashion news and features director until July 2010, when she became the editor of *T: The New York Times Style Magazine*, told Trebay, "Kim isn't just about big guys or big guys versus little guys. You could be Madonna or Beth Ditto or the next big thing in art or design. But you could just as easily be some adorable, highly androgynous club creature that's going to be a fun person to have at a party." More than 16 years ago, in an interview for the *New York Times* (January 2, 1994) with Amy M. Spindler, then the *Times Magazine's* style editor, Hastreiter and Hershkovits described *Paper* as a "mix"—"one page Pucci, one page homeboy," in Spindler's words. Hastreiter told *Current Biography*, the source of quotes for this article unless otherwise noted, "The world has changed, but we still look at it through the same kind of alternative way. Our [goal] is to support the creative underground community and shine a light on people who are doing amazing things."

Kim Hastreiter was born on November 12, 1951 to Walter and Gloria Hastreiter, who raised her and her younger sister in the suburbs of West Orange, New Jersey. Her mother collected art and had a taste for the avant-garde. As a high-school student, Hastreiter was a "square, suburban girl," her mother told Dana Goodyear for the *New Yorker* (September 24, 2007); by Hastreiter's own account, she was "kind of average." "I was a B student; I played tennis; I didn't get in trouble," she recalled. Two months after she enrolled at Washington University, in St. Louis, Missouri, in 1969, Hastreiter's parents went to visit her at college. According to Goodyear, when Hastreiter met them at the airport, her hair looked stringy and she was wearing workman's boots, second-hand carpenter's jeans, and an Indian-made shirt. Explaining her transformation, she told Goodyear that as an undergraduate, she "went right for the weird, crazy people. I was, like, I'm ho-ooome!" Due to the political and social turmoil of the time—including the civil rights struggle and demonstrations against the Vietnam War, one of which led to the killing of four student protestors by Ohio National Guardsmen at Kent State University in 1970—Hastreiter became somewhat "radicalized." She decided to study art, but the very traditional arts program at Washington University did not suit her. She transferred to the experimental Nova Scotia School of Art and Design, in Halifax, Canada, where she earned a B.F.A. degree in 1974. She then entered the California Institute of the Arts (CalArts), in Valencia, California, where she received an M.F.A. degree in 1976. At the Nova Scotia school and at CalArts, she studied mainly conceptual art involving videography and photography.

While she was living in Santa Monica, California (not far from Valencia), Hastreiter met Joey Arias, a drag performer and singer, in nearby West Hollywood. "I saw her coming down the street," Arias recalled to Goodyear. "She was wearing her hair in a bowl cut, with short, short bangs. She had this amazing figure, real burlesque-looking, and had on a Mao jacket, tight, tight jeans, cowboy boots. I was, like, Who *is* this woman?" The two became friends, and in 1976 they drove together to New York City, where they rented an apartment in Lower Manhattan. (Years later, through *Paper*, Hastreiter helped to boost Arias's career.) Hastreiter immediately got sidetracked from her goal of becoming an artist, because she had to find a job. She soon succeeded, securing one as a saleswoman at Betsey Bunky Nini, an Upper East Side boutique co-owned by the fashion designer Betsey Johnson. Johnson, who in the late 1960s had hung out with the likes of the artist Andy Warhol and the rock band the Velvet Underground, soon recognized that Hastreiter had an eye for fashion. Hastreiter herself said that she "fell in love with fashion." At the same time she became disenchanted with the art scene, mostly because—unlike other creative people she was meeting—the artists she knew showed little or no interest in music, fashion, film, theater, or any other creative pursuit other than art. "The art world, I thought, was very ghettoized and precious, and it took itself too seriously," Hastreiter said. "It didn't have anything to do with culture. It was rarefied. And I thought it was much more exciting to go hear a band in the middle of the night with graffiti artists painting the backdrop. It just felt more creative to me, more exciting."

One day as Hastreiter was walking to work, her unconventional outfit caught the eye of Bill Cunningham, the veteran *New York Times* "street-fashion" photographer. Their chance meeting led to friendship, and from Cunningham she learned that the *SoHo Weekly News*—launched in 1973 to compete with the *Village Voice*—needed a style editor. Although she had no academic credentials in journalism or fashion, Hastreiter got the job. What she lacked in formal training, she made up for in energy, imagination, a distinctive sense of fashion, and the insightful realization that the worlds of music and fashion were becoming far more closely connected than ever before. The fashion designer Stephen Sprouse, for example, was working with Debbie Harry, the lead singer of the rock band Blondie, and the punk and new-wave fashion designer Vivienne Westwood and her partner, Malcolm McLaren—the latter of whom went on to manage the band the Sex Pistols—owned a punk-clothing boutique called Sex, in London, England, and explicitly mixed music and fashion. Indeed, across a wide spectrum the creative arts were mixing and merging. As the fashion editor at the *SoHo Weekly News*, Hastreiter documented and thrived in that new cultural landscape and contributed to it as well. She created fashion shoots for such bands as Bow Wow Wow and the Pretenders; and she invited some of her friends—including the performer Ann Magnuson and the artists Keith Haring and Kenny Scharf—to write for the *SoHo Weekly News*.

In 1982 the *SoHo Weekly News* folded. Eager to continue reporting on and influencing the cultural and artistic environment of SoHo and other downtown New York neighborhoods, Hastreiter teamed up with David Hershkovits, who had been a writer and assistant managing editor at the *Weekly News*, to start a new publication. In May 1984, with $4,000 in savings, the two produced the first issue of *Paper*, working out of a loft near Soho that Hastreiter had bought. Hastreiter's mother handled the bookkeeping and subscriptions, and her father drove Hastreiter and Hershkovits to typesetters who were friends of theirs and willing to work overtime for them. Initially, *Paper* was printed as a black-and-white poster folded in quarters. "It looked like an elaborate note that a couple of high school kids might pass in art class," the fashion editor Robin Givhan wrote for the *Washington Post* (September 24, 2004). "The aesthetic," according to Goodyear, "was do-it-yourself punk rock, with an elegant, humorous twist." In an example of *Paper*'s humor, one of the early issues included in an "advice" column an effective way to remove a jun-

kie asleep on a couch. As quoted by Goodyear, *Paper* suggested that the unwilling host "purchase or borrow a sound effect record and tape the selection entitled 'Human Screams.' Place Walkman headphones securely over the ears of the nodding offender; shut all the lights in the room except one, trained on the exit (door or window). Turn up the volume to 10 and turn it on. You can also use any Yoko Ono record."

By 1986 *Paper* had assumed the form of a typical magazine, and its circulation had climbed to 10,000 a month. Each issue focused on a different theme, such as funny Christmas gifts or American fashion; in an example of the latter, *Paper* offered a fashion spread of people wearing clothes that bore images of such Communist leaders as Vladimir Lenin and Mao Zedong. Paper also included a great deal of information about New York City nightlife. Erica Spellman-Silverman, a William Morris Agency vice president, told Spindler that reading *Paper* was "a lot easier than going out eight nights a week until 3 in the morning to find out who's zooming who." In addition, each issue included an insert that served as an entertainment guide to downtown New York. The magazine's hip, off-beat, fashion-loving readership, mostly people in their 20s and 30s, and its influence in the field of fashion attracted prominent national advertisers, among them Absolut vodka, American Express, and such designers as Jean-Paul Gaultier, Geoffrey Beene, and Ted Muehling. By 1993 *Paper*'s circulation had reached 50,000; it was being sold nationwide at bookstores, newsstands, and boutiques and was no longer losing money, as it had in the beginning. Hastreiter, who had supported herself during the previous decade as a freelance journalist, now devoted all her working hours to the magazine.

At that point, for the first time, Hastreiter and Hershkovits hired an advertising director and several ad salespeople. They also established a consulting division, Paper Productions, whose services were offered to its advertisers at no charge and for $250 an hour to others. The magazine celebrated its first decade by publishing an issue called "The Annual Report 1994: Ten Years on the Cutting Edge." Spindler described the anniversary issue as "*Paper*'s keepsake guide to the city. The tone is very much like the one that carried the magazine from being a poster-size black-and-white fold-up tip sheet to a matte (studiously not glossy) color paper periscope on pop culture. *Paper* doesn't just try to reduce New York to a manageable small town with a lot of groovy inhabitants. It turns the city into a sort of high school for exceptional students, with all the rah-rah intensity of the class yearbook." In 1995 *Paper* became one of the first fashion magazines to publish on the Internet.

According to Spindler, although by 1994 Hastreiter and Hershkovits had lived in New York for years, both still "exude[d] the indefatigable eagerness of new arrivals." Similarly, Hastreiter continued to make sure that *Paper* maintained the same spirit with which it had come into existence. A half-year after the magazine's 15th anniversary, by which time circulation was around 100,000 a month, she told Marisa Fox for the *Chicago Tribune* (December 22, 1999) that contributors to the magazine did not have to be professional journalists—merely "fanatics" about something: "We never hire journalists and talk them into doing something we want," she said. "We always hire people who have an enthusiastic point of view about something. We don't like the bland tone of most magazines. I like having all these crazy different voices in one magazine." Although by then *Paper* had become profitable, its publishers still could not afford to pay its contributors much. "It's one of the things that keeps us young," Hastreiter told Fox. "We have just enough money to find up-and-coming talented people who are full of ideas. We train them, we teach them everything and then Condé Nast hires them. As torturous and painful a process as that may be, that's how we keep regenerating ourselves."

In 2004, the year of *Paper's* 20th anniversary, Horacio Silva noted for the *New York Times* (October 3, 2004) that since *Paper's* arrival many other alternative publications that had covered the city's downtown cultural scene had succumbed to insufficient readership and/or advertising and skyrocketing rent and other costs. *Paper*, by contrast, had not only flourished but was "feeling fresher than ever," he wrote. In addition, he noted, "the disillusioned will tell you there is no longer any difference between uptown and downtown (the Lower East Side is the new Upper East Side), or high and low (yo, even hip-hop's gone upscale!)," and that "the neobohemian spirit" had departed to other locales. Hastreiter, however, has consistently maintained that there is always something new and exciting awaiting discovery. "I hate when people say everything was so much better back then," Hastreiter told Trebay. "I live for the combustion that occurs when you bring together unlikely combinations of people and that's the same as it ever was."

With Hershkovits, Hastreiter has co-edited and co-written two *Paper*-inspired coffee-table books. The first, *From Abfab to Zen: Paper's Guide to Pop Culture* (1999), which has an introduction by John Waters, discusses the celebrities, fashions, trends, and oddities of the 1980s and '90s. The second, *20 Years of Style: The World According to Paper* (2004), recounts the evolution of fashion styles in the last two decades, as influenced by art, film, sports, music, and urban life. Hastreiter is the sole author of a third coffee-table book: *Geoffrey Beene: An American Fashion Rebel* (2008), about that high-end designer, who was best known for his women's apparel. Beene, who died in 2004, became friends with Hastreiter in 1986, after *Paper* published an article about him and his work.

In 2010 Hastreiter received the Eugenia Sheppard Award, presented by the Council of Fashion Designers of America to journalists who have had a profound influence on fashion. She lives in New York City with her Dandie Dinmont terrier, Romeo.

—D.K.

Suggested Reading: cityfile.com; *New York Times* A p20 Feb. 7, 1986, IX p1+ Jan. 2, 1994, C p8 Sep. 20, 1999, VI p34 Oct. 3, 2004, E p1 Apr. 8, 2010; *New Yorker* p114+ Sep. 24, 2007; papermag.com; *Washington Post* C p2 Sep. 24, 2004

Selected Books: *Geoffrey Beene: An American Fashion Rebel*, 2008; with David Hershkovits—*From Abfab to Zen: Paper's Guide to Pop Culture*, 1999; *20 Years of Style: The World According to Paper*, 2004

Hold Steady, The

Rock band

Finn, Craig
Aug. 22, 1971– Lyricist; singer; guitarist

Kubler, Tad
June 29, 1973– Guitarist; composer

Polivka, Galen
Dec. 31, 1970– Bassist

Drake, Bobby
1976(?)– Drummer

Address: c/o Shore Fire Media, 32 Court St., Suite 1600, Brooklyn, NY 11201

"I do think rock 'n' roll of any sort, whatever subgenre, when done correctly, is a religious experience, and it's akin to a religious experience in the joy and the celebration that it can create, as well as the escapism and the feeling that everything's going to be all right." Those words were spoken by Craig Finn, the guitarist, lead singer, and lyricist for the band the Hold Steady, during an interview with Saul Austerlitz for the *Boston Globe* (September 29, 2006). Formed in the New York City borough of Brooklyn, the Hold Steady has roots in the Midwest: Finn and the lead guitarist, Tad Kubler, who writes the band's music, were formerly members of the Minneapolis, Minnesota, group Lifter Puller, a regional favorite. Both musicians moved to Brooklyn after Lifter Puller broke up, in 2000, and two years later they formed the Hold Steady. Critics praised the group's debut album, *Almost Killed Me* (2004), for its unique mix of classic-rock instrumentation and punk-rock attitude, and they remarked on Finn's distinctive vocal style: rather than singing melodically, he barked out his lyrics in spoken-word rants, telling highly detailed stories about sex, drugs, drink, wild parties, sin, re-

Mark Seliger, courtesy of Ravenhouse Ltd.
The Hold Steady (l. to r.): Galen Polivka, Craig Finn, Tad Kubler, Bobby Drake

demption, and seedy underworld characters—topics that, along with Catholicism, have become Hold Steady trademarks. After a well-received sophomore effort, *Separation Sunday* (2005), the band released its breakthrough work, *Boys and Girls in America* (2006), which topped a number of publications' year-end lists of best albums. *Stay Positive* followed in 2008, again earning accolades and comparisons to the singer Bruce Springsteen, whom Finn has long cited as an influence. *A Positive Rage* (2009), the band's only live album to date, was recorded after two years of touring to promote *Boys and Girls in America* and was sold along with a documentary DVD. The Hold Steady's fifth studio album, *Heaven Is Whenever*, arrived in 2010. Franz Nicolay was the band's keyboardist from 2005 until early 2010. The drummer Judd Counsell played with the band for about three years, starting in 2002; his replacement, Bobby Drake, is currently the Hold Steady's drummer, and its bassist is Galen Polivka.

The Hold Steady's "music is loud, raucous, and fun, but the stories they tell ache of desperation and loneliness," the novelist Joshua Ferris wrote for *New York* magazine (July 21, 2008). "Their broad anthems are about small-bit players. And their sound, which is hard to pin down, confused by some for indie punk and by others for arena rock, obscures the universality of their appeal."

The son of a financial officer and his wife, a microbiologist, Craig Finn was born on August 22, 1971 in Boston, Massachusetts. He grew up in Edina, Minnesota, a suburb of the state's Twin Cities, Minneapolis and St. Paul. "I was a traditional kid—I was into books and sport, and there wasn't

a lot of rebellion," Finn told Adrian Thrills for the London *Daily Mail* (July 18, 2008). "But I got into music through friends and it took over my life." When Finn was an adolescent, his parents would drive him to see punk-rock shows. "I'm not sure they understood what it was," he told Joe Gross for the *Village Voice* (May 10, 2005), "but they knew I was a creative kid and this stuff seemed to foster creativity." In addition to local rock bands including the Replacements and Husker Du, a major influence on Finn's life (and eventual body of songs) was Catholicism. "I spent so much time in Catholic schools and going to church with my family, that it is a part of me," he told Simon Cosyns for the British newspaper the *Sun* (July 17, 2008, on-line). "The concepts of forgiveness and redemption interest me most." In 1989 Finn graduated from the private Breck High School, "where smart kids go," according to Chris Riemenschneider, writing for the Minneapolis *Star Tribune* (June 3, 2005). He enrolled at Boston College, where he earned a bachelor's degree in communications in about 1993.

Tad Kubler was born on June 29, 1973 and grew up in Janesville, Wisconsin. His introduction to music came through his father, who played records by the Beatles, Willie Nelson, and Peter, Paul, and Mary, among others. As a young boy he and his friends lip-synched to songs in his backyard. Kubler was an unfocused student, and music helped to keep him out of trouble. During elementary school he played the cello; by the time he entered Craig High School, in Janesville, he had switched to the guitar, impressing his teachers with his ability to learn songs by ear. Once, while performing with the school band during a basketball game, he played a Jimi Hendrix–like rendition of "The Star-Spangled Banner." Like Finn, he became a fan of punk rock, and in his late teens, he began driving to shows in larger cities. He graduated from high school in 1991. Before long he began playing in local rock bands, such as Doublespeak.

Finn was still living in Boston when, in 1994, he began recruiting musicians for Lifter Puller. He and the guitarist Steve Barone relocated to Minneapolis, and in 1997 the band released its first album, *Half Dead and Dynamite*. The following year Kubler joined the group, replacing Tommy Roach on bass. Lifter Puller's second album, *Fiestas + Fiascos*, appeared in 2000. "Musically, it was carfactory guitar clatter hopped up on funk and hip-hop, and it presented an illusion of spontaneity, as if the band were riffing, jazzlike, off lead 'singer' Craig Finn's sometimes deal-breaking Lenny Bruce–like rants," a reviewer wrote for the *Memphis (Tennessee) Flyer* (June 2, 2004). Finn had already developed the gruff vocal approach he would use in the Hold Steady, and many of Lifter Puller's songs dealt with the same topics. Despite its rabid local following, the group split up in 2000. (Several Lifter Puller MP3 albums have since been issued.) "With Lifter Puller, we worked hard," Finn said in an interview for the *Dallas (Texas) Ob-*

server (February 9, 2006), "but that was the exception more than the norm. In Minneapolis, it wasn't even cool to try. It's kind of like eighth grade or something—if you get good grades, you're a nerd. If you really went after something, it almost felt like you were halfway cheating."

That same year Finn moved to Brooklyn, "to get away from being that guy in Minneapolis from Lifter Puller," he told Riemenschneider. He took a job with an on-line music company and entertained thoughts of becoming a comedy writer. Kubler, after a brief stint with the Minneapolis band Songs of Zarathustra, also moved to Brooklyn, where he and Finn began jamming with each other on Tuesday nights. "When I moved [to New York], I found it really hard to keep in touch with people," Finn told the *West Australian* (July 10, 2008). "So, I said: 'Why don't we go and play music every Tuesday night and hang out and drink beer.'" After watching Martin Scorsese's film *The Last Waltz*, which documents the final concert by the influential rock group the Band, Finn and Kubler resolved to pay homage to the kinds of classic-rock songs they had heard on the radio as teenagers. Their decision was connected with the state of the local music scene: at that time many New York City bands were fixated on danceable 1980s-style rock music—the antithesis of what Finn believes rock and roll should be. In 2002 a friend of Finn's asked him to play classic-rock covers during performances by the friend's local comedy troupe. Finn and Kubler signed on and enlisted the bassist Galen Polivka (born on December 31, 1970) and the drummer Judd Counsell, both of whom had played in the Milwaukee, Wisconsin, band Punchdrunk. The comedy job "got us writing songs as a band," Kubler told Stephen Dalton for the London *Times* (January 12, 2007). "We just realised that this stuff is always going to sound good." In an interview with Donna Brown for the *Seattle Weekly* (June 8, 2005, on-line), Finn said that he wrote lyrics in a composition notebook every day. "When we write songs, Tad will have a riff, and I'll pull something out of the notebook. Sometimes, I'll use two things from two different days if I need something."

The Hold Steady made its live debut in January 2003, and before long the New York City label Frenchkiss asked the group to record an album. "Nothing was planned," Finn told Greg Kot for the *Chicago Tribune* (October 20, 2006). "We played one gig, then we got asked to play another, and the next thing you know we were making a record. The spirit of the band was to keep it loose and fun, and it's still that way." Finn asked Frenchkiss not to spend a lot of money on the recording sessions, since he doubted the band would perform much outside New York City. In 2004 the group released *Almost Killed Me*, which was met with widespread critical acclaim. Finn's prediction notwithstanding, the group began to tour widely in the U.S. and built a devoted following. "Mr. Finn was an unlikely lead singer: small and rumpled, with glasses that always needed adjusting and a guitar that rarely, it seemed, needed playing," Kalefa Sanneh wrote for the *New York Times* (October 1, 2006), describing the Hold Steady's early days. "No matter: it turned out that Mr. Kubler's beery guitar riffs went well with Mr. Finn's beery stories; both went better than well with actual beer." "Ultimately, the Hold Steady end up sounding like a bizarre amalgamation of Lifter Puller and Bruce Springsteen & The E-Street Band; when they're done with their assault, there's blood on the stage and everyone pours sweat," Amanda Petrusich wrote in a review for *Pitchfork.com* (March 25, 2004). *Almost Killed Me* was voted number 31 in the influential *Village Voice* "Pazz & Jop" music poll, and both *Rolling Stone* and *Spin* included it on their "best albums you didn't hear" lists.

In 2005, after adding the keyboard player Franz Nicolay (born on August 27, 1977), the Hold Steady released its sophomore album, *Separation Sunday*. (Around that time Counsell left the band. His replacement, Bobby Drake, played drums on half the album.) The disk was widely described as a "concept album," recounting the hard-luck adventures of Hallelujah (also known as Holly), Gideon, and Charlemagne—characters, introduced on the group's previous album, who Finn has said are composites of people he has known. The songs mentioned drug use, religion, and falling in with dangerous crowds—recurring themes in Finn's writing. (While Finn has admitted to experimenting with drugs as an undergraduate, he has maintained that the songs are not autobiographical.) "Like its predecessor, *Separation Sunday* is at once surreal and gloriously sweaty, as Craig Finn rails like a man who's seen too many late nights and too much bad TV, while his band plunders a seemingly endless supply of secondhand riffs," Christian Hoard wrote for *Rolling Stone* (May 19, 2005). *Separation Sunday* ranked eighth on the "Jazz & Pop" poll and 10th on *Spin*'s year-end list of bests.

Building on the buzz generated by its live shows and previous albums, the Hold Steady enjoyed something of a breakthrough with its next album, *Boys and Girls in America* (2006), released on the Vagrant label. The title comes from a line in Jack Kerouac's novel *On the Road*. "Love and relationships between guys and girls is something that, no matter how much smarter you get, it doesn't help you understand that part of life," Finn told Jim Carroll for the *Irish Times* (February 16, 2007). "Of course, you do think you know a lot more about love when you're 35 than when you're 17. There's been a million songs about love because it is such an interesting topic so that was how I framed everything on the album." Critics praised the group's increasingly Springsteen-like sound—for the first time Finn, who had recently taken singing lessons, sang rather than spoke his lyrics—and both *Magnet* magazine and the Web site the A.V. Club ranked the album the best of the year. In April 2007 the Hold Steady performed at a Bruce Springsteen tribute concert at Carnegie Hall, in New York City, and during the encore Springsteen and the band—as well as many of the other musicians on that evening's bill—offered a rendition of his song "Rosalita." That same month the band released *Live at Fingerprints*, a five-song acoustic EP recorded at a record store in Long Beach, California.

A *Details* magazine (July 2007) cover story in which the actor Daniel Radcliffe, of Harry Potter fame, extolled the Hold Steady greatly increased the band's celebrity overseas. In August 2007 the Hold Steady opened for the Rolling Stones in County Meath, Ireland. "It was, to be honest, pretty ironic—the band that set out to do nothing became a critics favorite and a touring machine," Finn wrote for the Vagrant Records Web site (April 21, 2008), marveling at his group's success. "The Hold Steady had become our lives." Due to touring commitments, the band had to write much of its next album while on the road. "As with each record, there was a desire to make it more musical than the last one," Finn wrote for Vagrant's Web site, describing *Stay Positive*, the band's fourth album, which was released in July 2008. "In this case, more musical meant an attempt at more dynamics, different instrumentation, more complex arrangements, and not always hiding behind raw volume." The second consecutive album not to center on the characters Holly, Gideon, and Charlemagne, *Stay Positive* earned enthusiastic reviews. A Hold Steady concert held on October 31, 2007 at Metro, a Chicago, Illinois, venue, was recorded for the album *A Positive Rage* (2009). The CD was sold along with a DVD containing footage of shows, backstage interviews, and comments from fans.

The Hold Steady's most recent studio album, *Heaven Is Whenever* (2010), was recorded without Franz Nicolay, who left the band amicably in early 2010 to launch a solo career. (The keyboardist Dan Neustadt and the guitarist Steve Selvidge are currently participating in the band's live shows.) Finn and Kubler worked on the songs face-to-face, creating new material together over a period of six months—far longer than for their previous records. "A lot of this record is written from the perspective of someone who's older, wiser and been through some stuff," the 38-year-old Finn told Chris Riemenschneider for the *Star Tribune* (July 1, 2010, on-line). In a representative review, Jon Dolan wrote for *Rolling Stone* (May 13, 2010), "On *Heaven Is Whenever*, the Hold Steady don't just show us how much they love classic rock—they make some of their own. It's their most polished record, nearly majestic at points, without scrimping on bloodshot angst or exuberance."

According to Brendan Vaughan, writing for *Esquire* (August 2008), the incomes of Hold Steady members are derived mostly from shows rather than record sales. Audience favorites include "Cattle and the Creeping Things," "Your Little Hoodrat Friend," and "Stevie Nix," from *Separation Sunday*; "Barfruit Blues," "Knuckles," and "Hostile, Mass.," from *Almost Killed Me*; "Chips Ahoy!," "Hot Soft Light," "Teenage Liberation," "Stuck Be-

tween Stations," "You Can Make Him Like You," and "Party Pit," from *Boys and Girls in America*; and "Sequestered in Memphis" and the title song from *Stay Positive*.

Writing for *pop-music.suite101.com* (July 9, 2010), Clarke Reader described Finn as "a delightfully fun mix of Woody Allen, Jack Sparrow and Elvis Presley" who gets audiences "revved up on his own energy alone, and gives his all to performance." Finn is a voracious reader. He and his wife, Angie, live in Brooklyn, where he receives communion at a neighborhood Catholic church (but does not go to confession); for Lent, he gives up alcohol. Kubler, who has a daughter, is a professional photographer (his work can be found on tadkubler.com) and occasionally does jury-selection consultations. "I do feel like a lot of people, just because we're kind of older dudes, and unassuming for rock guys, are sorta rooting for us . . . ," Kubler told Randy Harward for the *Salt Lake City (Utah) Weekly* in 2007. "Some of my friends, they're like, 'God—it's so cool you're doing this.'" Finn told Cosyns in 2008, "I see a lot of my friends from college and, because of all the touring we do, they're in such a different place to me." He added, "That isn't to say I'm not envious of them. I would like a family some day, more financial stability, but I think it's good to stay true to yourself."

—K.J.P.

Suggested Reading: *Boston Globe* D p14 Sep. 29, 2006; *Chicago Tribune* C p1 Oct. 20, 2006; *Irish Times* p8 Feb. 16, 2007; *Janesville (Wisconsin) Gazette* Apr. 19, 2007; (Minneapolis, Minnesota) *Star Tribune* E p1 June 3, 2005; *New York* p32+ July 21, 2008; *New York Times* II p1 Oct. 1, 2006; *Seattle Weekly* (on-line) June 8, 2005; (United Kingdom) *Sun* (on-line) Jan. 19, 2007, July 17, 2008; *Village Voice* p30 May 10, 2005

Selected Albums: *Almost Killed Me*, 2004; *Separation Sunday*, 2005; *Boys and Girls in America*, 2006; *Stay Positive*, 2008; *A Positive Rage*, 2009; *Heaven Is Whenever*, 2010

Ivey, Susan M.

Oct. 31, 1958– President and CEO of Reynolds American Inc.

Address: Reynolds American Inc., 401 N. Main St., Winston-Salem, NC 27102

As president, chief executive officer, and (until October 31, 2010) chairwoman of Reynolds American Inc., Susan M. Ivey is one of only 15 women leading companies included on the 2009 Fortune 500 list of the nation's top corporations. She has spent nearly three decades in the tobacco industry, work-

Susan M. Ivey

Courtesy of Reynolds American

ing her way up from a job as a sales representative in Kentucky. "People ask me how it feels to be a woman CEO," Ivey told Edward Martin for *Business North Carolina* magazine (April 1, 2005). "I say I don't know, because I have no idea what it feels like to be a male CEO."

In 2001 Ivey became the first woman to head a major tobacco company in the U.S., assuming the top post at Brown & Williamson (B&W) Tobacco Corp., the third-largest cigarette maker in the nation at the time, before it merged with R.J. Reynolds, in 2004, to form Reynolds American. "It is a real accomplishment to be a woman in this position, but the thing that drives me is my desire to see the company succeed," Ivey told Brent Adams for the Louisville, Kentucky, publication *Business First* (November 15, 2002). "A lot of employees and their families rely on the decisions I make, and as someone who has worked her way from the ground up, I want to see things [in the tobacco industry] turn around." Despite a drop in tobacco sales that started with the recent economic recession, Ivey has been able to maintain Reynolds American's market share.

Reynolds American employs more than 6,600 people and is the parent company of R.J. Reynolds Tobacco Co., American Snuff Co. LLC, Niconovum AB, and Santa Fe Natural Tobacco Co. Inc. The second-largest tobacco company in the U.S., R.J. Reynolds produces five of the nation's 10 top-selling cigarette brands: Camel, Kool, Pall Mall, Doral, and Winston. American Snuff (formerly Conwood Co.) is the second-largest manufacturer of smokeless tobacco products in the U.S., and Santa Fe Natural manufactures Natural American Spirit additive-free tobacco products. Ivey will

step down as president and chief executive officer of Reymonds American on February 28, 2011.

Born Susan Marie Hickok on October 31, 1958 in Schenectady, New York, Ivey was raised in Fort Lauderdale, Florida. Her father, Allan Hickok, worked as a manager for the General Electric Co., while her mother, Harriett (Mathis) Hickok, was a part-time secretary and school volunteer. Ivey graduated in 1976 from Fort Lauderdale High School, where she was voted "most likely to succeed," then enrolled at the University of Tennessee at Knoxville. Soon deciding to return to her home state, she transferred to the University of Florida at Gainesville, where she earned a B.S. degree in marketing in 1980. Shortly afterward Ivey followed her then-boyfriend to Louisville. To make ends meet she sold office supplies. "I hated it," she told Brian Lewis for the *Winston-Salem (North Carolina) Journal* (November 16, 2003), "because I had no affinity for the product category whatsoever."

Six months later, in 1981, Ivey began working in the tobacco industry by chance, after she was unable to obtain a carton of Barclay Menthol cigarettes—her favorite brand—which were manufactured by Brown & Williamson. "I couldn't find them anywhere, so I called [Brown & Williamson marketing officials] and they told me that they couldn't find a distributor for them locally," Ivey told Brent Adams. "They asked me if I would be interested in coming on board as a trade marketing representative, and that's how it all started. Believe it or not, I'm still smoking those cigarettes today." As a trade marketing representative, Ivey distributed cigarettes to retail outlets in Kentucky's Jefferson and Bullitt Counties. In 1983 she was promoted to district sales manager.

Ivey continued her education at Bellarmine University (then Bellarmine College) , in Louisville, earning an M.B.A. degree in 1987. She had worked her way up to become the Far East marketing director at B&W when, in 1990, Brown & Williamson's parent company—British American Tobacco—offered her a position as brand director in London, England, where the company was headquartered. With only a day to decide, Ivey accepted, serving in that post until 1994. She then moved to Hong Kong (now part of China), to become director of marketing for British American Tobacco. After two years she moved back to London to become manager of international brands for Brown & Williamson. She married an Englishman, Trevor Ivey, in 1997. "There was a period from 1994 to 1997 where I didn't think I'd ever come back to the states," Ivey told Adams. "I had gotten married . . . and I was content living abroad."

Nonetheless, Brown & Williamson lured Ivey back to the U.S. in 1999, when they offered her the position of senior vice president of marketing, as well as a spot on the company's executive committee. She returned to Louisville, where she was charged with promoting the company's cigarette brands, including Kool, Pall Mall, Lucky Strike, Capri, Barclay, Raleigh, and Viceroy. In November

2000 Brown & Williamson's CEO, Nick Brookes, and president, Earl Kohnhorst, announced their intentions to leave the company at the end of the year. Ivey was named to both posts, effective January 2001, becoming the first woman ever to run a major U.S. tobacco company.

Ivey took the helm at a time when Brown & Williamson was working to reduce its workforce and attract a larger number of consumers. The third-largest tobacco company in the nation at the time, it had suffered in previous years from a series of lawsuits. Brown & Williamson had come under fire in 1994 when it was discovered that the company had worked with a biotechnology firm, DNA Plant Technology Corp., to develop a genetically engineered tobacco plant, nicknamed Y-1, with twice the amount of nicotine found in other tobacco. When Congress investigated the matter, then-CEO Thomas Sandefur promised that the company would stop using genetically altered tobacco, though he denied manipulating nicotine levels. (Tobacco companies continue to dispute the fact, which is otherwise universally accepted, that nicotine is highly addictive.) It was discovered four years later that Brown & Williamson had continued to use the engineered tobacco in three of their cigarette brands and that Y-1 was being grown in Brazil and shipped into the U.S. In January 1998, during a government investigation into the tobacco industry, the DNA Plant Technology Corp. pleaded guilty to conspiring to grow high-nicotine tobacco abroad secretly so that Brown & Williamson could increase nicotine levels in its cigarettes. Brown & Williamson, however, denied that it had conspired secretly to manipulate nicotine levels in its products. Despite cooperation by DNA Plant Technology Corp. during the investigation, charges were never filed against Brown & Williamson. The following year, however, the Food and Drug Administration (FDA) filed suit against the tobacco industry, claiming that since the agency has the authority to regulate drugs, it should have the legal right to regulate cigarettes and smokeless-tobacco products, since they contain nicotine, an addictive substance. The 1999 U.S. Supreme Court case *Food and Drug Administration v. Brown & Williamson Tobacco Corp.* was the culmination of years of court battles between the FDA and the tobacco industry. (Brown & Williamson was the only company named in the FDA's lawsuit, due to its association with Y-1.) On March 21, 2000 the Supreme Court voted 5–4 in the tobacco industry's favor, ruling that the FDA did not have the jurisdiction to regulate tobacco products under the Food, Drug, and Cosmetic Act. The FDA, responsible for allowing only products they deem safe and healthy in the marketplace, had asserted that if tobacco products, which the FDA views as dangerous, were within its jurisdiction, the agency would ban the products entirely. That assertion, together with Congress's having passed several laws in recent years regulating tobacco—thus showing no intention to ban the product—shaped the decision by the court, which judged that the FDA sought to overstep the authority it had been given by Congress. (In June 2009, however, President Barack Obama signed the Family Smoking Prevention and Tobacco Control Act, which grants the FDA permission to regulate tobacco products but not ban them entirely.)

Prior to the Supreme Court case, Brown & Williamson, along with the three other top cigarette companies—Philip Morris USA, R.J. Reynolds, and Lorillard Tobacco Co.—agreed to pay a total of $206 billion to 46 U.S. states through the year 2025 as part of the Tobacco Master Settlement Agreement (MSA), adopted in November 1998. The settlement was reached after several court battles between the states and tobacco companies over who was responsible for the cost of smoking-related health care. (The four states not included in the MSA—Florida, Minnesota, Mississippi, and Texas—had already reached similar deals with the companies in the preceding year.) In addition to the monetary compensation, the tobacco industry agreed to invest money in anti-smoking campaigns, particularly ones aimed at youth, and to limit the marketing of their products. (Tobacco advertisements on billboards, apparel, and all forms of transportation were banned as part of the deal.)

The legal battles were part of the reason Ivey had been reluctant to return to the U.S. "I . . . had been watching the litigation craze and the court battles over limited personal responsibility in the U.S., and I was really apprehensive about what was happening," she told Adams. "I thought the whole place had gone mad." In an effort to compensate for the damage to sales after the MSA, Philip Morris and R.J. Reynolds heavily discounted their cigarettes. Brown & Williamson, which was not in a position to do so, saw its sales dip. When competition within the industry intensified and cost-cutting became a priority, R.J. Reynolds, the second-largest U.S. tobacco company at the time, struck a deal with British American Tobacco PLC in July 2004 to acquire Brown & Williamson for $4.1 billion. Together, R.J. Reynolds and Brown & Williamson created a new publicly traded parent company, Reynolds American Inc. (British American Tobacco received a 42 percent stake in the new company.) After the merger Reynolds American controlled about 30 percent of the tobacco market. (Altria Group, which owns Philip Morris, continues to hold the top spot, with 50 percent of the market.)

Ivey was named president and CEO of the new company, based in Winston-Salem, North Carolina. She made it clear to Edward Martin that her appointment was entirely due to her experience. "I'd spent 23 years in the industry and been successful as CEO of Brown & Williamson," she said. "In no way was it a gender-based decision." She was made chairwoman of Reynolds American in January 2006.

Reynolds American acquired Conwood, the nation's second-largest maker of smokeless tobacco, for $3.5 billion in May 2006. Citing 4 to 5 percent growth over the past five years in smokeless-tobacco products—which include chewing tobacco and snuff—due to smoking bans in public areas, Ivey stated, "We are excited about the growth prospects Conwood brings to Reynolds American. Conwood's strong, well-positioned brands are gaining share in the growing moist snuff market, and its high margins will enhance our ability to continue to provide an excellent return to our shareholders."

The following year Reynolds American garnered some criticism for launching a new line of cigarettes aimed at women. Given the slogan "Light and luscious," the brand, Camel No. 9, comes in fuchsia and teal packaging. Anti-smoking advocates were angered by Camel No. 9's aggressive marketing campaign, which included advertisements in several women's magazines, such as *Cosmopolitan* and *Glamour*, and lavish parties in bars and clubs that offered women free sample cigarettes, massages, and take-home gift bags. Though Reynolds American officials said they were careful to gear their message toward adults, critics argued that their tactics were aimed at younger people as well.

In 2010 Ivey unexpectedly announced that she would be retiring as chairwoman of Reynolds American Inc. at the end of October; Thomas C. Wajnert was named as her replacement. She will be stepping down as president, chief executive, and member of the board at the end of February 2011; she will be succeeded by Daniel (Daan) M. Delen, currently the chairman, president, and CEO of R.J. Reynolds Tobacco Co. According to the company, Ivey will be moving to Florida and plans to spend more time with her family.

Ivey, who is reported to have earned $8.8 million in 2008, has been named many times to *Forbes*'s list of the "100 Most Powerful Women in Business" (she was ranked number 59 in 2009) and *Fortune*'s "50 Most Powerful Women in Business" (she ranked number 23 in 2008). She has long been an active member of the United Way, serving as campaign chair of Metro United Way in 2003 and of United Way of Forsyth County in 2007; she is currently a member of the Women's Leadership Initiative for the United Way of America. Ivey is also a member of the Committee of 200, an international organization of female business leaders who provide mentoring, education, and support for aspiring female business executives, and she is on the board of trustees of Salem College, a private liberal-arts institution for women in Winston-Salem. In 2007 she created the Susan Ivey Professorship, an endowed chair, at the University of Florida's Warrington College of Business Administration.

Ivey enjoys reading suspense and crime novels in her limited spare time. She and her husband live in the Buena Vista neighborhood of Winston-Salem. Ivey is stepmother to her husband's two grown sons, Christopher and Richard, from a previous marriage. Ivey has said that her dedication to her career led her to decide against having her own children. She told Edward Martin, "Women actually carry the children, as opposed to men. I look forward to having grandchildren, but having the children was not for me."

—M.A.S.

Suggested Reading: *Business North Carolina* p32 Apr. 1, 2005; (Louisville, Kentucky) *Business First* p24+ Nov. 15, 2002; reynoldsamerican.com; *Winston-Salem (North Carolina) Journal* D p1 Nov. 16, 2003, A p1+ Oct. 16, 2010

Chip Somodevilla/Getty Images

Jackson, Lisa P.

Feb. 8, 1962– Administrator of the U.S. Environmental Protection Agency

Address: U.S. Environmental Protection Agency, Ariel Rios Bldg., 1200 Pennsylvania Ave., N.W., Washington, DC 20460

"We have a chance to expand the conversation on environmentalism, and welcome new voices and new ideas to the environmental movement. The inauguration of the first African American president, and my confirmation as the first African American Administrator of this Agency, has begun the process of changing the face of environmentalism in our country." Lisa P. Jackson wrote those words in an op-ed piece titled "Why We Need to 'Sell' Environmentalism," published in the *Huffington Post* (August 28, 2009, on-line), during her first year as the administrator of the Environmental Protection Agency (EPA), the federal agency charged with protecting human health and the environment through regulation. She added, "People are seeing more and more that environmentalism doesn't come in one shape, size, color, or income bracket." Prior to serving as EPA administrator, Jackson, a chemical and environmental engineer, worked for 16 years in the EPA's Superfund site-remediation program, developing regulations for the hazardous-waste cleanup projects mandated by the 1980 Comprehensive Environmental Response, Compensation, and Liability Act. Beginning in 2002 Jackson served in various positions within the New Jersey Department of Environmental Protection (DEP), becoming commissioner of the department in 2006. In 2008 she worked briefly as the chief of staff under New Jersey governor Jon Corzine, before being named to President-elect Barack Obama's transition team and, shortly thereafter, to her current position as EPA administrator. She was sworn into office on January 26, 2009.

During her first year as EPA administrator, Jackson took major steps to reverse the environmental policies of the George W. Bush administration, policies that had infuriated many scientists and environmentalists. Jackson has promised to fulfill her agency's duty, as designated by the 1970 Clean Air Act and a 2007 U.S. Supreme Court decision, to protect public health by regulating greenhouse-gas emissions. In December 2009 Jackson began that process when she announced the EPA's finding that greenhouse gases produced by vehicles, power plants, and factories pose a threat to public health and must be strongly regulated.

Lisa Perez Jackson was born on February 8, 1962 in Philadelphia, Pennsylvania. She was adopted a few weeks later by Benjamin Perez, a postal deliveryman living in the French Quarter of New Orleans, Louisiana, and his wife, Marie, a homemaker and secretary. Growing up with two brothers in the middle-class, African-American area of Pontchartrain Park, Jackson was sheltered from much of the poverty and inequality that existed in other regions of the city's Ninth Ward. "When I was growing up, it wasn't like I looked around and said, 'Well, I gotta do something about this, I live next door to a factory,'" she told Dina Cappiello for the Associated Press (January 10, 2010). Her mother told Cappiello, however, that Jackson "knew that there were some people that didn't have the same things she had. She always realized that neighborhoods were different, she realized as she got older . . . our pollution and our canals and the oil refineries and the drilling [are] detrimental to people."

At Mary's Dominican High School, an all-girls Catholic institution, Jackson was the valedictorian of her class. Her father died when she was in 10th grade. She attended Tulane University, in New Orleans, where she was a standout student as well as the only African-American member of her class. She graduated summa cum laude in 1984 with a B.S. degree in chemical engineering and went on to earn an M.S. degree in chemical and environmental engineering from Princeton University, in Princeton, New Jersey, in 1986.

After graduating Jackson worked at Clean Sites Inc., a nonprofit organization funded by the chemical industry and charged with managing environmental-cleanup projects at sites identified in the 1980 federal Comprehensive Environmental Response, Compensation, and Liability Act, also known as the "Superfund" Act. (Designed to clean up abandoned hazardous-waste sites, that law charged the EPA with identifying parties responsible for contaminated areas of the country and compelling them to clean up the sites; in cases in which no parties could be found responsible, the EPA itself was to spearhead the cleanup, using federal funds.) After two years with that organization, Jackson became a staff engineer with the EPA's Superfund program, a job that required her to identify key sites containing hazardous-waste materials, develop methods of regulating those sites, and help oversee the multimillion-dollar cleanup projects. Over the years Jackson rose through the ranks of the EPA, serving as the deputy director and then acting director of regional enforcement divisions, first in Washington, D.C., and then in New York City. During that time she worked with business and community leaders and gained a reputation for her skill at dealing diplomatically with those who opposed her views.

In 2002 Jackson was hired by New Jersey governor Jim McGreevey, a Democrat, to work in the state's Department of Environmental Protection (DEP) under Commissioner Bradley Campbell. The DEP was established in 1970, the same year that the EPA was founded. (That year also saw the passage of the Clean Air Act, which outlines the EPA's responsibilities in regulating air pollution.) The DEP is charged with collaborating with the EPA to safeguard natural resources and address pollution problems in New Jersey. As assistant commissioner for the New Jersey Division of Compliance and Enforcement, Jackson was the department's chief enforcer of environmental regulations. Her responsibilities included investigating companies and organizations suspected of violating environmental laws. During her tenure Jackson and her inspectors conducted more than 2,100 investigations in the cities of Camden and Paterson, where many residences are located near regulated facilities, and uncovered more than 500 violations. In 2005 Jackson was hired as the department's assistant commissioner for land-use management. One of her major duties in that position was to oversee the development of regulatory standards to preserve and protect the state's Highlands region, 800,000 acres in northwest New Jersey that contain an abundance of natural resources, including the source of drinking water for about half the state's population. The Highlands Water Protection and Planning Act, passed in August 2004, had established the Highlands Water Protection and Planning Council to develop those regulations and monitor compliance with them.

In 2006 Jackson was chosen by the newly elected Democratic governor, Jon Corzine, to become the commissioner of the DEP. Jackson's selection was widely endorsed by community leaders. In her new position she was charged with directing a staff of several thousand professionals in protecting and improving the quality of New Jersey's water, air, and land, preserving its natural resources, and managing the cleanup of the state's Superfund sites. With its long history of heavy industry, New Jersey is home to more federal Superfund sites than any other state in the country. Over the years the New Jersey DEP has followed a national trend—removing fewer contaminants from sites while putting more impermeable caps over polluted areas, which is less costly and more appealing to the business community but leaves many environmental concerns unaddressed.

In the fall of 2006, Jackson and the rest of the DEP came under criticism when it was revealed that a day-care center known as Kiddie Kollege had been allowed to open in 2004 on land that had formerly been the site of a thermometer factory and was on the state's list of contaminated areas due to the unsafe levels of mercury vapors detected there. Shortly after that news became public, it was reported that the department did not know which contaminated sites on its list were in the most need of attention and had allowed developers and polluters to hire unlicensed consultants to oversee the waste sites' cleanup. In October Jackson announced plans to overhaul the department's $60 million cleanup program, which was responsible for more than 16,000 contaminated sites. Jackson's plan called for prioritizing sites that required cleanup, establishing a licensing board for consultants, and creating incentives for companies to clean up their listed sites within a year.

In April 2007 the U.S. Supreme Court ruled that under the terms of the Clean Air Act, the EPA has the duty to regulate greenhouse-gas emissions, unless it can prove that the greenhouse gases do not contribute to climate change or provide some other reasonable explanation why regulation is not necessary. (The matter had been brought to the court after the EPA refused a request by officials in California, New Jersey, and other states to regulate those states' greenhouse gases, arguing that the agency had discretion to decide how to respond to the threat of global warming; in response 11 states sued the EPA to force it to act.) The EPA under Bush ignored the decision. In June 2007 Governor Corzine signed into law the Global Warming Response Act, which set the ambitious goals of cutting the state's greenhouse-gas emissions 20 percent by 2020 and 80 percent by 2050, "in the absence of leadership on the federal level," as Corzine stated in an official press release. Also in 2007 New Jersey joined a group comprising 11 states, Washington, D.C., New York City, and several environmental organizations in a lawsuit against the Bush administration over the Highway Traffic Safety Administration's new fuel-efficiency standard, which increased by less than two miles per gallon the minimum required for new vehicles. The parties in the suit charged that the new regulations violated federal law by ignoring both the impact of oil use on the environment and the country's dependence on imported oil. In reference to New Jersey's participation in the lawsuit, Jackson said, as quoted in the *New York Times* (December 11, 2008), "When it comes to the auto industry, the E.P.A. apparently is the Emissions Permission Agency." In 2007 Jackson was named the state's cabinet member of the year by the New Jersey Conference of Mayors.

By early 2008 New Jersey faced a major budget crisis and was forced to make drastic cuts to its workforce; by the end of Jackson's term, 400 state jobs were eliminated. In January Jackson announced her department's environmental goals for the year, which included repairing state parks, enacting the Highlands preservation plan, reducing vehicle emissions, and slowing environmentally destructive land development. At that time, however, Jackson stated that the budget concerns were requiring her to "do more with less" and would inevitably hinder a number of projects. In March 2008 Jackson announced plans to close nine state parks and reduce services at three others, in order to save the state $4 million. Environmental and conservation groups, as well as much of the general public, protested so vigorously that Jackson decided to keep the parks open with money that had been set aside to restore state beaches. That move, in turn, angered residents of many towns along the New Jersey coastline.

In October 2008 Governor Corzine appointed Jackson as his new chief of staff, citing her "leadership, work ethic and skills at handling complex issues," as quoted by Claire Heininger and Josh Margolin in the Newark, New Jersey, *Star-Ledger* (December 11, 2008). The next month the president-elect of the United States, Barack Obama, named Jackson to his 12-person transition team devoted to energy and natural resources. During the Democratic presidential primaries, Jackson, along with Governor Corzine, had endorsed U.S. senator Hillary Rodham Clinton of New York; she switched her support to Obama when it became clear that he would be the Democratic nominee. In December, just days after Jackson had taken her post under Corzine, Obama announced his nomination of Jackson to become EPA administrator. His appointment of Jackson was praised by most environmentalists. John McKeon, the chairman of New Jersey's Assembly Environment Committee, who had worked with Jackson, told Heininger and Margolin, "The best part about [Jackson] was her practical sense of always keeping the environment first and also being realistic and reasonable, and that's a recipe for getting things done, and that's why I'm so thrilled she's going to Washington." Some observers, however, blamed Jackson for a number of environmental reversals that took place in New Jersey during the Corzine administration, such as the weakening of environmental protections for streams. "New Jersey is number one in toxic waste sites in the country, number one in Superfund sites, number one in population densities," Robert Spiegel, the executive director of the Edison Wetlands Association, told Brian T. Murray for the *Star-Ledger* (January 11, 2009). "We needed someone who was going to fight for environmental policies based on sound science. What we got was a soldier for Corzine."

At her confirmation hearings before the U.S. Senate, Jackson promised to pursue the five environmental objectives that had been identified by President-elect Obama, which were to "reduce greenhouse-gas emissions, reduce other air pollutants, address toxic chemicals, clean up hazardous-waste sites and protect water," as listed in the *Star-Ledger* (January 15, 2009). Jackson's predecessor, the career scientist and federal legislator Stephen Johnson, had frequently been accused of basing his decisions on White House preferences rather than scientific findings. Despite the reservations of some Senate Republicans that the increased regulations Jackson promised to enact would not be in the interest of business, Jackson was confirmed by the Senate on January 23, 2009, becoming the first African-American leader of the EPA. Shortly after taking office Jackson pledged to establish a new direction for the agency, reviewing policies to determine if they had slowed the government's ability to respond to global warming and other environmental concerns. Chief among her priorities was to fulfill the EPA's responsibility to regulate greenhouse-gas emissions, as articulated in the 2007 Supreme Court decision.

In March Jackson issued a memorandum to stop the agency's decade-old "Performance Track" program, whereby corporations could set their own standards for environmental responsibility. The program had been deemed ineffective; recent articles had reported that many well-known corporations involved in the program were also the nation's biggest polluters. The next month Jackson made headlines when she released a 130-page report showing that the projected levels of greenhouse gases emitted by automobiles presented a danger to "current and future generations." Because the EPA could move on its own to enact greenhouse-gas regulations following a mandatory 60-day "public comment" period, the report put pressure on Congress to implement automobile regulations during that time, rather than leave the matter to the EPA. In May Jackson announced that the EPA would reestablish the procedures used prior to the Bush administration for examining the threat of air pollutants such as carbon monoxide. As part of those procedures, the EPA would begin issuing "staff papers" to clarify choices for policymakers to consider when drafting legislation regarding air quality, a practice that had been deemphasized under the Bush administration.

On December 7, 2009 Jackson announced that greenhouse gases produced by power plants and factories, in addition to vehicles, presented a danger to public health, expanding the EPA's April 2009 finding. The announcement was the first step in a legal process that would allow the EPA to develop rules to control greenhouse-gas emissions from those sources under the Clean Air Act. "The vast body of evidence not only remains unassailable, it's grown stronger, and it points to one conclusion," Jackson said in her announcement, as quoted by Christi Parsons and Jim Tankersley in the *Los Angeles Times* (December 8, 2009). "Greenhouse gases from human activity are increasing at unprecedented rates, and are adversely affecting our environment and threatening our health." She went on to note that the administration "will not ignore science or the law any longer, nor will we avoid the responsibility we owe to our children and grandchildren." Her announcement came on the first day of the 2009 United Nations Climate Change Conference, in Copenhagen, Denmark, which was attended by representatives of 170 countries with the goal of establishing a new global agreement to counter global warming and slow climate change. A few days after her announcement, Jackson delivered a speech at the Copenhagen conference, in which she promised that both the EPA and the U.S. Congress would work to establish regulations to control greenhouse-gas emissions.

Jackson has also asked Congress for the power to ban the use of certain chemicals, many of which are unregulated. As reported in the *Dallas Morning News* (September 30, 2009), House and Senate Democrats were expected to introduce bills to strengthen the Toxic Substances Control Act (the 1976 law under which chemicals are currently regulated) in the near future, particularly with regard to chemicals and processes introduced to the marketplace in recent years. Jackson has also called for better labeling and more rigorous testing of household products in order to protect children from dangerous chemicals. In January 2010 she announced her intention to set a new limit on smog-producing emissions, from 75 parts-per-billion, the limit approved by Bush in 2008, to about 60 to 70 parts-per-billion, which was more in keeping with the recommendation of a panel of scientists appointed by the EPA. "EPA is stepping up to protect Americans from one of the most persistent and widespread pollutants we face," Jackson told Randy Lee Loftis for the *Dallas Morning News* (January 8, 2010). "Using the best science to strengthen these standards is a long-overdue action that will help millions of Americans breathe easier and live longer." The announcement was applauded by environmentalists but was criticized by many conservative members of Congress, who viewed it as overzealous and a threat to jobs in the already struggling economy.

In China in mid-October 2010, Jackson met with Zhou Shengxian, the head of China's Ministry of Environmental Protection. Jackson and Shengxian signed a Memorandum of Understanding to reaffirm the U.S. and China's joint commitment to environmental protection.

In 2005, when Jackson was under consideration to become New Jersey's DEP commissioner, the flooding from Hurricane Katrina destroyed her childhood home, along with most homes in her New Orleans neighborhood, filling it with six to eight feet of water. Like thousands of other New Orleans residents, Jackson's mother, who still lived in that house and had no flood insurance, was forced to sell her home to the state. That experience strengthened Jackson's commitment to achieving social justice through environmental improvements. "After the hurricane I kept saying if I were rich, I would knock this house down, and rebuild an energy-efficient, elevated house for my mother," Jackson told Cappiello. "But then to be able to come back as the head of the EPA and say maybe I couldn't help my mother in her one instance, and thank God she is OK, but maybe I can help some people and help my city and help the Gulf Coast." Throughout her career Jackson has also been an outspoken advocate for civil rights; in 2007, as New Jersey's DEP commissioner, she rescinded a Methodist group's tax-exempt status after it denied the use of its seaside property for a same-sex civil-union ceremony.

Jackson is a member of the New Jersey Outdoor Women's League. With her husband, Kenneth Jackson, she has two teenage sons, Marcus and Brian.

—M.R.M.

Suggested Reading: *Dallas Morning News* Metro B p1 Jan. 8, 2010; *Huffington Post* (on-line) Aug. 28, 2009; *Los Angeles Times* A p1 Dec. 8, 2009; *New York Times* (on-line) Dec. 11, 2008; (Newark, New Jersey) *Star-Ledger* New Jersey p19 Sep. 18, 2007, News p1 Dec. 11, 2008, News p1 Jan. 1, 2009, New Jersey p17 Jan. 11, 2009; U.S. Environmental Protection Agency Web site

---

Jenike, Michael A.

(JEH-nih-kee)

May 8, 1945– Psychiatrist; specialist in obsessive-compulsive disorder

Address: Dept. of Psychiatry, Massachusetts General Hospital–East, Ninth Fl., Bldg. 149, 13th St., Charlestown, MA 02129

Michael A. Jenike is a psychiatrist specializing in the treatment of obsessive-compulsive disorder (OCD). An obsession is an intrusive and irrational thought or fear; a compulsion is the repetitive behavior adopted to reduce the anxiety caused by the obsession. According to the Obsessive Compulsive Foundation, OCD affects between 2 and 3 percent of people around the world and a similar percentage in the United States, where OCD sufferers number about seven million. The discomforting superstitious beliefs or mild worries that most people harbor do not affect their day-to-day lives in any major ways; the obsessions and compulsions of people diagnosed with OCD interfere significantly with their lives. For example, those without OCD who are concerned with the spread of the H1N1 virus might wash their hands after touching public banisters or doorknobs; people with OCD who obsess about the virus might wash their hands dozens or hundreds of times daily. In another example, a person might lock her front door after coming home and then, a little while later, check to make sure that she remembered to lock it; a person with OCD might recheck the lock over and over for hours on end. Among the most common types of obsessions are fears of being contaminated by germs or dirt, of harming oneself or others, and of losing control of powerful urges. Others include disturbing sexual thoughts, agonizing religious or moral doubts, and a persistent need to have one's environment in perfect order. Repetitive actions, also called rituals, are among the most common compulsions. They include continual counting of objects (passing cars, for example) or motions (steps as one walks).

Jenike began treating people diagnosed with OCD in the 1970s, at Massachusetts General Hospital (MGH), in Boston. He later founded an outpatient facility at MGH that offered a then-new treatment for OCD: a form of cognitive-behavioral therapy known as exposure and response prevention therapy, which was used in combination with medication. In 1997 Jenike established a residential treatment facility for patients with unusually severe OCD at McLean Hospital, in Belmont, Massachusetts. A professor of psychiatry at the Harvard Medical School, in Cambridge, Massachusetts, Jenike is unusual in his willingness to treat, at their homes, sometimes free of charge, sufferers of the most severe forms of OCD—those whose obsession-driven rituals demand virtually all their time, so that they no longer leave their homes or, in some cases, wash or dress. Jenike's treatment of a college student named David, whose obsessions regarding cleanliness led him to remain locked in his parents' bathroom for years, was featured in a series that aired on the TV newsmagazine *60 Minutes* between 1999 and 2001. His work with another sufferer of crippling OCD, Edward E. Zine, is described in *Life in Rewind: The Story of a Young Courageous Man Who Persevered Over OCD and the Harvard Doctor Who Broke All the Rules to Help Him* (2009), co-written by Jenike, Zine, and the journalist Terry Weible Murphy. Jenike has co-edited several books for professionals on the man-

Courtesy of Michael Jenike

Michael A. Jenike

agement and treatment of OCD and has written books, also for specialists, about geriatric psychiatry and psychopharmacology.

Michael Andrew Jenike was born on May 8, 1945 in Edinburgh, Scotland. He has a younger brother, Ian. Jenike's father, Andrew Jenike, was born in Poland; he earned a B.S. degree in mechanical engineering from the Warsaw Polytechnic Institute in 1939, before fighting with the Polish Army in World War II. He met Jenike's mother, Una, a British model, in England, where, in 1949, he earned a Ph.D. in structural engineering from the University of London. When Michael Jenike was about five years old, his family moved from Canada to the United States, briefly living in Niagara Falls, New York, before moving to Salt Lake City, Utah. Jenike's mother devoted herself to homemaking. His father was a pioneer in the field of bulk-solids flow—the movement of solids contained in silos or the hopper cars of freight trains, for example; he established the Bulk Solids Flow Laboratory at the University of Utah. The family relocated several times during Jenike's childhood, and he was a frequent target for bullies. In response he developed a defiant streak and became a troublemaker in school. When he was 11 years old, Jenike's disciplinary problems led his parents to enroll him in an extremely harsh religious school, where he grew even bolder in his questioning of authority figures. Although he was brighter than average, school did not interest him, and he worked only hard enough to get by. He was close to his mother and would often attend to her when she was incapacitated with migraine headaches. In 1963, when he was a senior in high school, the family moved to Winchester, Massachusetts, where his

father co-founded Jenike & Johanson, a consulting engineering company specializing in bulk-solids flow. (The company has continued to flourish since his death, in 2003.)

Jenike's father encouraged him to attend the Massachusetts Institute of Technology and prepare to take over Jenike & Johanson one day, but that prospect held no appeal for Jenike; rather, he dreamed of riding across the country on a motorcycle. He enrolled at Tufts University, in Boston, where, as before, he studied only enough to pass his exams. He and his classmates "would just sit in big lecture halls, memorize things, and spit it back," Jenike said in an interview with *Current Biography*, the source of quotes in this article unless otherwise noted. He found college "very boring," he said. "No, I wasn't too enthused about college at all. I was glad to get out." He graduated in 1967, with a B.S. degree, and then, in an effort to avoid being drafted into the U.S. Army and sent to serve in the Vietnam War, he enrolled in a Ph.D. program in biology at the University of Massachusetts. When he learned that student deferments had been abolished and that he would probably be drafted, Jenike took the necessary exams to earn a master's degree, in 1969, and, envisioning a career as a pilot, enlisted in the U.S. Air Force. He remained in the air force for about four and half years, during which he served in Vietnam for about 15 months. His heroic actions during a troop-evacuation mission on January 3, 1972 earned him a Distinguished Flying Cross. Jenike's experiences in Vietnam awakened in him a desire to help people as a physician. Those experiences also resulted years later, as he revealed in *Life in Rewind*, in symptoms of post-traumatic stress disorder. During his last year in the air force, while stationed at Langley Air Force Base, in Williamsburg, Virginia, he took courses at the College of William and Mary to qualify for admission to medical school. His hard work paid off: his score on the Medical College Admission Test (MCAT) was in the 99th percentile.

After he left the air force, with the rank of captain, in 1973, Jenike entered the University of Oklahoma Medical School, in Oklahoma City. Having always liked "to jump in and fix things," Jenike first intended to become a surgeon. At that time he was not at all interested in psychiatry, mainly because he assumed that treatment usually required years of talk therapy, and the criteria for determining when an individual's treatment was successful were indefinite. Those ideas changed when, while at medical school, Jenike became acquainted with several psychiatrists, among them Ronald King, Gordon Deckert, and John Rush, who seemed to approach psychiatry with the sort of initiative and pragmatism he associated with surgery. "That made an impression on me," Jenike said. "So I decided I would go learn psychiatry and then probably do something else." When he graduated from medical school, in 1978, Jenike was at the top of his class, and he earned the Solomon Papper Humane Scholar Award. He then completed a one-year internship in internal medicine at the University of Oklahoma College of Medicine. Acting on the advice of one of his professors, he applied successfully for a psychiatry residency at Massachusetts General Hospital (MGH), in Boston. During his residency (1978–81), he was also a clinical fellow in psychiatry at Harvard Medical School.

Jenike remained at MGH after he completed his residency. In his first job there, he managed the inpatient psychiatric facility. In 1982 he co-founded the hospital's Memory Disorders Dementia Clinic, for patients with memory problems associated with Alzheimer's disease and dementia. At that clinic Jenike, for the first time, examined people who suffered from OCD. "I found the patients fascinating, but they had a quality that seemed quite unique—their symptoms consisted of pure suffering," Jenike said in an undated interview for the *OCF Newsletter*, published by the Obsessive Compulsive Foundation. "The patients were for the most part very nice and competent people, but they were tormented by obsessions and rituals that they knew did not make sense (usually) but nonetheless they felt like they were unwilling slaves to the OCD." At that time the medical community knew little about OCD; the disorder was thought to be extremely rare, and it was treated mainly with a form of talk therapy whose aim was to reveal the subconscious causes or motivations for the patients' symptoms. With few exceptions, such therapy did little or nothing to diminish those symptoms; indeed, it often exacerbated them, because the patients were forced to ruminate on thoughts that were already obsessive. Some specialists held unproven theories about the causes of OCD; for instance, some thought that OCD was caused by bad parenting or poor toilet training. Jenike's colleagues told him that OCD sufferers were not likely to get better.

In the early 1980s Jenike appeared on TV in an installment of *Larry King Live* with a man who had suffered from depression and OCD until a suicide attempt in which a bullet injured a nonvital part of his frontal lobe. Following that televised discussion of OCD, Jenike "got bombarded by thousands and thousands of calls" from OCD sufferers and their family members. "I realized that almost nothing was known [about OCD] and that so many people were suffering and that as a profession, we were not helpful," Jenike said during an interview broadcast on *48 Hours* (January 5, 2001). At MGH Jenike assembled a team of researchers and doctors who began to reexamine OCD from biological and behavioral standpoints. In early 1983 Jenike established an outpatient clinic at MGH that focused exclusively on screening and treating patients with OCD. There he used what was then a fairly new treatment: a type of cognitive-behavioral therapy called exposure and response prevention therapy, which was based on a learning principle called habituation. Patients undergoing such therapy are asked to write lists of the situations that trigger anxiety and ritualized behaviors. Starting with the

least severe source of stress on an individual's list, the patient is exposed to that stressor and then restricted from performing the compulsive rituals he or she normally uses to cope with the stress. "You start with something fairly low-down and you get them to do the things that cause them a little bit of anxiety and then they'll become anxious and you just keep them in that situation for a while and then the anxiety goes down," Jenike said. For example, patients who repeatedly wash their hands might be exposed to an object perceived to be a little dirty, such as a well-thumbed library book, and then prevented from washing their hands for several hours. In later sessions such patients might be exposed to items that provoke greater stress—more heavily soiled or germ-laden objects, such as the dirty sole of a shoe. The aim of the sessions is to persuade the patients intellectually and physiologically that their anxiety can decrease without any rituals. Once patients complete exposure-and-response sessions with the help of therapists, they attend self-directed sessions; Jenike has said that their responses in those sessions are the best predictors of how they will fare after they have left the program.

To treat patients who suffer primarily from obsessive thoughts, Jenike uses similar methods. Jenike has said that it is particularly helpful for patients to understand that all people have disturbing thoughts at times and that their own are not as strange as they may seem. "Everybody has the thought that they want to smack somebody . . . or poke someone's eye out," Jenike said. "If you have OCD [the thoughts] get stuck there and go 24 hours a day. So what you need to try to do is not to try to force the thoughts out of your head, because that just makes them come in stronger. If you try not to think of something, even without OCD, it comes in stronger." To "let [patients'] thoughts pass naturally," Jenike and his colleagues often record the patients describing their obsessive thoughts; then each must listen to his or her own tape repeatedly. "After they do that, after a while it sounds kind of boring to them," Jenike said. "And if they can hear their own voice saying it, when they get the thought, they don't get all paralyzed."

The results of research published in the late 1980s and 1990s increased the medical community's understanding of OCD. Those studies revealed that between 2 and 3 percent of people suffered from OCD—far more than anyone had expected. Mounting evidence also suggested that OCD is linked to biological abnormalities and that it is not connected to child-rearing practices. In 1990 the Food and Drug Administration approved the first drug to treat OCD: clomipramine, which is sold under the trade name Anafranil and is one of a family of substances called selective serotonin reuptake inhibitors, or SSRIs. (That drug, as well as other medications that affect the brain's levels of serotonin, had been prescribed for years to treat OCD, without FDA approval for that particular use. It had been used to treat depression in Canada and

Europe, where its effectiveness in cases of OCD was discovered inadvertently.)

Although many OCD sufferers were helped tremendously at the MGH outpatient facility, many others got no relief from the treatment provided there. Due to budget constraints, MGH administrators rejected Jenike's proposal to set up a residential treatment program for people in the latter category. Later, Jenike discussed his idea for the facility with Arnold Hiatt, then the chief executive officer of the Stride Rite Corp. and the father of one of Jenike's patients. Hiatt provided the start-up funds for the facility, and in 1997 the Obsessive Compulsive Disorder Institute (OCDI) opened, at McLean Hospital, in Belmont, Massachusetts. Affiliated with both MGH and the Harvard Medical School, it was the nation's first privately funded residential facility for OCD patients. (At present, there is only one other, at Rogers Memorial Hospital in Oconomowoc, Wisconsin.) Early on, some patients stayed at the institute for more than a year, but after a while, Jenike recalled in the *OCF Newsletter*, "we noted that if patients had not gotten actively into treatment and started to improve within the first month of treatment, they were not going to be able to utilize our approach no matter how long we kept them." Currently, on average, patients remain at OCDI for three months.

Since his days as a resident, Jenike has occasionally visited and treated patients with severe cases of OCD at their homes for no charge—a practice that has sparked criticism from many of his colleagues, who reject such tactics as unprofessional and as evidence of what they consider to be overinvolvement with patients. One such patient was Ed Zine, whom Jenike treated in the mid-1990s. In his early 20s Zine became obsessed by an intense fear of death. He dropped out of college, where he had played on the football team, and returned home. In an effort to stop or reverse time so that no one close to him would die (he had already lost his mother, when he was nine, and several friends), he developed an elaborate set of rituals, which included constant counting and "rewinding," or repeating backwards, all of his actions on any day, doing so an even number of times—sometimes upwards of 16,000. Although, like the vast majority of OCD sufferers, Zine knew that his goal was unattainable, the rituals quelled his anxiety. After repeated failed attempts to help him with medication, his family had him admitted to a mental institution. After his release, that same year, Zine retreated to the basement of his father's house. He remained there for the next two years, repeating and "rewinding" the few actions of which he was still capable. He never bathed or brushed his teeth; the little that he ate or drank came in Ziploc bags and plastic bottles that members of his family brought him. He would defecate and urinate in the bags and bottles to avoid having to visit the bathroom, an act that had become insurmountably onerous for him.

After months of effort Jenike gained Zine's trust; then, for more than a year in Zine's home, he treated Zine with a variety of medications and cognitive-behavior therapy. Nothing helped, and one day in 1998, in Zine's presence, Jenike wept out of frustration and hopelessness. He left Zine's house that day thinking that from then on, he would communicate with Zine only by phone. But his tears turned out to be Zine's salvation: they sparked in Zine the determination to stop hurting those he loved (including Jenike) by overcoming his OCD. Using the methods Jenike had taught him, and with the help of a concerned postal worker who visited him nearly every day, Zine began to improve. When Jenike visited Zine in 1999, he did not recognize the clean-cut, healthy-looking man who greeted him. Zine now works in construction and is married and the father of two daughters. *Life in Rewind* describes not only Zine's illness and treatment but also Jenike's experiences in Vietnam and his bouts with depression and post-traumatic stress disorder in the 1990s—problems that for some time he did not want to reveal in the book. In an interview with Neal Conan for the National Public Radio program *Talk of the Nation* (May 13, 2009), he explained why he changed his mind: Zine, he said, "was willing to go forward with his life, his traumas and living there in filth and all kinds of embarrassing things. So I figured maybe I needed to step up to the plate, too." Jenike told Joseph P. Kahn for the *Boston Globe* (May 16, 2009), "Part of the book's message is that we psychiatrists have to step back a bit, that the relationship is much more important than we thought. A 15-minute conversation and prescribing meds is never going to work for some people."

Along with several behavioral therapists on staff at the OCDI, Jenike continues to treat patients with severe OCD, sometimes at their homes and, for the many who cannot afford to pay for treatment, free of charge. Jenike has witnessed the dramatic improvement of many of his patients; some of those who were housebound have married and become parents and hold jobs, a few as doctors or lawyers. In recent years researchers have made advances in determining the causes of the disorder and in developing new treatments. Evidence indicates that OCD is a physiological disorder related to an imbalance of serotonin in the brain; such an imbalance may be triggered by a traumatic experience, a bout of strep throat, encephalitis, or other conditions that affect parts of the brain. Researchers are currently examining thousands of genetic samples from OCD sufferers from all over the world, in an effort to discover whether the disorder has a genetic component. Deep-brain stimulation, using electrodes, is among the new treatments for cases in which all other methods have proven ineffective.

Jenike has served as the associate chief of psychiatry at MGH since 1986 and has held the title of professor of psychiatry at Harvard since 1995; for the last 15 years he has also chaired the scientific advisory board and sat on the board of directors of the National Obsessive Compulsive Foundation. Papers he has written or co-written have been published in the *New England Journal of Medicine*, the *Journal of the American Medical Association*, and the *American Journal of Psychiatry*. Jenike lives in Stow, Massachusetts, a suburb of Boston, with his partner of seven years, Carla Kenney, an OCD therapist. In his spare time he plays basketball, swims, runs, reads, and writes. From his marriage to the former Julie Ann Ryan, which ended in divorce, he has three adult children—Lisa, Eric, and Sara. Eric Jenike co-wrote, with his father and Evelyn Stewart, the chapter on the biological treatment of OCD in the *Oxford Handbook on Anxiety and Related Disorders* (2008). He has worked since 2005 at MGH, as a research assistant on projects concerning the genetic predictors of OCD, schizophrenia, and other mental disorders.

—M.R.M.

Suggested Reading: *Boston Globe* G p15 May 16, 2009; National Public Radio's *Talk of the Nation* (on-line) May 13, 2009; (New York) *Newday*

Health & Discovery B p19 July 11, 1995; *Newsweek* Lifestyle p71 Mar. 27, 1989; United Press International Nov. 9, 1983; Jenike, Michael A., Edward E. Zine, and Terry Weible Murphy. *Life in Rewind: The Story of a Young Courageous Man Who Persevered Over OCD and the Harvard Doctor Who Broke All the Rules to Help Him*, 2009

Selected Books: *Handbook of Geriatric Psychopharmacology*, 1985; *Geriatric Psychiatry and Psychopharmacology: A Clinical Approach*, 1989; *Life in Rewind: The Story of a Young Courageous Man Who Persevered Over OCD and the Harvard Doctor Who Broke All the Rules to Help Him* (with Edward E. Zine and Terry Weible Murphy), 2009; as co-editor—*Obsessive Compulsive Disorders: Theory and Management*, 1986, 1990; *Manual of Clinical Problems in Psychiatry*, 1990; *Obsessive-Compulsive Disorders, Practical Management*, 1998

Jha, Sanjay K.

(jah)

1963– Telecommunications executive

Address: Motorola Inc., 1303 E. Algonquin Rd., Schaumburg, IL 60196

In 2008 Sanjay K. Jha was appointed co–chief executive officer (CEO) of Motorola, one of the communication industry's most recognizable brand names, and also CEO of that company's faltering Mobile Devices business. Jha, who has a doctorate in electronic and electrical engineering, is "one of the stars of the wireless world," analysts at the investment bank Cowen and Co. told Wailin Wong for the *Chicago Tribune* (August 5, 2008), and according to Wong, Motorola recruited him to save the company from bankruptcy. Jha "can be the Lee Iacocca of the mobile industry, bringing an iconic brand back to life," Roger Entner, an executive at the marketing-research firm Nielsen IAG, told Wong, referring to Iacocca's success at rescuing the Chrysler auto company when it was on the brink of extinction. "And if it goes south, he can say: 'Sorry, this thing was so messed up when I got there that there was nothing I could do.'" Before he arrived at Motorola, Jha spent 14 years with Qualcomm, rising from senior engineer to executive vice president and chief operating officer (COO). During that time the firm became the world's biggest supplier of wireless-phone chips. Jha has been described as an engineering genius with both technological and corporate foresight, one who champions unproven technologies and software that

Courtesy of Motorola

emerge as industry standards. He is also known for his blunt, forceful, and decisive leadership style. "There's no ambiguity about who's in charge," Dale Stone, who worked with Jha at both Qualcomm and Motorola, told John Pletz for *Crain's Chicago Business* (December 22, 2008). Jeffrey Belk, a former head of strategy at Qualcomm, told Pletz that Jha is "a force of nature. He's not going to slow himself down for everyone else." In the past year and a half, Jha has put most of his efforts into developing a new generation of "smart phones," powered on an open-source Google platform. In late 2009 Motorola, in partnership with Google, launched a new smartphone, the Droid— which quickly became competitive with Apple's iPhone. In February 2010 Motorola confirmed its plans to divide into two independent companies by the first quarter of 2011. Jha will lead Motorola Mobility, which will focus on mobile devices and home business. (The other company, Motorola Solutions Inc., will focus on networks and enterprise radio systems operations.)

Sanjay K. Jha was born in 1963 in Madhubani, in Bihar, a state in eastern India. Very little about his personal life has been made public, and on the very rare occasions that he has granted interviews, he has spoken almost exclusively about the technology and telecommunications industries. According to Anna Marie Kukec, writing for the Chicago, Illinois, *Daily Herald* (August 5, 2008), Jha grew up in India. He earned a B.S. degree in engineering from the University of Liverpool, in England, and a Ph.D. in electronic and electrical engineering from the University of Strathclyde, in Scotland. During the next few years, he held engineering positions at the GEC Hirst Research Center, in London, England, a specialized industrial-research laboratory owned by the General Electric Co., and at the Brooktree Corp., a semiconductor company in San Diego, California. In 1994 Jha began working at Qualcomm, also in San Diego, as a senior engineer, initially working on the Globalstar satellite phone. In the early 1990s the company's founders had developed code division multiple access (CDMA), which became a standard in wireless communications, allowing multiple mobile-phone users to share the same frequency and enabling high-speed data transmissions. "It was a gamble, but it has worked out well for those of us who started out early," Jha told Vikas Bajaj for the *Dallas Morning News* (October 29, 2000). "We used to call this Qualcomm University because there is a very academic environment here. That was very appropriate when we were fighting for our technology." Jha, who had been in the industry for a few years, decided to take a chance on the company and its potentially groundbreaking technology. In the late 1980s and 1990s, Qualcomm became a major player in championing new-generation technologies (from 1G to 4G and beyond—the difference between the generations being the technology used to divide the spectrum, or frequency used to send data and sound over the airwaves); many of its employees became millionaires in the process. In the 1980s 1G, or first-generation technology, used an analog wave form and was primarily devoted to voice transmission. In the 1990s, when Jha was involved, the move to digital, or 2G (GSM), offered higher speed and greater efficiency and also allowed the transmission of data packets (e-mail messages and text). The next generation, 2.5, had higher download speeds. The digital 3G technology provided yet another jump in speed, and most telecom providers used CDMA technology. The next technology, 4G, was expected to be commercially available in late 2009 or 2010.

Jha moved quickly up the ladder at Qualcomm. In 1997 he was promoted to vice president of engineering, with responsibility for overseeing the company's development of cell-phone chips and software. In that capacity he led the development of application-specific integrated circuits, which were integrated into Qualcomm's chipsets, and oversaw the creation of several generations of modem and cell-site chipsets as well as system software. In 1998 Jha was promoted to senior vice president of engineering. In 2002 he launched Qualcomm's new investment division, Qualcomm Technologies & Ventures, managing both the technology-investment portfolio and the new technology group. In 2003 he became president of Qualcomm CDMA Technologies (QCT), the company's chipset, semiconductor, and software division, and he was named executive vice president of Qualcomm. In 2006 he was named COO, overseeing corporate research and development as well as the company's Flarion unit (QFT), which was creating advanced fourth-generation wireless technology that would make it easier and faster for wireless customers to surf the Internet. "He doesn't get a lot of headlines, but he is one of the key players at Qualcomm," Roger Entner, a Nielsen IAG telecommunications analyst, told Laura M. Holson for the *New York Times* (August 5, 2008). In addition to his roles at Qualcomm, Jha served in important positions in two of the industry's most influential organizations: in 2005 he was elected to the board of directors of the Semiconductor Industry Association, and he is currently vice chairman of the Fabless Semiconductor Association. Fabless companies focus on design and development of semiconductors while outsourcing the production of the silicon wafers that constitute the hardware.

On August 4, 2008 Motorola announced that starting that day Jha had assumed the positions of CEO of the Motorola Mobile Devices division and co-CEO, with Greg Brown, of the Illinois-based Motorola mother company, and that he would serve on the latter's board of directors. In an unusual power-sharing agreement, Jha was to be responsible for overseeing the mobile-devices unit— which at that time accounted for 41 percent of the company's revenue—and spinning it off into an independent, publicly traded company within a year. Brown was to oversee the company's more successful Broadband Mobility Solutions division, which sells radio equipment, set-top boxes, and wireless gear.

Founded in 1928 as a manufacturer of radios and radio-related products, Motorola introduced the world's first mobile phone in 1984. An industry leader for the better part of the next two decades, it had in the years before Jha's arrival lost market share and profits to such groundbreaking products as Apple Inc.'s iPhone, Palm Inc.'s Pilot, and Research in Motion's BlackBerry. According to most accounts, its leaders had become complacent, ignoring the firm's loss of its reputation for innovation and design. While some of Motorola's products had remained profitable—among them its wireless-infrastructure networks, set-top boxes, digital video recorders, and hardware for video and high-definition broadcasting—by 2008 its money-hemorrhaging cellular-phone division was in danger of becoming peripheral at best. Motorola's last cell-phone success had been its ultrathin Razr phone, introduced in 2004; since then iPhones and BlackBerries had overtaken Motorola's products, eating into the company's market share considerably. According to analysts, Motorola had rested on the success of the Razr model for too long and had not offered competitive products in the extreme high and low ends (technologically and with regard to design) from which most of the market growth of the preceding years had come. As Sascha Segan reported for Extremetech.com (May 1, 2009), the company's market share had dropped from 23.3 percent, with 65.7 million phones sold in the fourth quarter of 2006; in the first quarter of 2009, it had 6 percent of market share, with 14.7 million phones sold. "Motorola's history is marred by marketing missteps," Roger O. Crockett and Olga Kharif wrote for *BusinessWeek Online* (August 5, 2008). "When the industry shifted from analog phones to digital in the mid-1990s, executives and engineers at Motorola underestimated the significance of the shift, stumbled in introducing digital phones, and then lost their lead in the market to a Finnish upstart called Nokia (NOK). Then as the pace of product cycles quickened in recent years, Motorola's plodding culture contributed to its inability to deliver new phones to market as quickly as competitors."

The hiring of Jha was seen by many investors and other observers as a last-ditch effort to turn the company around. The value of shares of Motorola stock jumped 11 percent after his appointment was made public. It did so despite doubts voiced by those who, as Holson noted, felt that Jha was a curious choice given that his expertise was in cell-phone semiconductors and not mobile-phone design; after all, they contended, Motorola's main problems regarding its phones were their unappealing "look and feel." "For all of Jha's experience, he faces one huge challenge: Motorola's corporate culture," Roger O. Crockett and Olga Kharif wrote. "For the cell-phone unit to recover, Jha will have to fully cleanse Motorola of its sluggish, bureaucratic ways and teach a company that has long let engineers drive product development to think more like marketers, in tune with consumer tastes. It's a challenge that has proved insurmountable for several top Motorola executives."

To attract Jha, Motorola had offered him a $104.5 million pay package, most of it in stock and options that would materialize only if the company's financial situation improved. He was assigned the task of splitting the Mobile Devices division from Motorola's more-profitable units and taking it

public; if he succeeded by November 2010, he would be given a 3 percent stake in the new company, and if he failed, he would be forced out but given a $30 million payout. According to *Wall Street Journal* and *New York Times* surveys, that deal made Jha the highest-paid executive in the U.S., in terms of total compensation. Within months, though, the onset of what proved to be the worst recession in many decades significantly decreased its value. Still, the munificence of the package outraged many observers, especially after Jha began cutting thousands of jobs. An article in *Crain's Chicago Business* (May 25, 2009) noted that Jha's income was 653,193 times the average income of residents in his native Bihar and 3,690 times the average in Cook County, Illinois, where Motorola is headquartered, in the town of Schaumburg. In December 2008 Jha announced that he would voluntarily take a 25 percent salary reduction and forgo his 2009 bonus. Other critics pointed to the fact that the incentives in his contract might lead to excessive risk taking: that is, to maximize his compensation, he might resort to engineering a spin-off at all costs. Others argued that the promised $30 million payout, which in effect would reward failure, was egregious. Offering a different perspective was Elizabeth Woyke, who wrote for *Forbes.com* (September 10, 2009), "tasked with rebuilding the company's strength in cellphones, Jha is often described as having one of the hardest jobs in the wireless industry."

Jha placed the spin-off on hold temporarily because of the ailing economy. He quickly set about attempting to cut costs, by producing fewer but more-competitive, high-end models (rather than large volumes of cheaper ones) as well as slashing thousands of jobs, and focused on creating groundbreaking "smart phones"—one of the few strong markets in the cell-phone industry. He asked for and received more investment funds from the board and promised that his division would break even in 2010. "Put simply, Jha knew that Motorola's future depended on his ability to change the company from a mere manufacturer of phones to a provider of software and services," Jesse Hempel wrote for *Fortune* (September 29, 2009). "Analysts think a spin could happen in late 2010—if the new handsets succeed." Observers also noted Jha's insistence on instilling a sense of urgency within Motorola and on acting with transparency and realism. "He made the real problems public and did a very commendable job," Bonny Joy, an analyst at Strategy Analytics, told Phil Carson for *RCR Wireless News* (November 10, 2008). "It's always better to stand up and fight than to undergo a slow and painful death." While Jha was reluctant to criticize the engineering culture at Motorola, he indicated that change was needed. "I think the engineering culture is a tremendous asset to Motorola," he told Crockett and Kharif. "I think the challenge is to make that culture stay in tune with the marketplace. When it's a problem is when it gets disconnected with the marketplace. And my job is to keep it connected." In an attempt to differentiate their products from the iPhone, Jha announced that Motorola's cell phones would use software from Google. Analysts and other observers noted that Jha had made an "all-or-nothing" bet on developing fewer (both in models and units), better, more user-friendly multi-application smart phones based primarily on Google's untested Android software platform, or operating system (which would also be cheaper than having to customize different platforms for different wireless carriers). Jha had decided not to unveil phones in early 2009, as was originally planned, and to concentrate instead on a game-changing new line that would debut during that year's Christmas-shopping season. On September 10, 2009 Jha and Motorola introduced one new product, the Cliq, a touchscreen cell phone based on Google's Android system but also powered with custom Motoblur software, which allows social-networking sites and such applications as Gmail and Microsoft Outlook to update information directly and efficiently into a phone in the form of an instant message.

The launch of the Droid smartphone, in November 2009, generated a lot of interest. Based on Google's Android software, the Droid was the result of a partnership among Google, Motorola, and the wireless-service-provider Verizon. (The software company Adobe was later added to the partnership so as to acquire its Flash software, which the iPhone does not have.) After the second quarter of 2010, Motorola reported a profit of $162 million for that period. Third-quarter profits were expected to get a boost from sales of Droid X, the latest Droid phone—and a strong competitor of Apple's iPhone 4. "Sanjay Jha has plenty to crow about: Motorola Inc.'s Droid smartphones are generating sales and buzz the company hasn't enjoyed since the Razr," John Pletz wrote for *Crain's Chicago Business* (August 9, 2010). "But swamped by the tsunami of marketing generated by archrivals Apple Inc. and Research in Motion Ltd., Motorola's advertising looks like a drop in the bucket. Unless Mr. Jha dramatically steps up his marketing game, Motorola risks losing sales going into the critical fourth-quarter holiday shopping season." In the fall of 2010, Microsoft filed suit against Motorola, alleging that the latter's Android-based phones violate nine Microsoft patents. Jha has said that such suits are merely a part of doing business in a competitive environment. Some technology experts suggested that the suit could be an attempt by Microsoft to slow Google's expansion into the mobile-telephone business.

Jha and his wife, Fiona Mackin-Jha, married in 1991; the couple have three young sons—Kieran, Rohan, and Devon. Macklin-Jha is active in charitable activities in San Diego, where the couple maintain a home and their children attend school. Jha spends weekends in San Diego and weekdays in Schaumburg. An avid golfer, Jha plays so-called Type A golf, which, according to Pletz, "involves walking 18 holes, then being showered and at his desk in under four hours."

—M.M.

Suggested Reading: *BusinessWeek Online* Aug. 5, 2008; *Chicago Tribune* C p1+ Aug. 5, 2008; *Crain's Chicago Business* p1 Dec. 22, 2008; *Forbes* (on-line) Sep. 10, 2009; *New York Times* B p1+ May 1, 2009, (on-line) Aug. 5, 2008; *RCR Wireless News* (on-line) Nov. 10, 2008

Christian Petersen/Getty Images

Johnson, Andre

July 11, 1981– Football player

Address: Houston Texans, Two Reliant Park, Houston, TX 77054

Andre Johnson, a wide receiver for the Houston Texans of the National Football League (NFL), "has an amazing gift for going unnoticed," David Fleming wrote for *ESPN The Magazine* (November 30, 2009, on-line). "What the world will see" when it pays attention, Fleming added, "is a chiseled, [six-foot three-inch], 228-pounder with 4.35 speed who can trample linebackers, run past corners and leap over safeties—sometimes on the same play. Among the current pantheon of NFL pass-catchers, Torry Holt is known as the most precise route-runner, Santana Moss as the fastest speed demon, Reggie Wayne as having the best hands, and Hines Ward as the gutsiest going over the middle. But in crunch time . . . [Johnson] is the only wideout with all of those tools." In his seven seasons with the Texans, Johnson has quietly established himself as the NFL's best receiver. A four-time Pro Bowl selection, he led the NFL in receptions (103) in 2006 and then returned from an injury-plagued 2007 campaign to top the league in both receptions (115) and receiving yards (1,575) in 2008. During the 2008 season Johnson became the first player in history to record seven games with at least 10 receptions each (the New England Patriots' receiver Wes Welker became the second, in 2009). In 2009 Johnson eclipsed the 100-reception mark for the third time in his career, with 101, and again led the NFL in receiving yards, with 1,569, becoming only the second player in the Super Bowl era (after the Hall of Fame receiver Jerry Rice) to place first in the league in that category in consecutive seasons. He has also led the NFL in receiving yards per game (an average of 90.7) since 2006 and was named to the Associated Press First-Team All-Pro team in 2008 and 2009. (That annual list, compiled by a nationwide panel of Associated Press members, recognizes the best NFL players in each position.)

In contrast to the selfish behavior and "diva-receiver" boastfulness of many of the NFL's top receivers, Johnson has approached the game with a team-first mentality, earning a reputation for humility and professionalism as well as competitiveness. "I just don't get caught up in who gets the most attention," he told Fleming in an article for ESPN.com (November 23, 2009). "It's not that I don't care or don't have an opinion, I'm just not the kind of person who really worries about that kind of thing." For the same article, Johnson dismissed the word most often used over the years by journalists to describe his off-the-field manner. "I. Am. Not. Quiet," he said. "Mess with me, talk junk to me, challenge me. I won't run my mouth back at you. But on the next play I'm gonna do everything I can to embarrass you in front of the whole world."

Andre Lamont Johnson was born on July 11, 1981 in Miami, Florida. With his younger brother, Willie Pope, he grew up in a rough-and-tumble Miami neighborhood known as "the Bajas," where "drug deals and trouble always were within walking distance," John P. Lopez wrote for the *Houston Chronicle* (December 26, 2004). Johnson was raised by his mother, Karen, who worked as a letter carrier, and Karen's older brother Andre Melton, for whom he was named. His biological father, Leroy Richardson, deserted the family when he was born. Johnson met him only once for a few hours when he was eight years old, while Richardson was passing through Miami. (In 2002 Johnson's father was shot and killed in Mississippi.) Johnson's uncle Andre stepped in as a father figure and helped guide him in the right direction. "I never really had a chance to know my dad, but I couldn't have done anything without hard work and what my family taught me about things," Johnson told Lopez.

Growing up a mile and a half from Joe Robbie Stadium (now known as Sun Life Stadium), Johnson developed a passion for football early on and rooted for his hometown team, the Dolphins. Another of his mother's older brothers, Keith Francis,

who was a star football player at Miami Senior High School in the 1970s, began throwing passes to Johnson when the boy was four year old and quickly recognized his "freakish athletic potential," as David Fleming noted in the November 23, 2009 ESPN article. (Johnson's mother, too, was an athlete—a sprinter at Tennessee State University.) Francis, who had served time in prison for dealing drugs, was also a living example of the dangerous lure of the streets. "Because of him, [my family was] on me about everything," Johnson told Fleming (November 23, 2009). "Every conversation I ever had with him ended the same way: Don't make the same mistakes I made." (Francis was murdered in August 2004.)

Johnson played on youth-league teams from the age of five and further honed his skills in street pick-up games and on local Miami playgrounds. After graduating from North County Elementary School, in Opa-Locka, Florida, he attended Miami Senior High School. Like his uncle Keith, Johnson became a star on the school's football team and also excelled in basketball and track. He first garnered attention as a football player during his junior year, when he recorded 25 passes for 618 yards (an average of 24.7 yards per catch) and scored 11 touchdowns. As a senior Johnson made 31 receptions for 908 yards (29.3 yards per catch, on average) and 15 touchdowns. He was subsequently an All-America selection of *Parade* magazine and earned first-team all-state honors. In addition, he was named to the National Top 100 among high-school players by the *Dallas Morning News*. Johnson was heavily recruited by a number of colleges but, choosing to remain close to home, enrolled at the University of Miami (UM), in Coral Gables, Florida. (Informally referred to as "The U," the school has one of the best football programs in the nation and has produced a slew of current and former NFL stars, including Ray Lewis, Ed Reed, Jeremy Shockey, Santana Moss, and Reggie Wayne.)

At the University of Miami, Johnson emerged as one of the best wide receivers in American college football. As a sophomore he helped lead Miami to the 2001 national title against the University of Nebraska with seven receptions for 199 yards and two touchdowns at the Rose Bowl; he shared Rose Bowl Most Valuable Player honors with the quarterback Ken Dorsey. (Miami's 2001 team is considered to be one of the greatest in college-football history, with a record 11 players earning first-round selections in that year's NFL Draft.) Despite being double-teamed for most of the 2002 season, Johnson recorded 52 catches for 1,092 yards (an average of 21.0 yards per catch) with nine touchdowns and became just the second player in UM history to gain 1,000 or more receiving yards in a single season. The Hurricanes again reached the national title game but lost to Ohio State, 31–24, in double overtime at the Fiesta Bowl; Johnson was held to only four catches for 54 yards in the game. Already one of the nation's top prospects at the wide-receiver position, Johnson (who by that time was being called "Superman" by his teammates) decided to forgo his senior year to enter the NFL Draft. (He insisted that his decision was unrelated to his having been caught cheating in two classes and barred from summer school in 2002. He told reporters for the January 14, 2003 edition of the *Miami Herald* that that episode "made me a better person. It was a big steppingstone. Like a lot of people, I learned from my mistakes.") Johnson finished his college career at UM ranked fifth in career receiving yards (1,831) and tied for third in career touchdown receptions (20). In addition to his accomplishments on the football field, Johnson ran for UM's track-and-field team and won the 2002 Big East track title in the indoor 60 meters (6.83 seconds) and outdoor 100 meters (10.59 seconds).

The Houston Texans selected Johnson in the first round, and as the third overall pick, of the 2003 draft. He was the second receiver chosen in the draft, after Michigan State's Charles Rogers. "I always told my mom that some day I would be in the NFL," Johnson recalled to Lopez. "I didn't want to break that promise." That July he signed a six-year, $39 million contract with the Texans. Johnson made his debut as a professional on September 7, 2003, as a starter in the season opener against the Miami Dolphins. In the game, which the Texans won, 21–10, he recorded a team-high six receptions for 76 yards. The following week Johnson gained a team-high 71 receiving yards on five catches in a contest with the New Orleans Saints. In a week-three match against the Kansas City Chiefs, he made a game-high seven catches for 102 yards and scored his first two NFL touchdowns, which tied the Texans' single-game record. Then, in the following week, Johnson earned NFL Rookie of the Week honors for his performance in a win over the Jacksonville Jaguars, in which he made a game-high eight catches for 97 yards. He was named NFL Rookie of the Week for the second time in week eight, when he led the Texans with four receptions for 28 yards in a loss against the Tampa Bay Buccaneers. Johnson started all 16 games that season and led the Texans with 66 receptions for 976 yards and four touchdowns.

The year 2004 brought a breakout season for Johnson. Teaming up with the quarterback David Carr, he recorded 79 receptions for 1,129 receiving yards and six touchdowns and earned his first Pro-Bowl selection. He also led the Texans with four 100-yards-receiving games, which broke his own team record of three from the 2003 season. The Texans finished the season with a 7–9 record, improving on their win total from the previous year by two games. Johnson's numbers dropped in 2005 due to a calf-muscle injury that affected his play all season. Missing three games, he made 63 catches for 688 yards and two touchdowns in 13 starts. Johnson's injury had a disastrous effect on the Texans, who posted a 2–14 record, the worst in the league and in franchise history. The head coach, Dom Capers, was fired in the following off-season and replaced with the Denver Broncos' offensive

coordinator Gary Kubiak, who immediately overhauled the Texans' offense with the so-called West Coast system—a more pass-heavy approach that made the most of Johnson's abilities. "You come across good players and great players, and the thing that separates great players from good players is their work ethic," Kubiak said to Megan Manfull for the *Houston Chronicle* (February 10, 2007). "In my first season with Andre, he's as good as I've ever been around in all my years of coaching, and I've been around a lot of guys like Jerry Rice and Rod Smith."

During the 2006 season Johnson returned to form and emerged as one of the best all-around receivers in pro football. That year he led the NFL with 103 receptions for 1,147 receiving yards and five touchdowns and was the only receiver in the league to record 100 or more receptions. He earned his second career Pro Bowl selection and was named to the Associated Press's All-Pro second team. During that season Johnson completed plays despite being double- and even triple-teamed. His offensive output also helped the Texans improve on their record from the previous year; they finished the season with six wins and 10 losses.

In the 2007 off-season, Johnson signed an eight-year, $60 million contract extension that included a guaranteed $15 million. He started the year in top form, recording a 77-yard touchdown catch—the longest of his career—in the season opener, against the Kansas City Chiefs, and registering seven receptions for 120 yards and two touchdowns in a week-two contest with the Carolina Panthers. Then he suffered a knee injury that forced him to miss seven games. Johnson returned mid-season to finish with 851 receiving yards and eight receiving touchdowns. In spite of his injury, he was first in the NFL that year in receiving yards per game, with 94.6. The Texans improved on their record again, with a respectable eight wins and eight losses. Fully recovered from his knee injury, Johnson returned in 2008 to post the best numbers of his career. That season he recorded career highs in receptions (115, good for third-most in the NFL since 2000) and receiving yards (1,575), both of which led the league. Johnson also scored eight touchdowns and caught 10 or more passes in seven games, making him the first player in NFL history to accomplish that feat. He earned his third career Pro Bowl selection and, at the end of the season, was named a first-team All-Pro by the Associated Press.

Following another 8–8 season in 2008, Johnson entered the 2009 season with high expectations, and the Texans nursed realistic hopes of making the play-offs, thanks in large part to the starting quarterback Matt Schaub. During the course of the year, Schaub and Johnson proved to be one of the most successful duos in the NFL. Johnson finished the season with 101 catches for 1,569 yards and a career-high nine touchdowns, and Schaub led the league in several passing categories, which helped him earn his first career Pro Bowl selection. Johnson, meanwhile, finished tied for third in the league in receptions and became only the second player in NFL history (after Jerry Rice) to lead the league in receiving yards in consecutive seasons; he also became the second player in league history to have back-to-back seasons with at least 1,500 receiving yards. He was named to the Pro Bowl for the fourth time in his career and earned his second consecutive first-team All-Pro selection. The Texans achieved their first winning season in franchise history, with a 9–7 record, and narrowly missed their first year of postseason play. Johnson said to Megan Manfull for the *Houston Chronicle* (January 10, 2009), "I don't set personal goals anymore. My goal is getting this organization to the playoffs." On August 5, 2010 Johnson signed a new, two-year, $38.5 million contract extension that included a guaranteed $13 million. The deal will keep him with the Texans through the 2016 season and will make him the highest-paid receiver in the NFL.

In his November 23, 2009 article, Fleming wrote, "The only label Andre Johnson hates is 'quiet.' Why? Probably because he's not. He simply doesn't warm up to everyone immediately, and because that makes our job in the media a little harder, a little more complicated, we tend to dismiss players like Johnson as 'quiet.'" Fleming added that while profiling Johnson for *ESPN The Magazine*, "I found him to be thoughtful and funny and an unquestioned leader in Houston." Johnson has homes in Houston and Fort Lauderdale, Florida. Making good on a promise to his mother, he returned to the University of Miami for the 2010 spring semester to complete his degree. In 2003 Johnson launched the Andre Johnson Foundation, which is dedicated to helping children and teens in single-parent homes.

—C.C.

Suggested Reading: *Austin (Texas) American-Statesman* D p1 Aug. 8, 2003; ESPN.com (online) Nov. 23, 2009; *ESPN The Magazine* (online) Nov. 30, 2009; *Houston Chronicle* p8 Sep. 8, 2003, p1 Dec. 26, 2004, p1 Oct. 5, 2006, p3 Jan. 10, 2009; Houston Texans Official Web site; *Miami Herald* D p5 Jan. 14, 2003

Johnson, Chris

Sep. 23, 1985– Football player

Address: Tennessee Titans, Baptist Sports Park, 460 Great Circle Rd., Nashville, TN 37228

In only two seasons with the National Football League (NFL), the Tennessee Titans' running back Chris Johnson has established himself as one of his sport's most dynamic players. Widely considered to be the best running back currently playing, Johnson has often been seen on TV-news highlight reels, turning running plays into dazzling touchdown runs. A multi-threat player, he has drawn the most attention for his speed: his record-tying time of 4.24 seconds in the 40-yard dash at the 2008 NFL Scouting Combine gave him a reputation as the NFL's fastest man. Johnson is "unique," the Titans coach, Jeff Fisher, told Chris Harry for the *Orlando (Florida) Sentinel* (December 6, 2009). "The combination of speed, change of direction, and acceleration? Defenses just can't prepare for it. There's been no one like this before." In 2009 Johnson became only the sixth running back in NFL history to gain at least 2,000 rushing yards in a single season. He also became the only player in league history with at least 2,000 rushing yards (2,006) and 500 receiving yards (503) in the same season; broke Marshall Faulk's record of total yards from scrimmage, with 2,509; and became the first player in NFL history to record three touchdown runs of 85 or more yards (85, 89, 91) in the same season. At the end of 2009, Johnson was the only unanimous selection to the Associated Press First-Team All-

Elsa/Getty Images

Pro team and was named the NFL Offensive Player of the Year. He has also been named a Pro Bowl starter in each of his two seasons. Referring to three celebrated basketball players (LeBron James, Michael Jordan, and Kobe Bryant), he told a writer for the *Carleton Place (Ontario, Canada) Weekender* (November 14, 2009), "I'm just trying to make the whole world recognize that I'm one of those type players like a LeBron or Jordan or Kobe."

Christopher Duan Johnson was born on September 23, 1985 in Orlando, Florida. With his four older brothers, he grew up in Orlando's Mercy Drive neighborhood. "It was rough," his brother Pernell told Chris Harry. "We didn't have much." Johnson has seldom spoken to reporters about his childhood. His brother Antonio told Gary Estwick for the *Nashville (Tennessee) Tennessean* (January 30, 2010, on-line), "A lot of our friends, I hate to say, went down the wrong path and we pretty much followed them. I guess [Chris] was lucky enough to get that right group to hang around." Johnson grew interested in sports early on. As a youth he developed a passion for football and played on city-league teams.

In 2001 Johnson enrolled as a sophomore at Olympia High School, a new public school in Orlando. Despite his relatively small size, he immediately became a star on the school's varsity football and track teams. In the first quarter of a preseason game during his senior year, he broke a leg, forcing him to miss his team's first seven games. Mike Cullison, then the coach of the Olympia Titans, told Harry that despite the cast, "he would come to practice every day. . . . He not only was there, he'd have on his shoulder pads and helmet, you know, just to feel a part of it all. When he got better, he began to jog." In the three games in which Johnson played that season, he rushed for more than 400 yards—enough to earn all-county honors. He participated in the Orange County, Florida, All-Star Game and was named its Most Valuable Player (MVP).

Meanwhile, Johnson was racking up achievements in track. As a high-school senior (2003–04), he recorded the seventh-best time in the U.S. in the 100-meter race that year and ran the anchor leg on the nation's fastest 4 x 100-meter relay team. He made the Florida state championships in the 100-meter race and finished second to Walter Dix, who went on to win bronze medals in both the 100- and 200-meter dashes at the 2008 Beijing Summer Olympics. Johnson's only other loss during his high-school track career was to Xavier Carter, the National Collegiate Athletic Association (NCAA) champion in the 100- and 400-meter runs. "People thought of me as a track guy," Johnson recalled to Lee Jenkins for *Sports Illustrated* (December 9, 2009). "But I only ran track four years. I played football all my life." The "track guy" label may have hurt Johnson's college-football prospects: he was offered only one football scholarship, from East Carolina University (ECU), in Greenville, North Carolina. He turned down walk-on opportunities at two other schools with solid football programs—the University of Connecticut and Eastern Kentucky University—and accepted ECU's offer, because John Thompson, the coach of ECU's team, the Pirates, guaranteed him an opportunity to compete for a starting position. Noah Brindise, then the team's offensive coordinator, told Harry that Johnson was "skinny, and really quiet, but in two-a-days [two practice sessions in one day] you could

see he could make big plays. After three practices, I knew the guy was our best running back. I also knew he had no business being at East Carolina."

As a freshman Johnson performed outstandingly as a running back, receiver, and return specialist. He played in all 11 games, making seven starts, and led the Pirates in rushing yards (561), kickoff return yards (765), and all-purpose yards (1,562). At the end of the season, Johnson was selected to the Conference USA All-Freshman squad as a running back and return specialist. As a sophomore his duties increased; under a new coaching regime, led by Skip Holtz, Johnson started all 11 games at tailback and again led the team in rushing yards (684) and all-purpose yards (1,499). He also made 35 receptions for 356 yards. During his junior year, despite a series of injuries, Johnson led the Pirates in all-purpose yards, with 972 (314 rushing, 176 receiving, and 482 kickoff returns), while playing in 12 games and making five starts. He shined on kickoff returns and was selected to the All-Conference USA first team as a kick-return specialist. That season Johnson made a 96-yard kickoff-return touchdown in a game against Southern Mississippi, a feat labeled one of the top college-football plays of 2006 by the TV network ESPN.

During his senior year Johnson emerged among the top all-purpose running backs in American college football. He started all 13 games at running back and amassed 1,423 yards on 236 carries with 17 touchdowns. Johnson also added 37 receptions for 528 yards and six touchdowns and 36 kickoff returns for 1,009 yards and one touchdown. By the end of the season, he led the nation in all-purpose yards per game, with an average of 227.7, had been named to the All-American first team by *Pro Football Weekly*, and had earned an honorable mention All-American from *Sports Illustrated*. Johnson capped his collegiate career in a noteworthy way: in the 2007 Hawaii Bowl, in which ECU defeated Boise State, 41–38, he set the NCAA Division I record for most all-purpose yards in a bowl game, with 408 (223 rushing yards, 32 receiving yards, and 153 return yards) and was named the game's MVP. Johnson finished his college career at ECU as the school's all-time third-place leader in rushing, with 2,982 rushing yards, while setting Pirates records among running backs in career receptions (125) and receiving yards (1,296). He also became the school's all-time leader in total touchdowns (44), kickoff-return yards (2,715—a Conference USA record), and all-purpose yards (6,993—third in conference history). All told, Johnson set or tied 18 ECU game, season, and career records.

His record-breaking numbers notwithstanding, scouts predicted that Johnson would be a second- or third-round pick in the NFL draft, because of his relatively diminutive size—five feet 11 inches and 200 pounds. His draft stock rose considerably after he participated in the 2008 NFL Scouting Combine—an annual weeklong event in which NFL coaches, general managers, and scouts subject college-draft prospects to a battery of physical and mental tests. Johnson completed the 40-yard dash at that event in 4.24 seconds, the fastest time ever recorded for a running back in the combine. His time also tied the record set by Rondel Melendez, a wide receiver from Eastern Kentucky University, in 1999, when the combine started using electronic timing. Johnson performed outstandingly in other tests as well, posting a standing broad jump of 10 feet 10 inches and a 43.5-inch vertical jump—the third- and fourth-highest among running backs, respectively, that year. At the 2008 NFL Draft, the Tennessee Titans selected Johnson in the first round, as the 24th overall pick. Johnson was the fifth running back chosen in the draft, after Darren McFadden, Jonathan Stewart, Felix Jones, and Rashard Mendenhall. "People say I was only a first-round draft pick because of the combine," Johnson told Chris Harry. "But if you put on my film [from ECU], it was as good as any of the backs picked in front of me." Most scouting analysts said that Johnson would probably serve best in the role of a third-down back, because of his size; responding to those assessments, the Titans coach, Jeff Fisher, told Harry, "That was never an issue for us. We saw the inside moves and the outside runs, but we saw lead blocks against the linebacker on draw plays and pass-blocking responsibilities, too. Toughness and size just weren't considerations." Johnson graduated from ECU in 2008, with a bachelor's degree in communications. That July he signed a five-year, $12 million contract with the Titans.

Johnson made his debut as a professional on September 7, 2008, as a starter in the season opener against the Jacksonville Jaguars. In the game, which the Titans won, 17–10, Johnson rushed for a game-high 93 yards on 15 carries and scored his first NFL touchdown, on a seven-yard pass from the quarterback Vince Young. The following week he recorded a 100-yard rushing effort (109 yards on 19 carries), in a contest with the Cincinnati Bengals. In a week-four match against the Minnesota Vikings, Johnson recorded a rushing touchdown and racked up 75 all-purpose yards (61 rushing, 14 receiving) and two touchdowns. He was named the NFL Offensive Rookie of the Month for September, after totaling 402 yards from scrimmage and 337 rushing yards in the first four games of his pro career. During the course of the season, Johnson split his carries with the power runner LenDale White. One of the most dynamic running-back duos in the NFL, Johnson and White earned the nickname "Smash and Dash" for their complementary running styles. Anchored by that powerful rushing attack, the Titans won their first 10 games of the season and finished with an NFL-best 13–3. They won home-field advantage throughout the play-offs before losing to the Baltimore Ravens in the American Football Conference (AFC) divisional round, 13–10. Johnson ended the season with 1,228 rushing yards, good for third place in the AFC and eighth in the NFL. His 1,488 yards from scrimmage was good for fifth in the AFC and 10th in the NFL. Johnson was the only rookie selected to the AFC

Pro Bowl squad and finished second, to the Atlanta Falcons quarterback Matt Ryan, in the Associated Press Rookie of the Year voting.

Johnson got off to a slow start in 2009. In the season opener he rushed for only 57 yards in a last-minute, 13–10 loss to the Pittsburgh Steelers, the defending Super Bowl champions. During week two, in a 34–31 loss to the Houston Texans, he ran 197 yards and became the first player in NFL history to record touchdowns of 50-plus, 60-plus, and 90-plus yards in the same game, including a franchise-tying 91-yard touchdown run. He also recorded nine receptions, 87 receiving yards, and 284 scrimmage yards. Johnson failed to surpass 100 yards rushing in the next four games, all Titan defeats. In a game in week six against the New England Patriots, at the Patriots' Gillette Stadium during a snowstorm, Johnson ran for a game-high 128 yards on 17 carries. Overshadowing his performance was the Titans' humiliating defeat, 59–0, the worst loss since the start of the franchise, in 1960. During a bye that week, Fisher replaced the veteran quarterback Kerry Collins with Vince Young, known for his outstanding running and passing abilities. That change helped Johnson, who surpassed the 100-yard rushing mark in each of the team's last 10 games.

Earlier, in his first game after the bye, Johnson rushed for 228 yards and scored two touchdowns in a game against the Jaguars. He then ran for at least 125 rushing yards in six consecutive games, tying an NFL record shared by Earl Campbell and Eric Dickerson. Neither Campbell nor Dickerson, however, achieved Johnson's average of at least 5.0 yards per carry in each of those six games. During week 12, in a game against the Arizona Cardinals, Johnson ran for an 85-yard rushing touchdown, his third rushing touchdown of at least 85 yards that year—another NFL record. He also recorded 22 rushes of 20 or more yards, breaking the previous record of 20 set by the Minnesota Vikings' Adrian Peterson during the 2008 season, and he set the record for most rushing yards in a calendar month in NFL history, with 800 in November. Going into the final game of the regular season, Johnson was only 128 yards shy of 2,000 rushing yards—a total achieved or surpassed until then by only five players in NFL history (O.J. Simpson, Eric Dickerson, Barry Sanders, Terrell Davis, and Jamal Lewis). With a 134-yard effort against the Seattle Seahawks, bringing his regular-season total to 2,006, he joined those five. (In recognition of the part played by the Titans' offensive linemen, who serve as his main blockers, Johnson gave each a Rolex watch engraved with "CJ2K" and "2,006.") In the process Johnson also broke Marshall Faulk's record of 2,429 yards from scrimmage by finishing with a total of 2,509 yards (2,006 yards rushing and 503 yards receiving). Meanwhile, the Titans experienced a turnaround, winning eight of their last 10 games to finish the season with an 8–8 record. At the end the season, Johnson was named the NFL Offensive Player of the Year, earning $38^{1}/_{2}$ votes from a nationwide panel of 50 sportswriters and broadcasters who cover the NFL. He was also the only unanimous choice to the Associated Press All-Pro First Team and was named a Pro Bowl starter for the second consecutive year.

Before the start of the 2010 season, Johnson declared that he hoped to eclipse his 2,006-yard campaign by accumulating 2,500 yards rushing, 395 yards more than Eric Dickerson's NFL record. As of week six of the season, Johnson was on pace to exceed 1,500 yards rushing.

Johnson is known for his dreadlocks and gold-plated teeth. He has homes in Orlando, Florida, and Glendale, California.

—C.C.

Suggested Reading: Associated Press (on-line) May 22, 2009; *Los Angeles Times* C p1+ Dec. 4, 2009; (Nashville, Tennessee) *Tennessean* (on-line) Sep. 2, 2008, Jan. 30, 2010; (Ontario, Canada) *Carleton Place Weekender* p1+ Nov. 14, 2009; (Orlando, Florida) *Sentinel* C p6+ Dec. 6, 2009; *San Diego Union-Tribune* D p1+ Dec. 23, 2009

Johnson, Mat

Aug. 19, 1970– Writer

Address: Creative Writing Program, University of Houston, 229 Roy Cullen Bldg., Houston, TX 77204-5008

Mat Johnson is an award-winning writer who has used the mediums of fiction, creative nonfiction, and, more recently, the graphic novel to explore—in profoundly personal ways—often underrepresented aspects of African-American experience. His debut work, *Drop* (2000), a highly autobiographical coming-of-age story about a self-loathing Philadelphian who dreams of living in England, catapulted Johnson from aspiring writer to acclaimed novelist. His second book, *Hunting in Harlem* (2003), part hardboiled thriller, part satire, won the Zora Neale Hurston/Richard Wright Legacy Award for novel of the year in 2004. *The Great Negro Plot* (2007), Johnson's work of historical nonfiction, uses a dose of narrative license to recreate a slave revolt in 18th-century New York and the resulting hysteria. While doing research for that book, Johnson found part of the subject matter for his first foray into comics: a series focusing on the character Papa Midnite. Johnson's graphic novel, *Incognegro* (2008), dramatizes the true story of a light-skinned black journalist who "passed" as a white man in order to report on the lynching of blacks in the American South in the 1930s. His next graphic novel, *Dark Rain* (2010), is about two former convicts who plan to rob a temporarily abandoned bank in New Orleans in the aftermath of Hurricane Katrina, which devastated large parts of the U.S. Gulf Coast in 2005. Johnson, who was named a James Baldwin Fellow by the U.S. Artists Foundation in 2007, has taught creative writing and literature at several institutions, including Bard College and the University of Houston.

Mat Johnson was born in Philadelphia, Pennsylvania, on August 19, 1970, to an Irish-American father and an African-American mother. His parents divorced when he was young, and he was raised by his mother, a social worker, in the predominantly black neighborhood of Germantown, in northwest Philadelphia. He described the environment there to Nina Shengold for *Chronogram* magazine (January 25, 2007) as "not the roughest neighborhood, but not the best" and as "racially stratified." He added, "When I was a little kid, I looked *really* white—I was this little Irish boy in a dashiki." He told Shengold that his mixed race contributed to his feelings of alienation while he was growing up and that he spent a lot of time indoors, taking comfort in reading. He began with comic books and then "realized that for the same 75 cents I spent on an *Incredible Hulk* comic, I could buy a whole *book* of science fiction that would last three or four days." As a teenager Johnson enrolled at a private school, Abingdon Friends, in a wealthier neighborhood, where for the "first time I was around a lot of white people. I suddenly realized I had an ethnic identity, and started to think about race," he told Shengold. "African-American literature felt like an intellectual home, this place where I fit and belonged." Shengold observed that Johnson appears to embrace his black heritage rather than the other aspects of his lineage; the novelist explained, "African-American is a Creole culture" that "embraces the mix."

A poor student, Johnson spent much of his time reading books that were not on his course syllabuses. Nevertheless, he was admitted at a local state college, West Chester University, in West Chester, Pennsylvania, where he did well enough to be accepted as a sophomore to a yearlong foreign-exchange program at the University of Wales at Swansea. In his junior year he transferred to Earlham College, a Quaker institution in Richmond, Indiana, and served as the president of the school's black student union. Graduating in 1993 with a B.A. degree in English, he earned a Thomas J. Watson fellowship, which allowed him to go abroad to conduct research for a thesis on the effects of experiences in other countries, particularly in Europe and West Africa, on African-Americans. He lived in London, England, in the predominantly black Brixton neighborhood, which he later compared to the traditionally African-American area of Harlem, in New York City. After his stay there Johnson reluctantly returned to Philadelphia, where, in need of money, he worked at a series of low-paying jobs, including one at an electric company. He has called that period one of struggle and desperation, in which he became obsessed with returning to London. During that time he attempted to write a nov-

Courtesy of Bloomsbury USA

Mat Johnson

el, hoping to sell it and pay for his relocation to England. "I realized I wasn't good enough to write a good book, and [was] too proud to write one bad enough to sell," he told Shengold.

In the mid-1990s Johnson was accepted to the master-of-fine-arts program in creative writing at Columbia University, in New York City. He moved to nearby Harlem, which he described to Natalie Hopkinson for the Washington Post (May 21, 2003) as "the most romanticized ghetto in the world." According to several profiles of Johnson, he also worked as a copywriter for MTV at the time. Johnson shared an apartment with another student and aspiring writer, Victor D. LaValle, while each worked on his first book. (LaValle's was Slapboxing with Jesus.) "Before, I'd been trying to do Toni Morrison Knockoffs; that was my idea of what a writer should be," Johnson told Diane Baroni for Interview magazine (September 2000). In writing the book he started at Columbia, he discovered his own voice. He told Baroni, "With this book I was like, I'm $50,000 in debt, I'm not good at anything but writing stories, I have to give it everything."

Johnson earned his M.F.A. degree in 1999, and his debut novel, Drop, was published the next year. The book follows a young black man, Chris Jones, who is desperate to leave West Philadelphia for London. While the story's similarities to Johnson's life are clear, the novelist told Kenya Nyota Lee for Mosaic Literary Magazine (June 30, 2001): "Drop is semiautobiographical in the same way a dream is. You might have a dream, you might recognize some of the people, some of the places, but everything is screwed up and turned upside down. . . . So you wouldn't call a dream of yours truth." In Drop, Jones narrates: "Me: poor and broke, alone,

thirty-one-years-old and only just finishing as an undergrad at a third-rate Pennsylvania state college." Jones cannot stand the alienation of his life. "I was not a thug, I was not a baller, I was not a mack, I was not paid," Johnson wrote. "I was not a comedian, even though I inspired great mirth. All I was was clever and creative, and unless you had a ball in your hand or your mouth in front of a microphone, this place had no respect for either one of those things." Jones escapes Philadelphia and breaks into the advertising world in London, but events do not unfold as he had hoped, and he is forced to return to Philadelphia, to a job answering phones at an electric company. Ultimately, with the help of a friend, Jones finds peace and reaches the conclusion: "Funny how much nicer this town was when you couldn't feel it sitting on you."

Drop was well received and established Johnson as a hip, up-and-coming writer. "Johnson's talent is obvious from the get-go," Jabari Asim wrote for the Washington Post (October 17, 2000). "I especially like the way he injects snappy jazz into his sentences, successfully deconstructing Big Ideas while resisting the urge to show just how smart he is." Johnson received some criticism for what some felt was an unfair representation of Philadelphia, American inner cities, and African-Americans in general. "Some people who first read the book said, 'It's about this guy who hates being black,'" he told Baroni. "And I was like, no, it's not that. He loves being black; he just doesn't like being poor." "Chris is not the stereotypical Black male," Johnson explained to Lee. "Here's the exploitation of what we are supposed to be: athletic, sexually dominant, negative. Chris' struggle is that he isn't any of those things. He may hate himself but it's not a 'Black hatred.' . . . There is no stereotype for him to fit into." Johnson also told Natalie Hopkinson for the Washington Post (February 21, 2002), "There's so much aggrandizing of ghetto culture, affirmation of negative attributes. It's considered good to call yourself a murderer and a robber. . . . I'm . . . reacting to that." The book also focuses on the issue of class and addresses many of the topics Johnson studied during his stay in England. "I used to live with Nigerians, and it was a huge lesson, of class and of history," he explained on About.com (December 2000), adding that his roommates would sometimes tease him about slavery and "cotton picking." Johnson wrote, "I had never been around solidly upper-class black folks before who didn't care about slavery, had no concept of black as an identity. . . . Drop in many ways, not directly, is about looking at an international Black world, one you rarely see."

Johnson's next novel, Hunting in Harlem, was published in 2003. "It took me a year to calm down enough to start another book after the first one . . . ," Johnson told Neal Conan for the National Public Radio program Talk of the Nation (June 23, 2003). "So much about writing is just hiding, you know, in your little room just trying to come up with your own ideas, falling into your own world.

And when you have your book actually published, you know, you get pulled out into the light and poked and prodded. And it takes a while to get the ability to pull within your mind like that again. . . . With *Hunting in Harlem*, I pretty much thought about the book for two years and then I kind of wrote it in two months, and I'd just had a daughter and, you know, I'd strapped her to my chest in the Baby Bjorn and stayed up all night and typed it out." *Hunting in Harlem* follows a black real-estate agent who has poor Harlem residents killed in order to provide homes to upwardly mobile professionals for handsome fees. Although not as obviously autobiographical as *Drop*, the novel was inspired by Johnson's experiences in Harlem. After he graduated from Columbia, Johnson, his wife, and their baby daughter had been forced to move to Philadelphia as a result of gentrification-fueled rent increases. Johnson told About.com that he set the novel—part satire, part thriller—in Harlem because "I love the creepiness of the brownstones" there. He again defended his critique of the African-American community, telling Hopkinson: "If my work is about anything, it's about self-criticism, which doesn't happen enough in the black community." *Hunting in Harlem* marked another critical success for Johnson, with the noted African-American writer Walter Mosley calling it "righteously terrifying . . . a cautionary tale for our time," according to Shengold. The book won a 2004 Zora Neale Hurston/Richard Wright Foundation Award.

In 2007 Johnson published *The Great Negro Plot*, a work of creative nonfiction that he wrote, as he told Shengold, "like a novel." The book recounts real-life events: an unsuccessful rebellion by black slaves in colonial Manhattan in 1712 led citizens in 1741 to blame the slaves for a number of acts of arson; the result was a witch hunt against Manhattan's slaves. An indentured servant, Mary Burton, who was promised freedom in exchange for testifying, began implicating dozens of blacks. More than 150 slaves were jailed and dozens executed; Burton was declared unreliable only after she began implicating wealthy whites, including some of the trial judge's relatives. The prosecutors, according to Johnson, described the slaves as ingrates. As quoted by Nancy Klingener in the Key West, Florida, *Solares Hill* (March 2, 2007), Johnson depicted the prosecutors as saying: "[The blacks'] slavery among us is generally softened with great indulgence. They live without care, and are commonly better fed and clothed and put to less labour than the poor of most Christian countries." Johnson then offered his own analysis: "Within the paradigm of the English language there are some acknowledged great words: Hypocrisy. Gall. Delusion. Perversion. Grotesquery. Really, one could choose from any number of these words to give character to the views that were spewed on the part of the court that day."

Some critics accused Johnson of taking too much narrative license in *The Great Negro Plot* and blurring the line between fact and fiction. "Johnson is a novelist, and I have a sneaking suspicion that what he really wanted to write was a novel . . . ," Jessica Warner wrote for the *Toronto Star* (February 18, 2007). "Whole sentences rise up in rebellion, demanding to know why they have been placed in a work of non-fiction and not in the novel they so richly deserve. . . . The irony is that Johnson's [detour] into fiction subverts his real purpose: to bring home the sheer evil of slavery. He simply assumes that fiction is more eloquent than non-fiction, when often the opposite is true. There is no need to put words into people's mouths when the facts are already so damning." "With my fiction, I take pieces of reality and twist them around and turn them into collage and make them a fictional tale," Johnson told Tony Cox on the National Public Radio show *News & Notes* (February 7, 2007). "So what I wanted to [do] was look at a real event and apply a narrative strategy . . . used in novels and short stories to a real event."

In interviews Johnson drew parallels between the 1741 events and the U.S. "war on terrorism," launched after the terrorist attacks of September 11, 2001, which Johnson witnessed firsthand from his home in northern New Jersey. "I remember thinking, 'I wish I had a history book from 50 years from now that could tell me what the hell's happening,'" Johnson told Shengold. "Not just the attack, but the heightened insanity afterward . . . people wanting to bomb and raze entire countries just out of fear. *The Great Negro Plot* was the first terrorist attack on New York [and was] met with the same hysteria and militant xenophobia." "What interests me first about this book, was looking at a point in time where America was scared and how we dealt with this outside, unseen fear . . . ," he told Cox. "The most dangerous thing to our culture is usually not the initial attack but the reaction afterwards, which tends to multiply and be the real effect of what terrorism can do."

In 2005, while doing research for *The Great Negro Plot*, Johnson—in collaboration with the illustrators Tony Akins and Dan Green—had published a five-issue comic-book miniseries, a spin-off of DC Comics' popular *Hellblazer* franchise focusing on the villainous black character Papa Midnite. "I grew up reading comics—the first thing I ever read on my own was a reprint of Hulk #1 (minus cover, ghetto style)," Johnson was quoted as saying on the African American Literature Book Club Web site. "I pitched an idea based around my *Great Negro Plot* research, and [the publisher] went for it, asking that I use Papa Midnite as a character, who came complete with an existing audience." "I was always disappointed with Midnite, particularly his original incarnation . . . ," he told Jonah Weiland for the Comic Book Resources Web site (February 2, 2005). "To me Midnite was this two dimensional archaic black stereotype—the Noble Savage. Wearing a grass skirt like out of a 1930s

Tarzan movie, with a top hat and tails over his naked body just to emphasize through contrast how primitive he was, how uncivilized, how less than human. I love the series so I wanted him to be a fuller character, not just a racist fantasy. . . . What we see today is still a leftover of the idea that if something is African, or black, it is corrupt and inferior." Johnson's series recounts the origins of Papa Midnite, known as "New York's kingpin of voodoo and crime," and traces his curse of immortality to his role in sabotaging the slave rebellion of 1712 and in attempting to foment and profit from one in 1741. Johnson described the experience of writing a graphic novel instead of conventional fiction, telling Edward Nawotka for the *Houston Chronicle* (May 4, 2008) that with comics, "you have to ask yourself odd questions, such as how do I structure the story so that all the big 'reveals'—key events—appear on even-numbered pages, so a reader sees them only after turning a page. . . . You're fitting the story into the form." Johnson also described the preconceptions many have about traditional novels as opposed to graphic novels. "It's interesting to consider the different ways people look at the literary stuff and the graphic stuff," he told Nawotka. "People expect literary stuff to be smart and sophisticated, but not necessarily a good read, while the graphic novel is supposed to be a good read but not smart and sophisticated. In recent years, graphic novels have been gaining respect."

Johnson continued to work in that medium, publishing the graphic novel *Incognegro* in hardcover in 2008; the work appeared in paperback in June 2009. *Incognegro*, illustrated by Warren Pleece, tells the story of a light-skinned African-American reporter, Zane Pinchback, who goes undercover, "passing" for white in the American South in the 1930s to expose lynchings. After another risky but successful mission for the *New Holland Herald*, Pinchback returns to Harlem determined to give up the "Incognegro" beat and publish under his real name. His plan is put on hold when he learns that his brother has been arrested and charged with a crime in the South; Pinchback must then find the true culprit, before his brother falls victim to mob violence. "If this sounds like the setup for a preachy history lesson, fear not," Nawotka wrote. "Johnson has used this historical material as the basis for a classic noir crime story, one that includes satisfying doses of deceit, moral ambiguity and plenty of R-rated violence."

Johnson told Steve Bunche for *Publishers Weekly* (February 19, 2008) that "passing for white is a part of [African-American] mythology" and that as a very light-skinned child growing up in a mostly black neighborhood, he often dreamed about a time when his skin color would be "an asset instead of a burden." In college he learned of Walter White, an intrepid anti-lynching journalist and head of the NAACP (1931–55), who was also light-skinned and who went undercover in the South in the 1930s to investigate race-related crimes, including lynchings, writing about them for New York newspapers. While the author has said that White was the primary inspiration for *Incognegro*, Johnson's own past, as well as the births of his twin children in 2005—one lighter in skin tone than the other, as George Gene Gustines noted for the *New York Times* (March 3, 2008)—were also contributing factors. "Race doesn't really exist," Pinchback says in the book, as quoted by Gustines. "Race is just a bunch of rules meant to keep us on the bottom. Race is a strategy. The rest is just people acting. Playing roles." As Nawotka pointed out, "Johnson so closely identified with the main character" that the publisher, Vertigo, an imprint of DC Comics, "photographed him to use as the cover image." Johnson decided to tell the story in the graphic-novel format rather than in a series of comic books, to allow, according to Bunche, "for a stronger story flow unfettered by the need for cliffhangers and other conventions required by the monthly comics serial."

Johnson's most recent book, the graphic novel *Dark Rain* (2010), is set in New Orleans in 2005, in the days after Hurricane Katrina created a humanitarian crisis in a large part of the Gulf Coast. "Under the guise of a heist story in which two ex-cons plan to loot an abandoned bank during post-Katrina flood-induced chaos," Web Behrens wrote for *Time Out Chicago* (September 2–8, 2010), "Johnson spins a yarn that's really about the multiple human failures that helped wreak such destruction upon the city in the wake of the crumbling levees."

Johnson's work has appeared in several anthologies, including *Gumbo: An Anthology of African American Writing* (2002); *Not Guilty: Twelve Black Men Speak Out on Law, Justice, and Life* (2002); *Mixed: An Anthology of Short Fiction on the Multiracial Experience* (2006); and *The Darker Mask: Heroes from the Shadows* (2008). While teaching at Bard College for four years in the mid-2000s, Johnson worked on an as-yet-unpublished experimental spin-off of Edgar Allan Poe's only novel, *The Narrative of Arthur Gordon Pym of Nantucket*. Johnson has written columns for *Time Out New York*, among several other publications, and from 2006 to 2007 he authored the blog Niggerati Manor, which took its name from the term used by Wallace Thurman, Zora Neale Hurston, and others to describe the Harlem Renaissance intelligentsia; the blog discussed topics in African-American literature and culture.

The six-foot four-inch Johnson is currently a faculty member in the University of Houston's creative-writing program. He lives in Houston with his wife, Meera Bowman, previously an art director at *Essence* magazine, and their three children.

—M.M.

Suggested Reading: *Chronogram* (on-line) Jan. 25, 2007; *Houston Chronicle* p15 May 4, 2008; *Interview* (on-line) Sep. 2000; *Mosaic Literary Magazine* p11 June 30, 2001; *Toronto (Ontario,*

Canada) *Star* D p6 Feb. 18, 2007; *Washington Post* C p2 Oct. 17, 2000, C p9 May 21, 2003

Selected Books: *Drop*, 2000; *Hunting in Harlem*, 2003; *The Great Negro Plot*, 2007; *Incognegro*, 2008; *Dark Rain*, 2010

Tyron Francis, courtesy of Daniel Johnston

Johnston, Daniel

Jan. 22, 1961– Singer; songwriter; artist

Address: c/o Dick Johnston, 6117 Magnolia, Katy, TX 77493

Little known among the general public, the work of the 49-year-old singer/songwriter Daniel Johnston is admired by David Bowie, Tom Waits, and many other professional musicians. The late Kurt Cobain, too, lauded Johnston's melodies and lyrics—for some time he always wore a Johnston T-shirt in public—and Matt Groening, the creator of the TV series *The Simpsons*, has compared Johnston to the renowned singer/songwriter Bob Dylan. Johnston's songs have often been described as strange, childishly naïve ramblings, many containing hallucinatory images and references to the Beatles or cartoon characters, but they are also said to be unusually forthright, powerful expressions of feeling. In the early 1980s his homemade, low-fidelity tapes, with his amateurish piano or guitar accompaniments, gained local celebrity for Johnston in Austin, Texas, where an independent-music movement known as the New Sincerity was thriving. His appearance in 1985 in a televised documentary about Austin's music scene led to the commercial release of some of his recordings. Kathy McCarty's album of Johnston covers, *Dead Dog's Eyeball* (1994), struck Michael Azerad, writing for *Spin* (November 1994), as "gorgeous, throat lump–inducing music . . . an eclectic assortment of torch ballads, guitar rockers, beer-hall sing-alongs, and beguiling art pop," which at times reminded Azerad of the Beatles' *White Album* or the work of the Broadway composer/lyricist Stephen Sondheim. Johnston has since made a dozen solo albums and joint recordings. He has also won recognition for his cartoonlike artwork. Some of his drawings were included in the 2006 Whitney Biennial, in New York City, and the 2008 Liverpool Biennial, in England.

Johnston has occasionally toured or performed at music festivals, but severe mental illness has frequently stunted his ability to work or prevented him from working altogether, sometimes for years at a stretch. The toll his disorder has taken on his life and career is revealed in the prize-winning documentary *The Devil and Daniel Johnston* (2005). "Much has been made of Daniel Johnston's bouts with mental illness," Jason Nickey wrote for *Pitchfork.com* (October 1, 2001). "But the point is that they are 'bouts' as in the boxing term; they are battles. And out of these battles are born songs that reveal much about human nature in general, and not just the mind of a manic depressive. . . . Johnston's mental illness does not make up his central characteristic as a songwriter, though it does color it significantly. But if that's all his songs are—just expressions of mania and lunacy—there would be little recognition and identification with them, and they wouldn't be as moving as they so often are. Their main concerns are universal human concerns." "Johnston's world may seem small, but it's much bigger and friendlier than that of your wildest imagination," John Dougan wrote for the All Music Guide (2010, on-line).

Johnston's song "Come See Me Tonight" was on the soundtrack of the TV series *My So-Called Life*, and three of his songs are on movie soundtracks: "Casper," for *Kids*; "Adjective," for *Schoolhouse Rock*; and "Careless Soul," for *Return of the Texas Chainsaw Massacre*. The choreographer Bill T. Jones's dance *Love Defined* (1992), commissioned by the Lyon Opera Ballet, a French troupe, is set to six songs from Johnston's album *Yip/Jump Music*. Jason Nodler's rock opera *Speeding Motorcycle*, made up entirely of songs by Johnston, debuted in a highly praised performance by the Houston, Texas–based theater company Infernal Bridegroom Productions in 2006. "Hi, How Are You," an iPhone game based on Johnston's drawings and music, went on sale in 2009.

The last of the five children of William "Bill" Johnston and Mabel Johnston, Daniel Dale Johnston was born on January 22, 1961 in Sacramento, California. His father, a World War II fighter pilot, is a retired engineer, his mother a homemaker. Writing for the *Austin Chronicle* (March 19, 1999, on-line), Ken Lieck described Johnston's parents as "a devoutly God-fearing . . . fastidiously old-fashioned couple." Johnston is much younger than his brother and three sisters. When he was about three, the family settled in Chester, West Virginia. During Johnston's childhood his frequent bursts of hyperactivity exhausted his mother; when calmer, he mostly read comic books and drew his own comics. His favorite characters were the Incredible Hulk, Captain America, and Casper the Friendly Ghost. "I've always identified with Casper," he told Michael Hall for *Texas Monthly* (February 2005). "I try to be the good guy, and pure." In his early teens Johnston began keeping a taped record of his life; he also shot many home movies, often playing different roles himself. In one clip, for example, included in *The Devil and Daniel Johnston*, he cast himself as his mother and showed her berating him. With the help of siblings, he learned to play the piano, though poorly; he later learned the fundamentals of playing the guitar and the harmonica and developed a passion for the Beatles. While at Oak Glen High School, in New Cumberland, near Chester, he "started playing music by ear" and writing songs, he told Lieck.

Johnston attended Abilene Christian University, in Texas, for a year, then transferred to a branch of Kent State University near Chester, where he studied art and met an undergraduate named Laurie. "I made up some songs just to please her," he told Hall. "And she liked them. And I just flipped out. I was at the piano banging away every day, writing songs. And I turned into a maniac and I never gave up." The music journalist Paul Du Noyer wrote for his Web site that Johnston's feelings for Laurie, who was engaged to a mortician, inspired Johnston to write "literally hundreds of songs of unrequited love." Johnston recorded some on cassettes, with hand-drawn cartoons on their covers. He gave most of the tapes to passersby; others he bartered for comic books. Sometimes he succeeded in copying the tapes; more often he re-recorded them. *Songs of Pain*, *More Songs of Pain*, *Don't Be Scared*, and *The What of Whom* were made between 1980 and 1983. The lyrics for "More Dead Than Alive," from *More Songs of Pain*, contain the lines "He played the game but he failed the test / . . . / he said I can't live without her / she said too bad about that and left with the undertaker / now he just sits at the piano / singing I'll never grow up / I'll never grow up / more dead than alive." During that period, Lieck wrote, "anxious and often teary admonitions" voiced by Johnston's mother "became a staple of the tapes. . . . Typical motherly screeds of 'You'll never amount to anything!' pepper albums as between-song patter."

Meanwhile, Johnston's grades had plummeted, and at his parents' urging, he quit college. In 1983 he moved into his brother's home, near Houston, Texas, and got a job at AstroWorld, a Six Flags theme park. In his free time he wrote songs, often accompanying himself on his nephew's toy chord organ. When he recorded "Speeding Motorcycle" and the other works contained in *Yip/Jump Music*

(1983), he told David Wolinsky for the *A.V. Club* (February 28, 2008, on-line), he "never really thought that it was going to be an album that was going to be sold to the world—I thought it was just another tape for my friends."

Within a few months Johnston had moved again, this time into a sister's house in San Marcos, Texas, and got hired as a pizza deliveryman. While in San Marcos he recorded "Desperate Man Blues," "Keep Punching Joe," and other songs for *Hi, How Are You*. (Joe, a recurring character in his songs, is said to be a stand-in for Johnston.) Then he suffered a nervous breakdown. His discovery of a letter from his mother to his sister, which he interpreted as a suggestion that he be placed in a mental institution, led him to flee San Marcos. He found work with a touring carnival, but feeling unhappy that he had little time to devote to music or art, he quit five months later, when the carnival arrived in Austin. There, he worked at a McDonald's restaurant and lived in a church near the University of Texas campus. He again passed around his tapes; new ones included *Retired Boxer* (1984) and *Respect* and *Continued Story* (both 1985).

One of Johnston's tapes impressed Kathy McCarty, a member of the band Glass Eye. At the Glass Eye's invitation, Johnston opened for them at a local show in 1985. Michael Hall, who was present, recalled the audience's enthusiastic response to Johnston's performance of "The Marching Guitars," which, Hall wrote, "soared over a repeating circle of chords: No one can stop them / The marching guitars. [Austin] was full of . . . guitar bands intent on conquering America, and this sounded like an anthem." Later that year an MTV crew came to Austin to document the city's music scene for the show *I.R.S. Records Presents The Cutting Edge*, hosted by Peter Zaremba of the Fleshtones. According to Paul Du Noyer, Johnston "ambled onto the set" while MTV's cameras were rolling, and the documentary included footage of him introducing himself and waving around a copy of *Hi, How Are You*. Thanks to that film and his growing reputation in Austin, Johnston acquired a manager, Randy Kemper. In March 1986 Johnston ranked first among songwriters in an *Austin Chronicle* readers' poll.

That year Jeff Tartakov's Stress Records released *Hi, How Are You* and *Yip/Jump Music*. Around that time Johnston's behavior became increasingly erratic. His psychological problems worsened when he began to use illegal drugs. One day an LSD-induced hallucination in which Kemper turned into the devil led Johnston to strike his manager's head with a lead pipe. Kemper survived the attack but ended his association with Johnston; Tartakov succeeded him as Johnston's manager. A few nights later, after Johnston was found shouting about baptism while standing in a creek, he was admitted into Austin State Hospital, a psychiatric facility. At a court hearing he promised never to take LSD again, then returned to his parents' home. During the next few years, he took antipsychotic medications. His next tape was *Merry Christmas* (1988).

That year *Songs of Pain* and *More Songs of Pain*, on the Stress Label, went on sale. Both albums were later remastered by Dual Tone and sold as the two-CD set *Early Recordings Volume 1* (2003). The first disc includes the song "Grievances," which Johnston described to Lieck as his "Song of Songs." Referring to Laurie, it contains the lines "I saw you there at the funeral / You were standing there like a temple / I said, 'Hi, how are you? Hello' / Then I pulled up a casket and crawled in." The second disc includes "Phantom of My Own Opera," "You Put My Love Out the Door," and "True Grief." "They were strange, low-fi collections," Hall wrote, "with Daniel banging haphazardly on the piano. Most young songwriters try to be tough, cynical, or something they aren't. These songs . . . were naked and honest, full of longing and need, sung in a high twang that sounded as though his heart were breaking. It was as if he were exposing himself. . . . The melodies were sunny one song and aching the next, the kind of pure pop concoctions that Lennon and McCartney wrote."

Sometime in 1988 Johnston stopped taking his medications and moved to New York City to record for the Shimmy Disc label, founded in 1987 by Mark Kramer, a member of the Butthole Surfers and other bands. In 1990 Shimmy Disc released Johnston's *1990*, a $33^1/_3$ vinyl album. Its 12 songs include "Spirit World Rising" (for which Sonic Youth's Steve Shelley and Lee Ranaldo joined Johnston), "Don't Play Cards with Satan," "Devil Town," "Lord Give Me Hope," and Johnston's idiosyncratic cover of the Beatles' "Got to Get You into My Life." "On *1990*, Johnston's songs took a darker turn," Justin Crane wrote for a 2003 essay posted on his Web site. "The optimism of [his] cassette recordings was all but gone. Johnston had talked about pain before, but it wasn't until *1990* that he made you really feel it. He wasn't a lovesick kid anymore; he was an adult with some real issues." Shimmy Disc made *1990* available as a cassette in 1993; Instinct Records' and Hire Wire Music's *1990* CDs went on sale in 2004 and 2008, respectively. In 2008 Hire Wire also released a two-vinyl-record set containing *1990* and Johnston's *Artistic Vice* (1991), the latter being his second and last album for Shimmy Disc. Brett Hartenbach described *Artistic Vice* for the All Music Guide (on-line) as "rough-hewn pop/rock that despite its lo-fi exterior was [Johnston's] most accessible release to date." Hartenbach also wrote, "*Artistic Vice* is a consistently strong collection of songs that at times recalls the innocence of Johnston's work prior to his breakdown, while at the same time dealing both with where he had been and where he was heading."

Earlier, while he was in New York, Johnston's mental state had deteriorated. Sometimes he slept in a homeless shelter on the Bowery, a haunt of down-and-outers in Lower Manhattan. Caught painting Christian fish symbols in the stairwells of the Statue of Liberty, he was arrested and admitted to the psychiatric division of Bellevue Medical Center. A clerical error led to his release, and that same night he opened for the band Firehose at the Manhattan club CBGB. He then moved in with a woman he had met in Bellevue. When he and the woman split up, he returned to West Virginia. His parents arranged for his admission into a mental hospital, where he was diagnosed with manic depression. Also known as bipolar disorder, manic depression is incurable, but with proper medication victims can lead normal lives. Doctors at the hospital started Johnston on another regimen of drugs.

Johnston took part in the 1990 Austin Music Awards ceremony at the SXSW (South by Southwest) music festival. His father, who owned a plane, flew him there. During the flight back to West Virginia, Johnston read a comic book whose cover showed Casper clutching an open parachute. Suddenly, Bill Johnston recalled to Hall, Daniel shouted, "Let's bail out!," pulled the key from the plane's ignition, tossed it out the window, and grabbed the control stick. The plane went into a tailspin and crash-landed in a grove of trees, but neither father nor son was injured. Soon after the crash Johnston's parents moved with him to Waller, Texas, near Houston, to be closer to other family members.

In 1992 Kurt Cobain, the lead singer and guitarist of the band Nirvana, appeared at the MTV Music Awards ceremony (and repeatedly in public afterward) wearing a Johnston T-shirt printed with the words "Hi, How are you" above a drawing of Johnston's trademark cartoon frog. Nirvana's celebrity spilled over onto Johnston, leading two major record labels to court him. Johnston, who was in a mental hospital, turned down a lucrative deal with Elektra, asserting that the band Metallica, which recorded for that label, was satanic. He fired Tartakov and accepted a deal with Atlantic for a fraction of what Elektra had offered.

In 1994 Atlantic released Johnston's album *Fun*, produced by Paul Leary, the Butthole Surfers' guitarist. Johnston's medications had impaired his ability to play an instrument, so Leary and others had performed much of the music. "The collaboration enhances rather than compromises Johnston's music, as the settings reinforce the strengths of the songs," Don McLeese wrote for the *Austin-American Statesman* (October 6, 1994). McLeese also declared, "The spirit of this album is pure, unadulterated Daniel. 'Happy Time' offers a performance so rich in its bittersweet complexity that it forces a reassessment of how knowing the supposedly naive Johnston is, while 'Psycho Nightmare' and 'Delusion + Confusion' plumb the darker sides to maximum musical advantage." *Fun*'s poor sales—under 13,000 copies—led Atlantic to drop Johnston.

The year 1994 also saw the release of Kathy McCarty's album of Johnston covers, *Dead Dog's Eyeball: Songs of Daniel Johnston*, produced by

Brian Beattie. (Its title refers to a recurring image in Johnston cartoons.) McCarty told Michael Roberts for the Denver, Colorado, *Westword* (June 21, 1995) that in making that record, she hoped to display Johnston's songwriting talents to those who found his own singing and accompaniments unlistenable. In a review of the album for *Entertainment Weekly* (November 25, 1994, on-line), Steven Mirkin wrote that McCarty "fleshes out Johnston's stark recordings, unearthing veins of compassion and sadness not heard on the originals and proving Johnston is more than a primitive curiosity."

During the next few years, mental illness often incapacitated Johnston. On the rare occasions when he left home, he toured with the help of his brother (who has served as his manager for years) and Brian Beattie. His collection *Rejected Unknown* (2001) came out on Beattie's label, Gammon. Then came *Fear Yourself* (2003), produced by Mark Linkous of the band Sparklehorse, followed by *The Late Great Daniel Johnston: Discovered Covered* (2004), which contains two discs: one with Johnston singing and the other with covers of the same songs by 18 artists or duos, among them Tom Waits (singing "King Kong"), TV on the Radio ("Walking the Cow"), Beck ("True Love Will Find You in the End"), Sparklehorse and the Flaming Lips ("Go"), and Vic Chestnutt ("Like a Monkey in a Zoo"). In 2006 the Johnston family's newly launched label, Eternal Yip Eye Music, released a greatest-hits compilation, *Welcome to My World*.

That year also saw the worldwide release of the documentary *The Devil and Daniel Johnston*, produced by Henry Rosenthal and directed by Jeff Feuerzeig, the latter of whom told Mark Moring for *Christianity Today* (April 11, 2006), "I believe very strongly that the music [Johnston] created in '81, '82, '83 . . . is the most raw, unfiltered, beautiful emotion that's been laid to tape. . . . I've seen it touch people all over the world." Four years in the making, *The Devil and Daniel Johnston* won the award for documentary direction at the 2005 Sundance Film Festival.

The Devil and Daniel Johnston led to wider interest in Johnston's music and an increasing number of tours. In 2010 Johnston performed in Australia, New Zealand, Japan, and Europe and appeared at the All Tomorrow's Parties festival in Minehead, England, at the invitation of the festival's curator, Matt Groening. His most recent albums are *Is And Always Was* (2009) and *Beam Me Up!* (2010), the latter of which includes tracks made with Beam, an 11-piece Dutch orchestra. Johnston has also made albums with musicians including Jad Fair and Don "Jack Medicine" Goede.

In the past decade sales of some of Johnston's thousands of drawings have greatly boosted his income. (Jeff Tartakov, with whom he eventually reconciled, serves as his representative.) Reminiscent of doodlings or panels in comic books, many depict weird creatures, distorted human figures, and dreamlike or nightmarish scenarios, often accompanied by ambiguous text, exclamations, or imperatives. Johnston's drawings have been exhibited at galleries and museums in the U.S. and overseas. Some date from the 1970s, when he was giving his work away; they now command prices as high as several thousand dollars apiece.

Since the early 2000s medication has helped to keep Johnston's bipolar disorder and other health problems under control. Johnston recently moved into his own house, next door to his parents, in Waller. His mother and father, who are in their late 80s, remain his primary caregivers. Johnston lives with his cat, Spunky, and has a huge collection of pop-culture artifacts. He does not own a phone; his parents notify him via an intercom if a call comes for him on their phone. According to his official Web site, hihowareyou.com, which his brother maintains, printouts of e-mail messages for him are brought to him weekly. Johnston likes to get letters, his brother has said, but he has never answered any.

—W.D.

Suggested Reading: All Music Guide Web site; *Austin (Texas) Chronicle* (on-line) Mar. 19, 1999; *Christianity Today* (on-line) Apr. 11, 2006; hihowareyou.com; justincrane.com; rejectedunknown.com; *Salon.com* Mar. 31, 2006; Second Hand Songs (on-line); *Slant Magazine* (on-line) Apr. 18, 2006; *Texas Monthly* 124+ Feb. 2005

Selected Recordings: *Songs of Pain*, 1981; *Don't Be Scared*, 1982; *The What of Whom*, 1983; *More Songs of Pain*, 1983; *Retired Boxer*, 1984; *Respect*, 1985; *Continued Story*, 1985; *Hi, How Are You*, 1986; *Yip/Jump Music*, 1986; *Merry Christmas*, 1988; *1990*, 1990; *Artistic Vice*, 1991; *Fun*, 1994; *Rejected Unknown*, 2001; *Fear Yourself*, 2003; *Early Recordings Vol. 1*, 2003; *The Late Great Daniel Johnston: Discovered Covered*, 2004; *Welcome to My World*, 2006; *Is and Always Was*, 2009; with Jad Fair—*It's Spooky*, 1989; with Don "Jack Medicine" Goede—*The Electric Ghosts*, 2006; with Beam—*Beam Me Up!*, 2010

Jordan, Philippe

(zhor-DAN, fil-EEP)

Oct. 18, 1974– Musical director of the Paris Opera

Address: c/o Peter Wiggins, IMG Artists, 31 Rue du Temple, 75004 Paris, France

"He takes the stage with the air of someone intent on extruding every shred of profundity from every note in a score," the music critic Joshua Kosman wrote for the *San Francisco Chronicle* (October 29, 2007) about the Swiss conductor Philippe Jordan.

Stephane De Sakutin/AFP/Getty Images

Philippe Jordan

In 2009 Jordan was hired as the musical director of the Paris Opera, becoming, at 35, the youngest person ever to hold that title at the prestigious French company. He has also guest-conducted for several other prominent European companies, including the Berlin Philharmonic, the Vienna Philharmonic, the National Academy of St. Cecilia, and the London Philharmonic Orchestra, to name a few. In the United States Jordan has worked with the orchestras of Seattle, Dallas, Cleveland, Philadelphia, Washington, Minnesota, New York, and San Francisco, among others. For *Opera News* (August 2010), Matthew Gurewitsch wrote about the conductor, "When Jordan is presiding in the pit, one senses him listening rather than micromanaging, inspiring the musicians to listen, inviting the audience to listen actively, too."

Philippe Jordan was born on October 18, 1974 in Zurich, in central Switzerland, where German is spoken. His father, the acclaimed conductor Armin Jordan (who died in 2006), used to take Philippe to opera rehearsals during his childhood. Philippe told Matthew Gurewitsch, "My father's influence was tremendous. All my music-making is somehow linked to him—to his recordings, to the rehearsals I attended when I wasn't in school, to his performances. Everything about his work fascinated me. I wanted to experience his world. In our family, everything revolved around music and the theater. My mother, Käthe Herkner, was a ballet dancer. My younger sister Pascale Jordan is an actress in Switzerland. So none of us has turned away from the arts." Jordan, whose mother is of Irish descent, grew up learning English as his first language. He is fluent in German and French as well as English; he also speaks some Italian. Jor-

dan's formal musical education began when he took piano lessons at age six, followed by his joining the Zurich Boys' Choir at age eight and taking up the violin at 11. When he was a teenager, he attended the Zurich Conservatory and earned his diploma, with honors, as a piano instructor. While working as an assistant to Jeffrey Tate on the German composer Richard Wagner's *Ring* cycle at the Théâtre du Châtelet, in Paris, Jordan studied theory and composition with Hans Ulrich Lehmann, a Swiss composer. He also played piano in solo recitals and in chamber-music concerts. He considered becoming a stage director—at nine he constructed a model set for the Wagner opera *Das Rheingold*, part of the *Ring* cycle—until he decided that he wanted to become a conductor.

Although he never officially studied the art of conducting music, Jordan began his career in 1994 as *kapellmeister* (German for "music director") of the Ulm Theater, in Germany. "There are so many ways to become a conductor," he said in an interview for *Andante* magazine, as quoted on the New York Philharmonic Web site. "A violinist has his violin, a pianist has his piano to practice, [but] the chance for a conductor to practice on his own orchestra, that's very rare. It's difficult to say how you learn conducting. But my way has been the solid German way, learning through experience." He told William R. Braun for *Opera News* (July 2005), "It's very important for a conductor to find his own sound, and in the long term it's only possible with your own orchestra." Jordan served as an assistant to Daniel Barenboim, a pianist and conductor, at the Berlin State Opera, in Germany, from 1998 until 2001. For the next three years, he served as chief conductor of Austria's Graz Opera and Graz Philharmonic Orchestra. He told the music critic Scott Cantrell for the *Dallas (Texas) News* (November 3, 2005, on-line), "If you go to a conservatory, you're lucky to conduct two pianists or a string quartet. Once a year you may get to conduct a high school orchestra. In the opera, you just get thrown in. You start with musicals, then operettas, then operas. . . . The orchestra is the best and hardest teacher at the same time. They will tell you very clearly if something is right or wrong, technically, and how a first-level orchestra will react." Jordan had been hired by Karen Stone, the former general director of both Graz companies, who eventually left to lead the Dallas opera. Referring to Jordan, Stone told Scott Cantrell, "At the time he was a very young man with an enormous talent. . . . He just has extraordinary sensitivity and theatricality."

While serving as a conductor in Graz, Jordan also conducted at many other opera houses and festivals. In the early and mid-2000s, he made his debuts at the Houston Grand Opera (in Texas), the Glyndebourne Festival (in England), and New York City's Metropolitan Opera (commonly referred to as the Met). In the interview with William R. Braun, Jordan compared the experience of conducting at the Met to "driving a great Ferrari," adding, "At the end of the day you have to give the key back, because it's not your own." Anthony Tommasini, reviewing Jordan's direction of Mozart's *Nozze di Figaro* (*The Marriage of Figaro*) at the Met, wrote for the *New York Times* (December 8, 2007), "There was youthful vitality in his performance but also poise, spaciousness and refinement: qualities that typically come only with maturity."

Jordan has also served as a guest conductor at the New York Philharmonic, the Bavarian State Opera (in Munich, Germany), the Royal Opera House at Covent Garden (London, England), the Salzburg Festival (Salzburg, Austria), the Vienna State Opera (Vienna, Austria), and the Baden-Baden Festival Theatre (Baden-Württemberg, Germany), among others. In an interview with Hugo Shirley for MusicalCriticism.com (February 17, 2008), he said, "Free-lance music is a great thing. You get to see lots of great orchestras, great opera houses, great cities . . . but I've spent four years already doing that. In the long term, it's not very healthy and it's not very satisfying. Of course you can introduce some ideas and certain colours but it's difficult to really make your mark, you can't do anything long term where you can grow and develop with a group." In 2007 Jordan was given the opportunity to "grow and develop with a group" when he was named the next musical director of the Paris Opera, which had been led by guest conductors ever since the American maestro James Conlon left, in 2004, to head the Los Angeles Opera. Jordan's post became effective in 2009; his contract is for six years.

Before he began his tenure at the Paris Opera, Jordan conducted Wagner's *Ring* cycle, produced by Robert Wilson at the Zurich opera, from 2008 to 2009. *Der Ring des Nibelungen* (*The Ring of the Nibelung*) consists of four operas that, with intermissions, run for more than 15 hours in total. The plot involves an epic struggle among the gods, who rule the world as the possessors of a magical ring taken from the dwarf Alberich, who later places a curse on it. Jordan told Hugo Shirley, "It's always a dream for a conductor to do the *Ring*, you don't normally do the *Ring* when you're 33 or . . . 27. It was not even something for me to consider in my Graz years. . . . With Wagner, though, it's not only a thing of age but of experience. All the great conductors did it when they were very young—even Mahler was in his twenties when he did it—and you only can be good at this stuff when you do it and experience it. . . . I'm really glad to have the opportunity." In the interview with Matthew Gurewitsch, Jordan said, "Doing my first *Ring* in Zurich was very helpful for developing my conception of the whole cycle. I'm interested in a transparent, sometimes Impressionistic orchestral language, which the small house in Zurich simply demands. You can't play the music there as you would at the Met or in Berlin. It's just not possible. Playing the *Ring* in Zurich helped me find a way that is clearer, which helps the singers come

through more easily. The text becomes easier to understand. The textures and motifs register more clearly. And yet you don't have to sacrifice the grandeur of the drama, which we need as well." Around the same time that he conducted the *Ring*, Jordan also debuted at La Scala, a famous opera house in Milan, Italy.

In 2009 Jordan became the youngest-ever musical director of the Paris Opera, where he began collaborating with Nicolas Joël, the company's general manager, on directing the chorus and orchestra in performances at the Paris and Bastille opera houses. Jordan was happy that he would be able to establish a more personal connection with an orchestra. He told Hugo Shirley, "Although it's fantastic to work with an orchestra like the [London] Philharmonia, with them you get three rehearsals if you're lucky, so you can't really get across your own view of the piece—it's impossible. You can produce a good performance together but it's not really you." His first and second seasons concentrated on works by Mozart and Wagner (including another production of the *Ring* cycle), with the second also including the opera *Il Trittico*, by the Italian composer Giacomo Puccini. When asked about his plans in terms of presenting Parisian operas, Jordan told Matthew Gurewitsch, "It's been so long since this orchestra has had a music director, I thought it was crucial to begin with demanding work that would establish a way of working together—a sound, a style as a basis for our future work. . . . As general manager, Nicolas Joël has made it very clear that we'll do at least one new production of a French opera a year. But cultivating the Parisian repertoire isn't a project for us now. . . . We don't regard it as an obligation."

In the interview with Gurewitsch, Jordan discussed his belief that music derives from silence. "Every great composer has to immerse himself in silence to develop his thoughts, and to build from there. For performers it is the same. When I work with the orchestra and with singers, I always try to develop our sound from silence and from piano. We can always raise the volume to a big fortissimo, but the base—for the sake of a good dynamic and a good shape to the sound—is always a piano, which is related to silence." He added, "We have to listen to each other. At night in the mountains or the desert, the silence can be very loud! It's amazing music, very impressive and strong. It forces you to listen, to calm down. Silence is very healing. It centers you." When asked how he felt about the speed with which his career was progressing, Jordan told Gurewitsch, "It feels to me that I've moved forward very methodically, step by step. . . . I feel young for the work I am doing, but not too young." Asked by Hugo Shirley what he wants to accomplish, Jordan said, "As exciting [as] all my conducting work is, I do ask myself sometimes 'is this what I'm going to be doing for the rest of my life?' I think I might want to do something different in the way of writing and composing. . . . As a conductor you're always the composer's advocate, you're always interpreting, which is fantastic because you're getting to know the music, getting closer to the composer. But sometimes I ask myself what's coming out of *me*? What's actually inside me?" He went on to say, "It would be really exciting just to sit there at the piano with a blank sheet and just have one idea—not even an exact idea, especially if you don't have experience—and then a second idea and then a third idea and suddenly something is coming up and at the end of the day you can look at it and ask, 'Where's that coming from? Did I invent that?' And so you start to hear music that's inside you but you haven't experienced it, you haven't heard it. I think that's a very, very interesting process and I hope one day to have more time to do that."

Jordan has recorded on CDs the Beethoven piano concertos and on DVDs the operas *Carmen* (performed at Glyndebourne), *Werther* (Vienna), *Salome@* (Covent Garden), *Tannhäuser* (Baden-

Baden), and *Doktor Faust* (Zurich). In addition to his work with the Paris Opera, he is the principal guest conductor of the Berlin State Opera.

—J.P.

Suggested Reading: *Dallas (Texas) News* (on-line) Nov. 3, 2005; MusicalCriticism.com Feb. 17, 2008; *New York Times* B p7 Dec. 8, 2007; *Opera News* p16+ Aug. 2010; *San Francisco Chronicle* E p3 Oct. 29, 2007

Selected Recordings: *Beethoven Piano Concertos nos. 1 & 5*, 2008; *Beethoven Piano Concerto no. 4*, 2008; *Beethoven Piano Concertos nos. 2 & 3*, 2009; *Eine Alpensinfonie*, 2010

Selected Films: *Carmen*, 2003; *Werther*, 2005; *Doktor Faust*, 2006; *Salome@*, 2008; *Tannhäuser*, 2008

Stephen Lovekin/Getty Images

King, John

Aug. 30, 1963– Television news anchor

Address: One CNN Center, Atlanta, GA 30348

On November 11, 2009, with no warning, the host of the CNN program *Lou Dobbs Tonight* declared that the show—and Dobbs's 29-year association with the network—would end that evening. The next day CNN announced that starting in early 2010, John King, a 25-year veteran of journalism who joined CNN in 1997, would anchor a new program devoted to political news in the time slot vacated by Dobbs—7:00 to 8:00 p.m. on weeknights; the new show, *John King, USA*, made its debut on March 22. Dobbs's decision to leave CNN came after he rejected requests from network executives to curb his vehement criticisms of U.S. immigration policies and his opinion-laden discussions of other issues. King, who hosted the CNN Sunday-morning political-news show *State of the Union with John King* from January 2009 until early February 2010, has distanced himself from those who, like Dobbs, practice so-called advocacy journalism. "I don't think you have to give up your objectivity and give up being a reporter to be part of a very lively, provocative, feisty conversation about the issues of the day, as long as it is built around facts and information," King told Matea Gold for the *Los Angeles Times* (November 12, 2009, on-line). "I think people are hungry for it." On the same day he told Richard Huff for the New York *Daily News*, "I will convey what I learn in reporting, not what I think. I'm not an advocate for any person, any issue, any party. I'm a reporter [who] believes there's an amazing thirst for information, presented in an entertaining way."

King began his career in journalism as an Associated Press (A.P.) reporter, right after he graduated from college, in 1985. During the last six of his dozen years with the A.P., he served as the news agency's chief political correspondent. When CNN offered him a job, he had misgivings about leaving print journalism for cable-TV news. "I think most print guys have a skepticism or worse about television," he told Jacques Steinberg for the *New York Times* (April 22, 2008). "When you switch from print to television, most guys say, 'Oh yeah, the pretty people.'" He wondered whether, on TV, he might have to abandon the activities he enjoyed as a reporter—"working the phones" and "going places and seeing things." As it turned out, what troubled him after he arrived at CNN was his extreme nervousness in front of the camera. That problem steadily lessened, and before long "he fell in love" with the job, Bella English wrote for the *Boston Globe* (December 8, 2009, on-line). King held the post of CNN's senior White House correspondent from 1999 to 2005, when he was named chief national correspondent—a title that he still holds. As a contributor to CNN's "America Votes 2008," King attracted a lot of attention for his use of a huge screen, reminiscent of those of TV weather reporters, to provide viewers with poll results and other data connected to the 2008 elections. Often referred to as the "Magic Wall," the screen is used regularly on *John King, USA*. According to Jon Friedman, writing for *MarketWatch.com* (November 20, 2009), "King has prided himself on being part Walter Cronkite and part Charles Kuralt— an anchor who can do it all, from reading news headlines to interviewing guests and going on the road in search of great human-interest stories." The widely respected journalist Tim Russert, who hosted *Meet the Press* on NBC for more than 16 years until his death, in 2008, described King to Steinberg as "a tenacious, terrific reporter."

The third boy among his parents' five sons and two daughters, John King was born on August 30, 1963 in Boston, Massachusetts, and raised in the Dorchester section of that city. CNN's political director, Sam Feist, told English that King "comes from a place a lot of Washington people don't: a working-class neighborhood in Boston, and I think that keeps him grounded." King's father, a prison guard at the now-defunct Charles Street Jail, in Boston, "worked so hard," King told Marisa Guthrie for *Broadcasting & Cable* (February 2, 2009). "He didn't go to college, but we all got to go because he and my mom worked so hard and gave up so much for us. And that's the basic blue-collar work ethic: work hard and be fair and be honest, and it will be OK." He told English, "They were magicians. They gave us everything with nothing." King's father died of colon cancer at the age of 55, and his mother of emphysema at 59. "At least once a day," he said, he wishes that his parents were alive so that he could treat them to a cruise or other luxuries that he could easily afford now.

As a youngster King delivered newspapers. When he was older he worked in Copperfield's Bar and Down Under Pub, near Fenway Stadium, the home of the Boston Red Sox. He also washed dishes at the landmark Jacob Wirth Restaurant, in downtown Boston, where he accidentally sliced off the tip of his index finger. King attended Boston Latin School, an elite public school that admits students on the basis of scores on an entrance exam. After high school he entered the University of Rhode Island at Kingston. As an undergraduate he interned at the Providence, Rhode Island, bureau of the Associated Press—"the largest and oldest news organization in the world," according to its Web site. He landed a full-time job as an A.P. re-

porter after he graduated, with a B.A. degree in journalism, in 1985. In 1987 he transferred to the agency's Boston bureau, where he worked for two years. In 1988 he was assigned to report on the presidential campaign of Michael S. Dukakis, who was then the governor of Massachusetts, and he traveled with Dukakis and his entourage. King told Guthrie, "I was 24 years old when I was running around the country with Dukakis and I just thought, 'Wow, this is great! They pay people to do this?' I was incredibly lucky to have the opportunity." After Dukakis won the Democratic nomination, King broke the story of the governor's selection of U.S. senator Lloyd Bentsen of Texas as his running mate. In an article for the A.P. (December 2, 1988) after Dukakis's defeat, King wrote, "The trip to the nation's capital was far different from the last time Dukakis came, near the end of the campaign, when he still had Secret Service protection and was accompanied by a phalanx of aides. This time he took a commercial flight, accompanied by only two aides, and traveled around town in a crowded rental car. He met with Washington-based campaign workers before heading home to Boston."

In 1991 King became the A.P.'s chief political correspondent, based in Washington, D.C. In one of his first articles in his new post, he discussed Virginia governor L. Douglas Wilder's plans to seek the 1992 Democratic presidential nomination, and he mentioned that Governor Bill Clinton of Arkansas was also considering a run for the White House. In 1992, after Clinton became the Democratic nominee, King scooped his media colleagues with the news of Clinton's selection of U.S. senator Al Gore of Tennessee as his running mate. In 1996, in other scoops, he reported on General Colin Powell's decision not to seek the presidency and on the attempt by the Republican presidential nominee, Senator Bob Dole of Kansas, to secure the endorsement of the Texas businessman Ross Perot. (Perot had run as a third-party presidential candidate in 1992, and he did so again in 1996.)

King also reported on events in the Persian Gulf after Iraq invaded its neighbor Kuwait, in August 1990, and seized Kuwaiti oil fields. The United Nations ruled Iraq's actions illegal and imposed sanctions on that nation, but the Iraqi dictator, Saddam Hussein, ignored its demands that Iraqi troops withdraw from Kuwait and Saudi Arabia by January 15, 1991. On January 17 a coalition of forces from the U.S., Great Britain, France, and 31 other nations began bombing positions held by Iraq, and on February 23 they mounted a ground assault. King, along with another A.P. journalist and an A.P. photographer, provided so-called unilateral reporting from Saudi Arabia during the battle of Khafji (January 29–February 1, 1991)—that is, they were not part of the pool of reporters who shared information. He also reported from Kuwait City on February 27, after Iraq relinquished its hold on that city and a day before a cease-fire was declared. "Almost constant gunfire sounded today as Kuwaitis celebrated by shooting captured Iraqi AK-47 rifles," King wrote. "It was impossible to tell if any Iraqi remnants were shooting as well. Nearby, fires from oil wells set alight sent bright orange flames into the sky, which was black with thick clouds. Greasy and oily rain fell. Resistance fighters, witnesses and Kuwaiti officials recounted Iraqi atrocities." The A.P. Managing Editors' Association gave King a top-performance award for his coverage of the Gulf War.

In 1997, at the invitation of Frank Sesno, who was then CNN's Washington, D.C., bureau chief, King—reluctantly, by his own account—joined CNN as the network's White House correspondent. "I had the traditional print view of TV journalists: Those are pretty people who get paid a lot of money and don't do any work," he told English. "It turned out I was wrong." The job required King to report live on camera. "I had been a guest on programs before," he told Guthrie. "But I had never been a correspondent. I had never tracked pieces. I had never done a live shot. I was brand-new at it. And if you went back and dug up all the tapes, you would know that I was brand-new at it. It was rough and it was humbling and, at times, humiliating. It's like anything, when you're new at it you're going to fall down, but the important thing is to get up." He made his debut in a broadcast about the waning support for House Speaker Newt Gingrich among Republican Party leaders. "I was humiliatingly bad at it," he told Bella English. "My knees were shaking, and I hoped the sweat didn't go all the way up to my collar. After a few weeks, I went from a full shake to a slight tremble." On one occasion, on May 16, 1998, King conducted an exclusive joint interview with President Clinton and the prime minister of Great Britain, Tony Blair.

In 1999 CNN promoted King to senior White House correspondent. In November 2000 he conducted the only one-on-one interview with President Clinton during his trip to Vietnam. King was CNN's lead reporter during the latter part of Vice President Al Gore's 2000 presidential campaign; he covered the inconclusive results of balloting in Florida, which led to a recount of votes that the U.S. Supreme Court halted, in effect making Governor George W. Bush of Texas the president-elect. In 2002, when the Bush administration was attempting to build support for its later invasion of Iraq, King accompanied Vice President Richard B. "Dick" Cheney on a diplomatic mission to the Middle East. In an interview with Cheney that aired on CNN's *American Morning with Paula Zahn* (September 9, 2002), King asked the vice president if there was evidence that Iraq was building nuclear, chemical, and biological weapons. Cheney told King, "There is no question, [that] the evidence is there to support those conclusions, that his weapons of mass destruction capability is growing more robust. We also have circumstances now that are different than before September 11th. What happened on September 11th was an attack that was launched on the territory of the United States

against us. We know our vulnerabilities, and when we think about these weapons of mass destruction, and when we know, as we do, the Al Qaeda organization that hit on September 11th is doing everything they can to acquire chemical, nuclear and biological weapons. . . . So we have to be concerned now about the possibility that we're vulnerable to an attack the likes of which we did not experience prior to last September 11th with a far more deadly weapon. We have to worry about the possible marriage, if you will, of a rogue state like Saddam Hussein's Iraq, with a terrorist organization, like Al Qaeda. And we have to worry about the possibility that Saddam Hussein, for his own reasons, can use growing capability on our friends and allies in the region, on U.S. forces in the region or on the United States itself." The Bush administration pointed to Iraq's possession or imminent acquisition of "weapons of mass destruction" to justify its invasion of Iraq in March 2003. Investigations later turned up no evidence of such weapons or programs to build such weapons in Iraq.

In 2004 King accompanied Secretary of State Colin Powell to South Asia in the wake of the tsunami that claimed more than 175,000 lives. The next year he was named CNN's chief national correspondent. He was one of several CNN reporters who reported on conditions in Louisiana and other Gulf Coast states in the aftermath of Hurricane Katrina. In 2006 he was among journalists who traveled with George W. Bush to Baghdad, Iraq's capital, where the president met with Iraq's prime minister, Nouri al-Maliki. King also reported on the 2006 midterm elections in the U.S., for CNN shows including *The Situation Room* and *Lou Dobbs Tonight*, and he hosted an hour-long CNN special called *Broken Government: Power Play*, about the Bush administration's attempts to increase the power of the White House. During that period King also interviewed the president, First Lady Laura Bush, and Condoleezza Rice, the secretary of state during Bush's second term.

During the 2008 presidential-election season, King became known as "the man at the Magic Wall," as Guthrie put it: he often appeared in the studio with CNN's new "multi-touch" board behind him, summoning data in real time "from obscure precincts at the touch of a finger," as Guthrie wrote. In an instant the device, which Steinberg dubbed King's "electronic sidekick," provided the kind of information that King used to spend hours collecting as an A.P. reporter—and it was interesting to watch. "Nothing against white guys, but I'm a white guy talking in a box," King told Steinberg. "If all I'm doing is saying, '6 percent, 8 percent, 10 percent, 12 percent,' there's that glaze-over factor at home. You've lost them." He added, "The wonder of this [electronic screen] is that you can show it. You can make the math accessible." King visited many U.S. towns and cities while following various candidates' campaigns. His reports were aired on installments of the CNN series *America Votes 2008*. "My travel is very important to me as a political reporter," King told Guthrie. "You can't sit in Washington, D.C., and understand the country. You just can't. You have to go out and touch it and feel it and see it." King's conversations with ordinary Americans led him to report on various other issues. In September 2008, for example, when the White House and Congress were working on a multibillion-dollar federal bailout of troubled banks, King transmitted to CNN viewers the resentment some Montana Republicans expressed regarding their congressman's support of the plan. King presented "a completely different story on the bailout that was completely unexpected," Sam Feist told Guthrie. "You have to be out there to catch those moments."

January 18, 2009 marked the debut of *State of the Union*, which replaced Wolf Blitzer's longrunning *Late Edition*. (The change was made in part to lighten Blitzer's singularly heavy workload.) The show, which aired from 8:00 a.m. to noon on Sundays, offered news analyses and commentary and interviews with business and political leaders and other newsmakers. Regular features included "Reliable Sources," in which Howard Kurtz, a longtime *Washington Post* staff writer and columnist, discussed the media, and an hour of highlights from other news and interview programs, with a team of CNN journalists pointing out "what's real and what's just rhetoric," according to the show's Web site. Also in that hour King chatted with customers in diners, "listen[ing] to the opinions of people like you—raw and unfiltered," as the Web site's blurb put it. On the first installment of *State of the Union*, King interviewed David Axelrod, the chief strategist for Barack Obama's campaign for the presidency and now the president's senior adviser. A prerecorded interview that King had conducted with Obama also aired that day.

On November 12, 2009 CNN announced that early the next year, King would become the anchor of a new, one-hour program that would fill the weeknight time slot vacated by Lou Dobbs at the end of his show the day before. *John King, USA*, as it is called, premiered on March 22, 2010. (On February 7, 2010 Candy Crowley, CNN's senior political correspondent, succeeded King as the host of a shortened version of *State of the Union*.)

The hour-long *John King, USA* offers interviews, news analyses, commentary, and information displayed on the "Magic Wall." The show is characterized by a middle-of-the-road take on politics and King's unassuming, friendly manner; the set includes Boston Red Sox memorabilia and jugs of Vermont maple syrup. To date it has failed to win a large audience and thus has failed to help reverse CNN's falling prime-time ratings. In an interview with Eric Deggans for *Tampabay.com* (October 25, 2010), King said, "There's no question we have a challenge now when it comes to ratings. I've made some mistakes and CNN faces some broader challenges that we're caught up in. Do we need to abandon everything and go into the world of partisanship? I don't think so. I think we have some soul searching to do about how we do things. When you're having a rough stretch, you can do one of two things; you can sulk, or you can figure it out."

In his November 20, 2009 *MarketWatch* article, Jon Friedman wrote, "When CNN delivers unvarnished journalism, its anchors can seem mealymouthed. But King is a unique presence. He also takes the middle ground, but his grittiness and intensity are uncommon at genteel CNN." King told Friedman, "Lou [Dobbs] passionately believed in advocacy journalism. I passionately believe in steering conversations, not shaping them. That makes us different—doesn't make one right and one wrong." Sam Feist described King to Bella English as "a great moderator, a great interviewer," and then remarked, "I've been working with him for over a decade, and I have no idea what his views are." King told Friedman, "My overriding vision is born of my travels this year: give people more details, substance, information about the big questions of the day, empty our reporters' notebooks and have hopefully interesting and compelling interviews and debates. The overriding challenge of our business is relevance—helping people make their own decisions by exploring their questions in a language they understand. Be passionate about what we do, and also have a little fun along the way." Andrew Tyndall, who has monitored television news for two decades, told Paul Farhi for the *Washington Post* (November 13, 2009, on-line) that King is "part of a new generation of interviewers. He hasn't yet got a style and a voice; that takes years. He's a work in progress."

Before his marriage to the CNN reporter and anchorwoman Dana (Schwartz) Bash, in 2008, King converted from Roman Catholicism to Judaism, Bash's religion. King has a teenage son and daughter from his first marriage. Bash's previous marriage ended in divorce. Her father, Stuart Schwartz, was an ABC-TV producer for 40 years.

—W.D.

Suggested Reading: *Boston Globe* (on-line) Dec. 8, 2009; *Broadcasting & Cable* p22 Feb. 2, 2009; cnn.com; danabash.com; *MarketWatch.com* Nov. 20, 2009

Selected Television Shows: as host—*State of the Union with John King*, 2009–10; *John King, USA*, 2010–

Kings of Leon

Rock band

Followill, Nathan
June 26, 1979– Drummer

Followill, Caleb
Jan. 14, 1982– Singer; songwriter; guitarist

Followill, Jared
Nov. 20, 1986– Bass guitarist

Followill, Matthew
Sep. 10, 1984– Guitarist

Address: c/o RCA Records, 550 Madison Ave., New York, NY 10022

For a time the raw, country- and punk-infused, classic-style rock of Kings of Leon earned the band critical accolades and legions of fans overseas but only minor recognition in the U.S. That changed when the band's fourth album, *Only by the Night* (2008), featuring a cleaner, larger, modern-rock sound, found immediate commercial success and became the first record by Kings of Leon to go platinum in their own country. It also earned the band a total of four Grammy Awards in 2009 and 2010—cementing their rock-star status at home and abroad. The Nashville-based four-piece group is now one of the world's most popular and successful touring rock bands, packing arenas and heard in steady rotation on mainstream radio. Music journalists have taken note. Neil McCormick wrote for the London *Telegraph* (September 17, 2008, online), "The Kings of Leon possess the charisma, swagger, intensity, pop hooklines and dirty rock sensibility to make them all-time greats," and Ann Powers declared in the *Los Angeles Times* (January 31, 2010), "Kings of Leon has become the emblematic band of the new decade by resurrecting the sound and spirit of rock's classic era for a generation that doesn't view the music as necessarily heroic or transformative."

Kings of Leon's first full-length album, *Youth & Young Manhood*, appeared in 2003. At the time classic-rock-revival acts such as the Strokes were gaining critical and popular recognition; as a result Kings of Leon's ragged southern rock, 1970s-style long hair, mustaches, and vintage clothing, and uniquely American back story—which involved three of the four members, all brothers, raised by a strict, alcoholic preacher—helped propel the band to instant stardom in the United Kingdom and other parts of Europe. With a second album, *Aha Shake Heartbreak* (2004), Kings of Leon solidified their standing overseas and status among the leaders of the rock revival. The band opted for a more slickly produced sound on their next release, *Because of the Times* (2007), which reached a wider audience and signaled the new aesthetic that would be fully evident on *Only by the Night*. In

2010 the band released *Come Around Sundown*, which largely followed the successful modern-rock approach of *Only by the Night*.

The three brothers and one cousin who make up Kings of Leon are all known by their middle names. The brothers are the drummer, Ivan Nathan Followill, born on June 26, 1979; the lead vocalist and rhythm-guitar player, Anthony Caleb Followill, born on January 14, 1982; and the bass player, Michael Jared Followill, born on November 20, 1986. Cameron Matthew Followill, born on September 10, 1984, is the brothers' cousin and lead-guitar player. Caleb and Jared were born in Mount Juliet, Tennessee, while Nathan and Matthew were born in Oklahoma City, Oklahoma. The brothers spent much of their childhood crammed into a purple 1988 Oldsmobile with their mother, Betty-Ann, a church pianist, and their father, Ivan Leon Followill, a traveling United Pentecostal Church preacher who led revival meetings throughout the southern United States. During those road trips—which would last between three days and 12 weeks—the brothers were home-schooled by their mother or enrolled in small parochial schools. They often slept in the car, in churches, or in the homes of strangers. Except for five years in Jackson, Tennessee, the family spent most of its time on the road. "When you grow up in the back seat of a car, the window is your television," Caleb told Powers. "It was just about, where do you want to go with your mind?" "People picture this great travelling lifestyle," he told Lindsay Baker for the London *Guardian* (November 23, 2003). "There were moments that were awesome, and then there were moments that we don't think were that awesome. I guess it was tough, and it shows more on us now than it did then, because at the time it was just our lives and we didn't know it was weird." He also told Baker that the brothers' itinerant lifestyle made it difficult to maintain friendships outside the family: "It kind of made us colder, it made it easier for us to walk away from people." At the same time, the experience brought the brothers closer to one another. "We grew on love," Nathan told Vicky Davidson for the *Glasgow (Scotland) Evening Times* (December 11, 2003). "That's why we're all so close. Most people, if they got a chance to be in a band, they wouldn't want to be with their brothers. That's not how it is with us. We didn't have anything, so all we had was each other. . . . It's totally a family chemistry. Whenever we get together, somehow we all click."

Although generally forbidden to listen to secular music, the brothers were occasionally exposed to rock music when their father put on a Rolling Stones or Neil Young cassette in the car. For the most part they spent their early childhood listening to gospel music and church choirs. They also began to play music at a young age, with both Caleb and Nathan backing their mother on drums during church services. "It was more like black gospel music, like Aretha Franklin, Al Green—fun music to play," Nathan told Denise Quan for CNN.com

(September 28, 2009). "Most people hear, 'Oh, you played in church,' and they picture an organ, and just very quiet. It was very lively and wild." Caleb told her, "The thing that inspired me about the music we grew on is that it was human music. The people that got up to play, they basically just got up there and told the story of what happened to them that day."

In 1997 Ivan Leon Followill resigned from the church—he was reportedly asked to leave because of a drinking problem—and divorced his wife, taking Nathan and Caleb with him to live in a town outside Nashville, Tennessee. Jared settled in Oklahoma with his mother, where he made friends at public schools and discovered alternative rock bands, including the Pixies and the Velvet Underground. The divorce effectively ended the family's ban on rock and generally signaled the waning of the influence of religion on the family. "We were out of the church," Jared told Aaron Beck for the *Columbus (Ohio) Dispatch* (February 17, 2005). "We started to re-evaluate our lives." As the 2000s dawned, "I was the only one who wasn't an adult. Caleb was almost 18. Nathan was 21. I was 13. We just started to believe that it wasn't right for us. It wasn't right for anyone, I don't think." Nathan told Jenny Eliscu for *Rolling Stone* (February 24, 2005, on-line), "Our parents' divorce shattered the whole mirage of this perfect little existence the outside world couldn't touch and couldn't pollute. We realized that our dad, the greatest man we ever knew, in our eyes, was only human. And so are we. People are gonna f**k up. They're gonna want to experiment with drugs, have premarital sex. This whole new world was open to us." Without religion to deter them, the Followill brothers began to use drugs and drink alcohol, which, coupled with their newfound passion for rock music, led them down a new path. "Our friend Mary Jane showed up," Nathan told Eliscu, using a slang term for marijuana. "Someone bought us the Led Zeppelin box set, and we spent a week smoking as much pot as we could, listening. Our minds were blown."

Nathan and Caleb soon began to discuss forming their own band. In 2000 they met a local singer who inspired them—though perhaps not in the way he intended—to give it a try. "[Caleb and I] were working in the mall, and this guy came in talking about how he had just got a publishing deal for $15,000," Nathan told Powers. "We were making $5.50 an hour, and we thought, we could live for a year off of that! And he would play us his music, and it was horrible! We used to sing in church, and . . . so we just started writing." Their environment also inspired them, as Nashville is the home of the country-music industry. Nathan told Powers, "It's the songwriting capital of the world, so we were like, 'It's a sign.' This is our sign. We're gonna go out there and we're just gonna get a record deal, you know. We're going to get like the biggest publishing deal ever."

Around that time the two brothers came into contact with a manager, Ken Levitan, who introduced them to the songwriter and producer Angelo Petraglia. Petraglia became a mentor to the brothers, assisting them in their songwriting and introducing them to more music once forbidden to them. "Caleb and Nathan were doing a much different thing when I met them," Petraglia told Powers. "I was hearing them as this Southern soul Everly Brothers. They shared a lead vocal. They had the sibling harmony, and it wasn't a rock band. It was a duo, and they just knew how to sing together. I turned them on to [the Rolling Stones record] *Exile on Main Street* and the Velvet Underground and the Clash, and they were like, 'Wow.'" Once Caleb began to write songs, he realized the need to focus on themes beyond his personal concerns. He recalled to Eliscu, "Once I heard the Stones and Dylan, I thought, My God, why should we be held to our own experiences? Why not do like our dad did as a preacher: Every day, he saw something that inspired him and told a story about someone different. I had to put myself in other people's shoes." Levitan helped the brothers approach record labels; nine labels expressed interest, and Nathan and Caleb decided in 2002 to sign with RCA Records. The label asked them to recruit two more members to complete the lineup, so the brothers brought in Jared as bass player—although he was still in high school and did not yet know how to play bass. After their cousin Matthew agreed to join them as lead guitarist, the brothers named the band after their father and paternal grandfather, whose first name was Leon. Kings of Leon spent the next few months writing and rehearsing, and soon had the five songs that would comprise their debut, the 2003 EP *Holy Roller Novocaine*.

Petraglia and Ethan Johns (the son of Glyn Johns, a producer for the band Led Zeppelin) produced *Holy Roller Novocaine*, which got a generally positive critical response. A writer for the *Rolling Stone* Web site (March 11, 2003) observed, "These three brothers and their cousin play Southern boogie with a garage-rock twist on this debut EP. If the Strokes played [Lynyrd] Skynyrd songs, it might sound a bit like 'Molly's Chambers' or 'Wasted Time.' It adds up to five songs and not a weak moment among them." Amanda Petrusich, writing for the music Web site *Pitchfork Media* (July 2, 2003), noted, "For all their throwback styling, the Kings of Leon are exceptionally twenty-first century. Contemporary music has, for the most part, become about ticking off impressive, heavily-annotated lists of influences, and squeezing old sounds into vaguely novel templates; the new game is how well you can pull off the pilfering—how dynamic you can make a record's re-contextualization. *Holy Roller's* five songs mix late 60s garage/psychedelia with sprawling 70s guitar rock, and while the resulting sound is new enough, its underpants are still showing. It's not hard to see the colors of Kings past here: Steppenwolf, the Kinks, Neil Young, the Band, even skimpy traces of the Velvet Underground."

Kings of Leon (l. to r.): Matthew, Nathan, Caleb, Jared Followill

The band's first full-length album, *Youth & Young Manhood*, which contained four songs from the EP and seven others, was released later in 2003. While it received mostly positive reviews in the U.S., the reception there paled next to that in the U.K., where rave reviews in mainstream newspapers and the music press turned the band into an overnight sensation. As Laura Barton wrote for the London *Guardian* (November 17, 2003, on-line), "When they first arrived in the UK, a group of lithe young men in tight trousers wearing big beards who also happened to be sons of a preacherman from Tennessee, they brought with them a whiff of Lynyrd Skynyrd, of swamp rock and JJ Cale, and departed with not only a troop of committed followers but also a trail of swooning ladies in their wake. Stylistically and musically, they offer an alluring mix of the Strokes and archetypal southern rockers the Allman Brothers." The band sold a comparatively modest 100,000 copies of the album in the U.S. but 750,000 overseas. In a review of *Youth & Young Manhood*, Betty Clarke wrote for the *Guardian* (July 4, 2003, on-line), "Using and abusing passionate gospel, country sweetness and filthy guitar licks, the Kings of Leon are the kind of authentic, hairy rebels the Rolling Stones longed to be. Driving, fuzzy rhythms grind under Dylanesque phrasing, with singer Caleb Followill's whiskey-woozy voice and good-time attitude never obscuring his obvious fears." Not all critics were impressed by the album. Scott Hreha wrote for the Web site Popmatters (July 7, 2003) that the band "imbues its performances with an admirable jolt of energy, but the songs are so generic that the only thing left at the record's conclusion is the feeling of how hollow and insubstantial the whole thing is."

In 2004 Kings of Leon released their second album, *Aha Shake Heartbreak*, in the U.K., where it debuted at number three on the charts, with three songs later entering the singles charts. (The album was released n the U.S. in 2005 and reached the *Billboard* 200.) The band's new sound, which had moved away from southern rock and taken on a taut, post-punk-influenced angularity, reflecting the influences of bands including Wire and the Strokes, was welcomed by critics and fans alike. The album's success greatly expanded the band's popularity at home and abroad, and Kings of Leon received a further boost in visibility when they embarked on a tour supporting the hugely popular Irish band U2. They added to that momentum when they opened shows for Bob Dylan prior to the release of their album *Because of the Times* (2007).

That work saw the band moving even further from the roots and garage rock of earlier material. Partly influenced by the reverb- and delay-heavy aesthetic of U2, the band turned to atmospheric instrumentation and less-conventional song structures; the resulting album got mixed reviews. Clark Collis wrote for *Entertainment Weekly* (March 30, 2007, on-line) that *Because of the Times* is "a more sonically ambitious beast, as evidenced by album opener 'Knocked Up,' which is nicely loose and seven minutes long. Indeed, with the exception of the relatively straightforward 'Black Thumbnail,' all the tracks here find the band experimenting, successfully, with spacey atmospherics. If less accessible on first hearing than its predecessors, the result is an epic wide-screen movie of a CD and the band's best to date." Andrew Beaujon, on the other hand, wrote for *Spin* (March 31, 2007, on-line), "What these guys need now is songs, and this LP sounds too close to unfocused jamming. Even when a tune really pops, like the single 'On Call,' it's just a feeling. The Kings have the potential to reach nirvana, but enlightenment is a long way off."

Caleb told the *Village Voice* (September 22, 2008, on-line) that *Because of the Times* represented the band's attempt to form a new musical aesthetic. "We wanted it to have a more professional feel than anything we've ever done," he said. "We've always thought that, you know, the music that we write, it all feels big to us but the production styles that have been used in the past, when we come out of the studio the songs felt smaller than when we were writing them. So this is the first record that we literally rolled up our sleeves and said, 'All right, man, we're not going to come out of here again and have a song that can't get played on the radio because it's so lo-fi that, you know, people can't put it up next to other music. We want it to be bigger.' And I don't mean popularity-wise. I mean, we want it to feel bigger and more professional."

In 2008 the band entered the studio to record its fourth album, *Only by the Night*, produced by Petraglia and Jacquire King. The album became the band's most commercially successful release, debuting at number four in the U.S.; reaching the top of the album charts in the U.K., Ireland, and New Zealand; and becoming the biggest-selling album of the year in Australia. It sold 220,000 copies in its first week, and the single "Sex on Fire" ranked at number one in Ireland, the U.K., Finland, and Australia and on *Billboard's* U.S. Hot Modern Rock Tracks. That song also brought the band its first Grammy Award, for best rock performance by a duo or group with vocals, at the 51st Grammy Awards, in 2009—a hint of the success the rockers would achieve the next year. The album's second single, "Use Somebody," reached number two in the U.K. and Australia and became the band's first Top 10 hit in the U.S. *Only by the Night* eventually achieved platinum status in eight countries, and the band toured extensively in 2008 and 2009.

Most critics had mixed responses to the larger sound of *Only by the Night*, which built on the expanded sonic palette Kings of Leon had forged with *Because of the Times*. Christian Hoard wrote for *Rolling Stone* (October 2, 2008, on-line), "The revamped sound doesn't always work: Cuts like the slow-burning murk-fest 'Cold Desert' feel like sub-John Mayer soul—bland and overly ponderous. But when the Kings find a gussied-up groove with teeth—like the effects-laden [Led] Zeppelin stomp of 'Crawl' or the pulsating, New Wave 'Sex on Fire'—they sound like rock heroes experiencing the joy of well-manicured sound." Some critics were wholly disappointed with the album, taking to task the band's simplified songwriting and more radio-friendly sound as well as Caleb's lyrics. Ian Cohen complained for *Pitchfork Media* (September 16, 2008, on-line), "Followill is more than happy to hoist himself on his own petard, doling his typical mix of stock characterization, open misogyny, and bizarre non-sequiturs. . . . 'Sex on Fire' turns out to be disturbingly literal, while the dopey travelogue of 'Manhattan' has Caleb waxing with the naïve enthusiasm of a senior yearbook quote."

In response to critics' use of the term "arena rock" to characterize *Only by the Night*, Nathan told Lauren Salazar for *New York* magazine (September 23, 2008, on-line), "Going into this record, I don't know if we necessarily set out to make a record that would sound good in stadiums or arenas, but we had the fortune of touring with bands like U2, Pearl Jam, and Bob Dylan, and we got to play to crowds that were much bigger than we've ever played before, especially in America. I think it's kind of hard not to subconsciously go to that place when it comes time to start the process of making a new record. We definitely wanted to keep it in mind that we would still be playing to smaller crowds in America—as opposed to the crowds in Europe, Glastonbury, all that stuff—so we didn't want to make a record that would alienate our audiences over here by songs that are way too big-sounding for the size of the room we're playing."

The band released a DVD, *Live at the O2 London, England*, in November 2009. In 2010, at the 52nd Annual Grammy Awards, Kings of Leon won the award for record of the year (not too be confused with album of the year), one of the most coveted of the Grammys, for "Use Somebody." The song, which reached number one on the U.S. pop charts, also brought the band awards for best rock performance by a duo or group with vocals and best rock song. (Kings of Leon was also nominated for best rock album of the year, but the award went to the pop-punk band Green Day for the record *21st Century Breakdown*.)

The popularity of *Only by the Night* and the subsequent Grammy wins confirmed that Kings of Leon had finally become as successful in the U.S. as they were overseas. Nonetheless, a backlash among some longtime fans and critics, who were disappointed in the band's new mainstream direction, coupled with the frequent pop-radio play of "Sex on Fire" and "Use Somebody," made the band members hesitant to embrace their recent success fully. "We definitely got bigger than we wanted to be," Caleb told Peter Gaston for *Spin* (December 4, 2009, on-line). "You feel like you've done something wrong. That woman in mom jeans who'd never let me date her daughter? She likes my music. That's f***ing not cool. You almost start doing damage control: When people ask you to do stuff, you're like, 'No, because I can already tell this record is going to get to a level where people will f***ing hate us.'"

In October 2010 the band released *Come Around Sundown*, the follow-up to *Only by the Night*. Produced by Petraglia and King, the album was somewhat less pop-oriented than its predecessor—a response to the backlash generated by that last release—but still boasted a sprawling sound and penchant for infectious hooks. The record earned mixed reviews. Andre Leahey wrote for the All Music Guide Web site, "This is super-sized, guitar-driven, modern rock pomp, a sort of *Only by the Night: The Sequel* aimed at those who prefer their KOL songs big and bombastic. Kings of Leon haven't gotten to the point where 'Use Somebody' is their default setting, but it *has* become their benchmark, and *Come Around Sundown* attempts to replicate that song's success while still giving the middle finger to Top 40 radio. Sometimes, it works. Other times, Kings of Leon sound like they've flatlined their sound while trying to streamline their appeal."

The members of the band all reside in Nashville. Nathan married the singer and songwriter Jessie Baylin in 2009. Caleb told Korina Lopez for the Vineland, New Jersey, *Daily Journal* (November 23, 2009) that although the members of Kings of Leon have strayed from Christianity, they still believe in God. "I had once wanted to be a preacher, but I got burned by a lot of people in organized religion," he said. "But we're spiritual; I pray and thank God for everything I have every day." McCormick observed, "That conflict between the spiritual and the earthly, between the promise of eternal redemption and the temporal pleasures of sex and drugs has been at the heart of some of the greatest rock and roll since Elvis Presley and Jerry Lee Lewis. And it is still there in the Tennessee genes of the Kings of Leon."

—W.D.

Suggested Reading: All Music Guide Web site; (Glasgow, Scotland) *Evening Times* p24 Dec. 11, 2003; (London) *Guardian* p38 Nov. 29, 2003; *Los Angeles Times* E p1 Jan. 31, 2010; *Rolling Stone* (on-line) Feb. 24, 2005

Selected Recordings: *Holy Roller Novocaine*, 2003; *Youth and Young Manhood*, 2003; *Aha Shake Heartbreak*, 2004; *Because of the Times*, 2007; *Only by the Night*, 2008; *Come Around Sundown*, 2010

Eric Piermont/AFP/Getty Images

Kirk, Ron

June 27, 1954– U.S. trade representative; attorney

Address: Office of the U.S. Trade Representative, 600 17th St., N.W., Washington, DC 20508

In 2009, according to data compiled by the Foreign Trade Division of the United States Census Bureau, the U.S. exported more than 18,000 commodities worth a total of approximately $1.5 trillion and imported some 24,000 commodities whose value totaled about $1.9 trillion. As the U.S. trade representative, Ron Kirk heads the 200-member federal agency responsible for enforcing trade agreements, ensuring that the nation's trading partners abide by them, and negotiating new agreements. Also known as the U.S. trade ambassador, he serves as President Barack Obama's principal adviser, negotiator, and spokesperson on trade issues. Kirk has served on the boards of directors of three companies, but until he joined the Obama administration, he devoted his professional life not primarily to business but to the practice of law and to politics: among other positions he has served as an assistant to a U.S. senator, as the Texas secretary of state, and as the mayor of Dallas, Texas. He won his first term as mayor with 62 percent of the vote and his second with more than 74 percent, "at a time when conservative Dallas was also voting for George Bush [for governor of Texas], and for much the same reason," Peter J. Boyer wrote in a profile of Kirk for the *New Yorker* (August 12, 2002): "pro-business policies and a personal affability that complemented a powerful instinct for building consensus." A Democrat who has described himself as a centrist, Kirk lost his bid for a seat in the U.S. Senate in 2005. For four years after that, he was a partner at Vinson & Elkins, one of the world's largest international law firms. In 2008 the *National Law Journal* named him among the 50 most-influential minority lawyers in the U.S. The first African-American to hold the post of U.S. trade representative, Kirk was confirmed by the U.S. Senate on March 18, 2009 and sworn into office two days later. He has stated his commitment to free trade, the right of workers everywhere to form and join labor unions, and the environmental protections included in current trade agreements. He is working to open new markets for U.S. businesses and, in the process, to see the creation of new jobs for Americans.

The youngest of the four children of Lee Andrew Kirk and Willie Mae "Ankie" Kirk, Ronald Kirk was born on June 27, 1954 in Austin, the capital of Texas. His family lived a short walk from the state capitol building, where, in the 1950s, as he has recalled, there were still separate water fountains for blacks and whites. Kirk has two sisters: Saundra Kirk, a Texas state employee, and Connie Kirk, a musician; his brother, Lee A. Kirk Jr., is deceased. His parents met as students at the all-black Huston-Tillotson College, in Austin. His mother taught at the elementary-school level in Austin's public-school system for more than 30 years. She was active in the Austin chapter of the National Association for the Advancement of Colored People (NAACP); later, as a member of the Austin public-library board, she successfully fought to prevent the closing of the only branch library in Austin located in a black neighborhood. Kirk's father had "a brilliant mind for science," Ron Kirk told Christine Biederman for the *Dallas (Texas) Observer* (March 7, 2002); he gained acceptance to several black medical schools after he completed his military service, but with a wife and child to support, he could not afford the tuition. Instead, he joined the

U.S. Postal Service as a mail carrier; after many years he became a postal clerk—the first black to hold that position in Austin. "My dad was smart as a whip," Kirk told Biederman. "He took all these civil service exams. And they'd let him take them, but then they'd burn his test. But they'd keep a corner so he could see his score[s]—95, 99." Suffering from a lack of intellectual stimulation on the job and harassment from white postal workers, Lee Kirk Sr. developed a drinking problem. He "was in some ways the most curious alcoholic you'll ever see," Kirk told Biederman. "He always made the house payment, put his kids through college, never slapped around his wife. All we knew as kids was, when we came home we had to be quiet, 'cause he was asleep. He hid it pretty well. . . . But when he got older, into his 50's, it got to be harder to hide." His father died in 1982, at 59.

Kirk's parents instilled in him and his siblings the importance of tolerance of other people. "I taught them to love everyone, to have respect for everyone's feelings and to be concerned about the welfare of any individual, regardless of who it is," Willie Mae Kirk told Jim Schutze for the *Houston Chronicle* (April 21, 1996). She also imposed strict rules of behavior on her sons and daughters. They were forbidden to chew gum or sip soda from cans while outside, for example, or use slang or so-called Black English, and they had to attend church and Sunday school every week. "Willie Mae's home was the sort where friends of her teenage children would stop and tuck in their shirttails before knocking on the door," Peter J. Boyer wrote.

Ron Kirk attended an all-black elementary school. He was bused to a middle school where African-Americans were a small minority. White children at his school often made racist remarks in his presence; then, when he returned home at the end of the school day, black children who attended black schools in his neighborhood taunted him: "They assumed you were an Uncle Tom and thought you were better than they were, because you went to school with white kids," Kirk told Biederman. At John H. Reagan High School, also in Austin, Kirk was again one of a small number of black students, but racism there was far less overt. Kirk earned good grades, sang with the school choir, played cello in the school orchestra, played basketball, and won election as president of the student council. As a high-school student—at the urging of this mother, according to Boyer—he also served as president of the Texas chapter of the Teenage March of Dimes and belonged to Jack and Jill of America, which encouraged community service among black teens. He graduated from Reagan in June 1971.

Kirk next enrolled at Austin College, a predominantly white liberal-arts school in Sherman, Texas, that is affiliated with the Presbyterian Church. While there he began to struggle with issues of racial identity. His inner turmoil led him to leave college in his sophomore year and return home (temporarily, as it turned out). With the help of Sarah Weddington, a friend of his mother's and an Austin lawyer (best known for successfully representing the prosecution in *Roe v. Wade*, which led in 1973 to the U.S. Supreme Court's legalization of abortion), he secured an administrative internship with Price Daniel Jr., the speaker of the Texas House of Representatives. Daniel was the president of the Texas Constitutional Convention that met for seven months in 1974 with the aim (which was not fulfilled) of drawing up a new state constitution. During that time, Kirk told Christy Hoppe for the *Dallas Morning News* (March 11, 1994), "I got my first taste of Texas politics, and I've been fascinated and in love with it ever since." He also became acquainted with Ann Richards, Weddington's administrative assistant, who later won election as the Texas state treasurer (1983–91) and governor (1991–95).

Kirk next returned to Austin College, graduating with a B.A. degree with honors in political science and sociology in 1976. He earned a J.D. degree from the University of Texas School of Law in 1979. In October 1981, after less than two years as an attorney for a private law firm in Dallas, he moved to Washington, D.C., to work as a legislative assistant to U.S. senator Lloyd Bentsen, a Texas Democrat. His job with Bentsen launched his "evolution to what I call practical politics, away from partisanship and from the worry about whether you define me as a conservative or a liberal," he told Boyer. In 1983 Kirk returned to Dallas, where he had a dual job: chief lobbyist for Dallas and assistant to the Dallas city attorney. In the former post he became a familiar figure among state legislators as he worked to secure funds and other benefits for Dallas; according to a University of North Texas press release (April 19, 1999, on-line), 90 percent of the proposed legislation he pushed for was passed. During that period he became friendly with Rodney Ellis, who served on the Houston city council then. "Ron never asked me to vote for something without giving me both sides of the story. He would give me the pros and the cons, and the political analysis, and that's the sign of a good lobbyist," Ellis recalled to Lori Stahl and Sylvia Moreno for the *Dallas Morning News* (June 4, 1995). "He had access above and beyond others, but he never abused that," Ellis continued. "Even when he knew that I probably wouldn't vote with him, he still would be around to advise me on other issues. He had the ability to develop trust with members of the Legislature. Clearly, he was one of the most effective lobbyists in Austin."

In 1989 Kirk became a shareholder with Johnson & Gibbs, one of Dallas's largest law firms. His job entailed lobbying for corporations, among them Southwest Airlines, the Dallas Area Rapid Transit Authority, the Coors Brewing Co., and the Texas Association of Builders. Lobbying, he told A. Phillips Brooks for the *Austin American-Statesman* (March 20, 1994), "has given me an understanding that government is about balancing competing interests and coming up with a fair, efficient way of providing services." Kirk left Johnson & Gibbs in 1994. (The firm folded the next year.)

Earlier, in 1992, Governor Ann Richards had appointed Kirk to the Texas General Services Commission, the state's main purchasing agency; he chaired the commission in 1993. His service as a commissioner ended in March 1994, when Richards asked Kirk to replace John Hannah as Texas's secretary of state, after Hannah resigned to take a federal judgeship. Despite having to take a pay cut and commute to Austin daily, Kirk agreed to fill the rest of Hannah's term. Sworn in on April 4, 2004, Kirk was the first black man to serve as Texas secretary of state, an appointed position. (An African-American woman, Myra McDaniel, held the post from 1984 to 1987.) Kirk's primary responsibility was to ensure the proper implementation of election laws in Texas. He also tried to increase voter turnout.

In September 1994, two months after Steve Bartlett announced that he would not seek a second term as the mayor of Dallas, Kirk threw his hat into the ring for the mayoralty. "I became convinced some time ago that the most dynamic job in American politics was being the mayor of a big city, and I had decided a long time ago that if I ever did run, that there was only one job that I was interested in, and that was being mayor of Dallas," Kirk told Hans J. Massaquoi for *Ebony* (September 1995). When his term as secretary of state ended, he began campaigning for mayor.

Dallas, which is home to about 1.2 million people, is the eighth-most-populous city in the U.S. Its day-to-day administration is handled by the city manager, who is appointed by the city council; the mayor serves mainly as the head of the council, the city's policy-making body. The council, whose members are elected, meets only two evenings a month. Its members—including the mayor—were paid only $50 a week in 1994, and all had other jobs as well. In January 1995 Kirk had joined the Dallas law firm Gardere & Wynne (now Gardere Wynne Sewell) as a partner, leading some Dallasites to oppose his candidacy because they believed that his work with the firm (as well as the connections he had made as a lobbyist) would influence his decisions as mayor. Addressing such fears, Kirk told Lori Stahl for the *Dallas Morning News* (April 28, 1995) that one of the reasons he had joined Gardere & Wynne was that it seldom handled cases linked to the city, and he promised that he would recuse himself from any that were. In his campaign he talked about his intention to bring civility back to city-council meetings, which were known for constant bickering among members and even, on occasion, fistfights. He also pledged to assist the city's small businesses, keep jobs in Dallas, lure more companies to the Dallas area, and strengthen the police force.

On May 6, 1995, with his name and those of six other candidates on the ballot, Kirk captured 62 percent of the vote to win the election. His closest competitor, Darrell Jordan, a white lawyer, received 23 percent. Overall, 97 percent of the blacks, 42 percent of the whites, and 14 percent of the Hispanics who came to the polls that day chose Kirk to be Dallas's next mayor. About a quarter of registered African-Americans turned out to vote, nearly double the usual number. Kirk was reelected in 1999 with more than 74 percent of the vote.

During his tenure as mayor, Kirk restored order to city-council meetings and secured annual salaries for himself and other council members. By 1999, according to a University of North Texas press release (April 10, 1999, on-line), he had lowered taxes and attracted nearly 20,000 new jobs to the Dallas area. He had also campaigned successfully for the passage of a multimillion-dollar public-works bond measure, including $246 million for a project that will transform land along the Trinity River into the nation's largest urban park. The project includes the construction of three bridges designed by the renowned Spanish architect Santiago Calatrava. In addition, Kirk had successfully pushed for the construction of a $230 million sports arena to guarantee that the Dallas Mavericks, a basketball team, and the Dallas Stars, a hockey team, would remain in the city for the next 30 years. "As mayor," Jim Yardley wrote for the *New York Times* (July 16, 2002), "he avoided confrontational politics and cultivated a reputation for building alliances with the city's powerful white business establishment."

Kirk resigned from his mayoral post in November 2001 to run for the U.S. Senate seat held by the Republican Phil Gramm, who had announced that he would not seek reelection to a fourth term. He won the Democratic primary and in the general election faced John Cornyn, the Texas attorney general. During Kirk's years as the mayor of Dallas, he and the then–Texas governor, George W. Bush, a Republican, had maintained friendly relations, and he had "often voiced his support for Mr. Bush," Jim Yardley wrote for the *New York Times* (November 6, 2002). But President Bush repeatedly criticized Kirk during the latter's Senate campaign. "He's not the right man for the United State Senate as far as I'm concerned," Bush said, as quoted on abc.com (October 2, 2002). "I don't need an obstructionist, I need a positive influence." Bush, who had remained extremely popular in his home state, left Washington, D.C., several times to campaign for and raise funds for Cornyn in Texas, as did First Lady Laura Bush. Kirk positioned himself as a centrist, but the lead he enjoyed early on in polls narrowed, and on Election Day Cornyn triumphed, with 53 percent of the vote to Kirk's 43 percent. "The Democrats faced long odds," Yardley wrote the next day, noting that Republicans held every state office in Texas that year and had "dominated" statewide elections in Texas for the last decade. No African-American has won election to the U.S. Senate from any southern state since 1881.

After the election Kirk joined Vinson & Elkins as a partner. He represented Kohlberg Kravis Roberts and the Texas Pacific Group when, in 2007, along with Goldman Sachs, they purchased the energy company TXU for $45 billion, in the largest leveraged buyout to date. In addition, a national coalition of energy companies known as Compete hired Kirk as its co-chairman, to assist in its efforts to maintain the deregulation of Texas's retail-electricity market. In the six years that followed that deregulation, consumers had complained with growing anger about steadily rising costs. "Thus far, all of the debate about competition and open markets has been relative to what's happened to prices, without a lot of thought or attention to the fact that since we've gone to an open and competitive market, the amount of investment and potential for innovation has increased," Kirk declared to Elizabeth Souder, a *Dallas Morning News* (January 22, 2008) reporter. In 2007, 2008, and 2009 Kirk was cited among the nation's top government-relations attorneys by *The Best Lawyers in America*, a peer-reviewed guide.

President-elect Obama announced his nomination of Kirk as the U.S. trade representative on December 19, 2008. "As Mayor of Dallas, Ron helped steer one of the world's largest economies," Obama said. "He has seen the promise of trade, but also its pitfalls. And he knows there is nothing inconsistent about standing up for free trade and standing up for American workers. As a leader, negotiator, and principled proponent of trade, Ron will help make sure that any agreements I sign as President protect the rights of all workers, promote the interests of all Americans, and preserve the planet we all share." While many of Kirk's Dallas colleagues applauded the nomination, some others greeted it with trepidation. Union leaders expressed displeasure with what they viewed as Kirk's tendency to favor business rather than labor, and though he had publicly supported the North American Free Trade Agreement (NAFTA), some trade experts voiced uncertainty about his stances regarding labor laws and environmental standards. At the nomination press conference, Kirk tried to put such worries to rest, pledging to work toward stronger labor and environmental standards. "My responsibility as the president's U.S. trade rep is to administer all aspects of our trade policy, including that part of our policy that meets our environmental objectives and takes care of America's workers," he said. "My agenda is the president's agenda."

In March 2009, during the Senate Finance Committee's confirmation hearings for him, the public learned that Kirk owed nearly $10,000 in back taxes. (Kirk had claimed excessive deductions for season tickets to Dallas Mavericks games while mayor and for tax-preparation fees, and he had failed to report as income speaking fees he had donated to Austin College.) Kirk agreed to pay the back taxes and was confirmed by the Senate by a vote of 92 to five.

In its purest sense, "free trade" means trade with no restrictions imposed by governments, but in reality barriers to completely free trade exist everywhere, in such forms as tariffs, import quotas, and agricultural subsidies (which artificially inflate prices). The U.S. and the 152 other nations that are members of the World Trade Organization account for all but about 3 percent of international trade. The U.S. has signed a half-dozen regional trade agreements (among them, in addition to NAFTA, the Dominican Republic–Central America–United States Free Trade Agreement and the Asia-Pacific Economic Cooperation Forum) and bilateral agreements with 20 countries—Australia, Bahrain, Canada, Chile, Colombia, Costa Rica, Dominican Republic, El Salvador, Guatemala, Honduras, Israel, Jordan, Mexico, Morocco, Nicaragua, Oman, Panama, Peru, Singapore, and South Korea. (The pacts with Colombia, Panama, and South Korea have not yet gone into effect, because Congress has not approved and implemented them.) Canada and Mexico buy about one-third of U.S. exports, and China, Japan, and the United Kingdom about 15 percent. A third of the items the U.S. imports come from Canada and China; another one-fifth come from Mexico, Japan, and Germany. In 2009 the U.S. trade deficit was $380.7 billion—that is, the value of commodities imported exceeded the value of commodities exported by $380.7 billion. Much of the trade deficit stems from imports of petroleum products, cars, and consumer goods including clothing, electronic devices, and furniture. The U.S. also exports services—all economic activities other than those related to agriculture, mining, and manufacturing, in such areas as tourism; transportation; engineering, architecture, and construction; data processing and exchange and other information-related activities; education and training; entertainment; finance and insurance; and legal, accounting, advertising, and other professional endeavors. With regard to services, U.S. exports exceed imports in value.

In a year-end report posted on the U.S. trade representative's Web site (ustr.gov, December 21, 2009), Kirk's office listed its many accomplishments in the nine months since his appointment. "We know that trade policy that expands export opportunities can create jobs in American communities and put dollars in the pockets of American families," Kirk stated, as quoted in the report. "This year, USTR's efforts have focused on doing just that. We seized new opportunities for American businesses and workers in the global marketplace, tackled long-standing trade barriers and trouble spots, advanced U.S. interests through cooperation with our partners around the world, and sought to open a new conversation on trade here at home. In 2010, we will redouble our efforts to employ trade as a powerful tool for American job creation and economic growth." Accomplishments in 2009 included the opening or reopening of markets for U.S. exports of beef, poultry, and pork and the lifting of some overseas restrictions on their sales;

the negotiation of several agreements with China to prevent Internet piracy and theft of other intellectual properties, for example, and remove obstacles to sales to China of American-made products including medical devices and green-energy hardware; the strengthening of trade ties with countries including Turkey, Sri Lanka, Mauritius, the Maldives, Egypt, Pakistan, Afghanistan, Mongolia, and the Central Asian nations of Kazakhstan, Kyrgyzstan, Tajikistan, Turkmenistan, and Uzbekistan.

According to Christine Biederman, the six-foot two-inch Kirk "has charisma, a strange magnetism that makes people want to be near him, to shake his hand, to be acknowledged by him." For his extensive charitable activities, Kirk has earned honors including the Volunteer of the Year award from the Dallas chapter of Big Brothers/Big Sisters, in 1992, the Woodrow Wilson Center Award for Public Service, in 2000, and the Anti-Defamation League's Jurisprudence Award, in 2004. He and the former Matrice Ellis married in 1987. His wife is currently a managing partner at Heidrick & Struggles, an executive search firm. The Kirks have two daughters, Elizabeth Alexandra and Catherine Victoria.

—M.A.S.

Suggested Reading: *Dallas Morning News* A p1 June 4, 1995; *Dallas Observer* Columns May 18, 1995, Featured Stories Mar. 7, 2002; *Ebony* p32 Sep. 1995; *Houston Chronicle* A p1 Apr. 21, 1996; *New Yorker* p30+ Aug. 12, 2002; *Texas Monthly* p78 Aug. 2002; ustr.gov

Attila Kisbenedek/AFP/Getty Images

Kiviniemi, Mari

(kee-vee-NYEH-mee, MAH-ree)

Sep. 27, 1968– Prime minister of Finland

Address: Prime Minister's Office, Snellmaninkatu 1 A, Helsinki, P.O. Box 23, FIN-00023 Government, Finland

On June 22, 2010 Mari Kiviniemi became only the second woman ever to be elected prime minister of Finland, a northern European country located between Sweden and Russia. (The first, Anneli Jaatteenmaki, served briefly in 2003, before stepping down in the wake of a scandal over leaked government documents.) Currently, Finland is unusual in having two women in its top leadership posts; the presidency is held by Tarja Halonen, now in her second term. The pair govern a country that enjoys not only gender parity (more than a century ago, Finland became the first nation in the world to grant women both the right to vote and the right to run for Parliament) but a relatively high standard of living, an enviable educational system, and a strong social-security net. Among the challenges they face are an aging populace, high unemployment, and a fluctuating economy.

Kiviniemi is a member of Finland's Centre Party (Suomen Keskusta, commonly called Kesk), which currently holds 55 of the 200 seats in the Eduskunta, or Parliament. As prime minister she heads a coalition government that includes three other centrist parties in addition to Kesk—the National Coalition Party (Kansallinen Kokoomus r.p., usually called Kok); the Swedish People's Party (Suomen ruotsalainen kansanpuolue, or RKP), which represents the country's Swedish-speaking minority; and the Green League (Vihreä liitto).

A recent campaign-finance scandal, as well as friction between Kesk's liberal urban-based members and its more conservative rural members, has led to declining public support for the party. Party members hope that Kiviniemi will be able to reinvigorate Kesk and strengthen its image before the next parliamentary elections, due to be held in March 2011. "Does the 41-year-old Ms Kiviniemi have what it takes to put an end to her party's decline?" a reporter for the EIU ViewsWire (June 29, 2010) wrote. "On the one hand, she has an untainted public image, which many older Kesk heavyweights lack. She has the capacity to boost party support in urban constituencies, as she is likely to appeal to those at the centre who see the National Coalition Party—the other main governing party, alongside the smaller Green Party and Swedish People's Party—as too conservative and to whom the Social Democrats (SDP) are too far on the left. On the other hand, her liberal opinions will alienate many rural Kesk voters, who may channel their frustration by voting for the rightist populist party, True Finns. At the end of the day, the future of Kesk will be affected by not only what their leader represents, but also what kind of political decisions she makes and the policy programme she advocates at next year's election. If Ms Kiviniemi manages to revamp the party's image, there is a chance that she will succeed in reversing its decline in the polls."

Mari Johanna Kiviniemi was born in Seinäjoki, a city in Southern Ostrobothnia, Finland, on September 27, 1968 to Antti Toivo Iisakki Kiviniemi and Kaija Maija (Vihinen) Kiviniemi. Some sources state her father's occupation as agronomist and agricultural counselor; others say that he was a chicken farmer. Kiviniemi attended school in the Finnish municipality of Jalasjärvi, and as a teenager she spent a year as an exchange student in Germany. In 1988 she moved to Finland's capital to study economics and political science at the University of Helsinki, where she served as the secretary general for the Centre Party's student union. In 1994 she earned a master's degree.

From 1990 to 1992 Kiviniemi served as vice chair of the Nordic Centre Party Youth League, and in 1991, while still a student, she made an unsuccessful parliamentary run. In 1993 she worked as a trainee for the Finnish Competition Authority, a government organization that monitors competition among businesses. The following year she became the vice chair of the South Ostrobothnia Region Centre Party, a post she held until 2000.

In 1995, by a margin of nearly 10,000 votes, Kiviniemi was elected to represent the largely rural Vaasa constituency, which includes the administrative regions of Ostrobothnia, Central Ostrobothnia, and Southern Ostrobothnia, in Parliament. She served on several parliamentary committees and was also a member of the Finnish Delegation to the Nordic Council (1995–99), an organization that brings together delegates from the legislatures of the Nordic countries—Denmark, Iceland, Norway, and Sweden as well as Finland—to address issues affecting them.

Kiviniemi was reelected to Parliament for the Vaasa constituency in 1999 and 2003, and in 2007 she was elected to represent the Helsinki constituency. Over the course of her parliamentary career, she held numerous posts, including vice chair of the Commerce Committee (1999–03); member of the Grand Committee (2003–05 and 2006–07), which focuses on European Union affairs; vice chair of the Foreign Affairs Committee (2003–04 and 2006–07); and deputy member of the Finance Committee (2007). During her third term she chaired the Parliamentary Supervisory Council, which oversees the Bank of Finland. She was also a supervisory board member of various businesses, including the federally owned transportation company VR Group Ltd; Lännen Tehtaat Oyj, a food-production company; and Leonia Bank.

In 2003 Kiviniemi was made vice chair of the Centre Party's parliamentary group, and until 2008 she served as the deputy party leader. In 2004, the year she was elected to the Helsinki City Council, she advised Prime Minister Matti Vanhanen on economic policy. She subsequently spent half a year, from September 2005 to March 2006, filling in for the minister for foreign trade and development, who was on maternity leave. That post put Kiviniemi in charge of economic relations between Finland and its neighboring countries.

Kiviniemi became minister of public administration and local government in April 2007. She was the only Centre Party candidate in the 2007 election to win a seat for the Helsinki constituency.

In December 2009 Vanhanen announced his retirement as leader of the Centre Party, citing pending surgery as his main reason. Some believed, however, that the release of a tell-all book by a former girlfriend of his contributed to his decision, while others pointed to a recent campaign-financing scandal surrounding Vanhanen and the Centre Party as a major factor. (In 2008 the public had learned that both the Centre Party and the National Coalition Party had received large contributions from businesses seeking favors.)

After Kiviniemi, a relatively unknown yet experienced politician, announced her intention to run for leader of the Centre Party in early 2010, she quickly became the front-runner. Her direct approach to politics, her youth, and her scandal-free record made her a popular choice among her peers. Her two main opponents were Economic Affairs Minister Mauri Pekkarinen and Trade and Development Minister Paavo Väyrynen, both of whom were significantly older.

On June 12 the Centre Party elected Kiviniemi as chair. "I firmly believe that they [voters] wanted to look into the future, and therefore they gave the burden of responsibility to the younger generation," Kiviniemi told reporters following the vote, as quoted by Matti Huuhtanen for the Associated Press (June 12, 2010, on-line). "A new person always brings something new . . . and I want to reunite the party." According to a reporter for Agence France-Presse (June 13, 2010, on-line), Finland's leading daily newspaper, the *Helsingin Sanomat*, called Kiviniemi a "humble person who does not always take a me-me attitude," but also accused her of lacking charisma, asserting, "In her, the Centre Party got a leader and Finland a prime minister who can, at high level meetings, laugh in the right spot at jokes made in nearly all of Europe's main languages and sitting next to any leader. As long as she doesn't have to crack jokes herself."

Ten days later, on June 22, President Halonen appointed Kiviniemi to succeed Vanhanen as prime minister. The Parliament confirmed Kiviniemi by a vote of 115–56. (In Finland, the president nominates a prime minister only after the Parliament has negotiated the composition of the government and distributed seats to the various parties. The members of Parliament then vote on the nominee, who must receive more than half of the votes cast in order to be confirmed.)

Kiviniemi, who will be up for reelection in the parliamentary elections scheduled for March 2011, stated that she intended to follow the policies set forth by her predecessor and would concentrate on strengthening Finland's economy, which has suffered during the recent global economic downturn. In a poll conducted in October 2010 by the Finnish Broadcasting Co., only 19 percent of voters expressed support for the Centre Party. According to a writer for *Helsingin Sanomat* (October 19, 2010, on-line), voter dissatisfaction with the party stems from controversies involving rural sewage systems, among other issues. Nevertheless, Kiviniemi remained outwardly optimistic regarding the party's future. "There have been some bruises, but they come and go," she said, as quoted in *Helsingin Sanomat*. "There is no division in this party."

Kiviniemi plays the piano and the flute. A passionate opera fan, she served on the board of the Finnish National Opera Foundation from 2004 until 2007. She has been the chair of the Young Finland Association, which promotes youth fitness, since 2006. She enjoys running, in-line skating, and cross-country skiing. In addition to her native Finnish, she speaks Swedish and English fluently.

Kiviniemi married Juha Mikael Louhivuori, a businessman, in 1996. They have two children: Hanna, born in 1997, and Antti, born in 2000. Their family also includes two sons from Louhivuori's previous marriage.

—M.A.S.

Suggested Reading: BBC News (on-line) June 22, 2010; *BusinessWeek* (on-line) June 12, 2010, July 10, 2010; *Chicago Tribune* (on-line) May 28, 2008; *Washington Post* (on-line) June 28, 2010

Andrew H. Walker/Getty Images for Sunshine Sachs

K'Naan

(KAY-nahn)

Apr. 18, 1979– Rapper; poet

Address: c/o A&M/Octone Records, 113 University Pl., New York, NY 10003

"With his gentle nature, earnest lyrics and lack of flashy bling, K'Naan is somewhat of an anomaly on today's rap scene," Angela Pacienza wrote for the Canadian Press News Wire (June 29, 2005, on-

line). At the age of 13, the rapper and poet K'Naan fled Somalia—where he was born—during the start of that country's civil war. Now a Canadian citizen, he has used his music and poetry to shine a light on the struggles taking place in Somalia, and, on a personal level, to cope with the horrors he witnessed as a boy in that African nation's capital city, Mogadishu. "I think that my experiences have been . . . steering," he told Matilda Egere-Cooper for the London *Independent* (June 30, 2006). "They are not background experiences, but more the forefront of my life. I lived in Canada and the U.S. for half my life, but really I lived there as a [Somali]. . . . My longing for home had always been there with me. And I always felt, regardless of what citizenship they were able to afford me, that I was still in exile. I still feel that way because . . . home is not a geographical location. It's a feeling. So for me, that was the thing that really contributed to my poetry, my writings, and my music being the way it sounds."

Since the release of his debut album, *The Dusty Foot Philosopher*, in 2005, K'Naan has been a rising star in the hip-hop world. The record won the 2006 Juno Award for rap recording of the year and was shortlisted for the inaugural Polaris Prize, an annual award honoring the year's best Canadian album. In 2007 K'Naan received the BBC Radio 3 Award for world-music newcomer of the year. He has toured extensively over the past few years with such artists as Damian and Stephen Marley (sons of the famed Jamaican musician Bob Marley), Matisyahu, Mos Def, the Roots, Nelly Furtado, and Dead Prez. Speaking about the social relevance of K'Naan's music, Jarvis Church, a co-producer of *The Dusty Foot Philosopher*, told Angela Pacienza, "It's such an important part of what's missing from hip hop right now." He added that K'Naan conveyed his message in a way "that doesn't sound preachy." One of K'Naan's more well-known songs from that album, "Soobax" (pronounced "soo-bah," the word means "come out" in Somali), targets the warlords who terrorize his homeland. In Somali he urges, "Come out of my country / you've spilled enough blood / you have killed too many people / you have caused a ton of trouble / come out of my country." He then says in English, "I wanna talk to you directly / Somalia needs no gunmen / Mogadishu used to be a place / where the world would come to see / what to do / where to go / I got to be a refugee."

Though K'Naan has often referred to the dangerous environment in which he grew up, he has deplored the way in which American "gangsta" rappers, including 50 Cent, boast about their violent neighborhoods. In his song "What's Hardcore," K'Naan proclaims, "If I rhymed about home and got descriptive / I'd make 50 Cent look like Limp Bizkit." (Limp Bizkit, a metal-rap group from Florida, is not known for its "street cred.") "America has places like New Orleans with real struggles, and I respect those struggles," K'Naan told Chris Riemenschneider for the Minneapolis, Minnesota, *Star Tribune* (August 8, 2008). "But I'm talking about Mogadishu. It's a different level. That song is me talking to rappers who glorify their 'hood like it's the end of the world. [Somalis] are happy if we even get to live in their 'hood. Their 'hood is our salvation." K'Naan also explained to Adam Radwanski for the Toronto, Canada, *National Post* (August 5, 2005), "There are some artists that I think are ridiculous when they speak [about urban violence]. Kids I grew up with have the same feelings about it. . . . Imagine someone complaining about how rough it is because it's normal for them to hear gunshots in their neighbourhoods. And most of the kids I hung out with are talking about, 'Well, I've been shot. My parents [were] killed.' The tragedy level is so different." He added, "We can kind of see a certain exploitative aspect of [North American rap], which terrifies you when you're from my sort of background. To see anyone ever using it to their leverage is a problem. Our struggle is not something to be displayed as 'Hey, look at us, we're tougher,' or something like that. I like to present it as a matter of survival, rather than a matter of boasting." Following the release of his second studio album, *Troubadour* (2009), K'Naan won the awards for artist of the year and songwriter of the year at the 2010 Juno Awards ceremony.

K'Naan was born Keinan Abdi Warsame on April 18, 1979 in Mogadishu. He has an older brother, Liban, and a younger sister, Sagal. From birth K'Naan was surrounded by creative family members: his mother wrote poetry, his grandfather Haji Mohamed was a nationally celebrated poet, and his aunt, who performed as Magool, was one of East Africa's most popular singers. K'Naan wrote his first poem at age seven. "For [Somalis], our language is the memory bank of our community," K'Naan explained to Wade Hemsworth for the *Hamilton (Ontario, Canada) Spectator* (December 15, 2005). "We have installed every event, every important step of progress, every ideological change in our language. Our language is something we use for every purpose there is. It is the beginning and end, and poetry extends from that language."

K'Naan grew up in Mogadishu's Wardhiigleey neighborhood. Though that area would later be known as one of the most dangerous places in the world and earn the nickname "the river of blood," K'Naan told Robin Denselow for the London *Guardian* (May 25, 2007) that he can remember when, during his early childhood, his environment was "amazing, peaceful, and almost beautiful to a fault." His father, Abdi, immigrated to the U.S. when K'Naan was five years old and settled in New York City's Harlem neighborhood. Working as a cab driver, he would send money to his family. Soon he began sending K'Naan hip-hop albums, including Eric B. and Rakim's *Paid in Full* (1987). Though K'Naan did not understand English at the time, he memorized the raps phonetically, unconsciously learning the diction and technique that would later influence his rapping style.

In the late 1980s violence began to spread across Mogadishu, leading to the overthrow of the Somali dictator Siad Barre, as rival clans fought for control of the government. The unrest soon reached K'Naan's neighborhood. One day when K'Naan was 10, he and two friends found outside their school "what they thought was a rotten potato," Kathy McCabe reported for the Australian *Daily Telegraph* (December 22, 2005). The friends tossed the object around until a pin fell from it, revealing the object to be a grenade. K'Naan quickly tossed it away, blowing up part of the school. (No one was hurt.) Not long afterward militiamen chased K'Naan and three friends through the streets; K'Naan escaped, but his friends were killed. K'Naan's brother, who was jailed for bombing a federal building, narrowly escaped a firing squad thanks to his famous aunt, who pleaded for his release.

As the violence escalated, K'Naan's mother, Marian Mohamed, became determined to get her family out of the country. She walked to the U.S. embassy every day for a year seeking visas. Then, in January 1991, on the day before the embassy closed, a civil servant granted Marian Mohamed visas for her family. "We were from a poor neighborhood, probably the poorest and most violent in the country," K'Naan told Egere-Cooper. "She had no rights as far as the world is concerned to think that she could get us to New York City. How does someone come up with that ambition? But she did." K'Naan recalled to Nicholas Davis for the *Toronto Sun* (February 7, 2005), "We had to sell everything in our house just so we could buy plane tickets. We ended up getting on one of the last planes to leave Somalia before the country collapsed." K'Naan and his family joined his father in Harlem. He said to Egere-Cooper about his first impression of New York: "I remember asking my father, 'So this is America, huh?' How is it possible that there's this great big building that's vacant and there's homeless people sleeping in front of it?"

The family remained in Harlem for only a few months before moving to Canada. "There was a large influx of Somalis who were leaving New York to head to Toronto," K'Naan recalled to Nicholas Davis. "Canada was just a lot more open to immigration and it made it easier for relatives to stay together." They moved to Rexdale, a community in the northwestern corner of Toronto, Ontario. There, they lived on Dixon Road, in an area known as "Little Mogadishu" due to its large Somali population. In the beginning K'Naan found it difficult to adjust to his new life. "The first thing that kind of blew me away was that here I was 14 years old and I was expected to be a kid," he recalled to Davis. "I already had a very grown-up experience trying to survive a civil war. [In Toronto] my peers were running around and had few responsibilities and there was an expectation I would do the same. It was a huge disconnect for me trying to be a kid again."

K'Naan began to learn English and attended high school at the Kipling Collegiate Institute. "I was in school and wanted to learn and I would see the other kids making fun of the teacher. I thought this was crazy," K'Naan told Davis. "Here you have people who have the privilege to go to school and learn, something that wasn't always an option where I came from, and they were abusing the privilege." K'Naan dropped out of school after his sophomore year and became involved in a local gang; he has said that the gang—the Dixon Crew—formed less out of a desire to commit crime than as a way for culturally isolated Somali youth to find comradeship. The Dixon Crew's altercations with other gangs drew the attention of the police. K'Naan was arrested more than a dozen times on charges related to fighting and weapons. He was determined to better his life, though, and began to concentrate on writing poetry and songs. "I was an ambitious kid," he told Gerald Hannon for *Toronto Life* (December 2008). "I wasn't going to spend my life running from cops and living in these bad neighbourhoods. I didn't leave Somalia to make another Somalia for myself in Canada."

As he approached age 20, K'Naan, whose given name, Keinan, means "traveler" in Somali, decided to travel the world. While in Europe, perhaps on the strength of poems he had placed on Somali Web sites or local recordings he had made, he was asked to perform a spoken-word piece at a December 2000 concert held by the United Nations High Commissioner for Refugees in Geneva, Switzerland, to celebrate the organization's 50th anniversary. In his performance K'Naan criticized the U.N.'s policies in Somalia and its failure to publicly disclose what had been happening in the country. "I thought, 'This is the end of my career,'" he recalled, with laughter, to Chris Riemenschneider. "I could've just been the good entertainer and everybody would have been happy, but I had to say

something. How many kids who came from where I did, the streets of Mogadishu, would ever get that kind of chance?" Despite his harsh words, the audience gave K'Naan a standing ovation. Among them was the Senegalese singer Youssou N'Dour. N'Dour was so impressed with K'Naan that he flew the young poet to Dakar, Senegal, to record two songs for his 2001 compilation album *Refugee Voices—Building Bridges*. After touring with N'Dour's band throughout 2001, K'Naan returned to Rexdale. During that same year K'Naan met his manager and business partner, Sol Guy. (Guy, a big name in the Canadian hip-hop industry, has also managed the rappers K-OS and Kardinal Offishall.)

In October 2002 K'Naan contributed to a theme song for the Canadian arm of War Child, an organization that works to help children affected by war. Other Canadian artists involved in the project included the rapper Jelleestone, the singer Esthero, Jarvis Church of the R&B group the Philosopher Kings, and Red1 of the hip-hop group Rascalz. K'Naan's work on the song caught the attention of Church, who, along with the Philosopher Kings' guitarist Brian West, had formed the Grammy Award–winning production team Track and Field. (They had produced the singer Nelly Furtado's debut album, *Whoa, Nelly!* in 2000.) With Track and Field at the helm, K'Naan recorded *The Dusty Foot Philosopher*. Released in June 2005, the album combines K'Naan's poetic raps with hip-hop beats and African rhythms. "[K'Naan's] debut album is a rare masterpiece," Kathy McCabe wrote in her review. "A remarkable confluence of great beats, laidback fusions of reggae, rock, folk and African traditions and politically charged, socially conscious lyrics which actually have meaning."

K'Naan explained the meaning behind the album's title to Matilda Egere-Cooper: "It's one part dedication to a friend of mine, who I thought of as the dusty-foot philosopher, who died. But the second part is that I was thinking of how the West portrays Africa. When they show Africa, especially in those programmes that come on late at night, pleading for help, they often show children. And when they show children, they often pan the camera to their feet, and it's always dusty which is to portray poverty. But, I thought, I used to have those same feet. And now the people who are filming and making these statements to their culture, they respect me. I now have a place in their lives, the very people who are portraying the same child. I wanted to call that child The Dusty Foot Philosopher, the one who is articulate about the universe, but doesn't have anything." In 2007 K'Naan recorded a live album, *The Dusty Foot on the Road*.

On the subject of media representations of Somalis, K'Naan—like many others from his country—has objected to the depiction of people there in the 2001 film *Black Hawk Down*. Based on the journalist Mark Bowden's book *Black Hawk Down: A Story of Modern War* (1999), the film recounts the Battle of Mogadishu (or Battle of the Black Sea), in which several groups of American soldiers were stranded in the city—during the Somali civil war—after their Black Hawk helicopters were shot down in October 1993. Initially sent on a mission to capture two senior subordinates of the warlord Mohamed Farah Aideed, the soldiers were caught in a firefight that lasted more than 15 hours. In the end, 18 Americans and around 500 Somalis were killed. Unlike the book it was based on, the film, which focuses entirely on the struggles of the American soldiers, leaves out the fact that U.S. forces had orchestrated a missile attack months earlier on the home of an official who worked for Aideed. Known as Bloody Monday to Somalis, the attack had occurred during a meeting that included many opponents of Aideed, killing many important Somali religious figures and clan leaders and greatly impairing chances of a peaceful resolution to the war. Ultimately, *Black Hawk Down* fails to explain the reasons behind the Somali population's resistance to U.S. forces in their country. As Wade Hemsworth wrote, "By focusing on the individual sacrifices of the American servicemen instead of the hundreds of Somalis who died, and oversimplifying the context of the times, Somalis believe [the film] created a stereotype of their people as savages." K'Naan told Hemsworth, "Africa has always been portrayed in Western media in a way that makes African people cringe."

K'Naan's second studio album, *Troubadour*, was released in 2009. Most of the songs were recorded in Jamaica at the legendary Tuff Gong studios and in Bob Marley's home studio. (K'Naan is close friends with Damian and Stephen Marley.) As with his debut album, *Troubadour* provides insight into culture and conditions in Somalia. In the song "ABC's," K'Naan raps about the current situation of Somali children, raised in an atmosphere of violence: "More pistols, Russian revolvers / We shootin' all that is normal / But it ain't just because we want to / We ain't got nowhere we can run to / Somebody, please press the undo / They only teach us the things that guns do." K'Naan told Elizabeth Blair for the National Public Radio program *Morning Edition* (January 6, 2009, on-line), "So it's called ABC's, and it's about how, you know, being born in a certain place changes everything in your destiny. When you hear the song, I got the kids choir singing, 'They don't teach us the ABCs, we play on the hard concrete, all we got is life on the streets.' And for [Somalis], that is very true." K'Naan also comments on the recent surge of Somali pirates, who earn money by holding ships hostage and demanding ransom. In "Somalia" he raps, "So what you know about the pirates terrorize the ocean? / To never know a single day without a big commotion / It can't be healthy just to live with such a steep emotion / And when I try and sleep, I see coffins closin'."

In early 2010 K'Naan's song "Wavin' Flag," from *Troubadour*, was rerecorded by a group of Canadian musicians to raise money for the people of Haiti following the devastating January 12 earthquake. "Wavin' Flag," with references to war, poverty, and hunger, was rewritten to include lyrics specific to Haiti. In addition to K'Naan, the 57 artists who participated in the recording included Nelly Furtado, Avril Lavigne, Drake, Fefe Dobson, and Justin Bieber. The single debuted at number one on the *Billboard* Canadian Hot 100 chart on March 12; proceeds have gone to Haitian relief efforts via the Free the Children, War Child Canada, and World Vision Canada charities. "Wavin' Flag" was again reworked in March 2010—to invoke a more joyous, celebratory mood—when Coca-Cola chose K'Naan's song as the official anthem for its 2010 FIFA World Cup ad campaign.

On October 20, 2010, K'Naan was honored with the British MOBO Award for best African act. According to mobo.com, since they were introduced, in 1996, the awards have "played an instrumental role in elevating black music and culture to mainstream popular status in the UK." An estimated 250 million people worldwide watched the televised awards ceremony.

K'Naan participates in the Messenger of Truth project for the United Nations Human Settlements Programme (UN-HABITAT), the U.N. agency that promotes sustainable urban development and shelter for people around the world. In that capacity the rapper works to raise public awareness of the agency's goals and provide a voice for the world's disadvantaged youth. He has also appeared in an installment of *4REAL*, a documentary television series (co-created by Sol Guy) that follows celebrity guests as they travel the world to meet young men and women who are effecting positive change in their regions. K'Naan's installment focused on Kibera, the largest slum in Nairobi, Kenya, and in all of East Africa.

A slim, soft-spoken man, K'Naan is an observant Muslim who abstains from smoking, drinking, using drugs, and eating pork. He is also an avid reader. K'Naan's wife, Deqa, is a pharmacist. The couple live in Toronto with their two young sons.

—M.A.S.

Suggested Reading: *Calgary (Alberta, Canada) Herald* E p3 July 23, 2005; knaanmusic.ning.com; (London) *Independent* p14 June 30, 2006; thedustyfoot.com; (Toronto, Canada) *Globe and Mail* R p1 Apr. 2, 2007; *Toronto Life* p72+ Dec. 2008; *Toronto Sun* p20 Feb. 7, 2005

Selected Recordings: *The Dusty Foot Philosopher*, 2005; *The Dusty Foot on the Road*, 2007; *Troubadour*, 2009

Matt Carr/Getty Images

Korine, Harmony

(kor-EEN)

Jan. 4, 1973– Filmmaker

Address: c/o Endeavor Agency, 9601 Wilshire Blvd., Third Fl., Beverly Hills, CA 90212

"What I hate is the middle ground," the filmmaker Harmony Korine told Simona Chiose for the Toronto, Canada, *Globe and Mail* (September 11, 1997). "People should love your films, or people should hate your films. . . . The best reaction is to make people feel confused about what's funny and not funny . . . to make people feel guilty about their reaction. I like people to question their reaction." Since the photographer Larry Clark discovered him, when Korine was 17, the filmmaker has indeed provoked reactions that range from revulsion among mainstream critics to admiration from an avant-garde community that labeled him a "wunderkind" and identified him as representative of a new generation of auteurs with original, raw perspectives. Korine made his name as the screenwriter for *Kids* (1995), a realistic depiction of rampant sex and drug use among a group of urban youths, some of whom were spreading HIV. He made his directorial debut with *Gummo* (1997), a surrealistic portrayal of amorality among residents of an impoverished rural American town, which earned him immense respect from the independent-film community. Two years later he wrote and directed *Julien Donkey-Boy* (1999), which he made according to rules prescribed in the Danish Dogme 95 manifesto, which were intended to preserve "purity" in film. In 2007, after a troubled ab-

sence from filmmaking, Korine wrote and directed *Mister Lonely*, the most conventional and biggest-budgeted film of his career, which centers on a community of celebrity impersonators. At the 2009 Copenhagen Film Festival, Korine's most recent film, *Trash Humpers*, won the DOX Award, which honors the festival's best documentary. Korine is a longtime fan of independent films, especially those of the avant-garde filmmaker Werner Herzog. He famously told Sean O'Hagan for the London *Guardian* (March 13, 1999), "Plot disgusts me. Real life doesn't have plots."

Harmony Korine was born on January 4, 1973 (or 1974, according to the Library of Congress) in Bolinas, California, and spent most of his childhood in Nashville, Tennessee. When asked about his family and early life, he has offered mostly vague responses. In various interviews he has claimed that his parents were Marxist propagandists, children's-clothing vendors, or fur traders. It has been verified that his father, Sol Korine, was an Iranian-Jewish émigré who produced documentaries about the American South for the PBS television network in the 1970s. In some articles his mother's name is given as Eve Korine. Harmony Korine, who has an older brother, Avi, and, according to some sources, a sister, has described his childhood as "solitary." He attended "a progressive school that catered to people who were a little out of the ordinary," he told O'Hagan. In his teens he was diagnosed with attention-deficit disorder and was prescribed the drug Ritalin. He told Werner Herzog for *Interview* magazine (November 1997) that he had little contact with his parents: "It's not that they weren't good, they were just doing something else and I didn't know where they were." Nevertheless, his father was responsible for Korine's early exposure to film. "We didn't talk much when he was around, but every day after school, when I guess most kids would go home and do their homework, we'd go to the movies," Korine told Herzog. "By the time I was sixteen, I was seeing three or four films a day, including a lot of art films"—including works by the experimental filmmakers Rainer Fassbinder, Jean-Luc Godard, and Herzog. Korine was especially inspired by Herzog's surreal *Even Dwarfs Started Small* (1968), in which a prison is taken over by its inmates, all of them dwarfs. Korine told Herzog, "It was when I heard the girl screaming in the cave and saw the monkey being crucified in that film that I knew I wanted to make movies."

After graduating from high school, Korine moved to the New York City borough of Queens to live with his paternal grandmother, Joyce Korine. He went by the name "Harmful," in order to seem tougher. Unsupervised in the city, he spent much of his time in movie theaters, watching European and American avant-garde films; he also read voraciously about the influences of his favorite filmmakers. "It was exactly like falling in love," Korine told a reporter for the London *Guardian* (November 5, 1999). Korine also liked to skateboard and party with friends. He enrolled at New York University and studied English for one semester, then dropped out because he felt his creativity was being constricted. Korine worked as a production assistant on a couple of films, among them Paul Schrader's *Light Sleeper* (1992).

One day in 1993 Korine was skateboarding in Washington Square Park, adjacent to New York University, when he attracted the attention of Larry Clark, a photographer (born in 1943) best known for his portraits of alienated and debauched teenagers. The two struck up a friendship, and Korine showed Clark a short script that he had written in high school, about a 13-year-old boy whose father brings him to a prostitute. Impressed, a couple of years later, Clark asked Korine to write a full-length screenplay for him. Korine devoted three weeks to writing *Kids*, about a day in the lives of a group of New York teenagers as they skateboard, casually take drugs, skinny-dip, fight, party, and engage in unprotected sex, inadvertently spreading HIV. The events, which culminate in a drug- and alcohol-drenched party and a rape, were based on incidents in the lives of Korine's friends, some of whom appeared in the movie. "When we were casting the film," Korine told Edward Guthmann for the *San Francisco Chronicle* (August 9, 1995), "I was like 'Why should we use actors? My friends are right here.' There aren't many actors that I like anyway." Clark, who directed the film, used jerky camera work, which, coupled with the absence of well-known actors and what struck many as the naturalness of the dialogue, gave the movie the aura of a documentary.

Kids premiered in May 1995 at the Cannes Film Festival, in France, where it won the Golden Palm Award. It opened in the U.S. on July 28, 1995 to strong and conflicting reactions. "Take your choice," Roger Ebert wrote for the *Chicago Sun-Times* (June 4, 1995), "[*Kids*] is either (1) a searing and accurate cry for help from a generation without hope, or (2) a cynical exploitation film that skirts the edges of kiddie porn. Both views had their defenders at Cannes; I tend toward the first choice." In a review representative of the latter, Rita Kempley wrote for the *Washington Post* (August 25, 1995), "*Kids*, a disturbingly voyeuristic look at adolescent promiscuity, is virtually child pornography disguised as a cautionary documentary. . . . Except for pedophiles, it's hard to imagine who'll be drawn to this irresponsible Little Bo Peep show." Many critics, however, like Ebert, appreciated the film's harrowing portrayal of lost, amoral youths. "*Kids* makes no effort to sentimentalize," Guthmann wrote for the *San Francisco Chronicle* (July 28, 1995). "It doesn't flavor its story with sweet scents or mellow strings or false optimism; it doesn't twinkle and blush; and it never softpedals the immaturity, casual cruelty or toughness of these street kids." While the film failed to draw large audiences, perhaps because of its NC-17 rating (which was later changed to "unrated"), *Kids* became a cult classic, earning three Independent

Spirit Award nominations, including the one for best first screenplay (the two others were for best first feature and best actress for Chloë Sevigny), and one win, in the category of best debut performance, for the actor Justin Pierce.

Kids stirred the admiration of the Hollywood producer Cary Woods, who agreed to fund Korine's next project. Korine was also joined by the award-winning French cinematographer Jean-Yves Escoffier for his directorial debut, *Gummo* (1997), which was named after the fourth of the five Marx Brothers, of vaudeville and film-comedy fame. (The real Gummo Marx had been a child performer alongside his brothers, but his younger brother, Zeppo, replaced him when he joined the U.S. Army during World War I. Upon returning, he did not return to performing; instead, he went into business selling dresses and managing his brothers' careers.) The film consists of a series of vivid, often disturbing vignettes set in the small, rural town of Xenia, Ohio, which has failed to recover from a devastating tornado 20 years earlier and whose residents have sunk into extreme poverty, boredom, and amorality. (Though the real town of Xenia, Ohio, was damaged by tornados in 1974 and 2000, the settings and events in Korine's film are not drawn from that Xenia.) The film's main characters, Solomon (portrayed by Jacob Reynalds) and Tummler (Nick Sutton), sniff glue, torture and kill stray cats that they sell to a local butcher, and have sex (paid for by the minute) with the mentally handicapped relative of a local pimp. Korine had discovered Sutton on an installment of the *Sally Jessy Raphael Show* about children addicted to sniffing glue and spotted Reynalds in a Ritz Crackers commercial. Of the 40-person cast, only four were experienced actors, among them Sevigny; most of the others were nonactors from the Nashville area (where the film was shot), many of whom Korine knew from high school. "What I'm concerned with is the presentation of reality," Korine told O'Hagan. "I want people to feel like the images fell out of the sky."

Gummo debuted at the Telluride Film Festival, in Colorado, in August 1997 and was released in theaters in the U.S. the following October. Many reviewers criticized the film harshly for its lack of narrative direction or what they deemed to be its needlessly shocking images and freak show–like exploitation of poor, ignorant, or disabled people. In a scathing indictment written for the *New York Times* (October 17, 1997), Janet Maslin described *Gummo* as the "worst film of the year." In a similar assessment for *Newsday* (October 17, 1997), John Anderson wrote, "*Gummo* is a series of exercises in gross-out humor and outright depravity, all of which are nothing but what they say they are: postcards from hell. It's button-pushing, pure and simple, made on the cynical assumption that the only way to get our attention is to make a mess." By contrast, *Gummo* earned respect from such influential voices in independent cinema as the filmmakers Gus Van Sant and Herzog. Writing for the *Toronto Sun* (October 22, 1997), Bruce Kirkland called the film "an incredibly powerful social document" that lacks "a stated moral position, [and is] totally neutral in its depiction of the degradations inflicted on its subjects." Though it did not attract many moviegoers, *Gummo* earned accolades from independent-film festivals; it earned the Rotterdam Film Festival's KNF Award, granted to the best feature film that does not yet have distribution in the Netherlands. *Gummo* solidified Korine's reputation as a credible voice in independent filmmaking.

A Crackup at the Race Riots, Korine's fragmented, nonlinear novel, was published in 1998. Widely described as an antinovel, the book contains jokes, sketches, graffiti, lists, quotations, and suicide notes. Also in 1998 Korine directed a video for the song "Sunday," by the band Sonic. The video starred Macaulay Culkin and his then-wife, Rachel Miner. A series of manipulated photographs taken during the shooting of "Sunday" were exhibited at Taka Ishii Gallery, in Tokyo, Japan, and were published in a companion volume, *The Bad Son*. That same year Korine's film *The Diary of Anne Frank Part II* premiered at Ret.Inevitable, a one-night film "happening" presented in the anchorage of the Brooklyn Bridge, in New York City. The 40-minute film consisted of various images that were inherently unsettling: that of a handicapped man in a soiled diaper, for example, and another of a person burying a dead dog.

As Korine was preparing to make his next full-length film, he was contacted by Thomas Vinterberg, a founding member of Dogme 95, a collective of Danish filmmakers organized in 1995. ("Dogme" means "dogma" in Danish.) The filmmakers aimed to counter commercial, bourgeois elements in film by creating works in accordance with strict rules: no artificial sets, no props, no separately recorded music or sounds, no special lighting, and the use of handheld digital cameras rather than stationary cameras. Vinterberg, an admirer of *Gummo*, suggested that Korine make the first-ever American "Dogme" film. Korine had already written a script for his next film, *Julien Donkey-Boy*, but he abandoned it and worked only with an outline. The film was shot in Joyce Korine's home with dozens of cameras, which were either handheld, imbedded in the house, or hooked to characters' clothing or eyeglasses. Korine shot more than 100 hours of film and did not look at any of it until the editing process began. "It's like pouring chemicals in a bottle and shaking them up until they explode," Korine told Kevin Thomas for the *Los Angeles Times* (October 18, 1999). "What I'm doing is setting up and then documenting an explosion. I like movies you can live in. . . . I want to make everything look and feel as organic as possible."

Julien Donkey-Boy (1999) is a distorted, fragmented portrayal of a schizophrenic man and his highly dysfunctional family. The title character (played by Ewen Bremner) was based on Korine's schizophrenic uncle Eddie, who as an adult lived with his mother, Joyce Korine, for years before being institutionalized. Korine cast Joyce herself as the unnamed grandmother, a silent but constant presence in the film, and Herzog as the abusive, cough-syrup-addicted father, who regularly blasts his younger son (Evan Neumann), an aspiring wrestler, with cold water from a hose. Sevigny played Julien's sister, a pregnant amateur ballerina. Deliberately blurring the lines between reality and Julien's reveries, Korine attempted to paint a realistic picture of mental illness. "Any time I would see anyone depicted as mentally ill in movies, it was like *Rain Man*, this sort of cute, lovable eccentric," Korine told Chris Vognar for the *Dallas Morning News* (November 13, 1999). "I was disgusted by that. I wanted this film to show it how it really is." He dedicated the film to his uncle.

Julien Donkey-Boy premiered at the Venice Film Festival on September 7, 1999 and was released in Los Angeles, California, on October 15, 1999. While it received mixed reviews, it appealed to quite a few critics, who saw it as artistically superior to *Gummo*. "Without its highly expressive jagged, stylized quality, the film, in its raw emotional intensity, might well have been unbearable," Kevin Thomas wrote for the *Los Angeles Times* (October 15, 1999). "So steady is Korine's gaze, and of such a depth of compassion and understanding, that *Julien Donkey-Boy* acquires a spiritual dimension that allows it ultimately to become an act of redemption." Others found fault with the film's nonlinear structure or its grotesqueries. *Julien Donkey-Boy* was nominated for a number of awards at international film festivals, and Korine took home an Independent Spirit Award in the category of best director.

In the early 2000s Korine took part in at least two ultimately unfinished film projects. For a film to be called "Fight Harm," Korine harassed men bigger and seemingly stronger than himself on the streets of Manhattan until they attacked him physically. After a half-dozen fights, during which he sustained several broken bones and was arrested twice, he set the project aside. In 2000 Korine wrote a three-part film, to be called "Jokes," based on one-liners in the repertoire of the comedian Milton Berle (1908–2002). Each section was to be shot by a different director. After Van Sant completed the first part, called "Easter," financial problems ended the project. The screenplay for "Jokes" is included in the book *Harmony Korine: Collected Screenplays 1* (2002), along with those for *Gummo* and *Julien Donkey-Boy*.

Using a script that Korine wrote for him in 1995, Larry Clark directed *Ken Park* (2002), which was promoted as a sequel to *Kids* and premiered at the Telluride Film Festival in August 2002. Korine was not involved with the production of the film, which is about a sexually promiscuous group of skateboarding teenagers. Changes that Clark made to the script and Clark's claims to some of its ideas as his own infuriated Korine, and he and Clark had a public falling-out. Later, in interviews, Korine expressed regret about having agreed to write *Ken Park*.

Sometime after the release of *Ken Park*, Korine became unwilling or unable to maintain the life he had been leading. "I just wanted to disappear," he told O'Hagan. He also said to O'Hagan, "Looking back, it's hard to say what went wrong. I had come straight out of high school at 19 and wrote *Kids* and suddenly, a few years later I was burned out. I didn't really care about films or filmmaking." Rumors circulated that he and Sevigny had had a painful breakup and that he had deliberately set fire first to one house and then to another. (Both houses, which he had lived in, were severely burned.) Korine also drank heavily and, according to some sources, abused drugs as well. He went to France, where, not knowing French, he grew more depressed and isolated; rumors sprang up that he got caught with a crack pipe in a restaurant. He told Lorna Allen for *Film Ireland* (November/December 2007) that he next traveled to Panama and Peru and, with a group of fishermen, spent seven months traveling in search of a magical musical fish. Korine said that he eventually left the fishermen and returned to Nashville, where he quit drinking and began writing again.

In early September 2003 Korine reappeared in public in London, England. There, his friend David Blaine, the magician, undertook a stunt in which, suspended in a transparent Plexiglas case near Tower Bridge on the River Thames, he survived for 44 days straight without food and a with limited amount of plain tap water. Along with the director Steve Smith, Korine filmed Blaine and the actions of some of the thousands of spectators whose presence under the enclosure caused traffic jams in central London: hooligans throwing eggs and golf balls at the case, a Michael Jackson impersonator, a remote-control plane taunting Blaine with a hamburger. The resulting visual diary, called *David Blaine: Above the Below* (2004), aired on British television in December 2003. "The truly amazing thing is that Harmony seemed to capture all the things that I saw that stuck in my mind . . . ," Blaine told O'Hagan. "He's the only person I trusted to be true to the original vision I had."

Korine wrote his third feature film, *Mister Lonely*, with his brother, Avi. "If his art is a reflection of his emotional state," Lorna Allen wrote, "*Mister Lonely* is significant in that it is much more hopeful and poetic." Shot in France, Scotland, and Panama, *Mister Lonely* is about a commune of celebrity lookalikes or impersonators. The main characters are "Mr. Lonely," a Michael Jackson impersonator (portrayed by Diego Luna) and a Marilyn Monroe impersonator (Samantha Morton); others impersonated include Abraham Lincoln, Sammy Davis Jr., the Three Stooges, Charlie Chaplin, Shirley Temple, and the Pope (Werner Herzog). The highly anticipated film premiered at the Cannes Film Festival in 2007 and reached U.S. theaters in 2008. Reviewers noted its likable quirkiness and the limitations of its story. "*Lonely* is uneven and doesn't really go anywhere, but it has a wacky kind of charm with some good visual gags," Ray Bennett wrote for the *Hollywood Reporter* (May 25, 2007, on-line). "It's never clear what it all means or even if it's supposed to mean anything. Music and silliness get the picture through to its circular ending."

Korine told Paul O'Callaghan for an article on the British Film Institute Web site (October 29, 2009) that he felt exhausted and creatively stifled by the bureaucratic production process for *Mister Lonely*, and in its aftermath he wanted a more spontaneous filmmaking experience. The result was *Trash Humpers* (2009), a nonnarrative 78-minute film that follows a group of masked social misfits—including Korine and his wife—as they gallivant around the streets and alleyways of Nashville and take part in bizarre, perverse, and destructive activities, including "humping" trash. Korine shot the film on a VHS tape and edited it using two VCRs (rather than a professional editing machine), in an effort to approximate randomness, with the goal of "mak[ing] something that had its own logic and more closely resembled a found artifact or old VHS tape that someone had buried in a ditch somewhere," as he told O'Callaghan. When the film was shown on the festival circuit, critics reacted in by-now predictable ways, with combinations of disgust and confusion along with some praise.

In 2007 Korine married the former Rachel Simon, who turned 23 in 2009. Now known as Rachel Korine, she appeared in *Mister Lonely* as well as *Trash Humpers*. The couple live in Nashville with their daughter, Lefty, who was born in 2008. Though Korine remains committed to his vision of capturing reality through images on film, he is no longer quite as critical of conventional films as he was at 17. He told Sean O'Hagan for the London *Observer* (December 7, 2003, on-line), "I guess I'm not as angry and as confrontational as I was back then. I worked all that out the hard way."

—M.R.M.

Suggested Reading: *Dallas Morning News* C p9 Nov. 13, 1999; *Film Ireland* p32 Nov./Dec. 2007; *Hollywood Reporter* (on-line) May 25, 2007; *Interview* p88 Nov. 1997, p66 Nov. 1, 1999; (London) *Guardian* p10 Mar. 13, 1999; (London) *Observer* p5 Dec. 7, 2003; *Los Angeles Times* F p20 Oct. 15, 1999, F p4 Oct. 18, 1999; *New York Times* E p12 Oct. 17, 1997, E p1 Sep. 29, 1999; (Toronto, Canada) *Globe and Mail* C p5 Sep. 11, 1997

Selected Films: *Kids*, 1995; *Gummo*, 1997; *The Diary of Anne Frank Part II*, 1998; *Julien Donkey-Boy*, 1999; *David Blaine: Above the Below*, 2004; *Mister Lonely*, 2007; *Trash Humpers*, 2009; as writer—*Ken Park*, 2002

Selected Books: *A Crackup at the Race Riots*, 1998; *Harmony Korine: Collected Screenplays 1*, 2002; *The Collected Fanzines* (with Mark Golzales), 2008; *Harmony Korine: Pigxote*, 2009

Courtesy of Daniel Sieradski

Krauss, Nicole

Aug. 18, 1974– Writer

Address: c/o Louise Brockett, W. W. Norton & Co., 500 Fifth Ave., New York, NY 10110

"What is literature, really?" Nicole Krauss mused in an interview for *Bold Type* (May 2002, on-line), a Random House publication. "Boiled down to a single sentence, I'd say it's this: an endless conversation about what it means to be human. And to read literature is to engage in that conversation." With her first two novels, *Man Walks into a Room* (2002) and *The History of Love* (2005), Krauss invited readers to consider how nostalgia—that exclusively human sense of longing for people, places, occasions, and conditions from times past—can affect our ability to enjoy life and form meaningful connections in the present; she depicted characters whose only hope for attaining satisfaction in their current lives requires them to reexamine their complex relationships with the past. Profiled for the *New Yorker*'s "20 under 40" fiction issue, and asked to identify the elements that make for successful fiction, Krauss pointed to fiction's "ability to remind us of ourselves, of who we are in our essence, and at the same instant to deliver a revelation"—suggesting that fiction and memory can serve a similar purpose in our quest to understand who we are and how we relate to the world. "Art has the chance to offer us consolation," Krauss said to Ann Marsh in an interview for *Stanford* magazine (September/October 2005, on-line). "I mean to create out of the difficult and pedestrian experience of reality something that transcends, that is familiar but at the same time new." The novelist's most recent book is *Great House* (2010).

Nicole Krauss was born on August 18, 1974 in New York City and raised primarily in Old Westbury, on Long Island, New York, where her family moved a few years after her birth. She has an older brother and a younger sister; her mother is English, and her father, who trained during Krauss's childhood to become an orthopedic surgeon, is American. In Krauss's neighborhood the houses were far enough apart that she "didn't really know" her neighbors, as she told Gaby Wood for the London *Observer* (May 15, 2005), so she spent much of her childhood entertaining herself. That was not difficult for Krauss, whose vivid imagination and love of books kept her constantly occupied. "I read like an animal," Krauss said to the *Bold Type* interviewer. "I read under the covers, I read lying in the grass, I read at the dinner table. While other people were talking to me I read." By the age of 12, Krauss had read, among other works, a biography of the writer Henry Miller and the novels *The Fountainhead*, by Ayn Rand, and *Portnoy's Complaint*, by Philip Roth.

Krauss began to write at an early age. She said to the *Bold Type* interviewer, "My first opus was a book of poems put down in a spiral notebook at five or six, handsomely accompanied by crayon illustrations. But I guess I really started to write—and knew that's what I wanted to do—when I was thirteen or fourteen. There was a boy (isn't it always the way?) who was a few years older, and he wrote poems to me, and I wrote them back. . . . Why does one begin to write? Because she feels misunderstood, I guess. Because it never comes out clearly enough when she tries to speak." On the subject of writing verse, Krauss said in a 2005 interview with *Publishers Weekly* that was posted on her Web site, "Something about the directness and heightened emotional state a poem often demands appealed to me." Starting when she was in her teens, Krauss's poetry was published in literary magazines including *DoubleTake*, *Ploughshares*, *PN Review*, and the *Paris Review*.

After graduating from high school, Krauss headed west to study English at Stanford University, in Palo Alto, California. During her freshman year she attended a lecture given by the Russian-born Joseph Brodsky, who in 1991 became the U.S. poet laureate. After the lecture she gave Brodsky some poems she had written, not expecting him to respond. The next morning, however, Brodsky called her, and the two spent the next seven hours talking about and working on Krauss's poems. Krauss said in an interview with John Freeman for the Melbourne, Australia, *Age* (September 10, 2005), "[Brodsky] did the best thing a poet could ever do. He gave me a reading list." After graduating from Stanford with B.A. and M.A. degrees in English, in 1996, Krauss continued to read the works Brodsky had recommended; meanwhile, she attended Oxford University and the Courtauld Institute, both in England, on a Marshall scholarship. Brodsky also helped arrange for Krauss to curate a series of readings at the Russian Tea Room, in New York City.

Krauss has cited Brodsky as one of the greatest influences on her life and work.

Krauss was 25 years old, and had just finished working on a radio documentary about Brodsky for the BBC, when she decided to put her poetry aside indefinitely to experiment with longer forms. "I loved the feeling of waking up every morning and knowing there was something on my desk to return to," she told the *Bold Type* interviewer. "Something that was becoming larger and more complex over time, gaining weight and mass in my mind. When [the Brodsky documentary] was finally finished I suppose I felt a little empty. So I sat down and decided to try to write something bigger, and that became *Man Walks into a Room*." For Krauss, writing the novel was a completely new experience. "I felt in poetry that there was a possibility for perfection, and that was something that haunted me," she explained in an interview with Marya Spence for *Publishers Weekly* (August 9, 2010). "When I started to write *Man Walks into a Room*, I began to understand that novels are necessarily imperfect. And for whatever reason, that spoke to my nature. As I've gotten to know myself better as a writer, I've gotten very comfortable with the idea of working very close to the line of potential failure. Maybe because I feel that in that place, there's a potential for enormous discovery." Making the switch from poetry to prose meant learning a new set of rules, as Krauss explained to *Bold Type*: "Once I knew that it was going to be a novel, I started to read a lot of contemporary fiction—especially American—to try to figure out how to do it. *This is how you write a short sentence* (when reading [James] Salter), or *this is how you do good dialogue* (when reading [Philip] Roth), etc. It was very important to me NOT to write what some people call a 'poet's novel'—something driven largely by the momentum of language. I wanted a plot. I wanted characters that sounded like real people. I still wanted to use everything I'd learned writing poetry, but to a totally different effect."

Published in 2002, *Man Walks into a Room* is the story of Samson Greene, a Columbia University English professor who, after going missing for a week, is found wandering in the Nevada desert with no memory of an earlier time. The reason, the reader discovers, is that an operation to remove a tumor pressing on his brain has eliminated Greene's memory of his life after the age of 12. When Greene's wife, Anna, flies to Nevada to be by his side, she is devastated to find that her husband of over a decade does not recognize her. Greene lets Anna take him back to New York, but before long his inability to reconcile the details of his former and current circumstances proves too much for either of them to bear. He retreats to the blankness of the Nevada desert in which he was found, where a sinister neurosurgeon persuades him to participate in memory-swapping experiments.

Man Walks into a Room received mostly favorable reviews and was named as a finalist for the *Los Angeles Times* Book Award for First Fiction. Joy Press wrote in her review of the novel for the *Village Voice* (May 28, 2002, on-line), "Krauss is a fluent, thoughtful writer who takes on a lot of complex ideas and rarely loses her grip on them. . . . *Man Walks Into a Room* is a chilling addition to the annals of amnesia lit. It's a novel that grapples with the ephemeral experience of being human and the realization that we create a lifetime of memories that vanish when we do." Still, some reviewers felt that Krauss had failed in her stated goal of not writing "a poet's novel." Meredith Blum, for example, wrote for the *New York Times* (July 28, 2002), "Krauss seems to want to make every paragraph a poem: nearly every page contained a strained simile on the order of 'the dog crouched between them like a small country,' or 'Samson took out the Jack Daniel's that he'd been clutching to his chest like a wounded baby rabbit.'" Boris Kachka wrote that *Man Walks into a Room* has "the feeling of being too perfect," the quality Krauss had forsaken with her switch from poetry to prose.

In the months that followed the publication of her first book, Krauss signed a two-book, six-figure contract with the publisher W.W. Norton. Although *Man Walks into a Room* had brought Krauss the immediate success that most writers dream about, it also made her think differently about her approach to writing. "Getting a book published made me feel a little bit sad," she said to Kachka. "I felt driven by the need to write a book, rather than the need to write. I needed to figure out what was important to me as a writer." When Krauss finally sat down to start writing her next book, "there was a real loosening of control. There was no end in sight, no synthesis at all until finally there it was." She started by experimenting with writing in different voices, or from the points of view of different characters from her imagination; some of those voices led to dead ends, but one, that of Leo Gursky, an old man living in a dilapidated New York apartment, seemed to Krauss to have a story to tell. As a young man Leo was living in Poland when it was invaded by Nazi Germany. (Krauss's grandparents on both sides of her family escaped the Holocaust.) For two years he hid from the Nazis in the woods, afraid of being seen. Now his biggest fear is of dying on a day when no one has seen him; to combat his fear he makes sure that every day someone notices him, by dropping all his change on the floor at the grocery store, for example, or posing nude for an art class. Leo first appeared in 2004 as the narrator of a short story, "The Last Words on Earth," published in the *New Yorker*. After writing the short story, Krauss did not feel she was done with Leo, or he with her. "His voice felt very familiar to me," Krauss said, as quoted by Ann Marsh. "I don't remember scratching my head and thinking, 'What would an old man say here?' Leo's voice was a way of throwing my own voice. In his voice I can say things I simply couldn't say in my own. If you can imagine a fishing line casting out: everyone pays attention to the splash, but I'm over here turning the dial."

The story that resulted, which, in Krauss's own words, is "about the way in which books can change people's lives," was inspired in part by the life of Krauss's paternal grandmother. In *The History of Love* Leo Gursky has loved Alma Mereminski ever since he was a 10-year-old boy living in Poland before World War II. He even wrote a manuscript about their relationship, entitled *The History of Love*. When the Nazis occupy their hometown, Alma, pregnant with Leo's child, flees to America. Leo entrusts his manuscript to a friend and goes into hiding. Years pass and Alma, convinced that Leo has died at the hands of the Nazis, marries a man who will raise Leo's son as his own. When Leo locates Alma in America, he is heartbroken to find that she has married another man. Hesitant to disrupt his young son's life, he agrees to let the boy, Isaac, go on thinking that Alma's husband is his father. Leo becomes a locksmith and goes on with his life but vows never to love again. Decades later, an Israeli man traveling in Chile comes across Leo's book, which has been translated into Spanish by the friend to whom Leo entrusted it and published under the friend's name. The Israeli is so moved by the story that he names his daughter Alma. As a teenager growing up in Brooklyn with her mother and brother following the death of her father, the younger Alma comes into contact with the book herself, when her mother is hired by a mysterious stranger to translate it into English. Ultimately, Leo and the young Alma are brought together by the book.

Some reviewers admitted to thinking initially that Kraus had bitten off more than she could chew. Still, most felt that Krauss had succeeded in bringing the novel's different elements together by the end. In a review for the *San Antonio Express-News* (May 15, 2005, on-line), Steve Bennet wrote, "Krauss' imagination is more than huge enough to encompass this tightly woven contemplation of life, literature, loneliness and death. It's a book about family ghosts and their relative proximity, their cohabitation of our space, about 'the lives we could have led and the lives we led.' Krauss' writing is so engrossing, at once so fragile and brittle and sharp and pulsing with life, and the voices she creates are so real, that we are quickly absorbed into this mournful yet ultimately life-affirming novel."

The History of Love won the William Saroyan International Prize and the Edward Lewis Wallant Award. The Mexican film director Alfonso Cuarón, whose movies include *Y Tu Mama También* and *Harry Potter and the Prisoner of Azkaban*, is reportedly producing a film adaptation of the book, with a screenplay by the playwright Sabina Berman. According to imdb.com, the film's projected release date is in 2012.

Krauss's latest book, *Great House* (2010), came about through a process very similar to the one behind *The History of Love*, as Krauss explained to Marya Spence: "I wrote for a year or so, tons and tons of stuff, and lots of it ended up in the trash.

What emerged out of that were just these four voices." Just as the lives described in *The History of Love* intersect because of a book, the stories in *Great House* are connected by a desk that touches the lives of a disparate group of people. Krauss said in her interview with Spence, "In *Great House*, it wasn't so much the desk that mattered, but the burden of inheritance—emotional inheritance. This is one among many of the things I was writing about: what we inherit from our parents and what we pass down to our children. When I started *Great House*, I had just given birth to a child, and I had all these questions about, not only, what do we pass to our children literally through the umbilical cord, but also what we pass psychologically. I felt that heavily. . . . And so, somehow, the desk became imbued with all of that."

Krauss has been married to the writer Jonathan Safran Foer since 2004. The couple, who were introduced by their Dutch publisher, have two young sons. The Safran Foer Krauss family, as some publications have taken to calling them, live in a multimillion-dollar brownstone that occupies three lots in the Park Slope section of Brooklyn, New York. Because Foer and Krauss both published their second novels around the same time (Foer's was *Extremely Loud and Incredibly Close*), some critics were quick to point out similarities between the two books and to speculate on whether the two writers had helped shape each other's work. Krauss has insisted that she and Foer do not even read each other's fiction until it is in proof form. "These comparisons are laughable," she told Boris Kachka for *New York* (May 21, 2005, on-line). "People find what they're looking for." For the most part, Krauss avoids talking in interviews about her relationship with Foer.

In her interview for *Bold Type*, Krauss described her writing process: "I pace, I sit, I stand, I lean, I lie on the rug in a shaft of sunlight. I try not to answer the phone and then answer the phone. I also run. [The writer Norman] Mailer once said something about physically training, as if for a marathon, before beginning a novel. I'm a little like that, only during the process rather than before. I ran many, many miles while writing *Man Walks into a Room*. I probably ran all the way to Canada. It helps the ideas to come more easily, and also to release some of the tension. When I'm actually sitting at my desk chair, I write with one knee up, crunched into a little ball that would strike anyone who saw me as extremely uncomfortable. I try to write first thing in the morning. . . . And I use a computer." For Krauss, the most exciting part of writing is the feeling of liberation it offers, as she explained to Marsh: "A white page is a place that is totally uncensored. I have a way to exercise my freedom that I don't have in life."

—H.R.W.

Suggested Reading: *Bold Type* (on-line) May 2002; (London) *Guardian* (on-line) May 15, 2005; *New York* (on-line) May 21, 2005; *New Yorker* (on-line) June 14, 2010; *Publishers Weekly* p35+ Aug. 9, 2010; *Stanford Magazine* (on-line) Sep./Oct. 2005; (Toronto, Canada) *Globe and Mail* (on-line) Nov. 29, 2007

Selected Books: *Man Walks into a Room*, 2002; *The History of Love*, 2005; *Great House*, 2010

Stephen Lovekin/Getty Images

Lady Gaga

(gah-gah)

Mar. 28, 1986– Pop singer; songwriter

Address: c/o Interscope Records, 2220 Colorado Ave., Santa Monica, CA 90404

The Grammy Award–winning musician Lady Gaga has become as famous for her distinctive fashion sense and theatrical stage shows as she has for her pop dance music, and in less than two years, she has established herself as one of the most interesting and provocative pop artists to appear in the past decade. In November 2009 she became the first artist in the 17-year history of *Billboard*'s pop-songs chart to see four singles from a debut album reach the number-one spot ("Just Dance," "Poker Face," "LoveGame," and "Paparazzi"). At the 2010 MTV Video Music Awards ceremony, held on September 12, Lady Gaga won eight awards, including the prize for video of the year for her single "Bad Romance." She also shocked members of the audience and TV viewers by appearing onstage in a dress made entirely of raw meat—a garment similar to one that she wore for the cover photo of the

September 2010 issue of *Vogue Japan*. As of that month Lady Gaga had sold more than 15 million albums and 51 million singles worldwide.

"Instead of engaging the idea of 'realness,'" as other pop stars tend to do nowadays, Lianne George wrote for *Maclean's* (June 8, 2009), Lady Gaga has "created an absurdist alternate reality . . . where music, fashion, performance art and sex collide to create a commercial art supernova." "I always loved rock and pop and theater," Lady Gaga has said, as quoted on her Web site. "When I discovered Queen and David Bowie is when it really came together for me and I realized I could do all three. I look at those artists as icons in art. It's not just about the music. It's about the performance, the attitude, the look; it's everything. And, that is where I live as an artist and that is what I want to accomplish." A classically trained pianist, Lady Gaga dropped out of college to pursue music full-time. By the age of 20, she had written songs for pop artists including Britney Spears and Fergie, and by 21 she had signed a recording contract with Interscope Records.

Although Lady Gaga has often been described as being like nobody else in the American music industry, she has admitted that much of her persona has been shaped by the public characters and works of David Bowie, Freddie Mercury (the lead singer of the British rock band Queen), Andy Warhol, and other music and fashion icons. She told Fiona Sturges for the London *Independent Magazine* (May 16, 2009), "Some people say everything [in music and fashion] has been done before, and to an extent they are right. I think the trick is to honour your vision and reference and put together things that have never been put together before. I like to be unpredictable, and I think it's very unpredictable to promote pop music as a highbrow medium." Sturges also wrote, "Listening to . . . *The Fame*, a disco-tinged, sexually charged critique of modern pop culture, it's hard to distinguish Lady Gaga's sound from that of her chart-friendly contemporaries, from Pink to Christina Aguilera. Her songs are undoubtedly catchy but there is a gulf between how she perceives them and what the rest of us actually hear. What really sets Gaga apart from her contemporaries is that she is responsible for every part of her act. She directs her own shows, designs the sets, chooses the clothes and writes the songs. She never, ever lip-synchs. . . . She retains complete control over everything. If Gaga has spent the past two years fending off suggestions that she is nothing more than the product of a record-company brainstorm, she is not offended: 'It's exactly the kind of discussion that I want to start.'" Lady Gaga told Sturges, "I have found that my work has to be both deep and shallow. All of my songs have meaning, all of my clothing has iconography buried into it. But by the same token, it's just as special if you look at it in its shallowest form. A quick moment of melody, a beautiful dress. People think, 'Gaga's so sweet,' or 'Gaga sucks.' The point is that it's memorable. For commercial art to be taken seriously as fine art is a very unusual and difficult task. I think that a lot of people don't get it and a lot of people don't know what to make of me. And, you know what? I'm OK with that."

Lady Gaga was born Stefani Joanne Angelina Germanotta on March 28, 1986. (According to several sources, her birthplace is Yonkers, New York, but she has said that that is false.) She is the first of the two daughters of Joseph Germanotta, an Internet entrepreneur, and Cynthia (Bissett) Germanotta, a telecommunications assistant. She grew up in the New York City borough of Manhattan and began playing piano by ear at the age of four. She attended the Convent of the Sacred Heart, a prestigious, private, all-girls, prekindergarten-through-12th-grade Catholic school on Manhattan's Upper East Side. A straight-A student in high school, she was often scolded for wearing too much makeup and unacceptably short skirts. "When we had off-days where we didn't have to wear uniforms, I used to wear my [own] outfits and I would really get made fun of," she told a *China Daily* (April 27, 2009, on-line) interviewer. "It lost me my self-confidence and I suppressed myself for a while." A woman claiming to be one of Lady Gaga's school friends, however, told Michael O'Keeffe for the New York *Daily News* (February 7, 2010) that despite Lady Gaga's assertions that she was a social outcast in school, she was popular and often starred in student plays and musicals. "As soon as she would get in costume, she would be in character and would never break," the woman said.

Lady Gaga penned her first piano ballad at the age of 13 and at 14 had started to perform during open-mike nights at the Bitter End, a rock club in the Greenwich Village section of Manhattan. At 17 she was one of only 20 young people to gain early-admission to New York University's Tisch School of the Arts. After two years there she dropped out. She made a demo and, pretending to be her own manager, booked gigs at clubs around the city. "I know what I want; I know how to get it," Lady Gaga told Vanessa Franko for the Riverside, California, *Press Enterprise* (April 10, 2009). "I've sown my oats in every nightclub, every theater, community club from here to Ibiza. I became a pop artist the way rock bands become rock bands."

The singer and musician Wendy Starland attended one of Lady Gaga's performances in 2006. Afterward, she praised Lady Gaga's talents to Rob Fusari, a producer and songwriter who had worked with such popular artists as Beyoncé, Will Smith, and Whitney Houston. Fusari had been searching for a female lead for a rock band he hoped to set up, and he invited Lady Gaga to his Parsippany, New Jersey, studio to audition for that spot. With her bouffant hairdo and dark eyeliner, Lady Gaga, who was then still using her real name, did not impress Fusari at first. Then, at the piano, she sang one of her songs. "It was like the Earth had stopped," Fusari recalled to Michael O'Keeffe. "I'm listening to the lyrics and I'm thinking, 'holy s***, this is something new.' She was amazing."

Every day for four months, Stefani Germanotta commuted to Fusari's studio, where she was transformed into Lady Gaga. That name is derived from the Queen song "Radio Gaga." Fusari would greet his protégé with the song each day when she arrived at his studio. She had been trying to come up with a new name for herself when Fusari sent her a text message reading "Lady Gaga." "It was actually a glitch. I typed 'Radio Ga Ga' in a text and it did an autocorrect so somehow 'Radio' got changed to 'Lady,'" Fusari explained to Lisa Rose for the Newark, New Jersey, *Star-Ledger* (January 22, 2010). "She texted me back, 'That's it.' After that day, she was Lady Gaga."

Fusari, who knew that dance music was more commercially viable than rock, encouraged Lady Gaga to add dance beats to her songs. He overcame her unwillingness to do so by convincing her that Queen and other great bands had used drum machines without compromising their musical integrity. In a single day the two completed the song "Beautiful, Dirty, Rich," which was later included in *The Fame*. "That song opened the floodgates," Fusari told Lisa Rose. "We never went back to the rock stuff." After hearing her new demo, Island Def Jam signed her to a contract. Months later the company dropped her with no explanation. Undeterred, Lady Gaga continued to write songs and work with Fusari.

Meanwhile, Lady Gaga had become a frequent performer in clubs on Manhattan's Lower East Side. During one of her gigs, when her audience became too rowdy, she stripped down in order to get their attention. "I was sitting at the piano in my underwear and they shut up. It was spontaneous, but a turning point; I realised something about my nerve and I liked it," Lady Gaga told Jane Hutchinson for the Australian *Sunday Telegraph Magazine* (June 21, 2009). After that night she usually appeared in public scantily clad and often arrived for recording sessions wearing only her underwear.

In 2007 she formed a revue, called the Ultimate Pop Burlesque Rockshow, with the disk jockey and performance artist Lady Starlight. During their shows Lady Gaga, clad only in decorated bikini tops and hot pants or leather G-strings, would sing and dance while setting hairspray on fire. In August 2007 Lady Gaga and Lady Starlight performed at the annual music festival Lollapalooza, in Chicago's Grant Park. (Lady Gaga received a citation for indecent exposure while walking around the concert grounds in hot pants.) During that period Lady Gaga wrote songs for Fergie, the Pussycat Dolls, Britney Spears, and New Kids on the Block.

Offstage, Lady Gaga began to experiment with drugs. "I made a commitment to my dark side. I wanted to live the lifestyle of the artists I respect— to know what Jimi Hendrix went through, how Edie Sedgwick got that look," she told Hutchinson. "I don't want to encourage 11-year-olds to devote their lives to cocaine so they might become Lady GaGa, but I did go through that and it helped my creativity. I'm a stronger woman and artist because of it." Lady Gaga gave up drugs and hard partying after her father, angered by her behavior, refused to speak to her for months. "He let me know that he knew what I was doing, and the embarrassment and shame I felt was so great, I had to stop," Lady Gaga admitted to Hutchinson. "People can say whatever they want about me. The truth is, I'm so secure in my work [that] I don't give a damn. But if my father were to call me right now and be upset about something I did—it would ruin my night. I'm a daddy's girl."

In late 2007 Lady Gaga was signed to Streamline Records, a new imprint of Interscope Records headed by the producer and songwriter Vincent Herbert. Streamline arranged a songwriting partnership for her with the R&B singer Akon; Akon later persuaded Interscope Records to sign Lady Gaga to a joint deal with his own label, Kon Live Distribution. Lady Gaga then focused on making an album of her own. "She wrote almost all her hits in a week," Herbert told Cortney Harding for *Billboard* (August 15, 2009). "She flew to L.A. and sat in a studio with [the producer] RedOne and just cranked it out."

Lady Gaga was also working to develop a sense of fashion that would attract a lot of attention She dyed her dark-brown hair platinum blond and recruited a number of stylists who later became known collectively as the "Haus of Gaga." Emulating the pop artist Andy Warhol's Factory, the group collaborates with Lady Gaga to design her clothing, stage sets, and props. Lady Gaga has cited David Bowie, Grace Jones, Madonna, and Cher as her fashion influences. She rarely wears pants, regardless of the weather, preferring leotards, hot pants, or tights. She has worn everything from a porcelain bikini to a dress made of clear plastic bubbles to a metal outfit with rings that orbit her body as she performs. She is known for her signature huge hair bows, made with hair extensions; heavy makeup; and hats, wigs, veils, masks, or sunglasses that hide half her face.

Thanks to her growing celebrity, Lady Gaga has gotten the chance to wear creations by Hussein Chalayan, Alexander McQueen, Valentino, and some of her other favorite designers. She saves the more outrageous outfits for her performances and public appearances but dresses in similar styles at other times. She sometimes makes her own garments and shops in the clothing section of porn stores in Times Square, in Manhattan. "The most I dress down in is a leotard. . . . I'm not a T-shirt and jeans girl at all, not even at home on the couch," she told Kim Dawson and Nadine Linge for the London *Daily Star* (January 21, 2009).

Despite her affinity for provocative clothing, Lady Gaga—whose strong nose and prominent front teeth do not fit current conventions of beauty—has insisted that she is not trying to be a sex symbol. "I'm not super-sexy. A girl's got to use what she's given and I'm not going to make a guy drool the way a Britney [Spears] video does," she told Dawson and Linge. "So I take it to extremes.

I don't say I dress sexily on stage—what I do is so extreme. It's meant to make guys think: 'I don't know if this is sexy or just weird.' They start off thinking it's freaky then realise it's sexy because I'm having such a good time up there." "My album covers are not sexual at all, which was an issue at my record label," she told Miranda Purves for *Elle* (January 2010). "I fought for months, and I cried at meetings. They didn't think the photos were commercial enough. . . . The last thing a young woman needs is another picture of a sexy pop star writhing in sand, covered in grease, touching herself."

Lady Gaga's debut album, *The Fame*, was released in August 2008. Incorporating elements of disco, 1980s pop, R&B, and 1990s club music, it contains songs "about how anyone can feel famous," Lady Gaga wrote for her Web site. Kevin Courtney, who reviewed *The Fame* for the *Irish Times* (January 24, 2009), wrote that it is "an unashamed celebration of stardom in all its hedonistic, solipsistic glory. . . . The sound is an insistent mix of electro-disco and grimy R[&]B, delivered with an attention-seeking urgency, and spiced up with raps, techno beats and highly charged sexual energy." Stephen Thomas Erlewine wrote for the All Music Guide (on-line), "Gaga's got the outrageous outfits and dance moves down to a science, but underneath it all, the music is aggressive and authoritarian in ways that most other Top 40 tunes are not." He concluded that *The Fame* functions "simultaneously as glorious pop trash and a wicked parody of it."

The Fame's single "Just Dance" is about being intoxicated at a club: "What's going on on the floor? / I love this record, baby but I can't see straight anymore." "Just Dance" became an international hit, reaching the top spot on charts in seven countries, including the U.S., Australia, Canada, and the Netherlands, and was nominated for the 2009 Grammy Award for best dance recording. *The Fame*'s second single, "Poker Face," was another hit, reaching number one on charts in nearly 20 countries. That infectious pop song is about the mind games people play in gambling and sex. Other singles from the album are "LoveGame," about lusting after a stranger at a dance club—"Let's have some fun, this beat is sick / I wanna take a ride on your disco stick"—and "Paparazzi," which draws a parallel between the singer's determination to "chase down" a man she loves and the paparazzis' stalking of celebrities.

In late 2008 and early 2009, Lady Gaga toured as an opening act for New Kids on the Block and the Pussycat Dolls, respectively. With the worldwide success of *The Fame*, she headlined her first tour, beginning in March 2009. The Fame Ball Tour, as she called it, made stops in North America, Europe, and Asia.

Lady Gaga's second album, *The Fame Monster*, was released in November 2009. It contains only eight songs, among them the singles "Telephone," a duet with the R&B singer Beyoncé; "Bad Romance"; "Teeth"; "Speechless"; and "Alejandro."

Simon Price opened his review of *The Fame Monster* for the London *Independent* (November 22, 2009) by describing Lady Gaga as "the out-of-the-blue planetary pop phenomenon of 2009. At the age of 23, Stefani Germanotta, the funny-looking girl from Yonkers, has established herself as a self-created autonomous star, an avatar of avant-garde freako fashion and the queen of state-of-the-art electronic dance-pop. And, given that she writes or co-writes her material (unlike the majority of rivals in her field), a frighteningly prolific artist." He continued, "This eight-track stand-alone disc is a whole new piece of art in its own right," and concluded, "If this is [Lady Gaga's] idea of a stopgap release, we're looking here at a major talent indeed. On the evidence available so far, Lady Gaga isn't flesh and blood like the rest of us. She is made of amazingness." In an assessment for *Pitchfork.com* (January 13, 2010), Scott Plagenhoef wrote that in *The Fame Monster*, Lady Gaga's music "has become subtler, more playful, and more well-rounded, extending the electro-pop bubble she lived in on her debut. And instead of shoehorning references to celebrity into some tracks, she's borrowing elements and templates and simply focusing on quality control. The weird result is that, despite her flitting between personalities and personas, her music feels more like her own here than it did on her debut LP. The songs feel like they were written for Lady Gaga rather than simply for any modern pop star." Plagenhoef added, "It's refreshing to have a big pop star communicating to us from afar, like pop stars used to. . . . All of a sudden, . . . she's the only real pop star around." Many of Lady Gaga's fans complained that one or another of *The Fame Monster*'s labels—Streamline, Konlive, Cherrytree, or Interscope—censored the lyrics to some of the songs. In late 2009 *The Fame Monster* was re-released as an expanded edition of *The Fame*.

Among her many honors, in 2009 Lady Gaga won two International Dance Music Awards, for best breakthrough artist (solo) and best pop dance track for "Just Dance"; three MTV Video Music Awards; the MuchMusic Video Award for best international artist video, for "Poker Face"; and the MTV Europe Music Award for best new act. She was also named *Billboard*'s rising star in 2009. In 2010 she received the People's Choice Awards for favorite pop artist and favorite breakout artist. At the 52nd Annual Grammy Awards ceremony, on January 31, 2010, Lady Gaga was nominated for five awards—including album of the year—and won two, for best dance recording, for "Poker Face," and best electronic/dance album, for *The Fame*. On September 12, 2010, at the annual MTV Video Music Awards ceremony, she won the awards for video of the year, best pop video, best female video, best dance-music video, best choreography, best direction, and best editing, all for "Bad Romance," and best collaboration, with Beyoncé, for "Telephone."

Lady Gaga arrived at the MTV awards ceremony in a long white and aqua wig, and during the course of the evening, she wore three different outfits: an Alexander McQueen–designed gold, red, and dark-green dress, whose enormous flounce trailed the floor in back, an outfit she had worn in the "Bad Romance" video; a Giorgio Armani–designed black-rubber strapless dress with black spikes protruding from the bust and a billowing floor-length skirt, which was so heavy that two men held it while she mounted the stairs to the stage; and a Franc Fernandez dress made entirely with slabs of raw beef, which left her legs bare above the tops of her boots, also made of meat. Atop the wig she wore a spray of large gold feathers, as an accessory to the McQueen dress; an arc of tall lack spikes, with the Armani dress; and a piece of meat, with the Fernandez dress. The next day, during an appearance on Ellen DeGeneres's NBC-TV talk show, in response to a question from DeGeneres (who is a vegan) about the meat dress, Lady Gaga said, according to *USA Today* (September 13, 2010, on-line), "Well, it is certainly no disrespect to anyone that is a vegan or vegetarian. As you know, I am the most judgment-free human being on earth. However, it has many interpretations. . . . If we don't stand up for what we believe in and if we don't fight for our rights, pretty soon we're going to have as much rights as the meat on our own bones. And, I am not a piece of meat."

An album of remixes, *Lady Gaga—The Remix* (2010), debuted at number six on the *Billboard* charts. In October *Forbes* ranked Lady Gaga seventh among the 100 most powerful women in the world. Also in 2010 Lady Gaga launched her worldwide Monster Ball Tour; she was expected to continue the tour in 2011. Her next album, *Born This Way*, was scheduled to be released in 2011.

In the summer of 2010, Lady Gaga began to appear at gay-rights rallies and other events that called for repeal of the U.S. military's "Don't ask, don't tell" policy. At a rally in Portland, Maine, on September 20, 2010, she wore little makeup and an understated outfit and identified herself by her real name. In her speech she declared, as quoted by James Montgomery on mtv.com (September 20, 2010), "I'm here today . . . to say that, if the Senate and the president are not going to repeal this 'don't ask, don't tell' policy, perhaps they should be more clear with us about who the military is fighting for, who our tax dollars are supporting. . . . This equality stuff, I thought equality meant everyone. . . . Doesn't it seem to be that 'don't ask, don't tell' is backwards? Doesn't it seem to you that we should send home the prejudiced? The straight soldier who hates the gay soldier? The straight soldier who has prejudice in his heart in the space where the military asks him to hold our core American values? . . . I would like to propose a new law; a law that sends home the soldier that has the problem. Our new law is called 'if you don't like it, go home.' If you are not committed to perform with excellence as a United States soldier because you don't believe in full equality, go home. If you are not honorable enough to fight without prejudice, go home. If you are not capable of keeping your oath to the Armed Forces to defend the Constitution of the United States against all enemies foreign and domestic . . . then go home."

"In eight to 10 years, I want to have babies for my Dad to hold, grandkids," Lady Gaga told Miranda Purves. "And I want to have a husband who loves and supports me, just the way anyone else does. I would never leave my career for a man right now, and I would never follow a man around."

—M.A.S.

Suggested Reading: (Australia) *Sunday Telegraph Magazine* p12 June 21, 2009; *Elle* p139+ Jan. 2010; ladygaga.com; (London) *Observer Magazine* p16 June 28, 2009; (London) *Sunday Times* Culture p30+ Dec. 14, 2008, Style p8+ Feb. 22, 2009

Selected Recordings: *The Fame*, 2008; *The Fame Monster*, 2009; *Lady Gaga—The Remix*, 2010

LaValle, Victor

Feb. 3, 1972– Writer

Address: c/o Spiegel & Grau, Random House Inc., 1745 Broadway, New York, NY 10019

The celebrated poet, essayist, and novelist Ishmael Reed told Jeffrey A. Trachtenberg for the *Wall Street Journal* (July 24, 2009, on-line) that Victor LaValle is one of a group of African-American writers who have "reintroduced a fiction with comic possibilities, entertaining fantastical situations without losing a sharp social message." In the last decade LaValle has authored a short-story collection, *Slapboxing with Jesus* (1999), and two acclaimed novels, *The Ecstatic* (2002) and *Big Machine* (2009). *Slapboxing with Jesus*, whose 12 tales focus on the hardscrabble lives of African-American and Latino men coming of age in New York during the early 1980s, won the 2000 PEN/Open Book Award and brought its author the key to Jamaica, Queens. The collection, according to *Kirkus Reviews*, helped establish LaValle as one of the "most eloquent new voices of the approaching century." His novels have garnered equal praise: *The Ecstatic*, a semiautobiographical novel about an obese college dropout in the grip of schizophrenia, was a finalist for both the 2003 PEN/Faulkner Award for fiction and the 2003 Zora Neale Hurston/Richard Wright Legacy Award for debut fiction; and *Big Machine*, about a middle-aged recovering heroin addict who travels to Vermont to fulfill a promise he made years before, has earned comparisons to works by such renowned authors as Thomas Pynchon and Ralph Ellison. La-

Valle's writing focuses largely on people at the fringes of society. The writer explained to Tom Vitale for the National Public Radio (NPR) program *All Things Considered* (February 23, 2003), "I feel like the people who are considered truly monstrous in our society are somehow the people I always gravitate to, whether it's child prostitutes, fat schizophrenics, ugly women, ugly men. Those are the people I love to write about. And thus far in my mind, they're mostly colorless because everybody looks down on them. And that's who I love." While acknowledging the significance of race in African-American life, LaValle has expressed more interest in capturing the individuality of his characters. He explained to Joshunda Sanders for the *San Francisco Chronicle* (November 22, 2003), "I write about black people living their lives, while 90 percent of other black writers write about their lives as affected by racism. I thought I'd take a shot at the other 95 percent of their lives." The acclaim he has received notwithstanding, LaValle's genre-mixing approach to storytelling has made it difficult for him to garner a mainstream audience. The novelist Mat Johnson, a friend of LaValle's, told Trachtenberg, "Vic does horror movies with literary fiction. It's Thomas Pynchon with the Sunday afternoon double matinee. There's no section in the bookstore for that. But the work is transcendent." Chris Jackson, executive editor of Spiegel & Grau, which published *Big Machine*, said to Trachtenberg, "In the Obama era, Vic represents what might come next in American literature."

The older of two children, Victor Durmot LaValle was born on February 3, 1972 in the New York City borough of Queens to an Irish-American father and Ugandan-born mother. LaValle's parents, James and Damali, divorced when he was an infant; his mother and grandmother, Kezia, raised him and his sister, Shana, in the Jackson Heights, Flushing, and Rosedale neighborhoods of Queens. (LaValle also has a half-brother, Paul, from his father's second marriage.) His mother supported the family by working as a secretary. Commenting on his mother's influence on him, LaValle told *Current Biography*, "Besides working as a legal secretary she was a talented artist herself, she drew, made small clay structures, sewed, and played piano. She didn't do any of these things with the hopes of becoming famous, or making a living from her creations, she just enjoyed making beautiful things for our home. I think that's how the idea of being an artist stopped seeming foreign to me."

When LaValle was growing up, various members of his family suffered from mental illnesses, including schizophrenia and bipolar disorder. He had to be careful to avoid innocent acts that might exacerbate his relatives' conditions; as Lonnae O'Neal Parker reported for the *Washington Post* (December 2, 2003), "Simply pointing a pen could be interpreted" by a family member "as a secret message." Despite the atmosphere of mental instability around him, he had what he described to Sanders as a "pretty normal" childhood. He told

E. Raboteau, courtesy of Random House

Victor LaValle

Current Biography, "In fact, it was a surprise to me when I learned that other families didn't sometimes receive calls from people who'd been voluntarily or involuntarily hospitalized." Fond of heavy-metal music and works in the horror genre, LaValle "was a big reader, a nerdy kid in an aggressive neighborhood," as he recalled to Susan Morgan for the Web site unitedstatesartists.org.

LaValle first developed an interest in writing as a grade-school student. He recalled to *Current Biography*, "I used to write love letters for some of the kids at my grade school. This started around fifth or sixth grade and continued on to junior high. I used to charge two dollars per letter. They'd tell me a few things about their girlfriends and I'd go off and write something tailored to each one. I even learned to copy some of their handwriting so it really seemed authentic. I made decent money, it seemed to me then, and it made me see just how much of an effect writing could have on people." His biggest literary influences when he was growing up included the writers Shirley Jackson, Clive Barker, Ambrose Bierce, Stephen King, and Stephen Crane. By the time LaValle reached his teens, his family had moved from Flushing to Rosedale, which had a more suburban flavor. Treated as an outsider by his peers, he became depressed and comforted himself by overeating. In the opening lines of an essay for *Nerve* magazine (December 2000/January 2001, on-line) that addressed his weight problem, LaValle wrote, "I made it self-destruct. My body. I destroyed it." Around that time LaValle returned to writing as an escape from his emotional difficulties. He wrote poetry as well as book and movie reviews for his high-school newspaper. Then, after having his first story reject-

ed by a horror magazine, he did not write again for years.

Upon graduating from Long Island's Woodmere Academy (now known as Lawrence Woodmere Academy), in 1990, LaValle enrolled at Cornell University, in Ithaca, New York, where he studied English. He paid for his schooling through loans and grants, but money was so scarce at times that he often shoplifted junk food to satisfy his eating addiction. During that time LaValle's life began to unravel, as his weight ballooned to nearly 400 pounds. He wrote in the essay for *Nerve*, "Though I made friends, socialized, I often found myself marching spitefully through a dining hall, my tray loaded with donuts and imitation Philly cheesesteaks, as if I could hide from the collective grimaces and smirks in my rising pile of candied treats. You think I'm nasty, well watch this. That was my battle cry. The more my friends went to play basketball or jog or shotput, the more bags of Doritos, jars of peanut butter and three-liter Pepsi's I consumed. It was self-destruction, just not as sexy as cocaine or alcohol. With liquor you become loose and loquacious, but no one has ever turned charming after downing a whole bucket of extra-crispy fried chicken." To compound his problems, LaValle also started having psychotic delusions. He recalled to Tom Vitale, "I had this idea that I had to map all the mountains of the Finger Lakes region at some point during college. So I got on buses and I just would go around the Finger Lakes region mapping all these mountains. Only about two years later, when I was in a better state, I found these maps again and the thing that was amazing to me to find was that there are no mountains in the areas that I was traveling, you know. And I'm telling you, I had, like, animals; I had flora and fauna, everything for these places."

In the midst of his psychological breakdown, LaValle stopped attending classes and was kicked out of Cornell. He recalled to *Current Biography*, "The Dean who brought me in explained that my grades hadn't been impressive and that I hadn't really stood out in any other way in campus life. As a result he was rescinding all my financial aid and expelling me. He told me, in no uncertain terms, that he would never approve my return to Cornell." Instead of returning home, LaValle remained in Ithaca and worked for various temp agencies. When the dean who had expelled him went on sabbatical, LaValle was able to appeal his case to another dean, who allowed him to return to Cornell to complete his degree requirements. After making up a semester's worth of work during the summer of 1994, LaValle completed his undergraduate degree there in 1995. By that time he had decided on a career as a writer. He was accepted into the master-of-fine-arts program in creative writing at Columbia University, in New York, where he became a roommate and friend of the writer Mat Johnson, who went on to write the acclaimed novels *Drop* (2000) and *Hunting in Harlem* (2003). Johnson, the only other African-American man in Columbia's graduate creative-writing program at the time, noted to Joshunda Sanders about LaValle, "There's this vulnerability to him that makes you want to save him. The best writers stand inside but somewhat outside society at the same time."

LaValle's master's thesis contained stories that would appear in his debut work, *Slapboxing with Jesus* (1999), published by Vintage Contemporaries. Out of fear that the publicity photo of him used to promote the book would be widely circulated, LaValle, who still weighed in excess of 300 pounds, began a strict diet-and-exercise regimen. He told *Current Biography*, "I lost a little weight but was having some trouble so then I joined Jenny Craig. I stuck to their diet and I bought a refurbished Stairmaster which I used five days a week and I lost over a hundred pounds." He recalled to Lonnae O'Neal Parker that selling the book provided "the boost I needed to say, 'Maybe I can do this other stuff, maybe I can lose the weight.'" By the time *Slapboxing with Jesus* was published, LaValle had gotten his weight down to 200 pounds. (He later lost even more weight.) His story collection, set in gritty sections of New York during the early 1980s, follows young men through their day-to-day struggles. (The title of the collection was taken from a rap song by Ghostface Killah, a member of the New York City–based rap group Wu-Tang Clan.) Written in a deliberately disjointed prose style and featuring graphic depictions of sex and violence, the collection comprises two parts. The first, "The Autobiography of New York Today," features five stories about young characters in the Bronx and Queens. The second, "One Boy's Beginnings," tells the story of Anthony James and chronicles, in seven episodes, his development from a prepubescent boy into a sexually driven teenager.

Slapboxing with Jesus received unanimous praise from critics. Andrew Roe, assessing the book for the *San Francisco Chronicle* (February 6, 2000), wrote, "The people we meet [in the stories] are forever marked—and often muted—by their environment. . . . Along with the book's documentary-like portrait of the boroughs, LaValle also skillfully sketches out the lives of those who inhabit these bleak, forgotten cityscapes. The kind of spiritual and emotional paralysis that pervades Joyce's turn-of-the-century *Dubliners* (appropriately enough, the book opens with an epigraph from 'The Dead') likewise afflicts LaValle's cast of young men and boys (primarily African American) struggling to make sense of their edgy world, a place 'where mourning seemed like a lifestyle' and a teenager can wearily proclaim that 'it didn't seem strange that I was fifteen and already feeling ancient.' . . . Throughout, LaValle's revelatory run-on prose burns with ferocity and raw insight while also conveying a breathtaking poetry: At twilight 'the setting sun's flames were running down to an orange gasp on the horizon'; a chain-link fence 'swayed loosely, its rattle a language'; a pair of sneakers were old 'but their bright blue skin stood out like life on a desolate planet.' . . . But even if a few stories are somewhat flawed and less compelling than others, LaValle's energy and vision are enough to make every page, every sentence, sing. It's a sure sign of a writer's skill when you're willing to follow him anywhere, and LaValle is one such writer. Even his errant steps amaze." *Slapboxing with Jesus* received several awards, including the 2000 PEN/Open Book Award, given to writers of color, and the key to Jamaica, Queens.

LaValle spent the next three years on his next work, a picaresque novel called *The Ecstatic* (2002). That book's title alludes to religious movements whose members believe in the notion of being taken over mentally and physically by God. *The Ecstatic* continues the story of Anthony James, who is now an obese 23-year-old Cornell dropout suffering from recurring bouts of schizophrenia and living with his mentally unstable mother, nonagenarian grandmother, and 13-year-old sister in the Rosedale section of Queens. The story follows James as he accompanies his family to a Virginia beauty pageant for chaste girls that his younger sister has entered. Along the way he experiences hallucinatory episodes and encounters characters including a neighborhood loan shark, Ishkabibble, and the diminutive Uncle Arms, who is in charge of the pageant. LaValle, by his estimate, wrote at least 30 drafts of the novel before its completion. He said to Neal Conan for the NPR program *Talk of the Nation* (December 23, 2002), "People always think, when they're starting out anyway, 'My first draft is the one that has all the energy and the immediacy and the power, and so that's the one I've got to keep.' But that's almost entirely wrong. And, in fact, that's the one that's full of cliches and easy answers and simplistic endings, and you have to go back and ask yourself again and again: Could this be more complex?" In the case of *The Ecstatic*, the original draft was "self-indulgent," as LaValle admitted to Conan, portraying the character based on himself as having few flaws. He recalled that when he showed that version to friends, their response was, "Why don't you be a little more honest?" LaValle nonetheless noted to John Freeman that *The Ecstatic* is a "sort of love letter to my fat self. I still really love the good person I was then. I am not much different now, except I write books. I go on dates. I bathe more." He said to Tom Vitale, "I was very fat and very crazy for a good long time, and I wanted to write about it. Now that I've recovered from a lot of those problems, I really wanted to write about the person that I was then, both as this creature and a beast that people saw, but also as this tangible and complex human being inside that."

Like *Slapboxing with Jesus*, *The Ecstatic* garnered high praise from critics. A reviewer for *Publishers Weekly* (September 23, 2002) wrote, "Not since Chief Bromden [from Ken Kesey's 1962 novel *One Flew Over the Cuckoo's Nest*] has there been a misfit narrator as large and compelling as 315-pound Anthony. . . . The narrative shimmers with his self-deprecating wit and unexpected images ('Her hair was a big loose spray of black semi-curls emanating from her skull like the sound waves of her rollicking conversation'). LaValle's first book left critics divided over whether it had the substance to match its mannered style. Similar questions may be raised this time around, but La-Valle's sympathetic and original narrator is a remarkable creation." Richard Gehr, in a review for the *New York Times* (December 15, 2002), commented, *"The Ecstatic* is a valiant, if not entirely successful, attempt by LaValle to update the boy he introduced three years ago. Where the stories in *Slapboxing with Jesus* bristled with the energy of dire hip-hop singles, *The Ecstatic* lapses into long, torpid subplots—such as the extended Uncle Arms–Pretty Damn Mad episode, or Anthony's obsession with an imprisoned activist based on Mumia Abu-Jamal. Back home in Queens, though, Anthony feels as familiar as that large, fragrant man everyone avoids on the subway but whom Victor LaValle—who now appears, based on his photograph on this novel's dust jacket, to be rather thin—is empathetic enough to portray with strangely moving affection as a giddy, doomed 'Maxi Me.'" In 2003 *The Ecstatic* was a finalist for both the PEN/Faulkner Award for fiction and the Zora Neale Hurston/Richard Wright Foundation Legacy Award for debut fiction; each honor came with a $5,000 prize. In 2004 LaValle was the recipient of a Whiting Writers' Award for Fiction, which came with a $35,000 prize. (Ten Whiting Writers' Awards are given annually to emerging writers of fiction, nonfiction, poetry, or plays.)

LaValle's second novel, *Big Machine*, tells the story of Ricky Rice, a not-quite-former heroin addict who leaves his job as a janitor at a bus depot in Utica, New York, after a cryptic message arrives beckoning him to Vermont. There, Rice is enlisted in an all-black band of paranormal investigators, made up of petty thieves and ex-junkies, known as the Unlikely Scholars. Together, they sift through stacks of old news articles in search of clues about a higher power called the Voice. Rice is then sent with another scholar to San Francisco's East Bay to stop a rogue member of the group from launching a holy war. Underlying the story are questions about religion, doubt, faith, and parenting: at one point Ricky discovers that he will soon, in a highly unusual manner, become a parent. For *Big Machine* LaValle drew inspiration from the detective fiction of the legendary author Raymond Chandler as well as from works in the horror genre (the epigraph for *Big Machine* is from John Carpenter's 1982 cult remake of the movie *The Thing*).

Big Machine strengthened LaValle's reputation as a writer able to integrate elements from a variety of genres into a single work. The novel was generally well-received by critics. Elizabeth Hand, writing for the *Washington Post* (September 8, 2009), observed, "In Victor LaValle's spectacular new novel, *Big Machine*, race and religion are the subterranean tributaries that threaten to destroy America's underclass, even as they help to sustain it.

Along with Junot Diaz, Lev Grossman, Kelly Link and Kevin Brockmeier, LaValle is part of an increasingly high-profile and important cohort of writers who reinvent outmoded literary conventions, particularly the ghettos of genre and ethnicity that long divided serious literature from popular fiction." She added, "Despite its steady pulse of dark humor, its supernatural Voice and the presence of some creepy entities known as the Devils of the Marsh, *Big Machine* is a novel about faith and the ways in which religion can create monsters far more terrifying than anything dreamed up by H.P. Lovecraft."

LaValle told Amy Minton for *hobartpulp.com* (November 2009) that he was working on a short novel called "The Devil in Silver." "It's the story of a haunted house, in a sense," he said, "but I guarantee no one's ever written a haunted house story quite like this."

LaValle lives in the Washington Heights neighborhood of Manhattan. He is currently an assistant professor in the graduate writing program at Columbia University. LaValle has also taught at Warren Wilson College, in Asheville, North Carolina, Mills College, in Oakland, California, and the North Country Institute for Writers of Color of the State University of New York (SUNY) at Plattsburgh. He will serve as a visiting writer at Adelphi University, in Garden City, New York, in the spring of 2010. LaValle has received grants and fellowships from institutions including the Fine Arts Work Center, the Bread Loaf Writers Conference, and the United States Artists Foundation. He has written essays and book reviews for publications including *GQ, Essence, Paste Magazine,* the *FAD-ER,* and the *Washington Post.* In his spare time La-Valle enjoys traveling.

—C.C.

Suggested Reading: (Denver, Colorado) *Post* EE p2 Jan. 26, 2003; National Public Radio's *Weekend Edition Saturday* (on-line) Oct. 3, 2009; *Publishers Weekly* p154+ Aug. 12, 2002; *San Francisco Chronicle* D p1+ Nov. 22, 2003; Victor LaValle Web site; *Wall Street Journal* (on-line) July 24, 2009; *Washington Post* C p1+ Dec. 3, 2002

Selected Books: *Slapboxing with Jesus,* 1999; *The Ecstatic,* 2002; *Big Machine,* 2009

LeDoux, Joseph

(le-DOO)

*Dec. 7, 1949– Neuroscientist; educator; writer;
musician*

*Address: Center for Neural Science, New York
University, 4 Washington Pl., Rm. 809, New
York, NY 10003*

As recently as a few decades ago, nearly all psychologists, psychiatrists, and neuroscientists
thought that emotions could not be studied as biological, chemical, physical, or physiological phenomena. Insights regarding emotions, they believed, could be gained only through analyses of
people's descriptions of their thoughts and dreams
(the kind of work conducted by such pioneering
psychiatrists as Sigmund Freud, Carl Jung, and Karen Horney) or analyses of observed behavior
among nonhuman animals (research associated
with the naturalist Charles Darwin and such animal psychologists as Konrad Lorenz and Harry F.
Harlow). The neuroscientist Joseph LeDoux—
along with a few others—has overturned those beliefs. "His investigations of the links between the
brain's structure and emotions have helped to give
this field scientific respectability," the University
of Toronto psychologist Keith Oatley wrote for
New Scientist (January 4, 1997). LeDoux embarked
on his search for such links in the 1980s, at Cornell
University Medical College, in New York City. As
a postdoctoral fellow there, he devised a series of
experiments based on learned behavior in rats and
deliberate changes he made to the rats' brains. Focusing on fear, an emotion present from birth and
expressed similarly in virtually all animal species,
LeDoux conditioned (or, in a sense, "taught") rats
to respond fearfully to a harmless stimulus and
then observed their responses after he had made
specific parts of their brains inoperative. LeDoux's
first major discovery was that the rats displayed
fear of the stimulus even in the absence of a functioning cerebral cortex, the part of the brain required for higher-level, conscious processes, such
as reasoning. Thus, he concluded, the cortex is not
necessary for conditioned emotional learning to
take place; rather, the brain can register and store
such information subconsciously, using lower-level structures. LeDoux's second major discovery
involved a twin group of subcortical cells called
the amygdalae (ah-MIG-dah-lay), which are small,
almond-shaped clusters of neurons (brain cells) in
the temporal lobes, one in the left hemisphere of
the brain, the other in the right hemisphere; the
amygdalae, he found, play a crucial role in the unconscious response to fear. He has also elucidated
cellular and molecular changes that occur in and
between brain cells during the storage and retrieval
of fear memories. LeDoux's revolutionary work on
fear and the thousands of studies it has inspired
have shed light on the neurological bases of fear-

related disorders in humans, including phobias
and post-traumatic stress disorder (PTSD), and
have pointed to potential treatments as well.

LeDoux's work with rats has led him to conclude that attempts to locate in the brain a single,
"all-purpose" emotional system (long known as
the limbic system) have failed because most likely
a single system does not exist. "I've come to think
that emotions are products of different systems,
each of which evolved to take care of problems of
survival, like defending against danger, finding
mates and food, and so forth," LeDoux explained
to John Brockman for the *Edge* (February 17, 1997,
on-line). "These systems solve behavioral problems of survival. Detecting and responding to danger requires different kinds of sensory and cognitive processes, and different kinds of motor outputs, different kinds of feedback networks, and so
on, than finding a mate or finding food. Because of
these unique requirements, I think different systems of the brain are going to be involved in the different kinds of emotions." LeDoux also emphasizes
that so-called emotional memories, which are unconscious, are distinct from memories of emotions
and feelings, which are conscious. He told Brockman, "I think it's safe to say fear behavior preceded
fear feelings in evolution. . . . In this sense, animals were unconscious, unfeeling, and nonlinguistic before they were conscious, feeling, and
linguistic. . . . I'm trying to understand the things
about emotions that are similar in humans and other animals so that I can work on emotions through
the brain."

In 1989 LeDoux joined the faculty of the Center
for Neural Science and the Department of Psychology at New York University (NYU). He was promoted to professor in 1991 and was named the
Henry and Lucy Moses Professor of Science in
1996; since 2005 he has also held the title University Professor. In addition, since 2007 he has directed the Emotional Brain Institute, in Orangeburg,
New York, whose work is supported by both NYU
and the Nathan Kline Institute for Psychiatric Research. LeDoux is the co-author of *The Integrated
Mind* (1978), the co-editor of books including *Mind
and Brain: Dialogues in Cognitive Neuroscience*
(1986), and the author or co-author of more than
300 professional papers, book chapters, and review
articles (which summarize particular findings of
his and others' research). LeDoux has also written
two books for informed lay readers and specialists
alike: *The Emotional Brain: The Mysterious Underpinnings of Emotional Life* (1996) and *Synaptic
Self: How Our Brains Become Who We Are* (2002).
The Emotional Brain offers a history of the scientific study of emotion and a detailed survey of LeDoux's work, insights, and hypotheses up to that
point. According to Keith Oatley, the book is "in
tune with what psychologists know about emotions and learning, . . . and . . . directly applicable to understanding anxiety, the most common ingredient of emotional disorders. It's a terrifically
good book." Years later a writer for the *Economist*

Quentin Huys, courtesy of Joseph LeDoux
Joseph LeDoux

(July 26, 2008) noted that *The Emotional Brain* had "helped to inspire what is today one of the liveliest and most controversial areas of economic research: neuroeconomics," which combines psychology, economics, and neuroscience to determine how people make financial decisions. In *Synaptic Self* LeDoux described in detail the functioning of the brain at the cellular level—in particular, the thousands of tiny gaps, called synapses, between one neuron and its neighbors, where signals are transmitted from one to another, and he discussed how the connections among brain cells contribute to conscious and unconscious aspects of our personalities. In a blurb for its book jacket, Daniel Goleman, the author of *Emotional Intelligence*, described *Synaptic Self* as "a brilliant manifesto at the cutting edge of psychology's evolution into a brain science . . . [from] one of the field's preeminent, most important thinkers." "Covering an avalanche of neuroscientific research," Gilbert Taylor wrote for *Booklist*, as quoted on Amazon.com, *Synaptic Self* "is surely the most accessible contemporary work for those interested in the brain's effect on personality."

LeDoux is also the guitarist, lead singer, and songwriter of the rock band the Amygdaloids, a quartet of neuroscientists. The band's latest album, *Theory of My Mind* (2010), features guest musicians including the singer/songwriter Roseanne Cash. The lyrics in the Amygdaloids songs focus on such brain-related topics as memory, emotion, and free will.

Joseph Edward LeDoux Jr. was born on December 7, 1949 in Eunice, a town in Louisiana's Cajun country. He has a younger sister, Bonnie. His father, J. E. "Boo" LeDoux, and mother, the former

Elizabeth Priscilla Buller, owned a butcher shop; his mother kept the accounts and wrapped the meat that his father cut. Until LeDoux was about 12, the family lived above the shop. As a child LeDoux would ride his bike through the neighborhood, selling pigs' feet for a nickel. In the shop he prepared cow brains for sale, each time peeling away the outer membranes and then, with his fingers, removing the bullet, deep within, that had killed the cow. LeDoux thought about what the animals felt during their last moments. "I had a sense of soul or spirit and wondered about the cow— even though religion taught that animals don't have souls, it still kind of perplexed me," he recalled to *Current Biography*. "Did they feel anything? Did they think anything?" Young LeDoux greatly feared the venomous water moccasins ubiquitous in the bayous. Another of his fears, David Dobbs wrote for *Scientific American Mind* (February/March 2006, on-line), was that he might get "stuck" in "sleepy" Eunice forever.

LeDoux, whose parents were strict Roman Catholics, attended Catholic schools, served as an altar boy in his church, and until age 13 planned to enter the priesthood. "In eighth grade," he told *Current Biography*, "I guess the hormones kicked in and I got interested in girls. And the priest thing was out the window." Next he aimed at a career as a folk musician and then, after hearing the Beatles and other pioneering rockers, as a rock musician. Soon he was playing electric guitar for his high-school rock-and-roll band, the Countdowns; he also served as a disc jockey at a local radio station. LeDoux's parents, however, who grew up poor during the Great Depression, wanted him to become a businessman and told him that they would pay for his college education only if he studied business. LeDoux earned a B.S. degree in that field at Louisiana State University (LSU) in Baton Rouge in 1971 and remained at LSU to pursue a master's degree in marketing, which he considered to be the least boring aspect of business. He became interested in human psychology—for example, "why people bought stuff they didn't really need," he told Dobbs. While enrolled in a class taught by Robert Thompson, he grew fascinated by the psychology of learning, memory, and motivation. Before long LeDoux began helping with research on rats in Thompson's lab, and his name appeared as a co-author on four of Thompson's published papers. LeDoux earned an M.S. degree from LSU in 1974.

Determined to pursue a doctorate in neuroscience, LeDoux read widely in psychology. In part because he had almost no training in biology, he was rejected by all but one of the dozen graduate schools to which he applied. The acceptance came from the State University of New York (SUNY) at Stony Brook, after Thompson recommended LeDoux to an acquaintance of his—Michael S. Gazzaniga, who taught at SUNY–Stony Brook from 1973 to 1978. Gazzaniga told Dobbs that LeDoux had "a long-hair ponytail, and maybe some wouldn't have thought him impressive. But there are people who walk in and you see right away they have it. Joe was one." Gazzaniga became Le-Doux's adviser.

A few years earlier Gazzaniga had made a revolutionary discovery through his research on split-brain patients—people who had undergone a surgical procedure in which the corpus callosum, the largest bundle of nerves that connects the two hemispheres, was completely severed, to reduce the symptoms of severe epilepsy; thus, the higher-level portions of the two hemispheres could no longer communicate. As with all people, external signals sent from the left eyes of those with split brains go to the brain's right hemisphere, and signals from the right eye go to the brain's left hemisphere, the latter of which contains the brain's language center (the part responsible for reading, writing, and speech). Both hemispheres of split-brain patients are aware of what is being seen, but the patients can talk only about objects that the right eye has observed. When Gazzaniga covered the right eyes of split-brain patients, they were not able to express verbally what they were looking at. But, he discovered, they *could* respond *nonverbally*. For example, if the patients were looking at a picture of an apple only through their left eyes—which transmit the visual signal to their right hemispheres—they are not able to say, "That is an apple." But if given a bag containing various objects, they were able to select the object (the apple) that matched the picture if they used their left hands, which received a signal from their right hemispheres.

One day, LeDoux recalled to Carlin Flora for the *NYU Alumni Magazine* (Spring 2008, on-line), Gazzaniga remarked to him, "Gee, there's not much research on emotion out there." Keeping in mind the results of the split-brain experiment, LeDoux and Gazzaniga designed a similar experiment that focused on emotions. Their split-brain patient was unusual in that although he could speak only "through his left hemisphere," he could read with both. When the patient's right eye (and left hemisphere) were shown words, he could say the word aloud and convey its emotional significance—that is, how he felt about it ("good" or "bad"). Predictably, when the patient's right eye was covered and only his brain's right hemisphere received visual signals, he could not say the word. Nevertheless, he could convey how the word made him feel. For example, he said "good" when he saw "mother" and "bad" when he saw "devil," even though he could not say "mother" or "devil" aloud to identify those words. The emotional information (the way the stimuli made him feel) traveled from one hemisphere to the other hemisphere because the anterior commissure—which connects the left and right amygdalae, which are crucial for emotional processing—was still intact. The emotional processing occurred without the patient's being consciously aware of what the stimulus (the printed word, in that case) was. In other words, the processing occurred unconsciously. Those findings are described in LeDoux's Ph.D. dissertation, "The Split Brain and the Integrated Mind," as well as in the book *The Integrated Mind* (1978), which he co-wrote with Gazzaniga, and in *The Emotional Brain*.

After he received his Ph.D. degree in psychology from SUNY–Stony Brook, in 1977, LeDoux joined Cornell University Medical College, in New York City, as a National Institutes of Health (NIH) postdoctoral fellow in the Department of Neurology. He became an instructor at the college in 1979 and was promoted to assistant and then associate professor in 1980 and 1986, respectively. Earlier, in 1978, he had started working in the laboratory of the world-renowned neurobiologist Donald J. Reis, who told him, he recalled to John Brockman, that he "could do whatever I wanted as long as I recorded blood pressure" on his study animals—rats—as a contribution to Reis's investigations of the brain's influence on the autonomic nervous system. LeDoux chose rats as subjects in his study of the neurological basis of emotion, because for both ethical and practical reasons, he could not use humans in studies in which parts of brains were deliberately rendered nonfunctional. More recently LeDoux has also made use of functional imaging of brains—scans that record brain activity over specified periods of time—which can supplement but not replace work with nonhumans. "The animal work . . . gives the framework for interpreting the snapshots we get from human imaging studies," LeDoux told Brockman.

With his physiological studies of rats, LeDoux "launched into a new field alone," Gazzaniga told Carlin Flora. "His training with me was in testing patients, so he had to go back and learn basic neuroscience, learn how to make lesions in the brain. It was like getting another Ph.D." LeDoux's first application for a grant, in the mid-1980s, which offered as the title of his research project "The Neural Basis of Emotion," was rejected on the grounds that emotion cannot be studied physiologically. In 1985, after LeDoux changed the title to "The Neural Pathways Underlying Emotional Conditioning"—indicating the behavioral component of his project—and made a few other small changes, the National Institute of Mental Health (NIMH), a division of the NIH, awarded him the grant. (The NIMH has renewed that grant ever since. LeDoux's work has also been supported by other NIMH grants, along with funding from sources including the National Science Foundation and the American Heart Association.)

As he discussed in *The Emotional Brain*, among the many emotions that have been identified, Le-Doux chose to study fear, because the outward and physiological expressions of fear in the face of sudden threats are present among most animal species. For example, the sudden appearance of a predator will cause a prey animal to become motionless (freeze in place) for a fraction of a second and then flee, with an accelerated heartbeat and the release of stress hormones into the bloodstream. "All animals have to be able to detect and respond to danger, regardless of the kind of cognitive architecture they have," LeDoux told John Brockman. "This is as true of bees and worms and snails, as it is of fish, frogs, birds, rats, and people." Physiological manifestations of such emotions as love or hope, by contrast, are as yet difficult or impossible to pin down. In his experiments on rats, LeDoux used conditioned learning, a technique introduced by the Russian physiologist Ivan Pavlov in the 19th century. Pavlov would repeatedly give dogs meat right after ringing a bell, and within a short time the dogs would start salivating immediately upon hearing the bell, before or without smelling the meat. The odor of meat elicits salivation automatically; salivation in response to a ringing bell is called a conditioned response. In LeDoux's experiments with conditioned learning, the rats would soon ignore a repeated, nonthreatening tone; they would freeze and arch their backs and their hearts would beat faster when their feet were subjected to mild electric shocks accompanied by the sound; after a sufficient number of repetitions of sound and shock, they would freeze, and their heartbeats accelerate, upon hearing the sound alone, without the shock.

LeDoux set out to determine which parts of the brain's auditory system are involved in that sort of conditioning. "It's a matter of connecting the dots in the brain," he said to *Current Biography*. In rats, humans, and other vertebrate species, sound waves move through the ear and are converted to electrochemical signals that travel to three parts of the brain in succession: the auditory midbrain, the auditory thalamus, and the auditory cortex (that is, the parts of the midbrain, thalamus, and cortex connected with hearing). When LeDoux disrupted the functioning of the last part of the auditory pathway, the auditory cortex, in his rats' brains (by means of induced lesions), fear conditioning proceeded exactly as it had before. That result showed that, contrary to what scientists had universally believed, the auditory cortex—which is necessary for *consciousness* of an external auditory stimulus—is not necessary for producing an emotional response to a sound. That discovery was LeDoux's first major contribution to neuroscience. Like the study he conducted on split-brain patients, his series of experiments with rats showed that emotions (as revealed physiologically) can operate outside the realm of consciousness and without the involvement of higher brain centers, which are involved in thinking and reasoning.

As spelled out in a series of papers in the mid-1980s co-authored by Reis and others, LeDoux discovered that destruction of the auditory thalamus and of the auditory midbrain *did* prevent learned conditioning in rats. Next, by means of a tracer chemical injected into each rat's thalamus, he determined that an auditory signal is carried to several subcortical regions. By cutting off the connections between the thalamus and each of those regions, LeDoux found that only one of them was necessary for fear conditioning in rats. That single exception was the amygdala—in particular, the part known as the lateral amygdala—in either of the hemispheres. (Subsequent studies, some of which used brain-scan technology, have linked the amygdalae to additional emotions, including anger, sadness, and disgust, and LeDoux and others have detected subtle differences in the functions of the left and right amygdalae.)

In subsequent studies of conditioned learning, LeDoux and his colleagues focused on a portion of the cortex called the prefrontal cortex, which in humans is associated with complex cognitive functions. Normally, after a rat develops an association between, say, the sound of a bell and an electric shock, the association can be unlearned (that is, forgotten) if the rat repeatedly hears the bell without being shocked. In that circumstance, in scientific jargon, "extinction" of the learned response has occurred. LeDoux discovered that cutting the connections between the prefrontal cortex and the systems that bring auditory signals to the brain did not interfere with fear conditioning, but that without those connections, the stimulus never lost its power—extinction became impossible. In the latter case, LeDoux and others later found, every time the rats were subjected to the stimulus (the sound of the bell), thus triggering the retrieval of their "fear" memory, particular neurons in the amygdala underwent molecular changes, including the synthesis of new proteins—changes that could be detected after the memory went back into storage. Thus, during the recall process a memory is affected by the person's mood as well as cognitive and emotional information (conscious and unconscious) acquired since the event that is being remembered. The new proteins, in effect, "update" the memory when it is stored again.

Those findings have had major implications for the treatment of an array of anxiety disorders in humans. Scientists in other labs have used LeDoux's discoveries of "evolving" memories to help war veterans or victims of violent assaults who suffer from PTSD. The scientists instructed their patients to write about their traumatic experiences in detail and then read silently what they had written. Immediately afterward, the patients were given a drug that interfered with protein synthesis involving the memory they had actively recalled. The next time the patients read their accounts of their traumas, their memories were less intense, indicating that the memories had reentered storage in a weakened state. Theoretically, given sufficiently potent drugs and enough time, their painful memories can be erased altogether.

After leaving Cornell, in 1989, LeDoux joined New York University, where he taught courses in neuroscience and psychology and continued his research. His investigations have greatly expanded knowledge about the amygdala: its structure and functions at the macroscopic level (parts observable with the naked eye); its structure and functions at the microscopic level, including its various populations of neurons, how they are organized, and how they function; projections that connect the amygdala to other parts of the brain; changes that take place in it during conditioned learning, including protein synthesis during retrieval and storage of memories; its modes of chemical and electrical signaling at synapses; its receptors for glucocorticoids and other hormones; and patterns of gene expression within it. In the past two decades, LeDoux has published upwards of 120 peer-reviewed professional papers with dozens of colleagues, among them Claudia R. Farb, Lizabeth M. Romanski, Glenn E. Schafe, and Karim Nader. The papers have appeared in an array of publications whose names indicate the breadth of LeDoux's work—*Brain Research*; *Journal of Neuroscience*; *Journal of Comparative Neurology*; *Genes, Brain and Behavior*; *Learning and Memory*; *Journal of Traumatic Stress*; *Neuropharmacology*; *Current Molecular Pharmacology*; *Synapse*; *Frontiers in Neural Circuits*; and *Psychoneuroendocrinology*, to name a few.

LeDoux's book *The Emotional Brain* earned glowing reviews. Paul Gross described it for the *Wilson Quarterly* (Winter 1997) as "an outstanding specimen of the accessible science book" and concluded, "I have not seen a more readable and compelling account of ongoing brain science and its implications for what it means to be human." In an assessment for the *American Journal of Psychiatry* (April 1998), Sergio Paradiso wrote that although *The Emotional Brain* is about "hard science," it "reads like a novel with a plot as thrilling as those of Agatha Christie." Using as examples experiences familiar to nonexperts, such as fears associated with car accidents, LeDoux explained that connections from the amygdala to the cognitive systems of the brain are stronger than connections from the cognitive systems to the amygdala. That is why, while conscious control of emotion and feeling is weak, emotion and feeling can easily overwhelm consciousness; in other words, it is much easier for feelings to overwhelm our thoughts than for our thoughts to push away unwanted feelings. There is "an imperfect set of connections between cognitive and emotional systems in the current stage of evolution of the human brain," LeDoux wrote in *Synaptic Self*. "This state of affairs is part of the price we pay for having newly evolved cognitive capacities that are not yet fully integrated into our brains." "Our brain has not evolved to the point where the new systems that make complex thinking possible can easily control the old systems that give rise to our basic needs and motives, and emotional reactions . . . ," he further explained. "Doing the right thing doesn't always flow naturally from knowing what the right thing to do is."

The theme of *Synaptic Self*, in LeDoux's words, is "You are your synapses. They are who you are," or, as William Calvin put it in an admiring review for *Nature* (June 13, 2002), "The synapses are the seat of self." In another enthusiastic assessment,

Richard J. Davidson wrote for *Science* (April 12, 2002), "The book's central message is that the self is the product of patterns of interconnectivity among neurons in the brain. Who we are is in large part learned through experience and much of this information is stored implicitly, in ways that affect our behavior but are not fully accessible consciously." LeDoux told *Current Biography* that one major point in *Synaptic Self* is that "nature and nurture are not different but two ways of doing the same thing, which is wiring synapses. The synapse is both the way through which nature operates on personality and through which experience operates on personality. . . . The brain is adaptive and malleable. To say that personality is a function of the brain does not mean that it's a hardwired function. Learning is an important part of brain wiring, as is genetics."

At present, LeDoux is seeking to find out more about what happens to memories in the brain after they are retrieved, how the brain goes from unconscious reaction to conscious action, and components of individual differences in fear reactions. He is working on a textbook titled "An Introduction to Brain, Mind and Behavior."

LeDoux is a fellow of the New York Academy of Sciences and the American Academy of Arts and Sciences. His other honors include awards from the NIMH, the American Psychological Association, and the Fyssen Foundation. He lives in New York City with his wife, Nancy Princenthal, an art critic and contributing editor at the magazine *Art in America*. Their son Milo is a student at Merton College, Oxford University, in England. Their first son, Jacob, is deceased.

—D.K.

Suggested Reading: amygdaloids.com; cns.nyu.edu/ledoux; *Economist* (on-line) Dec. 23, 2006; (London) *Sunday Telegraph* p12 Mar. 24, 2002; *New Scientist* (on-line) Jan. 4, 1997; *New York Times* C p1+ Nov. 5, 1996; *NYU Alumni Magazine* (on-line) Spring 2008; *Scientific American Mind* (on-line) Feb./Mar. 2006; *Talk of the Nation*, National Public Radio (on-line) July 9, 2010

Selected Books: as author—*The Integrated Mind* (with Michael Gazzaniga), 1978; *The Emotional Brain: The Mysterious Underpinnings of Emotional Life*, 1996; *Synaptic Self: How Our Brains Become Who We Are*, 2002; as co-editor—*Mind and Brain: Dialogues in Cognitive Neuroscience*, 1986; *The Self: From Soul to Brain*, 2003; *PostTraumatic Stress Disorder: Basic Science and Clinical Practice*, 2009

Courtesy of CNN

Lemon, Don

Mar. 1, 1966– Television news anchor; journalist

Address: CNN, 190 Marietta St., Atlanta, GA 30303-2762

Don Lemon is a co-anchor and journalist for *CNN Newsroom*, which airs every day of the week. Since he joined that cable news network, in 2006, he has covered a wide variety of subjects and events. He has interviewed President Barack Obama and the president's chief of staff, Rahm Emanuel, and reported on disasters including the bridge collapse in Minnesota in 2007 and Hurricane Gustav in 2008. A one-time model, Lemon worked as a trainee at a Fox television station in New York City while attending college full-time. "I loved it," he told a reporter for Brooklyn College (2005, on-line), speaking of his hectic schedule as an undergraduate. "When you make up your mind that you want to do something, it makes everything easier." After he completed his formal education, Lemon continued working for the local Fox station in New York. He next became a news reporter for a local Birmingham, Alabama, TV station; an investigative reporter for a St. Louis, Missouri, station; and a weekend anchor and reporter for WCAU-TV, an NBC affiliate in Philadelphia, Pennsylvania. In 2002 he joined NBC as a national correspondent and substitute anchor for NBC's show *Weekend Today*. For three years beginning in 2003, he co-anchored a news program and served as a reporter for the Chicago, Illinois, TV station WMAQ. While with WMAQ he visited places in Africa where AIDS had killed tens of millions of people and left millions of orphans, and he reported from Louisi-

ana in the wake of the devastation caused by Hurricane Katrina. "Journalism has afforded me the opportunity to see the world and to see things that many people will never see," Lemon told Lenox Magee for the Chicago weekly *N'Digo* (August 31–September 6, 2006). "And, to experience things that many people will never experience. It's a part of who I am. I am Don Lemon the journalist. And, because of those experiences, my entire life is integrated as a journalist. Africa helped me realize that. Hurricane Katrina helped me realize that."

Don Lemon was born in Baton Rouge, Louisiana, on March 1, 1966. (Various sources differ regarding his year of birth.) His mother, Katherine Lemon-Clark, raised him and his older sisters, Yma and Leisa. His sisters founded and run a company that bakes and sells pralines, a confection associated with New Orleans. As a child Lemon watched TV news and interview programs as well as sitcoms and cartoons. "I never saw that many people on TV that were like me," Lemon told Magee. "And, I didn't see a lot of people on TV that looked like my family. One day, I was watching the news and there was this African American woman on, Jean West," a longtime Louisville, Kentucky, television reporter. "She looked good, she dressed nicely, and she spoke professionally. That's when I knew what I wanted to do." Even at a young age, Lemon considered the professionalism of TV journalists and commentators to be of the utmost importance. Most of all he admired Peter Jennings and Bryant Gumbel. "Bryant," Lemon told Magee, "is a smart man that knows how to ask questions and get the answer. Peter Jennings just had a knack. He would be reading the teleprompter and reading the news, but you wouldn't think he was reading." Lemon also watched and admired Max Robinson, who in 1978, as a co-host (with Jennings and Frank Reynolds) of ABC's *World News Tonight*, became the first black person to anchor a network news broadcast in the U.S. Robinson was also one of the founders, in 1975, of the National Association of Black Journalists.

After graduating from Baker High School, in 1984, Lemon entered Louisiana State University, in Baton Rouge. He took courses in journalism, but his friends told him that he would "never make any money" in that field, Lemon told Judy Bergeron for the Baton Rouge *Advocate* (November 3, 2002). Instead, he chose marketing and economics as his major. But after a while the journalism classes won him over. He not only enjoyed them, he found that writing and reporting on-camera came naturally to him. The process of editing proved to be difficult for him, though, and after a professor told him that without editing skills he would never succeed as a journalist, he became very discouraged. At that time Lemon was also working as a model, on runways and for TV, newspaper, and magazine ads. He also did some modeling for a local department store, where a talent agent noticed him and offered him a contract. Lemon soon signed with the agency, dropped out of college, and moved to New York City. "Oh, I was scared when he first left here for that big city," Lemon's mother told Bergeron. "He just jumped in his Jeep and on his way he went."

Lemon modeled in New York for several years. Then he enrolled at Brooklyn College, a division of the City University of New York, as a full-time journalism student. One of his professors, Adrian J. Meppen, a co-author of the book *Broadcast News Writing, Reporting, and Producing*, encouraged Lemon, assuring him that he had the right qualities for a career in television. Lemon's response was to laugh, because he knew that TV journalism is extremely competitive. Lemon graduated from Brooklyn College with a bachelor's degree in television, radio, and broadcast journalism in 1996. Earlier, as an undergraduate, he had landed a trainee job at Channel 5, WNYW, the local Fox Network affiliate. At around the time he earned his degree, Lemon had a chance meeting at the studio with a WNYW news director who, after learning that Lemon wanted to become an on-air reporter, asked him for a demo tape. Impressed by the tape, the director offered Lemon a job. Soon Lemon was appearing on the air during segments of the *McCreary Report*, an urban-affairs program anchored by the award-winning journalist Bill McCreary, a Fox vice president who also executive-produced the show. Occasionally, on other programs, Lemon filled in for Channel 5 reporters who were on vacation. After a while he left New York and moved to the South, where he won steady work, first in Birmingham, Alabama, as a weekend TV anchor for about a year, and then in St. Louis, Missouri, as a general-assignment reporter for about a year and a half. Then, in 1999, Lemon secured a job as the weekend anchor and general-assignment reporter at WCAU, an NBC affiliate in Philadelphia.

In the summer of 2002, having declined job offers from ABC and CNN, Lemon returned to New York City, to serve as a correspondent for Tom Brokaw's *NBC Nightly News*, the weekly newsmagazine *Dateline*, and MSNBC programs as well as an anchor for *Weekend Today* and MSNBC. He soon began to travel far afield, spending "a few weeks here, a few weeks there, at bureaus across the country"—an agenda he found "grueling," he told Bergeron. In Louisiana he covered the devastation caused when Hurricane Lili hit Houma, a town near Baton Rouge; in Miami, Florida, he investigated the high rates of HIV infection and AIDS within the black community; in Chicago, Illinois, he interviewed Iraqi-Americans and reported on their lives; and in the Washington, D.C., metropolitan area, he followed what came to be known as the Beltway sniper attacks, in which two men, over the course of a few weeks in October 2002, killed 10 people and injured three others.

In the summer of 2003, Lemon returned to local news, joining NBC's Chicago-based Channel 5, WMAQ, as the co-anchor of the 5:00 p.m. weekday newscast. "After leaving local news for the network, I never imagined I'd miss being part of a community so much," Lemon told Robert Feder for the *Chicago Sun-Times* (July 11, 2003). "Chicago is an amazing, world-class city. Now I get to work and live there. What more can I ask for?" But after less than a year with Channel 5, Lemon found himself in trouble with the station's management and the focus of articles in Chicago newspapers, stemming from an incident that occurred in March 2004. During that time Lemon, accompanied by a camera crew, had arrived at the scene of a fatal stabbing of a 16-year-old boy near a high school in Park Ridge, a Chicago suburb. After he learned the circumstances of the murder, he refused to cover the story because, he believed, it was not sufficiently newsworthy. WMAQ higher-ups sent another reporter to cover the story, and Lemon was suspended for three days. He was unapologetic, however. "I am a journalist, not a news robot," he told Gail Shister for the *Philadelphia Inquirer* (March 18, 2004). "I get paid to ask questions. As a journalist, I can question the content of what goes on our air and what I'm sent out to do. Any journalist worth their salt would." Despite the strained relationship with station executives that followed, Lemon stayed with WMAQ for another two and a half years. During that time he worked on two of the biggest stories of his career: the AIDS epidemic in Africa and the aftermath of Hurricane Katrina.

Lemon's story about the disproportionate number of new AIDS cases in Miami's black community had never been aired. He pitched the story again to WMAQ decision makers, but without success. After he learned more about the AIDS crisis in some sub-Saharan African nations, which have a disproportionately high percentage of the world's cases of AIDS and HIV infection, Lemon told Magee, he resolved to "go broader than just the community." At his own expense and with his own equipment, he traveled to Africa with an assistant (a student at Columbia College, in Chicago). In hospitals, orphanages, and community centers, Lemon saw the deadly and horrendous consequences of the AIDS crisis. In a typical example, a woman whose daughters had died or were dying of AIDS had become the sole caretaker of her four grandchildren, who were now living with her in a mud hut. Lemon sent some of his footage to Chicago's local NBC station, which posted it on a video blog. The full story aired after Lemon returned, as a three-part series on the 10:00 p.m. news. The series generated praise from viewers and fellow journalists, and it earned Lemon honors including three local Emmy Awards. What he saw and experienced in Africa, Lemon told Bergeron, "didn't only change me personally, it changed my career, it changed everything, how I view the world, what I put importance on as far as life. I think it not only made me a better journalist, but it made me a better person. I don't complain as much."

Hurricane Katrina hit the American Gulf Coast in late August 2005, devastating parts of Florida, Mississippi, and especially Louisiana, where breaches in the levees and failure of the floodwalls along Lake Ponchartrain caused massive flooding in New Orleans. "When we [NBC-5] found out that the levees were about to break, I just kept begging the news management to send me," Lemon told Magee. "They knew that I was from there, so I just kept saying 'hey guys, send me!' I wouldn't let up. And, when the levees were about to break, they said 'pack your bags.'" Getting into New Orleans was extraordinarily difficult, so for several weeks Lemon and his camera crew stayed in Mississippi, mostly in and near the city of Biloxi. After Lemon arrived in New Orleans, he filed stories for Channel 5 and wrote about his experiences on a blog. Lemon told Magee that the Katrina survivors' "story needed to be told because they needed help. And, probably the main way that was going to happen was through the media. We were there to tell a story, even if you have a personal connection with the subject. I knew millions of people were counting on me to tell that story."

Lemon left NBC in September 2006 to become a co-anchor of *CNN Newsroom*. He reported from Chicago prior to the 2008 presidential election; after the election he interviewed then-congressman Rahm Emanuel on the day he accepted the position of chief of staff for President-elect Barack Obama. Lemon has also interviewed Obama; Anne Cooper, a 106-year-old black woman who voted for Obama; the singer Michael Jackson's father, Joe Jackson; the rapper Nas; and many others. He covered the bridge collapse in Minnesota in 2007 and Hurricane Gustav, which devastated parts of the Atlantic Coast in 2008.

In an article for the *Huffington Post* (September 30, 2010, on-line), Trish Kinney discussed an interview that Lemon had recently conducted for CNN with three young African-American members of the New Birth Missionary Baptist Church in Atlanta, Georgia. The three talked about allegations that their church's leader, Bishop Eddie Long, had made unwanted sexual advances toward some young congregants. During the interview Lemon revealed that as a child he had been a victim of sexual abuse by an "older pedophile," in Kinney's words; he added that he had not told his mother about what had happened to him until he was 30 years old. "How very few role models we have in our society for 'telling,' especially when it is the abuser who is perceived to have, or actually does have, the power in such relationships," Kinney wrote. "Mr. Lemon . . . changed the game by being a successful survivor with a powerful voice of his own."

Lemon lives in Atlanta.

—D.K.

Suggested Reading: (Baton Rouge, Louisiana) *Advocate* p25 Nov. 3, 2002; brooklyn.cuny.edu; cnn.com; *N'Digo* p6 Aug. 31–Sep. 6, 2006; *Philadelphia Inquirer* D p8 May 20, 2002

Levy, Andrea

(LEE-vee)

Mar. 7, 1956– Novelist

Address: c/o Farrar Straus & Giroux, 19 Union Square West, New York, NY 10003

As a young woman Andrea Levy sought out literary fiction that would shed light on her experiences as a black person growing up in London, England—only to find that very little existed. Therefore, as she told Jackie McGlone for the Glasgow, Scotland, *Herald* (January 31, 2004), "I wrote the books I wanted to read." While her first three novels, *Every Light in the House Burnin'* (1994), *Never Far from Nowhere* (1996), and *Fruit of the Lemon* (1999), were well-reviewed, it was her fourth, *Small Island* (2004), that brought Levy prizes and widespread recognition. That book, in which each of the protagonists tells his or her story, centers on the lives of two couples—one black Jamaican, one white British—living in the same house in late-1940s London. Levy's latest novel is *The Long Song* (2010), which takes place in Jamaica in the early 19th century, during the days of slavery. *The Long Song* has received consistently good reviews.

The youngest of four children, Andrea Levy was born on March 7, 1956 in London to Jamaican immigrants. She was raised in a council estate—public housing—in Highbury, in north London, where hers was the only black family in the neighborhood. Her parents were part of the first wave of Caribbean immigrants to come to the United Kingdom after World War II. Her father, Winston, was one of the 492 people who in 1948 sailed from Jamaica to England on a onetime troop ship, the *Empire Windrush*, whose arrival was a significant step toward British multiculturalism. A few months later Levy's mother, Amy, arrived in England on another vessel. A teacher by training, she worked as a seamstress in London because her teaching credentials were rejected there; with additional training, she later served as a deputy headmistress of a school. Winston, who had been a bookkeeper in Jamaica, worked as an accounts clerk for the postal service. England was not what the couple had envisioned it to be. In Jamaica they were both educated members of the middle class and were considered "colored" (a designation given to light-skinned blacks), attributes they expected to bring them a certain amount of privilege in England; instead, they were considered simply black and at times suffered discrimination as a result. In the Levy house race and racism were never discussed. Neither was Jamaica. "I was not at all curious about Ja-

Christopher Furlong/Getty Images

Andrea Levy

maica as a child," Levy told Gary Younge for the London *Guardian* (January 30, 2010). "We were told, not in so many words, to be ashamed of it." Levy's parents valued education and tried to make sure their children worked hard in school. Levy, who was not very interested in schoolwork or reading, preferred to watch TV.

Ironically, it was by watching television that Levy discovered something of her father's history. When she was 17, in 1973—the 25th anniversary of the *Windrush* voyage—Levy happened to be watching a program about it when her father, ironing in the same room, casually remarked that he had been on the ship. At the time that information meant little to Levy, though, as she told Jackie Mc-Glone, it made her father "impossibly glamorous for about 10 seconds." Her father never brought the subject up again (he died in the 1980s), and Levy remained uninterested in her parents' past or in issues of race.

At Middlesex University, in London, Levy studied textile design and weaving. She later worked in the costume departments of the BBC and the Royal Opera House. One day when she was 26 and working for a volunteer organization, the volunteers were asked to split into a black group and a white group, as part of a race-awareness exercise. Levy—whose tan skin and black, curly hair sometimes led people to think she was Jewish, Spanish, or Italian—went to the white side. When someone pointed out that she was black, she innocently suggested that she was "half-caste," or of mixed race, and was told in response that that term was outdated and offensive. At that moment a seed of racial awareness was planted in Levy. After attending a lecture by the civil rights activist Angela Davis, Levy be-

gan to read voraciously, consuming the work of such black American female authors as Maya Angelou, Alice Walker, Audre Lorde, and Toni Morrison. She wanted, however, to read books reflecting her experience of growing up black in Britain. "You couldn't just go into a bookshop and say, 'I'll have your finest book on being Black British.' It was hard," Levy told Maggie O'Farrell for the London *Independent* (February 28, 1999). "So I thought I'd try writing."

After attending writing workshops, Levy, in her mid-30s, turned to fiction to discuss the black British experience. Her first novel was taken on by an agent, only to be rejected by publishers for the next year. "Publishers have a herd mentality," Levy said to Raekha Prasad for the *Guardian* (March 4, 1999). "They were worried that I'd be read only by black people—less than a million [in Britain] and they don't read anyway. . . . There was nothing to show I'd sell. But it's grist to my mill. My attitude is, I'm gonna get these [expletive]s. I'd love to have them pawing at my door. No one had been really successful as a black British writer writing about everyday things." The book company Headline Review signed her in 1994.

Levy's first three novels, all semiautobiographical, were generally well received. They explore the lives of children of Jamaicans in a constantly changing London, revealing how their experience is different from that of their parents—and how issues of race, family, and identity collide and overlap. Levy's first book, *Every Light in the House Burnin'* (1994), tells the story of Angela Jacob, a young black woman born and raised in north London's public housing during the 1960s. The narrative moves frequently between the present and past. Angela's father is seriously ill with cancer and, with his wife at his bedside, expresses bewilderment over the brashness of his children. Sitting with her father Angela remembers her childhood, during which her parents did their best to blend in and assimilate, while the children wanted equal rights and respect from the country of their birth. Critics commended Levy for her ability to delicately balance the comic and the tragic. "Their family story is told in a series of quick, impressionistic scenes, often hilarious, sometimes deeply moving," Aisling Foster wrote for the London *Independent* (November 27, 1994). "Play-ground skirmishes, hair straightening . . . a visit by relatives from Jamaica are told with such assured economy it is clear that Levy has plenty more to say about being British, or just about life."

Levy did have more to say: her next book, *Never Far from Nowhere* (1996), told the story of two very different sisters growing up in London's housing projects during the 1970s. The sisters, Olive and Vivien, narrate the book in alternating chapters—which, as the book progresses, illuminate how differently they see the world. While the girls' mother does not want to acknowledge the fact of race, her daughters' encounters in the outside world make it impossible to ignore. The main characters in the book, compared with those in Levy's first novel, are not very sympathetic, and the narrative tone is generally harsher. "*Never Far from Nowhere*," Christina Patterson wrote for the *Independent* (February 18, 1996), "is as much about the painful, messy reality of family life—too much envy, too little love—as it is about race and identity. In this lively, crisp, raw voice, young black Londoners may have found their Roddy Doyle"—the Irish novelist who has written about the lives of young residents of Dublin, Ireland, in such books as *The Commitments* (1987).

When Levy's third book, *Fruit of the Lemon* (1999), was published, Raekha Prasad wrote in the *Guardian* profile that the author was "the most prolific black female British-born novelist." In light of Levy's having published three well-received books in five years, the headline of the Prasad profile posed the question: "So why isn't she better known?" Like her first two books, *Fruit of the Lemon* focuses on the life of a second-generation Jamaican Londoner. Unlike the characters in those books, the protagonist—Faith Jackson—is interested in her heritage, journeying to Jamaica to learn about it. The first part of the book, titled "England," covers by-now-familiar, semiautobiographical territory. A reviewer for the *Independent* (March 13, 1999) called that part of the book "a disappointingly flat read" and argued that Levy's portrait of the "typical" Jamaican family is stereotypical. That view was not unanimous among reviewers; still, the core of the novel appeared to be its second half, titled "Jamaica," in which Faith goes to her parents' country of birth and meets Aunt Coral, who shares with her some of the family's history. That part of the book, the *Independent* reviewer noted, "is bright and inventive, brought alive by the moving and humorous creation of Faith's colourful extended family, and its extraordinary history."

Five years later Levy published *Small Island* (2004), which brought her unanimous praise, prestigious awards, and international recognition. *Small Island*—the name refers to both Jamaica and Britain—was a first for Levy in several ways: two of its four main characters are white, and its writing required substantial research (including interviews with her mother), because much of the narrative is set in late-1940s London, before Levy's birth. In *Small Island* Levy provided an elaborate account of cross-cultural ignorance, intimacy, understanding, and misunderstanding. Having served in the British air force during World War II, Gilbert, a Jamaican, returns to his home country; a few years later he joins hundreds of his countrymen on the *Empire Windrush*, bound for England. Soon Hortense, his wife, sails to London, where she joins her husband in a shabby apartment they rent from Queenie, a white working-class Englishwoman. Queenie's husband, Bernard, who also served in the war, returns to London from India and is displeased to find that his wife has a job and that there are black people living in his home. The tenants are also displeased: Gilbert would like to study law but instead drives a post-office truck, while his wife, proud, snobbish, and disappointed by their living conditions, cannot find work as a teacher, her former profession. As in Levy's previous book, her characters take turns telling their stories, which are set during, before, and after World War II.

In a review for the London *Guardian* (February 14, 2004), Mike Phillips called *Small Island* "honest, skilful, thoughtful and important." He also observed: "The interaction between the couples is, to a certain extent, predictable, but a notable feature of the book is that the entire narrative and the stories within it clearly emerge from the memories of the period's survivors. If ever there was a novel which offered a historically faithful account of how its characters thought and behaved, this is it. But the sheer excellence of Levy's research goes beyond the granddad tales of 50-year-old migrant experience, or the nuts and bolts of historical fact. Her imagination illuminates old stories in a way that almost persuades you she was there at the time." The book sold more than one million copies in England and was published in 22 other countries. It also inspired a BBC television miniseries that attracted millions of viewers in Britain and the U.S.

Levy was commended for her realistic rendering of speech—both English and Jamaican—and for her ability to create interesting characters who could arouse both sympathy and contempt. "What makes Levy's writing so appealing is her even-handedness," Marianne Brace wrote for the *Independent* (June 12, 2004). "All her characters can be weak, hopeless, brave, good, bad—whatever their colour." The book also received many notable literary honors, including the 2004 Orange Prize for Fiction, the 2004 Whitbread Novel Award, and the 2005 Commonwealth Writers Prize. By the time the book was published in the U.S., in 2005, American critics had become well aware of the hype surrounding it, which they addressed directly in their reviews. "We steel ourselves for reader backlash," Mameve Medwed wrote for the *Boston Globe* (July 3, 2005). "Can Levy's fourth novel be this good? It can. It is."

Levy's latest novel is *The Long Song* (2010), which is set in Jamaica in the early 19th century. The book's narrator is Miss July, who was conceived when a plantation's Scottish overseer raped her mother. Decades later, when she is an old woman, her long-lost son (a well-off publisher) brings her to his home in England and persuades her to share her life's story. As a child, the light-skinned Miss July was taken in by the plantation owner's sister and became her maid. Renamed Marguerite, she worked in her owner's house, minding the proprieties of British decorum while other slaves struggled on the plantation—until the Baptist War of 1831, the 10-day slave revolt that led to the eventual end of slavery in Jamaica. After the uprising Miss July became the mediator between the plantation's new owner and the recently freed slaves; but the owner quickly forgot his good intentions and used violence to control his workers. "It's clear that Levy has done her research, but this work never intrudes upon the narrative, which travels at a jaunty pace," Tayari Jones wrote for the *Washington Post* (May 8, 2010). "Levy's sly humor swims just under the surface of the most treacherous waters. (For example, a shocking suicide is preceded by a delightful farce.) Her refusal to reduce her characters to merely their suffering does not trivialize the experience of enslavement, but underscores the humanity of all involved."

Levy and her husband, Bill Mayblin, a graphic designer, live in London. Levy is stepmother to Mayblin's daughters, Maya and Hannah.

—D.K.

Suggested Reading: andrealevy.co.uk; (London) *Independent* p38 Nov. 27, 1994, p32 Feb. 18, 1996, Feb. 28, 1999, June 12, 2004; *New York Times Book Review* p17 Apr. 3, 2005, p9 May 9, 2010

Selected Books: *Every Light in the House Burnin'*, 1994; *Never Far from Nowhere*, 1996; *Fruit of the Lemon*, 1999; *Small Island*, 2004; *The Long Song*, 2010

Courtesy of Lisa Lillien

Lillien, Lisa

Dec. 31, 1966– Founder and CEO of Hungry Girl; cookbook author; Web entrepreneur

Address: 18034 Ventura Blvd., Suite 503, Encino, CA 91316

"I'm not a nutritionist. I'm not a doctor. I'm just someone who loves to eat," Lisa Lillien told Susan Young for the *Contra Costa (California) Times* (May 19, 2008). "I'm someone who decided to share some knowledge about how to eat the right way. You can have snacks; you just have to eat everything in moderation." Lillien is the founder and CEO of Hungry Girl, a free, daily e-mal subscription service that provides eating tips and low-calorie recipes for such popular foods as pizza and

onion rings. Since it was launched, in early 2004, the service—along with its Web site spin-off, Hungry-Girl.com—has evolved into a word-of-mouth phenomenon, spawning an empire that includes such best-selling cookbooks as *Hungry Girl: Recipes and Survival Strategies for Guilt-Free Eating in the Real World* (2008), *Hungry Girl 200 Under 200: 200 Recipes Under 200 Calories* (2009), and *Hungry Girl 1-2-3: The Easiest, Most Delicious, Guilt-Free Recipes on the Planet* (2010).

Lillien's e-mail service currently has nearly a million subscribers, and what started out as a modest endeavor is now a lucrative business. Hank Stuever wrote for the *Washington Post* (April 24, 2009), "In an online cacophony of self-started Web sites offering strong opinions about what to eat-buy-do, Lillien is one of those rare profitable breakouts. Hungry Girl occupies a new frontier between consumer news and retail sales, blowing past traditional media." The mass appeal of the Hungry Girl newsletter and books can be attributed in large part to their unpretentious style, which is both personal and informative. Lillien liberally sprinkles her writing with her pet expressions ("Two Yums Up") and tempting recipe names ("Chocolate Pudding Crunch Explosion"). She told Lauren F. Friedman for the *Philadelphia Daily News* (July 13, 2009), "I'm a very casual person. The voice of Hungry Girl is basically me." The same could be said for Hungry Girl's colorful logo, which features an appealingly drawn caricature of Lillien. In a profile for the *Los Angeles Times* (July 22, 2009), Rene Lynch wrote that the Hungry Girl CEO "looks disconcertingly like her cartoon image sprung to life, including the feline-green eyes, gleaming white teeth, and swing-y brown locks."

Lisa Lillien was born on December 31, 1966 and grew up on Long Island, New York. At an early age she was exposed to the problems that come with quick-fix weight-loss programs. "I grew up in a dieting household," Lillien recalled to Lisa Ryckman for the Denver, Colorado, *Rocky Mountain News* (May 13, 2008). "My mom was a yo-yo dieter, always trying the latest fad diets." As a teenager,

Lillien, wanting to lose a few pounds, joined her mother, Florence, in a succession of fad diets, with few discernible results. Lillien's sister, who attended a weight-loss camp one summer, had similar problems. Their brother, however, overate with impunity. Lillien noted to Stuever that it was not uncommon for him to consume "an entire box of Lucky Charms, in a salad bowl, with a carton of whole milk," but he remained "a stick with a big head, who never gained weight."

After graduating from Lawrence High School, in Cedarhurst, New York, in 1983, Lillien entered the State University of New York (SUNY) at Albany, where she majored in communications. Upon earning her bachelor's degree, in 1987, she became an editor at the now-defunct teen fan magazine *Tutti Frutti.* Lillien then entered the television industry, working as an executive producer for the on-line arm of the TV Land network and later as the director of convergence development for Nickelodeon's on-line concerns. She has also worked as an executive in on-line development at Warner Bros.

While enjoying enviable career success, Lillien found herself struggling to lose weight. "I was that person who would sit at the computer and eat an entire bag of fat-free pretzels and think I was doing a good thing," she told Stuever. "[But] I wasn't." Lillien subsequently gave up bread, pasta, and potatoes and began eating more fruits, vegetables, and lean meat. She also walked for an hour on the treadmill five times a week and ultimately lost about 30 pounds. She realized, however, that her spartan regimen was unsustainable, and she became determined to incorporate snacks and treats into her routine.

Wary of the nutritional information posted on products, one day Lillien drove 40 miles from her home in Los Angeles, California, to have her favorite pastries tested at an independent lab. "I was obsessed with them because they were fantastic and supposedly very low-calorie," she recalled to Ryckman. "I have since learned that if it tastes too good to be true, it probably is." Lillien began playing "mad scientist in the kitchen," as she has phrased it, concocting low-calorie snacks and modified versions of cake and brownies. In 2003 she began sending recommendations for preparing low-fat dishes and for finding healthy food in mainstream supermarkets to a handful of contacts. She was soon receiving enthusiastic feedback. "I knew I was on to something," she told Lynch.

In early 2004 Lillien quit her job and launched Hungry Girl with $10,000 of her own money. She explained to Lynch, "I told my husband, 'If after a year, this is just an expensive hobby, I will go back to work.'" Starting out with fewer than 200 subscribers—mostly friends and family members—the free e-mail service quickly expanded. Lillien recalled to Meghan Casserly for *Forbes* (October 20, 2009, on-line), "When I started, I hired one person. We e-mailed everyone we knew and said, 'This is what is happening: Hungry Girl is going to be this

and this, and if it's interesting to you, sign up—but *only* if it's interesting.' From day one, I wanted that list to be pure, filled with people who really liked the content." She continued, "We started getting new subscribers every day. At first it was nine subscribers, and then 20 a day and then 30, 50. The more people we had on the list, the more people were seeing it and subscribing every day." Currently Hungry Girl has nearly one million subscribers, and it attracts hundreds of new readers a day. Hungry Girl content can also be found on such social-networking sites as Facebook (where it has more than 200,000 fans) and Twitter (where it has attracted some 48,000 followers).

While companies often aggressively vie for notice on the Hungry Girl Web site or in the daily e-mails, Lillien—who now employs a staff of graphic designers, recipe testers, and others—refuses to accept payment in exchange for a product review or mention. She will tout an item only if she feels that it tastes good and provides what she has called "a lot of bang for your calorie buck." She explained to Natalie Haughton for the *Los Angeles Daily News* (April 18, 2006), "I write about what I love and I'm not afraid to name names." Lillien does accept payment for ads on her site, but only from manufacturers whose products she actually uses.

Some of the products whose sales have skyrocketed as a result of being mentioned by Lillien include Fiber One cereal, which she grinds to make crispy coatings for such items as oven-baked chicken or onion rings; PopChips, a low-fat alternative to conventional potato chips; and Vitalicious Vita-Tops, nutritious, low-calorie muffins. One previously little-known company, House Foods America, could barely keep up with demand after Lillien wrote of its Tofu Shirataki noodles: "We're gonna be straight with you here. We had completely given up on pasta until we were introduced to the wonders of Tofu Shirataki. Made of tofu and yam flour (it tastes better than it sounds), these noodlicious creations are high in fiber [and] VERY low in calories. . . . It's essentially 'pasta' with hardly any carbs or calories. That's complete and total insanity! Add these to your favorite soups, salads, or anywhere else you'd normally use pasta. We cannot possibly begin to explain to you how much we love and cherish these noodles. They WILL change your life."

Although Lillien sometimes receives criticism from nutrition professionals for her recommendations of processed foods, she has not changed her approach to her work. She explained to Friedman, "There are always going to be the purists who don't believe in any packaged food, but people are going to eat packaged foods anyway, and they need help." She added, "Someone needs to be the bridge between the complete 'shop the perimeter of the store' [where the produce, meat, and dairy sections are located] people and the full-on 'I'm eating a giant package of Oreos every day' people. There's got to be a happy medium."

In 2008 Lillien published *Hungry Girl: Recipes and Survival Strategies for Guilt-Free Eating in the Real World*. The book, a compilation of her most popular recipes and tips, debuted at number two on the *New York Times* "how-to"-books best-seller list and quickly sold more than 600,000 copies. "This is not a typical cookbook. If you're looking for fancy, formal 'chef-like' recipes you've definitely come to the wrong place," Lillien told an interviewer for MSNBC.com (May 1, 2008). "This book is filled with simple, fun, easy recipes that use lots of packaged foods and shortcuts to make great-tasting guilt-free snacks and meals. If you aspire to be a gourmet chef, there are more appropriate books out there for you. But if you want to prepare awesome, tongue-pleasing foods that won't send you out shopping for bigger pants, you've got the right book!"

The following year Lillien published the equally popular *Hungry Girl 200 Under 200: 200 Recipes Under 200 Calories*, which debuted at number one on the *New York Times* how-to best-seller list, and she followed that in March 2010 with *Hungry Girl 1-2-3: The Easiest, Most Delicious, Guilt-Free Recipes on the Planet*. The latest Hungry Girl book, *Hungry Girl Happy Hour: 75 Recipes for Amazingly Fantastic Guilt-Free Cocktails and Party Foods*, arrived in bookstores in June 2010 and spent three weeks on the *New York Times*'s paperback "Advice" best-seller list. In 2011 Lillien will begin hosting a Hungry Girl television show on the Cooking Channel, a recently launched spin-off of the Food Network.

Lillien, who collects kitschy memorabilia from the 1970s and 1980s, lives in Encino, California, with her husband, Dan Schneider, whom she married in 2002. Schneider is a former actor who played the role of Dennis Blunden, an overweight chemistry whiz, on the hit ABC sitcom *Head of the Class* (1986–91). Now a television writer and producer, Schneider is responsible for such hit Nickelodeon series as *Zoey 101*, *Drake & Josh*, and *iCarly*.

—C.C.

Suggested Reading: *Contra Costa (California) Times* Spotlight p8 May 19, 2008; (Denver, Colorado) *Rocky Mountain News* p8 May 13, 2008; *Forbes* (on-line) Oct. 20, 2009; (Fort Lauderdale, Florida) *Sun-Sentinel* p5 May 18, 2006; *Los Angeles Daily News* U p12+ Apr. 18, 2006; *Los Angeles Times* E p1+ July 22, 2009; (Philadelphia, Pennsylvania) *Daily News* p29 July 13, 2009; *Washington Post* A p1+ Apr. 24, 2009

Selected Books: *Hungry Girl: Recipes and Survival Strategies for Guilt-Free Eating in the Real World*, 2008; *Hungry Girl 200 Under 200: 200 Recipes Under 200 Calories*, 2009; *Hungry Girl 1-2-3: The Easiest, Most Delicious, Guilt-Free Recipes on the Planet*, 2010; *Hungry Girl Happy Hour: 75 Recipes for Amazingly Fantastic Guilt-Free Cocktails and Party Foods*, 2010

Jed Jacobsohn/Getty Images

Lincecum, Tim

(LIN-seh-kum)

June 15, 1984– Baseball player

Address: San Francisco Giants, AT&T Park, 24 Willie Mays Plaza, San Francisco, CA 94107

The pitcher Tim Lincecum, who turned 26 in June 2010, has played only three full seasons with the San Francisco Giants, and he is already one of the most dominant pitchers in Major League Baseball (MLB). Since he began playing the sport, Lincecum has been known for two things: his small stature relative to other power pitchers—officially listed as five feet 11 inches and 170 pounds, he was nicknamed "Seabiscuit" by major-league scouts, after the undersized champion racehorse—and his unusual if not unique pitching style, taught to him by his father as a way to reduce stress on his arm. "Most pitchers are taught a delivery in segments, such as a step back, a gathering of the limbs while balanced over the rubber, the loading of the ball in a cocked position behind the head and then a fast uncoiling of the body as the arm comes forward . . . ," Tom Verducci wrote for *Sports Illustrated* (July 7, 2008). "Lincecum, by contrast, pitches with the intentions of a drag racer: It's go time from the start. His delivery gives the illusion of being one movement rather than the cobbling of several separate ones." Greg Bishop, writing for the *Seattle Times* (April 25, 2006), described Lincecum's pitching as incorporating "feet, ankles, knees, hips, chest, shoulders, elbow and then wrist. Each body part in the throwing motion as important as the one before. The key is rhythm and centering the body to the core in the lower back. The idea is to make the body into a whip, relying on the motion and not the arm." Known for his dominant fastball, which regularly reaches speeds between about 95 and 100 miles per hour, Lincecum won the National League (NL) Cy Young Award in 2008—his second major-league season—and again in 2009, leading the league in strikeouts and earning a spot on the All-Star team in both seasons. In 2010 he led the NL in strikeouts for the third consecutive year and earned his third career All Star selection. Lincecum's pitching dominance extended into the 2010 postseason, in which he compiled a 4–1 record and helped the Giants clinch their first World Series title since 1954.

The second son of Chris and Rebecca Lincecum, Timothy LeRoy Lincecum was born on June 15, 1984 in Bellevue, Washington. His brother, Sean, is four years older. Chris Lincecum, an inventory-parts specialist at the Boeing aircraft company, was a pitcher on teams in junior college and in a semi-professional baseball league. He learned to pitch—in the same unusual style now used by Tim—from his uncle and his father, Leo. After Leo Lincecum's death, Chris Lincecum regretted not having spent more time throwing the baseball with his father and decided that he would not make the same mistake with his own children. He gave Sean backyard pitching lessons, teaching him to rely on more parts of the body and to use a lengthier, slower windup and a longer stride than most pitchers employed. "Basically, it's a sequence of leverages from toes to fingertips," Chris Lincecum explained to Ron Kroichick for *Baseball Digest* (October 1, 2008). "You use all your small muscles. His body does almost all the work and his arm comes along for the ride." Before he was old enough to pitch, Tim Lincecum would hang around during his brother's lessons, imitating what he saw. When he recognized Tim's interest and natural talent, Chris began teaching his younger son, too, to pitch. Unlike Sean, Tim Lincecum was always small for his age; his size sometimes led to his being overlooked for teams, despite his superior skills on the field. Chris Lincecum recalled to Gary Estwick for the *Fresno (California) Bee* (April 6, 2007) that there were times when, as a Little League player, Tim was selected for the all-star team but did not get to play during the game because the coach thought he was too small. "It's been that way my whole life," Lincecum told Bishop for the *Seattle Times* (June 5, 2006). "I always had to deal with [people thinking] that I was too small, this and that. It's just really old to me."

In his first two years at Liberty High School, in Renton, Washington, Lincecum played for the junior-varsity teams. "At the time [as a sophomore], he was probably 5-foot-4 or 5-foot-5 and weighed 120 pounds," Bret Grandstrand, one of Lincecum's high-school teammates, told Mark Purdy for the *San Jose (California) Mercury News* (June 1, 2008). "He was throwing a lot of breaking pitches, and the coach said, 'He doesn't throw it hard enough.' I

said, 'I don't care. He's getting people out.' He always had a live arm. That season, he shut out everybody in J.V. but they still never brought him up." As he grew and gained weight, Lincecum's pitches gained speed. Playing for the varsity team during his junior year, Lincecum earned a 4–2 record and a .73 earned-run average (ERA) and was selected for the first-team All-Eastside team. As a senior Lincecum posted a 12–1 record, an ERA of .70, and 183 strikeouts, helping to lead his team to a 20–7 record and a class-3A state championship victory. Lincecum won the state's 2003 Gatorade Player of the Year award and the 3A Most Valuable Player (MVP) award and was selected to play on the first-team All-State. He also played in the state's All-Star series in Wenatchee, where he received MVP honors. Lincecum graduated from high school in 2003, with a 3.25 grade-point average; at that time he stood five feet 11 inches and weighed 138 pounds.

After graduating Lincecum, who had been overlooked by major-league scouts, enrolled at the University of Washington (UW). He had impressed Craig Parthemer, the assistant baseball coach at UW, while playing for Parthemer's summer-league team as a high-school junior. Parthemer told UW's head coach, Ken Knutson, about Lincecum's talent, and Knutson agreed to watch him pitch. Upon meeting Lincecum, Knutson was surprised by the pitcher's lack of bulk and thought Parthemer "must have been kidding," he told Bishop (April 25, 2006). But Knutson was impressed, telling Bishop: "I don't know what to tell you. I've been coaching for almost 25 years, and he's got the best stuff I've ever seen." As a freshman Lincecum posted a 10–3 record, led all teams in the Pac-10 Conference in strikeouts (161)—a UW single-season record—and achieved the fourth-best ERA in the Pac-10 (3.53). Lincecum also ranked first in called strikeouts (60) and fourth in wins (10) and held opposing batters to the second-lowest batting average (.207) of any Pac-10 pitcher that year. He was the first player to receive both the Pac-10 Freshman of the Year and the Pac-10 Pitcher of the Year awards (and the first UW player to win either award). *Collegiate Baseball* named Lincecum the national freshman of the year and first-team freshman All-American. *Baseball America* identified Lincecum as the number-one prospect to be drafted to play in the Pacific International League (PIL), a competitive amateur league that serves as a developing ground for college players. During the summer Lincecum pitched for the Seattle Studs PIL team, helping lead them to the National Baseball Congress World Series.

During his sophomore year Lincecum, as UW's number-one starting pitcher, tied the school's second-place record for strikeouts (131) in a single season (falling behind only his own freshman-year record) and earned All Pac-10 honors for the second straight season. He led the conference with the lowest opponent batting average (.179), and his strikeout total ranked second in the Pac-10. Lincecum's statistics—as well as his 100-mph fastball and his impressive breaking ball—caught the attention of major-league scouts, but many were dismayed by the pitcher's size and technique. In the 2005 MLB draft, the Cleveland Indians selected Lincecum in the 42d round, as the number-1,262 pick. "There aren't too many comparables at his size, especially as starting pitchers," the Indians' general manager, Mark Shapiro, told Verducci about the team's decision to select Lincecum so late in the draft. Scouts, Shapiro noted, were worried that Lincecum's size and pitching style would result in a career marked by injuries and early retirement: "It looks like his head is going to snap off and his arm is going to fly off. Body type has something to do with it, but the way he throws too." Lincecum declined the Indians' offer, thinking he could secure a better contract if he played one more year in college. Spending the summer pitching for the Harwich Mariners, in the amateur Cape Cod League, Lincecum impressed major-league teams, posting a .69 ERA, a record of 2–2, 68 strikeouts, and an opposing batting average of .104 in 39.1 innings. He was named Cape Cod League All-Star and the Mariners' Pitcher of the Year. "That was probably the best decision I made, going to the Cape and not signing," Lincecum recalled at a press conference, as quoted by Bishop (June 5, 2006). "I had the best outings of my life there. Everything just kind of came together."

By the end of Lincecum's junior year at UW, he had secured single-season records for wins (12) and strikeouts (199) and college-career records for wins (30), starts (51), innings played (342.0), and strikeouts (491). His strikeout total was also the best of any Pac-10 player in history. He was named Player of the Week by *Collegiate Baseball* six times and appeared on the College Baseball Foundation's weekly honor roll seven times. He was also nominated for the 2006 Golden Spikes Award, which honors the nation's best amateur baseball player. Addressing the lingering reluctance of major-league scouts to accept Lincecum's unorthodox throwing style, Knutson told Bishop (April 25, 2006): "I don't expect him to break down, because of the way he takes care of his body. . . . If you project out, he's going to be an All-Star, a dominant major-league pitcher." *Baseball America* ranked Lincecum the number-two draft prospect, and most baseball observers predicted that he would be drafted in the top 10. Lincecum was selected 10th in the 2006 MLB draft by the San Francisco Giants, a struggling franchise that had not reached the play-offs since 2003. (Two other Pac-10 pitchers with noticeably weaker sets of accomplishments, Stanford University's Greg Reynolds and Brandon Morrow, from the University of California at Los Angeles, were drafted before him.) Lincecum received a $2.1 million bonus for signing with the Giants—the largest ever received by an amateur player. During spring training Lincecum was affectionately nicknamed "the Franchise" by his teammates for his expected dominance on the fledgling team.

Lincecum's minor-league career was brief but impressive. He played four innings on the Salem-Keizer Volcanoes rookie-league team, striking out 10 batters and giving up only one hit. Playing with the single-A San Jose Giants in August 2006, Lincecum threw 48 strikeouts in 27.2 innings. He entered the 2007 season ranked by *Baseball America* as the number-one prospect to join the Giants' major-league squad. In five starts and 31 innings with the Giants' triple-A affiliate, the Fresno Grizzlies, Lincecum struck out 48 batters and allowed just 12 hits and one run, with a 4–0 record. He made his major-league debut on May 6, replacing Russ Ortiz, who had landed on the disabled list with an irritated nerve in his elbow. Lincecum threw for his first major-league win on May 11, defeating the Colorado Rockies (8–3). In a July 1 game against the Arizona Diamondbacks, he threw 12 strikeouts, the fourth-highest single-game total by a rookie in Giants' history. In July he logged a career-high four-game winning streak, and on August 21, in a game against the Chicago Cubs, Lincecum pitched all nine innings for the first time in his major-league career. Giants' coaches removed Lincecum from the team's roster in September in order to preserve his strength for the upcoming season. He finished the 2007 season with 24 starts, a 7–5 record, a 4.00 ERA, 150 strikeouts, and an opponent's batting average of .226. His strikeout total was the highest among all National League rookie pitchers, and his opposing-batter average was second-best. The Giants finished the season with a 71–91 record.

In 2008—Lincecum's first full season in the major leagues—he was restricted from throwing in the bullpen before spring training (as most pitchers do), in an effort to protect his arm from overuse and prevent injury. Once he began pitching, Lincecum was almost unbeatable. By July 6, 2008 he had achieved a record of 10–1 and was selected for the National League All-Star team. (He was unable to play in the All-Star Game, however, because of a flu-like illness.) On September 13 Lincecum pitched his first complete-game shutout, against the San Diego Padres; in nine innings he gave up just four hits and struck out 12 batters, helping the Giants to a 7–0 win. Lincecum's winning streak ended at his next appearance, in a 2–3 loss against the Arizona Diamondbacks on September 18, a game in which he allowed three runs and six hits. Following that match the Giants' general manager, Bruce Bochy, announced that he would rearrange the pitching rotation in order to give Lincecum an extra start in the season's last game, on September 28, against the Los Angeles Angels. (Many observers interpreted that adjustment as an effort to pad Lincecum's statistics to help him earn the Cy Young Award.) In that contest Lincecum earned his 18th season win, with 13 strikeouts, including nine strikeouts in the game's first three innings—becoming the first pitcher to achieve that feat since Sid Fernandez in 1986.

While the team struggled throughout the season, finishing with a record of 72–90, Lincecum ended the season with stellar figures. He had the second-most quality starts (26) of any pitcher in the National League; his ERA (2.62) was the second-lowest; and his opponents' batting average (.221) was the lowest. He was the major-league leader in total strikeouts (265); his record (18–5) was second in the major leagues; and he led the majors with the most strikeouts (10.5) and the fewest home runs (.44) per nine innings. On November 11, 2008 Lincecum was named the National League's best pitcher by the Baseball Writers' Association of America and was given the Cy Young Award. In the vote to determine the winner, Lincecum had received 23 first-place votes, seven second-place votes, and one third-place vote. At 24 he was the youngest pitcher to win the award since 1986. He was only the second Cy Young Award–winning Giant in history (after Mike McCormick in 1967) and only the fourth player in history to win the award after his first full season in the major leagues.

Lincecum continued to dominate the National League in 2009. In six starts in June, he achieved a 4–1 record and a 1.38 ERA, pitched three complete games, and was named the National League Pitcher of the Month for June. Along with one of his teammates, the pitcher Matt Cain, Lincecum earned a position on the National League All-Star team, as the starting pitcher. In a game on July 27, against the Pittsburgh Pirates, Lincecum set a career-high single-game strikeout total of 15. (He was the first Giant to strike out 15 batters since Jason Schmidt, who struck out 16 in a game on June 6, 2006.) Lincecum finished the 2009 season as the league-leader in strikeouts (261), with a 15–7 record and a 2.48 ERA. His opponents' batting average (.206) and his walk total (268) each marked an improvement over 2008. The team's performance as a whole improved as well; the Giants finished the season with an 88–74 record.

On October 30, 2009 Lincecum faced a misdemeanor charge for possession of 3.3 grams of marijuana; he had turned the substance over to a police officer, who had detected the smell of the drug during a traffic stop. Though Lincecum initially pleaded not guilty to the charge of marijuana and paraphernalia possession, on November 6 his attorneys reached a plea bargain, as a result of which the charge was reduced to a civil infraction and the punishment to a fine of $250. The same month it was announced that Lincecum had won his second Cy Young Award, becoming only the eighth pitcher in major-league history to win back-to-back Cy Young Awards and the first pitcher ever to do so in his first two full major-league seasons. Unlike his 2008 win, the vote was one of the closest in Cy Young Award history; Lincecum received 11 first-place votes and 100 points, edging out Chris Carpenter (who received nine first-place votes and 94 points) and Adam Wainwright (12 first-place votes and 90 points), both of whom pitch for the St. Louis Cardinals. Both Carpenter (17–4) and Wainwright

(19–8) had win–loss records superior to that of Lincecum (15–7), whose win total was the smallest in history for a Cy Young winner in a non-strike-shortened season. Observers noted that Lincecum had won due to his league-leading strikeout total (261) and his dominance in more obscure categories. (For instance, he had the most starts in which he did not allow an earned run in eight innings and the most double-digit strikeout appearances.) In accepting the award, Lincecum issued his first public apology for his marijuana possession. In widely quoted remarks, he said, "I made a mistake and I regret my actions earlier this month in Washington. I want to apologize to the Giants organization and the fans. I know as a pro athlete I have a responsibility to conduct myself appropriately on and off the field. I certainly learned a valuable lesson from all of this. I promise to do better in the future."

After the 2009 season Lincecum's agent, Rick Thurman, began negotiations with the Giants organization over the pitcher's salary for 2010. Lincecum had earned $650,000 in 2009, and many considered him to be one of the most underpaid players in the major leagues. In February 2010 Lincecum and the Giants agreed to a two-year, $23 million contract that would pay Lincecum $8 million in 2010 and $13 million in 2011, with a $2 million bonus. Lincecum will be eligible for free agency in 2013.

Despite occasional control problems in 2010, Lincecum again put up solid numbers. He finished the year with a 16–10 record and an ERA of 3.43, leading the NL in strikeouts (231) for the third consecutive year and earning a spot on the All Star team for the third time. After struggling in August, posting a career-worst 0–5 record, Lincecum won five games and lost one, with a 1.94 ERA, in September. His performance played a pivotal role in the Giants' late-season play-off push, as they clinched the NL West Division title on the final day of the regular season, with a 3–0 victory over the San Diego Padres; they finished the regular season with a record of 92–70.

On October 7, 2010 Lincecum pitched a two-hit shutout against the Atlanta Braves in Game One of the National League Division Series. He struck out 14 batters, breaking the Giants' all-time record for strikeouts in a postseason game. In his next postseason start, on October 16, Lincecum recorded eight strikeouts and allowed three earned runs in seven innings, in a 4–3 Giants victory over the Philadelphia Phillies, in Game One of the National League Championship Series. He outperformed the opposing pitcher, the Phillies' ace Roy Halladay, who had pitched the second no-hitter in postseason history in his previous start, against the Cincinnati Reds. When the two superstar pitchers squared off again, on October 21, in Game Five, Halladay prevailed, despite another strong performance from Lincecum, who struck out seven batters and allowed only four hits and two earned runs in seven innings. The Phillies won that game,

4–2. The Giants went on to victory in Game Six, 3–2, their fourth win of the championship series, thus clinching their first World Series berth since 2002. On October 27 Lincecum started Game One of the World Series, allowing the Texas Rangers four runs on eight hits in five and a third innings. While his performance was sub-par by his standards, the Giants gave him ample run support, earning him the win with an 11–7 victory. Lincecum did not need much run support in his next start, on November 1, in Game Five: in eight masterful innings he struck out 10 batters and allowed only three hits and one earned run, leading the Giants to a 3–1 victory. The win, the Giants' fourth of the series, brought their first World Series title since 1954 (when the team was known as the New York Giants) and ended their 56-year championship drought. It also marked the Giants' first-ever title in San Francisco, where the team has played since 1958. Holding the World Series trophy, Lincecum was asked if he had dreamed as a boy of becoming a championship pitcher, to which he quipped, in a widely quoted remark, "No, I was dreaming about being a championship hitter, but I'll take this."

"A free spirit who wears his skater-boy knit cap even in formal surroundings, Lincecum has a reputation among teammates as someone who likes to have a good time away from the field," Andrew Baggarly wrote for the *San Jose Mercury News* (November 5, 2009). Lincecum is known among his teammates for being uncannily relaxed prior to pitching, giving casual interviews to journalists and singing along to songs on his iPod. "He's an enigma," the Giants infielder Rich Aurilia told an Associated Press (March 13, 2009) reporter. "Something I've never seen before in a ballplayer, as far as how relaxed and laid back he is." Lincecum is said to have memorized the lyrics to a staggering number of songs; he has "a little Rain Man in him," Knutson told Bishop (April 25, 2006), referring to the movie in which Dustin Hoffman portrayed an autistic idiot savant. For the same article, Lincecum's teammate Richie Lentz said about him, "He's the goofiest kid I know."

Lincecum lives in San Francisco.

—M.R.M.

Suggested Reading: Associated Press Feb. 18, 2010; *Baseball Digest* p40+ Oct. 1, 2008; *Fresno (California) Bee* D p1 Apr. 5, 2007; MLB.com Sep. 20, 2007; *San Jose (California) Mercury News* Sports June 1, 2008, Sports Nov. 5, 2009; *Seattle Times* D p1 Apr. 25, 2006, D p1 June 5, 2006; *Sports Illustrated* Baseball p36 July 7, 2008

Lopez, George

Apr. 23, 1961– Comedian; actor; talk-show host

Address: c/o Ron DeBlasio, SDM Inc., 740 N. La Brea Ave., Los Angeles, CA 90039

George Lopez is known for his stand-up comedy albums, popular self-titled sitcom, best-selling autobiography, and, most recently, the late-night talk show *Lopez Tonight*, which began airing in late 2009. Lopez has been called a pioneer: a Mexican-American, he addresses issues of ethnicity and race head-on in his comedy, and though Latinos are now the nation's largest minority group, his is one of relatively few Latino faces seen widely on American television. As Mark Sachs wrote for the *Los Angeles Times* (August 4, 2004), Lopez's "specialty" is "biting humor tinged with sadness." Lopez has drawn inspiration from his troubled heroes, Freddie Prinze and Richard Pryor, and like those trailblazing comedians, he has combined intensely personal material with frank and politically incorrect observations about race and racism, in ways that have resonated with legions of fans.

Lopez's sitcom, *George Lopez* (2002–07), the first series with a predominantly Latino cast to become a hit on network television, was set in a blue-collar Latino neighborhood in California—"a place not normally seen on network TV," as Charlie McCollum observed for the *San Jose (California) Mer-*

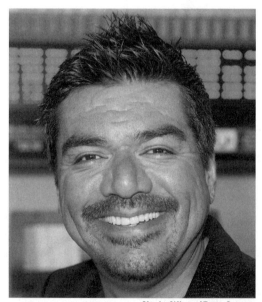

Kevin Winter/Getty Images

cury News (November 8, 2002). By contrast, his stand-up routines are "earthier and less restrained than on TV. He also makes greater use of Spanglish—sliding comically from Spanish to English to a mixture of the two languages." Phillip Rodriguez, a senior fellow at the Annenberg School for Communication at the University of Southern California and director of the 2007 documentary *Brown Is the New Green: George Lopez and the American Dream*, told Susan King for the *Los Angeles Times* (November 6, 2007), "George has been an agent, you could argue, for the normalization of the Mexican-American identity in America the same way Bill Cosby was [for African-Americans]. We have had very little of that." Lopez's hour-long, live, late-night talk show, *Lopez Tonight*, which premiered in November 2009, has attracted large numbers of viewers in its first few months, consistently outperforming competitors in the same time slot.

Lopez, who has won humanitarian awards for his work in Latino communities, has been outspoken in his disapproval of characters in television and movies who stereotype or reflect badly on Latinos. He has also sought to counter many Americans' fears surrounding the issue of immigration in the U.S. "I don't agree . . . that [Mexicans are] coming over and bankrupting the school system and taking jobs away from hard-working Americans," he told Michael Oriccho for the *San Jose Mercury News* (March 3, 1995). "You can't really tell me that people are working in the Silicon Valley just until something in produce opens up." In an article by Maria Elena Fernandez for the *Los Angeles Times* (October 12, 2005), the actor Freddie Prinze Jr.—whose father was among the first Latinos to break into mainstream American television comedy—was quoted as saying, "Desi [Arnaz] unlocked the door, [my] dad opened it and George kicked it down."

George Lopez was born on April 23, 1961 in Mission Hills, a suburb of Los Angeles, California. His father, Anatasio, a migrant worker, deserted his mother, Frieda, soon after Lopez was born. Lopez and his mother then moved in with Frieda's parents, who raised him in the San Fernando Valley. Lopez was told that his father had died; he later found out that Anatasio was alive but uninterested in a relationship with his son. His mother remarried when Lopez was 10, leaving him alone with his grandparents. "Hard as I try, I can't conjure up a single happy memory of my mom," Lopez wrote in his autobiography, *Why You Crying?: My Long, Hard Look at Life, Love, and Laughter* (2004), written with Armen Keteyian. According to Sachs, Lopez's grandfather died before long, and his grandmother, Benita, a worker at an airplane-manufacturing plant, then married Refugio Gutierrez, a construction worker from Mexico. "We were kind of assimilated . . . ," Lopez told Patricia Sheridan for the *Pittsburgh Post-Gazette* (August 27, 2007). "My neighborhood was predominantly white." Lopez and the few other Latino children in the neighborhood, he added, "were raised as Americans. Not Mexican-Americans."

Much of the material in Lopez's comedy comes out of the feelings of loneliness and abandonment he knew as a child; his relationship with his grandmother, in particular, has often found its way into his routines. "My grandmother was not a bad person, but she didn't have an enjoyable life, and she wanted to toughen me up for the things that she thought I was going to go through," he told Robert P. Laurence for the *San Diego Union-Tribune* (September 15, 2002). Often left alone by his grandparents, Lopez was so lonely that, according to Barry Koltnow, writing for the *Orange County (California) Register* (October 3, 2008), "he retreated into a fantasy world." Lopez told Neil Baron for the *Seattle Times* (December 5, 2003), "I developed this relationship with TV, and when I saw Freddie Prinze in 1973, it really changed my life because not only was he a stand-up comedian, he also had his own show [*Chico and the Man*]. So from the time I was 11, I wanted my own show and I wanted to be a comedian." He had already shown a gift for comedy, sometimes teasing classmates mercilessly. "What I initially thought was a God-given talent turned out to be a wall that I'd put up to deflect emotions from penetrating and actually hurting," he told Luaine Lee for the *Miami Herald* (May 5, 2004). "So you created humor to dispel the pain, like a shield. The comedy was a shield to deflect why I didn't have a jacket, why I was cold and why I didn't have a mother and father—because kids would ask. So it became a device that I used to disconnect."

Lopez began doing stand-up comedy when he was 18 years old. According to Sachs, writing for the *Los Angeles Times* (January 12, 2003), he performed at an open-mic night at a Los Angeles comedy club on the night of his high-school graduation, in 1979, "but the experience so spooked him that he didn't return to performing for four years, doing various odd jobs in the meantime." Those included one as a gofer in the aircraft plant where his grandmother worked. By 1984 "things weren't going very well in life," he told Lee. Because of Lopez's "horrible relationship" with an older woman, his grandmother's husband "had thrown me out of the house. . . . I ended up living on my friend Arnold's couch." At that point he decided to try stand-up comedy again. "I vowed I was not going to quit anymore," he said to Lee. "Because I'd quit at everything else—I'd quit accordion, on baseball, which I loved, quit on friends, on jobs—I was a quitter. And I didn't like that part of my personality."

Lopez started performing at small venues, working his way up to larger crowds until, in 1987, he quit factory work and became a full-time, touring comedian. By 1989 he had made enough of an impression that he was cast in the 1990 feature-film comedy *Ski Patrol*. The comedian Arsenio Hall saw Lopez's act at the Improv club in Los Angeles, and several months later, after Hall had begun hosting his own late-night talk show, he booked Lopez for the first of the 16 appearances he made during the *Arsenio Hall Show*'s five-year run. In 1993 Lopez appeared in a small role in the Carl Reiner film *Fatal Instinct* (a spoof of the femme-fatale thrillers *Basic Instinct* and *Fatal Attraction*). His first comedy album, *Alien Nation*, appeared in 1996. Nevertheless, for much of the 1990s Lopez was frustrated, feeling that he was not performing as well as he wanted to or doing anything meaningful. According to Sachs, it was the comedian Chris Rock's manager who helped Lopez regain a sense of purpose, advising him "to lose the generic ethnic-comedian approach and mine his own experiences."

In 1999 Lopez became the first Latino to host a major English-language morning (or "drive-time") radio show for Clear Channel Communications in Los Angeles, the country's top radio market. "Everything in L.A. radio has always been very black and white and the Latino part has always been Spanish-speaking," Lopez told Phil Davis for the *Los Angeles Times* (January 19, 2001). "It's the right time for someone like me." Within months the show was rated among the top 10 in the city. In 2000 Lopez played a part in the critically acclaimed Ken Loach film *Bread and Roses*, about the hardships of low-paid janitorial workers in the U.S. Lopez played the role of a company supervisor at odds with immigrant workers who are trying to form a union. In 2002 he earned praise for his performance as an inspirational teacher in the HBO film *Real Women Have Curves*, a coming-of-age story about a Mexican-American teenage girl living in East Los Angeles. Meanwhile, Lopez had released *Right Now Right Now* (2001), his second live stand-up comedy album, following it up with *Team Leader* (2002), which received a Grammy Award nomination for best comedy album. Also in 2002, along with Cheech Marin, Paul Rodriguez, and several others, Lopez was featured in the stand-up comedy film *The Original Latin Kings of Comedy*.

In 2000 the actress Sandra Bullock, who had been interested in producing a show that would give Latinos added presence on television, approached Lopez with her idea after hearing one of his records and seeing him perform a stand-up routine. The resulting sitcom, *George Lopez*, catapulted its star to household-name status and ran for 120 episodes over six seasons, from 2002 to 2007. The show's premise was highly autobiographical, depicting a blue-collar Mexican-American family living in Los Angeles, with the father, George, working in an airplane-parts plant; the character inspired by Lopez's grandmother was Benny, George's mother on the show (played by Belita Moreno). Some plot lines were lifted wholesale from Lopez's life, while others were based on his experiences in the entertainment world. In one episode, for example, George discovers, contrary to what his mother has always told him, that his father is alive. In another he finds out he is going to be offered an executive position at the plant, then learns that it is only because the company wants to fill a racial quota. "We wanted to touch on selling yourself out, which I could have done years ago [in Hollywood]," Lopez told Laurence. In 2007 ABC announced that the show would be cancelled after its

sixth season. That same year the Nickelodeon cable channel publicized plans to air the show in syndication. *George Lopez* has since been a ratings success for Nickelodeon.

During the run of his sitcom, Lopez also appeared in several movies, including *Where's Marty?* (2006) and *Tortilla Heaven* (2007), released the popular stand-up album *El Mas Chingon* (whose title translates as "The Baddest"), and published his autobiography, *Why You Crying?*, which was also the title of his first televised comedy special, broadcast on the Showtime network in 2004. A second comedy special, *America's Mexican*, aired on HBO in 2007. Also in 2007 the documentary *Brown Is the New Green: George Lopez and the American Dream* was broadcast on the PBS network. The film's director, Phillip Rodriguez, had wanted to use Lopez's story to illustrate how little the country as a whole knew about a group that comprised roughly 15 percent of its population; he also explored how corporations and advertisers were trying to tap into the so-called Latino market, in the process portraying Latinos as an undifferentiated mass of people. "I am trying to sell that we are diverse, we're important and we should be included in America," Susan King quoted Lopez as saying. "That means included in Honda commercials, in a Maytag commercial and a Bud Light commercial—not just for the Southwest but for the United States."

In 2008 Lopez appeared in the films *Swing Vote* and *Henry Poole Is Here* and lent his voice to a character in the comedy *Beverly Hills Chihuahua*. In the following year he was seen in the made-for-television movie *Mr. Troop Mom* and the TV series *Reno 911!* Also in 2009 Lopez's third comedy special, *George Lopez: Tall, Dark, & Chicano*, was broadcast live on HBO. In 2010 Lopez appeared in the films *The Spy Next Door* and *Valentine's Day* and lent his voice to the movie *Marmaduke*.

On November 9, 2009, after months of promotions declaring that Lopez would be "bringing change to late night TV"—an allusion to the campaign slogan of President Barack Obama—his hour-long, four-night-a-week show, *Lopez Tonight*, debuted on the TBS network. (Lopez had campaigned for Obama and had appeared as a featured performer at the president's inaugural celebrations in January 2009.) Lopez and TBS announced that they would be targeting a younger audience than his competitors on other late-night talk shows, as Arsenio Hall had in the early 1990s, and that the format of the show would reflect that aim. While he would, like other late-night hosts, deliver a few minutes of stand-up at the start of the show and interview guests afterward, the all-but-mandatory host's desk would be abandoned, and the studio audience would be large—about 400 people—to give the program an energy level more like that of a concert or a party than a talk show. The show's theme song, played by the Ese Vatos house band, is "Low Rider," by the group War, which has become an anthem of sorts for Lopez (it was also the theme song of his sitcom and some of his stand-up shows). Lopez again made history by becoming the first Latino to host an English-language late-night talk show on U.S. network TV. "Lopez is a brown face in a sea of white ones on late-night talk shows . . . ," Christine Granados wrote for the *Dallas Morning News* (December 12, 2009). "For someone like me, born and raised in El Paso, [Texas,] with a population that's about 85 percent Hispanic, it is a cathartic, heartwarming experience to watch *Lopez Tonight*. . . . I grew up with Johnny Carson, David Letterman and, later, Jay Leno. I noticed these men grow visibly uncomfortable when their guests were minorities. Our family, and many families like mine, joked about the talk show hosts' obvious unease." While the show attracted millions of viewers and outperformed rivals in its time slot in its first few weeks, not all reviews were glowing. "Mr. Lopez said he was 'bringing change to late-night TV,' but the only significant change was a coarsening of the already crass atmosphere . . . ," Mike Hale wrote for the *New York Times* (November 14, 2009). "Lopez scattered Spanish words and phrases through his monologues. . . . Beyond that, the only thing Mr. Lopez appeared to be adding to late night was a new freedom to exploit ethnic stereotypes for laughs."

Lopez has won much praise for his community service and humanitarian efforts. He has funded grants and scholarships for the needy through the organization CARE (Community and Arts Resources for Education) and has raised funds for the victims of earthquakes in Central America. He was named honorary mayor of Los Angeles and has won awards from the Manny Mota Foundation and People for the American Way. In 2004 he was named artist of the year by the Harvard Foundation for "his outstanding artistic work in television and film, and his humanitarian efforts to prevent youth violence and support community arts resources and education." In 2005 *Time* magazine named Lopez one of the "25 Most Influential Hispanics in America." An avid boxing fan, Lopez also enjoys golf and has hosted the Bob Hope Chrysler Classic.

In 1993 Lopez married Ann Serrano, a Cuban-American independent-film and television producer, with whom he has one daughter. "I named her Mayan after the Mexican culture," Lopez told Batia Rabec for the *San Jose Mercury News* (December 31, 1999). "I want her to be herself and be proud of who we are." In 2005 Lopez's wife donated one of her kidneys to him, after doctors told him he would need a transplant; Lopez had long suffered from a narrowing of the ureters, a disorder that caused urine to back up into his kidneys, gradually poisoning him. (As a result he had often wet the bed—and irritated his grandparents—as a child and endured hypertension as an adolescent and chronic fatigue as an adult.) "I credit my wife with literally saving my life," he told Bob Strauss for the *Los Angeles Daily News* (June 16, 2005). "Without her being a match, I would have gone from deterio-

ration to deterioration with practically no option. . . . Like she said, we had [gotten married] for richer or poorer, and now we were into . . . in sickness and in health." On September 27, 2010 the Associated Press reported that Lopez's publicist, Ina Treciokas, had revealed Lopez and his wife's mutual decision to end their marriage. Lopez and his ex-wife remain partners in their charitable work. Both also serve as voluntary representatives of the National Kidney Foundation.

—M.M.

Suggested Reading: imdb.com; *Los Angeles Times* p36 Jan. 12, 2003, E p1 Oct. 12, 2005; *Miami Herald* E p4 May 5, 2004; *Orange County (California) Register* Arts Oct. 3, 2008; *San Diego Union-Tribune* F p1 Sep. 15, 2002; Lopez, George, with Armen Keteyian.*Why You Crying?: My Long, Hard Look at Life, Love, and Laughter,* 2004

Selected Television Shows: *George Lopez Show*, 2002–07; *Lopez Tonight*, 2009–

Selected Comedy Albums: *Alien Nation*, 1996; *Right Now Right Now*, 2001; *Team Leader*, 2002; *El Mas Chingon*, 2006; *America's Mexican*, 2007; *Tall, Dark, & Chicano*, 2009

Selected Films: *Ski Patrol*, 1990; *Fatal Instinct*, 1993; *Real Women Have Curves*, 2002; *Valentine's Day*, 2010

Louis C.K.

(LOO-ee)

Sep. 12, 1967– Comedian

Address: Comedy Central, 1775 Broadway #10, New York, NY 10019-1903

Louis C.K.'s name is not a household term, but many comics, writers, and critics have called him one of the best stand-up comedians in the country, with some going even further. "Ask almost any comic who's the best stand-up working today," a *Los Angeles Times* (October 18, 2009) writer asserted, "and this balding redhead with no internal filter will most likely top their list." As Eric Spitznagel reported for *Vanity Fair* (March 2, 2009), the British comedian Ricky Gervais called C.K. "the funniest standup working in America." C.K. has written and starred in several televised stand-up comedy specials, most recently *Louis C.K.: Shameless* (2007) and *Louis C.K.: Chewed Up* (2008), the latter bringing his fourth Emmy Award nomination. His act is mostly about parenting, relationships, and the small things in life, subjects he dissects in ways that have the ring—sometimes the sting—of truth. C.K. has also written material for

Gabriel Bouys/AFP/Getty Images

Louis C.K.

some of the biggest names in comedy, as part of the writing staffs for *Late Night with Conan O'Brien* and the *Late Show with David Letterman*, and he won an Emmy Award for his work on the *Chris Rock Show*.

The comedian was born Louis Szekely on September 12, 1967 in Washington, D.C. (or New York City, according to some sources), to a father of Mexican and Hungarian-Jewish ancestry, Luis Szekely, and a mother of Irish descent, Mary Szekely. ("C.K." is an approximate phonetic spelling of "Szekely," a common Hungarian surname pronounced "SEK-kay.") Soon after C.K.'s birth, his parents moved to Mexico, where C.K. spoke Spanish. After about six years the family moved back to the U.S. and eventually settled in Newton, a suburb of Boston, Massachusetts. C.K.'s parents divorced when he was about 10, and he and his three siblings were raised by their mother. "When I was growing up, we had no money," C.K. told Terry Gross for the National Public Radio program *Fresh Air* (June 15, 2006). "And a memory that my sisters and I always laugh about is saying to my mother, 'Mom, I'm hungry.' And she'd say, 'Well, make yourself a bologna sandwich.' And I'd go, 'Well, I don't like bologna.' 'Well, then you're not that hungry.' So that's how we were raised. And notice that I'm making myself the bologna sandwich. My mother never made us any. We had a microwave, which meant we made our own meals. And it was just that we fended for ourselves. She worked all day; she had a huge amount of work to do raising us. So everyone had to sort of pitch in." An undistinguished high-school student, C.K. did not seriously consider going to college. Also, he told Gross, his mother could not have easily afford-

ed his tuition, and he did not want to "cost her the money." Instead, he found work as an auto mechanic. He enjoyed fixing cars and at one point thought about doing so as a career.

C.K. also greatly enjoyed stand-up comedy. One day while still in high school, he heard a radio announcement about an open-mic night at a Boston comedy club. He went to the club and appeared on stage for what turned out to be, according to C.K.'s official Web site, a "terrible experience," after which he did not perform for two years. Trying again, C.K. eventually joined the budding comedy scene in Boston. In 1989 he moved to New York City, where he performed in comedy clubs and on televised shows, including *MTV Half Hour Comedy Hour* and *Star Search*. During those years he made two short films, *Caesar's Salad* and *Ice Cream*.

C.K.'s big break came when he joined *Late Night with Conan O'Brien* as a writer during the show's first season, in 1993. He often wrote absurd skits with touches of social commentary, and some bits of his were used long after his departure from the program. He was also the first person to perform stand-up on the show. In 1995 he fulfilled a long-held dream by doing his act on the *Late Show with David Letterman*. According to many accounts, Letterman was so impressed with C.K's performance that he hired him as a writer, but C.K. told Gross that the reverse is true: after he left *Late Night with Conan O'Brien*, Letterman's representatives wanted to hire him based on his reputation as a writer. "And I said, 'You got to let me be a stand-up on the show first.' Because that was my dream to do standup on *Letterman*. So they let me do standup on the show first, and the following week, I was hired as a writer." C.K. spent three months with the *Late Show*, after which he became the producer and head writer of the *Dana Carvey Show*, a sketch-comedy program on ABC hosted by the *Saturday Night Live* veteran. The *Dana Carvey Show* was cancelled after only six weeks, a decision C.K.'s Web site attributes to the program's irreverence.

In 1996 C.K. became a writer and producer for the *Chris Rock Show*, on HBO. At first he was not sure what sort of material to write for Rock, an African-American whose stand-up comedy revolved largely around race. "When I started writing at *Chris Rock*, I think a lot of us, the white writers, were conscious of it," C.K. told Gross. "And at one point, Chris said, 'Stop thinking of this as a black show. This is not a black show. Just write the weird stuff you did at Conan and write it here.' And once I started thinking that way, I did." Although the overall focus of the show was on humor rather than race, there were many skits in which race was the subject. In one skit written by C.K., a black man is interviewed for a position and insists that black people still suffer discrimination and segregation. He then shows hidden-camera footage of himself trying to get into a restaurant and being turned away. The joke is that the man is completely naked; during the interview, though, he maintains, "They threw me out because I'm black." He then tries to catch a taxi, with similar results. In another sketch by C.K., a black man and a white man walk toward each other on a dark street. Each man is nervous, thinking about the other, "What is he doing in my neighborhood?" and "Is he going to rob me?" When they meet face-to-face, they ask each other, "What do you want?" and "You want something?" Then, suddenly, they start kissing passionately. The voice-over says: "Gay sex brings men together of all races." C.K. told Gross that that skit "got about four minutes of sustained laughter and screaming from [Rock's] audience. That was one of my favorite moments of my life, probably, when we first showed that to Chris' audience, and they just went berserk. It was great."

In 1997 C.K. produced, wrote, and directed his first feature-length film, *Tomorrow Night*. Shot in black and white, the film has as its main character a bespectacled nerd who has a fetish for sitting naked on tubs of ice cream and who falls in love with a widowed retiree. Despite some praise on the film-festival circuit—at the Sundance Film Festival and South by Southwest, for example—the film did not attract a distributor and got little popular notice. C.K. then went back to the *Chris Rock Show*, receiving his first Emmy Award nomination for his work on the program in 1998. The following year he won the Emmy Award for outstanding writing for a variety or music program, which he shared with 12 other *Chris Rock* writers. He was nominated again the following year. C.K. left the *Chris Rock Show* in 1999. Also that year he created and starred in *Louis C.K.'s Filthy Stupid Talent Show*, on Comedy Central. In 1999 and 2000 C.K. did a substantial amount of writing for *Late Night with Conan O'Brien*.

In 2000 C.K. wrote and directed his second movie, *Pootie Tang*, based on a skit he had created for the *Chris Rock Show* about a black folk hero who speaks in a made-up slang. The film—which by the end of production had been removed from C.K.'s control to be partly reshot and recut—was not widely seen and received mostly negative reviews. Still, what some perceived to be the film's idiocy and arbitrariness was viewed by others as entertaining absurdity, and the film later became a cult hit. Years after its release C.K. told Jon Waterhouse for the *Atlanta Journal-Constitution* (September 18, 2008) that he was surprised to learn about *Pootie Tang*'s popularity among prominent musicians and filmmakers: "I was at the Bonnaroo Music Festival recently, and Jack White of the White Stripes came up to me and said that *Pootie Tang* was his favorite movie. It's his tour bus movie. And John Mayer told me that, too, and so did Metallica, the entire band. Jack White told me he was working with Jim Jarmusch and told him that he should see *Pootie Tang*. And he said Jarmusch said Tom Waits had just told him the same thing. So when Tom Waits is telling Jim Jarmusch how great your movie is 10 years later, all the pain was worth it. It was

a difficult experience, and I don't think it was a particularly good movie. But I learned how to make films from it."

In 2001 C.K. started spending a lot of time on the road, performing at comedy clubs and comedy festivals. He created two TV-show pilots, one for CBS and another for Fox, but neither made it on the air. Then, in 2005, he wrote and produced *Lucky Louie*, the HBO channel's first sitcom, which was shot in front of a live audience and premiered in 2006. Although the sitcom's humor, tone, and situations were influenced by a number of classic sitcoms—*The Honeymooners*, *Roseanne*, and especially *All in the Family*—*Lucky Louie* exhibited a new level of bluntness and crudeness, all inspired by C.K.'s stand-up routines. C.K. played a part-time mechanic married to a full-time nurse, with whom he raises a daughter. Airing on a subscription-only channel, the sitcom had adult language and frank discussions (as well as portrayals) of sex, drug use, and questionable parenting methods. Reviews of the show were mixed. Brian Lowry wrote for *Variety* (June 5–11, 2006), "The multi-camera sitcom format has a half-century of history behind it, so seeing HBO attempt to turn the genre on its head through sheer rauchiness is initially jarring—almost like hearing children curse. The novelty, not surprisingly, wears off quickly, though there are still some extremely funny moments in this blue-collar comedy, a wildly uneven half-hour built around acerbic standup Louis C.K. Hardly everyone's cup of tea, *Lucky Louie* will have its loyalists, though likely as a narrow cult confection." After airing 13 episodes, HBO canceled the show, citing low ratings.

C.K. went back to stand-up. In January 2007 he starred in an hour-long stand-up special, *Louis C.K.: Shameless*, which aired on HBO. The exposure he got from that program led to sold-out dates at comedy clubs and theaters. In 2008 C.K. starred in an HBO stand-up special that featured all-new material, *Louis C.K.: Chewed Up*, for which he received an Emmy nomination. In *Chewed Up* he spoke about life in his trademark, harshly honest manner. Perhaps most controversially, he described his relationship with his young children: "Kids are like buckets of disease that live in your house," he said. "And you get sick from them all the time. Last week I had a flu because my daughter—coughed into my mouth. She did this, by the way, because she was trying to tell me a secret. And she thinks you tell secrets into people's mouths— which is inconsiderate, borderline-retarded behavior, if you ask me. And by the way, she's five. What secret does she have that I really need to hear? Like she's gonna tell me a secret and I'm gonna go, 'Holy [expletive], are you serious?'" After C.K. appeared on *Late Night with Conan O'Brien* in early 2009, the four-minute clip of his comic rant to O'Brien, usually referred to as "Everything's Amazing; Nobody's Happy," became a YouTube hit: "I read things like 'the foundations of capitalism are shattering.' . . . Maybe we need that. Maybe we need some time where we're walking around with a donkey with pots clanging on the sides. . . . Everything is amazing right now, and nobody's happy. . . . I was on an airplane and there was high-speed Internet, the newest thing that I know exists. . . . It's fast and I'm watching YouTube. . . . Then it breaks down and they apologize. Then the guy next to me goes, 'Pffff, this is bulls**t.' How quickly the world owes him something he knew existed only 10 seconds ago." Also in 2009 C.K. co-starred in his first feature film in wide release, Ricky Gervais's *The Invention of Lying*, in which C.K. played the Gervais character's best friend. The film, set in a world where no one is familiar with lying, was widely praised for its clever premise but criticized by some for failing to realize its potential. In addition to the above-mentioned TV shows, C.K. has written for the programs *Cedric the Entertainer Presents*, *Saint Louie*, and *Saturday Night Live* and the jazz "mockumentary" *The Legend of Willie Brown*, and he has acted in episodes of *Home Movies* and *Parks and Recreation*. He is also credited as a co-writer on two films written and directed by and starring Chris Rock—*Down to Earth* (2001) and *I Think I Love My Wife* (2007)—but he has said in interviews that after various stages of production and rewrites, his contributions to those films did not turn out to be significant. The film of *Louis C.K.: Hilarious*, a stand-up comedy special,

was screened at selected theaters starting in September 2010. Also in 2010 a new TV series, *Louie*, aired on the FX cable network; it has recently been scheduled for a second season. C.K. writes, directs, and acts in that show and occasionally produces it as well.

C.K. and his wife divorced in 2008. They have two young daughters.

—D.K.

Suggested Reading: *Atlanta (Georgia) Journal-Constitution* p22 Sep. 18, 2008; louisck.net; National Public Radio *Fresh Air* (on-line) June 15, 2006; *Vanity Fair* (on-line) Mar. 2, 2009

Selected Television Shows: as full-time writer—*Late Night with Conan O'Brien*, 1993–2000; *Late Show with David Letterman*, 1995; *The Dana Carvey Show*, 1996; *The Chris Rock Show*, 1997–99; *Lucky Louie*, 2006–07; as writer—*MTV Movie Awards*, 2002; *Cedric the Entertainer Presents*, 2002–03; as writer, actor, and director—*Louis*, 2010– ; stand-up comedy specials—*Louis C.K.: Shameless*, 2007; *Louis C.K.: Chewed Up*, 2008; *Louis C.K.: Hilarious*, 2010

Selected Films: as writer and director—*Tomorrow Night*, 1997; *Pootie Tang*, 2000

Lurie, John

Dec. 14, 1952– Saxophonist; composer; actor; painter

Address: c/o Author Mail, PowerHouse Books, 180 Varick St., New York, NY 10014

For the past three decades, John Lurie has amassed an idiosyncratic body of work—as a musician, actor, painter, and producer of music and television programs—that straddles the line between popular entertainment and the avant garde and reflects both his offbeat sense of humor and his penchant for experimentation. A veteran of the 1970s arts and music scene of downtown Manhattan, Lurie gained attention in 1979 as an alto saxophonist and leader of the experimental jazz band the Lounge Lizards. First conceived as a tongue-in-cheek homage to 1950s "cool jazz" and film music, the band eventually grew out of its ironic posturing to produce a unique brand of jazz that channeled world influences and received critical praise (though little commercial success); the Lounge Lizards released nine albums and played concerts all over the world in the 1980s and '90s. In 1984 Lurie became a minor celebrity when he appeared in and scored the music for Jim Jarmusch's groundbreaking independent film *Stranger Than Paradise*. He went on to establish a significant film career, most

Courtesy of Nesrin Wolf

notably starring in Jarmusch's acclaimed 1986 film, *Down by Law*, and scoring the 1995 crime film *Get Shorty*, for which he received a Grammy Award nomination. Lurie wrote and directed the short-lived satirical sportfishing television show *Fishing with John*, which became a cult classic, and in 1998 he founded his own independent record label, Strange & Beautiful. For much of the last decade, due to a mysterious, debilitating illness that Lurie has identified as advanced Lyme disease, Lurie's music and acting careers have been sidelined, and he has devoted much of his time to painting, one of his longtime passions. Lurie's paintings have become popular in the art world, and since 2004 he has exhibited them in galleries and museums in the U.S. and abroad. A book of reproductions of his paintings, titled *A Fine Example of Art*, was published in 2008.

John Lurie was born on December 14, 1952 in Minneapolis, Minnesota. Not long after his birth, his family moved to New Orleans, Louisiana, and then to Worcester, Massachusetts, where he spent most of his youth. His brother, Evan, was born in 1954, and he has a sister, Elizabeth. Lurie's mother, Theda Jones, who was Welsh, taught art at a school in Liverpool, England, before she immigrated to the U.S. His father, David Lurie, had been a poet and writer in college but produced little work while John Lurie was growing up. David Lurie's death from emphysema, when his older son was a junior in high school, greatly affected John. "When he died, I thought he was a failure for never having written anything," Lurie told Damien Love for the London *Guardian* (May 21, 1998). "He went to NYU [New York University] and wrote the whole literary magazine under pseudonyms. They thought he was going to be the next [James] Joyce or something. Then, instead of writing, he went to the South and organised farm workers for the socialists. . . . I went to my cousin's wedding about a year after my dad died, and all these old guys were coming up to me going, 'You're David Lurie's kid? He was my hero.' I guess he was really brave, and really altruistic."

Lurie delivered newspapers as a youth and attended Doherty High School in Worcester. When he was 15 he borrowed his brother's harmonica, and within a year he had become a skilled player. At that time John and Evan Lurie listened primarily to the work of blues musicians, including the innovative harmonica player Little Walter, the guitarist and singer Muddy Waters, and the pianist Otis Spann. Lurie's talents on the harmonica eventually led to his impromptu performances with two prominent blues artists: according to Lurie, he was invited by Fred McDowell to join him onstage at a concert after Lurie was egged on to do so by members of the audience. Another time Lurie and his brother hitchhiked to a New York City performance of the blues-revival band Canned Heat. After the show Lurie approached the singer, Bob Hite, and asked if he could perform with the band during the next show. Lurie and his brother then hitchhiked to Philadelphia, Pennsylvania, where a surprised Hite gave Lurie the opportunity to play. Lurie said in an interview with Tim Broun for the Web magazine *Perfect Sound Forever* (December

2006): "They were actually excited to see me, which was odd. . . . Hite goes, 'Okay, first two songs are in E.' I played with them in front of 20,000 people. It was quite surreal." Lurie also began painting at a young age and has continued to do so.

Lurie had previously envisioned becoming a professional basketball player, a writer, and the owner of a snake farm. As graduation approached, however, the young man—who did not want to serve in the Vietnam War or attend college—found himself with few prospects. Lurie has said that a bizarre encounter with a man on the streets of Worcester changed the direction of his life. "I was walking around about four one morning, and I run into this weird guy who's got a wheelbarrow full of dirt," Lurie told Love. "And he tells me he's just seen a statue turn into an angel. I was really looking for this kind of thing at this point in my life. He had something, this guy. He was insane, but he had something. So he brought me to his house and he gave me a bicycle and a saxophone, and that's when I started." Lurie spent the next several years hitchhiking around the country and practicing the saxophone. He spent time in Berkeley, California, and Boston, Massachusetts—where he played in a blues band called Crud—before settling in New York City.

When Lurie arrived in New York, in 1974, he sought out such jazz artists as Sam Rivers and Sirone and, as he later told Broun, "was shocked that heroes of mine, people I saw as celebrities, were absolutely poor and struggling." Lurie spent a few years in London, England, with his brother, during the inception of punk. When he returned to New York's East Village neighborhood in 1978, he found a hotbed of bohemian culture and an artistic community that combined the experimentation of the jazz scene with the rebellious attitude of New York punk. He recalled to Broun: "I came back to New York, to the Lower East Side and met all these very wild, creative people. Just ferocious. . . . The attitude was so, so real." Characterizing the music scene, Lurie continued: "The jazz thing was just lost. It was over somehow, there was no big voice. So either musicians were playing this very polite music so people could eat their meals in an atmosphere or they were playing this very indulgent, frenzy stuff, where clearly nobody was listening to each other and then they would come off stage and complain they weren't getting any grants. So I got caught up in this scene that was not exactly punk but held a giant amount of irreverence, which to me made a lot of sense." "No wave," a play on "new wave," the era's more radio-friendly brand of rock music, was the name applied to much of the alternative music being made in the East Village's grungy warehouses during that time, which incorporated elements of punk, chaotic noise, jazz, blues, and funk.

Lurie became involved in experimental film, and found his first acting role, with *Rome '78*, directed by James Nares. He also wrote, directed, produced, and starred in the 1979 film *Men in Orbit*. Through his circle of filmmaker–musicians, Lurie met Arto Lindsay, a member of the band DNA, and the two began to play music together, along with a revolving door of other East Village artists. "It was quite amazing, we would just switch instruments at random, these guys didn't really know how to play but it didn't matter because I would be playing the drums part of the time," Lurie told Broun. "These jams were amazing. To that point it was the best music I had ever played with people. And for sheer energy, it was the most powerful music that I ever played in a group." Lurie and Lindsay formed an avant-garde jazz group called the Lounge Lizards, along with Evan Lurie and the former Crud member Steve Piccolo on bass and Anton Fier on drums. At the first Lounge Lizards show, held on June 4, 1979 at the now-defunct Hurrah club, the band's drug-influenced performance was well received by the audience. Lurie told Broun, "I had been writing music for a movie I wanted to make called *Fatty Walks*. We had two rehearsals and did the gig. We also bought as much cocaine as we could possibly afford. Drugs have ruined a lot of gigs and of course a lot of other things but they made that gig better than could possibly be expected." The band began to book shows regularly in New York and elsewhere, receiving praise for its innovative sound and retro-kitsch look, which, as Lurie informed Broun, included "1950s suits with gaffers tape holding part of the shoe together."

The Lounge Lizards' early sound—consisting of Lindsay's atonal guitar playing coupled with Lurie's amateurish saxophone noise, both driven by a punk intensity—was as closely tied to the "no wave" aesthetic as it was to the 1950s "cool jazz" songs they played. The songs' wild improvisations and dissonant chords resulted in part from the band's efforts to approach their instruments from new directions, but also from the reluctance of band members to accept formal music lessons. "Steve Piccolo is sort of a jazz player," Lurie told Robert Palmer for the *New York Times* (February 13, 1981). "But the rest of us . . . well, I can't run through complex chord changes the way jazz musicians are supposed to be able to do." The music became known as "fake jazz," after Lurie used the term during an early interview to describe the band's sound. Lurie came to regret the "fake jazz" tag, as he felt it trivialized the music and reduced his group to a novelty. Many critics praised the Lounge Lizards. "Their intent is partly satirical; the Lounge Lizards affectionately recreate the clichés of 1950s jazz and then explode them with startling bursts of electronic noise," Palmer wrote. "But these musicians are also searching for fresh sounds and novel juxtapositions, using an existing body of American popular music as their raw materials. In effect, they are conceptual artists who enjoy toying with the form and content of musical idioms and sometimes satirizing the associated behavioral stances. The Lounge Lizards don't just sound like a 1950s band gone berserk, they even look like one."

The band released its all-instrumental, self-titled debut album in 1981 to mixed reviews. In an article for the *Washington Post* (July 10, 1981), in which he criticized an entire generation of musicians for being unoriginal, Boo Browning described the album as "13 snippets of ersatz '50s jazz played with varying degrees of energy and skill, whose accidents (as opposed to accidentals) are far more interesting and amusing than the intentional concept behind them." He noted that Lurie "overblows and honks, slides with drunken unctuousness from note to note and generally sounds as if he's using a reed that's as old and misbegotten as the tune itself." In a contrasting review posted on the All Music Guide Web site, Sean Caruthers wrote that although the album could be mistaken for traditional jazz on first hearing, it ultimately "neatly straddles both worlds, whether it's the noir-ish 'Incident on South Street,' the art-funk of 'Do the Wrong Thing,' or the thrash-bebop found in 'Wangling.'"

After the release of the Lounge Lizards' debut album, Lindsay and Fier left to pursue other projects, and the band—with John and Evan Lurie and a different lineup—released *Live from the Drunken Boat* in 1983. In 1985 Evan Lurie took a hiatus to record a solo piano album, and the Lounge Lizards released a live EP, *Live 79–81*. The Lurie brothers soon found a new lineup in saxophonist Roy Nathanson, trombonist Curtis Fowlkes, guitarist Marc Ribot, bassist Erik Sanko, and drummer Dougie Bowne and recorded the live album *Big Heart: Live in Tokyo* (1986) and the studio LP *No Pain for Cakes* (1987), the latter of which included the band's first vocal number. Palmer wrote for the *New York Times* (October 7, 1986), "The present-day Lounge Lizards are not faking anything. They have staked their claim to a musical territory that lies somewhere west of Charles Mingus and east of Bernard Hermann and made it their own."

In 1989 the Lounge Lizards released the self-produced album *Voice of Chunk*. It garnered generally positive reviews and helped the band begin to distance itself from the "fake jazz" stigma. Containing tracks influenced by Moroccan gnawa and other world music, the album was noted for its eclectic sounds and songs that lacked the satirical edge of those on the band's previous albums. "Lurie seemed to take the music out of quotation marks," Fernando Gonzalez wrote for the *Boston Globe* (November 28, 1991). "Emotions, often expressed with surprising directness, broke through the ironic posing. The overall sound drew from an even larger pool of sources, yet it was more focused." Lurie initially made the album unavailable in record stores and attempted to sell it exclusively through a mail-order service advertised on television commercials, which, like so much of Lurie's work, were noted for their surreal and subtle humor. According to Amy Duncan, writing for the *Christian Science Monitor* (April 28, 1990), one commercial showed Lurie reclining in bed surrounded by junk, saying, "If you're like me, you like to get things through the mail. I don't know why, but maybe it makes me feel less lonely."

After *Voice of Chunk* the Lounge Lizards released two live albums, both recorded in Germany in 1991. Over the next seven years the band suffered financial difficulties and struggled to find a record deal. In 1993 Lurie released *The John Lurie National Orchestra's Men with Sticks*, an album of material he recorded with a percussion ensemble. The John Lurie National Orchestra went on to perform several live shows and also provided music for some of Lurie's later television projects.

In 1998 Lurie, having grown frustrated with the music industry, started his own record label, called Strange & Beautiful. Later that year the Lounge Lizards, now a nine-piece unit with Michael Blake, Steven Bernstein, Jane Scarpantoni, David Tronzo, Erik Sanko, Ben Perowsky, Calvin Weston, and the Lurie brothers, released what would be the band's last album, *Queen of All Ears*, on the new label. It was warmly received by critics. Scott McLennan observed for the Massachusetts *Telegram and Gazette* (September 24, 1998), "The Lounge Lizards may not get an invitation from Wynton Marsalis to play the Lincoln Center anytime soon, but the nine-piece jazz orchestra will certainly find favor among fans of John Coltrane, Sun Ra and Gil Evans. The band can build majestic tunes from a variety of sources, from Middle Eastern sounds to blues laments, all the while sounding intense but never too serious."

Concurrently with his work with the Lounge Lizards, Lurie appeared in a number of independent films during the 1980s and '90s. He had small roles in Jim Jarmusch's existential film *Permanent Vacation* (1980), Amos Poe's *Subway Riders* (1981), and Wim Wenders's drama *Paris, Texas* (1984). In 1984 Lurie starred in Jarmusch's low-budget feature *Stranger Than Paradise*. The film, shot in gritty black and white, follows a New York hustler, Willie (Lurie), his cousin Eva (Eszter Balint), and his friend Eddie (former Sonic Youth drummer Richard Edson) as they set out on the road in a boredom-driven effort to discover something better than the urban wasteland that surrounds them. The subtle, deadpan humor of Lurie and Edson, coupled with Jarmusch's use of lengthy, static shots, made for a realistic and pensive film that stood out from that year's Hollywood fare and became an international hit. Vincent Canby wrote for the *New York Times* (December 30, 1984), "*Stranger Than Paradise* gives us a picture of America that you'll never see in *New York* magazine or *People*. It's not chic or hip or upwardly mobile. If it moves at all, it moves sideways. The picture is not pretty. It is, in fact, very bleak, but *Stranger Than Paradise* is so witty that the effect is not depressing but immensely invigorating." *Stranger Than Paradise* won many independent film awards, including the Special Jury Prize at the 1985 Sundance Film Festival. Lurie also composed the film's soundtrack, released in 1986.

Lurie starred in Jarmusch's popular dark comedy *Down by Law* (1986), playing a jailed pimp who bonds with his eccentric cellmates, portrayed by the Italian actor Roberto Benigni and the alternative-blues musician Tom Waits. Lurie next appeared in the Benigni-directed comedy *The Little Devil (Il piccolo diavolo*, 1988) and in Martin Scorsese's controversial film *The Last Temptation of Christ* (1988). He also had roles in David Lynch's romantic crime comedy *Wild At Heart* (1990); the crime comedy *Just Your Luck* (1996); the science-fiction film *New Rose Hotel* (1998); and the drama *Sleepwalk* (2000). From 2001 to 2003 Lurie had a recurring role as the troubled inmate Greg Penders on HBO's popular prison drama series *Oz*. Lurie also composed several film soundtracks. His score for the popular crime comedy *Get Shorty* (1995) was nominated for a Grammy Award and appeared on the *Billboard* Top Contemporary Jazz Albums chart that year. Ryan Gilbey wrote for the London *Independent* (March 14, 1996) that Lurie's *Get Shorty* score "nails the mood: a funky stroll with brassy blasts of jazz and samba." Lurie also composed the soundtracks for such films as Jarmusch's *Mystery Train* (1989); the teen dramas *Manny and Lo* (1996) and *Excess Baggage* (1997); *Clay Pigeons* (1998); Steve Buscemi's prison film *Animal Factory* (2000); and the downtown-Manhattan art-scene documentary *Face Addict* (2005), in which Lurie also appeared. Additionally, Lurie has composed music for television; he scored theme songs for NBC's *Late Night with Conan O'Brien* (1993–2009) and the short-lived *Late Show with Conan O'Brien* (2009–10).

Lurie had the idea of creating a deadpan parody of a sportfishing show while fishing with his friend the actor Willem Dafoe. With funding from a Japanese production company, Lurie wrote, directed, and produced the six-episode television series *Fishing with John* in 1991, though it did not premiere until 1998 on Bravo. In each episode Lurie and one of his celebrity friends—Tom Waits, Dennis Hopper, Matt Dillon, Dafoe, and Jarmusch—embark on a fishing trip to different locales, such as Thailand, Jamaica, and northern Maine, where they attempt to fish while engaging in meandering conversations and making pointless existential observations. Their adventures, which often include comically awkward situations, are narrated by Robb Webb, who injects "narrative hints onto what is otherwise straight documentary, introducing a tension between artifice and reality," as Damien Love wrote. In one episode featuring Lurie and Jarmusch hunting a shark along the coast of Montauk, New York, for example, Webb stated, "Today's program and fishing adventure could prove to be fun—but it could also prove to be very, very dangerous. When it comes to the shark, man is on his menu. It's a wonderful world we live in." Though never popular with mainstream audiences, the show gained a cult following. Lurie also composed the show's soundtrack, for which he intentionally mismatched music with locations, with African music accompanying a scene in Thailand, for example.

In 1999 Lurie released *The Legendary Marvin Pontiac's Greatest Hits*, which purported to be a posthumous collection of the work of Marvin Pontiac, a fictional creation of Lurie's. The album's 13 blues and soul songs were written and performed by Lurie and several collaborators, including some former Lounge Lizards members. To substantiate Pontiac's legend, Lurie posted a detailed biography of him on the Strange & Beautiful Web site, which described him as "one of the most enigmatic geniuses of modern music" and recounted several bizarre events that led to Pontiac's being committed to a mental hospital and later hit by a bus. A reviewer of the album for *Time Out* (July 25, 2001) noted, "As a concept this is superb, as an album it is wonderful, but flawed; a sort of minor thing of major delights. As an addition to Lurie's varied canon, though, it is hugely enthralling and coolly essential."

In 2002 Lurie began to experience an array of symptoms, including "flashing lights and roaring sounds, a sensation of rain pouring on his skin, a Kryptonite-like reaction to Windex, an inability to hold so much as a skillet in his left hand," as Tad Friend wrote for the *New Yorker* (August 16–23, 2010). Lurie's neurological problems worsened, and he soon found himself physically weak and unable to concentrate or play an instrument. Lurie consulted many doctors and eventually received a diagnosis of advanced Lyme disease. Because of his condition, Lurie confined himself to his New York apartment for several years, where he managed his production company and attempted to work on his memoir, which is expected to be titled "What Do You Know About Music, You're Not a Lawyer?"

When problems with concentration and motor control made writing too difficult (his physical condition has since improved), Lurie began painting full-time. He has produced many paintings in gouache and oils on paper, canvas, and wood panels. His first solo art show, held in 2004 at the Anton Kern Gallery in New York City, sold out. Since then his work has been shown in galleries and museums all over the world and earned positive assessments from art critics. "Lurie's compositions are filled with colorful, cartoonish figures, usually accompanied by absurdist captions tinged with sexual references; some are witty and profound, others convey an intentionally juvenile posturing," David Ebony wrote for *Art in America* (May 2005, on-line). "The images might be farcical, but the approach and use of materials are serious. The work impresses on an abstract level, especially in the crisp line, the textural play of translucent washes, and the unusual and engaging color relationships that Lurie employs." Lurie has published two books of art: *Learn to Draw* (2006), a collection of his black and white drawings, and *A Fine Example of Art* (2008), which features full-color reproductions of his work. Lurie's most recent show,

The Invention of Animals, was held at Gallery Brown, in Los Angeles, from June to August 2010. He also sells prints of his paintings through the Strange & Beautiful Web site.

According to Tad Friend's *New Yorker* article, Lurie has spent much of the last year and a half hiding from a former friend, the visual artist John Perry, who he believed was trying to kill him. The two reportedly had a major falling out in 2008, beginning with an argument over an instructional television pilot Perry was pitching to PBS, titled "The Drawing Show." (Since the publication of the *New Yorker* article, Friend's accounts of that argument and other details have been disputed by Lurie and others.)

Lurie lives in New York City's Soho neighborhood and is reportedly in a relationship with Jill Goodwin, who has worked as his personal assistant.

—W.D.

Suggested Reading: All Music Guide Web site; *Boston Globe* Calendar p10 Nov. 28, 1991, C p3 Sep. 26, 1998; (London) *Guardian* p15 May 21, 1998; (London) *Independent* Film p10 Mar. 4, 1996; (Massachusetts) *Telegram & Gazette* C p1 Sep. 24, 1998, E p3 June 3, 2008; *New York Times* C p1 Feb. 13, 1981, Arts and Leisure Dec. 30, 1984, C p17 Dec. 8, 1993, (on-line) Feb. 4, 2005; *New Yorker* p50+ Aug. 16–23, 2010; *Perfect Sound Forever* (on-line) Dec. 2006; Strange & Beautiful Web site; *Time Out* p115 July 15, 2001; *Washington Post* Recordings p41 July 10, 1981

Selected Recordings: with the Lounge Lizards— *The Lounge Lizards*, 1981; *Live from the Drunken Boat*, 1983; *Live 79-81*, 1985; *Big Heart: Live in Tokyo*, 1986; *No Pain for Cakes*, 1987; *Voice of Chunk*, 1989; *Queen of All Ears*, 1998; other projects—*The John Lurie National Orchestra's Men with Sticks*, 1993; *The Legendary Marvin Pontiac's Greatest Hits*, 1999

Selected Films: *Paris, Texas*, 1984; *Stranger Than Paradise*, 1984; *Down By Law*, 1986; *The Little Devil*, 1988; *The Last Temptation of Christ*, 1988; *Wild at Heart*, 1990; *Just Your Luck*, 1996; *New Rose Hotel*, 1998; *Sleepwalk*, 2000

Selected Film Soundtracks: *Stranger Than Paradise*, 1984; *Mystery Train*, 1989; *Get Shorty*, 1995; *Manny and Lo*, 1996; *Excess Baggage*, 1997; *Clay Pigeons*, 1998; *Animal Factory*, 2000; *Face Addict*, 2005

Selected Television Shows: *Fishing with John*, 1991

Selected Books: *Learn to Draw*, 2006; *A Fine Example of Art*, 2008

Frederick M. Brown/Getty Images

Lynch, Jane

July 14, 1960– Comic actress

Address: c/o Domain, 9229 Sunset Blvd., Suite 415, Los Angeles, CA 90069

For years people thought they recognized Jane Lynch when she was out in public, though not necessarily as a character actress from the many television shows and movies she had appeared in since her late twenties; all they knew was that she looked familiar. "Did we go to high school together?" they might ask. "This one woman was convinced I was the provost of a small southern Florida university," Lynch recalled to Novid Parsi for *Time Out Chicago* (December 3–9, 2009). That has recently changed: the rush of media attention Lynch has received for her Emmy Award–winning portrayal of the wicked, misfit-loathing cheerleading coach Sue Sylvester on the popular television show *Glee* is finally getting the actress the recognition many feel she has long deserved. Prior to winning that role, the openly gay Lynch—who turns 50 in July 2010—appeared to critical acclaim in several film comedies directed by Christopher Guest (including *Best in Show* and *A Mighty Wind*) and Judd Apatow (*The 40 Year Old Virgin, Talladega Nights,* and *Walk Hard*). "Jane has an unbelievable intelligence, and it really goes to strange and dark and great places," Guest told Mark Olsen for the *Advocate* (November 21, 2006, on-line). "She's always surprising to me and always exactly right on the mark."

Jane Lynch was born on July 14, 1960 in Dolton, Illinois, a suburb just south of Chicago. Her mother was a homemaker, her father a banker. In Dolton the "main pastimes," Lynch told Danielle Berrin for the London *Guardian* (January 9, 2010), were "beer, whiskey and story-telling"; Lynch was raised in an Irish-Catholic family that valued thrift and hard work but was more lax when it came to observing other social mores, such as that against underage drinking. "This is going to make my parents sound *terr-i-ble*, but all through high school, we were the drinking house. We'd sit around the kitchen table with my parents and drink beer," she said to Berrin. As a student at Thornridge High School in Dolton, the already six-foot-tall Lynch preferred to stay "under the radar," as she recalled to Novid Parsi; she floated between social groups, remaining on the periphery of each, to avoid drawing too much attention to herself. "I think always deep down I wanted to be a central player," Lynch told Parsi. "Maybe I was too afraid." While Lynch knew early on that she wanted to be an actor, she was banned from acting in school plays after walking away from her first role, in a high-school production of *The Princess and the Pea*. "I got so scared because I knew this was what I wanted to do with my life," she said to Berrin. "I got a reputation as a quitter, so I didn't get cast in anything in high school." Lynch did, however, muster the courage to sing as a member of the school choir, which performed throughout Illinois. Although Lynch's parents both loved to sing, and her mother often played records such as the *Funny Girl* and *Sound of Music* soundtracks for her, they were less than happy when their daughter announced that she wanted to be a professional performer. Lynch's mother, who was worried that her daughter would not find work in the notoriously competitive profession, suggested she learn how to type. To appease her parents Lynch enrolled at Illinois State University, in Normal, as a mass-communications major, but had switched to acting by the end of freshman year. "I changed my major, and I don't think I even bothered to tell anybody," Lynch told Kari Forsee for Oprah.com (December 21, 2009).

After graduating from Illinois State University, in 1982, with a bachelor's degree in acting, Lynch took intensive, graduate-level acting classes at Cornell University, in Ithaca, New York, where she earned an M.F.A. degree. At Cornell, she told Sarah Warn for *AfterEllen.com* (November 15, 2004), she studied with only six other people and "got on stage a lot. I was just thrown into parts I would never have played otherwise; I was stretched to within an inch of my life and it really revealed that I had more talent than I thought I did. It was like boot camp: whatever you have rises to the surface. I played ingénues, I played old ladies; I learned how to fence, to dance, to sing." Lynch returned to Chicago confident that she was ready to play any role she was given. She spent the next 10 years performing with the prestigious Chicago Shakespeare Theater and Steppenwolf Theatre Company and touring with the storied improvisational comedy troupe Second City, whose many notable alumni include Bill Murray, Dan Aykroyd, and Steve Carell. In 1988 Lynch made her feature-film debut with a small role in the body-switching comedy *Vice Versa*.

In the early 1990s Lynch spent about a year and a half performing in Chicago, New York City, and Los Angeles, California, as Carol Brady in *The Real Live Brady Bunch*, a tongue-in-cheek, independent-theater staging of episodes of the popular 1970s TV sitcom. "Flying by the seat of your pants is what you learn doing Second City and *The Real Live Brady Bunch*. It's being open to things not going like you thought they were going to be, and to be able to flow with that and roll with that," she told Forsee. "You never knew what was going to happen, and that was part of the fun too." It was around that same time that Lynch's agent in Chicago began netting the actress small roles in feature films, television shows, and commercials. In 1993 Lynch appeared opposite Harrison Ford, in a small part as a doctor, in the action movie *The Fugitive*. Lynch's participation in that high-profile film, combined with the agent's having an office on the West Coast as well as in Chicago, gave the actress the encouragement she needed to move to Los Angeles and try to make a living in TV and movies.

In 1998 Lynch wrote and starred in the award-winning play *Oh Sister, My Sister*. That play was later brought back to life to launch the Lesbians in Theater program at the L.A. Gay and Lesbian Center in 2004. Throughout the 1990s and early 2000s, Lynch racked up a considerable number of guest spots on popular network television shows, appearing in everything from *Married with Children* and *Party of Five* to *JAG* and *Boston Legal*. During that period she also did a significant amount of voice-over work. "I was a voice-over person for years, before the Christopher Guest movies came along," she told Roger Moore for the *Orlando Sentinel* (May 16, 2010, on-line). "That's how I made my living back then." She also continued to appear in commercials, including a pitch in the late 1990s for Kellogg's Frosted Flakes breakfast cereal. The director of the commercial was Christopher Guest, who had developed a following with the ensemble film comedies *This Is Spinal Tap* (1984) and *Waiting for Guffman* (1997). By that point Lynch had come close to giving up acting, feeling that she had progressed as far as she could, but meeting Guest "changed my life," she told Berrin. Guest was impressed with Lynch's improvisational skills, and when the two ran into each other six months after shooting the commercial, the director offered the actress a part in his upcoming film.

The 2000 "mockumentary" *Best in Show* follows five contestants in the prestigious Mayflower Kennel Club dog show and the slightly surreal interactions among the dogs' owners, trainers, and handlers. Lynch played Christy Cummings, the no-nonsense trainer of Rhapsody in White (a.k.a. Butch), a standard poodle and two-time "best in show" winner. Over the course of the film, Lynch's character becomes romantically involved with the dog's owner, Sherry Ann (Jennifer Coolidge). Guest

is known for giving his actors a lot of freedom in portraying their characters. Lynch described to Mark Olsen the process of acting in a Guest film: "They give us a really good thumbnail sketch [of a character], and then we just take it from there. We improvise all the dialogue; there's no written dialogue. The script looks like a regular script with no dialogue. It's probably 13 or 14 pages, just scene after scene and what happens in each scene. What's great about his movies is that they're very actor-centric. The set designer comes up to you and asks what you want your office to look like or what your house should look like, and the wardrobe designer asks what you think your character would wear, and then you go shopping together. You have basically 100% say on what you wear and do, whether you want an accent. We get to choose all that stuff." The film was a critical hit.

After *Best in Show* Lynch added to her already lengthy list of guest spots on network TV shows, appearing in such popular dramas as *Judging Amy* and *7th Heaven*. In 2002 she was given her first starring role, as Dr. Aileen Poole on ABC's short-lived medical comedy *MDs*. She also landed a recurring role as a gay civil rights lawyer on Showtime's *The L Word* (2002–08), about lesbian characters. Around that same time Lynch was again called on by Guest, to play the ex-porn-star-turned-folk-singer Laurie Bohner in his next film, the folk-music satire *A Mighty Wind* (2003). Now a bona fide featured actor in Guest's stable of comedy players, Lynch received extra praise for her performance in the film because she sang and played her own ukulele and guitar parts.

Lynch's growing reputation for slightly off-kilter comedy got her parts in TV shows including *Arrested Development* and *Monk*. Her career on the big screen was picking up as well; she took roles in the comedies *Sleepover* (2004) and *Lemony Snicket's A Series of Unfortunate Events* (2004), and she poked fun at reality television as a cocaine-abusing producer in the indie film *Surviving Eden* (2004). In 2005 she took the role of a lecherous electronics-store manager keen on deflowering one of her employees, the title character (played by Steve Carell), in the hit *The 40 Year Old Virgin*. Lynch's part was originally written for a man, but Carell's wife, the Second City alum Nancy Walls, thought Lynch would be perfect for it and introduced her to the movie's director, Judd Apatow. After *The 40 Year Old Virgin*, Apatow began using Lynch as a regular member of his comedy ensemble (which includes Carell, Paul Rudd, Seth Rogen, and James Franco), casting her in *Talladega Nights: the Ballad of Ricky Bobby* (2006) and *Walk Hard: the Dewey Cox Story* (2007). Lynch again teamed up with Guest to play a tabloid-entertainment TV-show host in *For Your Consideration* (2006).

Even as movie offers began to pour in, Lynch continued to take guest spots and recurring roles on popular television shows, appearing in four episodes of *Boston Legal*, starring in the improvised-comedy series *Lovespring International*, and playing Dr. Linda Freedman, the therapist of the Charlie Sheen character, in *Two and a Half Men*. Lynch lent her voice to animated characters in the *Family Guy* spin-offs *American Dad!* and *The Cleveland Show* and the films *Space Chimps* (2008), *Ice Age: Dawn of the Dinosaurs* (2009), and *Shrek Forever After* (2010). In *Role Models* (2008) Lynch was paired with her fellow *40 Year Old Virgin* cast member Paul Rudd to play Gayle Sweeney, the director of a Big Brother–style program for troubled youth called Sturdy Wings. Rudd said to Laura Fitzpatrick for *Time* magazine (April 26, 2010, online) about working with Lynch: "There are only a few people out there who are universally beloved. Everybody knows how funny [Lynch] is. The biggest challenge is not laughing while you're doing a scene with her." In 2009 Lynch took a brief break from comedy to play Julia Child's sister in Nora Ephron's film *Julie & Julia.*

Also in 2009 Lynch was cast on the STARZ channel's *Party Down,* a show about actors who moonlight as waiters for a caterer. Lynch played Constance Carmell, a nice but spacy struggling actress. Of Lynch's portrayal of Constance, the show's executive producer, John Enbom, said to Maureen Ryan for the *Chicago Tribune* (May 15, 2009, on-line), "She's taken a character who could have been merely an oddball outsider and turned her into someone you root for despite her rather large disconnect from reality. I think she brings a wonderful sense of warmth and lightness to the show. Her Constance is so grounded and satisfied in her delusions." Lynch remained with the show through its first season but was unable to return for a second because she was busy with her latest role, that of Sue Sylvester, the taskmaster high-school cheerleading coach and nemesis of the glee club, in the hugely popular TV musical comedy-drama *Glee.*

Lynch started on *Glee* as a guest star in the pilot episode, broadcast on May 19, 2009 on Fox. When the show was picked up for a full season, Lynch took on a permanent role, playing a lead character on a successful series for the first time in her career. Playing McKinley High's "queen of mean" proved to be a cathartic experience for Lynch, as she explained to David Martindale for the *Charlotte (North Carolina) Observer* (May 4, 2010): "When I put on that track suit, I have a license to say anything I want. . . . That kind of contemptuousness and heinous behavior (which Sue exhibits every day) is just very shallowly below the surface for me. I don't have to dig deep for it. But it's great I can do it on the set, so I don't have to do it at home." The series won the 2010 Golden Globe Award for best television series—musical or comedy, and Lynch was nominated for best supporting actress. Also in 2010 she earned an Emmy Award as outstanding supporting actress in a comedy. The show also received a People's Choice Award for favorite new comedy, a Peabody Award, and an Emmy for best direction of a comedy.

Lynch, who did not realize she was gay until after high school, found that her homosexuality was a nonissue in the theater world, which she described to Olsen as "teeming with the gays." Still, she did not come out to her parents until she was 31: "I didn't want to be gay . . . ," she said to Tracey Perkins for the *Mirror UK* (January 30, 2010), the on-line version of the London *Daily Mirror*. "I wanted an easy life. And you know what? I am gay and I still have an easy life." Lynch has said that her being gay has not affected her professionally because she is not a leading actress. She told Berrin, "I think if I were an ingénue—if I were Kate Winslet—it probably would hurt my career, but because I'm Jane Lynch and I'm a character actor, the world isn't projecting their romantic fantasies on me." On Memorial Day 2010 Lynch married her partner, Lara Embry, a psychologist, in a brief ceremony in Massachusetts. The women are raising Embry's young daughter, Haden.

Lynch's next film, *Paul*, is currently in postproduction and slated for release in 2011. Lynch believes her success, in both her acting career and her love life, comes from working hard and accepting herself for who she is. She has said that being in touch with every aspect of her personality helps her to relate to the characters she plays on screen and the people she aims to entertain. "Making people laugh is a really fabulous thing because it means you're getting deep inside somebody, into their psyche, and their ability to look at themselves," she said to Berrin. "You have to get through a lot of ego to get there. You have to get through a lot of self-protection that says, 'I'm cool,' to get down to the stuff that says, 'I'm just a goof.'"

—H.R.W.

Suggested Reading: *AfterEllen.com* Nov. 15, 2004; *Chicago Tribune* (on-line) May 15, 2009; (Durham, North Carolina) *Herald Sun* (on-line) May 5, 2010; (London) *Guardian* (on-line) Jan. 9, 2010; *New York Times* (on-line) May 18, 2009; *Time Out Chicago* (on-line) Dec. 3–9, 2009

Selected Films: *Best in Show*, 2000; *Sleepover*, 2004; *Lemony Snicket's A Series of Unfortunate Events*, 2004; *A Mighty Wind*, 2003; *The 40 Year Old Virgin*, 2005; *For Your Consideration*, 2006; *Talladega Nights*, 2006; *Walk Hard: The Dewey Cox Story*, 2007; *Role Models*, 2008; *Julie & Julia*, 2009

Selected Television Shows: *The L Word*, 2005–08; *Party Down*, 2009; *Glee*, 2009–

Kevin Winter/Getty Images

MacFarlane, Seth

Oct. 26, 1973– Animator; voice actor; writer; producer

Address: c/o Greater Talent Network, 437 Fifth Ave., New York, NY 10016

"The real beauty of animation is that there are no boundaries to the types of stories you can tell or rules on how you can tell them," Seth MacFarlane told Bruce Newman for the *New York Times* (January 24, 1999). In the late 1990s, only three years after graduating from the Rhode Island School of Design with a degree in animation, MacFarlane created *Family Guy*, an enormously popular animated TV series with several characters voiced by Mac-Farlane himself. The show has been lauded by many for its cultural satire and mix of highbrow and lowbrow humor, and maligned by many others, who view it as tasteless. *Family Guy* aired on the Fox network for three seasons before being cancelled due to comparatively low ratings; however, strong DVD sales, highly rated reruns, and the show's popularity among young males—an audience highly coveted by advertisers—persuaded Fox to bring the series back after a hiatus of three years. In 2005 MacFarlane launched a second show, *American Dad!*, which follows the exploits of a family headed by a jingoistic CIA employee and features more political humor than *Family Guy*. MacFarlane's third animated series, *The Cleveland Show*, debuted in the fall of 2009. In one of the first deals of its kind, in 2008 MacFarlane signed an agreement with Google to create content directly for the Internet. MacFarlane has won many honors for *Family Guy*, including Emmy Awards in 2000 and 2002.

Seth Woodbury MacFarlane was born on October 26, 1973 in Kent, Connecticut. His younger sister, Rachael, is an actress who voices a character on *American Dad!* MacFarlane's father, Ronald, was a history teacher; his mother, Perry, was a guidance counselor and admissions adviser at the private Kent School, which MacFarlane attended. MacFarlane described his parents to Bruce Newman as former hippies who were "just coming out of it"; they raised him in a liberal household. "The style of humor that you'll see in the show is the same kind of tasteless humor that you'd find around my house when I was growing up," he told Newman. "Some of the foulest jokes that I ever heard came from my mother." MacFarlane showed a penchant for drawing at a very young age. At eight he began publishing a comic strip, *Walter Crouton*, in the *Kent Good Times Dispatch*, a local newspaper. The thought of animation, however, intimidated him, until he saw a television show about an animated film created by a college student. "I started experimenting with animation after that," MacFarlane told Newman. As a boy he also participated with his sister in local musical theater.

MacFarlane graduated from Kent in 1991, then enrolled at the Rhode Island School of Design, in Providence, from which he graduated in 1995 with a B.A. degree in animation. MacFarlane initially wanted to work for the children's-animation giant Disney but later decided that he would rather make cartoons geared toward adults. (By then he had become a fan of the long-running animated prime-time show *The Simpsons*, created by Matt Groening.) While still a student MacFarlane had created an animated short, "The Life of Larry." One of his professors sent it to executives at Hanna-Barbera, the studio responsible for many of the animated programs that have appeared on American television since 1960. Impressed, the studio's executives invited MacFarlane to work for them, with the result that he moved to Los Angeles, California, shortly after graduating from college. Over the next few years, he worked on several Hanna-Barbera shows, including *Johnny Bravo* and *Dexter's Laboratory*. During that time the Fox network's program *MAD TV* showed an interest in airing "The Life of Larry," but that deal ultimately fell through. Soon, though, executives at Fox invited MacFarlane to create and pitch an animated series. Over the course of six months, he singlehandedly wrote, animated, and did all the voices for an eight-minute presentation in 1998 that laid the groundwork for *Family Guy*. Fox was sold. "That the network ordered a series off of eight minutes of film is just testimony to how powerful those eight minutes were," Sandy Grushow, president of 20th Century Fox Television, told Newman. "There are very few people in their early 20's who have ever created a television series." At 24, MacFarlane was the youngest creator and executive producer in television.

Family Guy, which debuted in 1999, is set in Quahog, Rhode Island, and follows the adventures of the overweight, bumbling Peter Griffin, his considerably smarter and more attractive wife, and their two misfit teenage children. The family also includes Stewie, an evil toddler bent on matricide and world domination, and Brian, an Ivy League–educated, martini-swilling, talking dog. MacFarlane voiced most of the male characters, including Peter, Stewie, the lecherous neighbor Glenn Quagmire, and Brian, the last of whom, many journalists have reported, has the speaking voice closest to his creator's. MacFarlane told *People* (November 29, 2004) that of all the characters he voices, he has the most in common with Brian: "We're both liberal, enjoy a good Scotch and tend to get in awkward situations with women." He revealed to Gloria Goodale for the *Christian Science Monitor* (February 12, 1999) that his inspiration for the character Peter was the father of a friend, who fell asleep and began snoring in a theater during a showing of the film *Philadelphia* (about the political and social implications of AIDS)—behavior that "just appalled his family." As Goodale reported, that act of "innocent political incorrectness" appealed to MacFarlane.

Family Guy drew both praise and condemnation for its willingness to make jokes about any and all topics, often in the form of sudden asides unassociated with the plots. "MacFarlane's pell-mell wit recalls *The Simpsons*' fevered early-'90s creative peak," Michael Krantz wrote for *Time* (January 11, 1999). "Punch lines spill out furiously as the show spirals into multilayered flashbacks and inventive fantasies." The *Entertainment Weekly* (April 9, 1999, on-line) writer Ken Tucker, however, likened *Family Guy* to "the *Simpsons* as conceived by a singularly sophomoric mind that lacks any reference point beyond other TV shows." MacFarlane asserted his right to pull humor from any milieu, high or low. "Hopefully, people will think of us as a smart show," he told Jefferson Graham for the *Financial Post* (February 15, 1999). "If we do a penis joke, we'll back it up with a Norman Mailer joke. We want a wide variety of humor." MacFarlane also denied charges of being intentionally offensive. "We're not out to simply piss people off," he told Ray Richmond for the *Hollywood Reporter* (October 31, 2007, on-line). "It's not about being as offensive as we can be. It's about being funny."

MacFarlane took ribbing not only from some critics but from his peers in prime-time animation. In an episode of *The Simpsons* in which the family of the title travels to Italy, a shot zooms in on a police blotter, which says that Peter Griffin is wanted for the crime of "plagiarismo." Matt Stone and Trey Parker, the creators of the raunchy cartoon show *South Park*, devoted two full episodes to mocking MacFarlane's work, ending with the report that *Family Guy* is actually written by manatees. *South Park* also poked fun at the seemingly random content and timing of the humorous asides on *Family Guy*. "If something is funny enough, we do step out

of the story," MacFarlane responded, as quoted by Alex Strachan for the Can West News Service (November 1, 2007). "I mean, who the hell watches a sitcom for the story? You watch it because you want to laugh." He added that he had found the *South Park* episodes about *Family Guy* to be very funny.

Family Guy impressed most critics and struck a chord with young male viewers. It won several honors, including Emmy Awards for outstanding voice-over performance (2000) and outstanding music and lyrics (2002), for the lyrics written by MacFarlane. The show suffered, though, from several programming missteps on the part of the network, which rescheduled the show many times—a proven way to lose viewers—and put it opposite such formidable competition as World Wrestling Entertainment offerings, the hit sitcom *Friends*, and the popular reality-TV show *Survivor*. *Family Guy* came close to cancellation in 2000 but was revived at the last minute, only to be axed in 2002.

Following the show's cancellation, Fox responded to popular demand and released the three seasons of *Family Guy* on DVD. It also licensed reruns to appear on the Cartoon Network as part of the channel's late-night "Adult Swim" lineup. The DVD *Family Guy: Volume One* sold more than 2.2 million copies, and *Family Guy* was the highest-rated show on "Adult Swim" during that time. In 2005 executives at Fox approved new episodes of the series after three years—the longest hiatus of any network show ever to be brought back to life.

Family Guy returned to the airwaves in January 2005, along with *American Dad!*, a new show MacFarlane had created for the network during *Family Guy*'s hiatus. Like the first show, *American Dad!* followed a nuclear family, headed this time by a bumbling CIA employee, Stan Smith. The more outlandish family members were a German-speaking goldfish and a junk-food-loving alien, both of whom Stan had rescued from government experiments at Area 51 (the Nevada military base where some conspiracy theorists believe the U.S. government is hiding bodies of space aliens who crash-landed on Earth). The humor on *American Dad!* was more overtly political than that of *Family Guy*, satirizing current events, such as the George W. Bush–led "war on terror." MacFarlane told Bridget Byrne for the Associated Press (April 20, 2005) that the show's concept "sprang from the climate during the [2004 presidential] election . . . a very politically charged time, with the whole country split in half."

Although MacFarlane is liberal, he told Virginia Rohan for the Bergen County, New Jersey, *Record* (May 1, 2005), "We do try and satirize both sides—the knee-jerk flag-waving personality of Stan and the [daughter] Haley personality, the type who will burst into applause if [the liberal comedian and commentator] Bill Maher even sneezes." *American Dad!* received relatively good ratings but did not come close to the popularity of *Family Guy*, perhaps, some suggested, because it addressed issues about which the American public was not yet ready to laugh. "Stan's cluelessness approximates that of Peter Griffin's, only with the potential of a body count," David Kronke wrote for the *Daily News of Los Angeles* (May 1, 2005). Nonetheless, the series has continued to air on Fox.

In 2006 MacFarlane helped create and voice a *Family Guy* video game, in conjunction with Take-Two Interactive Software Inc. He has created four *Family Guy* specials. *Family Guy Presents: Stewie Griffin . . . the Untold Story* (2005) was the first straight-to-DVD movie ever made from a television series. *Blue Harvest* (2007), the hour-long premiere episode of the show's sixth season, recast *Star Wars* with the Griffin family and friends and used the premise of that famous science-fiction film as a jumping-off point for numerous gags. An uncut version of *Blue Harvest* was released on DVD in 2008. *Family Guy Presents: Seth & Alex's Almost Live Comedy Show*—which was dropped by its original sponsor, Microsoft, because of the program's controversial content—aired in the fall of 2009, sponsored by Warner Bros. In that same year *Family Guy: Something, Something, Something, Dark Side*—a spoof of *The Empire Strikes Back*, the second film in the *Star Wars* series—was released on DVD.

Meanwhile, in 2008 MacFarlane had signed a deal with Google to create *Seth MacFarlane's Cavalcade of Cartoon Comedy*, an original series of animated shorts distributed by Google AdSense to various Web sites whose users are thought to be *Family Guy* viewers. That project represents the first original content that Google has underwritten for the purposes of on-line distribution. In early 2009 Priceline signed on as an additional partner, sponsoring MacFarlane's on-line animated short "Ted Nugent Is Visited by the Ghost of Christmas Past."

Also in 2009 MacFarlane introduced a third animated prime-time series. *The Cleveland Show* focuses on a character from *Family Guy*, Cleveland Brown; the first episode of the new program found Cleveland and his son leaving Rhode Island for California. "Cleveland is African American, which needs to be mentioned here because the other characters in the show never stop mentioning it . . . ," Tom Shales wrote about the show for the *Washington Post* (September 29, 2009). "The humor doesn't necessarily promote racial stereotypes, but whenever a crude joke can be made out of it, Cleveland's race is mentioned—over and over, in scene after scene. The message that young viewers receive is that racial minorities are different, separate, apart from the norm." (The character Cleveland is voiced by a white actor, Mike Henry.) *The Cleveland Show* airs on Fox on Sunday nights, along with *The Simpsons*, *American Dad!*, and *Family Guy*.

MacFarlane's animated shows have been highly successful both despite and because of their edgy humor. As Ray Richmond noted, gags on *Family Guy* have included a character identified as a "loveable pedophile"; a Pez dispenser, modeled on the slain U.S. president John F. Kennedy, that disgorges candy from its head; and an abandoned baby singing about having been left in a Dumpster. The humor has occasionally drawn complaints, as when Chris Griffin, a character on *Family Guy*, went on a date in a February 2010 episode with a woman with Down syndrome, who claimed to be the daughter of "the former governor of Alaska." The real-life former Alaska governor Sarah Palin, the 2008 Republican vice-presidential nominee, has a young son, Trig, with Down syndrome; Palin strongly criticized the airing of the episode and quoted her daughter Bristol as asking, "Shouldn't we be willing to say that some things just are not funny?" As quoted by the *Los Angeles Times* (February 17, 2010), MacFarlane responded in a statement, "From its inception, *Family Guy* has used biting satire as the foundation of its humor. The show is an equal-opportunity offender."

MacFarlane lives in Los Angeles. In 2008 he signed a four-year, $100 million deal with Fox, making him the highest-paid writer-producer working in television. "I get a lot of pleasure out of making shows," MacFarlane told Nellie Andreeva for Reuters News Service (May 5, 2008). "It's a bonus to be getting paid well for it, and it's a double bonus to be getting paid exorbitantly for it."

—J.E.P.

Suggested Reading: (Canada) *National Post* Arts & Life p9 Nov. 1, 2007; *Christian Science Monitor* Features p18 Feb. 12, 1999; *New York Times* II p38 Jan. 24, 1999, (on-line) Sep. 3, 2000; *Washington Post* C p1 Sep. 29, 2009

Selected Television Shows: as writer—*Dexter's Laboratory*, 1997–98; *Johnny Bravo*, 1997–2003; as creator, writer, and producer—*Family Guy*, 1999– ; *American Dad!*, 2005– ; *The Cleveland Show*, 2009– ; *Seth MacFarlane's Cavalcade of Cartoon Comedy*, 2009

Selected Films: *Family Guy Presents: Stewie Griffin . . . The Untold Story*, 2005; *Family Guy Presents: Seth & Alex's Almost Live Comedy Show*, 2009; *Family Guy Presents: Something, Something, Something, Dark Side*, 2009

Malcolm, Ellen R.

Feb. 2, 1947– Political activist; co-founder and former president of EMILY's List

Address: EMILY's List, 1120 Connecticut Ave., N.W., Suite 1100, Washington, DC 20036

In 1985, when 25 women gathered in Ellen Malcolm's home to start the organization EMILY's List, no Democratic woman had been elected to the U.S. Senate in her own right (although a handful had

Ellen R. Malcolm

Max Whittaker/Getty Images

been appointed to fill seats left vacant by the deaths of their husbands). Additionally, no woman had been elected governor of a large state, and the number of female members of the U.S. House of Representatives was in decline. The founders of EMILY's List, a donor network and political action committee (PAC), saw that promising pro-choice female candidates often struggled to obtain sufficient campaign money in the male-dominated political arena, and they wanted to devise an efficient way to offer financial assistance. (The acronym "EMILY" stands for "Early Money Is Like Yeast," because "It helps the dough rise," according to the organization's Web site.)

EMILY's List has grown into one of the nation's biggest PACs, boasting more than 100,000 members. Since its inception the group has helped elect almost 100 women to Congress and numerous others to state and local offices. Malcolm, a founder of the organization and for 25 years its president and public face, is widely credited for her pioneering work in organizing on behalf of female political candidates. Amanda Spake wrote for the *Washington Post* (June 5, 1988), "Malcolm was really the first person to believe it could happen, that women like herself—who came of age in the late '60s and early '70s, who went to work and who now have both money and a mission—would organize and ante up to elect other like-minded women."

The success of EMILY's List stems in part from its unique approach to fundraising. As a donor network, it provides members with information about candidates it has endorsed and encourages members to write checks directly to those running for office. The organization then bundles the members' checks and sends them to the individual can-

didates. Each member of EMILY's List is asked to contribute $100 to the group itself and to pledge $100 each to at least two endorsed politicians. That successful fund-raising model has made EMILY's List one of the Democratic Party's main allies. In 2008 alone, for example, the organization and its members contributed more than $9 million to candidates for federal and gubernatorial office. Bara Vaida and Jennifer Skalka wrote for the *National Journal* (June 28, 2009), "EMILY's List has won wide praise over the years for leveraging the power of women at the polls and building an unprecedented network of progressive female donors." As quoted on the group's Web site, Jennifer Granholm, then running for governor of Michigan, once stated in a speech: "EMILY is every working mom who's managed to balance a checkbook, who's managed a clean house, a corporate budget and a 12-year-old's basketball tournament in one day. . . . She's every candidate who's ever been asked how she can run for office and have a family at the same time. She is every African American woman who has had to work three times as hard to be considered as good as her white male colleague. She is every Jewish woman who has ever been called a princess. She is every Hispanic woman who has been asked how long her family has been in this country. She is every woman who has been called too soft or too strong or too aggressive or too nice or too ambitious to get the job done. She is every woman who has ever been measured against a glossy picture in a magazine. . . . She is you. . . . And EMILY doesn't get mad—she gets elected!"

Malcolm stepped down as president of EMILY's List at the end of January 2010. She has continued to chair its board of directors.

Malcolm was born Ellen Reighley on February 2, 1947 in Hackensack, New Jersey. She was raised in the nearby suburb of Montclair. Her parents met while working for the International Business Machines (IBM) Corp; her father, William Reighley, was employed as a salesman, and her mother, Barbara, as an assistant in the sales department.

When Malcolm was six months old, her father died of cancer. As a result, Malcolm became the sole heir to her paternal great-grandfather's fortune, to which she was granted access when she turned 21. Her great-grandfather, A. Ward Ford, was one of the founding partners of the Bundy Manufacturing Co., which eventually became part of IBM. Although Malcolm has never publicly revealed exactly how much she inherited, Laurie Kretchmar wrote for *Fortune* (April 6, 1992, online) that the heiress once admitted to having "millions upon millions upon millions."

When Malcolm was three her mother married Peter Malcolm, another IBM salesman. Her half-brothers, Doug and Andy, were born soon afterward. Despite the money she stood to inherit when she was older, Malcolm recalled to Spake that her family had a modest lifestyle. "We were not a jet-setter family," she said. "We had a station wagon and two golden retrievers."

When Malcolm, who was raised in a Republican household, was encouraged by her mother to hone her typing skills so that she could one day become an executive secretary, she chafed at the idea. In an opinion piece she wrote for the *Washington Post* (May 10, 2008, on-line) in support of Hillary Clinton's 2008 presidential campaign, Malcolm recalled, "When I was growing up in the 1960s, I wanted to play basketball. In those days, the rules said girls could dribble only three steps and then had to pass the ball. To make sure we didn't overexert ourselves, we weren't allowed to cross the half-court line. It's a wonder our fans (our mothers) could stay awake when a typical game's final score was 14-10." She continued, "It's remarkable that my generation of women entered the workforce and began to compete in business, politics and the hurly-burly of life outside the home. How did we ever learn to locate, much less channel, our competitive instincts in a world that made us play half-court and assumed that we would be content staying home to iron the shirts? It's a tremendous tribute to women of my generation that we sucked it up and learned to compete in the toughest environments."

Malcolm attended Hollins College, a women's school in Virginia that had a reputable experimental-psychology program. (The institution has since been renamed Hollins University.) While she initially hoped to become a clinical psychologist, Malcolm disliked many of the required lab courses. Although she earned a bachelor's degree in psychology in 1969, Malcolm—inspired by the liberal friends and professors she had met in college—decided instead to pursue a career in political activism. (In 1968 she had worked on the unsuccessful presidential campaign of the Democrat Eugene McCarthy.)

In 1970 Malcolm moved to Washington, D.C., and began working with Common Cause, a nonprofit advocacy group that encourages open government and political accountability. Volunteering at first, she was soon offered a post as a salaried field coordinator. By 1976, however, she had become "completely burned out," as she told Spake. After working briefly on the failed presidential campaign of the Democrat Morris "Mo" Udall, she found herself with little direction or ambition. "I think when you have enough money that you don't have to work for a living, in some kind of backward way, it makes the choices very difficult," she told Spake. "It did for me. I didn't want having wealth to define who I was." Malcolm bought a home and earned a real-estate license, which she did not use. "Like a clock spring, I unwound until the most exciting thing in life was being able to go out and get the groceries," she recalled to Spake.

In 1977 a bored and dispirited Malcolm decided to return to political activism and found a position as a project director with the National Women's Political Caucus (NWPC), a nonpartisan grassroots organization dedicated to increasing women's involvement in politics. There she met Lael Stegall,

then the organization's director of development. Until then Malcolm had not disclosed information about her fortune to anyone outside her family or her group of financial advisers, but after hearing that Stegall was looking for a way to branch out on her own and fund progressive women's organizations, Malcolm revealed her wealth.

Together, Stegall and Malcolm devised a way to channel Malcolm's money to various advocacy groups anonymously. They set up the Windom Fund (named after the street on which Malcolm lived) and moved their operation to an office in the Dupont Circle section of Washington, D.C. The fund easily found progressive organizations to back, and operations proceeded smoothly—until some groups began to ask who was responsible for the largesse. Malcolm responded to the inquiries by naming an imaginary philanthropist, Henrietta C. Windom. Meanwhile, she kept busy as a speechwriter for Esther Peterson, the special assistant for consumer affairs in the administration of President Jimmy Carter.

By 1980 Malcolm had begun to realize that if she were better able to channel and invest her money, she could wield considerable political influence. She entered the M.B.A. program at George Washington University, in Washington, D.C., graduating in 1984. "I ended up loving business, understanding how to make money and being successful at it," she told Spake.

In 1985 Malcolm and Stegall convened a meeting of women with whom they had worked at the NWPC. They discussed forming an organization to help pro-choice female Democrats adequately fund their campaigns early in the election process. The idea for the organization was largely inspired by the 1982 defeat of U.S. Senate candidate Harriett Woods, who lost partly because she ran out of campaign money before the election. Several of the women at the meeting, including Malcolm, had participated in Woods's campaign, and they understood that the key to keeping female candidates competitive was to donate money to them at the start. The late Ann Richards, a founding member of the group and an EMILY's List–endorsed candidate who was elected governor of Texas in 1990, told Connie Koenenn for the *Los Angeles Times* (October 9, 1991), "Women's races are lost early. You have to be a player early on. Texas has 19 major media markets and you have to make media buys early. It takes sophisticated crafting and planning. We needed money for focus groups, for polling necessary to shape the message. It takes early money to do all that." "You see, what happens to women is that people say they can't win," Joan Mondale, the wife of former U.S. vice president Walter Mondale and an EMILY's List advisory-board member, told Spake. "So they won't give them money. Then they can't raise money. And then they can't win. It's a vicious cycle."

Other prominent founding members of EMILY's List include the late Anne Wexler, a former aide to Carter and founder of a major lobbying firm; Barbara Boxer, now a Democratic U.S. senator from California; and Donna Shalala, the secretary of health and human services under President Bill Clinton and now president of the University of Miami. Journalists have sometimes commented on the perceived whimsicality of the group's name; Koenenn wrote, "[It] might sound like a tea party invitation, but the cuteness is deceptive." Malcolm explained to Spake, "If we had decided to become the Democratic Women's Early Money Fund, we probably would have raised $1.98 by now."

To build the organization's membership, Malcolm and the other founding women sent out personal letters to potential donors, and Malcolm visited 30 cities, talking to gatherings of women at events jokingly referred to as "the ultimate Tupperware parties," according to Koenenn.

EMILY's List was registered as a PAC because any organization or group that donates more than $1,000 to a political candidate must register as such. However, EMILY's List does not function in the same way as many other PACs. A typical PAC collects fees from members and then sends a single check to each candidate. (A PAC, according to law, can donate no more than $5,000 to a candidate in a federal race.) EMILY's List, on the other hand, endorses several candidates and asks each member to write a check for at least $100 each to at least two of the candidates. The organization then bundles the checks and sends them to the candidates. (There is no law limiting how many individual contributions can be made through an organization, as long as the checks are not written to the organization or cashed by it.)

By the 1986 elections, a year after the founding of EMILY's List, the organization had raised $545,000 to fund the campaigns of two Senate candidates and pay its own operating expenses. One of the organization's candidates, Barbara Mikulski of Maryland, became the first female Democrat elected to the U.S. Senate in her own right. In 1988 the organization recommended nine congressional candidates to members and raised more than $900,000. EMILY's List members donated to the successful campaigns of Nita Lowey of New York and Jolene Unsoeld of Washington State; the two victories reversed the long decline in the number of Democratic women serving in the House. (The pair boosted the number of female representatives to 14, the most since 1972.) In 1990 the organization claimed more than 3,500 members and broke the million-dollar mark for the first time, with members contributing $2.7 million. That year two governors and seven members of Congress who had been endorsed by EMILY's List won office. Two years later 20 new congresswomen and four new pro-choice female U.S. senators endorsed by EMILY's List were elected to office. Membership reached more than 23,000 members that year, and contributions totaled $10.2 million.

EMILY's List soon became, according its Web site, "a full-service political organization that raises money for women candidates, helps them build strong campaigns, and mobilizes women voters." In 2000, with the election of four new Senate members and four new House members, EMILY's List helped produce a record 10 female senators and 41 House members, and two years later the group helped to elect three new governors and two new House members. Every incumbent it supported also won reelection.

In 2006, however, EMILY's List suffered several losses. The group endorsed 31 House and Senate candidates, but only eight won office. Some political analysts believed that the influence of EMILY's List had waned because reproductive rights remained the group's main issue. They argued that the organization, in order to stay viable, should endorse women who were moderate on abortion rights but progressive on other issues. Marcy Kaptur, a Democratic U.S. representative from Ohio, told Vaida and Skalka in 2009 that the organization's focus was "too narrow." "I represent women who organize unions, carry mail on their backs, raise children, fight harassment in the workplace," she said. "They love their husbands and their sons. And with EMILY's List, I always felt there was a class-based, gender-based divide."

In 2008 EMILY's list rebounded somewhat, raising more than $43 million and contributing to the successful elections of 12 new female House members and two senators. It also played a role in the victory of the first female governor of North Carolina, and all the incumbents up for reelection remained in office. The group faced criticism from some progressives, however, for its ardent support of Hillary Clinton during the 2008 Democratic primaries. As a popular pro-choice Democratic senator from New York, Clinton was a fitting candidate for EMILY's List. Malcolm co-chaired Clinton's campaign and stumped for the candidate, and EMILY's List was one of the top five donors to the campaign, bundling roughly $850,000 and spending another $1.5 million on efforts to mobilize voters. However, a rift between the organization and its political allies was revealed when Malcolm announced that EMILY's List might not donate to those running for other offices if they supported Clinton's chief opponent for the Democratic nomination, Barack Obama. According to Vaida and Skalka, Malcolm's proclamation "incensed many in progressive Democratic circles, who viewed it as a threat." Malcolm later said to the *National Journal* that she had meant only to convey that EMILY's List donors who were unhappy with a List-backed candidate's support for Obama might cease making donations to that candidate.

Tensions were also exacerbated when EMILY's List questioned Obama's commitment to the pro-choice cause and criticized abortion-rights groups, such as NARAL Pro-Choice America, for endorsing him. The political pollster Celinda Lake told Vaida and Skalka, "I think one thing that EMILY's List has demonstrated is that they can play as bare-knuckles as the boys." Despite the organization's skepticism about Obama, it threw support behind the future president after he triumphed over Clinton for the Democratic Party nomination.

According to Vaida and Skalka, among other observers, the tension caused by EMILY's List's ardent support for Clinton reflected a large generational gap. The authors noted that during the primaries, "Baby Boomer moms continually resuscitated Clinton's candidacy while their daughters backed the more youthful Obama." That clash of values between younger female voters, who have typically faced less sex discrimination and have always had choice with regard to reproduction, and those who recall a less-tolerant era, is one that the group will have to contend with as it continues to expand. Nonetheless, Malcolm told Vaida and Skalka that younger voters are not her "market segment." "People who are donors to politics across the board are older, because they have the wherewithal to do it," she said. "Am I going to craft a message for 18-year-olds right now and try to raise money from them? No."

In November 2009, when the U.S. House passed a health-care reform bill that included the Stupak-Pitts Amendment, which prohibits taxpayer funding for abortions, many pro-choice groups, including EMILY's List, voiced frustration. "The assault on women's reproductive rights continues with a vengeance," Malcolm said, as quoted by Phillip Klein for the *American Spectator* (November 9, 2009). A petition to stop the amendment was made available on the EMILY's List Web site.

The end of January 2010 marked the end of Malcolm's service as president of EMILY's List; she has retained her post as chairwoman of its board of directors. Her successor as president, Stephanie Schriock, has a great deal of hands-on political experience, most recently as the chief of staff for Democratic U.S. senator Jon Tester of Montana and as the campaign manager for Al Franken's successful run for the U.S. Senate in Minnesota. "We've set the stage for history," Malcolm said a few weeks before she stepped down, as quoted by Philip Rucker in the *Washington Post* (January 7, 2010). "We've had astonishing victories. The U.S. House is a very different place today than it was when we began. The world has changed." Noting one major change, Malcolm said of Schriock, "She views politics through the lens of the Internet, which is what we will need going forward."

Malcolm has often been sought out for commentary related to political campaigns and has appeared on CBS's *60 Minutes* and NBC's *Today Show*, among other TV programs. She has been featured in such magazines as *People* and *Fortune*, and her opinion pieces have been published in the *Washington Post*, the *Los Angeles Times*, the *New York Times*, the *Chicago Sun-Times*, and other newspapers. She was named one of America's most influential women in a 1998 issue of *Vanity Fair*, and the following year she was selected as one of the 100 most important women in the nation by *Ladies' Home Journal*.

In 2003 Malcolm co-founded America Coming Together (ACT), a national organization devoted to voter mobilization. She was also involved in the creation of America Votes, a coalition of progressive organizations—including ACT and EMILY's List—that works to energize voters.

—W.D.

Suggested Reading: *Los Angeles Times* E p1 Oct. 9, 1991; *National Journal* (on-line) June 28, 2008; *Washington Post* A p1 Dec. 25, 1984, (on-line) May 10, 2008; *Washington Post Magazine* W p32 June 5, 1988

Courtesy of David All, via Creative Commons 2

Malkin, Michelle

Oct. 20, 1970– Political commentator; columnist

Address: c/o Creators Syndicate, 5777 W. Century Blvd., Suite 700, Los Angeles, CA 90045

Over the last decade the political commentator Michelle Malkin has become a major spokesperson for hard-core conservatives in the U.S. A former editorial writer for both the *Los Angeles Daily News* and the *Seattle Times*, Malkin is a syndicated columnist whose musings appear in more than 150 newspapers across the nation. Her four books include *Invasion: How America Still Welcomes Terrorists, Criminals, and Other Foreign Menaces to Our Shores* (2002); the highly controversial *In Defense of Internment: The Case for 'Racial Profiling' in World War II and the War on Terror* (2004), in which she argued that the internment of Japanese-Americans during World War II was justified and vital to national security; and *Culture of Corruption* (2009), an attack on the administration of President Barack Obama. Malkin maintains a blog, MichelleMalkin.com, which receives millions of page views per month; she founded the successful conservative multimedia blog Hot Air in 2006 and is a frequent guest on and contributor to such television programs as *The O'Reilly Factor*, *Hannity and Colmes*, and *20/20*. She is currently a commentator for the Fox News Channel.

In her column Malkin has voiced her opinions on a wide range of topics. On September 3, 2008 she wrote about what she saw as the mistreatment of conservative women by liberals: "Liberals hold a special animus for constituencies they deem traitors. Minorities who identify as social and economic conservatives have left the plantation and sold out their people. Women who put an 'R' by their name have abandoned their ovaries and betrayed their gender. As female Republican officeholders and female conservative public figures have grown in number and visibility, so has the progression of Conservative Female Abuse. The astonishing vitriol and virulent hatred directed at GOP Alaska Gov. [and former vice-presidential candidate] Sarah Palin is the most severe manifestation to date." In her November 19, 2008 column, Malkin criticized the opponents of California's Proposition 8, a constitutional amendment—passed during the November 2008 general elections—determining that the state will recognize a marriage only when the parties are a man and a woman. She wrote, "The sore losers who opposed Prop. 8 responded with threats, fists and blacklists. . . . [These] activists have published on the Internet an 'Anti-Gay Blacklist' of Prop. 8 donors. If the tables were turned and Prop. 8 proponents created such an enemies list, everyone in Hollywood would be screaming 'McCarthyism' faster than you could count to eight. . . . Corporate honchos, church leaders and small donors alike are in the same-sex-marriage mob's crosshairs, all unfairly demonized as hate-filled bigots by bona fide hate-filled bigots who have abandoned decency in pursuit of 'equal rights.'" Responding to charges that civil rights have been sacrificed in the name of national security during the war or terrorism, Malkin wrote on September 22, 2009, "Political correctness remains the handmaiden of terrorism." Malkin has been criticized by many for the polarizing nature of her views. She has also won awards for her work and praise from such conservative publications as *National Review*.

Malkin was born Michelle Maglalang on October 20, 1970 in Philadelphia, Pennsylvania. Her parents, Apolo and Rafaela Maglalang, had immigrated to the U.S. from their native Philippines earlier that year to escape the increasingly authoritarian and repressive rule of President Ferdinand Marcos and to seek opportunities not available to them in their home country. After Michelle was born the family settled in Absecon, in southern New Jersey. Malkin has a younger brother; her father was a neonatalogist at the Atlantic City Medical Center, in Atlantic City, New Jersey, and her mother worked as a schoolteacher in neighboring Pleasantville. Malkin told reporters for the Cherry Hill, New Jersey, *Courier-Post* (August 5, 2004) that though her parents were not outspoken in their political views, they were "huge, rock-ribbed Reagan Republicans." Her mother and father instilled in her "a unique perspective on being American," she told the *Courier-Post*. "They constantly reminded" their children "that we needed to be grateful for all we have." In addition, a visit to the Philippines with her parents in 1982 revealed to her "such utter destitution throughout the entire country," she told the *Courier-Post*, "and really shaped my world view."

While growing up Malkin studied music; her mother hoped that she would become a concert pianist. A Catholic, she attended Holy Spirit High School in Absecon, graduating in 1988. She then enrolled at Oberlin College, a liberal-arts institution in Oberlin, Ohio, known for its music conservatory. She took classes in government and English while continuing her classical-music studies. "I soon realized that I couldn't cut it with piano," Malkin admitted to Sarah Maserati for *National Review* (February 13, 2003, on-line). "I wrote for the regular student-run weekly and ended up majoring in English." During her college years Malkin was an intern for U.S. senator Bill Bradley of New Jersey, a Democrat.

While at Oberlin, which is famous for its liberal student body, Malkin joined a new right-of-center newspaper that had been started by a fellow student, Jesse Malkin, her future husband. She told Maserati, "My first piece, which I teamed up with my now-husband to write, was on affirmative-action policies on campus. It was a moderate, rather tepid report. It was seeing the violent paroxysms it caused on the Left that really put me on my way to a career in opinion journalism." Their article, which argued that admitting students based on racial preferences could harm those who arrive on campus without sufficient academic training, caused an uproar among the student body. Minority groups on campus shunned the couple, with some students going so far as to compare them to Adolf Hitler and Eva Braun. "It was such a profound and simple lesson to learn at Oberlin, and it has lasted me a lifetime," Malkin told Jonathan Pitts for the *Baltimore Sun* (March 9, 2008). "I've lived among many different kinds of people in this country, and it has always been the case—in life or on the Internet—that the most vicious attacks I've faced have not come from the archetypal red-necked bigots on the right. It's always been the people who profess to have the best intentions for me and my race and my gender. The loudest cheerleaders for tolerance are the most intolerant of all." Malkin has said that few of the students who expressed outrage over the article addressed the specific points it made. She told Pitts, "What's funny is that minority conservatives are almost universally accused of being self-loathing. That needs to be turned on its head. We're the ones who love what [the U.S.] has allowed us to do. There's nothing self-loathing about me. I love my life. I love my family. I love this country."

Malkin graduated from Oberlin in 1992. She then served an internship at NBC. Also in 1992 an article she had written in defense of the four white Los Angeles, California, police officers accused of beating Rodney King, an African-American, caught the eye of Tom Gray, then an editor at the *Los Angeles Daily News*. (The beating, which took place after King was stopped on a local street after speeding on a freeway, was captured on videotape; the acquittal of the officers triggered riots in Los Angeles.) Malkin soon joined the *Daily News* staff as an editorial writer. During her two years with the paper, she wrote on a wide range of topics, from school-board meetings to Mexican street gangs in the San Fernando Valley. In 1995 she was named a Warren T. Brookes journalism fellow at the Competitive Enterprise Institute (CEI), a libertarian think tank dedicated to the ideals of free enterprise and limited government, in Washington, D.C. (Every year the CEI selects a young journalist for the program, to bolster his or her knowledge of environmental issues and free-market economics.)

Malkin moved with her husband in 1996 to Seattle, Washington, where she wrote for the *Seattle Times*. She won several journalism awards during that time, including the 1998 Council on Governmental Ethics Laws (COGEL) national award for her investigative columns exposing campaign-finance abuses by Washington State Democrats, Republicans, and political organizations. Malkin left the *Seattle Times* in 1999, when she became a nationally syndicated columnist with the Creators Syndicate. Her twice-weekly column now appears nationwide in more than 150 newspapers, including the *Atlanta Journal-Constitution*, the *Miami Herald*, the *Detroit News*, the *Washington Times*, the *Chicago Sun-Times*, and the *New York Post*. She has also freelanced for such publications as the *Wall Street Journal*, the *Weekly Standard*, and *Reason*. In 2004 she launched her blog, Michelle-Malkin.com, on which she posts brief musings on current events.

Malkin's first book, *Invasion: How America Still Welcomes Terrorists, Criminals, and Other Foreign Menaces to Our Shores* (2002), argues that the U.S.'s immigration system threatens its national security by allowing terrorists and criminals to enter the country easily—legally or illegally—and stay. "[Advocates of open immigration] think it's possible to overlook the fact that we have 9 [million] to 11 million people in this country who have flouted our immigration laws, and still make sure we don't have another September 11," Malkin said to Robert Stacy McCain for the *Washington Times* (September 10, 2002). "I'm saying that's impossible. It's a deadly delusion." In *Invasion* Malkin pointed to several instances of how the current immigration system has failed, noting that one of the

9/11 hijackers entered the U.S. using a student visa but never enrolled in classes and that foreign criminals, such as a Mexican serial killer who murdered 12 Americans, have been able to enter the U.S. and evade the Immigration and Naturalization Service (INS). Sarah Maserati wrote about *Invasion*, "Malkin's book, and her many articles and columns, form a hall of shame of sorts—not just of the criminals and terrorists who make their way here, but also of the American officials at [the State Department] and the INS who are most responsible for letting them in." She added, "A lot of people—State Department and INS officials, immigration lawyers, 'unreconstructed open-borders advocates,' and the like—would love to see Malkin go away. But she's here to stay, fortunately. That hall of shame will keep expanding, and we'll have Malkin to thank for keeping tabs."

In 2004 Malkin stirred up a great deal of controversy with her second book, *In Defense of Internment: The Case for 'Racial Profiling' in World War II and the War on Terror*. Her book stands in stark contrast to a widely accepted view of history, which calls the relocation and detention of more than 120,000 Japanese-Americans during World War II a shameful result of wartime hysteria and racism. Malkin argued, rather, that the internment of Japanese-Americans was justified by the MAGIC cables, a set of intercepted, classified, decrypted messages indicating Japan's plan to install a spy network within the U.S., made up of Japanese immigrants and their U.S.-born children. Malkin used the example of the cables to defend the racial profiling of Arabs following the September 11, 2001 terrorist attacks. (She has not, however, advocated a mass internment of Arab-Americans.) "I was compelled to write this book after watching ethnic activists, historians, and politicians repeatedly play the World War II internment card after the September 11 attacks," Malkin explained on her Web site (February 6, 2006). "The [George W.] Bush Administration's critics have equated every reasonable measure to interrogate, track, detain, and deport potential terrorists with the 'racist' and 'unjustified' World War II internment policies of President [Franklin D.] Roosevelt. To make amends for this 'shameful blot' on our history, both Japanese-American and Arab/Muslim-American activists argue against any and all uses of race, ethnicity, nationality, and religion in shaping current homeland security policies. Misguided guilt about the past continues to hamper our ability to prevent future terrorist attacks." Unsurprisingly, *In Defense of Internment* caused uproar among Japanese-American groups. "Malkin claims to set the record straight when in reality she is distorting selected facts to fit her political position," Tom Ikeda, the executive director of Densho, a Seattle-based nonprofit organization that aims to preserve the histories of Japanese-Americans who were incarcerated during World War II, told John Iwasaki for the *Seattle Post-Intelligencer* (August 6, 2004).

In an op-ed piece for the *Boston Globe* (August 23, 2004) regarding *In Defense of Internment*, the reporter Cathy Young wrote, "Disputing the idea that the ethnic Japanese were selectively targeted, Malkin notes that people of German and Italian descent were also interned or evacuated from high-risk areas. But she glides over crucial differences. The targeted German and Italian ethnics were aliens, not American citizens. . . . And most internees of European origin were targeted on suspicion of specific subversive activities, not solely for their ancestry." Young added, "Ironically, the profiling measures Malkin advocates today, such as selective monitoring of aliens and visitors from countries with terrorist links, are moderate and fairly sensible. She is right that it's ludicrous to invoke Japanese internment as a parallel. But surely, defending something as extreme as mass internment can only undermine her case."

Malkin's book even sparked protest from some of her fellow conservatives. Aaron Goldstein, writing for the Web site Intellectual Conservative (December 17, 2004), maintained that while there are legitimate arguments to be made for racial profiling, "what was not legitimate was arbitrarily and capriciously removing hundreds of thousands from their homes who had little in common with each other, other than their ancestry, and taking their livelihoods away, when we knew that virtually all of the people in question had nothing to do with acts that threatened the national security of our country. . . . Michelle Malkin is wrong to pretend that the Japanese internment was of any service to the security of the United States. She is also wrong to believe that the Japanese internment will somehow better inform the United States in how to fight [the] War on Terror." In a review for the December 2004 issue of *Reason*, Eric Muller wrote, "Over the last several decades, historians have shown that the chief causes of the Japanese American internment were ingrained anti-Asian racism, nativist and economic pressures from groups in California that had long wanted the Japanese gone, and the panic of wartime hysteria. . . . Malkin contends that this history is a big lie—a 'politically correct myth' that 'has become enshrined as incontrovertible wisdom in the gullible press, postmodern academia, the cash-hungry grievance industry, and liberal Hollywood.' That passage alone should tell the reader this book is not a trustworthy work of history but a polemic—*The O'Reilly Factor* masquerading as the History Channel."

In 2005 Malkin published *Unhinged: Exposing Liberals Gone Wild*, in which she pointed to the actions and comments of some liberal-minded Americans as proof of the "utter hypocrisy of Democrats who fashion themselves as role models of tolerance and civility," as quoted on Amazon.com. Malkin's book "is a case study in uncensored hatred," Erin Montgomery wrote for the *Washington Times* (December 6, 2005). "As she shows, this hatred goes far beyond some Democrats' distaste for President Bush, the war in Iraq and conservative jour-

nalists. The Democrats who claim to value peace, tolerance and compassion have become violent, bigoted and just plain bizarre—and Mrs. Malkin has done a thorough job of chronicling their disturbing behavior." The *Publishers Weekly* reviewer, by contrast, judged that Malkin "makes no distinction between moderate and extreme liberals; everyone left of right is a nut. . . . Malkin uses extremist bloggers and airheaded celebrities as exemplars of the left, cherry picking the most egregiously tasteless examples of ill-conceived commentary or inflammatory behavior to bolster her case that liberals, as a whole, have gone off their rockers. Right-wingers looking for affirmation will enjoy."

In an article posted on the news Web site *Crosscut Seattle* (November 6, 2009), Ross Anderson, a former colleague of Malkin's at the *Seattle Times*, wrote that when he worked with her, she was not the combative, unyieldingly partisan figure she is known as today. At the time, Anderson wrote, she was less a hardline conservative than a libertarian, one who engaged in friendly debate. (Libertarians believe that individual freedoms are vital to the well-being and prosperity of the nation's people and that there should be little government intrusion in citizens' private lives.) Anderson claimed that Malkin was conflicted, for example, on the issue of abortion (which she now condemns as the "mass destruction of human lives"). Pointing to her current status as what he called a "conservative attack dog," Anderson wrote, "She snarls at Democrats, at any Republican . . . who dares associate with them, and at rival columnists such as David Brooks, whose sin is to harbor some admiration for his president [Obama]. This is not the intellectual debate [Malkin and I] once engaged in. It's tribalism, my people versus your people. I'm right and anybody who disagrees is ignorant or corrupt or both." Anderson went on to suggest that Malkin's increasingly conservative stance may have reflected her desire for success more than it did her actual beliefs. "Ideas are risky," he added. "Tell readers what you think, and you're liable to make at least half of them mad. Tribalism is easy, and it sells—albeit mostly to the choir. . . . Libertarian ideals don't sell on TV, and they won't get her back on the best-seller lists."

Malkin's most recent book, *Culture of Corruption: Obama and His Team of Tax Cheats, Crooks, and Cronies* (2009) spent six weeks at the top of the *New York Times* hardcover nonfiction best-seller list. Delving into the records of members of President Obama's staff, *Culture of Corruption* purports to reveal "the culture of corruption that surrounds Team Obama's brazen tax evaders, Wall Street cronies, petty crooks, slum lords, and business-as-usual influence peddlers," according to the book's jacket copy.

Malkin's husband, Jesse, whom she married in 1993, formerly worked as an associate for the Rand Corp. and is now a stay-at-home father and health-care consultant. The couple have two young children and live near Colorado Springs, Colorado.

—M.A.S.

Suggested Reading: (Cherry Hill, New Jersey) *Courier-Post* G p6 Aug. 5, 2004; michellemalkin.com; *National Review* (on-line) Feb. 13, 2003; *Washington Times* A p2 Sep. 10, 2002

Selected Books: *Invasion: How America Still Welcomes Terrorists, Criminals, and Other Foreign Menaces to Our Shores*, 2002; *In Defense of Internment: The Case for 'Racial Profiling' in World War II and the War on Terror*, 2004; *Unhinged: Exposing Liberals Gone Wild*, 2005; *Culture of Corruption: Obama and His Team of Tax Cheats, Crooks, and Cronies*, 2009

Courtesy of Roam Agency

Mamdani, Mahmood

Apr. 23, 1946– Expert on African affairs; writer; educator

Address: 401 Knox Hall, Columbia University, 606 W. 122d St., New York, NY 10027

Mahmood Mamdani is one of the world's most prominent social critics and scholars on Africa, particularly with regard to that continent's history and politics and the legacies of colonialism. Born in the African nation of Uganda, of Indian descent, Mamdani is probably best known for his provocative explanations of regional conflicts in Africa and elsewhere and his ability to frame such issues in historical context, in ways that lead even his critics to reexamine their views. Mamdani's ability to describe the forces behind developments, often challenging conventional wisdom (and, he would

argue, politically expedient explanations), has earned him the label of dissident. Frequently involved in controversial debates over the causes of and solutions to many of the region's biggest challenges, Mamdani has been dismissed by some as a dogmatic leftist; but in the eyes of admirers his skill in drawing connections from colonial institutions to contemporary wars, and from Cold War policies to present-day crises, has made his work an indispensable guide to understanding the how and why of conflicts in regions from Darfur to Iraq. Mamdani's work is not seen as merely critical: his nuanced views on past and present circumstances have also been helpful in finding constructive ways to move forward—for instance, in seeking to effect reconciliation between rival groups after civil wars—and he has served on several important advisory boards in Africa. Mamdani, who in 2008 was called one of the leading public intellectuals in the world by both *Prospect* and *Foreign Policy* magazines, is the author of books including *Citizen and Subject: Contemporary Africa and the Legacy of Late Colonialism* (1996); *When Victims Become Killers: Colonialism, Nativism, and the Genocide in Rwanda* (2001); *Good Muslim, Bad Muslim: America, the Cold War, and the Roots of Terror* (2004); and *Saviors and Survivors: Darfur, Politics, and the War on Terror* (2009). The director of Columbia University's Institute of African Studies from 1999 to 2004, he is currently professor of government in the university's Department of Anthropology and Political Science and the School of International and Public Affairs; he has held several top teaching posts at universities in Uganda, Tanzania, and South Africa. Mamdani told Bernard Tabaire for *Africa News* (August 12, 2004), "I have been pre-occupied with the institutional legacy of previous eras of the colonial world, of empires and how they tend to treat people as insiders or outsiders." In that regard, Mamdani has sometimes been compared to his colleague, friend, and mentor at Columbia, the late Palestinian intellectual and activist Edward Said.

A third-generation East African, Mahmood Mamdani was born on April 23, 1946 in Kampala, Uganda. Many of the Indians who made up the minority entrepreneurial classes in East Africa had arrived under British colonialism, a system that manipulated various race and class cleavages in order to function effectively. Upon finishing his O-level examinations at Senior Secondary School, in the Old Kampala district, in 1962—the year Uganda won its independence from Great Britain—Mamdani was one of a handful of students there offered scholarships to study in the U.S. "The scholarships were part of America's independence gift to Uganda. . . . Certainly, without a successful struggle for independence, I would not have got the higher education that I did," Mamdani wrote for the Uganda publication *New Vision* (April 28, 2007). During his years as a student at the University of Pittsburgh, in Pennsylvania, in the 1960s, Mamdani was a debater and a participant in the

American civil rights movement, then at its height. He wrote for the *New Vision* article, "In less than a year, I was among busloads of students going from northern universities to march in Birmingham, Alabama, in the south. . . . I and scores of other students were thrown in jail. Allowed to make one phone call from jail, I called the Uganda ambassador in Washington DC. 'What are you doing interfering in the internal affairs of a foreign country?' he asked. 'This is not an internal affair. This is a freedom struggle. How can you forget? We just got our freedom last year,' was my response."

Mamdani received a B.A. degree in 1967, then earned an M.A. and an M.A.L.D. (master of arts in law and diplomacy) from the Fletcher School of Law and Diplomacy at Tufts University, in Medford, Massachusetts, in 1969. Staying in the Boston area, Mamdani then pursued a Ph.D. in government at Harvard University, where he led a student strike to protest increases in tuition. He earned his doctorate in 1974.

Meanwhile, Mamdani had returned to Uganda in early 1972, to work as a teaching assistant at Makerere University, in Kampala. By the end of that year, he had become one of the 70,000 Ugandans of South Asian descent deported and dispossessed by the country's leader, Idi Amin; having mounted a successful military coup the previous year against the dictatorship of President Milton Obote, Amin claimed with the deportations to be finishing the work of independence by empowering black Africans. "I returned home . . . as a convinced Pan-African nationalist, but was thrown out later in the year as an Asian," Mamdani wrote for *New Vision*. In November 1972 he fled the country and was admitted to a refugee camp in London, England. "The British press was full of stories about Amin and the Asian expulsion," he wrote. "Every story talked of Amin not as a dictator, but as a black dictator. With few exceptions, the British press racialised Amin. His blackness was offered as the primary explanation for his brutality. Fresh from civil rights struggles in the American south, and anti-Vietnam war struggles in the American north, I had seen brutality in the white and was unwilling to accept this explanation." Nine months after he had arrived in England, a disillusioned Mamdani left for Tanzania to begin a teaching job at the University of Dar es Salaam, then a fertile environment for leftist and radical African activism; some of his colleagues and students there would go on to join anticolonial guerrilla groups around Africa, and some went on to become presidents and rebel leaders, among them Yoweri Museveni, who became Uganda's president in 1986; Laurent Kabila, who assumed power in the Congo (formerly Zaire) in 1997; and Ernest Wamba dia Wamba, who went on to become a member of the Congo Senate.

"Although my physical being was in Dar-es-Salaam where both my parents had been born," Mamdani wrote, "my mind was preoccupied with Uganda: Why Amin? Why the support for Amin?"

While he found black Africans' support for Amin painful on a personal level, Mamdani attempted to understand it. He has said that he fully understood the dynamics of the political situation in Uganda only after he returned there from exile, in 1979, following Amin's ouster. "Every Ugandan understood in his or her guts that the secret of Asian business success lay not just in hard work, but also in a racially unjust colonial system which made it difficult for black people to enter trade, thereby confirming Asian dominance in trade . . . ," Mamdani wrote for *New Vision*. "The demand for political independence went alongside another—that for social justice for those who had been the victims of colonial racial discrimination." Even after independence, elites—many of them Asian—had maintained their positions in Uganda by entering into lucrative alliances with bureaucrats. "Pointing to this informal apartheid in a complacent post-Independence Uganda, Amin asked uncomfortable questions, even if in a coarse and racist language. . . . I realised that Amin spoke the language of justice, however crudely, and that was the reason he was able to ride the crest of a historic wave of popular protest." In a controversial article for the *London Review of Books* (December 4, 2008) in which Mamdani tried to contextualize the recent policies of forcible land redistribution (in which land was taken from white farmers and given to blacks) carried out by Robert Mugabe in Zimbabwe, he wrote: "What distinguishes Mugabe and Amin from other authoritarian rulers is not their demagoguery but the fact that they projected themselves as champions of mass justice and successfully rallied those to whom justice had been denied by the colonial system. Not surprisingly, the justice dispensed by these demagogues mirrored the racialised injustice of the colonial system. In 1979 I began to realise that whatever they made of Amin's brutality, the Ugandan people experienced the Asian expulsion of 1972—and not the formal handover in 1962—as the dawn of true independence. The people of Zimbabwe are likely to remember 2000-3 as the end of the settler colonial era. Any assessment of contemporary Zimbabwe needs to begin with this sobering fact."

In 1979, as Obote and others were preparing a violent campaign to regain power from Amin, Mamdani left the University of Dar es Salaam and returned to teach political science at Makerere University, where he would remain until 1993. In the *New Vision* article, he recalled the decade after 1979 as "one of coming to political age for a second time." At Makerere Mamdani became a leading expert on the rural–urban divide in postcolonial Uganda as well as on agrarian policies and their relation to unrest in the nation. He also became an outspoken critic of Uganda's government and participated in literacy programs and campaigns for workers' rights. In 1985, in the midst of another civil war—which would bring Museveni to power—Mamdani was once again exiled for his criticisms of the government. Returning to teach at

Makerere in 1986, Mamdani was made chair of the Ugandan Commission of Inquiry into Local Government, a post he occupied until 1988, and was also the founding director of the Center for Basic Research in Kampala, where he served from 1987 to 1996. In the latter year he moved to postapartheid South Africa, where he was made director of the Center for African Studies at the University of Cape Town. He remained in the position until 1999, when he was made director of the Institute of African Studies at Columbia University in New York. There, he taught courses in the school's Anthropology and Political Science Departments and in its School of International and Public Affairs. Mamdani was also the president of the Council for the Development of Social Research in Africa, the continent's most important social-science body, based in Dakar, Senegal, from 1999 to 2002. From 2005 to 2006 Mamdani was a chief adviser to the U.N. High Level Group of the Alliance of Civilizations.

Mamdani is a prolific writer whose works have become staples in the field of postcolonial and African studies. His early works include *From Citizen to Refugee* (1973), *Politics and Class Formation in Uganda* (1976), and *Imperialism and Fascism in Uganda* (1983). The book that first brought him widespread attention, *Citizen and Subject: Contemporary Africa and the Legacy of Late Colonialism* (1996), is regarded as a seminal work in both African and postcolonial studies; it won several awards and was named by a jury in Ghana in 2002 as one of the 20th century's most important books on Africa. In the book Mamdani offered a new perspective on what he saw as the failures of postcolonial states in Africa. He described the newly independent countries as being incapable of reforming the old colonial system of rule through that system's methods, or via elites and tribal structures. During colonialism, while elites became the citizens through whom the ruling country could exercise direct control, the indigenous and rural masses became subjects, to be ruled indirectly via decentralized despotism—that is, through tribal structures managed from the outside. Mamdani referred to that arrangement as the bifurcated state. Its legacy, in the era of independence, is either centralized despotism (one-party or military) or states in which there is a massive and disastrous disconnect between urban and rural life. The book also examines the nature of resistance movements, particularly in South Africa.

Mamdani's book *When Victims Become Killers: Colonialism, Nativism, and the Genocide in Rwanda* (2001) traces the root causes of the 1994 genocide in the African nation of Rwanda by viewing it in the contexts of colonialism and regional conditions. Mamdani argued that the Belgian colonial authorities, acting through a divide-and-conquer policy, had defined the Tutsi minority as a privileged alien population through which they could rule the indigenous Hutu majority. The revolution of 1959, through which the Hutus overthrew the

Tutsi monarchy, sending thousands of Tutsis into exile, reproduced and ossified those colonial identities. When the exiled Tutsis, who felt like foreigners in Uganda, repatriated to Rwanda in 1990, the Hutu fear of a Tutsi return to power sparked in 1994 a state-sanctioned policy of genocide. Mamdani wrote, "In its motivation and construction, I argue that the Rwandan genocide needs to be understood as a natives' genocide. It was a genocide by those who saw themselves as sons—and daughters—of the soil, and their mission as one of clearing the soil of a threatening *alien* presence. This was not an 'ethnic' but a 'racial' cleansing, not a violence against one who is seen as a neighbor but against one who is seen as a foreigner; not a violence that targets a transgression across a boundary into home but one that seeks to eliminate a foreign presence from home soil, literally and physically." Mamdani made the point that the atrocities in Rwanda were not the results of inherent tribal conflict but arose from specific historical contexts.

Similarly, in *Good Muslim, Bad Muslim: America, the Cold War, and the Roots of Terror* (2004), Mamdani tried to debunk the notion that Islam was at the root of much of contemporary nonstate-sponsored terrorism, including the 9/11 attacks; he identified the source instead as the Cold War. "However awful, unpleasant and tragic 9/11 was, I hoped some good [would] come out of [discussions about it]," Mamdani told Arthur Pais for *India Abroad* (May 14, 2004). "But the lid over the debate was put back in no time and amnesia has been created about American responsibilities for creating terrorism. I used to think before 9/11 tragedies could bring people together in a way prosperity does not. Prosperity could isolate people but tragedy could connect. I was proved wrong by the American response to 9/11." In a direct attack on the notion of a "clash of civilizations" advanced by the scholars Samuel Huntington, Bernard Lewis, and others, according to which "good Muslims" are pro-American and "bad Muslims" are anti-American, Mamdani argued that religion had little to do with terrorism. Looking at what he called the late Cold War, which began after the U.S. defeat in Vietnam, in 1975, Mamdani argued that the U.S.— unable any longer to get citizens' support or financial backing for more overseas military interventions—decided to back proxies to fight the Cold War on its behalf. As the theater of the Cold War shifted from Asia to Africa with the fall of the Portuguese empire in Africa, in 1975, the U.S. began supporting nonstate, privatized combatants (financed, Mamdani wrote, through underground economies such as the drug trade, since Congress would not approve payments for wars that had not been officially declared). "The simple fact the government had to face was that if you decide to wage war without legislative consent, then you are likely to be short of funds," Mamdani wrote in *Good Muslim, Bad Muslim*. "Time and again, the agencies pursuing covert wars seemed to arrive at the same solution to their financial problems: collude with drug lords." In Angola, Mozambique, and later Nicaragua, the U.S. backed nonstate groups against leftist governments. (Mamdani pointed to the neoconservative U.S. diplomat Jeane Kirkpatrick's notion that there were two types of dictatorships in the Third World—left-wing totalitarian and right-wing authoritarian. "The difference, she argued, was that totalitarian dictatorships were incapable of reforming from within and so needed to be overthrown forcibly from without, whereas authoritarian dictatorships were open to internal reform, which could be tapped through constructive engagement," Mamdani wrote for the February 17, 2004 issue of the Nigerian newspaper *This Day*. "The political importance of Kirkpatrick's argument cannot be overstated. By giving a rationale for why it is fine to make friends with dictators while doing everything to overthrow left-wing governments, she solved the moral problem with [President Ronald] Reagan's foreign policy.") According to Mamdani, the lessons learned from taking that approach in Africa and Central America were later applied to Afghanistan, whose population the U.S. armed to fight the Soviets—then abandoned after the fight was won; Afghanistan became a base of operations for the terrorist group Al Qaeda, which was responsible for the 9/11 attacks. "Official America learned to distinguish between two types of terrorism—'theirs' and 'ours'—and cultivated an increasingly benign attitude to ours," Mamdani wrote in *Good Muslim, Bad Muslim*. "But then it turned out that their terrorism was born of ours." He told Nermeen Shaikh of the Asia Society (May 5, 2004, on-line), "The point of the book is that terror is a strategy to which the US turned to win the Cold War, that non-state terror was born of state terror, and that Islamist terror represents only the final and concluding outcome in this relationship, that its earlier outcomes, whether with [the armed conservative political group] Renamo in Mozambique or the Contras in Nicaragua, have little if anything to do with Islamist terror." With the help of Edward Said, Mamdani's book was picked up by a division of Random House and sold well in 2004, as the anti–Iraq war movement grew in force and a significant number of people began to question the official rhetoric of the "war on terrorism." Mamdani joked to Andrew Rice for the *New York Observer* (April 4, 2005) that the book sold well because people misunderstood the title, taking it to be "a directory of good Muslims and bad Muslims—you know, which ones to avoid." The book was criticized by some for downplaying the economic goals of Cold War geopolitics, notably the opening of markets.

In *Saviors and Survivors: Darfur, Politics, and the War on Terror*, Mamdani examined the conflict in the Darfur province of Sudan, in Africa, in the context of colonial history. He argued that, contrary to most Western accounts of the conflict—which he dismissed as dangerously simplistic—the genocide in Darfur was not a race-based conflict but a war over land, climate change, and de-

sertification. As with the Belgians in Rwanda, the British colonial tactic in Sudan was to divide the region into tribal homelands, assigning the label "native" to the groups given rights to the land, while outsiders, often nomads, were forced to pay tribute. "The British engineered the grand narrative . . . ," Mamdani told Joel Whitney for *Guernica* magazine (May 2009). "Tribe became the basis of systematic discrimination. So you got settler and native as a tribal distinction." Decades of severe drought drove nomads from the previously fertile lands in the north to Darfur, making the colonial-land rights an even more contentious issue. In addition, neighboring Chad became the site of a proxy Cold War fight that supplied the region with guns. That combination of factors, Mamdani wrote, led to a civil war in Sudan in the late 1980s, which intensified in the following decades with the government attempting unsuccessfully to create new tribal homelands and then engaging in a brutal counterinsurgency against rebel tribes. Mamdani also strongly criticized the "Save Darfur" campaign in the West as embracing a misguided, ahistorical account of events that relied on stereotypes of Arabs reinforced by the "war on terrorism." The assumption that one set of evil people, Arabs—somehow "less African"—were committing genocide against another, native blacks, was, according to Mamdani, an attempt to simplify a complex problem. In his view, the crisis was less a genocide than the story of a civil war, or, more specifically, an insurgency and a counterinsurgency, with killing on both sides. "I need to convince [supporters of the Save Darfur movement] that there is a politics around this—not simply good intentions and moralism and a fight against evil," Mamdani told Christopher Lydon, as broadcast on Radio Open Source (April 2, 2009). "I need to tell them that there is no such thing as a trans-historical evil in the world in which we live; that, in fact, all violence without exception has causes, and the causes are historical. And if you want to do something about the violence, we need to do something about the causes. The idea that violence is its own explanation is an idea which will take us nowhere except into a cycle of violence." Mamdani told Peter Hart and Steve Rendall on the radio show *Counter-Spin* (March 16, 2007) that the Western media, "because of the way they have reported Darfur," have "obscured the fact that there is a civil war going on. They have obscured the fact that the only way to stop the violence against the civilians is to settle this civil war. Instead, they have promoted the idea of an external military intervention as a possible solution. And the very prospect of an external military intervention has given hopes to the rebels that they may in fact end up with the entire cake, and instilled fears among the government that they may end up with no power whatsoever. So on both sides, it has reinforced those who think military and violence is the only way for them to safeguard their own position."

Mamdani argued that the words "humanitarian" and "genocide" have political meanings of their own—that the former, once used to protect victims, now serves the goals of foreign intervention; that the latter is used to demonize enemies of the West, particularly in the "war on terrorism"; and that its use aggravates conflicts by marginalizing key groups from peace talks. The solution, according to Mamdani, is not to call for the one-sided enforcement of criminal justice but to reform the colonial land-rights system. "The only conflicts in Africa that we have managed to resolve successfully are those conflicts where criminal justice took a second seat to political reform," he told Cheryl Chorley for the National Public Radio program *Tell Me More* (March 5, 2009). "I think the turnaround was in South Africa with the end of apartheid. The end of apartheid was predicated on an agreement between the ANC [African National Congress] and the apartheid government, whereby the apartheid government agreed to political reforms in return for impunity."

Mamdani, who speaks nine languages, is married to the Indian filmmaker Mira Nair, whose movies include *Salaam Bombay!*, *Mississippi Masala*, *Monsoon Wedding*, and *Amelia*. The two met when Nair interviewed him in 1989 in Uganda as part of her research for *Mississippi Masala*, about a romance between an Indian-American woman and an African-American man from the South. Mamdani and Nair live in Kampala and New York and have a son, Zohran.

—M.M.

Suggested Reading: *Boston Globe* p7 Mar. 22, 2009; *Guernica* May 2009; *India Abroad* p22 May 14, 2004; *London Review of Books* (on-line) Mar. 8, 2007; *New York Observer* p1 Apr. 4, 2005; *New Yorker* p100 Dec. 9, 2002; (Uganda) *New Vision* Apr. 28, 2007

Selected Books: *From Citizen to Refugee*, 1973; *Politics and Class Formation in Uganda*, 1976; *Imperialism and Fascism in Uganda*, 1983; *Citizen and Subject: Contemporary Africa and the Legacy of Late Colonialism*, 1996; *When Victims Become Killers: Colonialism, Nativism, and the Genocide in Rwanda*, 2001; *Good Muslim, Bad Muslim: America, the Cold War, and the Roots of Terror*, 2004; *Saviors and Survivors: Darfur, Politics, and the War on Terror*, 2009

Mayer, John

(MAY-er)

Oct. 16, 1977– Singer; songwriter; guitarist

Address: c/o Creative Artists Agency, Attn.: Scott Clayton, 3310 West End Ave., Fifth Fl., Nashville, TN 37203

The seven-time Grammy Award–winning recording artist John Mayer has been widely praised for his poetic songwriting and his virtuosity on the guitar. Identified initially with a string of sappy soft-rock hits, including "Your Body Is a Wonderland," from his 2001 album, *Room for Squares*, and "Daughters," from his 2003 release, *Heavier Things*, Mayer has since reestablished himself as one of the more substantive figures in contemporary pop music. After forming the John Mayer Trio, in 2005, he turned for inspiration to the classic blues he listened to as a child in Connecticut. He has since released two other successful albums: *Continuum* (2006), which merged his love of blues with his pop style, and *Battle Studies* (2009).

John Clayton Mayer was born on October 16, 1977 to Margaret Mayer, a middle-school teacher, and Richard Mayer, a high-school principal. (His parents divorced in 2009.) He has an older brother, Carl, and a younger brother, Ben. Mayer spent his first seven years in Bridgeport, Connecticut, then moved with his family to Fairfield. As a child he dreamed of becoming a radio announcer, often

Ian Gavan/Getty Images

practicing a patter for his imaginary radio station, WJOHN. His love of music blossomed after a neighbor exposed him to the work of the blues guitarist Stevie Ray Vaughan. When Mayer was 13 his father rented a guitar for him. At first he taught himself some notes by playing along with recordings; he then took lessons from Al Ferrante, who had once been a guitarist in the pop star Cyndi Lauper's band. Meanwhile, he listened to the records of such artists as Vaughan, Albert King, Bonnie Raitt, and Robert Cray. Mayer has Vaughan's initials tattooed on his upper left arm.

While attending Fairfield High School, Mayer formed a band with his fellow students Joe Beleznay, Tim Procaccini, and Rich Wolf called Villanova Junction. (Mayer named the band after a Jimi Hendrix song.) "We weren't doing anything extremely serious. . . . We were just doing covers at that time, fooling around," Beleznay recalled to Sean Spillane for the Bridgeport *Connecticut Post* (February 13, 2005). "John played so well. When I first saw him play, when I was 17 or 18, the level he was playing at was [so advanced that] a 50-year-old musician would have been jealous. Someone that had been doing it for years would have just loved to be at his caliber." Although Villanova Junction performed live only a few times, the band recorded an eight-song tape following Mayer's high-school graduation and made 300 copies to sell locally. "[The tape is] not a very listenable piece of work right now as it stands, but as it stood when I was 17, I had a record," Mayer told Spillane. "Forget about the fact that it was eight songs and they weren't very good, it was a record and it had a cover and it had shrink-wrap on it and they were original tunes."

When Mayer was 17 years old, he suffered an episode of heart arrhythmia—or an irregular heartbeat—that resulted in a weekend hospital stay. Before correcting the problem through less drastic measures, Mayer's doctors reportedly considered stopping his heart and restarting it. "It was so frightening at the time to be seventeen and have heart monitors hooked up to you," Mayer recalled to Brian Hiatt for *Rolling Stone* (September 21, 2006). "That was the moment the songwriter in me was born. I discovered a whole other side of me. I came home that night and started writing lyrics. I discovered it all at once: It was like opening up a lockbox, and inside was a depth that I didn't even know I had as a person, or a writer—incredible creativity and vision and neurosis, complete neurosis. They all go together in a package."

After high school Mayer spent 15 months working as a counter clerk at a Fairfield gas station. He saved his earnings to buy a guitar. Determined to become a successful musician, Mayer enrolled at the Berklee College of Music, in Boston, Massachusetts, in 1997; he dropped out of the school after only two semesters. "I went there with the idea of becoming the kind of guitar player who made everybody go, 'Whoaaa, he's better than me,'" Mayer confessed to Billy Watkins for the Jackson, Mississippi, *Clarion-Ledger* (February 21, 2003). "Then I thought about it, and I decided that all I wanted to be was listenable."

With a friend Mayer relocated to Atlanta, Georgia, where he became a frequent performer at the city's numerous blues clubs. "Atlanta's my musical home, it really is," he told Nick Marino for the *Atlanta Journal-Constitution* (November 20, 2003). "When somebody says to me, 'You're from Atlanta, right?' I don't really want to change their mind, because I am a hometown boy in that sense. I didn't play a single live show under my name until I got into Atlanta, and it really was the place where I really came alive." He recorded an acoustic album, the self-released *Inside Wants Out*, in 1999. The following year he performed at the well-known South by Southwest Music Festival, held annually in Austin, Texas. There, Mayer attracted the attention of Aware Records, a subsidiary of the major recording label Columbia Records. He signed with Aware soon afterward.

Mayer's major-label debut album, *Room for Squares*, was released in June 2001. The album featured four songs from his self-released album as well as eight new tracks. (Mayer co-wrote three of the album's songs with his friend Clay Cook; he wrote the others alone.) *Room for Squares*, whose title is a play on that of the 1963 Hank Mobley album *No Room for Squares*, is dominated by simple, mellow pop melodies. After striking a deal with Aware Records, Columbia signed Mayer and released a remixed version of the record, adding a song and changing the album cover to display Mayer's boyishly handsome face prominently. *Room for Squares* was well received; critics agreed that Mayer was a promising talent. "*Room for Squares . . .* is instantly likable and accessible. But it's no less smart and affecting for that," the *Rolling Stone* critic Anthony Decurtis wrote in his review (November 13, 2001, on-line). "These thirteen songs are a travelogue of discovery—of love, identity and purpose. They may chronicle what Mayer wryly terms a 'quarter-life crisis,' but they trade on energy rather than angst, wonder instead of pain. The arrangements, which are reminiscent of the deft pop of Elvis Costello and the Police, are built around Mayer's guitar but make free use of a rhythm section and keyboards. His singing, meanwhile, recalls David Gray and Dave Matthews."

Mayer's album eventually climbed to number eight on the *Billboard* 200 chart and sold more than four million copies. His first single, "No Such Thing," peaked at number 13 on the *Billboard* Hot 100 chart and number 11 on the *Billboard* Hot Adult Contemporary Tracks chart. In it Mayer criticized the notion that everyone must attend college and choose a practical career: "They love to tell you / Stay inside the lines / But something's better / On the other side / I wanna run through the halls of my high school / I wanna scream at the / Top of my lungs / I just found out there's no such thing as the real world / Just a lie you've got to rise above." The song was inspired by Mayer's parents—who did not support his dream of becoming a rock star and had urged him to focus on school—as well as by Mayer's friends who were still in college. Those friends "were living in dorm rooms paid for by their parents," Mayer told Billy Watkins. "They had their parents' credit cards in their wallets. I was like, 'So is this the real world they were warning us about?' I mean, when you think about it, how real is that?"

Mayer's second single, "Your Body Is a Wonderland," is a soft acoustic ballad in which he praises the body of a female lover. It was far more commercially successful than Mayer's previous single and brought the musician his first Grammy Award, for best male pop-vocal performance, in 2003. (The song has been rumored, incorrectly, to be about the actress Jennifer Love Hewitt, whom Mayer dated briefly in 2002.) Despite its success, "Your Body Is a Wonderland" has also been subject to plenty of criticism. It was included on several "worst song" lists, including *Blender* magazine's rundown of the "50 worst songs ever" (2009, on-line), on which it came in at number 28. *Blender* staffers wrote, "Drool never sounded as sweet as it does on this slow-stirred ode to daytime sex—but even from the otherwise charming Mayer, it's still drool."

Mayer's sophomore album, *Heavier Things*, debuted at the top of the *Billboard* 200 chart in September 2003 and eventually sold 2.7 million copies. The album's first two singles, "Bigger Than My Body" and "Clarity," had been popular on the radio, but it was the third single, the sentimental acoustic tune "Daughters," that proved the most commercially successful. "Daughters" considers the way relationships between fathers and their young girls affect the girls' future relationships with men. In the chorus Mayer urged, "Fathers, be good to your daughters / Daughters will love like you do / Girls become lovers who turn into mothers / So mothers, be good to your daughters too."

"Daughters" went on to win two Grammy Awards, for best male pop-vocal performance and song of the year. Despite its success, Mayer, who feared the song would pigeonhole him as a writer of sappy ballads, was not happy that his record company had chosen it as a single. He told Clark Collis for *Entertainment Weekly* (February 16, 2007), "A single becomes your quarterback for your record. Putting the ball in the hands of 'Daughters' and saying, Push this record? It just seems pandering." He said to Brian Hiatt, "I saw that as career death."

After the success of "Daughters," Mayer spent about a year trying to distance himself from his teeny-bopper image. He performed with such music greats as Buddy Guy, Herbie Hancock, B.B. King, and Eric Clapton and formed the John Mayer Trio, a blues-rock band. "It was, 'let me take a year and get myself on track,'" he explained to Hiatt. "I've met people who didn't realize they were off target, and they looked up and they were forty—they had six failed records, but everyone told them they were great. And they're . . . miserable." The John Mayer Trio, which included the bassist Pino Palladino, who had toured with the Who, and the drummer Steve Jordan, who had recorded with Clapton and Bob Dylan, toured small venues around the U.S. and recorded the 2005 live album *Try! John Mayer Trio Live in Concert.* "In a trio, there's nowhere to hide," Jordan told Clark Collis.

"And it was different for John [Mayer], not being the best guy in the band. He'd never worked so hard in his life. But he more than held his own. He's a fantastic musician. Here's a guy that knows about tone; he's constantly tweaking his guitar tone. That's something he shares with Clapton, with all the great guitarists."

Though not as commercially successful as his prior work, *Try!* helped Mayer overcome his association with treacly love songs and showcase his musical talent. "There are no two ways about it: anybody who dismissed Mayer as a lite Dave Matthews wannabe based on his first two records will be forced to reassess him on the basis of this excellent record . . . ," Stephen Thomas Erlewine wrote for the All Music Guide Web site. "[The songs on *Try!*] are his strongest, most ambitious set of tunes yet. And that's what's most impressive about *Try!*—Mayer has expanded what he can do as a musician and a writer and in the process has definitely separated himself from the pack of sensitive, jammy modern singer/songwriters. Based on this, he has more heart, soul, ambition, and chops than the rest of them combined."

Mayer went solo in 2006 to record his third studio album, *Continuum.* (He recruited Jordan and Palladino to play on the album; Jordan also co-produced it with Mayer.) For *Continuum* Mayer combined the bluesy rock of the John Mayer Trio with his signature pop-music style to create a heavier, more soulful sound. "*Continuum* is kind of like my thesis paper," he said to Clark Collis. "It's the one I feel best about. I've finally got it right. There's a little bit of me that's, like, now I can die proverbially." *Continuum* was markedly different from Mayer's previous albums in not only sound but content. In the album's single "Waiting on the World to Change," for example, Mayer tried to explain the seeming political apathy of his generation: "Now we see everything that's going wrong / With the world and those who lead it / We just feel like we don't have the means / To rise above and beat it. . . . It's not that we don't care / We just know that the fight ain't fair." In another song, "Stop This Train," Mayer sang about the brevity of life and his reluctance to accept that his parents will eventually die. "Gravity" is a bare-bones blues song about resisting self-destructive behavior.

Continuum received positive reviews and debuted at the number-two spot on the *Billboard* 200 chart. *Rolling Stone* selected it as the 11th-best album of 2006, stating (December 11, 2006, on-line), "*Continuum* is Mayer's most assured album yet, channeling familiar gifts—fluid guitar-playing, sexy white-boy croon, strong tune sense—with more subtlety, more focus and less lady-baiting cheese than ever. The result is a breezy pop-rock record that surrounds supremely crafted songs." *Continuum* was nominated in the category of album of the year at the 49th Annual Grammy Awards, in 2007, and won the awards for best male pop-vocal performance, for "Waiting on the World to Change," and best pop-vocal album. Mayer was also included on *Time* magazine's "Time 100" list of the "100 men and women whose power, talent and moral example" are "transforming the world."

In 2008 Mayer released *Where the Light Is: John Mayer Live in Los Angeles*, a recording of his December 8, 2007 performance at the Nokia Theatre in Los Angeles, California. That year he won the Grammy Award for best solo rock-vocal performance for the version of "Gravity" on the album. He also won the Grammy for best male pop-vocal performance for the single "Say," which he recorded for the 2007 Rob Reiner film comedy *The Bucket List*. Released as a single in November 2007, "Say" saw more than 1.2 million downloads and reached number 12 on the *Billboard* Hot 100 songs-of-the-year chart, becoming Mayer's highest-peaking Hot 100 single to date.

Mayer's most recent album, *Battle Studies*, was released on November 17, 2009. The songs on the album revolve around heartbreak and Mayer's skepticism about love. Despite debuting at the top spot on the *Billboard* 200 chart, *Battle Studies* has received mixed reviews. "John Mayer is clearly loaded with a plethora of not only talent, but creative intent, and it's . . . the realization that he's got the chops to pull it off that makes the album as disappointing as it is," Anthony Lombardi wrote for *PopMatters* (November 25, 2009, on-line). "It just seems that, in his muddled desire to strive for substance instead of allowing for a natural communication of the same goals, he's gotten lost in the haze. It would be unfair to call *Battle Studies* an outright misfire, but it's undoubtedly a regression on his winding, forward-moving path toward artistic maturity."

The six-foot-three-inch Mayer has dark brown hair and brown eyes. He is known as something of a ladies' man; in addition to Jennifer Love Hewitt, he has dated the singer Jessica Simpson and the actress Jennifer Aniston. For several years beginning in June 2004, Mayer wrote a column titled "Music Lessons with John Mayer" for *Esquire* magazine, in which he provided his often humorous take on various topics.

Mayer has homes in Los Angeles and New York City. He enjoys performing raunchy stand-up comedy; he appeared on a 2004 installment of the sketch-comedy program *Chappelle's Show* and had his own VH1 comedy special, *John Mayer Has a TV Show* (2004). Mayer collects watches; one is a Patek Philippe with a Sky Moon Tourbillon, generally valued at between $1.1 million and $1.5 million.

—M.A.S.

Suggested Reading: (Bridgeport) *Connecticut Post* (on-line) Feb. 11, 2007; *Entertainment Weekly* p38 Feb. 16, 2007; johnmayer.com; *New York Times* C p1 Nov. 21, 2009; *Rolling Stone* p66+ Sep. 21, 2006, (on-line) Feb. 22, 2007; *Ventura County (California) Star* G p29 Aug. 8, 2002

Selected Recordings: *Inside Wants Out*, 1999; *Room for Squares*, 2001; *Heavier Things*, 2003; *Continuum*, 2006; *Where the Light Is: John Mayer Live in Los Angeles*, 2008; *Battle Studies*, 2009; with John Mayer Trio—*Try! John Mayer Trio Live in Concert*, 2005

Selected Television Specials: *John Mayer Has a TV Show*, 2004

Sean Gallup/Getty Images for Burda Media

Mayer, Marissa

(MY-er)

May 30, 1975– Internet executive

Address: Google Inc., 1600 Amphitheatre Pkwy., Mountain View, CA 94043

"Two out of three web searches in the United States today go through Google, and few dispute that [Marissa] Mayer has a lot to do with that," Julian Guthrie wrote for *San Francisco Magazine* (March 2008, on-line). Google, founded in 1998 by two Stanford University students, Larry Page and Sergey Brin, is today by far the world's most-used Web browser, and its name has become synonymous with searching the Internet. Mayer joined the company as a programmer and software engineer in 1999, as roughly its 20th employee. In a series of promotions, she rose to project manager, director of consumer Web products, vice president of search products and user experience, and, in October 2010, a new position in which she will oversee "geographic and local services," as many sources put it—that is, finding ways to expand Google's influence in local business markets. She also joined Google's operating committee, a group of top executives who make the company's most important decisions; at 35, she is the committee's youngest member. Since her arrival at Google, Mayer has played a crucial role in the design and development of Google's search interface as well as the products and features that appear on the Web site. "Just about everything that goes on" at Google, Guthrie noted, "falls under Mayer's lens." "Almost every new feature or design, from the wording on a Google page to the color of a Google toolbar, must pass muster with her or legions of Google users will never see it," Laura M. Holson wrote for the *New York Times* (February 29, 2009).

When Google hired Mayer, the company was "very small. . . . There was a tremendous amount of energy, scruffy entrepreneurialism and a sense of hope," Mayer told Oliver Lindberg for *.net Magazine* (September 12, 2008). "We really felt we were working on something that might change the world. We were all very excited to be working on such an important problem and we thought it would really have an impact. Even from that vantage point, though, it wasn't clear to us what type of impact it would have." Google now employs more than 20,000 people in the U.S. and abroad and earned more than $23.6 billion in 2009. (The company generates most of its revenues from advertising.) Mayer has overseen the development, code-writing, and launch of Gmail, Google's free e-mail service; Google News, which aggregates headlines from news sources worldwide; Google Maps; and Google Product Search (formerly called Froogle), a price-comparison service, among many other innovations. Several patents have been filed for her work in artificial intelligence and interface design, including the design of Google's home page. A tall, photogenic blond with blue eyes, the outspoken Mayer has also become an information-technology celebrity: one of Google's few public faces, she has often provided interviews and appeared at events on the company's behalf. Mayer has been named among *Newsweek*'s "10 Tech Leaders of the Future," *Red Herring*'s "15 Women to Watch," and *Business 2.0*'s "Silicon Valley Dream Team." She has also been profiled in such publications as *Business Week*, *Fortune*, and *Fast Company*. Guthrie called Mayer "the most closely watched woman in the most closely watched company in the world."

Marissa Ann Mayer was born in Wausau, a city in central Wisconsin, on May 30, 1975. Her mother, Margaret, was an art teacher and homemaker; her father, Michael, worked as an environmental engineer for water-treatment plants. (She has an older half-brother and a younger brother.) Among many other activities, as a child she participated in ballet, ice-skating, and swimming and played the piano. As a student at Wausau West High School, she was a member of the precision dance team and helped the debate team win the state championship in her senior year.

Mayer graduated from high school in 1993 and then enrolled at Stanford University, in Palo Alto, California. She had originally intended to become a doctor but found the requisite coursework to be boring. Instead, Mayer earned a bachelor's degree in symbolic systems and a master's degree in computer science. Interested in logic and how it could be replicated in computers, she specialized in artificial intelligence. Prior to her final year in graduate school, Mayer spent nine months at the Union Bank of Switzerland's Ubilab research lab in Zurich, where she was one of 30 researchers working to build an Internet-based recommender system, similar to the Amazon.com system that uses customers' previous purchases to suggest additional selections. "I like to do things that I'm a little not ready to do, like moving to Switzerland when I don't speak German," Mayer told Michael Krauss for the magazine *Marketing News* (April 1, 2007). She added, "When you do something that you're not ready to do, you learn whole new skill sets."

While completing work for her master's degree, Mayer received 12 job offers, which ranged from a teaching post at Carnegie Mellon University, in Pittsburgh, Pennsylvania, to a consulting job with McKinsey & Co., a global management-consulting firm. Two months before her graduation, in June 1999, Mayer received an e-mail message about a job opportunity at Google. As she read the message, she remembered a conversation she had had with her computer-science teacher the previous fall; he had told her that there were two Stanford students who were working on a system much like the one she had helped to build in Switzerland. Though the teacher did not know any specifics of the system being built, he mentioned that the venture had a funny-sounding name. ("Google" is an accidental misspelling of the word "googol," which refers to a number that is equal to the numeral 1 followed by 100 zeros.)

Mayer interviewed three separate times with Google's co-founders, Page and Brin, and two of the company's employees. Still very much in its infancy, Google at the time had fewer than 10 employees, and Page and Brin used a ping-pong table as their conference table. Mayer was impressed by the level of intelligence she found at Google and thought she could learn more from working there—even if Google ultimate failed—than at any of the other places where she had been offered jobs. On May 7, 1999 Mayer signed on to work at Google. She was only about the 20th person hired by the company—and its first female engineer.

In the beginning of her tenure at the company, Mayer wrote codes and oversaw the teams of engineers, helping to develop and design Google's search offerings. (She has admitted that during her first month at Google she secretly used InfoSeek, a search engine popular at the time.) In their free time Google employees often attended Silicon Valley launch parties, where Mayer liked to gauge Google's popularity based on the reactions she got by saying that she worked there. It was not until she had been in her position for two months that she met someone who had heard of Google, but within two years Mayer began meeting people who frequented the site. By August 2003 the site was handling 77 percent of all U.S. Internet search requests.

It has been written that when Mayer started with Google she was one of few employees who had a keen sense of style; her fondness for bright colors against a white background inspired the spare look of the Google home page. Shona Brown, Google's vice president of business operations, told Sally Singer for *Vogue* (August 2009), "[Mayer's] fingers are all over the actual designs [of Google products], their simplicity and intuitive ease of use, their clean use." "It used to be people would come over to my apartment and say, 'Does your apartment look like Google or does Google look like your apartment? . . .'" a laughing Mayer told Laura M. Holson for the *New York Times* (March 1, 2009). "I really love color. I'm not very knick-knacky or cluttery. My place has very clean, simple lines. There are some elements of fun and whimsy. That has always appealed to me."

Mayer worked her way up Google's ladder, from engineer to project manager to director of consumer Web products to vice president of search products and user experience. She helped to internationalize the site, making searches possible in more than 100 languages, and is now what is often called the "gatekeeper" for new Google products and services: holding an average of 70 meetings per week, she makes assessments that determine whether projects will be pitched to Brin and Page, who are the final decision makers. Google employees refer to Mayer's process of critiquing new projects as "the Marissa Gauntlet." Mayer grants each team of developers 10 minutes to present their projects; a four-foot-high digital clock is projected on a wall to keep the teams focused on making their presentations efficiently. "I look for the insight and innovation that's baked into the idea," Mayer explained to Oliver Lindberg. "I also look at the overall energy and strength of the team that's presenting it. Then I develop an overall sense of confidence that it's both a good product idea and that we have a good team who are interested in moving it forward. If those two things come into alignment, it's going to be a successful product."

In order to avoid the appearance of favoritism, Mayer chooses designs based on data, not her personal feelings toward employees or proposed products. For instance, when team members on a certain project could not decide on what shade of blue to use for their design, Mayer had them test every shade of blue possible in HTML. "As it turns out there were 41 shades of blue that you can express in HTML. And we tested them all," she told John Donvan for *ABC News* (April 8, 2009). "We gave 2.5% of our users each a different shade of blue and we have been looking at their metrics to understand which . . . is the optimal shade of blue on the Google interface to promote clicking and overall user happiness."

Mayer has received criticism for her data-reliant approach, most notably from the Silicon Valley gossip blog ValleyWag, which often refers to her as "mechanical" and "robotic." (ValleyWag has also pointed out more than once that Mayer dated Page during the early years of the company.) In March 2008 the blog posted an e-mail message from an anonymous Google employee that read, "[Mayer] is by far the largest bottleneck in the company, and she likes it that way. She keeps people waiting outside her office for hours, she only focuses on projects that will generate her PR, and she will make compromises to those projects to ensure she maximizes her personal PR." ValleyWag also pointed to Doug Bowman, Google's visual designer, who resigned in March 2009 and wrote on his personal Web site, Stopdesign.com, about his decision to leave: "When a company is filled with engineers, it turns to engineering to solve problems. Reduce each decision to a simple logic problem. Remove all subjectivity and just look at the data. . . . And that data eventually becomes a crutch for every decision, paralyzing the company and preventing it from making any daring design decisions." He added, "I had a recent debate over whether a border should be 3, 4 or 5 pixels wide, and was asked to prove my case. I can't operate in an environment like that. I've grown tired of debating such minuscule design decisions."

Oliver Lindberg, however, suggested in his article that if Mayer seems "robotic," it may be because "she has to be to stay on top of it all." In addition to overseeing 150 product managers, Mayer is tasked with deciding the fate of at least 10 major product pitches each month and reviewing thousands of outside projects as well. She also approves every hire for the products group at the company. John Battelle, a founder of *Wired* magazine and the author of *The Search: How Google and Its Rivals Rewrote the Rules of Business and Transformed Our Culture*, told Julian Guthrie, "[Mayer's] character mirrors the culture of Google quite closely. Everything at Google depends on how intelligent you are and how well you defend a point of view, and Marissa's demeanor is very consistent with that. She speaks insanely quickly and has no patience with people who can't keep up."

In October 2010 Mayer was made responsible for guiding Google's efforts to compete with Yelp, Groupon, and other such companies in gathering geographically-based information to serve local markets. "They basically took one of our strongest generals and put her on the front lines of another important front," an unnamed Google staffer told Claire Cain Miller for the *New York Times* (October 12, 2010, on-line). "Frankly, in part it's because things in search are stable and in flux in local." As an example of "how to take on the Yellow Pages business in a new way," Miller paraphrased the informant as saying that "if Google knows what type of sushi you like and a Japanese restaurant nearby has a canceled reservation, Google could alert you on your cellphone." At the time of her latest promotion, Mayer became a member of Google's operating committee, composed of the firm's highest-level decision-makers.

Mayer, who has admitted to an obsession with cupcakes, is a co-owner of I Dream of Cake, a bakery in San Francisco, California. "I've always loved baking," she told Guthrie. "I think it's because I'm very scientific. The best cooks are chemists." Her hobbies also include scuba diving, snowboarding, running, and kiteboarding. She serves on the board of trustees for both the San Francisco Ballet and the San Francisco Museum of Modern Art. She collects work by famous artists including Robert Bechtle, Roy Lichtenstein, Andy Warhol, Sol LeWitt, and Robert Rauschenberg and owns a commissioned work by Dale Chihuly. She also has an interest in fashion; her favorite designers include Oscar de la Renta and Carolina Herrera. In addition

to her position at Google, Mayer has taught introductory computer-programming classes at her alma mater, Stanford University, which recognized her contribution to education with its Centennial Teaching Award and Forsythe Award in 2009.

Mayer owns a $5 million penthouse at the Four Seasons hotel in San Francisco and a home in Palo Alto. In December 2009 she married Zachary Bogue, a real-estate investment manager and lawyer.

—M.A.S.

Suggested Reading: Google.com; (London) *Guardian* p30 Aug. 25, 2006; *New York Times* BU p1 Mar. 1, 2009; *San Francisco Magazine* (on-line) Mar. 2008; *Vogue* p142 Aug. 2009

Fred Tanneau/AFP/Getty Images

McCann, Colum

Feb. 28, 1965– Writer; educator

Address: c/o Random House Inc., 1745 Broadway, New York, NY 10019-4343

With his eighth book, *Let the Great World Spin*, the novelist and short-story writer Colum McCann won the 2009 National Book Award for fiction. "Like the funambulist at the heart of this extraordinary novel, Colum McCann accomplishes a gravity-defying feat," the judges declared in the citation accompanying the award: "from ten ordinary lives he crafts an indelibly hallucinatory portrait of a de-

caying New York City, and offers through his generosity of spirit and lyrical gifts an ecstatic vision of the human courage required to stay aloft above the ever-yawning abyss." "It is my philosophy that we shouldn't write what we know," McCann, a native of Ireland, told Bret Anthony Johnston for the National Book Foundation Web site. "That's boring and ordinary. Rather, we should write towards what we want to know." The wide diversity of topics, settings, characters, and voices in his works reflects McCann's curiosity and the enormous amount of research he has undertaken: extensive reading, visits to many places in the U.S. and overseas, and face-to-face interviews. For his book *This Side of Brightness*, for example, McCann spent nights with homeless people on New York City streets; for *Zoli*, he studied the history and culture of the peoples known collectively as the Roma, or Gypsies, traveling in Slovakia to gain insights and information firsthand. For *Dancer*, he steeped himself in accounts of the Russian ballet dancer Rudolf Nureyev; educated himself on subjects including World War II, Soviet economics, Russian poetry, and dance; interviewed dozens of gay men and others who had known Nureyev or his circle of friends in Paris and New York; spent two months in Russia; and attended a ballet performance for the first time. For *Let the Great World Spin*—whose action begins on August 7, 1974, when Philippe Petit crossed between the towers of the World Trade Center eight times on a wire a quarter-mile above the ground—McCann researched "tightrope walking and computers and Vietnam and theology and all these things that the book tries to look at," he told Johnston. In addition, to "soak up a language that would relate to the streets," he said, he spent days in the Bronx (a New York City borough), chatting with homicide detectives and other police officers and following them on the job. He also scrutinized stacks of rap sheets, watched many films, studied old photos, and sat in the stairwells of some of New York City's roughest housing projects. "There was a sinister edge to the stairwell, as if anything could happen there," McCann told *Current Biography*. "It was the raw edge of New York. Needles and pills and graffiti and every form of despair you can think of. A laboratory of sorts. I would sit, sometimes terrified by the sound of footsteps, and conjure up some of the characters in the book." "I love research," he told Johnston. "I feel that I go to university each time I write a new book. I revel in getting away from myself."

The fourth of the five children of Sean and Sally McCann, Colum McCann was born on February 28, 1965 in a suburb of Dublin, Ireland. He has two sisters, Siobhan and Oonagh, and two brothers, Sean and Ronan. His mother was a homemaker. His father, a journalist and editor, worked for the BBC and publications including the *Irish Press*, a now-defunct daily; a one-time professional soccer player, he has also written more than 25 books, on subjects ranging from Irish wit to roses. McCann grew up with a love for reading. "The house was full of books," he told Travis Mahmout, whose article about him is posted on McCann's Web site. "You could run your hands along the spines and just keep going." McCann attended St. Brigid's National School, an elementary school in Foxrock, a Dublin suburb. When he was about eight, he and his father visited his paternal grandfather—whom until then he had never met—at a nursing home in London, England. "I sat on the bed beside and he told me stories," McCann told Mahmout. "Mostly tall tales, if I recall rightly, about love and war and drink—in other words, good Irish stories. He was dying, though I didn't know it at the time. I went back to school the following Monday and my teacher asked us to write an essay. It's the first time I remember being conscious of the power of story telling. I worked for hours and hours, crawling over every word." At 12 McCann entered Clonkeen College, a Catholic secondary school in Deansgrange, a Dublin suburb, whose faculty were from the Christian Brothers order. Among several influential teachers, he cited one, Brother Kelly, as outstanding. "He was the sort of teacher who could transform a class, turn words into living things," he told Mahmout. "His passion was extraordinary. He wasn't my English teacher, but he taught me a whole way of thinking."

After his high-school graduation, McCann enrolled in the only journalism program in Ireland, at Rathmines College, in Dublin. (Rathmines prepares students for various professions but does not confer bachelor's degrees.) One year the school named him the Young Journalist of the Year, for his investigations into the lives of abused women in Dublin. "I had to go into the flats in a part of the city I didn't know at all," McCann told Mahmout. "I was a middle-class kid. I had to learn to talk, or rather how to listen, I suppose. It was an eye-opener. Heroin needles on the stairs. Junkies hanging out down by the lifts. . . . After I'd written the article there was a questions and answers period in

the Irish parliament, the Dail. I began to recognize the odd power in the word." McCann completed the Rathmines program in 1984. He then traveled to New York City, where for a few months he worked for Universal Press Syndicate, first as an errands intern and then as a reporter.

Back in Ireland he worked as a reporter and columnist for various newspapers, including the now-defunct *Evening Press*. After two years he returned to the U.S., with the goal of writing "the great Irish-American novel," he told Mahmout. He spent one summer in Hyannis, Massachusetts, but wrote virtually nothing. "That's when I knew it was time to get some experience beyond my immediate white-bread world," he told Mahmout. For the next year and a half, he rode a bicycle some 12,000 miles, visiting all but about 10 states. His experiences left him with "a whole lifetime of stories," he recalled. He then found work at Miracle Farm, a residential ranch for troubled boys in Brenham, Texas, between Austin and Houston; among other jobs, he guided groups of boys in wilderness forays of as long as three months; at night he would read to them from J. D. Salinger's novel *The Catcher in the Rye* and other stories that he thought would please adolescents and teens. While employed at Miracle Farm, McCann wrote two books; they were never published (and never should be, he has said). "My brother, Sean, back in Ireland, bought one of the books from me for $10 a page," he recalled to Mahmout. "And that kept me going. That kept me writing. Certain things prop up your heart in the most unusual way."

McCann next enrolled at the University of Texas, where he was as fascinated by his physics and astronomy classes as he was by his English courses. In 1992 he earned a B.A. degree in English and, newly married, moved with his wife to Kitakyushu, Japan, where she studied Japanese. Feeling somewhat isolated, he completed work on at least a dozen short stories and started writing *Songdogs*, his first novel. The couple left Japan in 1994 and settled in New York City. A collection of 12 of McCann's short stories was published in England and Ireland that year. Called *Fishing the Sloe-Black River*, it contains tales about a gay man and his dying lover, an ex-prizefighter's obsession with a former girlfriend, and other stories of love, loss, exile, and everyday struggles. The book won the 1994 Rooney Award for Irish Literature.

Songdogs was published in the U.S. in 1995. Its title refers to the coyotes that, according to a Native American creation myth, howled the universe into existence. The main character is Conor, whose Irish father and Mexican mother traveled together through the United States in the 1950s and 1960s before settling in Ireland, where their son was born. When Conor was 12, his mother suddenly abandoned him and his father. Determined to find her, Conor, a storyteller, investigates his family history through stories, memories, and photographs. *Songdogs* sparked much critical acclaim. "This is not a flawless novel," Hermione Lee wrote for the *New Yorker* (November 6, 1995). "McCann can indeed be sentimental. . . . But the weaknesses are tied in to the book's immensely promising virtues—its eloquent intensity, its passionate image-making, its magical feeling for space and place and time." The next year, when *Fishing the Sloe-Black River* appeared in the U.S., several reviewers made note of McCann's abilities. Among them was Dan Cryer, a *Newsday* (November 22, 1996) critic, who felt that although "not every story here sparkles," McCann's "lyric gift, whether in long form or short, is to combine Irish poetry and American swagger."

McCann set the two alternating narratives in *This Side of Brightness* (1998) in New York City. One story, which takes place in the 1990s, is about Treefrog, a homeless, jobless man who has no family and lives in a subway tunnel. The other begins in 1916, during the building of a subway tunnel under the East River from Manhattan to Brooklyn. One day an accident in the tunnel kills several men, among them Con O'Leary, a friend of a black man from Georgia named Nathan Walker. Walker regularly visits O'Leary's widow and eventually marries her daughter. "McCann has blessed his novel with irony and despair and the curse of memory, finding within these shadows of history the 'brief rage of brightness' that enables us all to go on," Gail Caldwell wrote for the *Boston Globe* (March 22, 1998). "Marked by irrevocable loss, it is nonetheless one of the few novels in recent memory that I mourned ending even as I read." In a review for the London *Observer* (January 25, 1998), Lorna Sage concluded that although *This Side of Brightness* is "just an inch away from sentimentality, . . . it works."

Everything in This Country Must (2000) contains two very short stories and one novella, each about social and political issues in Northern Ireland, all told from the viewpoint of young people. In the title story an Irish farmer and his daughter, while trying to rescue their drowning horse, get an offer of help from passing British soldiers. The father is unable or unwilling to separate their actions from those of other British soldiers who, years earlier, had been involved in the car accident that killed his wife and son. In "Wood," in the absence of their incapacitated father and husband, a boy and his mother work at night in the family lumber mill, making poles for the banners of Protestant marchers in a political protest. The 13-year-old in the novella, "Hunger Strike," thinks about his father, who is dead, and his mother's brother, a member of the outlawed Irish Republican Army, who is on a hunger strike in prison. The boy, Kevin, and his mother have camped near the prison, where Kevin has little to keep him occupied until he meets a Lithuanian exile, who takes him under his wing. "In each of the pieces, the miracle is how McCann, with prose so terse and spare, is able to create worlds so emotionally complex and moving," Brian Kenney wrote for *Library Journal* (January 2000).

The idea for his next novel came to McCann when his friend Jimmy told him about the day that his working-class Irish father, who regularly beat his children, came home with a television but could not get a picture. Later that evening, when Jimmy turned it on, a clear image of the ballet dancer Rudolf Nureyev appeared on the screen, and Jimmy immediately fell in love. That incident, McCann told Julie Wheel Wright for the London *Independent* (January 11, 2000), is a "brilliant illustration of how the dancer's power transcended every possible barrier of culture or understanding." It inspired McCann to write an imagined biography of Nureyev, with real and fictionalized characters and events, and glimpses into aspects of the dancer's often tumultuous life that had rarely if ever been included in published accounts. The product of voluminous research, *Dancer* (2003) struck Peter Kurth, in a review for the *New York Times* (January 9, 2003), as a "beautiful, floating novel about Nureyev's life and art. . . . Images of water and weather, memory, motion and time, are the essence of *Dancer*, because they're the essence of Nureyev." "It's hard to tell what a reader unfamiliar with the outlines of Nureyev's life might make of *Dancer*," Kurth, a biographer of the great dancer Isadora Duncan, concluded. "Much, deliberately, is left unsaid. Reduced to words, the dance evaporates—only passion and the personal can make it move again. McCann makes no mistake in this regard, not stopping even to explain the terms of classical ballet, because they really don't matter." *Dancer* was named the 2003 Irish Independent Hughes and Hughes/Sunday Independent Novel of the Year.

Gail Caldwell, in a review for the *Boston Globe* (January 14, 2007), chose the word "riveting" to describe McCann's next novel, *Zoli* (2007), whose title character is a Romani poet. The story begins in Czechoslovakia in the 1930s, when the six-year-old Zoli and her grandfather witness the extermination of their family and the rest of their village. Zoli and her grandfather flee; later they join another Romani community. Partly for cultural reasons, literacy levels among Gypsies was low then (and now), but Zoli's grandfather teaches her to read and write. Zoli proves to be a gifted songwriter. After World War II Communist Party members discover her talents and set out to use her skills to their political advantage. Her fellow Gypsies banish her, and once again Zoli takes flight. McCann's description of her journey through Eastern Europe "gives us a tapestry of an entire culture, one shrouded and then marginalized into near extinction," Caldwell wrote. "But it is the thick interiors of Zoli's life that provide such resonant heft and beauty to the novel: her walk across Eastern Europe, scorned and starving, her psychological shrinking into an animal bent on survival." In one of the few negative reviews of *Zoli*, Richard Eder, writing for the *New York Times* (January 8, 2007), complained that the characters in the novel "fall short"; but he also wrote that the story "contains passages of stunning lyricism and sharp ironic force."

In his latest novel, *Let the Great World Spin* (2009), McCann used Philippe Petit's astounding feat of August 7, 1974—walking and cavorting on a wire strung between the roofs of the World Trade Center towers—as a metaphorical focal point to tell "a set of larger and smaller stories that approach, intersect, and diverge," in the words of Richard Eder, writing for the *Boston Globe* (June 21, 2009). The stories are those of 10 disparate people, among them an indigent monk from Ireland; the monk's brother, a more-recent Irish immigrant; a recovering drug addict; an aging African-American prostitute; a young wife and artist; a wealthy criminal-court judge and his stay-at-home wife, whose son was killed in Vietnam; and the tightrope walker himself, who is unnamed in McCann's novel. "Like a great pitcher in his prime, McCann is constantly changing speeds, adopting different voices, tones and narrative styles as he shifts between story lines," Jonathan Mahler wrote for the *New York Times Book Review* (August 2, 2009). "Inevitably, some of his portraits work better than others. . . . It is a mark of the novel's soaring and largely fulfilled ambition that McCann just keeps rolling out new people, deftly linking each to the next, as his story moves toward its surprising and deeply affecting conclusion. In a loose sense, what connects everyone in this novel is the high-wire walker; the day of his stunt is a pivotal one in all of their lives. But they are bound more powerfully by something else: grief. *Let the Great World Spin* is an emotional tour de force. It is a heartbreaking book, but not a depressing one. Through their anguish, McCann's characters manage to find comfort, even a kind of redemption." Mahler extolled the book as "one of the most electric, profound novels I have read in years." When the *Current Biography* interviewer asked McCann whether researching and writing about New York changed his awareness of the city and its myriad facets, he replied, "This city constantly surprises me. It wasn't just this novel that opened up the city for me. It opens itself up. . . . There's something new that pops into the landscape every single day. It's an image riot."

McCann co-wrote the screenplays for short films based on two of his books—*Fishing the Sloe-Black River* (1996) and *Everything in This Country Must* (2004), the latter of which received an Academy Award nomination—and for the full-length crime drama *When the Sky Falls* (2000). He has written fiction and nonfiction for periodicals including the *New Yorker*, the *New York Times Magazine*, *GQ*, the *Atlantic Monthly*, the *Paris Review*, *Paris Match*, the London *Guardian*, and the London *Independent*. He has taught in the M.F.A. creative-writing program at Hunter College, a division of the City University of New York, since about 2005. In addition to the National Book Award, the Rooney Prize, and the *Irish Independent* award, McCann's honors include the Hennessy Award for Irish Literature (1990), the Ireland Fund of Monaco

Princess Grace Memorial Literary Award (2002), and the Deauville Festival of Cinema Literary Prize (2009). In 2009, in addition to the National Book Award, he won two honors overseas: France named him a chevalier in the Ordre des Arts et des Lettres, and the Arts Council of Ireland inducted him into Aosdána, whose membership "is limited to 250 living artists who have produced a distinguished body of work."

McCann listens to music while he writes—recently, to recordings by Van Morrison, the French-Nigerian singer Asa, and the singer/songwriters David Gray, Damien Rice, and Brian Kennedy, a friend of McCann's. He is currently working on a new novel and other projects: he is collaborating with the choreographer Alonzo King on a ballet and with the musician Joe Hurley, also a friend of his, on songs inspired by *Let the Great World Spin*. McCann hopes to write a play someday.

McCann and his wife, Allison, a teacher, live in New York City with their three children: Isabella, an adolescent, and her younger brothers, John Michael and Christian.

—D.K.

Suggested Reading: *Boston Globe* D p6 Jan. 5, 2003; colummccann.com; nationalbook.org; *New York Times Book Review* p9 Aug. 2, 2009; *New Yorker* p174 Nov. 6, 1995

Selected Novels: *Songdogs*, 1995; *Fishing the Sloe-Black River*, 1996; *This Side of Brightness*, 1998; *Everything in This Country Must*, 2000; *Dancer*, 2003; *Zoli*, 2007; *Let the Great World Spin*, 2009

McDonald, Trevor

Aug. 16, 1939– British broadcast journalist

Address: c/o Capel & Land, 29 Wardour St., London W1D 6PS, England

"His silky and measured tones had a reassuring effect on the great British public . . . ," Tony Kane wrote for the London, England, publication *Time and Leisure* (April 22, 2010, on-line), referring to the well-known and respected British broadcast journalist Trevor McDonald. "No matter how alarming the news was, Trevor somehow made it seem all right—or at least palatable." McDonald, who moved to Britain from Trinidad in 1969, when he was 30 years old, was knighted in 1999 for his service to journalism and has received more awards than any other British broadcaster. With reporting experience on six continents, he is noted for his encounters with historic figures; he interviewed, for example, the South African activist and statesman Nelson Mandela after his release

Gareth Cattermole/Getty Images

Trevor McDonald

from prison, and he conducted the only British television interview with the Iraqi dictator Saddam Hussein immediately prior to the first Persian Gulf War. He has also interviewed the Libyan leader Muammar Al-Gaddafi, the Palestine Liberation Organization leader Yasir Arafat, the First Lady, U.S. senator, and U.S. secretary of state Hillary Clinton, and U.S. presidents Bill Clinton and George W. Bush. Retired from nightly-news broadcasts, McDonald remains a presence on British television. In 2010 he held an interview with David Cameron, prior to the election that made Cameron Britain's prime minister.

McDonald is most recognized for his work with the national British network Independent Television News (ITN), specifically for his lengthy tenure as the anchor of *News at Ten*. He is known for maintaining a very diplomatic style with a dedication to neutrality. According to Michael Deacon, writing for the London *Daily Telegraph* (June 27, 2009), "He always seems anxious to be fair, balanced, to see both sides." Deacon added, "It's hard to imagine an issue that would make him blow his top." One such issue might be broadcasters' failure to observe the journalistic code of objectivity, which McDonald takes very seriously. "The viewer doesn't need my indignation. That is something I have got from England: the importance of absolute balance. I hate that need to parade yourself; throwing your head about," he told Jasper Gerard for the London *Sunday Times* (July 25, 2004). Gerard wrote about McDonald, "Perhaps it is his lack of arrogance in a flashy trade that underpins his popularity."

The oldest of four children, Trevor McDonald was born on August 16, 1939 in San Fernando, Trinidad (in what is now Trinidad and Tobago), then a British colony. "We lived in a terribly small house with cracks in the walls, which we used to paper over with newspaper, and an outside loo," he said, as quoted by Gerald Kaufman in the London *Independent* (February 28, 1999). He has attributed his success to his father, who worked in an oil refinery and raised pigs, and his mother. "I cannot conceive, even in principle, of two better people. They were wonderful, wonderful people," he said to Gerard. McDonald told Kaufman, "I am what I am because of my parents." That statement notwithstanding, when the BBC World Service reports he heard on his family's wireless radio got him interested in broadcasting, his parents—who wanted him to be a doctor, lawyer, or engineer— were less than pleased. An article in the Scotland *Sunday Herald* (April 7, 2002, on-line) quoted McDonald as saying, "My father was beside himself with horror at this concept of being a journalist, he had no idea what it meant and didn't think much of it anyway. I'm very grateful that he lived long enough to feel that I hadn't entirely wasted my life, but I had fallen in love, very early on, with the business of wanting to communicate ideas."

Despite his parents' wishes, McDonald received little formal education. On his own, though, he read works by Charles Dickens, William Makepeace Thackeray, and William Hazlitt, among other great British writers, and by listening to BBC broadcasts, he perfected his diction, which helped him to win public-speaking contests. In the early 1960s he began his career in media by working as a radio reporter, news presenter, and sports journalist in Trinidad. "I was very lucky," he said, according to the *Sunday Herald* article, "because about 50% of the West Indies population seemed to think that they could be broadcasters at the time." He was sent to London in 1962 for his first significant story, covering the talks that resulted in the date being set for Trinidad to gain independence from Britain that year.

McDonald moved to London in 1969 to work as a producer for BBC World Service. In 1973 he was hired by ITN as a general reporter, becoming the network's first black journalist. His earliest major assignment was to report on the "Troubles" in Northern Ireland, the name given the conflicts between British forces and those seeking the country's independence from Britain and the hostilities between the minority Catholics and the majority Protestants. In 1978 McDonald became an ITN sports correspondent, covering that year's 1978 World Cup, among other events. Two years later he was assigned as an ITN diplomatic correspondent.

For five years beginning in 1982, McDonald served as diplomatic correspondent and newscaster for *Channel Four News*, ITN's main evening-news program. In that post he reported from nations including Egypt, Israel, Syria, Lebanon, Libya, India, Pakistan, Japan, New Zealand, Mexico,

South Africa, China, and the U.S. He also covered U.S. presidential and congressional elections as well as the Philippine elections of 1985, winning the station a British Academy of Film and Television Arts (BAFTA) Award. McDonald served as diplomatic editor with *Channel Four News* for two years before becoming the presenter of ITN's early-evening news, in 1989. In 1990 he conducted an exclusive interview with the Iraqi dictator Saddam Hussein, prior to Iraq's defeat by the U.S. and its allies in the 1991 Persian Gulf War. In the same year he interviewed the veteran South African antiapartheid leader and future president Nelson Mandela upon the activist's release from prison.

In 1992 McDonald was named an Officer of the Order of the British Empire. That same year he was promoted to sole presenter of ITN's *News at Ten*, making him one of the most familiar faces on British television. He remained in that position until the program went off the air, in 1999—the year he was knighted—and then assumed the role of anchor for the *ITN Evening News*. McDonald presented *News at Ten* from 2001, when it was relaunched, until it was canceled again, three years later. Afterward he presented the *ITN News at Ten Thirty* until he stepped down, of his own accord, in 2005, and was replaced by Mark Austin. When it was announced that *News at Ten* would be going back on the air for a third time, McDonald was persuaded to return once again, in 2008, and co-hosted the show with Julie Etchingham. McDonald told Kane (April 22, 2010), "I was politely black-mailed by [ITN executive chairman] Michael Grade to come back. He said 'We need you, we can't do what we want without you,' so I went back. But of course the Americans have a saying: 'You can never go back home again.' And I think that's true—I shouldn't really have gone back." He resigned from *News at Ten* less than a year later, after the 2008 U.S. presidential election.

In addition to hosting television news programs, in the late 1990s McDonald presented the series *Undercover Customs* (produced by Granada Television for ITN), which featured dramatic reenactments of some of Britain's largest real-life smuggling operations. In 2006 he hosted an installment of *Have I Got News for You*, an irreverent television political quiz show on the BBC. He also hosted his own talk show, the ITN-produced *Trevor McDonald Meets . . .* , from 1998 to 2000, and emceed the National Television Awards ceremony, broadcast on ITN, annually from 1996 to 2008. McDonald was also the host of ITN's current-affairs program *Tonight with Trevor McDonald* (later known as *Tonight*) from 1999 to 2007.

In 2007 McDonald hosted a satirical series on ITN, *News Knight with Sir Trevor McDonald* (often referred to as *News Knight*), on which he was joined by guest comedians in reflecting on the news of the past week. (The concept for *News Knight* came about after McDonald proved to be humorous as the host of *Have I Got News for You*.) *News Knight* received mixed reviews and aired for only seven installments. In an article entitled "Trevor McDonald Should Stick to Newsreading," Jim Shelley wrote for the London *Guardian* (June 27, 2007, on-line), "A legendary, great man . . . he's surely too dignified to be introducing sections like Saudis Do the Funniest Things, or Gay Or Blind?"

In July 2008 McDonald himself became the subject of news stories—of the tabloid variety. In an interview with *Decanter* magazine published that month and quoted by a number of media outlets, the journalist admitted to being a binge drinker who often consumed a significant amount of wine before bed. "The problem with that is that it's never just a glass," he said, as quoted by the London *Evening Standard* (July 4, 2008). "I get home at 11pm and then look at my watch and it is approaching midnight and I'm on my fourth glass." McDonald also confessed to having drunk heavily with his colleagues during the early days of his career. "There was a bar across the street and most people could be found there day and night," he said. Later in July 2008 it was reported that Mc-Donald's son Tim had accepted a job as the new editor in chief of the sexually explicit magazine *Hustler.* "Dad thinks this is a wonderful opportunity for me—at least that's what he says," Tim said in an interview with the London *Evening Standard* (July 20, 2008).

Within the past few years, McDonald has hosted ITN shows including *Britain's Favourite View*, which toured several places in the United Kingdom, including Hadrian's Wall and the Cornish coast; *The Secret Caribbean*; and *The Secret Mediterranean*, the last two of which featured McDonald exploring the locales of the titles. "It's so nice to get away from the news—it's unrelenting and there is that feeling of helplessness—disasters that one is helpless to do anything about," McDonald admitted to Kane. In 2010 he presented a short film on global warming, *Last Chance*. McDonald drew attention in March 2010 when he conducted an ITN interview with the Conservative Party leader David Cameron, before Cameron became the new prime minister of the United Kingdom. The interview, which included comments from Cameron's wife, Samantha, attracted close to three million viewers.

McDonald frequently visits Trinidad but has no intention of moving back there. Some critics have accused him of neglecting his West Indian roots by so easily adopting upper-class British culture, from his accent to his posh lifestyle. He has also weathered criticism for not using his fame as a platform to denounce racism or focusing more of his work on black themes. "I accept their criticism," he told Gerard. "It was entirely deliberate. I did not want to become the token black reporter, blathering about life in Brixton [a largely black district in south London]. I wanted to make my way." He added, "I am fascinated by English life even though I have been here donkey's years." He has claimed to have experienced very little racism in his adopted country. "My impression is that relations [among different races] are very good," he told Deacon. To Gerard, he said, "If you don't want to integrate, why come to Britain? I am an unashamed integrationist."

McDonald has received numerous awards. In 1997 he was presented with an honorary doctorate in journalism from the Open University in a ceremony at the University of Exeter. The following year he won a Royal Television Society Gold Medal for outstanding contributions to television news. His other honors include the Newscaster of the Year Award (1993, 1997, 1999) from the British Television & Radio Industries Club (TRIC), the Richard Dimbleby Award for outstanding contribution to television from BAFTA in 1999, and the National Television Award for outstanding commitment to television, presented by British prime minister Tony Blair in 2003. He is also chancellor of London South Bank University, a member of the Survey County Cricket Club, chairman of the Nuffield Foundation, and a governor of the Kings College Junior School, in Wimbledon.When asked by Rifkind in 2007 if he planned to retire, McDonald, then 67, responded, "I don't really see the point. I don't see what one does." He added, quoting the British poet Alfred Lord Tennyson, "How dull it is to pause, to make an end, to rust unburnished, not to shine in use!"

McDonald's autobiography, *Fortunate Circumstances*, was published in 1993. He has also written the books *Viv Richards—A Biography* (1984), *Clive Lloyd—A Biography* (1985), and *The Queen and the Commonwealth* (1986). He edited the poetry volumes *Trevor McDonald's Favourite Poems* (1997) and *Trevor McDonald's World of Poetry* (1999).

McDonald divorced his first wife, Beryl, in 1985. From that union he has two children, Timothy and Joanne. He married his second wife, Josephine, in 1986; the couple have a son, Jamie. McDonald is passionate about the game of cricket. He lives in southwest London with his family. The profile of McDonald in the *Sunday Herald* (April 7, 2002) stated about him, "For an entire generation he will remain the face of world events, the friendly voice translating the important issues as well as the trivial ones."

—J.P.

Suggested Reading: (London) *Daily Telegraph* (on-line) June 27, 2009; (London) *Independent* (on-line) Feb. 28, 1999; (London) *Sunday Times* (on-line) July 25, 2004; (Scotland) *Sunday Herald* (on-line) Apr. 7, 2002; *Time & Leisure* (on-line) Apr. 22, 2010; McDonald, Trevor. *Fortunate Circumstances*, 1993

Selected Books: *Viv Richards—A Biography*, 1984; *Clive Lloyd—A Biography*, 1985; *The Queen and the Commonwealth*, 1986; *Fortunate Circumstances*, 1993; as editor—*Trevor McDonald's Favourite Poems*, 1997; *Trevor McDonald's World of Poetry*, 1999

Selected Television Shows: *Channel Four News*, 1982–87; *News at Ten*, 1992–99, 2001–04, 2008; *Undercover Customs*, 1997–99; *Trevor McDonald Meets . . .*, 1998–2000; *Tonight with Trevor McDonald* (later known as *Tonight*), 1999–2007; *ITN News at Ten Thirty*, 2004–05; *News Knight with Sir Trevor McDonald*, 2007; *Britain's Favorite View*, 2007

Courtesy of DC Comics, under GNU Free Documentation License

McDuffie, Dwayne

Feb. 20, 1962– Writer and producer of animated cartoons; comic-book writer

Address: c/o Cartoon Network, 1050 Techwood Dr. N.W., Atlanta, GA 30318

Justice League: Crisis on Two Earths, a direct-to-DVD animated film, was released by Warner Bros. on February 23, 2010. Based on an original story by the award-winning comics writer Dwayne McDuffie, the video created buzz among animation fans because of its inclusion of a virtuous Lex Luthor. (In the story, Luthor, voiced by the actor Chris Noth, normally the evil archenemy of Superman, arrives from an alternate universe to recruit the popular DC Comics superheroes known collectively as the Justice League to help save his planet from wrongdoers.)

Justice League: Crisis on Two Earths does not mark the first time McDuffie has shaken up the comics industry. In the early 1990s he co-founded Milestone Media, with the goal of bringing diversity to the comic-book world. "There is a revolution going on in a Manhattan high-rise," Carolyn M. Brown wrote for *Black Enterprise* (November 1994). "On the fourth floor, a small army is busy creating a new universe. It is a world not unlike ours, full of colorful heroes and sinister villains: *Blood Syndicate, Hardware, Icon, Kobalt, Shadow Cabinet, Static, Xombi*. The denizens of this world are made in the image of their creators—a band of artists, editors and writers of backgrounds not limited by race, age or gender. It's a strange new world, one you may not have heard of yet." Brown continued, "Welcome to Milestone Media Inc., a . . . black-owned comic book company [whose] operating philosophy is based on the premise that comic book characters with 'powers and abilities far beyond those of mortal men,' as well as the artists and writers that tell their stories, should be African-American, Asian, Latino and female—as well as white and male."

While Milestone Media has since disbanded, McDuffie has kept busy as a writer (and sometimes producer) for such animated TV shows as *Justice League* and *Ben 10: Alien Force*, and he remains a popular and respected figure among fans of the superhero genre.

Dwayne Glenn McDuffie was born on February 20, 1962 in Detroit, Michigan, to Edna Earle Hawkins Gardner and Leroy McDuffie. With the help of a scholarship, he attended the Roeper School for gifted and talented children, in Bloomfield Hills, a wealthy area northwest of Detroit. "Roeper was the place where I started figuring out what was possible for myself," McDuffie told Cassandra Spratling for the *Detroit Free Press* (April 19, 1996). "Lots of kids don't go anywhere because they don't know anywhere to go. You have to stand on a hill to see what's around you. Roeper gave me that opportunity. Roeper taught me that 'No, you're not weird. You're smart, and maybe you can do something about it.'" He continued, "I got a chance to be around people from different backgrounds and different worlds who had things I didn't know existed."

With the emergence of the civil rights and black-pride movements of the 1960s, black characters were increasingly being featured in the comics that McDuffie read as a youth. Without exception, however, the characters—including the Black Panther, an African king with the speed and strength of his animal namesake; Infantryman Gabe Jones of Marvel Comics' *Sgt. Fury and His Howling Commandos*; and Joe Robertson, a newspaper editor who appeared regularly in *Spider-Man*—were written and drawn by white men. In an interview with the *New York Times* (August 4, 1993), McDuffie said: "You only had two types of characters available for children. You had the stupid angry brute and the he's-smart-but-he's-black characters. And they were all colored either this Hershey-bar shade of brown, a sickly looking gray or purple. I've never seen anyone that's gray or purple before in my life. There was no diversity and almost no accuracy among the characters of color at all."

Always creative, McDuffie began making rudimentary comic books in elementary school, and later, in high school, he wrote a film as a class project. He went on to study at the University of Michigan, where he received a B.A. degree in literature (in 1983, according to some sources) followed by an M.S. degree in physics, another area of intense interest for him. He then moved to New York City to attend New York University's Tisch School of the Arts, where he studied filmmaking. McDuffie ran out of money for tuition, however, and did not graduate from the program.

In 1987, after a brief stint as a copy editor at a financial publication, McDuffie was hired as a special-projects editor at Marvel Comics, the venerable company responsible for such iconic characters as Spider-Man, the Fantastic Four, and Captain America. McDuffie soon came up with an innovative idea for a new comic book. Because superhero-versus-supervillain battles generally cause damage to surrounding buildings, sidewalks, parks, businesses, and vehicles, McDuffie envisioned a multifaceted corporation (with construction, engineering, and insurance divisions) that would step in to clean up the mess. He called the company Damage Control and named its fictitious founder Ms. Hoag, after a Roeper School administrator whom he remembered fondly. Damage Control made its first, brief appearance in a 1988 Marvel annual and was the subject of a story in a Marvel anthology the following year. Over the next few years, the company was featured in its own series of comic books and was also mentioned in several other series, including Marvel's popular *Civil War*.

McDuffie left Marvel in 1990 to work as a freelance comics writer. He soon teamed with Derek T. Dingle (a business journalist with considerable financial savvy), Denys Cowan (a fellow artist with whom McDuffie had worked at Marvel), and Michael Davis (another veteran artist) to co-found Milestone Media. The quartet pooled some $300,000 in savings to get their new company off the ground. "From a creative standpoint, we decided to show a range of multicultural super-heroes," Dingle explained to Carolyn M. Brown. "From a business standpoint, we wanted to be extremely competitive, so we decided to create a line of books with a shared universe of characters." They called the shared milieu, which was centered on a fictitious city in the American Midwest, the "Dakota Universe." Having a wide stable of characters not only contributed to the company's financial viability but allowed for greater creative freedom. "If you do a black character or a female character or an Asian character, then they aren't just that character," McDuffie explained to Les Daniels for the book *DC Comics: Sixty Years of the World's Favorite Comic Book Heroes* (1995). "They represent that race or that sex, and they can't be interesting because everything they do has to represent an entire block of people. You know, Superman isn't all white people and neither is Lex Luthor. We knew we had to present a range of characters within each ethnic group, which means that we couldn't do just one book. We had to do a series of books and we had to present a view of the world that's wider than the world we've seen before."

In addition to featuring diverse characters in their titles, Milestone's founders were intent on creating comics that had redeeming social value. "I try to put superheroes in situations where being strong, or being able to fly or fight aren't the answers," McDuffie told Spratling. "We've dealt with teen pregnancy, abortion, racism and anti-Semitism. Being able to hit somebody harder doesn't help you deal with that." Milestone's first superhero comics reached newsstands in 1993.

One of the company's most popular early series featured a brilliant African-American scientist, Curtis Metcalf, who works for a powerful industrialist. Denied a share of the revenue from his inventions, Metcalf creates a number of innovative devices that transform him into a high-tech superhero named Hardware. (McDuffie has told journalists that the premise was a commentary on his reasons for leaving Marvel.) Among other popular series were *Icon*, which featured a politically conservative black superhero with an eager 15-year-old female sidekick, and *Static*, about an inner-city high-school student who is sprayed with an experimental chemical during a gang war and subsequently exhibits electromagnetic powers. (The character Static later spawned an animated TV show, *Static Shock*, which ran from 2000 to 2004.)

Milestone's business model resembled that of an independent record company under the umbrella of a major label: Milestone retained artistic and managerial independence, hiring its own artists and writers and creating its own stories and graphics, and DC Comics handled printing, marketing, and distribution. "Milestone's titles definitely benefit from being under the DC imprint," John Miller, the editor of *Comic Retailer*, a trade magazine, told Brown. "[Milestone] gets better shelf space and a higher profile than other African-American publishers." The potency of the partnership was proven by the success of *Worlds Collide*, a 14-book series featuring characters from both the Milestone and the DC universes, which sold almost two million volumes when it was published, in 1994. *Worlds Collide* helped boost Milestone's visibility with comics fans of all races, and sales of the company's other titles jumped dramatically. Despite that, later in the decade the comic-book industry as a whole began to suffer declining sales, and Milestone folded in 1997.

McDuffie found ample work, however, in the wake of Milestone's demise. He wrote several episodes of *Static Shock*, which premiered on the WB network and was later syndicated on the Cartoon Network. The show revived interest in the comic book, which led to reissues of the older volumes as well as an additional four-volume series, *Static Shock: Rebirth of the Cool*.

In 2002 McDuffie joined the creative staff of *Justice League* (also known as *Justice League of America* or *JLA* and in later seasons called *Justice League Unlimited*), a Cartoon Network series featuring several notable DC Comics characters, including Batman and Superman. The program, which he began producing as well as writing in 2003, was a big hit with fans and aired until 2006. (McDuffie also wrote the story for an associated video game, *Justice League Heroes*.)

The following year McDuffie, who remained affiliated with the *Justice League* franchise as a comic-book writer after the animated show went off the air, returned to Marvel Comics as a temporary writer. This time he worked on the *Fantastic Four* comic-book series, which had long been one of the company's most beloved titles. (The original quartet included Mr. Fantastic, who can stretch his body like elastic; the Invisible Woman; the Human Torch, who can fly and burst into flame at will; and the Thing, who has superhuman strength and endurance and orange, bricklike flesh.) "*Fantastic Four* is my all-time favorite comic book," McDuffie told Kurt Anthony Krug for *Mania* (June 24, 2009, on-line). "Marvel asked me to come in for four issues and they needed time for [the next creative team] to get ahead, then they needed a bit more time, so I did more issues. . . . It was the ultimate joy; I'd stay forever if I could."

In mid-2008 McDuffie began writing and editing for the Emmy Award–winning animated TV show *Ben 10: Alien Force*, whose protagonist is a young boy with the power to become several different superheroes. The series continues the adventures of the characters from *Ben 10*, which ran from December 2005 to April 2008. A third series, *Ben 10: Ultimate Alien* (developed under the title "Ben 10: Evolution"), premiered in the U.S. and the U.K. on April 23, 2010, following the series finale of *Ben 10: Alien Force*, on March 26, 2010.

In May 2009 McDuffie was fired by DC Comics from his post as writer of the *Justice League* comics. Although widely credited with revitalizing the franchise, which now includes three black characters and several females, McDuffie had angered DC executives by complaining publicly about his lack of artistic freedom and the frustrations of working with corporate overseers. "I'm told my removal had nothing to with either the quality of my work or the level of sales, rather with my revelation of behind-the-scenes creative discussions," he wrote on his Web site's message board.

McDuffie is reportedly working on a variety of projects, including the series *Milestone Forever*, which will continue the saga of Static, Icon, Hardware, and the other Milestone characters; a videogame script; and a new direct-to-DVD feature for Warner Bros.

McDuffie has received many honors, including more than 10 Parents' Choice Awards, a 2003 Humanitas Prize (for work that best communicates and encourages human values) for an episode of *Static Shock* dealing with gun violence, and a 2009 Comic-Con International Inkpot Award.

In 2009 McDuffie married Charlotte Fullerton, a native of Haverhill and fellow writer, whose credits include episodes of *Ben 10: Alien Force*, *Fairly OddParents*, *Kim Possible*, *Power Rangers*, and *Care Bears*, among other animated shows.

—D.K.

Suggested Reading: *Black Enterprise* p80 Nov. 1994; *Detroit Free Press* F p1 Apr. 19, 1996; *Mania* (on-line) June 24, 2009; *New York Times* C p1 Aug. 4, 1993

Selected TV Shows: *Static Shock*, 2000–04; *Justice League*, 2002–06; *Ben 10: Alien Force*, 2008–10; *Ben 10: Ultimate Alien*, 2010–

Courtesy of the American Red Cross

McGovern, Gail J.

Jan. 12, 1952– Organization official; former business executive

Address: American Red Cross National Headquarters, 2025 E St., N.W., Washington, DC 20006

"This is a brand to die for," Gail J. McGovern said to Ben Gose for the *Chronicle of Philanthropy* (April 8, 2008, on-line) about the American Red Cross (ARC). "It creates a visceral reaction. When people see it, they know that help is on the way." She made that comment on the day the ARC's board of governors announced that it had chosen her from among 170 candidates as the organization's new president and chief executive officer (CEO); McGovern assumed her new post on June

23, 2008. "One of the reasons I'm attracted to the position is that it does have challenges, and I'm hoping that I can bring my background and experience to the organization and help lead us to financial stability and growth," she told Phillip Rucker for the *Washington Post* (April 8, 2008, on-line). "I feel that so much of what I've done in my life and business and in volunteerism has really trained me for this opportunity, and I look at it as a capstone for my career." McGovern spent the first 28 years of her professional life in the world of business. She went to work as a computer programmer at Bell Telephone of Pennsylvania in 1974, right after her college graduation, and six years later joined its parent company, AT&T, as a district manager. In 1998, when she left AT&T, she held one of the corporation's top positions, that of executive vice president of the consumer-markets division. "Her efforts to bundle long-distance with other products, such as wireless and Internet services, helped slow [AT&T's] long market-share slide," Geoffrey Smith and Steve Rosenbush wrote for *BusinessWeek* (February 21, 2000), paraphrasing Alex J. Mandl, an AT&T executive in the 1990s. For four years beginning in 1998, she served in executive posts with Fidelity Investments. She next spent a half-dozen years in academia, as a professor of marketing at the Harvard Business School. In addition to her reputation for parlaying her expertise in marketing into handsome profits for AT&T and Fidelity, McGovern is known for her dedication to volunteerism and her skill as a fund-raiser. As a trustee of her undergraduate alma mater, Johns Hopkins University, she helped raise $3.2 billion for that school, $1.2 billion more than its original goal. She has also helped fund-raising efforts by Children's Hospital Boston, the Dana-Farber Cancer Institute, and the United Way of Boston.

In the decade before McGovern arrived at the ARC, its presidency had changed hands five times. That instability reflected fierce conflicts between the board of governors and the president, in at least two cases, and a series of errors, lapses, and actions that brought accusations of irresponsibility, dishonesty, and even immorality. Widespread public disenchantment with the ARC after 9/11 led donations to shrink drastically, leaving it $215 million in debt in 2008 and forcing it to lay off many employees. McGovern's "mandate is clearly to make the organization clean up its act and become truly transparent and all we're hearing is that they truly intend to do that," Ken Berger, the president and CEO of Charity Navigator, which monitors and evaluates charitable groups, told David Crary for the Associated Press (January 21, 2010). The earthquake that struck Haiti on January 12, 2010, killing or injuring half a million people and leaving upwards of a million homeless, was a major test of the ARC's ability to act swiftly, effectively, and honorably. "This could be a turning point, if they walk the walk that they say they're going to do. Everybody is watching very closely," Berger told Crary. In the 10 days following the earthquake, the ARC received $137 million for Haitian relief efforts—"by far the largest share of Haiti-inspired donations from the American public," according to Crary. McGovern told him, "We have been working very hard to gain the trust of the American public. This outpouring of generosity is a sign of that trust." By January 2011 the cost of its relief and rebuilding efforts in Haiti was reportedly going to reach $200 million. Although the ARC was criticized for a lack of transparency about precisely where the money was being spent, it has continued to receive substantial contributions from the public for its work. McGovern told Phillip Rucker, "I would like to live in a world where we're not fundraising episodically with each storm. Our mission is so much bigger than these epic storms. Our mission is to be there for the American people every day."

Gail J. McGovern was born on January 12, 1952 in the New York City borough of Brooklyn and grew up in Springfield, New Jersey. As a 12-year-old she began solving crossword puzzles with her father. "It was very special for us," she said during an ARC on-line chat (July 27, 2009). She has also recalled her father's enthusiasm for the volunteer work to which he devoted his retirement years. McGovern attended Boston University, in Massachusetts, for a year, then transferred to Johns Hopkins University, in Baltimore, Maryland, in 1971, when it became co-educational. "Professors thought it would be great to have women, but the men were very against it," McGovern told Sarah Capponi for the *Johns Hopkins University News-Letter* (October 1, 2009, on-line). "At the time, there were only 1,900 students, so girls stuck out like sore thumbs. . . . The school wasn't ready for us." But some male students welcomed her: "All of my friends were guys," McGovern told Capponi. "I'd go out on the weekends with platonic guy friends." Those experiences, she said, "taught me how to maneuver in an all-male world" and made her "direct, decisive and rough around the edges." She graduated with a B.A. degree in quantitative sciences and mathematics in 1974.

McGovern then moved to Philadelphia to work as a computer programmer for Bell Telephone Co. of Pennsylvania (now Verizon Pennsylvania), an AT&T subsidiary. As a developer of large-scale software systems, she "fell in love with work," she told Capponi. In 1979 she transferred to the company's directory division, where she headed the yellow-pages advertising department. She served as district manager for long-range systems planning at AT&T's Basking Ridge, New Jersey, site from 1980 to 1984, then as a district sales manager in New York City for three years. In 1987 she earned an M.B.A. degree from Columbia University, in New York, became an AT&T branch manager, and then transferred back to Basking Ridge, where she held the title of division manager for industry marketing until 1989. During the next three years, she was promoted to director of product marketing for the communications-services group and then to director for outbound networking services. She was in charge of AT&T's toll-free services in 1992 and 1993. In the latter year she was named vice president of strategic planning for the communication-services group. In 1994 and 1995, as vice president for business services, she was responsible for marketing to small and midsize firms. Her next titles were executive vice president for business markets (1995–96) and executive vice president of the consumer-markets division (1997–98), with responsibility for 40,000 employees and for overseeing residential long-distance and Internet services for 75 million customers. At the beginning of 1997, the consumer-markets division brought in $26 billion annually and accounted for 60 percent of the company's total revenues.

In September 1998 McGovern left AT&T to join Fidelity Investments, headquartered in Boston, Massachusetts. The largest money-management firm in the U.S., Fidelity provides investment-management, retirement, brokerage, and shareholder services to individuals and institutions. "I was looking for a fresh new learning curve in a brand new industry—to leverage my skills from AT&T, advance my career and expand my mind," she told Beth Fitzgerald for the Newark, New Jersey, *Star-Ledger* (August 20, 1998). She also felt that she had had little chance of becoming AT&T's president in "the next five or ten years," because John D. Zeglis, who had assumed that post in 1997, was only 51 years of age. McGovern began her stint at Fidelity as the president of distribution and services, which encompassed 77 branch offices and more than 3,200 phone operators. In what Geoffrey Smith and Steve Rosenbush described as "her first move," she suggested to 30,000 of the most frequent callers to Fidelity service centers that they use the Internet and Fidelity's automated phone system to get the information they wanted. "It was hardly the 'Reach Out and Touch Someone' approach made famous by AT&T," Smith and Rosenbush wrote. "Even so, most customers switched to automated services, and none pulled their account, McGovern claims. . . . It put a shine on McGovern's star inside Fidelity."

In 2000 McGovern was named president of Fidelity's personal-investments division—the firm's third-highest executive position and top consumer-marketing post, with responsibility for advertising and Fidelity's on-line brokerage operations. "I think of power and influence synonymously," she told Patricia Sellers and Alynda Wheat for *Fortune* (October 16, 2000) while in that post. "There's the type of power that's related to control—you know, I say, 'Jump!' and you say, 'How high?' But real power is influence. My observation is that women tend to be better in positions where they can be influential." In 2001 McGovern was named president of Fidelity's personal-investments group and joined the company's operating committee. She assisted in Fidelity's transition to wireless technology and worked to advance the company's on-line business. At the end of 2001, according to a Fidelity press release (April 10, 2002, on-line), McGovern's division "held total retail customer assets of $473.8 billion, and served 8.7 million retail accounts." The same on-line release announced that McGovern had decided to leave Fidelity, and it quoted Kevin J. Kelly, president of the Fidelity Brokerage Co., as saying of her, "She has helped to build Fidelity Personal Investments and its retail brokerage business into one of the major drivers of Fidelity's success." The press release offered McGovern's long interest in teaching as the reason for her departure. In both 2000 and 2001 *Fortune* listed McGovern among the most influential women in corporate America.

McGovern and her family retained their residence in Boston when she joined the faculty of the Harvard Business School, in Cambridge, Massachusetts, as the MBA Class of 1966 professor of marketing. In addition to teaching, she wrote or cowrote papers for professional journals, with titles including "Bringing Customers into the Boardroom" (about many boards' lack of awareness of their customers' needs and opinions), "Outsourcing Marketing," and "Companies and the Customers Who Hate Them," for the *Harvard Business Review* (November 2004, March 2005, and June 2007, respectively).

In April 2008 the board of governors of the ARC voted unanimously to name McGovern the organization's new president and CEO. The American National Red Cross (its official name) was founded in 1881, after years of effort by Clara Barton, a nurse who aided soldiers during the American Civil War and the Franco-Prussian War. In addition to helping victims of wars and natural disasters within the U.S., the organization provides "community services that help the needy; support and comfort for military members and their families; the collection, processing and distribution of . . . blood and blood products; educational programs that promote health and safety; and international relief and development programs," as stated on its Web site. As a so-called federal instrumentality, the ARC sporadically receives funds or other aid from the federal government and, sometimes, state governments. The ARC is the U.S. affiliate of the International Committee of the Red Cross (founded in 1864), the blanket agency for all the national and international humanitarian groups allowed to identify themselves with a red cross, a red crescent (a Muslim symbol), or a red Star of David (a Jewish symbol).

McGovern received a $65,000 signing bonus when she accepted the position of the ARC's president and CEO, at an annual salary of $500,000. She succeeded an interim head, who had taken over after revelations in 2007 that Mark W. Everson, after less than six months as the ARC's top executive, was having an extramarital affair with the head of a Mississippi ARC chapter. Everson was the fourth ARC president and CEO to resign since 1999, when Elizabeth Dole stepped down. When Dole assumed the ARC's top executive position, in 1991, the ARC was making an effort to correct serious problems in

blood-collection procedures and record-keeping uncovered by Food and Drug Administration (FDA) investigators. Those problems included failure to elicit necessary information from donors, failure to follow standard procedures in swabbing donors' arms before inserting needles, and failure to discard possibly unsafe blood—problems potentially life-threatening to recipients of blood transfusions. In 1993 the FDA secured a federal court order that demanded improvements in the ARC's blood-collection and -distribution operations; the court authorized the FDA to impose fines for failure to comply. Since then the FDA has issued dozens of critical reports and imposed on the ARC millions of dollars in fines, including a $1.7 million fine on June 11, 2008, two weeks before McGovern's arrival. The ARC was fined $16 million in June 2010 for violations that occurred in 2008 and 2009. Nevertheless, the FDA commended the ARC and its leadership for recent efforts to reach full compliance.

Dole's eight-year tenure included allegations that she had politicized the ARC in an effort to improve the chances of her husband, Republican U.S. senator Robert J. "Bob" Dole of Kansas, of winning the presidency in 1996. According to Linda Heller, writing for the *Nation* (July 1, 1996), "Shortly after her appointment . . . Mrs. Dole assembled a special team of longtime political advisers . . . to vet important Red Cross actions, both managerial and scientific, with a political sensitivity to what might help or hurt Bob Dole's presidential ambitions." In one example, to "cater to Christian right orthodoxies," Heller reported, an AIDS-prevention manual was rewritten to emphasize abstention from premarital and homosexual sex. According to Heller, "Mrs. Dole's special team interfered in day-to-day Red Cross decisions, frustrating the charity's professional staff and contributing to an exodus of many senior technicians, volunteers and other crucial personnel."

Dole's successor at the ARC, Bernadine Healy, was forced to resign; she left at the end of 2001, after less than two years at her post, in the wake of severe criticism of the ARC's actions following the September 11, 2001 terrorist attacks on the U.S. In particular, the ARC was denounced on the floor of Congress and elsewhere for allegedly deceiving the public by setting aside for other, future uses nearly half of the $564 million pledged to its Liberty Fund, created to help the families of victims of the attacks. It was also criticized for mounting a huge blood-collection drive after the attacks and continuing the drive even after it became clear that little blood would be needed for those injured—and that, with far too little storage space available for the amount of blood that was donated, most of that blood would have to be discarded.

Interim directors preceded and followed the ARC's next president and CEO, Marsha J. Evans, who served from 2002 through 2005. Evans's resignation followed another storm of criticism, for the ARC's mishandling of rescue efforts in New Orleans, Louisiana, and other areas of the Gulf Coast devastated by Hurricane Katrina in late August 2005. Although the ARC received more than $1.89 billion of the $2.6 billion collected in private donations for hurricane victims, "evacuees, public officials, and even some of its own volunteers . . . said the organization responded too slowly, often seemed disorganized, and failed to assist many remote Gulf Coast communities," Margaret Warner said on the December 14, 2005 edition of PBS-TV's *Online NewsHour.* Paul C. Light, a professor of public service at New York University, told Warner, "I think that Marsha Evans has become, to some extent, a scapegoat for all that ails the organization, and was having tremendous conflict with the board and eventually came under fire herself for being too much of an over promiser and an apologist for what had been going wrong down in the Gulf states." "The board seems to think it is a hiring and firing agency, and does not see its role as building a strong Red Cross," Light told Stephanie Strom for the *New York Times* (December 14, 2005). "The constant change in leadership is debilitating and does nothing to address the real problem, which is years and years of underinvestment in telecommunications, technology and other infrastructure to help the organization with its mission." In his conversation with Warner, Light also mentioned "a very serious lack of investment in volunteer training." "We saw tremendous weaknesses in the organization that have been years in the making come to the fore in the days and weeks after Katrina," he said.

The ARC board took 18 months to find a replacement for Evans, and its firing of Everson, her successor, brought the organization fresh criticism. Some observers felt that Everson's affair might have warranted a reprimand or temporary suspension, not dismissal, and that in ousting him the ARC's board was clinging to a "bizarrely antediluvian" code of morality, as Meghan Daum wrote for *latimes.com* (December 1, 2007). Moreover, in his few months in office, Everson had "brought a level of stability to the Red Cross that it had not experienced in more than a decade," according to Stephanie Strom, writing for the *New York Times* (November 20, 2007), and had overseen an overhaul of the board and gained the ARC's greater independence from its chairperson in day-to-day management. Also, the ARC's response to the wildfires that devastated large areas of Southern California in October 2007 had "won generally high marks," Strom reported. Diana Aviv, the president and chief executive officer of Independent Sector, which works to strengthen nonprofit organizations, said to Strom, "The tragedy of this is that the American Red Cross is probably the best-known nonprofit organization in this country. When the stories about it are more about governance and management and less about how it saves lives, it's sad and not just for the Red Cross." Paul C. Light predicted that replacing Everson would be difficult. "You need someone like Colin Powell to step in," he said to Strom. "But there aren't that many national figures like that who'll take the job, and within that pool, there aren't any who know anything about disaster relief, let along blood. And who would take this job under these circumstances, anyway?"

The answer to that question was Gail McGovern, who told Gose, "If this were going to be easy, it wouldn't be worth moving my family, changing my life, and jumping into something new. If it isn't hard, it's not worth doing." She told Rucker, "I feel so strongly about the mission that I want to scream it off the rooftops. We live in a very generous society, and I'm confident people will help." At the end of June 2008, a week after she assumed office as ARC's president and CEO, McGovern traveled to Sichuan Province, in China, where the previous month an earthquake of magnitude 7.9 on the Richter scale had killed approximately 70,000 people, among them thousands of children in shoddily built schools; the bodies of about 18,000 people were never found. The quake also injured many thousands of Chinese and destroyed thousands of houses and other buildings as well as schools. "It made me so committed to the mission," McGovern told Rucker. "And here's the corny part: It really restores your faith in humanity." Later that summer the ARC aided victims of Hurricanes Gustav and Ike, along the Gulf Coasts of Texas and Louisiana, respectively.

On January 12, 2010 an earthquake of magnitude 7.0 struck Haiti, destroying much of the capital city, Port-au-Prince, and surrounding areas. An estimated 230,000 of that impoverished nation's nine million inhabitants were killed, at least 300,000 were injured, and more than a million people were left homeless. The destruction of Port-au-Prince's airport, roads, hospitals, and water-supply system created a huge humanitarian crisis—and, for the ARC, "a dramatic chance to prove it learned from its flawed responses to Hurricane Katrina and the 9/11 terror attacks," David Crary wrote. By January 21 the ARC had raised $137 million in donations from people in the U.S., with $25 million from those who made text-message donations from their mobile phones—by far the largest amount of any American nonprofit group and "a remarkable show of confidence in an organization that irked many donors" after 9/11 and Hurricane Katrina, in Crary's words. McGovern assisted personally in relief efforts in Haiti and met with Haitian Red Cross and Haitian government officials, reassuring them that the organization would work closely with them and with other groups. "We learn from every single disaster," she told Crary. "What we learned from Katrina is that we can't do this alone."

According to a three-month progress report that the ARC posted on-line in April 2010, the organization had delivered tarpaulins and tents to more than 90 percent of those it had aimed to help. It had also "provided relief items for 400,000 people. Distributed 60 million liters of clean drinking water. Built more than 1,300 latrines. Treated more than

86,000 people at Red Cross hospitals or mobile clinics. Helped vaccinate more than 152,000 people against deadly diseases. Coordinated the shipment of more than 2,100 units of blood to medical facilities. Registered more than 28,400 people with missing loved ones on its family linking Web site." Nevertheless, journalists, members of Congress, and others have criticized the ARC not only for failing to disclose in detail its spending in Haiti but also for reducing its efforts after the first few months following the disaster. Writing for the *Miami Herald* (April 28, 2010), Frances Robles reported that, according to ARC officials, the slowdown reflected a change in focus from immediate relief to long-term infrastructure improvements. The outbreak of cholera in Haiti in October 2010 required a sudden diversion of funds. As of that month the ARC had collected about $300 million in donations since the earthquake and was expected to spend more than $200 million in Haiti by January 2011.

In 2010 the ARC also responded to the effects of a catastrophic earthquake in Chile, severe flooding in Pakistan, and a tsunami and a volcanic eruption in Indonesia, among other disasters.

McGovern has also worked to increase the American public's awareness of the ARC's everyday activities, among them managing the collection, storage, and distribution of almost half of the nation's blood supplies, offering instruction in first aid and cardiopulmonary resuscitation (CPR), and, every year, responding to thousands of fires in residential buildings. "Too often people think of the Red Cross only when there's a national disaster," McGovern told Gose. "We help people every day." On another front, as of the first few months of 2010, the ARC had cut its deficit to about $33 million.

McGovern and her husband, Donald E. McGovern, who works for Hewlett Packard, live in the Washington, D.C., area and own a beach house in New Jersey. Their daughter is a student at Johns Hopkins University.

—W.D.

Suggested Reading: American Red Cross Web site; *BusinessWeek* p146 Feb. 21, 2000; *Chronicle of Philanthropy* p39 Apr. 17, 2008, p51+ Sep. 18, 2008; *Johns Hopkins University NewsLetter* (online) Oct. 1, 2009; PR Newswire Apr. 8, 2008; WhoRunsGov.com; *Working Woman* p226+ June 1997; *Who's Who in America*

Mehretu, Julie

(merit-too)

Nov. 28, 1970– Artist

Address: c/o Marian Goodman Gallery, 24 W. 57th St., New York, NY 10019

"If, 100 years from now, a historian needs an illustration of our era, one picture worth a thousand words to describe both the collaborative sophistication of the Internet and the random brutality of terrorism, they couldn't do much better than to select one of Julie Mehretu's abstract paintings," Meisha Rosenberg wrote in a review of Mehretu's show City Sitings for the Albany, New York, weekly *Metroland* (May 22, 2008). Rosenberg continued, "Her jazzlike, large-scale paintings . . . are philosophical, passionate, and dynamic. These paintings capture our particular Zeitgeist through kinetic depictions of geopolitical forces and disruptions." Mehretu is known for producing massive, complex paintings that incorporate architectural plans, maps, signs, and symbols into abstract images that bring to mind cities in transition, aspects of warfare, and sociopolitical networks. Charles Bonenti wrote for the Pittsfield, Massachusetts, *Berkshire Eagle* (April 25, 2008) that Mehretu "has developed a way to codify the visual language of politics, architecture and art history into what are being called 'psychogeographic' landscapes. Her elaborately layered canvases read like archaeo-

Sarah Rentz, courtesy of Marian Goodman Gallery

logical excavations of our own era." Mehretu requires a team of assistants to complete many of her larger works and uses a technique that is "labor-intensive, in the way Old Masters were produced," as Bonenti put it. Mehretu begins by painting or drawing an initial image or set of images—often derived from a map or another preexisting document that has been manipulated on a computer and projected on the canvas. She then covers that image with a layer of translucent acrylic paint and sands it smooth before applying more painted layers, to create what Bonenti described as a "palimpsest with new images overlaying old ones, like memories seen through layers of time."

Mehretu began to garner attention in the art world in the early 2000s, when her work was included in exhibitions in New York City galleries and museums. Her paintings sold quickly—sometimes before a show opened—to museums and collectors who kept them rather than auctioning them, prompting Jeffrey Deitch, the director of the Los Angeles Museum of Contemporary Art, to observe to Calvin Tomkins for the *New Yorker* (March 29, 2010), "Julie is not a market artist. She belongs to the museum part of the art world." A biography of Mehretu on the PBS Web site noted about her work, "Architectural renderings and aerial views of urban grids enter the work as fragments, losing their real-world specificity and challenging narrow geographic and cultural readings. The paintings' wax-like surfaces—built up over weeks and months in thin translucent layers—have a luminous warmth and spatial depth, with formal qualities of light and space made all the more complex by Mehretu's delicate depictions of fire, explosions, and perspectives in both two and three dimensions. Her works engage the history of nonobjective art—from Constructivism to Futurism—posing contemporary questions about the relationship between utopian impulses and abstraction."

Julie Mehretu was born on November 28, 1970 in Addis Ababa, Ethiopia. She is the first child of Assefa, an Ethiopian college professor, and Doree, a white teacher from Alabama. She has a brother, David, now a lawyer, and a sister, Neesham. Her parents met in Washington, D.C., when Assefa was taking graduate classes at Johns Hopkins University, in nearby Baltimore, Maryland. In 1969 the family moved to Ethiopia; they returned to the U.S. in 1977 to escape the repressive Soviet-backed Socialist regime—known as "the Derg"—that had come to power in 1974. They settled in East Lansing, Michigan, where Mehretu's father had been offered a job teaching economic geography at Michigan State University and her mother found a teaching position at a local Montessori school. Mehretu easily adapted to life in the U.S. and excelled at school. She "came out" as a lesbian during her junior year of high school but did not inform her parents until she was in college. According to Tomkins she explained her sexual orientation to her parents "so cogently that they both became stronger enthusiasts for gay rights."

Mehretu attended Kalamazoo College, in Michigan. She had always been interested in drawing, and her experiences in college solidified her desire to create art. She spent her junior year studying at Cheikh Anta Diop University, in Dakar, Senegal (also known as the University of Dakar), where she learned to speak Wolof, the local language, and became acquainted with batik, a fabric-dyeing technique. When she returned to the U.S., she persuaded her professors to allow her to forgo classes and spend her last two semesters in Ann Arbor, Michigan, working on her senior project—a series of figurative portraits of several female friends.

After graduating, with a B.A. degree, in 1992, Mehretu and two friends moved to San Francisco, California. "Two of us were gay, and alternative, and we thought that was the place to be," Mehretu told Tomkins. "But within a week we'd decided it wasn't. San Francisco didn't have the edge, didn't feel like a place that was making culture in a way that interested us." They moved to New York City, where Mehretu lived for the next three years, working at the Coffee Shop, an upscale diner in Manhattan's Union Square neighborhood, and painting every day. The paintings she produced during her years in New York, which Tomkins called "messy and abstract," were "the kind of thing you do when you think you're making art, but you're not," she told Tomkins. "I finally realized I needed to go back to school."

Mehretu attended the Rhode Island School of Design (RISD), in Providence, on a full scholarship, and graduated with an M.F.A. degree in 1997. She was particularly inspired by one of her professors at RISD, Michael Young. "Michael wouldn't even talk to you about what you were working on," Mehretu recalled to Tomkins. "He'd talk to you about who you were as a person. I found that frustrating at first, but without him I don't know if I would have found my practice in the way I did." Young encouraged Mehretu to draw continuously until she found her creative voice and aesthetic. She soon discovered that she had a tendency to draw abstract groupings of shapes that resembled maps or architectural plans. "I began thinking of [the shapes] as little communities," she told Tomkins, "and then they started to look like maps, or aerial views of cities." Though many have pointed to her father's job as a geographer as a possible influence on her style, Mehretu told Tomkins, "I don't think there was an aesthetic link. It was more a subconscious awareness of his way of dissecting the world, to try to make sense of it."

During her second year at RISD, she completed a large black and white painting with nine layers of drawings, each separated by clear acrylic paint; that was the first of her paintings to feature layering and geographic shapes. As a student Mehretu had several small solo exhibitions in Providence and in Amherst, Massachusetts. From 1997 to 1998 she was a resident of the CORE Program, which provided a postgraduate fellowship at the Glassell School of Art at the Museum of Fine Arts in Houston, Texas. Around that time she began to use the computer as a drawing tool, taking images from the Internet, altering them, and re-creating them with paint and ink on canvas. In 1999 Mehretu returned to New York City, where two of her paintings and several of her drawings appeared in a show at the gallery Exit Art, in Manhattan's SoHo neighborhood. Her work at that show attracted the interest of art dealers, and Mehretu received offers to show her work at a number of prominent galleries and museums. In 2000 Mehretu was an artist-in-residence at the Headlands Center of the Arts, in Sausalito, California. The same year her work was featured in several group exhibitions, including the Museum of Modern Art (MoMA) show Greater New York, held at the P.S.1 Contemporary Arts Center in Queens. In 2001 Mehretu was an artist-in-residence at the Studio Museum in Harlem; that year she was one of 28 young African-American artists whose work was included in the museum's Freestyle exhibition. In a review of that show for the New York Times (May 11, 2001), Holland Cotter called Mehretu "a star on the rise" and observed, "Abstraction takes on a kind of cool, new cosmic poetry in Julie Mehretu's drawings."

In November 2001 Mehretu had her first New York City solo show, at the Project, a new Harlem gallery founded by Christian Haye, a young black art critic. (Haye faced legal troubles over the next several years, and the gallery closed in 2009.) All four of the paintings included in that show sold before the opening. "[Mehretu's] success came so fast that there was no time to even doubt it," Haye told Tomkins. Over time Mehretu produced larger and more detailed paintings; her 2001 painting Retopistics: A Renegade Excavation is 18 feet long and eight and a half feet high. Tomkins described that piece as "wildly colorful, almost violent, with several tower-like forms partially obscured by marks that resembled explosions." Mehretu's paintings were included in the 2001 group exhibition Painting at the Edge of the World, at the Walker Art Center, in Minneapolis, Minnesota, and in 2002 Mehretu had a solo show at the prestigious White Cube Gallery in London, England, which featured her painting Renegade Delirium and several smaller drawings. Writing for the Los Angeles Times (June 2, 2004), Christopher Knight described the experience of viewing Renegade Delirium: "From the bottom, your eye rises on a pair of escalators drawn in black ink, pushed along by a blast of shrapnel marks from behind. You arrive at what appears to be a classical amphitheater. From there, space expands laterally across the 12-foot-wide canvas. Architectural renderings of schematic stairways, corridors and colonnades merge with abstract French curves, clouds of smoky gray, scattered geometric shapes and fire."

In 2002 Mehretu's paintings and drawings were shown at the Busan Biennale in South Korea; the Eighth Baltic Triennial in Vilnius, Lithuania; and the group show Drawing Now: Eight Propositions, at MoMA. At the culmination of a 2003 residency at the Walker Art Center, Mehretu presented four large paintings and seven smaller works of paint and ink in the solo exhibition Drawing into Painting. That exhibit traveled to the Redcat Gallery in Los Angeles, California, and the Albright-Knox Art Gallery in Buffalo, New York. One of the show's large paintings, Transcending: The New International, is nine feet high and 20 feet long and features "an underlayer of architectural details representing the capitals of every post-colonial African nation," as Tomkins wrote. Another of the large paintings, Looking Back to a Bright New Future, contains a small white trapezoid in the center of the canvas "surrounded by an exuberant burst of puddle-shaped color-forms woven into a rich vaporous web of blueprint-like architectural drawing," Knight wrote in his review of the Redcat Gallery show. Knight further observed that Mehretu's paintings, "although abstract and absent topical subject matter . . . clearly speak of experience in a world shaken to its foundations by the events of Sept. 11, 2001" and "address big themes of history, calamity, germination and spiritual interdependence."

Two of Mehretu's paintings were included in the 2004 Whitney Biennial, the prestigious contemporary-art show held at New York City's Whitney Museum of American Art every other year. One of those paintings, Empirical Construction, Istanbul (2003), was purchased by MoMA for its permanent collection. Over the next few years, Mehretu's work was included in the 2004 São Paolo Biennial; the 2004 Carnegie International exhibition, held at the Carnegie Museum of Art, in Pittsburgh, Pennsylvania; the 2006 Biennale of Sydney, Australia; and the 2006 Contemporary Art Museum of Castilla and Leon, in Spain. Her solo show City Sitings, which included "recent works that speak of contemporary urban experience," in Rosenberg's words, premiered at the Detroit Institute of Arts in 2007 before traveling to other locations in 2008. That show included the painting Black City (2007), which, Rosenberg wrote, "comments on American cities post-9/11" and "uses three-dimensional plans of military fortifications such as Hitler's Atlantic bunkers. Seen up close, a painting like Black City evokes a dizzying chaos of black lines dense as smoke. From a distance, the tight layering and symbols—stars in a military flight pattern, a satellite, colored dots and bars—suggest the claustrophobia of heavy surveillance and the erasures of war."

From October 2009 to January 2010 Mehretu presented her solo show Grey Area at the Deutsche Guggenheim in Berlin. (It traveled to the Solomon R. Guggenheim Museum, in New York, in May 2010.) The show included seven paintings inspired by the city of Berlin, where Mehretu spent a six-month residency at the American Academy in 2007. The paintings, which were influenced by Romantic-era paintings of ancient ruins as well as images of the aftermath of earthquakes, bombings, and other disasters, were made primarily with ink, and, unlike her previous works, they feature large portions that have been smudged or erased. Mehretu took up the practice of erasing after suddenly deciding that she did not like the colorful canvas she had been working on. "The color had destroyed all the black-and-white drawing underneath," she told Tomkins. "So I sanded out a whole section in the middle of the painting, and walked to the back of my studio to look at it, and the painting was—done! The erasure had become the main action, the void was making all these other things happen." A press release for the show on the Guggenheim Museum's Web site read, "Asking what it means to be an American artist in Germany during the Iraq and Afghanistan wars of the [George W.] Bush years, Mehretu's canvases meditate on the idea of the modern ruin." In his review of the exhibition for the London *Guardian* (December 5, 2009, on-line), Brian Dillon described the painting *Middle Grey*: "Buried somewhere at the pale heart of the picture are the source drawings, but the canvas has erupted on several other planes at the same time. An immense variety of lines, dots, lozenges, half-figurative hints and starkly abstract shapes radiate from the mysterious centre; here and there they come together to form clumps and crowds, like sporadic settlements in some alien cartography." Referring to Mehretu's use of erasing, Dillon wrote: "Such disappearances seem melancholy at first, as if some aspect of historical witness were being vanished. But what they leave behind, typically, is a pale patch of grey: a void waiting to be refilled—and grey, as these paintings also prove, is the colour of potential, the colour of hope."

In 2006 Mehretu won a commission to create a piece to hang in the lobby of the office building of the financial firm Goldman Sachs, in Lower Manhattan. To create the 80-foot-by-23-foot painting, entitled *Mural*, the artist secured studio space in a former arms factory in Berlin (she was completing the Grey Area paintings simultaneously) and worked with a team of some 30 studio assistants, who traced images, selected and manipulated by Mehretu, onto the enormous canvas. The painting's first four layers contain images that "implicitly refer to the history of finance capitalism—maps, trade routes, population shifts, financial institutions, the growth of cities," Tomkins wrote. The first layer is composed of "part of a maplike network shooting through the whole painting," the artist explained to Tomkins. The next two layers consist of architectural images of historic financial institutions, such as the New Orleans cotton exchange and the New York Stock Exchange. Mehretu covered the fourth layer with the sorts of ink brushstrokes that appear in many of her pieces. In 2009, when the painting was affixed to a wall in the Goldman Sachs building, she added new shapes and adjusted the colors (there are 215 colors in total). She also added references to modernist art, including shapes reminiscent of the stained-glass window in the American Airlines terminal at New York's John F. Kennedy International Airport, which had been dismantled in 2008. "I was thinking back to the modernist tradition of painting as part of architecture, and I was also thinking about the narrative of lower Manhattan, how this was the source of the city and the core of how New York became what it is," Mehretu told Tomkins. "All these many layers." The painting was completed in 2010 and is visible from the street through the building's large street-level front window.

In 2009 Goldman Sachs was accused of having used investment tactics that contributed to, and allowed the firm to profit from, the recent economic recession, and in 2010 the Securities and Exchange Commission charged the company with subprime-mortgage fraud. Asked whether she would have accepted the commission had she known about the company's apparent role in the economic downturn, Mehretu told Tomkins, "Without hesitation." She continued, "I don't see [Goldman Sachs] as an evil institution, but as part of the larger system we all participate in. We're all part of it. And, anyway, for me it was about making something—it was about the art. . . . I was more concerned about participating in the legacy of painting. You just hope it will feel O.K. over time."

In 2010 Dodie Kazanjian, the director of the Metropolitan Opera's Gallery Met (an exhibition space in the Met's lobby), commissioned Mehretu to create a work inspired by Robert Lepage's production of Wagner's opera *Das Rheingold*, the first of the four operas that make up Wagner's Ring cycle, which were to be performed that year. "When I'm working I am usually listening to music," Mehretu told Carol Vogel for the *New York Times*, "and I have always been interested in the juxtaposition of looking at images and listening." Kazanjian told Vogel, "Julie's work is symphonic and continuous in the same way as Wagner's is." Kazanjian also said that Mehretu's "layered compositions—sometimes as many as four, five or more layers laid on top of one another—give the work great complexity and depth." Mehretu's piece, *Auguries*, was unveiled after *Das Rheingold*'s premiere, in September 2010, as the centerpiece of the Notations After the Ring exhibit in the gallery.

Many critics have noted in Mehretu's work the influence of a wide variety of art movements, including elements of Expressionism, Futurism, Geometric Abstraction, and even computer art. Observers have also interpreted Mehretu's aesthetic as a response to her global travels—including her immigration to the U.S.—and to her understanding of the connections among the world's social, financial, and political structures. Cate McQuaid wrote for the *Boston Globe* (May 25, 2008) that Mehretu "makes paintings and drawings that capture and scrutinize layer upon layer of social systems. They examine immigration, militarization, and economics, among other topics. Mehretu works organically and intuitively. She borrows from maps, blueprints, and corporate logos, then invigorates her surfaces with brushy, accumulating gestures that gather and swell into movements, and sometimes explosions, to make paintings that crackle with spontaneity." Amy White wrote for the Durham, North Carolina, *Independent Weekly* (September 17, 2008) that Mehretu "inhabits her own work like a citizen of an imaginary city, role-playing alternately as urban planner, itinerant vandal, mercenary soldier and intellectual theorist, commenting on the myriad complexities of socio-political space." Mehretu told White, "My aim is to have a picture that appears one way from a distance almost like a cosmology, city or universe from afar—but then when you approach the work, the overall image shatters into numerous other pictures, stories and events."

Mehretu's paintings are part of the public collections of numerous museums, including MoMA, the Brooklyn Museum of Art, and the Whitney; the Museum of Fine Arts in Boston; the National Gallery of Art and the Smithsonian Institution, in Washington, D.C.; and the Philadelphia Art Museum. Mehretu has received many honors, including a 2001 Penny McCall Award; a 2003 Joan Mitchell Foundation Grant; a 2005 American Art Award from the Whitney; and a 2007 Berlin Prize. In 2005 she received a MacArthur Fellowship—often called the "genius grant"—from the John D. and Catherine T. MacArthur Foundation.

Mehretu and her partner, the Australian-born artist Jessica Rankin, live in New York City. In 2005 Rankin gave birth to their son, Cade Elias Mehretu-Rankin.

—W.D.

Suggested Reading: (Albany, New York) *Metroland* Art p27 May 22, 2008; *Boston Globe* Living Arts N p2 May 25, 2008; (Durham, North Carolina) *Indepen-dent Weekly* Visual Art p38 Sep. 17, 2008; (London) *Guardian* (on-line) Dec. 5, 2009; *Los Angeles Times* E p1 June 2, 2004; *New York Times* E p36 May 11, 2001; *New Yorker* p62+ Mar. 29, 2010

Selected Paintings: *Retopistics: A Renegade Excavation*, 2001; *Renegade Delirium*, 2002; *Transcending: The New International*, 2003; *Empirical Construction, Istanbul*, 2003; *Black City*, 2007; *Mural*, 2010; *Auguries*, 2010

Courtesy of Myra Melford

Melford, Myra

Jan. 5, 1957– Jazz pianist; composer

Address: Dept. of Music, University of California, 104 Morrison Hall # 1200, Berkeley, CA 94720-1200

"In the realm of truly spur-of-the-moment improvised music there is hardly anyone better than Myra Melford," Thomas R. Erdmann wrote for *jazzreview.com* (2009). "To be brought into her au-

ral world is to be treated to sounds and colors unlike any other performer or composer alive." For more than 20 years, the pianist and composer Myra Melford has been considered one of the most innovative and bold musicians in experimental jazz, with a body of work that reflects her early training in classical piano and her study of the music of India and Eastern Europe as well as her immersion in boogie-woogie, the blues, and modern jazz. "Melford's is a muscular, ringing attack that sounds as true as a sledgehammer hitting a rail peg. Hers also is a diaphanous delicacy that breathes deeply within the music and creates an atmosphere fruitful for meditation," Robert Spencer wrote for AllAboutJazz.com (November 19, 2003), in a review of one of the more than 30 albums she has made, most as bandleader or co-leader. Melford has given concerts in 30 countries and performed and recorded with a virtual who's who of experimental jazz of the late 20th century—artists including the saxophonists Henry Threadgill, Joseph Jarman, and Marty Ehrlich, the violinist Leroy Jenkins, and the drummer and percussionist Han Bennink. In recent years she has also collaborated with acclaimed up-and-comers in experimental jazz, such as the pianist Satoko Fujii.

Melford's debut album, *Jump* (1990), and its successors have earned nearly unanimous praise from jazz critics. Two common themes of the reviews have been Melford's extraordinary ability to create experimental music that remains accessible and her constant breaking of new musical ground—with nearly every album after *Jump* being called her "best effort yet." By the mid-1990s, a decade after she came to New York City to become active in the "downtown" jazz scene, Melford had achieved a new level of recognition, attracting increasing attention in the mainstream American media as well as in Europe. "Her secret weapon is originality, something that has been dangerously close to going out of fashion in the conservative Eighties and Nineties," Stuart Nicholson wrote for the London *Observer* (November 24, 1996). "Ever since jazz emerged . . . it has been a music in flux. But the revolutionary zeal that's part of the music's credo became strangely muted in the [1980s]. Where jazz was once a flight from the status quo, the current generation of jazz musicians have come to represent a flight back to it. So welcome Myra Melford who's arrived in time to prick jazz's conscience with a timely reminder that it's time to move forward, not retreat into the past." Since 2004 Melford has taught courses in improvisation and jazz at the University of California at Berkeley.

Myra Melford was born on January 5, 1957 in Evanston, a suburb of Chicago, Illinois. She grew up in nearby Glencoe in a house designed by the master architect Frank Lloyd Wright. "It was our—especially my father's—pride and joy," Melford told *Current Biography*, the source of quotes in this article unless otherwise indicated. (The house was one of six that made up Ravine Bluffs, a subdivision Wright designed for middle-income buyers.) Both of Melford's older siblings (a brother and a sister) played the piano, and at the age of three, Melford began playing, too, making up little songs on her own. For five years beginning when she was in kindergarten, she took piano lessons from Erwin Helfer, a friend of the family. Although Helfer is best known as a jazz, boogie-woogie, and blues pianist, he taught Melford mostly from the classical repertoire—music ranging from works by Johann Sebastian Bach, from the early 1700s, to those of Béla Bartók and other 20th-century composers. After some time Helfer exposed her to blues and improvisation; she loved both, but he limited that kind of fun to a few minutes at the end of her lessons, when the two would play "four-hand blues," with Helfer supplying the bass notes and Melford the melody.

While in junior high school, Melford started taking classical piano lessons as a student in the extension program at Northwestern University, in Evanston. She practiced some very difficult pieces, notably ones by the early-20th-century Russian composers Rachmaninoff and Prokofiev. Such works were particularly challenging for her because her hands are much smaller than those of most professional pianists. Although she liked the music of such composers as Bach, Bartók, and Stravinsky, Northwestern's teachers emphasized pieces by Rachmaninoff and other Romantic works. That music, she recalled, "didn't really speak to me." By ninth grade she had abandoned her piano studies—without any inkling that one day she would return to them with renewed zeal.

After high school Melford enrolled at Evergreen College, in Olympia, Washington, as an environmental-science major. One day at a local restaurant, she noticed a flyer advertising jazz-piano lessons. Knowing little about jazz other than that it in-

volved improvisation, which she had enjoyed so much as a child, she began taking piano lessons again and soon changed her major to music. Olympia had a small jazz community, and Melford worked at a local club—a stopover for artists who had gigs in bigger cities nearby, including Seattle, Washington, and Portland, Oregon. At the club she met the avant-garde jazzmen Leroy Jenkins, Anthony Braxton, and Oliver Lake. Jenkins and Braxton were part of the Chicago-based Association for the Advancement of Creative Musicians (AACM), a collective dedicated to making innovative music. They introduced Melford to works by Cecil Taylor, Ornette Coleman, and various AACM musicians. Although Melford had come to enjoy the bebop of Thelonious Monk and Charlie Parker and other 1940s and '50s jazz, before long she realized that she felt far more strongly drawn to contemporary and avant-garde jazz from the 1960s onward. Melford also became interested in various kinds of world music; she took classes in African percussion and other aspects of world music at the Cornish Institute of the Arts, in Seattle. With others at the institute, she performed in a Gamelon—an ensemble that specializes in Indonesian music. ("Gamelon" also refers to the Indonesian instruments such groups play.) Melford received a B.A. in music from Evergreen College in 1980. She then moved to the East Coast, to submerge herself in experimental jazz and study with AACM musicians.

Earlier, Leroy Jenkins had given Melford his telephone number in New York City. After she moved to New York from Boston, Masschusetts, in 1983, she called him, and Jenkins invited her to his weekly workshop. "That workshop . . . was pretty instrumental in getting me going," she recalled. Others who attended included musicians who, like her, wanted to find ways of expressing themselves with new musical languages. Melford developed a close bond with the flutist Marion Brandis, with whom she would attend concerts as well as perform. After Brandis began to study under Henry Threadgill, a bandleader and flutist as well as a saxophonist, Melford took lessons in composition with Threadgill for a year. To prepare for a Thelonious Monk piano competition, she took lessons with the pianist Don Pullen and then continued to study with him, too, for about a year. Among the many other contemporary jazz musicians Melford met in the downtown Manhattan jazz scene were Butch Morris, Marty Ehrlich, the saxophonist John Zorn, the pianist Wayne Horvitz, and the guitarists Elliot Sharp and Fred Frith. Melford would frequently attend their concerts, at many of which they would play their own compositions. "They opened me up to new sonic possibilities and ways of organizing music," she said; some also invited her to play with them, and gradually she became known to downtown audiences.

In 1989 the Knitting Factory, a club that had opened two years earlier and had become the downtown Mecca of experimental jazz and rock, included Melford's performance of her solo piano composition "Some Kind of Blues" on its second live album, *Live at the Knitting Factory, Vol. 2*. On the strength of that recording, Melford was invited to join the first Knitting Factory–organized tour of Europe the following year. She toured with the bassist Lindsey Horner and the drummer Reggie Nicholson, and after the trio's first performance, both an agent and a representative of the recording company Enemy approached her; the former booked the trio, and Melford signed a record contract with the latter.

Jump (1990), with the Myra Melford Trio, marks Melford's debut album as a bandleader and composer. It was the first of the three albums that she would make with Horner and Nicholson. The style of *Jump* mirrors that of the trio on their Knitting Factory European tour. Although the influence of Cecil Taylor can be detected, the seven tracks exhibit Melford's signature mix of order and chaos. "Taylor's influence," Mark Miller wrote in a review of *Jump* for the Toronto, Canada, *Globe and Mail* (April 29, 1991), "is comfortably integrated into a broader, bluesier approach that gives a warmth and appealing accessibility to even the most abstract of her solos." For her trio's next album, *Now & Now* (1991), Melford again offered bluesy, free-jazz themes. In an assessment of *Now & Now* for the *Chicago Sun-Times* (August 16, 1992), Lloyd Sachs described the Myra Melford Trio as "one of the most invigorating and entrancing threesomes currently at work." "As a leading light of the new music, Melford brings the usual classical and free jazz influences to bear, but in a rhythmically arresting, melodically intoxicating manner," Sachs continued. "Waves and clusters of notes push her themes restlessly forward, a rhapsodic intensity lifts them and an unusually direct meditative quality opens them up." Several reviewers noted that although Melford's compositions were experimental and avant-garde, listeners would not find them difficult to respond to.

Eager to broaden her "sonic palette," in her words, Melford invited Marty Ehrlich and the trumpeter Dave Douglas to join her trio for her next studio album. Titled *Even the Sounds Shine* (1995), it marked both a continuation of what she had achieved on her first two albums and an exploration of new musical territory. Some reviewers considered it her best effort; she herself was happy with the record, but she realized, she said, "that if I wanted to have a quintet, I'd really like to change up the personnel and get some new energy—a different kind of approach to improvising." The Same River, Twice was the name of Melford's new quintet, which included Dave Douglas, the saxophonist/clarinetist Chris Speed, the cellist Erik Friedlander, and the drummer Michael Sarin. (The name of the quintet refers to an observation made by the Greek philosopher Heraclitus, who, about 2,500 years ago, wrote that one cannot step into the same river twice, because the water is always moving.) While the music she had composed for her trio, Melford explained, "was largely song-form

based, even though I was kind of creating my own song forms," with her new quintet she "started thinking about more extended, episodic kinds of compositions. The major pieces I did with the quintet were longer forms that went through a lot of different areas. It was really about setting up structures where smaller units of the quintet could do some improvising, so there were lots of duets and trios and solo sections that were kind of bridges between the composed material." With *The Same River, Twice* (1996), which appeared on the Salem, Massachusetts, Gramavision label, Melford turned far more heads in the U.S. than she had in the past. On October 8, 1996, in the first review of a Melford album to appear in the *New York Times*, Ben Ratliff lauded *The Same River, Twice* as her "most accomplished recording yet" and the five instrumentalists as "restless explorers of changing timbre." Like other reviewers Ratliff pointed out both the appeal and the complexity of Melford's music: "Her chromatic themes throughout the record use tricky odd meters, and Michael Sarin's drumming brings out the dance rhythms inside them. But it's a players' record as much as a composer's; though the written material guides the music, her improvising bursts with enthusiasm, prompting heated, fast and flexible responses from her band." Melford made her next recording, *Above Blue* (1999), with the same quintet.

Supported by a Fulbright scholarship, Melford spent September 2000 through May 2001 in Calcutta, India. She attended many concerts and, under Sohanlal Sharma, studied the harmonium, a keyboard instrument that is used primarily in northern Indian music. (Several Western composers and musicians, among them Mahler and the Beatles, also incorporated it into their works.) Melford said that she devoted herself to "developing my vocabulary on that instrument, which was starting to complement what I was doing on the piano." She also studied Hindustani music, a classical, North Indian form that is based on the raga, a scale consisting of seven notes, only two of which remain constant. "It really enriched my idea of what modal music could be and the importance of melody," she said.

All the while, beginning in the 1980s, New York jazz musicians and connoisseurs had been engaging in a lively debate about the nature of jazz. Those from the uptown jazz scene, with Lincoln Center as its focal point, favored mainstream, or traditional, jazz; the downtown faction championed experimental jazz of the sort offered at venues including the Bottom Line and CB's 313 Gallery (a performance space next to the hardcore punk-rock club CBGB) as well as the Knitting Factory. In 1987, the year the Knitting Factory opened, the trumpeter Wynton Marsalis co-founded a jazz program at Lincoln Center. Marsalis (who has won seven Grammy Awards and the 1997 Pulitzer Prize for music and is the artistic director of the Lincoln Center Jazz Orchestra) is a jazz classicist, or purist, whose definition of "real" jazz excludes the

AACM's varieties and others that have emerged since the 1960s. "I remember people like Wynton—whether it was Wynton per se or some other people—saying that my music wasn't jazz," Melford said. "I never set out to be a 'jazz musician.' I just set out to play music. Certainly the influence from the AACM was creative, improvised music, and experimental composition, and that dovetailed with the whole downtown aesthetic. . . . I became known as a jazz musician. I just naturally fell into that genre. . . . I play at jazz venues, I play at jazz festivals, my music is sold in the jazz department of the record store, I'm played on jazz radio stations, I'm reviewed by jazz journalists. And yet there are still some more mainstream jazz musicians that claim I don't play jazz. And I'm fine with that." Melford concluded that those who insist that jazz should have certain characteristics—such as what is known as an eighth-note swing feel—will not think of most of her music as jazz. Melford, along with many others, however, thinks of jazz as music that "incorporates a lot of possibilities, that's always incorporated other kinds of music." Among those who hold a similar view is the historian and musician Ted Gioia, who wrote in his book *The History of Jazz* (1997), "Impure at its birth, jazz grew ever more so as it evolved. Its history is marked by a fondness for musical miscegenation, by its desire to couple with other styles and idioms, producing new, radically different progeny. In its earliest form, jazz showed an ability to assimilate the blues, the rag, the march and other idioms; as it evolved, it transformed a host of even more disparate sounds and styles. It showed no pretensions, mixing as easily with vernacular musics—the American popular song, the Cuban son [a style with roots in both Spain and Africa], the Brazilian samba, the Argentinean tango—as with concert-hall fare. Jazz in its contemporary form bears traces of all these passages. It is the most glorious of mongrels."

After Melford returned to New York, "the filter of my Indian experience," as she called it, influenced her compositions. Her works did not sound like Indian music, but they differed from what she had written before her residency in Calcutta: they were, she said, "denser and had a lot more levels and layers of activity going on." Her new compositions reflected to some degree the out-of-doors cacophony that is ever-present in Calcutta, the second-largest metropolitan area in India and the ninth-largest in the world, where the constant honking of car horns, ringing of bicycle bells, and other traffic noise and the shouts of merchants and hagglers added up to an "overload of the senses," in her words.

In the last decade Melford has recorded a variety of albums and toured with many musicians. Prominent among the latter, for about five years, were Leroy Jenkins and Joseph Jarman. Their collaboration was important for her, Melford said, "because I was actually on the bandstand with two people who had been my mentors." The trio's only album

was titled *Equal Interest* (2000). Melford has recorded two highly acclaimed duet albums with Marty Ehrlich: *Yet Can Spring* (2001) and *Spark!* (2007). Early in 2006 Melford joined the bassist Mark Dresser and the drummer Matt Wilson to form Trio M (for their first initials); they released *Big Picture* in 2007. Although its members are busy with many other projects, the group is still active. After attending one of their live performances, Nate Chinen wrote for the *New York Times* (February 2, 2008), "Trio M is a band with a loving commitment to the jazz avant-garde, especially as it was expressed in the 1970s, a sort of frontier era." Melford describes Trio M's music as merging "groove-based music" with "experimental music." She said that she and her partners rarely talk of arrangements; rather, they have a nearly telepathic rapport. "It's one of my favorite projects right now," Melford said. No date has been set for the release of Trio M's most recent album.

Melford is a member of various other bands as well, including the experimental, electro-acoustic, Indian-influenced Be Bread, which has released two albums: *The Image of Your Body* (2006) and *The Whole Tree Gone* (2010). She occasionally performs live with the group Happy Whistlings, which formed in 2008. She has also released albums, as bandleader, with the Crush Trio (*Dance Beyond the Color*, 2000) and the quintet the Tent (*Where the Two Worlds Touch*, 2004).

Melford joined the avant-garde pianist and composer Satoko Fujii to make *Under the Water* (2009). Entirely improvised, the album was Melford's first two-piano project; it contains three duets and a solo by each woman. Among many other enthusiastic reviewers of *Under the Water* was *Lucid Culture*'s (May 21, 2009, on-line), who described it as "one of the most exciting piano albums of recent years" and as "an intense, often ferociously haunting yet sometimes extremely funny album." "Both pianists use the entirety of the piano, rapping out percussion on the case and manipulating the inside strings for effects ranging from something approximating an autoharp, to a singing saw," the writer noted. Jordan Richardson, the reviewer for blogcritics.org (August 10, 2009), wrote, "Those used to standard song progressions and delicate piano chords might be put off by Fujii and Melford's unstructured and tense playing, but the process is ultimately satisfying. . . . Fujii and Melford perform with urgency and honesty, conducting their individual performances as responses to the other and allowing true imagination to bloom through the splendour of sound." Thomas R. Erdmann wrote for *jazzreview.com* (2009), "For Melford fans this disc is yet another essential tome in her legacy, for fans of totally improvised music this recording shows how it should be done, and for practitioners of free jazz let this recording guide and show you the errors so many of you create."

Melford has received many grants and commissions; the latter include several from dance companies. In 2004 she left New York City to join the Music Department at the University of California at Berkeley as an assistant professor of improvisation and jazz. That job, she said, has not put a damper on her touring. Melford lives in Berkeley.

—D.K.

Suggested Reading: allaboutjazz.com; *Chicago Sun-Times* p16 Oct. 13, 1996; jazzreview.com; music.berkeley.edu; myramelford.com; *New York Times* C p18 Oct. 8, 1996

Selected Recordings: as leader/composer—*Jump*, 1990; *Now & Now*, 1991; *Even the Sounds Shine*, 1995; *The Same River, Twice*, 1996; *Above Blue*, 1999; *Dance Beyond the Color*, 2000; *Where the Two Worlds Touch*, 2004; *The Image of Your Body*, 2006; as co-leader/collaborator—*Eleven Ghosts*, 1997; *Equal Interest*, 2000; *Yet Can Spring*, 2001; *Spark!*, 2007; *Big Picture*, 2007; *Under the Water*, 2009

Miller, Geoffrey

1965– Psychologist

Address: University of New Mexico, Psychology Dept., MSC03 2220, Albuquerque, NM 87131-1161

Evolutionary psychology is a relatively new field of study that seeks "to discover and understand the design of the human mind," according to an online primer published on the Web site of the University of California at Santa Barbara. "Evolutionary psychology is an *approach* to psychology, in which knowledge and principles from evolutionary biology are put to use in research on the structure of the human mind. . . . In this view, the mind is a set of information-processing machines that were designed by natural selection to solve adaptive problems faced by our hunter-gatherer ancestors. This way of thinking about the brain, mind, and behavior is changing how scientists approach old topics, and opening up new ones."

In 2000 the evolutionary psychologist Geoffrey Miller gained international recognition among scientists and the general public with the publication of his first book, *The Mating Mind: How Sexual Choice Shaped the Evolution of Human Nature*. In his book Miller made the important distinction between natural selection (the competition to survive in an ever-changing environment) and sexual selection (the competition to reproduce). Each process is a part of evolution, and Charles Darwin wrote extensively about both. But since Darwin, evolutionary biologists, in their attempts to understand the unique characteristics of the human brain, have focused mainly on the process of natural selection—even though, when it came to animals, they considered both natural and sexual se-

lection. Through research and many experiments, Miller developed the theory that the elements that distinguish humans from animals—for example, the tendency to create art, poetry, and music, and the capacity for wit, humor, and kindness—were shaped largely by the process of sexual selection, or courtship. *The Mating Mind* received fairly good reviews, although some critics expressed their reservations about the speculative nature of Miller's theory. That theory was sometimes misunderstood or oversimplified by the general public and various journalists, some of whom argued that it makes no allowances for people's free will. In fact, Miller does not disregard choice but examines its complex biological and psychological nature. The question he examines is not whether people choose but how and why they do so.

In *The Mating Mind* Miller wrote, "The time is ripe for more ambitious theories of human nature. Our species has never been richer, better educated, more numerous, or more aware of our common historical origin and common planetary fate. As our self-confidence has grown, our need for comforting myths has waned. Since the Darwinian revolution, we recognize that the cosmos was not made for our convenience. But the Darwinian revolution has not yet captured nature's last citadel—human nature." He continued, "In the 1990s the new science of evolutionary psychology made valiant attempts. It views human nature as a set of biological adaptations, and tries to discover which problems of living and reproducing those adaptations evolved to solve. It grounds human behavior in evolutionary biology. Some critics believe that evolutionary psychology goes too far and attempts to explain too much. I think it does not go far enough."

In 2009 Miller published *Spent: Sex, Evolution, and Consumer Behavior*, which elaborates on his theory, particularly with regard to how sexual selection manifests itself in consumer behavior. In short, Miller argued, people buy things not only to show off their wealth or taste but also to demonstrate such personality traits as kindness or a sense of humor. Whether such a consumerist approach is effective—it is not, according to Miller—is beside the point; he is interested in consumerism as a manifestation of sexual selection. *Spent*, like Miller's first book, was written for lay readers, and it received a fair amount of attention in the press. Kate Douglass, writing for *New Scientist* (June 13, 2009), called the book "intelligent, engaging, exasperating and funny." Miller is an associate professor in the Psychology Department at the University of New Mexico at Albuquerque.

Geoffrey Miller was born in 1965 in Cincinnati, Ohio. He studied biology and psychology at Columbia University, in New York City, earning a B.A. degree in 1987 with an honors thesis titled "Cognitive Mechanisms of Metaphor Comprehension." He then attended Stanford University, in California, where he met some of the seminal figures in the field of evolutionary psychology: David Buss, John Tooby, and Leda Cosmides. While at

Norman Johnson, courtesy of Random House

Geoffrey Miller

Stanford Miller became interested in the question of why the human brain had tripled in size over the last two million years. He reasoned that natural selection alone—that is, the competition to survive—could not explain the size increase. His doctoral dissertation, "Evolution of the Human Brain Through Runaway Sexual Selection," offered an explanation. "Miller's theory . . . suggests that humans may have ended up with big, creative brains for similar reasons that a male peacock has a gigantic showy tail. Both may be the results of the irrational force of 'runaway sexual selection,'" Rosie Mestel wrote for *New Scientist* (December 23, 1995). "According to Miller, the story goes something like this: A few million years ago, we had brains a third the size of the 1,350 cubic centimeter whoppers we carry around today. But somewhere, in some group of our ancestors, females began to prefer males [who] could do creative, novel things—amusingly imitate a member of the clan, perhaps, or come up with a new idea. The creative males found more mates than competitors and they passed on both their creative genes and the preference for creative mates. Their creative sons had even more success in finding mates, and so evolution 'ran away,' creativity and the preference for it locked together."

Miller was awarded his Ph.D. degree in 1993 and conducted his postdoctoral research at the School of Cognitive and Computing Sciences at the University of Sussex, in Brighton, England, where he was part of the Evolutionary and Adaptive Systems Group. He then took on a series of academic posts, lecturing at the University of Nottingham for several months in 1995 and then joining the Max Planck Institute for Psychological Research, in Mu-

nich, Germany, where he remained until August 1996. Miller next returned to England and spent four years as a senior research fellow at the Centre for Economic Learning and Social Evolution at University College London. In 2000 he moved back to the U.S. briefly, to join the faculty of the University of California, Los Angeles (UCLA), where he served as a visiting associate professor. Upon his return to Great Britain, in January 2001, he became an associate researcher at the Centre for the Philosophy of the Natural and Social Sciences at the London School of Economics. In August 2001 Miller joined the faculty of the University of New Mexico as an assistant professor, and he was promoted to associate professor in 2008. A popular professor, he has remained at the university ever since, with the exception of a 2009 sabbatical during which he worked as a visiting scientist at the Queensland Institute of Medical Research, in Australia.

In his first book, *The Mating Mind*, Miller asserted that the process of sexual selection has greatly shaped the human mind over time. He wrote in the first chapter, "The human mind evolved somehow. The question scientists have asked for over a century is: How? Most people equate evolution with 'survival of the fittest,' and indeed most theories about the mind's evolution have tried to find survival advantages for everything that makes humans unique. . . . The survival advantages of better technology, trade, and knowledge seem obvious, so many believe the mind's evolution must have been technophilic and survivalist. Ever since the Darwinian revolution, this survivalist view has seemed the only scientifically respectable possibility. Yet it remains unsatisfying. It leaves too many riddles unexplained." While biologists have established that many traits—such as a fear of snakes or an aversion to bitter tastes—provided an evolutionary advantage to our ancestors, Miller asserted that from a purely biological perspective, elaborate language, love of art and music, humor, and morality seem to be wastes of energy in that they have little or nothing to do with finding acceptable sources of nutrition or avoiding predators. "This book proposes that our minds evolved not just as survival machines, but as courtship machines," he wrote. "Every one of our ancestors managed not just to live for a while, but to convince at least one sexual partner to have enough sex to produce offspring. Those proto-humans [who] did not attract sexual interest did not become our ancestors, no matter how good they were at surviving. Darwin realized this, and argued that evolution is driven not just by natural selection for survival, but by an equally important process that he called *sexual selection through mate choice.* Following his insight, I shall argue that the most distinctive aspects of our minds evolved largely through the sexual choices our ancestors made."

The book received largely mixed reviews. In an assessment for the *Financial Times* (April 29, 2000, on-line), Galen Strawson called the author "consistently penetrating and ingenious," but wrote, "Miller's book will probably be misunderstood in every possible way. The passion with which he traces almost everything about the human mind to sexual selection will annoy many, and he offers plenty of hostages to critics, mixing outstanding sober exposition of the mechanisms of sexual selection with speculations about its role in our capacities for morality, language and creativity that range from deep to wild. There's nothing wrong with exuberance in a snapshot of a provisional theory, and I am confident that Miller is largely right in his conclusions, but he does generalize most incautiously."

In *Spent* Miller examined consumerism and argued that the goods we buy are meant to display not only our wealth and status but such qualities as intelligence, creativity, kindness, and wit—the same traits that he had previously characterized as being the result of sexual selection. "Suppose, during a date, you casually say, 'The sugar maples in Harvard Yard were so beautiful every fall term.' Here's what you're signaling, as translated by Dr. Miller: 'My S.A.T. scores were sufficiently high (roughly 720 out of 800) that I could get admitted, so my I.Q. is above 135, and I had sufficient conscientiousness, emotional stability and intellectual openness to pass my classes. Plus, I can recognize a tree,'" John Tierney explained for the *New York Times* (May 18, 2009, on-line). "Or suppose a young man, after listening to the specifications of the newest iPhone or hearing about a BMW's 'Servotronic variable-ratio power steering,' says to himself, 'Those features sound awesome.' Here's Dr. Miller's translation: 'Those features can be talked about in ways that will display my general intelligence to potential mates and friends, who will bow down before my godlike technopowers, which rival those of Iron Man himself.' Most of us will insist there are other reasons for going to Harvard or buying a BMW or an iPhone—and there are, of course. The education and the products can yield many kinds of rewards. But Dr. Miller says that much of the pleasure we derive from products stems from the unconscious instinct that they will either enhance or signal our fitness by demonstrating intelligence or some of the Big Five personality traits: openness, conscientiousness, agreeableness, stability and extraversion."

Miller pointed out in the book, however, that people greatly overestimate how much others are influenced by such consumer displays. "We evolved as social primates who hardly ever encountered strangers in prehistory," he wrote, according to Tierney. "So we instinctively treat all strangers as if they're potential mates or friends or enemies. But your happiness and survival today don't depend on your relationships with strangers. It doesn't matter whether you get a nanosecond of deference from a shopkeeper or a stranger in an airport."

Spent, like *The Mating Mind*, attracted mixed reviews. In an assessment for *Time* (May 21, 2009, on-line), M.J. Stephey wrote: "Like Sigmund Freud, Miller sees sex everywhere; all our acquisitions of personal goods, according to Miller, are motivated by the primal desire for procreation, pleasure or both. Though he advocates abolishing income taxes in favor of a 'consumption tax' and learning to buy secondhand, he isn't a utopian hippie radical either. 'Unlike many malcontents,' Miller writes, 'I consider the three best inventions of all time to be money, markets and media.' But while Miller does his best to avoid sounding too academic . . . his broad, rambling arguments read at times like a college professor's lecture notes. Worse still, his ideas don't seem particularly groundbreaking. In fact, some seem downright antiquated: Men buy Porsches to project power, women use eyeliner to look pretty, and everyone seeks attention without realizing they're going about it all wrong. But if Miller's ideas don't quite hit the mark, don't blame him. 'Consumerism is hard to describe when it's the ocean and we're the plankton,' he argues in his defense." In a review for *Seed Magazine* (May 15, 2009, on-line), Jonathan Gottschall opined, "Miller is an entertaining and charming guide, moving with a nimble insouciance across domains of science, popular culture, and high and low art. And there is an undeniable power in his analogy between the way that animals—including humans—market themselves via sexually selected traits, and the way that people try to send exaggerated signals of their personal merits through the products they display. For Miller the process of runaway sexual selection that gave rise to energetically wasteful ornaments like the peacock's tail and antlers of the Irish Elk is precisely what gives rise to Hummers and McMansions."

As with his previous book, Miller engaged in some speculation, but he also cited many experiments. In one experiment he and his fellow researchers divided their test subjects into two groups, each made up of males and females. Those in the first group were shown photos of buildings and asked to write about the weather; those in the second group were shown photos of good-looking members of the opposite sex and asked to describe in writing an ideal date with someone whose picture they had seen. Then the individuals in each group were asked two questions: what would they do with $5,000 in extra cash, and how many of 60 hypothetical hours of leisure time would they devote in a single month to volunteering. In the group asked to write about an ideal date, women expressed a higher interest than men in engaging in volunteer work (as indicated by the number of hours per month), which would be considered displays of kindness, while men expressed a greater interest than women in purchasing flashy items, such as expensive watches (as indicated by the amount of money they would spend on such things), which would be considered displays of wealth, taste, or style. Neither the men nor the women in the group that wrote about the weather expressed significant interest in lavish spending or doing volunteer work. "Based on this result, it looks as though the sexes do, indeed, have different strategies for showing off," a writer for the *Economist* (August 4, 2007) concluded. "Moreover, they do not waste their resources by behaving like that all the time. Only when it counts sexually are men profligate and women helpful."

Miller, who has been hired as a consultant by various major companies, including Proctor & Gamble and Coca-Cola, is currently on the editorial boards of the journals *Intelligence* and *Evolutionary Psychology*. In 2007 he co-edited *Mating Intelligence: Sex, Relationships, and the Mind's Reproductive System*, which includes such chapters as "Mating Intelligence in Personal Ads," "Deception and Self-Deception as Strategies in Short- and Long-Term Mating," and "How Having Children Affects Mating Psychology."

In 2008 Miller received an Ig Nobel Prize in Economics for his article "Ovulatory Cycle Effects on Tip Earnings by Lap Dancers: Economic Evidence for Human Estrus?" Published in the journal *Evolution and Human Behavior*, the article posited that exotic dancers earn higher tips when they are ovulating. The Ig Nobel Prizes, according to the official Web site, "honor achievements that first make people laugh, and then make them think. The prizes are intended to celebrate the unusual, honor the imaginative—and spur people's interest in science, medicine, and technology."

—D.K.

Suggested Reading: (London) *Guardian* p9 May 6, 2000, p6 Aug. 8, 2009; *New Scientist* p28 Dec. 23, 1995, p47 June 13, 2009; *New York Times* (on-line) June 11, 2000, May 19, 2009

Selected Books: *The Mating Mind: How Sexual Choice Shaped the Evolution of Human Nature*, 2000; *Spent: Sex, Evolution, and Consumer Behavior*, 2009; as co-editor—*Mating Intelligence: Sex, Relationships, and the Mind's Reproductive System*, 2007

Alberto E. Rodriguez/Getty Images

Mo'Nique

(moh-NEEK)

Dec. 11, 1967– Comedian; actress; talk-show host

Address: c/o The Collective, 9100 Wilshire Blvd., Suite 700, West Beverly Hills, CA 91202

Since the late 1980s the Academy Award–winning actress, comedian, and talk-show host Mo'Nique has used her sassy, raucous humor to attack the limiting beauty standards set by the entertainment and fashion industries. At around 220 pounds (her height has been reported as everything from five-foot-two to five-foot-six), the African-American star makes no apologies for her size-20 figure. "Hollywood says [that] to be beautiful, you must be white, a size zero, blonde hair and blue eyes, and that's what beauty is . . . ," Mo'Nique told Kimberly C. Roberts for the *Philadelphia Tribune* (April 7, 2006). "That's crazy!" Plus-size women, Mo'Nique said to Ed Bark for the *Dallas Morning News* (August 6, 2005), are "going to take the word ['fat'] back. We're going to make it our word. I am a fat girl, which means I'm fabulous and thick and not ashamed of it. So when someone says to me, 'Hey, fat girl,' I go, 'Thank you very much. You noticed.' I'm very proud of that."

For her stand-up comedy routines, Mo'Nique mines her personal life for material. "I have never written a joke—ever . . . ," she told Bob Longino for the *Atlanta Journal-Constitution* (September 2, 2001). "I'm not the typical joke teller. I don't tell why the dog crossed the street. I just talk about my life. I talk about being a big woman, being married, having kids. Just everything that every day affects Mo'Nique." "If you can laugh at yourself and your situation I think people find that funny," she told Bridget Byrne for the BPI Entertainment News Wire (April 6, 2000, on-line). Mo'Nique first gained national recognition when she starred as Nikki Parker on the television comedy series *The Parkers* (1999–2004). A spin-off of the 1990s sitcom *Moesha*, *The Parkers* followed the antics of Nikki and her daughter, Kim (played by Countess Vaughn), as both attended college. Although the spin-off was conceived as a vehicle for Vaughn, who had portrayed one of the most popular characters on *Moesha*, Mo'Nique's performance as the wild, straight-talking Nikki soon became the show's main attraction. Ralph Farquhar, the executive producer and co-creator of *The Parkers*, told David Zurawik for the *Baltimore Sun* (August 30, 1999) about Mo'Nique, "She's fresh, she's just completely fresh. The thing about Mo'Nique is that there's an honesty there that truly comes across on stage. You can't manufacture that. Either a performer has it or she doesn't."

After a series of mostly comedic roles in television and movies, Mo'Nique landed the part of Mary Jones, a horrifically abusive mother, in the 2009 independent film drama *Precious*, adapted from the 1996 novel *Push*, by Sapphire. Directed by Lee Daniels, the film follows an illiterate, obese 16-year-old, Claireece Precious Jones (played by Gabourey Sidibe), through her daily struggles in the Harlem neighborhood of New York City. Pregnant for the second time by her own father, she is also subjected to constant physical, mental, and sexual abuse from her mother (Mo'Nique). The film has been lauded for its realistic portrayal of abuse and its ultimately inspirational message; Mo'Nique, too, has been praised, for her ability to add dimension to such a vile character. "Given her range of leisure interests—smoking, cursing, channel surfing, baby tossing, munching pigs' feet, and throwing televisions down the stairs—there is no reason that the character [Mary Jones] should be more than a vicious cartoon," the *New Yorker* critic Anthony Lane wrote in his review (November 9, 2009). "But Mo'Nique gives tremendous life to this dead soul, makes you wonder where her own misery sprouted from, and closes the proceedings with a monologue of selfishness so storm-driven that for a second, despite ourselves, we are almost swept away."

Mo'Nique, who has said that she was sexually abused by the elder of her two brothers as a young girl (she has long been estranged from him), had no hesitation about portraying the monstrous Mary. "Sapphire's book was the most honest book I have ever read. . . . I thought doing this part would be healing for me and for others," she explained to Joy Sewing for the *Houston Chronicle* (November 2, 2009). "Sexual and verbal abuse is happening to our children every day, but we continue to keep very quiet. This movie will hopefully start people talking." Mo'Nique has won numerous awards for her portrayal of Mary Jones, including the 2010 Golden Globe for best performance by an actress in a supporting role in a motion picture and the 2010 Academy Award in the same category.

Mo'Nique currently hosts her own late-night talk show. The *Mo'Nique Show* premiered in October 2009 on Black Entertainment Television (BET).

The actress and comedian was born Monique Imes on December 11, 1967 in Woodlawn, Maryland, just outside Baltimore, the youngest of the four children of Steven Imes Jr., a clinical psychologist and drug counselor, and Alice Imes, an engineer. Mo'Nique—who added an apostrophe to her name when she began performing in public—has

attributed her wit and foul mouth to her relatives. "My Aunt Bessie, Uncle Whip and my Aunt Tina are the funniest people I know," she told Bob Longino. "Bessie is the best cusser in the United States. She does combos you wouldn't believe." Mo'Nique says that she has been overweight since birth. "I was a fat baby coming out, and I'm going to be a fat baby leaving," she told Bob Longino. "I've always been comfortable with that. When I was in school, I was always the most popular, the best-dressed. I had boyfriends. There are a million size 2s in Hollywood, but how many 22s?" She has credited her healthy self-image to her father. "I never thought I was different. My father always told me I was beautiful and that was all I knew," she told Shantella Sherman for the *Philadelphia Tribune* (September 5, 2004). "He said, 'Hold your head up. You are the prettiest girl in the world. Let people see that face.' So all these years later, I'm still holding it up."

Mo'Nique graduated from Milford Mill High School (now Milford Mill Academy) in 1985. She then enrolled at Morgan State University, in Baltimore, which she left without graduating. In those years she worked a series of jobs, ranging from bank teller to plus-size model to phone-sex operator. ("I monitored the calls to see if the girls were doing their job right," she explained to Walt Belcher for the August 30, 1999 edition of the *Tampa [Florida] Tribune*. "I was like quality control.") She later found steady work as a customer-service representative for the telecommunications company MCI. During that time Mo'Nique married Shalon Watkins, with whom she had a son, Shalon Jr.

Although Mo'Nique claims that she has always loved attention, she said to Tom Feran for the Cleveland, Ohio, *Plain Dealer* (August 30, 1999), "I was never the class clown, I was always very prissy. I just wanted to be cute and fabulous and sit there and let the little boys look at me. I never realized I was funny until my brother [Steven III], who is now my manager, told me that I was funny." It was only after Steven was booed off stage during an open-mike night at Baltimore's Comedy Factory Outlet in the late 1980s that Mo'Nique discovered her comedic talent. After she teased her brother about his poor performance, "he dared me to go out and do it, and the following week, I went out . . . and my first night on stage I got a standing ovation," she recalled to Feran. "Someone offered to pay me $25 to do a show the following week and my brother negotiated $30, so I became a professional comedian."

Mo'Nique soon began to perform in small comedy clubs. Deciding that Baltimore was not a hospitable place for a young, black, female comic, she applied at MCI for a transfer to Atlanta, Georgia, known for fostering the talent of black artists and entertainers. After moving, Mo'Nique performed in comedy clubs around that city and along the East Coast. "I would get in my car and drive [to the gigs]. I would do comedy Friday, Saturday and Sunday and have to be back at work on Monday," she recalled to Sandra Crockett for the *Baltimore Sun* (November 19, 1994). "I played everything from red, redneck barnyards to deep and dank places where the people were so drunk they didn't even know I was there, to . . . concert halls. Wherever there was a show, I would go. I was out there by myself and I was saying prayers all across the country."

After a year of working full-time during the week and performing every weekend, Mo'Nique left MCI to pursue comedy. She moved back to Baltimore with her young son; by that time her marriage to Watkins, who had physically abused her, had ended. Explaining why she had stayed with Watkins for years, Mo'Nique told Nicholas Fonseca for *Entertainment Weekly* (May 2, 2003) that she mistakenly believed she could reform her husband. The comedian later incorporated her experience as an abused wife into her stand-up routines. The abuse "was something that happened to me, and I almost appreciate that it happened because I know now that I will never allow it to happen again," she told Steve Hedgpeth for the Newark, New Jersey, *Star-Ledger* (April 29, 2001). "In loving someone, sometimes you do things that you don't think you'll do. I never thought that I would allow a man to hit me, and I stayed long enough to get my lip busted. So when I talk about it [on stage], I'm saying to women, 'Baby, there's a way out. You can still be powerful and successful.'"

Upon Mo'Nique's return to Maryland, she and her brother, along with a business partner, opened Mo'Nique's, a comedy club and restaurant in downtown Baltimore. She soon became co-host, with Sonny Andre, of a morning radio show on WWIN (95.9 FM). In 1989 Mo'Nique made her television debut, performing her stand-up act on *Showtime at the Apollo* and later appearing on *Russell Simmons' Def Comedy Jam* and the BET channel's *Comic View*. After appearing at the Montreal Comedy Festival in 1997, Mo'Nique was offered a talk-show deal by the Fox television network, but plans for the show fell through. Meanwhile, she had caught the attention of Larry Lyttle, then president of the production company Big Ticket Television. (Big Ticket, which produced the shows *Moesha* and *The Parkers*, was absorbed by Paramount after Lyttle's departure, in 2003.) "He watched my tape for 10 seconds and he said, 'You're a sitcom star. If you can act, you'll have your own show,'" Mo'Nique recalled to Tom Feran.

In 1999 Mo'Nique made guest appearances on two episodes of the sitcom *Moesha*. The title character of the show, which ran from 1996 to 2001, was a Los Angeles, California, high-school student (played by the R&B singer Brandy). Mo'Nique's role was that of Nikki Parker, the loud, uninhibited mother of Moesha's best friend, Kim (Countess Vaughn). Later that year Vaughn and Mo'Nique were given their own spin-off series, *The Parkers* (1999–2004). Its premise was that Nikki had been forced to drop out of high school when she became

pregnant with Kim; she later earned her G.E.D. and enrolled, to her daughter's mortification, at the same college as Kim.

Soon after its debut *The Parkers* eclipsed *Moesha* in ratings, and by 2000 it had become the number-one network-television series among African-American viewers. (By contrast, the show tied for last place, number 144, among white viewers.) During its first season the show brought a 68 percent increase in viewership for its time slot. *The Parkers* remained hugely popular among African-American and teenage viewers throughout its run. For her performance as Nikki, Mo'Nique earned a BET Comedy Award nomination and won four NAACP Image Awards for outstanding actress in a comedy series, in 2001, 2002, 2004, and 2005.

Despite the show's success, many television critics—most of whom were white—criticized *The Parkers* for its stereotypical depiction of loud, crass, oversexed black characters. The critic Ken Parish Perkins, who is African-American, wrote for the *Fort Worth (Texas) Star-Telegram* (June 13, 2000), "The major problem with *The Parkers* is the same old story when it comes to sitcoms where the cast is largely black and the jokes are steeped in the tradition of black humor: raunchy, over-the-top, loud. . . . Mo'Nique, as Nikki, and Vaughn, as Kim, massacre the English language with 'dats' for 'that' and 'gons' for 'gone,' and usually to loud, animated squeals of studio audience laughter." Mo'Nique countered the criticisms by pointing to sitcoms comprised largely of white cast members. "I just don't understand why Michael Richards [who played Kramer on the much-lauded sitcom *Seinfeld*] can be silly and exaggerated and be called a great slapstick star, but as soon as black people show the same mannerisms, we're a disgrace to the race," she complained to Perkins. "So you're telling me that if people see five characters playing over the top . . . that we will be perceived, as an entire race, as over-the-top people? That's insane." In another interview, when a reporter commented on Nikki Parker's outrageous behavior, Mo'Nique, as she recalled to Bob Longino, grew indignant. "I said, 'Now, you're . . . telling me that [Nikki Parker,] a black woman who is a single mother, who had a child when she was young and is now going back to college and is a major, major player at this makeup firm . . . What's buffoonery about that?'" She went on to question why shows such as *The Parkers* are "always labeled as a black show" while the sitcom *Friends*, for example, is never called a "white" show. "It's just *Friends*, which makes no sense," because the characters on *Friends* are "in the heart of New York City. And you never see any other nationality of people. Well, come on!"

Mo'Nique made her first film appearance in the 2000 comedy *3 Strikes*. The following year she appeared in the comedy/drama *Baby Boy* (2001) and the romantic comedy *Two Can Play That Game* (2001), starring Vivica A. Fox. During the summers of 2001 and 2003, Mo'Nique toured with her fellow stand-up comedians Laura Hayes, Sommore, and

Adele Givens as the Queens of Comedy, the female counterpart to the Kings of Comedy, made up of Steve Harvey, Bernie Mac, D.L. Hughley, and Cedric the Entertainer. Segments of their first tour were filmed and broadcast on Showtime as the *Original Queens of Comedy* in 2001. An audio recording of the same name was nominated in 2001 for a Grammy Award for best comedy album.

Mo'Nique continued to take small roles in films, including the Steven Seagal action picture *Half Past Dead* (2002); the comedy *Good Fences* (2003), with Whoopi Goldberg and Danny Glover; and *Soul Plane* (2004). In 2004 she starred in the comedic film *Hair Show*, in which she played Peaches, who must win a hair-styling contest in order to keep her salon. Mo'Nique took on her first prominent dramatic role in Lee Daniels's independent thriller *Shadowboxer* (2005). She portrayed Precious, a crack addict in love with a white doctor. Mo'Nique later revealed that her sister had once struggled with drug addiction, and that the actress had drawn on memories of her sister's experience to play the role.

After another dramatic turn in the 2005 action film *Domino*, Mo'Nique had her first starring role, in *Phat Girlz* (2006). (She also served as executive producer.) That comedy follows Jazmin Biltmore (Mo'Nique), an aspiring fashion designer who struggles with her self-esteem and eventually finds romance with a handsome Nigerian doctor. Despite praise for Mo'Nique's acting ability, *Phat Girlz* failed to win over critics. "Equal parts low-mileage star vehicle and heavy-handed fantasy fulfillment, [*Phat Girlz*] isn't likely to advance budding film career of top-billed Mo'Nique, a vet standup and sitcom performer whose sassy, brassy shtick isn't nearly enough to support material this insubstantial," Joe Leydon wrote in his review for *Daily Variety* (April 10, 2006). Comparing the film to a "scrumptious-looking" cake that turns out to be made with artificial sweetener, Kathy Cano Murillo wrote for the *Arizona Republic* (April 8, 2006, on-line), "*Phat Girlz* has the same disappointing effect. It's a chick flick with good intentions about self-image and body size, yet it leaves an icky aftertaste. . . . Mo'Nique and her co-stars deliver an arsenal of laughs, and the overall message of triumph and learning to accept one's self is admirable. Unfortunately, those elements are not strong enough to cleanse the *Phat Girlz* palate." Many reviewers criticized the film's poor production quality (the multiple flaws included visible microphone packs and bad lighting), and more than one pointed out a major contradiction: "In a movie dedicated to the idea that skinny is not the only kind of beautiful," Chris Hewitt wrote for the *Saint Paul (Minnesota) Pioneer Press* (April 7, 2006), "why are all the men uniformly buff, shirtless and oiled?"

Mo'Nique, whose attempt to start her own clothing line had failed, signed on to become a spokeswoman for the plus-size women's fashion line JMS (Just My Size) in 2005. As part of their partnership, JMS sponsored Mo'Nique's reality-television program *Mo'Nique's Fat Chance*, which aired on the Oxygen network. From 2005 to 2007 Mo'Nique hosted and executive-produced the program, on which 10 plus-sized women per season competed in a beauty pageant, whose winner was crowned Miss F.A.T. ("Fabulous and Thick"). The show quickly became Oxygen's highest-rated original program, attracting more female viewers in the coveted 18-to-49-year-old demographic than any of the network's previous series. *Fat Chance* "was the first full-figure reality television beauty pageant," Mo'Nique told Aldore D. Collier for *Jet* (August 8, 2005). "One reporter asked, 'Why are you promoting women to be unhealthy?' At no time am I promoting anyone being unhealthy. People just think that because we're big women that we're automatically unhealthy. I've always promoted being healthy, exercising and walking." Pointing to the acceptance of very thin women in entertainment and fashion, she added, "It goes both ways. A woman weighing 98 pounds is unhealthy, but that's our society. My whole point is, 'Love the skin you're in.'"

In 2007 Mo'Nique performed in the televised comedy special *Mo'Nique: I Coulda Been Your Cellmate*. The stand-up show was filmed at a women's correctional facility in Ohio. She also hosted the VH1 show *Flavor of Love Girls: Charm School*, on which she attempted to teach etiquette to 13 women who had been contestants on the VH1 reality dating series *Flavor of Love*. *Charm School* became VH1's third-highest-rated series ever and drew in 4.1 million viewers for its finale. The following year Mo'Nique had a role in the Martin Lawrence comedy *Welcome Home, Roscoe Jenkins*.

The intensity of Mo'Nique's performance as an abusive mother in *Precious: Based on the Novel Push by Sapphire* has won her a new level of attention. She received near-universal praise and an Oscar for her work. She won more than a dozen other awards as well, including best-supporting-actress honors from the Stockholm International Film Festival, the Los Angeles Film Critics Association, the New York Film Critics Circle, and the National Society of Film Critics. She was honored with the Special Jury Prize at the Sundance Film Festival in January 2009 and, a year later, received both the Golden Globe Award and the Screen Actors Guild Award for outstanding performance by a female actor in a supporting role. Upon accepting the Golden Globe Award, Mo'Nique dedicated it to victims of abuse. "I celebrate this award with all the Preciouses, with all the Marys—I celebrate this award with every person that's ever been touched," she said at the awards ceremony, on January 17, 2010. "It's now time to tell. And it's okay."

Controversy has arisen among Mo'Nique's fans in recent years over reports that she has lost weight. She revealed that in 2006, when she was 262 pounds, doctors diagnosed her with high blood pressure and warned that her excess weight would shorten her life. Mo'Nique explained to

Margena A. Christian for *Jet* (June 8, 2009), "I decided I had to get some of that [weight] off of me. . . . I had to do something, because I want to be here for a lifetime and enjoy my family." In 2007 the comedian cut red meat from her diet and began exercising. She has firmly insisted, however, that she is not trying to conform to Hollywood beauty standards. "I want to say to big people, 'let's be healthy big people,'" she told Christian. "Everybody can't be a size 0 . . . but let's be healthy." Mo'Nique has since lost more than 40 pounds and has said that she is working on a fitness DVD for larger women who want to become healthier without aspiring to be thin.

The hour-long, late-night *Mo'Nique Show*, which premiered in the fall of 2009, opens with a monologue or skit and features interviews with celebrity guests and musical performances. Mo'Nique tapes the program in Atlanta with her co-host and announcer, the comedian Rodney Perry. She told David Hiltbrand for the *Philadelphia Inquirer* (November 12, 2009, on-line) that she intends to offer viewers a "penthouse party," complete with a house band, Big Jim and the Penthouse Players. Guests on the program have included the actors Danny Glover, Vivica A. Fox, and Terrence Howard and the musicians Lenny Kravitz, Jill Scott, Lil Wayne, and Patti Labelle. In February 2010 the program won an NAACP Image Award for outstanding talk show.

Mo'Nique has co-authored three books with Sherri McGee McCovey (formerly Sherri A. McGee): the memoir *Skinny Women Are Evil: Notes of a Big Girl in a Small-Minded World* (2003); a cookbook, *Skinny Cooks Can't Be Trusted* (2006); and, for young adults, *Beacon Hills High: A Novel* (2008), about a chunky 13-year-old girl from Baltimore who, after moving because of her father's work, struggles to fit into the thinness-obsessed culture of Los Angeles.

Following her divorce from Shalon Watkins, Mo'Nique married Mark Jackson, a barber, in December 1997. The two divorced four years later. On May 20, 2006 she married Sidney Hicks, who had been a close friend of Mo'nique's since they attended high school together. Hicks, who previously worked in corporate sales, is now a television writer and serves as Mo'Nique's business partner. Mo'Nique has two sons, Shalon Jr. and Mark Jr., from her previous marriages. In October 2005 she gave birth to twin boys, Jonathan and David. The twins' father, Hicks, has another son, Michael, from a previous relationship. Mo'Nique and her family live outside Atlanta.

—M.A.S.

Suggested Reading: *Atlanta Journal-Constitution* L p1 Sep. 2, 2001; *Baltimore Sun* D p1 Nov. 19, 1994; *Ebony* p64+ Aug. 2007; *Jet* p60+ Aug. 8, 2005, p36+ June 8, 2009; *New York Times* Arts and Leisure p22 Aug. 5, 2007; *New York Times Magazine* p28 Oct. 25, 2009

Selected Television Shows: *Moesha*, 1999-2000; *The Parkers*, 1999–2004; *The Original Queens of Comedy*, 2001; *Mo'Nique: I Coulda Been Your Cellmate*, 2007; *Mo'Nique's Fat Chance*, 2005–07; *Flavor of Love Girls: Charm School*, 2007; *The Mo'Nique Show*, 2009–

Selected Films: *3 Strikes*, 2000; *Baby Boy*, 2001; *Two Can Play That Game*, 2001; *Half Past Dead*, 2002; *Good Fences*, 2003; *Soul Plane*, 2004; *Hair Show*, 2004; *Shadowboxer*, 2005; *Domino*, 2005; *Phat Girlz*, 2006; *Welcome Home, Roscoe Jenkins*, 2008; *Precious: Based on the Novel Push by Sapphire*, 2009

Selected Books: *Skinny Women Are Evil: Notes of a Big Girl in a Small-Minded World* (with Sherri McGee McCovey), 2003; *Skinny Cooks Can't Be Trusted* (with Sherri McGee McCovey), 2006; *Beacon Hills High: A Novel* (with Sherri McGee McCovey), 2008

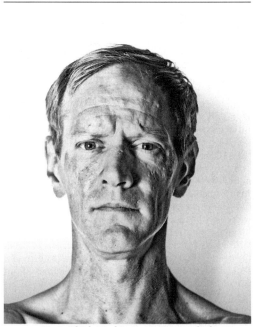

Devin Elijah Washington, courtesy of John Moran

Moran, John

1965– Composer; choreographer; performance artist

Address: c/o Galapagos Art Space, 16 Main St., Brooklyn, NY 11201

"My work is completely based on the idea that every sound in the world must have a melody and a rhythm to exist." Those are the words of John Moran, an experimental composer, choreographer, designer, director, and performer, quoted by Iris

Fanger in the *Boston Herald* (February 21, 1997). "We are surrounded by such beautiful melodies in the most mundane events from the moment we are born. That music comes together to make the experience we call our lives." Moran's works, frequently classified as operas, often do not contain coherent narratives, singing, or even live music, the elements that most people associate with the form. Rather, the scores typically consist of prerecorded sound and music samples, drawn from both everyday life and pop culture, which Moran carefully distorts, repeats, and arranges to create melodies and rhythms. In performances the scores, which can boast as many as 350 distinct sounds per minute, are coupled with painstakingly precise choreography and lip-synching by actors/dancers and are juxtaposed with often disorienting visuals; taken together, the innovative works are intended to produce the kind of excitement sparked by amusement-park rides. Moran has composed and choreographed more than a dozen works that have been performed on large and small stages, nationally and abroad, and has been credited with pioneering a new form of musical theater. In recent years, collaborating with Saori Tsukada, Moran has created works that center on dance.

John Moran was born in 1965 in Lincoln, Nebraska, and was adopted soon afterward. His father worked as a choral conductor and as the dean of arts and sciences at the University of Nebraska; his mother was an opera singer who later became a nurse. Early on Moran developed a taste for opera, performing the traditional children's parts in productions and listening to operas by Mozart and Wagner; as Joseph C. Koenenn reported for New York *Newsday* (July 15, 1990), his "first attempt at an opera was his own version of Wagner's *Parsifal*." He said to Koenenn, "I didn't have any instruments back then, so I did all the music on two cassette players. It wasn't music as much as sound—sound effects, ordinary sounds, a lot of television. I've always lifted a lot of television sounds." Moran was also significantly influenced by his first trip to Disneyland, when he was about seven. Mesmerized by the visual trickery and fantastic settings, he drew blueprints of an amusement park that he dreamed of building at home. (As an adult Moran continues to enjoy amusement parks, regularly visiting them to write and record sounds.)

By his own account Moran had quite a difficult childhood. He dropped out of school at age 13 and, due to what he has called his "violent" behavior, was sent to mental institutions. He later passed high-school equivalency tests. As a teenager Moran spent two years involved in a cult, an experience that would no doubt inform his work *The Manson Family*. "The thing about cult leaders that's so powerful," Moran told Koenenn, "is that they go for young, vulnerable, intelligent kids. . . . I know how powerful those techniques can be. I've lived a lot of my life in isolation. I know what that does, how you can really feel that you are the center of the universe. That's a cult technique." He attended the University of Nebraska but dropped out after two months, after failing in his music classes. "I was so frustrated [in college], because I had been writing pieces for orchestra and all, for a couple of years, but I was flunking out of Music Theory One-oh-one, because I had never really studied the scales and counterpoint techniques," Moran told Koenenn. "It was very embarrassing, to say the least. That was my whole self-worth, my music, and here I couldn't pass, so I quit, and that was my college career. Two months."

After leaving school Moran tape-recorded sounds from life and TV to create musical collages. When the famous avant-garde composer Philip Glass came to Lincoln in 1986 in connection with a performance of his music, Moran telephoned hotels around the city until he got in touch with Glass; he then gave him a tape of his recordings. Glass recalled to Allan Kozinn for the *New York Times* (November 19, 2000), "As I remember it this skinny kid came up and gave me a tape, like all the skinny kids with tapes do, and, believe it or not, I listen to them, at least in a haphazard way. And I was struck right away. This was a born theater creator, even at that age, which was about 20. This is a rare thing." Moran and Glass corresponded regularly for the next three years. At 23 Moran left Nebraska for New York City to pursue a musical career. On the train ride there, he lost all of his savings—$400—to a con artist. When he arrived in New York, with no money and no place to stay, he headed for Glass's apartment. "It sounds like he's exaggerating, but he really did show up on my doorstep," Glass told Patti Hartigan for the *Boston Globe* (February 23, 1997). "He was pretty green, but he had an unwavering devotion to his work. He wasn't just an ordinary kid; he came with a head full of ideas and a complete grasp of the theatrical event." Recognizing Moran's talent, Glass invited him into his home, where he ended up living for the next six years. With Glass's help, Moran met other musicians and composers, including the famous Beat poet Allen Ginsberg and the experimental performer and musician Laurie Anderson. "Philip is my mentor," Moran told Hartigan. "He not only taught me how to tie my shoes, but he taught me how to deal with people. He took a lot of time, and he's the kindest man I ever met."

Glass introduced Moran to Bob McGrath, the artistic director of the renowned avant-garde Ridge Theater Company. After listening to a tape of Moran's work, McGrath agreed to direct his first major opera, *The Jack Benny Program* (1989), performed at New York's LaMama Theater. The hour-long performance included a soundtrack composed entirely of audio samples from the run of the comedic television program *The Jack Benny Show* (1950–65), which Moran carefully edited and distorted with synthesizers, samplers, and tape decks. McGrath, who would go on to direct and showcase several of Moran's projects, told Kozinn, "When I heard John's tape, I didn't get it at all. But I thought it was just the greatest sounding stuff, so I played it for the group and told them that it was the next thing we were doing." Ridge Theater actors mouthed the prerecorded words while performing a variety of gestures and scenes, as period commercials and other images appeared on video monitors. Moran told Kozinn: "'I think of it as nightmarish. . . . There is humor in it, obviously. The jokes come from every direction. But they are non-sequiturs, clichés of jokes. They have nothing to do with reality. That's what attracted me to the show." McGrath told Kozinn, "The ancient Greek writers took barely remembered stories from the collective unconscious and recast them into myths that would get their points across. And in a way, that's what John has done. He has taken something from today's group unconscious—an old 1950's television show—and changed it around." Critics found the piece to be funny, eerie, engaging, and indicative of artistic talent. During that time Moran also composed two ballet scores, *Nuts (Homage to Freud)* and *Dairy*, performed by the XXY/Dance/Music ensemble.

In 1990, following the critical success of *The Jack Benny Program*, Moran and McGrath were commissioned by the Lincoln Center for Performing Arts to create a piece for the annual Serious Fun! experimental-theater festival. Moran composed and McGrath directed *The Manson Family: Helter Five-O*, an opera inspired by the real-life story of the infamous Charles Manson, who persuaded his cult followers to murder the actress Sharon Tate and six others in 1969, crimes that shocked the nation. The work was based on real events and interviews with Manson and included psychedelic imagery, a character from a TV police drama of the era, *Hawaii Five-O*, and a reference to the fifth-century B.C. Greek drama *Bacchae*, in which the god Dionysus leads the women of Thebes in performing deadly religious rites. Moran told a journalist from *Business Wire* (March 30, 1992), "I didn't want to tell the Manson story. I was more interested in the Manson characters. I think for many people, one of the most fascinating and frightening elements of the story is what it says about sexuality and society." Although the show played to sold-out audiences, it received mixed reviews. Many critics objected to what they saw as the cavalier, humorous treatment of the Manson murders and were made uncomfortable by Moran's take on Manson. "The moral confusions rest in Mr. Moran's clear fascination with Mr. Manson and his world and the composer's eagerness to suggest that American society is itself a kind of cult," John Rockwell wrote for the *New York Times* (July 22, 1990). "There is, of course, something to that parallel, but the way it is argued here serves to lend Mr. Manson a moral and mythic credibility most people would surely deny him." A recording of *The Manson Family*, produced by Glass, was released by Glass's record company, Point Music, in 1992. It was the first opera to be sold with parental-warning stickers for profanity.

In the 1990s Moran composed several more pieces for musical theater in his signature style, most of them directed by McGrath and performed by the Ridge Theater troupe. *The Hospital* (1991) was an opera with a score depicting the rhythms and chaos of a hospital, with sounds including those of typewriter keys, dial tones, heartbeats, elevator doors, and sirens and with rhythmic and repeated spoken elements. Jan Stuart wrote for *Newsday* (April 8, 1991), "The cumulative effect is strange, dramatic, exasperating and utterly compelling. Just like an emergency room, minus the purgatorial wait." Stuart added, "John Moran is a bonafide American original." In 1992 Moran and McGrath presented *The Haunted House*, a horror-film parody that follows three characters trapped in a haunted house, with a score consisting mainly of eerie sounds. In a positive review of that work, Kozinn wrote for the *New York Times* (April 16, 1992), "There are many ways one might describe Mr. Moran's operas, but operatic, in the word's traditional usage, is not a description that leaps to mind. They are unquestionably theatrical." *The Hospital* and *The Haunted House* were intended to be elements of a four-part "mega opera" called *Circus of Eternity*, whose other sections appear not to have been completed.

In 1993 Moran composed a three-part opera, *Every Day, Newt Burman (The Trilogy of Cyclical Existence)*. The first part, entitled "Every Day, Newt Burman," followed a clown caught in an inescapable, nightmarish ballroom scene. The second, "The Death Train of Baron von Frankenstein," with a minimalist score by Moran, featured passengers riding a doomed train and images of locomotives, landscapes, and magic-lantern figures projected on screens. "The Little Retarded Boy," the third section, focused on a disabled child watching television and dreaming of the outside world. Writing for the *New York Times* (March 22, 1994), Alex Ross called the work "a phenomenally imaginative evening of music theater." Moran's next project, *Mathew in the School of Life* (1995), also directed by McGrath, told the story of the education of an android, Mathew, and included Allen Ginsberg's voice as that of Mathew's tutor. The play caught the attention of Robert Brustein, the creative director of the American Repertory Theater (ART) in Cambridge, Massachusetts, who wrote for the *New Republic* (December 4, 1995): "The progress of Mathew, a holographic unit in a fiberglass white armored suit that gives him the appearance of a medieval knight, takes him from lobotomized infancy to agonized adulthood through a process of enforced education." Brustein praised that performance as well as the other collaborations of Moran and McGrath, writing, "Although both men [McGrath and Moran] are barely into their 30s, their collaboration may be potentially as important for American performing arts as that of Philip Glass and [the avant-garde playwright] Robert Wilson."

Brustein offered Moran and McGrath a commission on behalf of the ART to complete an operatic version of *The Cabinet of Dr. Caligari* (1920), the German director Robert Wiene's silent Expressionist film involving a murder mystery and a somnambulist who can predict the future. In their interpretation Moran and McGrath intended the show's sensory elements to resemble those of a fun house; Moran admitted to Hartigan, "Please don't tell anyone this, but the words don't really matter." (As Koenenn had noted, Moran "writes music and words at the same time but the words are secondary.") *The Cabinet of Dr. Caligari* opened in Cambridge in 1997, and while reviewers were impressed with Moran's use of audio and visual imagery, they criticized what they saw as the show's busyness and lack of coherence and depth, comparing it unfavorably with Wiene's film. The experience at ART was a frustrating one for Moran, not just because of the reviews, but because he felt creatively restricted throughout the process. "The piece in Cambridge was the first time I had ever done a work that wasn't my own idea of what to write about," Moran told Kozinn in 2000, "and I didn't enjoy it. There were a lot of talented people involved with it, and theoretically I could have done what I wanted. But I hadn't chosen the subject myself, and it just wasn't exciting to me." Moran was also upset by having been denied a directing credit, along with McGrath, despite what he saw as his significant contribution in that area. The show represented a creative split for Moran and McGrath.

Moran came up with the idea for his next piece, *Book of the Dead (Second Avenue)*—his first major work without McGrath—while watching passersby from a coffee shop on Second Avenue in New York. The score for the show, which debuted in 2000, featured Eastern and 19th-century operatic and Baroque music, rock and advertising jingles, and the recorded voice of the actress Uma Thurman, who provided narration. The performance, at New York City's Public Theater Martinson Hall, consisted of three parts. The second combined speech rhythms in ordinary settings, such as a fast-food restaurant and a singles bar, to create a symphony—or a cacophony—of the sounds of daily life; the first and third sections contained visual representations of the Egyptian and Tibetan versions of the *Book of the Dead*. Moran has called the performance "an attraction" (rather than an opera or a ballet), but insisted that, like all of his creations, the play was ultimately about death, as he told Kozinn: "I've always written about death. To me, it's the only thing worth writing about, really. So I decided to just get right down to it." While some reviewers felt the meanings of the scenes were not successfully conveyed to the audience, *Book of the Dead* received mostly positive reviews. "Most impressive about *Book of the Dead* is its celebration of the soundtrack of ordinary life," Michael Kuchwara wrote for the Associated Press (November 28, 2000). "The power of sound—

whether noise, music or conversation—affects everyone, Moran seems to be saying. All we have to do is listen."

In the early 2000s Moran toured with the German performer Eva Müller, performing scenes from Moran's previous works. In 2003 Moran met the Japanese dancer and choreographer Saori Tsukada, who happened to be his neighbor, while sitting on the stoop of his Brooklyn, New York, apartment building during a blackout. He had been looking for a new dancer for a performance and decided, based on her physical movements, that Tsukada was the dancer he had sought. She performed with him that fall. Soon afterward Moran was invited to Paris, France, where he worked for two years as the artist-in-residence for the mayor's office. Although he ended up contributing scores for a few projects, Moran admitted that his experience in Paris was not very fruitful. "I was very surprised at how they refused to ever mix mediums . . . ," Moran told Gia Kourlas for the *New York Times* (August 29, 2006). "So it ended up that I had nothing to do, and I was broke and I had to come home to save myself." When he returned to the U.S., Moran had little money and, at first, no place to live. He knew that he wanted to continue collaborating with Tsukada, who teamed up with him for performances at a variety of clubs, including Galapagos and P.S. 122, both in Brooklyn, under the title *John Moran and His Neighbor Saori* (2005). The show consisted of choreographed movements by Moran and Tsukada, a trained gymnast, playing exaggerated versions of themselves in a variety of strange and comical situations. The pair also performed at the Edinburgh Fringe Festival, in Scotland. "That show went really great, and I walked away from the final party, the last cheers, and realized I had nowhere to go," Moran told Kourlas. "All I'd been thinking about was work, work, work. It ended up that I had the keys to Galapagos, so I went there and fell asleep. The owner found me, and I was so embarrassed. He didn't say a word. He just gave me a blanket. And I saw him the next day, and he said, 'You know, you should do that again if you have to.'" Moran said that things seemed so grim at the time that he contemplated suicide. "I was going to call it in, and then I thought, no, no—just don't. I want to do my work," he said. After a few months he had saved enough money to rent his own place in the Bushwick area of Brooklyn.

Moran has continued to collaborate with Tsukada. In 2006 the pair presented *Zenith 5!*, a 45-minute lip-synched show, featuring snippets from several of his recent performances as well as new material. In a positive review for the *New York Times* (August 30, 2006), Rockwell described some of the scenes: "There was a man in an Aztec costume announcing that he was Ray Charles. There was a baldish woman in a shiny suit and tie making pronouncements and, toward the end, devolving into a protracted series of 'Yeah, I knows' as she talked to an imaginary person on the telephone. There was an old lady in a shiny robot-mask cackling in a rocking chair. . . . What did it all mean? Nothing, beyond a kind of stoned, floating wash of charm." In the fall of 2007, Moran and Saori presented, at P.S. 122, *What If Saori Had a Party?*. That 40-minute work, featuring the dancers Katherine Brook and Joseph Keckler, centered on the animated host of a Japanese children's show (played by Tsukada) who lives in a computerized bubble and wishes to have a birthday party; one day she receives a mysterious gift that threatens the stability of her existence. Alexis Soloski, who praised Tsukada's precise movement, wrote for the *Village Voice* (October 30, 2007, on-line) that the performance continued Moran's "longtime interest in representing characters not quite human or not quite whole. . . . Tsukada's gyrations, Moran's thorny score, and the air of candy-colored dread—what a swell party this is."

Moran and McGrath received an Obie Award (presented by the *Village Voice* for Off-Broadway theater productions) in 1994 in the category of special citation for sustained excellence, in recognition of their collaborations. Moran's 1993 show, *Everyday Newt Burman (The Trilogy of Cyclical Existence)*, received two Bessie Awards (for New York dance and performance), one for performance and one for visual design. "People's opinions come and go in the wind like leaves blowing past," Moran told Kourlas. "And it doesn't mean that the opinions aren't relevant, but I've seen everything, from way too much attention to being completely shut out to being let in again."

In 2008 and 2009 Moran and Tsukada toured Europe, performing their shows in venues and at festivals across England, Scotland, Poland, Germany, and the Netherlands. In May 2010 the duo were to premiere their most recent work, *John Moran and His Neighbour Saori . . . in Thailand*, at Mayfest—Bristol, England's festival of contemporary theater. The show was commissioned by the Arches theater in Glasgow, Scotland, and Theater Im Pumpenhaus in Munster, Germany.

With advances in technology, Moran's compositions have become increasingly intricate. Having long ago abandoned his tape-deck method, Moran now feeds hundreds of sounds into a digital sampler and edits them together so precisely that, for example, to present a traffic pattern, he records each car sound separately; according to Moran, the sound of opening a door can contain 35 separately recorded sounds. He told Kozinn: "I do the voices the same way. I record the actors separately from each other, and I have them say each line a variety of ways. Then I take bits and pieces from different takes, and I construct them into a melodic line. So I'm making something that's naturalistic, but also a composition. There is not a sound in this, or a phrase, that's not a purposely constructed melody." Of her close friend and artistic collaborator, Tsukada told Kourlas: "He's like a picture of a tortured artist. Probably to everybody else, also. I still get surprised by what he says and thinks. He is inspiring."

Moran lives in Brooklyn.

—M.R.M.

Suggested Reading: (New York) *Newsday* II p13 July 15, 1990, E p1 Aug. 29, 2006; *New York Times* C p15 Sep. 27, 1989, II p5 Nov. 19, 2000; *Village Voice* (on-line) Oct. 30, 2007

Selected Works: *The Jack Benny Program*, 1989; *The Manson Family: Helter Five-O*, 1990; *The Hospital*, 1991; *The Haunted House*, 1992; *Every Day, Newt Burman (The Trilogy of Cyclical Existence)*, 1993; *Mathew in the School of Life*, 1995; *The Cabinet of Dr. Caligari*, 1997; *Book of the Dead (Second Avenue)*, 2000; *John Moran and His Neighbor Saori*, 2005; *Zenith 5!*, 2006; *What If Saori Had a Party?*, 2007; *John Moran and His Neighbor Saori . . . in Thailand*, 2010

Ethan Miller/Getty Images for the Academy of Interactive Arts and Sciences

Morhaime, Michael

Nov. 3, 1967– Video-game executive

Address: Blizzard Entertainment, P.O. Box 18979, Irvine, CA 92623

"If *World of Warcraft* were a country, it would be the 75th most populated country in the world," Michael Morhaime, the co-founder and chief executive officer of Blizzard Entertainment, told a crowd of 15,000 "gamers" at the 2008 BlizzCon Festival, held in Anaheim, California, as quoted by Tamara Chuang in the *Orange County (California) Register* (October 16, 2008). The game Morhaime was referring to, *World of Warcraft* (*WoW*), produced by Blizzard Entertainment, is one of the most popular personal-computer (PC) games of all time. Unlike Blizzard's other game series, which include the best-selling *Warcraft*, *Diablo*, and *StarCraft*, *World of Warcraft* is a "massively multiplayer on-line role-playing game," or MMORPG, a genre of computer games in which a large number of players interact in an on-line world. Introduced in 2004, *WoW* boasted more than 12 million regular players by late 2010, each of whom had purchased the game package and signed up to pay a monthly subscription fee. Each player creates an avatar and helps it gain experience by completing often complicated and time-consuming quests, collecting weapons, and forming alliances with other virtual adventurers.

Morhaime, an avid gamer himself, studied electrical engineering at the University of California–Los Angeles (UCLA) and co-founded his company, then called Silicon & Synapse, in 1991 with his fellow UCLA graduates Allen Adham and Frank Pearce. Over the years the game-development enterprise changed its name to Chaos Studios Inc. and then Blizzard Entertainment. In 1998, when Adham vacated Blizzard's presidency to focus exclusively on game development as the company's chairman, Morhaime was elevated from executive vice president to president. Since then he has overseen the launch of many of Blizzard's most successful games, including *WoW*, and the vast expansion of the company's operations. In 2007 he helped to negotiate the merger of Blizzard with another major publisher, Activision, creating Activision Blizzard Inc., the largest video-game developer in the world. "It's a very social game," Morhaime told Sarah Tolkoff for the *Orange County Business Journal* (January 5–11, 2009), describing *WoW*. "It's not a very solitary experience unless you want it to be. Players are interactive with other real individuals and form real friendships. They come home from work and log in—it's almost like going to a local pub where everyone knows you."

Michael Morhaime was born on November 3, 1967 in Panorama City, in California's San Fernando Valley. As a child he was curious about "how stuff works," as he told Orion Tippens for the Web publication *Coast Magazine* (June 23, 2009). "Every time I got a new device, I would go through the manual and understand all the obscure features of pretty much everything I got. I wanted to know how it could work with other devices. That curiosity sort of led me to study mechanical engineering." Morhaime graduated from Granada Hills High School in 1985 and received his B.A. degree in electrical engineering from UCLA in 1990. He then took a job writing test software for the disk-drive maker Western Digital Corp., in Irvine, California. Around that time Adham, who had studied computer science at UCLA, began trying to recruit Morhaime to co-found a video-game company. After a year Morhaime agreed, and another UCLA graduate, Frank Pearce, joined them. For start-up funding Adham used $10,000 that his mother and father had given him for a trip to Europe, and Morhaime borrowed money from his own parents. They founded Silicon & Synapse, a small game-development company based in Irvine.

At that time scores of video-game publishers and producers were emerging as powerful players in a growing industry, among them Sunsoft Inc., Virgin Interactive Entertainment, and Interplay Productions. The earliest video games were invented in the 1950s and '60s; the first to become commercially successful was Pong, a game produced by Atari in the 1970s that led other companies to produce imitations. Video games became increasingly popular and sophisticated over the next several decades and were created for a variety of platforms, including arcade machines, personal computers, handheld devices, and consoles designed to be connected to television sets. Video games are today a multibillion-dollar industry and have had a significant impact on aspects of modern culture, including television, advertising, music, film, and technology, and debates about the positive and negative effects of video games on individuals and communities are ongoing.

Morhaime, Adham, and Pearce entered the industry as technical consultants for other companies, adapting games to fit different systems. For instance, for Interplay, they converted Nintendo games to other formats, such as Commodore Amiga. Silicon & Synapse earned $250,000 in its first year. As Morhaime, Adham, and Pearce gained experience in converting games to new formats, they began to better understand what went into designing successful games. Their company began to offer other services to game publishers, providing, for example, design, art, programming, and sound. They next began creating their own games and licensing them to publishers; early games included *The Lost Vikings* (1992) and *Rock N' Roll Racing* (1993), both published by Interplay. After playing an early version of *The Lost Vikings*, Brian Fargo, an executive at Interplay, asked that the characters be redrawn so that they would not look so similar to one another. It was difficult at first for the designers at Silicon & Synapse to accept such criticism; Morhaime told Colin Stewart for the *Orange County Register* (March 20, 2008) that the experience with Fargo "was our first painful iterative process, and it's happened with every game at Blizzard." Later the company developed multidisciplinary in-house "strike teams" to critique the latest version of each game in development. Sales of *The Lost Vikings* soon topped 300,000 units. In 1993 the company generated $750,000 in revenue from royalties on games that generated $20 million in sales for game-publishing companies.

In 1994, in order to gain more exposure and generate higher revenue, Adham, Pearce, and Morhaime sought a parent company that could help their game-design enterprise become a game publisher as well. That year they sold the company for $6.75 million to Davidson & Associates, a Torrance, California–based educational-software maker, choosing that firm because its owners, Jan and Bob Davidson, had agreed to give the game-makers complete creative freedom. At that point the video company—then called Chaos—had 19 employees, most of them artists and programmers, whose average age was 24.5 years. Each of the executives—Adham, who was then the company's president; Morhaime, the executive vice president; and Pearce, the company director and an executive producer—took part in several aspects of the company, including accounting, programming, and production. The founders prided themselves on employing only "gamers." "Everyone in our company is really passionate about video games," Adham told Dean Takahashi for the *Los Angeles Times* (March 13, 1994). "We are all fanatic game players. We *are* the target market, and that gives us an advantage in knowing what is going to sell." The company's Costa Mesa, California, offices had a laid-back, youthful corporate culture. "Comic super-heroes and fantasy monsters seem to spring from posters plastering the walls," Takahashi wrote of Blizzard's home base. "Beards, blue jeans, T-shirts and long hair are so common that the place looks more like a college campus than a corporation. At lunchtime, the staff plays cards or games." There was also a large game room, featuring a television equipped with Nintendo, and each desk was equipped with a video-game system.

Around that time Morhaime and programmers at Blizzard (the company's new name) began contemplating the creation of a "real-time strategy" (RTS) game, in which two players would compete against each other over the Internet in real time. (Most role-playing computer games at that time were "turn-based," meaning that each player performed actions separately during well-defined turns, allowing each player to have a period of analysis before making a move.) In 1994 the company began selling *Warcraft: Humans & Orcs*, a game whose action was set in the mythical kingdom of Azeroth, where each player—who has chosen to "live" as either a human or an orc (a tough and warlike humanoid creature)—is responsible for maintaining an economy while building a military to destroy the other player's economy. The description of the game on Blizzard's Web site reads: "By playing either the Humans or the Orcs in this saga, two separate story lines evolve with 12 scenarios per side telling the tale of the battle for Azeroth. From swords to sorcery, all the elements of classic fantasy are here to explore: rich forests, dark dungeons and bubbling swamps await the stalwart troops amassed to fight for dominance." *Warcraft: Humans & Orcs* was a best-seller. The next year Blizzard unveiled *Warcraft II: Tides of Darkness*, which allowed eight players to interact simultaneously. With each successor, the backstory of Azeroth became more complex.

In the next several years, the company went through a number of changes. In 1996 Blizzard acquired Condor Games, which for several years had been working on creating the dark-fantasy role-playing game *Diablo* for Blizzard. That same year Davidson, Blizzard's parent company, was acquired by CUC International, which later merged with a hotel, real-estate, and car-rental franchise, HFS Corp., to become Cendant. In 1998 Cendant's stock plummeted after it was revealed that CUC had engaged in accounting fraud prior to the merger. The company sold its consumer-software operations, Sierra On-line, which included Blizzard, to Havas, a French publisher, in 1998; Havas was purchased that year by Vivendi. In 1998 Morhaime became Blizzard's president when Adham decided to focus on game development. In his new post Morhaime dealt with the day-to-day running of the company. Adham told *PR Newswire* (April 21, 1998): "Mike was the natural choice to take over the reins as president. He has been a driving force in the company since day one. Mike is the right person to build on our successes and shape our future direction."

Earlier, in January 1997, Blizzard had introduced Battle.net, an on-line space that facilitated multiple-player war games. Battle.net was unlike other on-line services in several ways that made it popular among gamers; for instance, it was very easy to create an account, and there were no membership fees. Within six months the service had attracted 700,000 registered users, making it the largest on-line gaming network at the time. Blizzard introduced two more real-time strategy games—*Diablo* and *StarCraft*—in 1997 and 1998, respectively. By that time Blizzard had established a reputation for making graphically polished PC games, and the company prided itself on maintaining its high standards. Morhaime told Chuang for the *Orange County Register* (August 3, 2007): "We tried like crazy to get *Diablo* out by Christmas, but we missed it. But it didn't matter. Sacrificing high quality for speed, it just isn't worth it." In another example, Blizzard had postponed the release of *StarCraft* for two years; after the game received mediocre reviews at a game convention in 1996, Blizzard "scrapped the game and started over," in Chuang's words. Both games became best-sellers and also garnered awards from the gaming industry.

In about 1999 Morhaime noticed that *EverQuest*, a real-time role-playing game set in the medieval era, had become increasingly popular among the gamers on his staff. (It was jokingly referred to as "EverCrack" because of its addictive nature.) Published by Sony, *EverQuest* was one of the earliest and, at that time, most popular PC games in the MMORPG genre. Such games allow thousands of players around the globe to interact simultaneously. Morhaime saw the appeal of *EverQuest*, which at its peak attracted 450,000 subscribers, but found that the game provided very little guidance and was therefore not very accessible for casual players. "A lot of games that preceded [*WoW*] made the assumption that this type of game wouldn't appeal to gamers outside of the hard-core audience, so that's [who game developers] targeted," Morhaime explained to Robert Levine for *Fortune* (March 19, 2007). "We thought this type of game could appeal to more people if we made it easier to use." Some at Blizzard wondered whether a game like *Ever-Quest*, which, by its very design, could not be won or even completed, would attract more users. (The goal of *WoW* is not to win but to make one's character stronger and more resourceful as it navigates its way through the world.) Still, Morhaime was confident about his idea. He formed a creative team of about 100 designers, developers, and artists to begin writing the code for what would become *WoW*. Blizzard developed specific features to allure casual players. For instance, unlike many other MMORPG games, *WoW* allows users to play alone rather than with teams and also includes a "resting" feature that lets characters gain experience even if they have not been active in the game for days. In order to appeal to gaming cultures around the world, Blizzard also customized the interface for different countries; the company designed the version of the game distributed to South Korea, for example, so that it could be operated with one hand, since so many gamers in that country smoke cigarettes while playing. Meanwhile, Blizzard continued to release new editions of its existing games, including *Diablo II* (2000), *Warcraft III* (2002), and expansion packs for both.

A few months prior to the debut of *World of Warcraft*, Blizzard enlisted 100,000 people to test-play the game. By the time *WoW* appeared in stores, in 2004 (10 years after the first *Warcraft* game had gone on sale), the gaming community had been eagerly anticipating its arrival for years. Just before the game's midnight launch, Morhaime drove to Fry's Electronics store in Fountain Valley, California, and was surprised to see about 5,000 fans lining up to buy the game. "At that early point, we didn't even know if people knew about [the game]," Morhaime told Tolkoff. "There was a ton of traffic and all the parking lots nearby were full. . . . There were waves of people walking toward Fry's and we were wondering if something else was going on that night nearby." After the inventory at Fry's ran out, Morhaime went back to his office to retrieve his employees' copies of the game for the store to sell. "We didn't have any idea just how popular it would be," he told Tolkoff.

The action in *World of Warcraft* takes place within the world of Azeroth, two years after the events that concluded Blizzard's previous *Warcraft* game. When a player begins he or she must create an avatar, choosing one of 10 races (human, orc, or gnome, for example), each of which has unique characteristics. The player must also choose one of nine classes (such as warlock, warrior, druid, or priest), each of which is accompanied by different sets of skills and spells. (Each race has a different number of classes available to it.) Upon entering a realm, a character must embark on quests determined by various computer-controlled characters. Each quest provides charac-

ters with experience and skills, which in turn help it to accomplish more difficult tasks. Along the way characters meet and interact, collect rare items and weapons, enter professions (tailoring, blacksmithing, mining, and cooking, for example), and join guilds to accomplish broader and more difficult goals. *World of Warcraft*, which cost $70 for the start-up kit and requires a $15 monthly subscription fee, became the fastest-selling PC role-playing game in history. It was universally praised by gaming critics for its many innovations that eliminated a lot of downtime and helped players gain experience quickly. "The great thing about *World of Warcraft* is that you can sit down in your lunch hour and do a couple of quests and still feel like you've had a meaningful experience, rather than it feeling like you've got a second career," Morhaime told Rihanna Pratchett for the London *Guardian* (February 17, 2005).

As *World of Warcraft* gained popularity, Blizzard expanded its operations, hiring many more employees. In 2005, with 650 workers in Irvine, the company had grown to become Orange County's second-largest software company in terms of local employment, after the software maker FileNet Corp. Three hundred of those employees were "game masters," who provided 24-hour-a-day, seven-day-a-week technical support for players. By early 2007 the number of game masters managing the on-line universe had topped 1,200, and *WoW* boasted eight million subscribers, with analysts estimating that it had earned Blizzard $1 billion in 2006 alone. At the 2006 High Tech Innovation Awards, Morhaime was named the "high-impact" person of the year by the AeA (American Electronics Association) Orange County Council. In July 2006 *Business 2.0* named Morhaime to its list of "50 who matter now," which included executives, entrepreneurs, and innovators "whose ideas, products, and business insights are changing the world we live in today." In 2007 Morhaime was named runner-up for businessperson of the year by the *Orange County Business Journal*. Along with Sulka Haro, who created Habbo Hotel, an on-line role-playing community for teenagers, Morhaime delivered a keynote lecture at the 2007 Austin Game Developers Conference. That same year Blizzard Entertainment hosted its second fan convention (the first was held in 2005), known as BlizzCon, in Anaheim. The 8,000 attendees were able to meet Blizzard developers, artists, and designers and play new games scheduled to be released later that year, including *World of Warcraft: Wrath of the Lich King*, the second expansion pack for the 2004 game. When the first expansion pack, *World of Warcraft: The Burning Crusade*, went on sale, in 2007, it became the fastest-selling PC game of all time, with 2.4 million copies purchased in 24 hours; *Wrath of the Lich King* broke that record, selling three million copies in the first day.

In late 2007 Morhaime began talks with Bobby Kotick, the CEO of the video-game publisher Activision, the maker of such popular games as *Call of Duty* and *Guitar Hero*, about a possible merger of Activision and Blizzard. Kotick had approached Vivendi, Blizzard's parent company, about purchasing Blizzard outright, but Vivendi had refused to sell it. Vivendi had instead decided that merging its gaming division with Activision could help improve its console business. Both Blizzard and Activision had grown significantly in recent years, and their merger promised to pose the most formidable challenge to Electronic Arts, then the leader of the industry. In an effort to discuss the merger in a low-key setting, Morhaime arranged a dinner with Kotick at a steakhouse in Irving. Morhaime, however, booked a large banquet room by mistake. "We wanted to keep it low-key, which was pretty hard to do in this huge room with just the two of us there," Morhaime told Dan Gallagher for *Market Watch* (December 4, 2008). The complicated deal between Activision and Vivendi was announced in April 2008. The resulting company, Activision Blizzard Inc., with Kotick as president and CEO, is the biggest video-game developer in the world, with yearly sales of $4 billion. Because the merger resulted in Blizzard's playing a larger role in the new company than it had in Vivendi, it was expected to better highlight Blizzard's financial accomplishments. Previously, Blizzard's profits were not easily visible to shareholders because they were buried within reports of profits earned by Vivendi, its much larger parent company. "We've had a lot of experience running Blizzard as a division of a public company," Morhaime told Tolkoff. "The big difference [with the merger] is we are one step closer to the public markets. It requires that we spend more time than we used to in educating analysts and investors about Blizzard, where we used to be able to not deal with that side of the business."

Blizzard continued expanding in 2008, hiring both locally and abroad, becoming the biggest software company in Orange County in terms of sales. At the end of the year, *WoW*, which was Activision Blizzard's biggest money-maker, boasted 12 million subscribers. Morhaime received a Technology & Engineering Emmy Award for development of MMORPG and was inducted into the Academy of Interactive Arts and Sciences Hall of Fame. In June 2009 Morhaime and Paul Sams, Blizzard's chief operating officer, accepted awards on behalf of the company from Guinness World Records in the categories of largest MMORPG in the world, for *WoW*, and best-selling strategy game, for *StarCraft*, which had sold 9.5 million copies.

In August 2009 Morhaime confirmed that Blizzard was creating an updated version of the Battle.net server, which would allow gamers to interact in a shared space, no matter which Blizzard game they were playing. (As of early March 2010, Blizzard was beginning the first stages of beta testing for the Battle.net service, allowing it to be used by thousands of gamers.) According to Morhaime, as quoted in *Kotaku* (August 5, 2009), the revamped version will also include "social network-ing features, cross-game communication, unified account management," and other features. Blizzard is also updating *Diablo II*. The company recently began marketing toys, books, and apparel based on *WoW*, and there are rumors of a major motion picture inspired by the game. In 2009 Blizzard celebrated its success by erecting a 12-foot statue of an orc at its Irving offices. The following year saw the debut of *Starcraft II: Wings of Liberty* and the expansion pack *World of Warcraft: Cataclysm*.

Morhaime, who plays *WoW* as a Night Elf hunter, is also an avid poker player; he finished in second place in the 2006 Celebrity Poker Tournament, hosted by Design, Innovate, Communicate, and Entertain (DICE). Morhaime is single and lives in Irvine.

—M.R.M.

Suggested Reading: Blizzard Entertainment Web site; *Fortune* Features p151 Mar. 19, 2007; IGN.com Feb. 1, 2001; *(London) Guardian* Life Pages p20 Feb. 17, 2005; *Orange County (California) Business Journal* p8 Jan. 5–11, 2009; *Orange County Register* News A Mar. 20, 2008

Selected Games: *The Lost Vikings*, 1992; *Rock N' Roll Racing*, 1993; *Warcraft: Humans & Orcs*, 1994; *Warcraft II: Tides of Darkness*, 1995; *Diablo*, 1997; *StarCraft*, 1998; *Diablo II*, 2000; *Warcraft III: Reign of Chaos*, 2002; *World of Warcraft*, 2004; *World of Warcraft: Wrath of the Lich King*, 2007; *World of Warcraft: The Burning Crusade*, 2007; *StarCraft II: Wings of Liberty*, 2010; *World of Warcraft: Cataclysm*, 2010

Mueller, Robert

(MULL-er)

Aug. 7, 1944– Director of the FBI

Address: FBI, Hoover Bldg., 935 Pennsylvania Ave., N.W., Washington, DC 20535-3404

On September 4, 2001 Robert Mueller took over as director of the Federal Bureau of Investigation (FBI), becoming the sixth director in the agency's history. Just a week later the September 11 terrorist attacks transformed his job, as they did the jobs of all involved in maintaining the security of the United States. Prior to 9/11 a number of high-profile blunders had put the agency under intense public scrutiny, including the espionage case of the FBI-agent-turned-Russian-spy Robert Hanssen and the botched investigation of the Taiwanese-American nuclear scientist Wen Ho Lee, who was wrongly accused of stealing secrets about U.S. nuclear weapons for the People's Republic of China. The 9/11 attacks not only further revealed the FBI's weaknesses but pointed out the challenges Mueller faced upon taking the helm at one of the most

Mandel Ngan/AFP/Getty Images

Robert Mueller

widely recognized law-enforcement agencies in the world. Commenting on the beginning of Mueller's tenure as FBI director, Andrew Card, President George W. Bush's chief of staff on September 11, explained to Chitra Ragavan for *U.S. News & World Report* (May 26, 2003), "One can't even call it baptism by fire. It was baptism by conflagration." Since he took on the post, Mueller has helped lead one of the most extensive overhauls in the agency's storied history; he has also, in the aftermath of the 9/11 attacks, helped shift the FBI's focus from investigating and prosecuting crimes to preventing further attacks.

A former Marine who served in the Vietnam War, Mueller worked for a quarter-century as a prosecutor with the U.S. Department of Justice under Presidents Ronald Reagan, George H.W. Bush, and Bill Clinton, with brief forays in private practice, before serving as acting deputy attorney general in the initial months of the George W. Bush administration. As FBI director he is charged with overseeing more than 30,000 employees in the U.S. and overseas and an annual budget of nearly $7 billion. Mueller is known as "a soft-spoken but extremely intense manager who thrives on pressure," Tom Nugent wrote for *VFW Magazine* (October 1, 2002). Stacy Finz, writing for the *San Francisco Chronicle* (July 3, 2001), noted that he is "a man of few public words and is as no-nonsense as his dark suits." A former colleague, Michael Burt, described Mueller to Finz as "one of these Jimmy Stewart characters, with old-fashioned American values." Supremely devoted to his job, Mueller is on the verge of becoming the first FBI director to complete a 10-year term since J. Edgar Hoover, who reigned from 1924 to 1972, before the 10-year term

was introduced. Commenting on the FBI's international reputation, Mueller said to Garrett M. Graff for the *Washingtonian* (September 2008, on-line), "Anyplace we go in the world, when someone asks us what we do, we feel an immense pride in saying, 'FBI.'"

Robert Swan Mueller III was born on August 7, 1944 in New York City into an affluent family and was raised in an upscale neighborhood outside Philadelphia, Pennsylvania. He was influenced early on by his father, Robert, who served as the captain of a Navy submarine chaser during World War II and who taught him the importance of such values as honesty and integrity. "You did not shade or even consider shading with him," he noted to Graff for the *Washingtonian* (August 2008, on-line). "The most devastating thing that can happen to an institution is that people begin to shade and dissemble." Mueller attended St. Paul's School, an exclusive college-preparatory institution in Concord, New Hampshire, where he was known for his athletic skills. His 1962 graduating class included John Kerry, currently the senior U.S. senator from Massachusetts and the 2004 Democratic presidential nominee; the former *Philadelphia Inquirer* editor Max King; and Will Taft, who became a top lawyer for the U.S. State Department.

Following in his father's footsteps, Mueller attended Princeton University, in Princeton, New Jersey, where he continued to shine as a student and athlete, excelling at lacrosse. During his time there he became heavily influenced by a classmate, David Hackett, a popular athlete who, after his graduation, in 1965, volunteered for the Marines and died in the Vietnam War. Hackett inspired Mueller's move into public service. Mueller explained to Tom Nugent, "David Hackett was a good friend. . . . He was an example to many of us in my class. We admired his character. He was a strong leader and a model for the rest of us." Unlike many of his college peers, who used family connections to begin careers in banking and finance and avoid military service, Mueller joined the Marines and entered officer-training school shortly after receiving his B.A. degree, in 1966. He recalled to Nugent that in officer-training school "the first thing we learned was how to lead others by example. They taught us the importance of getting the job done, rather than talking about it. We learned to tackle the assignment before us, accomplish it, then move on to the next mission without fanfare—and I think that continues to be my approach today." Mueller received a master's degree in international relations from New York University in 1967 and he began his tour in Vietnam later that summer, serving from July 1968 to June 1969. He earned a Bronze Star while leading a rifle-platoon unit under fire in Vietnam's Quang Tri Province. Mueller's other military decorations include two Navy Commendation Medals, a Purple Heart, and the Vietnamese Cross of Gallantry. He said to Nugent that he "wouldn't be [FBI director] without the lessons I learned in the Corps."

After completing his military service, Mueller returned to the U.S. and enrolled at the University of Virginia's law school. There, he continued to play lacrosse and served on the school's law review. Upon graduating, Mueller tried unsuccessfully to land a job with the federal government as an assistant U.S. attorney. Instead, he spent three years as an associate at the San Francisco, California, law firm of Pillsbury, Madison & Sutro before being hired as an assistant U.S. attorney in San Francisco, in 1976. In that capacity Mueller "took on tough cases and got convictions," Graff noted, and rose through the ranks to become chief of the office's criminal division in 1981. He held that position for a year before being recruited by William Weld, then the Justice Department's U.S. attorney for Boston, Massachusetts, to become head of Boston's criminal division. In 1986 Mueller took over the Boston U.S. attorney's office when Weld was promoted to head the Justice Department's criminal division. It was during that time that Mueller developed a reputation for being closed-mouthed with the media. Commenting on Mueller's demeanor, Weld later recalled to Graff (August 2008), "You cannot get the words 'straight arrow' out of your head. He didn't try to be elegant or fancy; he just put the cards on the table." Mueller served as interim U.S. attorney for two years before briefly returning to private practice as a partner with the Boston law firm of Hill & Barlow, from 1988 to 1989.

In 1989 Mueller was hired by then–Attorney General Dick Thornburgh to work as an assistant on criminal matters. In that position he helped prosecute major international crime figures, including the deposed Panamanian leader Manuel Noriega, and other criminals, among them the New York crime boss John Gotti. Mueller also worked on the investigation of the Pan Am Flight 103 bombing over Lockerbie, Scotland (known in the media as the Lockerbie Bombing), which was the first major terrorist incident involving U.S. citizens. He rose to become the assistant attorney general in charge of the Justice Department's criminal division in 1990, remaining in that position for three years. His tenure there was marred by the Bank of Credit and Commerce International (BCCI) case, which involved large-scale fraud that deprived many people in Third World countries of their life's savings. He endured criticism for his handling of the investigation, which allegedly slowed after the discovery that CIA officials and numerous prominent U.S. politicians had been associated with BCCI. Following the criticism, top BCCI officials were indicted. President George H.W. Bush's defeat in the 1992 presidential election sent Mueller back to private practice for several years; he became a partner in the Washington, D.C., office of the Boston law firm of Hale & Dorr (now WilmerHale).

Unsatisfied with work in private practice, Mueller returned to public service as a homicide prosecutor with the U.S. attorney's office in Washing-

ton, which let him "get back in the trenches," as Finz put it. That more or less entry-level position in the country's largest U.S. attorney's office paid less than a quarter of his $400,000 law-firm salary. Mueller rose to become the department's homicide chief after only a year and a half and prosecuted a number of high-profile cases, including the so-called Georgetown Starbucks murders and a drunk-driving death involving a Georgian diplomat. Eric Holder, Washington's U.S. attorney at the time and now the U.S. attorney general under President Barack Obama, explained to Graff, "[Mueller] was just one of the guys. He didn't demand special treatment or receive it. He was doing what he wanted to do." Mueller said to Graff, "I've always loved investigations."

In 1998 Mueller was appointed by President Bill Clinton as a U.S. attorney in California. Returning to San Francisco, he fought what he saw as complacency among the staff, making lawyers and others reapply for their jobs. Mueller made the office much more efficient, in part through a complete overhaul of the antiquated computer systems; he also helped rebuild the office's case-management system, developing a program called Alcatraz, which was later used in other divisions around the country. Mueller was credited with doubling the number of criminal cases filed, from 672 in 1998 to 1,253 in 2000, and with increasing damages collected from $7 million in 1998 to $208 million in 2000. Beth McGarry, who served as Mueller's deputy in San Francisco, told Graff (August 2008), "Bob has this real rare combo of a practical day-to-day manager and a visionary at the same time. Most people are one or the other." Dianne Feinstein, the senior U.S. senator from California, told Gail Gibson for the Baltimore Sun (October 16, 2001), "Robert Mueller is a man who can come in, and whip an operation into shape—no nonsense, no excuses, just results."

Mueller was summoned back to Washington in 2001, when he was named acting deputy attorney general (DAG) during President George W. Bush's transition to the White House. In that position he helped oversee the day-to-day workings of Main Justice and the FBI (a branch of the Justice Department). Mueller was then offered a permanent DAG spot but turned it down to return to the San Francisco U.S. attorney's office. Then, when Louis Freeh announced his resignation as FBI director in June of that year, Mueller was quickly pegged as his likely successor. Freeh's resignation had come amid criticism that the FBI needed stronger leadership, particularly in the wake of a major espionage case involving the former FBI agent Robert Hanssen, who was charged with selling American secrets to Russia over more than two decades. Freeh's tenure had also seen other high-profile blunders, including the deadly standoffs between federal agents and others at the Ruby Ridge, Idaho, home of the white supremacist leader Randall Weaver and the Branch Davidian ranch of David Koresh outside Waco, Texas; the botched investigation of the Olympic Park bombing in Atlanta, Georgia; the mishandled case against the Taiwanese-American nuclear scientist Wen Ho Lee; the misplacement of hundreds of FBI firearms and laptop computers; and the withholding of thousands of pages of documents and other materials from Timothy J. McVeigh's defense lawyers during the Oklahoma City bombing trial, which led to a delay in McVeigh's execution.

On July 5, 2001, as expected, Mueller was nominated by President Bush to succeed Freeh. During his Senate confirmation hearings that month, President Bush said, as noted by Zachary Coile and Bob Egelko for the *San Francisco Chronicle* (July 6, 2001), "Bob Mueller's experience and character convince me that he's ready to shoulder these responsibilities. Agents of the Bureau prize three virtues above all: fidelity, bravery and integrity. This new director is a man who exemplifies them all." The same writers quoted Mueller as saying, "I look forward to working with the thousands of dedicated men and women who are agents and employees of the FBI to enforce our nation's laws fairly and with respect to the rights of all Americans." Mueller added, "We all know that the bureau's remarkable legacy of service and accomplishment has been tarnished by some serious and highly publicized problems in recent years. I will make it my highest priority to restore the public's confidence in the FBI, to re-earn the faith and trust of the American people," as reported by Michael Hedges for the *Houston Chronicle* (July 31, 2001).

On September 4, 2001 Mueller was officially sworn in, becoming the sixth director in the agency's history. One week later the 9/11 terrorist attacks transformed the nature of his leadership and the FBI's overall approach to law enforcement. Mueller immediately shifted the FBI's focus to fighting terrorism and centralized all terrorist-related investigations in the bureau's headquarters in Washington. (Previously, field offices oversaw terrorism investigations.) He also placed new emphasis on other areas, such as cybercrime, intellectual-property theft, and economic espionage, while maintaining the bureau's focus on such investigative mainstays as organized crime, health-care fraud, and public corruption. Other immediate actions included broadening the bureau's presence overseas, since the 9/11 plot had been formed on three continents; launching a command center within the FBI Strategic Information Operations dedicated to tracking terrorists around the globe; creating a new Office of Intelligence, which oversees two newly expanded counterterrorism and counterintelligence divisions; and upgrading the bureau's technology and information systems. (Immediately after the 9/11 attacks, FBI agents had had to express-mail photos of the airplane hijackers to one another because field offices lacked scanners.)

As FBI director Mueller has employed a corporate-like management style and has changed the face of the bureau by appointing nonagents with specialized skills to a number of high-ranking positions, such as general counsel and chief of staff. While he is generally admired, Mueller's demanding leadership style has resulted in a steady turnover at the bureau, especially with regard to chiefs of staff and special assistants. Lisa Monaco, his sixth (and current) chief of staff, told Graff (August 2008), "He's got one speed, and it's pretty relentless." She added, commenting on her daily briefings with him, "It's like appearing before a smart, tough judge every day. He wants to get information—and the right information—and he wants you to be on top of your game." Mueller's decision-making skills have been praised. James Comey, the deputy attorney general under President George W. Bush, said for the same article, "His gift is that he's decisive without being impulsive. He'll sit, listen, ask questions, and make a decision. I didn't realize at the time how rare that is in Washington."

In light of the FBI's longstanding reputation as an investigative agency, its strong focus on preventing terrorist attacks has brought Mueller criticism regarding a number of controversial policies. Those include the interrogation techniques practiced by agents on suspected terrorists or individuals detained at such facilities as the Abu Ghraib prison, in Iraq, and the Guantánamo Bay prison (sometimes called "Gitmo"), in Cuba. (The FBI was known until recently for developing nonviolent techniques in gathering information from detainees, often finding itself at odds with other groups, such as the CIA and military, which have frequently used more extreme interrogation tactics, including waterboarding. President Obama has repeatedly spoken out against those tactics, and in January 2009 he ordered a ban on harsh interrogation methods. He also ordered the closure of the Guantánamo Bay camp and shut all other overseas CIA prison camps for terror suspects. While as of October 2010, 176 detainees still remained at Guantánamo, President Obama has issued a presidential memorandum ordering their eventual extradition to the Thomson Correctional Center, in Thomson, Illinois.) In 2004, after the National Security Agency's planned implementation of a domestic-wiretapping and data-collection program that would have violated civil liberties on a grand scale—a program favored by the White House—Mueller, Acting Attorney General James Comey, and Attorney General John Ashcroft (who was hospitalized at the time) prepared to resign in protest of the unconstitutionality of the measures. The delay in the resignations caused by Ashcroft's hospitalization led to all sides' working out their differences, and the surveillance plan was dropped.

Mueller, who may well become the first FBI director to complete his 10-year term, has been widely credited with improving the bureau as a whole. However, he has acknowledged the threat of another terrorist attack. Mueller explained to Graff (September 2008), "It's an ongoing crisis. You can't sit back and say we've won. There will be another terrorist attack, and inevitably they'll find that we or the CIA or whoever could have done something to prevent it." In the wake of the failed terrorist attack on Christmas Day 2009, when the Al Qaeda–linked Nigerian student Umar Farouk Abdulmutallab tried to detonate plastic explosives hidden in his underwear while on board Northwest Airlines Flight 253, Mueller defended his bureau's handling of the matter and stated that subsequent interrogations of Abdulmutallab provided the government with valuable information. Nonetheless, he acknowledged the need to expand the No Fly List (names of those who are not permitted to board commercial aircraft flying to or from the U.S.), after it was revealed that Abdulmutallab had been on a list of people with known or suspected ties to terrorism. More recently, in response to the swift capture and arraignment of Faisal Shahzad, a Pakistani-American who attempted to detonate a car bomb in New York's Times Square on May 1, 2010, Mueller said, as quoted in a press release on the bureau's official Web site, "This investigation included a combination of traditional law enforcement techniques and intelligence-based authorities, with men and women from a number of agencies working side-by-side in support of a common goal." (On October 5, 2010 Shahzad was convicted and sentenced to life imprisonment without the possibility of parole after pleading guilty to 10 terrorism and weapons counts.)

Mueller and his wife, the former Ann Cabell Standish, his high-school sweetheart, live in the Washington, D.C., area. They have two adult daughters, Melissa and Cynthia, and two grandchildren. Mueller, a Republican, has a record of working effectively with colleagues on both sides of the political aisle.

—C.C.

Suggested Reading: *Baltimore Sun* A p10+ Oct. 16, 2001; *Boston Globe* A p1 July 6, 2001; *Christian Science Monitor* p1 Aug. 3, 2001; Federal Bureau of Investigation Official Web site; *Houston Chronicle* A p1 July 31, 2001; *San Francisco Chronicle* A p1+ July 3, 2001, A p1 July 6, 2001; *U.S. News & World Report* p14+ May 20, 2002, p18+ May 26, 2003; *VFW Magazine* p12+ Oct. 1, 2002; *Washingtonian* (online) Aug. 2008, Sep. 2008

Mugler, Thierry

(moo-GLAY, tee-AIR-ee)

Dec. 21, 1948– Fashion designer; photographer; perfumer

Address: Thierry Mugler Parfums, 1 Park Ave., New York, NY 10016

Since 1974 the French-born fashion designer Thierry Mugler has been known for using wit and fantasy to create clothing that places boldness and drama ahead of the human form. Mugler's inspirations have ranged from Hollywood glamour to sexual fetishism to Detroit car stylings of the 1950s; his work often stands in opposition to current fashion and intellectual trends, making Mugler a consistently controversial figure on the fashion scene. (Over the years, for example, he has been both celebrated for empowering women and criticized for objectifying them.) When the "power-dressing" fashions of the 1980s—prefigured by Mugler's work—were pushed aside by the bony elbow of waif-chic in the 1990s, Mugler took the opportunity to reinvent both himself and his empire, launching a line of perfumes and bringing his talents for direction and design to the theatrical stage. Today, Mugler's influence is stronger than ever; from hourglass shapes and exaggerated tailoring to metallic leggings, the impact of his work is visible throughout the fashion world.

Thierry Mugler was born on December 21, 1948 and raised in Strasbourg, in the province of Alsace, France. His father was a doctor, and in an inter-

Courtesy of James Alcock

view with Ian Phillips for the London *Independent* (December 5, 1998, on-line), Mugler described his mother as "the most elegant woman in town . . . a star"; Phillips noted that she was Mugler's "first muse." Still, Mugler was not close to either of his parents—"I was close to nobody," he told Phillips—and remembers his childhood as being "very, very difficult." "Nothing suited me," he said. "I found everything very, very boring, was very, very ill-at-ease and very, very lonely." As a child Mugler would skip school to wander around old areas of Strasbourg and spent his time writing plays, making costumes, and going to the movies. "I just had to create my own world, because I was too unhappy," he told Sheryl Garratt for the London *Telegraph* (May 21, 2009, on-line). At 14 Mugler was allowed to attend the Decorative Arts School in Strasbourg, even though he was two years younger than the usual minimum age of admittance. Although Mugler was a gifted artist, the school did not offer him the kind of stimulation he was looking for. Meanwhile, he had become interested in dance. After a couple of months at the Decorative Arts School, he stopped doing his work, leading his father to sign a contract so he could join the corps de ballet of the Rhine Opera. (His academic education ended at that point.) Dance served as a creative and emotional outlet for young Mugler, providing him with the discipline and structure he had been lacking in his life. Using the small salary he was afforded as a dancer, Mugler soon moved out of the family home and rented a small room with a fellow company member. While independence at such a young age was rewarding for Mugler, it also required hard work. He adhered to a grueling schedule with the Rhine Opera and struggled to support himself; he has recalled that with classes, rehearsals, and performances (he was on stage nearly every night), he worked 16-hour days.

In his scarce spare time, Mugler studied design on his own and began crafting his own clothing, often customizing flea-market finds. Of his earliest designs, Mugler told Phillips, "They were very colorful. I remember I had an old army coat which trailed on the ground and a pair of trousers, dyed in all the colors of the rainbow. I would also wear a huge plastic orchid in my lapel and had an acid-green jacket with royal blue buttons in the form of stars." He said to Garratt that his designs incorporated "all my fantasies. I had a medieval period, a Flash Gordon period, a superheroes period, a Renaissance period—but always very futuristic." Referring to the chameleonic rock icon, he said, "I was David Bowie before David Bowie!" Sporting his long, dyed hair and flamboyant clothes in the early 1960s, before that look and sensibility caught on with the public, he was often the target of physical violence. Still, he felt compelled to be himself. "It was loneliness," he recalled to Garratt. "But I always had something telling me to hold on. I was looking at my star, and I knew it was going to be fine."

When Mugler was 20 he auditioned successfully for the choreographer Maurice Béjart—and then, to the surprise of many, including himself, he turned the opportunity down. While the chance to work with Béjart was highly coveted among dancers, Mugler later came to understand why he had said no to the choreographer: the dance company, Ballet de l'Étoile, was based in Brussels, Belgium, and deep down Mugler knew that he needed to be in a place more connected with the new creative movements emerging in cities including New York, Paris, France, and London, England. Mugler chose Paris, and although he left Strasbourg with the intention of joining a contemporary dance company, he soon found himself becoming more and more involved in the world of fashion. The outfits that had sparked such violent reactions in Strasbourg got a very different reception in Paris; suddenly, people were stopping Mugler on the street to ask him where he shopped.

Almost immediately after coming to Paris, Mugler was hired as a window dresser for a boutique. He made some sketches to sell to hip local shops, and soon he was designing clothes for the hippest of them all, the Gudele boutique. Virtually overnight, Mugler had changed paths, moving away from dance to become a fashion designer. "I'd always had this idea of directing, of producing things on stage, and this was a way of having some control and some power," he told Garratt. "And at that time fashion was very important. People were expressing themselves through that. And it was fun!"

Over the next decade Mugler traveled, made clothes, and immersed himself in the hippie culture of the 1960s. In a reaction against the strictness of his ballet training, he studied the traditional Kathakali dance in India. He was even initiated into the Hindu faith, taking the name Ravi. "It was an incredible time," he said to Garratt. "We lived by trading things—there was no money involved. I'd trade clothes or ballet classes to get organic food. You were out all the time, and you'd meet people who had the same philosophy as you. I had a van, and I went to Afghanistan in it, all round Europe and Africa. You'd meet people on the road and share a week with them, then they'd go somewhere, you'd go another way. It was a completely new world." In 1968 Mugler made his way to the U.S., taking up residence for a time on the corner of Haight and Ashbury Streets—a center of the countercultural scene—in San Francisco, California. "There were all these white girls with their hair dyed with henna," he recalled. "And there were tattoos and piercings and saris. It was fabulous!"

As the 1960s came to a close, the hippie scene—with its rampant drug use—lost much of its appeal for Mugler, particularly after the highly publicized murders committed by the followers of Charles Manson. For the next few years, he worked as a freelance designer for fashion houses all over Europe. He perfected his craft by designing a variety of clothing, from children's fashions to leather garments. During that period Mugler split his time between a flat in the Notting Hill area of London and a houseboat in Amsterdam, the Netherlands. By 1973 he was ready to return to Paris and begin his first work for a clothing label. The line, called Café de Paris, featured muslin dresses trimmed with fox fur. The following year Mugler founded his own label, called simply Thierry Mugler, to great success. His first women's-wear collections were picked up by Browns in London and the department stores Neimann Marcus and Saks in the U.S. Ian Phillips wrote, "While the rest of the fashion world was still on a hippy trip, Mugler's clothes sculpted the body—the sexuality was overt and there was more than a touch of the military. . . . His style prefigured Eighties' power dressing, leading the way for a generation of designers, including Jean Paul Gaultier and Azzedine Alaïa." Talking with Phillips, Mugler explained his inspiration for the line: "I have always tried to sublimate the body and to make people dream." His interest lay in modifying the human form—padding shoulders, narrowing waists, and exaggerating curves. The designer has admitted that his clothes were never easy to wear; still, he has maintained, they made their wearers look good.

Mugler has also made a name for himself as a capable photographer. As the story goes, in 1976 Mugler hired the photographer Helmut Newton to shoot a campaign for him, but Newton soon grew annoyed by the demanding designer's excessive instructions and finally told Mugler to take the photos himself. Mugler happily took Newton's advice; he has since launched numerous fashion campaigns using his own photographs and has published several photo books. The design critic Gregory Votolato wrote for the *Modern Fashion Encyclopedia* (on-line), "Mugler's photographic talent may prove to be as important as his fashion designs." He added that Mugler's book of photographs *Thierry Mugler, Photographer* (1988) "contained images comparable in their artifice, explosive glamor, and formal control to the cinematic images of Peter Greenaway. His photographs exploit grand vistas, deep interior spaces, and heroic monuments as settings upon which models perch like tiny ornaments, strongly defined by the extravagant outline of their costumes and asserting their presence through dramatic pose and gesture. His fashion photographs provide a narrative framework for Mugler's clothes, while relegating them to the role of costume within a larger dramatic context."

By the 1980s Mugler had become one of France's biggest stars. He produced outrageous collections inspired by everything from insects to superheroes. To celebrate the 10th anniversary of his fashion house, in 1984, Mugler put on his first "super-show" for more than 6,000 spectators. That event was a huge undertaking for Mugler—predictably, considering how heavily involved he typically becomes in the execution of his runway shows. "I always was involved in everything, from the heels to the lashes, the storyboard to the music and sound effects," Mugler told Garratt. "It was done like a movie. We'd work on this, we'd work on that and at some point everything came together. We never did rehearsals. It was too complicated. So I discovered the show at the same time that you discovered it!" In 1985 Mugler designed the costumes for the children's stage musical *Emilie Jolie.*

The start of the 1990s brought about a change in the direction of fashion, away from the styles made popular by designers—Mugler among them—who had seen success in the previous decade. Mugler's designs, which epitomized the "power-dressing" 1980s style, were out of step with the minimalist stylings coming from the likes of Helmut Lang and Calvin Klein. The "grunge" and "waif" looks surfaced as a backlash to the 1980s' artifice and excess. While Mugler understood that reaction, he did not anticipate that the grunge look would soon amount to a full-blown fashion movement. "I totally understood the kids. It was a healthy reaction, and it was quite charming, very cute. But as soon as it became . . . a product, the whole thing was wrecked," he told Garratt. Also, as labels attempted to compete as global brands, the industry became more focused on money and marketing, and for Mugler, that was when the fun went out of designing. He also found the waif aesthetic boring and its models indistinguishable from one another.

As Mugler contemplated leaving the fashion world, he partnered with the French beauty-products company Clarins in 1992 to launch his first perfume. Called Angel, the blue-tinted fragrance is known for its distinctive chocolate and coffee tones and comes in a star-shaped bottle. Mugler explained to Garratt what he was trying to accomplish with the scent, and why creating it was not always a simple matter: "Something about tenderness, about childhood. That was the idea of the chocolate thing—like you want to eat the person you love. I made them create special essences of coffee and chocolate that had never been used before. I took a lot of risks. The name, the bottle, the colour—everything was a fight." Angel has since become one of the most popular perfumes in the world, often outselling the immensely popular Chanel No. 5 in Mugler's native France.

Always the showman, Mugler decided that if he was going to leave the fashion world behind and pursue his perfume line, he would "go out with a bang." In 1995 he celebrated the 20th year of the house of Mugler with a televised production featuring live music performed by James Brown and appearances by celebrities including Jerry Hall, David Bowie, and Diana Ross. In 1997 Mugler, who had become increasingly disengaged from the business side of his enterprise, was bought out completely by his Angel partner, Clarins. "I realized I was living in my own universe, with lots of assistants. I didn't have a cellphone, I didn't know how to use a computer. Everybody was doing everything for me. So I left, and moved to New York. It was the end of an era, and I must say I found myself a bit lost. I wasn't in the protected Mugler universe anymore," Mugler recalled to Garratt.

When Clarins shuttered the fashion line, in 2003, after significant losses, Mugler took some time to reinvent himself, away from the public eye. He succeeded in that effort: when Mugler reemerged, four years later, the former dancer, who had taken up bodybuilding, had bulked up to such an extent that he was barely recognizable. Mugler has said that that was his intention; he did not want to be recognized because he wanted to leave the past behind. "You don't want to be reminded that you did this or you did that," he said to Eric Wilson for the *New York Times* (April 30, 2010). "It is disturbing." Mugler also said, as paraphrased by Wilson, that in bodybuilding he found "a way of correcting the physical imbalances he developed as a professional ballet dancer in his teens, and of going within, extending the yoga and meditation practices he learnt in the 1960's." "It's about discovering yourself," he said to the writer. "It's very interesting, and it's infinite. The potential of your body is endless."

In recent years Mugler's main focus has been directing and staging theatrical shows. He was closely involved with the Cirque du Soleil's erotic revue *Zumanities* in 2003. Next, Mugler worked with his friend Joey Arias, a performance artist, to stage an award-winning Off-Broadway show called *Arias with a Twist*. In 2009 some of Mugler's classic fashion pieces, including his famous vintage motorcycle bustier, made with parts of a Harley Davidson motorcycle, were shown in the Superheroes exhibition at the Metropolitan Museum of Art in New York. That inspired the pop star Beyoncé to seek out Mugler to design the wardrobe for her "I Am Sasha Fierce" tour. Mugler told Garratt that the first time he saw Beyoncé, he thought, "'This girl has grace.' She's a real star, like they used to be. And she's thoroughly honest about it, and she's enjoying every minute of it. She doesn't piss on it by saying, 'Actually, in real life I'm a housewife.' She is an extremely talented and polished performer. She dances incredibly well, she acts, she sings—she's a complete artist. I was very touched that she asked me, because she could have asked younger people. But she recognised that I was pretty much the origin of this moment now about superheroes, the structured silhouette and the extreme silhouette, and she wanted that." Mugler created 58 costumes for Beyoncé, her backup dancers, and her band. The famously theatrical designer also directed several portions of Beyoncé's live show. Mugler found that aspect of his collaboration with the pop singer to be especially rewarding, because it helped him accomplish what he had wanted to do all along: intertwine fashion, music, and theater.

Although Mugler has no immediate plans to come out with a new clothing collection, his influence is apparent in the work of some of today's hottest designers. For example, Marc Jacobs's 2009 fall ready-to-wear collection featured accentuated shoulders and tapered waists; futuristic metallic leggings, inspired by Mugler, are selling out everywhere from Forever 21 to American Apparel to Bloomingdales; and during the opening ceremony of the 2010 World Cup Soccer games, in Soweto, South Africa, the recording artist Fergie appeared in a leotard by the Indian husband-and-wife team Shane and Falguni Peacock that brought to mind Mugler's alien- and insect-inspired collections of the 1980s.

Mugler, who is again using Paris as his home base, has said that he moved back to France for love, though he has refused to divulge any further information pertaining to his personal life. He is currently working with Joey Arias on a follow-up to *Arias with a Twist*. Mugler has continued to have success with the Thierry Mugler line of perfumes; a new fragrance, called Womanity, was introduced in 2010. Mugler expressed to Phillips his belief that fashion is meant to be a service—a belief that has helped him remain true to his ideals throughout his long career. "[Fashion] is supposed to improve people's lives and to help them. I am not trendy. I am not 'in fashion.' I am simply a positive human being, who has a positive outlook on life."

—H.R.W.

Suggested Reading: (London) *Independent* (online) Dec. 5, 1998; (London) *Telegraph* (on-line) May 21, 2009; *New York Times* (on-line) Apr. 30, 2010

Selected Books: *Thierry Mugler, Photographer*, 1988; *Thierry Mugler: Fashion Fetish Fantasy*, 1998; *Thierry Mugler: Galaxy Glamour*, 2010

Selected Theatrical Works: as costume designer—*Emilie Jolie*, 1985; *Zumanities*, 2003; *Arias with a Twist*, 2008

Murguía, Janet

(mer-GEE-yah)

Sep. 6, 1960– President and CEO of the National Council of La Raza

Address: National Council of La Raza, 1126 16th St., N.W., Washington, DC 20036

Janet Murguía is the president and chief executive officer of the National Council of La Raza (NCLR), which identifies itself as the largest nonprofit, nonpartisan Latino civil rights and advocacy organization in the U.S. "Demographics show that Hispanics are now the largest minority community" in the country, Murguía told Jerry LaMartina for the *Kansas City Business Journal* (November 26, 2004), when the U.S. Census Bureau estimated the number of people of Hispanic descent living in the U.S. to be about 40.5 million, or slightly under 14 percent of the total population. Murguía added, "Those numbers won't mean anything if we don't leverage those numbers into increased economic empowerment, political empowerment, and social advancement for the Hispanic community." In 2007—the most recent year for which the U.S. Census Bureau has provided data—descendants of Hispanics living in the U.S. numbered about 45.5 million, or about 15 percent of the total popu-

Kevork Djansezian/Getty Images

Janet Murguía

lation. Currently, in terms of income, educational level, home and business ownership, medical coverage, and other measures of achievement and well-being, Hispanics lag behind all other ethnic groups except African-Americans. The goal of the NCLR, according to its Web site, is to "improve opportunities for Hispanic Americans," by means of "applied research, policy analysis, and advocacy" that aim to "provid[e] a Latino perspective in five key areas—assets/investments, civil rights/immigration, education, employment and economic status, and health." Other areas in which the NCLR is active include the availability of affordable housing and bilingual programs. The NCLR does not provide help directly to people; rather, it offers training and funding to its affiliates, which currently number close to 300 and are located in 41 states, Puerto Rico, and Washington, D.C. "We need to have institutions like NCLR so that our Latino community can have a voice in Washington and across the country—wherever decisions and policies that affect us are made," Murguía told Frank DiMaria for the *Hispanic Outlook in Higher Education* (February 27, 2006). Murguía has spent much of her time as the leader of NCLR responding to false and malicious statements about the organization and about Hispanics in the U.S. "When I took this job, I thought I would be talking more about taking advantage of our opportunities rather than defending our civil rights," she told Michael Humphrey for the *National Catholic Reporter* (February 22, 2008, on-line). "We should be talking about housing and personal advancement, building community. Instead we are fighting hate speech and distortions."

Murguía, whose parents' education ended with elementary school, has two bachelor's degrees and a law degree. She began her professional life in Washington, D.C., in 1987, as an aide to a Democratic congressman, Jim Slattery of Kansas. From 1994 to 2000 she held a series of jobs at the White House, during the presidency of Bill Clinton. In 2000 she served as the deputy campaign manager and director of constituency outreach for the ultimately unsuccessful candidates on that year's Democratic presidential ticket, Vice President Al Gore and his running mate, U.S. senator Joseph Lieberman of Connecticut. For three years beginning in 2001, she held the post of executive vice chancellor for university relations at the University of Kansas, her alma mater. She became the chief operating officer of the NCLR in 2004 and was promoted to its top leadership position in 2005. "I've seen the American dream be a reality, and I want to make sure we can make it a reality for others as well," she told Teresa Watanabe for the *Los Angeles Times* (July 20, 2006).

The youngest, along with her twin sister, Mary, of the three sons and four daughters of a Mexican-American couple, Janet Murguía was born in Kansas City, Kansas, on September 6, 1960. She grew up in a Mexican-American community in the section of Kansas City known as Argentine. Her father, Alfredo Olivarez Murguía, was born in Oklahoma; during his childhood he returned to Mexico, then moved to Kansas after his marriage. He worked in a Kansas City steel plant; when he retired, in about 1990, after 37 years on the job, his salary was $18,000 a year (the equivalent of less than $30,000 in 2008). Murguía's mother, Amalia, operated an informal day-care facility in her home to supplement her husband's income. Amalia was a widow with a young daughter, Martha Hernandez, when she and Alfredo married. The children they had together, in addition to Janet and Mary, are Alfred Jr., Rosemary, Carlos, and Ramón. Janet Murguía told Janet Perez for *Hispanic Business* (April 2005) that her parents "set a terrific example" for her and her siblings. "The values that they imparted . . . reflect the positive aspects of our culture, the strong sense of faith, the strong sense of family, a strong sense of community that helps and supports one another." Her parents "scrimped" and "sacrificed" for their children, she wrote in a remembrance for *Newsweek* (October 15, 2007), and though neither had attended school beyond the sixth grade, they encouraged their children to excel academically. Murguía told Teresa Watanabe, "They always knew the importance of education. They knew . . . it was the key to the future for their kids." Six of the seven Murguía siblings have earned college degrees, and four have earned law degrees. Mary Murguía and Carlos Murguía are the first brother and sister in U.S. history to serve as federal judges; Ramón Murguía practices law privately in Kansas City. Alfred is a hotel caterer, and Martha works in a restaurant. Alfredo Murguía died in 2002; Rosemary quit her job at around that time to serve as her mother's caregiver and as the caretaker of the family house.

Janet Murguía attended Harmon High School, in Kansas City. During her years there she participated in Girls State, a citizenship-training program sponsored by the women's auxiliary of the American Legion. She was one of the two female students from Kansas chosen in 1977 to attend Girls Nation, another American Legion activity, in which participants visit Washington, D.C., for a week to learn firsthand about the workings of government.

According to Watanabe, Murguía and her twin sister earned "near-perfect" grades in high school. Both attended the University of Kansas (K.U.) and lived in the same dorm room. A worker in the school's financial-aid office, Murguía told Watanabe, helped her enormously in her successful search for the scholarships, loans, and grants necessary to cover her tuition and expenses. She received two bachelor's degrees from the university: a B.S. in journalism and a B.A. in Spanish, both in 1982. Three years later she completed a J.D. degree at K.U.'s School of Law. From 1987 to 1994 she worked in Washington, D.C., as an assistant to Jim Slattery, a Democrat who represented Kansas's Second Congressional District in the House from 1983 to 1995. (That district encompasses the state capital, Topeka, and much of eastern Kansas, excluding the Kansas City metropolitan area.) Slattery became a mentor to Murguía and steadily increased her responsibilities; as a result she gained experience in a wide range of areas. Murguía, Slattery told Janet Perez, "was deeply committed to trying to make the country a better place for all people. When you meet Janet you can't help but be impressed by the warmth of her personality, her enthusiasm, and her genuine concern and compassion for others."

Slattery opted not to seek reelection in 1994, deciding instead to run for governor of Kansas. At the recommendation of Bill Richardson, then a New Mexico congressman, Murguía was hired as a member of the White House Legislative Affairs Office under President Bill Clinton. Her titles during the next six years included deputy assistant to Clinton, deputy director of legislative affairs, and senior White House liaison to Congress. Murguía worked with First Lady Hillary Clinton's Task Force on National Health Care Reform. The extremely complex plan proposed by the task force never gained sufficient support among legislators and was abandoned in September 1994. Reflecting in 2007 on its failure, Murguía told Richard S. Dunham and Keith Epstein for *BusinessWeek* (July 3, 2007, on-line), "One of the big mistakes of the Clinton experience was to think that they could do this without business and industry. It was arrogance." (The Patient Protection and Affordable Care Act and the Health Care and Education Reconciliation Act were signed into law by President Barack Obama in March 2010.)

In 2000 Murguía served as a deputy manager of the presidential and vice presidential campaigns of the Democratic nominees, Vice President Al Gore and U.S. senator Joseph Lieberman of Connecticut, respectively; she was also the director of constituency outreach during their campaigns. In 2001, after the Republican George W. Bush assumed the presidency, she returned to Kansas to take on the post of executive vice chancellor for university relations at K.U. She was in charge of public and government relations and trademark licensing and managed the K.U. Visitor Center, KANU-FM (the campus radio station), and the Audio-Reader Network, a university-managed reading service for blind students. Her duties also included attending meetings of the Kansas state legislature in Topeka and raising funds through the K.U. Endowment Association. In addition, she toured the state to promote K.U. and spread the word about the importance of education and of "making it accessible and affordable," she told Michelle Adam for the *Hispanic Outlook in Higher Education* (February 24, 2003). "I saw those dismal statistics in Washington, D.C., not only about the lack of Latinos in higher education, but the fact that we have poor rates in terms of high school. We need to create higher expectations for our community. We have to keep the bar high. I feel that maybe I can help do my part in that regard." In a 2002 issue of *Hispanic Business*, Murguía was listed as one of the "100 Most Influential Hispanics."

In 2004 Murguía left K.U. to become the chief operating officer of NCLR. The organization was called the Southwest Council of La Raza when it was set up, in 1968, in Phoenix, Arizona, by Julian Samora, Ernesto Galarza, and Herman Gallegos, the last of whom was its first executive director. The group began helping Hispanic community organizations with voter registration, leadership development, and other activities, in the process linking up formally with groups including the Mexican American Unity Council (MAUC) and Chicanos Por La Causa Inc. (CPLC). In 1972, having drawn affiliates from all over the country, the organization changed its name to National Council of La Raza. In 1974 the NCLR board selected Raul Yzaguirre as NCLR's new executive director. Yzaguirre, who headed NCLR until the end of 2004, reorganized the group, obtained federal grants, and increased its involvement in public policy-making. Murguía became the head of the NCLR on January 1, 2005. Currently, NCLR has a staff of 120, a 21-member board, eight regional offices, and a budget of $1.3 billion. It receives funding from corporate partners, dues from affiliates, donations from individuals (who are considered members), and the federal government. Its corporate partners include Johnson & Johnson, Bank of America, PepsiCo, Wal-Mart, and State Farm Insurance. A few representative organizations among its approximately 300 affiliates are Academia Avance, in Los Angeles, California (one of the 115 charter schools that receive NCLR support); the

East Boston Ecumenical Community Council, in Massachusetts; the Hispanic Economic Development Corp., in Kansas City, Missouri; the Hispanic Women's Organization of Arkansas; the Michigan Commission on Spanish Speaking Affairs; the Mississippi Immigrants Rights Alliance; the Multicultural Career Intern Program, in Washington, D.C.; the Washington State Migrant Council; Valley Community Clinic, in North Hollywood, California (which, along with other NCLR-supported health centers, provided treatment to about 200,000 people in 2008); and Youth Development Inc., in Albuquerque, New Mexico.

Working with NCLR's affiliates is one of Murguía's most important duties. She also strives to strengthen the NCLR's ties to other civil rights advocacy groups—the National Association for the Advancement of Colored People (NAACP) and the National Urban League, for example. Another priority is the registration of new Hispanic American voters; in the months preceding the 2008 presidential election, about 200,000 Latinos registered for the first time with the NCLR's help. "One of the clearer roads that we have to move forward on as a community . . . is around civic engagement," Murguía told a reporter for th*e Denver Post* (September 2, 2007). "I don't think this is a policy debate anymore. I think we have to work on changing the political landscape for the community. . . . That means making sure that all folks who are eligible to be citizens are being naturalized . . . making sure that people go out and vote once they are registered."

Under Murguía, NCLR has been active in advocating for immigration reform, which has become one of the most polarizing political issues in recent years. In an interview broadcast on *NBC News* (March 28, 2006), Murguía said, "If we're going to deal with this problem sensibly, orderly, fairly and humanely, we need a solution that is comprehensive. It can't just be enforcement only. . . . That alone won't work. We need to offer guest worker options, and ultimately deal with those 11 to 12 million workers . . . [who do] back-breaking work that nobody else wants to do in this country. We need to recognize that they are contributing to the economic vitality of this country, and understand that they're already part of this country." According to the organization's Web site, "NCLR's immigration policy agenda supports a workable and humane immigration system that restores the rule of law and protects workers and families, measures that protect civil rights and due process and keep the nation safe, and integration strategies that help immigrants become fully participating and contributing Americans." The NCLR supported a bill proposed in 2007 by then–President George W. Bush that would have established a means for roughly 12 million undocumented immigrants to gain citizenship. It would also have toughened border security and established a guest-worker program. Critics of the bill complained that it offered illegal immigrants "amnesty," and it died in the

Senate. NCLR has expressed frustration with the failure of the administration of President Barack Obama to act on immigration reform. In a July 10, 2009 NCLR news release, Murguía complained, "It's time to stop the missteps, half-steps, and backsteps on immigration. The country wants immigration reform, the Latino community is waiting for it, our families are suffering, and we need to see some serious progress." She added, "NCLR urges the administration and Congress to demonstrate leadership by avoiding piecemeal attempts to address the country's broken immigration system and instead advance an effective, comprehensive solution."

The NCLR has been among the civil rights organizations strenuously fighting an Arizona law, signed by Governor Jan Brewer in April 2010, that requires immigrants to carry at all times documents regarding their status. Provisions of the law, which went into effect on July 29, 2010, made failure to provide such documents on request by law-enforcement officers a criminal offense and gave those officers the power to detain immigrants suspected of being in the U.S. illegally. On July 28, 2010 a federal judge blocked those provisions—the most controversial parts of the bill. The state of Arizona appealed the decision, and a hearing on the judge's injunction was scheduled for November 2010. The NCLR has argued that those provisions would open the door to legalized discrimination against Hispanics, regardless of their legal status, since they would permit police officers to demand to see anyone's documents in the course of questioning concerning possible infringement of other laws, and since the officers would be far more likely to demand documents if those stopped appeared to be Hispanic. The NCLR maintains the Web site boycottintolerance.org, which provides information about ongoing protests against the law and—as many other civil rights organizations have done—urges that people avoid vacationing or holding conferences in Arizona. The NCLR has also asked Major League Baseball officials to abandon plans to hold the 2011 All-Star Game in Phoenix, Arizona's largest city.

The NCLR's stance on immigration, along with many of its other stands, as well as its activities, mission, and even its name have been heavily criticized by conservative politicians and media figures. In an "open letter to the public" (October 26, 2006, on-line), Murguía wrote, "As an advocacy organization engaged in the public arena, we know that some will disagree with our views. As Americans committed to basic civil rights, we respect anyone's right to do so. But it is also clear that some critics are willfully distorting the facts and deliberately mischaracterizing our organization and our work." Murguía wrote the letter in response to remarks by Republican congressman Charlie Norwood of Georgia, who in a press release (September 20, 2006) had described the NCLR as "a pro-illegal immigration lobbying organization that supports racist groups calling for the secession of the western United States as a Hispanic-only homeland";

he had also charged that the NCLR had "mounted an all-out campaign to prevent state and local police from voluntarily aiding critically undermanned federal authorities" engaged in border patrols. "If Americans don't wake up now, they'll wake up one day soon to find their nation has been stolen by La Raza and pals," Norwood declared.

The conservative syndicated columnist Michelle Malkin has also demonized La Raza. Referring to the 2008 Democratic and Republican presidential candidates (and ultimate nominees), Malkin wrote (July 12, 2008, on-line), as posted on her Web site's archives, "Both Barack Obama and John McCain were scheduled to speak this week in San Diego at the annual conference of the National Council of La Raza, the Latino organization whose name is Spanish for, yes, 'The Race.' Can you imagine Obama and McCain paying homage to a group of white people who called themselves that? No matter. The unvarnished truth is that the group is a radical ethnic nationalist outfit that abuses your tax dollars and milks p.c. [politically correct] politics to undermine our sovereignty." She also wrote that NCLR "vehemently opposes cooperative immigration enforcement," "has consistently opposed post-9/11 national security measures," and "sponsors militant ethnic nationalist charter schools subsidized by your public tax dollars." During an interview with Rick Sanchez for CNN (May 28, 2008) two days after President Obama nominated federal judge Sonia Sotomayor for a seat on the U.S. Supreme Court, a third outspoken critic of the NCLR, the Republican former congressman Tom Tancredo of Colorado, characterized the organization as "a Latino K.K.K. without the hoods and the nooses." (He was referring to the Ku Klux Klan, a white-supremacist organization whose modus operandi has included violence and intimidation.) "If you belong to something like that, you've got to explain it in a way that's going to convince me and a lot of other people it's got nothing to do with race, even though the logo is 'All for the race, nothing for the rest,'" Tancredo declared, according to Ernest Luning, writing for the *Colorado Independent* (May 28, 2008, on-line).

The La Raza Web site rejects Norwood's, Malkin's, and Tancredo's claims as distortions or outright lies. For example, it declares that the NCLR "unequivocally rejects" the precept "All for the race, nothing for the rest" (in Spanish, "Por La Raza todo, Fuera de La Raza nada"), which "is not and has never been the motto of any Latino organization." Moreover, "race" is only one meaning of "la raza"; according to the NCLR, "La Raza" "has its origins in early 20th century Latin American literature and translates into English most closely as 'the people' or, according to some scholars, as 'the Hispanic people of the New World.' The term was coined by the Mexican scholar José Vasconcelos to reflect the fact that the people of Latin America are a mixture of many of the world's races, cultures, and religions. Mistranslating 'La Raza' to mean 'the race' implies that it is a term meant to exclude oth-

ers. In fact, the full term coined by Vasconcelos, 'La Raza Cósmica,' meaning the 'cosmic people,' was developed to reflect not purity but the mixture inherent in the Hispanic people. This is an inclusive concept, meaning that Hispanics share with all other peoples of the world a common heritage and destiny." Hispanics, Murguía has often said, "are an ethnic group, not a race."

In addition, the NCLR does not support separatist organizations or the idea that any part of U.S. territory should be returned to Mexico. It does not encourage illegal immigration; rather, it "has repeatedly recognized the right of the United States, as a sovereign nation, to control its borders. Moreover, NCLR has supported numerous specific measures to strengthen border enforcement, provided that such enforcement is conducted fairly, humanely, and in a nondiscriminatory fashion." Murguía herself was a member of the Independent Task Force on Immigration and America's Future, an independent, bipartisan committee chaired by former congressman Lee Hamilton, an Indiana Democrat, and former U.S. senator Spencer Abraham, a Michigan Republican, and she endorsed its recommendations for immigration reform, released in September 2006. As summarized on the Web site of the Migration Policy Institute, the recommendations included the creation of "an independent body in the Executive Branch that would introduce flexibility into the system by making regular recommendations to Congress and the President for adjusting immigration levels . . . based on ongoing analysis of labor market needs and changing economic and demographic trends." The committee also recommended the provision of "a path to legal status for unauthorized immigrants who can demonstrate steady employment, knowledge of English, payment of taxes, and passage of a background security check, among other requirements." The NCLR also maintains on its Web site, "It is in the best interests of the United States and of immigrants themselves to ensure that all immigration to the U.S. takes place legally."

Murguía has also responded to criticisms of NCLR, and discussed Latino affairs in general, on many television talk shows and news programs. As the head of the NCLR, she has testified before numerous congressional committees and subcommittees on matters directly affecting Hispanics. Murguía is a board member of the Independent Sector, a coalition of nonprofit groups and corporations; an executive-committee member of the Leadership Conference on Civil Rights; and a board member of both the Hispanic Association on Corporate Responsibility and the National Hispanic Leadership Agenda. Since 2003 several magazines, among them *Hispanic Business, the Washingtonian, Hispanic, NonProfit Times,* and *Newsweek,* have included her on their lists of the most influential or powerful women or Hispanics in the U.S. She received the Kansas University Law Alumni Association Distinguished Alumnus Award in 2005 and the Community Service Award of the Mexican

American Legal Defense and Educational Fund in 2008.

Like all her sisters, Murguía is unmarried.

—W.D.

Suggested Reading: *Hispanic* p32 June 2004; *Hispanic Business* p34+ Apr. 2005; *Hispanic Outlook in Higher Education* p17 Feb. 27, 2006; *Kansas City (Kansas) Star* p11 Feb. 8, 2004; *Los Angeles Times* p2 July 20, 2006; nclr.org; *Topeka (Kansas) Capital-Journal* A p1 Nov. 4, 2002

Myunghee Koh, courtesy of B. R. Myers

Myers, B. R.

Aug. 21, 1963– Literary critic; expert on North Korea

Address: Dongseo University, International Studies Dept., San 69-1 Churge-2-Dong, Sasang-Gu, Busan 617-716, South Korea

When former U.S. president Bill Clinton went to North Korea in the summer of 2009 to negotiate the release of two American journalists who had illegally entered that country, the world was watching. The U.S. perceived the North Korean ruler Kim Jong Il's invitation as a hint that he was willing to negotiate and, perhaps, seek better relations with the West—and viewed Clinton as having succeeded in freeing the journalists, who were facing long, harsh sentences in a labor camp. After more than five years of researching the pervasive domestic propaganda in North Korea, B. R. Myers understood that that nation's citizens viewed the incident very differently. Myers wrote in the preface to his best-selling book, *The Cleanest Race: How North Koreans See Themselves—And Why It Matters* (2010), as excerpted in the *New York Times* (January 28, 2010, on-line), "It is not in ideological treatises but in the more mass-oriented domestic propaganda that [North Korea's] official worldview is expressed most clearly and unselfconsciously. I stress the word domestic. Too many observers wrongly assume that the (North) Korean Central News Agency's English-language releases reflect the same sort of propaganda that the home audience gets. In fact there are significant differences. For example, where [North Korea] presents itself to the outside world as a misunderstood country seeking integration into the international community, it presents itself to its own citizens . . . as a rogue state that breaks agreements with impunity, dictates conditions to groveling U.N. officials, and keeps its enemies in constant fear of ballistic retribution." In an interview with *Current Biography*, the source of quotes for this article unless otherwise noted, Myers explained that North Korea, despite the popular perception, does not subscribe to Communist, Stalinist, or Confucian ideology; instead, it is a "paranoid, race-based, nationalist state which derives its legitimacy from the claim to be protecting this uniquely pure race from the 'Yankee' enemy." That people outside North Korea—including experts, politicians, and diplomats—are unaware of that phenomenon is no accident, according to Myers. "Generally speaking," he wrote in the preface, "the following rule of thumb applies: the less accessible a propaganda outlet is to the outside world, the blunter and more belligerent it will be in its expression of the racist orthodoxy." According to North Korea's domestic propaganda, Clinton's visit was an instance of the "Yankee jackals" sending one of their most prominent ambassadors to pay homage to the great Kim Jong Il. After the meeting Clinton and Kim, both sitting and neither smiling, posed for an official photo whose background was a painting of turquoise ocean waves crashing against rocks. Most Americans, Myers wrote in *The Cleanest Race*, probably saw the painting as ridiculous or kitschy, if they noticed it at all, but in North Korea the image is a common symbol of "the futility of the world's harassment of the motherland" and the country's unshakable determination to stand up to all outsiders.

In addition to being an expert on North Korea—he has a Ph.D. in North Korean studies and heads the international-studies program at Dongseo University, in Busan, South Korea—Myers is a literary critic. In the summer of 2001, then unknown in the literary world, Myers published an audacious essay titled "A Reader's Manifesto" in the *Atlantic Monthly* (July/August 2001). With little idea that he would generate passionate debate, he took issue with the "self-conscious, writerly prose" of contemporary novelists whom he accused of writing sloppily in their attempts to sound literary, poetic, or philosophical, and who, he wrote, try to "intimidate" both readers and critics into accepting incomprehensible passages as profound observations. He chose five big targets for his attack: Annie Proulx, Cormac McCarthy, Don Delillo, Paul Auster, and David Guterson. Within days the essay became a topic of conversation in literary circles nationwide. Critics, writers, and members of the general public—in newspapers, magazines, journals, and Web sites—were debating the merits of Myers's arguments, the worth of the writers whose work he had critiqued, and the general state of modern American fiction. Myers expanded his essay into the book *A Reader's Manifesto: An Attack on the Growing Pretentiousness in American Literary Prose* (2002). In his review of that work for the *New York Observer* (August 26, 2002), Adam Begley wrote, "Mr. Myers is particularly effective when he's dissing the 'cultural establishment'— the prize juries and book reviewers who puff up authors' reputations and pass off perfectly ordinary novels as miracles of writerly inspiration. If it rattles our critics, if it makes them think twice about claiming that a novel is 'beautifully written' without showing how, *A Reader's Manifesto* will have done good work. Mr. Myers will probably be assailed all over again for skewering the likes of Ms. Proulx. My advice to her many fans—and to McCarthy and Auster fans—is not to argue with Mr. Myers but to mimic him, though in a more generous mode: Pick apart the prose, make sure it merits every word of praise you offer."

Brian Reynolds Myers was born on August 21, 1963 in Fort Dix, New Jersey, on a military base where his father served as a chaplain. His parents divorced soon afterward. He and his mother then moved to her country of origin, Bermuda, a British island colony in the Atlantic Ocean. When Myers was 11 years old, his mother and stepfather decided to leave Bermuda; the governor, Richard Sharples, had been assassinated in 1973 by black militants, which had increased the racial tension on the island. Myers's parents looked to South Africa, which, Myers recalled in an e-mail message, "had the reputation among the white middle class in Britain and the rest of the commonwealth as being something of a land of opportunity." After moving to South Africa, Myers quickly became unhappy. Although he received a good education there— "lots of Shakespeare and essay writing," he recalled in an e-mail—he despised the strict environment, where corporal punishment ("with thin bamboo canes") was common. Myers attended high school in Kloof, a relatively well-to-do suburb on South Africa's east coast. Apartheid— institutionalized racial segregation—was still the law of the land there, with the white minority government denying the black majority basic rights. Myers recalled regularly hearing propaganda about the superiority of whites and inferiority of blacks. Whenever U.S. president Jimmy Carter publicly criticized South Africa, Myers—because he was American—would be "in for it the next day," sometimes getting beaten up by his fellow students. He was puzzled, for that reason, by the fact that some of those zealously racist students were big fans of reggae music. That taught him just how "sturdy" such nationalist racism can be: "It can absorb a lot of culture from the outside without being undermined by it"—a lesson, he would later realize, that also applies to North Korea.

After high school Myers went to Germany, where he majored in Soviet studies at Ruhr University, in Bochum, in pursuit of a master's degree. In 1985 he decided to take a year off to visit his father, who was stationed in South Korea. At the time Myers was interested in Japan (he even spoke Japanese). But during his yearlong visit to South Korea he became fascinated with that country, about which the Western world knew very little. He started learning Korean—helped by the grammatic similarities between Korean and Japanese—and in 1986 met the woman who would become his wife.

Myers later returned to Germany, where he received an M.A. degree in Soviet studies in 1989, a few months before the Berlin Wall came down. (After World War II the Soviet Union occupied East Germany, and in 1961 the Soviets built a wall to separate East and West Berlin. The dismantling of the wall marked the beginning of the reunification process for East and West Germany.) The fall of the Berlin Wall was seen as a sign that the Cold War between the United States and the Soviet Union was coming to an end. That development led Myers to change his career course; at Ruhr University he had minored in Korean studies, so at the University of Tübingen, in Germany, he shifted his focus to North Korea. Like most people he assumed that North Korea was a Stalinist state, and "it looked like one of the few Communist countries left that you could make a living in specializing in," Myers said. Because the German university system allowed him to complete his doctoral work independently, Myers left for Japan, where he taught German at a college. During that time he researched North Korean propaganda materials. Before long he concluded that North Korea was not what he had thought it was; the country's racist propaganda reminded him of what he had encountered in South Africa during his high-school years.

After a year in Japan, Myers moved to the United States and continued his research at the Library of Congress, in Washington, D.C. "I had of course begun, like everybody else, by reading English-language magazines that North Korea at that time still had the money to be sending around the world," Myers recalled. "Every university library in the West, at that time, was receiving huge bundles of North Korean propaganda materials in English." But the truly nationalist, racist propaganda was domestic, disseminated by the North Korean government only to its own people. Myers studied those materials in libraries, reading them in Korean. (He could both read and speak the language fluently at that point, conversing in Korean with his wife at home.) Myers received his Ph.D. degree from the University of Tübingen in 1994.

For three years beginning in 1995, Myers worked for the Mercedes-Benz auto company, which sent him to China. Myers spoke Chinese, but his wife did not, so the move was hard on her. In many ways it was also hard on him. "I wanted to go back to the States, to the English-speaking world," Myers said. "I felt like I was losing touch with my own language."

Myers returned to the U.S. in 1998 and immediately re-immersed himself in the English language, frequenting libraries and bookstores. In catching up on American literature, he noticed that many contemporary "literary" novels were adorned with hyperbolic blurbs. "These blurbs would rave about the book," Myers recalled, "and perhaps there was a prize stamped on the book, like the National Book Award or the Pulitzer Prize or something, and then I would open up the book and actually start to read it. And I thought, 'This is pretty horrible stuff.'" Myers read voraciously, eventually deciding to write some "straightforward literary criticism written in normal language, not academic jargon." His efforts led to the essay published in the *Atlantic* as "A Reader's Manifesto."

Myers did not criticize complex or challenging language generally—he wrote positively of Vladimir Nabokov, James Joyce, and Henry James—but he took exception to writers' use of sloppy, purposely opaque, or illogical passages to create the illusion of profundity. "At the 1999 National Book Awards ceremony," Myers wrote in the essay, "Oprah Winfrey told of calling Toni Morrison to say that she had had to puzzle over many of the latter's sentences. According to Oprah, Morrison's reply was 'That, my dear, is called reading.' Sorry, my dear Toni, but it's actually called bad writing. Great prose isn't always easy, but it's always lucid." Of the five modern American writers Myers attacked in the essay, he began with Annie Proulx, whose novel *The Shipping News* (1993) won both the National Book Award and a Pulitzer Prize. He quoted a sentence from Proulx's story collection *Close Range*: "In the long unfurling of his life, from tight-wound kid hustler in a wool suit riding the train out of Cheyenne to geriatric limper in this spooled-out year, Mero had kicked down thoughts of the place where he began, a so-called ranch on strange ground at the south hinge of the Big Horns." Myers wrote, "Like so much modern prose, this demands to be read quickly, with just enough attention to register the bold use of words. Slow down, and things fall apart. . . . [Proulx's] writing, like that of so many other novelists today, is touted as 'evocative' and 'compelling.' The reason these vague attributes have become *the* literary catchwords of our time, even more popular than 'raw' and 'angry' were in the 1950s, is that they allow critics to praise a writer's prose without considering its effect on the reader. It is easier to call writing like Proulx's lyrically evocative or poetically compelling than to figure out what it evokes, or what it compels the reader to think and feel." Myers then moved on to Cormac McCarthy. Mak-

ing an exception of McCarthy's first novel—*The Orchard Keeper* (1965), which Myers called a "masterpiece of careful and restrained writing"—he called attention to the "stern biblical tone that runs through all of McCarthy's recent novels. Parallelisms and pseudo-archaic formulations abound: 'They caught up and set out each day in the dark before the day was and they ate cold meat and biscuit and made no fire'; 'and they would always be so and never be otherwise'; 'the captain wrote on nor did he look up'; 'there rode no soul save he,' and so forth. The reader is meant to be carried along on the stream of language. . . . Like Proulx and so many others today, McCarthy relies more on barrages of hit-and-miss verbiage than on careful use of just the right words." Myers next took on Don Delillo, whose novel *White Noise* (1985) had made him a postmodern literary icon. "Not all contemporary writing is marked by the Proulx-McCarthy brand of obscurity," Myers wrote. "Many novels intimidate readers by making them wonder not what the writer is saying but *why* he is saying it." Citing a passage from *White Noise* that included a lengthy list of consumer goods, Myers concluded: "This is the sort of writing, full of brand names and wardrobe inventories, that critics like to praise as an 'edgy' take on the insanity of modern American life. It's hard to see what is so edgy about describing suburbia as a wasteland of stupefied shoppers, which is something left-leaning social critics have been doing since the 1950s. Still, this is foolproof subject matter for a novelist of limited gifts."

Next on the list was Paul Auster, who first gained acclaim with his trilogy of New York City–based novels, beginning with *City of Glass* (1985). "Anyone who doubts the declining literacy of book reviewers," Myers wrote, "need only consider how the gabbiest of all prose styles is invariably praised as 'lean,' 'spare,' even 'minimalist.' I am referring, of course, to the Paul Auster School of Writing." Myers argued that Auster's wordplay was unsuccessful and his philosophical insights shallow. "What gives Auster away is his weakness for facetious displays of erudition," Myers noted, adding: "Auster is commercially successful precisely because he offers so much cachet in return for so little concentration. Whole chapters can be skimmed with impunity." Last, Myers attacked the bestselling author David Guterson, whose novel *Snow Falling on Cedars* (1994), in which the husband of the main character's ex-lover is wrongly accused of murder, won the PEN/Faulkner book award. "Today's 'literary' novel," Myers wrote, "need only evince a few quotable passages to be guaranteed at least a lukewarm review. This reflects both the growing influence of the sentence cult and a desire to reward novelists for aiming high. It is perhaps natural, therefore, that the 'literary' camp now attracts a type of risk-averse writer who, under different circumstances, might never have strayed from the safest thriller or romance formulae. Many critically acclaimed novels today are no more than mediocre 'genre' stories told in a conformist amalgam of approved 'literary' styles. Every amalgam is a little different, of course; what unites these writers and separates them from the rest of the 'literary' camp is the determinedly slow tempo of their prose. They seem to know that in leaner and livelier form their courtroom dramas, geisha memoirs, and horse-whisperer romances would not be taken seriously, and that it is precisely the lack of genreish suspense that elevates them to the status of prize-worthy 'tales of loss and redemption.' The most successful of these writers is David Guterson." Myers concluded his essay by expressing the hope that literary critics begin reading more critically and "start toning down their hyperbole." The book *A Reader's Manifesto* appeared in 2002.

Starting in 2002 Myers wore two hats—North Korea expert and literary critic—writing primarily for the *Atlantic*, where he was eventually granted the title of contributing editor. Several months after "A Reader's Manifesto" was published, he moved to South Korea, where he taught classes on North Korea at Korea University, in Seoul. After four years he moved on to Dongseo University, in Busan, South Korea, where within months he became a tenured professor and director of the international-studies department.

During the first half of the 20th century, Korea, then one nation, was occupied by Japan and ruled harshly. Following World War II, in which the U.S. and its allies defeated Germany and Japan, Soviet troops temporarily occupied northern Korea, with U.S. troops in the south. In 1948 two separate governments—the Republic of Korea (or South Korea) and the Democratic People's Republic of Korea (DPRK, or North Korea)—were formed. In 1950, the year after U.S. and Soviet troops were withdrawn, the north invaded the south, beginning the Korean War (1950–53), in which the United States fought for South Korea. After the war differences between the two Koreas began to emerge, with the North developing into a totalitarian, nationalistic state and the South on the road to a free market and a form of democracy. Intermittent moves toward reunification in the following decades proved to be fruitless. Over the years North Korea's economy has fallen victim to a lack of resources and arable land, underinvestment, and a sustained focus on military spending, among other factors; the citizens suffer from malnutrition and generally substandard living conditions. While in South Korea Myers contributed articles to the *New York Times* and occasionally the *Wall Street Journal* in addition to the *Atlantic*; in his writing Myers stressed the profound difference between the ways North Korea and the West interpret diplomatic and international relations. He also noted the contrast between the way the North Korean leadership presented itself to the West, on the one hand, and to its own people, on the other.

"Last week's announcement," Myers wrote in an op-ed piece for the *New York Times* (February 13, 2005), "that North Korea has nuclear weapons, for example, said that while the country had 'manufactured nukes for self-defense,' it still sought only 'peaceful coexistence' with the United States. But the propaganda dinned every day into the North Korean people is of a different order. School textbooks, wall posters, literary works: all celebrate a cynical 'attack diplomacy' that makes a frightened and uncertain world dance to the drum of Kim Jong Il. Again and again, comic effect is derived from stories of stammering American and international officials trying to placate the relentless 'warriors' of the Foreign Ministry. Washington's refusal to follow through on veiled threats of military action is mocked as a failure of nerve." North Korea's version of events, according to Myers, is that after signing the Nuclear Nonproliferation Treaty, in 1985, North Korea withdrew from it in 2003—and that despite a lot of diplomatic dissatisfaction and grumbling, the United States not only did nothing in response (that is, took no military action), but provided North Korea with food aid. While the U.S. might see that course of action as arising from good will, North Korea's leadership tells its citizens that it constitutes appeasement. There was a similar interpretation gap in early 2008, when the New York Philharmonic was set to perform in Pyongyang, North Korea's capital. The hope expressed by many people, including the conductor, Lorin Maazel, was that bringing people together through music could bridge differences between nations. In the case of North Korea, Myers wrote in an op-ed piece for the *Wall Street Journal* (February 21, 2008), such a viewpoint is misguided, since the North Korean government has no interest in real negotiations with the West: "The North Koreans do know . . . that if they want to keep the [George W.] Bush administration in futile negotiation mode for the rest of its term, they must feign the occasional change of heart. The invitation to the orchestra serves this end." Furthermore, the North Korean government, Myers wrote, "will set about misrepresenting the performance as a tributary visit, the paper tiger's latest effort to curry favor from the iron-willed 'General'"—Kim Jong Il. When, in May 2009, North Korea conducted an underground nuclear test, it was condemned by leaders worldwide, including U.S. president Barack Obama. But North Korea cares less about what the world thinks, Myers wrote in an op-ed article for the *New York Times* (May 29, 2009), than about what its own citizens believe: because the North Korean people are becoming more concerned about their desperate economic circumstances, the Kim Jong Il regime "must justify its existence through a combination of radical nationalist rhetoric and victories on the military and nuclear front. This is why North Korea will never disarm, for to do so would be to declare itself irrelevant." The only way North Korea can inspire pride in its citizens, Myers argued, is by demonstrating its military might.

In preparation for writing *The Cleanest Race*, in addition to his research of North Korea's domestic propaganda, Myers spoke to North Koreans who had defected to South Korea, and he took two trips to North Korea. Because he is a high-profile scholar who does not write favorably about that country, he did not go to Pyongyang but instead to small towns and villages, where the poorest North Koreans live. Like all foreigners, he was accompanied by a "minder," a strict guide who was with him at all times. "The most important questions regarding North Korea are the ones least often asked," Myers wrote in the preface to *The Cleanest Race*. "What do the North Koreans believe? How do they see themselves and the world around them? Yes, we know the country has a personality cult, but this fact alone tells us little. Cuba has a personality cult too, yet the Castro regime espouses an ideology quite different from that of its counterpart in Pyongyang. On what grounds is the North Korean Leader so extravagantly acclaimed? What is the nature of his mission, and the purported destiny of his nation as a whole?" Not only are most Western media organizations and North Korea watchers not asking those questions, Myers wrote, but they also do not understand the country's dominant ideology, which Myers summarized as follows: "*The Korean people are too pure blooded, and therefore too virtuous, to survive in this evil world without a great parental leader.* More must be added perhaps, if only to explain that 'therefore' to an American reader, but not much more of importance. I need hardly point out that if such a race-based worldview is to be situated on our conventional left-right spectrum, it makes more sense to posit it on the extreme right than on the far left. Indeed, the similarity to the worldview of fascist Japan is striking. I do not, however, intend to label North Korea as fascist, a term too vague to be much use. It is enough for me to make clear that the country has always been, at the very least, ideologically closer to America's adversaries in World War II than to communist China and Eastern Europe. This truth alone, if properly grasped, will not only help the West to understand the loyalty shown to [North Korea] by its chronically impoverished citizens, but also to understand why the West's policy of pursuing late Cold War–type solutions to the nuclear problem is doomed to fail." *The Cleanest Race* received enthusiastic reviews. Christopher Hitchens, in a review for *Slate* (February 1, 2010, on-line), called the book "electrifying," "finely argued," and "brilliantly written." In the *New York Times* (January 27, 2010, on-line), Dwight Garner called *The Cleanest Race* "provocative" and referred to Myers's analysis of Kim Jong Il as "fascinating."

The biggest challenge the North Korean government will face in the near future, according to Myers, is the increasing amount of information from outside the country that conflicts with the government's propaganda—not about race but other matters. Myers cited three challenges: there is spreading awareness in North Korea, from Chinese and South Korean media and smuggled-in DVDs, that South Koreans are perfectly happy in their own state and have no desire to live under Kim Jong Il's rule; the North Korean regime has made the "very foolhardy and reckless decision to make the North Korean people think that the country will be transformed into a strong and prosperous one by the year 2012, and needless to say there is no way the government could live up to that promise," which makes Myers "nervous because it could lead the regime to engage in some kind of diversionary military tactics"; and, probably within the next few years, Kim Jong Il's successor will be appointed. Because he will be mostly unknown to the people, he may seek popular approval through military muscle-flexing—perhaps another nuclear test, a skirmish with the South Korean navy, or a more daring act.

Myers is often asked: What can the United States do with regard to North Korea? Is meaningful diplomacy possible? Although Myers has occasionally made suggestions—such as negotiating with China, which has business ties to North Korea, or negotiating simultaneously with North and South Korea—he insists that he is a researcher, not a strategist. The best scenario, he has said, would come about if experts, politicians, and diplomats study the way North Koreans see themselves. Before figuring out what should be, he has pointed out, Western politicians and diplomats must first figure out what is.

In addition to his other books, Myers is the author of *Han Sorya and North Korean Literature: The Failure of Socialist Realism in the DPRK* (1994). He and his wife, Myunghee, live in Busan, South Korea.

—D.K.

Suggested Reading: mhpbooks.com; *New York Times* (on-line) Jan. 27, 2010; *Slate* (on-line) Feb. 1, 2010; *Wall Street Journal* (on-line) Dec. 4, 2009; *Washington Post* C p2 July 2, 2001

Selected Books: *Han Sorya and North Korean Literature: The Failure of Socialist Realism in the DPRK*, 1994; *A Reader's Manifesto: An Attack on the Growing Pretentiousness in American Literary Prose*, 2002; *The Cleanest Race: How North Koreans See Themselves—And Why It Matters*, 2010

Adrian Dennis/AFP/Getty Images

Naidoo, Kumi

1965– Director of Greenpeace International; activist; environmentalist

Address: Greenpeace International, Ottho Heldringstraat 5, 1066 AZ Amsterdam, Netherlands

In November 2009 Kumi Naidoo became the director of Greenpeace International, a nearly four-decade-old organization committed to nonviolent activism to preserve the environment. A native of South Africa, a veteran of the antiapartheid struggle there, and a human-rights activist since his early teens, Naidoo has learned through sometimes bitter experience that meaningful change often takes time. Still, in his current post, in which he seeks to combat and raise awareness of global warming, he has emphasized that time is short. "We are talking about being in an extremely inconvenient moment of world history where the future is at stake and the present is already proving to be hugely painful," he said in an interview with David Smith for the London *Guardian* (November 18, 2009, on-line). The task of persuading world leaders to implement the changes required to reverse global warming is not easy; Naidoo, however, has made a career of going against the odds for causes he believes in. He said to Smith, "I think we will not make apologies for speaking truth to power and inconveniencing some political leaders." What will ultimately make the difference in our planet's future, Naidoo has said, is the involvement of ordinary citizens. "I strongly believe in the decency of ordinary men and women in rich and poor countries who all care about their children, and their grandchildren," he told Smith. "I think when they put the pictures of those kids in front of them and think [about] what kind of planet we [are] going to give them, I hope people will rise above whatever short-term economic and other interests they might have."

Kumi Naidoo, who is of Indian ancestry, was born in 1965 in South Africa. He was raised in a lower-middle-class family in the township of Durban. At that time apartheid, or officially sanctioned racial segregation, was brutally enforced in South Africa, where the white minority government relegated blacks and other nonwhites to second-class citizenship. Naidoo told Stephen Moss for the *Guardian* (November 30, 2009, on-line) that when he was 14, "the lights went on," and he saw the need to fight apartheid. As a 15-year-old student at a Durban secondary school that had no electricity or books, he marched as part of the national student uprisings of the 1980s. As a result, he was expelled. "We were shouting these ridiculous slogans, like 'You pay our teachers peanuts, no wonder we get a monkey education system,'" Naidoo told Annie Kelly for the *Guardian* (July 22, 2009, on-line). "It was like a big party, but three weeks later there were people being beaten all around me, people being hauled off into prison, being killed. It was then that I understood that we were up against something that was bigger than injustice in the education system. It was systematic. After that, there was no going back." Two weeks before those student demonstrations, Naidoo's mother had committed suicide. "She was 38 and had issues with my dad," Naidoo said to Stephen Moss. "She just reached a moment where it felt too much. During that apartheid period there were very high levels of suicide: there was no support for people. It was a surprise to us. She left a note, took an overdose, and was gone within hours. It feels like yesterday." Naidoo has said that he often wonders how his mother would have handled the repercussions of his activism, had she lived to see how tumultuous his life became as a result of it. "If you got involved in the struggle, the assumption was you'd end up dead, or in detention or exile," he told Kelly. "I spent much of my early life feeling like I was living on borrowed time, and it's a feeling I've carried around ever since." Following his expulsion, Naidoo studied at home and passed an entrance exam for the University of Durban-Westville, whose students were mainly South African Indians; he received a B.A. degree in law and political science, cum laude, in 1985.

For much of the 1980s, Naidoo was active in student and residents' associations, programs to foster youth leadership, and antiapartheid struggles. In 1986 he was arrested and charged with violating his country's state-of-emergency rules. Facing 15 years in prison, Naidoo spent one year underground before going into exile in Britain. (Afterward his younger brother was held in prison for a year without a trial.) Naidoo remained committed to the fight against apartheid, however, particularly after his good friend Lenny Naidu was murdered by South African special forces, in 1988. Naidoo recalled to Moss the last conversation he had with Naidu: "Before we fled in different directions into exile, he was very philosophical and asked me what was the best contribution you could make to the cause of humanity and justice. I said, 'That's very easy, it's giving your life.' He said, 'You mean participating in demonstrations and getting shot and killed.' I said, 'I guess so,' and he said, 'No, that's the wrong answer. It's not giving your life, but giving the rest of your life.'" Naidoo, then 22 years old, did not fully grasp at the time what his friend meant. "I still think deep and hard over what he was trying to say," Naidoo said to Nell Greenberg for the *Earth Island Journal* (Summer 2010). "What he was saying is that the struggle for justice—the struggle, whether it is gender justice, environmental justice—is a marathon, not a sprint. And the biggest contribution that any one of us can make is maintaining a lifetime of involvement until we win on those struggles."

While in exile in Britain, Naidoo was a Rhodes Scholar and earned a doctorate in political science from Magdalen College, at Oxford University. He remained in Britain until 1989. After the longtime antiapartheid activist Nelson Mandela was released from prison, on February 11, 1990, following decades spent behind bars, Naidoo returned to South Africa to work toward the legalization of the African National Congress (ANC). Mandela's release came as a shock to Naidoo and many of those involved in the antiapartheid movement. "Suddenly we had to think about a future, a career path, pensions, things that hadn't previously been in our vocabulary. It was quite an adjustment to have to make," Naidoo recalled to Moss. It was an exciting time, but also a difficult one. Not long after he returned to his newly liberated homeland, Naidoo lost another close friend, the social activist Joan Wright, in a car crash. Of that tragedy, Naidoo told Moss, "My story is an African story. We have to endure loss of loved ones on a much more regular basis [than in the West]. I've had more than my fair share of loss, but sadly it's not peculiar in the African context."

In 1993 Naidoo became the executive director of the National Literacy Co-operation of South Africa. That same year Walter Sisulu, a senior ANC member and one of Naidoo's heroes, had offered him a job as head of the ANC's media-production division. He chose to work instead in the area of literacy after a conversation with a mentor, Mary Mkwanazi, who told him, as Naidoo recalled to Moss, "If you want to be on TV and be famous then go and do the ANC job. If you really want to make a difference, go and do the adult literary job." Naidoo concluded that when it comes to achieving goals, activists have an advantage over politicians. "The constraints of election cycles and the compromises forced on you by the realpolitik of governing mean that often you can't speak truth to power. I think politicians are overrated, and the

role they play in society is disproportionately more valued than the role faith leaders, trade union leaders, NGO [nongovernmental-organization] leaders and media people play," he said to Moss. Naidoo headed the National Literacy Co-operation of South Africa until 1997.

During the 1994 democratic elections in South Africa, Naidoo served as the official spokesperson of the Independent Electoral Commission and was responsible for overseeing the training of all electoral staff in the country. The election, in which Mandela won South Africa's presidency, marked the beginning of universal adult suffrage in the country and the end of apartheid. "What I learned from that time, which is helpful now," Naidoo told David Smith for the *Guardian* (November 18, 2009, on-line), "is not to believe that things cannot change and not to underestimate the power of the voices and actions of ordinary people. We never thought change would come as fast as it came. In the mid-80s it just seemed that it was going to be another 20 years."

From 1996 to 1998 Naidoo was the executive director of the South African National NGO Coalition (SANGOCO). SANGOCO is an umbrella group created to incorporate the work of provincial and sectoral NGOs in governmental policy and ensure that the traditions of civil society continue to have a place in South Africa. In 1998 Naidoo became secretary-general and CEO of the Civicus World Alliance for Citizen Participation, whose mission, according to the official Civicus Web site, is to "empower citizens to participate in the processes of public decision-making that affect their lives." Civicus is made up of several programs, among them Civil Society Watch (CSW), whose actions include analyzing the effects of laws and policies on civil society, issuing press statements, and coordinating such civic actions as protest marches. In 2008 Naidoo was named honorary president of Civicus, a position he still holds. In April and July 2009, Naidoo was a visiting fellow at the Carnegie UK Trust—an organization that, according to its Web site, "investigates areas of public concern to influence policy and practice"—and an international adviser for the trust's inquiry into the future of civil society.

In February 2009 Naidoo embarked on a hunger strike in solidarity with the people of Zimbabwe. In Zimbabwe, agriculture, the backbone of the country's economy, has been crippled by the combined effects of drought, HIV/AIDS, and government land reforms. Unemployment is rampant, and inflation has made basic necessities unaffordable for many of Zimbabwe's citizens, who have fled to neighboring countries by the millions. The shared-government agreement between Zimbabwe's longtime president, Robert Mugabe, and Morgan Tsvangirai of the Movement for Democratic Change, negotiated in 2008 with South Africa as mediator, has reportedly been undermined by impropriety and foot-dragging, preventing the changes required to address the humanitarian crisis. The international community has accused South Africa of standing by passively instead of taking steps to ensure that the power-sharing agreement actually works.

Naidoo was on the 19th day of the 21-day hunger strike when he was contacted by a recruitment company on behalf of Greenpeace International. The recruiters wanted to know if he was interested in applying to become the organization's head. "I was OK, I was still compos mentis, but I was a little weak and had already lost 14kg [about 30 pounds]," he explained to Moss. "I said, 'Guys, this is not the best time to be thinking about jobs.'" That might have been the end of the matter, had Naidoo not happened to mention the call to his 17-year-old daughter, the product of his relationship with a young woman while he was a student at Oxford. (The couple never married but remain friends; Naidoo's daughter lives in Glasgow, Scotland.) Naidoo told Moss, "She said, 'Dad, I will not speak to you if you don't at least think about it because Greenpeace is one of the best NGOs in the world, and when I grow up I would love to work for them.' It has a kind of magic for young people." When the recruiting company called again a week later, Naidoo showed more interest. In November 2009, when Greenpeace's leader, Gerd Leipold, resigned after nearly nine years in the position, Naidoo stepped in to take his place. While some criticized Greenpeace's choice, arguing that Naidoo's success as a human-rights activist did not guarantee his competence as an environmentalist, Naidoo expressed the view that all aspects of activism are interconnected. "I can understand that people might see it as somewhat of a disconnect," he said to Robin Powell for the *Sydney (Australia) Morning-Herald* (February 22, 2010). "I'm not your traditional environmentalist. But I see it as a logical development, not an abrupt move. I've come to a revelation: I think the environmental crisis is, in a sense, at the centre and connected to all other crises." Naidoo has pointed out, for example, that while the genocide in Darfur is a "crisis of violence" and an ethnic conflict, the lack of water and arable land there have played a huge role in it.

Greenpeace International was founded in 1971, when a group of activists leased a small fishing vessel called the *Phyllis Cormack* and set sail from Vancouver, Canada, to Alaska to protest nuclear testing. Today, Greenpeace's efforts are focused on banning commercial whaling, with activists taking to the water to physically thwart whaling ships; putting an end to nuclear testing; and combating the threats of global warming and toxins in the environment. Responsible for 1,500 staff members in 28 offices worldwide and a budget of 200 million euros (currently equivalent to about $260 million), Naidoo took his post at a critical time for Greenpeace—the eve of the 2009 conference on climate change, held in Copenhagen, Denmark. The conference was organized by the United Nations in cooperation with the Danish government; in attendance were representatives of the member countries of the United Nations Framework Convention on Climate Change. Naidoo's first act as director was to gather the whole staff (about 150 people) at the Greenpeace headquarters, in Amsterdam, the Netherlands, for a meeting. "I told them I thought the moment we are living in right now can best be described as a perfect storm," he told Moss. "First, we had the fuel price crisis three years ago, that led to a food price crisis. We have an ongoing poverty crisis where 50,000 men, women, and children die every day from preventable causes. We've known about the climate crisis for some time now; and then the financial crisis was the final boot in the solar plexus. When you have such a convergence of crises, you have two options: you can get out a couple of Band-Aids, try to do a temporary fix and keep it as business as usual; or you can take a leaf out of Chinese culture, where the symbol for crisis is the same symbol for opportunity. I feel that we have to turn this moment into a point where humanity sobers up."

In the days leading up to the Copenhagen conference, Naidoo stressed its significance and attempted to convey to world leaders that their attendance was crucial. "The Copenhagen Summit offers the single greatest opportunity for leaders to come together and create a legally binding agreement to avert climate chaos," he told reporters at a press conference in Johannesburg, South Africa, as quoted on the Web site *7thSpace Interactive* (November 16, 2009). "Our leaders need to find the courage to do what is right instead of what is comfortable. They need to become the leaders we elected them to be by acting to save the climate. They must avert the threat of mass migration, mass starvation, and mass extinction, all of which will be inevitable if climate change goes unchecked." Naidoo pointed out that while global warming may seem to be a "slow-burning" issue for much of the developed world, other places are already experiencing serious consequences of the problem. "Developing countries are least responsible for the climate chaos we find ourselves in and also the ones paying the most brutal price. They should therefore receive significant financing to help them adapt to the impact of climate change, recognizing the historical responsibility," he said in an interview with Caroline Hartnell for *Alliance Magazine* (January 18, 2010, on-line).

When the summit came to an end, in December 2009, no international, legally binding agreement had been forged. Although deeply disappointed, Naidoo saw the need to move forward. "Part of what is critically needed right now is for us to actually build, if you want, the broadest possible awareness and understanding of citizens who are voters, in the hope that there can be a bottom up kind of pressure. With the Copenhagen summit, some might justifiably say that we put too much of our eggs into the COP15 [the 15th Conference of the Parties] basket. . . . So in the post-Copenhagen reflection we are saying we also need to continue to build other leverages of campaigning and resisting and popular mobilization," Naidoo said in his interview with Nell Greenberg. He told Hartnell, "History has shown us—the US slavery, anti-apartheid and so on—it's only when decent men and women are willing to stand up, put their lives on the line and take strong, vibrant action that the agenda can move forward. Citizens and civil society must recognize that governments will not act with the urgency that is needed unless they are pushed into it."

In July 2010 Greenpeace made headlines when it shut down between 30 and 50 British Petroleum (BP) gas stations in London, England, by disabling their pumps. That action was taken to protest BP's plans to continue deepwater drilling in the wake of the disastrous oil spill in the Gulf of Mexico, which was caused by the explosion of an offshore BP drilling rig the previous April. After BP announced that Robert Dudley would replace the firm's longtime chief executive officer, Tony Hayward, Naidoo declared, as quoted by *Press TV* (July 27, 2010, on-line), "Dudley should overturn current plans to extract oil from risky deepwater wells off Libya and in the Arctic, where a spill could have consequences even more devastating than in the gulf. A change in leadership is a key opportunity for BP to cut its losses in more ways than one, by turning away from high-cost and environmentally reckless sources of oil . . . towards an energy revolution based on clean energy sources."

In September 2010 Naidoo made public a letter he sent to Mark Zuckerberg, the chief executive officer of Facebook. The letter concerned Facebook's decision to buy electricity for its first data center, in Prineville, Oregon, from Pacific Power, which produces energy mainly by burning coal. In the letter Naidoo called upon Zuckerberg to turn to other, cleaner sources of energy and to use Facebook's enormous influence to spur other companies to do the same. "Greenpeace regularly uses Facebook to engage its supporters and their friends to hold corporations accountable for their environmental impact," Naidoo wrote, according to Targeted News Service (September 1, 2010, on-line). "Facebook is uniquely positioned to be a truly visible and influential leader to drive the deployment of clean energy." The news service reported that at least half a million Facebook users "have joined with Greenpeace to call on Zuckerberg and Facebook" to stop using coal-based energy.

Naidoo is currently based in Amsterdam. His longtime romantic partner remains in South Africa. Although the two have considered living together in Amsterdam, Naidoo travels so often that it would make little difference in terms of the time the couple spend together. Naidoo has acknowledged that life as an activist is difficult; change takes time, and sometimes even modest progress requires a seemingly disproportionate amount of work. He has learned to live with disappointment. Still, he has said that he would not trade his career path for anything. "If I were to turn the clock back, I wouldn't choose to do anything differently

. . . ," he told Greenberg. "When I reflect on my life now . . . I think that activism actually gave my life much more meaning than anything else could have given it. . . . My best friendships, you know, my best relationships with people. I mean, there are people who I worked with when I was in my teens, I don't see them for 20 years, and I bump into them and it's like a long lost relative. The depth, the closeness of that relationship is very different when you combine with people working for justice." When asked by Greenberg what advice he would give to young people who are considering activism but feel hopeless in the face of seemingly insurmountable problems, Naidoo responded, "To young people I would say, 'Activism can be fun, it can be sexy, it can be ethical, it can enhance your place in the world, it can help you with your education, it can help you with the quality of your relationships with family, friends, and community, and it's a path of life very well worth taking. And it's not a grind. When I think about my life as an activist, I've laughed a lot. Even though I have had to bury many, many people I still think that I got a lot of meaning, laughter, friendship, love out of activism.'"

—H.R.W.

Suggested Reading: *Alliance* (on-line) Jan. 18, 2010; *BBC News* (on-line) Mar. 14, 2010; *Earth Island Journal* (on-line) Summer 2010; (London) *Guardian* (on-line) July 22, 2009, Nov. 18, 2009, Nov. 30, 2009

Olsen, Mary-Kate and Ashley

Olsen, Mary-Kate
June 13, 1986– Actress; producer; fashion designer; entrepreneur

Olsen, Ashley
June 13, 1986– Actress; producer; fashion designer; entrepreneur

Address: Dualstar Entertainment Group, 1801 Century Park E., 12th Fl., Los Angeles, CA 90067; c/o Razorbill/Penguin Group Publicity, 375 Hudson St., New York, NY 10014-3658

Mary-Kate and Ashley Olsen have the distinction of becoming, at the age of six, the youngest film producers in history (though in name only), and, at 17, the youngest entertainers to receive a star (jointly) on the Hollywood Walk of Fame. Their company, Dualstar Entertainment Group, was formed in 1993 to produce the twins' television series, movies, videos, and albums. The Olsens made their TV debuts in 1987, when they were nine months old, playing the character Michelle Tanner on the ABC sitcom *Full House*. The sisters won three Young Artist Awards from the Young Artist

Evan Agostini/Getty Images for CFDA
Ashley (left) and Mary-Kate Olsen

Foundation, in 1989, 1990, and 1992, for their work on that show, which ran for eight seasons. *Full House* and the two other sitcoms in which the Olsens starred—*Two of a Kind* and *So Little Time*—have been widely syndicated. The twins parlayed their immense popularity as Michelle into one of the best-known brands in the U.S.—mary-kateandashley—whose products include everything from makeup, fragrances, clothing, and bedroom furniture to video games and books, made mostly for tweens, girls between the ages of about eight and 12. In terms of dolls produced by the toy-manufacturing giant Mattel, Mary-Kate and Ashley dolls are second in sales only to Barbie. In 2007 *Forbes* reported that Dualstar was selling $1 billion worth of products worldwide annually. With a combined net worth of $100 million, the Olsen sisters jointly ranked 11th on the magazine's 2007 list of the 20 richest women in entertainment. The next year they ranked 10th on *Forbes*'s list of the best-paid celebrities under 30.

The petite Olsen sisters are fraternal twins whose features are almost identical. (They reportedly prefer to be referred to as an "individual pair.") The right-handed Ashley is about one inch taller than the left-handed Mary-Kate. Each of the women has worked to establish her own identity, in part through styles of dress. Mary-Kate has continued to act, appearing on the Showtime comedy series *Weeds* in 2007 and in the independent film *The Wackness* in 2008. Ashley has focused on building a career in the fashion industry. She recently launched two high-end lines, the Row and then Elizabeth and James, for which she serves as a design consultant, with input from Mary-Kate. Merchandise that carries the Row or the Elizabeth

and James label is designed for teenagers and young adults.

Now 24, the Olsens are keenly aware of the special nature of their relationship. "Our bond is really beyond words," Ashley told Lucy Kaylin for *Marie Claire* (September 2007). "I know when [Mary-Kate's] hurting, I know when she's going through something. I know when she's happy—whether I'm with her or not, I know. We both carry the weight of each other. When she's doing really well, maybe I'm not doing so well. It's weird that we're never at the same place—we just kind of balance each other out."

Ashley Fuller Olsen and Mary-Kate Olsen were born on June 13, 1986 in Sherman Oaks, California, to David and Jarnette "Jarnie" (Fuller) Olsen. (Ashley is older by two minutes.) Their father, a former profesional golfer, is a mortgage banker and real-estate developer; their mother was a ballet dancer before becoming a homemaker. The Olsen sisters have an older brother, James (known to his family and friends by his middle name, Trent), and a younger sister, Elizabeth. When Mary-Kate and Ashley were nine, their mother and father divorced; their parents shared custody of the twins and their siblings. "To be honest, we were kind of busy at that point," Ashley told Michelle Tauber and Mark Dagostino for *People* (May 3, 2004). "We had so many people that loved us that we were like, 'That's okay. Things will be better this way.' We were very mature for our age." Their father later remarried; with his second wife, Martha Mackenzie-Olsen, he has a daughter, Taylor, and a son, Jake.

When the Olsen sisters were seven months old, their mother, urged by a friend who was a casting director, took them to an audition for *Full House*, an upcoming half-hour television sitcom. The show's executive producers, Jeff Franklin and Bob Boyett, were immediately charmed by the twins. "I thought they were unique," Boyett told Jefferson Graham for *USA Today* (October 2, 1998). "They had big, expressive eyes. They were friendly and would listen when you spoke to them." The Olsen sisters made their TV debut in September 1987. Both played the same character, Michelle Tanner. (Twins are often hired to play a single young character on TV series, because child-labor laws restrict the amount of time children can work, and if one twin is unwell or cranky, the other is often a ready substitute.) The Olsens did little in their early seasons but smile and look cute; if the script required them to crawl, they would be lured with candy placed out of camera range. As they learned to talk, they began to deliver lines. Their on-set teacher, Adria Later (who was more than a prompter; among other jobs, she made sure the twins were never in harm's way), would stand off-camera and tell whichever sister was on the set what to say, and then the child would repeat those words for the camera. Usually Ashley appeared in scenes heavy with dialogue, Mary-Kate in scenes in which action predominated. "But if there's a day when

Ashley is real tired, . . . I'll put Mary Kate in a dialogue scene and she pulls it off, too," Later told Jay Mathews for the *Washington Post* (February 3, 1991). In the latter years of the series, starting when the Olsens were six, they performed on their own, without prompting.

In its first year critics panned *Full House*, and it failed to attract a large audience. By its third season (1989–90), it ranked among the top 30 shows in terms of numbers of viewers. For the remainder of its run, *Full House* ranked among the top 25 shows, peaking at number seven in its fifth season (1991–92). Set in San Francisco, California, *Full House* was about a widowed father (Bob Saget) who raises his three young daughters (played by Candace Cameron, Jodie Sweetin, and the Olsen twins) with the help of his brother-in-law (John Stamos) and his best friend (Dave Coulier). Usually, when a baby or small child is introduced on a TV series, the part is later recast with an older child actor in order to age the character quickly. The Olsens, however, proved not only phenomenally popular with audiences but also highly competent; during the eight-year run of the show, their character grew older exactly as the twins did in real life. (The same was true of the Cameron and Sweetin characters.) Michelle Tanner became the series' most popular character, and according to their so-called Q Scores (measurements from zero to 100 of how well-known and well-liked particular celebrities, products, or shows are), the Olsen sisters became the second-most-recognizable and second-most-popular performers on television, after Bill Cosby.

Writing when Ashley and Mary-Kate were four and a half, Jay Mathews attributed the success of *Full House* in no small part to the appeal of the sisters. "For awhile they were little more than squirming props, with a precocious ability to move and smile on cue, but no more dramatic than trained seals. Yet, they had something," he observed. "To this day, having now met them and discovered that this mesmerizing quality is theirs and not just a product of good lighting and deft staging, I am not sure what it is they have. . . . But it is difficult to stop watching them, and as the producers of *Full House* began to realize the twins' power over an audience, and to invent dialogue and bits of business for them, the program became a must, a bit of usually mindless drivel that could not be easily removed from my family's weekend routine."

The Olsens' parents were careful to avoid the common pitfalls of childhood stardom; they hired lawyers and professional business managers to handle the twins' estates and refused to take a percentage of their pay (as parents of child stars are allowed to do by law). Instead, they deposited all the money the twins earned in trust funds, to remain untouched until the girls turned 18. The parents also tried to maintain a sense of normalcy in their home, giving their daughters an allowance of $10 a week, assigning them chores, and eschewing Hollywood parties. "We've never had stage parents," Ashley told Michelle Tauber and Mark Dagostino.

The Olsen sisters attended public school at least two days a week—they were tutored on other days—and were encouraged to participate in ballet, horseback riding, and other activities.

Despite the series' popularity, *Full House* was canceled in 1995, reportedly because of unmanageably high production costs. About 25 percent of households whose television sets were on watched the special, one-hour series finale, which aired on May 23, 1995. ABC had begun airing reruns of the show during the day as early as 1991; after the series ended it was widely syndicated, overseas as well as in the U.S. Currently, it airs on the ABC Family cable-TV network.

Earlier, in 1992, the Olsen sisters' careers had started to expand, when they starred in the made-for-television movie *To Grandmother's House We Go*, in which they played twin sisters who feel unwanted and leave home; along the way to their grandmother's they run into a pair of criminals (portrayed by Jerry Van Dyke and Rhea Perlman). That year the twins also recorded their first album, *Brother for Sale*, whose tracks include a song on the joys of eating peanut butter and another in which they plead to be given a dog. Their second album, *I Am the Cute One*, was released in 1993. Also in 1993 the Olsen sisters signed a deal with ABC to star in and produce their own TV series and a new TV movie. Dualstar Entertainment came into being at the same time. Based in Los Angeles, California, Dualstar was initially run by six attorneys, including the twins' manager and lawyer, Robert Thorne, and his collaborator, Greg Redlitz. After the Olsens turned 18, they bought out Thorne and Redlitz's stake in the company and, as of January 2005, became Dualstar's sole owners; their father is the chairman of its five-member board of directors.

In 1993 the sisters' second made-for-TV movie, *Double, Double, Toil and Trouble*, had premiered; their third was *How the West Was Fun* (1994). In addition to several other TV movies, the Olsens starred in more than two dozen videos. Among them was a series of musical mysteries all titled *The Adventures of Mary-Kate & Ashley* (1994–97), bearing subtitles including *The Case of the Fun House Mystery*, *The Case of the Christmas Caper*, and *The Case of Thorn Mansion*, in all of which the girls played little detectives. Each video in the *You're Invited to Mary-Kate & Ashley's* series (1995–2003) featured a different event: a birthday party or a fashion party, for example. Dualstar also produced compilations of videos in each series— for the *You're Invited* series, collections of the greatest parties, vacation parties, and favorite parties (2000, 2001, and 2003, respectively). By 2002 the Olsens' direct-to-video business (which included *Billboard Dad*, *Our Lips Are Sealed*, and other videos) had generated $500 million in retail sales. To date, sales have topped 30 million copies. Many of the videos were also adapted as short novels for young readers.

In 1995 the Olsens starred in their first feature film, *It Takes Two*, directed by Andy Tennant and co-starring Kirstie Alley and Steve Guttenberg. In it a social worker, Diane Barrows (Alley), grows close to a New York City orphan, Amanda Lemmon (Mary-Kate), but is unable to adopt her because she is unmarried and poor. Nearby, Alyssa Callaway (Ashley), the daughter of a billionaire, Roger Callaway (Guttenberg), is dreading her father's impending marriage to a mean, child-hating woman. When Amanda and Alyssa meet and notice their striking resemblance, they swap places in hopes of uniting Diane and Roger. Made for $14 million, *It Takes Two* received mixed reviews; it earned $19.5 million at the box office and $75 million as a home video.

The Olsen sisters continued to make straight-to-video films until 2002. During their teens their films often involved lightly sketched romances set in different parts of the world. *Passport to Paris* (1999) and *When in Rome* (2002) are representative of those movies. The sisters returned to television in 1998, with the ABC series *Two of a Kind*, in which they played scheming twins whose unmarried father (Christopher Sieber) hires one of his college students (Sally Wheeler) to serve as a part-time nanny. The show, on which Mary-Kate and Ashley portrayed polar opposites, highlighted some of the real-life differences between the sisters at that time. "Our personalities are different," Ashley said, as quoted by Richard Huff in the New York *Daily News* (July 20, 1998). "[Mary-Kate] likes sports. She likes basketball. She loves to play football with the guys. And I'll just hang around, sit down with my friends, and hang out and watch them." *Two of a Kind* was canceled after one season due to poor ratings.

The Olsens again turned to TV with *So Little Time*, a sitcom that aired on the Fox Family Channel during the 2001–02 season. They played twins being raised by their separated parents. Mary-Kate was nominated for the 2002 Daytime Emmy Award for outstanding performer in a children's series for her work in *So Little Time*. Despite its high ratings, the Olsen sisters left the series to focus on other pursuits.

The twins' second major feature film was made the year they turned 18: *New York Minute* (2004), a comedy directed by Dennie Gordon and produced by Warner Bros. Pictures and DiNovi Pictures as well as Dualstar Productions. The motion picture revolved around the straitlaced Jane (Ashley) and her wannabe-rocker twin sister, Roxy (Mary-Kate), during a single day in New York City. The film, which co-starred Eugene Levy, received a critical drubbing and failed to earn back the $30 million it cost to produce.

Also in 2004 the Olsen sisters enrolled at New York University (NYU). Mary-Kate abandoned her studies in 2005; Ashley remained for another year or so. Their departures seem to have been spurred by both eagerness to embark on new ventures and frustrations stemming from their fame; sometimes, for example, they would skip classes to avoid paparazzi.

In early 2005 the twins recruited the veteran apparel-company executive Diane Reichenberger to serve as Dualstar's chief executive officer, to oversee the design, marketing, and sale of products for their mary-kateandashley brand. Though they were only 19, Reichenberger recalled to Jim Hopkins for *USA Today* (May 6, 2005), the sisters displayed a solid grasp of marketing when they interviewed her. "Ashley wanted to know about Reichenberger's business experience," Hopkins reported. "Mary-Kate questioned her about management style: 'what kind of relationships I've built in the past and how I maintained them,'" Reichenberger told him, describing the sisters as "smart," "articulate," and "rational." Initially carried solely by the Wal-Mart chain, where the twins' photos were prominently displayed alongside merchandise, the mary-kateandashley brand is now available at Target stores.

During her time at NYU, Ashley had interned with the fashion designer Zac Posen, and she grew eager to design a line of clothing inspired by her newfound sense of style. "When we were growing up, it was always about being appropriate," Ashley told Amy Larocca for *New York* magazine (August 27, 2007). "[At NYU] I was studying architecture and psychology and I loved it, but I kept thinking about T-shirts and how to make the perfect one. It was my dad who said, 'You should do it.'" With the help of her friend Danielle Sherman, a designer, she launched the Row. An upscale line named for London's Savile Row, it debuted in 2007 (though it was not formally presented at a fashion show until February 2010) and offers mainly knit T-shirts, blazers, straight-legged pants, and long dresses in black, white, cream, or gray. Priced from $200 for T-shirts to upwards of $3,000 for coats, the apparel is currently carried by such high-end retailers as Bergdorf Goodman and Barneys New York.

With design help from Mary-Kate and in partnership with L'Koral Industries, a California–based sportswear manufacturer, Ashley introduced her next line, Elizabeth and James (named for the twins' sister and brother), in 2007. Inspired partly by the kinds of clothing the sisters have found in thrift shops around the world, Elizabeth and James apparel is more colorful and playful than the Row's. It is also more moderately priced, though considerably more expensive than low-end brands; in mid-July 2010 short-sleeved shirts with buttoned fronts, for example, cost more than $200. Spurred by strong sales, the Elizabeth and James line has grown more than 500 percent since its launch, having expanded to include jewelry, shoes, and men's apparel, and it is now sold in more than 200 stores. In early 2010 the Olsens unveiled a new jeans line, Textile Elizabeth and James. A year earlier the sisters had started a relatively inexpensive line of apparel for juniors, Olsenboye, which is carried by the J. C. Penney chain.

Mary-Kate is said to have invented the "Boho chic" or "Ashcan chic" look, a style characterized by layers of simple, oversized clothing that often make Olsen appear penniless, save for a few select couture accents—a Balenciaga handbag or Christian Louboutin shoes, for instance. The sisters' ability to mix and match fashions to create a unique, sometimes odd look has won plaudits from fashion-industry professionals. Karl Lagerfeld, who is currently Chanel's head designer and creative director, said of Mary-Kate to Robert Sullivan for *Vogue* (August 2006), "She has spirit, taste, and modernity. She mixes Chanel in her own way. It is very inspiring for a designer to see his designs interpreted by the right girl in this way." In 2006 the Olsens served as the faces of the upscale fashion line Badgley Mischka. That ad campaign marked the first time that the women represented a brand other than their own.

While Ashley devoted herself to the Olsens' fashion business, Mary-Kate focused on developing a serious acting career. "If you look at our career from 21 years ago to today, it was about entertaining a specific audience. It wasn't about acting. It was about pleasing other people and making kids smile," Mary-Kate told Karen Valby for *Entertainment Weekly* (September 14, 2007). She told Alun Palmer for the London *Daily Mirror* (August 29, 2008), "I made the decision to take acting seriously after high school. When I was in my freshman year at college I took some acting classes and found that I fell in love with it again. I was never challenged when it came to acting as a youngster. I sort of just did whatever was given to me without asking questions. I didn't really understand why I enjoyed it or why I did it." Mary-Kate appeared onscreen without her sister for the first time in an uncredited part in *Factory Girl* (2006), about Edie Sedgwick, the socialite and model who appeared in several of the artist Andy Warhol's films.

Two years later, after an eight-episode stint on the popular comedy-drama TV series *Weeds*, Mary-Kate won a role in the independent film *The Wackness*, written and directed by Jonathan Levine. Co-starring Ben Kingsley and Josh Peck and set in New York City in 1994, *The Wackness* follows a teenager (Peck) who spends his last summer before college selling marijuana and giving some to a psychiatrist (Kingsley) in exchange for treatment. Mary-Kate played a young hippie named Union. Her onscreen kiss with Kingsley, who is 42 years her senior, created a great deal of buzz. *The Wackness* won the Audience Award for Dramatic Film at the 2008 Sundance Film Festival, and the *New York Times* named Mary-Kate one of four actors to watch in 2008. "Although her role isn't much more than a cameo, she gives it such pungent specificity that it feels bigger," Karen Durbin wrote for the *Times* (May 4, 2008). Olsen will next be seen on the silver screen in *Beastly*, a contemporary version of "Beauty and the Beast"; written and directed by Daniel Barnz, it is scheduled for release in 2011.

The Olsens have long been fodder for tabloid news. That downside to their celebrity made itself felt when, in June 2004, after months of tabloid speculation about her health, Mary-Kate entered a treatment facility for anorexia nervosa, an eating disorder characterized by self-starvation. She was released in the next month and has since worked to maintain a healthy weight. The following year Ashley filed a $40 million defamation lawsuit against the *National Enquirer* after the paper ran a cover story headlined, "Ashley Olsen Caught in Drug Scandal." The article claimed that Ashley's then-boyfriend had been linked to alleged drug dealers but did not accuse Ashley of using or selling drugs. Still, Olsen believed that the misleading headline had damaged her reputation and that an accompanying photo in which she looked as if she might be under the influence of drugs had further sullied her name. The *National Enquirer* later published an apology.

Bimonthly issues of the short-lived *Mary-Kate and Ashley Magazine*, for which the sisters served as co–editors in chief, were sold beginning in April/May 2001. In 2008 the twins published *Influence*, a partly autobiographical coffee-table book of photos, reminiscences by the Olsens, and interviews the women conducted with people from the fashion world who have inspired them—Diane Von Furstenberg, Karl Lagerfeld, Francisco Costa, Richard Prince, and Lauren Hutton.

"Mary-Kate and Ashley are older than their years. Everyone says so," Cathy Horyn wrote for the *New York Times* (August 26, 2009). That year the Olsens were inducted into the Council of Fashion Designers of America, and in early 2010 their names appeared on *Women's Wear Daily*'s list of "People and Companies to Watch." Also in 2010 *Elle* magazine named them "Icon of the Year." The sisters live in New York City. Ashley told Horyn, "Our lives have been kind of backward. We never got that opportunity in high school to figure out what you want to do. We never had the time to discover, 'Oh, I love doing this . . . ' So for us this experience in fashion has been amazing."

—M.A.S.

Suggested Reading: elizabethandjames.us; *Los Angeles Times* F p21 Sep. 25, 1998; *Marie Claire* p168+ Sep. 2007; *New York* p72+ Aug. 27, 2007; *New York Times* E p1+ Aug. 27, 2009; *Premiere* p84+ May 2004; *Vogue* p262 Aug. 2006; *Washington Post* G p1+ Feb. 3, 1991; Olsen, Mary-Kate and Ashley. *Mary-Kate & Ashley: Our Story*, 2003, *Influence*, 2008

Selected Television Series: as actresses—*Full House*, 1987–95; *Two of a Kind*, 1998–99; *Weeds* (Mary-Kate only), 2007; as actresses and executive producers—*Fashion Forward: Spring 2001*, 2001; *So Little Time*, 2001–02; *Tough Cookie*, 2002

Selected Films: as actresses—*To Grandmother's House We Go*, 1992; *Double, Double, Toil and Trouble*, 1993; *The Little Rascals*, 1994; *How the West Was Fun*, 1994; *It Takes Two*, 1995; *Switching Goals*, 1999; *Our Lips Are Sealed*, 2000; *Charlie's Angels: Full Throttle*, 2003; as actresses and producers—*Passport to Paris*, 1999; *Our Lips Are Sealed*, 2000; *Winning London*, 2001; *Holiday in the Sun*, 2001; *Getting There*, 2002; *When in Rome*, 2002; *The Challenge*, 2003; *New York Minute*, 2004; Mary-Kate only—*Factory Girl*, 2006; *The Wackness*, 2008

Selected Videos: as actresses—*Our First Video*, 1993; *The Adventures of Mary-Kate & Ashley: The Case of the Logical I Ranch*, 1994; *The Adventures of Mary-Kate & Ashley: The Case of the Christmas Caper*, 1995; *You're Invited to*

Mary-Kate & Ashley's Sleepover Party, 1995; *The Adventures of Mary-Kate & Ashley: The Case of the Shark Encounter*, 1996; *You're Invited to Mary-Kate & Ashley's Hawaiian Beach Party*, 1996; *The Adventures of Mary-Kate & Ashley: The Case of the Volcano Mystery*, 1997; *You're Invited to Mary-Kate & Ashley's Favorite Parties*, 2001; *Mary-Kate & Ashley's Christmas Collection*, 2001

Selected Recordings: *Brother for Sale*, 1992; *I Am the Cute One*, 1993; *Give Us a Mystery*, 1994; *Cool Yule*, 1999; *Greatest Hits I*, 2003; *Greatest Hits II*, 2003

Selected Nonfiction Books: *Mary-Kate & Ashley: Our Story*, 2003; *Influence*, 2008

Theo Wargo/Getty Images for Time Inc

Olson, Theodore

Sep. 11, 1940– Lawyer; former government official

Address: Gibson, Dunn & Crutcher, 200 Park Ave. # 47, New York, NY 10166

From the early 1980s to 2009, the lawyer Theodore "Ted" Olson could reasonably have been called the top litigator of the Republican Party. He served as legal counsel in the administrations of two Republican presidents and dealt with many issues of importance to conservatives; his near-iconic status solidified when, in 2000, he represented then–

presidential candidate George W. Bush in *Bush v. Gore*, in which the Republican nominee and his Democratic opponent, Vice President Al Gore, contested the outcome of the election results in the swing state of Florida. Olson persuaded the U.S. Supreme Court to rule in favor of Bush, thus securing the Oval Office for the Republicans—and paving the way for Olson himself to serve as solicitor general of the United States from 2001 to 2004. Then, in 2009, in a move that shocked conservatives and liberals alike, Olson joined forces with his *Bush v. Gore* opponent, David Boies, to launch the lawsuit *Perry et al v. Schwarzenegger et al* to overturn Proposition 8, a 2008 California ballot initiative that amended the state's constitution to prohibit same-sex marriage. In August 2010 Olson and Boies argued successfully before a U.S. district court judge, who overturned the proposition, signaling the first step in a process that may lead to a landmark decision by the Supreme Court. (An appeals court in California has since kept Proposition 8 in place until an appeal is heard.)

Olson's arguments against the prohibition of same-sex marriage have landed him in hot water within his own party, some of whose members, as Gloria Borger wrote for CNN.com (August 5, 2010), have called his effort "an act of pure ego or even treason." Some supporters of same-sex marriage are concerned that Olson is taking up the cause too soon, since the Supreme Court currently has a conservative majority, and thus arguing before the court on behalf of same-sex marriage could result in a major setback for the gay-rights movement. Others believe that Olson is the perfect champion for the cause—that his conservative background lends credence to what is viewed as a liberal argument, and that Olson's legal record has prepared him to take such a controversial issue to the Supreme Court. "Mr. Olson's involvement stands out," Jo Becker wrote for the *New York Times* (August 19, 2009, on-line). "As one of the leading Supreme Court advocates of his generation, he commands wide respect in the legal community, and his views carry considerable weight with the justices." Steven G. Calabresi, a law professor at Northwestern University and a conservative, told Becker, "While some will think that this is an unpardonable error and rethink their views on Ted, I think it will cause others to take a second look at the argument he is making." For Olson the issue is not one of partisanship but of civil rights. He told Borger, "Civil rights battles are won by fighting for civil rights. . . . We're representing real people, who are being deprived of their constitutional rights, and we tell them to wait? For what? For how long?" A conservative with libertarian leanings, Olson does not view his defense of same-sex marriage as a step away from conservative values; on the contrary, he told Patt Morrison for the *Los Angeles Times* (July 25, 2009, on-line), "it is a conservative value to respect the relationship that people seek to have with one another, a stable, committed relationship that provides a backbone for our community, for our economy. I think conservatives should value that."

Olson is one of the top appellate lawyers in the U.S., with a focus on constitutional law and issues that arise at the state and federal levels; of the 56 cases he has argued before the Supreme Court, he has won 44. He has been an attorney with the law firm of Gibson, Dunn & Crutcher, which has 17 offices in the U.S. and abroad, since 1965, and is a member of the firm's executive committee as well as co-chair of its Appellate and Constitutional Law Group and Crisis Management Team.

Theodore Bevry Olson was born on September 11, 1940 in Chicago, Illinois, to Lester and Yvonne Olson. He was raised in Mountain View, California, in the San Francisco Bay Area. He attended Los Altos High School before earning a B.A. degree, cum laude, in 1962 from the University of the Pacific in Stockton, California. While traveling with his college debate team, Olson got a glimpse of discrimination when his African-American teammate was barred from a restaurant in Texas. The team's coach, Paul Winters, recalled to Becker that Olson "tore into" the restaurant's owner, saying that the team would not eat there unless everyone was served.

Olson attended the University of California (UC)–Berkeley School of Law (known more commonly as Berkeley Law or Boalt Hall), from which he received a degree in 1965. He was president of the Boalt Hall Republican group and a member of the *California Law Review*, the university's law journal; he also belonged to the Order of the Coif, a national honor society for law students who attend member schools. During the 1960s UC–Berkeley was a hotbed of liberal activism. Olson, who supported the 1964 Republican presidential nominee, Barry Goldwater, in his run against Lyndon Johnson, told Morrison, "I think there were five of us [in the Boalt Hall Republican group] during the Goldwater-Johnson election. . . . I don't

think [others] considered us much of a threat. I think the people in Berkeley thought of us as a sort of quirky novelty." According to a biography of Olson on the *New York Times* Web site, Olson "became active in the Republican Party as a college and law student . . . long before the rise of the religious right and its focus on social issues. He gravitated toward a particularly Western brand of conservatism that valued small government and maximum individual liberty."

Later in 1965 Olson joined the law firm of Gibson, Dunn & Crutcher as an associate. Over the next decade and a half, he represented a number of news-media clients, including Metromedia, the National Broadcasting Company (NBC), and the *Los Angeles Times*. He became a partner with his firm in 1972. In 1981, at the urging of Attorney General William French Smith, a former partner at Gibson, Dunn & Crutcher, he was tapped by the administration of Ronald Reagan to serve as assistant attorney general in the Office of Legal Counsel of the U.S. Department of Justice. In that post Olson put in 13-hour days, working with three deputies and 16 others to advise Smith. He often provided advice on constitutional issues to the heads of other executive-branch agencies.

As a legal adviser in the Reagan administration, Olson was limited to making recommendations on policy decisions. On a few occasions he disagreed with the decisions made by the administration— the result, as he explained to Leslie Maitland Werner for the *New York Times* (March 7, 1984), of his trying "to separate legal analysis from policy questions." In 1983, for example, in the case *Bob Jones University v. United States*, Olson believed it was the right of the Internal Revenue Service (IRS) to revoke the tax-exempt status of Bob Jones University, a private Christian school, because of its then-existing policies of racial discrimination. The Reagan administration disagreed and argued that Congress had never gave the IRS the power to deny tax exemptions to private schools because of such policies. The case was heard by the Supreme Court, whose decision was in line with Olson's opinion. "All you can do is give your legal opinion, your best legal analysis to the policy makers so they can understand the issues and options, and then let them make the decisions," Olson explained to Werner.

In 1985 Olson returned to private practice at Gibson, Dunn & Crutcher, where he began to develop an appellate practice. The next year he was the subject of an independent-counsel investigation for allegedly providing misleading testimony before a House Judiciary Committee subcommittee in 1983, when he was assistant attorney general. At that time a number of congressional committees were investigating potential wrongdoing in the management of the Environmental Protection Agency (EPA) "Superfund" program, which pays for toxic-waste clean-ups. The Reagan administration initially withheld EPA documents about the program from the committees, and Olson was later called upon—after some of the documents were turned over—to appear before the subcommittee to explain the administration's reasoning. (Olson and other senior officials had argued that the administration had the right, based on executive privilege, to withhold the documents.) During his testimony Olson had told the subcommittee that all papers pertaining to the investigation had been turned over, but it was revealed shortly thereafter that some, including a memo Olson wrote to Reagan, had not been. The memo in question contained Olson's assertions that no corruption on the part of the EPA was evident in the documents, and that the EPA supported the decision not to hand over those documents. Both assertions later proved false. The investigation lasted for 28 months, at the end of which the independent counsel decided not to charge Olson with perjury. However, a report by the independent counsel, Joe Conason wrote for *Salon.com* (February 6, 2001), suggested that Olson had "intentionally misled Congress even though his testimony had been 'literally true.'" Olson, for his part, has argued that his comments during the testimony were taken out of context; other conservatives saw the investigation as little more than a partisan attack. The investigation prompted Olson and others to challenge the constitutionality of appointing independent counsels, but the Supreme Court ruled in *Morrison v. Olson* (1988) that such appointments were permissible.

In 1986, meanwhile, Olson had represented Reagan during the Iran-Contra Affair, a major political scandal in which the Reagan administration was investigated for selling arms to Iran in exchange for the return of American hostages held by Iranian terrorists in Lebanon. The scandal widened when evidence surfaced that some of the money Iran paid for the weapons had been diverted to fund anti-communist "Contra" rebels fighting the left-wing Nicaraguan government. After the scandal broke, Reagan claimed that he had not been aware that members of his administration had diverted funds to the Nicaraguan rebels. An independent commission, appointed by the president, later determined that there was no evidence that Reagan had authorized the diversion of Iranian money. Nonetheless, Reagan was criticized in the media for violating national policy by sending weapons to Iran and for failing to keep members of his administration in check.

In 1991, before the U.S. Circuit Court of Appeals, Olson represented Jonathan Pollard, a naval intelligence analyst convicted of spying for Israel. Pollard, in a deal with U.S. government prosecutors to avoid a life sentence, had pleaded guilty in 1986 to a charge of conspiring to provide national defense information to a foreign government. In 1987, however, a judge imposed a life sentence. In the 1991 appeals case, Olson argued unsuccessfully that the life sentence violated the plea agreement, and that while prosecutors had not officially sought a life sentence, they had led the judge to that ruling through the use of such terms as "trai-

torous" and "treason." The Supreme Court subsequently refused to hear an appeal, and no president has been willing to commute Pollard's sentence, despite arguments by Olson and others.

In 1992, as a lawyer for *Newsday*, Olson defended the journalist Timothy Phelps, who had refused to disclose to a special counsel his source in a leak of FBI information. The leaked information—made public in an article by Phelps—pertained to an interview that the lawyer Anita Hill gave to the FBI, in which she accused then–Supreme Court nominee Clarence Thomas of sexually harassing her when she worked for him at the Equal Employment Opportunity Commission. When the special counsel attempted to compel Phelps and other reporters to reveal the source of the leak, a debate erupted over the rights of journalists under the First Amendment. Olson told Fred Bruning for *Newsday* (January 18, 1992), "The Constitution protects not only the dissemination of news but methods of gathering the news," and *Newsday* argued that it had a right to protect its sources in order to continue to cover the news and receive off-the-record information. The Senate Rules Committee agreed, denying the special counsel's request to force Phelps and other journalists to reveal their sources. Phelps told Jack Sirica for *Newsday* (March 26, 1992) that the decision was "a very important victory" that would "establish the principle that the work of reporters is indeed protected by the First Amendment."

In 1996, in *United States v. Commonwealth of Virginia*, Olson argued that the Virginia Military Institute (VMI), a state-supported military college, should be allowed to continue its men-only admissions policy. In his defense of the policy, Olson explained that there was an equal but separate state-funded military school for women already in place, and that the long-standing VMI program "would fundamentally have to be altered" if women were allowed in, as Jan Crawford Greenburg reported for the *Chicago Tribune* (January 18, 1996). Olson was unsuccessful, as the Supreme Court ruled that the policy violated the constitutional guarantee of equal protection under the law. In another landmark school-policy case, an appellate procedure that also took place in 1996, Olson successfully represented four white plaintiffs who had won a suit against the University of Texas School of Law over an affirmative-action policy they believed discriminated against them. The original case, *Hopwood v. Texas*, had been decided by the Fifth U.S. Circuit Court of Appeals, which ruled that the policy was unfair and that race should not be a factor in admissions. (The decision applied only to Texas, Louisiana, and Mississippi, the states within the appellate court's jurisdiction.) In 2003 the ruling was nullified when the Supreme Court decided in *Grutter v. Bollinger* (in which Olson was not involved) that race can be a factor in admissions as long as there is no racial quota.

Olson argued one of his most important cases in 2000, when he was tapped to represent George W. Bush before the Supreme Court in *Bush v. Gore*. On the night of the presidential election, November 7, news networks initially declared Bush the winner, but later retracted that declaration as votes continued to be counted into the next day. When it seemed as though Bush was indeed the victor, Gore conceded, but he later retracted his concession, after learning that Bush's lead in Florida was much smaller than it had appeared. For the next five weeks, Florida was the national center of attention, as a series of legal actions were taken, beginning with Gore's request for a manual recount of the ballots in four Democratic counties. Bush's legal team asked for the recount to be halted, but the Florida Supreme Court refused and gave the four counties five days to finish the manual recounts. The Florida secretary of state, Katherine Harris, a Bush supporter, did not extend the deadline for certification to allow all counties to complete their hand recounts. On November 26 Harris certified all votes tallied up to that point, pronouncing Bush the winner in Florida by 537 votes. Gore's team then contested the results of the election in Florida, first in a circuit court and then before the Florida Supreme Court.

At the same time, the U.S. Supreme Court began listening to the arguments of the Bush team, led by Olson, that Florida's Supreme Court had overstepped its authority by forcing Harris to include the manual recounts in the certified results. The U.S. Supreme Court then sent the case back to the Florida Supreme Court, asking it to clarify its reasoning for including manual recounts from specific counties. Several days later, on December 8, a divided Florida Supreme Court ordered manual recounts in all counties where there were a significant number of "under-votes," or punch-card votes that had not been registered by machine because the cards had not been punched through completely. The next day the U.S. Supreme Court, in a divided ruling, halted the manual recount and authorized a hearing on the matter, set for two days later.

In his arguments before the Supreme Court, Olson stated that the Florida court had violated the Equal Protection Clause of the 14th Amendment, as no standards had been set for each county to determine which ballots constituted legal votes, an oversight that potentially disenfranchised voters. David Boies, the opposing lawyer, argued for the Democrats that the Florida court was simply interpreting state law. On December 12, 2000, in a highly controversial, five-to-four decision, the U.S. Supreme Court ruled that the Florida Supreme Court had not set sufficiently clear rules for manually counting votes (the state court had said only to count as votes those ballots showing "clear intention"), and that any further delay in the certification of the votes would jeopardize their immunity from congressional reexamination after December 12, the date for final certification. In their majority opinion, the conservatives on the court contended that because different methods had been applied to recounts in different counties, the inexact standards prescribed by the Florida Supreme Court for manual recounts violated the Equal Protection Clause. Shortly after that decision was reached, Gore conceded the election to Bush. (Although Bush won the electoral vote, he had lost the popular vote by about a half-million ballots.)

In 2001 Olson was tapped by the Bush administration to serve as U.S. solicitor general, responsible for representing the federal government in Supreme Court cases. The confirmation process was far from smooth, as Democrats took Olson to task for his alleged involvement in efforts to undermine the Bill Clinton administration in the 1990s as part of the so-called Arkansas Project. That project, funded by the conservative businessman Richard Mellon Scaife, aimed to find evidence of illegal actions perpetrated by President Clinton and his wife, Hillary Rodham Clinton. With the help of Scaife's donations, the conservative magazine *American Spectator* printed articles on the Clintons. Olson became a lawyer for the magazine in 1994 and a member of its board in 1996. During Senate hearings Olson downplayed his involvement in the project and said he had even attempted to shut it down; he was nonetheless described by some news-media outlets as one of its main figures. Olson was confirmed by a vote of 51–47.

On his 61st birthday—September 11, 2001—Olson suffered the loss of his wife, Barbara, who was on the hijacked plane that struck the Pentagon building as part of an orchestrated series of attacks by the terrorist group Al Qaeda. Olson dealt with the loss in part by immersing himself in his work, spending the next few years defending the Bush administration's policies regarding suspected terrorists. Neil A. Lewis wrote for the *New York Times* (August 4, 2002, on-line) that after 9/11 Olson "assumed a new role that channels his need to be involved in the fight. He has become the legal field general coordinating the administration's strategy in several courts across the nation as civil libertarians challenge the Justice Department's new policies." Those controversial policies included detaining suspects indefinitely without specifying the charges or allowing them to challenge their detention, and withholding the names of those arrested in investigations related to the September 11 attacks. Olson was criticized by civil-liberties groups for his involvement in defending the administration's policies, although he privately advised the administration to afford more basic legal rights to suspects. (In 2004 the Supreme Court ruled that U.S. citizens and foreign nationals detained as suspected terrorists have the right to challenge their treatment in U.S. courts.)

During his tenure as solicitor general, Olson led the Justice Department to win more than 80 percent of its cases before the Supreme Court. Some of the most important of those victories include defenses of the Pledge of Allegiance in public schools, child-pornography laws, school vouchers, and the McCain-Feingold Act, which regulates political-campaign financing. In 2004 the Bush administration endorsed an amendment to the U.S. Constitution to define marriage as a union between one man and one woman; although Olson disagreed with the move, he did not do so publicly. (The amendment did not pass.) Later that year he resigned from his post as solicitor general and returned to Gibson, Dunn & Crutcher.

In 2009 Olson shocked both conservatives and liberals when he joined his former *Bush v. Gore* opponent, David Boies, to challenge Proposition 8, the California constitutional amendment that banned same-sex marriage when it was passed as a ballot initiative by voters in 2008. In the case, *Perry v. Schwarzenegger*, Olson and Boies argued that Proposition 8 amounted to discrimination based on sexual orientation and a violation of the due-process and equal-protection clauses found in the 14th Amendment to the U.S. Constitution. Olson told Becker, "For conservatives who don't like what I'm doing, it's, 'If he just had someone in his family [who is gay] we'd forgive him.' For liberals it's such a freakish thing that it's, 'He must have someone in his family, otherwise a conservative couldn't possibly have these views.' It's frustrating that people won't take it on face value." In a piece he wrote for *Newsweek* (January 9, 2010, on-line), Olson explained, "Many of my fellow conservatives have an almost knee-jerk hostility toward gay marriage. This does not make sense, because same-sex unions promote the values conservatives prize. Marriage is one of the basic building blocks of our neighborhoods and our nation. . . . The fact that individuals who happen to be gay want to share in this vital social institution is evidence that conservative ideals enjoy widespread acceptance. Conservatives should celebrate this, rather than lament it."

Perry v. Schwarzenegger resulted when a gay couple and a lesbian couple in California sued state officials, including Governor Arnold Schwarzenegger and California attorney general Jerry Brown, when they were not allowed to marry. (Neither Schwarzenegger nor Brown is a proponent of Proposition 8, and neither attempted to defend the law in court.) In lieu of a defense from state officials, the group that sponsored the ballot initiative, Protect Marriage, defended it through the Washington, D.C., lawyer Charles J. Cooper. Olson became involved when he was contacted by the filmmaker and liberal activist Rob Reiner, who, with other Democrats and activists, was contemplating a legal challenge to Proposition 8 shortly after it passed. Reiner had been informed by a chance encounter with Olson's former sister-in-law that Olson might be willing to get involved. To ward off any fears that, as a conservative, he was actually hoping to undermine the same-sex-marriage cause, Olson asked Boies to join him, and both lawyers waived portions of their usual fees. "I wanted to convey the message that this was not Republican or Democrat, conservative or liberal, that this is about human rights and human decency and constitutional law," Olson told Morrison. "David was my opponent in *Bush v. Gore*, but he's someone for whom I have great respect and affection."

During the trial, held before the U.S. District Court for the Northern District of California, Olson and Boies argued that sexual orientation is not a choice and that denying gay couples the right to marry deprives them of a fundamental right. They noted that the state of California did not benefit from banning same-sex marriage, and that denying homosexuals the right to marry one another did not encourage them to enter into heterosexual marriages. The defense argued that marriage had traditionally been between a man and a woman for the purpose of procreation, and that same-sex marriage would harm society. Judge Vaughn Walker, in striking down Proposition 8 on August 4, 2010, said that it was unconstitutional under both the due-process and equal-protection clauses. Walker issued an injunction against enforcing Proposition 8 as well as a stay to permit Proposition 8 supporters to mount an appeal. On August 12 Walker announced that the stay—and enforcement of Proposition 8—would end on August 18, but on August 16 the Ninth U.S. Circuit Court of Appeals in San Francisco extended Walker's stay until an appeal could be heard. That move effectively prevented any new same-sex marriages in California for the time being. The appeal was expected to be heard in December, and many expect the issue to reach the U.S. Supreme Court.

For their work on the landmark lawsuit, Boies and Olson were named to *Time*'s list of the 100 "people who most affect our world" for 2010. In his piece in *Time* (April 29, 2010, on-line) on the two lawyers, Joel Klein wrote, "In today's debates, polarization and personal attacks have replaced civility and excellence. It says a lot about Boies and Olson that they can disagree profoundly about legal issues without losing respect for each other. They remind us that the ideas binding us together in our constitutional democracy are far more important than those separating us."

Olson is a member of the conservative Federalist Society, which seeks to reform the U.S. legal system in accordance with a strict interpretation of the U.S. Constitution, and is a former president of the society's Washington, D.C., division. He is also a fellow of the American College of Trial Lawyers and the American Academy of Appellate Lawyers. He is a two-time recipient of the United States Department of Justice's Edmund J. Randolph Award, and he is also a recipient of the Department of Defense's highest civilian award. From 2006 to 2008 he served on the President's Privacy and Civil Liberties Oversight Board. In 2007 he was a visiting scholar at the National Constitution Center. He is co-chair of the Knight Commission on the Information Needs of Communities in a Democracy, as well as a member of the Board of Trustees on the Ronald Reagan Presidential Foundation and a member of the Steering Committee for the Sandra Day O'Connor Project on the State of the Judiciary.

Olson has been listed as one of the top lawyers in America by the *National Law Journal*, the *American Lawyer,* and *Legal Times*. In 2007 he was named the top lawyer in Washington, D.C., by *Washingtonian* magazine. In July 2010 Olson was appointed by President Barack Obama to serve as a member of the Council of the Administrative Conference of the United States (ACUS), which, according to the Gibson, Dunn & Crutcher Web site, is "a public-private partnership charged with providing nonpartisan, practical assessments and recommendations to improve agency procedures and operations."

Olson has been married four times and has two children. His third wife, Barbara, was a lawyer and prominent conservative commentator who often appeared on CNN and the Fox News Channel. In the 1990s she was a major critic of the Clinton administration, and she penned a book critical of the then–First Lady, *Hell to Pay: The Unfolding Story of Hillary Rodham Clinton* (1999). During the hijacking of American Airlines Flight 77, on September 11, 2001, Barbara Olson called her husband from the plane twice. Olson told Morrison that the day of his wife's death was "a very difficult day. I think our memories tend to fade a little bit. I guess we think after so many years that [the attack] was an aberration and could never happen again. Sadly, it could happen again. It's important for people to remain vigilant and remember what did happen that day was an assault on America's values." In 2006 Olson married Lady Booth, a Democrat 20 years his junior. When asked by Morrison if his wife has influenced his political leanings, Olson responded, "Well, she thinks that she has! She's working on me. It's important to be surrounded by people who think differently than we do. We don't learn anything if we surround ourselves by people who think the same way we do."

—W.D.

Suggested Reading: *Boston Globe* A p38 Dec. 13, 2000; gibsondunn.com; *Los Angeles Times* (online) July 25, 2009; *New York Times* B p8 Mar. 7, 1984, (on-line) Aug. 19, 2009; *Newsweek* (online) Jan. 9, 2010; *Salon.com* Feb. 6, 2001; *Washington Post* (on-line) June 14, 2010

Orender, Donna

1956(?)– Sports-association executive

Address: WNBA, Olympic Tower, 645 Fifth Ave., New York, NY 10022

When Donna Orender assumed the presidency of the Women's National Basketball Association (WNBA), in 2005, she became the only head of an American professional sports league whose resumé included playing time in the same sport. For four years in the 1970s, Orender was a standout guard with the Lady Knights, the Queens College women's basketball team, then one of the nation's top squads; an All-American, she took part in the first-ever women's basketball competition to be held at Madison Square Garden, in New York City. After she completed her bachelor's degree, in 1978, she played for three years with a series of teams in the short-lived Women's Professional Basketball League (WBL), becoming an All-Star in her second year, as a member of the New Jersey Gems. Then, for seven years or so, Orender worked as a producer for sports television, for two of those years as the head of her own company, Primo Donna Productions. For 17 years after that, she was employed by the PGA (Professional Golfers' Association) Tour, rising from vice president for PGA Tour Productions to senior vice president of strategic development in the office of the commissioner. In the latter post she was recognized as the most powerful woman in the golf business. Orender was being considered for the top leadership post of the Ladies Professional Golf Association when, in early 2005,

Christian Petersen/Getty Images

David J. Stern, the longtime commissioner of the National Basketball Association (NBA), announced that she would succeed Valerie B. "Val" Ackerman to become the second head of the WNBA. Orender, Stern told Eli Gelman for the Newark, New Jersey, *Star-Ledger* (April 10, 2005), is an "expert in all matters of sports marketing. Her energy is extraordinary. She's extraordinarily intense and competitive and truly understands what

[WNBA players] have gone through to get to this level."

"If you look at the origin of women's basketball, it started as a halfcourt game because it was not thought that women's hearts were strong enough to handle it . . . ," Orender told Mick Elliott for the *Tampa (Florida) Tribune* (March 3, 2008). "Think about a society that told women they were not strong enough, they were not capable enough, and how you would internalize that as a young woman and how that plays out in your everyday life. Now here we are, people standing and cheering for women who sweat and get dirty and throw themselves on the floor and are physical. It's remarkable. That's important because inherent to basketball are so many values that life demands to succeed." She also said, "There is a lot of research that shows how young girls and women benefit from participating in sports: health, diminishing breast cancer, the rise of self-esteem, better grades in school. That enhanced self-esteem, that ability to master the challenge, understanding how to compete, it all makes you a better corporate citizen."

The first of the three daughters of Jerry and Sherry Chait, Orender was born Donna-lyn Chait in about 1956 in New Hyde Park, on Long Island, New York, and grew up in nearby Elmont. Her father, a sports lover, headed an industrial-coating company; her mother was an art broker. One of her sisters is an artist, the other a teacher. Her parents also have two children adopted from China when Orender was an adult. Orender has said that she became interested in sports early on, in part to win her father's attention and approval. "My dad was all about being the best and nothing else," she told Liz Robbins for the *New York Times* (September 14, 2005). "Second place wasn't an option." Starting at about age seven, she participated in athletic games whenever she could. One day her father told her that she had been a tomboy long enough and that she must stop playing stickball in the street. "I continued to play stickball, but when I heard my dad's car coming, I would sit on the curb," she recalled to a *Newsweek* (October 15, 2007) interviewer. "My dad would pull in the driveway and I would say, 'I'm just sitting here cheering, Dad.'" Orender started playing basketball at a summer camp at age 12. At Elmont High School she played on the girls' varsity basketball, field hockey, volleyball, and softball teams and on the boys' varsity tennis team (there was no girls' team). Basketball became her favorite sport. "I preferred a team environment," she told Mick Elliott. "I like the collaborative process. I just seemed to have that physical ability to shoot and I loved to run. There was poetry in basketball for me." As a 14-year-old, Mark Herrmann wrote for *Newsday* (May 17, 2005), Orender would "sneak out of the house and go to Harlem to play basketball." She told Elliott, "I loved being able to go to a playground and have the guys say, 'What do you want?' and I say, 'I want to play.' Then [have] them question me and be able to prove myself."

After she completed high school, Orender attended Queens College, a division of the City University of New York, where she became an All-American guard on the women's basketball team. The team was guided by the famously determined and intense Lucille Kyvallos, one of the first coaches to introduce undergraduate women to aerobic conditioning and weight training as well as tactics for highly aggressive, fast-paced play. Orender was on the court when the Lady Knights competed against one of the nation's best teams, Immaculata College, at Madison Square Garden on February 22, 1975—the first-ever women's basketball game to take place there. Some 12,000 spectators witnessed Queens's defeat, with 61 points to Immaculata's 65.

Orender earned a B.A. degree in psychology from Queens College in 1978. She then enrolled in the graduate program in social work at Adelphi University, in Garden City, New York. She abandoned her studies soon afterward, to play for the New York Stars of the Women's Professional Basketball League during the inaugural season (1978–79) of the league, the first such organization for women in basketball. (From then until her second marriage, in 1994, Orender was known as Donna Chait Geils.) After one season she was traded to the New Jersey Gems. While with the Gems she played an average of more than 40 minutes per game (topping all but seven other WBL players) and ranked second in the WBL that season in total minutes played. Also in 1979–80, according to wblmemories.com, she placed in the WBL's top 10 in points, steals, and free-throw percentage and missed the 10th spot in assists by only two-10ths of a percentage point. She was selected for the league's All-Star team that year. Howie Landa, who coached the Gems in 1980, recalled to Liz Robbins, "She was so hard-nosed, it was unbelievable. She was a New York City kid. She played to win, not only just to play." Her Gems' teammate Ann Meyers told Robbins, "She was confident as a player. There was probably a competitiveness between us because we didn't get the recognition they get today, and you wanted to prove how good you were. We were competing against ourselves." After that season Orender moved to the Chicago Hustle. She supplemented her salary—$5,500, equivalent in buying power to about $14,500 in 2010—as the host of her own local radio and cable-TV shows. Years later she told Eli Gelman, "Basketball gave me an avenue to achieve success at a level I never would have thought possible. It built confidence, commitment. I didn't know what it would mean to spend three hours in a gym at a minimum. That feeling is still with me today."

The WBL folded at the end of the 1980–81 season, because of insufficient funding and a lack of public interest. In an article published in the Sunday Sports section of the *New York Times* (November 15, 1981) a few days later, Orender wrote, "In three seasons a league identity still had not developed, and the undercapitalized owners were skimping on the area they could least afford—marketing and public relations. No one promised that the WBL would be an easy sell, but no one promised that it could sell itself."

Orender told Helen Wheelock for the Women's Sports Foundation, as posted on fraser61.wordpress.com (September 7, 2008), "Competing at the highest level in sports taught me the fundamentals of how to succeed in business. No. 1 was about absolute commitment—if you want to be the best, you've got to focus on being the best and put in the time to be the best. No 2. taught me about determination—that clearly the easiest path between you and the basket was not easy at all, and if I was going to get there, I was going to be more determined than anyone else was to stop me. And lastly, it taught me about passion and joy, that when you really love what you're doing, your ability to succeed grows exponentially." She told the *Newsweek* interviewer, "As a professional athlete, I always felt I was part of a unique group of individuals on the planet who get paid to play a sport. I knew that the experience of competing on that high level would take me wherever I wanted to go. I also knew that it allowed me to compete in a male world. Many of these guys were sports wanna-bes. Well, I wasn't a wanna-be."

Earlier, starting in 1980, Orender had begun to work at a series of sports-related production jobs. She served as an assistant specializing in college football at ABC Sports, the sports-programming division of the ABC television network (now known as ESPN on ABC). She also worked for Cablevision's SportsChannel America and managed her own company, Primo Donna Productions, before joining NBA Entertainment (the production arm of the NBA).

In 1988 Orender got a job in the front office of the PGA Tour, which manages the main professional men's golf tournaments held in the U.S. every year. (Currently, there are 43 such events.) Among her first assignments, Orender produced *Inside the PGA Tour*, a weekly half-hour TV show. She was soon promoted to vice president of PGA Tour Productions and later, in 2001, to senior vice president of strategic development. In the latter post she supervised production for all PGA Tour televised events. In the last few years of her tenure, she negotiated record-breaking contracts worth hundreds of millions of dollars with television networks, far exceeding the value of earlier agreements and increasing TV coverage of PGA events many times over. According to Ryan Herrington, writing for *Golf World* (February 25, 2005), "Many credit Orender for devising the idea of splitting up the tour schedule and packaging events to maximize revenue." Orender was also in charge of management of the PGA Tour brand and ventures into new media, including the Internet. Paul Johnson, the senior vice president of new media for the PGA Tour, told Eli Gelman, "She wants things to be great. She doesn't want them to be good. . . . She's tough because she has very high expectations. The

flip side of tough is occasionally you get a punch in the nose, but you'll walk away and she'll have her arm around you and you'll say, 'Okay, this wasn't good enough and we have to do better.'"

In February 2005 Orender was selected to succeed Val Ackerman (also a former basketball player) as the president of the Women's National Basketball Association. The WNBA star Lisa Leslie told Liz Robbins, "When Val left, we were like: 'Oh my gosh, this is going to be the fall of us. Who are we going to find to replace her?' Donna, I didn't know her before, but I don't think we could have picked a better person, a woman who is familiar with sports, played basketball, who understands the struggle of trying to find our place in the sports world."

Founded in 1996 as the women's counterpart to the NBA, the WNBA started with eight teams, all owned by the NBA and operated by NBA owners. Changes made in 2002 allow teams to be owned independently. As president of the WNBA, Orender is responsible for overseeing all league operations and business. Soon after her arrival, in April 2005, she visited each WNBA team at its home stadium. Since then she has broadened the league's exposure in the media, including television, newspapers, magazines, and the Internet, and seen an increase in attendance at games. She has also expanded the league: with the addition of two franchises—the Chicago Sky, in 2006, and the Atlanta Dream, in 2008—there are currently a total of 12 teams in the Eastern and Western Conferences. The former, in addition to Chicago and Atlanta, includes the Indiana Fever, the Washington, D.C., Mystics, the Connecticut Sun, and the New York Liberty; the latter includes the Seattle Storm, the Phoenix Mercury, the Minnesota Lynx, the San Antonio Silver Stars, the Los Angeles Sparks, and the Tulsa Shock (formerly, until 2009, the Detroit Shock). Eight of the 12 teams are owned by the NBA; the other four are independently owned. Except for those four, each team shares an arena with an NBA club and is considered its "sister" team.

In 2006 Orender oversaw a season-long celebration of the WNBA's 10th anniversary, which marked the first time that a women's professional sports league had survived for a decade. (The women's American Basketball League, which did not have NBA support, folded in 1998, after two seasons.) Also in 2006 the league named 10 players to its All-Decade Team: Sue Bird and Lauren Jackson of Seattle; Lisa Leslie of Los Angeles; Tamika Catchings of Indiana; Katie Smith of Minnesota; Dawn Staley of the now-defunct Charlotte Sting; Cynthia Cooper, Sheryl Swoopes, and Tina Thompson of the now-defunct Houston Comets; and Yolanda Griffith of the now-defunct Sacramento Monarchs. (Thompson is now with the Sparks, Griffith with the Fever.)

In 2007 Orender helped to negotiate a new, eight-year television contract with ESPN/ABC. The agreement gave the WNBA rights fees for the first time and included digital-media rights. "It's a tremendous vote of confidence," Orender said, as quoted by Vin A. Cherwoo, an Associated Press (July 16, 2007) reporter. "It's a tremendous vote of affirmation and validation of 11 years of hard work of the athletes of the WNBA, the consistent growth of talent that we have and the growth in our fan base." The deal went into effect in 2009. The WNBA has enjoyed a steady rise in television viewership under Orender's watch, with regular-season games on ESPN2 averaging 269,000 viewers during the 2009 season, marking an 8 percent increase from the previous year. The WNBA Live Access, which was launched in 2009, allows fans to watch more than 200 games in real time through the Internet. The WNBA is also on Facebook, with at least 250,000 fans. Orender's goals include securing higher salaries for WNBA players; the current average is about $100,000 per year. (The average for NBA players is $5 million per year.)

On July 19, 2010 President Barack Obama spoke to Phoenix Mercury members at the White House, after the team secured its second WNBA championship. According to an Associated Press (July 19, 2010, on-line) reporter, the president "thanked the players for setting a good example" for his daughters and other young women.

Orender, who is Jewish, is a member of the boards of the Beth El–The Beaches Synagogue, in Ponte Vedra Beach, Florida (a suburb of Jacksonville), where she lives; the UJA Sports for Youth Initiative; and the Hadassah Foundation. She also sits on the executive committee of Maccabi USA/Sports for Israel. Orender was the captain of the U.S. women's basketball team at the 1985 Maccabiah Games, in Israel, and co-chaired the American women's basketball team for the 2001 Maccabiah Games. She sits on the boards of the Monique Burr Foundation for Children and the V Foundation for Cancer Research, serves on the Jacksonville Film and Television Advisory Council and the University of North Florida College of Arts and Science Advisory Council, and has participated in the National Minority Golf Foundation Mentor Program. She has received the March of Dimes Sports Leadership Award (2006); the Women in Sports and Events (WISE) Woman of the Year Award (2007); and an honorary doctoral degree from Adelphi University (2007). In 2006 she was inducted into the National Jewish Sports Hall of Fame and honored by the UJA-Federation of New York's Entertainment, Media, and Communications Division.

In 1994 Orender married Morgan Guy "M.G." Orender, the co-founder and president of Hampton Golf Inc., which runs a dozen golf clubs in the southeastern U.S. and the Hampton Golf Academy, in Jacksonville, Florida; for several years in the early 2000s, M.G. headed PGA of America. The couple's twin sons, Jacob and Zachary, were born in 1997. Orender has a stepson, Morgan, and a stepdaughter, Colleen, from her husband's previous marriage. When in New York City, where the WNBA maintains its headquarters, or on the road

for WNBA business, she maintains daily contact with her twins, while their father has the primary responsibility for their care, and for some time she coached their youth-league basketball team. By her own account, she has no culinary skills, so her husband serves as the family cook. Orender has often publicly expressed her gratitude for her husband's encouragement and support.

—C.C.

Suggested Reading: Associated Press July 8, 2005; fraser61.wordpress.com (Sep. 7, 2008); (Jacksonville, Florida) *Times-Union* E p1 Feb. 16, 2005, C p1 May 9, 2005; nba.com; *New York Times* D p7 Sep. 14, 2005; (Newark, New Jersey) *Star-Ledger* p10 Apr. 10, 2005; *Sports Illustrated* G p10+ Dec. 4, 2000; (Tampa, Florida) *Tribune* p1 Mar. 3, 2008; wnba.com; *Women's Digest* (on-line) 2002

Frederick M. Brown/Getty Images

Pacelle, Wayne

(puh-SEL-ee)

Aug. 4, 1965– President and CEO of the Humane Society of the United States

Address: Humane Society of the United States, 2100 L St., N.W., Washington, DC 20037

Wayne Pacelle is the president and chief executive officer (CEO) of the Humane Society of the United States (HSUS), the largest organization working in the U.S. to "create a humane and sustainable world for all animals," according to its on-line mission statement. Pacelle is a vegan: he does not eat meat, fish, or fowl or consume or use any products obtained from animals, including milk, eggs, leather, wool, and items stuffed with goose down. But neither he nor HSUS expects others to emulate him. "I'm . . . conscious of the cultural complexities of this issue," he told Karen MacPherson for the *Pittsburgh (Pennsylvania) Post-Gazette* (December 20, 2004). "People are raised to think of animals in a certain way, and to use animals in some ways. I try to see where people are and give them encouragement to get to a place where they view animals not as tools for research or game to be harvested, but as individual beings that have the same spark of life that all of us have." Before he joined the HSUS, in 1994, Pacelle worked for six years with the Fund for Animals, a group whose main goal was to end sport hunting. He served as the HSUS's senior vice president for communications and government affairs until 2004, when he rose to its top position. "The arrival of Wayne Pacelle as head of the Humane Society in 2004 both turbo-charged the farm animal welfare movement and gave it a sheen of respectability," Kim Severson wrote for the *New York Times* (July 25, 2007). She also wrote, "Pacelle has retooled a venerable organization seen as a mild-mannered protector of dogs and cats into an aggressive interest group flexing muscle in state legislatures and courtrooms." In 2008 *Supermarket News* named Pacelle to its annual Power 50 list of influential people in food marketing, declaring, "There's no denying his growing influence on how animal agriculture is practiced in the United States."

The HSUS was founded in 1954; currently, it has 10 million members. It works in both the U.S. and—through a subsidiary, the Humane Society International (HSI), established in 1991—the world over "to forge a lasting and comprehensive change in human consciousness of and behavior toward all animals in order to prevent animal cruelty, exploitation, and neglect and to protect wild habitats and the entire community of life." Thanks in part to images that have appeared in its ads and on address labels that have often accompanied its mailed fund-raising appeals, the HSUS is widely associated with the well-being of dogs and cats, but the welfare of pets is only one of its many concerns. (Indeed, the HSUS does not own or maintain any animal shelters, including those operated by local humane societies. It acts as an advocate for animal shelters when necessary, however, and publishes *Animal Sheltering*, a magazine regarded as the most comprehensive resource for shelter professionals.) High on HSUS's agenda is the reversal or slowing of global warming, which, if it continues unabated, according to the Intergovernmental Panel on Climate Change, will likely cause the extinction of up to a third of Earth's plant and animal species by 2050 (and have disastrous consequences for humans as well). Significantly contributing to global warming are the ways in which the 11 billion farm animals in the U.S. and more than

70 billion overseas are raised, the ways products are derived from them, and the ways those products are distributed. The HSUS and HSI urge major changes in the farm-animal industries and in the consumption of animal products. Toward that goal they have adopted what they call the "three R's" approach: "the refinement of production methods, the reduction of consumption, and the replacement of animal products with non-animal alternatives," according to the HSUS "Statements of Policy" (July 2009, on-line).

The top priorities of the HSUS include putting an end to the cruel treatment of animals in factory farms, in many of which pigs or calves raised for veal, for example, spend their entire lives in pens too small for them to turn around, and the beaks of chickens and turkeys are chopped off to prevent them from injuring or cannibalizing one another in their severely overcrowded enclosures. Among the other concerns of the HSUS are the use and treatment of animals in biomedical research and testing, in high-school and college classes, and in the entertainment industry, which encompasses film, television, greyhound races, horse races, rodeos, and circuses. Other matters of importance to the organization are the treatment and uses of companion animals—those trained to assist people with physical, visual, or hearing impairments; the handling of animals by pet stores and pounds; policies regarding pets during disasters, such as Hurricane Katrina, which struck the Gulf Coast of the U.S. in 2005; the operations of so-called puppy mills; the lawful (in some states) and illegal (in most states) operations of "blood" sports, including dog fighting and cock fighting; hunting practices that HSUS regards as inhumane, including the use of certain types of traps and hunting on enclosed properties or from airplanes; trapping and ranching animals for the fur industry; activities of the fishing industry that threaten the existence of some marine species and cause the inadvertent destruction of others; and conditions at zoos and aquariums. In terms of individuals, the HSUS, Pacelle told Bridget Kelly for the *Hartford (Connecticut) Courant* (August 30, 2004), is "simply asking people to expand their sensitivity and to exhibit greater mercy and kindness to the less powerful. If you're concerned about the well-being of animals, then you inevitably should think about your food choices, your clothing choices, your recreational pursuits."

Some critics of the animal-rights movement believe Pacelle is a radical who is determined to ban all forms of hunting and force the American public into a vegetarian lifestyle. By contrast, some within the movement think that Pacelle is not radical enough. Pacelle contends that he understands both sides of the animal-rights debate. Although HSUS is energetically engaged in animal-rights activism, Pacelle has rejected the use of illegal or in-your-face tactics to achieve the goals of the HSUS—the sorts of methods sometimes employed by representatives of People for the Ethical Treatment of Animals (PETA), for example, or the more radical Animal Liberation Front, which advocates, according to its Web site, "radical abolitionism: total liberation by any means necessary." Rather, HSUS devotes its efforts to awakening the public to its philosophy and lobbying for the passage of legislation that would help to achieve its goals. Nevertheless, in press releases from organizations of furriers, livestock or poultry farmers, and dog owners (in particular, those whose members own breeds commonly involved in dog fighting, such as pit bulls), HSUS is commonly and incorrectly equated with PETA or more-extreme groups. Pacelle has been quick to point out how they differ. He told Guy Raz for the National Public Radio (NPR) program *All Things Considered* (June 2, 2000), "There's no question that [PETA has] had some very significant victories in terms of getting major corporations to stop testing on animals. At the same time, I think it's clear that they have helped to contribute to the image of animal activism as sometimes a little too quirky and sometimes a little too radical." Pacelle told Alison Stewart for the NPR program *The Bryant Park Project* (November 6, 2007), "Really, our focus [at HSUS] is about human responsibility and less about animal rights. I mean, we're less concerned about whether animals have an inherent right than we are about what human responsibilities are in terms of our relationship with animals. . . . We have all the power in the relationship over animals, and we think . . . being a good person means being decent and responsible in our care of animals."

The youngest of the four children of Richard and Patricia Pacelle, Wayne Pacelle was born on August 4, 1965. He grew up in New Haven, Connecticut. His father, who is of Italian descent, was a high-school gym teacher and football coach; his mother, whose ancestors were Greek, worked as a secretary for an uncle's construction business. "Ever since I was a kid I've been focused on animals," Pacelle told Patricia R. Olsen for the *New York Times* (December 24, 2006). "I dog-eared the pages with the animal entries in our encyclopedia and memorized everything about them, from a polar bear to a pronghorn antelope." Every week he watched the TV show *Wild Kingdom* and dreamed of meeting its host, Marlin Perkins. The family had pet dogs during Pacelle's childhood; one of them, he learned later, was a product of a puppy mill—in effect, a factory for producing what were touted as pure-bred dogs, for sale to dealers or pet stores. Typically, females at such facilities are overbred; that is, they are impregnated every time they go into heat and are often killed when they no longer produce litters of sufficient size or stop producing altogether. Also common in puppy mills is inbreeding, which results in increased frequencies of genetic defects; many of those problems do not become evident until long after the retail sale of the dogs. In addition, the animals are often inadequately fed and are kept in cramped, overcrowded cages. Many weaken or die during transport to dealers or shops. "There are millions of healthy adoptable dogs in shelters that are fine dogs," Pacelle told Don Oldenburg for the *Washington Post* (August 9, 2004). "And shelters end up killing dogs because our society fails to provide homes to them and people fail to sterilize their animals properly."

Pacelle planned to become a lawyer when he enrolled at Yale University, in New Haven, Connecticut, in 1983. The summer following his sophomore year, he interned as a ranger at the Isle Royale National Park, an island park in the part of Lake Superior that lies within the Michigan border. He has said his devotion to the animal-rights cause was sparked late one night as he canoed on the lake. "You're in this pristine environment," he recalled to Carla Hall for the *Los Angeles Times* (July 19, 2008). "Inside this area, the animals could be protected. It just spoke to me. I could be part of the larger process of protecting animals and the environment."

Pacelle became a vegan shortly after that experience. As a junior at Yale, he established the Student Animal Rights Coalition. The group spurred the introduction of vegan meals in the school's dining halls and protested the Yale Medical School's use of animals in research. Pacelle made connections to other animal advocates, among them the writer Cleveland Amory, who founded the Fund for Animals in 1967. When Pacelle was home from school, he would lecture family members about the inhumane slaughter of food animals. "I was kind of strident," he told Hall. "But I've changed."

Pacelle graduated from Yale with a B.A. degree in history and environmental studies in 1987. He then got a job as a writer for the *Animals' Agenda*, a magazine published by the Fund for Animals. He became associate editor and, soon, was named president of the fund's board. At 23 he assumed the post of national director. Five years later, in 1994, he joined the Humane Society of the United States as its vice president for communications and government affairs, a position he held for the next decade. During that time Pacelle figured in the successful campaigns for the passage of 15 pieces of animal-friendly legislation in various states, including laws banning the use of bait and dogs in the hunting of bears, cougars, and bobcats in Oregon, Massachusetts, and Washington State; outlawing cockfighting in Arizona, Missouri, and Oklahoma; and forbidding the use in Arizona of crates that make movement impossible for veal calves. He also campaigned successfully for the defeat of several measures deemed to be injurious to animal protection, including Proposition 197 in California (1996), which would have repealed mountain lions' status as specially protected mammals under the California Wildlife Protection Act of 1990, and State Question 698 in Oklahoma (2002), which sought to increase the number of voters needed to propose an amendment to the state's laws dealing with permissible methods for hunting, fishing, and trapping.

In the past two decades, Pacelle has also been instrumental in the passage of federal statutes to protect animals. Among them are the Great Apes Conservation Act of 2000, which aims to protect apes (chimpanzees, gorillas, bonobos, orangutans, and gibbons) in their native habitats in Africa (the first three) and Asia (the last two); the Captive Wildlife Safety Act (2003), which bans commerce in such exotic animals as lions, tigers, leopards, cheetahs, jaguars, and cougars for purposes of private ownership; and the 2008 farm bill (officially, the Food, Conservation, and Energy Act of 2008), part of which banned the import of dogs from overseas puppy mills.

In the wake of Hurricane Katrina, which flooded large parts of New Orleans, Louisiana, in August 2005 and caused widespread damage elsewhere along the Gulf Cost, HSUS tried to rescue some of the tens of thousands of pets that were left stranded. The Federal Emergency Management Agency and the U.S. Coast Guard, however, declaring that only people would be rescued, prevented HSUS volunteers from entering New Orleans in the days after the storm. "Government policies forced people to make an awful choice—to be rescued and leave behind their pets or to stay in a stricken city and risk their lives," Pacelle told Marsha Ginsburg for the *San Francisco Chronicle* (September 16, 2005). "We want to see a rescue policy that recognizes the incredible bond between people and their pets." As reported in *Time* (June 6, 2007), 44 percent of the New Orleanians who refused to leave their homes did so because they would not part with their pets, according to a survey conducted by the San Francisco–based nonprofit Fritz Institute. Eventually the HSUS, which raised more than $34 million for relief efforts, coordinated the rescue of more than 10,000 animals in the Gulf Coast region and reunited some 2,500 of them with their owners. For the HSUS's role in the rescue and relocation of pets following Hurricane Katrina, Pacelle, along with the leaders of several other rescue organizations, was named Executive of the Year by the *NonProfit Times* (a magazine for executives of nonprofit organizations) in December 2005. The following year Pacelle and the HSUS campaigned for the passage of the federal Pets Evacuation and Transportation Standards (PETS) Act, which was signed into law by President George W. Bush on October 6, 2006. The law requires that in planning for disasters, all local, state, and federal agencies must include provisions for pets and service animals.

The Humane Society's clout within political circles increased in 2008, when its two-month investigation into unlawful activities at a slaughterhouse and meatpacking plant sparked the largest recall of beef in U.S. history. In October 2007 an HSUS investigator (without identifying himself as such) had secured a job at the Westland/Hallmark Meat Packing Co. in Chino, California. The undercover agent videotaped workers kicking sick cows, applying shocks to them, and using forklifts to force them to walk. The federal government has banned the use of sick, or "downer," cows as food because of an increased risk of infection in consumers caused by bacteria or prions, the latter of which cause bovine spongiform encephalopathy, known colloquially as mad cow disease, that infection causes deterioration of the brain and spinal cord and is often fatal. In February 2008, following further investigations by Chino police and agents of the U.S. Department of Agriculture (USDA), the USDA called for the recall of 143 million pounds of ground beef that had originated at the Westland/Hallmark slaughterhouse. Several of the workers caught on videotape were prosecuted, and the plant was shut down. Pacelle and the HSUS also appealed to the USDA for the closure of a loophole in the ban on downer cows as sources of food. A partial ban on the cows was implemented after the nation's first reported case of mad cow disease, in 2003, but a loophole allowed cows that had already passed federal inspection and later were unable to walk to enter the food supply after further examination. In March 2009 the USDA ruled that all nonambulatory cows, including those who had passed inspection, must be humanely euthanized and their deaths reported to proper officials.

In May 2009 Pacelle announced that the HSUS would work with the former Atlanta Falcons quarterback Michael Vick to campaign against dogfighting. Organized dogfighting is a felony in every U.S. state. Nevertheless, fights between two dogs, most commonly pit bulls, continue to be staged for purposes of entertainment and gambling. The dogs are often seriously injured, and some are killed. Often the owner of the losing dog will kill or abandon it if it is injured. In August 2007 Vick pled guilty to funding and operating a dogfighting ring at a home he owned in Virginia. Four months later he was sentenced to 23 months in a federal prison. (Vick was released from prison on May 20, 2009, and served the final two months of his sentence in his Virginia home.) Speaking to William C. Rhoden for the *New York Times* (May 22, 2009) about HSUS's collaboration with Vick, Pacelle said, "I understand that there are people who don't want to work with Michael Vick. I want to end dogfighting. And he may be a very important role player in that process. . . . If he's sincere, and if he's committed in the long run to this goal for whatever reasons, he can be an agent of change, he can steer young kids in urban communities' vile activity toward more productive interactions with dogs. Our goal is not endless punitive treatment of Michael Vick. Our goal is to eradicate dogfighting in America."

Pacelle has written for publications including *Human Dimensions of Wildlife* and the *George Wright Forum*, the latter of which is "devoted to interdisciplinary inquiry about parks, protected areas, and cultural sites," according to its Web site. His op-ed pieces have appeared in dozens of major newspapers, among them the *Washington Post*, the *Los Angeles Times*, the *New York Times*, and the *San Francisco Chronicle*. He also writes an occasional column for *Bark* magazine. He is a board member, co-founder, and former chairman of Humane USA, a nonpartisan organization, formed in 1999, whose goal is the election of animal-rights advocates to political office. In 2006 Pacelle co-founded the National Federation of Humane Societies (NFHS). He currently serves on its board.

Pacelle's marriage to Kirsten Rosenberg, the former managing editor of the now-defunct magazine *Animals' Agenda*, ended in divorce. He lives in Washington, D.C., with his girlfriend, Christine Gutleben, and her cat, Libby. Gutleben directs the HSUS's Animals and Religion program, which, ac-

cording to the HSUS Web site, "seeks to engage people and institutions of faith with animal protection issues, on the premise that religious values call upon us all to act in a kind and merciful way toward animals."

—M.A.S.

Suggested Reading: *Hartford (Connecticut) Courant* B p1 Aug. 30, 2004; hsus.org; *Los Angeles Times* A p1 July 19, 2008; *New York Times* III p9 Dec. 24, 2006; *New York Times Magazine* p47 Oct. 26, 2008; *Washington Post* C p1 Aug. 9, 2004

Robin Holland, courtesy of Nell Irvin Painter

Painter, Nell Irvin

Aug. 2, 1942– Historian; educator; author; artist

Address: c/o W.W. Norton, 500 Fifth Ave., New York, NY 10110

Nell Irvin Painter is one of the most respected scholars of African-American history in the U.S. A professor emeritus at Princeton University and a fellow of the American Academy of Arts and Sciences, she has also served as president of both the Organization of American Historians and the Southern Historical Association. Nellie Y. McKay, a friend and fellow professor of history, told Karen J. Winkler for the *Chronicle of Higher Education* (September 13, 1996), "[Painter is] a black woman scholar who—because her work can't be ignored—makes it easier for other black women to have access to scholarly attention. She's a pioneer."

Painter's many books include *Exodusters: Black Migration to Kansas after Reconstruction* (1976), about the migration of freed southern slaves to Kansas in 1879 and 1880; *Standing at Armageddon: The United States 1877–1919* (1987), a comprehensive account of the political and labor shifts that occurred within the U.S. between the end of Reconstruction and the end of World War I; and *Creating Black Americans: African American History and Its Meanings, 1619 to the Present* (2005), a wide-ranging survey. When Hollie I. West, writing for the *Washington Post* (February 27, 1980), pointed out that Painter "doesn't write about the great heroes of black American history or speculate about the grand achievements in Afro-Americana," Painter responded, "My generation doesn't have to do that job. My generation is talking about diversity within the race . . . about class and region and educational level, and even color of skin, because that's important too. Historians of the past didn't do this because of racism. Their burden was rehabilitating the race in terms of American thought, which was incredibly racist. The whole point used to be to write books and talk about how black people were really people."

Painter's most recent book, *The History of White People*, was published on March 15, 2010. She told Thomas Rogers for *Salon* (March 22, 2010, on-line) that when she was planning the book, many people expressed skepticism about a black scholar's tackling the topic. She asserted, however, "We've spent so much time in this country on various racial issues. It's our national sport, in a way, and it's always as if there is only one side: nonwhite. But this is one of those binaries where you need both sides to make sense of it."

The historian was born Nell Elizabeth Irvin on August 2, 1942 in Houston, Texas, at the Houston Hospital for Negroes, a segregated facility set up to serve the city's growing black population. Painter's family moved to California shortly after her birth. Her father, Frank Edward Irvin, a trained chemist, worked as an administrator in the Chemistry Department of the University of California (UC) at Berkeley, and her mother, Dona L. (McGruder) Irvin, was a homemaker who later worked in the personnel office of the Oakland public-school system. (Dona L. Irvin later wrote two books: *The Unsung Heart of Black America: A Middle Class Church at Midcentury*, published in 1992, which recounts the history of the Downs Memorial United Methodist Church in Oakland, and *I Hope I Look That Good When I'm That Old: An Older African-American Woman Speaks To All Women in All of America*, published in 2002.) Painter had an older brother, Frank Jr., who died when he was five years old, during a tonsillectomy.

As a student at Oakland Technical High School, Painter had little interest in her American-history classes. "I remember reading books about the United States, where the author would go into a hymn about how much better it was to be in America than Russia," she recalled to West. "What did I care about Russia? They would always leave out Alabama and lynchings and Emmett Till"—an African-American boy murdered in Mississippi in 1955, reportedly for whistling at a white woman. "They would leave out the whole side of the United States that spoke to me most clearly."

Painter won admission to UC Berkeley, where she majored in anthropology. During her junior year (1962–63) she studied French medieval history at the University of Bordeaux, in France. Returning to UC Berkeley, she earned her bachelor's degree with honors in 1964. She then spent a year in Africa, as a French lecturer at the University of Ghana's Institute of African Studies, in Legon. There, she met her first husband, Colin Painter, a linguistics professor at the school. They married in 1965 and divorced a year later.

Painter earned a master's degree in African history from the University of California at Los Angeles (UCLA) in 1967 and a Ph.D. degree in American history from Harvard University, in Cambridge, Massachusetts, in 1974. She then continued her lengthy and varied teaching career. Upon obtaining her doctoral degree, she joined the History Department of the University of Pennsylvania, in Philadelphia, as an assistant professor (1974–77); she was promoted to associate professor in 1977. During that time she won fellowships at Harvard's W.E.B. Du Bois Institute, the American Council of Learned Societies, and the National Humanities Center, among other prestigious institutions.

From 1980 to 1988 Painter taught American and Afro-American history at the University of North Carolina at Chapel Hill. She also served as the Russell Sage Visiting Professor of History at the City University of New York's Hunter College from 1985 to 1986. In 1988 she joined the History Department at Princeton University, in Princeton, New Jersey, where she served as director of the African-American studies program from 1997 to 2000. From 1991 until 2004, when she retired from teaching, Painter served as Princeton's Edwards Professor of American History. Upon her retirement, the university hosted a conference, "Constructing the Past, Creating the Future: The Legacy of Nell Irvin Painter," in her honor. The confer-

ence, whose participants discussed changes in the fields of women's and African-American studies over the years, as well as Painter's influence on those fields, included a number of leading scholars, including Robin D. G. Kelley, of Columbia University; Evelyn Brooks Higginbotham, of Harvard University; and David Levering Lewis, of New York University.

In addition to being a popular teacher, Painter was a prolific writer. Her doctoral dissertation at Harvard had focused on the Exoduster migration (also known as the Exodus of 1879 or the Kansas Exodus), in which freed African-American slaves fled the South for Kansas in order to escape racially oppressive laws. Her dissertation evolved into *Exodusters: Black Migration to Kansas after Reconstruction*, published in 1976. Margo Jefferson wrote in her review of the volume for *Newsweek* (January 17, 1977), "Painter examines [the] exodus in fascinating detail. In the process, she offers a compelling portrait of the post-Reconstruction South and the desperate efforts by blacks and whites in that chaotic period to 'solve the race problem' once and for all." In the *New York Times Book Review* (January 30, 1977), whose editors selected *Exodusters* as a Notable Book of the Year, David H. Donald called the volume "one of first serious historical studies produced by a young black scholar influenced by the doctrines of black nationalism." Donald continued, "Most previous students have focused on nationally recognized black leaders; she calls for attention to the black masses. Most earlier writers have emphasized black patterns of accommodation to the white world; she urges that the emphasis be placed upon widespread black rebelliousness."

Painter's second book, *The Narrative of Hosea Hudson: His Life as a Negro Communist in the South*, was published in 1979. (The book was later republished under the title *The Narrative of Hosea Hudson: The Life and Times of a Black Radical*.) In it, Painter recounted the life of Hudson, a steel-mill worker who became an active member of the Communist Party and a local union official in Birmingham, Alabama, during the 1930s and '40s. Painter had heard about Hudson while chatting at a party, and in 1976 she had driven to his home in Atlantic City, New Jersey, to speak to him. "I had no thought of writing a book," she recalled to West. "I just wanted to talk to an interesting man." Intrigued, however, Painter repeatedly returned to interview Hudson (who died in 1988) and wrote the book as a collaborative oral autobiography. "[Painter] fills a gaping hole in the history of this country," the historian John Hope Franklin told West. "We [historians] all try to go to the source, but she's gone to the people themselves." *The Narrative of Hosea Hudson* was selected as a Notable Book of the Year by the editors of the *New York Times Book Review*, who called it "an invaluable record of the black experience in the South during the Depression," in an assessment published on April 5, 1981. In her review of the book for the *Na-*

tion (January 5, 1980), Benita Eisler wrote, "Moving, fearful, and funny, Hudson and Painter's *Narrative* is [as] valuable an American life as has ever been wrested from anonymity."

Standing at Armageddon: The United States 1877–1919 (1987; an updated second edition was published in 2008) explores the class conflicts and political changes that occurred in the U.S. during that period. "Throughout the book, Painter shows a knack for recognizing [fine] details, and she draws on recent scholarship in social history without letting its complexity mar the enthralling story she tells," Michael Kazin wrote for the *Washington Post* (November 22, 1987). Like Painter's earlier books, *Standing at Armageddon* was named a *New York Times Book Review* Notable Book of the Year, and it additionally won the Letitia Woods Brown Book Award from the Association of Black Women Historians.

Painter examined the legacy of an iconic African-American abolitionist and women's-rights activist in *Sojourner Truth: A Life, A Symbol* (1996). Truth was born Isabella Van Wagenen in the 1790s and later took on the name with which she is famously associated. A slave until she was granted freedom in 1826, Truth was illiterate; thus, much that had been written about her had been filtered and interpreted by other people. Painter's *Sojourner Truth* describes the ways in which Truth's image was often distorted by the African-American and feminist communities to fit their ideal of a strong black woman. "I'm as much interested in the symbol of Sojourner Truth as in her life," Painter told Karen J. Winkler. "It tells you a lot about the way race functions in our society." Studying the historical documentation of Truth's life, including *The Narrative of Sojourner Truth*, an autobiography dictated to a friend and published in 1881, Painter applied modern psychological analysis to the topic. In one example, Painter pointed to Truth's involvement with the often-abusive religious impostor Prophet Robert Matthias and explained to Winkler, "[Psychological] theories about how children become attached to people who have been mean to them help us understand this period in Truth's life. They show us that Sojourner Truth came out of slavery very insecure." Painter's critically acclaimed book won the Black Caucus of the American Library Association (BCALA) Literary Award for nonfiction.

Painter next wrote *Southern History Across the Color Line* (2002), a collection of essays that address such issues as interracial sex and white supremacy. She followed that with *Creating Black Americans: African American History and Its Meanings, 1619 to the Present* (2005), a study that opens with life in Africa before slavery and extends to modern hip-hop culture. The volume included more than 150 works of African-American art, and while many critics applauded Painter for the ambitious undertaking, some felt that her inclusion of art detracted from the book as a whole. "[Painter's] primary purpose in including art

works is to illustrate historical points and to show black Americans as creators of their own history. Nevertheless, readers will likely be frustrated by the lack of analysis accompanying the images—Painter simply summarizes most of the art works, leaving much of their complexity and ambiguity unexplored," a *Publishers Weekly* (September 12, 2005) reviewer wrote, in a mixed assessment echoed by others. "Painter is clearly adept at writing straightforward history, however, and on this front the book is lucid, engaging and topical. It does an excellent job revealing both the African and the American dimensions of African-American history."

Painter's most recent book, *The History of White People*, spans from antiquity, when populations were distinguished by culture and geographic location rather than physical features, to the present—a time when the U.S. has elected its first African-American president but is still plagued by issues surrounding race. "Nell Irvin Painter's title, *The History of White People*, is a provocation in several ways: it's monumental in sweep, and its absurd grandiosity should call to mind the fact that writing a *History of Black People* might seem perfectly reasonable to white people," Linda Gordon wrote for the *New York Times Book Review* (March 25, 2010, on-line). "But the title is literally accurate, because the book traces characterizations of the lighter-skinned people we call white today, starting with the ancient Scythians."

Painter explained to an interviewer for the Big Think Web site (April 7, 2010): "The [idea of the] American [in the 1800s] was a Saxon and he was a man and he was educated. By the twentieth century the American . . . [was] still pretty much male, still definitely white, but not a Saxon anymore. We [currently] live in a world in which it's harder to talk about 'the American' in the singular. . . . We have several different people who represent the United States, so in that sense whiteness, the salience, the importance of whiteness is kind of tamping down some." She continued, "On the other hand, the idea of blackness, that is poor dark-skinned people, I think we will have that with us always."

In her review of *The History of White People* for the *Boston Globe* (March 21, 2010), Kate Tuttle wrote, "From skull-measuring to IQ testing, science has long been complicit in the ugliest racial politics, and the best parts of *The History of White People* manage to both soberly assess the damage and almost gleefully highlight the craziness behind it. It's shocking that a book about such ugliness should be such fun to read. Avoiding the dense thickets of academic jargon and the cinematic-uplifting tone of so many history books, Painter maintains a calm, ironic, almost bemused tone—a wise choice, when the material speaks for itself in such bizarre voices."

Painter has served on several editorial boards, including those of the *Journal of Women's History* and *Encyclopedia Americana*, and she is a member of numerous professional groups, including the American Historical Association, the Organization of American Historians, the American Antiquarian Society, the Association for the Study of Afro-American Life and History, and the Association of Black Women Historians. Her many accolades include the Candace Award from the National Coalition of 100 Black Women (1986), the Alumnus of the Year title from UC Berkeley's Black Alumni Club (1989), and the Association of Black Princeton Alumni's Dr. Carl A. Fields Memorial University Service Award (1998). She has received honorary doctoral degrees from Wesleyan University, Dartmouth College, the State University of New York (SUNY) at New Paltz, and Yale University.

Painter's next book, *Personal Beauty: Biology or Culture?*, will be published by W. W. Norton. Painter received a B.F.A. degree in painting from the Rutgers University Mason Gross School of the Arts, in New Brunswick, New Jersey, in 2009. She is currently the virtual artist in residence at the Creative Research Center of Montclair State University, in New Jersey. She is also an M.F.A. student at the Rhode Island School of Design, in Providence.

Painter married her second husband, Glenn R. Shafer, a Rutgers University business professor, on October 14, 1989. The couple live in Newark, New Jersey. Painter has two adult stepsons, Rick and Dennis, from her marriage to Shafer.

—M.A.S.

Suggested Reading: Big Think Web site Apr. 7, 2010; *Chronicle of Higher Education* A p18+ Sep. 13, 1996; *Journal of Blacks in Higher Education* p119+ Oct. 31, 2000; *New York Times* (on-line) Mar. 25, 2010; *Washington Post* B p1 Feb. 27, 1980

Selected Books: *Exodusters: Black Migration to Kansas after Reconstruction*, 1976; *The Narrative of Hosea Hudson: His Life as a Negro Communist in the South*, 1979; *Standing at Armageddon: The United States 1877–1919*, 1987; *Sojourner Truth: A Life, A Symbol*, 1996; *Southern History Across the Color Line*, 2002; *Creating Black Americans: African American History and Its Meanings, 1619 to the Present*, 2005; *The History of White People*, 2010

Paper Rad

Multimedia artists

Ciocci, Jacob
1977–

Ciocci, Jessica
1976–

Jones, Benjamin
1977–

Address: c/o Audio Dregs, 2418 N.E. Oregon St., Portland, OR 97232

In January 2008 audiences at the Sundance Film Festival, in Park City, Utah, watched the popular Nintendo video-game character Mario suffer an existential crisis, as the façade of his pixilated world (that of the 1985 game *Super Mario Bros.*) broke down around him into distorted graphics and mismatched, kaleidoscopic shapes and colors. Mario's inability to grapple with his digital existence is the crux of *Super Mario Movie*, a video short screened at the festival and created by Paper Rad, a trio of artists who have won international acclaim for their appropriation of pop-culture imagery for their myriad projects. Combining clips of iconic cartoon characters from the 1970s and '80s with found video footage, Web-based animation, and Pop Art illustrations, Paper Rad is considered a pioneer in the "new low-tech" genre of avant-garde art and has had exhibitions at such prominent museums as the Metropolitan Museum of Art (MoMA), in New York City, and the Tate Britain, in London, England.

The members of Paper Rad are Benjamin Jones and the siblings Jacob and Jessica Ciocci, who met in Boston, Massachusetts, in around 2000 and began to work together on handmade art books. Paper Rad's art involves collages of disparate pop-culture symbols juxtaposed to create vibrant, colorful, neo-primitive landscapes. Informed by the products and images of the artists' childhoods in the 1980s, Paper Rad's work, as Adam Strohm wrote for *Dusted* magazine (August 6, 2006, on-line), "taps into the collective childhood of an entire generation."

Benjamin Jones was born in Pittsburgh, Pennsylvania, in 1977 and earned a B.F.A. degree from the Massachusetts College of Art, in Boston. Jessica Ciocci was born in 1976, and Jacob Ciocci in 1977, in Lexington, Kentucky; Jacob earned a B.A. degree in computer science and art from Oberlin College, in Oberlin, Ohio, and Jessica received a B.A. in psychology and art from Wellesley College, in Wellesley, Massachusetts. The three have credited the television shows, comic books, and pop culture of their youth as being integral to the content and context of Paper Rad's work; Jacob told Leslie Hoffman, writing for the Pittsburgh publication *Whirl* (October 2005), "In the 70's and 80's, cartoons and consumer electronics were bigger and scarier than ever and freaked out a whole generation of kids. Now, those kids are getting older and freaking everybody else out with that same throwaway junk culture. . . . Corporate companies make this garbage and then send it out into the world, and then culture makes sense of it and uses it productively."

Paper Rad

Detail of Get Well Soon Card, *created by Paper Rad*

According to Hoffman, the artists grew up in households with parents who were reluctant to let their children watch television. Nonetheless, the three found ways to absorb it; the Cioccis watched television in secret, and Jones told Hoffman that he would "negotiate about five hours' worth per day" with his parents.

In 1998 Jones and his friend Chris Forgues, who were then in college and living in the student-populated Boston neighborhood of Allston, started *Paper Radio*, a handmade print publication consisting of comics and other drawings. While others also contributed to its content, Jones and Forgues were responsible for assembling each issue at a local copy shop, folding, stapling, and distributing them weekly. *Paper Radio* was influenced by the work of artists in nearby Providence, Rhode Island, who often gathered at a performance and exhibition space called Fort Thunder; those artists, in turn, were inspired by *Paper Radio* to make their own publication, *Paper Rodeo*, to which Jones and Forgues contributed. After Forgues moved to Providence, Jones met Jacob and Jessica Ciocci; their shared interest in comic books and pop culture led them, in about 2000, to collaborate on issues of *Paper Radio*, later shortening its name to *Paper Rad*, which became the name by which the artists were known collectively. Jones told Ben Tarnoff for the *Harvard Advocate* (Summer 2005), "The lines between [Paper Rad, *Paper Radio*, and *Paper Rodeo*] just aren't that important because I feel like there is collaboration between us and what Chris and *Paper Radio* [are] doing, and what the kids from *Paper Rodeo* are doing."

Soon Jones and the Cioccis also began to work with the animation software program Adobe Flash, created by Adobe Systems Inc. They compiled video collages from television programs they had recorded onto VHS cassettes, then incorporated that footage into the Flash animation to complete the media pastiche whose look has become the group's trademark. "We'd make these VHS mixes and in between all of our animation I started to collage found-footage," Jacob Ciocci said in an interview for the art blog sfbg.com (January 28, 2008). "It's almost as if the footage formed commercials between our animations." One of the group's first VHS mixes, according to Ciocci, was made up of "layers and layers of TV being dubbed on top of each other. It mixes original stuff, stuff from cable and more for that treasure trove experience of when you put an unlabeled VHS tape in the VCR and you don't know what you're going to get." He added, "I like looking at a tape as a completed piece of art, so there will be ruptures and then a return to the narrative. To think of it like that—that everything on it is there for an intentional purpose—is a fun way to watch."

In 2001 Paper Rad began to exhibit its art and animation in the Boston area, at such venues as the Somerville Comix Festival and the Boston Cyber Arts Festival, as well as at the Picture Star Film Series, in Providence. In 2002 Paper Rad participated in Project: Bookmobile, a U.S.- and Canada-wide exhibition of self-published comics. By the end of that year, Paper Rad had gained minor recognition in the mainstream art world through exhibitions and festivals. "Every few decades, young artists take to working in collaborative or communal groups . . . ," Holland Cotter noted for the *New York Times* (December 29, 2002). "The emergence of digitally savvy but low-tech multimedia groups like . . . Paper Rad . . . is by far the most interesting development in new art."

In 2003 Paper Rad designed an interactive installation, A Smiling Hunger, at the Future Tenant Gallery, in Pittsburgh. The piece consisted of a tent made from children's bedsheets and lit by a rotating wheel of colored light. Visitors were encouraged to crawl inside the tent to watch a television display of Paper Rad's animated work, read their comics, and listen to cassette tapes of music the artists had compiled. The *Pittsburgh City Paper* (June 18, 2003) noted that the artists had "left nothing out and the effect is unnerving. If you sit there long enough, that all-too-familiar-experience of vegging out in front of the TV, practically drooling, transforms into a more self-conscious experience of being inundated with images and information so that you come to understand how close the connection is between your memories of yourself and what you consumed as a child. It's a shared history, and also a shared method of thinking." That year Paper Rad also exhibited work at Tate Britain and the Institute of Contemporary Art, both in London, and at the New York Underground Film Festival, in New York City, among other venues and events.

In 2004 Paper Rad released the cartoon series Gumby: Graffiti Bridge Is Fading Down, whose title character originated on an old claymation children's show. Writing for C: International Contemporary Art (March 22, 2005), Jenifer Paparo observed that the work's "somewhat nostalgic characters are put through quasi self-searching journeys." For example, in one short in the series, Gumby: Life Is a Mister-E, Gumby is seen questioning his existence; as a lump of clay frequently taking on new shapes, he expresses frustration over his inability to learn who he is. Paparo wrote that despite the potential distractions of the ever-changing colors and shapes in the cartoons, "whatever [Paper Rad] put together, they're bound to find some meaning in the mix." That year Paper Rad also took part in a traveling show of artist-made T-shirts and exhibited work at several galleries. They created an interactive, live and on-line art project, tuxdog.org, in collaboration with the nonprofit arts group Electronic Arts Intermix; the work featured a digital character, Tux Dog, designed by Paper Rad. The computer code used to create Tux Dog is publicly available for others to download and incorporate into their art.

Paper Rad next worked with the Brooklyn, New York, multimedia artist Cory Arcangel in 2005 to make Super Mario Movie, based on the popular children's video game. Arcangel and Paper Rad worked directly with the game cartridge, removing the chip that controlled the workings of the game and manipulating the remaining chip's data. Super Mario Movie was first shown at the Deitch Projects gallery in New York City. Roberta Smith, writing for the New York Times (February 4, 2005), called it "a single, ambitious work" in which "the image component of the early Super Mario Brothers Nintendo game is rerouted to create a narrative about the program's erosion and its effect on one of the perpetually dazed brothers. An admiration for formalist painting is evident here, too, with extraordinary patterns pulsating in time to music." Paparo wrote that "emblematic of their art practice in general," the work "invigorates dead media and neglected characters, and communicates an underlying quest that Paper Rad approaches with awkward irony and self-conscious sincerity." Describing the artists' intention, Arcangel told Nick Chordas for the Columbus (Ohio) Dispatch (January 10, 2007), "We designed the game to look exactly like it does when the game crashes. It's Mario trying to deal with his own existential crisis."

In 2005 Paper Rad also created Facemaker, a short video of mutating cartoon-character faces. In a review for the Dallas Observer (April 20, 2006) of an exhibition of the video at the And/Or gallery in Dallas, Texas, Charissa N. Terranova wrote that "at its best this video offers an overview of the vocabulary of bright colors and animated form central to PR's work. At its worst, it brings to mind the mutating and eliding faces" of the pop singer Michael Jackson's video for his song "Black and White." The Dallas show also featured another Paper Rad

and Arcangel collaboration, Ever Danced with Garf?, which merged animated Paper Rad characters with footage of people singing karaoke. Paper Rad's first book, Paper Rad, B.J. & da Dogs (2005), features photographs of the group's art installations and paintings as well as two graphic novellas. A reviewer for Publishers Weekly (October 17, 2005) wrote that "the humor, when it exists, is scatological, but with an innocent, childlike quality. The art has a charmingly low-tech, drawn-in-a-notebook feel. It aims for the surreal but hits the nonsensical far more often. The haphazard nature of this collection will appeal mainly to fans of art comics."

According to Bill Van Siclen, writing for the Providence Journal (February 16, 2006), by 2006 Paper Rad's "art-world profile" was "growing by leaps and bounds." That month an exhibition of the group's non-animated work was held at Gallery Agniel, in Providence; it also included work by fellow artists from the Providence art-exhibit space Fort Thunder. Paper Rad's paintings, print work, and comic art dominated the show. Works including Jessica Ciocci's colorful two-part painting The Pigs Come Out at Night and Jones's comic-book-style panel Where Is the Plot were on display, as well as wallpaper derived from a video installation called Where Are They Now? Van Siclen wrote that "though Paper Rad clearly revels in the flotsam and jetsam of the digital age, the group's work also raises timely questions about everything from copyright law to the nature of artistic collaboration to the increasingly fluid meaning of words such as 'art' and 'originality.'"

Exhibitions of work by the Cioccis were also held in 2006. Jessica's show, P.E.A.C.E, and Jacob's, Inspiration Superhighway, opened at the Foxy Production gallery in New York City. Jessica's exhibit consisted of Pop Art–like renditions of a pig character represented in various mediums, from fabrics to paintings. Ken Johnson, writing for the New York Times (July 28, 2006), saw the work as an indictment of consumerism, writing that it "parodies the simple-minded visions of personal empowerment, passionate lifestyle and spiritual bliss that are constantly foisted on infantilized consumers of all ages." Jacob's show focused on a character he created, Little Dude. At the show audiences could enter a massive cube, built by the artist, that displayed animation of Little Dude as he sought, in vain, to find meaning in life. Jacob's exhibition was also held at Carnegie Mellon University's Regina Gouger Miller Gallery, in Pittsburgh; Kurt Shaw wrote for the Pittsburgh Tribune-Review (March 31, 2005) that it was like an "acid trip" and noted that it was "fun and way out there."

Paper Rad's DVD collection of animated shorts, Trash Talking, was released in 2006 to a mixed response from critics. The DVD consists of numerous visual sequences that combine the group's signature color palette with pop-culture references, clips of forgotten cartoon characters, and original Paper Rad creations. Grant Brissey observed for the

California publication *SF Weekly* (August 2, 2006) that *Trash Talking* was "another practice in confusion, non sequitur, and pop-culture references picked from the past 30 years" and that "moments of hilarity exist throughout this otherwise pleasantly baffling visual excursion." Adam Strohm observed, "*Trash Talking* tends to leave the viewer without footholds, like an amusement park ride whose erratic motions make all attempts at sensible consideration of one's surroundings absolutely moot." He also pointed out that even if some viewers accused the group of engaging in "cheap thrills" and of "mining their generation's retro-happy subconscious," Paper Rad, "at their best, can be just plain fun."

MoMA hosted Paper Rad and Arcangel in June 2007 as part of its PopRally series. Their event, Paper Rad Featuring Cory Arcangel, consisted of both multimedia art and musical performances by Paper Rad, individually and with other artists. Jones, for example, performed as the character Dr. Doo, drumming along to synthesized music and interacting with an animated cartoon wizard projected on a screen behind him. Zach Baron, writing about the event for the *Village Voice* (July 26, 2007), observed that the concert was unusual for MoMA. "The undercurrent of self-hate, the kind which requires the world's foremost museum curators to listen to noise music louder than they'd like, and to smile when the inevitable drunken mosh pit breaks out in their place of business, cuts both ways. As Jacob Ciocci incited the crowd to storm the stage, basically to riot, throw drinks and crowd-surf—which it did—he could've been screaming 'Spring Break!' to a passing car of Jersey frat brothers for all he had in common with the dressed up masses dancing to his band's freak-scene, industrial town rave-ups. 'A lot of times in my life, I've felt like a weirdo,' Ciocci said, closing out the set, 'and tonight made me feel like it was OK.' Whether it was because he finally had company, or merely revenge—he didn't say." The members of Paper Rad have also performed in bands and as solo acts apart from the MoMA event, making electronic and "noise" music. Those bands (which include members not generally affiliated with Paper Rad's visual art) include Extreme Animals, Fortress of Amplitude, Paz, Star Kings, Pajama Boys, and Gay Nerds. The bands' albums have been released on independent record labels.

A second Paper Rad book, *Cartoon Workshop/Pig Tales Digest*, was published in 2007. That November a new Paper Rad cartoon, *Umbrella Zombie Datamosh Mistake*, was listed by *New York* magazine as number two on the publication's list of the top five on-line art videos of the year. In January 2008 Paper Rad and Arcangel put on a multimedia performance, similar to that held at MoMA, at the Sundance Film Festival. There, the collective also screened its most recent animated piece, *Problem Solvers*, as well as *Super Mario Movie*. In August 2009 Jessica and Jacob Ciocci exhibited solo work, as well as Paper Rad work, at the show Deterioration, They Said, at the Migros Museum Für Gegenwartskunst, in Zurich, Switzerland. The next month they exhibited work in the show Rapture Heap, at Liberty Corner, in Dublin, Ireland. Jacob Ciocci and Cory Arcangel participated in Smoke and Mirrors, at the Wood Street Galleries in Pittsburgh, in June 2009.

Paper Rad is also affiliated with Wyld File, a multimedia production company that Jones, Arcangel, and others created in 2004. Wyld File animates music videos in Paper Rad's signature style, using Adobe Flash to create crude, pixilated landscapes for musical artists including Beck and the Gossip.

In November 2009 Audio Dregs Records released Jacob's solo album, *ROTFLOL* (the widely used e-mail acronym for "rolling on the floor laughing out loud"). A DVD of Jacob's work, *Music Is a Question with No Answer*, came out on the Audio Dregs label in 2010. Its release coincided with a U.S. tour by Jacob's duo, Extreme Animals—a "noise/techno/pop band," in his words—whose other member is David Wightman. In their performances Jacob, on keyboards, and Wightman, on drums, presented videos as well as music. Jacob teaches courses in video art at Carnegie Mellon. He earned a master of fine arts degree from that school in 2005.

The independent publishing house Nieves brought out *Centuries of Music* (2009), a collection of photographs and other images compiled by Jessica Ciocci. Jones has animated and directed motion-graphics segments for shows on MTV, Nickelodeon, and VH1. He has also had solo shows of his visual art. In 2009 Art Basel Miami Beach, in Florida, exhibited his furniture installation, Beehaven, and Deitch Projects, in New York City, showed his installation New Dark Age.

—W.D.

Suggested Reading: *C: International Contemporary Art* p36 Mar. 22, 2005; chiefmag.com; harvardadvocate.com; *Pittsburgh (Pennsylvania) City Paper* p35 June 18, 2003; *Providence (Rhode Island) Journal* L p13 Feb. 16, 2006; Surhone, Lambert M. and others, editors. *Paper Rad*, 2010

Selected Books: *Paper Rad, B.J. & da Dogs,* 2005; *Cartoon Workshop/Pig Tales Digest* (with Donald Baechler), 2007; by Jessica Ciocci—*Centuries of Music,* 2009

Selected Videos and DVDs: *Super Mario Movie*, 2005; *Facemaker*, 2005; *Trash Talking*, 2006; *Umbrella Zombie Datamosh Mistake*, 2007; by Jacob Ciocci—*Music Is a Question with No Answer*, 2010

Paul Ellis/AFP/Getty Images

Park Ji-Sung

Feb. 25, 1981– Soccer player

Address: Manchester United, Sir Matt Busby Way, Old Trafford, Manchester M16 0RA, England

The South Korean soccer player Park Ji-Sung's story "is one his compatriots sense mirrors their nation's tale; overcoming adversity, battling to prove your worth to bigger, stronger neighbours and eventually becoming a significant world player . . . ," Ian Chadband wrote for the London *Telegraph* (May 22, 2009). "He has also made a country extraordinarily proud by helping banish old preconceptions, even in Korea, that Asian players are too lightweight to make it in the big leagues." Park represents a number of firsts in international soccer competition. A member of England's storied Manchester United team since 2005, he is the first Asian to play in the final of Europe's Champions League (the most important annual club-championship tournament, featuring the top teams from each country's top leagues) and the only one to be a member of a winning team. He is also the first Asian to win an English Premier League medal, with three to his credit. Park is known less for his scoring than for his unselfish teamwork: through his constant running and his understanding of how to use space on the field, he opens opportunities for his teammates even when he does not have the ball, and he is seemingly always available to receive a pass. "He does dirty work for the bigger stars . . . ," Guus Hiddink, Park's former coach in South Korea and the Netherlands, told Jamie Jackson for the London *Observer* (March 1,

2009). "He is tireless, can go for 90 minutes, he's a smart player and is very determined." Rio Ferdinand, who has captained both the English national team and Manchester United, told Jackson that Park is "a real players' player. Up there with [the best in the] world for movement, and so intelligent and direct with runs off the ball. His work-rate is unreal, he adds a dimension no other player brings to the team. He's underrated, a real top player." Park, by all accounts a chronically shy and self-effacing star who is uncomfortable with celebrity, has become a cult hero and fan favorite on each team he has played for, due as much to his perseverance and boundless energy as to his inspirational story.

Park Ji-Sung was born on February 25, 1981, in Seoul, South Korea, the only child of Park Seong-Jong and Jang Myeong-Ja. He grew up in Suwon, an industrial city 20 miles south of Seoul. According to his parents, Park was a small, physically weak child who nonetheless, from a very early age, expressed the desire to play professional soccer. His parents, worried for his health and safety, refused at first to let him play. In response Park refused to eat until they gave in. According to a documentary about Park's life, *Do You Know Park Ji-Sung?*, which was broadcast on the South Korean network MBC on April 19, 2009 and quoted by Chadband, Park's father asked, "If I let you play, will you try hard and not quit?" To which Park replied: "I am never going to quit." It is Park's determination to succeed where others expected him to fail that his parents, coaches, and friends have recalled when discussing his childhood (during which Park idolized the unglamorous but hard-working Brazilian midfielder Dunga). Recognizing his dedication as well as his natural talent for the game, Park's father left his job in a metals factory to work as a butcher, hoping to help his son grow stronger by providing him with better cuts of meat. Another food Park consumed was one that, his father had heard, helped people grow: frog soup. Park said in the documentary, as quoted by Chadband, "There were times I threw up because of the taste, but I kept going because the heart of wanting to become a better footballer was greater than having a good tasting meal everyday. I was willing to do anything to become better."

At Suwon Technical High School, Park was the smallest player on the soccer team but also the fittest, and his work ethic, discipline, and team-oriented approach endeared him to his coach, Lee Hak-jong. "His drive to become a good athlete was immense, I still remember," Lee told the South Korean publication *Yonhap* (May 23, 2008). "But he was also a quiet boy who clearly knew what to do and what not to do. . . . As a manager, the more you know him, the more you can't help liking him. Park's as devoted as you can imagine." Toward the end of high school, Park was rejected by all the professional clubs he approached in the South Korean K-League, again due to concerns over his strength and size (even though he had had a significant growth spurt at age 17; he now stands about five-foot-nine). But Lee was so impressed with Park that he recommended the young man to a university coach, and Park began playing for Myung Ji University, in Seoul, in 1999. "It wasn't until another player turned down an offer . . . that the school decided to allow Park in," Lee said, as quoted in *Yonhap*.

In one game at Myung Ji University, against the South Korean under-23 national team, Park caught the eye of the country's Olympic coach and was named to the squad for the 2000 Olympics, held in Sydney, Australia. That same year Park signed with Kyoto Purple Sanga, a Japanese team that had just been relegated to that country's second division. Playing as a striker in 2001, he immediately became one of the key players on the team and led them to the top of their division and to promotion to the first division. "The thing that impressed me the most was that he was very stable and very cool . . . ," Gert Engels, Park's coach at Kyoto Purple Sanga, told Jeremy Walker for the *South China Morning Post* (July 10, 2005). "He listens and understands, and is a very quick learner." His play also attracted the attention of Pim Verbeek, who was then scouting players for the South Korean national-team coach, Guus Hiddink, prior to the 2002 World Cup. Hiddink, a Dutchman whom many South Koreans revere for his tactical prowess and ability to inspire players, quickly integrated Park into the national team.

Park had played in the Olympics as a defensive midfielder; Hiddink was responsible for his becoming a versatile, attacking winger. "It was Guus Hiddink who turned my career around," Park told reporters in 2007, as quoted by Agence France Presse (September 10, 2007). "By believing in me, he made me believe in myself. That is such an important thing for a young footballer." Park scored in pretournament warm-up games against France and England, as the South Koreans began to develop confidence that they could compete against the most celebrated teams in world soccer. Few, if any, however, predicted the soccer fervor that would grip South Korea in the summer of 2002. Park, who played in every game in the underdog host nation's fairy-tale–like run to the semifinals, scored one of the most memorable goals of the tournament, in South Korea's June 14 victory over Portugal. That win knocked the Europeans out of the competition and sent South Korea to the elimination stages of the tournament for the first time in history. In the game against Portugal, after arresting a long aerial pass with his chest, outmaneuvering a defender, and volleying the ball into the back of the net in front of an ecstatic home crowd, Park ran to the sidelines and jumped into Hiddink's arms. "Koreans watching Park outmaneuvering bigger players during the Cup saw his performance as a metaphor for South Korea itself—a small country whose survival has depended on outsmarting bigger and often sharper-elbowed neighbors," Donald Macintyre wrote for *Time* (October 3, 2005). Mostly un-known—even to his countrymen—before that goal, Park was a national hero afterward. While South Korea lost in the semifinals to Germany, and again in the consolation game to Turkey, they finished fourth, higher than any Asian nation before or since.

After the tournament Hiddink returned to the Netherlands to coach PSV (Philips Sport Vereniging) Eindhoven and made it clear that acquiring Park was his priority. Park and PSV negotiated the terms of his joining the team; meanwhile, Park led Kyoto Purple Sanga to its only-ever victory in Japan's premier tournament, the Emperor's Cup (Tenno Hai), with a goal and an assist in the final, capping off a pivotal year in his career. "On a personal level, I will always appreciate what he did for the team at the end of the 2002 season," Engels told Walker. "We were still in the Emperor's Cup, but Park had an Achilles tendon injury. He had agreed to sign for PSV in the new year, and many players would not have risked the injury as the transfer might have fallen through. But Park played in the last three games, and Kyoto won the Emperor's Cup on New Year's Day 2003. No one will forget that."

Park moved to Eindhoven with his South Korean teammate Lee Young-Pyo in 2003. Park had a disappointing first season, marred by injury and difficult cultural adjustments, including a language barrier and the move from "a tradition of communality to a western culture built around the importance of the individual," as Anna Kessel put it for the London *Observer* (October 23, 2005). A couple of months after making the move, Park injured his knee and was in so much pain that he was forced to undergo surgery. Unable to play much, he could not show his ability, and fans booed him. "It's really different in Europe," his father told Jackson. "When Ji-sung couldn't do well people threw their drinks at him, insulted him. He thought that was strange." Park also received criticism from coaches and teammates. He told Kessel: "In Korea if a player doesn't play well, you would never criticise him, but in European countries fans criticise their own teams. Sometimes they boo them off the pitch. In Korea if a player makes a mistake, the other players don't like to point it out, rather they try to embrace it. They take the attitude: 'Let's do better next time.' But in the West if you do something wrong another player will make a point of saying something and you will have to fix it immediately." Park told Jackson that Hiddink was also less supportive at that time: "Hiddink was very different in Holland, the way he treated me and Lee Young-pyo. Having been like a grandfather in Korea, he was more boss. When I'd heard of Holland, I was actually frightened because it's not at all familiar. I had to adjust myself."

By the end of the following season (2003–04), a fully recovered Park proved to players, fans, and coaches alike that he was a multifaceted midfielder and an integral element in the team's improved play. "I was at PSV Eindhoven when Park and Lee

Young-Pyo came," Pim Verbeek told Shintaro Kano for the Tokyo, Japan, *Daily Yomiuri* (May 20, 2008). "I know the PSV players looked at [them] and thought, 'Korean players?' There was a lot of skepticism about those players but that changed very, very soon because they saw what they could do—not only with the ball, but without the ball. They saw the work rate, the unbelievable mentality, the commitment to the game and they changed the mentality in the PSV squad. What they showed was a top professional attitude." The year 2005 was as significant for Park as 2002 had been: he contributed crucial goals and assists as PSV won the domestic-league title and the domestic-cup tournament (KNVB Cup) and made it to the Champions League semifinal. Park was also named to the league's best-11 team that year. The highlight of Park's PSV career—and one of his greatest matches aside from the game against Portugal in 2002—came in the Champions League semifinal, as the underdog PSV team took on AC Milan. While PSV lost the series, Park's play (including a goal) got him named to that year's Champions League All-Star team. Perhaps the biggest indicator of Park's new status on his team was that PSV's fans composed an anthem for him, "Song for Park" (essentially a repetition of the words "Ji-Sung Park"). Meanwhile, his popularity in South Korea, where all of his matches were broadcast live, had continued to grow.

In June 2005 Park scored a goal in a World Cup qualifier against Kuwait, which South Korea won, securing a spot in the following summer's World Cup competition in Germany. Also that month the public learned that one of the most successful soccer clubs in the world, Manchester United, had been scouting Park for about a year. "We identified a player with great understanding of space," Manchester's legendary manager, Sir Alex Ferguson, was quoted as saying by Jamie Dunn on Goal.com (July 24, 2009). "His movement was always very clever—especially in attacking areas—and we felt we needed somebody who could penetrate in the final areas." Park had long maintained that he wanted to play for Manchester United, whose players are among the best in the sport, "even if I have to sit on the bench," as he said, according to Jackson. "I want to learn." Park Seong-Jong said in the documentary about his son, as quoted by Jeré Longman in the *New York Times* (May 26, 2009), "For the first time in a century, a Korean entered the team. And people said there might not be another one for the next hundred years. That's how hard it is to join that team. I told him: 'Go for it. Even if you only play one game a year, go for it.'" Hiddink at first refused to let Park go to United, then placed a prohibitively high price tag on his standout player. Ferguson nonetheless acquired Park at the end of June 2005 for a reported £4 million (more than $7 million at that time). "When I made my mind up for Manchester I felt that I had betrayed [Hiddink]," Park told Jackson. "I knew that Hiddink wanted me to stay, so I found it difficult."

Once again, through newspaper headlines such as "Park Bench," Park's abilities were publicly questioned by critics who felt that the Asian player could not compete in the faster-paced, more-physical English Premier League. Others, taking a more cynical view, argued that United had signed Park as a strategy to raise its profile in the lucrative Asian markets. "When I came first I heard about that," Park later told reporters, as quoted in the *Manchester Evening News* (June 11, 2008). "People said that I was here for merchandising, but I couldn't say anything because I am a football player and had to show my ability on the pitch. I kept showing that and now everybody knows I'm not here to sell T-shirts." Park figured in all but four games in his first season (August 2005–May 2006) in Manchester, demonstrating both humility and a capacity for hard work. In the summer following that season, Park scored a goal in the World Cup to secure a 1–1 draw against one of the eventual finalists, France. "Park has fought for himself in a battlefield far from Asia and he has survived," Hiddink told Moon Gwang-lip for the *Korea Times* (May 17, 2006). "Park is not the oldest in the team but he has become the most influential player." Park's next two seasons in Manchester were marred by injuries. A hurt ankle in September 2006 kept him out of action for three months; then, in March 2007, he suffered a serious injury to the cruciate ligaments in his knee, forcing him to undergo career-saving surgery in the U.S. while his team went on to win the league championship. (Park became the first Korean member of a winning British-league team.) Upon his return to play, in 2008, Park proved himself to be a key regular player in a year in which United took home the Premier League trophy and the coveted Champions League trophy. In late April 2008 United beat Barcelona in the semifinal of the Champions League, with Park—who was voted Man of the Match—turning in a celebrated performance in the second game. When he was excluded from both the starting line-up and the bench in the Champions League final game, against Chelsea, in Moscow, Russia, in May 2008—which United won in penalty kicks—he called it "the biggest disappointment in my career so far," as quoted by Neil Custis in the England *Sun* (May 22, 2009). "I've had crucial injuries but this was the hardest thing." He added, "I used it as motivation." Many believed that Park's form and performances in the lead-up to the game had earned him a place in the final, and South Koreans, eager for him to become the first of their countrymen to play in the Champions League final, referred to the snub as "the Moscow nightmare." For his part Ferguson called the decision to leave Park out "the most difficult" of his managerial career. Many felt that, to the contrary, it had been the easiest move for Ferguson to make, as Park was the most humble player on an ego-heavy team.

In the summer of 2008, Park again underwent minor surgery on his knee, keeping him from playing for South Korea in that year's Olympic Games, held in Beijing, China. Observers agreed that the season that followed, 2008–09, was Park's best yet: he played a major part in United's winning the Premier League title (for the third time in a row), the Carling Cup, and the FIFA Club World Cup. He made his 100th appearance for United in December 2008, and in May 2009 he scored a goal and provided an assist to defeat Arsenal in the semifinal of the Champions League and send Manchester to the final for the second year in a row. He was named a starter for the team in the final against Barcelona in Rome, Italy, that year; United lost the game, 2–0. A month later Park, who had been named captain of the South Korean national team in October 2008, led that squad as top scorer in an undefeated World Cup qualification campaign, ensuring them a seventh straight appearance in the World Cup, held in 2010 in South Africa.

In their first group match at the 2010 World Cup, on June 12, South Korea defeated Greece, 2–0, with Park scoring the second goal of the game. The team lost the second group match to Argentina, 4–1, and tied 2–2 in a third match, against Nigeria. For the first time ever, South Korea advanced beyond the group stage to the knockout stage, where they fell to Uruguay, 2–1. Returning to Manchester United, Park netted his first goal of the 2010–11 season in a 5–2 win against Scunthorpe United, in the third round of the Carling Cup, on September 22, 2010.

Park has won several lucrative endorsement deals, with companies including Nike. His 2006 autobiography, whose title means "Infinite Challenge," topped Asia's best-seller lists. He signed a three-year contract extension with manchester United in September 2009. In his hometown of Suwon, residents have named a park and a street after him, making him the first soccer player in the country to be so honored.

Park has been described by his teammates as being very polite. Off the field his hobbies include playing as the Park Ji-Sung character on PlayStation soccer video games. He remains very close to his parents, who still cook traditional Korean medicinal soups for him. Park lives in Wilmslow, in the English county of Cheshire.

—M.M.

Suggested Reading: (London) *Daily Telegraph* (on-line) May 22, 2009; (London) *Observer* S p8 Oct. 23, 2005, S p12 Mar. 1, 2009; *manutd.com*; *New York Times* B p9 May 26, 2009; *Time* (on-line) Oct. 3, 2005; Park Ji-Sung. *Infinite Challenge*, 2006

Paulus, Diane

July 3, 1966– Theater director

Address: American Repertory Theater, Loeb Drama Center, 64 Brattle St., Cambridge, MA 02138

Diane Paulus was already an accomplished director of musicals and operas when, in 2008, she gained a new level of acclaim for her Off-Broadway production of the 1960s musical *Hair*. A year later, when the show moved to Broadway—winning a Tony Award and a Drama Desk Award for best revival of a musical—Paulus again received near-unanimous praise. Ben Brantley, a theater critic for the *New York Times* (April 1, 2009), observed that the show delivered "the intense, unadulterated joy and anguish of that bi-polar state called youth." (As of October 2010 *Hair* was still running on Broadway.) Also in 2009 Paulus fulfilled a long-held goal when she was named artistic director of the American Repertory Theater (ART), in Cambridge, Massachusetts.

Since she began her career as a theater director, Paulus has sought to create a dynamic connection between her actors and audience members. Paradoxically, she has managed to be both populist and experimental. "I mean, what could be more commercial and presentational than a Broadway show?" Paulus said in an interview with *Current Biography*, the source of quotes for this article unless otherwise noted. "But really, to me, the only reason why I'm interested in *Hair* and why I think *Hair* is doing as well as it is, is because it's relating to an audience. What did it mean to be alive in the '60s? What does it mean to be an American? What does it mean to be a young person today? These questions are alive in the piece." A decade before her debut at the helm of a Broadway musical, Paulus began her New York directing career with two very different shows: *Running Man*, a work about a family mourning a young man's disappearance (which was a finalist for the Pulitzer Prize and won an Obie Award), and *The Donkey Show*, a disco-musical version of Shakespeare's *A Midsummer Night's Dream*—a dance-club-meets-theater event. For *Running Man* Paulus worked with the jazz composer Diedre Murray and the poet Cornelius Eady; she collaborated with them again a few years later on the jazz/poetry musical *Brutal Imagination* (2002). Paulus said that *The Donkey Show* was not only her most successful show to date—it ran Off-Broadway for nearly six years—but also her most "intense experiment" with audience participation. "But, to me, it was less about audience [participation]. It was more about night life. . . . Everybody thinks theater has to be where you go inside a certain kind of architecture where you sit in a chair that's bolted to the floor and you look at a stage that has a proscenium. That is a very small piece of theater history. You know, theater was festival, theater was nightclubs; I really believe rock concerts and the way certain rock stars commune with an

Dmitry Kiper

Diane Paulus

audience is closer to what the Greek festivals were like."

Surprisingly, Paulus's populist approach brought her an opportunity to enter the world of opera—"high art" not generally known for appealing to a mass audience. In 2000, having liked the concept of *The Donkey Show*, Brian Dickie—then the newly appointed director of the Chicago Opera Theater—asked Paulus if she would be interested in directing an opera. She has since mounted three operas by Monteverdi, including *Orfeo*, and three by Mozart, including *The Marriage of Figaro*. She has also directed several other Shakespeare-based musicals, including *The Karaoke Show* (based on *The Comedy of Errors*) and *The Best of Both Worlds* (based on *The Winter's Tale*). "I never try to make art. I don't know what that is," Paulus said. "I try to make a theatrical event that engages an audience. Theater cannot happen without an audience. Theater is the actual transaction between a performer and a spectator." There is a human need, she added, for story, spectacle, ritual, and learning. "If I can create a theater event that starts to do all of those things, call it whatever you want to call it. That's going to be entertaining. It's probably art. But whatever it is, it's vibrant. It's alive."

One of three children, Diane Marie Paulus was born on July 3, 1966 in New York City. Her brother Steve Paulus, a television journalist, is the regional vice president and general manager of NY1 News, a cable-TV channel. Beginning when she was about three, Diane Paulus would sing along to her siblings' Beatles albums and other music from the 1960s; there was also a lot of classical music in the family's home. Paulus's father, Lawrence, worked for CBS, later retiring as an executive producer of public-affairs programming; her mother ran an interior-decorating business. The arts were a big part of life for Paulus's family, who often took her to dance, theater, and music performances. Her father was "theatrically inclined," Paulus recalled, and his passion for performance extended to the everyday world: Paulus said that he would make her read the newspaper out loud, so she could practice "elocution and diction."

Paulus began taking piano lessons at the age of seven and continued to study classical music until she graduated from high school. At that point she gave it up, knowing that becoming a professional pianist meant many hours of practice by herself and that she wanted to do something collaborative instead. Paulus had also studied ballet; at the age of eight, she started training at the School of American Ballet, which is associated with the New York City Ballet. After about four years of intense training, she had to choose whether she wanted to devote herself to ballet full-time. She decided against it, preferring yet another creative pursuit: acting. In her early teens she was a member of the children's company Theaterworks/USA, which required rehearsals every day, four shows on weekends, and occasional out-of-town performances. At Brearley, an all-girls private high school on Manhattan's Upper East Side, Paulus appeared in such plays as *Hay Fever* and *She Stoops to Conquer* and such musicals as *Wonderful Town* and *The Pajama Game*. Although she loved both forms of theater, she was more drawn to musicals. (She told Adam Green for the July 2008 issue of *Vogue* that even as a girl she was a big fan of *Hair*, calling its cast album "the hymnal of our generation.") Paulus loved the combination of acting, dancing, and singing in musicals, and with her training she could do all three.

Paulus had still another ambition, one removed from the artistic world: becoming mayor of New York City. While she did not have a passion for politics per se, she loved New York and wanted to improve conditions in the city. New York in the 1970s and '80s was a city of rampant crime, heavy drug use, and racial tension, dramatized in works such as Martin Scorsese's film *Taxi Driver* (1976) and Tom Wolfe's novel *Bonfire of the Vanities* (1988). "I looked at the city," Paulus recalled, "and I couldn't understand why it couldn't be a better place to live. . . . Even back then I was a director: I wanted to organize people." She organized neighborhood cleanups with her friends, participated in and made signs for marches in favor of nuclear disarmament, and petitioned for passage of the Equal Rights Amendment. Eventually she realized that in politics she would have a remote relationship with those she wanted to help and that she preferred being, as she said to Megan Tench for the *Boston Globe* (September 28, 2008), "in the trenches." Paulus's high-school years were not devoted only to activism, schoolwork, and theater; in the early to mid-1980s, Paulus and a few of her friends would sneak into Studio 54, the New York City club known (mostly in the late '70s) as a center of drugs, disco, and decadence—and as a hangout for such celebrities as Mick Jagger, Michael Jackson, Rudolf Nureyev, Al Pacino, and Elton John.

Paulus attended Harvard University, in Cambridge, Massachusetts, where she majored in social studies. She remained active in theater—mostly acting—and wrote her thesis on the Living Theatre, an experimental company founded in New York in 1947. After receiving her B.A. degree, in 1988, Paulus moved to New York, where she studied acting with the improvisation specialist and director Paul Sills before deciding that it was not a good use of her talents; most actors she knew were waiting tables while hoping for callbacks, a path she was too impatient to take. She recalled, "I thought, 'This is nuts.' I started directing out of an impulse to make work."

At Sills's invitation, Paulus moved to the farm Sills owned in Wisconsin, with the idea of organizing a theater group that would function somewhat like a commune. During her first summer in Wisconsin, Paulus staged a relatively traditional version of *A Midsummer Night's Dream*. A year later Edward Randall "Randy" Weiner—her future husband, whom she had met in high school—came from New York to join her. Weiner wanted to mount a rock-musical version of *The Tempest*, and he and Paulus looked for a local bar band to write music for the show and perform in it. The members of the band they found, Big Mouth, were excited about the idea but so busy with band practice, gigs, family life, and their day jobs that they did not think they would have time for rehearsal. Weiner and Paulus proposed that during the less-crowded first sets of their gigs, the band could practice *The Tempest* songs at the bar with the cast. Big Mouth agreed, with the unexpected result that some of the songs soon became local pop hits. "So by the time we actually did the show," Paulus said, "which was late July or early August, there was a whole feeling [in the community] about the show. . . . It just taught me how you make theater in a way that feels organically grown. In other words, how can you make a show that has relevance for a community? And I think that's been a theme with everything I've done."

In Wisconsin "we were really gaining momentum . . . ," Paulus said. "We had people showing us abandoned cheese factories and telling us, 'We'll buy this for you and you can turn it into an international arts center.'" Paulus, however, did not want to settle in Wisconsin, which she felt "would never be my home. New York was my home. I mean, I really feel connected to New York City." She and Weiner decided to come back to New York, where her desire to direct led her to study at Columbia University. After receiving her M.F.A. degree there, she began directing original shows. Although the 1999 production of *Running Man* was staged Off-Off-Broadway, in a small performance space in Manhattan's SoHo neighborhood, Paulus received an enormous amount of crit-

ical acclaim, and the show was selected as a finalist for the Pulitzer Prize. "It's one of those crazy things where you're doing this little show at a hole-in-the-wall," Paulus recalled. "And it just blew up." The show combined music by Diedre Murray and poetry by Cornelius Eady. "Operating at the exotic juncture where chamber musical, jazz session and opera might converge, the piece, performed spectacularly by a cast of six and a five-member orchestra, taps a well of feeling so deep at times it seems spiritual," Peter Marks wrote for the *New York Times* (March 5, 1999). "By no means is this a conventional musical—there are no show tunes in this show—but it shares with the successful versions of more mainstream forms an eloquence in structure and storytelling." The story revolves around Tommy, a young black man full of hope and promise who, after his disappearance, has become only a memory to his mother, father, and sister. Their memories, fantasies, and daydreams about him form a theatrical collage, one that Paulus, Marks wrote, directed with "a spare sophistication."

Over the years Paulus continued to work with Eady and Murray. *Brutal Imagination* (2002), a two-person musical based on Eady's long poem of the same name, was adapted by Eady and Paulus with music by Murray. The incident that inspired Eady to write the poem involved a South Carolina woman, Susan Smith, who in 1994 claimed that a black man had stolen her car while her two children sat inside. The national news media repeated that version of events until it was discovered that Smith had made up the story about the black kidnapper after murdering her children. *Brutal Imagination*, directed by Paulus, featured a character based on Smith as well as Mr. Zero, who, as Ben Brantley wrote for the *New York Times* (January 10, 2002), is "the ultimate imaginary accomplice and adversary—the menacing black man as scapegoat—programmed both to live forever and never to exist at all." Brantley added, "It's the sort of concept that grabs you instantly and ferociously, and a corresponding excitement glitters through the opening moments. . . . The excitement, however, is intellectual, which in theater is enough to arouse interest but not to sustain it. Despite a highly polished performance by Joe Morton as Mr. Zero, this production registers as an elegant but often frozen abstraction. . . . You are always aware of these people as conceptual tools."

Around the time that Paulus was working on *Running Man*, she and Weiner were directing another musical, which in some ways was *Running Man*'s polar opposite. One day it occurred to Weiner to stage a disco version of *A Midsummer Night's Dream*. The result, *The Donkey Show*, made for an experience that was closer to that of going to a dance club than seeing a play: a bouncer let audience members into the club, where, before the show, drinks were served, disco music blasted from speakers, and the cast casually interacted with the audience. The characters, as the audience soon discovered, were based very loosely on Shakespeare's; for example, Puck, instead of being a mysterious elf, was a drug dealer on roller skates. There was no dialogue—rather, the songs moved the plot, with the actors singing along to such disco hits as "Car Wash," "I Love the Nightlife," and "You Sexy Thing." The musical brought the audience and actors into intimate contact: most of the audience members stood on the dance floor— many of them drinking, dancing, or smoking—and watched as the actors performed all over the club and moved around and through the crowd. One of the reasons the show became so successful was that people who came to see it used the Internet, a relatively new phenomenon at the time, to spread word about it. Paulus was working on several other shows at the time and was used to having an audience of fewer than 10 people, but those for *The Donkey Show* far exceeded that. "People would come week after week after week," Paulus said, "and it just showed me what it means when a show finds its audience—and what that energy, what that kind of communion is. So we just started realizing that's the show we want to keep doing. We could be doing all these other little shows, but let's really do *The Donkey Show*." After starting out in a small venue on Manhattan's Lower East Side, the show moved to a big dance club, El Flamingo, in the Chelsea neighborhood, where it ran for more than five years. "People were coming because it was like nothing they had ever seen before," Paulus wrote in an e-mail message. "[The show] had the power to transform an audience as they were invited into the ecstatic and dangerous fantasy world of the enchanted woods of Shakespeare's play brought to life as Studio 54." In his review for the *New York Times* (August 27, 1999), Peter Marks wrote that although *The Donkey Show* "might have been a garish mismatch," it was instead "an exuberant and witty splicing of disparate sources." The show later toured in England, Scotland, Spain, and France.

In 2002 Paulus had another New York opening: her musical *Swimming with Watermelons*, which told the true story of how her parents met and fell in love. Prior to serving in the U.S. Army during World War II, her father had been an actor; after the war he was stationed in Japan, where he worked as a theater director for the U.S. Army. In Japan he met the woman he would one day marry. The play, which was written and directed by Weiner and Paulus, had an all-female cast of four who played all seven roles. Although *Swimming with Watermelons* was set in the 1940s—the characters sang along to tunes recorded by Ella Fitzgerald and Hank Williams—there was a modern aspect to the show, which mocked racial and gender stereotypes and offered altered lyrics of jazz standards. Reviews were mixed. "It's cheery and cute, and even oddly sexy," Bruce Weber wrote for the *New York Times* (April 19, 2002). "And besides, the gender element, with its implicit argument for tolerance, gently underscores the play's noble if not exactly complex or original theme: that love ought to find a way and that it generally does." Writing for *Variety* (April 29, 2002), Charles Isherwood called the show a "sweet but insubstantial karaoke musical." A year later Paulus directed *The Karaoke Show*, a musical version of Shakespeare's *Comedy of Errors*. Set in a karaoke lounge, the show included old and new pop hits, including U2's "With or Without You" and the Beatles' "Yesterday." The musical ended with several members of the audience belting out karaoke tunes.

In 2004 Paulus (as writer and director), Weiner (as lyricist), and Murray (as composer) collaborated on yet another musical version of a Shakespeare play, one that received more attention and critical praise than *The Karaoke Show*. Based on Shakespeare's *The Winter's Tale*, *The Best of Both Worlds* told the familiar story in an unfamiliar fashion, with a lively R&B soundtrack. "If the writing isn't always inspired (after all, there are only so many rhymes for 'sweet caress')," Paulus and Weiner "take a playful attitude to the source material with fairly happy results . . . ," Alexis Soloski wrote for the *Village Voice* (December 28, 2004). "Paulus directs in broad but effective strokes, though perhaps she relies too heavily on audience participation. The . . . crowd, though apparently enjoying themselves, were reluctant contributors."

Paulus's attempt to connect the audience to the performers reflects her view of theater's rightful place in contemporary culture. "I'm very interested in giving the audience ownership in a theatrical event," she said. "And it's really not 'interactive.' I kind of resist that word. I'm interested in the idea of freedom for an audience, where an audience feels like at a sporting event, that they can voice their feeling, that that's acceptable behavior. In the modern theater if you start booing or if you say anything, you'll be asked to leave; that's the etiquette. But that wasn't the etiquette of theater when theater was created." Paulus pointed out that in the early days of the famed Globe Theatre, in London, England, in the first part of the 17th century, the groundlings—audience members who stood in the tightly packed yard just below the stage—would occasionally yell at the actors or even throw tomatoes to express their dissatisfaction. "That's the live event for me. And if theater's going to survive it has to embrace what's live—because we have too much film, and TV, and Internet, and technology. What will always be necessary about the theater is that absolute moment between a performer and an audience, where as an audience member you think, 'I got it tonight. And I got it 'cause I was here.'"

Earlier, in 2000, Brian Dickie, the director of the Chicago Opera Theater, had asked Paulus if she wanted to direct an opera. "I had been desperately wanting to direct opera," Paulus said, "so it was an amazing opportunity." She directed what many consider to be the world's first great opera: Monteverdi's *Orfeo*, which premiered in 1607. *Orfeo* the story of a young man who travels to the underworld to bring back his recently deceased wife. Paulus's production, which opened in Chicago in October 2000, was set in a modern apartment in Manhattan. The production was a success, and in 2002 it was brought to the Brooklyn Academy of Music, in New York, as part of a Monteverdi festival. Paulus went on to direct two more Monteverdi operas: *Poppea*, which premiered in Chicago in 2004, and *The Return of Ulysses*, which opened there three years later. Although Paulus had plenty of experience directing musicals, she found directing opera to be a very different process. While the director must "bring a performance" out of a theater actor, she said, "I find opera singers—especially young opera singers—easier to work with than actors because they're so eager do something theatrical with their work that they jump at the opportunity to be given direction." Paulus also directed three Mozart operas for the Chicago Opera Theater. After her 2002 mounting of *Così fan tutte*, a tale of romance and deception that Paulus set in a chic nightclub, in 2005 she took on *The Marriage of Figaro*, setting it in South Beach in Miami, Florida—an attempt, she said, to make the audience feel that "the opera is relevant to them." In 2008 Paulus finished the Mozart trilogy with *Don Giovanni*, which she set in an elite, private nightclub, not, she said, merely for the sake of modernization. "When Mozart and [his librettist Lorenzo] da Ponte premiered this work in Prague 230 years ago," she told Andrew Patner for the *Chicago Sun-Times* (April 27, 2008), "they intentionally set it in the here and now. They knew that their audience expected something very contemporary—they even included a satire of one of Mozart's tunes from their *Marriage of Figaro*, which had been the international hit of the year before." Paulus's stagings of the operas were highly successful both commercially and critically.

Paulus's biggest hit to date has been the revival of the Broadway musical *Hair*, which premiered on Broadway in 1967 under the title *Hair: The American Tribal Love-Rock Musical*, a song-driven show about a group of hippies living in the East Village neighborhood of Manhattan. Four decades later, in the summer of 2008, Paulus directed a production of *Hair* in the outdoor Delacorte Theater, in Manhattan's Central Park. Staging the production outdoors was thought to be a natural fit, as was having Paulus direct it: her freedom-embracing, populist approach matched the show's aesthetic. "What's so excitingly eye-opening about Diane Paulus's interpretation of *Hair* isn't that it's fun," Ben Brantley wrote for the *New York Times* (August 8, 2008). "Put a bunch of kids with decent pipes, lithe bodies and adolescent energy on a stage and let 'em loose on Galt MacDermot's abidingly infectious score, and a certain amount of giddy pleasure is guaranteed. . . . [Paulus] does full justice to this show's madcap friskiness. But she also locates a core of apprehension in *Hair* that reveals it to be much more than a time-capsule frolic." Bradley noted that Paulus not only showed the fun-loving

hippies "struggling against a nascent sense that no party can last forever, and that they have no place to go once it's over," but did so "without ever imposing the irony of hindsight." The show quickly became a smash hit with critics and audiences alike and brought Paulus a new level of renown. When, a year later, *Hair* moved to Broadway's Al Hirschfeld Theater, it received nearly unanimous praise from critics.

In addition to the above-mentioned shows, Paulus has directed the Obie Award–winning *Eli's Comin'* (2001), a musical with songs by Laura Nyro; *Another Country* (2007), based on a novel of the same name by James Baldwin; *Kiss Me, Kate* (2008), the Cole Porter musical based on Shakespeare's *The Taming of the Shrew*; and *Lost Highway* (2008), an opera adaptation of a David Lynch film of the same name. As the CEO and artistic director of the American Repertory Theater since the beginning of the 2009–10 season, Paulus has revived *The Donkey Show* and *The Best of Both Worlds*, and in June 2010 she directed *Johnny Baseball*, a musical about the Boston Red Sox and the integration of African-Americans into Major League Baseball.

In the first few months of 2011, Paulus is scheduled to direct *Prometheus Bound*, a musical inspired by Aeschylus's Greek tragedy, with music composed by Serj Tankian, the lead singer of the popular Armenian-American hard-rock band System of a Down. She is also slated to direct *Death and the Powers: The Robots' Opera*, a futuristic work by Tod Machover, which will feature a chorus of robots.

Paulus, a petite woman, has long brown hair and intense blue eyes. She and Weiner live in New York City and Cambridge with their two young daughters.

—D.K.

Suggested Reading: *Boston Globe* N p1 Sep. 28, 2008; dianepaulus.net; *New York Times* E p3 Mar. 5, 1999, E p5 Jan. 10, 2002, E p5 Apr. 19, 2002, E p9 Dec. 15, 2004, C p1 Apr. 1, 2009; *New Yorker* p82 Apr. 13, 2009; *Vogue* p44 July 2008

Selected Musicals: *Running Man*, 1999; *The Donkey Show*, 1999; *Brutal Imagination*, 2002; *Swimming with Watermelons*, 2002; *The Karaoke Show*, 2003; *The Best of Both Worlds*, 2004; *Hair*, 2008– ; *Johnny Baseball*, 2010

Selected Operas: *Orfeo*, 2000; *Così fan tutte*, 2002; *Poppea*, 2004; *The Marriage of Figaro*, 2005; *The Return of Ulysses*, 2007; *Don Giovanni*, 2008

Courtesy of University of Michigan

Payton, John

Dec. 27, 1946– President and director-counsel of the NAACP Legal Defense and Educational Fund

Address: NAACP Legal Defense and Educational Fund, 99 Hudson St., Suite 1600, New York, NY 10013

"Despite the progress we have seen since the Civil Rights Movement and the passage of the 1964 Civil Rights Act, the 1965 Voting Rights Act, and the 1968 Fair Housing Act, the 21st century still continues to present significant challenges. In many ways, the problems of race have grown more challenging." John Payton made those remarks during an interview with the *Civil Rights Monitor* (Winter 2008, on-line), several months after he was named the president and director-counsel of the NAACP Legal Defense and Educational Fund (LDF). The LDF's name was the NAACP Legal Defense Fund when it was founded, in 1940, as an arm of the National Association for the Advancement of Colored People, with the aim of fighting racial discrimination in the nation's courts. In one of the greatest triumphs for civil rights in U.S. history, the NAACP–LDF filed the six lawsuits known collectively as *Brown v. Board of Education of Topeka, Kansas*, in which in 1954 the U.S. Supreme Court ruled as unconstitutional the state-sanctioned segregation of public schools. Payton himself argued civil rights cases before the Supreme Court in 1988 and 2003, during his years with the firm Wilmer, Cutler & Pickering. He practiced with the firm as a general litigator from 1978 to 1991 and then as a partner, from 1994 to 2008; in the interim he served as the corporation counsel for the District of Columbia.

As the head of the LDF, he has appeared before the Supreme Court once, on February 22, 2010, in the case of *Lewis Jr., et al. v. City of Chicago*. Payton has been a board member and co-chair of both the National Lawyers' Committee for Civil Rights Under Law and its Washington, D.C., chapter, and he was the president of the bar association of Washington, D.C. in 2001 and 2002. He has taught at the law schools of Harvard, Georgetown, and Howard Universities.

The primary mission of the LDF, according to the organization's Web site, is "to see that African Americans become full, equal and thriving participants in our democracy." Operating independently of the NAACP since 1957, the LDF has worked to improve the quality of education for children of all races in low-income areas where schools lack adequate funding and where huge numbers of young people never graduate from high school. It has also strived to end all forms of discrimination in employment, business, housing, public transportation, and health care; to remove barriers to voter registration; to ensure that at every polling station, citizens can be confident that they will enjoy the protections of state and federal voting laws; to overturn state laws that disenfranchise for life anyone ever convicted of a felony; and to end inequalities in the criminal-justice system, including inadequate legal representation for the poor, the persistence of far harsher sentencing for people of color than for whites, and the disproportionately high number of blacks and Hispanics on death row. (The LDF seeks to end the death penalty altogether.) The organization is also fighting to end "environmental" injustice, because of which low-income and minority populations have suffered far more harm than others from hazardous substances released into the environment by various industries. "The problems of race and inequality in our country have proven to be enduring and deep-seated in nature," Payton told the *Civil Rights Monitor* interviewer. "Long term solutions for these problems of justice and equality will require far-reaching change. LDF has a unique role to play and decades of experience in developing strategies that have had a profound impact on our society. But we must recognize that this is a marathon and not a race if we are to find solutions that will work. The challenge is figuring out how to best leverage the momentum of communities across the country in the broader fight for equality and human rights. In my view, our democracy has never needed LDF more than it needs it today to achieve promises and possibilities not yet realized."

John A. Payton was born on December 27, 1946 to an insurance agent and his wife. With the exception of the two years his family lived on Guam, which he described to an interviewer for the *Washington Lawyer* magazine (June 2001) as "an island paradise," he grew up in Los Angeles, California. "I think everyone remembers childhood as rather idyllic," he told that interviewer. "That's certainly true for me." As a high-school student, Payton considered a career in science. In 1965 he entered Pomona College, in Claremont, California, where he was one of very few African-American students in the five colleges in the Claremont Colleges system. As an undergraduate he became more interested in social activism than in science. "Everybody was worried about the draft and the Vietnam War. We were all worried about civil rights and issues of equality and justice. I was among the students who were very active," he recalled to the *Washington Lawyer*. Payton co-founded the Black Student Association at Pomona and organized various protests. As a senior he helped lead a successful student effort to persuade Claremont Colleges administrators to create an Intercollegiate Department of African-American Studies, as one way to increase enrollment of African-Americans. He told the interviewer, "During those years I became interested in pursuing something that would have the possibility of helping to create social change, and that was how I became interested in becoming a lawyer." Payton majored in literature and wrote his undergraduate thesis about the civil rights activist, historian, sociologist, and writer W. E. B. DuBois and his important role in the Harlem Renaissance of the 1920s and 1930s, when African-American writing, composing, and other cultural activities flourished. Because his limited funds prevented him from attending college full-time, Payton did not earn a B.A. degree until 1973, after eight years at Pomona.

That year Payton worked briefly at the Claremont Colleges in the African-American-admissions office, which he had helped to create. He then traveled to West Africa to study the literature and other aspects of that region, financed by a Thomas J. Watson fellowship, which supports one year of independent scholarship abroad with the goal of enhancing the recipients' "capacity for resourcefulness, imagination, openness, and leadership and to foster their humane and effective participation in the world community," according to the Watson Foundation's Web site.

After Payton returned to the U.S., he entered Harvard Law School, in Cambridge, Massachusetts. At that time Boston, across the Charles River from Cambridge, was embroiled in a controversy regarding the city's attempt to end racial imbalances in its public schools by busing many pupils to schools outside their own neighborhoods. The issue was extremely contentious among Boston residents, and violence erupted on several occasions. As a law student Payton took affidavits from African-American students who had been victims of the violence. In his first year at Harvard, Payton was the comments editor for the *Harvard Civil Rights–Civil Liberties Review*, and he and other students wrote briefs for a civil rights lawyer. "My view was that the law didn't work well on its own," he told the *Washington Lawyer*. "Therefore, it was important for people who cared about these issues to get involved, to push, to put in time, and to make the law work right." Payton earned a J.D. degree from Harvard in 1977.

Payton then moved to San Francisco, California, to serve as a law clerk for U.S. District Court judge Cecil F. Poole, the first African-American to serve as a federal judge in Northern California. Next, in 1978, Payton joined the venerable, nationally known Washington, D.C., law firm of Wilmer, Cutler, and Pickering (since 2004, Wilmer, Cutler, Pickering, Hale, and Dorr, and known informally as WilmerHale). At that time the firm was representing the NAACP in its appeal of the Mississippi Supreme Court's verdict in *NAACP v. Claiborne Hardware Co*. The plaintiffs in that case were a group of white Claiborne County, Mississippi, merchants who had sued the NAACP in 1966 for damages resulting from an NAACP-organized boycott of their businesses, launched with the goal of ending various forms of discrimination against Claiborne County's black residents. The Mississippi Supreme Court had ruled against the NAACP, which was represented by Wilmer, Cutler lawyers. Payton, who during his job interview with the firm had expressed interest in the case, was hired as a general litigator. Payton and seven other Wilmer, Cutler lawyers assisted Lloyd N. Cutler in preparing the NAACP's appeal, and in 1982 the U.S. Supreme Court decided unanimously (without Justice Thurgood Marshall, who had recused himself) in the organization's favor. "I don't think there's any question about the fact that our legal system has been affected by race, and that Mississippi in the 1960s and 1970s was affected by its legacy of racism and discrimination," Payton told the *Washington Lawyer*. "But at the same time, I think there were other factors at play, too. States routinely try to protect their local business interests, their merchants, and the U.S. Supreme Court was not subject to those pressures. So race was a factor, but it wasn't the only factor."

Payton also assisted in litigation involving many other clients, among them such major corporations as Cigna Insurance and ABC; the Nigerian government; the American Legacy Foundation, an antismoking foundation created after a 1998 agreement between the tobacco industry and 46 states; the Federal National Mortgage Association (Fannie Mae); and, without charge, injured parties in cases of racial discrimination. He appeared before the U.S. Supreme Court for the first time in 1988, arguing in defense of a Richmond, Virginia, law that required 30 percent of municipal-construction contracts to be awarded to minority-owned businesses. Six members of the court ruled in favor of the defendant, the J. A. Croson Co.; Justice Thurgood Marshall, who wrote the minority opinion, was joined by Justices Harry Blackmun and William J. Brennan, the last of whom wrote, "I join Justice Marshall's perceptive and incisive opinion revealing great sensitivity toward those who have suffered the pains of economic discrimination in the construction trades for so long. I never thought that I would live to see the day when the city of Richmond, Virginia, the cradle of the Old Confederacy, sought on its own, within a narrow confine, to lessen the stark impact of persistent discrimination. But Richmond, to its great credit, acted. Yet this Court, the supposed bastion of equality, strikes down Richmond's efforts as though discrimination had never existed or was not demonstrated in this particular litigation." According to Michael Abramowitz, writing for the *Washington Post* (January 21, 1991), Payton's demonstration of the discrimination and his skillful arguments received "high marks" from other lawyers.

In 1991 Payton was tapped by the administration of the newly elected mayor of Washington, D.C., Sharon Pratt Dixon, to serve as the corporation counsel for the District of Columbia (now called the office of the attorney general). Among his many duties in that post, which he held until early 1994, Payton handled all civil cases brought by or against the district; prosecuted juvenile criminal cases and adult misdemeanor cases; conducted or helped with criminal investigations involving government fraud; and supervised attorneys working for the district's dozens of agencies. At that time the nation's capital was experiencing a soaring number of crimes, increasing drug use among young people, and severe racial tensions as well as a budget crisis. "It was a daunting task, no doubt about that," Payton told the *Washington Lawyer.* "Once I was on the job, I realized I had completely underestimated the problems. So it was very, very challenging. And also very rewarding."

In 1993 leaders of Washington's civil rights groups urged President Bill Clinton to nominate Payton to head the Civil Rights Division of the U.S. Department of Justice. Before Clinton did so, Payton met with members of the Congressional Black Caucus to discuss his possible appointment. During that meeting he angered many caucus members when he refused to assure them that the Voting Rights Act of 1965 allowed the intentional creation of black-majority congressional districts. The members were further upset when they learned that during his 16 years as a district resident—he lived in the Mount Pleasant section—he had never voted. Having lost the caucus's support, Payton withdrew his name from consideration for the Justice Department job.

Earlier, in 1991, Payton had married Gay McDougall, a lawyer who starting in 1980 had directed the Southern Africa Project of the Lawyers' Committee for Civil Rights Under Law (a group organized at the request of President John F. Kennedy in 1963). In 1994 McDougall was appointed to the Independent Electoral Commission, set up in anticipation of the April 27, 1994 presidential election in South Africa. As a member of the lawyers' committee, Payton joined a team of international observers who monitored the voting, in which more than 18 million black South Africans voted for the first time and which resulted in the election of Nelson Mandela as South Africa's first black president.

Later in 1994 Payton returned to Washington and resumed his practice of law with Wilmer, Cutler, and Pickering. He remained with the firm for the next 14 years, serving from 1998 to 2000 as the head of its litigation department. In 2003 he appeared before the Supreme Court a second time, to argue for the defense in *Gratz et al. v. Bollinger et al.* In that case, filed by the Center for Individual Rights, a politically conservative organization, Jennifer Gratz and Patrick Hamacher, white applicants to the University of Michigan, accused the school's then-president, Lee C. Bollinger, and other school administrators of racial discrimination in their use of a points system that favored less-qualified African-American applicants. Payton, representing the university, argued that affirmative action was necessary to ensure that a "critical mass" of minority students attended the school, to create an atmosphere in which students of all races could become acquainted with one another as individuals and also broaden their knowledge of the world in a multicultural atmosphere. The court considered that case in conjunction with one brought by Barbara Grutter, a white applicant to the University of Michigan School of Law who had similarly accused the school of illegally discriminating against her. The court ruled against the university in the Gratz/Hamacher case but in its favor in the Grutter case, on the grounds that diversity in schools is a compelling state interest and that affirmative action is constitutional—that is, universities may legally take into account an individual's race in their admissions processes; the consideration of race by the law school, the court ruled, was legal, but the point system used by the undergraduate division was not. While the undergraduate division and Payton lost their case, civil rights leaders hailed the court's decision regarding the necessity and legality of affirmative action.

On December 6, 2007 the LDF announced that Payton had accepted its offer of the job of president and director-counsel. He succeeded Theodore M. Shaw, its fifth president (and the lead counsel for the defense in the *Gratz* case). The LDF's first president was Thurgood Marshall, its founder, who held the post for 21 years. In 1952 and 1953 Marshall argued for the plaintiffs before the Supreme Court in *Brown v. Board of Education*, and later, in 1967, he became the first African-American to be seated on the U.S. Supreme Court. "This is both a very exciting and a very humbling moment for me . . . ," Payton said, as quoted in an LDF press release (December 6, 2007, on-line). "Racial justice and equality are issues that I deeply care about, and being at LDF will allow me to be involved in that fight every day."

In 2009 Debo P. Adegbile, the LDF's director of litigation, argued for the defense in a case that challenged an important provision of the Voting Rights Act of 1965. The case—*Northwest Austin Municipal Utility District No. 1 v. Eric H. Holder Jr., et al*—arose when an Austin, Texas, utility filed a lawsuit against the U.S. Justice Department (headed by

Eric Holder) charging that a section of the Voting Rights Act of 1965 is unconstitutional. Section 5, the so-called pre-clearance provision, requires Justice Department approval of proposed changes in voting procedures or any other aspects of voting (including, for example, location of polling stations) in 16 specifically named states or localities that in 1965 were found to have a history of racial discrimination. The lawyers for the utility argued that conditions in the South had changed significantly since 1965, making Section 5 irrelevant; Adegbile maintained that continuing racial discrimination made it necessary, noting that Congress voted to renew the Voting Rights Act in 2006 after considering more than 16,000 pages of evidence of voting-related discrimination since 1965. The court ruled, 8–1, that "we are now a very different nation" compared with the U.S. in 1965, in Chief Justice John G. Roberts Jr.'s words, but that "whether conditions continue to justify such legislation [i.e., Section 5] is a difficult constitutional question we do not answer today," as Adam Liptak reported for the June 23, 2009 edition of the *New York Times*. (Justice Clarence Thomas cast the dissenting vote.) Roberts also suggested that the Austin utility might be able to take advantage of the Voting Rights Act's "bailout" provision, which enables "political" entities to avoid seeking Justice Department approval for voting-related changes; the bailout provision, he wrote, deserved a "broader reading." "This is one of the most important civil rights cases decided this year," Payton said in an LDF press release (May 30, 2008, on-line). "The Voting Rights Act does not stand at the periphery of the nation's long march to greater equality—it lies at its core. That a small utility district would think that it could take us off the path to political fairness by rehashing previously discredited arguments is unfortunate, but the Court declined that invitation." A lawyer for the utility company, however, described the court's ruling as "a complete victory as far as we're concerned," according to Liptak.

In September 2008 LDF was successful in persuading the 11th Circuit Court of Appeals to overturn the death penalty imposed on Herbert Williams, who had been on death row for 20 years. Williams's attorneys, the LDF argued, had failed to provide an adequate level of defense in his trial, as guaranteed by the Constitution. The next year the LDF persuaded the U.S. District Court for the Southern District of Texas to grant a prisoner named Mariano Rosales a new trial, because prosecutors had unconstitutionally excluded African-Americans and Hispanics from serving as jurors in his original trial. After his conviction Rosales had spent 23 years on death row. In 2008 the LDF filed with the U.S. Supreme Court a "friend of the court" brief in support of Andrew Cuomo, the attorney general of New York State, who in 2005 had attempted to investigate apparently discriminatory lending practices of many national banks, whereby those banks issued "a significantly higher percentage of high-interest predatory loans . . . to African-

American and Hispanic borrowers than to white borrowers," according to an LDF press release (March 4, 2009, on-line). A district court and then the U.S. Court of Appeals for the Second Circuit agreed with the argument presented by the Clearing House Association, a consortium of national banks, that state fair-lending laws cannot be imposed on national banks. In *Cuomo v. The Clearing House Association* (June 2009), the Supreme Court ruled in favor of Cuomo 5–4 (with Justice Antonin Scalia joining the four members of the court usually identified as liberals—John Paul Stevens, David Souter, Ruth Bader Ginsburg, and Stephen Breyer), noting, in Scalia's words, that states "have always enforced their general laws against national banks—and have enforced their banking-related laws against national banks for at least 85 years."

In February 2010 Payton appeared before the Supreme Court in the case *Lewis Jr., et al. v. City of Chicago*. He was representing African-American firefighters who had won a Federal District Court case against the city of Chicago for discrimination in the use of a job-placement test. According to a press release on the NAACP-LDF Web site (February 22, 2010), "The test was designed so that anyone who scored above a 65 was qualified for a firefighter job. But the City invented an arbitrary cut-off score of 89 and hired only applicants who scored above, even though, as the district court found, the cut-off score was statistically meaningless and bore no relationship to job performance as a firefighter. By hiring from the falsely named 'well qualified' pool, which was mostly white, African-American applicants were disparately and unjustifiably denied employment opportunities." On appeal, the U.S. Court of Appeals for the Seventh Circuit had reversed that ruling, on the grounds that the firefighters failed to file their complaint with the Equal Employment Opportunity Commission within the federally mandated 300-day limit. Thus, although the city of Chicago admitted to discriminatory hiring practices, the date of the plaintiffs' filing became the issue. The city argued that the 300-day window began when the results of the test scores were revealed; the plaintiffs claimed that a new act of discrimination occurred each time the test scores were used to hire, thus beginning the 300-day time period over again. On May 24, 2010 the Supreme Court ruled in favor of the firefighters. "Today, the Supreme Court affirmed that job-seekers should not be denied justice based on a technicality," Payton said, as quoted on TheDefendersOnline.com (May 24, 2010). "This victory goes well beyond the immediate results in Chicago. It should ensure that no other fire department or employer uses a discriminatory test, and LDF will go the extra mile to make sure that they do not." That month Payton was awarded the Charles Hamilton Houston Medallion of Merit by the Washington Bar Association.

On another front, in December 2009 the LDF, in a joint effort with the NAACP, the National Urban League, and the National Coalition of Black Civic

Participation, launched Count on Change 2010, a national public-awareness campaign whose goal is an accurate count of African-Americans and other members of minorities in the 2010 census. "The 2000 Census overlooked 1 million people of color, more than 600,000 of whom were African American," Payton said, as quoted in *TheDefendersOnline* (January 5, 2010). "The distribution of federal funds to state, county and municipal governments and the distribution of political power at every level of government depend on the Census. . . . We cannot afford to be excluded from the count again in 2010."

Recent cases in which the NAACP-LDF has been involved include *Davis v. City of New York*, a class-action lawsuit against the allegedly unlawful trespass policies in New York City Housing Authority projects; and *Georgia v. Holder*, in which the state of Georgia is suing to alter its voting laws. According to the NAACP-LDF Web site, with Georgia's proposed change, "qualified voters would be ineligible to register if the information they provide on their voter registration applications does not exactly match information maintained by the Georgia Department of Driver Services or the Social Security Administration. Eligible voters who are not perfectly matched must successfully navigate a series of steps before they can cast a regular ballot on Election Day. If they cannot complete the process before Election Day, but still turn out to vote, they must appear at a hearing to make sure the ballot they cast on Election Day counts. If the court will not allow Georgia to implement this voting change, the state asks the court to invalidate the federal preclearance provision of the Voting Rights Act, known as Section 5"—the same provision the NAACP-LDF successfully defended in *Northwest Austin Municipal Utility District No. 1 v. Eric H. Holder Jr. et al.*

Payton and his wife, Gay McDougall, live in New York City. The couple have no children. McDougall was the executive director of Global Rights, a U.S.-based international human rights advocacy group, from 1994 to 2006. In 2005 she was appointed as the first United Nations independent expert on minority issues.

—W.D.

Suggested Reading: *Civil Rights Monitor* (on-line) Winter 2008; District of Columbia Bar (on-line) June 2001; *Journal of Blacks in Higher Education* p43 July 31, 2002; naacpldf.org; *New York Times* A p18 Sep. 8, 1993; *Washington Post* B p1+ Jan. 21, 1991; *Contemporary Black Biography*, 2005; *Who's Who in America*, 2009

Peavy, Jake

May 31, 1981– Baseball player

Address: Chicago White Sox, 333 W. 35th St., Chicago, IL 60616

The Chicago White Sox pitcher Jake Peavy is "a stiletto in the sock drawer, a pistol beneath the pillow. Uncommonly armed. Deeply dangerous," Tim Sullivan wrote for the Copley News Service (October 4, 2005). With an impressive pitching repertoire that includes two-seam and four-seam sinking fastballs (which travel at 90 to 97 miles per hour), a hard slider (83–88 mph), a tailing change-up (80–84 mph), and an occasional curveball (74–76 mph), Peavy is considered one of the most talented pitchers in Major League Baseball (MLB) today. His former teammate Greg Maddux, a four-time Cy Young Award–winning pitcher, told Albert Chen for *Sports Illustrated* (June 11, 2007) that Peavy, a two-time All-Star, was "one of the best in the game." Maddux added, "He could be the best." Peavy spent the first nine seasons of his career with the San Diego Padres before being traded to the White Sox in a multi-player deal midway through the 2009 season. His best year to date came in 2007, when he led the National League (NL) in wins (19), earned-run average (ERA, 2.54), and strikeouts (240) and became only the second NL pitcher in 22 years to achieve the "Triple Crown" of pitching.

Ezra Shaw/Getty Images

(Randy Johnson did so in 2002.) That season Peavy was unanimously selected as the winner of the NL Cy Young Award, becoming only the 10th NL player in history to win in a unanimous vote. While his susceptibility to injury and emotionalism on the mound have caused concern among his coaches, and while he is severely nearsighted and relatively small for a power pitcher (six feet one inch and 182 pounds), Peavy has improved his game considerably since he entered the majors, in 2002. "He's old school," the former Padres pitcher David Wells noted to Chen. "He's got a lot of passion. He shows his emotions on his sleeve—unlike a lot of other young guys. . . . He knows he's good, that he can be one of the great ones, but still, he's really humble about it. He's not going to show anyone up. He knows how to do things the right way."

The older of the two sons of Danny and Debbie Peavy, Jacob "Jake" Edward Peavy was born on May 31, 1981 in Mobile, Alabama. His father (whose name is said to be "Donny" in some sources) owned a woodshop, and his mother was a mail carrier; they raised their sons in the Southern Baptist faith. Peavy grew up with his brother, Luke, in Semmes, a small suburb of Mobile, next door to the homes of his paternal grandparents and other relatives. Young Peavy enjoyed watching Atlanta Braves baseball games broadcast on TV. He studied that team's ace pitching staff, among them Tom Glavine, John Smoltz, and Greg Maddux, while idolizing the legendary pitchers Roger Clemens and Nolan Ryan. By all accounts, Peavy showed talent in every sport he played during his youth. At one point he longed to become a professional racecar driver on the NASCAR circuit. One of his early mentors was his grandfather Blanche Peavy, who instilled in him the importance of perseverance, hard work, and competitiveness; his grandfather also discovered Jake's extreme nearsightedness and bought him his first pair of eyeglasses. He drove Jake to school most days; evenings, the two would study the videotapes he made of Jake pitching from his backyard mound and taking swings in his homemade batting cage. Peavy noted to Chen, "He's the biggest reason I was always so serious about baseball." One day in 1994 his grandfather, then 58, had a freak accident in his cabinet shop; he remained in a coma for three weeks, until his family asked the hospital to end life support. "When he died, it put a different spin on things for me . . . ," Peavy told Kevin Acee for the *San Diego Union-Tribune* (February 13, 2006). "I want to live every day like it could be my last. We're not promised tomorrow. Every time I pitch it might be the last time I go out on a baseball field."

Peavy attended St. Paul's Episcopal High School, a private school in Mobile known for its outstanding sports program. During his first three seasons as a pitcher on the team's varsity baseball squad, he posted a 31–1 record. He won all 10 of the games he pitched as a senior and led the school team to the state championship. Many major-league scouts expressed an interest in him, but he "wanted to go to college and everybody kind of knew that," Peavy told Jim Short for the Riverside, California, *Press Enterprise* (July 28, 2001). His first choice would have been the University of Alabama, but the school offered him only a partial scholarship. Peavy won a full scholarship to Auburn University, also in Alabama, then turned it down in favor of a lucrative offer from the San Diego Padres, which chose Peavy in the 15th round of the major-league draft, held in early June 1999, shortly after his high-school graduation. The Padres gave him a $100,000 signing bonus, an above-average amount for such a late draft pick.

After three years in the minor leagues, Peavy made his major-league debut on June 22, 2002, three weeks after his 21st birthday. That nationally televised game, against the New York Yankees at Qualcomm Stadium, in San Diego, was played before a crowd of 60,021, the largest in baseball that season. Peavy gave up one run in the first inning, then retired 12 straight batters, allowing only three hits in six-plus innings before suffering a 1–0 loss. Commenting on his performance, Peavy told Bernie Wilson for the Associated Press (April 6, 2005), "I remember before taking the mound, I had it in my mind, 'I'm going to find out if I'm good enough to be here, or not, facing these boys.' I started getting them out, and you realize, 'Hey, I can get these guys out.' You've just got to try to do it on a consistent basis." Peavy won a permanent spot on the Padres' five-man rotation. He went on to suffer losses in his next two starts despite posting a 3.60 ERA. He picked up his first career win (5–1) on July 16, 2002, in a contest with the Colorado Rockies, allowing only five hits in seven innings. In his next outing, on July 21, facing the Arizona Diamondbacks, the Padres won, 11–9. In that game Peavy belted a two-run double against Randy Johnson. At the end of the season, Peavy had six wins and seven losses and a 4.52 ERA. He had fared better at home, with four wins and one loss and a 2.56 ERA in seven starts; on the road he won two and lost six, with a 6.23 ERA in 10 starts. On average, he held other teams' batters to an ERA of .216 at home, but against him in their own home stadiums, their average ERA was .318.

Peavy amassed 8–7 and 4–5 records during the first and second halves of the 2003 season, respectively. He also made 156 strikeouts in 194 innings pitched and gave up 33 homers in 32 starts; batters who faced him averaged an ERA of only .238. The Padres finished the season with a 66–96 record.

The year 2004 saw a breakthrough for Peavy. He not only emerged as the Padres' ace starting pitcher but also established himself as one of the best pitchers in Major League Baseball. Despite starting the season with an inflamed flexor tendon in his forearm, which forced him to remain on the disabled list for 15 days, he compiled a 15–6 record and allowed one run or none in 14 of his 27 starts. He struck out a career-high 173 batters in $166 1/3$ innings, while giving up only 53 walks. He posted a major-league-leading 2.27 ERA, thus becoming, at age 23, the majors' youngest ERA champion since the New York Mets' Dwight Gooden, who achieved a 1.53 ERA in 1985, when he was 21. He was the second pitcher in Padres' history to lead the National League in ERA and the first to lead the majors in that category. The Padres also made significant headway as a team that season, the first in which they played in their new stadium, Petco Park; their 87–75 record left them only six games out of first place and five wins shy of a wild-card berth. The San Diego chapter of the Baseball Writers' Association of America (BBWAA) named Peavy the Padres' 2004 Pitcher of the Year. During the off-season Peavy played with the MLB All-Star team in Japan.

Before the start of the 2005 season, Peavy signed a four-year, $14.5 million contract with the Padres. He pitched one of his shutout victories that year despite having bruised the middle finger of his throwing hand; in another winning game he pitched $6^2/_3$ innings despite having recently had four injections of Novocain when his wisdom teeth were pulled. He also played in several games while suffering a respiratory-tract infection. Such problems notwithstanding, he led the National League in strikeouts, with 216 in 203 innings, bettered only by Johan Santana of the Minnesota Twins, who had 238 strikeouts. His 2.88 ERA ranked seventh in the league. He compiled a 13–7 record while pitching three complete shutout games. He also appeared in the National League All-Star Game for the first time. The Padres ended the season with 82 wins, thus claiming the National League West Division title. Peavy started the first game of the NL Division Series against the heavily favored St. Louis Cardinals, but he was removed after $4^1/_3$ innings, in which the Cardinals scored eight runs. The public later learned that he had pitched with a fractured rib, apparently suffered during the Padres' celebrations after securing the NL West championship a week earlier. The Cardinals ended up sweeping the Padres in the division series.

In March 2006 Peavy took part in the first World Baseball Classic, an international tournament launched by Major League Baseball and other professional baseball associations around the world. He was selected as one of the captains of Team USA and started the opening game for the U.S.; he gave up only one hit over three innings in a contest with Mexico that the U.S. won, 2–0. In the second round, facing Japan, he gave up three runs in five innings and took a no-decision in the U.S.'s 4–3 victory. The U.S. was later eliminated in the second round, after losing to Korea, 7–3. Peavy had shoulder tendonitis and bursitis for most of the 2006 season and finished with an 11–14 record and a 4.09 ERA. He nevertheless ranked second in the league in strikeouts, with 215 in $202^1/_3$ innings, in addition to posting a league-best ratio of 9.56 strikeouts per nine innings. Opponents hit .242 off him, placing him seventh among NL starters. During a game against the Atlanta Braves in May, he set a franchise record by striking out a career-high 16 batters, tied for the highest total in the majors that year by Jason Schmidt, then with the San Francisco Giants.

During the 2006–07 off-season, on the advice of the Padres' conditioning coach, Jim Malon, Peavy strengthened his legs and scaled back his shoulder exercises. He also worked closely with the Padres' pitching coach, Darren Balsley, to refine his pitches, particularly regarding the path of his fastball: because of his recurring shoulder problems in 2006, he had begun to place more emphasis on power than on placement with his pitches, which often resulted in his heaving the ball over the plate. In addition, Peavy started meeting regularly with the Padres' newly acquired starter Greg Maddux, a veteran right-hander. Considered one of the most efficient and accurate pitchers ever to play the game, Maddux instructed him on the importance of various mental aspects of pitching. Peavy noted to Scott Miller for CBS SportsLine.com (May 30, 2007), "I think the biggest influence he's had on me is talking about pitch selection, how you should be 100 percent committed to every pitch you throw and know it's the right pitch at the right time. He told me, 'Hey, man, don't ever step on the rubber without knowing exactly what you're going to throw and why you're going to throw it.'" Peavy added, "There were a number of times in the past where I'd just shake my head yes to what the catcher wanted and heave it in there."

Peavy's intense training paid off. That year he led the National League in wins (19), strikeouts (240), and ERA (2.54)—the so-called Triple Crown of baseball. He was only the second National League pitcher in 22 years to achieve that feat. (There have been only three dozen Triple Crown pitchers in the history of the game.) He led the majors with his on-the-road winning percentage—.909—losing only one game out of 11. In July he was named the starter of the National League All-Star team. In May alone, he won four games and lost none in five starts and yielded only three runs, posting an astonishing 0.79 ERA—a major-league best for one month. In August he set a career high for wins in one month (five, with no losses), with a 1.56 ERA. From late July to early September, he had a career-high seven-game winning streak, posting a 1.17 ERA with 70 strikeouts. Mike Maddux, the pitching coach of the Milwaukee Brewers (and Greg Maddux's brother), told Albert Chen at that time, "He commands his fastball down and away as good as anybody. The way he's throwing, you'd have to say he's the best in the league right now." The Atlanta Braves' manager, Bobby Cox, told Chen, "He comes at you with everything hard. He's as good as it gets."

In early August 2007, in a game against the Diamondbacks, Peavy recorded his 1,000th career strikeout. A little over three weeks later, he became the Padres' all-time strikeout leader, after racking up his 1,037th strikeout in the first inning in another game against Arizona. That October the Padres were forced into a wild-card tiebreaker against the Colorado Rockies. Peavy, who started the game, gave up six runs and 10 hits in $6^1/_3$ innings, and the Padres lost, 9–8, in 13 innings. As expected, though, in November 2007 Peavy was the winner of the National League Cy Young Award, capturing first-place votes by all 32 voting members of the BBWAA. Only nine other players have won that award unanimously. (The Los Angeles Dodgers pitcher Sandy Koufax was unanimously selected three times.) The *Sporting News* named Peavy National League pitcher of the year, and his peers honored him with the Players' Choice Award for National League pitcher of the year. Peavy told an Associated Press (December 12, 2007) reporter, "I'm excited where I'm at, but I'm not happy where I'm at. I want to win a world championship, bottom line. I don't even care if I win another Cy Young Award. I want to be a world champion." In December 2007 the Padres added a $52 million, three-year extension to his contract, in the biggest deal in franchise history. His former teammate Woody Williams told Tom Krasovic for the *San Diego Union-Tribune* (November 16, 2007), "He's just scratching the surface of what he can do. He is only 26 years old. He's still figuring things out."

Peavy racked up a 10–11 record during the 2008 season. He suffered largely from a lack of run support and finished the year with the fourth-lowest run-support average in the NL (3.63). Nevertheless, he achieved a major-league-leading 1.74 home ERA and an overall 2.85 ERA, third in the NL. Peavy also recorded 166 strikeouts and 59 walks in 173.2 innings pitched. The San Diego chapter of the BBWAA again named him the Padres 2008 Pitcher of the Year. Because of efforts by the Padres to reduce salaries and build a team with players from their farm system, Peavy was the subject of many trade rumors during the 2008–09 offseason. He was courted by various teams but chose to remain with the Padres; then, at the 2009 regular-season trade deadline, he agreed to be traded to the Chicago White Sox. That year he made 16 combined starts with San Diego and Chicago while posting a 9–6 record with a 3.45 ERA. A strained tendon in his right ankle led to his spending most of the season on the disabled list. He resumed play in September and won in his White Sox debut in a game against the Kansas City Royals, in which he gave up three earned runs in five innings. Peavy closed out the season by winning his next two starts.

During the first two months of the 2010 baseball season, Peavy started 17 games and posted a record of seven wins and four losses, with an ERA of 4.63. Then, on July 6, he suffered a season-ending injury: during the second inning of a game against the Los Angeles Dodgers, the latissimus dorsi muscle in his right shoulder became detached. After surgery, a week later, he underwent months of rehabilitation. In October doctors predicted that the earliest he might begin training would be January 2011.

Peavy lives in Mobile with his wife, the former Katie Alford, whom he married when he was 19, and their three sons—Jacob Edward II (born in 2001), Wyatt (2004), and Judson (2009). His recreational pursuits include hunting and fishing.

—C.C.

Suggested Reading: Associated Press Apr. 26, 2007; (Riverside, California) *Press Enterprise* C p1 June 29, 2007; *San Diego Union-Tribune* D p1+ Feb. 13, 2006, A p1 Nov. 16, 2007; *Sports Illustrated* p60+ June 11, 2007; *Sports Illustrated for Kids* T p10 Sep. 2005

Peirsol, Aaron

July 23, 1983– Swimmer

Address: c/o USA Swimming, One Olympic Plaza, Colorado Springs, CO 80909

Aaron Peirsol is perhaps the greatest backstroke specialist in the history of competitive swimming. With his lanky, six-foot four-inch, 175-pound frame, Peirsol was described by Eddie Reese—the head coach of the 1992, 2004, and 2008 U.S. men's Olympic swim teams—as "the quintessential backstroker," as noted by David Woods for the *Indianapolis Star* (April 3, 2005). For much of the 2000s, Peirsol has virtually monopolized the 200-meter and 100-meter backstroke events: after winning the silver medal in the 200 meters at the 2000 Olympic Games, in Sydney, Australia, while still a teenager, he went undefeated in the event for nearly seven years; he holds the world record in the 100-meter backstroke and became the first man to break 52 seconds in that event, at the 2009 U.S. National Championships. He currently owns six of the eight fastest times ever recorded in the 200 meters and six of the fastest times ever recorded in the 100 meters. Peirsol has accumulated hundreds of victories, including seven individual world championships; he achieved a gold-medal sweep of his events at the 2004 Olympic Games, in Athens, Greece, and won another gold medal in the 100-meter backstroke at the 2008 Olympic Games, in Beijing, China. Over the years he has also been one of the few to consistently beat the swimming phenomenon Michael Phelps—arguably the greatest all-around swimmer in the history of the sport—who became the first American ever to win eight medals in a single Olympics. (It took until May 2008 for Phelps to end his years-long drought against Peirsol, defeating him in the 100-meter backstroke at the Santa Clara Grand Prix, a race that marked Peirsol's first loss in a final for the 100 meters in nearly six years.) "I'm more of a racer than an individual swimmer," Peirsol told Amy Shipley for the *Washington Post* (August 20, 2006, on-line). "I relish those moments. . . . I know, no

Toby Canham/Getty Images

Aaron Peirsol

matter what, [Phelps] is going to push me the entire race. It's not every day that I have enough energy to pull away from the guy." Peirsol has effortlessly balanced his down-to-earth, "surfer-dude" persona with the fiery competitiveness that has made him a dominant force in a sport normally characterized by anonymity. His fellow Olympian Ian Crocker said to Dave Matter for the *Columbia (Missouri) Daily Tribune* (February 19, 2008), "He's one of those guys that you want on your team because he's got more guts. He's got that mentality that most of us wish we had. He does not get beaten. He just won't let it happen. . . . He's got the ability to dig deeper than anyone I know."

The older of the two children of Scott and Mary Louella ("Wella") Peirsol, Aaron Wells Peirsol was born on July 23, 1983 in Irvine, California. His paternal grandfather was a world-class swimmer at Cornell University, and his father is a swimming enthusiast; as a result Peirsol began swimming at an age when most children learn to crawl or walk. When he was barely a year old, his father started taking him to a neighborhood pool in Newport Beach, California, and bathing him in a portable pool. At two Peirsol was able to swim the butterfly stroke, often called one of the hardest strokes in swimming. His mother wrote in his baby book "that he should be the next Mark Spitz," as she told Maria Speidel for *Sports Illustrated for Kids* (August 2004). Peirsol's parents divorced when he was very young, and he lived for a time in Jacksonville, Florida, before returning to California to live with his mother and sister, Hayley, who is also an accomplished competitive swimmer. At seven, back in Newport Beach, he signed up for the swim team at the local YMCA, quickly demonstrating above-

average swimming skills and joining the elite Irvine Novaquatics swimming club three years later. Peirsol initially excelled in the freestyle, but his age-group coach at the time, Brian Pajer, suggested to Peirsol and his mother that the boy switch to the backstroke. "We didn't believe him, so I kept saying that I was a freestyler," Peirsol recalled to Erik Hamilton for *Swimming World and Junior Swimmer* (February 1999). "Besides freestyle, I loved the fly; I never thought of myself as a backstroker. I wanted to be a freestyler and break some records. But things changed, and backstroke was my stroke."

Of the four strokes in competitive swimming, only the backstroke starts with the swimmer already in the water. The stroke requires the swimmer to lie flat on his or her back, arms stretched behind the head and legs extended, then use a strong circular motion of the arms toward the hips to travel the length of the pool. When Peirsol was 10 he set the national age-division record for the 100-meter backstroke, and at 11 he broke the national age-division record in the 200-meter backstroke. He would continue to set the standard in both events throughout his youth. It was watching his then-14-year-old Novaquatics teammate Amanda Beard win medals at the 1996 Olympics, in Atlanta, Georgia, that got him thinking about competing in the Games himself.

Instead of enrolling at Irvine High School, which had one of the top swimming programs in the area, Peirsol chose to attend Newport Harbor High to be with his non-swimming friends, explaining to Hamilton that he would probably have gotten "sick" of the sport if he saw mainly his fellow competitors. Upon entering high school, Peirsol started training under the renowned swim coach Dave Salo at Irvine Novaquatics. Salo, currently the head coach of the University of Southern California (USC) swim team, is responsible for steering the Olympic careers of Lenny Krayzelburg, Amanda Beard, Jason Lezak, Gabrielle Rose, and Staciana Stitts, among others. Under Salo, Peirsol began a training regimen that required him to wake up at 5 a.m. for a two-hour swim practice before school each day; his training currently entails swimming 10,000 yards per day, three hours a day, six days a week. Salo told Speidel about Aaron and Hayley Peirsol, "You step away from the [pool] deck and you'd never know that these were two of the best athletes in the world. They're not outwardly competitive. . . . They save all that energy for when they get up and compete." At the summer U.S. nationals in 1998, when he was 15, Peirsol became the youngest American to break the two-minute mark in the 200-meter backstroke, recording a time of 1:59.88. The following year, as the youngest male on the U.S. team at the 13th Pan American Games, in Winnipeg, Canada, he came in second in the 200-meter backstroke with a time of 1:59.77. Though many criticized the U.S. for sending its "B" team to the event while many of its more high-profile athletes took part in professional events, the competition drew comparisons to the 1967 Pan American Games, also held in Winnipeg, which had showcased such rising stars as Mark Spitz. By that time Peirsol was ranked 10th in the world in the 200-meter backstroke.

In 1999 Peirsol made the U.S. national "A" team; he has been a National "A" team member every year since then. In July 2000 he became the first swimmer in two years to beat Lenny Krayzelburg, then the world record-holder, winning the 200-meter backstroke at the Janet Evans Invitational. Peirsol repeated the same feat a week later, in the semifinals of the Olympic trials, in Indianapolis, Indiana, setting a trials record with a time of 1:57.93 in the 200-meter backstroke. He then garnered the second spot on the U.S. Olympic swimming team by placing second in the same event in the finals, with a time of 1:57.98; he finished just .67 seconds behind Krayzelburg's time of 1:57.31. He had also come close to qualifying in the 100-meter backstroke, coming in fourth with a time of 55.14. At age 17 Peirsol became the second-youngest male on the U.S. Olympic swimming team, behind only Michael Phelps, who was 15. At the 2000 Olympic Games, in Sydney, Peirsol earned a silver medal in the 200-meter backstroke with a personal-best time of 1:57.35; Krayzelburg took home the gold with a time of 1:56.76. After receiving his medal, Peirsol noted to Scott M. Reid for the *Orange County (California) Register* (September 22, 2000), "Standing there listening to the national anthem, it almost felt like I had the gold medal."

At the 2001 World Championships in Fukuoka, Japan, Peirsol won the gold medal and set a course record in the 200-meter backstroke with a time of 1:57.13. Krayzelburg, who is Jewish, had skipped the championships to participate in the Maccabiah Games in Jerusalem, Israel, which were held at the same time. Several months later Krayzelburg was forced to take a year off from swimming after badly injuring his knee on a treadmill. By the time he returned to training, Peirsol had succeeded him as the premier swimmer in the 200. In April 2002, at the FINA Short Course World Championships in Moscow, Russia, Peirsol broke world records to win the gold medal in the 200-meter backstroke (1:51.17) and the 400-meter medley relay (3:29.00), in addition to receiving a silver medal in the 100-meter backstroke (51.71). At the 2002 U.S. Spring National Championships, he set his first world record in the 200-meter backstroke (1:55.15), won the 100-meter backstroke, and placed sixth in the 200-meter freestyle. Despite a demanding schedule of year-round training and competitive swimming meets, Peirsol graduated from Newport Harbor High in 2002. He took home first-place finishes in the 100-meter and 200-meter backstroke events at that year's High School Championships. That summer Peirsol won the 100-meter and 200-meter backstroke events at the Janet Evans Invitational and swept those events at the 2002 Pan Pacific Swimming Championships in Yokohama, Japan.

At the latter he was also a member of the world-record-setting 400-meter medley-relay team (3:33.48).

In the fall of 2002, Peirsol enrolled at the University of Texas at Austin, a school long considered to have one of the best swimming programs in the nation. There, he began training under the legendary swim coach Eddie Reese, an eight-time National Collegiate Athletic Association (NCCA) coach of the year who is credited with helping to set the standard in collegiate swimming. As a freshman Peirsol went undefeated in the 200-yard backstroke, posting a perfect 7–0 record. While dominating his backstroke events throughout the season, he also became valuable to the Texas team in the 100-, 200-, and 500-yard freestyle events. One of his most impressive achievements took place during the 2003 NCAA Championships, which were hosted by the University of Texas. He first set a new U.S., NCAA, U.S. Open, and school record in the preliminaries of the 200-yard backstroke with a time of 1:40.01, then broke his own record in the finals of the same event—becoming the first person ever to go under 1:40.00 in the 200, clocking in at an astonishing 1:39.16. He also won three additional NCAA titles as a leg of the 200- and 400-yard medley-relay squads and as a member of the 800-yard freestyle-relay team; the first two teams set NCAA, American, U.S. Open, and school records with times of 1:24.46 and 3:04.47, respectively. Peirsol's other honors at the NCAA Championships included finishing second in the 100-yard backstroke (45.71), fourth as a member of the 400-yard freestyle relay (2:53.01), and 10th in the 500-yard freestyle (4:18.15). He capped off the 2002–03 season by being named the NCAA Swimmer of the Year, after setting four NCAA and American records, earning six NCAA All-America honors, and receiving one NCAA All-America Honorable Mention.

At the 2003 World Championships, in Barcelona, Spain, Peirsol captured three gold medals (100- and 200-meter backstroke and 400-meter medley relay) and a silver medal (800-meter freestyle relay). In the 100-meter backstroke, he set a course record and finished within .01 second of Lenny Krayzelburg's world-record time of 53.61, and in the 200-meter he clocked in at 1:55.92, then the fourth-fastest time ever in the event. His 400-meter medley relay team set a world-record time of 3:31.54, and his silver-medal-winning 800-meter freestyle-relay team set an American record time of 7:10.26. During the 2003–04 NCAA swimming season, Peirsol extended his undefeated streak in the 200-meter backstroke to 11 and defended his title in the event at the 2004 NCAA Championships, in East Meadow, New York, with a world-record time of 1:50.64. He was also a member on the first-place-finishing 400-meter medley relay team and came in third in the 100-meter backstroke. (NCAA-sanctioned races and championship events are normally held in 25-yard pools, with the exception of years in which the Olympic Games take place, when they are held in 25-meter pools.) In April 2004, at age 20, Peirsol decided to forgo his last two years of college eligibility at the University of Texas to turn professional, after agreeing to a multi-year endorsement contract with the sportswear company Nike. That May, at the Santa Clara Invitational, held at the George Haines International Swim Center in Santa Clara, California, he eked out close victories in the 100- and 200-meter backstroke events against the swimming wonder Michael Phelps. Before the summer, Phelps had expressed a desire to challenge Peirsol in his signature 200-meter backstroke event as part of his quest to equal or surpass Mark Spitz's record of seven gold medals at the 1972 Olympics, in Munich, Germany. Though he had come within several tenths of a second of Peirsol's world-record times in the 100- and 200-meter backstroke events in the months leading up to the Olympic trials in Long Beach, California, Phelps had never previously beaten him. While Phelps had one of the best meets of his career at the trials, becoming the first American swimmer to qualify for six individual events at the Olympics, Peirsol prevailed in the 200-meter event, with a world-record time of 1:54.74 to Phelps's 1:55.86, taking .41 of a second off the record he set in March 2002. After beating Phelps, Peirsol told Lynn Zinser for the *New York Times* (July 13, 2004), "I don't ever want to lose [the 200-meter] race. It's like anything that really means a lot to you; it becomes your baby and you want to take care of it." He also qualified in the 400-meter medley relay and the 100-meter backstroke, finishing that race almost half a second ahead of the second-place finisher, Krayzelburg, with a time of 53.64.

Not surprisingly, Peirsol entered the 2004 Olympics in Athens, Greece, as a heavy favorite in the 100-meter and 200-meter backstroke events. (The Athens Games marked the first time since the 1992 Barcelona Games that the swimming competition was held outside; athletes faced 90-plus-degree weather and water temperatures in excess of 80 degrees.) After winning the gold medal in the 100 meters, narrowly defeating the Austrian Markus Rogan with an Olympic-record time of 54.06, Peirsol cruised to a gold-medal victory in the 200 meters with another Olympic-record time, 1:54.95, nearly two and a half seconds ahead of Rogan's second-place finish (1:57.35). Though his victory was one of the rare routs at the Olympics that year, with many races being decided by only hundredths of a second, it was also controversial. Despite Peirsol's having dominated the race from the beginning, one of the judges ruled that he had used an errant flip turn going into his last lap, and his victory was disqualified. (In the backstroke the swimmer, upon flipping onto his or her stomach, is allowed to use forward momentum only when going into a flip turn, with any type of extra kick or hand stroke being prohibited. However, illegal-kick rulings in the backstroke are rare, in part because they are almost impossible to detect.) Eddie Reese said to a writer for the *Belleville (Illinois)*

News-Democrat (August 20, 2004), "It's almost something you can't see. To call Aaron on that, you would've had to disqualify the other seven guys in backstroke for the same thing." At the time some felt that the unidentified judge was getting back at Peirsol for his criticism of one of the judges' rulings earlier in the meet; Peirsol had questioned the legality of a kick by the Japanese breaststroker Kosuke Kitajima, who won the gold in the 100-meter breaststroke, beating Peirsol's teammate and friend Brendan Hansen. Roughly a half-hour after the race, the technical committee of FINA, the world's governing body for competitive swimming, reversed Peirsol's disqualification and gave him the gold medal, after calling the unidentified official's explanation of the first ruling inadequate. Rogan was awarded the silver medal, Razvan Florea of Romania received the bronze, and James Goddard of Britain was pushed into fourth place. While Austrian and British officials staged protests on behalf of their swimmers, the matter was resolved after Peirsol won the support of his fellow competitors, most notably Rogan, who said to Jerome Solomon for the *Houston Chronicle* (August 20, 2004), "My friendship with Aaron is more important than a medal. As far as I'm concerned, I didn't care about getting silver. I know he's a better swimmer than me. I would have just been a nominal champion, not a real champion." Once the reversal was official, Peirsol became the fifth male swimmer to sweep both backstroke events in one Olympics, joining Krayzelburg, who pulled off the same feat at the Sydney Games in 2000; Rick Carey of the U.S. at the Los Angeles Games in 1984; John Nabor of the U.S. at the Montreal Games in 1976; and Roland Matthes of East Germany in Mexico City (1968) and Munich (1972). In addition to his sweep of the backstroke events, Peirsol took home a third gold medal and helped set a new world record as a member of the 400-meter medley-relay team (3:30.68); his split time of 53.45 leading off the relay also set a new individual world record in the 100-meter backstroke.

Following the Olympics, Peirsol continued to dominate his events. That October, at the Short Course World Championships in Indianapolis, he won three gold medals and set two world records, first in the 200-meter backstroke (1:50.52) and then in the 400-meter medley relay (3:25.09), while adding a silver medal in the 50-meter backstroke. In April 2005, at the World Championship Trials in Indianapolis, Peirsol cut .28 of a second off his own world record in the 100-meter backstroke, with a time of 53.17, and recorded his third-fastest time in the 200-meter backstroke (1:55.13). Then, at that summer's World Championships in Montreal, Canada, he easily won gold medals in his signature events, taking home his third straight world title in the 200-meter backstroke and knocking .08 seconds off his world record, with a time of 1:54.66. Rogan, the second-place finisher, took more than half a second off his own best time in the 200 meters but still came in 1.97 seconds behind

Peirsol. "In swimming that's like a mile and a half," Rogan noted to Amy Shipley for the *Washington Post* (July 30, 2005). Peirsol told Shipley, "As time goes on, you seem to realize that every race you win, two more guys are trying to bring you down. All of those 14- and 15-year-old kids who are looking up to you are saying, 'I want to beat that guy.' When you are at the top, you are trying to fend everybody else off, and you only have two hands." At the 2006 Pan Pacific Games in Victoria, Canada, Peirsol set a course record in the 100-meter backstroke (53.32) and took another .22 seconds off his world record in the 200-meter backstroke, for a time of 1:54.44. (By that time he had owned seven of the fastest times in the 200-meter backstroke in history.) In the latter event Peirsol extended his winning streak against the second-place finisher, Phelps, who trailed him by over two seconds (1:56.81). In the spring of 2006, Peirsol graduated from the University of Texas with a degree in government.

At the 2007 World Championships in Melbourne, Australia, the University of Florida alumnus Ryan Lochte became the first man to beat Peirsol in the 200-meter backstroke in seven years, clocking in at a world-record time of 1:54.32, ahead of Peirsol's 1:54.80. While the two were neck-and-neck for most of the race, Lochte was able to pull away during the last 50 meters. Lochte recalled to Christopher Clarey for the *International Herald Tribune* (March 29, 2007, on-line) that he was "in shock" when he looked at the scoreboard. Peirsol said to Clarey, "The last 50, I cramped up. I didn't have it where I usually have it, but that's the name of the game. Usually it's there; that race it wasn't. For Ryan it was. He definitely pushed hard." Prior to his upset loss in the 200 meters, Peirsol won the gold medal and set a new world record in the 100-meter backstroke, becoming the first man ever to break 53 seconds in the event, with a time of 52.98. In May 2008, at the Santa Clara Grand Prix, Phelps ended his winless streak against Peirsol, defeating him in the 100-meter backstroke.

At the 2008 Olympics, in Beijing, Peirsol won the gold medal in the 100-meter backstroke with a world-record time of 52.54, which marked the fifth time he had set a world record in the event. He then got a chance to settle the score with Lochte in the 200-meter backstroke but again finished behind his teammate, claiming a silver medal with a time of 1:54.33. (Lochte's time of 1:53.94 was then a world record in the event.) Two days after that race, Peirsol won the third Olympic gold medal of his career and helped set a new world record as a member of the 400-meter medley-relay team (3:29.34), which included Brendan Hansen, Michael Phelps, and Jason Lezak.

Following the Olympics, Peirsol took a six-month break from swimming and vacationed in such places as Costa Rica and the Big Sky resort in Montana. Upon returning to competition in early 2009, he landed a new contract with the European-based swimsuit maker Arena. (Peirsol had been under contract with Speedo during the 2008 Olympics.) That May, at the Charlotte UltraSwim Grand Prix in North Carolina, Peirsol handed Michael Phelps his first defeat in nearly a year, edging him out in the final of the 100-meter backstroke for a first-place time of 53.32. After the race, Phelps, whose last loss in a final had also come against Peirsol in the backstroke, told Paul Newberry for the Associated Press (May 17, 2009), "This is going to come back with me. It doesn't matter what stroke it is or what event it is, I don't like to lose. Aaron has got the upper hand on me in pretty much all of our races." On the subject of Phelps's eyeing new events to compete in during the 2012 Olympics, in London, England, including the 100-meter backstroke, Peirsol said to Newberry, "By no means is anybody giving anything to anybody." About the May 2009 event, he added, "I definitely wanted to win that race."

At the 2009 U.S. National Swimming Championships in Indianapolis, Peirsol won the gold medal and lowered the world record in the 100-meter backstroke for the sixth time (51.94), becoming the first man ever to break 52 seconds in the event. Three days later he lowered Ryan Lochte's world record in the 200-meter backstroke by more than eight-tenths of a second with a gold-medal-winning time of 1:53.08. Then, at the 2009 World Championships in Rome, Italy, Peirsol broke his own record in the 200-meter backstroke by more than a second, with a time of 1:51.92, to win the gold medal. Despite shocking many by failing to qualify for the final of the 100-meter backstroke, largely due to his miscalculation of his position in the semifinals, Peirsol was able to redeem himself in the 400-meter medley-relay final by leading off his 100-meter backstroke leg with a world-record split time of 52.19. The relay team also set a new world record in the event, with a time of 3:27.28.

At the 2010 U.S. National Swimming Championships, which were held in early August in Irvine, Peirsol was upset in the 100-meter backstroke, losing by .03 seconds to David Plummer, whose winning time was 53.60; previously, he had won the event in every nationals competition he had entered since 2000. He also finished second to Ryan Lochte in the 200-meter backstroke, with a silver-medal-winning time of 1:56.28. Later that month Peirsol competed at the Pan Pacific Championships, also in Irvine. He set a course record in the 100-meter backstroke with a winning time of 53.31. He failed to qualify for the final heat of the 200-meter backstroke.

Peirsol, who plans on competing in the 2012 Olympics, has an opportunity to become the first man in history to win the same event (100-meter backstroke) in three consecutive Games. Undaunted, he explained to Mike Gustafson for the Swim Network Web site (April 29, 2010, on-line), "When I'm done swimming in a pool, there are countless number of things that I can do in the water that don't have to be me swimming over a black line. It's a very narrow way for me to express my love for the water."

Peirsol lives and trains in Austin. In addition to his busy swimming schedule, he has been actively involved with several eco-friendly charities and foundations. Since 2005 he has served as an ambassador for the Surfrider Foundation, a nonprofit environmental organization that works to protect the world's oceans and beaches, and since 2006 he has been the primary spokesperson for Oceana, the world's largest international organization advocating ocean protection. Peirsol created the Web site racefortheoceans.com, which allowed fans to pledge money for every mile he swam leading up to the Beijing Olympics. All proceeds went toward research performed by Oceana scientists or various lobbying efforts. "Every river leads to an ocean, so it kind of encompasses everything," he explained to Dave Matter. "From overfishing to mercury within fish to water pollution to the red tides, every single year, there's more and more days you can't get into the water. It's just those things I wanted to help out with."

—C.C.

Suggested Reading: Aaron Peirsol Official Web site; *Austin (Texas) American-Statesman* (online) July 30, 2007; *Indianapolis Star* C p7 Apr. 3, 2005; *New York Times* D p1 Aug. 20, 2004; *Orange County (California) Register* A p1 Sep. 22, 2000, Sports Mar. 23, 2004; *Swimming World and Junior Swimmer* Feb. 1999; *Washington Post* E p3 July 30, 2005

Courtesy of CCCEH

Perera, Frederica

Dec. 19, 1941– Molecular epidemiologist; director of the Columbia Center for Children's Environmental Health

Address: CCCEH, 100 Haven Ave., Tower 3, Apt. 25F, New York, NY 10032

While the phrase "security of the womb" has often been used as a metaphor for a place that is totally peaceful and safe, the womb, or uterus, does not protect a developing fetus from all dangers. Scientists have known since the early 1900s, for example, that the babies of mothers infected with syphilis may contract that disease while in the womb, and they discovered in the 1980s that babies of pregnant women infected with the AIDS virus may carry the same infection at birth. For the past three decades, the molecular epidemiologist Frederica Perera has been gathering mounting evidence that pregnant women who live in polluted environments pass along to their fetuses not only nutrients essential to life but also harmful substances in the air they breathe. Perera is a professor at the Columbia University Joseph L. Mailman School of Public Health (CSPH, also known as the Mailman School), in New York City. She has served since 1998 as the founding director and principal investigator of the Columbia Center for Children's Environmental Health (CCCEH) and since 2006 as the director of Columbia's Disease Investigation Through Specialized Clinically-Oriented Ventures in Environmental Research (DISCOVER) Center, an initiative sponsored by the National Institute of Environmental Health Sciences.

In the late 1970s and early '80s, Perera pioneered the field of molecular epidemiology, a novel interdisciplinary approach to understanding the causes of disease. In 1982 she and I. Bernard Weinstein wrote the seminal paper on molecular epidemiology; published in the *Journal of Chronic Diseases*, it offered a conceptual framework for incorporating biological markers, or biomarkers, into epidemiology studies (a proposal later adopted by the National Research Council). A biomarker, according to the National Institutes of Health, is in part "a characteristic that is objectively measured and evaluated as an indicator of normal biologic processes [or] pathogenic processes." In her research Perera relied on techniques invented by molecular biologists, who search for biomarkers in tissues or body fluids from animals that have been exposed to unnatural or uncustomary chemicals. Perera initially focused on biomarkers known as carcinogen-DNA adducts, which form when chemicals bind to biological molecules, such as cellular DNA or proteins. Some adducts result in genetic mutations. Such mutations increase the probability that cancer will develop. Ideally, if a biomarker linked to pathology is identified in an individual before symptoms of disease can be detected, physicians and policymakers can take steps to prevent the disease. Perera's doctoral thesis was entitled "Report of a Pilot Project in Molecular Epidemiology: A Preliminary Study of Carcinogen-DNA Adducts in Human Subjects"; a paper constituting the first report of carcinogen-DNA adducts in a human population based on that research appeared in the journal *Carcinogenesis* in 1982 with Perera as the lead author.

Molecular epidemiology incorporates "molecular, cellular, and other biologic measurements into epidemiologic research," according to the introduction to *Molecular Epidemiology: Principles and Practices* (1993), a groundbreaking work that Perera edited with the epidemiologist Paul A. Schulte; it is a discipline in which laboratory scientists, primarily molecular biologists, collaborate with epidemiologists, who study the incidence and distribution of diseases within groups of people. In particular, Perera studies the effects of environmental pollutants on chromosomes, genes, and other cell molecules in human populations.

At present there are tens of thousands of pollutants in Earth's air, soil, and water, produced by industry, agriculture, and other activities of humans; according to the World Health Organization, an arm of the United Nations, an estimated one-quarter of the diseases that strike people today can be traced to prolonged exposure to environmental pollution. Perera's long-term studies of thousands of pregnant women and their babies in New York City, Poland, and China have produced evidence that babies born to mothers who breathe polluted air may be harmed physically and mentally. "Early-life exposures, even occurring in the womb, appear to be important determinants of that child's respiratory health and development later on," Perera told Melissa Lee Phillips for *Environmental Health Perspectives* (October 2005). "We have enormous opportunities to prevent these diseases and conditions." Perera has also studied the effects of polluted air on smokers and nonsmokers and has investigated the roles of particular genes in individuals exposed to carcinogens—substances that cause cancer. She has been recognized internationally not only for her scientific work but also for her efforts to reduce children's exposure to pollutants, notably in several low-income New York City neighborhoods as well as at sites in China and Poland, and for her repeated attempts to awaken policy makers to the serious hazards of environmental pollution on children and adults. Perera's honors include the first Irving J. Selikoff Cancer Research Award from the Ramazzini Institute, in Bologna, Italy, in 1995; the first Children's Environmental Health Award from the Pew Center for Children's Health and the Environment, in 1999; an honorary doctoral degree from Jagiellonian University, in Cracow, Poland, in 2004; the Children's Environmental Health Excellence Award from the U.S. Environmental Protection Agency, in 2005; and the

Measure of Children Award from the Healthy Schools Network, in 2008.

The second of the four children of Davis Clapp Drinkwater and the former Frederica Plimpton, Perera was born Frederica Plimpton Drinkwater in Boston, Massachusetts, on December 19, 1941. Beginning at age 12, she grew up on her parents' farm, in Panton, Vermont, with two sisters, Susan and Polly, and a brother, Davis Drinkwater Jr., now a cardiothoracic surgeon in Nashville, Tennessee. Her father, a Harvard University graduate, served as a commander in the U.S. Navy during World War II before becoming a farmer. In Vermont her mother held an elected position in the town, helping people in need; she was also a longtime Planned Parenthood volunteer.

Perera graduated magna cum laude from Harvard University, in Cambridge, Massachusetts, with a B.A. degree in 1963. She married that year, and during the next decade she gave birth to three sons and a daughter. She earned a master's degree and a doctorate, with honors, in public health at Columbia University in 1976 and 1981, respectively. In the latter year Perera joined the faculty of the Mailman School as an assistant clinical professor; she was promoted to assistant professor in 1983, associate professor in 1988, and full professor in 1995. From 1989 until 2004 Perera was associate director of the Division of Epidemiology, Prevention and Control at the Columbia-Presbyterian Cancer Center (now part of New York-Presbyterian Hospital/Columbia University Medical Center), and from 1990 to 1991 she served as acting head of the Division of Environmental Sciences at the Mailman School.

In the late 1970s Perera began to investigate the suspected causal connections between chemicals in cigarette smoke and air pollution and the occurrence of cancer. Cigarette smoke inhaled by smokers and people nearby (those breathing so-called secondhand smoke) is among many thousands of environmental pollutants. The vast majority have been introduced into the world's air, water, and soil since the start of the Industrial Revolution, in the 19th century, and most of those since World War II. They include polycyclic aromatic hydrocarbons (PAHs) and other emissions from fossil-fuel combustion in vehicles, factories, homes, and power plants; waste from industrial processes; chemical fertilizers and pesticides in soil runoff that enters water supplies; motor oil, paint, batteries, electronic devices, and other things discarded improperly on land or in water; particles produced by incineration of garbage; and microscopic particles and vapors released from synthetic items such as carpets or plastics.

When Perera began her studies, most researchers used rats and mice to determine the effects of toxic substances on humans. Using the results of such studies—for example, the percentages of the animals that developed diseases, tumors, or organ abnormalities—the researchers would hypothesize about the results of exposure to those toxic substances in human populations. They would then conduct epidemiological studies of human communities exposed to those substances to find out the rates at which similar diseases, tumors, or abnormalities occurred in those people. Perera, however, wanted to work with human tissue and human populations directly. "Humans have a very different molecular response to the environment than rodents. But tests treat us like rodents, in a very uniform way," she told Jordana Hart for the *Boston Globe* (September 24, 1989).

In her early research Perera collected samples of tissues and body fluids (blood and urine) from human volunteers exposed to cigarette smoke and air pollution. Cigarette smoke contains not only nicotine and tars but chemicals including formaldehyde, ammonia, carbon monoxide, hydrogen cyanide, and PAHs. Perera focused on PAHs, a group of compounds released by the burning of organic matter including fossil fuel, many of which are used in industry; PAHs do not break down easily into their component parts and thus tend to persist in the environment for a long time. At least 15 PAHs are undoubtedly carcinogenic, and others have been implicated in high rates of cancer in workers whose exposure to them is direct, heavy, and prolonged. Perera searched for biomarkers in her subjects' tissues, blood, and urine that indicated exposure to PAHs. In the course of her research, she discovered that after PAHs enter a person's lungs, they pass into the bloodstream and damage blood cells by binding to the cells' DNA. With the aim of comparing damaged blood cells to healthy ones, she examined blood cells from the umbilical cords of newborn infants, thinking that such cells must be "pure"—that is, uncontaminated by environmental toxins. When she analyzed such blood, however, she found PAH molecules attached to some of the cells' DNA. "I was pretty shocked," she told Jerome Groopman for the *New Yorker* (May 31, 2010). "I realized that we did not know very much about what was happening during this early stage of development."

In the early 1990s, in collaboration with Kari Hemminki, Regina Santella, and other scientists and physicians from the U.S., Poland, and Scandinavia, Perera investigated cell damage in people living and working in Silesia, a highly industrialized part of Poland where there were high levels of air pollution, including the presence of PAHs from the combustion of coal. The researchers examined blood samples from adult volunteers from urban areas and, for comparison, from "a rural, less polluted area of Poland," according to the paper in *Nature* (November 19, 1992) in which they described their findings. Analyses of the volunteers' PAH-DNA adducts revealed that the quantities of adducts in their blood cells were significantly higher in the urban industrial area and coincided with seasonal fluctuations in air pollution. (Byproducts of coal combustion were greatest during winter months, when buildings were heated.) In measurements of the presence of adducts, the researchers also found huge variations among individuals: the presence of adducts in some people's cells was 200 times greater than in those of others. That finding supported the hypothesis that genes play a role in the extent to which environmental pollutants affect cells.

Also in the early 1990s, in a study of 87 Hispanic and African-American mothers and their preschool children, aged two to five years, in New York City, Perera found that exposure to mothers' cigarette smoke greatly increased the presence of PAHs in the children's systems. In another study during that period, Perera examined tissue samples taken from 15 women being treated for breast cancer at the Columbia-Presbyterian Medical Center and from four women who had undergone breast-reduction surgery. Of the 15 women with cancer, the tissues of five longtime smokers showed a pattern of adducts associated with exposure to tobacco smoke. None of the tissues from nonsmokers showed that pattern. Those findings suggested that the formation of adducts in the female breast is associated with exposure to environmental carcinogens. Perera described those findings and other results of her research up to that point in a 12,800-word article, entitled "Molecular Epidemiology: Insights into Cancer Susceptibility, Risk Assessment, and Prevention," published in *JNCI: Journal of the National Cancer Institute* (April 17, 1996). Perera and her team then carried out a case-control study of breast cancer and in 2000 reported a significant relation between PAH-DNA adducts in breast tissue and cancer risk.

In 1998, with support from the National Institute of Environmental Health Sciences (an arm of the National Institutes of Health) and the U.S. Environmental Protection Agency, Perera established the Columbia Center for Children's Environmental Health. Her aim, she told Jenn Preissel for the *Columbia Daily Spectator* (March 25, 2005), was to try to decrease the incidence of "serious childhood diseases through the identification of environmental risk factors that by their nature are preventable." As the director of the CCCEH since its founding, Perera has guided one of the largest and longest-standing studies of mothers and children in the U.S. At any one time the subjects include more than 700 women, who enter the study during pregnancy, and their newborn children, who are followed until age eight. The women and their families all live in New York City, some in the Washington Heights or Harlem neighborhoods of Manhattan and others in the South Bronx—places whose air contains greater levels of toxic substances than the air in many other parts of the city. All but a tiny percentage of the residents of those neighborhoods are low-income Hispanics or African-Americans, among whom the incidence of respiratory problems, notably asthma, and learning difficulties are significantly greater than in residents of neighborhoods with cleaner air. After concentrating on exposure to PAHs in the early years of her study, Perera expanded her research to include many more chemical compounds and other materials, such as insecticides and pest allergens. Toward the end of their pregnancies, the women in the study wear backpacks containing devices that monitor the air they breathe, and the women provide the researchers with urine samples. When their babies are delivered, a sample of umbilical-cord blood is drawn and the cells examined. The newborns are weighed and their head circumferences measured. As the babies grow, the researchers assess the children's physical and cognitive development and health.

Perera and her co-workers have conducted similar studies, though with fewer subjects, in other places with high levels of air pollution: Cracow, Poland's second-largest city, and Tongliang, a city in the municipality of Chongqing, China, where a local power plant burned more than 20,300 tons of coal each year before it was shut, in 2004. In another project, Perera focused on 330 infants born in Lower Manhattan on September 11, 2001 or up to half a year after that date, when Al Qaeda terrorists attacked the World Trade Center. The resulting fires and the collapse of the center's twin towers produced enormous clouds of smoke and dust—a mixture of particles of thousands of compounds— that continued to pollute the air in Lower Manhattan for more than four months. Scientists who monitored PAHs in the area during the six months following 9/11 recorded levels of pollution up to 65 times higher than normal.

Among other findings, Perera's research has produced evidence that babies whose mothers were exposed to higher-than-usual levels of PAHs from tobacco smoke or other forms of air pollution have lower birth weights and smaller heads than unexposed babies. Typically, newborns whose weights at birth are significantly lower than average are more likely than other newborns to experience respiratory disorders and other health problems in infancy and later on, and babies born with smaller-than-normal heads are more likely to experience learning difficulties as they get older. Although animal studies had suggested that the placenta filters out many of the PAHs to protect the fetus, Perera and her team found that mothers and infants had similar levels of PAH-induced DNA damage; babies with mothers who had been exposed to greater levels of pollutants had about 50 percent more persistent genetic abnormalities than babies with mothers exposed to lower levels of pollutants. "What gets across [the placenta] is not detoxified and the damage to the DNA is not repaired in the fetus as it is in the mother," Perera told Anna Gosline for *New Scientist* (July 3, 2004). Furthermore, Perera found, the babies had similar or higher adduct levels than their mothers, indicating that fetuses and newborns are especially susceptible to air pollutants, which can also lead to a greater risk of developing cancer later in life, many scientists believe. "We already knew that air pollutants significantly reduced fetal growth, but this is the first time we've seen evidence that they can change chromosomes in utero," Perera said, as quoted by

Karen Matthews for the Associated Press (February 15, 2005). She added, "While we can't estimate the precise increase in cancer risk, these findings underscore the need for policymakers at the federal, state and local levels to take appropriate steps to protect children from these avoidable exposures."

To learn whether PAHs from the World Trade Center disaster may have affected pregnant mothers and their fetuses, Perera and her collaborators measured PAH-DNA adducts in cord blood among newborns of mothers living near the site of the attacks in the following months. Levels of cord-blood adducts were higher the closer the mother lived to the site, and higher adducts in combination with in-utero exposure to secondhand smoke were associated with a reduction in birth weight and head circumference. The study in Tongliang revealed that infants born before the power plant was shut down—those whose mothers were exposed to combustion-related power-plant pollution during their pregnancies—had higher levels of DNA adducts and had less favorable birth measurements than babies born after the plant was shut down. At two years of age, children who had had the most exposure to PAHs, as evidenced by PAH-DNA adducts, performed significantly worse than others on neurodevelopment tests. The CCCEH's studies in Poland during the past decade have produced similar results. In 2009 Perera and colleagues reported that elevated prenatal PAH exposure in New York City was significantly associated with lower IQ scores at age five, a finding that was confirmed in the Polish study population.

In 2006 the CCCEH launched the DISCOVER initiative, four studies funded by the National Institute of Environmental Health Sciences that seek to further elucidate the relationships between air pollutants and childhood asthma, abnormal neurocognitive development, and cancer. An integral component of the project is community involvement: Perera and her team work with both families and neighborhood organizations to reduce residents' exposure to harmful pollutants, by means of educational efforts such as workshops and newsletters and visits to people's homes to advise on the best methods of controlling infestations of household pests.

Perera's first husband, Phillips Perera, served as a U.S. deputy assistant secretary of commerce, then as a vice president of American Express, before becoming the founder and president of Interfin, a New York financial-services company for international food businesses. From that marriage, which ended with her husband's death, in 1992, Perera has four children—Frederica, Christopher, Alexander, and Phillips Perera Jr., who is the director of ultrasound at the University of Southern California Department of Emergency Medicine. In 1996 Frederica Perera married Frederick A. O. Schwarz Jr., the great-grandson of the founder of the famous Fifth Avenue toy emporium, F.A.O. Schwarz. Frederick Schwarz Jr., chief counsel at New York University Law School's Brennan Center for Justice, has a son and two daughters from his previous marriage. Perera lives in Manhattan with her husband.

—M.A.S.

Suggested Reading: ccceh.org; *Discover* p60+ Mar. 2006; *Environmental Health Perspectives* A p664+ Oct. 2005; Mailman School of Public Health Web site; *New Yorker* p26+ May 31, 2010; *Newsweek* p56 Oct. 21, 1991

Selected Books: *Respirable Particles: Impact of Airborne Fine Particulates on Health and the Environment* (with A. Karim Ahmed), 1979; as co-editor—*Risk Quantitation and Regulatory Policy*, 1985; *Molecular Epidemiology: Principles and Practices*, 1993

Frederick M. Brown/Getty Images

Pierce, Wendell

Dec. 8, 1962– Actor

Address: c/o Paradigm Talent Agency, 360 N. Crescent Dr., North Building, Beverly Hills, CA 90210

"The world is not fair. Theater is not fair. We are not fair." Those words were written on a blackboard by the teachers of Wendell Pierce, then a high-school student, during his first day at the New Orleans Center for Creative Arts. While many students might have found that message to be highly discouraging, the now-successful actor told David Cuthbert for the New Orleans, Louisiana, *Times-Picayune* (March 21, 1993) that his reaction was,

"Well, I'm going to force you to respect me by doing good work." In the opinion of critics and audiences, he has done that and more. Since his graduation from the Juilliard School, in 1985, the 47-year-old New Orleans native has had an extensive presence on screen as well as on stage, acting in around 40 movies; working with directors including Woody Allen, Spike Lee, Brian De Palma, Barry Levinson, Sidney Lumet, and Paul Schrader; performing in more than a dozen plays; and making appearances on about 40 television shows. Pierce told Shelby J. Jones for *BlackFilm.com* (May 2000), "I love working on television because you get to play a character in a multitude of different situations, unlike theater and film where the challenge is to play the same events many times over while trying to keep it spontaneous." Pierce is most likely best known for his role as Detective William "Bunk" Moreland in all five seasons of the HBO police drama *The Wire*. His work on the show was twice nominated for an NAACP Image Award, and in 2008 he won that award for his role in the HBO movie *Life Support*, starring Queen Latifah. Pierce is currently seen on the HBO show *Treme*, which premiered in April 2010. In it, he portrays a trombone player, Antoine Batiste, who is struggling to make a living in New Orleans after the devastation wrought by Hurricane Katrina in 2005. "The connection that Pierce feels for his fellow townsmen is evident in his portrayal of Antoine Batiste," Regina R. Robertson wrote for *Venice* (May 2010).

Wendell Pierce was born on December 8, 1962 in New Orleans. He was raised in a neighborhood called Pontchartrain Park, one of the first New Orleans subdivisions to allow African-Americans to purchase homes. His mother, Althea, was a teacher, and his father, Amos, a World War II veteran, worked as a maintenance engineer. Reflecting on how his parents raised him, Pierce told Cuthbert, "They gave me values, along with unconditional love, which wasn't always easy, because I was a little hellion—always looking for the easy way out. They forced me to do it right." After attending Benjamin Franklin High School, Pierce transferred to the New Orleans Center for Creative Arts (NOCCA). "I was interested in many different things, like law and engineering before I realized the craft"—acting—"that would let me do it all," Pierce told Jones. While at NOCCA Pierce produced and hosted a television show for teens called *Think About It* and also hosted a weekly radio jazz show on WYLD FM98, *Extensions from Congo Square*. He graduated in 1981 and became his school's first Presidential Scholar, receiving a medallion in a White House ceremony. Pierce went on to study drama at the Juilliard School, in New York City. "NOCCA catches people right at the point where they want to express themselves. You learn that acting is not just a job, it's a way of life, and that you are responsible for the consequences of your actions. You learn to make decisions for yourself . . . ," Pierce explained to Cuthbert. "NOCCA prepared me for New York and Juilliard, where I learned that technique and training lead to opportunity."

While at Juilliard Pierce spent his days studying and his nights going to jazz clubs; his roommates were the jazz musicians and fellow New Orleans natives Wynton and Branford Marsalis. "That was an education in itself," Pierce told Shelby J. Jones. "I learned to act from jazz musicians because they understood how to have freedom within form. That's what acting is for me." Shortly after graduating from Juilliard, in 1985, Pierce landed his first movie role, as a paramedic in *The Money Pit*. That 1986 comedy, starring Tom Hanks and Shelley Long, was about a couple who purchase a million-dollar home for a low price, then realize it is not the bargain they thought. The next year Pierce appeared in one episode of the HBO series *Vietnam War Story*. For most of the late 1980s, he had small roles in such films as *Casualties of War* (a war drama starring Michael J. Fox and Sean Penn) and *Family Business* (a crime comedy starring Sean Connery, Dustin Hoffman, and Matthew Broderick). He also made cameos on such television shows as the crime drama *A Man Called Hawk*, starring Avery Brooks and Moses Gunn (based on a character created by the novelist Robert B. Parker), and *The Equalizer*, a crime drama starring Edward Woodward. In 1989 Pierce appeared on stage at the New York Public Theater in the Shakespeare romance *Cymbeline*.

In 1990 Pierce was given a leading role in the movie *A Matter of Degrees* (co-starring Arye Gross), a drama about a college student who is trying to gain self-knowledge. That same year he had a regular role as Conrad White on *Capital News*, a short-lived television drama about Washington, D.C., newspaper reporters. The following year Pierce was featured in a made-for-TV movie, *The 10 Million Dollar Getaway*, which told the true story of the largest cash robbery in American history. Pierce also had a small role, as the assistant to an undertaker, in the gangster film comedy *A Rage in Harlem* (based on Chester Himes's novel of the same name), starring Forest Whitaker, Danny Glover, Badja Djola, Robin Givens, and Gregory Hines. Over the next couple of years, Pierce had roles in various television shows, including *I'll Fly Away*, *Unnatural Pursuits*, and *New York News*. He also had small parts in such films as *Malcolm X*, *Manhattan Murder Mystery*, *Strapped*, *Bye Bye Love*, and *Hackers*. In 1993 Pierce appeared in a stage production of *Antigone*, the Greek tragedy by Sophocles, about the daughter of King Oedipus. The year after that Pierce secured a more substantial role, in the movie *It Could Happen to You*. In that romantic comedy, a police officer (played by Nicolas Cage) is unable to tip his waitress (played by Bridget Fonda) after a meal, so he instead offers her half of his prize money if he wins the lottery—which he does. Pierce played the role of Bo Williams.

Up until that point in his career, Pierce had appeared in a long list of movies and television shows but was still not well-known in the industry. That changed in 1995, when he was offered a supporting role in Forest Whitaker's *Waiting to Exhale*, a romantic comedy—with a dose of drama—based on a novel by Terry McMillan. Pierce played the part of Michael Davenport, the co-worker and love interest of one of the main characters, Robin, played by Lela Rochon. In a review for the *New York Times* (December 22, 1995, on-line), Stephen Holden, while praising the movie's performances, wrote that *Waiting to Exhale* "is little more than a collection of vignettes strung around [a] candy-sweet soundtrack." In spite of that and other poor reviews, the movie was a big hit in theaters, and Pierce gained recognition as a result. Pierce told Mark Lorando for the *Times-Picayune* (November 23, 1997), "All of a sudden I became this hot comedic actor. You never know what's gonna pop. . . . It took me to a different level of exposure."

In 1996 Pierce was cast as a district attorney, Cal Patterson, in five episodes of the CBS series *Moloney*. Also in that year he had small roles in the movies *Never Give Up: The Jimmy V Story*, *Sleepers*, and *Get on the Bus*—a movie about 12 African-American men on their way by bus to the Million Man March in Washington, D.C. In the film, directed by Spike Lee, Pierce portrayed Wendell, a wealthy Republican car salesman from Memphis, Tennessee, who gets kicked off the bus after offending the other characters. As mentioned by Janet Maslin in the *New York Times* (October 16, 1996), Pierce provided "some comic relief" in the film.

In 1997 Pierce procured his first regular comedic role, as Carl, the brother of Ben Stevenson (played by Gregory Hines), in 18 episodes of the *Gregory Hines Show*, a CBS program that was canceled after one year. In 1998 Pierce won a role on *The Brian Benben Show*, on which he played Kevin La Rue in seven episodes over the span of two years. Within the next few years, Pierce began to have slightly bigger roles in movies, including *Bulworth*, *The 24 Hour Woman*, and *Abilene* (also known as *Shadows of the Past*). He also continued to have smaller roles on television shows, among them *The Expert*, *God, The Devil and Bob*, and *413 Hope St.* In 1999 Pierce performed at New York's Delacorte Theater in the Richard Wilbur translation of the Molière play *Tartuffe*. According to Ben Brantley in the *New York Times* (August 23, 1999), Pierce did "wonders in rejuvenating the sermonizing speeches of Elmire's brother, Cleante."

At around that time Pierce started a production company. Called Jinja Media, the company had as its debut project a play by August Wilson, *Jitney* (co-starring Pierce), which was staged in Los Angeles, California, and New York City in 2000. Pierce's company also co-produced a short film, *The Date*, in which Pierce acted. Around the same time, Pierce began guest-starring as the crooked police officer Conrad "Candyman" Jones in five episodes of the popular NBC drama *Third Watch*. He was also on one episode of *City of Angels*, an unsuccessful medical drama on CBS.

In 2001 Pierce offered $2,000 to anyone with information about the shooting death of a 15-year-old boy in Pontchartrain Park. His pledge came in addition to the monetary reward already being offered by Crime Stoppers. Pierce wanted to help out because of his remaining connection to his hometown. "I was that kid 20 years ago, growing up in that idyllic neighborhood," he recalled in an interview with the Baton Rouge, Louisiana, *Advocate* (May 4, 2001). That same year Pierce played the role of Dr. Boucher on the pilot episode of the ABC sitcom *My Wife and Kids*. He also starred in all 17 episodes of the short-lived NBC sitcom *Cursed* (also known as *The Weber Show*) and acted in a movie called *The Gilded Six Bits*, a screen adaptation of the classic story by Zora Neale Hurston. The following year Pierce appeared on one episode of the UPN sitcom *Girlfriends*, and in 2002 he showed up in the romantic movie *Brown Sugar*, starring Taye Diggs and Sanaa Lathan.

Also in 2002 Pierce began appearing on the HBO drama *The Wire*, which would prove to be the biggest success of his career thus far. Referring to his luck in winning the role on *The Wire*, Pierce told Bret McCabe for the *Baltimore City Paper* (October 26, 2005), "I definitely won the lottery." In that show, created by the former police reporter David Simon, Pierce starred as the Baltimore, Maryland, homicide detective William "Bunk" Moreland, based on a retired Baltimore detective named Rick Requer. Pierce's character has a wife and three children as well as problems resulting from his infidelity and alcohol abuse. "I love Bunk. It's hard to play a character that you don't love. No matter who it is, you have to find their humanity. As much as we want to demonize people, when we're playing evil villains, they're people, like you and me, who are dysfunctional," Pierce said to Mekeisha Madden Toby for the *Detroit News* (March 8, 2007). The show aired for five seasons, each of which concentrated on a different aspect of Baltimore. The first season focused on the city's illegal drug trade; the second dealt with its port system; the third highlighted city government and bureaucracy; the fourth was about the school system; and the fifth season zeroed in on print news media. Teresa Wiltz, writing for the *Washington Post* (March 11, 2008), described *The Wire* as "reality in the form of a five-season visual novel set in the mean streets of Baltimore, marinated in Old Bay seasoning and a hefty dose of skepticism and rage against the systems that fail us." Though the drama often struggled in the ratings, critics praised it unanimously. Pierce was twice nominated for an NAACP Image Award for outstanding actor in a drama series for his work on show.

While filming *The Wire*, Pierce pursued several other projects. In 2003 he had a small role as Reverend Lewis in the romantic/musical film *The Fighting Temptations*, starring Cuba Gooding Jr. and Beyoncé Knowles. In 2006 Pierce spoke about the experiences of his family in New Orleans in the aftermath of Hurricane Katrina in Spike Lee's documentary *When the Levees Broke*. Also in 2006 Pierce performed in *Waiting for Godot in New Orleans*, a unique reimagining of the classic absurdist play by Samuel Beckett, staged in New Orleans. Pierce had a big part in the 2007 movie *Life Support* (loosely based on a true story), in which he played Slick, a former drug addict and the HIV-positive husband of Queen Latifah's character. That role won Pierce an NAACP Image Award for outstanding actor in a television movie, miniseries, or dramatic special. Around the same time Pierce made appearances in the television shows *Law & Order: Trial by Jury*, *Judging Amy*, *Close to Home*, *Women's Murder Club*, *In Plain Sight*, *House of Payne*, *Numb3rs*, *Fear Itself*, *Hawthorne*, *Drop Dead Diva*, and *Tim and Eric Awesome Show, Great Job!*.

Around 2008 Pierce helped create the nonprofit Pontchartrain Community Development Corp., to help rebuild homes in the actor's old neighborhood, which had been badly damaged by the flooding from Hurricane Katrina. Pierce wanted to help give young families the chance to become first-time homebuyers and "to buy into the American dream," as he told Becky Bohrer for the Associated Press (August 8, 2008); he hoped to help restore the quality of life that existed in Pontchartrain Park prior to the disaster. "We didn't come here to just build one home or two homes," Pierce informed Michelle Krupa for the *Times-Picayune* (May 15, 2010). "We want to do 500 or more, and we're in a position now to do 50 starts a month."

In 2009 Pierce appeared in *Broke-ology*, a stage drama about a family's struggles, mounted at the Mitzi E. Newhouse Theater of New York City's Lincoln Center. Misani wrote for the *New York Amsterdam News* (October 2009), "In this touching, reflective, clear-cut play, *Broke-ology* lovingly portrays this endearing African-American family with strong work ethics, pride, and great love and tenderness for each other."

Pierce currently appears in the HBO drama *Treme*, which premiered in April 2010. *Treme* is about the residents of New Orleans—musicians, chefs, and others—who are trying to put their lives back together three months after Hurricane Katrina. *Treme* was picked up for a second season just days after the series premiere. Pierce's character is a struggling trombone player, Antoine Batiste. Pierce described Antoine to Susan Young for *Daily Variety* (June 11, 2010) as "a man reacting to the depression of the devastation around him by acting out." Pierce also told Regina R. Robertson for *Essence* (May 18, 2010), "While [Antoine is] certainly flawed in many areas, the one thing he does have together is his music."

Treme was co-created by David Simon (creator of *The Wire*), who wrote Antoine's character with Pierce in mind. At the same time Ray Romano had written a role for Pierce for the TNT comedy/drama

Men of a Certain Age (for the character ultimately played by Andre Braugher), but Pierce declined, feeling it would be more appropriate for him to be in a show about his birthplace. "This was an opportunity to share the spirit of New Orleans and the culture of New Orleans, and more than any other place in the world, we understand culture. We lived through a lot and we're trying to go to a better place, to recover, renew and get to a place of success. To have this show where art imitates life and life imitates art, it's one of the most cathartic moments of my life," Pierce told Bill Burke for the *Boston Herald* (May 9, 2010). "I was honored when [Simon] told me that he wrote a role for me," Pierce told Brett Johnson for *TheGrio.com* (April 9, 2010). "To do a new series about this great city, my hometown, it's kismet." Music is an important part of *Treme*, and Pierce sings in it occasionally. To better prepare for the role, Pierce starting taking trombone lessons. "I didn't want to look like an actor who knows absolutely nothing about music, so I'm continually working with a trombone teacher . . . ," Pierce said to Johnson. "The goal is—as years go by—to play [the instrument] myself." David Zurawik wrote for the *Baltimore Sun* (April 9, 2010), "I have never seen music used as powerfully, organically or eloquently as it is in the pilot of *Treme*." According to Susan Young, a woman stopped Pierce on the street to say that after watching the show, she and her friends had planned a trip to New Orleans. Pierce told Young, "I'd love to get Emmys for *Treme*, but ultimately when a woman says 'I saw your show and bought a ticket to New Orleans,' that's the greatest award ever."

In August 2010 Pierce appeared in *New Orleans Rising*, a CNN documentary marking the fifth anniversary of Hurricane Katrina. The special focused on the actor's efforts as head of the Pontchartrain Community Development Corp. That same month he was seen in Spike Lee's *If God Is Willing and Da Creek Don't Rise*, which aired on HBO. Pierce will next be seen in the film *The Mortician* (which moviegoers will have the option of seeing in 3D), an urban thriller starring Method Man. His other upcoming films include the dramas *To Hell and Back* and *Bolden!* and the horror film *Foreclosure*.

Pierce divides his time among New York, Los Angeles, and New Orleans, where he remains involved in Pontchartrain Park redevelopment efforts.

—J.P.

Suggested Reading: Associated Press (on-line) Aug. 8, 2008; (Baton Rouge, Louisiana) *Advocate* (on-line) News May 4, 2001; *Boston Herald* The Edge p035 May 9, 2010; *Detroit News* E p6 Mar. 8, 2007; (New Orleans) *Times-Picayune* D p2 Mar. 21, 1993

Selected Films: as actor—*The Money Pit*, 1986; *Casualties of War*, 1989; *Family Business*, 1989; *A Matter of Degrees*, 1990; *The 10 Million Dollar Getaway*, 1991; *A Rage in Harlem*, 1991;

Malcolm X, 1992; *Manhattan Murder Mystery*, 1993; *Strapped*, 1993; *It Could Happen to You*, 1994; *Bye Bye Love*, 1995; *Hackers*, 1995; *Waiting to Exhale*, 1995; *Never Give Up: The Jimmy V Story*, 1996; *Sleepers*, 1996; *Get on the Bus*, 1996; *The Advocate's Devil*, 1997; *Bulworth*, 1998; *The 24 Hour Woman*, 1999; *Abilene*, 1999; *The Gilded Six Bits*, 2001; *The Date*, 2002; *Brown Sugar*, 2002; *The Fighting Temptations*, 2003; *When the Levees Broke*, 2006; *Life Support*, 2007; *New Orleans Rising*, 2010; *If God Is Willing and Da Creek Don't Rise*, 2010; as producer—*The Date*, 2002

Selected Television Shows: *Vietnam War Story*, 1987; *The Equalizer*, 1988–89; *A Man Called Hawk*, 1989; *Capital News*, 1990; *I'll Fly Away*, 1991; *Unnatural Pursuits*, 1992; *New York News*, 1995; *Moloney*, 1996–97; *413 Hope St.*, 1997; *The Gregory Hines Show*, 1997–98; *The Brian Benben Show*, 1998–2000; *The Expert*, 1999; *God, the Devil and Bob*, 2000; *Third Watch*, 2000; *City of Angels*, 2000; *Cursed*, 2000–01; *My Wife and Kids*, 2001; *Girlfriends*, 2002; *The Wire*, 2002–08; *Judging Amy*, 2004; *Law & Order: Trial by Jury*, 2005–06; *Close to Home*, 2006; *Numb3rs*, 2007–08; *Women's Murder Club*, 2008; *In Plain Sight*, 2008; *House of Payne*, 2008; *Fear Itself*, 2009; *Hawthorne*, 2009; *Drop Dead Diva*, 2009; *Tim and Eric Awesome Show, Great Job!*, 2010; *Treme*, 2010–

Selected Plays: as actor—*Cymbeline*, 1989; *Antigone*, 1993; *Tartuffe*, 1999; *Waiting for Godot in New Orleans*, 2006; *Broke-ology*, 2009; as actor and producer—*Jitney*, 2000

Piñera, Sebastián

(peen-YAIR-uh, seh-bass-CHYAN)

Dec. 1, 1949– President of Chile; businessman; former educator

Address: Office of the President, Palacio de la Moneda, Morandé 130, Santiago, Chile

The inauguration of the billionaire businessman Sebastián Piñera as president of Chile, on March 11, 2010, coincided with one of the many powerful aftershocks of the devastating earthquake that had struck central Chile less than two weeks earlier. While Piñera's election as president cannot be described as a political upheaval, it did symbolize a sea change in Chilean politics: running as a member of the center-right National Renewal Party, Piñera ended the reign of the leftist coalition that had controlled the government since 1990. Moreover, he is the first non-leftist to be democratically elected since 1958 and the first to overcome the suspicions that have shadowed conservative and right-

Andrew Harrer-Pool/Getty Images

Sebastián Piñera

leaning politicians since the start of the brutal military dictatorship of Augusto Pinochet, in 1973. Said to have a personal fortune of some $1.3 billion, Piñera greatly outspent his rivals in the first round of the presidential elections in December 2009 and during the weeks of campaigning that preceded the January 17, 2010 runoff election. But most observers, Alexei Barrionuevo wrote for the *New York Times* (January 18, 2010), "did not see the vote as a reflection of a major conservative shift among voters as much as a sign of disenchantment with what they saw as stale ideas and a desire for renewal." Piñera has described himself as a compassionate conservative and a Christian humanist. His positions on social and economic issues are a mix of liberal and conservative stances. He supports the legalization of civil unions for gay and unmarried couples, for example, but opposes gay marriage. He has called for both a greater role for the private sector in industry and also for tax increases, albeit temporary ones, to cover the cost of the multibillion-dollar relief and reconstruction efforts undertaken by the government in the wake of the February 27 earthquake, which affected about 80 percent of Chile's population.

Piñera served in the national Senate for eight years, beginning in 1990, first as a political independent and then as a member of the National Renewal Party. He failed in his first bid for the presidency, in 2005, when he lost to the socialist candidate, Michelle Bachelet, a pediatrician, who became Chile's first female head of state. He amassed his wealth by introducing credit cards to Chile and acquiring big stakes in Chile's national airline, LAN, and the TV station Chilevision, among other businesses. Piñera holds a doctorate in economics

from Harvard University, and he taught that subject for many years in several Chilean universities.

The third of the six children (two daughters and four sons) of Joseph Piñera Carvallo and the former Magdalena Echenique Rozas, Miguel Juán Sebastián Piñera Echenique was born on December 1, 1949 in Santiago, Chile. His brother José Piñera Echenique, an economist, served as minister of labor under Augusto Pinochet, who came to power after a military coup, in 1973; he is currently the co-chairman of the Project on Social Security Choice at the Cato Institute, a libertarian Washington, D.C., think tank. Another brother, Miguel "Negro" Piñera Echenique, is well known in Chile as a nightclub owner and musician. In 1950 the Piñera family moved to the U.S., after Piñera's father was appointed a representative of the Chilean Economic Development Agency. In 1955 they returned to Chile, where Piñera attended the Colegio del Verbo Divino (the Divine Word School), run by German priests. He studied there until 1964, when Chilean president Eduardo Frei Montalva appointed Piñera's father ambassador to Belgium, and the family moved to Brussels. (Later, beginning in 1967, his father served as Chile's ambassador to the United Nations.) After three years as a student at St. Boniface College, a Brussels secondary school, Piñera returned to Chile, where he finished his high-school education at Verbo Divino.

Piñera then entered the Pontifical Catholic University of Chile, in Santiago. He earned an undergraduate degree in commercial engineering (that is, business, or commerce) in 1971 and won the Raúl Iver Award for having the highest grade-point average in his class. Next, he attended Harvard University, in Cambridge, Massachusetts, where he received a master's degree and, in 1976, a Ph.D. degree in economics. His doctoral thesis was entitled "The Economics of Education in Developing Countries." In 1975 and 1976 he worked as a teaching fellow at Harvard. Concurrently, he was a consultant for the Inter-American Development Bank (1974–76), which supports efforts by Latin American and Caribbean countries to reduce poverty and inequality, and for the World Bank (1975–78), which provides financial and technical assistance to developing nations. He also worked for the United Nations Economic Commission for Latin America and the Caribbean, where he helped with a project aimed at decreasing poverty in Latin America.

Piñera returned to Chile in 1976. According to his entry in *Who's Who in America*, he taught economics at Catholic University in Chile, the University of Chile, and the Adolfo Ibañez University until 1990. In the 1980s Piñera made a substantial amount of money by introducing credit cards to Chile via two credit-card companies he founded—one of them the giant Bancard S.A.—and then sold. He headed Chile-based offices of several American companies (notably Citicorp and Apple) as well as the real-estate company Las Americas and the publishing house Los Andes. He also amassed wealth by investing in LAN-Chile, the national airline, in which he bought a 27 percent stake. In addition, he was a major shareholder in the TV station Chilevision and the popular soccer team Colo-Colo. By the mid-1990s his personal fortune was said to total about $300 million.

Chile stretches 2,700 miles along the western coast of South America, from Cape Horn, at the continent's southern tip, to the southern border of Peru, where the land begins to swell to the west. It is extraordinarily narrow, not wider than 150 miles across at any point. Some 70 percent of the country's 16.6 million inhabitants are Roman Catholic. (Although officially there is separation of church and state in Chile, the Catholic Church sometimes receives special treatment.) Starting in 1958 the balance of political power in Chile was almost equally divided among the left, the center, and the right. After the election of the socialist president Salvador Allende in 1970, and the subsequent nationalization of the coal, steel, and copper industries and the international boycott of Chilean copper it triggered, the country's economy quickly deteriorated. In 1973 General Augusto Pinochet led a coup d'état in which the military took over the government, and the following year he appointed himself president. Pinochet's brutal reign ended in October 1988 after a national plebiscite in which a majority of Chileans rejected the continuation of his regime and called for new elections. Piñera publically supported the referendum, a position he later cited repeatedly during his campaigns for political office as evidence of his democratic, center-right credentials. In 1989, as an independent, he won a seat in the 38-member Chilean Senate as a representative of east Santiago. (Chile's bicameral legislature also has a 120-member Chamber of Deputies. Deputies serve for four years, senators for eight.) Piñera began serving his term in 1990. He later joined the center-right National Renewal Party (Renovación Nacional, or RN). During his time in office he focused on human rights, health care, the treasury, and environmental issues. He introduced the Environment and Nature Protection Bill as well as a measure to allow independent candidates to run against party-member candidates in national and local elections. (As an independent candidate in 1989, Piñera had the backing of the party Democracy and Progress Pact.) He was also one of the leaders of a movement to end the interference of Chile's powerful military in politics.

To the chagrin of some critics, during his Senate stint Piñera remained active in his entrepreneurial pursuits in aviation, real estate, telecommunication, and finance. He did not sit on the boards of any corporations, since it was illegal for senators to do so, but people in the corporate world acted on his behalf. For example, in 1996, Piñera, through a partner, paid $30 million for a 6 percent share of the holding company Cruz Blanca S.A. His activities were not illegal, however.

In 1993, as a member of the RN, Piñera made his first attempt to run for the presidency, but his plans were cut short after the public learned of a conversation in which he had talked about ways of forcing one of his rivals, Evelyn Matthei, a member of the House of Deputies, to quit the race. The conversation had been secretly (and illegally) recorded and the tape given to Matthei by an army official who favored her candidacy. After the tape aired on national television and the way in which Matthei had acquired the tape became known, both she and Piñera dropped out of the race. When his Senate term ended, Piñera considered becoming a presidential candidate in 1999, but ultimately, in a move that was seen as a defeat for centrists, he ceded his party's nomination to Joaquin Lavin of the ultra-conservative Independent Democratic Union (UDI). Lavin lost the election that year to Ricardo Lagos of the center-left Coalition of Parties for Democracy. Piñera regained political prominence in 2001, when he was unanimously voted president of RN; he held that position until 2004. During that time the RN, according to opinion polls cited in the *Santiago Times* (May 28, 2001), was very unpopular: support among the public had dropped to a low of 8 percent, while the UDI had 24 percent. Piñera worked to steer the RN in a more moderate, centrist direction.

In 2005 Piñera came close to winning the presidency. That year the RN and the UDI had joined in opposition to the ruling party, with the UDI perceived as more disciplined, determined, and politically savvy. To the surprise of many observers, at a meeting called in May 2005 to rally behind Lavin, RN leaders instead voted for Piñera as the party's presidential nominee. Piñera's wealth was considered both an advantage, since he could finance his own campaign, and a disadvantage, because his ownership of sizable stakes in LAN as well as other companies posed potential conflicts of interests (although Piñera insisted that he would sell those assets if he was elected). On the day of the elections in December 2005, Piñera faced Lavin and Michelle Bachelet, the Socialist Party candidate, who was endorsed by the center-left Coalition of Parties for Democracy (CPD). No candidate received more than 50 percent of the vote, so the names of the top two winners, Bachelet and Piñera (with 45.96 percent and 25.4 percent of the votes, respectively), appeared on the ballot in a runoff election held in January 2006. Bachelet won—with 53.5 percent of the vote—and became the first female president in Chile's history. A single mother and a self-described agnostic, she also "shattered the mold of traditional Chilean politicians in a Roman Catholic stronghold," according to a *New York Times* (March 11, 2010) writer.

The Chilean economy was flourishing when Bachelet took office. According to statistics cited in the *Economist* (September 19, 2009), in the previous 20 years, the poverty rate had fallen from 45 percent of the population to 13.7 percent. During her administration Chile fared better than its South American neighbors after the start of the worldwide economic recession in 2008, in part by making a balanced national budget mandatory. In addition, the country's substantial revenues and savings from copper—its main export—enabled the Bachelet administration to launch a big fiscal stimulus. In the last two years of her presidency, Bachelet's approval ratings reached a high of 70 percent. Her popularity did not affect Bachelet's immediate political prospects, however, because Chilean law forbids consecutive presidential terms. Had she been permitted to seek reelection, many observers believe, she would have had an excellent chance of winning a second term.

In August 2009 the RN named Piñera its presidential candidate. Other conservative parties soon followed suit, forming a coalition that included UDI and newer parties, among them Chile First, Christian Humanism, and Greater North. As campaigning got underway the following month, polls showed Piñera in the lead, with 37 percent of the public behind him. His two rivals—the Christian Democrat Eduardo Frei, who was president of Chile from 1994 to 2000, and Marco Enríquez-Ominami, a former Socialist Party member who was running as an independent—trailed him, with 28 percent and 17 percent of those polled, respectively. During his campaign Piñera acknowledged Bachelet's accomplishments but maintained, according to the *Economist*, that her administration had stymied Chile's entrepreneurs. He promised that he would raise the country's annual growth rate to 6 percent (at the time it was 4 percent) by granting tax breaks for investment, among other measures. He also vowed to create a million jobs, get tough on crime (particularly drug trafficking), and privatize a part of Codelco, the state-owned copper company (the world's largest copper producer). His campaign benefited from infusions of large sums of his own money—a total of at least $13.6 million, Michael Smith and Sebastian Boyd wrote for bloomberg.com (January 18, 2010). According to a writer for Earthtimes.org (January 17, 2010), during the campaign Piñera organized raffles, with winners receiving household appliances. He also attracted centrist and center-left voters with his stances on some social issues: for example, he supported the legalization of gay civil unions and the availability of the morning-after contraceptive pill. (As health minister in the early 2000s, Bachelet had introduced free distribution of the pill to victims of sexual abuse.) He opposed gay marriage and abortion, however, both of which are illegal in Chile.

In the first round of the presidential election, held on December 11, 2009, Piñera won 44 percent of the vote and Frei 30 percent. In the runoff, held on January 17, 2010, he defeated Frei, with 52 percent of the ballots cast. On March 11, 2010 he was sworn in as the first democratically elected conservative president of Chile since 1958. After the election many journalists and political analysts speculated whether Piñera would be able to deliver on his campaign promises and pointed out continuing concerns over conflicts of interest stemming from his business investments. He placed many of his smaller investments in the control of investment banks and promised to sell his 26 percent stake in LAN.

National priorities changed drastically on February 27, 2010, after Chile was hit by a powerful, 8.8-magnitude earthquake that killed hundreds of people and caused widespread damage to housing, infrastructure, and some industries, notably forestry, fishing, wine, and fruit. (Copper mines were unaffected because they are located north of where the earthquake occurred.) A monthlong series of aftershocks followed. During the presidential swearing-in ceremony, two weeks later, Chile was hit by a 7.2-magnitude quake. Piñera—mindful of what many called Bachelet's unacceptably slow response to the disaster—promised to take quick, effective action to help victims, clear rubble, and rebuild. After being sworn in he viewed damaged areas from the air, piloting his own helicopter.

Nine days after the inauguration, the *Economist* (March 20, 2010) reported, "Having set up an emergency committee under his interior minister to handle the disaster, Mr Piñera is doing much of the work himself, holding cabinet meetings late into the night and making whistle-stop visits to the worst-affected areas in south-central Chile." The quake killed some 520 people and left 200,000 homeless. In late March Piñera announced that the government, over the course of the next 24 months, would spend more than $2.5 billion to rebuild the homes destroyed or damaged in the quake. A few weeks later he unveiled an $8.4 billion federal reconstruction plan. (The total cost of rebuilding was estimated to be $30 billion.) To help pay for the reconstruction, the government would impose a temporary 3 percent increase in the corporate tax and raise other taxes as well. "Despite the complaints," the *Economist* (April 24, 2010) reported, "the plan looks balanced." Even with the humanitarian crisis and its heavy economic toll, Piñera insisted that Chile's growth rate would reach 6 percent by the time he left office.

To quell charges of conflict of interest, Piñera sold his $1.5 billion stake in LAN. In August 2010 the U.S. media giant Time Warner was reportedly set to purchase Chilevision, but as of mid-October the deal had not been approved by Chile's antitrust office. Moreover, additional conflicts of interest arose, related to reconstruction efforts. According to the Associated Press (June 14, 2010), Piñera "gave $15 million in no-bid contracts to three giant building-supply companies formerly run or represented by cabinet members and [a] political appointee—cutting out local vendors who desperately needed the sales after the quake. And he's given private construction firms a leading role in designing new master plans for destroyed cities." In response to such criticism, Piñera pointed out how quickly schools and shelters were being built. That observation triggered new complaints, with skeptics questioning whether the government was subjecting privately built structures to sufficiently rigorous inspections.

During the summer of 2010, Piñera rejected the request by members of Chile's Roman Catholic hierarchy that he pardon long-term prisoners convicted of committing murder, rape, or other crimes against humanity during the more than 16 years that General Pinochet ruled the nation. Such a proposal, he said, according to BBC News (July 25, 2010, on-line), has "reopened old wounds and the rancours of the past." In September Piñera announced that government officials would begin talks with members of the Mapuche, Chile's largest indigenous minority, regarding antiterrorism laws dating from the Pinochet years. The approximately one million Mapuche make up about 5 percent of Chile's population. Some of the Mapuche who took part years earlier in a land dispute in southern Chile, where about half of the group live, are behind bars, awaiting trial on charges of terrorism under those laws. In July 38 prisoners began a hunger strike to pressure the government to retract those charges. Piñera has pledged to spend billions of dollars in economic aid for the Mapuche, but he has refused to recognize the prisoners as representatives of the Mapuche people. Amnesty International, other organizations, and James Anaya, the United Nations Special Rapporteur for the rights of indigenous peoples, "have urged the government not to use the anti-terrorism law to try Mapuche activists, and to consider all possible legal and political alternatives to find a solution to the conflict over land," Daniela Estrada wrote for the Inter Press Service (September 29, 2010, on-line).

Piñera has set up several foundations, whose missions include conserving Chile's environment, strengthening civil rights and other aspects of the nation's democratic system, supporting the economic aspirations of poor women, and finding ways to provide restitution to victims of the human-rights abuses of the Pinochet regime. He has been married to Cecilia Morel Montes since 1973. The couple have two daughters and two sons— Magdalena, a teacher; Cecilia, a pediatrician; Sebastián, a commercial engineer; and Cristóbal, a psychologist—and four grandchildren.

—D.K.

Suggested Reading: Associated Press (on-line) June 14, 2010; *Economist* (on-line) May 21, 2005, Sep. 19, 2009, Dec. 19, 2009; Gobierno de Chile Web site; *New York Times* I p3+ Jan. 15, 2006, A p4 Jan. 18, 2010

Pisani, Elizabeth

(puh-ZAH-nee)

Aug. 7, 1964– Epidemiologist; consultant; founder and director of Ternyata Ltd.

Address: Ternyata Ltd., 28 Smalley Close, London N16 7LE, England

"When people ask me what I do for a living, I say, 'Sex and drugs.' I used to say I was an epidemiologist, which is also true, but most people looked blank. . . . Saying I do sex and drugs saves me explaining that epidemiology is the study of how diseases spread in a population. . . . And it is a good conversation starter." Those words are from the preface of Elizabeth Pisani's book, *The Wisdom of Whores: Bureaucrats, Brothels and the Business of AIDS* (2008). *The Wisdom of Whores* grew out of Pisani's more than 10 years of work as an epidemiologist for the nonprofit organization Family Health International in Indonesia and as a consultant in epidemiology for UNAIDS—the United Nations Joint Programme on HIV/AIDS, based in Geneva, Switzerland. The book is also a product of her years as a journalist for the news agency Reuters and the newspaper *Asian Times* and her experiences of "debate, passionate disagreement, moments of enlightenment, misery and laughter shared with people in many countries," as Pisani wrote in *The Wisdom of Whores* (the source of quotes in this article unless otherwise noted).

Marit Miners, courtesy of Elizabeth Pisani

According to the latest figures from UNAIDS (2009), in the last three decades, an estimated 60 million people were infected with HIV (the virus that causes AIDS) and about 25 million died of AIDS. The amount of money wealthy countries have spent to combat the HIV/AIDS pandemic in developing nations has increased dramatically in recent years—from $300 million to $500 million annually in the late 1990s to over $13 billion in 2008. Yet in 2008 an estimated 33.4 million people worldwide were infected with HIV, among them 22.4 million in sub-Saharan Africa. That year an estimated two million people died of AIDS, and another 2.7 million were newly infected with HIV.

In *The Wisdom of Whores*, Pisani argued that a huge portion of the billions of dollars spent to stop or slow the spread of HIV/AIDS has been wasted, because of factors that are ubiquitous on what she calls Planet Politics: "hypocrisy, shame and prejudice," "ideology and religion and culture," and "the self-interest of bloated institutions." But on Planet Epidemiology, where, in her scenario, scientific findings and humanitarian impulses prevail, there are effective weapons to be used in the continuing fight against HIV/AIDS: "We have the knowledge, the tools and the money to beat the HIV and many other diseases besides. The armies on Planet Epidemiology and Planet Politics have been waging their battles in isolation from one another, the one fighting for things that are effective but unpopular such as clean needles [for drug users], the other fighting for things which are ineffective but popular such as abstinence [from sex]. But we are beginning to see signs that common sense and common humanity are gaining the upper hand. If politics and epidemiology got off their separate planets and stood shoulder to shoulder in the war against disease, we'd have a better Planet Earth." One such sign: in December 2009 the U.S. Congress repealed the 21-year-old ban on federal funding of needle-exchange programs, through which drug users receive clean needles in exchange for their used needles, so that a needle possibly contaminated with HIV-laden blood could never be used by another person.

The Wisdom of Whores received positive reviews. Rachel Holmes, writing for the London *Times* (May 24, 2008), described it as "an engaging, well-written and entertaining confessional. . . . Weaving anecdotes drawn from a rich cast of drug addicts, hookers, dive bars and street corners, the book investigates how these human stories are—or are not—effectively translated into the flip charts, colourful graphs and budgetary funding models that should influence and define global health policies." Stephen Lewis, a co-director of the U.S. advocacy group AIDS-Free World and a former United Nations envoy on AIDS in Africa, wrote in his review for the Toronto, Canada, *Globe and Mail* (July 19, 2008), "This is an utterly fascinating book. . . . Elizabeth Pisani writes with enormous verve and acerbity, her prose alive with anecdote and metaphor." He concluded, "The sad, sad truth about the Pisani book is that the rude language and controversial nostrums will allow it to be dismissed by policy makers at all levels. But it should be mandatory, not voluntary, reading." In January 2010 Pisani founded Ternyata Ltd., a London-based public-health consultancy firm. (The names means "an unexpected finding" or "a surprising re-

sult" in Bahasa Indonesian.) One of her hopes is that information about HIV/AIDS and other diseases that is compiled by government researchers, university scientists, and others will be openly shared, to aid in coming up with the best approaches to prevention of infection.

Elizabeth Pisani was born on August 7, 1964 in Cincinnati, Ohio, to an American father, Roger Pisani, and a British mother, Julie Pisani, both corporate executives. "My parents met when my father was hitchhiking around the world and my mother was hitching around Europe. Perhaps not surprising, then, that they bred into me curiosity, a love of travel and a tendency to talk to strangers in immigration queues." (Pisani dedicated her book to her mother and father, and in its acknowledgments she mentioned the enormous help she received from her brother, Mark, in writing it.) Her family is Roman Catholic. During her childhood the Pisanis moved often, mainly in Western Europe, and she became fluent in Spanish and French. When she was 15 she visited a school friend who lived in Hong Kong (then a British territory). "I absolutely loved it," she told Lucy Knight for the *New Statesman* (August 11, 2008, on-line). "Up until that point home had been wherever we were living but here was my first sense of foreignness. I was taken with the idea that there was a quarter of humanity in one country [China] and that I couldn't communicate with them." Also while in Hong Kong she "discovered that everyone has something interesting to say," she wrote in her book, and she became "hooked on Asia, hooked on nightclubs and girlie bars, hooked on chatting to anyone who would chat." For a time the Pisanis lived in England, where Elizabeth attended a sixth-form college (analogous to an academically rigorous U.S. high school) for students ages 16–19 in Richmond, a London suburb.

For a year between high school and college, starting in about 1981, Pisani worked for a fashion-advertising agency in New York City. It was then that the public began hearing about a never-before diagnosed disease, called GRID, or Gay Related Immune Deficiency. (It was renamed AIDS in 1982 after scientists and lawmakers discovered that the disease was not exclusive to the gay community.) "Within a year, GRIDS had worked its way into New York's consciousness," Pisani wrote. "Cafés grew hushed when yet another skeletal figure shuffled in. Drinks with friends in the city's gay bars were often interrupted by volunteers from the Gay Men's Health Crisis, handing out leaflets and condoms."

Pisani next enrolled at Oxford University, England, where she studied classical Chinese and became fluent in Mandarin Chinese. She earned an M.A. degree in 1986. (Since then her proficiency in Mandarin has waned. "I can speak it when it comes to discussing the contraction of AIDS but then I'll have trouble remembering the word for spoon," she told Knight.) After her graduation Pisani traveled in China and Tibet and settled in Hong Kong for a time. In 1987 she joined the news agency Reuters as a foreign correspondent. She was posted to Reuters bureaus in Hong Kong, New Delhi, India, and Jakarta, Indonesia, and was sent to cover stories not only in Asia but in Latin America as well. She also wrote regularly for the *Economist* and contributed articles to the *International Herald Tribune* and the *Financial Times*. The many topics and events she wrote about included the Indonesian stock market, Hong Kong nightclubs, and wars of liberation. She was among the few foreign journalists present in Tiananmen Square, in Beijing, China, in the early-morning hours of June 4, 1989, when Chinese troops attacked pro-democracy protesters.

While with Reuters Pisani became interested in the politics of population control, an important issue in India, China, and other Asian nations. In 1993 she quit her job and, having followed a boyfriend who had moved to London (David Fox, whom she married in 1998), enrolled at the London School of Hygiene and Tropical Medicine; known informally as the London School, it is a college of the University of London. She concentrated on medical demography—the study of population dynamics and their influence on public-health problems—and became fascinated with epidemiology, the study of the many factors affecting the health of populations: everything from the spread of disease through contaminated water, air pollutants, or insect bites and malnutrition to dangerous working conditions and unsafe toys. "The more I thought about it, the more I liked epidemiology," Pisani wrote. "It's actually not unlike investigative journalism. You need to ask the right questions of the right people. You need to record the answers carefully, analyse them correctly and interpret them sensibly, and in context. And you have to communicate the results clearly to people who might do something about them." More specifically, she was drawn to the study of HIV/AIDS. "AIDS didn't make it to the London School of Hygiene's curriculum until I was there, in 1994," she wrote. "By then we knew that almost all HIV-infected adults got their infection when having anal or vaginal sex, or while injecting drugs with shared needles. . . . Sex, drugs and plenty of squeamish politicians. AIDS was the disease for me."

Pisani earned an M.S. degree in medical demography in 1994. In 1995 she returned to journalism, to work for the newly launched newspaper *Asia Times*, based in Bangkok, Thailand. Pisani served as the bureau chief for Indochina, covering Vietnam, Cambodia, and Laos, with an office in Hanoi, Vietnam. In 1996, while still with *Asia Times*, she was hired as a consultant writer by the United Nations Joint Programme on HIV/AIDS—UNAIDS—based in Geneva. UNAIDS was launched in January 1996 in an effort to accelerate, coordinate, and expand the global response to the HIV/AIDS pandemic. Its partners, or co-sponsors, are the World Health Organization (WHO), the International Labour Organization, the World Food Programme (all

three are U.N. agencies), the U.N. Refugee Agency, the U.N. Children's Fund (UNICEF), the U.N. Development Programme, the U.N. Population Fund, the U.N. Office on Drugs and Crime, the U.N. Educational, Scientific and Cultural Organization (UNESCO), and the World Bank.

AIDS is caused by the human immunodeficiency virus (HIV), which attacks the immune system and leaves the body susceptible to infection. AIDS is the final stage of an HIV infection—when the immune system has been so badly damaged that it can no longer fight infections. Generally, people develop AIDS symptoms about 10 years after they are infected with HIV. The virus is transmitted through direct contact of a mucous membrane or the bloodstream with a bodily fluid containing HIV, including blood, semen, vaginal fluid, or breast milk; it can occur during unprotected anal, vaginal, or oral sex, while using a contaminated hypodermic needle, and through blood transfusion. Mothers can pass HIV to their babies during pregnancy, childbirth, or breastfeeding.

Pisani's work for UNAIDS involved preparing reports that emphasized the importance of addressing the spread of HIV/AIDS and acquiring funds from governments and nongovernmental sources for that purpose. Pisani wrote the first two editions of UNAIDS' biennial report on the AIDS pandemic. She admitted in her book that a common practice among UNAIDS consultants was "beating up" the story, or exaggerating the severity of the situation. "We weren't making anything up," she wrote. "But once we got the [statistics], we were certainly presenting them in their worst light. We did it consciously. I think all of us at that time thought the beat-ups were more than justified, they were necessary. We were pretty certain that neither donors nor governments would care about HIV unless we could show that it threatened the 'general population.'" The reports of Pisani and her colleagues tried to convince politicians that AIDS was endangering innocent civilians rather than "wicked" people—drug users and prostitutes. "All the evidence . . . suggested that governments don't like spending money on sex workers, gay men or drug addicts. . . . There are no votes in being nice to a drug addict," she wrote. In order to secure government support, "AIDS couldn't be about sex and drugs. So suddenly it had to be about development, and gender."

In 2001 Pisani took a job in HIV surveillance with Family Health International, which was working with the Indonesian government. (She is fluent in Bahasa Indonesian, Indonesia's official language.) Her assignment involved determining how many people were infected with HIV among Indonesia's most at-risk populations. Such work involved late-night visits to remote railway stations to talk to people who injected illicit drugs into their bloodstreams—"injecting drug users," as they are known—and trips to red-light districts to interview prostitutes, waria (males who dress and live like women and sell sex to men), soldiers, sailors, and civil servants about their sexual habits. Pisani also worked for the ministries of health in China, East Timor, and the Philippines and conducted HIV policy research for WHO and UNAIDS. She quit her job in 2005. "I was like, I didn't need to do this job anymore because everyone knows what I'm going to say. Even though nothing changes," she told Prodita Sabarini for the *Jakarta Post* (November 23, 2008, on-line). Pisani completed her Ph.D. in infectious-disease epidemiology at the London School in 2006; her dissertation was entitled "Back to Basics: Putting the Epidemiology Back into Planning and Monitoring HIV Prevention Programmes: Case Studies in Indonesia."

The next year Pisani became a consultant for the Wellcome Trust, a London-based, global charitable organization that supports biomedical research and activities "with the ultimate aim of protecting and improving human and animal health," according to its Web site. Around that time Pisani decided to write a book that would detail her experiences in Asia, sum up her criticisms of the global response to HIV/AIDS, and channel for the good of others the frustration and despair she had felt in the field. Written in only three months, *The Wisdom of Whores* was published in 2008 by W.W. Norton. The title refers to Pisani's realization that many of the Asian sex workers she met knew more about HIV/AIDS prevention and transmission than many bureaucrats and people with power.

According to Pisani, many of the billions of dollars that have been spent to combat HIV/AIDS have been wasted on misguided programs and policies. One of the most persistent myths about AIDS, she has repeatedly said, is that everyone is at risk of contracting HIV, but that is true only in Africa, particularly sub-Saharan Africa. Everywhere else, AIDS "is confined to sections of society where there are clearly defined risk factors," she told Rosita Bolad for the *Irish Times* (May 16, 2008). "But governments generally aren't that keen to be seen to be spending tax money on drug injectors and sex workers and gay guys—these aren't hugely politically popular. So it's much easier to peddle the myth that everybody is at risk and that way, you can spend money on pregnant women and schoolchildren and other more popular groups and feel like you are addressing the problem, when in fact you are not."

Pisani and many of her colleagues have advocated a simple and relatively cheap solution to slow or stop the spread of HIV: provide the most at-risk populations (injecting drug users, gay men, sex workers and their clients) with clean needles and condoms. Every major study of needle-exchange programs has shown that such programs cut transmission of HIV and other viruses and do not increase the prevalence of drug use. Moreover, many studies have shown that condoms are 80 to 90 percent effective in preventing HIV transmission; among couples in which one partner is HIV positive and the other is not infected, the correct and consistent use of latex condoms results in an infec-

tion rate below one percent per year. Nevertheless, in most countries those who urge the distribution of clean needles among drug users and condoms among prostitutes have been stymied because of religious beliefs, pervasive ideas regarding morality, and—in democratic nations—politicians who would rather remain popular with their constituents than support controversial programs. "The science tells us, for example, that making clean needles universally available to drug injectors can more or less wipe out HIV transmission in this group," Pisani wrote in an opinion piece for CNN.com (April 6, 2010). "The ideology tells us that providing such services for injectors is tantamount to condoning an illegal behavior that wrecks lives and families and increases crime. If you were running for election, faced with the choice of paying for clean needles and health services for injectors or with putting more cops on the streets and cells in the jails, which do you think would play best with the voters?"

Pisani has also charged that many HIV/AIDS programs and organizations have focused too much on treatment of people infected with HIV and not enough on preventive measures. In recent years antiretroviral therapies have maintained the well-being of many HIV-infected people who in the past would have succumbed to AIDS. Antiretroviral drugs (ARVs) suppress the replication of HIV in the body and reduce the viral load—that is, the quantity of the virus in the infected person's blood—thus delaying or even preventing the onset of AIDS. Pisani told Vicky Allan for the *Sunday Herald Magazine* (May 4, 2008), a Scottish periodical, "There aren't all these people with these whole clusters of symptoms that are in your face. It used to be that someone would shuffle into a bar with black blotches all over their face and you'd think, 'Oh, there's another one.' There were 10 years where it was a very visible thing and it has ceased to be so in developed countries." In *The Wisdom of Whores* she wrote, "Treatment makes HIV much, much less scary, because it makes it less fatal. There are fewer cadaverous people around, fewer funerals to go to. With treatment, people who were at death's door leap up and march back to the office and the nightclub." For that reason the advent of ARVs has a downside, because while the drugs lower the risk of transmitting the virus, many people have forgotten or choose to ignore the fact that they do not remove that risk entirely.

The gay community in San Francisco, California, illustrates that problem. By 1985, with the AIDS crisis becoming more acute, condom use among gay men in San Francisco rose from virtually zero to 70 percent. Condom use remained at that level until 1994, around the time that ARVs were introduced. By 2001, researchers found, half of the HIV-positive men within the community no longer used condoms, and of those men, a third were not using condoms even if their partners were HIV-negative or did not know if they were infected. In 1999 the rate of new HIV infections tripled. (Similar patterns were recorded in London, England; Amsterdam, the Netherlands; and Vancouver, Canada.) ARVs keep people "alive longer, and healthy enough to want to have sex," Pisani explained to Decca Aitkenhead for the London *Guardian* (May 13, 2008). "You only have to look at the experience of the UK or US gay communities where we've had more or less universal access to ARVs for at least eight or nine years, and the number of new infections are rising. More people are living longer with HIV, and there is what we call behavioural disinhibition: '[Forget] the condoms, I don't need them any more, because if he's positive he'll be on drugs, so he probably won't infect me. And if I do get infected, it would be annoying, but not the end of the world.'" Pisani added, "Yes, it's great that all this stuff on treatment is happening. But it becomes all the more urgent to have effective prevention. And that's not happening."

The situation in Africa is very different, but social scientists often ignore that difference, according to Pisani, for fear that they will be labeled racist. "Essentially there are two epidemics in the world," she explained to Terry Gross for the National Public Radio program *Fresh Air* (June 10, 2008). "One is . . . in east and southern Africa particularly. And one is in all of the rest of the world. . . . In most of the world HIV is spread mostly in behaviors that are fairly well defined as high risk, and that is: among people who buy and sell sex, among gay men who have many partners, and among people who inject drugs. In Africa, because of different patterns of sexual behavior, HIV spreads among men and women in the general population." Although Africans and people outside Africa may have the same total number of sexual partners in their lifetimes, non-Africans generally have a series of monogamous relationships ("sex in strings," as Pisani puts it), while Africans—both males and females—are more likely to have two or three partners at once ("sex in nets"). The crucial factor when it comes to transmission of the AIDS virus is that HIV is highly infectious, and most contagious, during the two or three months immediately following a new infection. After that period, thanks to the production of antibodies, the newly infected person is less likely to infect another person. "So the likelihood that you spread HIV essentially depends on how many partners you have in that very infectious period," Pisani told Gross.

In the African nations that have openly addressed their citizens' penchant for extramarital sex and concurrent, multiple sexual partners, and have promoted the use of condoms and assisted in their distribution, the occurrence of new HIV infection has dropped dramatically. Authorities in Senegal, in West Africa, took such action when HIV prevalence was low, and in 2006 fewer than 2 percent of adults in that country were infected. Similarly, in Uganda, in east-central Africa, HIV prevalence peaked at around 15 percent in 1991 and was down to 7 percent by 2006. Those nations are the exceptions. More commonly, according to Pisani, AIDS organizations working in Africa and many African leaders have tended to ignore patterns of sexual behavior and instead talk about the spread of HIV/AIDS as a problem stemming from poverty and insufficient economic development. But there is evidence that refutes such assertions. In 2008 the central African nation of Niger ranked 163d in per capita income among 168 nations, and India's neighbor Bangladesh ranked 144th, but in those countries, according to the World Bank, fewer than 1 percent of adults are infected with HIV. By contrast, in the southern African nation of Botswana, which ranked 51st—higher than any other African country—the rate of HIV infection is 24 percent.

The Republic of South Africa, which ranks second in per capita income behind Botswana among Africa's 52 nations but whose gross domestic product is the highest on that continent, is home to the world's largest population of people infected with HIV: 5.7 million in 2007. Thabo Mbeki, who served as president of South Africa from 1999 to 2008, and his health minister, Manto Tshabalala-Msimang, were notorious for openly casting doubt on the causes of AIDS; Tshabalala-Msimang advised people to avoid taking ARVs and to eat foods including garlic and beetroot to treat HIV infection. "You don't need to dream up complex economic formulae to explain why HIV prevention in Africa is failing," Pisani wrote in *The Wisdom of Whores*. "Look at the leadership."

In 2003 the administration of President George W. Bush initiated the President's Emergency Plan for AIDS Relief (PEPFAR), committing $15 billion from the U.S. over five years to fight the HIV/AIDS pandemic, with most of the funding allocated for treatment. PEPFAR has greatly increased the amount of ARVs available to HIV-infected Africans, but Pisani and others have criticized it for its moral agenda: one-third of the program's HIV-prevention money was specifically dedicated to programs that promoted abstinence until marriage, and all organizations and governments that received PEPFAR funding were banned from using any of the money for needle-exchange programs and were required to sign an "anti-prostitution pledge." Those who sign such pledges, Pisani explained to Terry Gross, agree not to "recognize commercial sex as an industry or a legitimate activity" or to "engage in anything that promotes commercial sex or recognizes it in any way." Thus, no PEPFAR funds may be used to distribute condoms in brothels or for any other purposes aimed at preventing HIV infection among those prostitutes and their clients. (Except for the anti-prostitution pledge, those requirements were lifted when PEPFAR was renewed in 2008.) "It fills me with rage that the same people who will not spend a couple of cents on clean needles are perfectly happy to spend thousands of dollars on expensive and toxic antiretroviral drugs," Pisani told Brian Hutchinson for the *Canadian National Post* (June 14, 2008). "'I won't give you the means to avoid infection, but once you do become infected, I'll come over all compassionate and care for you.' That pisses me off."

Ternyata, the consulting firm Pisani founded in 2010, provides training in infectious-disease epidemiology, surveillance methods, data management and analysis, and other vital skills. Pisani serves as a senior adviser to Wellcome Trust on matters related to public-health research in developing countries. She is an honorary senior lecturer at the London School. In 2010 she was a featured speaker at the TED Conference (named for the increasing convergence of technology, entertainment, and design), held in Long Beach, California. (In June 2010 a video of her talk was posted on her Web site, wisdomofwhores.com.) She has also lectured at institutions including Harvard University, the Massachusetts Institute of Technology, the University of Oxford, and the Royal Tropical Institute, in Amsterdam.

"Behind all the sex and drugs talk, I'm just a giant data nerd," Pisani has said. Pisani, who is divorced, lives in London. In her free time she enjoys sea kayaking.

—M.A.S.

Suggested Reading: (London) *Guardian* p10 May 13, 2008; *New Statesman* (on-line) Aug. 11, 2008; (Scotland) *Sunday Herald Magazine* p14 May 4, 2008; wisdomofwhores.com; Pisani, Elizabeth. *The Wisdom of Whores: Bureaucrats, Brothels and the Business of AIDS*, 2008

Selected Books: *The Wisdom of Whores: Bureaucrats, Brothels and the Business of AIDS*, 2008

Ethan Miller/Getty Images

Podesta, John D.

Jan. 8, 1949– Organization official; former government official

Address: Center for American Progress, 1333 H. St., N.W., 10th Fl., Washington, DC 20005

John Podesta is the president and chief executive officer of the Center for American Progress (CAP), the liberal think tank he founded in 2003 with the aim of countering the policies of the George W. Bush administration and the work of CAP's counterpart on the right, the Heritage Foundation. With a staff of more than 200, CAP has worked to influence the public debate over issues including health care and the environment. A political veteran, Podesta served in the Bill Clinton White House as, successively, staff secretary, deputy chief of staff, and chief of staff—positions in which he found himself in charge of damage control amid scandals ranging from the Whitewater investigation to the Monica Lewinsky affair. Since the election of Democratic president Barack Obama, CAP has played an influential role in crafting liberal policy positions and designing programs to address the many challenges facing the nation and the world, in areas including economic stimulus, financial regulation, sustainable energy, health-care reform, immigration reform, and international affairs. During the congressional debates over the health-care reform bill in the winter of 2009, as some liberal Democrats joined Republicans in opposing the bill because of the many compromises made in order to prevent its defeat, Podesta was among those who continued to push for its passage. In one of his current projects, he is working with Al Gore, the vice president of the U.S. under Bill Clinton, and Reed E. Hundt, the head of the Federal Communications Commission for several years during the Clinton administration, to come up with ways to make clean energy more affordable and desirable than continued reliance on carbon and other fossil fuels.

John David Podesta was born on January 8, 1949 in Chicago, Illinois. He is the grandson of Italian and Greek immigrants, and his family was both working-class and staunchly Democratic. His father, John Podesta, who left high school after his first year to help support his family, operated a cutting machine in a factory during Podesta's youth; his mother, Mary (Kokoris) Podesta, worked nights for an insurance company. The family, which included Podesta's older brother, Anthony, lived in northwest Chicago. "I was a blue-collar, hang-out-on-the-street-corner kind of kid," Podesta told Katharine Q. Seelye for the *New York Times* (July 2, 2001). Podesta earned his undergraduate degree in psychology from Knox College, in Galesburg, Illinois, in 1971. During his college years he was a member of the student senate, a participant in the student movement against the Vietnam War, and a volunteer for the presidential campaign of Eugene McCarthy. He received his law degree from Georgetown University Law Center in 1976.

In 1970 Podesta was a campaign worker for Joseph Duffy, who ran unsuccessfully for a seat in the U.S. Senate. During that campaign Podesta met and worked alongside Bill Clinton. In 1972 Podesta worked for the campaign of U.S. senator George McGovern of South Dakota, that year's Democratic presidential nominee, who lost in a landslide to the incumbent, Richard Nixon. In the years after he earned his law degree, Podesta worked as a trial attorney in the U.S. Justice Department's Land and Natural Resources Division and as the special assistant to the director of the federally run volunteer agency ACTION. In the late 1970s and 1980s, he forged a career as a congressional staffer, occupying a number of positions on Capitol Hill. He was the chief minority counsel for the Senate Judiciary subcommittees on patents, copyrights, and trademarks; security and terrorism; and regulatory reform. From 1979 to 1981 he served as counsel on the majority staff of the Senate Judiciary Committee, and from 1987 to 1988 he was the chief counsel for the Senate Agriculture Committee. In the latter year he directed opposition research for Michael Dukakis, the Democratic presidential nominee.

Also in 1988 Podesta and his brother founded Podesta and Associates (now known as the Podesta Group), a Washington, D.C.–based consulting firm specializing in technology, government relations, and public affairs. Podesta worked from 1988 to 1993 as the firm's president and general counsel. He served in the 1990s as a member of the council of the Administrative Conference of the United States and on the United States Commission on Protecting and Reducing Government Secrecy.

In 1993 the newly elected Democratic president, Bill Clinton, recruited Podesta as his staff secretary, a position in which he was responsible for overseeing the paper flow between the president's office and those of his advisers. Podesta's official duty was to see to it that the president heard all advisers' relevant views on a given topic and that documents were suitable to be shown to the president; he also made sure that all public statements and actions being considered were consistent with the administration's policies. In practice, however, Podesta became what John F. Harris described for the *Washington Post* (December 19, 1996) as "the administration's designated 'cleanup man,'" responsible for coordinating the White House's responses to controversies or scandals that arose. Working in that capacity, Podesta, despite his well-known preference for operating behind the

scenes, soon became a fixture in the political media, making regular appearances on the Sunday-morning political talk shows.

The first controversy Podesta had to handle, known as "Travelgate," erupted in May 1993, when seven longtime employees of the White House Travel Office were fired after a brief investigation by the FBI, and a number of friends and associates of the Clintons were hired in their places. While the Clintons claimed that the employees had been fired due to financial improprieties, critics accused them of practicing patronage. Podesta investigated the episode and wrote a report that revealed, to the displeasure of First Lady Hillary Clinton, that she had closely monitored the decisions that led to the firings. (Following heavy media attention given to the controversy, the Clintons rehired most of the employees. Investigations that took place over the next several years led to embezzlement charges against the travel-office director, Billy Dale, of which he was eventually acquitted.) Podesta also served as the White House spokesman regarding the investigations of the Whitewater controversy, the basis of which was a real-estate and land-development venture—the Whitewater Development Corp.—involving Bill and Hillary Clinton and their friends James and Susan McDougal in the 1970s and 1980s. In January 1994 Attorney General Janet Reno appointed an independent counsel, Robert B. Fiske Jr., to investigate the Clintons' political and financial relationship with the McDougals, who were convicted in 1996 of fraud in relation to the Whitewater deal. The investigation, later taken over by Kenneth Starr, also came to encompass the Clintons' actions during the independent counsel's probe as well as many other matters. Podesta assembled and headed a "Whitewater control team," which coordinated the White House's responses to the allegations. Though Starr's investigation continued until 1998, the Clintons were never charged with a crime with regard to Whitewater. Podesta was subpoenaed to testify before a grand jury regarding both the Travelgate and Whitewater matters but was not implicated in either affair.

In 1995 Podesta left the Clinton White House to join the faculty of his alma mater, Georgetown University Law Center. He also returned to his position with Podesta Associates and worked as counsel for Democratic Senate minority leader Tom Daschle. Following Clinton's successful reelection bid, in 1996, the president selected Podesta as one of his two deputy chiefs of staff. (The other was Sylvia Mathews.) Working under Clinton's chief of staff, Erskine Bowles, who was known to delegate many duties, Podesta had to immerse himself in a wide array of issues, from NATO expansion to government policy regarding encryption, the process of converting information into code for security purposes. Podesta told Chris Bury for *Frontline* (September 2000, on-line) that one of Clinton's greatest accomplishments during that time was the passage of legislation for a child health-insurance program, a bill that congressional Republicans had long opposed.

In January 1998 Clinton was questioned before a grand jury about his relationship with Paula Jones and other women, as part of a sexual-harassment lawsuit filed by Jones in May 1994—a case that came to involve accusations that Clinton had lied about an extramarital affair with Monica Lewinsky, a onetime White House intern. In his now-infamous testimony, Clinton alleged that he had never had "sexual relations" with Lewinsky. Reports about the alleged relationship had surfaced in the mainstream press the same month, and the president repeated his forceful denial in a White House press conference. Taking Clinton's word that the allegations were false, Podesta began working with a team of advisers to address the situation publicly. In February 1998 Podesta was one of many staffers subpoenaed to testify before a grand jury about the relationship between Clinton and Lewinsky. In three different testimonies Podesta stated that in 1997, at the request of Clinton's personal secretary, Betty Currie, Podesta had asked Bill Richardson—then a U.S. ambassador to the U.N.—to consider Lewinsky for a position. Podesta also said that he had been involved in strategy deliberations after the scandal came to light, claims that were consistent with Clinton's testimony.

In August 1998, after Starr obtained testimony from Lewinsky and DNA evidence that confirmed the affair, Clinton admitted to having had "an improper physical relationship" with Lewinsky. Podesta told Bury that, like the rest of Clinton's staff, he was deeply disappointed in the president's actions but felt that it was "a situation in which we needed to pull up our socks and move on, and that's what we did." Podesta also told Bury that he felt Clinton's televised speech to the nation about the Lewinsky affair should have been more conciliatory. "I think he was still dealing with anger about the way this whole independent counsel matter had taken," he told Bury. "He was dealing with the anger of what he thought, and I think, was a politically motivated lawsuit, which was at the underpinning of this—the Paula Jones case—and which was thrown out." In October 1998, when Starr publicly released the report that included detailed accounts of each of the president's encounters with Lewinsky, Podesta was one of the most visible and vocal advocates for Clinton. He represented the White House in a number of interviews, explaining the legal implications of the Starr reports. "I got to sit in the dunking tank while your colleagues threw baseballs at me," he quipped to Bury. Explaining what made the Lewinsky scandal so difficult to handle, he said, "From a press perspective, we were constantly battling with the fact that it was difficult to talk about anything else or that Washington's attention was totally focused on the Lewinsky matter in early 1998 and then, of course, into the fall. I think that one of the reasons that the American public stuck with the president was that he and we were able to keep our focus on

the people's business. He was able to . . . keep working on the issues that were important to the public." Podesta noted that during the period in which he was being investigated by Starr, Clinton negotiated a free-trade agreement with China, continued his work on a balanced budget, negotiated a peace agreement between the Republic of Ireland and Northern Ireland, and delivered a well-received State of the Union address.

In early October 1998 Bowles announced that he would step down from his position as White House chief of staff, and on October 20 Clinton named Podesta as his successor. In that post Podesta directed all policy development and staff activity at the White House as well as the executive branch's dealings with Congress. In the run-up to the 1998 congressional elections, Podesta worked to reinvigorate the party and strengthen the White House's ties to members of the House and Senate. In the November elections, to the surprise of many party leaders, Democrats gained five seats in the House. Podesta interpreted those gains to be an expression of the public's desire to move beyond the Lewinsky scandal and deal with more pressing issues. Congress did, however, pursue impeachment hearings that fall, to decide whether to bring charges of perjury, obstruction of justice, and abuse of power against the president. (In addition to lying under oath, Clinton was charged with asking Lewinsky to lie to investigators.) Clinton was impeached by the House of Representatives on December 19, 1998 but was acquitted by the Senate on February 12, 1999. Both votes were divided for the most part along party lines.

Clinton managed to maintain high approval ratings during the last year of his presidency among the public despite the politically divisive atmosphere in Washington. Many attributed that to Podesta's ability to oversee an array of complex issues and communicate the president's policy messages amidst the media frenzy. In the last six months of Clinton's presidency, in the hope of achieving Democratic victories in the November 2000 elections, Podesta and his staff made a concerted effort to challenge congressional Republicans in policy areas in which Clinton felt that their views contrasted with those of most of the American public, such as the $792 billion tax cut proposed by Republicans that summer, which Democrats considered irresponsibly large. "With the primaries coming to an end and the nominations being settled, we have an opportunity now to press our case for action," Podesta said in an interview quoted by the Washington Post (March 16, 2000). "We're still hopeful that on a number of fronts we can accomplish some important things." Despite Podesta's efforts, the 2000 elections saw Republican gains in both the legislative branch and the executive branch: Texas governor George W. Bush became the 43d president of the United States.

On March 2, 2001 Podesta and other former Clinton aides testified before a panel as part of an investigation by the House Government Reform

Committee of the 140 pardons and 36 sentence commutations that Clinton issued on January 20, 2001, his last day in office. Many of the pardons were criticized by members of both parties, because they gave the appearance of having been granted in exchange for gifts or donations. One of the most controversial pardons was that of Marc Rich, who had been living as a fugitive in Switzerland since his 1983 indictment for tax evasion and fraud and whose wife, Denise, had contributed $450,000 to Clinton's presidential library and $7,375 worth of furniture to the Clintons. Podesta testified that he had strongly advised Clinton against granting several of the pardons but did not know of any pardons that had been issued in exchange for contributions. A day before his testimony, Podesta expressed his hope that the controversy, which had become known as "Pardongate," would not cloud the public's overall view of the Clinton administration. "We're looking at this giant tree [of pardons] and missing the forest," Podesta told John F. Harris for the *Washington Post* (March 1, 2001), "which is that Clinton never governed for the wealthy and special interests."

In February 2001 Podesta rejoined the faculty of the Georgetown University Law Center, where he helped launch the school's Center on Law and Technology. Podesta, who had had a longtime passion for environmental issues, also took a position that year on the board of directors of the League of Conservation Voters, one of the nation's most politically active environmental-lobbying groups. He promised to engage in aggressive political action to prevent the Bush administration from undoing the accomplishments with regard to the environment that he had helped bring about under Clinton.

In the wake of the 2002 elections, which made the Democrats the minority party in both the House and the Senate, Podesta decided that progressive Democrats needed to establish a think tank that could successfully challenge the Heritage Foundation, a prominent conservative think tank, and create a new generation of spokespeople for the liberal agenda. In 2003 Podesta founded the Center for American Progress, an organization made up of scholars, policy experts, bloggers, and others, whose aim is to develop, promote, and defend progressive policy ideas and counter the agenda of conservatives. Over the next five years, CAP became one of the most vocal critics of the Bush administration and a leader in researching and promoting the liberal policy agenda.

In March 2007 Podesta testified before the House Judiciary Subcommittee on Commercial and Administrative Law on the subject of how to ensure executive-branch accountability in light of the revelation that Attorney General Alberto Gonzalez had fired U.S. attorneys allegedly because of their political leanings. Podesta identified Gonzalez's actions as an example of "the larger campaign that has occupied the Bush administration from the moment the president took office: to increase the power of the executive at the expense of other branches of government," as quoted in a CAP news release (March 29, 2007). He further pointed out that "the greater the power that the White House accumulates, the greater is the need for congressional access to White House documents and personnel."

In March 2008, during the Democratic presidential primaries (Republican U.S. senator John McCain of Arizona had secured enough delegates earlier that month to be his party's presumptive nominee), CAP launched the Hyde Park Project, an effort to create "a mandate for progressive action" in the key policy issues of health care, economic mobility, national security, and climate change. One aspect of the project is the Wonk Room, a rapid-response policy blog, on which CAP bloggers can respond quickly to policy issues that come up in public debate. The Hyde Park Project also disseminates content to radio stations and publishes an e-newsletter, the *Progress Report*; sponsors some 60 liberal American college newspapers; and commissions new academic analyses and studies that support progressive policy.

Podesta supported Hillary Rodham Clinton, then a U.S. senator from New York, in the Democratic primaries, but shifted his support to Senator Barack Obama of Illinois after June 3, 2008, when Obama secured enough delegate votes to be the presumptive Democratic nominee. In September 2008, at Obama's request, Podesta created a transition board, composed of many former members of the Clinton administration, and began a full-scale review of the federal government, compiling lists of potential members of an Obama administration. By the time Obama was elected the 44th president of the United States, in the historic election of November 4, 2008, separate policy groups within Podesta's transition board had already begun extensively evaluating various issues that would be of vital importance as soon as Obama entered the Oval Office. On November 5, 2008 Obama named Podesta co-chairman of his transition team, along with Obama's longtime advisers Valerie Jarrett and Pete Rouse.

In 2009 CAP's experts published the findings of numerous studies in reports that promoted liberal policy solutions to the nation's problems. Environmental policy has been a main focus of CAP's. In June 2009, four months after Obama signed into law the American Recovery and Reinvestment Act of 2009, which provided abundant funding for "green-collar" jobs, CAP—along with the Political Economy Research Institute (PERI) of the University of Massachusetts—released a study estimating that, as quoted in the *New York Times* (June 18, 2009, on-line), "a $150 billion investment in clean energy could create a net increase of 1.7 million American jobs and significantly lower the national unemployment rate." Later that year CAP released the results of another study that received a lot of attention, one about the changing societal roles of women, produced in conjunction with Maria Shriver, a journalist and California's First Lady. The study, titled "The Shriver Report: A Woman's Nation Changes Everything," revealed that in 2009, for the first time in history, American women constituted half of the country's work force—but that businesses, government agencies, religious institutions, and other segments of American society had yet to adjust to accommodate the new reality. (For example, as Podesta noted in the preface to the report, "schools still let kids out in the afternoon, long before the workday ends, and they shut their doors for three months during the summer, even though the majority of families with children are supported by a single working parent or a dual-earning couple.") Podesta wrote, "At one level, everything has changed. And yet so much more change is needed." CAP has also been a major supporter of reform during the congressional health-care debates, regularly posting on its Web site articles explaining aspects of the debate and recommending solutions. On December 24, 2009, the day the U.S. Senate passed its version of a health-care reform bill, Podesta wrote for the CAP Web site, "It is critical that a final bill ensures that the subsidies provided are sufficient to make insurance truly affordable for working families. But if enacted, health reform along the lines of what the House and Senate have passed will represent the most historic reform of our health care system in the more than 40 years that I have been in politics. We still have a way to go, but today's passage represents a major step forward."

Known for his intensity, sardonic wit, and moodiness, Podesta earned the nickname "Skippy" from his colleagues in the Clinton administration for the days when he seemed to them to have been replaced by his more grumpy twin. He is a fan of science fiction and roller coasters and harbors what some have described as an "obsession" with UFOs as well as the science-fiction television show *X-Files*. Podesta is both a marathon runner and a cooking enthusiast; he once wrote a monthly cooking column for a Washington magazine. Podesta and his wife of 31 years, the former Mary Spieczny, have three grown children—Megan Rouse, Mae, and Gabriel—and two grandchildren.

—M.R.M.

Suggested Reading: pbs.org Sep. 2000; *New York Times* A p10 July 2, 2001, P p3 Nov. 6, 2008, A p22 Nov. 7, 2008; *Washington Post* A p25 Dec. 19, 1996, A p6 Mar. 16, 2000, A p2 Mar. 1, 2001

Prokhorov, Mikhail

(PRO-hor-ov)

May 3, 1965– Russian financier

Address: Nets Sports & Entertainment, 390 Murray Hill Pkwy., East Rutherford, NJ 07073

When the Russian entrepreneur Mikhail Prokhorov announced in the fall of 2009 that he wanted to become the principal owner of the New Jersey Nets of the National Basketball Association (NBA), Michael Idov wrote for *New York* (June 7, 2010), "he leaped into the city's collective consciousness with a speed unusual for any foreigner, let alone a Russian. The Nets are not a trophy skyscraper, whose ownership ultimately matters only to the kind of people who keep track of trophy skyscrapers. They are a ticket to instant popular-culture importance. By becoming the first foreign owner of an NBA team, Prokhorov simultaneously established himself as a major figure in one of the world's most glamorous businesses (in the world capital of the sport, no less) and a central player in New York's biggest real-estate drama after ground zero."

"I never accept the risk I can't control," Prokhorov told Anita Raghavan for *Forbes* (March 30, 2009). A year later *Forbes* noted that with a net worth of $13.4 billion, Prokhorov ranked 39th on the magazine's list of the world's richest people; in May 2010 the *New York Times* reported that his fortune totaled an estimated $17.8 billion. Pro-

Mike Stobe/Getty Images

khorov himself has claimed ignorance of the exact amount. "I'm lucky to have enough money to be really independent," he told Steve Kroft, who interviewed him for the March 28, 2010 installment of the CBS-TV newsmagazine *60 Minutes*. But, he added, he has no desire to count his money or think about it; rather, "it's only a side effect of what

I'm doing in business." In terms of acquiring wealth, Prokhorov has often been the right man at the right place at the right time, helped by his inborn drive, management and organizational talents, social skills and charm, abundance of energy, fluency in English, and mastery of international finance—as well as by the enormous changes in his nation's political, economic, and social systems, which transformed Russia from a Communist state into a capitalist nation around the time that he earned his undergraduate degree. Now 45 years old, Prokhorov has also benefited greatly from luck and, in subtle ways, from his commanding height—six feet eight inches.

Prokhorov launched his first, highly profitable business as an undergraduate in Moscow, Russia's capital, selling blue jeans. In 1992, after three years as an employee at a bank run jointly by Communist-led governments, Prokhorov and a partner, Vladimir Potanin, founded their own bank and a venture-capital and investment firm. In 2001 they bought from the Russian government, at a bargain price, Norilsk Nickel, a previously state-run mining and smelting operation that is among the world's largest producers of nickel and palladium and is a leading producer of platinum and copper. Increasingly serious disagreements between Prokhorov and Potanin, and an incident that landed Prokhorov in a French jail for several days in 2007, led the partners to split; soon after Prokhorov sold his shares in Norilsk to Potanin for billions in cash, the worldwide recession led commodity prices to plummet and Norilsk's stock to lose much of its value. Prokhorov's current assets include a nearly 50 percent share in Polyus Gold, Russia's biggest producer of gold and one of the world's top dozen; a major share of UC Rusal, the world's biggest aluminum producer; two banks; an insurance company; a media conglomerate; and a great deal of real estate, including the mansion in which he lives with his older sister, who manages the Mikhail Prokhorov Foundation, which he set up in 2004. Prokhorov is well known in Russia as an adventurous, sports-loving bachelor who regularly hosts lavish parties at resorts and restaurants, where his guests invariably include beautiful women. "I don't understand small businesses, only big ones," he told Louise Armitstead for the London *Sunday Times* (July 29, 2007). "Marriage is the hardest small business."

In 2002 Prokhorov bought the basketball team CSKA Moscow; during his six years of ownership, CSKA won the Euroleague championships twice. In May 2010 the owners of the National Basketball Association (NBA) approved Prokhorov's offer of $200 million to acquire an 80 percent share of the New Jersey Nets and a 45 percent share of the Nets' future home, Barclays Center, which—after bitter controversy and several lawsuits—is currently under construction in Brooklyn, New York City, as part of a sports/commercial/residential complex. In an illustration of his newfound prominence in the Big Apple, on May 19, 2010 Prokhorov had breakfast with New York City's mayor, Michael Bloomberg, and the hip-hop artist and entrepreneur Jay-Z, a Brooklyn native who owns a minority stake in the Nets.

The second of two children, Mikhail Dmitrievich Prokhorov was born on May 3, 1965 in Moscow, Russia, in what was then the USSR. His parents were members of a Russian social elite: his father, Dmitry, headed the international-relations department of the Soviet government sports committee; his mother, Tamara, was a chemist, teaching and conducting research at a Moscow university. The family was not rich but lived relatively well in a small Moscow apartment. "Parties were a big part of my growing up," Prokhorov told Louise Armitstead. "Every day my parents had friends around to the house." His father's job required him to take occasional trips to Europe and the U.S. "Dmitry would tell his son tales of life in the West and bring him gifts, including Lee jeans and a Sharp radio/cassette player," Stephanie Baker wrote for Bloomberg.com (March 28, 2010). "The items gave young Prokhorov a cool edge among his peers and a taste for capitalism." Prokhorov told Armitstead that he started playing sports on the street at the age of four. During his childhood his peers nicknamed him "Giraffe." He played basketball at his high school, in Moscow, where many classes were taught in English. He next enrolled at the prestigious Moscow Finance Institute (later renamed the Finance Academy). After a year there he voluntarily joined the Russian army (mandatory conscription had ended by then; it was later reinstated, with new requirements), because, he told Armitstead, he "wanted to experience the hardships of real life."

When Prokhorov completed his military service, he returned to the Finance Institute, where he concentrated on international economic relations and studied capitalism, a subject foreign to most Russians then. Around that time, in the late 1980s, thanks to President Mikhail Gorbachev's introduction of the policy of perestroika ("restructuring"), the citizens of the Soviet Union were gaining more economic and social freedoms. One major change was the lifting of the ban on privately owned businesses. In 1988, while still in college, Prokhorov—after working briefly as a stevedore—started a business himself. He would buy ordinary new jeans, soften and fade them by means of a special process he had acquired, and then sell them as stone-washed jeans. After decades of scarcity of virtually all consumer products within the Soviet Union, there was an extremely high demand for Western goods among Russians at that time—especially for garments as symbolic of hipness and freedom as soft, faded blue jeans. Prokhorov's business thrived; according to Stephanie Baker, the young entrepreneur made a profit of 14 rubles for every ruble he spent. (The ruble was then worth about $6.30 in U.S. currency.) Eventually hundreds of people were working for him. "We got very rich," Prokhorov told Armitstead. "I bought a second-hand Lada [a popular car] and spent my money on girls and parties. It was the last time I felt real joy at having money." When he graduated from the Moscow Finance Institute, in 1989, with a B.S. degree with honors, he bequeathed his jeans business to friends.

Prokhorov next got a job with the International Bank for Economic Cooperation (IBEC), whose members included a dozen Communist countries in Europe and Asia. According to Baker, "He started out as a bond dealer and eventually rose to run the currency department." For his part, Prokhorov told Armitstead, "I spent three years as a clerk, working 14 hours a day finding out about different areas." During that period he met Vladimir Potanin, who had graduated from the Moscow Institute of International Relations in 1983 and had worked since then for the Soviet Union's Ministry of Foreign Trade. Prokhorov soon realized that he and Potanin shared an entrepreneurial spirit and a determination to take advantage of the profound changes afoot in the Russian economy. In 1992—months after the collapse of the Soviet Union—Prokhorov quit his job. With Potanin he then co-founded an investment company, Interros Foreign Trade Association, and also the MFK Bank, which he served as chairman. He lured many of his IBEC clients to do business with the bank. Prokhorov and Potanin, Baker wrote, "complemented each other. Potanin was the public face, the one who schmoozed government officials and often took a lead in business negotiations. Prokhorov was the banker, manager and headhunter for the group." In 1993 Prokhorov and Potanin co-founded a second bank, the United Export/Import Bank, or UNEXIM. UNEXIM later merged with Rosbank Moscow, as a division of the Interros Group.

By the mid-1990s the Russian economy had become mired in a serious depression. In an effort to raise funds, the federal government, under President Boris Yeltsin, introduced a privatization program known in the West as "loans for shares": in return for loans from banks, the banks gained control of shares in state-owned companies. If the government failed to repay a loan by September 1996—as it invariably did—the creditor bank acquired ownership of the shares. According to Baker, in 1995, in what was ostensibly an equal-opportunity auction, Prokhorov and Potanin "lent" the government $170 million in exchange for the right to manage a 38 percent stake in the government-run Norilsk Nickel, in Norilsk, the northernmost city in Siberia. Like many other transactions in the "loans for shares" program, that transaction was rigged. (During the 1990s much of the business activity in Russia was steeped in corruption and lacked transparency. Many of the records from that period are inaccurate, incomplete, or nonexistent; and information disseminated by the Russian media, which with few exceptions is controlled either by the state or by oligarchs, is also generally unreliable.) "Yes, it was rigged," Yulia

Latynina, a leading Russian business journalist, told Steve Kroft. "But it cannot be explained in normal economic terms to an outsider, especially an American." In 1997 Prokhorov and Potanin in effect bought that stake in Norilsk for $250 million—far less than its value; at that time, however, the company was poorly run, with "$2 billion of loans, a cashflow of minus $1 billion a year and six months of unpaid wages," Prokhorov told Armitstead. For the next few years, Prokhorov and Potanin worked successfully to make Norilsk Nickel efficient and profitable, and they oversaw its first public offering. Concurrently, in 1998, Prokhorov became UNEXIM's president while remaining chairman.

In 2000, when Vladimir Putin (a former member of Russia's secret police, the KGB) was elected president of Russia, he told the country's wealthiest men to stay out of politics. Those who did not obey ended up either in exile or in prison. Prokhorov and Potanin heeded Putin's message. They also avoided being murdered, the fate of hundreds of other businessmen in the vicious, amoral competitive environment that existed in Russia then. ("It was Wild West. It was a territory with no sheriff. No rules," Prokhorov told Kroft.) In 2001 Prokhorov became the general director and chairman of the management board at Norilsk Nickel, where in 2003 he also became the chairman of the board of directors. Norilsk was the most valuable holding of Interros, which was making both Prokhorov and Potanin very rich. They each owned approximately 25 percent of Norilsk Nickel. In 2006 Prokhorov also became the chairman of the board of Polyus Gold, of which Interros held many shares. By that point Prokhorov was said to be the 89th richest person in the world. In 2007 he launched a new investment company, ONEXIM Group.

In January 2007 Prokhorov was arrested by police in Courchevel, a ski resort in the French Alps, where he had organized a long weekend for friends. He was charged with flying in prostitutes from Russia for the benefit of his party guests. Prokhorov denied the charges, explaining that the many beautiful women with his group were not call girls. He spent three days in jail, he told Kroft (most sources say four), then was released and cleared of all charges; he also told Kroft that French president Nicolas Sarkozy, who had criticized his behavior, later apologized to him. Media outlets across the world carried the story, reportedly causing Potanin severe discomfort, not least because some Russian government officials ordered him to tell Prokhorov to use better judgment. According to Prokhorov, for some time prior to the Courchevel incident, he and Potanin had repeatedly disagreed regarding their business activities. Afterward, their relations deteriorated further, and in April 2007, at Potanin's request, Prokhorov sold his stake in Norilsk to the oligarch Oleg Deripaska, at that time Russia's wealthiest man. In addition to billions of dollars, Prokhorov gained a stake in the aluminum giant Rusal. The timing of that transaction proved to be extremely fortuitous for Prokhorov: in December 2007 the worldwide recession hit Russia. In less than a year, the value of Norilsk stock fell more than 70 percent. "It's a part of any business to be lucky," Prokhorov told Kroft, calling what had happened, in terms of his financial situation, a "miracle."

Rumors that Prokhorov wanted to purchase an NBA team became public in the summer of 2009. At that time no NBA owners were non-Americans; Steve Kroft noted that "twenty years ago, a Russian would never have been allowed to buy an American sports franchise." David Stern, the commissioner of the NBA, told Kroft, "America is the only place where the question gets asked, 'What about the foreigners?' [Basketball] is a global sport; our games are televised in 215 countries and in 43 languages. So it was really a natural import of globalization." As the NBA's bylaws require, Prokhorov's professional and personal lives underwent investigation. Speaking of Prokhorov to Kroft, Stern said, "I think he's a man who has passed a very tight security check and nobody has come up with any reason why he shouldn't be an NBA owner." In May 2010 the owners of 29 of the 30 NBA teams voted to approve Prokhorov's purchase of an 80 percent share in the New Jersey Nets. (One team did not participate in the vote.) As part of the deal, Prokhorov agreed to take on 80 percent of the Nets' debt—some $207 million—and to cover up to $60 million of the team's future losses. The Nets' minority owners are the rapper and businessman Jay-Z and Bruce Ratner, the real-estate developer who, after a six-year legal battle with local residents who fiercely opposed his plans, is building the Nets' future home in Brooklyn. The construction of the Barclays Center, on a 22-acre site in the Atlantic Yards, in downtown Brooklyn, is scheduled to be finished in 2012. The day the Nets play their first game in that arena will mark the first time since 1957 that any major professional-league team in the U.S. has competed in Brooklyn. Although in recent years the Nets have performed poorly—the team finished the 2009–10 season with 12 wins and 70 losses and both the 2007–08 and 2008–09 seasons with 34 wins and 48 losses—Prokhorov has expressed confidence about its future. "I'm real excited to take the worst team of the league and turn it to be the best," he told Kroft.

In 2008 Prokhorov launched a Russian-language magazine, Internet social network, and television station, all bearing the name "Snob." According to Andrei Schmarov, the project's general manager, in Russia "snob" refers to those who are self-made and therefore, unlike those with inherited wealth, are justified in feeling superior. The targeted readers of the magazine and viewers of the TV shows are successful people and those who hope to become successful. Schmarov told the Moscow Times, according to Lewis Wallace, writing for Wired.com (April 28, 2004), that only about 3,000 professionals "leading a sophisticated way of life"

will be invited to join the Facebook.com-like Snob social network. The magazine Snob is widely available in Russia, and plans are being developed to introduce it in New York, London, and Paris.

Prokhorov heads the Russian Biathlon Union; in that capacity he attended the 2010 Winter Olympics, in Vancouver, Canada. By his own account, he works out two hours daily without fail; his home includes a gym and an indoor swimming pool. He also skis, jet skis, plays basketball, and trains regularly in kickboxing with the coach of the Russian national kickboxing team. "I am addicted to sport," he told Steve Kroft. "Without sport, I feel bad. In this case it's some kind of drug." Most nights Prokhorov enjoys partying, often in private sections of restaurants or clubs. A wine connoisseur who eschews vodka (the Russian national drink), he has claimed that he never gets drunk.

In July 2008 Prokhorov deposited into an escrow account 10 percent of the equivalent of $525 million that he had offered to Lily Safra, the widow of the financier Edmond Safra, for her 20-acre estate on the French Riviera. After the legal time limit set for such contracts, he tried to back out of the deal, but a French court ruled against him and ordered the deposit plus interest to be released to the owner. (Safra, who said she had not planned to sell the property but had found Prokhorov's offer to be irresistible, announced that she would donate the money to 10 charities.)

In 2006 Prokhorov earned Russia's Order of Friendship for his contributions toward the realization of his nation's economic potential. He promotes Russian culture locally and internationally through the Mikhail Prokhorov Foundation, which he set up in 2004. His sister, Irina Prokhorova, who heads the foundation, is an important figure in cultural circles in Russia. A specialist in English and American literature who earned a doctorate in philology, she founded the Moscow publishing house New Literary Observer (NLO) in the early 1990s. NLO organizes scholarly conferences and cultural events. Its publications include a journal with the same name, for which Prokhorova serves as editor in chief; a magazine called Theory of Fashion; and dozens of books of nonfiction and fiction.

—D.K.

Suggested Reading: Bloomberg (on-line) Mar. 28, 2010; CBS-TV 60 Minutes (on-line), Mar. 28, 2010; Economist (on-line) Mar. 15, 2008; Forbes p109+ Mar. 30, 2009; (London) Observer Business p6 Apr. 13, 2008; (London) Sunday Times Business p11+ July 29, 2007; New York p22+ June 7, 2010; New York Times III p1+ July 8, 2007, D p1+ Oct. 19, 2009, (on-line) Sep. 24, 2009; New Yorker (on-line) Sep. 23, 2009

Courtesy of Bernard Purdie

Purdie, Bernard

June 11, 1939– Drummer

Address: Purdie Good Co., P.O. Box 230133, Portland, OR 97281

Bernard "Pretty" Purdie is one of the few who arguably can claim to be, as his Web site calls him, "the world's most recorded drummer." Although the accuracy of his assertion has never been proved, the drummer's presence on dozens of iconic and genre-defining 20th-century songs and albums—works of jazz, soul, pop, rock, and acid jazz—and the myriad studio sessions he took part in during the 1960s, '70s, and '80s certainly place him in the running for that distinction; his Web site notes performances on more than 3,000 albums, among them works by James Brown, Aretha Franklin, Steely Dan, and Louis Armstrong. Purdie told George Kanzler for the Newark, New Jersey, *Star-Ledger* (September 11, 1998) that he has recorded and performed so frequently because "I do it all." "I have never wanted to be categorized, yet I have been all my life," he said. "I've been called a funk drummer, a rock drummer, a soul drummer, an R&B drummer, a Latin drummer, a jazz drummer— but all I've ever wanted to be known as was a drummer, a good, soulful drummer." In addition to his work with others, Purdie has released original studio and live albums over the past few decades, among them *Soul Drums* (1969), *Soul Is . . . Pretty Purdie* (1972), *Soul to Jazz* (1997), and *Purdie Good Cookin'* (2007).

Purdie has a long-established reputation for his near-perfect musical timing and his innovative signature beat, the "Purdie Shuffle," a half-time groove created with six high-hat, bass-drum, and snare-drum tones and augmented with "ghost notes"—accents added by lightly brushing or tapping the snare drum. Purdie has performed his beat, or variations of it, on recordings of many popular songs, including "Home at Last," from the 1977 Steely Dan album, *Aja*. The beat has become a musical standard, one many drummers aspire to duplicate. David Segal wrote for the *New York Times* (March 30, 2009, on-line), "For bowlers the ultimate test is the 7–10 split. For card sharks it's the hot shot cut. For drummers it's the funky little miracle of syncopation known as the Purdie Shuffle." The Purdie Shuffle is challenging to play, and many drummers concede that only the beat's creator can pull it off perfectly. Jason McGerr, the drummer for the indie-pop band Death Cab for Cutie, told Segal, "It doesn't matter how much I practice, I will never play that shuffle like Purdie. It's because he has an attitude that seems to come through every time. He always sounds like he's completely in charge."

The 11th of 15 children, Bernard Purdie was born on June 11, 1939 in the town of Elkton, Maryland, near the Delaware border. At the age of six, he took up drumming, banging out rhythms on an improvised drum set comprised of his mother's kitchenware. "I knew right away that's what I wanted to do with the rest of my life," he told Segal. "No matter what happened, I wanted to play the drums." When he was 11 his mother died, and at 13 he lost his father as well; afterward Purdie's grandparents and "people all over town" raised him, as he told Bradley Bambarger for Newhouse News Service (June 8, 2006). Purdie was given music lessons early on by a drummer named Leonard Hayward (spelled "Heywood" in some sources), who played in a local orchestra. Hayward started Purdie out on trumpet and flute—not the drums— and while that teaching method initially confused the young musician, it paid off. As quoted in the transcript of a 2004 interview for the traveling Red Bull Music Academy, Purdie said that Hayward "wouldn't let me play the drums and I didn't understand this. Then one day [another musician] said: 'He wants you to learn music, dummy.' I'm like: 'Yeah, I knew that. [Of] course I knew that, this is the way you do it.' Boy, I was really dumb, but it worked. I learnt how to play the notes and when you hear notes you play the rhythms, patterns, all horn players play patterns. . . . Also what happened for me, instead of trying to give me a drum chart . . . I would take the horn chart and use that to follow where the music was going and it was the easiest thing in the world for me, 'cause I'm an ex-trumpet player." Purdie's early idols were such big-band jazz drummers as Sid Catlett, Louie Bellson, Gene Krupa, Cozy Cole, Papa Jo Jones, and Chris Columbus. He would eventually adopt the swinging high-hat technique used by those drummers. "Those swing drummers were timekeepers, and keeping time was what I was taught as my job," he told Bambarger. "To this day, that's what it's all about for me—keeping that beat happening and everybody's feet moving." When Purdie was 14 or 15, he used money he made by distributing advertising circulars to purchase his first drum set.

In addition to teaching Purdie music, Hayward let the young musician accompany his band to shows. One of Purdie's jobs was to keep alcohol away from Hayward, a heavy drinker. Purdie took advantage of that situation in order to sit in on the drums. He said in the Red Bull Music Academy interview, "Everyone was always watching [Hayward] to make sure that he never got hold of any alcohol when the gig was going. So he'd bring me along to make sure he didn't drink anything, stuff like that, and I'd have to walk around with this big tall glass of water—'I got your water Mr. Hayward, I got it!' Only the big tall glass of water was filled with either vodka or gin. So everytime after one or two songs, he'd need a drink of water, and I'd be standing there. . . . So by the time of the first break. . . . Mr. Hayward would have to go out to the station wagon and fall right to sleep. And I'd go inside and sit at the drums and I'd have to finish the gig, big band with 14-piece orchestra." In his teens Purdie also played with a host of local country and bar bands, including one called Jackie Lee & the Angels. According to Purdie's Web site, he became his family's biggest breadwinner through his frequent gigs, which also allowed him to "feel my way into nearly every kind of music, 'cause I had to know all styles and was never afraid to try something new."

Purdie attended George Washington Carver High School until the 12th grade, when community efforts to integrate public schools led him to enroll voluntarily in a previously all-white school. After graduating he attended Morgan State University (then Morgan State College), in Baltimore, Maryland. In the early 1960s, after two years at Morgan State, Purdie moved to New York City with a band, which played its first show at a club where the uncle of one of the group's members worked. Mickey Baker and Sylvia Robinson, who performed as the R&B duo Mickey and Sylvia, were in attendance—and were impressed by Purdie's drumming. After the show they asked him to play on a re-recording of their 1957 hit song "Love Is Strange." He was paid $80 for four hours of work. (He told Bambarger that the song "ended up making millions, but I felt rich with that 80 bucks, even though it was all gone by Tuesday, what with me buying drinks for everybody.") Purdie then found work at a laundry and spent the hours after work outside the nearby Turf Club, asking the musicians for a chance to play. That led to further session work, and soon Purdie was working up to four sessions a day, six days a week. He became known in the New York recording industry as a "fixer," a drummer on call to play session drums and add needed over-dubs. He established himself as an eager and available musician, and the professionally made signs he set up while working, which read

"You done hired the hit maker" and "If you need me, call me, the little old hit maker," added to his reputation as something of an eccentric. (He stopped displaying the signs toward the end of the 1960s, after a friend lectured him about his ego. "When she was done with me, I felt about an inch high and my behavior changed 180 degrees," the drummer told Bambarger.)

In the late 1960s Purdie became the house drummer for the jazz record label CTI (Creed Taylor International), owned by the producer Creed Taylor. He also played drums on numerous recordings for artists on Atlantic Records during that period. The first hit among the songs on which Purdie played during those years was the 1967 instrumental song "Memphis Soul Stew," by the saxophonist King Curtis (born Curtis Ousley). Purdie has credited Curtis with helping him find much of his recording work in the 1960s and early 1970s and with introducing him to Aretha Franklin. He told the Red Bull Music Academy interviewer that meeting Curtis in 1962 was "a highlight" in his life. "I didn't realise how big King Curtis was," he said. "All I knew was that he had the best band in the land. He had a 10-piece orchestra that was a funk band, a pop band, a classical band—whatever it took, the band smoked. . . . Meeting him elevated me automatically, 'cause he was the one who called me for 90% of the records that were done for Atlantic Records. He brought me in, he liked what I was doing."

The late 1960s were some of Purdie's most prolific years: he played drums on one or more tracks on James Brown's *Ain't That a Groove* (1965), Gabor Szabo's *Jazz Raga* (1966), Nina Simone's *Nina Simone Sings the Blues* (1967), Jimmy Smith's *Respect* (1967), David Newman's *Bigger and Better* (1968), and Gary McFarland's *America the Beautiful* (1969). He also played on two songs on the iconic soul singer Brown's groundbreaking album *Say It Loud—I'm Black and I'm Proud* (1969), "I Guess I'll Have to Cry, Cry, Cry," and "Let Them Talk." That year Purdie also released his own album, *Soul Drums*, as "Pretty Purdie." Reviewing a reissue of that record, Chris Ziegler wrote for the *OC Weekly* (June 10, 2005), "*Soul Drums*' monstrous production and Purdie's ferocious style make for a widely recognized but rarely available classic."

In 1970 Purdie played drums on the song "Soul Kiss" on the Dizzy Gillespie album *The Real Thing*. The next year he played on Gil Scott-Heron's *Pieces of a Man* and Galt MacDermot's *The Nucleus*. He also released the album *Stand by Me (Whatcha See Is Whatcha Get)* on the Flying Dutchman label. That album, recorded with his band, Pretty Purdie and the Playboys, featured guest performances by a host of well-known musicians, among whom were Gil Scott-Heron, Harold Wheeler, and Chuck Rainey. Several of the tracks were instrumental versions of soul songs; some had vocals provided by Purdie, Norman Matlock, and Scott-Heron. Purdie also released *Purdie Good! & Shaft*, an album of covers he recorded with other musicians that featured a version of "Theme from Shaft," the popular Isaac Hayes song from the cult "blaxploitation" film *Shaft*. According to a review on the Web site MustHear.com, "Far from groundbreaking, *Purdie Good! & Shaft* simply crackle with a raw uncluttered funk that is seldom heard in the age of technocratic music producers and $10,000 a day studios."

Purdie's profile was also given a major boost in the early 1970s when he was asked by Curtis to join his band, King Curtis and the Kingpins, who were to perform as Aretha Franklin's backing band for a series of shows. Purdie accepted the offer and later took over Curtis's spot as Franklin's music director, a position he held until 1975. (Curtis was murdered by a drug addict in the summer of 1971.) Among the band's members were Cornell Dupree on guitar and Billy Preston on organ. The concerts were recorded and preserved on the album *Live at Fillmore West* (1971). Purdie also played Curtis's original material as part of the Kingpins; a recording of the performance was released in 1971, also as *Live at Fillmore West*.

In 1972 Franklin's album *Young, Gifted, and Black* was released to popular and critical acclaim. It contained the song "Rock Steady," which includes one of Purdie's best-known drum performances, complete with his signature 16th-note high-hat beat. In 1972 another album of Purdie's work, *Soul Is . . . Pretty Purdie*, was released on the Flying Dutchman label. The album found Purdie and numerous studio musicians playing covers as well as originals, such as Purdie's "Song for Aretha." A description of the album on the Dusty Groove America Web site reads, "Purdie breaks out here in a compelling album of soul jazz tracks done in a number of styles. The approach is sort of big studio funk—with some cuts that have a harder sound, and others that open up in a groove that's gotten a lot more complicated than the early days."

In 1970 Purdie had played on Louis Armstrong's *Louis Armstrong and His Friends* (1970), which featured the popular song "What a Wonderful World" and was re-released in 1988 with that title. Later in the decade Purdie played on the soundtrack of the animated film *Fritz the Cat* (1972) and the albums *Abandoned Luncheonette* (1973), by Hall & Oates; *Bolivia* (1973), by Gato Barbieri; and *Foreigner* (1973), by Cat Stevens. Among the noteworthy songs from that period featuring Purdie's work are B.B. King's "The Thrill Is Gone" and Percy Sledge's "When a Man Loves a Woman." Purdie is also known as one of the session drummers for the 1977 album *Aja*, by the jazz-rock band Steely Dan. The album was a critical success and reached number three on the U.S. album charts. Purdie played on the songs "Deacon Blues" and "Home at Last," the latter famously showcasing the Purdie Shuffle. Other Steely Dan albums with Purdie's work include *The Royal Scam* (1976) and *Gaucho* (1980).

In 1980 Purdie recorded with Dizzy Gillespie at the Montreux Jazz Festival in Switzerland, which resulted in the album *Digital at Montreux* (1980). In 1983 Purdie toured with Gillespie. He played on B.B. King's *There Must Be a Better World Somewhere* (1981) and recorded frequently during the 1980s with the jazz and funk saxophonist Hank Crawford, performing on *Indigo Blue* (1983) and *Mr. Chips* (1987). He played on two songs on Dizzy Gillespie's *Rhythmstick* (1990) and teamed up with Chuck Rainey and the percussionist Pancho Morales, among others, for the 1993 release *Coolin' Groovin' (A Night at On-Air)*, which was recorded live in Japan. Also in 1993 he also played on three songs each for Al Green's *Don't Look Back* and *The Fugs Second Album*, by the garage-rock band the Fugs. In 1995 he contributed drums to the critically acclaimed *Pushing Against the Flow*, by the acid-jazz group *Raw Stylus*; that album, the only one by the group, brought together a large number of contributing musicians and merged soul, jazz, and hip-hop. Purdie also recorded drums for the electronic group Coldcult's 1997 album, *Let Us Play*.

The year 1996 saw the release of *Soul to Jazz*, the first recording in the U.S. in more than 20 years to be released under Purdie's name. The album, which included several soul and jazz covers, was followed by *Soul to Jazz II* (1998). For the follow-up recording Purdie enlisted guests from his past, Hank Crawford and Cornell Dupree. Douglas Payne wrote for the All About Jazz Web site (July 1, 1998), "*Soul to Jazz II* isn't as earth-shattering or hip-shaking as the premise promises. But the ultimate joy is hearing three soul sax giants (Hank Crawford especially) waxing eloquently in their own mighty soulful way."

Purdie has generated criticism and controversy for his claim, made at least as long ago as the late 1970s, that he was paid to provide, dub over, or "fix"—without credit—the percussion work on roughly 20 tracks by the Beatles. (He has said that he will make the case for that claim in a forthcoming autobiography.) His claim is still brought up in interviews, and he has stood by it. He told the Red Bull Music Academy interviewer, "People don't understand that fixing records was a way of life in the '60s and the '70s. 98% of self-contained groups are not on their own albums and I was one of the few drummers that could go in, join the group and make the records. . . . It was just a job to me, and the Beatles' music was just another job for me. . . . Half of the songs that I played on, I played on 21 of the Beatles tracks—half of them had no drums." He added that the Beatles' manager, Brian Epstein, "spent an amount of money to promote the Beatles that was unheard of in the '60s. [The Beatles' drummer, Ringo Starr,] had his place in the Beatles 'cause that's who they wanted and that's who they could control. . . . He looked the part and he's the one they chose, but when it came to those records and the fixing of those records, 98% of them were first recorded early in England and brought to the USA to be fixed. . . . There are four drummers on the Beatles music, and Ringo's not one of them." Purdie's assertion has brought him death threats.

While most of the recordings for which Purdie played in the late 1990s and 2000s were reissues and compilations, he has performed recently on a few original releases. He played on the song "Modern Jive" on Sugarman & Co's *Pure Cane Sugar* (2002), released by Daptone Records, and on *Steel Reelin'*, a 2006 record by the Steely Dan collaborator Elliot Randall. In 2007 Purdie released *Purdie Good Cookin'*, a live album that featured several musicians from Portland, Oregon. Since the early 1990s Purdie has also played occasional shows with the New Jersey–based R&B band the Hudson River Rats, fronted by Rob Paparozzi, who has since become a friend and business partner of Purdie's. Paparozzi played harmonica and provided vocals for *Purdie Good Cookin'* and has also served as Purdie's music director on tours of Europe and Japan. Purdie contributed to the Hudson River Rats' albums *Get It While You Can* (2003) and *First Take* (2007). In March 2009 Purdie began playing drums in the Broadway revival of *Hair* and is credited on the musical's cast recording. Purdie also appeared as Uncle Bill in the independent 2008 crime film *Priceless*.

The Purdie Shuffle, according to Purdie, was influenced by the rhythmic sounds of the train that regularly passed his childhood home. He told Segal, "When I first started working this out, I was 8 years old, and I called it the locomotion because that's what I was trying to capture: whoosh, whoosh, whoosh." The beat began as a standard drum shuffle, but as Purdie developed it he added lightly brushed "ghost notes," and instead of tapping the high-hat, he used a pattern in which he moved his right hand up and down to strike the side of the high-hat and then the top in repetition, creating what Segal described as a "tock-tick tock-tick sound." Purdie described his shuffle to the Red Bull Music Academy interviewer as "quarter notes, eighth notes, 16th notes, 32nd notes, dotted notes, triplets, half notes, whole notes, everything except 64th notes. A combination of high-hats and kick drums, putting it all together with the dotted feel, the loping feel, and allowing it to breathe in a two bar phrase. Not one bar, 'cause the worst thing you can do is trying to put all this into one bar, it's a two bar phrase, and if you put it into half time, you automatically fall into what is necessary for the shuffle." He noted that the reason the shuffle challenges drummers is that most, instinctively, want to play it faster than it should be played. "The best part of it is, the slower you do it, the better it is. Which is why it's so hard for people to do, 'cause a lot of people don't want to play slow," he said. Segal wrote about the Purdie Shuffle, "If you can listen without shaking your hips, you should probably see a doctor." The shuffle is a versatile beat; the Steely Dan member Donald Fagen told Segal that the beat unexpectedly fit the song "Babylon Sisters," from *Gaucho*. "I guess we expected more of a regular shuffle, and he started playing

something very complex," Fagen said. "We were amazed, because it was perfect for the tune. 'Babylon Sisters' has this dark mood to it, and the beat seemed to accentuate the floating dark mood that the song required."

Purdie has seven children, including three with his second and current wife, Barbara. He also has 12 grandchildren and 10 great-grandchildren. He has shown no sign of retiring soon from live performances. Paparozzi told Bambarger, "Bernard just loves playing music for people; it doesn't matter what it is—a giant concert, a serious recording session, a drum clinic or someone's wedding. He's played with some heavy cats, and he's got great stories to tell. But he's never intimidating; he's good at just being one of the guys."

—W.D.

Suggested Reading: allmusic.com; bernardpurdie.com; *New York Times* C p1 Mar. 31, 2009; Newhouse News Service June 8, 2006

Selected Solo Recordings: *Soul Drums*, 1969; *Stand by Me (Whatcha See Is Whatcha Get)*, 1970; *Purdie Good! & Shaft*, 1970; *Soul Is . . . Pretty Purdie*, 1972; *Soul to Jazz*, 1996; *Soul to Jazz II*, 1998; *Purdie Good Cookin'*, 2007

Radcliffe, Daniel

July 23, 1989– Actor

Address: c/o Artists Rights Group, Talent 4, Great Portland St., London W1W 8PA, England

When he was not yet 12 years old, Daniel Radcliffe was cast as the bespectacled title character in *Harry Potter and the Sorcerer's Stone* (2001), the big-screen adaptation of the first book in J. K. Rowling's phenomenally popular series. As the books in the series were made into films, Radcliffe reprised his role. He has appeared thus far in the sequels *Harry Potter and the Chamber of Secrets* (2002), *Harry Potter and the Prisoner of Azkaban* (2004), *Harry Potter and the Goblet of Fire* (2005), *Harry Potter and the Order of the Phoenix* (2007), and *Harry Potter and the Half-Blood Prince* (2009). (*Harry Potter and the Deathly Hallows*, the final book in the series, is scheduled to be released in two parts, the first on November 19, 2010 and the second on July 15, 2011.) Moviegoers who have followed the experiences of Harry and his friends at Hogwarts School of Witchcraft and Wizardry have at the same time seen Radcliffe and his co-stars go through adolescence. Rebecca Miller wrote for the *St. John's (Newfoundland) Telegram* (June 5, 2004), "Children sporting wizard capes and round glasses flocked to theaters [to see the first movie]; at a recent premiere here, many were replaced with screaming teenage girls, some holding signs say-

Bryan Bedder/Getty Images

Daniel Radcliffe

ing, 'Marry us, Dan!'" Radcliffe told Terry Lawson for the *Detroit Free Press* (July 13, 2007, on-line), "People are always asking me if I get bored or pigeonholed playing the same character for so long, and I don't get it. This is one of the rarest opportunities any actor has ever had, to play one person not only coming of age, but dealing with so many different issues. . . . I learn more about him, and myself, every time I come on to the set." Radcliffe has also appeared in other films as well as on television and onstage. He earned highly laudatory reviews for his performance in Peter Schaffer's drama *Equus* in a London, England, theater in 2007.

Daniel Jacob Radcliffe was born on July 23, 1989 in London. His mother, Marcia Gresham, is a casting agent who has often worked on BBC productions; his father, Alan Radcliffe, was a literary agent until he became his son's full-time chaperone and adviser. "I was never very good at school," Radcliffe told Joanne Hawkins for the Perth, Australia, *Sunday Magazine* (July 1, 2007). "I wasn't very sporty or particularly academic and if you aren't either of those things, then generally school isn't easy." His mother helped him get a role in a BBC television production of *David Copperfield* that aired in 1999. "I think Mum just thought, well if we send him for the *David Copperfield* audition, he won't get it, but he'll have done something that none of the other kids [at school] has," Radcliffe told Hawkins.

Radcliffe next won a small part in the film *The Tailor of Panama* (2001), a spy thriller starring Pierce Brosnan, Geoffrey Rush, and Jamie Lee Curtis. As Radcliffe was filming his first big-screen role, Chris Columbus, who had been hired to direct *Harry Potter and the Sorcerer's Stone*, was searching for young actors to populate J. K. Rowling's imaginary world. (The film was released in Great Britain as *Harry Potter and the Philosopher's Stone;* the book had originally been published in Great Britain, in 1997, with that title.) Impressed with Radcliffe's performance in *David Copperfield*, Columbus had his casting director approach Radcliffe's parents regarding a role in the Potter film. Realizing the magnitude of the project, they initially refused to let Radcliffe audition, fearful that he would be overwhelmed and disappointed if the role went to another boy. In what has become an oft-repeated story, the film's producer, David Heyman, who knew Alan Radcliffe slightly, bumped into the family at the theater one night and persuaded Radcliffe's parents to change their minds. (Heyman has told reporters that he could barely enjoy the play that night, because he was so busy focusing on how well Radcliffe fit his vision of the fledgling wizard.) Although a reported 400,000 boys had vied for the role, J. K. Rowling agreed that Radcliffe was perfect, and in August 2000 it was announced that he would play Harry, an orphaned wizard with a lightning-bolt-shaped scar on his forehead. Rupert Grint, a red-headed boy with no professional acting experience but with sharp comic sensibilities, was hired to play Harry's friend Ron Weasley, and Emma Watson, a nine-year-old girl from Oxfordshire, was given the part of their studious friend Hermione Granger.

Filming began the following month. The young actors were joined by a cast of veterans, including Richard Harris as Albus Dumbledore, the head of Hogwarts; Maggie Smith as Minerva McGonagall, the strict but kind professor of transfiguration; Alan Rickman as Severus Snape, a glowering potions professor; and Robbie Coltrane as Rubeus Hagrid, the dragon-loving giant who serves as Hogwarts's groundskeeper. Radcliffe quickly gained a reputation for playing harmless pranks on his cast mates, and with one-on-one tutoring in school subjects on the set, he flourished academically.

Harry Potter and the Sorcerer's Stone was released on November 15, 2001. "Who does not know of Harry Potter, or of his debut, this week, on the big screen?" Anthony Lane wrote for the *New Yorker* (November 19, 2001). "Anthropologists returning from the Amazon Basin have whispered excitedly of tiny, pre-industrial clans, clustered along minor tributaries, who have never heard of Harry or of his creator, J. K. Rowling, but I think we can dismiss such rumors as patronizing fantasy." The film went on to become the juggernaut Lane and many others had predicted: in the U.S. alone it opened in more than 3,500 theaters and took in a reported $90 million during its first weekend; it has since grossed more than $300 million domestically. While critics were divided about the merits of the film, most agreed that Radcliffe was an inspired choice to play Harry. Todd McCarthy wrote for *Variety* (November 9, 2001, on-line), "We are swept off into a magical world that has been physicalized to an extraordinarily appealing degree by the work of production designer Stuart Craig and his vast team, the locations, the effects and actors. Most important among the latter, of course, is Radcliffe. The boy's regular features, slightly shaggy dark hair, clear eyes and round specs make him instantly embraceable as Harry, and his performance goes on to strike the right balance between normal, but not exceptional, brightness and the gradual understanding of the extraordinary powers he possesses." "As the 11-year-old title character, Daniel Radcliffe is the embodiment of every reader's imagination," Bob Graham wrote for the *San Francisco Chronicle* (November 16, 2001, on-line). "It is wonderful to see a young hero who is so scholarly looking and filled with curiosity and who connects with very real emotions, from solemn intelligence and the delight of discovery to deep family longing."

Filming on *Harry Potter and the Chamber of Secrets* began within days of the first picture's premiere. Radcliffe told Alec Cawthorne for the BBC (October 29, 2002, on-line) that he particularly enjoyed doing the action sequences in *Chamber of Secrets*. "In the scene when I'm hanging out of the [flying] car window, that was actually me. I was hanging 25–30 feet up in the air, and it was just really cool. I do as many of the stunts as possible." Like *Harry Potter and the Sorcerer's Stone*, the new film received mixed reviews, with many critics expressing the view that no movie could live up to the hype and expectation surrounding that one. Several reviewers pointed out that Radcliffe's voice had deepened considerably since the first film and wondered if he was aging too fast to continue playing the character. (A rumor circulated that some of his lines had to be dubbed by another actor, because of his voice cracking.) Despite such concerns fans flocked to see the film, which was an unqualified box-office success, grossing almost $90 million in its first weekend.

When *Harry Potter and the Prisoner of Azkaban* was released, two years later, it was even more evident that its young stars were maturing. "The actors playing Harry, Ron and Hermione have outgrown their childhoods in this movie, and by the next film will have to be dealt with as teenagers, or replaced by younger actors," Roger Ebert wrote for the *Chicago Sun-Times* (June 3, 2004, on-line). "If they continue to grow up, I'm afraid the series may begin to tilt toward less whimsical forms of special effects violence, but on the other hand I like Radcliffe, Grint and Watson." A. O. Scott, writing for the *New York Times* (June 3, 2004, on-line), expressed no such fondness, however: "Mr. Radcliffe, arriving at puberty, may also have reached the limit of his range as an actor. When called upon to convey deep or complex feelings, he has a tendency to blink and look nervous. To be fair, Harry is an especially treacherous role, since he is both the charismatic center of the drama and the character everyone watching imagines him- or herself to be. This means he has to be heroically distinguished from his peers without having too distinct

a personality of his own, a paradoxical demand very few young actors could ever satisfy." Radcliffe has said that one of the most fulfilling aspects of working on that installment was the chance to act with Gary Oldman, who joined the cast as Sirius Black, Harry's godfather; Black is wrongly accused of murder and imprisoned at Azkaban, the notorious prison for criminal wizards. "I've watched probably 90 percent of Gary Oldman's films and I just have so much respect for him as an actor," Radcliffe told Joey Berlin for the Copley News Service (June 6, 2004). "It was a complete inspiration to work with him. He's actually the nicest guy as well. He's a really great bass player and he gave me a bass lesson." (Radcliffe is an avid music fan; in his interviews with teen-oriented publications, he has often chatted about his favorite bands, including the Darkness, the Hold Steady, and Jane's Addiction.)

The book *Harry Potter and the Goblet of Fire* was widely considered to have marked a turning point in Rowling's series. The characters, in their fourth year at Hogwarts, must deal with romantic crushes and adolescent angst—along with darkening plot twists. "*Goblet of Fire*, nobly faithful to its source material, is an end-of-childhood picture," Stephanie Zacharek wrote for *Salon* (November 17, 2005, on-line) of the film, directed by Mike Newell. "This is a brooding, somber story, a metaphor for the painful segue from childhood to adolescence. It balances the exhilaration of independence—one of the great joys of growing up—with the sobering realization that being a grown-up means there's no one around to protect you." Zacharek continued, "[One] of the series' pleasures has been watching the actors who play the three leads, Radcliffe, Grint and Watson, grow out of their childish mugging and develop a greater range of subtle emotions. Newell is especially sensitive, as Rowling is, to that strange, underwater period in which girls and boys begin to realize what they want out of life, coupled with the miserable recognition that other girls and boys—sexually elusive, maddening creatures that they are—hold the key." "Isn't that just like kids? One minute they're mounting broomsticks and lifting off into the wild blue yonder, vanishing inside invisible cloaks, ministering to werewolf bites and making objects fly with a swish and flick of their wrists. Then—without so much as an abracadabra—they reach puberty and become hot and bothered by the opposite sex," Ruthe Stein wrote for the *San Francisco Chronicle* (November 16, 2005, on-line). "The truly magical moments in *Harry Potter and the Goblet of Fire* illuminate the transition of Harry and chums Ron and Hermione into adolescence, made no less bumpy by powers attained at Hogwarts. . . . A magic wand can't shoo away butterflies in your tummy." During the film's New York City premiere, at Radio City Music Hall, thousands of cheering fans lined the streets, with one enthusiastic girl tossing her underwear at the young male actors.

Around the time that the movie *Harry Potter and the Order of the Phoenix* was released, on July 11, 2007, Radcliffe turned 18 and gained control of his earnings—about $40 million at that point. (Soon after he had been cast in the first Harry Potter film, his parents had set up a company called Gilmore Jacobs to manage his finances.) Shortly before his birthday Radcliffe had told Hawkins, "I know I'm in an incredibly fortunate position, but I don't plan to be one of those people who, as soon as they turn 18, suddenly buy themselves a massive sports car collection or something similar. I don't think I'll be particularly extravagant with my money at all. The things I like buying are things that cost about [$25]—books, CDs and DVDs."

Radcliffe's physical and professional development was frequently mentioned in reviews of *Harry Potter and the Order of the Phoenix*. In an assessment for *Entertainment Weekly* (July 20, 2007), Lisa Schwarzbaum praised his "increasingly chiseled" physique, and Richard Corliss, in an article for *Time* (July 5, 2007, on-line), wrote, "Radcliffe measures up to his character; his bold shadings reveal Harry as both a tortured adolescent and an epic hero ready to do battle." Other journalists focused on the Harry's first on-screen kiss, with Katie Leung, who played Cho Chung, Harry's first crush. Radcliffe told Bob Strauss for the *Daily News of Los Angeles* (July 13, 2007), "Obviously, lots of chewing gum was had [before the kiss]. I didn't want to inflict anything nasty on Katie. But it was fine. We did quite a few takes on it. After the first two, when we had been, possibly, a little nervous, [and] didn't know quite what to say to each other—it was absolutely fine. I think it's a very, very sweet scene."

In early 2007 the public learned that Radcliffe, Grint, and Watson would all return for the final Potter films. Earlier, Watson had expressed fatigue and told reporters that she might not sign on to complete the seven-part series. *Harry Potter and the Half-Blood Prince* was released in 2009 and, like its predecessors, drew sell-out audiences, earning almost $80 million during its opening weekend and bringing in more than $300 million by the end of the year. Most reviewers appreciated the movie's darker, more mature themes. "*Harry* is better than ever, a triumph of visual wonder and emotional storytelling. Only Muggles [non-wizard humans], who wouldn't know Slytherin from Gryffindor, will dismiss it as kid stuff for the multitudes who drank the Kool-Aid of J. K. Rowling's seven books," Peter Travers wrote for *Rolling Stone* (July 14, 2009, on-line). "What makes *Half-Blood Prince* top-tier is the descent of darkness on the lives of these characters. . . . All the actors excel at pulling us into the film's mysteries. Radcliffe's growing maturity as Harry gives the role a touching gravity." In a review for the *San Francisco Chronicle* (July 15, 2009), Amy Biancolli wrote, "In appearance and tone, *Harry Potter and the Half-Blood Prince* is much more stylishly gothic than the earlier films. It oozes doom. Violins shimmer dissonantly; storm clouds gather ominously; Hog-

warts, for once, looks like the gray and forbidding castle it always was. This is dark, difficult stuff."

Radcliffe, who has acknowledged that he will forever be associated with the orphaned wizard, has taken on other roles between filming the Potter movies. In 2006 he shot a well-received guest appearance on the British sitcom *Extras*, playing a self-absorbed teenager who makes sexual advances on every woman he meets. In 2007 he appeared in the West End revival of Peter Schaffer's 1973 play, *Equus*, about a disturbed stable boy who blinds the horses in his care; he appeared naked on stage for about 10 minutes of the production. When asked by Christy Lemire for the Associated Press (September 10, 2007, on-line) why he thought that brief period of nudity attracted so much attention from the press, he answered, "Maybe they want me to be Peter Pan and stay young forever." He also told Lemire that he was taking the tabloid headlines in stride: "They've used 'Hairy Botter' about five or six times now. . . . [And] the wand puns, yeah, you can have lots of fun with them." Most serious critics, however, were impressed by Radcliffe's performance. Charles Spencer, for example, wrote for the London *Telegraph* (February 3, 2007, on-line), "Daniel Radcliffe brilliantly succeeds in throwing off the mantle of Harry Potter, announcing himself as a thrilling stage actor of unexpected range and depth. Those of us who have watched the Potter films with our families have always liked Radcliffe, who has a rare natural charm about him, and he has improved greatly as an actor as the series has progressed. Despite minimal previous theatrical experience Radcliffe here displays a dramatic power and an electrifying stage presence that marks a tremendous leap forward." Radcliffe reprised the role on Broadway from September 2008 to February 2009, to equally laudatory notices.

Radcliffe also appeared in the film *December Boys*, released in September 2007. Set in Australia in the 1960s, the movie follows four orphans—Radcliffe plays the oldest—as they compete for the affections of a prospective family. Most reviews of the film were tepid. Roger Ebert wrote for the *Chicago Sun-Times* (September 21, 2007, on-line), "The sight of Harry Potter smoking [in the film] is a little like Mickey Mouse lighting up, but the period detail is accurate, and Radcliffe is convincing as the young man; he proves he can move beyond the Harry role, which I guess is the objective of this movie." Noting that Maps, Radcliffe's character, loses his virginity in the picture, Russell Edwards wrote for *Variety* (September 12, 2007, on-line), "Destined to be forever known as 'Harry Potter Gets Laid,' the visually well-mounted but narratively muddled *December Boys*, featuring Daniel Radcliffe, is an occasionally touching but rarely convincing coming-of-ager." Also in 2007 Radcliffe starred as Jack Kipling, the son of the famed writer Rudyard Kipling, in the television drama *My Boy Jack*. Set during World War I, the fact-based drama depicted Jack's disappearance during the Battle of Loos and his parents' desperate, futile search for him.

Fans worldwide have expressed their eagerness to see both parts of *Harry Potter and the Deathly Hallows*; the first installment is scheduled to open in American theaters on November 19, 2010 and the second—and final—picture in the series, which has already been filmed, will follow in mid-2011. Radcliffe has been cast in several other film projects in various stages of completion, including "The Woman in Black," an adaptation of a ghost tale by Susan Hill, due in 2011, and "The Journey Is the Destination," a biopic of the photojournalist Dan Eldon, who was stoned to death in Somalia in 1993.

Radcliffe has said that he has no plans to attend college, preferring to focus on his acting career. He is reportedly dating Olive Uniacke, David Heyman's stepdaughter. In 2010 Radcliffe was ranked among the highest-paid actors. His total net worth is said to be about $65 million.

—M.R.

Suggested Reading: Associated Press (on-line) Sep. 10, 2007; *Chicago Sun-Times* (on-line) Sep. 21, 2007; *Detroit Free Press* (on-line) July 13, 2007; (London) *Telegraph* (on-line) Feb. 3, 2007; (Perth, Australia) *Sunday Magazine* p15 July 1, 2007; *Variety* (on-line) Nov. 9, 2001, Sep. 12, 2007

Selected Films: *Harry Potter and the Sorcerer's Stone*, 2001; *Harry Potter and the Chamber of Secrets*, 2002; *Harry Potter and the Prisoner of Azkaban*, 2004; *Harry Potter and the Goblet of Fire*, 2005; *December Boys*, 2007; *Harry Potter and the Order of the Phoenix*, 2007; *Harry Potter and the Half-Blood Prince*, 2009; *Harry Potter and the Deathly Hallows: Part 1*, 2010

Selected Television Dramas: *David Copperfield*, 1999; *My Boy Jack*, 2007

Selected Plays: *Equus*, 2007, 2008–09

Courtesy of Stefan Rahmstorf

Rahmstorf, Stefan

Feb. 22, 1960– Climatologist; oceanographer; physicist; activist

Address: Potsdam Institute for Climate Impact Research, P.O. Box 60 12 03, 14412 Potsdam, Germany

Along with all but a tiny fraction of his colleagues worldwide, the climatologist Stefan Rahmstorf is certain that Earth's climate is warming. The dan-

gerous rates at which the temperatures of the oceans and the atmosphere are rising can be traced, most scientists believe, directly to the activities of humans since the start of the Industrial Revolution, in the 1700s—and primarily to the growing use of fossil fuels. A native of Germany, Rahmstorf is a physicist and an oceanographer as well as a climatologist; in Potsdam, Germany, he holds the title of professor of physics of the oceans at the University of Potsdam, and he heads the department devoted to the analysis of Earth systems at the Potsdam Institute for Climate Impact Research (known by the acronym PIK). In 1999 he received from the James S. McDonnell Foundation a $1 million Centennial Fellowship Award, one of the world's most prestigious science prizes, for his work on the role of the oceans in climate change, including the ways in which the movements and temperatures of ocean currents affect temperatures in Earth's atmosphere. His work entails the gathering and interpreting of vast quantities of data disseminated by other scientists, not only to determine forces at work on Earth's climate at present but also to shed light on climate changes over thousands of years in the past. He has used such information to create computer simulations to predict changes in climate in the future.

For some years Rahmstorf was a member of the Abrupt Climate Change Panel of the National Oceanic and Atmospheric Administration (NOAA), a U.S. agency, and he currently sits on the German Advisory Council on Global Change. He was a principal author in 2007 of the Fourth Assessment Report of the Intergovernmental Panel on Climate Change (IPCC, established in 1988 by the World Meteorological Organization and the United Nations Environment Programme). The report concluded that global warming was "unequivocal" and has almost certainly resulted from human-induced emissions of so-called greenhouse gases—particularly carbon dioxide (CO_2, which consists of one atom of carbon, whose chemical symbol is "C," and two atoms of oxygen, "O"). Rahmstorf has written or co-written some 60 scientific papers, including 14 published in *Nature* or *Science*; 20 book chapters, in such reference works as *Encyclopedia of Ocean Sciences* (2001); and more than two dozen articles for *New Scientist* and other publications for laypeople. He has also co-authored three books: *Der Klimawandel* ("Climate Change," 2006), *Our Threatened Oceans* (2008), and *The Climate Crisis: An Introductory Guide to Climate Change* (2009). He is a co-founder and regular contributor to Real-Climate, a blog written by climate scientists for both experts and laypeople that has had over two million visits in the past five years. In 2005 the blog won a Science and Technology Web Award from *Scientific American*. In an October 3, 2005 on-line post, the magazine's editors described RealClimate as "a refreshing antidote to the political and economic slants that commonly color and distort news coverage of topics like the greenhouse effect, air quality, natural disasters and global warming" and "a focused, objective blog written by scientists for a brainy community that likes its climate commentary served hot."

In recent years Rahmstorf has become prominent among scientists who are vigorously challenging the views of so-called climate-change deniers, contrarians, and skeptics. He has strived to convince the public that a vast and growing body of evidence proves beyond doubt that the activities of humans have caused significant rises in oceanic and atmospheric temperatures; that failure to reverse that trend in the next few years will be catastrophic for hundreds of millions of humans and many other species of animals and plants; and that as many as a third of those species may well die out. "I wish [the skeptics and deniers] were right," he told *Current Biography*. "But unfortunately the recent data show that we have not exaggerated but underestimated the problem thus far. Arctic sea ice is vanishing much faster and sea levels are rising more rapidly than we expected just a few years ago." "I believe we will stop global warming," he said. "The question is just: how fast and at what level? I am less optimistic that we have enough political will and courage to curb emissions fast enough to limit warming to below 2 degrees Celsius, as is the goal that has now become a global consensus. . . . I won't give up hope, but I worry that we will do too little, too late."

Stefan Rahmstorf was born on February 22, 1960 in Karlsruhe, Germany, to Rolf Rahmstorf, a manager in the pharmaceutical industry, and his wife, Hildegard, a pharmacist. Six years later his family, which includes his brother and sister, moved to the Netherlands. Rahmstorf has said that by the age of 12 he knew that he wanted to become a scientist. "I always wanted to understand how the world works," he told *Current Biography*. "I was particularly interested in astronomy and physics. I started to learn about oceanography in 1982, mid-way in my physics studies. I'd always loved the oceans and knew right away that oceanography was going to be the right field for me."

Rahmstorf attended the University of Ulm and then the University of Konstanz, both in Germany; at the latter he wrote a thesis on general relativity theory and earned a diploma in physics. During his undergraduate years he also studied physical oceanography at the University of Wales (now Bangor University) in Bangor. He next pursued a Ph.D. degree in oceanography at Victoria University of Wellington, New Zealand. He conducted research while on several cruises in the South Pacific. After he earned his doctorate, in 1990, Rahmstorf worked briefly as a scientist at the New Zealand Oceanographic Institute in Wellington. In 1991 he joined the Institute of Marine Sciences at the University of Kiel, in Germany. He has been working at the Potsdam Institute for Climate Impact Research since 1996 and has taught at the University of Potsdam since 2000.

Most of Rahmstorf's research on the role of ocean currents in climate change concerns what is known as the thermohaline circulation (THC) of the ocean (the world's connected seas). As Rahmstorf explained in a fact sheet posted on the PIK Web site (2002), the THC is different from wind-driven currents and tides, which occur at or near the surface and are controlled by the forces of gravity exerted on the ocean by the moon and the sun. The THC is linked instead to differences in seawater temperature and density; denser, colder seawater sinks below seawater that is warmer and less dense. The density of seawater depends on its salinity—the concentration of salt in it. Salinity increases as seawater evaporates and sea-ice forms; it decreases with rainfall, snowfall, runoff (water from rivers and rain, snow, and irrigation that is not absorbed into land but flows into the ocean), and the addition of meltwater, from melting glaciers, ice sheets, and other ice. Thermohaline circulation—sometimes called the ocean conveyor belt or the global conveyor belt—involves the sinking of huge masses of water (in a process known as deep-water formation) in particular areas—the Mediterranean Sea, the Greenland-Norwegian Sea, the Labrador Sea, the Weddell Sea, and the Ross Sea; the spreading and upwelling of deep water; and the movements of certain near-surface currents, including the North Atlantic Drift (or North Atlantic Current). The North Atlantic Drift and the Gulf Stream (the latter of which is mostly wind-driven) bring warm water from the Gulf of Mexico up along the eastern coast of the U.S. and across the Atlantic Ocean. The warm water releases heat that has kept the climate of Western Europe temperate for the past 10,000 years—since the last ice age. As the water grows colder, it grows denser and sinks; that sinking drives the currents. By the time the deep, cold water has returned south, it has reached depths of one to two miles below the surface.

"The crux of the matter is that the strength of the circulation depends on small density differences, which in turn depend on a subtle balance in the North Atlantic between cooling in high latitudes and input of rain, snowfall, and river runoff," Rahmstorf explained in an article for *UNESCO Sources* (December 1997). Continued global warming, he has maintained, will upset that subtle balance. With an abnormally large input of freshwater from melting ice, for example, seawater will become less salty and thus less dense, deep-water formation in the Atlantic will slow, and the movement of the "conveyor belt" will slow and eventually stop entirely. "We can see that such breakdowns have happened before in climate history . . . ," Rahmstorf wrote for *UNESCO Sources*, although precisely what caused them is not yet known. "Pulses of freshwater entered the Atlantic, causing cold spells lasting for hundreds of years. The last cooling occurred about 11,000 years ago. . . . So the possibility of a circulation breakdown is not just in the computer, it is real." The evidence comes from painstaking examinations of cores of ice extracted from Greenland and cores of sediments extracted from the floor of the ocean. The cores, from drillings to depths of thousands of feet, show the accumulations of yearly deposits, the contents of which can be analyzed to reveal climate conditions at the time that each deposit settled. (Such analyses are analogous to those of tree rings, which are added annually and reveal periods of drought, for example.)

The presence in Earth's atmosphere of carbon dioxide and other so-called greenhouse gases—methane, nitrous oxide, carbon monoxide, and (for the past 250 years or so) others produced by various industrial operations, such as sulfur hexafluoride—is not inherently harmful. On the contrary: such gases are vital for life, because—in a process dubbed the greenhouse effect in the mid-1800s—they trap long-wave radiation escaping from Earth into space, which normally balances the energy coming from the sun. In a self-regulating, natural system, the trapped radiation heats the atmosphere and keeps air temperatures at levels favorable to life as we know it. As humans began to burn fossil fuels (coal and liquid-petroleum products) to provide energy to run machinery in factories and, later, to run power plants, cars, and planes, unnatural amounts of CO_2 and other greenhouse gases were emitted into the atmosphere. Scientists' understanding of climate and the forces that control it is incomplete (as is their understanding of weather—climatic conditions in small locales minute by minute). However, they know without any doubt that the burning of fossil fuels (and, to a much lesser extent, deforestation) has led to the increased concentration of CO_2 in the atmosphere. It is also known that increases in CO_2 concentrations lead to an increase in trapped long-wave radiation, a rise in atmospheric temperatures near Earth's surface, and higher temperatures in the surface waters of the ocean. By the early 1990s, according to Rahms-

torf, global temperatures on average were 0.5 degrees Centigrade (0.5_oC) higher than they were before the Industrial Revolution, and since then they have risen another 0.3_oC.

Some of the effects of global warming are already apparent. Among the most dramatic is the loss of summer sea ice in the Arctic Ocean. "Ice extent in 2007 and 2008 was only about half of what it [was] in the 1960s," Rahmstorf wrote in his article "Climate Change—State of the Science," posted on the PIK Web site in 2009; "ice thickness has decreased by 20–25% just since 2001, and in 2008 the North-East Passage and North-West Passage were both open for the first time in living memory." One consequence of that melting of sea ice is that, in the past four decades, "sea levels have increased about 50 percent more than the climate models predicted," Rahmstorf told an Agence France Presse (December 14, 2006) reporter. (Rahmstorf provided evidence for that conclusion in a paper, co-written with six others, that was published in the May 4, 2007 issue of *Science*.) If sea levels were to continue to rise, land at or slightly above sea level would disappear under water, leaving homeless many of the millions of people who live on low-lying islands or in coastal areas. Another result of global warming is that the acidity of the oceans is increasing along with higher levels of CO_2. Such acidity threatens the well-being and even survival of marine ecosystems and fish and crustacean populations in many parts of the world.

The reality of anthropogenic (human-caused) global warming has been accepted as fact by the IPCC, the NOAA, the U.N. Environment Programme, the World Meteorological Organization, the National Academy of Sciences of the U.S., the American Geophysical Union (the world's largest association of Earth scientists), the National Aeronautic and Space Administration of the U.S., and dozens of other scientific government agencies as well as climatologists from around the world and the leaders of many nations. Despite that consensus, Rahmstorf complained in his paper "The Climate Sceptics" (2005, on-line), published in conjunction with a conference sponsored by the organization Munich Re, the media continue to convey to the public the false idea that the main conclusions of the scientific community regarding global warming "are still disputed or regularly called into question by new studies." In light of the voluminous evidence produced by thousands of studies, he wrote, "it is almost inconceivable" that those conclusions "could be overturned by a few new results." The media's persistent propagation of false ideas, in his view, "is mainly due to the untiring PR [public relations] activities of a small, but vocal mixed bag of climate sceptics . . . who vehemently deny the need for climate-protection measures." Prominent among that "vocal mixed bag" are representatives of, lobbyists for, or politicians who have benefited from the contributions of corporations that sell petroleum products or other commodities whose manufacture and/or use leads to the emission of greenhouse gases. In "The Climate Sceptics" and elsewhere, Rahmstorf has shown that there is no scientific evidence to support any of their arguments but that there is a huge body of evidence to refute them. He has pointed out the fallacies in arguments that global temperatures are not rising; that natural processes account for nearly all the increase in CO_2; that CO_2 plays little or no role in global warming; that greater solar activity has caused increased temperatures on Earth; that the potential effects of global warming are negligible; and that the costs of measures proposed for stopping or reversing global warming by limiting CO_2 emissions would be prohibitively high.

The last-mentioned argument was presented in an article for *Newsweek* (August 29, 2009, on-line) by Bjorn Lomborg of Denmark, whose academic training is in political science and who teaches at the Copenhagen Business School. According to Lomborg, "Even if all industrialized nations succeeded in meeting the most drastic emissions goals, it would likely come at a huge sacrifice to prosperity." Referring to figures offered by the economist Richard Tol of the Economic and Social Research Institute in Ireland, he wrote, "Using carbon cuts to limit the increase in global temperature to 2 degrees Celsius . . . would cost 12.9 percent of [the world's gross domestic product, or GDP] by the end of the century. That's $40 trillion a year. . . . Yet, such measures would avoid only $1.1 trillion in damage due to higher temperatures. The cure would be more painful than the illness." Lomborg suggested as far more cost-effective the use of "climate engineering": "For instance, automated boats could spray seawater into the air to make clouds whiter, and thus more reflective, augmenting a natural process. Bouncing just 1 or 2 percent of the total sunlight that strikes the Earth back into space could cancel out as much warming as that caused by doubling pre-industrial levels of greenhouse gases. Spending about $9 billion researching and developing this technology could head off $20 trillion of climate damage." Rahmstorf has rejected such approaches. "First of all they do nothing to stop ocean acidification, which by itself would be enough reason to cut down our CO_2 emissions, unless we want to destroy our ocean ecosystems," he told *Current Biography*. "Secondly they would make the climate system inherently unstable and requiring [of] human control, which would have to be maintained for thousands of years because of the long lifetime of the CO_2 that is building up in the atmosphere. If you let those cooling measures slip for just a few years, the full force of CO_2 warming would hit us immediately. I just don't trust humans can reliably manage such a complex system for millennia—I'd much rather keep it the relatively stable self-regulating system it is now." Rahmstorf has endorsed the work of the British economist Nicholas Stern, who, after a review of other economists' studies, has estimated that the cost of cutting emissions would total 2 percent of global wealth (as measured by the gross domestic product of all nations), while the damage resulting from inaction would cost anywhere from 5 to 20 percent of global wealth, and possibly far more. In an interview posted on the Allianz Knowledge Web site (June 9, 2009), Rahmstorf suggested that people could "build an energy system over the next decades based primarily on renewable resources"—biofuels, solar power, and wind power—and thus avoid the use of fossil fuels, at least to a significant extent.

On November 18, 2008, in taped remarks that Rahmstorf has sometimes quoted, President-elect Barack Obama addressed the Bi-partisan Governors Global Climate Summit, held in Los Angeles, California. Obama told some 30 U.S. governors and representatives of many nations, "Few challenges facing America—and the world—are more urgent than combating climate change. The science is beyond dispute and the facts are clear. . . . Now is the time to confront this challenge once and for all. Delay is no longer an option. . . . The stakes are too high. The consequences, too serious." The U.S, which in recent years has been responsible for at least 21 percent of greenhouse-gas emissions, did not join the 185 countries that ratified the Kyoto Protocol, drawn up by 37 industrialized nations and the European Union during the U.N. Framework Convention on Climate Change held in Japan in 1997. A legally binding treaty that went into effect in 2005, the protocol aimed to reduce greenhouse-gas emissions from 1990 levels by an average of 5 percent between 2008 and 2012. In December 2009, when the U.N. held its 15th conference on climate change, in Copenhagen, CO_2 levels were continuing to increase, in part because of China's rapidly rising use of fossil fuels and the failures of nearly every other nation to cut emissions. Government heads and other delegates from 192 countries (among them Obama and Rahmstorf) attended that gathering. The agreement that resulted, known as the Copenhagen Accord, "fell short of even the modest expectations for the summit . . . ," according to the *New York Times* (December 18, 2009, on-line). "The accord drops what had been the expected goal of concluding a binding international treaty by the end of 2010, which leaves the implementation of its provisions uncertain. It is likely to undergo many months, perhaps years, of additional negotiation before it emerges in any internationally enforceable form." The *Times* also reported, "The maneuvering that characterized the final week of the talks was a sign of [global leaders'] seriousness; never before have [they] come so close to a significant agreement to reduce the greenhouse gases linked to warming the planet." The leaders agreed that global warming must never exceed 2°C above preindustrial levels and that by the end of January 2010, wealthy nations must register the emissions cuts they will implement by 2020. Those nations also pledged to fund efforts by poorer nations to reduce greenhouse-gas emissions and adapt to consequences of climate change.

In his free time Rahmstorf enjoys photography, yoga, and dancing. His first marriage, in 1991, to the New Zealand–born actress Dulcie Smart, ended in divorce. He lives with his second wife, Stefanie, and their two children in Potsdam, where his wife owns a jewelry-design shop. The couple sell sterling-silver jewelry of their own design; each piece reads "OCO" or in some other way refers to CO_2. The Rahmstorfs use the money from each sale to buy one of the limited number of CO_2-emission credits issued by the European Union. They stamp each piece of jewelry with the serial number of the credit, to serve as evidence that with that purchase, the buyer has prevented the emission of one ton of CO_2 into the atmosphere.

—M.A.S.

Suggested Reading: Allianz Knowledge (on-line) June 9, 2009; Copenhagen Climate Council (online) Aug. 5, 2009; PIK Web site; realclimate.org; Stefan Rahmstorf Web site; *Washington Post* A p3 Apr. 12, 1999

Selected Books: *Der Klimawandel* (with Hans Joachim Schellnhuber), 2006; *Our Threatened Oceans* (with Katherine Richardson), 2008; *The Climate Crisis: An Introductory Guide to Climate Change* (with David Archer), 2009

Jack Miller, courtesy of Basic Books

Ravitch, Diane

July 1, 1938– Historian; writer; educator; former federal-agency administrator

Address: New York University, Steinhardt School, 82 Washington Sq. E., New York, NY 10003

"The single biggest problem in American education is that no one agrees on why we educate." Diane Ravitch, who expressed that conviction in a brief statement for the *New York Times Magazine* (September 27, 2009) about the future of American schools, has studied the history and politics of education in the United States for more than four decades and is one of the nation's most prominent and respected scholars in her field. "Faced with this lack of consensus," Ravitch continued in the same piece, "policy makers define good education as higher test scores. But higher test scores are not a definition of good education. Students can get higher scores in reading and mathematics yet remain completely ignorant of science, the arts, civics, history, literature and foreign languages. Why do we educate? We educate because we want citizens who are capable of taking responsibility for their lives and for our democracy. We want citizens who understand how their government works, who are knowledgeable about the history of their nation and other nations. We need citizens who are thoroughly educated in science. We need people who can communicate in other languages. We must ensure that every young person has the chance to engage in the arts. But because of our narrow-minded utilitarianism, we have forgotten what good education is." Ravitch elaborated on those ideas in her book *The Death and Life of the Great American School System: How Testing and Choice Are Undermining Education* (hereafter referred to as *Great American School System*). Published in 2010, it is the most recent of the 10 books Ravitch has written as sole author. She has also co-written two books and edited or co-edited 14.

In her books and many of her approximately 500 published articles and reviews, Ravitch has often referred to the succession of educational philosophies and fads that have seized the imaginations of educators, politicians, and the public in the U.S. since the 1800s; those ideas have led to repeated and sometimes radical changes both in the way school systems are organized and in instruction. In reviewing her writings in 2007, as she explained in *Great American School System*, she recognized two themes: "One constant has been my skepticism about pedagogical fads, enthusiasms, and movements. The other has been a deep belief in the value of a rich, coherent school curriculum, especially in history and literature, both of which are so frequently ignored, trivialized, or politicized. . . . I have consistently warned against the lure of 'the royal road to learning,' the notion that some savant or organization has found an easy solution to the problems of American education. . . . I have consistently warned that, in education, there are no shortcuts, no utopias, and no silver bullets." Yet in recent years she herself, she realized, "had fallen for the latest panaceas and miracle cures," in the form of inflexible, poorly constructed standardized tests, financial incentives (for both schools and teachers) for improving test results, rigid criteria for teacher and school performance, and "school choice," with the creation of charter schools as alternatives to public schools—in effect, turning education into a market-driven business.

Those measures started to become the basis of federal educational policy during the administrations of President George H. W. Bush (1989–93) and President Bill Clinton (1993–2001), who endorsed a "reinvention" of the federal bureaucracy that called for "adapt[ing] private sector management techniques to the public sector," in Ravitch's words. Similar changes were embraced by President George W. Bush (2001–09), who signed into law the Elementary and Secondary Education Act (known as "No Child Left Behind") in 2002, and by President Barack Obama, who introduced the federal "Race to the Top" initiative. Ravitch herself served in the federal government: she was assistant secretary in the Office of Research and Improvement in the U.S. Department of Education and counselor to the secretary of education, Lamar Alexander, for 18 months (1991–93); she was also a member of the National Assessment Governing Board (1997–2004), which supervises the National Assessment of Educational Progress, a federal testing program. "I wanted to believe that choice and accountability would produce great results," Ravitch wrote in Great American School System. "But over time, I was persuaded by accumulating evidence that the latest reforms were not likely to live up to their promise." Empirical evidence, she concluded, has shown that those "reforms" have seriously worsened the nation's education system. She wrote Great American School System to explain why she has come to think of them as "deforms."

The passionately civic-minded Ravitch has also worked actively with such groups as the Brookings Institution, a nonprofit, Washington, D.C.–based think tank, where she held the Brown chair in education studies (1995–2005) and edited Brookings Papers on Education Policy. In 1982, with Chester E. Finn Jr., she co-founded the Educational Excellence Network. Ravitch taught at Columbia University's Teachers College, in New York City, from 1975 to 1991 and has held the title of research professor at New York University since 1994. Every week since 2007 Ravitch and the educator Deborah Meier have contributed individual essays on their shared blog, "Bridging Differences," which appears on the Education Week Web site.

The third of eight children, Ravitch was born Diane Rose Silverstein on July 1, 1938 in Houston, Texas. (According to Sarah Kershaw's profile of her in the December 1, 1996 edition of the New York Times, her parents later shortened their last name to Silvers; many sources state that her surname at birth was Silvers.) Her father, Walter, and mother, the former Anna (or Ann) Katz, who were Jewish, owned a liquor store or sometimes, depending on the economy, two or three small ones. Ravitch attended Houston public schools and graduated from San Jacinto High School (now part of the Houston Community College–Central Campus) in 1956. She earned a B.A. degree from Wellesley College, in Massachusetts, in June 1960.

Later that month Ravitch married Richard Ravitch, a lawyer, and moved with him to New York City. During their marriage, which ended in divorce in 1986, Richard Ravitch became a prominent, public-spirited developer and government official; he chaired the New York State Urban Development Corp. in the 1970s and the city's Metropolitan Transit Authority from 1979 to 1983. Diane Ravitch spent the early years of their marriage as a homemaker. Her first son, Joseph, was born in 1962; her second son, Steven, in 1964. In 1966 Steven died of leukemia, at age two and a half. "Needless to say, I was devastated . . . ," she wrote for her Education Week blog (February 26, 2007). "I had another son as soon as I could." That child, Michael, was born in 1967.

After Steven's death, Ravitch recalled to Karen De Witt for the New York Times (November 19, 1991), "I just had a kind of a sea change in my outlook toward work and life, and felt that I wanted to commit myself to something that was important, that I really cared about. And I guess because I was a young mother it was education." Within months of Michael's birth, the Carnegie Corp. of New York hired Ravitch as a freelance writer. In her first published article, "Programs, Placebos, Panaceas," which appeared in the now-defunct Urban Review (1968), she questioned the value of short-term attempts to help failing students.

Her work for the Carnegie Corp. led Ravitch to meet Lawrence A. Cremin, a professor of education (and later president) of the Teachers College of Columbia University. Through his intercession she gained acceptance into the college's doctoral program despite her lack of a master's degree. While she was fulfilling her course requirements for her doctorate, Ravitch wrote her first book, The Great School Wars: New York City, 1805–1973; A History of the Public Schools as Battlefield of Social Change. The book, published in 1974, was later accepted as her dissertation. Ravitch was awarded a Ph.D. degree in history in 1975.

The Great School Wars, an account of the politically charged history of New York City's public-school system, "asks us to recognize that the public schools cannot solve all the problems of society, and asks us to reconsider catchwords of the moment by reminding us that they echo the slogans of past failures," according to a New Yorker (April 15, 1974) reviewer, who judged the book to be "excellent." Other assessments were similarly enthusiastic. The book led Delta Kappa Gamma, an organization of female educators, to honor Ravitch with its Educators' Award in 1975, and 20 years later the *New York Times* listed *The Great School Wars* among the 10 best books about New York City. Updated editions were published in 1988 and 2000 with the subtitle *A History of the New York City Public Schools*.

In 1975 Ravitch joined the faculty of Teachers College, where she taught courses in history and education for 16 years. She was a Guggenheim Foundation fellow in 1977–78. Urged on by Cremin, she wrote her second book, *The Revisionists Revised: A Critique of the Radical Attack on the Schools* (1978), in response to "a group of leftist historians who attacked the underpinnings of public schooling" and claimed that public schools were "devised by elites to oppress the poor," as she put it in *Great American School System*. Ravitch maintained, rather, that "schools were never an instrument of cultural repression. . . . They are a primary mechanism through which a democratic society gives its citizens the opportunity to attain literacy and mobility" and "are necessary and valuable for individuals and for the commonweal."

In her third book, *The Troubled Crusade: American Education, 1945–1980* (1983), Ravitch discussed the effects on schools of such phenomena as the G.I. Bill, which enabled World War II veterans to attend college or vocational schools; McCarthyism—the vicious, highly publicized effort to oust suspected Communist Party members or sympathizers from schools (as well as government and the entertainment industry); efforts to improve education for members of minority groups, through affirmative action, busing, and bilingual classes; and attempts to combat educational handicaps associated with poverty, through Head Start programs, for example. "At times [Ravitch's] narrative assumes the aspect of a very dark comedy, and one fully expects her to pronounce some dire moral at the end," Christopher Lehmann-Haupt wrote in his review of *The Troubled Crusade* for the *New York Times* (September 7, 1983). "But she never does. What seems to have happened" is that "having set out to write such an objectively detailed account of the period that the villains would betray themselves, she discovered that there really were no villains. Everyone behaved with the best of motives, she seems to be saying—from proponents of progressive education in the 1930's to defenders of the rights of the handicapped in the 70's. It was just that the winds of history kept shifting and changing the landscape." *The Troubled Crusade* earned Ravitch a second Delta Kappa Gamma Educators' Award and an Ambassador Book Award from the English-Speaking Union of the United States.

For two years beginning in 1985, at the invitation of Louis "Bill" Honig, California's elected superintendent of public education, Ravitch helped to develop a new state kindergarten-through-12th-grade history curriculum, along with guidelines for "a substantial infusion of history and biography in the elementary grades," she wrote in *Great Ameri-*can School System. Aspects of geography, social studies, and the humanities were incorporated in the new curriculums, which, with minor revisions to bring them up to date, are still used in California.

The year 1985 also saw the publication of *The Schools We Deserve: Reflections on the Educational Crises of Our Times*, which contains 21 essays that Ravitch wrote during the preceding decade. They deal with topics that remain controversial, such as the abandonment of classic literature in favor of basal readers; the tendency to blame teachers disproportionately for students' poor performance; the question of whether tax credits for private-school tuition are justified; and the role of the federal government in setting educational standards.

Ravitch wrote *What Do Our 17-Year-Olds Know?: A Report on the First National Assessment of History and Literature* (1987) with Chester E. Finn Jr., who at the time was an assistant secretary in the U.S. Department of Education. Their book discussed the results of the National Assessment of Educational Progress, multiple-choice tests administered for the first time to nearly 8,000 high-school students. The results were troubling: the average scores on the history and literature tests were 54.5 percent and 51.8 percent, respectively. "Recognizing one's ignorance is the beginning of wisdom," Paul Piazza wrote for the *Washington Post* (November 3, 1987). "To Ravitch and Finn we owe a great deal for starting us down the road, if not to wisdom, at least to a knowledge of our failure, perhaps even to the beginnings of educational reform."

In 1989 and 1990, as a representative of the American Federation of Teachers, Ravitch traveled in Czechoslovakia, Hungary, Poland, and Romania—former Soviet satellite nations that had become fledgling democracies—to advise educators about the formation of teachers' unions. Her work as an adviser to Poland's Teachers Solidarity trade union earned her a medal from the Polish government in 1991.

Around that time in the U.S., a willingness to allow federal officials to enter an area long regarded as the purview of the states—standards for student performance—had emerged nationwide because of a growing conviction that state standards had been set too low. In April 1991 the U.S. secretary of education, Lamar Alexander, asked Ravitch to serve as assistant secretary in his department's Office of Educational Research and Improvement (OERI), which conducted and sponsored research on education and work to develop voluntary educational standards. (The OERI has since been replaced by the federal Institute of Education Sciences.) Ravitch, a registered Democrat (in 2000 she registered as an Independent), hesitated to take the job. "It had been almost a personal conviction of mine never to go into government, because I wanted to be free as possible to say what was on my mind and never to curry favor with politicians and never to worry about whether someone would like what I had to say," she told Kenneth J. Cooper for the

Washington Post (August 22, 1991). Alexander and his deputy secretary, David Kearns, won her over with their apparent openness to new ideas. The U.S. Senate confirmed her, and she was sworn into office in July 1991.

In her new post Ravitch organized a series of seminars in which Education Department officials met with prominent educators to discuss their ideas regarding voluntary national standards for students. With funds allocated by federal legislation known as Goals 2000, OERI and other federal agencies awarded grants to major organizations of teachers and scholars to develop standards in science, history, geography, economics, civics, the arts, English, physical education, and foreign languages. Their efforts came to naught, mainly because of opposition from conservative Republicans. Ravitch left the Education Department in 1993, when President Clinton took office. In her book *National Standards in American Education: A Citizen's Guide* (1995), Ravitch provided "a sophisticated, evenhanded introduction to the complex issues associated with the effort to set national standards for education," Michael W. Kirst wrote for *Issues in Science and Technology* (Winter 1995–96).

In 1997 President Clinton's secretary of education, Richard Riley, appointed Ravitch to the National Assessment Governing Board, which oversees the National Assessment of Educational Progress. In 2001 he reappointed her to the board, where she served until 2004. Although Ravitch was widely branded a "neoconservative" for her views during that period, she has always rejected such labels, on the grounds that the roots of her educational philosophy are democratic and pedagogical principles and not those of any particular political group. "Ravitch is an intelligent and sophisticated thinker who manages to blur the boundaries between progressivism and conservatism," the educator Herbert R. Kohl wrote for the *Los Angeles Times* (September 10, 2000).

The central argument of Ravitch's seventh book, *Left Back: A Century of Battles Over School Reform* (2000), was that in a democracy, students destined for vocational training as well as those bound for college should receive instruction that fosters their intellectual development, and that in general U.S. school systems had failed in that task, in part because, in adopting a so-called progressive agenda, many had "dethroned" academic curricula and instead had dedicated themselves to "socializing students, teaching them proper attitudes and behaviors, and encouraging conformity to the norms of social life and the workplace," in Ravitch's words. *Left Back* received an extraordinary amount of media attention. Its admirers included Alan Wolfe, who wrote for the *New Republic* (December 11, 2000), "*Left Back* is the most important book written in many decades about America's most important public institution." Detractors of *Left Back* faulted Ravitch for, among other things, focusing on the failures of American education and downplaying its successes and for giving short shrift to vocational and industrial education.

For some years before and after the publication of *Left Back*, Ravitch "argued that certain managerial and structural changes—that is, choice, charters, merit pay and accountability—would help to reform our schools," as she wrote in *Great American School System*. Ravitch supported the "No Child Left Behind" legislation of 2002, which requires states to develop educational standards in the areas of reading and math for elementary-, middle-, and high-school students. It also requires schools to measure students' progress, through annual standardized tests, and to meet yearly progress goals set by the state. All students must meet their state's proficiency requirements by the 2013–14 school year. Schools that consistently fail to meet standards face punitive action, including decreased funding and the replacement of the entire teaching and administrative staffs.

Based on mounting evidence of severe problems, Ravitch came to believe that "No Child Left Behind" has failed to improve schools. For example, many schools focused on "teaching for the test"—that is, they emphasized practice in choosing the desired answers on standardized multiple-choice tests rather than an understanding of subject matter and the abilities to make reasoned conclusions and distinguish fact from opinion. In an interview for the National Public Radio (NPR) program *Morning Edition* (March 2, 2010), Ravitch told Steve Inskeep, "The basic strategy [of 'No Child Left Behind'] is measuring and punishing. And it turns out that as a result of putting so much emphasis on the test scores, there's a lot of cheating going on; there's a lot of gaming the system. Instead of raising standards, it's actually lowered standards because many states have dumbed down their tests, or changed the scoring of the tests, to say that more kids are passing than actually are. There are states that say that 80 to 90 percent of their children are proficient readers and proficient in math. But when the national test is given, the National Assessment of Educational Progress, the same state will have not 90 percent proficient, but 25 or 30 percent."

In addition, Ravitch no longer advocates competition among schools, which the "Race to the Top" initiative promotes. "There should not be competition," she told Inskeep. "Schools should operate like families. The fundamental principle by which education proceeds is collaboration. Teachers are supposed to share what works; schools are supposed to get together and talk about what's succeeded for them. They're not supposed to hide their trade secrets, and try to have a survival of the fittest competition with the school down the block." Furthermore, because "No Child Left Behind" addresses competency in reading and math only, many schools offer far too little instruction (and in some cases none) in many other subjects, including science, history, literature, art, music, foreign languages, and physical education. Ravitch also rejects as "absurd" the goal of "achieving universal proficiency by 2014," she wrote in an op-ed piece for the *New York Times* (October 3, 2007). "Given that no nation, no state and no school district has ever reached 100 percent math and reading proficiency for all grades, it is certain that the goal cannot be met. . . . Unless we set realistic goals for our schools and adopt realistic means of achieving them, we run the risk of seriously damaging public education and leaving almost all children behind."

In *Great American School System*, Ravitch explained why she had come to disagree with her ideas from the 1990s about standardized testing, accountability, and charter schools. In the last chapter, "Lessons Learned," she wrote, "A democratic society cannot long sustain itself if its citizens are uninformed and indifferent about its history, its government, and the workings of its economy. Nor can it prosper if it neglects to educate its children in the principles of science, technology, geography, literature and the arts. The great challenge to our generation is to create a renaissance in education, one that goes well beyond the basic skills that have recently been the singular focus of federal activity. . . . Indeed, much of what policymakers now demand will very likely make the schools less effective and may further degrade the intellectual capacity of our citizenry."

Ravitch's other books include *The Language Police: How Pressure Groups Restrict What Students Learn* (2003) and *Edspeak: A Glossary of Education Terms, Phrases, Buzzwords and Jargon* (2007). Her many honors include the Henry Allen Moe Prize in the humanities from the American Philosophical Society (1986), the Leadership Award of the Klingenstein Institute at Teachers College (1994), and the National Education Association's Friend of Education Award (2010).

Ravitch lives in Brooklyn. Her son Joseph worked until recently as an investment banker. Her son Michael is a writer and the co-editor, with Ravitch, of *The English Reader: What Every Literate Person Needs to Know* (2006). Ravitch has three grandsons.

—M.A.S.

Suggested Reading: "Bridging Differences" blog, *Education Week* (on-line) Feb. 27, 2007; *College Board Review* p42+ May 2001; Diane Ravitch Web site; *Education Week* p1+ Mar. 10, 2010; *New York Times* A p22 Nov. 19, 1991, City Weekly Desk p3 Dec. 1, 1996, A p13 Mar. 3, 2010; *Salon.com* May 17, 2010; Ravitch, Diane. *The Death and Life of the Great American School System: How Testing and Choice Are Undermining Education*, 2010; *Who's Who in America*

Selected Books: *The Great School Wars: New York City, 1805–1973*, 1974, 2000; *The Revisionists Revised: A Critique of the Radical Attack on the Schools*, 1978; *The Troubled Crusade: American Education, 1945–80*, 1983; *The Schools We Deserve: Reflections on the Educational Crises of Our Times*, 1985; *What Do Our 17-Year-Olds Know?: A Report on the First National Assessment of History and Literature* (with Chester E. Finn, Jr.), 1987; *National Standards in American Education: A Citizens Guide*, 1995; *Left Back: A Century of Battles Over School Reform*, 2000; *The Language Police: How Pressure Groups Restrict What Students Learn*, 2003; *Edspeak: A Glossary of Education Terms, Phrases, Buzzwords, and Jargon*, 2007; *The Death and Life of the Great American School System: How Testing and Choice Are Undermining Education*, 2010; as editor—*The American Reader: Words That Moved a Nation*, 1990; *Debating the Future of American Education: Do We Need National Standards and Assessments?*, 1995; *Brookings Papers on Education Policy* (annual editions, 1999–2004); as co-editor—*Educating an Urban People: The New York City Experience*, 1981; *The School and the City: Community Studies in the History of American Education*, 1983; *Against Mediocrity: Improving the Teaching of the Humanities in America's High Schools*, 1984; *Challenges to the Humanities*, 1985; *The Democracy Reader*, 1992; *Learning from the Past: What History Teaches Us about School Reform*, 1995; *New Schools for a New Century: The Redesign of Urban Education*, 1997; *City Schools: Lessons from New York City*, 1999; *Making Good Citizens: Education and Civil Society*, 2001; *Kid Stuff: Marketing Sex and Violence to Our Nation's Children*, 2003; *The English Reader: What Every Literate Person Needs to Know*, 2006; *Beyond the Basics: Achieving a Liberal Education for All Children*, 2007

Richardson, Robert

Aug. 27, 1955– Cinematographer

Address: c/o Skouras Agency, 1149 Third St., Third Fl., Santa Monica, CA 90403

Robert Richardson is the two-time Academy Award–winning cinematographer of 30 motion pictures. But in the opinion of Oliver Stone, with whom Richardson has worked on 11 feature films, Richardson is not simply a cinematographer; he is, like Stone, a filmmaker. "He's totally involved—on the script, the characters, the editing," Stone told Steve Chagollan for *Daily Variety* (February 24, 1994). "When we go on scouts together, I generally do my shot lists and he does some of his own and we compare. Bob is a 360-degree photographer. It's not a job for him, it's a way of life." For several years after he earned a master's degree in cinematography from the American Film Institute, Rich-

Frank Micelotta/Getty Images
Robert Richardson

ardson assisted in the making of documentaries and handled assignments as a member of second-unit film teams. His work for a 1983 documentary about the civil war in El Salvador led to his collaborations with Stone on the fictional *Salvador* as well as *Platoon, Born on the Fourth of July, JFK*—for which he won his first Oscar—and *Natural Born Killers*. Richardson has also served as the cinematographer for the filmmakers Martin Scorsese, on movies including *Casino* and *The Aviator*, the latter of which earned him his second Oscar; Errol Morris, on the documentaries *Fast, Cheap & Out of Control* and *Standard Operating Procedure*; and Quentin Tarantino, on *Kill Bill: Vol. 1, Kill Bill: Vol. 2*, and *Inglourious Basterds*. In 1992, by invitation, Richardson became a member of the prestigious American Society of Cinematographers (ASC).

Also known as a director of photography—or D.P., in movie-industry jargon—a cinematographer is charged with composing each shot of a film: choosing which film stock and lens to use, deciding how to frame the shot and which camera movements to use, and designing all aspects of lighting. Richardson has earned a reputation within the industry and among film aficionados for his signature "halo" lighting, for which he uses a single strong light aimed straight down to create a pool of light that bounces off the actors' faces. In an interview with Bob Fisher for the *International Cinematographers Guild Magazine* (October 2003, online), Richardson said that his role is "to give birth to what the director imagines. It is a confounding relationship. Sometimes there is a catastrophic collision of egos and at other times it's a marriage of shared artistic interests that are as pure as poetry. Each film has a singular identity that begins with

the director and the script. From there, I facilitate—beginning with the director and stretching outward to the story—the plot and characters." "One has to be a chameleon," Richardson told Aljean Harmetz for the *New York Times* (March 25, 1990). "The story has to come first. I'm not making a wonderful book of still images." A cinematographer, he continued, "must bend to the director's vision, contend with the crew, massage the actors, listen to the producer telling you you're spending too much money, and hear your wife complain because you're away so much."

Robert Bridge Richardson was born in Hyannis, Massachusetts, on August 27, 1955 to Edward E. "Eliot" Richardson and Berry Delahanty Richardson. He had a younger brother, James, who died in 1998. He was raised in Brewster on Cape Cod, Massachusetts. For over 60 years his mother, who died in 2007, operated the Cape Cod Sea Camps, summer camps founded by her parents in 1922. She was an early proponent of the establishment of strict standards for summer camps and led both the American Camp Association and its New England affiliate.

Richardson attended the Proctor Academy, a boarding school in Andover, New Hampshire, where, by his own admission, his main concern was acquiring illegal drugs. He also fought with his brother there; he told Harmetz that he thinks those conflicts brought his first gray hairs, when he was 13. After his graduation, in 1973, he entered the University of Vermont (UVM) at Burlington. Undecided about a career, he took classes in everything from Chinese history to jazz to Russian literature. A screening of the 1956 Swedish drama *The Seventh Seal (Det sjunde inseglet)* during his second semester sparked his interest in filmmaking. Written and directed by Ingmar Bergman, *The Seventh Seal* is about a knight who returns home to Sweden after 10 years on the battlefields of medieval Europe to find that the bubonic plague has spread across his country. When Death, in human form, appears to claim the knight, he fights for his life by challenging Death to a game of chess. During the game the two discuss the meaning of life and the existence of God. "That movie forced me to question my identity," Richardson told Susan Green for the *Burlington Free Press* (February 9, 2005). "I dropped almost all my other classes and concentrated on film studies."

Having decided that UVM's film program was inadequate, Richardson left the college in 1975. He briefly moved back to Cape Cod, where he ushered at a movie theater and joined a local theatrical troupe. The following year he matriculated at the Rhode Island School of Design, in Providence, where he enrolled in the school's film, animation, and video program. There he was influenced by Peter O'Neal, who "opened his eyes to the diversity of film as art," in Bob Fisher's words, as exemplified by films as different as *Nanook of the North*, *Salesman*, and *The Red Shoes*. Richardson graduated with a B.F.A. degree in 1979 and within the next year earned a master's degree in cinematography at the American Film Institute (AFI), in Los Angeles, California. During his time at AFI, he was mentored by the film producer and editor George Folsey, who, he told Bob Fisher, "inspired me to analyze the men who photographed the films that were instrumental in my life"; they included Sven Nykvist, Jack Cardiff, Giuseppe Rotunno, Raoul Coutard, Gregg Toland, Stanley Cortez, and Néstor Almendros.

Richardson spent several years working on documentaries and served as a camera operator on such films as Alex Cox's *Repo Man* and Dorian Walker's *Making the Grade*, both released in 1984. In 1983 he was a cameraman for "Crossfire in El Salvador," an episode of the PBS documentary series *Frontline* about the civil war in that Central American nation. That perilous assignment, during which Richardson narrowly missed being hit by a barrage of bullets, paid off two years later, when Oliver Stone, then a fledgling writer/director, hired the soundman from the *Frontline* documentary, Ramon Menendez, as a consultant for his fictional film *Salvador*. Menendez introduced Richardson to Stone, who hired Richardson as the cinematographer for the film. *Salvador* follows an American journalist, played by James Woods, who becomes increasingly involved with both leftist guerrillas and members of the right-wing military. Richardson's work on *Salvador* (1986) was nominated for the 1987 Film Independent Spirit Award for cinematography.

Richardson next worked with Stone as the director of photography for *Platoon* (1986). Co-starring Charlie Sheen, Tom Berenger, and Willem Dafoe, the film was based on Stone's experiences as an infantryman during the Vietnam War. Shot in the Philippines in 54 days with a budget of only $6.5 million, *Platoon* has been hailed as one of the best Vietnam War movies ever made. David Elliot wrote for the *San Diego (California) Union-Tribune* (January 29, 1987), "Stone and his wonderful cinematographer, Robert Richardson, . . . dipped into the stew of male-bonded pain, weariness, bewilderment and fear to serve the best view that we (us lucky stiffs who missed the war) may ever get of our famous sojourn in hell." *Platoon* won the 1987 Academy Award for best motion picture and the Golden Globe Award for best motion picture in the drama category. It earned Richardson the Film Independent Spirit Award for best cinematography in 1987 as well as Academy Award and British Academy of Film and Television Arts Award (BAFTA) nominations.

The third film Richardson made with Stone, the critically acclaimed *Wall Street* (1987), explores the greed and corruption that taints the world of high finance in the U.S. Richardson then worked on John Sayles's *Eight Men Out* (1988), a dramatization of the real-life scandal that occurred when poorly paid members of the Chicago White Sox baseball team accepted bribes to deliberately forfeit the 1919 World Series. He reunited with Stone

for *Talk Radio* (1988), based on Eric Bogosian's play of the same name, about a radio talk-show host whose program will soon be broadcast nationally.

Stone and Richardson's next film, *Born on the Fourth of July* (1989), earned Richardson his second Oscar nomination for best cinematography and his first ASC Award nomination. Starring Tom Cruise, the film presents the true story of the army veteran Ron Kovic, whose service in the Vietnam War ended when a bullet left him paralyzed from the waist down; back in the States he became an anti–Vietnam War activist. Richardson feared that, because "we're so inundated by horrors today," as he said to Harmetz, Americans had become inured to the awfulness of the war in Vietnam. "*Born* wanted to make people feel a break in their lives, feel the loss," he recalled. Toward that goal, Richardson had the camera move rapidly while shooting the title sequence, during which Kovic is seen celebrating the Fourth of July as a child. "The movie provides a vicarious ride," he explained. "We could have avoided so much camera motion at the beginning, but all that motion sets the audience ill at ease immediately. They're acclimated to the style of the movie by the end of the title sequence, so they don't suddenly become ill at ease in the Vietnam and veterans' hospital sequences."

In 1991 Richardson worked on Stone's *The Doors*, in which Val Kilmer portrayed Jim Morrison, that rock group's frontman; Sayles's drama *City of Hope*; and Stone's *JFK*, the last of which mixes fact and fiction regarding the assassination of President John F. Kennedy and diverges sharply from the official account of the murder (as spelled out in the so-called Warren Commission Report of 1964). In shooting *JFK* Richardson used 14 kinds of film stock and formats to re-create historical footage and produce grainy, fictional home videos. "The result: viewers can't tell in this cinematic collage where the actual, grainy Abraham Zapruder footage of Kennedy's assassination ends and Richardson's new material begins," John Horn wrote for the Associated Press (March 25, 1992). He added, "It is Richardson's verisimilitude that has made *JFK* as powerful—and controversial—as it is." The American Academy of Motion Picture Arts and Sciences agreed, and in 1992 Richardson won his first Oscar for best cinematography. He also earned his second ASC award nomination.

Richardson captured two more ASC nominations in the following years, for Rob Reiner's Oscar-nominated drama *A Few Good Men* (1992) and *Heaven & Earth* (1993), the last installment in Stone's Vietnam War trilogy. He then worked on *Natural Born Killers* (1994), directed by Stone from a story by Tarantino, which follows two psychopathic lovers, Mickey (played by Woody Harrelson) and Mallory (Juliette Lewis), on a killing spree in New Mexico. According to Laurent Bouzereau, in his book *Ultraviolent Movies: From Sam Peckinpah to Quentin Tarantino* (2000), "Stone used a fast-cut style which mixes video, documentary film techniques, animation, rear projection images, black and white, and mock documentary reportage to draw the viewer into the interior world of Mickey and Mallory." To give *Natural Born Killers* structure, Richardson explained to Stephen Pizzello for *American Cinematographer* (November 1994), he and Stone came up with the idea "to break the film down, piece by piece, into textures. The most obvious way of doing textures is with production design—walls, colors, and so forth. But that always left me with a fear that financially, or simply because of logistics, we wouldn't be able to control those textures to the degrees that were necessary. . . . What started to get driven in as . . . our minds got stretched further and further, was going back to 16 mm black & white, and figuring out how we could utilize the grain structure, how we could break down into Hi8 or Super 8." In a review for *Rolling Stone* (September 8, 1994, online), Peter Travers wrote, "For a while, the fireworks dazzle. Say this for Stone: He knows what to do with a camera. The movie is a technical marvel, stunningly photographed by Robert Richardson." For the most part, however, widespread denunciations of *Natural Born Killers* by critics and ordinary moviegoers who felt that it glorified meaningless violence overshadowed discussions of the film's aesthetic merits. Travers himself concluded his review with the remark, "By putting virtuoso technique at the service of lazy thinking, Stone turns his film into the demon he wants to mock: cruelty as entertainment."

Years earlier Scorsese had considered hiring Richardson as the cinematographer for his thriller *Cape Fear* (1991), based in part on photographs Richardson had sent him. The pictures were "fragmented, interesting pieces of images, like faces that he felt dealt with the subject matter of the film," Scorsese recalled to Bob Fisher for *Daily Variety* (October 17, 1995). "I thought it was interesting the way his mind worked. He wasn't trying to be literal in suggesting a specific look. He was conveying a theory or a philosophy in terms of the way the film would look. I was impressed with somebody who would go into that sort of detail." Several years later Scorsese tapped Richardson as cinematographer for the crime drama *Casino* (1995).

Richardson next worked with Stone on *Nixon* (1995) and *U Turn* (1997), Barry Levinson on the political satire *Wag the Dog* (1997), and Errol Morris on the multi-award-winning documentary *Fast, Cheap & Out of Control* (1997). The last-named film focuses on a lion and tiger tamer, a topiary gardener, a robot scientist, and a zoologist who studies naked mole rats (a species of mammal whose societies resemble those of social insects), each of whom is totally immersed in his work. With Morris, according to the filmmaker's Web site, Richardson used "numerous film formats and resolutions—including black & white, color, 35mm, 16mm, Super 8 and video, as well as stock footage, old movies and cartoons." Richardson's work for Scott Hicks's romantic drama *Snow Fall-*

ing on Cedars (1999), which was based on an internationally best-selling novel by David Guterson, earned him both Oscar and ASC Award nominations.

The cinematographer's professional relationship with Oliver Stone ended when Richardson agreed to work on Scorsese's thriller *Bringing Out the Dead* (1999). His acceptance of that job left him unavailable to work on Stone's next project, *Any Given Sunday* (1999). "Oliver felt a bit betrayed," Richardson told Susan Green, after describing Stone as "a brother to me." "I've tried to patch it up without much success. I'd love to work with him again." (Though Richardson has since said that he and Stone have reconciled, the two have not worked together again.)

Following *Bringing Out the Dead* and Shekhar Kapur's *The Four Feathers* (2002), Richardson was hired as the director of photography for Quentin Tarantino's two-part revenge drama, *Kill Bill: Vol. 1* (2003) and *Vol. 2* (2004). The films tell the story of the Bride, played by Uma Thurman, a former member of the Deadly Viper Assassination Squad, led by Bill. She becomes pregnant and leaves the group to start a new life, only to be gunned down by Bill and others in the squad. When she wakes from a coma four years later, she sets out to hunt down and kill each of the squad members. In typical Tarantino fashion, the *Kill Bill* films pay tribute to Hong Kong martial-arts movies, exploitation films, and Italian "spaghetti" Westerns and tell their stories in chapters. "One of the first statements Quentin made was that he wanted each chapter of the script to feel like a reel from a different film," Richardson told John Pavlus for *American Cinematographer* (October 2003). To prepare for shooting *Kill Bill*, Richardson watched hundreds of films of different genres. "What I'm going after in [any genre] is what that genre represents: the attitude toward the filmmaking, rather than the filmmaking itself," he told Pavlus.

Richardson won his second Academy Award for his work on Scorsese's historical drama *The Aviator* (2004). Starring Leonardo DiCaprio, the film is based on the life of Howard Hughes (1905–76), an aviator, industrialist, film producer and director, philanthropist, and one of the wealthiest people in the world. Richardson was presented with the task of re-creating the Technicolor film processes that were commonplace during the period when Hughes was active in aviation and filmmaking (the 1920s to the 1950s). For the early scenes of *The Aviator* he reproduced two-strip Technicolor (in which only red and green were used); for later scenes he introduced the three-strip scheme (red, green, and blue), invented in the mid-1930s. "The most complex element of *The Aviator* was creating and maintaining the purity of the color palette," Richardson told Jack Egan for *Daily Variety* (January 7, 2005). The colors were created by means of digital intermediate, a process that digitalizes motion pictures and allowed Richardson to give two-color and three-color looks to the film. For some of the flight sequences a radio-controlled model air-plane was used. Richardson's work on *The Aviator* received widespread praise from film critics. Clarissa Cruz and Michelle Kung, for example, wrote for *Entertainment Weekly* (February 4, 2005), "The flight sequences in *The Aviator* make you feel like you're in Howard Hughes' cockpit, while the lush set pieces transport you to Holly-wood's golden age." In addition to his Oscar win, Richardson was nominated for both the BAFTA and ASC awards for cinematography.

In recent years Richardson has worked on Rob-ert De Niro's *The Good Shepherd* (2006); Scor-sese's *Shine a Light* (2008), a documentary about the rock band the Rolling Stones; and Errol Mor-ris's documentary *Standard Operating Procedure* (2008), about the abuse and torture of captives at Abu Ghraib, a prisoner-of-war camp run by the U.S. military in Iraq. Richardson's most recent film, *Inglourious Basterds*, premiered at the Cannes Film Festival in Cannes, France, in May 2009 and opened in U.S. theaters three months lat-er. Written and directed by Quentin Tarantino, the fictional *Inglourious Basterds* is set during World War II and follows a group of Jewish-American sol-diers, known as the "Basterds," who brutally kill and scalp Nazi soldiers.

Recent films on which Richardson worked in-clude Scorsese's thriller *Shutter Island* (2010) and the adaptation of Elizabeth Gilbert's best-selling memoir *Eat, Pray, Love* (2010). His upcoming proj-ects include a documentary, to be called "Living in the Material World: George Harrison," about that member of the Beatles, and another Scorsese film, "Hugo Cabaret," set in 1930s Paris. Both films are scheduled for release in 2011. He is also slated to work on "Pinkville," a drama about the My Lai massacre, in which U.S. soldiers murdered hun-dreds of unarmed civilians during the Vietnam War.

When Richardson is between projects he often works on commercials; he has shot ads for such companies as Budweiser, American Express, and Harley-Davidson. Richardson sports a beard and long white hair; his dark eyebrows, Aljean Har-metz wrote, "give his lean face a Mephistophelean look." His marriage to Monona Wali, who directed the film *Maria's Story* (1990), ended in divorce in 2003. Richardson has three daughters. He lives in Santa Monica, California.

—M.A.S.

Suggested Reading: *American Cinematographer* (on-line) Oct. 2003, (on-line) Jan. 2005; *Boston Globe* E p1 Mar. 24 2000; *Burlington (Vermont) Free Press* C p1 Feb. 9, 2005; *New York Times* II p17 Mar. 25, 1990; tcmdb.com

Selected Films: *Salvador*, 1986; *Platoon*, 1986; *Wall Street*, 1987; *Eight Men Out*, 1988; *Talk Radio*, 1988; *Born on the Fourth of July*, 1989; *The Doors*, 1991; *City of Hope*, 1991; *JFK*, 1991; *A Few Good Men*, 1992; *Heaven & Earth*, 1993;

Natural Born Killers, 1994; *Casino*, 1995; *Nixon*, 1995; *U Turn*, 1997; *Fast, Cheap & Out of Control*, 1997; *Wag the Dog*, 1997; *The Horse Whisperer*, 1998; *Snow Falling on Cedars*, 1999; *Bringing Out the Dead*, 1999; *The Four Feathers*, 2002; *Kill Bill: Vol. 1*, 2003; *Kill Bill: Vol. 2*, 2004; *The Aviator*, 2004; *The Good Shepherd*, 2006; *Shine a Light*, 2008; *Standard Operating Procedure*, 2008; *Inglourious Basterds*, 2009; *Shutter Island*, 2010; *Eat, Pray, Love*, 2010

Linda LaBranche, courtesy of Random House

Rideau, Wilbert

(rih-DOH)

Feb. 13, 1942– Journalist; memoirist

Address: c/o Alfred A. Knopf Publishing, 1745 Broadway, New York, NY 10019

In 1961, during a botched robbery in Louisiana, Wilbert Rideau—a 19-year-old African-American—shot three white bank employees, one of whom he also stabbed fatally. Found guilty of murder by an all-white, all-male jury who includ-ed a cousin of one of the victims, Rideau was sen-tenced to death. While on death row Rideau began reading voraciously and, by his own account, came to understand the seriousness and finality of what he had done. After his sentence was commuted to life in prison, following a 1972 U.S. Supreme Court decision barring capital punishment, Rideau, wanting to make a contribution to society, devoted himself to exposing injustices in the U.S. correc-tional system. As the editor of the Louisiana State

Penitentiary news magazine, the *Angolite*, he inspired widespread prison reforms through articles detailing horrific conditions among inmates, in the process winning prestigious journalism awards. In 1993 *Life* magazine pronounced Rideau to be "the most rehabilitated prisoner in America." In his fourth trial, in 2005, he was cleared of the murder charge and convicted of manslaughter; having already served twice the maximum sentence for manslaughter, he was released, after 44 years in prison. Rideau then began writing his memoir, *In the Place of Justice*, published in 2010. David Oshinsky observed for the *New York Times Book Review* (June 3, 2010, on-line) that Rideau is "the rarest of American commodities—a man who exited a penitentiary in better shape than when he arrived."

One of the five children of Gladys and Thomas Rideau, Wilbert Rideau was born on February 13, 1942 in Lawtell, Louisiana. When he was six years old, he moved with his family to the city of Lake Charles, Louisiana, approximately 30 miles from the Texas border. To their neighbors the Rideaus appeared to be an upstanding Catholic family headed by a hard-working husband and father; they were always in church on Sundays, and the children rarely missed a day of school. In reality, Thomas Rideau, a manual laborer whose jobs included work in oil refineries, was a controlling brute who regularly beat his wife and children after nights spent drinking in bars with his friends. Soon after their arrival in Lake Charles, Thomas Rideau abandoned the family, leaving his pregnant wife to raise the couple's children on a maid's salary; Gladys Rideau was eventually forced to go on welfare. Growing up in the pre–civil rights era South, Rideau attended the all-black Second Ward Elementary School before transferring to the W.O. Boston Colored High School in the eighth grade. Around that time Rideau started skipping school. He committed his first crime when he stole $40 and some costume jewelry (gifts for girls at his school) from a Piggly Wiggly supermarket near his home. When he tried to steal a second time, he was caught and sent for psychiatric counseling; too ashamed to return to school, where everyone had heard about his attempted theft, he dropped out. At 13 he got a job at a local grocery store.

At 16 Rideau learned that his brother and another boy had committed burglary. When the two were caught, Rideau—as an accessory—was sent with the other boys to the State Industrial School for Colored Youths, a reform school, where he spent five months. After his release he landed a job, with the help of a cousin, in a fabric shop. He found the atmosphere there pleasant but became embittered when, after he had assumed the responsibilities of an assistant manager who had left, the store's white owner offered him a raise of $2.50 per week, much less than he thought he had been promised. "I was fed up with a white society that marginalized me," he wrote in *In the Place of Justice*. "I brooded about that, and about the fact that I had no real friends,

only some people who would become chummy when they hit me up for cash. I felt my life was empty, and I despaired of things ever being different." On February 15, 1961, a day on which he was paid, Rideau bought a .22-caliber pistol. He has said that he bought the gun for protection; Rideau, who stood five feet seven inches and weighed less than 120 pounds, was frequently hassled by blacks and whites alike. "What pushed me over the edge," he wrote, "was having been slapped and threatened in front of others at a nightclub by a guy with a knife a week earlier. . . . I vowed that would never happen again." Meanwhile, Rideau had heard that there were job opportunities for blacks in California, but he lacked the money to get there.

On the evening of February 16, 1961, Rideau, then 19, walked into a branch of the Gulf National Bank, carrying a suitcase and his concealed pistol and hunting knife. He approached the manager, Jay Hickman, telling him that there was a woman outside who wanted to speak with him. Hickman was not initially alarmed; he recognized Rideau from the times the young man had come into the bank to make change for his boss. Hickman followed Rideau to the rear of the bank, where Rideau revealed that he had a gun and ordered Hickman into a small side room. Rideau instructed Hickman to call to the two tellers working at the time, Julia Ferguson and Dora McCain, and have them lock the doors and draw the front curtain. McCain, who had always been wary of Rideau, could tell from the sound of Hickman's voice that something was wrong and made a phone call to the bank's main branch. The two women were then called to the back of the bank. As Hickman, following Rideau's instructions, emptied money from the tellers' drawers into the robber's suitcase, the phone rang; Rideau told Hickman not to pick up, but when Hickman suggested that it would seem suspicious if no one answered, Rideau allowed him to take the call. The caller was the bank's vice president, who asked if the police should be called; Hickman responded, "It might be a good idea," then hung up. Rideau, unaware of the caller's identity but suspicious nonetheless, told Hickman to put the rest of the money in the suitcase quickly. He then forced all three employees out the back door and into Ferguson's car. From the back seat, he ordered Ferguson to drive.

At his 2005 trial Rideau said that his original plan was to lock the workers inside the bank's safe, where they would not be discovered before he had a chance to make his getaway. Even after the unexpected phone call, Rideau said, he did not intend for anyone to get hurt; he planned to let the three hostages out of the car a few miles outside of town, then simply drive away. It was only when one of the employees tried to escape from the vehicle, he maintained, that he panicked and opened fire, hitting all three. He then fatally stabbed Ferguson. Next, he fled, driving her car north on Highway 90. Later he was stopped by two troopers and taken into custody.

News of the crime and Rideau's arrest spread, and by the time Rideau arrived at the local prison to be booked, an angry mob of several hundred had gathered there. In April 1961, following Rideau's confession—which was made without benefit of legal counsel, videotaped without his knowledge, and aired repeatedly on a local news station—he was tried by an all-white jury, including two deputy sheriffs, Julia Ferguson's cousin, and a man who knew Hickman personally. At the trial, in testimony that was later discredited, McCain said that after the robbery Rideau ordered Ferguson to stop the car, had the hostages get out and stand in a line, then shot all three. McCain further testified that Ferguson begged for her life as she tried to stand up and that Rideau grabbed her by the hair and said, "Don't worry. This will be quick and cool," before stabbing her several times in the chest and slitting her throat. The jury found Rideau guilty of murder and sentenced him to death. He was placed on death row at one of the nation's most notorious prisons, the Louisiana State Penitentiary, better known as Angola—the largest maximum-security facility in the U.S.

Because he was usually kept in solitary confinement at Angola, Rideau had relatively little contact with the rest of the prison population during his first 12 years there. To keep himself occupied, he began to read. Through books from the prison library, Rideau began to educate himself and see life from a different perspective. "Reading ultimately allowed me to feel empathy, to emerge from my cocoon of self-centeredness and appreciate the humanness of others. . . . It enabled me finally to appreciate the enormity of what I had done," he wrote in In the Place of Justice.

In the 1972 case Furman v. Georgia, the U.S. Supreme Court ruled that the death penalty, because of the arbitrary way it was applied at the time, constituted cruel and unusual punishment and would be banned until the court's concerns could be addressed. Along with those of the nation's other condemned criminals, Rideau's death sentence was changed to life imprisonment. While his life was spared, Rideau would be confined with Angola's general population—among whom, as he told Terry Gross for the National Public Radio program Fresh Air (April 26, 2010, on-line), "there was violence literally every day. You had people getting killed and gang wars. You had drug traffickers rampant. You had sexual violence [and] enslavement of prisoners. Guys would rape you, and that was a process that redefined you, not as a male but as a female and also as property. Whoever raped you owned you, and you had to serve him . . . as long as you were in prison, unless you killed him or he gave you away or sold you or you got out of prison."

Rideau was spared that treatment because of the respect accorded him among the prisoners for having survived death row. Soon, however, he felt the need not only to survive but to find a sense of purpose. Specifically, "I wanted to leave something behind that would contribute to furthering a better understanding of the criminal, and the only way to do it is to write it," he told David Gilson in an interview for Mother Jones (May/June 2010, on-line). "I didn't have any other forums, so I had to teach myself to write. I concluded that the books I was reading were written by people who didn't come into the world writing with a pen in their hand, so that means they learned it. And if they can learn it, I can learn it. So I started reading books differently." Slowly, Rideau taught himself to write. In an interview with Erin Moriarty for the CBS-TV show Sunday Morning (April 25, 2010, on-line), he said, "If you had given me paint and brush and an easel and canvas, I might have become a painter, but I didn't have any of that. All I had were a pencil, paper and books. And that's the way I learned to express myself."

After Rideau left death row, he had asked if he could be assigned to work on the prison newspaper, the Angolite, whose censorship by prison authorities, he recalled to Gilson, made it "the equivalent of a boarding school newsletter." His request to join the all-white Angolite staff was initially denied; Angola was a segregated prison at the time. Determined to be heard, Rideau started his own newspaper, the Lifer, which grew to be popular among the inmates because of its honest portrayal of life in Angola. Rideau even started writing a weekly column for a chain of black newspapers and then began freelancing for other outside publications, including Penthouse. When, in 1975, a federal court ruled the conditions in Angola to be unconstitutionally cruel, the prison underwent a transformation, including the installation of a new administration. The new secretary of corrections, C. Paul Phelps, realized that a prison publication had the potential to take the place of the prison's rumor mill. Impressed by the quality of Rideau's column, "The Jungle," Phelps appointed Rideau as the Angolite's new editor—making him the first black editor of a prison publication in the U.S.—and agreed to publish the paper uncensored as long as Rideau and the rest of the inmate staff adhered to professional journalism standards. Rideau devoted himself to exposing the violence that prisoners of Angola lived with every day. "What I really wanted to do was tell . . . ," he said to Terry Gross. "I just couldn't believe that society would accept . . . the barbarity, the horrible things that were going on. And . . . I can write. And I felt it was incumbent upon me to tell society. . . . I couldn't make things right, but I [could] give something back. I [could] contribute something to society." It soon became clear that not everyone valued Rideau's candor as much as Phelps did. Rideau, however, refused to change his approach to editing the Angolite. "The first thing I realized was that the prisoners no more wanted 'tell it like it is' than the guards," he told Gilson. "You had to tread lightly in the beginning, but gradually the concept took root and they began to appreciate it. The thing is, you have to try and treat both sides the same way.

It doesn't matter what you write; somebody will be offended by it. But once you acquire a reputation for fairness, for impartiality, and knowing what you're talking about, and you always try to be right, people will respect that."

Under Rideau's direction the *Angolite* became the first prison publication to be nominated for a National Magazine Award; in all it was nominated for that prestigious award seven times. Rideau himself became known outside the prison for his groundbreaking exposés, including "The Sexual Jungle," a detailed essay about sexual assault and slavery in prison, and a piece called "Conversations with the Dead," about prisoners who had served their sentences but were still behind bars, that led to the release of many inmates. Rideau's inclusion in a 1990 issue of previously unpublished post-mortem photos of an inmate who had sustained severe burns when he was executed in a defective electric chair in 1983 prompted Louisiana to change the method of execution to lethal injection. Under Rideau the *Angolite* received some of journalism's most coveted awards, including the Robert F. Kennedy Journalism Award and the Sidney Hillman Award, and Rideau won the George Polk Award. In 1979 he became the first prisoner to win the American Bar Association's Silver Gavel Award. Together with the *Angolite* associate editor Ron Wikberg and University of Louisiana professor Burk Foster, Rideau published *The Wall Is Strong* (1991), a textbook on criminal justice. Rideau collaborated with Wikberg again to compile an annotated anthology of *Angolite* articles, *Life Sentences: Rage and Survival Behind Bars* (1992).

In the 1990s Rideau became a correspondent for National Public Radio and worked with the radio documentarian Dave Isay on a program called *Tossing Away the Keys*. He produced a segment for the ABC-TV newsmagazine *Day One* that won the CINE Award; co-created the documentary *Final Judgement: The Execution of Antonio Jones*, which aired in 1996 and won the Thurgood Marshall Award and the Louisiana Bar Association's award for overall excellence; and served as a co-director of the 1998 documentary *The Farm: Angola, USA*, which won the Grand Jury Prize at the Sundance Film Festival that year and was nominated for an Academy Award as best documentary feature in 1999. An exemplary prisoner, Rideau was permitted to lecture widely in Louisiana, accompanied by one unarmed guard. He also made two trips to Washington, D.C., to address a group of newspaper editors on the subject of prison journalism.

Meanwhile, Rideau was recommended for release by the Louisiana pardon board several times, only to be denied clemency by the sitting governors. An investigation by the ABC-TV show *20/20* revealed part of the reason why: former Louisiana governor Edwin Edwards had reportedly made a promise to Rideau's victim Dora McCain that neither he, nor any of his successors if he could help it, would ever release Rideau. Over the years Rideau had exhausted every legal avenue to gain his freedom. His first conviction was appealed, and in the landmark 1963 decision *Rideau v. the State of Louisiana*, the U.S. Supreme Court ruled that Rideau had been denied his right to a fair trial; the 1961 conviction was overturned, with Justice Potter Stewart calling Rideau's first trial a "kangaroo court proceeding" and noting that there had been "no lawyer to advise Rideau of his right to stand mute," among other blatant violations of Rideau's rights. At his second trial, in 1964, Rideau was again found guilty of murder by an all-white, all-male jury and sentenced to death. Rideau appealed that decision as well, and in 1970 he was convicted and sentenced to death a third time. Following the *Furman v. Georgia* decision, in 1972, the Louisiana Supreme Court vacated his death sentence but upheld his murder conviction. In an interview with Adam Liptak for the *New York Times* (January 17, 2005), Rideau admitted that he had all but given up hope for a fair trial when he learned that he would be tried a fourth time. "When you've been turned down and ridden that hope train for so long and keep getting knocked back, you stop making plans," he said.

During Rideau's fourth and final trial, in 2005, many of the highly sensational details from testimony at previous trials were discredited. In particular, there was new testimony from a forensic pathologist, Werner Spitz, who stated that the wound in Julia Ferguson's neck appeared to be from a doctor's emergency-room procedure rather than from a stabbing—and thus that Ferguson's throat had not been slit by Rideau. The defense successfully argued that Rideau's violent actions had been the result of panic, not premeditation. The mixed-race jury of 10 women and two men convicted Rideau of manslaughter rather than murder. Because the maximum sentence for manslaughter in 1961 was 21 years and Rideau had already served nearly 44, he was immediately released.

Having spent his entire adult life behind bars, Rideau had to learn how to function as a free man. He explained to Gilson, "Prison is all sort of planned out, and you can pretty much predict what you're going to be doing five years from now. But out here's it's totally different, totally a different ball game. You can have the best-laid plans—and then your car doesn't start. Those are the things you don't think about when you're fantasizing about freedom." Finding work is hard for an ex-convict, even one as well-known as Rideau. He told Liptak in 2005, the year he was released, "Most people my age are retired, and I have no health insurance, no pension, no Social Security. I've got to start producing. I've got to get a job. I'd like to write. I've got so much to say. I'm going to continue, to the extent that I can, to be a journalist." Most of all, Rideau had to adjust to no longer being a big fish in a small pond. "Somebody recently asked me was there anything I missed, you know, not being in prison?" he recalled to Moriarty. "I said, 'Yeah, I miss being a big shot!' Out here, I'm just a nobody, you know?"

Rideau's memoir, *In the Place of Justice: A Story of Punishment and Deliverance*, was published by Random House in 2010. The book received good reviews. "Rideau tells his story in riveting detail, beginning with how he grew up . . . ," Mary Foster wrote for the Durham, North Carolina, *Herald-Sun* (May 2, 2010). "The amazing part of Rideau's story, however, is his transformation from an uneducated, prejudiced teen to a thoughtful, well-read adult who became so well-respected by prison wardens that they began calling on him for help and advice. . . . Now he has provided a wonderful chance to share his remarkable life." In another assessment, Steve Weinberg wrote for the *San Francisco Chronicle* (May 2, 2010): "Perhaps no book written by an inmate has ever conveyed so much factual and emotional information about day-to-day prison life. . . . Rideau is a first-rate stylist, a man of letters despite sparse formal education."

Rideau has committed himself to educating people about life behind bars. He often speaks at training sessions and seminars devoted to continuing legal education for lawyers already admitted to the bar; he also offers his services as a consultant to legal-defense teams in capital-offense cases.

Rideau lives in Baton Rouge with his wife, Linda LaBranche. During Rideau's incarceration, LaBranche became familiar with the criminal-justice system while conducting research for Rideau, and she helped engineer the legal strategy that led to his release. "I know I've been the recipient of a lot of good fortune," Rideau told Erin Moriarty. "I like to believe that it's all for a reason, that somehow or another I was chosen, so to speak, to live this long for a good reason. And because I believe in that, that's what I try to do." Near the end of his memoir, Rideau wrote, "I wake up in heaven every day. . . . I rise early because I don't want to miss a thing."

—H.R.W.

Suggested Reading: *Mother Jones* (on-line) May/June 2010; *New York Times* (on-line) Mar. 21, 1999, Jan. 17, 2005, May 4, 2010, June 3, 2010; *Nation* Jan. 21, 2002; New Orleans *Times-Picayune* National p4 Jan. 15, 2005; *CBS Sunday Morning* (on-line) Apr. 25, 2010; Rideau, Wilbert. *In the Place of Justice: A Story of Punishment and Deliverance*, 2010

Selected Books: *The Wall Is Strong* (with Ron Wikberg and Burk Foster), 1991; *Life Sentences: Rage and Survival Behind Bars* (with Ron Wikberg), 1992; *In the Place of Justice: A Story of Punishment and Deliverance*, 2010

Selected Films: *The Farm: Angola, USA*, 1998

Roberts, Michael V. and Steven C.

Entrepreneurs

Roberts, Michael V.
Oct. 24, 1948– Entrepreneur

Roberts, Steven C.
Apr. 11, 1952– Entrepreneur

Address: The Roberts Companies, 1408 N. Kingshighway, St. Louis, MO 63113

Since the founding of their first company, Roberts-Roberts & Associates (RRA), in 1974, Michael V. Roberts and Steven C. Roberts have built an empire worth an estimated $1 billion. Roberts-Roberts is now part of a family of concerns that comprise the Roberts Companies and function as umbrellas for a total of 76 businesses. Those involve real estate, including the construction and management of residential, retail, and commercial properties; broadcasting; wireless telecommunications; aviation; public relations; custom cabinetry; and hotel management. The brothers also own a historic theater in St. Louis, Missouri, where they have lived since birth and where they maintain their headquarters. "We are diversified," Michael Roberts told Pam Droog for *St. Louis Commerce Magazine* (May 2003). "I always felt that's important. If you limit yourself to one sector of business opportunities in this economy, you die." Michael Roberts, the older of the brothers, is the chairman and chief executive officer of the Roberts Companies; Steven is the president. Both men are lawyers, and both have served on St. Louis's board of aldermen, the city's legislative body—Michael from 1977 to 1983 and Steven from 1979 to 1991. In the course of their careers, the Robertses have contributed beyond measure to the well-being of thousands of St. Louisans through job creation and urban-renewal projects and, in both those spheres, initiatives aimed at increasing the presence of women and members of minority groups in all facets of private enterprise. The brothers' affirmative-action efforts have also helped many people living in and around Washington, D.C., New York City, and Atlantic City, New Jersey. Kay Gabbert, the conglomerate's senior vice president, who has worked with Michael and Steven Roberts since 1982, listed on the Roberts Companies Web site three major reasons for the brothers' success: "They are very aggressive; they never say they can't do something; [and] they are always looking for opportunities." Michael Roberts is the author of the self-published book *Action Has No Season: Strategies and Secrets to Gaining Wealth and Authority* (2005).

The first of the four children of Victor and Delores (Talley) Roberts, Michael Victor Roberts was born on October 24, 1948; Steven Craig Roberts, the

Courtesy of the Roberts Companies

Michael (left) and Steven Roberts

second child, was born on April 11, 1952. Their brother, Mark, and sister, Lori, work for the Roberts Companies. The Robertses' paternal grandfather was a physician. Their father served in World War II as a member of one of the nation's all-black infantry units; he held the job of night-shift supervisor when he retired from the U.S. Postal Service after working there for 39 years and is now the chief financial officer of the Roberts Companies (but refuses to take a salary). Delores Roberts was a homemaker who later became a schoolteacher. "We were pretty much sheltered as a middle-class African-American family," Michael told Shelley Smithson for St. Louis's *Riverfront Times* (March 17, 2004). "We were taught traditional work habits and values. We were altar boys in the Episcopal Church." Their mother saw to it that her children engaged in educational extracurricular activities, such as Saturday-morning science classes held in a local park.

The Robertses lived with the children's paternal grandmother in north St. Louis until 1958. That year, along with a dozen other African-American families, they moved into their own home in a newly built enclave in that part of the city. The residents of houses surrounding their small development were white, and as boys the Roberts brothers were subjected both to institutionalized racism and, occasionally, racist acts by individuals. They were not permitted to swim with whites in public pools and were permitted to sit only in a designated area behind right field at home games of the St. Louis Cardinals baseball club, and even after the Supreme Court, in 1954, ruled unconstitutional the enforced segregation of public schools, the public schools the boys attended remained all

black. One day when Steven was about six, "I was playing baseball with these kids who were white," he recalled to Smithson. "We were in my backyard and there was this big redneck-looking guy who came out of this four-family flat behind our home. He comes out and grabs his son and says, 'You can't play with him because he's a n*****.' I didn't even know what a n***** was." As the boys got older, they witnessed so-called white flight from the neighborhoods adjacent to their enclave: when a few black families bought homes from whites on those streets, realtors warned other white homeowners that the value of their property was going to decline as a result. The realtors would then buy the whites' homes at below market value and sell them to black families at a handsome profit.

According to Michael Roberts, he and Steven "were always linked," as he told Pam Droog. "We were pretty much interested in achieving our goals, and in working." The boys earned money by shoveling snow, mowing lawns, and delivering newspapers. "By the age of 11 or 12, I was making about a buck a week mowing the yard for my parents," Michael recalled to Gary Pettus for the Jackson, Mississippi, *Clarion-Ledger* (March 25, 2007). "Then I was invited to cut a neighbor's yard, and they paid me $5 for the same work. That's when the light bulb went off: I realized I could make more money working for myself." He added, "Ownership, in my opinion, is the key to the success of the abundant lifestyle. I did not want to be a part of someone else's destiny. I wanted my own. Whether I was making a lot of money was beside the point."

In 1967 Michael Roberts graduated from Northwest High School, St. Louis's first desegregated secondary school. He spent the first part of his college career at the University of Central Missouri, in Warrensburg, and then St. Louis Community College at Forest Park; at the latter he helped to found the Black Students Association. One summer he attended Camp Winnewanka, an American Youth Foundation facility founded by William H. Danforth (who established the St. Louis–based Ralston Purina Co.). At that camp, which aimed to instill feelings of Christian brotherhood in teenagers, Michael met Danforth's grandson John "Jack" Danforth, an Episcopal minister and Missouri politician (and later, for two decades, a U.S. senator). Armed with a Danforth fellowship, Michael transferred to Lindenwood University, in St. Charles, Missouri; money he earned by selling dashikis helped to pay his expenses. He received a B.S. degree in English literature and communications in 1971. Earlier, he had briefly considered studying medicine or becoming an Episcopal priest, "because in that role I could pontificate to people on Sunday mornings," he told Droog. "But I realized if I went to law school and got into politics I could pontificate every day." Roberts attended the Saint Louis University School of Law. As a law-school student, he also took classes at the International Institute of Human Rights in Strasbourg, France, in 1972, and the Hague Academy of International

Law in the Netherlands, in 1973. He earned a J.D. degree in 1974. Meanwhile, in 1970, Steven Roberts had entered Clark University, in Worcester, Massachusetts, also as a Danforth fellow. He majored in both sociology and economics and earned a B.A. degree in 1974. He, too, toyed with the idea of becoming a doctor or a priest, then decided to study law. In 1978 he earned both a master's of law degree in urban law and a J.D. degree at Washington University, in St. Louis. He also studied law abroad. According to Michael Roberts, neither he nor Steven ever planned to practice law; rather, he told Droog, they attended law school because they believed that it offered "a great extended liberal arts education that also teaches you a new language, how to think, how to perceive opportunities more quickly."

Earlier, in 1974, Michael and Steven Roberts had launched Roberts-Roberts & Associates, as a business-consulting and construction-management company. The impetus, Michael told Droog, was the growing number of multimillion-dollar class-action lawsuits being brought against large companies and government agencies for alleged discrimination against women and members of minority groups. The danger of being sued or fined for noncompliance with government-mandated affirmative-action rules led corporate and public entities to seek advice from RRA on ways to increase the participation of so-called disadvantaged business enterprises (DBEs) and minority- and women-owned businesses (MBEs and WBEs) in construction projects, which typically involve many suppliers and contractors. Among other accomplishments listed on the RRA Web site, thanks to RRA such St. Louis–based companies as the food wholesaler Wetterau Inc. and Southwestern Bell (now AT&T Southwest) paid $63 million (between 1974 and 1983) and $167 million (in 1983 and 1984), respectively, to MBEs and/or WBEs, and, nationally, Anheuser-Busch companies paid $2.2 billion to MBE or WBE construction companies between 1983 and 2003. Other major DBE, MBE, or WBE contracts negotiated with RRA's assistance were connected with Missouri Department of Transportation and Metropolitan Washington Airports Authority projects, the Lambert–St. Louis International Airport, the Woodrow Wilson Bridge Project (in Washington, D.C.), and the St. Louis Cardinals' new stadium.

Also in 1974, with a $7,000 loan from his father, who had borrowed the money from the credit union set up for U.S. Postal Service workers, Michael began to acquire real estate. He would buy dilapidated inner-city houses, have them renovated, and sell them at a profit. In addition to amassing capital, he used the renovated properties as collateral for loans for additional purchases. In 1982 Michael and Steven formed Roberts Brothers Properties (RBP) and purchased a three-story, 200,000-square-foot building in Fountain Park, an economically depressed area of St. Louis. After the renovation of the building, which had once been a Sears

Roebuck outlet, they moved RRA and RBP offices to the top floor and gradually leased spaces on the other floors to a total of 50 government agencies and businesses, including retail stores and eateries. By 1985 the Victor Roberts Building, as the brothers had named it, had become a destination for some 3,000 shoppers and others daily. Nevertheless, in 2000 and 2001, when the Robertses attempted to get loans to build a mall adjacent to their building, every bank turned them down on the grounds that the site was not a "good location," as Michael told Droog. The brothers proceeded with construction nevertheless, using $4 million of their own funds. Called the Shops at Roberts Village, the mall opened in 2003. That year Roberts Brothers Properties bought the seven-story St. Louis Board of Education Building, in the historic Old Post Office District in the city's downtown, and had it converted into 47 luxury rental apartments and lofts and 8,000 square feet of retail space. The first tenants moved there in 2005. In 2006 the brothers broke ground on Roberts Place, a gated community in St. Louis's Upper West End that will consist of 72 rental apartments and 24 single-family homes. The homes, which were still under construction at the end of 2009, were designed to meet the Leadership in Energy Efficient Design (LEED) standards for environmentally responsible building design. In addition to other properties in St. Louis, the Roberts brothers own Roberts Isle, a 76-unit gated condominium development in Nassau, Bahamas.

Following their purchase of the historic Mayfair hotel in downtown St. Louis, in 2003, and the Crowne Plaza in Marietta, Georgia, in 2006, the brothers established the Roberts Hotels Group LLC. In addition to St. Louis and Marietta, their portfolio includes hotels in Dallas and Houston, Texas; Tampa and Fort Myers, Florida; Shreveport, Louisiana; Jackson and Memphis, Mississippi (which borders Memphis, Tennessee); and Spartanburg, South Carolina. In 2007 the Roberts Hotels Group were named an Ernst & Young 2007 Entrepreneur of the Year, and their extensively renovated Crowne Plaza in Marietta, jointly managed by the InterContinental Hotels Group, won the top award at InterContinental's annual meeting. It was also honored as the best-managed of InterContinental's more than 400 Crowne Plaza hotels. In 2003 Michael and Steven also purchased the Historic American Theater, in St. Louis. The renovated building, which they renamed the Roberts Orpheum Theater, reopened in 2005.

In 1989, with the purchase of the St. Louis television station WRBU, the Roberts brothers launched the Roberts Broadcasting Co. Originally an affiliate of the Home Shopping Network, the station became an affiliate of UPN in 2003 and of the Fox-owned MyNetwork TV in 2006. As of late 2009 the brothers owned three television stations—WRBU in St. Louis, WZRB in Columbia, South Carolina, and WRBJ in Jackson, Mississippi—as well as WRBJ-FM, a hip-hop radio station in Jackson. In

April 2007 the Robertses announced that their stations would no longer be permitted to broadcast anything that they deemed unacceptably violent, sexist, or racist.

In the late 1990s the Roberts brothers entered the emerging wireless-communication market. They launched Roberts Wireless Communications, and along with the telecommunications company Sprint (now Sprint Nextel Corp.), they built wireless networks in Missouri, Kansas, and Illinois. Lucent Technologies (now Alcatel-Lucent) lent $56 million to the project, whose cost totaled $78 million. In 2001 Alamosa Holdings, a Sprint affiliate at that time, bought out Roberts Wireless Communications for $300 million. The Roberts Companies retained ownership of communication towers in Missouri, Oklahoma, Illinois, and Kansas, and later, the brothers having formed the Roberts Tower Co., added towers in Missouri, Utah, New Mexico, and Tennessee. The demand for the Roberts brothers' rural cellular-phone towers, which they had purchased when most other companies were focused on urban markets, increased significantly as telecommunications companies including AT&T, Verizon, and T-Mobile expanded their services. The Roberts Tower Co. is currently the second-largest privately held tower concern in the U.S.

Roberts Aviation, founded in 2000, "fit with our other companies, because we had made a big sale and needed an appropriate tax shelter," Michael told Pam Droog. The two jets that Roberts Aviation owns and leases, a 12-passenger Gulfstream II and an eight-passenger Hawker, "earn their keep," he said.

For many years the Roberts brothers were also active in politics. In 1976 Michael Roberts assisted Jimmy Carter's successful run for the presidency as the manager of the Carter campaign in St. Louis. After Carter's inauguration Michael became a regular guest at the White House. According to Pam Droog, "He played tennis with Hamilton Jordan, Carter's chief of staff, and hob-nobbed with cabinet members." In 1976 Michael was elected to the St. Louis board of aldermen, the equivalent of a city council. He was the youngest person ever to win a seat on the board until 1979, when Steven won the contest for alderman in another district. The board of aldermen had major problems to contend with at that time: because of the loss of manufacturing jobs and the boom in suburban development that accompanied a huge increase in highway construction outside the city during the decades following World War II, St. Louis had suffered the exodus of half its residents. Many of the St. Louisans who remained lived in deteriorating housing in rundown neighborhoods. During Michael's four two-year terms as an alderman and Steven's six, the brothers worked to reverse the city's declining fortunes while creating opportunities for minority- and women-owned businesses. In the process they "met the city's most powerful developers and learned how to use incentives such as tax-increment financing and tax abatements to lure investments," Droog wrote. Each brother has made an unsuccessful bid for the mayoralty of St. Louis, Michael losing the Democratic primary in 1989 and Steven doing so in 1993. In his conversation with Droog, Michael blamed their failures on the decision of William Lacy Clay Sr., who represented various parts of St. Louis in the U.S. Congress from 1969 until 2001, to support their opponents for reasons connected with the Democratic St. Louis political machine.

In 2010 the Robertses acknowledged that their businesses, like countless others, had been affected by the worldwide economic downturn that began in 2007. "As we began to get hit hard [by] the recession, we looked at what are the better assets for us to sell in order to create liquidity, and this year we sold our communications tower company for about $90 million," Michael told Brandon Clements for CNN (October 16, 2010, on-line). "Your businesses are like your children. As you grow them and mature them, at some point you may feel you have to let them go." He also said, "We are in a time like no other. . . . It's the best time to start a business."

Among other honors, in 2002 and 2003 the Robertses were listed among the *St. Louis Business Journal*'s "100 Leaders to Watch," and in 2007 and 2008 they received that magazine's Top 50 Award. In 2009 Michael Roberts received the Trumpet Award for business from the Trumpet Awards Foundation, in Atlanta, Georgia.

Michael and his wife, Jeanne Gore, a former schoolteacher, have four grown children—Michael Jr. and Jeanne, who are twins, Fallon, and Meaghan. Steven and his wife, Eva L. Frazer, a physician, have three children—Steven Jr., Christian, and Darci, who ranged in age from 15 to 21 in 2009. The brothers and their families live within a block of each other in St. Louis.

—M.A.S.

Suggested Reading: *Black Enterprise* p169+ June 2000; *Chicago Defender* p3 Apr. 25, 2007; *Forbes* p170+ Oct. 16, 2000; (Jackson, Mississippi) *Clarion-Ledger* F p1 Mar. 25, 2007; Michael V. Roberts Web site; roberts-companies.com; *St. Louis Commerce Magazine* (on-line) May 2003; (St. Louis, Missouri) *Riverfront Times* (on-line) Mar. 17, 2004; *Southern Style* F p1+ Mar. 25, 2007; Steven C. Roberts Web site; TheHistoryMakers.com

Selected Books: Roberts, Michael. *Action Has No Season: Strategies and Secrets to Gaining Wealth and Authority*, 2005

Courtesy of Ariel Investments

Rogers, John W. Jr.

Mar. 31, 1958– Business executive; investment manager

Address: Ariel Investments, 200 E. Randolph Dr., Suite 2900, Chicago, IL 60601

"I'm a natural contrarian. If you're going to be above average, you can't do the things the average person does," the business executive, entrepreneur, and investor John W. Rogers Jr. told Lauren Young for *SmartMoney* (March 2002). In 1983, at the age of 24 and less than three years after he completed college, Rogers founded Ariel Capital Management, the first money-management firm started by an African-American and the largest minority-run mutual fund in the U.S. Inspired by Aesop's fable "The Tortoise and the Hare," Rogers included on Ariel's logo an image of a tortoise holding a huge loving-cup trophy; on the company's home page, an animated illustration shows a triumphant tortoise and displays Ariel's motto: "Slow and steady wins the race." The chairman, chief executive officer, and chief investment officer of Ariel Investments, as it was renamed in 2008, Rogers built his firm by adopting a conservative approach to investing, one that focused on well-managed but lesser-known and undervalued companies—a strategy associated with the legendary investor Warren Buffett, one of his heroes. "We do not subscribe to flashy investment styles," Rogers told Lynn Norment for *Ebony* (August 2004). "We do not chase today's hot stocks, which can turn out to be tomorrow's laggards. Instead, we utilize patient investing—the disciplined analysis of businesses and the methodical search for good companies

with the potential for earnings and share price growth." "Ariel is driven by Rogers' style of management," Matthew S. Scott wrote for *Black Enterprise* (June 30, 2002). "His strategic vision, competitiveness, and passion for precision have taken root in all operations of the firm. He has built the enterprise slowly, handpicking many employees himself while crafting a team culture that breeds loyalty, productivity, and performance." Rogers's column, "The Patient Investor," has appeared in *Forbes* magazine since 2002.

Inspired by Martin Luther King Jr.'s "Letter from Birmingham City Jail" (1963), in which King called for nonviolent, direct action to end racial injustice, Rogers has long engaged in social activism. In doing so he has become part of what Peter Slevin, writing for the *Princeton Alumni Weekly* (October 10, 2007), characterized as "a potent African-American elite that is carving a growing role in civic and cultural affairs" in Chicago, Illinois, Rogers's home since birth and the home of Ariel Investments. One of his major projects is the Ariel Education Initiative, which supports a Chicago public school, the Ariel Community Academy, whose curriculum emphasizes financial literacy. For six years in the 1990s, he served as the president of the Chicago Park District's board of commissioners, and he is a vice chair of the Chicago Urban League board of trustees. In 2002 he co-founded the annual Black Corporate Directors Conference, which aims to "promote a comprehensive commitment to corporate diversity," as Rogers's office wrote to *Current Biography*. As a board member of two Chicago-based firms, the Aon Corp., an insurance holding company, and Exelon, a utilities company, and of the McDonald Corp., whose headquarters are in Oak Brook, a Chicago suburb, he has worked to increase racial diversity among employees and to increase employee investments in savings and retirement accounts. For more than two decades, Rogers has been a Democratic Party fundraiser, supporting politicians including Chicago mayor Richard M. Daley, one-term U.S. senator Carol Moseley Braun, and former U.S. senator Bill Bradley, during Bradley's unsuccessful bid for the 2000 Democratic presidential nomination. A longtime friend of Barack Obama's, he backed Obama's voter-registration drive in Chicago in 1992 and his run for the U.S. Senate, in 2004; later, he co-chaired presidential-candidate Obama's campaign-finance committee in Illinois and the 2009 Presidential Inaugural Committee. In 2008 Princeton University, his alma mater, conferred on him its most prestigious honor, the Woodrow Wilson Prize, for his efforts to further the common good. In 2010 the *Financial Times*–sponsored Outstanding Directors Exchange, a gathering of boards of directors of publicly traded companies, named Rogers one of six outstanding directors, for his "invaluable guidance, investor insights, management mentoring and an unflagging commitment to diversity."

An only child, John W. Rogers Jr. was born on March 31, 1958 in Chicago to John W. Rogers Sr. and the former Jewel Stradford. Rogers's maternal great-grandfather, J. B. Stradford, was an attorney and at one time the only black person to own a hotel in Tulsa, Oklahoma. J. B.'s son, Cornelius Francis Stradford, also a lawyer, co-founded the National Bar Association and the bar association of Cook County (which encompasses Chicago); he represented J. B. and other African-American victims of the horrific race riots that took place in Tulsa in 1921, and in 1940 he appeared before the U.S. Supreme Court to argue for the defendant, Carl A. Hansberry, in a famous case whose ruling effectively declared racially restrictive housing covenants to be unconstitutional. Rogers's father flew more than 100 missions during World War II, as a member of the Tuskegee Airmen, a group of African-American pilots whose contributions to the war effort were not recognized until decades later. After the war he earned a law degree and maintained a private practice with his wife until he became a juvenile-court judge in Cook County, serving in that position for 21 years. Rogers's mother was a founding member of the Congress of Racial Equality (CORE) and the first woman to earn a doctor of laws degree (in 1946) from the University of Chicago Law School. A critic of Democratic machine politics in Chicago, she became a Republican Party loyalist. She was the first woman to be named (by President Dwight D. Eisenhower) assistant U.S. attorney for the Northern District of Illinois (1955–58); she seconded the presidential nomination of then–Vice President Richard M. Nixon at the 1960 Republican National Convention and under President Nixon became the first woman to serve as the U.S. deputy solicitor general (1972–75), a post in which she argued many cases before the Supreme Court. In the Lyndon B. Johnson White House, she served on the Council on Minority Business Enterprise (1965–67). In 1989 President George H. W. Bush appointed her ambassador-at-large and, at the U.S. State Department, U.S. coordinator for refugee affairs. She served on numerous committees and commissions and on 20 corporate boards, among them those of Trans World Airlines, Continental Bank, Mobil, Revlon, and the U.S. Chamber of Commerce; she held leadership posts in the National Association for the Advancement of Colored People (NAACP), the American Civil Liberties Union, the Illinois Humane Society, and other organizations and earned dozens of awards for her legal, civic, and humanitarian work.

In 1961, when Rogers was three, his parents divorced. That same year his mother married H. Ernest LaFontant, a lawyer; that union ended with her husband's death, in 1976. At the time of her death, in 1997, she was married to Naguib S. Mankarious, an Egyptian-born international business consultant. Rogers's father also remarried; his second wife, Gwendolyn, is a director of the charitable organization Family Focus.

After his parents' divorce Rogers lived with his father on weekends and during the week with his mother (or with his grandmother Aida Stradford, when his mother's work kept her away from Chicago)—an arrangement that made him "half crazy," he told Lauren Young. As a boy he attended GOP events with his mother and helped his father, a Democratic Cook County precinct captain, distribute fliers for Democratic candidates and causes. Starting the year John Jr. turned 12, his father gave him shares of stock as birthday and Christmas gifts and opened a bank account for him to deposit his dividends. "I knew the stock market was the future for blacks," John Sr. told Young. "They don't know whether you are black, blue or green if you are trading in stocks." In his teens Rogers followed stock-market reports in newspapers and on TV and also discussed the market with his father's broker, Stacy Adams, one of the first African-American stockbrokers in Chicago. "With parents with such strong backgrounds, it was important for me to have something of my own," he told Albert Chen for *Sports Illustrated* (November 6, 2000, on-line). He spent six summers selling snacks at home games of Major League Baseball's Chicago Cubs and Chicago White Sox and invested some of his earnings in the stock market.

Rogers attended the University of Chicago Laboratory School, a private high school. As a senior he also played on the Illinois Class A All-State Hall of Fame basketball team. After his graduation, in 1976, he enrolled at Princeton University, in New Jersey, where he majored in economics. He played basketball on the men's varsity team, the Tigers, whose coach at that time, Pete Carril, emphasized "precision and teamwork," Rogers told Chen. Carril, one of Rogers's role models, recalled to Chen that Rogers was "very steady and always a hard worker." One of Rogers's teammates was Craig Robinson, whose sister, Michelle, later married Barack Obama. In 1979–80, his senior year, Rogers was the team's captain; he "led the Tigers to a share of the Ivy League championship that season," according to a press release on the Tigers' Web site (November 8, 2007) that announced Rogers the winner of Princeton's Woodrow Wilson Prize. As an undergraduate Rogers studied Burton G. Malkiel's *A Random Walk Down Wall Street: The Time-tested Strategy for Successful Investing* (1973), now considered a classic. As a contestant on the TV game show *Wheel of Fortune*, he won $8,600 and invested all of it. After he graduated from Princeton, with an A.B. degree in 1980, he took a job as a stockbroker with the Chicago-based investment firm William Blair & Co. He was the first person in four years whom the firm hired directly out of college as well as the first African-American to fill a non-clerical and non-janitorial position at the 400-employee company.

Two and a half years later, the 24-year-old Rogers left William Blair to start his own financial firm, Ariel Capital Management, with money he had collected from friends and family, a two-page prospectus, and his mother as part-owner. (Rogers's office informed *Current Biography* that he chose the name Ariel "because it is one of his favorite names" and is "derived from a character on the television show *The Waltons* from Rogers's teen years.") According to the company's Web site, "Ariel began as little more than an idea that wealth can be created by investing in great companies at bargain prices, whose true value would be realized over time." Rogers's earliest accounts included $100,000 from Howard University, a traditionally black school in Washington, D.C., that his mother served as a trustee, and $75,000 from the Chicago-based Johnson Publishing Co., the world's largest black-owned and -operated publishing house. In 1984 he landed his first million-dollar account, the Municipal Employees of Chicago pension fund. He started a newsletter, *The Patient Investor*, to publicize the launch, in 1983, of a mutual fund that invested in so-called growth stocks. Currently, the *Patient Investor* is both an award-winning quarterly shareholder report and a regular column Rogers writes for *Forbes* magazine. Rogers recruited a Maryland-based firm, the Calvert Group Ltd. (now Calvert Investments), to serve as the fund's distributor and transfer agent for another instrument, the Calvert-Ariel Growth Fund.

By the end of 1986, Ariel had over $113 million in managed assets. A year later the total had risen to $264 million. Thanks to Rogers's mother's many contacts in the business world, high-profile corporations including Revlon and Mobil became Ariel clients. The firm was also hired to manage the Los Angeles, Detroit, and Washington, D.C., municipal-employees' retirement funds, whose managers had learned of Ariel's knack for identifying companies not likely to be affected to any great extent by modest economic downturns—small and mid-size companies that manufactured toothbrushes, plastic binders, desktop stacking trays, hospital uniforms, and other widely used products. "We were successful during the '80s because we picked some good, reasonably priced small stocks," Rogers told Carolyn M. Brown for *Black Enterprise* (April 1992). "We avoided the go-go, glamorous small stocks that soared in 1980 and then plunged by 1985. Instead, we stuck with low-expectation stocks that didn't go up as much, but also didn't suffer as much."

In 1988 *Venture* magazine and the international auditing firm Arthur Young named Rogers the Entrepreneur of the Year, and *Sylvia Porter's Personal Finance Magazine* named him Mutual Fund Manager of the Year. In 1989 the Illinois District of the U.S. Small Business Administration named him Minority Small Business Person of the Year. In the early 1990s the performance of mutual funds weakened, and in 1994 Rogers decided to gain independence from Calvert, paying $4 million to sever their partnership. As a result Ariel lost $1.2 billion of its $2.3 billion in assets. "It was extraordinarily uncomfortable and frightening," Rogers recalled to Matthew S. Scott. To heighten Ariel's visibility, Rogers sponsored a stock ticker at Chicago Bulls basketball games and collaborated on occasion with the Black MBA Association and other professional organizations. Before long Ariel gained back what it had lost and as of the end of 1994 had $2 billion in managed assets. In 1994 Rogers was featured in *Time* as one of 50 "future leaders" under 40.

Unlike many of his competitors, in the late 1990s Rogers ruled out investments in Internet firms and technology stocks, and for that reason the Ariel Fund did not perform as well as many other funds. Then, in 2002, the so-called dot-com bubble burst. "It was very easy two years ago for people to get pulled away from their principles if they were value managers," Rogers told Scott in 2002. "People found excuses to add this tech stock, this dotcom company, or this new issue to their portfolio. We didn't succumb to any of that pressure. When value came back in favor we benefited completely, while a lot of our peers only partially benefited because they had moved away from their core strategy during the growth stock bubble of the late '90s." By the end of 2002, Ariel had more than 120 corporate and institutional clients, including ChevronTexaco, United Airlines, and the California State Teachers' Retirement System. By April 2004 both Ariel mutual funds had received four-star ratings from Morningstar. At the end of the year, the firm had 73 employees and was managing $21 billion in assets. Rogers introduced the Ariel Focus Fund in 2005.

On November 30, 2007 a writer for gurufocus.com reported that in the past decade, Ariel Capital Management had "earned nearly 14 percent a year, beating the market by more than five percentage points annually." The next month saw the start of the worst economic recession since the Great Depression of the 1930s. The recession severely hurt Ariel, along with the rest of the financial industry. The company lost investors and was forced to lay off 20 percent of its staff. In 2009 its assets totaled $3 billion—only one-seventh the amount five years earlier. "Ariel weathered the crisis by doubling down on stocks it viewed as cheap at a time when competitors sought the safety of cash and more-conservative holdings," Rogers told Lynne Marek for *Crain's Chicago Business* (May 17, 2010). For example, when shares of the newspaper publisher Gannet traded as low as $1.85, Ariel—confident that Gannet would recover—purchased more; by April 2010 the value of its shares had reached as high as $19.69.

According to the Ariel Web site, as of March 31, 2010 the company held stock in 112 companies. As of September 30, 2010, its managed assets totaled $5 billion. As of June 30, 2010, the value of an investment of $10,000 in the Ariel Fund made in 1986 was worth $100,692, while an equal investment in stocks listed in the Standard & Poor (S&P) 500 Index had risen, on average, to $71,943. Also as of June 30, 2010, the figures for a $10,000 investment in 1989 in the Ariel Appreciation Fund and in the average S&P 500 Index stock were $65,881 and $46,288, respectively. The Ariel Focus Fund performed somewhat worse than S&P 500 Index stocks, on average, with a $10,000 investment in 2005 in the former worth $8,961 on June 30, 2010 and in the latter, $9,542. In his *Forbes* column (June 28, 2010, on-line), Rogers wrote that he advised fearful investors not to worry over "the day-to-day movement of stocks. It's a kind of 'Don't sweat the small stuff' approach to stock volatility. In fact, sharp downswings offer the chance to buy great companies at bargain prices."

To gather market-related information, Rogers relies not on the Internet but on print media (for example, trade publications, newspapers, magazines, and newsletters) and what he described to Brown as "tire kicking"—"going out and visiting the companies, getting to know the employees and management, and talking to the customers, competitors and suppliers." "I don't even have a computer in my office," he told Jason Zweig for CNN.Money.com (June 19, 2007). "If I had e-mail, I'd never take the time to read research or absorb information. I want to think about what I'm doing, and that takes time." In recent years he has gone further afield in his investment choices, embracing such companies as Sotheby's, Citigroup, and Bio-Rad Laboratories. As Rogers's office informed *Current Biography*, "Ariel Fund, Ariel Appreciation Fund, and Ariel Focus Fund do not invest in corporations whose primary source of revenue is derived from the production or sale of tobacco products or the manufacture of handguns." Ariel believes that "all of the aforementioned industries are more likely to face shrinking growth prospects, draining litigation costs and legal liabilities that cannot be quantified." Since Ariel believes that "ethical decisions impact long-term success," it also considers "a company's environmental policies when evaluating a stock for purchase in . . . portfolios. Although this is not a formal screen, it plays a role in [Ariel's] decision making process."

Outside of business hours, Rogers, as a corporate-board member and the organizer of the yearly Black Corporate Directors Conferences, has worked to strengthen civil rights in the corporate world and to promote the appointment of members of minority groups to positions of power. "Often people are shy and uncomfortable talking about race," Rogers told an interviewer for the Outstanding Directors Exchange (2010, on-line). "If you as a black director don't bring it up, you in effect are giving cover for the status quo to stay the same." Rogers has also used his seat on corporate boards to encourage greater numbers of African-Americans to save and invest. The Ariel-Schwab Black Investor Survey has shown that black workers save significantly less for retirement than their white counterparts. Thanks to efforts McDonald's has made since Rogers joined its board, in 2003, black employees' participation in the company's 401(k) plan has increased by more than 20 percent. "It comes down to public education . . . ," Rogers

told Zweig. "Financial literacy is just as important in life as the other basics."

Financial literacy is stressed at the Ariel Community Academy, a kindergarten-through-eighth-grade public school in Chicago's South Side that opened in 1996 and has received more than $3 million in support from Ariel Investments since then. Created with the assistance of Rogers's friend Arne Duncan (currently the secretary of the U.S. Department of Education), the school incorporates finance-related material in coursework beginning in the first grade. Each year Ariel and Nuveen Investments invests $20,000 in the stock market in the name of the entering class of first-graders. The children (and their parents) receive information about the purchased stocks every year and attend stockholders' meetings. Beginning in the six grade, the students themselves choose stocks in which to invest. From the total amount accumulated by the time they graduate, $20,000 goes to the next semester's incoming first-grade class. Half of the profits are donated to the school, and the rest is divided among the graduates. Nearly all of the graduates deposit their portions in college savings accounts. If they choose to do so, Ariel and Nuveen add $1,000 to each child's contribution. Close to 70 percent of the graduates go on to attend specialized Chicago high schools.

Rogers's marriage, in 1988, to the former Desirée Glapion, a businesswoman, ended in divorce. Desirée Rogers served as the White House social secretary during the first year of the Obama administration. In 2002 John Rogers married Sharon Renee Fairley, a businesswoman and lawyer who is currently an assistant U.S. attorney in Chicago. From his first marriage Rogers has one daughter, Victoria, a Yale University undergraduate who is studying art history. As a volunteer with a refugee-resettlement agency near Yale, in New Haven, Connecticut, Victoria Rogers has assisted refugees from Iraq and other nations. In March 2010, with other Yale students, she worked in a youth village set up for children orphaned during the 1994 genocide in Rwanda.

In 2004 Lynne Norment described Rogers as "humble and unpretentious." "He's a person who develops longterm friendships," Desirée Rogers told the whorunsgov.com writer. Arne Duncan told another whorunsgov.com interviewer that Rogers "treats the homeless guys exactly how he treats Barack. I think that's so rare." Craig Robinson described him to Lauren Young as "quirky" but "very consistent." During their years as Princeton Tigers basketball players, Robinson recalled, Rogers ate nothing on the road except hamburgers, french fries, and pizza. Virtually every day for many years, Rogers has eaten at least one McDonald's meal. "I like the way McDonald's feels," he told Young. "It's comfortable. It's an oasis for me." Young also reported that he wore one of his eight identical custom-made gray pinstripe suits to work every day. "John is constantly figuring out ways to narrow his choices to manage his life," Robinson told her. For years Rogers, Robinson, and Duncan played three-on-three basketball together, sometimes in tournaments. Rogers and Robinson were among a small number of former basketball players with whom Michael Jordan practiced in the winter of 2001, when he was contemplating a comeback. On Election Day 2008 Rogers played basketball with Obama. Recalling that experience, he told the whorunsgov.com interviewer, "You pinch yourself sometimes."

—W.D.

Suggested Reading: Ariel Investments Web site; *Barron's* p18+ Jan. 15, 1996; *Black Enterprise* p46 Apr. 1992, p239 June 30, 2002; *Crain's Chicago Business* p1+ May 17, 2010; *Fortune* p186+ Feb. 16, 1998; *Princeton Alumni Weekly* (on-line) Oct. 10, 2007; *SmartMoney* p110+ Mar. 2002; whorunsgov.com June 2, 2010

Courtesy of Getty Images

Rospars, Joe

Apr. 14, 1981– Founding partner of Blue State Digital; former director of new media for Barack Obama's 2008 presidential campaign

Address: Blue State Digital, 734 15th St., N.W., Suite 1200, Washington, DC 20005

Named on *Rolling Stone*'s list of "100 People Who Are Changing America" (March 18, 2009, on-line), Joe Rospars is a founding partner of the on-line consultancy firm Blue State Digital (BSD). The company develops Web sites and provides custom Internet applications and communications strate-

gies to nonprofit organizations, advocacy groups, Democratic political candidates, and corporations, both in the U.S. and overseas. Rospars established BSD in 2004 with three others who, like him, had worked that year in the presidential campaign of former Vermont governor Howard Dean. In 2007, at the age of 25, Rospars was appointed director of new media for the presidential campaign of then– U.S. senator Barack Obama of Illinois. Rospars managed the campaign's digital presence, integrating design and branding, Web and video content, mass e-mails, text messaging, and on-line advertising, organizing, and fund-raising. Explaining the appeal of a Web-based campaign, Rospars told Jose Antonio Vargas for the *Washington Post* (May 4, 2007), "TV is a passive experience, and the Internet is all about interactivity, all about making a direct connection." At the heart of the new-media campaign was My.BarackObama.com, a social-networking Web site that gave Obama supporters many ways to participate in the campaign, from creating a fund-raising page to organizing local gatherings to maintaining blogs. "We've tried to bring two principles to this campaign," Rospars explained to Joshua Green for the *Atlantic* (June 2008, on-line). "One is lowering the barriers to entry and making it as easy as possible for folks who come to our Web site. The other is raising the expectation of what it means to be a supporter. It's not enough to have a bumper sticker. We want you to give five dollars, make some calls, host an event. If you look at the messages we send to people over time, there's a presumption that they will organize." Rospars told Michael Learmonth for *Advertising Age* (March 30, 2009, on-line), "There are lots of organizations and campaigns that say, 'We're going to have a whiz-bang digital presence.' But the point isn't for people to come to your [Web] site and do cool stuff; it's to help you accomplish your core goals." The London *Independent* named the Obama campaign's use of the Internet as one of the 10 best ideas of 2008. "Every future political campaign, in the US, Britain and beyond, will learn from the internet strategies of the Obama campaign," David Usborne wrote for that newspaper (December 31, 2008). Joe Trippi, who served as Howard Dean's national campaign manager and as a senior adviser to U.S. senator John Edwards's 2008 presidential campaign, told Josh Schwartz for *Rolling Stone* (March 18, 2009), "A new era of politics empowered by the people exists in no small measure because of Joe's effort." Following President Obama's inauguration, on January 20, 2009, the successful digital campaign headed by Rospars was turned over to the Democratic National Committee (DNC) and was transformed into the group Organizing for America. His enormous contributions to Dean's and Obama's campaigns notwithstanding, Rospars preferred to keep out of the spotlight and refused to put his name on official campaign e-mails or take credit for many of his ideas. "If he wanted [them] to, 13 million people could know the name Joe Rospars," Sam Graham-Felsen, who ran the Obama campaign's blog and is a former Blue State Digital employee, told Amy Harder for *National Journal* (April 14, 2009, on-line).

Based in Washington, D.C., BSD has grown to include offices in Boston, Massachusetts; Los Angeles, California; New York City; and London. It has worked with more than 200 clients, among them several U.S. senators, five labor unions, Planned Parenthood, the Global AIDS Alliance, Hearst Publishing, and the European Council on Foreign Relations. As of late March 2010, BSD had helped to raise over $500 million in on-line contributions for its nonprofit clients and to generate "tens of millions of online signups and actions," according to its Web site. The firm has won many Internet awards; in September 2009 *Inc. Magazine* named it one of the fastest-growing private companies in the U.S., and in 2006 *Fast Company* listed it among the year's 50 most innovative companies.

The youngest of four siblings, Joseph L. Rospars was born on April 14, 1981 and raised in Oyster Bay, on Long Island, New York. He was a student at St. Dominic High School, a Roman Catholic school in Oyster Bay. He then attended George Mason University, in Fairfax, Virginia, for one year after his high-school graduation, in 1999. In 2000 he took courses at Erasmus University in Rotterdam, the Netherlands, and in 2001 he entered George Washington University, in Washington, D.C., where he majored in political science. He earned a bachelor's degree at that school in 2003.

Rospars spent the next year teaching English in Stockholm, Sweden, in part to be near his Swedish-born girlfriend. While there he began keeping a blog that discussed U.S. politics and became active from afar in the fledgling presidential campaign of Howard Dean. In the summer of 2003, Rospars returned to New York for a visit; through the Internet he found that a van of Dean supporters was headed to Burlington, Vermont, to witness Dean's official announcement of his candidacy. "Up until that point I was working for the campaign, but I had really never had any face-to-face conversations about Howard Dean with anybody other than my girlfriend. So it was a pretty intense six-hour ride," Rospars recalled to Joe Garofoli for the *San Francisco Chronicle* (November 3, 2007).

That experience, Rospars told Garofoli, opened his eyes to the effectiveness of on-line organizing and fueled his passion for politics. Dean's announcement "was an amazing speech; it changed my whole life," he told Jon Sawyer for the *St. Louis (Missouri) Post-Dispatch* (January 11, 2004). Soon afterward Rospars left his job, as well as his girlfriend, in Sweden, moved to Vermont, and joined Dean's campaign full-time as a writer and Web strategist.

Dean, a physician who had served as governor of Vermont for nearly 12 years, had no national profile and was considered a long shot for the White House. He quickly gained popularity, however, by capitalizing on Democrats' anger regarding the war in Iraq and other actions and policies of the administration of the incumbent Republican president, George W. Bush. The idea for Dean's strong Internet presence came out of Meetup, a Web site that allows users to organize social groups or find existing groups and arrange local meetings. In early 2003 Dean and his staffers found out that supporters were organizing gatherings using Meetup. "We fell into this by accident," Dean told Gary Wolf for *Wired* (January 2004). "I wish I could tell you we were smart enough to figure this out. But the community taught us. They seized the initiative through Meetup. They built our organization for us before we had an organization." In March 2003 a Dean campaign worker, Mathew Gross, created Blog for America (a play on the name of Dean's Web site, Dean for America), the first presidential campaign blog. Blog for America linked supporters to Meetup, allowing them to organize events in support of Dean. Campaign staffers—including Rospars, who wrote for Blog for America from July 2003 to February 2004—communicated with supporters by posting updates on Dean's activities, his organization, and his views on certain issues. "Nobody reads my stuff before [I post it on-line]. I just hit publish," Rospars told Edward Cone for *eWeek* (November 18, 2003, on-line). "The blog is about humanizing [the] campaign, not just Dean but the staff and supporters." Without interference from campaign staffers, volunteer Dean workers, too, created blogs chronicling their experiences.

Thanks to the Internet Dean attracted a network of dedicated followers and thousands of first-time voters. Overall, more than 800,000 people signed up on his Web site. Dean's Internet team used the Web to organize volunteers to go door-to-door, write personal letters to potential voters, and distribute flyers. Moreover, Dean raised $50.3 million, more than anyone among his Democratic opponents up to that time. The campaign was the first to concentrate on young donors who contributed relatively small amounts: a quarter of the contributors to Dean's campaign were under 30 years of age, and the average contribution was around $80. One day in August 2003, when Vice President Dick Cheney hosted a $2,000-a-plate lunch to raise funds for President Bush's reelection campaign, Dean used his Web site to ask his backers to join him for lunch in front of their computers. Cheney raised $250,000 while Dean received more than $500,000 over four days, with donations averaging $53. While Dean had been seen at the start of the presidential primary season as the Democratic candidate to beat, he lost three of the first four primary elections, and on February 18, 2004, he dropped out of the race.

Soon after Dean ended his candidacy, Rospars and three other former Dean staffers—Clay A. Johnson, Jascha Franklin-Hodge, and Ben Self—founded Blue State Digital. In 2005 BSD helped to create a set of social-networking tools for the DNC. Called Party Builder, the software allowed DNC supporters to post personal profiles and blogs, create or join groups of people with shared interests, organize local events, and upload fund-raising pages. Rospars served as the Internet director for that project.

In early 2007 Jim Brayton, then–Senator Obama's Internet director, approached Rospars about joining Obama's presidential campaign. The ideas Rospars heard when he met with Obama and his campaign director, David Plouffe, thrilled him. The campaign "was going to be something organic. It was going to be bottom-up," Rospars told Amy Harder. "Naturally, that would have to go through the digital space." Rospars signed on to become Obama's media director, and within weeks he had assembled nine team leaders. They included 23-year-old Chris Hughes, one of the co-founders of the popular social-networking Web site Facebook, who became coordinator of on-line organizing; Kate Albright-Hanna, an Emmy Award–winning producer, who left CNN to help direct and produce videos for the campaign; and Scott Goodstein, who temporarily closed his Washington, D.C., public-relations consulting firm to run the campaign's text-messaging and mobile-communications arm. Speaking of Rospars, David Plouffe told Harder, "The ability to hire people who have more expertise than you do is always a good sign you're a good leader."

Obama's on-line operations, known as the "Triple O," included My.BarackObama.com, a site that allowed supporters to create their own profiles, join local groups, plan gatherings, sign up for campaign updates, blog, and set up personal fund-raising pages. Also on the site was an on-line list of names and phone numbers of potential voters; those who made calls recorded on the site information about each call. Rospars and his colleagues compiled an e-mail list that grew to contain the names of 13.5 million Obama supporters and undecided voters—a resource that proved to be one of their most valuable tools. In June 2008, after U.S. senator Hillary Clinton of New York abandoned her bid for the Democratic nomination, Obama staffers sent out a mass e-mail encouraging those on their list to host "United for Change" house parties, as a way of reaching out to those who had favored Clinton. Nearly 4,000 such parties were held across the nation.

Text messaging via mobile phones was another tool extremely useful to Obama's campaign. Goodstein collected names, phone numbers, and e-mail addresses of supporters and potential supporters by means of texts, then sent texts periodically to supporters, updating them on campaign news, reminding them to watch televised debates, and asking for feedback. Before the start of a Columbia, South Carolina, rally in December 2007, Obama's state field director asked the roughly 29,000 people in attendance to use their mobile phones to text "SC" to 62262, the campaign's short code. (Short codes are special telephone numbers that can receive text messages.) In the weeks after the rally, Goodstein sent texts to the cell-phone numbers he had amassed and asked supporters to make phone

calls to urge people to vote and volunteer in their election precincts during the Democratic primary in South Carolina, held on January 26, 2008. Obama won 55 percent of the vote, more than twice Clinton's 27 percent. "South Carolina was a defining moment in what we were going to do with text messaging—not just with young voters but with all voters," Goodstein recalled to Jose Antonio Vargas for the *Washington Post* (August 20, 2008). The Obama campaign also used social networking Web sites—Facebook, MySpace, and BlackPlanet—and the video-sharing site YouTube.

By Election Day, November 4, 2008, the Obama campaign had raised $500 million in on-line contributions from three million donors, most in amounts of less than $100; MyBarackObama boasted 1.5 million individual members and some 35,000 groups; 1,800 campaign videos had been posted to YouTube, garnering 50 million views; and Obama's Facebook page had more than 3.4 million "friends," more than six times the number recorded on the Facebook page of Obama's main rival, John McCain, the Republican U.S. senator from Arizona. Since January 23, 2009 the 13.5 million people on Rospars's mailing list have received e-mail messages via Organize for America, most prominently regarding health-care reform. Rospars has applauded such ties between the White House and Obama's grassroots supporters. "The relationships didn't end on Election Day," he told Amy Harder. "We built those relationships in a way that it was never really about Election Day or a candidate. It was about a common sense of purpose and what the people wanted the country to be."

After Obama was elected president, Rospars returned to Blue State Digital. His title is "founding partner." The firm's other executives are Jascha Franklin-Hodge, chief technology officer; Thomas Gensemer, managing partner; and Rich Mintz, vice president for strategy. BSD has grown steadily, attracting a roster of clients that includes the film-production company Focus Features and Hearst Publishing. BSD's clients also include politicians, among them the Democratic U.S. senators Harry Reid and John Kerry; Congressman Steny Hoyer; and Ken Livingstone, a member of Britain's Labor Party and the mayor of London, England, from 2000 to 2008. Among other clients are five labor unions, notably the AFL-CIO (American Federation of Labor and Congress of Industrial Organizations) and the American Federation of State, County, and Municipal Employees (AFSCME).

Rospars is a member of the Commission on Smart Global Health Policy of the Center for Strategic and International Studies. The center, which is nonprofit and bipartisan, "provides strategic insights and policy solutions to decision makers in government, international institutions, the private sector, and civil society," according to its Web site. In March 2010 the commission published a report, "A Healthier, Safer and More Prosperous World," which urges U.S. decision-makers to embrace a strategic global-health policy that includes the continuation of the fight against HIV/AIDS, malaria, and tuberculosis, and investment in multilateral institutions, to better the lives of people around the world and strengthen ties between the U.S. and other nations.

Rospars lives in Washington, D.C., and New York City.

—M.A.S.

Suggested Reading: *Advertising Age* (on-line) Mar. 30, 2009; bluestatedigital.com; *National Journal* (on-line) Apr. 14, 2009; *Newsweek* p30 May 21, 2007; *St. Louis (Missouri) Post-Dispatch* E p3 Jan. 11, 2004; *Washington Post* A p1+ May 4, 2007, C p1+ Aug. 20, 2008

Courtesy of Kevin Daley

Roth, Gabriel

1974– Founder of Daptone Records; songwriter; bass player

Address: 115 Troutman St., Brooklyn, NY 11206

The songwriter, musician, arranger, and producer Gabriel Roth is the co-founder of the Brooklyn, New York–based Daptone Records, a label that specializes in music modeled on the funk and soul sounds of the 1960s and 1970s. Released on vinyl, recorded using vintage analog equipment, and packaged in retro cardboard sleeves, Daptone's albums emulate the look, spirit, and sound of those released by such genre-defining labels as Stax and Motown.

In an age of assembly-line pop recordings, Roth has succeeded (somewhat paradoxically) in satisfying people's desire for authenticity by manufacturing it: Daptone's strategy, informed by the discriminating tastes of Roth and his collaborators, shrewdly addressed the biases of consumers to carve out a niche market. "I think we've had a lot of luck as far as people not being able to judge us on who we are but on how they like the music," Neal Sugarman, Roth's partner, told Michaelangelo Matos for *Seattle Weekly* (May 18, 2005, online). "At the beginning, we'd get people thinking they were old records. . . . And they made unbiased decisions on it, not saying, 'Oh, this is a new record by a bunch of young white kids.' It was a record they already liked; when they found out, I think it impressed them more." When one of the label's most popular acts, Sharon Jones and the Dap-Kings, covered Janet Jackson's 1986 hit "What Have You Done for Me Lately" in 2001, performing the tune in their distinctive soulful style, the track was done so well that listeners erroneously assumed that Jackson had been covering a (nonexistent) 1970s-era Sharon Jones tune.

Some critics have accused Roth of fetishism, exploitation, and "wholesale appropriation of black tradition," as Saki Knafo, writing for the *New York Times Magazine* (December 7, 2008), reported. Others, however, have credited Roth and his artists for reviving interest in beloved but neglected music that was being forgotten in the current cultural landscape. "I've always just tried to make records that sound like . . . the records I like," Roth told Terry Gross for the National Public Radio program *Fresh Air* (November 28, 2007). "I never had too much of a very specific agenda that we were going to try to . . . ape something or try to pass something off. We just wanted to make records that felt good to us and sounded good to us." Dan Daley wrote for *Sound On Sound* magazine (June 2008): "I believe [Roth] when he says that [he is] not willfully making retro records for the sake of it. Daptone [is] not some super-cool karaoke cover factory . . . but a place where people who really love a certain kind of music use the tools of the time to continue to make new editions of that music." Knafo pointed out: "In an age of MP3s and computer-generated sounds, [Roth] has distinguished himself by making vinyl records featuring actual musicians manipulating real-life instruments. He has rejected the music industry, and in doing so, he has aroused its interest."

Gabriel Roth was born in 1974. His parents, Diane and Andrew Roth, are lawyers, as is his sister, Samra. Roth grew up in Riverside, California, and attended Ponderosa High School. When he was a teenager, his parents, who frequently worked on civil rights and discrimination-related cases, began opening their home to children from varied racial and socioeconomic backgrounds who needed a place to stay; several became part of the extended family. While some journalists have assumed that the ethnic diversity of Roth's home predisposed him to enjoying soul music, he has denied a connection, pointing out that his African-American foster brother was a fan of the Caucasian pop musician Phil Collins.

Roth attended New York University (NYU), where he studied sound engineering, listened to records by the soul singer James Brown, and, by most accounts, smoked large amounts of marijuana. He also formed a short-lived band, "Dine-O-Matic," and began collecting rare funk and soul recordings. One of the labels that interested him was Pure Records, which had been established in the late 1980s in Paris, France, by a wealthy record collector, Philippe Lehman. Roth arranged to meet Lehman when the latter visited New York City. "Philippe and I just had a vision for the same style and sound—hot and nasty, '70s funk in the James Brown tradition," Roth was quoted as saying on the Drumsuite Web site. The pair began recruiting musicians and recording tracks in a small studio on Manhattan's Lower East Side. By 1997—the year after Roth earned a bachelor's degree, cum laude, from NYU—they had moved to an office on West 41st Street, under a store called Desco Vacuum. Borrowing the name, they dubbed their enterprise Desco Records. A highly specialized independent soul and funk label, Desco released music only on vinyl. Their first single was "Let a Man Do What He Wanna Do," performed by the Soul Providers, a house band that included Roth on bass. They quickly realized that their own "classic-funk stuff" was "only commercially viable if you lied about how classic the funk was exactly," Ezra Gale wrote for the *Village Voice* (March 4, 2009). As a result, they began misrepresenting their releases as lost vintage recordings. "I was about 19, 20 years old, and we were really into these old records," Roth told Terry Gross. "And we would make kind of these fake old records, you know, reissues of a sound. The first record album we did was a reissue of a soundtrack to a Kung Fu movie that never existed. You know, we just kind of made this stuff up. . . . And people were buying them. And then we said, 'Oh, great, man, people really like this music.' So . . . we'd do a real name and say, 'OK, this is a new record we just recorded.' And nobody was interested. We couldn't give them away. So we got kind of more into this fake thing." (In keeping with that strategy, Roth himself uses several aliases, including Bosco "Bass" Mann.) The Kung Fu record was called *The Revenge of Mr. Mopoji*. "We put the 'soundtrack' out as a reissue and took it around to record stores," Roth explained to Dan Daley. "These stores would never have touched a funk or soul record by a new band, but when they saw a 're-issue' they scooped it up. We heard people saying, 'Oh, yeah, my cousin had that movie on VHS.'"

Roth used similarly deceptive tactics when he released *Soul Explosion* (1998) by the Daktaris, who were described by Steve Huey for the All Music Guide Web site as "an Afro-beat group . . . recording compact, Fela Kuti-style grooves that sounded as though they'd come straight out of

1970s Nigeria." Huey continued, "At first, Desco did nothing to discourage that perception, packaging . . . *Soul Explosion* to look like an authentically African collector's dream, and even giving some of the band members Nigerian aliases. But in reality, the Daktaris were Brooklyn-based studio musicians, many of them white." Roth admitted to Daley, "[People] just created their own assumptions. We had an ethnomusicologist in LA tell us that he had other Daktari records! It's kind of disconcerting, seeing how much bias people look at things through." Members of the Daktaris went on to form the Antibalas Afrobeat Orchestra, which also recorded on Desco.

During the late 1990s Roth and Lehman hosted a weekly radio show, *Across 110th Street*, on WKCR, a station based at Columbia University, in Upper Manhattan. They continued to build the Desco roster as well. In addition to their young house musicians, the two recruited a handful of soul and funk veterans, including Lee Fields, who had made a name for himself in the 1970s. During that period Roth also forged a working relationship with the artist who would become the most successful in his future roster, Sharon Jones. Jones had sung in talent shows and funk groups during the early 1970s and later participated in church choirs and wedding bands. She made her living, however, as a prison guard, among other such jobs. Jones's boyfriend (some sources say husband) was playing saxophone on a session with Fields and suggested they bring her in for backup vocals. Roth was impressed and began recording additional tracks with her, including a fiery prison rant called *Switchblade*. "Gabe had faith in me," Jones told Mike Greenhaus for Jambands.com (January 23, 2008). "Everyone else told me I was too old and didn't have the look. I was too fat and too black. But he really believed."

Although Desco was slowly building a following of record fans, by 2000 Lehman and Roth were arguing about money, and they decided to dissolve the company. Lehman went on to form Soul Fire Records, but Roth's debts, which included student loans, were so large that he was forced to take a job in the distribution division of Sony Records. "It was the last place in the world I wanted to be," Roth told Knafo. "They would joke about how awful the songs were, and how the [artists] were singing out of tune and how formulaic it was and blah, blah, blah, and when they were finished joking they'd put together a two- [or] three-million-dollar budget to promote the next video." Roth spent much of his time at Sony planning the resurrection of his own company, sketching possible logos and making long-distance calls at his desk. Despite his lack of loyalty to Sony, he was offered a promotion, which he declined.

In 2002 Roth partnered with the saxophonist Neal Sugarman, who had been one of the cornerstone artists in the Desco stable, to found Daptone. Many of the other musicians who had comprised the Desco collective rejoined them to form a new house band, the Dap-Kings, which was often fronted by Jones. *Dap Dippin' with Sharon Jones and the Dap-Kings* was the first album to be released on the fledgling label. Daptone initially recorded in a sublet basement studio in the Williamsburg section of Brooklyn, but after learning that a royalty check was due from distributors, Roth and Sugarman signed a long-term lease on a house in Bushwick, another section of Brooklyn, intending to convert it into an office and studio. When the royalties never arrived, the pair renovated the space themselves, with the help of other Daptone artists and Roth's parents. The studio, equipped with a 16-track tape machine rather than a digital setup, as well as other vintage equipment, was ready by 2003.

One night, after a session spent recording Sharon Jones and the Dap-Kings' second album, *Naturally*, Roth was involved in a car accident on the way home from the studio. His eyes were badly damaged when an airbag exploded in his face, temporarily blinding him; he has worn dark protective sunglasses ever since. Roth's recuperation took several months, and *Naturally* was not completed until early 2005. The band then embarked on a grueling 267-show tour, slowing down only briefly in the winter of 2006 to record a third studio album, *100 Days, 100 Nights*, which they released in October 2007. The album, whose cover features a glamorous shot of Jones in a vintage cocktail dress, has since sold more than 100,000 copies and remains among Daptone's most successful releases to date.

Some of the other main groups on the Daptone roster are the Menahan Band, the Budos Band, the Sugarman Three, the Mighty Imperials, the Daktaris, and Binky Griptite. Their work includes funk, soul, Afrobeat, boogaloo, and sometimes a fusion of all those musical styles and more, usually produced by Roth and backed by permutations of the same loose pool of musicians who still form the bulk of the label's session artists. During the late 1990s Roth had become interested in gospel music after meeting Cliff Driver, the organist and bandleader of Naomi Shelton and the Gospel Queens, a Brooklyn-based group. Roth eventually began playing bass and writing songs for the Gospel Queens, who later joined the Daptone roster. Some journalists have commented on the irony that Roth, who is Jewish by birth and now an atheist, writes gospel music. "Such is Roth's skill at creating a sense—or, some would say, an illusion—of authenticity," Knafo wrote, "that Driver, a consummate perfectionist, has incorporated the songs into his church repertory, regularly trotting them out before some of the more discriminating and faithful gospel audiences in the world." *What Have You Done, My Brother?*, Naomi Shelton and the Gospel Queens' first Daptone album, was released in 2009. (It does not mark the label's first foray into gospel. The previous year Daptone had released *Como Now*, a stirring album recorded at the Mount Mariah Church in Como, Mississippi.)

Daptone's rising profile and sales are due in large part not only to Sharon Jones and the Dap-Kings but also to the label's contributions to mainstream pop and hip-hop hits. When the producer Mark Ronson was trying to manufacture a classic retro sound for the British singer Amy Winehouse using computers and sampling, he found that Daptone studios and the Dap-Kings provided a better solution. "We were using every computer trick in the book to make it sound old," Ronson told Ben Sisario for the *New York Times* (September 29, 2007). "But it was just so ridiculous. [As soon as we used the Dap-Kings] it just sounded a million times better." The resulting album, Winehouse's platinum, Grammy Award–winning *Back to Black* (2006), featured the Dap-Kings on six of its 11 tracks, including the hit single "Rehab." (Roth also served as sound engineer on the project.) The Dap-Kings then backed Winehouse on tour, and other popular British singers, including Lily Allen and Robbie Williams, began hiring the band. "The pop stuff is cool and it opens a lot of doors for us," Roth told Oliver Wang for *LA Weekly* (July 17, 2008), "[but] that's not really our meat and potatoes." In the U.S. several hip-hop artists—including Kanye West, Ghostface Killah, and Jurassic 5—also drew upon the Daptone roster, and the Dap-Kings have backed such performers as Al Green and Rod Stewart as well.

In February 2009 Daptone's Bushwick premises were burglarized, with thousands of dollars' worth of equipment stolen, including most of Roth's collection of rare, vintage microphones. His Trident series 65 mixing board and eight-track reel-to-reel tape machine remained, however.

Sharon Jones and the Dap-Kings' latest album, *I Learned the Hard Way* (2010), earned positive reviews. "The Dap-Kings succeed through attention to detail," Joe Tangari wrote for *Pitchfork.com* (April 5, 2010). "While a lot of music makes aesthetic or stylistic nods to the 60s, almost none of it actually captures the sonic character of the era. But on each of their albums, Jones and her collaborators, led by Gabriel Roth, have done just that." Daptone also distributes music under the imprints Ever-Soul Records and Dunham Records.

Roth and his wife, Veronica, have a daughter, Penelope.

—M.M.

Suggested Reading: *Big Daddy* p72+ Summer 2000; *LA Weekly* (on-line) July 17, 2008; *New York Times Magazine* p38 Dec. 7, 2008; *Pop Matters* (on-line) Mar. 7, 2008; *Seattle Weekly* (on-line) May 18, 2005; *Sound on Sound* (on-line) June 2008

Selected Recordings: as producer and performer—with Sharon Jones & the Dap-Kings: *Dap Dippin' with Sharon Jones and the Dap-Kings*, 2002; *Naturally*, 2005; *100 Days, 100 Nights*, 2007; *I Learned the Hard Way*, 2010; with the Budos Band: *The Budos Band I*, 2005;

as producer—with the Budos Band: *The Budos Band II*, 2007; *The Budos Band III*, 2009; with the Daktaris: *Soul Explosion*, 2004; with the Menehan Band: *Make the Road by Walking*, 2008; with the Mighty Imperials: *Thunder Chicken*, 2003; with Naomi Shelton and the Gospel Queens: *What Have You Done, My Brother?*, 2009; with the Sugarman Three—*Pure Cane Sugar*, 2002; *Soul Donkey*, 2003; *Sugar's Boogaloo*, 2006

Selected Radio Programs: *Across 110th Street* (1990s)

Jim McIsaac/Getty Images

Ryan, Rex

Dec. 13, 1962– Football coach

Address: New York Jets, 1000 Fulton Ave., Hempstead, NY 11550

"Rex Ryan makes headlines with his brash statements, often sounding like the bully in the schoolyard, but that's only one side of the Jets coach," Rich Cimini wrote for the New York *Daily News* (January 17, 2010). Cimini continued: "There's also this side: The Xs-and-Os whiz, the coach who transformed an average defense into the best unit in the NFL." Greg Bishop observed in an article for the *New York Times* (January 22, 2009), "Underneath the bluster, Ryan remains the quintessential football coach, a brash, tough, confident teacher who inspires players with simple instruction of a complex scheme." Considered one of the top defensive masterminds in the National Football

League (NFL), Rex Ryan—the son of the legendary NFL coach Buddy Ryan—spent 10 seasons with the Baltimore Ravens, serving as defensive-line coach (1999–2004) and defensive coordinator (2005–08) under head coach Brian Billick, before joining the New York Jets in 2009. Ryan helped shape a Ravens' defense that consistently ranked sixth or better and was among the most feared in the league for its ability to stop runners. Ryan's tenure with the Ravens also coincided with the team's first—and only—Super Bowl victory, in 2000, and a second American Football Conference (AFC) Championship appearance, in 2008. Upon joining the Jets, Ryan promised to deliver a more physical team and boldly predicted a Super Bowl victory within the next few years. Though some have interpreted Ryan's off-the-cuff statements as crossing the line between confidence and arrogance, his player-friendly coaching style and unabashed belief in the long-struggling franchise quickly won over players and fans. In his first season with the Jets, Ryan helped to transform what had been an average defense into the top-ranked defense in the NFL and led the team to its first AFC Championship game since 1998. Though the Jets lost that game to the heavily favored Indianapolis Colts, 30–17, Ryan was praised for helming the Jets through a surprisingly successful season.

Rex Ryan was born on December 13, 1962 in Ardmore, Oklahoma, along with his fraternal twin brother, Rob. Ryan has another brother, Jimmy, who is six years older. At the time of Ryan's birth, his father, Buddy, then an assistant football coach at the University of Buffalo, was away on a recruiting trip. Buddy Ryan went on to coach in the NFL and became known for his original defensive strategies as well as his outspoken and unpredictable behavior. He served as the linebackers' coach for the New York Jets (1968–75) during their win over the Baltimore Colts in Super Bowl III, in 1969. That stunning upset is one of Rex Ryan's earliest memories. Buddy Ryan told Sam Borden for the *Westchester County (New York) Journal News* (January 25, 2009), "Rex was 6 years old when we won that ring. He wanted to be a football coach since he was 7." Ryan's parents divorced when he was two years old, and his mother, Doris, moved with the children to Toronto, Ontario, Canada, where Ryan spent much of his youth and adolescence. Doris Ryan, who had earned a doctorate in education administration from the University of Chicago, served as a professor at the University of Toronto and later became vice president at the University of New Brunswick. Buddy Ryan, who made frequent visits to Toronto to see his children, went on to serve as defensive coordinator for the Minnesota Vikings (1976–77) and the Chicago Bears (1978–85) and head coach of the Philadelphia Eagles (1986–90), the Houston Oilers (1993), and the Arizona Cardinals (1994–95).

Wild and energetic, Rex Ryan and his twin brother began playing football in the fourth grade. They were soon kicked out of the local youth league, however, for their propensity for violent play. "We were probably using our helmets as weapons. Something like that," Ryan told Mike Zeisberger for the *Toronto Sun* (December 2, 2009). Along with his brother, Rex Ryan took up hockey (playing goalie), baseball (playing catcher), and curling and became a fan of the city's National Hockey League (NHL) team, the Toronto Maple Leafs. To earn money the Ryan brothers delivered newspapers on one route in the morning and another in the afternoon. A poor student, Rex Ryan was frustrated in school and often skipped class when the opportunity presented itself. He has attributed his early academic difficulties to dyslexia—which affects a person's ability to read, write, and spell—though he was not diagnosed with the condition until adulthood. "I just struggled. It was brutal," he recalled to Zeisberger. "Maybe it drove me to follow athletics. We'd have a spelling test and I'd have no chance. Even now, I'll mess up a vowel in a second. Here's my mom, a Phi Beta Kappa, and I'm having all this trouble [reading and writing]. It was embarrassing. It got to the point that, if there wasn't floor hockey or some other sport going on at school, there wasn't much motivation for me to go."

In the fall of 1977, Rex and Rob Ryan went to live with their father in Edina, Minnesota, where Buddy Ryan was beginning his second season as the defensive coordinator for the Minnesota Vikings. In 1978 Buddy Ryan was hired for the same job with the Chicago Bears, and the family moved to Illinois. Rex Ryan attended Stevenson High School, in Prairie View, Illinois, and often accompanied his father to Bears' home games, where he served as a ball boy and befriended several professional players, including the franchise's legendary Hall of Fame running back Walter Payton. After graduating from high school, Ryan and his brother attended Southwestern Oklahoma State University, in Weatherford. The two played the defensive end position on the university's football squad, which was helmed by Bob Mazie, an acquaintance of Buddy Ryan's. Although Rex Ryan possessed only marginal natural talent on the field, Cecil Perkins, then the university's athletic director, told Bishop for the *New York Times* (January 21, 2009) that he "hit harder than his bones were supposed to." Perkins added, about the two brothers: "They were just great people. Ornery as heck. If you were to insult their girlfriends, they might just swat you on the nose. I happen to think that's the way it should be done, so I have a lot of respect for them." Ryan struggled with injuries during much of his college football career, and as a result he saw very little playing time. Doris Ryan told Bishop (January 21, 2009), "I don't think he particularly cared. He was ready to get out and start coaching."

Both Rex and Rob Ryan were determined to become football coaches. So in the spring of 1987, during his tenure as head coach of the Philadelphia Eagles, Buddy taught his sons the 46 defense, a defensive scheme he had designed in which eight de-

fenders are positioned at or near the line of scrimmage, in order to confuse the quarterback, stop the running game, and disguise various coverages. Though the 46 defense is not often used in today's game, it was widely credited with reinventing defensive football in the 1980s and played an integral part in the Chicago Bears' 1985 Super Bowl victory. With his father's help Ryan obtained a graduate-assistant position for the 1987 season as the defensive-end coach under head coach Roy Kidd, at Eastern Kentucky University (EKU). Ryan helped the Colonels advance to the Division I-AA quarter-finals in 1987 and the semifinals in 1988. Ryan also earned a B.S. and, in 1988, an M.S. degree, both in physical education, from EKU. In 1989 Ryan served as the assistant head coach and defensive coordinator for the Division II New Mexico Highlands University football team, in Las Vegas, New Mexico. The next season he became the defensive coordinator for the Division I-AA school Morehead State University, in Kentucky. During Ryan's four-season tenure there, the Eagles' defense consistently ranked among the best in the nation.

In 1994 Ryan left the college-coaching ranks to work in the NFL under his father, who was then the head coach of the Arizona Cardinals. He became an assistant defensive line coach, and his brother Rob served as a defensive backs coach. That season the Cardinals' defense ranked in the NFL's top five in every major statistical category. In the 1995 season Ryan served as the team's linebackers' coach. That season the Cardinals finished with a dismal 4–12 record, and their scoring defense ranked last in the league. Along with both his sons, Buddy Ryan was fired, marking the end of his coaching career. After being dismissed from the Cardinals, Rex Ryan was unable to find a coaching position with an NFL team and instead accepted a job as the defensive coordinator at the University of Cincinnati, in Ohio, under head coach Rick Minter. During the 1996 season the Bearcats posted a 6–5 record and ranked 13th in the nation in overall defense. The following season the Bearcats' defense was ranked fifth against the rush, and the team defeated Utah State University, 35–19, in the Humanitarian Bowl, the team's first bowl appearance in 50 years. In 1998 Ryan became defensive coordinator for the University of Oklahoma Sooners, a Division I-A team. That season, under Ryan's defensive game planning, the Sooners finished sixth in the nation in total defense.

In 1999 Ryan returned to the NFL, joining the Baltimore Ravens as a defensive-line coach under the new head coach, Brian Billick. Upon joining the organization, Ryan boldly predicted that the Ravens' defense would soon be considered one of the best in league history and that people would talk about them 100 years in the future. The former Ravens tackle Tony Siragusa, now an analyst with the Fox Network, recalled to Bishop for the *New York Times* (January 22, 2009), "I thought, 'Either this guy is nuts or really thinks we're going to be the best defense ever.' Soon enough, you start believing." After finishing the 1999 season ranked second in the league in overall defense, the Ravens' defense posted one of the best all-around performances in league history in 2000, finishing the season ranked number one against the run and second in overall performance. That season the defense also set a 16-game league record by allowing only 970 total yards rushing and just 2.68 yards per rushing attempt; it also set the league record for fewest points allowed in a 16-game season, with 165. The Ravens' record-setting defense, led by the All-Pro linebacker Ray Lewis and the All-Pro cornerback Rod Woodson, helped the team advance to Super Bowl XXXV, in Tampa, Florida, in January 2001. The Ravens crushed their opponents, the New York Giants, 34–7, notching the franchise's first and only Super Bowl win to date.

The Ravens followed up their Super Bowl–winning season in impressive fashion, compiling a 10–6 season record and finishing second in the NFL in overall defensive performance. The team advanced to the divisional round of the play-offs and lost to the Pittsburgh Steelers, 27–10. During that off-season the Ravens' heralded defensive coordinator, Marvin Lewis, left the team to take the same position with the Washington Redskins. Ryan interviewed for the Ravens' defensive-coordinator position, but Billick chose Mike Nolan, the team's wide-receivers' coach, to replace Lewis. Disappointed but determined, Ryan continued to work relentlessly under Nolan. On top of the coaching change, other difficulties, including salary-cap issues that forced the Ravens to part with several key players, contributed to a disappointing 7–9 record in 2002. That year, despite holding opponents to an average of only 3.7 yards per carry—the fewest in the AFC—the team's defense finished the season ranked 22d in overall performance. They bounced back in the 2003 and 2004 seasons, with overall defensive performances ranking third and second, respectively, in the league.

In 2005 Nolan was hired as the head coach of the San Francisco 49ers, and Ryan was promoted to become the Ravens' defensive coordinator. That season the Ravens' defense ranked fifth in the NFL, allowing an average of only 284.7 yards per game. The 2006 Ravens defense proved even more dominant, finishing the season ranked first in the NFL in points allowed (201) and in overall defensive performance (allowing an average of only 264.1 yards per game). Ryan's defense thrived especially in turnover situations; they ranked second in the league in takeaways (40) and scored six defensive touchdowns, including five interceptions and one fumble recovery. At the end of the season, six defensive players earned Pro Bowl honors, and Ryan was named NFL Assistant Coach of the Year by *Pro Football Weekly* and the Pro Football Writers' Association of America. The Ravens, meanwhile, finished with a franchise-best record of 13–3 but lost in the divisional play-off round to the Indianapolis Colts, 15–6. Ryan was praised for his imaginative and flexible defensive schemes, which seemed to

be reinventions of those his father had taught him. Doris Ryan explained to Bishop (January 21, 2009), "He plays a version of Buddy's defense, but he made it his own. Particularly with the Ravens. That defense is all Rex." Ryan described his defensive style to Jamison Hensley for the *Baltimore Sun* (January 10, 2009) as "organized chaos," noting, "There is a method to the madness."

Although the Ravens finished the 2007 season with a disappointing 5–11 record, the team's defense, despite being riddled with injuries, had a strong performance, finishing second in the league against the run—allowing only 2.8 yards per rushing attempt—and sixth in the league in overall defense. Nevertheless, Billick and the entire coaching staff were fired at the end of the season. Billick was replaced by the longtime Philadelphia Eagles assistant coach John Harbaugh, who promptly rehired Ryan as assistant head coach and defensive coordinator. (Ryan, who had also interviewed for the Ravens' head-coaching position, was the only member of Billick's coaching staff to be rehired.) Despite facing one of the toughest schedules in the NFL, the Ravens enjoyed a major turnaround in 2008, finishing with a record of 11–5. In the postseason the Ravens defeated the Miami Dolphins in the wildcard round and the Tennessee Titans in the divisional play-off round, before losing to the Pittsburgh Steelers in the AFC Championship Game, 23–14. The Ravens were anchored by their defense, which finished second in the league in yards allowed (an average of only 261.1 per game), third in fewest points allowed (244), and first in takeaways (34, including 26 interceptions).

On January 19, 2009 Ryan signed a four-year, $11.5 million contract to become the New York Jets' head coach, replacing Eric Mangini, who had been fired following the Jets' disastrous late-season performance in 2008. The Jets' general manager, Mike Tannenbaum, was impressed with Ryan's preparation—he brought to his interview a notebook containing detailed plans for the whole season—and the respect Ryan commanded from his colleagues in the Ravens' organization. Tannenbaum recalled to Bishop for the *New York Times* (January 24, 2010), "What was unbelievable was the passion in which people believed in this guy and how much they rooted for him. It was shocking." In his first news conference, Ryan—who with his outspoken demeanor contrasted greatly with the notoriously stone-faced Mangini—outlined his vision for the Jets, a team that had been characterized for decades by disappointment. Ryan promised to turn the Jets into the most physical team in the league with a "ground and pound" strategy—a mode of football that relies primarily on a strong defense and running game—and even predicted that the Jets would meet President Barack Obama at the White House within a couple of years as Super Bowl victors. Ryan made many other bold statements during the off-season, some of which earned him criticism. In an interview with the New York sports radio station WFAN, Ryan explained that he was not intimidated by the three-time NFL champions, the New England Patriots, stating, as quoted in the New York *Daily News* (June 3, 2009, on-line), "I did not come here to kiss [Patriots coach] Bill Belichick's rings. I came here to win, let's put it that way." During the summer Ryan engaged in a long-distance exchange with the Miami Dolphins linebacker Channing Crowder after the famously chatty player lambasted Ryan for his bravado. Ryan said in jest during a press conference, as quoted by Tim Layden for *Sports Illustrated* (June 22, 2009): "I've walked over tougher guys going to a fight than Channing Crowder."

Attention-grabbing headlines aside, Ryan's impact on the Jets was immediate. The team started out strong, winning its first three games. In a roller-coaster-like season, they went on to lose six out of their next seven games. Several of those losses were attributed to the many interceptions thrown by the Jets' young but promising rookie quarterback, Mark Sanchez. The Jets bounced back with three consecutive victories, before suffering another heartbreaking loss in week 15 to the Atlanta Falcons in the game's final minutes. After that loss Ryan declared that the Jets, whose record was then 7–7, were out of play-off contention, despite the fact that a postseason berth was still possible—albeit unlikely. A series of fortuitous circumstances allowed the Jets to advance to the play-offs. Both of the Jets' final two opponents, the Indianapolis Colts and the Cincinnati Bengals, had already secured their play-off positions and, as is common practice in the NFL under such circumstances, decided to bench their starting players, in order to avoid needless injuries in the season's last games. Likely helped to a great extent by the fact that their opponents' best players had little playing time, the Jets defeated the Colts and the Bengals and captured the wildcard play-off spot. The Jets finished the regular season with the league's number-one-ranked rushing offense and overall defense. The Jets' defense also led the league in two of the most important defensive categories, fewest yards allowed (4,037) and fewest points allowed (236).

As the Jets entered the postseason, sports analysts gave them the longest odds of any postseason team to advance to the Super Bowl. Ryan, however, confidently echoed his preseason predictions by proclaiming that the Jets should be the tournament favorites, going so far as to map out the route for the parade that would follow the team's Super Bowl victory. The Jets surprised many observers by winning back-to-back road victories, defeating the Bengals in the wildcard round and the San Diego Chargers in the divisional play-off round. In the AFC Championship game, the Jets faced the heavily favored Indianapolis Colts. After winning the first half, 17–13, the Jets lost the game, 30–17. In a press conference held the day after the loss, Ryan predicted, as noted by Rich Cimini, that the Jets would be "a definite contender these next several years." The Jets opened the 2010 season in a brand-new, $1.4 billion stadium. In July 2010 Ryan signed a contract extension that will keep him with the Jets until 2014.

A week after the Jets' AFC Championship loss, on January 30, 2010, Ryan made headlines for giving the middle finger to a Miami Dolphins fan during a mixed martial-arts event in Sunrise, Florida. The Dolphins fan apparently began taunting Ryan after the coach gave a ringside interview that was shown on the venue's big screen, in which Ryan declared, as quoted by Cimini for the New York *Daily News* (February 2, 2010, on-line): "I want to just tell everybody in Miami, 'Hey, we're coming to beat you twice next year.'" Ryan was fined $50,000 by the league and later issued an apology.

Often ridiculed for his rotund physique, Ryan once admitted to consuming an average of 7,000 calories a day. In March 2010 he underwent lap-band surgery, a weight-loss procedure in which a plastic band is used to create a smaller, adjustable stomach area that limits food intake. As of late October 2010, Ryan had reportedly lost 70 pounds.

During the summer of 2010, Ryan and the Jets were the subject of the Emmy Award–winning HBO reality-television series *Hard Knocks*, which documents NFL teams' preseason practice and preparation. Ryan's frequent use of expletives in several episodes drew heavy criticism from the former NFL coach and current NBC football analyst Tony Dungy. Thanks to the exposure he and his team received through *Hard Knocks*, the Jets opened the 2010 season under intense scrutiny. Then, during the opening weekend of the season, the Mexican TV Azteca reporter Ines Sainz accused the Jets players and staff of sexually harassing her when she visited their training facility to interview Mark Sanchez. Sainz claimed that players purposely threw footballs toward her and that she was subjected to rude comments. Following an NFL investigation the league commissioner, Roger Goodell, criticized the Jets' behavior but concluded that they had not sexually harassed or physically harmed Sainz. The Jets' owner, Woody Johnson, issued a statement of apology and has since been commissioned to underwrite a sensitivity-training program for the entire league.

The Jets lost their 2010 season opener, at home, against the Baltimore Ravens, 10–9. They soon earned more negative media coverage, when their often-troubled starting wide receiver Braylon Edwards was arrested on a DWI charge on the day after the team's 28–14 week-two victory over the New England Patriots. The decision to bench Edwards for only one-quarter of the next game, a 31–23 win over the Miami Dolphins, was heavily criticized, with many sports analysts and others complaining that he should have been disciplined far more seriously. Such charges led Ryan to hold a team meeting in which he made an impassioned plea to his players to stop embarrassing the organization. In terms of their on-the-field performance, the Jets had the best record in the NFL (5–1) going into their bye week in mid-October.

Ryan is collaborating with Don Yaeger, a former *Sports Illustrated* editor, on a book about his life and coaching philosophy. Doubleday plans to publish the book in 2011.

Ryan and his wife, Michelle, live in Summit, New Jersey. They have two teenage sons, Payton and Seth. Rex Ryan's brother Rob is the defensive coordinator for the Cleveland Browns.

—C.C.

Suggested Reading: *Baltimore Sun* D p1 Jan. 10, 2009; (New York) *Daily News* Sports p56+ Jan. 17, 2010; New York Jets Web site; *New York Times* B p9 Jan. 21, 2009, B p11 Jan. 22, 2009, A p1 Jan. 24, 2010; *Sports Illustrated* p46+ June 22, 2009; *Toronto Sun* S p4+ Dec. 2, 2009; (Westchester County, New York) *Journal News* C p1 Jan. 25, 2009

Courtesy of CNBC

Santelli, Rick

July 1956– Financial journalist

Address: c/o CNBC Business News, 1025 Connecticut Ave., N.W., Washington, DC 20036-5405

Until early 2009 Rick Santelli was known to television audiences mainly for his daily appearances on CNBC. Reporting live from the trading floor, Santelli, a financial-industry veteran, was popular with viewers for his colorful and easy-to-understand explanations of interest rates, futures, and the Federal Reserve, among other such topics. Then, on February 19, 2009, while broadcasting

live, he began railing against President Barack Obama's proposed plan to help homeowners facing foreclosure. "The government is promoting bad behavior," Santelli asserted. "This is America! How many people want to pay for your neighbor's mortgages that has an extra bathroom and can't pay their bills? Raise their hand! President Obama, are you listening?" Making reference to the 1773 Boston Tea Party, during which American colonists threw a shipment of tea into the Boston Harbor to protest being forced to pay British taxes without representation in Britain's Parliament, Santelli exclaimed, "We're thinking of having a Chicago Tea Party in July. All you capitalists that want to show up to Lake Michigan, I'm gonna start organizing." The clip quickly went viral on the Internet, and a group of viewers took Santelli's pronouncements as a call to action. Santelli is thus sometimes known as the catalyst or founder of the populist Tea Party movement, which stages anti-government-bailout rallies around the country and is promoted extensively on such conservative outlets as Fox News.

"So many outlets . . . seemed to acknowledge that the movement began with those four minutes of airtime," Santelli later said, according to Phil Rosenthal, writing for the *Chicago Tribune* (February 18, 2010). "We were a lightning rod, and it sparked a groundswell." He continued, "I have no desire to be [the movement's] leader, but I'm proud as hell . . . to have been a part of creating it." While Santelli was encouraged by supporters to seek political office in the wake of his newfound fame, he instead renewed his CNBC contract and continues to report several times a day on financial matters. "In hindsight, those could have been the best four minutes of my life, but I think we all know what we're good at in life," Santelli said, as quoted in Rosenthal's piece. "My passion's what I did before February 19, and what I've continued to do since then and hopefully will continue to do for many more years. I love the markets."

Rick Santelli was born in July 1956. He grew up in Chicago, Illinois, and attended the University of Illinois at Urbana-Champaign, where he majored in political science and earned a B.A. degree in January 1979. Although he considered entering law school, a trip to the floor of the Chicago Mercantile Exchange (CME) to visit the father of a friend changed his mind. "It was his first taste of life in a business infamous for its wild bargaining and pressure-cooker environment," Shareen Mani wrote for the *Chicago Daily Herald* (March 9, 2003). "Santelli, a high-energy guy who could easily win a speed-walking contest, was hooked."

Santelli found a low-paying job as a "runner," delivering market orders from the brokers to the floor traders. Soon he had worked his way up to trader and order filler, becoming involved in a variety of markets, including gold, lumber, foreign currencies, and livestock. Santelli admitted to Mani that he sometimes lost money during that period. "There were a lot of times I had to count pennies to go buy breakfast," he recalled.

Santelli went on to hold various positions in the financial industry. He served as a vice president of interest-rate futures and options at Drexel, Burnham, Lambert—one of the largest investment firms in the country before its declaration of bankruptcy in 1990—and then as a managing director at the Derivative Products Group of Geldermann Inc., a Chicago-based firm. In 1993 he joined Rand Financial Services as a vice president in charge of institutional futures and options, remaining there until 1997. (In financial-industry jargon, the term "futures" refers to the practice of buying or selling a specified commodity at a date in the future at a market-determined price.) When he was tapped by CNBC to provide commentary, in 1999, he was working as a vice president for institutional trading and hedging at Sanwa Futures LLC, a subsidiary of the Tokyo, Japan–based Sanwa Bank.

Santelli had occasionally appeared on television before being hired by CNBC. During the early 1990s television cameras were allowed onto the exchange floor for the first time, and Santelli was asked by a friend who ran media operations for the Chicago Board of Trade (CBOT) to help out. He began providing expert commentary for several news outlets. "I found it very invigorating; it hit a chord with me," Santelli told Frank Ahrens for the *Washington Post* (November 13, 2008, on-line). "I liked trying to open up this fascinating insider world to the public and thought I could make a positive difference. It was right around that time that I started to see the industry was changing in a way that was not beneficial to me and my family—the amount of risk and effort had gone up and the reward had slipped a bit."

In June 1999 Santelli became a full-time on-air editor at CNBC, reporting live from the CBOT floor. (In 2007 the CBOT merged with the CME to form the CME Group.) He joined "a growing cadre of financial professionals going into business broadcasting, specifically on cable TV," Jim Kirk wrote for the *Chicago Tribune* (June 22, 1999). Bruno Cohen, a CNBC executive, explained to Kirk: "We think those people who have had direct experience have been more effective. We're looking for a combination of reporting and an ability to analyze information from a historical perspective." Santelli's reports aired several times a day—starting at 7:30 in the morning—five days a week. "In a world that's notorious for being cutthroat and highly stressed, Santelli's down-to-earth, personable nature is a relief," Mani wrote. "His desire to help average people understand otherwise esoteric business jargon is unmistakable." Ahrens offered similar praise: "Santelli . . . is CNBC's automatic bull-poop detector. In his native Chicago accent, the former trader and financial executive is terrible, absolutely terrible, at hiding his contempt for a bad idea, whether it comes from a Fed chairman or one of his CNBC colleagues." Ahrens continued, "Santelli . . . is usually perched in a lower corner of the TV screen and is filmed from above, shouting up from a trading pit at the Chicago Board of Trade. It gives his rants a classic plain-speaking-little-man-against-the-system feel."

Santelli achieved a new level of recognition after February 19, 2009, when he gave a reportedly unscripted reaction to the Obama administration's proposed Homeowner Affordability and Stability Plan, a $275 billion initiative aimed at helping millions of families to restructure or refinance their mortgages to avoid foreclosure. Speaking on camera from the exchange floor, Santelli said: "You know, the new administration's big on computers and technology. How about this, president and new administration: Why don't you put up a website to have people vote on the Internet as a referendum to see if we really want to subsidize the losers' mortgages? Or would we like to at least buy cars and buy houses in foreclosure and give them to people that might have a chance to actually prosper down the road, and reward people that could carry the water instead of drink the water?" Traders on the floor began cheering and applauding, and referring to them, Santelli said, "These guys are pretty straightforward, and my guess is, a pretty good statistical cross-section of America, the silent majority." The video of the "Santelli Rant," as most labeled it, quickly became an Internet hit. Within 24 hours more than one million people had viewed the clip on the CNBC Web site, and it soon logged millions more views on the video-sharing site YouTube. While many observers took issue with Santelli's characterization of those who could not pay their mortgages as "losers" and scoffed at the notion that floor traders provided "a pretty good statistical cross-section of America," others concurred with his views.

The clip received so much attention that the White House felt compelled to address the issue. The following day, in response to a question about Santelli, White House press secretary Robert Gibbs said, as quoted by Josh Gerstein for Politico.com (February 20, 2009), "I've watched Mr. Santelli on cable the past 24 hours or so. I'm not entirely sure where Mr. Santelli lives or in what house he lives but the American people are struggling every day to meet their mortgages, stay in their jobs, pay their bills, send their kids to school. I think we left a few months ago the adage that if it was good for a derivatives trader that it was good for Main Street. I think the verdict is in on that." In an article for *Slate* (February 21, 2009, on-line), John Dickerson pointed out: "It's definitely not White House policy to elevate cable talking heads. But Gibbs had to push back against the blanket coverage Santelli was getting. . . . Politically, Gibbs wants this fight because his bet is that Santelli is a good face for the opposition. He's a member of the media, and people don't like us very much. And Santelli's persona is well short of huggable." "Plus," Dickerson concluded, alluding to the belief that Santelli and other CNBC commentators had been overly enthusiastic or careless in providing investment advice, "he can easily be tied to the financial interests that people blame for the current mess." (That comment referred to subprime-mortgage lending, or banks' practice of extending credit to home buyers who could not afford their purchases; that widespread practice has been blamed for the recent economic downturn.)

Within weeks of Santelli's comments, Tea Party protests were taking place all over the United States. On March 2, 2009 Santelli posted a piece on the CNBC Web site headlined, "I Want to Set the Record Straight," in which he wrote: "I have NO affiliation or association with any of the websites or related tea party movements that have popped up as a result of my comments on February 19th, or to the best of my knowledge any of the people who organized the websites or movements." He continued, "Anyone who has watched my thousands of appearances on CNBC is well acquainted with my aggressive and impassioned style. . . . As a financial reporter I have never shied away from trying to promote discourse and dialogue of the important issues that affect markets and therefore our lives. The one spot in particular that occurred on February 19th at roughly 8:15 [Eastern Standard] time and maybe lasted for a minute probably wasn't even in my top 5 in terms of intensity, energy, or controversy. It was unique in that it obviously struck a chord with the public thus inciting what can only be described as a groundswell of feedback from the public, the White House, the Internet, and the media at large. The President's plan addressing issues in the housing market was the topic; but only the tip of the iceberg in fact. The real nerve struck seems to be the pent up emotions felt by millions of Americans regarding spending TRILLIONS of dollars to fix the housing market, the banks, and the economy." Addressing concerns that had arisen about the authenticity of his speech, he wrote, "The 'rant heard around the world' (as it has been named by the media) on February 19th was spontaneous . . . not scripted . . . and any person, organization, or media outlet that claims otherwise IS INACCURATE."

Whether or not Santelli intended to instigate the Tea Partiers, the movement snowballed. "As spring passed into summer," Ben McGrath wrote for the *New Yorker* (February 1, 2010), "the scores at local Tea Party gatherings turned to hundreds, and then thousands, collecting along the way footloose Ron Paul supporters, goldbugs, evangelicals, Atlas Shruggers, militiamen, strict Constitutionalists, swine-flu skeptics, scattered 9/11 'truthers,' neo-'Birchers,' and, of course, 'birthers'—those who remained convinced that the President was a Muslim double agent born in Kenya." In September 2009 tens of thousands of protestors marched in Washington, D.C., in support of the movement. "Some [of their] signs, reflecting the growing intensity of the health care debate, depicted President Obama with the signature mustache of Nazi dictator Adolf Hitler. Many made reference to Obama as a socialist or communist, and another imposed his face on that of the villainous Joker from *Batman*. Other protesters waved U.S. flags and held signs

espousing fiscal conservatism, declaring 'I'm Not Your ATM' and 'Go Green Recycle Congress,'" an article posted on the Fox News Web site (September 12, 2009) stated. "The rally, and others like it, have been billed as 'tea parties,' part of a movement that takes its cue from the Boston Tea Party and other imagery from the days of the founding fathers. On Saturday, men wore colonial costumes as they listened to speakers who warned of 'judgment day'—Election Day 2010."

Despite the encouragement of his fans, Santelli has ruled out making a bid for public office. "There's so much compromise in politics," he told Paul Bedard for the *U.S. News & World Report* (January 25, 2010, on-line). "I'm not a good compromiser." Still, he told Bedard, he is happy to have inspired others: "It's very gratifying to me that four minutes out of my life made a difference. It seems to me that any reason for people getting more active in running or taking part in politics and government . . . is just terrific." Santelli is reportedly working on a book, which will not focus exclusively on the incidents of February 2009.

Santelli met his wife, Terri, when she was a young CME runner. They now live in a suburb of Chicago and have three daughters.

—D.K.

Suggested Reading: *Chicago Daily Herald* Business p1 Mar. 9, 2003; *Chicago Tribune* N p2 June 22, 1999, C p25 Feb. 18, 2010; *New Yorker* p40 Feb. 1, 2010; Politico.com Feb. 20, 2009; *Slate* (on-line) Feb. 21, 2009; *U.S. News & World Report* (on-line) Jan. 25, 2010; *Washington Post* (on-line) Nov. 13, 2008

Scannell, Herb

(SKAN-il)

Jan. 11, 1957– Broadcasting executive

Address: BBC America, 747 Third Ave., Sixth Fl., New York, NY 10017

In June 2010 the British Broadcasting Corp. (BBC), one of the world's most famous media networks, announced that Herb Scannell would head its U.S. commercial arm, BBC Worldwide America. Scannell is best known for the innovations he brought to children's television programming as the president of Nickelodeon from 1996 to 2006. Under his leadership the network bucked the trend of airing shows that were little more than ads for toys, introducing original programs including the animated hits *SpongeBob SquarePants* and *Dora the Explorer*; in the process Nickelodeon became a ratings juggernaut. Scannell left Nickelodeon to co-found Next New Networks (NNN), an Internet-based umbrella of smaller networks aimed at fostering innovative shows. At BBC Worldwide America Scan-

Frank Micelotta/Getty Images

Herb Scannell

nell will be responsible for overseeing such existing British imports as *Doctor Who* and *BBC World News* while also developing original content.

The youngest of four children, Herb Scannell was born on January 11, 1957 in Huntington, on the north shore of Long Island, New York. His father, a Boston, Massachusetts, native of Irish descent, was a social worker, and his mother, born in Puerto Rico, was a case worker for Catholic Charities. Scannell told Lawrie Mifflin for the *New York Times* (June 17, 1999), "My mother and father were like Ricky and Lucy, only in reverse," referring to the married couple on the classic American sitcom *I Love Lucy*, on which the husband was Latino and the wife Caucasian. As a boy Scannell was taught Spanish by his mother and, beginning at about age eight, spent every summer in Puerto Rico. As a result he developed a strong interest in Puerto Rican culture. Scannell also took a liking to pop culture as a child, perhaps an indicator of his future career; he memorized the Top 40 music countdowns on the radio and circled his favorite shows in *TV Guide*. Scannell graduated from high school in 1975 and attended Boston College, where he worked as the manager of WZBC, the campus radio station. He graduated with a B.A. degree in English and history in 1979, and then, unable to find a job in radio, worked in the admissions office of Baruch College, in New York City. A year later he landed a job at radio station WHN, in New York. "Shortly after I got there," he wrote in a reminiscence for the *New York Times* (May 8, 2005, on-line), "the vice president of the department left the company, as did the promotion director and promotion manager. I became the de facto head of the department at age 22. I learned a lot." In 1981 Scannell was hired

at the Movie Channel (which later merged with Showtime), where he held several positions in promotion and marketing, eventually becoming the director of program promotion.

In 1988 Scannell began to work in the marketing department of Nickelodeon, a cable-television network owned by MTV Networks, which is a division of Viacom International. He worked his way up to become Nickelodeon's director of programming that same year, a post in which he supervised the scheduling of shows. In 1989 Scannell became vice president for programming, and in 1995 he was named executive vice president of the Nickelodeon Network and U.S. Television. In an interview with John Flinn for *Brandweek* (April 29, 1996), Scannell explained his efforts to differentiate Nickelodeon's offerings from those of other children's networks, which often aired programs based on real-life music acts. "New Kids on the Block, MC Hammer, they all had cartoons—I don't know why," he said. "The question it really begged for us was, what happened to original ideas in animation?" Scannell and his team set out to create what Flinn called "shows for the smart set on the playground." During those years Scannell oversaw the making of *Nick News* (an educational program for children and teens), *Snick* (a two-hour Saturday-night programming block), and *Nicktoons* (Sunday-morning cartoons, created in response to other networks' Saturday-morning cartoons). In addition, he oversaw the creation of the popular shows *Blue's Clues*, *Doug*, *Rugrats*, and *The Ren & Stimpy Show*. As quoted in *BusinessWire.com* (December 15, 1995), Tom Freston, then the chairman and CEO of MTV Networks, said, "Herb Scannell's great instincts and ability to develop innovative programming franchises has made Nickelodeon the number-one-rated basic cable network and the recognized leader in children's television."

In February 1996 Scannell succeeded Geraldine Laybourne as the president of Nickelodeon. Laybourne, who had held the title for 15 years, left to become president of the Disney/ABC Cable Networks. "He's a guy with a whole lot of heart and brains and cares deeply about kids, so it doesn't get much better than that," Laybourne said of Scannell to Verne Gay for *Newsday* (February 18, 2001). "I don't think there's any way I could have left Nickelodeon if he hadn't been there." Many wondered if Scannell could do as effective a job as his predecessor. "People felt he was a behind-the-scenes kind of guy. People thought he would have a tough time," Jack Irving, the executive vice president and media director for the advertising agency Saatchi & Saatchi New York, explained to Lawrie Mifflin. Tom Freston even moved into Laybourne's old office for six weeks and served temporarily as Nickelodeon's president, while watching Scannell in action to make sure he knew what he was doing.

Scannell proved himself not only qualified to do the job but capable of making Nickelodeon even more successful. The network's chief operating officer, Jeffrey D. Dunn, told Mifflin, "For Herb, it wasn't just, 'How does this work?' but 'How are we going to win, how are we going to take it to the next level?' It was empowering." Within his first five years as the company's president, the competitive Scannell tripled Nickelodeon's profits through his hard work. Several high-level executives at Nickelodeon, unhappy with the high expectations Scannell set for them, left the company. "He made people deliver," Cyma Zarghami, the network's general manager, said to Mifflin. "The ones who were delivering were the ones who stayed." Scannell told Verne Gay, "Some people left, and I might have ruffled some feathers, but it was important to me and the company that we move on, and that's what I was determined to do." He added, "When I first got here there was a lot of 'we've never done this before . . .' and I thought, 'You may have never done it, but a lot of other people have.'" While Scannell was always aware of what other networks were doing, he did not emulate their programming in order to draw viewers, because he was confident that Nickelodeon's shows would enable the network to stand out among its competitors, notably Warner Bros. and Walt Disney. Scannell told John Flinn, "If you make successful series, people will come back week in and week out to watch them." In Scannell's opinion, another factor that made Nickelodeon superior was that it was not "driven by a toys-first" mentality, as he told Donna Petrozzello for *Broadcasting & Cable* (February 2, 1998). "At Nickelodeon, we don't think of kids as little consumers."

During his tenure Scannell doubled Nickelodeon's animation production, building the first new animation studio in Los Angeles in four decades—a $350 million facility that enabled Nickelodeon to create several noteworthy series, including *Fairly Odd Parents, Hey Arnold!*, and one of the network's biggest hits, *SpongeBob SquarePants*. Building on the success of the nighttime-programming block Nick at Nite, in 1996 Scannell launched a 24-hour channel called TV Land, to air reruns of classic variety shows, sitcoms, and dramas; the channel later added original content and movies to its schedule. In February 1999 Scannell arranged to have Nickelodeon team up with Children's Television Workshop (which produces *Sesame Street*) in order to create a commercial-free educational channel for children called Noggin. The channel, intended for preschoolers and slightly older children, was renamed Nick Jr. in 2009. Scannell also encouraged the new network to explore other areas, including feature films, magazines, consumer products, and live theatrical shows.

During his career at Nickelodeon, Scannell was responsible for launching three shows aimed at attracting Hispanic viewers: *Taina; The Brothers García*, based on *Los García*, a show that Scannell watched as a child in Puerto Rico; and the extremely successful *Dora the Explorer*. In 2000 Scannell took over The Nashville Network (TNN), a country-music-themed television channel, which was subsequently renamed The National Network (still referred to as TNN). The new TNN featured less country music and more content that would appeal to a broader audience. "Our goal was to make it a national network with national distribution," Scannell said in an interview with *Brandweek* (June 24, 2002). In 2003 TNN was transformed into the first television network for men and renamed Spike TV.

In June 2003 Scannell, while remaining president of Nickelodeon Networks, was named vice chairman (some sources say group president) of MTV Networks, becoming responsible for the company's creative and business operations. On the occasion of Nickelodeon's 25th anniversary, in 2004, Scannell spoke about why Nickelodeon had been the number-one children's and basic-cable network for eight consecutive years, and why the company was ahead of Disney in the ratings. He told David Faber and Jim Cramer of the *Kudlow & Cramer* show on CNBC (March 15, 2004), "[Disney was] more concerned about movies, not about television, so Nickelodeon really kind of took advantage of that and really kind of delivered and brought new characters to television. . . . Disney I think had a period where they were resting on their laurels, we really were a vibrant entity in kids' television." In 2005 Scannell took part in the State of Hispanic America National Conference, for which he was an Executive Roundtable member. That same year Nickelodeon acquired the Web site NeoPets, which allows visitors to take care of virtual pets in a virtual world called Neopia. Scannell also led the effort to launch an on-line broadband channel, TurboNick (also known as Nick Video).

On January 5, 2006 Scannell resigned from his position with Nickelodeon and MTV Networks and was replaced by Cyma Zarghami. He then co-founded an Internet media company, Next New Networks, that was created to air programs of micro-networks. (A micro-network is an on-line brand that targets niche viewers—for example, aficionados of cars, comics, or fashion—and allows viewers to share and distribute content. As of 2008 NNN had 16 micro-networks and hoped to double that number.) The other co-founders of NNN included Emil Rensing, Fred Seibert, Timothy Shey, and Jed Simmons—all former TV executives. "We want to be the next wave of media company," Scannell told Mike Shields for *Mediaweek* (April 14, 2008). "This is not intended to be a traditional media company run by traditional media guys," he added. "This is really embracing what the Web does best. We are looking for a certain Web aesthetic." The official Web site for NNN describes the company as "TV for the Internet" and as "the leading independent producer of online television networks." NNN's networks include VOD Cars, Fast Lane Daily, and Channel Frederator.

In 2009 Scannell was elected to WNYC Radio's board of trustees. The popular, New York–based National Public Radio affiliate found itself struggling financially and hoped that Scannell's extensive experience in media would contribute to a recovery. "We're honored to have Herb, with his invaluable digital experience, at the helm during a time of rapid change and tremendous possibilities," WNYC's president, Laura Walker, said in a press release quoted on *Mediabistro.com* (June 3, 2009). "I'm thrilled to be a part of WNYC," Scannell said. "Unknown to many, my first job in media was in radio, and I've always been passionate about the immediacy and intimacy of the medium." Also in 2009 Scannell joined the board of Sí TV, an English-language cable network geared toward bicultural Latinos.

In June 2010 the 53-year-old Scannell was hired as the president of BBC Worldwide America, replacing Garth Ancier. As president Scannell is in charge of the U.S. arm of the world-famous British network, with responsibility for BBC America HD, BBC Worldwide Productions, and the U.S. arm of BBC.com as well as sales and distribution, home entertainment, and licensed consumer products for the U.S. market. The audience for BBC America is small but growing. The channel shows such British imports as *Torchwood*, *Top Gear*, *Doctor Who*, and *BBC World News America*. Scannell told Brian Stelter for the *New York Times* (June 2, 2010) that he hoped to make BBC America "an expanded and more diversified producer of television." He also told Stelter that he would like to have more "made in America programs," but that he will maintain "the D.N.A. of the BBC, which is smart, innovative and irreverent."

In an interview with Michael Schneider for *Variety* (June 2, 2010), Scannell said, "The thing about the BBC that's most appealing to me is it's probably the most innovative force in television. They just do things differently. And they always have." Scannell has praised the BBC for striving for objectivity in its news coverage, which distinguishes it from many other news providers. He told Schneider, "I have great respect for the institution and the way they report. I listen to them on the radio, and they are a voice of reason. My sense is it's part of what makes the BBC great." Scannell's experience as president of a children's network for 10 years will be directly relevant to his new duties, as BBC Worldwide America has announced plans to introduce an American version of its preschool children's channel, CBeebies. Scannell said to Schneider, "Having been in kids' television, I have a total respect for the kids programming from the BBC and CBeebies." In a BBC America press release (June 2, 2010), Scannell was quoted as saying, "I've been associated with innovative brands and businesses throughout my career, and there's none more innovative in television than BBC. It's a world renowned brand with a great portfolio of businesses in the U.S. that have tremendous prospects. I'm excited to be bringing these businesses together to make America an even bigger success for BBC Worldwide." Scannell has appointed a few new executives, among them Perry Simon, general manager, channels; Ann Sarnoff, chief operating

officer, BBC Worldwide America; and Sandy Ashendorf, executive vice president, network distribution, BBC Worldwide America.

Over the course of his career, Scannell had received many honors, including the Campaign of the Year award, presented by the Cable & Telecommunications Association for Marketing; the Broadcast Promotion and Marketing Executives' Award; the National Association for Multi-Ethnic Diversity in Communications Vision and Image Award; and the Amnesty International Award.

Scannell lives with his wife, Sarah Reetz, and two daughters in Manhattan. He also spends time in London, England.

—J.P.

Suggested Reading: *Broadcasting & Cable* p28+ Feb. 2, 1998; *Crain's New York Business* p33 Mar. 11, 1996; *Mediaweek* p26+ Apr. 14, 2008; (New York) *Daily News* p64 Nov. 6, 2000; *Newsday* D p17 Feb. 18, 2001

Jason Merritt/Getty Images

Sigismondi, Floria

1965– Music-video director; filmmaker; photographer; artist

Address: c/o William Morris Agency, 1325 Ave. of the Americas, New York, NY 10019-6047

The path that led the photographer and music-video director Floria Sigismondi to write and direct her first feature film—*The Runaways* (2010), about the 1970s rock band of the same name—is not an example of a typical route to Hollywood. A native of Italy, Sigismondi first established herself in Canada, as a photographer and music-video director. In 1996 she gained instant recognition in the U.S. with the "Beautiful People" video she made for the rock star Marilyn Manson. During the following year, on the strength of the next three videos that she directed—"Tourniquet," for Manson, and "Little Wonder" and "Dead Man Walking," for David Bowie—she became one of the most acclaimed music-video directors in the world. In a recent e-mail message to Sia Michel for the *New York Times* (March 14, 2010), David Bowie wrote, "Floria is a real force of nature, never short of ideas, and meticulous in the way she brings them into play." In the past decade and a half, Sigismondi has directed dozens of music videos, for acts including Jimmy Page and Robert Plant (formerly of the 1970s rock band Led Zeppelin), Leonard Cohen, Björk, Sarah McLachlan, Sheryl Crow, Christina Aguilera, Interpol, the Cure, Muse, the White Stripes, the Raconteurs, the Living Things, and the Dead Weather. The distinctive style of her videos can be traced to her academic training as a painter and photographer, her experience as a fashion photographer, and her adaptations of otherworldly aesthetics associated with the photographer Joel-Peter Witkin, the painters Hannah Hoch and Francis Bacon, and the film directors Federico Fellini, Tim Burton, and David Lynch.

Sigismondi had never written or directed a feature film when, a few years ago, the Hollywood producer Art Linson and his son and fellow producer, John Linson, approached her with the proposal that she make a film about young female rock stars. The producers' preference for a female director who was steeped in the music scene made Sigismondi an excellent candidate, since, in the course of her work as a videographer, she had become familiar with musicians' grueling touring, rehearsing, and recording schedules. "When we met Floria she was undeniable . . . ," Art Linson told Sia Michel. "If you've met her and you've seen her work, you see that she's got a spectacular eye, she's got great style and she's got the heart of a girl." *The Runaways* earned mixed reviews. Among the more enthusiastic was that of A. O. Scott, who wrote for the *New York Times* (March 19, 2010) that the film "evokes its moment and milieu with affectionate, almost uncanny fidelity." He concluded, "Ms. Sigismondi infuses crucial scenes with a rough, energetic spirit, and shows a willingness to accept the contradictions inherent in the material without prurience, moralism or too much sentimentality. The movie may be a little too tame in the end, but at its best it is just wild enough." Similarly, Frank Wilkins wrote for *ReelTalk* (May 8, 2010, on-line), "On the surface, *The Runaways* is a movie about a rock band that flamed out too early. But the real story being told—that of an unlikely bunch of girls who captured lightning in a bottle—is so well handled by all involved, the movie will likely become a rock n' roll staple alongside such classics as *Velvet Goldmine* and *Almost Famous*."

Sigismondi has published two books of photographs: *Redemption* (1999), which includes shots from her music videos, surreal self-portraits, and photos shot in a museum of medicine, and *Immune* (2005), which contains images from her music videos as well as self-portraits and other photos. Her work, including mixed-media installations, has been exhibited in galleries in Canada, England, Germany, Mexico, France, Italy, Canada, Denmark, and, in the U.S., Los Angeles, California, and New York City. A solo show of her paintings, sculptures, photos, and music videos was mounted at the Museum of Contemporary Canadian Art (MOCCA), in Toronto, in 2001.

Floria Sigismondi, whose given name is that of the title character in Puccini's opera *Tosca*, was born in 1965 in Pescara, a small city on Italy's east coast. Her parents, Domenico and Lina Sigismondi, were opera singers. Sigismondi told an interviewer for *Border Crossings* (August 2001) that being "raised on Italian folklore and story and on the films of Fellini" along with "the tragedies of the operas" helped to make her unafraid to "explore the different sides of life." Her father's atheism, her mother's devotion to Catholicism, and Sigismondi's own grapplings with faith-linked guilt, she has said, underlie some of her work. The Sigismondi family, which included her sister, Antonella, moved to Hamilton, a city in Ontario, Canada, when Floria was two years old. According to the interviewer for *Border Crossings*, as a child she spent a great deal of time "attending opera rehearsals, wearing fanciful clothes sewn by her mother, and being encouraged to become an artist." From a very young age, Sigismondi loved to draw and paint. "As far as I can remember," she told Nick Krewen for the *Toronto (Ontario) Star* (February 5, 1997), "I would just look at paint brushes and go, 'Ohhh!' Art was just part of me." (Antonella has also loved art since childhood; she is now a sculptor, working mainly with metal and glass. Under the name Julia Mondi, she appeared in a small role in *Runaways*.) After high school Sigismondi enrolled at Sheridan College, in a Toronto suburb, to study painting. A year later she transferred to the Ontario College of Art and Design, in Toronto. There she switched her focus to photography because she found it to be far more intimate and immediate than painting. (Even then—long before digital photography became widespread—taking photos, having the film developed, and getting prints made was much faster than completing most paintings.) "By the end of [the program]," Sigismondi told Krewen, "I ended up with a whole portfolio of photographs instead of paintings. It was wild! I became obsessed with it." She received her bachelor's degree in 1988.

Sigismondi then began to establish herself as a professional photographer, beginning as a fashion photographer. Two of her major influences, she told the *Border Crossings* interviewer, were Sarah Moon and Deborah Turbeville: "Those are the two women who actually inspired me to realize you could do something that wasn't just about the clothes, that could be about creating a mood." Sigismondo's fashion-lingerie photo spread in a 1990 edition of the Toronto *Globe and Mail Magazine* brought her national recognition. Soon after it appeared she began to get photography opportunities from other corporate clients, among them art, lifestyle, and fashion magazines including *Flare, Fashion*, and *Toronto Life*. Her passion for painting strongly influenced her work. Painting, she told Leo Rice-Barker for *Playback* (July 29, 1996), led her to take "more of an organic approach than a technical approach." She elaborated: "It's more theatrical—a pushing of colors and makeup—than journalistic. This whole thing comes from my parents' background in opera. We've always been in the theater." Sigismondi, a music fan from as far back as she can remember, found the theatrical side of rock very appealing, so the transition to music videos seemed to be a perfect melding of her love for music and her aesthetic preferences. "I've never taken pictures on a tripod," she told Rice-Barker. "It has always been more about movement, so the transition [to film] was easy for me." In the early 1990s Don Allan, the owner of the Canadian company Revolver Films, hired Sigismondi to direct music videos, notably for the Canadian rock bands the Tea Party, Harem Scarem, 13 Engines, Pure, and Victor. In making music videos, she told Adriana de Barros for scene360.com (February 11, 2003), "it is most important that the song move me." "I call it being 'plugged in,'" she told Mark Dillon for *American Cinematographer* (August 1998). "When you're plugged in, images appear."

Sigismondi was little known in the U.S. when, in the mid-1990s, she pitched her ideas for a video of "Beautiful People" to Marilyn Manson. "Beautiful People"—a hard-rock song produced by Trent Reznor of Nine Inch Nails—is about the homogenization of the concept of beauty in the U.S. and the people who shape that concept, whom Manson equated with totalitarian leaders. For the video, which was shot by the cinematographer Christopher Soos, Sigismondi used a lot of grotesque and surreal images, in the manner of the photographers Hans Bellmer and Joel-Peter Witkin and the film directors Tim Burton and David Lynch. Because the video had to be far shorter than a feature film, Sigismondi sped everything up: the camera was often moving or shaking, shots were usually held for no more than a second or two, and scenes rapidly changed, with Manson performing with his band, then walking around on stilts and proselytizing to crowds, then in various forms of physical restraint, including a metal dental device that forced his mouth to remain open. Manson "gave me an opportunity to create with no boundaries imposed, allowing me the chance to torture him at length quite freely," Sigismondi told Adriana de Barros. Speaking to Terry Kattleman for *Advertising Age* (February 1, 1997), she explained the metaphorical significance of some of the images in the video. The restraints are symbolic, she said, of how "leaders"

who espouse a very limited concept of beauty "try to handicap their followers both physically and mentally. That's why I chose physical restraint with medical devices, and not bondage or the typical sort of video thing." She included images of Manson on stilts, looking reminiscent of Benito Mussolini (the fascist dictator of Italy from 1922 to 1943), because "that's what these people end up becoming: larger than life. The followers are all brainwashed, zombielike. It's not that there was a storyline, but you can get the gist of the idea from the lyrics." The work was nominated for an MTV Music Award for best music video. Sigismondi's next video for Manson, "Tourniquet," also shot in 1996, included images of worms, rotting teeth, and charcoal-black eyeballs. "I find those things very beautiful," she told Nick Krewen. "I'm so close to them, I can't even imagine what a reaction from a stranger who has seen it for the first time might be."

Also in 1996, again working with Soos, Sigismondi directed her first music video for David Bowie, for the song "Little Wonder." That video contains fast-moving images of an urban environment, shots made with a shaking camera, out-of-focus as well as in-focus shots, and such archetypal Sigismondi images as an eyeball in a teaspoon and an alien-like woman sitting in a subway car and removing the head of her alien-like baby. "I'm interested by how the idea of beauty would change if you had anything at your disposal, and it is possible," she told Adriana de Barros. "I'm also interseted in deconstructing the body. And after you've taken it apart, the next step is to create a new one." In 1997 Sigismondi directed Bowie's "Dead Man Walking," a dance track with unsteady camera shots and quickly changing scenes that showed Lynchian influences, particularly the use of bold shades of red, green, orange, and blue. Sigismondi has said that many of her ideas come from her dreams and the semi-hallucinatory thoughts that pass through her mind before she falls asleep. Krewen wrote that she "has no problem describing her work as dark and intense, eerie and haunting. . . . But Sigismondi stops short of calling them nightmarish." "To me, it all makes sense," she told him. "It's all actually very passionate and very emotional, so I don't think of them as nightmares. If I did, I don't think I could do them."

By the late 1990s Sigismondi was receiving worldwide recognition and offers to direct feature films. She was also directing videos for well-known musicians, including the trip-hop artist Tricky ("Makes Me Wanna Die"), the electronica group the Crystal Method ("Trip Like I Do"), the singer/songwriter Sheryl Crow ("Anything but Down"), and the rock legends Jimmy Page and Robert Plant ("Most High"). Toward the end of that decade, *Time* (September 27, 1999) declared that Sigismondi's "brilliant iconography and swirling imagination have made her one of North America's most influential video makers, and she promises to be one of the most significant imagemakers of pop culture."

Sigismondi started off the 2000s by directing a video for the Icelandic composer/musician Björk's song "I've Seen It All," which also featured the vocals of Radiohead's lead singer, Thom Yorke. Much of the video consists of images of Björk singing and others dancing slowly on a railroad flatcar as it passes through a pastoral landscape of lush grass, deep-green foliage, and a light-blue sky. With its steady pace, long-held shots, and complete lack of surreal or grotesque imagery, the video was quite different from most of Sigismondi's earlier ones. The following year she directed a video for Leonard Cohen's song "In My Secret Life," in which Cohen, dressed in black, is a shadowy figure who secretly observes members of a family with huge, smooth, featureless, ovoid heads. Sigismondi went on to direct videos by the Jon Spencer Blues Explosion, Interpol, Living Things, Incubus, the Cure, Fiona Apple, and Muse. Her video for Sigur Rós's "Untitled" (2003) earned both an MTV European Award, as best international video, and a New York Underground Film Festival Award; her video for Christina Aguilera's "Fighter" (2003) brought her, in Canada, a 2004 Juno Award and a Special Merit Award at the Advertising and Design Awards ceremony in Toronto.

Sigismondi's video for Muse's "Supermassive Black Hole," from the band's album *Black Holes and Revelations* (2006), displays her fondness for surreal, Lynch-inspired images, colors, and textures: intense reds and blues, owls, closeups of owls' eyes, tattooed faces, mask-like faces, and shots of the band performing—first in a dream-like environment, then in a room, with the band members wearing fashionable retro suits. Sigismondi had Jack and Meg White, of the White Stripes, wear late-19th-century outfits for the video of "Blue Orchid," a song from their album *Get Behind Me Satan* (2005). That video also offered manically moving camera shots, occasional sideways shots, many slithering white snakes, a thin white horse, white high heels, a white deer-horn chandelier, a white bathtub (a Sigismondi motif), stacks of white plates used as drums, and Jack White dancing with a white cane. The following year Sigismondi directed the music video for the song "Broken Boy Soldier," by the Raconteurs—another band that Jack White had joined. The video, à la Tim Burton, shows doll parts assembling themselves into a figure dressed in full military garb; the doll proceeds to move across piano keys, a guitar neck, and natural landscapes. In 2010 Sigismondi directed a video for "Die by the Drop," by the Dead Weather, which includes members of the Raconteurs, the Kills, and Queens of the Stone Age. With its themes of witchery and black magic, the video focuses on Jack White and Alison Mosshart (the lead singer of the Kills) facing the camera as they performed, their images quickly—and hauntingly—overlapping.

By her own account, Sigismondi had wanted to make a feature film at least as far back as 1997. The first project to capture her interest came her way more than a decade later, when Art and John Linson recruited her to write and direct a film about the 1970s all-female rock band the Runaways. The members of the Runaways, all teenagers, were Cherie Currie, lead vocalist and keyboardist; Joan Jett, vocalist and rhythm guitarist; Lita Ford, lead guitarist; Sandy West, drummer; and a frequently rotating lineup of bass players. Sigismondi based the script on Currie's memoir *Neon Angel: The Cherie Currie Story* (1989), written with Neal Shusterman, and on conversations she had with Currie and Jett, both of whom were present on the set during filming. (Jett was also a co-producer.) *The Runaways* (2010) focuses on the life stories of Currie (played by Dakota Fanning) and Jett (Kristin Stewart) and their relationship from the time the band formed, in 1975, the year Currie turned 16 and Jett 15. The singers got their break when the promoter Kim Fowley (played by Michael Shannon)—who has invariably been described in such unflattering terms as "highly manipulative," "obnoxious," and "ruthless"—decided to manage them. "Here he's an evil Svengali, who teaches rock 'n' roll as an assault on the audience; the girls must batter their fans into submission or admit they're losers," Roger Ebert wrote for the *Chicago Sun-Times* (March 17, 2010, on-line). "He's like a Marine drill sergeant: 'Give me the girl. I'll give you back the man.'" Fowley also demanded that the singers use their sexuality to promote their careers.

Sigismondi, film critics generally agreed, proved adept at evoking in *The Runaways* a genuine, gritty 1970s rock aesthetic: the film looked grainy, the music performances looked and sounded realistic, the dialogue was often coarse, actors' hair was messy and their skin spotty, and sex, drugs, and alcohol—the inevitable trappings of the rock-and-roll lifestyle—were on display. In his review for the *New York Times*, A. O. Scott wrote that Sigismondi "has a good ear and a sharp eye for period detail." He added, "Acknowledging the brazen, rebellious energy of rock 'n' roll at the dawn of punk, Ms. Sigismondi also tallies the costs that an ardent, ambitious love of the music can exact . . . [and] is astute in recognizing that the rise of the Runaways was fueled by a volatile blend of empowerment and exploitation." The film critic Karina Longworth wrote for the *Village Voice* (March 16, 2010) that *The Runaways* is "a movie worth taking seriously." "Sigismondi gets the most mood out of chiaroscuro lighting, invisibly elliptic editing, and well-chosen source cues, but actually saying something is harder. All that artsy, abstracted imagery is painted over the skeleton of a predictable rock movie." Longworth also wrote that *The Runaways* is "at its best when working through the contradictions of teen sex-for-sale, when it's both turn-on and creep-out. And Sigismondi's nearly avant-garde visual choices elevate what would be junk food into something more." Some critics were harsher. A reviewer for the *Atlantic* (April 19, 2010, on-line) called the film "a stylish, but sanitized biopic." Sigismondi "does focus some attention on sexism and exploitation," the reviewer wrote, but she missed an opportunity to examine more deeply the abuse, neglect, and exploitation of the teenage girl rockers. (For example, Fowley forced some of the bandmates to watch him have sex with a young woman as part of their "education.") The film also "steers clear of some of the uglier aspects of Currie's experience"—such as the drug problem Currie had for years before she joined the Runaways and the abortion she underwent after getting pregnant by a much older Runaways crew member. As a rock movie, the *Atlantic* reviewer concluded, *The Runaways* "hits all the right notes. But a story about abused, neglected and exploited teenage girls deserves to be more than just a genre film."

Sigismondi is currently set to direct Lady Gaga in a film about Madonna, tentatively titled "Madonna: From a Virgin to a Phenomena [sic]," set for a 2012 release. In addition to the artists mentioned above, Sigismondi has directed music videos for Pure, Fluffy, Barry Adamson, Amon Tobin, and Shivaree. She has directed TV commercials for Coca-Cola, Converse, the National Basketball Association, Target, Adidas, and other corporations and organizations.

Sigismondi is married to Lillian Berlin (born Jason Rothman), the lead singer and guitarist for the band Living Things. The couple's daughter, Tosca,

was born in 2004. Sigismondi divides her time among New York, Los Angeles, and Toronto.
—D.K.

Suggested Reading: *American Cinematographer* p60+ Aug. 1998; *Border Crossings* p12+ Aug. 2001; *Creative Review* p36+ June 1999; floriasigismondi.com; imdb.com; *Los Angeles Times* P p3 Mar. 14, 2010; *New York Times* AR p1+ Mar. 14, 2010, C p12 Mar. 19, 2010; *Playback* p25 July 29, 1996; scene360.com Feb. 11, 2003; (Toronto, Ontario) *Globe and Mail* R p1 Feb. 26, 2003

Selected Films: *The Runaways*, 2010

Selected Music Videos: "The Beatiful People," 1996; "Tourniquet," 1996; "Little Wonder," 1996; "Dead Man Walking," 1997; "Makes Me Wanna Die," 1997; "Trip Like I Do," 1997; "Most High," 1998; "Anything but Down," 1999; "I've Seen It All," 2000; "In My Secret Life," 2001; "Untitled," 2003; "Obstacle 1," 2003; "Fighter," 2003; "Blue Orchid," 2005; "Supermassive Black Hole," 2006; "Broken Boy Soldier," 2006; "Die by the Drop," 2010

Selected Books: *Redemption*, 1999; *Immune*, 2005

Sigurdardottir, Johanna

(SIG-oor-thar-DOHT-teer, yoh-HAN-ah)

Oct. 4, 1942– Prime minister of Iceland

Address: Althingi, Austurstraeti 1, 150 Reykjavik, Iceland

"My time will come!" the Icelandic politician Johanna Sigurdardottir exclaimed in 1994—on the day when, after 16 years as a Social Democratic legislator in the Althingi, her nation's parliament, she lost her bid to lead her party. Her prediction came true some 15 years later: on February 1, 2009 Sigurdardottir was appointed interim prime minister of Iceland, and then, on April 25, 2009, she assumed that post as a result of the national elections. She is Iceland's first female prime minister and, as far as is known, the first openly gay elected head of government in the modern world. She is also the chairperson of the Social Democratic Alliance, created in 1995. Now 67 years old, Sigurdardottir entered politics after nine years as a stewardess, another seven as a corporate office worker, and years of activity as a member of Iceland's flight-attendants' and commercial-workers' unions. Her extensive union work helped her win a seat in the Althingi in 1978, as a representative from a district

in Reykjavik, Iceland's capital, and she has won re-election ever since; currently, she is the longest-serving legislator in her country's history. As a unionist, a lawmaker, and, twice, Iceland's minister of social affairs, Sigurdardottir built a reputation as a tireless fighter for gender equality, champion of the underprivileged, and advocate of progressive social-welfare policies. "There has never been anything remotely scandalous about Sigurdóttir," Kolfinna Baldvinsdóttir wrote for *European Voice* (June 11, 2009, on-line); "social affairs is her area of expertise and to Iceland's poor, sick and elderly, she is beyond criticism."

Sigurdardottir's rise to the highest position in the government came four months after Iceland, then one of the world's most prosperous nations, plunged into its most serious economic recession since World War II. The downturn was a direct result of the burst of the financial bubble in the U.S. in the fall of 2008, which led to the burst of a similar bubble in Iceland. Within weeks the country experienced the failure of many businesses, a huge rise in unemployment, massive stock-market losses, severe weakening of the krona (Iceland's currency), and the near-failure of the nation's three largest banks. For a while many within Iceland and outside observers, too, feared that the country as a whole might be driven into bankruptcy. As many as 10 percent of the citizenry engaged in peaceful isn't tainted by the economic crisis." The Sigurdardottir government has acted aggressively to combat the impact of the recession, restore confidence in the nation's economy, and establish "a clear path towards renewed economic growth," in the words of an Icelandic Government Information Centre online post. The prime minister has also been promoting the benefits of joining the European Union, a step opposed by a significant number of Icelanders.

Johanna Sigurdardottir was born on October 4, 1942 in Reykjavik, Iceland's capital, to Sigurdur Egill Ingimundarson (1913–78) and Karítas Gudmundsdóttir (1917–97). In Icelandic, her name is spelled Jóhanna Sigurðardóttir. (With a few officially approved exceptions, the last names of both male and female Icelanders are patronymics, derived from their fathers' given names, with the suffix "dottir" indicating a daughter. Icelanders typically refer to one another by their given names, never by their patronymics alone; lists of names— for example, those of members of the Althingi as posted on the parliament's Web site and those in telephone directories—are alphabetized by first names rather than surnames. Among Icelanders the head of state is referred to as Johanna, not as Prime Minister Sigurdardottir; her official e-mail address is johanna@althingi.is.) One of Sigurdardottir's grandmothers was among the earliest of Icelandic female labor leaders, in the 1920s and '30s; her father served in the Althingi from 1959 to 1971.

An island nation about the size of Virginia, Iceland lies in the North Atlantic Ocean just south of the Arctic Circle. About three-quarters of its surface is covered by glaciers, ice fields, a mountainous lava desert, and other land inhospitable to human settlement and agriculture. Nearly all Icelanders, who currently number between 310,000 and 320,000 (a figure approximately equal to the population of Bakersfield, California), live along the coast, almost two-thirds in the Reykjavik metropolitan area. Some 80 percent of Icelanders are Lutherans, and of those, 85 percent belong to the Evangelical Lutheran Church, the national state church. Fewer than 3 percent of Icelanders work on farms (most food is imported). About 7 percent of workers earn their livings from fishing or fish processing; fish and fish products account for about 70 percent of the nation's exports. According to the U.S. State Department (on-line), "Because of its small size and relative homogeneity, Iceland holds all the characteristics of a very close-knit society." It is the only member of NATO that does not maintain a standing army, air force, or navy.

By all accounts, Sigurdardottir has never talked to any media representative about her childhood or any other aspect of her private life. She attended the Commercial College of Iceland, a private, nonprofit school in Reykjavik that offers high-school-level courses for two years and then, for another two years, courses considered college level. Sigurdardottir took secretarial classes and earned a di-

Olivier Morin/AFP/Getty Images
Johanna Sigurdardottir

but extremely noisy public demonstrations to protest the actions of bank and government officials. The single occasion on which the police used tear gas to control the crowds marked the first time that law-enforcement officers had deemed it necessary to resort to such force since 1949, when thousands of Icelanders had taken to the streets to protest the government's decision to join NATO (the North Atlantic Treaty Organization). The 14 weeks of demonstrations that began in October 2008 ended with the appointment of Sigurdardottir as interim prime minister. "The job she is about to take on is both the most difficult and most critical that any Icelander of our generation has taken on," Runólfur Ágústsson, a former rector of Bifröst University, told Jonas Moody for *Time* (January 30, 2009). "The future of this society depends on how she handles this position."

Hailed for her plainspokenness and honesty, Sigurdardottir has repeatedly topped all other politicians in Icelandic popularity polls in recent years, and her approval ratings remained high even after the start of the recession in 2008. "According to political analysts, she has that priceless gift— people trust her and believe what she says," Paola Totaro wrote for the Melbourne, Australia, *Age* (April 25, 2009). "It's a question of trust, people believe that she actually cares about people," Olafur Hardarson, a University of Iceland political-science professor, told David Stringer for the Associated Press Online (January 28, 2009). Eyvindur Karlsson, a 27-year-old translator from Reykjavik, told Stringer, "If there's anyone who can restore trust in the political system it's her. People respect her because she's never been afraid of standing up to her own party. They see her as someone who ploma in 1960; she completed her academic studies in 1962. That year she became a stewardess with Loftleidir Icelandic Airlines (which later merged with another airline to become Icelandair). During her nine years as a stewardess, she became active in the Icelandic Cabin Crew Association, serving on the union's board from 1966 to 1969 and as the board's chair in both 1966 and 1969. According to Baldvinsdóttir, "During a flight-crew strike she showed her skills as an uncompromising trade union leader, forcing the management to sign up to a generous deal." Sigurdardottir married in 1970 and gave birth to her first child in 1972. Earlier, in 1971, she had been hired as an office worker with Kassagerd Reykjavikur, Iceland's largest manufacturer of corrugated-cardboard boxes and other packaging; she remained with the firm until 1978. She was a board member of the Commercial Workers' Union from 1976 to 1983. From 1974 to 1976 she sat on the board of Svölurnar, the Association of Former Stewardesses, chairing that board in 1975.

In 1978 Sigurdardottir was elected to the Althingi as a Social Democratic representative of a Reykjavik district. (Founded in the year 930, the Althingi is the oldest parliamentary entity in the world. It is unicameral and, currently, has 63 members.) Sigurdardottir quickly impressed her colleagues, winning a post as one of several deputy speakers in 1979. She served as a deputy speaker again from 1983 to 1984 and from 2003 to 2007. She was a member of the Althingi Presidium (which handles issues affecting the parliament) in 1979, 1983–84, and 2003–07. Between 1994 and 2007 Sigurdardottir served on a half-dozen Althingi committees, including those that dealt with foreign affairs, industry, the economy and trade, social affairs, and general affairs. Three times between 1995 and 2007, for a total of about nine years, she was also a member of the Althingi Special Committee on Constitutional Affairs. She was a member of the national Board of Social Security from 1978 to 1987 and the board's chair from 1979 to 1980. Sigurdardottir served as Iceland's minister of social affairs from 1987 to 1994 and from 2007 until her rise to prime minister. In that position she continued her unwavering efforts to increase assistance for the elderly, people suffering from mental and physical disabilities, and victims of domestic violence; to promote gender equality; to provide better housing for the poor and educational opportunities for adults; and to ensure the fairness of social-security policies. She also became known for eschewing certain government privileges; for example, she refused to have a chauffeured government limousine bring her to her office, driving herself in her old car instead. In time many people began to refer to her by the nickname "Saint Johanna."

Earlier, in 1984, Sigurdardottir had been elected vice chairman of the Social Democratic Party, a post she held until 1993. In 1994 she ran for her party's top leadership post. She lost decisively,

and during her concession speech, she punched her fist in the air and exclaimed, "*Minn tími mun koma!*"—"My time will come!"—a declaration that became a catchphrase in Iceland. As she had threatened to do if she were not chosen to head her party, she resigned as minister of social affairs. She then formed a new political organization, Thjodvakinn, the National Movement Party. In the 1995 general elections, the National Movement Party captured four seats in the Althingi. Sigurdardottir rejoined the Social Democrats five years later, when the National Movement merged with the Social Democratic Party and two other center-left parties to form the Social Democratic Alliance, which was recognized as the opposition party to the dominant, center-right Independence Party.

In 2007 the Social Democratic Alliance joined with the Independence Party to form a coalition government, and Sigurdardottir was again appointed Iceland's minister of social affairs. Her approval rating among her compatriots stood at 73 percent when, in the fall of 2008, a disastrous economic crisis occurred in Iceland. In the two decades preceding the recession, Iceland's economy had turned from one of the poorest in the developed world into one of the wealthiest (in terms of per-capita income). That transformation, within a single generation and with few setbacks, was due to factors including the privatization of some industries, economic reforms, deregulation of the banking industry, and manipulation of the krona. With an unprecedented explosion of consumerism, many individuals and families took out second mortgages and accumulated huge credit-card debts, and companies borrowed in high-yielding foreign currencies in amounts far greater than ever before. Meanwhile, taking advantage of lower interest rates elsewhere, Iceland's three largest banks—Landsbanki, Kaupthing, and Glimir—expanded their businesses exponentially (and often recklessly) not only at home but in Great Britain, Scandinavia, and other places. By September 2008 the three banks had acquired assets whose total value was at least 10 times Iceland's gross domestic product.

That month the venerable New York–based global financial-services company Lehman Brothers filed for bankruptcy, for reasons that sparked panic among investors the world over. The Icelandic banks were deluged by demands for funds that had suddenly become unavailable to them and found themselves on the brink of defaulting on their loans. By October the government had taken control of Landsbanki and Kaupthing, and Glimir had been placed in receivership, in the hands of the national Financial Supervisory Authority. The situation worsened when the British government, on the grounds of certain provisions of its Prevention of Terrorism Acts, froze the assets of Landsbanki's on-line operations (called IceSave) in Great Britain, which included deposits made by 300,000 British savers and many millions of British pounds invested by British borough councils and other local government groups. (IceSave's Dutch customers were also affected.) That action followed the public declaration by David Oddson, a former Icelandic prime minister and a governor of the Central Bank of Iceland, that Iceland "[did] not intend to pay the debts of the banks that have been a little heedless," as quoted in the *Wall Street Journal* (October 17, 2008, on-line). Moreover, the European Union refused a request for assistance made by the government of Iceland's prime minister, Geir Haarde. In a nationally televised address on October 6, 2008, Haarde, a member of the Independence Party, declared, "There is a very real danger . . . that the Icelandic economy, in the worst case, could be sucked with the banks into the whirlpool and the result could be national bankruptcy." During the next weeks Haarde's government obtained loans totaling about $10 billion from the International Monetary Fund and a few countries, among them Poland, Norway, and the Faroe Islands.

Meanwhile, with Iceland's financial industry in turmoil, the value of the krona had fallen by 30 percent against the euro, foreign-currency transactions had been halted, and the country's stock market had suffered immense losses. Inflation reached 14 percent, with further rises probable, and the cost of loans increased by 50 percent. Construction firms and many other businesses were forced to close their doors, thus pushing the unemployment rate from about 3 percent to nearly 9 percent. (At its peak, in February 2009, it reached 9.4 percent.) Suddenly faced with imminent personal bankruptcies, inability to make substantially higher payments on cars or homes, or other severe economic troubles, thousands of fearful and distraught Icelanders took to the streets to express their anger toward the banks and the government, yelling through loudspeakers and banging on pots and pans with kitchen utensils in what was dubbed the "saucepan revolution."

On January 26, 2009 Prime Minister Haarde resigned—partly, he said, because he was scheduled to begin treatment for esophageal cancer in the Netherlands—and the government disbanded. After discussions with representatives of the Social Democratic Alliance and several other political parties, Olafur Ragnar Grimsson, Iceland's president, asked Ingibjorg Gisladottir, the leader of the Social Democratic Alliance and the country's foreign minister, to form an interim government, to rule until national elections in April. Gisladottir, who was undergoing treatment for a benign brain tumor, declined, suggesting that Sigurdardottir be named to the post. "What is needed straight away is to try to restore trust between the political establishment and the general public," the Social Democrat Thorunn Sveinbjarnardottir, Iceland's environment minister and a Sigurdardottir supporter, told David Stringer for the Associated Press (January 26, 2009). "What we need is for the general public to believe that the politicians are working in their interests." With the exception of some conservative politicians, who warned that she would

spend too much, particularly on social-service initiatives, and might raise taxes, the appointment of Sigurdardottir was greeted with enthusiasm. Sigurdardottir "is a good choice . . . ," an unnamed government worker told Peter Popham for the London *Independent* (January 29, 2009, on-line). "Getting Johanna to become Prime Minister was a way of saying trust is an issue. Politicians want a fresh mandate from the electorate and, before they get it, they need to rebuild trust.'"

From 1980 to 1996 a woman, Vigdís Finnbogadóttir, served as Iceland's president, a post that in Iceland is largely ceremonial. When Sigurdardottir was sworn in as interim prime minister, on February 1, 2009, she became the first female Icelander to hold that position. She retained her position after the national elections held on April 25, 2009, in which the Social Democratic Alliance won 20 seats in the Althingi. Her party then formed a coalition government with the Left-Green Movement, which won 14 seats. "The nation is settling the score with . . . the Independence Party, who have been in power for much too long," Sigurdardottir said to reporters, as quoted by Herdis Sigurgrimsdottir and Gudjon Helgason on the Associated Press Financial Wire (April 26, 2009). "The people are calling for a change of ethics. That is why they have voted for us." In addition to the total of 34 Social Democratic Alliance and Left-Green representatives, the current Althingi is composed of 16 Independence Party members, nine from the centrist Progressive Party, three from the Movement (an offshoot of the now-defunct Citizens' Movement, whose main concern is fisheries management), and one independent member. The 11 members of Sigurdardottir's cabinet include more women (five) than in any previous Icelandic cabinet.

In its first few months, the new administration forced out the chief executive officers of Landsbanki, Kaupthing, and Glimir and reorganized the management of the Central Bank, ruling that its governors must have postgraduate degrees in economics and a great deal of relevant experience. Sigurdardottir also adopted what she termed an "ambitious austerity program," decreasing spending and increasing taxes with the aim of balancing Iceland's budget by 2013. Her government has also undertaken a major reform of the financial-market regulatory system and is working to restructure debts for families and companies. Among other measures to aid cash-strapped Icelanders, the Althingi has approved legislation whereby people may withdraw money from certain pension savings accounts. The government has also engaged in complex negotiations regarding the losses suffered by IceSave customers in Great Britain and the Netherlands, a thorny problem that has not yet been resolved. In a referendum (labeled "meaningless" by Sigurdardottir) held on March 7, 2010, more than 90 percent of Icelandic voters rejected a government-proposed plan whereby the nation would offer those depositors a total of $5.3 billion. The question of membership in the European Union is also unresolved. Although many Icelanders fear that membership would jeopardize Iceland's supremacy over its fishing grounds, polls indicate that a majority of adults are open to further discussion of the matter. According to the *CIA World Factbook*, from 2008 to 2009 Iceland's GDP (in terms of purchasing power) fell 6.6 percent, from $13.01 billion to an estimated $12.15 billion (or from about $42,700 to about $39,600 per person), and in the same period the public debt rose from an estimated 56.5 percent to an estimated 95.1 percent of GDP. In December 2009 8.2 percent of workers were unemployed.

Clouds of ash from the eruption of Iceland's volcano Eyjafjallajökull on March 20, 2010 severely disrupted air travel to and from Europe but had minimal consequences on the ground in Iceland. In September 2010 the Althingi voted to ask a special court, the Lansdomur, to consider whether Geir Haarde should be tried for his failure to prevent the financial crisis. (The court was set up years earlier to consider cases of government ministers charged with crimes, but to date it has never held a trial.) Some Icelanders complained that Haarde was not the only one to blame and demanded that other former ministers also stand trial for their roles in the crisis. The next month, speaking before the Althingi, Sigurdardottir promised to make a greater effort to help the country recover from the crisis. In her speech she acknowledged criticisms of her government and called for opposing voices to unite to come up with solutions. While she spoke, an estimated 7,000 protestors gathered outside the Althingi building, in Reykjavik, to demand that the government do more to help those in financial trouble. The protestors beat oil drums and set a bonfire but otherwise behaved peacefully.

Johanna Sigurdardottir has been described as intense, serious, and extremely hard-working; she has been called a loner because, on the job, she sometimes prefers to work in solitude. She is said to be fluent in English, but in talks with English-speaking diplomats, she speaks Icelandic and relies on an interpreter. Her marriage to Torvaldur Johannesson, a banker, ended in divorce in 1986. From that union she has two sons, Sigurdur Egill and Davíd Steinar, and six grandchildren, with whom she spends much of her free time. In 2002, in a civil ceremony, Sigurdardottir married Jonina Leosdottir, a playwright, novelist, and journalist. Leosdottir is the divorced mother of one adult son, Gunnar Hrafn Jonsson. Sigurdardottir's homosexuality has not been an issue in Iceland, which legalized civil partnerships in 1996 and granted same-sex couples the right to adopt children and other parental rights in 2006. "Johanna is a very private person," the unnamed government worker told Peter Popham. "A lot of people didn't even know she was gay. When they learn about it people tend to shrug. . . . That's not to say they are not interested; they are interested in who she's living with— but no more so than if she was a man living with

a woman." Frosti Jónsson, a spokesperson for Samtökin '78, Iceland's National Queer Association, told Moody, "There are so many openly gay prominent figures in both the public and private sector here that it doesn't affect who we select for our highest offices. Our minds are focused on what counts, which is the current situation in the country." Jónsson told John F. Burns for the *New York Times* (February 2, 2009), "Iceland is a small society, and the public knows what Sigurdardottir stands for as a politician, and that's the only thing that is important."

—W.D.

Suggested Reading: Althingi Web site; Associated Press Online Jan. 26, 2009, Jan. 28, 2009; eng.forsaetisraduneyti.is; *European Voice* (on-line) June 11, 2009; Iceland.org; (London) *Guardian* (on-line) Jan. 30, 2009; (Melbourne, Australia) *Age* p14 Apr. 25, 2009; *New York Times* A p6 Apr. 27, 2009; *Scandinavian Press* p13 Spring 2009; *Time* (on-line) Jan. 30, 2009

Getty Images

Simpson, John

Aug. 9, 1944– Journalist; writer

Address: BBC, Broadcasting House, Portland Pl., London W1A 1AA, England

"I am a traveler by profession, and commute to work; but my job tends to be carried out in outlandish and difficult places—Afghanistan, the Middle East, the darker parts of Africa, and Latin America. As a result I have had a rather larger acquaintance with deranged dictators, ethnic cleansers, bandits, and terrorists than seems altogether reasonable." That thumbnail personal sketch appears in *Unreliable Sources* (2010), the latest book by the British journalist John Simpson. Simpson has worked for the British Broadcasting Corp. (BBC) since 1966, and his face has become one of the most familiar in televised world news. He has reported from more than 130 countries and several dozen war zones and has interviewed hundreds of regional, national, and international heads of state and others of prominence. He was at the scene during many of the historic events of the last third of the 20th century and the first decade of the 21st, including the Soviet and U.S. invasions of Afghanistan (1979 and 2001, respectively) and the rise of the Taliban in the years in between; the fall of the Berlin Wall, in Germany (1989); the massacre of student protestors at Tiananmen Square, in Beijing, China (1989); the South African leader Nelson Mandela's release from prison and the beginning of the end of apartheid in South Africa (1990); and the wars involving the republics of the former Yugoslavia (1990s). A quarter-century into his career, Flammetta Rocco wrote for the London *Independent* (September 6, 1992) that although Simpson was "undramatic, unactorish, [and] underplayed," he had become a "personality." "The reason may be that the audience trusts and respects him," she continued; he "appears wise," "looks reflective, a thinker in a complicated world, and yet comfortable and ordinary." A decade later Craig Williams wrote for *Scotland on Sunday* (September 29, 2002), "Even if he were to pack it in tomorrow, John Simpson would be remembered as one of the greatest foreign correspondents Britain has ever produced. His reporting has brought many of recent history's most extraordinary events into our living rooms." "No international crisis—a war, an uprising, a famine—now seems real until we have heard the mellifluous tones of the BBC's grandly titled world affairs editor," Peter Wilby wrote, in a somewhat tongue-in-cheek tone, for the London *Guardian* (October 20, 2007), when Simpson's career with the BBC had passed the four-decade mark. "So measured and authoritative is John Simpson's style that it seems presumptuous to form any opinions before he delivers his verdict to microphone."

Simpson started as a BBC Radio subeditor before he was promoted to correspondent. He went on to hold, successively, the TV-news posts of diplomatic correspondent, political editor, presenter of the *Nine O'Clock News*, diplomatic editor, foreign-affairs editor, and, since 1988, world-affairs editor; in the last position he works more or less as a freelancer, with a new contract every year. John Dugdale wrote for the *Guardian* (June 21, 1999) that Simpson often takes advantage of his "star reporter's privilege" by "big-footing"—arriving at the center of a crisis zone and sidelining BBC journalists already there. According to Allan Laing, a Glasgow, Scotland, *Herald* (November 17, 2001) reporter, Simpson "has helped to change the rules of engagement" in journalism: "In effect, he pushes the boundaries of the BBC's reputation for balance and objectivity by venturing strong and trenchant opinions in his news reports." That tendency has led at times to severe criticism of Simpson (and the BBC) by members of Parliament and others for what they called the anti-British bias of his reportage and its undermining of support for official British policies. On the other hand, through the years Simpson has also been accused, particularly by rival journalists, of toeing the government line and parroting establishment views as well as dangerously oversimplifying issues and drawing unnecessary attention to himself. In a profile of Simpson for the *Independent* (November 17, 2001, on-line), for example, his BBC colleague Martin Bell wrote that as far back as the mid-1970s, Simpson had "a rare ability . . . to locate himself at the centre of the story. He not only reported the story. He was the story." Nevertheless, Simpson has twice (in 1991 and 2000) been named Journalist of the Year by the Royal Television Society.

Simpson has written 15 books, many of them heavily autobiographical, about his observations and impressions as a journalist. He has been an op-ed columnist for the *Spectator* (1991–96) and the London *Telegraph* (since 1996). For some years he has hosted his own television show, *Simpson's World*, which currently airs in some 200 countries and is among the BBC's most popular programs.

John Cody Fidler-Simpson was born on August 9, 1944 in Cleveleys, Lancashire, England, and grew up first in the Norwood section of London and then in Dunwich, Suffolk. His maternal grandfather, Samuel Franklin Cody, a pioneer aviator, made the first powered flight in Great Britain, in 1908. Simpson's mother, the former Joyce Cody, was a widow with two children when she married his father, Roy Fidler-Simpson; a onetime cruise-ship steward, his father made a precarious living in real estate, dabbled in genealogy, and, like his wife, believed firmly in Christian Science. Simpson told Lynn Barber for the London *Observer* (February 24, 2002, on-line) that his father retained the habits of an irresponsible teenager and would alternately bully and charm; politically, he supported anarchism and, for a time, communism. By his own account, Simpson's early childhood was unhappy, mostly because of his parents' marital discord. One day when he was seven, his mother packed several suitcases and left for good. She intended to take all three children with her, but just as she was exiting the house with them, her husband demanded that John decide which parent he preferred to live with. He chose to stay with his father, he has said, because it did not seem fair to leave one parent childless. Simpson had little contact with his mother after that and often felt lonely. He told Barber that an unmarried, emotionally stable, scholarly friend of his father's, Brian Brooks, who lodged with them for years, became his mentor. "I think he was the prime intellectual influence on my early life," he told Barber. Simpson often felt embarrassed by his unusual domestic situation; sometimes he would tell others that his mother still lived at home. His father died in 1980.

Simpson's formal education began at the Crispin School, a private facility in Penge, in South London. The Crispin uniform was highly conspicuous, and during his two-mile walk to and from school through a working-class area of Norwood, Simpson would try to avoid the rough neighborhood children who teased or attacked him whenever they had the chance. At age 10 he transferred to Dulwich College Preparatory School, where he enjoyed classes in English and history. Then, from 1957 to 1963, on a scholarship, he attended the prestigious, 500-year-old St. Paul's School in London. There, he edited the student newspaper and headed the debating society. A history teacher, Philip Whitting, took a special interest in him— "He liked rebels and people who didn't quite fit the mould," Simpson wrote for Unreliable Sources, as quoted in the London Daily Mail (October 10, 2009)—and encouraged him to meet the so-called Oxbridge standard, the requirements necessary to gain admission to Oxford or Cambridge University. Math was Simpson's weakest subject, and one math teacher often taunted him, "but this turned to my advantage," he wrote for Unreliable Sources, "because I learnt how to make people laugh and . . . I'd use humour as a weapon to counter his sarcasm." After he graduated from St. Paul's, Simpson enrolled at Magdalene College, one of Cambridge University's 31 schools. He majored in English literature and co-edited, with Nicholas Snowman, the influential literary magazine Granta (a Cambridge student publication from 1889 until 1979, when it became independent). In 1965 he was a contestant on the long-running British quiz show University Challenge (based on the U.S. series College Bowl). He earned an M.A. degree from Magdalene College in 1966. The Best of Granta, 1889–1966, compiled and edited by Simpson, Snowman, and Jim Philip, was published in the same year.

Immediately after he completed his degree, Simpson joined BBC Radio as a trainee subeditor, a job that, he told Maggie Brown for the Guardian (August 17, 1998), he "loathed and detested." Others employed there "kicked me around, it was a ferocious place where people queued up to tell you that having a university degree meant nothing . . . ," he continued. "It left me with a really serious deep lack of confidence." After two years he was promoted to regional reporter and then, after another two years, a national news reporter for BBC Radio. In one of Simpson's first assignments, during what was meant to be a photo op, he asked Prime Minister Harold Wilson whether he planned to call an early election (rather than wait the officially sanctioned maximum of five years between parliamentary elections); Wilson responded by punching Simpson. "It was a short jab to the solar plexus," Simpson told Jason Gagliardi for the South China Morning Post (September 10, 2000).

"[Wilson] was small but tubby. I thought a bit more of him afterwards, when the anxiety settled. . . . I used to be a boxer at school so I kind of appreciate a decent punch." Simpson told an interviewer for the Independent (November 29, 2004) that he was powerfully influenced by Costa-Gavras's 1969 film, Z, which was based on events surrounding the military coup that toppled a democratically elected government in Greece in 1967; the victorious military junta exonerated those who had been found responsible for the assassination of a left-wing political leader four years earlier, while the people who had helped to identify the murderers were suddenly denounced as criminals. Z, Simpson said, "showed that journalism could be a way of defending political freedom."

When Simpson secured the position of BBC foreign correspondent, in late 1971 or early 1972, he was posted to Dublin, Ireland. It was during the period of the Troubles in Northern Ireland, and at around the time of his arrival, that a horrific incident occurred: on January 30, 1972 British soldiers shot and killed 13 Irish-Catholic civilians (later found to be unarmed) engaged in a march in Londonderry, Northern Ireland, to protest British rule. An official parliamentary inquiry into the Londonderry tragedy—known ever since as Bloody Sunday—led to the publication on April 18, 1972 of the so-called Widgery report, which exonerated the military in the shootings and further inflamed the rage of anti-government Northern Irelanders. In 1975 Simpson was transferred to Brussels, Belgium, to serve as the BBC's Common Market correspondent. In that position he distinguished himself as a fearless reporter with an instinct for breaking stories. On his own, soon after a civil war broke out in Angola following its gaining independence from Portugal, he "followed a group of mercenaries into Angola," the veteran BBC reporter Charles Wheeler told Oliver Burkeman for the Guardian (November 14, 2001). "He got past emigration at Brussels airport by crawling along the floor and got on to a plane without a ticket," according to Wheeler. "He disappeared for weeks, but he got the story." (Strangely, given Simpson's official post as a Common Market reporter, many sources state that the BBC assigned him to cover the civil war in Angola.) In 1977 and 1978 Simpson served as BBC Radio's Southern Africa correspondent.

In 1978 Simpson moved to television, as the diplomatic correspondent for BBC TV News. His next promotion, to political editor, in 1980, put him in an important decision-making role that covered both TV and radio. He hated that job, however—it was "ghastly," he told Maggie Brown, because it made him feel "like a battery hen, like a Strasbourg goose, someone stuffs a bloody great tube down your neck and pumps you with information." Within a year he took a demotion, to that of co-anchor of the BBC's Nine O'Clock News, with the journalist John Humphrys. Simpson was soon dismissed from that post, for reasons that remain unclear. Some suspected that it was because the prime minister, Margaret Thatcher, had been incensed at a report that Simpson aired, three days prior to his dismissal, that focused on government failures in the days leading up to the controversial Falklands War. Simpson himself has implied that there were political reasons for his dismissal but has also said that he was simply not a good newsreader. "I belong on the streets," he told Brown. "I don't belong in a studio." In 1981 Simpson published the thriller *Moscow Requiem*. His second novel made its appearance in 1983. Called *A Fine and Private Place*, it is about a Polish defector to England who, after an absence of 15 years, returns to his native land to visit his dying father and becomes enmeshed in the affairs of the non-Communist Solidarity trade union.

Earlier, in 1982, the BBC had named Simpson its diplomatic editor. With Jana Bennett, an American-born BBC producer, he wrote a book about the thousands of people who vanished in Argentina during the rule of a series of military dictators from 1976 to 1983. On orders of the dictators and high-ranking military officers, at least 11,000 left-wing opponents of the government (and possibly as many as 30,000), most of them in their 20s or 30s, were abducted and killed, many by being thrown from planes flying high above the Atlantic Ocean. For decades the mothers of some of the "disappeared" have marched weekly in a plaza in Argentina's capital, Buenos Aires, seeking information about their missing children and punishment for those responsible for their fates. Simpson and Bennett's book, entitled in Great Britain *The Disappeared: Voices from a Secret War*, was published in the U.S. in 1985 as *The Disappeared and the Mothers of the Plaza: The Story of the 11,000 Argentinians Who Vanished*. An unnamed reviewer for the *Economist* (June 29, 1985) wrote that the book "seems to have been written for television news. It is fast, racy, colourful, full of short episodes and fleeting impressions. It jumps from point to point without a clear direction. Those who persevere will, however, find it to be a moving account of the bravery of those few Argentines who were prepared to oppose what was happening." The *Library Journal* (November 15, 1985) reviewer, Virginia L. Muller, described the book as "a superbly written account of the human rights violations that occurred under Argentina's military regime. . . . The authors avoid lurid sensationalism by balancing their factual treatment of victims' cases with general insights into Argentina's political climate. Their story of the 'Dirty War,' in which political moderates as well as extremists were kidnapped, tortured, and murdered, documents the military government's systematic program of state repression and institutionalized corruption."

In 1988 Simpson's job title changed again, to foreign-affairs editor. The precipitating factor, according to Simpson, was a report released in October 1986 by Norman Tebbit, who was then the chairman of the Conservative Party and a member of the cabinet of the Conservative prime minister Margaret Thatcher—and who had long criticized the BBC as institutionally biased in favor of the Labour Party. The Tebbit report attacked as "riddled with inaccuracy, innuendo and imbalance" the BBC journalist Kate Adie's coverage of the U.S. bombing of sites in Tripoli and Benghazi, Libya, on April 14, 1986, in retaliation for a Libyan-backed terrorist bombing two days earlier of a German nightclub frequented by American servicemen. The British were involved in the U.S. action, too, in that they granted permission for American bombers to take off from British air bases. At the behest of Ronald "Ron" Neil, the editor of BBC News, Simpson analyzed the Tebbit report, concluding that it contained an "incredible lack of accuracy" and "obvious bile," as he told Brown. "That was when I started back on the road with Ron Neil," he added. "I think I rescued myself." Later in 1988, championed by the BBC's new deputy director-general, John Birt, Simpson was named world-affairs editor, a title he has retained ever since. Also in 1988 Simpson's next book appeared: *Inside Iran: Life Under Khomeini's Regime*. It was followed two years later by *Despatches from the Barricades: An Eye-Witness Account of the Revolutions That Shook the World, 1989–1990*. In *Despatches* Simpson described his observations and experiences during the student demonstrations in Tiananmen Square, in May 1989, and the Chinese military's brutal suppression of the students' fledgling prodemocracy movement; the nonviolent collapse of the Communist government in Czechoslovakia in November 1989, in the so-called Velvet Revolution; and the release on February 11, 1990 of Nelson Mandela, a leader of the African National Congress (ANC), after 27 years' imprisonment in South Africa, followed by the recognition of the ANC as a legitimate political party and the dismantling of apartheid.

Simpson published a revised and updated edition of *Despatches*, called *The Darkness Crumbles: Despatches from the Barricades*, in 1992. In a review for the *Independent* (July 12, 1992), Tony Barber wrote, "As foreign affairs editor of the BBC, John Simpson comes across on television as a man of experience, honesty and good sense. In contrast to some of his breathlessly inarticulate colleagues, he has often provided welcome insight into the problems of the former communist countries. He is, in short, the last person of whom one would expect a glib and misleading account of the 1989 revolutions and their aftermath. All the more distressing, then, that his latest work, *The Darkness Crumbles* . . . , consistently misspells names, misdates events and, in attempting to render expressions in their original German, Russian and Romanian, displays a grasp of foreign languages that is, to say the least, shaky." Simpson's account, he added, "arouses the suspicion that he simply barged into one country after another, camera crew and interpreter in tow, and barged out again a week or two later, pausing in the meantime to dip into an O-level reference work on Eastern Europe."

By that time, Simpson's reporting of the first Persian Gulf War, in 1990–91, had catapulted him to the front ranks of international journalists. Simpson had filed stories from that part of the world before, during the war between Iraq and Iran (1980–88); in *Behind Iranian Lines* (1989), Simpson had offered his firsthand impressions of that conflict. He was one of only a handful of foreign reporters in Iraq in the weeks following that nation's invasion of its neighbor Kuwait in August 1990. Despite orders from BBC higher-ups to leave, he remained in Baghdad after a coalition of 34 nations joined to evict Iraqi forces from Kuwait. The coalition began that effort in January 1991with an aerial bombardment and continued it with a ground invasion the next month. Simpson told Gagliardi that he had been the victim of more than a few "stolen scoops" earlier in his career and that he had learned not to "leave a place . . . always stay." The harsh criticism that rained down on him and the BBC by Conservative members of Parliament, who branded them the "Baghdad Broadcasting Corp." for showing the war on the ground in Iraq and its effects on ordinary Iraqis, helped not only to raise Simpson's profile but to bring him public approbation: in 1991, along with the BBC's political editor John Cole, he was named Television Journalist of the Year by the Royal Television Society, and in the same year he was named a Commander of the British Empire (CBE) in Queen Elizabeth II's Gulf War Honours List. Some media insiders viewed his acceptance of the CBE as a breach of journalistic ethics. "Giving gongs [slang for 'medals'] to journalists causes more than a passing sense of unease," an editorial in the London *Guardian* (June 29, 1991) warned. "Journalism is, of necessity, a profession of outsiders. It is the journalist's job to get up the noses of people in authority, to question and ferret out what's going on from a position of untrammelled independence. Once journalists become part of the system they are supposed to be invigilating, murk enfolds." Simpson himself later expressed regret for accepting the CBE, telling Flammetta Rocco, "I don't like the idea that the Establishment has handed me down something."

The year 1991 also saw the publication of *From the House of War: John Simpson in the Gulf*. In an assessment for the *Jerusalem Post* (June 5, 1992), Jonathan Freedland wrote, "Mostly written on the spot, with the benefit of only a few months' hindsight, this book cannot be more than a polished version of the 'first draft of history' that good journalism represents." With the journalist and TV producer Tira Shubart, Simpson wrote *Lifting the Veil: Life in Revolutionary Iran* (1995). A more personal account appears in his book *The Wars Against Saddam: Taking the Hard Road to Baghdad* (2003). In early 2010 Simpson revisited Rasheed Street, a central Baghdad artery that has witnessed major events in Iraqi history, and on the March 19, 2010 edition of *Simpson's World*, he talked about changes that had occurred there since the start of the second Gulf War.

Earlier, in late summer 1992, Simpson had traveled to Peru with the goal of producing a documentary about that nation. Several months earlier Peru's president, Alberto Fujimori, with the support of the military, had suspended the constitution, disbanded the congress, and taken control of the judiciary, thus assuming dictatorial powers. Simpson also hoped to interview Abimael Guzmán Reynoso, the founder and leader of the Sendero Luminoso, or Shining Path, a Maoist guerrilla organization that by 1990 had gained control of a large part of Peru, murdered thousands of peasants and others, and crippled the nation's economy. The elusive Guzmán had seldom been interviewed, and even people high up in his organization had reportedly never seen him. Within days of Simpson's arrival, Guzmán was captured in an upper-class section of Lima, Peru's capital—an event that presented "a rare journalistic opportunity," as Sam Dillon wrote in an assessment for the *New York Times Book Review* (September 25, 1994) of Simpson's book about Peru, published in the U.S. in 1994 with the title *In the Forests of the Night: Encounters in Peru with Terrorism, Drug-Running, and Military Oppression*. "Simpson brings to his project a correspondent's courage and pluck, sharp analytic powers and a keen, at times elegant, narrative ability," Dillon wrote, after citing examples of several "gripping passages." "Unfortunately," he continued, "his book fails to provide many new insights into the character of either Mr. Guzmán or, for that matter, Peru itself." In a review for the *Washington Post Book World* (October 16, 1994), the Peruvian journalist Gustavo Gorriti complained that Simpson's "brief glance of Peruvian history" in his book was "rife with inaccuracies" and his "rendering of the facts about the present . . . frequently incorrect." "Yet, for all its inaccuracies and the often outsized presence of the writer . . . , I found myself liking the book and turning the pages with undiminished attention, often with fascination and enjoyment. If you want a very well-written, compassionate description of a journalistic expedition through a tortured, rough, immensely diverse country in a decisive historical moment, Simpson's book is instructive reading."

Simpson was among only a handful of journalists who reported firsthand from Belgrade, in the former Yugoslavia, in 1999, during the bombing of Serbian military strongholds in the province of Kosovo. The goal of the bombing, launched under the auspices of the North Atlantic Treaty Organization (NATO), was to stop the so-called ethnic cleansing of Albanians by Serbs in Kosovo. The British government accused Simpson of becoming "a mouthpiece for Serb propaganda" by reporting on the bombings, which killed civilians as well as armed fighters, and by interviewing Serb noncombatants who claimed that the bombing had strengthened their support for the Serbs' leader, Slobodan Milosevic, whose promotion of Serbian nationalism had sparked the warfare in the Balkans a decade earlier. "I'm amused by the idea that I'm too simple-minded to understand these things and I'm bamboozled by the Serb government and its tricks," Simpson declared in response to such charges, as quoted by Janine Gibson in the *Guardian* (April 17, 1999). "Impartiality of telling what's happening in front of you is bred into me. I've been in the BBC for 34 years now, I know how to have control over what I say or write." According to Mark Lawson, writing for the *Guardian* (April 17, 1999), the British government's accusations amounted to more than an attack on the integrity of a single journalist: "The dispute is more interesting and subtle: a disagreement between politicians trying to maintain an old definition of wartime reporting and broadcasters trying to move towards a new interpretation."

In a widely publicized stunt connected with the American and British invasion of Afghanistan in October 2001, in the wake of the September 11 terrorist attacks on the U.S., Simpson smuggled himself into Afghanistan by disguising himself in a burka. On November 13, 2001 Simpson and his photographer, Joe Phua, and several other BBC reporters arrived in Kabul, the Afghan capital, ahead of any allied troops. He recalled to David Lister for the *Independent* (November 27, 2002) that during an interview that day for *BBC Radio 4 Today*, Sue MacGregor asked him, "I don't quite understand this, but Northern Alliance troops stopped at the entrance to Kabul and the Taliban have fled: who liberated Kabul?" Simpson responded by saying, "It's an exhilarating feeling to be liberating a city. Yes, the BBC has liberated Kabul. . . . We got in ahead of the Northern Alliance"—remarks that led the British media to ridicule him. Simpson, describing himself on David Frost's BBC Radio program as "very, very, very embarrassed," expressed his regret for his failed joke. "I walked down through this vast great crowd and they were so delighted to see us," he told Frost, as quoted by Lucy Ward in the *Guardian* (November 19, 2001). "I got a bit carried away really. I got excited. I can't help it. It was a fantastic moment. What I should have said of course was that we brought the news to people in Kabul that they had been liberated." He told Lister, "Until you're on the receiving end of the violent spite of journalists, you don't know how dreadful it is." Simpson and Phua won International Emmy Awards in 2002 for their coverage of the fall of Kabul.

During the second Persian Gulf War, which began with the U.S. invasion of Iraq in March 2003, Simpson accompanied a military convoy on duty in northern Iraq. One day he and the convoy were bombed by American F-15 planes in one of the worst incidents of friendly fire to occur in that conflict. Sixteen people were killed, including Simpson's Kurdish translator, Kamaran Abdurrazaq Mohammed; the 45 injured included Simpson, who sustained shrapnel injuries to his hip and leg and was left deaf in one ear. Simpson blamed the deaths on the U.S. and British militaries' official policy of embedding journalists with ground forces. According to Ewen MacAskill, writing for the *Guardian* (November 29, 2003), Simpson claimed that "the US military felt no obligation towards—or awareness of—those journalists like himself [who] were not embedded and [were] operating independently."

In addition to *Unreliable Sources*, Simpson's autobiographical or semi-autobiographical works include *A Mad World, My Masters: Tales from a Traveller's Life* (2000), *News from No Man's Land: Reporting the World* (2002), *Simpson's World: Dispatches from the Front Lines* (2003), *Days from a Different World: A Memoir of Childhood* (2005), *Not Quite World's End: A Traveller's Tales* (2007), and *Twenty Tales from the War Zone: The Best of John Simpson* (2007).

Simpson married an American Christian Scientist, Diane Petteys, in 1965. From that union, which ended in divorce in 1984, he has two daughters, Julia and Eleanor, and several grandchildren. He maintained a decade-long relationship with Tira Shubart before his marriage, in 1996, to Adele "Dee" Kruger, a South African, who produces *Simpson's World*. Sources report variously that the couple maintain homes in Dublin, London, and Paris. Their son, Rafe, was born in 2006.

—M.M.

Suggested Reading: *Irish Times* Features p15 Dec. 10, 1998; (London) *Guardian* Media p104 Aug. 17, 1998, Features p2 Nov. 14, 2001; (London) *Independent* p21 Sep. 6, 1992, (online) Nov. 17, 2001; (London) *Observer* (on-line) Feb. 24, 2002; nyt.co.uk/john-simpson; *South China Morning Post* Agenda p3 Sep. 10, 2000; Simpson, John. *Days from a Different World: A Memoir of Childhood*, 2005, *Twenty Tales from the War Zone: The Best of John Simpson*, 2007

Selected Books: nonfiction—*The Disappeared: Voices from a Secret War* (published in the U.S. as *The Disappeared and the Mothers of the Plaza: The Story of the 11,000 Argentinians Who Vanished*) (with Jana Bennett), 1985; *Inside Iran: Life Under Khomeini's Regime*, 1988; *Despatches from the Barricades: An Eye-Witness Account of the Revolutions That Shook the World, 1989–1990*, 1990; *From the House of War: John Simpson in the Gulf*, 1991; *In the Forests of the Night: Encounters in Peru with Terrorism, Drug-Running and Military Oppression*, 1994; *Lifting the Veil: Life in Revolutionary Iran* (with Tira Shubart), 1995; *A Mad World, My Masters: Tales from a Traveller's Life*, 2000; *News from No Man's Land: Reporting the World*, 2002; *Simpson's World: Dispatches from the Front Lines*, 2003; *The Wars Against Saddam: Taking the Hard Road to Baghdad*, 2003; *Days from a Different World: A Memoir of Childhood*, 2005; *Not Quite World's End: A Traveller's Tales*, 2007; *Twenty Tales from the War Zone: The Best of John Simpson*, 2007; *Unreliable Sources*, 2010; as editor or co-editor—*The Best of Granta*, 1966;

The Oxford Book of Exile, 1995; fiction—*Moscow Requiem*, 1981; *A Fine and Private Place*, 1983

Ronald Martinez/Getty Images

Sizemore, Grady

Aug. 2, 1982– Baseball player

Address: Jacobs Field, 2401 Ontario St., Cleveland, OH 44115

"There is a superstar player on our team, but if you walked into our clubhouse, you'd have no idea who it is," Mark Shapiro, the Cleveland Indians general manager, told Tom Verducci for *Sports Illustrated* (May 14, 2007). Shapiro was referring to Grady Sizemore, the Indians' leadoff hitter and center fielder, who in 2000, at age 17, turned down a college football and baseball scholarship to join the Montreal Expos. After setting records as an Expo and then, beginning in 2002, playing with Cleveland's minor-league teams, Sizemore emerged in 2005 as one of the Indians' strongest and most versatile players. In 2007 he helped lead Cleveland to its division-series victory over the New York Yankees and also helped give the Boston Red Sox a run for their money in the American League Championship Series. He continued to impress in 2008, earning his first Silver Slugger Award and his second consecutive Golden Glove Award and committing only two errors in the field. That year he signed a $23.5 million, six-year contract with the Indians. Though he spent much of the 2009 and 2010 seasons battling injuries, he remains one of the Indians' most valuable assets, thanks to his high-percentage fielding, his ability

to earn base hits consistently, and his remarkable speed in rounding the bases. According to his family and teammates, the unusually hard-working, six-foot two-inch, 200-pound Sizemore is also modest and laid-back and avoids the spotlight. "Individual attention? Oh, he just runs from that," Sizemore's father told Verducci. "I tell him, 'You've got to accept a little bit of that. Some of the people are genuinely happy for you. They're sincere, and you don't want to turn away from that.' He understands, but he's not really interested. He's always been that way." Sizemore's humility, talent, and passion for the game—along with his good looks—have made him a fan favorite in Cleveland. The Indians hitting coach Derek Shelton told Allison Glock for the ESPN Web site (October 24, 2008), "Grady is what every boy in America should grow up to be. I wish you could bottle what he has and give it to every guy you draft. Full effort, every time. Old-school. The real deal."

The first of two children, Grady L. Sizemore III was born on August 2, 1982 in Mill Creek, Washington, a suburb of Seattle, to Grady L. Sizemore II, an insurance-claim investigator, and his wife, Donna, a bookkeeper. His father is African-American, his mother white. Sizemore's athletic ability and competitiveness were apparent when he was very young. While playing baseball in his neighborhood cul-de-sac, the five-year-old Grady would repeatedly tag out his three-year-old brother, Corey, despite his parents' requests that he allow the younger boy to reach base once in a while. "He only knew one way to play: the right way," his father told Verducci. No matter what the weather, Grady would often pull his father—who was also his Little League coach—from his chair in front of the TV with the request, "Let's go hit!" The elder Sizemore spent hours pitching buckets of balls to his son in the backyard or at a nearby park. "I knew he was going to be a major leaguer from the time he was eight years old," his father told Verducci. As a student at Cascade High School, in nearby Everett, Sizemore was a baseball, basketball, and football star. He was the basketball team's starting point guard. On the football team he played cornerback, defensive back, wide receiver, quarterback, and, usually, running back, setting school records with 16 interceptions and 3,081 rushing yards in four years and winning the Defensive Player of the Year award as a senior. On the baseball field Sizemore pitched and played center field. In his senior year he had a .457 batting average, seven home runs, 20 runs batted in (RBIs), 24 stolen bases, and 32 hits, 10 of them doubles. He also scored 43 runs, a school record. In center field he did not commit a single error.

As a senior Sizemore had been pursued by many universities for both his football and baseball skills. He signed a letter of intent to play football and baseball at the University of Washington. Rich Neuheisel, a former University of Washington football coach, told Verducci that he expected Sizemore to start as quarterback, because the quarterback Marques Tuiasosopo had recently left the school to join the National Football League (NFL). "I thought [Sizemore] might be the next Tuiasosopo," Neuheisel said. "He had great instincts, is a great competitor and has a very athletic body. If he'd been a track guy, he'd have been a decathlete." But in June 2000 the Montreal Expos selected Sizemore in the third round of the draft, forcing him to decide between college and baseball. "You're still in high school and you're making these big decisions . . . ," he told Daniel Jimenez for *Young Money* (2007, on-line). "I just decided that baseball was where I was leaning anyway as far as my career. It was what I loved more." His father agreed, advising him that "if it didn't work out," his baseball earnings would leave him with "enough to fall back on," as quoted by Jimenez. Sizemore's contract with the Expos came with a $2 million signing bonus, thanks to his agent from Octagon, which represents athletes worldwide. He spent a little of the money on the purchase of a 2001 Chevy Suburban, saving and investing the balance.

Sizemore played with the Expos' minor-league teams for nearly four years. As a member of the Gulf Coast League (GCL, a rookie league) Expos in 2000, Sizemore racked up a batting average of .293, with one home run, eight doubles, and 16 stolen bases out of 18 attempts. Ranked eighth among GCL prospects, he moved to the Clinton, Iowa, Lumberkings, in the single-A Midwest League, in 2001. With the Lumberkings Sizemore stole 32 bases in 43 attempts in 123 games and finished the season with 81 walks, the second-highest number in the league.

Sizemore began 2002 with the Florida Manatees, another single-A team. Although he had hit only three home runs in his 912 at-bats until then in the minor leagues, he was considered a good "gap hitter" and quickly became known for his maturity as well as his athleticism. "He was the most disciplined teenage hitter I have ever seen," the Indians' farm-club director, Tony LaCava, told Verducci. "Twenty-pitch nights were not uncommon for him. And he played the game the right way from Day One. He ran hard 90 feet to first base all the time and had a quiet confidence and determination. The package was all there." In late June, in a six-player deal, Sizemore, the Expos' first baseman Lee Stevens, and two other minor-league players, the pitcher Cliff Lee and the shortstop Brandon Phillips, were traded to the Cleveland Indians in exchange for the Expos' starting pitcher Bartolo Colon and their minor-league pitcher Tim Drew. Occurring in the wake of a disappointing season for Cleveland—it began with 11 wins in 12 games and ended with a third-place finish in their conference—the trade was largely interpreted as an investment in the future. In the 47 games Sizemore played with one of the Indians' class-A affiliates, the Kinston, North Carolina, Indians, in 2002, he batted .343, with nine doubles, three triples, three home runs, 20 RBIs, and 14 stolen bases out of 21 attempts. That year he was named to the SportsTicker All-Teen Team.

Sizemore shined as a player with the Indians' double-A team, the Akron Aeros, in 2003. He made no errors in his first 84 games. In the 15 games he played in August, his best month that season, his batting average was .330, with two doubles, five triples, and four home runs. The Aeros won the Eastern League crown that season, while Sizemore led all the Cleveland farm teams in runs (96) and hits (151), had the third-best batting average (.304), and hit 10 triples. He was named to the Team USA 2004 Olympic squad and won the Lou Boudreau Award as the Indians' Minor League Player of the Year. He also won the Larry Doby Award as the MVP in the RadioShack All-Star Future's Game, in which the U.S. team defeated the world team, 3–2.

After an impressive spring-training performance, Sizemore began the 2004 season with the triple-A Buffalo Bisons and as the number-one prospect in the Indians' minor-league system, according to *Baseball America*. A stomach illness hampered him at the beginning of the season; between April 8 and May 19, he had a .228 average, with two home runs and 19 RBIs.

Sizemore made his major-league debut on July 21, 2004, as a defensive replacement in the ninth inning of a game against the Chicago White Sox. On July 22 he started for the Indians, and on July 23 he recorded his first major-league hit—an RBI double—against the Kansas City Royals' pitcher Mike Wood. The next day his was the game-winning, ninth-inning hit, against the Kansas City pitcher Rudy Seanez. On July 25 Sizemore hit his first major-league home run, and on July 28 he stole his first major-league base. On August 5, after failing to hit in 26 consecutive at-bats, Sizemore made a game-winning, two-run double in a contest with the Toronto Blue Jays. "He's had some tough at-bats," the Indians' manager, Eric Wedge, told Bob Matuszak for MLB.com (August 5, 2004). "But he doesn't let a tough at-bat or game faze him. He's even keel and very strong mentally already."

Nevertheless, his hitting slump led Cleveland to send Sizemore to the triple-A Buffalo Bisons for more practice. "I went back down there with the same approach I've always had. I wanted to learn from the mistakes I made," he told Burt Graeff for the Cleveland, Ohio, *Plain Dealer* (September 27, 2004). He finished that triple-A stint as the team's leadoff hitter, with an impressive .320 batting average, six home runs, and 32 RBIs in 62 games. In September Sizemore was summoned back to the Indians. In the team's last 13 games of the regular season, he averaged .306, with two doubles, two triples, two home runs, and nine RBIs. Sizemore hit leadoff in a handful of those games, and he thrived defensively; for the 38 games in which he started for the Indians that year, he made only one error, finishing with a .991 fielding percentage. With an 80–82 record the Indians failed to make the play-offs.

Slated to start the 2005 season with the Bisons, Sizemore was instead called up to replace the injured Indians' right fielder Juan Gonzalez. He proved himself to be a reliable, powerful hitter and a smart, speedy base runner. "Sizemore . . . was somewhere between a blur and a good rumor circling the bases in the sixth inning of the Indians' 8–0 victory" over the White Sox, Phil Rogers wrote for the *Chicago Tribune* (September 22, 2005). The team's hopes of reaching the play-offs were dashed when the Indians lost six of their last seven games. The downward streak started when, in a game against the Royals, Sizemore lost a fly ball in the sun in the ninth inning, allowing Kansas City's winning run. He was the Indians' last out that season: in a game against the White Sox, he was thrown out at first base after hitting a weak ground ball. In an out-of-character moment of frustration, Sizemore threw his helmet to the ground. "It was such a tough week and a frustrating time," he told Jorge Arangure for the *Washington Post* (October 3, 2005). "I wanted to come through and I didn't. A lot was going through my head." Sizemore's 2005 offensive statistics placed him in the company of several earlier Indian record-setters. He became only the second member of the team to hit at least 20 doubles (he ended up with 37), 10 triples (11, finally), 20 home runs (22), and 20 stolen bases (22) in the same season. He was the seventh Cleveland player to hit at least 20 home runs and steal 20 bases in the same season and was one of only five in Major League Baseball (MLB) who did so in 2005. On the road he made 103 hits, the most for an Indian since 1959 (when that statistic was first recorded).

On March 30, 2006 Sizemore signed a six-year contract with the Indians worth $23.45 million, more money than any player with under two years of experience in the major leagues had ever been promised. He told his parents that they could retire and used some of his money to buy a 1966 Lincoln automobile and a house in Scottsdale, Arizona.

In 2006 Sizemore played in all 162 games, becoming the first Indian to do so since Joe Carter, in 1989, 1990, and 1991. He was the first major leaguer in nearly 70 years to hit at least 50 doubles, 10 triples, and 25 home runs in one season. He led the American League in doubles (53) and the major leagues in runs scored (134), the fifth-highest total in Cleveland history. He also led the major leagues in extra-base hits (92), a club record. On September 24, 2006, for the first time, he scored two home runs in a single game, one of which was his first inside-the-park home run. Overall, Sizemore reached base in 136 of 162 games. He also compiled the ninth-best fielding percentage among major-league outfielders that year. Members of the Cleveland chapter of the Baseball Writers Association of America named him the Indians' Man of the Year, an honor that recognizes the player or executive in the franchise who consistently performs well in the world of baseball and beyond. Although the team won eight out of their last nine games, they fell short of making the play-offs.

Sizemore was a major factor in the Indians' excellent 2007 season. The team started off well, struggled in midseason, then won nine of their last 10 games, decisively capturing their division title and earning a spot in the play-offs. Their opponents in the American League Division Series were the Yankees, widely considered to be the better team. The Indians won the first two games, played in Jacobs Field; in the second, Sizemore stole home in the sixth inning, tying the score before Cleveland triumphed, 2–1. The Yankees handily won Game Three, 8–4. In Game Four Sizemore hit a homer on the third pitch of the first inning, and with a score of 6–4, his team won the series. Pitted against the Boston Red Sox in the seven-game American League Championship Series, the Indians lost the first game on the road, 10–3. They won the second away-game, 13–6, with Sizemore contributing three base hits. Back in Cleveland the Indians won the next two games. With only one game between the Indians and their first World Series since 1997, they lost the next three games. In Games Four through Seven, Sizemore made only three hits in 17 at-bats; his troubles mirrored those of his teammates throughout the series. In the last three games, the Indians scored only five runs, while Boston racked up 30. "I thought we played well, we just weren't able to get the big hit . . . ," Sizemore told T. R. Sullivan for MLB.com (October 22, 2007). "I thought we played hard, they just played better." With a .277 batting average, 174 hits, 118 runs, 34 doubles, five triples, 24 home runs, 78 RBIs, and 33 stolen bases, Sizemore performed slightly less well in 2007 than he had the previous year.

On April 27, 2008 Sizemore's streak of consecutive games played (382) ended when he sprained his ankle in a loss to the Yankees. By the season's end Sizemore had become the first Indian to rack up four consecutive seasons that included at least 20 home runs (he had 33) and at least 20 stolen bases (38). He led the team in hits for the fourth year in a row, becoming the first Indian to accomplish that feat since "Shoeless" Joe Jackson, in 1911–14. For the third consecutive year, Sizemore was named to the American League All-Star team; he also won his first Silver Slugger Award and his second consecutive Golden Glove Award for his impressive fielding percentage—.995, second among American League center fielders. The Indians finished second in the American League Central Division and did not make the play-offs. Sizemore struggled with elbow and groin injuries through much of 2009; playing through the pain he batted a career-low average of .248, with 18 home runs, 44 extra-base hits, 60 walks, 64 RBIs, and 13 steals over 106 games. He stopped playing on September 4 (the Indians were already out of play-off contention) and then underwent surgical procedures on his elbow and also his abdomen, to repair a hernia related to his groin injury. The 2009 season was disappointing for the Indians, who finished fourth in their division, with a record of 65–97.

Sizemore's 2010 season was cut short due to injury. After playing in 33 games, he underwent microfracture surgery on his left knee and remained on the sick list for the remainder of the season. The Indians finished fourth in their division for the second consecutive year, with a record of 69–93.

With his boyish good looks and quiet confidence, Sizemore is a Cleveland fan favorite. The team and apparel companies have capitalized on Sizemore's bachelor status and popularity among girls and women by selling T-shirts reading "Mrs. Sizemore." Sizemore has received admiring letters and marriage proposals from scores of fans, among them members of an on-line club, Grady's Ladies, launched by Hallie Sheck, a Dayton, Ohio, schoolteacher. (Grady's Ladies' on-line store carries three dozen items emblazoned with Sizemore's number, 24, and initials.) Despite such attention, Sizemore has remained modest. "I think I drive my agent cra-zy with the [endorsements] I turn down," Sizemore told Verducci. "I just want to go out on the field and play. I'm not comfortable in front of the camera. I don't like seeing this mug on TV." The infielder Aaron Boone (then with Cleveland) told Steve DiMeglio for *USA Today* (May 8, 2006), "He just has a great way about him. For one thing, he's good. And he just has that personality, and you see it right away that he is who he is and he's not going to change."

Sizemore lives with his brother in Scottsdale, where his parents also own a home.

—M.R.M.

Suggested Reading: ESPN.com Oct. 24, 2008; MLB.com Aug. 5, 2004, Oct. 22, 2007; *Seattle Times* D p10 June 2, 2000; *Sports Illustrated* p74 Apr. 3, 2006, p56 May 14, 2007, p58 Nov. 21, 2007; *USA Today* C p9 Mar. 30, 2006, C p3 May 8, 2006; *Washington Post* E p5 Oct. 3, 2005

Chris Graythen/Getty Images

Smith, Mike

June 13, 1959– Football coach

Address: Atlanta Falcons, 4400 Falcon Pkwy., Flowery Branch, GA 30542

When Mike Smith was hired as the head coach of the Atlanta Falcons, on January 23, 2008, the team was at a low ebb. In 2007 Michael Vick, the Falcons' star quarterback, had been suspended indefinitely by the National Football League (NFL) and sentenced to nearly two years in a federal prison; the team's head coach, Bobby Petrino, had resigned after only 13 games, and at the season's end the Falcons had posted a 4–12 record. Smith was a relatively obscure but well-respected assistant coach with more than a quarter-century of experience in football when he joined the Falcons. He quickly won over the team's owner, Arthur Blank, general manager, Thomas Dimitroff, and players with his no-nonsense style. After rebuilding the team during that off-season through free agency and the NFL draft, Smith helped guide the Falcons to an 11–5 record and a berth in the 2008 National Football Conference (NFC) play-offs. The team's striking turnaround earned Smith the Associated Press 2008 Coach of the Year Award. The Falcons finished the 2009 season with a 9–7 record, thus failing to make the play-offs but marking the first time ever that the team posted consecutive winning seasons. "I think I'm different than I was in my first game last year," Smith told Charles Odum for the Associated Press (November 9, 2009). "I can assure you I was very, very nervous in my first game. But in terms of how I coach, I've been coaching for a long time and I've always coached this way, with a lot of enthusiasm, and I want our players to have that same enthusiasm and the same drive."

An award-winning undergraduate football player, Smith spent the first 17 years of his coaching career with a succession of three college football teams, including a dozen years with the Tennessee Technological University Golden Eagles. His association with the NFL began in 1999, when he was hired as the Baltimore Ravens' defensive assistant coach/defensive line coach. In his second year with the Ravens, the team won the 2001 Super Bowl. Two years later Smith was named the Jacksonville Jaguars' defense coordinator. He held that position for the next five seasons, earning a reputation for getting the most out of players with average talents. "Nobody works harder," Jacksonville's head coach, Jack Del Rio, said of Smith, as posted on the Atlanta Falcons Web site. "He's got a great mind for football." "It's great to have a coach who gets fired up on the sideline and gets mad about things and wears his heart on his sleeve pretty much when he's coaching a football game," the Falcons' safety Thomas DeCoud said of Smith to Charles Odum. "You like to play with that kind of passion and that kind of fire, and it's great to have a coach who emulates the same kind of sentiments and you can feed off his energy." The former NFL lineman Jeff Lageman, a friend of Smith's, told Jeff Schultz for the Atlanta (Georgia) Journal-Constitution (January 24, 2008), "The thing I like most about him is he's organized. He's detailed. He understands football and he knows opposing coaches and what they're trying to accomplish. He understands playing to strengths and eliminating weaknesses. Most coaches would love to have him as a consultant just because he understands the game so well." The Falcons' general manager, Thomas Dimitroff, told Schultz, "He is a football coach, not a carnival act. He is straightforward, X's and O's, respected by players, admired by peers."

The oldest of the four sons and four daughters of Sam and Carol Smith, Mike Smith was born on June 13, 1959 in Chicago, Illinois, and raised in Daytona Beach, Florida. At an early age he became a role model for his siblings. He learned the importance of diligence and responsibility from his parents, both of whom pursued careers in education. His father is currently the principal of an alternative high school in Daytona Beach; his mother is a part-time special-education teacher. "I've always just been very task-oriented," Smith told Kent Somers for the Arizona Republic (Decemer 31, 2008). "My dad always told me if you work hard, people will take notice. Just do the best you can do every day. That's how I've tried to approach this profession." Smith was introduced to sports by his father, who coached student football teams in the Daytona Beach area. In his teens Smith also spent some of his leisure time fishing and surfing.

Rather than a public school, Smith chose to attend Father Lopez Catholic High School, in Daytona Beach, where he was an excellent student and an All-State linebacker. His father insisted that Mike pay half the tuition, and, as Sam Smith noted to Steve Hummer for the Atlanta Journal-Constitution (January 27, 2008), his son "always came up with the money." Despite his being somewhat undersized for a football player, Smith's passion and determination made him a standout. When a broken arm relegated him to the sidelines during his senior year, he continued to work with the team as a voluntary coach. "He loved football," his high-school coach, Phil Richart, told Hummer. "He came to me and said, 'Coach, I've got to do something to be a part of the team.' So I let him coach the other linebackers." Carol Smith told Hummer that her son "used to tell me he could go to sleep and play the game in his head."

Smith earned a football scholarship to East Tennessee State University (ETSU), in Johnson City. As a linebacker he lettered each of his four years with the ETSU Buccaneers and was named the team's defensive Most Valuable Player (MVP) twice. Smith led the team in tackles during his junior and senior years, with 120 and 186, respectively. His senior-season tally of tackles (91 solo, 95 assists) helped set an ETSU single-season record that still stands. (East Tennessee discontinued its football program after the 2003 season.) A former ETSU offensive-line coach, Robert McGraw, told Brian T. Smith for the Bristol (Virginia) Herald-Courier (February 10, 2008), "Mike was a good kid and a tough son of a gun. I've coached for 47 years, and you remember the tough ones. He was a great teammate, tougher than hell and very determined." Smith's Buccaneers teammate Donnie Cook, a defensive back, told Hummer, "He could go sideline-to-sideline quicker than anyone I ever saw at that position." After Smith graduated, in 1981, he was invited to try out with the Winnipeg Blue Bombers of the Canadian Football League. Randy Rorrer reported for the Daytona Beach News-Journal (September 5, 2008) that he reached the final cut but failed to win a place on the team. According to Who's Who in America, however, he was a linebacker with the team in 1982.

Smith's coaching career began in 1982, when he landed a part-time assistant-coaching job at San Diego State University, in California. The entry-level position came with a very small salary, which forced him to moonlight as a night watchman. During his first year at San Diego State, Smith met Brian Billick, then the school's tight-ends coach. In 1983 Smith was made a full-time member of the coaching staff and promoted to linebackers coach. He held that post for the next three seasons, before moving on to serve as the defensive-line coach and recruiting coordinator at Morehead State University, in Kentucky, in 1986. After one season at Morehead State, Smith joined the coaching staff at Tennessee Tech University, in Cookeville, where he stayed for 12 seasons. He spent one season as the defensive-line coach of Tennessee Tech's Golden Eagles before being promoted to special-teams coordinator, in 1988. Smith held that position for eight seasons. In 1996 he was named the Golden Eagles' defensive coordinator. He held that post for his final three years there. The Golden Eagles finished in the top 10 in total defense in 1997 and 1998 among teams in the Football Championship Subdivision (formerly known as Division I-AA). Concurrently in his final year at Tennessee Tech, Smith served as assistant head coach.

When Brian Billick became the head coach of the Baltimore Ravens, in 1999, Smith secured his first NFL coaching job, as a Ravens defensive assistant/defensive-line coach, with responsibility for breaking down game films. He served in that capacity for three seasons, among them the team's first Super Bowl–winning season, in 2000. During that year the Ravens won 16 games and lost four, and its defense surrendered only 165 points, which set an NFL record for a 16-game season; they defeated the New York Giants, 34–7, in Super Bowl XXXV. In 2002 Smith was promoted to linebackers coach. That season he guided the All-Pro linebacker Ray Lewis and the Pro Bowl linebackers Adalius Thomas and Peter Boulware; under Smith Boulware enjoyed one of the best seasons of his career, recording 57 tackles, seven sacks, one interception, and four passes defensed. Adalius Thomas, who started 12 games at the defensive-end position for the Ravens that season (and played with the New England Patriots from 2007 until he was let go, in April 2010), described Smith for the Falcons Web site as "a hard worker who is known as a football coach's coach. He demands the best of you as a player, but he also gives you the best as a coach."

In 2003, after Jack Del Rio was hired as head coach of the Jacksonville Jaguars, Smith left the Ravens to become the Jaguars' defense coordinator. With Smith's help the Jaguars' defense quickly turned into one of the best in the NFL, and Smith became known for getting the best out of players with only average talent. From 2003 to 2006 the Jaguars ranked fourth in the NFL in overall defense (with an average of 296.6 yards per game), third in offensive points allowed (an average of 16.1), and fifth in rushing defense (an average of 99.3 yards per game). In 2006 the Jaguars ranked second in the league in total defense: their average of 283.6 yards per game was the most in franchise history. The squad also picked up a team-record average of 20 interceptions at home and an NFL-low average of 11 points per game for their opponents at home, while posting two shutouts. The success of the Jaguars' defense that season was largely credited to Smith, who succeeded despite injuries to three of the unit's starters (the defensive end Reggie Hayward, the safety Donovin Darius, and the linebacker Mike Peterson) that placed the men on the disabled list. Smith told Pete Prisco, "You just have to play with what you have. The guys went out and did the job. You have to have contingency plans for when they go down. That's why we cross-train our guys so they're ready to play other positions and have comfort level when they do." During his tenure in Jacksonville, Smith also helped develop several players into Pro Bowlers: defensive tackle Marcus Stroud (who played in the Pro Bowl three times, in 2003, 2004, and 2005), defensive tackle John Henderson (2004, 2006), and cornerback Rashean Mathis (2006). In 2007 the Jaguars dropped to 12th in the league in total defense but finished sixth in the American Football Conference in rushing defense, after holding opponents to 100.3 yards per game, on average. The Jaguars finished the season with an 11–5 record and reached the play-offs for the sixth time. They defeated the Pittsburgh Steelers in the first round of the play-offs, then lost to the New England Patriots in the divisional play-off round.

On January 23, 2008 Smith signed a four-year contract (reportedly worth between $8 million and $10 million) with the Atlanta Falcons. He replaced the interim head coach, Emmitt Thomas, to become the 14th head coach since the Falcons' debut, in 1966, and the sixth since 2003. He was hired as part of a major overhaul led by the team's owner, Arthur Blank, and the new general manager, Thomas Dimitroff. Prior to Smith's arrival the Falcons had been in disarray: in 2007 they won four games and lost 12—placing them last in the National Football Conference (NFC) South. Their disastrous showing was attributed mostly to the loss of the quarterback Michael Vick, who spent 21 months in prison after his conviction for operating an illegal interstate dog-fighting ring. The Falcons' head coach, Bobby Petrino, had been hired in January 2007 partly to develop Vick into a more complete quarterback. In Vick's absence Petrino struggled to implement his offense-heavy philosophy; he resigned after 13 games, when the team's win–loss record stood at 3–10.

"Mike came in and he was a real football coach," Dimitroff told Jeff Schultz for an *Atlanta Journal-Constitution* blog (June 29, 2009). "There's no pretense about him at all. He came in and it was all about communicating with his players. There were no ulterior motives." "My philosophy is that we were starting anew," Smith told Kent Somers. "It was a fresh, clean slate. 2007 was history. It was 2008, and we were going to move forward." Along with Dimitroff, Smith worked to create a tough, disciplined team. Several months after his arrival in Atlanta, Smith declared, according to Steve Wyche, a Cox News Service (April 2, 2008) reporter, "We're going to be physical. We're going to try and control the line of scrimmage, and if we do that, we have a chance to be successful." Describing desirable players, he added, "You look for mental toughness. Do they play hard? Are they consistent in the effort they put out? . . . That, first and foremost, is the thing you look at. You also have to look at how they respond when things are going well and when things are going poorly." That off-season Smith released a few veteran players and acquired several others, including the running back Michael Turner. Then, in the third overall pick of the 2008 NFL draft, he selected the Boston College quarterback Matt Ryan. In the weeks leading into training camp, Smith strived to create an atmosphere of fervor and accountability among the players. He told D. Orlando Ledbetter for the *Atlanta Journal-Constitution* (September 25, 2008), "When you have that accountability, you're going to be a disciplined football team."

In his first season with Atlanta, Smith led the Falcons to an 11–5 record, thus achieving one of the greatest single-season turnarounds in NFL history. The Falcons' success stemmed in part from Ryan's stellar performance and a newly improved running game under Turner. The Falcons finished a close second in the NFC South Division and earned their first play-off berth since 2004. In the first round of the play-offs, they lost to the Arizona Cardinals, 30–24. Smith was named the Associated Press (AP) Coach of the Year, edging out the Miami Dolphins' Tony Sparano by one vote, and the AP named Matt Ryan Offensive Rookie of the Year.

In 2009 the Falcons finished with a 9–7 record, marking the first time in franchise history that the team had back-to-back winning seasons. In November of that year, during a contest with the Washington Redskins, Matt Ryan was hit out of bounds by the Redskins' LaRon Landry, and Smith promptly got into a scuffle with several Redskins players. His behavior led the league to impose a $15,000 fine on Smith. "That's the type of coach you want," the Falcons' defensive tackle Jonathan Babineaux told Charles Odum. "You want a coach who's going to stand in there for us and have our back just like we have his back." The longtime Falcons' center Todd McClure said to Odum, "He's always like that. I love playing for him. I think everybody in this locker room does. . . . He is always looking out for his guys." In a news conference later that week, Smith refused to express regret or apologize for his actions; as quoted on ESPN.com (November 12, 2009), he stated, "I want to reiterate that I'm always going to have my players' backs and I'm going to take care of them."

Smith and the Falcons began the 2010 season with high expectations. They entered week seven of the season tied for first place in their division with the New Orleans Saints, the defending Super Bowl champions, with a record of 4–2.

Smith and his wife, the former Julie McDonald (Brian Billick's sister-in-law), live in Suwanee, Georgia. They have one daughter, Logan. Since he joined the Falcons, Smith and his wife have participated in a Gatorade-sponsored campaign called "Beat the Heat," which aims to prevent potentially fatal dehydration and heat exhaustion among professional and amateur athletes. In his scarce spare time, Smith enjoys kayaking and fly-fishing.

—C.C.

Suggested Reading: Associated Press Nov. 9, 2009; Atlanta Falcons Web site; *Atlanta Journal-Constitution* E p1+ Nov. 16, 2008, C p1+ Jan. 5, 2009, C p1+ May 31, 2009, C p1+ Nov. 9, 2009; CBSSports.com Oct. 18, 2007; *Dallas (Texas) Morning News* C p4 Oct. 24, 2009; (Ontario, Canada) *Guelph Mercury* p1+ Nov. 9, 2009

Spalding, Esperanza

1984– Jazz bassist; singer; composer

Address: Heads Up, 23307 Commerce Park, Cleveland, OH 44122

In the world of jazz instrumentalists, where women make up a small minority, female bandleaders are rare, and female standup-bass players rarer still. At the age of 25, Esperanza Spalding has won high acclaim as both. Influenced as much by R&B artists, including Stevie Wonder and Erykah Badu, as by such jazz icons as Wayne Shorter and Ron Carter, Spalding has performed with many jazz greats and recorded three albums as a bandleader, showcasing her eclectic sensibilities along with her vocal and compositional talents. After graduating from the prestigious Berklee College of Music, in Boston, Massachusetts, at the age of 20, Spalding was offered a teaching position there, making her the second-youngest person in the school's 60-year history (after the jazz guitarist Pat Metheny) to be hired as an instructor; she taught at Berklee for three years. While her tendency to cross musical boundaries has led some to question whether her music is really jazz, Spalding told *Current Biography*—the source of quotes for this article, unless otherwise noted—that she is not concerned with how people label her music: "I know that I like what I'm doing, and people seem to have a great time at the shows. And people that I really respect have invited me to play in their bands, only because of the music, not because of any hype or titles."

Sandrine Lee, courtesy of Heads Up International

Esperanza Spalding was born in 1984 in Portland, Oregon. Her mother raised Spalding and her older brother in a lower-middle-class Portland neighborhood called King. Because Spalding's mother was the only provider for her children, working a number of jobs, the family struggled financially, sometimes coming close to homelessness; Spalding remembers little about that, recalling mainly that she grew up with a loving and caring mother. From an early age Spalding loved music. She enjoyed listening to an oldies radio station, which played songs by Stevie Wonder, Sam Cooke, the Monkees, and others. One day she heard her mother trying, with difficulty, to play a relatively simple classical piece on the family's piano; Spalding, then four years old, went to the piano bench and played the piece by ear. During those years Spalding saw the famed cellist Yo-Yo Ma perform on the children's TV show *Mister Rogers' Neighborhood*, and she was transfixed. "Oh, I want to do that," Spalding remembers thinking. "That's what I want to do."

Because the local, free music program had no cellos, Spalding settled for a violin. Though she did not like to practice, her ability to play by ear allowed her to develop her music skills. She eventually joined the Chamber Music Society of Oregon, a nonprofit program that included a children's chamber orchestra, in which Spalding played, and a summer camp, where she took group lessons. Around the age of 12, she started getting private instruction. By age 15 she was the orchestra's concertmaster, or lead violinist. During those years, from fifth to eighth grade, Spalding was homeschooled, in part because she had a poor immune system and was often ill, and in part because her mother generally disliked the public-school environment. Since her mother worked full-time, Spalding mostly educated herself—borrowing books from the library, having her mother check her work, and taking tests administered by the state. One of the most important lessons Spalding learned during that time, one that she applies today, was the importance of time management: with no schedule in place, she realized that the only way to get work done was to structure her own time.

Spalding attended the Northwest Academy, a private arts high school in Portland, on a full scholarship. One day during her freshman year, while walking through the halls of her school, she spotted a new standup bass on the floor of an empty classroom. She instinctively went inside, picked it up, and started to play. "I remember distinctly," she said, "the first thing you notice [about a bass] is the vibration is so powerful, particularly compared to a violin—or any other instrument. I felt it resonating through my whole system. I said, 'Wow. This is pretty hip.' And I just kept noodling around." Brian Rose, a jazz-improvisation teacher, came into the room and explained the concept of a walking bass line (a steady rhythm of quarter notes) and then showed Spalding a simple blues progression. That was an illuminating moment for Spalding. "I was like, 'Oh, cool, so you can just make up some accompaniment that fits into the harmony, but it can be whatever you *hear*.' And I really am an ear player on a lot of different levels, so that was really encouraging, because I always felt so behind everyone else in the classical world. My brain just never worked in a mathematical way,

and it was really discouraging, because I loved music, and I felt I was good at it." After a few minutes of playing blues on the standup bass, Spalding felt she had found "something I can relate to."

Within a few months Spalding was playing live gigs with a variety of bands—jazz, blues, rock, funk, and hip-hop groups. One that contributed significantly to her development as a singer and songwriter was the indie-rock band Noise for Pretend. The members of that already established group, both men, needed a bass player who could also sing backup; Spalding had not done much singing, let alone while playing bass, but she said she could do it. Soon after joining the band, she started contributing lyrics and compositions, and before long she was writing most of the group's songs. "Composition is a huge part of my musical identity," Spalding said. She added that most teenagers "don't get a platform like that, that you can write stuff and have it played by these awesome grown-up musicians who are not only going to play it and take it seriously but contribute to it and give constructive feedback, and help make the arrangements better, etcetera." At the suggestion of a record-label owner, Spalding, at age 16, also became the band's lead singer. While with Noise for Pretend, she improved her composition, singing, and playing as well as the coordination required to sing and play bass at the same time. She also got better at commanding the attention of a live crowd, usually people in their 20s, 30s, and 40s "getting drunk and wanting to party." During that period Spalding was officially in four bands—including a jazz group, Trio Esperanza—and played with many others, among them a 14-piece jazz ensemble. At the suggestion of a band member, she learned to sing and play several jazz standards. Spalding's transition to jazz was not deliberate. "It wasn't like, Oh, I want to be a jazz musician now," she said. "It was like, I want to do this some more, because I'm really good at it and it's fun." The pace of her evolution as a musician was rapid. She told Marty Hughley for the *Oregonian* (August 16, 2002), "I feel like I've tried to cram 10 years of development into two years."

At 15 Spalding dropped out of high school. Later, after getting a GED, she spent a year in a conservatory program at Portland State University. Because her studies there were very intense, and because she already had a wealth of musical experiences, she had an easy time when she arrived on a full scholarship at the Berklee College of Music, in 2002. "I didn't really dig most of the classes at Berklee," she confessed. "Of course there were some teachers that opened my mind and taught me so much, but most of the curriculum I found to be pretty dry—compared to what I wanted to do." Spalding nonetheless enjoyed the environment at Berklee, where she could meet and play with gifted musicians from more than 50 countries. Spalding was also performing four or five nights a week, appearing with famous and influential musicians who included Pat Metheny, the saxophonist Joe

Lovano, the singer Patti Austin, and many others. One encounter with Metheny made a lasting impression on her. At the time he was producing a recording of a student ensemble led by the vibraphonist Gary Burton. "Everybody had left the studio," Spalding recalled, speaking to Thomas Peña for jazz.com (May 28, 2008), "and I was there, probably practicing and Mr. Metheny walked in and asked me what I was planning to do with my life. I told him that I was thinking of leaving school and pursuing a degree in political science. He told me that he meets a lot of musicians, some great, some not so great and that I had [what he called] the 'X Factor.' Meaning, that if I chose to pursue a career in music and I applied myself, my potential was unlimited." Spalding graduated in 2005 and then, at the age of 20, accepted a teaching position at the school, which she held until 2008.

As she was finishing her studies at Berklee, Spalding recorded her first album, *Junjo* (2006), an instrumental-jazz record with bebop and Latin elements. Spalding had not envisioned the album as her debut. In Boston she had been playing Latin and improvisational music with the pianist Aruan Ortiz and the drummer Francisco Mela and asked them to record with her, "purely as a project for our enjoyment, and the desire to capture the music we were making." The resulting record, released on a small Spanish label, won attention from jazz fans, critics, and other musicians that far exceeded her expectations. Writing for allmusic.com, Michael G. Nastos called the album "an exercise in joy and freedom. . . . For sure, [Spalding] is an accomplished bassist, musician, and original thinker. *Junjo* is an auspicious beginning that should catch the ears of any lover of great music." Spalding wrote or co-wrote four of the nine tracks; the rest were her versions of songs by such jazz greats as Chick Corea ("Humpty Dumpty") and Jimmy Rowles ("The Peacocks"). Along with her bass playing, Spalding provided wordless vocals for nearly all the songs. In a short review for the *New York Times* (July 9, 2006), Ben Ratliff called the record "charming."

Late in 2007 Spalding began recording her full-fledged, self-titled debut album. *Esperanza* (2008) was more diverse and ambitious than her first record, encompassing a wider variety of sounds and styles, a gumbo of jazz, samba, bossa nova, neo-soul, and R&B. Spalding wrote the music and words for nine of the 12 songs and sang in English, Portuguese, and Spanish. She put unique twists on other people's songs; one of the three covers on the album is "Cuerpo y Alma," her version of the jazz standard "Body and Soul." The opening bass line provides a hint of the original tune, which vanishes when all the elements—the nonstandard time signature (5/4), Latin rhythm, and Spanish lyrics—come together to form an entirely new song. Other tracks, especially "Precious" (composed by Spalding), are much closer to neo-soul and pop than to jazz or Latin music. Still others, such as "I Know You Know," another Spalding original, float in be-

tween: the song begins with a funky bass line accompanied by drums and spare piano; Spalding sings the verse in a cool, neo-soul style, showing the influence of Erykah Badu, and then delivers the partly scatted chorus over a Latin rhythm. "She Got to You," another Spalding original, is also sung in English, between and along with bursts of alto-sax melodies. A mellow and soulful samba is heard on the album's last track, "Samba em Preludio," a song by the celebrated Brazilian guitar player Baden Powell. *Esperanza* debuted at number three on *Billboard*'s top contemporary jazz albums chart, quickly moved up to number two, and remained on the chart for over a year.

"The ambition on display on *Esperanza*," Thom Jurek wrote for allmusic.com, "is not blind; it's deeply intuitive, and her focus brings out the adventure on the album in all the right ways. By a lesser musician, even attempting something like this would have been disastrous." The fact that Spalding was only 23 years old did not go unnoticed by Jurek or other critics. "In sum," Jurek concluded, "*Esperanza* sounds like the work of a much older, more experienced player, singer, and songwriter. Spalding not only has these gifts in natural abundance but is disciplined in her execution as well." Writing for the *Chicago Tribune* (July 10, 2008), Ed Morales described Spalding's album as "picking up where the jazz fusion of the 1970s left off." He added: "The songs pulsate with complex arrangements, Spalding's uniquely expressive vocals and fat-bottomed bass playing, and challenging melodies and harmonies." The positive reception, however, was not unanimous. Some critics, among them Ben Ratliff of the *New York Times* (May 26, 2008), argued that Spalding's attempt to blend the various genres and styles was ambitious but ultimately unsuccessful. Ratliff, who conceded that Spalding's talent is "beyond question," argued: "This is mostly acoustic music played by jazz musicians and owes as much to Stevie Wonder as Wayne Shorter. It's an attempt at bringing this crisscrossing to a new level of definition and power, but its vamps and grooves are a little obvious, and it pushes her first as a singer-songwriter, which isn't her primary strength."

Acknowledging how different the songs on *Esperanza* are from one another, Spalding called the album an "appetizer sampler of all the elements that made up my musical identity." She conceded that the record is "all over the place" but said that that is because "I only got however many songs to make a statement about who I was." The album, she said, was meant to be an introduction to her various styles. "I really think I have a lot to offer long-term," she said, "and I want people to pay attention and experience my music." Because jazz artists and other musicians now make most of their money through touring rather than record sales, *Esperanza* was also meant to be an advertisement for music fans to see her in live performance, which, she said, is "where the magic happens."

At the request of President Barack Obama, Spalding performed for him three times in 2009: twice at the White House—once for a tribute to Stevie Wonder and again as part of an evening of music and poetry—and once in Oslo, Norway, where Obama accepted the Nobel Peace Prize. Spalding's latest album, *Chamber Music Society*, a modern chamber-music record with elements of classical, folk, and world music as well as early-20th-century jazz, was released in 2010. In a review for the *Washington Post* (August 17, 2010), Bill Friskics-Warren wrote that the album's "fusion of jazz, contemporary classical and other sources, including some understated funk, is as lively as it is original." In early fall Spalding began an international tour in support of the album. Another album, as yet untitled, will be what she called a "rocking funky singer-songwriter" jazz record; it is due out in the spring of 2011. Spalding's bass playing can also be heard on Joe Lovano's *Folk Art* (2009), a critically acclaimed post-bop album of original tunes by Lovano's band Us Five. Spalding has said that she would like to collaborate with the singer/songwriter Paul Simon and the hip-hip artist Andre 3000 of the rap group OutKast. She would also like to act in films and write music for large ensembles.

Spalding lives in Austin, Texas, and New York City.

—D.K.

Suggested Reading: allaboutjazz.com; allmusic.com; *Boston Globe* D p11 Apr. 22, 2005; esperanzaspalding.com; *New Yorker* p32 Mar. 15, 2010; *Oregonian* p38 Aug. 16, 2002

Selected Albums: *Junjo*, 2006; *Esperanza*, 2008; *Chamber Music Society*, 2010

Doug Benc/Getty Images

Sparano, Tony

Oct. 7, 1961– Football coach

Address: Miami Dolphins, 7500 S.W. 30th St., Davie, FL 33314

"I never came into this league to be a position coach," the football coach Tony Sparano told Jeff Darlington for the *Miami Herald* (November 9, 2008), referring to the National Football League (NFL). "I came . . . to be a head coach." Sparano achieved his goal in 2008, when he was named the head coach of the Miami Dolphins. In his first season with Miami, Sparano led the Dolphins to the greatest single-season turnaround in NFL history: the team compiled an 11–5 record, winning nine of their last 10 games and becoming the only team in the league's history to reach the play-offs after losing all but one of their 16 games the previous season. That achievement earned Sparano the NFL's Alumni Coach of the Year Award, and in balloting for the Associated Press 2008 Coach of the Year Award, he finished only one vote behind the Atlanta Falcons' first-year head coach, Mike Smith.

Sparano spent the first 14 years of his career working with college football teams: from 1984 to 1987, and again from 1994 to 1998, with the University of New Haven Chargers, with whom he had played as an undergraduate, and from 1988 until 1993 with the Boston University Terriers. His association with the NFL began in 1999, when he was hired as the offensive quality-control coach for the Cleveland Browns. After two years with the Browns, he worked for the Washington Redskins (2001), the Jacksonville Jaguars (2002), and the Dallas Cowboys (2003–07). Sparano's coaching style has been described as player-friendly and as characterized by an aggressive but encouraging no-nonsense approach. "There are no antics," the Dolphins cornerback Will Allen told Greg Stoda, writing for the *Palm Beach (Florida) Post* (August 3, 2009). "He's just a hard worker. As a player, you appreciate that." The Dolphins linebacker and team co-captain Joey Porter told Stoda, "He's the voice. We follow him. We're the carriers of his message." Sparano is also "so meticulous that he makes other perfectionists look sloppy," Karen Crouse wrote for the *New York Times* (December 28, 2008). "He has a screenwriter's eye for detail, picking up tendencies on game tapes that nobody else notices, and a director's sense of pacing."

The first of three children, Anthony Sparano III was born on October 7, 1961 in West Haven, Connecticut, to Anthony Sparano Jr. and Marie Sparano, who both came from tight-knit Italian-American families. At different times his father held jobs at a metal foundry, as the driver of a liquor truck, and as a furniture upholsterer; his mother worked variously as a waitress, a school crossing guard, and a sewing-machine operator. His father, Sparano told Edgar Thompson for the *Palm Beach (Florida) Post* (July 20, 2008), "worked really hard for the money he got. There were no shortcuts in what you had to do. That's what he taught me." Sparano and his younger sisters were raised in a three-story row house that his family shared with both sets of grandparents in a working-class section of West Haven. As a child Sparano "organized marbles instead of playing with them" and "cleaned his room like a good soldier, no sheet untucked, no shirt unfolded," Greg Bishop wrote for the *New York Times* (September 6, 2008). A sports lover, he rooted for the New York Giants of the NFL and worked in 1973 and 1974 as an usher at the Yale Bowl, in nearby New Haven, when the Giants played there.

Sparano attended the now-defunct Richard C. Lee High School, in New Haven, where he was an excellent student and a standout offensive lineman. He "always had a fascination . . . with helping people," he told Karen Crouse, and fostered dreams of becoming a football coach or a police officer. As a teenager he lost his sight for several weeks after hot grease spattered his face while he was at work in a restaurant. Since then his eyes have been extremely sensitive to light, and he often wears sunglasses indoors and at night as well as outdoors. After his high-school graduation, he attended the University of Central Florida for a semester, then transferred to the University of New Haven, in West Haven. He was a four-year letterman on the school's football team, the Chargers, where he started at the center position. He received a B.A. degree in criminal law in 1982.

Sparano's coaching career began in 1984, when he was hired by the University of New Haven to work with the Chargers' offensive line and serve as the school's recruiting coordinator. Categorized as a part-time employee, he earned only $2,000 a year (about $4,000 in 2008 dollars). He got married that year, too; his wife's earnings enabled the couple to make ends meet. When the Chargers' head coach, Larry McElreavy, left to take over the football program at Columbia University, in 1985, McElreavy's successor, the future Cleveland Browns coach Chris Palmer, made Sparano a full-time member of the staff. For the next three years, Sparano served as New Haven's offensive-line coach and recruiting coordinator. In 1988 he followed Palmer to Boston University, in Massachusetts, where he stayed for six years. He spent two seasons as the Boston Terriers' offensive-line coach, recruiting coordinator, and academic liaison, before being promoted to offensive coordinator, in 1990. He held that post for his final four years there, which included an 11–0 season, in 1993.

In 1994 Sparano returned to the University of New Haven to head the school's football program. In gradually overhauling the program to reflect his no-nonsense style, he introduced a zero-tolerance policy regarding unacceptable behavior on and off the field. In his four years as head coach, he compiled a 41–14–1 overall record and led the Chargers to two National Collegiate Athletic Association (NCAA) Division II play-off appearances. In 1997 the Chargers finished with a 12–2 record and advanced to the Division II championship game, where they lost to Northern Colorado University, 51–0. That year Sparano was named the New York Metropolitan Football Writers Division II Coach of the Year; he was named the New England Football Writers Division II/III Coach of the Year in both 1995 and 1997.

When Chris Palmer became the head coach of the Cleveland Browns, in 1999, Sparano secured his first NFL coaching job, as an offensive quality-control coach, with responsibility for analyzing game films. In 2000 he was promoted to offensive-line coach; under his guidance the team allowed 20 fewer sacks (40) than in the previous season. Palmer was fired at the end of that season, after posting a dismal two-year record of 5–27; Sparano was let go soon afterward. In 2001 the Washington Redskins' coach, Marty Schottenheimer, brought Sparano on board as the tight-ends coach. That job, too, lasted only one season, which the Redskins finished with an 8–8 record. In 2002 the Jacksonville Jaguars' coach, Tom Coughlin, hired Sparano as the tight-ends coach. That season the Jaguars' tight ends performed well, totaling 69 receptions for 712 yards and six touchdowns. Coughlin told Matt Mosley for ESPN.com (July 10, 2008, on-line) that Sparano was "incredibly organized. He's just the type of person who doesn't leave a stone unturned. It was pretty obvious he had some of the characteristics that a head coach needs." Nevertheless, in yet another staff overhaul, Sparano received a pink slip after the 2002 season's end.

In 2003 Sparano accepted the job of tight-ends coach with the Dallas Cowboys, who had lost 11 games and won five in each of the last three seasons. His boss, the Cowboys' new head coach, Bill Parcells, recalled to Mosley, "Tom [Coughlin] told me that Tony was one of the two best assistants he'd ever had. And it didn't take long to figure out what he was talking about." For his part, Sparano recalled to Tom Yantz, "I've coached for a lot of people and worked for a lot of great coaches. Coach Parcells has taught me the most and prepared me the most for this job." In his first year with the Cowboys, Sparano helped develop the team's rookie tight end Jason Witten, a third-round draft choice, into an outstanding All-Pro. During the 2003 season Witten caught 35 passes for 347 yards and a touchdown, tying for fourth among all NFL rookies in receptions and finishing first among the league's rookie tight ends.

After the 2004 season Parcells promoted Sparano to offensive-line coach, a position in which he continued to develop young players. After the 2005 season the New Orleans Saints' new head coach, Sean Payton, who had served as the Cowboys' assistant head coach under Parcells during the previous season, offered Sparano the job of offensive coordinator. In response, Parcells, who was determined to keep Sparano, promoted him to assistant head coach. While serving as the Cowboys' primary play-caller in 2006, Sparano turned their offense into a powerhouse: at the end of that season, they ranked fifth in the NFL in total offense (an average of 360.8 yards per game) and fourth in total points scored (425). He also served as the Cowboys' running-game coordinator that season and helped establish one of the top running attacks in the league, with the running back Julius Jones surpassing the 1,000-yard rushing "barrier" by 84 yards. The Cowboys finished with a 9–7 record that year and earned a play-off appearance, in which they lost to the Seattle Seahawks in the National Football Conference (NFC) wild-card game. Shortly after that loss Parcells retired (for a third time) and was replaced by Wade Phillips, who kept Sparano on as the Cowboys' assistant head coach and offensive-line coach. (Sparano was the only holdover from the Parcells regime.) The Cowboys went on to post an NFL-best 13–3 record during the 2007 season, but they were beaten by the eventual Super Bowl champions, the New York Giants, in the divisional play-off round.

On January 16, 2008 Sparano signed a four-year, $11 million contract to become the Miami Dolphins' head coach, replacing Cam Cameron. He arrived as part of a major overhaul led by Parcells, who had come out of retirement in December 2007 to join the Dolphins as executive vice president of football operations. Parcells had earned a reputation as a "turnaround specialist" for his ability to transform losing franchises into play-off contenders. The Dolphins were in dire need of help: in 2007 they compiled one win and 15 losses—the league's worst record that year and the worst in Dolphins history. Perennial play-off contenders under the legendary coach Don Shula (1970–95), the team had made only one play-off appearance (in 2000) and undergone four coaching changes in the previous eight seasons. Sparano resolved to create a team with a winning mentality; in his first meeting with the players, he conveyed his conviction that Miami would become a winner again. The Dolphins running back Patrick Cobbs recalled to Greg Stoda, "The guy walks into the room, and from his first couple of words you knew that he commands respect. First time he gave a speech, we knew. It doesn't matter who you are, what position you play, what kind of money you make . . . he's the same with everybody. He's going to be that same guy with every single player." As quoted by Jeff Darlington, Sparano said in his introductory press conference, "I think discipline is critical. We'll have discipline here with the Dolphins, there is no question about that. At the same time, we'll treat each other with respect. That's a two-way street. That just doesn't mean that I need the players to respect me, I need to respect the players as well."

In his first season with Miami, Sparano led the Dolphins to the greatest single-season turnaround in NFL history. After losing their first two contests, the team compiled an 11–5 record, winning nine of their last 10 games and becoming the only team in the league's history to reach the play-offs after losing all but one of 16 games the previous season. The Dolphins joined the 1999 Indianapolis Colts as the only two teams in NFL history to win 10 more games than they had the previous year. Observers credited the Dolphins' success to their having taken a smart approach to the game, characterized by minimal penalties and a low turnover ratio; indeed, with 13 turnovers, they set an NFL record (along with the 2008 New York Giants) for fewest turnovers allowed in a single season. The team also used a widely publicized offensive scheme known as the Wildcat, or single-wing offense, in which the running back lines up in the shotgun formation with the option of handing off, running, or throwing; many other teams incorporated the scheme into their playbooks during the course of the season. After defeating the New York Jets, 24–17, in the regular-season finale, the Dolphins won their first American Football Conference (AFC) East title since 2000 and earned their first play-off berth in seven seasons. Then, in the first round of the play-offs, they lost to the Baltimore Ravens, 27–9. Sparano was named the NFL Alumni Coach of the Year and missed by a single vote being selected by the Associated Press as the Coach of the Year.

Going into the 2009 season with the NFL's toughest schedule (based on teams' winning percentages from the previous year), Sparano's Dolphins found it difficult to repeat the Cinderella heroics of 2008. Despite losses in their first three games, a season-ending shoulder injury suffered by their starting quarterback, Chad Pennington, and several other team injuries, the team stayed in the thick of the play-off race going into December, after winning seven of their next 10 games under the promising second-year starting quarterback Chad Henne. The team's play-off hopes, however, faded after they lost their last three games, ending the season with a 7–9 record.

During the 2010 off-season, the Dolphins made two major free-agent acquisitions, signing the linebacker Karlos Dansby, formerly with the Arizona Cardinals, and the Pro Bowl wide receiver Brandon Marshall, formerly with the Denver Broncos. One week before the start of the 2010 season, Bill Parcells stepped down as the Dolphins' executive vice president of football operations, and all decisions regarding the team were handed to the Dolphins' general manager, Jeff Ireland; Parcells has remained with the team as a consultant. Sparano and the Dolphins entered week seven of the 2010 season with a record of 3–2.

"In the high-powered world of the NFL, it's rare to run across a man without pretense, but . . . Sparano might be the exception," Matt Mosley wrote. Greg Stoda described Sparano as being "no frills. He's about as subtle as a punch in the mouth, or the gut. There isn't much room for delicate on the docks, and Sparano has a longshoreman's grit." Sparano "speaks with the thick accent of a Queens cab driver" and "looks like an extra from *The Sopranos*, with a thin mustache, a compact build and a barrel chest," Greg Bishop wrote, referring to the popular 2000s television series. Sparano and his wife, Jeanette, make their home in the Stonebrook Estates community of Davie, Florida. They have two sons, Tony and Andy, and a daughter, Ryan, a high-school softball player. In 2010 Tony Sparano joined the United Football League's Hartford Colonials (whose coach is Chris Palmer) as an assistant defensive-line coach.

—C.C.

Suggested Reading: Associated Press Dec. 18, 2008; ESPN.com (on-line) July 10, 2008; (Fort Lauderdale, Florida) *Sun-Sentinel* Jan. 16, 2008, Aug. 29, 2008; (Hartford, Connecticut) *Courant* C p8 Jan. 17, 2008, C p1 Apr. 12, 2008; Miami Dolphins Official Web site; *Miami Herald* D p1 Nov. 9, 2008; *New York Times* D p7 Sep. 6, 2008, p1 Dec. 28, 2008; (Palm Beach, Florida) *Post* B p1+ July 20, 2008, C p1 Aug. 3, 2009; (St. Petersburg, Florida) *Times* C p8 Jan. 4, 2009

Stuart Wilson / Getty Images

Swanberg, Joe

Aug. 31, 1981– Filmmaker

Address: IFC Films, 323 6th Ave., New York, NY 10014

"One of the more interesting if obvious effects of the digital revolution is that it has become easier for moviemakers of comparatively modest means to get their work into the world than at any other time," Manohla Dargis wrote for the *New York Times* (March 14, 2009, on-line). "These days, all you need is a (relatively) cheap camera and some software to call yourself a filmmaker. You don't even need an actual film print, just a disc you can feed into that ravenous maw called the independent film world, where upstart festival programmers, microdistributors, critics and bloggers are clamoring for directors they can discover, brand and champion as their very own. Hence Joe Swanberg." The director of five feature-length films as well as a Web series, Swanberg is a pioneer of "do-it-yourself" filmmaking, a method based more on practicality than on any philosophy or aesthetic; he has shot most of his films with comparatively inexpensive digital video cameras, enlisted friends to serve as cast and crew, and financed the projects with his own money. Those elements, along with his focus on the everyday concerns of young adults, make him a quintessential member of the so-called "mumblecore" movement, whose films concern the ennui and social anxiety experienced by recent college graduates often unable to express what they feel.

Swanberg initially garnered attention at the South by Southwest (SXSW) Film Festival for his first two features: *Kissing on the Mouth* (2005), a sexually explicit look at post-college relationships, and *LOL* (2006), a study of young men addicted to Internet-based social networks. With *Hannah Takes the Stairs* (2007) and *Nights and Weekends* (2008), two intimate portrayals of fractured relationships, he received further acclaim and fully established himself in the independent-film world. In making all four films, Swanberg relied heavily on improvisation, one of his trademarks; the latter two movies starred the actress and frequent Swanberg collaborator Greta Gerwig, who became known as the "queen" of the mumblecore scene. As a result of his relative success, Swanberg's 2009 film, *Alexander the Last*, made use of a professional producer and cast, prompting some to wonder if the filmmaker had left mumblecore behind.

Joe Swanberg was born on August 31, 1981 in Detroit, Michigan, to Greg and Joan Swanberg. His father worked for a military contractor, and as a result the Swanberg family moved often, eventually settling in Naperville, Illinois. Swanberg attended Naperville Central High School before enrolling at

Southern Illinois University at Carbondale. He told Chris Gore for *chinashopmag.com* (April 2, 2009), "The first thing I can remember from my life is seeing [the movie] *Revenge of the Nerds* when I was just shy of three years old. My dad would reach around me and cover my eyes and ears anytime there was something inappropriate on the screen and it made movies seem exciting and dangerous. I have been in love with them ever since." During high school he worked in a video store and "fell asleep in class every day because I was up late watching movies," he told Gore. In his freshman year Swanberg saw the eccentric film comedy *Raising Arizona* (1987), made by Joel and Ethan Coen; he told the *Chicago Reader* (October 7, 2005), "Making movies is all I've ever wanted to do since." (Before he became committed to making movies, the now six-foot three-inch filmmaker aspired to play professional basketball.)

In 2003 Swanberg graduated from Southern Illinois University at Carbondale with a bachelor's degree in film. That summer he found himself living in his parents' home and worrying that he would not succeed as a filmmaker. Then, in August of that year, he secured a job with the Chicago International Film Festival as a travel coordinator. Through discussions with a fellow film-festival colleague, his then-girlfriend and future wife, Kris Williams, he began to flesh out his position on the state of modern independent cinema. "I was frustrated with a lot of films I was seeing about young people at the time," he told Gore. "I didn't feel that our lives were being accurately represented or that filmmakers were taking enough risks in the way they depicted adults. A lot of things seemed taboo, especially sex and nudity, and that seemed silly to me. I wanted to make a film that was natural and funny and truthful and didn't shy away from anything that my friends and I talked about or did." Swanberg began to write a screenplay in an attempt to reflect his post-collegiate experiences accurately.

The result was a true independent film, with no studio or investor backing of any kind. *Kissing on the Mouth* was made as efficiently and inexpensively as possible: Swanberg tapped Williams (who also served as assistant director) and his friends Kate Winterich and Kevin Pittman to act in the film and cast himself as the male lead. The actors also doubled as the film's crew. "I made the film with my own money, for about $1,200 . . . ," Swanberg recalled to Gore. "I . . . wanted total control over the project and I knew that meant using my own money. I was very realistic about the slim chances of the film finding distribution, and I knew the sexual aspect of the project would keep us out of mainstream theaters, so it didn't make sense to me to try and approach anyone." After a positive response to a screening of the film—then a work in progress—for friends and Carbondale film students, Swanberg completed *Kissing on the Mouth* and posted clips of it on an Internet site, avary.com, for filmmakers seeking and offering advice. An Austin, Texas–based filmmaker, Dan Brown, saw the clip and contacted Swanberg, requesting a DVD of the movie to pass along to a friend at the South by Southwest Film Festival, held annually in Austin. The movie was accepted for the festival, where it had its world premiere in 2005. "It was fun for us to watch the film with an audience for the first time," Swanberg told Gore in 2009. "To this day I have not had a better learning experience as a filmmaker than that first screening. I watched the film in a much more detached, critical way, and it was an important experience. It made me a better filmmaker, and I have been able to see my own work more clearly since then."

Kissing on the Mouth follows four characters as they struggle through the ups and downs of life after college. Swanberg played Patrick, who becomes jealous when Ellen (Winterich), his roommate and longtime friend, begins to date her ex-boyfriend again. The dialogue is almost completely improvised (the other actors received "writing" credits), and the film contains several sexually explicit scenes. It also includes interviews with 20-something nonactors about their lives. For its frank portrayal of early adulthood and its realistic sex scenes, *Kissing on the Mouth* became one of the most talked-about films at SXSW, but subsequent reviews were mixed. "Intended as riposte to the usual frivolous or sensational portraits of American youth, no-budget *Kissing on the Mouth* earns points for being more like real life, even though, generally speaking, truth is duller than fiction," Dennis Harvey wrote for *Variety* (September 19–25, 2005). After viewing the film at the Chicago International Film Festival, Michael Wilmington described it for the *Chicago Tribune* (October 7, 2005) as "an unvarnished, unprotected look at sex in the city—among a quartet of sexually active or wishful post-collegiates—that almost makes up in audacity what it lacks in conventional polish."

Buoyed by his newfound status as a successful underground filmmaker, Swanberg made his second feature film, *LOL*, for $3,000. Released in 2006, *LOL* concentrates on the effects of Internet and cell-phone use on social interactions; its three protagonists, the recent college graduates Alex, Tim, and Chris, are so obsessed with chat rooms and camera phones that they cannot form or maintain personal relationships. (The film's title is an abbreviation for "laughing out loud," commonly used in Internet communication.) A synopsis on the film's Web site reads, "This up-to-the-second feature intimately explores masculinity in the new millennium, a time when young men are trying to decipher the mixed messages of modern relationships and technology." Swanberg, who was also the film's producer, editor, and director of photography, played Tim; he shared writing credits with C. Mason Wells and Kevin Bewersdorf. (Only Winterich returned from *Kissing on the Mouth*, in the role of Tessa.) *LOL* also marked the debut of Gerwig, who was brought into the film by chance: Gerwig's then-boyfriend, Wells, played Chris, who is in a long-distance relationship, and Wells asked Gerwig if he could use a voice-mail message she had left on his phone as a message from Chris's girlfriend. Swanberg later expanded the role of the girlfriend and asked Gerwig to play the part via cellphone photographs and conversations.

LOL was relatively well received, earning accolades at SXSW. In a review for the *New York Times* (April 23, 2006, on-line), Nathan Lee wrote, "The impact of technology on social relations has received subtler analysis elsewhere (see the films of David Cronenberg), but this small-scale, microbudget indie speaks the theme with a fresh voice. . . . Authentic in texture if narrow in scope, *LOL* is a movie about the way we live—or rather about the way white, urban, heterosexual circuit boys are failing to live."

Swanberg met Gerwig in person when both attended a screening of *LOL*, and he was so impressed by her that he cast her as the title character in the 2007 film *Hannah Takes the Stairs,* which Swanberg also co-wrote with her and the actor Kent Osborne. (Additional material in the screenplay was provided by other cast members.) In the film Hannah, an aimless recent college graduate, shares an office—and pursues romances—with two men while still harboring affection for her former boyfriend. *Hannah Takes the Stairs* elevated Swanberg and Gerwig to fame in independent-film circles and brought the mumblecore genre more mainstream recognition. Matt Zoller Seitz observed for the *New York Times* (August 22, 2007, on-line), "For newcomers to D.I.Y. [do-it-yourself], the movie's snappy but unadventurous style— episodic structure, deadpan performances and raggedy, improvisational dialogue—makes it a less-than-ideal introduction. . . . [But] for devotees of recent D.I.Y. moviemaking, *Hannah* will evoke melancholy feelings, and not just because the heroine finds (probably temporary) bliss without seriously examining her preconceptions." Discussing his preference for improvised dialogue, Swanberg told Robert Levin for filmschoolrejects.com (March 14, 2009), "The reason that I've stayed away from a script is because . . . all of the characters [might] end up just sounding like me." In his films, he added, the actors are "always saying things that they would actually say. They're not ever having to interpret my words."

Swanberg seemed to have found an ideal collaborator and muse in Gerwig, and the two worked together as co-directors and co-writers of *Nights and Weekends* (2008). In that film Gerwig and Swanberg played a couple, James and Mattie, who attempt to maintain a long-distance relationship. An official selection of the SXSW, Stockholm, and London film festivals, *Nights and Weekends* continued the theme of emotional uncertainty Swanberg had explored in his previous films; James and Mattie have difficulty being open with each other after having spent time apart. Critics were split in their opinions of the film. Andrew O'Hehir, writing for *Salon.com* (March 10, 2008), described it as "a vastly leaner and more elliptical film than *Han-*

nah Takes the Stairs." He wrote, "We watch James and Mattie thrown together and torn apart, thrown together and torn apart, in a sort of erotic molecular action. There's an intimacy and a universality to these characters that feels a world away from the post-collegiate claustrophobia of *Hannah Takes the Stairs.*" Comparing the movie to the work of iconic filmmakers of the past, O'Hehir added, "Take away their cell phones and throw some different outfits on them, and James and Mattie could be characters from [John] Cassavetes or the French New Wave or [Ingmar] Bergman." Noel Murray wrote for the *A.V. Club* (October 16, 2008, on-line), "To some extent, if you've seen one Swanberg film, you've seen them all; *Nights and Weekends* contains the usual mix of frank, awkward sex scenes and couples talking passive-aggressively around each other. . . . But Swanberg and Gerwig also have a gift for constructing the kind of moments rarely seen in contemporary American independent film. When Gerwig cheerfully shoos Swanberg out of her apartment so she can change for their not-quite-a-date, then crumples into sobs as soon as he steps out, it's both a powerful, beautifully acted scene and a critical study of what becomes of the noncommittal."

Swanberg parted ways with Gerwig after *Nights and Weekends* to begin production of his latest directorial effort, *Alexander the Last,* for which he shared writing credits with several of the actors. The film marked his first use of a professional cast, which nonetheless continued his tradition of improvisation. *Alexander the Last* also found the director edging closer to the mainstream in other ways, as one of the film's producers was Noah Baumbach—himself an underground-film icon who achieved mainstream recognition for his 2006 sleeper hit, *The Squid and the Whale*, and the 2007 movie *Margot at the Wedding*. (Baumbach cast Gerwig in his 2010 comedy, *Greenberg*.) *Alexander the Last* premiered at SXSW in March 2009 and was made available on-demand via cable through the International Film Channel the same day.

An examination of a more mature theme, *Alexander the Last* focuses on marriage and "the challenges of monogamy amidst myriad sexual and creative temptations," according to the film's Web site. In the story Alex (played by Jess Weixler), a stage actress, begins to pursue a co-star, Jamie (Barlow Jacobs)—in competition with her sister— while Alex's husband, a musician, is away. Keith Phipps wrote for the *A.V. Club* (March 24, 2010), "Here, both filmmaker and characters have moved a little further along. Swanberg takes greater care with his compositions and the film's construction; one elegantly edited sequence flits between the rehearsal for a lovemaking scene and its offstage corollary. His protagonists play for higher stakes, too. As Weixler steps up her teasing campaign and Jacobs begins to respond, the film takes on a sense of mounting dread. There's more in the balance now than who goes home with whom at the end of the night." To the critic David Denby, the higher production values and emotionally mature content of the film signaled a shift away from mumblecore. In an article for the *New Yorker* (March 16, 2009), Denby wrote, "In the past, people in Swanberg's movies slept with one another without much consequence—the plots were not fully worked out, and many implications, not to mention relationships, were left hanging. The slapdash style of storytelling was part of Swanberg's cool contempt for mainstream filmmaking. But in *Alexander the Last* he's advancing toward a firmer structure and more emotionally explicit scenes. . . . [His actors] work up an emotion much more clearly than the earlier casts of amateurs did, though without the surprises. In brief, Swanberg is giving up some of the methods of mumblecore."

With his wife, Swanberg is the creator, writer, and star of a Web series called *Young American Bodies*. The series premiered in 2006 on nerve.com and has been available since its third season on IFC.com. In seven-minute episodes, the show follows the lives of 20-somethings living in Chicago. Swanberg has worked as a producer, actor, and crew member on the films of his wife and friends. He was a producer of a film by his wife (who now goes by the name Kris Swanberg), *It Was Great, But I Was Ready to Come Home* (2009); worked as the cinematographer for Kentucker Audley's romantic comedy *Open Five* (2010); acted in Michael Harring's *The Mountain, the River and the Road* (2009); and served as the second-unit director for David Lowery's drama *St. Nick* (2009). With Kent Osborne he wrote and directed the short comedy *Swedish Blueballs* (2008). His acting credits for 2010 include appearances in the films *Audrey the Trainwreck* and *Everyone Says I Look Just Like Her*. He will also be seen in "A Horrible Way to Die," scheduled for release in 2011.

Swanberg has also written and performed music. He has played in a group called the Electronic Toys Band, and mp3 files of his originals songs are available for free download on his Web site.

Swanberg, who lives with his wife in Chicago, considers the mumblecore tag associated with his films a mixed blessing. He told Levin, "I have a weird relationship to mumblecore and to the backlash just because they both are things that I feel like have been put upon me. . . . It's hard to have a bad attitude about it because in order for there to be a backlash about it there has to be generally praise and support. That stuff, all of it including the backlash, is all part of a general discussion that is the whole purpose of making the work in the first place." He also noted that as the original crop of mumblecore filmmakers age, their work will reflect their maturity, and the movement will take on new meaning. "I can only speak for myself, but my working method is changing and the work itself I feel like is changing, so the things that people used as the definition of mumblecore isn't necessarily true to the work anymore and especially won't be as the characters move into their 30's and 40's, but I think the term might stick with all of us and be

redefined as we change."

—W.D.

Suggested Reading: *Chicago Reader* p14 Oct. 7, 2005; *chinashopmag.com* Apr. 2, 2009; filmschoolrejects.com Mar. 14, 2009; *New Yorker* p114 Mar. 16, 2009

Selected Films: *Kissing on the Mouth*, 2005; *LOL*, 2006; *Hannah Takes the Stairs*, 2007; *Nights and Weekends*, 2008; *Alexander the Last*, 2009

Selected Internet Series: *Young American Bodies*, 2006–

Frederick Breedon/Getty Images

Swift, Taylor

Dec. 13, 1989– Singer

Address: Taylor Swift Entertainment, 242 W. Main St., PMB 412, Hendersonville, TN 37075

The singer Taylor Swift "is one of pop's finest songwriters, country's foremost pragmatist and more in touch with her inner life than most adults," Jon Caramanica wrote for the *New York Times* (December 21, 2008). Since she made her recording debut, in 2006, the 21-year-old Swift—who writes or co-writes nearly all of her own material—has not only sold more than 13 million albums; she has also seen more than 25 million paid Internet downloads of her songs, more than any other country-music artist to date. Her two studio albums, *Taylor Swift* (2006) and *Fearless* (2008), both cracked the Top 10 of the *Billboard* 200 album chart, and *Fearless* was the first album in nearly a decade to hold down the number-one spot on that chart for more than two months, making Swift the biggest-selling artist of 2008 in any genre. Her third studio album, *Speak Now*, was released on October 25, 2010. While critics have praised her lyrics and voice—which one writer called "airy," another "light and breathy"—Swift's success has been attributed largely to her use of the Internet, particularly the social-networking site MySpace.com, to attract publicity and build a fan base. Amy Raphael wrote for the London *Observer* (February 1, 2009), "Swift is unlike any country star before her, her mainstream pop aesthetic attracting a devoted young audience in what is traditionally a middle-aged market. . . . The appeal is not just smart pop with country roots; here's a star who doesn't believe in the us-and-them divide between artist and audience. In this, she is following a country music tradition that dictates strong contact with fans. . . . So, despite her success, Swift is still the girl next door, the clean-living role model who is an antidote to Britney [Spears], a tonic in these days of destructive, dramatic pop stars." While remaining grounded in the country tradition, Swift has also incorporated elements of other genres in her music, which has contributed to her mass appeal. Sasha Frere-Jones, writing for the *New Yorker* (November 10, 2008), called Swift a "prodigy," adding, "What is surprising about Swift is her indifference to category or genre. She is considered part of Nashville's country-pop tradition only because she writes narrative songs with melodic clarity and dramatic shape—Nashville's stock-in-trade. But such songs also crop up in R&B and rap and rock. It is evidence of her ear that she not only identifies with songs in other genres but performs them, even though Nashville is a musically conservative place. . . . Swift is not an agent of revolution; she, much like Beyoncé, is a preternaturally skilled student of established values. Her precociousness isn't about her chart success, but lies in the quality of her work, how fully she's absorbed the lessons of her elders and how little she seems to care which radio format will eventually claim her. Change the beat and the instruments around the voice, and her songs could work anywhere."

The daughter of Andrea and Scott Swift, Taylor Alison Swift was born on December 13, 1989 in Wyomissing, Pennsylvania. She has a brother, Austin, who is three years her junior. Swift's mother, who was a successful career woman before she began raising a family, chose the name "Taylor" to hide her daughter's gender—and avoid discrimination—from the girl's future prospective employers. Swift spent her early years on a Christmas-tree farm, which her father, who worked as a stockbroker, ran as a hobby. She was introduced to music by her grandmother Marjorie Finlay, who was an opera singer. After being exposed to a wide variety of musical genres, she felt particularly drawn to country music. "LeAnn Rimes was my first impression of country music," Swift recalled to Amy Ra-

phael. "I got her first album when I was six. I just really loved how she could be making music and having a career at such a young age." Early on Swift also developed a love of writing and started composing poetry. In the fourth grade she won a national poetry contest for a three-page poem titled "Monster in My Closet." Her mother noted to J. Freedom du Lac for the *Washington Post* (February 28, 2008), "She wrote all the time. If music hadn't worked out, I think she'd be going off to college to take journalism classes or trying to become a novelist. But her writing took an interesting twist when she picked up the guitar and applied her writing to music."

At the age of 10, Swift began performing at county fairs, festivals, and karaoke contests around her hometown. At 11 she gave her first major public performance, singing the national anthem at a Philadelphia 76ers basketball game. At 12 she learned to play the 12-string guitar; it has been noted that she would practice the guitar for hours at a time, until her calluses bled. (Swift now often plays a Swarovski-crystal-encrusted guitar.) She recalled to Bruce DeMara for the *Toronto Star* (January 12, 2008), "As soon as I picked up a guitar and learned three chords, I started writing songs. Songwriting just came as another form of expression." While attending Wyomissing Junior High School, Swift found it difficult to fit in with the other girls, which led her to channel her emotions through songwriting. One of her earliest songs, "The Outside," was later included on her debut album.

When Swift was 13 years old, her parents sold their Christmas-tree farm and moved the family to Hendersonville, Tennessee, near Nashville, the nation's unofficial country-music capital; there, Swift was able to focus on her music career. She recalled to Dan DeLuca for the *Philadelphia Inquirer* (November 7, 2007), "I literally walked up and down and knocked on doors and said: 'Hi, I'm Taylor. I want a record deal.' When you've got nothing to lose, you have everything to gain." After rejecting a deal at RCA that would have prevented her from recording her own songs, she became, at 14, the youngest staff writer ever hired at the Sony Tree publishing house. Swift was home-schooled in the mornings before heading off to Nashville each afternoon for various writing assignments; it was during that time that she honed her songwriting skills.

Swift received her big break while performing at Nashville's famed Bluebird Café. There, she caught the attention of a music-business veteran, Scott Borchetta, who quickly signed her to his newly formed independent label, Big Machine Records. Swift "has a real inner vision, a real inner directedness," Borchetta explained to DeLuca. He added, "I thought: This girl has the potential to be a really big star. Her songs have these extraordinary takes on everyday life. There's a certain slant, a sense of humor and a sarcasm to them." Wanting to be embraced by the country-music audience, Swift appeared in a series of film shorts that aired on the

Great American Country (GAC) cable network. She followed those in 2006 with her debut single, "Tim McGraw," named for her favorite male country-music star; the song reached number six on the *Billboard* country-singles chart. In October of that year, she released her debut album, *Taylor Swift*, which arrived on the *Billboard* 200 chart at number 19 and sold 39,000 copies in its first week. Albums sales rose dramatically after the release of her second single, "Teardrops on My Guitar," about a secret high-school crush. After reaching the number-two spot on the country-singles chart, the song achieved crossover status, peaking at number 13 on the *Billboard* Hot 100 chart. *Taylor Swift* went on to spawn three more Top 10 country singles ("Our Song," "Picture to Burn," and "Should've Said No"). The album reached number one on *Billboard*'s top country-albums chart (after 39 weeks) and peaked at number five on the *Billboard* 200 chart; it has since sold more than 4.3 million copies in the U.S. and has been certified quadruple-platinum by the Recording Industry Association of America (RIAA). It is also the longest-charting album by a female country artist in the era of Nielsen SoundScan (a sales-counting system established in 1991), with over 158 weeks logged on the *Billboard* 200 album chart.

Taylor Swift received widespread praise from critics. Nick Cristiano wrote in a review for the *Philadelphia Inquirer* (November 12, 2006), "[Swift] displays a maturity beyond her years while retaining the freshness of youth, just as her slightly husky voice balances between open-hearted innocence and life-scarred experience. There's a feistiness to country-rockers 'Picture to Burn' and 'Should've Said No,' but no bubblegum angst or melodrama. Much of the music has a bracing acoustic country texture that reflects the taste and restraint of the singing and writing." Jon Caramanica declared for the *New York Times* (September 7, 2008) that the album is "a small masterpiece of pop-minded country."

Swift spent most of 2007 touring in support of her first album, performing mainly as an opening act for such country stars as George Strait, Brad Paisley, Kenny Chesney, Tim McGraw, and Faith Hill. In May of that year, Swift was nominated for the honor of top new female vocalist by the Academy of Country Music Awards. (She lost to Miranda Lambert.) Later that year she took home the Horizon Award, given by the Country Music Association (CMA), making her the second-youngest CMA winner ever. (The award is given annually to up-and-coming artists; previous winners include Carrie Underwood, the Dixie Chicks, and LeAnn Rimes, who at 15 became the youngest winner.) On October 14, 2007 Swift released a promotional EP, *Sounds of the Season: The Taylor Swift Holiday Collection*, exclusively through the discount-department-store chain Target. Also in 2007 Swift won the songwriter-of-the-year award from the Nashville Songwriters Association.

Swift continued to tour in 2008, with such country acts as Alan Jackson and Rascal Flatts, and made high-profile appearances at a wide variety of events. On February 10, 2008 she appeared at the 50th Annual Grammy Awards ceremony, held at the Staples Center in Los Angeles, California; she received a Grammy nomination in the best-new-artist category but lost to the British crooner Amy Winehouse. Swift next gave a memorable performance at the 43d Annual Academy of Country Music Awards ceremony, which was held at the MGM Grand Garden Arena on May 18, 2008 in Las Vegas, Nevada, where she was named top new vocalist. After beginning her performance of the song "Should've Said No" in an unassuming sweatshirt-and-jeans ensemble, she revealed a short black halter dress underneath, concluding the song under a waterfall. During the summer of 2008, Swift released a CD/DVD set, *Beautiful Eyes*, which featured alternate versions of previously released tracks and was sold exclusively at Wal-Mart. The DVD portion of the set included the music videos of some of her best-known singles (among them "Tim McGraw" and "Teardrops on My Guitar"), as well as various extras. The album debuted at number one on *Billboard*'s top country-albums chart after selling 45,000 copies in its first week. During that same week Swift's debut album held the number-two spot, making her the first artist to hold the top two positions on the country-albums chart since LeAnn Rimes in 1997.

Swift released her much-awaited second album, *Fearless*, on November 11, 2008. The album debuted at number one on the *Billboard* 200 album charts and reportedly sold 592,304 copies in its first week of release. That figure marked the largest opening-week sales in the U.S. that year by a female artist in any musical genre and the fourth-highest overall, behind Lil Wayne, AC/DC, and Coldplay. *Fearless* went on to hold the top spot on the *Billboard* 200 album chart for 11 nonconsecutive weeks, marking the first time in a decade that an album had spent that much time at the top of the charts; it also topped the *Billboard* top country-albums chart for 26 nonconsecutive weeks. The album produced five Top 10 hits ("Change," "Love Story," "Fearless," "You Belong with Me," and "Jump Then Fall") and eight Top 20 hits (including "You're Not Sorry," "White Horse," and "Untouchable"). It also became the first album in music history to produce 12 Top 40 hits. As with her debut, Swift wrote or co-wrote every song on *Fearless*. By the end of that year, she had become the top-selling musical artist of 2008 and the first artist in the history of Nielsen SoundScan to have two albums in the Top 10 on the year-end album chart, with *Fearless* and *Taylor Swift* finishing at number three and six, respectively. *Fearless* has since been certified sextuple-platinum by the RIAA. (On October 26, 2009 the album was re-released as *Fearless: Platinum Edition*, with six new songs.)

Fearless was also a major critical success. Jody Rosen, in a review for *Rolling Stone* (November 13, 2008, on-line), which gave the album four stars, called Swift "a songwriting savant with an intuitive gift for verse-chorus-bridge architecture" and wrote that her music "mixes an almost impersonal professionalism—it's so rigorously crafted it sounds like it has been scientifically engineered in a hit factory—with confessions that are squirmingly intimate and true."

In January 2009 Swift made her first musical guest appearance on *Saturday Night Live*, becoming the youngest country singer to appear on the show since its premiere, in 1975. Her massive popularity helped draw *SNL*'s highest ratings since the vice-presidential candidate Sarah Palin's appearance on the show in November 2008. The following month Swift performed her song "Fifteen" with Miley Cyrus at the 51st Annual Grammy Awards ceremony. That April Swift launched her first North American headlining tour. Between the end of April and the beginning of October 2009, Swift performed in the U.S. and Canada at more than 50 concerts, all of which sold out, many in minutes; in November she performed several sold-out dates in England. The *Fearless* tour ran through June 2010 and included a series of concerts in Australia and three dozen additional shows in North America.

In 2009 Swift was showered with awards and accolades. In March she took home album-of-the-year honors for *Fearless*, the award for top female vocalist, and the video-of-the-year award (for "Love Story") at the 44th Annual Academy of Country Music Awards ceremony. She was also presented with the academy's Crystal Milestone Award, which is given for outstanding achievement in country music. (Swift is only the second artist to receive the prestigious award; Garth Brooks won it in 2007.) That summer Swift won two Country Music Television (CMT) Awards (video of the year and female video of the year for "Love Story") and two Teen Choice Awards (best album—*Fearless*—and best female artist). Then, on September 13, 2009, Swift became the first country singer in history to capture an MTV Video Music Award, when she won in the best-female-video category for her song "You Belong with Me." Her history-making win was largely overshadowed, however, by what happened immediately afterward. During Swift's acceptance speech the rapper and producer Kanye West came on stage and grabbed the microphone from her to declare that Beyoncé's video for the song "Single Ladies (Put a Ring on It)," nominated for the same award, should have won. He then handed the microphone back to Swift, who was visibly too shaken to finish her speech. When Beyoncé later won the award for best video of the year for "Single Ladies," she invited Swift back on stage to finish her acceptance speech. West, who was removed from the show for his actions, received thunderous criticism in the media the following day, even drawing a harsh comment from President Barack Obama. Following Swift's appearance on the daytime talk show *The View* two days later to address the matter, West contacted her to apologize personally; she has since forgiven him. On November 7, 2009 Swift returned to *Saturday Night Live*, as both host and musical guest. During her opening monologue, she made light of the Kanye West incident and poked fun at her personal life.

November 2009 brought Swift still more honors: she became the first solo female act in a decade to claim the entertainer-of-the-year award from the Country Music Association, and she picked up five prizes at the 37th Annual American Music Awards (AMA), including those for favorite female pop/rock artist, favorite female country artist, and AMA artist of the year. The following month Swift received eight Grammy nominations, including those for record of the year, song of the year, and album of the year.

On January 31, 2010 Swift performed with the singer Stevie Nicks and the singer-songwriter Butch Walker at the 52nd Annual Grammy Awards ceremony. Her album *Fearless* took home the Grammy for album of the year, making her, at 20 years of age, the youngest artist in history to win that prize. Swift also won Grammys for best country album, best country song ("White Horse," with co-composer Liz Rose), and best female country vocal performance ("White Horse"). The next month Swift made her feature-film acting debut, in Garry Marshall's romantic comedy *Valentine's Day* (2010), whose cast also included Julia Roberts, Ashton Kutcher, Anne Hathaway, Jessica Biel, Jamie Foxx, Kathy Bates, George Lopez, and Shirley MacLaine, among many others. Despite tepid critical reactions, the film was a box-office success, grossing more than $213 million worldwide.

Swift's third studio album, *Speak Now*, arrived in stores on October 25, 2010. Its lead single, "Mine," had been released the previous August; it has since sold over one million copies. Swift sang another, "Innocent," which is reportedly about Kanye West, at the 2010 MTV Music Video Awards ceremony on September 12. She wrote those and the 12 other tracks on *Speak Now*; like those on her first two albums, the songs are autobiographical, each representing a confession to a particular person. "Back to December," "Dear John," and "Better Than Revenge" are aimed at Taylor Lautner (who stars in the *Twilight* films), the singer-songwriter John Mayer, and Joe Jonas of the Jonas Brothers, respectively. Swift planned to tour internationally in support of the album in 2011.

Swift, who has blond hair and blue eyes and is five feet 11 inches tall, lives in Nashville. Among her many philanthropic efforts, she has donated tens of thousands of dollars to the American Red Cross. She has landed several endorsement deals: she currently serves as the face of the l.e.i. clothing brand and has lent her name to its line of sundresses, which are sold exclusively at Wal-Mart. She has also released her own line of fashion dolls through the toymaker Jakks Pacific. In July 2008 Swift graduated from Aaron Academy, a private Christian school in Hendersonville, Tennessee, which serves as a base for home-schooled students. In 2010 she ranked third on *Forbes*'s annual list of the highest-earning artists in country music, with an estimated $45 million in earnings.

—C.C.

Suggested Reading: All Music Guide Web site; (London) *Sunday Telegraph* p12+ Apr. 26, 2009; *Los Angeles Times* F p13+ Oct. 26, 2008; *New York Times* AR p1+ Nov. 9, 2008, AR p1+ Aug. 2, 2009; *New Yorker* p88+ Nov. 10, 2008; (Ottawa, Canada) *Citizen* B p6 Sep. 4, 2007; *Philadelphia Inquirer* E p1+ Nov. 7, 2007; Taylor Swift Web site; *Washington Post* C p1+ Feb. 28, 2008

Selected Albums: *Taylor Swift*, 2006; *Sounds of the Season: The Taylor Swift Holiday Collection* (EP), 2007; *Beautiful Eyes* (CD/DVD set), 2008; *Fearless*, 2008; *Speak Now*, 2010

Swiss, Jamy Ian

Nov. 30, 1952– Magician; writer

Address: c/o Magical Nights Inc., 70-72 108th St., Suite 2N, Forest Hills, NY 11375

"One of my great satisfactions in being a magician is that it is the most honest living I have ever made," Jamy Ian Swiss, who launched his career in magic when he was 29, declared on his Web site. "As Karl Germain, a world-famous conjurer at the turn of the century, said, 'The magician is the most honest of all professionals. He first promises to deceive you, and then he does.'" "The Honest Liar," as he likes to be called, the 58-year-old Swiss is among the world's masters of sleight-of-hand illusions, which rely on extraordinary manual dexterity and are usually performed with coins, cups, balls, or—Swiss's specialty and "overriding passion," in his words—playing cards. In an interview for penguinmagic.com (August 10, 2004), Swiss named among his favorite card illusions the "think-of-a-card effect," in which a card that is merely imagined by someone is revealed; that seemingly impossible feat appeals to Swiss "because it breaks down many of the audience's preconceptions about what might constitute a card trick when you can crawl into their heads without them even touching a card." He has also called himself a "sleight-of-mind" illusionist, whose apparent mind-reading abilities depend on "pure psychology, subtle influence, deft illusion, uncanny intuition, and a healthy dose of downright deception," according to an on-line blurb for a show of his at the headquarters of the American Associa-

tion for the Advancement of Science in October 2009.

Swiss, who has performed in hundreds of venues in a dozen countries and at many conferences and conventions of businesspeople and other professionals, is also a scholar and philosopher of magic, and he has studied its psychology in depth. He is the author of *Shattering Illusions: Essays on the History, Ethics and Presentation of Magic* (2002); monographs devoted to subjects including "invisible" thread, classic card routines, coin tricks, and psychological aspects of magic; and dozens of essays and book reviews for *Genii, the Conjurer's Magazine* and other trade journals. He co-authored *The Art of Magic* (1998), the book version of the same-titled PBS documentary, in which he appeared, and he has served as a consultant for, editor of, or contributor to books including *Magic for Dummies* (1998), by David Pogue; *Visual Explanations: Images and Quantities, Evidence and Narrative* (1997), by Edward R. Tufte; and *How to Play with Your Food* (1992) and *How to Play in Traffic* (1997), by Penn & Teller. Swiss has lectured widely on magic and held clinics for magicians at all skill levels. He has also advised law-enforcement agencies on street scams and casino operators on methods of gaming the system. A co-founder of the nonprofit organizations National Capital Area Skeptics and New York City Skeptics, he is an outspoken fraud-buster. Swiss performs regularly in New York City's longest-running Off-Broadway magic show, *Monday Night Magic*, which he helped to establish. "What magic is out to do isn't just to amaze you but to achieve what [the magician] Whit Haydn calls putting 'a burr under the saddle of the mind' . . . ," Swiss said to Adam Gopnik, writing for the *New Yorker* (March 17, 2008). "The mind starts working. . . . It's the situation of someone whose mind is alive! It's the state of the scientist, or the artist—and magic is a fringe art, but it's not a fringe subject. Truth, deception, and mystery are big material, and they're the natural, the intrinsic subject of magic. And I propose that it's the only art form where that's the intrinsic subject. And that's why, with all the indignities and absurdities of being a professional magician, we'll always need magic."

Jamy Ian Swiss was born on November 30, 1952 in the New York City borough of Brooklyn, where he grew up. According to Gopnik, Swiss was close to his father, Evans C. Reitman-Swiss, who worked for much of his adult life as an executive in the textile industry and later received a law degree, but not his mother. A self-described "extremely introverted" child who wore thick-lensed eyeglasses, he spent much time alone, reading, writing, and playing music. "I had all the qualifications to achieve excellence in magic," Swiss told Mike Guerra for the Web site cardmsg.com (September 2003). "I was a fat four-eyed kid with a speech impediment." One day when Swiss was seven, his father was fooled by a trick that a friend of his performed with a Color Vision Box. The still-popular device

Courtesy of Lee Graham

Jamy Ian Swiss

consists of a small covered box containing a cube decorated on each side with a circle, each a different color. The magician faces away while the spectator chooses a color, replaces the cube in the box with the chosen circle on top, and covers the box. The magician, by means of a rapid series of movements hidden from the spectator, places the cover on the side of the box, leaving the colored circle exposed, and holds the box so that he can see the color while the spectator sees only the covered box. In that way the magician can correctly name the chosen color. An examination of the box and the cube reveals nothing to the spectator. The elder Swiss bought a Color Vision Box at Lou Tannen's Magic Shop, a famous magicians' hangout in New York City, where the proprietor himself revealed the secret of the trick to him; he then performed it for young Jamy and taught him how to do it. "This is how I learned magic, one trick at a time, for the next several years," Swiss recalled to the penguinmagic.com interviewer. His love for magic blossomed under the tutelage of his father. At 11 he presented a magic show at his school. The next year he performed Amadeo Acrobatic Matchbox, Dizzy Dominoes, the Money Paddle, and other tricks at a friend's bar-mitzvah party.

As his interest in magic grew, Swiss began frequenting Lou Tannen's Magic Shop, first with his father and then on his own. "You just can't imagine the effect Tannen's could have in those days on a shy kid with a speech impediment," he told Adam Gopnik. "It was a scene! Everyone would be there! There were photographs of magicians from floor to ceiling, and shadow boxes filled with effects, and Tannen's symbol, a hat and a rabbit, was inlaid right in the linoleum. . . . The magicians were ev-

erywhere, and they were such elegant and resourceful men. They would all drop in and do work just for the pleasure of it. Lou Tannen himself was there, a kind man who loved magic and sympathized with kids." "Lou became my first sleight-of-hand instructor, over the counter," Swiss told the penguinmagic.com interviewer. He was thrilled the day that Tannen invited him "into the hallowed halls of the back room to have a look" at the misprinted or damaged books that Tannen would sell to youngsters at a discount. In that way Swiss began to build his own library of magic books, with such classics as *The Tarbell Course in Magic*, by Harlan Tarbell, *The Royal Road to Card Magic*, by Jean Hugard and Frederick Braue, and *Close-Up Card Magic*, by Harry Lorayne. Also at Tannen's Swiss met Earl "Presto" Johnson, a specialist in sleights involving cigarettes and coins. Johnson taught Swiss his first coin tricks, including the "palm to palm switch," now a magicians' standard, and several other techniques of Johnson's invention. Swiss regularly attended magic shows in New York City starring such experts as Lorayne, Frank Garcia, Slydini, Derek Dingle, and Albert Goshman. While in high school he earned money as a guitarist in a rock band, performing at clubs, weddings, and bar mitzvahs.

After he graduated from high school, Swiss held jobs in sales, mostly in pet shops or suppliers. In his early 20s he also began writing for a national pet-industry trade journal and made a name for himself in that field. "My real motivation was not in the retail business, although I was good at it, but rather the science and natural history education areas," Swiss told Guerra. Swiss was also a wildlife activist during those years, giving talks on wolf conservation. Swiss, who was largely self-educated in the subject, was turned down, after three interviews, for the position of director of education at the Staten Island Zoo. (The job was given to someone who already worked at the zoo.) "I realized that I would not have another opportunity to enter that industry without [professional] credentials, as the zoo and aquarium world was in the midst of professionalizing," Swiss told *Current Biography.* Swiss then left the pet and aquarium industry.

In the mid-1970s Swiss became the part owner of a private telephone company that sold, installed, and serviced business-telephone systems. Concurrently he resumed his contacts with the New York City magic community. He attended magic conventions, including the annual Tannen's Magic Jubilee, which offered lectures and demonstrations by professional magicians. At the 1976 convention Swiss became "fascinated" by Peter Samelson's "theatrical and intelligent approach to magic, unlike anything I had ever seen." "He did ten minutes of close-up magic that rocked my basic assumptions about magic," Swiss told the penguinmagic.com interviewer. At subsequent shows that Swiss attended, Samelson impressed him with his ability to incorporate drama and real-life subject matter into his presentations. After about a year Samelson accepted Swiss's invitation to join him for a meal, and the two became friends and professional associates. While retaining his daytime telephone-company job, Swiss devoted evenings and weekends to serving Samelson as a consultant, business adviser, and co-writer and co-director of his stage show. Swiss edited Samelson's book, *Theatrical Close-Up* (1984), and wrote its introduction. "It was . . . the first time I ever saw a contemporary, full-time magician up close and personal, as it were, making a living at magic," Swiss told Guerra. "So when I got out of the phone business, and it was time for a new career, magic came to mind."

Swiss was then 29. With his wife's encouragement and financial support, he left the phone company and took a year off from working in order to study magic full time. "My then-wife said that if I didn't try magic then, I would always wonder about it the rest of my life," Swiss told Guerra. He told Gopnik, "Mastering magic at twenty-nine is as late to begin seriously as it would be if you were studying violin." In what he has described as one of the most productive periods of his life, he did little else besides practice magic in front of a mirror for as many as 60 hours a week. He received help from Geoff Latta, a magician who specialized in close-up sleight-of-hand magic with coins and playing cards. "Whereas Peter Samelson influenced me significantly in my thinking about theater, Geoff became a lasting influence on my approach to technique," Swiss told Guerra. "Geoff is simply the best technician with both cards and coins I've ever known, and is an equally inventive originator with both, creating many original tricks as well as sleights." Among other tricks, Latta (who died in 2008) taught Swiss ways to perform the "classic pass," in which a deck of cards is secretly cut but the order of the cards appears to be undisturbed. After about a year of solitary practice, Swiss performed his first two gigs as a professional magician, both at corporate Christmas parties. Aware that he needed a steady source of income, he enrolled at a bartending school. As he told Gopnik, he had "heard somewhere that you could work as a magic bartender"—someone who, Eve Zibart wrote for the *Washington Post* (April 20, 1990), "not only pulls in the bartender's bag of palaver and the familiar implements of liquid amusement . . . but also withstands the strains of extreme audience mobility, erratic attention and even the occasional inebriated intervention." "I loved being a bartender . . . ," Swiss told Gopnik. "Magic was for me partly an art thing, partly a blue-collar artisanal thing, so being a magic bartender was ideal." Swiss recalled to Guerra that those early days as a performer were "a difficult but very useful period, as it got me some experience with real people."

In 1985 the comic magician Bob Sheets hired Swiss as the magic bartender at the Brook Farm Inn of Magic, near Washington, D.C., a venue for comedy and magic dinner-theater. The experience of entertaining guests at the inn five nights a week was "the crucible that made me a performer," Swiss told Guerra: "Magic bartending is like street magic—you survive or you die, that's it. I survived and I learned a lot." In 1987 Swiss performed a week-long gig as a magician at the Magic Castle, a well-known nightspot in Hollywood, California. The legendary Dai Vernon (a Canadian born David Verner who was widely known as the Professor) was the magician-in-residence there. In his early 90s then, Vernon and Swiss became friends, and sometimes the two "sessioned" together (analogous to jamming among musicians). "His friendship with Vernon led him in another direction as well—backward, in a sense, to try to define what it was that made magic matter, why the tradition counted, and what it meant," Gopnik wrote. "He began to think about magic as an entertaining form of skepticism rather than as a debased form of mysticism." In his first column for *Genii, the Conjuror's Magazine* (June 1993), called "Why Magic Sucks," Swiss wrote, "I love magic as a means more than as an end. I love what magic can be far more than I love what it is. . . . Magic has failed to achieve artistic standing because it has failed to transcend its technique. . . . When you fool the audience you indeed fulfill the essential mandate of your job. But you have in no way come even remotely close to completing the job. . . . Absent some larger substantive goal, the audience is left watching trick after trick after trick, each time receiving this most dreary of messages loud and clear: See, I fooled you." In his subsequent *Genii* columns, some of which are included in *Shattering Illusions*, Swiss used magic "as a lever into the human condition: perceptual, aesthetic, and ethical . . . ," Crispin Sartwell wrote in a review of the book for the *Los Angeles Times* (June 22, 2003). "At his best, he comes close to the heart of the issues magic raises about truth and art." For Swiss, magic is "an experiment in empathy," in his own words. In a recent issue of the quarterly magazine *Antimony*, according to Gopnik, Swiss wrote, "From the very start, the moment a magician looks into his practice mirror, he is envisioning an alien awareness—a mind other than his own, perceiving an illusion that he is creating but cannot actually experience for himself." Thus, Gopnik wrote, "Only by a command of intellectual empathy can the magician lead the viewer down an explanatory highway from which there is no exit, or better, from which there are six exits, all of them blocked. Magic is imagination working together with dexterity to persuade experience how limited its experience really is, the heart working with the fingers to remind the head how little it knows."

Swiss's work as a magic bartender led to a flourishing career as an entertainer, lecturer, teacher, consultant, and writer. As a performer he quickly became known for his wondrous card sleights and the humor that he incorporated into his shows. "Swiss's humor is both visible and risible," Zibart wrote after witnessing an early performance of his at Fatty's, a Rockville, Maryland, bar. "He's suave, he's smooth, he's sesquipedalian—he's a stitch. . . . He works the crowd, he works the cards . . . and he is in fact a superlative magician, almost more expert than his audience realizes." Swiss has performed in stage shows all over the world, on the Las Vegas Strip and the Ginza District in downtown Tokyo, at the Rainbow Room in New York City, and at the Magic Castle in Hollywood, among many other places. He has also performed magic at many trade shows and for such companies as Citibank, American Express, Chemical Bank, Prudential Insurance, the Lego Corp., Publicis, Adobe, Intuit, and Electronic Arts.

Like a great number of magicians, Swiss considers himself a rationalist and a skeptic. "I think these ideas of rationality and anti-superstition lie at the core of much of my interest in magic," he told Guerra. In 1987, along with his friend D.W. "Chip" Denman, a statistician at the University of Maryland, Swiss co-founded the National Capital Area Skeptics, a "nonprofit educational and scientific membership organization that promotes critical thinking and scientific understanding" through projects and events in and around the nation's capital, according to its Web site. He is the co-founder and vice president of New York City Skeptics, founded in 2007. Swiss has contributed many articles and book reviews to the magazine *Skeptic*, published by the Skeptics Society. A longtime admirer of the magician James Randi, who in recent years has concentrated on investigating and demystifying paranormal and pseudoscientific claims, Swiss has participated in Randi's annual "conference on critical thinking," known as The Amazing Meeting. He has often lectured on behalf of the Center for Inquiry, whose self-described mission is "to foster a secular society based on science, reason, freedom of inquiry, and humanist values."

In 1992 Swiss assisted New York City law-enforcement officials in a public-awareness campaign about street scams—in particular, the game called three-card monte, in which the dealer typically arranges and rearranges, faces down, two black spot cards (non-face cards) and one red card (often an ace), and the bettor must guess which card is the red one. The dealer, usually aided by one or two shills, is in reality a sleight-of-hand con artist, and he fools the bettor into believing that he is merely moving the cards in a straightforward manner. Swiss told Dana Kennedy for the Associated Press (November 10, 1992), "They've been playing it for 140 years and no one's won yet. If you do happen to win they'll mug you before you get off the block. It's a sucker's bet." Swiss's lecture "Don't Bet on It" exposes techniques used by professional cardsharps. In his talk "The Illusion of Psychic Powers," Swiss shows that the four main kinds of paranormal events—telepathy, precognition, clairvoyance, and psychokinesis—are in reality tricks performed by con artists. "I want to highlight the line between illusion and reality," he explained on his Web site. Swiss co-wrote and co-

executive-produced *Cracking the Con Game*, a documentary about swindles and frauds that aired on the Discovery Channel in 2000. Swiss was the head writer for, and associate producer of, *The Virtual Magician*, an eight-episode TV series starring the award-winning illusionist Marco Tempest, who has incorporated computer graphics and other high-tech phenomena in his act. The show aired in many countries in 2004 and 2005. Swiss himself has performed on television many times, on programs including NBC's *The Today Show*, the PBS program *Nova*, and CBS's *48 Hours*.

In his writings and interviews Swiss has expressed concern about the widespread dissemination of information about magic on videos and the Internet, the dwindling of personal interactions between teachers and students, the shrinking use of the literature of magic, and the concomitant increase in the number of magicians who are neither invested in the culture of magic nor committed to learning its history and the art of presentation. "I see young magicians who learn a lot of sleights— really a LOT—very early in the game," Swiss told the penguinmagic.com interviewer. "However, many seem to know very little about conjuring— little about what it takes to really create a magical experience rather than just a quick special effect. Conjuring theory cannot be taught from the video screen, it exists almost entirely in books." Swiss went on to say, "I also see an ever-growing lack of respect for the art, and one of the things I was fortunate to be able to learn in the tradition of magic in which I grew up was a fundamental respect—for the art, for its tradition, for its accomplished practitioners. . . . The way to improve in this world— the way to learn anything—is to seek out someone with more knowledge, experience, and taste than you have."

Swiss lives in San Diego, California, with Kandace Schultz, a writer and producer of television advertisements, and their twin sons, Dexter and Grayson.

—M.R.M.

Suggested Reading: cardmsg.com Sep. 2003; jamyianswiss.com; *Los Angeles Times* R p16 June 22, 2003; *New Yorker* p56+ Mar. 17, 2008; penguinmagic.com Aug. 10, 2004; *Village Voice* Theater p70 Aug. 29, 2000; *Washington Post* N p25 Apr. 20, 1990

Selected Books: *The Art of Magic: The Companion to the PBS Special* (with Carl Waldman and Joe Layden), 1998; *Shattering Illusions: Essays on the History, Ethics and Presentation of Magic*, 2002; as contributor— *Visual Explanations: Images and Quantities, Evidence and Narrative*, 1997; *Magic for Dummies*, 1998; as creative consultant—*Penn & Teller's How to Play with Your Food*, 1992; *Penn & Teller's How to Play in Traffic*, 1997; as editor—*Theatrical CloseUp*, 1984

Selected Films: as co-writer and co-executive producer—*Cracking the Con Game*, 2009

Selected Television Shows: as writer and associate producer—*The Virtual Magician*, 2004

Courtesy of Abigail Thernstrom

Thernstrom, Abigail

Sep. 14, 1936– Social critic; writer

Address: American Enterprise Institute, 1150 17th St., N.W., Washington, DC 20036

In her body of work, the conservative scholar and social critic Abigail Thernstrom has underscored the need for racial equality in the U.S., at the same time attacking as misguided the various government-sponsored programs aimed at achieving it. While she won a measure of recognition with her first book, *Whose Votes Count?: Affirmative Action and Minority Rights* (1987), it was her second, *America in Black and White: One Nation, Indivisible* (1997), written with her husband, Stephan Thernstrom, that put Thernstrom in the national spotlight and made her the darling of many conservatives and libertarians. In that book the Thernstroms argued that African-Americans as a whole were faring better than was commonly supposed and that affirmative action and even the civil rights movement have been less responsible than other factors for black advancement. Thernstrom followed that book with *No Excuses: Closing the Racial Gap in Learning* (2003). Her most recent work, *Voting Rights—and Wrongs: The Elusive Quest for Racially Fair Elections* (2009), tackles an issue—

modern applications of the Voting Rights Act of 1965—with which she has long been fascinated. From 1993 to 2009 Thernstrom was a senior fellow at the Manhattan Institute, a conservative think tank. She is currently an adjunct scholar at the American Enterprise Institute and the vice chair of the U.S. Commission on Civil Rights, a federal voting-rights agency.

Thernstrom was born Abigail Mann on September 14, 1936 in New York City to Jewish parents. She grew up on Finney Farm, a commune in Croton-on-Hudson, a town 30 miles north of the city. Her parents, while not members of the Communist Party, shared its beliefs and surrounded themselves with like-minded people. Thernstrom's father, she has said in numerous interviews, was a failed businessman. When Thernstrom was a year old, her mother was diagnosed with breast cancer; she died when her daughter was a teenager. Though Thernstrom received her education at communist-leaning schools, she never took to communism, and for a long time she resented her parents' willingness to overlook the Soviet Union's atrocities. She accepted one of her parents' beliefs, however: the equality of all people, regardless of race. "I grew up in a very racially integrated scene, and that was one of the very good things about communism," Thernstrom told Adam Shatz for the *American Prospect* (March 12–26, 2001). "I lived in a cocoon in which race didn't matter, and I think that was very influential in terms of the way I think about racial issues. I'm in deep rebellion against race consciousness."

After graduating from high school, Thernstrom enrolled at a succession of colleges, attending Reed College, in Portland, Oregon, for a few months, then New York University, in New York City, after which she settled on Barnard College, a women's liberal-arts institution, also in New York. She graduated in 1958 with a bachelor's degree in European history and moved that year to Cambridge, Massachusetts, where she began graduate work in Harvard University's Middle Eastern studies program. During her first year she attended a lecture by the liberal investigative journalist I. F. Stone; the event was also the setting of her first (blind) date with Stephan Thernstrom, a graduate student in history at Harvard. (At that point, Abigail Thernstrom has admitted, she was looking for a husband.) Two and a half months later, the two were married. The couple shared an interest in intellectual and political issues, none more important to them than civil rights: together they picketed Woolworth stores because blacks were not allowed at the chain's lunch counters in the South. Throughout the 1960s and early 1970s, while Stephan was gaining notice as a scholar, Abigail raised the couple's two children, Melanie and Sam. She later completed her dissertation and received her Ph.D. degree from Harvard's Department of Government, in 1975, after which she was offered a teaching position in the school's social-studies program, where she remained for three years. She lectured at Harvard again from 1988 to 1989 and has also taught at Boston College and Boston University.

Thernstrom's political and ideological shift began in the late 1970s and gained momentum in the 1980s. In his profile of the Thernstroms for the *American Prospect*, Shatz told the story of when, in 1978, Thernstrom had lunch with Nathan Glazer, an anti–affirmative-action Harvard University sociologist and author of the influential *Affirmative Discrimination: Ethnic Inequality and Public Policy* (1976). Thernstrom called Glazer "the single most important intellectual influence in my life," according to Shatz. (Glazer later softened his stance on affirmative action.) At the lunch meeting Glazer strongly suggested, as quoted by Shatz, that Thernstrom set out to "become the world's greatest authority on some one little topic." A few months later, after Thernstrom found her niche topic—the Voting Rights Act of 1965 and its later applications—Glazer suggested she write an article about it for the newly established (now defunct) neoconservative magazine the *Public Interest*. The following year she published an article about what she called the "odd" evolution of the act, signed into law by President Lyndon B. Johnson to guarantee that African-Americans in the South would be permitted to vote. "The evolution was 'odd' because the act was no longer being applied to eliminate obstacles that disenfranchised black voters—its original and sole purpose, in [Thernstrom's] view," Shatz wrote. Thernstrom argued that through gerrymandering, or the creation of black- or Hispanic-majority voting districts, the U.S. government was creating affirmative action in the world of electoral politics—and that despite its intentions the effect was segregation along racial lines. Conservative intellectuals who opposed then-current uses of the Voting Rights Act embraced Thernstrom's arguments.

Also around that time a movement toward optimistic, small-government, purportedly color-blind conservatism took hold, culminating in the election of the Republican Ronald Reagan to the presidency in November 1980. In 1981 Thernstrom received a grant from the Twentieth Century Fund, a New York City–based nonprofit public-policy research institution, to write a book about voting and race in America. In 1987 she published *Whose Votes Count?: Affirmative Action and Minority Rights*, her first book, which she dedicated to her husband. The book elaborated on the points in the article she had written for *Public Interest* nearly a decade earlier. In his review of the book for the *New York Times* (October 18, 1987), Adam Clymer asked with regard to the recent protections offered by the Voting Rights Act: "Can blacks get elected without such protections? Or, to put it more bluntly, will whites vote for black candidates? Here Ms. Thernstrom's research, admirable on the legal and administrative side, lets her down by not measuring political realities; she argues what she thinks, not what she can prove. The research of others indicates that, at the local level, cross-racial voting is rare, while last year's CBS and ABC exit polls implied that in Congressional races pitting a black against a white, blacks were more likely to vote for the candidate of their own race than whites were. But she doesn't tell us this. Ms. Thernstrom faults the civil rights community for an unwillingness to trust the system to do better by minorities without such extraordinary remedies. It would be nice, of course, if race meant less to most voters than it does. But in politics few serious participants have the luxury of dealing with an ideal world." On the other hand, Clymer wrote, when Thernstrom "complains that the issues have not been fought out in the open, she is on stronger factual ground. The law's shift in meaning never has been debated with the glare of public attention that surrounded its original passage." Thernstrom argued that one major factor preventing the debate from taking place is that both major political parties benefit from the status quo: the Democrats do not object (and civil rights lobbyists support) the manufacturing of black- or Hispanic-majority political districts because blacks and Hispanics generally vote for Democrats. The Republicans, Thernstrom argued, have their own reasons for not objecting: first, it may be safer to ignore gerrymandering than to criticize it and risk being labeled racist, and second, the more black voters are collected into a district, the fewer blacks there are in adjacent districts, where Republican candidates therefore have a better chance of winning. Voting-rights advocates, for the most part, accused Thernstrom of distorting evidence and using statistics selectively. Despite—or because of—the criticism, within a year of the book's publication Thernstrom had received national recognition.

That recognition paled in comparison with the attention Thernstrom and her husband would receive a decade later, with the publication of one of the late 20th century's most passionately debated and controversial books on affirmative action and other race-based programs. *America in Black and White: One Nation, Indivisible* represented seven years of research. (The book was written with the financial support of several conservative institutions, including the Lynde and Harry Bradley Foundation and the Smith Richardson Foundation.) The first third of the book is a history of the South from the late 1800s to the mid-1900s, when segregation was the law of the land. In that section the Thernstroms, while fully acknowledging the injustice and ill effects of segregation, made two arguments that relate to their overall thesis: that the civil rights movement and federal legislation did less for black economic and social progress than did World War II, which saw a robust economy and the migration of blacks from the South for jobs in the North; and that while government actions that legally demolished "separate-but-equal" segregation and created the Civil Rights Act of 1964 and the Voting Rights Act of 1965 were unquestionably good, the federal government should have stopped there. The book attacks not only affirmative action but also gerrymandered electoral districts, school busing programs, and other programs or initiatives through which the government tried—unsuccessfully, in the authors' view—to effect positive change as opposed to simply stopping legalized discrimination. *America in Black and White* led to the Thernstroms' appearances on national TV-news programs. In his piece on the book for the *New York Times Book Review* (September 7, 1997), Nicholas Lemann wrote, "It is irresistibly tempting to discern a split personality in a volume with two authors; whether or not that is the reason, this book veers back and forth between two sensibilities, one reasonable and large-spirited, the other pugnacious and angry to the point of occasional bitterness and sarcasm." In an interview with Shatz, in 2001, Thernstrom regretted the book's occasionally harsh tone: "There were points [in *America in Black and White*] that had a backlash tone that I would take out today."

The tone of the book aside, *America in Black and White* offered a great deal of data and analysis. Paul Magnusson wrote for *Business Week* (September 22, 1997): "In convincing statistical detail, [the authors] demonstrate that economic and social circumstances for African Americans have improved markedly. Well-written and thoughtful, the book never stoops to the exaggeration and bombast that plague much of the current debate on race." Lemann, while acknowledging the "sincerity of [the authors'] desire for better race relations and better conditions for African-Americans," argued that the Thernstroms often used data selectively, providing "many, many alarming statistics" regarding crime, unemployment, and poverty "when it serves their purposes" of emphasizing the failure of various government programs. Lemann, as well as other reviewers, found that the Thernstroms painted a distorted picture of racism in America: although at one point they conceded that "too much remains" of white racism, they generally suggested that it had become an insignificant societal factor, while viewing black racism as a larger problem. Tamala M. Edwards, writing for *Time* (September 8, 1997), accused the authors of having a double standard when it came to "black shortcomings and white attitudes": "For blacks, the Thernstroms have concrete data—marriage rates, test scores and employment figures. But a major part of their argument—that white racism has largely disappeared—rests on the answers that whites give pollsters when queried about intolerance. It's an axiom of the business that people give pollsters answers they believe to be socially acceptable." Edwards also pointed out that the Thernstroms did not try to investigate the reasons for "black discontent"—why so many black Americans at the time believed racism to be a big problem. (In an interview with *Time*, Abigail Thernstrom conceded the point.) Writing for the on-line magazine *Slate* (October 15, 1997), Randall Kennedy, himself an opponent of most public affirmative-action programs, took issue with the great significance the Thernstroms gave affirmative action: "There is something dreadfully wrong with a study of race relations in the United States that places affirmative action at the center of the drama. The imbalance is especially notable given that other significant phenomena—such as the lingering effects of racial oppression in the (recent) past, new eruptions of anti-black prejudice, and so-called rational racial discrimination (by which people, without malevolent intent, use black skin as a negative cue)—are relegated to the far margins of discussion."

The Thernstroms' next book, *No Excuses: Closing the Racial Gap in Learning* (2003), focused on increasing test scores for black and Hispanic students from kindergarten through high school. What is needed, they argued, is not only an improvement of the academic performance of minorities but the elimination of the racial gap: their scores, the Thernstroms argued, must rise until they are on par with those of white and Asian students. A significant part of the book aimed to dismantle the conventional arguments—such as bad teachers and insufficient funding—used to explain the relatively poor academic performance of many black and Hispanic students. The Thernstroms cited evidence that, contrary to widespread belief, white-majority school districts do not receive more money per pupil than predominantly black or Hispanic districts. (They acknowledged, however, that some schools are still much wealthier than others.) They pointed out that classroom overcrowding is actually slightly worse in mostly white schools. The authors also dismissed, due to lack of evidence, notions that either discrimination or genetics provides explanations for the racial gap. The real problem, they claimed, is culture in minority communities—the insufficient value placed on education and on what it takes for students to do better: going to class, doing homework, limiting TV viewing, and avoiding delinquent behavior.

In his review of the book for the *Washington Post* (November 30, 2003), Richard D. Kahlenberg found the Thernstroms' argument unconvincing, mostly because they had failed to consider the element of class: "In a chapter on black culture that the Thernstroms call a 'painful discussion,' they point to studies finding that black children 'appeared less eager to learn new things, and were less likely to pay close attention to the class than whites,' that blacks are 'far more likely than others to break school rules, disrupting their own and their classmates' education,' and that African Americans are much more likely to spend excessive time 'staring at a TV screen' than whites. Elsewhere, the authors note that robberies are much more common in majority-minority schools than in overwhelmingly white schools. These are all facts that cannot be wished away, but the authors' attribution of these patterns to 'black culture' is unconvincing, given numerous studies finding that such acts as cutting class, watching large amounts of television, and committing violent acts all track much more closely by socioeconomic class than by race." Timothy A. Hacsci, in his review for the *New York Times* (January 4, 2004), while noting that readers might be able to learn a "great deal" from the book, also observed that "like many who write on education, instead of letting the best research drive their argument, [the Thernstroms] cite the research that supports it." Despite Kahlenberg's many criticisms of the book, he admitted that the Thernstroms "are on to something": the learning environment in those charter schools—and even in good middle-class public schools—is something to strive for.

Thernstrom's latest book, of which she is the sole author, is *Voting Rights—and Wrongs: The Elusive Quest for Racially Fair Elections* (2009), a legal, political, and historical analysis of the 1965 Voting Rights Act. One of her main points is that racial gerrymandering actually diminishes black influence in the world of politics: majority-black districts often elect leftist (as opposed to centrist) politicians who do not concern themselves with moderate political positions among constituents or take into account a significant number of white voters; if a majority of black politicians are on the left, Thernstrom argued, then black constituents end up on the outskirts of the decision-making process.

In addition to writing books, Thernstrom contributed articles as a stringer for the *Economist* from 1989 to 1992.

—D.K.

Suggested Reading: *American Prospect* p32 Mar. 12 2001; *New York Times* p40 Oct. 18, 1987, p19 Jan. 4, 2004; *Slate.com* Oct. 15, 1997; thernstrom.com/bio; usccr.gov

Selected Books: *Whose Votes Count? Affirmative Action and Minority Rights*, 1987; *Voting Rights—and Wrongs: The Elusive Quest for Racially Fair Elections*, 2009; with Stephan Thernstrom—*America in Black and White: One Nation, Indivisible*, 1997; *No Excuses: Closing the Racial Gap in Learning*, 2003

Thomas, Sarah

1973(?)– Football referee

Address: c/o Conference USA, 5201 N. O'Connor Blvd., Suite 300, Irving, TX 75039

Sarah Thomas made sports history when, on September 15, 2007, she became the first woman to officiate for the National Collegiate Athletic Association (NCAA) Football Bowl Subdivision (formerly Division-1A)—the highest level of college football. Thomas worked a handful of Conference USA (C-USA) games that year and the next and was assigned to an officiating crew with a full schedule (11 games) in 2009. She made history again on December 26 of that year, as the first woman to officiate a bowl game, when she served as a line judge during the Little Caesars Pizza Bowl. A star athlete in high school and college, Thomas officiated for youth football leagues beginning in 1996; she reached the high-school level in 1999 and moved to college football in 2006. She has called practice games at training camps of the New Orleans Saints of the National Football League (NFL) and is widely regarded as the most likely woman to officiate at NFL games someday. NFL officials "have got to look at her. She's too good," Gerald Austin, an NFL referee since 1982 and director of officials for C-USA since 2004, declared to Joe Drape for the *New York Times* (September 19, 2009). Austin told Thanh Truong for *NBC Nightly News with Brian Williams* (September 28, 2009, on-line), "I think if she continues to develop the way she has the first three years, I think [the NFL is] in her future."

Courtesy of the University of Mobile Athletics

Thomas has won the respect of players and coaches for her preparedness, excellent judgment, strong-mindedness, agility, and unobtrusiveness on the field. Keeping her hair hidden under her cap during games has helped her to blend in with her male colleagues. (The feminine quality of her voice, of course, cannot be concealed.) "Most of the time [players] are so focused on what they are doing, they don't notice me," she told Drape. "And that is what every other official strives for. Our best games are the ones that no one knows we're there."

"I'm not doing this for recognition or wanting to break a glass ceiling or whatever," Thomas told Teresa M. Walker for the Associated Press (November 27, 2009, on-line). "I'm going at it the same way [men are] going at it. There's a job to be done. It just so happens I'm a female." Thomas has also built a career as a pharmaceutical-company representative.

The second of the three children and the only daughter of Spencer and Donna Bailey, Thomas was born Sarah Bailey in around 1973 in southern Mississippi. Her older brother, Spencer Lea Bailey, is known by his middle name; her younger brother is Scott Bailey. Committed Christians, her parents raised their children with "tough love" and "an unrelenting belief in their potential," Peter Jackel wrote for *Referee.com* (February 2009), and the rule that they could never quit anything they had started. Thomas grew up in Pascagoula, a small city on the Mississippi Gulf Coast. A tomboy, she became interested in sports—and a fan of the Saints—at an early age, largely through the influence of her father and her older brother, who both played football. She recalled to Catherine Fredman for *Ladies' Home Journal* (September 2009, on-line), "My mother says that as a kid I was always on a field or a court playing basketball, baseball, whatever. But I loved football the best." Thomas played on the boys' basketball team in the fifth grade (there was no girls' team). "I always just played with the boys," she told Lindsay Mott for the *Mobile (Alabama) Register* (March 15, 2009). As an eighth grader she began playing with the Pascagoula High School girls' softball team. She was the first girl to earn five letters in softball (or any other sport) at that school. She also played basketball at Pascagoula High, not only as a student but with her father when school was out. Starting when she was very young, she recalled to Peter Jackel, her father always told her, "Don't depend on a man or anyone else to help you get through." "I just went through life knowing I couldn't make excuses," she told Jackel. "If I got the opportunity, I was the one who had to perform, I was the one who had to show myself." "I always told her to dwell on the positive instead of the negative," her father told Jackel. Thomas graduated from high school in 1991.

Thomas then entered the University of Mobile (UM), a Baptist-affiliated institution in Pritchard, Alabama, a Mobile suburb, which had awarded her a full basketball scholarship. She was a standout guard on the women's basketball squad, the Lady Rams of the Gulf Coast Athletic Conference, and helped the team win the 1993 National Association of Intercollegiate Athletics (NAIA) District 30 championship. At the end of four years at UM, Thomas ranked fourth on the school's career steals list and earned All-American honors as a student athlete. She earned a B.A. degree in communications in 1995.

After college Thomas played basketball as a member of a Mississippi church basketball league for men for about two years, until "the pastor, God love him, voted I couldn't play," she told Renee Busby for the *Mobile Register* (October 1, 2009). Her interest in officiating was sparked during a phone conversation with her brother Lea one day in 1996. Lea, who wanted to train to become a referee, told her that he was going to a meeting of the Gulf Coast Football Officials Association (GCFOA) that night. "I said, 'Can girls do that?' He said, 'Meet me at the meeting and we'll see,'" Thomas recalled to Busby. While most of those in attendance "thought I was someone's wife checking up on them," she told Teresa M. Walker, what she learned about the team-oriented nature of refereeing appealed to her, and the depth of football knowledge required of officials surprised her. After she passed a criminal-background check and displayed her expertise on game rules and regulations, Thomas became an official in training. "Some of the older guys took me under their wing and showed me from scratch where to start," she told Busby.

Thomas spent her first year working pee-wee-level games, then passed the tests for middle-school and junior-varsity officials. In 1999 she reached the high-school level, becoming the first female referee in the Mississippi High School Activities Association. That season she worked the game clock. The next year she was assigned to an officiating crew. During the six years in which she refereed at high-school games, she gave birth to two sons. "The spouses of my crew made me a maternity referee shirt," she recalled to Joe Drape. "Standing out there, big and in stripes has been the only time I've ever felt out of place." Thomas earned top assignments working high-school playoffs and All Star games, including the 2005 Alabama-Mississippi All-Star Classic and the 2006 Class 4A state championship game. That year, thinking that she would never rise further in the officiating ranks, she considered retiring to focus on her family and her fledgling career as a pharmaceutical sales representative. Around that time Thomas was contacted by a scout, Joe Haynes, who had been impressed with a tough call she had made during a state championship game he had attended. Haynes then put her in touch with Gerald Austin, a longtime NFL referee and director of officials for C-USA, a 12-university league, since 2004. At Austin's invitation, Thomas attended an annual C-USA officials camp in Reno, Nevada. "There were 12 people at each position, and I felt like Sarah was as good as anyone else at her position when I saw her," Austin said to Walker. He told Antonio Gonzalez for the Associated Press (September 13, 2007) that Thomas had "a good presence and demeanor" and "the ability and courage to make a call, and the guts to not make one, too." Several months later Thomas was hired as an alternate official for C-USA games.

At the college and pro-football levels, officiating crews consist of a head referee, or crew chief, who wears a white cap, and a head linesman, a line judge, an umpire, a back judge, a side judge, and a field judge, all of whom wear black caps. Thomas made her debut as an official for the NCAA's Football Bowl Subdivision (as Division I-A became known in 2006) on September 15, 2007, serving as a line judge in a game between the University of Memphis Tigers and the Jacksonville State University Gamecocks at Liberty Bowl Memorial Stadium, in Memphis, Tennessee. Thomas told Caitlin Moscatello for *Sports Illustrated* (October 1, 2007), "I felt extra pressure because of the media attention on the game. But as my supervisor told me, 'When the game starts, it's just 60 minutes of football.' That's where my concentration was." When Moscatello asked Jacksonville's head coach, Jack Crowe, about Thomas, he praised her performance and noted her obvious ease around football players.

Thomas worked a nonconference Football Bowl Subdivision game in 2007 and a handful of games in 2008. She was assigned to a crew with a full schedule in 2009. That season she became the first woman to officiate a bowl game, serving as a line judge during the Little Caesars Pizza Bowl (formerly the Motor City Bowl) between Ohio University and Marshall University, held in Detroit, Michigan, on December 26, 2009. As with all other college-level football officials, Thomas's performance is evaluated after every game; she is "critiqued, coached, and constructively criticized," Drape noted. She is one of only five women working games in the Football Bowl Subdivision; two of her female colleagues work in the Southwestern Athletic Conference and the other two in the Mid-Eastern Athletic Conference. Thomas has also worked scrimmages in New Orleans Saints' training camps. She is said to have a strong chance of becoming the first woman to officiate for the NFL. (Qualifications for that job include at least 10 years of officiating experience, including five years at the Bowl Subdivision level or with another professional league.) "My goal is to just be the best I can be every time I'm given the opportunity to work," she told Walker. "I know it sounds so cliché, but it's just the mindset of officials." She told Drape, "I am learning something every week. I just can't imagine not being on a football field in the fall."

The five-foot 11-inch Thomas lives in Mississippi with her husband, Brian, a medical-supplies salesman, and their two young sons, Bridley and Brady. Brian Thomas, who coaches a youngsters' travel-baseball team, said to Drape of his wife's two jobs, "I wasn't going to stand in her way. We've figured out a way to make our schedule work for the kids. I'm hustling in the fall, and she is in the spring and summer."

—C.C.

Suggested Reading: Associated Press (on-line) Nov. 27, 2009; Associated Press Mississippi (on-line) Oct. 12, 2007; (Auburn, West Virginia) *War Eagle Reader* (on-line) Nov. 18, 2009; *Detroit Free Press* (on-line) Dec. 26, 2009; *Ladies' Home Journal* (on-line) Sep. 2009; *(Mobile, Alabama) Register* A p11 Mar. 15, 2009, A p1 Oct. 1, 2009; *New York Times* D p1 Sep. 19, 2009; *Referee.com* Feb. 2009

Amy Sussman/Getty Images

Thompson, John Douglas

1964– Actor

Address: Shakespeare & Company, 70 Kemble St., Lenox, MA 01240

In the early 1990s John Douglas Thompson worked as a salesman for a computer-technology company before deciding to pursue his dream of becoming an actor. Though he struggled with long periods of unemployment during the first years of his stage career, Thompson is now one of the most in-demand stage actors in the New York area and has won an Obie Award and a Lucille Lortel Award for his performances. The *New York Times*'s chief theater critic, Ben Brantley, called Thompson "one of the most compelling classical stage actors of his generation." Tina Packer, the founder and artistic director of the theater group Shakespeare & Company, told Catherine Foster for the *Boston Globe* (November 18, 2001), "John is very intelligent, very hardworking, very good with the language, and he's a company player—he doesn't cuss around about things, but doesn't take any nonsense either. It's a rare combination, and when you have that, you want to put [the person] in leading roles."

A "Shakespeare specialist," in one writer's words, Thompson—who is black—is best-known among theatergoers for his portrayal of the title character in William Shakespeare's *Othello*. Since he debuted in the role, with the Trinity Repertory Company in its 1999–2000 season, Thompson has performed Othello on multiple occasions, including an award-winning Off-Broadway run in 2009. In his review of Thompson's second portrayal of Othello, at the American Repertory Theater (ART) in the 2001–02 season, Ed Siegel wrote for the *Boston Globe* (November 30, 2001), "Thompson is a magnificent physical actor and leaves the audience all but gasping at his frenetic and epileptic energy. But he has learned how to command a stage in subtle ways as well." Thompson has appeared in a variety of other plays, too, including Eugene O'Neill's *The Emperor Jones*, Sophocles' *Antigone*, and Bertolt Brecht's *Mother Courage and Her Children*.

John Douglas Thompson was born in 1964 in Bath, England, to Jamaican parents. His family, which includes two sisters and a brother, immigrated to Montreal, Quebec, Canada, when he was a toddler. When Thompson was 12 they settled in Rochester, New York, where his father worked as a technician for Bausch & Lomb, a supplier of eye-health products, and his mother was a nurse. Following Jesuit high school, Thompson studied marketing and business at Le Moyne College, in Syracuse, New York, graduating in 1985.

Thompson found work with a computer-software company, which, following a merger in September 1986, became Unisys Corp. One of the company's few African-American salesmen, he sold Unisys equipment to financial institutions around New England. "I didn't see a salesperson who looked like me," he told Catherine Foster for the *Boston Globe* (November 18, 2001). "After awhile you realize it's an aspect of your life as you live in this country. Sometimes it gives you a lot of freedom to be unique, to be unapologetically yourself." Because of his job Thompson lived, at different times, in Hartford and New Haven, Connecticut, and Providence, Rhode Island. Speaking of his six years as a salesman, he told Monica Drake for the *New York Times* (October 4, 2009), "I didn't feel passionate about it, so much as, 'This is what I'm supposed to be doing?'"

One night, in 1986, Thompson planned to take a date to see the Yale Repertory Theater's production of August Wilson's play *Joe Turner's Come and Gone*, which starred Delroy Lindo. "When my date didn't show up, I decided to go myself to see the play, one of the first theater pieces I had ever seen by the way. And what I saw blew my mind," Thompson recalled to Rita Charleston for the *Philadelphia Tribune* (April 30, 2004). "I had never been exposed to that type of entertainment, that type of art. And I knew from the moment I saw it that's what I wanted to do with my life. . . . I knew

I wouldn't make a lot of money so I had to keep working as a salesman. But I was interested in the craft, in exploring humanity and I understood it was a noble profession."

In 1991 Thompson was laid off from Unisys due to restructuring. With a severance package from the company, he felt secure enough to pursue acting. After reading an advertisement in the *Boston Phoenix* regarding casting for *World Do for 'Fraid*, a black contemporary version of *Hamlet* written and produced by Nabie Swaray for the Boston Playwrights' Theater, Thompson drove to Boston, Massachusetts, to audition. At his first-ever audition, without formal training or even a headshot, he won the lead role.

Thompson continued to audition, for plays and television commercials. At one point a casting director suggested that he get formal training. "I had no idea there was a school for actors or ones that taught drama," Thompson admitted to Charleston. He revealed to Foster that at the time, while he was able to draw from life experience for the roles he played, he "didn't know who the playwrights were, what famous plays were out there. I knew who Shakespeare was, but only vaguely, from an English class in college." Thompson successfully auditioned for the Trinity Repertory Conservatory and graduated from the two-year acting program in 1994. A couple of years later, the actor—by then well-versed in major theatrical works—offered advice to other black actors, saying, as quoted by Rita Charleston in the *Philadelphia Tribune* (November 1, 1996), "Study the classics. Study a lot of Shakespeare because when theaters are casting Shakespeare plays there seems to be what we call 'color-blind' casting as opposed to other productions. So there appears to be many more parts for African-Americans in your classic plays."

Thompson's work over the next several years included roles in *Richard III*, *The Merchant of Venice*, and *All's Well That Ends Well* at Shakespeare & Company; *Romeo and Juliet* at Commonwealth Shakespeare Company, in Boston; and *The Idiots Karamazov*, *The Ohio State Murders*, *The Winter's Tale*, *Antigone*, *Mother Courage and Her Children*, *Richard II*, and *Henry V* at the American Repertory Theater. With the Trinity Repertory Company he played Othello and performed in *Measure for Measure* and *The Good Times Are Killing Me*. He also had roles with the Huntington Theatre Company, in Boston, Hartford Stage, in Connecticut, Portland Stage, in Portland, Maine, and Philadelphia Theatre Company, in Pennsylvania. Thompson's first Off-Broadway role was in the Tectonic Theatre Project's *Marlowe's Eyes* at the Theater at St. Clement's Church in March 1996. Those years, Thompson told Drake, included periods without work, during which he "ate a lot of Ramen Pride and pasta." He continued his training at Shakespeare & Company and joined the American Repertory Theater in 1999.

In the 1999–2000 theater season, Thompson first appeared as Othello, with the Trinity Repertory Company. *Othello* is about a Moorish general in the army of Venice who has recently wedded Desdemona, the young daughter of a Venetian senator. When Othello's trusted ensign Iago is passed over for a promotion, Iago plots revenge against his superior, manipulating Othello into thinking that Desdemona has not been faithful; in a fit of rage, Othello kills his wife. When Othello later realizes that Desdemona was innocent, he kills himself out of grief. Othello is "the most dynamic role, I believe, that Shakespeare ever wrote for any actor of any color," Thompson told Kay Bourne for the Boston *Bay State Banner* (November 22, 2001). (Though there remain a number of scholars who disagree, Othello is widely believed to be a dark-skinned Moor of African descent, which adds another layer of tension to the play.)

In the beginning of *Othello*, the title character is at "the top of the world in his career, he's a general, and a man who has married the first woman he has ever been in love with," Thompson explained to Bourne. "The downfall occurs within two weeks. Think of the journey he takes. It doesn't get much better for an actor than that." He added, "There's love, hate, betrayal, being a foreigner, being black in a white society trying to assimilate because you feel that's the right thing to do. It's an old play, but very contemporary." For the *Boston Globe* (September 11, 1999), Anne Marie Donahue wrote about Thompson's first performance as Othello, "Nothing short of a firebomb could steal the limelight from John Douglas Thompson, who's riveting in the title role."

Thompson's work in the 2000s included his role in 2004 as the killer Lucius Jenkins in Stephen Adly Guirgis's *Jesus Hopped the 'A' Train*, at Philadelphia's Wilma Theater; his performance won the Theatre Alliance of Greater Philadelphia's Barrymore Award for outstanding supporting actor in a play. Later that year he appeared Off-Broadway as Judge Brack in Henrik Ibsen's *Hedda Gabler* at the New York Theater Workshop. Thompson made his Broadway debut as Flavius in Daniel Sullivan's production of the Shakespeare tragedy *Julius Caesar*. Starring Denzel Washington as Brutus, the limited engagement ran from April through June 2005 at New York's Belasco Theatre. In 2006 Thompson appeared Off-Broadway as Edgar in *King Lear* at the Harlem School for the Art Theatre; his performance earned a nomination for the 2007 Vivian Robinson/AUDELCO Recognition Award for supporting actor. He then appeared as Le Bret in Edmond Rostand's *Cyrano de Bergerac* on Broadway from November 1, 2007 to January 6, 2008. The production starred Kevin Kline in the title role and Jennifer Garner as Roxane.

Thompson was again nominated for the AUDELCO Award for supporting actor after his Off-Broadway run as Orombo in Thomas Southerne's *Oroonoko* from February 10 to March 9, 2008. The following month he began a month-long Off-

Broadway run as Enobarbus in Shakespeare's *Antony and Cleopatra*. Thompson again won critical praise for his Othello during Shakespeare & Company's month-long production of the tragedy in Lenox, Massachusetts, in the summer of 2008. "Thompson . . . brings the same majestic physicality to his Othello that made him unforgettably charismatic on the ART stage," Louise Kennedy wrote for the *Boston Globe* (July 31, 2008).

Six months later Thompson brought his Othello to Theater for a New Audience's Off-Broadway production of the play at the Duke on 42nd Street. *Othello* ran from February 22 to March 7, 2009, and Thompson's performance won the Lucille Lortel Award for outstanding lead actor, the Obie Award for performance, and the Joe A. Calloway Award, given annually by the Actors' Equity Association to honor a male and a female actor for the best performance in a classical play in the New York metropolitan area. He was also nominated for the Drama League Award for distinguished performance and for the AUDELCO Award for lead actor. In the February 24, 2009 edition of the *New York Times*, Charles Isherwood wrote that Thompson's performance "is carefully paced and wrought with care. The tenderness of Othello's love for Desdemona feels as palpably real as the violence that surges through his body when Iago's poison begins to infect his blood."

Thompson then starred in Eugene O'Neill's *The Emperor Jones* at the Irish Repertory Theatre in New York City. That controversial drama centers on Brutus Jones, an African-American man who is sent to prison for murder. He escapes and flees to a Caribbean island, where, as the play's action begins, he has made himself emperor. When the island's inhabitants stage a rebellion against Jones's rule, he attempts to escape through the forest, where parts of his life's story are revealed in flashbacks. The play has been criticized for its use of dialect and for portraying black people as violent, superstitious, and lazy. For those reasons, *The Emperor Jones* is rarely staged. Ciaran O'Reilly, the producing director and co-founder of the Irish Repertory Theatre, has admitted that it took some time to persuade Thompson—who, he told Drake, he thinks is "one of the great actors we have"—to take on the role of Brutus Jones. Thompson agreed only after he had researched the influences behind O'Neill's decision to write *The Emperor Jones*. "I saw Brutus Jones as Everyman," Thompson told Patricia Cohen for the *New York Times* (October 14, 2009), calling Jones's ascent to power the story of "a member of the disenfranchised who wants to become enfranchised by any means. The universal themes in the play are not constricted by color or race. I found great humanity in this story."

In her review of the production for the November 1, 2009 issue of *Variety*, Marilyn Stasio wrote, "The primitive dialect, the native superstitions and all the other supposedly racist elements in Eugene O'Neill's 1920 tragedy that make sensitive [audiences] squirm nowadays are simply brushed aside by John Douglas Thompson. This astonishingly gifted thesp[ian] . . . confers dignity, intelligence, canniness and a sly sense of humor on the psychologically complex character of Brutus Jones." *New York* (December 21, 2009) cited Thompson's 2009 performances as one of its "reasons to love New York" that year.

The Emperor Jones enjoyed a sold-out run from October 18 to December 6, 2009. Due to high demand, the production returned for a seven-week run starting on December 22 at the Soho Playhouse. Thompson's critically lauded performance was nominated for the Drama League's distinguished performance award, the Drama Desk Award for outstanding actor in a play, and the Lucille Lortel Award for outstanding lead actor. For the second time, he received the Joe A. Calloway Award.

In addition to theater, Thompson has appeared on television, in episodes of the crime dramas *Law & Order* and *Law & Order: SVU* and the soap opera *All My Children*. He has also been seen in movies, including the Spike Lee film *Malcolm X* (1992), the short film *Midway* (2007), and the legal drama *Michael Clayton* (2007), starring George Clooney.

In May 2010 Thompson starred alongside Dianne Wiest in the Classic Stage Company's Off-Broadway production of Alexander Ostrovsky's *The Forest*. That comedy-drama centers on Raisa Pavlovna (Wiest), a scheming, middle-aged widow who sells off parcels of forest land to finance a marriage between her niece, Aksyusha (Lisa Joyce), and a peasant's son, so that Raisa can be with the young man Aksyusha would prefer to marry. The situation is complicated when two out-of-work actors, including Raisa's long-lost nephew, Gennady (Thompson), arrive at her door asking for money. The production received mixed reviews, though the majority of critics felt that Wiest and Thompson gave strong performances.

Thompson's portrayal of the title character in Shakespeare & Company's August 2010 production of *Richard III* again impressed critics. Ben Brantley wrote for the *New York Times* (August 23, 2010), "As portrayed by John Douglas Thompson, this monarch-in-the-making quickly establishes himself as a man who is almost never still and who takes absolutely nothing lying down. To call Mr. Thompson's superkinetic Richard III a force of nature doesn't quite get it. He suggests instead a force of history, a juggernaut that keeps charging relentlessly forward, sweeping up and mowing down whatever's in its path." In another assessment of the same performance for the *Times* (September 9, 2010), Brantley wrote, "Mr. Thompson was, in a sense, history incarnate. . . . And *Richard III* as, above all, a history play suddenly made fresh sense to me." In October 2010 Thompson played opposite Kate Mulgrew in Shakespeare's *Antony and Cleopatra* at the Hartford Stage, in Connecticut. The show opened to positive reviews. After citing Brantley's assertion that Thompson is "one of the most compelling classical stage actors of his gener-

ation," Anita Gates wrote for the *New York Times* (October 22, 2010), "If you don't see that throughout his performance here, it will hit you hard in the agonizingly powerful scene in which he orders a servant to help him die and then takes things . . . into his own hands."

Speaking to Kay Bourne for the *Bay State Banner* (May 4, 2000), Thompson said that Shakespeare's appeal for many black actors lies in "the humanity that Shakespeare allows the actors who do his plays to explore," in his opinion. "That quality of writing is consistent throughout his work," he continued. "The language [Shakespeare] uses is not what we speak every day or what people in his time spoke every day but it captures so perfectly moods and feelings. He wrote for the human soul."

Tall, muscular, and dark-skinned, Thompson shaves his head and keeps a neatly trimmed, Van Dyke–style beard. He lives in the Bedford-Stuyvesant neighborhood of Brooklyn, in New York City.

—M.A.S.

Suggested Reading: *(Boston) Bay State Banner* p20 May 4, 2000; *Boston Globe* C p4 Nov. 18, 2001; *New York Times* Arts & Leisure p6 Oct. 4, 2009; *Philadelphia Tribune* E p35 Apr. 30, 2004

Selected Broadway Performances: *Julius Caesar*, 2005; *Cyrano de Bergerac*, 2007–08

Selected Off-Broadway Performances: *Marlowe's Eyes*, 1996; *Othello*, 1999, 2009; *Jesus Hopped the 'A' Train*, 2004; *Hedda Gabler*, 2004; *King Lear*, 2006; *Oroonoko*, 2008; *Antony and Cleopatra*, 2008, 2010; *The Emperor Jones*, 2009–10; *The Forest*, 2010; *Richard III*, 2010

Selected Television Shows: *Law & Order*; *Law & Order: SVU*; *All My Children*

Selected Films: *Malcolm X*, 1992; *Midway*, 2007; *Michael Clayton*, 2007

Venkatesh, Sudhir

(soo-DEER)

Aug. 19, 1966– Sociologist; writer

Address: Institute for Social and Economic Research and Policy, Columbia University, 420 W. 118th St., Rm. 813, New York, NY 10027

One day in the early 1990s, when he was a second-year graduate student in sociology, Sudhir Venkatesh entered the Robert Taylor housing projects of Chicago, Illinois, with a list of questions for the residents. When he left, the next day—having been

Courtesy of Sudhir Venkatesh

Sudhir Venkatesh

held in a stairwell by a gang of drug dealers—he had few answers but a whole new set of questions, which he explored over the next half-dozen years as a guest, friend, and confidant of the projects' residents, who ranged from gang leaders to struggling parents. In writing about his experiences and observations, Venkatesh provided a new model for sociologists, one based on a close identification with his subjects. His book *American Project: The Rise and Fall of a Modern Ghetto* (2000) is an analysis of life in the Robert Taylor Homes from 1962 to the time of the book's publication, while *Off the Books: The Underground Economy of the Urban Poor* (2006), his next book, focuses on the complex web of legal and illegal businesses in the ghetto, involving preachers, drug dealers, prostitutes, store owners, and many others. The subject of the latter book had also surfaced in Steven D. Levitt and Stephen J. Dubner's best-selling 2005 volume, *Freakonomics: A Rogue Economist Explores the Hidden Side of Everything*, which featured Venkatesh's work and brought the sociologist a new level of attention. The subtitle of *Freakonomics* informed that of Venkatesh's own best-seller, *Gang Leader for a Day: A Rogue Sociologist Takes to the Streets* (2008). Venkatesh, a professor of sociology at Columbia University, in New York City, has also written essays for the *New York Times* and the on-line magazine *Slate*. In 2009 *Rolling Stone* included Venkatesh on its list of 100 "agents of change."

Sudhir Alladi Venkatesh was born on August 19, 1966 in Madras, India. A few years later his father, Alladi, moved to the United States to pursue a master's degree at Syracuse University, in upstate New York. In 1971, after a year in the U.S., Alladi Venkatesh sent for his wife and son. In Syracuse "I

learned English in two weeks and completely forgot how to speak my native tongue," Sudhir Venkatesh told Robert L. Kaiser for the *Chicago Tribune* (December 10, 2000). One day when Venkatesh was in third grade, his gym teacher had a hard time pronouncing his name during roll call, giving up after the fourth try and calling him "Sid"—a name that stuck. In 1981, after his father received an offer to teach at the University of California's Graduate School of Management, in Irvine, the family moved to Southern California, where Venkatesh attended University High School; there, he kept up a good grade-point average and played soccer, tennis, and basketball, meanwhile having no idea what he wanted to do for a career. At the University of California at San Diego–La Jolla, he majored in math, but it was later in his college career, when he was inspired by his interest in race, class, and other social issues to take philosophy and sociology courses, that he discovered what he wanted to pursue. After graduating, in 1988, with a B.A. degree in mathematics, Venkatesh enrolled in graduate school at the University of Chicago, to study sociology.

During Venkatesh's second year of graduate school, his professor William Julius Wilson—a respected sociologist and the author of *The Truly Disadvantaged* (1987), a study of inner-city poverty—sent Venkatesh to collect data at the Robert Taylor Homes, on Chicago's South Side, whose 28 high-rise buildings comprised the nation's largest housing project. Full of fear, naiveté, and curiosity, Venkatesh walked among the dilapidated buildings, approaching residents with the questions in the survey he had been given, which included "How do you feel about being black and poor?" (The answers in the multiple-choice survey ranged from "very bad" to "very good.") As Levitt and Dubner reported in *Freakonomics*, Venkatesh went inside one building and told the gang of young black crack dealers he found shooting dice there, "I'm a student at the University of Chicago, and I am administering—" One of the young men cut him off with "F**k you, ni**er, what are you doing in our stairwell?" After figuring out that Venkatesh was neither a police officer nor a rival gang member, the young men argued over what to do with him, one of them excitedly waving a gun. Soon J.T., the gang's leader, showed up and calmed everyone, but the terrified Venkatesh was nonetheless forced to spend the night on the stairwell with the drug dealers. Released the next day, Venkatesh was both relieved and intensely curious about the men he had met. He also realized how misguided his academic approach to his subjects had been and how little was known by supposed experts about the lives of the people he had encountered. He decided to go back to the Robert Taylor Homes, this time with questions he had written himself.

Venkatesh persuaded J.T. to let him spend time with the gang and observe their activities. He applied to live in the housing project in order to be fully immersed in the environment, but he was turned down; nonetheless, over the next six years, Venkatesh got to know the members of J.T.'s gang and spent many nights in the homes of various families in the housing project, sharing their meals, engaging the parents in discussions, helping wash dishes, playing with children, and sleeping on floors. He quickly began to understand the complicated nature of the connection between the drug gang and the community. He explained to Terry Gross for the National Public Radio program *Fresh Air* (January 31, 2001, on-line): "At the end of the 1980s when the crack cocaine economy started to flourish in Chicago, one of the things the street gangs had to do at the very local level was to make sure that they were staying out of the eyes of police . . . a very difficult thing to do. . . . The tenants really rejected their offers for a long time, for bribes and so on, but they were also experiencing a great deal of frustration because it was at this very time, right after the second term of [President] Ronald Reagan, that the Housing Authority's budget started to decline. Their social services in the wider community were not actively reaching the public housing residents. . . . One of the needs that they wanted to take care of was making sure their kids got to school safely. Well, it just so happened that the street gang was interested in a type of public safety as well"—that is, protection from notice by the police—"because that helped them to sell their drugs more smoothly. So the tenants and the street gangs started to engage in these community meetings where they would try and find compromises. And one of the ones that they struck was that . . . a tenant leader would say, 'OK. You, the street gang leader—you can't sell your wares, sell your drugs on these corners and in front of the buildings between the hours of three and seven when kids are coming home from school and playing. And you can't do it in the morning. But if you do it late at night and you do it in the afternoon, well, we'll look the other way.'" Venkatesh told Gross that there was real debate and disagreement surrounding the ad-hoc alliance with the gangs: "I'd have dinner on numerous occasions with families. . . . And the street gang leader would show up for dinner and they'd talk to them. And they'd use that as opportunities to inveigh against that person and say, 'Look. Look what you're doing to our community.' And, you know, they'd get in arguments and so on, but they did so with a sense of compassion and with a real sincere wish to try and steer that person away from the street gang back into the mainstream labor force and to pursue their education and so on."

Following the gang around, Venkatesh witnessed a lot of crime, including drug deals, harassment, and acts of violence. As he told Gross, his romantic view of his situation—as a young, intrepid field worker exploring and documenting the dangerous and exciting world of black urban poverty—was shattered on the day he saw a young man get killed right in front of him in a drive-by shooting. The young man was not a gang member; he was

simply in the wrong place at the wrong time. "And you see something like that, and . . . you couldn't help but think that there's something wrong here," Venkatesh told Gross. "The task now becomes how to explain and how to figure out exactly what it is and what we can do about it."

Venkatesh received his M.A. degree in sociology in 1992 and his Ph.D. in 1997. He participated in the Junior Fellowship program at Harvard University, in Cambridge, Massachusetts, from 1996 to 1999; in the latter year he joined the faculty of Columbia University.

The experiences and data Venkatesh amassed during his six years of studying the Robert Taylor Homes led to the publication of three books, the first of which was *American Project: The Rise and Fall of a Modern Ghetto* (2000). That work received laudatory reviews, which focused not only on the book but on the author's having immersed himself in the Chicago neighborhood and interacted with the community. In his profile of Venkatesh, Robert L. Kaiser cited several sociologists who agreed that, not despite but because of his unorthodox methods, Venkatesh "in some ways, changed the rules, raised the bar and expanded the parameters of sociological research." *American Project* won the 2000 Best Book Award from the American Association of Publishers.

After the book was published, Venkatesh maintained an interest in the lives of the people he had met. Starting around 2001 he began working with Steven Levitt, a young economist at the University of Chicago, on a follow-up study. They were primarily concerned, Venkatesh told Gross, with two questions: "What happens after people have had long-term exposure to gang activity, to criminal activity, at a formative period in their lives? 'If you see them 10 years from that date, are they working? Are they still alive? Are they in school? Are they in prison?' and so on. The other [question] relates to public housing: Where do people go when they leave public housing, especially young people?" For about 18 months he and Levitt tried to "track down . . . 118 youth who were living in this housing development," Venkatesh told Gross, and ask them "a series of questions about their lives and what [they were] doing." According to his follow-up research, Venkatesh said, 25 percent of those involved in gang activity in the Robert Taylor Homes would probably be killed within four years of joining gangs. Venkatesh and Levitt continued to work together, and as *Freakonomics* became a bestseller, Venkatesh received a lot more exposure.

In *Off the Books: The Underground Economy of the Urban Poor* (2006), Venkatesh examined both the legal and illegal businesses practiced by residents of the Robert Taylor Homes. The underground economy, he wrote in the preface, amounted to a web of off-the-books accountants, house burglars, car thieves, painters, musicians, gun traders, prostitutes, mechanics, store owners, gypsy-cab drivers, preachers, police, and gang members. In examples of how the network functioned, an owner of a corner store, instead of paying for a security guard, might give a homeless man food in exchange for guarding (i.e., sleeping near) his store at night; the owner of a restaurant or gas station might, for a fee, look the other way as prostitutes solicit customers nearby; or a preacher might accept a "contribution" to resolve disputes between the local crack-dealing gang and the block's neighborhood association. (The gang might agree to stop dealing crack in the park after school in exchange for permission to do so in the parking lot of a local store.) Harold Henderson wrote of *Off the Books* for the *Chicago Reader* (December 15, 2006) that Venkatesh "paints a detailed picture that reflects his close acquaintance with the neighborhood, moving from businesses that are legal but off the books to those that are entirely outside the law. . . . This is a Chicago you don't know, told in readable prose that puts most other sociologists to shame." Venkatesh observed that such an economy, with both its legal and illegal components, lends a measure of order to the neighborhood—one that he did not sentimentalize. "If Venkatesh sometimes marvels at the ingenuity of the people he writes about," Patrick Radden Keefe wrote for *Slate.com* (December 8, 2006), "he does not overlook the essentially tragic nature of the story he is telling. The depredations of daily life mean that for many residents, what Venkatesh calls the 'perceptual horizon' does not extend beyond the neighborhood. Sadder still, it doesn't reach beyond the struggles of the day to day." *Off the Books* won best-book honors from *Slate.com* and the American Political Science Association; it also won a 2007 C. Wright Mills Award.

Venkatesh's next book, *Gang Leader for a Day: A Rogue Sociologist Takes to the Streets* (2008), is his most personal to date—a memoir of sorts as well as the story of the Black Kings gang in the Robert Taylor Homes. In assessments of the book, Venkatesh was both praised and criticized— sometimes by the same reviewer—for his method of near-total immersion. A reviewer for the *Economist* (January 5, 2008) called the book "a rich portrait of the urban poor" and added: "The author's tone is self-deprecating, self-righteous and rather guilty in turn. By the end of the book he sees himself as a hustler like the rest, bending the rules to get what he wants—in his case, information." In his attempt to form an objective picture of the relationship between the gang and the residents, the sociologist faced a barrier: "Mr. Venkatesh fails to gauge the feelings of project residents about the Black Kings," William Grimes wrote in a review for the *New York Times* (January 16, 2008), "probably because he is perceived as part of them and therefore someone to steer clear of. Most residents avoid him, he writes, or limit their conversation to 'a quick hello or a bland comment about the weather.' This is a glaring omission. On the other hand, Mr. Venkatesh, through sheer persistence, does unravel a complex, intertwined system of political and economic relationships that makes the housing

project run in the near-total absence of city services." Like several other reviewers, Grimes observed that Venkatesh "ridicules his own naiveté but just as often fails to rise above it." Grimes and other critics observed that Venkatesh was smitten by J.T. and his world—even after J.T. suggested he conduct a study of the residents' collective economy and then tricked him into giving him the information so that J.T. could further "tax" the residents. Most conceded, though, that Venkatesh had conducted important research. Grimes wrote, "[Venkatesh] writes what might be called tabloid sociology, but it rests on a solid foundation of data, like records of the gang's finances turned over to him by T-Bone, its treasurer." Still, the book focused less on such statistics than on the stories of people in the Robert Taylor Homes and their relationships to one another. (The housing development was demolished beginning in the mid-2000s.)

By the time that book was published, Venkatesh had begun studying a particular aspect of the underground economy: prostitution. Again working with Levitt, Venkatesh hired former prostitutes to obtain information from those who were still active, immediately after they had seen clients—for example, information concerning the sorts of sexual act performed, whether or not violence had occurred, and the professions of the clients. (About 160 working prostitutes in Chicago were interviewed.) One of the questions Venkatesh and Levitt sought to answer was why some of the women became prostitutes instead of finding legal minimum-wage work; one answer was that prostitutes earned approximately $27 an hour on average, substantially more than minimum wage. Along with greater earnings, however, came the risk of violence, arrest, extortion, and sexually transmitted diseases. (Condom use among prostitutes and clients was under 25 percent, and an encounter between a prostitute and a policeman in Chicago was more likely to end with sex than with an arrest.) Some of that research on prostitution was incorporated into Levitt and Dubner's book *SuperFreakonomics: Global Cooling, Patriotic Prostitutes, and Why Suicide Bombers Should Buy Life Insurance* (2009). Venkatesh's next book, according to his Web site, "will focus on the role of the black market in the revitalization of New York in the last decade."

Venkatesh is the co-editor, with Ronald Kassimir, of the book *Youth, Globalization and the Law* (2006). He has produced and directed a number of documentaries, including *Dislocation*, about families leaving condemned public housing, which aired on PBS in 2005, and a National Public Radio documentary, *Transformation* (2005), on the history of public housing. His most recent, the film *At the Top of My Voice* (2008), concerns two people who return from the U.S. to their native country of Georgia to promote democracy and human rights; that work has been screened at several festivals and theaters.

Venkatesh is married to Katchen Locke, a lawyer.

—D.K.

Suggested Reading: *Chicago Tribune* C p14 Dec. 10, 2000; *Economist* p81 Jan. 5, 2008; *New York Times* E p8 Jan. 16, 2008; sociology.columbia.edu; sudhirvenkatesh.org

Selected Books: *American Project: The Rise and Fall of a Modern Ghetto*, 2000; *Off the Books: The Underground Economy of the Urban Poor*, 2006; *Gang Leader for a Day: A Rogue Sociologist Takes to the Streets*, 2008

Doug Pensinger/Getty Images

Vonn, Lindsey

Oct. 18, 1984– Skier

Address: c/o FIS, Marc Hodler House, Blochstrasse 2, CH-3653 Oberhofen/Thunersee, Switzerland

"The Olympics are something that, as a little kid, I always dreamed about winning," the skier Lindsey Vonn told Michael C. Lewis for the *Salt Lake (Utah) Tribune* (October 11, 2009, on-line). The 26-year-old Vonn, who has been perfecting her techniques on the slopes for 24 years, was the top-ranking female alpine, or downhill, skier on the World Cup circuit in the 2007–08, 2008–09, and 2009–10 seasons. With her three consecutive overall World Cup titles, she was recognized as the best all-around skier among the few women who have triumphed in all five traditional alpine events: the

downhill race, the slalom, the giant slalom, the super giant slalom (or super G), and the combined race (one downhill run followed by two slalom runs). Acquiring that level of skill "has been a lot of hard work," she told Sonia Gardner for *International Racer* (January 8, 2009, on-line). Vonn competed in both the 2002 and the 2006 Olympic Games but did not win a medal at either. At the 2010 Winter Olympics, held in February 2010 in Canada, Vonn achieved her childhood dream, winning one gold and one bronze medal.

In the months leading up to the Games, Vonn was an object of much American media attention. That was because, according to Andrew Longmore, writing for the London *Times* (February 8, 2009, on-line), "from being a gifted but erratic downhill specialist, Vonn has matured into the most complete skier in the sport." Vonn has received invaluable help in that process from experts who travel with her full-time. She and Thomas Vonn, her husband since 2007 and a racer with the U.S. men's ski team in the 2002 Olympics, have dubbed those specialists the Vonntourage: a physiotherapist, a fitness trainer, and an equipment expert. Their services, along with that of the coach Robert Trenkwalder, have been provided to her since 2005 by the Austrian energy-drink company Red Bull, one of her half-dozen corporate sponsors. Thomas Vonn, too, devotes himself full-time to her career, as her manager, unofficial coach and technical adviser, and source of emotional support. "Thanks to Thomas, I can focus entirely on my sport," Vonn has said, as quoted on redbull.com. "He comes to all my races, he can console me, motivate me, or take my mind off things when it's not going so well." In the 10-plus years between mid-November 1999, when Vonn was 15, and March 2010, she competed in more than 450 races, in events including—in addition to World Cup events and the Olympics—the Nor-Am Cup, the U.S. National Championships, the European Cup, the International Ski Federation (FIS) Junior World Ski Championships, and the FIS World Ski Championships.

According to *The Physics Factbook* (on-line), "Speed skiing is the fastest, most intense non-motorized sport in the world." Alpine skiers typically reach speeds in excess of 60 miles per hour after 15 seconds; speeds exceeding 80 miles an hour after another five to 10 seconds are common. (The record to date, set by Sanna Tidstrand of Sweden in Les Arcs, France, on April 20, 2006, is 150.74 miles per hour.) During any competition wind and light conditions and air quality may change (for example, sometimes fog rolls in), presenting greater challenges for individual skiers. All downhill courses, no two of which are exactly alike, extend from about one and a half to three miles in length, with skiers beginning their races at or near the highest point of each slope. For female racers, that point may range, vertically, from about 1,640 feet to more than 2,600 feet above the end point; the grade, or angle, of the slope may range from about 14 degrees to close to 30 degrees.

According to abc-of-skiing.com, "A good course consists of the following elements: long icy paths, challenging turns, extreme steeps, flats, uneven slopes, and large airs for challenging jumps." The icy condition of the course is maintained through human intervention, usually with water. Downhill skis are about 30 percent longer than those used in other alpine events, and many alpine skiers use curved rather than straight poles.

The five-foot 10-inch, 160-pound Vonn is taller and heavier than most of her peers. "It's a pretty big disadvantage," she told Sonia Gardner. "When you're taller, you have a lot more problems with balance. It's harder to control what you're doing. The movements are so quick. When you're bigger, there are a lot more opportunities to make mistakes." Vonn was born Lindsey Kildow on October 18, 1984 in Burnsville, a suburb of St. Paul, Minnesota. She is the oldest of the five children of Alan Kildow and Linda Krohn. (Her mother resumed the use of her maiden name after she and her husband divorced, in 2002.) Her father, a onetime competitive ski racer (as was his father), is a lawyer; he is now a partner in a Minnesota firm. Her mother, also a lawyer, worked as a public defender and then as a welfare-appeals referee; currently, she is an administrative assistant at a Presbyterian church in Minnesota. Vonn's siblings are a sister, Karin, and triplets (two boys, Dylan and Reed, and a girl, Laura), who are about four and six years her junior, respectively. Vonn began skiing at the age of two. "She was so good, right away," her mother recalled to Lewis. "She just loved skiing. You can't make somebody like it so much." Within a few years Vonn had started training at Buck Hill, in Burnsville, under the veteran coach Erich Sailer. At the age of seven, she began to enter races in the U.S., and at nine she began to compete in international events. At that time, she wrote for a school assignment, she aspired "to win more medals than anyone ever did," as her mother recalled to David Leon Moore for USA Today (February 21, 2008, online). During that period Vonn began commuting to Vail, in the Rocky Mountains of Colorado, to train on slopes far more challenging than any in Burnsville, where the highest hill is about 310 feet—less than one-10th the average height of Vail peaks. A meeting with the champion alpine ski racer Picabo Street at an autograph signing when Vonn was 10 reinforced her goal of skiing in the Olympics one day. That same year, to advance Vonn's career, the Kildow family moved to Vail, where she trained at the Ski and Snowboard Club Vail.

During her teens Vonn was home-schooled, so that she could ski as much as possible. In 1999, at the age of 14, she became the first American female to win the slalom race at Trofeo Topolino, in Italy, a prestigious competition for skiers ages 11 to 14. At 15 Vonn participated in several events in the Northwest Funds Coupe Nor-Am Cup Series, the top-level racing competitions in North America. In 2001 she took home the bronze medal in the combined event at the U.S. National Championships.

That season she also skied in the FIS World Cup slalom race for the first time. In the super-G in Val d'Isère, France, on December 15, 2001, she came in 26th and won her first World Cup points. At 17 she raced in the 2002 Winter Olympics, in Salt Lake City, Utah, and placed sixth in the combined event. After those Games Picabo Street took Vonn under her wing, and despite their 13-year age difference, they became friends.

Vonn's teens were also marked by family problems. The move to Vail, and the growing costs of supporting Vonn's training and travel, proved to be extremely stressful for her parents, and their marriage suffered. In addition, Vonn's relationship with her father, who served as her manager, became increasingly strained, and she stopped communicating with him in 2005. "He always supported me when I did well, which was 90 percent of the time, but when I didn't, he didn't handle it very well," Vonn told Karen Crouse for the New York Times (December 9, 2005). "It was so hot and cold. It was so much criticism and so much negativity, and it was really hard for me to balance emotions." The difficulties between father and daughter worsened as Vonn grew closer to Thomas Vonn, whom she met when she was 18 and he was 27. According to Vonn, her father made plain to her that he disapproved of their deepening friendship. The moral support she received from her mother and from her great-aunt Doris Rudsill Kildow, who lived near Aspen, helped to boost her spirits. "Many who know Vonn believe that breaking away from her father's influence was a pivotal moment in her development and has allowed her to flourish," Michael C. Lewis wrote. According to Lewis, Vonn does not want her father to attend any of her races.

On March 4, 2003 Vonn won the silver medal in the downhill race at the Junior World Ski Championships in Puy St. Vincent, France. The following March 20 and 21, she earned gold medals in the super G and the slalom, respectively, at the U.S. National Championships in Alyeska, Alaska. On December 3, 2004, in her first World Cup victory, she placed first in the downhill at the FIS races in Lake Louise, Alberta, Canada; two days later, in the same series, she took home the bronze in the super G. On December 21, 2004 she placed second in the super G in the World Cup race in St. Moritz, Switzerland. On January 15, 2005 she placed third in the World Cup downhill competition in Cortina d'Ampezzo, Italy. By the end of the 2005 season, she had to her credit 13 top-five finishes—six of them in the top three—in World Cup and World Championship events. At that point she ranked sixth overall in the world among female alpine skiers.

Earlier that year, by invitation, Vonn had joined Red Bull's Athletes Special Project, and she came under the tutelage of several experts: Robert Trenkwalder, a famous Austrian ski coach; Martin Hager, a fitness trainer (who checks Vonn's blood chemistry several times a day); Oliver Saringer, a physiotherapist; and Heinz Heammerle, an equipment specialist. "At first I would question every new suggestion," she recalled, as quoted on the Red Bull Web site. "During power training, for example, I wanted to know the exact benefits of each individual exercise. Gradually I saw my strength and performance improve, so my confidence in the programme grew." Hager told Marc Peruzzi for *Outside* (November 2008) that in the off-season, Vonn works out in a gym for six to eight hours daily. Her regimen includes four hours on an exercise bicycle, two hours of weight-lifting or running hurdles, and an hour of maneuvers with an exercise ball (also called a Swiss ball or physio ball). Vonn told Alex Crevar for *Outside Online* (November 2009), "Physically, having a solid core is huge. Having strong ab[dominal] and back muscles allows you to ski the angles you want and be in the position you want. Hamstring strength will help prevent knee injuries. As far as technique is concerned, the most important thing is to be in a good body position: hips forward, arms up, and a generally good athletic stance. Mentally, I have a big advantage with my husband around because I keep the right mindset. I try to always be a glass-half-full person anyway. The most important thing for me is to think about skiing and not the finish line . . . like I did when I was younger. It is me and the course: hands up, be dynamic, stay aggressive." Vonn also trains under Alex Hoedlmoser, the U.S. Ski Team's head women's downhill, or speed, coach since 2004.

In December 2005 Vonn was victorious in the downhill World Cup races in Lake Placid and Val d'Isère. The traditional prize in the latter contest is a cow, which virtually all winners exchange for prize money. Vonn, though, kept hers; named Olympe, the cow lives on a farm in Kirchberg, Austria, near a U.S. Ski Team training facility.

During a practice run on February 18, 2006 in Sestriere, Italy, during that year's Winter Olympics, in what observers described as a "spectacular" and "harrowing" crash, Vonn "lost her balance and came down bruisingly hard on her hip and rear end," Charles McGrath reported for the *New York Times* (February 19, 2006, on-line). She was airlifted to a nearby hospital, where acute pain led her to fear, erroneously, that she might have broken her back. Her mother, who remained by her side, described to David Leon Moore Picabo Street's visit to the hospital that night: after learning that tests had ruled out broken bones or other serious damage, Street declared to Vonn, "A *real* champion would get up and race." Two days later, still experiencing what Moore characterized as "excruciating" pain, Vonn returned to the slopes, finishing seventh in the super-G, on February 20, and 14th in the slalom, on February 22. Her courage earned her a 2006 U.S. Olympic Spirit Award, which had never before been given to a female non-medal-winner at the Games. On her Web site Vonn wrote that she believed her accident had "happened for a reason. It was a lost opportunity, but it gave me the fuel and motivation that I need." Later in 2006 Vonn won two gold medals in the giant slalom in FIS races at Coronet Peak in Japan; a silver and a gold in the downhill and a silver in the super G at the World Cup races in Lake Louise; and a gold and a bronze in downhill races at the World Cup races in Val d'Isère.

In February 2007 Vonn won silver medals in the downhill and the super-G at the FIS World Ski Championships in Åre, Sweden. Soon afterward she pulled a tendon in her right knee during training, ending her 2006–07 season prematurely. In 2007–08 her achievements included first-place finishes in the downhill races in Lake Louise (on December 2, 2007), St. Anton am Arlberg, Austria (on December 21 and 22, 2007), Cortina d'Ampezzo (January 19, 2008), Sestriere (February 9, 2008), and Crans-Montana, Switzerland (on March 8 and 9, 2008). Her March 8 win brought Vonn's 10th career World Cup downhill gold medal. Also in St. Anton Vonn won the super-combined event (one downhill or super-G run and one slalom run)—a race that, on her Web site, she described as "a brutal test of courage." In that season's World Cup circuit, she ranked first in points, thus earning her the overall World Cup title. She was only the second overall winner among American female downhill skiers (after Tara McKinney, in 1983). The prize accompanying that honor is a large crystal globe atop a crystal pedestal.

On February 3, 2009 Vonn won the gold medal in the super-G at the FIS World Ski Championships in Val d'Isère—her first gold medal in that series and the first for an American woman. "It was a struggle the whole way," she said during a teleconference after the event, as quoted by Amy Donaldson in the Salt Lake City, Utah, *Deseret News* (February 4, 2009, on-line). "From top to bottom, I was just fighting the whole way." She completed the race with a time of 1:20.73, .34 seconds ahead of the second-place winner. On February 6 Vonn finished second in the super combined event at Val d'Isère, but 10 minutes later the judges disqualified her for having missed one of the gates in the slalom—an error of which she had been unaware. Learning that she had lost that race, she told Philip Hersh for the *Chicago Tribune* (March 17, 2009), was both "shocking and disappointing," and she cited the disqualification as her worst memory of that season. Then, on February 9, at the same series, she won first place in the downhill race. She thus became the first American woman in 57 years to win two World Championships golds in the same year. (Andrea Mead Lawrence won the slalom and the giant slalom World Championships honors in 1952.) At a party held to celebrate Vonn's successes, she accidentally severed a tendon in her thumb on the broken rim of a champagne bottle. The tear was surgically repaired the next day, and thanks to a special splint and to tape her husband used to secure her gloved hand to the ski pole, she raced on February 14 in the slalom (but did not finish). Overall during the 2008–09 season, Vonn captured 16 podium wins, among them nine first-place wins (in every event except the giant slalom)—a U.S. record for men as well as women; her five consecutive super-G wins set an international record for women. She also racked up more points than any of her competitors, thus earning her second overall World Cup title, in Åre, Sweden, on March 13, 2009. "I give my whole life for the sport and to be able to win something like this for a second time in a row, it means a lot to me," she said that day, as quoted by an Associated Press (March 13, 2009, on-line) reporter. "It's why I work hard, it's what I live for." Vonn triumphed despite her thumb injury, which had not yet healed. "It still hurts and it makes my starts a lot more weak, which has definitely cost me time," she observed. "But, during my run I feel like it is almost normal. It's a little awkward with the tape and I can't quite put my pole exactly where I want it, but I think that I've gotten used to it."

In 2009 World Cup races, Vonn placed ninth in the giant slalom in Sölden, Austria, on October 24; second in the slalom in Levi, Finland, on November 11; first in downhill races in Lake Louise, on December 4 and 5; and second in the super G in Lake Louise on December 6. On November 28 in Aspen she ended in 39th place in a giant-slalom run after hitting a rock with her right ski. On a downhill run in Lake Louise on December 4, she hit a bump in the course and bit her tongue when a knee butted her chin, but she finished in first place nevertheless. "My mouth guard was the only reason I didn't completely chop off my tongue," she told reporters, as quoted by Bill Pennington in the *New York Times* (December 7, 2009, on-line). She achieved a second downhill victory in Lake Louise the next day, and the day after that, she came in second in the giant slalom, losing to Elisabeth Goergl of Austria by only .03 seconds. On December 12 in Åre, she crashed during the giant slalom, and the following day she finished eighth in the slalom. She attributed some of her problems on the slopes in recent weeks to a change in her equipment: the previous September, after a cut in her funding, she dropped the equipment company Rossignol as a sponsor in favor of Head, signing a contract to use Head skis, bindings, and boots for the next five years.

On December 28, 2009 Vonn bruised her arm during the opening run of the World Cup giant slalom in Lienz, Austria. The injury occurred a few days after the skier finished first in the super combined and third in the super-G at Val d'Isère, which had propelled her to the lead spot in the World Cup rankings. On January 10, 2010 in Haus Im Ennstal, Austria, she won the World Cup super-G race, her 28th World Cup win. At the same competition she also won two downhill races. Later in the month Vonn won the women's World Cup super-G title after a victory in St. Moritz, Switzerland. She won the overall World Cup title for the season after winning the super-G at Garmisch-Partenkirchen, Germany, in March 2010. With that victory she be-

came the American with the most World Cup wins (33) and the first woman to win three back-to-back overall titles since Petra Kronberger of Austria (1990–92).

At the 2010 Winter Olympics, despite an injured shin, Vonn captured a gold medal in the downhill—her leadoff event—thus becoming the first American woman to win the downhill in the Olympics. In her second race she crashed into a gate during the slalom portion of the combined event. Vonn placed third, behind Austria's Andrea Fischbacher and Slovenia's Tina Maze, in her third event, the super-G. She crashed and broke a finger in the fourth race, the giant slalom, and was thus disqualified. In her final race, she was disqualified after she straddled a gate. Although her performance was "not the quintuple-golden Games everyone was hoping she would have," Brandon Penny wrote for skiing.teamusa.org (October 25, 2010), it was admirable. "Yes, Vancouver was her third Games, but it was the first time she was a definite medal contender," Penny noted. Vonn remained a celebrity in the U.S. after the Games, appearing on television shows, ringing the opening bell at the NASDAQ Stock Market, and attending the White House Correspondents' Association Dinner, and her image appeared on magazine covers. She received two ESPY Awards from ESPN, for best female athlete and best female U.S. Olympic athlete.

In October 2010, at the first World Cup event of the season, in Sölden, Austria, Vonn began with an 18th-place finish. She remained optimistic, however, as the giant slalom is not her specialty. In a Facebook.com post Vonn wrote, as quoted by Penny, "I came into the race training very well and with high expectations[;] unfortunately I wasn't able to execute when it counted. Sometimes that is just how it goes especially at the beginning of the season. As many of you know over the past year alot [sic] of my GS races have ended with a DNF [did not finish] and trip to the hospital with X-rays, so in a strange way yesterday[']s race was slightly successful."

In addition to Rossignol, Vonn's corporate sponsors are Vail Resorts, the apparel firm Under Armour, the protective-eyewear company Uvex, the bakery-products company Oroweat, Alka-Seltzer Plus, and the *magazine SkiRacing*. Vonn and her husband own a home in Park City, Utah. "Thomas and I are a great team," she has said, as posted on her Web site, "and skiing is actually the one thing that we hardly ever have conflicts over. He understands the stresses and sacrifices of skiing and he's the one who can get me through the day when I am feeling down." Vonn has learned German; she sometimes converses in that language with Hager, Saringer, and Heammerle, and she can hold her own in German-language interviews.

—W.D.

Suggested Reading: FIS Web site; Lindsey Vonn Web site; (London) *Times* (on-line) Feb. 8, 2009; NBC Olympics Web site; Red Bull Web site; *New*

York Times Magazine p26+ Feb. 7, 2010; *Salt Lake (Utah) Tribune* (on-line) Oct. 11, 2009; skiing.teamusa.org Oct. 25, 2010; *Slytech Protection* (on-line) Mar. 13, 2009; *Sports Illustrated* p52+ Mar. 10, 2008, p52+ Feb. 8, 2010; *Vogue* p218+ May 2010; *Washington Post* (on-line) Dec. 9, 2005; LeMaster, Ron. *Ultimate Skiing*, 2009

Harry How/Getty Images

Weir, Johnny

(weer)

July 2, 1984– Figure skater

Address: c/o U.S. Figure Skating Headquarters, 20 First St., Colorado Springs, CO 80906

The three-time national figure-skating champion Johnny Weir has attracted as much media coverage for his flamboyant attire and outsized personality as for his sports record. Covering the 2006 Olympic Games, in Turin, Italy, Amy Shipley wrote for the *Washington Post* (February 7, 2006): "Weir has contemplated dyeing his hair blue and decorating himself with feathers to capture the essence of his music. He has worn crimson streaks in his hair, a massive sequined broken heart on his chest, sheer purple fabric, off-the-shoulder necklines. At the mid-January U.S. championships in St. Louis, he performed with one arm covered with fishnet and sequins, part of a silver-and-white cascade of glitter and sparkle designed to evoke his choice of music, from the ballet *Swan Lake*, right down to a red glove on his right hand that represented the head

of the swan. . . . Even when he is wearing street clothes, Weir's eccentricity shines through."

Weir finished in fifth place overall in Turin, and after his second bid for an Olympic medal, at the 2010 Games, in Vancouver, Canada, he landed in an even more disappointing sixth place overall. Weir, who designs all his own skating costumes, has said that in the near future he will leave the ice to pursue a career in fashion. "In figure skating your body can only last for so long. I can't be 50 and trying to skate but I can be 50 and be in fashion, so I have to look to my future and what I want to achieve," he told Martin Rogers for the Yahoo! Sports Web site (February 19, 2010). "I want to create art more than anything and the way I want to do it is through fashion. I want to go to the Fashion Institute of Technology in Manhattan and really learn the basics of fashion from the ground up."

Weir starred in a documentary film, *Pop Star on Ice*, which was shown on the Sundance Channel in late 2009. In early 2010 the channel began showing *Be Good, Johnny Weir*, an eight-part reality series that continues the narrative of the film, following the skater both on and off the ice. In a review of the show for the *New York Times* (January 17, 2010, on-line), Neil Genzlinger wrote, "There is drama in the series: the relationship with the tough new coach; a roommate issue in Mr. Weir's private life; the recurring rivalry with another American skater, Evan Lysacek. Whether that's enough to hold your interest will depend on your personal Weir tolerance level." Weir typically dismisses those who claim to have a low tolerance for his antics. "Figure skating is very old fashioned and staid," he told Marnie Hanel for *Vanity Fair* (February 11, 2010, on-line). "The people in power are several decades older than the people they are judging, which makes things tense when somebody like me comes along. I respect my elders, but I don't feel a need to appease them. I don't play by anyone's rules but my own. That's why it's controversial when I say and wear things that are deemed inappropriate. I hope in my own way that I've helped the next generation of athletes to feel comfortable being themselves and flying their freak flags high."

Johnny Weir was born in Coatesville, Pennsylvania, on July 2, 1984 to Patti and John Weir, workers at the Peach Bottom Atomic Power Plant. John Weir had been the captain of his high-school football team, while Patti Weir had been a star cheerleader. As a child Johnny Weir, who has one brother, Brian, enjoyed skiing and competitive horseback riding. After watching Oksana Baiul perform her winning routine at the 1994 Olympic Games, in Lillehammer, Norway, Weir developed an interest in figure skating. Wearing a pair of roller skates, he began trying in the basement of the family home in Quarryville, Pennsylvania, to replicate Baiul's moves. After his parents gave him a pair of used ice skates one Christmas, Weir began practicing in a frozen-over cornfield behind his house. Visiting the local ice rink, he was tormented by the hockey players, who threw pucks at him. "We always knew Johnny was a little bit different," John Weir told Shipley. "We were aware he had a tough time now and then."

In 1996, at the age of 12, Weir took his first group figure-skating lesson and astonished his instructor by performing a single axel (a difficult jump during which the skater rotates in the air) after only one week. Encouraged to pursue more advanced training, Weir went several times a week to Newark, Delaware—driven two hours round-trip by his mother—to work with Priscilla Hill, the first American woman to land the triple loop in competition. Unable to afford both horseback riding and skating, Weir gave up competing in equestrian events.

The Weirs soon moved to Delaware to be closer to Hill, who paired Weir with a young female skater, Jodi Rudden. The couple qualified for the Junior Olympics for two consecutive years, but Rudden quickly grew taller than her new partner. "I'm tiny," Weir told Lynn Zinser for the *New York Times* (January 14, 2005, on-line). "It was obvious I'm not going to be doing any lifts." Abandoning pairs skating, Weir earned a bronze medal in the novice division at the 1998 U.S. Championships, held in Philadelphia, Pennsylvania. The following year he moved to the junior division, finishing fourth at the championships in Salt Lake City, Utah. He next competed at two Junior Grand Prix events, finishing second and seventh. Although Weir finished first in the short program at the 2000 U.S. Championships, held in Cleveland, Ohio, he struggled during the freeskate portion of the competition and finished fifth overall.

In 2001 Weir recorded his first major victory, winning the World Junior Championships. He also made his senior debut, coming in at a respectable sixth place overall at the U.S. Championships, in Boston, Massachusetts. The following season he began competing internationally at the senior level, and he drew attention by finishing in the top 10 at such prestigious events as the Goodwill Games, Skate Canada, and Trophée Lalique (now known as the Trophée Eric Bompard). At the 2002 U.S. Championships, held in Los Angeles, California, Weir improved on his previous record at that event, finishing fifth overall. He was subsequently named an alternate on the World Championship and Olympic teams and narrowly missed the podium with his fourth-place finish at that year's Four Continents Championships.

Weir dropped out of his scheduled Grand Prix events early in the 2002–03 season due to injury. He surprised many in the skating world at the 2003 U.S. Championships, in Dallas, Texas, when he placed second in the short program, right behind Timothy Goebel. (Goebel was known as the "Quad King" for his ability to perform quadruple-rotation jumps; in 1998 he had become the first person ever to land a quadruple jump in competition.) "I wasn't really expecting to be in the top three after the short program," Weir told Shannon Ryan for the *Philadelphia Inquirer* (January 17, 2003). "I'm very excited to be where I am." Weir's short pro-

gram, skated to a zydeco tune, included a triple lutz–triple toe, a triple axel, and a triple flip, all of which he landed cleanly. The performance was especially impressive given that he had only recently recovered from a fractured tibia. His triumph was tarnished, however, by his performance in the long program: Weir fell just 23 seconds into his routine by skating too close to the boards and catching his blade in the rink barrier. He then botched a triple axel, smashing his kneecap. Forced to leave the ice in pain, he withdrew from the competition.

The following year Weir returned to the U.S. Championships, held in Atlanta, Georgia, hoping to redeem himself. He had endured a particularly difficult period after the embarrassment of the 2003 nationals. "He was called a quitter," Amy Rosewater wrote for the *Washington Post* (January 11, 2004). "He was called Johnny Weird. At times, he simply was known as the guy who skidded into the boards. [For] a year after his infamous crash during the opening seconds of his program at the U.S. Figure Skating Championships in Dallas, Johnny Weir was the laughingstock of the figure skating world." In preparation for the 2004 event, Weir had left the University of Delaware rink where he had been training in order to work at a less crowded local facility, where he studied for six weeks with the legendary Russian skating coach Tatiana Tarasova.

On January 10, 2004 Weir—wearing a heavily sequined blue costume and skating to music from the film *Dr. Zhivago*—landed eight triple jumps and garnered a perfect 6.0 score for artistry to win his first U.S. National Championship. He told Todd Zolecki for the *Philadelphia Inquirer* (January 24, 2004), "I really put all the naysayers in their place. I'm just excited that I could re-prove myself and make people eat their words." He was admonished by United States Figure Skating Association (USFSA) officials for describing his self-designed costume as "an icicle on coke," but that minor controversy passed quickly, and two months later Weir traveled to Dortmund, Germany, for his first world figure-skating championships, where he finished fifth overall. A rising star on the international scene, he next took home the NHK Trophy, part of the International Skating Union (ISU) Grand Prix of Figure Skating series, as well as the Trophée Eric Bompard; he placed second at the Cup of Russia.

At the 2005 U.S. National Championships, held in Portland, Oregon, Weir successfully defended his title, this time causing an uproar by likening his attire to that of a "Care Bear on acid." The competition was the last in which Weir participated to use the traditional 6.0-point judging scale. A new system was adopted by the ISU, in which each technical element is given a base mark, which is then modified based on the quality of its execution. Additional marks are given for such elements as transitions, choreography, and interpretation. The new system was meant to decrease the level of subjectivity involved in judging, but some observers felt that it placed excessive emphasis on technical prowess rather than artistry. Weir found himself under increasing pressure to add a quadruple jump to his routine in order to stay competitive. He told Frank Fitzpatrick for the *Philadelphia Inquirer* (January 13, 2005), "I really try to focus on the whole package of the program, the steps and the spins, not just jumping to music. I focus on the details. I'm not driven by medals." He acknowledged to Philip Hersh for the *Chicago Tribune* (January 13, 2005), "As far as studying [the new system's rules] and making sure I get the maximum points, it's not that interesting to me. It may mean the difference between Olympic gold and fifth place, but it's my performance and that's what I like to focus on." Hersh pointed out, "All three medallists at the 2002 Winter Olympics landed quads [and] all four of the men who finished ahead of Weir at last year's world championships landed at least one quad in competition."

When Weir arrived in Moscow for the 2005 World Championships, he suffered a flare-up of sesamoiditis, an irritation of a group of small bones in the foot. Before skating his first program, he was given two injections of lidocaine to numb the pain. (The reigning world champion, Evgeni Plushenko, also skated while injured and eventually withdrew from the competition.) In too much distress to attempt a quad, Weir ultimately placed fourth in the competition, behind Stephane Lambiel of Switzerland, Jeffrey Buttle of Canada, and his U.S. teammate Evan Lysacek. Weir injured his ankle at the Skate Canada event in October 2005 but took home a bronze medal from the Cup of Russia later in the season, finishing behind Plushenko and Lambiel.

Defending his national title at the 2006 U.S. Championships, Weir caused a sensation, skating his short program to Camille Saint-Saëns's "The Swan" and wearing a costume appliqued with feathers. The routine earned him his personal best short-program score: 83.28 points, almost six points ahead of the second-place finisher, Michael Weiss. Following the short program Weir entertained reporters by introducing "Camille," as he called his single red glove, which was meant to represent a swan's beak. (His outfit was broadly parodied in the 2007 Will Ferrell film comedy, *Blades of Glory*.) Weir again raised the ire of skating officials by telling reporters that during his elegant short program the audience could have "sat back and had their cognac and cigarettes and relaxed and watched," while his competitor Ryan Bradley's performance was "more a vodka shot, let's-snort-coke kind of thing." In his long program Weir recorded 225.34 points to retain his title and gain a berth on the Olympic team, alongside Matt Savoie and Lysacek. After that victory he was widely quoted as saying, "My mother is [celebrating by] getting drunk already."

Although the USFSA was not pleased with Weir's comments, reporters reveled in them. "Johnny Weir is a gold-medal talker . . . ," Filip Bondy wrote for the New York *Daily News* (January 15, 2006). "There is a very good chance that he will say something deliciously naughty once he arrives in Italy, cause a riotous scandal with his tongue," Juliet Macur reported for the *New York Times* (January 15, 2006) that Weir considered himself a role model only for children who "feel different or stifled or squashed" and that he explained his candor by saying, "No one is Jesus. I'm not for everyone. . . . I don't make statements just to make them. I mean every single word I say regardless of if it's offensive or mean-spirited. I'm not going to sugarcoat it in any way."

When Weir arrived in Turin, wearing a vintage Communist Party jacket, his refusal to censor himself was apparent. He told John Powers for the *Boston Globe* (February 14, 2006), "I think people are very wary about what's going to come out of my mouth and very worried about the kind of image I'm portraying for figure skating. . . . That's cool. People should stay scared."

Weir turned in a clean performance in the short program, leaving him in second place, behind Plushenko and ahead of Lambiel. Hersh wrote for the *Chicago Tribune* (February 15, 2006), "Weir, who has never attempted a quad in competition, was more aesthetically pleasing [than Plushenko], not a surprise for a skater with his sensibilities. . . . Weir was subsumed into his music, Camille Saint-Saens' 'The Swan,' with his spins, head positions and arm movements. Plushenko merely was doing jumps and spins with 'Tosca' playing in the background." Still, Weir was dogged by questions of whether or not he would include the quad in his long program.

The night of the long program, Weir missed a bus to the arena and arrived late. He felt, as he told a reporter for the *Washington Post* (February 17, 2006), "black inside." Though he successfully completed some difficult elements, including a triple axel–triple toe loop combination, Weir omitted several other triples and never attempted a quad. He finished the Games in fifth place overall.

Despite his poor performance at the Olympics, Weir's star power grew following the Games. In the September 2006 issue of *Blackbook* magazine, he modeled a Gucci dress and high heels. Weir told Amy Rosewater for ESPN.com (January 27, 2007), "It wasn't like I went in and said, 'Oh my God, I want heels. I want fur. I want glitter. . . . I think the pictures are very interesting. They're not gaudy. They're not campy. They're just me modeling clothes." The skater also modeled at the Heatherette fashion show during New York Fashion Week.

During the 2007 national championships, criticism arose about Weir's off-the-ice activities and his new long program, skated to "Child of Nazareth." Weir defiantly told Frank Fitzpatrick for the *Philadelphia Inquirer* (January 25, 2007), "It's more exciting to walk in a fashion show or portray Jesus than it is to sit at home learning how to play the piano or skating to *The Nutcracker*." Despite the criticisms Weir skated a clean short program, putting him in second place, only .85 points behind Lysacek. In the long program, however, he made mistakes on three jumps and fell to third place; Lysacek took the title, with Ryan Bradley in second place. At that year's world championships, Weir was not considered a major contender and finished in eighth place.

After his lackluster season Weir moved to New Jersey, leaving his longtime coach, Priscilla Hill, to train with the famed Galina Zmievskaya, the Russian coach who had taught Oksana Baiul. Weir began the 2007–08 season with wins at the Cup of China and the Cup of Russia. He also performed at an awards show in Moscow, where he was presented with the Love of Russia prize, for his often-expressed respect for Russian culture.

During his seventh trip to the U.S. Figure Skating Championships, held in St. Paul, Minnesota, Weir told Pat Borzi for the New York Times (January 25, 2008), "I feel prepared and happy. That's the biggest thing. I got here and I was excited to be here." His confidence was not misplaced: he ended his short program with first-place marks. Weir followed up with a conservative long program in which he omitted the second jump in one of his combinations. While the decision cost him points, at the end of the competition he and Lysacek were tied. Lysacek ultimately triumphed, because of an obscure rule that in the event of a tie, the winner of the long program is the overall victor. The rivalry between Weir and Lysacek was widely seen as representative of a larger tension in the sport of figure skating, between artistry and athleticism. "The lingering feeling in the building was these two skaters were about as even as two peas in a pod. Albeit an odd pod, since they are stylistic opposites when they skate," E. M. Swift wrote for Sports Illustrated (January 27, 2008, on-line). "Asked about his rivalry with Lysacek, Weir said he respects him as a competitor but that he doesn't consider him a friend. 'We don't sit around doing each other's hair,' Weir explained."

Weir next won the bronze medal at the World Championships in Gothenburg, Sweden, the only medal won by a member of the U.S. team at that competition. His 2009–10 season was noteworthy for his silver-medal win at the NHK Trophy competition and his third-place finish at the Grand Prix Final in Tokyo, Japan.

Weir then placed a respectable third at the 2010 U.S. National Championships in Spokane, Washington. He attracted widespread media attention for his exhibition routine at the event, skating to the pop tune "Poker Face," by Lady Gaga, a recording star who has become something of an icon in the gay community. Weir also attracted the attention of animal-rights activists, who objected to his use of fox fur in his skating costume. Facing threats from People for the Ethical Treatment of Animals (PETA), among other groups, he moved into the heavily guarded Olympic Village during the 2010 Games, instead of off-site accommodations, as he had originally planned. He also elected to remove the fur from his outfits, which stood out nonetheless for their corset-like lacing, tassels, and lavish crystals. "I do not want something as silly as my costume disrupting my second Olympic experience and my chance at a medal, a dream I have had since I was a kid," he wrote for his Web site. Those dreams remained unrealized, however. Weir—who skated his short program to "I Love You, I Hate You" by the Argentinean jazz artist Raúl DiBlasio and choreographed his freeskate program around the theme of "Fallen Angels"—finished the Games sixth overall, albeit with a new personal-best combined score of 238.87. His rival, Lysacek, took home the gold. "I skated two programs I can be proud of for the rest of my life, medal or not," Weir told Maria Elena Fernandez and Denise Martin for the Los Angeles Times (March 8, 2010, on-line). "But still, I am an athlete, and at the end of the day, nobody likes to lose."

Weir was slated to compete at the World Championships in Torino, Italy, in late March 2010, but he dropped out at the last minute. In a written statement he thanked his friends, family, fans, and coaches and said that he planned to reassess his career goals. He later decided to take a break from competing in 2010–11 in order to revise his approach to skating. In an interview with Jessica Flint for Vanity Fair (July 8, 2010, on-line), he said, "If you look at the [female figure skaters], they are maxing out at age 17, 18; for guys, it's 24, 25, 26. I'm right around those golden years. I still have so much passion to perform. . . . That's who Johnny Weir is: I'm a figure skater, I'm an athlete. I want to have fun and enjoy it. . . . The time away from performing will be great to revamp my skating style. In sports, you get very little time to reinvent yourself . . . in the style of Madonna and Lady Gaga. You need to constantly evolve and fix your flaws. A lot of people get by saying, I have no flaws to fix. It's about enhancing the things I do well while changing the things I don't. Figure skating is all very cookie-cutter and nuts-and-bolts. People always do the same thing. No one does anything fresh and new. I want to come out with a new style of skating."

In May 2010 Weir embarked on his first music venture, recording a dance/pop track called "Dirty Love" with the producer Lucian Piane. The next month the Sundance Channel aired the finale of the documentary series Be Good, Johnny Weir. Weir recently completed an autobiography, titled "Welcome to My World," which will be published by Gallery Books in 2011. He hopes to compete in the 2014 Winter Olympic Games, in Russia.

—T.O.

Suggested Reading: Boston Globe D p1 Feb. 17, 2006; Chicago Tribune N p3 Jan. 17, 2003, C p16 Mar. 21, 2004; Los Angeles Times (on-line) Mar. 8, 2010; New York Times D p5 Feb. 16, 2006; Philadelphia Inquirer E p1 Jan. 17, 2005, D p1 Jan. 25, 2007; San Francisco Chronicle D p3 Jan. 13, 2006; USA Today (on-line) Jan. 12, 2006, Jan. 28, 2008; Washington Post E p8 Jan. 11, 2004

Wilco

Music group

Tweedy, Jeff
Aug. 25, 1967– Singer; songwriter; guitarist

Stirratt, John
1967– Bass guitar player

Cline, Nels
Jan. 4, 1956– Guitarist

Kotche, Glenn
1970– Drummer

Sansone, Pat
June 21, 1969– Multi-instrumentalist

Jorgensen, Mikael
1972(?)– Keyboardist

Address: c/o Nonesuch Records, 75 Rockefeller Plaza, New York, NY 10019

After the popular "alternative-country" music act Uncle Tupelo disbanded, in 1993, its co-founder Jeff Tweedy launched Wilco, which has earned critical recognition and commercial success and is one of the few contemporary groups that appeal to teenagers, their parents, and the generation in between. Wilco has cultivated its audience through an idiosyncratic mix of "roots" country, experimental yet accessible pop, psychedelia, and classic-style rock. It has won praise from the music press for its seven studio albums, collaborations with Billy Bragg on two collections based on songs by Woody Guthrie, and live album. Tweedy, the band's main vocalist and primary songwriter, is the face of Wilco. Bob Mehr wrote for the *AmericanWay* Web site, "Tweedy has continually challenged both his audience and himself musically. A somewhat reluctant rock star, he's managed to toe the fine line between underground respect and mainstream success and has become one of contemporary music's most compelling and revered figures in the process."

Wilco has gone through several lineup changes, with Tweedy and John Stirratt being the only constant members; the band currently includes, in addition, the guitarist Nels Cline, the multi-instrumentalists Pat Sansone and Mikael Jorgensen, and the drummer Glenn Kotche. Joe Klein wrote for the *New York Times* (June 13, 2004), "Through it all, Tweedy has produced some terrific (and not so terrific) music. Each Wilco album is different from the last. Tweedy is a classic autodidact, inhaling books, constantly pushing himself to grow and change. Over time, he has become a better guitar player and learned how to mess with the computerized gimmickry of the modern recording studio. Most important, he has figured out how to sing in an entirely distinctive and compelling way.

Like [Bob] Dylan, Neil Young and others, Tweedy has a scratchy, nasal, good-bad voice, which depends on his emotional intelligence and phrasing, rather than timbre, for its effectiveness. His delivery is purposefully nervous, artfully irresolute. He will bend or slur a phrase, pause uncomfortably, allow a note to shatter in mid-attack; at times, it sounds as if he's very close to a nervous breakdown. There is a terrible sadness to it."

The youngest of four children, Jeffrey Scott Tweedy was born on August 25, 1967 in Belleville, Illinois, a working-class suburb of St. Louis, Missouri. His father, Bob, was a switching-yard supervisor with the Alton & Southern Railroad; his mother, Jo Ann, was a kitchen designer. Tweedy showed an inclination toward music at a very young age. "My mom put records on for me before I could operate the turntable," he told Steven Chean for *USAWeekend.com* (April 7, 2002). "Before I could speak, she says, I would point to it." Tweedy's siblings, Debra Ann, Steven, and Robert, all born in the 1950s, "were more like doting aunts and uncles" to their younger brother, according to Greg Kot, in his book *Wilco: Learning How to Die* (2004). When they left for college, he picked through their record collections, discovering bands including Herman's Hermits and the Beatles. Soon he was also listening to punk rock, absorbing the sounds of X and the Clash. In eighth grade, while confined to his bed for several weeks with a leg injury he suffered in a bicycle accident, Tweedy picked up the acoustic guitar his mother had given him when he was six. "I saw the life my dad had, and I knew I didn't want it," he told Kot. "He had to take care of a family basically since he was seventeen, and the only real outlet he had was a twelve-pack after working all day. I saw the guitar as my outlet."

While a freshman at Belleville Township High School West, Tweedy saw his first live rock show, performed at a junior-high-school dance by the Plebes—a band consisting of Tweedy's classmate Jay Farrar and his older brothers, Wade and Dade. "I just went nuts . . . ," he told Kot. "I was just completely blown away in awe—in awe of Jay, in awe of his brothers, in awe of the idea that this could be happening, that I was part of their inner circle in some way. . . . They were empowered in the way that I imagined myself to be empowered." Tweedy began to spend time with the Farrar brothers and took over on bass guitar when Dade left the band. Before departing Dade had brought in a new drummer, Mike Heidorn, for a lineup that now included Wade on vocals and Jay on guitar. The band changed its name to the Primitives (sometimes spelled "Primatives") and began to play raw, fast-paced covers of garage-rock, punk, and country songs. When Wade became too busy at college to practice regularly, the remaining trio re-formed as Uncle Tupelo, taking its name from two words randomly chosen from two columns of nouns they had written. (Tupelo, Mississippi, is the birthplace of Elvis Presley.) Uncle Tupelo began to write its own

Taylor Hill/Getty Images

Jeff Tweedy, Wilco's frontman

material, inspired by such punk bands as Husker Du and the Minutemen and by Neil Young, the Canadian singer-songwriter and guitarist known for his unique brand of acoustic folk and harder, guitar-heavy rock. Richard Byrne, then a music columnist for the St. Louis weekly the *Riverfront Times*, told Kot, "[Uncle Tupelo was] hearing the country and folk stuff that they grew up around, and they were listening to all their . . . punk records, and Neil crystallized it for them."

After high school Tweedy enrolled in courses at Southern Illinois University–Edwardsville and Belleville Area College. Less passionate about school than about playing in the band, however, he failed to graduate. To support themselves the members of Uncle Tupelo worked odd jobs; Tweedy found work as a clerk at a St. Louis music store, Euclid Records. Although the store's manager, Tony Margherita, was unmoved the first time he saw a live performance by Tweedy's band, a later acoustic show—free of the feedback and distortion Uncle Tupelo created during a regular set—so impressed him that he became the band's manager, booking shows and talking the band members into recording a demo tape. Soon Uncle Tupelo was playing regularly at Cicero's, a St. Louis "dive" bar that was quickly becoming the center of a growing independent-music scene. The band developed a small but devoted following.

In 1989 Uncle Tupelo signed with the independent label Gasatanka/Rockville/Crepescule. Their debut album, *No Depression* (1990), has been widely credited as the catalyst for "alt-country"— music that merged the energy of punk with traditional Americana and country. Jason Ankeny wrote for the All Music Guide Web site, "The most

rock-centric of Uncle Tupelo's releases, its songs were meditations on small-town, small-time life, candid snapshots of days spent working thankless jobs and nights spent in an alcoholic fog."

Uncle Tupelo's sophomore effort, *Still Feel Gone* (1991), expanded on the sound of its predecessor. *March 16–20, 1992*, released the next year, was named for the five days over which it was recorded. Consisting of all-acoustic originals and covers of traditional folk songs, the album was a critical success. Shortly after its release, Heidorn left the band and was replaced by the drummer Ken Coomer. Around that time Tweedy and Farrar recruited Max Johnston to play violin and mandolin at live shows and added John Stirratt (born in 1967) to the road crew, to maintain the conditions of the guitars. Stirratt also played bass for Uncle Tupelo occasionally, freeing Tweedy to play guitar.

Uncle Tupelo signed to Sire Records before the release of *Anodyne* (1993), which is considered to be the band's most accomplished and cohesive work. Ankeny wrote for the All Music Guide that Uncle Tupelo "never struck a finer balance between rock and country than on *Anodyne*." Although the record was not supported by mainstream radio or MTV, it sold more than 150,000 copies and became an alt-country staple. Not long after its release, however, differences between Farrar and Tweedy led Farrar to break up the band. Since the release of Uncle Tupelo's first recording, the two had been vying to have songs included on the albums. "It just seemed like it reached a point where Jeff and I really weren't compatible," Farrar told the alt-country magazine *No Depression*, according to a *Los Angeles Times* article (January 20, 2005) by Randy Lewis. "It had ceased to be a symbiotic songwriting relationship." Tweedy told Kot, "I thought it could go on for a long time, with each of us contributing our six best songs to an album, and I would have been happy to continue on that way. I was naïve."

Intent on continuing to write and record music, Tweedy—with Coomer, Johnston, and Stirratt— formed a new group. After briefly considering the name "National Dust," the band members settled on "Wilco"—short for "will comply," a term used in two-way radio communication. Tweedy told Deborah Solomon for the *New York Times* (July 5, 2009, on-line) that the name "struck me as an ironic name for a rock band, which is historically responsible for not complying." Under Margherita's management, Wilco signed with Reprise, a Warner Bros. subsidiary.

Wilco's debut, *A.M.*, recorded less than a year after Uncle Tupelo dissolved, included the work of the guitarist Brian Henneman of Missouri's Bottle Rockets and the pedal-steel player Lloyd Maines. *A.M.* received generally positive reviews, with some critics noting the continuation of Uncle Tupelo's sound and themes. Holly George-Warren wrote for *Rolling Stone* (February 2, 1998), "The band's back-porch groove is the perfect underpinning for Tweedy's laconic baritone; he leaves wide-open spaces with his laid-back phrasing and the plain-spoken poetry of his lyrics. Maines' lovesick pedal steel and Johnston's nimble offerings on mandolin, banjo, dobro and fiddle add plaintiveness, while Henneman's Neil Young–inspired guitar antics provide muscle."

In 1995 Wilco married a booking agent, Sue Miller, bought a home in Chicago, Illinois, and became a father, and the emotions stirred by those developments came through in Wilco's next album, *Being There* (1996). "I was a later bloomer," Tweedy told Kot. "I was in my thirties before I even came to terms with the idea that I was making a living as a recording artist. . . . [With Uncle Tupelo] I was a bass player in a band making fifty dollars a night, paying eighty dollars a month in rent . . . and having this naïve sense of well-being that I would always do this and never have much more responsibility than that. I went from that to being a dad and a major label-recording artist who had the pressure of supporting a family and also making something I felt good about artistically." A 19-song double album, *Being There* won critical acclaim. It featured the work of a recently recruited second guitarist, Jay Bennett, who replaced Henneman, and the pedal-steel player Bob Egan of the band Freakwater on two tracks. *Being There* was regarded by the music press as a bit of a departure from the alt-country sounds of *A.M.*, as many of the songs had off-the-wall lyrics, improvised moments, and other experimental elements. For example, in a portion of the opening track, "Misunderstood," the band members can be heard in the background playing one another's instruments. In an article for the *Chicago Tribune* (October 18, 1996), Kot wrote, "The first sound heard on Wilco's new record, *Being There*, suggests studio meltdown: amplifiers buzzing, violins sawing, noise swelling. It's a cacophonous introduction that says, put away all your preconceptions and enjoy the ride, because the band's friendly Midwestern twang has taken on some new accents." The album fared better than *A.M.* commercially, peaking at number 73 on the *Billboard* 200 album chart and landing on several "best-of-the-year" lists. The single "Outtasite (Outta Mind)" received a moderate amount of play on college radio stations.

Not long after the release of *Being There*, Johnston left Wilco to play music with his sister, Michelle Shocked; he was replaced by Egan. In 1998 Wilco collaborated with the British singer-songwriter Billy Bragg on a collection of songs based on previously unrecorded material by the iconic folk singer Woody Guthrie, who died in 1967. The recording sessions were organized by Guthrie's daughter, Nora, who had approached Bragg in 1995 about recording her father's songs for a new audience. Bragg told Kot that the influence of traditional music on Wilco's sound appealed to him: "With a lot of American roots bands, it doesn't go back much beyond the 1950s, but Wilco gives you the feeling that they go back to the '30s and even into the last century."

Although Wilco and Bragg had creative clashes during the recording sessions, the results—*Mermaid Avenue* (1998) and *Mermaid Avenue, Vol. 2* (2000)—were critically acclaimed, and *Mermaid Avenue* was nominated for a Grammy Award for best contemporary folk album. On the albums Bragg performed Guthrie's more overtly political material, while Tweedy chose to record the singer's more personal songs. In a 1998 review posted on his Web site, the music critic Robert Christgau wrote of the first release, "It's the music, especially Wilco's music, that transfigures the enterprise. Projecting the present back on the past in an attempt to make the past signify as future, they create an old-time rock and roll that never could have existed. Finally—folk-rock!" Mark Guarino wrote for the Chicago *Daily Herald* (July 10, 1998), "The timeless sound of *Mermaid Avenue* prevents it from being a novelty knockoff and instead surrounds Guthrie's words with lively arrangements and an unholy playfulness. Here, there's the clunky pianos, honking harmonicas, shout-along choruses, wheezy slide guitars and the unpretentious production heard on Wilco's acclaimed double-album *Being There*. Not only demonstrating the breezy interplay between folk and rock styles, the new album clearly links Guthrie to modern times without damaging nor deifying him."

Wilco's *Summerteeth* (1999), recorded prior to the *Mermaid Avenue* sessions, won rave reviews for songs that largely eschewed country influences in favor of densely layered pop. Jason Ankeny wrote, "While lacking the sheer breadth and ambition of . . . *Being There*, *Summerteeth* is the most focused Wilco effort yet, honing the lessons of the last record to forge a majestic pop sound almost completely devoid of alt-country elements; the lush string arrangements and gorgeous harmonies of tracks like 'She's a Jar' and 'Pieholden Suite' suggest nothing less than a landlocked Brian Wilson [of the Beach Boys], while more straightforward rockers like the opening 'I Can't Stand It' bear the influence of everything from R&B to psychedelia." Christgau included *Summerteeth* in the Top 10 of his annual "Pazz and Jop Critics Poll" in the *Village Voice*. Nonetheless, *Summerteeth*'s failure to sell as well as *Being There* caused strained relations between Wilco and the band's record label.

Wilco recorded its fourth album, *Yankee Hotel Foxtrot*, at a Chicago loft converted into a recording studio. Tweedy tapped the experimental solo musician Jim O'Rourke to serve as producer, added the multi-instrumentalist Leroy Bach to the lineup, and hired the drummer Glenn Kotche (born in 1970) to replace Coomer, whom he had fired. Coomer learned of his dismissal from Margherita and was taken by surprise. "I made a decision to honor inspiration as opposed to honoring loyalty to a friend," Tweedy told Kot. "It was about loyalty to the music and to the band, and making the band better. It's not that Ken wasn't a good drummer. But he wasn't the right drummer anymore." He added, "I should have called him. . . . By the time

I did make the call, I don't think he wanted to talk to me." *Yankee Hotel Foxtrot* comprised quirky pop songs with sound textures and collages provided by O'Rourke and Bennett. Despite the album's pop hooks and lush instrumentation, Reprise—under pressure to cut costs—rejected *Yankee Hotel Foxtrot* as uncommercial. Instead of reworking the album, Wilco bought out its $50,000 contract with Reprise and gained the rights to *Yankee Hotel Foxtrot*. While shopping for a new label, Wilco streamed the album on the Internet, generating anticipation among fans and critics and drumming up negative publicity for Warner Bros. and Reprise executives, who were demonized by journalists for seemingly placing profit above artistic integrity. *Yankee Hotel Foxtrot* was released in 2002 by Nonesuch Records, another Warner Music Group subsidiary. It is the biggest popular success of Wilco's career to date, debuting at number 13 on the *Billboard* pop-album chart and selling more than 400,000 copies within two years. It was named the best album of 2002 in the *Village Voice's* annual critics' poll and otherwise lavished with praise. Jeff Gordinier wrote for *Entertainment Weekly* (April 26, 2002) that it was "a subliminal album. Spin it once and it barely registers. Play it five or six times and its vaporous, insinuating, rusty-carousel melodies start to carve out a permanent orbit in your skull." Ben Wener wrote for the *Orange County (California) Register* (April 26, 2002), "[*Yankee Hotel Foxtrot*] is entrancing, uplifting rock 'n' roll that embodies the yin and yang of love, the exuberant joy of it all and the inevitable insecurity and tension that brings."

Although Bennett had contributed heavily to the songwriting and production of *Yankee Hotel Foxtrot*, he was asked to leave Wilco shortly after the album's release. Tweedy told Kot that during the sound-mixing process for *Yankee Hotel Foxtrot*, Bennett's controlling approach made for a tense atmosphere and undermined the group's creativity. Although Bennett initially said, as quoted by Kot, that he believed he was fired because "Jeff was threatened by me," he later acknowledged that the band's decision had been the right one. The contentious relationship between Bennett and Tweedy was captured in the 2002 documentary about the making of *Yankee Hotel Foxtrot*, Sam Jones's *I Am Trying to Break Your Heart*.

Wilco's next release, *A Ghost Is Born* (2004), was written and recorded with the help of Mikael Jorgensen, who provided sound manipulation and later joined the band as a keyboardist and live-sound manipulator. The album, like its predecessor, sprinkled Tweedy's idiosyncratic pop songs with experimental flourishes. It was also influenced by Tweedy's longtime struggle with addiction to painkillers, which he developed in an attempt to treat migraine headaches and depression. In a piece for the *New York Times* Web site (March 5, 2008) about the making of the album, Tweedy wrote, "For a lot of that record I was just trying not to be too drugged out and as a result I was suffering from enormous migraine type throbbing pain. Quite a bit of that came out on *A Ghost Is Born*. . . . In particular there's a piece of music—'Less Than You Think'—that ends with a 12-minute drone that was an attempt to express the slow painful rise and dissipation of migraine in music." (Tweedy shook his addiction after a period of rehab in 2004.) The album was a critical success and earned Wilco its first two Grammy Awards—one for best alternative-music album and another for best recording package. It also reached number eight on the *Billboard* 200 chart.

Wilco's next release, *Sky Blue Sky* (2007), included playing by the guitarist Nels Cline (born on January 4, 1956) and the multi-instrumentalist Pat Sansone (born on June 21, 1969). (Bach had left the band, amicably, after *Yankee Hotel Foxtrot*.) *Sky Blue Sky* was a more laid-back and straightforward collection, with songs reminiscent of those written during earlier incarnations of the band. *Wilco (The Album)* (2009) offered experimental tracks such as the dissonant "Bull Black Nova" along with pop-rock fare, such as the George Harrison–inspired "You Never Know," the band's second number-one song on the *Billboard* Triple A (adult album alternative) chart in 12 years. (The first was "Outtasite [Outta Mind]," in 1997.) The album also found the band poking fun at itself and reflecting on its reputation for playing emotionally charged music. For example, the opening track, "Wilco (The Song)," features Tweedy singing the sarcastic lines, "Do you dabble in depression? / Is someone twisting a knife in your back? . . . Wilco will love you, baby." *Wilco (The Album)* received generally positive reviews. David Fricke wrote for *Rolling Stone* (June 29, 2009, on-line), "Wilco's seventh studio album is a triumph of determined simplicity by a band that has been running from the obvious for most of this decade."

Tom Breihan, writing for *Pitchfork.com* (July 7, 2010), reported that in an interview with an ex-pressnightout.com reporter, Cline revealed that Wilco would be leaving Nonesuch Records and would launch its own label. The following month Wilco organized its own three-day independent festival, the Solid Sound Festival, at the Massachusetts Museum of Contemporary Art (Mass MoCA), in North Adams. The festival included performances by Wilco and each Wilco member's side groups, including the Nels Cline Singers; Glenn Kotche's On Fillmore; the Autumn Defense, with both Stirratt and Sansone; and Mikael Jorgensen's Pronto.

Tweedy has sometimes been criticized for the control he exerts over the band—as when he fired Bennett. That criticism arose again in May 2009, when Bennett sued Tweedy over royalty payments and noncompensation for his appearance in *I Am Trying to Break Your Heart*. In statements to the media, Tweedy denied that he owed Bennett money and noted that he was not the producer of the documentary. That same month Bennett died after an accidental overdose of prescription painkillers.

Tweedy told Romesh Ratnesar for *Time* (June 30, 2009) about Bennett's death, "It's a real hard thing to talk about. . . . It's been eight years since he's been in the band, and our situation was very tenuous and not very well connected. But it's a tragic end to a brilliant and gifted guy and musician. And that's really sad."

Tweedy described his singing voice to Solomon as being "somewhere between Gordon Lightfoot and a tea kettle. I would not get past the first round of *American Idol*." In addition to Wilco and Loose Fur, Tweedy has performed in the "super group" Golden Smog. He lives in Chicago with his wife and two young children, Spencer and Sam. When Ratnesar asked him what had inspired the more optimistic songs on *Wilco (The Album)*, Tweedy said, "I don't think there's any reason to feel guilty about having joy in your life, regardless of how bad things are in the world. Even the most dismal and

hopeless-sounding Wilco music, to my ears, has always maintained a level of hope and consolation. I think art is a consolation regardless of its content. It has the power to move and make you feel like you're not alone. And ultimately that's what everybody wants to know."

—W.D.

Suggested Reading: All Music Guide Web site; *Rolling Stone* Web site; *USA Weekend* (on-line) Apr. 7, 2002; Kot, Greg. *Wilco: Leaning How to Die*, 2004

Selected Recordings: *A.M.*, 1995; *Being There*, 1996; *Summerteeth*, 1999; *Yankee Hotel Foxtrot*, 2002; *A Ghost Is Born*, 2004; *Sky Blue Sky*, 2007; *Wilco (The Album)*, 2009; with Billy Bragg— *Mermaid Avenue*, 1998; *Mermaid Avenue, Vol. 2*, 2000

Frederick Breedon/Getty Images

Womack, Lee Ann

Aug. 19, 1966– Country singer

Address: c/o Erv Woolsey Co., 1000 18th Ave., South Nashville, TN 37212

Lee Ann Womack is known for her signature twang and old-fashioned musical style, which have earned her comparisons to such country-music legends as Dolly Parton and Tammy Wynette. Womack burst onto the country-music scene in 1997 with an eponymous debut album that achieved instant critical and commercial success, and she

went on to even greater fame with the hit crossover recording *I Hope You Dance* (2000), which reached the number-one spot on the *Billboard* country-album chart and sold nearly four million copies in the U.S. Womack "is one of the few mainstream female country artists left in Nashville who continues to remain successful by maintaining a traditional influence in her music," Michael A. Capozzoli Jr. wrote for the BPI Entertainment News Wire (June 29, 2000).

The daughter of Aubrey and Ann Womack, Lee Ann Womack was born on August 19, 1966 in Jacksonville, Texas. She has a sister, Judy, who is six years her senior. Her father, who was the principal of an East Texas high school, worked as a part-time country-music disc jockey at KEBE-AM, a local radio station, and her mother, a teacher, loved show tunes. As a child Womack listened to country music on the radio and often accompanied her father to the station, where she helped select the records he played. "My dad had a lot of Ray Price and Bob Wills and Tommy Duncan records," she recalled to Chet Flippo for *Billboard* (April 5, 1997). "And then, of course, Tammy Wynette and Dolly Parton." Womack soon began dreaming of becoming a country-music star. "She always wanted to go to Nashville," Ann Womack told Steve Dougherty for *People* (July 31, 2000). "We never dissuaded her. We wanted her to follow her dreams."

At her parents' suggestion, Womack began taking piano lessons. "At first I hated every minute of it," she explained to Dougherty. "My teacher made me play classical music, and I wanted to play country. I used to sit and play these sad little songs, wishing I was in Nashville." She skipped her high school's senior class trip and used the money for a trip to Nashville, to visit Music Row and other iconic sites.

After graduating from Jacksonville High School, in 1984, Womack attended South Plains Junior College, in Levelland, Texas, where she studied music. (The school was one of the first in the nation to offer degrees in bluegrass and country music.) Shortly after entering South Plains, Womack became a vocalist in Country Caravan, a college band that toured the country. She left junior college after a year, however, and moved to Nashville to pursue her musical career. In order to satisfy her parents, Womack entered Nashville's Belmont University, where she studied the commercial aspects of the music industry. During that time she landed a student internship in the A&R department of MCA Records.

Womack remained at Belmont until 1990, when she left to marry her college sweetheart, the country-music artist Jason Sellers. (She was just three courses shy of earning her degree.) The following year she gave birth to her first daughter, Aubrie Lee. While putting in hours as a waitress and child-care worker, Womack remained focused on her music career. Craig Seymour wrote for the *Atlanta Journal-Constitution* (August 25, 2002), "Unable to afford a babysitter, she would stroll down Music Row holding her baby with one hand and a demo tape with the other." Womack's persistence paid off in 1995, when she was offered a songwriting deal at Sony/ATV Music Publishing. As a staffer at the company's subsidiary Tree Publishing, she co-wrote songs with such prominent country-music names as Ed Hill, Bill Anderson, Sam Hogin, and Mark Wright. Ricky Skaggs recorded Womack's composition "I Don't Remember Forgetting" for his 1995 album *Solid Ground*.

In early 1997 Womack's songwriting abilities and strong desire to sing landed her an audition with MCA Nashville's chairman, Bruce Hinton, who quickly signed her to a contract with MCA's sister label, Decca Records. "She came into the office and performed acoustically, and it was a very special moment," Hinton recalled to Chet Flippo. Shortly after signing with Decca, Womack showcased her talents at the Country Radio Seminar, an annual convention held in Nashville that was attended by more than 2,000 industry insiders. That performance helped bolster the release of her debut single, "Never Again, Again," which made the *Billboard* country-singles chart and received heavy radio airplay.

In May 1997 Womack released her eponymous debut album, which was produced by Mark Wright and consisted of both original material and songs written by Mark Chesnutt, Ricky Skaggs, and Tony Brown. The traditional style of the album, which included the hit singles "The Fool," "You've Got to Talk to Me," and "Buckaroo," struck a chord with fans; it peaked at number nine on the *Billboard* country-album chart and reached gold status within months. "*Lee Ann Womack* is a rarity in modern Nashville—an authentic honky-tonk debut album," the music critic Geoffrey Himes wrote in a review available on Amazon.com. "Producer

Mark Wright has refused to bury Womack's small-town, East Texas drawl under the Hollywood soft-rock cloaking that Music Row favors these days. As a result, the young singer's soprano projects an attitude too unsophisticated to hide any emotion. On the first single, 'Never Again, Again,' you can hear in quivering high notes the dilemma of a woman who keeps breaking her own promise to never take her ex-lover back. Not every song is that sharply focused, and the obligatory boot-scootin' dance numbers and string-smothered ballads dilute the album's impact. But you can hear Womack's potential." In recognition of her debut, Womack was named best new female vocalist by the Academy of Country Music (ACM), top new artist of the year by *Billboard*, and favorite new country artist at the American Music Awards (AMAs). Additionally, she was nominated for a Horizon Award from the Country Music Association (CMA); that prize ultimately went to the teenage singer LeAnn Rimes.

Womack brought out her sophomore album, *Some Things I Know*, in 1998. The recording, which was also produced by Wright, featured the hit singles "A Little Past Little Rock" and "I'll Think of a Reason," both of which reached the number-two spot on the country-singles chart. *Some Things I Know* peaked at number 20 on the *Billboard* country-album chart and later achieved gold status.

In 1999 Decca Records folded, and Womack moved to MCA Records. The following year her third album, *I Hope You Dance*, appeared. The title track, a crossover hit, reached number one on the *Billboard* country-singles chart, topped the adult-contemporary chart, and peaked at number 14 on the *Billboard* Hot 100 chart. The recording as a whole debuted at number one on the *Billboard* country-album chart and entered the *Billboard* 200 chart at number 17; it has since sold almost four million copies in the U.S. Womack landed six CMA nominations for the album and won awards for single of the year and song of the year. She also received two ACM awards, in the same categories, and took home a Grammy Award for best country song.

Because of the uplifting theme of "I Hope You Dance," which includes the lyrics "Promise me you'll give faith a fighting chance / And when you get the choice to sit it out or dance / I hope you dance," Womack was asked to perform at the 2000 Nobel Peace Prize concert (an annual event honoring the year's laureate) and on an installment of the widely watched *Oprah Winfrey Show*. The track has been played at countless proms, graduations, and weddings. "[The song] made me think about my daughters and the different times in their lives," Womack told Chuck Taylor for *Billboard* (July 1, 2000, on-line). "But it can be so many things to different people. Certainly, it can represent everything a parent hopes for their child, but it can also be for someone graduating, having a baby, or embarking on a new path. It fits almost every circumstance I can think of."

I Hope You Dance, which also featured the Top 40 country singles "Ashes by Now," "Why They Call It Falling," and "Does My Ring Burn Your Finger," received widespread attention from critics. In a review for the All Music Guide Web site, Maria Konicki Dinola called the recording "one of the finest albums to hit country music [since] Shania Twain" and added, "Womack possesses such a sweet, melodious voice and its distinctiveness graces every one of the 12 tracks like they were chosen just for her vocals." In an assessment for *People* (June 19, 2000), Ralph Novak wrote, "With its rueful tone, evocative songs and emotion-drenched, sweet-voiced vocals, this could have been mistaken for a Dolly Parton album. Who would have guessed it's the erstwhile Texas firebrand Womack in a new mode less suited to honky-tonks than to wedding receptions." In a review featured in the *Quincy (Massachusetts) Patriot Ledger* (June 14, 2000), Ken Rosenbaum expressed untempered praise: "Womack's sweet, crystalline voice blends a wide assortment of country song types into a craftsmanlike, cohesive, and satisfying package. She glides from painful laments and torchy sizzlers to fiddle-drenched waltzes and bouncy honky-tonkers, leaving in her wake a profound feeling that something special has just been heard."

In 2002 Womack's album *Something Worth Leaving Behind* reached stores. Despite reaching number two on the *Billboard* country-music album chart and peaking at number 16 on the *Billboard* 200 chart, the recording failed to produce a Top 10 country hit and received tepid notices from reviewers, who criticized Womack for abandoning her signature sound in favor of a more pop-oriented style and for sporting a new, more glamorous look than before. In a review published in the *Bergen County (New Jersey) Record* (September 6, 2002), Nick Cristiano wrote, "*Something Worth Leaving Behind* contains too many pedestrian songs that are further burdened by schlocky, play-it-safe production. The title track, done in two equally unsatisfying versions, is a prime example. With its inspirational message, it is an obvious attempt to repeat the success of *Dance*'s title song, but it is much triter."

In the summer of 2002, Womack toured with the country legend Willie Nelson, and in October of that year, she released a Christmas album, *The Season for Romance*, featuring a rendition of the popular standard "Baby It's Cold Outside," which she performed with Harry Connick Jr. Womack next collaborated with Nelson on his single "Mendocino County Line," which won a 2003 Grammy Award for best country collaboration. The single also garnered awards from the ACM and the CMA.

In early 2003 Womack made her acting debut, with a small guest role on the CBS drama *The District*. She returned to the record stores in 2004, with the appearance of a greatest-hits collection, which also included two new songs, the Top 40 country hit "The Wrong Girl" and "Time for Me to Go." That year Womack performed "I Hope You Dance" at the Republican National Convention and collaborated with the country band Cross Canadian Ragweed on the song "Sick and Tired," which became a minor hit.

In 2005 Womack released *There's More Where That Came From*. The album, which included a duet with the country icon George Strait called "Good News, Bad News," marked a return to the singer's traditional roots. The lead single, "I May Hate Myself in the Morning," cracked the Top 10 on the *Billboard* country-singles chart and featured background vocals by Jason Sellers, with whom Womack had split amicably in 1997. Two additional singles, "He Oughta Know That by Now" and "Twenty Years and Two Husbands Ago," became Top 40 country hits. Womack told Mikel Toombs for the *San Diego Union-Tribune* (February 17, 2006), "Everybody has different definitions of what traditional country music is. To me, traditional country music is twin fiddles and steel guitars, and the hardcore country [songs]. There are some people out there who love it. I'm from Texas, and that's where a lot of them are." She also discussed the topic with Michael A. Capozzoli Jr., asserting, "Even though it's been hard to stay grounded in the real traditional music with radio the way it is right now, I love very real country music. . . . That will always be a priority to me."

Critics were almost universally impressed with *There's More Where That Came From*. Anthony Easton wrote for *Stylus* magazine (March 23, 2005, on-line), "The brilliance of this album is that it knows its history, but collapses and expands it into a universe all its own." Making mention of the hazy, vintage-looking portrait of Womack that adorned the album jacket, Stephen Thomas Erlewine wrote for the All Music Guide Web site, "*There's More Where That Came From* . . . is still firmly within the country-pop confines, but there's a notable difference—as the rather brilliant cover art suggests, this hearkens back to the sound and style of early-'70s country-pop albums from the likes of Barbara Mandrell, Loretta Lynn, and Dolly Parton. Not that this is a retro effort, or anything like a stab at neo-traditionalist country. Instead, Womack takes her inspiration from these records, crafting a record that's laidback but never lazy, smooth but never too slick, tuneful without being cloying." He concluded, "All this adds up to an album that's not only the best album that Lee Ann Womack has yet made, but one that does suggest that there is indeed more where this came from." *There's More Where That Came From* was named album of the year by the CMA, and "I May Hate Myself in the Morning" garnered song-of-the-year honors. "Good News, Bad News" also took home the CMA award for best "musical event" of the year. (The association uses the term "event" to refer to a collaboration between artists.)

In the summer of 2006, Womack released the single "Finding My Way Back Home," on the Mercury Nashville label. The single debuted at number

46 on the *Billboard* country-singles chart and peaked at number 37. Womack had intended to include the song on a studio album of the same name, but those plans fell through when she left Mercury and returned to MCA Nashville. In 2008 she released *Call Me Crazy*, which debuted at number four on the *Billboard* country-album chart. Produced by Tony Brown, the Grammy-nominated record included the single "Last Call," which became Womack's first Top 20 hit in nearly three years. Another single, "Solitary Thinkin'," cracked the Top 40 of the country charts. Like its predecessor, the album included a duet with Strait ("Everything but Quits") and also featured a cover of the Strait classic "The King of Broken Hearts."

Call Me Crazy received largely mixed reviews. Expressing sentiments echoed by other critics, Jonathan Keefe wrote for *Slant Magazine* (October 19, 2008, on-line), that *Call Me Crazy* is "characterized by a stylistic diversity and an insistence on playing against her strengths." He added, "Though her voice sounds thin when compared to that of Patty Loveless or Trisha Yearwood, Womack is a first-rate stylist and one of the finest interpretative singers of her generation, so she is able to carry the album even when the production and the songwriting fail her." Christian Hoard wrote for *Rolling Stone* (November 13, 2008, on-line), "The album sounds way more professional than crazy, but tunefulness this pleasant works out just fine."

Womack is currently putting the finishing touches on her next studio album. The lead single from the album, "There Is a God," was released in late 2009 and debuted at number 60 on the *Billboard* country-singles chart. Womack has since revealed the titles of other songs on the album, including "Talking Behind Your Back" and "You Do Until You Don't."

Womack, who spent the early months of 2010 touring with Strait and Reba McEntire, has been married to the record producer Frank Liddell since November 1999. In addition to Aubrie Lee, her daughter with Sellers, she has one daughter with Liddell, Anna Lise.

—C.C.

Suggested Reading: *Atlanta Journal-Constitution* L p1+ Aug. 25, 2002; *Billboard* p67 Aug. 10, 2002; BPI Entertainment News Wire June 29, 2000; *Chicago Tribune* C p7 Oct. 1, 2000; *Miami Herald* G p5 Dec. 2, 2005; *People* p129 July 31, 2000

Selected Recordings: *Lee Ann Womack*, 1997; *Some Things I Know*, 1998; *I Hope You Dance*, 2000; *Something Worth Leaving Behind*, 2002; *The Season for Romance*, 2002; *Greatest Hits*, 2004; *There's More Where That Came From*, 2005; *Call Me Crazy*, 2008

Zandi, Mark

May 28, 1959– Economist; entrepreneur; writer

Address: Moody's Economy.com, 121 N. Walnut St., Suite 500, West Chester, PA 19380

Mark Zandi's name "may sound familiar," David Leonhardt wrote for the *New York Times* (December 23, 2008, on-line)."He is probably the most quoted economist in the country. His ubiquity sometimes causes journalists to be afflicted by Zandi syndrome—a sudden onset of fear that we are quoting him too much. But we inevitably get over it because he is a master of digging up data and then explaining it in a language foreign to most economists: plain English." Zandi—an economist whom legislators, too, often consult—is the cofounder of Moody's Economy.com, an economic-forecasting firm that sells tailored packages of economic data to investors including banks and other businesses and government agencies. He is the chief economist of Moody's Analytics, a subsidiary of Moody's Corp., where he is the director of research and consulting. On its Web site Moody's Economy.com offers economic data and analyses free of charge, in language easy for laypeople to understand; for a monthly subscription the company offers its on-line newsletter, the *Dismal Scientist*.

Brendan Smialowski/Getty Images for *Meet the Press*

Economic forecasting involves collecting thousands of pieces of information, known as economic indicators (examples include total jobless claims, number of home foreclosures, and sales at particular retail chains during a given period), designing computer models that generate likely future economic scenarios, plugging data into the models, and interpreting the results. "If I can't explain [the results] to myself in clear, simple terms, then I can't explain [them] to anyone else," Zandi told Susan Warner for the *Philadelphia Inquirer* (December 9, 2001). "It's a very painful process, but for me it's the most necessary thing I do." Zandi founded the forerunner to Moody's Economy.com, called Financial Regional Associates, in 1990, with his brother Karl and his friend Paul Getman. The company's popularity grew during the economic boom that took place in the next decade. In 1999 Zandi and Getman purchased the domain name Economy.com; the "Moody's" was added in 2005, when their firm was purchased by the investment-management firm Moody's Investors Service. Zandi strongly supported the federal stimulus package signed into law by President Barack Obama in February 2009. The previous year Zandi had published his first book, *Financial Shock: A 360 Degree Look at the Subprime Mortgage Crisis*, in which he analyzed the factors that led to the recent recession.

The first of the five children of Iraj Zandi and the former Annette M. Grantham, Mark Mansur Zandi was born on May 28, 1959. He grew up in Gulph Mills, a suburb of Philadelphia, Pennsylvania, with his three brothers (Richard, Karl, and Peter) and one sister (Meriam). His father, an Iranian immigrant, was a professor of civil and urban engineering at the University of Pennsylvania (UPenn). As a child Zandi spent a lot of time with his father on campus. After he completed high school, he attended UPenn's Wharton School, the oldest college to focus on business. He had little aptitude for accounting or management, he discovered, but enjoyed economics. He earned a B.S. degree in economics in 1981. He then pursued graduate studies at the school, becoming something of a protégé of Lawrence R. Klein, an economist known for his revolutionary work in economic forecasting. Klein—who won the Nobel Prize in Economic Science in 1980—embraced Keynesian economics, a theory, proposed by the British economist John Maynard Keynes (1883–1946), that advocates government involvement in the private market to create efficient and stable macroeconomic conditions. (Macroeconomics is the study of the economy as a whole. Microeconomics examines the behavior of individual consumers and companies.) Zandi completed his doctoral dissertation in 2006.

While he was a graduate student, Zandi worked at an offshoot of UPenn: Wharton Economic Forecasting Associates (WEFA), a leading forecasting and consulting organization founded by Klein. Zandi also worked at another major economics-forecasting firm, Chase Econometrics, an independent subsidiary of Chase Manhattan Bank that was purchased by WEFA in 1987 and became known as the WEFA Group. Along with another Wharton graduate student and Chase staff member, Paul

Getman, Zandi grew critical of WEFA's and Chase's products: high-priced packages that offered the fruits of the employees' research and were sold to banks and other businesses without any modifications to meet their particular needs. Zandi and Getman believed that they could develop a more "customer-friendly" means of disseminating economic information. They proposed to their superiors that Chase create customized packages of economic information, each focusing on a particular aspect of the global economy and each priced individually. Their idea was rejected. Getman recalled to David Whitford for *Fortune Small Business Magazine (FSB)* (March 2003), "We said, 'Fine, you can stay the way you are. We're going to take our marbles and start our own firm.'"

In 1990, in the midst of an economic recession, Zandi and Getman left Chase and, with Zandi's brother Karl, set up a financial-services company; called Financial Regional Associates (FRA), it was housed in Getman's basement in West Chester, a Philadelphia suburb. Mark Zandi used his personal credit card to fund the firm's start-up expenses, while Getman, who became CEO, cashed in his 401(K) retirement account. "I didn't breathe for a year," Zandi told Christopher Dinsmore for the *Virginian-Pilot* (January 22, 2004). Around that time personal computers were gaining in popularity, and within a few years the Internet had become widely available. Zandi, FRA's chief economist, and Getman, its CEO, took advantage of those phenomena by creating both an open company Web site and a members-only site. Its public site, the *Dismal Scientist*—a reference to the "dismal sciences," a derogatory term for economics coined in the 19th century—allowed users to compare economic data, such as housing prices and unemployment figures, associated with different states and regions. At first FRA earned most of its revenue from sales of consulting services to businesses and government agencies and the balance from on-line sales of small, individualized packages of data. By 1997 FRA had 40 employees, most in their 20s, who analyzed information regarding 250 metropolitan areas in the U.S. and provided their findings to banks, utilities, real-estate firms, and government agencies. (By 2003 most of the company's revenue was coming from subscriptions to its on-line newsletter.)

In the 1990s Zandi became a source of expertise for journalists writing about the economy. During that decade the U.S. economy expanded greatly, along with the proliferation of Internet-based companies (so-called dot-coms). From 1992 to 1993 lenders' interest rates declined to their lowest point in about 20 years, prompting many people to take out home loans and many homeowners to refinance their mortgages. As more Americans acquired wealth, many became first-time investors, and the market for low-cost, reliable, easily understood economic information grew. In the early 1990s Zandi was one of the few economists who identified the phenomenon that became known as the "wealth effect"—an increase in home buying and renovation not because of higher wages but because of wealth derived from stock-market profits. At the same time housing prices, government tax revenues, and individual spending rose dramatically. "This relationship between retail sales and consumer activity and the stock market is very, very strong," Zandi told an interviewer for the *Massachusetts Telegram & Gazette* (May 26, 2000).

By the latter part of the 1990s, Zandi had detected some disturbing trends. In 1997, for example, he noted an increase in sub-prime loans: high-interest loans approved for borrowers with poor credit histories. In many cases lenders had lured such borrowers by leading them to assume, mistakenly, that their monthly mortgage fees would always remain unusually low. When, as inevitably happened, the monthly rates increased, many of the borrowers would find themselves unable to keep up with their payments. Their debts would mount, and some would default on their loans; some would be forced to file for bankruptcy. For that reason Zandi predicted that an economic slowdown, or even a recession, would occur in five to seven years.

Six times between 1999 and 2000, Alan Greenspan, the chairman of the Federal Reserve System, the country's central banking system, raised the interest rates imposed on banks. By raising the cost of borrowing, those moves exacerbated a number of problems within the economy that were not apparent to most people, because of the low unemployment rate and other conditions that seemed to indicate prosperity. Indeed, at one point in early 2000, the unemployment rate fell to 3.9 percent, the lowest rate since 1970. At that time Zandi agreed with a minority of economists when he warned that the present combination of such phenomena as overvalued dot-com stocks and high interest rates would lead to a situation in which the economy was no longer sustainable. The result, Zandi argued, would be an economic downturn in the near future. Though many observers later credited him for those early warnings, Zandi in retrospect described his pronouncements on the tech-boom's demise as premature. But he had correctly concluded that many of the Internet-based companies were not sustainable and that traders had overvalued such businesses' stocks. In March 2000 the dot-com "bubble" burst; stock prices plummeted, investments dried up, many jobs ceased to exist, and the housing market slowed.

Eager for information about the economy and advice, hundreds of thousands of people turned to Zandi and Getman's company, which by then was called Economy.com. "When things are eroding and uncertain, it sends a wake-up call, and people are more interested in the economy," Zandi told Charles J. Whalen for *BusinessWeek* (April 23, 2001). Zandi established a reputation as an economic expert, appearing with increasing frequency as a guest on television and radio news programs. While Greenspan kept insisting that the U.S. would not face a recession anytime soon, Zandi

and other economists issued warnings that a full-blown national recession was imminent.

After Al Qaeda terrorists attacked the World Trade Center, in New York City, and the Pentagon, in Washington, D.C., on September 11, 2001, the *New York Times* commissioned Zandi to predict which areas of the country would suffer the worst economic losses in the wake of the attacks. With information from 318 metropolitan areas and an elaborate economic model, Zandi predicted that the areas of the country that had been most prosperous before the event would be hit the worst. Noting that a large percentage of the public now feared flying, Zandi concluded that the worst-affected cities would be those whose economies depended on tourism: for example, Las Vegas, Nevada; Honolulu, Hawaii; Fort Worth, Texas; and Miami, Florida. He predicted that the places that would be most "cushioned" from economic peril included communities with colleges (because students tend to remain in school during recessions) and locales with military bases, information-technology firms, and other enterprises of potential interest to intelligence agencies. In October, about one month after the attacks, Zandi predicted that the dampening in consumer confidence would continue for weeks or months. However, the economic downturn that followed 9/11 was neither as severe nor as long-lasting as Zandi, and most other economists, had feared. The U.S. economy began improving in early 2002, and on September 11, 2002, the first anniversary of the attacks, Zandi estimated that the recession caused by the attacks had cost the U.S. economy around $60 billion. (For comparison, in 2002 the gross domestic product, or GDP, was more than $10,000 billion, or $10 trillion; the federal budget totaled almost $1,800 billion, or $1.8 trillion.) Zandi attributed the resilience of the economy to various actions and activities of the federal government, including the lowering of interest rates for banks and the early successes of the U.S. military in Afghanistan. He also observed that some economic problems, such as the weak stock market, stemmed not from the terrorist attacks but from conditions dating to before 9/11, such as the burst of the dot-com bubble.

In January 2003 Zandi observed, as quoted in the Burlington, Vermont, *Free Press* (January 11, 2003), that the economy had recovered from the recent downturn but had stalled due to the public's uncertainty about the U.S. involvement in a war with Iraq. In an interview with David Whitford, Zandi credited the recovery to federal stimulus programs and suggested that the best long-term step the government could take to help small businesses would be to reform the nation's health-care system. The U.S. economy continued to expand in 2004 and 2005. In January 2005 Zandi stated publicly that for the first time in four years, every state in the union was out of a recession.

In November 2005 Moody's Investors Service, which describes itself on its Web site as "among the world's most respected and widely utilized sources for credit ratings, research and risk analysis," bought Economy.com for $27 million. Renamed Moody's Economy.com, the company remained an independent operation with the same staff.

In April 2006, after the Federal Reserve Board raised interest rates, Zandi identified places (Washington, DC; Atlantic City (and nearby Ocean City), New Jersey; Phoenix, Arizona; Las Vegas; and Miami and Orlando, Florida) where housing prices exceeded what prospective buyers were willing to pay, and where a "correction"—or a drop in home prices—was imminent. Zandi predicted that, because of the increasing interest rates, many first-time buyers—who had previously made up about 40 percent of homebuyers—would be shut out of the market. Zandi said that the problems with the housing market would worsen when low-income and low-credit borrowers began to default on their mortgage payments. Over the next several months, the housing market continued to shrink. Because the mortgages had been backed by securities (financial instruments that represent the value of debts), the shrinking housing market led to a shrinking market for securities and other investment tools. As a result banks were less able to lend, and borrowers had a difficult time obtaining the loans they needed to make big purchases, such as those of homes or cars (in the case of individuals), or to expand and hire new employees (in the case of businesses). As Zandi had warned, unemployment rates soared.

On July 16, 2007 Bear Stearns, a major global investment bank, disclosed that two of its major hedge funds had lost nearly all of their value, due to their dependence on the sub-prime-mortgage market. That news sent stock markets plummeting worldwide. Zandi told David Nason for the *Weekend Australian* (July 28, 2007) that another event of similar magnitude could "have a profound psychological impact on investor confidence." (Almost a year later two Bear Stearns hedge-fund managers, Matthew Tannin and Ralph R. Cioffi, were arrested on charges of lying to investors. In November 2009 a federal jury found them not guilty; after the verdict some jurors expressed the view that the men had been scapegoated and that far larger forces had led to Bear Stearns's near-bankruptcy.) Zandi also told Nason that based on his economic modeling, sub-prime-mortgage delinquencies would peak in mid-2008 and would continue at the peak rate until 2009. He predicted that investors' losses would total $100 billion to $125 billion in the next two or three years and that home prices would decrease but by no more than 10 percent. By January 2008 much of the nation had fallen into a recession. At a speech he delivered in Norfolk, Virginia, that month, Zandi praised the $150 billion worth of incentives and services included in proposed federal economic-stimulus legislation, which was making its way through Congress at that time (it was signed into law by President George W. Bush in February 2008). He said that there was no

way to predict the length of the current economic downturn, and he warned that banks' reluctance to lend would likely affect all aspects of the economy.

In August 2008 Zandi published *Financial Shock: A 360 Degree Look at the Subprime Mortgage Crisis*, in which he described the factors that had led the U.S. economy into its greatest downturn since the Great Depression of the 1930s. "In *Financial Shock*, [Zandi] walks through the three great causes of the crisis—the housing bubble, Wall Street's underestimation of risk and regulators' failure to intervene," Leonhardt wrote in his *New York Times* assessment. "He notes that more than 30 percent of homeowners with adjustable rate mortgages were not even aware of crucial terms of their loan, like how much their rate could rise, the Federal Reserve found. He compares Wall Street managers, who believed that the slicing and dicing of mortgages into securities somehow meant the mortgages couldn't go bad, to S.U.V. owners who speed down the highway believing that they are protected from injury. And he explains exactly what Alan Greenspan and other regulators could have done differently." Zandi also proposed 10 ways to help prevent a financial crisis in the future. The Obama administration is currently attempting to adopt many of them, including an overhaul of financial-industry regulations. Zandi also offered a number of other ideas, such as creating a federal code to make uniform the many state rules regarding foreclosure proceedings. Critics praised Zandi's book for its lucid interpretation of a complex event; it was especially popular among lawmakers. In April 2009 Zandi published a revised and updated edition. He is donating the royalties from the book to the Reinvestment Fund, which invests in inner-city projects in Pennsylvania, New Jersey, Delaware, Maryland, and Washington, D.C.

A registered Democrat, Zandi served as an economic adviser to the Republican presidential candidate John McCain in 2008. "My policy is I will help any policymaker who asks, whether they be a Republican or a Democrat," he told Shailagh Murray for the *Washington Post* (February 3, 2009). After the election, in late 2008 and early 2009, when Congress discussed the provisions of a proposed economic-stimulus act, Zandi was a vocal supporter of a generous package; he testified before congressional committees many times and was among the economists most often quoted by Democrats in support of their plans. During testimony before the Senate Budget Committee in November 2008, Zandi said that nearly every dollar spent by the government on infrastructure, food stamps, extended unemployment benefits, and other such programs would generate $1.50 or more in economic activity. That "multiplier effect," however, would be absent if the stimulus came entirely in the form of a tax break, as most Republicans proposed. At that time Zandi stated his support for an economic stimulus plan worth about $400 billion. By February 2009, however, after economic indicators had grown measurably worse, Zandi expressed his support for a stimulus plan worth $1 trillion. "This may be where my Democratic leanings come out," Zandi told Murray. "Government needs to be extraordinarily aggressive at this point in time, because there's a huge hole in the economy. The only player in the economy with resources is government." The American Recovery and Reinvestment Act, a stimulus package totaling $787 billion in expanded benefits and social-welfare programs, funding for education, health care, and infrastructure, and tax cuts, was signed into law by President Obama in February 2009. In March 2009 Zandi predicted that, thanks to the effects of the stimulus package, unemployment would peak at 9.5 percent in the second quarter of 2010, resulting in a total job loss of about seven million from December 2007 to early 2010, when he predicted the economy would begin to expand again.

By the fall of 2009, in light of several improved economic indicators—including rising stock prices, increased home sales, a decline in the rate at which unemployment figures were growing, and a generally expanding economy—Zandi, along with congressional Democrats and President Obama, declared that the recession was over and that, thanks to the stimulus plan, the economy was on its way to recovery. Conservative Republicans, however, complained that jobs were still being lost and that the stimulus plan had not yet added new jobs to the economy. Zandi, along with other supporters of the bailout plan, have responded to such criticisms by noting that many aspects of the stimulus plan have yet to go into effect. In October Zandi revised his prediction for the country's peak unemployment rate. "10.5 percent is a very reasonable expectation for the peak in unemployment, but I think it would be measurably higher if not for the stimulus package," Zandi told an interviewer for *Fox News Sunday* (October 11, 2009, on-line). "The stimulus in my view is working. It's just gotten overwhelmed by the magnitude of the economic crisis." In an op-ed piece for the *New York Times* (November 3, 2009), Zandi warned that the recovery is fragile because of high unemployment, and he outlined several steps the government should take to stem job losses in small businesses, which account for 25 percent of all jobs. His suggestions included extending certain provisions in the current stimulus bill that allow failing firms to receive refunds of the taxes they paid in previous years and providing financing for state-run work-share programs.

In 2001 Warner wrote that Zandi "has the look of a perpetual graduate student. He's a neat-desk person, with a single note stuck to his computer monitor, a cheat sheet listing the official U.S. government industrial codes. But despite Zandi's knack for grounding clients and reporters lost in the economic haze, there is much of the absent-minded professor about him." Zandi and Getman received a Paradigm Award at the Chester County Economic Development Council's 2009 Business Achievement Awards Dinner, which honors small businesses located in Chester County, Pennsylvania. At present Moody's Economy.com has about 125 employees and maintains offices in Sydney, Australia, and London, England, as well as West Chester. Zandi's wife, the former Ava Nelson, earned a doctorate from UPenn in 1983. The couple live in Malvern, Pennsylvania, with their three children—Bill, Anna, and Lily.

—M.R.M.

Suggested Reading: *Fortune Small Business Magazine (FSB)* p72 Mar. 2003; *Mortgage Banking* p21 Jan. 2006; *New York Times* Business p1 Sep. 30, 2001, (on-line) Dec. 24, 2008, Nov. 3, 2009; *Philadelphia Inquirer* Business C p1 Feb. 10, 2009; *Philadelphia Inquirer Magazine* p16 Dec. 9, 2001; *Time* p38 Apr. 20, 2009

Selected Books: *Financial Shock: A 360 Degree Look at the Subprime Mortgage Crisis*, 2008

Alex Wong/Newsmakers

Zelnick, Strauss

June 26, 1957– Founding partner of ZelnickMedia; chairman of Take-Two Interactive Software

Address: ZelnickMedia, 19 W. 44th St., 18th Fl., New York, NY 10036

"The cynical might describe Strauss Zelnick's glittering resume as a chronology of relentlessly upward opportunism," Michael Schrage wrote for

Brandweek (July 3, 2000), two years after Zelnick was promoted to president and chief executive officer (CEO) of BMG Entertainment and six months before he launched his own company, ZelnickMedia. "The more upbeat interpretation would cast him as a profitable embodiment of digital convergence. His wunderkind career has been an unusually broad blend of managing operations, exploiting technologies and building a brand." Zelnick is a notable example of a 21st-century media-business expert, one who has gained in-depth knowledge and executive-level experience regarding the production, marketing, and dissemination of nearly every contemporary form of mass communication—from print to cable television to the Internet. An aspiring rock-and-roll artist in his youth, Zelnick realized as an undergraduate that his devotion to music exceeded his artistic and creative gifts and changed his goal to fostering talent in others. Immediately after he earned both a master's degree in business and a law degree from Harvard University, in 1983, he joined Columbia Pictures, where he rose to vice president of Columbia's international TV division. He then spent three years (1986–89) with Vestron, a leading independent film producer and distributor. He held the title of executive vice president there in 1987, the year Vestron's sleeper hit *Dirty Dancing* was released, and in 1988–89 served as the company's president and CEO. Next, for four years, he was the president and chief operating officer (COO) of the film division of 20th Century Fox; one of the nation's major motion-picture studios, its releases during his tenure included the first two *Home Alone* movies, *Die Hard 2*, and *Speed*.

In 1993 Zelnick left Hollywood to seek his fortune as a Silicon Valley entrepreneur. After 15 months as president and CEO of Crystal Dynamics, a start-up that produced and distributed interactive entertainment software, Zelnick served for four years as the president and CEO of the North American division of BMG (Bertelsmann Music Group) Entertainment and then for three years, until the end of 2000, as the head of BMG Entertainment worldwide. His purview included some 200 record labels (among them Arista and RCA) representing such music superstars as Whitney Houston, Carlos Santana, Christina Aguilera, and Toni Braxton. During his time with BMG Entertainment, the firm generated record profits; according to David Carr, writing for the *New York Times* (January 12, 2004), Zelnick "became known as something of a turnaround artist after taking the company's music division to second place from fifth among the top five music companies." In the process Zelnick became recognized as a spokesperson for the music industry. In 2000, for example, he testified before the Senate Committee on the Judiciary in an investigation of possible connections between juvenile violence and depictions of violence in the media.

Zelnick spoke before a congressional committee again in 2007, in his capacity as chairman of Take-Two Interactive Software, the maker of such video-game series as *Grand Theft Auto*, *Manhunt*, *BioShock*, and *Red Dead Redemption* and one of the top video-game publishers. Take-Two is among a changing bevy of media enterprises owned (wholly or in part) and managed by ZelnickMedia. "Strauss is one of the rare [corporate executives] who has been able to make the transition to entrepreneurial life, and he's done it spectacularly," Barry Diller, a one-time Hollywood executive who currently chairs two thriving Internet-based enterprises, told Peter Lauria for the *New York Post* (May 11, 2008). Zelnick is the CEO of ZelnickMedia, which has acquired businesses including the Lillian Vernon Corp., Time Life, UGO Networks, Threshold Sports, National Lampoon, Airvana, Cannella Response Television, and ITN Networks, the last of which Zelnick also chairs. According to David Carr, "Many former media executives are on the prowl for deals, but ZelnickMedia is unusual because in addition to investing in properties, the group has made deals in which it has received significant equity in return for its expertise and management." According to a blurb posted on the Web site of Greater Talent Network, a speakers' bureau, Zelnick "believes that the success of any organization, and of any actor within that organization, is driven by sales, not just the selling of products to customers, but the selling of the mission to employees, investors and other stakeholders. His philosophy is built on the principle that consumer behavior is not static, but evolves over time. Zelnick believes that the best way to succeed in a highly competitive environment is to stay true to proven models while always keeping [an] eye trained on future trends."

Zelnick was born Harry Strauss Zelnick on June 26, 1957 in Boston, Massachusetts, to Allan Zelnick and Elsa Lee Strauss. His father is a partner in the New York law firm Fross Zelnick Lehrman & Zissu, which specializes in intellectual-property litigation. His mother immigrated to the U.S. from the Dominican Republic. Zelnick grew up in his father's hometown, East Orange, New Jersey. According to Calvin Sims, writing for the *New York Times* (June 22, 1993), Zelnick "once said that he had dreamed of working in Hollywood since the age of 3." Zelnick's love of music led him to learn to play the guitar and write songs. "Like every teenage boy in America, I wanted to be a rock and roll star," he told Beverly Schuch for CNN's *Pinnacle* (November 16, 1996). He graduated from Columbia High School, in Maplewood, New Jersey, in 1975 and then enrolled at Wesleyan University, in Middletown, Connecticut. By then it had become apparent to him that "my passions for creating were limited by the fact that I didn't have an enormous amount of creative talent," he told Schuch, "and I'm nothing if not a realist. . . . So I realized . . . the right thing to do and the most exciting thing to do would be to be on the business side and I really started focusing on that pretty early." He graduated from Wesleyan with a B.A. degree, summa cum laude, in English and psychology in 1979 and then entered the joint business and law program at Harvard Law School, in Cambridge, Massachusetts. He earned a J.D. degree, cum laude, and an M.B.A. degree in 1983. He was admitted to the New York State bar in 1984.

Immediately after he completed his law and master's degrees, Zelnick was hired as the director of international television at Columbia Pictures International Corp. He was promoted to vice president of the department in 1985. He left Columbia Pictures the next year to become the senior vice president of corporate development at Vestron Inc., an independent motion-picture producer and distributor based in Stamford, Connecticut. The company's best-known production is the romantic coming-of-age movie *Dirty Dancing* (1987), starring Patrick Swayze and Jennifer Grey; the unexpectedly very popular *Dirty Dancing* has to date grossed about 35 times the $6 million it cost to produce, and, according to Anita Singh, writing for the London *Telegraph* (September 16, 2009), it was "the first film to sell over one million copies on video." Zelnick was promoted to executive vice president of Vestron in 1987 and to president and COO in 1988.

In 1989 Zelnick moved to Los Angeles, California, to take on the posts of president and COO of the film division of 20th Century Fox, which is owned by Rupert Murdoch's News Corp. As head of Fox Films' worldwide production and distribution, Zelnick reigned over a $2 billion business with 1,200 employees. During the next three years, Fox distributed such popular movies as *Die Hard 2*, *Home Alone*, and *Edward Scissorhands* (all 1990 releases), and *My Cousin Vinny* and *Home Alone 2* (1992). By 1993 Zelnick had become "frustrated by his lack of creative input and limited opportunities for further advancement at Fox," Calvin Sims reported that year, in particular when he was passed up to succeed Joe Roth as the chairman of the Fox Entertainment Group in 1992. In addition, although he had achieved one of his goals—running a studio—he also wanted to have his own business. "I always had one eye open for entrepreneurial opportunities," he told Sims for the *New York Times* (February 13, 1994).

Zelnick recognized that opportunity in Crystal Dynamics, a start-up producer and distributor of interactive entertainment software (both its own and others') in Palo Alto, California. In mid-1993, a few days before he turned 36, he came on board the company as president and CEO, supervising 28 computer programmers and video-game creators. Crystal Dynamics had negotiated an exclusive deal to develop games for 3DO's Interactive Multiplayer gaming system (manufactured by Matsushita), one of the first 32-bit central-processing units (CPUs) to be sold in the U.S. Crystal Dynamics' first original game, called *Crash and Burn*, involved car races—a perennial favorite with young men. However, with a price of between $700 and $800, the 3DO device failed to attract many consumers. Zelnick told Sims in February 1994 that he was not disappointed by its sluggish sales—"We have been able to achieve a position of market dominance, which has been quite profitable for us," he said. Bruce Ryon, a multimedia analyst, told James Bates for the *Los Angeles Times* (September 14, 1994, on-line) that Zelnick had succeeded in leading the company "away from its attachment to 3DO," and that Zelnick had also raised his company's "profile in a crowded field of competitors," in Bates's words, thereby attracting investors. On the day Bates's article was posted, Zelnick started a new job. He had enjoyed working at Crystal Dynamics, he told Bates, but wanted "to take advantage of a new opportunity," as Bates put it.

That opportunity came from BMG Entertainment, the music and entertainment branch of the German firm Bertelsmann AG, the world's fourth-largest media company. Zelnick assumed the titles of president and CEO of BMG Entertainment's North American operations. In those positions he was in charge of BMG Music Publishing, which owned the rights to more than 700,000 songs and, for fees, approved their use in radio and TV, films, videos, video games, cellphone ringtones, and other products. In addition, Zelnick oversaw BMG's 200 or so record labels, whose contracted artists included Whitney Houston, Sarah McLachlan, Kenny G, Carlos Santana, Christina Aguilera, Sean Combs, and the Dave Matthews Band. Zelnick's responsibilities extended to upcoming ventures in the arenas of film and new technologies, notably the Internet.

When Zelnick joined BMG all but three of the North American division's two dozen sectors were losing money. Zelnick scaled back spending by selling or shutting down most of the units operating at a loss, reducing manufacturing costs by $50 million, and laying off 16 percent of the staff. "I perceive my role first of all as leading by example, and leading the company to focus with passion on creating great music," Zelnick told Timothy Middleton for *Chief Executive* (November 1997). "Secondly, it is to operate the company as efficiently as possible. The bottom line is, we have the lowest cost structure in our industry." At the urging of Kevin Conroy, BMG's president for new technology and chief marketing officer, Zelnick supervised the launching of a series of Web sites designed to raise the profiles of artists and albums—for example, Peeps.com for rhythm and blues and hip-hop and Rockuniverse.com for rock-and-roll.

Zelnick's achievements led to his appointment as president and CEO of BMG Entertainment in July 1998. Under his watch BMG Entertainment earned record revenues; the portion of albums released on their labels grew from 13 percent in 1994 to 20 percent in 2000, and the number of BMG's platinum- or multiplatinum-selling albums in the U.S. rose from 44 in 1995 to 85 in 2000. In 1999 BMG Entertainment's revenues totaled about $4.6 billion; the firm maintained operations in more than 50 countries, and five of the year's 10 best-selling albums carried one of its labels. Additionally, under Zelnick's guidance, the BMG Direct division became the world's leading direct-to-consumer retailer of recorded music, through its music clubs and, to a lesser extent at that time, Internet sales, starting in late 1999. Zelnick was a pioneer in advocating the establishment of legal alternatives to the growing problem of music piracy (the illegal duplication and distribution of music) by the file-sharing site Napster and many other enterprises. In 1999, in partnership with the Universal Music Group, BMG formed the Web site GetMusic.

In 2000 BMG and other music companies sued Napster for copyright infringement. Then, on October 30, 2000, before the suit was brought to trial or settled, Zelnick learned that Bertelsmann's top management had negotiated an agreement with Napster, whereby Napster would compensate music-copyright holders; moreover, Bertelsmann and Napster had formed an alliance whereby BMG would offer through Napster a file-sharing service to paid subscribers. Zelnick fiercely opposed that move, reportedly on the grounds that Bertelsmann would be seen as rewarding Napster for its illegal activities while withdrawing support from the efforts of the other plaintiffs in the lawsuit to end illegal file-swapping. His opposition also stemmed from his conviction that BMG should use the Internet primarily to support its artists, and that nobody could show how the deal with Napster would generate more profits for BMG. Zelnick's superiors dismissed his concerns and on the following day publicly announced the deal with Napster. The next month Zelnick announced his resignation from BMG, effective on December 31, 2000. "I didn't like what Thomas [Middlehoff, Bertelsmann's CEO] was doing with Napster, but it's not why I left," Zelnick told David Carr, adding, in Carr's words, "that he was ready to go into business for himself."

The following day Zelnick, Ben Feder, and two others launched ZelnickMedia, "a partnership of experienced media executives and investors" that manages and owns various businesses. The company "invests in media companies in which the partnership's capital resources, industry contacts and operational experience can meaningfully enhance growth and value," its Web site states; since 2008 it has done so through a private investment fund called ZM Capital. "What we try to do is add value from a management point of view," Zelnick told Bill Griffeth for CNBC/Dow Jones (January 6, 2004). "We are very hands-on and we are willing to buy assets that are troubled. Where they require a lot of work, we put that work in and hope to build value that way." For a while the partners worked without pay. "I essentially traded a salary for equity in what I do but I wanted to play for equity and that [is] terribly important to me," Zelnick told Diane Mermigas for *Advertising Age* (March 5, 2004, on-line). He also told her, "Being autonomous and entrepreneurial is its own reward."

When Mermigas interviewed Zelnick, his firm owned interests in companies including the gaming-software firm Arkadium; the fantasy-entertainment on-line network UGO; the Pro Cycling Tour; National Lampoon; and WFX Rights Group. The previous year, with financial backing from Ripplewood Holdings, ZelnickMedia had paid $60 million to acquire Lillian Vernon, a mail-order and on-line retailer of household, gardening, and gift items. With Ripplewood, ZelnickMedia set up Direct Holdings Worldwide, which in 2004 purchased Time Life, the direct-marketing music and video branch of Time Warner. (Time Life's famous books division, founded in 1961, closed in 2003.) Direct Holdings Worldwide, which also became the umbrella for Lillian Vernon, was sold to the Reader's Digest Association in 2007 for $91.8 million. Other Zelnick projects have included an alliance with Threshold Sports, a company that organizes professional cycling races, with the aim of increasing the popularity of bicycling in the U.S.; Naylor Inc., a business-to-business media service; OTX, a provider of on-line research; and ITN Networks, which develops TV, digital, and broadband-video networks. In 2007 ZelnickMedia acquired a 2 percent stake in Take-Two Interactive, along with the power to manage and operate it—for a hefty fee. (As of early 2008 the fee was nearly $210,000 per month, with an annual bonus, linked to performance goals, of up to $2.5 million, and Take-Two's board of directors had agreed to continue paying a percentage of the fee through 2012 even in the event that ZelnickMedia had ended its association with the firm.) "We're operators who invest rather than just investors," Zelnick told Peter Lauria. "So far the strategy has paid off," Lauria wrote: as of May 11, 2008, ZelnickMedia "ha[d] yet to lose money on an investment," and the five companies it then managed (earlier it had eight) generated $2.5 billion in total annual sales. In December 2009 ZelnickMedia, in partnership with several other investments groups, paid $530 million to acquire Airvana, which manufactures equipment for mobile broadband networks. More recently, in June 2010, ZelnickMedia paid about $126.5 million to purchase Alloy, the originator of the teen-oriented *Gossip Girl*, *Vampire Diaries*, and *Sisterhood of the Traveling Pants* franchises.

In his congressional testimony in September 1999, in hearings regarding possible connections between violent behavior in youth and references to violence in song lyrics or depictions of violence in films and video games, Zelnick said, "There is no question that the First Amendment would allow us to do whatever we want, but I believe we are all editors, and editors have a social responsibility and responsibility to themselves to decide what they want to publish. . . . There's clearly a line that we won't cross." In his statement before the U.S. House Subcommittee on Commerce, Trade and Consumer Protection on September 25, 2007, Zelnick asserted that "there is no link between the use of [interactive video games] and violence. . . .

In seeking the root of violent behavior in America today, we must therefore look elsewhere: to the easy access to guns, as well as factors such as domestic abuse, weakening community values, an inadequate educational system, and gang activity." He also noted that 85 percent of video games were "appropriate for young players" (for example, his company's products *Dora the Explorer* and *Rockstar Games Presents Table Tennis*), that the average age of a gamer was 33, and that while the use of video games had risen exponentially between 1990 and 2006, the homicide rate in the U.S. had dropped during that period from about 10 to about 5.6 per 100,000 U.S. residents. Moreover, although video games were enormously popular overseas, in Japan and South Korea, for example, the incidence of violent crime in those nations was only a fraction of that in the U.S. He also maintained that Take-Two's highly successful series *Grand Theft Auto*, which had been widely criticized as unacceptably violent, "includes instant feedback that demonstrate the dire results of antisocial acts: the player immediately increases his 'wanted level,' which can make the game not just hard, but actually impossible to play. At the highest level, the National Guard is mobilized against the player and there is no escape from the long arm of the law. There are also explicit rejections of drug use and racism—and a strong moral center in the African-American hero."

Zelnick serves on the board of trustees of Wesleyan University and on the boards of directors of Naylor Publications and Blockbuster Inc. In his leisure time he enjoys skiing, bicycling, sailing, and playing squash. He engages in strenuous workouts daily, explaining to David Kushner for *Men's Fitness* (November 2008)—which ran a cover story about him in that issue—"I schedule exercise as though it's a meeting and treat it the same way." In 1990 Zelnick married Wendy Belzberg, a onetime TV producer who for several years wrote the syndicated advice column "Ask Wendy." Zelnick and his wife have a home in Westchester County, New York, where they live with their two sons, Cooper and Lucas, and a daughter, Leigh. They also maintain an apartment on the Upper East Side of Manhattan.

—M.A.S.

Suggested Reading: *Advertising Age* (on-line) Mar. 5, 2004; *Brandweek* p27+ July 3, 2000; *Chief Executive* (on-line) Nov. 1997; *New York Post* p35 May 11, 2008; *Westchester (County, New York) Magazine* p25+ Jan. 2004; ZelnickMedia.com

---

Ziegler, Jean

Apr. 19, 1934– Member of the Advisory Committee of the U.N. Human Rights Council

Address: c/o Office of the U.N. High Commissioner for Human Rights, Palais Wilson, 52 rue des Pâquis, CH-1201 Geneva, Switzerland

A former Socialist member of the Swiss parliament, Jean Ziegler was until recently the United Nations (U.N.) special rapporteur, or judicial reporter, on the right to food. Currently a member of the Advisory Committee of the U.N.'s Human Rights Council, Ziegler has for the last several decades been an outspoken proponent of economic and social equality and an acerbic critic of capitalism and imperialism. A provocative polemicist, he has been called a "Marxist demagogue," "Switzerland's Noam Chomsky," and "sociology's Rambo" by his detractors and, by those who admire him, a courageous crusader for the underprivileged and a "post-modern [Émile] Zola, an angry man of letters." A reporter for Radio Suisse Romande (October 29, 2007) commented that Ziegler "leaves no one indifferent. . . . He continues to sound the alarm. He is controversial, but he is heard."

Jean Ziegler was born on April 19, 1934 in Thun, in the Swiss canton of Berne. His Swiss-German father, Hans, was the president of a district court—a "merciful judge who fought against poverty," ac-

Michael Gottschalk/AFP/Getty Images

cording to Radio Suisse Romande. His mother's name was Léa. Ziegler spent large portions of his youth at his maternal grandfather's farm, where he learned about subsistence agriculture. At age 16 he enrolled at the University of Berne. He subsequently studied sociology, economics, law, and political science at a series of other schools, among them the University of Geneva, in Switzerland; the Sorbonne, in Paris, France; and Columbia University, in New York City. In Paris, where he arrived with only a rudimentary knowledge of French, Ziegler met the founder of the nonprofit Emmaüs organization, dedicated to helping the underprivileged; he would later head its Geneva chapter. Ziegler also joined the Communist movement in Paris, becoming an unofficial pupil of Jean Paul Sartre. "Sartre taught me a critical Marxism," he told Burton Bollag for the *Chronicle of Higher Education* (October 23, 1998, on-line). "He said one should follow one's conscience, not the Communist Party."

Ziegler earned doctoral degrees in sociology and law, and he later taught those subjects at the University of Grenoble and the Sorbonne. He also later began a long-term affiliation with the University of Geneva, where he established and directed the Laboratory of Sociology for the Study of the Societies of the Third World, focusing his work on the plight of developing nations.

After completing his doctoral work, Ziegler was hired in 1961 as a U.N. assistant in war-ravaged Congo. The experience reaffirmed his conviction to fight global injustice. In an interview given to the Geneva Tribunal in 2005, as quoted on Radio Suisse Romande, he said, "I vowed never again, not even by chance, to side with the hangmen." He explained to Bollag, "My love of certainties was shattered. I saw that not all whites were bad. There were doctors, Jesuit priests, and others working themselves to death to help. And not all blacks were victims. Look at Mobutu!"

Another pivotal moment for Ziegler came when he met the Cuban revolutionary Ernesto "Ché" Guevara. In 1964 Ziegler acted as a chauffeur for Guevara, then Cuba's minister of industry, while he was in Geneva for an international conference. Ziegler explained to Guevara that he wanted to immigrate to Cuba in order to participate in building a more just society. As Ziegler recounted to Bollag, Guevara, gazing at the wealthy city around them, told the young idealist: "Here is the brain of the monster. Your fight is here." Ziegler has told reporters that he did not realize until later that it would be more efficient to combat global injustice from his privileged position in Switzerland than from the developing world. He did, however, "spend some time working in the sugar fields of Cuba," as he told Samantha McArthur for Reuters (August 19, 1990). "That was my romantic phase."

From 1963 to 1967 Ziegler was a municipal councilman in Geneva. In 1967 he was elected to the National Council, one of the two chambers in Switzerland's bicameral parliament, known as the Federal Assembly. (The other chamber is the Council of States.) Ziegler remained an outspoken council member until 1983, when he did not win reelection, but four years later he returned, serving until 1999.

During his years as a politician and professor, Ziegler became known for his unrelenting attacks on his country's apolitical neutrality and its secretive banking laws. He published numerous books on the topics, including *Switzerland Exposed* (first published in 1976 and translated into English two years later) and *Switzerland Washes Whiter: The Financial Hub of International Crime* (originally published in 1990). "Switzerland invented the beautiful concept of 'neutrality' which serves to protect the Swiss banks," Ziegler told a journalist for the *Hindu* (May 28, 2000, on-line). "Switzerland is not a member of the United Nations. It is not even in the European Commission. . . . This gives the banks a free hand to stick to their numbered accounts and secrecy laws. It is all perfectly legal. . . . There are two things that are profoundly indecent about all this. The first is the sabotage of the banking process, allowing criminals to keep money in Swiss banks. The second is the hypocrisy of the Calvinist bankers of Switzerland who put on a show of moral rectitude, preferring to talk about the humanitarian work of the Swiss Red Cross." He asserted, "Switzerland is the richest country. Not in absolute wealth but in terms of per capita income. . . . Yet, the country has no natural resources. Its only resource is foreign money." Ziegler has charged that such foreign wealth comes largely from criminals, members of the tax-evading ruling class, and despots—including the former dictators Mobutu Sese Seko of Zaire (now the Democratic Republic of Congo), Ferdinand Marcos of the Philippines, and Augusto Pinochet of Chile. "Many dictators bleed the poor in their countries and stash the money in Swiss banks," Ziegler explained. "If the Swiss banks were not there it would be that much more difficult to rob the poor on such a massive scale."

Ziegler wrote in *Switzerland Exposed* that the Swiss system, at its core, allows the "imperialist oligarchy to safeguard and then to re-invest profitably their accumulated plunder." His claims that Switzerland was hiding behind its façade of neutrality in order to engage in global money laundering made Ziegler a target of the country's powerful banking establishment. At one point he was stripped of his parliamentary immunity, and almost half his salary was garnisheed to cover the legal fees incurred in the many libel suits brought against him by traders, businessmen, and arms dealers, among others.

Ziegler has been accused by many observers, particularly those on the right of the political spectrum, of gross exaggeration and even treason. According to McArthur, editorialists for the German newspaper *Blick* referred to him as a "bird which fouls its own nest." The Swiss historian Beatrix Mesmer told Carolyn Henson for the Associated Press (July 3, 1997), "Much of what Ziegler says is true. But the trouble is, there are so many mistakes in the [details] of what he writes that he loses credibility. His real gift is to provoke." Ziegler responded to Henson: "I don't mind what people say. I am in a privileged position. . . . I have an international publishing house so they cannot censor me. I have academic protection, political protection and international protection. I can say things that everyone thinks and no one dares to say." That comment notwithstanding, Ziegler has received numerous death threats and periodically lives under police protection.

Ziegler leveled perhaps his most inflammatory and damaging accusation against the Swiss establishment in *The Swiss, the Gold, and the Dead: How Swiss Bankers Helped Finance the Nazi War Machine* (originally published in 1997 and translated into English the following year). In that book he argued that throughout World War II, under the pretext of neutrality, Switzerland had acted as Hitler's banker, buying stolen gold from the Nazis, who then used the proceeds to fund their war efforts. He additionally charged that Swiss banks had misappropriated the assets of Jews who had deposited them in Switzerland for safekeeping at the start of the war. (Although happy to receive the assets, Ziegler pointed out, the Swiss had turned away Jewish asylum seekers.) After the war, although the Allies had agreed that all confiscated assets would serve as reparations, the Swiss banks endeavored to block the proceedings, citing their secrecy laws. As the *Hindu* reported, at roughly the same time that *The Swiss, the Gold, and the Dead* was published, New York City sought a public loan worth $1 billion, and UBS, Switzerland's largest bank, made a bid to provide the funds. The city's comptroller, Allan G. Hevesi, rejected the offer and organized a broad-based coalition to impose economic sanctions on Swiss banks, which had recently denied compensation to the families of Holocaust survivors from the former Soviet bloc. Ziegler was the only Swiss official to agree to testify before the U.S. Senate Banking Committee. He learned soon after his testimony that a group of conservative Swiss politicians, lawyers, and bankers (several of them stockholders in UBS) was attempting to charge him with treason and with endangering national security. Switzerland's Federal Court ultimately decided against prosecution, judging the matter to be a freedom-of-speech issue. The Swiss banks, for their part, quickly agreed to pay Jewish survivors a $1.25 billion settlement. Ziegler told Henson that the issue had a personal dimension for him: "During the war, parliament wasn't working and there was press censorship. The Swiss believed in the ridiculous myth that the Swiss army was so strong that Hitler didn't dare to attack. My own father, he was a colonel in the Swiss army. He was a cultivated man. But he believed until he died he guarded Switzerland with his troops against the aggression of Hitler. I want to put an end to this lie. I want my children to know the truth."

During his closing statement to the U.S. Senate Banking Committee, Ziegler touched upon an issue that would provide the focus for the next phase of his career, saying, "Hundreds of millions of children, women and men live in hunger, misery and sickness. In 1998, according to the World Bank, Switzerland is the richest country on Earth (per capita income). Banking secrecy is playing a central role. . . . The present act of reparation . . . could be the first step for the necessary reform of certain fundamental aspects of the Swiss financial system."

In 2000 the U.N. Human Rights Commission established the position of special rapporteur on the "right to food." (The Human Rights Commission has special rapporteurs assigned to a variety of other issues as well, including housing, child prostitution, arbitrary executions, and the right to education.) Ziegler was nominated for the new post, which involved traveling to countries around the globe and reporting to the commission on government response to hunger. He explained to a journalist for *Africa News* (March 3, 2004), "Preventing global hunger and ensuring the right to food should not be a moral obligation, but a legal one."

"My mandate is fascinating," Ziegler told Gian Paolo Accardo for the left-leaning newsletter *Counterpunch* (December 19, 2005, on-line). "I have to make a new human right justifiable, through statutory or conventional rights: the right to food. It is a Sisyphus task! It advances millimeter by millimeter. The essential center of this struggle is the collective conscience. For a long time, the destruction of human beings by hunger has been tolerated with a kind of ice-cold acceptance. Today, it is regarded as intolerable." According to the U.N.'s International Covenant on Economic, Social and Cultural Rights, the right to food will be "realized when every man, woman and child . . . has physical and economic access at all times to adequate food or means for its procurement. It implies the availability of food in a quantity and quality sufficient to satisfy the dietary needs of individuals. . . . It is indivisibly linked to the inherent dignity of the human person." Ziegler believes that far from being an inevitable plague, the world's hunger crisis arises from poor political and economic decisions. He equated the effects of stock-market speculation on agricultural products and the overarching system of unequal capitalist globalization with "crimes against humanity," responsible for mass starvation. "We are going towards a new feudalization of the world," Ziegler told Accardo, asserting, "September 11, 2001 did not only provide George W. Bush with the pretext for extending the influence of the United States over the world, the event also served as justification for the staging of organized economic destruction of the people of the Southern hemisphere by the large private transcontinental corporations." He called for developing nations to fight back by investing in infrastructure that would guarantee adequate food, instituting land reform, halting privatization, and establishing protections against multinational corporations.

Even the production of biofuels—considered by many to be an environmentally friendly way of weaning the world from oil—came under Ziegler's scrutiny, because policymakers (particularly in the U.S. and Brazil) had granted huge subsidies to farmers to replace food crops with biofuels. Some observers concurred with him. Javier Rulli, a Latin American biologist and activist, told a reporter for the *Ottawa (Canada) Citizen* (April 30, 2008), "Farmers in our countries pay with their blood so that people in rich countries can feed their cars. The grain used to fill one SUV tank with ethanol could feed a person for a year." Ziegler thus called for a five-year moratorium on biofuel production, by the end of which scientific research would presumably have produced alternatives, such as energy sources from agricultural waste products. To date, such a moratorium has not been put in place.

During his tenure as special rapporteur, Ziegler was heavily criticized for his praise of the Cuban model of food provision and his call for an end to U.S. sanctions against that country. He was also derided for his outspoken statements on Israel and on American foreign policy. In 2003, for example, he called for a boycott of Caterpillar tractors, on the grounds that they were being used by Israeli defense forces to destroy Palestinian farms, "further limit[ing] the sustainable means for the Palestinian people to enjoy physical and economic access to food." "The consequences of the ways in which current security measures are applied in the Occupied Palestinian Territories are entirely disproportionate in the sense that they jeopardize the food and water security of the great majority of the Palestinians and thus amount to collective punishment," he wrote in a report, as quoted by Jim Lobe for the Inter Press Service (IPS) news agency (November 12, 2003). "The confiscation of land, extension of settlements and settler-only roads, and the building of the security fence/apartheid wall, where this deprives thousands of Palestinians of their lands, homes, crops and means of subsistence, is a violation of the right to food." The response from Israel and its allies was swift, and calls were made for the U.N. to dismiss him. (Israel has repeatedly called for Ziegler's firing. One such call came after an incident in 2005, during which he compared Israeli soldiers in Gaza to concentration-camp guards; another came in 2006, when he called for an international investigation in response to Israel's invasion of Lebanon and the targeting of that country's food and water supplies.)

Long a critic of the crippling sanctions on Iraq, which he has said left 500,000 people dead from hunger-related causes, Ziegler warned that the 2003 invasion would result in "catastrophe." He took aim at the military tactic of cutting off food and water supplies to areas populated by insurgents, pointing to the Geneva Conventions, which ban the use of hunger as a weapon. He has also criticized the American-led war on terrorism for worsening global inequalities; he told a reporter for Agence France-Presse (March 31, 2005), "The amount of aid being provided for development and famine relief is falling, as money is redirected towards strengthening national security and the fight against terrorism. Yet the fight against terrorism should incorporate efforts to reduce hunger, poverty and inequality."

In March 2008 Ziegler was elected as one of the 18 expert members of the Advisory Committee of the U.N. Human Rights Council. (He was replaced as special rapporteur by Olivier De Schutter.) His new mandate is to promote and protect broader economic and social rights in addition to the right to food.

Among Ziegler's most recent books are *L'Empire de la honte* (whose title translates as "The Empire of Shame," 2005) and *La Haine de l'Occident* (whose title translates as "The Hatred of the West," 2008). A chevalier in France's Ordre des Arts et des Lettres, he has received many other honors, including the Adlai Stevenson Peace Award (1964) and the Bruno Kreisky Peace Prize (2000). He lives in Switzerland with the art historian Erica Deuber Ziegler and has one son.

—M.M.

Suggested Reading: *Africa News* (on-line) Mar. 3, 2004; Associated Press (on-line) July 3, 1997; *Chronicle of Higher Education* (on-line) Oct. 23, 1998; *Counterpunch* (on-line) Dec. 19, 2005; *Der Spiegel* (on-line) Apr. 23, 2008; *Hindu* (on-line) May 28, 2000; Reuters (on-line) Aug. 19, 1990; *Washington Post* (on-line) Mar. 27, 1978

Selected Books in English Translation: *Switzerland Exposed*, 1978; *Switzerland Washes Whiter: The Financial Hub of International Crime*, 1990; *The Swiss, the Gold, and the Dead: How Swiss Bankers Helped Finance the Nazi War Machine*, 1998

Zuberbühler, Klaus

(ZOO-ber-byew-ler, klowss)

Dec. 30, 1964– Psychologist; primatologist; educator

Address: School of Psychology, University of St. Andrews, St. Andrews, Fife KY16 9JU, Scotland

From his recordings of "Krak krak!" "Hok hok hok!," "Boom boom!," "Pyow!," "Hack!," and other calls of forest-dwelling Old World monkeys, and his observations of how other monkeys respond to such sounds, the primatologist and psychologist Klaus Zuberbühler has shed new light on the intriguing cognitive and linguistic abilities of nonhuman primates. "It's a humbling experience to realize there is so much more information being passed in ways which hadn't been noticed before," Zuberbühler commented to Nicholas Wade, a *New York*

Courtesy of Gina Zuberbühler-McClung

Klaus Zuberbühler

Times (January 12, 2010) science writer. His discoveries have also provided clues to the ways in which language may have evolved among humans. His hundreds of hours of research on the African continent—in Tai National Park, in Ivory Coast (Côte d'Ivoire), Gashaka Gumti National Park, in Nigeria, and the Budongo Forest, in Uganda—have led Zuberbühler to conclude that some species of Old World monkeys are capable not only of conveying information by means of specific sounds but also of using primitive syntax. Put differently, they can link sounds in particular sequences to transmit information different from that communicated by repetitions of single sounds. Zuberbühler studied zoology, anthropology, psychology, and primatology at the University of Zurich, in Switzerland, where he was born, and at the University of Pennsylvania, in Philadelphia. He has worked at the Zoological Institute of the University of Zurich and the Max Planck Institute for Evolutionary Anthropology, in Leipzig, Germany; since 2001 he has been a faculty member of the University of St. Andrews, in Scotland, where he is now a full professor. In 2004 he won a Distinguished Scientific Award for Early Career Contribution to Psychology from the American Psychological Association.

Klaus Zuberbühler was born on December 30, 1964 in Basel, Switzerland, to Eugen Zuberbühler, a high-school teacher, and Heidy Zuberbühler-Stricker, a primary-school teacher. His brother, Karim Koch Zuberbühler, is an archaeologist and museum curator. Klaus Zuberbühler grew up in St. Gallen, in northeastern Switzerland. His curiosity about animals began at an early age. When he was in his teens, he kept two pet boa constrictors. "I often sat in front of their cage, wondering what it's

like to be a snake," he told *Current Biography*. While in high school he spent a year in Wilson, North Carolina, as an exchange student. After he completed secondary school, he attended the University of Zurich, where he studied anthropology and zoology (though he never felt "completely at home" with the latter subject, in his words) and became interested in psychology. A course in animal behavior taught by Hans Kummer, a prominent primatologist who specializes in primate ethology and cognition, was "a revelation," he told *Current Biography*. Kummer was then engaged in a decades-long field study of a species of baboon, and Zuberbühler was fascinated by what the professor had learned about their rigid social structure, the skill with which dominant males led their harems, and their decisionmaking processes. "I instantly knew that this is what I wanted to do," he recalled to *Current Biography*. "It became obvious how much there was to learn about the biological roots of our own human behavior by studying non-human primates."

In 1990 Zuberbühler undertook a nine-month study of the vocal behavior of various species of Old World monkeys in the Tai National Park of Ivory Coast, where Kummer has worked. In the park, which protects one of the last areas of undisturbed rainforest in West Africa, he "could hear the calls of the Diana monkeys, but the babble held no meaning for him," Nicholas Wade wrote. By the time he had completed his master's thesis, in 1993, Zuberbühler had gained some understanding of the monkeys' calls and their importance in communicating to others in their groups the presence of predators nearby. Zuberbühler next worked as a research assistant in the Department of Ethology and Wildlife Research at the University of Zurich's Zoological Institute. Supervised by Kummer, he studied captive long-tailed macaques, Old World monkeys that live primarily in Asia. In particular, he investigated the macaques' use of tools and the transfer of information about tool use among individuals. (In captivity such macaques have been seen flossing their teeth with hair and cracking the shells of crustaceans with rocks.) A paper about that research, which Zuberbühler wrote with Kummer and two others, was published in the journal *Primates* in January 1996.

In 1994 Zuberbühler was admitted to the Ph.D. program in psychology at the University of Pennsylvania. For his doctoral research he returned to Tai National Park to study the vocalizations of free-ranging Diana monkeys. He completed his dissertation, entitled "Natural Semantic Communications in Wild Diana Monkeys: Proximate Mechanism and Evolutionary Function," in 1998. He also presented his findings in papers, written alone or with others, that appeared in the next few years in scholarly periodicals including *Ethology*, the *Journal of Comparative Psychology*, *Animal Behaviour*, *Proceedings of the Royal Society of London*, *Cognition*, *Behavioral Ecology and Sociobiology*, and the *Journal of Human Evolution*. After he earned his Ph.D. degree, Zuberbühler received funding from the National Geographic Society, the University of Zurich, and the Swiss National Science Foundation to conduct postdoctoral research at the Max Planck Institute for Evolutionary Anthropology. There, he worked with a group headed by the developmental psychologist Michael Tomasello. Their research was in the field of developmental and comparative psychology; their subjects were children ages four and under and members of the great-ape family (which includes chimpanzees, gorillas, orangutans, and bonobos). In particular, they studied social cognition, which refers to thinking and behavior involved in interpersonal relationships, and social learning and communication, which are aspects of culture and its transmission. "Primate Vocal and Gestural Communication," a paper in which Tomasello and Zuberbühler described their observations, was published as a chapter in the book *The Cognitive Animal* (2002), edited by A. Collin and others.

In early 2001 Zuberbühler got a job as a lecturer (equivalent to an assistant professor in the U.S.) in the School of Psychology of the University of St. Andrews, in St. Andrews, Scotland, about 50 aerial miles northeast of Edinburgh. He was promoted to reader (associate professor) in 2005 and to full professor in 2008. Shortly after he arrived at St. Andrews, he was appointed head of a team of St. Andrews researchers who studied the vocalizations of the Campbell's monkey (also known as Campbell's mona monkey or Campbell's guenon) and the Diana monkey. In their field research, conducted in Tai National Park, they concentrated on the distinct cries with which the monkeys warned their fellows of impending danger in the form of specific predators—primarily leopards, which are agile tree-climbers, and crowned eagles (also known as crowned hawk-eagles), birds of prey up to three feet in length whose diet consists largely of monkeys. The scientists discovered that a Campbell monkey's repeated cry of "Krak krak!" led the other monkeys in the group to look down at the ground to spy a leopard, while a cry of "Hok hok hok!" led them to look toward the sky to spot an eagle. Zuberbühler and his team also discovered that male Campbell's monkeys sometimes preceded their alarms with a "boom" call. Playing the calls recorded in the rainforest, they found that when the "boom" call was used in conjunction with one of the other calls, it seemed to indicate that the monkeys sensed danger but were unsure of the identity of the feared attacker. "The use of the 'boom' could be compared to man's use of the word 'maybe'," Zuberbühler told Paul Kelbie for the London *Independent* (February 27, 2002). "[The sound] modified the meaning of the alarm calls and transformed them from highly specific warnings, requiring immediate anti-predator responses, into more general signals of disturbance. Although the analogies to human language remain suggestive, the results show that monkeys can . . . implement the same sentence structure rules that humans

use." Further research uncovered evidence that the Campbell's monkeys add the sound "oo" to their warning calls when they hear alarm calls issued by Diana monkeys. The "oo" modifier thus seems to differentiate between an alarm call from a member of their own group and one that comes from an individual from another monkey species. Zuberbühler and his colleagues Karim Ouattara and Alban Lemasson, both of the University of Rennes, in France, published those findings in *Behaviour* (December 2009) in their paper "Anti-predator Strategies of Free-Ranging Campbell's Monkeys."

In the early 2000s Zuberbühler collaborated in a study of primate vocalization from an anatomical and physiological perspective, in an attempt to provide part of the answer to the complex question of why Homo sapiens is the only primate species that generates more than a few distinct sounds. His co-workers in that project were Tobias Riede, a researcher with the National Center for Voice and Speech who studies the physiology and mechanisms of sound production in verte-brates; Ellen Bronson, a veterinarian with the Maryland Zoo; and Haralambos Hatzikirou, who uses advanced computing to tackle problems in biomedicine. The researchers focused on the primate vocal tract—the cavity and organs that produce and regulate sound. Scientists had long believed that in humans, the vocal tract "consists of various flexible tubes of different sizes," while in other animal species, "the vocal tract was like a uniform tube," Zuberbühler told Paul O'Hare for the Scottish Press Association (December 23, 2004). The complexity of Diana monkey calls led him and his colleagues to suspect that that species must possess a more complicated vocal tract than was previously believed. To test that hypothesis, they examined the vocal tracts of three adult Diana monkeys, by radiation-derived images and physical dissection. They then used their data to construct a computer model of a vocal tract capable of simulating the sounds produced by wild Diana monkeys. "The model performed best when it combined a nonuniform vocal tract consisting of three different tubes with a number of articulatory manoeuvres," Zuberbühler reported. Although humans and Old World monkeys evolved from different branches of the primate family tree millions of years ago, that finding indicates possible steps in the evolution of Homo sapiens' vocal tract. (Since the tract consists of soft tissues, evidence of its structure in past eons is not present in fossilized remains.)

With Kate Arnold, a psychologist who teaches at the University of St. Andrews, Zuberbühler conducted studies of the alarm calls of puttynosed monkeys in the Gashaka Gumti National Park, in Nigeria. Puttynosed monkeys have two distinct calls: "pyow" calls, which warn of nearby leopards, and "hack" calls, which indicate the presence of crowned eagles. Zuberbühler and Arnold learned that the males of the species also combine the two to produce a "pyow-hack" call—an example of simple syntax. Using global positioning equipment and playback techniques, they found that the monkey groups that had produced the "pyow-hack" call series had traveled significantly farther from their original locations than groups that had not used that vocalization. They concluded that the "pyow-hack" sequence must convey a different message from "pyow" or "hack" used alone—perhaps, "Move faster and farther." "What we showed is that it was this call sequence alone that was sufficient to trigger group travel," Zuberbühler said, as quoted by Steve Connor in the London *Independent* (March 11, 2008). He and Arnold published their results in *Animal Behaviour* and *Nature* in 2006 and (with Yvonne Pohlner) in *Behavioural Ecology and Sociobiology* in 2008. In their paper "Meaningful Call Combinations in a Nonhuman Primate" (*Current Biology*, March 11, 2008), the researchers challenged the belief that combining signals, an essential step in the evolution of human language, occurs only after the development of a large repertoire of sounds. "Our research shows that these assumptions may not be correct," Zuberbühler said, according to a University of St. Andrews press release (March 10, 2008, on-line). "Putty-nosed monkeys have very small vocal repertoires, but nevertheless we observe meaningful combinatorial signaling." He continued, "Most primates are limited in the number of signals they can physically produce due to their lack of tongue control. The only way to escape this constraint may be to combine the few calls they have into more complex sequences. In other words, it may be harder for non-human primates to evolve large repertoires than to evolve the ability to combine signals. Hence, the evolution of combinatorial signalling may not be driven by too many signals but rather by too few."

Zuberbühler's more-recent investigations indicate that adult male Campbell's monkeys produce six distinct calls and arrange them in particular sequences to convey information about a variety of events or situations, including the falling of a tree nearby or the presence nearby of other monkey groups, specific predators, nonspecific predators, or nonpredatory animals. Each of the sequences seems to contain at least three pieces of information: the nature of the event or situation, the caller's identity, and whether the caller intends to travel. In a paper that appeared in the December 22, 2009 issue of the *Proceedings of the National Academy of Sciences of the United States of America*, Zuberbühler, Karim Ouattara, and Alban Lemasson wrote, "Within the responses to predators, we found that crowned eagles triggered four and leopards three different sequences, depending on how the caller learned about their presence." They concluded, "As the different sequences were so tightly linked to specific external events, the Campbell's monkey call system may be the most complex example of 'protosyntax' in animal communication known to date."

With the St. Andrews psychologist Simon Townsend and Tobias Deschner of the Max Planck Institute, Zuberbühler carried out a 16-month study of chimpanzee behavior in the Budongo Forest, in Uganda. One of their particular interests was what is known as the copulation call—a sound voiced during the act of mating. In primate species other than the chimpanzee, calls from females tend to come more often than not while they are copulating. The function of such calls in female primates has been debated for years. According to one of the more widely held theories, females use the calls to notify males in their groups that they have entered their most fertile periods. By analyzing the hormones of female chimpanzees in their study group, Zuberbühler and his colleagues showed that the female chimpanzees' calls were not related to their periods of greatest fertility. Instead, the female chimpanzees called out while mating with high-ranking males—their partners during about one-third of copulations; when high-ranking females were nearby, they suppressed their calls. This behavior led the researchers to conclude that female chimpanzees try to minimize competition with high-ranking females in the group while advertising their receptivity to and mating with various high-ranking males, which confuses paternity—important since male chimpanzees sometimes kill baby chimpanzees that they know are not their own—and secures protection from the group's socially important members. Zuberbühler, Townsend, and Deschner presented their findings in a report published in *PLoSOne* (Volume 3, Number 6, 2008), the Public Library of Science, a peer-reviewed, open-access on-line journal.

With five other researchers, Zuberbühler also conducted an experiment to study tool use among two neighboring chimpanzee populations in Uganda: Kanyawara chimpanzees, of the Kibale Forest, and Sonso chimpanzees, of the Budongo Forest. The chimpanzees were observed in their efforts to obtain honey that the scientists had poured into specially drilled holes in horizontal logs. In a report published in *Current Biology* (October 22, 2009), Zuberbühler and his colleagues wrote, "Kanyawara chimpanzees, who occasionally use sticks to acquire honey, spontaneously manufactured sticks to extract the experimentally provided honey. In contrast, Sonso chimpanzees, who possess a considerable leaf technology but no food-related stick use, relied on their fingers, but some also produced leaf sponges to access the honey. Our results indicate that, when genetic and environmental factors are controlled, wild chimpanzees rely on their cultural knowledge to solve a novel task."

Zuberbühler is currently conducting research on the psychological aspects of animal communication as part of a fellowship at the Institute for Advanced Study in Berlin, Germany. His other ongoing projects include research on the alarm-calling behavior in white-handed gibbons, vocal communication in chimpanzees and bonobos, attention-getting and gaze-following in captive chimpanzees, and food-locating skills of free-ranging mangabeys.

Zuberbühler was one of only seven researchers to receive a Distinguished Scientific Award for Early Career Contribution to Psychology from the American Psychological Association in 2004. The $1,000 award recognized his contributions to the study of animal learning and behavior. Zuberbühler is the director of the Tai Monkey project, scientific director of the Budongo Conservation Field Station, deputy director of the Living Links to Human Evolution Research Centre at the University of St. Andrews, and a member of the Scottish Primate Research Group. In 2002 he served as a science adviser to David Attenborough's BBC documentary series *Life of Mammals*.

Zuberbühler is married to Jennifer McClung, an American from Texas. The couple live outside Dundee, Scotland, with their four young children—Gina, Nikolai, Aidan, and Julien.

—M.A.S.

Suggested Reading: *American Psychologist* p724+ Nov. 2004; *Hindustan Times* (on-line) Mar. 11, 2008; *National Geographic News* (online) May 17, 2006; *New York Times* D p1+ Jan. 12, 2010; psy.st-andrews.ac.uk; wiko-berlin.de

Obituaries

ASHLEY, THOMAS L. Jan. 11, 1923–June 15, 2010
Former U.S. representative. The Democrat Thomas
L. Ashley, who represented Ohio's Ninth Congressional District in the U.S. House for 13 terms, was
known for his work on housing issues and toward
ending the 1970s energy crisis. According to Ashley's obituary in the Traverse City, Michigan, *Record
Eagle* (June 16, 2010, on-line), "In some ways Mr.
Ashley's life was one of contrasts. He was extremely
popular in the largely blue-collar area he represented; yet he moved easily in the circles of privilege that
dated back to his youth." Thomas William Ludlow
"Lud" Ashley was born in Toledo, Ohio, to William
Meredith Ashley, an attorney and businessman, and
Mary Alida (Ludlow) Ashley. Ashley was the great-
grandson of James M. Ashley, the radical Republican
congressman who introduced the resolution to im-
peach President Andrew Johnson in 1867 and later
served as the territorial governor of Montana. Immediately after his high-school graduation, in 1942,
Thomas Ashley enlisted in the U.S. Army, and he
served in the Pacific theater until the end of World
War II. Discharged in 1946, he entered Yale University. He received an A.B. degree two years later and
an LL.D. degree from Ohio State University in 1951.
Ashley practiced law in Ohio for about a year and
then accepted a position in New York City as an assistant director of special projects for Radio Free Europe. In 1954 he made a successful run for a U.S.
House seat. As a member of Congress, Ashley became a top advocate for public housing. Serving on
the housing subcommittee of the Banking and Currency Committee (now the Committee on Financial
Services), he pushed for a reexamination of existing
housing programs and persuaded his committee to
authorize hearings on national urban growth. Those
hearings provided the impetus for the passage of the
Housing and Urban Development Act of 1970, which
secured grants for cities and counties for the continued improvement of low- and moderate-income
housing. Many of Ashley's constituents benefited directly from his efforts on the housing subcommittee.
The urban-renewal measures that he supported provided much of the funding for the revitalization of
Toledo's central business district and decaying residential neighborhoods. Voters regularly returned
Ashley to Congress by impressive majorities; his
only serious challenge in 13 general elections came
in 1974, after his arrest on a drunk-driving charge.
He won that election by only a few thousand votes.
In 1977 Ashley was appointed to an ad hoc committee on energy. The bipartisan committee was responsible for passing several bills to decrease oil consumption and to encourage the exploration of alternative energy sources. In 1980 Ashley was defeated
by a Republican opponent. He subsequently
founded a consulting firm and became a successful
lobbyist. From 1988 to 1993 he headed the Association of Bank Holding Companies, a major trade organization. He died at his home in Leland, Michigan,
at the age of 87. Ashley, who was a longtime friend
of President George H. W. Bush, is survived by his
two sons, Meredith and Mark; a daughter, Elise; and
a brother, Charles. He was predeceased by his wife,
Kathleen, in 1997. The federal courthouse in Toledo
is named in honor of both Ashley and his great-
grandfather. See *Current Biography* (1979). —W.D.

Obituary *New York Times* (on-line) June 16,
2010

AUCHINCLOSS, LOUIS Sep. 27, 1917–Jan. 26, 2010
Writer; lawyer; civic leader. Although Louis Stanton
Auchincloss (AW-kin-klos) enjoyed the privileges of
being born into a wealthy and prominent New York
City family, he gained recognition for dissecting and
criticizing the trappings of the upper class. In addition to his work as an attorney and the chair of the
City Hall Restoration Committee and such institutions as the Museum of the City of New York, Auchincloss was a prolific author. During a writing career that spanned more than five decades, he penned
some 60 volumes of fiction and nonfiction, including the well-regarded novels *The Rector of Justin*
(1964), *The Embezzler* (1966), *The Education of Oscar Fairfax* (1995), and *East Side Story* (2004). "Of all
our novelists, Auchincloss is the only one who tells
us how our rulers behave in their banks and their
boardrooms, their law offices and their clubs," Gore
Vidal once wrote, as quoted by Holcomb B. Noble
and Charles McGrath in the *New York Times* (January 27, 2010, on-line). "Not since Dreiser has an
American writer had so much to tell us about the role
of money in our lives." The title of his final book,
The Last of the Old Guard (2008), "in many ways
ways fit the author himself," according to Noble and
McGrath: "Mr. Auchincloss had a beaky, patrician
nose and spoke with a high-pitched Brahmin accent.
He had elegant manners and suits to match, and he
wrote in longhand in the living room of an antiques-
filled apartment on Park Avenue." Auchincloss was
born in Lawrence, Long Island, the third of the four
children of Priscilla (Stanton) and Joseph Howland
Auchincloss, a Wall Street lawyer. Like his parents,
grandparents, and great-grandparents, he lived in
New York City, as part of an aristocratic clan of Dix-
ons, Howlands, Stantons, and Auchinclosses, whose
antecedents uniformly made their fortunes in the
professions and in the higher echelons of corporations. His childhood was characterized by private
clubs; summer homes on Long Island and in Bar Harbor, Maine; numerous household servants; and,
when he reached his teens, debutante parties and
foreign travel. During the 1920s he attended the
Bovee School for Boys on Manhattan's Fifth Avenue,
and in 1929 he entered the exclusive Groton School,
in Massachusetts. A hopeless athlete and unmotivat-
ed student, Auchincloss was at first unpopular at
Groton, but he eventually achieved a measure of sta-

tus as a scholar, editor of the school's literary magazine, and president of the drama society. In 1935 Auchincloss entered Yale University, in New Haven, Connecticut, where he wrote stories for the school magazine. He attempted, unsuccessfully, to have a novel published during his junior year. Discouraged, he skipped his senior year at Yale and entered the University of Virginia's law school. He earned his law degree in 1941 and subsequently joined the firm of Sullivan and Cromwell. During World War II he joined the U.S. Navy and was deployed to the Panama Canal Zone, among other locales. He returned to Sullivan and Cromwell after the war ended. Despite the demands of serving in the military and practicing law, Auchincloss continued to write. His first novel, *The Indifferent Children*, appeared under the pseudonym Andrew Lee in 1947. He did not publish the book—which followed the adventures of a patrician protagonist in New York, Panama, and London— under his own name because his parents found the novel vulgar and feared that it would damage his legal career. Soon, however, the *New Yorker*, *Esquire*, and the *Atlantic*, among other periodicals, began publishing some of Auchincloss's short fiction under his own name. Auchincloss left Sullivan and Cromwell in 1951 to undergo psychoanalysis—"to find out, once and for all, who I am," he wrote in his autobiography, *A Writer's Capital* (1974)—and to write full-time. Three years later, while continuing to write, he returned to practicing law, becoming a partner at Hawkins, Delafield, and Wood. Among Auchincloss's most well-known and best-selling books is *The Rector of Justin*, which follows the charismatic character Frank Prescott, the headmaster of a New England boys' school. Auchincloss's 1966 novel, *The Embezzler*, was critically acclaimed, but it generated heated controversy among his fellow upper-class Manhattanites for its disapproving take on the city's wealthy elite. His other well-known novels include *The House of Five Talents* (1960), *Portrait in Brownstone* (1962), *A World of Profit* (1968), *I Come as a Thief* (1972), *Honorable Men* (1985), *Diary of a Yuppie* (1986), *The Golden Calves* (1988), *The Lady of Situations* (1990), *Tales of Yesteryear* (1994), *Her Infinite Variety* (2000), and *The Headmaster's Dilemma* (2007). Auchincloss also wrote several biographies of prominent historical figures, including Theodore Roosevelt and Woodrow Wilson. Recognized as a skillful critic of both literature and the social scene, he also edited such volumes as *An Edith Wharton Reader* (1965) and penned several books of essays and commentary, including *The Vanderbilt Era: Profiles of a Gilded Age* (1989), *Love Without Wings: Some Friendships in Literature and Politics* (1991), and *The Style's the Man: Reflections on Proust, Fitzgerald, Wharton, Vidal, and Others* (1994). Auchincloss, who served as a president of the American Academy of Arts and Letters, was awarded the National Medal of Arts in 2005. He died from complications of a stroke at New York City's Lenox Hill Hospital. He is survived by his sons, Andrew, John, and Blake; his brother Howland; and seven grandchildren. His wife, Adele, an artist and environmentalist, died in 1991. See *Current Biography* (1978). —W.D.

Obituary *New York Times* (on-line) Jan. 27, 2010

BLANDA, GEORGE Sep. 17, 1927–Sep. 27, 2010
Professional football player. Hall of Fame quarterback and placekicker George Blanda played 26 seasons of professional football (from 1949 to 1975), the most of any player in history. George Frederick Blanda was the second of the four sons of Michael and Mary Blanda, who were both of Czech heritage. He was born in Youngstown, a coal-mining town in western Pennsylvania that was also the birthplace of Hall of Fame quarterbacks John Unitas, Joe Namath, and Joe Montana. Blanda's father, who worked 10 hours a day in a coal mine, made sure his sons attended high school, where all of them became outstanding athletes. George Blanda was an all-county halfback and also did all of his team's kicking and punting. After graduating from high school, in 1945, he attended the University of Kentucky on an athletic scholarship and played quarterback under the notoriously hard-driving coach Paul "Bear" Bryant, who taught him, as Blanda put it, "discipline, respect, and dedication." Blanda graduated from college with a bachelor's degree in education and was selected by the Chicago Bears in the 12th round of the National Football League (NFL) draft. However, the Bears already had two star quarterbacks on their roster and had little use for a third. Blanda was traded to the Baltimore Colts just before the 1950 season, then was sent back to the Bears after the Colts' first game. Blanda spent the next 10 years with the Bears, mainly as a starting kicker and a third-string quarterback. He played in 115 games, kicked 88 field goals, and made 247 out of 250 attempted extra points, which totaled 511 points on conversions and field goals—a team record. Blanda had an uneasy relationship with owner and coach George Halas, who refused to consider Blanda for the job of quarterback for much of his time with the Bears. He saw more playing time as a quarterback in 1952, and he began the 1953 season as a starter in the position but lost the job due to an injury. His quarterback appearances during his 10 years with the Bears resulted in 48 touchdown passes and 5,936 yards. In 1959 Halas refused to let Blanda into the Bears' lineup or to trade him to any other NFL team, forcing him into early retirement. After threatening to sue, Blanda was allowed by Halas to join the Texas Oilers in the then-fledgling American Football League (AFL). In Houston, Blanda's talents were finally put to full use. In his first three years with the Oilers, Blanda, as quarterback, led the team to three division titles and two league championships. He led the AFL in yards gained by passing (3,330) and touchdown passes (36) in 1961 and in extra points in both 1961 and 1962 (64 and 48, respectively). For three consecutive years, from 1963 through 1965, he led the league in passing, with a total of 1,370 throws and 672 completions, and he played in the All-Star games following the 1961, 1962, 1963, and 1967 seasons. In the mid-1960s the Oilers, dizzy from a succession of coaches, began to falter, and the local press made Blanda the scapegoat, pointing out that year after year he had more throws intercepted than any other passer in the AFL, an observation that fueled suspicions that he was being paid by gamblers to throw interceptions. (An investigation by the AFL commissioner cleared him of all allegations.) After the 1966 season the Oilers traded Blanda to the Oakland Raiders, where he

became the backup quarterback to starter Daryle Lamonica and the first-string placekicker. In 1967 Oakland won the AFL championship by beating Houston 40–7, in a game that saw Blanda kick four field goals. The next season the Raiders won the AFL Western Division title only to be beaten in the championship game by the New York Jets. Again in 1969, Oakland won the Western Division title but lost the championship, this time to the Kansas City Chiefs. During those years Blanda saw little action outside of placekicking. A misunderstanding regarding some remarks about fellow players and management publicly attributed to Blanda after the 1969 season seemed to threaten his tenure in Oakland, but the problem ultimately evaporated. In 1970, as part of a newly unified NFL, Blanda replaced the injured Lamonica. His "miracle finish"—five straight weeks in which he favorably altered the course of the game in its last minutes—began on October 25, when he threw three touchdown passes and kicked a field goal as Oakland beat Pittsburgh, 31–14. A week later a 48-yard field goal by Blanda in the last three seconds of the game brought the Raiders from behind to tie Kansas City, 17–17, and in the last 90 seconds of a game against Cleveland on November 8, Blanda threw a touchdown pass and kicked a field goal to defeat Cleveland, 23–20. On November 15 a 20-yard pass from Blanda to Fred Bilentikoff with two minutes and 28 seconds remaining brought Oakland to a 24–19 victory over Denver. The string of brilliant performances that gave Oakland the divisional championship was capped on November 22, when Blanda kicked a 16-yard field goal in the last seven seconds to vanquish San Diego, 20–17. That season the Raiders lost in the second round of the play-offs to the Colts. Blanda retired prior to the 1976 season, when he was 48 years old. In 1981 he was inducted into the Pro Football Hall of Fame. He is one of only two players to compete in four separate decades. (Punter Jeff Feagles is the other.) Blanda ran for nine career touchdowns and threw for 236 more. He kicked 335 field goals and more extra points (943) than any other player in football history. Upon his retirement Blanda held the record for scoring, with 2,002 points. After his professional football career was over, Blanda spent his time giving speeches, playing in celebrity golf competitions, and following horse racing. He is survived by his wife, Betty, and his two children. See *Current Biography* (1972). —W. D.

Obituary *New York Times* (on-line) Sep. 27, 2010

BOURGEOIS, LOUISE Dec. 25, 1911–May 31, 2010 Artist. Louise Bourgeois was one of the most celebrated and enduring sculptors of modern times, known for her deeply psychological and "confessional" work. Some of her most famous pieces, including the towering spider series she called *Maman*, were produced when Bourgeois was well into her 80s. Because of her independence and uncompromising allegiance to her own vision, it was not until the mid-1970s, as trends in art changed, that the importance of her work began to be more fully recognized. Richard Dorment wrote for the London *Telegraph* (June 1, 2010, on-line) that if one is "equipped with intimate knowledge of her life's story . . . the symbolism of her materials was easy to interpret. Tapestries refer to the family business, cages to imprisonment; marble houses to the security of her early childhood, guillotines to its brutal end. This literal, one-to-one, indexical symbolism turned each new work into a fragment of a psychoanalytical case history seething with oedipal angst." A native of Paris, France, Bourgeois was born in the Left Bank's St-Germain-des-Prés district to Louis and Josephine (Fauriaux) Bourgeois. The family owned a tapestry gallery and an apartment on the Boulevard St-Germain in Paris and, beginning in 1919, maintained a workshop for the restoration of Aubusson tapestries in Antony, five miles south of Paris, on the Bièvre River. Recovered from stables and old houses in the countryside, many of the tapestries had been damaged. From about the age of 10, Bourgeois earned her parents' praise by drawing in the missing parts of the tapestries. Bourgeois never described her youth as idyllic. She considered her father a womanizer; he had an ongoing sexual relationship with a tutor ostensibly hired to teach English to Bourgeois and her siblings. The jealousy, resentment, and rage that Bourgeois felt as an intermediary in the liaison motivated much of her work in later years. Bourgeois studied mathematics and philosophy at the Sorbonne until 1935, when she turned her attention more fully to art, studying at the École du Louvre (1936–37), the Académie des Beaux-Arts (1936–38), and the Académie Julian and the Atelier Fernand Léger (1938), among other schools. In 1938 Bourgeois met the American art historian Robert Goldwater. They were married in September of that year and left the following month for New York City. (Bourgeois became a naturalized U.S. citizen in 1953.) For some years Bourgeois produced paintings, drawings, and prints in a style that reflected her interest in geometry, supported by a familiarity with the principles of cubism. She exhibited her work for the first time in the U.S. in 1939, in a group show of prints at the Brooklyn Museum. Her first solo exhibition consisted of a dozen paintings displayed at the Bertha Schaefer Gallery in New York in 1945. By 1949, when her collection of expressive pole-like figures—based on family and friends—debuted at the Peridot Gallery, Bourgeois had given up painting in favor of sculpting. In the 1960s she turned to a variety of materials, including plaster, plastics, rubber latex, marble, and bronze. By the late 1970s she had begun using steel, either alone or in combination with other materials. Between 1978 and 1981 Bourgeois mounted five solo shows in New York City, as well as several others elsewhere. In 1982 the Museum of Modern Art (MoMA) staged a retrospective for the sculptor—a sign that she was now fully established. In 1989 Bourgeois had her first retrospective in Europe, in Frankfurt, Germany, and in 1993 she represented the U.S. at the Venice Biennale. The sculptures with which Bourgeois is perhaps most associated, her *Maman* spider structures, began appearing in 1999. Versions of *Maman*, in steel or cast in bronze, can now be found at museums in Bilbao, Spain; Washington, D.C.; London, England; and Boston, Massachusetts, among other locales. "This spider is an ode to my mother," she said in a prepared statement quoted in the *New York Times* (October 4, 2007, on-line). "She was my best friend. Like a spider, my mother was a weaver. Like spiders, my mother was very clever. Spiders are friendly presences that eat mosquitoes. We know that mosquitoes spread diseases and are therefore unwanted. So, spiders are helpful and protective, just like my mother." Bourgeois was a fellow of the American Academy of Arts and Sciences, and she taught at various institutions, including Brooklyn College, Pratt Institute, Goddard College, New York City's School of Visual Arts, Columbia University, the Cooper Union, Rutgers University, the New York Studio School, and Yale University. She was named an Officer of the Order of Arts and Letters by the French government in 1983 and received the National Medal of Arts from President Bill Clinton in 1997. In 2008 Bourgeois saw career retrospectives mounted at the Guggenheim Museum, in New York City; the Tate Modern, in London; and the Centre Pompidou, in Paris. That year she was also the subject of a feature-length documentary, *Louise Bourgeois: The Spider, the Mistress and the Tangerine.* Bourgeois died of a heart attack at her home in New York City. She is survived by her sons Jean-Louis and Alain, two grandchildren, and a great-granddaughter. (Her other son, Michel, died in 1990.) See *Current Biography* (1983). —W.D.

Obituary *New York Times* (on-line) May 31, 2010

BRAZAUSKAS, ALGIRDAS Sep. 22, 1932–June 26, 2010 Lithuanian politician. In 1993, two years after the dissolution of the Soviet Union, Algirdas Brazauskas (pronounced al-HEER-dahs bran-ZOW-skas) became the first elected president of Lithuania since 1940, when the country was forcibly annexed by the Soviets. He later served as prime minister, and in both those roles he skillfully navigated the complex tangle of economic and social problems facing his newly democratic nation. Brazauskas was born in Rokiskis, Lithuania. His father worked as a teacher, accountant, and civil servant; his mother was a notary public, barrister, and judge. In 1956 Brazauskas graduated from the Kaunas Polytechnic Institute (now the Kaunas University of Technology) with a degree in civil engineering. In 1965 he was appointed minister of the Building Materials Industry, and two years later he was made deputy chair of the State Planning Committee. While serving in the latter capacity, Brazauskas studied economics, and in 1974 he earned a doctoral degree in that field. In 1977 those credentials helped him land his first job in the Lithuanian Communist Party, as the Central Committee's secretary for economic affairs. Brazauskas emerged as a strong political force in the 1980s, as the Soviet Union (of which Lithuania was a constituent republic) ushered in a period of radical reform. Following years of economic stagnation and declining morale, Soviet leader Mikhail Gorbachev launched the policies of glasnost and perestroika ("political openness" and "economic restructuring," respectively). The ensuing climate of political and economic freedom roused Lithuania's slumbering national consciousness and gave rise to a popular national front movement, called Sajudis (SAH-you-dis), from the Lithuanian term for "the movement." Brazauskas was known as a reform-minded Communist who advocated greater autonomy from Moscow, so in 1988 the Kremlin, struggling to show that it would bend but not break, appointed him, in a spirit of compromise, as first secretary of the Central Committee of Lithuania. On December 20, 1989 the Lithuanian Communist Party voted to break with the Soviet Communist Party, and on January 15, 1990 Lithuania's legislature overwhelmingly elected Brazauskas as the country's president. Soon Lithuania was preparing for its first multi-party legislative elections in decades, to be held on February 24; Sajudis was favored to win. The Communists, sensing that their ties to the past were a political liability, downplayed party ideology, and Brazauskas avoided even mentioning the word "communist" in his campaign. Despite his best efforts, Brazauskas was unable to escape his party's unpopular legacy: when the Communists were swept from power in the February elections, he was replaced as president of Lithuania by his Sajudis opponent, Vytautus Landsbergis. On March 11, 1990 Brazauskas joined other members of the Lithuanian Parliament in voting 124–0 for a unilateral declaration of independence from Moscow. Brazauskas, recognized as a savvy negotiator who might be able to reason with Moscow, was subsequently appointed deputy prime minister. In 1991 the Soviet confederation disintegrated, leaving a multitude of independent republics in its wake; Lithuania officially gained its independence on September 7, 1991. In October 1992 the Lithuanian electorate voted Sajudis out of power and returned Brazauskas and his party (now operating under the rubric of Social Democratic Labor Party, or DLP) to a leadership role in the newly independent country. With the national legislature, the Sejm, brimming with supporters, Brazauskas was a shoo-in to become acting president of Lithuania, and in February 1993 he won a popular mandate to continue on as president for a full term. He did not seek reelection in 1998 but returned to politics in 2001, to be elected head of the Social Democrats. He was named prime minister in July of that year and served until 2006, helping to bring Lithuania into the North Atlantic Treaty Organization (NATO) and the European Union. Brazauskas died of lymphoma and prostate cancer. Divorced from his first wife, Julia, he is survived by two daughters from that union and by his second wife, Kristina. See *Current Biography International* (2002). —D.K.

Obituary *New York Times* (on-line) June 28, 2010

BUECHNER, THOMAS S. Sep. 25, 1926–June 13, 2010 Museum director. Thomas Scharman Buechner (pronounced BEEK-ner) made substantial improvements to New York City's Brooklyn Museum during his tenure as director (1960–71), including the addition of a sculpture garden and a program to modernize the building. Buechner also served two notable stints, in the 1950s and 1970s, as the director of the Corning Museum of Glass, in Upstate New York. He was born in New York City to Thomas Buechner, an advertising executive, and Anne Buechner. He and his two sisters were raised in the suburban community of Bronxville, New York. Buechner attended preparatory school in Lawrenceville, New Jersey, where he founded the Easel Club, played on the soccer team, served as an art director of student publications, and was the Bibliophile Prize winner. After graduating, in 1944, he enlisted in the U.S. Navy and studied at the V-5 Naval Air Corps Training Program at Princeton University, in New Jersey. Discharged from the navy shortly after the end of World War II, he spent a year in Puerto Rico, because he wanted to learn Spanish and interact with another culture; there, he worked at the island's tourist board and at a series of other jobs. Upon returning to New York City, in 1946, he enrolled at the Art Students League. He then studied at the École des Beaux Arts, in Paris, during the summer of 1947, and spent 1948 studying painting with M. M. van Dantzig in the Netherlands. He returned to the Art Students League in 1949 for an additional year of study. By that point Buechner had come to the conclusion that he was a "very bad painter," in his words. After briefly holding a job at a New York City department store, he joined the staff of the Metropolitan Museum of Art as assistant manager of the display department, a position that required him to design posters and covers for museum publications and to handle the details of some exhibitions. In 1950 he became the director of the Corning Museum of Glass, in Corning, New York. During the decade he served as director, the museum became an outstanding showplace for demonstrating the beauty and versatility of glass as a creative as well as functional medium, and Buechner mounted a number of exhibitions of ancient and contemporary glass that were subsequently shown at leading museums around the country. He also redesigned the museum's layout so as to retain the interest of visitors for longer periods. In 1960 Buechner became the director of the Brooklyn Museum. Some of his most important accomplishments as director were his efforts to modernize the museum building itself; he installed temperature and humidity controls and created study galleries for all of the departments. He also took hundreds of paintings out of storage and made them available for the public to see in an open-study gallery, and he oversaw the creation of a sculpture garden that held a number of architectural gems. (It was renamed the Steinberg Family Sculpture Garden after a museum renovation was completed in 2004.) Buechner resigned from his post in 1971 and returned to the Corning Museum of Glass, where he served as president of the Steuben Glass division from 1973 to 1982 and as the musuem's director from 1973 to 1980. After retiring from Corning, in 1987, Buechner resumed painting. Buechner, the founder of the professional journals *New Glass Review* and the *Journal of Glass Studies*, also authored several books, including *Norman Rockwell: Artist and Illustrator* (1970) and *How I Paint* (2000). He died of lymphoma at his home in Corning and is survived by his wife, Mary Hawkins; his daughter, Barbara; two sons, Thomas and Matthew; two sisters, Nancy and Betsy; and seven grandchildren. See *Current Biography* (1961).—D.K.

Obituary *New York Times* (on-line) June 17, 2010

BUTLER, ROBERT N. Jan. 21, 1927–July 4, 2010 Gerontologist. Known as the father of modern gerontology, Robert Butler devoted most of his professional life to championing the rights of the elderly, and he is widely credited as one of the first medical professionals willing to discuss the realities of growing old within the context of a culture that places exceptional value on youth. Butler worked to dispel widely held misconceptions about old age and shed light on the problem of "ageism," a term he coined in the late 1960s to describe the discriminatory treatment of the elderly. Instead of what he characterized as the "quiet despair, deprivation, desolation and muted rage" often associated with growing old in the U.S., Butler presented the possibility of an alternate aging experience that could ease our anxieties about death and dying. "There is no way to avoid our ultimate destiny," he wrote in his Pulitzer Prize–winning book, *Why Survive?* (1975), which was published with the subtitle *Being Old in America*. "But we can struggle to give each human being the chance to be born safely, to be loved and cared for in childhood, to taste everything the life cycle has to offer, including . . . a secure old age." He concluded, "After one has lived a life of meaning, death may lose much of its terror. For what we fear most is not really death but a meaningless and absurd life." Robert Neil Butler was born in New York City to Fred and Easter (Dikeman) Butler. After his parents' separation, when he was 11 months old, he was sent to live with his maternal grandparents in Vineland, a rural town in southern New Jersey. Butler became particularly close to his grandfather, a chicken farmer, and delighted in hearing the older man's stories as they cared for the poultry together. At seven, Butler was bewildered when his grandfather, who had been nearly 70 when Butler joined the household, disappeared without explanation. Later, Butler learned that his beloved grandfather had died; no one had wanted to tell the boy. In his struggle to come to terms with his loss and with the finality of death, he thought about his family's physician, Dr. Rose. "I had cherished him for his reassuring presence and care through my serious [childhood] bout with scarlet fever. If Dr. Rose had been there with the right medicine, I would certainly have had my grandfather with me longer. To be a doctor was clearly the answer. For the first time [since my grandfather's death], my anxiety eased," Butler wrote in *Why Survive?* Forced to give up the farm, his grandmother found work as a seamstress, and Butler helped out by selling newspapers and repairing bicycles. When he was 11, a fire destroyed the rooming house where he and his grandmother were living, and they lost everything they owned. "We started again," Butler wrote. "And what I remember even more than the hardships of those years was my grandmother's triumphant spirit and determination." He asserted, "If love of my grandfather and old Dr. Rose brought me to medicine, it was my grandmother in the years that followed who showed me the strength and endurance of the elderly." In 1945 Butler entered Columbia University, in New York City, and after receiving a B.A. degree, in 1949, he studied medicine at the Columbia University College of Physicians and Surgeons, earning an M.D. degree in 1953. During his internship, at St. Luke's Hospital, he tended many elderly patients and realized how little he had been taught in medical school about the aged. To make up for that gap in his knowledge, he began reading widely on such subjects as the biology of aging and attempts to lengthen the life spans of laboratory animals through diet. After completing a residency at the University of California, San Francisco, Butler served as a research psychologist for the National Institute of Mental Health (NIMH), where he began work on a long study on aging and, with the consumer activist Ralph Nader, helped investigate nursing-home conditions. In 1975 he became the founding director of the National Institute on Aging. He was also a founder of the American Association for Geriatric Psychiatry, the Alzheimer's Disease Association, and the International Longevity Center. In 1982 he persuaded the Mount Sinai School of Medicine, in New York City, to create a department specifically devoted to gerontology, and it became one of the first medical schools in the nation to do so. In addition to *Why Survive?*, Butler wrote several other books, including the best-selling *Sex After Sixty* (1976), later published under the title *Love and Sex After Sixty*. Butler was appointed by President Bill Clinton to chair the advisory committee of the 1995 White House Conference on Aging, and he served on a number of other such bodies, including the Commonwealth Fund Commission on Elderly People Living Alone, the advisory board of the National Women's Health Resource Center, and the national advisory committee of the group Physicians for Human Rights. Among his many honors were the U.S. Public Health Service Distinguished Service Medal; the Claude Pepper Award, from the New York Foundation for Senior Citizens; and the Sandoz Prize for Gerontological Research, from the International Association of Gerontology. Butler, ill with leukemia, worked until three days before his death. He was predeceased in 2005 by his second wife, Myrna Lewis, the co-author of *Sex After Sixty*. (His first marriage, to Diane McLaughlin, ended in divorce.) Butler is survived by his four daughters (Christine, Cynthia, Alexandra, and Carole) and several grandchildren. See *Current Biography* (1997). —H.R.W.

Obituary *New York Times* A p13 July 7, 2010

BYRD, ROBERT C. Nov. 20, 1917–June 28, 2010 U.S. senator from West Virginia. A Democrat whose positions ranged from conservative to liberal, Robert C. Byrd held a seat in the U.S. Senate for 51 years, making him the longest-serving member in the history of that body. He wrote in his autobiography, *Robert C. Byrd: Child of the Appalachian Coalfields* (2005), that it was his "constant desire to improve the lives of the people who have sent me to Washington time and time again." In a tribute after Byrd's death, President Barack Obama said, "America has lost a voice of principle and reason," and he described the senator as "generous with his time and advice, something I appreciated as a young senator." Byrd was born Cornelius Calvin Sale Jr. in Wilkesboro, North Carolina. After his mother, Ada Mae Kirby Sale, died from influenza the next year, he was sent to live on the West Virginia farm of an uncle and aunt, Titus and Vlurma Byrd, who renamed him Robert Carlyle Byrd. Byrd suffered a hardscrabble childhood; the

farmhouse had no electricity or indoor plumbing, he had only one toy (a small peddle car), and he could attend Sunday school only because a local shopkeeper donated suitable clothing for him. The valedictorian of the 1934 graduating class of Mark Twain High School, he could not afford to attend college. Instead, he took jobs as a gas-station attendant and grocery clerk. He later trained himself to be a butcher. In the early 1940s Byrd moved to Baltimore, Maryland, to work as a shipyard welder. After World War II ended, he returned to West Virginia and opened his own grocery store. A born-again Baptist, Byrd taught Bible classes whose popularity led a local radio station to broadcast his weekly lessons. At about that time Byrd organized a 150-member chapter of the Ku Klux Klan in Sophia, West Virginia. One Klan head, impressed by Byrd's leadership skills, suggested that he go into politics. "Suddenly, lights flashed in my mind," Byrd recalled. "Someone important had recognized my abilities." In 1946 Byrd was elected to the West Virginia state House, and two years later he won a state Senate seat. In 1952 Byrd won a seat in the U.S. House, where he represented West Virginia's Sixth Congressional District, whose voters were unconcerned about his former Klan membership. (While Byrd always insisted that his Klan chapter had never engaged in hate speech or racial violence, he admitted that as a young man he had "reflected the fears and prejudices" of the era, and later he repeatedly apologized for his actions in that period in his life.) He won re-election in 1954 and 1956, and in 1958 he was elected to the U.S. Senate, where he remained until his death. During his early years in the Senate, his voting record on civil rights was inconsistent. When the sweeping Civil Rights Act came before Congress in 1964, he joined his fellow southern Democrats in arguing that it infringed upon states' rights. It was only after Byrd became a Senate party leader in 1977 that he began to consistently back civil rights legislation. (Whereas in 1964 officials with the liberal organization Americans for Democratic Action determined that his views reflected theirs only 16 percent of the time, in 2005 they judged the correspondence to be 95 percent.) Byrd served as Democratic leader until 1989. For many years he sat on the powerful Appropriations Committee, chairing it from 1989 to 1995, 2001 to 2003, and 2007 to 2009. Known for carrying a copy of the U.S. Constitution with him, Byrd was described in the *Almanac of American Politics* as perhaps "[coming] closer to the kind of senator the Founding Fathers had in mind than any other" and by some others as "an institution within the institution." Unfailingly devoted to his constituents, he attracted billions of dollars in funding and initiatives to West Virginia. In 1963, after attending night classes for 10 years at the American University in Washington, D.C., he earned a law degree, despite his lack of an undergraduate degree. (In 1994 Marshall University, in Huntington, West Virginia, awarded him a B.A.) Byrd was lauded for his dedication to educational causes. In 1985, for example, he launched the first federally funded merit-based scholarship program. A supporter of the Vietnam War, Byrd joined the small number of senators who opposed the U.S. invasion of Iraq in 2003. In his long Senate career, Byrd had a 98 percent attendance record and cast

18,555 roll-call votes—more votes than any other senator in U.S. history. On June 12, 2006 he became the longest-serving U.S. senator in history, and on November 18, 2009 he became the longest-serving member of Congress, surpassing the previous record of 20,775 days. At the time of his death, he was serving as president pro tempore of the Senate, that body's second-highest-ranking official (after the nation's vice president, who casts tie-breaking votes); by tradition, the Senate elects the most senior member of the majority party to that post. In his last few years, Byrd suffered from failing health; he died at a Virginia hospital after being admitted for exhaustion and dehydration in the midst of a Washington-area heat wave. He is survived by two daughters, Mona and Marjorie, as well as by five grandchildren and seven great-grandchildren. He was predeceased in 2006 by his wife of 68 years, the former Erma Ora James, his high-school sweetheart. In addition to his memoir, Byrd wrote books including *Losing America: Confronting a Reckless and Arrogant Presidency* (2004); *Letter to a New President: Commonsense Lessons for Our Next* Leader, 2008; a four-volume history of the U.S. Senate; and a treatise on Roman constitutionalism. A skilled fiddle player, he released the LP album *Mountain Fiddler* in 1978. See *Current Biography* (1978). —H.R.W.

Obituary *New York Times* A p1+ June 28, 2010

CALDERA, RAFAEL Jan. 24, 1916–Dec. 24, 2009 Former president of Venezuela. Rafael Caldera served two terms, roughly 20 years apart, as the president of the South American republic of Venezuela. Each tenure was notable for a significant event in Venezuela's history. Caldera's first term, from 1969 to 1974, marked the first time that a Venezuelan government peacefully relinquished power to the opposition party since the nation won its independence from Spain, in 1821. During his second term, which lasted from 1994 to 1999, Caldera pardoned Hugo Chavez for his role in a failed military coup. (The pardon paved the way for Chavez's later rise to power; Chavez is the current president of the country and a frequent critic of U.S. foreign policy.) During his two terms Caldera also worked to uphold democracy and nurture political stability. A native of the mountainous region of north central Venezuela, Rafael Caldera Rodriguez was born in San Felipe, in the state of Yaracuy. He was one of the two sons of Tomas Rafael Caldera Izaguirre, a lawyer, and Rosa Sofia Rodriguez Rivero de Caldera. At the Central University of Venezuela, Rafael Caldera became one of the leaders of the conservative, anti-Communist Roman Catholic youth movement. In 1936 he helped found the Union Nacional Estudiantil (UNE), a student organization based on Christian social principles. Caldera graduated in 1939 with degrees in both law and political science. He soon became one of the youngest men ever elected to the Venezuelan National Congress, where he represented the Acción Nacional (Democratic Action) party as a deputy for the state of Yaracuy from 1941 to 1944. From 1944 to 1945 he was Venezuela's attorney general. In 1946 Caldera left Acción Nacional and became the co-founder of a new party, the right-of-center Comité de Organizacion Política Electoral Independiente

(COPEI or Christian Democratic) party. He ran in Venezuela's 1947 presidential election but lost to the Accion Nacional candidate, despite being endorsed by the Roman Catholic Church, which supported his platform to make "the rich less rich and the poor less poor." (Caldera opposed the Marxist concept of class struggle, however, and called for social harmony.) In 1957 Caldera was imprisoned for four months by the dictator Marcos Perez Jimenez, who had seized power in 1953. Upon his release, he went into exile. In 1958, after Jimenez was deposed, Caldera returned and took part in signing a landmark deal that guaranteed democratic elections. The agreement, known as the Punto Fijo pact, called for all parties to respect election results. Caldera successfully ran in Venezuela's 1968 presidential election, and upon taking office in March 1969, he persuaded armed leftists to stand down, forged ties with the Soviet Union, and budgeted generously for public works. Caldera won reelection in 1993, backed by a coalition of 17 parties known as the Convergence movement. During that term he took on Venezuela's banking crisis—unsuccessfully, as the country was forced to accept the assistance of the International Monetary Fund (IMF). He also pardoned Chavez for his part in a failed 1992 coup. (Had he not been pardoned, Chavez, a populist figure, would have been unable to succeed Caldera as president.) During his final years, however, Caldera, who wrote a weekly newspaper opinion column, voiced his criticism of Chavez and his administration. Caldera was multilingual, an accomplished writer, and an expert on Venezuelan literature. He is survived by his wife, Alicia Pietri de Caldera, and his three sons and three daughters. See *Current Biography* (1969). —W.D.

Obituary *New York Times* (on-line) Dec. 24, 2009

CALLAHAN, JOHN Feb. 5, 1951–July 24, 2010 Cartoonist. John Callahan was noted for his rude and politically incorrect sense of humor, and his syndicated cartoons, which appeared in more than 200 publications at the height of his popularity, often poked fun at women, African-Americans, and disabled people. Among Callahan's best-known single-panel comics is one in which a posse on horseback has halted next to an empty wheelchair in the middle of a desert. "Don't worry, he won't get far on foot," the head of the posse is saying to the other men. (That gag provided the title for Callahan's 1989 memoir.) In another well-known cartoon, a man holding a cane and a beggar's cup stands at a street corner; a sign hanging from his neck reads "Please help me. I am blind and black but not musical." Bruce Weber wrote for the *New York Times* (July 28, 2010, on-line), "[Callahan] viewed the world through a dark and wicked lens." The cartoonist's mother abandoned him to a Roman Catholic orphanage immediately following his birth. Shortly thereafter, he was adopted by David Callahan, who worked for a grain company, and his wife, Rosemary, who believed she was unable to conceive but went on to bear five children after she and her husband adopted John. The family lived in Dalles, Oregon, where Callahan attended a very strict Catholic school. The nuns who instructed him inspired some of his very first cartoons. "I showed my work around and it made me pretty popular with the other students," he recalled to Jeff Lyon for the *Chicago Tribune* (January 2, 1994). After high school he spent some time working as an orderly at a state mental hospital and then at an aluminum plant. Callahan had first tasted alcohol at the age of 12, and by his late teens he had developed a major drinking problem. Although he had an aptitude for drawing and humor, his drinking held him back from working up to his potential or from pursuing any kind of career in drawing or writing. In 1972, after a day of heavy drinking, he allowed an intoxicated man to drive his car. While Callahan was in the passenger seat, the driver crashed into a telephone pole at 90 miles per hour, causing Callahan to suffer a severe spinal injury that left him paralyzed below the diaphragm, with only partial use of his hands and arms. His injury rendered him unable to dress himself or control his bodily functions, which caused him to become depressed and drink even more heavily. With therapy, he relearned how to draw, and in 1978 he joined Alcoholics Anonymous. With his addiction under control, he earned a bachelor's degree in English from Portland State University and began to create cartoons on a regular basis. Callahan's cartoons were first published in the early 1980s, in some of Oregon's alternative newspapers. Later *Penthouse*, the *New Yorker*, and other widely read national magazines began publishing them. In 1988 his work went into syndication, appearing in more than 200 newspapers around the world. In addition to *Don't Worry, He Won't Get Far on Foot: The Autobiography of a Dangerous Man*, Callahan wrote a second book based on his life, *Will the Real John Callahan Please Stand Up?: A Quasi Memoir* (1998). Some of his cartoon collections include *Digesting the Child Within and Other Cartoons to Live By* (1991), *Do What He Says! He's Crazy!!* (1992), *What Kind of God Would Allow a Thing Like This to Happen?!!* (1994), *Freaks of Nature* (1995), and *Levels of Insanity* (2004). His work was the basis for two short-lived animated series: *Pelswick*, a family-friendly show about the life of a boy in a wheelchair, and *John Callahan's Quads*, an adult-oriented program featuring characters with a variety of disabilities. Callahan died in Portland, Oregon, due to respiratory problems and complications from his quadriplegia. He is survived by his adoptive mother, Rosemary, and his five siblings. At the time of his death he was enrolled in a Portland State University master's-degree program in counseling. See *Current Biography* (1998). —J.P.

Obituary *New York Times* (on-line) July 28, 2010

CARONE, NICOLAS June 4, 1917–July 15, 2010 Artist. Nicolas Carone, an Abstract Expressionist, is often mentioned alongside Jackson Pollock and Willem de Kooning as one of the early members of what came to be called the New York School. Abstract Expressionism was a post–World War II movement influenced by surrealism and characterized by a free-form, subconscious-driven approach to painting. Although widely recognized during the height of the movement, Carone, as Roberta Smith observed for the *New York Times* (July 29, 2010, on-line), demonstrated his "best work . . . long after the style faded,

in the large paintings in shades of black, white and gray that he made during the last two or three decades of his life. The shifting lines and layered brushwork of these works most completely integrated the classical figurative tradition he absorbed during his earliest art studies and the instinctive painting processes of Abstract Expressionism." The second of six children, Nicolas Carone was born in New York City and raised in nearby Hoboken, New Jersey, by parents who had immigrated from Italy. When he was about 11, he began attending the rigidly academic Leonardo da Vinci Art School in Manhattan. He then studied at the Art Students League, the National Academy of Design (now the National Academy Museum and School of Fine Art), and the Hans Hoffman School of Fine Arts. Under Hoffman's tutelage Carone began producing increasingly abstract work. From 1947 to 1951 Carone lived in Italy, using funds from a Fulbright Fellowship. His first solo exhibition was held in Rome in 1949, and he had his first show in New York City in 1954, at the Stable Gallery. In 1951 Carone and a number of other painters held a show in a small space at 60 East Ninth Street, in Manhattan. Now referred to as the Ninth Street Exhibition (or Ninth Street Show), it has come to be considered by art historians as one of the most important exhibitions of American art of the 20th century, highlighting a distinctively American approach to painting and bringing together a group of Abstract Expressionists who for the next decade or so commanded worldwide attention. Carone himself enjoyed a strong period of sustained public exposure for his work, which appeared at the Venice Biennale, two Whitney Museum Annuals, and other prestigious museums and galleries. He was also represented at a show of Abstract Expressionists at the Solomon R. Guggenheim Museum, in New York City, in 1962. Between 1962 and about 1999, Carone's work was shown in public only intermittently, although he continued to sell it privately. In 1978 and 1993 he mounted solo shows in Florida, exhibiting a type of painting that he had been doing for decades: portraits, often of people in simple clothes, with firm gazes and wide noses—subjects that were not glamorous but suggested deep sensuality. In addition to those paintings, whose subjects were not based on live models, Carone carved heads out of stones he found outside his home in Italy. Mysterious yet evocative, the heads became important examples of Carone's work in sculpting, an art he had taken up in the mid-1960s at the suggestion of a friend. The beginning of the 21st century brought a renewed interest in Carone and his work. In addition to his participation in a variety of group exhibitions, in 2003 he had a solo show at the Butler Institute of American Art, in Youngstown, Ohio, that focused on his works on paper, especially gouaches, paintings made with a rich type of watercolor that resembles oil-based paint. A more wide-ranging exhibit of Carone's works on paper opened in October 2005 at the Lohin Geduld Gallery, in New York City. That exhibition brought enthusiastic reviews from the city's critics. Lance Esplund wrote for the New York *Sun* (November 17, 2005) that Carone's work was "rich and absorbing—a rhythmic tumble of classicism, eroticism, and ambiguity." Esplund continued, "Looking at his works, most of which, though fresh and alive, feel as if, half-baked, they had fallen straight out of mid-century, I could not help but think that here is an artist who is not anxious about what 'must-see' exhibition is currently showing. Here is an artist focused on his work who, moving picture to picture, line by line, is taking his own sweet time." In later years Carone's work was shown at the Washburn Gallery, in New York City. Carone was a founding faculty member of the New York Studio School, which opened in 1964, and taught there for some 25 years. He also taught at the Cooper Union, Columbia University, and the National Academy Museum and School of Fine Arts. In 1988 he launched an art school in Doglio, Italy, where he maintained a home. Carone died at his residence in Hudson, New York. His two marriages, to Nell Mager and Adele Bishop, ended in divorce. He is survived by his three sons (David, Claude, and Christian) and one grandson. See *Current Biography* (2006). —W.D.

Obituary *New York Times* (on-line) July 29, 2010

CHABROL, CLAUDE June 24, 1930-Sep. 12, 2010 Filmmaker. Claude Chabrol, who was often referred to as the "Gallic Hitchcock" for his highly stylized suspense thrillers, directed nearly 60 films over a career that spanned more than half a century. Along with his contemporaries Jean-Luc Godard, François Truffaut, Eric Rohmer, and Jacques Rivette, Chabrol was one of the founders of La Nouvelle Vague. (Also known as the French New Wave, that influential film movement emerged in the late 1950s and 1960s and was derived from the Italian neorealist and classic Hollywood styles.) Born in Paris, Chabrol was the only child of Yves Chabrol, a pharmacist, and the former Madeleine Delarbe. He grew up in the country village of Sardent, in the Limousin region of central France. Chabrol developed a passion for film as a child and overcame the misery of World War II by running a film club in a barn in Sardent. It was at that time that he became drawn to thrillers, detective stories, and other such popular genres. After the war, Chabrol returned to Paris and entered the Sorbonne to study pharmacology and literature. Upon graduating with a degree in literature, he became a habitué of Paris movie houses and befriended such other cineastes as Godard, Truffaut, Rohmer, and Rivette. Chabrol fulfilled his compulsory military service in the French medical corps, serving for a time in Germany and rising to the rank of sergeant. After leaving the army he wrote film criticism for *Arts* magazine before joining the influential French film journal *Cahiers du Cinema*, which had been founded by the renowned critic and theorist André Bazin in 1950 and also counted among its writers Godard, Truffaut, Rohmer, and Rivette. There, Chabrol wrote reviews and an array of seminal pieces that analyzed the merits of various directors and their respective oeuvres. Eschewing the work of most of their predecessors in the French cinema, with the exception of Jean Renoir, Chabrol and his contemporaries championed such directors as Roberto Rossellini, Ingmar Bergman, Fritz Lang, Alfred Hitchcock, Howard Hawks, Nicholas Ray, and Otto Preminger, which helped give rise to the auteur theory—that is, the idea that a director's body of work reflects his personal creative vision. Chabrol and his colleagues yearned for a new, more personal brand of cinematic expression, free from the limitations imposed by the Hollywood studio system, and that longing ultimately resulted in the launch of their own film careers. In 1955 Chabrol went to work as the Paris publicity officer for Twentieth-Century Fox, but he left the job after only a year, having been told he was "the worst press officer they'd ever seen," as he once noted; his replacement, Godard, was reportedly even worse. In 1957 Chabrol's first wife, the former Agnes Marie-Madeleine Goute (whom he had married in 1952), came into an inheritance, which allowed him to form a production company and make his first film, *Le Beau Serge* ("Handsome Serge," 1958). Shot on location in Sardent with nonprofessional actors, the low-budget, black-and-white film, about a man who returns to the village of his youth and tries to save his former best friend from self-inflicted ruin, was the first full-length feature to express the ideas of the French New Wave, and it proved to be both a critical and commercial success. The success of that film allowed Chabrol to begin work on a second feature, *Les Cousins* ("The Cousins," 1958), which won the prestigious Golden Bear award at the Berlin Film Festival. Chabrol used the proceeds from his first two box-office triumphs to launch the careers of his friends. Chabrol had small acting roles in several of their films and served as the technical adviser for Godard's landmark picture *Breathless* (1960). Chabrol's third film, *A Double Tour* (1959, released in the U.S. under the title *Leda* in 1961), marked his first foray into color and centered on the murder of a wealthy wine-grower's mistress. That film would serve as a precursor to other suspense thrillers—including *La Femme infidèle* ("The Unfaithful Wife," 1968), *Le Boucher* ("The Butcher," 1970), *Juste avant la nuit* ("Just Before Nightfall," 1971), and *Les Noches Rouges* ("Wedding in Blood," 1973)—many of which starred his second wife, the actress Stéphane Audran. Some of Chabrol's best films in later years featured the actress Isabelle Huppert, among them *Une Affaire de Femmes* (1998), *Madame Bovary* (1991), *La Cérémonie* (1995), and *Comedy of Power* (2006). While he failed to reach the same level of prominence as some of his contemporaries, namely Godard and Truffaut, Chabrol was easily the most prolific of the French New Wave directors. His final film, the police thriller *Bellamy*, was released in France in 2009 and starred Gerard Depardieu in the title role; the film was released in the U.S. in October 2010. Chabrol also lent his talents to television, directing two films in 1973 based on short stories by Henry James and a documentary about occupied France, *The Eye of Vichy* (1993), among other such projects. He was the recipient of numerous honors for his contribution to the arts, including the European Film Prize in 2004. Chabrol died of complications from anemia in a Paris hospital. He is survived by his third wife, Aurore Pajot, who had been his longtime script supervisor, and four children. See *Current Biography* (1975). —C.C.

Obituary *New York Times* A p29 Sep. 13, 2010

COFFIN, FRANK M. July 11, 1919–Dec. 7, 2009 Former U.S. representative; federal judge. Frank Morey Coffin was a Democratic politician who served on the U.S. Court of Appeals for more than 40 years. Coffin was born into a political family in Lewiston, Maine. His maternal grandfather, Frank M. Morey, served as mayor of Lewiston and in 1911 was appointed the speaker of the Maine House of Representatives; his grandmother Maude Morey and his paternal grandfather were also members of the Maine State Legislature; and his mother served on Maine's Democratic State Committee. Coffin was educated in Lewiston public schools before enrolling at Bates College, in his native city. Upon receiving a bachelor's degree, in 1940, he began studying at Harvard's Graduate School of Business Administration. Coffin served in the U.S. Navy during World War II, working in the Pacific theater as a supply-corps officer. By the time he returned to civilian life, in 1946, he had achieved the rank of lieutenant. Coffin earned an LL.B. degree with honors from the Harvard Law School and gained admission to the Maine bar in 1947. His honors record brought him an appointment as law clerk to Judge John D. Clifford Jr., of the U.S. Circuit Court for the District of Maine. He served as a law clerk for two years before entering into private practice. At about that time Coffin became active in local politics, and in 1954 he was elected chair of Maine's Democratic State Committee. He went on to play a pivotal role in Edmund S. Muskie's election as governor later that year. In 1956 Coffin won a seat in the U.S. House of Representatives, becoming the first Maine Democrat to join Congress in more than two decades. He won reelection in 1958, and in 1960 he made an unsuccessful gubernatorial run. After that failed bid Coffin became a deputy administrator with the U.S. Agency for International Development (AID), where he served until 1964. The following year he was appointed to the U.S. Court of Appeals for the First Circuit by President Lyndon B. Johnson. Coffin served on the bench for the next four decades, spending 11 years (1972–83) as chief justice. He assumed senior status (indicating semi-retirement) in 1989 and continued to be involved in rulings until his full retirement, in 2006. As a federal judge, he delivered more than 2,500 opinions on a wide range of issues and became known for his unbiased manner. Coffin, a recipient of the Edward J. Devitt Distinguished Service to Justice Award, was also the author of four books: *Witness for AID* (1964), *The Ways of a Judge: Views from the Federal Appellate Bench* (1980), *A Lexicon of Oral Advocacy* (1985), and *On Appeal: Courts, Lawyering and Judging* (1994). Coffin died at Maine Medical Center, in Portland, of complications from surgery to repair an aortic aneurysm. He is survived by his wife, Ruth; four children; and several grandchildren. See *Current Biography* (1959). —C.C.

Obituary *New York Times* B p13 Dec. 17, 2009

COSSIGA, FRANCESCO July 26, 1928-Aug. 17, 2010 Politician. Francesco Cossiga was a former president and prime minister of Italy. He made international headlines in 1978, while Italy's minister of the interior, for his failed attempt to save the life of Aldo Moro, a kidnapped colleague. He stepped down from his post after Moro was killed, thus becoming the first Italian Cabinet minister to voluntarily leave office since World War II. Cossiga was born on the island of Sardinia to Giuseppe Cossiga, a bank director, and Maria (Zanfarino) Cossiga. Involved in Roman Catholic Church activities since childhood, Cossiga joined the newly reconstituted Partito Democrazia Cristiana (DC), or Christian Democratic Party, at the end of World War II, when he was 16. He then acquired a law degree from the University of Sassari and subsequently became a professor of constitutional law there. In 1958 Cossiga became a member of the DC's national council and won election to Parliament as a deputy from the city of Sassari. He soon became identified with the liberal wing of his party and began a gradual rise to prominence, eventually becoming chair of the DC Parliamentary group. From 1966 to 1970 Cossiga occupied the post of undersecretary of defense. Then, in 1974, he achieved Cabinet status as minister without portfolio and was made responsible for organizing public administration, a job that entailed reforming the government's complex and inefficient bureaucracy. In February 1976 Cossiga became minister of the interior. In that role he inherited the Herculean task of curbing the epidemic of political terrorism that had ravaged Italy since the late 1960s. On March 16, 1978—the day on which the Italian Parliament was to ratify a new measure for parliamentary cooperation among Christian Democrats, Communists, Socialists, Social Democrats, and Republicans—the DC party president and former prime minister Aldo Moro, who deserved much of the credit for creating the new alliance, was kidnapped by Red Brigade terrorists. On May 9, 1978 Moro was found murdered in central Rome. Moro's kidnapping had placed a grave burden on Cossiga. The interior minister had been officially put in charge of the search for his close friend, and Moro's family had been counting on him. Cossiga, however, had upheld the government's policy of rejecting all bargaining with the kidnappers and had instead organized police and army forces in a massive manhunt. On May 10, after Moro's body was found, Cossiga resigned. Observers noted that Cossiga's decision was almost unprecedented: no Italian Cabinet minister had voluntarily resigned since the end of World War II, and the move earned him admiration and respect among Italy's citizens. In 1979 Cossiga was asked to form a government coalition after a number of administrations had failed to win the support of the Parliament. As prime minister, Cossiga was warmly received by his constituents, and he quickly moved to impose harsher punishments on terrorists. He also emphasized pro-American and pro-European policies. In 1980, however, the Socialist Party withdrew its support for Cossiga's coalition, and the prime minister resigned. In 1983 Cossiga was elected president of the Italian Senate, and in 1985 he was elected by the Parliament to serve as president of Italy. As president—a largely ceremonial role—he became an outspoken critic of the government and even of his own party. He was nicknamed *picconatore* (pickaxe-wielder) for his sharp rhetoric. Cossiga resigned as president in 1992 when it was revealed that he was involved in Gladio, a secretive NATO-sponsored, anti-Communist organization. As a former president, he became a senator for life. Cossiga, who was married to his wife, Giuseppa Sigurani, from 1960 to 1998, when the marriage was annulled, died at a Rome hospital of cardiovascular disease. He is survived by his two children: Anna Maria, a writer, and Giuseppe, a politician. See *Current Biography* (1981). —W.D.

Obituary *New York Times* (on-line) Aug. 17, 2010

COSTANZA, MIDGE Nov. 28, 1932–Mar. 23, 2010 Former presidential adviser; social and political activist. Margaret "Midge" Costanza served as a special assistant to President Jimmy Carter from 1977 to 1978, earning a reputation as a passionate proponent of equal rights for women and minorities as well as a strong defender of the gay community. Costanza, one of the four children of Philip Joseph and Concetta (Granata) Costanza, immigrants from Sicily, was born in LeRoy, New York. She grew up in Rochester, where her parents ran a sausage-making business. After graduating from the local high school, Costanza ended her formal education and began working in a series of clerical jobs. She eventually became an administrative assistant to John Petrossi, a real-estate developer and the head of a cement business in Rochester. Costanza spent two decades working with Petrossi, during which she also served on the boards and advisory committees of a number of organizations, including the Community Savings Bank of Rochester, the Women's Council of the Rochester Chamber of Commerce, and the American Cancer Society. Costanza's entry into political circles came in 1954, when she volunteered for W. Averell Harriman's successful gubernatorial campaign. From 1959 to 1964 she served as the executive Democratic committeeperson for Rochester's 22d ward. In 1964 she helped oversee Robert F. Kennedy's senatorial campaign in Monroe County, New York. Costanza then served as vice chair of the Monroe County Democratic Committee, from 1966 to 1970, and chair of the New York State Democratic Women's Conference, in 1968. In 1972 she became a member of the Democratic National Committee and was named an alternate delegate to the Democratic National Convention. The following year Costanza was elected to the Rochester City Council, becoming the first councilwoman in the city's history. Despite winning a record number of votes, she was passed over for mayor by her fellow council members, who named her to the ceremonial post of vice mayor instead. Undaunted, Costanza remained an active voice on the council and emerged as an effective rabble-rouser. In 1974 she ran for a Rochester-based seat in the U.S. House of Representatives but lost to the popular Republican incumbent Barber Conable. It was during Costanza's congressional campaign that she met Jimmy Carter, who was then the governor of Georgia and chair of the Democratic National Committee. Costanza subsequently became the first prominent Democrat in New York State to support his bid for the U.S. presidency. She became co-chair of Carter's presidential campaign in New York and gave a speech for him at the 1976 Democratic National Convention. Following Carter's election as president, Costanza was appointed to be his liaison with such organized special-interest groups as the American Israel Public Affairs Committee (AIPAC) and the U.S. Chamber of Commerce. The first woman ever to serve as an assistant to the president, she held the official title of assistant to the president for public liaison. (The Office of Public Liaison was later renamed the Office of Public Engagement.) Costanza worked in the West Wing, in an office adjacent to that of the president. During her tenure she was often referred to as Carter's "window to the nation," and she became known for her outspokenness on issues related to women and minority groups. Her actions—which included holding the first White House meeting with gay activists and urging top-level women in the administration to write letters in protest of Carter's stance on providing federal funding for disadvantaged women seeking abortions—frequently rankled the president and his other advisers. Carter soon stripped her of most of her responsibilities, cut her staff, and banished her to a basement office. Costanza resigned from her post in August 1978, just 20 months after stepping into the role. She then moved to Los Angeles, California, where she teamed up with a friend, the actress Shirley MacLaine, to run a series of seminars on spirituality. In 1990 Costanza moved to San Diego, where she began working as an adviser to prospective political candidates. She was instrumental in both the successful Senate campaign of Barbara Boxer and the successful congressional campaign of Lynn Schenk. From 2000 to 2003 Costanza served as a special assistant to California governor Gray Davis as a liaison to women's groups. In 2003 she founded the Midge Costanza Institute for the Study of Politics and Public Policy, a San Diego–based nonprofit organization whose aim is to encourage civic participation. In 2005 she began working as a public-affairs officer for the San Diego District Attorney's Office, where she focused on aiding the elderly. Costanza, who never married, died at a hospital in San Diego after a long battle with cancer. She is survived by her brother, Anthony. See *Current Biography* (1978). —C.C.

Obituary *New York Times* (on-line) Mar. 24, 2010

CREWE, ALBERT V. Feb. 18, 1927–Nov. 18, 2009 Physicist. Albert Crewe came to international fame in 1970, when he presented the first images of an individual atom ever taken with an electron microscope. (An atom is approximately four billionths of an inch in diameter.) He achieved that seemingly impossible feat by creating the scanning transmission electron microscope (STEM), which used focused beams of electrons instead of light waves for magnification. Crewe's pioneering work has benefited a number of fields, including biology, chemistry, medicine, and genetics. Albert Victor Crewe was born in Bradford, Yorkshire, England. At age 15, after passing a national entrance exam, he became the first member of his working-class family to attend high school. He then received a scholarship to the University of Liverpool, where he earned a B.S. degree in physics in 1947 and a Ph.D. degree in the same subject three years later. Crewe was an assistant lecturer at the University of Liverpool from 1950 to 1952, when he was named a full lecturer. In 1955 Crewe, who was then doing pioneering work with particle accelerators, accepted a post as a visiting research associate at the University of Chicago. After moving to the U.S., he began working on a new cyclotron built under the direction of Enrico Fermi and Herbert Anderson. (A cyclotron is a type of particle accelerator that consists of two D-shaped cavities sandwiched between two electromagnets.) In 1958 Crewe joined the staff of the Argonne National Laboratory, outside Chicago. There, he led a research team that developed a more advanced particle accelerator, and from 1961 to 1967 he was the director of the laboratory's particle-accelerator division. Crewe became interested in electron microscopy in the 1960s. His goal was to develop technology that could reach resolutions of up to a single angstrom, a unit of measurement equal to 0.1 nanometers. He left Argonne and his managerial position in 1967 to return to the University of Chicago, where he became a full professor. (From 1971 to 1981 he was the dean of physical science at the university, and he retired in 1996 as professor emeritus.) Crewe, who had jotted down his initial plans for an improved microscope when he found himself without a book to read while on a plane flight, developed STEM while at the university; in June 1970 he published the results of his work in *Science*. Along with his article, "Visibility of Single Atoms," the journal published his groundbreaking photographs of uranium and thorium atoms magnified one million times. The photos caused widespread excitement in the scientific world. (One of Crewe's daughters was a middle-school student at the time, and when she announced his achievement to her science teacher before the news officially broke, she was accused of making up stories.) In 1976 Crewe received further praise when he strung together a series of still photos to make a rudimentary film that showed that atoms were in constant motion. Crew later collaborated with the Hitachi Corp. on the development of commercial electron microscopes, and today the devices are fixtures in the semiconductor industry and laboratories of all types. Crewe, who held almost 20 patents and published hundreds of scientific papers, died from complications of Parkinson's disease at his home in Dune Acres, Indiana. He is survived by his wife, Doreen, to whom he had been married since 1949; his four children, Jennifer, Sarah, Elizabeth, and David; and his 10 grandchildren. See *Current Biography* (1964). —W.D.

Obituary *New York Times* (on-line) Nov. 21 2009

CURTIS, TONY June 3, 1925—Sep. 29, 2010 Actor. Tony Curtis reached the height of his fame and popularity in the late 1950s, when he appeared alongside Sidney Poitier in the prison-escape drama *The Defiant Ones* (1958) and co-starred with Jack Lemmon and Marilyn Monroe in Billy Wilder's iconic comedy *Some Like It Hot* (1959). In a tribute published in the *New York Times* (September 30, 2010, on-line), Dave Kehr praised Curtis as "one of the last survivors of Hollywood's golden age." The son of Jewish immigrants from Hungary, Bernard Schwartz, as he was named at birth, grew up in a tough neighborhood in the New York City borough of the Bronx. He and his brothers, Robert and Julius, shared a single cramped bedroom behind his parents' tiny tailor shop. All three boys were often beaten by their mother, who suffered from schizophrenia. During the Great Depression, Curtis and Julius were placed in a boys' home by their desperate parents. Upon his return home, Curtis found himself the victim of anti-Semitic bullies, and he soon joined a gang that offered some protection. Just months before his high-school graduation, in 1944, Curtis joined the U.S. Navy, serving as a submarine signalman until a winch chain snapped and injured him while he was loading torpedoes at Guam. For four weeks he lay in a hospital with his legs paralyzed. He subsequently returned to New York City and earned his high-school diploma in 1946. Already a movie fan, Curtis enrolled via the G.I. Bill in a drama workshop at the New School for Social Research, where his fellow students included the actor Walter Matthau. He then joined a stock company that toured the so-called Borscht Belt, in New York State's Catskill Mountains. Discovered by a casting agent for Universal Pictures, he signed a $75-a-week contract and moved to Hollywood. There, he took courses in dramatics, voice, gymnastics, horsemanship, and pantomime; thought up his stage name; and waited for the studio to award him a role. Curtis was finally given a bit part in *Criss Cross* (1949), which starred Yvonne De Carlo. Although it was a small role, fan mail began to pour in, and Curtis was assigned increasingly more prominent roles, including those of the title characters in the costume drama *The Prince Who Was a Thief* (1951) and the biopic *Houdini* (1953). Playing a venal, ambitious publicist in Alexander Mackendrick's *Sweet Smell of Success* (1957), Curtis turned in a performance that many critics still call one of the best of his career. Among his other critically acclaimed films are *The Defiant Ones* (1958), in which he portrayed an embittered escaped convict—a role that earned him an Oscar nomination—and *Some Like It Hot* (1959), in which he famously appeared in drag. After he appeared in Stanley Kubrick's costume drama *Spartacus* (1960), set in ancient Rome, Curtis became the object of some derision for not modulating his Bronx accent; he proclaims at one point, "I'm uh singa of sawngs." Curtis's other films include *The Outsider* (1961), *Goodbye Charlie* (1964), *The Great Race* (1965), and *The Boston Strangler* (1968). Throughout the 1970s and 1980s he appeared frequently on television, starring in the short-lived series *The Persuaders* (1971–72) and *McCoy* (1975–76) and making guest appearances on such shows as *Vega$*. Later in life Curtis took up painting and co-wrote *Tony Curtis: The Autobiography* (1994) and *American Prince: A Memoir* (2008). Curtis, who struggled on occasion with alcoholism and drug addiction, was married six times. From 1951 to 1962 he was the husband of the popular actress Janet Leigh, famed for her role in Alfred Hitchcock's *Psycho* (1960). His other wives were the actress Christine Kaufmann, whose underage affair with Curtis had precipitated his divorce from Leigh; the model Leslie Allen; the actress Andrea Savio; the lawyer Lisa Deutsch; and the horse trainer Jill Vandenberg, to whom he was married at the time of his death. Curtis died at age 85 of cardiac arrest at his home near Las Vegas, Nevada. He is survived by Vandenberg and five children: Jamie Lee and Kelly Lee (from his union with Leigh); Alexandra and Allegra (from his marriage to Kaufmann); and Benjamin (from his union with Allen; Curtis and Allen had another son, Nicholas, who died of a drug overdose in 1994). Jamie Lee Curtis followed her father into acting; she is particularly known for her starring roles in John Carpenter's *Halloween* franchise. See *Current Biography* (1959). —D.K.

Obituary *New York Times* (on-line) Sep. 30, 2010

DALY, CAHAL B. Oct. 1, 1917–Dec. 31, 2009 Theologian. Cahal Daly was a leading figure in the Irish-Catholic Church for more than four decades and one of the most outspoken critics of the Irish Republican Army (IRA). Born in the parish of Loughguile, in County Antrim, Northern Ireland, Daly was the third of seven children. His father, Charles, struggled to support the family on a teacher's salary, and their home had no running water. Although Catholics and Protestants enjoyed relatively good relations in Loughguile, Daly was exposed at an early age to the violent tensions brought on by sectarianism. When he was four years old, IRA members burned down his family's cottage as a retaliatory measure against the British Auxiliary Police, who had occupied the adjacent, vacant home. In his autobiography, *Steps on My Pilgrim Journey: Memories and Reflections* (1998), Daly wrote, "All my parents' wedding presents, all their first pieces of furniture and possessions, went up in flames." His family lived with relatives before finding a new home on a small farm in Tully, also in County Antrim. Daly went on to study the classics and theology at St. Malachy's College in Belfast. He then earned bachelor's and master's degrees from Queen's University Belfast, in 1936 and 1937, respectively. Drawn to the clerical life through the influence of his devoutly religious mother, Daly studied for the priesthood at St. Patrick's College in Maynooth and was ordained a priest in 1941. He earned a doctorate in divinity from St. Patrick's College three years later and began pursuing an academic career. He worked as a classics master at his alma mater St. Malachy's for a year before joining the faculty of Queen's University as a lecturer in scholastic philosophy in 1946. Daly taught there for the next two decades, during which he acted as an adviser at the Second Vatican Council (1962–65) in Rome and published two books on Catholic theology: *Morals, Law, and Life* (1962) and *Natural Law Morality Today* (1965). In 1967 he was named bishop of Ardagh and Clonmacnoise, in the Republic of Ireland. Daly's appointment came amidst rising tensions between Protestants and Catholics in Northern Ireland, which set off a wave of violence that initiated the period known as the Troubles (1968–98). The target of a thwarted terrorist plot by IRA members, Daly frequently used the pulpit to condemn IRA-related violence and worked tirelessly to improve relations between Northern Ireland's Protestants and Catholics. Daly was widely credited with writing the speech given by Pope John Paul II during his 1979 visit to Ireland. The speech strongly denounced violence and pleaded with the IRA to end its bloody campaign. In 1982, after recovering from a heart attack, Daly was appointed the bishop of Down and Connor, a diocese in Northern Ireland that included the war-torn city of Belfast. He remained in that post until 1990, when he was appointed the archbishop of Armagh and the Roman Catholic Primate of All Ireland.

Daly was elevated to cardinal in 1991. He retired as cardinal in 1996 but continued to write on a number of topics. Sometimes criticized for the perceived half-heartedness of his response to the Church's sex-abuse scandals of the 1980s and 1990s, Daly was nonetheless widely praised for his peace efforts. Former British prime minister Tony Blair told reporters that Daly's life should be considered "a real and lasting example of effective religious leadership working to build peace and resolve conflict in the most challenging of circumstances." Daly died surrounded by his family and friends at Belfast City Hospital, in Northern Ireland. He is survived by his brother Paddy and sister Rosaleen. See *Current Biography International Yearbook* (2002). —C.C.

Obituary *New York Times* p6 Jan. 2, 2010

DEAN, JIMMY Aug. 10, 1928–June 13, 2010 Country-music star; entrepreneur. Jimmy Dean enjoyed a lengthy career as a singer, radio and television host, and actor. He was also widely known as the pitch-man for an eponymous line of pork products, making commercials in which he exhibited the folksy, homespun quality that had been his hallmark as an entertainer. Jimmy Ray Dean was born in Seth Ward, a community northeast of Plainview, on the Texas panhandle. During Dean's youth his father deserted the family; his mother, Ruth, supported Dean and his younger brother, Don, by operating a local barber shop. Dean sang in his church's choir; learned how to play the piano, guitar, harmonica, and accordion; and picked cotton and cleaned chicken coops, among other jobs, to help the family survive. At the age of 16, he dropped out of high school and spent two years in the U.S. Merchant Marine. He then entered the air force and was stationed at the Bolling Air Force Base, in Washington, D.C. There, Dean began to play the accordion at a local tavern in the evenings and formed his first band, the Tennessee Haymakers. After leaving the air force, in 1948, Dean joined a musical group called the Texas Wildcats, whose first single, "Bummin' Around," became a Top 10 hit in 1953. Dean and the Wildcats found themselves in great demand on local television and radio, and in 1957 CBS began airing the *Jimmy Dean Show*, a national morning program that featured such musical stars as Roy Clark and Patsy Cline. Although the show received tens of thousands of fan letters a week and ratings were high, CBS soon canceled it. Dean remained with the network, however, appearing in various time slots until 1959, when he was dropped from the roster. In response to a suggestion made by Dean, his fans flooded the CBS mailroom with 12,000 wrappers from a sponsor's soap product, but that demonstration of the strong following he commanded left network officials unmoved, and his employment was terminated as planned. Although not on television, Dean remained busy, performing concerts and making sold-out personal appearances at county fairs and other venues. In 1961 he released "Big Bad John," a ballad about a heroic coal miner who dies saving his co-workers in a mine collapse. The song spent five weeks at the top of the *Billboard* chart and earned Dean a Grammy Award. On December 21, 1962 the *Jimmy Dean Show*, a new variety program, began airing on ABC. The show proved to be highly popular and remained on the air until 1966. Dean—whose other hit singles include "P.T. 109," "Sam Hill," and "I.O.U."—subsequently found additional screen work. He appeared regularly, for example, on the hit TV series *Daniel Boone*, played a millionaire in the 1971 James Bond film *Diamonds Are Forever*, and served as a guest host on the *Tonight Show*. He was perhaps best known to audiences in later decades for his commercials on behalf of the Jimmy Dean Meat Co., a successful pork-processing business that he had founded in the early 1960s and sold to the Sara Lee Corp. in 1984. Even after his company was acquired by that large conglomerate, Dean remained a spokesman for two decades, assuring consumers of the purity and wholesomeness of his sausages and other products. In 2004 Dean published an autobiography, *30 Years of Sausage, 50 Years of Ham*. He was named to the Country Music Hall of Fame in February 2010, just months before his sudden death at his home in Virginia. He is survived by Gary, Connie, and Robert, his three children with his first wife, Sue Wittauer, whom he divorced acrimoniously in 1991, after 40 years of marriage. He is also survived by his second wife, Donna Meade, a singer/songwriter 25 years his junior. See *Current Biography* (1965). —J.P.

Obituary *New York Times* (on-line) June 14, 2010

DOBRYNIN, ANATOLY F. Nov. 16, 1919–Apr. 6, 2010 Soviet diplomat. Anatoly F. Dobrynin had a 24-year tenure as the Soviet ambassador to the United States, during which he served under six Soviet leaders, worked with six American presidents, and played a vital role in the resolution of a number of conflicts, most notably the Cuban Missile Crisis of 1962. Robert D. McFaddin wrote for the *New York Times* (April 8, 2010, on-line): "To a generation of Washington officials in a perilous nuclear age, Mr. Dobrynin was the pre-eminent channel for Soviet-American relations: a tough, nuanced, charming ambassador who was, as admirers and detractors put it, no more duplicitous than he had to be." Dobrynin was born in Krasnaya Gorka, near Moscow, Russia, to a Ukrainian plumber and an "essentially unlettered" mother, as he once referred to her. He graduated from a technical college before the outbreak of World War II, and during the war he served as an engineer at an aircraft plant run by the Russian aeronautical engineer A. S. Yakovlev. In 1944 Dobrynin, who knew English, was chosen to study at a diplomatic training school in Moscow. After the war ended he assumed increasingly important positions in the Soviet Foreign Ministry. He served as an assistant to the deputy minister of foreign affairs from 1949 to 1952 and was then sent abroad to the Soviet Embassy in Washington, D.C. He remained there for three years, rising to become the embassy's number-two-ranking official. In 1955 he returned to the Soviet Union to join the ministry of foreign affairs, where he held the rank of ambassador extraordinary and plenipotentiary. In that capacity he attended several international conferences, including the 10th anniversary celebration of the United Nations and the Geneva summit conference, both held in 1955. In 1957 Dobrynin traveled to New York City to serve as un-

dersecretary without portfolio to the U.N. secretary general Dag Hammarskjold. He enjoyed a close relationship with Hammarskjold, and his tenure marked a period of relative cooperation between the secretary general and Soviet leadership. In 1962 Soviet premier Nikita S. Khrushchev, whom he had accompanied on his historic visit to the U.S. three years earlier, appointed Dobrynin ambassador to the United States. As ambassador, Dobrynin often met privately with President John F. Kennedy to discuss diplomatic affairs and the possibility of securing a "durable peace with justice" between the Soviet Union and the U.S. Unlike other Soviet diplomats of the time, Dobrynin immersed himself in American culture and spoke without the help of interpreters. His tenure as ambassador saw him involved in addressing such Cold War matters as the Cuban Missile Crisis of 1962, the Soviet invasions of Czechoslovakia and Afghanistan, in 1968 and 1979, respectively, and American and Soviet participation in the Vietnam War. He was also involved in drafting the Anti-Ballistic Missile Treaty of 1972. After leaving the ambassadorship, in 1986, Dobrynin returned to Moscow and became a senior official in the Communist Party's Central Committee. He retired two years later but continued to advise Premier Mikhail Gorbachev until the collapse of the Soviet Union, in 1991. In 1995 Dobrynin published a memoir, *In Confidence: Moscow's Ambassador to Six Cold War Presidents*. His death, at the age of 90, was announced by the Kremlin. Dobrynin is survived by his wife of 68 years, Irina; his daughter, Yelena, and a granddaughter, Yekaterina. See *Current Biography* (1962). —C.C.

Obituary *New York Times* (on-line) Apr. 8, 2010

FEOKTISTOV, KONSTANTIN PETROVICH Feb. 7, 1926–Nov. 21, 2009 Cosmonaut; spacecraft engineer. Konstantin Feoktistov, an engineer who became the first Soviet civilian to orbit the Earth, has a crater on the moon named in his honor. He was born to Pyotr, a retired bookkeeper, and Maria Feoktistov in the southwestern Russian city of Voronezh. His older brother, Boris, was killed by German forces in 1941. When Voronezh came under Nazi occupation following year, Feoktistov, then 16, joined the Red Army and helped conduct reconnaissance missions. After leading several successful assignments, he was captured and sentenced to death by firing squad. Shot through the neck, Feoktistov feigned death and escaped from the burial trench after the German officers left the site. Sympathetic townspeople then helped him reach safety behind Soviet lines. Following World War II Feoktistov attended the Bauman Moscow Higher Technical School. Upon graduating, in 1949, he worked as a factory engineer in Zlatoust, a city in the Ural Mountains. In 1955 Feoktistov earned a doctoral degree in physics. Although he was not a member of the Communist Party, which made him highly unpopular in many quarters, Feoktistov was enlisted to work in the Soviet space program. He joined the renowned spacecraft engineer Mikhail Tikhonravov's Experimental Design Bureau, where he became part of the team responsible for the *Sputnik*, *Vostok*, *Voskhod*, and *Soyuz* space capsules. When the *Voskhod*, a seven-ton multi-seat craft, launched on October 12, 1964, Feoktistov was aboard—along with Dr. Boris B. Yegorov, a young lieutenant in the Soviet Army's medical corps, and the Soviet Air Force commander Vladimir M. Komarov. The flight, which lasted just over 24 hours and covered 494,700 miles, was the first to include a civilian, the first to carry a three-person crew, and the first in which the cosmonauts did not wear space suits (because room in the small capsule was severely limited). The three, who had performed various scientific experiments while orbiting Earth, were widely credited with proving the viability and benefits of multidisciplinary teams in space. After that flight Feoktistov trained for further space missions, but he was eventually forced to retire due to medical reasons. Although he never again flew in one of his crafts, he continued to work in space engineering, and he took part in the development of the special suit worn by cosmonaut Aleksei Leonov during the flight of *Voskhod II* in 1965. (Leonov earned renown during that mission for being the first man to step outside an orbiting spacecraft to float in space.) Feoktistov later became the head of the Soviet space-design bureau, a position he held until 1990. During his tenure there, he helped design the space shuttles *Progress* and *Mir* and the station Salyut and made preliminary plans for an ion-powered vessel capable of taking humans to Mars. After stepping down as head of the Soviet space-design bureau, Feoktistov taught at Bauman Moscow Higher Technical School. Feoktistov, a recipient of the Order of the Red Banner of Labor, the Order of Lenin, and the Gold Star Medal, among other honors, died of unspecified causes in Moscow. His wife and four children survive him. See *Current Biography* (1967). —C.C.

Obituary *New York Times* B p7 Nov. 23, 2009

FISCHER, JOHN H. July 16, 1910–Dec. 18, 2009 Educator. In the early 1950s, when Baltimore, Maryland, became the first large city in the nation to integrate its public schools, John H. Fischer, then the superintendent of the school system, was given much of the credit. Later, as the head of Columbia University's Teachers College, in New York City, from 1959 to 1974, he oversaw a teacher-training center that has influenced educational ideas and practices throughout the world. Fischer was born in Baltimore and attended the Maryland State Teachers College, in Towson, earning a diploma in 1930. He then began his career in education as an elementary-school teacher in Baltimore. From 1933 to 1935 he taught in a city junior high school and then, in his first administrative appointment, he became an assistant junior-high principal. In 1938 he was made special assistant in charge of Baltimore's Benjamin Franklin Junior High School. At the same time that Fischer was acquiring practical experience, he was also gaining formal academic training. He earned a B.S. degree from Johns Hopkins University, in Baltimore, in 1940. Later, at Columbia's Teachers College, he was awarded a master's degree in 1949 and an Ed.D. degree in 1951. During his years of study, Fischer continued to advance in the Baltimore school system to director of attendance and child guidance in 1942 and to assistant superintendent for general administration in 1945. He became deputy superintendent of schools in 1952 and superintendent of public instruction in

1953. One of the most challenging problems with which Fischer had to deal as superintendent was that of racial integration, especially after the ruling of the U.S. Supreme Court in May 1954 outlawing the segregation of white and black pupils in public schools. In June he met with the city's teachers to announce that he would be complying with the ruling and that anyone opposed to his actions was welcome to step down. Despite protests and boycotts on the part of some Baltimore residents, the new policy of integration was implemented relatively smoothly and peacefully. In 1959 Fischer was named dean of Columbia University's Teachers College, which had been founded in 1888 to train teachers, guidance counselors, and educational administrators. (At the time he assumed the post, it was estimated that half of the large school systems in the nation were headed by graduates of Teachers College.) In 1962 he was appointed college president. At Columbia, Fischer stressed the importance of serving minority students and instilling a sense of intellectual competence in all pupils. Additionally, he fostered cooperation between Teachers College and Columbia's other departments, and he toughened the standards for admission and graduation. During his tenure Fischer oversaw the establishment of the Institute for Urban and Minority Education and the Institute of International Studies at Teachers College, and he was a major supporter of the school's efforts to build an education system in Afghanistan, traveling to Kabul each year to measure its progress. (The Teachers College Afghanistan Program had been established in 1954.) Fischer, who also chaired the National Commission on the Education of the Disadvantaged for several years, retired from Teachers College in 1974. He died at his Massachusetts home from congestive heart failure at the age of 99. Fischer was predeceased by his wife, Norma, in 2002. He is survived by his sons, David and Miles; five grandchildren; and six great-grandchildren. See *Current Biography* (1960). —M.R.

Obituary *New York Times* (on-line) Dec. 26, 2009

FISHER, EDDIE Aug. 10, 1928–Sep. 22, 2010 Singer; entertainer. Eddie Fisher, one of the most popular performers of the 1950s, was known for his golden voice and movie-star looks—as well as for his romantic relationships with a string of Hollywood actresses. With hits including "Wish You Were Here," "I'm Walking Behind You," "Oh My Pa-Pa," and "I Need You Now," Fisher wooed an entire generation of teenage girls only to alienate them with the very public dissolution of his marriage to the actress Debbie Reynolds, whom he left for Elizabeth Taylor in 1959. Edwin Jack Fisher was born in Philadelphia, Pennsylvania, one of seven children. He grew up in a poor section of South Philadelphia. As a boy Fisher sang at synagogue services and competed in talent contests sponsored by local radio stations. After winning a competition on the *Horn and Hardart Children's Hour* when he was 13, Fisher became a regular performer on Philadelphia radio. At 17 he was hired as a singer for the trombonist Buddy Morrow's band, a job that brought him to New York City and led to an engagement with the saxophonist Charlie

Ventura's band. A few months shy of 18, Fisher auditioned for Monte Proser, then the director of the Copacabana nightclub. Although he could not yet hire the young performer due to age requirements, Proser helped Fisher land a summer gig as a staff singer at a resort in the Catskills. There, Fisher made a number of contacts, including Bob Weitman, the manager of the Broadway Paramount Theatre, and Eddie Cantor, who booked him for a cross-country tour in 1949. The tour was successful, and Fisher signed a recording contract with RCA Victor soon afterward. "In one year, this boy will be America's most important new singer of popular songs," Cantor predicted, and indeed, within a year, three of Fisher's songs had made it to the Top 20 charts, including "Thinking of You," which peaked at number five. In 1950 Fisher was named "America's Most Promising New Male Vocalist" in an annual nationwide poll of disk jockeys conducted by Billboard magazine. Fisher, who the summer before was making $75 a week as an "intermission singer" at the Paramount Theater, now commanded $1,000 a week to appear at the Paramount as a headlining act. Inducted into the U.S. Army in April 1951, Fisher performed as part of an Armed Forces Review, taking part in more than 150 shows while touring Hawaii, Wake Island, Japan, Korea, Alaska, and the Aleutian Islands, as well as locations in mainland Europe, Iceland, and Greenland. In an article for the New York Daily Mirror (April 16, 1953), Sidney Fields quoted Fisher as saying, "The Army gave me a lot more than I gave it. Why, I did shows I never would have done. In the rain, the mud, off the backs of trucks, without a mike, and sometimes even without music." During his two years in uniform, Fisher continued to make records, scoring 10 hits that sold more than seven million copies collectively. Back in New York he booked a three-week engagement at the Paramount and was met with a frenzied reaction from young fans. By 1956 Fisher had released a total of 50 Top 40 hits, 24 of which had made it to the top 10. From 1953 to 1957 he hosted his own musical variety television show, Coke Time with Eddie Fisher (which was sponsored by the soft-drink company), and then starred in another program, The Eddie Fisher Show, which aired on NBC from 1957 to 1959. At the height of his popularity, Fisher was romantically linked to a number of leading Hollywood stars, including Marlene Dietrich and Kim Novak. He married the actress Debbie Reynolds in 1955 and quickly started a family. Together the two were hailed as Hollywood's golden couple, and they appeared together in the musical-comedy film Bundle of Joy in 1956. When Fisher left Reynolds, in 1959, to marry the actress Elizabeth Taylor, the widow of his late best friend (the producer Mike Todd, who had died a year earlier), the singer suffered a major blow to his public image from which his career never fully recovered. NBC canceled The Eddie Fisher Show that year, and he was dropped by RCA in 1960. Clouded by scandal, his marriage to Taylor ended in divorce in 1964, when she left him for her Cleopatra co-star, Richard Burton. Fisher's last major hit was the song "Games that Lovers Play" from the successful album of the same name, recorded with the arranger Nelson Riddle in 1966. He released only a handful of minor albums over the next few years, including a Christmas-themed record in 1969. In 1967 Fisher married his third wife, the actress and singer Connie Stevens. As Fisher's career slowed, he began a descent into drug and alcohol addiction, and in 1970 he filed for bankruptcy. Fisher divorced two more times. He penned two memoirs, Eddie: My Life, My Loves (1984) and Been There, Done That (1999), both of which focus more on his love life than his singing career. Fisher died at his home in Berkeley, California, shortly after having hip-replacement surgery. He is survived by his daughters Tricia Leigh and Joely, from his marriage to Connie Stevens; a son, Todd, and a daughter, Carrie, from his marriage to Debbie Reynolds; and six grandchildren. All of Fisher's daughters are actresses; Carrie Fisher is a well-regarded writer as well. See Current Biography (1954). —H.R.W.

Obituary New York Times D p7 Sep. 25, 2010

FLEMING, ROBBEN W. Dec. 18, 1916–Jan. 11, 2010 Lawyer; former university president. Robben Wright Fleming served as the president of the University of Michigan from 1968 to 1978, a period of unprecedented student unrest and social ferment on American college campuses. During that time he became known for his ability to quell campus uprisings while protecting the rights of students and preserving intellectual freedom. Born in Paw Paw, Illinois, to Edmund Palmer Fleming, a general-store owner, and the former Emily Jeannette Wheeler, a teacher, Fleming was active in sports, theater, music, and public speaking while in high school. He graduated from Beloit College, in Wisconsin, with a bachelor's degree in political science in 1938 and received a law degree from the University of Wisconsin in 1941. He began his career as an attorney for the Securities and Exchange Commission in Washington, D.C., and after the U.S. entered World War II, he worked briefly as a mediator on the National War Labor Board. Fleming served for four years (1942–46) in the U.S. Army, traveling to North Africa and Western Europe to help restore order in cities under Allied control. After his discharge he worked as an adviser to the Veterans Emergency Housing Program and as the director of the Industrial Relations Center at the University of Wisconsin. In 1952 Fleming, who was gaining a strong reputation as an expert in labor relations and workplace issues, became the director of the Institute of Labor and Industrial Relations at the University of Illinois, and six years later he accepted a position as a professor of law at the university. In 1961, at a White House Conference on National Economic Issues, he called for a study of the effects of automation (the use of automated processes to control industrial machinery in production lines, thus reducing the need for human labor) on the national economy. In 1962 Fleming was appointed by President John F. Kennedy to lead a three-person board in resolving a dispute between the International Longshoremen's Association and its members' employers. The board succeeded in preventing a strike by the dockworkers and effectively mediated the subsequent negotiations. In 1964, amidst the increasing unrest on college campuses regarding the Vietnam War, Fleming's work caught the attention of officials at the University of Wisconsin, who hired him as a professor of law and a chancellor at the school's 30,000-student Madison campus. Fleming displayed his diplomatic skills in February 1967, when students staged demonstrations to protest the presence of on-campus recruiters for the Dow Chemical Co., a manufacturer of napalm (used by U.S. forces in Vietnam). Although Fleming was blockaded in his office at one point, he harbored no ill will and wrote a personal check to pay the bail of students who had been arrested during the demonstrations. In mid-1967 Fleming was chosen to serve as the ninth president of the University of Michigan, which had in recent years been the setting of some of the most radical youth demonstrations in the U.S., many of them led by the left-wing protest group Students for a Democratic Society. He took his oath of office in March 1968. Fleming's willingness to negotiate with students and his resistance to notifying the police unless absolutely necessary made him an admired figure among his young charges. For example, in March 1969, when a group of students protesting against military personnel on campus barricaded a navy recruiter in a small room, Fleming refused to call the police, and the matter was soon resolved. In 1970 members of the Black Action Movement threatened violence unless the university increased its enrollment of African-Americans from 3 to 10 percent; the organization led a 12-day student strike. In response, Fleming, a supporter of affirmative action, negotiated an agreement with student leaders and called for an increase in the recruitment of black applicants. When four student protestors at Ohio's Kent State University were killed by members of the National Guard, also in 1970, and two students were killed at a protest at Mississippi's Jackson State University later that year, Fleming testified before the President's Commission on Campus Unrest and was lauded for his commonsense appeals to limit the use of force against young people. After leaving his position at Michigan, Fleming served for two years as the president of the Corporation for Public Broadcasting; in 1988 he returned briefly to the university, to serve as its interim president. Fleming, who died after a long period of declining health, is survived by his son, two daughters, five grandchildren, and great-grandson. See Current Biography (1970). —M.R.M.

Obituary New York Times (on-line) Jan. 22, 2010

FOOT, MICHAEL July 23, 1913–Mar. 3, 2010 British politician; writer. Michael Foot was an influential radical-left member of the Labour Party, which he led at a time when Margaret Thatcher and the Conservative Party were gaining power in England. "He knew—as I knew, which is why I counseled him against doing it—that he was letting himself into purgatory in becoming leader of the Labour Party in its darkest, grimmest hour," Neil Kinnock, the leader of the party after Foot, said, as quoted by William Grimes in an obituary for the New York Times (March 3, 2010, on-line). "But if he hadn't done it, I don't think Labour would have survived as a political force." Michael Mackintosh Foot, one of seven children, was born in Plymouth, England. His father, Isaac Foot, was a solicitor, a Methodist preacher, and a Liberal Party politician. Michael Foot studied at Wadham College, in Oxford, where he was active in student political organizations and president of the

Oxford Union. After graduating with honors, in 1934, with degrees in philosophy, politics, and economics, Foot worked for a time at a shipping office in Liverpool. Moved by the suffering he saw during the Great Depression and inspired by Aneurin Bevan, the controversial leader of the radical wing of the Labour Party, Foot made a bid for Parliament in 1935, but he was rejected by voters. He then pursued journalism, working as an assistant editor at the Tribune, a political weekly founded by Bevan, beginning in 1937. Starting in 1938 he worked as an editorial writer for Lord Beaverbrook's right-wing Evening Standard and became the acting editor in 1942. He resigned in 1944, because of political differences with Beaverbrook, and joined the Daily Herald as a political columnist, a post he held for two decades. In 1945 Foot, among the foremost young intellectual spokesmen of the Labour Party at that time, made a bid for the parliamentary seat for the Devonport Division of Plymouth. As part of a nationwide Labour Party landslide, Foot won by a wide margin. That year he rejoined the Tribune as managing director, serving in that capacity until 1974. Concurrently he served stints as the Tribune's editor, from 1948 to 1952 and from 1955 to 1960. For a decade beginning in 1964, he was also a literary critic for the London Evening Standard. In the House of Commons, he was an outspoken advocate of policies that were so far left that even many of his Labour Party colleagues considered them extreme, such as the nationalization of British industry and commerce, disengagement from the Cold War and from Britain's alliance with the U.S., complete nuclear disarmament, and nonparticipation in the developing European Economic Community. Foot lost his parliamentary seat in the 1955 election, but through his writing, for the Tribune and other publications, he continued to play an important role in the Labour Party. During the 1950s he also became one of British television's most familiar political personalities, serving as a regular panelist on two public-affairs programs, Free Speech and In the News. After Bevan's death, in 1960, Foot returned to Parliament, succeeding his mentor as a leader of the Labour Party's radical faction. (Foot penned a two-volume biography of Bevan, publishing the first volume in 1962 and the second in 1973.) On the floor of the House of Commons throughout the 1960s, Foot showed himself to be, in the eyes of some political observers, an uncompromising and doctrinaire ideologue more given to criticizing his moderate colleagues than to formulating a compromise program that could win elections and solve Britain's economic problems. Following the Conservative Party victory in the 1970 election, the Labour Party elected 12 members to the Shadow Cabinet in Parliament, headed by Harold Wilson, the party's acknowledged leader. In 1974 Foot accepted the position of secretary of state for employment in Wilson's Cabinet. Two years later Foot became deputy leader of the party and the leader of the House of Commons. Inflation, rising unemployment, and other economic and political problems, among them the financial drain imposed by Britain's continuing military presence in strife-torn Northern Ireland, catapulted the Conservative Party, headed by Margaret Thatcher, back into power in the general election of 1979. Despite the efforts of Foot, who was elected Labour Party leader in 1980, to unite the party's radical-left and moderate wings, in 1981 the moderate Labourites split from the party to form the Social Democratic Party. In the early 1980s Foot continued to work for such goals as the nationalization of the banks and unilateral disarmament. It was clear after the 1983 election—a decisive victory for Thatcher and the Conservative Party—that Foot's influence had dwindled, and in 1992 he retired. In addition to the biography of Bevan, he is the author of *Another Heart and Other Pulses: The Alternative to the Thatcher Society* (1984), *The Politics of Paradise: A Vindication of Byron* (1988), and *H. G.: The History of Mr. Wells* (1995). Foot died at his home in Hampstead, North London. His wife of many years, Jill Craigie, a writer and documentary filmmaker, died in 1999. See *Current Biography* (1981). —D.K.

Obituary *New York Times* (on-line) Mar. 3, 2010

FORRESTER, MAUREEN July 25, 1930–June 16, 2010 Opera singer. Maureen Forrester, known for her down-to-earth, "anti-diva" attitude, was a popular Canadian contralto who was particularly acclaimed for her performances of works by Gustav Mahler. Anthony Tommasini described her range for the *New York Times* (June 17, 2010): "Though Ms. Forrester sang the broader mezzo-soprano repertory, she rightly considered herself a contralto, the lowest and rarest female voice. In her prime she was a classic contralto with a plummy, deep-set sound. Yet she had a full-bodied upper voice and could sing passagework in [George Frideric] Handel arias with agility. She sang Mahler and German lieder with impeccable diction." Maureen Katherine Stewart Forrester was born in Montreal, Canada, the youngest of the four children of Thomas, a cabinetmaker of Scottish descent, and his wife, Mae, who was of Irish descent. In her late teens Forrester, a basketball-loving tomboy who had dropped out of school at age 13 because she was bored with academics, began to take voice lessons with the Dutch baritone Bernard Diamant, her only vocal teacher. Forrester's formal debut as a recitalist took place at the YWCA in Montreal in March 1953. That quickly led to a performance with the Montreal Symphony, conducted by Otto Klemperer, and the following year she made her debut with the Toronto Symphony. In 1955 she debuted in Paris, France. That year she also gained the sponsorship of Les Jeunesses Musicales du Canada (JMC), which arranged for her to give several recitals in Quebec and Ontario and subsidized a three-month tour of Europe. Her success in Europe made it possible for her to extend her stay there for a full year, during which she worked extensively on learning German lieder. Forrester made her New York City recital debut at Town Hall in 1956, accompanied by the pianist John Newmark, who would serve as her accompanist throughout her career. That performance was greatly praised by critics. Writing for the *New York Times* (November 13, 1956), Edward Downes observed, "Miss Forrester has a superb voice of generous compass and volume. Its color ranges from a darkly resonant chest register to a brilliantly focused top with a middle register that she makes velvet soft or reedy according to her expressive intent." While in New York, Forrester auditioned for Bruno Walter, who invited her to appear under his direction at a February 1957 performance of Mahler's Symphony no. 2 (known as the "Resurrection") with the New York Philharmonic Orchestra. That date marked not only her American debut as a soloist with a symphony orchestra but also her first performance of Mahler's music, and a recording of the event is now considered iconic. Forrester's New York City Opera debut occurred in 1966 in a production of Handel's *Giulio Cesare*. In 1975 she performed several times at the Metropolitan Opera, singing the roles of Erda in Richard Wagner's *Das Rheingold* (part of his "Ring" cycle) and Ulrica in Giuseppe Verdi's *Un Ballo in Maschera*. Forrester, who chaired the Voice Department at the Philadelphia Music Academy for several years, made more than 130 recordings. A fervent supporter of Canadian composers, she also chaired the Canada Council for the Arts from 1983 to 1988 and was honored with a star on Canada's Walk of Fame. Forrester married the violinist and conductor Eugene Kash in 1957; the couple had four daughters (Gina, Paula, Linda, and Susan) and a son (Daniel) before divorcing, in 1976. Forrester, who suffered from alcoholism and dementia in the years preceding her death, is survived by her five children and several grandchildren. See *Current Biography* (1962). —W.D.

Obituary *New York Times* (on-line) June 17, 2010

FORSYTHE, JOHN Jan. 29, 1918–Apr. 1, 2010 Actor. John Forsythe is perhaps best known to audiences for starring in the highly rated television series *Charlie's Angels* (1976–81) and *Dynasty* (1981–89). Born John Lincoln Freund in Carney's Point, New Jersey, the actor was the son of Samuel Jeremiah and Blanche Materson (Blohm) Freund. (Some sources give his place of birth as nearby Penn's Grove, New Jersey.) When he was six years old, his father, a stockbroker, moved the family to New York City. Forsythe later studied at the University of North Carolina at Chapel Hill for a time and spent a few summers as a sports announcer at Ebbet's Field, in the New York City borough of Brooklyn, then the home of the Dodgers. His announcing job led to acting assignments on such long-running radio soap operas as *Helen Trent* and *Stella Dallas*. Forsythe made his theatrical debut in 1939, as a member of a traveling troupe that performed plays for children. In addition to acting in the troupe, he drove a truck and served as an assistant stage manager. Forsythe made his Broadway debut in 1942, as a replacement in *Vickie*, a farce. His stage roles brought him to the attention of executives from Warner Bros., who cast him in *Destination Tokyo* (1943) and *Northern Pursuit* (1943). After completing those movies he served a tour of duty in the U.S. Army Air Corps. Following his discharge from the air corps, in 1945, Forsythe obtained a release from his Warner Bros. contract and returned to New York City. In 1947 he was chosen by Elia Kazan to succeed Arthur J. Kennedy as Chris Keller in Arthur Miller's seething drama of family tensions *All My Sons*. Forsythe performed in that play for a year, during which he became a charter member of Lee Strasberg's Actors' Studio. In 1949 Forsythe took on the title role in the first national road company of the hit play *Mister Roberts*, and in October 1950 he succeeded Henry Fonda in the Broadway production of that long-running World War II comedy. Meanwhile, he interspersed his stage appearances with roles on such television dramatic programs as *Studio One*, *Philco Playhouse*, *Kraft Theatre*, and *Robert Montgomery Presents*, and in 1952 he was named television actor of the year by *TV Guide*. He also found success on the big screen, in such films as *It Happens Every Thursday* (1953) and *The Ambassador's Daughter* (1956), both of which paired him with Loretta Young; *Everything but the Truth* (1956), in which his leading lady was Maureen O'Hara; Alfred Hitchcock's *The Trouble with Harry* (1956); *In Cold Blood* (1967); Alfred Hitchcock's *Topaz* (1969); and *The Happy Ending* (1969). Television historians seeking to describe the medium's so-called "Golden Age" often mention Forsythe's starring role in the acclaimed two-part TV movie *What Makes Sammy Run?* (1959), which aired on NBC's anthology series *Sunday Showcase*. From 1957 to 1962 Forsythe played a dashing lawyer who is pressed into service to care for his young niece in the popular TV series *Bachelor Father*. His next major recurring role came on *Charlie's Angels*, a hit series about three attractive female private eyes. (At various times, the trio included the actresses Farah Fawcett, Kate Jackson, Jaclyn Smith, Cheryl Ladd, and Shelley Hack.) Forsythe's character, the wealthy and mysterious Charles Townsend, is never seen but gives his "angels" instructions via speaker-phone at the start of each episode. Forsythe next played the suave oilman Blake Carrington on the long-running nighttime soap *Dynasty*, a show whose glitzy fashions and over-the-top storylines made it an indelible part of 1980s pop culture. Forsythe's last TV appearance came in May 2006, during *Catfights & Caviar*, a special *Dynasty* cast reunion. Forsythe was an avid horseracing enthusiast throughout his life. He died at his California home as a result of pneumonia. He is survived by his third wife, Nicole Carter, whom he wed in 2002. (He was married to the actress Parker McCormick from 1939 to 1943. The year they divorced, he married the actress Julie Warren. That union lasted until her death, in 1994.) Forsythe is also survived by his son, Dall (from his marriage to McCormick); two daughters, Page and Brooke (from his marriage to Warren); six grandchildren; and five great-grandchildren. See *Current Biography* (1973). —D.K.

Obituary *New York Times* (on-line) Apr. 3, 2010

FRANCIS, DICK Oct. 31, 1920–Feb. 14, 2010 Writer; former jockey. Dick Francis was a champion steeplechase jockey who later became the author of more than 40 mystery and crime thrillers set in the high-stakes world of horse racing. His novels have collectively sold some 60 million copies. Francis was born to George Vincent and Catherine Mary (Thomas) Francis in Lawrenny (some sources say Tenby), in southern Wales. His father was a professional steeplechase rider and a stable manager, and Francis learned to ride at an early age. In 1933 he accepted an offer to ride for Bertram Mills, a circus owner with a string of show horses. Francis made his hunter-class debut two years later when, at the last minute,

he replaced his father, who had been stricken with sciatica right before a horse show. To the surprise of almost everyone, he rode to a first-place finish. During World War II Francis joined the Royal Air Force, and when he returned to civilian life, he became an amateur jockey. He turned professional in 1948 and was the top-ranking jockey of the 1953–54 racing season. In 1956 he was chosen by the Queen Mother to serve as her jockey for the Grand National at Aintree, one of the top steeplechasing races in the United Kingdom. Initially in the lead, Francis's horse, Devon Loch, dramatically collapsed near the finish line. Francis wrote in his autobiography, *The Sport of Queens* (1957), that he feared that he would always be known as "the man who didn't win the National." Francis retired from racing soon afterward, having grown weak from the many injuries he had suffered over the course of his riding career. Within months of his retirement, Francis had been hired as a racing correspondent by the London *Sunday Express*, a job he held for 16 years. He published his first mystery novel, *Dead Cert*, a tightly constructed story about a steeplechase jockey who infiltrates an organized-crime racket in pursuit of a murderer, in 1962. *Dead Cert* was well received and kicked off its author's lengthy literary career. After *Dead Cert* Francis regularly wrote a book a year and in the process acquired a worldwide following and a reputation as a master of the mystery genre. His last three novels, *Dead Heat* (2007), *Silks* (2008), and *Even Money* (2009), were co-authored with his son Felix, a former physics teacher. Francis also wrote a collection of short stories, *Field of Thirteen* (1998). Francis, who was named to the Order of the British Empire (OBE) by Queen Elizabeth II, received numerous other honors during his lifetime. He is survived by his sons, Felix and Merrick (who works as a horse trainer), as well as five grandchildren and a great-grandson. His wife of 53 years, Mary, died in 2000. See *Current Biography* (1981). —W.D.

Obituary *New York Times* A p19 Feb. 15, 2010

GARDNER, MARTIN Oct. 21, 1914–May 22, 2010 Writer specializing in mathematics, science, and pseudoscience. "I think of myself as a journalist who writes mainly about math and science, and a few other fields of interest," Martin Gardner once said. Gardner authored more than 70 books, including some two dozen on recreational mathematics and others on science, pseudoscience, philosophy, and religion; he has also written fiction, poetry, literary criticism, and puzzle books for young people. He may be best known as the creator of *Scientific American*'s monthly "Mathematical Games" column, which he produced for 25 years beginning in 1957, and as the author of *The Annotated Alice: Alice's Adventures in Wonderland & Through the Looking Glass*, in which he revealed the word games, parodies, and references that Lewis Carroll had concealed within his classic fantasies. A co-founder of the Committee for the Scientific Evaluation of Claims of the Paranormal, Gardner spent much of his career "debunking bad science," in his words; according to the Pulitzer Prize–winning scientist Stephen Jay Gould, Gardner was "the single brightest beacon defending rationality and good science against the mysticism and anti-intellectualism that surround us." Gardner was born in Tulsa, Oklahoma, to James Henry Gardner, a petroleum geologist who started an oil company, and his wife, Willie (Spiers) Gardner. As a child Gardner enjoyed playing chess, practicing magic tricks, and reading, especially the work of L. Frank Baum, the author of the Wizard of Oz series. In high school Gardner was on the gymnastics team and also played tennis. In 1932 he enrolled at the University of Chicago, earning a bachelor's degree in philosophy in 1936. He then returned to Oklahoma and worked briefly as an assistant editor for the *Tulsa Tribune*; he soon went back to Chicago, where he worked in press relations and sold magic kits. During World War II Gardner served as a yeoman aboard the destroyer escort *USS Pope*; he was at sea when Japan surrendered to the allies in August 1945. With his military service completed, Gardner embarked on a career as a freelance writer after selling a humorous story called "The Horse on the Escalator" to *Esquire* magazine. In the early 1950s Gardner moved to New York City, where he found steady employment penning features for *Humpty Dumpty's Magazine for Little Children* and other such periodicals. In 1956 he sold an article to *Scientific American* magazine about hexaflexagons—three-dimensional hexagons made from flat strips of paper that reveal different faces when flexed in different directions. Impressed by the article, the magazine's publisher asked Gardner to write a regular column featuring similar material. Gardner had not taken a single mathematics course since high school, but he agreed to try. To compensate for the gaps in his understanding, he bought every book he could find on recreational mathematics, immersing himself in puzzles and logic. The "Mathematical Games" column, featuring puzzles and brain-teasers, ran in *Scientific American* for 25 years and earned Gardner the American Mathematical Society's Prize for Mathematical Exposition. Some have suggested that Gardner's lack of mathematical expertise, and his consequent reliance on cross-cultural references, jokes, and anecdotes, rather than technical jargon, was precisely what made "Mathematical Games" so engaging and accessible to laypeople. Gardner also wrote fiction and books on philosophy, physics, magic, religion, and word games; his most popular work, *The Annotated Alice*, was published in 1960 and has never gone out of print. He also wrote popular annotated versions of other classic works, including "The Rime of the Ancient Mariner" and "The Night Before Christmas." In 1976 Gardner—increasingly bothered by people's readiness to believe in the existence of such supernatural phenomena as faith healing, extrasensory perception, alien abduction, psychic surgery, and astrology—cofounded the Committee for the Scientific Evaluation of Claims of the Paranormal (now known as the Committee for Skeptical Inquiry), with Carl Sagan, Isaac Asimov, and others. From 1983 to 2002 Gardner penned the column "Notes of a Fringe Watcher" for the committee's bimonthly publication, the *Skeptical Inquirer*. Gardner, along with his wife, the former Charlotte Greenwald, and their two sons, lived for many years in Hastings-on-the-Hudson, in New York's Westchester County; in 1981, after Gardner retired from *Scientific American*, they moved to

Henderson, North Carolina. After Charlotte's death, in 2000, Gardner returned to Oklahoma, where one of his sons is a professor at the University of Oklahoma. Gardner continued to write until the time of his death. His most recent published article, on what he saw as the pseudoscience championed by Oprah Winfrey, appeared in the March 2010 issue of the *Skeptical Inquirer*. Gardner is survived by his two sons, James and Thomas, and three grandchildren. See *Current Biography* (1999). —H.R.W.

Obituary *New York Times* (on-line) May 23, 2010

GINZBURG, VITALY Oct. 4, 1916–Nov. 8, 2009 Nobel Prize–winning physicist. Renowned for helping to develop the first Soviet hydrogen bomb, Vitaly Lazarevich Ginzburg (whose first name is often transliterated as "Vitalii") also garnered worldwide recognition for his study of superconductivity—the ability of materials to conduct electricity with little or no resistance. Ginzburg's "pioneering contributions to the theory of superconductors and superfluids" earned him the 2003 Nobel Prize in Physics, an honor he shared with Alexei A. Abrikosov and Anthony J. Leggett. Ginzburg was born in Moscow, Russia, just months before the Bolshevik Revolution of 1917, which ended the tsar's reign. Ginzburg was the only child of Russian-born Lazar Efimovich Ginzburg, a water-purification engineer, and Avgusta Veniaminovna Vil'dauer-Ginzburg, a Latvian-born doctor. Following his mother's death from typhoid, in 1920, Ginzburg was raised by his father and maternal aunt, who lived with them. His father initially kept him out of school because of his concern about the poor quality of Russian education. "I was sent to school in 1927 when I was 11. Education was not compulsory at the time," Ginzburg wrote in an autobiographical profile for *Physics World* (November 3, 2009, on-line). "But in 1931, after I had been at school for only four years, the Soviet Union imposed another round of . . . school reforms, abolishing all upper secondary schools, which used to be for 16-18-year olds. It was recommended that all pupils who had been at school for seven years should transfer to the factory school (the school for 'working people') and that only then should they try to find a way to enroll in a university." Ginzburg avoided factory school when a friend of his aunt's helped him find a job as an assistant in an X-ray laboratory, where he first became interested in science. (He has also cited O. D. Hvolson's book *The Physics of Our Days* as an influence.) In 1934 Ginzburg won admission to Moscow State University, after passing a competitive college-entrance examination the year before. In 1938, a year after marrying his classmate Olga Zamsha, Ginzburg earned a bachelor's degree in physics. He remained at Moscow State, where he obtained a Ph.D. degree in 1940 and D.Sc. degree two years later. Also in 1942 Ginzburg joined the Communist Party and began working for the P. N. Lebedev Physics Institute of the Russian Academy of Sciences, in Moscow. In 1945 he was a visiting professor at Gorky State University, where he met Nina Ermakova, who had been exiled to Gorky after serving three years in a labor camp for her alleged role in a plot to kill Joseph Stalin. In 1946 Ginzburg divorced Zamsha, with whom he had a daughter, Irina, and married Ermakova. After the end of World War II, Ginzburg returned to Moscow without his still-exiled wife, but frequently visited her in Gorky, where he continued to teach. In 1948 Ginzburg was recruited to work with three other Russian scientists, including the famed nuclear physicist Andrei Sakharov, to develop a hydrogen bomb for the Soviet Union. According to Frank Close, writing for the London *Guardian* (November 15, 2009), "A gas is hard to control in hydrogen bombs, and Ginzburg's insight was that it could be made, within the device, by bombarding solid lithium deuteride with neutrons." As a result of one of Stalin's anti-Semitic purges, in 1953, Ginzburg, Jewish by birth, was removed from the hydrogen-bomb project, despite his contributions. His fears about being sent to a labor camp ended after Stalin's death later that year. Ermakova, who was granted amnesty, joined her husband in Moscow. Also in 1953 Ginzburg, a member of the Russian Academy of Sciences, earned the State Prize for his work on the hydrogen bomb. At about this time Ginzburg also began researching superconductivity. Along with fellow Russian physicist Lev Landau, Ginzburg "successfully predicted that, under certain circumstances, superconductors can tolerate magnetic fields," according to Close. This finding contributed to various technological breakthroughs, including the development of more powerful electromagnets used in particle accelerators and magnetic resonance imaging (MRI) devices. Ginzburg also made the significant discovery that cosmic radiation in space is the result of the acceleration of high-energy electrons in magnetic fields, rather than thermal radiation, and along with Iosif S. Shklovskii, he identified the remnants of exploding stars, or supernovas, as the source of cosmic rays located near the Earth. In 1968, when his teaching stint at Gorky University ended, Ginzburg founded and headed the Academic Department of Physics and Astrophysics Problems at the Moscow Institute of Physics and Technology. He oversaw the I. E. Tamm Theory Department at the P. N. Lebedev Physical Institute from 1971 to 1988, after which he remained an adviser at the institute. From 1989 to 1991 Ginzburg was a deputy of the Supreme Soviet of the USSR, then the nation's highest legislative body. After the collapse of the Soviet Union, Ginzburg, an atheist, spoke out about the increasing influence of the Russian Orthodox Church in state affairs. In 2007, along with 10 other distinguished scholars, he signed an open letter to President Vladimir Putin, denouncing the church's influence in state schools and elsewhere. In addition to the Nobel Prize in Physics, Ginzburg received several other prestigious awards, including the Mandelstam Prize (1947), the Lenin Prize (1966), the Wolf Foundation's Physics Prize (1994–95), the Vavilov Gold Medal (1995), the Lomonosov Gold Medal of the Russian Academy of Sciences (1995), the UNESCO-Niels Bohr Gold Medal (1998), the American Physics Society's Nicholson Medal (1998), the Humboldt Prize (2001), and the Triumph Prize (2002). He was a member of the American Academy of Arts and Sciences, the American National Academy of Sciences, and the Royal Society of London, among other international organizations. Ginzburg died of a heart attack in Moscow. He is sur-

vived by Ermakova and his daughter from his first marriage. *See Current Biography International Yearbook* (2007). —W.D.

Obituary *New York Times* (on-line) Nov. 9, 2009

GODDARD, JAMES L. Apr. 24, 1923–Dec. 18, 2009 Physician; former government official; company executive. During his short tenure as commissioner of the U.S. Food and Drug Administration (FDA), James L. Goddard reorganized the administration, introduced modern scientific research methods, and changed the public's image of the agency from that of a weak handmaiden of the pharmaceutical industry to that of a strong, effective champion of the consumer. Goddard was born in Alliance, Ohio. He served in the U.S. Army from 1943 to 1946, and upon his discharge from the military, he entered the George Washington University School of Medicine, in Washington, D.C. After graduating, in 1949, he interned for a year at the U.S. Public Health Service Marine Hospital in Cleveland, Ohio, and then set up a private practice in Kalida, Ohio, a small town near Lima. Within a year he had become discontented with his career as a private practitioner, and in 1951 he rejoined the Public Health Service, as the medical officer in charge of the Federal Employee Health Service at the Denver Federal Center. There, he launched the nation's first on-the-job medical program for the center's 6,000 employees. In 1953 Goddard moved to Chapel Hill, North Carolina, to administer health services in two county districts. A year later he left to work for a master's degree in public health at Harvard University. After receiving that degree, magna cum laude, in 1955, he served for a year in the Office of Program Development and Evaluation of the State Department of Health in Albany, New York, where he developed a driver research and testing center. In 1956 he was called to Washington, D.C., to set up and direct a national accident-prevention program to minimize deaths, injuries, and disabilities from accidents of all types, especially automobile collisions. In 1959 Goddard became the first civil air surgeon of the Federal Aviation Agency, a government bureau that Congress had established only two years before in an effort to streamline nonmilitary flying and to modernize the air-navigation system. In 1962 he was appointed assistant surgeon general and given the post of chief of the Public Health Service's Communicable Disease Center in Atlanta, Georgia. On January 17, 1966 Goddard was sworn in as commissioner of the FDA. Within weeks of taking office, he had begun to move swiftly to counter long-standing complaints from Congress about the FDA's laxity in policing the drug industry. He announced, for example, that clinical testing of MK-665, an oral contraceptive suspected of causing cancer, was being suspended, and soon after, with characteristic decisiveness, he gave the CIBA Pharmaceutical Co. 24 hours to remove Elipten, an anticonvulsant with harmful side effects, from the market. During the following months he removed additional drugs from the market for being unsafe; banned approximately 250 antibiotic preparations, particularly throat lozenges, from the market because drugmakers had not proved their effectiveness; sought to curb misleading drug advertising;

and started an investigation of possible criminal violations in the testing of new drugs. In the face of almost continual controversy and criticism from the drug industry, Goddard left the FDA on July 1, 1968, to become vice president of EDP Technology, a company engaged in medical and industrial systems analysis. He later spent two years as an adviser to the Ford Foundation in India, and he did consulting work well into his 70s. Goddard died of a brain hemorrhage at his California home. He was predeceased in 2004 by his wife of almost three decades, Marjorie Geraldine Raitt, as well as by his stepson Steve, who died in April 2009. He is survived by his children, Bruce, Margaret, and Tricia; his stepchildren, Bonnie and David; eight grandchildren; and three great-grandchildren. (Bonnie Raitt, his stepdaughter, is a popular singer.) See *Current Biography* (1968). —M.R.

Obituary *New York Times* (on-line) Jan. 2, 2010

GORDON, LINCOLN Sep. 10, 1913–Dec. 19, 2009 Diplomat; political economist; educator. Lincoln Gordon enjoyed a long career in both academia and government service. Born in New York City to Bernard Gordon, a lawyer, and the former Dorothy Lerner, a media moderator, Abraham Lincoln Gordon (who never used his first name) attended Ethical Culture–affiliated schools before entering Harvard University, from which he graduated summa cum laude in 1933. Awarded a Rhodes Scholarship, he next studied at Balliol College, part of the University of Oxford, which awarded him a Ph.D. degree in 1936. After he returned from Great Britain, Gordon joined the faculty of Harvard, teaching government studies until 1941, when he took a leave of absence to work with the War Production Board during World War II. He returned to the university as an associate professor of business administration in 1946, and from 1947 to 1950 he held a full professorship at the Harvard Graduate School of Business Administration and the Graduate School of Public Administration. Concurrently, in 1946 and 1947 he was a member of the U.S. delegation to the United Nations Atomic Energy Commission. During the immediate postwar years, he was also a consultant to the Army and Navy Munitions Board and to the State Department in its development of the European Recovery Program (commonly known as the Marshall Plan). From 1948 to 1950 he worked with the Economic Cooperation Administration, which oversaw that ambitious plan, whose goal was to rebuild Western Europe's economies and infrastructure. Gordon resigned from the faculty of Harvard in 1950 to devote himself solely to U.S. government posts. He was named economic adviser to the special assistant to President Harry S. Truman in 1950, and in 1951 he served as an alternate on the North Atlantic Treaty Organization (NATO) temporary council committee. From 1952 to 1955 Gordon served at the American Embassy in London as the U.S. minister for economic affairs and the director of American operations missions in the United Kingdom. In October 1961 President John F. Kennedy appointed Gordon as the U.S. ambassador to Brazil, a post he held until 1966. His tenure was marked by tension and controversy. It was a time of high inflation in Brazil, which had just seen the left-wing João Goulart assume the presidency. When Goulart was deposed after a right-wing military coup in 1964, Gordon and the Central Intelligence Agency were widely suspected of involvement in the coup. (Although he repeatedly denied those claims, later in life Gordon admitted that the Lyndon B. Johnson administration had been prepared to use military force to prevent a leftist takeover of the new government.) In 1967 Gordon became president of Johns Hopkins University. Like many schools of the era, Johns Hopkins was being rocked by widespread faculty dissatisfaction and student rebellion, and Gordon resigned after four years. (He is remembered as the first administrator to admit female students to the previously all-male undergraduate program.) Until 1975 Gordon served as a fellow at the Woodrow Wilson International Center for Scholars, and from 1984 until his death, he was affiliated with the Washington, D.C.–based Brookings Institution. Gordon, the author of such books as *A New Deal for Latin America* (1963) and *Brazil's Second Chance* (2001), died at an assisted-living home in Maryland. He was predeceased by his wife, Allison, in 1987. He is survived by his sons, Robert and Hugh; his daughters, Sally and Amy; seven grandchildren; and two great-grandchildren. See *Current Biography* (1962). —D.K.

Obituary *New York Times* (on-line) Dec. 21, 2009

GUCCIONE, BOB Dec. 17, 1930–Oct. 20, 2010 Publisher. Bob Guccione was best known for publishing the erotic magazine *Penthouse*, which made its American debut in 1969. By 1972 there were Penthouse clubs, resorts, and franchises—23 companies in all, including a casino in Yugoslavia—and by the early 1980s, *Penthouse*'s parent company, General Media International, had evolved into a $300 million publishing empire that encompassed several other magazines, including the respected science title *Omni*, in addition to more than a dozen foreign editions of *Penthouse*. In later years Guccione suffered serious financial losses: General Media filed for bankruptcy in 2003, and he resigned soon after from his posts as chairman of General Media and chief executive officer and chairman of Penthouse International. Despite spending his final years fending off creditors and watching others take advantage of the openness about sex he had helped to bring about, Guccione remained an iconic figure, widely credited (or vilified in some quarters) for helping usher in a new age of sexual freedom. "I think we made a very serious contribution to the liberalization of laws and attitudes," Guccione once told a reporter. "Much that has happened now in the Western world with respect to sexual advances is directly due to steps we took." Of Sicilian descent, Robert Charles Joseph Edward Sabatini Guccione was born in the New York City borough of Brooklyn and raised in suburban Bergenfield, New Jersey. An altar boy at his Roman Catholic church, he briefly considered entering the priesthood. In 1948 Guccione, who had by then discovered a talent for art, graduated from high school, married his first wife, Lilyann, and set out for Europe. For about 12 years he eked out a living, selling caricatures and pencil sketches to tourists and doing odd jobs. In the early 1960s, having settled in London—where he produced syndicated cartoons, served as managing editor of the London *Daily American*, and operated a dry-cleaning concern—Guccione entered the mail-order business, selling back issues of men's magazines. Because his initial mailing of a brochure containing eight full-color nudes used outdated lists of addresses, the erotica reached many inappropriate targets, including at least one member of Parliament, who complained in a speech to the House of Commons. British authorities intercepted a quarter of a million brochures, and Guccione was made to pay a fine. Partly because of all the publicity generated by the wayward mailing, the first issue of *Penthouse*, launched in London with a bank loan of $1,170 in 1965, sold out its debut issue in five days, with advance sales of 120,000 copies. In September 1969 Guccione introduced an American edition of his magazine. It was an immediate success, with a circulation of 375,000 for its first edition. Compared with the photos in its direct competitor, Hugh Hefner's popular *Playboy*, which had been launched in late 1953, Guccione's subjects, whom he often photographed himself, appeared more realistic and less idealized and exhibited more variety in body type and look. *Penthouse* also left less to the imagination; in a first, Guccione dared to show full frontal nudity in his sold-out April 1970 issue, and *Playboy* was forced to follow suit in December of that year, despite Hefner's long opposition to such explicitness. Over the next few years, *Penthouse* steadily gained on *Playboy* in circulation: by 1975 *Penthouse* was selling three copies for every five of *Playboy* sold, and by 1978 *Penthouse*'s newsstand sales had surpassed *Playboy*'s by 37 percent. Business, however, did not always run smoothly for Guccione. *Viva*, an erotic magazine for women that he launched in 1973, failed to find an audience and folded within a few years; *Caligula*, a sex-and-violence-filled film he financed in 1979, proved to be a colossal flop; a scandal ensued after his publication, in the mid-1980s, of graphic nude photographs of the reigning Miss America, Vanessa Williams; he was subject to various suits and countersuits for libel; and he failed to obtain financing to build a hoped-for casino in Atlantic City. In addition to those troubles, Guccione saw a drop in *Penthouse*'s circulation, from a high of 4.7 million in the 1970s to about 1.5 million in the early 1990s, thanks in large part to the emergence of numerous imitators and the rising popularity of video pornography. Guccione, who was at one time said to have a net worth of $400 million, also found himself facing enormous bills for back taxes from the IRS, and the federal government indirectly took another chunk of his revenues in 1986, when it published a strongly worded anti-pornography report that resulted in *Penthouse*'s being withdrawn from many newsstands. *Penthouse*'s fortunes faded even further as free pornographic content became readily available on the Internet, and in 2001 the magazine recorded a $10 million loss. General Media filed for bankruptcy in 2003, and Guccione resigned as chair and CEO of Penthouse International soon after. In 2006 he was forced to move out of his art-filled mansion when it went into foreclosure. *Penthouse*, which under Guccione's direction had featured writing by such luminaries as Stephen King, Philip Roth, and Joyce Carol Oates, continues to be published by a different media conglomerate; it can be found predominately in adult bookshops rather than in more mainstream outlets. Guccione, who had been ill for several years with cancer, died at a hospital in Plano, Texas. He had one daughter, Tonia, with his first wife. In 1955 he married his second wife, Muriel, with whom he had four children: Bob Jr., Nina, Anthony, and Nick. (Bob Jr., estranged from his father for years, is a well-known editor and publisher.) In 1988 Guccione married his longtime girlfriend and business partner, Kathy Keeton, who predeceased him in 1997. At the time of his death he was married to his fourth wife, April. See *Current Biography* (1994). –M.R.

Obituary *New York Times* (on-line) Oct. 20, 2010

HAIG, ALEXANDER Dec. 2, 1924–Feb. 20, 2010 Four-star military general; presidential aide; business executive. Alexander Haig, who served during several conflicts as a member of the U.S. military and commanded North American Treaty Organization (NATO) forces for five years (1974–79), was also an adviser to President Richard Nixon during the Watergate scandal and a key Cabinet member in President Ronald Reagan's administration. Alexander Meigs Haig Jr. was born to a lawyer and a homemaker in Bala-Cynwyd, Pennsylvania, a suburb of Philadelphia. He graduated from West Point in 1947, and two years later he served as an aide to General Douglas MacArthur's deputy chief of staff in occupied Japan. During the Korean War he saw combat in five campaigns and earned three medals. Haig earned a master's degree in international relations from Georgetown University, in Washington, D.C., in 1961. In subsequent years he worked on European and Middle Eastern affairs at the Pentagon and held a post in the office of the deputy chief of staff for military operations. In 1964 Haig became the military assistant to Secretary of the Army Cyrus R. Vance, and two years later he was assigned to command a brigade in Vietnam. He received the Distinguished Service Cross and the Purple Heart for his service in that war. In 1969 Haig was appointed military assistant to Henry Kissinger and assistant to President Nixon, and later he was named the deputy assistant to the president for national security affairs. Haig was promoted to four-star general in 1972, and following a brief stint as vice chief of staff of the army, he was named White House chief of staff under President Nixon in 1973. That year the Watergate scandal erupted, and Haig is said to have played a major role in persuading Nixon to resign as well as in President Gerald Ford's pardon of Nixon. Amid public outrage at the scandal and its aftermath, Haig left the White House in 1974 to resume his military career; he served as supreme allied commander in Europe, a post that put him in command of NATO forces. In 1979 he left NATO and retired from the military. Haig then served as president of the defense contractor United Technologies for a year before becoming President Reagan's secretary of state in January 1981. When, on March 30, 1981, Reagan was seriously wounded in an assassination attempt, Haig—fearing that misleading actions and statements by the confused White House staff might have serious repercussions—explained in response to reporters' questions about who was running the government: "As of now, I am in control here, in the White House, pending return of the vice president, and in close touch with him." The comment was seen in segments of the media as an improper attempt by Haig to assume authority during the absence of Vice President George H.W. Bush, who was flying back from Texas to the nation's capital. (Under the Constitution, the secretary of state is preceded in the order of succession for the presidency by the Speaker of the House of Representatives and the president pro tem of the Senate. But, as was explained later, since the president had not surrendered his authority and the vice president was only temporarily absent, the secretary of state, as the administration's most senior officer, was authorized to take charge of the "emergency watch" at the White House.) Haig's hawkish and forcefully expressed views on U.S. foreign policy often put him at odds with other members of the Reagan administration, and he resigned on June 25, 1982. (He was succeeded as secretary of state by George P. Shultz.) After leaving politics, Haig founded the Washington-based business consultancy firm Worldwide Associates Inc. He also served on the boards of several other companies, including America Online Inc. (AOL), MGM Grand Inc., and Metro-Goldwyn-Mayer Inc. Haig ran as a Republican candidate in the 1988 presidential race, but he drew little public support. He wrote a book about his time in the Reagan White House, *Inner Circles: How America Changed the World* (1992). Haig died at Johns Hopkins Hospital, in Baltimore, Maryland, of complications from an infection. He is survived by his wife of nearly 60 years, Patricia; two sons, Alexander and Brian; a daughter, Barbara; a brother, the Reverend Francis R. Haig; and eight grandchildren. See *Current Biography* (1987). —M.A.S.

Obituary *New York Times* A p1 Feb. 21, 2010

HARDIN, CLIFFORD Oct. 9, 1915–Apr. 4, 2010 Former U.S. secretary of agriculture; university administrator. During his short tenure as U.S. secretary of agriculture, which lasted from 1969 to 1971, in the Richard M. Nixon administration, Clifford M. Hardin successfully pushed for passage of the Agricultural Act of 1970, which limited the subsidies paid to the nation's largest farmers, and he was also credited with extending the government's food-stamp program. The son of a Quaker farmer, Clifford Morris Hardin was born near Knightstown, Indiana. During the Great Depression his father worked in Florida for half the year to supplement his income, leaving the younger Hardin to manage the family farm during his absences. Hardin received a 4-H scholarship to attend Purdue University, in Lafayette, Indiana, where he earned a bachelor's degree in 1937, a master's degree in 1939, and a Ph.D. degree in 1941. Upon earning his doctoral degree, he joined the faculty of the University of Wisconsin, in Madison, where he taught agricultural economics, and in 1944 he moved to Michigan State College (now Michigan State University). Within two years he was appointed chair of his department. In 1947 he went to Western Europe on behalf of Michigan State College and Michigan farm associations to investigate possible ways of assisting with the Marshall Plan. Also in 1947 he was a member of the U.S. delegation to the International Conference of Agricultural Economists. The following year President Harry S. Truman named him to a group studying development in South America. When he was named chancellor of the University of Nebraska, in 1954, Hardin, then 38, was the youngest university head in the nation. In that post he quadrupled enrollment, successfully lobbied the state legislature to raise professors' salaries, and introduced international-studies programs to the curriculum. He also continued to be involved in national governance. In 1962 he was appointed by President John F. Kennedy to sit on a committee reviewing the American foreign-aid program, and the following year he was a member of the president's Committee to Strengthen the Security of the Free World. In June 1966 President Lyndon B. Johnson named him to the policymaking section of the National Science Foundation. During the summer of 1968, he chaired a task force at the U.S. Department of Agriculture. Hardin took office as secretary of agriculture in January 1969. Although his 1970 farm bill passed with bipartisan support, it greatly angered major farm groups, which complained about the limits it imposed on government subsidies. Hardin sometimes found himself at odds with Nixon during his tenure. In one notable example, the president overturned Hardin's decision to cap federal price supports for dairy farmers in exchange for a large donation to his campaign fund from the Associated Milk Producers. In November 1971 Hardin resigned and was replaced by Earl L. Butz. Hardin went on to become vice chair of research for the Ralston Purina Co. (now known as Nestlé Purina PetCare Co.) and chair of Ralston Purina of Canada. He later directed the Center for the Study of American Business at Washington University, in St. Louis, Missouri, and served as vice president and board member of the St. Louis–based investment firm Stifel Nicolause. Hardin, who suffered from heart and kidney disease, died at his home in Lincoln, Nebraska. He is survived by his wife of more than 70 years, Martha Love Wood; three daughters, Sue, Cynthia, and Nancy; two sons, Clifford and James; and several grandchildren and great-grandchildren. See *Current Biography* (1969). —M.A.S.

Obituary *New York Times* B p18 Apr. 6, 2010

HAWKINS, PAULA Jan. 24, 1927–Dec. 4, 2009 Politician; activist. In 1980 Paula Hawkins was elected by the voters of Florida to a single term as a U.S. senator. Although she refused to label herself a feminist, Hawkins was the state's first female senator. She was also the first woman to be elected to a full term in the U.S. Senate whose career was not based on her relationship to a husband or other male relative. A conservative Republican, Hawkins opposed the Equal Rights Amendment, drawing scorn from the National Organization for Women. She did, however, champion legislation that helped stay-at-home wives enter the job market after being widowed or divorced. Hawkins was also the leading sponsor of the Missing Children's Act of 1982, which requires the Federal Bureau of Investigation to enter a missing child's descriptive information into a national computer database that can be used by law-enforcement agencies across the country. The daughter of a naval officer, she was born Paula Fickes in Salt Lake City, Utah. Her family moved frequently until her father left the military, in 1934, when they settled in Atlanta, Georgia. Her parents divorced 10 years later, and she moved to Logan, Utah, with her mother and three younger siblings (Carole, Karma, and Llewellen). She attended Utah State University for a time but, unable to decide on a major, left without earning a degree. In 1947 she married her high-school sweetheart, Gene Hawkins, and moved back to Atlanta, where he found employment as an electrical engineer, and she supplemented their income by working as a model for local department stores and as a secretary. A devout Mormon who was committed to traditional family roles, Hawkins dedicated much of her time to raising the couple's three children. In 1955 the family moved to Florida, where Hawkins became active in several civic organizations. In 1966 she joined the Orange County Republican organization's finance committee. In 1968 she was selected to co-chair Richard Nixon's presidential-campaign activities in Florida and served as a delegate to the first of what would be four successive Republican National Conventions. In 1972 Hawkins was elected to the State Public Service Commission. Reelected in 1976, she served a total of seven years on the commission, the last three as its chair. (In the interim she made unsuccessful bids for elective office: the U.S. Senate in 1974 and Florida's lieutenant governorship in 1978.) In 1979 Hawkins, who had a reputation as a staunch consumer advocate, was hired as vice president of consumer affairs for a small Florida airline. She resigned the following year, after deciding once again to enter the Republican senatorial primary. After winning a primary runoff with 62 percent of the vote, she went on to defeat Democrat Bill Gunter in the November 1980 election by a slim margin. Hawkins, who quickly became known for her forceful manner, chaired the Senate Labor and Human Resources Committee's Subcommittee on Investigation and Oversight during her term. In 1982 a television-studio backdrop fell and struck Hawkins. The accident resulted in chronic neck and back pain, and she underwent surgery in 1986. Her reelection campaign was severely hampered by her forced recuperation, and she was defeated by the Democratic Florida governor, Bob Graham. Hawkins, who suffered a series of health problems later in life, died at a hospital in Orlando, Florida, from the complications of a fall. She is survived by her husband, two daughters, a son, a sister, 11 grandchildren, and 10 great-grandchildren. See *Current Biography* (1985). —M.A.S.

Obituary *New York Times* B p8 Dec. 5, 2009

HEIGHT, DOROTHY I. Mar. 24, 1912–Apr. 20, 2010 Activist. Dorothy Height, sometimes called the "godmother" of the civil rights movement, brought attention to the lack of equality accorded both women and African-Americans. Although she often went unacknowledged due to her gender, Height was active alongside such towering figures as Martin Luther King Jr., James Farmer, John Lewis, and A. Philip

Randolph. As a leading member of the Young Women's Christian Association (YWCA) in the 1940s, she worked to desegregate that organization, and from 1957 to 1988 she led the nonprofit National Council of Negro Women. Dorothy Irene Height was born in Richmond, Virginia, to James Edward Height, a building contractor, and Fannie (Burroughs) Height. When she was four years old, the family, which included her younger sister, moved to Rankin, Pennsylvania, where she attended integrated schools. In childhood she suffered from asthma and shyness, both of which she later overcame. Height graduated from high school with a college scholarship, her prize for winning a national oratorical contest sponsored by the Elks National Foundation. Her first choice among colleges was Barnard, in New York City, but when she applied there she was informed that the school already had two African-American students and that she would have to wait for admission. She then turned to New York University (NYU), where she was accepted because of her superior scholastic record. As a student at NYU she helped organize the all-black Rameses Club. She earned her B.S. degree in 1933, followed by a master's degree in educational psychology in 1934, and she later pursued further postgraduate studies at the New York School of Social Work. Upon leaving NYU Height became a caseworker for New York City's welfare department. She also became passionate about civil rights activism through her association with Adam Clayton Powell Sr., the pastor of the Abyssinian Baptist Church in Harlem, and his son, Adam Clayton Powell Jr., a future U.S. congressman. In 1933 she became a leader of the United Christian Youth Movement of North America, which she later served as vice president. At about the time she was beginning her work with the YWCA, in 1938, Height gave testimony before the New York City Council about a situation then occurring daily at intersections in the city. In what she termed a "slave market," young African-American women were bargaining with passing motorists for a day's housework at subsistence wages. Height's testimony helped drive the street market away for a brief period. In 1946, as part of the national leadership team of the YWCA, Height worked to desegregate the organization's national facilities. She was the president of Delta Sigma Theta, an international sorority of African-American women, from 1947 to 1956, and in 1965 she founded the Y's Center for Racial Justice, which she ran until 1977. During the civil rights movement of the 1960s, the National Council of Negro Women, over which she presided, contributed money and volunteer hours to voter-registration drives in the South and voter-education drives in the North, and it provided financial aid for students who interrupted their education to work in the movement. Height personally worked at establishing communication between black and white women in several Alabama communities, and she sent regular reports on evidence of the harassment and intimidation of prospective voters in Selma, Alabama, and elsewhere. She was present on the platform when Martin Luther King Jr. gave his legendary "I Have a Dream" speech in front of the Lincoln Memorial, in Washington, D.C., in 1963. During the early 1970s Height worked with such figures as Gloria Steinem and Betty Friedan to establish the National

Women's Political Caucus. Height, who advised several U.S. presidents on civil rights issues, died at Howard University Hospital, in Washington, D.C. The recipient of the Presidential Medal of Freedom in 1994 and the Congressional Gold Medal in 2004, she was the National Council of Negro Women's president emeritus at the time of her death. She never married and is survived by a sister, Anthanette Aldridge. See *Current Biography* (1972). —W.D.

Obituary *New York Times* A p25 Apr. 21, 2010

HICKEL, WALTER Aug. 18, 1919–May 7, 2010 Former governor of Alaska; former U.S. secretary of the interior. During his tenures as governor (1966–68 and 1990–94) and interior secretary (1969–70), Walter J. "Wally" Hickel's views on environmental conservation shifted dramatically. Among Alaskans he is probably best remembered as a visionary who helped Alaska achieve statehood and helped establish safe conditions for the construction of the trans-Alaska pipeline. The oldest of 10 children, Walter Joseph Hickel was born in Ellinwood, Kansas, to Robert A. and Emma (Zecha) Hickel, tenant farmers of German descent. After attending public schools in Claflin, Kansas, he ended his formal education at the age of 16 and left the family farm three years later for California, where he worked for a time as a carpenter before trying to arrange passage to Australia. When he learned that he could not get a passport until he was 21, he decided to travel to Alaska (which was then still a territory) and spent $41 for a steerage ticket. According to lore, Hickel arrived in Alaska in 1940 with just 37 cents in his pocket. After holding various jobs as a bartender, a railroad worker, and a construction worker, he built a house, sold it at a profit, and then repeated the venture. In 1947 Hickel founded the Hickel Construction Co. of Anchorage. Over the years the company constructed housing developments, apartments, hotels, and shopping centers and made Hickel a millionaire. A lifelong Republican, Hickel served two terms (1954–64) as Alaska's Republican National Committeeman, during which he led the campaign for Alaskan statehood (proclaimed in 1959) and became acquainted with Richard M. Nixon. Hickel supported Nixon in his unsuccessful 1964 bid for the Republican presidential nomination. Two years later Hickel made his own bid for public office, challenging the Democratic incumbent William A. Egan in the race to become governor of Alaska. Despite the fact that registered Democrats outnumbered registered Republicans two-to-one in the state, Hickel won the general election by about 1,000 votes and was sworn in as Alaska's first Republican governor on December 5, 1966. Hickel's plans for Alaska's economic development centered on mining the state's vast Arctic areas, building railroads, and drilling for oil. Before the end of Hickel's first term as governor, Nixon, who was elected president in 1968, tapped him to become U.S. secretary of the interior, a Cabinet post in which he was charged with protecting and developing public lands and resources. At his first Washington, D.C., press conference, on December 18, the governor ignored Nixon's request that his Cabinet nominees remain silent on policy matters until the new administration took office. "I think we have had a

policy of conservation for conservation's sake," Hickel told the press. "Just to withdraw a large area for conservation purposes and lock it up for no reason doesn't have any merit in my opinion. We should expand the size of the area in a way to benefit the American people, both in recreation and development of natural resources." Hickel's remarks drew much criticism from concerned environmentalists. After five days of public and private hearings that included adverse testimony from conservation groups, the Senate Interior Committee announced that Hickel had "met the minimum standards" to become secretary, and he took the oath of office on January 25, 1969. By the time Hickel addressed the National Petroleum Council in Washington in July 1970, his views on conservation seemed to have radically shifted; he was quoted as saying, "Let's find new ways, better ways of doing business so that our industries can prosper and our environment flourish at the same time. The right to produce is not the right to pollute. America must prove to itself as well as to others worldwide that it has the ability to clean up the garbage it has left in its wake." During his 22-month tenure as interior secretary, Hickel filed suits against companies accused of discharging mercury into the water, issued stricter offshore drilling regulations, blocked plans to build a jet airport in the Florida Everglades, and authorized an investigation of the energy company Chevron after a company platform caught fire in the Gulf of Mexico and spewed more than 40,000 barrels of oil into the ocean. (The investigation revealed that Chevron had failed to install certain required safety devices on 90 oil wells.) Hickel also made efforts to delay construction of the trans-Alaska pipeline—the 800-mile oil-pipe construction project he had supported as governor—after hearing geologists' arguments against it. Hickel ultimately succeeded in persuading oil companies to include in the pipeline's construction plans a number of major safety alterations. Hickel was also outspoken in policy areas outside of his purview, and in November 1970 he was fired by Nixon for airing his thoughts on the Vietnam War. Hickel returned to Alaska, where he reinvigorated his business empire and re-adopted his pro-business and pro-development stances, supporting oil drilling in the Arctic National Wildlife Refuge and once again championing the proposed plans for the trans-Alaska pipeline, which was completed in 1977. In 1990 Hickel was elected a second time as governor of his state, as a member of the secessionist Alaskan Independence Party. Once in office, however, he renounced the notion that Alaska should secede and re-registered as a Republican. Hickel's term, which lasted until 1994, was so turbulent that he sometimes telephoned reporters to rebut charges that he was mentally unstable. The author of several books on Alaska, Hickel remained a powerful presence in Alaskan life and politics for many years after his retirement and was an early supporter of Republican Sarah Palin during her successful 2006 bid to become governor. His support for Palin waned, however, after she was selected by John McCain as his running mate for the 2008 presidential election. Hickel died of natural causes at an assisted-living facility in Anchorage. He is survived by his wife, six sons, 21 grandchildren, and seven great grandchildren. See *Current Biography* (1969). —H.W.R.

Obituary *New York Times* A p24 May 9, 2010

HOOKS, BENJAMIN L. Jan. 31, 1925–Apr. 15, 2010 Civil rights leader; minister; attorney. Benjamin L. Hooks is perhaps best known for his 16-year tenure as executive director of the National Association for the Advancement of Colored People (NAACP), the country's oldest and largest civil rights group. He was also the first African-American to serve on the Federal Communications Commission (FCC). Hooks was born in Memphis, Tennessee, the fifth of seven children. His father, Robert, operated a successful photography business, and the family enjoyed a stable, middle-class standard of living. Hooks and his siblings were strictly disciplined, and both Robert and Hooks's mother, Bessie, instilled in their children a belief in hard work and education. Hooks's paternal grandmother, Julia Britton Hooks, was only the second black woman in the U.S. to graduate from college. Drawn to the ministry in his youth but discouraged from pursuing that vocation by his father, who opposed organized religion, Hooks pursued a career in law. He enrolled at LeMoyne College, in Memphis, in 1941 and studied there for two years before being drafted into the U.S. Army. He served in the all-black 92d Infantry Division in Italy and rose to the rank of staff sergeant. Upon completing his military service, Hooks used the G.I. Bill to attend DePaul University, in Chicago, where he continued his law studies. (At the time he was prevented from enrolling in law school in his home state of Tennessee because of segregation.) He earned his law degree from DePaul in 1948 and then returned to Tennessee to establish his own practice. Driven by a commitment to social change, Hook spent most of the 1950s overcoming racial barriers in the segregated Memphis courts. He told Robert A. Deleon in an interview for *Jet* (December 21, 1972): "At that time you were insulted by law clerks, excluded from white bar associations and when I was in court, I was lucky to be called 'Ben.' Usually it was just 'boy.'" Hooks participated in NAACP-sponsored restaurant sit-ins and other boycotts during the late 1950s and early 1960s. In addition to becoming a lifetime member of the NAACP, he served on the board of directors of the Southern Christian Leadership Conference (SCLC), the iconic civil rights organization headed by Martin Luther King Jr. Hooks had never lost his interest in the ministry, and in 1956 he was ordained as a Baptist minister. He served as the pastor of two churches simultaneously while maintaining a busy law practice. In 1961 he became the assistant public defender of Tennessee's Shelby County, but he had little chance, as a black man, of becoming chief public defender. In 1965, however, Hooks was appointed to fill a vacant judgeship in the Shelby County criminal court. He thus became the first black criminal-court judge in Tennessee history, and the following year he won election to a full term in the post. Hooks resigned his seat on the criminal-court bench in 1968, to focus on his church duties and to try his hand at business, overseeing a fried-chicken chain in Memphis. In 1972 Hooks was appointed by President Richard M. Nixon to serve on the Federal Communications Commission (FCC). He was the first black commissioner in the history of the agency. Hooks resigned from the commission in 1976, when he was elected to serve as executive director of the NAACP, succeeding Roy Wilkins, who was retiring. Hooks spent much of his 16-year tenure battling policies of presidents Ronald Reagan and George H. W. Bush. "I've had the misfortune of serving eight years under Reagan and three under Bush," he said in 1992. "It makes a great deal of difference about your expectations. We've had to get rid of a lot of programs we had hoped for, so we could fight to save what we already had." After retiring from the post, in 1992, Hooks became a professor at the University of Memphis, and he continued to serve as a resident minister at both of his churches. Hooks, who received the Presidential Medal of Freedom in 2007, died at his home in Memphis after a long battle with cancer. He is survived by his wife, Frances; his daughter, Patricia; his sister, Mildred; his brother, Raymond; and two grandsons, Carlos and Carlton. See *Current Biography* (1978). —C.C.

Obituary *New York Times* A p19 Apr. 16, 2010

HOPPER, DENNIS May 17, 1936–May 29, 2010 Actor; director; photographer. Dennis Hopper was one of Hollywood's most notorious bad boys in the 1960s, wild men in the 1970s, and, it appeared, burnout cases in the mid-1980s. By the late-1980s, however, a clean and sober Hopper had begun acting and directing once again, and he worked steadily until the time of his death. Celebrated for the iconic picture *Easy Rider* (1969), which established him as a kind of guerrilla genius among independent filmmakers and as a hero of the counterculture, Hopper was last seen on screen in the TV series *Crash* (2008–09) and completed a handful of projects that will be released posthumously. Hopper was born in Dodge City, Kansas, and was raised primarily by his grandparents, who lived on a working 12-acre farm. In the late 1940s his parents moved the family to San Diego, California, where Hopper—against his mother's wishes—turned to acting. He won a scholarship to the National Shakespeare Festival at San Diego's Old Globe Theatre, where he played Montano in *Othello*, Sebastian in *Twelfth Night*, and Lorenzo in *The Merchant of Venice*. After playing an epileptic man in an episode of the TV series *Medic* in the mid-1950s, Hopper was courted by several movie studios and ultimately signed with Warner Bros. He had a small part in *Rebel Without a Cause* (1955), starring James Dean, and worked with the troubled young Dean again on *Giant* (1956), a saga about a Texas cattle-ranching family that also starred Rock Hudson and Elizabeth Taylor. Hopper viewed Dean, who died in an auto accident shortly before filming was completed on *Giant*, as a friend and mentor. Devastated by Dean's death, Hopper traveled to New York City to study with Dean's teacher, Lee Strasberg, the foremost exponent of the Stanislavski style of acting (also known as method acting), in which the actor draws on the resources of his own psyche in creating a role. When Hopper appeared in Henry Hathaway's film *From Hell to Texas* (1958), the two men clashed bitterly, and Hopper gained a reputation for being uncooperative and insubordinate. His Hollywood career appeared to be over, and he returned to New York, where he worked on the stage and appeared in some 140 episodes of various television shows. At the same time he wrote poetry and took up painting and photography. After marrying Brooke Hayward—whose family was considered Hollywood royalty—in 1961, Hopper began to win prominent film roles again; even Hathaway cast him in two John Wayne Westerns, *The Sons of Katie Elder* (1965) and *True Grit* (1968). Hopper had become close to his wife's childhood friend Peter Fonda, and the two men subsequently appeared together in the low-budget biker movie *The Glory Stompers* (1966) and in Roger Corman's *The Trip* (1967), an exploitation film about LSD. In 1968 Hopper and Fonda began work on the film that would make cinematic history and inaugurate Hopper's short-lived reputation as a Hollywood genius. Produced by Fonda and directed by Hopper, *Easy Rider* told the story of two drug-loving, freedom-seeking motorcyclists on a road trip across the U.S. The film, which won the 1969 Cannes Film Festival prize for best picture by a new director, put Hopper in the spotlight as the leader of a new independent film movement. By that time Hopper, who divorced Hayward in 1969, was abusing alcohol and drugs—not only marijuana and hallucinogens, which he had been using for over a decade, but also cocaine. Armed with an $850,000 budget furnished by a major studio, in 1970 Hopper gathered a large cast and crew and headed for Chinchero, a remote Indian village in central Peru, to make his own film. The project showed signs of trouble almost as soon as he arrived in Peru, with stories being widely circulated in the press about clashes with right-wing Peruvian authorities, violence on the set, orgies, and what one writer called bouts of "drug-induced pandemonium." In addition, when Hopper returned to Taos, New Mexico, where his home had become a kind of Mecca for hippies, it took him almost a year to edit the film, a process that was hampered by his frequent use of psychedelics to invoke his muse. Appalled by the nonlinearity of the film, Universal Pictures studio executives ordered him to recut it, but he refused. Although *The Last Movie* (1971) was the grand prize winner for best film at the Venice Film Festival, it opened domestically to generally dismal notices. After a brief run in New York and Los Angeles, it was hastily withdrawn from commercial release, and Hopper was blackballed by Hollywood once again. Hopper spent the next decade in a self-destructive downward spiral. He worked occasionally as an actor, most notably as the co-star (with Bruno Ganz) of *The American Friend* (1977), a critically acclaimed film by the German director Wim Wenders, and as the babbling, drug-crazed journalist in *Apocalypse Now* (1979), Francis Ford Coppola's Vietnam War epic. By the early 1980s Hopper was snorting large amounts of cocaine and consuming almost a gallon of rum every day. In 1983 he succumbed to the delusion that one of his underworld drug associates had put out a contract on his life, and he fled Taos for Los Angeles, where he began to shoot cocaine directly into his bloodstream. After spending a few months in a rehabilitation program, Hopper stopped drinking alcohol but continued to use cocaine. He was well enough, however, to portray an alcoholic father in Coppola's *Rumble Fish*

(1983), and after joining Alcoholics Anonymous he staged a major comeback with two film roles in 1986: as an alcohol-ravaged ex-basketball star in *Hoosiers* and as a drug-warped maniac in *Blue Velvet*. In 1987 Hopper again delivered a well-received performance as a psychotic drug dealer, in the film *River's Edge*, and once more played a drunken, irresponsible father in *The Pick-up Artist*. That year Hopper, who had been taking photos since he was given a camera by Hayward during their marriage, mounted an exhibition of his work at a gallery in New York. The photos—compelling shots of civil rights marches and portraits of such artists as Andy Warhol—were collected in the book *Out of the Sixties* (1987). When Hopper returned to directing, with *Colors* (1988), an urban police drama starring Sean Penn and Robert Duvall, he was met with generally admiring reviews. He had several notable roles in the 1990s, including parts in the films *Paris Trout* (1991), *Red Rock West* (1993), and *True Romance* (1993). One of his most visible roles of the decade was that of the sociopathic ex-cop in the blockbuster *Speed* (1994), which starred Sandra Bullock and Keanu Reeves. He then appeared in such films as *Waterworld* (1995), *Space Truckers* (1996), *Basquiat* (1996), *The Good Life* (1997), *Road Ends* (1997), *Meet the Deedles* (1998), *EdTV* (1999), and *Jesus' Son* (1999). Hopper found himself equally in demand in the new millennium, appearing in *The Spreading Ground*, *Luck of the Draw*, a television production of *Jason and the Argonauts*, and *Held for Ransom*, all released in 2000. While appearing in such films as *The Piano Player* (2002), *Land of the Dead* (2005), and *Swing Vote* (2008), Hopper could be seen most often during those years on the small screen, where he appeared in several episodes of the series *Flatland*, the immensely popular *24*, and *E-Ring*. From 2008 to 2009 he portrayed Ben Cendars, a maverick music producer, on *Crash*, a TV series about racial tensions in Los Angeles. (The program was based on the 2004 Oscar-winning film of the same name.) In 2009 Hopper was diagnosed with prostate cancer. He died at his home in Venice, California. His voice can be heard in the animated film *Alpha and Omega*, released in September 2010, and he was cast in the lead role in the comedy "The Last Film Festival," which was in the post-production stage in the fall of 2010. An avid and prescient collector of modern art, Hopper reportedly bought Andy Warhol's first soup-can painting for $75. He is said to have once purchased a Jean-Michel Basquiat painting for $17,000 and to have turned down a million-dollar offer for it less than a year later. Hopper was married five times. His second marriage, to the singer Michelle Phillips, lasted for only eight days. He was in the process of divorcing his last wife, the actress Victoria Duffy, at the time of his death. He is survived by four children: Marin, born of his union with Brooke Hayward; Ruthanna, daughter of Hopper and Daria Halprin, Hopper's third wife; Henry, son of Hopper and the actress Katherine LaNasa; and Galen, from Hopper's marriage to Duffy. See *Current Biography* (1987).
—D.K.

Obituary *New York Times* (on-line) May 30, 2010

HORNE, LENA June 30, 1917–May 9, 2010 Actress; singer. Among the first black women to sign a major film-studio contract, Lena Horne broke new ground for African-Americans in Hollywood. As a singer, the multitalented Horne won international acclaim and several Grammy Awards, including one in 1989 recognizing her lifetime achievements. Lena Calhoun Horne was born in the New York City borough of Brooklyn. Her paternal grandparents, Edwin and Cora Horne, were prominent members of the NAACP; her maternal grandfather was the first black member of the Brooklyn Board of Education; and an uncle, Frank Smith Horne, was a scholar, educator, and government administrator who served occasionally as an unofficial adviser on race relations to President Franklin D. Roosevelt. Horne's father, Edwin F. "Teddy" Horne, a numbers runner and gambler, left his family when she was three. Her mother, the former Edna Scottron, then became a touring actress with a black theater troupe. As a result Horne lived with her grandparents for four years until her mother was able to resume her care. At age 16 Horne left school to help support her ailing mother. She landed a job as a chorus girl at Harlem's famed nightspot the Cotton Club, which was run by white racketeers. (The other chorus members were mainly, like Horne, young and light-skinned.) A year later, in 1934, she made her Broadway debut, performing a voodoo dance in the short-lived production *Dance with Your Gods*. When Horne was 19 she married 28-year-old Louis Jones and moved to Pittsburgh, Pennsylvania, with him. They had two children together before they split up, in 1940. After returning to New York City, Horne was hired as a vocalist with Charlie Barnet's orchestra, becoming one of the first African-American performers to sing with a major white band. She then landed a spot singing jazz tunes at Café Society, a Manhattan club. She began recording with Teddy Wilson, who led the house band, as well as with Artie Shaw and Henry Levine's Dixieland Jazz Group. Later that year Horne, who was often a featured vocalist on various radio programs, made her first solo records for RCA Victor. In 1942 she left for Los Angeles, California, where she appeared in a show at the Little Troc nightclub in Hollywood. There, she was discovered by Roger Edens, a composer and arranger at Metro-Goldwyn-Mayer (MGM), who helped her secure a seven-year film contract with the studio. Despite reservations about pursuing a film career, Horne signed the contract at the urging of friends, including the NAACP executive secretary Walter White and the bandleader Count Basie, who felt that in doing so she might inspire other African-Americans. (Because blacks were not allowed at that time to live in Hollywood, a white friend signed a lease on a house for her, greatly angering neighbors when they found out.) After making her MGM debut with a small part in *Panama Hattie* (1942), which featured music by Cole Porter, Horne had her first major role, that of Georgia Brown, a temptress, in the all-black musical *Cabin in the Sky* (1943). That year she also starred in another all-black musical, *Stormy Weather*, loosely based on the life of the tap dancer Bill "Bojangles" Robinson. The film's title number became one of Horne's best-known songs. Despite her strong performances in those early films, Horne was often cast in large-scale musicals in which she performed only one or two songs, so that the studio could cut her from versions of the pictures shown in the Deep South. Her credits from that period include *Thousands Cheer* (1943), *Broadway Rhythm* (1944), *Two Girls and a Sailor* (1944), *Ziegfeld Follies* (1946), and *Words and Music* (1948). During World War II Horne performed frequently at army bases and became a favorite pin-up girl for African-American soldiers. However, Horne soon grew critical of the army's poor treatment of its black service members, and she refused to perform for segregated audiences or for audiences in which German POWs were afforded better seating than African-American servicemen. As a result, she was blacklisted from Hollywood for the next several years, although she was able to find work on television shows in the 1950s. She also continued to sing and record, releasing the live 1957 album *Lena Horne at the Waldorf-Astoria*, which became the best-selling effort by a female artist in the history of RCA Victor. During the 1960s Horne was active in the civil rights movement, often taking part in marches and protests. In 1970 and 1971 she endured the deaths of her father; her son, who had been suffering from a kidney ailment; and her second husband, Lennie Hayton. (Hayton was white, and the couple had kept their 1947 wedding, which had taken place in France, a secret for three years.) Horne made her final film appearance as Glinda the Good Witch in *The Wiz* (1978), an all-black musical based on *The Wizard of Oz*. In 1981 she created a hugely successful one-woman show, *Lena Horne: The Lady and Her Music*, which ran on Broadway for more than a year, toured internationally, and earned a Tony Award. In it she performed her most popular songs and discussed her life and career. Horne, who continued to release albums as an octogenarian, died at New York-Presbyterian Hospital. She is survived by her daughter, Gail Lumet Buckley; six grandchildren; and three great-grandchildren. See *Current Biography* (1985). —W.D.

Obituary *New York Times* (on-line) May 9, 2010

HOUK, RALPH Aug. 9, 1919–July 21, 2010 Professional baseball manager. During his first seasons as a Major League Baseball manager, Ralph Houk led the New York Yankees to three consecutive American League (AL) pennants (1961–63) and two World Series victories (1961–62). Houk, the fourth of five children, was born on his father's 160-acre farm near Lawrence, Kansas. Four of his uncles, who lived nearby, played on a semiprofessional baseball team, the Belvoirs, which was managed by his uncle Charlie Houk. At the age of 11, Ralph Houk tried out for a team in the local Twilight League, for players aged 11 to 17, and soon settled behind home plate in the position of catcher. Houk attended Lawrence High School, which at that time had no baseball team, and he ended up playing football, as a quarterback and a defensive fullback, and made the All-State team in his senior year. Several colleges offered Houk football scholarships, but he turned them down so that he could continue to play baseball with the Belvoirs, which he had joined at age 16. He also played on a Lawrence team in the Ban Johnson League. During a national tournament game in which the Lawrence team competed, Yankee scouts recognized Houk's talent and signed him up. He began his professional baseball career in the minor leagues in 1939. His progress toward the major leagues was interrupted by the outbreak of World War II. In early 1942 Houk and his brother Harold joined the U.S. Army. Taking part in the invasion of Normandy, in June 1944, and the Battle of the Bulge the following December, Houk earned a Silver Star, a Bronze Star, and a Purple Heart. He left the army at the end of 1945 with the rank of major and returned to baseball in 1946, playing with the Kansas City club of the triple-A American Association and the Beaumont club of the double-A Texas League. He made three hits in his major-league debut with the Yankees, on April 26, 1947, in a game against the Washington Senators. That season, Houk's best as a player, he was a third-string catcher and batted .272 in 41 games. After another stint in the minor leagues, Houk played with the Yankees from 1950 through 1954, serving mainly as a reserve catcher and spending much of his time in the bullpen. "I used to sit out there with pitchers who weren't in the starting rotation," Houk once said, "and I learned exactly what went through their minds." He also kept written records over the years analyzing each play, each player, and each game in detail. Recognizing his flair for leadership and his thorough knowledge of baseball, Yankee officials appointed Houk manager of the Denver Bears, in the Yankees' triple-A American Association, in 1955. He held that position for three seasons (1955–57), during which time the team was consistently in the running for the pennant. Houk's success with the Bears led the Yankees to hire him as the team's first-base coach, a position he held from 1958 to 1960. When he became the 16th manager of the Yankees, on October 20, 1960, Houk made it clear from the start that he had no intention of imitating the management style of his predecessor, Casey Stengel, who had won 10 pennants and seven World Series titles during his tenure. During Houk's first season as manager, he led the team to win the AL pennant over the Detroit Tigers and to defeat the Cincinnati Reds in the World Series. The following year, under Houk's leadership, the Yankees won a second World Series title, defeating the San Francisco Giants in seven games. In 1963 the Yankees won the AL pennant yet again but lost in the World Series to the Los Angeles Dodgers. Houk is one of two managers in the American League to have led their teams to pennants three seasons in a row. He won the respect and affection of his players by abandoning Stengel's system of "platooning" (alternating players at the same position, instead of allowing each to appear at one position regularly), by keeping his criticism of their mistakes private, and by showing sympathy for their personal problems. After the 1963 season Houk was promoted to general manager. The following year the Yankees won the pennant yet again, but the team struggled for much of the rest of the decade. Houk remained with the Yankees until the end of the 1973 season, less than a year after the team had been purchased by a syndicate headed by George Steinbrenner. Houk served as the manager of the Detroit Tigers organization for five seasons before retiring. He returned to baseball in 1981 to manage the Boston Red Sox for four seasons, and in 1986 he became vice president of the

Minnesota Twins. Houk died in his home in Winter Haven, Florida. He is survived by his daughter, Donna; his son, Robert; four grandchildren; and 10 great-grandchildren. His wife, Bette, died in 2006. See *Current Biography* (1962).—D.K.

Obituary *New York Times* (on-line) July 21, 2010

HOVING, THOMAS Jan. 15, 1931–Dec. 10, 2009 Museum director; art historian. From 1967 to 1977 Thomas Hoving was the director of the Metropolitan Museum of Art (known informally as the Met) in New York City. During his tenure he was credited with reshaping the iconic institution by establishing new departments, wings, and galleries and mounting several "blockbuster" exhibitions. He maneuvered to obtain the Met's famed Temple of Dendur, despite the fact that officials at the Smithsonian Institution were equally intent upon the acquisition, and he helped painstakingly reassemble an entire Prairie House living room by Frank Lloyd Wright in the American Wing. He earned a reputation in the museum world for purchasing pieces that might have been obtained illegally by the sellers. In 1972, for example, art experts began to voice concern that a Greek vase the museum had purchased for $1 million had been smuggled out of Italy. In his 1993 memoir, *Making the Mummies Dance: Inside the Metropolitan Museum of Art*, Hoving admitted to knowing that the piece, which the Met ultimately returned to Italian authorities, had likely been obtained through illicit means, and he unabashedly called his collecting style "pure piracy." Thomas Pearsall Field Hoving was born in New York City to Walter and Mary Osgood (Field) Hoving. His father was president of the department store Bonwit Teller and later became chair of Tiffany & Co. His parents divorced when he was five. Hoving and his sister lived with their mother, who died in 1954. He attended New York City's Buckley School but was expelled for poor behavior and was sent to the Eaglebrook School, in Deerfield, Massachusetts. He moved on to the exclusive Phillips Exeter Academy, in New Hampshire, but was expelled for insubordination. He next enrolled at the Hotchkiss School, in Lakeville, Connecticut, graduating cum laude in 1949. The summer before he entered Princeton University, Hoving worked as a copy boy for the columnist Sidney Fields at the now-defunct New York *Daily Mirror*. At Princeton, Hoving studied art and archaeology, and he earned a B.A. degree summa cum laude in 1953. After leaving Princeton he served in the Marine Corps for three years and then returned to the university as a graduate student, receiving a master's degree (1958) and a doctoral degree (1959) in art history. In 1958, at the annual student symposium of the New York Institute of Fine Arts, Hoving attracted the attention of the director of the Metropolitan Museum of Art, who offered him a job. In 1959 Hoving began working as a curatorial assistant at the Cloisters, the Met's world-renowned collection of medieval art, in upper Manhattan. He impressed museum officials when he pointed out that a marble relief carving that had recently been rejected by the museum was, in fact, a sought-after piece of a 12th-century pulpit. Soon afterward Hoving became the museum's chief liaison with the world art market for works from the period 300 to 1500 A.D. He made many trips to Europe in search of art treasures; one of his most notable finds came in 1962, when he identified a 12th-century whalebone ivory cross from Bury St. Edmunds in England. Hoving was named the Met's curator of medieval arts and of the Cloisters in 1965. He left the post within a few months, when the recently elected mayor John V. Lindsay, for whom he had campaigned, appointed him New York City parks commissioner. Hoving, although unfamiliar with parks administration, was successful in the post, orchestrating a series of well-attended gatherings known as "Hoving's Happenings" and closing parts of Central Park to traffic on Sundays. Following the death of James J. Rorimer, the director of the Met, in May 1966, speculation arose that Hoving, despite his popularity as parks commissioner, would be tapped to replace him. Official confirmation of the appointment was made in December of that year, and Hoving returned to the Met in April 1967. At age 35, he was the youngest director in the museum's history. Hoving, who continued to consult with Lindsay on the city's parks and various cultural matters, introduced a number of changes to the Met; he established a contemporary-art department, galleries for Islamic art, an expanded American wing, and a wing for African art and art from the Pacific Islands, among other innovations. He also reopened the Egyptian wing and extended the museum's massive front steps, which have proven to be a popular spot for New Yorkers and tourists to rest and watch the passing traffic on Fifth Avenue. Hoving has been credited with introducing the concept of "blockbuster" museum shows, such as the Tutankhamun exhibition, which opened in 1978 and brought in $1.3 million in just four months. Although he was instrumental in changing the public perception of the Met and was widely praised in most quarters, Hoving was sometimes criticized by traditionalists. In 1977 he left the Met. The following year he became an arts correspondent for the ABC newsmagazine *20/20*, and he appeared on the show until 1984. He also edited *Connoisseur* magazine from 1981 to 1991 and wrote several books, including *Tutankhamun: The Untold Story* (1978), *False Impressions: The Hunt for Big-Time Art Fakes* (1996), and *Master Pieces: The Curator's Game* (2005). Hoving died of lung cancer at his Manhattan home. He is survived by his wife, Nancy, and their daughter, Petrea. See *Current Biography* (1967). —W.D.

Obituary *New York Times* (on-line) Dec. 10, 2009

JONES, JENNIFER Mar. 2, 1919–Dec. 17, 2009 Actress. Jennifer Jones rose to stardom with her Academy Award–winning performance in *The Song of Bernadette* (1943). While she went on to receive further critical acclaim and additional Oscar nominations, she also came under media scrutiny for her tumultuous personal life and high-profile marriages. The actress was born Phylis Lee Isley in Tulsa, Oklahoma. Her parents, Phil and Flora, were the owners and stars of the Isley Stock Company, a tent-show theatrical troupe that performed in towns across the Midwest. (They later became the owners of a chain of Texas movie theaters.) As a child, Jones sold refreshments, took tickets, and sometimes performed on stage. She studied dramatics at Northwestern University, in Chicago, Illinois, for one year, and in 1938 she transferred to the prestigious American Academy of Dramatic Arts, in New York City, where she met the aspiring actor Robert Walker. The two married in 1939 and traveled to Hollywood, where they won a few bit parts. (Jones appeared in the 1939 movie *New Frontier* and the serial *Dick Tracy's G-Men*, while Walker had two lines in the 1939 Warner Bros. film *Winter Carnival*.) Discouraged, they returned to New York. There, Jones gave birth to two sons, Robert Jr. and Michael, and worked occasionally as a hat model, while Walker found work as a radio actor. Jones met David O. Selznick, the acclaimed producer of *Gone with the Wind* (1939), when she auditioned for the lead part in the film *Claudia*. Jones did not win the role, which Selznick gave to Dorothy McGuire, a young actress already in his stable. Still, the studio executive was taken by the young, dark-haired beauty and signed her to a personal contract. Coining her stage name, he cast her in *The Song of Bernadette*, a film based on Franz Werfel's best-selling novel about a French peasant girl who has a vision of the Virgin Mary. Jones recieved universal acclaim and a best-actress Oscar for her part in the film. One reviewer wrote, "[Jones's] large, sad eyes and soft face, her wistful mouth and luminous smile are a thoroughly appealing exterior for the innocence which shines from within." Shortly after that success, Jones, who had become romantically involved with Selznick, announced her divorce from Walker, whose own acting career had also taken off, with roles in *Bataan* (1943), *Madame Curie* (1943), and *See Here, Private Hargrove* (1944). In 1944 Jones appeared opposite her estranged husband in the World War II drama *Since You Went Away*, receiving an Academy Award nomination for her supporting role. She received another Oscar nod—this time for best actress—for her performance as an amnesiac in *Love Letters* (1945) and next appeared in the films *American Creed* (1946) and *Cluny Brown* (1946). A fourth Oscar nomination came for her part in the Western *Duel in the Sun* (1946), in which she starred as Pearl Chavez, a biracial girl who is sent to live with distant white relatives in Texas, after her father is hanged for shooting his wife and her lover. In 1949 Jones married Selznick, whose wife had left him in 1945, partly because of his relationship with the young actress. Selznick took total control of his new wife's career, arranging for her to star in several films, including *The Wild Heart* (1952), *Carrie* (1952), *Ruby Gentry* (1952), and *Good Morning, Miss Dove* (1955). She received her fifth Oscar nomination for her part as a Eurasian doctor who falls in love with an American war correspondent in *Love Is a Many-Splendored Thing* (1955), followed by roles in *The Man in the Gray Flannel Suit* (1956), *The Barretts of Wimpole Street* (1957), the screen adaptation of Ernest Hemingway's classic *A Farewell to Arms* (1957), and the film version of F. Scott Fitzgerald's *Tender Is the Night* (1962). Jones's career slowed considerably after Selznick's death, in 1965. She appeared in *The Idol* (1966) and the low-budget film *Angel, Angel, Down We Go* (1969), before winning a small part in the ensemble drama *The*

Towering Inferno (1974), which marked her final acting role. Jones occasionally made headlines for reasons unrelated to her professional accomplishments. Walker, who died at the age of 32, publicly blamed their divorce for the emotional problems and alcoholism that plagued him in the years preceding his demise, and in 1967 Jones was discovered close to death on a Malibu beach after having swallowed a bottle of sleeping pills. In 1971, after only a three-week courtship, Jones married Norton Simon, a multimillionaire who had headed a series of conglomerates, including Hunt Foods and Canada Dry, before retiring to amass art for an eponymous private museum. Simon died in 1993. Jones was also predeceased by her 21-year-old daughter, Mary Jennifer Selznick, who committed suicide in 1976 by jumping out of a Los Angeles building. Her son Michael died in 2007 of undisclosed causes. Jones, who spent her later years overseeing a renovation of Simon's museum and doing philanthropic work relating to mental-health issues, is survived by her son Robert Jr., an actor, as well as by eight grandchildren and four great-grandchildren. See *Current Biography* (1944). —M.R.M.

Obituary New York Times (on-line) Dec. 17, 2009

JORDAN, MICHAEL H. June 15, 1936–May 25, 2010
Businessman. Michael H. Jordan is best known for turning the long-established Pittsburgh, Pennsylvania–based Westinghouse Electric Corp., a manufacturer of power equipment and refrigeration units, into a media juggernaut that included CBS and Infinity Broadcasting. Jordan was born into a middle-class family in Kansas City, Missouri. A scholarship student at Yale University, he received a B.S. degree in chemical engineering in 1957 and an M.S. degree in the same field from Princeton University two years later. After a brief stint at Procter & Gamble in Kansas City, he served a four-year tour of duty with the U.S. Navy, reaching the rank of lieutenant. As a member of Admiral Hyman G. Rickover's staff, he spent six months at the Westinghouse Bettis Atomic Power Laboratory, near Pittsburgh, where he was certified as a nuclear engineer. He then returned to civilian life. Jordan spent 10 years (1964–74) as a consultant and principal with McKinsey & Co., a New York–based management consulting firm. In 1974 he joined PepsiCo Inc. as the beverage giant's director of financial planning. Steadily climbing the corporate ladder, he served as chief executive officer and president of PepsiCo Worldwide from 1987 to 1992. In that capacity he closed deals with Mexico, Canada, and various countries in Europe, and he was credited with expanding overseas snack-food operations from $300 million, in 1986, to $1.8 billion by the end of his tenure. In June 1992, despite his being considered one of the two most likely candidates to succeed PepsiCo Inc.'s chairman, Jordan resigned from the company, citing weariness with his grueling travel schedule and his desire for change. He subsequently joined Clayton Dubilier & Rice, a private investment firm in New York City specializing in leveraged buyouts. Jordan's association with the investment firm lasted only a year; in June 1993 he was named chairman and chief executive officer of Westinghouse. Jordan, who took over the head position five months after investors had pressured the previous CEO, Paul E. Lego, to resign, became the first outsider to head Westinghouse since 1929. Founded in 1886 as a maker of air brakes for trains, Westinghouse manufactured equipment for electrical and nuclear generators, mobile cooling equipment, and electronic devices, and it also operated radio and television stations. During the two years preceding Jordan's arrival, it had lost nearly $2.4 billion, largely because of its disastrous foray in the 1980s into the arena of junk bonds, leveraged buyouts, and commercial real estate via Westinghouse Financial Services. Upon his arrival, Jordan laid off 7,000 of the company's 105,000 employees and sold off several divisions. Jordan saw potential for the company in Asia, and in the summer of 1994, he accompanied U.S. secretary of commerce Ronald H. Brown to China, where he reached an agreement with the Shanghai Electric & Engineering Corp. for a $100 million joint venture to build steam turbines. During the early 1990s Group W, Westinghouse's broadcast division, which included 16 radio stations, five television stations, satellite communications, and programming divisions, was a reliable source of revenue. Still, most of the firm's business relied on low-growth industrial holdings, so it surprised industry analysts when Jordan announced in mid-1994 that Westinghouse would enter into a joint venture with CBS to produce programming and invest in new television and radio stations. A year later he announced Westinghouse's plan to purchase CBS, the last independent television network. Westinghouse thus became the nation's largest broadcast owner, with control of more than 15 television stations and 39 radio stations and access to about 35 percent of the nation's households. In 1998 Jordan left Westinghouse and joined Electronic Data Systems, a technology-services company. There, he streamlined operations by shifting work abroad and expanded the company's technology consulting business. By 2005 Jordan had turned Electronic Data Systems around completely, and in 2008 Hewlett-Packard purchased the revived company for $13.9 billion. Jordan, who served for a time as the chair of the United Negro College Fund, died in New York City of neuroendocrine cancer at the age of 73. He is survived by his second wife, Hilary Cecil-Jordan; two children from his first marriage, which ended in divorce; two stepchildren; and six grandchildren. See *Current Biography* (1998) —H.R.W.

Obituary *New York Times* A p33 May 27, 2010

KACZYNSKI, LECH June 18, 1949–Apr. 10, 2010
President of Poland. After establishing himself as an anti-Communist lawyer and political activist, Lech Kaczynski was elected president of Poland in 2005. During his tenure he was known for his social conservatism and his efforts to strengthen ties with the U.S., often frustrating member nations of the European Union. Lech Aleksander Kaczynski, along with his twin brother, Jaroslaw, was born in Warsaw. Both his father, an engineer by training, and his mother, a philologist at the Polish Academy of Sciences, were members of Polish resistance organizations during the Nazi occupation. As a youth, Kaczynski

was deeply affected by learning about the Nazi defeat of the 1944 Warsaw Uprising and the consequent blow to Poland's national dignity. At the age of 12 Kaczynski and his brother attained national fame when they starred in the popular 1962 film version of the Polish children's book *The Two Who Stole the Moon*. The twins did not pursue acting, however; instead they studied law at Warsaw University, and Lech Kaczynski earned a degree from that institution in 1971. Five years later he received a doctoral degree in law from the University of Gdansk. He then became involved in the labor movement, providing unions with legal services, and in 1980 he began to represent the newly established labor union Solidarity, which quickly expanded to include millions of Polish workers. In 1981 state leaders, believing they faced a threat to public and economic order, declared martial law and arrested a number of Solidarity leaders, including Kaczynski, who was sent to a prison camp. After spending about 10 months at the camp, Kaczynski was allowed to return to Gdansk, where Solidarity had been officially banned. Still, Lech and Jaroslaw Kaczynski continued to meet with Solidarity leaders; Lech Kaczynski undertook formal roles within the union, serving terms as secretary of its provisional coordinating commission and secretary of its national executive committee. Both brothers were also involved in an underground international human rights organization. After strikes destabilized the country politically and economically in 1988, Kaczynski took part in meetings between Solidarity and Poland's Communist government. The Communist Party agreed not only to officially recognize Solidarity, but to establish a democratic government, reinstating the Senate and creating a presidency that would take the place of the Communist Party–run council that had previously overseen the government's executive functions. In June 1989 Kaczynski won a position in the newly created Senate, representing the Elblag district, on the country's northern coast. In March 1991 he was appointed minister of state for defense and security by Poland's president Lech Walesa, a former member of Solidarity who in 1990 had become the country's first democratically elected president. (Jaroslaw Kaczynski was also serving as an adviser in the Walesa administration.) Lech Kaczynski resigned from his position in November, however, over political disagreements with Walesa. In 1992 the Polish legislature appointed Kaczynski to lead the NIK, a government division whose responsibilities include certifying the practices of private and public organizations. That position gave Kaczynski the freedom to investigate the type of waste and corruption on which he would focus in his 2005 presidential campaign. His aggressive efforts were met with disapproval by the president, and in June 1995 he was removed from that post. Kaczynski spent the next five years in relative obscurity, working for some time as a professor of law at the Academy of Catholic Theology, in Warsaw. He reemerged on the national political scene in June 2000, when then–Prime Minister Jerzy Buzek appointed him justice minister. Kaczynski was fired from that post in 2001 over—among other political reasons—his blunt criticism of Poland's penal system, which he considered too lenient. In 2002, in the first election ever held for

mayor of Warsaw, Kaczynski, who had long been popular with the electorate, won the post by campaigning on his crime-fighting credentials. As mayor he united the city's autonomous boroughs under one municipality and increased the number of police officers; he received criticism when he refused to grant permits for two gay-rights demonstrations and when he named a public square after Dzhokhar Dudayev, a Chechen rebel, whom the Russian government regarded as a terrorist. In 2005 Kaczynski, running under the conservative Law and Justice Party that he had founded with his brother in 2001, was elected president of Poland. In his first speech as president, he promised to bring a "moral revolution" to the country and to purge the government of corruption. In a controversial move, he attempted to achieve a parliamentary majority by forming a coalition government with two far-right parties, the Self-Defense Party and the League of Polish Families. Kaczynski also embarked on an effort to remove all government officials with ties to the Communist Party. His actions on the international front drew concern from many European governments, who opposed his apparent homophobic and ultranationalistic attitudes. Kaczynski was generally suspicious of the European Union, which Poland had joined in 2004, and did not pursue diplomatic relations with other member nations. Kaczynski, along with his wife, Maria, and dozens of top-level Polish political and military officials, were killed in a plane crash. He is survived by his brother; his mother; his daughter, Marta; and two granddaughters, Ewa and Martyna. See *Current Biography International* (2006).—D.K.

Obituary *New York Times* (on-line) Apr. 10, 2010

KILPATRICK, JAMES J. Nov. 1, 1920–Aug. 15, 2010 Newspaper columnist; editor; author; television personality. James J. Kilpatrick—who once described himself as "ten miles to the right of Ivan the Terrible" in the view of some liberals, but "only a little to the south of John C. Calhoun" to those who loved him—was a nationally syndicated columnist and author known for his strong conservative views on politics, law, and language. Kilpatrick's thrice-weekly political column, "A Conservative View," appeared in hundreds of newspapers across the country from 1964 to 1993. Prior to launching that column, Kilpatrick served as the editor of the *Richmond (Virginia) News Leader*. James Jackson Kilpatrick was born in Oklahoma City, Oklahoma, where his father worked as a lumber dealer. As a white boy reared in the southern consciousness, he readily accepted racial segregation as a way of life and from a young age embraced the idea of white supremacy. A precocious child, Kilpatrick learned to read at the age of four and taught himself to type by practicing on an old Remington typewriter in his father's office. By the time he was seven, he was determined to become a journalist. At Oklahoma City's Classen High School, from which he graduated in 1937, Kilpatrick served as editor of the school paper. He was forced to pay his way through journalism school at the University of Missouri after his father's business failed. During that time Kilpatrick spent his summers working as a copy boy with the *Oklahoma City Times*. After earning a journalism degree, in 1941, he started working as a cub reporter for Virginia's *Richmond News Leader*. Kilpatrick's energy and enthusiasm pleased the paper's editor, Douglas Southall Freeman, who took him under his wing and groomed him to become his successor. Kilpatrick worked his way up to become an investigative reporter before being named the paper's chief editorial writer in 1949, the same year Freeman retired. In 1951 Kilpatrick took over as the paper's editor in chief, a position he held until 1966. During that time he led several notable crusades. In 1953 Kilpatrick helped win a pardon for an African-American handyman who had been sentenced to life in prison for killing a police officer, after a *News Leader* investigation revealed he had been wrongly charged. In 1959, after becoming incensed over an incident in which a Richmond pedestrian was fined for climbing across the hood of a car whose driver had persisted in blocking a busy intersection, Kilpatrick founded the Beadle Bumble Fund (inspired by a character in Charles Dickens's novel *Oliver Twist*). The purpose of the fund, which used contributions from readers to pay the legal fees of those who had broken laws that Kilpatrick deemed purposeless, was, as he wrote at the time, "to deflate an occasional overblown bureaucrat, to unstuff a few stuffed shirts and to promote the repeal of foolish and needless laws." During the 1950s Kilpatrick began to articulate his views on issues of race and became an outspoken opponent of desegregation. Following the U.S. Supreme Court's landmark 1954 decision in *Brown vs. Board of Education*, which declared school segregation unconstitutional, Kilpatrick wrote a series of editorials condemning the court's ruling, framing his arguments around a 19th-century doctrine called interposition, according to which states had a right and duty to override federal mandates that impinged upon their sovereignty. Kilpatrick elaborated on that subject in the 1957 book *The Sovereign States: Notes of a Citizen in Virginia*, in which he attempted to rally support for the doctrine outside the South. He followed that book with *The Southern Case for School Segregation* (1962). Kilpatrick's views gained a wider audience when in the 1960s he engaged in a series of public debates with prominent civil rights leaders, including James Farmer and Martin Luther King Jr. In 1964 he began writing the political column "A Conservative View" for the Newsday Syndicate, which allowed him to work on his columns without leaving the *Richmond News Leader*. The following year he began writing his column for the Washington Star Syndicate, which later became the Universal Press Syndicate. In 1966 Kilpatrick left the *News Leader* and moved to Washington, D.C., to devote all of his energy to his column, which by that time was nationally syndicated. It appeared every week in more than 400 newspapers across the country until 1993, when he began writing another weekly column, "Covering the Courts," which ran until January 2008. His most recent column, "The Writer's Art," devoted to lambasting poorly written prose, ended in January 2009. Kilpatrick gradually moderated his views on race, which had drawn much criticism over the years, and he eventually reexamined his original analysis of it. In 1978 he defined his view of conservatism in *Nation's Business* magazine, writing, "Conservatives

believe that a civilized society demands orders and classes, that men are not inherently equal, that change and reform are not identical, that in a free society men are children of God and not wards of the state." He continued, "Self reliance is a conservative principle. The work ethic is a conservative ethic. The free marketplace is vital to the conservative's economic philosophy." In the 1970s he broadened his exposure by engaging in intellectual boxing matches with the liberal journalist Shana Alexander and Nicholas von Hoffman on the "Point-Counterpoint" segment of CBS's *60 Minutes*; their debates were later parodied on NBC's *Saturday Night Live* by Dan Aykroyd and Jane Curtin. In addition to his columns, Kilpatrick was a contributing editor to the *National Review* and wrote more than a dozen books, including *The Writer's Art* (1984), about his love of language. He recieved numerous journalism awards and honors and was among only a handful of columnists ever to be named as a fellow of the Society of Professional Journalists. Kilpatrick died of congestive heart failure at a Washington, D.C., hospital. He was married to his first wife, the former Marie Louise Pietri, from 1942 until her death, in 1997. Kilpatrick is survived by his second wife, the Washington columnist Marianne Means; three sons; four stepdaughters; seven grandchildren; nine stepgrandchildren; and seven great-grandchildren. See *Current Biography* (1980). –C.C.

Obituary *New York Times* (on-line) Aug. 16, 2010

KIRCHNER, NÉSTOR Feb. 25, 1950–Oct. 27, 2010 Argentinean politician. As president of Argentina from 2003 to 2007, Néstor Kirchner steered his country out of an economic crisis and paved the way for his wife, Cristina Fernández de Kirchner, to succeed him. He was expected to run for president again in 2011, as part of what political observers called the couple's "leapfrog" strategy to pass the presidency back and forth between them, in order to create a strong dynasty. The son of a postal worker, Néstor Carlos Kirchner was born in Río Gallegos, the capital of Santa Cruz Province, in the Patagonian region of Argentina. In the early 1970s he joined the Juventud Perónista, the youth branch of the Perónist movement. (Perónism, a political ideology derived from the practices of the former president Juan Perón, is generally associated with a heavily nationalized economy, a mixture of socialist and capitalist policies, and strong authoritarian leadership.) In 1976 Kirchner received a law degree from the Universidad Nacional de La Plata, outside Buenos Aires. He then returned to Santa Cruz and opened a law firm with his wife, whom he had married the previous year. Kirchner served as mayor of Rio Gallegos from 1987 to 1991. In the latter year, when the governor of Santa Cruz was impeached, Kirchner was elected to replace him; he was reelected in both 1995 and 1999. Argentina was in dire financial straits prior to the 2003 presidential elections; it had defaulted on its foreign debt the year before, and many banks had closed. During his campaign Kirchner called for income redistribution and increased government intervention to strengthen national industry. His supporters pointed to his success as governor of Santa Cruz, which had achieved the lowest unemployment and infant-mortality rates among Argentina's 23 provinces during his tenure, while his detractors noted his authoritarian streak. Kirchner's main opponent was Carlos Menem, who had served as the country's president from 1989 to 1999. Menem, however, withdrew from a second-round runoff when polls showed Kirchner pulling far ahead (thanks in large part to the popularity of his wife, who had been a member of the national Senate for the last several years). As a result, Kirchner won the presidency despite receiving only 22 percent of the popular vote. He was sworn in on May 25, 2003. Once in office, Kirchner, who was nicknamed "the Penguin"—a reference to the penguins that live in Patagonia—fired several corrupt police officials and judges and pressed for prosecutions of human-rights abuses that had taken place during Argentina's military dictatorship (1976–83). He renegotiated Argentina's foreign debt, helped to decrease unemployment, and led the country out of its severe economic crisis. Many predicted that he would have easily won reelection in 2007 if he had not stepped aside to allow his wife to run in his place. After Cristina Fernández de Kirchner became the first female president in Argentinean history, her husband remained an influential adviser and the president of the Partido Justicialista, their Perónist party. In May 2010 he also began serving as the head of the Union of South American Nations (UNASUR), an organization modeled on the European Union. Kirchner died of a heart attack at a hospital in Santa Cruz, shortly after complaining of flu symptoms. Many expect that his death will lessen his wife's chances of reelection in 2011. Alexei Barrionuevo wrote for the *New York Times* (October 27, 2010, on-line), "As president, Mrs. Kirchner was more often the public face of their partnership, while he was the master political operator, pulling the levers of the Peronist machinery." In addition to his wife, Kirchner is survived by the couple's two children, Maximo and Florencia. See *Current Biography International* (2004). —W.D.

Obituary *New York Times* (on-line) Oct. 27, 2010

KLUGE, JOHN W. Sep. 21, 1914–Sep. 7, 2010 Businessman. John Werner Kluge (pronounced KLOO-gee) was the founder of the Metromedia Co., the first major independent communications conglomerate of its kind in the United States. Kluge was born in Chemintz, Germany, to Fritz Kluge, an engineer, and Gertrude (Donj) Kluge. Fritz Kluge died in 1922. That same year John Kluge and his mother and new stepfather, Oswald Leitert, immigrated to Detroit, Michigan. As a youth Kluge worked as a payroll clerk for Leitert's contracting business. While attending Wayne State University, in Detroit, Kluge worked on an assembly line for the Ford Motor Co. He later transferred to Columbia University, in New York City, after being offered a full scholarship. As a student at Columbia, Kluge earned extra income by selling shoes; doing secretarial work for the son of the president of China, who was also a student there; and playing poker. After graduating with a bachelor's degree in economics, in 1937, he took a job as a shipping clerk at Otten Brothers, a small paper company in Detroit, and within three years he had

become the sales manager, vice president, and partial owner of the company. Kluge served in the U.S. Army Intelligence unit during World War II, working his way up to the rank of captain. After leaving the army, in 1945, he used his discharge money to purchase the WGAY radio station in Silver Spring, Maryland, with a partner; in the 1950s he bought several other radio stations around the country. During that decade he served as the president of the Mid-Florida Radio Corp., in Orlando, Florida, and as the treasurer of its television operation; as president of the St. Louis Broadcasting Corp., the Pittsburgh Broadcasting Co., and the Capitol Broadcasting Co. in Nashville, Tennessee; and as a partner in the Western New York Broadcasting Co. in Buffalo. Around the same time he began investing in real-estate and food-brokerage businesses. In 1956 Kluge, with his business partner, David Finkelstein, founded the Maryland-based wholesale operation Kluge, Finkelstein and Co., which sold products made by such companies as Coca-Cola and General Foods. Three years later Kluge purchased a controlling interest in the Metropolitan Broadcasting Corp.—which at the time consisted of a radio station in Cleveland, Ohio, and television stations in New York City and Washington, D.C.—and ousted the company's president, Richard Buckley. In 1961 Kluge renamed the company Metromedia and started adding stations in Boston, Massachusetts; St. Louis, Missouri; Los Angeles, California; and other cities. It soon became the fastest-growing group broadcaster in the country, and by the 1980s the conglomerate was the nation's largest group of independent television and radio stations. The Metromedia Co. came to include 14 radio stations and seven television stations, along with such entertainment franchises as the Ice Capades and the Harlem Globetrotters, and products such as mobile phones and radio pagers. In 1984 Kluge, who went through with many of his acquisitions against the advice of financial analysts, borrowed $1.2 billion to purchase all the outstanding shares of Metromedia in what was touted as one of the riskiest leveraged buyouts in the history of the communications industry. Over the next few years, as he sold some of his holdings to pay off the debt he had acquired in the deal, Kluge amassed one of the largest fortunes in the United States. By 1992 Kluge had sold almost all of his original holdings and had accumulated a net profit of some $3.4 billion. Kluge, who was a master of taking advantage of tax-code intricacies, was named the richest person in the U.S. in 1989, 1990, and 1991. By 2010, however, he had dropped to number 109, with an estimated fortune of $6.5 billion. Kluge, who rarely gave interviews, said in 1987, "Taking a business risk is where I get my kicks. I'm like a kid in a candy store. It's got my adrenaline going like crazy." He served on the boards of such companies as Occidental Petroleum, Orion Pictures, Conair, and the Waldorf-Astoria Corp., and he was a collector of fine art as well as a generous philanthropist who donated substantial sums to Columbia University, Ellis Island, and the Library of Congress. Kluge, a convert to Roman Catholicism, died in his family home near Charlottesville, Virginia. His first three marriages ended in divorce. He is survived by his fourth wife, Maria Tussi Kuttner; three stepchildren from his first marriage; one daughter from his second marriage; one adopted son from his third marriage; and one grandson. See *Current Biography* (1993). —J.P.

Obituary *New York Times* (on-line) Sep. 8, 2010

KOIRALA, GIRIJA PRASAD 1925–Mar. 20, 2010 Former prime minister of Nepal. The scion of a respected political dynasty, Girija Prasad Koirala served several stints as the prime minister of Nepal (1991–94, 1998–99, 2000–01, and 2006–08) and is celebrated for his role in the success of the 2006 Comprehensive Peace Accord (CPA), which declared a formal end to the 10-year Nepalese civil war between government forces and Maoist rebels. Koirala, the youngest of four bothers, was born in Bihar, India. His father—sometimes described as the "Nepali Gandhi"—was a businessman and activist who had been banished from Nepal by the Rana family, an autocratic dynasty that controlled the country from 1846 until 1953. As a young man Koirala fought for Indian independence from Britain, and in 1947, after India gained its independence and was partitioned, he moved to Biratnagar, Nepal, where he came to prominence as a trade-union leader. He was arrested and exiled by the Rana family numerous times for championing democracy. Two of Koirala's brothers, Matrika Prasad Koirala and Bishweshwar Prasad Koirala, had remained in India and founded the Nepali National Congress, which in 1950 became the Nepali Congress (N.C.) Party. The party formed an alliance with Nepal's monarchy to rid the country of the Rana regime, and after an armed revolution, in 1951, the Ranas were deposed. Matrika Prasad Koirala was appointed prime minister by the king, and Koirala assumed the presidency of the Morang district Nepali Congress. Power in Nepal was ostensibly shared between the monarch and Parliament until 1960, when King Mahendra Bir Bikram Shah dissolved the government and assumed complete control over Nepal, banning political parties and beginning decades of absolute monarchy. Many members of Parliament, including Koirala and his brother Bishweshwar Prasad Koirala, who was then prime minister (the second Koirala brother to assume that post), were jailed. After some seven years in prison, Koirala was released, and he continued to protest the king's reign until 1971, when he was once again arrested for participating in the pro-democracy movement and fled to India. In 1979 King Birendra Bir Bikram Shah, who had ascended to the throne in 1972 after Mahendra died, offered amnesty to political refugees, and the N.C. leaders returned to Nepal. In 1982 Koirala was elected the secretary-general of the N.C. Massive protests continued throughout the 1980s to pressure the king to restore a parliamentary democracy. (He had instituted a system of panchayats, or councils, with power concentrated in the hands of a few.) In 1990, in the face of intensifying rioting in the streets, Birendra dropped his ban on political parties, and in May 1991, after the country's first democratic elections in more than 30 years, the N.C. triumphed, winning 106 out of 205 parliamentary seats; Koirala became the third of Krishna Prasad Koirala's sons to become prime minister of his country. Koriala served in the post from 1991 to 1994, 1998 to 1999, 2000 to 2001, and 2006 to 2008.

Although his tenure was often tumultuous—marked by allegations of corruption, no-confidence votes, occasional house arrest, and the chilling 2001 massacre of most of Nepal's royal family by one of its members—Koirala cemented his legacy as a statesman in late 2006, when he helped to broker a deal that brought together Nepal's Maoist insurgents and its democratic political parties. Joining forces, they unseated the nation's monarchy, establishing Nepal as a republic and allowing the Maoists to enter mainstream politics. Koirala, who had long been in ill health, died at his daughter's home in Katmandu. His wife, Sushma, died in 1968, after being injured in a kerosene-stove explosion. Nepalese leaders declared the day of his funeral a national holiday and ordered the flag to be flown at half-staff. See *Current Biography International* (2006). —M.A.S.

Obituary *New York Times* A p24 Mar. 22, 2010

KREPS, JUANITA MORRIS Jan. 11, 1921–July 5, 2010 Former U.S. secretary of commerce. When Juanita Kreps was appointed secretary of commerce under President Jimmy Carter, in 1977, she became the first woman, and the first economist, to serve in a Cabinet post traditionally held by men with business backgrounds. Juanita Morris Kreps was born in the coal-mining town of Lynch in Harlan County, Kentucky. Of Scotch-Irish parentage, she was the sixth child of Elmer M. Morris, a struggling mine operator, and Larcenia (Blair) Morris. Her parents divorced when Juanita was four, and she lived with her mother until she entered a Presbyterian boarding school at the age of 12. Of her experiences during the Great Depression, she recalled many years later, "Everyone was having economic problems, and we weren't any worse off than anyone else." Morris studied English at Kentucky's Berea College as part of a work-study program for poor Appalachian students. She graduated with high honors in 1942 and went on to earn a master's degree (1944) and a doctoral degree (1948) in economics from Duke University, which she attended as a scholarship student. Kreps enjoyed a long career in academia, teaching and serving in administrative posts at such institutions as Hofstra College (now University) and Queens College, as well as at her alma mater Duke. In 1968 she became the last dean of Duke's Women's College, overseeing the merger of the men's and women's divisions. She was named Duke's vice president in 1973. The year before Kreps had become the first female director in the history of the New York Stock Exchange. (Over the course of her career, she also served as a director of some of the country's biggest corporations, including J.C. Penney, Citicorp, and AT&T.) Kreps had a particular interest in labor demographics. In one of her best-known books, *Sex in the Marketplace: American Women at Work* (1971), she pondered such questions as why women entered the same limited number of occupations year after year, why they earned fewer advanced degrees than men, and why so many were willing to exchange the monotony of housework for equally dull office jobs. The many other books she wrote or edited include *Automation and Employment* (1964), *Lifetime Allocation of Work and Leisure: Essays in the Economy of Aging* (1971), and *Women and the American Economy: A*

Look to the 1980s (1976). Kreps—who had worked in Washington as part of the National War Labor Board in the mid-1940s—met Jimmy Carter late in 1976, after his election as president, when she was invited to brief him on economic issues. Soon afterward reports began to circulate that she was under consideration for a governmental post. At first she did not take the reports seriously since she had not campaigned for Carter and had not been looking for a job in Washington, which would separate her from her family in Durham, North Carolina. But on December 20 the president-elect announced her nomination to be secretary of commerce. She was confirmed by the Senate, and on January 23, 1977 she was sworn in at the White House. In her new post Kreps managed some 38,000 Commerce Department employees, promoted international trade, recorded trademarks and patents, and oversaw billions of dollars in public-works projects. While in Washington Kreps lived in an apartment overlooking the Potomac, commuting to the family home in Durham on weekends to be with her husband, the economics professor Clifton H. Kreps Jr., whom she had married in 1944, and their three children. In 1979, the year she negotiated an historic trade agreement with China, Clifton Kreps attempted suicide. Anxious about her family, Kreps resigned from the Carter administration and returned to her post at Duke. She retired from the school as vice president emeritus. The Juanita and Clifton Kreps chair in economics was established there in 1985. During her later years Kreps served on a number of government commissions, and by the time she died, at age 89, from complications of Alzheimer's disease, she had received more than a dozen honorary degrees and numerous other accolades. Kreps is survived by a daughter, Laura Anne; a son, Clifton III, and four grandchildren. Her husband died in 2000, and Kreps was also predeceased by her daughter Sarah. See *Current Biography* (1977). —H.R.W.

Obituary *New York Times* A p22 July 8, 2010

LAMBSDORFF, OTTO Dec. 20, 1926–Dec. 5, 2009 German politician. Otto Lambsdorff, who served as West Germany's minister of economics from 1977 to 1984, became known later in life as the architect of an historic program that offered reparations to Nazi-era slave laborers. A member of the Free Democratic Party (FDP), a minor party that provided the swing vote in several coalition governments, he was an ardent free marketer who fought for lower corporate taxes and opposed trade unions. Otto Count Lambsdorff—whose full name was Otto Friedrich Wilhelm von der Wenge Graf Lambsdorff—was a native of the Rhineland industrial city of Aachen, although his family domain was in the Baltic region, where his ancestors had moved from Westphalia some 700 years ago. He was the son of Herbert Count Lambsdorff and his wife, the former Eva von Schmid. After spending his early years in Berlin, Lambsdorff studied for three years in the Spartan atmosphere of the Ritterakademie Dom, in Brandenburg on the Havel, a school where the sons of the aristocracy were groomed for careers in the civil service, the military, or agriculture. Lambsdorff was drafted into the Wehrmacht (German military) in 1944. He was in-

jured in a Soviet air attack in March 1945, and his left leg was subsequently amputated at the upper thigh. Freed as a prisoner of war after Germany's surrender, Lambsdorff learned to walk again, at first with the aid of crutches and later with an artificial leg and a cane. From 1947 to 1950 he studied law and political science at the universities of Bonn and Cologne, and in 1950 he passed his first state bar examination, qualifying as a junior barrister. In 1952 Lambsdorff obtained a doctorate in jurisprudence at Cologne University, and three years later he passed his second state examination and qualified as an assistant judge. However, he decided on a more lucrative career in banking instead. Lambsdorff was a fiscal conservative and was known for his fierce support of the free market. A member of the FDP since 1951, he was elected to the Bundestag (parliament) for North Rhine-Westphalia in 1972. In Bonn (which was the capital of West Germany from 1949 to 1990 and then the seat of government for a united Germany from 1990 to 1999) Lamsbdorff became a spokesman on economic affairs. He was selected by Helmut Schmidt, the leader of the Social Democratic Party, to become the minister of economics in 1977; the party hoped he would bring a pro-business slant to the left-leaning coalition government. During the early 1980s Lambsdorff, dismayed at what he saw as a drift toward a welfare state, persuaded his party to ally with the conservative Christian Democrats, and in 1982, under the new chancellor, Helmut Kohl, he retained the economics ministry. In 1984 it was revealed that FDP members had received illegal political contributions from a major conglomerate. Although Lambsdorff was acquitted on corruption charges, he was fined for tax evasion and resigned his ministry. Nonetheless, he retained his popularity within the FDP and served as chair of the party from 1988 to 1993. In 1998 Chancellor Gerhard Schroeder selected him to negotiate with the U.S. in the matter of Nazi-era slave-labor reparations. A number of German companies were then confronting class-action lawsuits filed in U.S. courts on behalf of those who were forced into slave labor under the Nazis. The talks, which lasted for two years, resulted in a reparations package worth some $5 billion. Former slave laborers received $7,500 each, and a group of non-Jewish laborers who had been forced to work for minimal pay received $2,500 each. "It was imperfect justice," Stuart Eizenstat, a Bill Clinton administration official who had worked with Lambsdorff on the package, told Dennis Hevesi for the *New York Times* (December 9, 2009, on-line), "but without the settlement the victims would have had great difficulty ever recovering in a court of law. Count Lambsdorff made it possible for people to be paid within their lifetimes, and for their suffering to be recognized." Lambsdorff married Renate Lepper in 1953; the couple had two daughters and a son. From 1995 until his death, in Bonn, he was married to Alexandra von Quistorp. See *Current Biography* (1980). —W.D.

Obituary *New York Times* (on-line) Dec. 9, 2009

LÉVI-STRAUSS, CLAUDE Nov. 28, 1908–Oct. 30, 2009 Anthropologist. Claude Lévi-Strauss was designated "the father of modern anthropology" for his theory that primitive and modern societies share common thoughts and behaviors. "A powerful thinker, Lévi-Strauss, in studying the mythologies of primitive tribes, transformed the way the 20th century came to understand civilization itself," Edward Rothstein wrote for a *New York Times* obituary (November 4, 2009) of him. "He became the premier representative of 'structuralism,' a school of thought in which universal 'structures' were believed to underlie all human activity, giving shape to seemingly disparate cultures and creations." Lévi-Strauss was born to Raymond and Emmy (Lévy) Lévi-Strauss, both Jewish artists, in Brussels, Belgium. His great-grandfather was the renowned violinist Isaac Strauss. Lévi-Strauss grew up in Paris, France, attending the Lycée Janson-de-Sailly, where he was introduced to the writings of the German political philosopher Karl Marx. In 1927 he studied law and philosophy at the University of Paris (also known as the Sorbonne), graduating in 1932, the year he married Dina Dreyfus. Upon completion of his studies, he returned to the Lycée Janson and taught alongside Jean-Paul Sartre and Simone de Beauvoir. In the mid- to late 1930s, Lévi-Strauss began teaching sociology at the University of São Paulo, in Brazil. In his quest to become an anthropologist, he conducted fieldwork in the country's Amazon rainforest, studying the language, rituals, and myths of indigenous tribes including the Caduveo, Bororo, Nambikwara, and Tupi-Kawahib, who were viewed as savages by the "civilized" world. "I was envisaging a way of reconciling my professional education with my taste for adventure," he recalled to Didier Eribon for *Conversations with Lévi-Strauss* (1988). "I felt I was reliving the adventures of the first 16th-century explorers." Lévi-Strauss returned to France in 1939, prior to the start of World War II, and was conscripted into military service, serving as a French army officer, handling liaison with the British. In 1941, after the fall of France to the Germans, he fled the country by boat and settled in New York City, after accepting a visiting professorship funded by a Rockefeller Foundation grant. While teaching ethnology at the New School for Social Research, he spent hundreds of hours at the New York Public Library. "What I know of anthropology I learned during those years," Adam Kufer quoted him as saying in the London *Independent* (November 4, 2009). Lévi-Strauss also befriended several intellectuals, including Roman Jakobson, who introduced him to structural linguistics, which examines the formation and structures of languages and the relationships among words. Lévi-Strauss would apply this method of analysis to human culture. Appearing on the National Public Radio program *All Things Considered* (November 2, 2009), Neil Chudgar, a cultural and literary professor at Macalester College, explained: "[Lévi-Strauss] teaches us to believe that culture in general works very much the way language does; that all kinds of cultural forms from myths, to structures of kinship, to novels and movies work in the way that language does, by organizing individual elements and systems, so that any individual element—a word or a practice or a ritual or an event—derives its meaning from its relationship to all the other elements in the same system." After World War II ended, Lévi-Strauss worked as a cultural attaché for the French government before returning to France in 1947. In 1949, a year after earning his doctorate in letters from the University of Paris, he wrote *The Elementary Structures of Kinship (Les Structures Élémentaires de la parente@)* in which he explored human kinship systems. He was named assistant director of the Musée de l'Homme in Paris, a post he held until 1950, when he became director of anthropology studies at the École Pratique des Hautes Études (also in Paris), where he remained until 1974. Lévi-Strauss, who also chaired the social-anthropology department at the Collège de France (1959–82), received international recognition with the publication of the memoir *Tristes Tropiques* (1955), which chronicles his travels in Brazil. His subsequent books include *Structural Anthropology* (1961), *The Savage Mind* (1962), and *Totemism* (1962). Next came his main anthropological work, the four-volume *Mythologiques* (the final volume was published in 1971), which explores the origins of cooking and the uses of tobacco and honey in relation to culture and also focuses on the parallel development of North and South American tribal customs and myths, among other topics. Lévi-Strauss was a member of the prestigious Académie Française, the National Academy of Sciences, the American Academy and Institute of Arts and Letters, the American Academy of Arts and Sciences, and the American Philosophical Society, among other institutions. His honors included the Légion d'honneur (1964), the Wenner-Gren Foundation's Viking Fund Medal (1966), the Erasmus Prize (1975), the Meister-Eckhart Prize for philosophy (2003), and the James Smithson Bicentennial Medal (2009) from the Smithsonian Institution. Lévi-Strauss suffered a fatal heart attack at his home in Paris. He is survived by his third wife, Monique Roman, and their son, Matthieu, as well as another son, Laurent, from his second marriage, to Rose-Marie Ullmo. His first two marriages ended in divorce. See *Current Biography* (1972).—W.D.

Obituary *New York Times* (on-line) Nov. 4, 2009

LEVINE, DAVID Dec. 20, 1926–Dec. 29, 2009 Caricaturist, illustrator, artist. David Levine was described by the famed cartoonist Jules Feiffer as "the most important political caricaturist [of his day]," according to Bruce Weber, writing for the *New York Times* (December 30, 2009, on-line). The art critic Robert Hughes told Michael Kimmelman for the *New York Times* (December 31, 2009, on-line): "Most caricature is no more than cartooning. But with Levine you always knew there was some truth emanating from the drawings. You always had the sense he was telling a truth, even when it was most unwelcome." Levine's work appeared in such periodicals as *Esquire*, *Rolling Stone*, the *New York Times*, the *New Yorker*, *Playboy*, and *Time*, and from 1963 to 2007 he contributed close to 4,000 pen-and-ink caricatures to the *New York Review of Books*, the venerable publication with which he was most closely linked. "His cerebral, brooding faces quickly became identifiable as, well, the cerebral, brooding face of the publication," Weber asserted. Levine's career constituted, according to David Margolick, writing for *Vanity Fair* (November 2008), "one of the most remarkable runs in the history of journalism and art. . . . In the course of it, more than anyone before him, Levine put together a facebook of human history." Levine was born in the New York City borough of Brooklyn. His father, Harry, ran a small garment shop, and his mother, Lena, was a nurse and political activist with Communist sympathies. After a two-year stint in the U.S. Army, Levine earned a degree from Temple University's Tyler School of Art, in Philadelphia, Pennsylvania. Concurrently, he obtained an education degree from Temple. Upon graduating, in 1949, he moved back to New York City, where he studied painting at the Pratt Institute and came under the influence of the renowned Abstract Expressionist Hans Hofmann. Levine's watercolor paintings of factory workers and ordinary people at the beach in Coney Island stood in stark contrast to his biting caricatures. In 1958, along with the artist Aaron Shikler, Levine founded the Painting Group, a salon that met for the next several decades. Because he could not earn enough money with his paintings to make a living, Levine also found work drawing Christmas cards and making illustrations for such publications as *Gasoline Retailer*. His career as a caricaturist began in the early 1960s, when he found work making political illustrations for *Esquire*. Levine's first piece appeared in the *New York Review of Books* in 1963, a few months after the publication's inaugural issue. Margolick described Levine's working relationship with the left-leaning, intellectual periodical: "A remarkable ritual quickly developed. Pretty much every other Thursday for the next 40 years, a messenger from the *Review* would drop off an envelope at the Heights Casino, on Montague Street, where Levine played tennis, a few blocks from his apartment. In it were photographs of the people he was to draw for the next issue, along with the articles about them. . . . Tuesdays, the messenger would return to the Casino to pick up what he'd drawn." While his most famous drawing was based on a well-known photo of U.S. president Lyndon B. Johnson pulling up his shirt to reveal a scar from an operation, which Levine drew in the shape of Vietnam, his most frequent subject was Richard Nixon, whom he sketched more than 60 times. "Especially in his political work, his portraits betrayed the mind of an artist concerned, worriedly concerned, about the world in which he lived," Weber wrote. "Mr. Levine's drawings sent out angry distress signals that the world was too much a puppet in the hands of too few puppeteers." Another of his frequent subjects, the writer John Updike, was quoted on the *Review*'s Web site: "Besides offering us the delight of recognition, his drawings comfort us, in an exacerbated and potentially desperate age, with the sense of a watching presence, an eye informed by an intelligence that has not panicked, a comic art ready to encapsulate the latest apparitions of publicity as well as those historical devils who haunt our unease. Levine is one of America's assets. In a confusing time, he bears witness. In a shoddy time, he does good work." After being diagnosed with macular degeneration, an eye disease that leads to blindness, Levine found it increasingly difficult to create new works. His last original drawing (of the novelist Howard Norman) appeared in the *Review* in April 2007. Levine's name continued to appear on the masthead of the publication. Some 2,500 of Levine's caricatures are archived on the *New York Review of Books* Web site. His work

is included in the permanent collections of New York City's Metropolitan Museum of Art and London's National Portrait Gallery, among other institutions. It has been collected in several books, including *Pens and Needles* (1969), *The Arts of David Levine* (1978), and *American Presidents* (2008). Levine—whose many laurels included the Louis Comfort Tiffany Foundation Award, the George Polk Memorial Award, a Guggenheim Fellowship, the Childe Hassam Purchase Prize from the American Academy of Arts and Letters, and the French Legion of Honor—died of prostate cancer at New York Presbyterian Hospital. He is survived by his second wife, Kathy Hayes; two children, Matthew and Eve; and two stepchildren, Nancy and Christopher. See *Current Biography* (1973) —M.M.

Obituary *New York Times* (on-line) Dec. 29, 2009

LINCOLN, ABBEY Aug. 6, 1930–Aug. 14, 2010 Jazz singer; songwriter; actress. Abbey Lincoln was a daring jazz singer and poetic songwriter who worked with such jazz legends as Max Roach, her husband for many years, and Sonny Rollins. She was born Anna Marie Wooldridge in Chicago, Illinois, and raised on a farm in rural Calvin Center, Michigan. Her father, who worked as a handyman, frequently borrowed records from his customers to bring home and play on the family's Victrola phonograph, which was housed in a cabinet. The family, while poor, owned an upright piano, and at the age of five, Lincoln began to play. The 10th of 12 children, she found solace in music. At 14 she became enchanted with a Billie Holiday recording and began listening to other great jazz singers, including Ella Fitzgerald, Sarah Vaughan, and Lena Horne. After winning a local singing contest at age 19, she travelled west and spent two years as a nightclub singer in Honolulu, Hawaii, where she met her idol, Billie Holiday, and Louis Armstrong. Performing at the Moulin Rouge in Los Angeles, California, she met the lyricist Bob Russell, who became her manager and suggested that she adopt the stage name Abbey Lincoln. She recorded her first album, *Affair: A Story of a Girl in Love*, in 1956. Later that year she appeared in the film *The Girl Can't Help It*, starring Jayne Mansfield. Although she had only a small singing role, Lincoln attracted attention for wearing a dress that Marilyn Monroe had worn in *Gentlemen Prefer Blondes*, prompting *Ebony* magazine to feature her on the cover of its June 1957 issue. As her profile as a sex symbol grew, Lincoln began to worry that it might undermine her singing career. Her relationship with the jazz drummer Max Roach, whom she met in the mid-1950s and married in 1962, helped convince her of the importance of her music. In the late 1950s, on the advice of Roach, she moved to New York City, where she met and worked with such jazz legends as John Coltrane, Sonny Rollins, and Thelonious Monk. In 1957 Lincoln recorded for the Riverside label what is considered to be her first real jazz album, *That's Him*, with an ensemble that included Roach, Rollins, and others. She followed that up with *It's Magic* (1958) and *Abbey Is Blue* (1959). Lincoln meanwhile found herself drawn to the emerging civil rights movement, particularly after witnessing, while on tour, the extent to which many African-American communities were mired in poverty. In an expression of pride in her cultural heritage, she began wearing her hair in an Afro, becoming one of the first stage singers to do so. In 1960 she sang on Roach's controversial civil rights album, *We Insist! Freedom Now Suite*. One of the tracks on that avant-garde record features Lincoln screaming along with Roach's drumming—a performance that shocked many listeners. During that period she began to write lyrics, mostly for other jazz composers' previously wordless tunes. She supplied lyrics, for example, for John Coltrane's "Africa" and Thelonious Monk's "Blue Monk," the latter of which she recorded on her 1961 album, *Straight Ahead*. Although that effort proved her talent as a songwriter, it alienated some critics because of its outspoken racial politics. As a result, Lincoln received fewer record offers in the years that followed. In the mid-1960s the door to a promising film career opened for Lincoln, beginning with a starring role in Michael Roemer's 1964 film, *Nothing But a Man*, about racial relations in Alabama. Four years later she starred as a white family's maid, opposite Sidney Poitier, in Daniel Mann's romantic comedy *For the Love of Ivy*. After a painful divorce from Roach, in 1970, and a subsequent mental breakdown, she moved to Los Angeles, California, where she took minor parts in television shows, read a great deal, learned to paint, and wrote poetry. A two-month trip to Africa in 1972 inspired her, and upon her return to the U.S., she composed the songs for the album *People in Me* (1973). She continued to write lyrics and train as a vocalist for the next several years, all to the apparent indifference of the music industry. Lincoln moved back to New York City in 1981 and started performing in nightclubs again. In 1983 she recorded *Talking to the Sun*. Two other albums followed—volumes one and two of *Abbey Sings Billie*—but it was *The World Is Falling Down* (1990) that marked the beginning of her highly celebrated comeback. The record was notable not only for her singing but also her emotional, poetic songwriting. In 1990 the director Spike Lee cast her in a small role in his film *Mo' Better Blues*. Lincoln's next release, *You Gotta Pay the Band* (1991), which paired her with the eminent jazz saxophonist Stan Getz, fared even better than her previous album. *Devil's Got Your Tongue* (1992), for which Lincoln wrote nine of the 11 songs, also reached the top of the jazz charts. The highly acclaimed *A Turtle's Dream* (1994), also featuring nine original songs, earned Lincoln a Grammy Award nomination and appeared on numerous critics' album-of-the-year lists. Lincoln wrote seven of the 10 songs on *Wholly Earth* (1998), which was followed by *Over the Years* (2000) and *Abbey Sings Abbey* (2007). Lincoln, who never remarried, lived her last years on Manhattan's Upper West Side. She is survived by her brothers, David and Kenneth, and a sister, Juanita. See *Current Biography* (2002). —D.K.

Obituary *New York Times* (on-line) Aug. 14, 2010

LINKLETTER, ART July 17, 1912–May 26, 2010 Radio and television personality. Art Linkletter entertained millions of people as the host of *People Are*

Funny and *House Party*, long-running shows that aired in the 1950s and '60s. Although he was sometimes accused by critics of being bland and uncharismatic, he had a particular talent for interacting with children, and he was perhaps best known for a *House Party* segment called "Kids Say the Darndest Things," in which his young interview subjects often gave unintentionally amusing answers to his questions. The entertainer was born Arthur Gordon (some sources say Gordon Arthur) Kelly in Moose Jaw, Saskatchewan, Canada. Before he was one month old, he was abandoned by his parents and adopted by Fulton John Linkletter, a one-legged shoemaker and itinerant evangelist, and his wife, Mary. When Linkletter was three years old, the family moved to California. There they held revival meetings, with Linkletter playing the triangle during hymns. Following his high-school graduation, Linkletter traveled around the country taking odd jobs, including stints as a busboy in Chicago, a stevedore on the New Orleans docks, a meatpacker in Minnesota, a clerk on Wall Street during the historic days of the 1929 stock-market crash, and a merchant seaman on a Buenos Aires–bound freighter. He later returned to California to study at San Diego State Teachers College (now San Diego State University), earning his tuition as a switchboard operator, bouncer, ranch hand, and lifeguard, among other occupations. Because of his talkative nature, Linkletter was hired as an announcer for KGB, a radio station in San Diego, during his junior year of college. After graduating, in 1934, Linkletter continued to work at KGB and ultimately became the station's chief announcer. In 1937 he became the radio director for the San Francisco World's Fair, for which he wrote two theme spectacles, *Cavalcade of the Golden West* and *Cavalcade of a Nation*. He left two years later to become a freelance radio announcer and master of ceremonies. Linkletter moved to Hollywood in 1942 and landed a job hosting the NBC radio program *People Are Funny*, which featured ad-libbing, contests, gags, and audience participation. The program could be heard on the radio from 1942 to 1960, and a television version aired from 1954 to 1961. Linkletter also hosted the CBS variety and talk show *House Party*, which aired on the radio from 1945 to 1967 and on television from 1952 to 1969. *House Party*, like *People Are Funny*, featured gags and contests, as well as the popular "Kids Say the Darndest Things" segment. (Linkletter's book *Kids Say the Darndest Things* was illustrated by the popular cartoonist Charles M. Schulz and published in 1957. A sequel, *Kids Still Say the Darndest Things*, was published in 1961.) In 1969 Linkletter's daughter Diane, then 20 years old, jumped to her death from her sixth-floor apartment. Linkletter maintained that LSD had contributed to her death. Although an autopsy revealed no evidence of the drug in her system, Linkletter began to speak out against drug use and later served on President Richard Nixon's National Advisory Council for Drug Abuse Prevention. After Linkletter left broadcasting, he became an in-demand lecturer and commercial spokesperson. He also wrote several books, including: *Women Are My Favorite People* (1974), *How to Be a Super Salesman: Linkletter's Art of Persuasion* (1974), *Public Speaking for Private People* (1980), *Hobo on the Way to Heaven* (1980),

My Child on Drugs?: Youth and the Drug Culture (1981), *Old Age Is Not for Sissies* (1990), and *How to Make the Rest of Your Life the Best of Your Life* (2006). Additionally, he chaired Linkletter Enterprises, which invested in oil wells, manufacturing plants, restaurants, real estate, mobile storage units, a bowling alley, and a skating rink, among other ventures. He also served as a spokesman for USA Next (a conservative lobbying group devoted to privatizing Social Security) and as a successful fundraiser for various Republican candidates. A TV show called *Kids Say the Darndest Things*, hosted by the comedian Bill Cosby, aired from 1998 to 2000, and Linkletter made regular appearances on the program, introducing himself to a new generation of viewers. Linkletter died at his home in Bel Air, California, at the age of 97. He was predeceased by three of his five children. In addition to Diane, his son Robert died in a 1980 car accident, and his son Jack died of lymphoma in 2007. Linkletter is survived by his wife, the former Lois Foerster; his daughters Sharon and Dawn; and several grandchildren and great-grandchildren. See *Current Biography* (1953). —J.P.

Obituary *New York Times* (on-line) May 26, 2010

MANDELBROT, BENOÎT Nov. 20, 1924–Oct. 14, 2010 Mathematician. Benoît Mandelbrot is known for his pioneering work in the field of fractal geometry, considered one of the most important developments in modern mathematics. The term fractal refers to a group of shapes whose irregular contours mimic those found in coastlines, clouds, snowflakes, and brain tissue; the behavior of earthquakes, the patterns of the weather, the growth of the human brain, and even the distribution of galaxies in space are a few of the irregular or chaotic phenomena that have begun yielding the secrets of their structures thanks to the new geometry. Mandelbrot, who was of Jewish descent, was born in Warsaw, Poland, to Bella (Lurie) Mandelbrot, a doctor, and Charles Mandelbrot, a clothing manufacturer. At the start of World War II, the family moved to France to escape the Nazis. After Paris was liberated, in 1944, Mandelbrot attended two of the country's leading science schools, the École Normale Supérieure and the École Polytechnique. After earning an undergraduate degree, in 1947, he traveled to the U.S. and entered the California Institute of Technology, in Pasadena, earning an M.S. degree in aeronautics the following year. After a stint in the French air force, Mandelbrot studied at the University of Paris, where in 1952 he received a doctoral degree in mathematics. He subsequently won a one-year fellowship to work with the renowned mathematician John von Neumann at the Institute for Advanced Study in Princeton, New Jersey. After his year in Princeton, Mandelbrot spent three years in Europe, first in Geneva and then in France, where he taught mathematics at the University of Lille and the École Polytechnique and continued an association that he had begun in 1949 at the Centre National de la Recherche Scientifique (National Center for Scientific Research) in Paris. In 1958 Mandelbrot joined the staff of the technology giant IBM, while working at the company's Yorktown Heights, New York–based Thomas J. Watson Research Center

as a faculty adviser. In 1962 Mandelbrot, whose interests were so wide-ranging that he sometimes despaired of finding a permanent home in any single university department, began serving as a visiting professor of economics, a research fellow in psychology, a visiting professor of applied mathematics, and a staff member of the Joint Committee on Biomedical Computer Science at Harvard University. In 1987 he began to teach at Yale, where he earned tenure in 1999. Fractal geometry, which he is credited with developing, has been applied to the fields of biology, physics, finance, geology, and engineering, among others. The author of such seminal works as *Fractals: Form, Chance, and Dimension* (1977) and *The Fractal Geometry of Nature* (1982), Mandelbrot died in Cambridge, Massachusetts, of pancreatic cancer. He is survived by his wife, Aliette; his two sons, Laurent and Didier; and three grandchildren. See *Current Biography* (1987). —J.P.

Obituary *New York Times* (on-line) Oct. 16, 2010

MANKILLER, WILMA Nov. 18, 1945–Apr. 6, 2010 Former chief of the Cherokee Nation. When Wilma Mankiller was sworn in as principal chief of the Cherokee Nation, in December 1985, she became the first woman ever to serve as leader of a major North American Indian tribe. Mankiller was born to a Caucasian mother and a full-blooded Cherokee father in Tahlequah, Oklahoma. (The surname Mankiller comes from a high Cherokee military rank that a male ancestor had adopted.) She spent her early childhood on a 160-acre tract known as Mankiller Flats. The land was given to her grandfather as part of a settlement the U.S. government made with the Cherokee after they were forced, in 1838, to march on what became known as the Trail of Tears from their traditional home in the southeastern part of the country to "Indian territory" in Oklahoma. Further hardship followed when the federal government dismantled the Cherokee tribal government in 1907 and reapportioned their lands. The Cherokee Nation was legally reconstituted in 1971, on 7,000 square miles in northeastern Oklahoma. Mankiller's family, which included 11 children, lived in abject poverty, without indoor plumbing or electricity. After their farm was ruined by two years of drought, Mankiller, then 12 years old, moved with her family to San Francisco, California, under a Bureau of Indian Affairs relocation program. During the 1960s Mankiller, who eventually adjusted to city life, studied sociology, worked as a social worker, married a wealthy Ecuadorian accountant, and gave birth to two daughters, Gina and Felicia. In 1969, inspired by a group of young activists who had taken over the property that once housed Alcatraz prison, in San Francisco Bay, she became active in the Native American rights movement. She later found work as the Native American programs coordinator for the Oakland, California, school system, and in the mid-1970s she divorced her husband and returned to Oklahoma to claim her grandfather's land. In 1977 she got a job as economic-stimulus coordinator for the Cherokee Nation. Concurrently, she continued her studies, earning a B.A. degree in social science from Flaming Rainbow University, in Stilwell, Oklahoma. In 1979 the car she was driving crashed head-on into another vehicle that was driven by a friend. The friend was killed, and Mankiller was so badly injured that she required 17 surgeries. Despite such trials, in 1981 she founded the Community Development Department of the Cherokee Nation and became its director. In that post she instituted several innovative programs meant to foster community self-help, including the development of rural water systems and the rehabilitation of housing. Her work drew the attention of Ross O. Swimmer, then the principal chief of the Cherokee Nation, who selected her as his running mate in the tribal elections of 1983. The ticket was successful, and Mankiller became the first woman to serve as deputy chief of the Cherokee people. Two years later Swimmer was appointed head of the Bureau of Indian Affairs in Washington, D.C., and Mankiller was sworn in as principal chief on December 15, 1985, becoming the first woman to hold that position. Despite initial skepticism on the part of some members of the Cherokee Nation, she was elected in her own right in 1987, and in 1991 she retained her post by an overwhelming margin. Sam Howe Verhovek wrote for the *New York Times* (April 6, 2010, on-line) that as the leader of the Cherokee Nation, Mankiller served as "both the principal guardian of centuries of Cherokee tradition and customs, including legal codes, and chief executive of a tribe with a budget that reached $150 million a year by the end of her tenure." Mankiller—who suffered at various times from lymphoma, myasthenia gravis, and kidney problems that necessitated a transplant—stepped down in 1995 because of failing health, but she remained active in tribal affairs in an advisory capacity. In 1998 she was awarded the U.S. Medal of Freedom. Mankiller died at her home in Oklahoma of pancreatic cancer and is survived by her second husband, Charlie Soap; her daughters; her mother; several siblings; and four grandchildren. See *Current Biography* (1988). —M.R.

Obituary *New York Times* (on-line) Apr. 6, 2010

MATHIAS, CHARLES July 24, 1922–Jan. 25, 2010 Former U.S. legislator. During his four terms in the U.S. House of Representatives (1961–69) and three terms in the U.S. Senate (1969–87), Charles Mathias, a liberal Republican from Maryland, played an influential role in drafting civil rights legislation and in ending the Vietnam War. The first of three children of Charles McCurdy and Theresa McElfresh Mathias, Charles McCurdy Mathias Jr., known as "Mac," was born in Frederick, Maryland. The family was prosperous up until the Great Depression. Mathias attended Haverford College, in Pennsylvania, but left in 1942 to enlist in the U.S. Navy. He was sent to the V-12 naval-training unit at Yale University and to the Midshipmen's School at Columbia University. The credits he earned at those schools were accepted by Haverford, which awarded him a bachelor's degree in 1944. Commissioned as an ensign in 1944, Mathias served in the Philippines and Japan during World War II, before being discharged in 1946. He then earned a law degree from the University of Maryland in 1949. After several years of practicing law in Frederick, Mathias was appointed assistant attorney general of Maryland in 1953 and then served as Frederick's city attorney from 1954 to

1959. He successfully ran for the Maryland House of Delegates in 1958, and two years later he defeated the Democrat John R. Foley in the election for Maryland's Sixth Congressional District seat in the U.S. House. As a member of the Judiciary Committee, Mathias was involved in shaping the 1964 Civil Rights Act. Mathias pledged his support to the civil rights leader Martin Luther King Jr. and fought to achieve voting and housing rights for African-Americans. He was elected to the U.S. Senate in 1968, defeating the Democratic incumbent Daniel Brewster, a friend and former classmate. Though he supported President Richard Nixon early in his administration, Mathias was a vocal critic of Nixon's Vietnam War policies and his involvement in the Watergate scandal. In the 1970s Mathias was an advocate of public campaign financing and of capping campaign contributions, measures that were enacted in 1974. During the presidential administration of Ronald Reagan, Mathias criticized the increasingly right-leaning policies of the Republican Party and fought Reagan's efforts to repeal civil rights victories. Over the course of his legislative career, Mathias also worked to strengthen ties with Europe and was influential in the preservation of the Chesapeake Bay and the construction of the Vietnam Veterans Memorial in Washington, D.C. After Mathias retired from the Senate, in 1987, he practiced law in Washington, D.C. Mathias, who died from complications of Parkinson's disease at his home in Chevy Chase, Maryland, is survived by his wife of more than 50 years, Ann Bradford Mathias; his two sons, Robert and Charles; two grandchildren; a sister; and a brother. See *Current Biography* (1972). —M.A.S.

Obituary *New York Times* B p18 Jan. 26, 2010

MCCLANAHAN, RUE Feb. 21, 1934–June 3, 2010 Actress. Rue McClanahan was best known for her role as Blanche Devereuux—an aging southern belle—on the TV sitcom *The Golden Girls*, which aired from 1985 to 1992 and still runs in syndication. "People always ask me if I'm like Blanche," McClanahan often joked to reporters. "Well, Blanche was an oversexed, self-involved, man-crazy, vain southern belle from Atlanta—and I'm not from Atlanta." Of Irish and Native American ancestry, Eddi-Rue McClanahan was born in Healdton, Oklahoma, the older of the two daughters of William Edwin McClanahan, a building contractor, and the former Dreda Rheua-Nell Medaris, a beautician. (Her given name is a contraction of her parents' middle names.) She made her stage debut at the age of four, appearing in a local production of *The Three Little Kittens*, and by age 12 she was determined to make a living as an actress one day. Turning down offers of dance scholarships, McClanahan majored in drama at the University of Tulsa, in Oklahoma. After graduating, in 1956, she headed for New York City. She made her professional debut the following year as Rachel in *Inherit the Wind* at the Erie Playhouse in Pennsylvania. She appeared there in several other productions before heading for the West Coast, where she enrolled in a four-week course at the Pasadena Playhouse and also won one of its scholarships. Among her roles was that of Blanche DuBois in *A Streetcar Named Desire*. After assignments at the Pasadena

Playhouse became scarce, she interspersed small roles in movies and television with odd jobs as a waitress, secretary, and clothing saleswoman. In 1964 a director asked her to come to New York City to play Hazel in an Off-Broadway musical production of James Thurber's short story *The Secret Life of Walter Mitty*, and over the next several years McClanahan compiled an impressive list of theater credits. She made her Broadway debut in 1968, in the supporting role of the prostitute Sally Weber in *Jimmy Shine*, a comedy that also starred Dustin Hoffman. In 1970 she took on the role of Caroline Johnson, a nanny who becomes so enamored of her boss that she tries to poison his wife with a variety of cream soups, on the NBC soap opera *Another World*. She later appeared in the soaps *Where the Heart Is* and *Love of Life*. Concurrently she remained in demand for film work, taking on roles in such pictures as *The People Next Door* (1970), *They Might Be Giants* (1971), and *The Pursuit of Happiness* (1971), as well as on the stage, where she appeared in a 1970 Off-Broadway revival of *Dark of the Moon* and a 1972 production of *Dylan*, a biographical play about the writer Dylan Thomas, among other such assignments. McClanahan achieved the most visibility that decade for her work on the groundbreaking TV series *Maude*, which starred Bea Arthur as an opinionated feminist. McClanahan co-starred as Vivian, Maude's traditionally minded neighbor. The program, which was directed by Norman Lear, ran from 1972 to 1978. McClanahan's next notable TV role was that of the high-strung spinster Aunt Fran in the NBC sitcom *Mama's Family*, on which she appeared from 1983 to 1985. In the latter year McClanahan was cast in *The Golden Girls*, which premiered on September 14, 1985. The show, which revolved around four aging single women who share a house in a retirement resort in Miami, co-starred Bea Arthur as the strong-willed Dorothy; Estelle Getty as Dorothy's feisty mother, Sophia; and Betty White, as the kind-hearted but dim-witted Rose. Consistently one of the top-rated programs in its time slot, *The Golden Girls* attracted a loyal audience that continues to view it in syndication. "Rue McClanahan . . . had the toughest role on *The Golden Girls*. Most of the sly punch lines went to Dorothy (Bea Arthur) and Sophia (Estelle Getty); Betty White's Rose got all those delightfully daffy little asides, all those opportunities to tell winding tales of [her midwestern home-town of] St. Olaf," Linda Holmes wrote for npr.org (June 3, 2010). "Blanche didn't get the best jokes, really; much of the humor there was in the sheer relish with which McClanahan played her. She was charged with being a woman of a kind we are *still* socially unskilled at handling: a sexually confident and aggressive woman over 50." After *The Golden Girls* discontinued production, McClanahan remained busy, guest-starring on such shows as *Murphy Brown*, *Safe Harbor*, and *Touched by an Angel*. In 2008 she also starred in *Sordid Lives: The Series*, a short-lived sitcom about a dysfunctional Texas family that aired on Logo, a network with programs intended for gay, lesbian, bisexual, and transgender communities. McClanahan, who· was divorced five times, is the author of a 2007 memoir, *My First Five Husbands . . . and the Ones Who Got Away*. While recovering from bypass surgery and a recent stroke,

she suffered a massive brain-aneurysm rupture at her New York City apartment and died shortly thereafter. She is survived by her sixth husband, Morrow Wilson, from whom she was separated at the time of her death; her son, Mark Bish; and her sister, Melinda Lou McClanahan. See *Current Biography* (1989). —D.K.

Obituary *New York Times* (on-line) June 3, 2010

McLAREN, MALCOLM Jan. 22, 1946–Apr. 8, 2010 Band manager; music promoter; punk-rock musician. Malcolm McLaren's role in the British punk movement earned him the moniker the "Godfather of Punk." He first became widely known as the manager of the influential punk band the Sex Pistols. After the band's breakup, in 1978, McLaren managed such musical acts as Adam and the Ants and Bow Wow Wow, made numerous television and film appearances in which he tried to explain the punk ethos, released four of his own studio albums, and took part in several other creative projects. Malcolm Robert Andrew McLaren was born in Stoke Newington, London, England. He spent very little time with his parents as a child; after his father left the family, when McLaren was two years old, he was raised by his wealthy maternal grandmother, Rose Corre Isaacs, whose motto was, "To be bad is good, to be good is simply boring," according to McLaren's obituary in the London *Independent* (April 10, 2010, on-line). In grade school he demonstrated a talent for manipulating his classmates, on one occasion luring them to a Dumpster and persuading them to get into a cardboard box so that they could be a part of his "box gang." A "brilliant but erratic art student," as Liam Lacey wrote for the Toronto *Globe and Mail* (February 2, 1985), McLaren attended as many as seven art schools before the age of 25, including St. Martin's School of Art, Harrow Art College, Chiswick Polytechnic (which expelled him in 1966), Croydon College of Art (whose administrators attempted to commit him to a mental hospital), and Goldsmiths College, where he ended his academic career, in 1971. McLaren's interests during his college years included rock music, a London-based group of anarchist pranksters called King Mob, the subversive art of Andy Warhol, and the French situationist philosophers, who instigated their chaotic "situations" to expose the injustices of class and power. After college McLaren decided to bring his art-school sensibilities to the area of capitalism. He and his fashion-designer business partner (and sometime girlfriend) Vivienne Westwood took over a clothing store in London's Chelsea neighborhood in 1971, called it Let It Rock (later renamed Too Fast to Live, Too Young to Die), and sold "Teddy boy" and punk-rock-style clothing, much of which was designed by Westwood. After a stay in New York City a couple of years later, during which he managed the proto–punk rock group the New York Dolls, McLaren returned to London intent on putting together a rock act. In the mid-1970s McLaren, working out of his and Westwood's store (then called Sex and selling fetishistic clothing), began working with a band called the Swankers. He ejected one of the band's members and helped the remaining three become famous, providing them with a new name, the

Sex Pistols, and a new singer—a skinny, slightly hunchbacked Cockney youth named John Lydon, whom McLaren gave the stage name Johnny Rotten because of the state of his teeth. McLaren found in Rotten the perfect figurehead for both the group and a rebellious new youth movement. With such socially provocative songs as "Anarchy in the U.K." and "God Save the Queen," which expressed a sense of nihilism and anger, the Sex Pistols gained a following while waging war against a stodgy British society. McLaren continued to attack traditional symbols by arranging for the band to sign its contract with A&M Records outside Buckingham Palace and organizing a performance of "God Save the Queen" on a boat situated on the Thames River outside the Houses of Parliament. The stunt was quickly halted by the police, and McLaren was arrested. The band released just one album, *Nevermind the Bullocks: Here's the Sex Pistols* (1977), which reached the number-one spot on the album charts. After the band's breakup, in 1978, McLaren briefly managed Adam Ant, the lead singer of the New Wave/post-punk group Adam and the Ants, before putting together the band Bow Wow Wow with Ant's backing musicians and the 14-year-old Burmese singer Annabella Lwin. McLaren tried his hand as a recording artist himself, releasing the influential album *Duck Rock* (1983), a blend of world music and hip-hop. McLaren recorded three more albums—*Fans* (1984), *Darling* (1989), and *Paris* (1994)—and remained a presence in the music, art, fashion, and film worlds. He produced the film *Fast Food Nation* (2006) and was also involved with two series on BBC2 Radio, *Malcolm McLaren's Musical Map of London* and *Malcolm McLaren's Life and Times in L.A.* McLaren was diagnosed with mesothelioma, a rare form of cancer that develops in the lining of internal organs, in October 2009. He died at the age of 64 in Switzerland. McLaren is survived by his son with Westwood, Joseph Corre, the founder of the lingerie company Agent Provocateur; his brother, Stuart Edwards; a grandchild; and Young Kim, a 37-year-old Korean-American fashion historian who was his companion for the last 12 years of his life. See *Current Biography* (1997). —H.R.W.

Obituary *New York Times* (on-line) Apr. 8, 2010

MCQUEEN, ALEXANDER Mar. 17, 1969–Feb. 11, 2010 Fashion designer. Alexander McQueen's designs were often unconventional and intentionally controversial. His futuristic and eccentric clothing is worn by such pop stars as Lady Gaga, Björk, and Rihanna, and he was designated British Designer of the Year four times. Lee Alexander McQueen was born in London, England, to a cab driver and a teacher. Along with his two older brothers and three older sisters, he grew up in the shabby Stratford section of London's East End. McQueen became aware of his homosexuality at a young age, and he was often teased by his classmates at the all-boys Rokeby School, who reportedly gave him the derogatory nickname "McQueer." Although McQueen's father wanted him to become a plumber or an electrician, he always knew he wanted to work in the fashion industry, and he left school at age 16 to take an apprenticeship on Savile Row, a street famous for its men's custom tailoring. He worked for a succession of London tailors, theatrical costumers, and designers before moving to Italy to work for nine months as a pattern cutter for the designer Romeo Gigli. Upon his return to London, McQueen entered the Central St. Martins College of Art and Design. His graduate collection greatly impressed the style icon and arts patron Isabella Blow, who subsequently became his unofficial public-relations representative. He graduated in 1992 and mounted a show in October of the following year. Industry observers were shocked and excited by the event, which featured dresses that appeared to be covered in blood as well as "bumsters," a term McQueen coined for his revealingly low-slung jeans and trousers. He continued to shock in subsequent years. In March 1995, for example, he mounted a show he dubbed "Highland Rape" (a reference to the forced uprooting, in the late 17th and early 18th centuries, of tens of thousands of Scots and the clearing of their land by English noblemen who used it to raise sheep). The models, whose eyes were hidden by opaque contact lenses, walked down a runway covered with heather and bracken in dresses with violently ripped bodices and hems. A later show, called "Dante," featured apparel printed with images of war (including portrayals of American soldiers and crippled Vietnamese civilians). Another show included models with their heads heavily bandaged, stumbling clumsily around a glass-walled room. In 1996 Moët Hennessy Louis Vuitton (LVMH), the world's largest and most successful luxury-goods conglomerate, announced that the company had signed McQueen to a five-year contract to head the much-celebrated fashion house of Givenchy, in Paris, France. McQueen's collections for Givenchy were not well received, and he often clashed with LVMH management. He left in 2001 to join the Milan-based Gucci Group, LVMH's major competitor, to whom he sold a majority stake in his own label. McQueen subsequently opened boutiques in London, New York City, Milan, Las Vegas, and Los Angeles. He also licensed his name for use on perfumes, created a lower-priced clothing line called McQ, and designed athletic shoes and suitcases for Puma. In 2009 McQueen—who once claimed to have sewn hanks of human hair into a group of jackets, as a reference to the 19th-century serial killer Jack the Ripper—attracted attention by sending models down a garbage-strewn runway as a commentary on the fashion industry's decline during the current economic downturn. McQueen had long suffered periods of depression and was reportedly despondent over the death on February 2, 2010 of his mother, Joyce, always one of his strongest supporters. McQueen was found hanged in his London apartment, the day before his mother's funeral. His death was ruled a suicide. He is survived by his father, Ron, and five siblings. See *Current Biography* (2002). —W.D.

Obituary *New York Times* (on-line) Feb. 11, 2010

MIHAJLOV, MIHAJLO Sep. 26, 1934–Mar. 7, 2010 Political dissident; writer. Mihajlo Mihajlov was an outspoken figure in the former Communist stronghold of Yugoslavia and was jailed for many years for his inflammatory writings about the government.

Mihajlov was born in Pancevo, Yugoslavia, near Belgrade. His parents were Russian émigrés who had met and married in Yugoslavia. Mihajlov studied comparative literature at the University of Belgrade and the University of Zagreb, receiving a degree from the latter institution in 1959. Following a period of service in the Yugoslav army, he worked in the city of Zagreb as a translator, wrote for several Yugoslav periodicals, and delivered lectures over the radio. Through those activities he became known as an expert on the writer Fyodor Dostoyevsky and post-Stalin Soviet literature. In December 1963 Mihajlov was appointed assistant professor in the philosophy department of the Zadar branch of Zagreb University, where he taught Russian literature while working on his doctoral dissertation. A collection of Mihajlov's literary, political, and philosophical essays, written over a five-year period beginning in 1961, was translated into English by his sister and published in 1968 under the title *Russian Themes*. In those essays Mihajlov used the works of Russian writers as a springboard for discussions of his own views on social and political issues. During the summer of 1964, Mihajlov spent five weeks in Moscow and Leningrad under a cultural-exchange program. He recounted the conversations he held with Russian writers during that visit in an essay that was published in two installments, both under the title "Moscow Summer 1964," in the January and February 1965 issues of the Belgrade literary periodical *Delo*. (In 1965 the essay was published as a book called *Moscow Summer*.) Mihajlov asserted that death camps had first been established not by the Nazis but by the Soviets, after the 1917 October Revolution, and that shortly before World War II, Stalin had committed genocide in regions along the Turkish-Iranian border. Mihajlov's assertions offended the Russian ambassador to Yugoslavia, and in 1966 Yugoslavia's president, Josip Broz Tito, denounced Mihajlov and sentenced him to three and a half years in prison. In 1975 Mihajlov was imprisoned again for publishing a spate of essays and articles that were critical of Tito's leadership. While in prison Mihajlov began a hunger strike, which brought him international attention and support from the West. He was given amnesty and released from prison in 1977, and the following year he was presented with an award from the International League for Human Rights. In 1978 he moved to the U.S., where he lived for the next several years, teaching Russian literature and philosophy at such institutions as Yale University, the University of Virginia, and Ohio State University and delivering lectures around the world. He returned to Europe in 1985 and became an analyst for Radio Free Europe, a U.S.-funded radio service that broadcasts in locations with heavy state censorship. In 2001 he settled in Serbia, following the resignation of President Slobodan Milosevic and the end of a string of ethnic conflicts, and became a prominent public figure, giving frequent television interviews and writing for various publications about social and political issues. He was active until the time of his death, the causes of which were unreported. Mihajlov's books, which have been published in many languages, include *Underground Notes* (1976), *Unscientific Thoughts* (1979), *Planetary Consciousness* (1982), and *The Homeland Is*

Freedom (1994). See *Current Biography* (1979). —W.D.

Obituary *New York Times* (on-line) Mar. 7, 2010

MILLER, MITCH July 4, 1911– July 31, 2010 Music impresario. In the 1960s Mitch Miller, instantly recognizable because of his trademark goatee and moustache, exhorted television audiences to "follow the bouncing ball," during *Sing Along with Mitch*, a popular show on which he and a chorus sang such traditional favorites as "The Yellow Rose of Texas" and "It's a Long Way to Tipperary." (The lyrics to the songs were superimposed along the bottom of the screen, much as in modern karaoke, and the "ball," which bounced from word to word, allowed viewers to follow along.) *Sing Along with Mitch* was considered old-fashioned even during its heyday but was beloved by those who had little interest in the burgeoning rock-and-roll scene. Mitchell William Miller was born in Rochester, New York, the son of Russian-Jewish immigrants. His father, Abram, was a wrought-iron worker, and his mother, Hinda, was a seamstress. Miller attended the Eastman School of Music at the University of Rochester on a full scholarship. He graduated cum laude in 1932. He began his career as a solo oboist, first with the Rochester Philharmonic Orchestra, then with the CBS Symphony Orchestra, with which he performed during Orson Welles's notorious "War of the Worlds" broadcast in 1938. In 1947 Miller was hired to oversee the classical division of Mercury Records; he was soon promoted to artists and repertoire (A&R) director. Concurrently he directed the children's label Little Golden Records. In 1950 Miller left Mercury to head the popular-music division at Columbia Records. While at Columbia Miller established himself as a hit-maker, and he helped shape the careers of such singers as Tony Bennett, Johnny Mathis, and Doris Day. His decision to feature a relatively unknown Rosemary Clooney on a tune based on an old Armenian folk melody, "Come On-a My House," with lyrics written by the playwright and novelist William Saroyan and his cousin Ross Bagdasarian, put Clooney on the map. Miller's uncanny ability to match talent with hit songs was integral to Columbia's emergence as a top-selling label. He had an especially good ear for novelty hits, including Jimmy Boyd's "I Saw Mommy Kissing Santa Claus" and Frankie Laine's "Mule Train," and he was known for using unorthodox instrumentation in his recordings. Miller came up with the concept for a series of sing-along albums in 1958. Featuring "the Gang," an all-male chorus led by Miller, the albums contained selections of standards and had the lyrics to each song printed on the record jacket. Mitch Miller and the Gang went on to release more than 20 *Sing Along with Mitch* albums, many of which hit the charts. (By 1966 the series had sold some 17 million copies.) In 1960 the concept was adapted for a one-time television special on NBC. The episode received such high ratings that the network arranged for Miller to have a weekly show, which aired from 1961 to 1964. (Reruns were shown in 1966.) After the show went off the air and the fad for sing-along music had declined, Miller worked sporadically on Broadway. Throughout the 1980s and 1990s, he made regular appearances as a guest conductor for orchestras across the country. Miller died in New York City at age 99, after a short illness. He is survived by two daughters, a son, two grandchildren, and two great-grandchildren. His wife of 65 years, the former Frances Alexander, died in 2000. See *Current Biography* (1956). —H.R.W.

Obituary *New York Times* A p16 Aug. 3, 2010

MOSBACHER, ROBERT Mar. 11, 1927–Jan. 24, 2010 Former U.S. secretary of commerce, business executive, and political fundraiser. Following a successful career in the oil industry, Robert A. Mosbacher served as the U.S. secretary of commerce under President George H. W. Bush, from 1989 to 1992. He was also one of the Republican Party's most prolific fundraisers. Robert Adam Mosbacher was born in Mount Vernon, New York, the youngest of the three children of Gertrude (Schwartz) and Emil Mosbacher Sr. His father was a trader at the American Stock Exchange. Emil Mosbacher Sr. managed to salvage the family fortune after deciding to sell his stock in oil, natural gas, and real estate holdings before the Wall Street crash of 1929, which was followed by the Great Depression. As a result, Robert Mosbacher and his two siblings enjoyed a privileged childhood in New York, where the family divided their time between an apartment on Park Avenue in Manhattan and a 43-acre estate in the suburb of White Plains. After graduating from the Choate School (now called Choate Rosemary Hall), an elite preparatory school in Wallingford, Connecticut, in 1944, Mosbacher studied business administration at Washington and Lee University, in Lexington, Virginia. At age 19 he married Jane Pennybacker. In 1947 Mosbacher earned a bachelor's degree. The following year the couple moved to Houston, Texas, where Mosbacher managed his father's oil investments and launched the Mosbacher Energy Co., an independent oil and gas exploration/production business that he funded with $500,000 of his father's money. Mosbacher had success in 1954, finding his first million-dollar field of natural gas in southern Texas; he later drilled additional wells in such locales as Louisiana, Montana, and western Canada. After awhile Mosbacher diversified into ranching, real estate, and banking and amassed a fortune that has been estimated at more than $200 million. In the late 1950s Mosbacher formed a close friendship with George H. W. Bush; the two formed a venture to provide barge and tug services to the offshore oil and gas industry. Mosbacher first became involved in politics during the 1960s, serving as a fundraiser for Republican politicians. He helped raise money for George H. W. Bush's successful campaign for Texas's Seventh Congressional District seat, in 1966, as well as Bush's failed U.S. Senate bids in 1964 and 1970. Mosbacher also served as the Harris County chair for Richard M. Nixon's successful presidential bid in 1968 and the finance chair for Gerald R. Ford's unsuccessful 1976 presidential campaign. In 1980 Mosbacher was the chief fundraiser for Bush's presidential bid. After Bush's poor showing in the New Hampshire primary, Mosbacher, along with James Baker, another campaign adviser, helped persuade Bush to leave the race early. The decision proved

fruitful for Bush, whom Ronald Reagan selected as his running mate at the Republican National Convention. After serving two four-year terms in the White House, Bush made another run for the presidency, aided by Mosbacher, who was instrumental in raising an estimated $75 million for the successful 1988 bid. Bush named Mosbacher to head the U.S. Commerce Department. During his tenure Mosbacher worked to foster closer ties between government and industry. He also played a key role in promoting and negotiating the North American Free Trade Agreement (NAFTA), a pact abolishing taxes on products and services to stimulate trade among the U.S., Canada, and Mexico; NAFTA was signed into law in December 1993. Mosbacher also oversaw the 1990 U.S. census. He stepped down from his post as U.S. commerce secretary in 1992 to raise capital for Bush's unsuccessful reelection campaign. In 2008 he served as the general chair for Arizona senator and unsuccessful presidential candidate John McCain. In 2009 Mosbacher founded the Odyssey Academy Charter School in Galveston, Texas; that same year Texas A&M University unveiled the Robert Mosbacher Institute for Trade, Economics, and Public Policy, which is located in the Bush School of Government and Public Service. An accomplished sailor, Mosbacher was the recipient of several sailing awards. Mosbacher, who died of pancreatic cancer at a Houston hospital, is survived by his fourth wife, the former Michele McCutchen. He was previously married to Sandra Gerry (1973–84) and Georgette Paulsin (1985–98). With Pennybacker, who predeceased him in 1970, Mosbacher had three daughters and a son, who also survive him. Among his other survivors are six grandchildren and one step-grandchild. See *Current Biography* (1989). —M.A.S.

Obituary *New York Times* (on-line) Jan. 25, 2010

MUZOREWA, ABEL TENDEKAI Apr. 14, 1925–Apr. 8, 2010 Religious and political leader. When Rhodesia (now known as Zimbabwe) was run by a white-dominated government, Bishop Abel Muzorewa fought for the inclusion of black politicians. Unlike Joshua Nkomo and Robert Mugabe—African leaders who conducted guerrilla warfare campaigns—Muzorewa rejected violence and instead engaged in talks with Rhodesian prime minister Ian Smith to allow black-led parties in the national government. For a short time in 1979, Muzorewa, as head of the United African National Council (UANC), served as prime minister of an interim government. Muzorewa, the eldest of eight siblings, was born in an American Methodist settlement near what was then known as Umtali, Rhodesia (now Mutare, Zimbabwe). He taught school for three years before becoming a lay preacher in the late 1940s. Following his graduation from a theological college in 1952, Muzorewa became an ordained minister and served as a village pastor before traveling to the U.S. in 1958 to further his theological education. Upon receiving a master's degree, in 1963, he returned to Rhodesia, where he was appointed national director of the Christian Youth Movement, youth secretary of the Christian Council, and traveling secretary of the Student Christian Movement. In 1968 he was consecrated as bishop of Rhodesia in the United Methodist Church. Three years later Muzorewa established the UANC political party. His negotiations with Smith resulted in an internal settlement that allowed black parties to enter parliamentary elections but reserved one-third of the seats in the Parliament, one quarter of the Cabinet, and control of the nation's police, army, civil service, and judiciary for whites. In its first all-race election in 1979, the UANC won the majority, making Muzorewa the first black prime minister of the newly renamed Zimbabwe-Rhodesia. Radical nationalists condemned Muzorewa, however, characterizing him as Smith's puppet, and civil war between the government and insurgents raged. A new election was held in 1980, and the UANC was defeated by Mugabe's Zimbabwe African National Union (ZANU). Muzorewa served as a minority legislator for several years and remained an outspoken opponent of Mugabe. Muzorewa's wife of 58 years, Maggie Chigodora, died in 2009. The couple had five children (Blessing Tendekai, Philemon Dairai, Wesley Tanyaraduzwa, Charles Scarritter Chido, and Charity Rufaro) and five grandchildren. See *Current Biography* (1979). —M.A.S.

Obituary *New York Times* A p22 Apr. 11, 2010

NEAL, PATRICIA Jan. 20, 1926–Aug. 8, 2010 Actress. Patricia Neal's life "alternated almost surreally between triumph and tragedy," Aljean Harmetz wrote for the *New York Times* (August 9, 2010, online). Patsy Louise Neal, as she was named at birth, was born in a mining camp in Packard, Kentucky. Her father, William, who worked for the South Coal and Coke Co., moved the family to Knoxville, Tennessee, while Neal was in grammar school. She displayed a talent for acting at a young age, reciting monologues at church events. While attending Knoxville High School, Neal performed with the Tennessee Valley Players, a community theater group, and won the Tennessee State Award for dramatic reading. She was then chosen to apprentice at the Barter Theater, in Virginia. After graduating from high school, she enrolled at Northwestern University, where she majored in drama. While still a student she served as an understudy in a road company production of *The Voice of the Turtle*, and after filling in one evening for an ill Vivian Vance, she was offered the chance to play the role for two weeks at the Morosco Theater, on Broadway. Neal subsequently quit school to pursue her acting career. While auditioning for roles she held such jobs as jewelry-store clerk, photographer's model, and cashier. She met the playwright Eugene O'Neill while auditioning for a production of *A Moon for the Misbegotten*, and although she did not get the part, O'Neill arranged for her to appear in a new summer-stock production, *Devil Takes a Whittler.* In November 1946, Neal, not yet 21, began appearing in Lillian Hellman's *Another Part of the Forest* at the Fulton Theatre in New York City. For her portrayal of an amoral southern belle, she won a Tony Award, among several other accolades, and her photo was featured on the cover of *Life* magazine. Praised for her strong facial features and distinctive, husky voice, Neal quickly landed a Hollywood contract and made her screen debut in the poorly received 1949 film *John Loves Mary.* The next

films in which she appeared, *The Fountainhead* (1949) and *Bright Leaf* (1950), were both dismissed as fatuous and pretentious by the majority of reviewers. A thaw in critical hostility set in with *The Hasty Heart* (1950), which found her cast as a nurse trying to ease the last days of a dying soldier, and as she became more at home in the new medium, her natural talent began to assert itself. A relatively warm critical reception greeted her performance as an amiable tramp in *The Breaking Point* (1950), which was loosely based on Hemingway's *To Have and Have Not.* The rapid succession of films that followed gradually established her as a screen actress of range, power, and perception, although she seemed permanently condemned to roles that gave little scope for her talents. The films included *Three Secrets* (1950), *Operation Pacific* (1951), *Raton Pass* (1951), *The Day the Earth Stood Still* (1951), *Weekend with Father* (1951), *Diplomatic Courier* (1952), *Something for the Birds* (1952), and *Washington Story* (1952). At that point Neal abandoned Hollywood to return to the New York stage. She opened in December 1952 in a revival of Lillian Hellman's *The Children's Hour*, playing Martha Dobie, the teacher who is driven to suicide by a sadistic child's allegations that she is a lesbian. Stage roles in such plays as *The School for Scandal, A Roomful of Roses, Cat on a Hot Tin Roof*, and *The Miracle Worker* followed. In a better position to choose her screen roles, she appeared in Elia Kazan's *A Face in the Crowd* (1957), winning almost universal acclaim for her portrayal of an Arkansas radio reporter who falls in love with a drunken musician (played by Andy Griffith). In 1963 came the film that removed any lingering doubts about Neal's mastery of screen acting: *Hud*, in which Paul Newman starred as the hedonistic son of a Texas rancher and Neal played Alma, the housekeeper, described by Bosley Crowther for the *New York Times* (May 29, 1963) as "a rangy, hard-bitten slattern with a heart and a dignity of her own." Neal's performance won her an Academy Award for best actress, as well as recognition from the British Academy of Film and Television Arts (BAFTA) and the New York Film Critics Circle, among other groups. A year after that triumph, Neal suffered a series of strokes, leaving her in a coma for nearly a month. When she regained consciousness she was partially paralyzed and unable to speak, but she ultimately recovered, thanks in large part to the tough-love ministrations of her husband, the writer Roald Dahl, whom she had married in 1953. (The two had already endured the near-death of their son Theo, who was left brain-damaged when his baby carriage was crushed between two vehicles in 1960, and the death in 1962 of their oldest daughter, Olivia, from measles encephalitis.) Although she was left with an impaired memory after the strokes, Neal returned to acting, appearing in the film *In Harm's Way* (1965) and making an Oscar-nominated appearence in a screen version of *The Subject Was Roses* (1968). A rehabilitation facility for brain-injured patients in Knoxville was named in her honor in 1978. Later in life Neal, who divorced Dahl in 1983, after discovering that he was engaged in an affair with one of her friends, made guest appearances on such television shows as *Murder, She Wrote* and *Little House on the Prairie.* In 2009 she had a small part in the TV movie *Flying By*, which starred Billy Ray Cyrus. Neal died at her home in Edgartown, Massachusetts, from lung cancer. She is survived by four of her five children: Tessa, Ophelia, Theo, and Lucy. See *Current Biography* (1964). —J.P.

Obituary *New York Times* (on-line) Aug. 9, 2010

NEWMAN, EDWIN Jan. 25, 1919–Aug. 13, 2010 Writer; broadcast journalist. Edwin Newman, a news anchor and panelist on NBC for over three decades, was one of the most distinguished and respected journalists of the 20th century. A familiar face to many who watched the news between 1952 and 1984, he won praise for his commentary, his cultural criticism, and his meticulous attention to grammar. "Ed Newman was never preachy or pedantic," *NBC Nightly News* anchor Brian Williams said in a statement quoted by Duane Byrge in the *Hollywood Reporter* (September 15, 2010, on-line). "He was approachable, elegant and precise. He was a teacher, a broadcaster and above all a superb journalist. To those of us watching at home, he made us feel like we had a very smart, classy friend in the broadcast news business." Edwin Harold Newman was born in New York City, the second of the three children of Myron Newman and Rose (Parker) Newman. His brother, M. W. Newman, who died in 2001, was a reporter for the *Chicago Daily News* and the *Chicago Sun-Times*. Newman attended local primary schools and studied at George Washington High School in upper Manhattan, where he worked on the school newspaper and graduated in January 1935. He then entered the University of Wisconsin, where he majored in political science and obtained a B.A. degree in 1940. Awarded a fellowship for the 1940–41 school year, Newman spent a semester studying in the Department of Government at Louisiana State University before leaving to pursue journalism. He became a dictation boy with the Washington bureau of the International News Service in 1941 and then found work with the United Press. In 1942 he joined the U.S. Navy; he did not see any combat and was discharged with the rank of lieutenant in October 1945. He then returned to United Press, where he remained until late 1946. He worked briefly with the Washington bureau of the liberal New York daily *PM* before joining the staff of the Tufty News Service. From the spring of 1947 to the summer of 1949, Newman prepared nightly radio broadcasts for the anchor Eric Sevareid at the CBS Washington bureau. He then went to London, England, to work on a freelance basis and spent the next few years writing magazine articles and broadcasting stories for NBC and the BBC, as well as writing articles published in the U.S. for the European Recovery Program (the Marshall Plan). In 1952 he became a full-time correspondent for NBC in London, and in 1956 he was made NBC news-bureau chief there. The following year he was transferred to head NBC's news bureau in Rome, and in 1958 he took charge of NBC's Paris bureau. During his time reporting abroad, Newman visited some 25 countries and covered stories in all the major European cities, as well as many in Africa, the Middle East, and Southeast Asia. In 1960 Newman returned to the U.S. to cover the presidential election and to host his own show, *Edwin Newman Report-*

ing, on NBC. After briefly returning to Paris later that year, he moved back to the U.S. and settled in New York City, where he filled in as an anchor on NBC's *Today Show* and appeared on numerous other NBC television and radio programs. He also hosted several documentaries, including *Japan: East Is West* (1961), which examined the impact of the U.S. upon Japanese manners and morals since the end of World War II; *California—The Most* (1963), a study of the diversity of life in California, for which he had written the script; *Who Shall Live?* (1965), about the high cost of artificial kidney machines; and *Politics: The Outer Fringe* (1966), which focused on extremism. Newman also hosted specials on such subjects as the Orient Express, the first anniversary of the assassination of President John F. Kennedy, and the bombing raids on North Vietnam. He moderated presidential debates between Gerald Ford and Jimmy Carter in 1976 and Ronald Reagan and Walter Mondale in 1984. With NBC's local affiliate, WNBC-TV, Newman served as a drama critic beginning in 1965—riling many Broadway theater producers with his often scathing reviews—and also hosted the affiliate's interview program *Speaking Freely*. He won seven New York Emmy Awards for his work at WNBC-TV. Among his other honors are a 1961 Overseas Press Club Award and a 1966 Peabody Award. In the 1970s Newman, who was known for his penchant for correcting others' grammar and his enthusiasm for the English language, began publishing books about language, most notably *Strictly Speaking: Will America Be the Death of English?* (1974) and *A Civil Tongue* (1976). He also published a comic novel, *Sunday Punch*, in 1979. After leaving NBC in 1984, Newman narrated several PBS programs and served as a moderator for a number of televised events. In his later years Newman delivered lectures on news and the English language. Newman died of pneumonia in Oxford, England, where he had moved with his wife in 2007 to be closer to his daughter. He is survived by his wife, the former Rigel Grell; his daughter, Nancy Drucker; and a sister, Evelyn Newman Lee. See *Current Biography* (1967). —W.D.

Obituary *New York Times* (on-line) Sep. 15, 2010

NIRENBERG, MARSHALL WARREN Apr. 10, 1927–Jan. 15, 2010 Biochemist. Marshall W. Nirenberg, a Nobel laureate, was celebrated for his discovery of a procedure that helped crack the genetic code. Born in New York City, Nirenberg developed rheumatic fever as a child. His father, who ran a shirt-manufacturing company in New York, moved the family to the warmer climes of Orlando, Florida, when Nirenberg was 10 years old, in an effort to improve his son's health. Surrounded by marshland filled with a wide variety of wildlife, Nirenberg developed an interest in biology. He attended the University of Florida, where he earned bachelor's and master's degrees in biology, in 1948 and 1952, respectively. Nirenberg earned a doctoral degree in biochemistry from the University of Michigan in 1957. He then completed a postdoctoral fellowship at the National Institutes of Health (NIH) in Bethesda, Maryland. In 1960 he became a research biochemist in an institute section whose focus was metabolic enzymes. Working with a colleague, Johann Heinrich Matthaei, Nirenberg began investigating the relationship between deoxyribonucleic acid (DNA), ribonucleic acid (RNA), and the production of proteins. (The genetic instructions—or genetic code—used in the development and functioning of all cells are contained in DNA. The genetic code is also needed to assemble other parts of cells, including proteins and RNA.) Nirenberg and Matthaei discovered how RNA transmits the "messages" that are encoded in DNA and directs how amino acids, the building blocks of proteins, link to form the many protein molecules that exist in the human body. By 1959 scientists knew, theoretically, that the code must consist of a sequence of three of the nucleotides of which DNA is composed, a trio called a codon. To the shock of many in the scientific community, Nirenberg and Matthaei identified the first codon. The discovery, presented to a small group at the International Congress of Biochemistry in Moscow, in August 1961, rocked the scientific community. Most had predicted that a finding of such importance would have been the work of the renowned molecular biologist Francis Crick, who had helped demonstrate the double-helix structure of DNA in 1953, or a scientist from his inner circle. Nirenberg, who was named chief of the NIH biochemical-genetics section in 1962, identified the other 63 codons in the genetic code, despite heated competition from other, better-funded scientists. In 1968 he shared the Nobel Prize in physiology or medicine with Har Gobind Khorana and Robert W. Holley for their monumental work on deciphering the genetic code. In the wake of his new-found fame, Nirenberg was offered positions at other institutions around the world, but he remained at the NIH for the rest of his career. He later shifted his focus to neurobiology, where he made a variety of significant contributions. His important later discoveries included a fruit-fly gene essential for heart development. Nirenberg, a recipient of the National Medal of Science and the National Medal of Honor, died of cancer at his home in New York City. His first wife, the biochemist Perola Zaltzman, died in 2001. He is survived by his second wife, Myrna Weissman, a Columbia University professor of epidemiology and psychiatry; four stepchildren; and seven grandchildren. See *Current Biography* (1965). —C.C.

Obituary *New York Times* A p30 Jan. 21, 2010

NOLAND, KENNETH Apr. 10, 1924–Jan. 5, 2010 Artist. Kenneth Noland was a master of the post–World War II style of abstraction known as Color Field painting, and his boldly colored canvases of chevrons, circles, and stripes are still highly sought. Noland was born in Asheville, North Carolina. During World War II he served in the armed forces as a glider pilot and a cryptographer. After the war he enrolled at Black Mountain College, near Asheville, where his teachers included the abstractionists Ilya Bolotowsky and Josef Albers. The avant-garde style of Black Mountain College owed much to the teaching of Bauhaus-trained Albers, whose use of color in geometric abstractions greatly influenced Noland's work. In 1948–49 Noland studied in Paris with the experimental sculptor Ossip Zadkine. Upon his return to the United States, Noland settled in Washing-

ton, D.C., where he taught at the Institute of Contemporary Arts from 1950 to 1952 and at Catholic University from 1951 to 1960. He also supported himself during a lean decade or more in Washington by teaching ceramics to children and driving a taxi. During that period Noland began producing a large series of paintings that depicted circles within squares, using the target, or bull's eye, not as a symbol or representation of any object, but as a means of creating countless dazzling color combinations. In the early 1960s he began incorporating ovals, and he subsequently experimented with chevrons, stripes, and dramatic crisscrossing lines. His work fell somewhat out of favor in the 1970s, with the rise of such movements as minimalism and postmodernism. Still, he continued producing Color Field works, and in the 1990s he returned to circular motifs. His work can be found in the permanent collections of such well-regarded venues as the Art Institute of Chicago; the Hirshhorn Museum and Sculpture Garden, in Washington, D.C.; the Metropolitan Museum of Art, in New York City; and the Tate Gallery, in London. Noland died of cancer at his home in Maine. He is survived by his fourth wife, Paige Rense, a longtime editor of *Architectural Digest*; two sons, William and Samuel; two daughters, Cady and Lyn; and one grandchild. See *Current Biography* (1972). —M.R.

Obituary *New York Times* (on-line) Jan. 6, 2010

PARKER, ROBERT B. Sep. 17, 1932–Jan. 18, 2010 Writer. As the creator of Spenser, one of the most popular and enduring detectives in contemporary American fiction, Robert B. Parker added new elements to the hard-boiled crime novel while remaining true to many of the traditions established by such earlier masters of the genre as Raymond Chandler and Dashiell Hammett. (So effectively did he embody those traditions that in 1988 the Chandler estate asked Parker to complete a 30-page manuscript that Chandler had left uncompleted when he died; Parker later also wrote a sequel to Chandler's classic mystery *The Big Sleep*.) Robert Brown Parker was born in Springfield, Massachusetts, the only child of Carroll Snow Parker, a telephone-company executive, and Mary Pauline (Murphy) Parker. He attended Colby College, in Waterville, Maine, where he received a B.A. degree in English in 1954. He then entered the U.S. Army and was stationed in Korea as a radioman. After returning to civilian life, in 1956, Parker worked as a technical and advertising writer for various companies in New York City and Massachusetts—jobs he found highly unsatisfying. He earned an M.A. degree in English literature from Boston University in 1957, and about four years later he enrolled in a Ph.D. program at that institution, concentrating on American and English literature. For his doctoral dissertation Parker focused on detective fiction, a genre with which he had become fascinated as a teenager, and set about substantiating his thesis that the private eye was a direct descendant of the "cowboy frontier hero." While fulfilling the requirements for a Ph.D. degree, which he received from Boston University in 1971, Parker taught English at Boston University (1962–64) and at the Massachusetts state colleges at Lowell (1964–66) and Bridgewater (1966–68). In 1968 he joined the

English Department of Northeastern University, in Boston, as an assistant professor. By the time he resigned from Northeastern, in 1979, to devote himself to writing full-time, he had risen to the position of professor. Parker introduced Spencer (he never divulged the detective's given name) in *The Godwulf Manuscript* (1974), naming his protagonist after the 16th-century English poet Edmund Spenser. Several other volumes followed in quick succession, including *God Save the Child* (1974); *Mortal Stakes* (1975); *Promised Land* (1976), for which he received the Edgar Allan Poe Award for best novel of the year from the Mystery Writers of America; and *The Judas Goat* (1978). The Boston-based Spenser, who narrated the books in first person, became known for his athleticism, impatience with pretentiousness, and loyalty to Susan Silverman, his longtime romantic partner. (Like his creator, he was also a skilled amateur chef; publishers often tried to coax Parker into compiling a cookbook.) Spenser was featured in some 40 books, among them *Looking for Rachel Wallace* (1980), *Early Autumn* (1981), *Love and Glory* (1983), *Taming a Seahorse* (1986), *Pale Kings and Princes* (1987), *Playmates* (1989), *Double Deuce* (1992), *Thin Air* (1995), *Hush Money* (2000), *Hugger Mugger* (2000), *Back Story* (2003), *Cold Service* (2005), *Now and Then* (2007), and *The Professional* (2009). The character was adapted for television audiences in the popular ABC series *Spenser: For Hire*, which starred Robert Urich and aired from 1985 to 1988. (Spenser's sidekick, Hawk, was the subject of a spin-off series, *A Man Called Hawk*, which ran for 13 episodes in 1989.) Urich later reprised his role in several made-for-television movies, including *Spenser: Pale Kings and Princes* (1994), *Spenser: The Judas Goat* (1994), *Spenser: A Savage Place* (1995), and *Spenser: Small Vices* (1999). Parker also wrote a series of books featuring Jesse Stone, an alcoholic police chief. Those included: *Night Passage* (1997), *Trouble in Paradise* (2000), *Death in Paradise* (2001), *Sea Change* (2006), *High Profile* (2007), *Stranger in Paradise* (2008), and *Night and Day* (2009). Stone was portrayed by Tom Selleck in a series of TV movies, the latest of which, *Jesse Stone: Thin Ice*, aired in early 2009. Parker, whose many honors included the Mystery Writers of America's Grand Master Award (2002) and Mystery Ink's Gumshoe Award for Lifetime Achievement (2007), created another protagonist—Sunny Randall, a female private eye with romantic woes—at the request of the actress Helen Hunt, who hoped to portray a Parker heroine on screen. While no films have yet been made, Randall is featured in several novels, including *Family Honor* (1999) and *Spare Change* (2007). Parker, who also penned several Westerns and young-adult novels, died while working at his desk in his Cambridge, Massachusetts, home. Until the time of his death, he unfailingly wrote five pages a day, five days a week, 50 weeks a year. He is survived by his wife, Joan, and two sons, David and Daniel. Several new books, including at least one featuring Spenser, are scheduled to be published posthumously. See *Current Biography* (1993). —D.K.

Obituary *New York Times* (on-line) Jan. 20, 2010

PEKAR, HARVEY Oct. 8, 1939–July 12, 2010 Comic-book writer. Harvey Pekar was the author of *American Splendor*, an unconventional comic book about the mundane experiences of an ordinary person—Pekar himself. It gained a cult following during its 32-year run, from 1976 to 2008. In *American Splendor* Pekar "applied the brutally frank autobiographical style of Henry Miller to the comic-book format, creating a distinctive series of dispatches from all-too-ordinary life," William Grimes wrote for Pekar's *New York Times* obituary (July 12, 2010, on-line). "His alter ego . . . trudged on from episode to episode, quarreling with co-workers, dealing with car problems, addressing family crises and fretting over money matters and health problems." "Harvey was like the original blogger, before there was an internet," Dean Haspiel, an artist who worked with Pekar, said, as quoted by Grimes. "He was *Seinfeld* before *Seinfeld*. Comics, which had been power fantasies for 12-year-old boys, could now be about anything." The older of two boys, Harvey Lawrence Pekar was born in Cleveland, Ohio, to Jewish immigrants from Poland. His father, Saul, a Talmudic scholar, and his mother, Dora, ran a grocery store. As a child Pekar was "extroverted to the point of obnoxiousness," as he once put it, and was regularly bullied by the other children in the mostly black neighborhood where he spent his early years. An athlete who developed a love for jazz early on, Pekar attended Case Western Reserve University, in Cleveland, for one year and then enlisted in the U.S. Navy, before being discharged due to his many anxieties. He returned to Cleveland, where he held a series of low-paying jobs before finding employment as a filing clerk at a Veterans Administration medical center. (Despite his later success, Pekar held that same position, turning down all offers of promotion, until his retirement, in 2001.) As a sideline, Pekar wrote music criticism for such magazines as *Downbeat* and *Jazz Review*. In the early 1960s he met and befriended the 19-year-old alternative-comics artist Robert Crumb. One day, while complaining to Crumb that there were no comic books about regular people, Pekar realized that he could write his own. "I always wanted praise and I always wanted attention; I won't lie to you," Pekar told Michael Malice for *Interview* magazine (October 13, 2009). "I was a jazz critic and that wasn't good enough for me. I wanted people to write about me, not me about them." He began creating comic-book storyboards, using stick figures and basing the stories on his own life. When he showed the drawings to Crumb, the artist agreed to provide illustrations for his stories. Early comic strips by Pekar and Crumb appeared in such collections as *The People's Comics* and other underground titles. Eager to write longer, more in-depth stories, Pekar decided to self-publish his work; the result was *American Splendor*, an autobiographical collection of short comics in which Pekar, as the main character, deals with life's everyday annoyances. Pekar lost money on the first issue, which appeared in 1976, but he soon gained a cult following. He self-published the first 15 issues of the annual comic book, each of which ran about 60 pages. Though Crumb illustrated most issues of *American Splendor*, over the years Pekar also worked with such artists as Frank Stack, Jim Woodring, Joe Zabel, Gary Dumm, Greg Budgett, and Mark

Zingarelli. *American Splendor* won a 1987 American Book Award, and by the early 1990s it had printings of 10,000 copies per issue. Meanwhile, in the early 1980s, Pekar, who had been married and divorced twice, began corresponding with one of his readers, the Delaware writer and teacher Joyce Brabner. The two bought rings on their second date and married on their third. In 1990 Pekar received radiation treatment and chemotherapy for non-Hodgkins lymphoma, after which the disease went into remission. He chronicled that experience in *Our Cancer Year* (illustrated by Stack, 1994), a comic book he cowrote with Brabner. (Pekar received treatment for the disease again in 2002.) In 2003 *American Splendor* was adapted into a film starring Paul Giamatti as the adult Pekar. The film, in which Pekar himself appeared, was critically acclaimed and won several prizes at the Cannes and Sundance film festivals. Pekar was pleased with the film and wrote about the experience in *American Splendor: Our Movie Year* (illustrated by Crumb, Zingarelli, and others, 2004). His other books include *American Splendor Presents Bob & Harv's Comics* (illustrated by Crumb, 1996); *American Splendor: Unsung Hero* (illustrated by David Collier, 2003); *The Quitter* (illustrated by Dean Haspiel, 2005); *Ego & Hubris: The Michael Malice Story* (illustrated by Dumm, 2006); *Macedonia* (with Heather Roberson, illustrated by Ed Piskor, 2007); *Students for a Democratic Society: A Graphic History* (illustrated by Dumm, 2008); *Studs Terkel's Working: A Graphic Adaptation* (illustrated by Dumm, Sharon Rudahl, Terry LaBan, and others, 2009); *American Splendor: Another Dollar* (illustrated by Zachary Baldus and others, 2009); and, as editor, *Best American Comics 2006*. Pekar also worked freelance as a writer and as a radio storyteller and commentator. *Harvey Pekar: Conversations*, edited by Michael G. Rhode, a collection of interviews spanning 25 years, was published in 2008. Pekar died at his home in Cleveland. Though no cause of death was initially determined, he reportedly had prostate cancer, asthma, and high blood pressure. He was also said to suffer from depression. He is survived by his wife; their adopted daughter, Danielle; and his brother, Allen. See *Current Biography* (2004). —J.P.

Obituary *New York Times* (on-line) July 12, 2010

PEMBERTON, JOHN DE J. JR. Apr. 21, 1919–Oct. 21, 2009 Civil rights leader. As the executive director of the American Civil Liberties Union (ACLU) during the 1960s, John de Jarnette Pemberton Jr. broadened the organization's focus, doubled its membership, and more than tripled its budget. A descendant of Captain de Jarnette, a French army officer who fought in the American Revolution, and of Richard Pemberton, who emigrated from England to the United States at about the time of the Revolution, Pemberton was born in Rochester, Minnesota, to Dr. John de J. Pemberton Sr. and Anna (Hogeland) Pemberton. Pemberton attended Rochester public schools and Swarthmore College, in Pennsylvania. He received a B.A. degree in 1940. Having what he later described as "some uncertain leanings toward pacifism," he served with Quaker-sponsored American Field Service ambulance units in the Middle East and India

during World War II. As a student at Harvard Law School, Pemberton served on the board of editors of the *Harvard Law Review* during his final academic year. After earning an LL.B. degree cum laude at Harvard in 1947, he taught commercial and bankruptcy law at Duke University until 1950. From 1950 to 1962 he practiced law in Rochester as a member of the firm Pemberton, Michaels, Bishop and Seeger. While in Rochester he also served on the Minnesota advisory committee of the U.S. Civil Rights Commission and on the Minnesota Fair Employment Practices Commission. Pemberton's interest in the ACLU began in the early 1950s, when a friend became executive director of the Illinois chapter, and he soon joined. From 1955 to 1958 Pemberton chaired the organization's Minnesota branch and was a member of the branch's executive board until 1962. One of the civil-liberty suits on which he worked in Minnesota involved a Swedish-American and his Indian wife, who had purchased a cemetery lot but were then denied its full use on the grounds that the cemetery was for Caucasians only. Pemberton won the case in the state's Supreme Court. In April 1962 he became the ACLU's executive director, a position he held until 1970. During his tenure he oversaw a variety of cases, including those involving free speech, the death penalty in Georgia and Texas, the loyalty oath provision of the Medicare law, and the racial integration of juries in the Deep South. He represented Tom Hayden (a future politician and husband of the actress Jane Fonda) and Staughton Lynd, two critics of the Vietnam War whose passports were revoked after they violated a Department of State ban on travel to Hanoi, North Vietnam. Pemberton also appealed the case of students in Richmond, Virginia, who had been denied registration at a state school because of their beards and long hair. One of the most dramatic and sweeping of his projects was "Operation Southern Justice," through which the Lawyers Constitutional Defense Committee of the ACLU rallied the chief legal officers of various religious and civil rights organizations to the defense of African-Americans and civil rights workers. Working out of Jackson, Mississippi, Operation Southern Justice, with five full-time, salaried lawyers and some 200 volunteer lawyers, handled thousands of criminal-defense suits over the course of the project. Under his leadership the ACLU also advocated for a sometimes surprising variety of defendants, including Ku Klux Klan members and Lieutenant William A. Calley Jr., who was convicted of ordering the infamous My Lai massacre during the war in Vietnam. (Pemberton held that because graphic photos of the slaughtered Vietnamese civilians had been made public, Calley could not get a fair trial.) In 1970 Pemberton stepped down from his ACLU post and became the acting general counsel for the U.S. Equal Employment Opportunity Commission and regional attorney for the commission's San Francisco branch. He also taught at the University of San Francisco. Pemberton died of congestive heart failure at the age of 90. He is survived by his daughters, Nancy, Sally, Ann, and Caro; his son, James; his second wife, Frances Werner; four grandchildren; and nine great-grandchildren. See *Current Biography* (1969). —D.K.

Obituary *New York Times* (on-line) Oct. 30, 2009

PENN, ARTHUR Sep. 27, 1922–Sep. 28, 2010 Filmmaker. Arthur Penn was best known as the director of the landmark Hollywood film *Bonnie and Clyde* (1967), which revolutionized the depiction of violence in cinema and opened the floodgates for a pioneering new generation of moviemakers. Of Russian-Jewish heritage, Penn was born in Philadelphia, Pennsylvania, where his father owned a small watch-repair business and his mother worked as a nurse. When Penn was three years old, his parents divorced. He and his older brother, Irving (who later earned renown as a photographer), moved with their mother to New York. Because of her meager wages, the three were forced to move to a succession of ever-cheaper apartments, and Penn ultimately attended at least 12 different grammar schools. At the age of 14, he returned to Philadelphia to live with his father, whose health was failing. Penn helped the older man run his watch-repair shop and studied horology (the science of measuring time), with the intention of following in his father's footsteps. He was frequently diverted, however, due to his growing love of the theater. He acted in student productions at Olney High School and got his first chance to direct, at the Neighborhood Playhouse, an amateur venue near his home. Penn became fascinated by the artistic possibilities of film while watching Orson Welles's groundbreaking *Citizen Kane* (1941). Soon after his father died, in 1943, Penn was drafted into the U.S. Army. Toward the end of World War II, Penn was transferred to Paris, where he performed with Joshua Logan's Soldiers Show Company; he also served as a civilian director of productions for occupation troops in Germany for a year after his discharge. Penn returned to the U.S. in 1946 and used the G.I. Bill to attend Black Mountain College, in North Carolina, where he focused on performing arts and literature. He also studied for two years at the Universities of Perugia and Florence, in Italy. Penn subsequently studied with Michael Chekhov, a proponent of the acting technique known as "the Method," at the Los Angeles branch of the Actors Studio. In 1951 he got a job as a floor manager with NBC-TV in New York City and was assigned to *The Colgate Comedy Hour*, a top-rated show that featured such stars as Bob Hope, Dean Martin, and Jerry Lewis. Penn later began directing teleplays for the live drama programs *First Person*, *Philco Television Playhouse*, and *Playhouse 90*. Penn's 1957 *Playhouse 90* production of William Gibson's *The Miracle Worker*, about the relationship between Helen Keller and her determined teacher, Annie Sullivan, received widespread critical praise and earned him Emmy nominations for writing and directing. On the strength of his television success, Penn next ventured onto Broadway in 1958 to direct Gibson's play *Two for the Seesaw*, which starred Henry Fonda and Anne Bancroft (in her Broadway debut). That year marked Penn's film debut as well, with the release of *The Left Handed Gun*, which starred Paul Newman as Billy the Kid. Penn continued to direct critically acclaimed stage dramas, including Lillian Hellman's *Toys in the Attic* and *An Evening with Mike Nichols and Elaine May*, before returning to Hollywood in 1962 to direct the film version of *The Miracle Worker*, which won Academy Awards for Anne Bancroft and Patty Duke. Penn next directed the films *Mickey One* (1965) and

The Chase (1966). The former starred Warren Beatty as a nightclub comedian on the run from mobsters, and the latter starred Marlon Brando as a Texas sheriff trying to protect a recently escaped convict (played by Robert Redford) from a gang of vigilantes. Both of those films were heavily edited by their producers, and a disgruntled Penn returned to Broadway in 1966 to direct the thriller *Wait Until Dark*, with Lee Remick and Robert Duvall. He was quickly lured back to Hollywood by Warren Beatty, who asked him to helm *Bonnie and Clyde*, a film project that had been turned down by Jean-Luc Godard and François Truffaut. Starring Beatty and newcomer Faye Dunaway as the notorious 1930s bank robbers Clyde Barrow and Bonnie Parker, the film became a worldwide sensation that shocked critics and audiences alike with its graphic violence; it is particularly known for its bloody, slow-motion climax, during which Beatty and Dunaway are riddled by machine-gun bullets. *Bonnie and Clyde* earned 10 Oscar nominations, winning for best cinematography (Burnett Guffey) and best supporting actress (Estelle Parsons). The picture, which was strongly influenced by the French New Wave, paved the way for what would become known as the New Hollywood generation of filmmakers—including Robert Altman, Hal Ashby, Sam Peckinpah, Martin Scorsese, and Paul Schrader. Penn's subsequent films included the quirky *Alice's Restaurant* (1969), the revisionist Western *Little Big Man* (1970), the detective thriller *Night Moves* (1975), the offbeat comedy *The Missouri Breaks* (1976), and the reflective drama *Four Friends* (1981). His last big-screen film, *Inside*, centered on South African apartheid and was released in 1996. Penn spent his later years working in theater and television. He served as an executive producer for the popular crime series *Law & Order* in the early 2000s, and in 2002 he made a return to the stage with the Broadway production *Fortune's Fool*, which earned Tony Awards for the actors Alan Bates and Frank Langella. Penn's final Broadway production was a 2004 revival of the comedic play *Sly Fox*. Penn died of congestive heart failure at his home in Manhattan. He is survived by his wife of over five decades, the actress Peggy Maurer; his children, Matthew and Molly; and four grandsons. Penn's brother, Irving, died in 2009. See *Current Biography* (1972). —C.C.

Obituary *New York Times* A p1 Sep. 30, 2010

PLAIN, BELVA Oct. 9, 1915–Oct. 12, 2010 Writer. During her decades-long career, the best-selling author Belva Plain wrote sprawling works about American-Jewish life. A third-generation American of German-Jewish descent, Plain was born Belva Offenberg in New York City. (There have been conflicting reports as to the year of her birth, with most sources stating 1915 but some claiming 1919.) The only child of Oscar Offenberg, a contractor, and his wife, Eleanor, Plain attended Barnard College, an academically rigorous women's school affiliated with New York City's Columbia University. Shortly after graduating with a degree in history, she married Irving Plain, an ophthalmologist. As a young housewife, Plain spent her spare time writing and sold dozens of short stories to various women's magazines, including *Cosmopolitan* and *Good Housekeeping*. In the early

1960s she stopped writing in order to focus on her family. (She had given birth to three children in quick succession.) Plain resumed writing fiction in the 1970s after becoming discontented with the depictions of Jews in contemporary fiction. "I got sick of reading the same old story, told by Jewish writers, of the same old stereotypes—the possessive mothers, the worn-out fathers, all the rest of the neurotic rebellious unhappy self-hating tribe," she once said, as quoted by Elsa Dixler in the *New York Times* (October 17, 2010, on-line). "I wanted to write a different novel about Jews—and a truer one." Plain's debut novel, *Evergreen*, published in 1978, was based on people she knew. Set in the early 20th century, the novel follows a courageous Polish immigrant, Anna Friedman, as she toils as a maid, copes with tragedy, and wrestles with forbidden love. The multigenerational saga, which also follows the travails of Friedman's employers, members of the Werner family, became an immediate success, spending 41 weeks on the *New York Times* best-seller list and selling 3.5 million copies. (The book was made into a miniseries by NBC in 1985.) Plain became a major name in popular fiction and produced a steady stream of novels over the next three decades. They include three more volumes featuring the Werner family— *Golden Cup* (1986), *Tapestry* (1988), and *Harvest* (1990). Among her other popular books are *Blessings* (1989), *Random Winds* (1980), *Eden Burning* (1982), *Crescent City* (1984), *Treasures* (1992), *Daybreak* (1994), *The Carousel* (1995), *Homecoming* (1997), *After the Fire* (2000), *Her Father's House* (2002), and *The Sight of the Stars* (2004). Her most recently published novel, *Crossroads*, appeared in 2008. A final book, *Heartwood*, is scheduled to be published in 2011. While her work, which has been published in 22 languages, was generally panned by reviewers, who likened her plots to those of soap operas, Plain dismissed such critics as snobs. At the time of her death, from natural causes, there were nearly 30 million copies of her books in print. Plain's husband died in 1982. She is survived by two daughters, Barbara and Nancy; a son, John; six grandchildren; and three great-grandchildren. See *Current Biography* (1999). —C.C.

Obituary *New York Times* (on-line) Oct. 17, 2010

REDGRAVE, LYNN Mar. 8, 1943–May 2, 2010 Actress; playwright. Born into a family that had been active in theater, film, and television for generations, Lynn Redgrave was twice nominated for an Academy Award, for her captivating performances in the films *Georgy Girl* (1966) and *Gods and Monsters* (1998). She was also nominated for three Tony Awards for her work in the theater world, where she was particularly praised for her performances in Shakespearean plays. During the last two decades of her life, Redgrave established a career as a playwright, basing her scripts on her family's history as an acting dynasty. Lynn Rachel Redgrave was born in London, England, the youngest of the three children of the actors Sir Michael Redgrave and Lady Redgrave (better known by her stage name, Rachel Kempson). Her sister, Vanessa, and her brother, Corin (who died in April 2010), also took up acting. Though she was initially reluctant to become an ac-

tress, Lynn Redgrave changed her mind after a visit to Stratford-on-Avon, the birthplace of William Shakespeare. She attended the Central School of Speech and Drama in London, and her stage debut was as Helena in a 1962 production of Shakespeare's *A Midsummer Night's Dream* in the Royal Court Theater. (The play's director was Tony Richardson, who later married Redgrave's sister, Vanessa.) In 1963 Lynn Redgrave made a brief appearance (alongside her mother) in the film *Tom Jones*. Her performance impressed the legendary actor, director, and producer Laurence Olivier, who asked her to audition for the National Theater (now the Royal National Theater), which he was organizing. She joined the theater in its first season, and during her three-year tenure there, Redgrave performed in plays directed by such luminaries as Franco Zeffirelli, Noel Coward, and Olivier himself. Some of her most noteworthy roles included those of a flapper in Coward's *Hay Fever* and Margaret in *Much Ado About Nothing*. She was also greatly praised for her performance in the Bertolt Brecht play *Mother Courage*. In 1964 Redgrave appeared with Peter Finch and Rita Tushingham in the movie *Girl with Green Eyes*. The role that brought her film stardom was that of Georgina in *Georgy Girl*, directed by Silvio Narizzano. In that part, for which she gained several pounds, Redgrave played "a previous generation's Bridget Jones, a pudgy, gawky young woman whose painfully uncertain self-image leads her to sublimate her own desires to those of her acquaintances," Bruce Weber wrote for her *New York Times* obituary (May 3, 2010). The film was well received by most reviewers, and Redgrave's performance earned unanimous praise. Bosley Crowther wrote for the *New York Times* (November 6, 1966), "It is [Redgrave's] exceeding sensitivity to the nuances of this girl and her dexterity in expressing these nuances that are the core of the film." In her review for the New York *World Journal Tribune* (October 18, 1966), Judith Crist observed, "Miss Redgrave has magic in the very way she transforms face and figure from scene to scene, bringing inner beauty and grace to physical terms, contracting and expanding for the size of passion, for the grand laugh at life's ironies and the takeoff on its pretenses. . . . Hers is a beautiful performance." Redgrave was nominated for an Academy Award, putting her in competition with her sister, who was nominated that year for her performance in *Morgan!* (Both lost to Elizabeth Taylor.) In 1967 Redgrave made her Broadway debut in Peter Shaffer's *Black Comedy*. Critics praised Redgrave's performance as the British debutante fiancée of an eccentric sculptor. She appeared in numerous other Broadway plays, winning the title roles in *Mrs. Warren's Profession* in 1976 and *Saint Joan* in 1977. She continued to appear on the big screen, in such pictures as the Sidney Lumet spy thriller *The Deadly Affair* (1966), the comedy *Smashing Time* (1967), Woody Allen's *Everything You Always Wanted to Know About Sex But Were Afraid to Ask* (1972), and *The Happy Hooker* (1975), in which Redgrave played the real-life ex–brothel owner Xaviera Hollander. She appeared mostly in television films and shows in the 1980s, including a role in the short-lived sitcom *Chicken Soup* in 1989, then had a career revival in the 1990s, with roles in the films *Shine*

(1996) and *Gods and Monsters* (1998), the latter of which brought her a second Oscar nod. From 1998 to 2001 Redgrave portrayed Trudy Frank on the Showtime comedy series *Rude Awakening*. In 2009 she appeared in episodes of *Law & Order: Criminal Intent* and *Ugly Betty*. During the 1990s Redgrave had begun writing one-woman plays about her family's history, an activity she said was therapeutic. Those works include *Shakepeare for My Father*, *The Mandrake Root*, *Nightingale*, and *Rachel and Juliet*. Redgrave, who died of breast cancer, is survived by her son, Benjamin, and her daughters, Pema and Annabel. She divorced her husband, the theater producer John Clark, in 2000, following his revelation that he had, years prior, fathered a child with his secretary, Nicolette. (Adding to the soap opera–like aspects of the incident, Nicolette had later married and divorced Benjamin Redgrave, making her, for a time, Lynn Redgrave's daughter-in-law.) See *Current Biography* (1969). —W.D.

Obituary *New York Times* (on-line) May 3, 2010

RINES, ROBERT Aug. 30, 1922–Nov. 1, 2009 Inventor; patent lawyer; cryptozoologist; composer. "Robert Rines was a true Renaissance man whose many talents ranged from composing music for Broadway musicals to pioneering work in patent law," according to an obituary writer for the Brisbane, Australia, *Courier Mail* (December 2, 2009). "But he was best known as a prodigious inventor whose advances in sonar technology paved the way for the discovery of the wreck of the [ships] *Titanic* in 1985 and the *Bismarck* in 1989. He was even better known for using that technology to try to find the Loch Ness monster." The younger of two children, Robert Harvey Rines was born in Boston, Massachusetts. His father, David, was an attorney specializing in patent law. Robert Rines displayed a knack for inventing as early as the age of six, when he suggested adding a fork, spoon, and scissors to a pocket knife. An impressed David Rines researched his son's idea but discovered that a patent already existed. Robert Rines also had a talent for music, beginning to play the violin by the age of four; once, at 11, he performed a duet with the renowned physicist Albert Einstein while at summer camp. While attending Brookline High School, Rines founded the Six Aces of Rhythm band, for which he arranged the music. In 1939 the academically gifted Rines graduated early from high school and began studying physics at the Massachusetts Institute of Technology (MIT), in Cambridge. He stopped attending classes and intentionally flunked out, however, when he was not allowed to transfer to Harvard. Rines's father threw him out of the house, and he temporarily moved in with an aunt while working as a janitor at MIT—a job he had landed, unbeknownst to him, thanks to his father's influence. When Rines made the discovery, he returned to MIT, and in 1942 he graduated at the top of his class with a B.S. degree. By the following year Rines had begun serving as a radar operator in the U.S. Army Signal Corps. His experience working in the MIT radiation laboratory led him to help develop the Army's Microwave Early Warning System, which is instrumental in detecting aircraft movement in overcast skies. After World War II Rines worked as an examiner at the U.S. Patent Office, while juggling night classes at Georgetown University Law School. He earned a J.D. degree in 1947. (Rines also earned a Ph.D. degree in physics and microwave technology from the National Chiao Tung University, in Taiwan.) In 1963 Rines founded the nonprofit Academy of Applied Science (AAS), in Concord, New Hampshire, "for the purpose of promoting creativity, invention, and scientific achievement," according to the organization's Web site. From the early 1970s to the late 2000s, Rines and a group of AAS researchers oversaw investigations into the existence of an underwater cryptid reportedly inhabiting the murky Loch Ness, a lake in Scotland. (Rines claimed to have first seen the creature in the late 1950s, while on vacation.) Using high-resolution sonar equipment, underwater cameras suspended from two boats, and strobe lighting designed by Rines, the researchers captured a series of underwater images that they claimed showed the so-called Loch Ness monster. Although the photos were not clear enough to prove conclusively that the creature existed, they were published in *Nature* magazine in December 1975. Rines spearheaded subsequent investigations, returning to Scotland in 1997 (with his son Justice) to take part in a documentary that aired on the PBS series *Nova*. After expeditions in 2001 and 2002 failed to yield sightings of the creature, Rines concluded during a final visit in 2008 (as part of a joint project with the History Channel documentary series *MonsterQuest*) that the Loch Ness monster had become extinct. Over the course of his inventing career, Rines amassed numerous patents "for electronic apparatus that improve the resolution of radar and sonar scanning." Additionally, Rines played a key role in helping to develop the patent systems for Taiwan and the People's Republic of China. Considered a leading contributor to the field of intellectual property, Rines established the Franklin Pierce Law Center in Concord, New Hampshire, and lectured on patent law at Harvard and MIT. He taught at the latter school for more than 50 years, before retiring in May 2008. Rines, a member of the U.S. National Inventors' Hall of Fame, also garnered recognition as a composer, whose credits include the stage productions *Blasts and Bravos*, *Drums Under the Windows*, *Long Voyage Home*, and *Creditors*. Rines's score for *Hizzoner the Mayor*, a television special about New York City mayor Fiorello LaGuardia, earned him a 1987 Emmy Award. Rines died of heart failure at his home in Boston. His first marriage, to Dorothy Kay, ended in divorce, and his second wife, Carol Williamson, died in 1993. He is survived by his third wife, the former Joanne Hayes; his sons, Justice and Robert; his daughter, Suzi; a stepdaughter; and four grandchildren. *See Current Biography* (2003). —W.D.

Obituary *New York Times* (on-line) Nov. 7, 2009

ROBAINA, ALEJANDRO Mar. 10, 1919–Apr. 17, 2010 Cuban tobacco grower; cigar manufacturer. Alejandro Robaina, considered Cuba's top tobacco grower for many years, was credited with producing some of the world's finest cigars. Lisa J. Adams, writing for the Associated Press (February 23, 2004), dubbed him "Cuba's unofficial tobacco ambassador to the world" and "king of [Cuba's] tobacco growers." In 1998 the Cuban government—which owns Cuba's cigar industry—recognized Robaina's standing as one of the country's most celebrated tobacco farmers (or *vegueros*, as they are known) by naming a line of cigars after him, making him the only living Cuban with a cigar bearing his name. In *Cigar Aficionado* (October 1, 2006, on-line), James Suckling described Robaina as "a legend in Cuba, and the dean of its cigar industry. He has dedicated his life to growing the best wrapper tobacco in Cuba, if not the world." "Don" Alejandro Robaina, the son of Maruto Robaina and Maria Pereda, was born into one of Cuba's premier tobacco-farming families. In 1845 Robaina's paternal grandfather, a Spanish immigrant to Cuba, began growing tobacco in San Luis, about 125 miles from Havana, in the Pinar del Río region. Maruto Robaina later inherited the plantation, called Finca la Pina, from his father, and Alejandro began working in the fields when he was 10 years old (and began smoking cigars—secretly—when he was 11). The family grew tobacco leaves that were used in Havana cigars, a world-famous product whose devotees have included the British prime minister Winston Churchill. Robaina took over the plantation from his father in the late 1940s. During the 1950s he supported the armed struggle against the Cuban dictator Fulgencio Batista by distributing propaganda, assisting in the sale of bonds to fund the revolution, and allowing the rebels to use his plantation for refuge. After Fidel Castro rose to power, in 1959, and the Cuban government nationalized most of the country's tobacco farms, Robaina managed to maintain his status as an independent grower. He explained to Suckling, "I told Fidel I did not like cooperatives or state farms and that the best way to grow tobacco was through family production. He wanted me to join a cooperative and I told him no. I would not do it and that I would remain working with my family." Castro later promoted independent ownership of tobacco farms, and today the vast majority are privately owned, though the government, which closely regulates the industry and oversees cigar exports, is the only buyer. In the mid-1990s Robaina was named Cuba's top tobacco grower by the Cuban government, and in 1997 that government and Britain's Imperial Tobacco Group launched the joint venture Habanos S.A., to distribute Vegas Robaina (which translates as "Robaina's Fields"), a brand of cigar that features Robaina's likeness as well as his name on the boxes. In the years after the launch of the brand, Robaina, who was previously a relative unknown to most of the world, gained a sizeable following. Tourists flocked to his plantation, hoping to meet with the grower and to obtain his autograph on cigar boxes. He was touted as the elder statesman of Cuba's tobacco industry; a Danish documentary on Robaina's life, *The Love of Don Robaina*, was released in 2003, and a biography of him was made available at the 2004 Habanos Cigar Festival. Despite the popularity of the Vegas Robaina brand, the cigar's flavor was sometimes panned by cigar critics. Robaina told a correspondent from the Cigars-of-Cuba Web site (September 29, 1998) that he felt the negative reception was "due to political reasons." For several years before Robaina's death, which followed a long illness, his tobacco operations were managed by his grandson, Hiroshi. In addition to Hiroshi, Robaina is survived by four children, several grandchildren, and a dozen great-grandchildren. See *Current Biography International* (2004) —W.D.

Obituary *New York Times* (on-line) Apr. 19, 2010

ROBERTS, ORAL Jan. 24, 1918–Dec. 15, 2009 Pentecostal evangelist. Oral Roberts was among the first American religious leaders to recognize the potential of television to reach a wide audience. A proponent of the prosperity gospel—the belief that Christians who pray frequently and donate to their churches generously will be rewarded with good health and wealth—Roberts was a controversial figure. Granville Oral Roberts was born near Ada, Oklahoma, to Ellis Roberts, an impoverished Pentecostal preacher, and his wife, Claudius, a deeply devout woman who was part Cherokee Indian. Roberts had two older sisters—Velma, who died at age 19 from complications of epilepsy, and Jewell—as well as two older brothers, Elmer and Vaden. When he was 16, Roberts nearly died from an advanced case of tuberculosis. He regained his health after his family visited a traveling evangelist who had pitched a tent in Ada. The evangelist reportedly prayed with Roberts and commanded the disease to leave his body. Roberts said that during that experience, he felt called to the ministry. Beginning at age 18, when he delivered his first sermon, Roberts spent several years serving as a pastor of churches in various southern towns. During the mid-1940s he attended the Oklahoma Baptist University in Shawnee and Phillips University in Enid, Oklahoma, and in 1948 he established a nonprofit organization called Healing Waters Inc., which would later become the Oral Roberts Evangelistic Association, Inc. Roberts began to broadcast his worship services (edited before they aired) on television in 1955. Toward the end of each service, Roberts, who claimed that God was working through him, would touch each worshipper who had lined up and pray for him or her to be healed. Other religious leaders questioned the authenticity of the healings, and his television programs were criticized for omitting the instances in which his prayers had apparently been unsuccessful. Although Roberts could not provide concrete, medical proof of his efforts' success, many of his followers asserted that they had been cured of their ailments by his hand. Even more controversial were the televangelist's appeals for monetary donations to his ministry. During a televised service in 1987, for example, Roberts proclaimed that God would "call him home" if he did not raise several million dollars for his City of Faith Medical Center in Tulsa, which he had built in 1981. Although he quickly became the butt of jokes by late-night talk-show hosts and was ridiculed by mainstream religious leaders, he met his fundraising goal. (Despite the infusion of funds, the troubled medical center closed in 1989.) More successful was Oral Roberts University, which Roberts founded in 1963. The school, accredited in 1971, now boasts more than 3,000 students and is the world's largest charismatic Christian university. Roberts died from complications of pneumonia at a hospital in Newport Beach, California. He was predeceased by his wife, the former Evelyn Lutman Fahnestock, a schoolteacher, whom he had married in 1938. He was also predeceased by his first daughter, Rebecca, who died in a plane crash in 1977, and his second son, Ronald, who committed suicide in 1982. Roberts is survived by a daughter, Roberta; a son, Richard; 12 grandchildren; and several great-grandchildren. See *Current Biography* (1960). —M.A.S.

Obituary *New York Times* A p1+ Dec. 16, 2009

ROBERTS, ROBIN Sep. 30, 1926–May 6, 2010 Baseball player. During the 1950s Robin Roberts was one of the most respected baseball pitchers in the National League. A member of a group of star players informally known as the "Whiz Kids," he helped lead the Philadelphia Phillies to a National League pennant in 1950. During 19 seasons in the majors, Roberts, considered a "control pitcher" with a reliable fastball, pitched 305 complete games and racked up 286 wins, including 20-plus wins per season between 1950 and 1955. He also had 45 career shutouts, an earned run average (ERA) of 3.41, and 2,357 strikeouts, and he was named to the All-Star team seven times. "I stood out there in total isolation," Roberts once told Donald Honig, the author of *Baseball Between the Lines* (1976). "Nothing bothered me. I would concentrate to the point where I would not even see the batter; I would only see the bat as he swung. When I was pitching well, I saw only the catcher." Robin Evan Roberts, the fifth of six children of Welsh immigrants Thomas and Sarah Roberts, was born on the outskirts of Springfield, Illinois. Thomas Roberts, who had worked in coal mines in Wales, was a night foreman with the Sangamo Electric Co., in Springfield. The elder Roberts was also a baseball fan who took his sons to watch the St. Louis Cardinals' home games whenever possible. During his senior year at Lanphier High School, Robin Roberts qualified as an Army Air Force cadet, and in 1944 he was sent by the air force to the Student Training Reserve Unit at Michigan State College (now Michigan State University), in East Lansing. There, he played basketball for an airforce team and so impressed college officials that he was given an athletic scholarship. He remained at East Lansing until his transfer from reserve to active status in March 1945. Later that year he received his military discharge and returned to Michigan State, where he earned a B.S. degree in physical education. While in college Roberts refined his pitching skills by playing in a nonprofessional summer league in Vermont. In 1947 he signed with the struggling Phillies organization. After pitching in the minor leagues for half a season, he made his major-league debut, on June 18, 1948, in a 2–0 loss to the Pittsburgh Pirates. Four days later Roberts had his first major-league victory, a 3–2 win over the Cincinnati Reds. Roberts finished the 1948 season with a 7–9 record and a respectable ERA of 3.18. The next season he pitched in 34 games and notched a record of 15–15. In 1950 Roberts achieved sports stardom when he became a member of the "Whiz Kids"—a nickname given to a group of youthful Phillies players who led their team to the National League pennant. Before the 1950 regular season was over, Roberts had taken the mound in 304 innings and notched 146 strikeouts and only 77 walks. He clinched the team's first-place finish in

the National League in the last game of the season, in which he allowed just five hits in a 4–1, 10-inning win over the Brooklyn Dodgers, who finished as the league's second-ranked team. That victory gave the Phillies their first National League pennant in 35 years and also gave Roberts a 20–11 record, making him the first Phillies pitcher to win 20 games since Grover Cleveland Alexander won 30 in 1917. (The Phillies went on to lose the 1950 World Series to the New York Yankees.) Roberts had his best statistical season in 1952, when he completed 30 out of 37 starts and notched a 28–7 record and a 2.59 ERA. In his 14 seasons with the Phillies, Roberts had 234 wins—an especially impressive number because the team lost more games than it won between 1948 and 1961. Roberts was sold to the Yankees in 1961 but was released the following year without playing a game. He went on to pitch for the Baltimore Orioles, the Houston Astros, and the Chicago Cubs. During his career Roberts, a founding member of the players' union, allowed 505 home runs, a record that still holds today. (It has been tied, however, by Jamie Moyer.) His major-league career ended in 1966, and he went on to become a stockbroker and also served as a baseball coach at the University of South Florida. In 1976 he was elected to the Baseball Hall of Fame. Roberts, who died of natural causes at his home in Temple Terrace, Florida, is survived by his brother, four sons, seven grandchildren, and one great-grandson. His wife, Mary, predeceased him. See *Current Biography* (1953). — W.D.

Obituary *New York Times* (on-line) May 6, 2010

ROHMER, ERIC Dec. 1, 1920–Jan. 11, 2010 Filmmaker; critic. Eric Rohmer, known for his philosophical, dialogue-driven films, was, along with his compatriots Jean-Luc Godard and François Truffaut, an important member of the French New Wave. He was born to Lucien and Mathilde (Bucher) Scherer. There is a dispute among sources as to whether his name at birth was Jean-Marie Maurice Scherer or Maurice Henri Joseph Scherer. His place of birth is also in contention—sources are divided as to whether it was in the French town of Nancy or of Tulle—as is his date of birth; while most sources have it as December 1, 1920, others assert that it was April 14, 1923 or April 4, 1920. At about the age of 20, he adopted the name Eric Rohmer. Educated in Paris, he earned an advanced degree in history and taught school in Clermont-Ferrand. Rohmer began writing professionally during World War II, and in 1946 he published a novel, *Elisabeth*, under another pseudonym, Gilbert Cordier. In about 1950 he moved to Paris, where he met Godard, Truffaut, and others in that circle. Later in the decade, Rohmer became a film reviewer for the venerable magazine *Les Cahiers du Cinéma*. His first feature-length film, the tale of an American expatriate in Paris titled *The Sign of Leo*, was released in 1959. The film was not a success, and Rohmer resumed his duties at the film magazine, retaining his post there until 1963. Between 1964 and 1966 Rohmer directed more than a dozen documentaries for French television, including several studies of major literary figures, among them Victor Hugo, Blaise Pascal, and Stéphane Mallarmé. For his feature films, to set his work apart, Rohmer decided to orchestrate variations on a single theme, renewing the subject by changing casts, settings, and social milieus. He elected as his theme the conflicts within a man who, although he flirts with one woman, is already irrevocably committed to another. The films that comprise the resulting Six Moral Tales series are *The Bakery Girl of Monceau* (1962), *Suzanne's Career* (1963), *The Collector* (1967), *My Night at Maud's* (1969), *Claire's Knee* (1970), and *Chloe in the Afternoon* (1972). *My Night at Maud's*, which was nominated for an Academy Award as best foreign-language film, remains among his best-loved pictures in the U.S. Michael Atkinson, reviewing a later, DVD release of *My Night at Maud's* for the *Village Voice* (August 1, 2006, on-line), wrote: "[It] remains, to all eyes, the masterpiece in the middle [of the Six Moral Tales]. Rohmerians do not need to be told, but for others, [you should] begin with this snowy eclogue pitting righteous piety against bohemian freedom." Atkinson wrote of the series as a whole, "Don't be misled: These magical, yackety films are not parables of moral struggle, but episodes of egotistic and romantic folly, missiles of fond social critique aimed at the French man, in all his self-analytical jerkiness." Rohmer chose as his next project the dramatization of *The Marquise of O . . .* (1976), based on a short story by the German writer Heinrich von Kleist. Set in 1799, the tale follows an Italian noblewoman who is rescued from rape by a heroic Russian officer, who then rapes her himself while she is unconscious. Widely admired by critics, the film won the Special Jury Prize at the 1976 Cannes Film Festival. Rohmer's other film series include "Comedies and Proverbs," which was comprised of movies that illustrated traditional sayings or quotes from famous authors, and "Tales of the Four Seasons," a quartet of romances. Among his final films are *The Lady and the Duke* (2001), *Triple Agent* (2004), and *The Romance of Astrée and Céladon* (2007). Rohmer died in a Paris hospital. He is survived by his wife and two sons, as well as a younger brother, the philosopher René Schérer. See *Current Biography* (1977). —D.K.

Obituary *New York Times* (on-line) Jan. 12, 2010

ROSS, JERILYN Dec. 20, 1946–Jan. 7, 2010 Psychotherapist. Jerilyn Ross was renowned for her treatment of anxiety disorders, the most common type of mental illness in the United States. Ross was born in the New York City borough of the Bronx and was predisposed to anxiety from an early age. (She once clung to her mother so hard when left at school, for example, that she pulled her mother's skirt off.) After earning a B.A. degree from the State University of New York (SUNY) at Cortlandt, Ross took a job as a math teacher in New York City. She first experienced a crippling panic attack while at a party on the rooftop terrace of a 20-story building in Salzburg, Austria; then 25 years old, Ross suddenly felt a powerful urge to jump off the roof, and for years after returning home to New York City, she was terrified to be on the 10th floor or higher in any building. While pursuing a master's degree in psychology at the New School for Social Research in the early 1970s—at a time when the medical community knew very little about phobias and anxiety disorders—she sought

treatment for her phobia at New York's Roosevelt Hospital. There, she was introduced to an innovative technique called cognitive-behavioral therapy (CBT), which involves gradually introducing a patient to anxiety-inducing objects or situations while teaching the patient ways of managing his or her symptoms of anxiety. The treatment worked for Ross, and after completing the M.A. degree, she joined the staff of the Center for Behavioral Medicine in Rockville, Maryland, as a senior clinical associate. She worked with the psychiatrist Robert L. Dupont, who specialized in the same sort of treatment that Ross had received in New York. In 1981 Ross, DuPont, and several of their colleagues launched the Phobia Program of Washington, with the aim of using CBT to treat patients. At about the same time, they also founded the Phobia Society of America (later renamed the Anxiety Disorders Association of America); in 1987 Ross succeeded DuPont as the president of that advocacy organization. From 1985 to 1991 Ross served as an associate director at the Roundhouse Square Psychiatric Center, in Alexandria, Virginia. Beginning in 1987 she hosted a weekly radio talk show focusing on phobias and anxiety disorders on Washington, D.C.–based WRC Radio, where she became known as "the phobia lady." She also appeared regularly on television shows and wrote numerous newspaper and magazine articles explaining how to live with and manage persistent anxiety. In 1991 Ross founded the Washington, D.C.–based Ross Center for Anxiety and Related Disorders, an outpatient facility that provides treatment for obsessive-compulsive disorder, post-traumatic stress disorder, and panic disorder, among other such problems, using the CBT method. The center also treats children and adolescents as well as adults and offers an intensive, accelerated program for people who do not live within easy traveling distance of the facility. Ross was the author of *Triumph Over Fear: A Book of Help and Hope for People with Anxiety, Panic Attacks, and Phobias* (1995). She wrote her next book, *One Less Thing to Worry About: Uncommon Wisdom for Coping with Common Anxieties* (2009), in response to growing public fears about the economy, the environment, and terrorism. In 2004 Ross earned the American Psychiatric Association's Award for Patient Advocacy. Ross, who died from cancer, is survived by her husband, the real-estate developer Ronald Cohen; Cohen's three children from a previous marriage; and seven step-grandchildren. See *Current Biography* (2009) —M.R.M.

Obituary *New York Times* (on-line) Jan. 22, 2010

ROSTENKOWSKI, DAN Jan. 2, 1928–Aug. 11, 2010 Politician. Daniel "Dan" Rostenkowski was a U.S. representative from Illinois who served in the House from 1959 to 1995. Although he was arguably one of the most prominent and powerful House members of his generation, his legacy was tarnished by his later imprisonment on charges of fraud. Rostenkowski was born in Chicago to Joseph P. and Priscilla Rose (Dombrowski) Rostenkowski. His father served in the Illinois House of Representatives and was for many years a Chicago alderman and ward committeeman. Rostenkowski and his two sisters, Marcie and Gladys, grew up in the four-story brick house that his paternal grandfather had built in the city's 32d Ward. Rostenkowski attended St. John's Military Academy in Delafield, Wisconsin, where he won letters in baseball, football, basketball, and track. After receiving his high-school diploma from St. John's, in 1946, he enlisted in the U.S. Army and served for two years as a private with the Seventh Infantry Division in Korea. Encouraged by his army buddies, Rostenkowski tried out for the Philadelphia Athletics baseball club in the spring of 1949, but his father persuaded him to give up his dream of becoming a professional athlete and to undertake night classes in business at Loyola University, in Chicago. In 1952 Rostenkowski won his father's former seat in the Illinois House of Representatives. Two years later he was elected to the state Senate, and in November 1958 he ran for the Eighth Congressional District seat in the U.S. House being vacated by the retiring Democratic incumbent, Thomas R. Gordon. In the general election he won 75 percent of the vote and became, at 30, the youngest member of the 86th Congress. During his first decade in Congress, Rostenkowski gradually attained a position of great influence. With the help of Thomas J. O'Brien, the leader of the Democratic delegation from Illinois, he secured an assignment to the important Interstate and Foreign Commerce Committee during his freshman term. He sat on that committee until O'Brien's death, in 1964, at which time he inherited his colleague's seat on the influential Ways and Means Committee. He served on Ways and Means for most of his time in office and was chair from 1981 to 1994. Rostenkowski's standing rose even more when he was elected chair of the House Democratic Caucus in both 1966 and 1968. From early on, Rostenkowski's record was typical of that of a northern Democrat with close ties to a powerful big-city political organization. He used his influence to obtain key committee assignments for Illinois Democrats, and he made sure that Chicago received its full share of funds under such programs as the Law Enforcement Assistance Act. On the House floor he supported civil rights legislation and the social-welfare programs that made up President Lyndon B. Johnson's War on Poverty. He also argued in favor of federal funding of inner-city renewal projects and urban mass-transit networks. In 1966 Rostenkowski was involved in crafting the legislation that established Medicare. In 1983 he was involved in a deal to reform Social Security, and in 1986 he worked on a compromise that helped enact a major tax-reform act. Throughout his time in the House, Rostenkowski was known for working with both Democrats and Republicans, and he forged positive working relationships with Presidents Ronald Reagan, Bill Clinton, and George H. W. Bush. In 1992 Rostenkowski was investigated for abusing the House post office. In 1994 he was charged with abusing the congressional payroll and his office expense account, as well as obstructing justice. As a result, he was defeated in the 1994 midterm elections. He pleaded guilty to two counts of mail fraud and served 15 months behind bars. He was pardoned by Clinton in 2000. Rostenkowski later worked as a commentator for a Chicago television station and as a college instructor. He was also the head of a consulting firm, Danross Associates. He

died at his vacation home in Wisconsin. He is survived by his wife, LaVerne, and three daughters: Gayle, Dawn, and Kristie. (His youngest daughter, Stacy, died of liver cancer in 2007.) See *Current Biography* (1982). —W.D.

Obituary *New York Times* (on-line) Aug. 11, 2010

RUDD, PAUL May 15, 1940–Aug. 12, 2010 Actor. Although his acting career lasted less than two decades, Paul Ryan Rudd made his mark in movies, on television, and on stage. The actor was born Paul Kenneth Rudd in Boston, Massachusetts. His father, Frank Stanley, was of Irish descent, and his mother, the former Kathryn Frances Ryan, was of Norwegian descent. (Rudd later replaced his given middle name with his mother's maiden name.) Rudd's father worked as a milkman before moving up within his company to become a district manager and then the president of a subsidiary; as a result of his father's changing positions, Rudd's family moved often, mainly in Massachusetts and New Hampshire. Rudd attended Roman Catholic schools and then enrolled at Fairfield University, in Connecticut. There, he helped organize student support for John F. Kennedy's 1960 presidential campaign. After graduating with a bachelor's degree in psychology in 1962, Rudd studied for the priesthood at the Maryknoll Seminary in Ossining, New York. It was not long before he decided that he "wasn't meant for that kind of life," as he once told a reporter. He moved to New York City, where, following some graduate study at Fordham University, he worked for the Madison Avenue firm of Compton Advertising for two years. At the relatively late age of 27, Rudd began pursuing an acting career, accepting any roles he could get. He began performing at such venues as the Repertory Theater of Lincoln Center, the Hartford Stage in Connecticut, and the Arena Stage in Washington, D.C. In 1969 Rudd landed a part in the Boston production of *The Boys in the Band* and went on to perform with the play's New York company. In 1970 he had a small role in the film *Tell Me That You Love Me, Junie Moon*, and in 1972 he appeared in such theatrical productions as *Love's Labour's Lost* and *The Changing Room*. The turning point in Rudd's career came in 1974, when he appeared in Peter Nichols's play *The National Health*, about a terminal-patient ward in a British hospital. Rudd's performance, as the victim of a motorcycle crash, helped the play advance to Broadway. The performance also helped Rudd secure his first television role, on the CBS series *Beacon Hill* (1975), about a wealthy Boston household in the 1920s. To prepare for his role, as a cocky Irish immigrant who works as a chauffeur in America, Rudd traveled to Ireland to improve his accent and pick up some colloquialisms. Despite early positive reviews, *Beacon Hill* was cancelled after eight episodes, and Rudd returned to the Broadway stage, appearing in productions of *Ah, Wilderness!* (1975); *The Glass Menagerie* (1975); *Streamers* (1976), for which he received the Outer Critics Circle Award for best actor; and *Bosoms and Neglect* (1979). He also played the title roles in *Henry V* (1976) and *Romeo and Juliet* (1977), both part of the New York Shakespeare Festival. "Paul Rudd makes a taut-nerved Romeo, his handsome face either tense with pain or almost consciously relaxed and sunny," Clive Barnes wrote in a *New York Times* (March 19, 1977) review of *Romeo and Juliet*. "He speaks the verse very well, with intelligent nuances, and his ardent death wish at the end is most impressive." Rudd played John F. Kennedy in the television film *Johnny We Hardly Knew Ye* (1977) and appeared in the 1978 movie *The Betsy*. During the early 1980s he made guest appearances on the television shows *Moonlighting, Hart to Hart*, and *Knots Landing*, among others. In the mid-1980s Rudd retired from acting in order to help raise his children with his second wife, Martha Bannerman. (Rudd had divorced his first wife, Joan Mannion, in 1982.) He later worked as a theater instructor at Sarah Lawrence College and the New School for Drama. Rudd, who died of pancreatic cancer at his home in Greenwich, Connecticut, is survived by his mother, his second wife, and his three children: Eliza, Kathryn, and Graeme. See *Current Biography* (1977). —J.P.

Obituary *New York Times* (on-line) Aug. 14, 2010

SALINGER, J. D. Jan. 1, 1919–Jan. 27, 2010 Writer. The success of J. D. Salinger's 1951 novel, *The Catcher in the Rye*, which captured the alienation and disillusionment of post–World War II American youth, catapulted him to literary fame. Despite that, Salinger chose to retreat into a life of seclusion, shunning the spotlight and avoiding the attentions of his devoted readers. Today, Holden Caulfield, the troubled narrator and protagonist of *The Catcher in the Rye*, is recognized as an American literary icon as significant as Mark Twain's Huckleberry Finn. Jerome David Salinger was born in New York City, the second child and only son of Sol Salinger, a food importer of Jewish descent, and Miriam (Jillich) Salinger, a Catholic of Scots-Irish heritage. By the early 1930s the upwardly mobile family was living on Park Avenue, a tony Manhattan thoroughfare. As a teenager, Salinger was expelled from prep school and sent to Valley Forge Military Academy, in Pennsylvania. After graduation he entered New York University (NYU) but left after a few weeks to travel to Europe with his father, who hoped to teach him the food-exporting business. In the fall of 1938, Salinger enrolled at Ursinus College, in Pennsylvania, where fellow students have recalled that he proclaimed his intention to write the Great American Novel. Salinger returned to New York City after only one term and completed his education at Columbia University, in evening classes. Whit Burnett, a Columbia teacher and the editor of the literary magazine *Story*, encouraged him to publish his work. Salinger's short stories were soon being published in *Story, Esquire*, and the *Saturday Evening Post*, but he had to put his writing career on hold when he was drafted into the U.S. Army. He served with the Counter-Intelligence Corps of the Fourth Infantry Division and took part in D-Day and the Battle of the Bulge. (Two of his short stories, "A Perfect Day for Bananafish" and "For Esme—With Love and Squalor," feature soldiers deeply affected by war.) In 1945 Salinger was hospitalized for battle fatigue. He remained in Europe for a brief period and married a German wom-

an, Sylvia, whom he soon divorced. Salinger then returned to New York and, while living in his parents' apartment, began writing again. "A Perfect Day for Bananafish" was published in the *New Yorker* in 1948. In it, Salinger introduced the troubled Glass family, whose members he would revisit repeatedly in his fiction. "A Perfect Day for Bananafish" culminates when Seymour, the oldest Glass son, commits suicide while on his honeymoon. The story, along with "For Esme—With Love and Squalor" and several others, was republished in *Nine Stories* (1953). In 1951 *The Catcher in the Rye* was published, and it quickly turned the literary world on its head. The novel was noteworthy for its youthful cynicism, contemporary slang, and occasionally coarse language. (Although reviews were generally positive, many schools banned the book.) The novel follows 16-year-old Holden Caulfield in his picaresque ramble around Manhattan, where he interacts with taxi drivers, a prostitute, nuns, an elevator operator, a former teacher, and others. The young narrator is on the verge of dropping out of Pencey Prep (modeled on Valley Forge Military Academy), and he sees his odyssey as an affirmation of youthful integrity against the "phony" adult world, a cry that would resonate throughout U.S. schools and universities for decades after the book's initial publication. The novel continues to sell more than 250,000 paperback copies per year and has been translated into 30 languages. Salinger's other books, *Franny and Zooey* (1961) and *Raise High the Roof Beam, Carpenters and Seymour: An Introduction* (1963), continued the saga of the eccentric Glass family. Although Salinger's name became a household word in the U.S. during the 1950s and 1960s, Salinger the man became more and more reclusive. In 1953 he had moved to the small town of Cornish, New Hampshire, to avoid the media spotlight. He remained there until his death, turning down requests for interviews and socializing only with the town's residents. He reportedly instructed his literary agents, Harold Ober Associates, to discard his fan mail. In 1986 Salinger took the British writer Ian Hamilton to court to prevent him from quoting unpublished letters in a Salinger biography he was writing. The case went to the U.S. Supreme Court, which ruled in Salinger's favor. In 2009 Salinger sued the Swedish author Fredrik Colting, who had written an unauthorized sequel to *The Catcher in the Rye*, and a federal judge halted publication of the book. Despite his attempts at absolute privacy, Salinger was not able to stop the publication of two memoirs: one, penned by Joyce Maynard, an ex-lover, appeared in 1998, and the other, written by his daughter, Margaret, was published in 2000. Both women described Salinger as eccentric, personally abusive, and eerily obsessed with his health. Salinger's first wife was Claire Douglas, the daughter of the British art critic Robert Langton Douglas. The couple had two children, Matthew and Margaret, before divorcing, in 1966. In 1972 Salinger began his affair with Maynard, then a Yale University freshman. In the early 1980s Salinger was involved with the actress Elaine Joyce, and later in the decade he married Colleen O'Neill, a nurse. Salinger is survived by O'Neill, his two children, and three grandsons. The cause of his death was not revealed and, in keeping with Salinger's penchant for privacy, no public service was held. See *World Authors 1900–1950* (1996). —W.D.

Obituary *New York Times* (on-line) Jan. 28, 2010

SAMARANCH, JUAN ANTONIO July 17, 1920–Apr. 21, 2010 Spanish sports official; diplomat. Juan Antonio Samaranch served for 21 years (1980–2001) as the president of the International Olympic Committee (IOC), during which he transformed the Olympics from a struggling, almost-bankrupt enterprise into a successful and profitable entity, by brokering broadcasting and sponsorship deals and by reigniting the public's interest in the Games in a variety of ways. Samaranch was born in Barcelona, Spain, the third son among six siblings. His father owned and operated a highly successful textile business. Samaranch was fond of soccer and roller hockey in his youth and later became a champion table-tennis player. He attended two business institutes in Barcelona and received further schooling at the city's German College. According to some sources Samaranch served briefly with the leftist Popular Front army during the Spanish Civil War (1936–39) before deserting; he then reportedly spent time in France before returning to Spain and joining the forces of the nationalist leader Francisco Franco. (Other sources claim he did not fight in the war.) After the war Samaranch worked as a manager in his family's textile business. According to some reports he also became involved in the real-estate, banking, and construction industries. His first experience in the professional sports world came in the early 1950s, when he established and managed Spain's national rink-hockey team, which later won the world championship. He became a member of the Spanish Olympic Committee in 1954 and was vice president of the committee that organized the 1955 Mediterranean Games (a multi-sport event held every four years involving nations bordering the Mediterranean Sea). Samaranch led the Spanish delegation to the 1956 Winter Olympics as well as the 1960 and 1964 Summer Olympics. In 1966 Samaranch became a member of the IOC; the same year he was appointed by Franco as Spain's national sports minister, a position he held for four years, and he was named chief of protocol for the 1968 Summer Games. He became a member of Franco's national Parliament in 1971 and served as vice president of the IOC from 1974 to 1978. During that time he also held various political positions within Franco's regime, including that of president of Catalonia's regional council (1973–77); his tenure in that post included a period of civil unrest in Spain following Franco's death in 1975. Spain established a democracy under King Juan Carlos I, who appointed Samaranch to serve as Spain's ambassador to the Soviet Union and to the People's Republic of Mongolia. In the former post Samaranch played a crucial role in helping the Soviets organize the 1980 Summer Olympics, in Moscow. (The U.S. boycotted those games in response to the Soviet Union's invasion of Afghanistan.) Samaranch stepped down from his ambassadorships in 1980, when he was elected president of the IOC, becoming the first person of Spanish heritage to head the organization. At the time, the IOC was in financial shambles, with reportedly only $200,000 in cash reserves.

Samaranch used his negotiating skills to help turn the Olympics into a multibillion-dollar industry. During his 21-year reign, he became known for his autocratic leadership style and unrelenting work ethic. He encouraged several countries to participate in the Games following periods of national or international turmoil, including South Africa after the end of apartheid. He also established a program called Olympic Solidarity, which provided financial aid to underdeveloped nations to help them participate in the Games. Samaranch helped broker lucrative broadcasting deals with television companies and with corporations wanting to benefit from association with the Olympics, and by allowing professional athletes to compete in the Games, he heightened the aura of glamour surrounding the events. Additionally, he broke down barriers by allowing women to become members of the IOC, and he was credited with increasing the participation of female athletes in the Games by more than 40 percent. Samaranch's tenure, however, was not without controversy; he faced several bribery scandals involving committee members as well as a rise in doping scandals. Many Olympic officials have cited Samaranch's failure to adequately address the issues of performance-enhancing drugs as the most significant blight on his reign. After stepping down, in 2001, Samaranch was succeeded by Jacques Rogge of Belgium and was named an honorary president for life of the IOC—as is the custom with outgoing IOC heads. Samaranch, who remained active in the committee and played a vital role in Madrid's unsuccessful bids for the 2012 and 2016 Olympic Games, died at a Barcelona hospital. Samaranch was married to the former Maria Teresa Salisachs Rowe for more than 50 years. She died in 2000. He is survived by his son, Juan Antonio Jr.; his daughter, Maria Teresa; and his companion, Luisa Sallent. See *Current Biography* (1994). —C.C.

Obituary *New York Times* (on-line) Apr. 21, 2010

SAMUELSON, PAUL A. May 15, 1915–Dec. 13, 2009 Economist. Paul A. Samuelson was the author of one of the the the best-selling economics textbooks of all time, *Economics: An Introductory Analysis*, published in 1948. In 1970 he became one of the first recipients of the Nobel Prize in Economic Sciences. (The category had been introduced the previous year.) Samuelson spent most of his career as an economics professor at the Massachusetts Institute of Technology (MIT), and he advised several presidents on economic policy. According to an obituary on the MIT News Office Web site (December 13, 2009), "In a career that spanned seven decades . . . [Samuelson] transformed his field, influenced millions of students, and turned MIT into an economics powerhouse." Paul Anthony Samuelson was born in Gary, Indiana, to Frank Samuelson, a pharmacist, and Ella (Lipton) Samuelson. His father lost much of his money after World War I, and the family relocated to Chicago. Samuelson graduated from high school at the age of 16 and went on to obtain a B.A. degree from the University of Chicago in 1935. He then took graduate courses in economics at Harvard University, in Cambridge, Massachusetts, where he studied under Alvin Hansen, then one of the leading proponents of the economic theories of John Maynard Keynes. (Keynes held that in the event of depression, modern market economies would need government intervention in the form of spending or tax cuts; that idea contrasted sharply with earlier views that a troubled market would repair itself.) Samuelson received an M.A. degree in 1936 and a Ph.D. degree in 1941. In 1940 Harvard offered Samuelson an instructorship, but a month later MIT countered with an assistant professorship. Harvard administrators made little effort to persuade him to stay. As quoted by Michael Weinstein in the *New York Times* (December 13, 2009, on-line), Robert M. Solow, another Nobel laureate, once said of the Harvard Economics Department of that era: "You could be disqualified for a job if you were either smart or Jewish or Keynesian. So what chance did this smart, Jewish, Keynesian have?" Samuelson became an associate professor at MIT in 1944. Three years later he was promoted to full professor, and he was named institute professor—the school's highest faculty position—in 1966. Samuelson is credited with elevating the MIT Department of Economics to its current status as one of the world's finest. Samuelson, a Democrat, also famously provided economic advice to the newly elected Democratic president John F. Kennedy in a 40-minute session on the beach at Hyannis Port, Massachusetts. During the meeting he recommended that the president employ a Keynesian tax cut to boost the economy. Samuelson went on to advise Lyndon B. Johnson, Kennedy's successor, and during an economics seminar with President Gerald Ford in 1974, Samuelson coined the term "stagflation," which refers to a period of rising unemployment and inflation. Samuelson received the Sveriges Riksbank Prize in Economic Sciences in Memory of Alfred Nobel (known informally as the Nobel Prize in Economics) in 1970. According to the Nobel Web site, Samuelson had "done more than any other contemporary economist to raise the level of scientific analysis in economic theory." After officially retiring, in 1985, Samuelson continued to work in the Economics Department at MIT. In 1996 he was awarded a National Medal of Science. A past president of both the American Economic Association and the Econometric Society, Samuelson authored hundreds of articles and served as an associate editor and adviser for several professional journals. His collected scientific papers have been published by MIT Press. Samuelson died at his home in Belmont, Massachusetts. His first wife, Marion, whom he married in 1938, died in 1978. He is survived by his second wife, Risha; six children from his first marriage—Jane, Margaret, William, and triplets Robert, John, and Paul; and 15 grandchildren. (It has been said that he was motivated to write *Economics: An Introductory Analysis* after the birth of the triplets, in order to pay the expenses of the newly expanded household.) Samuelson is also survived by a brother, Robert Summers, a professor emeritus of economics at the University of Pennsylvania. (Lawrence Summers, a former director of the White House National Economic Council and former presi-dent of Harvard, is Samuelson's nephew.) See *Current Biography* (1965). —W.D.

Obituary *New York Times* (on-line) Dec. 14, 2009

SANCHEZ JUNCO, EDUARDO Apr. 26, 1943–July 14, 2010 Publishing executive. Eduardo Sanchez Junco owned the multimillion-dollar publishing company behind *Hola!*, a Spanish-language gossip magazine that has spawned numerous editions in different languages as well as two sister publications—the popular British magazine *Hello!* and the French magazine *Oh La!*. Margalit Fox wrote for the *New York Times* (June 17, 2010, on-line), "Since its founding in 1988, *Hello!* has flourished as the antithesis of the scandal sheet, airing no dirty linen and offering not a jot of titillation. In many ways it is a throwback, recalling the mid-20th-century American movie magazines in which stars were dreamily photographed with their glamorous houses, adoring spouses and rosy-cheeked children." Sanchez Junco's publishing company often paid large sums of money for exclusive interviews with famous figures. According to the London *Telegraph* (July 15, 2010, on-line), "*Hello!* featured carefully-posed, pin-sharp colour pictures and anodyne interviews with celebrities who knew that not only would the magazine refrain from digging for dirt but it would also put them in control." Today there are 14 editions of the magazine published in 10 languages, selling a collective 10 million copies weekly. Eduardo Sanchez Junco was born in Palencia, Spain. His parents, Antonio Sanchez Gomez and Mercedes Junco Calderon, launched *Hola!* in 1944. (Antonio managed the business until his death, in 1984, when his son took over.) At the time of *Hola!*'s founding, Spain was under the rule of the fascist dictator General Francisco Franco, who was in power from 1939 until his death, in 1975. Antonio took no chances with satire or negative remarks about Spain's elite in his inexpensive, four-page publication. Instead, he devised a technique of "building fantasy around the famous and then peddling the fantasy in full color," as Roula Khalaf wrote for *Forbes* (November 8, 1993). By 1963 *Hola!* had become Spain's most popular magazine, with a weekly circulation of 250,000. The family relocated the business to Madrid that year, at about the same time that Sanchez Junco left for college. His father insisted that he earn a degree in something other than journalism, and he elected to study agronomy at the University of Madrid. After graduating, however, Sanchez Junco returned to work in the family business. In 1986, when Spain joined the European Union, Sanchez Junco expanded the magazine's circulation to other European countries, using local journalists when needed. In 1988 he launched *Hello!* in Britain, with content specifically focused on British figures. *Hello!* proved popular, and by 1992 it had reached a circulation of 1.3 million. *Oh La!*, the French version, was launched in 1998. Sanchez Junco developed a reputation for his expert handling of celebrity contacts. For instance, he was known to purchase unflattering photos of celebrities from paparazzi simply to keep them from being published. He also paid exorbitant amounts of money for interviews; in 1990, for example, he paid £250,000 for an interview with Prince Andrew and his wife, Sarah Ferguson. When *Hello!* lost an exclusive bid to photograph the wedding of the Welsh actress Catherine Zeta-Jones and the American actor Michael Douglas, in 2000, one of the magazine's photographers infiltrated the event anyway, and by the next day, the grainy, low-quality images had found their way into a new issue. In 2003 Douglas and Zeta-Jones sued *Hello!*, and the company was ordered to pay damages to the couple and a competitor, *OK!*—the magazine that had won the bidding war. Sanchez Junco, who had stakes in the wine, dairy, and farming industries, was a part-owner of Spain's Antena 3 television network. While he was sometimes featured in the business news, he kept his personal life private, avoiding interviews and public appearances. European newspapers reported that Sanchez Junco died of cancer. He is survived by his mother, an honorary president of the business, as well as his wife, Mamen Perez Villota, and three children: Eduardo, Mamen, and Cheleles. Eduardo is the current editor of *Hello!*. See *Current Biography International* (2003). —W.D.

Obituary *New York Times* (on-line) July 17, 2010

SARAMAGO, JOSÉ Nov. 16, 1922–June 18, 2010 In 1998 José Saramago became the first Portuguese author to win the Nobel Prize for Literature. In awarding the prize, the Swedish Academy praised Saramago as a writer "who with parables sustained by imagination, compassion and irony continually enables us once again to apprehend an illusory reality." Saramago—whose writing is often characterized as magical realism—has drawn comparisons to the literary giants Gabriel Gárcia Márquez and Franz Kafka. He published his first novel, *The Land of Sin*, in his early 20s and spent the next several decades working various jobs, as a mechanic, a bureaucrat, a printer, a proofreader, and a literary critic, publishing fiction only sporadically, before becoming a full-time writer in his 50s. His body of work, which includes more than 15 novels as well as a collection of short stories, several books of poems, newspaper articles, plays, opera libretti, diaries, and travelogues, has been translated into more than 25 languages. José de Sousa Saramago was born to José de Sousa and Maria de Piede, poor, landless peasants in the village of Azinhaga in the Ribatejo section of Portugal. In 1924, when Saramago was two years old, his father, a World War I veteran, found work as a policeman and moved the family to Lisbon, the capital city. Saramago was 14 years old when the family moved into their first house; until that point, they had shared living quarters with other families. Though Saramago excelled in grammar school, his parents could not afford to pay additional school fees, so he was sent to technical school to be trained as a mechanic. Saramago became interested in writing after enrolling in a literature course offered by the technical school. After completing school he worked for two years as a mechanic, using the public library in Lisbon in the evenings after work. Saramago was employed as a civil servant for the Social Welfare Service, in Lisbon, when he married his first wife, Ilda Reis, in 1944. In 1947—the same year his daughter, Violante, was born—Saramago published his first book, *The Land of Sin*. (Unless otherwise mentioned, all publication dates refer to the year the work was first published in Portuguese.) Around that time Saramago began work on two other novels, both of which he eventually abandoned. He then disappeared from the Portuguese literary scene for the next 19 years. Saramago has stated that the long period of silence was not because of the repressive regime of Antonio de Oliveira Salazar, whose right-wing government ruled Portugal from 1932 to 1974, as some have suggested; rather, he simply had nothing of interest to write. Beginning in the late 1950s, Saramago worked at the publishing company Estudios Cor, where he befriended some of the most prominent Portuguese writers of the time. Concurrently Saramago earned extra income by translating the work of such writers as Baudelaire and Tolstoy, and he also briefly worked as a literary critic. His return to the literary world was marked by the publication of two books of poetry, *Possible Poems* (1966) and *Probably Joy* (1970), followed by two collections of newspaper articles, *From This World and the Other* (1971) and *The Traveller's Baggage* (1973). After leaving his publishing job, in 1971, Saramago worked at the newspaper *Diario de Lisboa* and the morning paper *Diario de Noticias*. He was fired from the latter paper in 1975, in the wake of a politico-military coup, for holding leftist political views. (He had been a member of the Portuguese Communist Party since 1969.) At 53 Saramago, now considered unemployable because of the country's political situation, decided to devote himself to literature. "It was about time to find out what I was worth as a writer," Saramago wrote in a short autobiography for the official Web site of the Nobel Foundation. In early 1976 he spent several weeks of intense reflection in Lavre, a rural village in the Alentejo Province, which Saramago described as a "period of study, observation and note-taking that led, in 1980, to the novel *Risen from the Ground* where the way of narrating which characterizes my novels was born." That novel, a love story inspired by memories of the writer's parents and grandparents, won Saramago the City of Lisbon Prize for literature. In 1978 he published a collection of short stories entitled *Quasi Object*, and after that, several plays. Saramago won international acclaim in 1982 when, at age 60, he published *Baltasar and Blimunda*, a story that intertwines an account of the building of the convent of Mafra, outside Lisbon, and an anachronistic fantasy involving two lovers as they try to flee the Inquisition in a flying machine. The book earned rave reviews from American critics when it was published in English translation, in 1987. Saramago later adapted the novel for the libretto of the opera *Blimunda*, with music by the Italian composer Azio Corghi. Other novels published by Saramago during the 1980s include *The Year of the Death of Ricardo Reis* (1984), considered one of Saramago's masterpieces, about Salazar's reign; *The Stone Raft* (1986); and *The History of the Siege of Lisbon* (1989). Saramago, who divorced his first wife in 1970 and had a long-term relationship with the Portuguese writer Isabel da Nobrega, married the Spanish journalist Pilar del Rio in 1988. Throughout their marriage del Rio devoted herself to translating Saramago's works into Spanish. The Portuguese government vetoed the nomination of Saramago's 1991 book, *The Gospel According to Jesus Christ*, for the

European Union's Ariosto Literary Prize on the grounds that the book was offensive to Catholics. Many were offended by the book, which retells the Gospel stories from an ironic point of view, imagines new prophesies, depicts God as something of a villain, and describes Jesus's sexual relationship with Mary Magdalene. Because of the Portuguese government's opposition to the book, which it later retracted, Saramago left Portugal with his wife and moved to Lanzarote in the Canary Islands, a Spanish archipelago. In 1995 Saramago published *Blindness*, an allegory about the horrors of 20th-century society, which was later adapted into a film starring Mark Ruffalo and Julianne Moore. Saramago published new work at a steady rate up until his death, including *All the Names* (1997), *The Cave* (2000), *The Double* (2002), *Seeing* (2004), and *Death with Interruptions* (2005). In 2006 he published the childhood memoir *Small Memories*. He also published several volumes of his journal, which he had begun in 1993. In addition to the Nobel Prize, Saramago received several other prestigious literary awards, including Portugal's Luis de Camoes Prize. Saramago died of multiple organ failure in the company of family and close friends at his home in the Canary Islands. He is survived by his wife, his daughter, and two grandchildren. At the time of Saramago's death, more than two million copies of his books had been sold. His novel *The Elephant's Journey* was published in the U.S. in 2010. See *Current Biography* (2002). —H.R.W.

Obituary *New York Times* A p19 June 19, 2010

SAXBE, WILLIAM June 24, 1916–Aug. 24, 2010 Former U.S. senator and attorney general. William B. Saxbe was a disillusioned "law and order" Republican in the U.S. Senate when the so-called "Saturday night massacre" occurred, on October 20, 1973. On that occasion Elliot Richardson, President Richard Nixon's third attorney general, resigned and Richardson's deputy, William D. Ruckelshaus, was discharged, when in turn they refused to obey the president's order to fire Special Watergate Prosecutor Archibald Cox, who had recently subpoenaed Nixon. The White House sought to fill the Justice Department vacancy with a person who was not an avowed enemy of Nixon but who was also not overtly partial toward him either, because it wished to avoid a prolonged and politically damaging confirmation battle in the Senate. It found such a man in Saxbe, a GOP maverick who tried during his tenure to support the administration when possible—despite his private judgment that the Nixon administration was one of the most inept in American history. Of English descent, Saxbe was born in Mechanicsburg, Ohio, the town where his great-grandfather settled in 1825. Saxbe attended Ohio State University, from which he graduated with a B.A. degree in political science in 1940. A member of the Ohio National Guard, he served for five years stateside in the Army Air Forces during World War II. (Called up again during the Korean War, he was discharged as a colonel.) In 1946, while still studying law at Ohio State University, Saxbe was elected to the Ohio House of Representatives, where he spent four terms. (He earned a J.D. degree in 1948.) After stepping down, in 1954, he be-

came a partner in the Columbus, Ohio, law firm of Saxbe, Boyd & Prine. After three years in the private sector, practicing law and raising cattle on his farm in Mechanicsburg, he ran for the post of state attorney general. He was elected to four terms in that office, for a total of eight years (1957–58 and 1963–68). In November 1968 Saxbe triumphed in a closely fought race against the liberal Democrat John J. Gilligan to represent Ohio in the U.S. Senate. He soon became disenchanted with the slow pace of the legislative process and increasingly critical of the Nixon administration. In September 1973 Saxbe announced that he did not intend to seek reelection. Scarcely a month later Nixon offered him the job of attorney general. Saxbe was sworn into his new post on January 4, 1974. Saxbe was at first skeptical about Nixon's innocence in the Watergate scandal, but he gradually became more willing to accept Nixon's version of the affair. Saxbe promised the Senate, however, that he would not interfere with the impeachment process on Nixon's behalf unless the House was proceeding on "obviously political grounds" and not on "criminal charges." (Nixon resigned in August 1974.) Although most closely associated in the public eye with the Watergate matter, Saxbe's tenure was also notable for a landmark 1974 antitrust lawsuit that put an end to the longstanding Bell system telephone monopoly. After Gerald Ford replaced Nixon as president, Saxbe remained at the Justice Department for several months. He stepped down in early 1975 and accepted a post as ambassador to India. In 1977 he returned to Mechanicsburg to practice law. He died at the age of 94 and is survived by his wife, Ardath, who is known by the nickname Dolly; his children, Charles, Juli, and William; nine grandchildren; and four great-grandchildren. See *Current Biography* (1974). —M.R.

Obituary *New York Times* (on-line) Aug. 25, 2010

SCHILLEBEECKX, EDWARD Nov. 12, 1914–Dec. 23, 2009 Catholic theologian. Edward Cornelius Florentius Schillebeeckx (pronounced "SKIL-uh-bakes") was known for his contributions to the Second Vatican Council and for his controversial writings on theology. Born in Antwerp, Belgium, Schillebeeckx was the sixth of 14 children in a middle-class Flemish family. He attended Mass every day with his devoutly Catholic father, who worked as an accountant in the public-records office. Schillebeeckx attended a Jesuit-run secondary school in Turnhout, Belgium, and in 1934 began studying philosophy at a Dominican institution in Ghent. After three years there he completed a compulsory term of service in the Belgian military. He was ordained to the priesthood in 1941 and continued his studies at the Sorbonne, in Paris, France, and later at Le Saulchoir, a Dominican house of studies in Etiolles, near Paris. At Le Saulchoir he earned his doctoral degree in theology and encountered Marie-Dominique Chenu and Yves Congar, pioneering theologians who introduced him to modern Catholic thought and the Calvinist teachings of Karl Barth, which would serve as a major influence. Schillebeeckx went on to publish several books over the next decade before joining the theological faculty at the Catholic University of Nijmegen (now Radboud University) in 1958, where he remained until his retirement, in 1983. Schillebeeckx was widely recognized for his contributions to the Second Vatican Council, a landmark reassessment of Catholic life that was held in Rome from 1962 to 1965. There he served as a theological expert with the Dutch Episcopal delegation, lecturing and leading discussions of the council's documents at conferences that included not only the Dutch prelates but also the Polish, Indian, and Brazilian bishops. Those documents eventually allowed for such changes as permitting celebration of the Mass in modern languages rather than Latin and breaking barriers separating Catholics, Protestants, and members of other faiths. Schillebeeckx continued to espouse radical changes after the Second Vatican Council, and many of his writings were met with derision from church officials, who investigated him repeatedly for heresy. All such investigations ended with no formal censures or penalties imposed. (His admirers often mentioned that he was questioned by the Congregation for the Doctrine of the Faith—the church office that had overseen the Inquisition.) In 1989 the Edward Schillebeeckx Foundation, which aims to collect and preserve his work, was established in Nijmegen. Schillebeeckx continued to write until shortly before his death, at the age of 95. See *Current Biography* (1983). —C.C.

Obituary *New York Times* A p26 Jan. 17, 2010

SCHORR, DANIEL Aug. 31, 1916–July 23, 2010 Journalist; broadcaster. Daniel Schorr covered the news for more than half a century, serving as a commentator for CBS (1953–76), CNN (1979–85), and National Public Radio (1985 until the time of his death). He was known for his brash demeanor, hard-hitting reporting, and outspoken liberal views, all of which often brought him into conflict with various media officials. Daniel Louis Schorr was born in the New York City borough of the Bronx, to Louis and Tillie Schorr, Russian-Jewish immigrants. His father died when he was six, and his younger brother, Alvin, suffered from a series of childhood illnesses, including polio and scarlet fever. As a result, Schorr was forced to supplement the meager income his mother earned as a seamstress by working as a paperboy. Schorr was unhappy and awkward as a child. He sold his first story at the age of 12, after witnessing a woman jump to her death from his apartment building. (He was paid $5 by the *Bronx Home News* for calling in the tip.) He subsequently edited the student newspaper and the yearbook at DeWitt Clinton High School, in the Bronx, and in his spare time he worked as a stringer for the *Bronx Home News* and the *Jewish Daily Bulletin*. Upon graduating from high school, in 1933, Schorr attended the City College of New York, where he majored in sociology and wrote for the school newspaper. During his college years he also contributed articles to several New York dailies and to the Jewish Telegraphic Agency (JTA). After receiving a B.S. degree, in 1939, Schorr became a full-time assistant editor at the JTA. He subsequently worked for a brief time at the *New York Journal-American* before joining the Netherlands-based news agency ANETA in 1941, as its New York news editor. In 1943 Schorr was drafted into the U.S Army. He served as a public-relations officer at Camp Polk, Louisiana, and worked in intelligence at Fort Sam Houston, in Texas, before being discharged, with the rank of sergeant, in 1945. After completing his military service, Schorr returned to ANETA and moved to the Netherlands to reorganize the agency's news operations in Europe. He left ANETA in 1948 to work as a freelance foreign correspondent, and over the next few years, he contributed pieces to such publications as the *New York Times*, the *Christian Science Monitor*, the London *Daily Mail*, *Time*, and *Newsweek*. Upon returning to the U.S. in 1952, Schorr landed a tryout on the city desk of the *New York Times*. His reporting caught the attention of the preeminent broadcast journalist Edward R. Murrow, who offered him a job at CBS News. When a long-term job offer at the *New York Times* fell through, Schorr joined CBS's Washington bureau. (Schorr later discovered that the managing editor of the *Times*, Turner Catledge, had ordered a freeze on hiring Jewish reporters out of fear that they might bias the paper's coverage of the Middle East.) At CBS News Schorr became a protégé of Murrow but continued to exhibit the values of a no-nonsense print reporter, scoffing at the laborious set-up of camera angles and the practice of wearing makeup. In 1955, after learning how to operate a camera himself, Schorr moved to Russia to open the first CBS News bureau in Moscow. In 1957 he helped plan the first U.S. television interview with Soviet premier Nikita S. Khrushchev, on *Face the Nation*. He repeatedly defied the Soviet Union's censorship rules, however, and was denied readmission into the country after a holiday visit to the U.S. later that year. Schorr spent the next several years working as a roving diplomatic correspondent, incurring the wrath of Presidents Dwight D. Eisenhower and John F. Kennedy, as well as Republican presidential nominee Barry Goldwater, for his investigative reports. (Kennedy, for example, so objected to Schorr's inclusion of German criticism of U.S. foreign policy in dispatches from Bonn that he asked CBS to transfer the reporter.) In the 1970s Schorr won three Emmy Awards for his reporting on the Watergate scandal, which was often punctuated by no-holds-barred criticisms of the Richard M. Nixon administration. Schorr later took pride in discovering his name on Nixon's infamous "enemies list." In 1976 Schorr came under intense scrutiny after he leaked a suppressed report by the House Permanent Select Committee on Intelligence that exposed illegal CIA and FBI operations. Although he characterized his actions as "an inescapable decision of journalistic conscience," Schorr's reporting duties at CBS News were revoked, and he resigned from the network later that year. In 1979 Schorr was hired by the television magnate Ted Turner to join his nascent cable news network, CNN. As the network's first news anchor, Schorr was responsible in great part for the resounding success of the enterprise. He and Turner frequently clashed, however, over assignments and issues of journalistic integrity, and in 1985 Schorr was dismissed from the network. That year he joined National Public Radio (NPR) as a commentator on such programs as *All Things Considered* and *Weekend Edition*. In 2001 Schorr, who also wrote a column for the *Christian Science Monitor* for several decades, penned the memoir *Staying Tuned: A Life in Journalism*. Schorr, who used a typewriter rather than a computer until the year before his death, was the last surviving member of the "Murrow Boys," a group of legendary reporters hand-picked by Murrow. Schorr is survived by his wife of 43 years, the former Lisbeth Bamberger; their son, Jonathan; their daughter, Lisa; and one grandchild. See *Current Biography* (1978). —C.C.

Obituary *New York Times* (on-line) July 23, 2010

SEGAL, ERICH June 16, 1937–Jan. 17, 2010 Writer. Erich Segal is best known for his debut novel, *Love Story*, published in early 1970. The book follows Oliver Barrett IV, a wealthy, Harvard-educated man who falls in love with Jennifer Cavalleri, a working-class beauty. Despite objections from his family, the pair marry, but soon after the wedding, Jennifer becomes ill and dies. Though *Love Story* received few wholly positive critical reviews, it sold tens of millions of copies and was translated into more than 20 languages. A poll taken soon after its publication revealed that one in five Americans had read the book. A film adaptation, also written by Segal, was released in late 1970. Starring Ryan O'Neal and Ali MacGraw, the romance grossed nearly $200 million and earned seven Academy Award nominations, including one for Segal's screenplay. Erich Wolf Segal was born in the New York City borough of Brooklyn to Samuel Segal, a rabbi, and Cynthia (Shapiro) Segal. He graduated from Harvard University, where he was both class poet and Latin salutatorian, in 1958. Segal obtained a master's degree (1959) and a doctoral degree (1964) in comparative literature, also from Harvard. He joined the faculty of Yale University as an assistant professor in 1965 and became an associate professor three years later. Segal taught classics at Yale until the 1980s and later held visiting professorships at various insitutions, including Princeton, Oxford, and the University of London. Prior to penning *Love Story*, Segal helped write the screenplay for the animated Beatles movie *Yellow Submarine* (1968), wrote the scholarly book *Roman Laughter: The Comedy of Plautus* (1968), and co-wrote, with Joe Raposo, *Sing Muse!* (1961), a musical comedy based on the story of Helen of Troy. *Love Story* had originally been written as a screenplay, but after every major studio rejected it because of its sentimentality, Segal rewrote the story as a novel, which was quickly purchased by Harper & Row. Only later did Ali McGraw, who knew Segal from her student days, persuade Paramount Pictures to make *Love Story* with her in the lead role of Cavalleri. One of *Love Story*'s taglines, "Love means never having to say you're sorry," was listed by the American Film Institute (AFI) as one of the top movie quotes of all time. Segal's later works include the screenplay for *A Change of Seasons* (1980), which stars Shirley MacLaine and Anthony Hopkins, and the novels *Oliver's Story* (1977), *The Class* (1985), *Doctors* (1988), *Acts of Faith* (1992), and *Only Love* (1997). Segal died of a heart attack in his London home after having been ill with Parkinson's disease for 25 years. He is survived by his wife, the former Karen James; two daughters, Francesca and Miranda; his mother, Cyn-

thia Zeger; and two brothers, David and Thomas. See *Current Biography* (1971). —M.A.S.

Obituary *New York Times* (on-line) Jan. 20, 2010

SIEPI, CESARE Feb. 10, 1923–July 5, 2010 Opera singer. Known for his rich bass voice and masculine stage presence, Cesare Siepi was widely considered one of the most brilliant opera stars of his day. He was especially celebrated for his portrayal of the title character in Mozart's *Don Giovanni*, a role he reprised numerous times. Anne Midgette wrote for the *Washington Post* (July 7, 2010, on-line), "He was one of the few Giovannis who could both sing with the sensuous, seductive ease the role requires and look the part of the irresistible seducer." Siepi (pronounced see-EP-ee) was born in Milan, Italy. He harbored early ambitions to be a boxer, but during one amateur bout his face was cut so badly that his mother made him promise never to step into the ring again. Siepi was a member of his school's choir and also participated in a madrigal-singing group. At the age of 18 he entered a vocal competition in Florence, and although he knew only two arias, he won. He made his operatic debut two months later, in Venice, singing the role of Sparafucile in *Rigoletto*. World War II brought his singing career to a temporary halt. In 1943, when Nazi troops entered Milan and Siepi was to be drafted into the army to fight alongside Germany, he went into hiding until he could escape from Italy into Switzerland. There, he gave concerts in detention camps. He returned to Italy in 1945 and participated in a benefit concert to raise funds for the rebuilding of La Scala, in Milan. He also returned to opera, as Zaccaria in *Nabucco* at the Teatro la Fenice, in Venice. So spectacular was his success that he was asked to help reopen the rebuilt La Scala in *Nabucco* in 1946. He continued appearing at La Scala in major bass roles, not only in the Italian repertory but also in several Wagnerian roles. Guest appearances in other major European opera houses together with concert appearances in Spain, Switzerland, Scandinavia, England, and Mexico spread his fame throughout most of Europe. Siepi made his American debut on November 6, 1950 at the Metropolitan Opera House, in New York City, singing the role of King Philip II in Verdi's *Don Carlo*. He sang the role of Don Basilio in *The Barber of Seville* at the Met the following month. He quickly became a favorite with American audiences, and his name often appeared in the gossip columns of New York City's newspapers, as an escort for a succession of beautiful women around town. During his more than two decades with the Metropolitan Opera, Siepi commanded admiration in still other roles: Silva in a 1956 revival of *Ernani*; Zaccaria in the Met's first performance of *Nabucco* on October 24, 1960, the opening night of the season; Alvise in *La Gioconda*; Oroveso in *Norma*; Sparafucile in *Rigoletto*; Fiesco in *Simon Boccanegra*; Sarastro in *The Magic Flute*; Don Fernando in *Fidelio*; and Gurnemanz in *Parsifal*. Along with King Philip II and Don Basilio, his most frequently performed roles were the lead in *Don Giovanni*, which he first performed in 1952; Figaro in *The Marriage of Figaro*; Mephistopheles in *Faust*; and Colline in *La Bohème*. In all, Siepi made almost 500 appearances at the Met. He also appeared regularly at London's Covent Garden and with the Vienna State Opera. Siepi continued to perform on stage until he was in his mid-60s. After his retirement he led a quiet life in Atlanta, Georgia. He suffered a stroke in late June 2010 and died the following month. Siepi is survived by his wife, Louellen, a former ballet dancer to whom he had been married since 1962; his son, Marco; his daughter, Luisa; and two grandchildren. See *Current Biography* (1955). —D.K.

Obituary *New York Times* (on-line) July 6, 2010

SIMIONATO, GIULIETTA May 12, 1916–May 5, 2010 Opera singer. From the 1930s to the 1960s, the Italian-born Giulietta Simionato was recognized as one of the world's leading opera stars. A mezzo-soprano who regularly appeared in works by Rossini, Bellini, and Donizetti, among many others, Simionato won acclaim around the world for her highly lyrical bel canto performances. In a *New York Times* obituary (May 6, 2010, on-line), Margalit Fox wrote that Simionato was "praised for her firm, agile voice; her smooth phrasing; and a vocal range so wide it encompassed the register of a soprano while retaining the meaty lower notes of a mezzo. She was also known for a commanding stage presence that belied her petite stature." Simionato was born in Forli, a town near Bologna, to Felice and Giovanna (Truddaiu) Simionato, neither of whom was musically inclined. Her father, a Venetian who was one of 24 brothers, was the director of a local prison. Her mother was a native of Sardinia, where Giulietta spent most of her childhood. There she received early vocal training at a convent and briefly considered pursuing a monastic life herself. Her mother forbade her to pursue secular singing, insisting that she devote her talents to "singing for Madonna." Her father moved the family to Rovigo, near Padua, after her mother's death, when Simionato was 15. There, the dark and vibrant quality of her voice was soon recognized, and with her father's permission, she obtained professional voice lessons. While still a student she made her debut as Lola in Pietro Mascagni's *Cavalleria Rusticana*, and at age 18, she debuted in the role of Maddalena in Giuseppe Verdi's *Rigoletto*. Her father died not long after that performance. In 1933 she won a singing competition in Florence, and in 1938 she appeared in a small role in Ildebrando Pizzetti's *Orseolo*. Over the next few years, Simionato regularly performed as a member of the company at La Scala but soon struck out on her own in search of bigger roles. She had some success, performing in Bizet's *Carmen* and Verdi's *Azucena*, and in 1947 she was called back to La Scala to play the title role in Ambroise Thomas's *Mignon*, which proved to be her breakthrough performance. (Simionato would return to La Scala several times for performances over the course of her career.) Her roles over the next few years included those in Rossini's *Il Barbiere di Siviglia*, Leonore in Donizetti's *La Favorite*, and Preziosilla in Verdi's *La Forza del Destino*. She was especially well received for her 1950 performance in the role of Marfa in Modest Mussorgsky's *Khovanshchina*. Simionato debuted at the Royal Opera House in London as Adalgisa in Vincenzo Bellini's *Norma* in 1953. The opera featured Maria Callas, one of Si-

mionato's good friends, in the title role, and was widely praised. The next year Simionato appeared in *Norma* at the Lyric Opera of Chicago, where she would spend six seasons. (Some sources claim that that performance was Simionato's U.S. debut, but a correction in her *New York Times* obituary puts Simionato's debut in 1953 at the San Francisco Opera.) In 1957 Simionato appeared with Callas again, playing Giovana Seymour in the Donizetti opera *Anna Bolena*. She made her debut at the Metropolitan Opera, in New York City, in 1959 as Azucena in Verdi's *Il Trovatore*. The *New York Times* reviewer, Howard Taubman, wrote of that performance, "The Italian mezzo-soprano brings a rich, secure and cultivated voice to the Met. Her range is formidable; the high tones have accuracy and brilliance, and the low are firm and vibrant. She sings with stirring ardor and moves with intelligence." Simionato went on to sing 28 performances at the Met. In 1966 she retired after a final performance at La Scala's Piccola Scala, as Servilia in Mozart's *La Clemenza di Tito*. That year she married Cesare Frugoni, a retired physician who was roughly 30 years her senior. He died in 1978. (She was reportedly married several other times, although specific information about those unions is not readily available.) Simionato died in Rome. See *Current Biography* (1960).—W.D.

Obituary *New York Times* (on-line) May 6, 2010

SIMMONS, JEAN Jan. 31, 1929–Jan. 22, 2010 Actress. Over the course of her career, which spanned more than six decades, Jean Simmons amassed nearly 100 credits on the big and small screens. Jean Merilyn Simmons was born in Crouch Hill, London, the youngest of the four children of Charles and Winifred Ada (Loveland) Simmons. Her father was a physical-education teacher and a former gymnast who competed at the 1912 Olympics. Simmons grew up in Golders Green, a London neighborhood, where she attended the Orange Hill School for Girls. Following the outbreak of World War II, in 1939, Simmons and her three older siblings were sent to live in Somerset. Upon returning to London in 1943, the 14-year-old Simmons was enrolled in the Aida Foster School of Dancing, and within the first two weeks, she attracted the attention of the film producer Val Guest, who invited her to audition for the role of Margaret Lockwood's precocious younger sister in the film *Give Us the Moon* (1944). Despite a lack of acting experience, Simmons's innate natural talent helped her win the part. She subsequently landed a succession of minor roles in the dramas *Mr. Emmanuel* (1944), *Kiss the Bride Goodbye* (1945), and *Meet Sexton Blake* (1945). Following her appearance as a singer in the 1945 war drama *The Way to the Stars*, she was offered a seven-year contract with the J. Arthur Rank Studio, which has been credited with launching the careers of Vivien Leigh, Deborah Kerr, and Christopher Lee, among others. Her first film with the studio was the historical epic *Caesar and Cleopatra* (1945), in which Simmons played a harpist; the movie starred Leigh (in the role of the Egyptian queen) and Stewart Granger. Simmons's big break came a year later, with her role as a young Estella in David Lean's critically acclaimed adaptation of Charles Dickens's novel *Great Expectations*, which earned Academy Award nods in the best-director, best-picture, and best-screenplay categories. Following less-than-memorable roles in *Black Narcissus* (1947) and *Hungry Hill* (1947), Simmons made her debut as a leading lady in Charles Frank's *Uncle Silas* (1947). She starred in *The Woman in the Hall* (1947) and the 1948 adaptation of Shakespeare's *Hamlet*, in which she played Ophelia, opposite Sir Laurence Olivier as the title character. For her performance in the last-named film, Simmons earned her first Academy Award nomination, in the best-supporting-actress category; she was also honored with the Volpi Cup at the 1948 Venice Film Festival. After appearing alongside Donald Houston in *The Blue Lagoon* (1949), Simmons starred opposite Granger in the romantic comedy *Adam and Evelyn* (1949). Simmons and Granger, who was almost 16 years her senior, married in 1950. Her other movie credits in 1950 included *Trio, So Long at the Fair, Cage of Gold*, and *The Clouded Yellow*. Early the next year the wealthy, reclusive tycoon Howard Hughes, who owned RKO Pictures, purchased the remainder of Simmons's contract from the J. Arthur Rank Studio; Hughes had professed unrequited feelings for the newly married Simmons, who spent considerable time warding him off. Hughes prevented Simmons from appearing in films made by other movie studios; in response the actress filed a lawsuit against RKO in 1951. During the year-long legal battle, Simmons appeared in the forgettable *Androcles and the Lion* (1952) and Otto Preminger's critically acclaimed film noir *Angel Face* (1952), in which she had a memorable role as a psychopathic femme fatale. When the suit was settled, in 1952, Simmons was freed from her contract with RKO, permitting her to make movies for other film studios. In 1953 she appeared in two films produced by Metro-Goldwyn-Mayer (MGM): the costume drama *Young Bess*, in which she co-starred opposite Granger; and the lighthearted comedy *The Actress*, in which Simmons starred as a teenage girl who aspires to be a movie star, despite her disapproving father (played by Spencer Tracy, with whom she became close friends). After the release of *She Couldn't Say No* (1954), Simmons appeared in a string of unmemorable costume dramas, including *The Robe* (1953), *The Egyptian* (1954), and *Desiree* (1954). In 1955 she reunited with Frank Sinatra, her *Desiree* co-star, for the musical comedy *Guys and Dolls*, in which she had the opportunity to display her singing and dancing talents. Also that year she starred opposite Granger in the thriller *Footsteps in the Fog*. During the rest of the decade, Simmons starred in six films: *Hilda Crane* (1956); *This Could Be the Night* (1957); *Until They Sail* (1957), in which she co-starred with Paul Newman; *The Big Country* (1958), a Western in which she appeared opposite Gregory Peck and Charlton Heston; *Home Before Dark* (1958); and *This Earth Is Mine* (1959). In 1960 Simmons had roles in two of the year's biggest-grossing films: *Elmer Gantry*, with Burt Lancaster, and the period drama *Spartacus*, which featured Kirk Douglas, Laurence Olivier, and Charles Laughton; she also appeared in *The Grass Is Greener*, with Cary Grant. In 1960 Simmons divorced Granger after falling in love with *Elmer Gantry*'s director, Richard Brooks, whom she married later the same year. Next came roles in *All the Way Home* (1963), *Life at the Top* (1965), *Mister Buddwing* (1966), *Divorce American Style* (1967), and *The Happy Ending* (1969). Simmons earned an Oscar nomination for the last-named movie, which was directed by Brooks and in which she played an alcoholic wife—a performance that mirrored her real-life troubles. Over the next decade Simmons struggled to land feature-film roles. After starring in *Say Hello to Yesterday* (1971), the actress amassed mainly small-screen credits, with parts in several made-for-television movies, including *Decisions! Decisions!* (1972), *The Easter Promise* (1975), *Beggarman, Thief* (1978), *Golden Gate* (1981), the 1981 adaptation of the Jacqueline Susann novel *The Valley of the Dolls*, and *A Small Killing* (1981), as well as guest appearances on the TV shows *The Odd Couple* and *Hawaii Five-O*. In 1983 Simmons starred in the hit ABC miniseries *The Thorn Birds*, for which she won an Emmy Award in the category of outstanding supporting actress in a limited series or special. In 1985 she appeared as Clarissa Main on another popular ABC miniseries: the Civil War drama *North and South*. A year later Simmons reprised that role in the sequel, *North and South, Book II*. Also in 1986 the actress entered the Betty Ford Clinic to treat her alcoholism; she later spoke publicly about her addiction. Following treatment, Simmons resumed her acting career, landing roles in the little-seen films *Yellow Pages* (1988) and *The Dawning* (1988) and guest appearances on episodes of the television programs *Murder, She Wrote* and *Alfred Hitchcock Presents*. In 1989 Simmons played Miss Havisham in a Disney television adaptation of *Great Expectations*. During the 1990s she remained a fixture on the small screen, with roles on the revived horror-themed soap opera *Dark Shadows*, as well as the series *Star Trek: The Next Generation* and *In the Heat of the Night*. Her television credits also included the made-for-television movies *Laker Girls* (1990), *They Do It with Mirrors* (1991), *One More Mountain* (1994), *Daisies in December* (1995), and *Her Own Rules* (1998). On the big screen she starred alongside Winona Ryder, Ellen Burstyn, and Anne Bancroft in *How to Make an American Quilt* (1995). During the next decade Simmons remained active with voice work; her credits included the animated films *Final Fantasy: The Spirits Within* (2001), *Howl's Moving Castle* (2004), and *Through the Moebius Strip* (2005). In 2009 the actress played a dying poet in *Shadows in the Sun*, her last film role. Simmons died of lung cancer at her home in Santa Monica, California. She is survived by her two daughters: Tracy (named after Spencer Tracy), from her marriage to Granger, and Kate (named after Katharine Hepburn), from her marriage to Brooks. See *Current Biography* (1952). —W.D.

Obituary *New York Times* (on-line) Jan. 23, 2010

SIMONS, DAVID G. June 7, 1922–Apr. 5, 2010 Physician; member of the U.S. Air Force. David G. Simons was the first man to spend an appreciable length of time (32 hours) in the stratosphere, reaching an altitude of more than 19 miles in a pressurized gondola attached to a research balloon on August 19, 1957. The ascent proved that humans could survive at that altitude and, as William Grimes wrote for the *New York Times* (April 17, 2010, on-line), "helped put the United States on the road to manned space flight." David Goodman Simons was born in Lancaster, Pennsylvania, to Samuel Simons, a physician, and his wife, the former Rebecca Katherine Goodman. In 1943 Simons received a B.S. degree in chemistry from Franklin and Marshall College, in Lancaster, and three years later he earned an M.D. degree from the Jefferson Medical College, in Philadelphia. After a year-long internship at the Lancaster General Hospital, Simons joined the U.S. Air Force. Working at the Aero-medical Laboratory at Wright-Patterson Air Force Base, in Dayton, Ohio, he studied the physiological responses of monkeys to weightlessness. In 1949 Simons took an advanced course in aviation medicine and subsequently served in the Korean War as a flight surgeon. When that conflict ended, in 1953, he became chief of the space-biology branch of the Aero-medical Field Laboratory, which was located at the Holloman Air Development Center, in New Mexico. There, using mice and guinea pigs that were floated by balloons for extended periods of time, he engaged in a series of experiments to evaluate the biological hazard of primary cosmic radiation at altitudes above 85,000 feet. The idea of sending a human being high into space to test the conditions from the standpoint of human tolerance and space medicine was first suggested by Colonel John P. Stapp, chief of the Aero-medical Field Laboratory at Holloman. For the experiment, which was known as Project Man High, a vehicle was assembled consisting of an aluminum-alloy gondola or capsule, a heavy-load plastic polyethylene balloon, and a parachute. The vehicle's first manned test flight, which was supervised by Simons, was made on June 2, 1957 by Joseph W. Kittinger, an Air Force captain who reached 96,000 feet and remained there for an hour and 50 minutes. On August 19, 1957 Simons ascended in the capsule from a deep open-pit iron mine in Crosby, Minnesota. For 32 hours he traveled above Earth in the capsule, reaching an altitude of 102,000 feet. During that time he performed two dozen experiments, and according to a report in *Newsweek* (September 2, 1957), "he was sort of a one-man stand . . . keeping alive with one hand, watching dials, conducting experiments and snapping cameras with the other." Simons touched down in a flax field in South Dakota with a wealth of data he had collected using several cameras, a telescope, a tape recorder, and other instruments that had been crammed into the capsule. Among the most important discoveries of the flight, Simons told the *New York Times* (August 25, 1957), was that "no physiological or psychological bars to a stay in space were found." In recognition of his service, Simons was awarded the Distinguished Flying Cross on August 24, 1957. Three years later he published an account of the flight in the book *Man High*. In 1965 Simons retired from the air force with the rank of lieutenant colonel. He began conducting research on neuromuscular function at Veterans Administration hospitals, and in 1983 he co-authored the book *Myofascial Pain and Dysfunction: The Trigger Point Manual*. (His co-author was Janet G. Travell, who had served as the personal physician to President John F. Kennedy and had treated his chronic back pain.) Simons, who died of heart failure, is survived by his sister, Elizabeth; two sons, Sam and Scott; two daughters, Susan and Sally; four grandchildren; and five great-grandchildren. See *Current Biography* (1957). —D.K.

Obituary *New York Times* (on-line) Apr. 17, 2010

SMITH, ELINOR Aug. 17, 1911–Mar. 19, 2010 Aviation pioneer. At the age of 15, Elinor Smith became the youngest woman to complete a solo flight. Earning the nickname "The Flying Flapper of Freeport," she went on to break numerous endurance and altitude records throughout her aviation career in the 1920s and '30s. Smith was born Elinor Patricia Ward in New York City and grew up in Freeport, on Long Island, New York. Her father—Tom Ward, a vaudeville comic and dancer who adopted "Smith" as a stage name—had an interest in airplanes and often took his son and daughter to the airfield. Smith took her first flying lesson with her father when she was eight years old, and as a young girl she flew frequently. "I remember so vividly my first time aloft that I can still hear the wind swing in the wires as we glided down," Smith wrote in her 1981 memoir, *Aviatrix*. "By the time the pilot touched the wheels gently to earth, I knew my future in airplanes and flying was as inevitable as the freckles on my nose." Not long after completing her first solo flight, Smith, at 16, became one of the youngest people of either gender to receive a pilot's license. In 1928, in response to a challenge from a male pilot, she flew under all four of the bridges that span the East River of Manhattan: the Queensboro, Williamsburg, Manhattan, and Brooklyn bridges. She remains the only pilot who has accomplished that stunt. In 1929 Smith set the solo endurance record for women when she flew for 13 hours, 16 minutes, and 45 seconds. That year Louise Thaden exceeded Smith's endurance record by nine hours, but a month later Smith broke Thaden's record, with a flight lasting 26 hours, 23 minutes, and 16 seconds. Also in 1929 she became, at 18, the youngest person to receive a transport pilot's license and the first woman to pilot a military aircraft. She also became the first female executive pilot employed at the Irving Air Chute Co., which manufactured parachutes; in that capacity she traveled with a tour that staged parachuting demonstrations. In 1929 Smith teamed with Evelyn "Bobbi" Trout in an effort to set a new aviation endurance record for women. The 42-hour journey not only accomplished that goal, but also marked the first time a plane had been refueled by female pilots in midair. In 1930 Smith became the first female test pilot at the Long Island–based Fairchild Aviation Corp. That same year, while working for Fairchild, she set a new altitude record (27,418 feet) for a female pilot; she was named the best female pilot in the country by the American Society for the Promotion of Aviation. In 1931 Smith became the first woman to fly at an altitude exceeding 30,000 feet; the same year she broke her own record by several hundred feet. In 1932 she set the straight-course speed record for women, clocking in at 229 miles per hour. From 1930 to 1935 Smith served as an aviation commentator for NBC Radio. Four years later she became the first woman featured on a Wheaties cereal box; she endorsed other products as well, among them flight goggles and motor oil. During that period she also served as an adviser to the New York State Aviation Committee. Meanwhile, in 1933, she married Patrick H. Sullivan II, a lawyer, New York State aviation commissioner, and assemblyman. At the age of 29, pregnant with her third child, she retired. Smith returned to work after her husband died, in 1956, writing and editing articles on aviation for several magazines. At the age of 60, she flew with the U.S. Naval Reserve Force in a successful effort to save Floyd Bennett Field (in Brooklyn, New York) from developers. At 89 she participated in a simulated landing of a space shuttle at NASA's Ames Research Center. Smith died at the age of 98 at a nursing home in Palo Alto, California. She is survived by her son, Patrick; her daughters, Patricia, Pamela, and Kathleen; five grandchildren; and four great-grandchildren. See *Current Biography* (2001). —D.K.

Obituary *New York Times* (on-line) Mar. 26, 2010

SMITH, VIRGINIA B. June 24, 1923–Aug. 27, 2010 Lawyer; economist; college president. Virginia Beatrice Smith is best known for her role as president of Vassar College, a post she held from 1977 to 1986, and as a proponent of quality higher education for all. One of six children, Smith was born in Seattle, Washington. After attending Seattle public schools and earning B.A., M.A., and J.D. degrees at the University of Washington, in Seattle, she did further work at Columbia University, in New York City. Her major academic focus, outside of law, was labor economics. After a stint as an economist at the Seattle district Office of Price Adminstration, from 1944 to 1946, she completed a year-long research fellowship at the Institute of Labor Economics at the University of Washington. From 1947 to 1949 she taught economics and business at the College of Puget Sound, in Tacoma, Washington, and practiced law part-time. In 1952 Smith joined the faculty of the University of California's Berkeley Extension as an instructor and coordinator of public programs in the Institute of Industrial Relations. She later became an administrative analyst on the staff of the president of the university, and starting in 1965 she served as an assistant vice president in charge of policy development. Concurrently, she also worked as a labor-management arbitrator, and she chaired the California State Wage Board and served on the women's advisory council of the California Fair Employment Practices Commission. In 1967 Smith joined the Carnegie Commission on Higher Education, a newly created think tank. The first of the commission's reports proposed a $200 million federal foundation to expand educational opportunities through grants and scholarships to those who might not otherwise have an equal opportunity for higher education. Another commission report explored the "unfocused" relationship between university campuses and the cities in which they are located. In 1973 Smith left her post to become the first director of the Fund for the Improvement of Postsecondary Education, in Washington, D.C. During her four-year tenure, Smith was responsible for dispensing more than $43 million in grants. In April 1977, after an 11-month search in which 450 candidates were considered, it was an-

nounced that Smith was the unanimous choice for the presidency of Vassar College, a prestigious liberal-arts school in Poughkeepsie, New York. (She was Vassar's second female president; the first, Sarah Gibson Blanding, served from 1946 to 1964.) As president, Smith led a $100 million fundraising drive, emphasized the school's commitment to minorities, and recruited students from all walks of life. She came out of retirement for a year in 1990 to serve as president of Mills College, an all-female school in Oakland, California. Smith died at her home in Alamo, California. She is survived by her longtime partner, Florence Oaks; her sister, Bessie Francis; and her brother, Frank. Since 1999 the Virginia B. Smith Innovative Leadership Award—an annual prize named in her honor and administered jointly by the National Center for Public Policy and Higher Education and the Council for Adult and Experiential Learning—has been given to visionary educators. See *Current Biography* (1978). —D.K.

Obituary *New York Times* (on-line) Sep. 7, 2010

SMYSLOV, VASSILY Mar. 24, 1921–Mar. 27, 2010 Russian chess grandmaster. Vasily Smyslov, whose name has been transliterated by the Western media in a variety of ways, sometimes as Vassilii Smyslov, was among the game's best players in the 1950s and '60s. He was the World Chess Champion from 1957 to 1958 and a contender for the World Chess Championship on eight other occasions. He won a total of 17 Chess Olympiad medals, an all-time record, and his victory at the 1953 Zurich Candidates Tournament, during which he lost only one game, is considered one of the great feats in chess history. Born in Moscow, Vassily Vassilyevich Smyslov was taught to play chess at the age of six by his father, one of the leading chess strategists in the Soviet Union. After defeating an uncle in a non-handicapped match a year later, Smyslov reportedly became obsessed with the game. At age 13 he beat his father for the first time, and the following year he participated in his first tournament. Smyslov became a first-category chess player in 1936, and two years later he won the USSR Junior Chess Championship. In late 1938 he tied for first place in the Moscow Championship and became a chess master. He placed third in the 1940 Soviet Championship, and the following year he finished third in a national six-master event, earning him the title of grandmaster. Smyslov had enrolled at the Moscow Aviation Institute in 1939 but was excused from service at the start of World War II due to his poor eyesight. He instead spent the war years working on his game. In addition to his win in 1957, he vied for the World Chess Championship in 1948, 1950, 1953, 1956, 1959, 1965, 1983, and 1985. (At the 1948 event Smyslov finished second to Mikhail Botvinnik, beginning a longtime rivalry between the men.) Smyslov, who was honored with the Order of Lenin after his 1957 triumph, remained active in competitive chess as late as 1991, when he won the inaugural World Senior Championship. Though Smyslov loved chess, he had originally hoped to become an opera singer and had dedicated his life to the game only after failing an audition for the Bolshoi Theatre in 1950. Smyslov, who wrote several books on chess strategy, died of heart failure at a

Moscow hospital. He is survived by his wife, Nadezhda Andreevna. See *Current Biography* (1967). —M.A.S.

Obituary *New York Times* (on-line) Mar. 28, 2010

SÖDERSTRÖM, ELISABETH May 7, 1927–Nov. 20, 2009 Opera singer. Elisabeth Söderström was one of the most versatile and beloved figures in the opera world. She was widely celebrated for her interpretations of the music of Leoš Janáček and Richard Strauss, and she was one of the few singers ever to have performed all three lead roles (the Marschallin, Octavian, and Sophie) in Strauss's acclaimed opera *Der Rosenkavalier*. "Söderström was not so much a great soprano—though she was one—as a great actor and a remarkable woman," Martin Kettle wrote for the London *Guardian* (November 23, 2009, on-line). "The feeling that touched an audience in a Söderström performance . . . was not the response to the voice, lovely though that was. It was the response to the person. Söderström possessed a remarkable ability to communicate the personality of the character she was portraying by drawing on things within her own personality. . . . What you always got from her was intelligence and empathy. You cared about her character because you cared about Söderström." The eldest of three daughters, Söderström was born in Stockholm, Sweden. She suffered from asthma and assorted allergies but was otherwise healthy. Her father, a businessman and Swedish naval captain, sang as a tenor in his spare time, and her mother, who had fled Russia during the 1917 revolution, was a concert pianist. As a young child Söderström was taught hymns by her caregiver and frequently performed for her parents' dinner guests. Söderström began taking voice lessons at age 14 and later entered Stockholm University, where she studied languages and literature. Aspiring to a career in the theater, Söderström applied to the Stockholm Academy of Dramatic Arts. Out of hundreds of applicants, she ranked ninth, but only the top eight students gained admission. After that disappointment she decided to focus instead on singing. Söderström enrolled in Stockholm's prestigious Royal Academy of Music and Opera School and made her professional debut at age 20, at the Drottningholm Court Theater, where she sang the role of the shepherdess Bastienne, in Mozart's one-act opera *Bastien und Bastienne*. In 1950 Söderström became a member of the Swedish Royal Opera and also married Sverker Olow, an officer in the Royal Swedish Navy. Söderström—who was becoming a fixture at such annual events as the Salzburg Festival, the Glyndebourne Festival, and the Edinburgh Festival—was named the royal court singer by King Gustave VI of Sweden in 1959. She also made her debut that year at New York City's Metropolitan Opera (known informally as the Met), singing the role of Susanna in Mozart's *Marriage of Figaro*. Söderström went on to perform at the Met several times over the next few years, singing in Italian, French, and German. In 1962 she received rave reviews from New York audiences when she replaced the scheduled soloist, Irmgard Seefried, with only three days' notice, at a Town Hall concert. Starting in 1964, with her husband frequently away at sea, Söderström reduced her travels abroad and remained in Sweden with her school-age children. She used her reduced radius of movement to broaden rather than narrow her range of activities. Although the Swedish Royal Opera's schedule encompassed 10 months out of the year, she was not content merely to fulfill a rigorous commitment there, highlighted by occasional command performances for the king and guest appearances in northern Europe. She told Stephen Godfrey for the Toronto *Globe and Mail* (January 31, 1980): "In my own country I try to spread opera wherever I can—in factories, prisons, hospitals, mental institutions. I'm preaching; I admit it. I'm always on the barricades." Söderström also became a member of the board of the Swedish Broadcasting Corp., and she co-produced and co-starred in the television show *The Prima Prima Donnas*, aimed at demystifying classical music for a mass audience. As she described the show to Godfrey, "We mix classical and pop. For example, in a scene from *The Marriage of Figaro*, where Cherubino jumps out of the window, we cut to him landing in a bathtub, and the next song is 'I'm Gonna Wash That Man Right Out of My Hair.'" During the 1960s and 1970s Söderström made a number of influential recordings, including definitive versions of the complete operas of Janáček (with the Australian conductor Charles Mackerras). Söderström returned to the U.S. to sing in 1977, in the San Francisco Opera production of Janáček's *Katya Kabanova*. (Though she did not display the same vocal range as she had in earlier years, critics enthused about her dramatic ability and emotional expression.) By the early 1980s, with her children fully grown and independent, Söderström had revived her international career, appearing with such companies as the State Opera of South Australia, the Chamber Music Society of Lincoln Center, and the Houston Grand Opera, among many others. From 1993 to 1996 Söderström served as the director of the Drottningholm Court Theater. She made her final stage performance in 1999, playing the aging countess in Tchaikovsky's *Queen of Spades* at the Met, where she was greeted by a tumultuous ovation. During the last years of her life, Söderström suffered from ill health and the effects of a stroke. She is survived by her husband, her three sons (Malcolm, Peter, and Jens), and several grandchildren. See *Current Biography* (1985). —M.R.M.

Obituary *New York Times* (on-line) Nov. 22, 2009

STEINBRENNER, GEORGE July 4, 1930–July 13, 2010 Owner of the New York Yankees. In the process of transforming the Yankees into a billion-dollar baseball empire, George Steinbrenner became an iconic figure. During his 37 seasons as owner, he led the team to seven World Series championships, 11 American League pennants, and 16 American League East titles. Steinbrenner made the Yankees the richest team in baseball history and is credited with changing the economics of the sport. The scion of a Great Lakes shipping family, George Michael Steinbrenner 3d was born in Rocky River, Ohio. His mother, Rita (Haley) Steinbrenner, who was of Irish descent, imbued him, he once said, with compassion for the underdog; his father, of German ancestry, instilled in him a steely will to win. Trained to be self-reliant, Steinbrenner earned his own pocket money delivering eggs in Bay Village, the Cleveland suburb where he grew up. Steinbrenner's father, who idolized such Yankees players as Joe Dimaggio, took him to see the Yankees play the Cleveland Indians whenever they were in town. At Culver (Indiana) Military Academy, Steinbrenner was an all-around athlete, and at Williams College, in Williamstown, Massachusetts, he ran hurdles on the track team and was president of the glee club. After graduating from Williams, in 1952, with a bachelor's degree in English, Steinbrenner served as an officer in the U.S. Air Force. After being discharged from the military, he worked as a high-school football and basketball coach and as an assistant coach at Northwestern and Purdue universities before returning to Cleveland in 1957 to join the family shipping firm, Kinsman Marine Transit Co. While working as the company treasurer, Steinbrenner made his first move as a sports entrepreneur when he formed a partnership in 1960 to buy the Cleveland Pipers, a semiprofessional basketball team. The attempt to turn the Pipers into a pro team cost Steinbrenner a reported $250,000, and when the team folded in 1962 with a debt of $125,000, he ignored advice to file for bankruptcy and paid off the debt over the course of the next three years. In 1967 Steinbrenner bought stock in the American Shipbuilding Co. of Lorain, Ohio, later merging it with Kinsman. Business had improved considerably by the time Steinbrenner and his investment group bought the Yankees from the Columbia Broadcasting System (CBS) for some $10 million in 1973. In succeeding years he bought out his investment partners, acquiring 55 percent ownership. During that time the value of the Yankees rose 150 percent, to $25 million; the club's annual receipts reached $12 million; and the Yankees became the first team in the history of the American League to draw an annual attendance of two million both at home and on the road. During his early years as owner, Steinbrenner concentrated his efforts on ending a long string of pennant losses by taking advantage of the new "free agent" system to sign such high-quality players as Jim "Catfish" Hunter and Reggie Jackson. In November 1974 Steinbrenner was suspended from baseball for two years (the term was later reduced) by Commissioner Bowie Kuhn after pleading guilty to making illegal corporate contributions to President Richard Nixon's 1972 reelection campaign. Although he did not serve any jail time in the criminal case, Steinbrenner was ordered to pay a fine of $15,000. (He was later pardoned by President Ronald Reagan.) In 1977, the year after Steinbrenner's return to baseball, the Yankees claimed their first World Series title since 1962. The following year they won their second consecutive championship. While the Yankees were enjoying a string of high-profile wins, Steinbrenner became notorious for making the club a revolving door of management personnel; by 1990 he had switched managers 18 times and hired 13 different general managers. Billy Martin was hired (and fired) by Steinbrenner five times and was preparing to manage the team a sixth time when he died, in 1990. Five years later Steinbrenner hired Joe Torre to manage the Yankees, who went on to win World Series titles in 1996, 1998,

1999, and 2000. Steinbrenner involved himself with even the smallest details of ballpark maintenance, earning himself the nickname "the Boss." Former team manager Lou Piniella once said, "George is a great guy, unless you have to work for him," and the sports tycoon was famously parodied on the hit sitcom *Seinfeld*. Steinbrenner's larger-than-life presence inarguably revolutionized the franchise. After a lucrative partnership with Madison Square Garden revealed the earning potential in cable television, Steinbrenner created the Yankees Entertainment and Sports (YES) network. Later he started his own ballpark-food company and secured a number of high-profile marketing contracts, including a $95 million clothing and apparel deal with the sportswear and sneaker manufacturer Adidas. In 2008 Steinbrenner, who was widely acknowledged for his strong philanthropic streak in addition to his business acumen, ceded day-to-day control over the Yankees to his sons, Hank and Hal, but he retained the title of senior club owner. In 2009 the Yankees' payroll, estimated to be about $210 million, was by far the largest of any team in baseball. Steinbrenner spent his later years in Tampa, Florida, but he returned to the Bronx to attend the April 2009 opening of the new, $1.5 billion Yankee Stadium. He was also on hand at the 2010 home opener, at which team captain Derek Jeter presented him with a 2009 World Series ring. Steinbrenner died of a heart attack at a Tampa hospital. At the time of his death, which came just days after the demise of the longtime stadium announcer Bob Sheppard, the Yankees were worth a reported $1.6 billion. In addition to his sons, Steinbrenner is survived by his wife, Joan (pronounced Jo-Ann); his daughters, Jessica and Jennifer; and several grandchildren. *See Current Biography* (1979). —H.R.W.

Obituary *New York Times* A p1+ July 14, 2010

STEVENS, TED Nov. 18, 1923–Aug. 9, 2010 Former U.S. senator from Alaska. Ted Stevens, whose tenure lasted from 1968 to 2008, was the longest-serving Republican in the history of the U.S. Senate. He was credited with helping to shape modern Alaska by securing billions of dollars in federal funding for the state's oil and fishing industries, military bases, infrastructure, and other projects. (For the same reason, he was often criticized for being among the Senate's most notorious pork-barrel spenders.) In 2000 the state legislature named Stevens the Alaskan of the Century, noting that he "represents Alaska's finest contribution to our national leadership." Theodore Fulton Stevens was born in Indianapolis, Indiana, the third of four children. When he was a young boy, his family moved to Chicago, Illinois, where his father, George A. Stevens, worked as an accountant before the 1929 stock-market crash. His parents divorced in the early years of the Great Depression, and Ted Stevens traveled to California to live with his aunt. He attended Oregon State University, in Corvallis, and Montana State University, in Bozeman, before leaving college in 1943 to join the U.S. Army Air Corps. Stevens spent the next three years in Asia, flying transport planes, and he was awarded two Distinguished Flying Crosses and two Air Medals. He left the army in 1946 with the rank of first lieutenant and earned a bachelor's degree from the

University of California, Los Angeles (UCLA) the following year. In 1950 he earned an LL.B. degree from Harvard Law School, in Cambridge, Massachusetts. After working in both private practice and as a legislative counsel to the U.S. Department of the Interior, Stevens served as an assistant to the secretary of the interior from 1958 to 1960, playing a key administrative role when Alaska achieved statehood, in 1959. He then established a private law practice in the new state and subsequently made a few unsuccessful bids for the U.S. Senate. In 1964 he won a seat in the Alaska House of Representatives. Four years later, after Alaska's U.S. senator E. L. "Bob" Bartlett died while in office, Stevens was appointed to replace him by the state's governor, Republican Walter J. Hickel. In 1970 Stevens won a special election to retain the seat for the remainder of Bartlett's term; he was returned to office by voters in the next six contests. In 1968 huge oil reserves were discovered in Prudhoe Bay and the North Slope of Alaska, a finding that reshaped the state's economy. Recognizing the potential of the petroleum industry to bring much-needed money, jobs, and infrastructure to Alaska, Stevens emerged as a key ally of "big oil," backing industry leaders in their efforts to gain access to wilderness land believed to contain deposits of oil and natural gas. Stevens also took a strong interest in native Alaskan issues; he played a key role, for example, in the passage of the Native Claims Settlement Act of 1971, which not only resolved the longstanding land-ownership dispute between Alaska's indigenous tribes and the federal government, but also cleared the way for the lease or sale to commercial interests of large tracts of federally controlled Alaskan land. In 1972 Stevens was named to the Senate Appropriations Committee, the powerful body that controls the spending of federal tax dollars, and the following year he used his influence to facilitate the construction of the Trans-Alaska Pipeline, which connects the oil-producing and shipping regions of the state. Stevens, a harsh critic of environmentalists throughout his Senate tenure, repeatedly lobbied for oil drilling in the Arctic National Wildlife Refuge (ANWR), which was set aside as wilderness land by the federal government in 1978. Over the years, while still focused primarily on his Alaskan constituency, Stevens began to assert himself more forcefully on the national political stage, in part by emphasizing America's need to strengthen its military. However, in 1982 and again in 1984, Stevens raised some Republican eyebrows when he advocated trimming President Ronald Reagan's proposed military budget to comply with general budget guidelines. By the early 1980s Stevens had been Alaska's senior senator for more than a decade, and his grasp on power was secure. While environmentalists continued to decry his coziness with the petroleum industry, his role in facilitating the unprecedented growth of the Alaskan economy could not be denied. As a high-ranking member of the Appropriations Committee, Stevens was able to funnel hundreds of millions of dollars in federal tax revenues directly to Alaskans, primarily by inserting spending provisions into existing bills just prior to Senate votes, thus avoiding debate for the most part. Alaska thus gained funds for road-building and other regional infrastructure projects; rural and Native American

medical clinics, museums, and historical societies; and fishermen, craftspeople, and other groups. In 1989 the oil tanker *Exxon Valdez* crashed in Prince William Sound, in southern Alaska, and spilled more than 11 million gallons of crude oil, causing terrible environmental damage. In the wake of that disaster—the largest oil spill in U.S. history up to that point—Stevens sponsored the Oil Pollution Act of 1990, which strengthened regulations and provided financial compensation to Alaskans affected by the spill. Stevens became chair of the Senate Appropriations Committee in late 1996 and held the position until 2001. In 1998 he secured a record $300 million in federal appropriations for Alaska. Stevens continued to bring federal money to his home state and fight for the interests of Alaskan industry during the first years of the new millennium. In 2008 he was tried for corruption, and after being convicted on all counts, he lost the November 2008 election. The following year, however, the conviction was overturned by Judge Emmet G. Sullivan, at the request of Attorney General Eric Holder, when it was revealed that prosecutors had withheld crucial evidence during the trial. Stevens—who had been one of just two passengers to survive the December 1978 crash of a twin-engine Lear jet that took the life of his first wife, Ann—died at age 86 in a plane crash in southwest Alaska while on a fishing trip. He is survived by his second wife, Catherine Chandler, whom he married in 1980; their daughter, Lily; five children from his first marriage, Susan, Elizabeth, Walter, Theodore Jr., and Ben; and 11 grandchildren. See *Current Biography* (2001).—D.K.

Obituary *New York Times* (on-line) Aug. 10, 2010

STEVER, H. G. Oct. 24, 1916–Apr. 9, 2010 Scientist; presidential adviser. Horton Guyford Stever, who served as a chief science adviser to U.S. presidents Richard M. Nixon and Gerald Ford, was highly influential in shaping the nation's space program. Stever was born to Ralph Raymond Stever, a merchant, and Alma (Matt) Stever in the glass-manufacturing city of Corning, New York. Both of his parents died of tuberculosis when he was young, and he and his sister were raised largely by their maternal grandparents. Stever attended Colgate University, in Hamilton, New York, and, aided by scholarships and part-time jobs, he earned an A.B. degree, with a major in physics, in 1938. He undertook graduate work, also in physics, at the California Institute of Technology (Caltech), where he received a Ph.D. degree in 1941. Returning to the East Coast, Stever briefly held a staff position at the Massachusetts Institute of Technology (MIT) radiation laboratory. When the U.S. entered World War II, Stever joined the Office of Scientific Research and Development as a civilian science-liaison officer and was assigned to assess Germany's radar capabilities. After the Allied invasion of Europe, he was also a member of several intelligence missions. In 1945 he returned to MIT, as a professor in the Department of Aeronautical Engineering. He headed MIT's Department of Mechanical Engineering and its Department of Naval Architecture and Marine Engineering from 1961 to 1965. Concomitant with his teaching and research activities, Stever held a number of appointments to government and military advisory committees. The Special Committee on Space Exploration, which Stever chaired, prepared the report that provided the first guidelines for the National Aeronautics and Space Administration (NASA) in its development of a civilian space program. In 1965 Stever left MIT to take over the presidency of the Carnegie Institute of Technology, in Pittsburgh, Pennsylvania. His tenure there lasted until 1972, when he became the director of the National Science Foundation under the Nixon administration. Stever became a party to controversy when Nixon eliminated the White House Office of Science and Technology in the spring of 1973 and failed to replace his science adviser, Edward E. David Jr., when Davis resigned in January of that year. Instead Nixon named Stever his unofficial adviser. After Nixon's resignation, on August 9, 1974, Stever remained in the role of director of the National Science Foundation and became the official science adviser to President Gerald Ford. An editorial writer for the *New York Times* (August 24, 1976) asserted, "Science has now returned to the White House," and a piece in the journal *The Sciences* stated, "Stever has been the conscientious shepherd of the American scientific community during a time when zealots in and out of the community have been afire with wildly conflicting schemes concerning the scope, role and responsibilities of science." At the end of the Ford administration, Stever left his White House post and was self-employed as a consultant for various corporations and organizations. He returned briefly to public service in 1986, when the space shuttle *Challenger* exploded shortly after lift-off, killing its entire crew. The accident was caused by an equipment malfunction, and Stever was appointed by the National Research Council to oversee the redesign of the faulty rocket booster. Stever died in his home in Gaithersburg, Maryland, at the age of 93. He is survived by a sister, Margarette Johnson; his sons, Guy Jr. and Roy; his daughters, Sarah and Margarette; and seven grandchildren. See *Current Biography* (1981). —H.R.W.

Obituary *New York Times* (on-line) Apr. 13, 2010.

STUART, GLORIA July 4, 1910–Sep. 26, 2010 Actress. Gloria Stuart, who appeared in dozens of films in the 1930s, was in her 80s when she was nominated for an Academy Award for her role in James Cameron's blockbuster film *Titanic* (1997), which exposed her to a new generation of fans. As a young girl Stuart, who was born in Santa Monica, California, dreamed of being a writer. She met her first husband, the sculptor Gordon Newell, while attending the University of California at Berkeley in the early 1930s. The young couple settled in Carmel, a community of artists in northern California, where Stuart began to study acting and performed at the small but highly regarded Theatre of the Golden Bough. During that time she also worked for the *Carmelite*, a well-respected local newspaper. When Stuart acted in a production of Anton Chekhov's *The Seagull*, a friend volunteered to get his film-industry connections to see her performance. Subsequently, representatives from both Universal Studios and Para-

mount Pictures offered her contracts. She signed with Universal, but during the 1930s, it was common for studios to loan out their actors, and her first film, *Street of Women* (1932), was made under the auspices of Warner Bros. She worked frequently throughout the rest of the decade, appearing in such films as *The Old Dark House* (1932), a thriller in which Boris Karloff played an insane butler; *The Invisible Man* (1933), an adaptation of an H. G. Wells novel that starred Claude Rains as the title character; the musical comedy *Roman Scandals* (1933), which co-starred Eddie Cantor; and *Here Comes the Navy* (1934), alongside James Cagney. After her contract with Universal expired in 1935, Stuart signed with Twentieth Century-Fox. Her high hopes for her career were soon dashed. "For the most part I played girl reporters, girl detectives, girl reporters, girl detectives," she told Lee Server for *Films in Review* (February 1988). "There was no chance to do what I would have called acting." Stuart worked with Shirley Temple in *Poor Little Rich Girl* (1936) and *Rebecca of Sunnybrook Farm* (1938), and she later lamented that she was given little to do in those films other than smile as she held the young star's hand. Nor did her role in a successful remake of *The Three Musketeers* (1939) challenge her. "I loved to act, but it wasn't worth the crying every day in the dressing room over these stupid, clichéd parts," Stuart told Server. "When my contract with Fox was up, I quit. I pulled the curtain down and decided to travel and entertain and raise my daughter and enjoy myself." With her second husband, the screenwriter Arthur Sheekman, Stuart traveled around the world, and in the early 1950s the couple, whose friends included such luminaries as Humphrey Bogart and the Marx Brothers, settled in Europe, where Stuart took up painting. During the 1970s Sheekman began to exhibit the symptoms of Alzheimer's disease, and as a respite from her arduous duties at home, Stuart returned to acting on occasion, making guest appearances on such television series as *Murder, She Wrote* and taking on a role in the film *My Favorite Year* (1982), which starred Peter O'Toole. She also began making and illustrating hand-printed books. In 1983 she began a late-life romance with the artist Ward Ritchie that lasted until Ritchie's death, in 1996. (Sheekman had died in 1978.) In her mid-80s Stuart was rediscovered by the director James Cameron, who cast her as Rose, a 101-year-old shipwreck survivor, in *Titanic*. Still youthful-looking, Stuart underwent two hours of makeup application on each day of shooting in order to portray the elderly Rose. (Kate Winslet portrayed the 17-year-old version of Rose, a wealthy girl who becomes romantically involved with the poor but dashing Jack, played by Leonardo DiCaprio.) *Titanic* became one of the highest-grossing films of all time, and Stuart, who received a best-supporting-actress nod, became the oldest person ever to be nominated for an Academy Award in an acting category. Stuart, who was known throughout her life as an exceptional cook and hostess, died at her home in Los Angeles, California, at age 100. She is survived by a daughter, Sylvia Vaughn Thompson, a cookbook author; four grandchildren; and 12 great-grandchildren. See *Current Biography* (1998). —H.R.W.

Obituary *New York Times* B p19 Sep. 28, 2010

SUTHERLAND, JOAN Nov. 7, 1926–Oct. 10, 2010 Opera singer. Joan Sutherland was one of the most celebrated sopranos of the 20th century. Nicknamed "La Stupenda," for her enormous vocal range and agile singing voice, Sutherland was a major force in the revival of the Italian bel canto operas of the early 19th century. Sutherland was born in Sydney, Australia, where her Scottish-born father worked as a tailor. He had fathered four children with his first wife, who had died of influenza, and Joan Sutherland was her parents' only child. Her mother, Muriel, was a trained opera singer who was too shy to pursue a professional career; instead she vocalized with her daughter daily. On the day she turned six, Sutherland's father died of a heart attack, forcing Sutherland, her mother, and her youngest half-sister to live with an aunt and uncle in the Sydney suburb of Woollahra. Sutherland learned the finer points of opera from her mother, who recognized her talents early on, and she was also influenced by her cousin, John, who introduced her to the recordings of such great operatic singers as Enrico Caruso and Luisa Tetrazzini. At age 12 she vowed to become an opera singer after seeing her first concert at the Town Hall in Sydney. She graduated from St. Catherine's Church of England School, in the Sydney suburb of Waverly, and then worked a series of office jobs to support herself. She began receiving formal vocal lessons in her late teens after winning a two-year voice scholarship from John and Aida Dickens, two of the leading Australian voice instructors of their time. They convinced Sutherland that she was a dramatic soprano and suggested she enroll at the Rathbone Academy of Dramatic Art to study languages and stage deportment. Sutherland made her concert debut in Sydney in 1947, as the female lead in Henry Purcell's *Dido and Aeneas*. Over the next few years, she made several other stage appearances and won various vocal competitions, including one sponsored by the Australian newspaper the *Sun* in 1949. Winnings from that and other competitions enabled Sutherland to move to London, England, in 1951. There she attended the Opera School of the Royal College of Music, in England, where she became reacquainted with Richard Bonynge, a pianist and conductor she had met and befriended at a youth concert in Sydney; Bonynge became Sutherland's greatest musical influence, and the two married in 1954. In 1952, after auditioning unsuccessfully three times, Sutherland was accepted into the Royal Opera at Covent Garden, where she made her debut as the First Lady in Mozart's *Zauberflöte* (*The Magic Flute*). At Covent Garden she sang a wide range of parts, including the Countess in Mozart's *The Marriage of Figaro*, Frasquita in Bizet's *Carmen*, and Penelope Rich in Britten's *Gloriana*. At the urging of Bonynge, Sutherland began learning the signature roles of bel canto operas by Vincenzo Bellini, Gaetano Donizetti, and Gioachino Rossini and making the transition from mezzo-soprano to coloratura soprano. Sutherland earned international renown when she appeared as Lucia in a Covent Garden production of Donizetti's *Lucia di Lammermoor* in 1959. The production, directed by Franco Zeffirelli and conducted by Tullio Serafin, marked the first time that the opera had been staged in London in 70 years, with the exception of a single presentation in 1925. Following

that performance Sutherland became a bona fide star and went on to resurrect other forgotten bel canto operas, including Bellini's *I Puritani* and *La Sonnambula*. In 1960 she made her debut in Italy, in a Zeffirelli production of Handel's *Alcina*, and was subsequently given the nickname "La Stupenda" ("The Stupendous One") after wowing Italian critics and audience members with her performance. That same year she made her U.S. debut, at the Dallas Opera in Texas, appearing in the title role of the first American production of *Alcina*. In 1961 Sutherland reprised her portrayal of Lucia for her New York City debut, at the Metropolitan Opera (known informally as the Met). She later sang at other renowned opera houses around the world, and she formed a longtime relationship with the Met, where she delivered more than 200 performances over three decades. Sutherland made numerous recordings for the Decca label during her career and often performed and recorded with her friends Marilyn Horne, the renowned American mezzo-soprano, and Luciano Pavarotti, the Italian operatic tenor. The latter singer once referred to Sutherland as "the greatest female voice of all time." Both Horne and Pavarotti joined her on stage for her last performance at Covent Garden, in 1990. The final performance of her career came in October of that year, in a Sydney production of Giacomo Meyerbeer's *Les Huguenots*. While Sutherland was sometimes criticized for lacking dramatic flair in her performances, her vocal expertise and knack for comedy overshadowed her shortcomings as an actress. With Bonynge, Sutherland settled in Switzerland but maintained close ties to her native Australia; Bonynge served as music director of the Australian Opera from 1975 to 1986, and the singer frequently performed there. After she retired Sutherland made very few public appearances, spending the bulk of her time at her home in the village of Les Avants, Switzerland. In 1994 she published *The Autobiography of Joan Sutherland: A Prima Donna's Progress*. Sutherland, who was appointed a Dame Commander of the Order of the British Empire by Queen Elizabeth II in 1978 and was honored by the Kennedy Center in 2004 for her enormous contribution to the arts, died at her home in Les Avants. She is survived by her husband; their son, Adam; and two grandchildren. See *World Musicians* (1998). —C.C.

Obituary *New York Times* (on-line) Oct. 11, 2010

SUTTON, PERCY E. Nov. 24, 1920–Dec. 26, 2009 Civil rights lawyer, politician, and business executive. Percy E. Sutton was a trailblazing figure in several fields. He first rose to prominence during the civil rights era, as the lawyer to the activist Malcolm X and his family. From the late 1960s to the late 1970s, Sutton had the distinction of being Manhattan's longest-tenured borough president to date. He was also a successful business mogul who was instrumental in revitalizing the borough's Harlem neighborhood, including the restoration of the famous Apollo Theater. Percy Ellis Sutton was born in San Antonio, Texas, the youngest of the 15 children of Samuel J. and Lillian (Smith) Sutton. His mother was a teacher, and his father was a high-school principal and civil rights activist who also managed various business enterprises, including a mattress factory, a skating rink, a funeral home, and a cattle farm. From an early age Sutton milked cows and often accompanied his father during his milk deliveries to the poor. His crusade for racial equality began when he was 13, after he was assaulted by a police officer for passing out pamphlets from the National Association for the Advancement of Colored People (NAACP) in an all-white neighborhood. After attending local public schools, Sutton studied at several historically black colleges—Prairie View A&M University, in Texas; Tuskegee University, in Alabama; and Hampton University, in Virginia—but never earned a degree. While in college Sutton learned to fly and then worked as a stunt pilot at county fairs. During World War II Sutton, who met his future wife, Leatrice O'Farell, in late July 1943, joined the Tuskegee Airmen, the groundbreaking all-black fighter squad, as an intelligence officer. He saw combat in Italy and the Mediterranean as a member of the 332d Fighter Group's all-black 99th Pursuit Squadron. His accomplishments earned him combat stars, and he was discharged with the rank of captain. He next attended Columbia University, in New York City, on the G.I. Bill, and then entered the Brooklyn College School of Law, where he studied part-time while holding down full-time jobs as a postal worker and a subway conductor. Sutton earned a J.D. degree in 1950 and passed the New York bar exam the following year. He reenlisted in the military during the Korean War, serving as an airforce intelligence officer and the first-ever black trial judge advocate. In 1953, following the end of his second military stint, Sutton, along with a brother and another partner, founded a law practice in Harlem. In the 1950s, while working at the local branch of the NAACP, Sutton heard about a charismatic black activist named Malcolm X; to build up his law practice, Sutton took him on as a client and continued to represent him until his assassination, in 1965. During the early 1960s Sutton served as the president of the New York branch of the NAACP (1961–62) and as an adviser to the Student Nonviolent Coordinating Committee (SNCC); in the latter role he represented more than 200 civil rights protesters who had been arrested for taking part in demonstrations in the South. Along with David Dinkins, Basil Paterson (the father of New York State's governor David Paterson), and Charles Rangel, Sutton formed the Gang of Four, an influential group of local black politicians. In 1964, after numerous failed political bids, Sutton was elected to the New York State Assembly. (Dinkins, Paterson, and Rangel were also elected to local or state offices.) Sutton became the spokesperson of the State Legislature's black caucus. He was also responsible for securing state funding to build the New York Public Library 's Schomburg Center for Research in Black Culture and establishing the Search for Education, Elevation, and Knowledge (SEEK) program, which provides talented but disadvantaged students the opportunity to go to college. In 1966, when Manhattan borough president Constance Baker Motley was appointed to a federal judgeship, the New York City Council selected Sutton to finish the remaining three years of her term. Sutton was reelected to two four-year terms (in 1969 and 1973); during the 11 years that he held the post,

he was the state's highest-ranking black elected official. In 1977 Sutton unsuccessfully ran for the office of mayor, losing in a seven-way Democratic primary. By then the budding entrepreneur was building his fledgling business empire. Earlier in the decade he had invested in several media companies, including the *New York Amsterdam News*, among the nation's largest black newspapers; the AM radio station WLIB, New York City's first black-owned radio station; and the FM radio station WBLS. He also helped found the Inner City Broadcasting Corp.; in 1981 Inner City, then chaired by Sutton, purchased Harlem's Apollo Theater for $250,000, had it designated as a landmark, and oversaw its $20 million renovation. Sutton also produced the TV series *Showtime at the Apollo*. By the early 1990s Sutton had put his son, Pierre, and daughter, Cheryl Lynn, in charge of Inner City Broadcasting, where he retained emeritus status; he had also turned over managerial duties of the Apollo Theater to the theater's foundation board, which was chaired by Rangel. In 1998 Sutton and Rangel were subjected to a state investigation regarding mismanagement of the theater's finances; the two were cleared of wrongdoing in September of the following year. Sutton's accolades include the NAACP's Spingarn Medal (1997), the Arthur G. Gaston Lifetime Achievement Award (2000), and the American Heritage Award (2005). Sutton died in a Manhattan nursing home. In addition to his two children, Sutton is survived by his wife, Leatrice; his sister, Essie Mae Sutton; and four grandchildren. See *Current Biography* (1973).

Obituary *New York Times* (on-line) Dec. 28, 2009

TERHORST, JERALD F. July 11, 1922–Mar. 31, 2010 Former U.S. press secretary; journalist. Jerald F. terHorst was appointed White House press secretary by President Gerald R. Ford, terHorst's longtime friend, in 1974, shortly after President Richard M. Nixon resigned in the wake of the Watergate scandal. The new press secretary resigned just four weeks into his term, however, when Ford pardoned Nixon for any crimes he had committed against the U.S. while in office. Despite the brevity of his tenure as press secretary, terHorst, along with other members of the Ford administration, was credited with cultivating a more honest and press-friendly atmosphere in the White House. He was also praised for his principled decision to resign. "If justice is to be even-handed and administered to the rich and the poor, the weak and the powerful alike," he told a *New York Times* reporter shortly after his resignation, "then mercy, I thought, when administered by a president who sets the tone for the country, also should be an act of [a] similar kind." Jerald Franklin terHorst was born in Grand Rapids, Michigan, to Dutch immigrant parents. He dropped out of school in 10th grade to work on his uncle's dairy farm. His high-school principal eventually persuaded him to return to school, and he earned a diploma. He then attended Michigan State University (MSU), in East Lansing, on an agricultural scholarship and served as a writer and editor for the daily campus newspaper, the *Michigan State News*. In 1943 he left college to join the U.S. Marine Corps Reserve, and he served as a captain during World

War II. After the war ended he resumed his education and earned a bachelor's degree in 1947. He had joined the *Grand Rapids Press* as a city-hall reporter the previous year and was assigned to cover Ford's successful bid for the U.S. House in Michigan's Fifth Congressional District in 1948. (Ford served in that office until 1973, when he was appointed vice president by Nixon after the resignation of his predecessor, Spiro Agnew.) After serving a tour of duty with the Marines in Korea, from 1951 to 1952, terHorst began working for the *Detroit News*, and three years later he was appointed chief of the newspaper's Washington, D.C., bureau, a post he held for more than a dozen years. When Ford became president following Nixon's resignation, in August 1974, he promptly named terHorst White House press secretary. In early September, however, shortly after Ford announced that he was granting Nixon a full pardon for his connection to Watergate—which was still being investigated—terHorst, who had not been informed of the pardon and did not agree with the decision to grant it, resigned. "I cannot in good conscience support your decision to pardon former President Nixon even before he has been charged with the commission of any crime," terHorst wrote in his resignation letter to Ford. "As your spokesman, I do not know how I could credibly defend that action in the absence of a like decision to grant absolute pardon to the young men who evaded Vietnam military service as a matter of conscience and the absence of pardons for former aides and associates of Mr. Nixon who have been charged with crimes—and imprisoned—stemming from the same Watergate situation." The former press secretary was applauded by members of the media for his honesty, and he became the first recipient of the American Association of Journalists and Authors' Conscience-in-Media Award in 1975. He subsequently returned to the *Detroit News*, where he worked as a senior correspondent and columnist for many years, before leaving in 1981 to work as the Washington public-affairs director for the Ford Motor Co. He authored a biography of Ford, *Gerald Ford and the Future of the Presidency*, which was published in late 1974. In 1979 he published *The Flying White House: The Story of Air Force One*, which he co-wrote with Air Force One pilot Ralph Albertazzie. He died of congestive heart failure in his Asheville, North Carolina, home. His wife, Louise Roth terHorst, died in 2009. He is survived by a son, three daughters, and eight grandchildren. See *Current Biography* (1975). —M.A.S.

Obituary *New York Times* (on-line) Apr. 1, 2010

THEBOM, BLANCHE Sep. 19, 1915–Mar. 23, 2010 Opera singer. Mezzo-soprano Blanche Thebom, one of the first American-born opera singers to gain international acclaim, gave more than 350 performances at the famed Metropolitan Opera, in New York City. Thebom was born in Monessen, Pennsylvania, and raised in Canton, Ohio. (There are conflicting reports as to the year of her birth, with most reliable sources stating 1915 but some asserting that it was 1918.) Her parents, who had immigrated to the U.S. from Sweden, were both musically inclined. Her mother has been described as a fine amateur singer, and her father played the accordion. In Canton her father (and

later her two brothers) worked in the steel mills. Thebom began to study the piano at age eight, sang in her school's glee club and her church choir, and on one occasion appeared in a school production of the opera *Martha*. She hoped to attend college and eventually to teach, but by the time she graduated from Canton's McKinley High School, the Great Depression had begun. Financially strapped, she enrolled instead in a business course and subsequently obtained a position as a secretary in a real-estate office, where she worked for seven years. During an ocean voyage to Sweden with her parents in 1938, she was asked to entertain on the ship—her father having made no secret of his pride in her ability. The pianist Kosti Vehanen was in the audience, and, impressed by her natural ability, he arranged for her to study in New York City. Among Thebom's teachers were Edyth Walker, formerly of the Metropolitan Opera (often called the Met), and Lothar Wallerstein, a Czech-born composer and opera director. In 1940 Thebom auditioned for the impresario Sol Hurok, who signed her to a contract. She made her professional debut at a recital in Sheboygan, Wisconsin, in October 1941. That was followed by an engagement to sing the solo part in Brahms's *Alto Rhapsody* with Eugene Ormandy and the Philadelphia Orchestra in November 1941. A coveted Metropolitan Opera contract was offered to her in the fall of 1944. Her first role with the company was that of Brangane in Richard Wagner's *Tristan und Isolde*, sung in Philadelphia on November 28, 1944, and on December 14, 1944, she sang the role of Fricka in Wagner's *Die Walkure*, in New York City. (Because the former engagement occurred in Philadelphia, the latter appearance is often listed as her Metropolitan debut.) In addition to the Wagner roles for which she became celebrated, Thebom appeared in the title role in Bizet's *Carmen* and as Amneris in Verdi's *Aïda*, among others. Her last performance at the Met took place in 1967. She went on to direct an opera program at the University of Arkansas, in Little Rock, and later she moved to San Francisco, California, where she taught privately and helped found a training program for young singers. Thebom, whose nine-year marriage to Richard Metz, a banker, ended in divorce in 1960, died at her San Francisco home at the age of 94, leaving no immediate family. See *Current Biography* (1948). —D.K.

Obituary *New York Times* A p26 Mar. 28, 2010

TODD, RICHARD June 11, 1919–Dec. 3, 2009 Actor. During his lengthy screen career, Richard Todd played British war heroes in such memorable films as *The Hasty Heart* (1949), *The Dam Busters* (1955), and *The Longest Day* (1962) and won acclaim for his roles in such pictures as *A Man Called Peter* (1955) and *The Virgin Queen* (1955). He was also known for turning down a chance to play James Bond in the first Bond film, *Dr. No* (1962), due to prior commitments. Richard Andrew Palethorpe-Todd was born in Dublin, Ireland, the son of Major A. W. and Marville Palethorpe-Todd. In 1925 the family moved to Devon, England. Wanting to become a playwright, Todd enrolled at the Italia Contri Academy, a drama school in London. During the late 1930s many theatrical companies were forming in Scotland, and in

December 1939 he helped to found a repertory company in the town of Dundee. Todd found that he enjoyed acting—so much that he abandoned his ambition to become a playwright. World War II interrupted his acting career. After serving in a number of units, including the Armored Calvary and the Airbourne, he was discharged in 1946. Seeking more financial security than the Dundee theater scene could offer, Todd traveled to London in 1948 to find work in film and was quickly signed to a contract with the Associated British Picture Corp. His first picture was the melodrama *For Them That Trespass* (1949), in which Todd played a man punished for a murder he did not commit. The critical consensus was that the young star's acting was almost the sole redeeming feature of the film. The next year Todd received an Academy Award nomination in the category of best actor for his work in *The Hasty Heart*, a drama set in Burma during World War II. In 1955 Todd starred in *The Dam Busters*, based on the real-life raids of the Royal Air Force Squadron 617, which destroyed important German dams during World War II. In the film Todd played squadron leader Guy Gibson. That year Todd was also praised for his performance in the biopic *A Man Called Peter*, in which he played Reverend Peter Marshall, a Scottish-born minister who immigrated to the U.S. and became chaplain of the U.S. Senate. In 1955 Todd also appeared as Sir Walter Raleigh, the British aristocrat and explorer, in *The Virgin Queen*, which starred Bette Davis. In *The Longest Day* (1962) Todd returned to playing war heroes, portraying Major John Howard, a British officer who led the seizure of the Pegasus Bridge prior to the D-Day invasion in Normandy. (Todd had been one of the first World War II paratroopers in Normandy, where he had been sent to help Howard defend the bridge.) Some of Todd's other well-known film credits included roles in Alfred Hitchcock's *Stage Fright* (1950), *D-Day the Sixth of June* (1956), and *Saint Joan* (1957). Later he made occasional guest appearances on such TV programs as *Doctor Who* and *Murder, She Wrote*. His final role came in a 2007 episode of the popular British crime show *Heartbeat*. Todd wrote two memoirs, *Caught in the Act* (1986) and *In Camera* (1989). In 1993 he received the Order of the British Empire. Suffering from cancer, Todd died in his sleep at his home in England. His two marriages, to Catherine Grant-Bogle and Virginia Mailer, both ended in divorce. He is survived by Fiona, his daughter from the first marriage, and Andrew, a son from the second. His son Peter, from his first marriage, committed suicide in 2005, and his son Seumas, from his second marriage, committed suicide in 1997. See *Current Biography* (1955). —W.D.

Obituary *New York Times* (on-line) Dec. 4, 2009

TSHABALALA-MSIMANG, MANTO Oct. 9, 1940–Dec. 16, 2009 Former South African minister of health. Manto Tshabalala-Msimang (pronounced cha-buh-LA-lum zih-MANG) was a controversial South African health minister who drew international censure for her views on AIDS. Born Mantombaza Botloane in Durban, South Africa, she graduated from Inanda Seminary School in 1959 and subsequently attended the University of Fort Hare, South Africa, where she became a member of the African National Congress (ANC) Youth League. She earned a bachelor's degree before fleeing the country, in 1962, with a number of other student activists, including South Africa's future president Thabo Mbeki. The students were arrested in Zimbabwe and spent six weeks in a Bulawayo prison before being detained in Botswana. Avoiding deportation back to South Africa by fleeing to Tanzania (then called Tanganyika), Tshabalala-Msimang later traveled to the Soviet Union, where she enrolled at the First Leningrad Medical Institute, in Moscow. There, Tshabalala-Msimang learned to speak Russian and earned a medical degree in 1969. She then returned to Tanzania, settling in Dar es Salaam to practice medicine and to attend the University of Dar es Salaam, where she earned a diploma in obstetrics and gynecology in 1973. That year she became the medical superintendent of a hospital in Botswana but was soon fired for stealing a watch from the wrist of an anesthetized patient. She was later treated for kleptomania. In 1977 Tshabalala-Msimang, who had remained active with the ANC, helped to set up the group's health department, which held the First International Conference on Health and Apartheid in 1980. By that time she was in Belgium, where she had completed a master's degree in public health at the University of Antwerp, also in 1980. Tshabalala-Msimang spent the next decade living in Tanzania and Zambia, working for the United Nations and the Organization of African Unity as well as continuing to serve the ANC. Among the projects she completed for the ANC were a 1981 survey on the nutritional status of the children of ANC exiles in Tanzania; a 1983 study of the incidence of resistant malaria among members of the ANC communities in Angola, Mozambique, and Tanzania; and a 1986 mental-health survey of those living in ANC communities in Angola, Mozambique, Tanzania, and Zambia. During those years she also began working with people infected with HIV/AIDS. In 1990 (some sources state 1991), after nearly three decades in exile, Tshabalala-Msimang returned to South Africa to help coordinate the ANC's health plan. With the end of apartheid in 1994, she was named chair of the National Assembly's committee on health. She held that position until 1996, when she was appointed deputy minister of justice. After Nelson Mandela stepped down from the South African presidency, in 1999, Tshabalala-Msimang was appointed health minister under the newly elected president, Thabo Mbeki. Her tenure was tarnished by frequent scandals and controversy: she repeatedly denied that HIV caused AIDS (as did Mbeki) and (also like Mbeki) was lambasted in the international press for her belief in treating South African victims of HIV and AIDS epidemic with garlic, beetroot, and lemons, rather than with antiretroviral drugs. That approach earned her the derisive nickname Dr. Beetroot. In 2005 more than 80 scientists and academics signed a letter asking Mbeki for "the immediate removal of Dr. Tshabalala-Msimang as Minister of Health and for an end to the disastrous, pseudoscientific policies that have characterized the South African government's response to HIV/AIDS," according to the London *Independent* (September 7, 2006). When Mbeki was forced to resign by the ANC in 2008, Tshabalala-Msimang was stripped of her position. It has been estimated that during her tenure the number of HIV-infected people in South Africa rose to more than five million and that her reluctance to distribute antiretroviral drugs was responsible for hundreds of thousands of premature deaths. Tshabalala-Msimang, who was widely suspected of being an alcoholic, underwent a liver transplant in 2007. (Officials claimed that her liver damage had been caused by hepatitis.) She never fully recovered and was awaiting a second transplant when she died at a hospital in Johannesburg. She is survived by her second husband, Mendi Msimang, the former treasurer of the African National Congress, and two daughters, Phulane and Zuki. Her first husband, Mandla Tshabalala, also survives her. See *Current Biography International Yearbook* (2007).—C.C.

Obituary *New York Times* A p41 Dec. 18, 2009

UDALL, STEWART L. Jan. 31, 1920–Mar. 20, 2010 Former U.S. secretary of the interior; former U.S. representative. Stewart L. Udall is best known for his eight-year tenure as the U.S. secretary of the interior in the presidential administrations of John F. Kennedy (1961-63) and Lyndon B. Johnson (1963-69), during which he pioneered environmental preservation efforts. Prior to holding that position, Udall represented the Second Congressional District of Arizona in the U.S. House. Udall was born in the desert town of St. Johns, Arizona. His family had deep roots in the region; his father's father, David King Udall, moved to the town in 1880 as a missionary with the Church of Jesus Christ of Latter-day Saints and established a Mormon colony there. His mother, Louise Lee Udall, was the granddaughter of John Doyle Lee, who was executed for his involvement in the 1857 Mountain Meadows Massacre, in which a group of migrant workers on a wagon train bound for California were murdered by Mormon militia members. Udall's father, Levi Stewart Udall, served as an elected judge in the Arizona Superior Court and as a justice on the Arizona Supreme Court. Udall and his siblings (his two brothers, Morris and David, and his sister, Elma) were raised in the Mormon faith and learned the importance of hard work by helping with chores on the family farm. Udall studied for one year at Eastern Arizona Junior College, in Thatcher, before transferring to the University of Arizona in Tucson. He interrupted his education to serve for two years as a Mormon missionary in Pennsylvania and New York. In 1944 he enlisted in the U.S. Air Force and saw combat in Italy as a gunner on a B-24 bomber. Upon completing his military service, he returned to the University of Arizona, where he was an all-conference guard on the 1946 varsity basketball team. Udall received a bachelor of law degree from the University of Arizona in 1948 and then established a law practice with his brother Morris in Tucson. Udall entered national politics in 1954, when he was elected to Arizona's Second Congressional District seat in the U.S. House of Representatives. He represented the district for three consecutive terms, during which he supported such progressive causes as civil rights and school integration and forged a close relationship with then-senator John F. Kennedy. Udall was elected to a fourth term in 1960 but relinquished his seat to accept an appointment to serve in Kennedy's presidential administration, as U.S.

secretary of the interior; he retained his Cabinet post under Lyndon B. Johnson. (His brother Morris "Mo" Udall was elected to replace him in the House and ultimately represented Arizona's Second Congressional District for three decades.) During Stewart Udall's tenure as secretary of the interior, he became a leader of the modern environmental movement, presiding over the acquisition of 3.85 million acres of new land holdings, including four national parks, six monuments, nine national recreation areas, 20 historic sites, 50 wildlife refuges, and eight national seashores. In addition to championing several important pieces of environmental legislation, most notably the Wilderness Act of 1964, which protected from development some nine million acres of land, Udall helped publicize the department by hosting special events that featured such public figures as the poet Carl Sandburg and the actor Hal Holbrook. Udall penned the book *The Quiet Crisis* (1963), which called upon Americans to adopt a new "land conscience" when it came to protecting the environment and preserving the natural beauty of the American landscape. Udall's influence in the department lasted longer than his own tenure; much of the environmental legislation enacted in the 1970s and 1980s, including the Endangered Species Act, was at least in part a result of Udall's efforts. "That was a wonderful time, and it carried through into the Nixon administration, into the Carter administration," Udall once said. "It lasted for 20 years. I don't remember a big fight between Republicans and Democrats. . . . There was a consensus that the country needed more conservation projects of the kind that we were proposing." After leaving office Udall became a professor at Yale University, in New Haven, Connecticut, and also practiced law. In 1979 he returned to Arizona and became an advocate for those whose health had been adversely affected by the U.S. nuclear program. He brought two lawsuits against the government, one on behalf of Navajo Indians who had developed lung cancer after mining for uranium and another for people who were exposed to radiation from nuclear-weapons manufacturing and testing in Nevada. Although both lawsuits failed in court, Udall's efforts were credited with helping to lead President George H. W. Bush to sign the 1990 Radiation Exposure Compensation Act. In 1994 Udall published *The Myths of August: A Personal Exploration of Our Tragic Cold War Affair with the Atom*, about the effects of uranium mining and nuclear-weapons development on humans and the environment. He was also the author of *The Forgotten Founders: Rethinking the History of the Old West* (2002), among numerous other volumes. Udall, who remained a dedicated outdoorsman well into his 80s, spent the last two decades of his life in New Mexico surrounded by his family. He died at his home in Santa Fe, about a week after injuring himself in a fall. Udall's wife, the former Irmalee Webb, died in 2001. He is survived by six children—Tom, Scott, Lynn, Lori, Denis, and Jay—and eight grandchildren. See *Current Biography* (1961). —C.C.

Obituary *New York Times* A p25 Mar. 22, 2010

VOZNESENSKY, ANDREI May 12, 1933–June 1, 2010 Poet. Andrei Voznesensky gained recognition as one of the Soviet Union's most talented and courageous poets, "burst[ing] onto the stage in the cultural thaw that followed [Communist leader Joseph] Stalin's death in 1953," according to Raymond H. Anderson, who wrote Voznesensky's obituary for the *New York Times* (June 1, 2010, on-line). Asserting that the Moscow-born Voznesensky had "helped lift Russian literature out of its state of fear and virtual serfdom," Anderson continued, "[His] poetry epitomized the setbacks, gains and hopes of the post-Stalin decades in Russia. His hundreds of subtle, ironic and innovative verses reflected alternating periods of calm and stress as the Communist Party's rule stabilized, weakened and then, in 1991, quickly disintegrated." Voznesensky's father, also named Andrei, was a designer of hydroelectric-power stations and a professor of engineering. His mother, Antonina, was a scholar who specialized in the history of Russian literature. From 1941 to 1944 Voznesensky lived with his mother in Kurgan, in the Urals, while his father helped evacuate factories during the German army's siege of Leningrad. After World War II ended, Voznesensky returned to Moscow to continue his education. Interested predominantly in painting and drawing, in 1951 he enrolled at the Moscow Architectural Institute and received a degree in engineering six years later. Concurrently, Voznesensky dabbled in poetry, and one of his pieces, "Fire in the Architectural Institute," was based on an actual occurrence. One of the greatest influences in Voznesensky's literary life was Boris Pasternak, the Russian author of *Doctor Zhivago*. Their relationship began in the 1950s, when Voznesensky showed some of his poetry to Pasternak, who became his mentor and encouraged him to pursue writing, despite the strict censorship enforced during Stalin's dictatorial regime. The situation for writers improved little under Nikita S. Khrushchev, and in 1963 Voznesensky was rebuked by official critics for "formalism [experimentalism] in style that departed from the officially approved style of socialist realism." In 1967 Soviet authorities forbade him to fulfill a poetry-reading engagement in New York City. In response he wrote a fiery letter to *Pravda*, which that Soviet newspaper refused to print but which appeared in several foreign journals. "I am a Soviet writer," he said, "a human being made of flesh and blood, not a puppet to be pulled on a string. It is not a question of me personally, but of the fate of Soviet literature, its honor and prestige in the outside world. How much longer will we go on dragging ourselves through the mud?" For that and other transgressions, Voznesensky was threatened with expulsion from the Soviet Writers' Union but escaped that punishment, without making the apology demanded, by leaving on a two-month tour of Siberia until tensions had calmed. There were further attacks on him in 1973, centering on two new groups of poems, published in magazines, which satirized the shallowness, falsity, and conformity of Soviet literary life and seemed to suggest (in a poem ostensibly about the French Revolution) that the ideals of the Bolshevist Revolution had been betrayed. Despite such official censure, poetry readings by Voznesensky, his compatriot Yevgeny Yevtushenko, and oth-

ers were enormously popular with ordinary Russian citizens, and such events were among the principal social functions in Moscow and the surrounding areas. Voznesensky drew crowds numbering in the thousands to recitals held in the Luzhniki Stadium, at museums, and in concert halls. Describing one of the readings, Paul Wohl wrote in a profile of the poet for the *Christian Science Monitor* (April 7, 1966): "As he speaks his poems, Voznesensky, who in the street might pass for a clerk or book salesman, is transfigured and shaken by the drama which he seeks to convey." Among Voznesensky's most famous poems is "Ya Goya" ("I Am Goya"), which expressed his childhood fear of war and read, in part, "I am Goya / of the bare field, by the enemy's beak gouged / till the craters of my eyes gape / I am grief/ I am the tongue / of war, the embers of cities / on the snows of the year 1941." Raymond H. Anderson explained the power of the piece in its original Russian: "The poem creates its impressions of war and horror through a series of images and interrelated variations on the name of the painter, which echo throughout in a series of striking sound metaphors in Russian: Goya, glaz (eyes), gore (grief), golos (voice), gorod (cities), golod (hunger), gorlo (gullet)." Voznesensky's work was widely translated, and among his popular collections published in English are *Dogalypse* (1960), *Selected Poems of Andrei Voznesensky* (1964), *Voznesensky: Selected Poems* (1966), *Antiworlds and the Fifth Ace* (1967), *Story Under Full Sail* (1974), and *An Arrow in the Wall* (1985). Eventually, Voznesensky was recognized by Soviet authorities as a national treasure, and in 1978 he was awarded the USSR State Prize. He was later given a seat on the board of the Soviet Writers' Union. Of the poet's later years, Anderson wrote, "After the collapse of Communism, Mr. Voznesensky the rebel became Mr. Voznesensky the writer for the Russian version of *Playboy* magazine and the organizer of provincial poetry festivals." Voznesensky, who had suffered multiple strokes, died at his home in Moscow. He is survived by his wife, Zoya Boguslavskaya, a writer and literary critic. See *Current Biography* (1967). —J.P.

Obituary *New York Times* (on-line) June 1, 2010

WARNECKE, JOHN CARL Feb. 24, 1919–Apr. 17, 2010 Architect. John Carl Warnecke designed numerous important buildings and structures during his decades-long career, including President John F. Kennedy's grave site in Arlington National Cemetery. Warnecke's eponymous architecture firm established a reputation for "contextualizing" each of its structures, paying close attention to local surroundings during the design process. Warnecke was born in Oakland, California, to Carl I. Warnecke, an architect, and Margaret (Esterling) Warnecke. At Stanford University Warnecke played left tackle on the school's undefeated football team, which won the 1941 Rose Bowl. He graduated that year with a B.A. degree and then entered Harvard University's architecture school, where he studied under Walter Gropius, the German architect who founded the Bauhaus School of architecture. Completing the three-year curriculum in just one year, Warnecke earned a master's degree in architecture in 1942.

Warnecke, who was unable to serve in World War II because of a football injury he had sustained in college, then took a job as an assistant technical director of the housing authority in Richmond, California. In 1944 he became a draftsman at his father's firm, Miller and Warnecke, and in 1947 he struck out on his own, although he continued to collaborate with his father on occasion. Some of Warnecke's early projects included designs for the Mira Vista Elementary School in El Cerrito, California; the post office and bookstore at Stanford University; residence halls and the earth-sciences building at the University of California at Berkeley; and a state office building in Oakland. The design for the Mira Vista Elementary School, completed in 1951, demonstrated Warnecke's sensitivity to his buildings' surroundings: the classrooms climb the hills in rows and are topped by broad, slanting roofs with enormous skylights. Warnecke garnered international attention in 1956, when he received a commission from the U.S. State Department to design the American Embassy building in Bangkok, Thailand. His proposed structure, which won critical praise but was never built, was "a light pagoda-like building with slender white stilts that seemed to rise, miragelike, from a lake," as William Grimes described it in Warnecke's *New York Times* obituary (April 22, 2010, on-line). In 1962 Warnecke (a longtime friend of the Kennedy family) won a commission from the Kennedy administration to redesign Lafayette Square in Washington, D.C. In the space, whose structures were initially set to be razed, Warnecke managed to accommodate two new office buildings—the National Courts Building and the New Executive Office Building—while retaining the square's historic rowhouses and overall aesthetic. In 1963 Kennedy appointed Warnecke to the U.S. Commission of Fine Arts, which approves new federal building projects. After President Kennedy's assassination, in 1963, Jacqueline Kennedy chose Warnecke to design her husband's grave site. (Warnecke reportedly engaged in a romantic relationship with the former First Lady during their collaboration for the memorial site.) The completed site, which hugs the contours of an Arlington National Cemetery hill, includes a circular walkway leading to an overlook and steps that rise to a marble platform featuring an eternal flame. The simple monument was praised by architecture critics and members of the general public. "Never have the complexities of a design problem and the difficulties of a site been so painfully and publicly clear, and rarely have results been greeted with such general praise obviously motivated by relief," the architecture critic Ada Louise Huxtable wrote for the *New York Times*. (The site also contains the graves of two Kennedy children, a daughter who was stillborn and a son who died after two days, and upon her death, in 1994, Jacqueline Kennedy Onassis was laid to rest there.) By the late 1970s John Carl Warnecke and Associates had become the largest architectural firm in the country, with offices in New York City, San Francisco, Los Angeles, Boston, Honolulu, and Washington, D.C. Some of Warnecke's most significant projects from that decade included the AT&T Long Lines Building in New York City; the Soviet Embassy in Washington, D.C.; and the South Terminal at Boston's Logan Airport. In the 1980s he designed the

Hart Senate Office Building in the nation's capital. During the latter part of that decade, Warnecke retired to his ranch along California's Russian River. There, he grew grapes for wine and worked on his memoir, which he completed just before his death. Warnecke, who died of pancreatic cancer at the age of 91, is survived by a sister, Margaret Putnam; his daughter, Margo; his sons, Rodger and Fred; and four grandchildren. See *Current Biography* (1968).—W.D.

Obituary *New York Times* (on-line) Apr. 22, 2010

WILD, EARL Nov. 26, 1915–Jan. 23, 2010 Pianist. "Earl Wild . . . was one of the greatest pianists of the 20th century. With the extraordinary catholicity of his repertoire, his role as a pianist-composer and his charismatic stage presence, Wild came closer than most to being the complete virtuoso," Jeremy Nicholas wrote for the London *Guardian* (February 3, 2010). "It is hard to name another pianist who has been as successful in the works of such a diverse range of composers, from Dietrich Buxtehude, Bach and Mozart through to Paul Hindemith, Walter Piston, Aaron Copland, Gian Carlo Menotti and Paul Creston." Wild was born in Pittsburgh, Pennsylvania, the third of four children of Royland and Lillian Wild. His father worked in the invoice department at Pittsburgh Steel, and his mother was a hat designer. Wild, who had two older sisters and a younger brother, showed an affinity for music at an early age. "Practice was my refuge," he once said, explaining that the sound of the piano drowned out his parents' quarrels. With no formal study, Wild could discern the melody and pitch of the operas blaring from his parents' Edison phonograph. "The first record I learned was the overture to Bellini's opera *Norma*," he recalled to Barrymore Laurence Scherer for the *Wall Street Journal* (November 29, 2005). "It started with a G-minor chord. And when I was about three, I was able to reach up to the keyboard of our upright piano and play along in the same key." At the age of four, he started taking piano lessons. Two years later Wild, who possessed perfect pitch and an uncanny ability to sight-read sheet music, entered the Pittsburgh Musical Institute. When he was 11 years old, Wild studied under Selmar Janson, a music professor at Pittsburgh's Carnegie Institute of Technology (now called Carnegie Mellon University); a year later Wild performed a recital at KDKA, the first commercially licensed radio station in the U.S., and was later invited to be the house pianist. He joined the Pittsburgh Symphony as a 14-year-old (the youngest member in that symphony's history) and toured with the Minneapolis Symphony when he was 15. During his early teens he became the breadwinner, after his father abandoned the family. "I did everything," he told Andrew Druckenbrod for the *Pittsburgh Post-Gazette* (January 26, 2010). "I played popular music and anything that was available. That was the only way to make a living. I didn't think. I just went from one thing to the next." At age 17 Wild was awarded a scholarship to attend a program for artistically gifted young people at Carnegie Tech, where he reunited with Janson and learned to play various other instruments, including the flute, the bass, and the cello. In 1935 Wild took a year-long leave of absence from Carnegie and moved to New York City, where he studied with the Dutch pianist Egon Petri, who is credited with helping to develop Wild's improvisational style, which became his trademark. After obtaining a bachelor's degree, in 1937, Wild returned to New York and joined NBC as a radio pianist and as a member of the network's symphony orchestra, then under the direction of Arturo Toscanini. Two years later, when NBC transmitted its first experimental telecast, Wild became the first American pianist to perform on television. On the program he played Felix Mendelssohn's "Rondo Capriccio" and Maurice Ravel's "Jeux d'eau" ("The Fountain"). In 1942 Wild garnered national attention after delivering a flawless interpretation of George Gershwin's "Rhapsody in Blue" for an NBC radio broadcast. During World War II he played the flute with the U.S. Navy Band and performed piano solos at White House recitals and other notable events. After receiving his military discharge, in 1944, Wild joined the newly formed American Broadcasting Company (ABC) television network as a house pianist, conductor, and composer. While working at ABC he was commissioned by the network to compose the Easter oratorio "Revelations," which contained a libretto by William Lewis and which the network televised in 1962. He also toured extensively around the world and collaborated with other performers, including the violinist Mischa Elman and the singers Maria Callas, Jan Peerce, and Robert Merrill. Wild also composed and performed music for *Caesar's Hour*, a variety show hosted by the comedian Sid Caesar. After leaving ABC, in 1968, Wild focused mostly on concerts and recordings. His vast body of work includes such original compositions as "The Turquoise Horse" and the "Doo-Dah" Variations. His discography consists of more than 35 piano concertos by various composers; 26 chamber music recordings; and more than 700 solo piano works, including highly regarded interpretations of the major works of Liszt, Chopin, Rachmaninoff, Beethoven, Brahms, Copland, Gershwin, and Debussy. Wild also helped to revive lesser-known virtuoso works by Mily Balakirev, Leopold Godowsky, Henri Herz, Nikolai Medtner, and Sigismond Thalberg. Wild recorded for some 20 record companies; starting in 1997 his recordings, both old and new, were issued on his own label, Ivory Classics. Also in 1997, Wild won a Grammy Award for his album *The Romantic Master*. Credited with sparking a revival of interest in the work of the Hungarian composer Franz Liszt, Wild was awarded the Liszt Medal by the Hungarian government in 1986 for his long association with the composer's music. From 1992 to 2006 Wild served as an artist-in-residence at Carnegie Mellon's School of Music. He also had teaching posts at the Juilliard School, the Eastman School of Music, Penn State University, Ohio State University, and the Manhattan School of Music. In 2005 Wild's final performance at New York City's famed venue Carnegie Hall took place on his 90th birthday; that same year he released his last album, *Living History*. In 2007 he received an honorary doctorate of fine arts from Carnegie Mellon. A year later Wild was awarded the Presidential Medal of the Academy of Recording Arts and Sciences; the presentation was held at Disney Hall, in Los Angeles, following his final public

performance. Wild, who continued to teach well into his 90s, died of congestive heart failure at his home in Palm Springs, California. He is survived by his companion of 38 years, Michael Rolland Davis. Wild's memoirs were scheduled to be published by Carnegie Mellon University Press in 2010. *See Current Biography* (1988). —C.C.

Obituary *New York Times* B p8 Jan. 25, 2010

WIRTZ, W. WILLARD Mar. 14, 1912–Apr. 24, 2010 Former U.S. secretary of labor; attorney; law professor. W. Willard Wirtz served as the secretary of labor in the presidential administrations of John F. Kennedy (1962–63) and Lyndon B. Johnson (1963–69), during which he established a reputation as a champion of the unemployed. Prior to holding that position, he worked as a professor of labor law at Northwestern University, in Chicago, Illinois, and as a mediator and an arbitrator in labor disputes. William Willard Wirtz was born in Dekalb, Illinois, where his father worked as a teacher at the Northern Illinois State Normal School. After graduating from the local high school, Wirtz spent two years studying at Northern Illinois State Teachers College and one year at the University of California at Berkeley, before transferring to Beloit College, in Wisconsin, where he played football and was president of the student body. An academic standout, Wirtz was elected to Phi Beta Kappa and graduated in 1933 with a bachelor's degree in sociology. He taught high school in Illinois for one year before enrolling at Harvard University Law School, where he earned a degree in 1937. After teaching law for several years at the University of Iowa and Northwestern University, Wirtz relocated to Washington, D.C., in 1942 to become an assistant general counsel to the Board of Economic Warfare, an agency that provided goods for the U.S. and its allies during World War II. Soon afterward he became chair of the appeals committee of the National War Labor Board (1943–45), a federal agency whose purpose was to arbitrate labor disputes in order to ensure economic productivity during wartime. In 1946 Wirtz became the chair of the Wage Stabilization Board, the organization that replaced the War Labor Board after the war ended. In that role he helped oversee a change in wage scales during the country's transition to peacetime. Later that year, when wage and price controls had been lifted and the Wage Stabilization Board was no longer needed, he returned to Northwestern University, where he served as a professor of labor law until 1954. During the 1950s Wirtz also worked under the governor of Illinois, Adlai E. Stevenson, serving as a top strategist and a speechwriter for Stevenson's 1952 and 1956 presidential campaigns. Following Stevenson's defeat in the latter race, the men established the law firm of Stevenson, Rifkind & Wirtz. During that time Wirtz worked as an arbitrator in hundreds of labor-management disputes. Wirtz left his law practice in 1961 to serve as the under secretary of labor, when Arthur J. Goldberg was the U.S. labor secretary, in the Kennedy administration. In 1962, after Goldberg was nominated to the U.S. Supreme Court, Wirtz was appointed by Kennedy to replace him as labor secretary; he retained that post when President Johnson took office in 1963, after Kennedy's assassination. During Wirtz's tenure he established programs to promote literacy and provide assistance and job training to the unemployed. He also implemented a number of important antidiscrimination measures signed into law by Johnson—most notably the Age Discrimination in Employment Act of 1967. As labor secretary Wirtz also continued, albeit reluctantly, to take part in resolving a wide range of labor disputes. Disagreements with Johnson over the Vietnam War hampered his relationship with the administration near the end of his tenure. Wirtz stepped down from his post in January 1969, when President Richard Nixon took office, and returned to his Washington, D.C., law practice. He began serving as a trustee on the financially plagued Penn Central Transportation Co. and as president of the Manpower Institute, which worked to resolve labor problems by uniting labor, industry, and government. In 2008 Wirtz published a memoir, *In the Rearview Mirror*. At the time of his death, from natural causes, he was the last surviving member of the Kennedy Cabinet. Wirtz was married for 66 years, to the former Jane Quisenberry, who died in 2002. He is survived by two sons, Philip and Richard; three grandchildren; and his sisters, Frances and Kathyrn. See *Current Biography* (1963). —C.C.

Obituary *New York Times* A p15 Apr. 26, 2010

WOLPER, DAVID L. Jan. 11, 1928–Aug. 10, 2010 Film and television producer. David Wolper once stated, "I can possibly say I have entertained and educated more people than anyone else in the world." At the time of his death, Wolper had been involved in more than 300 projects, many of which had won Oscars, Emmys, and Golden Globes. Wolper was born in New York City, the only child of Irving S. Wolper, a commercial real-estate broker, and his wife, Anna. Wolper, who was not given a middle name, adopted the initial L to distinguish himself from an uncle who was also named David Wolper. As a student at Columbia Grammar and Preparatory School, Wolper was already developing into an entrepreneur. When he was 15 he and his friend Jimmy Harris, whose father was a successful film financier, acquired the rights to an Italian B movie—doing so in the belief that any involvement in movies impresses girls. Wolper and Harris invited critics to a private screening of the film at Harris's apartment and sold the film, which they renamed *Fear No Evil*, to a small New York theater for a short run. The experience taught Wolper that there was money to be made in the acquisition and distribution of old film footage. After graduating from high school, Wolper spent a year at Drake University, in Des Moines, Iowa, before transferring to the University of Southern California (USC). Eager to start making money, Wolper left USC at the end of his junior year and began buying old movies with the intention of selling them to television stations across the country. An expert salesman, Wolper traveled from city to city, convincing television executives that they needed whatever he happened to have on hand, from B movies to dubbed Soviet cartoon versions of *Pinocchio*. The personal relationships he developed with television stations and Soviet film suppliers helped Wolper years later, when, in 1958, he bought 6,000 feet of footage dealing with the Soviet space program and used it as the basis for his first documentary, *The Race for Space: The Missile*. That documentary, which Wolper sold to more than 100 television stations, was screened at the Metro Theater as part of the 1959 San Francisco International Film Festival and was nominated for an Academy Award in the category of best documentary. By the mid-1970s Wolper Productions, which had started out with only two employees in a single-room office, had grown to more than 200 employees using 40 cutting rooms. Wolper's 1971 production *The Hellstrom Chronicle*, which combined elements of the documentary with science fiction to explore mankind's relationship with the insect world, won an Academy Award for best documentary feature. Wolper is perhaps best known for producing the miniseries *Roots*, based on the best-selling book by Alex Haley and shown on ABC in 1977. Besides being one of the highest-rated programs in television history, *Roots*, which tells the story of an African man and his descendants, beginning when the African is abducted from his village and sold into slavery in America, won nine Emmy Awards and prompted a national discussion about race. Another successful Wolper-produced miniseries was *The Thorn Birds* (1983), a drama set in Australia and based on the same-titled best-selling 1977 novel by Colleen McCullough. Though many of Wolper's big-screen productions were critical and commercial flops, many others, including *Willy Wonka and the Chocolate Factory* (1971) and *L.A. Confidential* (1997), were well received. Some of Wolper's other notable television projects over the years included the Emmy Award–winning documentaries *The Making of the President 1960* (1963), based on Theodore H. White's best-selling book, and *The Undersea World of Jacques Cousteau* (1966) and the popular 1970s sitcoms *Chico and the Man* and *Welcome Back, Kotter*. Wolper, who also served as a high-profile event organizer, coordinated the 1984 Summer Olympic Games ceremonies, which included sky divers, break dancers, and 84 pianists playing music of George Gershwin in unison. To commemorate the 100th anniversary of the dedication of the Statue of Liberty in New York Harbor, on July 4, 1986, Wolper organized a ceremony that included thousands of skyrockets set off in the largest fireworks display in history and 265 tall ships on parade. Wolper was inducted into the Academy of Television Arts and Sciences Hall of Fame in 1989. He published his autobiography, *Producer*, written with David Fisher, in 2002. Wolper died in his Beverly Hills home from congestive heart failure and complications of Parkinson's disease. He is survived by his third wife, the former Gloria Hill; two sons and a daughter from his second marriage, to the former Margaret Dawn Richard; and 10 grandchildren. See *Current Biography* (1986). —H.R.W.

Obituary *New York Times* A p28 Aug. 12, 2010

WOODEN, JOHN Oct. 14, 1910–June 4, 2010 College basketball coach. During the 26 years that John Wooden served as head coach of the men's basketball team at the University of California, Los Angeles (UCLA), the Bruins never had a losing season. In his last 12 seasons as head coach (1964–75), Wooden led the Bruins to win a remarkable 10 National Collegiate Athletic Association (NCAA) championship titles, seven of which were in consecutive seasons (1967–73). Under Wooden the Bruins also won 88 consecutive games between 1971 and 1974—still an NCAA record—and won an impressive 38 consecutive NCAA tournament games between the 1963–64 and 1973–74 seasons. Wooden, known as an old-fashioned disciplinarian, was revered not only as a skilled coach but as a teacher of life lessons. The UCLA chancellor Gene Block told Claudia Luther for the UCLA Newsroom Web site (June 4, 2010), "Coach Wooden's legacy transcends athletics; what he did was produce leaders. But his influence has reached far beyond our campus and even our community. Through his work and his life, he imparted his phenomenal understanding of leadership and his unwavering sense of integrity to so many people." John Robert Wooden, the son of Joshua and Roxie Wooden, was raised on a 60-acre farm near Centerville, Indiana. Despite its size, the farm, which had no electricity or indoor plumbing, provided the Woodens with only a meager living, and life was austere for the Wooden children, who had a stern upbringing. Throughout his career John Wooden carried in his wallet a credo penned for him by his father that read, "Be true to yourself. Make each day a masterpiece. Drink deeply from good books. Make friendship a fine art. Build a shelter against a rainy day." In 1924 the Woodens, facing bankruptcy and the prospect of losing their farm, moved to Martinsville, a small town famous throughout Indiana for its high-school basketball team. Wooden excelled on his high-school squad, earning a spot on the All-State basketball team three times. At Purdue University, where he majored in engineering, Wooden won the Big Ten Medal for excellence in athletics and scholarship, and in 1932 he led the Boilermakers to the Helms Athletic Foundation's unofficial national championship and was named national college player of the year. After graduating he began his coaching career at Dayton High School in Kentucky, where he compiled the only losing record of his career. The following year he moved back to Indiana and coached at South Bend Central High School, where he also taught English. Wooden spent several years playing professionally in the National Basketball League, which existed from 1937 to 1949 before merging with the National Basketball Association (NBA). He served as a physical-education instructor in the U.S. Navy from 1943 to 1946 and was then hired by the Indiana State Teachers College (now Indiana State University) as an athletic director and a basketball and baseball coach. He was hired by UCLA in 1948 to coach the Bruins, which were then considered the weakest team in the Pacific Coast Conference. In Wooden's first year as coach, he predicted that the Bruins would win only about half their games; the team well exceeded Wooden's prediction, with a 22–7 record. The following season UCLA won the first of many conference championships under Wooden. During his tenure at UCLA, the Bruins had a remarkable record of 620–147. Wooden's overall win–loss record during his 40 years as a coach, 885–203, is also unmatched. Wooden retired in 1975 after the Bruins defeated the University of Kentucky in the NCAA championship game, earn-

ing Wooden his 10th NCAA title. Some of the well-known players coached by Wooden are Kareem Abdul-Jabbar (called Lew Alcindor while with the Bruins), Bill Walton, Willie Naulls, Gail Goodrich, Walt Hazzard, Jamaal Wilkes, and Marques Johnson. Wooden's success has been attributed, in part, to his life philosophy, which he called the "Pyramid of Success." Describing the pyramid, Luther observed: "At the base of the five-level pyramid are industriousness, friendship, loyalty, cooperation and enthusiasm. The next levels up are self-control, alertness, initiative and intentness; condition, skill and team spirit; and poise and confidence. At the pinnacle is competitive greatness, which he defined as performing [to] one's best ability when one's best is required, which, he said, was 'each day.'" Wooden was inducted into the UCLA Athletics Hall of Fame (1984), the Pac-10 Basketball Hall of Honor (2002), and the National Collegiate Basketball Hall of Fame (2006). In 2003 President George W. Bush presented Wooden with the Presidential Medal of Freedom. Wooden was the first person to be inducted into the Naismith Memorial Basketball Hall of Fame as both a player and a coach, in 1960 and 1973, respectively. During his retirement Wooden regularly attended UCLA home games and could be seen sitting behind the Bruins' bench. Wooden, who died of natural causes at Ronald Reagan UCLA Medical Center, is survived by his son, James; his daughter, Nancy; seven grandchildren; and 13 great-grandchildren. See *Current Biography* (1976). —W.D.

Obituary *New York Times* (on-line) June 4, 2010

YAR'ADUA, UMARU Aug. 16, 1951–May 5, 2010
Nigerian leader. When Umaru Musa Yar'Adua became president of Nigeria, in 2007, he pledged to end rampant corruption, improve the country's infrastructure, reform the electoral process, and stop oil-related violence in the Niger Delta. His untimely death came before he could achieve those goals. Yar'Adua was born into an aristocratic Fulani family in the northern Nigerian state of Katsina. The younger of two sons, he earned the equivalent of a high-school diploma in 1971 and then enrolled at Ahmadu Bello University (ABU). He earned a B.S. degree in 1975 and returned to ABU in 1980 to complete a master's degree in analytical chemistry. While completing his studies Yar'Adua taught at the Katsina College of Arts, Science and Technology until 1979 and then took a similar position, which he held until 1983, at Katsina Polytechnic. At both of those institutions, he was a member of the governing council and also an active member of the now-defunct People's Redemption Party (PRP), which was considered a progressive organization. After years of involvement in academia, Yar'Adua entered the private sector, and he spent much of the next two decades working in banking and real estate, among other fields. As a student Yar'Adua had professed Marxist beliefs, but when he began to pursue politics more seriously, he followed family tradition and became a member of the People's Front, which was then under the leadership of his older brother, Shehu. The People's Front later merged with other parties to become the Social Democratic Party (SDP). Umaru Musa Yar'Adua rose through the ranks to be-

come Katsina's SDP secretary, and in 1991 he ran for governor but lost to Alhaji Saidu Barda from the National Republican Convention (NRC). Shehu Yar'Adua was running for president that same year, and many within the SDP believed that conflict would arise if both brothers held high political office. The question became moot after neither of them won, but the younger Yar'Adua gained a reputation as a tireless grassroots activist and campaigner. In 1998 Yar'Adua founded the political party K34 (Katsina State has 34 local governments), and after K34 gained political strength, it merged with the People's Democratic Party (PDM). In 1999 Yar'Adua ran for state governor once more and was victorious. As governor he was successful in eradicating Katsina's debt and for improving education, health care, and infrastructure. Nonetheless, he was criticized internationally when Katsina became the fifth Nigerian state to adopt Sharia (Islamic religious law), and a public outcry arose when a woman was sentenced to death for adultery (the sentence was overturned on appeal). Yar'Adua was reelected governor in 2003. In 2007 he was chosen as the PDM's presidential candidate, and he swept the primary elections despite criticism that he was a puppet of the incumbent, Olusegun Obasanjo. The Nigerian presidential elections began on April 14, 2007, and during the following week, which was marked by police violence and protests, a relatively small percentage of the population went to the polls. Yar'Adua reportedly received more than 24.6 million votes—at least 70 percent of those tallied—and although there were immediate accusations of fraud, Yar'Adua was ultimately sworn in as president, marking the first civilian-to-civilian transfer of power since Nigeria gained its independence, in 1960. Among the most pressing issues facing the new administration was the situation in the Niger Delta, at the southern tip of Nigeria, where there were huge reserves of oil. Various multinational companies had been extracting it for decades, under contracts with the government, and oil had been Nigeria's principal export since the 1970s. It brought tremendous wealth to the country, but the distribution of that wealth was radically uneven—villagers in the area suffered from extreme poverty and the effects of industrial pollution. An indigenous guerrilla group, the Movement for the Emancipation of the Niger Delta (MEND), took to kidnapping foreign oil workers and bombing rigs and storage facilities. Yar'Adua brokered periodic ceasefires, and by 2009 tensions had calmed to some degree. Still, the situation was not fully resolved when he departed the country in November of that year for medical treatment in Saudi Arabia. He had long suffered heart and kidney problems, and his health was a source of constant media speculation. Yar'Adua did not transfer power before setting off, leaving Nigeria in a state of confusion, with no central authority. In February 2010 the National Assembly tapped Goodluck Jonathan, the vice president, to serve as acting president. Upon his return Yar'Adua did not seek to regain the powers that had been transferred to Jonathan. Yar'Adua died at his villa in the capital city, Abuja. He is survived by his two ex-wives: Turai, with whom he had seven children; and Hajiya Hauwa, with whom he had two children. *See Cur-*

rent Biography International Yearbook (2007). —W.D.

Obituary *New York Times* (on-line) May 5, 2010

ZINN, HOWARD Aug. 24, 1922–Jan. 27, 2010 Historian; social activist; educator; writer. Howard Zinn's best-selling *A People's History of the United States: 1492–Present* (1980) was a groundbreaking and revisionist work that chronicled American history from the perspectives of people who Zinn believed had been exploited politically and economically by the U.S. government and social structure—namely ethnic and racial minorities, women, and workers. For example, in the volume's opening chapter, Zinn told the story of Christopher Columbus's landing from the point of view of the Arawak Indians, who were among the first indigenous peoples Columbus met in the West Indies. In another example of Zinn's approach, he explained the technological and economic boom of the Industrial Revolution from the standpoint of the men, women, and children who labored in unsafe factories and barely earned a living wage. Lauded by some as a voice for justice and champion of the disenfranchised and derided by others as a mere social agitator, Zinn awakened several generations of students to his belief in the need for social responsibility and the dangers of irresponsible authority. Zinn was of Jewish descent. His father, Edward, had immigrated to the U.S. from Austria, and his mother, the former Jenny Rabinowitz, came from Siberia, Russia. Zinn and his three brothers were raised in the slums of the New York City borough of Brooklyn. His father struggled to support the family with whatever work he could find, including washing windows, peddling ties from a pushcart, and, later, operating a candy store. Zinn's boyhood pastime of playing in the street ended when he discovered books, and he fondly recalled to journalists the first book he ever owned: a tattered copy of *Tarzan and the Jewels of Opar* that he found on the street. At the age of 17, Zinn participated in his first public protest, lured by the seemingly sophisticated young Communists who had invited him, as well as the chance to visit Times Square in Manhattan. During the demonstration Zinn was knocked unconscious by a mounted police officer wielding a baton. "I was nursing not only a hurt head, but hurt feelings about our country," Zinn told David Barsamian in an interview for the *Progressive* (July 1997). "All the things these radicals had been saying were true. The state is not neutral, but on the side of the powerful." Upon graduating from high school, Zinn worked as a pipe fitter at the Brooklyn Navy Yard. During World War II he enlisted in the U.S. Army Air Corps and trained as a bombardier. His experiences, which included flying bombing missions over Europe in a B-17, left him convinced that there could be no moral justification for war. Thanks to the G.I. Bill, Zinn earned a B.A. degree from New York University, in 1951, and a Ph.D. degree from Columbia University, also in New York City, in 1958. Meanwhile, he and his wife, the former Roslyn Shecter, whom he had married prior to his military service overseas, had moved into a housing project on Manhattan's Lower East Side and had become the parents of two children. Two years before completing his doctoral dissertation, Zinn accepted his first full-time teaching post, at Spelman College, then a school attended solely by black women, in Atlanta, Georgia. (Among his students were the novelist Alice Walker and the activist Marian Wright Edelman.) Zinn's doctoral dissertation, *LaGuardia in Congress*, about the famed politician Fiorello LaGuardia, who became the mayor of New York City in 1934, after leaving the U.S. House, was published by Cornell University Press in 1959. While conducting research for the book, Zinn realized that there was an enormous gap between the popular historical perception of the 1920s—as the prosperous Jazz Age—and the reality: most of LaGuardia's constituents lived in poverty. "It suggested to me that we need to take another look at the way we label periods of American history," he explained to Shawn Setaro for *Instant* (1998, on-line). In 1964 Zinn was fired by Spelman's administrators, who objected to his increasing outspokenness and participation in student protests. Zinn joined the faculty of Boston University (BU), in Massachusetts, and quickly became a vocal member of the city's antiwar movement. Once again, he found himself at odds with his employers because of his extracurricular activities; his frequent, heated battles with BU's president, John Silber, became legendary. Zinn's academic writings, colored by concern for groups he saw as disenfranchised, struck Silber as distorted, unbalanced, and unscholarly. Silber continually refused to grant Zinn salary increases, so when Zinn retired,

in 1988, after 24 years of tenured service to BU, he was earning only $41,000 annually—far less than what colleagues with equivalent experience were getting. In addition to *A People's History of the United States*, which has sold an estimated two million copies, Zinn was the author of books including *Vietnam: The Logic of Withdrawal* (1967), *Disobedience and Democracy* (1968), *Declarations of Independence: Cross-Examining American Ideology* (1990), *You Can't Be Neutral on a Moving Train: A Personal History of Our Times* (1994), *Howard Zinn on War* (2000), *Howard Zinn on Democratic Education* (2004), *Original Zinn: Conversations on History and Politics* (2006), and *The Unraveling of the Bush Presidency* (2007). He also wrote the introductions to more than two dozen books by others (among them Noam Chomsky and Daniel Berrigan) and plays including *Emma* (about the activist Emma Goldman), *Daughter of Venus* (a drama that tackled the theme of nuclear disarmament), and *Marx in Soho: A Play on History* (in which the revolutionary theorist returns from the afterlife to clear his name). Zinn, the subject of several documentaries, including one hosted by Matt Damon on the History Channel, died of a heart attack while swimming. His wife died in 2008. Zinn is survived by his daughter, Myla; his son, Jeff; and five grandchildren. See *Current Biography* (1999). —D.K.

Obituary *New York Times* (on-line) Jan. 29, 2010

CLASSIFICATION BY PROFESSION—2010

ACTIVISM
Bryce, Quentin
Cheney, Liz
Daniels, Lee
Douglas, Emory
Gaspard, Patrick
K'Naan
Malcolm, Ellen R.
Mamdani, Mahmood
Murguía, Janet
Naidoo, Kumi
Pacelle, Wayne
Payton, John
Peirsol, Aaron
Perera, Frederica
Pierce, Wendell
Pisani, Elizabeth
Rahmstorf, Stefan
Ravitch, Diane
Sigurdardottir, Johanna
Ziegler, Jean

ANTHROPOLOGY
Dominy, Nathaniel J.
Fisher, Helen

ART
Dean, Tacita
Demand, Thomas
Douglas, Emory
Dumas, Marlene
Johnston, Daniel
Lurie, John
Mehretu, Julie
Painter, Nell Irvin
Paper Rad
Sigismondi, Floria

ASTRONAUTICS
Bolden, Charles F. Jr.

ASTRONOMY
Boss, Alan P.
Geha, Marla
Ghez, Andrea

BUSINESS
Agassi, Shai
Bewkes, Jeffrey L.
Bolden, Charles F. Jr.
Burch, Tory
Chang, David
Conde, Cristóbal
Daniels, Lee
Donoghue, John
Field, Patricia
Gorman, James P.
Gross, William H.
Ivey, Susan M.
Jha, Sanjay K.
Lillien, Lisa
Mayer, Marissa
McDuffie, Dwayne
McGovern, Gail J.
Morhaime, Michael
Mugler, Thierry
Olsen, Mary-Kate and
  Ashley
Orender, Donna
Piñera, Sebastián
Pisani, Elizabeth
Podesta, John D.
Prokhorov, Mikhail
Roberts, Michael V. and
  Steven C.
Rogers, John W. Jr.
Rospars, Joe
Roth, Gabriel
Santelli, Rick
Scannell, Herb
Zandi, Mark
Zelnick, Strauss

COMEDY
Goldthwait, Bobcat
Handler, Chelsea
Lopez, George
Louis C.K.
Mo'Nique

COMPUTERS
Agassi, Shai
Conde, Cristóbal
Morhaime, Michael

CONSERVATION
Agassi, Shai
Jackson, Lisa P.
Naidoo, Kumi
Rahmstorf, Stefan

DANCE
Fleming, Maureen
Fortier, Paul-André
Moran, John
Mugler, Thierry

ECONOMICS
Zandi, Mark

EDUCATION
Bair, Sheila C.
Benjamin, Regina
Bigelow, Kathryn
Blair, Dennis C.
Brockmeier, Kevin
Broder, David
Bryce, Quentin
Catlin, Don H.
Cole, Juan R. I.
Critchley, Simon
Dominy, Nathaniel J.
Donoghue, John
Dudamel, Gustavo
Dumas, Marlene
Ehrman, Bart D.
Fortier, Paul-André
Geha, Marla
Ghez, Andrea
Gioia, Ted
Gray, William M.
Haass, Richard N.
Jenike, Michael A.
Johnson, Mat
LaValle, Victor
LeDoux, Joseph
Mamdani, Mahmood
Mayer, Marissa
McCann, Colum
McGovern, Gail J.
Melford, Myra
Miller, Geoffrey
Myers, B. R.

Painter, Nell Irvin
Paper Rad
Perera, Frederica
Piñera, Sebastián
Podesta, John D.
Rahmstorf, Stefan
Ravitch, Diane
Spalding, Esperanza
Thernstrom, Abigail
Venkatesh, Sudhir
Ziegler, Jean
Zuberbühler, Klaus

FASHION
Atwood, Colleen
Brown, Scott
Burch, Tory
Field, Patricia
Hastreiter, Kim
Lady Gaga
Mugler, Thierry
Olsen, Mary-Kate and
  Ashley

FILM
Atwood, Colleen
Baumbach, Noah
Bewkes, Jeffrey L.
Bigelow, Kathryn
Boll, Uwe
Daniels, Lee
Dean, Tacita
Demand, Thomas
Favreau, Jon
Fenton, George
Field, Patricia
Fox, Megan
Gerwig, Greta
Goldthwait, Bobcat
Korine, Harmony
Lopez, George
Louis C.K.
Lurie, John
Lynch, Jane
Mo'Nique
Olsen, Mary-Kate and
  Ashley
Paper Rad
Pierce, Wendell
Radcliffe, Daniel
Richardson, Robert
Rideau, Wilbert
Sigismondi, Floria
Swanberg, Joe

Thompson, John Douglas
Zelnick, Strauss

FINANCE
Bair, Sheila C.
Gorman, James P.
Gross, William H.
Rogers, John W. Jr.
Santelli, Rick

GASTRONOMY
Chang, David
Deen, Paula
Lillien, Lisa

GOVERNMENT AND
  POLITICS, FOREIGN
Bryce, Quentin
Cameron, David
Kiviniemi, Mari
Naidoo, Kumi
Piñera, Sebastián
Sigurdardottir, Johanna
Ziegler, Jean

GOVERNMENT AND
  POLITICS, U.S.
Bair, Sheila C.
Benjamin, Regina
Blair, Dennis C.
Bolden, Charles F. Jr.
Brown, Scott
Cheney, Liz
Eikenberry, Karl W.
Gaspard, Patrick
Haass, Richard N.
Jackson, Lisa P.
Kirk, Ron
Malcolm, Ellen R.
Mueller, Robert
Murguía, Janet
Olson, Theodore
Podesta, John D.
Ravitch, Diane
Rospars, Joe

HISTORY
Cole, Juan R. I.
Painter, Nell Irvin
Ravitch, Diane

JOURNALISM
Anderson, Chris
Arellano, Gustavo
Broder, David

Brzezinski, Mika
Cole, Juan R. I.
Gregory, David
Grossman, Lev
Hansen, Chris
Hastreiter, Kim
King, John
Lemon, Don
Malkin, Michelle
McDonald, Trevor
Myers, B. R.
Pisani, Elizabeth
Rideau, Wilbert
Santelli, Rick
Simpson, John
Thernstrom, Abigail

LAW
Bair, Sheila C.
Brown, Scott
Bryce, Quentin
Cheney, Liz
Gorman, James P.
Kirk, Ron
Mueller, Robert
Murguía, Janet
Olson, Theodore
Payton, John
Podesta, John D.

LAW ENFORCEMENT
Mueller, Robert

LITERATURE
Bair, Sheila C.
Brockmeier, Kevin
Ferris, Joshua
Grossman, Lev
Johnson, Mat
K'Naan
Korine, Harmony
Krauss, Nicole
LaValle, Victor
Levy, Andrea
McCann, Colum
McDuffie, Dwayne
Mo'Nique
Simpson, John

MEDICINE
Benjamin, Regina
Catlin, Don H.
Donoghue, John
Jenike, Michael A.

Ravitch, Diane
Thernstrom, Abigail
Venkatesh, Sudhir
Zandi, Mark
Zuberbühler, Klaus

SPORTS
Arena, Bruce
Bosh, Chris
Bradley, Bob
Brown, Dustin
Cink, Stewart
Davis, Glen
del Potro, Juan Martin
Durant, Kevin
Ferguson, Alex
Goosen, Retief
Greinke, Zack
Johnson, Andre
Johnson, Chris
Lincecum, Tim
Orender, Donna
Park Ji-Sung
Peavy, Jake
Peirsol, Aaron
Prokhorov, Mikhail
Ryan, Rex
Sizemore, Grady
Smith, Mike
Sparano, Tony

Thomas, Sarah
Vonn, Lindsey
Weir, Johnny

TECHNOLOGY
Bolden, Charles F. Jr.
Donoghue, John
Grossman, Lev
Jha, Sanjay K.
Mayer, Marissa
Rospars, Joe

TELEVISION
Atwood, Colleen
Bewkes, Jeffrey L.
Brzezinski, Mika
Deen, Paula
Favreau, Jon
Fenton, George
Field, Patricia
Fox, Megan
Goldthwait, Bobcat
Gregory, David
Grossman, Lev
Handler, Chelsea
Hansen, Chris
King, John
Lemon, Don
Lopez, George
Louis C.K.

Lurie, John
Lynch, Jane
MacFarlane, Seth
Malkin, Michelle
Mayer, John
McDonald, Trevor
McDuffie, Dwayne
Mo'Nique
Olsen, Mary-Kate and
  Ashley
Pierce, Wendell
Radcliffe, Daniel
Santelli, Rick
Scannell, Herb
Simpson, John
Swiss, Jamy Ian
Thompson, John Douglas
Zelnick, Strauss

THEATER
Fenton, George
Lynch, Jane
Moran, John
Mugler, Thierry
Paulus, Diane
Pierce, Wendell
Radcliffe, Daniel
Swiss, Jamy Ian
Thompson, John Douglas

CUMULATED INDEX 2001–2010

This is the index to the January 2001–November 2010 issues. It also lists obituaries that appear only in yearbooks for the years 2001 to 2010. For the index to the 1940–2005 biographies, see Current Biography Cumulated Index 1940–2005.

3D *see* Massive Attack

Abakanowicz, Magdalena Jan 2001
Abel, Jessica Aug 2007
Abelson, Philip H. obit Yrbk 2004
Abizaid, John Oct 2003
Abraham, Spencer May 2001
Abrams, J.J. Jul 2009
Abrams, Jeffrey Jacob *see* Abrams, J.J.
Abrams, Jonathan Apr 2006
AC/DC Mar 2005
Acocella, Joan May 2007
Adams, Brock obit Yrbk 2004
Adams, Douglas obit Sep 2001
Adams, Edith obit Yrbk 2008
Adams, Ernie Jan 2009
Adams, William James Jr. *see* Black Eyed Peas
Adams, Yolanda Mar 2002
Aday, Marvin Lee *see* Meat Loaf
Addington, David S. Jan 2007
Adebimpe, Tunde *see* TV on the Radio
Adele Jul 2009
Adkins, Adele *see* Adele
Adler, Larry obit Oct 2001
Adler, Mortimer J. obit Sep 2001
Aerosmith Jul 2004
Agassi, Shai Sep 2010
Agatston, Arthur Mar 2007
Agnelli, Giovanni obit Jun 2003
Aigner-Clark, Julie Jan 2002
Ailes, Stephen obit Oct 2001
Aitken, Doug Apr 2007
Ajami, Fouad Feb 2007
Akers, Michelle Nov 2004
Akon Jan 2008
Aksenov, Vasilii *see* Aksyonov, Vassily
Aksyonov, Vasily *see* Aksyonov, Vassily
Aksyonov, Vassily obit Yrbk 2009
Albarn, Damon *see* Blur
Albert, Eddie obit Yrbk 2005
Aleksii II obit Yrbk 2009

Aleksy II *see* Aleksii II
Alexander, Christopher Oct 2003
Alexander, Donald C. obit Yrbk 2009
Alexy II *see* Aleksii II
Alfonsin, Raúl obit Yrbk 2009
Ali, Laylah Jul 2008
Alibek, Ken Jun 2002
Alibekov, Kanatjan *see* Alibek, Ken
Alito, Samuel Apr 2006
Alito, Samuel Jr. *see* Alito, Samuel
Aliyev, Heydar obit Jul 2004
Allen, Betsy *see* Cavanna, Betty
Allen, Betty obit Yrbk 2009
Allen, J. D. Nov 2010
Allen, John Daniel 3d *see* Allen, J.D.
Allen, Ray Jan 2009
Allen, Rick *see* Def Leppard
Allen, Steve obit Jan 2001
Allyson, June obit Yrbk 2006
Alterman, Eric Feb 2007
Altman, Robert obit Yrbk 2007
Alvarez Bravo, Manuel obit Jan 2003
Amado, Jorge obit Oct 2001
Ambani, Anil Feb 2009
Ambani, Mukesh Jun 2009
Amend, Bill Apr 2003
Ames, Jonathan Oct 2007
Amichai, Yehuda obit Jan 2001
Amies, Hardy obit Aug 2003
Amin, Idi obit Yrbk 2003
Ammons, A. R. obit Jul 2001
Anastasio, Trey *see* Phish
Anderson, Chris Jan 2010
Anderson, Constance obit Apr 2001
Anderson, Don L. Oct 2002
Anderson, Jack obit Yrbk 2006
Anderson, Ray C. May 2005
Anderson, Robert obit Yrbk 2009
Anderson, Robert O. obit Yrbk 2008
Anderson, Roy obit Mar 2004

Anderson, Tom and DeWolfe, Christopher Jul 2007
Anderson, Wes May 2002
Anderson, William R. obit Yrbk 2007
Anderson, Winston A. Mar 2007
Andre 3000 *see* OutKast
Angeles, Victoria de los obit Aug 2005
Angell, Marcia Nov 2005
Annenberg, Walter H. obit Jan 2003
Anthony, Carmelo Jun 2005
Antonioni, Michelangelo obit Yrbk 2007
Aoki, Rocky Jun 2005 obit Yrbk 2008
apl.de.ap *see* Black Eyed Peas
Appel, Karel obit Yrbk 2006
Appiah, Kwame Anthony Jun 2002
Apple, Fiona Nov 2006
Apple, R. W. Jr. obit Feb 2007
Applebaum, Anne Aug 2004
Aquino, Corazon obit Yrbk 2009
Arafat, Yasir obit Feb 2005
Arceneaux, Edgar Aug 2008
Archer, Michael D'Angelo *see* D'Angelo
Arellano, Gustavo Aug 2010
Arena, Bruce Sep 2010
Arenas, Gilbert Feb 2009
Arledge, Roone obit Apr 2003
Armitage, Kenneth obit May 2002
Armitage, Richard Oct 2003
Armstrong, Anne obit Yrbk 2008
Armstrong, Billie Joe *see* Green Day
Armstrong, J. Sinclair obit Mar 2001
Armstrong, Vic Aug 2003
Arnesen, Liv Jun 2001
Arnold, Eddy obit Yrbk 2008
Arnold, Eve Oct 2005
Aronofsky, Darren Feb 2009
Arpino, Gerald obit Yrbk 2008
Arrarás, María Celeste Aug 2002

Arthur, Bea obit Yrbk 2009
Arulpragasam, Mathangi *see* M.I.A.
Ash, Mary Kay obit Feb 2002
Ashanti Jan 2003
Ashley, Thomas L. obit Yrbk 2010
Ashwell, Rachel Oct 2004
Astor, Brooke obit Yrbk 2007
Atashin, Faegheh *see* Googoosh
Athey, Susan Sep 2007
Atkins, Chet obit Sep 2001
Atkins, Jeffrey *see* Ja Rule
Atkinson, Kate Feb 2007
Atwood, Colleen Oct 2010
Auchincloss, Louis obit Apr 2010
Auerbach, Arnold obit Yrbk 2007
Augstein, Rudolf obit Jan 2003
Austin, "Stone Cold" Steve Nov 2001
Auth, Tony Feb 2006
Avedon, Richard obit Mar 2005
Axelrod, David Apr 2009
Ayers, William Apr 2009
Azcona Hoyo, José obit Yrbk 2006

Bacher, Robert F. obit Yrbk 2005
Bahcall, John N. obit Yrbk 2007
Bailey, Glenda Oct 2001
Bair, Sheila C. Feb 2010
Baitz, Jon Robin Aug 2004
Baker, Dusty Apr 2001
Baker, James A. 3d Mar 2007
Baker, Mitchell Apr 2009
Baker, Winifred Mitchell *see* Baker, Mitchell
Bakula, Scott Feb 2002
Balaguer, Joaquín obit Yrbk 2002
Baldwin, Tammy Jun 2005
Ball, Robert M. obit Yrbk 2008
Ballard, J.G. obit Yrbk 2009
Balthus obit May 2001
Bampton, Rose obit Yrbk 2007
Bancroft, Anne obit Oct 2005 obit Yrbk 2007
Bandaranaike, Sirimavo obit Jan 2001
Banfield, Ashleigh Jul 2002
Banks, Tyra Apr 2007
Banksy Apr 2009
Bannister, Constance obit Yrbk 2005

Bánzer Suárez, Hugo obit Yrbk 2002
Barber, Patricia Sep 2007
Barber, Ronde *see* Barber, Tiki and Barber, Ronde
Barber, Tiki and Barber, Ronde Oct 2003
Barbieri, Fedora obit Aug 2003
Barker, Travis *see* blink-182
Barlow, Maude Feb 2009
Barnard, Christiaan N. obit Nov 2001
Barnes, Brenda May 2006
Barnes, Clive obit Feb 2009
Barnett, Etta Moten Feb 2002 obit Biography Reference Bank
Barney, Matthew Aug 2003
Barnouw, Erik obit Oct 2001
Barre, Raymond obit Yrbk 2007
Barris, Chuck Mar 2005
Barsamian, David Mar 2007
Bartiromo, Maria Nov 2003
Bartlett, Bruce Jun 2006
Barton, Jacqueline K. Sep 2006
Barzel, Rainer obit Yrbk 2006
Bassler, Bonnie Apr 2003
Bateman, Jason Oct 2005
Bates, Alan obit Yrbk 2004
Baudrillard, Jean obit Yrbk 2007
Baumbach, Noah Oct 2010
Bausch, Pina obit Yrbk 2009
Bavetta, Dick Mar 2008
Bawer, Bruce Jul 2007
Beach, Edward obit May 2003
Beame, Abraham D. obit Apr 2001
Beane, Billy Jul 2005
Bebey, Francis obit Sep 2001
Bechdel, Alison Jul 2009
Beck, Kent Jan 2007
Beckinsale, Kate Aug 2001
Beckman, Arnold O. Jan 2002 obit Yrbk 2004
Bedford, Sybille obit Yrbk 2006
Beehler, Bruce Aug 2006
Beene, Geoffrey obit Mar 2005
Beers, Rand Oct 2004
Behar, Ruth May 2005
Behe, Michael J. Feb 2006
Behrens, Hildegard obit Yrbk 2009
Beiser, Maya May 2009
Béjart, Maurice obit Yrbk 2008
Bel Geddes, Barbara obit Yrbk 2005
Belaúnde Terry, Fernando obit Yrbk 2002

Belcher, Angela Jul 2006
Belichick, Bill Sep 2002
Bell, Griffin B. obit Yrbk 2009
Bell, James A. Jul 2006
Bellmon, Henry obit Yrbk 2009
Bellow, Saul obit Aug 2005
Benchley, Peter obit Jun 2006
Benedict XVI Sep 2005
Benjamin, Andre *see* Outkast
Benjamin, Regina Jan 2010
Bennett, Lerone Jr. Jan 2001
Bennington, Chester *see* Linkin Park
Bentsen, Lloyd obit Oct 2006
Benyus, Janine M. Mar 2006
Benzer, Seymour May 2001 obit Yrbk 2008
Beresford-Kroeger, Diana Nov 2008
Berg, Patricia Jane obit Yrbk 2007
Berg, Patty *see* Berg, Patricia Jane
Bergeron, Tom Oct 2007
Bergman, Ingmar obit Sep 2007
Berio, Luciano obit Yrbk 2003
Berle, Milton obit Yrbk 2002
Berlin, Steve *see* Los Lobos
Berlitz, Charles obit Yrbk 2004
Berman, Lazar obit Yrbk 2005
Bernanke, Ben S. Mar 2006
Bernhard Leopold, consort of Juliana, Queen of the Netherlands obit Mar 2005
Bernstein, Elmer Jun 2003
Bernstein, William J. Nov 2009
Berri, Claude obit Yrbk 2009
Berrigan, Philip obit Mar 2003
Berryman, Guy *see* Coldplay
Berton, Pierre obit Yrbk 2005
Bertozzi, Carolyn R. Jul 2003
Bessmertnova, Natalia obit Yrbk 2008
Bethe, Hans obit Aug 2005
Bethune, Gordon M. Jun 2001
Bettis, Jerome Aug 2006
Bewkes, Jeffrey L. Nov 2010
Beze, Dante *see* Mos Def
Bhutto, Benazir obit Apr 2008
Bible, Geoffrey C. Feb 2002
Biden, Joseph R. Mar 2009
Big Boi *see* OutKast
Bigelow, Kathryn Mar 2010
Bigelow, Robert Aug 2008
Bilandic, Michael A. obit Apr 2002
Biller, Moe obit Yrbk 2004

Bing, Stanley *see* Schwartz, Gil

Birendra Bir Bikram Shah Dev, King of Nepal obit Sep 2001

Bishop, Eric *see* Foxx, Jamie

Bishop, Joey obit Yrbk 2008

Bittman, Mark Feb 2005

Björk Jul 2001

Black Eyed Peas Oct 2006

Black, Jack Feb 2002

Blackburn, Elizabeth H. Jul 2001

Blackman, Cindy Oct 2010

Blades, Joan and Boyd, Wes Aug 2004

Blaine, David Apr 2001

Blair, Dennis C. May 2010

Blake, James Mar 2006

Blakemore, Michael May 2001

Blanchard, Felix A. obit Yrbk 2009

Blanco, Kathleen Jun 2004

Blanda, George obit Yrbk 2010

Blankenbuehler, Andy Apr 2009

Blankenship, "Two-Tone" Tommy *see* My Morning Jacket

Blass, Bill obit Nov 2002

Blind Boys of Alabama Oct 2001

blink-182 Aug 2002

Blitzer, Wolf Feb 2007

Block, Herbert L. obit Jan 2002

Bloomberg, Michael R. Mar 2002

Blount, Winton Malcolm obit Jan 2003

Blum, William May 2007

Blunt, Roy Mar 2008

Blur Nov 2003

Blythe, Stephanie Aug 2004

Bocelli, Andrea Jan 2002

Boehner, John Apr 2006

Bogut, Andrew Jan 2008

Boland, Edward P. obit Feb 2002

Bolden, Charles F. Jr. Jul 2010

Boll, Uwe Sep 2010

Bollinger, Lee C. Feb 2008

Bolt, Usain Jul 2009

Bolten, Joshua Jul 2006

Bolton, John R. Feb 2006

Bond, Julian Jul 2001

Bontecou, Lee Mar 2004

Booker, Cory Feb 2007

Boorstin, Daniel J. obit Yrbk 2004

Boras, Scott May 2009

Borge, Victor obit Mar 2001

Borlaug, Norman E. obit Yrbk 2009

Borodina, Olga Feb 2002

Borowitz, Andy Jul 2007

Borst, Lyle B. obit Yrbk 2002

Bosch, Juan obit Feb 2002

Bosh, Chris Mar 2010

Boss, Alan P. Apr 2010

Bosselaar, Laure-Anne Sep 2006

Botha, P. W. obit Yrbk 2007

Botha, Pieter W. *see* Botha, P.W.

Boudreau, Lou obit Oct 2001

Boulud, Daniel Jan 2005

Bourdain, Anthony Jan 2006

Bourdon, Rob *see* Linkin Park

Bourgeois, Louise obit Yrbk 2010

Bourne, St. Clair obit Mar 2008

Bowden, Mark Jan 2002

Bowker, Albert obit Yrbk 2008

Boyd, John W. Feb 2001

Boyd, Wes *see* Blades, Joan and Boyd, Wes

Bracken, Eddie obit Feb 2003

Bradley, Bob Aug 2010

Bradley, Ed obit Yrbk 2007

Brady, Tom Aug 2004

Bragg, Rick Apr 2002

Branch, Michelle May 2005

Brando, Marlon obit Yrbk 2004

Bravo, Rose Marie Jun 2004

Brazauskas, Algirdas obit Yrbk 2010

Brazile, Donna Mar 2006

Breathitt, Edward T. obit Sep 2004

Breen, Edward D. Jul 2004

Brennan, Edward A. obit Yrbk 2008

Brewer, Roy M. obit Yrbk 2006

Bridges, Christopher *see* Ludacris

Bridgewater, Dee Dee Oct 2008

Brier, Bob Sep 2002

Brier, Robert *see* Brier, Bob

Brin, Sergey and Page, Larry Oct 2001

Brinkley, David obit Sep 2003

Brockmeier, Kevin May 2010

Broder, David Sep 2010

Brodeur, Martin Nov 2002

Brody, Adrien Jul 2003

Broeg, Bob May 2002

Broemel, Carl *see* My Morning Jacket

Brokaw, Tom Nov 2002

Brolin, Josh Feb 2008

Bronson, Charles obit Mar 2004

Brooks & Dunn Sep 2004

Brooks, David Apr 2004

Brooks, Donald obit Yrbk 2005

Brooks, Geraldine Aug 2006

Brooks, Gwendolyn obit Feb 2001

Brooks, Kix *see* Brooks & Dunn

Brooks, Vincent Jun 2003

Brower, David obit Feb 2001

Brown, Aaron Mar 2003

Brown, Campbell Nov 2008

Brown, Charles L. obit Sep 2004

Brown, Claude obit Apr 2002

Brown, Dan May 2004

Brown, Dee obit Mar 2003

Brown, Dustin Oct 2010

Brown, J. Carter obit Yrbk 2002

Brown, James obit Mar 2007

Brown, Jesse obit Yrbk 2002

Brown, Junior Nov 2004

Brown, Kwame Feb 2002

Brown, Lee P. Sep 2002

Brown, Robert McAfee obit Nov 2001

Brown, Ronald K. May 2002

Brown, Scott Aug 2010

Brown, Troy Oct 2007

Brownback, Sam Apr 2008

Browning, John obit Jun 2003

Broyhill, Joel T. obit Feb 2007

Brueggemann, Ingar Nov 2001

Brumel, Valery obit Jun 2003

Brunson, Doyle Sep 2007

Bryant, C. Farris obit Yrbk 2002

Bryce, Quentin Feb 2010

Brynner, Rock Mar 2005

Bryson, David *see* Counting Crows

Brzezinski, Mika Jul 2010

Bublé, Michael May 2009

Buchanan, Laura *see* King, Florence

Buchholz, Horst obit Aug 2003

Buchwald, Art obit May 2007

Buckingham, Marcus Aug 2006

Buckland, Jon *see* Coldplay

Buckley, Priscilla L. Apr 2002

Buckley, William F. Jr. obit Jun 2008

Budge, Hamer H. obit Yrbk 2003

Buechner, Thomas S. obit Yrbk 2010
Buergenthal, Thomas Jan 2009
Bujones, Fernando obit Yrbk 2006
Bumiller, Elisabeth Sep 2008
Bundy, William P. obit Feb 2001
Bunim, Mary-Ellis obit Yrbk 2004 see also Bunim, Mary-Ellis, and Murray, Jonathan
Bunim, Mary-Ellis, and Murray, Jonathan May 2002
Bunton, Jaleel see TV on the Radio
Burch, Tory Sep 2010
Burford, Anne Gorsuch see Gorsuch, Anne
Burgess, Carter L. obit Yrbk 2002
Burnett, Mark May 2001
Burns, Ed May 2008
Burns, Ursula M. Oct 2007
Burris, Roland Jun 2009
Burroughs, Augusten Apr 2004
Burrows, James Oct 2006
Burrows, Stephen Nov 2003
Burstyn, Mike May 2005
Burtt, Ben May 2003
Bush, George W. Aug 2001
Bush, Laura Jun 2001
Bush, Margaret Berenice see Wilson, Margaret
Bushnell, Candace Nov 2003
Busiek, Kurt Sep 2005
Butcher, Susan obit Yrbk 2006
Butler, R. Paul see Marcy, Geoffrey W., and Butler, R. Paul
Butler, Robert N. obit Yrbk 2010
Buttons, Red obit Yrbk 2006
Butz, Earl L. obit Yrbk 2008
Byrd, Robert C. obit Sep 2010
Byrne, John Keyes see Leonard, Hugh

Caballero, Linda see La India
Cabrera, Miguel Jul 2009
Cactus Jack see Foley, Mick
Cafferty, Jack Oct 2008
Caldera, Rafael obit Yrbk 2010
Calderón, Sila M. Nov 2001
Caldwell, Sarah obit Yrbk 2006
Calisher, Hortense obit Yrbk 2009
Callaghan, James obit Yrbk 2005

Callahan, John obit Yrbk 2010
Calle, Sophie May 2001
Cameron, David Aug 2010
Camp, John see Sandford, John
Campbell, Bebe Moore obit Yrbk 2007
Campbell, Douglas obit Yrbk 2009
Campbell, Viv see Def Leppard
Canada, Geoffrey Feb 2005
Canin, Ethan Aug 2001
Cannon, Howard W. obit Yrbk 2002
Cantwell, Maria Feb 2005
Canty, Brendan see Fugazi
Cao, Anh "Joseph" Jun 2009
Capa, Cornell Jul 2005 obit Yrbk 2008
Capps, Lois Mar 2008
Capriati, Jennifer Nov 2001
Caras, Roger A. obit Jul 2001
Card, Andrew H. Jr. Nov 2003
Carell, Steve Feb 2007
Carell, Steven see Carell, Steve
Carey, Ernestine Gilbreth obit Yrbk 2007
Carey, Ron obit Yrbk 2009
Carlin, George obit Oct 2008
Carlos, Walter see Carlos, Wendy
Carlos, Wendy Sep 2008
Carlson, Margaret Nov 2003
Carmines, Al obit Yrbk 2005
Carmona, Richard Jan 2003
Carney, Art obit Yrbk 2004
Carone, Nicholas see Carone, Nicolas
Carone, Nicolas Jul 2006 obit Yrbk 2010
Carroll-Abbing, J. Patrick obit Nov 2001
Carroll, Betty Jean see Carroll, E. Jean
Carroll, E. Jean Jul 2008
Carroll, Jim obit Yrbk 2009
Carroll, Vinnette obit Feb 2003
Carruth, Hayden obit Yrbk 2008
Carson, Anne May 2006
Carson, David Jul 2008
Carson, Johnny obit Jul 2005
Carter, Benny obit Oct 2003
Carter, Jimmy see Blind Boys of Alabama
Carter, Majora Oct 2007
Carter, Matthew Oct 2007
Carter, Regina Oct 2003
Carter, Shawn see Jay-Z
Carter, Vince Apr 2002

Cartier-Bresson, Henri obit Yrbk 2004
Cary, Frank T. obit May 2006
Casablancas, Julian see Strokes
Casey, George W. Jr. Mar 2006
Cash, Johnny obit Jan 2004
Cassini, Oleg obit Yrbk 2006
Castle, Barbara obit Yrbk 2002
Castro, Fidel Jun 2001
Cat Power Oct 2007
Catlin, Don H. Mar 2010
Cattrall, Kim Jan 2003
Catz, Safra A. Jan 2008
Cavanagh, Tom Jun 2003
Cavanna, Betty obit Oct 2001
Cave, Nick Jun 2005
Cedric the Entertainer Feb 2004
Cela, Camilo José obit Apr 2002
Celmins, Vija Jan 2005
Chaban-Delmas, Jacques obit Feb 2001
Chabrol, Claude obit Yrbk 2010
Chafee, Lincoln Jan 2004
Chaikin, Joseph obit Yrbk 2003
Chamberlain, Owen obit Jul 2006
Champion, Will see Coldplay
Chandler, Otis obit Yrbk 2006
Chandrasekhar, Sripati obit Sep 2001
Chang, David Aug 2010
Chao, Elaine L. May 2001
Chapin, Schuyler G. obit Yrbk 2009
Chapman, Duane Mar 2005
Chapman, Steven Curtis Oct 2004
Chappelle, Dave Jun 2004
Charisse, Cyd obit Yrbk 2008
Charles, Eugenia obit Yrbk 2006
Charles, Michael Ray Oct 2005
Charles, Ray obit Yrbk 2004
Charney, Dov Sep 2009
Chase, Alison Becker Nov 2006
Chase, David Mar 2001
Chauncey, Henry obit Mar 2003
Cheeks, Maurice Feb 2004
Chen, Steve; Hurley, Chad; and Karim, Jawed Jan 2007

Cheney, Liz Aug 2010
Cheney, Richard B. Jan 2002
Chertoff, Michael Oct 2005
Chesney, Kenny May 2004
Chestnut, Cyrus Jul 2009
Chiang Kai-shek, Mme. *see* Chiang Mei-Ling
Chiang Mei-Ling obit Mar 2004
Chieftains Mar 2004
Child, Julia obit Nov 2004
Chillida, Eduardo obit Yrbk 2002
Chinmoy, Sri obit Yrbk 2008
Chisholm, Shirley obit Apr 2005
Chu, Steven Mar 2009
Chung, Kyung-Wha Feb 2007
Church, Sam Jr. obit Yrbk 2009
Churchland, Patricia S. May 2003
Cink, Stewart Feb 2010
Ciocci, Jacob *see* Paper Rad
Ciocci, Jessica *see* Paper Rad
Claiborne, Liz obit Yrbk 2007
Claremont, Chris Sep 2003
Clark, Kenneth B. obit Sep 2005
Clarke, Arthur C. obit Yrbk 2008
Clarke, Richard May 2006
Clarkson, Kelly Sep 2006
Clarkson, Patricia Aug 2005
Clemens, Roger Aug 2003
Clement, Jemaine *see* Flight of the Conchords
Cleveland, Harlan obit Yrbk 2008
Click and Clack, the Tappet Brothers *see* Magliozzi, Tom and Ray
Cline, Nels *see* Wilco
Clinton, Hillary Rodham Jan 2002 Mar 2009
Clooney, George Jul 2008
Clooney, Rosemary obit Nov 2002
Clowes, Daniel Jan 2002
Clyburn, James E. Oct 2001
Coburn, James obit Feb 2003
Coca, Imogene obit Sep 2001
Cochran, Johnnie L. Jr. obit Oct 2005
Cochran, Thad Apr 2002
Coddington, Grace Apr 2005
Coffin, Frank M. obit Yrbk 2010
Coffin, William Sloane obit Yrbk 2006
Cohen, Richard Nov 2007
Cohen, Rob Nov 2002
Cohen, Roger May 2008

Cohen, Sasha Feb 2006
Cohn, Linda Aug 2002
Colbert, Edwin H. obit Feb 2002
Colbert, Gregory Sep 2005
Colbert, Stephen Nov 2006
Coldplay May 2004
Cole, Juan R. I. Oct 2010
Coleman, Cy obit Feb 2005
Coleman, Mary Sue Feb 2007
Coleman, Miasha *see* Miasha
Coleman, Norman Sep 2004
Coleman, Ronnie Feb 2007
Coleman, Steve Jul 2004
Coles, Dennis *see* Ghostface Killah
Collen, Phil *see* Def Leppard
Collier, Sophia Jul 2002
Collins, Jim Aug 2003
Collins, Patricia Hill Mar 2003
Columbus, Chris Nov 2001
Comden, Betty obit Yrbk 2007
Cometbus, Aaron Mar 2005
Como, Perry obit Jul 2001
Conable, Barber B. obit Sep 2004
Conde, Cristóbal Sep 2010
Conlee, Jenny *see* Decemberists
Conneff, Kevin *see* Chieftains
Connelly, Jennifer Jun 2002
Conner, Nadine obit Aug 2003
Connor, John T. obit Feb 2001
Conway, Gerry *see* Fairport Convention
Conway, John Horton Sep 2003
Cook, Richard W. Jul 2003
Cooke, Alistair obit Oct 2004
Coontz, Stephanie Jul 2003
Cooper, Anderson Jun 2006
Cooper, Chris Jul 2004
Cooper, Kyle Nov 2009
Coppola, Sofia Nov 2003
Corbijn, Anton Jun 2006
Corelli, Franco obit Mar 2004
Corsi, Jerome R. Nov 2008
Corzine, Jon Aug 2006
Cossiga, Francesco obit Yrbk 2010
Costanza, Midge obit Yrbk 2010
Cotto, Miguel Feb 2008
Coughlin, Tom Aug 2008
Coulter, Ann Sep 2003
Counsell, Craig Sep 2002
Counting Crows Mar 2003
Couric, Katie Apr 2008
Cowher, Bill Nov 2006
Cowles, Fleur obit Yrbk 2009

Cox, Archibald obit Yrbk 2004
Cox, Lynne Sep 2004
Coyne, Wayne *see* Flaming Lips
Craig, Daniel Apr 2007
Crain, Jeanne obit Sep 2004
Crandall, Martin *see* Shins
Crane, Eva obit Yrbk 2007
Cranston, Alan obit Mar 2001
Creed May 2002
Creeley, Robert obit Yrbk 2005
Crespin, Regine obit Yrbk 2007
Crewe, Albert V. obit Yrbk 2010
Crichton, Michael obit Apr 2009
Crick, Francis obit Yrbk 2004
Critchley, Simon Apr 2010
Crittenden, Danielle Jul 2003
Crocker, Ryan Oct 2007
Cromwell, James Aug 2005
Cronkite, Walter obit Sep 2009
Cronyn, Hume obit Yrbk 2003
Croom, Sylvester Jr. Aug 2004
Crosby, John obit Yrbk 2003
Crossfield, A. Scott obit Yrbk 2006
Crowe, William J. obit Yrbk 2008
Cruz, Celia obit Nov 2003
Cruz, Penelope Jul 2001
Cuban, Mark Mar 2001
Culpepper, Daunte Sep 2007
Cummings, Elijah E. Feb 2004
Cunhal, Álvaro obit Yrbk 2005
Cunningham, Merce obit Yrbk 2009
Currie, Nancy June 2002
Curry, Ann Jun 2004
Curtis, Tony obit Nov 2010

da Silva, Marta Vieira *see* Marta
Dacre of Glanton, Baron *see* Trevor-Roper, H. R.
Daddy G *see* Massive Attack
Daft, Douglas N. May 2001
Dallek, Robert Sep 2007
Daly, Cahal B. obit Yrbk 2010
Daly, Carson Nov 2009
Daly, Chuck obit Yrbk 2009
Daly, Maureen obit Yrbk 2006
Damasio, Antonio R. Oct 2007
Dan the Automator *see* Nakamura, Dan
Dancer, Stanley obit Yrbk 2005

D'Angelo May 2001

Dangerfield, Rodney obit Feb 2005

Daniels, Lee Jun 2010

Daniels, Leonardo see Daniels, Lee

D'Antoni, Mike Jun 2009

Darling, Sharon May 2003

Darman, Richard G. obit Yrbk 2008

Dassin, Jules obit Yrbk 2008

Dati, Rachida Apr 2009

Dausset, Jean obit Yrbk 2009

Davidson, Gordon Apr 2005

Davidson, Richard J. Aug 2004

Davis, Artur Feb 2009

Davis, Benjamin O. Jr. obit Yrbk 2002

Davis, Evelyn Y. Oct 2007

Davis, Glen Nov 2010

Davis, Glenn obit Yrbk 2005

Davis-Kimball, Jeannine Feb 2006

Davis, Nathanael V. obit Yrbk 2005

Davis, Ossie obit Yrbk 2005

Davis, Shani May 2006

Davis, Wade Jan 2003

Dawdy, Shannon Lee Apr 2006

Day, Laraine obit Yrbk 2008

De Bakey, Michael obit Yrbk 2008

de Branges, Louis Nov 2005

de Hartog, Jan obit Jan 2003

De Jong, Dola obit Sep 2004

de la Rúa, Fernando Apr 2001

de Meuron, Pierre see Herzog, Jacques, and de Meuron, Pierre

De Sapio, Carmine obit Yrbk 2004

De Valois, Ninette obit Aug 2001

de Varona, Donna Aug 2003

de Waal, Frans Mar 2006

Deakins, Roger May 2001

Dean, Howard Oct 2002

Dean, Jimmy obit Aug 2010

Dean, Tacita May 2010

Dearie, Blossom obit Yrbk 2009

DeBusschere, Dave obit Yrbk 2003

DeCarava, Roy Aug 2008 obit Aug 2009

DeCarlo, Dan Aug 2001 obit Mar 2002

Decemberists, The Aug 2007

Deen, Paula Mar 2010

Deep Throat see Felt, W. Mark

Def Leppard Jan 2003

del Naja, Robert see Massive Attack

del Potro, Juan Martin May 2010

Del Toro, Benicio Sep 2001

Delilah Apr 2005

Dellinger, David obit Yrbk 2004

Dello Joio, Norman obit Yrbk 2008

DeLonge, Tom see blink-182

DeLorean, John Z. obit Yrbk 2005

Deloria, Vine Jr. obit Yrbk 2006

Delson, Brad see Linkin Park

Demand, Thomas Mar 2010

DeMarcus, Jay see Rascal Flatts

DeMille, Nelson Oct 2002

Densen-Gerber, Judianne obit Jul 2003

Derrida, Jacques obit Mar 2005

Desai, Kiran Jan 2007

Deschanel, Caleb Feb 2008

Destiny's Child Aug 2001

Deutsch, Linda Apr 2007

Devi, Gayatri, Maharani of Jaipur obit Yrbk 2009

DeWolfe, Christopher see Anderson, Tom and DeWolfe, Christopher

Diamond, David obit Yrbk 2005

Diaz, Cameron Apr 2005

Dickerson, Debra Apr 2004

Dickinson, Amy Apr 2004

diCorcia, Philip-Lorca Apr 2008

Diddley, Bo obit Sep 2008

Diebold, John obit Yrbk 2006

Dillon, C. Douglas obit May 2003

Dimon, James Jun 2004

Dionne, E. J. Jr. May 2006

Dionne, Eugene J. Jr. see Dionne, E.J. Jr.

Dirnt, Mike see Green Day

Dith Pran obit Yrbk 2008

Djerassi, Carl Oct 2001

Djukanovic, Milo Aug 2001

DMX Aug 2003

Dobbs, Lou Nov 2006

Dobrynin, Anatoly F. obit Yrbk 2010

Dodge, Charles Aug 2007

Doerr, John May 2009

Domini, Amy Nov 2005

Dominy, Nathaniel J. Apr 2010

Don Alejandro Robaina see Robaina, Alejandro

Donald, Arnold W. Nov 2005

Donald, David Herbert obit Yrbk 2009

Donaldson, William Jun 2003

D'Onofrio, Vincent May 2004

Donoghue, John May 2010

Donovan, Billy Feb 2007

Donovan, Carrie obit Feb 2002

Donovan, Landon Jun 2006

Donovan, Shaun Mar 2009

Doubilet, David Mar 2003

Doudna, Jennifer Feb 2005

Douglas, Ashanti see Ashanti

Douglas, Dave Mar 2006

Douglas, Emory Feb 2010

Douglas, Jerry Aug 2004

Douglas, John E. Jul 2001

Douglas, Mike obit Yrbk 2007

Douthat, Ross Aug 2009

Downey, James Jun 2008

Downey, Jim see Downey, James

Drake, Bobby see Hold Steady, The

Drake, James Jul 2005

Drinan, Robert F. obit Yrbk 2007

Drozd, Steven see Flaming Lips

Drucker, Eugene see Emerson String Quartet

Drucker, Peter F. obit Apr 2006

Duany, Andrés see Duany, Andrés and Plater-Zyberk, Elizabeth

Duany, Andrés and Plater-Zyberk, Elizabeth Jan 2006

Dudamel, Gustavo Apr 2010

Dude Love see Foley, Mick

Duesberg, Peter H. Jun 2004

Duff, Hilary Feb 2006

Dugan, Alan obit Oct 2004

Duke, Annie Aug 2006

Dumas, Marlene Jan 2010

Duncan, Arne Mar 2009

Dungy, Tony Aug 2007

Dunham, Katherine obit Yrbk 2006

Dunlop, John T. obit Sep 2004

Dunn, Jennifer obit Nov 2007

Dunn, Ronnie see Brooks & Dunn

Dunne, Dominick obit Yrbk 2009

Dunne, John Gregory obit Yrbk 2004

Dunst, Kirsten Oct 2001

Dunwoody, Ann E. Nov 2008

Durant, Kevin May 2010

Durbin, Richard J. Aug 2006

Duritz, Adam see Counting Crows

Dutton, Denis Aug 2009

Dutton, Lawrence *see*
Emerson String Quartet
Dwight, Ed Jul 2007
Dworkin, Andrea obit Yrbk
2005

Eagleton, Thomas F. obit
Yrbk 2007
Earnhardt, Dale Jr. Jan 2007
Eban, Abba obit Mar 2003
Eberhart, Richard obit Yrbk
2005
Ebsen, Buddy obit Yrbk 2003
Ecevit, Bülent obit Yrbk 2007
Eckert, Robert A. Mar 2003
Eddins, William Feb 2002
Edwards, Bob Sep 2001
Edwards, John Oct 2004
Edwards, Ralph obit Yrbk 2006
Egan, Edward M. Jul 2001
Egan, Jennifer Mar 2002
Eggleston, William Feb 2002
Ehlers, Vernon J. Jan 2005
Ehrman, Bart D. Apr 2010
Eikenberry, Karl W. Mar 2010
Eiko *see* Eiko and Koma
Eiko and Koma May 2003
Eisner, Will obit May 2005
El-Tahri, Jihan Aug 2009
Elfman, Danny Jan 2007
Elgin, Suzette Haden Aug 2006
Elizabeth, Queen Mother of
Great Britain obit Jun 2002
Elling, Kurt Jan 2005
Elliott, Aaron see Cometbus,
Aaron
Elliott, Joe *see* Def Leppard
Elliott, Osborn obit Yrbk 2008
Elliott, Sean Apr 2001
Ellis, Albert obit Yrbk 2007
Ellis, Monta Feb 2008
Ellison, Keith Apr 2007
Elo, Jorma Jul 2009
Emanuel, Ari Jul 2009
Emanuel, Kerry A. Jan 2007
Emanuel, Rahm Mar 2009
Emerson String Quartet Jul
2002
Emin, Tracey Nov 2009
Eminem Jan 2001
Endara, Guillermo obit Yrbk
2009
Engibous, Thomas J. Oct 2003
Ensler, Eve Aug 2002
Epstein, Samuel S. Aug 2001
Epstein, Theo May 2004
Ericsson-Jackson, Aprille J.
Mar 2001
Estenssoro, Victor Paz *see* Paz
Estenssoro, Victor
Estern, Neil Nov 2008
Etherington, Edwin D. obit
Apr 2001

Eugenides, Jeffrey Oct 2003
Eustis, Oskar Oct 2002
Eustis, Paul Jefferson *see*
Eustis, Oskar
Evanovich, Janet Apr 2001
Evans, Dale obit Apr 2001
Evans, Donald L. Nov 2001
Eve Jul 2003
Everett, Percival L. Sep 2004
Everett, Rupert Jan 2005
Exon, J. James obit Yrbk 2005
Eyadéma, Etienne Gnassingbé
Apr 2002 obit Yrbk 2005
Eyre, Chris May 2003
Eytan, Walter obit Oct 2001

Faber, Sandra Apr 2002
Fadiman, Anne Aug 2005
Fagles, Robert Apr 2006 obit
Yrbk 2008
Fahd, King of Saudi Arabia
obit Yrbk 2005
Fahd, Prince of Saudi Arabia
see Fahd, King of Saudi
Arabia
Faidley, Warren Feb 2008
Fairclough, Ellen obit Yrbk
2005
Fairport Convention Sep 2005
Falco, Edie Mar 2006
Fallaci, Oriana obit Yrbk 2007
Fallon, Jimmy Jul 2002
Fallon, William J. Jul 2007
Falls, Robert Jan 2004
Falwell, Jerry obit Aug 2007
Fangmeier, Stefen Aug 2004
Farhi, Nicole Nov 2001
Farmer, Paul Feb 2004
Farmer-Paellmann, Deadria
Mar 2004
Farrell, Dave *see* Linkin Park
Farrell, Eileen obit Jun 2002
Farrelly, Bobby *see* Farrelly,
Peter and Bobby
Farrelly, Peter and Bobby Sep
2001
Fast, Howard obit Jul 2003
Fatal1ty *see* Wendel,
Johnathan
Fattah, Chaka Sep 2003
Faulk, Marshall Jan 2003
Faust, Drew Gilpin Jul 2007
Fausto-Sterling, Anne Sep 2005
Favreau, Jon [film director] Jul
2010
Favreau, Jon [speechwriter] May
2009
Favreau, Jonathan *see*
Favreau, Jon [speechwriter]
Fawcett, Farrah obit Aug 2009
Fawcett, Joy May 2004
Fay, J. Michael Sep 2001
Fay, Martin *see* Chieftains

Feifel, Herman obit Yrbk
2005
Feist Jun 2008
Feist, Leslie *see* Feist
Feith, Douglas J. Jul 2008
Felker, Clay S. obit Yrbk 2008
Felt, W. Mark Sep 2005 obit
Yrbk 2009
Fenton, Florence *see* Cowles,
Fleur
Fenton, George Jul 2010
Fenty, Adrian M. Mar 2007
Fenty, Robyn Rihanna *see*
Rihanna
Feoktistov, Konstantin
Petrovich obit Yrbk 2010
Fergie *see* Black Eyed Peas
Ferguson, Alex Jun 2010
Ferguson, Maynard obit Yrbk
2006
Ferguson, Stacy *see* Black
Eyed Peas
Ferré, Gianfranco obit Yrbk
2007
Ferré, Luis A. obit Mar 2004
Ferrell, Will Feb 2003
Ferrer, Rafael Jul 2001
Ferrera, America Sep 2007
Ferris, Joshua Oct 2010
Ferris, Timothy Jan 2001
Fey, Tina Apr 2002
Fidrych, Mark obit Yrbk 2009
Fiedler, Leslie A. obit Yrbk
2003
Field, Patricia Nov 2010
Fielder, Prince Jun 2008
Fields, Mark Apr 2005
Finch, Caleb E. Sep 2004
Finch, Jennie Oct 2004
Finckel, David *see* Emerson
String Quartet
Finn, Craig *see* Hold Steady,
The
Firth, Colin Mar 2004
Fischer, Bobby obit Yrbk 2008
Fischer, John H. obit Yrbk
2010
Fisher, Eddie obit Yrbk 2010
Fisher, Helen Oct 2010
Fishman, Jon *see* Phish
Fitzgerald, Geraldine obit
Yrbk 2005
Fitzgerald, Patrick J. Jan 2006
Flagg, Fannie Nov 2006
Flaming Lips Oct 2002
Flanagan, Tommy obit Mar
2002
Flay, Bobby May 2008
Fleming, Maureen Mar 2010
Fleming, Robben W. obit
Yrbk 2010
Fletcher, Arthur obit Yrbk
2005

Flight of the Conchords Mar 2008
Flint, Keith *see* Prodigy
Flowers, Vonetta May 2006
Foer, Jonathan Safran Sep 2002
Foley, Mick Sep 2001
Folkman, Judah obit Yrbk 2008
Followill, Caleb *see* Kings of Leon
Followill, Jared *see* Kings of Leon
Followill, Matthew *see* Kings of Leon
Folon, Jean-Michel obit Yrbk 2006
Foner, Eric Aug 2004
Fong, Hiram L. obit Yrbk 2004
Fong-Torres, Ben Aug 2001
Foot, Michael obit Yrbk 2010
Foote, Horton obit Yrbk 2009
Foote, Shelby obit Yrbk 2005
Ford, Gerald R. obit Feb 2007
Ford, Glenn obit Yrbk 2007
Ford, Harrison Jun 2008
Forrest, Vernon Jul 2002 obit Yrbk 2009
Forrester, Maureen obit Yrbk 2010
Forsberg, Peter Nov 2005
Forsee, Gary D. Oct 2005
Forsythe, John obit Yrbk 2010
Forsythe, William Feb 2003
Fortey, Richard Sep 2005
Fortier, Paul-André Nov 2010
Foss, Joseph Jacob obit Yrbk 2003
Foss, Lukas obit Yrbk 2009
Fossett, J. Stephen *see* Fossett, Steve
Fossett, Steve Apr 2005 obit Yrbk 2008
Fountain, Clarence *see* Blind Boys of Alabama
Fowles, John obit Apr 2006
Fox, Megan Feb 2010
Fox Quesada, Vicente May 2001
Foxx, Jamie May 2005
Fraiture, Nikolai *see* Strokes
Franca, Celia obit Yrbk 2007
Franciosa, Anthony obit Yrbk 2006
Franciosa, Tony *see* Franciosa, Anthony
Francis, Arlene obit Sep 2001
Francis, Dick obit May 2010
Francisco, Don Feb 2001
Franco, Julio Sep 2006
Francona, Terry Jul 2008
Frank, Reuven obit Yrbk 2006

Frankenheimer, John obit Oct 2002
Franklin, John Hope obit May 2009
Franklin, Shirley C. Aug 2002
Franks, Tommy R. Jan 2002
Franzen, Jonathan Sep 2003
Fraser, Brendan Feb 2001
Fraser, Douglas A. obit Yrbk 2008
Fredericks, Henry St. Clair *see* Mahal, Taj
Freed, James Ingo obit Yrbk 2006
Freeman, Lucy obit Yrbk 2005
Freeman, Orville L. obit Yrbk 2003
Freidman, Florence *see* Cowles, Fleur
French, Marilyn obit Yrbk 2009
Freston, Tom Aug 2003
Friedan, Betty obit May 2006
Friedlander, Lee May 2006
Friedman, Jane Mar 2001
Friedman, Milton obit Yrbk 2007
Friedman, Tom Oct 2008
Frist, Bill Nov 2002
Froese, Edgar *see* Tangerine Dream
Froese, Jerome *see* Tangerine Dream
Frum, David Jun 2004
Fry, Christopher obit Yrbk 2005
Fu, Ping Oct 2006
Fugazi Mar 2002
Fujii, Satoko Jun 2010
Fukuyama, Francis Jun 2001
Fuller, Millard obit Yrbk 2009
Funk, Chris *see* Decemberists

Gades, Antonio obit Yrbk 2004
Gagliardi, John Jan 2008
Gagne, Eric Jun 2004
Gaines, Donna Jun 2006
Gajdusek, D. Carleton obit Yrbk 2009
Galbraith, James K. Feb 2006
Galbraith, John Kenneth obit Yrbk 2007
Galinsky, Ellen Oct 2003
Gallagher, Ellen Feb 2009
Galloway, Joseph L. Sep 2003
Galtieri, Leopoldo obit Yrbk 2003
Gandy, Kim Oct 2001
Garcia, Sergio Mar 2001
Gardner, John W. obit May 2002

Gardner, Martin obit Yrbk 2010
Gardner, Rulon Nov 2004
Garfield, Henry *see* Rollins, Henry
Garner, Jennifer Apr 2008
Garofalo, Janeane Mar 2005
Garrels, Anne Mar 2004
Garrison, Deborah Jan 2001
Gary, Willie E. Apr 2001
Garza, Ed Jun 2002
Garzón, Baltasar Mar 2001
Gaskin, Ina May May 2001
Gaspard, Patrick Jul 2010
Gates, Melinda Feb 2004
Gates, Robert M. May 2007 Mar 2009
Gaubatz, Lynn Feb 2001
Gawande, Atul Mar 2005
Gayle, Helene Jan 2002
Gebel-Williams, Gunther obit Oct 2001
Geha, Marla Jun 2010
Geis, Bernard obit Mar 2001
Geithner, Timothy F. Mar 2009
Gelb, Leslie H. Jan 2003
Gennaro, Peter obit Feb 2001
George, Susan Jul 2007
Gerberding, Julie Louise Sep 2004
Gerbner, George obit Yrbk 2006
Germanotta, Stefani *see* Lady Gaga
Germond, Jack W. Jul 2005
Gerson, Michael Feb 2002
Gerwig, Greta Jun 2010
Gessen, Keith Sep 2008
Getty, Estelle obit Yrbk 2008
Ghez, Andrea Nov 2010
Ghostface Killah Jun 2008
Giamatti, Paul Sep 2005
Giannulli, Mossimo Feb 2003
Gibbs, Robert Apr 2009
Gibson, Althea obit Feb 2004
Gibson, Charles Sep 2002
Gibson, Lois Mar 2008
Gibson, Mel Aug 2003
Gierek, Edward obit Oct 2001
Gilani, Yousaf Raza Nov 2008
Gilbert and George Jun 2009
Gilbreth, Frank B. Jr. obit Jul 2001
Gillingham, Charles *see* Counting Crows
Gillis, John *see* White Stripes
Gilmore, James S. III Jun 2001
Ginzberg, Eli obit Yrbk 2003
Ginzburg, Vitaly obit Yrbk 2010
Gioia, Ted Jan 2010
Giordani, Marcello May 2008

Girardi, Joe May 2008
Giroud, Françoise obit Jul 2003
Giroux, Robert obit Yrbk 2008
Giuliani, Rudolph Jan 2008
Giulini, Carlo Maria obit Yrbk 2005
Gladstone, Brooke Jan 2009
Gladwell, Malcolm Jun 2005
Glass, H. Bentley obit Yrbk 2005
Glavine, Tom Oct 2006
Goddard, James L. obit Yrbk 2010
Goff, M. Lee Jun 2001
Goheen, Robert F. obit Yrbk 2008
Gold, Thomas obit Yrbk 2004
Goldberg, Bill Apr 2001
Golden, Thelma Sep 2001
Golding, Bruce Mar 2008
Golding, Orette Bruce see Golding, Bruce
Goldman-Rakic, Patricia Feb 2003
Goldovsky, Boris obit Aug 2001
Goldsman, Akiva Sep 2004
Goldsmith, Jerry May 2001 obit Nov 2004
Goldstine, Herman Heine obit Yrbk 2004
Goldthwait, Bobcat Sep 2010
Goldthwait, Robert see Goldthwait, Bobcat
Golub, Leon obit Yrbk 2004
Gomes, Marcelo May 2007
Gomez, Jaime see Black Eyed Peas
Gondry, Michel May 2007
Gonzales, Alberto R. Apr 2002
Gonzalez, Henry obit Feb 2001
Good, Mary L. Sep 2001
Good, Robert A. obit Yrbk 2003
Goodpaster, Andrew J. obit Yrbk 2005
Googoosh May 2001
Goosen, Retief Jun 2010
Gopinath, Suhas Jul 2008
Gopnik, Adam Apr 2005
Gopnik, Alison Jan 2007
Gordon, Bruce S. Oct 2005
Gordon, Cyrus H. obit Aug 2001
Gordon, Ed Jul 2005
Gordon, Edmund W. Jun 2003
Gordon, Lincoln obit Yrbk 2010
Gordon, Mike see Phish

Gordon-Reed, Annette May 2009
Gordon, Wycliffe Sep 2009
Gorman, James P. Jun 2010
Gorman, R. C. Jan 2001
Gorsuch, Anne obit Yrbk 2004
Gorton, John Grey obit Yrbk 2002
Gottlieb, Melvin B. obit Mar 2001
Gould, Stephen Jay obit Aug 2002
Goulet, Robert obit Yrbk 2008
Gourdji, Françoise see Giroud, Françoise
Gowdy, Curt obit Yrbk 2006
Gowers, Timothy Jan 2001
Gowers, William Timothy see Gowers, Timothy
Graham, Franklin May 2002
Graham, Katharine obit Oct 2001
Graham, Susan Oct 2005
Graham, Winston obit Yrbk 2003
Grandberry, Omari see Omarion
Granger, Clive W. J. obit Yrbk 2009
Granholm, Jennifer M. Oct 2003
Grasso, Richard Oct 2002
Graves, Florence George May 2005
Graves, Morris obit Sep 2001
Gray, L. Patrick obit Yrbk 2005
Gray, Simon obit Yrbk 2008
Gray, Spalding obit Yrbk 2004
Gray, William M. Jan 2010
Greco, José obit Mar 2001
Green, Adolph obit Mar 2003
Green, Darrell Jan 2001
Green Day Aug 2005
Green, Tom Oct 2003
Greenberg, Jack M. Nov 2001
Greene, Wallace M. obit Aug 2003
Greenstein, Jesse L. obit Yrbk 2003
Greenwald, Julie Nov 2009
Greenwood, Colin see Radiohead
Greenwood, Jonny see Radiohead
Gregory, David Oct 2010
Gregory, Frederick D. Oct 2005
Gregory, Wilton D. Mar 2002
Greider, Carol W. Feb 2008
Greinke, Zack Jul 2010

Griffin Jr., William Michael see Rakim
Griffin, Kathy Sep 2008
Griffin, Merv obit Yrbk 2007
Griffin, Michael Aug 2005
Griffiths, Martha W. obit Yrbk 2003
Grigg, John obit Apr 2002
Grizzard, George obit Yrbk 2008
Groban, Josh Aug 2009
Grohl, Dave May 2002
Groopman, Jerome E. Oct 2004
Gross, Bill see Gross, William H.
Gross, William H. Jul 2010
Grossman, Edith Mar 2006
Grossman, Lev Apr 2010
Gruber, Ruth Jun 2001
Gruber, Samuel H. Aug 2004
Grubin, David Aug 2002
Guarente, Leonard P. May 2007
Guccione, Bob obit Yrbk 2010
Gudmundsdottir, Björk see Björk
Guerard, Albert J. obit Mar 2001
Guerrero, Vladimir Jun 2006
Guggenheim, Davis Nov 2009
Guillen, Ozzie May 2006
Guillermoprieto, Alma Sep 2004
Guinier, Lani Jan 2004
Gunn, Thom obit Yrbk 2004
Gunn, Tim Oct 2009
Gunningham, Robin see Banksy
Gupta, Sanjay Aug 2006
Gursky, Andreas Jul 2001
Guthman, Edwin O. obit Yrbk 2008
Gwathmey, Charles obit Yrbk 2009
Gygax, Gary Mar 2007 obit Yrbk 2008

Haas, Jonathan Jun 2003
Haass, Richard N. Jun 2010
Habash, George obit Yrbk 2008
Hacker see Hackett, Buddy
Hackett, Buddy obit Oct 2003
Hadley, Jerry obit Yrbk 2007
Hadley, Stephen Nov 2006
Hagel, Chuck Aug 2004
Hagen, Uta obit Yrbk 2004
Haggis, Paul Aug 2006
Hahn, Hilary Sep 2002
Hahn, Joseph see Linkin Park
Haig, Alexander obit Yrbk 2010

Hailey, Arthur obit Yrbk 2005
Hailsham of St. Marylebone,
    Quintin Hogg obit Feb
    2002
Hair, Jay D. obit Jan 2003
Halaby, Najeeb E. obit Yrbk
    2003
Halasz, Laszlo obit Feb 2002
Halberstam, David obit Jul
    2007
Hall, Conrad L. obit May
    2003
Hall, Deidre Nov 2002
Hall, Edward T. obit Yrbk
    2009
Hall, Gus obit Jan 2001
Hall, Richard Melville see
    Moby
Hall, Steffie see Evanovich,
    Janet
Hall, Tex G. May 2005
Halladay, Roy Sep 2009
Hallahan, Patrick see My
    Morning Jacket
Hallaren, Mary A. obit Yrbk
    2005
Hallström, Lasse Feb 2005
Hamilton, Laird Aug 2005
Hamilton, Tom see
    Aerosmith
Hamm, Morgan see Hamm,
    Paul and Morgan
Hamm, Paul and Morgan Nov
    2004
Hammer, Bonnie Apr 2006
Hammon, Becky Jan 2003
Hammond, Albert Jr. see
    Strokes
Hammond, Caleb D. Jr. obit
    Yrbk 2006
Hammons, David May 2006
Hampton, Lionel obit Yrbk
    2002
Hancock, Graham Feb 2005
Hancock, Trenton Doyle Apr
    2006
Handler, Chelsea Oct 2010
Hanna, William obit Sep
    2001
Hannity, Sean Apr 2005
Hansen, Chris Jun 2010
Hansen, Liane May 2003
Hanson, Mark see Yusuf,
    Hamza
Harcourt, Nic Oct 2005
Harden, Marcia Gay Sep 2001
Hardin, Clifford obit Yrbk
    2010
Hardin, Garrett obit Apr 2004
Hardwick, Elizabeth obit Yrbk
    2008
Hargis, Billy James obit Yrbk
    2005

Hargrove, Marion obit Yrbk
    2004
Harjo, Joy Aug 2001
Harper, Ben Jan 2004
Harrer, Heinrich obit Yrbk
    2006
Harris, E. Lynn obit Yrbk
    2009
Harris, Eva Mar 2004
Harris, Mark obit Yrbk 2007
Harris, Richard obit Yrbk
    2003
Harrison, George obit Mar
    2002
Harrison, Gilbert A. obit Yrbk
    2008
Harrison, Marvin Aug 2001
Harrison, William B. Jr. Mar
    2002
Hart, Kitty Carlisle obit Yrbk
    2007
Hartford, Huntington obit
    Yrbk 2008
Hartigan, Grace obit Yrbk
    2009
Hartke, Vance obit Yrbk 2003
Hartmann, Heidi I. Apr 2003
Hartzog, George obit Yrbk
    2008
Harvey, David Aug 2008
Harvey, Paul obit Yrbk 2009
Harvey, PJ May 2008
Harvey, Polly Jean see
    Harvey, PJ
Hashimoto, Ryutaro obit Yrbk
    2006
Haskins, Caryl P. obit Feb
    2002
Hass, Amira Apr 2009
Hass, Robert Feb 2001
Hassenfeld, Alan G. Jul 2003
Hastings, Reed Mar 2006
Hastreiter, Kim Aug 2010
Hathaway, Anne Feb 2009
Hatton, Richard see Hatton,
    Ricky
Hatton, Ricky Oct 2008
Hauerwas, Stanley Jun 2003
Haughey, Charles obit Yrbk
    2006
Hawkins, A. F. obit Yrbk
    2008
Hawkins, Paula obit Yrbk
    2010
Hawkinson, Tim Aug 2005
Hax, Carolyn Nov 2002
Hayden, Melissa obit Yrbk
    2006
Hayden, Michael V. Nov 2006
Hayes, Bob obit Jan 2003
Hayes, Edward May 2006
Hayes, Isaac obit Yrbk 2008
Hayes, Tyrone B. May 2008

Haynes, Cornell Jr. see Nelly
Haynes, Todd Jul 2003
Haysbert, Dennis Nov 2006
Headley, Elizabeth see
    Cavanna, Betty
Heath, Edward obit Yrbk
    2005
Heath, James R. Oct 2003
Hecht, Anthony obit Yrbk
    2005
Heckart, Eileen obit Mar 2002
Hee, Dana May 2008
Height, Dorothy I. obit Jul
    2010
Heilbroner, Robert L. obit
    Yrbk 2005
Heilbrun, Carolyn G. obit Feb
    2004
Heiskell, Andrew obit Yrbk
    2003
Held, Al obit Yrbk 2005
Hellenga, Robert Mar 2008
Heller, Agnes Nov 2008
Helms, Jesse obit Yrbk 2008
Helms, Richard obit Yrbk
    2003
Henderson, Donald A. Mar
    2002
Henderson, Hazel Nov 2003
Henderson, Joe obit Oct 2001
Henderson, Skitch obit Apr
    2006
Hendrickson, Sue Oct 2001
Henriques, Sean Paul see
    Sean Paul
Henry, Brad Jan 2005
Henry, John W. May 2005
Hepburn, Katharine obit Nov
    2003
Herbert, Don obit Yrbk 2007
Herblock see Block, Herbert
    L.
Hernandez, Dave see Shins
Herndon, J. Marvin Nov 2003
Herrera Campins, Luis obit
    Yrbk 2008
Herring, Pendleton obit Yrbk
    2004
Herring Wonder see Ames,
    Jonathan
Hersch, Fred Apr 2006
Hertzberg, Arthur obit Yrbk
    2006
Herzog, Jacques see Herzog,
    Jacques, and de Meuron,
    Pierre
Herzog, Jacques, and de
    Meuron, Pierre Jun 2002
Heston, Charlton obit Jul
    2008
Hewitt, Angela Apr 2007
Hewitt, Don obit Yrbk 2009
Hewitt, Lleyton Oct 2002

Hewlett, Sylvia Ann Sep 2002
Heyerdahl, Thor obit Yrbk 2002
Heym, Stefan obit Mar 2002
Heymann, David L. Jul 2004
Hickel, Walter obit Yrbk 2010
Hickey, Dave Sep 2007
Hicks, Louise Day obit Jun 2004
Hidalgo, David see Los Lobos
Higgins, Chester Jr. Jun 2002
Higgins, Jack Feb 2007
Higgs, Peter Feb 2009
Hildegarde obit Yrbk 2005
Hill, Andrew Apr 2004 obit Yrbk 2007
Hill, Arthur obit Yrbk 2007
Hill, Dulé Jul 2003
Hill, Faith Mar 2001
Hill, George Roy obit Jun 2003
Hill, Grant Jan 2002
Hill, Herbert obit Yrbk 2004
Hillary, Sir Edmund obit Yrbk 2008
Hillenburg, Stephen Apr 2003
Hiller, Stanley obit Yrbk 2006
Hiller, Wendy obit Yrbk 2003
Hillerman, Tony obit Yrbk 2008
Hines, Gregory obit Yrbk 2003
Hines, Jerome obit Jun 2003
Hingle, Pat obit Yrbk 2009
Hinojosa, Maria Feb 2001
Hirschfeld, Al obit Jul 2003
Hirschhorn, Thomas Sep 2009
Hobson, Mellody Aug 2005
Hobson Pilot, Ann May 2003
Hockfield, Susan Apr 2008
Hoffman, Philip Seymour May 2001
Hogg, Quintin see Hailsham of St. Marylebone, Quintin Hogg
Hold Steady, The Sep 2010
Holden, Betsy Jul 2003
Holder, Eric H. Jr. Mar 2009
Holdsclaw, Chamique Feb 2006
Holl, Steven Jul 2004
Hollahan, Keenan see Savage, Dan
Holland, Dave Mar 2003
Hollander, Robert B. Sep 2006
Holm, Ian Mar 2002
Holmes, Odetta see Odetta
Honderich, Ted Feb 2009
Hondros, Chris Nov 2004
Hong, Hei-Kyung Nov 2003
Hooker, John Lee obit Sep 2001

Hooks, Benjamin L. obit Yrbk 2010
Hope, Bob obit Yrbk 2003
Hopkins, Bernard Apr 2002
Hopkins, Nancy May 2002
Hopper, Dennis obit Yrbk 2010
Hoppus, Mark see blink-182
Horne, Lena obit Aug 2010
Horsey, David Sep 2008
Horwich, Frances obit Oct 2001
Houk, Ralph obit Yrbk 2010
Hounsfield, Godfrey obit Yrbk 2004
Hounsou, Djimon Aug 2004
Houston, Allan Nov 2003
Houston, James A. obit Yrbk 2005
Hoving, Thomas obit Yrbk 2010
Howard, Ryan Jul 2007
Howard, Terrence Jun 2007
Howard, Tim Sep 2005
Howe, Harold II obit Yrbk 2003
Howland, Ben Jun 2007
Howlett, Liam see Prodigy
Hoyer, Steny H. Mar 2004
Hoyle, Fred obit Jan 2002
Hrawi, Elias obit Yrbk 2006
Hua Guofeng obit Yrbk 2008
Huckabee, Mike Nov 2005
Hudson, Jennifer May 2007
Hudson, Saul see Slash
Hughes, Barnard obit Yrbk 2006
Hughes, John obit Yrbk 2009
Hughes, Karen Oct 2001
Hugo, Chad see Neptunes
Hull, Jane Dee Feb 2002
Humbard, Rex obit Yrbk 2008
Hunt Lieberson, Lorraine Jul 2004 obit Yrbk 2006
Hunt, Swanee Mar 2006
Hunter, Charlie Nov 2007
Hunter, Evan obit Yrbk 2005
Hunter, Kermit obit Sep 2001
Hunter, Kim obit Yrbk 2002
Hurley, Chad see Chen, Steve; Hurley, Chad; and Karim, Jawed
Hussein, Saddam obit Apr 2007
Hutton, Betty obit Yrbk 2007
Hyde, Henry J. obit Yrbk 2008

Iakovos, Archbishop obit Yrbk 2005
Ifill, Gwen Sep 2005
Iijima, Sumio Nov 2009
Ilitch, Michael Feb 2005
Illich, Ivan obit Yrbk 2003

Immelman, Trevor Oct 2008
Immelt, Jeffrey R. Feb 2004
India.Arie Feb 2002
Inkster, Juli Sep 2002
Inskeep, Steve Jun 2009
Irvin, Nell see Painter, Nell Irvin
Irwin, Steve obit Yrbk 2007
Isbin, Sharon Aug 2003
Isley, Phylis Lee see Jones, Jennifer
Istomin, Eugene obit Feb 2004
Ive, Jonathan Oct 2006
Ivey, Susan M. Mar 2010
Ivins, Michael see Flaming Lips
Ivins, Molly obit Yrbk 2007
Iyengar, B. K. S. Jun 2007
Izecson dos Santos Leite, Ricardo see Kaká
Izetbegovic, Alija obit Jun 2004

Ja Rule Jul 2002
Jacir, Emily Aug 2009
Jackman, Hugh Oct 2003
Jackson, Alan Apr 2004
Jackson, Hal Oct 2002
Jackson, Lauren Jun 2003
Jackson Lee, Sheila Nov 2008
Jackson, Lisa P. Mar 2010
Jackson, Maynard H. Jr. obit Yrbk 2003
Jackson, Michael [beer connoisseur] Aug 2005 obit Yrbk 2007
Jackson, Michael [singer] obit Aug 2009
Jackson, Peter Jan 2002
Jackson, Thomas Penfield Jun 2001
Jacobs, Jane obit Yrbk 2006
Jacobs, Paul E. Feb 2007
Jaffee, Al Jul 2008
Jaffee, Allan see Jaffee, Al
Jagger, Janine Apr 2004
Jakes, T.D. Jun 2001
Jamail, Joe Sep 2008
James, Alex see Blur
James, Bill Jun 2004
James, Edgerrin Jan 2002
James, Jim see My Morning Jacket
James, LeBron Nov 2005
Jamison, Kay Redfield Feb 2009
Janeway, Elizabeth obit Yrbk 2005
Jarecki, Eugene May 2006
Jarrett, Valerie Apr 2009
Jarring, Gunnar obit Yrbk 2002

Jarvis, Erich D. May 2003
Jarvis, Jeff Aug 2009
Jastrow, Robert obit Yrbk 2008
Jay-Z Aug 2002
Jealous, Benjamin Todd Feb 2009
Jean, Michaëlle Jun 2009
Jeffers, Eve Jihan see Eve
Jefferts Schori, Katharine Sep 2006
Jeffery, Vonetta see Flowers, Vonetta
Jeffords, James Sep 2001
Jenike, Michael A. Jan 2010
Jenkins, Jerry B. see LaHaye, Tim and Jenkins, Jerry B.
Jenkins, Roy obit Yrbk 2003
Jennings, Peter obit Sep 2005
Jennings, Waylon obit Apr 2002
Jensen, Oliver O. obit Yrbk 2005
Jet see Urquidez, Benny
Jha, Sanjay K. Jan 2010
Jimenez, Marcos Perez see Pérez Jiménez, Marcos
Jin, Deborah Apr 2004
Jindal, Bobby Jan 2008
Jindal, Piyush see Jindal, Bobby
Jobert, Michel obit Yrbk 2002
Johannesen, Grant obit Yrbk 2005
Johansson, Ingemar obit Yrbk 2009
Johansson, Scarlett Mar 2005
John, Daymond Aug 2007
John Paul II obit Jun 2005
Johnson, Alexander Boris de Pfeffel see Johnson, Boris
Johnson, Andre Nov 2010
Johnson, Avery Jan 2007
Johnson, Boris Oct 2008
Johnson, Brian see AC/DC
Johnson, Chad see Ochocinco, Chad
Johnson, Chris Aug 2010
Johnson, Claudia Alta obit Oct 2007
Johnson, Eddie Bernice Jul 2001
Johnson, Elizabeth A. Nov 2002
Johnson, Eric see Shins
Johnson, John H. obit Yrbk 2005
Johnson, Lady Bird see Johnson, Claudia Alta
Johnson, Mat Mar 2010
Johnson, Philip obit Sep 2005
Johnson, Sheila Crump Jun 2007

Johnson, Simon Oct 2009
Johnson, Van obit Yrbk 2009
Johnson, Zach Jan 2008
Johnston, Daniel Sep 2010
Jolly, Alison Jan 2009
Jones, Benjamin see Paper Rad
Jones, Bobby Jun 2002
Jones, Chipper May 2001
Jones, Chuck obit May 2002
Jones, Cullen Aug 2008
Jones, Edward P. Mar 2004
Jones, Elaine Jun 2004
Jones, George L. Apr 2007
Jones, Jennifer obit Yrbk 2010
Jones, Larry Wayne Jr. see Jones, Chipper
Jones, Nasir bin Olu Dara see Nas
Jones, Norah May 2003
Jones, Sarah Jul 2005
Jones, Scott Jan 2006
Jones, Tayari Aug 2009
Jones, Van Apr 2009
Jonze, Spike Apr 2003
Jordan, Hamilton obit Yrbk 2008
Jordan, Michael H. obit Yrbk 2010
Jordan, Philippe Oct 2010
Jorgensen, Mikael see Wilco
Josefowicz, Leila May 2007
Joyner, Tom Sep 2002
Judd, Jackie Sep 2002
Judd, Jacqueline Dee see Judd, Jackie
Judson, Olivia Jan 2004
Juliana Queen of the Netherlands obit Yrbk 2004
July, Miranda Nov 2007

Kabila, Joseph Sep 2001
Kaczynski, Lech obit Yrbk 2010
Kael, Pauline obit Nov 2001
Kagan, Elena Jun 2007
Kagan, Frederick W. Jul 2007
Kainen, Jacob obit Aug 2001
Kaiser, Philip M. obit Yrbk 2007
Kaká May 2008
Kamber, Michael Jun 2009
Kamen, Dean Nov 2002
Kane, Joseph Nathan obit Nov 2002
Kani, John Jun 2001
Kann, Peter R. Mar 2003
Kantrowitz, Adrian obit Yrbk 2009
Kantrowitz, Arthur obit Yrbk 2009
Kao, John Oct 2008

Kaptur, Marcy Jan 2003
Kapuściński, Ryszard obit Yrbk 2007
Karbo, Karen May 2001
Karim, Jawed see Chen, Steve; Hurley, Chad; and Karim, Jawed
Karle, Isabella Jan 2003
Karon, Jan Mar 2003
Karpinski, Janis Apr 2006
Karsh, Yousuf obit Nov 2002
Karzai, Hamid May 2002
Kase, Toshikazu obit Yrbk 2004
Kass, Leon R. Aug 2002
Katchalski, Ephraim see Katzir, Ephraim
Katsav, Moshe Feb 2001
Katz, Jackson Jul 2004
Katzir, Ephraim obit Yrbk 2009
Kaufman, Charlie Jul 2005
Kaufman, Millard Jan 2008 obit Yrbk 2009
Kavafian, Ani Oct 2006
Kazan, Elia obit Yrbk 2004
Kcho Aug 2001
Keane, Sean see Chieftains
Keegan, Robert Jan 2004
Keener, Catherine Oct 2002
Keeshan, Bob obit Yrbk 2004
Keith, Toby Oct 2004
Kelleher, Herb Jan 2001
Keller, Bill Oct 2003
Keller, Marthe Jul 2004
Keller, Thomas Jun 2004
Kelly, Raymond Sep 2008
Kelman, Charles obit Yrbk 2004
Kemp, Jack obit Yrbk 2009
Kempthorne, Dirk Jun 2007
Kennan, George F. obit Yrbk 2005
Kennedy, Edward M. obit Oct 2009
Kennedy, Kathleen Feb 2009
Kennedy, Randall Aug 2002
Kennedy, Robert F. Jr. May 2004
Kennedy, Ted see Kennedy, Edward M.
Kent, Jeff May 2003
Kentridge, William Oct 2001
Kenyon, Cynthia Jan 2005
Kepes, György obit Mar 2002
Kerlikowske, R. Gil Nov 2009
Kerlikowske, Richard Guilford see Kerlikowske, R. Gil
Kerr, Clark obit May 2004
Kerr, Deborah obit Feb 2008
Kerr, Jean obit May 2003

Kerr, Mrs. Walter F *see* Kerr, Jean
Kerry, John Sep 2004
Kesey, Ken obit Feb 2002
Ketcham, Hank obit Sep 2001
Keys, Ancel obit Yrbk 2005
Keys, Charlene *see* Tweet
Khalilzad, Zalmay Aug 2006
Kid Rock Oct 2001
Kidd, Chip Jul 2005
Kidd, Jason May 2002
Kidd, Michael obit Yrbk 2008
Kiessling, Laura Aug 2003
Kilar, Jason Aug 2009
Kilbourne, Jean May 2004
Kilpatrick, James J. obit Yrbk 2010
Kilpatrick, Kwame M. Apr 2004
Kim Dae-Jung obit Yrbk 2009
Kim, Jim Yong Nov 2006
Kimmel, Jimmy Oct 2009
King, Alan obit Yrbk 2004
King, Coretta Scott obit Apr 2006
King, Florence Apr 2006
King, John Mar 2010
Kings of Leon Jul 2010
Kirchner, Leon obit Yrbk 2009
Kirchner, Néstor obit Yrbk 2010
Kirk, Ron Apr 2010
Kirk, Ronald *see* Kirk, Ron
Kirkpatrick, Jeane obit Yrbk 2007
Kitaj, R. B. obit Yrbk 2008
Kitchen, Michael Nov 2008
Kitt, Eartha obit Yrbk 2009
Kittikachorn, Thanom obit Yrbk 2004
Kiviniemi, Mari Oct 2010
Klaus, Josef obit Oct 2001
Kleiber, Carlos obit Yrbk 2004
Klein, Herbert G. obit Yrbk 2009
Klein, Naomi Aug 2003
Klein, William Mar 2004
Kleppe, Thomas S. obit Yrbk 2007
Klinkenborg, Verlyn Jul 2006
Klossewski, Balthazar *see* Balthus
Kluge, John W. obit Yrbk 2010
K'Naan Jun 2010
Knievel, Evel obit Yrbk 2008
Knievel, Robbie Mar 2005
Knipfel, Jim Mar 2005
Knoll, Andrew H. Apr 2006
Knowles, Beyoncé *see* Destiny's Child
Knox, Simmie May 2009
Koch, Kenneth obit Yrbk 2002

Koff, Clea Nov 2004
Koh, Jennifer Sep 2006
Kohl, Herb May 2008
Koirala, Girija Prasad obit Yrbk 2010
Koizumi, Junichiro Jan 2002
Kolar, Jiri obit Yrbk 2002
Kolff, Willem Johan obit Yrbk 2009
Kollek, Teddy obit Yrbk 2007
Koma *see* Eiko and Koma
Konaré, Alpha Oumar Oct 2001
Koner, Pauline obit Apr 2001
Kopp, Wendy Mar 2003
Korine, Harmony Feb 2010
Korman, Harvey obit Yrbk 2008
Kornberg, Arthur obit Feb 2008
Kos *see* Moulitsas Zúniga, Markos ("Kos")
Koster, Bo *see* My Morning Jacket
Kostunica, Vojislav Jan 2001
Kotche, Glenn *see* Wilco
Kott, Jan obit Mar 2002
Kournikova, Anna Jan 2002
Kovalchuk, Ilya Mar 2007
Kramer, Jack obit Yrbk 2009
Kramer, Jake *see* Kramer, Jack
Kramer, Joey *see* Aerosmith
Kramer, Stanley obit May 2001
Krause, David W. Feb 2002
Krauss, Nicole Nov 2010
Krauthammer, Charles Jan 2008
Krawcheck, Sallie Mar 2006
Kreps, Juanita Morris obit Yrbk 2010
Kreutzberger, Mario *see* Francisco, Don
Kripke, Saul Oct 2004
Kristof, Nicholas D. Feb 2006
Kristol, Irving obit Nov 2009
Krugman, Paul Aug 2001
Krupp, Fred Sep 2007
Kübler-Ross, Elisabeth obit Yrbk 2004
Kubler, Tad *see* Hold Steady, The
Kucinich, Dennis J. Jul 2008
Kuhn, Bowie obit Yrbk 2007
Kummant, Alexander Jan 2007
Kunitz, Stanley obit Aug 2006
Kurzweil, Raymond Sep 2008
Kushner, Jared Jun 2007
Kushner, Tony Jul 2002
Kusturica, Emir Nov 2005
Kuznetsova, Svetlana Mar 2008

Kyles, Cedric see Cedric the Entertainer
Kyprianou, Spyros obit May 2002

La India May 2002
La Montagne, Margaret *see* Spellings, Margaret
La Russa, Tony Jul 2003
LaBeouf, Shia Aug 2009
Labov, William Mar 2006
LaChapelle, David Jun 2008
Lacy, Dan obit Nov 2001
LaDuke, Winona Jan 2003
Lady Gaga May 2010
LaFontaine, Don Sep 2004 obit Yrbk 2008
Lagardère, Jean-Luc obit Aug 2003
Lagat, Bernard Oct 2008
LaHaye, Tim *see* LaHaye, Tim and Jenkins, Jerry B.
LaHaye, Tim and Jenkins, Jerry B. Jun 2003
LaHood, Ray Mar 2009
Laimbeer, Bill Jan 2006
Laine, Frankie obit Yrbk 2007
Laker, Freddie obit Yrbk 2006
Lally, Joe *see* Fugazi
Lamb, Willis Jr. obit Yrbk 2008
Lambsdorff, Otto obit Yrbk 2010
Lamont, Ann Huntress Feb 2007
Lampert, Edward S. Sep 2005
Landers, Ann obit Nov 2002
Lane, Anthony Nov 2008
Lang, Pearl obit Yrbk 2009
Lang, Robert J. Jul 2007
Lange, David obit Yrbk 2005
Langevin, Jim Aug 2005
Lanier, Cathy L. Mar 2007
Lantos, Tom Jul 2007 obit May 2008
Lanzone, Jim May 2007
Lapidus, Morris obit Apr 2001
Lapp, Ralph E. obit Feb 2005
Lara, Brian Feb 2001
Lardner, Ring Jr. obit Feb 2001
Laredo, Ruth obit Yrbk 2005
Larrocha, Alicia de obit Yrbk 2009
Lassaw, Ibram obit Yrbk 2004
Lauder, Estée obit Yrbk 2004
LaValle, Victor Jan 2010
Lavigne, Avril Apr 2003
Law, Ty Oct 2002
Lawal, Kase L. Nov 2006
Laws, Hubert Jr. Jul 2007
Lax, Peter D. Oct 2005

Layton, Jack Nov 2009
Le Clercq, Tanaquil obit Mar 2001
Leakey, Meave Jun 2002
Lederberg, Joshua obit Yrbk 2008
Lederer, Esther Pauline *see* Landers, Ann
Lederle, John obit Yrbk 2007
Ledger, Heath Jun 2006 obit Yrbk 2008
LeDoux, Joseph Oct 2010
Lee, Andrea Sep 2003
Lee, Barbara Jun 2004
Lee, Cliff Aug 2009
Lee, Debra L. Jun 2006
Lee, Geddy *see* Rush
Lee, Jeanette Oct 2002
Lee, Mrs. John G. *see* Lee, Percy Maxim
Lee, Peggy obit May 2002
Lee, Percy Maxim obit Jan 2003
Lee, Richard C. obit Jun 2003
Lee, Sherman obit Yrbk 2008
LeFrak, Samuel J. obit Yrbk 2003
Legend, John Feb 2007
Lehane, Dennis Oct 2005
Leiter, Al Aug 2002
Lelyveld, Joseph Nov 2005
Lem, Stanislaw obit Yrbk 2006
Lemmon, Jack obit Oct 2001
Lemon, Don May 2010
L'Engle, Madeleine obit Yrbk 2007
Leo, John Sep 2006
Leo, Melissa Jul 2009
Leon, Kenny Nov 2005
Leonard *see* Hackett, Buddy
Leonard, Hugh obit Yrbk 2009
Leone, Giovanni obit Feb 2002
Leslie, Chris *see* Fairport Convention
LeSueur, Larry obit Jun 2003
Lethem, Jonathan Mar 2006
Letterman, David Oct 2002
Letts, Tracy Oct 2008
Levert, Gerald Oct 2003 obit Yrbk 2007
Lévi-Strauss, Claude obit Jan 2010
Levin, Carl May 2004
Levin, Ira obit Feb 2008
Levin, Janna Jan 2008
Levine, David obit Yrbk 2010
Levine, Irving R. obit Yrbk 2009
Levine, Mel Nov 2005
LeVox, Gary *see* Rascal Flatts
Levy, Andrea Sep 2010

Levy, Eugene Jan 2002
Lewis, Ananda Jun 2005
Lewis, David Levering May 2001
Lewis, David S. Jr. obit Yrbk 2004
Lewis, Dorothy Otnow May 2006
Lewis, Flora obit Yrbk 2002
Lewis, John obit Jun 2001
Lewis, Kenneth Apr 2004
Lewis, Marvin Nov 2004
Lewis, Ray Jan 2007
Lewitt, Sol obit Yrbk 2007
Lhuillier, Monique Jun 2008
Li, Jet Jun 2001
Li Lian Jie *see* Li, Jet
Libeskind, Daniel Jun 2003
Lifeson, Alex *see* Rush
Lillien, Lisa May 2010
Lilly, John C. obit Feb 2002
Lilly, Kristine Apr 2004
Lima do Amor, Sisleide *see* Sissi
Lincecum, Tim Jun 2010
Lincoln, Abbey Sep 2002 obit Yrbk 2010
Lincoln, Blanche Lambert Mar 2002
Lindbergh, Anne Morrow obit Apr 2001
Lindgren, Astrid obit Apr 2002
Lindo, Allan Pineda see Black Eyed Peas
Lindo, Delroy Mar 2001
Lindsay, John V. obit Mar 2001
Ling, James J. obit Yrbk 2005
Lingle, Linda Jun 2003
Link, O. Winston obit Apr 2001
Linkin Park Mar 2002
Linkletter, Art obit Yrbk 2010
Linowitz, Sol M. obit Yrbk 2005
Lipinski, Anne Marie Jul 2004
Lippold, Richard obit Yrbk 2002
Little Steven *see* Van Zandt, Steven
Liu, Lucy Oct 2003
Llinás, Rodolfo R. Sep 2009
Lloyd, Charles Apr 2002
Locke, Gary Apr 2003
Lockhart, Keith Aug 2008
Logan, Lara Jul 2006
Lohan, Lindsay Nov 2005
Lomax, Alan obit Oct 2002
London, Julie obit Feb 2001
Long, Russell B. obit Yrbk 2003

Long, William Ivey Mar 2004
Lopez, Al obit Yrbk 2006
Lopez, George Mar 2010
López Portillo, José obit Yrbk 2004
Lord, Walter obit Yrbk 2002
Los Lobos Oct 2005
Loudon, Dorothy obit Yrbk 2004
Louis C.K. Feb 2010
Love, John A. obit Apr 2002
Lowell, Mike Sep 2003
Lozano, Conrad *see* Los Lobos Lobos
Lucas, George May 2002
Luce, Charles F. obit Yrbk 2008
Luckovich, Mike Jan 2005
Ludacris Jun 2004
Ludlum, Robert obit Jul 2001
Ludwig, Ken May 2004
Luke, Delilah Rene *see* Delilah
Lumet, Sidney Jun 2005
Luns, Joseph M. A. H. obit Yrbk 2002
Lupica, Mike Mar 2001
Lurie, John Oct 2010
Lustiger, Jean-Marie obit Yrbk 2007
Lynch, Jane Jul 2010
Lyng, Richard E. obit Jun 2003
Lynne, Shelby Jul 2001

M.I.A. May 2009
Mac, Bernie Jun 2002 obit Nov 2008
MacFarlane, Seth May 2010
Machado, Alexis Leyva *see* Kcho
MacKaye, Ian *see* Fugazi
MacKenzie, Gisele obit Jul 2004
Mackey, John Nov 2008
MacMitchell, Leslie obit Yrbk 2006
Maddow, Rachel Aug 2009
Maddox, Lester obit Yrbk 2003
Madsen, Michael Apr 2004
Magliozzi, Ray *see* Magliozzi, Tom and Ray
Magliozzi, Tom and Ray Jun 2006
Magloire, Paul E. obit Nov 2001
Maguire, Tobey Sep 2002
Mahal, Taj Nov 2001
Mahesh Yogi, Maharishi obit Yrbk 2008

Mahfouz, Naguib obit Yrbk 2007
Mailer, Norman obit Jan 2008
Makeba, Miriam obit Yrbk 2009
Maki, Fumihiko Jul 2001
Malaby, Tony Sep 2008
Malcolm, Ellen R. Feb 2010
Malden, Karl obit Yrbk 2009
Malina, Joshua Apr 2004
Malkin, Michelle Apr 2010
Malley, Matt see Counting Crows
Malone, Kyp see TV on the Radio
Maloney, Carolyn B. Apr 2001
Maloney, Walter E. obit Yrbk 2007
Maltin, Leonard Aug 2008
Mam, Somaly Jun 2009
Mamdani, Mahmood Jan 2010
Manchester, William obit Yrbk 2004
Mandelbrot, Benoît obit Yrbk 2010
Mankiller, Wilma obit Yrbk 2010
Mankind see Foley, Mick
Mankoff, Robert May 2005
Mann, Bosco see Roth, Gabriel
Mann, Emily Jun 2002
Manning, Eli Sep 2008
Mansfield, Michael J. see Mansfield, Mike
Mansfield, Mike obit Jan 2002
Marceau, Marcel obit Yrbk 2007
Marcinko, Richard Mar 2001
Marcus, Bernie Aug 2007
Marcus, George E. Mar 2006
Marcus, Stanley obit Apr 2002
Marcy, Geoffrey W. see Marcy, Geoffrey W., and Butler, R. Paul
Marcy, Geoffrey W., and Butler, R. Paul Nov 2002
Margaret, Princess of Great Britain obit May 2002
Markova, Alicia obit Yrbk 2005
Marks, Leonard H. obit Yrbk 2006
Marlette, Doug Jul 2002 obit Yrbk 2007
Marshall, Burke obit Yrbk 2003
Marshall, Chan see Cat Power
Marshall, Charlyn see Cat Power
Marshall, Grant see Massive Attack

Marshall, Rob Jun 2003
Marta Apr 2008
Martin, A. J. P. see Martin, Archer
Martin, Agnes obit Apr 2005
Martin, Archer obit Yrbk 2002
Martin, Chris see Coldplay
Martin, Demetri Oct 2009
Martin, Dick obit Yrbk 2008
Martin, George R. R. Jan 2004
Martin, James S. Jr. obit Yrbk 2002
Martin, Jesse L. Jul 2006
Martin, Kenyon Jan 2005
Martin, Kevin J. Aug 2005
Martin, Mark Mar 2001
Martin, Roland S. Jun 2009
Martinez, Pedro Jun 2001
Martinez, Rueben Jun 2005
Martinez, Vilma Jul 2004
Martz, Judy Mar 2005
Mary Kay see Ash, Mary Kay
Mashouf, Manny Feb 2009
Massive Attack Jun 2004
Masters, William H. obit May 2001
Mathers, Marshall see Eminem
Mathias, Bob see Mathias, Robert Bruce
Mathias, Charles obit Yrbk 2010
Mathias, Robert Bruce obit Yrbk 2007
Matisyahu Mar 2007
Matsui, Connie L. Aug 2002
Matsui, Robert T. obit Apr 2005
Matsuzaka, Daisuke Apr 2007
Matta obit Yrbk 2003
Mauch, Gene obit Yrbk 2005
Mauer, Joe Aug 2007
Mauldin, Bill obit Jul 2003
Mauldin, William Henry see Mauldin, Bill
May, Brian Oct 2008
Mayer, Jane Oct 2008
Mayer, John Mar 2010
Mayer, Marissa Jan 2010
Mayne, Thom Oct 2005
Mayr, Ernst obit May 2005
Mays, L. Lowry Aug 2003
Mayweather, Floyd Oct 2004
McAdams, Rachel May 2009
McBride, Martina Mar 2004
McCain, John S. Mar 2006
McCambridge, Mercedes obit Yrbk 2004
McCann, Colum Mar 2010
McCann, Renetta May 2005
McCarthy, Eugene J. obit Mar 2006

McCaw, Craig Sep 2001
McChrystal, Stanley Sep 2009
McClanahan, Rue obit Yrbk 2010
McClinton, Marion Jan 2009
McCloskey, Robert obit Yrbk 2003
McClurkin, Donnie Apr 2007
McColough, C. Peter obit Yrbk 2007
McConnell, Addison Mitchell see McConnell, Mitch
McConnell, John M. see McConnell, Mike
McConnell, Mike Apr 2007
McConnell, Mitch Feb 2008
McConnell, Page see Phish
McCourt, Frank obit Yrbk 2009
McCracken, Craig Feb 2004
McCrary, Tex obit Yrbk 2003
McCullough, Gary E. Nov 2009
McCurry, Steve Nov 2005
McDonald, Gabrielle Kirk Oct 2001
McDonald, Trevor Sep 2010
McDonough, William Jul 2006
McDuffie, Dwayne Feb 2010
McFate, Montgomery Aug 2008
McGhee, George Crews obit Yrbk 2005
McGill, Anthony Apr 2009
McGovern, Gail J. Mar 2010
McGrady, Tracy Feb 2003
McGrath, Judy Feb 2005
McGraw, Eloise Jarvis obit Mar 2001
McGraw, Phillip Jun 2002
McGraw, Tim Sep 2002
McGreal, Elizabeth see Yates, Elizabeth
McGruder, Aaron Sep 2001
McGuire, Dorothy obit Nov 2001
McIntire, Carl obit Jun 2002
McIntosh, Millicent Carey obit Mar 2001
McKay, Christopher P. Aug 2009
McKay, Jim obit Yrbk 2008
McKenzie, Bret see Flight of the Conchords
McKeon, Jack Apr 2004
McKinney, Robert obit Yrbk 2001
McLachlin, Beverley Sep 2009
McLaren, Malcolm obit Yrbk 2010
McLaughlin, John Feb 2004

McLean, Jackie Mar 2001 obit
Nov 2006
McLean, John Lenwood *see*
McLean, Jackie
McLurkin, James Sep 2005
McMahon, Ed obit Yrbk 2009
McMath, Sid obit Jan 2004
McNabb, Donovan Jan 2004
McNair, Barbara obit Yrbk
2007
McNair, Steve Jan 2005 obit
Yrbk 2009
McNally, Andrew 3d obit Feb
2002
McNamara, Robert S. obit
Yrbk 2009
McNeil, John Jun 2007
McNerney, James Mar 2008
McNerney, Walter James Jr.
see McNerney, James
McQueen, Alexander Feb
2002 obit Jun 2010
McWhirter, Norris D. obit
Yrbk 2004
McWhorter, John H. Feb 2003
Meat Loaf Nov 2006
Mechem, Edwin L. obit Yrbk
2003
Medvedev, Dmitry Jun 2008
Mehretu, Julie Jul 2010
Meier, Deborah May 2006
Meiselas, Susan Feb 2005
Melford, Myra Apr 2010
Mellers, Wilfrid obit Yrbk
2008
Meloy, Colin *see*
Decemberists
Melton, Douglas A. Jun 2008
Mendes, Sam Oct 2002
Menken, Alan Jan 2001
Menotti, Gian Carlo obit Yrbk
2007
Mercer, James *see* Shins
Merchant, Ismail obit Yrbk
2005
Merchant, Natalie Jan 2003
Meron, Theodor Mar 2005
Merrifield, R. Bruce obit Yrbk
2006
Merrill, Robert obit Feb 2005
Merton, Robert K. obit Yrbk
2003
Meskill, Thomas J. obit Yrbk
2008
Messick, Dale obit Yrbk 2005
Messier, Jean-Marie May 2002
Messing, Debra Aug 2002
Messmer, Pierre obit Yrbk
2007
Meta, Ilir Feb 2002
Metzenbaum, Howard obit
Yrbk 2008
Meyer, Cord Jr. obit Aug 2001

Meyer, Danny Jul 2007
Meyer, Edgar Jun 2002
Meyer, Stephenie Oct 2008
Meyers, Nancy Feb 2002
Meyers, Seth Apr 2009
Miasha Oct 2009
Michel, Sia Sep 2003
Mickelson, Phil Mar 2002
Middelhoff, Thomas Feb 2001
Mihajlov, Mihajlo obit Yrbk
2010
Millan, Cesar Jan 2009
Miller, Ann obit Yrbk 2004
Miller, Arthur obit Jul 2005
Miller, G. William obit Yrbk
2007
Miller, Geoffrey Jul 2010
Miller, J. Irwin obit Yrbk
2004
Miller, Jason obit Yrbk 2001
Miller, John Aug 2003
Miller, Judith Jan 2006
Miller, Marcus Feb 2006
Miller, Matthew *see*
Matisyahu
Miller, Mitch obit Yrbk 2010
Miller, Neal obit Jun 2002
Millionaire, Tony Jul 2005
Millman, Dan Aug 2002
Mills, John obit Yrbk 2005
Milosevic, Slobodan obit
Yrbk 2006
Milosz, Czeslaw obit Yrbk
2004
Mingus, Sue Jul 2008
Mink, Patsy T. obit Jan 2003
Minner, Ruth Ann Aug 2001
Mirabal, Robert Aug 2002
Mirvish, Edwin obit Yrbk
2007
Mitchell, Dean Aug 2002
Mitchell, Elvis Jul 2008
Mitchell, Jerry Oct 2007
Mitchell, Pat Aug 2005
Mitha, Tehreema May 2004
Miyazaki, Hayao Apr 2001
Miyazawa, Kiichi obit Yrbk
2007
Mlodinow, Leonard Jun 2009
Moby Apr 2001
Moen, John *see* Decemberists
Moffo, Anna obit Yrbk 2007
Mohammed bin Rashid Al
Maktoum Apr 2008
Mohammed, W. Deen Jan
2004 obit Yrbk 2008
Mohammed Zahir Shah *see*
Zahir Shah, Mohammed
Moiseiwitsch, Tanya obit Jul
2003
Moiseyev, Igor obit Yrbk 2008
Molina, Alfred Feb 2004
Molloy, Matt *see* Chieftains

Moloney, Paddy *see*
Chieftains
Mondavi, Robert obit Yrbk
2008
Monheit, Jane Feb 2008
Mo'Nique Apr 2010
Monk, T. S. Feb 2002
Monseu, Stephanie *see*
Nelson, Keith and Monseu,
Stephanie
Montagne, Renee Nov 2009
Monte, Elisa Jun 2007
Montero, Gabriela Jul 2007
Montresor, Beni obit Feb
2002
Moore, Ann Aug 2003
Moore, Dudley obit Yrbk
2002
Moore, Elisabeth Luce obit
Yrbk 2002
Moore, George E. obit Yrbk
2008
Moore, Gordon E. Apr 2002
Moore, Paul Jr. obit Yrbk
2003
Moore, Thomas W. obit Yrbk
2007
Moorer, Thomas H. obit Yrbk
2004
Moran, John Jun 2010
Morella, Constance A. Feb
2001
Moretti, Fabrizio *see* Strokes
Morgan, Tracy Mar 2007
Morhaime, Michael Apr 2010
Morial, Marc Jan 2002
Morris, Butch Jul 2005
Morris, Errol Feb 2001
Morris, James T. Mar 2005
Morris, Lawrence *see* Morris,
Butch
Morrison, Philip obit Aug
2005
Mortensen, Viggo Jun 2004
Mortenson, Greg Sep 2009
Mortimer, John obit Yrbk
2009
Mos Def Apr 2005
Mosbacher, Robert obit Yrbk
2010
Moseka, Aminata *see*
Lincoln, Abbey
Mosel, Tad obit Yrbk 2008
Moses, Bob *see* Moses,
Robert P.
Moses, Robert P. Apr 2002
Mosley, Sugar Shane Jan 2001
Mosley, Timothy *see*
Timbaland
Moss, Adam Mar 2004
Moss, Frank E. obit Jun 2003
Moss, Randy Jan 2006

Moten, Etta *see* Barnett, Etta Moten

Motley, Constance Baker obit Feb 2006

Mott, Stewart R. obit Yrbk 2008

Moulitsas Zúniga, Markos ("Kos") Mar 2007

Mousavi, Mir Hossein Sep 2009

Moynihan, Daniel Patrick obit Yrbk 2003

Mueller, Robert Aug 2010

Mugler, Thierry Aug 2010

Muhammad, Warith Deen *see* Mohammed, W. Deen

Mukasey, Michael B. Feb 2008

Mulcahy, Anne M. Nov 2002

Mullen, Michael *see* Mullen, Mike

Mullen, Mike Feb 2008

Murguía, Janet Jan 2010

Murkowski, Frank H. Jul 2003

Murphy, Mark Sep 2004

Murphy, Thomas obit Yrbk 2006

Murray, Bill Sep 2004

Murray, Donald M. Jul 2006

Murray, Elizabeth obit Yrbk 2007

Murray, Jonathan *see* Bunim, Mary-Ellis, and Murray, Jonathan

Murray, Ty May 2002

Musharraf, Pervaiz *see* Musharraf, Pervez

Musharraf, Pervez Mar 2001

Musk, Elon Oct 2006

Muzorewa, Abel Tendekai obit Yrbk 2010

Mwanawasa, Levy obit Yrbk 2008

My Morning Jacket Nov 2008

Mydans, Carl M. obit Yrbk 2004

Mydans, Shelley Smith obit Aug 2002

Myers, B. R. Jun 2010

Myers, Brian Reynolds *see* Myers, B. R.

Myers, Joel N. Apr 2005

Myers, Richard B. Apr 2002

Nabrit, Samuel M. obit Yrbk 2004

Nachtigall, Paul E. Jan 2006

Nagin, C. Ray Jan 2006

Naidoo, Kumi Sep 2010

Najimy, Kathy Oct 2002

Nakamura, Dan May 2007

Napolitano, Janet Oct 2004 Mar 2009

Narayan, R. K. obit Jul 2001

Nas Sep 2009

Nash, Steve Mar 2003

Nason, John W. obit Feb 2002

Nasser, Jacques Apr 2001

Nathan, Robert R. obit Nov 2001

Navratilova, Martina Feb 2004

Nawasha, Taboo *see* Black Eyed Peas

Ne Win obit Yrbk 2003

Neal, Patricia obit Yrbk 2010

Neals, Otto Feb 2003

Neeleman, David Sep 2003

Negroponte, John Apr 2003

Nehru, B. K. obit Feb 2002

Nelly Oct 2002

Nelson, Byron obit Yrbk 2007

Nelson, Don May 2007

Nelson, Gaylord obit Yrbk 2005

Nelson, Keith and Monseu, Stephanie Jun 2005

Nelson, Marilyn Carlson Oct 2004

Nelson, Stanley May 2005

Neptunes, The May 2004

Nerina, Nadia obit Yrbk 2008

Neto, Ernesto Oct 2009

Neuhaus, Richard John obit Yrbk 2009

Neustadt, Richard E. obit Yrbk 2004

Newkirk, Ingrid Apr 2008

Newkirk, Kori Mar 2008

Newman, Arnold obit Yrbk 2006

Newman, Edwin obit Yrbk 2010

Newman, J. Wilson obit Yrbk 2003

Newman, Paul obit Yrbk 2008

Newmark, Craig Jun 2005

Newsom, Lee Ann Oct 2004

Newton, Helmut obit Yrbk 2004

Nguyen Van Thieu *see* Thieu, Nguyen Van

Nicol, Simon *see* Fairport Convention

Nikolayev, Andrian obit Yrbk 2004

Nilsson, Birgit obit Sep 2006

Nimeiri, Gaafar Mohammed *see* Nimeiry, Gaafar Muhammad al-

Nimeiry, Gaafar Muhammad al- obit Yrbk 2009

Nimeiry, Jaafar Muhammad Al- *see* Nimeiry, Gaafar Muhammad al-

Nirenberg, Marshall Warren obit Yrbk 2010

Nitze, Paul H. obit Mar 2005

Nixon, Agnes Apr 2001

Nixon, Marni Oct 2009

Nofziger, Lyn obit Yrbk 2006

Nolan, Christopher obit Yrbk 2009

Noland, Kenneth obit Yrbk 2010

Nooyi, Indra K. Nov 2006

Norman, Christina Nov 2007

Norquist, Grover Oct 2007

Norris, Michele Mar 2008

Northrop, Peggy Nov 2009

Norton, Andre obit Yrbk 2005

Norton, Gale A. Jun 2001

Nottage, Lynn Nov 2004

Nouvel, Jean Sep 2008

Novacek, Michael J. Sep 2002

Nowitzki, Dirk Jun 2002

Nozick, Robert obit Apr 2002

Nugent, Ted Apr 2005

Nykvist, Sven obit Yrbk 2007

Obama, Barack Jul 2005 Mar 2009

Obama, Michelle Oct 2008

Obote, Milton obit Yrbk 2006

O'Brien, Ed *see* Radiohead

O'Brien, Soledad Nov 2009

Ochocinco, Chad Aug 2009

O'Connor, Carroll obit Sep 2001

O'Connor, Donald obit Apr 2004

O'Day, Anita obit Jan 2007

Odetta obit Jan 2009

Odierno, Ray Nov 2009

Odom, Lamar May 2009

Offit, Paul A. Apr 2009

Ogilvie, Elisabeth obit Yrbk 2007

O'Hair, Madalyn Murray obit Jun 2001

O'Hara, Kelli Oct 2008

Ohlin, Lloyd E. obit Yrbk 2009

Ohno, Apolo Anton Feb 2006

O'Horgan, Tom obit Yrbk 2009

O'Keefe, Sean Jan 2003

Okrent, Daniel Nov 2004

Olbermann, Keith Feb 2009

Olin, Lena Jun 2003

Olitski, Jules obit Yrbk 2007

Oliver, Garrett Nov 2008

Oliver, Pam Jul 2009

Ollila, Jorma Aug 2002

Olopade, Olufunmilayo Sep 2006

Olsen, Ashley *see* Olsen, Mary-Kate and Ashley

Olsen, Mary-Kate and Ashley Sep 2010
Olson, Ted *see* Olson, Theodore
Olson, Theodore Nov 2010
O'Malley, Sean Patrick Jan 2004
Omarion Feb 2008
O'Neal, Jermaine Jun 2004
O'Neal, Stanley May 2003
O'Neill, Joseph Jun 2009
O'Neill, Paul H. Jul 2001
O'Neill, William A. obit Yrbk 2008
Oppenheim, Chad Sep 2006
Orbach, Jerry obit Apr 2005
O'Reilly, Bill Oct 2003
Orender, Donna Sep 2010
Orlean, Susan Jun 2003
Orman, Suze May 2003
Ortega, Kenny Mar 2008
Ortiz, David Aug 2005
Ortner, Sherry B. Nov 2002
Osawa, Sandra Sunrising Jan 2001
Osborne, Barrie M. Feb 2005
Osbourne, Sharon Jan 2001
Osteen, Joel Jan 2006
Otis, Clarence Jr. Oct 2009
Oudolf, Piet Apr 2003
Ouma, Kassim Jun 2007
OutKast Apr 2004
Ovechkin, Alexander Jun 2008
Oz, Mehmet C. Apr 2003

Pääbo, Svante Feb 2007
Paar, Jack obit Yrbk 2004
Pace, Peter Jun 2006
Pacelle, Wayne Jan 2010
Page, Clarence Jan 2003
Page, Ellen May 2008
Page, Larry *see* Brin, Sergey, and Page, Larry
Paige, Roderick R. Jul 2001
Paik, Nam June obit Yrbk 2006
Painter, Nell Irvin Jun 2010
Palade, George E. obit Yrbk 2008
Palance, Jack obit Feb 2007
Paley, Grace obit Yrbk 2007
Palin, Sarah Jan 2009
Palmeiro, Rafael Aug 2001
Palmer, Keith *see* Prodigy
Palmer, Violet Nov 2006
Paltrow, Gwyneth Jan 2005
Pandit, Vikram Jun 2008
Panofsky, Wolfgang K. H. obit Yrbk 2007
Paper Rad Apr 2010
Pareles, Jon Nov 2008

Park Ji-Sung Apr 2010
Park, Linda Sue Jun 2002
Park, Rosemary obit Yrbk 2004
Parker, Mary-Louise Apr 2006
Parker, Robert B. obit Yrbk 2010
Parker, Robert M. May 2005
Parker, Tony Apr 2008
Parks, Gordon obit Jun 2006
Parks, Rosa obit Jan 2006
Parsons, Richard D. Apr 2003
Pascal, Amy Mar 2002
Passmore, George *see* Gilbert and George
Patchett, Ann Apr 2003
Paterson, David Jul 2008
Patrick, Danica Oct 2005
Patrick, Deval May 2007
Patterson, Floyd obit Yrbk 2007
Patty, Sandi Feb 2004
Patton, Antwan *see* Outkast
Pau, Peter Feb 2002
Paul, Chris Nov 2009
Paul, Les obit Yrbk 2009
Paul, Ron Jun 2008
Paulson, Henry M. Jr. Sep 2002
Paulus, Diane May 2010
Pavarotti, Luciano obit Nov 2007
Payne, Alexander Feb 2003
Payton, John May 2010
Paz Estenssoro, Victor obit Sep 2001
Pearman, Raven-Simone *see* Raven-Simone
Peart, Neil *see* Rush
Peavy, Jake May 2010
Peck, Gregory obit Sep 2003
Peck, M. Scott obit Yrbk 2005
Pegg, Dave *see* Fairport Convention
Peirce, Kimberly Aug 2008
Peirsol, Aaron Jun 2010
Pekar, Harvey Jan 2004 obit Oct 2010
Pelikan, Jaroslav obit Yrbk 2006
Pell, Claiborne obit Yrbk 2009
Pelosi, Nancy Feb 2003
Pelt, Jeremy Feb 2009
Peltz, Nelson Feb 2008
Pelzer, Dave Mar 2002
Pemberton, John de J. Jr. obit Yrbk 2010
Penn, Arthur obit Yrbk 2010
Penn, Irving obit Yrbk 2009
Pennington, Chad Oct 2009
Pennington, Ty Feb 2006
Pepperberg, Irene Sep 2008
Perdue, Frank obit Oct 2005
Perera, Frederica Oct 2010

Pérez Jiménez, Marcos obit Feb 2002
Pérez, Louie *see* Los Lobos
Perino, Dana Jan 2008
Perkins, Charles obit Feb 2001
Perkins, Elizabeth Jan 2007
Perle, Richard Jul 2003
Perry, Joe *see* Aerosmith
Perry, Tyler Jun 2005
Person, Houston Jun 2003
Perutz, Max obit Apr 2002
Petersen, Wolfgang Jul 2001
Peterson, Martha obit Yrbk 2006
Peterson, Oscar obit Yrbk 2008
Petraeus, David H. Apr 2007
Pettibon, Raymond Apr 2005
Pevear, Richard and Volokhonsky, Larissa Jun 2006
Peyroux, Madeleine Nov 2005
Phelps, Michael Aug 2004
Phillips, Peter *see* Rock, Pete
Phillips, Sam Apr 2001
Phillips, Scott *see* Creed
Phillips, William obit Yrbk 2002
Phish Jul 2003
Phoenix *see* Linkin Park
Piano, Renzo Apr 2001
Piccard, Jacques obit Yrbk 2009
Picciotto, Guy *see* Fugazi
Pickering, William H. obit Yrbk 2004
Piel, Gerard obit Feb 2005
Pierce, David Hyde Apr 2001
Pierce, John Robinson obit Jun 2002
Pierce, Paul Nov 2002
Pierce, Samuel R. Jr. obit Feb 2001
Pierce, Wendell Aug 2010
Pifer, Alan J. obit Yrbk 2006
Pincay, Laffit Sep 2001
Pineda Lindo, Allan *see* Black Eyed Peas
Piñera, Sebastián Nov 2010
Pingree, Chellie Jan 2005
Pinochet, Augusto obit Yrbk 2007
Pinter, Harold obit Jul 2009
Pisani, Elizabeth Aug 2010
Pitt, Harvey Nov 2002
Pitts, Leonard Jr. Oct 2004
Plain, Belva obit Yrbk 2010

Plater-Zyberk, Elizabeth *see* Duany, Andrés and Plater-Zyberk, Elizabeth

Plimpton, George obit Jan 2004

Plimpton, Martha Apr 2002

Plouffe, David Jun 2009

Podesta, John D. Feb 2010

Poehler, Amy Aug 2008

Poletti, Charles obit Yrbk 2002

Polgar, Susan Feb 2008

Polgár, Zsuzsanna *see* Polgar, Susan

Polivka, Galen *see* Hold Steady, The

Pollack, Sydney obit Sep 2008

Pollan, Michael Oct 2007

Pollitt, Katha Oct 2002

Polsfuss, Lester William *see* Paul, Les

Pomeroy, Wardell B. obit Yrbk 2001

Popeil, Ron Mar 2001

Posen, Zac Jul 2006

Posey, Parker Mar 2003

Poston, Tom obit Yrbk 2007

Potok, Chaim obit Yrbk 2002

Potter, Myrtle S. Aug 2004

Poujade, Pierre obit Yrbk 2004

Powell, Colin L. Nov 2001

Powell, Jody obit Yrbk 2009

Powell, Joseph Lester Jr. *see* Powell, Jody

Powell, Kevin Jan 2004

Powell, Michael K. May 2003

Power, Samantha Aug 2008

Prada, Miuccia Feb 2006

Prado, Edgar Sep 2007

Pressel, Morgan Nov 2007

Prigogine, Ilya obit Yrbk 2003

Prince, Charles O. III Jan 2007

Prince-Hughes, Dawn Apr 2005

Prinze, Freddie Jr. Jan 2003

Prodigy Oct 2009

Proesch, Gilbert *see* Gilbert and George

Profumo, John obit Jun 2006

Prokhorov, Mikhail Oct 2010

Prosper, Pierre-Richard Aug 2005

Proxmire, William obit Mar 2006

Pryor, Richard obit Apr 2006

Pujols, Albert Sep 2004

Purdie, Bernard Jan 2010

Pusey, Nathan M. obit Feb 2002

Pym, Francis obit Yrbk 2008

Queloz, Didier Feb 2002

Query, Nate *see* Decemberists

Quine, W. V. obit Mar 2001

Quine, Willard Van Orman *see* Quine, W. V.

Quinn, Aidan Apr 2005

Quinn, Anthony obit Sep 2001

Quinn, William F. obit Yrbk 2006

Rabassa, Gregory Jan 2005

Racette, Patricia Feb 2003

Radcliffe, Daniel Nov 2010

Radiohead Jun 2001

Rahman, A. R. Jun 2009

Rahmstorf, Stefan Feb 2010

Raimi, Sam Jul 2002

Rainier III, Prince of Monaco obit Yrbk 2005

Rakic, Patricia Goldman *see* Goldman-Rakic, Patricia

Rakim Aug 2008

Rakoff, David Nov 2007

Rakowski, Mieczyslaw obit Feb 2009

Rall, Ted May 2002

Ralston, Joseph W. Jan 2001

Rama Rau, Santha obit Yrbk 2009

Ramirez, Hanley Apr 2009

Ramirez, Manny Jun 2002

Ramirez, Tina Nov 2004

Ramonet, Ignacio Jun 2008

Ramos, Jorge Mar 2004

Rampling, Charlotte Jun 2002

Rampone, Christie Oct 2004

Randall, Lisa May 2006

Randall, Tony obit Yrbk 2004

Randolph, Willie Sep 2005

Rania Feb 2001

Rankin, Ian Jan 2008

Rao, P. V. Narasimha obit Yrbk 2005

Rascal Flatts Aug 2003

Ratzinger, Joseph *see* Benedict XVI

Rau, Johannes obit Yrbk 2006

Rauschenberg, Robert obit Aug 2008

Raven *see* Raven-Symone

Raven-Symone Sep 2008

Ravenstahl, Luke Aug 2008

Ravitch, Diane Nov 2010

Rawl, Lawrence obit Yrbk 2005

Rawls, Lou obit Oct 2006

Ray, Rachael Aug 2005

Reagan, Ronald obit Sep 2004

Reality, Maxim *see* Prodigy

Redd, Michael Mar 2005

Redgrave, Lynn obit Yrbk 2010

Redgrave, Vanessa Sep 2003

Redlener, Irwin Nov 2007

Reeve, Christopher obit Jan 2005

Reeves, Dan Oct 2001

Reeves, Dianne Jul 2006

Regan, Donald T. obit Yrbk 2003

Rehnquist, William H. Nov 2003 obit Yrbk 2005

Reich, Walter Aug 2005

Reichs, Kathy Oct 2006

Reid, Antonio *see* Reid, L. A.

Reid, Harry Mar 2003

Reid, L. A. Aug 2001

Reid, Whitelaw obit Yrbk 2009

Reilly, John C. Oct 2004

Reilly, Rick Feb 2005

Reinhardt, Uwe E. Mar 2004

Reinking, Ann Jun 2004

Reitman, Ivan Mar 2001

Rell, M. Jodi Sep 2005

Ressler, Robert K. Feb 2002

Reuss, Henry S. obit Mar 2002

Reuther, Victor obit Yrbk 2004

Revel, Jean Francois obit Yrbk 2006

Reyes, José Aug 2008

Reyes, Silvestre Sep 2007

Reynolds, Glenn Harlan Oct 2007

Reynolds, John W. Jr. obit Mar 2002

Reynoso, Cruz Mar 2002

Rhodes, James A. obit Jul 2001

Rhodes, John J. obit Yrbk 2004

Rhodes, Randi Feb 2005

Rhyne, Charles S. obit Yrbk 2003

Rice, Condoleezza Apr 2001

Richards, Ann obit Yrbk 2007

Richards, Cecile May 2007

Richards, Lloyd obit Yrbk 2007

Richardson, Robert Jan 2010

Richler, Mordecai obit Oct 2001

Richter, Gerhard Jun 2002

Rickey, George W. obit Yrbk 2002

Ricks, Thomas E. Nov 2007

Rideau, Wilbert Nov 2010

Ridge, Tom Feb 2001

Riefenstahl, Leni obit Yrbk 2004

Riesman, David obit Yrbk 2002

Rihanna Nov 2007

Riley, Terry Apr 2002
Rimm, Sylvia B. Feb 2002
Rimsza, Skip Jul 2002
Rines, Robert H. Jan 2003 obit Yrbk 2010
Rinfret, Pierre A. obit Yrbk 2006
Riopelle, Jean-Paul obit Yrbk 2002
Ripley, Alexandra obit Yrbk 2004
Ripley, S. Dillon obit Aug 2001
Risen, James Aug 2007
Ritchie, Robert James see Kid Rock
Ritter, John obit Yrbk 2004
Rivers, Doc Nov 2008
Rivers, Larry obit Nov 2002
Rizzuto, Phil obit Yrbk 2007
Roach, Max obit Nov 2007
Robaina, Alejandro obit Yrbk 2010
Robards, Jason Jr. obit Mar 2001
Robb, J. D. see Roberts, Nora
Robbe-Grillet, Alain obit Yrbk 2008
Robbins, Anthony see Robbins, Tony
Robbins, Frederick C. obit Yrbk 2003
Robbins, Tony Jul 2001
Roberts, John G. Feb 2006
Roberts, John G. Jr. see Roberts, John G.
Roberts, Michael V. and Steven C. Feb 2010
Roberts, Nora Sep 2001
Roberts, Oral obit Feb 2010
Roberts, Robin [baseball player] obit Yrbk 2010
Roberts, Robin [broadcast journalist] Feb 2008
Roberts, Steven C. see Roberts, Michael V. and Steven C.
Roberts, Tony Oct 2006
Robinson, Arthur H. obit Yrbk 2005
Robinson, Eddie obit Yrbk 2007
Robinson, Janet L. Mar 2003
Robinson, Marilynne Oct 2005
Robinson, Peter Sep 2007
Rochberg, George obit Yrbk 2005
Roche, James M. obit Yrbk 2004
Rock, Pete Aug 2009
Rockefeller, Laurance S. obit Yrbk 2004

Rockwell, Llewellyn H. Jr. Jun 2007
Roddick, Andy Jan 2004
Roddick, Anita obit Yrbk 2007
Rodino, Peter W. obit Yrbk 2005
Rodriguez, Alex Apr 2003
Rodriguez, Arturo Mar 2001
Rodriguez, Ivan Jun 2009
Rogers, Fred obit Jul 2003
Rogers, John W. Jr. Aug 2010
Rogers, William P. obit Mar 2001
Roh Moo Hyun obit Yrbk 2009
Roh Moo-hyun see Roh Moo Hyun
Rohmer, Eric obit Yrbk 2010
Rojas, Rudy Jan 2006
Rollins, Edward J. Mar 2001
Rollins, Henry Sep 2001
Romenesko, Jim Feb 2004
Romer, John Jul 2003
Romero, Anthony Jul 2002
Romney, Mitt Sep 2006
Rooney, Joe Don see Rascal Flatts
Rosas, Cesar see Los Lobos
Rose, Jalen Mar 2004
Rose, Jim Mar 2003
Rosenfeld, Irene B. Jul 2007
Rosenthal, A. M. obit Sep 2006
Rosenthal, Joe obit Yrbk 2007
Rospars, Joe May 2010
Ross, Alex Nov 2007
Ross, Gary May 2004
Ross, Herbert obit Feb 2002
Ross, Jerilyn Nov 2009 obit Yrbk 2010
Ross, Robert Oct 2002
Rostenkowski, Dan obit Yrbk 2010
Rostow, Eugene V. obit Yrbk 2003
Rostow, Walt W. obit Jul 2003
Rostropovich, Mstislav obit Aug 2007
Rotblat, Joseph obit Feb 2006
Rote, Kyle obit Yrbk 2002
Roth, Gabriel Feb 2010
Roth, William V. Jr. obit Yrbk 2004
Rothschild, Baron Guy de obit Yrbk 2007
Rothschild, Miriam obit Yrbk 2005
Rounds, Michael Jun 2006
Rowan, Carl T. obit Jan 2001

Rowland, Kelly see Destiny's Child
Rowley, Janet D. Mar 2001
Rowntree, David see Blur
Rubenstein, Atoosa Oct 2004
Rubin, Edward M. Jan 2006
Rubin, Rick Sep 2007
Rubin, William S. obit Yrbk 2007
Rucker, Rudy May 2008
Rudd, Paul obit Yrbk 2010
Rudd, Phil see AC/DC
Rukeyser, Louis obit Nov 2006
Rule, Ja see Ja Rule
Rumsfeld, Donald H. Mar 2002
Rus, Daniela Feb 2004
Rusesabagina, Paul May 2005
Rush Feb 2001
Russell, Anna obit Yrbk 2007
Russell, Harold obit Apr 2002
Russell, Kurt Nov 2004
Russert, Tim obit Yrbk 2008
Russo, Patricia May 2008
Rutan, Burt Jun 2005
Ryan, George H. Sep 2001
Ryan, Rex Oct 2010
Ryder, Jonathan see Ludlum, Robert
Ryer, Jonathan see Ludlum, Robert

Saab, Elie Aug 2004
Saakashvili, Mikheil May 2009
Sabah, Jaber Al-Ahmad Al-Jaber Al-, Sheik obit Yrbk 2006
Sabathia, C. C. Apr 2008
Safina, Carl Apr 2005
Safire, William obit Yrbk 2009
Sagan, Francoise obit Feb 2005
Said, Edward W. obit Feb 2004
Saint Laurent, Yves obit Oct 2008
Salazar, Ken Mar 2009
Sales, Soupy obit Yrbk 2009
Salinger, J. D. obit Yrbk 2010
Salinger, Jerome David see Salinger, J. D.
Salinger, Pierre obit Feb 2005
Samaranch, Juan Antonio obit Yrbk 2010
Samuelson, Paul A. obit Yrbk 2010
Sánchez, David Nov 2001
Sanchez Junco, Eduardo obit Yrbk 2010
Sandberg, Sheryl Jun 2008

Sanders, Ric *see* Fairport
Convention
Sandford, John Mar 2002
Sándor, György obit Yrbk
2006
Sandoval, Jesse *see* Shins
Sanger, Stephen Mar 2004
Sansone, Pat *see* Wilco
Santana, Johan Jul 2006
Santelli, Rick Jul 2010
Santos, José Nov 2003
Sapolsky, Robert Jan 2004
Sapp, Warren Sep 2003
Saramago, José Jun 2002 obit
Yrbk 2010
Sardi, Vincent Jr. obit Yrbk
2008
Sarris, Andrew Jan 2007
Saulnier, Raymond J. obit
Yrbk 2009
Savage, Dan Jul 2009
Savage, Rick *see* Def Leppard
Savimbi, Jonas obit Jun 2002
Saxbe, William obit Yrbk
2010
Sayles Belton, Sharon Jan
2001
Sayre, Francis Jr. obit Yrbk
2008
Scammon, Richard M. obit
Sep 2001
Scannell, Herb Aug 2010
Scaturro, Pasquale V. Oct
2005
Scavullo, Francesco obit Yrbk
2004
Scdoris, Rachael Jul 2005
Scelsa, Vin May 2006
Scelsa, Vincent *see* Scelsa,
Vin
Schaap, Phil Sep 2001
Schakowsky, Jan Jul 2004
Schell, Maria obit Yrbk 2005
Scheuer, James obit Apr 2006
Schieffer, Bob Aug 2006
Schillebeeckx, Edward obit
May 2010
Schiller, Vivian Oct 2009
Schilling, Curt Oct 2001
Schindler, Alexander M. obit
Feb 2001
Schirra, Walter M. obit Yrbk
2007
Schjeldahl, Peter Oct 2005
Schlein, Miriam obit Yrbk
2005
Schlesinger, Arthur M. Jr. obit
Aug 2007
Schlesinger, John obit Yrbk
2003
Schmidt, Eric Apr 2008
Schoenberg, Loren Feb 2005

Scholder, Fritz obit Yrbk
2005
Schorr, Daniel obit Yrbk 2010
Schott, Marge obit Yrbk 2004
Schriever, Bernard obit Yrbk
2005
Schroeder, Frederick R. obit
Yrbk 2006
Schroeder, Ted *see*
Schroeder, Frederick R.
Schulberg, Budd obit Yrbk
2009
Schultes, Richard Evans obit
Sep 2001
Schultz, Ed Aug 2005
Schwartz, Gil Aug 2007
Schwartz, Pepper Jun 2008
Schwartz, Tony obit Yrbk
2008
Schwartzman, Jason Oct 2009
Schwarzenegger, Arnold Aug
2004
Schwarzkopf, Elisabeth obit
Yrbk 2006
Scofield, Paul obit Yrbk 2008
Scorsese, Martin Jun 2007
Scott, Christian Jan 2008
Scott, George obit Yrbk 2005
see Blind Boys of Alabama
Scott, H. Lee Oct 2006
Scott, Jill Jan 2002
Scott, Robert L. Jr. obit Yrbk
2006
Scott, Tony Nov 2004
Scottoline, Lisa Jul 2001
Scully, Vin Oct 2001
Seacrest, Ryan Sep 2009
Seamans, Robert C. obit Yrbk
2008
Sean Paul Jan 2007
Sears, Martha *see* Sears,
William and Martha
Sears, William and Martha
Aug 2001
Seau, Junior Sep 2001
Sebelius, Kathleen Nov 2004
Sedaris, Amy Apr 2002
Segal, Erich obit Yrbk 2010
Seidman, L. William obit
Yrbk 2009
Seitz, Frederick obit Yrbk
2008
Selick, Henry May 2009
Selway, Phil *see* Radiohead
Sembène, Ousmane obit Yrbk
2007
Semel, Terry Jul 2006
Senghor, Léopold Sédar obit
Mar 2002
Serrano Súñer, Ramón obit
Yrbk 2004
Servan-Schreiber, Jean-
Jacques obit Yrbk 2007

Settle, Mary Lee obit Yrbk
2006
Setzer, Philip *see* Emerson
String Quartet
Seymour, Lesley Jane Nov
2001
Seymour, Stephanie Oct 2002
Shahade, Jennifer Sep 2005
Shaheen, Jeanne Jan 2001
Shales, Tom Jan 2009
Shalhoub, Tony Nov 2002
Shamsie, Kamila Sep 2009
Shapiro, Irving S. obit Nov
2001
Shapiro, Neal May 2003
Shaw, Artie obit Apr 2005
Shaw, Dash Jan 2009
Shawcross, Hartley obit Yrbk
2003
Shearer, Harry Jun 2001
Shearer, Moira obit Yrbk 2006
Sheehan, Cindy May 2007
Sheikh Hamad bin Khalifa al-
Thani Jul 2009
Sheldon, Sidney obit Yrbk
2007
Shepherd, Michael *see*
Ludlum, Robert
Shields, Mark May 2005
Shinoda, Mike *see* Linkin
Park
Shins Jun 2007
Shinseki, Eric K. Mar 2009
Shoemaker, Willie obit Apr
2004
Short, Bobby obit Nov 2005
Shriver, Eunice Kennedy obit
Yrbk 2009
Shriver, Lionel Sep 2005
Shubin, Neil Apr 2007
Shumway, Norman E. obit
Yrbk 2006
Shyamalan, M. Night Mar
2003
Siddons, Anne Rivers Jan
2005
Siegel, Robert Jul 2008
Siemionow, Maria May 2009
Siepi, Cesare obit Yrbk 2010
Sigismondi, Floria Jul 2010
Sigurdardottir, Johanna Jul
2010
Sills, Beverly obit Oct 2007
Silva, Daniel Apr 2007
Silver, Joel Nov 2003
Silverman, Sarah Jul 2006
Simionato, Giulietta obit Yrbk
2010
Simmons, Earl *see* DMX
Simmons, Jean obit Yrbk
2010
Simon, Claude obit Yrbk 2005
Simon, David Jun 2008

Simon, Herbert A. obit May 2001
Simon, Paul obit Yrbk 2004
Simone, Gail Nov 2008
Simone, Nina obit Yrbk 2003
Simons, David G. obit Yrbk 2010
Simpson, India Arie see India Arie
Simpson, John Jun 2010
Simpson, Lorna Nov 2004
Sin, Jaime obit Yrbk 2005
Sinclair, Cameron Apr 2008
Sinclair, David A. Sep 2008
Sinegal, James D. Aug 2007
Singer, Bryan Apr 2005
Singh, V.P. see Singh, Vishwanath Pratap
Singh, Vishwanath Pratap obit Yrbk 2009
Sinopoli, Giuseppe obit Sep 2001
Sisco, Joseph obit Yrbk 2005
Sissi Jun 2001
Sitek, David see TV on the Radio
Sittenfeld, Curtis Nov 2008
Sizemore, Grady Apr 2010
Sklansky, David Apr 2007
Slash Mar 2008
Slater, Kelly Jul 2001
Slaughter, Frank obit Yrbk 2006
Slavenska, Mia obit Apr 2003
Smathers, George A. obit Jun 2007
Smiley, Tavis Apr 2003
Smith, Ali Jun 2006
Smith, Amy Jun 2005
Smith, Chesterfield H. obit Yrbk 2003
Smith, Dante Terrell see Mos Def
Smith, Elinor Mar 2001 obit Yrbk 2010
Smith, Gary Jan 2009
Smith, Gerard see TV on the Radio
Smith, Howard K. obit Aug 2002
Smith, Ian obit Feb 2008
Smith, Jeff obit Yrbk 2004
Smith, Kiki Mar 2005
Smith, Lovie Sep 2007
Smith, Maggie Jul 2002
Smith, Mike Sep 2010
Smith, Orin C. Nov 2003
Smith, Roger B. obit Yrbk 2008
Smith, Steve Sep 2006
Smith, Virginia B. obit Yrbk 2010
Smits, Jimmy May 2006
Smuin, Michael obit Yrbk 2007

Smylie, Robert E. obit Yrbk 2004
Smyslov, Vasily see Smyslov, Vassily
Smyslov, Vassily obit Yrbk 2010
Smyslov, Vassily see Smyslov, Vassily
Snead, Sam obit Yrbk 2002
Snider, Stacey Apr 2008
Snodgrass, W. D. obit Yrbk 2009
Snow, John Aug 2003
Snow, Tony Sep 2006 obit Yrbk 2008
Snyder, Tom obit Yrbk 2007
Soderberg, Alicia M. Oct 2009
Söderström, Elisabeth obit Yrbk 2010
Soeharto obit Yrbk 2008
Soffer, Olga Jul 2002
Solis, Hilda L. Mar 2009
Solmonese, Joe Oct 2009
Solomon, Phil Oct 2007
Solomon, Susan Jul 2005
Solzhenitsyn, Aleksandr obit Nov 2008
Sontag, Susan obit May 2005
Sothern, Ann obit Aug 2001
Sotomayor, Sonia Oct 2009
Souzay, Gérard obit Yrbk 2004
Spade, Kate Apr 2007
Spahn, Warren obit Yrbk 2004
Spalding, Esperanza Aug 2010
Sparano, Tony Jan 2010
Spark, Muriel obit Yrbk 2007
Sparks, Nicholas Feb 2001
Specter, Arlen Aug 2009
Spektor, Regina Jul 2007
Spelke, Elizabeth Apr 2006
Spelling, Aaron obit Yrbk 2006
Spellings, Margaret Jun 2005
Spence, Hartzell obit Yrbk 2001
Spencer, John Jan 2001 obit Yrbk 2006
Spencer, Scott Jul 2003
Spergel, David Jan 2005
Speyer, Jerry May 2008
Spillane, Mickey obit Nov 2006
Spiropulu, Maria May 2004
Spitzer, Eliot Mar 2003
Sprewell, Latrell Feb 2001
Sprinkel, Beryl obit Yrbk 2009
Squyres, Steven Nov 2006
St. John, Robert obit Yrbk 2003

St. Laurent, Yves see Saint Laurent, Yves
St. Louis, Martin Feb 2007
Stabenow, Debbie Feb 2006
Stackhouse, Jerry Nov 2001
Stafford, Robert T. obit Yrbk 2008
Staley, Dawn Apr 2005
Stamberg, Susan Oct 2008
Stanfield, Robert Lorne obit Yrbk 2004
Stanley, Kim obit Jan 2002
Stanton, Andrew Feb 2004
Stanton, Bill May 2001
Stanton, Frank obit Yrbk 2007
Stapleton, Maureen obit Nov 2006
Stapp, Scott see Creed
Stargell, Willie obit Sep 2001
Starr, Chauncey obit Yrbk 2007
Stassen, Harold E. obit May 2001
Steele, Claude M. Feb 2001
Steele, Michael S. Jul 2004
Steig, William obit Apr 2004
Steiger, Rod obit Yrbk 2002
Stein, Benjamin J. Sep 2001
Stein, Janice Gross Aug 2006
Steinbrenner, George obit Yrbk 2010
Steingraber, Sandra Sep 2003
Steitz, Joan A. Jun 2007
Stephens, John see Legend, John
Stern, Isaac obit Jan 2002
Stern, Jessica May 2006
Stevens, Ted Oct 2001 obit Yrbk 2010
Stever, H. G. obit Yrbk 2010
Steves, Richard see Steves, Rick
Steves, Rick Jan 2009
Stew Sep 2007
Steward, David L. Nov 2004
Stewart, Alice obit Yrbk 2002
Stewart, James "Bubba" Feb 2005
Stewart, Jon Jul 2004
Stewart, Mark see Stew
Stewart, Thomas obit Yrbk 2007
Stewart, Tony Nov 2006
Stewart, William H. obit Yrbk 2008
Stiefel, Ethan Apr 2004
Stirratt, John see Wilco
Stockhausen, Karlheinz obit Yrbk 2008
Stoller, Debbie Aug 2007
Stoltenberg, Gerhard obit Mar 2002
Stolz, Mary obit Yrbk 2007

Stone, W. Clement obit Yrbk 2002

Storch, Gerald L. Jun 2007

Storr, Anthony obit Sep 2001

Stott, John May 2005

Straight, Michael obit Yrbk 2004

Stratton, Dorothy obit Yrbk 2006

Stratton, William G. obit Aug 2001

Straus, Roger W. Jr. obit Yrbk 2004

Streb, Elizabeth Apr 2003

Stringer, Howard Jan 2006

Stroessner, Alfredo obit Yrbk 2007

Strokes, The Feb 2007

Stroman, Susan Jul 2002

Struzan, Drew Mar 2005

Stuart, Gloria obit Yrbk 2010

Stuhlinger, Ernst obit Yrbk 2008

Stutz, Geraldine obit Yrbk 2005

Styron, William obit Yrbk 2007

Subandrio obit Apr 2005

Sucksdorff, Arne obit Sep 2001

Sugar, Bert Randolph Nov 2002

Sullivan, Daniel Feb 2003

Sullivan, Leon H. obit Sep 2001

Sumac, Yma obit Yrbk 2008

Summers, Lawrence H. Jul 2002

Summitt, Pat Jun 2005

Sun Wen Apr 2001

Sunstein, Cass R. Oct 2008

Supman, Milton *see* Sales, Soupy

Sutherland, Joan obit Yrbk 2010

Sutherland, Kiefer Mar 2002

Sutton, Percy E. obit Yrbk 2010

Suzman, Helen obit Yrbk 2009

Suzuki, Ichiro Jul 2002

Suzuki, Zenko obit Yrbk 2004

Swanberg, Joe Nov 2010

Swayze, Patrick obit Yrbk 2009

Swearingen, John obit Yrbk 2007

Sweeney, Anne Jun 2003

Swift, Taylor Jan 2010

Swinton, Tilda Nov 2001

Swiss, Jamy Ian Feb 2010

Syal, Meera Feb 2001

Szekely, Louis *see* Louis C.K.

Taboo Nawasha *see* Black Eyed Peas

Tainish, Juan *see* Watts, Jeff "Tain"

Taintor, Anne Jun 2005

Tajiri, Satoshi Nov 2001

Talese, Nan Sep 2006

Talley, André Leon Jul 2003

Talmadge, Herman E. obit Jun 2002

Tange, Kenzo obit Yrbk 2005

Tangerine Dream Jan 2005

Tao, Terence Sep 2007

Tarter, Jill Cornell Feb 2001

Tartt, Donna Feb 2003

Tarver, Antonio Jun 2006

Tattersall, Ian Aug 2007

Taufa'ahau, Tupou IV obit Yrbk 2007

Taurasi, Diana Nov 2007

Tauscher, Ellen O. Mar 2001

Taylor, Herman A. Jun 2006

Taylor, Jermain Apr 2006

Taylor, Jill Bolte Jan 2009

Taylor, John W. obit Apr 2002

Taylor, Koko Jul 2002 obit Yrbk 2009

Taylor, Lili Jul 2005

Taylor, Theodore obit Feb 2005

Tebaldi, Renata obit Apr 2005

Tebbel, John obit Mar 2005

Tejada, Miguel Jun 2003

Teller, Edward obit Sep 2004

Temple, Johnny Oct 2008

terhorst, Jerald F. obit Yrbk 2010

Terkel, Studs obit Yrbk 2009

Terkel, Louis *see* Terkel, Studs

Tethong, Lhadon Sep 2008

Tetley, Glen obit Yrbk 2007

Thain, John A. May 2004

Thaler, William J. obit Yrbk 2005

Thebom, Blanche obit Yrbk 2010

Thernstrom, Abigail Mar 2010

Theron, Charlize Nov 2004

Thiam, Aliaune *see* Akon

Thieu, Nguyen Van obit Jan 2002

Thomas, Dave *see* Thomas, R. David

Thomas, Michael Feb 2008

Thomas, R. David obit Apr 2002

Thomas, Sarah Nov 2010

Thomas, William H. Jan 2006

Thome, Jim Jun 2007

Thompson, Hunter S. obit Yrbk 2005

Thompson, John Douglas Sep 2010

Thompson, John III Nov 2007

Thompson, John W. Mar 2005

Thompson, Lonnie Jan 2004

Thomson, David Sep 2009

Thomson, James A. Nov 2001

Thomson, Kenneth R. obit Yrbk 2006

Thomson, Meldrim Jr. obit Sep 2001

Thurmond, Strom obit Nov 2003

Thyssen-Bornemisza de Kaszan, Baron Hans Heinrich obit Yrbk 2002

Tian, Hao Jiang Feb 2009

Tice, George A. Nov 2003

Tierney, John Aug 2005

Tigerman, Stanley Feb 2001

Tilghman, Shirley M. Jun 2006

Tillerson, Rex Sep 2006

Timbaland Mar 2003

Tisch, Laurence A. obit Yrbk 2004

Titov, Gherman obit Jan 2001

Tobin, James obit May 2002

Todd, Richard obit Yrbk 2010

Toledano, Ralph de obit Yrbk 2007

Toledo, Alejandro Nov 2001

Toles, Thomas G. *see* Toles, Tom

Toles, Tom Nov 2002

Tolle, Eckhart Feb 2005

Tomlinson, LaDainian Oct 2006

Tonatto, Laura Apr 2009

Tre Cool *see* Green Day

Tremonti, Mark *see* Creed

Trenet, Charles obit Sep 2001

Trenkler, Freddie obit Yrbk 2001

Trethewey, Natasha Aug 2007

Trevor-Roper, H. R. obit Jul 2003

Tridish, Pete Apr 2004

Trigère, Pauline obit Jul 2002

Tritt, Travis Feb 2004

Trotter, Lloyd Jul 2005

Trout, J.D. Jul 2009

Trout Powell, Eve May 2004

Trout, Robert obit Jan 2001

Trowbridge, Alexander B. obit Yrbk 2006

Troyat, Henri obit Yrbk 2007

Trudeau, Pierre Elliott obit Jan 2001

Truman, David B. obit Yrbk 2004

Truman, Margaret obit Yrbk 2008

Truss, Lynne Jul 2006

Tshabalala-Msimang, Manto obit Yrbk 2010
Tsui Hark Oct 2001
Tufte, Edward R. Nov 2007
Tull, Tanya Nov 2004
Tureck, Rosalyn obit Yrbk 2003
Turin, Luca Aug 2008
Turner, Mark Nov 2002
Turre, Steve Apr 2001
TV on the Radio Apr 2009
Tweedy, Jeff see Wilco
Tweet Nov 2002
Tyler, Steven see Aerosmith
Tyson, John H. Aug 2001

Udall, Stewart L. obit Yrbk 2010
Underwood, Carrie Mar 2007
Underwood, Cecil H. obit Yrbk 2009
Unitas, Johnny obit Yrbk 2002
Updike, John obit Yrbk 2009
Uris, Leon obit Yrbk 2003
Urquidez, Benny Nov 2001
Urrea, Luis Alberto Nov 2005
Ustinov, Peter obit Aug 2004
Utzon, Jorn obit Yrbk 2009

Valdes-Rodriguez, Alisa Jan 2006
Valensi, Nick see Strokes
Valenti, Jack obit Yrbk 2007
Valentine, Bobby Jul 2001
Van Allen, James A. obit Yrbk 2007
Van den Haag, Ernest obit Jul 2002
Van Duyn, Mona obit Nov 2005
Van Exel, Nick Mar 2002
Van Gundy, Jeff May 2001
Van Zandt, Steven Feb 2006
Vance, Cyrus R. obit Apr 2002
Vanden Heuvel, Katrina May 2009
Vandiver, S. Ernest obit Yrbk 2005
Vandross, Luther obit Yrbk 2005
Vane, John R. obit Yrbk 2005
Vargas, Elizabeth Apr 2006
Varnay, Astrid obit Yrbk 2007
Varnedoe, Kirk obit Yrbk 2003
Vaughn, Vince Sep 2006
Veneman, Ann M. Sep 2009
Venkatesh, Sudhir May 2010
Verdon, Gwen obit Jan 2001
Vick, Michael Nov 2003

Vickrey, Dan see Counting Crows
Vieira, Meredith Apr 2002
Viereck, Peter obit Yrbk 2006
Villa-Komaroff, Lydia Jul 2008
Villaraigosa, Antonio Aug 2007
Vilsack, Tom Mar 2009
Vinatieri, Adam Sep 2004
Virilio, Paul Jul 2005
Viscardi, Henry Jr. obit Yrbk 2004
Visser, Lesley Apr 2007
Vitale, Dick Jan 2005
Volokhonsky, Larissa see Pevear, Richard and Volokhonsky, Larissa
von Ziegesar, Cecily Jan 2008
Vonn, Lindsey Feb 2010
Vonnegut, Kurt obit Aug 2007
Voulkos, Peter obit Aug 2002
Voznesensky, Andrei obit Yrbk 2010

Wachowski, Andy and Larry Sep 2003
Wachowski, Larry see Wachowski, Andy and Larry
Wade, Dwyane Apr 2006
Waldheim, Kurt obit Oct 2007
Waldman, Ayelet Sep 2009
Wales, Jimmy Oct 2006
Walker, Mort Feb 2002
Walker, Olene S. Apr 2005
Wall, Art obit Feb 2002
Wallace, Ben Apr 2004
Wallerstein, Immanuel May 2009
Wallis, Jim Jul 2005
Walsh, Bill obit Yrbk 2007
Walsh, John Jul 2001
Walters, Barbara Feb 2003
Walters, John P. May 2008
Walters, Vernon A. obit Jul 2002
Walworth, Arthur C. obit Yrbk 2005
Ward, Benjamin obit Yrbk 2002
Ward, Paul L. obit Yrbk 2006
Ward, William E. Nov 2005
Ware, David S. Sep 2003
Warnecke, John Carl obit Yrbk 2010
Warner, Kurt Sep 2009
Warner, Mark R. Oct 2006
Warnke, Paul C. obit Feb 2002
Warren, Rick Oct 2006
Warsame, Keinan see K'Naan

Washburn, Bradford obit Yrbk 2007
Washington, Walter E. obit Yrbk 2004
Wasserman, Lew R. obit Yrbk 2002
Wasserstein, Wendy obit Yrbk 2006
Waters, Alice Jan 2004
Watkins, Donald Jan 2003
Watkins, Levi Jr. Mar 2003
Watson, Arthel Lane see Watson, Doc
Watson, Doc Feb 2003
Watson, Emily May 2007
Watts, Jeff "Tain" Apr 2008
Watts, Naomi Mar 2007
Waugh, Auberon obit May 2001
Wayans, Marlon see Wayans, Shawn and Marlon
Wayans, Shawn and Marlon May 2001
Weaver, Dennis obit Yrbk 2006
Weaver, Pat obit Yrbk 2002
Weaver, Sylvester see Weaver, Pat
Webb, Jim Nov 2007
Webb, Karrie Aug 2001
Webber, Chris May 2003
Weber, Dick obit Yrbk 2005
Weinberg, Alvin M. obit Yrbk 2006
Weinberger, Caspar W. obit Jul 2006
Weiner, Jennifer Jul 2008
Weinrig, Gary Lee see Rush
Weinstein, Allen Jun 2006
Weir, Johnny Apr 2010
Weis, Charlie Nov 2007
Weisberg, Jacob Oct 2007
Weiss, Paul obit Yrbk 2002
Weisskopf, Victor F. obit Yrbk 2002
Weitz, John obit Apr 2003
Weizman, Ezer obit Aug 2005
Weizsäcker, Carl F. von obit Yrbk 2007
Wek, Alek Jun 2001
Welch, Stanton Jul 2007
Weller, Thomas H. obit Yrbk 2008
Wells, David May 2004
Wells, Spencer Mar 2008
Wellstone, Paul D. obit Yrbk 2003
Welty, Eudora obit Nov 2001
Wendel, Johnathan Apr 2007
Wendrich, Willeke Jan 2007

Wesley, Valerie Wilson Jun 2002

West, Kanye Aug 2006

Westmoreland, William C. obit Nov 2005

Wexler, Haskell Aug 2007

Wexler, Jerry Jan 2001 obit Yrbk 2008

Weyrich, Paul Feb 2005 obit Yrbk 2009

Wheeldon, Christopher Mar 2004

Wheeler, John Archibald obit Yrbk 2008

Whipple, Fred L. obit Yrbk 2005

Whitaker, Mark Aug 2003

Whitcomb, Richard T. obit Yrbk 2009

White, Armond Oct 2006

White, Byron Raymond obit Jul 2002

White, Gilbert F. obit Yrbk 2006

White, Jack see White Stripes

White, John F. obit Yrbk 2005

White, Meg see White Stripes

White, Reggie obit Yrbk 2005

White Stripes Sep 2003

Whitehead, Colson Nov 2001

Whitford, Brad see Aerosmith

Whitford, Bradley Apr 2003

Whitmore, James obit Yrbk 2009

Whitney, Phyllis A. obit Yrbk 2008

Whitson, Peggy Sep 2003

Wick, Charles Z. obit Yrbk 2008

Widmark, Richard obit Yrbk 2008

Wiesenthal, Simon obit Yrbk 2005

Wiggins, James Russell obit Mar 2001

Wilber, Ken Apr 2002

Wilco Feb 2010

Wild, Earl obit Yrbk 2010

Wilder, Billy obit Yrbk 2002

Wiley, Kehinde Aug 2007

Wilhelm, Hoyt obit Yrbk 2002

Wilkins, Maurice H. F. obit Yrbk 2005

Wilkins, Robert W. obit Yrbk 2003

will.i.am see Black Eyed Peas

Williams, Armstrong May 2004

Williams, Cliff see AC/DC

Williams, Ev see Williams, Evan

Williams, Evan Jul 2009

Williams, Harrison A. Jr. obit Mar 2002

Williams, Juan May 2008

Williams, Lauryn Sep 2008

Williams, Michelle see Destiny's Child

Williams, Pharrell see Neptunes

Williams, Preston Warren II May 2007

Williams, Ronald A. Jul 2009

Williams, Roy Mar 2007

Williams, Serena see Williams, Venus and Williams, Serena

Williams, Tad Sep 2006

Williams, Ted obit Oct 2002

Williams, Venus and Williams, Serena Feb 2003

Williams, Wendy Oct 2009

Willingham, Tyrone Nov 2002

Willis, Deborah Sep 2004

Willis, Dontrelle Aug 2006

Wilmore, Larry Nov 2007

Wilson, August obit Feb 2006

Wilson, Heather Jul 2006

Wilson, James Q. Aug 2002

Wilson, Kemmons obit Yrbk 2003

Wilson, Luke Feb 2005

Wilson, Margaret obit Yrbk 2009

Wilson, Marie C. Sep 2004

Wilson, Owen Feb 2003

Wilson, Sloan obit Yrbk 2003

Winchester, Simon Oct 2006

Winsor, Kathleen obit Yrbk 2003

Winston, Stan Jul 2002 obit Nov 2008

Winters, Shelley obit Apr 2006

Wirtz, W. Willard obit Yrbk 2010

Wise, Robert obit Apr 2006

Witcover, Jules Apr 2008

Witherspoon, Reese Jan 2004

Woertz, Patricia A. Mar 2007

Woese, Carl R. Jun 2003

Wojciechowska, Maia obit Yrbk 2002

Wolfe, Art Jun 2005

Wolfe, Julia Oct 2003

Wolff, Maritta M. obit Yrbk 2002

Wolfowitz, Paul Feb 2003

Wolfram, Stephen Feb 2005

Wolfson, Evan Jul 2009

Wolper, David L. obit Yrbk 2010

Wolpoff, Milford Jul 2006

Womack, Lee Ann Apr 2010

Wong, Andrea Sep 2007

Wong-Staal, Flossie Apr 2001

Wood, Elijah Aug 2002

Wood, Evan Rachel Jun 2009

Wood, Kerry May 2005

Woodcock, Leonard obit Apr 2001

Wooden, John obit Yrbk 2010

Woods, Donald obit Nov 2001

Woodson, Rod Oct 2004

Woodward, Robert F. obit Yrbk 2001

Wooldridge, Anna Marie see Lincoln, Abbey

Wooldridge, Dean E. obit Yrbk 2007

Worth, Irene obit Aug 2002

Wright, David May 2009

Wright, Jeffrey May 2002

Wright, Steven May 2003

Wright, Teresa obit Yrbk 2005

Wright, Will Feb 2004

Wright, Winky Jul 2004

Wriston, Walter B. obit Aug 2005

Wrynn, Dylan see Tridish, Pete

Wyatt, Jane obit Yrbk 2006

Wyeth, Andrew obit Yrbk 2009

Wylde, Zakk Oct 2004

Wyman, Jane obit Yrbk 2007

Wyman, Thomas obit Yrbk 2003

Wyner, Yehudi Apr 2008

Xenakis, Iannis obit Jul 2001

Yagudin, Alexei Feb 2004

Yar'Adua, Umaru obit Yrbk 2010

Yard, Molly obit Apr 2006

Yashin, Aleksei see Yashin, Alexei

Yashin, Alexei Jan 2003

Yasin, Rania see Rania

Yassin, Ahmed obit Yrbk 2004

Yassin, Rania see Rania

Yates, Elizabeth obit Nov 2001

Yates, Sidney R. obit Jan 2001

Yeltsin, Boris obit Jun 2007

Yokich, Stephen P. obit Yrbk 2002

York, Herbert F. obit Yrbk 2009

Yorke, Thom see Radiohead

Young, Angus see AC/DC

Young, Kimberly S. Jan 2006

Young, Malcolm *see* AC/DC
Yuen Wo Ping Jan 2008
Yusuf, Hamza Mar 2007

Zagat, Nina *see* Zagat, Tim and Nina
Zagat, Tim and Nina Mar 2008
Zahir Shah, Mohammed obit Yrbk 2007
Zahn, Paula Feb 2002
Zaillian, Steven Oct 2001
Zambello, Francesca May 2003

Zandi, Mark May 2010
Zardari, Asif Ali Jan 2009
Zatopek, Emil obit Feb 2001
Zell, Sam Jan 2009
Zellweger, Renee Feb 2004
Zelnick, Strauss Nov 2010
Zerhouni, Elias Oct 2003
Zeta-Jones, Catherine Apr 2003
Zhao Ziyang obit Yrbk 2005
Zhu Rongji Jul 2001
Ziegler, Jean Jul 2010
Ziegler, Ronald L. obit Jul 2003
Zimmer, Hans Mar 2002

Zindel, Paul obit Yrbk 2007
Zinn, Howard obit Yrbk 2010
Zinni, Anthony C. May 2002
Zito, Barry Jul 2004
Zittel, Andrea Aug 2006
Zivojinovich, Alex *see* Rush
Zoellick, Robert B. Jul 2008
Zollar, Jawole Willa Jo Jul 2003
Zorina, Vera obit Yrbk 2003
Zuberbühler, Klaus Jul 2010
Zucker, Jeff Jan 2002
Zuckerberg, Mark Jan 2008
Zukerman, Eugenia Jan 2004